T0388690

Classroom Companion: Economics

The Classroom Companion series in Economics features fundamental textbooks aimed at introducing students to the core concepts, empirical methods, theories and tools of the subject. The books offer a firm foundation for students preparing to move towards advanced learning. Each book follows a clear didactic structure and presents easy adoption opportunities for lecturers.

More information about this series at ▶ http://www.springer.com/series/16375

Fabio Petri

Microeconomics for the Critical Mind

Mainstream and Heterodox Analyses

Volume 2

Fabio Petri
University of Siena
Siena, Italy

ISSN 2662-2882 ISSN 2662-2890 (electronic)
Classroom Companion: Economics
ISBN 978-3-030-62069-1 ISBN 978-3-030-62070-7 (eBook)
https://doi.org/10.1007/978-3-030-62070-7

© Springer Nature Switzerland AG 2021
This work is subject to copyright. All rights are reserved by the Publisher, whether the whole or part of the material is concerned, specifically the rights of translation, reprinting, reuse of illustrations, recitation, broadcasting, reproduction on microfilms or in any other physical way, and transmission or information storage and retrieval, electronic adaptation, computer software, or by similar or dissimilar methodology now known or hereafter developed.
The use of general descriptive names, registered names, trademarks, service marks, etc. in this publication does not imply, even in the absence of a specific statement, that such names are exempt from the relevant protective laws and regulations and therefore free for general use.
The publisher, the authors and the editors are safe to assume that the advice and information in this book are believed to be true and accurate at the date of publication. Neither the publisher nor the authors or the editors give a warranty, expressed or implied, with respect to the material contained herein or for any errors or omissions that may have been made. The publisher remains neutral with regard to jurisdictional claims in published maps and institutional affiliations.

This Springer imprint is published by the registered company Springer Nature Switzerland AG
The registered company address is: Gewerbestrasse 11, 6330 Cham, Switzerland

Preface (Mainly, But Not Only, For Teachers)

We should regret that the truth only progresses slowly,
but it shall surely triumph at last
(David Ricardo, letter to *Morning Chronicle*, 4 November 1810)

This is a textbook designed for first-year graduate lecture courses in microeconomics and suitable also for last-year honours undergraduate courses. It differs from other textbooks in that it aims at supplying as correct as possible a picture of the present state of the theory of value and distribution, arguably the most important part of the usual microeconomics curriculum because it gives the general picture of the functioning of market economies, which greatly conditions nearly all analyses, also in macroeconomics, growth theory, international trade.

Current micro textbooks are highly misleading on the state of the theory of value and distribution. They introduce students only to the supply-and-demand, or neoclassical, or marginal, approach (and, most of the time, trying not to mention the difficulties the approach encounters). The presentation of standard consumer theory, theory of the firm and partial-equilibrium analyses is a prelude to the presentation of general competitive equilibrium theory, that is, of the supply-and-demand approach to value and distribution. The chapters on oligopoly, imperfect information, externalities and public goods introduce several qualifications but do not question the basic insights derived from the general competitive equilibrium model. No other approach to value and distribution is presented. This is a misrepresentation of the present state of economic theory. The current situation in the theory of value and distribution (but then also, as a consequence, in the theories of the labour market, of growth, of taxation, of international economics, etc.) is one of frequent doubts about the correctness of the supply-and-demand approach to income distribution, employment and growth; and of attempts by a consistent and growing minority of economists to explore alternatives. The number of journals and of associations aiming at the exploration of non-neoclassical approaches (e.g. Post-Keynesian, Sraffian, Kaleckian, neo-Marxist, evolutionary, institutionalist approaches) has been growing rapidly in recent decades; also, even in Departments not greatly interested in these 'heterodox' approaches one observes a tendency to give the theory of general equilibrium very little space in graduate-level microeconomics courses, which suggests a tendency towards an agnostic stance on the validity of that theory (more on this below).

In this situation of scientific uncertainty and co-existence of competing approaches, the duty of serious teachers is to make students capable of understanding the writings of economists belonging to different schools of thought, and to stimulate them to form their own opinion as to which approach appears scientifically more promising. The situation requires open, critical minds. The present textbook is an attempt in this direction. Accordingly, its contents and structure are partly unusual.

The neoclassical (or marginal, or supply-and-demand) approach is explained in full detail, indeed in greater detail than elsewhere on many issues, because the need to compare it with other approaches requires careful discussion of aspects given little attention in other textbooks. For example, considerable space is given to the very important shift undergone by general equilibrium theory from traditional versions aiming at the determination of long-period prices to the nowadays dominant neo-Walrasian very-short-period versions. And the disappointing results on uniqueness and stability of general equilibrium are not only presented (contrary to the disconcerting choice, in some recent textbooks, to omit these topics completely, as if it were better for scientific progress to hide the problems under the carpet), but their relevance is discussed in greater depth than in any other textbook I am aware of.

But the neoclassical approach is not the sole approach presented. The classical or surplus approach of Smith, Ricardo and Marx is also presented, including its modern developments; and it is introduced *before* the marginal one: it has seemed opportune to start the book with the presentation of a non-neoclassical approach, so as to make it easier for students to look at the neoclassical approach (probably the sole approach they were previously introduced to) 'from the outside', that is, as only one possible way to explain the functioning of market economies, that must be compared with alternatives. The obvious choice has been the classical approach, not only because in this way students acquire a sense of the history of economic thought, but also because, when coupled with a Keynesian approach to the determination of aggregate output and employment, its framework appears capable of hosting many of the insights of other non-neoclassical schools of thought (e.g. Post-Keynesian, Kaleckian, evolutionary). The first chapter ends precisely with a simple sketch of how the classical approach to value and distribution can be combined with a Keynesian, demand-based approach to aggregate output. The reader is thus presented (albeit in simplified form) with a possible approach to the determination of quantities produced, income distribution and prices, against which the specificities of the neoclassical approach can be better perceived.

This has made it possible and opportune to contrast very early on (▶ Chap. 3) the marginal/neoclassical with the classical approach to value and distribution, and to highlight the central analytical difference between them. To such an end, in ▶ Chap. 3 the fundamental structure of the neoclassical approach to value and distribution is explained through very simple models *before* the chapters presenting advanced neoclassical consumer theory and producer theory, i.e. on the basis of simple intro-

Preface (Mainly, But Not Only, For Teachers)

ductory microeconomics only (which is itself concisely presented, so as to make the exposition accessible to readers coming from other disciplines). My teaching experience has shown that this is a very useful order of presentation; when, immediately afterwards, the student tackles rigorous consumer theory and producer theory and meets Kuhn–Tucker, upper hemicontinuity, Shephard's lemma, Gorman form, the weak axiom, etc., she/he has a stronger motivation and a greater capacity to grasp the role of the several assumptions.

The subsequent study of general equilibrium theory is unique at textbook level in that the various versions of the theory ('atemporal', long-period, intertemporal without and with overlapping generations, temporary) are distinguished, and the differences between the objections that can be advanced against them are clarified. In particular, care is taken to distinguish the criticisms based on the Sonnenschein–Mantel–Debreu results from the 'Sraffian' criticisms. These distinctions will spare students many confusions.

The several criticisms, when thus clarified, paint a rather negative image of the persuasiveness of the supply-and-demand approach. It would be misleading to hide this state of affairs, which is the reason behind important aspects of the present trend in scientific research and teaching. As one author has perceptively noticed,

> the Walrasian theory of market behavior or, as it is more commonly referred to, general equilibrium theory, has increasingly been abandoned by microeconomists ... an appropriately acceptable analysis of the uniqueness and global stability of Walrasian equilibrium has yet to be found ... The persistence of this gap along with the seemingly hopelessness of filling it has, to a considerable extent, led many microeconomists to forsake the general equilibrium conceptualization altogether. As a result, microeconomic theory has, by and large, been reduced to a collection of techniques and tricks for resolving narrow, isolated microeconomic problems and the study of, also narrow and isolated, strategic behaviors (Katzner 2006, p. ix).

This picture is correct; the content of many graduate microeconomics courses has indeed been evolving in this direction, avoiding discussion of the overall theory. The result is to leave students prisoners of whatever rather unrigorously presented picture of the functioning of market economies they absorbed as undergraduates. Nor is the present situation one in which either one teaches the supply-and-demand approach to value and distribution, or one can only remain silent, waiting for some new theory to emerge. Alternative approaches do exist. Thus, ▶ Chaps. 10, 12 and 13 go on to ask whether the classical approach to value and distribution, combined with a recognition of the importance of aggregate demand for the determination of quantities and employment, can be a fruitful alternative framework; they discuss in greater detail the notion of long-period prices (also in the presence of land rents), the functioning of competition in product markets, the determinants of the degree of utilization of capacity, the labour market, and some macroeconomic implications of the microeconomics thus surveyed. ▸ Chapter 14, on welfare economics, besides standard arguments includes an attempt to indicate elements for a non-neoclassical welfare economics. My own theoretical preferences inevitably emerge, but I have tried hard correctly to illustrate also the views I find unpersuasive. It is indispensable at present for prospective economists to understand all the main competing positions.

The aim of reflecting the richness (and uncertainties) of the present theoretical situation has suggested the inclusion of micro topics that are now generally relegated to 'macro' courses: efficiency wages and other theories of the labour market; the microtheory of the degree of capacity utilization; the investment decisions of firms. It would seem that the criterion for exclusion of these topics from standard microeconomics courses is not that they are not micro topics, but rather that they are associated with an admission of labour unemployment. This has historical reasons that appear now outdated. The distinction between microeconomics and macroeconomics was a consequence of the Keynesian revolution. Keynes did not question the marginalist/neoclassical 'real' factor substitution mechanisms behind the decreasing labour demand curve and the decreasing investment function; but he argued that those mechanisms were generally incapable of bringing about the full employment of labour, owing to various difficulties (on whose exact nature and relevance an intense debate has raged ever since). Anyway, in his theory, once investment and the multiplier determine aggregate production and hence labour employment, real wages are still determined by the marginal product of labour, and the marginal product of capital remains a fundamental determinant of investment. Keynesian theory became universally adopted for short-period macroanalyses, but the 'neoclassical synthesis' soon gave support to the faith that the long-run trend of the economy was reasonably well described by traditional marginalist analyses. The division between microeconomics and macroeconomics could then be proposed as a division between the study of the 'real' marginalist factor substitution forces determining long-run trends, and the study of the Keynesian mechanisms determining short-run deviations of labour employment and aggregate output from the full-employment long-run trend. Micro courses were accordingly confined, fundamentally, to the teaching of traditional marginalist/neoclassical 'real' theory, a theory of full-employment equilibrium, while the presentation of microeconomic mechanisms useful for the explanation of unemployment was mostly relegated to macro courses. The present existence of approaches that reject traditional marginalist 'real' theory (and thus also its predictions about long-run trends) obliges one to re-define the confines of microeconomics and macroeconomics. A considerable portion of modern economists argue that there is little reason to consider unemployment a regrettable but temporary lapse from a normal trend of roughly full employment, and that therefore the functioning of economies where significant unemployment is a normal state of affairs should be at least as central to micro courses as the study of full-employment situations. And this textbook wants to be an introduction to these views too.

The price to be paid for the inclusion of these topics is that less space is left for some other topics. For example auctions, and social choice, are treated in lesser detail than in other advanced micro textbooks; and regretfully there is nothing on the economics of crime, and too little on the economics of the Internet. Unfortunately space is a scarce resource; anyway given the enormous importance of these topics even a full chapter on each of them would not have done justice to their importance, they deserve full courses.

Much effort has gone into trying to make this text user-friendly, accessible to readers without advanced previous mathematical competences and/or without previous study of economic theory. Many graduate economics students do not have an undergraduate degree in economics; so this textbook does not assume a previously acquired familiarity with elementary microeconomics. ▶ Chapter 3 introduces the notions of production function, tangency between isoquant and isocost, utility function, tangency between budget line and indifference curve, marginal cost, in simple ways that should be understandable even to students totally new to economics. Simple models are used whenever possible to clarify the economic intuition before going on to more general formalizations. Even when more advanced mathematics are inevitable the treatment remains user-friendly, and this should make the textbook suitable also for semi-advanced third-year honours undergraduate courses.

The book should be of interest to economists too. ▶ Chapter 1 should help surmount misinterpretations of Marx. ▶ Chapter 7 should be of help if one wants better to understand why many heterodox economists attribute great importance to the Cambridge controversy in capital theory and dislike aggregate production functions. ▶ Chapter 8 clarifies the problems of intertemporal general equilibrium theory, including some which are seldom perceived, and can help to grasp the causes of the widespread dissatisfaction with modern general equilibrium theory. It also discusses temporary general equilibrium, a topic which has disappeared from modern teaching but cannot be totally neglected, younger economists must understand why it has been abandoned. ▶ Chapter 12 shows the enormous implications of variable capacity utilization for the effects of demand on aggregate production; in addition, it tries to bring sense back to the theory of investment, a field nowadays dominated in mainstream macroeconomics by theories in contradiction with all sensible microeconomics. ▶ Chapter 13 brings back to microeconomics the fundamental question, why wages do not decrease in the presence of unemployment. ▶ Chapter 14 presents a rather unusual view of welfare economics.

At the end of each chapter, before the exercises, the reader finds a list of review questions—the kind of questions that might be posed to students in traditional Italian university oral exams. I regret the general tendency to abandon oral exams, the preparation for this type of exams obliges students to become able to repeat the steps of each argument, aiding comprehension and rigour (and memorization too). The reader can check her/his grasp of the material by trying to answer these review questions in a loud voice.

This book has a web page on SpringerLink containing appendices that could not be included in the printed book for space reasons. My personal web page *fabiopetripapers* (that any search engine will locate) will contain a section dedicated to this book, where I will post errata and improvements suggested by the comments, criticisms, suggestions I hope I will receive.

I particularly thank for their comments Stefano Bartolini, Enrico Bellino, Christian Bidard, Ennio Bilancini, Sam Bowles, Mauro Caminati, Roberto Ciccone, Ariel Dvoskin, Heinz D. Kurz, Neri Salvadori, Antonella Stirati. I have not always followed their advice, and certainly many mistakes and weak points remain, but they would have been much more numerous without those comments. Again, thanks.

Siena, Italy
Fabio Petri

Reference

Katzner, D. W. (2006). *An introduction to the economic theory of market behavior. Microeconomics from a Walrasian perspective*. Cheltenham, UK: Edward Elgar.

Contents

1	**The Classical or Surplus Approach**	1
1.1	**A Very Brief Historical Introduction**	3
1.2	**Social Surplus and Income Distribution**	6
1.3	**Income Distribution, Wages**	12
1.3.1	The General Wage Level	12
1.3.2	Relative Wages	18
1.4	**The Other Data in the Determination of the Surplus**	19
1.4.1	Quantities	19
1.4.2	Technology	20
1.5	**Land Rent**	24
1.5.1	Extensive Differential Rent	24
1.5.2	Intensive Differential Rent	26
1.6	**Rate of Profit and Relative Prices**	30
1.7	**Corn Model, Luxury Goods, the Decreasing w(r) Function**	36
1.8	**The Labour Theory of Value**	39
1.9	**Marx**	46
1.9.1	Values, Surplus Values, Value of Labour Power	46
1.9.2	The Determination of the Rate of Profit	48
1.9.3	A Mistake in Marx's Determination of the Rate of Profit	51
1.10	**The Marxist Tradition**	52
1.11	**The Standard Commodity as the 'average' Commodity Marx Was Looking For**	57
1.12	**More on Marx**	59
1.12.1	Wages	59
1.12.2	Quantities	62
1.12.3	Growth, Technical Change, the 'law' of the Tendency of the Rate of Profit to Fall	64
1.12.4	Marx and the Future of Capitalism	69
1.13	**'Core' and 'Out-of-Core' Analyses in the Surplus Approach**	71
1.14	**A Modern View of the Determinants of Aggregate Production**	73
1.14.1	Going Beyond Marx on What Determines Aggregate Production	73
1.14.2	The Principle of Effective Demand	75
1.14.3	The Dynamic Multiplier	81
1.14.4	The Adaptability of Production to Demand	83
1.15	**Conclusions**	85
1.16	**Review Questions and Exercises**	85
References		88
2	**Long-Period Prices**	91
2.1	**Long-Period Prices: Matrix Representation**	93
2.2	**Eigenvalues and the Perron–Frobenius Theorem**	96
2.3	**Applying Perron–Frobenius. The Standard Commodity**	100

XII   Contents

2.4	Non-basic Commodities	105
2.5	Leontief's Open Model	106
2.6	The Hawkins–Simon Condition	109
2.7	The Interpretation of the Leontief Inverse	109
2.8	Subsystems; Labours Embodied as Employment Multipliers	110
2.9	Pricing with Vertically Integrated Technical Coefficients	112
2.10	The Relationship Between Rate of Profit and Rate of Wages	112
2.11	Choice of Technique	119
2.12	Non-basics and Choice of Techniques	127
2.13	Techniques Including Different Commodities	129
2.14	The Samuelson–Garegnani Model and the Champagne-Whiskey Model	130
2.15	Fixed Capital	137
2.16	Conclusions	147
2.17	Review Questions and Exercises	148
References		151

3	**Introduction to the Marginal Approach**	153
3.1	Introduction	156
3.2	Equilibrium and Gravitation	157
3.3	The Labour–Land–Corn Economy: Direct (or Technological) Factor Substitutability	159
3.3.1	Production Functions, Isoquants and Marginal Products	159
3.3.2	Factor Demand Curves, Cost Function and Equilibrium in Factor Markets	163
3.3.3	Importance of Factor Substitutability	174
3.3.4	Comparative Statics	175
3.4	The Role of Consumer Choice: The Indirect Factor Substitution Mechanism	177
3.5	The Simultaneous Operation of Both Substitution Mechanisms, and the Importance of Highly Elastic Factor Demand Curves	180
3.6	Money	184
3.7	Efficiency, the Forest Exchange Economy, Choice Curves and Equilibrium in the Edgeworth Box	185
3.7.1	Elements of Consumer Theory: Utility Function, Indifference Curves, MRS	185
3.7.2	Exchange Economy, Edgewort Box, Pareto Efficiency	190
3.8	Pareto Efficiency in the Production Economy. Marginal Cost	196
3.9	Robinson Crusoe and Market Valuation as Reflecting 'Natural' Laws	206
3.10	Introduction of the Rate of Interest and of Capital in the Marginalist Theory of Distribution	209
3.10.1	The Rate of Interest in the Exchange Economy	209
3.10.2	The Rate of Interest in the Corn Economy	211
3.10.3	Capital and the Indirect Factor Substitution Mechanism	213
3.11	Money and the Rate of Interest	217
3.12	Accumulation	218

Contents

3.13	A Comparison Between the Classical and the Marginal Approaches to Income Distribution: The Basic Analytical Difference and Some Implications	219
3.13.1	The Different Data When Determining the Rate of Return on Capital	219
3.13.2	The Role of Social and Political Elements. Competition in Labour Markets	222
3.13.3	Exploitation?	224
3.13.4	Technical Progress, Relative Wages, Unequal Exchange	226
3.14	Intensive Differential Rent and the Marginal Approach	228
3.15	Final Elements of Differentiation: Supply of Capital, Say's Law	236
3.16	Conclusion	240
3.17	Review Questions and Exercises	241
References		245

4	**Consumers and the Exchange Economy**	247
4.1	Introduction	250
4.2	The Consumption Set, Time and the Role of Equilibrium	250
4.3	Preferences and Utility	253
4.4	Convex Preferences, Quasi-Concave Utility, Typical Indifference Curves	259
4.5	Optimization	261
4.6	Demand, Continuity and Upper Hemicontinuity of Correspondences	264
4.7	The Two-Goods Exchange Economy and the Importance of Continuity of Demand	268
4.8	First-Order Conditions. Corner Solutions. The Kuhn–Tucker Theorem	272
4.9	Envelope Theorem	280
4.10	Indirect Utility, Expenditure Function, Compensated Demand	282
4.11	Roy's Identity, Shephard's Lemma, Some Dualities and Some Utility Functions	287
4.11.1	Roy's Identity and Shephard's Lemma	287
4.11.2	Homothetic Utility Functions and Homothetic Preferences	289
4.11.3	Quasi-Linear Utility	290
4.11.4	The Cobb–Douglas Utility Function and the Elasticity of Substitution	291
4.11.5	The CES Utility Function	293
4.12	The Slutsky Equation	295
4.13	Given Endowments: The Walrasian UMP, The Walrasian Slutsky Equation	301
4.14	Labour Supply. Saving Decision	305
4.15	Some Notes on the Usefulness of Consumer Theory for Empirical Estimation	310
4.16	Money Metric Utility Function, Equivalent Variation, Compensating Variation	313
4.17	Constant Marginal Utility of Money. Consumer Surplus. Reservation Prices	319
4.18	Price Indices and Inflation	324

XIV Contents

4.19	Hicksian Aggregability of Goods	326
4.20	Revealed Preference	328
4.21	Aggregability of Consumers: Gorman Aggregability and the Representative Consumer	333
4.22	General Equilibrium of Pure Exchange. Aggregability of Consumers	337
4.23	Aggregate or Market Demand and the Weak Axiom of Revealed Preference	341
4.24	Conclusions	344
4.25	Review Questions and Exercises	344
References		351

5	**Firms, Partial Equilibria and the General Equilibrium with Production**	353
5.1	Introduction	356
5.2	Production Possibility Sets, Netputs, Production Functions	357
5.3	Axioms on the Production Possibility Set	364
5.4	Returns to Scale	365
5.5	Differentiable Production Functions and Value Capital	368
5.6	Homogeneous Production Functions and Returns to Scale	369
5.7	Activity Analysis	372
5.8	Marginal Product, Transformation Curve	373
5.9	Profit Maximization and WAPM	376
5.10	Optimal Employment of a Factor	378
5.11	Cost Minimization	379
5.12	WACm; Kuhn–Tucker Conditions and Cost Minimization	382
5.13	Supply Curves: Short-Period Marshallian Analysis, Quasi-Rents	384
5.14	From Short-Period to Long-Period Supply	388
5.15	The Product Exhaustion Theorem with U-Shaped LAC	393
5.16	Aggregation	394
5.17	Shephard's Lemma	395
5.18	The Profit Function and Hotelling's Lemma	395
5.19	Conditional and Unconditional Factor Demands, Inferior Inputs, Rival Inputs, Substitution Effect and Output Effect	397
5.20	Functional Separability: Leontief Separability	402
5.21	Duality	403
5.22	Elasticity of Substitution	404
5.23	Partial Equilibrium	405
5.24	Stability of Partial Equilibria	408
5.25	Welfare Analysis of Partial Equilibria	409
5.26	Price Taking, Perfect Competition, Tâtonnement	413
5.27	The Number of Firms in Modern GE	419
5.28	The Equations of the Non-capitalistic General Equilibrium with Production	423
5.29	The 'Reduction' to an Exchange Economy	427
5.30	The Role of Demand in Determining Product Prices: Why General Equilibrium Product Supply Curves Are Upward Sloping	429

Contents

5.31	International Trade	430
5.32	On the Persistency of Preferences. Doing Without Demand Curves?	433
5.33	Conclusions	437
5.34	Review Questions and Exercises	438
References		441

6	**Existence, Uniqueness and Stability of Non-capitalistic General Equilibria**	443
6.1	Introduction. The Exchange Economy	446
6.2	Existence: Properties of the Market Excess Demand Correspondence	447
6.3	Continuity: Non-strictly Convex Preferences	450
6.4	Continuity: Non-convex Consumption Sets	453
6.5	Continuity: Survival	456
6.6	Continuity: The Zero-Income Problem	458
6.7	Continuity: Survival Again and Subsistence	460
6.8	Existence of General Equilibrium of Exchange: A Simple New Proof	463
6.9	Brouwer's Fixed-Point Theorem	465
6.10	Existence of Exchange Equilibrium with Strongly Monotonic Preferences	466
6.11	Uniqueness: The Non-uniqueness of Equilibrium in General. Possibility of Several Locally Stable Equilibria	469
6.12	Uniqueness: Regular Economies	471
6.13	The Sonnenschein–Mantel–Debreu Result	474
6.14	Uniqueness Through Conditions on Excess Demand: Gross Substitutes	475
6.15	Uniqueness Through Conditions on Excess Demand: WAM	478
6.16	Uniqueness: No-Trade Equilibrium and Index Theorem	481
6.17	Conditions on the Distribution of Characteristics	482
6.18	Stability: The Cobweb	483
6.19	Stability: The Samuelsonian Walrasian Tâtonnement	485
6.20	Stability: Some Mathematics and the WAM Theorem	488
6.21	Stability: Further Aspects of the Problem	492
6.22	On the Likelihood of Uniqueness and Stability	494
6.23	Production	498
6.24	Existence of a GE of Production and Exchange	499
6.25	Uniqueness of the Production Equilibrium	502
6.26	WAM and the Hildenbrand–Grodal Observation	509
6.27	Gross Substitutability not Sufficient for Uniqueness	511
6.28	Stability: The Tâtonnement in the Production Economy	512
6.29	Mandler's Factor Tâtonnement	515
6.30	Again on the Likelihood of Uniqueness and Stability	518
6.31	Conclusions	523
6.32	Review Questions and Exercises	523
References		527

XVI   Contents

7	**Capital: Long-Period Equilibria**	529
7.1	The Notion of Long-Period Equilibrium	531
7.2	The Endogenous Determination of Equilibrium Capital Endowments	534
7.3	The Equations of Long-Period General Equilibrium	539
7.4	The Quantity of Capital: Supply-Side Problems	548
7.5	The Quantity of Capital: Demand-Side Problems. Demand for 'capital' and Investment	551
7.6	Re-switching and Reverse Capital Deepening	558
7.7	More on Reverse Capital Deepening. Price Wicksell Effects	563
7.8	Stationary States and Hicks' Criticism of Long-Period Prices	569
7.9	The 'Austrian' Approach	572
7.10	On Substitutability in Modern and in Traditional Production Functions	575
7.11	Aggregate Production Functions	579
7.12	'Surrogate Production Functions' in a Non-Neoclassical Economy. Endogenously Determined Marginal Products	587
7.13	Perception of the Difficulties with 'Capital', and Shift Back to Walras—or Almost	591
7.14	Conclusions	595
7.15	Review Questions and Exercises	596
References		599

8	**Intertemporal Equilibrium, Temporary Equilibrium**	601
8.1	Introduction	605
8.2	The Intertemporal Reinterpretation of the Non-capitalistic Atemporal Model	606
8.3	Postponing to Chapter 9 on Uncertainty	609
8.4	The Consumer's Intertemporal Utility Function	609
8.5	Meaning of Prices; Own Rates of Interest	611
8.6	Production	612
8.7	The Reinterpretation Should not Hide a Difference	615
8.8	Different Own Rates of Interest and Effective Uniformity of Rates of Return	616
8.9	Uniform Effective Rate of Return Versus Long-Period Uniform Rate of Profit	618
8.10	UERRSP and URRSP	619
8.11	Radner Sequential Equilibria (Without Uncertainty)	620
8.12	Existence, Uniqueness, Stability	622
8.13	Really Only a Reinterpretation? Some First Problems	623
8.14	Money	625
8.15	Impermanence Problem, Price-Change Problem, Substitutability Problem	627
8.16	The Savings–investment Problem	632
8.16.1	The 'Further Assumption'	632

Contents

8.16.2	The Difference It Makes to Assume or Not the 'Further Assumption'	635
8.16.3	The Neoclassical Synthesis	640
8.17	**Equilibrium Over the Infinite Future**	641
8.17.1	The One-Good Growth Model	641
8.17.2	The Old Problems Remain, Plus a New One	648
8.18	**Behind the Neoclassical Reliance on Intertemporal Equilibria**	650
8.19	**Overlapping Generations**	652
8.20	**Multiple OLG Equilibria**	656
8.21	**The Core of Allocations in the Neoclassical Economy**	661
8.22	**The Core Equivalence Theorem is not Valid for OLG Economies**	668
8.23	**A Continuum of Equilibria in OLG Models**	669
8.24	**Summing Up on OLG Models**	675
8.25	**Temporary Equilibria. An Informal Presentation of Some Problems**	677
8.26	**An Introductory Pure-Exchange Model**	679
8.26.1	General Description of the Exchange Economy	679
8.26.2	A More Detailed Description of the Household's Behaviour	680
8.26.3	Problems with the Introductory Model	685
8.26.4	A Perplexing Aspect of Green's Equilibrium	689
8.27	**Extension to the Case of Economies with Production**	691
8.27.1	The Extended Model	691
8.27.2	Discussion of the Extended Model	697
8.28	**Temporary Equilibrium in Economies with 'Money'**	702
8.28.1	Introduction of Money	702
8.28.2	Existence of Monetary Equilibrium	707
8.28.3	Some Doubts on Grandmont's Characterization of the Function of Money	713
8.29	**Conclusions on the Marginal/Neoclassical Approach, with Special Emphasis on the Labour Demand Curve and on the Investment Function**	714
8.30	**Review Questions and Exercises**	718
References		723

9	**Uncertainty and General Equilibrium**	727
9.1	**Lotteries and Expected Utility**	730
9.2	**Axioms for Expected Utility**	734
9.3	**Existence of Expected Utility**	738
9.4	**Risk Aversion and Prospects**	742
9.5	**Risk Aversion and Convexity of Expected Utility**	746
9.6	**Comparing the Riskiness of Lotteries: Stochastic Dominance**	748
9.7	**The St. Petersburg Paradox**	749
9.8	**Cardinality of VNM Utility**	750
9.9	**Insurance**	752
9.10	**Actuarially Fair Insurance and Risk Premium**	753
9.11	**Unfair Insurance**	755
9.12	**Measuring Risk Aversion: Arrow–Pratt**	757
9.13	**Global Comparison of Risk Aversion**	759

XVIII   Contents

9.14   Decreasing Absolute Risk Aversion 760
9.15   Relative Risk Aversion.. 761
9.16   An Application of Arrow–Pratt: Efficient Risk Pooling in Absence
        of Wealth Effects 763
9.17   Diversification 767
9.18   Consumption and Saving Under Uncertainty 768
9.19   Firm Behaviour Under Uncertainty 769
9.20   Portfolio Selection: Two Assets 771
9.21   Portfolio Selection: Many Assets. Tobin 776
9.22   State-Dependent Utility.. 782
9.23   Subjective Expected Utility... 784
9.24   Risk or Uncertainty?... 787
9.25   Non-expected Utility: Allais' Paradox, Prospect Theory, Ellsberg's
        Paradox.. 790
9.26   Reducing Uncertainty Through More Information. Satisficing.
        Informational Cascades 796
9.27   Uncertainty and General Equilibrium in Traditional Marginalist
        Authors 801
9.28   Contingent Commodities 804
9.29   Equilibrium with Contingent Commodities 811
9.30   Radner Equilibrium (EPPPE) 814
9.31   Incomplete Markets.. 817
9.32   Conclusion. Final Considerations on the Supply-And-Demand
        Approach 821
9.33   Review Questions and Exercises 823
References 829

10   **Back to Long-Period Prices** 831
10.1   The Gravitation to Long-Period Prices in the History of Economic
        Theory, and Some Empirical Evidence................................. 833
10.2   Objections to the Uniform Rate of Profit 839
10.3   The Traditional Explanation 842
10.4   Cross-Dual Models 844
10.5   The Possibility of a High Price and a Low Profit Rate.................. 851
10.6   Joint Production and Sraffa 853
10.7   Graphical Representation: Single Production 858
10.8   Graphical Representation: Joint Production 865
10.9   Choice of Technique as a Linear Programming Problem 870
10.10   Piccioni's Contribution 879
10.11   No Gravitation to a Definite Technique? 885
10.12   Extensive Rent... 889
10.13   Intensive Rent 895
10.14   External Intensive Rent; Rent Due to Consumer Demand.............. 902
10.15   Given Quantities?.. 904
10.16   Constant Returns to Scale?... 906
10.17   Lack of Consistency?... 911

Contents

10.18	Conclusions	913
10.19	Review Questions and Exercises	913
References		916

11	**Games and Information**	919
11.1	Introduction, and Some Examples of One-Shot Simultaneous Games	921
11.2	Sequential or Dynamic Games	925
11.3	Extensive and Strategic (or Normal) Form	929
11.4	Mixed Strategies	931
11.5	Behavioural Strategies	933
11.6	Solutions. Elimination of Strictly Dominated Strategies. Some Doubts	935
11.7	Weakly Dominated Strategies, Dominance Solvable Games	939
11.8	Dominated Mixed Strategies	941
11.9	Nash Equilibrium in Pure Strategies	942
11.10	Nash Equilibria in Mixed Strategies	943
11.11	Existence of Nash Equilibrium. The Reasons for Interest in Nash Equilibria	944
11.12	Trembling-Hand Equilibria	950
11.13	Backward Induction and Subgame Perfection	951
11.14	Repeated Backward Induction and the Centipede Game	954
11.15	Infinitely Repeated Games	957
11.16	Finitely Repeated Games	962
11.17	Bayesian Games	963
11.18	Auctions as Bayesian Games. Revenue Equivalence Theorem. Winner's Curse	970
11.19	Dynamic Games of Imperfect Information	976
11.20	Sequential Rationality, Behavioural Strategies, Perfect Bayesian Equilibrium (PBE)	978
11.21	Limits of Perfect Bayesian Equilibrium. Sequential Equilibrium	983
11.22	Asymmetric Information. Signalling Games. Separating and Pooling Equilibria	985
11.23	Adverse Selection	994
11.24	Principal–agent Models	996
11.25	Screening	1003
11.26	Conclusions	1008
11.27	Review Questions and Exercises	1008
References		1019

12	**Product Markets: Pricing, Capacity, Investment, Imperfect Competition**	1021
12.1	Introduction	1023
12.2	Two Types of Markets. Primary Products	1024
12.3	Administered Prices and Capacity Utilization	1027
12.4	Unused Capacity	1029

XX   Contents

12.5	Time-Specific Input Prices	1030
12.6	Demand Variations	1035
12.7	The Investment Decision of Firms	1041
12.7.1	Neoclassical Investment Theory Without Full Labour Employment	1041
12.7.2	The 'Array-of-Opportunities' Approach	1046
12.7.3	The Adjustment Costs Approach	1050
12.7.4	Investment Determined by Profits?	1052
12.7.5	Investment and Sales Prospects	1060
12.8	Administered Prices, Differentiated Products, and Competition	1062
12.9	Full-Cost Pricing	1063
12.10	Monopoly	1067
12.11	Monopolistic Competition Versus Full-Cost Pricing	1073
12.12	Duopoly	1079
12.12.1	Cournot Duopoly	1079
12.12.2	Conjectural Variations	1086
12.12.3	Stackelberg (Quantity Leadership)	1086
12.12.4	Price Leadership	1089
12.12.5	Bertrand	1090
12.12.6	Bertrand-Edgeworth	1092
12.12.7	Capacity Constraints and Bertrand Competition	1094
12.12.8	Differentiated Products and Bertrand Versus Cournot Competition	1095
12.12.9	Price Matching and the Kinked Demand Curve	1096
12.13	Repeated Interaction, Cartels, Tacit Collusion, Folk Theorems	1098
12.14	Entry	1102
12.15	Conclusions	1109
12.16	Review Questions and Exercises	1110
References		1113
13	**Labour Markets and Income Distribution**	1115
13.1	Introductory	1117
13.2	The Labour Demand Curve Is Indeterminable	1118
13.3	Search Theory	1127
13.4	Implicit Contracts	1140
13.5	Insiders–Outsiders	1143
13.6	Efficiency Wages	1146
13.6.1	Five Versions	1146
13.6.2	Adverse Selection	1149
13.6.3	Turnover Costs	1150
13.6.4	Shirking	1152
13.6.5	Gift Exchange, Fairness, Morale	1164
13.7	Trade Unions	1165
13.8	The Solow or Solow–Hahn Approach	1180
13.9	Long-Period Theories of Wages: Four Approaches. The Cambridge School	1188
13.10	The Kaleckian Approach	1200
13.11	The Classical–Marxian Approach. Goodwin. Investment	1202

Contents

13.12	**Pivetti**	1214
13.13	**Concluding on Real Wages**	1216
13.14	**Review Questions and Exercises**	1220
References		1223

14	**Welfare, Externalities, Public Goods and Happiness**	1227
14.1	**Introductory**	1229
14.2	**Pareto Efficiency and Value Judgements**	1230
14.3	**Externalities**	1234
14.3.1	The Coase Theorem	1234
14.3.2	Production Externalities	1236
14.3.3	Pollution Rights	1241
14.3.4	Network Externalities and the Internet	1241
14.3.5	The Tragedy of the Commons	1246
14.3.6	Urban Segregation	1248
14.4	**Public Goods**	1249
14.4.1	Non-rival Goods and Non-excludable Goods	1249
14.4.2	When to Get an Indivisible Public Goods	1250
14.4.3	What Quantity of a Divisible Public Good?	1251
14.4.4	Lindahl Equilibrium	1254
14.5	**The Groves–Clarke Mechanism**	1255
14.6	**The Fundamental Theorems of Welfare Economics**	1258
14.6.1	Does Competition Produce Pareto Efficiency?	1258
14.6.2	The First Fundamental Theorem	1260
14.6.3	The Second Fundamental Theorem	1265
14.7	**Some Generally Accepted Limitations of the Two Fundamental Theorems**	1271
14.8	**Pareto Efficiency: A Non-neoclassical Perspective**	1277
14.9	**Cost–Benefit Analysis and the Compensation Principle**	1281
14.10	**Cost–benefit Analysis Run Amok**	1287
14.11	**Social Welfare Functions**	1292
14.12	**Three Applications of Social Welfare Functions**	1301
14.13	**Arrow's Impossibility Theorem**	1305
14.14	**Happiness, and Externalities Again**	1322
14.15	**Conclusions**	1330
14.16	**Review Questions and Exercises**	1330
References		1334

15	**Mathematical Review**	1337
15.1	**Sets, Relations, Functions, Convexity, Convex Combination of Vectors**	1338
15.2	**Logic: If, Only if, Contrapositive, Proof by Contradiction, Connection with Subsets**	1342
15.3	**Vectors, Matrices, Hyperplanes. Definite Matrices**	1343
15.4	**Analysis**	1353
15.5	**Correspondences**	1364

15.6	**Optimization**	1366
15.7	**Linear Programming and Duality**	1381
15.8	**Complex Numbers**	1382
15.9	**Integrals**	1384
15.10	**Probability and Statistics**	1385
15.11	**Poisson Process**	1391
References		1394

Uncertainty and General Equilibrium

Contents

9.1   Lotteries and Expected Utility – 730

9.2   Axioms for Expected Utility – 734

9.3   Existence of Expected Utility – 738

9.4   Risk Aversion and Prospects – 742

9.5   Risk Aversion and Convexity of Expected Utility – 746

9.6   Comparing the Riskiness of Lotteries: Stochastic Dominance – 748

9.7   The St. Petersburg Paradox – 749

9.8   Cardinality of VNM Utility – 750

9.9   Insurance – 752

9.10   Actuarially Fair Insurance and Risk Premium – 753

9.11   Unfair Insurance – 755

9.12   Measuring Risk Aversion: Arrow–Pratt – 757

Electronic supplementary material The online version of this chapter (▶ https://doi.org/10.1007/978-3-030-62070-7_9) contains supplementary material, which is available to authorized users.

© Springer Nature Switzerland AG 2021
F. Petri, *Microeconomics for the Critical Mind*,
Classroom Companion: Economics, https://doi.org/10.1007/978-3-030-62070-7_9

9.13	Global Comparison of Risk Aversion – 759	
9.14	Decreasing Absolute Risk Aversion – 760	
9.15	Relative Risk Aversion – 761	
9.16	An Application of Arrow–Pratt: Efficient Risk Pooling in Absence of Wealth Effects – 763	
9.17	Diversification – 767	
9.18	Consumption and Saving Under Uncertainty – 768	
9.19	Firm Behaviour Under Uncertainty – 769	
9.20	Portfolio Selection: Two Assets – 771	
9.21	Portfolio Selection: Many Assets. Tobin – 776	
9.22	State-Dependent Utility – 782	
9.23	Subjective Expected Utility – 784	
9.24	Risk or Uncertainty? – 787	
9.25	Non-expected Utility: Allais' Paradox, Prospect Theory, Ellsberg's Paradox – 790	
9.26	Reducing Uncertainty Through More Information. Satisficing. Informational Cascades – 796	
9.27	Uncertainty and General Equilibrium in Traditional Marginalist Authors – 801	
9.28	Contingent Commodities – 804	

9.29 Equilibrium with Contingent
Commodities – 811

9.30 Radner Equilibrium (EPPPE) – 814

9.31 Incomplete Markets – 817

9.32 Conclusion. Final Considerations on the
Supply-And-Demand Approach – 821

9.33 Review Questions and Exercises – 823

References – 829

730   **Chapter 9** · Uncertainty and General Equilibrium

This chapter presents the standard way to study choice under uncertainty, followed by how uncertainty is introduced into general equilibrium theory. You will learn about:

- the enlargement of the notions of preferences and choice to include lotteries or gambles;
- the definition of expected utility and the axioms that justify its form;
- how risk aversion explains insurance and diversification;
- portfolio selection among risky assets;
- subjective expected utility;
- some doubts about the realism of expected utility theory;
- informational cascades;
- general equilibrium with contingent commodities;
- Arrow securities;
- the notions of incomplete markets and of sunspot equilibria.

9.1 Lotteries and Expected Utility

Sections 9.1–9.26 of this chapter introduce to the standard microeconomic analysis of single-agent choice problems in the presence of uncertainty, followed by Sects. 9.27–9.31, plus an online appendix on Marshall, on how uncertainty is embodied into the supply-and-demand approach to value and distribution. The chapter ends with a final assessment, in ▶ Sect. 9.32, of the marginal, or supply-and-demand, or neoclassical, approach to value and distribution. For space reasons some proofs are in the online Appendix to this chapter in the book's website.

Let us start by enlarging the set of things, among which a consumer chooses, to include *lotteries*. A lottery (also *gamble* or bet) is a possible object of choice, consisting of a list of possible *outcomes*, or *payoffs*, or *prizes*, each one with a probability attached to it, and with the probabilities summing to 1. An example: suppose you consider whether to bet one dollar on number 1 at a roulette spin; the (European) roulette keeps the bet and pays 36 times the bet on a single number if the number comes out; so the lottery connected with betting 1 dollar on number one offers two possible outcomes: (1) winning 35 dollars net (i.e. 36 dollars minus the one you paid) with probability 1/37 (there are 37 equally probable numbers from 0 to 36), (2) losing 1 dollar with probability 36/37. Another example: you buy an insurance against a house fire; you have actually chosen a lottery with, as possible outcomes, (1) no fire happens, in which case you lose the downpayment, and (2) the fire happens, in which case you receive the insurance prize minus the downpayment; but the lottery is not fully specified yet, the probability of the two events must be indicated.

The outcomes of lotteries can be vectors of consumption goods, or sums of money, or happenings (e.g. that someone gets married; an accident), anything really; but I will generally consider payoffs that are consumption bundles, or sums of money.

A lottery or gamble with n outcomes can be represented in different ways: one is as a double vector, that lists first all the possible outcomes $x_1, ..., x_n$ and then, in the same order their probabilities of occurrence $p_1, p_2, ..., p_n$. (Actually only

9.1 · Lotteries and Expected Utility

the first $n - 1$ probabilities need be listed, since the n probabilities must sum to 1.) Another is as a vector of couples, $(x_1, p_1; \ldots; x_n, p_n)$. When several alternative lotteries must be compared, one way to proceed is to assume a given set X of *all possible* outcomes, univocally indexed, to be called the *outcome set*, and to assume that each lottery has a probability distribution over X, which identifies the lottery: if there is a finite number N of possible outcomes, with the outcomes known, ordered and numbered $1, \ldots, n, \ldots, N$, each lottery can be specified simply as a vector, an N-list of probabilities $p_1, \ldots, p_N$ summing to 1. This does not exclude lotteries contemplating just a few of the outcomes in X, it only means that all other outcomes in X are assigned zero probability. But if the outcomes in X are numerous, this procedure can make for a very cumbersome representation of lotteries with only few outcomes. So for simple examples it is preferable to adopt the representation that indicates the outcomes explicitly (Varian 1992):

$$L = p_1 \circ x_1 \oplus p_2 \circ x_2 \oplus \ldots \oplus p_n \circ x_n \quad \text{where} \quad \sum_i p_i = 1.$$

This means: if you choose this lottery, then you win one of n different outcomes $x_1, \ldots, x_n$ and outcome x_i can occur with probability p_i. Note that the example above of roulette lottery will be represented as $1/37 \circ \$35 \oplus 36/37 \circ -\$1$ if one is only interested in the *net* payoffs of that lottery, but if several lotteries must be compared to decide which one is preferred, their effects on wealth are generally the important thing, especially when wealth is considerably affected by the outcome, and then one must represent the prizes as *wealth after the result of the lottery*; then the roulette lottery must be represented as $1/37 \circ (W + 35) \oplus 36/37 \circ (W - 1)$ where W is initial wealth in dollars.

Among the outcomes or prizes of a lottery there can be other lotteries (some of whose outcomes can in turn be lotteries); e.g. one can have, with A, B, C three outcomes:

$$L = p_1 \circ A \oplus p_2 \circ (p_3 \circ B \oplus p_4 \circ C) \quad \text{where } p_1 + p_2 = 1, \quad p_3 + p_4 = 1.$$

For example, a lottery might have as one of its outcomes a lottery ticket.

A lottery where some prizes are lotteries (sometimes called *sublotteries*) is said **compound**, otherwise **simple**. The **completely reduced lottery** corresponding to compound lottery L is defined as the simple lottery L' stating the total probabilities of occurrence of each final or ultimate payoff, for example for the above lottery L:

$$L' = p_1 \circ A \oplus p_2 p_3 \circ B \oplus p_2 p_4 \circ C.$$

Reduction can also be only partial. Conversely a lottery with more than two outcomes can always be transformed into a compound lottery with only two outcomes, reducible to the original lottery, by having the two outcomes consist of compound lotteries; for example a lottery $L = p_1 \circ A \oplus p_2 \circ B \oplus p_3 \circ C \oplus p_4 \circ D$ (with $p_1 + p_2 + p_3 + p_4 = 1$) is the reduced form of the two-outcomes compound lottery

$$L' = (p_1 + p_2) \circ \left[p_1/(p_1 + p_2) \circ A \oplus p_2/(p_1 + p_2) \circ B \right]$$
$$\oplus (p_3 + p_4) \circ \left[p_3/(p_3 + p_4) \circ C \oplus p_4/(p_3 + p_4) \circ D \right].$$

The outcomes of a completely reduced lottery are not lotteries, but rather things to which usual consumer theory can be applied, e.g. consumption bundles, amounts of money.

Let us assume the following, perhaps too pompously called an axiom:

■■ Equivalence (or Reducibility) Axiom

The decision maker treats a compound lottery and all the partially or completely reduced lotteries derivable from it as the same lottery, or at least is indifferent among them.

Now assume that all lotteries L, L', L'', ... in a problem under examination assign probabilities to the N elements of the same finite set X of indexed outcomes and therefore can be represented simply by N-vectors of probabilities (see above). Then a compound lottery

$$\alpha \circ L \oplus (1 - \alpha) \circ L'$$

(also called a *mixture* of the two lotteries) can be represented as

$$\alpha\lambda + (1 - \alpha)\lambda'$$

where λ *and* λ' *now stand for the vectors of probabilities* that represent L and L'; indeed with $\lambda = (p_1,...,p_N)$, the list of probabilities $\alpha\lambda + (1-\alpha)\lambda'$ correctly lists the probabilities of the outcomes of the reduced lottery corresponding to the compound lottery $\alpha \circ L \oplus (1-\alpha) \circ L'$. Now suppose you decide that if $x_i \in X$ indicates an outcome, the *same symbol* also indicates the *degenerate* lottery that assigns probability 1 to this outcome and zero to all other outcomes in X; such a degenerate lottery too can be represented simply with its list of probabilities, all zero except for 1 in the i-th place; if you decide that this representation too can be indicated with the symbol x_i, then a lottery L over X represented by the list $(p_1,..., p_N)$ of probabilities can also be represented as

$$L = p_1 x_1 + ... + p_N x_N,$$

which would appear to make no sense unless the outcomes are different amounts of the same 'stuff', but makes sense if seen as a sum of vectors of probabilities, which actually comes down to the list $(p_1,..., p_N)$ but makes the names of the outcomes appear explicitly. When you find a lottery written as a sum, something like the above is assumed.

A lottery can also be over a continuum of outcomes, with their probabilities defined by a distribution function; but the mathematics required for a general formalization of choices in this case are much more advanced, requiring topological notions, so I will only consider the case of a finite number of possible outcomes.

The admission of degenerate lotteries allows us to assume, without loss of generality that *all* the alternatives among which a consumer chooses are lotteries. So traditional consumer choice can be considered a special case of choice among lotteries. However, the analogy has limitations: one must remember that the space of lotteries is different from the space of consumption bundles in that, differently from consumption goods or bundles, lotteries are not *quantities*, it does not generally make sense to add lotteries, or to divide or multiply a lottery by a scalar. Lacking divisibility, there are no continuous indifference curves among lotteries.

9.1 · Lotteries and Expected Utility

I will assume that the decision maker has preferences over lotteries, representable through a utility function. Now I describe the most widely assumed form for such a utility function and then I inquire what assumptions imply it.

■■ Definition

(***Expected Utility Form***) Given a finite set X of possible outcomes $\{x_1, \ldots, x_N\}$, the preferences of an agent over completely reduced lotteries on X are representable by an additively separable[1] utility function of **expected utility form** if numbers $u_1, \ldots, u_N$ exist such that these preferences are correctly represented by a utility function that assigns, to each lottery $L = \left(p_1^L, p_2^L, \ldots, p_N^L\right) = p_1^L \circ x_1 \oplus p_2^L \circ x_2 \oplus \ldots \oplus p_N^L \circ x_x$, utility

$$U(L) \equiv U\left(p_1^L, p_2^L, \ldots, p_N^L\right) = p_1^L u_1 + p_2^L u_2 + \ldots + p_N^L u_N \tag{9.1}$$

That is, for any two lotteries L, L' on X it is $L \succeq L'$ if and only if $U(L) \geq U(L')$.

Two immediate observations are important. First (dropping for brevity the suffix L in apex from the probability symbols) if the lottery is *not* a completely reduced one, that is if $L = (p_1 \circ L_1 \oplus p_2 \circ L_2 \oplus \ldots \oplus p_k \circ L_k)$, then if $U(L)$ has the expected utility form then the equality holds

$$\begin{aligned} U(L) &\equiv U(p_1 \circ L_1 \oplus p_2 \circ L_2 \oplus \ldots \oplus p_k \circ L_k) \\ &= p_1 U(L_1) + p_2 U(L_2) + \ldots + p_k U(L_k). \end{aligned} \tag{9.1'}$$

This follows immediately from the definition of $U(L)$ and the rule for reducing compound lotteries, as the reader will have no difficulty in proving. The formal similarity between (9.1) and (9.1$'$) should not induce one to forget that, although in (9.1$'$) each $U(L_i)$ is a number too, it is a number *derived* from the numbers u_i and from the probabilities that L_i assigns to the ultimate outcomes.

Second, if the ultimate outcomes $x_1, \ldots, x_N$ are elements of a consumption set as defined in ▶ Chap. 4, over which a usual consumer-theory utility function $u(\mathbf{x})$ is defined, then the numbers $u_1, \ldots, u_N$ are interpretable as the utility levels assigned to these elements by that utility function, in which case one can also write:

$$U(L) = p_1 u(\mathbf{x}_1) + p_2 u(\mathbf{x}_2) + \ldots + p_N u(\mathbf{x}_N). \tag{9.1''}$$

The formal similarity with (9.1$'$) is striking; still, one must not forget that in (9.1$'$) the utility function on the left-hand side is not a usual consumer-type utility function, because it depends on objects that are not consumption bundles. One distinguishes the utility function $u(\mathbf{x}_i)$ on the right-hand side of (9.1$''$) from the overall expected utility function U by calling $u(\cdot)$ the *basic utility* function, or *subutility* function, or sometimes *felicity* function. The overall utility function is

---

1 An *additively separable* function is an additive function of several variables where in each addendum there appears only one variable. E.g. $f(x, y) = x + xy^2$ is additive but not additively separable.

734 Chapter 9 · Uncertainty and General Equilibrium

called *expected utility function*, or also ***Von Neumann–Morgenstern (VNM) utility function*** from the name of the originators of the notion. The denomination 'expected utility function' reflects the fact that if the numbers u_i are interpreted as utility levels, then $p_i u_i$ is the expected value $E(u_i)$ of the utility level u_i.

If a VNM utility function correctly represents preferences, any increasing monotonic transformation of it (for example, raising it to the power of 3) correctly represents the same preferences; but if one wants to maintain the expected utility form (thus maintaining its convenient additive form) then only affine positive transformations are acceptable, from $U(\cdot)$ to $V(\cdot) = a U(\cdot) + b$ with a, b scalars and $a > 0$.

9.2 Axioms for Expected Utility

If preferences satisfy certain axioms, then they admit representation via a VNM utility function. I proceed to list a number of axioms that suffice to guarantee the expected utility form.[2] To decrease the number of indices, often I will indicate both lotteries and outcomes (that can be either ultimate outcomes or lotteries) with capital letters: A, B, C, etc. If the symbol refers only to ultimate outcomes, this will be made clear.

Some of the axioms are so universally accepted that some authors do not even call them axioms, but rather, less emphatically, assumptions; these are:

- that the decision maker doesn't care about the order in which a lottery is described, the lottery $p_1 \circ A \oplus p_2 \circ B$ and the lottery $p_2 \circ B \oplus p_1 \circ A$ are treated by the decision maker as the same lottery;
- that the decision maker considers the degenerate lottery that assigns probability 1 to one outcome as the same as getting that outcome for certain.

Empirical evidence is not always in accord with these assumptions. In particular, sometimes people choose differently depending on how a choice among lotteries (and not only among lotteries) is presented, an issue discussed under the

---

2 It must be said at the outset that the empirical evidence does *not* strongly support expected utility; we will see later some counterexamples, and one attempt (out of several) to construct an alternative theory more in accord with the empirical evidence, *prospect theory*. Just to give a hint of other possibilities, I mention here *worst-case-scenario preferences*: a lottery is preferred to a second lottery if, given a utility function over outcomes, the lowest utility that can be yielded by the first lottery is greater than the lowest utility that can be yielded by the second lottery. But VNM utility has been so dominant that most of game theory and of models in industrial economics and in labour economics that introduce uncertainty (some will be mentioned in ▶ Chaps. 12 and 13) assume VNM utility; certainly an enormous reconstruction would be necessary if VNM utility were discarded. For the moment, at least at textbook level not much can be told a critical mind beyond 'keep this caveat in mind, VNM utility might need replacement'. Of course the doubts about the empirical validity of VNM utility theory imply analogous doubts about the axioms, but it is difficult to understand which one of several axioms is responsible for the predictions that raise doubts about the theory.

9.2 · Axioms for Expected Utility

denomination 'framing'. This is a well-confirmed phenomenon but I will neglect it; it seems of limited relevance for usual economic choices.

To these assumptions, which are about the decision maker's perception of the lotteries open to her, assumptions/axioms are added that specify the structure of preferences. Normally one assumes:

— the *Equivalence Axiom*
— that preferences over lotteries are complete, reflexive, transitive, and, when among sure divisible outcomes (e.g. consumption bundles, money), they satisfy continuity as defined in ▶ Chap. 4.[3]

From this point on, different authors take different routes, starting from different axioms. To go deeper into this field the reader should compare the axioms in a number of different treatments, for example in Varian (1992), Owen (1995), Kreps (1990).

The minimal number of additional axioms is two:

— 1. Continuity axiom
— 2. Independence axiom.

■■ Continuity Axiom

The preference relation $\succsim$ over the space of simple lotteries $\mathcal{L}$ is continuous, that is, for any three lotteries A, B, $C \in \mathcal{L}$ *the sets* $\{p \in [0, 1]: p \circ A \oplus (1 - p) \circ B \succsim C\}$ and $\{p \in [0, 1]: C \succsim p \circ A \oplus (1 - p) \circ B\}$ are closed.

This axiom states that if a lottery $p \circ A \oplus (1 - p) \circ B$ is *strictly* preferred to another lottery or outcome, a sufficiently small change in p will not invert the preference order.[4] An example that illustrates its concrete meaning is the following: if a trip with zero probability of a serious accident (e.g. death) is strictly preferred to no trip, the same trip with a positive but sufficiently small probability of a serious accident is still preferred to no trip.

Remember that a lottery can also be a degenerate lottery that assigns probability 1 to a single ultimate outcome, in which case it is equivalent to the ultimate outcome for sure. Therefore A, B, $C...$ and the preference relations among them can refer both to single outcomes and to non-degenerate lotteries.

---

3   The assumption of completeness is here a stronger assumption than for choices under certainty, because one may have to compare rather complex compound lotteries, and it is more likely that one may find it impossible to compare their desirability. The assumption of transitivity can also be questioned, because people seem to have *fuzzy* preferences, i.e. to be unable to distinguish between lotteries that differ by less than a certain threshold; so a person may declare indifference between (A): obtaining 1000 dollars for sure or 3000 dollars with probability $p = 0.5$, and (B): the same but with $p = 0.501$; and she may declare indifference between (B) and a lottery (C) equal to B except that $p = 0.502$; but the increment of p from 0.5 to 0.502 may be above the threshold, so the same person may declare she strictly prefers (C) to (A), violating transitivity. This case too seems to have limited relevance in economic choices and I will neglect it.

4   This axiom concerns continuity *in probabilities* which is not the same continuity of preferences as in ▶ Chap. 4; but remember that the basic utility $u(\cdot)$ when defined over consumption bundles is a standard utility function, so it is assumed to satisfy the usual assumptions on preferences over sure consumption bundles, among them continuity in the sense of ▶ Chap. 4.

736   **Chapter 9 · Uncertainty and General Equilibrium**

■■ Independence Axiom

The preference relation $\succsim$ on the space of simple lotteries $\mathcal{L}$ satisfies independence, that is, for any three lotteries $A, B, C \in \mathcal{L}$ and for $p \in (0, 1)$ it is

$$A \succsim B \text{ if and only if } p \circ A \oplus (1 - p) \circ C \succsim p \circ B \oplus (1 - p) \circ C.$$

This is sometimes called the **substitution axiom**. It can be proved (cf. Sect. 1 in the online Appendix to this chapter) that from it one can derive the 'strong preference' and the 'indifference' versions of the same axiom:

$$A \succ B \text{ if and only if } p \circ A \oplus (1 - p) \circ C \succ p \circ B \oplus (1 - p) \circ C. \tag{9.2}$$

$$A \sim B \text{ if and only if } p \circ A \oplus (1 - p) \circ C \sim p \circ B \oplus (1 - p) \circ C. \tag{9.3}$$

The independence axiom and its implications (9.2) and (9.3) assume that if we have two lotteries A and B with $A > B$, then for *any* positive probability p and *any* third lottery C it is $p \circ A \oplus (1 - p) \circ C > p \circ B \oplus (1 - p) \circ C$, and the same preservation of ranking holds if $A \sim B$. Replacing the third lottery with any other one, even with A or B, does not alter this preservation of ranking.[5] This axiom is justified as follows: consider a lottery $p \circ x \oplus (1 - p) \circ y$ and a third outcome z such that the consumer is indifferent between x and z; whether the *lottery* $A = p \circ x \oplus (1 - p) \circ y$ is preferred to another lottery B should not be affected by replacing x with z, because the consumer is going to consume *either x or y*, and *either z or y*, so if the probability of y is the same in the two cases, it seems plausible that the consumer be indifferent between $p \circ x \oplus (1 - p) \circ y$ and $p \circ z \oplus (1 - p) \circ y$ if $x \sim z$.[6]

Another argument in support of the independence axiom is that if it is violated then one will accept so-called **Dutch books**, combinations of bets that cause a sure loss of money.[7] Indeed suppose two lotteries A and B and an individual T for whom $A > B$; the independence axiom then implies that $A > p \circ B \oplus (1 - p) \circ A$ for $0 < p < 1$; for brevity call D the latter compound lottery; assume that in contradiction of the independence axiom, T finds that $D > A$. Suppose T has acquired lottery A, i.e. the right to obtain the outcome of this lottery. Since she strictly prefers D to A, now we can persuade her to pay a small amount x of money to trade A with D. T accepts, and acquires the right to the outcome of D. Then the outcome of D is announced: it is either A, or B, whose outcomes are not known yet. If the outcome of D is A, T is back where she started and has lost x. If it is B, since T strictly prefers A to B, we can persuade T to pay a small amount of

---

5   Replacing C with A, one obtains $A \sim B$ if and only if $A \sim p \circ B (1 - p) \circ A$, which shows that the Independence axiom excludes the possibility that the presence of uncertainty in a lottery may be found by itself attractive, perhaps because one likes adrenalin. This is an important limitation of expected utility theory which makes it unfit to analyse phenomena like addiction to gambling.

6   And yet this axiom too has been criticized, see below ▶ Sect. 9.25.

7   A 'book' is a bet (hence 'bookmakers'). From the time when the Dutch were shrewd merchants competing with the British in international markets, the British seem to have derived a hostile popular image of the Dutch as swindlers, which explains the denomination.

9.2 · Axioms for Expected Utility

money z to trade B with A before the outcome of either A or B is announced: then T has lost $x+z$ to be back where she started, at ownership of A. And the process can be repeated. The argument then is that individuals, who do not respect the independence axiom in nearly all choices, will be exploited by others who understand Dutch books, and finally will go bankrupt and disappear from the market.

From these axioms one derives:

▪▪ Lemma 1

(Monotonicity-In-Probabilities (M-In-P for Short)) *If $A \succ B$ and $p'>p$ with p, $p' \in (0, 1)$, then*

1. $A \succ p \circ A \oplus (1-p) \circ B,$
2. $p \circ A \oplus (1-p) \circ B \succ B$
3. $p' \circ A \oplus \left(1-p'\right) \circ B \succ p \circ A \oplus (l-p) \circ B,$

and conversely if $p'>p$ with p, $p' \in (0, 1)$ and $A \succ p \circ A \oplus (1-p) \circ B$ or $p' \circ A \oplus (1-p') \circ B \succ p \circ A \oplus (1-p) \circ B$, then $A \succ B$.

Proof The trick is to use B or A in place of C in (9.4) and to remember that $A = p \circ A \oplus (1-p) \circ A$. Inequality (1) derives from the fact that $A \succ B$ and (9.2) imply $A = (1-p) \circ A \oplus p \circ A \succ (1-p) \circ B \oplus p \circ A$ for all $p \in (0, 1)$. Inequality (2) analogously derives from $p \circ A \oplus (1-p) \circ B \succ p \circ B \oplus (1-p) \circ B = B$. Now define a probability $\pi = (p'-p)/(1-p)] \in (0, 1)$, admissible since $p<p'<1$; then $p' \circ A \oplus (1-p')B = \pi \circ A \oplus (1-\pi) \circ (p \circ A \oplus (1-p) \circ B)$; let L stand for the compound lottery $p \circ A \oplus (1-p) \circ B$ which by (1) we know to be worse than A; then in (2) we can replace B with L, and p with π, obtaining $\pi \circ A \oplus (1-\pi) \circ L \succ L$, that is, $p' \circ A \oplus (1-p') \circ B \succ p \circ A \oplus (1-p) \circ B$, that proves (iii). Conversely, $A = p \circ A \oplus (1-p) \circ A \succ p \circ A \oplus (1-p) \circ B$ implies $A>B$ by 9.2, and $p' \circ A \oplus (1-p') \circ B \succ p \circ A \oplus (1-p) \circ B$ can be rewritten $\pi \circ A \oplus (1-\pi) \circ (p \circ A \oplus (1-p) \circ B) \succ p \circ A \oplus (1-p) \circ B$ with π defined as above, or $\pi \circ A \oplus (1-\pi) \circ L \succ L$ that implies $A \succ L$ and hence $A \succ B$. ▪

▪▪ Lemma 2

(Archimedean 'Axiom') *Let a, B, C be lotteries or outcomes such that $a \succ C \succ B$. then there exists some $P^* \in (0, 1)$ Such that $p^* \circ A \oplus (1-p^*) \circ B \sim C$.*[8]

Proof It is in the proof of this result that the continuity axiom is relevant. The two sets $\{p \in [0, 1]: p \circ A \oplus (1-p) \circ B \succsim C\}$ and $\{p \in [0, 1]: C \succsim p \circ A \oplus (1-p) \circ B\}$ are closed and nonempty (each one contains at least 0 or 1), and every point in $[0, 1]$ belongs to at least one of the two sets because of

---

8 'Axiom' is in inverted commas because here it is a derived result, but many treatments take it as one of the axioms (in place of the continuity axiom, which is then derived from the independence axiom and the Archimedean axiom). The qualification 'Archimedean' appears to have derived from the analogy with 'Archimedes' principle': given a number $x>0$ no matter how small, and a number $y>0$ no matter how big, there is an integer n such that $nx>y$.

738   **Chapter 9 · Uncertainty and General Equilibrium**

completeness of the preference order. Since the unit interval is a *connected set*,[9] there must be some p belonging to both sets, and at that p the lottery $p{\circ}A \oplus (1-p){\circ}B$ must be *equipreferred* to C since the weak inequality holds both ways. If the inequalities are strict, $A \succ C \succ B$, then the common p cannot be 0 or 1 because then the lottery $p{\circ}A \oplus (1-p){\circ}B$ would be equivalent to A for sure or to B for sure, which—given that $A \succ C \succ B$—would render the equipreference between the lottery and C impossible. ∎

■■ Lemma 3

(Uniqueness of the equipreference probability) *The p^* in the Archimedean 'axiom' is unique.*

Proof [10] For any number s in $[0,1]$ different from p^*, if $p^* > s$ then, by result (iii) in the M-in-P Lemma, $C \sim p^*{\circ}A \oplus (1-p^*){\circ}B \succ s{\circ}A \oplus (1-s){\circ}B$; and if $s > p^*$ then $s{\circ}A \oplus (1-s){\circ}B \succ C$. ∎

9.3 Existence of Expected Utility

Now I build a utility function for preferences satisfying these axioms and show that it has the expected utility form, following the proof method of Owen (1995).

■■ Theorem 4

(Expected Utility Theorem) *Let X be a set of N possible ultimate outcomes $\{x_1, x_2, \ldots, x_N\}$. If preferences satisfy the listed assumptions and the equivalence, independence and continuity axioms, then it is possible to assign numbers $u_1, \ldots, u_N$ to the ultimate outcomes such that the utility function $U(L) = p_1^L u_1 + p_2^L u_2 + \ldots + p_N^L u_N$, of expected utility form, that maps each reduced lottery $L = \left(p_1^L, \ldots, p_N^L\right)$ over X into the real numbers, satisfies, for any two lotteries L, L' over X:*

$$U(L) > U\left(L'\right) \text{ if and only if } L \succ L'. \text{[11]} \tag{9.4}$$

---

9   A set is *connected* if it is possible to connect any point of the set to any other point of the set with a continuous curvilinear segment consisting entirely of points of the set. Each point of a continuous curve is a point of accumulation along the curve from either direction; hence if a continuous curvilinear segment in a connected set S goes from a point internal to a subset F of S to a point not in F but in another subset H of S, with F and H both closed and connected and such that F H = S, then any point of the curvilinear segment not in F is in H, and there must be a point of it which is a frontier point of F and also an accumulation point for H, so by the definition of closed set it belongs to H, and therefore to both subsets.

10   To give the reader a feeling of the possibility of different derivations of expected utility, online Appendix to the chapter, in the book's website, in its Sect. 1 reports a different proof of Lemma 3.

11   *Exercise*: Prove that this implies that if $A \sim B$ then $u(A) = u(B)$.

9.3 · Existence of Expected Utility

Interpreting $U(x_j)$ as the degenerate lottery that assigns probability 1 to ultimate outcome x_j, the function U assigns utility u_j to $U(x_j)$ and in this way it correctly reflects the preference order over ultimate outcomes too. Therefore A in $U(A)$ can be interpreted to stand for an ultimate outcome or for a non-degenerate (reduced or non-reduced) lottery. U satisfies linearity in convex combinations:

$$U(p \circ A \oplus (1 - p) \circ B) = pU(A) + (1 - p)U(B), \tag{9.5}$$

whichever the type of lottery, degenerate or not, indicated by A, B.

U is unique up to an affine transformation; i.e. if there exists a second function V that satisfies 9.4 and 9.5 for the same preferences, then there exist real numbers $\alpha > 0$ and β such that for all outcomes (lotteries or ultimate outcomes) A:

$$V(A) = \alpha U(A) + \beta. \tag{9.6}$$

Proof *(partial)*. The complete proof is long and I shall only give parts of it, sufficient to point out its basic principle. Let us assume that there exist two reference outcomes E_1 and E_0 such that $E_1 \succ E_0$, and let us initially restrict ourselves to outcomes A (which can be lotteries or ultimate outcomes) such that $E_1 \succ A \succ E_0$.[12] Then by Lemmas 2 and 3 there exists a unique probability $s \in (0,1)$ such that $s \circ E_1 \oplus (1 - s) \circ E_0 \sim A$. This probability s is chosen as the numerical value of $U(A)$ relative to the reference outcomes E_1 and E_0. If there exists a best outcome and a worst outcome in the set of possible outcomes, it is possible to choose them as reference outcomes E_1 and E_0, and then all outcomes will either satisfy $E_1 \succ A \succ E_0$, or $E_1 \sim A$ in which case we put $U(A) = U(E_1) = 1$, or $E_0 \sim A$ in which case we put $U(A) = U(E_0) = 0$. One can then prove that U thus defined satisfies the theorem (see below). But one need not choose the best and worst outcomes (even when they exist) as reference outcomes, it is possible to choose any couple of outcomes such that $E_1 \succ E_0$, then an outcome A can also be preferred to E_1 or worse than E_0, but one can still assign, in the way shown below, values to $U(A)$ connected with probabilities determined by Lemmas 2 and 3. (This allows treating also the cases in which there is no best or no worst outcome.) In this way a number $s = U(A)$ is assigned to any lottery A. If now we let A stand for the degenerate lottery with probability 1 assigned to ultimate outcome x_j, the corresponding $s = U(A) = U(x_j)$ (where in the last expression x_j stands for the degenerate lottery with certain outcome x_j) is chosen to stand for u_j; thus we find the numbers $u_1, \ldots , u_N$ that yield the expected utility form of $U(L)$ and satisfy (9.4, 9.5 and 9.8) (The case in which there are no two outcomes E_1 and E_0 such that $E_1 \succ E_0$ is uninteresting, it is the case when for all outcomes A and B it is $A \sim B$, then we can simply assign $u(A) = 0$ for all outcomes, the conditions of the theorem are satisfied.)

---

12 These symbols E_1, E_0 should not be confused with the expectation operator.

740   **Chapter 9 · Uncertainty and General Equilibrium**

The rules to assign $U(A)$ for all the five possible cases are as follows:

(a) $A \succ E_1$. Then there exists a probability $q \in (0, 1)$ such that $q \circ A \oplus (1 - q) \circ E_0 \sim E_1$. Define $U(A) = 1/q$, which is > 1.

(b) $A \sim E_1$. Define $U(A) = U(E_1) = 1$.

(c) $E_1 \succ A \succ E_0$. Then there exists a probability $s \in (0, 1)$ such that $s \circ E_1 \oplus (1 - s) \circ E_0 \sim A$. Define $U(A) = s$.

(d) $A \sim E_0$. Define $U(A) = 0$.

(e) $E_0 \succ A$. Then there exists a probability $t \in (0, 1)$ such that $t \circ A \oplus (1 - t) \circ E_1 \sim E_0$. Define $U(A) = \frac{t-1}{t}$, which is negative.

By Lemma 3, the numbers q, s, t not only exist but are uniquely defined. The proof that U thus defined satisfies (9.4) and (9.5) for any two outcomes A and B is lengthy, differing (in details although not in the basic logic) according to which combination of cases the two outcomes belong to: there are 15 possible combinations. Only one combination will be examined here, (c, c). The other combinations except (e, e) are examined in Sect. 2 of the online Appendix to this chapter. Case (e, e) is left as an **Exercise**. Once it is shown that (9.4) and (9.5) are satisfied, U is easily shown to have the expected utility form.

Assume then case (c, c): $U(A) = s_A$, $U(B) = s_B$. If $s_A = s_B$ then $A \sim s_A \circ E_1 \oplus (1 - s_A) \circ E_0 \sim B$, so $A \sim B$. If $s_A > s_B$ then $s_A \circ E_1 \oplus (1 - s_A) \circ E_0 > s_B \circ E_1 \oplus (1 - s_B) \circ E_0$ and therefore $A \succ B$. Conversely if $A \succ B$ it must be $s_A > s_B$ where $s_A \circ E_1 \oplus (1 - s_A) \circ E_0 \sim A$ and $s_B \circ E_1 \oplus (1 - s_B) \circ E_0 \sim B$; otherwise it could not be $s_A \circ E_1 \oplus (1 - s_A) \circ E_0 > s_B \circ E_1 \oplus (1 - s_B) \circ E_0$. Therefore U satisfies (9.4).

To prove (9.5), treat the lottery $p \circ A \oplus (1 - p) \circ B$ as a possible outcome and ask what utility our rules assign to such an outcome. By the definitions of s_A, s_B and the equivalence axiom:

$$p \circ A \oplus (1 - p) \circ B \sim$$
$$\sim \left[p \circ (s_A \circ E_1 \oplus (1 - s_A) \circ E_0) \right] \oplus \left[(1 - p) \circ (s_B \circ E_1 \oplus (1 - s_B) \circ E_0) \right]$$
$$\sim (p s_A + (1-p) s_B) \circ E_1 \oplus \left[p(1-s_A) + (1-p)(1-s_B) \right] \circ E_0$$
$$= (p s_A + (1-p) s_B) \circ E_1 \oplus \left[1 - (p s_A + (1-p) s_B) \right] \circ E_0.$$

So $p \circ A \oplus (1 - p) \circ B$ is equipreferred to a lottery over the reference outcomes; hence the probability of E_1 in this lottery, i.e. $p s_A + (1 - p) s_B$, is the utility that our rules assign to $p \circ A \oplus (1 - p) \circ B$; but by definition, $s_A = U(A)$ and $s_B = U(B)$; hence we obtain (9.5):

$$U(p \circ A \oplus (1 - p) \circ B) = p U(A) + (1 - p) U(B).$$

If in (9.5) A, B refer to ultimate outcomes, and therefore $p \circ A \oplus (1 - p) \circ B$ is a reduced lottery L, our rule for assigning utilities gives us immediately the expected utility form of U:

$$U(L) = p u_A + (1 - p) u_B.$$

9.3 · Existence of Expected Utility

There remains to prove that U is unique up to an affine transformation with $a>0$. Let V be any other function satisfying (9.4) and (9.5). Since $E_1 \succ E_0$ it must be $V(E_1)>V(E_0)$. Define $\beta=V(E_0)$, and $\alpha=V(E_1)-V(E_0)$, so $V(E_1)=\alpha+V(E_0)=\alpha+\beta$ where $\alpha>0$. Consider an outcome A belonging to case (c), that is, such that $E_1 \succ A \succ E_0$. Let s be such that $A \sim s{\circ}E_1 \oplus (1-s){\circ}E_0$, and hence $U(A)=s$. By (9.4) $V(\cdot)$ must assign the same number to A and to $s{\circ}E_1 \oplus (1-s){\circ}E_0$, hence using (9.5):

$$V(A) = V(s \circ E_1 \oplus (1-s) \circ E_0) = sV(E_1) + (l-s)V(E_0)$$
$$= s(\alpha+\beta) + (1-s)\beta = s\alpha + \beta = \alpha U(A) + \beta.$$

Hence $V(\cdot)$ satisfies (9.6). With similar reasonings it can be shown that $V(\cdot)$ satisfies (9.6) also for A falling in the other cases (a), (b), (d), (e). For example in case (a) we define α and β in the same way, and from $E_1 \sim q{\circ}A \oplus (1-q){\circ}E_0$, $U(A)=1/q$, and $V(E_1)=V(q{\circ}A \oplus (1-q){\circ}E_0)=qV(A)+(1-q)V(E_0)$ we deduce

$$\alpha = V(E_1) - V(E_0) = qV(A) - qV(E_0) = qV(A) - q\beta;$$

$$V(A) = (\alpha + q\beta)/q = \alpha\frac{1}{q} + \beta = \alpha U(A) + \beta.$$

■

The above considerations extend straightforwardly to cases in which the outcomes are more than two but finite in number. If the probability of outcome x_i is p_i, with $i=1,\dots,N$, then the expected utility of this lottery is[13]:

$$\sum_{i=1}^{N} p_i U(x_i) = \sum_{i=1}^{N} p_i u_i.$$

The same extension holds for lotteries with several outcomes that are in turn lotteries.

It can be shown—but it requires considerably more advanced mathematics—that under essentially the same axioms, if a lottery consists of a continuous probability distribution $p(x)$ defined on a continuum of outcomes, then the expected utility of this lottery is the integral $\int U(x)p(x)dx$ defined over the interval of values of x.

Up to now, in order to help the reader not to forget the conceptual difference between utility of lotteries, and utility of ultimate outcomes such as consumption goods or money, I have used capital letters for the utility function of lotter-

---

13 Consider a lottery $L=p_A{\circ}A \ \ p_B{\circ}Bp_C{\circ}C$ where $p_C=1-p_A-p_B$; it was shown that L can be seen as the reduced form of a compound lottery $M=p_A{\circ}A \ \ p_D{\circ}D$ where $p_D=p_B+p_C$ and D is a lottery with B and C as outcomes with respective probabilities $p_B=p_B/p_D$ and $p_C=p_C/p_D$. If preferences satisfy the continuity and independence axioms then $u(M)=p_A u(A)+p_D u(D)$ and, D being a lottery, $u(D)=p_B u(B)+p_C u(C)$, which reduces to $u(M)=u(L)=p_A u(A)+p_B u(B)+p_C u(C)$.

742   **Chapter 9 · Uncertainty and General Equilibrium**

ies $U(A)$, and small letters u_i for the numbers that measure the utility of ultimate outcomes. But the formal identification of ultimate outcomes with degenerate lotteries that assign probability 1 to them, and the formal similarity—that achieves the expected utility form—between the determination of utility of a lottery and of a final outcome, allow us to indicate with the same symbol $u(x)$ or $u(A)$ both the overall expected utility of a lottery, and the utility of an outcome of a lottery, leaving to the context the task of clarifying whether the outcome is an ultimate outcome, or in turn a lottery.

9.4 Risk Aversion and Prospects

If offered (for free) a bet that gives a 50% chance of winning 1000 dollars and a 50% chance of losing 1000 dollars, experience shows that most people will refuse the bet. It must mean that the utility of the lottery $1/2 \circ (\textit{initial wealth} + 1000) \oplus 1/2 \circ (\textit{initial wealth} - 1000)$ is less than the utility of initial wealth; i.e. *the utility of the lottery is less than the utility of obtaining the expected value of the lottery (initial wealth, in this case) for certain.*

This empirical fact, called **risk aversion**, is not always verified (for example people buy lottery tickets or play roulette, in spite of knowing that the gambles associated with them are not *fair*, which means that the expected value of the variations in wealth associated with the gambles is negative); but it is verified in many cases of economic relevance, and it is argued to be the explanation of the existence of insurance, and of risk pooling and risk diversification. Let us see how preferences must look like in order to produce it.

Let us restrict ourselves to sets of lotteries with money (or wealth) payoffs, and to choices among two-outcome money lotteries, all lotteries being such that the first outcome obtains if a specified *event* occurs (the same for all the lotteries under consideration), the second outcome obtains if that event does not occur. Let us stop on this new notion a bit. Suppose a person must select an *act* today—a course of action among a set of possible actions, for example, a purchase or not of an insurance—that will yield tomorrow one out of a possible set of outcomes (payoffs, prizes or also *consequences*) of relevance to the person's well-being, depending not only on the act the person chooses today but also on things whose occurrence is beyond the person's control and not certain. Define a *state of nature* or *state of the world*, or for brevity a *state*, as a description of one possibility about what the world is or will be like, which is complete enough to determine, together with knowledge of the action, the payoff of the action if that state occurs. There is uncertainty about which state will occur. *Events* are subsets of the set of possible states of nature. If some states of nature have some relevant characteristic in common that makes them indistinguishable for the purpose of assessing preferences over the alternatives under examination, then one can assemble them in an event, and only distinguish the consequences of acts according to which event will be the case. Example of an event: all possible states of nature in which when tonight at 10:00 pm I gamble at roulette the ball will stop on number 36.

9.4 · Risk Aversion and Prospects

It is always possible to interpret the outcomes of lotteries as depending on some event occurring or not, because there must be some reason why one prize and not another one is obtained; in the roulette example in ▶ Sect. 9.1, the event was number 1 coming out; what we add here is the assumption that the event is the same for all the lotteries among which one is to choose. This is also expressed by saying that the lotteries concern **state-indexed outcomes**, because the outcomes depend on whether when the uncertainty is resolved one finds oneself in a *state of nature or state of the world* where the event has occurred, or in a state where the event has not occurred. Then for all lotteries the probabilities p and $1 - p$ are the same, where p is the probability of occurrence of the event. Examples of such sets of lotteries are the different bets that might be offered on a certain horse winning a horserace; or the possible house fire insurance contracts one can stipulate, which can differ in the refund and in the downpayments to the insurance company.

The payoffs of these lotteries can be represented as points (vectors) in R^2, a point $\mathbf{x} = (x_1, x_2)$ representing in abscissa the payoff if the event obtains (a situation I shall also call 'state 1') and in ordinate the payoff if the event does not obtain (state 2).

There are two possible states; the figure shows how, given the probability of the two states and a vector (a lottery) $\mathbf{x}$, one can derive the lottery's expected value $E(\mathbf{x})$ and, from the individual's indifference curve through $\mathbf{x}$, its *certainty equivalent* $C(\mathbf{x})$, that is, the vector of same payoff in both states the chooser finds equipreferred to the lottery. It also shows that if the individual starts on the certainty line then with strictly convex indifference curves she will not accept actuarially fair bets since these move the initial point to a new point with the same expected value (e.g. if she starts at $C(\mathbf{x})$ she will not accept a bet corresponding to point $\mathbf{y}$). Note that prizes need not be positive, a negative prize indicates a loss or a sum to pay.

These vectors $\mathbf{x}$ are formally analogous to usual consumption vectors. So we can assume that preferences over these vectors are complete, reflexive, transitive, continuous in the sense of ▶ Chap. 4[14]; let us further assume that they are monotonic. Then there will exist indifference curves in the plane, downward sloping because of monotonicity. Note that it is possible to postulate the existence of a preference order and hence of indifference curves over such vectors of outcomes *without having to assume known probabilities of the two states*; for example, a person might have a preference order over all the possible bets on a certain horse winning a horserace, without having a clear idea of what probability she assigns to the horse's victory. Then the points in R^2 represent **prospects**, that is, couples of state-indexed outcomes *without* a specification of the probability of the two states (we will see later that this is precisely the approach of modern general equilibrium theory). *If* the probabilities of occurrence of the two states *are* known, and if preferences can be represented by expected utility, then we can say something interesting about the slope of the indifference curves when they cross the 45° line, cf. ◼ Fig. 9.1 where state 1 has probability of occurrence p, and state 2 has probability $1 - p$.

---

14 Cf. footnote 3.

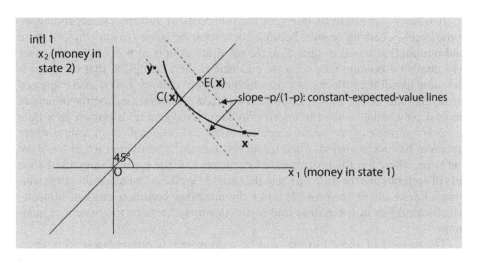

Fig. 9.1 Possible state-indexed outcomes of two-outcome money lotteries. The 45° line is the certainty line

Interpreting lotteries as describing state-indexed money outcomes, if preferences can be represented by an expected utility function, then the latter must have the same subfunction $u(\cdot)$ for all states, see (9.1″) in ▶ Sect. 9.2, which here means that the subutility of money is *state independent*. This assumption may be inappropriate: for example, if the event distinguishing the states is an accident that damages health, one may well question that the level of utility associated with a given amount of money will be the same in the two states. But for now let us assume state-independent utility of money. The subutility function $u(\cdot)$ can be plausibly assumed strictly increasing and continuous. This means that *potentially* the set of payoffs X is not finite; but we will only consider examples with a finite number of alternative payoffs.

The 45° line is called the **certainty line** because its points represent amounts of money that will be available independently of which state occurs, and therefore are certain or sure. The utility of any point $\mathbf{x}^* = (x_1^*, x_2^*)$ on the 45° line $(x_1^* = x_2^* = x^*)$ is therefore $U(\mathbf{x}^*) = pu(x^*) + (1-p)u(x^*) = u(x^*)$. Let us determine the slope at the certainty line of the indifference curve through $\mathbf{x}^*$, the curve $x_2(x_1)$ that satisfies $pu(x_1) + (1-p)u(x_2(x_1)) = u(x^*)$. Let us differentiate both sides of this equality with respect to x_1 in $x_1^* = x_2^*$. We obtain

$$p\frac{du(x_1*)}{dx_1} + (1-p)\frac{du(x_2(x_1*))}{dx_2}\frac{dx_2}{dx_1} = pu' + (1-p)u'x_2' = 0.$$

(The left-hand side can be rewritten as shown because the two derivatives $du(x_i)/dx_i$ are equal since determined at the point where $x_1 = x_2$.) This implies

$$dx_2/dx_1|_{x_1*} = -p/(1-p).$$

This is true at all points on the certainty line. Thus the absolute slope of all indifference curves at the certainty line is the same and measures the ratio between the probabilities of the two states. Tracing a straight line with that slope through any point $\mathbf{x}^*$ on the certainty line, all points $(x^* + dx_1, x^* + dx_2)$ along this line have

9.4 · Risk Aversion and Prospects

the same expected value because $dx_2/dx_1 = -p/(1-p)$ implies $(1-p)dx_2 = -pdx_1$, i.e. $E(d\mathbf{x}) = 0$ where E is the expectation operator.

Now let $\mathbf{x}$ indicate a point *not* on the certainty line; we can find its **expected value** $E(\mathbf{x})$ by tracing a line through $\mathbf{x}$ with slope $-p/(1-p)$ and finding the $\mathbf{x}^*$ at the intersection with the certainty line. On the other hand we can find the **certainty equivalent** $C(\mathbf{x})$ of any vector $\mathbf{x}$ as the amount of the good for sure that yields the same utility as $\mathbf{x}$, that is, as the $\mathbf{x}^{\wedge}$ where the indifference curve through $\mathbf{x}$ crosses the certainty line.

Thus, if indifference curves are strictly convex, the *expected value* of any vector not on the certainty line is greater than the *certainty equivalent* of that vector. This form of indifference curves seems to be a good way to explain the situations in which decision makers reject an **actuarially fair bet**, which is the name given to the payment of an amount of money M to buy the right to the outcomes of a lottery with money prizes whose expected value is M, so that the overall expected value of the bet's outcomes is zero. Example: you bet $10 dollars that the toss of a fair die will produce a 2, in which case you win $60, for any other result of the toss you win nothing; the probability of the toss producing a 2 is 1/6; hence the expected value of $60 is $10; the bet is fair. Acceptance of this bet can be formalized as a lottery where the consumer has initial wealth W, the downpayment is M, the win is either X or zero, and p is the probability of X (so $1-p$ is the probability of winning nothing): the lottery is $p\circ(W-M+X)\oplus(1-p)\circ(W-M)$, and its expected value is $W+pX-M = W$ if the bet is fair, i.e. if $pX = M$. A fair bet in the context of our two states displaces the consumer to a vector $\mathbf{y}$ with the same expected value as the initial situation $\mathbf{x}$, and therefore *below* the indifference curve through $\mathbf{x}$ if $\mathbf{x}$ represents a sure initial wealth and indifference curves are strictly convex: the agent rejects the bet. Cf. $\mathbf{y}$ in ◘ Fig. 9.1, relative to a sure initial wealth $C(\mathbf{x})$.[15] The analysis is obviously generalizable to cases where lotteries have more than two outcomes. This motivates the following definition:

■■ Definition
(*Risk aversion*) Preferences exhibit risk aversion if indifference curves (or, in the case of many states, indifference hypersurfaces) relative to prospects are strictly convex. The definition is local or global depending on whether the convexity of indifference curves holds locally or globally.

Note that this definition of risk aversion does not *need* the existence of well-defined probabilities for the states, only of preferences generating indifference curves over prospects; but it is *motivated* by its interpretability as rejection of fair bets when there are well-defined probabilities.

If probabilities exist and utility has the expected utility form, then risk aversion implies for two-state lotteries that if $\mathbf{x}$ is not on the certainty line and both states have nonzero probability, then $E(\mathbf{x}) > C(\mathbf{x})$. Since the utility of $C(\mathbf{x})$ is the same as the expected utility of the lottery,

---

15 Then does risk aversion *not* apply to roulette gamblers? It may well apply, and yet be compensated by the pleasure of gambling. We are implicitly assuming that only the money result of the lottery affects preferences, but this is often untrue.

746   Chapter 9 · Uncertainty and General Equilibrium

Implication of Risk Aversion   *Risk aversion means that if $p \in (0, 1)$ and outcomes differ, obtaining for sure the expected value of a lottery* L *is preferred to the lottery*: $u(E(L)) > u(L)$.

If one is indifferent between a lottery and obtaining its expected value for sure, one is **risk neutral**. If one prefers a lottery to its expected value, one is **risk loving**.[16] Risk neutrality means straight-line indifference curves, and risk love means strictly concave indifference curves.

9.5 Risk Aversion and Convexity of Expected Utility

With VNM utility, risk aversion implies a specific form of the basic utility function $u(x)$: it must be strictly concave; that is, the marginal utility of x (wealth or money) must be decreasing; thus when wealth (or more generally the amount of a single good) is the payoff, risk aversion and decreasing marginal utility are equivalent ways to characterize the situation.

◘ Figure 9.2 illustrates. A consumer faces a lottery L yielding wealth x_1 with probability p and wealth x_2 with probability $1 - p$. Draw utility as a function $u(x)$ of sure wealth x; A and B are the points on this function corresponding to x_1 and x_2; $u(x)$ must be drawn strictly concave to represent risk aversion, as I proceed to prove. The expected value or mean $E(L) = px_1 + (1 - p)x_2$ is a point between x_1 and x_2 in abscissa, whose position depends on p and moves towards x_1 as p increases; for brevity let us indicate it as x^*. The expected utility *of the lottery* is $u(L) = pu(x_1) + (1 - p)u(x_2)$ and is the height of the point vertically above x^* on the segment joining points A and B. The utility $u(x^*) = u(px_1 + (1 - p)x_2)$ *of a sure wealth equal to the expected value of the lottery* is the height of the point on $u(x)$ vertically above x^*. Risk aversion requires $u(x^*) = u(px_1 + (1 - p)x_2) > pu(x_1) + (1 - p)u(x_2)$ for any $p \in (0, 1)$, and this is precisely the definition of a strictly concave function.

If we indicate $x_1 = x^* + a$, $x_2 = x^* - b$, we can also interpret the lottery as resulting from an initial wealth $W = x^*$ plus acceptance of a fair bet offering a win a with probability p, or a loss b with probability $1 - p$. Thus risk aversion is shown to imply rejection of fair bets.

The figure also shows how to find the *certainty equivalent* $C(L)$ of lottery L: it is the point in abscissa that indicates the amount of sure wealth yielding the same utility as L. The difference $x^* - C(L)$ is called the **risk avoidance price**, or **risk premium**, or **willingness to pay** (to avoid risk), that is, the maximum amount of wealth the consumer starting with wealth x^* would be ready to give up in order to avoid the gamble $p \circ a \oplus (1 - p) \circ -b$. The risk premium is the segment in abscissa between point x^* and point $C(L)$.

◘ Figure 9.2 also illustrates the effect of a *mean-preserving spread* of the outcomes: assume that, with p constant, the two outcomes 'spread out', in the sense that their distance from the lottery's unchanged mean increases, that is, a and b increase while x^* remains unchanged. In ◘ Fig. 9.2 point A moves to point A' on

---

16 Note that being risk loving is not the same as deriving pleasure from gambling.

9.5 · Risk Aversion and Convexity of Expected Utility

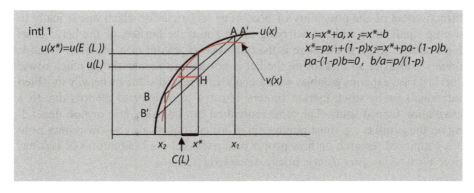

Fig. 9.2 Given a lottery $L = p \circ x_1 \oplus (1-p) \circ x_2$, the lottery's expected utility varies with p along the segment AB, from B for $p=0$, to A for $p=1$; the lottery's mean x^* reveals p graphically, and once determined it allows describing the prizes as $x_1 = x^* + a$ and $x_2 = x^* - b$. (In the figure, $p = 1/2$.) The certainty equivalent $C(L)$ is the quantity of wealth for sure yielding the same expected utility as L; the thick segment from $C(L)$ to x^* measures the *risk premium*. The line A'B' represents the shift the AB line would undergo with a *mean-preserving spread* consisting of an increase of x_1 and decrease of x_2: it shows that $u(L)$ decreases, to the altitude of point H. Also shown, in red, is a different more concave utility function $v(x)$ with $v(x^*) = u(x^*)$, chosen for graphical simplicity so that the segment connecting $v(x_1)$ and $v(x_2)$ lies on the same line as A'B'; so now H indicates $v(L)$, the risk premium is the thick red horizontal segment

its right and B moves to B' on its left on the $u(x)$ curve: the line connecting them shifts downwards, so $u(L)$ and $C(L)$ decrease: the risk premium (not shown) is now greater than before the spread.

The intuition for the effect of a mean-preserving spread can also be obtained from ◘ Fig. 9.1: a movement from any vector **x** to another vector **x'** with the same expected value but further *away* from the certainty line corresponds to the shift from line A-B to line A'-B' in ◘ Fig. 9.2, and it means a passage to a lower indifference curve.

In ◘ Fig. 9.2 an alternative utility function $v(x)$ (the red curve) has also been drawn, more concave than $u(x)$ but such that $v(x^*) = u(x^*)$ so as to favour comparison. For the same lottery L the greater concavity causes the A-B line to be lower than with $u(x)$, so the risk premium (the thick red horizontal segment) is greater. One then says that $v(x)$ shows *greater risk aversion* than $u(x)$.

Is risk aversion a universal phenomenon? Clearly not, for example it does not explain the acceptance of gambles known to be unfair, like buying tickets of lotteries known to give back in prizes much less than the total revenue from the sale of tickets.

Exercise Prove formally that if a ticket lottery with a single prize pays back to the winner the total amount earned by selling tickets, then the lottery is actuarially fair, and therefore a risk-averse individual should not buy a ticket.

Purchases of unfair lottery tickets or gambling with unfair slot machines can be explained as due to the excitement of gambling (i.e. one derives utility not only from the prizes but also from the activity itself of gambling); or as due to the

748   Chapter 9 · Uncertainty and General Equilibrium

attractiveness of the possibility of becoming very rich, for which one is ready to give up small sums without worrying much about the fairness of the bet;[17] or as due to desperation, if the prize is the only way to get out of a situation which is already a disaster so that losing the bet is not going to make things much worse (this last case explains gambles with a negative expected value by heavily indebted individuals or by stock market traders who try to recuperate the loss due to a speculation turned sour). The same individual can be risk averse or not, depending on the gamble, e.g. most purchasers of lottery tickets also buy insurance policies. Empirical research on how people concretely behave in situations of risk has given birth to *prospect theory*, briefly discussed later.

9.6 Comparing the Riskiness of Lotteries: Stochastic Dominance

Suppose the decision maker must choose between two different actions, 'F' and 'G', whose scalar outcomes (e.g. amounts of money) are two different random variables; what characteristics of the two different probability distributions allow one to conclude *unambiguously* that one action is preferable? Assume outcomes can take any value x on the continuous real line, and let $f(x)$ and $g(x)$ be the two density functions with associated cumulative density functions (distribution functions) $F(x)$ and $G(x)$. We can define two notions of 'better' distribution.

First-Order Stochastic Dominance $F(x)$ *first-order stochastically dominates* $G(x)$ if $F(x) \leq G(x)$ *for all x, and* $\exists\ x°$ *such that* $F(x°) < G(x°)$.

This means that the graph of $F(x)$ is always not above, and at least in a neighbourhood of a certain $x°$ is below, the graph of $G(x)$; that is, for each given outcome x, action 'F' has a not lower probability, and a higher one for some x, than 'G', of obtaining a better outcome. So the mean or expected value of the 'F' distribution is higher, and accordingly 'F' is preferred as long as the decision maker has an increasing utility function.

Second-Order Stochastic Dominance $F(x)$ *second-order stochastically dominates* $G(x)$ if *for all x it is* $\int_{-\infty}^{x} F(t)dt \leq \int_{-\infty}^{x} G(t)dt$ *and* $\exists\ x°$ *such that* $\int_{-\infty}^{x°} F(t)dt < \int_{-\infty}^{x°} G(t)dt$.

In words, for each possible outcome x the area included between the abscissa and the distribution function $F(x)$ from $-\infty$ to x is always not greater, and smaller at least for $x°$, than the corresponding area below $G(x)$. The economic meaning becomes evident if we assume that $F(x)$ and $G(x)$ have the same mean; then if $F(x)$ second-order dominates $G(x)$ it must be because for some interval of val-

---

17 There is reason to suspect that people tend not to calculate expected values when the gamble involves a very small loss versus a very large (although highly improbable) gain; most people have only the vaguest idea of the probability of winning the big prizes of important lotteries. The anticipation of a **regret** if one completely gives up the possibility, however improbable, of becoming very rich is probably an important reason why one buys lottery tickets.

9.6 · Comparing the Riskiness of Lotteries: Stochastic Dominance

ues of x it is $F(x) < G(x)$ and for some higher values of x it is $F(x) > G(x)$.[18] Then $G(x)$ can be viewed as a mean-preserving spread of $F(x)$, and we know that this reduces the utility of the associated lottery if there is risk aversion.

9.7 The St. Petersburg Paradox

An interesting example of risk aversion is the *St. Petersburg Paradox*. The following gamble is proposed: a fair coin is flipped until heads appears; if this happens at the nth flip, the prize is 2^n dollars. What sum M would you be ready to pay for the right to this uncertain prize? The following table illustrates the probability of the prizes and their expected values:

flip	1	2	3	4	5	n
prize if heads first comes out at this flip	2	4	8	16	32	2^n
probability p of heads first coming out at this flip	1/2	1/4	1/8	1/16	1/32	$1/2^n$
expected value of prize	1	1	1	1		1

The expected value of the gamble is the sum of the expected values of the prizes: $1 + 1 + 1 + \ldots = +\infty$! If one were risk neutral one should be ready to pay her entire wealth for the right to a single play of this gamble. On the contrary, people are only ready to pay a modest amount of money, not much above 4 dollars in most cases according to some experimental evidence. Bernoulli, one of the founders of probability theory, proposed to explain this paradox by assuming what was in fact expected utility, with wealth w having a decreasing marginal utility due to $u(w) = log \, w$. A naive way to approach the determination of M is to assume that the utility function $log \, w$ applies to the *wins*, and that a person will be ready to pay a maximum M equal to the certainty equivalent of the expected utility of the prizes; the latter can be calculated easily:[19]

$$\sum_{n=1}^{\infty} p_n u(prize_n) = \sum_{n=1}^{\infty} \frac{1}{2^n} log \, 2^n = \sum_{n=1}^{\infty} \frac{1}{2^n} n \, log \, 2$$

$$= log \, 2 \sum_{n=1}^{\infty} \frac{n}{2^n} = 2 \, log \, 2 = log \, 2^2 = log \, 4.$$

This implies the certainty equivalent is 4, so maximum $M = 4$. This is not far from the empirical evidence, so the procedure may be close to how people *actually* reach a decision in this case; but the correct way to approach the problem, if one

---

18 So second-order stochastic dominance does not imply first-order stochastic dominance. *Exercise*: Does first-order stochastic dominance imply second-order stochastic dominance?

19 This result requires finding the value to which the series $\Sigma n x^n$ converges, and then setting $x = 1/2$ in it. Consider the geometric series $1 + x + x^2 + \ldots + x^n + \ldots = 1/(1 - x)$ for $0 < x < 1$; differentiate both sides to obtain $0 + 1 + 2x + 3x^2 + 4x^3 + \ldots + n x^{n-1} + \ldots = 1/(1 - x)^2$; rewrite the left-hand side as $1 + x + x + 2x^2 + x^2 + 3x^3 + x^3 + \ldots = (1 + x + x^2 + \ldots + x^n + \ldots) + \Sigma n x^n$, hence $\Sigma n x^n = 1/(1 - x)^2 - 1/(1-x) = x/(1 - x)^2 = 2$ if $x = 1/2$.

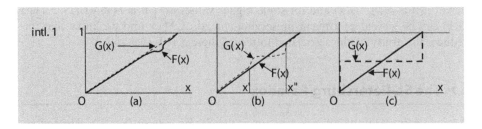

• **Fig. 9.3** Distribution functions of outcomes x. In **a** $F(x)$ first-order dominates $G(x)$; in **b**, $G(x)$ is a mean-preserving spread of $F(x)$ that has reallocated the probabilities of outcomes between x' and x'' from a constant probability to a greater probability for outcomes close to x' and to x'' and very little probability in between. (*Exercise*: imagine the possible outcomes in $F(x)$ and $G(x)$ in (**b**) or (**c**) in • Fig. 9.3 to be a high but finite number of regularly spaced outcomes, all with the same probability in $F(x)$; interpret the mean-preserving spread as a number of mean-preserving spreads applied to sublotteries of two outcomes equally distant from the mean. Then apply the reasoning used for the mean-preserving spread in • Fig. 9.2 to explain why $G(x)$ has lower expected utility.) It is second-order stochastically dominated by $F(x)$. In (**c**) the mean-preserving spread has been rendered extreme

assumes a concave utility of *wealth* in a VNM utility function, is to assume that the expected utility $u(L)$ of the lottery is the expected utility of the amounts of wealth one can obtain *taking into account the starting wealth and the payment of M*, so it is $u(w_n) = u(W - M + prize_n)$ where W is initial wealth, M is the payment for the right to the prizes, n the flip where heads first comes out; the maximum M one is ready to pay is determined as the one that renders $u(L)$ equal to initial utility $u(W) = \log W$, that is the M that satisfies the equality:

$$u(L) = \sum_{n=1}^{\infty} p_n u(w_n) = \sum_{n=1}^{\infty} \frac{1}{2^n} \log(W - M + 2^n) = \log W;$$

so M is a complicated implicit function of W. Deaton and Muellbauer (1980, p. 388) report that assuming, differently from the example above, that the prize at the nth flip is 2^{n-1}, and that initial wealth is $W = 100$, it is $M \cong 4.4$, nearly double what the empirical evidence shows (which would be around 2.5 for this case), indicating that people are even more risk averse than Bernoulli suggested.

9.8 Cardinality of VNM Utility

The meaning of 'decreasing marginal utility of wealth' may appear obscure to people accustomed to the usual utility function of consumer theory only defined up to an increasing monotonic transformation, so that for the same preferences marginal utilities can be decreasing or increasing depending on the transformation one applies. The fact that the subutility $u(\cdot)$ in the VNM expected utility function $U(\cdot) = \sum_s p_s u(x_s)$ is defined up to an affine transformation has induced some economists to say that the VNM axioms imply that utility has *cardinal* significance, rather than simply ordinal significance; that is to say, that like with length, weight or temperature, it makes sense to say that the amount by which the

9.8 · Cardinality of VNM Utilitys

utility or satisfaction or happiness or pleasure intensity yielded by two outcomes A and B differ is greater, or smaller, than the amount by which the utility or satisfaction or happiness or pleasure intensity yielded by two other outcomes C and D differs, which is what cardinality of a measure implies. Utility is shown to be after all something concrete whose quantity can be measured. This interpretation does not appear warranted, as explained in an excellent 1954 article by Daniel Ellsberg that I very strongly recommend. The number $u(x)$ assigned to a sure outcome x by a VNM utility function is, not a measure of the cardinal amount of satisfaction (or happiness or pleasure intensity) yielded by that outcome, but a probability: the probability which—given for example two reference outcomes E_1 and E_0 such that $E_1 \succ x \succ E_0$—must be assigned to the better outcome E_1 in the reference lottery $p \circ E_1 \oplus (1 - p) \circ E_0$ in order that the consumer be indifferent between x and this lottery. Therefore for example the fact that $u(x) = 2u(y)$ does not indicate that x yields twice as much satisfaction as y; it only indicates that the probability p_x that makes the reference lottery $p_x \circ E_1 \oplus (1 - p_x) \circ E_0$ equipreferred to x is twice the probability p_y that makes the same lottery equipreferred to y. Even if one thought that it makes sense to speak of the quantity of satisfaction yielded by x or by y as something cardinal, there would be no reason to think that because p_x is twice p_y the quantity of satisfaction is twice for x what it is for y. (Here I do not intend to discuss whether it makes sense or not to speak of a cardinal quantity of satisfaction. Certainly in some cases a person is ready to say that A is *much* more preferable to B than C is to D, e.g. that not losing a leg is immensely more important than not losing a thousand dollars, or perhaps that obtaining an income increase from 20,000 to 22,000 dollars a year would yield her less pleasure than an income increase from 50,000 to 80,000. What is not clear is whether such statements say more than that one would be ready to renounce to more of something else—which would have only ordinal significance—, and if so what importance this has for the explanation of economic choices.) Thus if x is income, a concavity of the utility of income $u(x)$ expressing risk aversion does not mean that additional units of income yield a smaller and smaller addition to subjective satisfaction or pleasure, it only says that the increase in the probability p_x in the reference lottery $p \circ E_1 \oplus (1 - p) \circ E_0$, required to maintain equipreference with an income increased by one dollar, becomes smaller and smaller as income increases. As pointed out by Baumol in another useful article on the issue, what this concavity expresses is only that there is a decreasing marginal rate of substitution between (i.e. a decreasing ratio of the marginal utilities of) income and the probability of winning E_1 instead of E_0; and the same would hold if instead of income we spoke of marginal VNM utility of apples: 'Only if we are prepared to assume that we know the behaviour of the denominator of the MRS, the marginal subjective utility of an increase in the probability of winning, can we go on to make deductions about the marginal subjective utility of apples from VNM index data' (Baumol 1959, p. 669).

Ellsberg's paper is also very nice as an indication of reasons why the VNM axioms, on the surface convincing, upon further examination are less so. For example, if you found the equivalence or reducibility axiom obviously acceptable, go and read Ellsberg's lively counterexample (Ellsberg 1954, p. 543).

752   Chapter 9 · Uncertainty and General Equilibrium

9.9 Insurance

The situation of ◘ Fig. 9.2 is used to explain why people accept insurance contracts. Consider insurance against, say, house fire. Interpret x_1 as wealth if no fire happens (i.e. initial wealth W), and x_2 as wealth if a fire happens, causing a loss or damage $D = x_1 - x_2$, reducing wealth to $x_2 = W{-}D$. The probability of a fire is known to be $1 - p$. Then

$$x^* = px_1 + (1 - p)x_2$$

is the expected value of the lottery the consumer faces without insurance,[20] while $C(L)$ is the certainty equivalent of the lottery, i.e. the sure amount of wealth that the consumer finds equipreferred to the gamble, $u(C(L)) = u(L)$. As ◘ Fig. 9.2 shows, owing to risk aversion it is $C(L) < x^*$, so if someone offers the consumer an insurance contract that assures the consumer a *certain* wealth $x^{\wedge}$ greater than $C(L)$ in exchange for the payment of $x_1 - x^{\wedge}$ as 'premium' (insurance price, or downpayment), the consumer accepts. The certainty of $x^{\wedge}$ is established by a contract stipulating that the consumer pays $x_1 - x^{\wedge}$ for sure, and receives $x^{\wedge} - x_2$ if and only if the fire happens. The maximum downpayment the consumer is ready to pay is the one corresponding to $x^{\wedge} = C(L)$, which means renouncing, relative to her initial *expected* wealth x^*, the amount $x^* - C(L)$; which explains why this latter amount is called **risk premium**[21] or *risk avoidance price*.

Suppose now for simplicity that all consumers and all fire insurance contracts are identical, and that the risks of house fire of different consumers are independent. The insurance company, by insuring a high number of consumers, owing to the law of large numbers can be practically certain to pay damages to a percentage $1 - p$ of insured customers on average, so it has little reason to be risk averse; if it had no expenses, it would be capable of guaranteeing its customers a certain wealth x^* by asking for $x_1 - x^*$ as 'premium' (downpayment); by offering only $x^{\wedge} < x^*$ (and asking for $x_1 - x^{\wedge}$ as premium) the insurance company obtains a difference between earnings and payments with which it can cover administrative expenses and earn a rate of profit on its capital. Thus one can say, as a first approximation, that *it is risk aversion that makes the existence of insurance companies possible*. If the company were a monopolist, it would offer an $x^{\wedge}$ for sure only infinitesimally greater than $C(L)$; with free entry and competition, $x^{\wedge}$ will tend to be the highest one allowing insurance companies to cover administrative expenses and to earn the normal rate of return on their capital.

---

20 One can also see x^* as initial wealth x_1 minus the *expected value* of the damage $x_1{-}x_2$, i.e. $x^* = x_1 - (1 - p)(x_1 - x_2)$. In an example below the expected value of the damage is indicated as d.

21 The term 'premium' can create confusion: it is used (without adjective) in commercial language to indicate what the customer pays for the insurance coverage, the downpayment, $x_1{-}x^{\wedge}$ in our example, it must not be confused with the 'risk premium'. To add to the risk of confusion, 'risk premium' is also used to mean a very different notion in portfolio theory, see below.

9.10 Actuarially Fair Insurance and Risk Premium

Let us see some further results in the theory of insurance, derivable from the assumption that consumers have preferences of expected utility form. Imagine an individual facing the possibility of a loss of money owing to some event, and considering whether to insure against this loss. Let us indicate with:

W – the given initial *wealth*,

D – the damage or loss of wealth (a single value, for simplicity) the insuree suffers if the bad event occurs, measured in money,

p – the probability of D occurring, assumed independent of the insuree's actions[22] (careful: I am now indicating the probability of the damage as p, while before it was $1 - p$),

q – the 'insurance coverage', i.e. the number of units of the *conditional good* 'one dollar the insurance company will pay in case D occurs',[23]

π – the given 'premium' or fee or dowpayment to be paid by the insuree to the insurance company *per dollar* of coverage.

P – the 'total premium' or total cost πq of the insurance contract.

If the individual insures for an insurance coverage q, she pays πq for sure and obtains wealth $W - \pi q$ if D does not occur, $W - D - \pi q + q$ if D occurs. The individual chooses q so as to maximize expected utility $(1 - p)u(W - \pi q) + pu(W - D - \pi q + q)$. The first-order condition is, with $u' = \partial u/\partial q$:

$$-(1 - p)\pi u'(W - \pi q) + p(1 - \pi)u'(W - D - \pi q + q) = 0,$$

that is,

$$\frac{u'(W - D - \pi q + q)}{u'(W - \pi q)} = \frac{\pi}{(1 - \pi)} \cdot \frac{(1 - p)}{p}.$$

Now suppose the insurance company offers an actuarially fair contract, that is, $p = \pi$, because competition with entry reduces expected pure profit to zero, and the insurance company—we assume for simplicity—has no costs other than the payment of coverages, in which case expected pure profit is, on each insurance contract, $p(\pi q - q) + (1 - p)\pi q = (p - \pi)q$, implying $p = \pi$ if expected pure profit is zero. An *actuarially fair gamble or bet* is, as already indicated, one that offers

---

22 In many cases the probability of the damage depends on the individual's actions: e.g. a house fire, or falling ill and in need of medical assistance, can depend on how careless one is. This problem of *moral hazard* (the decrease of the insuree's incentive to avoid actions favouring a bad event if the damage deriving from it is reduced by insurance, which makes the probability of the bad event depend on the extent of insurance), that requires a different approach and will be discussed in ▶ Chap. 11, is the reason why most insurance contracts do not offer 'full coverage' (full reimbursement of the damage); the difference between damage and reimbursement, called *franchise clause*, necessarily borne by the insuree, is intended to discourage her from acting carelessly.

23 A conditional good is a good to be delivered to the purchaser only if a certain event or state of nature obtains. Cf. below, ▶ Sect. 9.28.

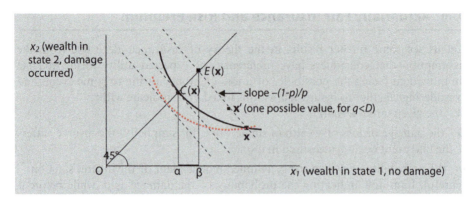

Fig. 9.4 This figure reproduces **Fig. 9.1**, adding the indication of the risk premium or risk avoidance price, segment $\alpha\beta$; it also shows that a more convex indifference curve through **x** (the dotted red one) would cause the risk premium to be greater because it causes the certainty equivalent to be smaller. With actuarially fair insurance, as q rises $\mathbf{x}'$ moves up the constant-expected-value line

a win whose expected value equals what one pays for the gamble; to accept a fair bet leaves the expected value of wealth unchanged. If the customer pays πq and receives q with probability $p = \pi$ the expected value of receiving q is $pq = \pi q$, the insurance contract is fair. If $p = \pi$ then the right-hand side of the second way of writing the above first-order condition equals 1, implying equality of the marginal utilities on the left-hand side and therefore, since u is strictly concave, a marginal utility determined at the same value of $u(\cdot)$ at the numerator and at the denominator, i.e. $(W - D - \pi q + q) = (W - \pi q)$, i.e. $D = q$. This shows that the individual chooses *complete insurance*: she pays πq and is left with $W - \pi q$, and in case D happens she receives $q = D$ and finds herself again with $W - \pi q$. So she obtains $W - \pi q$ for sure, and since the insurance contract is fair, this means $W - \pi q$ equals the expected value of the lottery $E(L) = p(W - D) + (1 - p)W$, corresponding to wealth x^* in **Fig. 9.2**.

A clear intuition for this result can be obtained from **Fig. 9.4**. Let **x** represent the payoffs of the lottery without insurance, with initial wealth in abscissa and, in ordinate, wealth in case the damage occurs: $x_1 = W$, $x_2 = W - D$; since p is now the probability of D occurring, in this figure it is x_2 that has probability p; therefore differently from the case in **Fig. 9.1**, the constant-expected-value lines have slope $-(1 - p)/p$; the expected value of this lottery is $E(\mathbf{x}) = p(W - D) + (1 - p)W$. If the customer buys q dollars of coverage, paying πq for it, the point representing the lottery with insurance becomes $\mathbf{x}' = (W - \pi q, W - \pi q - D + q)$, that is, as q increases $\mathbf{x}'$ moves North-West from **x** along a straight line of slope $-(1 - \pi)/\pi$. If insurance is actuarially fair, $p = \pi$, then this 'insurance line' coincides with the constant-expected-value line, so for any q the expected value of the lottery with insurance is the same as without insurance, $\pi(W - D - \pi q + q) + (1 - p)(W - \pi q) = p(W - D) + p(1 - \pi)q + (1 - p)W - (1 - \pi)\pi q = p(W - D) + (1 - p)W$. Then the customer finds it optimal to reach the point $E(\mathbf{x})$ on the certainty line. By insuring

9.10 · Actuarially Fair Insurance and Risk Premium

completely the individual obtains the utility of the expected value of the lottery for sure, and therefore avoids the loss in utility associated with risk aversion.

Example (Here ◘ Fig. 9.2 is more helpful.) A family with wealth m has utility $u(m) = m^{1/2}$ and the family has VNM utility relative to choices under uncertainty. The family's initial wealth is $m_1 = 100$, and there is a $p = 50\%$ probability of a damage $D = 64$, which would reduce wealth to $m_2 = 36$.

1. Determine the expected value $E(m)$ of the family's wealth without insurance.
2. Determine the expected utility of the lottery L describing the two possible wealths of the family if no insurance is purchased.
3. Determine the maximum total premium P the family is ready to pay for complete insurance, and the associated risk avoidance price R, i.e. benefit from elimination of risk, and show that $P = d + R$ (where d is the *expected value* of the damage reimbursement with complete insurance).

Solution. Expected value of wealth: $E(m) = 100(1 - p) + 36p = 68$. $L = 1/2 \circ 100 \oplus 1/2 \circ 36$, its expected utility is $u(L) = 1/2 \cdot 10 + 1/2 \cdot 6 = 8$. Certainty equivalent of L: $C(L) = 64$, the certain wealth that has utility 8. Maximum P payable for complete insurance: the one that reduces initial wealth 100 to the level yielding the same utility $u = 8$ as without insurance, therefore $P = 36$ that reduces wealth to $C(L) = 64$. $R = E(m) - C(L) = 4$; d is the *expected value* of the reimbursement, i.e. of the damage (because of full insurance), hence $d = pD = 32$; and $E(m) = m_1(1 - p) + (m_1 - D)p = m_1 - Dp = m_1 - d$, $C(L) = m_1 - P$, hence $R = E(m) - C(L) = P - d$.

9.11 Unfair Insurance

In order to cover administrative costs and, possibly, some risk aversion of the owners, insurance companies do not offer actuarially fair insurance contracts. We can understand the effect in terms of the two-states diagram (◘ Fig. 9.5).

Now $\pi > p$, so as q rises point $\mathbf{x'}$ moves North-West from $\mathbf{x}$ along an 'insurance line' (the continuous straight line through $\mathbf{x}$) less steep than the constant-expected-value line. If the consumer is free to choose q, and if at $\mathbf{x}$ the 'insurance line' is steeper than the indifference curve through $\mathbf{x}$, utility is maximized at the point $\mathbf{y}$ of tangency between the 'insurance line' and indifference curve, so she insures only partially.[24]

The analysis of the same case through ◘ Fig. 9.2 is as follows, cf. ◘ Figure 9.6. With fair insurance ($\pi = p$) we have seen that the consumer insures completely, that is, buys a coverage $q = D$, pays πq, and is left with $x^* = W - \pi q = W - \pi D$ for sure, which is the expected value of the original lottery. To understand the effect of $\pi > p$, start from the case $\pi = p$ but less than com-

---

24 If the insurance company is risk neutral and can decide both q and π, what is the choice that maximizes its profit?

756   Chapter 9 · Uncertainty and General Equilibrium

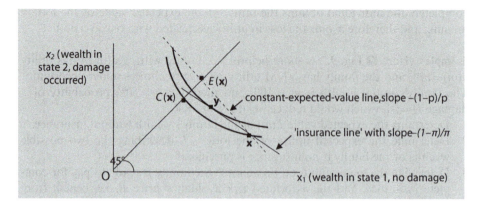

◘ Fig. 9.5   Unfair insurance

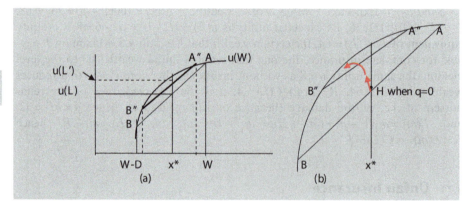

◘ Fig. 9.6   Figure a: $u(L')$ is utility when $q<D$ but $p=\pi$ and therefore the expected value of L' remains equal to x^*. b: enlarged portion of $u(x)$ with path of point H as q increases from zero, when $\pi>p$

plete insurance, the case shown in ◘ Fig. 9.6a: with $q<D$ and $p=\pi$ the expected value of the lottery $L'=p\circ(W-D-\pi q+q)\oplus(1-p)\circ(W-\pi q)$ remains equal to $x^*=W-pD$; hence $u(L')$ is the point in ordinate corresponding to where the vertical line that starts at x^* crosses the segment that connects the points A'' and B'' corresponding, respectively, on the curve $u(x)$, to $x=W-\pi q$ and to $x=W-D-\pi q+q$; A'' moves to the left, and B'' to the right, as q increases, so the segment $A''B''$ shifts upwards and becomes shorter, and $u(L')$ rises with q, which is why it is best for the consumer to go all the way to $q=D$, which causes A'' and B'' to coincide. If on the contrary $\pi>p$, for a given $q>0$ the points A'' and B'' are both more to the left than with $\pi=p$, and if q rose up to becoming equal to D, they would coincide, corresponding to $x=W-\pi L<x^*$; but the optimum is at $q<D$, because the first-order condition tells us that if $\pi>p$ it must be $u'(B'')/u'(A'')>1$ at the optimum, that is, q is such that B'' is to the left of A'' on the utility curve. The point is that now the expected value of L' equals $W-pD-(\pi-p)q$, which concides with x^* only if $q=0$; otherwise it is less, and

9.11 · Unfair Insurance

it decreases as q increases; there are therefore two effects on $u(L')$ as q increases from zero, a positive effect deriving from the A''-B'' segment moving upwards, and a negative one deriving from the leftward movement of the point $E(L')$ in abscissa, from which (going up vertically) one obtains the point on the A''-B'' segment, call it H (not shown in the left-hand figure), that determines $u(L')$. Thus as q rises, point H moves up and to the left.[25] Evidently as q increases the negative effect becomes stronger than the positive effect before A'' and B'' come to coincide; that is, as q increases point H traces a concave curve upwards and leftwards that turns *downwards* before touching the curve $u(x)$, as shown in red in ◼ Fig. 9.6b: the uppermost point of this path corresponds to optimum q.

9.12 Measuring Risk Aversion: Arrow–Pratt

For the case of scalar payoffs, ◼ Fig. 9.5 shows that the risk premium is the greater, the greater the convexity of indifference curves; ◼ Fig. 9.2 shows that the risk premium is the greater, the greater the concavity of the expected utility $u(x)$. In applications, the approach illustrated in ◼ Fig. 9.2 is the more frequent one; then a measure of the concavity of $u(x)$ can be useful; it must measure how fast the slope of $u(x)$ decreases if x increases. The most widely used measure is

$$-\frac{u''(x)}{u'(x)},$$

the absolute value of the ratio between second and first derivative of $u(x)$. This is called the ***Arrow–Pratt measure of absolute risk aversion***. When applied to the expected utility of wealth, it indicates how fast its slope decreases as wealth increases: the second derivative alone does not suffice, because it is altered by affine transformations of the expected utility function, which as we know do not alter preferences and maintain the expected utility form; division by u' makes the measure independent of such transformations. Its appropriateness as a measure of risk aversion can be shown in two ways. First, the utility curve in red in ◼ Fig. 9.2 has the same slope as the other one at x^* and is more concave; thus its Arrow–Pratt measure is greater, and indeed it causes a greater risk avoidance price (a smaller certainty equivalent) for the same lottery, indicating a greater loss of utility due to risk aversion. Second, the Arrow–Pratt measure indicates how convex the indifference curves of ◼ Fig. 9.1 are at the certainty line. Let us go back to indicating with p the probability of the state in abscissa. Consider the indifference curve through the point $\mathbf{w} = (w, w)$ indicating the initial sure wealth w of a consumer who is offered gambles consisting of a win x_1 with probability p, and a loss x_2 (a negative number) with probability $1 - p$; if the consumer accepts one such gamble, her wealth becomes a lottery $p \circ (w + x_1) \oplus (1 - p)(w + x_2)$. The set of gambles the consumer will accept is the set of points on or above the

---

25 This is so if the consumer finds it convenient to buy at least some insurance coverage; it is also possible that π be so high that the consumer does not insure at all: this is the case corresponding in ◼ Fig. 9.4 to an 'insurance line' through $\mathbf{x}$ not steeper there than the indifference curve.

758   **Chapter 9 · Uncertainty and General Equilibrium**

indifference curve through $\mathbf{w}$; this is called her *acceptance set*. The acceptance set will be the smaller, the more convex the indifference curve through $\mathbf{w}$, indicating that fewer gambles will be accepted. We can say then that risk aversion is (at least locally) the greater for small gambles from a certain initial wealth, the more convex the indifference curves at the certainty line. We have already seen that at the certainty line all indifference curves have slope $x_2'(x_1) = -p/(1-p)$; hence this holds at $x_1 = 0$, i.e. at point $\mathbf{w}$. Let us differentiate again with respect to x_1 in $x_1 = x_2 = 0$ both sides of the equality from which this result was derived:

$$p \frac{\partial u(w + x_1)}{\partial x_1} + (1-p) \frac{\partial u(w + x_2(x_1))}{\partial x_2} \frac{dx_2}{dx_1}$$
$$= pu' + (1-p)u'x_2'(0) = 0.$$

We obtain $\partial u^2/\partial x_1^2 = \partial u^2/\partial x_2^2 = u''(w)$ because both calculated where $x_1 = x_2$, hence:

$$pu''(w) + (1-p)\left[u''(w)x_2'(0)x_2'(0) + u''(w)x_2''(0)\right] = 0$$

from which, using the fact that $x_2'(x_1) = -p/(1-p)$ *at* $x_1 = 0$, one obtains

$$x_2''(0) = \frac{p}{(1-p)^2}\left(-\frac{u''(w)}{u'(w)}\right).$$

Thus the convexity of the indifference curve is the greater, the greater is the Arrow–Pratt measure of risk aversion; a consumer with a smaller Arrow–Pratt measure will accept all the gambles accepted by a consumer with a greater Arrow–Pratt measure, plus some more, indicating less risk aversion.

A property of this measure is that *for small bets it is approximately proportional to the risk premium or risk avoidance price*. Let us prove it.

Let the payoffs of a fair bet on wealth be a random variable h, with $E(h)=0$. Indicate the risk premium as R and the initial sure wealth as W, with the possible values of h small relative to W. By the definitions of certainty equivalent and of risk premium it is

$$E[u(W + h)] = u(W-R).$$

On the left-hand side we have the expected utility of the random wealth $W+h$; on the right-hand side we have the utility of the certainty equivalent $W-R$. Let us expand both sides in Taylor's series. For the right-hand side one can stop at the second term since R is a fixed amount:

$$u(W - R) = u(W) - Ru'(W) + higher\text{-}order\ terms.$$

For the left-hand side it is better to include the third term to allow for the variability of h:

$$E[u(W + h)] = E\left[u(W) + hu'(W) + \frac{h^2}{2}u''(W) + higher\text{-}order\ terms\right]$$
$$= u(W) + E(h)u'(W) + 1/2E\left(h^2\right)u''(W) + higher\text{-}order\ terms.$$

9.12 · Measuring Risk Aversion: Arrow–Pratt

Remembering $E(h)=0$, noting that $E(h^2)$ is the variance of h, and neglecting higher-order terms, we obtain $\frac{1}{2}E(h^2)u''(W) \cong -Ru'(W)$, i.e.

$$R \cong -\frac{u''(W)}{u'(W)}\frac{Var(h)}{2}. \tag{9.7}$$

The risk premium is approximately equal to the Arrow-Pratt measure of absolute risk aversion multiplied by half the variance of h.

The above was calculated assuming that the initial wealth was precisely the expected value of the lottery $(W+h)$. But the reasoning still holds when that is not the case, by replacing W with the expected value x^* of the random variable 'wealth'. The Arrow–Pratt measure must then be calculated at x^*. We can determine the (approximate) certainty equivalent of the random variable 'wealth' with expected value x^* as $x^* - R = x^* - \left[-\frac{u''(W)}{u'(W)}\frac{Var(x*)}{2} \right]$.

I illustrate with a numerical example. Take the kind of situation considered earlier that may induce one to buy insurance against a possible house fire causing a loss D. Assume *initial* wealth is $W^*=625$; $u(W)=W^{1/2}$; $D=225$ with a probability 10% of happening. The lottery the uninsured individual faces is $L=0.1 \circ 400 \oplus 0.9 \circ 625$; the expected value of wealth it implies is $x^*=E(W)=602.5$. The expected utility of the lottery is $u(L)=0.1 \cdot 400^{1/2}+0.9 \cdot 625^{1/2}=24.5$. The certainty equivalent is $C(L)=[u(L)]^2=600.25$. Therefore the risk premium is $R=E(W)-C(L)=2.25$ (did you expect it to be so small?). Now let us see what measure of the risk premium is obtained from the (9.7) approximation. With this utility function, $u''(x)/u'(x)=-1/(2x)$; the Arrow–Pratt measure must be calculated at x^* and therefore is $1/(2x^*)=1/1205$. The variance is

$$E\left((x-x^*)^2\right) = .9 \cdot (625-602.5)^2 + .1 \cdot (602.5-400)^2 = 4556.25.$$

Half this variance times the Arrow–Pratt measure yields 1.89. The true risk premium, 2.25, is 19% greater. The order of magnitude is roughly correct but the percentage of error is rather big, which shows that the (9.7) approximation is good only for random variables with very small deviations from the mean.

9.13 Global Comparison of Risk Aversion

The Arrow–Pratt measure of absolute risk aversion is a local one; sometimes one is interested in establishing whether an individual A is always more risk averse than another individual B. Three ways of establishing it come out to be equivalent (cf. Varian 1992, pp. 182–183).

The first one is that for *any* level of wealth, A's Arrow–Pratt measure is greater than B's.

The second way is that A's utility function, indicate it as $u_A(w)$, is a concave transformation of B's; that is, there exists some strictly concave increasing function $c(\cdot)$ such that $u_A(w)=c(u_B(w))$. (***Exercise***: The reader should prove (it is easy) that the concave transformation raises everywhere the Arrow–Pratt measure, by using the fact that the second derivative of a strictly concave function is negative.)

For the third way we need the following property:

Jensen's Inequality   *Let X be a random variable and $f(X)$ be a strictly concave function of X. Then $Ef(X) < f(EX)$.*

Or, '*the expected value is less than the value of the expectation*', for a strictly concave function of a random variable. I skip a rigorous proof. An intuition for the reason can be obtained as follows. A function $f(x)$ from a subset of R^n to R^n is strictly concave if, for $\alpha \in (0, 1)$, it is $f(\alpha x' + (1 - \alpha)x'') > \alpha f(x') + (1 - \alpha)f(x'')$. Repeated application of this condition can easily be shown to imply

$$f\left(\alpha_1 x^1 + \alpha_2 x^2 + \ldots + \alpha_k x^k\right) > \alpha_1 f\left(x^1\right) + \ldots + \alpha_k f\left(x^k\right)$$

for any collection of k points x^i in the domain of f and numbers $\alpha_1, \ldots, \alpha_k$ positive and summing to 1. Now interpret the α's as the probabilities that the respective x's occur: this yields Jensen's Inequality for a discrete random variable. The passage to a continuous distribution generalizes this property in an intuitively obvious way.

The third way is that, for any given level of wealth, A is ready to pay more than B to avoid a given risk. We prove that this is implied by a greater concavity of A's utility function. Let X be a random variable with expectation zero: $EX = 0$. The maximum amount of wealth individual A is ready to give up in order to avoid facing the random variable X is the risk premium R_A satisfying $u_A(w - R_A(X)) = Eu_A(w + X)$, where the right-hand side is the certainty equivalent of the random wealth $w + X$. Assume $u_A(w) = c(u_B(w))$ with $c(\cdot)$ strictly concave. Then

$$
\begin{aligned}
u_A(w - R_A) &= Eu_A(w + X) \\
&= Ec(u_B(w + X)) < c(Eu_B(w + X) \\
&= c(u_B(w - R_B)) = u_A(w - R_B).
\end{aligned}
$$

The inequality in this series of relationships follows from Jensen's Inequality. Comparison of the first and last term shows that $R_A > R_B$.

I refer the reader to Varian (1992, p. 183) for the proof that conversely, if A is ready to pay more than B to avoid a risk, then A's absolute risk aversion is greater than B's, which proves the equivalence of the three ways.

9.14 Decreasing Absolute Risk Aversion

A question of practical interest is whether an increase in wealth induces or not a readiness to accept bets that one refuses at a lower wealth level. This is connected with the behaviour of the risk premium, because if one starts with a *sure* wealth W and is offered a bet h that turns W into the random variable $W + h$, the individual with VNM utility will accept the bet if

$$E[u(W + h)] > u(W),$$

which is equivalent to (if we indicate the lottery with the random variable):

$$C(W + h) > W$$

9.14 · Decreasing Absolute Risk Aversion

i.e. to

$$E(W + h) - R(W, h) > W.$$

If the bet remains unchanged in payoffs and in probabilities as W changes, it is

$$E(W + h) = W + E(h)$$

so the bet is accepted if

$$E(h) > R(W, h).$$

One speaks of *decreasing absolute risk aversion* if as wealth increases one comes to accept bets that at a lower wealth level one would not accept, that is, if for any given h the risk premium R is a decreasing function of W. It seems intuitive that especially when comparing much lower with much higher levels of wealth and when considering a bet that, even though with a positive expected value, at the lower wealth level might endanger the individual's subsistence, the individual will be more disposed to accept the bet if rich. Indeed there is ample evidence supporting decreasing absolute risk aversion (except, of course, in cases of desperation). (However, buying lottery tickets with improbable big prizes may appear less attractive to very rich people than to poor people because of the smaller impact of a win on their life condition; how would you analyse this case?).

In some analyses the assumption is made of *constant absolute risk aversion*, abbreviated as *CARA*, meaning that for a given bet represented by the random variable h with expected value $E(h)$ the risk avoidance price R that renders the consumer indifferent between the random variable $(W + h)$ and the sure sum $W + E(h) - R$ does not change when W changes. One can also express this assumption as an assumption of *absence of wealth effects* on R (this is further explained below). It can be proved (I omit the proof) that the utility functions exhibiting CARA must be of the form

$$u(x) = -ce^{-\alpha x} + B$$

where c, α are positive constants, B is an arbitrary constant that can be put equal to zero, and x is the random wealth or income. This function is negative, increasing, concave and tending asymptotically to zero. With it one obtains— $u''(x)/u'(x) = \alpha$, so α is the Arrow–Pratt coefficient of absolute risk aversion. If one sets $c = 1/\alpha$ one obtains $u'(x) = e^{-\alpha x}$ which makes some analytical derivations easier.

9.15 Relative Risk Aversion

Suppose you are interested in knowing whether an increase in wealth makes an individual more or less averse to accepting a bet *whose payoffs are specified as proportional to wealth*. For example, suppose at wealth W the individual rejects a bet that yields 0.1 W with probability 55%, and –0.1 W with probability 45%: will he still reject this bet if W increases tenfold?

If at wealth W the bet is a random variable h, we have seen that the bet is accepted if $C(W + h) > W$. What is of interest now is whether $C(W + h)$ increases

762   **Chapter 9 · Uncertainty and General Equilibrium**

in the same proportion as W if h increases in that same proportion; we can describe the increase of W and of h as the result of multiplication by an increasing scalar b, so the question is how $C(bW + bh)$ behaves relative to bW. Since $C(bW + bh) = E(bW + bh) - R(bW, bh) = bW + bE(h) - R(bW, bh)$, the question turns on whether R changes in the same proportion as W and h, or not. So what is relevant is whether the *relative risk premium* R/W changes or not as W and h increase in the same proportion.

Let us then note that the approximation (9.7) can be rewritten

$$R/W \cong -\frac{u''(W)}{u'(W)} \frac{Var(h)}{2W}.$$

If X and Y are two random variables with $Y = bX$, then $Var(Y) = b^2 Var(X)$. So if the sure initial wealth W increases and becomes bW while the random variable h (the bet) becomes bh, the variance σ^2 of wealth if the bet is accepted becomes $b^2\sigma^2$. Therefore if we rewrite R/W as

$$R/W \cong -W\frac{u''(W)}{u'(W)} \frac{Var(W)}{2W^2}, \tag{9.8}$$

the second fraction on the right-hand side is invariant to proportional changes of sure wealth and of the bet payoffs (to see it, replace W with bW). So the behaviour of R/W as W and h increase is, at least locally, indicated by the behaviour of the Arrow–Pratt measure multiplied by W. For this reason, $-W\frac{u''(W)}{u'(W)}$ is called the **Arrow–Pratt measure of relative risk aversion**, and its increase or decrease as W increases indicates whether the relative risk premium is an increasing or decreasing function of W. Note that the often plausible assumption of decreasing *absolute* risk aversion is compatible with any behaviour of *relative* risk aversion, and it is much less clear what kind of behaviour one should expect for the latter; some people argue that a constant relative risk aversion is not too implausible an assumption.

Constant Relative Risk Aversion   (CRRA) obtains if

$$u(x) = \frac{x^{1-\rho}}{1 - \rho} \text{ with } \rho > 0.$$

If modified to $u(x) = \frac{x^{1-\rho}-1}{1-\rho}$ then $u(x) = ln\ x$ if $\rho = 1$, provable with L' Hôpital's rule.

The constant ρ is the coefficient of relative risk aversion. The CRRA function implies, as you can easily check, decreasing absolute risk aversion because the latter is ρ/x.

Note that if you have a lottery $L = p\circ x \oplus (1 - p)\circ y$ and the utility function is CRRA then

$$u(L) = p\frac{x^{1-\rho}}{1 - \rho} + (1 - p)\frac{y^{1-\rho}}{1 - \rho} = \frac{1}{1 - \rho}\left[px^{1-\rho} + (1 - p)y^{1-\rho}\right]$$

9.15 · Relative Risk Aversion

where the expression in square brackets is a CES utility function raised to the power $(1 - \rho)$, whose constant elasticity of substitution is $1/\rho$. A similar expression is reached, with rates of discount in place of probabilities, if in an intertemporal neoclassical growth model one assumes that the total utility of infinitely lived households is a sum of per-period 'felicity functions' of CRRA form; then one obtains that the elasticity of substitution between consumption in two periods is constant, which simplifies some analytical derivations (see, e.g. Blanchard and Fischer 1989, p. 51). But analytical simplicity is not sufficient to make an assumption economically reasonable; I leave to the macroeconomics lecturer the task of giving a more convincing motivation, if possible, for this frequent choice of 'felicity function' in neoclassical growth models.

Exercise Prove that in the graph of ◨ Fig. 9.1 or 9.4 if there is constant absolute risk aversion then along a straight line parallel to the certainty line all indifference curves have the same slope, while with constant relative risk aversion indifference curves have the same slope along rays from the origin.

9.16 An Application of Arrow–Pratt: Efficient Risk Pooling in Absence of Wealth Effects

I take from Milgrom and Roberts (1992) an example of application of approximation (9.7). This example is based on the assumption of *absence of wealth effects*, the assumption that, in choice without uncertainty, is expressed by quasi-linear utility (linear in wealth).

Absence of wealth effects holds if the following three conditions hold:

1. for each couple of alternative outcomes a and b that the individual can have access to, with a strictly preferred to b, there exists an amount of money m sufficient to compensate the individual for getting b instead of a (that is, getting b plus m is equipreferred to getting a);

2. given a, b, m as in (1), both the preference order between a and b and the compensating amount of money m are independent of the wealth of the individual; thus the individual is also indifferent between getting b, or getting a and *paying m*; and she is also indifferent between getting a plus an amount of money M, or getting b plus $m + $M;

3. for the choice under examination, the individual's wealth is greater than the reduction m in it that would compensates for the passage from b to a.

These conditions are obviously restrictive, and therefore not legitimate in many cases.[26] But when they can be assumed to be sufficiently close to reality, then the

---

26 One implicit assumption is that the capacity of money to yield utility is given, which implies that money prices are given, at least the money prices in markets other than the one under study (cf. in ▶ Chap. 4 the analysis of quasilinear utility and of consumer surplus). The analysis is necessarily a partial-equilibrium one. If the agents involved are firms, wealth effects are always absent because it is as if firms had quasilinear utility functions.

764   Chapter 9 · Uncertainty and General Equilibrium

utility function of the individual who, relative to the choice set of interest, has no wealth effect takes a quasi-linear form, linear in wealth. More formally: assume monotonicity; let x be the money wealth of the individual, and let $\mathbf{y}$ be a vector of variables relevantly influencing her decisions relative to that choice set; assume (1), (2) and (3); then $u(x,\mathbf{y})$ can be represented as $x+v(\mathbf{y})$.

To prove it, note that the additivity indicates that $v(\mathbf{y})$ too is a quantity of money, interpretable as the m such that the individual is indifferent between obtaining total wealth $x+m$, or obtaining wealth x plus the vector $\mathbf{y}$. Accordingly $v(\mathbf{y})$ can be called the *money equivalent* of $\mathbf{y}$. (If $\mathbf{y}$ is a 'bad', which reduces utility relative to having only x, then $v(\mathbf{y})$ is negative.) Because of (1) the money equivalent exists, therefore $u(x,\mathbf{y})=u(x+v(\mathbf{y}))$, which by monotonicity is an increasing function of wealth and therefore represents the same preference order as $x+v(\mathbf{y})$. Call $x+v(\mathbf{y})$ the *equivalent wealth*. In the absence of wealth effects, equivalent wealth can be chosen as a measure of utility.

Because of monotonicity $u(x, \mathbf{y}) > u(x, \mathbf{y}')$ if and only if $u(x+v(\mathbf{y})) > u(x+v(\mathbf{y}'))$ or equivalently if and only if $x+v(\mathbf{y})>x+v(\mathbf{y}')$. Because of (2) $v(\mathbf{y})$ is independent of x; therefore $v(\mathbf{y})-v(\mathbf{y}')$ is the m, independent of x, that compensates for obtaining $\mathbf{y}'$ instead of $\mathbf{y}$. Note that, like with quasi-linear utility for choices without uncertainty, absence of wealth effects requires that the initial wealth of the individual be greater than the greatest of the possible difference $v(\mathbf{y})-v(\mathbf{y}')$ for $\mathbf{y}, \mathbf{y}'$ in the relevant choice set.

When an economic problem involves the welfare of several individuals, if wealth effects are absent the equivalent wealths of different individuals can be added to obtain the *total equivalent wealth*, an amount of money; and—this is why absence of wealth effects simplifies many problems—*Pareto efficiency obtains if and only if total equivalent wealth is maximized*: indeed, if total equivalent wealth is not maximized in an initial situation, then it can be increased and then each individual can be made better off by dividing equally the increase of total equivalent wealth among all individuals, so the initial situation is not Pareto efficient; conversely, when total equivalent wealth is maximized, no further increase of the welfare of some individual is achievable without reducing the welfare of some other individual, because the equivalent wealth of some individual would have to be reduced, so the situation is Pareto efficient. Milgrom and Roberts call this result the *principle of value maximization*. Application of this principle does not determine how much equivalent wealth will go to each individual, because redistributions of wealth that leave total equivalent wealth at its maximum level do not disturb Pareto efficiency. *There is room, therefore, for side payments* among the involved individuals as incentives to behaviours conducive to 'value maximization'.

One of the possible interpretations of x and $\mathbf{y}$ is that $\mathbf{y}$ is the vector of possible values assumed in different states of nature by a random variable Y that measures *deviations* of wealth from a mean or expected value x, causing $x+Y$ to be itself a random variable. Then $u(x, Y)$ is the utility of the *random variable $x+Y$*, that is, the utility of the certainty equivalent $C(L)$ of the lottery defined by this random variable; we assume that u has the expected utility form, then in the absence of wealth effects the measurability of utility as equivalent wealth means that utility

9.16 · An Application of Arrow–Pratt ...

can be measured as *equal* to the certainty equivalent; we have seen that this certainty equivalent is $x - R$, where x is the expected value of wealth and R is the risk premium; it can also be expressed as $x + v(Y)$ where $v(Y)$ is *the negative of the risk premium*. Under the absence of wealth effects the risk premium associated with the random variable Y is independent of x; in other words, *there is constant absolute risk aversion*. *Proof*: If W is sure wealth and h a random variable, a risk-averse consumer prefers $W + E(h)$ for sure to the random variable $W + h$, so we can treat $W + E(h)$ as a and $W + h$ as b in the definition of absence of wealth effects; the risk avoidance price or risk premium R is the compensating amount of money m that makes the consumer indifferent between getting b, or a minus m; absence of wealth effects means that R does not change with W, which is the definition of CARA. ∎

In an uncertainty context with no wealth effects, the principle of value maximization becomes: *an allocation is efficient if and only if it maximizes the sum of the certainty equivalents of the random wealths of the individuals involved.* The certainty equivalent indicates the wealth for sure that the individual finds equipreferred to the lottery represented by her random wealth, and therefore it measures the equivalent wealth.

I come now to the example. ***Risk pooling*** occurs when individuals who face different risky income prospects agree to share in some way the total realized income. Suppose the incomes of two individuals A and B are two *independent* random variables Y_A and Y_B, with means y_A and y_B and variances $Var(Y_A)$, $Var(Y_B)$. Indicate with ρ_A, ρ_B the respective coefficients of constant absolute risk aversion. The principle of value maximization implies that we must allocate risk so as to maximize the certainty equivalent of total (random) wealth, that is, the expected value of total wealth minus the total risk premium. Without risk reallocation the sum of the risk premiums, using approximation (9.7), is

$$1/2 \, \rho_A Var(Y_A) + 1/2 \, \rho_B Var(Y_B).$$

Suppose the two individuals agree to share their incomes such that individual A will receive $\alpha Y_A + \beta Y_B + \gamma$, with $0 \leq \alpha \leq 1$, $0 \leq \beta \leq 1$ two constants, and γ a side payment (positive, negative or zero) whose role and possible size will become clear below; while B will receive $(1 - \alpha)Y_A + (1 - \beta)Y_B - \gamma$. This is a feasible contract, in that what is distributed in total is $Y_A + Y_B$.

Now the total risk premium is

$$1/2 \, \rho_A Var(\alpha Y_A + \beta Y_B + \gamma) + 1/2 \, \rho_B Var((1 - \alpha)Y_A + (1 - \beta)Y_B - \gamma).$$

The expected value of total wealth is $y_A + y_B$, and this *minus* the total risk premium is the total certainty equivalent that must be maximized; therefore we must minimize the total risk premium. Minimization must be with respect to α, β and γ; but γ does not influence the variances nor, as a consequence, the minimum, it is only relevant as possibly necessary in order to satisfy the ***participation constraints*** that require, in order for the contract to be acceptable to both individuals, that the expected utility to each individual of what the contract gives her be not inferior to what she can get without risk pooling; I will soon formalize this condition.

766   Chapter 9 · Uncertainty and General Equilibrium

Neglecting γ, the total risk premium can be rewritten as[27]:

$$1/2\, \rho_A Var(\alpha Y_A + \beta Y_B) + 1/2\, \rho_B Var((1 - \alpha)Y_A + (1 - \beta)Y_B)$$

$$= 1/2\, \rho_A \left[\alpha^2 Var(Y_A) + \beta^2 Var(Y_B) + 2\alpha\beta cov(Y_A, Y_B)\right]$$

$$+ 1/2\, \rho_B \left[(1 - \alpha)^2 Var(Y_A) + (1 - \beta)^2 Var(Y_B) + 2(1 - \alpha)(1 - \beta)cov(Y_A, Y_B)\right]$$

$$= 1/2 \left[Var(Y_A) \cdot \left(\rho_A \alpha^2 + \rho_B(1 - \alpha)^2\right) + Var(Y_B) \cdot \left(\rho_A \beta^2 + \rho_B(1 - \beta)^2\right)\right].$$

The first-order minimization conditions are that the partial derivatives of this expression relative to α and to β be set equal to zero, which produces:

$$\frac{\alpha}{1 - \alpha} = \frac{\rho_B}{\rho_A} = \frac{\beta}{1 - \beta}.$$

We obtain two results. First, α must be equal to β. This means that the closer is α to 1, the closer is A's income to $Y_A + Y_B + \gamma$, and the closer is B's income to $-\gamma$; in the extreme case $\alpha = 1$, A bears the entire variability of $Y_A + Y_B$ while B's income is certain and equal to $-\gamma$ (in this case γ must be negative; otherwise B gets nothing and rejects the agreement): one can say that A is bearing all the risk from total income variability, while B is bearing no risk at all because his income is certain. Conversely, the closer is α to zero, the closer A's income is to a sure income equal to γ and the closer is B's income to bearing all the variability of total income.

Second, α and β are greater than 1/2 if $\rho_A < \rho_B$, indicating that A is less risk averse than B, so the optimal 'allocation of risk' requires that the less risk-averse individual bear a greater portion of the risk.[28] The closer is A to risk neutral, the more the risk from the variability of total income must be borne by A.

We grasp here the reason for the necessity of the side payment γ: without it an optimal α (and β) close to 1 or to zero would cause one of the two individuals to get almost the entire joint income, and then the other individual would reject the risk pooling agreement. The *participation constraints* impose that each individual must obtain from the contract a utility not less than without the contract, that is,

$$u_A(\alpha Y_A + \beta Y_B + \gamma) \geq u_A(Y_A) \cong y_A - 1/2\, \rho_A Var(Y_A)$$

$$u_B((1 - \alpha)Y_A + (1 - \beta)Y_B - \gamma) \geq u_B(Y_B) \cong y_B - 1/2\, \rho_B Var(Y_B).$$

Generally these constraints determine an *interval* of feasible values that γ can take, inside which the value of γ is left indeterminate. Satisfaction of the principle of value maximization only determines the total certainty equivalent, not how it gets distributed between A and B; the participation constraints reduce but generally do not completely eliminate the indeterminacy. As normal in an interaction

---

27 Remember that if $Y = a + bX$ then $Var(Y) = b^2 Var(X)$, that $Var(X + Y) = Var(X) + Var(Y) + 2Cov(X, Y)$, and that Y_A and Y_B are assumed independent so $Cov(Y_A, Y_B) = 0$.

28 'Allocation of risk' is a common expression, which however can be given a precise meaning only under restrictive assumptions, for example it has no quantitative meaning when probabilities are not defined (see, e.g., ▶ Sect. 9.33 below).

9.16 · An Application of Arrow–Pratt ...

between only two individuals, how the indeterminacy gets resolved will depend on many things: different bargaining ability, different urgency of reaching an agreement, etc. Just to give an example, one way to determine γ is so as to *leave the expected value of the two incomes unchanged*: this is possible, because if $\alpha y_A + \alpha y_B + \gamma = y_A$, that is, if $\gamma = (1 - \alpha)y_A - \alpha y_B$, then $(1 - \alpha)y_A + (1 - \alpha)y_B - \gamma = y_B$: now each individual has the same mean income as before the risk pooling agreement, but with less risk; this favours the individual with greater risk aversion.

The reduction of risk can be seen even more clearly with the help of a new notion. Define *risk tolerance* as the reciprocal of the Arrow–Pratt measure of risk aversion, $1/\rho$ if ρ is the Arrow–Pratt coefficient. Then it can be proved that the share of risk assigned to A, α, is the ratio of A's risk tolerance to *total* risk tolerance (the sum of the individual risk tolerances). For example if $\rho_A = 2$ and $\rho_B = 4$, and hence $\alpha = 2/3$, it is $2/3 = \frac{\frac{1}{2}}{\frac{1}{2} + \frac{1}{4}}$. And the total risk premium is $\frac{\frac{1}{2} Var(Y_A + Y_B)}{\frac{1}{\rho_A} + \frac{1}{\rho_B}}$, as if all risk were borne by an individual with risk tolerance equal to the sum of the risk tolerances of A and B. Thus assume n individuals having the same independent random income Y and the same risk aversion coefficient ρ (the side payments can now be assumed equal to zero, since equal sharing in total income is the natural contract); the *total* risk premium expressed through risk tolerance is

$$\frac{1}{2} \frac{1}{n\frac{1}{\rho}} Var(nY) = \frac{1}{2} \frac{1}{n\frac{1}{\rho}} nVar(Y) \ (because\ the\ covariances\ are\ zero)$$

$$= \frac{1}{2}\rho\ Var(Y).$$

The total risk premium is the same as the risk premium R of a single individual on her own; this means that the total certainty equivalent is the sum of the certainty equivalents of the isolated individuals, *plus* $(n - 1)R$; an equal sharing of this total certainty equivalent yields therefore for each individual a certainty equivalent increase, relative to being on their own, equal to $R(n - 1)/n$.

9.17 Diversification

It is widely known that risk can be reduced by diversification. We can easily reach an explanation of why it is so for simple cases.

If x_i, x_j are two random variables, their covariance is defined as

$$\sigma_{ij} = E\big[(x_i - \mu_i)(x_j - \mu_j)\big]$$

$$= \int\limits_{-\infty}^{+\infty} \int\limits_{-\infty}^{+\infty} (x_i - \mu_i)(x_j - \mu_j)f(x_i, x_j)dx_idx_j$$

where μ_i, μ_j are the means of x_i and x_j, and $f(x_i, x_j)$ is the joint density function that yields the probability $P(a \le x_i \le b\ and\ c \le x_j \le d)$ as $\int_a^b \int_c^d f(x_i, x_j)dx_idx_j$. Two properties of covariance are:

$$cov\,(X,Y) = E(X \cdot Y) - E(X) \cdot E(Y)$$

$$Var(aX + bY) = a^2 Var(X) + b^2 Var(Y) + 2ab\,cov\,(X,Y).$$

Now consider a random variable obtained as a mixture of x_i and x_j, $z = \alpha x_i + (1 - \alpha) x_j$, with $0 \le \alpha \le 1$; z could represent the returns from investing a sum partly in asset i and partly in asset j, that is, from diversification. We obtain

$$\mu_z = \alpha \mu_i + (1 - \alpha) \mu_j$$

$$Var(z) = \alpha^2 Var(x_i) + (1 - \alpha)^2 Var(x_j)$$
$$+ 2\alpha(1 - \alpha)cov(x_i, x_j)$$

Let us consider the case $\mu_i = \mu_j$ and $Var(x_i) = Var(x_j)$: then the random variable z has mean $\mu_z = \mu_i$ and variance $Var(z) = [\alpha^2 + (1 - \alpha)^2]Var(x_i) + 2\alpha(1 - \alpha)Cov(x_i, x_j)$.

For $0 < \alpha < 1$ it is $\alpha^2 + (1 - \alpha)^2 < 1$; hence $[\alpha^2 + (1 - \alpha)^2]Var(x_i)$ is smaller than $Var(x_i)$ and is minimized for $\alpha = 1/2$ where it becomes half the variance of x_i or x_j; so if $Cov(x_i, x_j)$ is zero, or positive but small, the variance and hence the risk premium decrease with diversification; if the covariance is negative, the reduction of riskiness is even greater.

9.18 Consumption and Saving Under Uncertainty

No formalization will be needed for the little that will be said here on these topics. On aggregate consumption, the main effect of the presence of uncertainty as to future income is the following. Risk aversion implies that if future income becomes more uncertain without a change in its mean, that is, if future income is uncertain and its distribution undergoes a mean-preserving spread, then the utility of future income decreases, and therefore in the choice between consumption to-day and consumption in the future the consumer will behave *as if future income had decreased*. According to permanent income theory and to a majority of plausible formalizations of the intertemporal utility function the effect will be a reduction of current consumption, that is, an increase of savings in the current period. But this effect is not guaranteed; cf. Deaton and Muellbauer (1980, pp. 406–408) for a counterexample.

If it is the *return* on saving that is uncertain, then, again because of risk aversion, an increased uncertainty about this rate of return, i.e. a mean-preserving spread of its distribution, acts like a decrease of its mean; the effect on saving depends on whether intertemporal preferences are such that, in the absence of uncertainty, a lower rate of return on savings would induce a rise or a decrease of savings: as we know from ▶ Chap. 4, both cases are perfectly possible.[29]

---

29 For example, in all likelihood a decision to buy a house with the help of a mortgage stimulates savings; then if a higher rate of interest discourages from buying a house because the mortgage has become too expensive, this reduces savings.

9.19 Firm Behaviour Under Uncertainty

Firms face two types of uncertainty: *technological* uncertainty about how much output will be produced from the utilization of given amounts of resources, about quality of inputs, about external events (e.g. snowfall) preventing timely delivery of inputs; and *market* uncertainty, about prices (of outputs, but sometimes also of inputs if the production process cannot be stopped once started, and if the prices of the raw materials or labour to be utilized half-way through are uncertain when the production process starts), and/or about demand if the firm is demand-constrained.

As ▶ Sect. 9.28 will explain, if there were complete contingent futures markets firms would bear no risk deriving not only from market uncertainty (since all prices reach equilibrium at the initial date for the entire future covered by the equilibrium), but also from technological uncertainty (because separate contracts are specified for each possible future state of nature). But in the real world there aren't complete contingent futures markets; therefore firms bear risks relative to their decisions as to how much to produce; if they are price makers (imperfectly competitive markets), they also bear risks relative to their pricing decisions. However, the insights that one can draw from more detailed analysis of their decision problems are generally not surprising: for example, inventories will be held for precautionary reasons in excess of the amount needed to satisfy the expected value of sales, the excess depending on risk aversion and on the durability of the good produced.[30] Depending on the nature of the good sold, the possibility to postpone delivery of the good to some customers (that is, to have customers queue) must also be considered,[31] and it can be optimal for the firm to choose a dimension that entails some, perhaps periodic, queueing of customers, so that the firm produces largely to order. So much depends on the specifics of the firm's market that one does not expect general theoretical considerations to go beyond such rather intuitive conclusions.

A conclusion of some general interest can be reached by considering the influence of price uncertainty upon a price-taking firm. Assume a firm that produces a quantity q of output which costs a certain total cost $c(q)$ and will be sold at the uncertain price p_r not affected by q (in p_r and, below, y_r, suffix r indicates that the symbol refers to a random variable). Let us set aside the problem discussed in ▶ Chap. 8, ▶ Sect. 8.27, of who decides the objective of the firm if there are several owners with different expectations and different preferences and risk aversion, by assuming a single owner with expected utility function $u(y_r)$, where y_r is the owner's random income, the sum of the random profit of the firm $p_r q - c(q)$ and of other sure sources of income M. The owner chooses q to maximize

$$U = Eu(y_r) = Eu(p_r q - c(q) + M).$$

---

30 See, for example, McKenna (1986).
31 For example, customers are sometimes ready to wait even for a couple of months to get their preferred car model. Clearly, the good must have no very close substitutes more readily available.

The first-order condition, assuming $q > 0$, is

$$Eu'(y_r)dy_r/dq = Eu'(p_r q - c(q) + M)[p_r - c'(q)] = 0.$$

The second-order condition is

$$Eu''(p_r q - c(q) + M)[p_r - c'(q)]^2 - Eu'(p_r q - c(q) + M)c''(q) < 0.$$

If there were no uncertainty the maximand would be simply profit, $pq - c(q)$, the first-order condition would be $p - c'(q) = 0$, and, assuming this to be satisfied, the second-order condition would be $-c''(q) < 0$. Maximization of $u(pq - c(q) + M)$ would yield the same conditions, as the reader can check. Let us assume the typical Marshallian firm with U-shaped average cost curve (and therefore increasing marginal cost at least from a certain level of q onwards) so these conditions can be satisfied. The presence of uncertainty changes things, first, because the decision about how much to produce must be taken before p is known, and therefore the firm may find that it did not produce the *ex post* profit-maximizing quantity; second, because of the possible presence of risk aversion. If the firm owner is risk neutral, maximization of $Eu(y_r)$ is equivalent to maximizing the expected value of y_r, that is, with p^* the mean price (we must assume the distribution of p is known), to maximizing

$$E(p_r q - c(q) + M) = p^* q - c(q) + M.$$

The first-order condition is $p^* q - c'(q) = 0$: *the risk-neutral firm behaves as if it faced a sure price equal to the expected value of the price.* The similarity extends to the second-order condition: since with risk neutrality $u(y_r)$ is linear in y_r, $u'' = 0$ because u' is a constant, so in the second-order condition the first addendum disappears and the second addendum implies $-c'' < 0$, marginal cost must be increasing at the profit-maximizing output $q^*(p^*)$.

Risk aversion introduces some difference. Let us rewrite the first-order condition utilizing the covariance rule:

$$\begin{aligned} Eu'(y_r)[p_r - c'(q)] &= Eu'(y_r)E[p_r - c'] + Cov(c'(y_r), p_r - c') \\ &= Eu'(y_r)E[p * -c'] + Cov(u'(y_r), p_r) = 0. \end{aligned}$$

The covariance is negative, because a higher p_r raises y_r and under risk aversion $y'' < 0$. Therefore $Eu'(y_r)E[p^* - c']$ must be positive; since $u' > 0$ it is $Eu'(y_r) > 0$ so it must be $E[p^* - c'] > 0$, i.e.:

$$c'(q) < p^*.$$

Marginal cost must be less than the marginal cost, equal to p*, that would be optimal for the risk-neutral firm. As marginal cost is increasing at the optimal output $q^*(p^*)$ of the risk-neutral firm, we have shown that *the risk-averse competitive Marshallian firm chooses a smaller output than the risk-neutral firm.*

This is one instance of a general rule: when one must choose between lotteries with income (or wealth) as outcomes, a strictly concave utility of income (or wealth) induces the choice of a smaller expected income than with risk neutrality.

9.19 · Firm Behaviour Under Uncertainty

The decreasing marginal utility of income causes less weight to be given to the possibility of high incomes than to the possibility of low incomes, hence a precautionary attitude.

This rule is illustrated by the case of a mean-preserving spread of expected money outcomes: in ◨ Fig. 9.2 it was shown that with a strictly concave utility function of income, a mean-preserving spread reduces expected utility; on the contrary with risk neutrality the utility function is a straight line and the decision maker is indifferent between a first lottery, and a second one which is a mean-preserving spread of the first. Then a small increase of the payoffs of the second lottery will make it preferable to the first one for the risk-neutral decision maker, but not for the risk averter, who will prefer the first lottery in spite of its lower expected value.

The same general rule will appear in (non-financial) investment decisions: the more uncertain the future output price or, in imperfect-competition market forms, the more uncertain the future demand, the more cautious will be the investment decision of a risk-averse firm, which will prefer to build a smaller productive capacity than under risk neutrality although this reduces expected profit, in order to reduce the risk of incurring losses or even bankruptcy. Thus, *ceteris paribus increases of uncertainty must be expected to reduce aggregate investment if investors are risk averse.*

9.20 Portfolio Selection: Two Assets

Now let us study the optimal portfolio choice of a risk-averse individual faced with the possibility of investing income into assets with different expected returns and different riskiness.

Assume a two-periods time horizon, and suppose there are two assets: a safe one, which next period will return one sure dollar per dollar invested now (hence a zero *rate* of return: e.g. money), and a risky one, with a *gross* return of k dollars per dollar invested, a random variable with an expected value greater than 1, i.e. an expected positive *rate* of return $r = E(k-1)$. A given wealth W must be allocated between the two assets.[32] Let a and b be the *amounts* of wealth invested respectively in the risky and in the safe asset, $a + b = W$. Assume $0 \leq a \leq W$ (this excludes *short sales*, a notion to be explained shortly). Assume strict risk aversion. The individual's wealth next period is a random variable $w = ak + b = W + a(k-1) = W + ar$ where r, the random *rate* of return on the risky asset, has a known (or subjectively esteemed) distribution function $F(r)$ with mean $Er > 0$. If the individual has a

---

32 A more complete analysis would have to determine W on the basis of the overall utility maximization problem, which will determine which portion of the individual's income is allocated to immediate consumption and which portion is left for financial investment. We concentrate on a given W because for any W the consumer has the problem of getting out of it as much wealth as possible in the second period.

772   **Chapter 9 · Uncertainty and General Equilibrium**

VNM expected utility function with basic utility function $u(\cdot)$, her utility maximization problem is

$$\max_a Eu(W + ar) = \max_a \int u(W + ar)dF(r) \text{ s.t. } 0 \le a \le W.$$

Let a^* be the solution; I prove now that it must be $a^* > 0$ if the consumer is not satiated.

Proof The first-order Kuhn–Tucker condition suffices for an optimum because the objective function is concave owing to risk aversion. The derivative of the Lagrangian function must equal zero, where λ_1 is the multiplier of constraint $a \ge 0$ and $-\lambda_2$ is the multiplier of constraint $a \le W$:

$$\int u'(W + ar)rdF(r) + \lambda_1 - \lambda_2 = 0.$$

The complementary slackness conditions are $\lambda_1 a = 0$, $\lambda_2(W - a) = 0$. So if $0 < a < W$ then $\lambda_2 = \lambda_1 = 0$; if $a = 0$ then $\lambda_2 = 0$ and $\lambda_1 > 0$ and therefore $\int u'(W)rdF(r) < 0$, but this cannot be optimal because at $a = 0$ it is $dEu(W + ar)/da = \int u'(W)rdF(r) = u'(W) \int rdF(r) > 0$ because $\int rdF(r) = Er > 0$; so at $a = 0$ the derivative of expected wealth with respect to a is positive; this proves that the solution requires $a^* > 0$. The case $a^* = 0$ can only obtain if $Er \le 0$. ∎

This shows that *as long as a risky asset has actuarially favourable returns (and no asset has even more favourable returns), the optimal portfolio composition will include at least a small amount of it*. The optimal investment, if internal, will satisfy the first-order condition

$$Eu'(W + a^*r)r = 0, \tag{9.9}$$

the expected marginal utility of wealth must equal zero; in trying to reach this result it is possible to hit the boundary $a^* = W$.

The earlier analysis of actuarially unfair insurance conforms to this result, because one can treat the situation corresponding to complete insurance as the safe asset, relative to which the 'lottery' without insurance (point **x** in ◻ Fig. 9.4) is a risky asset with a greater expected value; and we saw that the optimal decision is not to insure fully, i.e. to accept some risk.

We can now ask about the effect on a^* of changes in W and of changes in Er.

It can be shown that da^*/dW is ambiguous, but positive if the Arrow–Pratt coefficient of absolute risk aversion is decreasing in wealth, i.e. if at a higher W one accepts bets that at a lower level of W one rejects. This is not surprising, and I skip the proof (cf. Varian 1992, p. 185; Cowell 2006, p. 213; whether a^*/W, the *proportion* of W invested in the risky asset, increases with W remains ambiguous). More interesting is what happens to a^* as Er rises. Let me follow Varian (1992) and maintain things simple by considering the case where the random variable r becomes $r(1 + h)$, with $h \ge 0$ a scalar: an increase of h from zero represents an equi-proportional rise of all possible net returns. The first-order condition (9.9) if

9.20 · Portfolio Selection: Two Assets

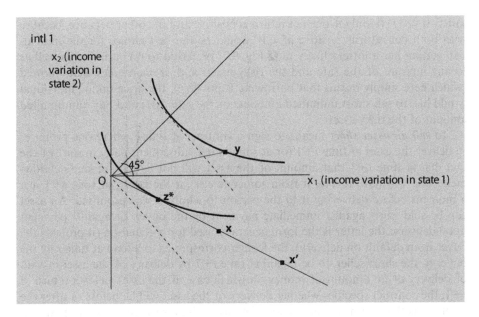

Fig. 9.7 Portfolio selection with two assets

the optimum is internal can be written, with $a^*(h)$ the demand for the risky asset as a function of parameter h, and with $(1+h)r$ in place of r:

$$E\big((1+h)r \cdot u'\big[W + a^*(h)(1+h)r\big]\big) = 0. \tag{9.10}$$

Since for each level of h we can treat h as a constant, the first term $(1+h)$ in (9.10) can be taken out of $E(\cdot)$ and neglected because of the equality to zero, so (9.10) becomes

$$Eu'\big[W + a^*(h)(1+h)r\big]r = 0. \tag{9.11}$$

Note that in (9.9) the a^* corresponds to $a^*(0)$ here; and that (9.11) coincides with (9.9) if $a^*(h) = a^*(0)/(1+h)$; hence optimization requires $a^*(h) = a^*(0)/(1+h)$. This means that at higher levels of h the individual decreases the amount held of the risky asset in exactly the same proportion as the rise of returns, so *the individual restores exactly the same pattern of returns as before the increase of h.*

This conclusion is strictly dependent on the assumption that the safe asset has zero expected net return (e.g. money in the absence of inflation, if checking accounts pay no interest). To see why, let us use in ◘ Fig. 9.7 a graphical representation as in ◘ Fig. 9.1; i.e. let us assume only two possible rates of net return of the risky asset per dollar invested in it, r_1 and r_2. Let the origin $O = (0, 0)$ represent *initial* wealth, and let us measure on the axes the *variation* in wealth (the total *net* return) if one invests the whole of W in a portfolio; a safe asset has returns on the certainty line; initially I assume the safe asset has rate of return $r_0 = 0$; therefore the return from investing W entirely in the safe asset $(a = 0, b = W)$ is indicated by the origin. The demand a^* for the risky asset will satisfy $0 < a^* < W$ only if one net return is positive and the other negative, because with both net returns positive $a^* = W$ would be the best choice for the individual, getting her a lottery like **y** in ◘ Fig. 9.7, preferred to no variation as well as to any mixture of the safe and the risky asset; and, if *short sales* were allowed (which here simply means that borrowing is possible), the price-taking individual would like to sell short unlimited amounts of the safe asset and buy an unlimited amount of the risky asset.

To **sell an asset short** means to sign a contract at time t where one promises to deliver the asset at time $t + 1$ (or at some other subsequent date) in spite of the fact that at time $t + 1$ that amount of the asset will not be part of one's endowment: one will have to buy it from someone else, at the latest, at time $t + 1$ just a moment before delivering it to the person to whom it was promised. An asset can be sold short against immediate payment by the buyer, or against payment upon delivery: the latter is the form generally used for speculation (it protects the buyer from default on delivery); the former corresponds to a loan at time t by the buyer to the short seller, to be repaid at time $t + 1$ by delivery of the asset instead of delivery of an amount of money; in which case, if the asset yields a return at $t + 1$, the contract specifies whether delivery of the asset will be before or after the asset earns the return, but either way the buyer obtains the return (why?). Speculation through short sales is based on the short seller believing that the value of the asset at time $t + 1$ will be less than the value at which the purchaser is ready to pay it on delivery; since financial transactions can be completed in the space of seconds, the individual who short sells the asset for delivery in exchange for a price P at $t + 1$ counts on buying the asset just a few seconds before delivery, at a lesser price P', pocketing the difference $P - P'$. Of course the purchaser accepts because she entertains the opposite expectation, that at time $t + 1$ the market price P' of the asset will be greater than P, so she will be able, by reselling the asset immediately, to pocket the difference $P - P'$.

Let us consider ◘ Fig. 9.7. It shows on the axes the *net* returns from the portfolio in the two states; the downward-sloping broken lines are equal-expected-value lines whose slope indicates the probabilities assigned to states 1 and 2. Point **x** indicates the net returns in the two states if all W is spent on a risky asset, $a^* = W$; the net returns are $x_1 = W \cdot r_1$, $x_2 = W \cdot r_2$, with $r_1 > 0$, $r_2 < 0$; the points on the O**x** segment are the portfolios corresponding to different values of a; the optimal portfolio is the one that generates tangency with an indifference curve, it is represented by net returns **z*** in the figure. But it is conceivable that the tangency be on the prolongation of the O**x** segment to the right of **x**, e.g. in **x**′, in which case if short sales are allowed the individual will sell the *safe* asset short against immediate payment (that is, will borrow, by assumption at a zero rate of interest), and will use the proceeds to spend *more* than W on the risky asset so as to reach the point of tangency with an indifference curve; reaching a point like **x**′ to the right of **x** means a negative holding of the safe asset. Point **y** represents the total net returns (with $a = W$) of a risky asset delivering a positive net return in both states: if such an asset were available, the individual would spend the whole of W on it; with a possibility of unlimited short sales of the safe asset the individual would demand an infinite amount of the risky asset. Indeed one dollar of

9.20 · Portfolio Selection: Two Assets

safe asset sold short against immediate payment at t allows buying one dollar of the risky asset, which will yield more than one dollar at $t+1$, while only one dollar will be enough at $t+1$ to buy one dollar of the safe asset and deliver it to the lender; hence an unlimited incentive to sell the safe asset short and buy the risky asset. However, in this case the given price of the assets becomes implausible: the excess demand for the risky asset will cause its price to rise, decreasing the expected rates of return; while the excess short sales at t of the safe asset of date $t+1$ will cause the price at t of a unit of that asset to fall, creating a positive rate of return on it.[33] The price of financial assets must be considered determined by the market; it can be taken as given only as a first step, useful to determine individual demands and thus the tendency of the asset price to vary.

The same figure allows us to understand why, in the case of the safe asset having zero net return, a rise of the return on the risky asset does not induce the individual to alter the pattern of returns, i.e. why she remains at z^*: the rise of h moves x to some x' along the same O-x line but further away from the origin: the optimal choice, the point of tangency with the indifference curve, remains z^*. This is obtained by reducing a^*: if a^* did not decrease, the portfolio returns would be represented by a point to the right of z^*, that touches a lower indifference curve.

If on the contrary the safe asset yields a positive rate of return r_0 (this may be the case of Treasury bonds) it will not be the case that $a^*(h)=a^*(0)/(1+h)$; a^* need not decrease with h. A graphical analysis is again sufficient. Assume the net returns from investing the whole of W in the safe asset are indicated by point s on the certainty line in ◻ Fig. 9.8, with $s_1=s_2=W{\cdot}r_0$. Now the condition $0<a^*<W$ does not prevent both rates of return r_1 and r_2 from being positive, and this is the case shown in ◻ Fig. 9.8. Assume $x=(Wr_1,\ Wr_2)$ is to the South-East of s. As a varies from 0 to W, the point representing net returns moves from s to x along the segment joining them.[34] Let z^* indicate the initial optimal portfolio, with $h=0$; now let h rise, causing x to move outwards to x'; the line representing the achievable portfolios (i.e. the line through s and x) rotates counterclockwise around s. If it were $a^*(h)=a^*(0)/(1+h)$ it would be $a^*(h)r_1(1+h)=a^*(0)r_1$, and the net returns from holding the risky asset would not change; therefore the new portfolio would be found (by the parallelogram rule) on the s-x' line at point c, which will generally *not* be the point of tangency between the s-x' line and an indifference curve; e.g. with CARA—the case shown—the slope of the indifference curve at c is the same as at z^* and the tangency must therefore be to the right of c; with CRRA, the tangency will be even farther to the right. Thus, apart from highly unlikely cases, $a^*(h)r_1(1+h)$ rises with h; a^* itself will rise, if the tangency between indif-

---

33 To help intuition, imagine the safe asset to be gold, with the money price of one ounce of gold at t and at $t+1$ equal to 1 dollar because it is legal tender; the attempt at t to short sell great amounts of titles promising the delivery of an ounce of gold at $t+1$ would cause the price of these titles to fall below 1 dollar.

34 *Exercise*: Show graphically how to build a riskless portfolio from two risky assets, using short sales if necessary.

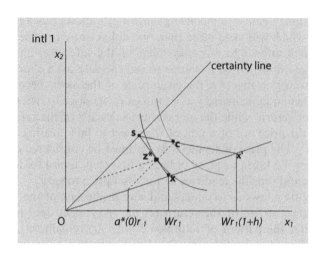

Fig. 9.8 Asset choice with the safe asset yielding a positive rate of return

ference curve and **s-x'** segment is to the right of the point on that segment corresponding to $a^*(0)(1+h)$.[35]

9.21 Portfolio Selection: Many Assets. Tobin

In order to extend the analysis of portfolio choice to many assets indexed as 0, 1, ..., i, ..., n it is convenient to focus on the *gross* returns, which will again be indicated as k_i dollars per unit of dollar value of asset i. Let us assume these returns are random variables except for the safe asset 0, which has a certain gross return k_0. Assume again a two-periods framework, the assets are purchased in the first period and deliver their returns in the second period. We assume a given wealth W to be spent on the portfolio. The prices of assets are given; now let α_i stand for the *share* of W spent on purchasing asset i. Wealth in the second period is a random variable w:

$$w = W \sum_{i=0}^{n} \alpha_i k_i.$$

The shares α_i must sum to 1; let us write this budget constraint as $\alpha_0 + \sum_{i=1}^{n} \alpha_i = 1$. Replacing in the expression for w we obtain:

$$w = \alpha_0 k_0 W + W \sum_{i=1}^{n} \alpha_i k_i = Wk_0 \left(1 - \sum_{i=1}^{n} \alpha_i\right)$$
$$+ W \sum_{i=1}^{n} \alpha_i k_i = Wk_0 + W \sum_{i=1}^{n} \alpha_i (k_i - k_0).$$

---

[35] This point is found by finding the point $(a^*(0)r_1(1+h), a^*(0)r_2(1+h))$ on the **Ox** line, and tracing from it toward the **s-x** segment a line parallel to the certainty line i.e. with slope 1.

9.21 · Portfolio Selection: Many Assets. Tobin

In this way we have embodied the budget constraint into the objective function, so we obtain an unconstrained maximization problem:

$$\max_{\alpha_1,\dots,\alpha_n} E\left\{ u\!\left(Wk_0 + W \sum_{i=1}^{n} \alpha_i(k_i - k_0)\right) \right\}.$$

The objective function can be indicated for brevity as $Eu(w)$. The first-order conditions are

$$\partial E(\cdot)/\partial \alpha_i = E\big(u'(w) \cdot (k_i - k_0)\big) = 0, \quad i = 1,\dots,n. \tag{9.12}$$

The equality may not be obtainable without short sales, but these can be admitted, at least within limits (obviously enormous short sales will not be accepted by the buyers because the risk of default of the seller would become excessive).

These rather opaque first-order conditions become more informative if we rewrite them as $E(u'(w)k_i) = k_0 E(u'(w))$ and we apply to the left-hand side of this equation the covariance identity $Cov(X,Y) = E(XY) - E(X)E(Y)$, rewritten as $E(XY) = Cov\,(X,Y) + E(X)E(Y)$, to obtain

$$Cov\big(u'(w), k_i\big) + E(k_i)E\big(u'(w)\big) = k_0 E\big(u'(w)\big),$$

which can be rearranged to yield:

$$E(k_i) = \frac{k_0 E(u'(w)) - Cov(u'(w), k_i)}{E(u'(w))} = k_0 + \frac{-Cov(u'(w), k_i)}{E(u'(w))}. \tag{9.13}$$

Expression (9.13) tells us that if a risky asset is held in a portfolio, it must yield the safe return plus an addition, usually called again 'risk premium' (not to be confused with the 'risk premium' of the insurance problem and of the Arrow–Pratt approximation, which will be called here *risk avoidance price*), which depends on the covariance between the marginal utility of wealth and the gross return of the asset. This 'risk premium' is positive if the covariance is negative, i.e. if the asset return is positively correlated with wealth (and hence negatively correlated with the decreasing marginal utility of wealth) and therefore to insert it into the portfolio increases riskiness relative to investing only in the safe asset; it is negative if the asset return is negatively correlated with wealth, and to insert it into the portfolio decreases the variability of wealth and therefore decreases the riskiness of the portfolio, making the investor willing to accept a lower rate of return than on the safe asset in exchange for the risk reduction.

What if the 'risk premiums' do not satisfy this condition? If the asset's return is greater than required, the single price-taking investor will prefer it to other assets and may end up investing only in it; if the asset's return is insufficient, the investor will not include it in the portfolio. But one must also consider market behaviour. If there is an excess demand or excess supply of the asset, the *price* of the asset (which we were taking as given because of our purpose of analyzing the choices of a price-taking investor) will change while its return doesn't, so the rate of return changes, altering the excess demand, plausibly towards equilibration. The ultimate purpose of the analysis, in other words, is *to determine the prices of assets.* Each k_i is the random gross return *per unit of money spent on asset i,* so it changes if the price of the asset changes while the return per physical unit of the asset does not. For example consider a share with random future dividends: the dividends are per share, but in order to obtain them one pays a price that depends on the price of the share. So one of the things that condition (9.13) tells us is that in order for an asset to be accepted in a portfolio the price of the asset must adjust until it falls in a range that makes it possible to satisfy that condition.

However, the condition itself can appear surprising because no explicit mention of the riskiness of the non-safe assets appears in Eq. (9.13). One might have expected some measure of the riskiness of each asset to appear in the condition, e.g. the risk avoidance price associated with the lottery represented by the asset's returns. Intuition suggests that risk aversion should imply that one will invest in a riskier asset only if the expected value of the asset's returns is sufficiently higher than for the less risky investments as to compensate for the greater risk. Is this intuition proved mistaken by Eq. (9.13)?

No, and we can understand what is going on by considering the case with only one risky asset (asset 1) besides a safe one (asset zero), cf. Eq. (9.9); however, now we assume $r_0 > 0$ and we express the choice in terms of the *share* α of invested wealth going to the risky asset, so the first-order condition is (9.12) applied to asset 1, which, remembering that $k_1 - 1 = r_1$, can be written

$$E\big(u'(w)(r_1 - r_0)\big) = 0.$$

Rewriting it as $E(u'(w)\cdot r_1) = r_0 E(u'(w))$ and applying the covariance identity we obtain

$$
\begin{aligned}
E(r_1) &= \frac{r_0 E(u'(w)) - Cov(u'(w), r_1)}{E(u'(w))} \\
&= r_0 + \frac{-Cov(u'(w), r_1)}{E(u'(w))} = r_0 +' \textit{ risk premium'}.
\end{aligned}
\tag{9.14}
$$

The 'risk premium' is positive, because r_1 is necessarily correlated positively with w, it is what makes w a random variable! The negative $Cov(u'(w), r_1)$ is the way the dependence of the randomness (and hence riskiness) of w on the randomness of r_1 reveals itself. So the 'risk premium' must be positive to compensate for the randomness of the returns of a mixed portfolio that includes the risky asset. The greater the share of W allocated to the risky asset, the greater the variability of the random variable $u'(w)$, therefore the greater the absolute value of the covariance: if $E(r_1)$ is given, expression (9.14) also determines the share of the risky asset in the portfolio.

Now we can understand better what is going on with many assets. A risky asset which, when added to a portfolio, increases the variability of total returns and hence of w will be accepted in the portfolio only if it has a higher expected rate of return than the portfolio without it. The 'variability' of w is a vague expression, and in more advanced texts the reader can find comparisons of the riskiness of different assets based on 'stochastic dominance' (briefly hinted at here in ▶ Sect. 9.6), but here we limit ourselves to using variance as the measure of 'var-

9.21 · Portfolio Selection: Many Assets. Tobin

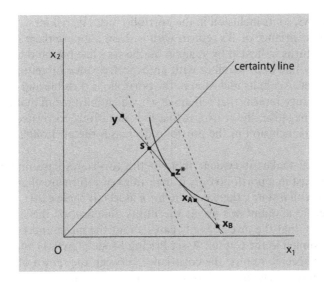

■ **Fig. 9.9** Two states of nature, the slope of the broken lines indicates the respective probabilities. Let s be the return of a safe asset, x_A the returns of risky asset A, and z^* the preferred combination; a second risky asset B can enter the portofolio and increase its variance only if its returns have greater expected value so as to compensate the increased variance.

iability' and hence of riskiness.[36] Every time an asset's returns are correlated with the general movement of the ensemble of returns to the point that its inclusion in the portfolio raises the variance of the total return, this increases the riskiness of the portfolio, and, owing to risk aversion, this makes the inclusion of the asset in the portfolio convenient only if it raises the average portfolio expected return.

Thus assume a safe asset (with net returns **s** if the whole of W were allocated to it) and two risky assets A and B, and suppose initially that only asset A (with net returns x_A if the whole of W were allocated to it) is included in the portfolio together with the safe asset. There results a certain riskiness of the portfolio, that implies a 'risk premium' on the risky asset which we indicate as $P_A = E(r_A) - r_0$. Now the investor considers the possibility of including the second risky asset in the portfolio. Assume only two states of nature, and hence two possible returns for each asset, and consider ■ Fig. 9.9, where as usual the broken lines are constant-expected-value lines whose slope indicates the probabilities of the two states. Suppose the second risky asset has net returns x_B that are on the line s-x_A but further away from the certainty line. The optimal portfolio remains the one yielding average returns z^*, which means that A and B can co-exist in the portfolio. Since B has a higher expected return than A, this must mean that the 'risk premium' P_B is greater than P_A. The reason is that B's returns have greater

---

36 There is no universally accepted *definition* of riskiness; the definition is implicitly supplied by how one measures it. One approach is to define the riskiness of a lottery by the risk avoidance price, or better (in order to be able to compare lotteries with different sizes of prizes) by the ratio of the risk avoidance price to the expected value of the lottery. Then which one, of two lotteries, is riskier can depend on the utility function one uses.

variance than A's, so its inclusion in the portfolio raises its riskiness; this shows up in the greater covariance of B's returns with w. Now suppose there is a third risky asset C with returns indicated by $\mathbf{y}$, again on the $\mathbf{s}$-$\mathbf{x_A}$ line but on the opposite side of the certainty line and therefore with an expected value of returns lower than for the safe asset. Again its inclusion in the portfolio is possible and does not alter the optimal average returns that remain at $\mathbf{z^*}$, which must mean that the 'risk premium' on C is negative; the reason is that C is negatively correlated with A or B and therefore its inclusion in the portfolio decreases the portfolio's variance and hence riskiness.

◘ Figure 9.9 makes it evident that, in the two-states case, more than two assets can co-exist in a portfolio only if their rates of return are aligned, like $\mathbf{s}$, $\mathbf{x_A}$, $\mathbf{x_B}$ and $\mathbf{y}$. But with n states, there is room for n assets (if these exist).

More specific assumptions about the utility function of the financial investor, for example that the investor only cares about the mean and the variance of returns (as assumed in the Capital Asset Pricing Model, CAPM), make it possible to reach more specific results; the covariance between the return of an asset and the portfolio return remains an important influence on the asset's risk premium because it reveals the extent to which inclusion of the asset in the portfolio affects the mean and the variability of its average return.[37] Still, it may be useful to see how the assumption that the investor measures risk simply by the variance of returns can allow a simple analysis of 'liquidity preference' (Keynes's 'speculative' demand for money) based on portfolio choice.

Assume, following Tobin (1958), that the agent must choose whether to hold a stock of idle money (which yields zero return) in excess of what is strictly required for transaction and precautionary purposes, or use all of her wealth (apart from the minimum portion to be held in transaction and precautionary money) to buy assets yielding a positive but uncertain return. Assume there is a single such asset, that yields a return $r+g$, where r is given and g is a random variable with mean zero and a normal distribution with standard deviation σ. Suppose the agent has already decided the total sum to allocate between idle money A_1 and return-yielding asset A_2, and normalize this sum to 1, so A_1 and A_2 indicate the share of the total sum going respectively to money and to the asset. In her choice of portfolio composition, the agent prefers more expected return to less, but is risk averse and therefore prefers less variance to more. Draw a Cartesian diagram with quadrants I and IV; in quadrant I, measure the portfolio expected return R in ordinate and the *portfolio's* standard deviation σ_p in abscissa, see ◘ Fig. 9.10. In the diagram we can draw the indifference curves of the agent as between expected return and risk; these are upward sloping because a higher expected return is required to compensate for more risk, i.e. more variance. If furthermore we assume that risk aversion increases as risk increases, the indif-

---

37 I leave to texts on finance the task of a more detailed introduction to portfolio choice and of a discussion of the limits of mean-variance analysis. A healthy dose of realism is certainly very useful in this field, inside stories written by financial market operators can be of help, for example, MacDonald (2009).

9.21 · Portfolio Selection: Many Assets. Tobin

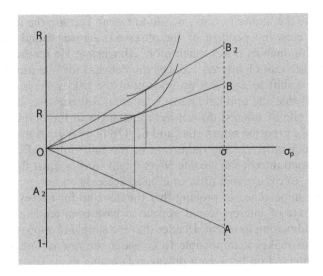

Fig. 9.10 Tobin's analysis

ference curves are convex. If $A_1=1$, the portfolio includes only money and has return zero and standard deviation zero. If $A_2=1$, the portfolio includes only the asset and has expected return and standard deviation equal to those of the asset's return, as indicated by point $B=(\sigma, r)$.

By changing A_1/A_2 the agent can reach any point on the straight line from the origin to point B: the line indicates R as a linear function of σ_p, because both R and σ_p change linearly with the share allocated to the asset, resulting from the linear combination of the zero return on money and the expected return r on the asset, and of the zero standard deviation and σ. If indifference curves are convex, it is possible that the agent chooses a mixed portfolio, at the point of tangency between indifference curve and the OB line; a 'corner' solution consisting of point B or the origin is also a possibility. If indifference curves are concave or straight lines (indicating that risk aversion does not increase with riskiness), the agent will choose a 'corner' solution.

In quadrant IV, which has again σ_p in abscissa, in ordinate let us have A_2 (measured downwards), that is the share of the asset in the portfolio; and let us draw a straight line OA from the origin with slope $-1/\sigma$. This line, once A_2 is given, determines σ_p which in turn determines R; so we obtain the portfolio's return as a function of its composition. Conversely, if there is internal tangency between the OB line and a convex indifference curve, we immediately obtain the corresponding portfolio composition.

This analysis was proposed by Tobin (1958) as a more solid microeconomic foundation for Keynes's claim that the demand for money is downward sloping in the rate of interest, a claim that Keynes had justified essentially by reference to the existence of expectations of a 'normal' level of the rate of interest, that induce a greater subjective probability of a shift of the actual rate of interest back towards that normal level, the greater the distance from it. Keynes's argument,

782   **Chapter 9** · Uncertainty and General Equilibrium

that could imply the 'liquidity trap', was found weak because the idea of a 'normal' rate of interest independent of the observed rate was found unpersuasive. However, Tobin's analysis is not much more convincing. He reaches the conclusion that a higher rate of interest reduces the demand for idle money balances, that is, induces a shift to a greater proportion of the risky asset in the portfolio, by assuming (1) that the optimal choice is internal (otherwise at least moderate changes in the rate of interest do not induce changes in the optimal portfolio), and (2) that if the expected return rises and the OB line becomes the OB_2 line, the point of tangency moves to the right, that is, the substitution effect dominates. But this is not guaranteed: the income effect might work against the substitution effect causing σ_p to change very little, or even to decrease.

Anyway the importance of proving that the demand for money is downward sloping in the rate of interest would appear to have been rendered obsolete by the increasing admission in recent decades that the supply of money is essentially endogenous: this makes it impossible to consider the rate of interest as determined by the intersection between a downward-sloping money demand schedule and a given money supply.

9.22 **State-Dependent Utility**

I leave now portfolio selection and return to some considerations on VNM utility theory.

A distinction relevant for the appropriate use of VNM utility is between state-independent and state-dependent utility.

We have already mentioned the possibility to consider the outcomes of a lottery as state-indexed, that is, as obtained depending on which state of nature (or on which event, that is, *set* of states of nature) comes out to be the case when uncertainty is resolved. Now consider a health insurance representable as a two-outcomes money lottery: suppose the probability of an invalidating accident is 50%; consider the two-states representation of payoffs as in ◻ Fig. 9.1; will the indifference curves at the certainty line have slope −1/2? It would mean that the consumer's overall utility is unaffected by the expectation of one less future dollar in the healthy state and one more future dollar when invalid; but the consumer knows that in the latter state she will be much less happy and less able to obtain pleasurable consumptions, so it is highly likely that she needs more than one more dollar in the unlucky state to compensate for one less dollar when healthy. The assumption, made in VNM expected utility, that the basic utility function $u(x)$ is the same for all outcomes, is only plausible when the events determining which outcome is realized do not affect the enjoyment that the good x, be it money or anything else, is capable of producing. Another example: a state-independent utility of money is not appropriate if the states differ significantly in the money prices of relevant consumption goods.

Let us consider a numerical example. Assume a lottery with two states, money as payoff, and state-specific utility functions. Suppose the decision maker judges that $u_1(x) = x^{1/2}$ and that she will be equally happy in

9.22 · State-Dependent Utility

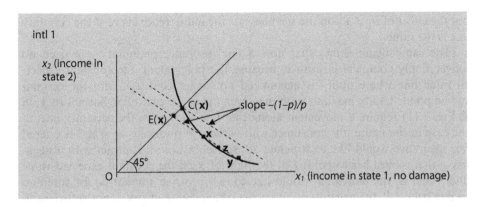

Fig. 9.11 State-dependent utility: the slope of the indifference curve at the certainty line differs from $-(1-p)/p$

state 2 as in state 1 if she has double the amount of money in state 2 than in state 1, hence $u_2(2x)=u_1(x)$, that is, $u_2(x)=x^{1/2}/2^{1/2}$, and suppose that, were it not for this, utility would have the expected utility form, that is, $U(x) = pu_1(x_1) + (1-p)u_2(x_2) = px_L^{1/2} + (1-p)x_2^{1/2}/2^{1/2}$. Then the slope of an indifference curve is

$$-(\partial U/\partial x_1)/(\partial U/\partial x_2) = -1/2px_1^{-1/2}/\left[1/2(1-p)x_2^{-1/2}/2^{1/2}\right].$$

At the certainty line $(x_1=x_2)$ this slope becomes $-2^{1/2}p/(1-p)$, different from $-p/(1-p)$; it depends not only on the probabilities but also on the different marginal utility of money in the two states.

This example has assumed that overall utility is still the sum of the expected values of the utility of the different payoffs, but that the subutility functions differ across states. This form of overall utility too can be derived from axioms, very similar in fact to the ones producing the VNM expected utility form, and we discuss them later. Now I only note some implications of the utility of a lottery having the form $U(L)=\Sigma_s p_s u_s(x_s)$.

Assuming for simplicity only two states, the slope of the indifference curve at the certainty line is

$$-\frac{\partial U/\partial x_1}{\partial U/\partial x_2} = -\frac{p_1}{1-p_1}\frac{\partial u_1/\partial x_1}{\partial u_2/\partial x_2} \text{ with } x_1 = x_2.$$

Thus $u_1' > u_2'$ causes the slope to be steeper than the constant-expected-value line, $u_1' < u_2'$ causes it to be flatter. Furthermore unless it is $u_2=\alpha u_1 + \beta$ the slope of indifference curves will not be constant along the certainty line.

Another important difference from VNM utility is that now strictly convex indifference curves no longer imply $E(x)>C(x)$ for x not on the certainty line, as
◘ Fig. 9.11 makes evident. If the figure is interpreted as applying to insurance, with $x=(W, W-D)$, and if p is the probability of the damage D (i.e. of state 2) as assumed earlier, then the slope of the constant-expected-value line is $-(1-p)/p$

Chapter 9 · Uncertainty and General Equilibrium

but the effect of $u'_1 \neq u'_2$ on the steepness of the indifference curve at the certainty line is the same.

The same figure shows that now a fair insurance premium $\pi = p$ need no longer imply complete insurance, because the point along the constant-expected-value line where utility is maximized no longer coincides with the certainty-line point. Utility maximization may even (as in the case of **x**, but not of **y**, in ◘ Fig. 9.11) require a movement along that line *away from* the certainty line; in the case in the figure, the consumer who without insurance is at **x** and is offered fair insurance would like to stipulate a 'reverse' insurance contract with a negative q that moved her to point **z** to the right of **x** on the constant-expected-value line,[38] that is, the individual would like to *receive* some amount pq for sure and to pay back q if the negative event occurs: the increase in risk is not sufficient to compensate for the greater marginal utility of income in state 1. The empirical evidence suggests that this case is unlikely. More interesting is the case $u'_1 < u'_2$ at the certainty line, which implies (confirm it graphically as an ***Exercise***) that the individual would like to *overinsure,* i.e. to move from an initial point **x** to the right of the certainty line to a point to the left, a case that may well happen when insuring against invalidating accidents.

9.23 Subjective Expected Utility

Up to this point we took the probabilities of outcomes or of states of nature as regarded by the decision maker as *objective, known*. This assumption is legitimate when one faces a well-defined randomizing device, such as fair dice, a roulette wheel, card shuffling, for which frequentist definitions of probability appear legitimate. Often this is not the case. The result of horse races, or of football (soccer) games, or of investment in research, are standard examples. For such non-repeated cases a frequentist might even deny that it makes sense to talk of *probability* of an event. But a tradition of thought started by Ramsey and De Finetti, and first completely formalized by Leonard Savage in 1954, has argued that when individuals choose among actions with uncertain outcome their choices *reveal* the likelihood they attribute to the occurrence of the states on which the outcome depends, and if these choices satisfy certain axioms then it is possible to view them as performed by an agent who behaves *as if* she/he were maximizing an expected utility function, in which the numbers that multiply the several sub-utilities have formally the same role as the probabilities in VNM utility functions,

---

38 Convex indifference curves now mean that the consumer will prefer to a lottery the lottery with the same expected value but where the slope of the indifference curve equals the slope of the constant-expected-value line (like point **z** relative to initial point **x** in ◘ Fig. 9.10), which means that the *marginal utility* of money is the same in the two states: this condition takes the place of certainty in the determination of the initial lotteries from which the consumer will refuse to move by accepting a fair bet.

9.23 · Subjective Expected Utility

and therefore are called *subjective probabilities*. I report a very clear passage that illustrates the perspective, from the textbook by Mas-Colell et al.:

>> Individuals make judgments about the chances of uncertain events that are not necessarily expressible in quantitative form ... If would be very helpful, both theoretically and practically, if we could assert that choices are made as if individuals held probabilistic beliefs. Even better, we would like that well-defined probabilistic beliefs be revealed by choice behavior. This is the intent of *subjective probability theory*. The theory argues that even if states of the world are not associated with recognizable, objective probabilities, consistency-like restrictions on preferences among gambles still imply that decision makers behave as if utilities were assigned to outcomes, probabilities were attached to states of nature, and decisions were made by taking expected utilities. (Mas-Colell et al. 1995, p. 205)

The basic idea of the approach can be supplied by reference to ◘ Fig. 9.1, after some terminology. Savage's basic framework distinguishes:

states of nature, one of which is going to occur but the decision maker does not know which one in advance; the states are mutually exclusive and exhaustive, and which one will occur is independent of the decision maker's choice; an *event* is a subset of the set of states of nature;

outcomes or *payoffs*, i.e. the *consequences* (the ones relevant to the decision maker's preferences) of the decision (the *act*) taken by her/him, consequences that, for the same act, will differ depending on the state of nature that obtains; the outcomes or consequences can be sums of money, vectors of goods, lotteries, anything really.

acts or decisions, i.e. courses of action (for example to sell a certain asset rather than keeping it, to sign an insurance contract and for what amount, to raise the bid or not at a game of poker, to choose a vacation resort without knowing what the weather will be like in that place, to choose to enrol for a university degree rather than taking a job immediately), which have different consequences depending on which state of nature obtains; formally, an act can be seen as a function from states to consequences, that specifies the payoff of that act for each state (the function itself, however, is an incomplete rendering of the intuitive idea of what an act is, because it does not clarify which concrete action *causes* the list of possible consequences indicated by the function). If the probabilities of the states are given, an act is like choosing a lottery, because it associates probabilities to consequences. By itself an act does not specify the probabilities of the consequences (i.e. of the states). Preference among acts, however, can only be specified when the probabilities of states are given.

Assume all outcomes can be represented by vector of divisible goods $\in R^n$. In order to help intuition you can interpret it as a vector of consumption goods. It might consist of a single element, e.g. money. We also assume a finite number of alternative states, indexed by $s = 1, ..., S$. A vector $\mathbf{x}_s$ indicates a consumption vector obtainable in state s.

A *prospect* is a vector of outcomes, one for each possible state; hence, if outcomes are vectors (e.g. consumption baskets), a prospect is a vector of S vectors $\mathbf{x}_s$ that are state-indexed outcomes. A prospect differs from a lottery in that

786   **Chapter 9** · Uncertainty and General Equilibrium

it is a list of outcomes *without* probabilities attached to them.[39] I will not use bold characters for prospects. Assume the decision maker faces a *known* (possibly infinite) set of prospects P, P', P'', ..., and can choose one of them, that is, can decide to *act* so as to make one of these prospects become the one that determines the outcomes she will obtain depending on which state of nature occurs. For example, she may sign a house fire insurance contract or not sign it, her choice determines the prospect that indicates the payoffs for the two alternative events 'house fire, no house fire'. An act is therefore, formally, a map that assigns to each state of nature s a payoff x_s; it differs from a prospect only in that it includes the idea of *choice* of a prospect, but otherwise it is formally identical to a prospect. (If one talks of events instead of states of nature, one interprets the prospect as assigning the same outcome to all states of nature grouped in the same event.)

Suppose the decision maker has *a preference order over prospects (or acts), which is complete, reflexive, transitive and continuous* in the same sense as for the vectors of consumption goods studied in ▶ Chap. 4; the definitions are the same, it suffices to apply them to the vectors of 'consumption goods' with $n \times S$ elements x_{is}, the first index indicating the type of good and the second one the state of nature.[40] Thus we are assuming that there exist continuous indifference curves or rather (hyper)surfaces that specify all prospects equipreferred to a given one.

To obtain an initial intuition of the approach, let us restrict ourselves for simplicity to one good (e.g. money) and two states, then the preference order implies indifference curves like in ◘ Fig. 9.1, *without* known probabilities attached to the two states. The basic idea of the subjective expected utility approach is that we can still define the 45° line as the certainty line, and *if* the preferences of the decision maker can be represented by an additively separable utility function $U(x_1, x_2) = \alpha u(x_1) + (1 - \alpha)u(x_2)$ with $u(\cdot)$ the same for the two states, *then* α is implicit in the slope of the indifference curve at the certainty line (because this slope is $-\alpha/(1 - \alpha)$ as shown earlier), and we can interpret α as equivalent to a probability assigned by the decision maker to the occurrence of state 1. Then we can call α the *subjective* probability implicitly assigned by the individual to state 1, as revealed by his preferences over prospects.

The question becomes, which axioms (in addition to the specified conditions of completeness, transitivity, etc., of preferences) can ensure that preferences over prospects can be represented by a VNM expected utility function. Savage (1954) obtains it with seven axioms. A complete presentation of his approach is beyond the aims of this textbook. The central axioms are:

- an axiom of *state irrelevance*, that is, that the individual only cares about outcomes and not about the states and the acts or prospects that yield them;
- an axiom of *revealed likelihood* that formalizes the idea that, if outcome $\mathbf{x}$ is preferred to $\mathbf{x'}$ under certainty, and if two prospects P and Q both offer $\mathbf{x}$ or $\mathbf{x'}$

---

39 This definition of prospect has no necessary connection with *prospect theory* which is a specific theory of the utility function in the presence of uncertainty and is briefly discussed later.

40 The continuity axiom specified in the derivation of VNM expected utility is unnecessary for the moment because prospects are not lotteries (i.e. do not include a specification of probabilities).

as the sole outcomes but in different events and prospect P is preferred, it must be because the events in which P offers **x** are considered by the chooser more likely to happen than the ones where Q offers x; thus suppose four states of nature, P offers **x** in states 1 and 2, and x' in states 3 and 4, while Q offers x in states 1 and 3, and **x'** in states 2 and 4, and P is strictly preferred: it must mean that (it is as if) the joint probability of the event 'states 1 or 2' is esteemed greater than the joint probability of the event 'states 1 or 3';

- the axiom called the *Sure Thing Principle* that assumes that the preference order among two prospects is independent of the payoffs in the states where the payoffs are the same. This axiom is the most famous one so I give a more precise statement:

The Sure Thing Principle.

Suppose two distinct prospects P and P' disagree on some of the payoffs in a subset of states whose generic index s without loss of generality we can assume goes from 1 to k, i.e. $x_s(P) = x_s(P')$ *for s = 1,…,k, while they agree on the payoffs in the remaining states of nature s = k + 1,…,S; and suppose that P is preferred to P'. If the payoffs* x_s *common to the two prospects for s = k + 1,…,S are changed in the same way for the two prospects, that is if, calling the new prospects Q and Q', for s = k + 1,…,S it is* $x_s(Q) = x_s(Q')$ *with at least one* $x_s(Q) \neq x_s(P)$*, while the payoffs for the other states s = 1,…,k are not changed [i.e.* $x_s(Q) = x_s(P)$ *and* $x_s(Q') = x_s(P')$ *for s = 1,…,k], then Q is preferred to Q' whatever the new common* x_s *payoffs for s = k + 1,…,S.*

This is similar to the independence axiom of VNM expected utility, and it is defended on the same basis.

Savage's approach produces the desired result, but the proof, besides using mathematical notions too advanced for this course, is *very* long: in a highly esteemed reference book, Fishburn (1970), it takes 19 pages! I defer the reader to Sect. 2 of the online Appendix to this chapter (in the book's website on Springer-Link) for a discussion of axioms that imply the existence of subjective expected utility, using the simpler approach of Anscombe and Aumann.

9.24 **Risk or Uncertainty?**

The subjective expected utility approach is sometimes argued to surmount the distinction, proposed by Frank Knight (1921), between *risk* and *uncertainty*. Risk refers to situations where the probabilities of the possible alternative events are known, objective, as with roulette. Uncertainty refers to situations where probabilities are not known, be it because of insufficient information by the chooser, or because of intrinsic impossibility, due to the event being unique, non-repeated and complex (e.g. the outcome of a football match), or due to the possible occurrence of logically unpredictable novelties (e.g. a scientific discovery). Nowadays the term 'uncertainty' is often used to cover risk too, and this usage has been accepted here. Then Knightian uncertainty can be distinguished by calling it 'radical uncertainty' or 'strong uncertainty'. Radical uncertainty is extremely important in Keynes's *General Theory* (1936):

> The outstanding fact is the extreme precariousness of the basis of knowledge on which our estimates of prospective yield have to be made. Our knowledge of the factors which will govern the yield of an investment some years hence is usually very slight and often negligible. If we speak frankly, we have to admit that our basis of knowledge for estimating the yield ten years hence of a railway, a copper mine, a textile factory, the goodwill of a patent medicine, an Atlantic liner, a building in the City of London amounts to little and sometimes to nothing". (*General Theory* p. 150)

In such a situation, Keynes argues, optimal choices are not determinable, and other influences must be considered in order to explain choices. Keynes stresses two, in particular. One is **animal spirits** (prerational impulses), such as the urge and pleasure to make things happen, to conquer a social position, to take risks: 'If human nature felt no temptation to take a chance, no satisfaction (profit apart) in constructing a factory, a railway, a mine or a farm, there might not be much investment merely as a result of cold calculation' (*ibid.*). Although Keynes has in mind above all the owner-entrepreneur who risks his own capital, these considerations apply to salaried managers too, whose social status depends on the success of their enterprise. The other influence is **conventions**, that is, rules of behaviour that have come to dominate a certain sphere of economic life, and produce 'a considerable measure of continuity and stability in our affairs' (*ibid.*, p. 152); as long as one follows them, one avoids the risk of being accused of extravagant and imprudent behaviour, which is very important if one is to go on being trusted in the community of investors. Sociology and psychology have a role here, because animal spirits and conventions, and their changes, in turn must have causes, which if understood will allow explanations and predictions and will perhaps permit policy insights.

Relative to these considerations, the argument of the subjective expected utility theorist is that, since a person makes choices in situations of radical uncertainty too, if these choices conform to the axioms of subjective expected utility then it is as if the person were assigning probabilities, revealed by the choices, to the alternative possible events, and therefore it is as if the person were considering the situation as one of measurable risk:

> Ramsey (1931), de Finetti (1931) and Savage (1954) showed that probabilities can be defined in the absence of statistics after all, by relating them to observable choice. For example, $P(E) = 0.5$ can be derived from an observed indifference between receiving a prize under event E and receiving it under not-E (the complement to E). Although widely understood today, the idea that something as intangible as a subjective degree of belief can be made observable through choice behaviour, and can even be quantified precisely, was a major intellectual advance. (Wakker 2008, p. 428).

Some have concluded that Knight's distinction between risk and radical uncertainty is obsolete (Hirshleifer and Riley 1979). This conclusion has not met general acceptance. On the one hand, from experimental evidence a clear difference has emerged between risk and radical uncertainty in that people exhibit **ambiguity aversion**, that is, they particularly dislike bets where probabilities are not clear (see below on the Ellsberg paradox). The dislike may be such that, on issues on which people have only the vaguest feelings about the likelihood of possible future events, they simply refuse to bet.

On the other hand, even if the choices in situations of radical uncertainty were formalizable as maximizing a utility function in which subjectively estimated probabilities play a role, still the subjective element producing the as-if probabilities would need explanation, because the objective data of the situation do not suffice to determine these probabilities: then the values of these subjective probabilities, and how they are arrived at, become the really important issue.[41] Which is another way of saying that in this case utility maximization is a nearly empty expression: what is important is how people deal with radical uncertainty so as to arrive anyway at decisions in spite of the impossibility of reaching an unambiguously optimal decision.[42] Which takes us back to Keynes's considerations.

For example, on animal spirits: the decision to build a tourist resort in a tropical nation which has known guerrilla episodes can seldom be based on a certainty that no further social turmoil will break out, or that no change in tastes and no new illness will discourage tourism in tropical climates: some self-assurance that one will find a way to deal with the unforeseeable difficulties that no doubt will turn up is often indispensable for taking such a decision. This self-assurance can be produced by social conditioning, education, a certainty of support by one's social group or by the state, etcetera. Thus there is a tradition that tries to explain differences in the growth rates of nations as due, at least in part, to differences in *entrepreneurship*, that is in the readiness to undertake investment projects with unclear returns, differences to be in turn explained by institutional and sociological differences that can be seen as influencing animal spirits (see, e.g., Chang and Kozul-Wright 1994).

As to conventions, the term broadly interpreted also includes routines and rules, that are developed to decrease the difficulty with taking decisions in complex or novel situations, and often acquire an inertia that makes them survive without clear indications that they are efficient. For example, in product-differentiated industries where continuous product innovation is important, there seems to be a widely accepted routine of investing in research and development 5 or 6 percent. of sales receipts, with no evident reason why not less nor more, except that most other firms in the industry follow this rule.

---

41 An important consequence is that, as Wakker (2008, p. 431) notes, differently from objective probabilities that 'are stable, and readily available for analyses, empirical tests and communication in group decisions', radical-uncertainty subjective probabilities 'can be volatile and can change at any time by mere further thinking by the agent'. Thus, like the expectations about future prices discussed in ▶ Chap. 8, *subjective probabilities suffer from the indefiniteness and the impermanence problems.*

42 Starting from this impossibility, Herbert Simon has stressed the need to abandon the assumption of rational optimization and to replace it with the study of *procedural rationality*, the set of procedures considered fruitful for the *search* for a *satisfactory* decision, a search that will stop at a certain point because further analysis would always be possible (as in scientific research!) but it would be costly in time and resources. Simon's insistence on limited rationality and satisficing rather than optimization has deeply affected the study of organizations (March and Simon 1958).

790   **Chapter 9** · Uncertainty and General Equilibrium

9.25 Non-expected Utility: Allais' Paradox, Prospect Theory, Ellsberg's Paradox

It is increasingly accepted that the way people actually choose in uncertain situations is not well depicted by expected utility and subjective expected utility. The proposed alternatives are still in an infant stage in the application to the kinds of problems discussed thus far in this chapter, but at least the most popular contender, Kahneman and Tversky's *prospect theory,* deserves to be illustrated. Before coming to it, I remember that the birth of new approaches to choice under uncertainty was greatly stimulated by two famous counterexamples to expected utility and to subjective expected utility: the Allais Paradox (Allais 1953) and the Ellsberg Paradox (Ellsberg 1961).

Here is one version of the Allais Paradox. You are offered a choice between:

» Gamble I. You receive $1 million for certain.
Gamble II. You receive 5 million with probability 10%, or 1 million with probability 89%, or nothing with probability 1%.

» Which gamble do you choose? Write it down.
Now you are offered a choice between two more gambles:

» Gamble III. You receive 1 million with probability 11%, or nothing with probability 89%.
Gamble IV. You receive 5 million with probability 10%, or nothing with probability 90%.

Which gamble do you choose? Allais's argument (applied to this example) was that, on the basis of introspection, it is perfectly reasonable to choose I over II (the 10% probability of obtaining 4 more million may not seem worth the 1% risk of getting nothing rather than the considerable sum of 1 million for sure), and IV over III (the increase by 1% of the anyway high probability of getting nothing may well appear a price worth paying for the possibility of obtaining not 1 but 5 million). Subsequent experimental evidence produced by Kahneman and Tversky and also by others has confirmed that this is indeed the choice of a majority of people. But it contradicts expected utility, because if one chooses I over II, then expected utility implies (the numbers in parentheses indicate millions of dollars):

$$u(1) > .10u(5) + .89u(1) + .01u(0)$$

which can be rewritten

$$.11u(1) > .10u(5) + .01u(0)$$

which by adding $0.89u(0)$ to both sides becomes $u(III) > u(IV)$:

$$.11u(1) + .89u(0) > .10u(5) + .90u(0).$$

Can we find a VNM axiom contradicted by Allais' Paradox? The example can be reformulated as proposing four gambles, all of them contemplating three possible

9.25 · Non-expected Utility ...

outcomes α, β, γ with respective probabilities 0.01, 0.10, 0.89, but differing in the payoffs associated with these probabilities. The payoffs (in millions of dollars) are as follows:

	α = 0.01	β = 0.10	γ = 0.89
I	1	1	1
II	0	5	1
III	1	1	0
IV	0	5	0

Gambles I and II have the same γ payoff; gambles III and IV too, except that the γ payoff is zero; furthermore if one looks only at the first two payoffs, these are the same in I and III, and in II and IV. So we can interpret these gambles as lotteries. Consider the following four outcomes: A and C yield payoff 1 for sure, D yields payoff 0 for sure, and B is a lottery with payoffs (0, 5) with respective probabilities 1/11 and 10/11. Also let p = 0.11. Then:

I − is equivalent to p∘A ⊕ (1 − p)∘C,

II − is equivalent to p∘B ⊕ (1 − p)∘C,

III − is equivalent to p∘A ⊕ (1 − p)∘D,

IV − is equivalent to p∘B ⊕ (1 − p)∘D.

The independence axiom in the strong version (9.2) states that A ≻ B if and only if p∘A ⊕ (1 − p)∘C ≻ p∘B ⊕ (1 − p)∘C, for any C; therefore replacing C with D should not alter the preference order, and since I is preferred to II, III should be preferred to IV: but it isn't. So Allais' Paradox violates the independence axiom.

One suggested explanation is that a 1% probability of losing an otherwise certain and considerable gain is valued differently from a 1% increase of the probability of losing an already highly improbable gain, because of different *regrets*: one anticipates a strong regret if the loss were to occur owing to having chosen II over I, while very little regret is anticipated if one chooses IV over III and does not win, since the probability of winning was low anyway.

Another suggested explanation is that people do not fully understand the gambles, and do not realize that their choices contradict the independence axiom, which they find rational if it is explained to them; so if they are shown the implication of their choice, they modify it. However, the empirical evidence shows that some, but only a minority, of the people who violated the independence axiom do reconsider their choice once they are illustrated the axiom and shown that they contradicted it.

Another suggested explanation, nowadays the more popular one, is offered by *prospect theory*. The latter, on the basis of considerable experimental evidence, argues that empirical choices under uncertainty differ from the usual analyses based on expected utility theory in several respects. I will discuss the more recent version called 'cumulative prospect theory', and restricted to scalar outcomes, e.g. amounts of money. Following Barberis (2013), consider the gamble

$$(x_{-m}, p_{-m}; x_{-m+1}, p_{-m+1}; \ldots; x_0, p_0; x_1, p_1; \ldots; x_n, p_n)$$

to be read as 'gain x_t with probability p_t, gain x_{t+1} with probability p_{t+1}, and so on', for $-m \leq t \leq n$, where the outcomes are arranged in increasing order, and $x_0 = 0$. Under expected utility theory, the utility of this gamble is $\sum_{t=-m}^{n} p_t u(W + x_t)$, where W is current wealth and u is the subutility function, strictly concave if the individual is risk averse.

Prospect theory on the contrary evaluates the gamble as

$$\sum_{t=-m}^{n} \pi_t v(x_t)$$

where $v(\cdot)$, called the 'value function', is an increasing function with $v(0) = 0$, that has the role of a subutility function but has a shape to be illustrated, and the π_t's are 'decision weights' that reflect a weighing (a 'deformation') of probabilities. The prospect theory approach is characterized by four main elements:

First, *reference dependence*. The gamble is evaluated on the basis of the gains and losses alone, not on the basis of the total wealth associated with each outcome; according to expected utility the same gamble would be evaluated differently depending on the W one starts from; not so according to prospect theory, which implies that what is relevant is the divergence the outcomes cause from a reference situation, the one corresponding to x_0 where $v = 0$ (usually, one's situation before accepting or not the gamble). Reread the distinction between two ways of assessing the outcomes of the St. Petersburg Paradox. But prospect theory adds that the same outcomes in terms of final wealth will be evaluated differently for different reference points.

Second, *loss aversion*. A decrease of wealth relative to the wealth of the reference point is disliked much more than the same *increase* in wealth relative to the reference point is appreciated.

Third, *risk aversion for gains, risk loving for losses, but with 'diminishing sensitivity'*.

The result of these three characteristics is that the typical value function has the shape of ■ Fig. 9.12, concave for gains, convex for losses, but less and less concave or convex as the payoffs become more removed from the reference point.

Fourth, *probability weighing*. The numbers multiplying the value function for each outcome are not the probabilities but a transformation of the probabilities according to a *probability weighing function* $\pi(p)$, which—empirical evidence is argued to show—gives greater weight to probability changes when probability is very small or very high, so that $\pi(p)$ has the form shown in ■ Fig. 9.12. This aspect has been given particular importance in a second version of the theory, called *cumulative prospect theory*, which insists on a relevantly overweight given to very small probabilities.[43]

(This can explain the Allais paradox, because in the example of the paradox given above the probability of winning a considerable prize decreases from 100 to 99% as between I and II, and from 11 to 10% as between III and IV, and accord-

---

43 Here this term has no negative connotation, it does not imply *excessive* weight, it simply means a greater weight than standard expected utility would assign to it.

9.25 · Non-expected Utility ...

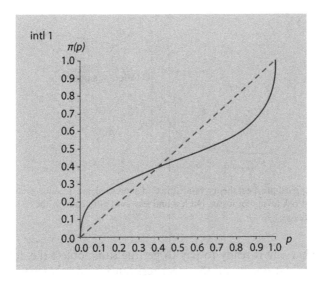

Fig. 9.12 According to prospect theory, the probability weighing function 'deforms' the relevance of differences in p, making them weigh more when p is close to certainty

ing to prospect theory much greater weight is attributed to the first decrease than to the second.)

Kahneman and Tversky have shown that the great majority of individuals who had manifested risk aversion relative to a choice between two gambles both offering a *positive* expected value, when offered a choice between the two gambles V and VI below, both with *negative* expected value, choose gamble VI over V:

> Gamble V: a certain loss of $ 750.
> Gamble VI: a loss of $ 1000 with probability 75% and zero loss with probability 25%.

The expected value of VI is—750, so risk-averse individuals should prefer the expected value for sure to the risky gamble VI; on the contrary about 80% of the interviewed people chose VI. This result is not by itself in contradiction with expected utility, but it shows that the utility of wealth may be a concave or a convex function depending on whether expected wealth is greater or less than an initial reference point (mostly, the wealth one starts from). Indeed Kahneman and Tversky on the basis of extensive evidence conclude that individuals are risk averse for most gains, but risk seeking for most losses; they also note that this pattern appears to switch for very small probabilities and very big gains or losses: people buy lottery tickets that imply very unfair bets (thus exhibiting risk seeking, or overvaluation of the probability of wins relative to expected utility theory), and buy unfair insurance for very-low probability losses (thus exhibiting risk aversion, or 'overvaluation' of the likelihood of loss relative to expected utility theory) (Fig. 9.13).

Prospect theory has been around for over thirty years, and it seems very realistic; it explains many observations that contradict expected utility, for example the relevant difference between what one wants in order to accept giving up an object one already has (i.e. to compensate for the loss of remaining without the

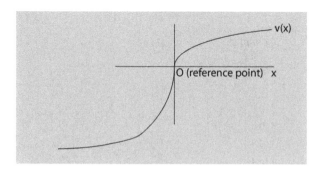

◘ **Fig. 9.13** This typical prospect theory value function shows risk aversion for gains above the reference point, and risk loving for losses, but less and less so in both cases as the distance from the reference point increases

object), and what one is ready to pay to get the same object (i.e. for the gain of having what one did not have); the great resistance to decreases in consumption levels; the readiness of the same individual to buy insurance (which shows risk aversion) and lottery tickets (which contradicts risk aversion because these lotteries are always far from fair). The overweighing of very small probabilities has an important implication for the theory of insurance: it suggests that often insurance might be due, more than to traditional risk aversion, to 'excessive' weight given to the very low probabilities of very unfavourable events; it is still unclear whether this suggestion has validity. Anyway prospect theory is far from having been incorporated into majority research and teaching. As we will see in Chapts. 11–13, not only the theory of strategic choice under uncertainty but also the models in industrial economics and in labour economics that admit uncertainty use only expected utility. Still, a number of stimulating applications of prospect theory are described by Barberis (2013), his survey is definitely worth reading. But will a generalized adoption of prospect theory imply fundamentally different conclusions from those of mainstream analyses based on VNM utility on the 'big' questions of interest for the welfare of people, such as unemployment, poverty, growth, environmental problems? On these questions, it does not seem that prospect theory can make much of a difference.

Now here is (one variant of) the other famous counterexample, the Ellsberg paradox, which questions subjective probability theory. There are two urns, each one containing 100 balls. In urn A it is known that there are 49 red balls and 51 blue balls. In urn B there are red and blue balls in unknown proportion. One ball, to be called A-ball below, is drawn randomly from urn A, and a second ball, to be called B-ball, is drawn randomly from urn B, and their colour is not revealed. Two choices must be made before the colour of the balls is disclosed. The first choice is:

» Choose either the A-ball or the B-ball; if the ball you choose is blue you win $ 100, if it is red you win nothing.

The second choice is:

» Choose either the A-ball or the B-ball; if the ball you choose is red you win $ 100, if it is blue you win nothing.

9.25 · Non-expected Utility ...

Most people choose the A-ball for the first choice, implying—if they are choosing on the basis of subjective probability—that they are assigning to the outcome 'the B-ball is blue' a subjective probability less than the 51% probability that the A-ball is blue; this implies a subjective probability 50% or greater that the B-ball is red; therefore in the second choice they should choose the B-ball or at most (if they believe the probability that it be red to be 50%) they should be indifferent and choose randomly; so in the second choice at most half the participants should choose the A-ball; but the experimental evidence shows that a clear majority choose again the A-ball. Evidently most people prefer a sure 49% probability of getting it right to an unknown probability. This result shows the existence (confirmed in numerous other situations) of *ambiguity aversion*: people dislike situations where the probability distribution of outcomes is itself highly uncertain. Some theorists argue that in a situation of complete ignorance where there is no reason to consider one value of the probability of an outcome (e.g. the number of red balls in urn B) more probable than other values, one should consider all values equally probable (this is called the *principle of insufficient reason* or the *Harsanyi principle*), and therefore in Ellsberg's example one *ought* to consider the situation of urn B analogous to a situation with probability 1/2 of extracting a red ball; others disagree, and the discussion is subtle and relevant for the foundations of probability; but on how people *actually* choose, the existence of ambiguity aversion appears indubitable.

We cannot ask which axiom of the Anscombe–Aumann approach is violated, because this approach requires the existence of lotteries with objective probabilities among the payoffs and cannot be applied to Ellsberg's example, where no consequence is a lottery. So we must refer to Savage's formalism, in spite of having barely hinted at it. Then a different Ellsberg example is easier to analyse. You observe 100 red balls are put into an urn, and then 200 more, whose colour you cannot observe; you only know they are blue or green, but you have no clue as to the proportion. Before one ball is drawn randomly from the urn, you must choose twice between two gambles. The first choice is between gamble A: you win \$100 if the draw is a red ball, and zero dollars otherwise; and gamble B: you win \$100 if the draw is a blue ball, and zero dollars otherwise. The second choice is between gamble C: you win \$100 if the draw is not a blue ball (that is, if it is either a red or a green ball), and zero dollars otherwise; and gamble D: you win \$100 if the draw is not a red ball (that is, if it is either a blue or a green ball), and zero dollars otherwise. Many people interviewed by Ellsberg declared they strictly preferred A to B, and D to C. The explanation is the same as for the previous example: the number of red balls is clear, the number of blue balls is 'ambiguous', and people dislike ambiguity.

To prefer A to B, and D to C, violates Savage's Sure Thing axiom, because A, B, C, D can be viewed as prospects over three possible states of the world distinguished by the colour of the drawn ball: red, blue, green. Let us list the payoffs:

	red	blue	green
A	100	0	0
B	0	100	0
C	100	0	100
D	0	100	100

It is evident that A and B have the same outcome for state 'green', and the same holds for C and D, and that A and C have the same outcomes for 'red' and 'blue', and the same holds for B and D. Therefore A and B are like prospects P and P', and C and D are like prospects Q and Q', in the definition of the Sure Thing axiom (▶ Sect. 9.23), which therefore would require that if A is preferred to B, then C must be preferred to D.

These and other choices contradicting the behaviour predicted by VNM theory or by subjective probability theory have stimulated the exploration of different theories of choice under uncertainty; one must add to prospect theory at least rank-dependent utility, and Choquet subjective utility. Wakker (2008) can be a starting point for the interested reader; also Starmer (2000).

9.26 Reducing Uncertainty Through More Information. Satisficing. Informational Cascades

One way to deal with uncertainty is to postpone decisions to after the uncertainty is resolved. For example, buying in advance a non-refundable train ticket for a one-day vacation may not be convenient if the weather is uncertain and it greatly affects the relative pleasurableness of different locations; then one can reasonably decide to renounce the discount for advance purchase and to wait and buy the ticket just before leaving. (This example assumes that it is not possible to buy advance train tickets conditional on the weather on the day of departure—but that is only too often the situation in the real world.)

Waiting for the uncertainty to be resolved can be seen as a way to obtain better information; of course it is not always possible to adopt this solution; but it is often possible to dedicate resources to obtaining better information, in contents and in probabilities, about what might happen, so as to reduce uncertainty. For example, better information about the products and research projects of competing firms can be costly, but useful to assess the convenience of purchasing a patent. Better information about the state of medical science, demography, and state of health of different social and age groups can permit a better assessment of the probability distribution of life expectancy, important for life insurance firms. In both cases, there is a decision to be made about how many resources to dedicate to acquiring better information.

One example of resources spent on obtaining better information is the frequent use by firms of *sensitivity analysis*: in order to determine the possible returns from a decision, a series of hypotheses is made about possible alternative values of relevant variables: the purpose generally is to determine within which *intervals* of values of these variables the decision does not gravely endanger the firm's survival. This analysis requires time and resources. The probability of possible events remains only vaguely defined, as in the previous example of investment in a tropical tourist resort (▶ Sect. 9.24), but one reaches a clearer understanding of the possibilities. And, as in that example, in deciding what 'gravely' means, Keynesian 'animal spirits' no doubt play a role.

9.26 · Reducing Uncertainty Through More Information ...

On the problem of *how much* to spend on the search for better information, the economist's training immediately suggests that one should equalize the marginal cost of extra information with its marginal benefit (i.e. increase in expected revenue). The problem is that the marginal benefit is not clear until you get the extra information; furthermore, there is no guarantee that the marginal benefit is decreasing. A laboratory looking for a new medicine may find zero benefit from additional units of expenditure, up to a big investment in new scientific instruments that allows new research and finds something that makes the firm enormously rich. One cannot know in advance. Only in very particular situations can one assign plausible probabilities to the marginal benefit from additional expenditure in information gathering. So it seems inevitable to admit *satisficing* rather than definite optimization. Satisficing is the term proposed by Herbert Simon to describe the behaviour of individuals who normally, against standard assumptions, owing to uncertainty and to limits of calculating capacity (bounded rationality) are logically unable to formulate definite maximization problems and must be content with 'satisfactory' decisions; for example firms because of "the uncertainty in the real world, the lack of accurate information, the limited time and limited ability of managers to process information, and other constraints, ... cannot act with the global rationality implied in the traditional theory of the firm. Indeed uncertainty makes impossible the maximization of anything. Given these conditions firms do not seek the maximization of profits, sales, growth or anything else. Instead they exhibit a *satisficing* behaviour: they pursue 'satisfactory profits,' 'satisfactory growth' and so on." (Koutsoyiannis 1975, p. 258). Of course then the definition of 'satisfactory' will result from a set of routines, wisdoms, conventions, susceptible of modification as time goes by; Keynes's observations on the importance of conventional behaviour (▶ Sect. 9.24) are again relevant. It can be argued, however, that satisficing rather than perfect optimization does not undermine the traditional realistic descriptions of the working of competition, firms with satisficing management will still prefer to invest in the more promising sectors, to adjust production to sales, to adopt innovations that reduce average cost ... Indeed one can argue that both in classical authors, and in the more realistic marginalist authors, e.g. Marshall, it is not perfect optimization but rather satisficing that is assumed. Still, the impossibility of perfect optimization, on which Simon was no doubt correct, points to the importance of finding other explanations for issues like how many resources are allocated by firms to trying to produce technical progress, but space constraints prevent a discussion of this fascinating topic.

A recent interesting development is the study of the acquisition of information from the observation of other people's choices, which are taken to reflect the information those other people have about the situation. The result can be *informational cascades* (or information cascades). These are sequences of decisions taken by different individuals, in which an individual takes a decision based on observation of the decisions of others, which is different from the decision suggested by her private information; the individual's decision, being observed by others, reinforces the incentive for subsequent individuals to take the same decision.

798   **Chapter 9 ·** Uncertainty and General Equilibrium

A concrete example is the following. Early in the evening you must choose between two nearby restaurants A and B where you have never been before; a friend has told you that he has learned from friends of friends that the two places cost the same but restaurant A is slightly better; but when you get to restaurant A you observe that it is empty, while in nearby restaurant B four tables are occupied, so you go to restaurant B, taking the fact that B is apparently found preferable to A by others as a more reliable information on the relative quality of the two restaurants than the friend's somewhat tepid recommendation. In fact the customers in restaurant B had chosen it by tossing a coin because they had no previous information. The cascade develops if subsequent customers reason in the same way as you; then starting from a situation where by pure accident restaurant B has some customers while A has none, B becomes full and A remains empty, while perhaps A's cuisine is superior. The tendency to imitate choices that one presumes were rationally based on private information certainly exists in many situations, and can produce non-optimal results.

The more formal study of one example will be a good exercise in the use of **Bayes' Rule**. Imagine a situation in which several risk-neutral individuals decide in sequence whether to choose between two actions A or B, and previous choices (but not payoffs) are observed by subsequent choosers; the payoff to B is known to be zero with certainty; the payoff to A, to be indicated as V, is known to be either $+1$ or -1, but nothing is known on the probability of the two payoffs except that it is known that, before choosing, each individual receives a private signal, not observable by the others, which can be High or Low, and it is known that the signal is High with probability $p > 1/2$ if $V = +1$, and with probability $1 - p$ if $V = -1$. (This signal could be information passed by friends on the quality of a restaurant.) Therefore if one assigns probability π to $V = +1$, then one assigns probability $\pi p + (1 - \pi)(1 - p)$ to receiving signal High.

Suppose the first individual, let us call her Prima, chooses A; the second individual, Secundo, infers that Prima received High. This is because Prima is known to use Bayes' Rule and to accept **Harsanyi's Principle** that, in the absence of reasons to believe otherwise, all possible events should be assigned equal prior probabilities, so she assigns prior probability $1/2$ to $V = +1$, and hence also to the prior probability of receiving High, $1/2$ being the sum of the probability $p/2$ of receiving High if $V = +1$, and of the probability $(1 - p)/2$ of receiving High if $V = -1$; hence, with H and L shorthands for receiving High, and receiving Low, for Prima it is

$$Pr(V = +1|H) = Pr(H|V = +1) \cdot Pr(V = +1)/Pr(H)$$
$$= 1/2p/1/2 = p > 1/2$$

and conversely $Pr(V = +1|L) < 1/2$. So, Secundo (and everybody else) concludes, Prima's choice of A unambiguously reveals that she received High; therefore it is somewhat more likely that $V = +1$. If Secundo receives High, he is even more certain than Prima that V is more likely to be $+1$ than -1, so he chooses A; but if his signal is Low, the two signals offset each other and he is indifferent between A and B; let us assume that in such a situation he chooses randomly by tossing a

9.26 · Reducing Uncertainty Through More Information ...

fair coin and this is known to everybody. Now consider a third chooser, Thirda, before she receives her signal. She observes either AA, or AB. AB leaves no ambiguity: Prima received High, and Secundo received Low and the toss of the coin produced B; so Thirda is in the same situation as Prima, her prior probability of $V = +1$ is 1/2, and she chooses according to her signal; then the fourth individual is in the same situation as Secundo. If Thirda observes AA, she does not know whether Secundo received H, or received L and tossed the coin obtaining A. But she can apply Bayes' Rule. She needs to estimate the probability that Secundo received High, conditional on knowing that he chose A. Then let A be the event 'Secundo chooses A', let H be the event 'Secundo receives High', and let $notH$ be the event complementary to Secundo receving High (that is, $notH$ is the same as Secundo receiving Low). Finally let Q be the probability of an event, conditional on Prima having received High. Thirda is interested in the probability $Q(H|A)$ that Secundo received High, given that he chose A; this by Bayes' Rule can be expressed as

$$Q(H|A) = Q(A|H) \cdot Q(H)/Q(A) = Q(A|H) \cdot Q(H)$$
$$/[Q(A|H) \cdot Q(H) + Q(A|notH) \cdot Q(notH)]$$
$$= \left[p^2 + (1-p)^2 \right] / \left\{ \left[p^2 + (l-p)^2 \right] + 1/2 \left[1 - \left(p^2 + (1-p)^2 \right) \right] \right\}$$
$$> 2/3 \text{ if } p > 1/2.$$

This is because $Q(A|H) = 1$ (Secundo certainly chooses A if he receives High); $Q(A|notH) = 1/2$ (if Secundo receives Low he chooses by tossing a coin); $Q(H)$ results from the following reasoning: on the basis of her certainty that Prima received High, Thirda's updated probability π that $V = +1$ before observing Secundo's decision is p, therefore the probability $\pi p + (1-\pi)(1-p)$ she attributes to Secundo receiving High equals $p^2 + (1-p)^2$, or more formally:

$$Q(H) = Q(H|V = +1)Q(V = +1)$$
$$+ Q(H|V = -1)Q(V = -1) = p^2 + (1-p)^2.$$

The resulting $Q(H|A)$ is $> 2/3$ because it is 2/3 if $p = 1/2$, and its derivative with respect to p is positive if $p > 1/2$. The implication is important: if after observing AA Thirda receives Low, she chooses A anyway, because, if she took into account only Prima's High signal and her own Low signal, she would conclude that V is equally likely to be $+1$ or -1; but she also knows that Secundo is more likely to have received a High than a Low signal; this tilts the decision in favour of A.

Thus if the first two choices are AA, Thirda's choice is A *irrespective of the signal she receives*. Hence, Thirda's choice reveals nothing to subsequent choosers on the signal she received; knowing this, the fourth individual has the same information as Thirda, *and makes the same choice*, A. The same holds for the fifth individual, and so on forever even if the subsequent signals are, all of them, Low! An informational cascade has started with Thirda. By symmetry, if the first two choices are BB, an informational cascade starts in which every successive individual chooses *B*. If the first two choices are *AB* or *BA*, Thirda is in the same position as Prima, and an informational cascade starts with the fifth individual if the fourth one makes the same choice as Thirda: a sufficient condition for this is that, when the first two signals differ, the third and fourth signal be the same. An informational cascade will start sooner or later with probability 1! But there is no guarantee that the cascade's choice corresponds to the truth: the initial sequence *AA* may be due to the signal's randomness, which does not prevent the first two signals from being High, High (or from being High, Low with then *A* the random choice of Secundo) even when $V = -1$. The reason for the continuation of the wrong choice is that once the informational cascade starts, there is no further accumulation of information.

Of course things would be different if the signals were publicly observable: then the signals, not the choices, would be the basis of subsequent choice. But situations in which the signals are not observable are numerous. Examples of informational cascades are:

- people panic and start running away when in a public occasion, e.g. a rock concert, they see other people panicking and running away, even if they have no idea of why they are running away;
- people prefer a product to another one because they observe that the product has been preferred by others (thus the appearance of a book on top of a best-seller list will nearly certainly increase its sales: this creates room for corruption and other tricks);
- doctors adopt a medical practice because they see that it is adopted by many colleagues;
- voters decide that a leader is trustworthy because they see that lots of people trust her/him (thus opinion polls can influence people's choices);
- buying and selling decisions of financial managers are influenced by their colleagues' decisions;
- 'tulip manias' (stock prices bubbles, housing prices bubbles) can start and continue because financial investors see that everybody believes that asset prices will increase, and 'follow the crowd'.

Since the basis of this type of 'herding' behaviour is learning, or presuming to learn, from the choices of others, an interesting implication of the theory is that the choice of individuals who are considered better informed can have great impact, starting an informational cascade immediately. A person like George Soros, the highly esteemed international investor and financial speculator, can start a wave of sales of a currency by starting to sell it, because many other financial operators will conclude that he has reasons to believe in a depreciation of the currency—which may then be caused by the informational cascade! (and Soros may have counted exactly on this happening...).

The tendency, in situations of this type, to imitate the observed choices of others is far from irrational: informational cascades can be rationally presumed to

9.26 · Reducing Uncertainty Through More Information …

hit on the best choice more often than not,[44] and since acquiring better information may be impossible or costly, to 'herd' or 'follow the crowd' is often a rational choice, that reduces the risk of a wrong choice. Still, wrong choices *can* result and continue; the policy implication is that people should be given incentives to look for information on the signals rather than only on the choices of others, and that such information should be made more widely available.

Incidentally, the examples given above illustrate one reason why there is little hope that the market mechanism be always capable of producing Pareto efficiency.

9.27 Uncertainty and General Equilibrium in Traditional Marginalist Authors

The remainder of the chapter completes the presentation of neo-Walrasian intertemporal general equilibrium theory by explaining how it deals with *environmental* uncertainty, that is, uncertainty about the circumstances (such as amount of rain, hurricanes, pests among farm animals, unexpected deaths) that general equilibrium theory must treat as data independent of economic choices.

But first, something on how traditional marginalist/neoclassical authors such as Marshall or Wicksell dealt with uncertainty. The theory of the consumer and the theory of the firm presented in ▶ Chaps. 4 and 5 were originally developed to deal with *normal* average decisions (in Alfred Marshall, also normal *short-period* decisions[45]): for example, for a consumer, average consumption of the several goods over a sufficiently long period. In the formalization of optimal decisions in those chapters, uncertainty did not explicitly appear; but this does not mean that uncertainty was supposed absent. To describe the 'atemporal' (in fact, long period) model of Ch. 5 and the explicitly long-period model of ▶ Chap. 7 as

---

44 This is almost not the case in the formal example given, where the probability of being in a correct cascade is very little above 1/2, it is only 0.5133 according to the calculation in Bikhchandani et al. (1992); but in real situations people have private information from multiple sources and the start of a cascade that overpowers contrary private signals generally requires the observation of many concordant choices. Also, if the sequence of decisions is long, people will most probably realize that previous choices are not very informative, and will then look for additional information, or will decide to trust their private signal more than the choices of others; a 'wrong' cascade will then probably come to an end. Indeed the theory of information cascades concludes that 'wrong' information cascades are generally fragile.

45 Marshall's short period is actually rather long, it refers to period lengths in which only the factors that require a rather long time for considerable alterations of their endowments (e.g. experienced fishermen, ships, fixed plants) are in given supply: to think of it as a couple of years will be often reasonable.

based on certainty would be a gross misinterpretation. The point is that normal decisions take uncertainty into account, because they describe normal *average* behaviour and results, the average over climate oscillations, accidents, thefts, default of debtors, oscillations of market prices, stochastic variations of demand, etcetera: an average behaviour that includes the actions that are deemed best to deal with these irregularities, including some precautionary buffer for unpredictable difficulties. Thus the normal price of the product of an industry where productivity is relevantly affected by random events (e.g. by the weather) is the one that yields the normal rate of profit, or normal rate of return on investment, *over a number of years*, account being taken of the random variability of productivity, of the occasional accident, of the extra costs due to workers' average absenteeism and turnover, etcetera.[46] As proof of awareness of these facts in traditional marginalist authors, one can cite Marshall who notes that this random variability is taken care of by calculating which product price, on an average of good and bad times, will yield the normal rate of return. Of course insurance contracts will exist, but Marshall goes on to observe that 'external' insurance (that is, provided by another firm) is used almost only in those cases where a bad event would cause the bankruptcy of the firm because the profits are not diversified: for example, a shipping company owning only one ship will prefer to insure the ship since the loss of the ship in a tempest would cause its bankruptcy, but if the company owns fifty ships it will prefer not to pay insurance and to set its prices so as to cover the average cost of ship loss and of precautionary internal funds. In this way insurance is internalized, and therefore in a theory of normal prices there will appear much fewer insurance contracts than if all contingencies were distinguished. Either way, the cost of external insurance, or of average losses plus precautionary internal funds, will enter the normal product price. In some industries where risks are particularly high, these extra costs will include higher-than-average insurance costs, as well as a higher rate of interest asked for by lenders owing to the greater risk that the borrower may be unable to repay the debt. The risk of default is never absent, and this explains the existence of an average excess of the rate of return on investment over the rate of interest on safe loans, an excess that will differ as between different industrial branches depending on the different riskiness of investments. This difference has been neglected for simplicity up to now, on the basis of Adam Smith's argument quoted in ▶ Chap. 1, ▶ Sect. 1.3, that whatever the reasons that explain persistent differences in rates of profit in different employments of capital, these reasons are not going to be relevantly affected by the general changes with which the theory of value and distribution

---

46 Similar considerations apply to uncertainty about demand for one's product: the average inventories or average extra costs incurred to face random changes of demand, or possibly the more expensive wage contracts including an agreement by the worker to accept variations in labour time when needed, are implicitly included in normal costs. In Appendix 1 to this chapter, this time at the end of the chpater and not in the website, you find a long quotation from Alfred Marshall's *Principles*, which illustrates the traditional approach to these issues.

9.27 · Uncertainty and General Equilibrium in Traditional Marginalist Authors

is mostly concerned, such as changes in wages, or extension of agriculture to less fertile land; therefore in order to understand, for example, the impact of a general rise of wages on rates of profit one may well assume *given* differences between the rates of profit of the different industries—and then the analysis is not altered in its important results relative to a situation of uniform rate of profit, and therefore in a general analysis one may well assume that the rate of profit is uniform. The same type of considerations explains why, in traditional *neoclassical* authors, rate of return (net of risk) and rate of interest were generally assumed to coincide: the normal and non-uniform difference between rate of profit (or of return) and rate of interest in the several types of economic activity could be assumed given and plausibly constant in the face of changes in average real wages or in the face of technical progress; competition would oblige entrepreneurs to be content with the minimum risk-and-trouble mark-up sufficient to make it worthwhile to stay in business, and once this normal mark-up was subtracted from the rate of return considered normal in that field, one obtained the rate of return net of risk, equal to the rate of interest asked for by lenders on safe loans.

Traditional neoclassical authors did not feel the need for a detailed study of what determined the magnitude of this mark-up. Walras, for example, includes the average cost of accidents in the cost of capital goods via the device of an insurance premium defined as follows: 'whatever sum is required as a contribution to the restoration of all similar capital goods annually destroyed by accident is deducted from the annual income of the capital good in question and reckoned as proportional to the price of that capital good' (Walras 1954, p. 268): this premium he takes as a *given* specific percentage for each capital good. Marshall distinguishes the net rate of interest from the one actually paid which includes an 'allowance for insurance against risk", a large part of which, he argues, is actually 'earnings of management of a troublesome business' because 'when, from the nature of the case, the loan involves considerable risk, a great deal of trouble has often to be taken to keep these risks as small as possible" (*Principles*, VI, vi, 4: 488–489);[47] but the remaining normal difference due to insurance against risk he does not attempt to determine. Wicksell mentions the existence of 'an increased risk premium for long-term loans' (1934: 161) but does not attempt to determine its magnitude, nor does he discuss its determinants. The reason appears to be, again, the one indicated by Adam Smith: for the comparative statics for which the theory of value and distribution is most useful, one can take the normal differences between rates of return (rates of profit) and rates of interest as constant, and to be studied, if necessary, at a second level of approximation.

---

47 Marshall notes that the payment of managerial activity is often out of 'profits', so activities that require more intense or more skilled managerial activities to take care of risk and of unexpected events will on average show a higher rate of profit because of accounting conventions, and this is another reason for the observation of persistent differences in the rates of profit. Adam Smith's excess of profit over interest to cover the 'risk and trouble' of enterprise analogously includes both risk coverage, and remuneration of entrepreneurial activity directly out of profits.

804   Chapter 9 · Uncertainty and General Equilibrium

Therefore, there appears to have been agreement between classical and traditional neoclassical authors on the thesis that what is important is what determines *normal* prices and outputs and *normal* income distribution, although the theories explaining these normal magnitudes were very different as explained in ▶ Chap. 3. The consideration of the specific effects of environmental uncertainty was believed to add only details to the grand view; Marshall, for example, has only a few pages on the issue (of which a relevant portion is quoted in Appendix 4 in the online Appendix to this chapter).

9.28 Contingent Commodities

We will be concerned, in the remainder of the chapter, with *environmental* uncertainty (uncertainty about future elements of the world independent of economic choices), not uncertainty *about decision variables,* i.e. about what other participants in the economy will decide to do and about the resulting prices, demands, etc. To understand the effects of this second type of uncertainty is part of the specific task of the theories of value, outputs, investment, employment, distribution and growth proposed by either overall approach.

The distinction between the two types of uncertainty is very important for modern general equilibrium theory: in this theory, the second type of uncertainty is not admitted, the assumption of complete markets or of perfect foresight about state-specific future prices eliminates it.

The first type of uncertainty is dealt with by a further reinterpretation of the 'atemporal non-capitalistic' model of ▶ Chap. 5 as now referring to *commodities* distinguished not only by type, location and date but also by the state of nature (of uncertain occurrence) in which they are available.[48] (I will only discuss intertemporal equilibria.)

The commodities are now ***contingent commodities***, that is, their availability is contingent on the realization of 'a particular state of nature, the one which must be realized in order that a stipulated delivery of this commodity should take effect' (Malinvaud 1971, p. 236, my transl.); the contract for delivery of a good or service at a certain date can contain a clause such as 'if I have broken a leg', or 'if I am in town', or 'if it rains' or 'if a war has broken out between India and Pakistan the day before'.[49]

---

48   The general equilibria discussed in Ch. 8 are accordingly described by modern neoclassical theorists as based on certainty. The term 'commodity' is used in this literature not in the old classical sense (good produced to be sold) but as broader than 'goods' in that also including contingent commodities, bonds, Arrow securities, etc. A physically specified type of good, e.g. potatoes, or gold, is sometimes called a basic good when it must be distinguished from a good or commodity also described by its date and state.

49   This last example illustrates the *danger of ambiguity* in the specification of a contingent commodity. What if—a frequent situation—no official declaration of war is issued but fighting is vigorous? In recent years, the danger of ambiguity has been particularly evident in determining when Credit

9.28 · Contingent Commodities

Let us distinguish three sets of variables in the description of the 'physical world':
1. environmental variables, which are decided by 'Nature';
2. decision variables, which are chosen by economic agents (e.g. consumption decisions);
3. all other variables, which are completely determined by decisions and environmental variables (e.g. equilibrium prices).

The contingent commodities contemplated by the theory are distinguished according not only to physical characteristics, location and date, but also according to the state of the world, or state of nature, in which they appear at their date. Assume that the intertemporal equilibrium extends over a finite number of periods distinguished by their initial date, from 0 to T. Each period is characterized by an environmental state, but except for date/period 0 it is not known which environmental state will come out to be the case. At the initial date 0 the environmental state is known, where 'environmental state' means a complete description of all aspects of the environment at the given date that are relevant to choice. The environmental state remains constant for the length of the period. Everybody knows that this environmental state limits the possible environmental states at date 1 to a set $\sigma(1)$; at date 1, uncertainty resolves and everybody sees that the environmental state is $s(1) \in \sigma(1)$. Everybody also knows that, if $s(1)$ is realized, the possible states at date 2 are a subset of the set $\sigma(2)$ of possible states at date 2, the subset compatible with the fact that at date 1 state $s(1)$ has been the case; this subset can be indicated as $\sigma(2, s(1))$; when date 2 is reached, a state $s(2)$ reveals itself to be occurring, which is one of the possible states in $\sigma(2, s(1))$. This in turn conditions the possible environmental states at date 3 to be elements of the subset $\sigma(3, s(2))$ of $\sigma(3)$. And so on down to date T. There is therefore a 'tree' of possible states, with only one node at date 0, from which as many branches depart to date-1 nodes as there are elements in set $\sigma(1)$ of possible states at date 1; from each one of these nodes which are the elements of $\sigma(1)$ as many branches depart to date-2 nodes as there are possible states at date 2 subsequent to that node, if that node is called $s(1)$ then the set of these possible states is set $\sigma(2, s(1))$, the total number of branches that reach date 2 being $\sigma(2)$; and so on. 'Nature' chooses a state at date 1, then chooses a state at date 2 among those compatible with the state chosen by 'Nature' at date 1, and so on. These possible states at each date are called in the literature states of nature, states of the world. By calling them environmental states I intend to stress that the description of any one such state of one period does not include the choices of agents in that period, but only the elements of the world which the agents must take as given, unaffected

---

Default Swaps become payable. Note also that not all differences among states of nature can be the basis for contingent contracts: for example, one's future mood, 'if I will be in a happy mood tomorrow', certainly is an important difference between possible future states, but it indicates a cause of uncertainty that cannot be a basis for contingent contracts, because not objectively ascertainable.

806　**Chapter 9** · Uncertainty and General Equilibrium

by their economic choices. The possible histories of states of the world from date 0 to the horizon date/period T coincide at date 0 and two of them may coincide for many more periods, even up to date $T - 1$. The number of elements in set $\sigma(t)$ grows very rapidly with t.

Then when distinguishing goods according to which physical or basic good they are (generic index h, which also distinguishes goods by their location), at which date (generic index t), and in which state of nature (generic index s), the set of states depends on the date.

The literature sometimes distinguishes and sometimes identifies states and *events*. The more common procedure is to consider an event at a given date as a *subset* of the set of environmental states. Delivery of a contingent commodity is conditional on the occurrence of an event. For example, delivery of an umbrella 'if it rains' depends on the event 'it rains', which includes many different states (distinguished, e.g. by temperature, or by who is alive) that may need distinguishing for other choice problems. But in the latter case the price of an umbrella will generally depend on which specific state is occurring, if it rains but taxis are not running because of absence of petrol the price of umbrellas will probably be different from the case with taxis. Therefore to determine equilibrium prices one must distinguish contingent commodities by the state, not the event, to which they are associated, if by event one means a subset of states. For this reason below there is little reference to events.

Commodities to be delivered only if a certain state occurs are called *contingent commodities*, and the corresponding contracts are called *contingent contracts*; the price paid (at the initial date) for a contingent contract is called *contingent price*. What is needed to include contingent commodities in general equilibrium theory is only a reinterpretation of the general equilibrium model as referring to contingent commodities and contingent prices. Contingent commodities of the same physical type (including location) and the same date are distinguished by the state which makes them deliverable. As the example above of umbrellas and the discussion of the notion of event made clear, the same physical good may be available in many states of a given date, but it must be considered as many contingent commodities.

The simplest picture to which the theory is meant to apply is that of an imaginary world where

- people distinguish among the possible future states of the environment in a thoroughly exhaustive and universally shared way and know that they will agree on which environmental state occurs at date t once that date arrives,
- markets for *all* possible contingent commodities indexed on environmental states exist at date zero, for all future periods over which the equilibrium extends.

This situation will be called one of **universal** contingent markets: the term '*complete* contingent markets' would be the natural extension of the term 'complete markets' used in ▶ Chap. 8, but for contingent commodities equilibria the literature uses the latter term in a different sense to be explained later. With the help of the auctioneer this economy can be imagined to reach at date zero an equilibrium

9.28 · Contingent Commodities

analogous to the intertemporal equilibrium discussed in ▶ Chap. 8, but now for all possible contingent commodities, and such that no subsequent reopening of markets is necessary: at subsequent dates people must only check which environmental state has occurred, and they must honour the corresponding contingent contracts, which were all paid for at date zero, with the auctioneer acting as a clearing house.

» A contract for the transfer of a commodity now specifies, in addition to its physical properties, its location and its date, an event on the occurrence of which the transfer is conditional. This new definition of a commodity allows one to obtain a theory of uncertainty free from any probability concept and formally identical with the theory of certainty developed in the preceding chapters. (Debreu 1959, p. 98; Debreu identifies events and states.)

To understand the words "free from any probability concept" in this quote, remember that the discussion earlier in this chapter has shown that it is possible to conceive event-indexed commodities (state-contingent commodities) and preferences over vectors of these commodities, independently of an assignment of probabilities to events.

Purchase of a contingent commodity is purchase of a *promise* of delivery of a (type-location-date) commodity if a certain state of nature comes out to be the case. If the relevant event does not occur, the seller of the contingent commodity has no obligation.

An example of purchase of a contingent commodity is a health insurance contract that will pay a sum to the insured person in case she falls ill of one of the stipulated illnesses. Or consider a contract of advance purchase of repair assistance for, say, five years in case a machine malfunctions: the service 'assistance and repair' will be delivered any day of those five years in which the state of nature exhibits malfunctioning of the machine; here one is purchasing 365×5 contingent commodities, promises of conditional delivery of the service 'assistance and repair', one for each day.

The enlargement of the definition of commodity to include indexing by state, so that traded commodities are contingent commodities, is argued to leave the formal structure of intertemporal general equilibrium theory unchanged because it does not make a difference to the formal structure of choice sets and of preferences of consumers or of firms.

Let us take a consumer. We specified her decisions in ▶ Chap. 4 as resulting from utility maximization over the intersection between a consumption set, and a budget set determined by endowments and prices. Now the consumption set and the endowments include contingent commodities. Therefore we must assume that consumers have complete, transitive, reflexive and continuous preferences over the possible vectors of contingent commodities.

If a consumer wants to purchase a unit of commodity h for sure at date t, the idea is that she will buy a unit of each contingent commodity (h, t, s) for all states s of date t. Of course there will generally be contracts selling 'commodity (h, t) for sure' that will avoid the need to sign a high number of contingent contracts.

808   **Chapter 9** · Uncertainty and General Equilibrium

In the intertemporal equilibrium with contingent commodities it is *not* required that consumers agree on the likelihood of the several states. Thus, if one passes to the interpretation (discussed below) of the intertemporal equilibrium as a Radner sequential equilibrium with perfect foresight, the latter term means correct foresight of what the equilibrium prices will be at date t for each possible state at that date, but not correct foresight of which state will occur nor of the probability that it occurs.

What the consumer must be assumed to choose is now a vector of excess demands for *each* possible succession of states. Again prices must be interpreted as discounted prices quoted at the initial date, when all consumers simultaneously decide their plans of action for all future periods (and now also for all possible states in those future periods) up to the economy's horizon. The auctioneer and its ultrafast tâtonnement are again necessary in order to visualize how an equilibrium might be reached (I do not repeat here the difficulties with the perfect foresight alternative, see ▶ Sect. 8.15).

No other restriction is imposed on the shape of the utility functions, they need not be VNM, nor additively separable; when additively separable, state-dependent basic utility functions are perfectly admissible; nor is it necessary to suppose that consumers attribute precise probabilities to states. All one needs is a preference order for each consumer over vectors of contingent commodities covering all periods and all environmental states. Different consumers can have different assessments of the likelihood that a certain state will occur. Of course if consumers attribute precise probabilities to states, these probabilities must be consistent, if a state s in period 1 has probability 1/3 of occurrence, then the states of period 2 compatible with state s having occurred in period 1 must have probabilities of occurrence that sum to 1/3.

As to firms, they too are assumed to distinguish perfectly among all possible states, and to know their possible feasible netput vectors depending on the state. If the output of a production process is uncertain, different output levels of a firm corresponding to the same inputs distinguish different states. For the moment, let us stay with the assumption of universal contingent markets and that all transactions are stipulated at the initial moment; this has an important consequence: in equilibrium, *firms' decisions entail no risk*, because in each possible state their output has purchasers (supplies have been brought by the auctioneer to equal demands), and the value of the production plan—that is, the present value, at the given discounted prices, of the contingent purchases and sales associated with all possible different outcomes of the plan the firm decides—is realized at the initial date. Thus, suppose at date t there are two states, it rains or it does not rain, date-t umbrellas are contingent on the state. A firm that produces umbrellas (with, let us suppose, the same production function in both states) does not know whether at date t it will rain or not, nor the probability, but at date zero it sells contingent umbrellas and is paid for them; it produces the number of umbrellas sufficient to satisfy the greater of the two demands, and charges prices such that the cost of producing those umbrellas is covered by the joint revenue from the two sales; if at date t the firm is left with a number of unsold umbrellas, this is not a cause of losses because the cost of producing them was covered anyway. Of course in real economies firms do bear risks, because there aren't complete contingent markets; hence the relevance of the brief considerations of ▶ Sect. 9.19.

9.28 · Contingent Commodities

Consumers on the contrary do bear risk, because they must decide how likely it is that a certain state will come about, and therefore they must decide how much they are ready to pay now in order to make sure that, if state s happens, they are going to get certain commodities. If one wants a unit of a future good for sure for a certain date, one must buy a unit of that contingent good for each state for that date; otherwise one risks remaining without the good.

Let me further clarify the meaning of prices in this model. Let us use two indices, the first one to indicate the (type-date) commodity and the second one the state. Let p_{hs} be the present price of commodity h in state s, that is, the price to be paid by the purchaser at the initial date for a promise from the seller of delivery of one unit of commodity h if and only if state s occurs. If any other state occurs, nothing is due from the seller. This is called a **contingent price**. The payment of this price is not conditional, it *must* be effected for the contract to come into existence, we can call it a *firm* payment (firm (adjective) = assured, certain, not contingent); only the delivery of the commodity is uncertain; the contract is called a **contingent contract**.

Contingent prices must be distinguished from what can be called (Malinvaud 1971, p. 237) a **conditional price**, that is, the price of a **conditional contract** defined as follows: the contract stipulates delivery by the seller and payment by the purchaser *both* conditional on the realization of a certain state. Here payment too is contingent. In real economies there are indeed contracts of this kind, in which both payment and delivery are conditional on some event happening. Stipulation of a real-world conditional contract does not entail any payment at the moment the contract is signed. In our intertemporal universal-markets world a *conditional* contract can be shown to be equivalent to the simultaneous stipulation of two *contingent* contracts, each one with payment of a firm price. To such an end, assume the contingent good to be bought is good (h, t, s) and that payments are in kind, they consist of (promises of) firm delivery of a physical good of a date not earlier than the date of the state on which good (h, t, s) is contingent; say, gold to be delivered in the last period—the horizon—of the economy; call it good N. Consider purchaser A wishing to stipulate with seller B a conditional contract establishing that, if state s is realized, B will deliver to A one unit of good h (of date $t \le N$, which for simplicity is omitted in the price symbols below) and A will pay to B the *conditional price* p^*_{hs}, a quantity of good N. This can be obtained by the simultaneous stipulation of two contingent contracts. According to the first contract, A pays p_{hs} (a quantity of good N) to B as the (firm) contingent price for delivery to A of one unit of good h if state s is realized (the relationship of p_{hs} to p^*_{hs} is clarified below). According to the second contract, B pays p_{hs} to A as the (firm) contingent price for delivery to B of p^*_{hs} units of good N if state s is realized,[50] which implies that B is paying for each unit of contingent commodity (N,s) the firm price.

$$p_{Ns} = p_{hs}/p^*_{hs}$$

---

50 It is not necessary that the state, on which delivery of a good at date t is conditional, be of date t; it can be of an earlier date, in which case the date-t good is delivered whatever the state of nature at date t.

810   **Chapter 9** · Uncertainty and General Equilibrium

The two firm payments p_{hs} are signed at the initial date and cancel out; if then state s is realized, A pays p^*_{hs} units of good N (or more rigorously of good (N, s)) to B, and B delivers one unit of good (h, s) to A. Note that the result is in line with the usual definition of relative price[51]:

$$p^*_{hs} = p_{hs}/p_{Ns}.$$

Of course the prices p_{hs} and p_{Ns} must be the same prices as practiced by other traders, so it is p^*_{hs} that must adapt to the right-hand side in the last equation.[52]

The (firm) contingent price of a delivery that depends on the realization of an *event,* that is, on the realization of any one of the states comprised in that event, will be the sum of all the prices of the contingent commodities corresponding to the states comprised in that event. If the event includes *all* possible states, then delivery of the good is certain, and we can define the price of *certain* or *firm* delivery of one unit of good h as (with S the number of possible states at the date in question):

$$\bar{p}_h = \sum_{s=1}^{S} p_{hs}.$$

This shows that in general the price of a contingent good will be less than the price of the certain delivery of that good.

---

51 The price p_{Ns} is not 1 even if good N is the numéraire, because it is the price for delivery of one unit of good N *if* state s is realized, while if good N is chosen as numéraire then 1 is the price of the *firm* delivery of one unit of good N in the last period, i.e. whatever the state of nature in the last period.

52 An example will help. Suppose there are two dates, 0 and 1, two states at date 1, α and β, and good N is gold of date 1 delivered for sure. Consumer A wants to buy 1 unit of good (2, 1, α), that is 1 unit of good 2 of date 1 conditional on state α occurring, with payment only if the good is delivered because state α occurs. B accepts, for a *conditional* price consisting of 4 units of good N. The two contingent contracts might be the following ones. A pays a *contingent* price of *3* units of N to B for the contingent delivery of 1 unit of good (2, 1, α); since this is a firm payment, it means a quantity of N going to B whatever the state at date 1. B pays a contingent price of 3 units of N to A for the contingent delivery of 4 units of N if state α occurs. The two contingent payments of 3 firm units of N cancel out and what is left is that if state α occurs, A delivers 4 units of N to B and B delivers 1 unit of good (2, 1,α) to A. Note that if the general numéraire is, for example, gold of date 0 and the discounted price of a unit of N delivered for sure is, say, 1/2 (an own gold rate of return of 100% for firm delivery), this allows us to say that the discounted value of the contingent payment of 3 *firm* units of N is 1.5, but can we calculate the discounted value of a unit of good (N, α), that is, N conditional on state α? Yes. We know that A and B are indifferent between 3 units of N for sure and 4 units of (N, α); this must mean that the two have the same discounted value, 1.5, which implies a discounted value of (N, α) equal to 0.333, and by implication a discounted value of (N, β) equal to 0.167.

9.29 Equilibrium with Contingent Commodities

The general intertemporal equilibrium of an economy with universal markets for contingent commodities up to a finitely far horizon is what is meant by an *Arrow–Debreu equilibrium*. (As explained in ▶ Chap. 5, actually this label should be associated with models with a given number of firms; but for simplicity, when the relevance of free entry is not the main object of discussion, here the same label will also cover general equilibrium models with the more acceptable assumption of CRS *industries* owing to free entry.)

As mentioned, the theory needs no specific assumption on attitudes to risk; it does not need, for example, that utility functions be VNM, nor that agents assign precise probabilities to the several possible states. Risk aversion will entail strictly convex indifference curves as between quantities of the same commodity available in different states or events, as illustrated in ◻ Fig. 9.1, but people may well be risk neutral or risk-loving.

Still, if we assume overall utility depends on the expected consumption of each period according to expected utility, we obtain a representation of consumer choice under uncertainty very similar to the standard one. Consider a single consumer with endowment vector $\omega = (\dots, \omega_{hts}, \dots)$ who faces a contingent goods (discounted) price vector $\mathbf{p}$ with generic element p_{hts}. Contingent claims are all paid at date 0; hence the consumer has budget constraint (assuming non-satiated preferences):

$$\sum_{h,t,ts} p_{hts} x_{hts} = \sum_{h,t,ts} p_{hts} \omega_{hts}.$$

(The double index ts in the summation is to indicate that for each date the sum is over only the states of that date; index s acquires precise meaning only when coupled with a date.) The consumer has utility function $U(U^0, U^1, \dots, U^t, \dots, U^T)$ where U^t indicates the expected utility of consumption in period t, determined by a felicity function (possibly specific to the period) $u^t(\mathbf{x}_{ts})$ according to VNM expected utility and therefore

$$U^t = \sum_{ts} \psi_{ts} u^t(\mathbf{x}_{ts})$$

where ψ_{ts} is the probability the consumer attributes to state s of date t, and the summation is over the states which are possible for the given t; $\mathbf{x}_{ts}$ indicates the vector of consumption goods in state s of date t. The consumer solves, under the above budget constraint,

$$max_{x_{hts}} \sum_{t,ts} \psi_{ts} u^t(\mathbf{x}_{ts}).$$

Assuming non-corner solutions, the Lagrangian is

$$\sum_{t,ts} \psi_{ts} u^t(\mathbf{x}_{ts}) + \lambda \sum_{h,t,ts} p_{hts}(x_{hts} - \omega_{hts})$$

and the first-order condition on good (h, t, s) is

$$\psi_{ts} u^{t\prime}(x_{hts}) + \lambda p_{hts} = 0.$$

Therefore if s, s' are two possible states at date t, as between good (h,t,s) and good (k, t, s') the consumer obeys

$$-\left(\psi_{ts} u^{t\prime}(x_{hts})\right) / \left(\psi_{ts\prime} u^{t\prime}(x_{kts\prime})\right) = -p_{hts}/p_{kts\prime}.$$

This is the standard equality between marginal rate of substitution and relative price, modified only in that marginal rates of substitution now include the probability of occurrence of states.

The basic idea is still that the factor-substitution mechanisms plus competition will tend to ensure the full employment of resources together with product prices equal to minimum average costs, composition of production reflecting the choices of consumers, and income distribution reflecting the indirect marginal utility of factors. The addition is that now one can also consider how exchanges of contingent commodities, and transfers of income from one state to another through contingent or conditional contracts (e.g. insurance), will cause a sort of generalized risk pooling.

We can obtain some intuition on this effect from the simplest case, the Edgeworth box of the exchange of a single good available in two states between two risk-averse individuals. Suppose individual A has a positive endowment of the good if state α occurs and zero endowment if state β occurs, while the opposite is the case for individual B. It will then generally be Pareto-improving for the individuals to make contingent contracts, under which individual A promises to give some amount of the good to B if state α occurs, in exchange for B promising to give some amount of the good to A if state β occurs. That is, A offers some amount of the state-contingent good $x(\alpha)$ in exchange for some amount of the state-contingent good $x(\beta)$. (As usual, we interpret the box as reflecting in fact the choices of an equally numerous multitude of type-A and type-B individuals, who can then be assumed to be price takers.)

In ◘ Fig. 9.14, amounts of the good in state α are in ordinate, those in state β in abscissa. Point Ω indicates the initial endowments; it is not on either of the 45° certainty lines (the broken lines in the figure), so for neither individual the endowment is certain: this is described by saying that there is *individual risk*. The sides of the Edgeworth box are of unequal length, indicating that the total endowment of the economy depends on the state: this is described by saying that there is *social risk*. (There is individual risk but no social risk if the total endowment is state independent, the state only determines who gets what portion of it.) Assuming risk aversion, the convex indifference curves of A and B through point Ω form a lens of allocations that constitute Pareto improvements. We know that these indifference curves need not reflect conscious probability assessments by the individuals; *if* the individuals have preferences of expected utility form and therefore state-independent basic utility functions, then the slope of an individual's indifference curves at the certainty line is constant and can be taken to indicate the subjective probability she attributes to the two states; but the analysis does not need such a form of preferences. It is possible to discuss Pareto improvements

Uncertainty and General Equilibrium

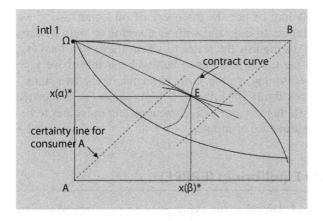

Fig. 9.14 Exchange of contingent commodities; single good, two states α and β

and Pareto efficiency in the same way as for an Edgeworth box with two goods and no uncertainty. The locus of tangency between indifference curves of A and B inside the lens of Pareto improvements is the contract curve. The equilibrium (assumed unique in the figure, but it need not be) is point E: it is clearly Pareto efficient, indicating an efficient 'allocation of risk' between the two individuals.

Indeed the formal equivalence of the model with the atemporal, non-capitalistic model entails the validity of the First Theorem of Welfare Economics, which now also means Pareto-efficient allocation of risk. The proof is omitted because identical, given the formal equivalence. Actually the expression *'allocation of risk'* can be inappropriate here, since there is no presumption of a *measurability* of risk: probabilities need not be given; but if they are given, then we can see this example as a generalization of the efficient 'risk pooling' studied in Sect. 9.16, a generalization because now not needing absence of wealth effects, nor preferences of expected utility form; the reaching of competitive equilibrium can be viewed as one way to determine the allocation of the gains from risk pooling, the γ that had been left largely indeterminate in ▶ Sect. 9.16.

An example might be the following. A ski station wants plenty of snow, a transport firm in the same area wants little snow because snow increases its costs; they can reach a mutually advantageous risk-sharing agreement by stipulating a contract whereby the ski station will receive money from the transport firm if it snows below average, and the transport firm will receive money from the ski station if it snows above average. But such types of contracts are very rare, because it is difficult to reach an agreement on the sharing of the gains when, as in most situations, it is just two firms facing each other, and because the random variable must be measurable, observable without ambiguity by all interested parties, and independent of the actions of the interested parties.

Contingent dated commodities also allow representing uncertain production plans. For example, suppose oil drilling to-day may or may not find oil tomorrow. Uncertainty is only resolved tomorrow. We can distinguish two states of the world, 1 and 2, which cover to-day and tomorrow and are identical for to-day and

814   **Chapter 9 ·** Uncertainty and General Equilibrium

differ as to including or not the discovery of oil tomorrow. If we indicate with $\mathbf{y}_0$ a vector of inputs to-day, and with $\mathbf{y}_1$ a vector of outputs tomorrow, adding index 1 or 2 to distinguish the states to which they refer, then $(\mathbf{y}_{01}, \mathbf{y}_{02}; \mathbf{y}_{11}, \mathbf{y}_{12})$ is a production plan, and in order to be feasible it must have $\mathbf{y}_{01} = \mathbf{y}_{02}$, since the input vector used to-day is necessarily the same in the two states, while $\mathbf{y}_{11} \neq \mathbf{y}_{12}$ will reflect the possibility of different outputs tomorrow associated with the two different states. In this way one can allow uncertain outcomes to be the result of a certain input or sequence of inputs.

9.30 Radner Equilibrium (EPPPE)

Only a fool could claim that the assumption of existence of universal markets in contingent commodities resembles the situation of actual economies.

But it was argued by Arrow (1953) and then by others that the absence of some contingent markets at the initial date need not prevent the establishment of the same equilibrium allocation as with universal markets. To see why, let us introduce the notion of ***Arrow real contingent security***, a promise of contingent delivery of one unit of good (h,t,s). (In ▶ Chap. 8 the notion of Arrow security had not been extended to include contingent commodities.) Assume a sequential exchange economy going from date 0 to T. At each date, after checking which state has occurred, spot markets open up, that allow delivery and exchange of the goods of that date–state. Suppose in this economy at date 0 there are no markets in contingent commodities for $t = 1,\dots,T$ except markets in Arrow real securities of good 1 (gold) for all future dates and states. Further *assume perfect foresight of the relative spot prices that will rule at each future date and state* (should that state occur); and assume that good 1, gold, has a positive spot price at all date–state pairs. Then each consumer, by buying and selling Arrow securities for the several date–state pairs, can transfer wealth from one date–state pair to another and achieve the same redistribution of purchasing power across date–state pairs as if all contingent markets existed at date 0. The principle is the same as illustrated in ▶ Sect. 8.11, extended from spot markets distinguished only by date to spot markets distinguished by date *and* state, with bonds replaced by Arrow securities in a contingent commodity. Therefore any equilibrium achievable with universal contingent markets can also be achieved with this reduced set of markets. Again the intuition is so clear that a complete proof is omitted; it will only be shown that for a simplified case the optimal consumption under universal contingent markets can also be achieved with Arrow securities.

Proof Assume only two dates, zero and one, so the alternative states only concern date 1. At date zero consumers buy and sell Arrow real securities that will deliver one unit of good 1 of date 1. Let $\alpha_s^{\,j}$ be the amount of Arrow security for state s *bought* by consumer j; if negative, $\alpha_s^{\,j}$ indicates a *sale* of α units of that Arrow security. Good 1 of date 1 is the numéraire for the spot prices of each date–state pair, and good 1 of date zero is the general numéraire. Demand for

9.30 · Radner Equilibrium (EPPPE)

consumption goods by consumer j in period 0 is a vector x_0^j; for state s at date 1 it is vectors x_{1s}^j. Spot prices at date zero are vector p_0 and in state s at date 1 are vectors p_s. The prices of Arrow securities at date zero are π_s. The consumer maximizes her utility, a function of $x_0^j, x_1^j, ..., x_S^j$, under the constraints[53]

1. $\Sigma_s \pi_s \alpha_s^j + p_0 x_0^j = p_0 \omega_0^j$

2. $p_s x_s^j = p_s \omega_s^j + \alpha_s^j$.

The first constraint indicates that the net value of purchases of Arrow securities at date 0 must equal that date's savings (positive or negative), that is the difference between the value of endowments and the value of consumption of that date. The second constraint says that in each state s the consumer can spend the value of her endowments in that state, plus the value of the amount of good (1, s) delivered by the Arrow securities she bought at date 0 for that state. Now note that if a unit of good 1 in state s costs π_s at date zero, then by purchasing good 1 in state s and using its value in the spot market of that state to buy good h at price p_{hs} one obtains this good at price $p_{hs}\pi_s$ in terms of the general numéraire at date zero. Therefore what we must ask is whether with universal contingent markets at date 0 a consumer facing the array of current and discounted prices $(p_0, \pi_1 \cdot p_1, ..., \pi_S \cdot p_S)$, will make the same choices as if facing the two above constraints. This consumer would maximize her utility under the budget constraint (where for brevity the suffix j is dropped):

$$p_0 x_0 + \Sigma_s \pi_s p_s x_s = p_0 \omega_0 + \Sigma_s \pi_s p_s \omega_s.$$

Once the optimal consumption vector $(x_0, x_1, ..., x_S)$ is chosen under this constraint, we can find, for each state, the difference between value of consumption and value of endowments in terms of good 1:

$$\pi_s p_s x_s - \pi_s p_s \omega_s = \pi_s \alpha_s.$$

The α_s's thus determined are feasible because they respect constraints (i) and (ii), and therefore if universal contingent markets are not available but Arrow securities for good 1 are, the consumer will buy the amounts α_s thus determined and will be able to achieve the same optimal consumption vector as with universal contingent markets. ∎

One thing worth stressing is that the quantities of Arrow securities are *not* given: the quantities of Arrow securities in existence in equilibrium are created by the agents who wish to sell them (i.e. to dissave) and who find purchasers. Obviously, equality of demand and supply means that in equilibrium for each Arrow security total trades sum to zero, $\Sigma_j \alpha_s^j = 0$ for each s.

---

53 In these formulas, the suffix 1 in x_1, π_1, p_1 refers to state 1 of date 1. I assume non-satiation. Also remember that the spot price of good 1 is normalized to 1 in all states.

816   **Chapter 9** · Uncertainty and General Equilibrium

(Actually, since the economy has a past, as noted in ▶ Sect. 8.29 one should admit that Arrow securities have been sold and bought in the past and therefore at date zero agents can have credits and debts, that is, their *endowments* can include positive or negative amounts of Arrow securities coming due at that date, and these should be included in date-zero budget constraints; but this issue is universally neglected in the literature.)

With only spot markets and Arrow contingent securities the number of required contingent markets decreases drastically relative to universal markets, only the markets for Arrow securities are contingent markets; but this is compensated by the need for correct forecast of the prices that will rule at each date–state pair in case that state occurs. The difficulties of the assumption of perfect foresight discussed in ▶ Chap. 8 are present here too,[54] with the additional burden that agents must have perfect price foresight for each possible future date–state couple.

The equilibrium thus established consists of:

- an allocation and prices for the initial (or 'current') period, inclusive of prices for the Arrow securities;
- unanimously expected prices for each subsequent contingent market;
- plans by the agents about what to supply and demand in each subsequent contingent market at those expected prices, plans that respect all budget constraints (thus there is here, as in the intertemporal equilibrium without uncertainty, an implicit assumption of *no default* on obligations) and assure equality between supply and demand on each current and possible future market.

This is the original *Equilibrium of Prices, Plans and Price Expectations*, EPPPE, also called *Radner equilibrium*, defined in ▶ Chap. 8 for the case of certainty, but originally formulated by Radner (1972) in the form described here including environmental uncertainty.

The expectations that cause such an equilibrium to come about have several names in the literature: correct expectations, self-fulfilling expectations, perfect foresight, rational expectations.[55]

We have assumed that markets for Arrow real securities are available only at date zero, and for all date–event pairs. One might alternatively assume that at each date, when markets reopen, there are markets for subsequent-dates Arrow

---

54   The unpredictability of novelties takes here the form of inability to list all possible future states of the world; states of the world may be realized that no one knew to be possible – universal contingent markets are then impossible.

55   There isn't complete agreement on the meaning of these terms. The term 'rational expectations equilibrium' occurs in the intertemporal macroeconomics literature in connection with economies without universal markets but where agents have somehow arrived at understanding the probabilities of the several states and therefore agents agree on these probabilities and hence on the probability distribution of the several equilibrium price vectors unanimously correctly associated with the different states. This agreement on the probabilities is not assumed in Arrow–Debreu equilibria, nor in Radner equilibria, and implies a rational expectations equilibrium can only be a long-period equilibrium (▶ Sect. 8.18).

9.30 · Radner Equilibrium (EPPPE)

securities (for the events that remain possible), then one's plans at date zero can also include plans of purchase or sale of securities in subsequent markets, and transfers of purchasing power across date–event pairs can also be obtained through repeated transaction in securities, for example one can transfer income from date zero to date two by buying securities for date one and then, when date one arrives, using their returns to buy securities for date two. This example shows that a possibility to transfer income across any date–event pairs will still exist even if, at each date–event pair (except at the last date, of course), there are markets for Arrow securities for only one date ahead. This is a first example of *missing markets* that do not prevent achieving all the income transfers across date–event pairs that might be achieved with universal markets. The literature has come to use the term *complete markets* to mean precisely this situation: some markets may be missing, but the existing ones are such that the *span* of possible income transfers (that is, the couples of state–event pairs between which income transfers are possible, directly or indirectly) is the same as with *universal markets*, the term with which I indicate here what was meant by complete markets in ▶ Chap. 8, namely existence at the initial date of markets for all future certain or contingent commodities. By *incomplete markets* it is meant that there are couples of date–event pairs between which it is not possible to transfer income.

9.31 Incomplete Markets

The issue of 'incomplete markets' has given rise in recent years to a voluminous literature; here only a minimal information will be supplied.

The term 'incomplete markets' is not used to denote the absence of some contingent markets, but rather as shorthand for the different notion of *incomplete asset structure*. An *asset* (sometimes also called a *security*) is a title to receive, at one or more future dates, *returns* that can be either physical goods, or fiat money, in quantities that depend on which states occur at these dates. If the returns are real commodities, the asset is called *real*. If the returns are quantities of fiat money, the asset is called *financial*. Arrow real securities in good 1 are one example of real assets. Any contingent contract promising delivery of a commodity at date t if and only if state s occurs is actually a real asset. But the notion of asset covers more general and more complicated cases, up to assets that specify a return for each possible state at each date. Ownership of a forest, that produces different quantities of timber depending on climate and tree illnesses, is an example of real asset with different returns in different states.

Financial assets introduce the need to specify the future purchasing power of money, which encounters the problem that the approach has difficulties with fitting fiat money into general equilibrium models and determining the price level, for the same reasons as discussed in ▶ Chap. 8, Sect.. 8.13. But the case most explored in the literature is precisely the one of financial assets, such as shares of firms, that promise different *monetary* dividends depending on future events. It would take too long to discuss how the value of money is determined in the different models; let it suffice to say that fiat money is generally assumed to have a

818　Chapter 9 · Uncertainty and General Equilibrium

correctly predicted positive value (the framework is a sequential Radner economy, of course with perfect price foresight).

An *asset structure* is a set of assets. Why certain assets exist and other ones do not is not an easy question, and the literature has mostly taken the asset structure as given.[56] Assume there is only one future date, date 1, and that all assets have returns specified in purchasing-power-parity dollars, that is, in dollars divided for each state by the (correctly forecasted) money price of a representative basket of goods, so returns are in fact in general purchasing power measured in units of that basket. Suppose the assets are all indexed, from 1 to K. For each asset k we have a vector of returns $(r_{1k}, ..., r_{Sk})$, one for each state 1, ..., s, ..., S that can occur at date 1, possibly zero for most states. Build an $S \times K$ *matrix of returns* with generic element r_{sk} that indicates the return of asset k in state s. The asset structure is said *complete* if the matrix of returns has rank equal to S, that is, if there are $K \geq S$ assets and some subset of them composed of S assets has linearly independent returns. A complete asset structure satisfies the *spanning requirement* that the possible wealth transfers across states span all possible couples of states.

If the asset structure is complete, then by buying and selling assets (including the possibility to sell them short, see ▶ Sect. 9.20) a consumer can transfer wealth from any state to any other state. Complete Arrow real securities for a good with positive price in all states are an example of complete asset structure. Indeed, suppose there is only one good, three states, and a different Arrow security for each state. Then the matrix of returns looks like:

$$
\begin{array}{c}
\text{Asset (Arrow security)} \\
\begin{array}{ccc}
1 & 2 & 3
\end{array}
\end{array}
$$

$$
\text{States} \quad
\begin{array}{c}
1 \\
2 \\
3
\end{array}
\begin{bmatrix}
r_{11} & 0 & 0 \\
0 & r_{22} & 0 \\
0 & 0 & r_{33}
\end{bmatrix}
$$

and clearly it has full rank.

It can be shown that the equivalence between Arrow–Debreu contingent equilibria with universal markets, and Radner sequential equilibria, mentioned earlier for the case of complete Arrow securities, can be generalized to complete asset structures.

Incomplete markets is used in the literature as synonymous with incomplete asset structure, that is, an asset structure that does not allow wealth transfers across all states (the matrix of returns has rank less than S), and therefore the span of possible wealth transfers is incomplete.

---

56 Laffont (1989) has attempted a list of reasons why markets are incomplete.

9.31 · Incomplete Markets

Incomplete markets are clearly the rule in actual economies. Ways of transferring general purchasing power across *dates*—saving and dissaving—regardless of states of nature[57] exist only for dates not too far into the future, and only for a very limited number of states. (For example, insurance companies refuse to insure against earthquakes or terroristic attacks.) There are many reasons for this incompleteness. The condition $K \geq S$, necessary for completeness of the asset structure, suggests a first reason why: the number of different possible states is enormous, it seems impossible to imagine an asset structure in which all of them are considered.[58] Another reason is that ascertaining, and agreeing on, whether a certain state has occurred, may not be easy and entails costs (possibly, relevant costs of litigation). Another reason is *transaction costs*: writing down a sufficiently unambiguous contract to which both parties will agree can take considerable time and resources; the distinction between possible environmental states must be maintained coarse, to avoid having to sign too many contracts; also, insurance companies have costs that must be covered and that can make the cost-covering supply price of insurance greater than the highest demand price in many instances. Other two reasons (to be studied in ▶ Chap. 11) are *moral hazard* and *adverse selection*: the absence of information about the actions of an agent or about the quality of a good or of a worker can make it impossible to have contingent contracts that distinguish states of the world depending on these actions or this quality. Then there are the reasons for absence of futures markets even independently of environmental uncertainty: the risk of *default* on promises; and the general reluctance to precommit because of the impossibility to be sure as to what one will want at a future date, owing to the likely emergence of unpredictable *novelties*.

A considerable and considerably subtle literature has developed that analyses the implications of incomplete markets for the existence, determinacy (i.e. uniqueness or multiplicity), and especially Pareto efficiency, of intertemporal general equilibria with contingent commodities. This literature assumes perfect price foresight (for each spot market in each state), perfect knowledge of all possible future states, no externalities, and continuous full employment of resources: but then whatever Pareto inefficiency may nonetheless result from inability to insure relative to certain events appears of little importance relative to the inefficiencies resulting from the non validity of those assumptions, in particular from the extensive presence of externalities (see ▶ Chap. 14) and the evident inability of

---

57 Formally, securities that promise a unit of money at a future date for sure, that is, regardless of the environmental state at that date.

58 For example, if for each possible aggregate output of apples next year one is to stipulate a different contingent contract for the purchase of apples, how many contingent contracts would have to be signed? As noted by Ciccone (1999, p. 91) 'Since altering the specification of even one single element of a state of the world defines a different state, and this procedure may in principle be repeated at will for any element, the number of possible states of the world is clearly infinite'. Then there is the impossibility of a complete list of all possible future states, owing to the unpredictability of novelties insisted upon in ▶ Chap. 8.

820   **Chapter 9** · Uncertainty and General Equilibrium

market economies to ensure the full utilization of resources. For this reason I only report without proof the two main results of this literature. First, in some rather exceptional cases the existence of equilibrium is endangered because the rank of the matrix of returns can change with changes in relative spot prices, causing discontinuities; for an example, see Sect. 3 in the online Appendix to this chapter. Second, if not all desired transfers of purchasing power across states are possible, unsurprisingly it may be impossible to reach a Pareto-efficient allocation *defined relative to complete assets*; but furthermore and more surprisingly, it can be that even *constrained* Pareto efficiency, that is, Pareto efficiency within the constraints due to the incomplete asset structure, cannot be reached (see Wilson 2008).

A curious possibility that has emerged in this literature is Pareto inefficiency due to **sunspot equilibria**. Imagine an exchange economy over two periods, 0 and 1, where there is a single date-0 state and at date 1 there are several alternative states which however differ only in elements irrelevant for consumer choice: each consumer has the same utility function and the same endowment in all these states. *Sunspots* is the term used to indicate differences that allow the states to be distinguished but are irrelevant to utility (for example, whether in the first minute of date 1 there is or not a pigeon on top of Nelson's statue). Consumers should be indifferent to sunspots; but suppose that, if one neglects the sunspot difference as between states and accordingly treats the economy as having only one date-1 state, this economy has multiple equilibria that differ in date-1 allocation and prices. For example suppose there are two equilibria, and two date-1 states identical in all utility-relevant aspects but distinguished by a pigeon being or not on top of Nelson's statue. It is then logically possible to imagine that consumers co-ordinate on one or on the other equilibrium depending on the sunspot signal. Then the Radner equilibrium of this economy will have different prices in the two states; this is called a *sunspot equilibrium*.

A sunspot equilibrium can be Pareto inefficient. To show it a simple case suffices. Suppose that all consumers have VNM utility functions, share the same estimates of the probability of the several states and are strictly risk averse. Under these assumptions in the assumed exchange economy *any Pareto-efficient allocation must be uniform across states, i.e. must be state independent*.

Proof. Assume two states that differ only in sunspots. Assume a Pareto-efficient allocation that assigns to each consumer i in state $s = 1,2$ a commodity vector $\mathbf{x}_{i,s}$, possibly different across states. Since the states are identical apart from sunspots, the subutility function is the same and the utility of consumer i is $\pi u_i(\mathbf{x}_{i1}) + (1 - \pi)u_i(\mathbf{x}_{i2})$, where π is the probability of state 1, not the price of an Arrow security. Now consider an allocation that assigns to each consumer i in both states her *expected* consumption vector $\mathbf{\varepsilon}_i = \pi\mathbf{x}_{i1} + (1 - \pi)\mathbf{x}_{i2}$. With risk aversion, u_i is strictly concave, hence $\pi u_i(\mathbf{x}_{i1}) + (1 - \pi)u_i(\mathbf{x}_{i2}) < u_i(\pi\mathbf{x}_{i1} + (1 - \pi)\mathbf{x}_{i2})$ as long as the two vectors are different. This clearly generalizes to $n > 2$ states. The state-independent allocation is feasible, because endowments are state independent, and

$$\Sigma_i \varepsilon_i = \Sigma_i \Sigma_s \pi_s \, x_{i,s} = \Sigma_s \pi_s \left(\Sigma_i x_{i,s} \right) \leq \Sigma_s \pi_s (\Sigma_i \omega_i) = \Sigma_i \omega_i.$$

So the state-independent allocation is a Pareto improvement relative to the original allocation if in the latter for any consumer the vector $\mathbf{x}_{i,s}$ is not the same in all states; but this means that the original allocation is not Pareto efficient. Therefore Pareto efficiency requires that the original allocation be state independent. ■

The implication of the above result is that, for this economy, sunspot equilibria are Pareto inefficient because they do not assign the same allocation to all states. This is not possible with complete markets: then Pareto efficiency obtains in equilibrium because Radner equilibria with complete markets generate the same allocations as Arrow–Debreu equilibria; each equilibrium (remember that there may be several of them) is *sunspot free*, that is, in this economy each overall equilibrium has the same allocation and relative prices in all date-1 states.

With incomplete markets, this need not obtain. It is now possible that consumers expect different prices in different states, and that these expectations are self-fulfilling. Then allocations are not the same in all states. The simplest example is the economy we have just considered, with the added assumption that there are no securities at all, so no transfer of income across states is possible. Then each state at date 1 is an independent one-period economy. If this one-period economy has multiple equilibria, it is possible that in an overall equilibrium different date-1 states are associated with different date-1 relative prices: then one has sunspot equilibria, and Pareto inefficiency. The interpretation is that, since the prices which at date 0 consumers expect to hold at date 1 in the different states are correct self-fulfilling expectations, the irrelevant sunspot differences that distinguish the states are used by consumers to co-ordinate their expectations on one or on another date-1 equilibrium.

It remains unclear how such co-ordination might possibly arise: why should *everybody agree* that, if two equilibria A and B are possible in either of the two date-1 states distinguished by starting with or without a pigeon on top of Nelson's statue, then equilibrium A is the one to be expected if date 1 starts with the pigeon, and equilibrium B if without the pigeon? (And this is, even conceding that everybody agrees that there are two equilibria and which prices will rule in each.)

9.32 Conclusion. Final Considerations on the Supply-And-Demand Approach

Relative to the intertemporal equilibrium studied in ▶ Chap. 8, one is adding here a new type of goods, contingent commodities, of which the two most important categories are insurance contracts, and conditional forward financial contracts of which there is a great variety which the reader will have to study in other courses. The analysis of the markets for insurance contracts does not seem to require reconsideration of the basic mechanisms determining relative prices, income distribution, outputs, according to the neoclassical approach; it can only introduce minor modifications to the basic 'vision'. No relevant obstacle seems to arise to analyzing these markets in a partial-equilibrium framework, with income distribution, and hence the incomes of consumers and the input prices faced by firms, taken as determined in another part of the overall theory and then modified if necessary to take risk margins into account. Then it is not necessary that these incomes and input prices be determined neoclassically. One can introduce the partial-equilibrium analysis of these markets into a non-neoclassical approach. For example the analysis in Sects. 9.9–9.11, of how risk aversion allows the existence of an insurance industry, is perfectly compatible with a classical determination of income distribution. The online Appendix to this chapter contains a passage by Marshall which is perfectly adaptable to an economy where real wages are determined by classical rather than neoclassical forces.

Financial contracts are a more delicate issue; speculation, bubbles, herd behaviour, excessive risk taking can cause financial crises and therefore also problems with aggregate demand and employment, and the framework inside which their study is located has more relevance for the conclusions on their implications; but certainly they do not add support to the mechanisms at the foundation of the supply-and-demand approach: if one accepts general equilibrium theory with perfect foresight they are just one part of it but deprived of the speculative component (remember, no bankruptcies are admitted in general equilibrium!); if one tries more realistic analyses then financial contracts can only introduce further instability possibilities, for example further doubts on the capacity of savings to determine investment.

Therefore the introduction of contingent commodities seems to add little to the supply-and-demand approach of neo-Walrasian intertemporal general equilibrium theory. Let us nonetheless ask, whether the introduction of contingent commodities reduces the strength of the criticisms advanced in ▶ Chap. 8.

Clearly, nothing changes with respect to the impermanence problem, the substitutability problem, and the savings–investment problem. The equilibrium still needs to be reached instantaneously, raising the problem of the distance between equilibrium path and actual path if such an instantaneous equilibration cannot be assumed; it still risks determining an implausible income distribution and implausible prices of most of the initial endowments of capital goods owing to insufficient substitutability; and it still simply *assumes* that investment adjusts to full-employment savings without adducing reasons to justify such an adjustment.

As to perfect price foresight (which is as necessary as in ▶ Chap. 8, if for no other reason, because of the impossibility to have not-yet-born consumers present at the initial date), it is still present and fundamental, and with an added requirement: perfect knowledge, in fact perfect foresight, of which future states are *possible*,[59] although not of their probabilities of occurrence. The uncertainty

---

59 So again the theory excludes by assumption *unexpectable* events, that is, *novelties*, things that could not have been imagined before they come about (e.g. scientific discoveries, and more generally new ideas). This fact has been used by Davidson (1991) to criticize the assumption that the future is quantitatively predictable at least stochastically: this assumption, he argues, requires that the paths followed by economic variables be *ergodic*, that is, roughly, that the statistical regularities observed up to the present continue to exist in the future. Davidson argues that this would require the absence of novelties; history does not repeat itself. I agree: some predictability of tendencies does exist (e.g. about the influence of cost on price, about production adjusting to demand, about multiplier processes), but the tendencies of growth and distribution depend on too many unpredictable influences to allow robust predictions reaching out into the future even only ten years.

9.32 · Conclusion. Final Considerations on the Supply-And-Demand Approach

is only about which state will occur; the equilibrium requires perfect foresight of the prices that will rule in each future state if it were to occur. The number of markets for which agents must be able to have correct foresight of future spot prices increases enormously relative to an Arrow–Debreu equilibrium without uncertainty: this adds, if possible, to the absurdity of the perfect foresight assumption, whose other difficulties are in no way diminished.

Let us take stock. The need to abandon the inconsistent conception of capital as a single factor of variable 'form', a quantity of exchange value, without abandoning a supply-and-demand determination of income distribution made it obligatory to turn to the treatment of the capital endowment as a given vector. The price-change problem raised by this shift obliged to imagine a totally unreal world already in order to *define* general equilibria. The impermanence problem obliged to assume that these equilibria are reached instantaneously, that is, that the economy is *continuously* in equilibrium. When one tries to understand on what basis the equilibrium path is believed to give indications about the actual path of economies without auctioneer nor complete futures markets nor perfect foresight, one discovers that in fact the old conception of the capital goods as embodiments of a single factor 'capital' is still present. The neo-Walrasian versions would have been long recognized as totally sterile, were it not for a continuing faith in adjustment mechanisms originally derived precisely from the conception of capital whose inconsistencies prompted the switch to these versions.

We saw in ▶ Chap. 3 that the marginal/neoclassical approach can be seen as the attempt to extend differential rent theory, from the explanation of the division of the net product between on one side land rents, and on the other side *the sum* of profits (income from property of capital) and wages, to the explanation also of the division of this second part between profits and wages. It seems necessary to conclude that this attempt 'shunted the car of economic science onto a wrong track' (to use the words Stanley Jevons applied to Ricardo).

In ▶ Chaps. 1 and 2 we saw that the main weakness of the classical approach—the imperfect determination of the rate of profit and of long-period relative product prices (prices of production)—can be surmounted in the case of single production and simple fixed capital. It seems worthwhile to explore, in the next chapter, whether this conclusion continues to hold more generally; a positive answer would open the way to attempting a reconstruction of the theory of value and income distribution on the basis of a modernized classical approach.

9.33 Review Questions and Exercises

? Review Questions

1. Explain what is meant by fuzzy preferences.
2. Recite by heart the continuity axiom and the independence axiom at the basis of VNM utility, and also the Archimedean 'Axiom'.
3. Ilustrate the difference between overall VNM utility and subutilities and explain why it is possible to use the same symbol for both.

824   **Chapter 9** · Uncertainty and General Equilibrium

4. Explain why risk aversion can be defined without needing the existence of well-defined probabilities for the states, and why ultimately this definition is motivated by its interpretability as rejection of fair bets.
5. Give the intuition for first-order and for second-order stochastic dominance.
6. Consider a lottery with two money outcomes. Assuming risk aversion, determine graphically the certainty equivalent and the risk premium.
7. Prove that the risk premium or risk avoidance price is approximately equal to the Arrow–Pratt measure of absolute risk aversion multiplied by half the variance of random variable h.
8. Explain the necessity of the side payment γ in risk pooling, using participation constraints.
9. Explain why diversification reduces risk.
10. Explain why in a contingent commodities intertemporal equilibrium firms bear no risk.
11. Show graphically how to build a riskless portfolio from two risky assets, using short sales if necessary.
12. Confirm the intuition that riskier assets require higher returns in order to be part of a mixed portfolio (unless the covariance ... ?)
13. Reproduce and explain the figure that illustrates Tobin's analysis of liquidity preference.
14. Argue that state-dependent utility is often a very realistic assumption.
15. Why can subjective probabilities be accused of suffering from the indefiniteness and the impermanence problem?
16. Prospect theory suggests that sometimes, perhaps often, insurance can be due, more than to traditional risk aversion, to excessive weight given to very low probabilities. Explain.
17. As a good exercise in the application of Bayes' Rule, learn by heart and repeat the proof that, in the informational cascade example in ▶ Sect. 9.26, if the first two choices are AA, Thirda's choice is A irrespective of the signal she receives, and the fourth individual will choose A too.
18. Distinguish a conditional contract from a contingent contract.
19. Explain why the theory of general contingent equilibrium does not need that agents assign precise probabilities to the several possible states of the environment.
20. Explain what ◨ Fig. 9.14 permits to illustrate.
21. Explain why one should admit that at date zero *there are* endowments of Arrow securities.
22. Explain why in a contingent-markets equilibrium firms' decisions entail no risk.

✅ Exercises

1. Assume lotteries can be represented as N-vectors of probabilities over a finite outcome set. Prove. for an outcome set X consisting of three outcomes, that the vector $\alpha\lambda + (1 - \alpha)\lambda'$ correctly describes the reduced lottery corresponding to the compound lottery $\alpha \circ L \oplus (1 - \alpha) \circ L'$.
2. Prove case (e,e) in the proof of existence of VNM expected utility.

9.33 · Review Questions and Exercises

3. (Cowell) Suppose you have to pay $2 for a ticket to enter a competition. The prize is $19 and the probability that you win is 1/3. You have an expected utility function with $u(x) = \log x$ and your current wealth is $10.
   (a) What is the certainty equivalent of this competition?
   (b) What is the risk premium?
   (c) Should you enter the competition?

4. A's utility function $u_A(w)$ is more risk-averse than B's if it is a strictly concave transformation of B's, that is, if there exists some strictly concave increasing function $c(\cdot)$ such that $u_A(w) = c(u_B(w))$. Prove that the concave transformation raises everywhere the Arrow–Pratt measure. (Hint: use the fact that the second derivative of a strictly concave function is negative.)

5. This exercise shows the similarity between intertemporal utility discounting and probability of survival if intertemporal utility has the usual additive form with discounting. A person lives for 1 or 2 periods (indexed period 0 and period 1). If she lives for both periods she has a utility function given by $U(x_0, x_1) = u(x_0) + \delta u(x_1)$ with $0 < \delta < 1$. The probability of survival to period 1 is γ, and the person's utility in period 1 if she does not survive is 0.
   (a) Show that if the person's preferences in the face of uncertainty are represented by the expected-utility functional form $\Sigma_i p_i u(x_i)$, then the person's utility can be written as $u(x_0) + \beta u(x_1)$. What is the value of β?
   (b) Assume the person can live up to period 3, the felicity function is the same for all periods, the rate of time preference is the same δ for any adjacent pair of periods, and the probability of survival to the next period given survival to the current period remains constant at γ. Prove that the person's utility can be written as $u(x_0) + \beta u(x_1) + \beta^2 u(x_2) + \beta^3 u(x_3)$.

6. Prove that in the graph of ■ Fig. 9.1 or 9.4 if there is constant absolute risk aversion then along a straight line parallel to the certainty line all indifference curves have the same slope, while with constant relative risk aversion indifference curves have the same slope along rays from the origin.

7. You must decide whether to advertise a product or not. For simplicity, either you advertise and spend $100, or you don't, and spend nothing. Not producing is not an option. Sales can be of two levels only: either low, yielding a loss (apart from advertising expenses) of $100, or high, with a profit (apart from advertising expenses) of $300. There are three possibilities: (1) customers respond to advertising and will buy low if you don't advertise, high if you do; (2) customers are insensitive to advertising and will buy low in any case; (3) customers are insensitive to advertising and will buy high in any case. Your utility depends on money only, and has expected utility form.
   (a) Find the condition on subjective probabilities that will make it convenient for you to advertise if you are risk neutral.
   (b) Find the condition on subjective probabilities that will make it convenient for you to advertise if you are risk averse, and your money utility function is $u(m) = (W + \Delta W)^{1/2}$, where: $W = 200$ is initial wealth, ΔW is its variation due to the realized consequence of the act you choose, and the probability of state (3) is zero.

Chapter 9 · Uncertainty and General Equilibrium

8. Modify ◼ Fig. 9.14 (in Sect. 9.B.5) to reflect the following assumptions: the endowment of the single good is the same for both consumers in both states. Then the Edgeworth box is square and the endowment point is the middle point of the main diagonal. Explain and show graphically why the two consumers can nonetheless find it convenient to exchange contingent-goods claims, and to reach an equilibrium not on the main diagonal.

9. In footnote 11.

10. Show graphically that a mean-preserving spread decreases the expected utility of the lottery in ◼ Fig. 9.2 if outcome x_2 is replaced by a lottery with prizes $x_2 + \varepsilon$ and $x_2 - \varepsilon$, both with probability 1/2.

11. In footnote 18.

12. Does first-order stochastic dominance imply second-order stochastic dominance?

13. With reference to prospect theory, show that, for the case of gambles over two possible outcomes, the following function $\pi(p)$ is a probability weighing function that generates the graph of ◼ Fig. 9.12:

$$\pi(p) = p^\beta / \left[p^\beta + (1 - p)^\beta \right], \quad \text{with } \beta \in (0, 1).$$

Also point out the form of $\pi(p)$ if $\beta = 0$ and if $\beta = 1$.

14. With reference to prospect theory, show that the function

$$v(x) = x^\alpha, \text{if } x > x_0$$
$$v(x) = -\lambda(-x)^\alpha, \text{if } x < x_0$$

with $\alpha \in (0, 1]$, generates the graph of ◼ Fig. 9.13.

15. What is *Harsanyi's principle*? Do you find it convincing? Do you think it is undermined by ambiguity aversion? (No 'correct' answer here, even economists don't agree; express your pondered opinion.)

16. Repeat exercise 6 of ▶ Chap. 8 (spot markets superfluous) with contingent commodities in place of dated commodities. Assume N goods and two states of the world, $s = 1, 2$. What is the interpretation of the assumption (analogous to that made in part (iv) of exercise 6 of ▶ Chap. 8) that if the consumer would have consumed bundle $\mathbf{x}_1$ had state $s = 1$ occurred, his utility of consuming any bundle $\mathbf{x}_2$ in state $s = 2$ is $u(\mathbf{x}_1, \mathbf{x}_2)$?

17. (Jehle and Reny) (Arrow Securities) This is a guided exercise that reexamines the role of Arrow securities in Radner equilibria, assuming now Arrow *financial* securities. An *Arrow financial security* for date t and state s entitles the bearer to one dollar at date t and in state s and nothing otherwise. In each spot market prices are in dollars.

    The exercise guides you towards confirming that if for an exchange intertemporal economy $\hat{p} > 0$ is a Universal Contingent Markets Equilibrium (UCME) price vector for N contingent commodities,[60] and if $\mathbf{x} \geq \mathbf{0}$ is the

---

60 That is, a price vector ensuring intertemporal contingent equilibrium when at the initial date it is possible to trade all contingent goods against each other – universal markets, in my terminology.

9.33 · Review Questions and Exercises

corresponding equilibrium allocation, then the same prices and allocation ensure equilibrium when at the initial moment only Arrow securities can be traded to transfer purchasing power across dates and states, and all other goods can only be traded on spot-markets, that is, each good only with goods of the same date and state. The argument assumes correct price foresight. The picture is as follows.

At date zero, there is a market for trade in Arrow financial securities contingent on any date and any state. The price of each Arrow security is one dollar, and each date-t and state-s security, or (t,s)-security for short, entitles the bearer to one dollar at date t and in state s, and nothing otherwise. Let a^i_{ts} denote consumer i's quantity of (t,s)-security, a negative quantity if the security has been sold (entailing a promise of payment of one dollar to someone else at some (t,s)). No consumer is initially endowed with any Arrow security. The purchase of an Arrow security can only be paid with income from sale of other Arrow securities: to purchase a date-1 security paying for it with a quantity of a good of date 0 would mean the seller of the security exchanges a promise to pay one dollar at date 1 with some date-0 good, violating the assumption that no good can be used for transfers of purchasing power across dates or states. Hence, consumer i's budget constraint for Arrow securities at date zero is $\sum_{t,s} a^i_{ts} = 0$.

At each date $t \geq 1$, event (t,s) is realised and all consumers are informed about it. Each consumer i receives her vector $e^i_{ts} \in \mathbf{R}^N_+$ of endowments of the N goods for that date–state. Spot-markets open for the N goods. If the spot price in dollars of good k is p_{kts}, then consumer i's date-t state-s budget constraint is $\sum_k p_{kts} x^i_{kts} = \sum_k p_{kts} e^i_{kts} + a^i_{ts}$.

Each consumer i is assumed correctly to forecast future spot prices for every good in every state. Consequently, at date zero consumer i can plan the trades to make in each subsequent (t,s) spot-market simultaneously with her date-0 trades. At date zero consumer i therefore solves,

$$\max_{(a^i_{ts})(x^i_{kts})} \quad u^i((x^i_{kts}))$$

subject to the Arrow security budget constraint $\sum_{t,s} a^i_{ts} = 0$, and subject to the spot-market budget constraint,

$$\sum_k p_{kts} x^i_{kts} = \sum_k p_{kts} e^i_{kts} + a^i_{ts} \geq 0,$$

for each date t and state s. (The inequality condition ensures that there is no bankruptcy.)

(a) Argue that the above formulation implicitly assumes that at any date t, current and future utility in any state is given by $u^i(\cdot)$ where past consumption is fixed at actual levels and consumptions in states that did not occur are fixed at the levels that would have been chosen had they occurred (no regrets! the consumer knows that she/he chose at date 0 as best she/he could).

(b) The consumer's budget constraint in the date-0-universal-contin-gent-markets exchange economy is $\sum_{k,t,s} p_{kts} x^i_{kts} = \sum_{k,t,s} p_{kts} e^i_{kts}$.

Show that (x^i_{kts}) satisfies this budget constraint if and only if there is a vector of Arrow securities (a^i_{ts}) such that (x^i_{kts}) and (a^i_{ts}) together satisfy the Arrow security budget constraint and each of the spot-market budget constraints.

(c) Conclude from (b) that any UCME price vector and allocation of the universal contingent commodity exchange model can be implemented in the spot-market model described here and that there will typically be trade in the spot-markets. Show also the converse.

(d) Explain how the price of each Arrow security can be one. For example, why should the price of a security entitling the bearer to a dollar tomorrow be equal to the price of a security entitling the bearer to a dollar in two days' time when it is quite possible that consumers prefer consumption tomorrow to the same consumption in two days' time? (Hint: Think about price levels in different spot markets.)

(e) Use the insight of (d) to conclude on what the price at date 0 of Arrow *real* securities would be if, instead of paying the bearer in dollars, one (t,s) security paid the bearer one unit of basic good 1 (a good, say bread, with a positive relative price in all spot markets) at date t in state s and nothing otherwise. Also specify how the budget constraints would be modified. Compare with Sect. 9.B.6.

18. Use ◘ Fig. 9.7 to show graphically that if there are two possible states and an agent can buy or sell and also sell short two *risky* assets (that is, both with positive return in one state and negative in the other state) whose return vectors are linearly independent, then it is always possible to obtain a composite asset which has positive payoff with certainty, that is the same positive payoff in both states. (Remember that short sales in ◘ Fig. 9.7 mean points to the left of the ordinate.)

Does this imply that, unless there are limits to short sales, the agent would expand the demand for the composite asset indefinitely? If so, (a) why doesn't this happen in reality? (b) does this problem have connections with the possible non-existence of temporary equilibrium due to non-overlapping expectations discussed in ▶ Chap. 8, Sect. 8.26?

19. (Gravelle and Rees) (Spanning and derivatives) Assume there are two future states and only one asset: the N shares of a firm with state-contingent total dividend prospects D_1 and D_2, with $D_1 > D_2$. The spanning requirement is not satisfied: buying and selling the shares does not allow transferring wealth from one state to the other. But suppose that a market in call options on the firm's shares is introduced. The call option entitles its holder to purchase one of the N shares in the firm at a fixed prespecified price p* after the state of the world is revealed and the firm announces its dividend, but before the dividend is actually distributed. If it is $D_1/N > p* > D_2/N$, the holder of an option will exercise it if and only if the firm announces a dividend D_1. Show that the market in the firm's shares plus the derivative market in options together satisfy the spanning requirement.

References

Allais, M. (1953). Le comportement de l'homme rationnel devant le risque, critique des postulats et axiomes de l'École Américaine. *Econometrica, 21,* 503–546.

Anscombe, F.J., & Aumann, R. J. (1963). A Defi nition of Subjective Probability. *Annals of Mathematical Statistics, 34* (1), 199–205.

Arrow K. J. (1953). Le rôle des valeurs boursières pour la répartition la meilleure des risques. In *The role of securities in the optimal allocation of risk-bearing. Review of Economic Studies, 31,* 91–96). Econométrie, Paris: CNRS.

Barberis, N. C. (2013). Thirty years of prospect theory in economics: A review and assessment. *Journal of Economic Perspectives, 27*(1), 173–195.

Baumol, W. (1958). The cardinal utility which is ordinal. *Economic Journal, 68* (272), pp. 665–672.

Bikhchandani S., Hirshleifer, D., Welch, I. (1992). A theory of fads, fashion, custom and cultural change as informational cascades. *Journal of Political Economy 100,* 992–1026.

Blanchard, O., & Fischer, S. (1989). *Lectures on macroeconomics.* Cambridge MA: MIT Press.

Chang, H.-J., & Kozul-Wright, R. (1994). Organising development: Comparing the national systems of entrepreneurship in Sweden and South Korea. *Journal of Development Studies, 30*(3), 859–891.

Chiu, A., & Wu, G. (2010). Prospect Theory. *Wiley Encyclopedia of Operations Research.* 7 ▸ https://doi.org/10.1002/9780470400531.eorms0687.

Ciccone, R. (1999). Classical and neoclassical short-run prices: A comparative analysis of their intended empirical content. In G. Mongiovi & F. Petri (Eds.), *Value, distribution and capital: essays in honour of Pierangelo Garegnani* (pp. 69–92). London: Routledge.

Cowell, F. (2006). *Microeconomics. Principles and analysis.* Oxford: Oxford University Press.

Davidson, P. (1991). Is probability theory relevant for uncertainty? A post keynesian perspective. *Journal of Economic Perspectives, 3*(1), 129–143.

Deaton, A., & Muellbauer, J. (1980). *Economics and consumer behavior.* Cambridge: Cambridge University Press.

Debreu, G. (1959). *Theory of value.* New York: Wiley.

Ellsberg, D. (1954). Classic and current notions of "measurable utility" . *Economic Journal, 64*(255), 528–556.

Ellsberg, D. (1961). Risk, ambiguity, and the Savage axioms. *Quarterly Journal of Economics, 75,* 643–669.

Geanakoplos, J., Polemarchakis, & H. (1991). Overlapping generations. In: W. Hildenbrand & H. Sonnenschein (Eds.), *Handbook of mathematical economics* (Vol. IV, pp. 1899–1960). Elsevier Science.

Hirshleifer, J., & Riley, J. G. (1979). The analysis of uncertainty and information: An expository survey. *Journal of Economic Literature, 17,* 1375–1421.

Karni E. (2008) Savage's subjective expected utility model. In *(The) New Palgrave dictionary of economics* (2nd ed.).

Keynes J. M. (1936) The *general theory of employment interest and money* (1967 Papermac repr.). Macmillan, London. Cited in the text as GT.

Koutsoyiannis, A. (1975). *Modern microeconomics.* London and Basingstoke: Macmillan.

Kreps, D. M. (1990). *A course in microeconomic theory.* New York: Harvester Wheatsheaf.

MacDonald, L. G., & Robinson, P. (2009). *A colossal failure of common sense: The inside story of the collapse of Lehman Brothers.* New York: Crown Business.

Laffont J.-J. (1989). A brief overview of the economics of incomplete markets. *Economic Record, 65*(1), 54–65.

Mas-Colell, A., Whinston, M. D., & Green, J. R. (1995). *Microeconomic theory.* Oxford: Oxford University Press.

March J. G., Simon H. A. (1958) *Organizations.* University of Illinois at Urbana.

Malinvaud, E. (1971). *Leçons de théorie microéconomique.* Paris: Dunod.

McKenna, C. J. (1986). *The economics of uncertainty.* Wheatsheaf Books, Chap. 4.

Milgrom, P., Roberts, J. (1992). *Economics, Organization and Management*. Hemel Hempstead, UK: Prentice Hall International

Owen, G. (1995). *Game theory* (3rd ed.). New York: Academic Press.

Radner, R. (1972). Existence of equilibrium of plans, prices, and price expectations in a sequence of markets. *Econometrica, 40,* 289–304.

Savage, L. (1954). *The foundations of statistics*. New York: Wiley.

Simon H. A. (1959). Theories of Decision-Making in Economics and Behavioural Science. *American-Economic Review*.

Tobin, J. (1958). Liquidity preference as behavior towards risk. *Review of Economic Studies, 25,* 65–86.

Varian, H. (1992). *Microeconomic analysis* (3rd ed.). New York: W. W. Norton.

Wakker P. P. (2008). Uncertainty. In (*The*) *New Palgrave, A dictionary of economics* (2nd edn.).

Walras, L. (1954). In Homewood, Ill. & R. D. Irwin (Eds.), *Elements of Political Economy* (*Jaffé translation*). New York: Reprinted, 1977 by Augustus M Kelley.

Wilson, C. (2008). Incomplete markets. In: (*The*) *New Palgrave: A dictionary of Economics* (2nd ed.).

Wicksell, K. (1934). *Lectures on Political economy* (Vol. I). London: Routledge and Kegan Paul.

Back to Long-Period Prices

Contents

10.1 The Gravitation to Long-Period Prices in the History of Economic Theory, and Some Empirical Evidence – 833

10.2 Objections to the Uniform Rate of Profit – 839

10.3 The Traditional Explanation – 842

10.4 Cross-Dual Models – 844

10.5 The Possibility of a High Price and a Low Profit Rate – 851

10.6 Joint Production and Sraffa – 853

10.7 Graphical Representation: Single Production – 858

10.8 Graphical Representation: Joint Production – 865

10.9 Choice of Technique as a Linear Programming Problem – 870

Electronic supplementary material The online version of this chapter (▶ https://doi.org/10.1007/978-3-030-62070-7_10) contains supplementary material, which is available to authorized users.

© Springer Nature Switzerland AG 2021
F. Petri, *Microeconomics for the Critical Mind*,
Classroom Companion: Economics, https://doi.org/10.1007/978-3-030-62070-7_10

10.10	Piccioni's Contribution – 879
10.11	No Gravitation to a Definite Technique? – 885
10.12	Extensive Rent – 889
10.13	Intensive Rent – 895
10.14	External Intensive Rent; Rent Due to Consumer Demand – 902
10.15	Given Quantities? – 904
10.16	Constant Returns to Scale? – 906
10.17	Lack of Consistency? – 911
10.18	Conclusions – 913
10.19	Review Questions and Exercises – 913
	References – 916

10.1 · The Gravitation to Long-Period Prices in the History ...

In this chapter we return to the theory of long-period prices as foundation of the method of long-period positions. You will learn about
- the discussion on whether there is gravitation to a uniform rate of profit;
- the enlargement of the theory to joint production and to more general rent theory;
- the discussion about the treatment of quantities as given in the 'core' of classical theory.

10.1 The Gravitation to Long-Period Prices in the History of Economic Theory, and Some Empirical Evidence

The problems of the marginal approach to value and distribution, problems partly different depending on the version, but extremely serious in all cases as argued in Chaps. from 6 to 9, have persuaded many economists to explore alternative approaches to the explanation of relative product prices, income distribution, and quantities produced.

On the theory of product prices, it has been argued that the theory of value should return to the traditional distinction between market prices—the prices established day by day in the markets—and the prices traditionally considered the centres of gravitation of market prices under free competition, and named *natural prices* by Smith and Ricardo, *prices of production* by Marx, *long-period normal prices* by Marshall, simply *equilibrium prices* by Wicksell.[1] As the names of these authors indicate, the distinction was accepted both by classical economists, and by all marginalist economists at least up to the 1930s, and was part of what is called the **method of long-period positions or normal positions**. This method argues that long-period normal prices—equal to minimum average cost inclusive of a uniform rate of return on capital—is what economic theory must first of all determine, because they indicate the average of market prices, and with their changes they indicate the trend of this average. It was of course accepted that elements of monopoly, or barriers to entry, or dynamical advantages such as learning by doing, could prevent the tendency towards a uniform rate of return on capital from fully displaying its effects, or could sometimes contrast it for long periods in certain sectors. The competitive normal or long-period relative prices were anyway seen as the basis, starting from which one could understand the rea-

---

1   Caution: Wicksell's term 'equilibrium prices' mixes two aspects: that they are long-period prices (uniform rate of return on supply price) *and* that they are (long period) *general-equilibrium* prices, reflecting the equilibrium income distribution as determined by the marginal approach. The two aspects should be kept distinct. The distinction becomes evident if the long-period general equilibrium is determined with a real wage fixed above the equilibrium level: the long-period prices are then different from the full-employment equilibrium prices. The distinction is also clear in Marshall's partial-equilibrium notion of long-period price, where input prices (i.e. income distribution) are given, and might be determined by non-neoclassical forces.

834 Chapter 10 · Back to Long-Period Prices

sons for the (limited) deviations due to such causes.[2] The present chapter argues that a return to this traditional method appears feasible.

Sections 10.1–10.5 of the present chapter discuss the stability of long-period prices, that is, the plausibility of the gravitation of market prices towards uniform-profit-rate prices (leaving aside joint production and land rent). Among classical and old neoclassical economists this stability was never doubted; but the recent loss of familiarity with the long-period method has made the claim that market prices gravitate towards long-period prices appear a novel claim, in need of reexamination. Sections 10.1–10.5 report on this reexamination. Then Sects. 10.6–10.14 extend the discussion of long-period prices of ▶ Chaps. 2 and 7 to general joint production and to differential land rent. The last four sections discuss how to treat produced quantities when the purpose is the determination of long-period prices. Competitive markets with free entry are assumed in the entire chapter.

In this chapter one distributive variable (the real wage, or the rate of profit) is taken as given but what determines it is not discussed; the non-neoclassical alternatives in the theory of income distribution will be discussed in ▶ Chap. 13.

The gravitation of market prices towards prices of production (the term for long-period prices preferred in this literature) was taken for granted by the classical economists. The well-known idea was that competition tends to render rates of wages the same for similar jobs, and rates of land rent the same for similar lands. For capital, the tendency towards a uniform rate of profits operates by having investment go in greater proportion to the industries where the rate of profits is higher: the supply increase reduces the product price and thus the rate of profit, which tends back to the average.[3] Only Marx argued that this process, although no doubt existing, might cause—instead of a smooth tendency of market price to approach price of production—excessive reactions and hence waves of bankruptcies in some industry, even possibly the start of a general economic crisis owing to the tendency of bankruptcies to cause other bankruptcies among the suppliers of the bankrupted firms. But this possibility did not induce Marx to deny that prices of production describe the average of market prices and that the tendency towards a uniform rate of profits is fundamental to explain observed average exchange ratios among produced commodities. Only, for Marx the average might be the average of great fluctuations accompanied by instabilities of employment and

---

2 Of course one must not expect a complete equality of rates of profits ever to be reached (even taking into account differences in risk), because change is continually occurring. Innovation, in particular, permits a higher-than-average rate of profit, then gradually eroded by imitation and further innovation. Hence, a complete equalization of the rate of profit is never reached. Market prices are always chasing, as it were, long-period prices which often change; but the existence of the chase makes long-period prices the best guide, at least as a first approximation, for the study of such general questions as the persistent effects of technical progress in an industry, or the effects of changes in real wages on the rate of profit.

3 From now on I go back to using 'profit' in the classical sense, using the term 'extra profit' to indicate profit in the marginalist sense, that is, profit in excess of the normal interest rate. I neglect here the differences e.g. in risk which can render differences in rates of return necessary in order to make investments in the different industries equally attractive.

10.1 · The Gravitation to Long-Period Prices in the History ...

growth. Historical evidence suggests that Marx was too pessimistic in this regard, capitalist economies do fluctuate and sometimes undergo violent general crises, but the cause does not seem to originate in destabilizing excessive investments in industries where the rate of profits is greater than the average. A partial exception is the 2007–2008 financial crisis, one of whose causes was excessive investment in the housing industry, but due to financial deregulations that allowed excessive concession of mortgages and excessive securitization, worsened by false credit ratings due to vested interests, rather than due to a too high rate of profits.

The gravitation of market prices towards long-period prices was also universally accepted by traditional marginalist economists. Marshall motivated it with his well-known partial-equilibrium argument that in the long period variation of the number and dimension of firms will cause the short-period supply curve to shift until its intersection with the given demand curve causes price to equal minimum average cost. The latter includes a normal rate of return that must cover the rate of interest opportunely increased to compensate for the 'risk and trouble' of starting and running firms, which can differ across industries. If one in a first approximation neglects these differences, Marshall's price equal to minimum average cost yields a uniform rate of return in all industries, the same thing as the classical uniform rate of profits.

In neo-Walrasian intertemporal equilibrium theory too, in a certain sense the gravitation to long-period prices is accepted (the moment the equilibrium is considered stable, i.e. reached by the economy), but in a very different form that some economists would not call 'gravitation' because not relying on trial-and-error time-consuming adjustments. In this theory one must distinguish three notions of price: (i) market price, (ii) equilibrium price which is not a long-period price, (iii) equilibrium price which is also a long-period price. Market prices are disequilibrium prices, which the theory seems to exclude from what can be observed in reality, owing to the assumption that the economy reaches equilibrium instantaneously (it was seen in ▶ Chap. 8, under the rubric 'impermanence problem', that the theory has serious troubles with admitting disequilibrium actions in the actual economy). The equilibrium, determined at date zero on the basis of whatever vector of endowments of capital goods the economy happens to have at date zero, determines prices that for the first periods are not, in general, long-period prices: given the absence of substitutability, inevitably some capital goods are so abundant that their rentals do not cover production costs, and they are not produced, so there isn't UERRSP (see ▶ Chap. 8, Sects. 8.8 and 8.9 on the difference between UERR and UERRSP, and Sect. 2 in the online Appendix to ▶ Chap. 8 for a numerical example). In these initial periods, prices are intertemporal-equilibrium prices but are not long-period prices, investments yield a uniform rate of return on demand price, not on supply price. But as one moves to subsequent periods along the unfolding of the intertemporal equilibrium path, more and more of the utilized capital goods become produced inside the equilibrium; their price is then determined by production cost, there is coincidence between supply price and demand price. If one goes far enough into the future, a period is reached in which all capital goods in use have been produced inside the equilibrium, hence for all utilized capital goods the UERRSP assumption is satisfied; now and from that moment on (in the absence of shocks) product prices are long-period relative prices. Generally they will not be perfectly constant, but the rates of return on their purchase at a price equal to production cost will be *effectively* uniform, in the sense that differences in own rates of return are compensated by changes in relative prices from one period to the next, so investment is equally convenient in the purchase of all capital goods (of the dominant technique). *These long-period relative product prices need not be strictly constant*, what defines them is the UERRSP condition, not an assumption of constancy in time (Garegnani 2003, Appendix). Still, if technical knowledge is given, the UERRSP (or long period) relative prices determined by intertemporal equilibria will at most change very slowly, so the change will be negligible as a first approximation, which is precisely the assumption made in traditional analyses: these did not assume strictly constant long-period relative prices but only that their endogenous changes were slow enough to authorize neglecting them in the price equations. To sum up, in intertemporal equilibrium theory the gravitation of market prices to equilibrium prices (which coincides with the assumption that the equilibrium is tâtonnement stable) is assumed unobservable in reality because ultrafast; but there is another 'gravitation' or more precisely convergence, of the equilibrium relative product prices towards equilibrium UERRSP prices, where the latter are the form taken in this theory by long-period prices. So if one goes enough into subsequent periods, intertemporal equilibria too realize long-period relative product prices which are practically constant if the other data (preferences, technical knowledge, population) are persistent.[4]

Thus if one neglects the reasons for persistent differences in rates of profit such as different riskiness of investment in different industries, one finds in the history of economic thought an impressive agreement on the tendency of competitive product prices to gravitate towards prices equal to average costs inclusive of a uniform rate of return on capital advances. The difference among schools of thought is on what determines the *level* of this uniform rate of return or rate of profit.

Such a unanimity in the history of economic thought is rare; it must have been due to very persuasive empirical evidence.

And the empirical evidence is indeed very persuasive. Consider that without the tendency to minimum average cost (inclusive of the normal, uniform rate of profit) there would be no reason why the decrease in the production cost of a good should – as it does – bring down its price (think, e.g., of computers). Essentially the same thing can be looked at from an even more enlightening viewpoint: *without the tendency to a uniformity of rates of profit, there would be no reason why rates of profit might not be persistently as different as 1% versus 10,000%: and such differences are simply not observed.*

Now, if such persistent differences are not observed, there must be a force that prevents them from occurring. This force can only be competition, which through price undercutting and entry tends to bring down the rate of return where it is higher than elsewhere. The empirical support for a *tendency* of rates of

---

4   See Duménil and Lévy (1985), Dana et al. (1989a, b).

10.1 · The Gravitation to Long-Period Prices in the History …

return towards uniformity is therefore indubitable. However, the tendency might produce instability (explosive oscillations), or might be impeded by obstacles that prevent it from bringing about its full effects. On the empirical evidence on instability I have already said something *à propos* Marx. On the obstacles, these certainly exist, but compared with the *theoretically possible* differences in profit rates, the observed persistent differences in profit rates appear nearly insignificant; and anyway, if one leaves aside legal or natural monopolies, usually they can be readily explained in terms of sluggish closing-down of loss-making firms (workers resist, governments subsidize, etc.), of the time required for competition via entry to operate, of economies of scale or other barriers to entry,[5] of dynamical advantages deriving from learning-by-doing, and perhaps of rent elements, e.g. associated with technological secrets or special skills of managers, illegitimately included into the rate of profit.[6]

In recent decades there has been some empirical enquiry on this issue. Semmler (1984) finds that differences in profit rates do not disappear completely, but argues (p. 147) that the empirical evidence on persisting differences of profit rates can be explained on the basis of barriers to the mobility of capitals within a dynamical classical theory of competition. Glick and Ehrbar (1990; also see Ehrbar and Glick 1988) find only a weak equalization of industry profit rates in the USA between 1948 and 1979, but they find that profit rates are included in a range of about 5 percentage points above or below the average: a range whose amazing narrowness (when compared with the *possible* differences in profit rates) can only be explained, I would contend, by postulating a powerful tendency of relevant differences in profit rates to disappear owing to competition. They propose to explain the persistence of differences in terms of different risk levels. Mueller's (1986) *Profits in the long run* studies the profit rates of almost 600 USA firms over the years 1950–1972, and finds that extremely few companies earn a rate of profits greater than twice the average for many years.[7] Mueller's study

---

5 Cases such as those of Microsoft or Google are precisely cases of particularly strong barriers to entry, due to strong network externalities or economies of scale, that would clearly require anti-monopoly interventions (see ► Chap. 12).

6 Nor is the assumption of a perfectly uniform rate of profit a necessary one in the method of long-period positions; to be able to say how one distributive variable depends on the level and changes of the other distributive variable and on technology, taking into account the dependence of relative prices on distribution, one only needs to be able to say how relative prices will change with distribution, and although the uniform rate of profits is the obvious first approximation, persistent differences in rates of profits can be admitted without difficulty. Cf. the quotation from Adam Smith in ► Chap. 1, Sect. 1.3.2. On the causes of persistent differences in profit rates Smith's Chapter 10 in Book I of *Wealth of Nations* is a very useful reading.

7 It is not clear, from Mueller's book, whether his definition of profits is gross or net of depreciation. The rate of profit that competition can be assumed to render uniform is the one *net* of depreciation. Glick and Ehrbar (1990) are clearer on the issue, and unfortunately their definition of profits is gross of depreciation. But this weakness of their analysis is irrelevant in the face of the absence of long-run increasing divergences of profit rates, and might on the contrary explain part of the persistence in differences of profit rates that they observe, as due simply to different 'organic compositions of capital'.

Chapter 10 · Back to Long-Period Prices

aims at finding out whether abnormally high or low rates of profits tend to return towards the mean as time passes: it finds clear evidence (in ▶ Chap. 2) that this is indeed so on average, although profit rate differences do not tend to disappear completely, rather tending to persistent differentials, and although there are cases where the difference has increased for some part of the period considered. But both the persistence of some profitability differences even over long periods, and the observation of cases where the profitability difference has increased for some period, in no way contradict the existence of a gravitation of prices towards uniform-rate-of-profit prices, given that barriers to entry and other obstacles to complete profit rate equalization are not absent in reality,[8] and given that new events creating possibly durable deviations of profitability from the average do occur. Mueller himself never doubts the existence of a tendency of unimpeded competition to eliminate profit rate differences in the long run unless novelties arise,[9] and his research aims at finding out the best explanation of why this tendency does not work itself out completely[10]: differences in the nature of the industry, or

---

8 And particularly so for the big companies which are the object of Mueller's study, most of them conglomerates operating in many differentiated, imperfectly competitive markets. The limited deviations from the mean and the tendency to return to the mean that Mueller finds for company profit rates appear to confirm that the effect of competition conforms to traditional expectations in these instances as well.

9 'In an economy subject to uncertainty, profits and losses signal the existence of excess demand or excess supply at long-run competitive price. If resources are free to respond to market signals, they should move into areas where profits are being earned and out of areas suffering losses. This movement of resources continues until returns are equalized across all markets (with appropriate adjustment for risk). Of course, each new period brings new uncertainties and new positions of profits and loss, so that a point in time when all firm or industry profit levels are equal never obtains. But if the market is capable of responding to the signals of profits and losses, the long-run movement of individual firm and industry profit rates should be toward a common competitive level. All observed profits and losses should be short-run deviations around this trend.... Although most studies of profit rate determinants have focused on industry profit levels, the competitive environment hypothesis of convergence on a single competitive level should be equally valid for firm-level profits and for industry profits. For a homogeneous product, all firms in an industry should charge the same price under competitive conditions. Free entry and exit should ensure that only the most efficient firms survive, that all firms have the same average costs as well as price' (Mueller 1986, pp. 8, 9). These lines appear to reflect the general opinion among industrial economists. Another example: 'In a dynamically competitive economy where entry and exit behavior is sufficiently strong, short-run deviations of profits should quickly disappear, and profits should stay near their normal levels' (Yamawaki 1989, p. 390).

10 Interestingly, when Mueller attempts to extend his enquiry to the year 1980, he interprets his results as indicating that the process of convergence toward normal levels of the rates of profit is continuing. 'The competitive environment hypothesis is sustained, provided one waits long enough. [...] The earlier results [relative to the period 1950–72] suggested that as much as 70 percent of the differences in profit rates across firms in 1950–52 is transitory; that is, 30 percent or more of any profit differences observed are permanent. Table 2.7 implies that some 75–80% of these 'permanent' profit differences also disappear over time and that the process of eroding profit differences continues until the job is done. But this process takes a long time' (Mueller 1986, p. 30). Because of firm mortality and other reasons, his sample shrinks and his data become less reliable, which is why Mueller only considers the issue briefly and restricts the main inquiry to the years 1950–72.

10.1 · The Gravitation to Long-Period Prices in the History ...

in the nature of firms? He finds truth in both these competing explanations, and considers reasons such as the ones mentioned above.

Further empirical evidence supporting the convergence of profit rates to uniformity, or at least limited and non-increasing differences in profit rates, is provided by Duménil and Lévy (1993, pp. 41–46).

10.2 Objections to the Uniform Rate of Profit

Now I discuss two objections advanced in recent decades against the assumption of a uniform rate of profit.

A strand of thought among radical Keynesian economists stresses absence of perfect foresight, volatility of expectations, variability of the general state of confidence, role of animal spirits, unpredictable novelties, and argues that these elements undermine the method of long-period positions; it is argued that investment is too irregular and unpredictable, and external circumstances change too often, for a gravitation towards uniform-rate-of-return prices to be a powerful determinant of relative prices.

These views are less popular now than some decades ago when they were energetically advocated by Joan Robinson. They seem to have been part of an attempt to defend Keynesian theory against the 'neoclassical-synthesis' reestablishment of the neoclassical orthodoxy at least for the long-run tendencies of the economy, by denying not the existence of the neoclassical long-period forces but their capacity to determine the path of the economy because impeded by uncertainty. Nowadays there is a clearer perception that acceptance of the long-period method need not mean acceptance of the neoclassical long-period forces, which therefore can be rejected while continuing to accept the gravitation of market prices to long-period prices, which as argued seems empirically solid. It must also be remembered that the determination of *aggregate* investment is a different question from the determination of the *composition* of investment. A worsening of the general state of confidence can cause a decrease of aggregate investment which, by causing a decrease of aggregate demand (Sect. 1.11), can cause a further decrease of investment, and a grave crisis; but even during this process it is highly likely that the decreasing *amount* of total *gross* investment will be directed in higher *proportion* towards the sectors with higher prospective rates of return; therefore aggregate output fluctuations do not impede the tendency towards a uniform rate of return.

The second objection might be seen as a variant of the first, but it does not stress animal spirits or uncertainty, it concentrates on the doubtful *persistence* of the data determining long-period prices. The argument is that innovations have become so quick that technical conditions of production as well as consumer products do not remain unchanged long enough for the gravitation to long-period prices to complete its operation.

But as argued by Cesaratto (1995, 1996) the usefulness of the long-period method requires, not that long-period prices be actually *reached*, but only that the economy tends to them all the time and therefore most prices are not far from their long-period values, even if they never completely catch up with the moving target. The assumption of a uniform rate of profits seems to be the best starting point on which if necessary to superpose, at a second stage of analysis, the reasons that may explain why in some cases that uniformity is not closely approached. Anyway the tendency of the price of a product to decrease when technical innovations reduce costs appears to be generally very quick in all markets where entry or imitation are not overly difficult.

The above objections have come above all from Post-Keynesian economists. They tend to prefer a different explanation of relative prices, and of their considerable persistence. This explanation is that the prices of industrial products[11] are generally determined according to a ***mark-up*** procedure which adds a certain percentage (specific to each firm) to variable costs, or to total average costs other than interest charges, and are generally not changed when demand changes, but are rather kept fixed while production adjusts to demand.

There is indeed abundant empirical evidence supporting a mark-up picture of how prices of differentiated industrially produced goods are set (see ▸ Chap. 12), but it would seem to confirm the usefulness of the notion of long-period prices. The mark-ups will reflect the market power of firms; the more competitive the industry (that is, the more substitutable the products and the easier the entry of competing producers), the more the mark-ups will have to reflect a ***full-cost pricing*** procedure that will add such a mark-up as to cover depreciation of fixed plant and other overhead costs and to guarantee in addition a normal rate of return on the capital invested when capacity utilization is normal[12]: a higher mark-up would encourage entry, or price undercutting by already existing competing firms; a lower mark-up would entail losses. If the industry is such that entry is difficult, the mark-up may guarantee a higher rate of return than the average one, but the difference is generally due to persistent causes, and then one can take the differences in profit rate as given, and the analysis of, for example, the effect of a rise in wages on rates of profits and on relative prices can proceed essentially in the same way as with a perfectly uniform rate of profits.

Both with mark-ups that guarantee a uniform rate of profits in all industries, and with mark-ups associated with given differences in rates of profit among industries, the gravitation of competitive relative prices to long-period prices *is guaranteed*, at least in the absence of joint production. I show this first for a uniform rate of profits. Suppose that all capital is circulating capital, all production processes last one period, and for simplicity assume that the given real wage is advanced and included in the technical coefficients; firms determine output prices

---

11 That is, not the prices of agricultural products, whose supplies are essentially given in the short period because their production processes take a year; and not the prices of some raw materials (e.g. oil) determined by a supply coming from official or informal near-cartels, and by a demand heavily conditioned by stock market speculation.

12 This is also called *cost-plus pricing*. Normal capacity utilization was briefly discussed in ▸ Chap. 1, Sect. 1.13.4. The tendency of prices not to change when demand changes will be further discussed in ▸ Chap. 12; here it suffices to say that frequent price changes are disliked by buyers, and also by sellers because they increase the danger of price wars.

10.2 · Objections to the Uniform Rate of Profit

at time t by charging on the input costs (determined by prices at time $t-1$) a mark-up equal to depreciation plus a nominal rate of return ρ. Then, with $\mathbf{C}$ the matrix of technical coefficients of inputs, inclusive of the real wages physically specified (cf. ▶ Chap. 2), prices obey

$$\mathbf{p}_t = (1 + \rho)\mathbf{p}_{t-1}\mathbf{C}. \tag{10.1}$$

This dynamical system causes *relative* prices to converge to long-period relative prices, while their absolute levels converge to a common rate of inflation π determined by $1+\rho=(1+\pi)(1+r)$, where r is the uniform rate of profits associated with long-period prices when there is no inflation, $\pi=0$; hence r is the real rate of profit.

▪▪ Proof

The proof is based on the following result of matrix theory, whose demonstration I omit (cf. Nikaido 1968, pp. 110–113):

Let $\mathbf{A}$ *be a non-negative square matrix such that* $\mathbf{A}^k > 0$ *for some integer* $k > 0$, *and let* λ *be the dominant eigenvalue of* $\mathbf{A}$. *Then the matrix* $\mathbf{B} = \lim_{t \to +\infty}(1/\lambda^t)\mathbf{A}^t$ *exists, and for any solution* $\mathbf{x}_t = \mathbf{A}^t\mathbf{x}_0$ *of the equation* $\mathbf{x}_{t+1} = \mathbf{A}\mathbf{x}_t$, *the vector* $(1/\lambda^t)\mathbf{x}_t$ *converges to* $\mathbf{Bx}_0$ *as* $t \to +\infty$. *Stated differently, all the component ratios* $x_{it}/(\lambda^t x_{i0})$ *converge to a common limit.*

Let $\mathbf{C}$ be the (viable) matrix of wage-inclusive coefficients of the basic commodities, hence indecomposable; then we know from Ch. 2 that $\mathbf{C}^k > 0$ for some k; let λ be the dominant eigenvalue of $\mathbf{C}$, with r defined by $(1+r)=1/\lambda$ the uniform rate of profits associated with long-period relative prices. The matrix $(1+r)\mathbf{C}$ has dominant eigenvalue equal to 1; then the above result means that if $\rho=r$ in $\mathbf{p}_t=(1+\rho)\mathbf{p}_{t-1}\mathbf{C}$, as t increases relative prices converge to $\mathbf{p}_0\mathbf{B}$, with $\mathbf{B}=\lim_{t \to +\infty}(1+r)^t\mathbf{C}^t$. If ρ is different from r, put $(1+\rho)=(1+\pi)(1+r)$; then $\mathbf{p}_t=(1+\pi)(1+r)\mathbf{p}_{t-1}\mathbf{C}=(1+\pi)^t\mathbf{p}_0(1/\lambda^t)\mathbf{C}^t$, which means that each price p_{it} equals $(1+\pi)^t$ times the p_{it} that *would* obtain if it were $\rho=r$; the *ratios* p_{it}/p_{jt} are unaffected by the multiplication by $(1+\pi)^t$ and therefore converge. The *relative* prices to which $\mathbf{p}_t$ converges must then be the long-period prices, since these are the sole ones that yield a uniform real rate of profits equal to r when relative prices are constant through time. The rate of change of each nominal price converges to a common rate of inflation π.

It is then easy to prove that the relative prices of non-basic commodities converge to their long-period levels too. Let us call $\mathbf{D}$ the rectangular matrix of (wage-inclusive) technical coefficients of basic commodities in the non-basic industries, and let $\mathbf{E}$ be the square matrix of technical coefficients of non-basics in the non-basic industries. Let $\mathbf{v}$ be the vector of non-basic prices. Then the full-cost pricing dynamical equations for non-basics are

$$\mathbf{v}_{t+1} = (1 + \rho)\mathbf{v}_t\mathbf{E} + (1 + \rho)\mathbf{p}_t\mathbf{D}.$$

Since we are only concerned with relative prices, let us assume $\rho=r$. Then $\mathbf{p}_t$ converges to $\mathbf{p}$, the long-period prices of basics; then $(1+r)\mathbf{p}_t\mathbf{D}$ converges to a vector,

842   Chapter 10 · Back to Long-Period Prices

let us indicate it as $\mathbf{c}$, and to ascertain whether $\mathbf{v}_t$ converges it suffices to study the behaviour of

$$\mathbf{v}_{t+1} = (1 + r)\mathbf{v}_t\mathbf{E} + \mathbf{c} = \mathbf{v}_t\mathbf{M} + \mathbf{c} \quad \text{where } \mathbf{M} = (1 + r)\mathbf{E}.$$

As usual we assume that the dominant eigenvalue of $\mathbf{E}$ is less than λ; hence the dominant eigenvalue of $\mathbf{M}$ (a non-negative matrix) is less than 1, and therefore by Perron–Frobenius theorem it is $(\mathbf{I}{-}\mathbf{M})^{-1} = \mathbf{I} + \mathbf{M} + \mathbf{M}^2 + \mathbf{M}^3 + ...$, which implies that $\lim_{t \to +\infty} \mathbf{M}^t = \mathbf{0}$. Since $\mathbf{v}_t = \mathbf{v}_{t-1}\mathbf{M} + \mathbf{c} = \mathbf{v}_{t-2}\mathbf{M}^2 + \mathbf{c}\mathbf{M} + \mathbf{c}$ $= \mathbf{v}_{t-3}\mathbf{M}^3 + \mathbf{c}\mathbf{M}^2 + \mathbf{c}\mathbf{M} + \mathbf{c} = ... = \mathbf{v}_0\mathbf{M}^t + \mathbf{c}(\mathbf{I} + \mathbf{M} + \mathbf{M}^2 + ... + \mathbf{M}^{t-1})$, then for t tending to $+\infty$, $\mathbf{v}_0\mathbf{M}^t$ tends to zero and $\mathbf{v}_t$ converges to $\mathbf{c}(\mathbf{I}{-}\mathbf{M})^{-1}$. ∎

If the rates of return implicit in mark-ups differ across industries, relative prices converge to the constant relative prices associated with the *vector* of rates of profits. Suppose that $(r_1,...,r_n)$ is a vector of profit rates and let $\mathbf{R}^*$ be a diagonal $n \times n$ matrix with diagonal terms $1 + r_1,...,1 + r_n$. Assume that $\mathbf{R}^*$ is compatible with $\mathbf{p} = \mathbf{p}\mathbf{C}\mathbf{R}^*$, i.e. that the dominant eigenvalue of $\mathbf{C}\mathbf{R}^*$ is 1 (differences in profit rates cannot be arbitrary; for a given $\mathbf{C}$ if one profit rate rises some other profit rate must decrease). Let r be the uniform profit rate determined by $\mathbf{p} = (1 + r)\mathbf{p}\mathbf{C}$, and let $\mathbf{D}$ be a diagonal matrix such that $\mathbf{R}^* = \mathbf{D}(1 + r)\mathbf{I}$; i.e., with $d_1,...,d_n$ the elements on the main diagonal of $\mathbf{D}$, it is $1 + r_i = d_i(1 + r)$. Then $\mathbf{p} = (1 + r)\mathbf{p}\mathbf{C}\mathbf{D}$, and the analysis of convergence proceeds as in the case of a uniform profit rate, with the matrix $\mathbf{C}\mathbf{D}$ taking the place of $\mathbf{C}$.

Mark-up pricing therefore strongly supports the role of long-period prices[13] as indicators of the averages of market prices. It adds that long-period prices often rule even when capacity utilization is different from the normal one for most firms in an industry, see ▶ Chap. 12.

It would seem therefore that there is no empirical reason to doubt the existence of a gravitation of market prices towards long-period prices as long as entry can be assumed; at most the question can be whether the *traditional explanation*—to be discussed presently—of this empirical *fact* reveals, upon further examination, deficiencies that oblige one to look for a different explanation.

10.3 The Traditional Explanation

In order to study the gravitation of market prices to long-period prices, to assume that the latter prices are associated with a uniform rate of profit or with given differences in profit rates makes essentially no difference, so I will assume the first case. In both classical and traditional marginalist authors it is esteemed that, in analysing the tendency towards the long-period price *in a single market*, one can assume that, if the quantity supplied is less (resp. greater) than the quantity forthcoming at the long-period price, then the price will be higher (lower) than

---

13 The notion of long-period relative prices as centres of gravitation of market prices can be extended to the case of given differences in rates of profit.

10.3 · The Traditional Explanation

the long-period price; that this will induce an increase (a reduction) in the *normal* quantity supplied, that is, an increase (a reduction) in the industry's productive capacity; and furthermore that the repercussions on other markets, and then from these back on the first market, of changes in price or quantity produced in the first market can be neglected. Thus Ricardo:

> I have already remarked, that the market price of a commodity may exceed its natural or necessary price, as it may be produced in less abundance than the new demand for it requires. This however, is but a temporary effect. The high profit on capital employed in producing that commodity will naturally attract capital to that trade; and as soon as the requisite funds are supplied, and the quantity of the commodity is duly increased its price will fall, and the profits of the trade will conform to the general level. (Ricardo 1951, p. 119)

An important difference is that in the generally accepted Marshallian version of marginalist analyses a demand curve and a short-period supply curve for the product are assumed that determine univocally a short-period partial-equilibrium price; in classical analyses it is only assumed that one can define an 'effectual demand' (the normal demand at the natural price) and that if supply is greater (less) than effectual demand the price will be less (greater) than the natural price, but with no precise determinability of a short-period price.

This traditional argument appears prima facie quite convincing, under the assumption (implicit in Ricardo's quote, and explicit in Marshall's partial equilibrium analyses) that the costs of the unspecialized inputs[14] are given or anyway only little affected by the change in demands for the inputs of a commodity, associated with change in the output of the commodity. This can be called the 'partial-equilibrium' assumption.

It might be thought that, even under such conditions, the stability of a product market may be endangered by production lags, which may cause 'cobweb cycles' or 'hog cycles', see Sect. 6.26. But the instabilities that can arise owing to this type of causes do not appear to endanger the theory, they can be argued to be short-lived.

The type of phenomenon illustrated by explosive cobwebs may well occasionally happen. One need not accept the precise formalization of cobwebs (with a definite demand curve and a definite supply curve, anyway partial equilibrium notions and therefore not as open to the capital-theory critique) in order to accept that if there is a lag in the adaptation of production to demand on, e.g. the market for a consumption good, then there may be an oscillation of the price, which might in certain circumstances be of increasing amplitude.

---

14 Specialized input prices adjust so as to maintain extra-profits equal to zero: e.g. if the production of a famous wine only grown in a restricted area is observed to yield a higher-than-average rate of profits, the attempt by competitors to enter that industry will result in a rise of the rate of rent in that area, which will cause the rate of profits to become the normal one, not because of a decrease in price caused by an increase in supply, but rather because of an increase in costs.

844   **Chapter 10** · Back to Long-Period Prices

But phenomena of this kind, although no doubt possible for perishable goods (if the product is durable, it will be possible to postpone sales and build up inventories when the price decreases significantly below the long-period normal level), will tend not to last. It is opportune to distinguish short-period output oscillations while industry's productive capacity is given, from long-period oscillations of the productive capacity itself. The short-period oscillations will be soon damped down by the producers realizing what is happening; the expectation of an inversion of the price movement will induce caution in the variation of supply; the diminished sensitivity of lagged supply to price will turn an unstable cobweb into a stable one. In the long period, the cobweb would have to arise owing to an excessive creation of new capacity in the industry, causing a subsequent bankruptcy of most firms nearly at the same time, with a consequent sharp reduction of productive capacity that causes a rise of price that starts a new wave of creation of new firms. But the bankruptcy (a *legal* event) of the owners of plants need not destroy the plants; these can be bought by other capitalists the moment it is realized that supply has decreased enough to make production profitable again; a repeated pronounced oscillation *of productive capacity* of a single industry is therefore extremely difficult to imagine.[15] One can add that the expansion of plants would presumably not be simultaneous for all firms, and even more so for the closing down of plants due to losses; the adjustment of capacity would in all likelihood be gradual.

When a market appears to be particularly prone to instabilities, institutional changes generally develop in order to mitigate the problem. For example, in agriculture it can happen that in a year the harvest of some perishable product is so abundant that free competition would cause the price to fall nearly to zero, with a risk of generalized bankruptcy of producers. In these cases usually the government intervenes to purchase and destroy part of the harvest, or the producers themselves by acting collectively find some way to prevent the price from falling too much.[16]

I conclude that, from the analysis of a single competitive market, no significant problem appears to emerge for the thesis of the long-period tendency of market price towards average cost. The problems can only come, if at all, from the interaction of markets.

10.4 **Cross-Dual Models**

A rather different picture emerges from most of the articles on the gravitation towards long-period prices, and in particular from the more widely followed approach, the so-called cross-dual models of gravitation. These are models where

---

15 Repeated oscillations of general productive capacity are on the contrary perfectly conceivable but as due to oscillations of aggregate demand (due to multiplier-accelerator interactions), which do not question a tendency of market prices to gravitate towards or around long-period prices.

16 Other examples might be given to show that when markets work well, this is often because some institutional change occurred to correct problems highlighted by previous historical experience. The history of banking is rich in such examples.

10.4 · Cross-Dual Models

the rate of change of relative quantities is made to depend on the difference between the sectoral rates of profit and the average or normal rate of profit, while the rate of change of relative prices is made to depend on excess demands. In the so-called pure versions of these models, where it is assumed that, owing to fixed proportions both in technical coefficients and in consumption, there is no 'substitution' in demand and the changes in the composition of demand depend exclusively on the changes in the composition of investment, one obtains instability. I present the simplest model of this kind (Lippi 1990).[17]

Consider a two-goods economy where the goods are both consumption goods and circulating capital goods, with production in yearly cycles. Real wages are given, advanced, and included in the input coefficients. Let P stand for the relative price p_1/p_2, and Q stand for the relative quantities produced q_1/q_2. P^* is the price ratio associated with the uniform rate of profit r^*. If relative prices are not changing through time, when $P > P^*$ then the rate of profit in industry 1 is greater than in industry 2, as easily shown by the price equations (based on the C-representation, see ▶ Chap. 2):

$$(c_{11}p_{1t} + c_{21}p_{2t})(1 + r_{1t}) = p_{1t}$$
$$(c_{12}p_{1t} + c_{22}p_{2t})(1 + r_{2t}) = p_{2t}.$$

These make it evident that if, starting from given values of p_1 and p_2, one raises P by raising p_1, then r_1 rises and r_2 decreases (assuming $c_{12} > 0$). These equations determine the rates of profits by assigning to the product the same price it has as an input: this might be criticized because if rates of profit are not the same entrepreneurs will try to take expectable changes in prices into account when deciding where to invest. But 'The requirement of the correct foresight necessary to make those price-changes relevant will not generally be fulfilled. And economic theory, which cannot be expected to determine actual prices, but only prices corresponding to averages of actual prices, can hardly be expected to determine the actual changes in actual prices as distinct from providing a guidance to the *sign* of those changes. Appreciation or depreciation of the capital stocks of each industry relative to its product seem accordingly to be best abstracted from in a first approximation – just as we abstract from, say, the non-unicity of the market price in any actual situation of the economy'. (Garegnani 1990c, p. 335). This view is reinforced by the observation that, when a product earns a lower-than-average rate of profit, the natural expectation is that its price will rise, but except in extreme and temporary cases this will only reduce the divergence of the expected rate of profit from the average rate of profit without changing its sign, nor therefore the sign of the tendential change of productive capacity in that industry (a tendency to decrease, in this case).

---

17 Discussion of more complex models of gravitation would require a mastery of the mathematics of dynamical systems, which this textbook does not presume. The interested reader can consult Caminati and Petri (1990), Boggio (1992, 1998), Garegnani (1990c, 1997), Bellino and Serrano (2017), and the literature there cited; for the mathematics, Gandolfo (1971) is a good starting point.

846 **Chapter 10 · Back to Long-Period Prices**

Assume workers don't save and capitalists invest all profits; hence, Lippi assumes that the normal long-period composition of demand is Q^* which is the balanced-growth composition associated with a rate of growth $g=r^*$.

Assume that one can formalize the adjustment process in discrete time. For quantities, we assume that when the rate of profit is higher in industry 1 than in industry 2, then the composition of production shifts in favour of commodity 1, and contrariwise, e.g.

$$Q_{t+1} - Q_t = \alpha(r_{1t} - r_{2t}). \tag{10.2}$$

with scalar $\alpha > 0$. The sign of $r_{1t} - r_{2t}$ is the same as the sign of $P - P^*$, so we can also use, with an opportune different α:

$$Q_{t+1} - Q_t = \alpha\left(P_t - P^*\right) \tag{10.3}$$

For prices, we are interested in *relative* prices; what is assumed is that when the *ratio* of demand to supply is greater (respectively, smaller) for good 1, then the *relative* price of good 1 rises (respectively, decreases), and its rate of profit moves in the same direction. A ratio of demand to supply for good 1 at time t greater than for good 2 is formalized as

$$(c_{11}q_{1,t+1} + c_{12}q_{2,t+1})/q_{1t} > (c_{21}q_{1,t+1} + c_{22}q_{2,t+1})/q_{2t}, \quad \text{or} \quad \frac{c_{11}q_{1,t+1} + c_{12}q_{2,t+1}}{c_{21}q_{1,t+1} + c_{22}q_{2,t+1}} > \frac{q_{1t}}{q_{2t}}$$

that is, in period $t+1$ supply of good i is q_{it}, and demand for it is determined by the outputs of the period; demand can well be greater (or less) than supply for both goods, but relative price changes depending on which excess demand is greater; this assumption can be written as follows (with β a positive scalar):

$$P_{t+1} - P_t = -\beta\left[\frac{q_{1t}}{q_{2t}} - \frac{c_{11}q_{1,t+1} + c_{12}q_{2,t+1}}{c_{21}q_{1,t+1} + c_{22}q_{2,t+1}}\right] = -\beta\left[Q_t - \frac{c_{11}Q_{t+1} + c_{12}}{c_{21}Q_{t+1} + c_{22}}\right]. \tag{10.4}$$

If we restrict attention to situations in which P_t and Q_t lie near P^* and Q^* respectively, and if furthermore we assume that α is small so that Q_{t+1} is very close to Q_t, then it is possible to assume that the sign of $\left[Q_t - \frac{c_{11}Q_{t+1} + c_{12}}{c_{21}Q_{t+1} + c_{22}}\right]$ is normally the same as the sign of $\left[Q_t - \frac{c_{11}Q_t + c_{12}}{c_{21}Q_t + c_{22}}\right]$. The latter expression is zero if and only if $Q_t = Q^*$ (check it!), and is positive or negative according as Q_t is greater or smaller than Q^*. Then in a neighbourhood of (P^*, Q^*) we can replace (10.3) with

$$P_{t+1} = P_t - \beta(Q_t - Q^*). \tag{10.5}$$

System (10.3)–(10.5) can be rewritten with, as variables, $\pi_t = P_t - P^*$ and $\chi_t = Q_t - Q^*$; it becomes (Duménil and Lévy 1990):

$$\begin{bmatrix} \pi_{t+1} \\ \chi_{t+1} \end{bmatrix} = A \begin{bmatrix} \pi_t \\ \chi_t \end{bmatrix} \quad \text{where } A = \begin{pmatrix} 1 & -\beta \\ \alpha & 1 \end{pmatrix}.$$

10.4 · Cross-Dual Models

This is an autonomous system of two linear difference equations of the first order in two variables, in normal form. The theory of dynamical systems (e.g. Gandolfo 1971, ▶ Chap. 8) tells us that this system converges asymptotically to a unique equilibrium if and only if all the eigenvalues of $\mathbf{A}$ are less than 1 in modulus. The eigenvalues of $\mathbf{A}$ solve

$$det(\lambda \mathbf{I} - \mathbf{A}) = \lambda^2 - 2\lambda + 1 + \alpha\beta = 0.$$

The product of the two eigenvalues[18] is equal to $1 + \alpha\beta$; i.e. it is larger than 1 for all non-negative values of α and β with at least one of them positive; therefore the modulus of at least one eigenvalue is larger than 1 and the equilibrium is not stable.[19]

Let us try to understand the origin of this result that seems to contradict the stability derived from the 'partial-equilibrium' assumption. Suppose that at time t relative prices are production prices, supplies are equal to normal effectual demands, and then for some reason (say, an earthquake) some plants in industry 1 are destroyed, the relative supply of good 1 discontinuously decreases and this creates an excess demand for good 1. By Eq. (10.4) or (10.5), p_1/p_2 increases, stimulating a change in the composition of production in favour of good 1. Assume that from one period to the next the composition of production only changes gradually, i.e. that several periods are required to reach again Q^*; this assumption is necessary in order for the model's behaviour not to be too far from a reality where most adjustments are closer to being a continuous than to being a discrete process. Then it is $Q_t - Q^* < 0$ for several periods; during all this time, the model assumes that p_1/p_2 keeps increasing. So when the composition of supply becomes again equal to the normal long-period one, $Q = Q^*$, we have that P is *not* equal to P^*, it is *higher*; hence $r_1 > r_2$, and thus the tendency to expand the relative production of good 1 is still there; indeed, it is at its strongest; so an *overshooting* of Q is inevitable. As Q becomes greater than Q^*, P starts decreasing, but it remains for several periods greater than P^*; that is for all these periods it is $r_1 > r_2$ and Q keeps increasing, starting to decrease only when P becomes smaller than P^*; so when in the course of its decrease P becomes equal to P^*, it is $Q > Q^*$, and P keeps decreasing. As 'one variable moves towards its equilibrium position, the other moves further away from it' (Boggio 1998, p. 354). The overshooting causes an oscillatory behaviour of the dynamical system, and the mathematics show that the system is unstable; that is, the oscillations are of increasing amplitude. It has been shown (e.g. Boggio 1992) that the result extends to the case with n goods.

A clear difference from the 'partial-equilibrium' verbal analyses of classical authors is that in the latter no overshooting is considered. Smith or Ricardo made the *level* (not the sign of the time derivative) of the price of a commodity depend on the 'proportion of supply to demand', where by 'demand' they intended the

---

18 The product of the two solutions $x = \left(-b \pm \sqrt{b^2 - 4ac}\right)/2a$ of a second-degree equation $ax^2 + bx + c = 0$ is c/a.

19 For the proof that the original system (10.1)–(10.3) is analogously unstable cf. Lippi (1990). For a detailed survey of results on cross-dual models of gravitation cf. Boggio (1992).

normal effectual demand, i.e. the quantity—a single quantity, not a function—demanded at the natural price, and by 'supply' they again intended a single quantity, the quantity supplied in the given short period.[20] The natural interpretation is that, when arguing that a supply less than demand (so conceived) means a market price higher than the natural price, the classical authors were arguing much the same as a Marshallian economist arguing that in the short period the price will be higher than the long-period price if the quantity supplied is less than the long-period equilibrium quantity.[21] It is implicit in such a view that price adjusts faster than productive capacity, and that there will be a price sufficiently high, or sufficiently low, as to make the quantity demanded temporarily equal to supply (which can also adapt, both because of changes in the degree of utilization of fixed plants, and because of inventory decumulation or accumulation) when productive capacity is not the one required to satisfy normal effectual demand at the natural price. Demand in turn can be influenced by temporary anticipations or posticipation of part of demand decisions in view of expectation of price changes.

The realism of this picture is not adequately grasped by the cross-dual formalization, owing above all to the rigidity of relative price in each period: as Eq. (10.4) makes clear, prices at date $t+1$ are not influenced at all by demand and supply in that period, they depend only on what happened in the previous period. This neglects the very plausible Marshallian assumption that productive capacity changes much slower than price; price in each period should be assumed to reach a level that brings about a temporary equality of production and sales, for example, by rising to stimulate a higher utilization of capacity and some discouragement of demand if production is less than sales, and contrariwise if sales are less than production. This radically changes the behaviour of prices relative to that assumed in cross-dual models: price overshooting disappears because if for a moment we assume given input prices the adjustment of industry capacity causes the product price to be the closer to the price yielding the normal rate of profit, the more industry capacity gets close to the level required to satisfy demand at that price.

Let me illustrate with an example. Suppose an economy where the production of toilet paper has become concentrated almost entirely in one town, and an earthquake destroys the toilet paper factories. Production of toilet paper falls

---

20 Flaschel and Semmler (1986) produce several quotations from classical authors to support their cross-dual approach, but do not notice that all those quotations talk about supply and demand 'regulating' the *level* of the market price, not its rate of change; e.g. they quote Marx (1977, vol. II, p. 208): 'supply and demand determine the market price', i.e. determine the *level* of the market price.

21 The difference from Marshall is that no attempt is made by classical economists to find a precise rule for the determination of the temporary or the short-period price of a commodity, consistently with the absence of supply or demand *functions* in their theories; these authors do not go beyond the observation of a tendency of the market price to be the higher, the greater the (effectual) demand relative to the quantity supplied, and always with added observations on the impossibility of reaching a more precise determination, owing to the influence of accidental elements: for example, how urgent is the need for some seller to sell off all her supply quickly, an urgency depending on the specific situation (see, e.g., *Wealth of Nations* I, VII, 9; 1975, vol. 1, p. 50).

10.4 · Cross-Dual Models

down to almost zero for the time required to rebuild the factories and/or convert some other paper factories to the production of toilet paper. (Toilet paper seems to be a good example of a consumption good with very rigid desired demand, as the simple cross-dual models assume.) The cross-dual model would have the price of toilet paper rise week after week during all the months required for toilet paper production to go back to the old level, and would have this price stop rising and start gradually to decrease only when finally the production capacity of the toilet paper industry became *excessive*, greater than the old normal capacity, as no doubt it would become given the persistence of a price considerably higher than normal. Clearly, this is not what is going to happen: the price of toilet paper will jump up to a high level immediately after the earthquake, will perhaps rise further as inventories in shops are exhausted, but will then gradually decrease as production gradually increases, and will go back to the old normal price when the productive capacity of the toilet paper industry goes back to the old normal one.

Other aspects of the simple cross-dual model are also open to criticism, for example as stressed by Duménil and Lévy (1993, p. 86), the determination of the rates of profit in the several industries assumes the normal utilization of capacities, because it is based on the given technical coefficients and on Sraffa-type equations, but this is not the appropriate measure of the incentive to reallocate investment if average capacity utilization in the industry is not normal. If for example there is excess supply of a good then, even if prices are production prices, firms in that industry will still wish to reduce their productive capacity because on average it is underutilized (the 'actual', ex-post profitability in that industry will be lower on average than the one on normally utilized plants). This can be shown to damp down the oscillations of the simple cross-dual model, making stability likely even if one preserves the unconvincing formalization of price changes. And what determines demands, and what happens when demand and supply differ would require more discussion. There are very many complex aspects of disequilibrium that one should pay attention to, a reading of Garegnani (1990c, or 1997) is very instructive on this issue. But the basic deficiency of these models is the formalization of price changes that neglects the capacity of prices quickly to change in response to the demand–supply situation within each period, thus avoiding overshooting.

Garegnani goes on to argue that the 'Marshallian' view appears to have considerable plausibility (independently of the right to draw demand *functions*,[22]) because of the processes which induce a decrease of the short-period demand for a good, and possibly an increase of supply from the short-period given capacity, when the good's price rises. These processes, on the demand side, will include not only the changes in the choices of purchasers that are usually qualified as 'substitution' in consumption or in production, but also postponements of purchases, often made possible by decumulations of buyers' inventories of that good.[23] On the supply side, there will be increases of supply associated with over-normal

---

22 See below on the general legitimacy of demand functions; also ▶ Chap. 4, Appendix 1.
23 Cf. Garegnani (1997, Appendix, pp. 167–8).

utilization of productive capacity, and, when the price has increased, possible decumulations of sellers' inventories in order to profit from the high price before the latter starts decreasing; a temporary accumulation of inventories in the opposite case in which demand is less than expected is a well-known way to avoid sharp price falls, while waiting for the reduction of production (plus, sometimes, temporary discounts) to bring inventories back to normal. These several adjustments suggest the correctness of the classical conception.

Bellino and Serrano (2017), by assuming as suggested by Adam Smith and by Garegnani that price is above (respectively, below) the natural price when output is less (respectively, greater) than effectual demand, do obtain a tendency of output towards effectual demand and hence a tendency of price towards the natural price. Of course the topic is still open, further contributions will no doubt come out, but my provisional conclusion is that the traditional argument is valid.

Some reluctance has been occasionally manifested by non-neoclassical economists towards admitting that changes in consumer choice induced by price changes may be one reason why a temporary adjustment between demand and supply can be reached in the market of a product, a reluctance deriving from a fear of falling into neoclassical modes of reasoning.[24] This reluctance does not appear warranted. To admit that, when the price of a product changes, there may be changes in the consumption choices of consumers, or in the technical choices of firms if the good is a capital good, does not mean adopting neoclassical assumptions; it only means admitting the facts, from which the marginalist/neoclassical approach wrongly thought that decreasing demand curves for factors could be derived. A classical approach need not—indeed, should not—deny that sufficient variations in the price of a consumption good will relevantly alter the demand for it. Raise the price of apples sufficiently, and most people will stop buying them. This is an undeniable element of reality; there is nothing specifically neoclassical about admitting it. The neoclassical element comes in when one argues that this undeniable fact justifies the assumption of well-defined, persistent and reversible demand functions for consumption goods from which one can derive decreasing demands for factors *as income distribution changes.* It is not the admission of some 'substitution' in consumption, but rather the way one derives from it decreasing demand curves for factors, that one should criti-

---

24 '…we do not want to confer the work of bringing about stability upon a suitable consumption function….At least in this respect we shall be immune to the criticism of being infected by neoclassical influences and their way of gaining stability results' (Franke, 1986, pp. 57–58). And more explicitly: '…one should then rely on price substitution effects and some additional assumption like gross-substitutability, whose Neoclassical flavour is certainly unpleasant for most students of the theory of production prices. It is also natural to notice that, by moving in this direction, the stability conditions for these models become very similar to those of orthodox general equilibrium theory' (Boggio 1990, p. 56). The 'very similar' does not appear acceptable; in the study of the gravitation to long-period prices, income distribution is given, so stability does not concern 'factor markets', which is where above all the neoclassical approach encounters problems and must introduce restrictive assumptions to exclude backward-bending factor supply curves, and 'perverse' operation of the indirect factor substitution mechanism. In a production economy with a given income distribution it is also unclear what gross substitutability might mean.

10.4 · Cross-Dual Models

cize: their derivation requires that one neglects not only the possibility of anti-neoclassical income effects (that not even the assumption of gross substitutability eliminates in economies with production, remember Sect. 6.37), but also the possible anti-neoclassical behaviour of relative prices and capital–labour ratio owing to reverse capital deepening when income distribution changes (Sect. 7.19), and the problems with specifying the endowment of capital, or of the several capital goods, without which consumer incomes cannot be determined. (Technical choices too no doubt depend on the prices of inputs, but there seems to be no reluctance among non-neoclassical economists about admitting this dependence.)

10.5 The Possibility of a High Price and a Low Profit Rate

With more than two goods, another possible worry about the gravitation of market prices towards long-period prices derives from the possibility that an industry, where the product market price is *higher* (relative to a sufficiently representative composite numéraire) than its long-period value, earns a rate of profits *below* the average rate of profit, because the prices of its inputs lie 'even more above' their long-period values (Steedman 1984a). Then the tendency will be to contract rather than to expand the industry's supply, plausibly causing a further rise of the market price rather than the decrease required by the gravitation towards its long-period level.

Here is a numerical example. Suppose three goods, with technical coefficients and market prices as in the table in ◘ Fig. 10.1. Goods 2 and 3 are non-basics, produced in small quantities; good 1, the sole basic good and the sole wage good, is the logical numéraire. The physical wage rate is 0.5 units of good 1, and it is advanced; hence the rate of profits in industry 1 is 25%. In the non-basic industries the rate of profits adjusts to it. Adopting Ricardian terminology, we can call it the natural rate of profit. The *long-period* prices of goods 2 and 3 can be calculated to be respectively 5 and 10; but assume the market prices initially are $p_2 = 10$, $p_3 = 14$. As a result, $r_2 = 2/3$, $r_3 = 0$. The market price of good 3 is above its long-period price, but the rate of profits in its production is below the natural rate of profit. It is plausible that in such a case the initial tendency will be to contract the production of good 3, which will likely cause a rise of p_3.

	industry j=1	industry j=2	industry j=3
a_{1j}	0.3	1.5	1.5
a_{2j}	0	0.4	1.2
a_{3j}	0	0	0
a_{Lj}	1	1	1
p_j	1	10	14

◘ **Fig. 10.1**

852   **Chapter 10** · Back to Long-Period Prices

But this rise can only be temporary, because in the meanwhile production of good 2 increases, and this will tend to lower p_2. This will reduce the costs of industry 3, and when p_2 gets sufficiently close to its long-period value 5, since we have assumed that p_3 has possibly increased but certainly has not decreased, it is still $p_3 > 10$ and the rate of profits of industry 3 becomes greater than 25%, inducing a reversal of the initial contraction of the industry, and finally a decrease of p_3 too. The gravitation towards the long-period prices eventually asserts itself.[25]

The above example was in terms of non-basic commodities; the possibility of a market price 'above' the long-period level while the rate of profits is 'below' the average rate also exists for basic commodities, and will be again due to the fact that the price of some inputs is even more 'above' their long-period level. But the argument that the gravitation towards the long-period prices will eventually assert itself can still be put forth, on the basis of the consideration that in all plausibility the rate of profits of the commodity (or the group of commodities) with the lowest rate of profits cannot further decrease: this would require a decrease of its own price relative to the average price of its inputs, which is highly unlikely, since its supply tends to decrease,[26] and in all likelihood faster than for any of its inputs (for many of these the supply will rather tend to increase). It is therefore highly plausible that the minimum one among the different rates of profits monotonically rises; this suffices to obtain convergence to a uniform rate of profits for all basic commodities, because if a rate of profits rises in a basic industry, some other basic rate of profits must decrease, and if the *minimum* basic rate of profits equals the natural rate of profits r^* then no basic rate of profits can be above r^* either.[27] (An analogously plausible reversed reasoning can be applied to non-ba-

---

25 In this example it has been implicitly assumed that aggregate demand is given. This assumption corresponds to the classicals' separate determination of the normal quantities produced, which includes a determination both of *aggregate levels* and of *proportions* (we have already made an assumption about normal proportions, but we had not said anything yet about the aggregate level of demand). This assumption can be dispensed with, but it spares us the need to specify every time that what is relevant for the behaviour of *relative* product prices is *relative*, and not absolute, excess demands.

26 Liquidation of inventories, which might cause a decrease of the price of the commodity and thus a further decrease of its rate of profit, is unlikely because 'it would occur for a commodity the value of which, relative to that of the mass of other commodities, could be expected to rise in the longer run' (Garegnani 1997, p. 148); its effect would be anyway only temporary and therefore negligible with respect to long-period tendencies. A decrease of the demand for the commodity even faster than the decrease in its supply is also possible, but it requires that the production of some other commodities is decreasing at least as fast, and this too cannot but be temporary, since the price of these other commodities will increase, rendering further decreases in their production less convenient.

27 Suppose advanced wages, included in the technical coefficients (if wages are in fact paid in arrears, assume an advanced wage equal to the wage rate divided by $(1 + r^*)$). By assumption the dominant eigenvalue is $\lambda = 1/(1 + r^*)$. Suppose that in no industry the rate of profit is below r^*, and in at least one industry the rate of profit is above r^*. In all industries where the rate of profit is above r^*, we can reduce the rate of profit to r^* without changing any price by increasing some technical coefficient. By the Perron–Frobenius theorem, this raises the value of the dominant eigenvalue of the matrix of technical coefficients, but then the uniform rate of profit can no longer be r^*: we obtain a contradiction.

10.5 · The Possibility of a High Price and a Low Profit Rate

sics, by assuming that the highest rate of profits in non-basic industries will tend to decrease as long as it is above r^*.)

Garegnani (1997), after advancing this argument, adds that what the assumption of a monotonic rise of the minimum rate of profits essentially excludes is 'the possibility of any but convergent oscillations in reaching the normal position of the economy': the lowest rate of profits r_i can well shoot up beyond the natural rate, and leave the role of lowest rate of profits to the rate of profits r_j of another commodity, but it is assumed that it cannot shoot up so much as to push down r_j to or below the previous level of r_i. But, Garegnani argues, 'there seem to be only two possible sources of those constant or divergent oscillations' assumed away by that assumption: time lags between production decisions and realized outputs, as in cobweb cycles; and inventory cycles due to the incentive to reaccumulate excessive inventories when the end of a liquidation of inventories causes the price to rise again, only to give rise to a new liquidation of inventories and a new price fall, and so on. Both phenomena are short-period phenomena that can only concern fluctuations in production from *existing* plants: this is particularly evident for inventory cycles; therefore these price fluctuations are not the ones, connected with decisions to alter productive capacity, with which the gravitation issue is concerned; furthermore, 'it would seem legitimate to suppose that in such cases individuals could and would learn from their experience and that any such endogenous oscillations in the markets of individual commodities would tend to decrease in amplitude' (Garegnani 1997, p. 160).

It would seem, in conclusion, that there is no reason to doubt the role of 'capital mobility' in bringing about the tendency of rates of profit towards uniformity, and therefore the tendency of competitive relative prices towards their long-period or 'natural' levels.

On this basis, we can proceed to study the determination of long-period prices in more complex cases than those studied in ► Chap. 2, which was limited to single-product systems and systems where the sole element of joint production is pure fixed capital.

10.6 Joint Production and Sraffa

Differently from Piero Sraffa,[28] Ian Steedman (1984b) has insisted that joint production is a *very* general phenomenon—that includes for example the many different products (milk, different meats, leather…) obtained from a cow, the many products obtained from crude oil, the travellers carried by the same train for different distances, the apartments differing in dimension and altitude in a high-rise

---

28 'The interest of Joint Products does not lie so much in the familiar examples of wool and mutton, or wheat and straw, as in its being the genus of which Fixed Capital is the leading species. And it is mainly as an introduction to the subject of fixed capital that the preceding chapters devoted to the intricacies of joint products find their place.' Sraffa, 1960, p. 63.

854   **Chapter 10 · Back to Long-Period Prices**

building,[29] the saleable side products of many production processes—and therefore joint production should be considered the normal and general case. This conclusion may be excessive, but certainly a theory of normal relative prices must be capable of dealing with joint production. The field has not been explored yet as much as models without joint production, there remains considerable room for research and PhD dissertations. What follows is a first introduction to the field that makes extensive use of geometrical illustrations to help intuition, and includes one long mathematical proof to give a taste of the tools needed in the field.[30]

Let n be the number of different produced commodities; assume that m different CRS methods are known to produce them that take one period; let these methods be arbitrarily numbered. Let b_{ij} be the output of good i in method j; the condition of zero extra profit for method j is then, with wages paid in arrears:

$$(1+r)\left(a_{1j}p_1 + \ldots + a_{nj}p_n\right) + wa_{Lj} = b_{1j}p_1 + \ldots + b_{nj}p_n. \tag{10.6}$$

Note that, if a method produces many commodities, the natural choice of the dimension of a method as the one that produces 1 unit of output is lost; a frequent choice is to fix the unitary dimension as the one that employs one unit of labour. Once some such choice is made that fixes the unitary dimension and hence the technical coefficients, the m methods available to produce the n different commodities are represented by

$$\mathbf{A} * \mathbf{a_L} \rightarrow \mathbf{B},$$

where $\mathbf{A}=(a_{ij})$ is the $n \times m$ matrix of input coefficients, $\mathbf{a_L}$ is the row m-vector of labour coefficients, that coincides with vector $\mathbf{e}^T=(1, \ldots, 1)$ if the unitary dimension of methods is the one that uses 1 unit of labour, and $\mathbf{B}=(b_{ij})$ is the $n \times m$ matrix of output coefficients.

If one can assume that there are as many activated methods as commodities, $n=m$, and that each commodity is produced by at least one of these methods, then there are n price equations in $n+2$ variables (the n prices, w, r), so as many equations as variables once a numéraire is chosen and either r or w is fixed, and therefore the $n–1$ relative prices and the other distributive variable can be determined (but see below on whether prices will come out positive). But can we assume $n=m$? In single production, it was necessary to have a method for each produced commodity, and it was natural to define a technique as a set of n different methods, each one producing a different commodity. Now a single method can produce many commodities; it is then conceivable that fewer processes than commodities may be activated because sufficient to satisfy effectual demands. This would mean fewer equations than variables to be determined.

It is for example possible to imagine an economy where wool and mutton are the only products, jointly produced in fixed proportion by a single process that

---

29 Steedman also notes the existence of cases of *intertemporal* joint production, for example crop rotation.

30 See Kurz and Salvadori (1995) and Bidard (1991, 2004) for extensive treatments closer to the frontier of research.

10.6 · Joint Production and Sraffa

uses wool, mutton and labour as inputs and produces positive net products of both goods. With, for example, mutton as the numéraire and a given real wage fixed in mutton, there would be a single price equation like (10.6) to determine two unknowns, the price of wool and the rate of profit. There is a degree of freedom. (And the degrees of freedom would be more than two, if more than two commodities are jointly produced by a single process.)

Acquaintance with neoclassical theory might suggest to eliminate this degree of freedom through some assumption making the composition of demand a variable dependent on the relative product price; this might allow the addition of an equation imposing that the relative product price be such that the composition of demand allows the products to be all sold, and then one would have two equations in two variables.

More formally, let mutton be good 1 and the numéraire, $p_1 = 1$; wool is good 2, and indicate as $\delta(p_2) = d_2/d_1$ the composition of demand for consumption purposes, assumed independent of the level of employment and of income distribution but a decreasing function of the relative price $p_2/p_1 = p_2$. Choose the unit dimension of the single productive process as the one that employs one unit of labour and assume a stationary economy (all net product goes to consumption). The suggestion would be to write:

$$b_{11} + p_2 b_{21} = (1 + r)(a_{11} + p_2 a_{21}) + w$$

$$\delta(p_2) = (b_{21} - a_{21})/(b_{11} - a_{11}).$$

$$w = w^* \text{given.}$$

Of course both net outputs must be supposed positive. The idea is that the relative price p_2 will adjust so as to bring the composition of demand into equilibrium with the composition of the net product,[31] and this will determine r too, because generally r is a function of p_2, the sign of its derivative depending on the technical coefficients and on the level of the wage.[32]

Sraffa does not consider such a possibility. Why? Waiting for a publication of his unpublished manuscripts hopefully helping to understand Sraffa's own reasons, in the meanwhile one can suggest two reasons that probably had a role:

(I) in a classical approach, especially when combined with the principle of effective demand, one does not have the possibility of a univocal determination of the changes in consumer incomes (from which demands should be derived) simultaneous with the changes in distribution and prices; aggregate output and employment can be affected by those changes in different ways depending

---

31 It is possible that not even a fall of p_2 to zero, or conversely of p_1/p_2 to zero (a possibility that our choice of numéraire makes it difficult to analyze, rather than $p_1 = 1$ one should put, for example, $p_1 + p_2 = 1$), may suffice to bring the composition of demand into equality with the composition of the net product; then one good will have price zero and become a free good.

32 **Exercise**: find the condition that makes r independent of p_2; prove that r is an increasing function of p_2 if $b_{21}/a_{21} > b_{11}/a_{11}$, and can still be an increasing function of p_2 even when the opposite inequality holds.

on the specifics of the situation[33]; so the basis univocally to determine how demands change with changes in distribution and prices is missing[34];

(II) consumer preferences are not like the reaction of a mercury column to temperature: the long dominance of the marginal/neoclassical approach should not make us blind to the fact that (a) often consumers themselves do not know how they would choose at prices different from the usual ones or with different incomes, and (b) preferences are relevantly altered by experience, fashion changes, advertising, experimentation of new products; therefore even independently of the problems under (I), preferences lack the definiteness, independence from relevant changes in prices, and reversibility, needed to derive from them demand schedules of sufficient generality and persistence.[35]

For both reasons, already at the age of 28 Sraffa wrote: 'The demand and supply schedules have no objective contents: nothing corresponds to them in the real world' (from unpublished manuscripts of 1926). He looks then for a more objective basis for the explanation of normal prices in the presence of joint production. He notes 'that there will be room for a second, parallel process that will produce the two commodities by a different method", and assumes that "in such cases a second process or industry does in fact exist'(1960, p. 43). His justification is[36]:

> Incidentally, considering that the proportions in which the two commodities are produced by any one method will in general be different from those in which they are required for use, the existence of two methods of producing them in different proportions will be necessary for obtaining the required proportion of the two products through an appropriate combination of the two methods. (1960, p. 43, Fn. 2)

---

33 E.g. remember from Chapter 1 the possible different effects of wage rises on the level of economic activity according to Marx.

34 Indeed the determination of the composition of demand δ in the above wool-mutton example is clearly too simple: it should be made to depend at least on the level of employment, since a given mutton wage does not univocally determine the composition of household expenditure if how many members of a household have a job on average is not determined. And the level of employment can relevantly depend on p_2 if the latter (through its influence on r) affects saving propensities and investment propensities.

35 Thus P. Garegnani has written: 'The received general concept of a dependence of the quantity demanded of a commodity on its price may be seen to run the risk of falling between two stools. If the effect of the price on the quantity bought is not appreciable, then the effect can be ignored without great error. Alternatively, when the effect is important enough to need general consideration, it seems it will often be the case that the effect constitutes an *irreversible* change, which is incompatible with its treatment in terms of a demand function. That is, the effect will entail a permanent change in the habits of consumers, which even marginalist authors would have to treat as a change of 'tastes' ... Think, for instance, of the increase in the demand for cars in the USA in the 1920s, as technical developments led to an appreciable fall in their price.' (Garegnani 1990b, p. 131). Also remember the observations on irreversible demand (that is, on hysteresis of preferences) in ▶ Chap. 5, Sect. 5.32.

36 Sraffa initially assumes that just two commodities out of *n* are jointly produced. On the difference between 'process' and 'method': here a process is simply a method applied on a certain scale.

10.6 · Joint Production and Sraffa

Generalizing this assumption, Sraffa assumes a number of activated methods equal to the number of commodities. Another way to fill the degree of freedom consists of having two different methods that *use* (at least one of) the two jointly produced commodities as inputs, in different proportions,[37] to produce a *third* product (Sraffa 1960, p. 44). But, does one have the right to assume that there will be enough alternative methods?

Actually, coexistence of alternative methods is frequent; for example, trains jointly produce many different transport services, but transport services are also supplied by buses, cars, airplanes, and all these methods coexist, which shows that they are profitable. Still, it might be the case that to produce wool and mutton only one method is known; or two methods might be known, but the requirements for use might be in a proportion not achievable with those methods; for example, if the first method produces wool and mutton in the proportion of two to one, and the second in the proportion of one to one, then a gross effectual demand rigidly in the proportion of three to one cannot be satisfied except by overproducing and throwing away some of the mutton. However, Marshall observed:

> » if straw were valueless, farmers would exert themselves more than they do to make the ear bear as large a proportion as possible to the stalk. Again, the importation of foreign wool has caused English sheep to be adapted by judicious crossing and selection so as to develop heavy weights of good meat at an early age, even at the expense of some deterioration of their wool. (*Principles of Economics*, 8th ed., V, vi, 5; reset and repr. 1949; London, Macmillan 1972, p. 323)

When a joint product is overproduced, research will often be directed at avoiding the waste, by looking for new production methods that produce less of that product, or for alternative ways to utilize it. Marshall's examples illustrate the first type of solution. Analogously, in fishing, many different species of fish are often caught together, but if one type of fish is in particularly high demand, new ways of fishing will be developed, particularly aimed at that catch, which will reduce the catch of other fish. Therefore, it can be presumed that in most periods there are enough co-existing methods as to allow producing jointly produced goods in the demanded proportions.

Bertram Schefold argues that the number of potential methods of production is indeed always in *excess* of the number of commodities, and out of them technical choice will select the number needed for a determinate system of normal prices on the basis of given quantities to be produced. He adduces two reasons why potentially available methods are more numerous than one tends to perceive. The first one is household production: cooking, for example, transforms raw food

---

37 An extreme case of different proportions is when only one of the two goods is used as an input in one method, and only the other in the other method. This is the case, for example, for petrol (gasoline) and diesel oil, produced by a single distillation process of crude oil, and used by different engines to produce the same output: energy to move vehicles.

into dishes in a great variety of ways.[38] The second reason is 'the fact that most processes of production are not rigid in that some substitution between outputs is possible' (Schefold 2003, p. 458): one example he gives concerns precisely wool and mutton: 'if wool and mutton are produced jointly, usually varying the age at which the sheep are slaughtered will suffice to adapt the amount of wool and mutton to the given composition of output by choosing an appropriate combination of old and young sheep' (ibid., p. 456).

It is of course possible, and confirmed by reality, that for some side products of the production process of a main commodity (e.g. rubbish from housebuilding or building roads) no useful employment exists capable of absorbing their output and allowing them to have a positive value: these side products either have a zero price, or can be considered to have a *negative* price if they are a cause of *disposal costs*. The explicit treatment of disposal costs or of negative prices will not be attempted in this book because it causes significant formal complications and is not fully studied yet: it will be implicitly assumed that disposal costs can be included in the production costs of the main product, and the side product to be disposed of can then be given a zero price, or cancelled from the list of jointly produced outputs. For the commodities with a positive price, the assumption of a great number of potential alternative processes makes it plausible that given gross demands for outputs can be exactly satisfied by opportune linear combinations of a subset of the available processes; then, as Schefold (1997, ▶ Chaps. 5–7) proves, apart from extremely improbable flukes the number of operated processes is generically *equal* to the number of commodities with positive price; prices can be determined from the sole side of production (once the quantities to be produced are given).

10.7 Graphical Representation: Single Production

So far we have assumed rigid proportions of requirements for use. The production of commodities in those exact proportions with a number of methods inferior to the number of commodities can only happen by a fluke of probability zero; the *generic* case will be that if the number of methods is less than the number of commodities, then at least one commodity is produced in excess; its price can then be set at zero; if this is done for all overproduced commodities,

---

38 It might be argued that a sufficient number of alternative processes is missing in the determination of the different prices of the many different meats obtained from pigs or cows, so one must take into account demand, i.e. preferences, in order to explain these prices. However, these meats are cooked each one in a different way (or in more than one way) to produce nutrition, so household production provides the missing processes. Socially determined average tastes produce a hierarchy of esteem for foods, with many dishes considered in general equally good, hence substitutable; then the different meats required for their production will have to differ in price depending on the other costs, in time and other ingredients, required for the production of these equally attractive dishes. So even in this field, price differences would appear to be largely reducible to differences in costs of production, inclusive now of household production costs.

10.7 · Graphical Representation: Single Production

the number of positive prices is equal to the number of methods. Therefore if we restrict ourselves to consideration of commodities with positive prices, there will be as many price equations as commodities; the system of price equations is then called *square* because matrix $\mathbf{A}$ (and therefore also matrix $\mathbf{B}$) is square. With wages paid in arrears, it looks like this:

$$\mathbf{pA}(1+r) + w\mathbf{a_L} = \mathbf{pB}, \quad \mathbf{pv} = 1, \tag{10.7}$$

where $\mathbf{v}$ is the column vector of goods chosen as numéraire; if, say, the numéraire is good 1, then $\mathbf{v} = (1, 0, \ldots, 0)^{\mathrm{T}}$; $\mathbf{p}$ is a row vector. If r or w is given, number of equations equals number of variables.

It remains to show that a 'square system' is what the economy will generally[39] arrive at, if it starts with a number of production methods (possibly greater than the number of commodities) and with given requirements for use.

Let us approach the issue through a graphical representation that will be initially applied to the case of single production and then extended to joint production. Assume two commodities are produced in single-product industries by the use of themselves and labour, with technical coefficients:

$$a_{11} * a_{21} * a_{L1} \rightarrow 1 \text{ unit of commodity 1}$$

$$a_{12} * a_{22} * a_{L2} \rightarrow 1 \text{ unit of commodity 2}$$

Let us represent graphically on the Cartesian plane the net product vector per unit of labour of *each* industry:

$$\boldsymbol{\beta}^1 \equiv 1/a_{L1} \cdot \left[(1, 0)^{\mathrm{T}} - (a_{11}, a_{21})^{\mathrm{T}} \right] = [(1-a_{11})/a_{L1}, -a_{21}/a_{L1}]^{\mathrm{T}}$$

$$\boldsymbol{\beta}^2 \equiv 1/a_{L2} \cdot \left[(0, 1)^{\mathrm{T}} - (a_{12}, a_{22})^{\mathrm{T}} \right] = [(1-a_{12})/a_{L2}, -a_{22}/a_{L2}]^{\mathrm{T}}$$

The geometric representation of each one of these vectors can be obtained, through the usual parallelogram rule, as the sum of the vector of outputs per unit of labour with the negative of the vector of inputs per unit of labour; for example for commodity 1 the vectors to be summed are $(1/a_{L1}, 0)^T$ and $-(a_{11}/a_{L1}, a_{21}/a_{L1})^T$.

Let us choose units for the several products, such that the production of one unit of a commodity requires one unit of labour[40]; then $a_{L1} = a_{L2} = 1$. Let us use the symbols $\mathbf{e}^1 = (1, 0)^{\mathrm{T}}$, $\mathbf{e}^2 = (1, 0)^{\mathrm{T}}$, $\mathbf{a}^1 = -(a_{11}, a_{21})^{\mathrm{T}}$, $\mathbf{a}^2 = -(a_{12}, a_{22})^{\mathrm{T}}$. Then $\boldsymbol{\beta}^1 = \mathbf{e}^1 + \mathbf{a}^1, \boldsymbol{\beta}^2 = \mathbf{e}^2 + \mathbf{a}^2$. Therefore, if we measure commodity 1 on the abscissa and commodity 2 on the ordinate, $\boldsymbol{\beta}^1$ is in the fourth quadrant and $\boldsymbol{\beta}^2$ is in the second quadrant, cf. ◼ Fig. 10.2.

---

39 Of course the possibility remains, that the number of methods is greater than the number of positive prices because at the prices and rate of profit at which n processes are equally profitable another process is also equally profitable, in analogy with switch points of two w(r) curves in the single-products case. But it will be a fluke.

40 Of course this is only possible if there is only one available method per industry.

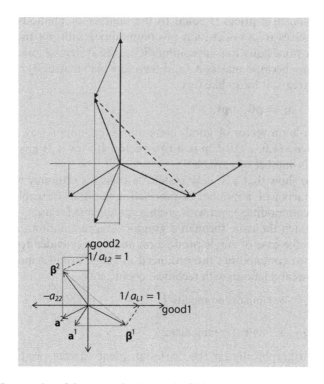

Fig. 10.2 Construction of the net-product (per unit of labour) segment

Let us now assume that total labour employment in the economy is one unit (again, this is simply a matter of choice of units). Then the non-negative linear combination of β^1 and β^2, graphically the straight-line segment connecting β^1 and β^2, represents all net outputs obtainable by varying the dimension of the two industries while leaving total labour employment at one unit. In other words, it is the locus of the possible vectors of net output per unit of labour that this economy can obtain, assuming adaptability of inputs to the industry requirements. Let us call it the *net product segment*. Its equation is $\lambda_1\beta^1 + \lambda_2\beta^2$, where $\lambda_1, \lambda_2 \geq 0$ and $\lambda_1 + \lambda_2 = 1$. The scalar λ_i represents both the labour employment and the quantity produced in industry i.

If $\lambda_1 = 1$, $\lambda_2 = 0$, then the economy's net product vector is β^1; as λ_1 decreases, the net product vector moves towards β^2 along the net product segment. If the net product segment has a portion in the positive quadrant, the economy is viable, i.e. capable of positive growth (if wages are zero) (◘ Fig. 10.3).

Let us now define *growth-diminished net product industry vectors* (per unit of labour) as follows:

$$\beta^1(g) \equiv (\beta_{11}(g), \beta_{21}(g))^T \equiv \left[(1 - (1+g)a_{11})/a_{L1}, -(1+g)a_{21}/a_{L1}\right]^T$$

$$\beta^2(g) \equiv (\beta_{12}(g), \beta_{22}(g))^T \equiv \left[(1 - (1+g)a_{12})/a_{L2}, -(1+g)a_{22}/a_{L2}\right]^T$$

10.7 · Graphical Representation: Single Production

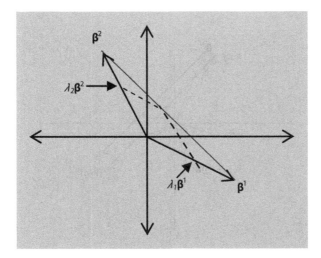

◘ **Fig. 10.3** Any point on the segment connecting β^1 and β^2 represents a possible net product vector per unit of labour, reachable by an opportune linear combination of the two methods

Graphically, $\beta^1(g)$ and $\beta^2(g)$ are obtained from β^1 and β^2 by prolonging vectors $\mathbf{a}^1$ and $\mathbf{a}^2$ by a percentage g. The straight-line segment $\lambda_1\beta^1(g) + \lambda_2\beta^2(g)$ is the locus of the possible consumption vectors per unit of labour, if both industries are to grow at a common rate g.

The segment connecting $\beta^1(g)$ and $\beta^2(g)$ will be called the ***growth-diminished net product segment*** or ***GD-segment*** for short.

Suppose that consumption consists of the two commodities in given proportions, and choose a basket $\mathbf{v} = (v_1, v_2)^T$ that includes the commodities in those proportions. Then consumption per unit of labour can be expressed as a scalar function of the rate of growth, $c = c(g)$, that indicates how many units of this basket per unit of labour the economy is capable of producing as growth-diminished net product; graphically, $\mathbf{v}$ is a vector in the non-negative quadrant, and $c\mathbf{v}$ is the same vector prolonged or shortened so as to reach the GD-segment (cf. ◘ Fig. 10.7). It is immediately evident that c is a decreasing function of g, because the GD-segment shifts in a south-westerly direction (generally also changing its slope) as g increases.

If one chooses the same basket as numéraire, then if $r = g$ it is also $c = w$. Now I prove this result for the general case of n commodities. Suppose the economy's residual net product, after allowing for an increase of all inputs by g, consists entirely of goods in the proportion of the numéraire $\mathbf{v} = (v_1, \ldots, v_n)^T$. Then, with $\mathbf{y} = \mathbf{x} - \mathbf{A}\mathbf{x}$ the net product vector, it is $\mathbf{y} - g\mathbf{A}\mathbf{x} = c\mathbf{v}$. Thus $\mathbf{x} = (1 + g)\mathbf{A}\mathbf{x} + c\mathbf{v}$, which implies

$$\mathbf{x} = [\mathbf{I} - (1 + g)\mathbf{A}]^{-1} c\mathbf{v}, \tag{10.8}$$

where $[\mathbf{I} - (1 + g)\mathbf{A}]^{-1}$ exists and is positive as long as g is less than $(1 - \lambda^*)/\lambda^*$ where λ^* is the dominant eigenvalue of $\mathbf{A}$. Let us fix the economy's dimensions by

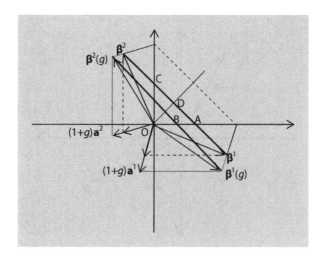

Fig. 10.4 Determination of the growth-diminished net product (per unit of labour) locus

assuming $\mathbf{a_L}\mathbf{x}=1$, where $\mathbf{a_L}=(a_{L1}, \ldots, a_{Ln})$, and $\mathbf{a_L}\mathbf{x}$ is total labour employment. Then

$$1 = \mathbf{a_L}\mathbf{x} = \mathbf{a_L}\left[\mathbf{I}-(1+g)\mathbf{A}\right]^{-1}c\mathbf{v} = c\mathbf{a_L}\left[\mathbf{I}-(1+g)\mathbf{A}\right]^{-1}\mathbf{v}.$$

Therefore the function, or curve, $c(g)$ is given by

$$c(g) = 1/\{\mathbf{a_L}\left[\mathbf{I}-(1+g)\mathbf{A}\right]^{-1}\mathbf{v}\}. \tag{10.9}$$

Now, we know (cf. Eq. (2.25) in ▶ Chap. 2) that the $w(r)$ curve is given by

$$w = 1/\{\mathbf{a_L}[\mathbf{I}-(1+r)\mathbf{A}]^{-1}\mathbf{v}\}.$$

This shows that $w(r)$ and $c(g)$ are the same function, if one assumes that consumption consists of units of the same basket used to measure the real wage rate. Then $c(g)$ derived as shown above can be reinterpreted as the real wage rate associated with $r=g$. For example, if commodity 1 is the numéraire, that is if $\mathbf{v}=(1,0)^T$, then the real wage rate is the intercept of the GD-segment with the abscissa, $\overline{OB}$ in ◘ Fig. 10.4 if $r=g$, $\overline{OA}$ if $r=0$. If the physical wage is a vector containing the two goods in equal proportions, then for $r=0$ it is represented by point D.

Another proof, perhaps of clearer economic meaning, that $w=c$ is as follows. The value of the net product vector goes either to wages (to one wage, since we assume that labour employment is one unit) or to profits, i.e. to the rate of profits times the value of capital, therefore

$$\mathbf{py} = w + r\mathbf{pAx}.$$

10.7 · Graphical Representation: Single Production

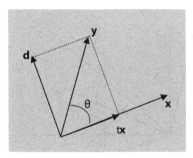

Fig. 10.5 Projection of **y** onto **x**. From $\mathbf{y}=t\mathbf{x}+\mathbf{d}$ we obtain, by the distributive property of the inner product, $\mathbf{x}\cdot\mathbf{y}=t\mathbf{x}\cdot\mathbf{x}+\mathbf{d}\cdot\mathbf{x}=t\|\mathbf{x}\|^2$ since $\mathbf{d}\cdot\mathbf{x}=0$; if **x** is chosen of unitary length, then $\mathbf{x}\cdot\mathbf{y}=t$

Suppose all profits are reinvested into increasing the stocks of capital goods by a proportion r, and that the remainder of the net product consists of baskets of the numéraire composite good **v**; then

$$\mathbf{y} = c\mathbf{v} + r\mathbf{A}\mathbf{x}.$$

Multiplying both sides by **p** we obtain $\mathbf{py} = c\mathbf{pv} + r\mathbf{pAx}$, and since $\mathbf{pv}=1$ we obtain

$$\mathbf{py} = c + r\mathbf{pAx}.$$

Hence $w=c$ or, perhaps more clearly, $w=c\mathbf{pv}$; now, since **p** and w are given once r is given, the purchasing power of the wage must equal $c\mathbf{pv}$ independently of what the capitalists actually buy.

We can also reach a geometrical determination of relative prices. The price vector $\mathbf{p}=(p_1, p_2)$ that satisfies the uniform-rate-of-profit condition can be represented in the same diagram.[41] It will be in the positive quadrant. Since we have put $a_{L1}=a_{L2}=1$, the price equations are

$$p_1 = (1+r)(a_{11}p_1 + a_{21}p_2) + w$$

$$p_2 = (1+r)(a_{12}p_1 + a_{22}p_2) + w.$$

These can be rewritten as

$$[1 - (1+r)a_{11}]p_1 - (1+r)a_{21}p_2 = w$$

$$-(1+r)a_{12}p_1 + [1 - (1+r)a_{22}]p_2 = w,$$

that is, with $r=g$ so that we can also indicate $\boldsymbol{\beta}^1(g), \boldsymbol{\beta}^2(g)$ as $\boldsymbol{\beta}^1(r), \boldsymbol{\beta}^2(r)$: (Fig. 10.5)

$$\mathbf{p}\boldsymbol{\beta}^1(r) = w$$

$$\mathbf{p}\boldsymbol{\beta}^2(r) = w.$$

---

41 In the geometrical representation it does not matter whether a vector is treated as a row or as a column vector.

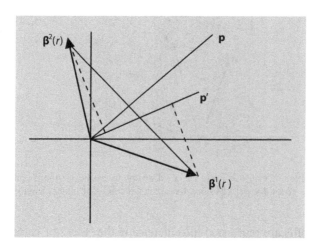

◼ **Fig. 10.6** The price vector is orthogonal to the GD-segment or wage line. Any other price vector, such as **p'**, would cause the projections onto it of $\boldsymbol{\beta}^1$ and $\boldsymbol{\beta}^2$ not to coincide. If the price vector is chosen of unitary length, the length of these projections is given by $\mathbf{p}\boldsymbol{\beta}^1$, $\mathbf{p}\boldsymbol{\beta}^2$

Hence $\mathbf{p}\boldsymbol{\beta}^1(r) = \mathbf{p}\boldsymbol{\beta}^2(r)$, that is, $\mathbf{p}\boldsymbol{\beta}^1(r) - \mathbf{p}\boldsymbol{\beta}^2(r) = 0$ or $\mathbf{p}[\boldsymbol{\beta}^1(r) - \boldsymbol{\beta}^2(r)] = 0$, which means that the vector **p** is orthogonal[42] to the vector $\boldsymbol{\beta}^1(r) - \boldsymbol{\beta}^2(r)$ and therefore also to the straight line through the vertexes of $\boldsymbol{\beta}^1(r)$ and $\boldsymbol{\beta}^2(r)$, the straight line that includes the GD-segment. This straight line, the locus of points $\lambda\boldsymbol{\beta}^1(r) + (1-\lambda)\boldsymbol{\beta}^2(r)$, also satisfies equation $p_1 x_1 + p_2 x_2 = w$, where x_1 and x_2 are quantities of each product, measured along the horizontal and vertical axis respectively. Indeed $\mathbf{p}\boldsymbol{\beta}^1(r) = w$ means that if $x_1 = \beta_{11}(r)$ then $x_2 = \beta_{12}(r)$ and analogously for $\boldsymbol{\beta}^2(r)$; hence the straight line $p_1 x_1 + p_2 x_2 = w$ goes through the vertexes of $\boldsymbol{\beta}^1(r)$ and $\boldsymbol{\beta}^2(r)$. The economic interpretation is simple: the points on that line must have total value w because they represent the possible real wage *vectors* if the rate of profits is r. Therefore we can call this straight line the *real wage line* (not to be confused with the wage *curve*) and the intercept of this straight line with the abscissa indicates the purchasing power of the wage in terms of good 1, i.e. the real wage if we choose good 1 as numéraire (also interpretable as the amount of good 1 that can be bought with the wage if the latter is used to purchase only good 1); and analogously for the intercept with the ordinate, and good 2 (◼ Fig. 10.6).

The direction of **p** determines relative prices only. The length of **p** is arbitrary and is fixed by the normalization chosen, e.g. by the choice of a numéraire or by a condition such as $p_1^2 + p_2^2 = 1$ that makes the length of **p** equal to 1. In this latter case the length of the projection of any vector **x** of goods onto **p** is the exchange value of **x**; more generally, if the length of **p** is α then the value of a vector **x** of goods is the length of the projection of **x** onto **p**, multiplied by α. The choice of a

---

42 See the Mathematical Appendix, M.A.3, for the proof that, given two vectors **x**, **y** that form an angle θ, it is $\mathbf{x} \cdot \mathbf{y} = \|\mathbf{x}\| \|\mathbf{y}\| \cos \theta$. Thus the dot product $\mathbf{x} \cdot \mathbf{y}$ equals 0 if the two vectors are orthogonal ($\cos 90° = 0$), it is > 0 if the angle is acute, < 0 if the angle is obtuse.

10.7 · Graphical Representation: Single Production

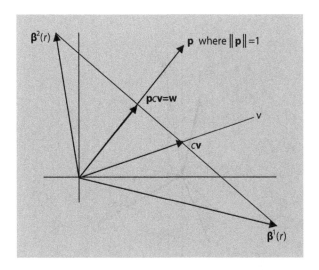

■ **Fig. 10.7** Determination of the price vector and measurement of the real wage as c units of the numéraire vector **v**

numéraire **v**, i.e. the condition $\mathbf{pv}=1$, means that the length of **p**, α, must be such that the length of the projection of **v** onto **p** is $1/\alpha$.

The result reached earlier, that $w=c$ if real wage rate and consumption per labour unit are measured in terms of the same basket and if $r=g$, means that $w\mathbf{v}$ too lies on the GD-segment (i.e. on the real wage line), and that increases of r cause a decrease of w because the segment shifts closer to the origin. Thus we have reached a geometrical demonstration that $w(r)$ is a decreasing function.[43] Unless the conditions hold for the validity of the pure labour theory of value, as r increases the slope of the segment changes. As r keeps increasing, finally the GD-segment touches the origin: at that point $w=0$ and $r=R$ (■ Fig. 10.7).

10.8 Graphical Representation: Joint Production

Let us now extend this graphical representation to joint production. Assume there are two methods, both of which produce both products jointly. Take as unitary dimension of each method that dimension that uses 1 unit of labour. Then:

$a_{11} * a_{21} * a_{L1} \rightarrow b_{11} * b_{21}$ where $a_{L1} = 1$

$a_{12} * a_{22} * a_{L2} \rightarrow b_{12} * b_{22}$ where $a_{L2} = 1$

---

43 Note that the reasoning is easily extended to n > 2 commodities: the vectors $\beta^1(g), \beta^2(g),...,\beta^n(g)$ are defined without problems and their connection defines a simplex in R^n which is the locus of all possible growth-diminished net product vectors per unit of labour, and which moves closer to the origin as g = r increases.

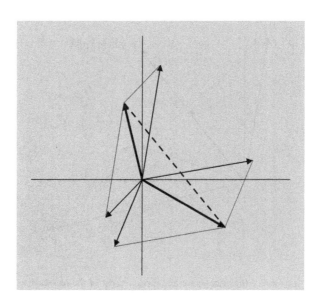

Fig. 10.8 An all-productive all-engaging technique

The vectors of growth-diminished net products per unit of labour of each method are now—I put directly r in place of g—:

$$\beta^1(r) \equiv [b_{11} - (1+r)a_{11}, b_{21} - (1+r)a_{21}]^T$$

$$\beta^2(r) \equiv [b_{12} - (1+r)a_{12}, b_{22} - (1+r)a_{22}]^T$$

and it is no longer guaranteed that they lie in the II or IV quadrant: one or both might lie in the positive quadrant (Figs. 10.8 and 10.9).

If this case does not arise, i.e. if (after renumbering methods if necessary) for method 1 the growth-diminished net product is positive only for commodity 1, while for method 2 it is positive only for commodity 2, then the graphical representation is similar to that for single production: $\beta^1(r)$ and $\beta^2(r)$ are respectively in the IV and in the II quadrant; the GD-segment is negatively sloped, goes from the II to the IV quadrant, has a portion in the positive quadrant (if the economy is viable), and moves closer to the origin as r increases. The price vector has positive slope; i.e. both prices are positive; all possible proportions of the two commodities in the GD-net product can be achieved. If this situation arises when $r=0$, it means that, after an opportune renumbering of commodities, the square matrix $\mathbf{B}-\mathbf{A}$ has a strictly positive main diagonal and no other positive element; the technique is then called *all-productive*, and it can be shown to have the property that $(\mathbf{B}-\mathbf{A})^{-1} \geq 0$. All-productive techniques are such that for each commodity it is possible to produce a net product consisting only of that commodity. If, whichever the commodity, in order to produce a net product consisting only of that commodity it is necessary to use all methods at positive levels, an all-productive technique is called *all-engaging*, and it can be shown to have the property that $(\mathbf{B}-\mathbf{A})^{-1} > 0$.

10.8 · Graphical Representation: Joint Production

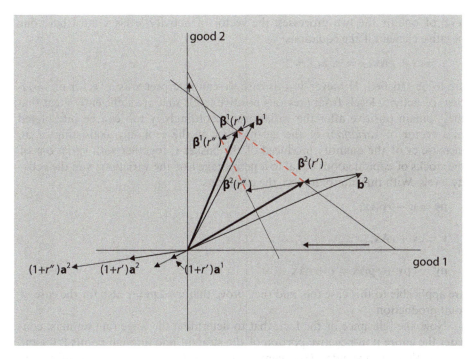

Fig. 10.9 Two wage lines corresponding to different levels of r can cross in the positive orthant, implying that the sign of the variation of the real wage can depend on the numéraire. The GD-segments are the bold broken-line red segments. If the numéraire is good 2, the real wage rate (measured by the intersection of the wage line with the ordinate) rises as r rises from r' to r''

▪▪ Exercise

Produce an example of a two-commodities technique with joint production, that is all-productive but not all-engaging.

If on the contrary one or both methods produce a positive net product of both commodities, then some possibilities arise that do not arise with single production.

Now consider ◘ Fig. 10.9, where $\beta^1(r)$ and $\beta^2(r)$ lie both in the positive orthant. The GD-segment does not touch the axes, if we restrict the levels of activation of the two methods to being non-negative. But if we want to use that segment in order to determine w, then we must consider its prolongation in both directions until we reach the positive axes, because there is no reason why the numéraire basket **v** should be internal to the cone spanned by $\beta^1(r)$ and $\beta^2(r)$; for example it might consist of only one commodity, and w is in any case the scalar such that $w\mathbf{v}$ is on the straight line through points $\beta^1(r)$ and $\beta^2(r)$.

This last statement needs proof, which can be easily reached on the basis of the second of the proofs given above, for single-production systems, that $w=c$. That proof might appear non-applicable, because if **v** lies outside the cone spanned by $\beta^1(r)$ and $\beta^2(r)$ then the production of a GD- (that is, growth diminished) net product consisting of a quantity of **v** requires a negative activation

868   Chapter 10 · Back to Long-Period Prices

level of one of the two processes; the vector of activity levels $\mathbf{x}$ must have one negative element if the equations

$$\mathbf{y} = c\mathbf{v} + g\mathbf{Ax}, \ g = r, \ \mathbf{a_L x} = 1$$

are to be satisfied. However, in this case we can interpret $\mathbf{x}$ as a vector of *variations* of activity levels from previous positive levels that are sufficiently great that they remain positive after the variations; accordingly, $\mathbf{y}$ too can be interpreted as a vector of *variations* of the net product of the economy, consisting of an increase $c\mathbf{v}$ of the quantity produced of the basket $\mathbf{v}$, together with variations of the stocks of capital goods equal to a percentage r of the variations $\mathbf{x}$ in the activity levels. With this interpretation, the equations

$$\mathbf{py} = w + r\mathbf{pAx},$$

$$\mathbf{y} = c\mathbf{v} + r\mathbf{Ax},$$

$$\mathbf{py} = c\mathbf{pv} + r\mathbf{pAx} = c + r\mathbf{Ax}$$

are applicable to this case too, and they prove that $w = c\mathbf{pv} = c$ also for the case of joint production.

Now, the relevance of the fact, that to determine the wage rate we must consider the entire non-negative portion of the straight line through points $\boldsymbol{\beta}^1(r)$ and $\boldsymbol{\beta}^2(r)$, is that this extended GD-segment or *wage line*, as we can also call it, can move with r such that wage lines corresponding to different levels of r can cross in the positive quadrant, something impossible with single production. Then the sign of the variation of the wage rate depends on the numéraire. This possibility is shown in ◘ Fig. 10.9. In the case drawn, where $r'' > r'$, at r'' the wage rate w is higher that at r' if measured in terms of commodity 2, it is lower if measured in terms of commodity 1. The reason why this can happen is that with joint production it is no longer true that all prices rise relative to the wage rate when the rate of profit rises; the presence of more than one price on the output side of some methods makes it possible for a (labour-commanded) price to decrease when the rate of profit rises, because the other price can increase so as to compensate. This means that in some cases and with some numéraires the $w(r)$ curve can have upward-sloping portions.

◘ Figure 10.10 highlights another difference from single production: with joint production it can happen that the wage line is negatively sloped at a certain level of r, and positively sloped at a different level of r. Since the price vector must still be perpendicular to the GD-segment if the rate of profits is to be uniform (the reader is invited to check it as an exercise), when the segment is negatively sloped one of the two prices is negative (p_2, in the case of ◘ Fig. 10.10); this is economically impossible, so the two methods cannot be equally profitable, but then one of the two methods should not be in use. This is not necessarily incompatible with satisfaction of the requirements for use, if the surviving method has a positive net product of both commodities and if it is admissible to overproduce one of the commodities, whose price will then fall to zero.

10.8 · Graphical Representation: Joint Production

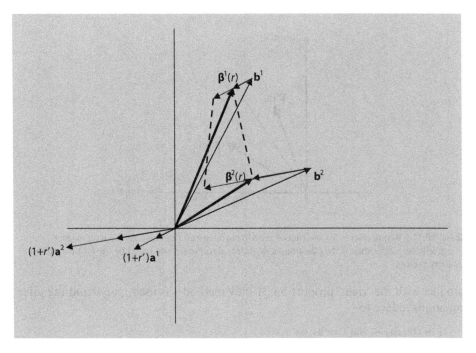

Fig. 10.10 The GD-segment is negatively sloped at the initial level of r, but it becomes positively sloped as r increases to r', indicating that one price becomes negative

If a method produces positive net products of both commodities, it might suffice to use that method alone, throwing away the excess production of one of the two products. For example, if both methods produce a positive net output of both commodities, assuming that the net-product requirements for use are rigidly determined and assuming free disposal of the overproduced commodity, the requirements might be satisfied with method 1 alone, with method 2 alone, or with a combination of both methods. In this case there is a problem of choice of technique in spite of the equality between the number of known methods and the number of commodities: there are three alternative 'techniques' among which the market 'chooses'. The choice-of-technique process in this case cannot be separated from the specification of the requirements for use, because the latter contribute to the determination of whether a good is overproduced (in which case its price becomes zero). The choice of techniques for a given r will have to be studied by determining, for each technique, whether some price becomes zero, and by studying whether at the resulting prices and income distribution there exists some method, not used in that technique, that yields extra profits (Fig. 10.11).

For example let us assume that the requirements for use can be specified in terms of net products and are in the proportions of vector D in Fig. 10.11. Then method 1 overproduces commodity 1, method 2 overproduces commodity 2, while an opportune combination of the two methods can produce a net

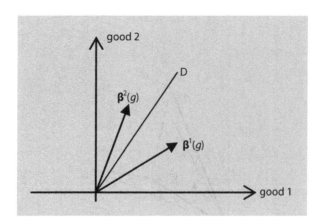

◘ **Fig. 10.11** Requirements for use (net of growth requirements) can be satisfied without any overproduced commodity, if they lie along a ray internal to the cone spanned by the GD-net product industry vectors

product with the 'right' proportion. If only method 1 is used, $p_1 = 0$ and the price equations reduce to

$$(1 + r)a_{21}p_2 + wa_{L1} = b_{21}p_2$$

$$p_2 v_2 = 1, \; p_1 = 0.$$

Care must be taken in the choice of the numéraire basket: if $v_2 = 0$ (the numéraire consists only of commodity 1), then $\mathbf{pv} = 1$ has no solution. To avoid problems once one admits that a price can become zero, one must choose as numéraire a basket $\mathbf{v}$ including positive amounts of both commodities.

The choice to determine requirements for use as gross products, or as net products, can entail a different determination of the technique adopted. Sraffa takes the *gross* products as given, but the majority of the subsequent literature has preferred to specify the requirements for use in terms of net products. It is to be hoped that the study of Sraffa's unpublished papers will clarify his reasons, so far little understood, for his apparent preference for the other option. Anyway also see below, ▶ Sect. 10.16.

10.9 Choice of Technique as a Linear Programming Problem

Linear programming results have come out to be useful for the analysis of the problem of choice of technique that arises with joint production. I largely follow Lippi (1979) and Schefold (1988).

A *linear programming problem* is a problem where one is asked to minimize or to maximize a linear combination of n non-negative variables, subject to linear inequality constraints. Consider the following linear programming minimization problem, where $\mathbf{M}$ is a given $m \times n$ matrix, $\mathbf{u}$ is the *row* m-vector to be determined, $\mathbf{b}$ is a given *column* m-vector, $\mathbf{d}$ is a given *row* n-vector:

10.9 · Choice of Technique as a Linear Programming Problem

(P) $\text{Min}_u \mathbf{ub}$ subject to $\mathbf{uM} \geq \mathbf{d}$, $\mathbf{u} \geq \mathbf{0}$. $\hspace{2cm}$ (10.10)

A vector $\mathbf{u}$ satisfying the constraints $\mathbf{uM} \geq \mathbf{d}$, $\mathbf{u} \geq \mathbf{0}$ of problem (P) is called a *feasible solution*, while a vector $\mathbf{u}^*$ solution of (P) is called an *optimal* solution or simply a solution.

To such a problem one can associate another problem called *dual* of the first one (which is then called *primal* relative to the dual), where $\mathbf{v}$ is the *column n-vector* to be determined:

(D) $\text{Max}_v \, \mathbf{dv}$ s. to $\mathbf{Mv} \leq \mathbf{b}, \mathbf{v} \geq 0$. $\hspace{2cm}$ (10.11)

Here too, a solution or *optimal* solution $\mathbf{v}^*$ of (D) is an element of the set of *feasible* solutions $\mathbf{v}$ satisfying the constraints $\mathbf{Mv} \leq \mathbf{b}, \mathbf{v} \geq 0$.

A basic result in the theory of linear programming, often called the Fundamental Theorem of Linear Programming, whose proof I omit, states:

Fundamental Theorem of Linear Programming. *If feasible solutions exist for both (P) and (D), then optimal solutions $\mathbf{u}^*$ and $\mathbf{v}^*$ exist for both (P) and (D) and they are such that $\mathbf{u}^* \mathbf{b} = \mathbf{dv}^*$. Either both problems (P) and (D) have optimal solutions, or neither does (which means that at least one of them has no feasible solution). If the optimal solution $\mathbf{u}^*$ is not unique, the set of optimal solutions is convex.*

Because of this Fundamental Theorem, problem (P) has a solution (equivalently, problem (D) has a solution) if and only if the following set of inequalities has a solution $\mathbf{u}^*$, $\mathbf{v}^*$:

$$\mathbf{uM} \geq \mathbf{d} \hspace{4cm} (10.12)$$

$$\mathbf{Mv} \leq \mathbf{b} \hspace{4cm} (10.13)$$

(P′) $\mathbf{ub} = \mathbf{dv}$ $\hspace{5cm}$ (10.14)

$$\mathbf{u} \geq \mathbf{0} \hspace{4.5cm} (10.15)$$

$$\mathbf{v} \geq \mathbf{0}. \hspace{4.5cm} (10.16)$$

The proof is obvious and left to the reader as an ***Exercise***. Notice furthermore that condition (10.14) in (P′) can be replaced by

$$\mathbf{um}^i > d_i \text{ implies } v_i = 0 \text{ and } \mathbf{m}_i \mathbf{v} < b_i \text{ implies } u_i = 0, \quad \text{all } i \hspace{1cm} (10.17)$$

where $\mathbf{m}^i$ and $\mathbf{m}_i$ are respectively the ith column and the ith row of $\mathbf{M}$.

Now consider the following primal and dual problems where the symbols have the interpretation in terms of technical coefficients, prices and activity levels adopted earlier in the chapter, and there are n different commodities:

(PX) $\hspace{1cm}$ $\text{Min}_x \, \mathbf{a}_L \mathbf{x}$ subject to $[\mathbf{B} - (1+r)\mathbf{A}]\mathbf{x} \geq \mathbf{c}, \ \mathbf{x} \geq \mathbf{0}$, $\hspace{1cm}$ (10.18)

(DP) $\hspace{1cm}$ $\text{Max}_p \, \mathbf{pc}$ subject to $\mathbf{p}[\mathbf{B} - (1+r)\mathbf{A}] \leq \mathbf{a}_L, \ \mathbf{p} \geq \mathbf{0}$. $\hspace{1cm}$ (10.19)

The primal problem (PX), where the variables are the m activity levels, asks to minimize the total employment necessary, in an economy where m

872   **Chapter 10** · Back to Long-Period Prices

joint-production methods are known and are all listed in $(\mathbf{A}, \mathbf{B}, \mathbf{a}_L)$, to produce a growth-diminished net product at least equal to the given vector $\mathbf{c}$, with $g = r$. Matrices $\mathbf{A}$ and $\mathbf{B}$ are $n \times m$. The dual problem (DP), where the variables are the n prices, asks to maximize the value of $\mathbf{c}$ subject to the condition that prices (implicitly measured in labour commanded, $w = 1$; I assume that the real wage rate is positive) must be such as not to yield extra profits with any method, i.e. $\mathbf{pB} \leq (1 + r)\mathbf{pA} + w\mathbf{a}_L$ with $w = 1$.

In these two problems the transposes of $[\mathbf{B} - (1 + r)\mathbf{A}]$, $\mathbf{a}_L$, $\mathbf{x}$, $\mathbf{c}$, $\mathbf{p}$ have exactly the same mathematical roles as, respectively, $\mathbf{M}$, $\mathbf{b}$, $\mathbf{u}$, $\mathbf{d}$, $\mathbf{v}$ in (P) and (D). Feasible solutions of (DP) certainly exist because $\mathbf{p} = \mathbf{0}$ is one such feasible solution. Therefore if (PX) has feasible solutions, i.e. *if it is possible for the economy to produce a net product at least equal to* $\mathbf{c}$ *when the input matrix* $\mathbf{A}$ *is replaced by input matrix* $(1 + r)\mathbf{A}$, *then (PX) and (DP) have solutions* $\mathbf{x}^*$ *and* $\mathbf{p}^*$, *such that* $\mathbf{p}^*\mathbf{c} = \mathbf{a}_L\mathbf{x}^*$.

What is the relevance of this result for the problem of choice of techniques? It shows that, under the stated assumption, there exists a set of methods of production capable of satisfying the requirements for use (increase of all inputs by the percentage r and, in addition, production of the consumption vector $\mathbf{c}$) and such that no method (activated or not activated) yields extra profits. In particular, the application of (3′) to our economic problem means that if (PX) and (DP) have solutions, then the condition $\mathbf{p}^*\mathbf{c} = \mathbf{a}_L\mathbf{x}^*$ is equivalent to (remember that $w = 1$):

$\mathbf{b_i}\mathbf{x}^* - (1 + r)\mathbf{a_i}\mathbf{x}^* > c_i$ implies $p_i = 0$, i.e. *overproduced commodities have zero price*,

$\mathbf{pb^i} < (1 + r)\mathbf{pA^i} + a_{Li}$ implies $x_i = 0$, i.e. *loss-making methods are not activated*.

Since the solution $\mathbf{p}^*$, $\mathbf{x}^*$ is such that none of the non-activated methods is capable of yielding extra profits, *the activated methods constitute a cost-minimizing technique* relative to the specified requirements for use.[44]

As in single production, it is possible that at the given r two cost-minimizing techniques can coexist, because at the prices of one cost-minimizing technique there is a method not belonging to it that yields the same r; it is like being at a switchpoint of the $w(r)$ curves (except that with joint production $w(r)$ curves require further consideration, see below). It has been demonstrated[45] that under the assumption $g = r$ (called the *Golden Rule* assumption), apart from this case the solution is unique in the methods activated and, given the assumed rigidity

---

44 For single-product economies too, the problem of choice of techniques might have been formulated in this way, directly as a problem of finding a technique and associated prices and real wage, such that none of the methods not included in the technique is capable of yielding extra profits. Formally, the sole difference is that matrix $\mathbf{B}$ would have all columns with only one nonzero element (equal to 1 with an opportune choice of units), that is, each method would have a positive net product for only one good; therefore a cost-minimizing technique satisfying requirements for use positive for all commodities would in general include just n methods, one for each commodity; requirements for use would be exactly satisfied; and no price would be zero.

45 By Schefold (1998; cf. ibid., fn. 4, p. 194, for a correction of a mistake in previous work of the same author). I omit the proof.

10.9 · Choice of Technique as a Linear Programming Problem

of requirements for use, the number of commodities with positive prices is (apart from flukes of probability zero) equal to the number of activated methods; if one then cancels from the system the commodities with zero price (by considering them free goods, like air or sunlight) and only includes the activated methods, one obtains a 'square' system (number of methods equal to number of commodities), with all prices positive and uniquely determined. Another result is that as $r = g$ varies (and the technique with it), the real wage varies in the opposite direction for any numéraire. Thus one finds results extremely similar to the single-production case.

However, these pleasant results rest on the golden rule assumption, $g = r$: the specification of the gross requirements for use as $\mathbf{c} + (1 + r)\mathbf{Ax}$ is restrictive. An economy will generally be growing at a rate different from the rate of profit; also, the different sectors will be generally growing at different rates. More general specifications of the requirements for use (still assuming that they are rigid) are, for example, that the net product $(\mathbf{B} - \mathbf{A})\mathbf{x}$ must be at least equal to a given semi-positive vector $\mathbf{c}$ (now no longer interpretable as a consumption vector, unless the economy is stationary), or that the gross product must be at least equal to $\mathbf{c} + (1 + g)\mathbf{Ax}$ with $g \neq r$, plausibly $g < r$.

This changes things considerably. Several phenomena impossible with single production become possible.

First, it is possible that $(\mathbf{B} - \mathbf{A})\mathbf{x} \geq \mathbf{c}$ has solution while $[\mathbf{B} - (1 + r)\mathbf{A}]\mathbf{x} \geq \mathbf{c}$ doesn't. The fact that in this case (PX) does not have solution does not necessarily mean that prices and technical choice cannot be determined. ◘ Figure 10.12 (Lippi 1979, p. 53) shows a case in which at $r' > 0$, $g = 0$, requirements for use can be satisfied exactly and prices and the real wage rate are well determined and positive, while at $g = r'$ requirements for use cannot be satisfied.

Second, as the case drawn in ◘ Fig. 10.12 also illustrates, the possibility arises that at $r = 0$ one price is negative, while at $r = r'$ prices are all positive. This result has been interpreted by Steedman (1975) as meaning that labours embodied (equal to labour-commanded prices when $r = 0$) can be negative. That a labour embodied be negative may appear nonsensical; but if we accept the interpretation of the labour embodied in a commodity as 'employment multiplier', i.e. as indicating the total employment necessary to obtain one unit of that commodity as net product, then the labour embodied in a commodity can also be interpreted as the *variation* in total labour employment if the net output of that commodity increases by one unit, all other net outputs remaining unchanged; then in the case of ◘ Fig. 10.12 the rate of profit r', prices, and the real wage are all positive and requirements for use are satisfied, but the labour embodied in commodity 1 is negative: an increase in the sole net output of commodity 1 will entail a decrease in total employment. The reason is that industry 2 (the one using method 2, which has the higher ratio of net output of good 1 to net output of good 2) must be expanded, and industry 1 must be contracted so as to maintain the net output of commodity 2 unchanged; but method 2 also has a greater net output of commodity 2 per unit of labour, so the increase in employment in industry 2 is less than the decrease of employment in industry 1.

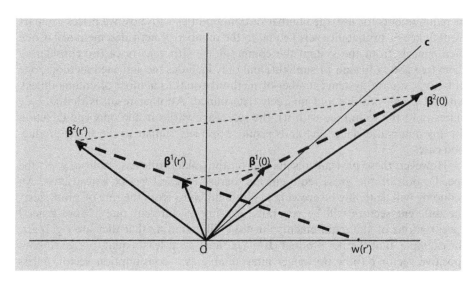

◧ **Fig. 10.12** A case in which a positive $r=r'$ renders the wage line (shown as a bold broken line) negatively inclined (prices are therefore positive) while it would be positively inclined (one price is therefore negative) at $r=0$. Note that it is $\beta^1(0)$ and $\beta^2(0)$ that indicate the physical net products, and hence the capacity to satisfy the requirement for use **c** when $g=0$

As ◧ Fig. 10.12 makes clear, this is only possible because method 1 produces a smaller net output per unit of labour of *both* commodities; if the rate of profit were zero, method 1 could not be equally profitable as method 2 at non-negative prices; but if, as the rate of profit rises, the costs of method 1 rise less rapidly than for method 2 because it uses fewer inputs per unit of output than method 2, then at a positive rate of profit the two methods can co-exist.[46]

---

46 Steedman's example assumes two goods, A and B, and two methods, I and II:

method	inputs			outputs	
	A	B	Labour	A	B
I	5	0	1 →	6	1
II	0	10	1 →	3	12

The real wage consists of 0.5 units of A and 5/6 units of B, and is paid in arrears. When both methods are in use, it is $r=20\%$, both prices are positive and $p_B/p_A = 3$. Labours embodied, or labour values, are (the reader is invited to check it as an exercise) $h_A = -1$, $h_B = 2$. When the rate of profit is not uniform let us indicate the two rates of profit as r_I and r_{II}. If the composition of final net demand is intermediate between the compositions of the net products of the two methods (Steedman obtains it by assuming that wages are consumed and profits are invested, hence the normal requirements for use are those of steady growth), then if only method II is used, A is overproduced, its price falls to zero, but then $r_{II} = 11.6$ while $r_I = +\infty$, and it is convenient to introduce method I; if only method I is used, B is overproduced, its price falls to zero and then $r_I = 10\%$, $r_{II} = +\infty$, and it is convenient to introduce method II: thus (I,II) is the sole (and stable) cost-minimizing technique. Steedman's example has shocked some Marxist economists because the surplus product has a negative labour value: steady growth at $g=20\%$ implies (the reader is invited to

10.9 · Choice of Technique as a Linear Programming Problem

Third, as shown earlier (cf. ● Fig. 10.9), it is not guaranteed that, as r rises, the real wage measured in any numéraire decreases: in some cases there can be numéraires in terms of which the real wage increases.

Fourth, the existence of a unique cost-minimizing technique satisfying the requirements for use is no longer guaranteed (see below, Bidard's example in ▶ Sect. 10.10); and it has been claimed that there may be no gravitation to a definite technique (see below, Bidard's example in ▶ Sect. 10.11; the question is under discussion).

However, it has been proved by Lippi (1979), Salvadori (1982), Schefold (1988) that a cost-minimizing technique exists under assumptions that, although slightly different in the three authors, amount essentially to positing that the economy must be capable of satisfying the given requirements for use **c** when the matrix **A** is replaced by $(1+r)$**A**; in other words, the available methods must be capable of producing **c** as consumption vector besides guaranteeing a uniform rate of growth equal to the rate of profit; this comes out to be essentially equivalent to assuming that $0 \leq g \leq r < R$, where R is the highest possible uniform rate of growth of the economy. [47] I reproduce Schefold's (1988) proof, which is largely inspired by Lippi (1979).

The result to be proved is the following.

Schefold–Lippi theorem on joint production. *Let m productive methods* ($\mathbf{a}^i$, $\mathbf{b}^i$, $\mathbf{a}_L^i$) *for the production of n commodities be given, with i* = 1, ..., m. *Indicate with* **A**, **B**, $\mathbf{a}_L$ *the corresponding n × m matrices of physical input and output coefficients and row vector of labour input coefficients; each good is produced by at least one method, each method uses at least one input, and* $\mathbf{a}_L > 0$. *Let* **c** *be a given semipositive column vector of commodities, and let* **x** *stand for a non-negative vector of activity levels, and* **p** *for a non-negative vector of labour-commanded prices. Assume that net requirements for use are given by* $\mathbf{c} + g\mathbf{A}\mathbf{x}$. *If* $0 \leq g \leq r < R$ *where R is the maximum rate of expansion (or maximum rate of profits that can be reached under a golden rule assumption), then there is a cost-minimizing technique fulfilling the following conditions:*

$$(1*) \quad (\mathbf{B} - (1+g)\mathbf{A})\mathbf{x} \geq \mathbf{c}$$

$$(2*) \quad \mathbf{p}\big[\mathbf{B} - (1+g)\mathbf{A}\big]\mathbf{x} = \mathbf{p}\mathbf{c}$$

$$(3*) \quad \mathbf{p}[\mathbf{B} - (1+r)\mathbf{A}] \leq \mathbf{a}_L \qquad\qquad (10.20)$$

$$(4*) \quad \mathbf{p}[\mathbf{B} - (1+r)\mathbf{A}]\mathbf{x} = \mathbf{a}_L\mathbf{x}.$$

Before proving this theorem, some clarificatory comments, and a mathematical tool. Equation (1*) formalizes the condition that it is possible to produce at least the net requirements for use; (2*) is another way to express the condition

---

check it as an exercise) that if total labour employment is e.g. 6 units, the surplus product is (5A, 2B) and its labour value is -1; hence the article's title, 'Positive profits with negative surplus value'. If this economy wanted to pass to producing a net product *exactly equal* to the sole consumption of workers, it would have to *increase* labour employment. This confirms that, as argued in ▶ Chap. 1, the rate of profit depends on physical quantities, not on labours embodied.

47 The equivalence will become clear shortly, when we clarify what R is.

that overproduced goods have price zero; (3*) imposes that no process yields extra profits; (4*) imposes that unprofitable methods are not used. The non-negativity of prices and of activity levels has been assumed in the statement of the result. A set of methods, for which the corresponding elements of a vector $\mathbf{x}$ solution of (1*) to (4*) are positive, is clearly a cost-minimizing technique associated with $(r, g, \mathbf{c})$. (For a given r, the cost-minimizing technique can depend on the requirements for use and therefore can change with changes in g or $\mathbf{c}$.) The maximum rate of growth R is determined by starting from $g=0$, then raising g, and studying all possible GD-segments or more generally GD-simplexes (in the general case of $n>2$ commodities) resulting from combinations of up to n different methods. At $g=0$ at least one of these simplexes must have at least a point in the non-negative orthant (otherwise the assumption $g\geq0$ causes the non-existence of solutions: the economy is not viable). Starting from $g=0$ one raises g; for a sufficiently high g, no $\beta^i(g)$ vector is in the non-negative orthant and no GD-simplex has a point in common with the non-negative orthant; the highest g for which a GD-simplex has a point in common with the non-negative orthant is the maximum rate of expansion R; the active methods are the ones associated with that GD-simplex if the point is in the origin, or otherwise they consist of the sole last method whose growth-reduced net product vector has not yet abandoned the non-negative orthant (the reader is invited to experiment with drawings in the two-commodities case). As long as $g<R$, the GD-simplex has some points strictly internal to the positive orthant, i.e. there is an $\mathbf{x}$ such that $(\mathbf{B}-(1+g)\mathbf{A})\mathbf{x}>\mathbf{0}$, and then, multiplying $\mathbf{x}$ by a sufficiently big scalar, any net product vector $\mathbf{c}$ can be overproduced; hence a solution to (1') exists. How restrictive is the assumption $g\leq r<R$? Notice that in ◼ Fig. 10.12 it is $r'>R$ (the GD-segment, from $\beta^1(r')$ and $\beta^2(r')$, is entirely outside the non-negative orthant); this case shows that, with joint production, it is not impossible that prices and the real wage be positive for $r>R$ (of course it must be $g<R$). However the case $g\leq r<R$ would seem to be the only empirically relevant one: in real economies, empirically, the *actual* average rate of growth is always inferior to the rate of profit,[48] and the *maximum* rate of growth R (the one associated with zero consumption!) would appear to be always higher than the rate of profit.[49]

The additional mathematical tool we need is a fixed-point theorem, a generalization of Brouwer's theorem to correspondences:

Kakutani's fixed-point theorem

Let set $A\subset R^n$ be non-empty, compact and convex and let $f:A\to A$ be an upper-hemicontinuous correspondence such that $f(\mathbf{x})$ is a non-empty and convex set for all $\mathbf{x}\in A$ (f is then said convex-valued). Then f has a fixed point, in the sense that $\exists\mathbf{x}$ such that $\mathbf{x}\in f(\mathbf{x})$.

---

48 The rate of growth can well be higher than the riskless interest rate, but the rate of profits is always considerably higher than the riskless interest rate, according to many authors it is usually above 10% and even above 20%.

49 A rough reasoning on this issue might go as follows: the normal rate of profit seldom goes above 15%; when the growth rate is around 5%, net investment is generally not above 20% of net national income; therefore a reduction of consumption to zero should permit a four-fold increase in the rate of growth, which means a maximum rate of growth above 15%.

10.9 · Choice of Technique as a Linear Programming Problem

Note that in this theorem the possibility of discontinuities that do not violate upper hemicontinuity, such as shown in ● Figs. 4.11–4.13 of ▶ Chap. 4, is *excluded* by the assumption that $f(\mathbf{x})$ is a convex set at all $\mathbf{x}$. With this we can prove the Schefold–Lippi theorem.

■■ Proof of the Schefold–Lippi theorem

Equation (2*) can be written $\mathbf{p}[\mathbf{B}-\mathbf{A}]\mathbf{x}-g\mathbf{p}\mathbf{A}\mathbf{x}=\mathbf{p}\mathbf{c}$, and Eq. (4*) can be written $\mathbf{p}[\mathbf{B}-\mathbf{A}]\mathbf{x}-r\mathbf{p}\mathbf{A}\mathbf{x}=\mathbf{a}_L\mathbf{x}$, thus they imply $\mathbf{p}\mathbf{c}-\mathbf{a}_L\mathbf{x}=(r-g)\mathbf{p}\mathbf{A}\mathbf{x}$ or

$$(5*)\quad \mathbf{p}\mathbf{c} = \mathbf{a}_L\mathbf{x} + (r-g)\mathbf{p}\mathbf{A}\mathbf{x}. \tag{10.21}$$

Conversely, (5*) implies (2*) and (4*) if (1*) and (3*) hold, for otherwise we get $\mathbf{p}[\mathbf{B}-(1+r)\mathbf{A}]\mathbf{x}<\mathbf{a}_L\mathbf{x}$ and/or $\mathbf{p}[\mathbf{B}-(1+g)\mathbf{A}]\mathbf{x}>\mathbf{p}\mathbf{c}$, hence $\mathbf{p}\mathbf{c}-\mathbf{a}_L\mathbf{x}<(r-g)\mathbf{p}\mathbf{A}\mathbf{x}$ contradicting (5*). Therefore Eqs. (1*), (3*) and (5*) are equivalent to Eqs. (1*) to (4*). Let us call *system S* the system (1*), (3*), (5*) plus the conditions $\mathbf{p}\geq 0$, $\mathbf{x}\geq 0$.

Consider now the following primal-dual problem pair, where $\mathbf{x}^*$ is an arbitrary given non-negative vector:

$$(P1)\quad \text{Min}_\mathbf{x}\ \mathbf{a}_L\mathbf{x}\quad \text{s.t. } [\mathbf{B}-(1+r)\mathbf{A}]\mathbf{x}\geq\mathbf{c}-(r-g)\mathbf{A}\mathbf{x}*, \mathbf{x}\geq 0, \tag{10.22}$$

$$(D1)\quad \text{Max}_\mathbf{p}\ \mathbf{p}(\mathbf{c}-(r-g)\mathbf{A}\mathbf{x}*)\quad \text{s.t. } \mathbf{p}[\mathbf{B}-(1+r)\mathbf{A}]\leq\mathbf{a}_L, \mathbf{p}\geq 0. \tag{10.23}$$

Suppose that the given $\mathbf{x}^*$ in P1 and D1 is chosen such that the solution $\mathbf{x}^\wedge$ of P1 coincides with $\mathbf{x}^*$: then $\mathbf{x}^\wedge$ and $\mathbf{p}^\wedge$, solution of (P1) with $\mathbf{x}^*=\mathbf{x}^\wedge$, fulfil the conditions of system S, because the constraint in (1*) can be rewritten $[\mathbf{B}-(1+r)\mathbf{A}]\mathbf{x}^*+(r-g)\mathbf{A}\mathbf{x}^*=(\mathbf{B}-(1+g)\mathbf{A})\mathbf{x}^*\geq\mathbf{c}$ which is (1*); (3*) is the constraint in P1; and by the Fundamental Theorem of Linear Programming, $\mathbf{a}_L\mathbf{x}^*=\mathbf{p}(\mathbf{c}-(r-g)\mathbf{A}\mathbf{x}^*)$ which is (5*). Therefore $\mathbf{x}^*$ selects with its nonzero elements a set of methods forming a cost-minimizing technique.

Thus in order to prove that a cost-minimizing technique exists, we have to prove that a vector $\mathbf{x}^*$, such that $\mathbf{x}^\wedge=\mathbf{x}^*$, exists. In other words, if we consider the correspondence $\mathbf{X}^\wedge$ that associates to each $\mathbf{x}^*$ the set $\mathbf{X}^\wedge(\mathbf{x}^*)$ of solutions $\mathbf{x}^\wedge$ generated by P1, we must show that this correspondence has a fixed point. To such an end I will use Kakutani's theorem.

I will consider not the entire correspondence $\mathbf{X}^\wedge$, but only a part of it, defined on a domain that is a closed, bounded and convex set to be called Q; if we can prove that $\mathbf{X}^\wedge$ thus restricted is upper hemicontinuous and associates to each $\mathbf{x}^*$ in Q a non-empty convex set $\mathbf{X}^\wedge(\mathbf{x}^*)$ whose elements are all in Q, then we have proved that $\mathbf{X}^\wedge$ has a fixed point.

Suppose $\mathbf{x}^*=\mathbf{0}$, which means that any feasible solution of P1 must satisfy $(\mathbf{B}-(1+r)\mathbf{A})\mathbf{x}\geq\mathbf{c}$. Since by assumption $r<R$, by the definition of R the GD-simplex with $g=r$ has a portion in the positive orthant; i.e. there is an $\mathbf{x}$ such that $(\mathbf{B}-(1+g)\mathbf{A})\mathbf{x}>0$, and then, by multiplying $\mathbf{x}$ by a sufficiently big scalar, any net product vector $\mathbf{c}$ can be overproduced. Therefore P1 has a feasible solution for $\mathbf{x}^*=\mathbf{0}$ and then, since $\mathbf{p}=\mathbf{0}$ is always a feasible solution in D1, by the Fundamental Theorem P1 has a solution; let us indicate it as $\mathbf{x}^+$. Note that if $\mathbf{x}^*\geq 0$ (i.e. $\neq 0$) then $\mathbf{x}^+$ is a feasible solution of P1 because $(\mathbf{B}-(1+r)\mathbf{A})\mathbf{x}^+\geq\mathbf{c}\geq\mathbf{c}-(r-g)\mathbf{A}\mathbf{x}^*$;

therefore $\mathbf{x}^+$ is always a feasible solution and, since $\mathbf{p}=\mathbf{0}$ is always a feasible solution in D1, then $X^\wedge(\mathbf{x}^*)$ is not empty for any non-negative $\mathbf{x}^*$. Now define the set Q as $Q \equiv \{\mathbf{x} \geq \mathbf{0}: \mathbf{a_L}\mathbf{x} \leq \mathbf{a_L}\mathbf{x}^+\}$: since $\mathbf{x}^+$ exists, Q is not empty. It is closed and convex, and it is bounded because we have assumed $\mathbf{a_L}>\mathbf{0}$; hence it is a compact set. $X^\wedge(\mathbf{x}^*)$ is entirely contained in Q because if $\mathbf{x}^\wedge \in X^\wedge(\mathbf{x}^*)$, then $\mathbf{x}^\wedge \geq \mathbf{0}$, and furthermore $\mathbf{a_L}\mathbf{x}^\wedge \leq \mathbf{a_L}\mathbf{x}^+$ because $\mathbf{x}^+$ is always feasible hence it is also feasible for the $\mathbf{x}^*$ for which $\mathbf{x}^\wedge$ is optimal, implying $\mathbf{a_L}\mathbf{x}^\wedge \leq \mathbf{a_L}\mathbf{x}^+$. Let us then restrict $\mathbf{x}^*$ to $\mathbf{x}^* \in Q$: we have shown that $X^\wedge(\mathbf{x}^*)$ defined over Q is not empty and contained in Q. It only remains to show that the set $X^\wedge(\mathbf{x}^*)$ is convex and that $X^\wedge$ defined over Q is upper hemicontinuous. That the solutions of a linear programming problem form a convex set is a standard result of linear programming theory. The upper hemicontinuity of $X^\wedge$ follows from the Theorem of the Maximum (cf. Beavis and Dobbs pp. 83–84, or the Mathematical Appendix), which states that if a continuous real-valued function is maximized over a compact set which varies continuously with some parameter vector, then the set of solutions is an upper hemicontinuous correspondence of the parameter vector, and the value of the maximized function varies continuously with the parameters.

Thus all assumptions of Kakutani's theorem are satisfied by the correspondence $X^\wedge$ defined over Q, and therefore this correspondence has a fixed point $\mathbf{x}^*=\mathbf{x}^\wedge$. This proves that a vector of activity levels $\mathbf{x}^*$ exists, which with its positive elements selects a cost-minimizing technique from among the methods appearing in $(\mathbf{A},\mathbf{B},\mathbf{a_L})$. Therefore a cost-minimizing technique exists for $0 \leq g \leq r < R$. ∎

The above proof makes use of the assumption $\mathbf{a_L}>0$, that is, all methods use a positive amount of labour. This assumption may appear restrictive, because some storage or ageing methods, resulting from the subdivision of a long production method into elementary one-period methods, for example the ageing of wine in cellars, may appear to require no labour input. However, even these processes usually require some surveillance labour. Furthermore, it is intuitive that, by adding a positive but extremely small amount of labour to the inputs of a method that uses no labour, one raises its cost of production by an amount that can be made as small as one likes and that therefore cannot but have a negligible effect on the overall results of the analysis; thus, since the general results reached by assuming that $\mathbf{a_L}$ is strictly positive also hold when some of the elements of $\mathbf{a_L}$ are extremely small, it is intuitive that these results must continue to hold if some of these elements are reduced to zero.[50] Indeed a different proof of the existence of a cost-minimizing technique, due to Salvadori (1982), dispenses with the assumption that the vector of labour inputs is *strictly* positive; but it relies on very different mathematical instruments (called Theorems of the Alternative), that the reader will definitely have to learn if she/he wants to become a specialist in this field, but that need not be explained for the purposes of this textbook.

---

50 Clearly, at least some of the basic commodities must use a positive amount of labour. But the extension of the notion of basic commodity to the case of joint production is a complex matter in which we do not enter.

10.9 · Choice of Technique as a Linear Programming Problem

The proof also applies to cases of non-uniform growth, because if one puts $g=0$, then $\mathbf{c}$ stands for the entire net output vector, which can well be the one of an economy with sectors growing at different rates.

10.10 Piccioni's Contribution

The existence of a cost-minimizing technique does not mean that it will be unique, nor that the economy will certainly gravitate to it. Some advance in the understanding of these complications has been achieved by Piccioni (1989) whose analysis I present now.[51]

Assume that only two commodities are produced; take the rate of profit as given; and assume that the requirements for use are in given *proportions* ($g=0$, $\mathbf{c}=t\mathbf{c}°$ with t a positive scalar and $\mathbf{c}°$ a given semipositive vector). Wages are paid at the end of the period. A number of production methods are known, indexed by $j=1, 2, ...$; choose as unit dimension of each method the one such that the labour coefficient is 1. The price equation of the jth method:

$$(1+r)\left(a_{1j}p_1 + a_{2j}p_2\right) + w = b_{1j}p_1 + b_{2j}p_2$$

can be rewritten as

$$w = \left[b_{1j} - (1+r)a_{1j}\right]p_1 + \left[b_{2j} - (1+r)a_{2j}\right]p_2.$$

The terms in square brackets would be the elements of the growth-diminished net product vector if it were $g=r$; let us indicate them here as $\beta_{ij}(r) \equiv b_{ij} - (1+r)a_{ij}$, then the price equation becomes

$$w = \beta_{1j}(r)p_1 + \beta_{2j}(r)p_2. \tag{10.24}$$

If we choose one of the two goods as numéraire, let us say good 1, then this equation expresses the real wage in terms of good 2 as a *linear* function of p_2 (because r is given), with intercept $\beta_{1j}(r)$ and slope $\beta_{2j}(r)$. That w is a function of p_2 in spite of the given r of course depends on the fact that we are considering method j in isolation, not introducing yet the condition that a second method must yield the same w. We can call this $w^j(p_2)$ function the **wage-price function** of method j, and we can draw in the same diagram the wage-price functions of the several methods among which the economy can choose.[52] One reaches useful results by jointly considering the wage-price functions and the net product vectors $\left(b_{1j} - a_{1j}, b_{2j} - a_{2j}\right)^{\mathrm{T}}$, which it is convenient here to indicate as $\mathbf{y}^j$ to avoid confusions.

---

51 In the remainder of this Part I also use some ideas from Piccioni's unpublished Ph.D. dissertation (1991). I thank the author for permission to use those ideas.

52 A different basket in terms of which to measure the real wage, i.e. a different numéraire, as long as it did not consist only of good 2, would still make it possible to arrive at linear wage-price functions $w^j(p_2)$, it would only change their slope, e.g. $p_1+p_2=1$ would mean – dropping for simplicity the indication of the dependence on r since r is given—$w = \beta_{1j}(1-p_2) + \beta_{2j}p_2 = \beta_{1j} + (\beta_{2j}-\beta_{1j})p_2$. The height of w in ordinate would then indicate how many baskets consisting of 1 unit of each good can be purchased with the wage rate.

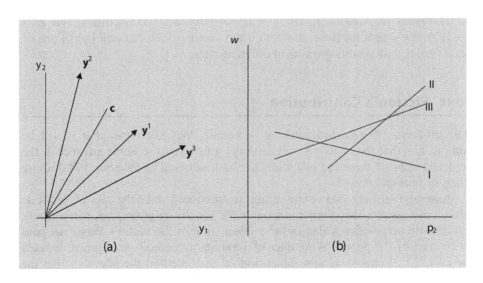

Fig. 10.13 Possible wage–price curves

For example consider the following situation. The economy is satisfying the given requirements for use by using methods 1 and 2, where method 1, if used alone, would overproduce commodity 1 relative to the requirements for use, while method 2 would overproduce commodity 2, as shown by their net product vectors relative to vector **c** in ◘ Fig. 10.13a. A third method is then discovered, method 3. We want to know whether it will be introduced. The corresponding wage-price functions are shown as respectively I, II, III in ◘ Fig. 10.13b. When methods 1 and 2 are the ruling methods—we then say that the economy is using technique (1,2)—, w and p_2 must correspond to the intersection of I and II. If at that level of p_2 the wage determined by the wage-price function of method 3, line III in ◘ Fig. 10.13b, is above the intersection, this means that at the *ruling* prices method 3 is capable of paying a higher wage; hence if it pays the same wage as the other two methods it yields extra profits; hence it is profitable to introduce it. This shows the usefulness of this graphical representation: for each p_2, the position of the wage-profit functions indicates which method can afford to pay the highest wage, i.e. will be more profitable if the wage rate is uniform.

We now ask, which method will be replaced by method 3? With simple production the answer is unambiguous—the method producing the same commodity as the new method—, but with joint production the answer may not be immediately clear. In ◘ Fig. 10.13b, the line III intersects both I and II in the positive orthant, so both technique (1,3) and technique (2,3) are a possibility.

However, from ◘ Fig. 10.13a we know that method 3, if used alone, overproduces commodity 1. Hence its introduction—which, when relative prices have not started changing yet, can be plausibly assumed initially not to cause a change in the relative proportion in which methods 1 and 2 are used[53]—will tend to shift the composition of the net product such as to cause an overproduction of commodity 1, and therefore a decrease of p_1/p_2, i.e. an increase of p_2. Therefore, in ◘ Fig. 10.13b, plausibly p_2 increases and we can conclude that the economy will tend towards the intersection of lines II and III, while method 1 disappears.

This approach allows a further observation. The initial position had to be characterized by a slope of II greater than the slope of I; otherwise it would have been unstable: with the reverse order of the slopes, any accidental deviation of the relative activity levels of I and II from the ones satisfying the requirements for use would have caused such a change of market prices, as to reinforce the deviation.

The same kind of considerations allows a graphical examination of an example due to Bidard (1997, example 2). The rate of profit is r = 100%. The requirements for use are that the net product must contain equal quantities of the two commodities. There are four methods with the following coefficients:

Method	a_{1j}	a_{2j}	a_{Lj}		b_{1j}	b_{2j}	y_{1j}	y_{2j}	$\beta_{1j}(r)$	$\beta_{2j}(r)$
1)	1	1	1	→	6	2	5	1	4	0
2)	1	3	1	→	5	8	4	5	3	2
3)	3	0	1	→	8	3	5	3	2	3
4)	1	2	1	→	2	8	1	6	0	4

The wage–price functions of the four methods, cf. ◘ Fig. 10.14b, exhibit three intersections on the upper envelope, A, B, and C, corresponding to techniques (1,2), (2,3), (3,4). All three techniques can satisfy the requirements for use exactly, as one can check from ◘ Fig. 10.14a. Since at each one of these intersections the other two wage–price functions are below the intersection, the excluded methods are not capable of yielding extra profits; i.e. all three techniques are cost minimizing: for example, at the relative prices and real wage associated with technique (1,2), methods 3 and 4 are both unprofitable; at the relative prices and real wage associated with technique (3,4), methods 1 and 2 are both unprofitable. This is a case of multiple cost-minimizing techniques. The reader is invited to check this result by explicitly calculating p_2 and w associated with each technique and checking that at those prices each one of the other two methods has production costs (inclusive of $r = 1$) higher than the value of its product. A complete search for cost-minimizing techniques must also examine the techniques consisting of a single method, which entail that one of the goods is overproduced and its price is zero. Method 1 and method 3 entail overproduction of good 1; hence

53 If, differently from what is assumed in ◘ Fig. 10.2a, $\mathbf{y}^3$ has a slope intermediate between those of $\mathbf{c}$ and of $\mathbf{y}^1$, it is perhaps conceivable that its introduction may induce such a quick contraction of the process adopting method 1, as to cause an initial underproduction of commodity 1. But since method 3 is more convenient than both the other methods, the process adopting method 2 will contract too, and eventually the composition of production will be dominated by method 3 and the overproduction of good 1 will assert itself.

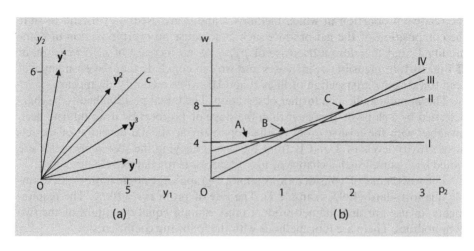

● Fig. 10.14 Bidard's example

$p_1=0$; method 2 and method 4 entail $p_2=0$. Then neither method 2 alone nor 4 alone are cost-minimizing because when $p_2=0$ method 1 is more profitable than either; and methods 1 or 3 alone are not cost minimizing because if either is alone adopted they cause p_2 to grow indefinitely and when it grows beyond $p_2=3$, they are both less profitable than method 4. Thus the sole cost-minimizing techniques are the three ones we have listed initially.

What Piccioni's reasoning adds is that not all these techniques can be centres of gravitation. Considerations similar to the ones already developed for the example in ● Fig. 10.13 show that technique (2,3) is 'unstable' in the sense that any accidental deviation, of the proportion between the two methods from the one required to exactly satisfy the requirements for use, will cause a movement away from point B that will induce the movement to continue. For example, if the proportion changes in favour of method 2, ● Fig. 10.14a shows that good 2 becomes overproduced relative to requirements for use; hence p_2 decreases; this causes method 2 to become more profitable than method 3, inducing a further expansion of method 2 and contraction of method 3, and therefore further decreases of p_2, until method 1 becomes more convenient than method 3 and replaces it; the economy gravitates towards point A. A deviation in the other direction would cause a gravitation towards point C. Techniques (1,2) and (3,4) on the contrary are 'stable' in the sense that, in each of them, if the proportion between one method and the other one rises relative to the one required to satisfy the requirements for use, this lowers the relative profitability of the method which has been expanded, and therefore pushes towards a restoration of the 'correct' proportion, as the reader can check.

For the two-goods economy Piccioni proves formally—but the thing can be easily deduced from the graphical representation—that if there are several cost-minimizing techniques, then (if one also includes the ones associated with a negative wage—see below) they are necessarily odd in number, with the inter-

10.10 · Piccioni's Contribution

sections on the upper envelope that represent 'stable' cost-minimizing techniques separated by intersections representing 'unstable' or, as he prefers to call them, 'watershed' techniques which cannot be viewed as centres of gravitation.

That, with joint production, there can be more than one cost-minimizing technique has been proved by several authors (see, e.g., the exercises of ▶ Chap. 8 of Kurz and Salvadori 1995); hence there can be more than one long-period position, to which the economy may converge; these long-period positions differ in relative prices, in the gross quantities produced, and in the value of the distributive variable determined residually (the real wage rate, in our examples; but it could be the rate of profit, if it is the real wage rate that is taken as given); once reached, a cost-minimizing technique will persist only as long as prices and the real wage do not fluctuate too widely.[54] Which technique the economy tends to gravitate towards can depend on the starting point. Thus if at different points in time two new methods become available, it can happen that the cost-minimizing technique finally adopted depends on the order in which they become available. The situation the economy tends towards can therefore depend to some degree on historical accidents, and it is not excluded that a temporary but significant change in the wage rate, followed by a return to the old wage rate, may not cause a return to the old technique. However, Piccioni argues that, at least for the two-goods case, once the initial methods are given, one can always uniquely determine the methods towards which the economy will tend, and the associated prices and wage, once a new method is introduced. It is not clear yet whether this result can be extended to economies with more than two goods (an example, intended to show that the answer is negative, is criticized below).

The possibility of some non-uniqueness of the distributive variable residually determined, that thus emerges, should not induce one to think that the classical approach is in the same situation, as regards non-uniqueness, as the neoclassical approach. Leaving aside for the sake of argument the logically prior problems with determining the data of a neoclassical equilibrium, a multiplicity of neoclassical equilibria renders *both* distributive variables *r* and *w* indeterminate, and possibly *gravely* indeterminate,[55] while here the indeterminacy a) only concerns the *residual* distributive variable, and b) is in all likelihood very limited. As to a), multiple cost-minimizing techniques in no way question the plausibility of the socio-political forces that according to the classical approach determine the real wage in a given historical period; nor do they question the plausibility

---

54 It is plausible, however, that it will rather be technical progress that will cause a change of the long-period position around and towards which the economy gravitates.

55 The reader will remember for example how different the equilibrium real wage can be as between different equilibria, when the multiplicity of equilibria derives from multiple intersections of the labour demand curve with a backward-bending labour supply curve. She will also remember the Sonnenschein–Mantel–Debreu results, that show that the economy might have so many different equilibria very close to each other, as to be close to having a continuum of equilibria.

of the approaches (e.g. Pivetti's, see ▶ Chap. 13) which argue that it is mainly through the rate of profit that the forces affecting income distribution more directly operate, for example by fixing the real rate of interest. As to b), when there is multiplicity of cost-minimizing techniques due to joint production the possible degree of indeterminacy of the residual distributive variable (the variation of the rate of profits—or of the real wage if it is the rate of profits that is given—between the minimum and the maximum of the values associated with the different cost-minimizing techniques when the other variable is given) is in all likelihood negligible when we consider realistic, highly complex economies rather than examples with two or three commodities. Plausible changes in the methods adopted in even some dozen of productive processes cannot but have a very limited effect on the rate of profit when those processes are only a small fraction of the thousands, if not hundreds of thousands, of processes influencing the rate of profit. Significant changes in the rate of profit when the real wage is given, or in the real wage when the rate of profit is given, would appear to require *generalized* changes in labour productivity, such as only generalized technical progress (or regress, due, e.g. to exhaustion of natural resources) appears capable of bringing about.

The possible multiplicity of cost-minimizing techniques also means that the gravitation towards a cost-minimizing technique need not maximize the distributive variable determined residually. In Bidard's example above, the wage rate in terms of good 2 is maximized at C, i.e. by technique (3, 4), but if the economy settles at technique (1, 2) there is no incentive to move towards C. This result does not appear to question in any way the classical approach, which nowhere needs that the endogenous distributive variable be maximized. Furthermore the argument that pointed out the restricted scope of the indeterminacy implies that in all likelihood the distance of the residual variable from its maximized value is negligible in real economies.

Another difference between single production and general joint production is that in the latter case the discovery and introduction of a new, more convenient method does not necessarily raise the real wage. The reason can be grasped through an example. Consider an economy producing many commodities and suppose that joint production only concerns commodities 1 and 2; these are both non-basics, and there are two methods producing them, the first one, let us call it method I, produces commodity 1 and 2 jointly, while the second one, method II, produces only commodity 2. We can conceive method I as producing commodity 1 as main product and commodity 2 as a by-product, while method II is the 'main' method producing commodity 2. The rate of profits is given. Now suppose that a new method is discovered that produces only commodity 2, at a lower cost. This method is introduced in place of method II, and it causes a lowering of the price of commodity 2. One result is that the earnings of method 1 decrease, and in order for the rate of profits earned by this method to remain unchanged the price of commodity 1 must increase. Hence if the real wage rate is measured in terms of commodity 1, it decreases.

For still other differences from the single-production economy, see Piccioni (1997, p. 116).

10.11 · No Gravitation to a Definite Technique?

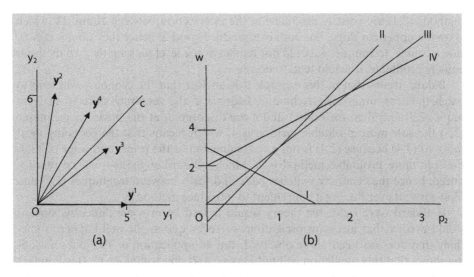

Fig. 10.15 Bidard's second example; no definite gravitation?

10.11 No Gravitation to a Definite Technique?

Will technical choice *converge* to some cost-minimizing technique, when at least one exists? It has been claimed that even this is not guaranteed. Bidard (1997, example 4, p. 692) has backed this claim with the example illustrated in the following table, of a two-goods economy with four methods, $r=1$, and equal quantities of the two commodities in the requirements for use. The techniques capable of satisfying the requirements for use, possibly overproducing one commodity, are (2), (3), (4), (1,2), (1,4), (2,3), (3,4). Let us look for cost-minimizing techniques utilizing ◘ Fig. 10.15b.

method	a_{1j}	a_{2j}	a_{Lj}		b_{1j}	b_{2j}	y_{1j}	y_{2j}	β_{1j}	β_{2j}
(1)	2	2	1	→	7	2	5	0	3	−2
(2)	2	2	1	→	3	8	1	6	−1	4
(3)	4	0	1	→	8	3	4	3	0	3
(4)	1	3	1	→	4	8	3	5	2	2

(2) overproduces good 2, hence p_2 tends to zero and all other methods become more profitable. (3) overproduces good 1, hence p_2 tends to grow, and then method 2 becomes more profitable. (4) too causes p_2 to tend to zero, which finally makes method 1 more profitable. (1,2) implies that p_2 and w are determined by the intersection of I and II, and then methods 3 and 4 are more profitable. (1,4) is on the upper envelope hence is cost minimizing. At the prices and wage of (2,3) method 4 is more profitable. At the prices and wage of (3,4) method 2 is more profitable. Hence the sole cost-minimizing technique is (1,4). (Note that the two

886   **Chapter 10** · Back to Long-Period Prices

methods (2,4) are equally profitable at the intersection between II and IV which is on the upper envelope, but both overproduce good 2; hence they do not constitute a 'stable' technique: p_2 could not remain at the level making the two methods equally profitable; it would tend to decrease.)

Bidard argues that in this example it is unclear that the economy will tend to reach the cost-minimizing technique, because if the economy starts with technique (2,3) and then methods 1 and 4 are discovered, at the prices of technique (2,3) the sole more profitable method is 4, which means that the economy must move to (3,4) because (2,4) is not a technique, but at the prices and wage of (3,4) the sole more profitable method is 2, which—Bidard suggests—will be reintroduced; hence the economy switches back and forth between techniques (2,3) and (3,4) without ever finding it convenient to introduce method 1.

If Bidard were right, the theory would indeed be in some difficulty, since it would predict that incessant oscillations of technique might well happen, something that does not seem to be observed. But an application of Piccioni's reasoning shows that this oscillation will not happen and that technique (1,4) will in fact be reached. If at the start the technique is (2,3) and method 4 is introduced, the effect is to overproduce good 2; hence p_2 decreases, and method 2 tends to disappear, but method 4 remains more profitable than method 3; therefore all firms tend to adopt it, and the overproduction of good 2 does not disappear, and p_2 continues to decrease towards zero. Technique (3,4) is not reached. If method 1 were not known, p_2 would go to zero, and the economy would settle at technique (4) with $p_2=0$; indeed, absent method 1, technique (4) would be the sole cost-minimizing technique. Since method 1 is available, p_2 decreases until IV intersects I, at which point the economy has reached technique (1,4), which is a 'stable' technique (as the reader can check). If on the other hand the economy starts with technique (3,4), then method 2 is more profitable, its introduction causes overproduction of good 2, and hence a decrease of p_2, which continues beyond the intersection of II and IV, and the end result is the same.[56]

Another implication of Piccioni's analysis deserves to be pointed out. Let us consider again the analysis illustrated by ◘ Fig. 10.13 but let us assume that now the methods and corresponding wage–price functions are as shown in ◘ Fig. 10.16. The technique initially adopted is (1,2), and, at the corresponding price and wage (p_2,w), method 3 yields extra profits and is introduced, but now method 3 is assumed to overproduce commodity 2 and therefore its introduction tends to cause a *fall* of p_2; it will be method 1 that will tend to be eliminated; but since both methods 2 and 3 overproduce commodity 2, we should expect the price of this commodity to fall to zero and the technique finally reached to consist of the sole method which is most profitable when $p_2=0$. But $p_2=0$ corresponds to a negative real wage (in terms of good 1) with either method. What happens in this case?

---

56 Schefold (1988, p. 205, 207) shows that another 2-goods example of oscillation back and forth between two techniques, produced by Salvadori (1985) in order to argue the possibility that no cost-minimizing technique exists, rests again on excluding the possibility of a technique consisting of only one method—the true cost-minimizing technique, to which in fact the economy would tend.

10.11 · No Gravitation to a Definite Technique?

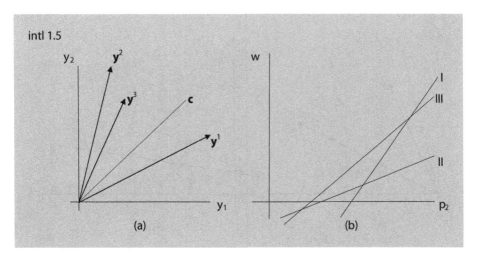

Fig. 10.16 Negative real wage?

This is still largely unexplored ground so we limit ourselves to some plausible observations. Clearly, we must introduce a lower limit to the real wage. The assumption of a given rate of profit is only acceptable as long as it does not contradict the fact that the real wage cannot fall below a historically determined minimum subsistence level. If there is a pressure on the real wage to decrease and in the course of its decrease the real wage reaches such a lower limit, then it is the real wage rate that must be treated as given, and the rate of profit becomes the residual variable. The analysis in successive stages, characteristic of the classical approach, enters then a second stage in which one asks what will plausibly happen with a given real wage. In the present example one can provisionally conclude, it would seem, that if (as, given our assumptions on the methods and on vector **c**, seems likely) the pressure on p_2 to decrease continues and p_2 becomes zero, then the technique will consist of the sole one, among methods 2 and 3, which yields the higher rate of profits when $p_2=0$ and the real wage rate is at its minimum (if we call r_j^o the rate of profit of method j when $p_2=0$ and the real wage rate is at its minimum, then which r_j^o will be higher is not deducible from Fig. 10.16).[57]

---

57 Suppose the lower limit of the real wage is below the wage rate associated with technique (1,2), but non-negative (even zero, if we interpret w as only the 'surplus part' of the real wage, the subsistence part being already included in the technical coefficients—an interpretation suggested by Sraffa 1960 pp. 9–10). When this lower limit is reached, method 3 is still the most convenient one, and our assumption as to the vector **c** of requirements for use implies that commodity 2 is still overproduced and therefore its price must be decreasing. The effect on the rate of profit can be derived from the assumption— in accord with our choice of commodity 1 as numéraire—that the minimum wage consists of z_1 units of commodity 1. Then $(1+r_j)(a_{1j}+a_{2j}p_2)+z_1=b_{1j}+b_{2j}p_2$. Then when $p_2=0$ it is $1+r_j=(b_{1j}-z_1)/a_{1j}$; and the numerator of $d(1+r)/dp_2$ is $(b_{2j}a_{1j}-b_{1j}a_{2j})+z_1a_{2j}$.

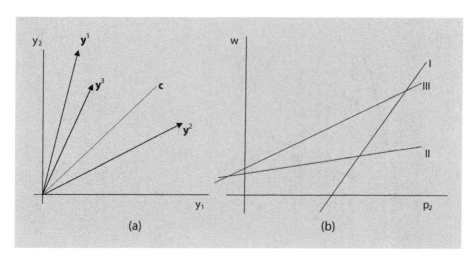

◘ **Fig. 10.17** A price goes to zero

Another possibility worth a brief mention is the case in which the gravitation is towards a technique formally associated with a negative price. In ◘ Fig. 10.17 if the initial technique is (1,2) the discovery and introduction of method 3 tends to cause an overproduction of commodity 2 and a decrease of p_2, but the overproduction can only be eliminated by technique (2,3), which would require a negative p_2. What will happen in this case is simply that p_2 goes to zero, and only method 3 is used. Indeed (3) is a cost-minimizing technique in this case.

In several of the examples discussed, a price has gone to zero, and it might be wondered whether this is a weakness of the theory, since in real economies prices are positive. The answer is no. First, in real economies many joint products do have a zero price: rubbish, for example, is a generic name for many joint products which have a zero price (and may even be a cause of disposal costs): sometimes part of them *is* used productively (e.g. the broken bricks and other rubbish of construction sites are sometimes used to fill holes in white roads), but they still have a zero price, because overproduced relative to the profitable uses. Second, in the above examples only a very restricted set of methods was assumed available; in real economies, the number of available methods is very high, and in many cases, when the price of a good decreases considerably, then previously unprofitable methods become convenient which absorb its excess production. For example domestic 'production' often finds ways to utilize oversupplied kinds of fish or meat or fruit when their prices become very low. One should also remember that methods are often found when they are looked for: research for innovations

---

If for example we assume that the minimum wage is zero because the subsistence wage is already included in the technical coefficients, then r rises or decreases with p_2 according as b_{2j}/a_{2j} is greater or smaller than b_{1j}/a_{1j}, and when $p_2 = 0$ then $r = b_{1j}/a_{1j}$. Let now $r°_j$ be the rate of profit with method j when $w = p_2 = 0$. The case assumed in ◘ Fig. 10.15 is compatible both with $r°_2 < r°_3$ and with $r°_2 > r°_3$.

10.11 · No Gravitation to a Definite Technique?

is directed towards targets, and it is seldom totally unproductive of innovations; a sharp decrease in the price, for example, of a raw material will generally stimulate research for new ways to utilize it.[58] In conclusion, the theory would appear to imply that it is unlikely that a jointly produced commodity with an initially positive price may become a free good because of technical innovations: the fall in price will be soon stopped by the convenience of introducing previously non-profitable, or newly discovered, methods utilizing the commodity. But even if the overproduction were to persist, the fall of the commodity's price to zero would not question the theory.

10.12 Extensive Rent

Now let us study the theory of differential rent in more general cases than the extremely simple one-good examples of ▶ Chap. 1, Sect. 1.5, and ▶ Chap. 3, Sect. 3.17, where, in land-using production, product and capital consisted of the same commodity.

Initially let us confine ourselves to a simple case of pure extensive rent, without joint production.[59] There are n produced commodities, and only the first one, corn, requires land to be produced. For each one of the other commodities only one production method is known. There are two types of land, A and B, and on each type only one method for the production of corn is known. We consider the effects of a gradual growth of the demand for corn. We assume that as long as a land is not fully utilized, competition brings the rent rate on it to zero.

Initially either A or B more than suffice to produce the quantity of corn demanded. Which land will be utilized? Rent is zero in either case, so costwise the two alternative methods on land A and on land B are just like methods that utilize no land, and the usual analysis of choice of technique applies. Having chosen a numéraire, we can derive the two decreasing $w(r)$ curves corresponding to the techniques differing in the sole corn method; as shown in ▶ Chap. 2 the tendency to adopt the cost-minimizing method will bring the economy onto the outer $w(r)$ curve, and this will decide which land is utilized.

Now assume there are three types of land, A, B and C, and A is utilized first; the demand for corn rises to a level such that A no longer suffices to satisfy it, and the rise in the price of corn allows a rent to be asked for utilization of land A. Formally, with corn as the numéraire, this has the same effect as a decrease

---

58 We have quoted Marshall to such an effect in ▶ Sect. 10.1; Kurz (1986, p. 6) writes that this is precisely the perspective of several classical authors, according to whom 'the overproduction of certain products triggers off the search for alternative ways to use or to produce the products', so that the overproduction is only temporary.

59 Actually, production with land can be seen as an instance of joint production too, the special instance of production with a durable capital (land) that is eternal and of constant efficiency and therefore reappears among the outputs identical to (and with the same price as) itself as an input. Cf. the next footnote. The price of land is the capitalized value of its rent according to the usual capitalization formula for endless revenue streams, that is, rent divided by rate of interest.

in the amount of output per unit of land A, that is, as a proportional increase of all technical coefficients; the $w(r)$ curve associated with land A shifts inwards. The $w(r)$ curves associated with B and C are unaffected, and the one of these two curves which is outermost for the given level of w (if it is the real wage that is given) or of r (if it is the rate of profit that is given) is the one that is utilized; suppose it is land B; the rate of rent on land A rises until its wage curve, shifting inwards, comes to yield the same r if w is given as on land B (or the same w if r is given). The same reasoning holds for successive lands. Thus the order in which lands are put to use, the *order of utilization, or of profitability,* can be gauged from the drawing of all $w(r)$ curves without rent, and it corresponds to the decreasing order of the rates of profit associated with the given real wage rate, or the decreasing order of the real wage rates associated with the given rate of profit. If these no-rent $w(r)$ curves intersect, the order of profitability changes with changes in the level of the distributive variable taken as given.

In Ricardo the order of utilization of lands is independent of the real wage rate, because capital is treated as if consisting entirely of advanced wages, and then the no-rent $w(r)$ curves do not cross (prove it!). The same would be the case if a lower-quality land always required more of *all* inputs per unit of output. But with multiple inputs there is no reason why it should be so, and then the order of utilization can depend on the real wage rate.

The order of utilization or of profitability must be distinguished from the *order of rentability*, or of rent per acre. Ricardo implicitly assumes that all land requires the same amount of labour (and hence of capital advances) per acre, so a higher (gross or net) product per unit of corn capital also means a higher product per acre, and also (the real wage being given) a higher rate of profits in the absence of rent; the order of profitability then coincides with the order of rentability. The simple numerical example with three lands in ▶ Chap. 1, Sect. 1.5.1, shows that the two orders need not coincide when a land, which is less productive that another per unit of corn-capital, is more productive per unit of land. A still different order is the *order of fertility*, which can be defined on the basis of the gross, or of the net, or (once the real wage is given) of the surplus product per acre; in Ricardo it coincides with the other two orders however it is defined, but in the general case it does not, and the precise definition (plus whether wages are advanced or paid post factum) can make a difference.[60]

■■ Exercise

Show with a simple numerical example that the order of rentability can depend on the real wage. (Hint: use the example of extensive differential rent of ▶ Chap. 1 with three lands and make assumptions about how capital is composed of seed-corn and of advanced wages such as to cause the total wage bill per acre to rise faster on one land that on another land when the wage rate rises.)

---

60 I disagree with Kurz and Salvadori's (1995, p. 287) use of the term 'order of fertility' to mean order of profitability; 'fertility' traditionally has a quantitative connotation independent of exchange values (a more fertile land produces a more abundant harvest).

10.12 · Extensive Rent

The above picture implies that with extensive differential rent, except during the transitional period when the last land becomes fully used but no further land has started being utilized yet, there is always a land which is only partly utilized and where therefore rent is zero. Small variations in the demand for corn will not cause a change in the lands in use, there will be only a change in the utilized fraction of the no-rent land. When the no-rent land becomes fully utilized and it becomes necessary to cultivate an inferior land that becomes the new no-rent land, for a given real wage the rate of profit decreases, as Ricardo argued.[61]

The possible dependence of the order of utilization on the level of the given distributive variable means that, if we are told which lands are *at least partially* in use but we are not told which lands are *fully* used, then in order to discover the no-rent land, or *'marginal' land*, we should determine the order of profitability and thus discover the least profitable land. In the case of n commodities of which only one, corn, uses land, this can be avoided by writing down as many price equations as commodities other than corn, plus as many corn price equations as lands in use for the production of corn, with these latter equations including among the costs a different unknown rate of rent for each land, plus a final equation imposing that at least one of the rent rates must be zero. With k different lands in at least partial use, one has $n-1+k+1=n+k$ price equations, in $n+k+2$ variables: the n product prices, the k rates of rent, w, r. The choice of a numéraire adds one equation (e.g. $\mathbf{pv}=1$ with $\mathbf{v}$ a semipositive vector of commodities), so there remains the usual degree of freedom, to be 'closed' by taking the real wage, or r, as given. Let us list these equations.

Apart from the fact that I write the conditions of production in terms of technical coefficients and not, like Sraffa, in terms of total quantities employed with each method, the equations below are Sraffa's. Let λ_j^s be the surface of land of type s needed to produce one unit of commodity j, and let β_s be the rate of rent per unit of land of type s; let a_{ij}^s, a_{Lj}^s stand respectively for the technical coefficient of input i, and of labour, in the production of commodity j on land of type s. Corn, commodity 1, is the numéraire and is the sole commodity requiring land; it is produced on k different lands; wages and rents are paid post factum. The rates of rent are assumed non-negative; also, all no-rent $w(r)$ curves are assumed to yield a positive r for the given w (and vice versa, of course). The $n+k+1$ equations are[62]:

---

61 Marx argued against Ricardo that new lands brought into cultivation are not necessarily worse lands, they may have been left uncultivated for various reasons (e.g. for lack of a road, then built by public intervention; or because of a need for preliminary investments e.g. a canal for irrigation, or deforestation) and when brought into cultivation they may come out to be better than other already cultivated lands. This is fully acceptable, and it can imply that in some historical cases the extension of agricultural production need not have caused a reduction of the rate of profit (or of the real wage) even in the absence of technical progress.

62 Notice that the first k equations could also be written in harmony with the interpretation of production with land as a special case of joint production, suggested in the previous footnote. For example let T_1 be the price of land 1; the first equation can be rewritten $(1+r)\left(a_{11}^1 p_1 + a_{21}^1 p_2 + \ldots + a_{n1}^1 p_n\right) + wa_{L1}^1 + (1+r)T_1\lambda_1^1 = p_1 + T_1\lambda_1^1$, which coincides with the equation in the text because $T_1 = \beta_1/r$ by capitalization.

892   Chapter 10 · Back to Long-Period Prices

$$p_1 = (1+r)\left(a_{11}^1 p_1 + a_{21}^1 p_2 + \ldots + a_{n1}^1 p_n\right) + wa_L{}_1^1 + \beta_1 \lambda_1^1$$
$$p_1 = (1+r)\left(a_{11}^2 p_1 + a_{21}^2 p_2 + \ldots + a_{n1}^2 p_n\right) + wa_L{}_1^2 + \beta_2 \lambda_1^2$$
$$\ldots\ldots\ldots\ldots\ldots\ldots\ldots\ldots\ldots\ldots\ldots\ldots\ldots\ldots\ldots\ldots\ldots\ldots\ldots\ldots\ldots$$
$$p_1 = (1+r)\left(a_{11}^1 p_1 + a_{21}^1 p_2 + \ldots + a_{n1}^1 p_n\right) + wa_L{}_1^k + \beta_k \lambda_1^k$$
$$p_2 = (1+r)(a_{12}p_1 + a_{22}p_2 + \ldots + a_{n2}p_n) + wa_{L2}$$
$$\quad (10.25)$$
$$\ldots\ldots\ldots\ldots\ldots\ldots\ldots\ldots\ldots\ldots\ldots\ldots\ldots\ldots\ldots\ldots\ldots\ldots\ldots\ldots\ldots$$
$$p_n = (1+r)(a_{1n}p_1 + a_{2n}p_2 + \ldots + a_{nn}p_n) + wa_{Ln}$$
$$p_1 = 1$$
$$b_1 \cdot b_2 \cdot \ldots \cdot b_k = 0$$

The last equation establishes that at least one rate of rent is zero. More than one rate of rent *might* be zero: it would mean that, by a fluke, two lands yield zero-rent $w(r)$ curves that cross at exactly the given w or given r; then producing corn on either land is equally profitable, and it suffices that one of the two lands is not fully utilized for both rates of rent to be zero: if on the fully utilized land a positive rent arose, capitalists would move to the zero-rent land and the first land would become underutilized. If w, or r, is given, there are as many equations as variables to be determined. That the solution of the system is economically acceptable can be verified by viewing it as resulting from the following iterative process.

■■ Proof of existence of economically acceptable solution

Set one rate of rent, say β_1, as equal to zero and neglect the other land-using equations: you obtain a system of n price equations identical to the one studied in ▶ Chap. 2; assuming viability, you obtain (as long as the given distributive variable is not too high) positive prices and a non-negative value of the residual distributive variable. Now you can determine the rates of rent that satisfy the other k-1 corn price equations on the basis of w, $\mathbf{p}$, r thus determined. If one of these rates, say β_2, comes out negative, repeat the procedure replacing $\beta_1 = 0$ with $\beta_2 = 0$, which means moving to a 'lower' $w(r)$ curve (that is, lower for the given value of the exogenous distributive variable). Repeat the procedure until you reach a rent rate β_s at which no other rent rate is negative: the 'lowest' $w(r)$ curve has been reached, to which the (if unique) no-rent land corresponds; all prices are positive, and (apart from the fluke of coexistence of two no-rent lands) all other rent rates are positive. Such a rent rate $\beta_s = 0$ exists and will be reached, because a 'lowest' $w(r)$ curve exists and at each replacement of a zero rent rate with a negative one, one moves to a 'lower' $w(r)$ curve. ■

Once the no-rent land is ascertained, the other price equations with land are superfluous for the determination of relative prices and of w (if r is given) or of r (if w is given); their sole role is to determine the rates of rent on the respective lands. A tax levied on some of these rent-yielding lands, as long as rent suffices to pay it, does not alter relative prices nor income distribution between wages and profits.

The above proof assumes that the lands in (at least partial) use are already known, they do not consider the problem of choice of which lands to put to use. This is what Sraffa assumes, as part of his resumption of a classical method that starts from the *observed* situation. If what is known is, on the contrary, the quan-

10.12 · Extensive Rent

tity of corn to be produced (for example, in order to inquire into the effect of future increases in the demand for corn), then which lands will be used is part of the problem, but the order of utilization or profitability is univocally determined, it depends only on the technical coefficients on each land, then one assumes that lands are fully utilized in that order until with the last land production becomes greater than the quantity to be produced, this last land will be only partly utilized and will have rent zero. Let us number lands in order of utilization, and let the marginal land be the k-th land; then we can directly put $\beta_k = 0$ and, assuming that r is given, the first $k-1$ equations become irrelevant for the determination of w and of prices; the other equations can be solved first, and then in the first $k-1$ equations with land the sole variables to be determined are the rates of rent. (The lands beyond the marginal one in the order of utilization would yield negative rates of rent and obviously are not utilized, so their price equations need not be considered.) [63]

The classical view, that as corn production is extended to previously unutilized lands the price of corn rises relative to that of other goods, and r decreases, is confirmed. It suffices to reverse the result indicated at the end of ▶ Sect. 2.11 that a more convenient method appearing in industry j reduces the price of good j relative to all other commodity prices: the passage to the next no-rent land, say land C, replaces the production method on the previous no-rent land B with a method which at the previous r was capable of yielding that r only by imputing a negative rate of rent to land C; with this negative rate of rent, the method on B and the one on C are equiprofitable, the price equations would determine the previous r with either method for corn production; the rise of rent to zero on land C is like a loss of efficiency, that is, like having to adopt an inferior method for the production of corn.

We can see further aspects of the issue by examining the form of the relationship between r and w when rent is present. To such an end let us suppose two lands A and B whose corresponding zero-rent $w(r)$ curves (with wage measured in any commodity) are depicted in ◼ Fig. 10.18 as respectively blue, and broken red. For simplicity they are assumed to cross only once. Let us take r as given. (This example is from Mainwaring, 1984, pp. 146–8.). If initially A alone or B alone more than suffices to produce the required quantity of corn, then rents are zero and the relationship between r and w is the outer envelope of the two $w(r)$ curves, i.e. is the curve JKR_B. For $0 \leq r < r_2$ land A is preferred, for $r_2 < r \leq R_B$ land B is preferred; for $r = r_2$ both lands can be in use.

Let us now suppose $r \neq r_2$ and that demand for corn grows until the land in use becomes insufficient. If $r < r_2$ the land initially in use was A, and as B starts being used β_A becomes positive but $\beta_B = 0$ so w is determined by $w_B(r)$; if $r > r_2$ it was B that was initially in use, as A starts being used β_B becomes positive but $\beta_A = 0$ so w is determined by $w_A(r)$. If it is exactly $r = r_2$, rent is zero on both lands and it stays at zero as long as at least one of them is not fully utilized. The relationship between r and w is given by the curve HKR_A.

---

63 For a more complete formalization, including non-negativity constraints etc., the interested reader can consult Kurz and Salvadori (1995, pp. 280–85).

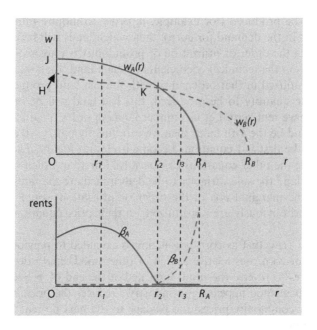

Fig. 10.18 Relationship between w and r with a switch in rent-yielding land

The lower diagram in Fig. 10.18 shows what happens to the rates of rent: β_A (blue curve) is positive to the left of r_2, β_B (red curve) to the right. As r rises the qualitative behaviour of the rates of rent (when positive) in the lower diagram derives from whether, in the upper diagram, the vertical distance between the two $w(r)$ curves increases or decreases (make sure you understand why).

So far we have taken r as given and compared situations where corn demand differs. Now let us ask what happens if corn demand is given and r changes.

If r does not pass from one side to the other side of r_2, the existence or absence of rent on each land is not disturbed, and w moves along the corresponding section of the JKR_B curve if there was no rent to start with, and along the corresponding section of the HKR_A curve if there is rent.

If r passes from one side of r_2 to the other side, we must also know whether A alone or B alone suffices to produce the required quantity of corn. If both A and B are more than sufficient, then there is no rent before and after the change of r. If A is more than sufficient while B is not, then if r rises from less to more than r_2, e.g. from r_1 to r_3 in Fig. 10.18, before the change rents were both zero; after the change land B is more convenient, corn production is gradually transferred on it until B becomes fully utilized, then β_B becomes positive while land A (partially utilized) earns no rent; a passage of r from r_3 to r_1 on the contrary causes β_B, initially positive, to go to zero. The relationship between r and w is the curve JKR_A, and in the lower diagram both rents are zero for $0 < r \leq r_2$, while for $R_A \geq r > r_2$ rents are as shown in the lower diagram. Analogous behaviour, with the two lands in inverted roles, if B is more than sufficient while A is not. If neither land alone is sufficient, and demand does not exceed the maximum production obtainable by fully using both lands, then there is always rent on only one land, the passage of r from one side to the other side of r_2 changes the no-rent land, the relevant curve in the upper diagram is HKR_A, and rents behave as described in the lower diagram.

The above shows that, given the amount of corn to be produced, the existence itself of rent in an economy can depend on the level of r. It also shows that, as r rises, the overall amount of rents can increase, decrease, or alternate increasing and decreasing behaviour: in the last case illustrated (neither land alone sufficient), as r rises from zero the total amount of rents first rises, then decreases, becoming zero for $r=r_2$, then rises again. Significant changes in income distribution can cause rents to change a lot, and in unexpected ways.

Some final considerations on extensive rent: First, the existence of extensive differential rent alone (without joint production) does not disturb the inverse relationship between real wage rate and rate of profit when the amount of corn to be produced is given: as r rises the relevant 'envelope' w(r) curve is composed of a series of portions of w(r) curves, all of them decreasing.

Second, we have assumed so far that only one method is known for each non-land-using commodity and for each type of land. We could introduce choice of techniques for the commodities that do not utilize land, but it would not add much to the theory. Suppose the real wage rate is given; the sole difference would be that in order to determine the order of utilization of lands, for each land treated as no-rent land one would have to determine the no-rent w(r) curve (in fact, an envelope) by finding the most convenient methods for the non-land-using commodities for each level of the distributive variable treated as given. On the contrary, admitting that more than one method is known for the production of corn on some land changes the theory radically, because it becomes possible to use one method on part of the surface of that land and another method on the remaining surface, but then we have *intensive* differential rent, to be discussed later. Pure extensive differential rent requires that only one method is *used* for each type of land, and one cannot be certain that it will be so unless only one method is *known* for each type of land.

Third, it is possible that the quantity of corn to be produced is such that it requires the utilization of lands so little productive that for the given real wage rate the rate of profit becomes negative. This is not a weakness of the theory: it only means that the assumptions made are economically incompatible; in the real economy, either the real wage rate will have to decrease, or the quantity of corn produced will not rise to that amount (people will find other ways to satisfy their nutritional needs).

10.13 Intensive Rent

Coming to intensive rent, we meet a problem. It was shown in ▶ Chap. 1, Sect. 1.5, that in the presence of intensive rent it is possible to derive a method that pays no rent, the 'differential' method, which has formally the same role in the determination of prices and profit rate as 'marginal' land in the presence of extensive rent. But when there is more than one input, the input vector of the

896   **Chapter 10 · Back to Long-Period Prices**

'differential' method, being the difference between two non-negative vectors, can contain negative elements. Then the square matrix of technical coefficients that uses the 'differential' method for the corn industry is no longer non-negative and the Perron–Frobenius theorem no longer applies. Even the labour coefficient of the 'differential' method might be negative. Then, will prices be positive?

I maintain things simple by assuming again single production, only one method known for each non-land-using commodity, and that only commodity 1, corn, requires land for its production. Now there is only one type of land, fully utilized, and two different methods, call them α and ε, are employed on it. The rate of rent per acre is β. The condition of equal profitability of the two methods is

$$
\begin{aligned}
p_1 &= (1+r)(a_{11}^\alpha p_1 + a_{21}^\alpha p_2 + \ldots + a_{n1}^\alpha p_n) + w a_L{}_1^\alpha + \beta \lambda_1^\alpha \\
p_1 &= (1+r)(a_{11}^\varepsilon p_1 + a_{21}^\varepsilon p_2 + \ldots + a_{n1}^\varepsilon p_n) + w a_L{}_1^\varepsilon + \beta \lambda_1^\varepsilon.
\end{aligned}
\tag{10.26}
$$

To these one must of course add one price equation for each one of the $n-1$ non-land-using commodities, and a numéraire equation, in all $n+2$ equations for $n+3$ variables: n product prices, β, w, r; there is the usual degree of freedom. For this simple case we can prove without difficulty that if r is given at the level r^*, if prices and the wage rate are positive with either method when $\beta=0$, and if $\beta^* \geq 0$ exists which, at the given r^*, renders the two methods equally profitable for $w \geq 0$, then prices at r^* are all positive.

▪▪ Proof

For $\beta=0$ we can determine, in the same way as in the absence of land, relative prices and real wage rate for either of the two techniques differing only in the method, α or ε, used for the production of corn. If the two techniques yield the same prices and wage rate, the two methods are equally profitable and the proof ends here. If the two techniques yield a different wage rate, then let $(\mathbf{A}_\alpha, \mathbf{a}_{L\alpha})$ be technique α. The system of price equations without rent $\mathbf{p}_\alpha = (1+r^*)\mathbf{p}_\alpha \mathbf{A}_\alpha + w_\alpha \mathbf{a}_{L\alpha}$ yields positive prices and wage rate. Choose corn as numéraire. To introduce a positive β and therefore an additional cost $\beta \lambda_1^\alpha$ in the first of these price equations is equivalent to increasing the technical coefficient of corn of method α to $a_{11}^\alpha + \beta \lambda_1^\alpha/(1+r*)$. By Perron–Frobenius, this decreases the maximum rate of growth associated with matrix $\mathbf{A}_\alpha$ and shifts the entire $w_\alpha(r)$ curve closer to the origin, but as long as $w_\alpha(r^*,\beta)$ remains non-negative, $\mathbf{p}_\alpha$ remains positive. The same argument holds for $(\mathbf{A}_\varepsilon, \mathbf{a}_{L\varepsilon})$ and $\mathbf{p}_\varepsilon = (1+r^*)\mathbf{p}_\varepsilon \mathbf{A}_\varepsilon + w_\varepsilon \mathbf{a}_{L\varepsilon}$. If the two methods are equally profitable for $\beta=\beta^*>0$ we have two techniques differing in only one method and equally profitable, and the theory of technical choice tells us that if $w_\alpha(r^*, \beta^*) = w_\varepsilon(r^*, \beta^*) = w(r^*, \beta^*) \geq 0$ then $\mathbf{p}_\alpha = \mathbf{p}_\varepsilon > 0$, thus the two methods can co-exist and prices are positive. ▪

When corn is the sole input, and two methods co-exist on the land that produces corn at the rent rate β^*, the one of the two methods that becomes more profitable if β decreases is the less fertile one; that is, the method which is more profitable at $\beta=0$ would not suffice alone to satisfy the demand for corn. This is no longer necessarily true in the general case.

10.13 · Intensive Rent

We can show it through the following numerical example due to D'Agata (1983). There are three commodities, only the third one of which, corn, requires land for its production; there is only one type of land and three methods A, B and C, are known to produce corn; only one method is known to produce commodities 1 and 2. The technical coefficients are shown in the following table. The economy is stationary and consumption demand is given in fixed quantities, 90 units of commodity 1, 60 units of commodity 2, and 19 units of corn. There are 100 units of land.

Method	Input 1	Input 2	Input 3 (corn)	Labour	Land		Output 1	Output 2	Output 3 (corn)
(1)	0	0	0.1	1	0	→	1	0	0
(2)	0	0	0.6	1	0	→	0	1	0
(3A)	0.1	0.4	0.1	1	1	→	0	0	1
(3B)	0.1	0.1	0.3	2.2	1	→	0	0	1
(3C)	0.1	0.1	0.4	1	1	→	0	0	1

We choose corn as numéraire, $p_3 = 1$. The price equations are:

$$p_1 = 0.1(1+r) + w$$
$$p_2 = 0.6(1+r) + w$$
$$1 = (1+r)(0.1p_1 + 0.4p_2 + 0.1) + w + \beta_A \qquad (10.27)$$
$$1 = (1+r)(0.1p_1 + 0.1p_2 + 0.3) + 2.2w + \beta_B$$
$$1 = (1+r)(0.1p_1 + 0.1p_2 + 0.4) + w + \beta_C.$$

Of the last three equations, only two can hold simultaneously.

By substituting in the last three equations the expressions for p_1 and p_2 given by the right-hand sides of the first two equations, we obtain for each alternative corn method a relationship between w, r and β, which becomes a decreasing linear relationship between w and β if r is taken as given:

$$w_A = [1 - \beta_A - 0.25(1+r)^2 - 0.1(1+r)]/[0.5(1+r) + 1]$$
$$w_B = [1 - \beta_B - 0.07(1+r)^2 - 0.3(1+r)]/[0.2(1+r) + 2.2]$$
$$w_C = [1 - \beta_C - 0.07(1+r)^2 - 0.4(1+r)]/[0.2(1+r) + 1].$$

Let us take r as given. We can calculate the values of w_A, w_B and w_C corresponding to $\beta = 0$, and the values of β_A, β_B, β_C corresponding to $w = 0$, for the given r; this gives us the intercepts of these linear relationships in a diagram with w in abscissa and β in ordinate. A line $\beta(w)$ above another means that the method yielding the first line can pay a higher wage for the same rent rate (or yields extra profit if it pays the same rent and wage) and therefore is more profitable. The intersections indicate that two methods are equally profitable.

Let us assume $r = 50\%$. The reader is invited to check that for $\beta = 0$ it is $w_A \cong 0.164$, $w_B \cong 0.157$, $w_C \cong 0.186$, while for $w = 0$ it is $\beta_A \cong 0.287$, $\beta_B \cong 0.392$, $\beta_C \cong 0.242$. The diagram is represented in ◗ Fig. 10.19. There are three intersec-

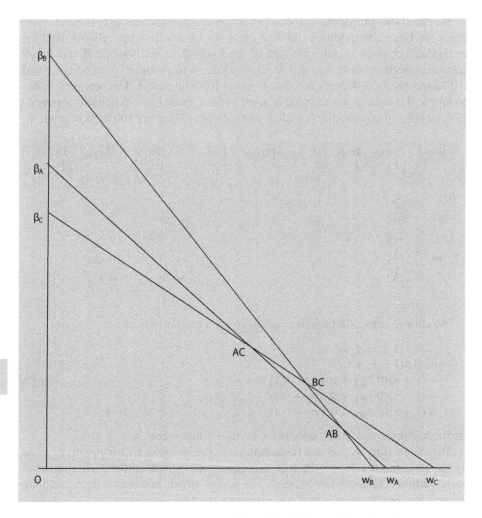

◘ Fig. 10.19 D'Agata's example. (The scale in abscissa is double the scale in ordinate.)

tions, labelled AB, BC, AC. To show that the order of profitability as rent rises does not coincide with the order of fertility (net corn product per acre), let us initially assume that method C is not available. Then for $\beta=0$ method A is the more convenient one; as rent rises, beyond point AB method B becomes more convenient. But method B is less fertile than A, its net product of corn per acre is 0.7 while that of method A is 0.9. Contrary to the simple examples of ▶ Chaps. 1 and 3 which were the foundation of the marginal approach, here the rise in the rent of land does *not* render relatively more profitable the method which uses less land per unit of net product of corn; the opposite is the case. This confirms what we have learnt from reswitching: in the presence of heterogeneous capital and of a positive rate of profit, technical choice does not behave in the way postulated by the marginalist/neoclassical approach.

10.13 · Intensive Rent

But the example has more to teach us, it is diabolical. Method A suffices alone to satisfy the net demand for corn, because if employed on the entire land it produces 100 units while consuming 10 units of corn; in order to satisfy consumption demands the gross productions of the other goods must be 100 units of commodity 1 (because 10 units are needed by corn production) and 100 units of commodity 2 (for the same reason), which implies the utilization of 70 units of corn, so the net product of corn is 20, greater than the consumption demand. (We are taking as given the demands for the three products as *net* products.)

Thus if A is initially used, land is not fully employed and rent is zero; unless for some strange reason rent were to arise and rise above the level corresponding to point AB, A will remain the sole method utilized. If, as assumed so far, only A and B are available, the peculiarity of the technical choice between A and B as rent rises does not cause strange phenomena. But it does, if we now admit that method C is discovered. If initially A is used and $\beta=0$, method C is more convenient and agricultural capitalists pass to it. But the adoption of C reduces the net product of corn; even when C is employed on the entire land, net corn production is insufficient: the gross production of corn is 100, of which 40 are required by C; the gross production of commodity 1 must be 100, that of commodity 2 must be 70, so the first two industries absorb 52 units of corn, and the net product of corn is only 8. Therefore rent arises and rises until we reach point BC where B and C can co-exist. But the use of B does not permit to produce enough corn either. B, used on the entire land, produces 100 and uses 30 units of corn; the needed gross products of the other two commodities are the same as with C, so the net product of corn is 18. Hence the combined use of C and B can only yield a net product of corn intermediate between 8 and 18: insufficient. Method A is the sole one which overproduces corn if used on the entire land; hence the combined use of A and B, or of A and C, would be capable of satisfying the demand for corn while employing land fully and thus determining positive values for w and β; but at both couples (w, β) corresponding to these two possibilities (points AB and AC) the method not in use is more profitable, so the economy cannot stop at either of these points.[64] In this example the given r, the rigid consumption demands, the assumption that the rate of rent rises (with w adapting passively) as long as the net demand for corn is greater than the net supply, plus the assumption that more profitable methods are preferred to less profitable ones, imply that *no cost-minimizing solution exists to the problem of satisfying the given demand for corn* (and this, in spite of the fact that a method exists that might satisfy it!): method A, even if initially adopted, is then discarded and never readopted, rent continues to rise, the economy tends to use the sole method B, so rent does not stop rising and the conclusion should be that w goes to zero. Of course in a real economy this would not happen, the given r loses credibility if the real wage becomes too low, but a rate of profit tending to become zero because

---

64   If method B were not available, the economy would unproblematically converge to J.

900 Chapter 10 · Back to Long-Period Prices

the real wage cannot decrease below a given lower bound is just as unlikely; the rise in the relative price of corn would soon prompt the recourse to alternative ways to satisfy the needs for which corn was demanded (that is, the composition of demand cannot be assumed rigid if this brings to implausible results), and most probably there would also be recourse to public intervention. (As in the case of public intervention that destroys part of an excessive harvest of a perishable agricultural product that would otherwise make its price so low as to cause a wave of bankruptcies among agricultural firms, one must be ready to accept the likelihood of public intervention in other cases too where the spontaneous working of markets would produce malfunctioning.) The implications of possibilities like the one highlighted by D'Agata have not been much discussed so far, the issue is waiting for further study.

Another peculiarity of intensive rent when compared with extensive rent is that the rate of profits and the real wage rate can move in the same direction: it can happen that a rise in the rate of profits causes such a decrease of rent as to leave room for an increase of the real wage rate. In order to show it, it suffices to consider a very simple example where corn is the only product. Suppose that corn is produced by seed-corn and labour on a single fully employed land with two methods, A and B, and that the methods *per acre* are:

A: $\quad$ 4 corn * 1 labour $\quad$ * 1 acre of land $\rightarrow$ 9 corn

B: $\quad$ 2 corn * 10 labour $\quad$ * 1 acre of land $\rightarrow$ 18 corn

(If the real wage were advanced, and equal to 1, this would be the first example of intensive rent in ▶ Chap. 1.) The 'differential method' per acre, B–A, has positive labour input but negative seed-corn input; assuming wages paid post factum, for it the zero extra profit equation is $-(1+r)2+9w=9$; hence $w=1+2(1+r)/9$: as r rises the rate of rent decreases considerably and allows w to rise; for $r=0$ it is $w=44/36$, $\beta=136/36$; for $r=25\%$ it is $w=45/36$ and $\beta=117/36$. In order for a rise of r to cause a decrease of w in this corn economy, the process introduced second (B in our example) must employ both more labour and more capital per unit of land (which is what Ricardo assumed, because of his view of advanced agricultural capital as consisting essentially of advanced wages).

A graphical representation (Mainwaring 1984, p. 158) shows that an indeterminacy can arise, if what is given is the real wage rate rather than r. Call the two methods in use α and ε. If at $\beta=0$ the two techniques obtained by including only one of the two corn methods do not yield the same real wage rate for a given r, from the analysis of choice of techniques we know that the corn method associated with the higher real wage is the more profitable one at the prices of either technique and so it is adopted. Suppose it is α, which does not suffice alone to satisfy the demand for corn, while methods α and ε together do. This implies that ε alone, if used on the entire land, would overproduce corn. Then there is a problem of choice of techniques in the following sense: the economy can satisfy the demand for corn by using both methods and paying a rent β which renders the two methods equally profitable, or by using only method ε on part of the land and paying a zero rent. But if rent is zero, by assumption α is more profitable, so it is preferred, then demand for land becomes greater than supply, giving rise to

10.13 · Intensive Rent

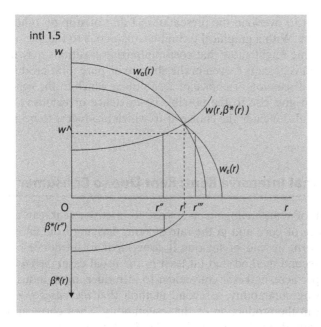

■ **Fig. 10.20** Two possible choices of technique with intensive rent when the wage rate $w_{\beta*}(r)$ increases with r, and what is given is the wage rate

a positive rent. Hence either a level $\beta > 0$ associated with a nonzero w exists that renders the two methods equally profitable, or rent rises up to its highest acceptable limit without method ε being adopted, and the considerations become relevant which were presented at the end of the discussion of D'Agata's example. However, the method more convenient at $\beta = 0$ may change as r changes.

Let us then represent in the same (r, w) diagram three $w(r)$ curves with the real wage rate in terms of corn, see the upper diagram in ■ Fig. 10.20: $w_\alpha(r)$, the real wage if corn were produced only with method α and the rent rate β were zero; $w_\varepsilon(r)$, the same with method ε in place of α; and $w(r, \beta^*(r))$, the real wage if both methods are used and the rent rate β renders the two methods equally profitable: let us indicate this rent rate as $\beta^*(r)$; it is not necessarily positive. We have seen that as long as $\beta > 0$ it is both $w(r, \beta^*(r)) < w_\alpha(r)$ and $w(r, \beta^*(r)) < w_\varepsilon(r)$, and that, while $w_\alpha(r)$ and $w_\varepsilon(r)$ are necessarily decreasing functions of r, $w(r, \beta^*(r))$ can be an increasing function of r. Let us suppose that this latter is the case; that $w_\alpha(0) > w_\varepsilon(0)$ and $\beta^*(0) > 0$; that at r' it is $w_\alpha(r') = w_\varepsilon(r')$, which implies that they are also equal to $w(r', \beta^*(r'))$ and that $\beta^*(r') = 0$; and that for $r > r'$ the more convenient method for $\beta = 0$ is ε (while $\beta^*(r)$ is negative). If what is given is $r > r'$, there is no problem; but if what is given is $w < w(r')$, there may be two possible choices of technique: in ■ Fig. 10.20 if the real wage rate is fixed at $w^\wedge$, the economy can use method ε alone and obtain $r = r'''$ and zero rent, or use both corn methods and obtain $r = r''$ and a rent $\beta^*(r'')$. In either situation there is no incentive to abandon it, so which one is established depends on the past history of the economy.

902 Chapter 10 · Back to Long-Period Prices

In order not to overload the presentation I do not stop on other peculiarities of intensive rent. With a graphical technique analogous to the one used for D'Agata's example one might show that cost-minimizing positions may not be unique even when what is given is r, even in the absence of pure joint production.[65] I also leave aside the discussion of choice of techniques, which in the general case with many lands can give rise to the possible co-existence of extensive and intensive rent, and must also include the choice as to which product is to be grown on each quality of land.

10.14 External Intensive Rent; Rent Due to Consumer Demand

Another form of rent, analogous in a sense to intensive rent, can arise when the rise in the price of corn and in the rate of rent, deriving from an increase in the demand for corn, instead of making it convenient to introduce on part of the same land a second method that (at least in the usual case) *increases the production* of corn per acre, makes it convenient to introduce, in an industry producing some corn-using commodity, a second method that *decreases the utilization* of corn as input in the production of that commodity. Then corn can be produced by a single method on the fully utilized land, while a corn-using commodity is produced by two different methods, one of which uses less corn per unit of product than the other one. This form of rent has been called '*external intensive rent*' because it is again due to the limited availability of a fully utilized land but it arises from the co-existence of two methods in another industry. We can give the basic intuition by having recourse again to a simple example. Suppose that corn (commodity 1) is produced by corn, labour and land, and is used together with labour to produce bread (commodity 2); bread can be produced with two methods A and B, the second one using less per unit of bread that the first one. Corn is the numéraire. The technical coefficients are as in the table below.

Method	Input 1	Input 2	Labour	Land		Output 1	Output 2
(1)	0.2	0	1	1	→	1	0
(2A)	2	0	1	0	→	0	1
(2B)	1	0	4	0	→	0	1

The price equations are three in the four variables r, w, β, p_2:

$$0.2(1 + r) + w + \beta = 1 \tag{10.28}$$

$$\text{(A)} \quad 2(1 + r) + w = p_2 \tag{10.29}$$

---

65 Examples illustrating these possibilities are supplied in the exercises to Ch. 10 in Kurz and Salvadori (1995), and in D'Agata (1983).

10.14 · External Intensive Rent; Rent Due to Consumer Demand

(B) $(1 + r) + 4w = p_2.$ (10.30)

If r is given at the level $r = 50\%$, then $w = 0.5$ and $\beta = 0.2$ render the two methods A and B equally profitable ($p_2 = 3.5$); when $\beta < 0.2$ (and $w > 0.5$), method B is less profitable than method A. The process making A and B equally profitable and at the same time establishing β may be clearer if we take both r and the *nominal* wage as fixed and treat the nominal price of corn p_1 as variable. A rise in the demand for corn, by raising p_1, also raises β as shown by the price equation for corn (10.28) written as

$$0.2(1 + r)p_1 + w + \beta = p_1;$$

if both r and w are given and p_1 rises, the left-hand side increases by a smaller percentage than the right-hand side unless β increases. In Eq. (2A) rewritten as $2(1 + r)p_1 + w = p_2$, the rise of p_1 causes the left-hand side to rise by a greater percentage than in Eq. (2B) rewritten in the same way, making method B more competitive. When the two methods are equally profitable it is possible to produce a given quantity of bread with a variable total input of corn, by varying the proportion of bread produced with the second method. In this way a given total output of corn can be made compatible with the gross demand for corn by adapting, not the output, but the gross demand.

In this simple example, the rise of external rent causes a change in the relative profitability of two methods analogous to the one at the basis of 'factor substitution' in the standard microeconomic analysis of cost minimization with activity-analysis kinked isoquants.[66] When the interrelations due to production of (many) commodities by means of commodities are taken into account, then, as with intensive rent, the analogy with marginalist factor substitution is lost; phenomena analogous to those arising with intensive rent, such as the relative profitability of alternative methods changing in an unexpected direction when rent rises, absence of solutions, or multiplicity of cost-minimizing positions, can arise here too.[67]

Then there is ***rent due to consumer demand***. Suppose that the wine obtained on a certain land is an absolutely unique high-quality wine and only one method for producing it is known that requires that special land. Then the maximum amount producible of this product is given, and the price that it can fetch is determined by what consumers are ready to pay for it. If property of this land is concentrated in the hands of a single firm, this firm will behave like a monopolist and may well decide to produce less than the maximum, leaving part of the

---

66 It must be remembered, however, that in the usual standard analysis of cost minimization (where the slope of the isocost is arbitrarily given) cost minimization with activity-analysis isoquants will normally entail the use of only one method (a point where the isoquant has a kink is chosen); here on the contrary the normal case is the co-existence of two methods, the isocost coincides with one of the segments of the isoquant). The reader is invited to try and grasp the basic reason for this difference. Reflection on the analysis of intensive rent in ► Chap. 3, Sect. 3.14, can be of help.

67 For numerical examples cf. again the exercises of ► Chap. 10 in Kurz and Salvadori (1995).

904   Chapter 10 · Back to Long-Period Prices

land not utilized. If property is dispersed among many small owners unable to organize into a formal or informal cartel, then (if rent is positive) the land will be fully utilized, wine production will be determined by the given method, and rent will be determined by the difference between the price that allows selling the wine output, and unit production costs other than rent. The price at which this wine will be sold will depend on the incomes of well-off people, on fashion, on the most recent evaluation of the wine in specialized wine journals, etc.; we have here one instance of those 'rare statues and pictures, scarce books and coins, wines of a peculiar quality', judged by Ricardo (re-read the quote in Sect. 1.6) of no relevance for the big questions that the theory of value must answer.

10.15 Given Quantities?

So far in this chapter we have followed Sraffa in taking the quantities produced as given (determined in another part of the overall analysis); in the terminology proposed by P. Garegnani, the analysis has been a 'core' analysis (Sect. 1.13), where one studies how

(i)   the real wage (or wages; or alternatively the rate of profits and *relative* wages),
(ii)   quantities produced, and
(iii) production methods adopted

deductively determine relative prices, the residual main distributive variable, and, when necessary, rates of rent (given tax rates can be introduced as necessary). In the reconstruction proposed by Garegnani (1960a, 1990b, 2007) of the implicit method of classical authors, these three groups of magnitudes are *intermediate* data of the overall analysis, that is, their determinants are *not* considered to fall outside economic science, but are considered of such a nature that they can be taken as given when attempting the determination of relative prices and of the rate of profit (or of the real wage, if it is the rate of profit that is taken as given).

Of course this taking them as given is only provisional, a first stage in a two-stages procedure which can be described as follows. I enrich here what was said on the 'core' in Sect. 1.13.

If the gravitation to normal prices operates, and a sufficient time length is considered, one can presume the observed average quantities and technologies to be sufficiently representative of normal conditions, and prices to be sufficiently close to normal, implying that average quantities demanded too are sufficiently close to the theoretical Smithian notion of **effectual demands**, the quantities demanded at the natural prices with the given income distribution and the given average level of aggregate output and employment. So the quantities taken as given in 'core' analyses can be taken from the observation of reality, using perhaps moving three-year averages to smooth out non-durable influences.

One can then proceed to comparative statics: the study in the 'core' of the effect of a *change* in one of the given 'core' magnitudes, for example the average real wage, on the residual distributive variables (rate of profit, land rents) and relative prices, while keeping the other given magnitudes unchanged. This study, Garegnani (1990b, 2007) warns, yields only *provisional* conclusions, that must then be reconsidered and possibly modified in the light of the plausible effects of the initial change in the rate of profit and land rents on quantities and on technology. The study of these 'out-of-core' effects constitutes the second stage, more inductive, owing to the dependence of these effects on many elements that differ from situation to situation, so that not only the magnitude of these effects but even their sign may not be determinable on the basis of a general theory and may need attention to the specificities of the situation. If these effects on quantities and technology are particularly strong, a second 'core' analysis will be used to assess how much the conclusions of the first 'core' analysis need to be modified. A need for this second 'core' analysis can be presumed to arise only infrequently; for example, it is unlikely that a rise in real wages will have such an effect on quantities produced and on methods of production as to considerably change the no-rent land.

In order to reach conclusions on this issue one needs some theory of how the change in wages affects quantities produced. The abandonment of the neoclassical approach, which seems necessary on the basis of the conclusions of previous chapters, does not leave economics helpless on this issue. We have the Keynesian multiplier, that allows determining aggregate income once the autonomous[68] components of aggregate demand (i.e. essentially, state expenditure, investment, exports) and saving propensities are ascertained. The size of the multiplier will relevantly depend on income distribution, since saving propensities differ as between social groups. As to the determinants of autonomous demand: state expenditure is clearly a matter of political decisions; and international competitiveness is clearly the main determinant of exports; but these issues fall largely outside the purpose of this textbook. There is more disagreement about the determinants of investment; on this something will be said in ▶ Chap. 12. Third, concerning the *composition* of aggregate output, the composition of the autonomous spending decisions of entrepreneurs, foreign importers, and the state can be studied case by case as determined by growth decisions, innovation, monetary policy, international competitiveness of the several industries (which also depends on exchange rate policies), political decisions, and of course the reproduction needs of the economy (replacement of the used-up capital goods). It seems clear that a well-informed Ministry of Industry would be capable of rather detailed indications on these issues, much more useful than the ideological aggregate production functions.

There remains the composition of consumer choices (including propensities to save). A rise in real wages will probably affect it, but probably not by so much as to considerably change the effects on aggregate demand derived by assuming it as unchanged. Anyway it must be stressed that there is little difference here between the position of the non-neoclassical and of the neoclassical economist. The latter postulates demand functions, but these are undermined by Marshall's observation that how consumers will choose at prices different from the usually experienced ones is not known to the consumers themselves, by the absence of full employment, by the essential irrelevance (argued in ▶ Sect. 4.15) of consumer

---

68 In the Keynesian sense of autonomous relative to the level of aggregate income.

906   Chapter 10 · Back to Long-Period Prices

theory for the behaviour of demand coming from heterogeneous consumers and for categories of (heterogeneous) goods (e.g. meat), by the doubtful persistence of consumption habits. The useful information is independent of which general approach to value and distribution one prefers. For example, on whether and by how much a rise in wages will raise the demand for imported consumption goods (this can be important for a nation with balance-of-payments problems) standard consumer theory is of no help, one must use whatever information is available on how income increases are spent at different income levels in the given economy, and combine it with the forecasts on the effect of the wage rise on unemployment.[69]

The two-stages procedure, Garegnani (1990b) insists, is the sole possible one because, once the marginal/neoclassical approach is abandoned, often even the *sign* of the relevant effects cannot be considered a priori certain on the basis of a general theory; one will have to try and find out, on the basis of whatever is known about the specificity of the situation; and sometimes one may even have to accept an inability to arrive at clear predictions. For example the effects, on the general level of activity, of a rise in real wages can depend on whether the dominant opinion among capitalists is, or isn't, that the rise is a prelude to further pretenses and to social turmoil; if yes, a possible reaction is an 'investment strike', a crisis with capital flights, etc. Analogously difficult to predict in general are the effects of a rise of real wages on propensities to save: in a situation of relevant indebtedness of the working classes, the income rise may cause a *decrease* of the average saving propensity of the working classes, a smaller saved proportion of income being now sufficient for the repayment of debts.

10.16 Constant Returns to Scale?

Another much-discussed question in the resumption of a classical approach to value is whether Sraffa's study of prices in *Production of Commodities by Means of Commodities* needs an assumption of constant returns to scale.

With all the evidence of a Preface, Sraffa denied it:

» Anyone accustomed to think in terms of the equilibrium of demand and supply may be inclined, on reading these pages, to suppose that the argument rests on a tacit assumption of constant returns in all industries. If such a supposition is found helpful, there is no harm in the reader's adopting it as a temporary working hypothesis. In fact, however, no such assumption is made. No changes in output and (at any rate in Parts I and II) no changes in the proportions in which different means of production are used by an industry are considered, so that no question arises as to the variation or constancy of returns. The investigation is concerned exclusively with such properties of an economic system as do not depend on changes in the scale of production or in the proportions of 'factors'. (Sraffa 1960, p. v)

---

69 On non-neoclassical consumer theory see the passage from Robinson and Eatwell in the online Appendix to the chapter, and then Lavoie (2014, ▶ Chap. 2), Earl (1986).

10.16 · Constant Returns to Scale?

This statement implicitly alludes to Sraffa (1925, 1926), two famous articles in which Sraffa had criticized Marshall's supply functions. In those articles Sraffa had argued that the sole assumption about returns of a competitive industry compatible with Marshall's *partial-equilibrium* determination of long-period prices is constant returns, that is, a horizontal supply curve of the industry: unchanging long-period price of the product of the industry because input prices do not change with the industry's output level ('returns' here has the third meaning discussed in Sect. 5.4). The two possible reasons for non-constant returns are increasing returns, or decreasing returns. But increasing returns refer to changes in the division of labour (Adam Smith!), a very-long-period change that requires increases in the general scale of the economy and on such a time scale that they are not confined to the industry under study, and therefore contradict the 'ceteris paribus' clause that renders partial-equilibrium analyses legitimate. And decreasing returns cannot be admitted since nothing prevents the entry of new firms with the same efficient technology as existing firms. There remain only two very special cases compatible with partial equilibrium, for decreasing returns the case of an industry which is the sole one to use a specialized scarce resource, and for both increasing and decreasing returns the case of *external economies or diseconomies* internal to the industry, so that the single firm behaves as if it had constant returns to scale but the efficiency of all firms in the industry (and only in that industry otherwise the 'ceteris paribus' clause is violated) is influenced by the scale of the industry (see Sect. 5.4 for some illustration, and ibid. fn. 11 on external economies). Sraffa considers these two cases so special and unlikely as to deserve the status of negligible exceptions; the only admissible *general* case in long-period partial equilibrium competitive analysis, he concludes, is constant returns, that is, a horizontal long-period supply curve. The 1960 Preface appears to have aimed at making clear that both increasing division of labour and external economies must be admitted in a realistic analysis of how economies function, but Sraffa intended his book as only a preliminary step to more realistic analyses, a preliminary step in which the complications of external effects and of increasing division of labour were left out, evidently for consideration in the second stage of a Garegnani-like two-stages method; and in order not to induce the reader to think that increasing returns and external effects can be left out of realistic analyses, Sraffa stresses that he is not assuming constant returns.[70]

Sraffa's Preface has raised perplexities. Paul Samuelson, for example, has repeatedly argued that Sraffa's analysis needs constant returns to scale. His arguments are presented in very quick allusive sentences that make it occasionally difficult to grasp their logic, but I agree with Sergio Parrinello (2002) that one can extract the following argument from Samuelson (2000, pp. 118–121). Assume an economy that produces two goods, in which the observed technical coefficients (that include advanced real wages) result from cost minimization from production functions that are (generalized) Cobb–Douglas:

---

70 For a slightly different view, see Panico and Salvadori (1994).

$$Q_1 = A \cdot Q_{11}^\alpha Q_{21}^\mu$$

$$Q_2 = B \cdot Q_{12}^\beta Q_{22}^\sigma.$$

Here Q_i is the total production of good $i = 1,2$, while Q_{ij} is the input of good i in industry j. Assume production takes one period, but the rate of interest or of profit is zero, as in the first chapter of *Production of Commodities*, because the economy is only capable of simple reproduction, with zero surplus. Then the price equations are

$$p_1 Q_{11} + p_2 Q_{21} = p_1 Q_1$$

$$p_1 Q_{12} + p_2 Q_{22} = p_2 Q_2.$$

Sraffa's equations in (Sraffa 1960 ▶ Chap. 1) indeed assume prices equal to costs of production, with zero profits. Since there is technical choice, one must assume cost minimization; but owing to the product exhaustion theorem, in this economy optimal factor employments (that is, input rentals equal to marginal revenue products) imply zero profit only if the production functions have constant returns to scale, that is only if $\mu = 1-\alpha$, $\sigma = 1-\beta$. So, Samuelson argues, if Sraffa's prices reflect cost minimization (as they must if they are to indicate normal prices resulting from competition), the assumption of zero profits or interest requires CRS. (With the rate of interest assumed equal to the rate of profits, the same argument could be advanced even with a positive rate of profits, and it would refer to the implication of zero *extra* profits.)

But Parrinello (2002) has countered as follows. Suppose that in each industry the same Cobb–Douglas function holds for all firms, and appears to the individual firm to have constant returns to scale, but because of *external effects* internal to the industry the multiplicative coefficients A and B depend on total industry output as follows:

$$A = Q_1^{1-\gamma}$$

$$B = Q_2^{1-\lambda}$$

where γ, $\lambda > 1$, respectively < 1, indicate respectively negative external effects (e.g. due to pollution) or positive effects (e.g. greater ease at finding spare parts or competent repairmen in case of malfunctioning of machines). The *industry* production functions are then

$$Q_1 = Q_1^{1-\gamma} Q_{11}^\alpha Q_{21}^{1-\alpha} = Q_{11}^{\alpha/\gamma} Q_{21}^{(1-\alpha)/\gamma} \quad \left(\text{because then } Q_{11}^\alpha Q_{21}^{1-\alpha} = Q_1^{1-(1-\gamma)}\right)$$

$$Q_2 = Q_2^{1-\lambda} Q_{12}^\beta Q_{22}^{1-\beta} = Q_{12}^{\beta/\lambda} Q_{22}^{(1-\beta)/\lambda}.$$

10.16 · Constant Returns to Scale?

Assume the industries are competitive, with firms small relative to total industry production; firms ignore the effect of their decisions on A and B; they treat A and B as given, they are *technology-takers*, an assumption as admissible as the assumption that they are price-takers, and in fact made by Marshall when studying external effects. Then cost minimization satisfies the same conditions as with CRS, and the product exhaustion theorem holds, because for each firm coefficient A, or B, is unaffected by changes in the quantity produced by the firm, so the firm treats A, or B, as given.[71] Still, the *scale* of the industries is relevant for the determination of technical coefficients and hence of relative prices and, in the presence of a surplus, of the rate of profits. In this type of economy, one needs the total quantities produced in order to determine relative prices and the rate of profits; the economy does not exhibit constant returns. But, assuming observation of quantities produced and of the adopted methods over a period sufficient for adjustments of quantities to demands and for cost minimization, the observed technical coefficients *would* allow a correct determination of normal prices. For this determination based upon observation, one would need no assumption as to whether there are or not external effects, or as to their sign.

Of course, a change in income distribution that caused relevant changes in the quantities produced *would* alter external effects and hence normal technical coefficients in such an economy; but then the two-stage procedure would allow their (approximate) determination if there were reason to believe the changes in external effects to be important.

A different argument has been put forward by Ian Steedman (1980). The need for constant returns to scale is due, he argues, to what is needed for a comparison of the convenience of alternative methods when there is technical choice. It is impossible, he argues, to keep the gross quantities produced unchanged when in an industry there is a change of method, because a different method, by using up different capital goods, requires different productions of new capital goods to replace the used-up ones. So the quantity produced by many industries must be admitted to change when an industry changes method. Then, if industry returns to scale are not constant, technical coefficients will change even in the industries where no new method has been really introduced; it is then impossible to determine the switch points between two techniques, because a switch point is a level of the real wage (if the real wage is the distributive variable taken as a parameter) at which relative prices and the value of the rate of profits are the same for both alternative techniques; and this requires that the methods other than the replaced one remain unchanged. Steedman concludes: 'the only non-arbitrary basis for the usual analysis of switches in production methods is the assumption of constant returns in *every* non-switching industry' (1980, p. 11).

Steedman's argument has been answered as follows. First, the relevant reasons why industry returns to scale (in Marshall's and Sraffa's sense) may not be

---

71 Nor is it necessary to assume that, for given A or B, each firm has a CRS production function; one can admit U-shaped average cost curves and variations in the number of optimal-sized firms, to obtain an industry that would exhibit CRS were it not for the external effects.

constant are three: (i) at the firm level, economies of increasing dimension or increasing division of labour; (ii) external effects; (iii) changes in utilization of scarce natural resources. Now, in order to need consideration, these effects must be relevant, otherwise one can neglect them.

》 'However, Ricardo treated decreasing returns from land, just as Smith had treated the increasing returns from division of labour: as relevant, that is, only for the comparatively large output changes involved in capital accumulation and growth... Smith and Ricardo could therefore leave physical returns to scale quite naturally aside when dealing with relative prices in a given position of the economy, with the kind of comparatively small output changes generally involved in that specific analysis' (Garegnani 2007, pp. 187–8).

These lines by Garegnani imply that, as long as one can assume 'comparatively small output changes', one is authorized to assume constant returns. Actually, in this case it is the changes in quantities themselves that can be neglected. The same considerations apply to external effects.

Second, the two-stages method will allow to proceed without need for a simultaneous determination of choice of technique and of quantities, even when there is reason to think that returns may be relevantly affected. If the 'core' analysis in the first stage, on the basis of the given gross quantities of the initial situation, suggests the introduction of a new method, this introduction will in all likelihood happen, because single investors must individually decide on new plants, and in a competitive economy they will act on the basis of the observed prices and methods, without being able to take into account final prices nor changes in external effects. If then the introduction of the new method causes relevant changes in quantities[72] that, for example by changing the no-rent land, make a new round of 'core' analysis of choice of techniques opportune, this analysis will again refer to given gross quantities, the new ones, and in this way it will reflect a dynamical process in all likelihood actually going on in the real economy. Piccioni (1989) stresses that in this way, each time, the comparison among methods is for given gross quantities produced, and therefore there is no need to abandon the assumption of given quantities in 'core' analyses.

A different argument in support of the need for a simultaneous determination of technical choice and quantities rests on joint production. It is sometimes argued that the dependence of demand composition on relative prices must be taken into account to explain why certain jointly produced goods have or do not have zero price, and even to explain technical choice since the non-substitution theorem does not hold. Assume two goods and two processes that can produce them jointly in different proportions. This can give rise to a limited interval of compositions of demand that supply can match; outside this interval, only one process will be used, and one good will be overproduced and will have price zero; but if the composition of demand depends on the relative price of the two goods,

---

72 These changes, for the reasons explained, will not be determinable a priori but will depend on circumstances.

10.16 · Constant Returns to Scale?

it is possible that only one process is used and yet both goods have a positive price. Thus it is theoretically possible that there be fewer processes than goods with positive price. However, the considerations advanced at the end of ▶ Sect. 10.11 suggest that this case is extremely unlikely and generally at most temporary, because there is always a (sometimes hidden) availability of alternative processes, e.g. in domestic production (the treatment of choice of domestic production methods as a choice among different consumption bundles obscures this fact), and furthermore there is continuous search for ways to reduce waste of side products.

10.17 Lack of Consistency?

A more intriguing possibility is that of a *lack of consistency* between long-period prices and composition of demand. The intuitively simple case of (extensive) differential rent will suffice to clarify the potential problem. Imagine the real wage is measured in corn, but consumers also demand another agricultural product, say rice, a non-basic good produced on specialized lands A, B, C... that are put to use in this order as demand for rice increases. Assume CRS industries, no joint production. For a given real wage and given no-rent lands, relative prices are given, and the production price of rice is determined. Suppose the rice market can be analysed in partial equilibrium, and that if rice production is above 100 tonnes, the no-rent land in rice production is C that causes the production price of rice to be 12; while if rice production is between 80 and 100 tonnes, the no-rent land is B, and the production price of rice is 10: thus the rice industry's supply curve is horizontal at $p = 10$ before $q = 100$, and horizontal at $p = 12$ after $q = 100$, with at $q = 100$ a vertical segment from 10 to 12. Now suppose that at price 12 the normal (or 'effectual') demand for rice is 90 tonnes, and at price 10, it is 110 tonnes. So when the production price is 12, demand is less than the minimum required for the price to be 12, and when the price is 10, demand is more than the maximum compatible with a price 10. (A similar problem can arise with joint production— try to explain why with an example, as an *Exercise*.)

The issue raised by this example is that of the existence of a long-period position. We have proved that a cost-minimizing technique exists under sufficiently general assumptions *if* the quantities produced are given or the uniform rate of growth and the composition of the growth-reduced net product are given; we would like to make sure that this proof is not undermined by a more general dependence of the quantities demanded on prices and income distribution.[73] The quantities demanded taken as given in 'core' analyses should be what Adam Smith called *effectual demands*, the quantities demanded when prices are at their natural levels: if these quantities depend on prices, then one should make sure

---

73 Extensions of the Schefold–Lippi approach to more general growth models with different consumption composition out of wages and out of profits have been performed by Franke (1986) and Bidard and Franke (1987); cf. also Bidard (2004, p. 256).

912   **Chapter 10** · Back to Long-Period Prices

that at least one combination of mutually compatible natural prices and quantities exists (or one should have some plausible theory of what happens when that is not the case).

The rice example just illustrated shows the kind of difficulties that can arise. Does this example endanger the approach, questioning the existence of a long-period position?

It would seem not. First, it is possible that at a price intermediate between 10 and 12, say at price 11, effectual demand is precisely 100; then at that price land B is fully utilized, production is 100, land rent on land B is positive, but the price is not high enough to make it convenient to bring land C into cultivation. It might be argued that, in this case, taking the quantity produced of rice as equal to 100 is not enough to determine the price of rice, which is indeterminate between 10.1 and 11.9: one would need to know the price below which demand for rice is greater than 100, and above which demand for rice is less than 100. But in actual economies the different qualities of land and the alternative methods on each land (that give rise to intensive differential rent) are so numerous that discontinuous jumps in price of production as big as in this example are not found; and a small residual indeterminateness does not disturb 'core' analyses, where anyway technical coefficients too must be considered approximate to some extent. Second, it is possible that the good is such that demand stays constant at 110 for a price less than 11, and jumps down to 90 and stays there as the good's price increases above 11; the reason will have to be that we are now talking about a non-basic good used as input in industrial productions, the demand for which in one of its industrial uses jumps to zero when its price makes the process α that uses it less convenient than an alternative process β that does not use it. In this case there must be a price—11 in our example—at which process α and process β are equally convenient, so they can be both used in variable proportion, and the quantity demanded of our good can be anything between 90 and 110. Then one can expect a continuous oscillation of the price of this product: suppose initially effective demand (and production) is above 100 at price 12, so initially price is 12; then something changes in the economy, demand at price 12 becomes 90, so price and production start decreasing, land C is no longer convenient (it is convenient only at prices not below 12) and is abandoned, production drops below 100 and price keeps decreasing until it drops below 11; then demand jumps up to 110, price tends to rise, and production too, but not beyond 100 (full utilization of land B) because to produce more than 100 would require using some land C but this requires price to reach 12, and in all likelihood it won't, because as it goes above 11, normal demand jumps back to 90. So plausibly the price will oscillate around 11, and the quantity produced will oscillate, with 100 as its maximum, going below 100 when the price goes above 11, then tending to return to 100 as the price goes below 11. So, as in the first case, we can consider 100 as the effectual demand at normal price 11, corresponding to the coexistence of processes α and β in such proportions as to permit the full utilization of land B, as required by the fact that at a price greater than 10 land B earns a positive rate of rent. Empirical observation will then in all likelihood indicate a production somewhat less than 100, but not by much, and theoretically 100 is its centre of gravitation.

10.17 · Lack of Consistency?

It seems therefore that even in the cases in which there seems to be a lack of consistency between effectual demands and long-period prices, further analysis shows that there is the possibility to reach a sensible definition of effectual demand, consistent with normal price, and such that one can expect it to be roughly revealed by observation because it is a centre of attraction for actual quantities, a centre of gravitation.

10.18 Conclusions

We can conclude that the theory of long-period prices, or prices of production, is able to determine these prices under sufficiently general conditions.

There seems little reason to doubt the traditional thesis that entry and the search for the highest rate of return on investment cause prices to gravitate towards long-period prices.

Some open issues persist with pure joint production and with intensive differential rent. But it must not be forgotten that in real economies there are thousands, perhaps millions, of different goods, so the possible multiplicity or non-existence of cost-minimizing techniques can only have localized effects that do not question the general relationship between real wage and rate of profits obtainable in the absence of joint production. If these cases imply, for example, that a price may remain indeterminate within, say, a 10% interval, this has next to no influence on most other prices and on the endogenously determined distributive variable. The basic difference from the neoclassical approach is that the forces, which fix the income variable on which the relative bargaining power of wage labour and capital first exerts its effect, are unaffected by these small price indeterminacies. In the neoclassical approach, on the contrary, it is precisely the forces supposedly determining income distribution that are unable to determine a well-defined, unique and stable result.

The possibility that, with joint production, as the rate of profit decreases, the real wage rises in terms of most goods but decreases in terms of some goods would create a significant indeterminacy in the behaviour of the real wage only if the goods in terms of which the wage decreases were a significant portion of the workers' expenditure. This case seems extremely improbable.

It would seem therefore that a return to the long-period method affords a robust theory of competitive value. To assess how far this theory applies to economies where oligopolistic elements are important is the next task. It will require first some elements of game theory.

10.19 Review Questions and Exercises

Review questions
1. Explain Garegnani's objection to cross-dual gravitation models.
2. Report how Steedman's (1984a) doubts about gravitation can be answered.
3. Report Schefold's arguments in favour of the number of processes exceeding the number of commodities.

914   Chapter 10 · Back to Long-Period Prices

4. Reproduce ◘ Fig. 10.9 and explain its implications.
5. Reproduce ◘ Fig. 10.10 and explain its implications.
6. Explain how the Fundamental Theorem of Linear Programming helps to show that a cost-minimizing technique exists under joint production, and that if $r = g$ one obtains a square system.
7. 'The possibility of some non-uniqueness of the distributive variable residually determined, that thus emerges, should not induce one to think that the classical approach is in the same situation, as regards non-uniqueness, as the neoclassical approach' (Sect. 10.B.16). Explain how this thesis is argued. Do you agree?
8. Explain why intensive rent confirms that in the presence of heterogeneous capital, technical choice does not behave in the way postulated by the marginalist/neoclassical approach.
9. Show that with intensive rent, rate of profit and real wage can move in the same direction.
10. Explain what is external intensive rent.
11. The text argues that 'from the analysis of a single competitive market, no significant problem appears to emerge for the thesis of the long-period tendency of market price towards average cost' (Sect. 10.A.7). Summarize the reasons in support of this claim.
12. Full-cost pricing is supportive of the thesis that market prices gravitate towards UERRSP. Explain.
13. Negative embodied labours need not make no sense. Give a sensible economic interpretation.
14. Illustrate Piccioni's approach graphically.

Exercises

1. Develop a numerical example to check the validity of the instability of the model discussed in ▶ Sect. 10.4.
2. In Footnote 32.
3. Produce an example of a two-commodities technique with joint production that is all-productive but not all-engaging.
4. Prove the statement in ▶ Sect. 10.7 (see ◘ Fig. 10.5) that the price vector must be perpendicular to the GD-segment if the rate of profits is to be uniform.
5. (Franke 1986). There are two commodities and the six processes of the table below

	Input 1	Input 2	Labour		Output 1	Output 2
(1)	1	2	1	→	5	7
(2)	2	1	1	→	7	5
(3)	1	2	1	→	5	0
(4)	1	2	1	→	0	7
(5)	2	1	1	→	7	0
(6)	2	1	1	→	0	5

The growth rate equals zero and commodities are consumed in the proportion of ten units of commodity 1 to 11 units of commodity 2.

(a) Show that if $0 \leq r < 1$, there is only one cost-minimizing technique consisting of processes (1, 2).

(b) Show that if $r = 2$ (actually, if $1 \leq r \leq 3$, but $r = 2$ suffices to see the aspect we are interested in) there are three cost-minimizing techniques: (1, 2), (1,3) and (2,6).

(c) Now notice that the last four processes in the table can be seen as existing as a consequence of an assumption of free disposal since the first two processes exist. On this basis, discuss why one speaks of the cost-minimizing techniques (1, 3), and (2, 6), rather than (1) alone, and (2) alone.

(d) Then use Piccioni's approach to conclude that at $r = 2$ technique (1,2) is a 'watershed' technique (see the 'further consideration' at the end of Sect. 10.B.13).

Also discuss what is implicit in consumer tastes when accepting that a price can go to zero.

6. (Land) Show with a simple numerical example that the order of rentability can depend on the real wage. [Hint: use the example of ▶ Chap. 1 with three lands and make assumptions about the proportion of seed-corn to advanced wages such as to cause the total wage bill per acre to rise differently on different lands when the wage rate rises.]

7. (Freni). Intensive rent. Corn can be produced on homogeneous land by either of three processes whose technical coefficients are as follows

	Seed-corn	Land	Labour		Gross corn output
(1)	7/10	1/5	2/5	→	1
(2)	7/24	1/2	2	→	1
(3)	21/32	1/7	1	→	1

Consumption consists of 35 units of corn. There are 24 units of land.

(a) Show that if $r = 1/7$, then there are three long-period positions made up respectively of processes (1 only), (1 and 2), (2 and 3).

(b) Assume the net demand for 35 units of corn was reached via a gradual increase from zero: then which long-period position is more plausibly reached?

(c) Find the long-period position if r is greater than 1/7 (and feasible).

8. Develop an example that may suggest for joint production a difficulty with lack of consistency as in the first paragraph of ▶ Sect. 10.17.

9. (Ricardian rent). Corn is produced by labour alone on different lands, the wage is advanced and consists of corn. Prove that the no-rent wage curves of different lands do not cross, and hence the order of utilization is independent of the wage level.

10. Produce an example in which order of utilization, order of rentability, and order of fertility differ.

916   Chapter 10 · Back to Long-Period Prices

11. Prove the statement immediately after the Fundamental Theorem of Linear Programming in ▶ Sect. 10.9.
12. (Bidard) (Choice of techniques) Consider a one-good model where corn and labour produce corn with a set of methods parameterised by $t > 0$ according to:

$$[1/(1+t)] \text{ quarters of corn} * \left[t^2/(1+t)\right] \text{ hours of labour} \rightarrow 1 \text{ quarter of corn}$$

Write down the equation of the envelope of wage curves $w(r)$. (Hint: remember that for a given r, the choice of technique - here the choice of method - must be such that w is maximized.)
13. (Bidard) (Choice of techniques) Same as in the previous exercise but now the family of methods is parameterised by $t > 0$ according to:

$$\frac{e^t}{1+e^t} qr \cdot corn * \frac{1}{256} \frac{e^{-3t}}{1+e^t} hr.labour \rightarrow 1 \text{ qr.corn.}$$

Prove that the solution is $w(r) = 27 \, r^{-3}$.

References

Bellino, E., & Serrano, F. (2017). *Gravitation of market prices towards normal prices: Some new results.* Centro Sraffa Working Paper no. 25, Centro Sraffa, Rome.

Bidard, C. (1991). *Prix, reproduction, rareté.* Paris: Dunod.

Bidard, C. (1997). Pure joint production. *Cambridge Journal of Economics, 21,* 685–701.

Bidard, C. (2004). *Prices, reproduction, scarcity.* Cambridge: Cambridge University Press.

Bidard, C., & Franke, R. (1987). On the existence of long-term equilibria in the two-class Pasinetti-Morishima model. *Ricerche Economiche, 41,* 3–21.

Boggio, L. (1990). The dynamic stability of production prices: A synthetic discussion of models and results. In Caminati & Petri (Eds.) (pp. 47–58).

Boggio, L. (1992). Production prices and dynamic stability: Results and open questions. *The Manchester School, 60*(3), 264–294.

Boggio, L. (1998). Gravitation. In H. D. Kurz & N. Salvadori (Eds.), *The Elgar companion to classical economics* (Vol. I, pp. 351–356). Aldershot: Edward Elgar.

Caminati M., & Petri F. (Eds.). (1990). Convergence to long-period positions. *Political Economy: Studies in the Surplus Approach, 6*(1–2).

Caminati M. (1990). Gravitation: an introduction. In: M. Caminati, F. Petri, eds., Convergence toLong-Period Positions. *Political Economy: Studies in the Surplus Approach 6*(1–2): 11–44.

Cesaratto, S. (1995). Long-period method and analysis of technical change: Is there any inconsistency? *Review of Political Economy, 7*(3), 249–278.

Cesaratto, S. (1996). Long-period positions and economic change. A rejoinder. *Review of Political Economy, 8*(4), 409–425.

D'Agata. (1983). The existence and uniqueness of cost-minimizing systems in intensive rent theory. *Metroeconomica, 35,* 147–58.

Dana, R. A., Florenzano, M., Le Van, C., & Lévy, D. (1989a). Production prices and general equilibrium prices: A long run property of a Leontief economy. *Journal of Mathematical Economics, 18,* 263–280.

Dana, R. A., Florenzano, M., Le Van, C., & Lévy, D. (1989b). Asymptotic properties of a Leontief economy. *Journal of Economic Dynamics and Control, 13,* 553–568.

Duménil, G., & Lévy, D. (1985). The classical and the neoclassicals: A rejoinder to Frank Hahn. *Cambridge Journal of Economics, 8,* 327–345.

References

Duménil, G., & Lévy, D. (1990). Stability in capitalism: Are long-term positions the problem? With an addendum. In M. Caminati, & F. Petri (Eds.), *Convergence to long-period positions. Political economy: Studies in the surplus approach* (Vol. 6(1–2), pp. 229–278).

Duménil, G., & Lévy, D. (1993). *The economics of the profit rate*. Aldershot, UK: Edward Elgar.

Earl, P. (1986). *Lifestyle economics: Consumer behaviour in a turbulent world*. New York: Wheatsheaf.

Ehrbar H., Glick M. (1988). Profi t Rate Equalization in the U.S. and Europe: An Econometric Investigation. *European Journal of Political Economy*, 4(1): 179–201.

Flaschel, P., & Semmler, W. (1986). The dynamic equalization of profit rates for input-output models with fixed capital. In W. Semmler (Ed.), *Competition, instability, and non-linear cycles* (pp. 1–34). Berlin and New York: Springer-Verlag.

Franke, R. (1986). Some problems concerning the notion of cost-minimizing systems in the framework of joint production. *The Manchester School, 52,* 298–307.

Franke, R. (1986). A cross-over gravitation process in prices and inventories. In W. Semmler (Ed.), *Competition, Instability, and NonLinear Cycles* (pp. 51–82). Berlin and New York: Springer-Verlag.

Gandolfo, G. (1971). *Mathematical methods and models in economic dynamics*. Amsterdam: North-Holland.

Garegnani P. (1960a), *Il capitale nelle teorie della distribuzione*. Milan: Giuffré.

Garegnani P. (1990b). Sraffa: Classical versus marginalist analysis. In K. Bharadwaj & B. Schefold (Eds.), *Essays on Piero Sraffa* (pp. 112–40). London: Unwin and Hyman (reprinted 1992 by Routledge, London).

Garegnani, P. (1990c). On some supposed obstacles to the tendency of market prices towards natural prices. In M. Caminati & F. Petri (Eds.), *Convergence to long-period positions. Political economy: Studies in the surplus approach*, (Vol. 6(1–2), pp. 329–359).

Garegnani, P. (1997). On some supposed obstacles to the tendency of market prices towards natural prices. In G. Caravale (Ed.), *Equilibrium and Economic Theory* (pp. 139–171). London: Routledge.

Garegnani, P. (2003). Savings, investment and capital in a system of general intertemporal equilibrium. In Petri & Hahn, (pp 117–173).

Garegnani, P. (2007). Professor Samuelson on Sraffa and the classical economists. *European Journal of the History of Economic Thought, 14*(2), 181–242.

Glick, M., & Ehrbar, H. (1990). Long-run equilibrium in the empirical study of monopoly and competition. *Economic Inquiry, 28,* 151–162.

Kurz, H. D. (1986). Classical and early neoclassical economists on joint production. *Metroeconomica, 38,* 1–37.

Kurz, H. D., & Salvadori, N. (1995). *Theory of production: A long-period analysis*. Cambridge: Cambridge University Press.

Lavoie, M. (2014). *Post-Keynesian economics: New foundations*. Cheltenham, UK: Edward Elgar.

Lippi, M. (1979). *I prezzi di produzione*. Il Mulino, Bologna: Un saggio sulla teoria di Sraffa.

Lippi M. (1990). Production prices and dynamic stability: Comment on Boggio. In M. Caminati & F. Petri (Eds.), Convergence to long-period positions. *Political Economy: Studies in the Surplus Approach, 6*(1–2), 59–68.

Mainwaring, L. (1984). *Value and distribution in capitalist economies. An introduction to Sraffian economics*. Cambridge: Cambridge University Press.

Marx, K. (1977). *Capital, a critique of political economy Volume III*. New York: International Publishers.

Mueller, D. C. (1986). *Profits in the long run*. Cambridge: Cambridge University Press.

Nikaido, H. (1968). *Convex structures and economic theory*. New York: Academic Press.

Panico, C., & Salvadori, N. (1994). Sraffa, Marshall and the problem of returns. *European Journal of the History of Economic Thought, 1,* 323–343.

Parrinello, S. (2002). Sraffa's legacy in economcs: Some critical notes. *Metroeconomica, 53*(3), 242–260.

Petri, F., & Hahn, F. (Eds.). (2003). *General Equilibrium: Problems and Prospects*. London: Routledge.

Piccioni, M. (1989). Distribuzione e quantità prodotte nell'impostazione classica. *Studi Economici, 44,* 179–218.

Piccioni, M. (1991). *Produzione congiunta e scelta della tecnica in Sraffa*. Unpubl. PhD dissertation,Università La Sapienza, Roma.

Piccioni, M. (1997). Joint Production and Gravitation. *Contributions To Political Economy*, 16, 103–118.

Ricardo D. (1951). *On the principles of political economy and taxation*. Vol. I of P. Sraffa, ed., *The works and correspondence of David Ricardo*. Cambridge: Cambridge University Press.

Salvadori, N. (1982). Existence of cost-minimizing systems within the Sraffa framework. *Zeitschrift für Nationalökonomie, 42*, 281–298.

Salvadori, N. (1983). On a new variety of rent. *Metroeconomica*, 35, 73–85.

Salvadori, N. (1985). Switching in methods of production and joint production. *The Manchester School, 53*, 156–178.

Samuelson, P. A. (2000). Sraffa's hits and misses. In H. D. Kurz (Ed.), *Critical essays on Piero Sraffa's legacy in economics* (pp. 111–151). Cambridge: Cambridge University Press.

Schefold, B. (1997). *Normal prices, technical change and accumulation*. London: Macmillan.

Schefold, B. (2003). Applications of the classical approach. In F. Petri & F. Hahn (Eds.), *General Equilibrium: Problems and Prospects* (pp. 439–469).

Schefold. (1997). The dominant technique in joint production systems. *Cambridge Journal of Economics, 12*, 97–123. (Also repr. in Schefold, 1997).

Semmler, W. (1984). *Competition, monopoly, and differential profit rates*. New York: Columbia University Press.

Sraffa, P. (1925). Sulle relazioni tra costo e quantità prodotta. *Annali di economia, 2*, 277–328. (English translation by J. Eatwell & A. Roncaglia, 'On the relations between cost and quantity produced', in L. Pasinetti, ed., *Italian Economic Papers*, vol III. Oxford University Press, London, and Il Mulino, Bologna, 1998).

Sraffa, P. (1926). The laws of returns under competitive conditions. *Economic Journal, 36*, 535–550.

Sraffa, P. (1960). *Production of commodities by means of commodities*. Cambridge: Cambridge University Press.

Steedman, I. (1975). Positive profits with negative surplus value. *Economic Journal, 85*, 114–123.

Steedman, I. (1980). Returns to scale and the switch in methods of production. *Studi Economici, 35*, 5–13.

Steedman, I. (1984a). L'importance empirique de la production jointe. In C. Bidard (Ed.), *La production jointe* (pp. 5–20). Paris: Economica.

Steedman, I. (1984b). Natural prices, differential profi t rates and the classical competitive process. *TheManchester School*, 52, 123–139.

Yamawaki, A. (1989). A comparative analysis of intertemporal behaviour of profits: Japan and the United States. *Journal of Industrial Economics, 37*(4), 389–409.

Games and Information

Contents

11.1   Introduction, and Some Examples of One-Shot Simultaneous Games – 921

11.2   Sequential or Dynamic Games – 925

11.3   Extensive and Strategic (or Normal) Form – 929

11.4   Mixed Strategies – 931

11.5   Behavioural Strategies – 933

11.6   Solutions. Elimination of Strictly Dominated Strategies. Some Doubts – 935

11.7   Weakly Dominated Strategies, Dominance Solvable Games – 939

11.8   Dominated Mixed Strategies – 941

11.9   Nash Equilibrium in Pure Strategies – 942

11.10   Nash Equilibria in Mixed Strategies – 943

11.11   Existence of Nash Equilibrium. The Reasons for Interest in Nash Equilibria – 944

11.12   Trembling-Hand Equilibria – 950

11.13   Backward Induction and Subgame Perfection – 951

11.14   Repeated Backward Induction and the Centipede Game – 954

© Springer Nature Switzerland AG 2021
F. Petri, *Microeconomics for the Critical Mind*,
Classroom Companion: Economics, https://doi.org/10.1007/978-3-030-62070-7_11

11.15	Infinitely Repeated Games – 957
11.16	Finitely Repeated Games – 962
11.17	Bayesian Games – 963
11.18	Auctions as Bayesian Games. Revenue Equivalence Theorem. Winner's Curse – 970
11.19	Dynamic Games of Imperfect Information – 976
11.20	Sequential Rationality, Behavioural Strategies, Perfect Bayesian Equilibrium (PBE) – 978
11.21	Limits of Perfect Bayesian Equilibrium. Sequential Equilibrium – 983
11.22	Asymmetric Information. Signalling Games. Separating and Pooling Equilibria – 985
11.23	Adverse Selection – 994
11.24	Principal–agent Models – 996
11.25	Screening – 1003
11.26	Conclusions – 1008
11.27	Review Questions and Exercises – 1008
	References – 1019

11.1 · Introduction, and Some Examples of One-Shot Simultaneous Games

This chapter introduces you to game theory, and to its applications to situations of asymmetric information. You will learn:

— a number of simple games, representative of typical social situations
— the difference between simultaneous and sequential games
— solution concepts for games: dominant strategies, Nash equilibrium
— backward induction and subgame perfection
— the difference it makes if a game is at least potentially infinitely repeated
— Bayesian games
— auctions and the winner's curse
— asymmetric information models: principal–agent problems, moral hazard, adverse selection, signalling, screening.

11.1 Introduction, and Some Examples of One-Shot Simultaneous Games

This chapter introduces to game theory, and to its application to situations of asymmetric information. Only concepts in *non-cooperative* game theory will be discussed.[1] *Cooperative* game theory is very different, it looks for the *consequences* of general principles on which 'deals' among several players might be struck, given a description of what players can achieve if they cooperate and if they don't; it does not ask how cooperation can be achieved and maintained; it assumes that the 'deals' are enforceable. Non-cooperative game theory starts from individualistic behaviour of each player; cooperation emerges, if at all, as a result of maximizing choices of the players, if the incentives supplied by the situation make cooperative behaviour self-enforcing.

After presenting the notions of dominance, backward induction, Nash equilibrium, mixed strategies, repeated games, subgame perfection, Bayesian games, sequential rationality, perfect Bayesian equilibrium, the chapter applies these notions to the study of hidden action and hidden information: moral hazard, adverse selection, auctions, the general principal–agent problem, simple cases of signalling and screening. Many of these notions will reappear in subsequent chapters.

Non-cooperative game theory studies the structure of strategic interactions formalizable as 'games', i.e. as situations in which two or more *players* choose *actions* (or *strategies*, out of a set of possible alternative actions or strategies) and these determine *outcomes*, and hence *payoffs* to each player, which depend

---

1 To the reader wishing to learn a bit more on game theory than explained here, I would suggest the lively chapters on game theory in Kreps' textbook (1990), and, among the books entirely dedicated to game theory, the refreshing and provocative Gintis (2000) at an intermediate level. If one wishes to go one or two levels up, there is ample choice, Osborne and Rubinstein (1994) is probably best for a start; as always, the entries on game theory and related topics in the *New Palgrave* offer ample bibliographic suggestions.

on the actions chosen by all involved players. A game is defined by a set of players, a set of possible strategies for each player, and a set of outcomes or payoffs for each combination of strategies, one for each player. Poker, contract bridge, chess, tic-tac-toe, Rock-Paper-Scissors, Monopoly are examples of parlour games with well-specified rules that entail definite payoffs depending on the chosen strategies of the players; many social situations can be similarly described, the 'rules' being the specification of the situation, of the alternatives available to each player, and of the outcomes of actions. A strategy can consist of a single action, or of a sequence of actions in a temporal succession, as will be explained. Game theory tries to determine general principles helpful to find the optimal course of action of each player, thus it has a *normative* connotation; but if it can be assumed that players do choose their optimal actions, then game theory becomes *predictive* of what individuals *will* do; thus it acquires the *explicative/predictive* connotation that largely motivates the interest of economists in game theory.

'One-shot' games (games of a single *simultaneous* move by players each one of whom must choose her move without knowing what move the other players are choosing) are an easy introduction to the subject. For simplicity, I consider two-player games.

There are two players, A and B. Assume each player has two possible moves or strategies, so there are four possible combinations of moves: (A1, B1), (A1, B2), (A2, B1), (A2, B2). Let A be the row player and B the column player, and build a matrix with as element i, j the two payoffs (first A's payoff, then B's payoff) resulting from A choosing strategy Ai ($i = 1, 2$) and B choosing strategy Bj ($j = 1, 2$). The result is a **bimatrix**, so called because in each place or 'box' i, j it has two elements.

For example, two fiancés, Art and Belle, must separately choose which cinema theatre to go to: in an age before telephones, they have agreed to meet at the cinema at 6 pm but have forgotten to agree on which one, and must choose without knowing to which of the two cinema theatres in town their fiancé/e will go. The choice is between a horror film (H), that he prefers, or a comedy (C) that she prefers. We can represent their possible choices, and the outcomes in terms of utility, through a bimatrix as in ◘ Fig. 11.1. Art is the row player.

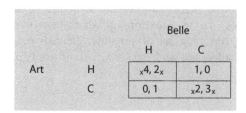

◘ **Fig. 11.1** Small x's are next to the payoff that is highest for the row player in that column, and highest for the column player in that row, so they indicate the payoff resulting from a strategy that is a *best response* to the strategy of the other player; for example, the best response for Belle to Art choosing H is to choose H, hence a small x next to Belle's payoff 2 in the (H, H) box. If in a box there are two x's, then the strategies are *mutual* best responses, and we will see later that such couples of strategies constitute a **Nash equilibrium**.

11.1 · Introduction, and Some Examples of One-Shot Simultaneous Games

The bimatrix of payoffs associated with the different combinations of strategies is called the ***normal or strategic form*** of the game. (Sometimes for brevity I shall speak simply of 'matrix' for a bimatrix.)

A ***strategy*** for a player in a game is a set of actions completely describing what he/she is to choose in all possible situations in which he/she might have to choose an action during the game. Here there is only one situation, the initial one, and the strategies are the same for either player: play H, or play C. *It is assumed that each player knows the bimatrix, and knows that the other player knows the bimatrix, and knows that the other player knows what she/he knows, and so on* ad infinitum. This is called the ***complete knowledge*** assumption.

This game is called ***Battle of the Sexes***. It is one of a number of ***coordination games***, in which it is important for players to converge on a common course of action but there is more than one course on which coordination makes sense, with a resulting uncertainty as to what other players will decide to do.

Many two-person simultaneous games nicely grasp typical situations of strategic interaction and for this reason the names of these games are used in order concisely to describe the type of interaction. In the ***Hawk-Dove*** game (also called ***Chicken*** game) each player can act either aggressively, hawk-like (H), or meekly, dove-like (D); playing Hawk against an opponent who 'chickens out' and plays Dove yields high payoff, but if both players play Hawk the result is a disaster for both, while if both play D they don't do so bad.

Examples are two cars aiming at each other at high speed, and the first driver who swerves loses in reputation, but if neither swerves both are maimed; or peasants with neighbouring fields who need a fence separating them (otherwise the animals of one peasant damage the harvest of the other), and either peasant can choose to act Hawk and not set the fence up, to induce the other peasant to bear the cost of the fence (both playing Dove would mean in this case that they share the cost of the fence). The bimatrix might be the one of ◘ Fig. 11.2.

Another frequently mentioned game is the ***Stag Hunt*** game. Two hunters have started together to hunt a stag (the cooperation of two hunters is indispensable for this type of hunt), but having got separated as required by the hunting tactics, they start wondering whether the other hunter will continue to go for the stag or will prefer to gather mushrooms, in which case to keep hunting for the stag is useless and it is better to go for mushrooms too (◘ Fig. 11.3).

This is another coordination game, without the conflict of the Battle of the Sexes; the difficulty is that each hunter cannot be certain as to what the other will

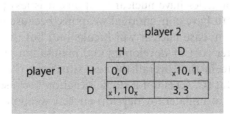

◘ **Fig. 11.2**   Hawk-Dove game

Chapter 11 · Games and Information

		player 2	
		S(tag)	M(ushrooms)
player 1	S	5, 5	0, 3
	M	3, 0	2, 2

▣ Fig. 11.3 Stag Hunt game (You are invited to locate the small x's yourself)

A \ B	Nuclear	Conventional
Nuclear	$_x1, 1_x$	$_x10, -5$
Conventional	$-5, 10_x$	1, 1

▣ Fig. 11.4 Arms Race game

choose to do, and the fear of being the only one to go for the stag can induce both to choose to go for mushrooms. This type of game is called an **_Assurance Game_** because each player may well decide to choose M in order to be assured that the risk is avoided of the very bad outcome in case she is the sole one to choose S. The fear of the result of bad coordination, coupled with the not-too-bad result of going for mushrooms, can cause the Pareto superior outcome (S, S) not to be achieved. In this type of game, if one player commits to one course of action and **_credibly_** announces it to the other player, she is assured that the other player will adopt the same course of action; the difficulty is being credible. For example, one might show that she signed a contract with a third person which obliges her to pay a penalty if she doesn't get a stag; but careful!, this means a change of payoffs, i.e. a modification of the game. Indeed the formalization of a game can help to understand why people try to modify it into a different game.

Now consider two countries A and B that can develop or not nuclear weapons. Suppose the bimatrix of payoffs is as in ▣ Fig. 11.4.

The payoffs can be motivated as follows. A country that is the sole to have nuclear weapons can dictate terms to the other country and obtain considerable advantages in several fields (e.g. commercial rules), because in case of war it will win easily; if both countries have nuclear weapons, it is less probable that a war breaks out than if both have conventional weapons, because of MAD (Mutually Assured Destruction) in case nuclear war breaks out, but this advantage is compensated by the greater cost of developing and maintaining nuclear weapons, so that both nations esteem that overall the two situations (N, N) and (C, C) are roughly equivalent. But (C, C) is not a stable situation because in it each country finds it advantageous to unilaterally develop nuclear weapons. And if one country develops them, then it is in the interest of the other country to develop them too. This explains why the USSR rushed to develop the atomic and the hydrogen

11.1 · Introduction, and Some Examples of One-Shot Simultaneous Games

bombs after seeing that the USA had them, and why now other countries are trying to do the same.

It might even be that (N, N) is actually considered worse than (C, C) by both countries, because it causes very high costs, yielding payoffs (0, 0) rather than (1, 1): the reasons for an arms race will still be there; but now we would have the game called **Prisoner's dilemma**. The name comes from the story with which this type of situation was first illustrated. Two criminals α and β have been arrested because suspected of having committed a grave crime, and put in separate cells; to each one the possibility is offered of confessing the crime and supplying details to confirm the confession, receiving a very mild sentence if the confession helps to convict the other criminal, but a less mild sentence if the confession is superfluous because the other confessed too; if one confesses and the other doesn't, the second criminal will receive a very harsh sentence; if neither confesses, they will be condemned for a minor crime, to less than if both confess but to more than a sole confessing prisoner will obtain. The payoffs are years of prison, with a minus sign in front to indicate that the smaller the number of years, the better, and are for example as in the table below. To be able later to apply this type of interaction to other situations, it is best to indicate the team-cooperative behaviour (here Not to Confess) with a C for 'Cooperate', and the non-cooperative behaviour with a D for 'Defect on cooperation' (here Confess); therefore don't get confused, C stands for Cooperate, i.e. *not* confess, and D for Defect, i.e. confess.

The important aspect of the situation is that, whatever one prisoner chooses, the other prisoner's payoff is better if she Defects by confessing, so there is an incentive to confess, but if both confess they end up worse off than if both had Cooperated by not confessing. This type of interaction is characteristic of many social situations. For example if going to work by bus always takes more time than going by car whatever the traffic level, then there is always an individual incentive to go by car, but if everybody goes by car, traffic is disastrous, and time lost and irritation are more than if everybody had chosen the bus. The Arms Race game with (0, 0) as payoffs for (Nuclear, Nuclear) is another example.

These examples give some initial feeling of the variety of possible situations that games can represent, but also of the frequent difficulty with deciding which is the best move.

11.2 Sequential or Dynamic Games

Now let us consider games where there is a *succession* of moves: a player moves first, then another player moves on the basis of a (perfect or imperfect) knowledge of the choice of the first player, and so on. These are called **dynamic** or **sequential** games.

An example is the well-known game of tic-tac-toe. The game is between players A and B. The two players take turns ticking squares from a 3×3 array of squares; the first one to form a row or a column or a diagonal of three squares,

β	Defect (i.e. confess)	Cooperate (i.e. not confess)
D	$_x$-5, -5$_x$	$_x$-1, -10
C	-10, -1$_x$	-3, -3

(α in left column)

◨ **Fig. 11.5** Prisoner's dilemma

wins; if neither succeeds by the time all squares have been ticked, it is a draw. Another example is chess. Still another is poker.

For these games, it is often preferable to adopt a description called the ***extensive form*** of the game. This specifies the order of play, the information and choices available to a player whenever it's her turn to play, the payoffs for all players (depending on all players' choices) when the game ends, and possibly a probability distribution if the initial situation, or the outcome of a choice, has a random component. The latter randomness is usually formalized as a choice by an imaginary agent called 'nature'.

The extensive form is usually depicted as a ***game tree***, with 'nodes' and (directed) 'branches' coming out of these nodes. A node is a situation in which one player has to make a choice; the branches coming out of a node indicate her/ his possible choices. Each branch goes to a different node, where another player (or sometimes the same player again) must make a choice. Each node is reached by only one branch. The paths from a node to another node cannot allow circles. Nodes corresponding to endings of the game have no branches coming out of them, and to them are associated the payoffs for each player if the game ends there.

Take tic-tac-toe; the two players are A, who is to move first, and B. I assume the reader knows the game; the squares are numbered 1 to 9. A partial depiction of its extensive form is given in ◨ Fig. 11.5. Suppose A moves first and chooses square 1; then B must choose among the remaining 8 squares, and if B chooses 5, then A must choose among the remaining 7 squares; and so on. It is evident that a complete graphical representation of the 'tree' of the game is impossible: there are eight branches out of each first move by A, i.e. 72 in all, and out of each one of them 7 branches go out ... (◨ Fig. 11.6).

It is possible that a player, when it is her turn to choose, does not know at which node she is. This might be because she does not know what was chosen by a player before her turn.[2] Consider the following two-person game—a simplified

---

2 Another possibility is that the player does not remember what has happened in previous stages of the game (for examples, her previous choices). This possibility is usually excluded by the assumption of ***perfect recall***, that assumes that at each information set the associated player, besides knowing which nodes belong to that information set (as implied by the assumption of perfect knowledge of the structure of the game), also knows that she is at that information set and knows which information sets the previous history of the game has reached.

11.2 · Sequential or Dynamic Games

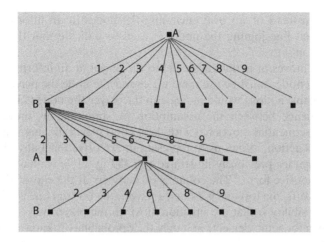

Fig. 11.6 A small part of the game tree of tic-tac-toe, assuming A's first move is to tick square 1, and B's first move is to tick square 5; then A must choose among the squares 2, 3, 4, 6, 7, 8, 9

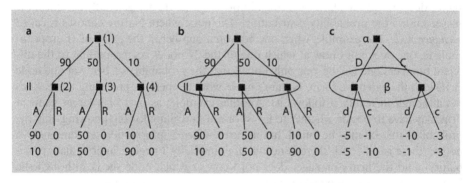

Fig. 11.7 Three examples of sequential games, the last two with imperfect information

version of the **Ultimatum Game**—where two players must split 100 dollars. Player First (*I*) moves first and can choose to offer player Second (*II*) 90 dollars, 50 dollars or 10 dollars. *II*, having *observed I*'s choice, chooses between Accept and Reject: if she accepts, she gets *I*'s offer and *I* gets the remainder of the 100 dollars; if she rejects, both get nothing. The tree is depicted in ◘ Fig. 11.7a. Now let us consider a different version of this game, in which *II* must choose between Accept and Reject *without knowing I*'s choice. In this case it is as if the two choices were simultaneous; an extensive-form representation is however still possible and is achieved as shown in ◘ Fig. 11.7b: the 'oval' or 'balloon' encircling the three nodes is used to indicate that the three nodes are part of the same **information set** of player *II*; an information set collects the nodes where *II* has the same information (which can only be the case if *II* does not know at which of the nodes in the information set she is). Nodes not included in ovals are information sets with only one element. A node is identified by the history of moves (choices) that bring to that node. The initial node is called the root node, also the empty-history node.

928 Chapter 11 · Games and Information

Sometimes instead of an oval encircling the nodes in an information set, a broken or dotted line joining the nodes is used to indicate that they are in the same information set.

Clearly, the moves or **actions** available to the player at an information set that includes several nodes must be the same whichever the node the player is at—otherwise the available actions would indicate to the player the node (s)he is at.

The equivalence between the assumption of simultaneous moves, and the assumption of sequential moves but with the second player moving while ignoring the first player's action, allows us to represent in extensive form any of the simultaneous-move games previously illustrated[3]; in ◧ Fig. 11.7c we have a Prisoner's Dilemma in extensive form.[4] The columns of numbers at the end of the branches indicate the payoffs, the top one is I's or α's payoff, the bottom one is II's or β's.

Another possibility is that the situation in which the player must choose is only partially known: for some elements in it only their probability is known. Then the situation is formalized as an information set containing as many nodes as there are possible states, with a node before that information set, where a fictitious player 'Nature' or 'Chance' chooses among the states according to a probability distribution, and the player does not know Nature's move, although (game theory generally assumes) the player knows the probability distribution. The node where Nature chooses is called a *chance node*. For example, when one bets on a number at the game of (European) roulette, one does not know at which one of the 37 nodes corresponding to the different numbers one will be, one only knows that the probability of being at one node is 1/37 (in the extensive form, Nature's move would appear as preceding the player's bet although in reality it follows it). Another example: as part of a larger game, a firm may have to decide whether to invest or not in drilling for oil, knowing only the probability that oil may be found. In this case the firm's information set contains two nodes, 'there is oil', and 'there is no oil' (for simplicity I neglect intermediate possibilities), and the firm's manager does not know at which node she is, although she knows (game theory assumes) the probability of being at either node.

When there is no oval that encloses nodes in the extensive form of a game, and all players are assumed to know the entire game tree, the game is *of complete and perfect information*. Chess is one such game.

A game is said to be of *incomplete* information when it is not true that each player knows all relevant information *about the other players* including their pay-

---

3 Clearly which player is assumed to move first makes no difference.

4 One might argue that it must be possible for α and β to reach an agreement to play (C, c), since in this way both are better off, obtaining (−3, −3) instead of (−5, −5). But if one player is convinced that the other will honour the agreement, then it is in his/her interest to defect on the agreement, which is therefore useless. If some punishment or side payment is available that makes it convenient not to defect on the agreement, then the game needs a different description, it is a different game. This is an important point, because it suggests that, when cooperation can improve results relative to individualistic choice, people will often try to *change* the game by introducing side payments that render cooperation convenient (organized crime will kill the prisoner who confesses). Actually the search for ways to change games is a crucial component of social life and it causes history seldom to repeat itself. An extremely important part of competition is precisely the continuous search by economic agents for ways to alter in their favour the strategic situations they are engaged in.

offs from the various outcomes of the game; it is said to be of *imperfect* information when players do not always know which node they are at when they reach an information set (of course not all information sets must contain a single node) but otherwise know everything about the game structure and the characteristics of the other player. One-shot simultaneous-move games are games of imperfect information (this is made evident by their representation in extensive form). Games in which one is not certain about preferences of other players, or about payoffs (e.g. an army general might not be certain about the result of battle because uncertain about the fire power of the enemy army), are games of incomplete information. A game can be of incomplete and imperfect information.

11.3 Extensive and Strategic (or Normal) Form

For all games it is possible to adopt either an extensive-form representation or a matrix-form representation as in ◘ Figs. 11.1, 11.2, 11.3 and 11.4 which is called the *normal* form or *strategic* form. The latter name derives from the fact that in this form one lists all possible strategies for each player. With $n > 2$ players, the n-matrix of the strategic form is not easily representable because it is in more than two dimensions, but the notion of strategic form is the same: it requires that, for each combination or '*profile*' of strategies (i.e. vector of strategies, one for each player), the payoffs of each player are listed.

A *strategy* for a player is a list of actions, one for each node in the extensive form of the game where it is the player's turn to choose; at each such node the player has a number of possible actions and must choose one of them, or must choose randomly among them with assigned probabilities: in the latter case the player is adopting a *random strategy*, but for the moment let us consider only *pure* (i.e. non-random) strategies. In the game of ◘ Fig. 11.7a the three possible strategies of *I* are the three choices 90, 50 and 10, at the sole node (the first one in the game) where it is *I*'s turn to play. For *II*, each strategy is a specification of an action at each of the three nodes (2, 3, 4) where *II* can be when it is her turn to choose, hence it is a vector of three choices; for example, 'Accept if First proposes 90, Accept if First proposes 50, Reject if First proposes 10' is one possible strategy. Since at each node there are two actions, *II* has eight possible strategies: four can be represented as (A, A, A), (A, A, R), (A, R, A), (A, R, R), the other four are the same but with R replacing A in the first place, where the letters indicate the action at node 2, at node 3, and at node 4. The *strategic* or *normal* form of the game is therefore a 3×8 bimatrix:

player II

		AAA	RAA	AAR	RAR	ARA	RRA	ARR	RRR
	90								
player I	50								
	10								

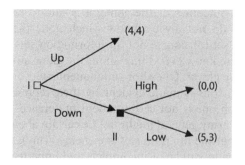

◘ **Fig. 11.8** A sequential game where player Second has no choice if First chooses *Up*

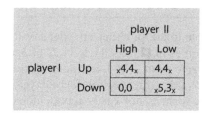

◘ **Fig. 11.9** Normal form of the game in ◘ Fig. 11.8

As an exercise, fill the boxes with the payoffs, deriving them from ◘ Fig. 11.7a. For the game of ◘ Fig. 11.7b, player *I* has the same three strategies, but *II*, who cannot distinguish which node she is at, has only two strategies, A and R, the strategic form is a 3 × 2 matrix; write it down.

Now consider the game of ◘ Fig. 11.8. How is one to pass from the extensive form to the strategic or normal form for this game? If player First chooses Up, the game ends and there is no node left where Second is to choose.

But the principle remains valid that a strategy profile must include a strategy for each player; here the strategies of Second are High and Low[5]; the strategic form bimatrix is accordingly as in ◘ Fig. 11.9.

The fact, that actually Second does not choose if First chooses Up, shows up in the irrelevance of Second's strategy to the payoffs in the first row.

In the above games the number of strategies open to a player was finite. It is also possible that the number of strategies be infinite; this is usually the case when some strategic variables are a continuum or at least are treated as such, e.g. quantity supplied of a perfectly divisible good, or price.

A game in normal form consists of:
- the list of players, numbered 1, ..., N;
- for each player i a set $S_i = \{s_j\}$ of strategies, with $S_i \in S$;

---

5 To be interpreted as "play High if *I* plays Down" and "play Low if *I* plays Down".

11.4 · Mixed Strategies

- for each player a payoff function $u_i(\mathbf{s}) = u_i(s_1, ..., s_N)$ that indicates the von Neumann–Morgenstern utility level associated with the (possibly random) outcome arising from each possible **strategy profile** $\mathbf{s} = (s_1, ..., s_N)$, a vector including one strategy for each player. See footnote 8 below.

Hence formally a game in normal form is representable as[6]

$$\Gamma_n = (N, S = \{S_i\}, \{u_i(\cdot)\}).$$

Extensive-form games can be indicated with Γ_e; what they consist of is a much longer list (the nodes, the actions available at each node, the information sets ...) that I will not detail (see, e.g., Mas-Colell et al. 1995, p. 227, or Kreps 1990, p. 363 and ff.), but the examples will suffice to render the idea.

11.4 Mixed Strategies

One distinguishes *pure strategies* from *mixed strategies*. A pure strategy is the choice by a player of an action (or—in sequential games—a series of actions, one for each information set where the player can be called upon to choose) with certainty. So far I have been talking of pure strategies, implicitly assuming that these were the only ones available to the players. It is also possible for a player to play a mixed strategy that consists of choosing randomly between two or more pure strategies via some randomizing device that assigns to these strategies probabilities summing up to 1. A mixed strategy for a player is a probability distribution over the set of feasible pure strategies of the player. A pure strategy is the special case of a mixed strategy where only one strategy has probability different from zero (and therefore equal to 1); it is sometimes called a *degenerate* mixed strategy.

In some cases recourse to a mixed strategy can be argued to be plausible. Consider the one-shot simultaneous-move game of *Matching Pennies*. There are two players, A and B; each one independently chooses Heads or Tails; if the two choices are the same, B pays A 1 dollar; if the choices do not match, A pays B 1 dollar (write the strategic form of this game). This is an example of a *zero-sum game*, where what one player wins is what the other player loses.[7] A wants to make the same choice as B, B wants the opposite. In this game it is convenient for a player to make it very hard for the other player to predict what she will choose, and then it may be convenient for her to choose randomly. In other cases, mixed strategies although theoretically definable do not appear to have a plausible real-life interpretation and then should not be considered among the available strategies.

In a sequential game, if at a node a player randomizes among several possible choices, since the aim is not to reveal one's action the subsequent player is at an

---

6 Γ is the Greek-alphabet letter 'capital gamma'. The small n stands for 'normal form'.

7 Historically, game theory started with the study of zero-sum games; but most games relevant for economists are not zero-sum games.

932 Chapter 11 · Games and Information

information set with as many nodes as there are possible results of the randomization performed by the first player.

The payoff of a mixed strategy (given the other players' strategies) is defined to be the sum of the *expected values* of the corresponding pure strategy payoffs, as standardly defined by probability theory. Of course this requires that the pure strategy payoffs are not simply ordinal rankings but have cardinal significance, like amounts of money; if they are utility levels, one must be speaking of expected utility, satisfying the von Neumann–Morgenstern axioms.[8] Let us see how one determines the payoffs; logically the thing is straightforward, but it is a bit complicated.

The strategic- or normal-form representation of a game only lists the pure strategies, mapping each *profile* of strategies (each vector of one pure strategy per player) into payoffs for each player. The set of mixed strategies open to a player is the set of all probability distributions over her set of pure strategies.

Suppose there are N players, numbered 1, ..., N. I assume that each player j has a finite number M_j of pure strategies $S_1^j, \ldots, SM_j^j$. A mixed strategy σ^j of player j is a probability distribution $(\sigma_1^j, \sigma_2^j, \ldots, \sigma_h^j, \ldots, \sigma M_j^j)$ that assigns a probability to each member of the set $\left(S_1^j, \ldots, S_h^j, \ldots, SM_j^j\right)$ of pure strategies of player j; in each mixed strategy at least one probability is positive, because the sum of probabilities is 1; a pure strategy is a degenerate mixed strategy that assigns probability 1 to that pure strategy. A **profile** of mixed strategies is a vector of mixed strategies, one per player, $\sigma = (\sigma^1, \ldots, \sigma^j, \ldots, \sigma^N)$. When one wants to highlight above all the behaviour of a certain player, say player j, one can represent a profile of mixed strategies as $\sigma = (\sigma^j, \sigma^{-j})$, where σ^{-j} stands for the profile of pure or mixed strategies of the $N-1$ players other than j (an $N-1$-vector of vectors of probabilities).

Given a profile $\sigma = (\sigma^j, \sigma^{-j})$ of mixed strategies, the probability of a profile of pure strategies $s = \left(s_i^1, \ldots, s_h^j, \ldots, s_k^N\right)$, and therefore also of the vector of payoffs $(u^1(s), \ldots, u^j(s), \ldots, u^N(s))$ associated with that s, is the product of the probabilities that σ assigns to each pure strategy in that s:

$Prob(s) = \sigma_i^1 \cdot \ldots \cdot \sigma_h^j \cdot \ldots \cdot \sigma_k^N$ *(where the $_h^j$ couples of indexes are the same as in s)*. Therefore the expected value of payoff $u^j(s)$ for player j is $u^j(s) \cdot Prob(s)$. If player j were the sole one to adopt a mixed strategy, the strategies of the other players being given, there would be M_j possible profiles s of pure strategies, and the expected value for player j of her mixed strategy would be the sum of the M_j expected payoffs $u^j(s) \cdot Prob(s)$ where each $Prob(s)$ would be simply the prob-

---

8 See ▶ Chap. 9 for these axioms. Here one encounters an important limitation of current game theory: it assumes agents' utility functions have the VNM expected utility form. Very little work has been done so far on how the theory would have to be modified if some other form of utility functions is assumed. The assumption that preferences among mixed strategies are based on comparison among expected values of payoffs appears to have been nearly universally adopted mainly because analytically easy to manipulate, in spite of protestations by many that individuals might well have other preferences, for example might take into account skewness of the probability distributions too, or might have peculiar risk aversions.

11.4 · Mixed Strategies

ability that σ^j assigns to j's strategy in that s. If all players play a mixed strategy the number of possible profiles of pure strategies is $M^* = M_1 \cdot \ldots \cdot M_N$, and the expected value of σ^j is the sum of the M^* expected payoffs $u^j(s) \cdot Prob(s)$. More formally, let S stand for the set (of cardinality M^*) of possible profiles of pure strategies; if s is one such profile (an N-vector of pure strategies, one per player), let us now indicate with s^j the pure strategy of player j in s, and with $\sigma^j(s^j)$ the probability assigned by player j to s^j according to the profile of mixed strategies σ; then the expected payoff of σ^j for player j, given that the mixed strategies of the other players are σ^{-j}, is

$$u^j\left(\sigma^j, \sigma^{-j}\right) = \sum_{s \in S} \sigma^1(s^1) \sigma^2(s^2) \ldots \sigma^N(s^N) u^j(s) = \sum_{s \in S} \left[\prod_{n=1}^{N} \sigma^n(s^n)\right] u^j(s).$$

A different formulation, closer to the above verbal exposition, is as follows. Assume all players apart from j play one pure strategy each, let s^{-j} represent this profile of $N-1$ strategies. Then there are M_j possible complete profiles of pure strategies (s^j, s^{-j}), all identical except for j's pure strategy, and $u^j\left(\sigma^j, s^{-j}\right) = \sum_{i=1}^{M_j} \sigma_i^j u^j(s_i^j, s^{-j})$. From now on for brevity suppose without loss of generality that player j is in fact player 1. Let S^{-1} be the set of all possible profiles s^{-1}; its cardinality is $M_2 \cdot \ldots \cdot M_N = M^* - M_1$. If a profile $s^{-1} = (s^2, s^3, \ldots, s^N)$ (where s^2, s^3 etc. are the pure strategies in the given s^{-1}) is played, not with certainty, but rather according to the probabilities of the mixed strategies σ^{-1}, the probability that it be played is $p^\wedge = \sigma^2(s^2)\sigma^3(s^3) \ldots \sigma^N(s^N)$; the expected payoff for player 1 is therefore $p^\wedge u^1(\sigma^1, s^{-1})$. The sum of these expected payoffs over all possible s^{-1} profiles must be again the expected payoff of the mixed strategy σ^1, which therefore can also be determined as

$$u^1\left(\sigma^1, \sigma^{-1}\right) = \sum_{s^{-1} \in S^{-1}} \left[\prod_{n=2}^{N} \sigma^n(s_n)\right] u^1(\sigma^1, s^{-1}). \tag{11.1}$$

This expression will be useful later, in ▶ Sect. 11.8.

11.5 **Behavioural Strategies**

When one uses the extensive form of a game, there is another, perhaps more intuitive way of describing randomization among strategies. The *behavioural strategy* of a player, instead of listing the probability attached to each strategy (as a mixed strategy does), lists separately the probability distribution over the possible actions at each information set where it is the player's turn to choose. To describe the behavioural strategy of a player we need:

(i) a list of *all* information sets in the game tree where it is the player's turn to choose (*including* the ones which, given the strategies, certainly will not be reached)

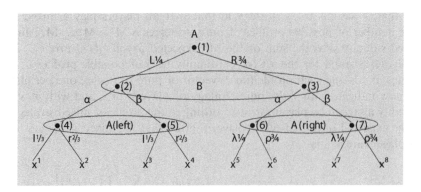

◻ **Fig. 11.10** Representation of behavioural strategies

(ii) for each information set, a list of the possible actions of the player at that set with the probabilities (summing up to 1) with which she randomizes among them.

Given a behavioural strategy one can define an associated mixed strategy of its normal-form counterpart, by finding a probability for each pure strategy, such that the implied mixed strategy is 'outcome equivalent' to the behavioural strategy, that is, generates the same probability distribution over final outcomes. *It suffices, for each pure strategy, to multiply all probabilities assigned by the behavioural strategy to the actions occurring in the pure strategy.* The resulting mixed strategy is called a *mixed strategy representation* of the behavioural strategy. Let us examine how one passes from one to the other with the help of an example. Assume the sequential game of ◻ Fig. 11.10 between two players A and B, where the behavioural strategy for A is indicated by the probabilities next to each action:

The ovals show that this is a game of imperfect information: A randomizes between Left and Right, B does not know at which node he is, B randomizes too; after B's action A knows whether she is at the left or at the right information set (she knows whether she played L or R), but does not know at which of the two nodes in that information set she is. A has 3 information sets and two actions at each one, so she has 8 pure strategies: (L, l, λ), (L, l, ρ), (L, r, λ), (L, r, ρ), and the same four with R in place of L. (Note that A's strategies specify her action at all three information sets even though the third one, A(right), cannot be reached if she chooses L at the initial node, and the second one, A(left), cannot be reached if she chooses R at the initial node. But B does not know at which information set A is located after B's action, and in order to decide his strategy he needs beliefs about A's choices at *all* information sets. Later we will see that the choices at unreached information sets can be important.)

Let us determine the mixed strategy corresponding to A's behavioural strategy. In determining the probability assigned to each pure strategy by the behavioural strategy one must take into account whether an information set can be reached or

11.5 · Behavioural Strategies

not, given the previous actions. Once B's choices are given, the choice between pure strategies (L, l, λ) and (L, l, ρ) makes no difference to outcomes because once L is chosen, the information set where A would have to choose between λ and ρ is not reached and the choices there cannot have an influence on the outcome; so the important thing is the *joint* probability of (L, l, λ) and (L, l, ρ) which is $1/4 \times 1/3 = 1/12$. Any distribution of this joint probability between the two pure strategies will bring to the same probability of the final outcomes x^1 and x^3 that can be reached with these pure strategies. This shows that the mixed strategy corresponding to a given behavioural strategy (in the sense of being 'outcome equivalent') need not be uniquely determined. But to fix ideas, one can decide that the total probability 1/12 is divided between the two pure strategies as indicated by the probabilities of λ and ρ, which sum to 1. So $P(L, l, \lambda) = 1/12 \times 1/4$ and $P(L, l, \rho) = 1/12 \times 3/4$. With the same method one assigns joint probability 9/16 to the two pure strategies (R, l, ρ) and (R, r, ρ), and assigns one-third of it to the first strategy and two-thirds to the second. So one obtains the probability with which a given pure strategy is played by multiplying the probabilities assigned by the behavioural strategy to each action at each information set where the player is the chooser.

A more formal analysis—omitted here—of the issue and also of the converse possibility of deriving a behavioural strategy from a mixed strategy would prove that if *perfect recall* is assumed (that is, complete memory of what has happened in previous stages of the game: I will always assume it), this passage from one representation of the game to the other representation is always possible (although in both directions the passage need not be uniquely determined, but with no consequence for the payoffs and the solution of the game).

11.6 Solutions. Elimination of Strictly Dominated Strategies. Some Doubts

A **solution** of a game is a profile of strategies, one for each player, that are reputed 'optimal' or 'rational' for each player, and therefore presumably will be adopted by rational players. Unfortunately, optimality criteria can generate more than one solution, and then unless some criterion is found that makes one and the same solution preferred to the other ones by all players, the analysis loses predictive capacity.

In order to determine the optimal strategy of each player, game theory has recourse to a series of assumptions. One such assumption is (for games of perfect information) that each player knows both the *extensive* and the *normal or strategic form* of the game, including the payoffs, and knows that the same is true of the other players. Another one is that each player is able to determine and follow her optimal strategy, if it exists, and knows that the same is true of the other players and is also able to determine the other players' optimal strategies; an implication is that each player assumes that the other players choose optimally or, as the terminology goes, rationally. The realism of these assumptions must be checked

936   **Chapter 11 · Games and Information**

case by case, if they do not apply the results of game theory have unclear predictive value.[9]

There are two criteria generally used by game theorists to arrive at solutions of a game. The first is elimination of dominated strategies. The second is restriction to Nash equilibria. I start with the first.

To make an optimal decision, a player must foresee how her opponents will behave. A nearly universal assumption is that each player assumes that the opponents will not play a ***strictly dominated strategy***. A strategy for a player is strictly dominated if there is a second strategy yielding strictly higher payoff whatever the strategies of the other players. The second strategy is said to ***strictly dominate*** the first strategy.[10] Whether a strategy is strictly dominated can be seen from the strategic form of the game. The standard argument is that it is irrational to play a strategy which is strictly dominated by a second strategy, since whatever your opponent chooses to do, the second strategy gets you a better outcome. (Later I will argue that this argument is not always convincing.) If this argument is accepted, then one can delete the strictly dominated strategy from the strategies that a player can choose, causing the corresponding row or column to disappear from the strategic form of the game.

A strategy is a ***best response*** to a given profile of the opponents' strategies if no other strategy of that player ensures her a strictly better payoff. If one strategy strictly dominates all other strategies of a player, it is called the ***strictly dominant strategy*** for that player; it is the ***unique best response*** to whatever strategy profile is played by the opponents. If each player has a strictly dominant strategy, their combined choice is the unique solution, and the game is said to have a ***strictly dominant strategy equilibrium***.[11]

Sometimes in the new game resulting from the elimination of a strictly dominated strategy some other strategy results strictly dominated, and therefore eliminable. One then proceeds to an ***iterated elimination of strictly dominated strategies***.

Thus consider the simultaneous game in normal form of ◘ Fig. 11.11. As usual in each box the payoff of the row player is given first. Strategy Alpha is dominated for player B by Delta, and Beta is dominated by Gamma. If we delete columns Alpha and Beta, the game reduces to the last two columns; now High is dominated by Low for player A; if we delete row High, the only player who has a choice is B, who chooses Delta. So we reach the solution (Low, Delta).

---

9   Take the well-known game of Rock, Paper, Scissors. This is a game where, as in Heads and Tails, it is convenient not to let the opponent guess what one is going to choose, so to randomize may look optimal; but in fact, because the game is played repeatedly and quickly, it is difficult purely to randomize, and then it is often better, in order to win, to assume that one's opponent does not randomize well and to try to detect a pattern in the sequence of moves of the opponent – i.e. it can be better *not* to assume that the other player plays optimally.

10   The strategy that dominates the dominated strategy must be the same whatever the opponents' strategies.

11   Why the solution is called 'equilibrium' will become clear later when we define the Nash equilibrium.

11.6 · Solutions. Elimination of Strictly Dominated Strategies. Some Doubts

		player B			
		Alpha	Beta	Gamma	Delta
player A	High	4, 0	8, 4	4, 5	1, 1
	Low	2, 2	6, 0	6, 1	2, 3

◘ **Fig. 11.11**   A game to study elimination of dominated strategies

This result can raise doubts about the correctness of elimination of strictly dominated strategies, because (High, Beta) and (High, Gamma) would have yielded a better payoff for both players. One might argue that player A should reason differently: 'B cannot remain blind to the fact that by playing (High, Gamma) we both reach a better payoff than with (Low, Delta) and that if I play High he has no better choice than Gamma. So I will play High, and B certainly can predict it and will play Gamma; in this way I obtain 4 instead of 2.' But there is a counterargument: the more A feels confident that B will choose Gamma, the more A is induced to choose Low instead of High, obtaining 6 instead of 4 but leaving only 1 to B. So B can legitimately mistrust A and choose Delta. On the other hand, B may believe on the basis of his past experience that in situations like this people generally go for the higher payoff compatible with a higher payoff for the opponent too, as a convention developed by society and generally interiorized, that favours cooperative behaviour, because the latter makes social life more pleasant and allows people to obtain the higher cooperative payoff; and so B may play Gamma (and for the same reason A may play High). And some experimental evidence suggests that indeed in situations of this type some players (not all, but often a majority) do choose a 'cooperative' behaviour corresponding in the present game to playing (High, Gamma). The reply of most game theorists is that then the game is not correctly represented, because besides the numbers representing the payoffs of the game the players also have information on the probability with which the opponent will choose a 'friendly' strategy. As you can see, if one tries to be realistic about how a game will be played things rapidly get complex.

Or consider the game of ◘ Fig. 11.5 (and ◘ Fig. 11.7c), the famous Prisoner's Dilemma. To play Defect is a strictly dominant strategy for both players; but the result is (1, 1) while if both players play Cooperate the payoffs are (4, 4). In this case, is it really rational to play D? Clearly it would be convenient for both players to find a way to achieve (4, 4). Consider this reasoning: 'I am as intelligent as my opponent, so, given the symmetric nature of the game, I can assume that we reach the same conclusions; now, the only way to achieve (4, 4) is for both of us to play C; well, if my opponent plays C and I play D, I get 5 instead of 4, but if I start reasoning like this I will conclude that I must play D and my opponent will reach the same conclusion and we will both play D which must be avoided, so I must not reason like this; and since I expect my opponent to be as intelligent as I am and to realize—just as I am doing—that we must avoid this line of reasoning otherwise we end up at (D, D) and obtain (1, 1), I will play C and I can expect my

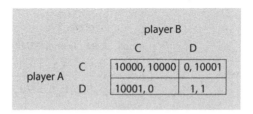

◘ Fig. 11.12 An extreme prisoner's dilemma game

opponent too to play C'. The counterargument is that if I expect my opponent to play C then it is better for me to play D. The counter-counterargument is that this way of reasoning is irrational and must be avoided, because it produces (D, D). This counter-counterargument appears particularly attractive for a Prisoner's Dilemma like the one of ◘ Fig. 11.12, where the payoffs are dollars.

Here, whatever my opponent chooses, the advantage from choosing D rather than C is so small (one dollar), and the loss relative to the payoff of (C, C) is so large if we both choose D, that avoiding the risk of ending up at (D, D) may well justify a neglect of the fact that, whatever my opponent chooses, playing D gets me one more dollar than playing C, and so may justify playing C. If you agree on this conclusion for this extreme set of payoffs, then you probably have to agree also for somewhat less extreme payoffs,[12] the certainty that it is always rational to eliminate strictly dominated strategies starts vacillating…

Debate among game theorists and philosophers continues on the thesis that choosing Defect is the only rational choice in Prisoner's dilemma games; an important recent contribution is Michael Bacharach, *Beyond Individual Choice* (2006), who argues that game theory is unable to prove such a thesis and argues that other criteria can be rational too. Consider the two-person one-shot extremely simple **Hi-Lo** game. A representative bimatrix for this game is in ◘ Fig. 11.13.

Bacharach (2006, pp. 43–58) persuasively argues that game theory offers no convincing reason for the players to converge to (Up, Left) rather than to (Down, Right); but most people would agree that reasonable people who think that their opponent is reasonable will, without hesitation, choose (Up, Left): now, Bacharach argues, this indicates the adoption of a broader criterion of rationality

---

12 Consider this Prisoner's dilemma game applying to the original story, so the numbers are years of imprisonment:

		B	
		Confess	Not confess
A	Confess	-30,-30	-3,-32
	Not confess	-32, -3	-4, -4

Does (Confess, Confess) appear to you to be the more probable way this game will be played, even apart from the danger of punishment by other criminals if one confesses?

11.6 · Solutions. Elimination of Strictly Dominated Strategies. Some Doubts

A \ B	Left	Right
Up	2,2	0,0
Down	0,0	1,1

◘ **Fig. 11.13** Hi-Lo game

than the ones considered by game theory, a criterion that looks at what can be achieved by counting on a possibility of co-operation; then why shouldn't similar broader criteria be adopted in other games too?

But to enter these debates is for a course where game theory can be given more space than here. For the moment a great majority of game theorists insist that it would be irrational to play strictly dominated strategies in *all* cases in which one can assume that the other players are rational, and I must introduce you to game theory as currently practised. Still, this thesis seems to me to be accepted as a dogma, rather than carefully defended.

Anyway in many cases a Prisoner's dilemma situation does result in the inferior, non-cooperative outcome; there is then a clear indication that some change in the game would be opportune, capable of incentivizing players to act cooperatively. In the case of a *true* Prisoner's dilemma, with criminals as prisoners, the game modification is generally present: punishment if you confess, administered by other criminals the moment you get out of prison, or even before.

11.7 Weakly Dominated Strategies, Dominance Solvable Games

A pure strategy s_2 of a player is **weakly dominated** by another pure strategy s_1 of the same player if the payoff from s_1 is at least as large as from s_2 for all possible strategy choices by the other players, and strictly larger for some but not for all. If the player attributes strictly positive probability of occurrence to all the other players' strategies and maximizes the expected value of payoffs, then the presumption that the player will not play a weakly dominated strategy is reasonable, the expected value of s_1's payoffs is certainly higher than for s_2. When iterated elimination of strictly and weakly dominated strategies results in only one strategy left for each player, this is considered the solution, and the game is said **dominance solvable**. But the deletion of one or more weakly dominated strategies when more than one player has weakly dominated strategies is admitted to be much more problematical than for strictly dominated strategies. Consider ◘ Fig. 11.14.

For B, Right weakly dominates Left; for A, Down weakly dominates Up. To conclude that A will not play Up, and B will not play Left, would not present problems if we could assume that A attributes positive probability, however small, to both B's strategies and that the same does B for both A's strategies. But

940 **Chapter 11 · Games and Information**

$_A \backslash {}^B$	Left	Right
Up	1,0	1,1
Down	2,0	1,0

Fig. 11.14 A game where elimination of weakly dominated strategies destroys it rationale

this assumption encounters a logical problem: the conclusion that A will certainly not play Up authorizes B to attribute probability zero to the occurrence of Up, in which case B is indifferent between playing Left and Right, and we can no longer be certain that Left will not be played; a symmetrical reasoning applied to A's certainty that B will not play Left brings to the conclusion that we cannot be certain that Up will not be played by A. Thus in this case the justification for simultaneous deletion is self-contradictory, while the deletion of only one of the two weakly dominated strategies is arbitrary.

Further problems are that the *iterated* deletion of weakly dominated strategies can result in the survival of different sets of strategies depending on the order of elimination, and that the removal of an action at some stage in the iterative deletion procedure may eliminate the rationale for the removal of some other action at an earlier stage.

In the example of Fig. 11.15 if we first eliminate L and then T the outcomes that survive are (B, C) and (B, R), yielding payoffs (1, 2). If we first eliminate R and then B, there survive (T, L) and (T, R) yielding payoffs (1, 1). If we first eliminate both L and R, the outcomes that survive are (T, C) and (B, C) where only the row player is called to choose, but is indifferent, so both payoff profiles (1, 1) and (1, 2) are possible. In the example of Fig. 11.16, Bottom is

$_A \backslash {}^B$	Left	Center	Right
Top	1,1	1,1	0,0
Bottom	0,0	1,2	1,2

Fig. 11.15 In this game iterated elimination of weakly dominated strategies produces different results depending on the order of elimination

	Left	Middle	Right
Top	2,2	2,1	1,0
Bottom	2,1	2,2	0,2

Fig. 11.16 Another example of debatable elimination of weakly dominated strategies

11.7 · Weakly Dominated Strategies, Dominance Solvable Games

weakly dominated by Top, but also Right is weakly dominated by Middle and if we eliminate Right the row player no longer has a reason not to choose Bottom.

However, 'Despite such examples, economists tend to use successive weak dominance when they can' (Kreps 1990, p. 398) (Rigour takes second place if it results in no result …).

11.8 Dominated Mixed Strategies

The notions of strict and of weak dominance are extended to mixed strategies by referring to their expected payoffs. The computation of strictly dominated strategies when mixed strategies are admitted is time-consuming and will not be examined in all details.

First, one finds out the pure strategies strictly dominated by other pure strategies. Here a helpful result is that, in order to ascertain whether a mixed or, as a special case, a pure strategy σ_1 of a player is strictly dominated by another mixed or pure strategy σ_2 of that player we only need to consider the payoffs of these strategies against the *pure* strategies of the player's opponents.

Proof Let s_i^j be the ith pure strategy of player j, let s^{-j} be a profile of pure strategies by j's opponents with S^{-j} be the set of such profiles, and let s be a complete profile of pure strategies with S its set; let $\sigma^{j\alpha}$, $\sigma^{j\beta}$ be two mixed strategies of player j, and let σ^{-j} be a profile of mixed strategies of j's opponents. Let $u^j(\sigma^j, \sigma^{-j})$ be the expected payoff of mixed strategy σ^j against strategies σ^{-j}. I wish to prove that $u^j(\sigma^{j\alpha}, \sigma^{-j}) > u^j(\sigma^{j\beta}, \sigma^{-j})$ for all σ^{-j} if and only if $u^j(\sigma^{j\alpha}, s^{-j}) > u^j(\sigma^{j\beta}, s^{-j})$ for all s^{-j}. I only prove this for the case of a finite number of feasible pure strategies $s_1^j, …, s_{Mj}^j$. From expression (11.1), ▶ Sect. 11.4, we can derive

$$u^j\left(\sigma^{j\alpha}, \sigma^{-j}\right) - u^j\left(\sigma^{j\beta}, \sigma^{-j}\right) = \sum_{s^{-j} \in S^{-j}} \left[\prod_{n \neq j} \sigma^n(s)\right] \left[u^j(\sigma^{j\alpha}, s^{-j}) - u^j(\sigma^{j\beta}, s^{-j})\right].$$

This expression is positive for all σ^{-j} if and only if $\left[u^j(\sigma^{j\alpha}, s^{-j}) - u^j(\sigma^{j\beta}, s^{-j})\right]$ is positive for all s^{-j}. ∎

Second, among the remaining pure strategies one looks for the pure strategies strictly dominated by some mixed strategy. That a pure strategy, not dominated by any other pure strategy, can be dominated by a mixed strategy is shown by ◧ Fig. 11.17 (from Mas-Colell et al. 1995, p. 241). No pure strategy dominates another for player A; but the mixed strategy consisting of playing Up and Down with probability 1/2 dominates the pure strategy Middle (it yields A an expected payoff of 5 whichever B's strategy, against 4 of Middle).

Third, having found the undominated pure strategies, one looks for the dominated mixed strategies; here a helpful result is that *all mixed strategies that assign positive probability to a dominated pure strategy are dominated* (the proof is easy and left as an *Exercise* for the reader), so one needs only look at mixtures of undominated pure strategies.

942 Chapter 11 · Games and Information

		player B	
		Left	Right
player A	Up	10,1	0,4
	Middle	4,2	4,3
	Down	0,5	10,2

◼ **Fig. 11.17** In this game A's middle strategy is dominated by a mixed strategy

All this can be very laborious; if you intend to become a specialist in this field it is strongly advisable that you learn some computer programming and develop a program capable of doing these tasks for you. A doubt arises: if the purpose of the analysis is explicative/predictive, can we assume people make all these calculations?

11.9 Nash Equilibrium in Pure Strategies

If a game is not dominance solvable, then one must look for some other 'reasonable outcome'. By far the most widely accepted notion of reasonable outcome is the *Nash equilibrium*. It can be defined in a variety of ways. A very intuitive one is the following.

■■ **Definition**
A Nash equilibrium is a profile of strategies, one for each player, such that no player regrets her strategy choice once she knows the strategies chosen by the other players.

In other words a Nash equilibrium is a profile of strategies such that no player can gain by *unilaterally* changing strategy, that is, while the other players' strategies do not change.

A Nash equilibrium can also be defined as a profile of strategies such that:
(i) each player's strategy choice is a best response given her beliefs about the other players' strategies,
(ii) furthermore these beliefs are correct.

This definition[13] applies to pure as well as to mixed strategies. But initially I restrict discussion to pure strategies. Slightly more formally, a profile of pure

---

13 It can be disputed that the second definition, that introduces beliefs, is really equivalent to the first, because it is not always necessary, for a player's strategy s^j to be a best response to the profile s^{-j} of strategies of her opponents, that s^{-j} was correctly predicted. E.g. in a two-players game in which both players have strictly dominant strategies, they may well play them and obtain the unique Nash equilibrium even though they expected the other player to choose another strategy. However, a Nash equilibrium is universally interpreted as a situation of correct expectations.

11.9 · Nash Equilibrium in Pure Strategies

	A \ B	Heads	Tails
player A	Heads	$_x$1,-1	-1, 1$_x$
	Tails	-1, 1$_x$	$_x$1,-1

☐ **Fig. 11.18** Matching Pennies

A \ B	Left	Right
Up	$_x$1,2$_x$	$_x$2,2$_x$
Down	$_x$1,3$_x$	0,1

☐ **Fig. 11.19** Many Nash equilibria

strategies $s = (s^1, ..., s^N)$ is a Nash equilibrium if for each player $j, j = 1, ..., N$, the payoff from $s = (s^j, s^{-j})$ is as high as the payoff from any other profile of strategies differing from s only in s^j.

A game can have more than one Nash equilibrium. This is the case, for example, for the Stag Hunt, for the Battle of Sexes, for Hi-Lo. A game can have no Nash equilibrium: a simple example is in ☐ Fig. 11.18 (it's the game of *Matching Pennies* already mentioned in ▶ Sect. 11.4).

These examples show that for two-player games in strategic form, to check whether a couple of pure strategies is a Nash equilibrium one must check that the column player does not obtain a higher payoff in the same row, and the row player does not obtain a higher payoff in the same column. Put a little x next to the highest payoff(s) of the column player in each row, and next to the highest payoff(s) of the row player in each column: the boxes where both payoffs have the x next to them are Nash equilibria. Check that in the game of ☐ Fig. 11.11 the only Nash equilibrium is (Low, Delta).

Note that the absence of an incentive to deviate does not exclude equal payoffs obtainable by deviating. In ☐ Fig. 11.19 only (Down; Right) is *not* a Nash equilibrium.

11.10 Nash Equilibria in Mixed Strategies

Now I allow players to randomize among the strategies available to them. A Nash equilibrium in mixed strategies is a profile of mixed strategies, such that for each player, if the mixed strategies of the other players are kept fixed, no other mixed strategy yields a higher expected payoff.

A necessary condition for a *strictly* mixed strategy (also called *proper* mixed strategy, i.e. one in which at least two pure strategies are played with positive probability) to be part of a Nash equilibrium is that it satisfies the following important property that I call the *Indifference Condition*:

Indifference Condition for mixed-strategy Nash equilibria. In a Nash equilibrium all the pure strategies appearing with positive probability in the mixed strategy of a player must yield the same expected payoff if played as a pure strategy against the given mixed strategies of the opponents.

If it were not so, the original mixed strategy would not be a best response, because attributing probability 0 to a pure strategy with lower expected payoff than some others and raising all probabilities of the remaining pure strategies in the same proportion until they sum up to 1 would yield a higher expected payoff than the original mixed strategy. The same kind of reasoning proves that each pure strategy given positive probability in the mixed strategy of a player must yield an expected payoff no worse than any of the pure strategies given zero probability.

Sometimes the Indifference Condition is sufficient to guarantee that there is a unique Nash equilibrium in mixed strategies. Consider Matching Pennies, which has no Nash equilibrium in pure strategies. Let $p_A < 1$ be the probability player A assigns to playing Heads and hence $1 - p_A$ the probability A plays Tails; we can use p_A to indicate A's mixed strategy. Analogously let p_B be the probability that B assigns to playing Heads. The expected payoff to B from playing the pure strategy Heads against p_A is $-p_A + (1 - p_A)$; the expected payoff to B from playing Tails against p_A is $p_A - (1 - p_A)$. In order for these payoffs to be equal it must be $p_A = 1/2$; this is the only mixed strategy by A that makes it possible for B to play a (proper) mixed strategy satisfying the Indifference Condition. The same reasoning shows that $p_B = 1/2$ is the only mixed strategy by B that makes it possible for A to play a proper mixed strategy satisfying the Indifference Condition. Thus Matching Pennies does have a Nash equilibrium, only one, and in mixed strategies $(p_A = 1/2, p_B = 1/2)$, yielding expected payoffs $(0, 0)$.

Or consider the Battle of the Sexes of ◘ Fig. 11.1. This game has two Nash equilibria in pure strategies, (H, H) and (C, C), but it also has a Nash equilibrium in mixed strategies. Let p_A, p_B, the probabilities of playing H, represent the mixed strategies of Art and of Belle. The expected payoff to Belle from playing H against p_A is $2p_A + (1 - p_A)$, the one from playing C is $3(1 - p_A)$, they are equal if $p_A = 1/2$; the analogous calculation for Art produces $4p_B + (1 - p_B) = 2(1 - p_B)$ i.e. $p_B = 1/5$; the unique Nash equilibrium in mixed strategies is $(p_A = 1/2, p_B = 1/5)$; the reader should check that it yields expected payoffs (8/5, 3/2). We see again that the need that one player satisfies the Indifference Condition determines the probabilities of the mixed strategy of the *other* player.

11.11 Existence of Nash Equilibrium. The Reasons for Interest in Nash Equilibria

It has been proved (1) that a Nash equilibrium always exists in mixed strategies if there is a finite number of pure strategies, and (2) that a Nash equilibrium in pure strategies always exists if for all agents the strategy sets are convex compact

11.11 · Existence of Nash Equilibrium. The Reasons for Interest in Nash Equilibria

subsets of R_n and the payoff functions are continuous and quasi-concave.[14] The proofs rely on fixed-point theorems and are rather similar to the proofs of existence of a general equilibrium of pure exchange.

When the pure strategies available to players are a continuum and the payoffs are *differentiable* functions of the strategies, then the condition that each player's pure strategy be a best response to the other players' pure strategies can be expressed in terms of a system of first-order conditions for a maximum. Suppose there are two players with strategies x for the player 1, and y for player 2, that consist of the choice of any real number, and differentiable payoffs $q(x, y)$ for player 1 and $\pi(x, y)$ for player 2; a Nash equilibrium (x^*, y^*) requires that $\partial q(x^*, y^*)/\partial x^* = 0$ and simultaneously $\partial \pi(x^*, y^*)/\partial y^* = 0$; this is a system of two equations in two unknowns; its solutions, if second-order conditions are satisfied, yield the Nash equilibria.

But these and other results are not very interesting unless there is reason to believe that the (or one) Nash equilibrium is how the game will be played. I turn to this issue.

The notion of Nash equilibrium is by far the most widely used indicator of how games will be played. On the basis of what arguments? There isn't an accepted general answer to this question, but rather a series of considerations that suggest that in *some* circumstances it is plausible that players will choose strategies forming a Nash equilibrium.

Hyper-rational inference, and rationalizability. One standard argument, very popular in the past, in support of the usefulness of the notion of Nash equilibrium relies on hyper-rationality. A Nash equilibrium is a strategy profile in which each player's strategy is a best response to the profile of strategies of the other players. The argument is that *if* there is only one Nash equilibrium, and *if* each player has complete knowledge of the game structure and is extremely intelligent and rational and knows that the other players know the game and are just as intelligent and rational, and *if* she also knows that the other players know that she knows this fact and so on indefinitely, *then* she can do all the reasonings of other players and the same is true of them, hence whatever conclusion she reaches about *her* optimal strategy will also be reached by all other players, so each one of them will find it optimal to play a best response to her optimal strategy, therefore a strategy cannot be optimal for her unless it is a best response to strategies each one of which is a best response—but then these strategies form a Nash equilibrium.

This elegant argument is not as watertight as it looks. It implicitly assumes that hyper-rationality (and common knowledge of hyper-rationality)[15] restricts

---

14 Note that it is not excluded that for some player the strategy set is a single point, i..e that the player has only one strategy. How come this does not exclude the existence of a Nash equilibrium in pure strategies?.

15 What I am calling hyper-rationality is generally named simply 'rationality', but the usual meaning of rationality does not imply that a rational person has all the immense analytical and computing capacity that may be necessary for the required reasonings. A 'rational' player as game theory intends it would know the winning strategy at chess.

946　Chapter 11 · Games and Information

	b_1	b_2	b_3
a_1	1, 8	2, 2	8, 0
a_2	2, 2	3, 3	2, 2
a_3	8, 1	2, 2	0, 8

□ Fig. 11.20 .

the possible strategies of players to being based on *correct* beliefs about what other players will play. Is this assumption legitimate? Consider a two-person game. The subjectively best response strategy $\alpha 1$ for player A depends on the strategy $\beta 1$ she believes player B will choose, where B's strategy $\beta 1$ must be a best response to the strategy $\alpha 2$ that A believes B believes A will play; $\alpha 2$ in turn must be a best response to the strategy $\beta 2$ that A believes B believes A believes B will play, and so on ad infinitum. The hyper-rationality argument implicitly assumes that this sequence of beliefs would reveal an inconsistency somewhere, unless $\alpha 1 = \alpha 2 = \alpha 3$ … and $\beta 1 = \beta 2 = \beta 3$ …, that is, unless the sequence was applied to strategies forming a Nash equilibrium. But this assumption is false. The following example proves it. Consider a simultaneous-move game in which players are restricted to pure strategies; A can choose among three strategies a_1, a_2 and a_3, and B can choose among three strategies b_1, b_2 and b_3. The payoffs are given by the normal-form matrix of □ Fig. 11.20:

This game has only one Nash equilibrium, (a_2, b_2), but there also exists a sequence of beliefs by A (on what B will play; on what B believes A will play; on what B believes A believes B will play; and so on ad infinitum), that, if held, would justify A's choice of a_1. To see that it is so, note the following succession of best responses, with '$a_i \leftarrow b_j$' meaning 'strategy a_i is a best response to strategy b_j' and therefore also interpretable as 'a_i will be played if it is believed that b_j will be played'[16]:

$$a_1 \leftarrow b_3 \leftarrow a_3 \leftarrow b_1 \leftarrow a_1 \leftarrow b_3 \dots .$$

This means that A will play a_1 if she believes that B will play b_3, and she will believe it if she believes that B believes that she will play a_3, and she will believe this if she believes that B believes that she believes that B will play b_1, and so forth. No contradiction arises in this infinite sequence of beliefs about beliefs.

A's choice of strategy a_1 is therefore *rationalizable*—this is the technical term used to indicate a strategy choice that can be justified by a sequence of internally consistent beliefs about what other players believe—but it is not part of a Nash equilibrium. Nash equilibrium strategies are always rationalizable, but we see here

---

16　In this example, best responses are unique, but the interpretation would be sustainable even if this were not so.

11.11 · Existence of Nash Equilibrium. The Reasons for Interest in Nash Equilibria

that there may be other rationalizable strategies too.[17] Note that the same reasoning, if started at b_3, or at a_3, or at b_1, shows that b_3, a_3, b_1 are also rationalizable. Thus in this example *any* couple of pure strategies can be played, depending on beliefs. Since there is no way to check the correctness of beliefs before the game is played, there is no guarantee that A's beliefs will be correct, in spite of their being internally consistent. We conclude that when in a game there are other rationalizable strategies besides the Nash equilibrium ones, the argument that hyper-rationality plus common knowledge of hyper-rationality must imply the choice of Nash equilibrium strategies is faulty.

But even when there are no other rationalizable strategies besides Nash equilibrium ones, the argument runs into problems if there are several Nash equilibria and there is no evident reason why players should 'converge' onto one of them: then it is impossible for a player to be certain about the other players' optimal strategies, and then the definition of optimal strategy becomes problematical.

Also problematical is the case when the Nash equilibrium requires excessively complicated calculations in order to be determined (chess is a standard example).

Focal equilibria. One way to surmount the problem caused by multiple Nash equilibria is to look for elements that may render one of these equilibria the one people spontaneously prefer. A standard example: suppose two persons are to meet on a fixed day at a fixed time in a town, but the meeting place is not specified. They will certainly try to think of a place that suggests itself as the most obvious meeting place in that town. In Venice, Piazza S. Marco most probably; in New York, the top of the Empire State Building (at least, if one is a tourist). These Nash equilibria are called **focal.** Unfortunately it is doubtful that focal equilibria can often be found: in Rome, Piazza S. Pietro, or the Coliseum?

Stable social convention. A different argument is that Nash equilibria are what players must have converged to, if a standard way of playing the game, a 'steady state' or stable social convention, has been reached in a population; individuals must have no preferred alternative behaviour otherwise they would not conform.

» Informally, the idea is … that the players have learned each other's strategies from their experience playing the game. In the idealized situation to which the analysis corresponds, for each player in the game there is a large population of individuals who may take the role of that player; in any play of the game, one participant is drawn randomly from each population. In this situation, a new individual who

---

17 Rationalizable strategies are what remains after iterated elimination of strategies that are never a best response; the reason, briefly, is that no belief about what other players intend to play can justify choosing a strategy that is never a best response. The distinction from Nash equilibrium strategies is very clearly put in the following lines: "In a Nash equilibrium, each player's strategy choice is a best response to the strategies *actually played* by his rivals. The italicized words distinguish the concept of Nash equilibrium from the concept of rationalizability. Rationalizability, which captures the implications of the players' common knowledge of each others' rationality and the structure of the game, requires only that a player's strategy be a best response to some reasonable conjecture about what his rivals will be playing, where *reasonable* means that the conjectured play of his rivals can also be so justified. Nash equilibrium adds to this the requirement that players be *correct* in their conjectures." (Mas-Colell et al. 1995, p. 246).

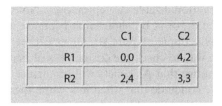

◘ Fig. 11.21 R2, C2 may be self-enforcing without being Nash

joins a population that is in a steady state (i.e. is using a Nash equilibrium strategy profile) can learn the other players' strategies by observing their actions over many plays of the game. As long as the turnover in players is small enough, existing players' encounters with neophytes (who may use nonequilibrium strategies) will be sufficiently rare that their beliefs about the steady state will not be disturbed, so that a new player's problem is simply to learn the other players' actions (Osborne 2004, p. 134).

An example is the convention that in Downtown Manhattan when speedily walking to work in the morning, one should keep to the right. This convention once established discourages from not adopting it (a unilateral deviant would find it almost impossible to proceed). Another example cited by Bowles (2003, p. 24) is peasants in Palanpur (India) who all wait for the very last useful day to sow their winter crops in their several fields, which is many weeks after the date when yields would be maximized: the reason is that simultaneous sowing reduces the quantity of seed eaten by birds, but collective ex-ante coordination is difficult, so no one wants to be first to sow, and it is the need not to lose the entire harvest that finally pushes to all families sowing on the same last useful day.[18]

The argument is plausible when applicable, but it leaves out most of the strategic interactions for which one hopes game theory can be useful, e.g. military strategies, or industrial strategies, which are generally not repeated.

Self-enforcing agreement. When players can talk to each other and form agreements as to how to play a game prior to the beginning of the game, and there is no enforcement mechanism providing independent incentives for compliance with the agreement, then agreements will appear acceptable only if each player has reason to respect them in the absence of external enforcement; it is then argued that the agreed strategies must form a Nash equilibrium.

But it has been objected that self-enforcing agreements need not necessarily be Nash equilibria. One example cited in the entry 'Game Theory' from the *Internet Encyclopedia of Philosophy* is reported in ◘ Fig. 11.21.

I report the comment: 'Let's imagine the players initially agreed to play (*R2, C2*). Now both have serious reasons to deviate, as deviating unilaterally would profit either player. Therefore, the Nash equilibria of this game are (*R1, C2*) and

---

18 This can be seen as the outcome of an Assurance game with many players, re-read the discussion of the Stag Hunt game in ▶ Sect. 11.2.

11.11 · Existence of Nash Equilibrium. The Reasons for Interest in Nash Equilibria

	c1	c2	c3	c4
r1	$_x$200, 6$_x$	3, 5	4, 3	0, −1000
r2	0, −10000	$_x$5, −1000	$_x$6, 3	$_x$3, 20$_x$

◘ **Fig. 11.22** A game submitted by David Kreps to students

($R2$, $C1$). However, in an additional step of reflection, both players may note that they risk ending up with nothing if they *both* deviate, particularly as the rational recommendation for each is to *unilaterally* deviate. Players may therefore prefer the relative security of sticking to the agreed-upon strategy. They can at least guarantee 2 utils for themselves, whatever the other player does, and this in combination with the fact that they agreed on ($R2$, $C2$) may reassure them that their opponent will in fact play strategy 2. So ($R2$, $C2$) may well be a self-enforcing agreement, but it nevertheless is not a Nash equilibrium.'[19]

Kreps (1990, pp. 391, 406) cites another game for which, he argues, Nash equilibrium does not appear to be the way people would play, see ◘ Fig. 11.22.

The game has two Nash equilibria, (r1, c1) and (r2, c4), but Kreps says that in discussing this game with students he found that most say they expect (r2, c3) will be played (and it is what they *would* play if called to be the players)—the reason being that other strategies are too dangerous for the column player in case the choice of the row player has not been correctly foreseen, and the row player sees this and guesses the column player will choose c3.

Kreps uses this as one of a series of considerations to conclude that a Nash equilibrium should be expected to be how players will act only if it is an *obvious* way to play the game.

For Nash equilibria in mixed strategies, an additional problem is that, since they presuppose the Indifference Condition, it is unclear why players should stick to them: if player A can be certain that player B is playing the Nash equilibrium mixed strategy, A can well decide not to randomize, since if she plays just any pure strategy the payoff is the same. But this makes B totally uncertain as to whether A will play the Nash equilibrium mixed strategy.

For these and other reasons, some of the best game theorists are very cautious on the justification of the interest in Nash equilibria. The entry 'Game Theory' in *Internet Encyclopedia of Philosophy* concludes that 'it seems that there is no general justification for Nash equilibria in one-shot, simultaneous-move games'. In

---

19 The reader is invited to note the difference between the game in ◘ Fig. 11.21 and a Prisoner's Dilemma, and yet the similitude in that in both there is a danger that the joint result of unilaterally choosing the apparently optimal strategy may produce a much inferior result. In the case of in ◘ Fig. 11.21 the argument for the non-optimality of deviating to the unilaterally superior strategy is made easier by the absence of a dominant strategy, but I leave it to the reader to decide whether that can be enough to conclude that in a Prisoner's Dilemma the reasoning should be different.

950   **Chapter 11 · Games and Information**

spite of these doubts, often Nash equilibria are considered the solution of games without much discussion of how well justified such an assumption is. Kreps (1990, p. 405) protests against this practice: 'In the great majority of the applications of non-cooperative game theory to economics, the mode of analysis is equilibrium analysis. And in many of those analyses, the analyst identifies a Nash equilibrium (and sometimes more than one) and proclaims it (them?) as 'the solution'. I wish to stress that this practice is sloppy at best and probably a good deal worse'.

11.12 Trembling-Hand Equilibria

The notion of Nash equilibrium is not of great help if there is more than one such equilibrium. Game theorists have looked for criteria that reduce the problem by showing that some Nash equilibria are not plausible choices. One such criterion is illustrated below.

In a Nash equilibrium the probability attributed to strategies not played in that equilibrium is zero. This implies that the existence of Nash equilibria in weakly dominated strategies is not in contradiction with the thesis that weakly dominated strategies cannot be optimal for a player if she attributes positive probability to all the opponents' strategies. But can one be really sure that the probability of strategies not played in a Nash equilibrium is zero? Players may fear that it is possible (although highly improbable) that *by mistake* their opponents play strategies other than the Nash equilibrium ones. This can render some Nash equilibria implausible. Two examples follow, where A is the row player, and B the column player.

In the game in ◘ Fig. 11.23b (Up, Left) and (Down, Right) are the Nash equilibria in pure strategies; the second one is in weakly dominated strategies for both players. But here one can use the Hi-Lo criterion (the payoff dominance criterion) to eliminate the inferior equilibrium. The game in ◘ Fig. 11.23a is more interesting. Here the Nash equilibria are again (Up, Left) and (Down, Right); and (Down, Right) is again in weakly dominated strategies, but it is superior to the other Nash equilibrium. So why can it be considered implausible? Because player A may be afraid of the bad payoff in case B plays Left by mistake while she plays Down, and analogously for B's fear of the (Up, Right) outcome; the strategies Up, and Left, are less risky.

Selten (1975) has proposed to consider as predictions in a game only those Nash equilibria that do not become implausible if players are not totally cer-

(a)	Left	Right		(b)	Left	Right
Up	$_x$-1,-1$_x$	$_x$0,-3		Up	$_x$1, 1$_x$	$_x$0, -3
Down	- 3, 0$_x$	$_x$0, 0$_x$		Down	-3, 0$_x$	$_x$0, 0$_x$

◘ **Fig. 11.23**   Two games with Nash equilibria in weakly dominated strategies

11.12 · Trembling-Hand Equilibria

tain as to which strategy their opponents will choose, e.g. because they admit the possibility of 'mistakes' by the other players. He has accordingly formulated the notion of ***trembling-hand perfect equilibrium*** (The name derives from the idea that a mistake can be due to a hand tremble that results in the wrong button being pushed on a terminal.) I only supply an intuitive idea of the notion.

A Nash equilibrium is trembling-hand perfect if each one of the strategies forming it remains an optimal response to a very small modification of the opponents' equilibrium strategies that consists of transforming them into *totally mixed* strategies in which the strategies not played at all in the original Nash equilibrium are played with a very small probability.

The consequence can be appreciated in the game of ◘ Fig. 11.23b where, if a positive probability however small is assigned by A to B playing Left, then A finds it optimal to play Up, and the Nash equilibrium in weakly dominated strategies (Down, Right) disappears. In the game of ◘ Fig. 11.23a one can apply the same reasoning, but it is less convincing because the players may be ready to run the risk of the −3 payoff because by playing (Up, Left) they would select an inferior equilibrium.

11.13 Backward Induction and Subgame Perfection

For finite dynamic games of perfect information, a powerful technique for determining optimal choices, which is also sometimes useful to reduce the number of Nash equilibria, is ***backward induction***. Consider the sequential game of ◘ Fig. 11.8, reproduced here in ◘ Fig. 11.24 for the reader's convenience. In this game, if First plays Down, Second will certainly play Low because more convenient than High; thus First can reason that the payoffs from playing Down are certainly (5, 3), and can limit herself to considering the 'reduced game' of ◘ Fig. 11.24, concluding that Down is for her better than Up. Therefore the solution is (Down; Low) (◘ Fig. 11.25).

More generally, in games of perfect information one can run a game tree 'backwards', imputing to preceding nodes the payoffs from optimizing decisions at subsequent nodes. Starting at *final decision nodes* (the ones for which the only successor nodes are *terminal* nodes, where no choice is made, the players simply

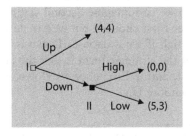

◘ Fig. 11.24 .

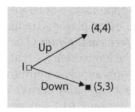

◘ Fig. 11.25

get payoffs), one can determine the maximizing choices there, and if these are unique one can impute the resulting payoffs to those nodes, eliminating the terminal nodes; the resulting game is called a *reduced game*. Proceeding backwards in this way (if possible[20]) up to the root node, one finds a succession of moves that is necessarily a Nash equilibrium.

A result called **Zermelo's Theorem**, which will not be proved here, states that every finite game of perfect information (hence without simultaneous moves!) has at least one pure strategy Nash equilibrium that can be derived through backward induction; moreover, if no player has the same payoffs at any two terminal nodes, backward induction locates only one Nash equilibrium.

Solutions resulting from repeated backward induction cannot always be trusted as predictions of how people will behave, because they can sometimes result in payoffs that are worse for all players than other payoffs obtainable with different, apparently 'irrational', strategies (more on this later). But in those cases where backward induction appears fully reasonable, it highlights a deficiency of the notion of Nash equilibrium in dynamic games.

When backward induction reaches a unique solution, that solution is necessarily a Nash equilibrium; but there may be other Nash equilibria of the game in normal form, that backward induction eliminates. One example is the game of ◘ Fig. 11.24. For this game, backward induction reaches the unique solution (Down, Low), but the normal form exhibits another Nash equilibrium: (Up, High). This second equilibrium has a defect that does not emerge from the normal form but justifies its elimination by backward induction. In the normal form, (Up, High) is a Nash equilibrium because First does not find it convenient to deviate to Down if she treats Second's strategy 'play High if First plays Down' as given; but if First were actually to choose Down, then Second would *not* find it convenient to play High, because Low yields a greater payoff. Note that Second prefers (Up, High) so we can imagine Second stating with great energy that she will play High whatever First chooses, but we can describe such a situation as 'Second's threat to play High if First chooses Down is *not credible*'. The difference from looking only at the strategic form is that the latter does not show that Second chooses after First, and if First chooses Down, Second would be stupid to stick to the promise to choose Up.

---

20 Sometimes backward induction is blocked by a player being indifferent between two actions, which makes the payoff for the other player indeterminate.

11.13 · Backward Induction and Subgame Perfection

In order to restrict the analyst's attention to the sole Nash equilibria not resting on non-credible threats, recourse is made to the notion of **subgame perfect Nash equilibrium**, usually shortened to SPNE. A *subgame* of a dynamic game is a portion of the original game tree from a certain node onwards that can be treated as a self-sufficient game in its own right, i.e. that:
(i) begins with an information set that contains only one node,
(ii) contains all and only the nodes to which one can arrive, under succession, from that node in the original game tree,
(iii) does not reach information sets that also contain nodes to which one cannot arrive from the first node of the subgame.

The last condition implies that in the game tree of ◘ Fig. 11.26 neither of the 'branches' starting at node 2 or at node 3 is a subgame; the branches starting at nodes 4 or 6 are subgames. These last two subgames are *single-decision-maker problems*: this is so when the subgame begins with a node whose successive nodes are all *terminal nodes* (also called *end-nodes*, payoff nodes where there is no decision to be taken, only payoffs to be obtained); by convention, the optimal decision of the decision maker at such a node is considered the Nash equilibrium of the subgame in spite of the absence of other players (if the decision maker is indifferent between several decisions then the Nash equilibrium of this subgame is not unique).

Note that the original game itself is one of its subgames; the other subgames are called *proper* subgames.

▪▪ Definition
Subgame perfect Nash equilibrium. *A SPNE is a profile of strategies, one for each player, such that in any subgame of the original game these strategies (truncated to this subgame) form a Nash equilibrium.*

If a game contains no proper subgame, then any Nash equilibrium of the game is subgame perfect.

In the game of ◘ Fig. 11.24 there are two subgames: the entire game, and the single-decision-maker subgame starting at the node reached after First chooses Down. The Nash equilibrium (Up, High) is not a SPNE because this strategy profile, truncated to the second subgame, consists of Second playing High, which is not a Nash equilibrium because it is not Second's best choice at that node. Thus the restriction to subgame perfect equilibria eliminates the implausible Nash equilibrium. *Backward induction selects subgame perfect equilibria.*

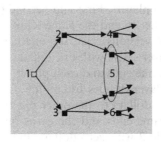

◘ **Fig. 11.26** A sequential game without proper subgames

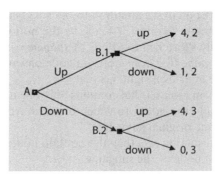

◘ Fig. 11.27

In dynamic games of perfect information where at each final decision node, and at each final decision node of each reduced game obtained by backward induction, there is always a single optimal choice for the player called upon to move, then there is a unique SPNE. But when at a node there are several equally optimal moves for the choosing player, then backward induction produces different reduced games depending on which move is chosen, and one can then obtain several SPNEs. One example is in ◘ Fig. 11.27.

Here player A cannot know how B will choose because B is indifferent between her two moves at either information set. The subgame perfect equilibria are found by assuming a strategy by B, and applying backward induction. For example if B plays 'down at B.1, down at B.2', then A chooses Up; if B chooses 'up at B.1, up at B.2' then A is indifferent between Up and Down, both are eligible as part of Nash equilibria. There are five Nash equilibria in pure strategies—find them!—all of them SPNEs, plus some in mixed strategies. This shows that the main advantage of backward induction is not to determine a unique equilibrium, but to eliminate Nash equilibria based on non-credible threats.

11.14 Repeated Backward Induction and the Centipede Game

Now I explain why solutions based on repeated backward induction cannot always be trusted as predictions of how people choose, and not because people act irrationally. I show it with a famous example, the ***Centipede game***. This is a dynamic game in which two players, First and Second (*I* and *II* in ◘ Fig. 11.28), take turns in deciding whether to end the game (choosing E for Exit), or to continue (choosing C). Several versions exist, the one here is the original long one (Rosenthal 1981). Each player starts with one dollar. First starts. If at her turn a player decides to exit, the game ends and each player wins the dollars she arrived at that node with; if the player decides to continue, the game master takes one dollar from her and gives 2 dollars to the other player. Thus if at the first node First decides to exit, the game ends and she earns one dollar; if she decides to continue she arrives at node 2 with zero dollars and Second with three dollars.

11.14 · Repeated Backward Induction and the Centipede Game

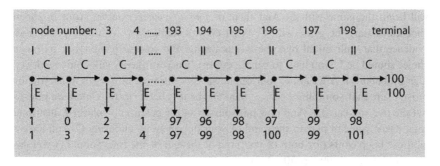

Fig. 11.28 The Centipede game: the drawing explains the name. The dots are the nodes, the choosing player is indicated on top of them as *I* or *II*; C = continues, E = exits; under the E's are indicated the payoffs if E is chosen at that node, player *I*'s payoffs are on top. Exiting at an even node $2n$ causes payoffs $(n-1, n+2)$; exiting at an odd node $2n-1$ causes payoffs (n, n)

If not before, the game stops after the 198th 'Continue', with final payoffs (100, 100). In Fig. 11.28 under each Exit decision the payoffs of the players are indicated, that is the dollars they arrived at that node with, First's payoff is indicated on top.

The tricky aspect of this game is that at each node, if the choosing player exits, she/he obtains more than by continuing *if* Exit is chosen by the other player at the next node. Then repeated backward induction implies that at the first node First chooses Exit, and the game ends there. This is because at node 198, if reached, certainly Second chooses Exit (101 is better than 100) and First obtains 98; knowing it, at node 197, if reached, First chooses E (thus obtaining 99 instead of 98); knowing it, at node 196, if reached, Second chooses E, and so on backwards to the first node. First's exiting immediately is the sole SPNE.

Here is how Kreps comments on this result:

> Since there are such lovely payoffs out at the end of the tree, this outcome seems rather a shame. More to the point, based on irregularly gathered evidence, it is a poor prediction. Asked to play this game, one typically finds even rather sophisticated players moving a fair way out to the end before one player or the other chooses E. There are two points to make in this regard. First, the prediction that player *I* will choose E to start the game is based on *200* rounds of iterated dominance.[21] It is rather hard to believe that players are so sure of their opponent's rationality and their opponent's certainty of theirs, and so on, that we can trust to a prediction so based. Second, suppose that you, and player *I*, are absolutely certain that your opponent is rational, and that your opponent is certain that you are, and so on, for as many iterations as this takes. So you are certain that your opponent

---

21 [*My footnote*] Kreps formulates the game slightly differently so that 200 nodes are required to reach the concluding payoffs (100, 100). Also, Kreps names the players 1 and 2, I have changed the names to *I* and *II* to fit my description.

956   Chapter 11 · Games and Information

will begin the game with E. And then, *despite all your certainties*, your opponent chooses to start the game with C. What do you think then? You have pretty good evidence that your initial hypothesis was wrong. But to justify that your follow-on choice should be E, you have to believe ex post that your theory still holds (with very high probability). After all, if your opponent isn't rational, or doesn't think you are, or isn't sure that you think he is, ... then maybe it is better to try C and see how far out the tree you can get. And now put yourself in the position of player *I*. Just think what havoc you can play in the mind of your opponent by choosing C. And look at all those big payoffs (for both of you!) out at the end of the tree. Shouldn't you give C a shot? (Kreps 1990, pp. 401–402).

I would argue that the implications of the observations following 'Second' in this quotation go even farther than Kreps admits. The standard conclusion reached via repeated backward induction rests on an assumption of supposedly 'rational' behaviour of both players; an initial choice of C by *I* undermines this assumption, also undermining the right to assume that at the second node rationality requires *II* to choose E, since having observed *I*'s initial choice *II* has no right to conclude that *I* will exit at the third node, and therefore it is not irrational for *II* to choose C: it suffices that *I* does not choose E at the next node, and *II* is better off choosing C rather than E at the second node. Now, since the result of repeating such an 'irrational' behaviour is higher payoffs than exiting immediately, clearly the irrational behaviour is to exit immediately. Kreps, when writing 'if your opponent isn't rational, or doesn't think you are...', keeps using 'rational' in the accepted game-theoretic sense that would imply that *I* exiting immediately is the rational solution if *I* is sure that *II* is rational; but in fact choosing E at the first node cannot be considered the rational behaviour, since choosing C opens the door to much greater payoffs. Hence the experimental evidence alluded to by Kreps (that shows on the basis of several experiments that players generally continue past node 180) does *not* show that players are imperfectly rational or do not assume that the other player is perfectly rational; it is rather game theory that in this instance cannot convincingly support the rationality of applying repeated backward induction all the way.[22] Similar considerations apply to repeated backward induction in finitely repeated Prisoner's Dilemma games, to be discussed in ▶ Sect. 11.16.

---

22 Aumann (1995) has proposed a formal proof that rationality plus common knowledge of rationality implies acceptance of repeated backward induction: that is, if both players are rational and know that the other player is rational, then in the Centipede game First exits at the first node. Aumann's proof uses *knowledge theory*, the way game theorists formalize that somebody knows something, an advanced topic that we cannot cover here (see Osborne and Rubinstein 1994, ▶ Chap. 5). I have not worked on this article enough to disprove Aumann, but I feel certain that there must be something debatable in the definition of rationality if it allows reaching Aumann's result. I am sure you reader are rational, then suppose you are player First in the Centipede game, would you exit at the first node? indeed, suppose you must hand in to a referee your complete strategy (your choice at each odd node if you get there) without knowing Second's strategy: at which node would you choose Exit? and what would you find irrational in First's adoption of the strategy "never choose Exit" (intended to discourage Second from exiting before node 198)?

11.15 Infinitely Repeated Games

A particular class of dynamic games is *repeated games*, in which the same game, called the *stage game*, is repeated a finite or infinite (or indefinite, see below) number of times. Knowledge that the stage game will be repeated may induce players to alter their strategy choice in some or all stage games relative to what they would have chosen if the stage game had been played only once. Therefore the several plays of the stage game in a repeated game must be treated as part of a single overall game, and a strategy must specify what a player chooses in stage game 1, in stage game 2, and so on, possibly depending on what was played by all players in previous stage games. The choice in a single stage game can be called *action*, in order to distinguish it from the strategy, that determines an action for each stage game. I only discuss repeated games in which at the beginning of each stage game the actions chosen in earlier stage games are known to all players (these are called *repeated games with observed actions*).

An example is supplied by the repeated Prisoner's Dilemma. Suppose that two players know that they are going to play an infinite number of times a one-shot simultaneous game with the structure of the game in ◘ Fig. 4. For the reader's convenience the game is reproduced here as ◘ Fig. 11.29.

The possibility now arises of Nash equilibria different from the repetition of (Defect, Defect), because there arises the possibility of proposing the adoption of the (Cooperate, Cooperate) repeated strategy and of punishing the opponent in case she deviates from it.

Consider, for example, the following strategy profile: both A and B adopt a *retaliatory trigger strategy*, consisting in playing C initially, and then playing C if in all previous stage games the opponent played C, and playing D for ever if in any previous stage game the opponent played Defect. (The name comes from the fact that the player choosing Defect triggers the response Defect by the opponent for ever.) We show that this strategy profile is a Nash equilibrium if players do not discount future payoffs too much.

Proof Suppose A adopts the retaliatory trigger strategy. We must prove that for B the retaliatory trigger strategy is a best response.

We need some premises. In order to ascertain whether a strategy is a best response, we must specify the payoffs in a way that is also applicable to infinitely repeated games. So far we assumed that in dynamic games the payoffs are obtained at the end of the game. For infinitely repeated games this is not sensible.

A \ B	Def	Coop
Def	1, 1	5, 0
Coop	0, 5	4, 4

◘ Fig. 11.29

958   Chapter 11 · Games and Information

Therefore we assume that payoffs are obtained after each stage game, and that for each player the total payoff is the *expected average discounted value* of the finite or infinite series of her payoffs. Let x_t be the expected payoff to a player from the tth play of the stage game. Let δ be the *discount factor*, constant, positive and ≤ 1, generally assumed common to all players, that applies to payoffs in future repetitions of the game, so that the discounted value of x_t is $\delta^{t-1}x_t$; this discount factor may reflect intertemporal impatience, the market rate of interest,[23] or the probability that the game will be repeated and hence that the future payoffs will be obtained, or a combination of both. For example, if the number of repetitions of the stage game is determined after each play by a random draw that assigns probability $p < 1$ to the game being repeated one more time, and if there is no impatience, then the discount factor is $\delta = p$. (This may correspond to some social interactions, for example between a firm and a customer, that are repeated but it is not certain for how long.) The sum of the discounted values might diverge to infinity; for this reason it is generally preferable to use the expected *average* discounted value of payoffs, defined to be

$$(1-\delta)\sum_{t=1}^{\infty}\delta^{t-1}x_t \quad \text{if } \delta < 1; \quad \lim_{T\to\infty}\frac{1}{T}\sum_{t=1}^{T}x_t \quad \text{if } \delta = 1.$$

If $\delta = 1$ the average value is simply the arithmetic average; if $\delta < 1$ and if $x_t = x$ is constant, then $(1-\delta)\sum_{t=1}^{\infty}\delta^{t-1}x = x$, because $\sum_{t=1}^{\infty}\delta_m^{t-1} = 1 + \delta + \delta^2 + \ldots = 1/(1-\delta)$.

Now we can examine whether the adoption by B of the retaliatory trigger strategy is a best response to A adopting it. If B too adopts it, both players play (C,C) for ever and obtain a payoff of 4. If B adopts a different strategy, then in at least one stage game her choice is D (while A plays C). Let t be the stage game where B first adopts D. From $t+1$ onwards A plays D, and B's best response is D. Thus B's payoff is 5 in t, and then no more than 1 for all subsequent periods. If B had continued to play C, her average payoff discounted to t would have been 4. The maximum average payoff discounted to t of her choice of D in t is

$$(1-\delta)\left(5 + \delta + \delta^2 + \delta^3 + \ldots\right) = (1-\delta)(5 + \delta/(1-\delta)) = 5 - 4\delta.$$

Thus continuing to play C is a best response if $4 \geq 5 - 4\delta$ i.e. if $\delta \geq 1/4$. If this condition is satisfied,[24] B cannot increase her payoff by deviating from the retaliatory trigger strategy, and the adoption of the retaliatory trigger strategy by both players is a Nash equilibrium. ∎

---

23 A discount *factor* δ is related to a discount *rate* or interest rate r by $\delta = 1/(1+r)$.
24 *Exercise*: Find the general relationship between the payoffs of a symmetric Prisoner's Dilemma and the condition on δ for the retaliatory trigger strategy to be a Nash equilibrium. Call a, b, c, d the four payoffs of the game, with $a < b < c < d$.

11.15 · Infinitely Repeated Games

Note that adoption of the retaliatory trigger strategy is *not* a subgame perfect equilibrium: if in the first period the actions are (C, D) then the infinitely repeated game starting the second period is a subgame, and the retaliatory trigger strategies as specified above require that B plays C at $t=2$; but since A will play D, B's best response at $t=2$ is D, not C.

Subgame perfection obtains if both players adopt the following slightly different trigger strategy, also called the *Grim strategy*: play C the first time, and then play C if *both* players have always played C in all earlier stage games, otherwise play D for ever. This strategy means that if at $t=1$ the actions are (C, D) then at $t=2$ the actions are (D, D). The proof of subgame perfection is left to the reader. Here too if both players adopt this strategy, they cooperate for ever.

But this is not the only subgame perfect Nash equilibrium. Another one is when both players play D whatever the other player does. In fact, a general result for infinitely repeated games is: the indefinite repetition of actions (that is, choices of strategies for the stage game) that are a Nash equilibrium of the stage game is a subgame perfect Nash equilibrium of the repeated game (can you prove it? it's not difficult). But a more interesting result is the possibility of subgame perfect Nash equilibria involving *limited-punishment strategies*. Suppose a player plays D once, perhaps by mistake. Should the players, only because of that, be obliged to play (D, D) for ever, renouncing for ever the possibility of higher payoffs? A strategy that threatens a finite-periods punishment sufficient to deter deviations from the cooperative strategy, but that proposes a return to cooperation after the punishment, may be able to reap higher payoffs. It has indeed been proved that, as long as players are rather patient (δ not far from 1), for repeated Prisoner's Dilemma games it is possible to devise Nash equilibrium strategies that embody threats of limited punishment, avoiding the danger that a mistake triggers off the loss of any hope of future cooperation. (On this I will only give some general information, the topic is advanced.)

It has been discovered that the number of such limited-punishment Nash equilibria is very large, and associated with average payoffs that can be any *individually rational payoffs* (as long as δ is sufficiently close to 1). A payoff for one of the n players *in the stage game* is defined to be *individually rational* if it is *feasible*, i.e. achievable by some feasible action profile $\mathbf{a} = (a^1, \ldots, a^n)$ (where the actions can be pure or mixed strategies of the stage game), and not less than the *minmax* payoff for this player, which is the minimum payoff that other players, by playing pure strategies, can force the player to get in the stage game. Assume that for each stage-game pure strategy profile of the opponents, player i plays a best response and therefore obtains the maximum payoff in the stage game conditional on that profile of strategies of the other players; among these best-response payoffs, the minimum one is the minmax payoff, the payoff below which the player will never go if she/he plays best-response strategies.

This result is called **Folk Theorem** because the basic idea (whose first proponent is unclear) had become 'folk wisdom' among game theorists much before a formal proof was published.

960   Chapter 11 · Games and Information

■■ Basic Folk Theorem

Consider an infinitely repeated game. Let Π be the set of payoff profiles $v = (v^1, ..., v^n)$ of its stage game, such that for each player i the payoff v^i is individually rational; for any $v \in \Pi$ such that, for all i, v^i is greater than player i's minmax payoff, if δ is sufficiently close to 1 there is a Nash equilibrium of the infinitely repeated game such that v is the average payoff profile.

Sketch of proof   I supply only the basic intuition of the proof. For any such $v \in \Pi$, let each player i play the following strategy s^i: play the action a^i in the action profile **a** that produces v (thus obtaining v^i in each repetition of the stage game) provided the other players do likewise; if a player j deviates (in a period that without loss of generality can be considered to be period 0), play the action that (if all players apart from j behave in this way) causes j to obtain the minmax payoff forever. Since v^j is greater than player j's minmax payoff, for a δ sufficiently close to 1 the gain for player j from the one-period deviation is more than compensated by the present value of the subsequent loss forever, due to obtaining only the minimax payoff rather than v^j, hence it is not convenient to deviate, and the profile of strategies s^i is a Nash equilibrium. ■

(The simplicity of this intuition explains why it could be widely believed that the theorem could be proved before the proof was actually supplied.)

The Nash equilibria whose existence is guaranteed by the Basic Folk Theorem need not be subgame perfect, so the punishment threat need not be credible. But a group of results, also known as *folk theorems*, have shown that for δ sufficiently close to 1 the possibility of obtaining any of a vast interval of payoffs can also be proved for subgame perfect equilibria. The first one of such results was published in 1971 by J. Friedman:

***Friedman's Folk Theorem for subgame perfect Nash equilibria.** Consider an infinitely repeated game whose stage game is a one-shot simultaneous-move game of complete information. Let $x = (x^1, ... x^i, ..., x^n)$ be the payoff profile of a Nash equilibrium action profile $b = (b^1, ..., b^n)$ of the stage game, and let v be another feasible payoff profile of the stage game with $v^i > x^i$ for all i. Then for δ sufficiently close to 1 there exists a subgame perfect Nash equilibrium of the repeated game with v as average payoff profile.*

Sketch of proof   The idea of the proof is similar to the previous one. For any such v, let each player i play the following strategy s^i: play the action a^i in the action profile **a** that produces v provided the other players do likewise; if a player j deviates, play b^i. If player j deviates, from the successive stage game her opponents play the action profile b_{-j} forever, to which her best response cannot get her more than x_j, which is less than v_j, with the same consequence as in the previous proof. ■

Later it has been proved that the new possibilities open by repetition do not necessarily mean an improvement of payoffs relative to the ones obtainable by repetition of the Nash equilibrium actions of the stage game; sometimes subgame perfect Nash equilibria with punishments can be found which let some player get on average less than in the worst Nash equilibrium of the stage game. The following example taken from Osborne (2004, p. 456) shows it.

11.15 · Infinitely Repeated Games

	A	B	C
A	$_x4, 4_x$	$_x3, 0$	$_x1, 0$
B	$0, 3_x$	$2, 2$	$_x1, 0$
C	$0, 1_x$	$0, 1_x$	$0, 0$

■ **Fig. 11.30** .

Consider the two-player symmetric stage game of ■ Fig. 11.30. It has a unique Nash equilibrium (A, A) yielding a payoff of 4 which is the highest possible payoff. Therefore one equilibrium of the infinitely repeated game is the repetition of (A, A), with average payoff 4. The minmax payoff is 1. As long as $\delta \geq \frac{1}{2}\sqrt{2}$ the infinitely repeated game based on this stage game has a subgame perfect Nash equilibrium where both players play the following strategy: if (B, B) was played in the preceding stage game, play B; if the actions in the preceding stage game were not (B, B) (unless they were (C, C) in the two previous stage games), play C and also play C in the next stage game; if the actions in the two previous stage games where (C, C), play B. (This is a strategy that punishes a player who deviated from playing B by playing C for two stage games, and then returns to playing B unless the other player deviated from playing C twice, in which case the two-period punishment strategy C starts again.) For the proof I refer the reader to Osborne. The average payoff from this equilibrium is 2, less than the payoff obtained by repeating (A, A).

In conclusion, in infinitely repeated games there often is an embarrassing richness of possible equilibria; the notion of subgame perfect Nash equilibrium does not significantly restrict the number of possible strategies nor the possible payoffs; the latter are any payoffs between the minmax payoffs and the maximum feasible payoffs.

Anyway the important result has been reached that the possibility of punishing the opponent for not cooperating implies that *cooperation can be sustained in an indefinitely repeated Prisoner's Dilemma*; for the same reason, we will see in the next chapter that repeated interaction can give stability to cartels which otherwise would dissolve. Furthermore the analysis draws our attention to some factors upon which the capacity of groups to sustain cooperation depends, e.g. the discount rate, and the probability that the stage game will be repeated. But often no definite prediction about payoffs is obtained.[25] It all depends, it would seem, on what kind of convention gets established.

---

25 Fudenberg and Tirole (1986 p. 160): "The various folk theorems show that standard equilibrium concepts do very little to pin down play by patient players. In applying repeated games, economists typically focus on one of the efficient equilibria, usually a symmetric one. This is due in part to a general belief that players may coordinate on efficient equilibria, and in part to the belief that cooperation is particularly likely in repeated games. It is a troubling fact that at this point there is no accepted theoretical justification for assuming efficiency in this setting.".

962   Chapter 11 · Games and Information

11.16 Finitely Repeated Games

A repeated game can consist of a *finite* number, known to the players, of repetitions of the stage game. This changes things considerably relative to infinite or indefinite repetition. In some cases this allows the application of backward induction to reach stark conclusions. An example is a Prisoner's Dilemma game played T times. Suppose we accept the standard analysis which argues that rationality requires both players to choose Defect in a single play of the game. Then in the last repetition of the stage game, the equilibrium actions can only be (Defect, Defect). But then in the preceding stage game no room is left for two-period strategies possibly justifying playing C in that stage game, and the equilibrium actions can only be (Defect, Defect). The same reasoning repeated for the preceding stage game and so on backwards proves that the sole Nash equilibrium is with both players playing Defect at all stage games.

However, empirical experiments show that, as in the Centipede game, people do not follow the indication coming from repeated backward induction and do not play the Nash equilibrium; in a vast majority of cases they start cooperating and continue to cooperate, often until the next-to-last stage game (and sometimes in the last stage game too). In one experiment carried out in Germany (Selten and Stoecker 1986), in which the repeated game—that included ten repetitions—was played 25 times against changing opponents, the average number of cooperations per game decreased a bit as players acquired experience, but remained at four or higher in nearly all the cases, and the mean *intended* cooperations (i.e. the intended number of choices of C if the other player did not defect earlier: these were cleverly deduced by the authors from the evidence) only went down from 9.2 (higher than 9, note!) to 7.4. This allowed the players to obtain significantly higher payoffs than by playing the Nash equilibrium strategy: thus, they were smarter than game theory!

Also interesting is what happened when political scientist Robert Axelrod (1984) twice organized a tournament based on a finitely repeated Prisoner's Dilemma game: he invited game theorists in mathematics, psychology, economics and other social sciences and, in the second tournament, other people too to propose a strategy, to be then computer-implemented against the strategies proposed by the other participants. In the first tournament the strategy that obtained the best overall payoff was the very simple *tit-for-tat* strategy proposed by psychologist Anatol Rapoport: start by cooperating, and then play the same action as played by the opponent in the previous stage game, which came nearly first in the second tournament too; the Grim strategy performed rather well too; but what interests us most is that *no one* proposed the Nash equilibrium strategy of always defecting! One must conclude that not even game theorists believe in repeated backward induction, when an initial readiness to cooperate looks promising. In the light of this, it is saddening that, in order to explain why people behave as in the German experiment or in Axelrod's tournaments, it is generally suggested that, either players do not perform all the necessary backward induction (i.e. they are not 'perfectly rational'), or players have preferences that include other aims besides maximizing the explicit payoffs of the game (e.g. a preference for cooperation). It seems evident to me that in this case (as in the Centipede game) players—

11.17 · Bayesian Games

including most game theorists!—are simply aware that there are better ways to maximize payoffs than Nash equilibrium behaviour, and *rationally* avoid the latter behaviour. But where precisely the mistake lies in the logic of repeated backward induction in these games is still not clear—a topic for research, if you are interested.

11.17 Bayesian Games

Now I pass to a different category of games, ***games of incomplete information***, in which a player is uncertain about the characteristics of the other players. For example, a firm may not know the cost functions of competing firms. I remember that games, in which an information set includes more than one node and the player who must choose at that information set does not know at which node she is, are called ***games of imperfect information***. Harsanyi (1967) proposed a way to transform the games of *incomplete* information into games of *imperfect* information, which has been universally adopted. The uncertainty of a player about the characteristics of a second player is assumed to be an uncertainty as to which *type* of second player a random move by Nature has caused to come into existence; then a move by the second player takes the first player to an information set where she does not know at which node she is because the node depends on which type of the second player came into existence. The game becomes well defined the moment one assumes each player has a prior probability distribution over the possible different types of each player. It is generally assumed that all the types of each player agree on the prior probability distribution of the different types of each player—in short, that these prior probability distributions are common knowledge. Of course each player knows which type she is, but the other players don't. Games of this sort are called ***Bayesian games*** because Bayes' Rule is very important in them as will become evident.

For example, a firm B may not know whether a competing firm A is a low-cost producer or a high-cost producer; if B esteems that the probability of the first case is 20% and of the second case is 80%, this is equivalent to assuming that, in the game tree, one or more steps before the first information set where B is to choose there has been a node where the fictitious player Nature (or Choice) has randomized over the choices 'I let a low-cost A-firm come into being' and 'I let a high-cost A-firm come into being' with respective probabilities 20 and 80%. After this random move by Nature, firm A knows its type, but B does not; therefore B must formulate her strategy taking into account the possible strategy of either type of A firm, and then must calculate its payoff in expectations[26] on the basis of the probabilities it attributes to facing the strategy of each type. The usual assumption is that firm A knows that B does not know A's type and also knows the probabilities 20 and 80% that B assigns to the two types, that B knows that A knows this, and so on.

---

26 If the player is not risk neutral, what she is assumed to maximize is the expected utility she derives from the payoffs, account being taken of risk. I will assume that players are risk neutral.

964   **Chapter 11** · Games and Information

The distinction among different types is intended to summarize everything that is relevant for the strategic behaviour of players. If a player is uncertain about the preferences of a second player over outcomes, then as many different types of the second player must be distinguished as the different possible preferences that according to the first player the second player might have. Thus nearly any uncertainty might be treated by distinguishing different types, although possibly at the cost of an increasing complexity of the game because of the increasing number of player types; a fundamental problem is rather, whether a well-defined belief about the probability of the types can be reasonably attributed to the players, and whether this belief can be assumed to be shared by all players. The theory we illustrate assumes that this is possible; in some cases (e.g. when official statistics illustrate the frequency of different types in a population) this is a legitimate assumption.

Let us define things more formally. Let us initially concentrate on games in strategic form. There are N players $1, \ldots i, \ldots, N$. The ith player can be of any one of K^i possible types from a set $\Theta^i = \{\theta^i_k\}, k = 1, \ldots, K^i$. For simplicity, assume that for each player the number of types is finite. A type *profile* is a vector of types, one for each player, $\theta = (\theta^1_h \cdots, \theta^N_m)$. For brevity let us drop the index that for each player indicates which type we are considering, let θ^j indicate a type of player j; and let θ^{-i} denote the type profile θ deprived of the element θ^i, that is $\theta^{-i} = (\theta^1, \ldots \theta^{i-1}, \theta^{i+1}, \ldots, \theta^N)$, where each θ^j is a specific type of player j; then we can also represent θ as (θ^i, θ^{-i}).

Initially Nature randomly chooses the type profile and reveals to each player and to her alone her type. This choice operates according to an objective known probability distribution $p(\theta)$ that determines the probability that a type profile θ be the one actually in existence. Let $p_i(\theta^i)$ be the probability that player i is of type θ^i, that is, the probability that Nature draws a type profile θ in which player i is of type θ^i; it is the sum of the probabilities of all type profiles in which the type of player i is θ^i, that is, $p_i(\theta^i) = \Sigma_{\theta^{-i}} p(\theta^i, \theta^{-i})$.

It is useless to include in Θ^i types that cannot occur, so I assume that $p_i(\theta^i)$ is positive for all i and all θ^i in Θ^i. I assume that $p(\theta)$ is *common knowledge* (a restrictive assumption, but without it, it is extremely difficult to get anywhere) and that, starting from it, having observed her type each player updates her subjective *beliefs* about the probability of the types of her opponents on the basis of the observation of her own type. These beliefs are represented by a conditional probability distribution that to each profile θ^{-i} of types of the other players assigns probability $p^\wedge(\theta^{-i}|\theta^i)$ determined according to ***Bayes' Rule***,[27] where $\theta = (\theta^i, \theta^{-i})$:

$$p^\wedge \left(\theta^{-i}|\theta^i \right) = p(\theta)/p_i \left(\theta^i \right).$$

---

27 Bayes' Rule (here P stands for 'the probability of'):

P(A|B) = P(B|A)·P(A)/P(B) = P(B|A)·P(A)/[P(B|A)·P(A) + P(B|notA)·P(notA)].

What is used here in the text actually is not Bayes' Rule but rather the property from which Bayes' Rule is derived, namely P(A|B) = P(A∩B)/P(B); but it has become common among game theorists to extend the term 'Bayes' Rule' to the latter property too.

This is why these games are called **Bayesian**. In one-shot simultaneous-move Bayesian games, this initial updating of beliefs is the only one to occur.

This updating will cause the subjective beliefs of player i about the probability of the types of her opponents to be different depending on her type whenever types are not independent, i.e. whenever the observation by player i of her own type suggests that for the other players certain types are more likely to occur than other ones. Suppose, to make an extreme example, that for all players the type univocally depends on the climate and this dependence is common knowledge; observing her type, player i can deduce the climate and then, with certainty, the types of the other players.[28] If on the contrary the probability distributions of players' types are independent, then a player's beliefs about the probabilities of the types of her opponents are independent of her type.

Let us come to strategies. In Bayesian games one must distinguish between *player strategies* and *type strategies*. The type strategies (if pure) correspond to what so far we have called pure strategies in games of perfect information, e.g. Heads in the game of Matching Pennies, or, in sequential games, the specification of an action for each information set where the player can be called upon to move. In Bayesian games a *pure player strategy* consists of a *vector* of type strategies, one for each possible type of that player; the type strategy that the player will in fact implement depends on which type that player is, therefore the action of a player at an information set is type-contingent. Hence a profile of pure player strategies, one per player, in fact is a profile of type strategies, one for each type of each player.

A mixed player strategy by player i is a vector of mixed type strategies, one for each of her types, each mixed type strategy being a randomization (a probability distribution) *by that type* over her possible actions (the possible actions may differ from type to type).

For example, suppose that in a one-shot simultaneous-move game there are two players 1 and 2, the first one can be of two types 1A or 1B, the second one can be of three types 2A, 2B, 2C, neither player can tell in advance the opponent's type, and each player has two possible single-move strategies, H or T. A pure strategy of player 1 is a vector of two moves, one for type 1A and one for type 1B; a pure strategy of player 2 is a vector of three moves.

A frequent question is, why one should worry about specifying the strategies of types that are not in existence, since the real moves are the ones chosen by the existing types. The answer is that game theory tries to understand how moves are (or should be) chosen, and to such an end one must consider that each player, not knowing for sure which types of other players she is facing, must ask what her optimal choice is, given the probabilities of facing the several possible pro-

---

28 Another example: suppose there are two oil companies which have looked for oil in nearby areas, each one knows the result of its research but ignores the other company's results, but each considers it more probable that the results are similar rather than divergent; then the probability the first firm will assign to the other firm's types "has found oil", "has not found oil" is not independent of the first firm's type.

966 Chapter 11 · Games and Information

files of her opponents' types, and to such an end she must formulate predictions about the choices of all types of the other players; and since the other players, not knowing for sure her type, will base their choices on their predictions about the choices not only of her actual type but also of her other possible types, she must also formulate predictions about what (each type of) each other player will predict each of her types would choose if in existence, and a necessary part in forming such second-order predictions is ascertaining what she would *in fact* choose if she were of types other than the one she is.

We can use the above example to clarify the payoffs to strategies. In a game of incomplete information one must distinguish between *outcomes* (i.e. actual payoffs *to players*), that depend on which types are in existence and which actions they choose, and *expected payoffs to types*, that are relevant in order to determine whether each type's strategy is a best response to given strategies of the other players/types. Suppose that, in the above game where 1A or 1B plays against 2A or 2B or 2C, there is a common knowledge prior probability distribution over independent types $\{p_{1A} + p_{1B} = 1, p_{2A} + p_{2B} + p_{2C} = 1\}$. Given a pure strategy profile, i.e. a strategy by player 1 and a strategy by player 2, the outcome of the game, i.e. the *actual* payoffs to the two players is a vector of 2 numbers, determined by the chosen strategies of the existing types and by the initial random move by Nature that determines which types are in existence; but in the strategic form of the game (a 4×8 matrix of boxes, in this case) the payoffs that appear in each box as the result of the corresponding profile of player strategies are vectors of 5 numbers, the *expected* payoffs going to *each* type, determined for each type by her action and by the probability of occurrence of the types of the *other* player. Thus suppose that $p_{1A} = 1/2$, $p_{1B} = 1/2$, $p_{2A} = 1/2$, $p_{2B} = 1/4$, $p_{2C} = 1/4$; that the strategy profile is (H,T; H,T,T); and that the possible outcomes caused by this strategy profile are:

1,1 if the types in existence are 1A (who plays H) and 2A (who plays H).
0,1 if the types in existence are 1A (who plays H) and 2B (who plays T).
1,0 if the types in existence are 1A (who plays H) and 2C (who plays T).
1,0 if the types in existence are 1B (who plays T) and 2A (who plays H).
1,1 if the types in existence are 1B (who plays T) and 2B (who plays T).
1,1 if the types in existence are 1B (who plays T) and 2C (who plays T).

Then the expected payoffs for this strategy profile are 3/4 for 1A, 1 for 1B, 1/2 for 2A, 1 for 2B, 1/2 for 2C. The expected payoffs calculated in this way also allow each type to calculate the expected payoff of a mixed type strategy against given mixed substrategies of the other player's types. Of course the outcomes, i.e. the payoffs to players, can in turn be expected outcomes if some player (i.e. for each player, her type actually in existence) adopts a mixed strategy.

Note that the example also shows that if two different couples (e.g. 1A, 2B and 1A,2C) choose the same couple of moves (here H;T), the outcome need not be the same, because the outcome can depend on the types choosing the moves (if two people must decide between fighting or retreating, and both decide to fight, the outcome will depend on their types, i.e. on whether each one is good or not at fighting).

11.17 · Bayesian Games

Exercise For the game just discussed, determine the expected payoff for 1A of a mixed type strategy where H and T are played with equal probability, if the same kind of mixed type strategy is played by each type of player 2 and if the outcomes of the cases not already listed are 1,0 if the couple of moves played by existing types is (H;H) or (T;T), and is 0,1 if the couple of moves is (H;T) or (T;H).

▪▪ Definition

A **Bayes-Nash equilibrium** for a simultaneous-move Bayesian game is a profile of pure or mixed normal-form strategies, one for each type of each player, that maximizes the expected utility of each type of player, given the (common-knowledge[29] and positive) prior probabilities of occurrence of each type of each player, and given the strategies pursued by the other players/types.

So it is as if each player were a *team* of players (her types); only one member of each team is called upon to play, and one does not know against which member of the opposing teams one is playing. A Bayes-Nash equilibrium requires that each member of each team is correct on the optimal strategy played by each member of the other teams, and plays a strategy that is a best response to these strategies, given the conditional probabilities that these strategies be played.

I illustrate with an example taken from the 1996 Internet pages on game theory by Jim Ratliff, ▶ https://virtualperfection.com/gametheory.

There are two firms, the first is the sole incumbent in a market, and the second is a potential entrant. Firm 1 must choose between M (secretly investing to Modernize) or A (remaining with antique technology), and if it chooses M, it knows for sure whether the cost of investment will be L (Low) or H (High); the choice must be taken before knowing whether firm 2 enters or not. Firm 2 (which knows that firm 1 is choosing between M and A) must decide between E (Entering) and N (Not entering), without knowing whether firm 1 has chosen M or A nor, in case the choice is M, whether the cost to firm 1 will be H or L; firm 2 attributes probability ρ to H (and of course $1-\rho$ to L) in case firm 1 chooses M, and firm 1 knows ρ. Firm 2 prefers not to enter if firm 1 modernizes, prefers to enter if firm 1 does not modernize; if firm 2 enters, firm 1 prefers not to modernize whatever the investment costs, while if firm 2 does not enter firm 1 prefers to modernize only if modernization is not very costly.

This can be represented as firm 2 being of a single type and firm 1 being of two possible types, a high-cost investor 1H, and a low-cost investor 1L, with ρ the common-knowledge probability that the initial move by the fictitious actor Chance causes 1H to be in existence. The game can be represented in extensive form as in ◘ Fig. 11.31; in the terminal payoffs firm 1's payoff is given first.

The strategic form is determined as follows. Firm 1's strategies must specify her choice between M and A if of type 1H and if of type 1L, hence are the 2-vec-

---

29 The common prior assumption need not be part of the definition of Bayesian games, but we only discuss games with a common prior.

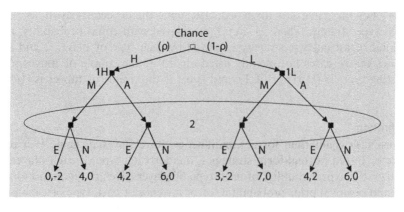

◘ Fig. 11.31 Ratliff's investment/entry game

	E	N
MM	0, 3; -2	4, 7; 0
MA	0, 4$_x$; $-2\rho+2(1-\rho)$	4, 6; 0
AM	4, 3; $2\rho-2(1-\rho)$	6, 7; 0
AA	4, 4; 2	6, 6; 0

◘ Fig. 11.32 Strategic form of Ratliff's game. Payoffs are in the order (1H, 1L; 2)

tors (where the choice of type 1H is given first) MM, MA, AM, AA. Firm 2's strategies are E and N. In each box of the 4×2 'trimatrix' of expected payoffs one lists 3 numbers, first the expected payoff of 1H, then (after a comma) the one of 1L, then (after a semicolon) the one of 2. For example if the strategy profile is (MA; E) the payoff of 1H is the one at the end of the history H, M, E hence 0, the payoff of 1L is at the end of the history L, A, E hence 4, while the payoff of firm 2 is -2 if it faces 1H, and 2 if it faces 1L, hence the expected payoff is $-2\rho + 2(1-\rho)$. The matrix is as in ◘ Fig. 11.32.

A Bayes-Nash equilibrium in pure strategies requires that each type's pure strategy be a best response to the other player's strategies. Hence firm 2's strategy must be a best response to the two strategies of 1A and of 1M, account being taken of their probabilities, which are already embodied in the way 2's payoffs are calculated in the strategic form matrix (it is as if firm 2 were facing a mixed strategy by a single-type player 1, playing 1H's strategy with probability ρ and 1L's strategy with probability 1-ρ). And both 1H's strategy and 1L's strategy must be best responses to 2's strategy; in other words, the strategy profile must be a Nash equilibrium both if one deletes 1H's payoffs from the matrix, and if one deletes 1L's payoffs. The reader can verify that this is the case for the profile (AA;E) for any value of ρ, and for the profile (AM;N) if $\rho \geq 1/2$.

11.17 · Bayesian Games

Alternatively, in order to determine the Nash equilibria, instead of separately indicating the payoffs of 1H and of 1L, in the matrix one might indicate only their joint expected value, dependent on ρ; for example for (AM, E), 1's payoff would be $4\rho + 3(1 - \rho)$. The point is that if both 1H and 1L play a best response to 2's strategy, the joint expected value of their payoffs too is a best response among joint expected values. But the separate indication allows a better grasp of the strategic form.

Now let us look for mixed-strategy equilibria. Suppose 2 plays E with probability ε, 1H plays M with probability α, and 1L plays M with probability μ. In the present case it is certainly $\alpha = 0$, because strategy A is strictly dominant for 1H. Thus what we must find is the couples (μ, ε) such that μ is a best response to ε and vice-versa. To such an end let us look for the best-response correspondences $\mu^*(\varepsilon)$ and $\varepsilon^*(\mu)$. The expected payoff to 1L from playing M is $3\varepsilon + 7(1 - \varepsilon) = 7 - 4\varepsilon$, the one from playing A is $4\varepsilon + 6(1 - \varepsilon) = 6 - 2\varepsilon$. These are equal if $\varepsilon = 1/2$; if $\varepsilon > 1/2$, the expected payoff from A is greater, hence certainly $\mu = 0$; if $\varepsilon < 1/2$ it is certainly $\mu = 1$; $\varepsilon = 1/2$ leaves μ undetermined between 0 and 1. Hence

$$\mu^*(\varepsilon) = \begin{cases} 1 & \text{if } \varepsilon < 1/2 \\ [0, 1] & \text{if } \varepsilon = 1/2 \\ 0 & \text{if } \varepsilon > 1/2 \end{cases}$$

Let us come to firm 2; if it plays E, with probability ρ it faces 1H with payoff 2, with probability $(1 - \rho)$ it faces 1L with payoff $-2\mu + 2(1 - \mu)$; thus the expected payoff from playing E is $2\rho + (1 - \rho)[-2\mu + 2(1 - \mu)] = 2 - 4(1 - \rho)\mu$, a decreasing function of μ. The expected payoff from playing N is zero. These two payoffs are equal if $\mu = 1/[2(1 - \rho)]$; call μ° this value, an increasing function of ρ; it cannot be less than 1/2; but it can be >1, which will be the case if $\rho > 1/2$ and will mean that $\mu = \mu^\circ$ is impossible. If $\mu < \mu^\circ$, E is preferred to N and $\varepsilon = 1$. We derive the correspondence $\varepsilon^*(\mu)$:

$$\varepsilon^*(\mu) = \begin{cases} 1 & \text{if } \mu < \mu^\circ \\ [0, 1] & \text{if } \mu = \mu^\circ \text{(only possible if } \mu^\circ \leq 1, \text{ that requires } \rho \leq 1/2) \\ 0 & \text{if } \mu > \mu^\circ \text{(only possible if } \mu^\circ < 1, \text{ that requires } \rho < 1/2). \end{cases}$$

The mixed strategy equilibria are triplets $(\alpha, \mu, \varepsilon)$ such that $\alpha = 0$, $\mu \in \mu^*(\varepsilon)$ and $\varepsilon \in \varepsilon^*(\mu)$. These (that will also include the pure strategy equilibria) can be found graphically by drawing both $\mu^*(\varepsilon)$ and $\varepsilon^*(\mu)$ in the same diagram; we need to distinguish the cases $0 \leq \rho < 1/2$ (◻ Fig. 11.33a), $\rho = 1/2$ (◻ Fig. 11.33b), $1/2 < \rho < 1$ (◻ Fig. 11.33c).

When $\rho < 1/2$, it is $\mu^\circ < 1$, and the two correspondences meet in three points: $(\mu = 0, \varepsilon = 1)$; $(\mu = \mu^\circ, \varepsilon = 1/2)$; $(\mu = 1, \varepsilon = 0)$; these correspond to the pure strategy equilibrium (AA;E), to a mixed strategy equilibrium $(\alpha = 0, \mu = \mu^\circ, \varepsilon = 1/2)$, and to the pure strategy equilibrium (AM;N). When $\rho > 1/2$, it is $\mu^\circ > 1$, $\mu \geq \mu^\circ$ is impossible, hence $\varepsilon^*(\mu) = 1$, and the only common point of the two correspondences is $(\mu = 0, \varepsilon = 1)$ i.e. the pure strategy equilibrium (AA;E). When $\rho = 1/2$, it is $\mu^\circ = 1$, and, besides the two pure strategy equilibria already mentioned, there is a continuum of mixed equilibria $(\alpha = 1, \mu = \mu^\circ = 1, 0 < \varepsilon < 1/2)$.

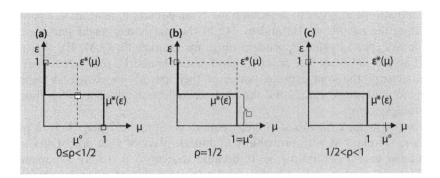

◻ **Fig. 11.33** Graphical determination of mixed strategies in Ratliff's investment/entry example. The small squares ◻ indicate Nash equilibria; in **b** there is a continuum of equilibria

As you can see, even a rather simple Bayesian game can require careful, detailed specification of the many possibilities, especially if one does not restrict the analysis to pure strategies only. Kreps (1990, ▶ Chap. 13) adds flesh onto this basic skeleton with many examples commented in detail.

11.18 Auctions as Bayesian Games. Revenue Equivalence Theorem. Winner's Curse

Now let us examine an example of Bayesian game with an infinite number of strategies. An *independent-private-values auction* is an auction for an indivisible object, in which each bidder has a clear idea about the value of the object to her and does not know the other bidders' valuations, and the bidders' valuations are statistically independent (that is, to learn about the other bidders' valuations would not affect each bidder's own valuation[30]). Assume each bidder perceives each other bidder's valuation as a draw from a common probability distribution, and knows that the other bidders have the same perception, and all bidders agree on the probability distribution. Consider a *sealed-bid first-price* independent-private-values auction,[31] in which two *risk-neutral* players A and B simultaneously submit their bids b_i, $i = A, B$, for an indivisible object they desire, and the highest bidder gets the object and pays the bid. The bids can be any non-negative real number; we need not really worry about the case $b_A = b_B$ because it has probability zero, but anyway we can assume that in this case the object is assigned

---

30 It is easy to think of cases where this assumption would not hold, for example how much one is ready to pay for a painting may well depend on how much one thinks one can obtain by re-selling it, which depends on how much others are ready to pay for it.
31 A sealed-bid first-price auction is one in which each bidder submits the bid in a sealed envelope, the object goes to the highest bid, and the winner must pay her bid. A second-price auction is one in which the object goes to highest bid but the amount to be paid is the second-highest bid.

11.18 · Auctions as Bayesian Games. Revenue Equivalence Theorem. Winner's Curse

randomly to one of the players. Assume quasi-linear utility; then player i's surplus is $t_i - b_i$ if she wins, zero if she loses. Both players try to maximize their expected surplus. The game is then said *symmetric* in that both players face the same problem (apart from the parameter t_i indicating the private valuation) and have the same objective function; therefore the relationship $b_i^* = \beta(t_i)$ tying the optimal bid to the valuation must be the same for both players; we only need look for symmetric-equilibrium strategies $b_i = \beta(t_i)$. The game can be formalized as a Bayesian game by assuming that each player can come in an infinity of types, each one identified by her valuation t_i.

Player i's expected payoff, when the player is of type t_i and bids b_i, is the expected value of the surplus, i.e.

$$v_i(t_i, b_i) = (t_i - b_i) Prob(b_i > b_j).$$

Let us assume that $\beta(\cdot)$ is a continuous and strictly increasing function. Then

$$Prob\,(b_i > b_j) = Prob(b_i \geq b_j) = Prob(\beta(t_i) \geq \beta(t_j)) = Prob\left(t_j \leq \beta^{-1}(b_i)\right) = F\left(\beta^{-1}(b_i)\right).$$

Let $v_i^*(t_i) := max_{b_i} v_i$. Because of the Envelope Theorem:

$$\partial v_i^* / \partial t_i = Prob(b_i^* \geq b_j) = F\left(\beta^{-1}(b_i^*)\right) = F(t_i)$$

where b_i^* is the optimal value of b_i. Integrating from $t_i = 0$ (the lowest possible value of t_i):

$$v_i^*(t_i) = \int_0^{t_i} F(x) dx$$

Rearranging $v_i^*(t_i) = \int_0^{t_i} F(x)dx = (t_i - b_i^*)Prob(b_i^* \geq b_j) = (t_i - \beta(t_i))F(t_i)$ we obtain the function $\beta(\cdot)$:

$$b_i^* \equiv \beta(t_i) = t_i - \frac{\int_0^{t_i} F(x)dx}{F(t_i)}.$$

For simplicity, assume F is the uniform distribution $F(t)=t$; then it is $\int_0^{t_i} F(x)dx = t^2/2$ so $b_i^* = t_i/2$: under our assumptions the Bayesian equilibrium (a *perfect* Bayesian equilibrium, in fact—this is defined in ▶ Sect. 11.20) is for each player to bid one half of her valuation. This result can be shown to extend to more than two bidders as follows: if the lowest possible valuation is zero and F is uniform and there are n bidders, then each bidder bids a fraction $(n-1)/n$ of her valuation. This means two things (that are true also for other distributions $F(t)$): first, for given valuations, bids are increasing functions of the number of bidders; second, considering the **order statistics** of the sample consisting of the valuations,[32]

---

32 Definition of an **order statistic**: consider a sample of n numbers randomly drawn from a distribution; having ordered the n elements of the statistical sample from smallest to largest, the first order statistic is the smallest number in the sample, the n-th order statistic is the highest number.

each bidder bids the *expected value* of the second highest order statistic conditional on her valuation of the object being the highest order statistic. In this example the valuations are known to be uniformly distributed over an interval [0, 1]; if a sample of n observations is drawn from a uniform distribution over [0,1], then the probability that the highest observation in the sample (i.e. the highest order statistic $X_{(n)}$) be not higher than a number y ($0 \leq y \leq 1$) is the probability that this holds for all observations x_i in the sample, i.e. $[p(x_i \leq y)]^n = y^n$. This is the distribution function of $X_{(n)}$. The density function of $X_{(n)}$ is therefore ny^{n-1}, and the expected value of $X_{(n)}$ is $\int_0^1 yny^{n-1} dy = n/(n+1)$; this result will be useful below.

The probability, that the second highest order statistic be not higher than a number z where $0 \leq z \leq X_{(n)}$, is $X_{(n)} z^{n-1}$. From this fact it can be analogously shown that for the uniform distribution $F(t) = t$ on the unit interval the expected value of the second highest order statistic is $E(X_{(n-1)}) = X_{(n)} \cdot (n-1)/n$ for the bidder who treats her bid as the nth-order statistic, or $E(X_{(n-1)}) = (n-1)/n+1$ for the external observer. The winner bids just enough not to be defeated by the *expected value* of the second highest valuation. (Or a very little bit above this, to make sure.) The assumption of risk neutrality is obviously crucial for this result; it is possible to remove it but this would complicate things considerably, taking us to advanced treatises on auctions. In the present case with two players, each bidder plays 1/2 her/his valuation.

Then the seller's expected revenue is one half of the higher valuation, that is, one half of the expected value of the highest order statistic, which we saw is $n/(n+1)$, that is 2/3, in our case of two bidders. Hence the seller's expected revenue is 1/3.

Let us compare this with the seller's expected revenue from a **second-price sealed-bid auction**[33] (also called a *Vickrey auction*) under the same assumptions.

To determine it, we start from a basic result: in this type of auction it is a weakly dominant strategy for bidders to submit their true valuation.

Proof In this proof we are not restricted to only two bidders. Choose a bidder, indicate with v her/his valuation of the object, and with b her bid. We want to compare the strategy of bidding a sum $b \neq v$ with the strategy of bidding v. There are two cases: $b < v$, $b > v$. Consider the first case. Let b^* be the highest rival bid. If $b^* > v$ it is also $b^* > b$ so our bidder does not win with either strategy. If $b^* < b$, our bidder wins with either strategy. So for these two cases the two strategies are equivalent. But if $b < b^* < v$, bidding v is superior to bidding b because with b the bidder does not win and obtains zero surplus, with v she/he wins and gains $v - b^*$. So bidding v is weakly superior to bidding $b < v$. With analogous reasoning one shows that bidding v is weakly superior to bidding $b > v$. (We can neglect the cases $b^* = b$ or $b^* = v$ because these are cases of zero probability for a continuous distribution.) ∎

---

33 Why should the seller prefer a second-price auction? doesn't this make the winner pay less than in a first-price auction? one consideration is, that the fact that the winner, the highest bidder, pays only the second-highest bid can induce bidders to bid more aggressively, because what the winner pays is independent of her/his own bid, it depends on the bids of the others. But the issue is more complex than we can exhaustively discuss here.

So we can assume the two bidders bid their true valuations: $b_1 = v_1$, $b_2 = v_2$. The seller's expected revenue is $E(min(v_1, v_2))$ because the winner pays the other bid. But $min(v_1, v_2)$ is the first-order statistic, coinciding in this case with the second highest order statistic, whose expected value was shown to be $(n - 1)/(n + 1)$, that is, in our case, 1/3: the same as for the sealed-bid first-price auction!

We have seen here one instance of a general result called the **revenue equivalence theorem**, which states that *if* the independent private-values model applies, and *if* the bidders are risk-neutral and adopt strategies that constitute a non-cooperative equilibrium, then the expected revenue from the four basic auctions (the sealed-bid first-price auction, the sealed-bid second-price auction, the ascending or English auction, and the descending or Dutch auction) is the same.[34]

The reasons for the seller to prefer one kind of auction over the others must be found outside the model considered here: for example bidders may not be risk-neutral, or different forms of auction may differ in the capacity to discourage collusion, or to elicit competition based on prestige or other emotions.

A different kind of auction is the **common-values auction**, in which the auctioned object has an objective value on which the bidders would agree if they knew it, but this value will only become clear after the object is auctioned, and the bidders have private guesses about this value that are known not to be statistically independent, so that the valuation of a bidder would likely change if she/he learned about the other valuations. A typical example is auctions for carpets or antiques or paintings when the bidders are merchants who want to resell the object and have different estimates of the market price the object will be able to fetch in the future. Sometimes the situation is not properly an auction but shares similar characteristics, e.g. teams competing for professional athletes whose future performance (which will influence the team owners' earnings) cannot be known for sure.

An important characteristic of this type of auction is the **winner's curse**: if the bids correspond to the valuations, and *if the valuations are correct on average* about the value of the auctioned object (that is, are the true value plus a random error with mean zero), then the winning bid reflects the most optimistic valuation, which is higher than the true value of the object. Winning is bad news for the winner because it reveals that everybody else valued the object less than the

---

34 This was proved for the first two auctions; for the other two, the rigorous proof will not be supplied here, but it should be intuitively clear that the Dutch auction and the first-price sealed-bid auction are strategically similar, both requiring an attempt to minimize the excess of the winner's bid over the second-highest bid, via some estimate of the expected value of the latter bid on the basis of whatever information is available; this will entail betting only slightly above the expected value of the second-highest bid (see below in the text on how to avoid the winner's curse in the common-value auction), so that the winner ends up paying (on average) as much as the winner of the second-price sealed-bid auction, who only pays the second highest bid. Analogously, it should be intuitively clear that the English auction and the second-price sealed-bid auction are strategically similar, in that in the English auction it is optimal to reveal the valuation – by dropping out only when the price becomes greater than the valuation—in which case usually the winner pays only very little more than the second-highest valuation. But the limits of this similarity would require extensive discussion, a task for a specialist course in auction theory.

974   Chapter 11 · Games and Information

winner, and this means that, if average opinion is roughly correct (that is, unless the winner has better information than the other bidders), she overestimated the value of the object and will therefore incur in losses. There is convincing empirical evidence that the winner's curse is a frequent phenomenon.

In the winner's curse, winning delivers new information. The implications can be very relevant in other contexts too. An example first proposed by Max Bazerman and William Samuelson imagines that firm A is considering whether to purchase firm B. The managers of firm A are certain that, whatever the value X of firm B as currently run, because of synergies with firm A the incorporation of firm B into A would raise that value by 50%. But X is not known by the managers of firm A who only know that X is a random variable uniformly distributed between 0 and 100; X is known to the owners of firm B but not divulged. There is room for only one take-it-or-leave-it offer by firm A to the owners of firm B. What maximum value P can firm A's managers offer for the purchase of firm B, if they know that the offer will be accepted if $P \geq X$ and rejected otherwise? The answer is: no P is convenient. The reason is that, if an offer P is accepted, this means that $X \leq P$ and X can be any value between zero and P, hence $E(X|X \leq P) = P/2$, thus the expected value of firm B after the purchase and the improved management is 0.75P which is less than P, and this is so for any P.[35]

The way to avoid the winner's curse is to reason as follows: if my bid wins, it is because it is higher than any other bid, which implies that the other bidders are valuing the object less than I do (under the reasonable assumption that bids are increasing functions of valuations, and under the assumption that all bidders reason in the same way and share the assumptions about the distributions from which the random variables that appear in their reasonings are drawn), which means, since I believe that the true value of the object is the average of the valuations, that I am overestimating the value of the object; this requires me to bid less than my valuation. But how much less? I must also remember that the other players too will bid less than their valuations, if conscious of the winner's curse.

Suppose, for example, that the valuations are known to be unbiased and to be uniformly distributed over an interval $(0, M)$ where M is unknown; then the correct expected value of the object is $M/2$. If there are n bidders and my valuation is x^*, then if x^* is the highest valuation it is the highest *order statistic* of the sample of n valuations; statistical theory teaches that the expected value of the highest order statistic in such a sample is $M \cdot n/(n+1)$; from this I can derive the expected value of M as $x^*(n+1)/n$. Hence I should bid not more than $M/2 = x * (n+1)/2n$. (Note that this upper limit on the bid is now a *decreasing* function of the number of bidders, because the more bidders value the object less than I do, the lower the probable value of the object.) But should I bid $x * (n+1)/2n$, or less? If my valuation is the highest, then it is higher than the second highest valuation, call it x_2

---

35   This example is not very plausible, firm A's management will normally be able to bargain. You ought always to ask how plausible an example is. But when we arrive at Akerlof's model of second-hand cars (in the section on adverse selection), we will see that the same problem arises in more plausible circumstances.

(its expected value for me can be derived from the expected value of the second highest order statistic once I conclude as to the value of M); since the bidder with valuation x_2 is not going to bid more than $x_2(n+1)/2n$, and since I am risk neutral by assumption, I need not bid more than just one cent above $x_2(n+1)/2n$.

Let us see how this logic brings to a Bayesian equilibrium, following the same route as for the independent-private-values case. Assume a sealed-bid first-price auction with only two players, 1 and 2, who have formed secret estimates x^*_1, x^*_2 of the value of the object; each one of these estimates is known to be drawn from an unbiased uniform distribution $F(x)$ on $[0, M]$ where M is unknown. Hence $F(x)=x/M$. From the previous reasoning we conclude that player 1 esteems the expected value of M, conditional on x^*_1 being the highest valuation, as equal to $x^*_1(n+1)/n = 3x^*_1/2$, hence the expected value of the object conditional on $x^*_1 > x^*_2$ is $t^*_1 = x^*_1 \cdot 3/4$. Since this is true for both players, player 1 considers x_2 to be drawn from a uniform distribution $F(x)$ on $[0, M(x^*_1)]$, hence $F(x)=2x/3x^*_1$; and she considers t_2 to be drawn from a uniform distribution $G(t)$ on $[0, 3 M(x^*_1)/4]$, hence $G(t) = 4t/3M = 8t/9x^*_1 = 2t/3t^*_1$. The game is again symmetric so we assume that $b_i=\beta(t_i)$ with $\beta(\cdot)$ a continuous and strictly increasing function. Player i's expected payoff, when of type x_i and if she bids b_i, is $v_i(t_i,b_i)=(t_i-b_i)Prob(b_i>b_j)$. Then

$$Prob(b_i > b_j) = Prob(b_i \geq b_j) = Prob(\beta(t_i) \geq \beta(t_j)) = Prob\left(t_j \leq \beta^{-1}(b_i)\right) = G\left(\beta^{-1}(b_i)\right).$$

Let $v_i^*(t_i):=max_{b_i}v_i$. Because of the Envelope Theorem,

$$\partial v_i^*/\partial t_i = Prob\left(b_i^* \geq b_j\right) = G\left(\beta^{-1}(b_i^*)\right) = G(t_i) = 4t_i/3M$$

where b_i^* is the optimal value of b_i. Integrating from $t_i=0$ (the lowest possible value of t_i):

$$v_i^*(t_i) = \int_0^{t_i} G(x)dx$$

Rearranging $v_i^*(t_i) = \int_0^{t_i} G(x)dx = (t_i - b_i^*)Prob(b_i^* \geq b_j) = (t_i - \beta(t_i))G(t_i)$, one obtains the function $\beta(\cdot)$:

$$b_i^* \equiv \beta(t_i) = t_i - \frac{\int_0^{t_i} G(x)dx}{G(t_i)}.$$

Since G is the uniform distribution $G(t)=4t/3M$, it is $\int_0^{t_i} G(x)dx = \frac{4}{3M} \int_0^{t_i} xdx = 2t^2/(3M)$, so $b_i^* = 1/2t_i = 3/8 \cdot x_i$.

Thus we see that the optimal strategy consists of bidding considerably less than the expected value of the object (conditional on winning), indicated above for a uniform distribution as $x^*_i(n+1)/2n$, which with two players boils down to $\frac{3}{4}x^*_i$; in the present case, the optimal bid is only one half of that. We find again that the optimal bid b_1 equals (i.e. is the minimum possible increase above) the expected value of the second highest valuation; but, here, not of the original valuation x^*_2, rather of the one conditional on winning t_2, because the expected value of x^*_2 conditional on $x^*_2<x^*_1$ is $x^*_1(n-1)/n=x^*_1/2$ which implies $t_2 = 3/4x^*2 = 3/8 \cdot x^*1$.

When as in the common-values auction the independent private-values model does not apply, the revenue equivalence theorem does not hold. In particular, when valuations are uncertain and not independent, the English auction appears to produce a greater revenue than the other ones because during its process one observes the other bidders' valuations as bidders gradually drop out, and this supplies information that can be used to correct one's valuation, decreasing the risk of incurring in the winner's curse and therefore decreasing the need to bid considerably less than the expected value of the object.

The field of the design and analysis of auctions is one where game theory has been usefully applied. The pioneering analyses of William Vickrey in 1961 did not receive much attention at first, but their practical use became apparent in the 1990s, when auctions of radio frequency spectrum for mobile telecommunication raised billions of dollars. Auctions for advertising slots on the Internet have since become even more important; Google has a team of specialists, headed by Hal Varian, working on how to improve its auction-based system of allocation of these slots. See McMillan (1994) and Klemperer (2004) for a broader view of the theory of bidding in auctions. So many are the details that can determine the revenue production capacity of auctions, and so considerable are the empirical teachings derivable from the experience with auctions so far, that it is best for this textbook to stop here on this topic, and to invite the interested readers to attend a full course on auctions.

11.19 Dynamic Games of Imperfect Information

For *dynamic* (or sequential) games of incomplete information, the definition of a Bayes-Nash equilibrium is the same as for simultaneous-move games, because it is defined for their strategic form.

If a game is one of imperfect information, the recourse to the representation based on types is equally possible. Thus consider the entry game of ◘ Fig. 11.34. Suppose B knows that firm A, if it decides to enter, randomizes between Fight

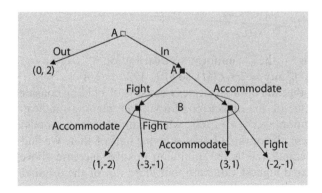

◘ Fig. 11.34

11.19 · Dynamic Games of Imperfect Information

and Accommodate assigning probability p to Fight. Then it is equivalent to assume that if A chooses In, it must hire a new manager, who can turn out with probability p to be a Fighting type and with probability $1 - p$ to be an Accommodating type. (It would only mean that the node reached by In is one where Nature, rather than A, chooses the manager type.) The converse is also possible. Thus below we will sometimes use games of imperfect information but with no 'types' to illustrate aspects also arising in games of incomplete information.

Before coming to Bayesian games we saw that the strategic form of a sequential-move game can indicate Nash equilibria that, upon further examination, are implausible, because based on non-credible threats; in order to eliminate them from the plausible solutions of a game, the notion of subgame perfection was introduced.

An analogous need to discard implausible Nash equilibria as solutions of sequential-move *Bayesian* games has stimulated the adoption of some restrictions that solutions should satisfy. These restrictions require defining the notion of **beliefs** of players.

When a player (or a 'type') must choose among actions at an information set that includes several nodes, the result of choice depends on which node the player actually is at, so the player must try to form as reasonable as possible an opinion on the probability of being at each one of these nodes. The probabilities she assesses are her *beliefs at that information set*. They depend of course on the probabilities of the several types, and on the strategy profile. The vector of beliefs for all information sets in the game is called the players' **belief system**.

The presence of several nodes in the information set can be due to not knowing which type of a player made the previous move, for example whether the poker player in front of you, who just raised the bet above yours, is a good bluffer or not; but it can also be due to the fact that a player randomized between two actions at the previous node, both nodes resulting from the random choice are in your information set, and you don't know which action came out.

Given a common prior on the probabilities of each type, and a strategy profile (a strategy for each type of each player), and assuming all players' types fully know both, for information sets that can be reached with positive probability the application of Bayes' Rule determines beliefs univocally; so given the profile of behavioural strategies, *if* beliefs are derived from Bayes' Rule all players can determine the beliefs at all the information sets reached with positive probability, even when the beliefs refer to another player's information set. And players would be irrational not to use correct probability theory to derive their beliefs; so it seems only rational to *use Bayes' Rule whenever possible*. But we must clarify how this rule is applied, and the 'whenever possible'.

Let H stands for an information set where player i is to move, and let x, x' stand for nodes at that information set. Let Prob(x|H, σ) mean 'probability that player i be at node x in information set H, conditional on the game having reached information set H, and conditional on σ being the strategy profile followed by all players'. Bayes' Rule states that, if A and B are two events, as long as Prob(B) > 0 it is

$$\text{Prob}(A|B) = \text{Prob}(A) \cdot \text{Prob}(B|A)/\text{Prob}(B)$$
$$= \text{Prob}(A) \cdot \text{Prob}(B|A)/[\text{Prob}(B|A) \cdot \text{Prob}(A) + \text{Prob}(B|notA) \cdot \text{Prob}(notA)].$$

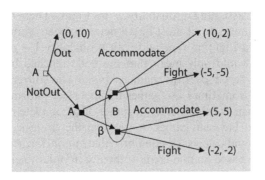

◘ Fig. 11.35

Then Bayesian updating (since Prob(H|x, σ)=1) requires that player *i* determines the conditional probability of being at x as:

$$\text{Prob}(x|H,\sigma) = \text{Prob}(x|\sigma) \cdot \text{Prob}(H|x,\sigma)/\text{Prob}(H|\sigma) = \text{Prob}(x|\sigma)/\sum_{x' \in H}\text{Prob}(x'|\sigma).$$

For example in the entry game of ◘ Fig. 11.35 if player A plays the totally mixed strategy σ_A that assigns probabilities 1/4, 1/2, 1/4 respectively to Out, α, β, and assuming that player B knows these probabilities, then the probability that B's information set is reached (that is, that A chooses NotOut) is 3/4 and Bayes' Rule allows us to calculate B's beliefs about being at nodes x_α or x_β:

$$\text{Prob}(x_\alpha|\text{NotOut}, \sigma_A) = (1/2)/(3/4) = 2/3; \quad \text{Prob}(x_\beta|\text{NotOut}, \sigma_A) = 1/3;$$

these are B's beliefs ***Bayes-consistent*** with σ_A.

But Bayes' Rule cannot be applied to information sets that, given the strategy profile, have zero probability of being reached. If in the game of ◘ Fig. 11.35 player A's strategy chooses Out at the root node with probability 1, then Prob(NotOut) is zero, and division by zero is not defined; the beliefs at B's information set are then considered unconstrained. This explains the words 'whenever possible'. We will see that beliefs about such unreached information sets can nonetheless influence the choice of strategies.

11.20 Sequential Rationality, Behavioural Strategies, Perfect Bayesian Equilibrium (PBE)

The notion of Bayes-Nash equilibrium defined in ▶ Sect. 11.17, when applied to sequential games of incomplete (or imperfect) information, does *not* require beliefs to be derived from application of Bayes' Rule whenever possible. But such a derivation is clearly required for an optimal choice of strategies, since it offers the best way to assess the likelihood of being at one node rather than at another when a player is at an information set comprising more than one node. So it seems logical to assume it. But it does not eliminate all implausible Nash equilibria.

11.20 · Sequential Rationality, Behavioural Strategies, Perfect Bayesian ...

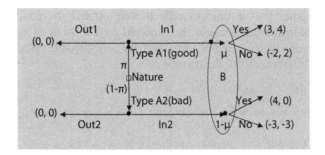

Fig. 11.36 A Bayesian game. Nature chooses the type of player A with probabilities π and $1 - \pi$; μ and $1 - \mu$ are B's beliefs

A ↓	B: Yes	B: No
Out1, Out2	0, 0; 0$_x$	$_x$0, 0$_x$: 0$_x$
Out1, In2	0, 4$_x$; 0$_x$	$_x$0, -3; -3+3π
In1, Out2	$_x$3, 0; 4π_x	-2π, 0$_x$; 2π
In1, In2	$_x$3, 4$_x$; 4π_x	-2, -3; -3+5π

Fig. 11.37 The strategic form of the previous game

An example is the game of **Fig. 11.36**. Firm A worked on developing an innovative product and can offer to firm B (action In) or not offer (action Out) the right to utilize the product; but it is unclear whether it developed a good product (type A1) or a product with hidden defects (type A2); firm B is unable to discover the quality of the product before the contract but assesses at π, $0 < \pi < 1$, the probability that the product is good. Firm A knows π. B's beliefs are described by the probability μ it assigns to being faced with the offer of a good product if it receives the offer, that is the probability of being at the upper node in the information set on the right in **Fig. 11.36**. B can accept or reject the contract, if offered.[36]

One can say, in Bayesian language, that firm A can be of two types, A1 and A2, and has four strategies each consisting of two choices, one for each type: (Out1, Out2); (Out1, In2); (In1, Out2); (In1, In2). The matrix in **Fig. 11.37** is the strategic form with the payoffs to A1, to A2 and to B listed in this order.

The best responses (indicated by the small x's in subscript) reveal two Nash equilibria in pure strategies: (Out1, Out2; No) and (In1, In2; Yes). But the first

---

36 The bad payoff for B of A2 choosing In and B choosing No might be due to the fact that firm A2 risks going bankrupt (it will be unable to place the product with other firms, while A1 can trust it will be finally able to persuade other firms that the product is good) and in revenge it sabotages the plant of firm B.

equilibrium assumes that if unexpectedly B were offered the contract, it would refuse it. This is irrational, because the expected payoff for B of choosing Yes is greater than the one of choosing No whatever B's belief, that is, whatever the probability μ that B attributes to be facing type A1:

$$EU_B(Yes) = 4\mu > EU_B(No) = 2\mu - 3(1 - \mu) = 5\mu - 3;$$

for the inequality *not* to hold it should be $5\mu-3 \geq 4\mu$, that is $\mu \geq 3$, impossible since $\mu \leq 1$.

In order to exclude implausible equilibria like this one, a condition has been proposed that has the same motivation as subgame perfection: the condition of **sequential rationality**. It requires that each player chooses an optimal action at each information set where she is the chooser, *given her beliefs* and given her opponents' strategies. Importantly, this condition must hold also at information sets with zero probability of being reached, where beliefs are unconstrained. Sequential rationality by itself does not require beliefs to have been derived whenever possible though correct application of Bayes' Rule, i.e. to be Bayes-consistent; but in general it is coupled with such a requirement (see below).

Let us define a number of notions and symbols that allow a more precise definition of sequential rationality.

(i)   When player j is at an information set H^j where she must move, let $p^j(H^J)$ be the vector of her **beliefs** at H^j, where the symbol p is motivated by the beliefs being the probabilities she assigns to being at each one of the nodes in that information set, their sum of course equal to 1.

(ii) Define a **system of beliefs** μ^* in a dynamic game in extensive form as an ordered numbering of all information sets in the game and, attached to each information set, the probability distribution over the nodes in it, that reflects the beliefs of the player active at that information set. (Of course if the information set contains only one node the belief is trivially that the probability of being at that node conditional on that information set being reached is 1.)

(iii) A **behavioural strategy** σ^j of player j defines, for each information set where player j is the chooser, the probabilities with which she will *play* the available moves at that information set. Do not confuse the probability the player entertains *of being at one node in an information set* (this is part of her beliefs) with the probability with which the player *intends to play one move* among those available to her/him at that information set (this is part of her behavioural strategy).

(iv) A **strategy profile** $\sigma = (\sigma^j, \sigma^{-j})$ in a dynamic game in extensive form is a set of behavioural strategies, one for each player; it is **sequentially rational at information set H^j** (an information set where player j is to move), **given a system of beliefs μ^***, if the expected utility of player j starting from H^j is maximized by the appropriate portion of σ^j, in the set of substrategies open to j from information set H^j onwards, against the given profile σ^{-j} of strategies of the other players.

(v)   If, for the given μ^*, σ is sequentially rational at *all* information sets, then we say σ is **sequentially rational, given belief system μ^***.

11.20 · Sequential Rationality, Behavioural Strategies, Perfect Bayesian Equilibrium (PBE)

Note then that sequential rationality is defined with reference to *given* beliefs. An equilibrium requires that these beliefs not be irrational. This idea is captured as follows:

A couple (μ^*, σ) consisting of a system of beliefs and of a strategy profile, also called an **assessment**, is called a **perfect Bayesian equilibrium** (**PBE**), or also an **assessment equilibrium**, if

(1) it is a Nash equilibrium,
(2) σ is sequentially rational for each admissible μ^*,
(3) μ^* is admissible, i.e. *Bayes-consistent with σ* in the sense that beliefs at successive information sets are determined by Bayesian updating whenever possible, no restriction being put on beliefs at information sets having probability zero of being reached under σ.

Note that if the probabilities with which Nature plays its moves (when Nature is one of the players) are common knowledge as generally assumed, then for each strategy profile, assuming it is common knowledge, each player can univocally determine the Bayes-consistent beliefs of *all* players for the information sets with positive probability of being reached. If the behavioural strategies are all given, then for each information set H reached with positive probability one can calculate for each node x in H the belief p(x) (of the player j who is to move at H), as

$$p(\mathrm{x}|\mathrm{H}) = \left[\mathrm{Prob(H|x)Prob}\left(\mathrm{x}|\sigma^j\right)\right] / \sum_{x_k \in H} \mathrm{Prob}\ (x_k|\sigma)$$

where Prob (H|x)$=1$, and Prob (x|σ) must be derived from the behavioural strategies and the initial chance choice by Nature.

Thus for these information sets beliefs are common knowledge for each strategy profile; this allows players to ascertain whether their strategies in that strategy profile are best responses.

In the game of ◘ Fig. 11.36, the Nash equilibrium strategy $\sigma^\wedge=$(Out1, Out2; No) leaves B's information set unreached, hence any belief of B is Bayes-consistent[37]; conditions (1) and (3) are satisfied, but condition (2) is not: strategy $\sigma^\wedge$ is not sequentially rational for any μ, because, as shown, if B's information set is reached then optimization from that point on requires B to choose Yes. The only PBE (in pure strategies) is (In1, In2; Yes). Sequential rationality has eliminated the implausible Nash equilibrium relying on a 'non-credible threat' by B to play No if called to move.

Given a strategy profile and a belief system, it is easy (although perhaps laborious) to check whether beliefs are Bayes-consistent.

---

37 Of course, Bayes-consistency of beliefs concerns only the beliefs at information sets with several nodes: the theory assumes that players know where they are, so when a player is at an information set with a single node the only possible belief is that she is at that node.

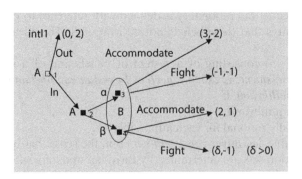

◘ Fig. 11.38

But if only the payoffs are given and the optimal strategies must be *found*, the thing is more complicated. For an example, consider the entry game of ◘ Fig. 11.38 (a modification of the one of ◘ Fig. 11.35). At node 2 there starts a proper subgame, but it has no Nash equilibrium in pure strategies as long as $-1 < \delta$ (check it by drawing the strategic form of this subgame). Assume $\delta > 0$. Let b_F be the probability that firm B plays Fight; let μ_α be the probability assigned by B to being at α (that is, the belief about being at α) if called to move, which coincides with the probability B assigns to A playing α after In; let us look for beliefs that are consistent with the strategies they induce. We must find a fixed point of the correspondence that sends from beliefs to optimal strategies and back from optimal strategies to beliefs consistent with them according to Bayes' Rule.

To find it, first notice that, after observing that A has played In, B will play Fight with probability $b_F = 1$ if its expected payoff, -1, is greater than the expected payoff from playing Accommodate which is $-2\mu_\alpha + (1 - \mu_\alpha)$, i.e. if $\mu_\alpha > 2/3$; while $b_F = 0$ if $\mu_\alpha < 2/3$. Now I show that either one of these two possibilities is incompatible with *mutually shared* beliefs: if A plays In and $\mu_\alpha > 2/3$ and hence $b_F = 1$, A must play β with probability 1 but then the PBE concept requires $\mu_\alpha = 0$; if A plays In and $\mu_\alpha < 2/3$ and hence $b_F = 0$, A must play α with probability 1 but then the PBE concept requires $\mu_\alpha = 1$. Therefore if A plays In with positive probability, a PBE requires $\mu_\alpha = 2/3$, i.e., having played In, A must randomize between α and β with probabilities 2/3 for α and 1/3 for β; for an equilibrium in mixed strategies, B must play Fight and Accommodate with probabilities that make A indifferent between α and β, which requires $-b_F + 3(1 - b_F) = \delta b_F + 2(1 - b_F)$, i.e. $b_F = 1/(\delta + 2)$. A's payoff from playing In is therefore $(3\delta + 2)/(\delta + 2) > 0$, hence preferable to playing Out. Thus In will be played with probability 1. We have thus found the unique PBE for $\delta > 0$, where A plays the mixed strategy (Prob(In) = 1; Prob(α) = 2/3) and B plays the mixed strategy $b_F = 1/(\delta + 2)$. The payoff to B is -1.

(Finding PBEs is clearly not trivial, but I will be content with this example; if you want to become a specialist in the field, clearly it is opportune you learn to develop or to master softwares that can find the PBEs of a game for you.)

11.21 Limits of Perfect Bayesian Equilibrium. Sequential Equilibrium

PBEs eliminate most Nash equilibria relying on non-credible threats, but not all. The point is that sequential rationality requires that choices be optimal at all information sets (reached or unreached) *given the beliefs*, and in certain cases the freedom of beliefs at unreached information sets can result in an implausible PBE.

An example is the entry game of ◘ Fig. 11.34 (taken from Mas-Colell et al. 1995, p. 290). Firm A must decide whether to enter a market where firm B is the sole incumbent; if A decides to enter, then both firms must simultaneously decide whether to fight, or to accommodate. The tree is the same as in ◘ Fig. 11.38, only drawn downwards, and the payoffs are different. In this game there are no 'types', but what we have seen about equivalence of incomplete information games and imperfect information games implies that the problem to be highlighted can arise in incomplete games too. The reader should draw the strategic form.

Suppose B assigns probability 1 to A playing Fight after entering. Then one perfect Bayesian equilibrium consists of A choosing the strategy 'Out, Accommodate if In' and B choosing 'Fight if In'. A's strategy means B's information set is not reached, hence B's beliefs are unconstrained, which authorizes our supposition on her belief; and *given B's belief, B's strategy is sequentially rational*; so we do have a PBE. But if A were actually to choose In, then the belief that A would certainly play 'Fight' would be very hard to defend, given that at that node 'Accommodate' would be the dominant strategy for A (by backward induction); and in fact this PBE strategy profile, when restricted to the subgame that starts after A chooses In, does not correspond to a Nash equilibrium, hence is not subgame perfect. We see here that *sequential rationality does not always eliminate non-credible threats, and need not ensure subgame perfection*.

Conversely, subgame perfection does not ensure sequential rationality. The best known example (Selten, 1975) is **Selten's Horse**, see ◘ Fig. 11.39, where the only subgame is the entire game so any Nash equilibrium is subgame perfect.

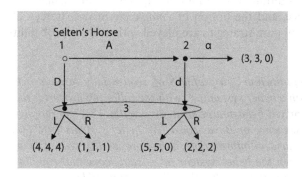

◘ **Fig. 11.39** Selten's Horse

984   **Chapter 11 · Games and Information**

There are three players, 1, 2 and 3; player 3, if called upon to choose, might be at either node, depending on the behavioural strategies of 1 and 2. If player 1 plays D with probability p, and player 2 plays d with probability q, then Bayes-consistent beliefs of player 3 require that she assigns probability $\mu = p/[p + (1-p)q]$ to being at the left node. There are two Nash equilibria in pure strategies, (A, α, R) and (D, α, L). They *are* Nash equilibria, that is, neither player can improve her/his payoff if those are the strategies of the other players (check it!). And they are subgame perfect because here we have a single subgame. But the second equilibrium is unpersuasive, because player 2's choice of α is hard to justify if 1 chooses D, because then 3 assigns probability 1 to being at the left node and chooses L, but then 2 should choose d; so 2's choice of α is not sequentially rational.

Why do we find player 2's choice of α debatable? Because the choices at an unreached information set should nonetheless be declarations of what one will choose *if* for some reason one is called upon to choose, given the subsequent nodes that can be reached from that information set and the optimal choices of the other players at those subsequent nodes. So since 3 will choose L, 2's choice should be d. Sequential rationality reduces the number of Nash equilibria to only one.

Why worry about having sensible choices at unreached information sets? One cannot neglect what a player decides to do at an unreached information set, because the other players may decide not to let the game reach that information set precisely because of what the player promises to choose in case that information set were reached. We saw this happening in the game of ◘ Fig. 11.34.

In Selten's Horse we see again that sequential rationality is helpful in reducing the number of plausible Nash equilibria. Unfortunately there remains the example of the entry game of ◘ Fig. 11.34, where sequential rationality is unable to eliminate a debatable PBE. That example helps one grasp why further '*refinements*' of Nash equilibria have been proposed, i.e. notions of Nash equilibrium imposing still further restrictions aimed to exclude the 'unreasonable beliefs' that even sequential rationality appears sometimes unable to eliminate.

Of these 'refinements', the more widely cited is ***sequential equilibrium*** (not to be confused with sequential rationality). I will only give a rather informal definition and an intuition. The definition requires the mathematical notion of converging sequence, and the notion of *completely mixed* strategy, that is, a mixed strategy where all pure strategies are played with positive probability.

■■ Definition

*A **sequential equilibrium** is a profile S of sequentially rational behavioural strategies coupled with a belief system μ^*, with the following property: there is a sequence of completely mixed behavioural strategy profiles $\{S^n\}$ converging to S, such that the associated sequence of Bayes-consistent belief systems $\{\mu^n\}$ (where no belief is unrestricted because no information set has probability zero of being reached) converges to μ^*. Then the belief system μ^* is said sequential-equilibrium-compatible, or also simply compatible (rather than Bayes-compatible).*

11.21 · Limits of Perfect Bayesian Equilibrium. Sequential Equilibrium

The motivations behind such a definition can be at least partly grasped by returning to the entry game of ❒ Fig. 11.34 with its implausible PBE. In that game the implausible equilibrium (Out, Accommodate; Fight if In) rests on B believing that if A plays In then A will certainly choose Fight (that is, B assigns probability 1 to being at the left node). But, given sequential rationality, this belief is made legitimate only by its being unrestricted because of the zero probability that A plays In. If there is a nonzero probability, however small, of A playing In, then after In sequential rationality obliges A to choose Accommodate (backward induction shows that Accommodate is always better for A), so Bayes' Rule assigns probability 1 to B being at the right node, conditional on B's information set having been reached. The notion of sequential equilibrium forbids B from changing this probability abruptly from 1 to zero when the probability that A plays In passes from extremely close to zero to exactly zero. This renders the Bayes-compatible beliefs behind the unsatisfactory Nash equilibrium not sequential-equilibrium-compatible.

However, the complicated reasonings required by these 'refinements'; the difficulty with formalizing anything but simple situations; the little plausibility of the assumption that the probability of each type is common knowledge; the doubts about Nash equilibria being what will really be played; the scarce practical relevance of mixed Nash equilibria; the fact that multiple Nash equilibria survive in many cases, which leaves players uncertain as to what to do; all these elements seem to have induced in recent years a slowdown of enthusiasm in going ahead with further refinements, and perhaps a slowdown of enthusiasm for the entire theory of games, because the latter has come out to be less powerful as a predictive tool than one hoped. However, the *forma mentis* one gets from game theory is certainly very useful, one immediately asks what kind of strategic interaction characterizes a situation, and game theory often does suggest what can be expected, and what can be done to decrease the danger of bad results: for example, prisoner's dilemmas require modifications of the game that introduce penalties for not cooperating; assurance games require that some institution ensures coordination. And there is no doubt that many applications, for example in auction theory, are very useful.

Now let us study a few more of these useful applications, in another field: asymmetric information.

11.22 Asymmetric Information. Signalling Games. Separating and Pooling Equilibria

In some strategic interactions *information is asymmetric*, that is, one of the players is not perfectly informed about the other player's actions or about the other player's characteristics (or type).

A first example is *signalling games* (also called sender-receiver games), one of the simplest categories of dynamic games of incomplete information. I restrict the presentation to two-players games. The first player to move can be of one of

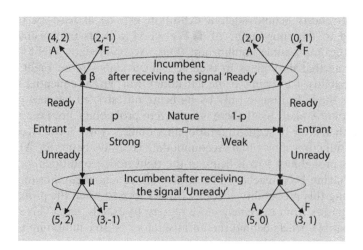

Fig. 11.40 A signalling game of entry. Entrant's payoffs are listed first

K possible *types* $t_1, t_2, ..., t_K$; the type is decided by an initial move by 'Nature' that selects the type according to a strictly positive probability distribution assumed to be common knowledge. The first player knows which type she is, but the second player doesn't. The first player chooses an action that is observed by the second player and that is described as 'sending a signal' to the second player; the first player is called the sender and the second player the receiver. The receiver then chooses her move on the basis of the signal and of the probabilities she assigns to the signal coming from each sender's type. The payoffs depend on the sender's type, on the signal, and on the strategy chosen by the receiver.

In certain signalling games the equilibrium strategies are such that the sender's signal reveals her type, because different types of sender choose different signals, and thus the receiver is certain as to which type she is facing and acts differently with different types; the equilibrium strategies are then said to form a ***separating equilibrium***. When this is not so, and different types of sender choose the same signal, then the receiver treats all types equally, the equilibrium strategies are said to form a ***pooling equilibrium***.

The entry game of ◘ Fig. 11.40 (from Osborne 2004, p. 333) can clarify some aspects of signalling games. The Entrant firm can be of two types, Strong or Weak, and it is common knowledge (the usual assumption—but how plausible?) that the Incumbent firm assigns probability p to the Entrant being Strong and $1 - p$ to Weak. The Entrant firm enters with either a clear signal that it is Ready to fight for a significant market share, or a clear signal that it is Unready to stand a fight (and therefore ready to exit if the Incumbent fights); not entering is not an option. The Incumbent can respond by either Accommodating or by Fighting. The first move is by Nature or Chance that chooses the type of Entrant with probabilities p and $1 - p$. The game 'tree' with the payoffs (first the Entrant's, then the Incumbent's) is in ◘ Fig. 11.40. I offer no explanation for the payoffs, which I take from Osborne.

The Incumbent receives either the signal 'Ready' or the signal 'Unready' without knowing whether the Entrant is Weak or Strong. The Entrant's strategy must specify a choice for each type, hence the Entrant's possible strategies (listing first the choice of the Strong type, and indicating for brevity Ready with R, and Unready with U) are: RR, RU, UR, UU. The Incumbent's strategy must determine the choice at each of its two information sets, so its possible strategies (listing first the response to 'Ready', with A for Accommodate and F for Fight) are AA, AF, FA, FF.

Let us look for the perfect Bayesian equilibria in pure strategies. The beliefs to be considered are those of the Incumbent, let us indicate them as β for the probability of being at the upper left node (signal Ready received from a Strong Entrant), $1 - \beta$ for the upper right node, μ for the lower left and $1 - \mu$ for the lower right node (signal Unready received from a Weak Entrant). First, it is good practice to look for dominated strategies. Do it, and you will note that, for a Weak Entrant, Unready is the dominant action; the Incumbent concludes that the Entrant's strategies can be only RU or UU.

Suppose that the Entrant's strategy is RU and the Incumbent believes this is indeed the Entrant's strategy; the Entrant's is a **separating** strategy, where each type sends a different signal; then the Incumbent's beliefs on the type she is facing are ($\beta = 1$, $\mu = 0$), in words: 'the Entrant is Strong with probability 1 if I receive the signal Ready, is Weak with probability 1 if I receive the signal Unready'; hence its strategy choice is AF; with this strategy of the Incumbent, the Entrant if Strong prefers to play Ready, and if Weak prefers to play Unready, thus the Incumbent's beliefs are correct; hence the strategy profile (RU; AF) coupled with Incumbent's beliefs ($\beta = 1$, $\mu = 0$) is a *separating* PBE.

Now suppose that the Entrant's strategy is UU and the Incumbent believes this is the Entrant's strategy: the Incumbent assigns probability zero to receiving the signal Ready. The Entrant's strategy does not separate the types, hence upon receiving the signal Unready the Incumbent believes that it comes from a Strong Entrant with probability p and from a Weak Entrant with probability $1 - p$; thus the Incumbent's expected payoff to A is $2p$ and to F is $1 - 2p$; hence A is preferred if $p > 1/4$, F is preferred if $p < 1/4$, both A and F are optimal if $p = 1/4$. If $p > 1/4$ the Incumbent plays A, and the Entrant finds it convenient to play Unready whether Strong or Weak and whatever the Incumbent decides to play against Ready. To avoid complications, let us not discuss the case when p is exactly 1/4, which would make the Incumbent's choice between A and F indeterminate, anyway an improbable fluke. Note that a Strong Entrant still prefers Unready even if the Incumbent plays F against Ready, which is not impossible since the Incumbent's beliefs at the unreached upper information set are unrestricted. Thus both (UU, AA) and (UU, FA) are *pooling* PBEs if $p > 1/4$.

If $p < 1/4$, then in order for a Strong Entrant to stick to Unready rather than play Ready, the Incumbent must play F against Ready, which it will do if its payoff $1-2\beta$ from playing F is greater than the payoff 2β from playing A, i.e. if the Incumbent believes that β is less than 1/4. Such a belief is ... hard to believe, because a Weak Entrant finds Unready to be the dominant strategy, so β should be 1, but the definition of PBE does *not* preclude the Incumbent from entertain-

988 Chapter 11 · Games and Information

ing the belief that $\beta < 1/4$ because the beliefs at information sets reached with probability zero are unrestricted. Hence the strategy couple (UU, FF) together with Incumbent's beliefs ($\beta < 1/4$, $\mu = p < 1/4$) is one more PBE in pure strategies.

But it is an implausible PBE; we see here again the reason for the search for further 'refinements' briefly mentioned earlier. A refinement proposed by Cho and Kreps (1987) for signalling games, that does the job of eliminating this equilibrium, is called the **Intuitive Criterion**. Its working can be informally explained as follows. Consider a PBE of a signalling game where player 1 can be of several types, in which (i) there is an information set of player 2 reached with probability zero because no type of player 1 chooses the action α that would take the game to that information set, and (ii) if that information set were reached, player 2 would not be certain as to which type chose α. Consider a type t of player 1 and call x the payoff this type obtains in this PBE. Indicate as Max(α) the maximum payoff that type t could possibly obtain by playing α (that is, the maximum among all possible payoffs resulting from all possible strategic choices of all players not incompatible with type t choosing α). If Max(α) $< x$, then the Intuitive Criterion stipulates that the belief of player 2 at the information set reached by α should assign probability zero to α having been chosen by type t. The reason is that type t could never possibly gain by playing α instead of her equilibrium action, since at best she would obtain Max(α) which is worse than x.

In the game we are examining, for the Weak Entrant $x = 3$ in the PBE (UU, FF; $\beta < 1/4$, $\mu = p < 1/4$) and Max(Ready) $= 2$, so the Intuitive Criterion imposes $\beta = 1$; this PBE **does not survive the Intuitive Criterion**. Nor does the PBE (UU, FA) when p > 1/4. These PBEs can be considered implausible, because based on beliefs which an intelligent player would find implausible.[38]

This example is rather typical, in that multiple equilibria are the rule in signalling games, some of them separating equilibria, and some of them pooling equilibria.

The Intuitive Criterion often eliminates some equilibria, but it is not always able to bring down the surviving equilibria to only one, as the above example shows: for $p > 1/4$, there are two PBEs, a separating one (RU; AF) coupled with Incumbent's beliefs ($\beta = 1$, $\mu = 0$), and a pooling one (UU,AA) coupled with any beliefs of the Incumbent.

Now let us study a well-known example of signalling game where there is an infinity of solutions, both of separating equilibria and of pooling equilibria. The game, originally proposed by Michael Spence (1973), will be presented here in a version close to the one in Varian (1992). Numerous firms must hire workers with a non-modifiable contract, without being able to establish their efficiency in advance; workers are known to be of one of two types, high productivity (subscript H) or low productivity (subscript L), with different given marginal products θ_H and θ_L; the probability λ that a worker be a hard-working type is assumed to be common knowledge. Firms are competitive and pay a worker her marginal product if the worker's type is clear; then a firm is indifferent about which type

---

38 For more on the Intuitive Criterion, see Peters (2015, pp. 81–82).

11.22 · Asymmetric Information. Signalling Games ...

to hire. A firm examines a worker and decides at which wage to hire her/him. The marginal product of each type of worker is given and independent of the level of education. If firms are totally unable to distinguish among types, they pay a wage equal to the expected marginal product, then the wage offered is $w = \lambda \theta_H + (1 - \lambda)\theta_L$. Workers can send a signal consisting of the level of education e they achieved (a continuous variable). To make matters particularly stark, it is assumed that education does not contribute to productivity, but high-productivity workers find education less costly (in psychological effort or time) than low-productivity workers. Getting education can therefore be a separating signal, if high-productivity people are the only ones to find it worthwhile to get a high level of education to signal their productivity, the cost of education being so high for low-productivity workers that they do not find it worthwhile to bear it.[39]

The cost of education is assumed to be $c_H(e)$ for H types and $c_L(e)$ for L types, both strictly increasing in the level of education e, with $c_H(0) = c_L(0) = 0$, $c_H(e) < c_L(e)$ for all $e > 0$, and $\partial c_H / \partial e < \partial c_L / \partial e$ for all e: both the cost and the marginal cost of positive levels of education are lower for the H type. The utility function is given by the wage minus the cost of education, $u_H = w_H - c_H(e)$, $u_L = w_L - c_L(e)$. Under these assumptions the indifference curves of a hard-working and of a lazy worker in $(e, w)_+$ space are upward-sloping, and have the **single-crossing property**: two indifference curves of two different types cross at most once, with the H-type indifference curve having smaller slope. All this is again assumed to be common knowledge.

All firms, having observed the level e of education of a worker, are assumed to have a common belief $\mu(e)$ representing the probability that the worker is of type H; competition forces them to offer a wage equal to the expected marginal product of the worker, $w = \mu(e)\theta_H + (1 - \mu(e))\theta_L$. This means a common wage schedule $w(e)$. The graph of this schedule is included between θ_H and θ_L, but apart from this it is difficult to determine (it need not even be continuous) because it depends on how firms evaluate the probability that the two types choose the level of education; but it will be seen that it is not important to determine it precisely, only its value at certain points in (e, w) space will be important. The worker knows that for each level of education the wage offer is the same from all firms; she accepts the wage offer unless she has a higher reservation wage; I assume that the reservation wage is zero so the wage offer is always accepted.

Let me now illustrate the multiplicity of possible PBEs. These will consist of a choice of education level by each type of worker, and of a wage schedule $w(e)$ derived from a belief function $\mu(e)$ which is common knowledge. We show that there exist both a multiplicity of separating equilibria, and a multiplicity of pooling equilibria.

---

39 The assumption that education does not contribute to productivity is of course extreme but it highlights an aspect that might well exist, to some degree, in reality (according to some studies, having completed a university course is appreciated by firms enormously more than having completed the same course except for one exam, plausibly because it signals, not so much greater competence due to that last exam, but a greater capacity for self-control, discipline, sticking to a goal).

In ◘ Figs. 11.41, 11.42 and 11.43, IC_H and IC_L stand for an indifference curve of type H, respectively of type L, drawn as straight lines only for simplicity (the reader is welcome to re-draw these Figures with convex indifference curves). A greater utility requires a higher indifference curve. In all three diagrams the indifference curve $IC_L{}^*$ is the one that starts at θ_L, the wage that type L worker gets if recognized ($\mu=0$). The wage function $w(e)$ could be different, e.g. in ◘ Fig. 11.41 it could be constant at level θ_L for $0 \le e \le e_1$, and constant at level θ_H for $e > e_1$, indicating that firms believe that an education level up to e_1 signals with certainty an L-type worker, while $e > e_1$ signals with certainty an H-type worker: this different first portion of $w(e)$ is drawn as a dotted red line. An analogous thing might be imagined for ◘ Fig. 11.42.

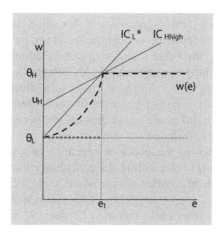

◘ Fig. 11.41

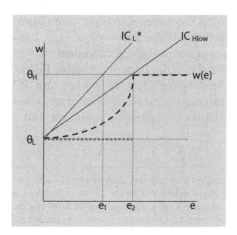

◘ Fig. 11.42

A separating PBE is shown in ◘ Fig. 11.41, where IC_{Hhigh} is the indifference curve of type H workers which reaches height θ_H infinitesimally to the right of the level of education e_1 where $IC_L{}^*$ reaches that same height. In this Figure the beliefs of firms $\mu(e)$ are such that $w(e)$ is as shown: $w(e)$ is always below $IC_L{}^*$ and below IC_{Hhigh}, except (i) at $e=0$ where $w(0)=\theta_L$, and (ii) infinitesimally to the right of e_1 where $w(e)$ touches IC_{Hhigh}. As a result, type L cannot reach a higher utility than by choosing $e=0$; and type H cannot reach a higher utility than by choosing $e=e_1+\varepsilon$ with ε very small. The beliefs of firms are correct, $e=0$ signals that the worker is of type L and therefore it is appropriate to offer $w=\theta_L$, and $e=e_1+\varepsilon$ signals that the worker is of type H and therefore to offer $w=\theta_H$ is appropriate. At levels of e intermediate between zero and e_1, the beliefs of firms are arbitrary because, given the workers' strategies, these levels of e are reached with probability zero; it is only required that the $w(e)$ function does not pass above either indifference curve, which would induce a type to change strategy. At levels of e greater than $e_1+\varepsilon$ the same holds, but since it is even more certain (if possible) that type L workers will never acquire those levels of education it is sensible (although not obligatory) to assume that $w(e)$ continues horizontally.

Another separating PBE is shown in ◘ Fig. 11.42, where IC_{Hlow} is the indifference curve of type H workers that starts from the vertical axis very slightly above θ_L; if in this case the form of the $w(e)$ function is as shown, this causes type-H workers to want to achieve level e_2 of education in order to signal their type. Again firms' beliefs are confirmed: type L workers cannot reach a higher utility level than with $e=0$, and type H workers reach a slightly higher utility level at e_2 than at $e=0$, so they acquire equcation level e_2, and this justifies the firms' belief that at $e=0$ all workers are type L and at e_2 all workers are type H.

In between these two separating equilibria we have the announced infinity (a continuum) of separating equilibria, with type-H workers on an indifference curve intermediate between IC_{Hlow} and IC_{Hhigh}, with the education level of type-H workers between e_1 and e_2, with type L choosing zero education, and with beliefs of firms that cause the $w(e)$ function to start at θ_L, to remain below both indifference curves, to rise to touch from below the type-H indifference curve at the point where the latter reaches height θ_H, and then to continue horizontally.

Now let me show that there are infinitely many pooling equilibria too. If the two types choose the same level of education, firms cannot distinguish among them and hence offer to each worker an equilibrium wage $w_P=\lambda\theta_H+(1-\lambda)\theta_L$. Thus the wage of a pooling equilibrium is uniquely determined. But the level of education is not. In ◘ Fig. 11.43 one possibility is shown: the level of education e_3 is the maximum one compatible with a pooling equilibrium, the one that causes type-L workers to be on the indifference curve that starts at θ_L. Any education level e' satisfying $0\leq e'\leq e_3$ is compatible with a pooling equilibrium, it only requires beliefs of firms such that the $w(e)$ curve starts at θ_L and reaches from below height $w_P=\lambda\theta_H+(1-\lambda)\theta_L$ at e'.

Pooling equilibria, since in their case education brings no wage improvement, can be strongly Pareto-ranked, with the best one being the no-education one, that avoids the waste of an education that has no productivity-enhancing effect. Separating equilibria can be weakly Pareto-ranked, because wages are the same in all

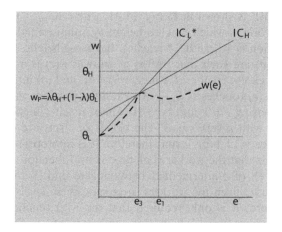

◻ Fig. 11.43

separating equilibria so type-H workers are better off the less education they get, hence the Pareto-superior equilibrium is the one of ◻ Fig. 11.41. It is also possible that the best separating equilibrium be strongly Pareto dominated by the no-education pooling equilibrium; this will be the case if $w_P = \lambda \theta_H + (1-\lambda)\theta_L$ yields a higher utility than the best separating equilibrium not only for type L workers (which is always the case) but also for type H workers, which will be the case if w_P is greater than the vertical intercept of the IC_{Hhigh} indifference curve, u_H in ◻ Fig. 11.41.

But, with reasonings that amount to the Intuitive Criterion, it can be argued that some of these equilibria are based on unreasonable off-the-equilibrium-path beliefs of firms. An example is the separating equilibrium of ◻ Fig. 11.42. Type-H workers choose education level e_2 because if they chose an education level intermediate between e_1 and e_2, firms would not be certain that they are type-H and would offer them a wage sufficiently lower than θ_H to make it preferable for type H workers to choose e_2. But type-L workers will never find it convenient to choose an education level greater than e_1, because it would yield them a utility level less than the one obtainable by choosing $e = 0$; firms cannot but know it and so they must assign probability 1 to a worker being of type H if her education is greater than e_1 even if less than e_2. Thus $w(e)$ must be horizontal at height θ_H for $e > e_1$. But then type-H best response is $e = e_1 + \varepsilon$ for ε positive and as small as possible,[40] and we can classify as unreasonable the beliefs motivating the wage schedule not only of the separating equilibrium of ◻ Fig. 11.42 but of all separating equilibria except the 'best' one of ◻ Fig. 11.41.

---

40 For $\varepsilon = 0$ there still is a separating equilibrium, with all type-L workers choosing $e = 0$; but since they are indifferent between $e = 0$ and e_1, the belief by firms that all workers who choose e_1 are type-H workers is arbitrary even when it is correct. This difficulty is surmounted by assuming, not without some plausibility, that e is not perfectly continuous, it can only be increased by finite although very small amounts ε, and that type-H workers choose education level $e_1 + \varepsilon$ in order to make their type absolutely clear.

11.22 · Asymmetric Information. Signalling Games. Separating and Pooling Equilibria

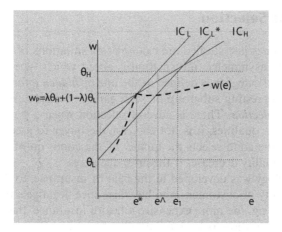

◘ **Fig. 11.44** Pooling equilibrium that does not survive the Intuitive Criterion

An analogous reasoning excludes the pooling equilibria yielding for type-H workers a lower utility than the 'best' separating equilibrium. Thus suppose u_H (◘ Fig. 11.41) is greater than $w_P = \lambda \theta_H + (1-\lambda)\theta_L$. Then it is convenient for a type-H worker to choose education level $e_1 + \varepsilon$, because then firms are certain of her type and therefore will offer her a wage $w = \theta_H$.

A further argument finds *all* pooling equilibria to be based on implausible beliefs. Consider any pooling equilibrium, even of the type not excluded by the previous argument. In ◘ Fig. 11.44 a pooling equilibrium of this type is considered; the type-L indifference curve through the pooling equilibrium is indicated as IC_L, higher than IC_L^*; u_H, the vertical intercept of type-H indifference curve through (e_1, θ_H), is below w_P. Now suppose that from the equilibrium education level e^* someone deviates to an education level slightly greater than $e^\wedge$ which is the education level that, if coupled with a wage θ_H, would yield a type-L worker the same utility as at the pooling equilibrium. Reasonableness requires firms to believe that this is a type-H worker, because the move could not possibly improve the utility of a type-L worker even if she were mistakenly considered a type-H worker and received the maximum wage θ_H. Therefore firms must offer such a worker a wage θ_H. But then for any type-H worker the education level e^* cannot be a best response to everybody else adopting it, her best response is the education level $e^\wedge + \varepsilon$, since in this way she reaches a higher indifference curve. The argument applies to any pooling equilibrium (you can easily check that it holds for the best and the worst ones). The conclusion is that no pooling equilibrium survives the Intuitive Criterion, which then implies they must be all eliminated from the set of reasonable equilibria.

So the sole equilibrium that survives the Intuitive Criterion is the 'best' separating equilibrium of ◘ Fig. 11.41.[41]

---

41 But this criterion is not universally accepted. For a criticism cf. Mailath et al. (1993).

994 Chapter 11 · Games and Information

11.23 Adverse Selection

The signalling games just studied are examples of situations of strategic interaction in which the asymmetric information is about which type of player one is facing. The general category is defined as the one of **hidden information or hidden type**. One very interesting subgroup of such games is characterized by the presence of **adverse selection**. There is adverse selection when a good (or a worker) can be of different qualities, it is not easy for the buyer to ascertain its quality, and the price of the good selects the quality of the goods on offer in such a way that the average quality decreases if the price decreases.

This terminology was developed in the field of insurance, to describe the tendency of the quality of customers who buy insurance negatively to depend on the cost of insurance, e.g. the more expensive a health insurance, the more likely it is that the people with a low risk of falling ill will not buy it, so the average riskiness of the pool of insured people rises. (This case fits the above definition if one views the insurance company as the buyer, *purchasing* the customer's premiums and *paying* with the promise of a sum if the illness occurs.)

Adverse selection must be distinguished from another possible influence of an insurance policy on the likelihood of the insured event: **moral hazard**. This term refers to the possibility that the insured customer is 'morally weak' and after getting insured against some damage starts caring less about avoiding the damage (e.g. an insurance against car theft can induce the car owner not to lock the car) and it is very difficult to ascertain whether the negligence occurred and to calibrate the refund on its occurrence. Moral hazard and adverse selection can both be seen as instances of asymmetric, or imperfect, information: but moral hazard is an example of **hidden action**, in that the insurer cannot ascertain the actions of the insured person; adverse selection is an example of **hidden information**, the buyer does not have access to the seller's information on the quality of the good.

In the field of insurance, moral hazard is generally dealt with by not insuring the full damage caused by the undesired event, e.g. guaranteeing the repayment of only 3/4 of the value of a stolen car so the customer retains an interest in avoiding car theft; or by having the health-insured persons bear a fraction of the cost of medical treatments (so-called *copay*) so they care more about avoiding illnesses. We will study later some other examples of hidden action as part of *principal–agent* problems.

Adverse selection is less easy to fight. The effects can be dramatic. Consider the following example due to Akerlof (1970) that concerns the market for second-hand cars. Suppose the quality of second-hand cars is clear to their owners but very difficult to ascertain for potential buyers, who are unable to distinguish a still good car (a 'peach') from a bad car (a 'lemon'). Suppose this quality can be indexed in some way representable via a number $q \in [0, 1]$ and that quality is uniformly distributed between 0 (the worst quality) and 1 (the best). There are many potential buyers and many potential sellers. Because the quality of each individual second-hand car cannot be ascertained, the price P is uniform. We look for the equilibrium price. Assume buyers are not interested in cars of quality zero and are ready to pay up to qX dollars for a car of expected quality $q > 0$, where

11.23 · Adverse Selection

the given X is what they are ready to pay for the top quality; assume owners of a second-hand car of quality q are ready to sell it for a price equal to $\frac{3}{4}qX$ dollars or greater, e.g. if $X=\$12{,}000$ and $P=\$4500$ only second-hand cars of quality $q=1/2$ *or less* will be put on sale (make sure you are clear as to why); and *buyers know it*. So if there were perfect information on the quality of cars, all second-hand cars could be easily sold at prices yielding a surplus to both buyer and seller. But buyers only know that if price is equal to or greater than $\frac{3}{4}X$, *all* second-hand cars will be on offer; while if $P<\frac{3}{4}X$ the cars on offer will be those of quality less than or equal to the highest quality sellers are ready to sell at that price, the quality $q^*(P)$ satisfying $P=\frac{3}{4}Xq^*$, which implies $q^*=4/3\cdot P/X$; given the assumption of uniform quality distribution, the *average* quality at price P will be $q^{\wedge}=\frac{1}{2}q^*=2/3\cdot P/X$. Buyers find that when $P\leq\frac{3}{4}X$ what they are ready to pay for a car is $q^{\wedge}X=X\cdot2/3\cdot P/X=2/3\cdot P<P$. (If $P>\frac{3}{4}X$ things are even worse, the buyers know that average quality is $1/2$ and so they are ready to pay only $\frac{1}{2}X$.) So for all $P>0$ buyers are not ready to pay P for the average quality of cars on offer, demand is zero. Price would fall endlessly tending to zero and average quality would also tend to zero, but we assumed that buyers are not interested in cars of quality zero, so $P=0$ is the only 'equilibrium', with both demand and supply equal to zero. The potential sales benefiting both buyer and seller are blocked by the imperfect information of buyers.

Nor can the owner of a car of quality $0<q\leq1$ go to a potential buyer and offer to accept a price equal to $\frac{3}{4}Xq$ dollars, because by assumption the buyer cannot trust the seller, the car might be a 'lemon' and the seller might be pretending that q is greater than it really is.

Of course the example is extreme, there are ways to reduce the problem; a frequent one is that firms selling second-hand cars offer **warranties** of refund if the car comes out to be a 'lemon'; private sellers generally accept to have the car examined by a mechanic chosen by the potential buyer. But the point is precisely that the price mechanism if unaided can be unable to operate efficiently.

In health insurance the problem can present itself in the following form (this example is taken from the excellent textbook by Milgrom and Roberts 1992). An insurance policy offers coverage of medical expenses of a certain kind. Buyers differ as to likelihood of needing medical expenses, but the insurance company cannot distinguish between them and must ask for the same price P from all potential buyers. Each buyer has a correct expectation x of her needed medical expenses, and—measuring utility in money—she obtains a utility increase v (for simplicity assumed the same for all customers) from the reduction, associated with the policy, of the risk of not being able to afford medical assistance. Neglecting time discounts for simplicity, a policy with price P will be bought by those individuals for whom $P\leq x+v$. Suppose x is uniformly distributed in the potential population of customers between 0 and x^*; then as P rises, the *average* x among the buyers of the policy rises, because the previous customers for whom now $P>x+v$ drop out: so it is the customers with the lower expected medical expenses that drop out. For each P, the potential buyers are those with $x=P-v$ or higher, up to x^*; since x is uniformly distributed, its average among willing buyers is $[x^*+(P-v)]/2$, an increasing function of P. Here we see the operation of adverse selection. Under some assumptions about numerical values of the variables, in this case too adverse selection can destroy the market. The average cost of a policy to the insurance firm is $[x^* + (P - v)]/2$ plus administrative costs, that we can assume are c dollars per dollar of medical expenses. For the policy to be convenient for the insurer, it must be

$$P_s \equiv (x^* + P - v)(1 + c)/2 \leq P$$

where P_s indicates the average cost of the policy, i.e. the minimum supply price of the policy for each level of P. The policy will be offered only if there is some level of P for which $P_s \leq P$. Such a level may not exist; it will not exist if $P_s > P$ both when $P = v$ (the level of P below which it does not make sense to reduce P, since everybody is buying the policy) and when $P = x^* + v$ (the limit upper level of P if one wants demand for the policy not to be zero): then since P_s is a linear function of P, it will stay above P in the entire relevant interval of possible values of P. This will be the case if $x^*(1 + c)/2 > v$, and $x^*(1 + c) > x^* + v$. So, it can happen.

The literature on adverse selection has produced many studies of ingenious ways in which the potential buyer can induce the supplier of the good of uncertain quality to reveal the quality by offering the supplier a choice among alternative contracts, such that the supplier's choice of one contract over the others reveals the type (the quality) of the good. This literature goes under the name of *screening*. We examined in the previous section cases in which the *suppliers* of better-quality goods want this better quality to be recognized, and take some action that signals this quality, so as to be able to ask for a better price: cases of *signalling*.

Two examples of signalling equilibrium have been already discussed, and an example of screening equilibrium is discussed below (see also exercises 24 to 26). The analyses are clever and interesting; however, in many instances it seems possible to obtain better information about quality differences by direct tests. The health of candidates to health insurance can be assessed by having them go through an array of medical tests. When adverse selection concerns the hiring of workers, the test can consist of watching the performance of the worker during a probation period, only at the end of which the worker is hired for good if her performance was satisfactory. When adverse selection concerns the fact that insurance against car accidents is found particularly attractive by bad drivers, information is supplied by the driver's accident record: insurance premiums can be, and indeed are, periodically updated on the basis of the number of accidents caused by the customer in recent years. For this reason, in this textbook signalling, screening, and separating and pooling equilibria receive only a comparatively short treatment.

11.24 Principal–agent Models

Now let us study the typical problem posed by *hidden action*. One person, the Principal, wants to induce another person, the Agent, to act in the way most convenient for the Principal, by offering the Agent an incentive to act as the Principal desires.

11.24 · Principal–agent Models

The Principal may be unable directly to observe the action of the Agent, but does observe the outcome of the Agent's action; but may be unable to deduce the Agent's action because the outcome also depends on random influences. The Principal's problem is to design an *incentive payment scheme*—a payment to the Agent dependent on the observables—that will induce the Agent to take actions that are optimal *for the Principal*. The Principal-Agent interaction can be seen as a game, but the Principal can choose the form of the game; we have here one instance of *mechanism design*, the design of rules of interaction so as to obtain a specific result.

For example a manager wants a worker to maximize effort so as to produce as much output as possible, while the worker wants to maximize utility given the effort and the incentive payment scheme. Let us examine this problem in simple terms.

Let x be the (value of) output, and let a be one of the possible actions of the Agent. Initially let us suppose there is no uncertainty. Output is a function of the action, $x = x(a)$.

Let $c(a)$ be the cost of action a for the Agent, measured in money. If x is observed, the sum $s(x)$ is paid by the Principal to the Agent. The function $s(x)$ is the **incentive payment function**. The Principal's utility function is $x-s(x)$; the Agent's utility function, which is known to the Principal, is $s(x(a)) - c(a)$.

The Principal's problem is to choose the incentive payment function $s(x)$ so as to maximize his/her utility, taking into account how $s(x)$ influences the Agent's action a. Typically this requires the Principal to take into account two constraints.

The **participation constraint**, PC, states that in order to accept to work for the Principal, the Agent must obtain at least her *reservation utility* $u^\wedge$, that is, the highest utility level she can obtain if she refuses to be an Agent for the Principal and engages in other activities. The **incentive compatibility constraint**, ICC, states that the action the Principal wants the Agent to perform must be the one that the Agent freely chooses, given the incentive payment function she faces.

Let us see the role of these constraints in the simplest case. The Principal has full information about the Agent's actions and costs, so she must simply determine which action she wants the Agent to choose, among the actions she can induce the Agent to adopt. Let b stand for this preferred action, while a stands for any one action of the Agent. The Principal's problem is

$$\max_{a,s(.)} x(a) - s(x(a))$$
such that, for b the optimal action,
$$s(x(b)) - c(b) \geq u^\wedge$$
$$s(x(b)) - c(b) \geq s(x(a)) - c(a), \quad a \neq b, \ \forall a \in A$$

where A is the set of actions available to the Agent, $u^\wedge$ is the exogenously given reservation utility of the Agent, measured in money, and $x(b)$ is the optimal level of x for the Principal. The first constraint is the participation constraint, PC. The second is the incentive compatibility constraint, ICC; it states that, given the function $s(\cdot)$, action b maximizes the Agent's utility. Actually both constraints should be strict, if the Principal wants to be certain that the Agent accepts to work for her and chooses action b; but the excesses need only be very small, and the literature has unanimously decided that one can treat them as in practice *negligibly* small.

998   **Chapter 11 · Games and Information**

The solution is very simple. For each x, the Principal wants $s(x)$ to be as small as possible. Therefore, if the ICC can be satisfied, $s(x(b))$ must satisfy the PC as equality. Then in the Principal's maximization one can replace $s(x(a))$ with $u^\wedge + c(a)$, and the Principal must find the action that maximizes $x(a) - (u^\wedge + c(a))$, that is, since $u^\wedge$ is given, the action that maximizes $x(a) - c(a)$ over all actions open to the Agent $a \in A$, and that satisfies the ICC. This can be done by maximizing $x(a) - c(a)$ forgetting about the ICC, by calling b the action that solves the problem, and then choosing any function $s(x)$ such that $s(x(b)) - c(b) > s(x(a)) - c(a)$ for all $a \neq b$ in A. For example, $s(x)$ could be

$$s(x) = u^\wedge + c(b) \text{ if } x = x(b); \quad s(x) = -\infty \text{ if } x \neq x(b).$$

Any other $s(x)$ would do such that if $x \neq x(b)$ then $s(x) < u^\wedge$. This type of incentive scheme, that guarantees a sufficiently large punishment for any output less than the one preferred by the Principal,[42] is called a *target output scheme*. A different incentive scheme that achieves the same result is the *linear incentive scheme*

$$s(x(a)) = x(a) - F,$$

where F is a lump-sum fee that the Agent must pay to the Principal, keeping for herself the remaining output, and the Principal chooses $F = x(b) - (u^\wedge + c(b))$. Then the Agent maximizes $x(a) - c(a) - x(b) + u^\wedge + c(b)$ which is equivalent to maximizing $x(a) - c(a)$, whose solution we know is $x(b)$; the Agent obtains $u^\wedge$, and the Principal obtains the same output as with the target output scheme. This arrangement makes the Agent the **residual claimant** to the output produced.

For example, if a land is rented out by a landlord to a farmer for a fixed annual sum F, then the farmer is the residual claimant. If yearly output x (measured in such units that its unit price is 1, so x is also total revenue) is a function of the farmer's expenses B inclusive of the value of the farmer's labour, with $x(B)$ increasing and strictly concave, and if the farmer has a reservation income $m^\wedge$, and the landlord knows both $x(B)$ and $m^\wedge$, then the landlord can calculate $F = x(b) - b - m^\wedge$, where b is the value of B that solves $max_B \, x(B) - B$. (One target output scheme, in a ferocious dictatorship, might consist of the farmer getting $x(b) - F$ if output is $x(b)$, and the farmer's left hand being cut off if output is less than $x(b)$, even only a little less.)

It is useful to clarify the difference between the above analysis and the implications of assuming long-period competitive partial equilibrium. Above we assumed a given $m^\wedge$, and no competition of the landlord against other landlords. If there are many landlords, the reservation income of the farmer is what he can get under other landlords; if there is excess supply of land, competition among landlords will tend to raise what is offered to farmers, so $m^\wedge$ becomes endogenous. Then one must turn to the theory of income distribution to understand what will happen. Let us consider the competitive case. The landlord rents out the land to an entrepreneur/farmer who employs labour and capital goods. We

---

42 Formally, for any output different from $x(b)$ in either direction; but the Agent if rational will never produce more than $x(b)$.

11.24 · Principal–agent Models

must assume, as required by partial-equilibrium analysis, that there are a given real wage, a given rate of profit (or rate of interest, neglecting risk), and given prices of produced goods; then it is best to interpret the function $x(B)$ on the given land as indicating the value of output (or quantity of output measured in such units that its unit price is 1) that can be obtained on this land with each level B of expenditure on labour and capital inputs. Then B is total cost *other than land rent*, $x(B)$ is the inverse of the function that specifies B as a function of output, and the single worker is now replaced by an entrepreneur who employs other inputs (hence $c(a)$ is now replaced by B) and because of competitive entry makes zero pure profit, hence $m^\wedge = 0$. If the land is a 'marginal' land in excess supply, F will be zero. If the land is a non-marginal land capable of earning a differential rent, the reason is that the land's output has a price (equal to minimum average cost on the marginal land) greater than the minimum average cost obtainable on this superior land, and this creates room for a rent. This is not in contradiction with the above analysis, it only means that $m^\wedge = 0$; for the rest, only some reinterpretation is needed, the role of $c(a)$ is taken by B, total cost other than land rent; and F is the land rent that results from the excess of revenue over total cost when one maximizes $x(B) - B$ with respect to B, which yields the well-known equality between marginal revenue (i.e. output price, in competitive markets) and marginal cost. The PC is now the condition that the entrepreneur's pure profit must be zero because of competitive entry. The ICC is now the condition that output must be at the profit-maximizing level (this condition, that maximizes the landlord's rent, is the condition for the farmer not to be bankrupted by competition—remember that the other farmers are ready to pay the maximum rent for the use of the land).

An illustration can help. In what follows, I will call B 'total cost' but it stands for 'total cost *apart from land rent*', and 'average cost' will mean B/x. In ● Fig. 11.45 physical output x obtainable from the landlord's land is in abscissa, and total cost $B(x)$ and total revenue $R(x)$ are in ordinate. Output price p is given and via an opportune choice of units for the output good it can be assumed equal to 1, then $R(x)$ is a straight line out of the origin with slope $+1$. Input prices other than land rent are given. As long as the land is only partially utilized, it is convenient to use on it the average-cost-minimizing method; then total cost

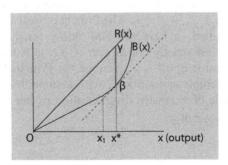

● **Fig. 11.45** Land rent $\overline{\gamma\beta}$ absorbs the maximum difference between revenue $R(x)$ and costs other than land rent

increases in proportion with output (and land use), and the total cost function is a straight line out of the origin, with slope less than 1 because of the assumption that this is a non-marginal land, where average cost is less than the average cost on marginal land (which is the one that determines output price). With this method, output is proportional to the portion of land put to cultivation, the maximum output (that utilizes this land completely) is x_1. Up to x_1 marginal cost is constant and equal to average cost. Following Marshall we can assume that further increases in production can be obtained only at a gradually increasing marginal cost[43]; then it is optimal to increase output up to the level x^* where marginal cost equals price. The difference $\overline{\gamma\beta}$ between total revenue and total cost at output x^* is absorbed by land rent, owing to competition that bids up land rent as long as (neoclassical) profit is positive.

Now assume the Agent's actions are not directly observable, and a random influence on the outcome of the Agent's action makes it impossible for the Principal to derive with certainty the action chosen by the Agent from observed output. We have a problem of **hidden action**.

Suppose the Agent can choose among n possible actions a_1, ..., a_n. These actions produce one among m results x_1, ..., x_m that we can interpret as revenues for the Principal, *gross* of the payment to the Agent. If the Agent chooses action a_i, the Principal observes result x_j with probability $\pi_{ij} > 0$. It is assumed that *these probabilities are known to both the Principal and the Agent*. This can be a highly disputable assumption; for example if the Agent is a manager of a multinational firm and the Principal is a committee that tries to look after the interests of shareholders, novelties (new laws, earthquakes, strikes, innovations ...) can arise in any one of the several nations where the firm operates, and it can be impossible to assess the probabilities π_{ij}, given that to at least some extent most situations will have never occurred before. But without this assumption, theoretical analysis gets nowhere. In some cases, e.g. insurance, this assumption can be acceptable because based on a vast number of observations in a situation that only changes very slowly.

The Principal can only observe the result x_j, not the action, and must choose a payment system or contract $\{w_j\}$ that assigns a 'wage' (more generally, a reward) $w_j(x_j)$ to the Agent that depends on the observed result x_j; having ordered and numbered the possible results from x_1 to x_m, a different contract associates to them a different vector $(w_1(x_1), ..., w_m(x_m))$. The Principal is left with a profit $x_j - w_j$.

The Agent is assumed to have a VNM utility function with the subutility strictly increasing and strictly concave in w, i.e. is risk averse. For simplicity, assume this function is $u(w_j) - a_i$. Assume the Principal *knows this function* (again, not always a credible assumption). Also assume that the Principal is risk neutral because capable of extensive diversification of her investments, and has utility function $u(x_j) = x_j - w_j$.

---

43 This was not illustrated in ▶ Chap. 1 because no assumption was made there of a gradually increasing marginal cost. Intensive rent was illustrated by assuming the coexistence of two methods, as also done at the end of ▶ Chap. 3.

11.24 · Principal–agent Models

Faced with a contract $\{w_j\}$, the Agent, who is risk averse, maximizes her VNM utility function by choosing the action that solves

$$\max_{i=1,\dots n} \sum_{j=1}^{m} \pi_{ij}(u(w_j) - a_i).$$

The Agent can also reject the contract and decide not to work for the Principal; acceptance of the contract requires that the participation constraint be satisfied, that is, if a_i is the action chosen by the Agent, that:

$$(PC) \quad \sum_{j=1}^{m} \pi_{ij}(u(w_j) - a_i) \geq u^\wedge$$

where $u^\wedge$ is the given reservation utility of the Agent. The Principal chooses the contract $\{w_j\}$ by solving:

$$\max_{(w_1,\dots w_m)} \sum_{j=1}^{m} \pi_{ij}(x_j - w_j).$$

subject to the participation constraint (PC) and to the n-1 incentive compatibility constraints implicit in the agent's choice of the best action a_i rather than of the other possible actions, that is, for each a_k different from a_i it must be:

$$(ICC_k) \quad \sum_{j=1}^{m} \pi_{ij}\left(u\left(w_j\right) - a_i\right) \geq \sum_{j=1}^{m} \pi_{kj}\left(u\left(w_j\right) - a_k\right), \text{ for all } k \in \{1,\dots,n\} \text{ and } k \neq i.$$

That is, the best contract $\{w_i^*\}$ must be such that (i) if it induces the Agent to select an action a_i then no other contract that induces the Agent to choose the same action a_i yields greater expected profits for the Principal, (ii) it induces the Agent to choose an action a_i such that greater expected profits cannot be obtained by inducing the Agent to choose a different action. Always, of course, under (PC).

This maximization problem can be approached in two steps: first, for each action a_i treated as given, the Principal finds the contract (if it can be found) that induces the Agent to choose that action while maximizing the Principal's expected profit; second, the Principal compares the expected profits obtainable for the different a_i's, and chooses the contract that induces the profit-maximizing a_i.

Little univocal conclusions can be derived from such a general approach, beyond the generic one that *there will have to be some risk sharing* between the Principal and the Agent. If there were no incentive problem, that is if the Agent's action were a constant independent of the contract, then the optimal contract would be to pay the Agent a fixed payment ensuring the Agent her reservation utility; in this way in effect the Principal would be ensuring the Agent completely, taking upon herself all risk—which is the efficient solution since the Principal is risk neutral and the Agent is risk averse. But if the Agent must be incentivized, then payment must depend on results, otherwise the Agent would produce very little effort; and since results also depend on a random element, the Principal cannot punish low output too much, because in that way she imposes too much risk on the Agent and the rise in the payment to the Agent required by PC becomes not convenient. With perfect knowledge of the Agent's utility function and of the random element in output the Principal, via techniques that borrow much from statistical inference, can find an optimum which is also an optimum allocation of risk; anyway since the Agent is risk averse, it is clear that in order to allow her/him to reach $u^\wedge$ the Agent will have to be paid more (on average) than if her action were perfectly observable.

We will not stop on a detailed presentation of some of the possible formalizations of the problem (see, e.g., Salanié 1994, Chap. 5). The reason is that without precise numerical estimates of the functions and of the probabilities involved, it is generally impossible to conclude as to the optimal contract and the associated risk sharing. The difficulty can be illustrated by considering the case when the Agent is the manager of a corporation. To try to induce the manager to work hard at maximizing profits, one can make her salary a function of profits, or of the value of the company's shares; or one can pay the manager with a bonus increasing in the firm's profits, or with shares; or one can threaten the manager with firing if profit goes below a certain level (but what level?); or one can promise future salary increases if the firm is prosperous; and so on. With such a vast array of tools at the Principal's disposal, and with their effects depending on so many uncertain elements (including uncertainty about the personal characteristics of the Agent), general theoretical analysis is unable to formulate precise practical indications: too much depends on the details of the case.

A typical example of principal–agent interaction with hidden action is ***moral hazard*** in insurance. As already briefly mentioned, the problem here is the risk that complete insurance raises the probability of occurrence of the insured bad event, because the customer has less incentive to allocate effort to trying to prevent the event from happening. For the insurance company it is generally impossible to ascertain the level of care the customer took to avoid the event, so the reimbursement cannot be made conditional on the level of care. This can make it convenient for the insurance company to find ways to induce the customer to care about avoiding the event. Formal analysis confirms the convenience, in many cases, of so-called ***coinsurance*** (also called *exemption clauses* or ***deductible payments*** or *copay*), that is, only partial coverage of the damage, so that the customer retains an interest in avoiding the event.[44] Empirical evidence shows that indeed insurance companies generally do not offer complete insurance. How to calibrate

---

44 The analysis is not exceedingly difficult but it requires pages and pages of algebraic derivation, in order to find the contracts inducing the customer to adopt different accident-preventing effort levels, so as to be able to calculate the profit for the company of each contract, and to choose the most profitable contract; in the end, even after making some restrictive assumptions generally one reaches a rather indeterminate result: that the convenience of offering coinsurance or not depends on the specifics of the case. See for example the very clear treatment in Jehle and Reny (2011, pp. 413–20); or Mas-Colell et al. (1995, pp. 478–88).

the extent of partial insurance coverage will depend on the specifics of the case, in particular on the available evidence about the influence of deductibles on the customers' behaviour; in each field, e.g. house fires, health insurance, car theft, there is a great mass of historical and statistical evidence, and it is on this basis that insurance companies choose their policies.

It can be that the insurance company faces customers who are of different types as to how much moral hazard arises with them. Then the company may derive advantage from ascertaining to which type the customer belongs, and proposing different contracts to different types. In this case the problem is also one of *hidden information*. It is therefore possible to meet problems that are both of hidden information and of hidden action, for example, in health insurance, types of persons whose health is imperfectly known and who are differently careful in avoiding health dangers. Then the company has two problems, first, how to recognize the customer's type, and second, the principal–agent problem of finding how best to minimize the cost of moral hazard. Now I concentrate on one way to deal with the first problem. Customers of different types are ready to pay different amounts for the same insurance contract; then insurance firms may find it convenient to propose a menu of contracts that *screens* the customers because different types prefer different contracts. To this I pass now.

11.25 Screening

In a situation in which a second player can be of several types and a first player is unable to observe the type of the second player, the first player instead of relying on signals sent by the second player can try to ascertain the type of the second player by offering her a menu of contracts, such that each type finds it convenient to choose a different contract. One speaks then of *screening* inducing *self-selection*. This may allow the first player to obtain better deals. Note that the aim of the first player is to find the most convenient menu of contracts, that is, *the structure of the game is not given*, and it is decided by the first player. We are again in the field of *mechanism design*, the study of how a player A can find a game structure that, in a class of possible situations, induces other players to behave in the way desired by player A. One standard example to be briefly discussed in ▶ Chap. 14 is the search for a game that induces individuals truthfully to reveal how much they are ready to contribute to the cost of a public good. An example we have already met is the principal–agent *hidden-action* subcase in which the principal cannot ascertain with certainty the action chosen by the Agent and looks for a most profitable contract to propose to the Agent. This is one example of a class of mechanism design problems characterized by asymmetric information in which the aim is to find an optimal *contract* or menu of contracts; their study is sometimes referred to as *Theory of Contracts* (e.g. Salanié 1994). Here we are interested in the *hidden-information* or *hidden-type* subcase of the principal–agent framework, in which the Principal is uncertain about which type of Agent she is facing.

1004   **Chapter 11** · Games and Information

I illustrate some of the aspects of this case with an example. Imagine a new manager is hired to run a firm that owns a large land surface, divided into fields assigned each one to a different tenant/worker/household. Custom makes it very dangerous to try to evict current tenants, violent collective protests might ensue, so the manager knows she must guarantee the current tenants enough income for them not to want to leave; but within this constraint she can modify the long-term contract with each tenant; nothing prevents the stipulation of different contracts with different tenants. The contract stipulates a wage and an effort level e; the latter is ascertainable, I assume now, and the manager is authorized not to pay the wage if the contract is not respected i.e. if e is less than the stipulated amount. She does not know how hard-working each tenant is, for simplicity I assume that she only knows a tenant can be of one of two types, the high-cost-of-effort type HC, tendentially lazy, and the low-cost-of-effort type LC. (Note that the meaning of H and L is now opposite than in the Spence model, here the HC type finds it more painful to work hence is the *less* productive worker.) Long experience indicates the probability that a tenant be of the better type LC as equal to P. For each field, the firm's profit function is

$$\pi(e, w) = x(e) - w$$

where x is output, e is the effort of the worker/tenant, w is the real wage in terms of output. Output is an increasing, differentiable and strictly concave function of effort. The univocal connection between effort and output allows the manager to derive e from x, but this can only be done *after* the contract is signed. The *(net)* utility functions $V(w,e) = u(w) - c(e)$, that measure for each type of tenant the increase in utility above reservation utility,[45] are, with $c(e)$ the disutility or subjective cost of effort:

$$V_{HC}(w, e) = u(w) - c_{HC}(e), \quad V_{LC}(w, e) = u(w) - c_{LC}(e).$$

For simplicity I assume a separable utility function with the $u(w)$ part the same for both types, $u'(w) > 0$, $u''(w) < 0$; below, at a certain point I will further simplify by assuming $u(w) = w$. The cost functions are different, both are increasing, differentiable and strictly convex, but $c_{HC}(e) > c_{LC}(e)$ and $c_{HC}'(e) > c_{LC}'(e)$ for every $e > 0$. The manager knows the form of the two utility functions.

If the manager could ascertain the worker's type—the case called *symmetric information*—she would solve, with $i = HC$, LC

$$\max_{w_i, e_i} x(e_i) - w_i$$
$$\text{subject to PC}: \quad u(w_i) - c_i(e_i) \geq 0.$$

This *participation constraint* imposes that the worker must not prefer to reject the contract and be evicted. For each e_i, the manager finds it advantageous to reduce

---

45 When the Participation Constraint binds, this net utility is assumed to be zero.

11.25 · Screening

w as much as possible, so PC can be taken to bind.[46] Hence $u(w_i) = c_i(e_i)$. The first-order conditions require, with

$$L = x(e_i) - w_i + \lambda[u(w_i) - c_i(e_i)]$$

the Lagrangian, that

$$\partial L/\partial w_i = -1 + \lambda u'(w_i) = 0, \quad \partial L/\partial e_i = x'(e_i) - \lambda c_i'(e_j) = 0$$

that is, $\lambda = 1/u'(w_i) = x'(e_i)/c_i'(e_i)$ which implies

$$x'(e_i) = c_i'(e_i)/u'(w_i).$$

With the two contracts satisfying the PC constraint and this condition, the firm extracts all surplus from each type of worker.

But the manager does not know the worker's type, so she can only try to maximize expected profit by designing a pair of contracts (w_{HC}, e_{HC}) and (w_{LC}, e_{LC}) that maximize the firm's expected profit under four constraints: a participation constraint for each type, and for each type an *Incentive Compatibility Constraint*, ICC, also called self-selection constraint, that requires that each type prefers the contract intended for that type to the contract intended for the other type. Formally:

$$\max_{w_L, e_L, w_H, e_H} P[x(e_{LC}) - w_{LC}] + (1 - P)[x(e_{HC}) - w_{HC}] \quad \text{subject to:}$$

$(\text{PC}_{HC}) \quad u(w_{HC}) - c_{HC}(e_{HC}) \geq 0$

$(\text{PC}_{LC}) \quad u(w_{LC}) - c_{LC}(e_{LC}) \geq 0$

$(\text{ICC}_{HC}) \quad u(w_{HC}) - c_{HC}(e_{HC}) \geq u(w_{LC}) - c_{HC}(e_{LC})$

$(\text{ICC}_{LC}) \quad u(w_{LC}) - c_{LC}(e_{LC}) \geq u(w_{HC}) - c_{LC}(e_{HC})$

In the ICC constraints, note carefully the indices on the right-hand side of the inequality. For example the first ICC constraint states that the utility the HC type derives from the (w_{HC}, e_{HC}) contract must be not less than the utility the HC type derives from the (w_{LC}, e_{LC}) contract.[47]

Via long algebraic derivations,[48] this constrained maximization can be shown to imply certain results, which I will more simply reach via a graphical analysis, see ◘ Fig. 11.46.

In a diagram with effort e in abscissa and real wage w in ordinate, each point represents a possible contract (w, e). In it let us draw *isoprofit curves* $w_\pi(e)$ representing how w must change with e in order to leave a given profit π of the firm unchanged, and *isoutility curves* $w_{LC}(e_{LC})$ and $w_{HC}(e_{HC})$ representing how w must change with e changes in order to leave a given net utility V (derived from accepting to work) unchanged, respectively for the LC type and for the HC type.

---

46 Actually the manager must allow $u(w_i) > c_i(e_i)$ by a very small amount if she wants to make sure that the worker prefers to accept the contract rather than tossing a coin, but the amount can be so small that one can neglect it.

47 Actually, 'not less than' should really be 'slightly more than' to avoid true indifference and then random choice, but the same argument holds as advanced in the previous footnote.

48 For the complete algebraic derivation see Muñoz-Garcia (2017, pp. 769–775).

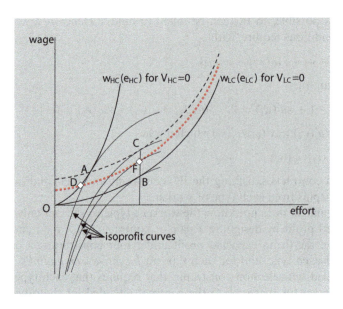

◘ **Fig. 11.46** Screening tenants who can be high-cost-of-effort or low-cost-of-effort types by offering different effort-wage contracts. Profit is the higher, the lower the isoprofit curve. It is assumed that the isoutility curves of type LC are vertical translations of one another. Points D and F are the screening equilibrium's contracts

Each $w_\pi(e)$ curve derives from $\pi = x(e) - w$, with π given; and since $x(e)$ is assumed increasing and strictly concave, the $w_\pi(e)$ curve is an increasing and strictly concave curve too. If the given π is increased, the curve undergoes a downwards parallel shift. So the lower the curve, the greater the profit. Its slope is $dw/de = x'(e)$ from the rule for the derivative of implicit functions.

First of all I draw in ◘ Fig. 11.46 the $w_{LC}(e_{LC})$ curve and $w_{HC}(e_{HC})$ curve corresponding to the participation constraint binding for both contracts, as one would obtain in the symmetric information case. The corresponding curves, that we can call *PC isoutility curves*, start at the origin, indicating that accepting a contract yields no net utility, $V_{HC} = V_{LC} = 0$. These curves result from $V = u(w) - c(e, \theta) = 0$; the derivative rule for implicit functions shows that the slope is $dw/de = c'(e,\theta)/u'(w)$, and they are increasing and are assumed to be strictly convex (e.g. because $u(w) = w$, so $u'(w) = 1$ is constant, while $c'(e)$ is increasing). A higher net utility requires a shift upwards of the curve (for a given level of effort, a higher utility requires a higher w). Since by assumption $c_{HC}(e) > c_{LC}(e)$ and $c_{HC}'(e) > c_{LC}'(e)$ for all levels of e, the PC isoutility curve of the LC type is always below, and less steep than, the PC isoutility curve of the HC type.

We have seen that in the symmetric information case, for each type the firm's profit is maximized by the contract (w, e) that satisfies $x'(e) = c'(e)/u'(w)$. Indeed, since a lower isoprofit curve indicates a higher profit, the firm looks for the point on the HC-type PC isoutility curve touched by the lowest isoprofit curve, and analogously for the LC-type PC isoutility curve; that is, the firm chooses on each PC isoutility curve the point of tangency with an isoprofit curve,

11.25 · Screening

confirming the equal-slope condition $x'(e) = c'(e, \theta)/u'(w)$ as the condition for each contract to be profit-maximizing. Let these tangency points, indicating the two profit-maximizing (w, e) contracts in the symmetric information case, be A for the HC type and B for the LC type.

If the firm can distinguish the types, it can offer to each type the respective profit-maximizing contract. The maximum profit from type LC is greater than from type HC because for any given w the participation constraint allows extracting a greater effort from type LC, hence more output. If the firm cannot distinguish the types and offers both contracts A and B to a worker, then the worker certainly chooses contract A even if of type LC, because the isoutility curve of type LC through point A (drawn as a broken curve) represents a higher net utility than at B. So with an LC-type worker the firm would make only the lower profit corresponding to the maximum profit from type HC.

One way to increase profit relative to this result is to offer a choice between two contracts: A, and C where (or better, very slightly above where) the type LC's isoutility curve through A is tangent to an isoprofit curve: the latter isoprofit curve, being lower than the isoprofit curve through A, indicates a higher profit. Type HC chooses contract A because C does not satisfy her participation constraint, type LC chooses C, and the firm's expected profit is a weighted average of the lower profit from type HC choosing A, and the higher profit from type LC choosing C, the weights being the probabilities of each type.

But profit can be increased further, by offering type HC a contract still on her PC isoutility curve, but closer to the origin. Since at A this isoutility curve and the tangent isoprofit curve have the same slope, for small movements downwards along HC's PC isoutility curve the profit from a type HC worker decreases very little, its small reduction is more than compensated by the fact that now the firm can reduce w_{LC} considerably without inducing type LC to switch to the contract intended for type HC. Each further 1\$ reduction of w_{HC} causes an increasing reduction in the profit obtainable from the HC type because the needed reduction of e_{HC} increases, so sooner or later a point D is reached where it is optimal to stop reducing w_{HC} (and to which will correspond a contract F offered to type LC). If it is assumed that the isoutility curve of type LC undergoes a *parallel* upward shift when V_{LC} is increased (this will be the case if one assumes $u(w) = w$), then the e_{LC} level in the optimal contract offered to type LC does not change when w_{HC} and hence w_{LC} are changed. This allows us to reach graphically the main conclusion we might have reached with four or five pages of algebra: type HC will be offered a contract D with both a lower w and a lower e than with symmetric information, and with the participation constraint binding, while type LC will be offered a contract F with the same e_{LC} ("no distortion at the top") and a higher w_{LC} than with symmetric information, so the 'better' worker gets a positive net utility, the participation constraint does not bind.[49] This is a general

---

49 Except in the special case in which to reduce w_H remains convenient down to zero, in which case the LC-type worker is offered contract B and no contract is offered to type HC. Whether this can happen depends on the specificities of the case.

result of this class of models: with asymmetric information, it is impossible to extract all surplus from the better type, because one must induce this type not to choose the less exacting contract intended for the worse type. The better type enjoys an **informational rent** due to the possibility to masquerade as a worse type.

This analysis does not apply to *hirings* of new workers, because a firm will generally have a given number of vacancies to be filled, and as long as there is sufficient supply of type LC workers a firm will find it convenient to fill the vacancies with only type LC workers, proposing only contract B, which screens out type HC workers. But the convenience of separating via screening and then hiring *both* types with different contracts will hold in other cases, for example the case of a movie theatre or an airplane, which as long as partly empty has convenience to admit both full-ticket customers who pretend a comfortable seat, and discount-ticket customers who would not enter at the full-ticket price but will at a lower price coupled with worse seating. In insurance cases too (these offered the initial stimulus to develop this kind of analyses) insuring low-risk people does not make it unprofitable to insure high-risk people too, as long as these are ready to pay more. In insurance, screening can be possible by offering either expensive nearly complete insurance, or cheaper but more partial insurance: the cheaper contract will be preferred by the low-risk type, who might prefer no insurance if it is not cheap; if the difference between the contracts is well calibrated, the only partial coverage offered by the cheaper insurance will discourage the high-risk type from preferring it to more complete but more expensive insurance. To go beyond these general statements is impossible except with detailed information on the specificities of each situation.

11.26 Conclusions

This chapter had the limited purpose of introducing you to how game theorists approach situations in which strategic thinking is required, and of supplying notions that will be useful in subsequent chapters, for example the theory of repeated games will be relevant for understanding the capacity of cartels to resist, and for the Solow–Hahn approach to wage rigidity. I think the chapter supplied numerous stimuli to critical thinking, I hope you are as puzzled as I am by the Centipede game, and as fascinated as I am by the subtleties of 'refinements', for example Cho and Kreps' Intuitive Criterion. Unfortunately, you will have to learn about interesting extensions of the theory such as mechanism design, evolutionary games, and applied auction theory in other courses. But with so much microeconomics still to explain, there was no space to deal with these topics too, sorry.

11.27 Review Questions and Exercises

- **Review Questions**
  1. Discuss the problem with repeated backward induction highlighted by the Centipede Game and by finitely repeated Prisoner's Dilemma games.

11.27 · Review Questions and Exercises

2. Explain why the theory of infinitely repeated games suggests that cartels may not be so unstable as static analysis would suggest.
3. Prove that the solution of infinitely repeated Prisoner's dilemma games *can* be cooperation.
4. Explain the difference, in infinitely repeated Prisoner's dilemma games, between the retaliatory trigger strategy and the Grim strategy.
5. Produce an example of a dynamic game (game in extensive form) with a non-credible threat.
6. Explain the difference between games of imperfect information and games of incomplete information and how they can be reduced to the same kind of game.
7. Define subgame perfection and produce an example in which it is missing.
8. Produce an example of a game with consistent beliefs (i.e. beliefs in harmony with strategies).
9. Explain the difference between a Bayes-Nash equilibrium and a perfect Bayesian equilibrium.
10. Why can't Bayes' Rule determine beliefs at information sets off the equilibrium path?
11. Explain the winner's curse.
12. Why is it found useful to assume sequential rationality?
13. Prove with an example that sequential rationality correctly defined (including 'given the beliefs') does not guarantee subgame perfection.
14. Explain why moral hazard is a problem of hidden action and adverse selection is a problem of hidden information. Can there be problems with both hidden information and hidden action?
15. Illustrate in ◘ Fig. 11.45 that the participation constraint does not bind for one of the two types.
16. Write the maximization problem of a firm which tries to screen good (low-cost-of-effort) workers L from less good (high-cost-of-effort) workers H by offering them separate (w, e) contracts; explain the four constraints; explain why the PC_L constraint is not binding; explain why this fact authorizes writing the Lagrangian without the PC_L constraint in it.
17. Explain why asymmetric information can have disastrous effects in certain markets.
18. Explain what are the Monotone Likelihood Ratio Property and the CFDC, what they are for, and why they are not of great help in practical problems.

▪ Exercises

1. Consider a more moderate version of the Arms Race game, where the alternative to Conventional is not Nuclear but only Increased armaments, which gives some bargaining advantage over a nation with only Conventional armaments but no crushing superiority, and entails such costs that both nations would prefer not to increase military expenditures, but hesitate to choose that course of action because the damage in case the other nation chooses Increased is considerable. Representative payoffs are:

A \ B	Improved	Conventional
Improved	$_x2, 2_x$	3, 0
Conventional	0, 3	$_x4, 4_x$

Discuss the similarity with the Stag Hunt game.

2. Consider the following simultaneous-move one-shot game. Discuss the effect of eliminating weakly dominated strategies. Does the order of elimination affect the result? Then return to the game without eliminations and discuss what you think is a reasonable way to play it. Does this game have elements of a Hi-Lo game?

			Player B	
		Left	Center	Right
	Top	3, 3	0, 3	0, 0
Player A	Middle	3, 0	2, 2	0, 2
	Bottom	0, 0	2, 0	1, 1

3. Exercise: prove that all mixed strategies that assign positive probability to a dominated pure strategy are dominated.

4. The game of Nim (simplest version) is played by two persons, A and B. Five matches are put on a table. The players take turns taking off from the table one or two matches. The player who is left with the last match loses. A starts. Draw the tree and find the solution by backward induction.

   Now assume the matches are six. You should be able to indicate the winning strategy without needing to re-draw the tree.

5. Find the general relationship between the payoffs of a symmetric one-shot Prisoner's dilemma and the condition on δ for the retaliatory trigger strategy to be a Nash equilibrium of the repeated game. Call a, b, c, d the four payoffs of the stage game, with $a < b < c < d$.

6. For the game discussed in Sect. 11.31, determine the expected payoff for 1A of a mixed type strategy where H and T are played with equal probability, if the same kind of mixed type strategy is played by each type of player 2 and if the outcomes of the cases not already listed are (1, 0) if the couple of moves played by existing types is (H; H) or (T; T), and is (0, 1) if the couple of moves is (H; T) or (T; H).

7. Consider the following simultaneous-move game. Can it be solved by elimination of strictly dominated strategies? Perhaps not if one restricts attention to pure strategies only, but if one considers the mixed strategies of player 2?

	L	M	R
Up	3, 0	0, –3	0, –4
Down	2, 4	4, 5	–1, 8

11.27 · Review Questions and Exercises

8. Consider the following simultaneous-move one-shot game. Discuss the effect of eliminating weakly dominated strategies. Does the order of elimination affect the result? Then return to the game without eliminations and discuss what you think is a reasonable way to play it. Does this game have elements of a Hi-Lo game?

		Player B		
		Left	BCenter	Right
	Top	3, 3	0, 3	0, 0
Player A	Center	3, 0	2, 2	0, 2
	Bottom	0, 0	2, 0	1, 1

9. Consider a two-player simultaneous-move game where each player has 3 pure strategies. Player 1's *maximin* utility level A1 is determined as follows: for each strategy of player 1, one determines the worst possible payoff that a (pure or mixed) strategy of player 2 can cause player 1 to obtain; then the strategy is chosen that maximizes this worst payoff. Player 1's *minimax* utility level B1 is determined by finding, for each possible strategy of player 2, the best-response payoff of player 1, and then assuming player 2 chooses the strategy that minimizes this payoff. With reference to the Matching Pennies game, show that they differ if only pure strategies are allowed, but are the same if mixed strategies are allowed.

10. In the simultaneous zero-sum game below, show that there is no Nash equilibrium in proper mixed strategies; then prove that maximin and minimax coincide for player 1.

	left	right
up	2, −2	1, −1
down	1, −1	0, 0

11. (More difficult) A game is called zero-sum if the players' payoffs always sum to zero. Let u(x, y) denote player 1's payoff when player 1 chooses x and player 2 chooses y in a two-person, zero-sum game with finite strategy sets X, Y. For this two-person zero-sum game, with m1, m2 mixed strategies respectively of player 1 and player 2 out of their possible (proper or degenerate) mixed strategies:

   (a) Indicate with A1 player 1's *maximin* utility level and with B1 player 1's *minimax* utility level (see exercise 9 for the definitions). Show that $B1 \geq A1$ for any game

   (b)* Prove the **minimax theorem**. That is, prove that there exists a pair of mixed strategies m1*, m2* such that:

$$A1 = \max_{m1} \min_{m2} u(m1, m2) = u(m1*, m2*) = \min_{m2} \max_{m1} u(m1, m2) = B1$$

   (c) Prove that in any mixed strategy Nash equilibrium of this game the expected utility of player 1 is $A1 = B1$.

12. In the game below, find consistent beliefs for B assuming $\gamma > 0$.

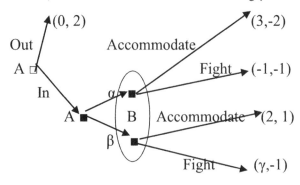

13. (a) The players are distinguished by Roman numerals I, II, III. In the game on the left, which one is the debatable Nash equilibrium and why? Does subgame perfection eliminate it?

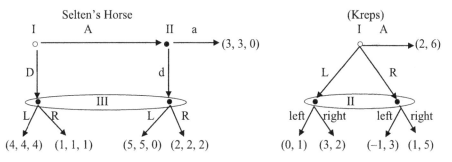

(b). In the Bayesian game on the right, which one is the implausible Nash equilibrium? Prove that subgame perfection does not eliminate it. Is a different tree representation possible that results in the same strategic form but avoids the implausible Nash equilibrium if subgame perfection is assumed?

14. In the game below, find consistent beliefs for player B and deduce her strategy. (Hint: let p be the probability that B plays 'down'. Find the value of p that makes A indifferent between Up and Down.)

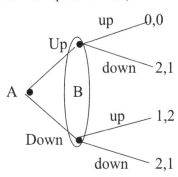

11.27 · Review Questions and Exercises

15. In the Dynamic Game Below, with Players 1 and 2, Prove that it is not optimal for Player 1 to choose Out.

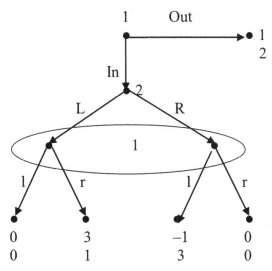

16. In the Dynamic Game Below, Find the Bayesian Nash Equilibrium if 3 plays the Mixed Strategy (a, d), distinguishing three cases: Prob(a) > 1/2, = 1/2, < 1/2.

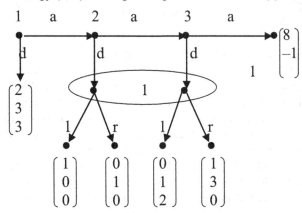

17. Explain what the notion of sequential equilibrium adds to sequential rationality.
18. Describe a game with an implausible SPBE not sequential-equilibrium-compatible.
19. Find the only Nash equilibrium in the game below from the strategic form, confirm it by backward induction, and show it can be a PBE.

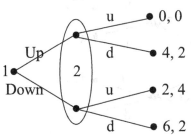

20. (Prisoner's dilemma with signalling) The risk-neutral Receiver must play against a Sender who can be either a petty criminal B, or, with probability p, a mafia member M (who can obtain a punishment for the Receiver's choice of Defect if M chooses to cooperate). The payoffs are

payoffs are

	R				R	
	Coop	Defect			Coop	Defect
BCoop	5, 5	0, 6		MCoop	,5, 5	0, 2
BDefect	6, 0	1, 1		MDefect	4, 0	1, 1

The extensive form: The risk-neutral Receiver is informed of the Sender's choice but does not know the Sender's type. The Receiver's upward arrows indicate Coop, the downward ones Defect.

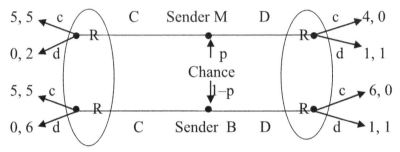

Establish whether there are separating or pooling equilibria in pure strategies, and whether p affects the result, assuming both players know p. For each equilibrium, specify the beliefs consistent with the equilibrium strategies.

21. (Mas-Colell et al.) Two opposed armies are poised to seize a strategically important island. Each army's general can choose either Attack or Not Attack. Each army is either Strong, or Weak, with equal probability (the draws for each army are independent), and an army's type is not known to the other army. Payoffs are: The island is worth M if captured. An army captures the island if it attacks and the other army doesn't, or if it attacks and is strong while the other army attacks but is weak. If two armies of equal strength both attack, neither captures the island. The cost of attacking for an army is s if it is strong and w if it is weak, with $s < w$, but is zero if the rival army is not attacking.

Identify all pure strategy Bayesian Nash equilibria of this game and derive its strategic form.

22. (Maskin) Consider the extensive-form game below.

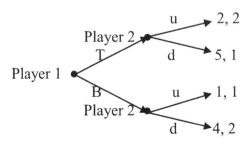

(a) Find a subgame perfect Nash equilibrium of this game. Is it unique? Are there any other Nash equilibria?
(b) Now suppose that player 2 cannot observe player 1's move. Write down the new extensive form. What is the set of Nash equilibria?
(c) Now suppose that player 2 has a glimpse at player 1's move which allows her to assess it correctly with probability $p \in (0, 1)$ and incorrectly with probability 1–p. Suppose p is common knowledge. What is the extensive form now? Show that there is a unique perfect Bayesian equilibrium. What is it?

23. Redo the example of winner's curse in the text assuming 4 players instead of two.

24. (Munoz-Garcia) (Signalling) Guided exercise on Spence-type signalling and the Intuitive Criterion. A worker, who knows whether she is a High-Productivity (HP) or a Low-Productivity (LP) worker, decides whether to pursue further education (Ed) or not (NoEd). Further education does not raise productivity and has a cost which is greater for the LPWorker. The firm observes whether the worker has Ed or NoEd but cannot ascertain the worker's productivity; it is common knowledge that the percentage of HPWorkers is 1/3. The firm can hire the worker either in a Top-level job requiring high productivity (call it choice T for a worker with Ed, choice T' for a worker with NoEd), or in a Bottom-level job requiring low productivity (choice B, or B' for a worker with NoEd). (The possibility of not hiring at all the worker is not considered.) The worker's payoff is listed first, the firm's payoff second. The further education costs 4 units of utility to the HPWorker, 7 units to the LPWorker. The symbol α indicates the belief of the firm, that is the probability the firm assigns to being at the top node (i.e. facing a HPWorker), in its information set N (the firm faces a NoEd worker); β indicates the same in information set E (the firm faces a worker with Ed).

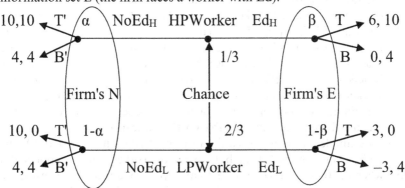

You are asked to find a separating PBE and a pooling PBE.

(a) For a separating PBE you need different educational choices of HP and of LP workers, which induce firms to recognize the type of workers and to assign them to different jobs: so the strategy profile might be (Ed_H, $NoEd_L$; T at E, B' at N), (that is, get education if you are a HPworker, don't get education if you are a LPworker; give the worker a top job if the worker has education, a bottom job if the worker has no education) if beliefs consistent with it support it. Prove with Bayes' Rule that $\beta = 1$, $\alpha = 0$ are firm's beliefs consistent with the worker's strategy. Prove that with those beliefs the firm's strategy is optimal. Prove that with this strategy of the firm, the worker's strategy is optimal. Conclude that this strategy profile is a PBE. Now check whether the other possible separating strategy of the worker, $(Ed_L, NoEd_H)$ can be part of a PBE. Now the firm's beliefs must be $\alpha = 1$, $\beta = 0$. The firm's optimal strategy with these beliefs is (B at E, T' at N). Prove that then for the LPWorker NoEd is preferable, and conclude that we do not obtain a PBE.

(b) For a pooling PBE you need the same educational choice of HP and of LP workers, which induces firms to assign probability 1/3 to facing a HPWorker. Suppose first that the common educational choice of both types of workers is NoEd and that this is an equilibrium. Then $\alpha = 1/3$ (prove it with Bayes' Rule). Prove that then the optimal choice for the firm is B'. Now you must check that it is not convenient for either type of worker to deviate. This creates the complication that if we indeed are at an equilibrium, then for the firm to meet a worker with Ed is off the equilibrium path, hence it is an event of probability zero, Bayes' Rule cannot be applied, the belief β can take any value between 0 and 1. The firm will then decide between T and B on the basis of their expected utility that depends on β. Prove that the firm chooses T if $\beta > 2/5$, chooses B if $\beta < 2/5$, is indifferent if $\beta = 2/5$ but with even an infinitesimal risk aversion will prefer to choose B, so to reduce complications you can assume that B is chosen for $\beta \leq 2/5$. You must check whether in one of these cases it is convenient for at least one type of worker to deviate from the supposed equilibrium behaviour. Prove that if $\beta > 2/5$ it is indeed convenient for a HPWorker to get Ed. Hence for $\beta > 2/5$ we do not get a pooling PBE. If $\beta \leq 2/5$, the firm chooses B. Prove that then for either type of worker it is better to choose NoEd than Ed. Conclusion: there is a pooling PBE with strategies $(NoEd_H, NoEd_L; B$ at E, B at N) and beliefs $\alpha = 1/3$, $\beta \leq 2/5$. (It is left to you to prove that the other possible worker's pooling strategy (Ed_H, Ed_L) doesn't generate a PBE.)

(The infinite number of equilibria in the Spence analysis does not arise here because there is only one possible cost of education.)

This example allows us to see the Intuitive Criterion of Cho and Kreps at work. The choice of NoEd for both types of worker can be supported as a PBE when off-the-equilibrium beliefs satisfy $\beta \leq 2/5$ (a probability less than 1/2 that the worker is HP type). Is such a belief reasonable? Go back to the case $\beta > 2/5$, and prove that a LPWorker does not find it convenient to get Ed in that case. Therefore the firm's belief β should be very close to 1 in this eventuality, $\beta \leq 2/5$ is very hard to justify. But then HPWorkers, knowing it, will prefer to acquire Ed, and the pooling equilibrium collapses.

11.27 · Review Questions and Exercises

25. (Salanie) (Screening) The Principal is a wine merchant who can offer buyers a better or a worse wine bottle at the same or at different prices. The Agent is a consumer who intends to buy zero or one bottle of wine, and can be of either of two types, refined or unrefined. His utility is $U = q\theta - p$, where p is price, q is an index of quality and θ is an index of how refined is his taste. $U = 0$ if no bottle is purchased, hence $U = 0$ is the reservation utility. The parameter θ can take two values, $\theta_1 < \theta_2$. The a priori probability that the consumer is of type 2 is π.

Draw a map of indifference curves (actually, indifference lines) of either type in (q, p) quadrant; check that the indifference curves of the two types cross only once, and that the steeper curves are those of type 2, the more refined one. Interpret in terms of different willingness to pay for an improvement of the quality of wine. Show that for each type utility decreases as one moves to higher-up indifference curves.

The Principal is a local monopolist; she can produce wine of quality $q \in [0, \infty]$. With per-bottle cost C(q), a twice differentiable and strictly convex function with $C'(0) = 0$ and $C'(\infty) = \infty$. Her utility from selling a bottle is the difference between revenue and cost, $p - C(q)$.

Draw in the same (q, p) quadrant a map of isoprofit curves for the Principal, $p = C(q) + R$ where R is profit per bottle. Argue that they are strictly convex and parallel vertical transpositions of any one of them, with higher profit the higher up they are. Deduce that if types were evident, the profit-maximizing quality of wine for each type, q_1^* and q_2^*, would be at the tangency of an isoprofit curve with the type's indifference curve corresponding to zero utility, and $q_1^* < q_2^*$. Prove that this arrangement would respect the PC and the ICC constraints. Conclude that in this case if the amount of wine the Principal can produce is limited, and if at either quality/price combination (q_1^*, p_1^*), (q_2^*, p_2^*) the Principal is able to sell all she can produce, then she chooses to produce only the higher-quality wine.

Now assume the Principal cannot distinguish the types and only knows that the probability of type 2 is π. Prove that if the Principal proposes the same price/quality combinations as with perfect information—call this Contract 1—both types choose the lower quality wine.

Now consider the type-2 indifference line through point (q_1^*, p_1^*). Show that a contract, offering to type 1 the same as in Contract 1 and to type 2 the quality q_2^* together with [a price a very little bit less than] the price associated to it by this indifference line, satisfies the constraints and is better for the Principal than Contract 1 for any $0 < \pi < 1$. Call it Contract 2. (Draw the figure.)

Call A the point in the (q, p) quadrant representing the contract offered to type 1. Relative to Contract 2, shift A a bit to the left along the zero-utility indifference line of type 1, draw the type-2 indifference curve through the new A, and show that offering this A to type 1 and q_2^* to type 2 together with the price associated to it by this indifference line satisfies the PC and

ICC constraints. Call it Contract 3. Show that relative to Contract 2, Contract 3 reduces profit if in fact the customer is type 1, but it increases profit, and by a greater amount, if in fact the customer is type 2. In expectations, the sign of the profit variation depends on the probability π that the customer is type 2, and on the relative size of the two variations. If for a small leftward shift of A Contract 3 offers a better expectation of profit, then a further small shift is in order. Show that as A shifts leftwards, shifts of equal length correspond to increasing profit reductions from facing a type 1 customer (hint: the difference in slope between indifference line and iso-profit curve increases). Conclude that if initially it is convenient to shift A to the left, it may be convenient to stop the shift before q_1 becomes zero, but it need not be so (which would imply that only the contract $(q_2{}^*, p_2{}^*)$ is offered), and that the case $q_1{}^* = 0$ is the only one in which type 2 enjoys no informational rent.

26. Screening (Luenberger). One of many competing insurance companies faces potential customers all with the same initial wealth W and identical preferences for wealth and risk aversion, who want to buy insurance against a financial risk. With no insurance an individual ends up either in state 1 corresponding to unchanged wealth W, or in state 2 corresponding to wealth $W - b$. The insurance contract has fixed coverage (reimbursement) y and premium h. With this contract the individual will have wealth $W_1 = W - h$ in state 1, and $W_2 = W - h - b + y$ in state 2. The insurance company is able to offer fair contracts and has no administrative costs. Competition with free entry means that profit is zero. The individual can be of one of two types, type H (high risk) and type L (low risk) with identical preference for wealth and facing the same possible loss b, but differing in the probabilities of loss, with $p_H > p_L$. The probability is λ that the individual be of type H.

(a) Draw a diagram as in ◘ Fig. 9.1 with wealth in state 1 in abscissa and wealth in state 2 in ordinate. Choose W on the certainty line and point A vertically below it, with the length of segment WA measuring b. Prove that the indifference curves of type L at the certainty line are steeper than those of type H (see Sect. 9.A.10) and the single-crossing property holds.

(b) If the insurance company cannot distinguish the two types but knows λ and point A, prove that a zero-profit pooling equilibrium must be on the fair-odds zero-profit line through A of slope determined by the average probability of loss $p^* = \lambda p_H + (1 - \lambda)p_L$.

(c) If in all points D along the segment of the zero-profit line from A to the certainty line (the 45° line) the two indifference curves of the H-type and of the L-type cross as in Figure (a), prove that there is no pooling equilibrium. (Would L accept a contract offering D?)

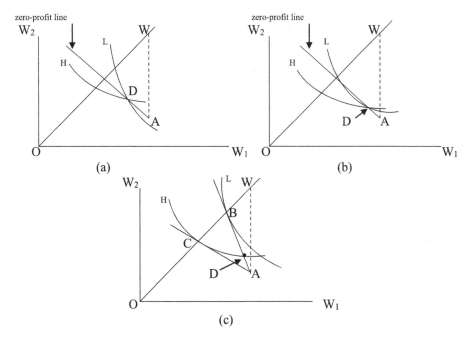

(d) If there is a point D along the zero-profit line as in Fig. (b), argue that that is a pooling equilibrium if the insurance companies offer only D.

(e) In Fig. (c), lines AB and AC are the fair-odds lines for contracts offered only to L-types, respectively only to H-types. Indicate their slopes and explain why there is tangency between these lines and respective indifference curves at the 45° line. Then explain why offering a choice between contracts B and C would not screen applicants and would cause a negative profit to the insurance companies. Finally argue that offering the choice between C and D (which is just a very little bit closer to A on the AB line than the point where this line crosses the H-type indifference line through C) is a separating equilibrium.

References

Akerlof, G. (1970). The market for lemons: Quality uncertainty and the market mechanism. *Quarterly Journal of Economics, 89*, 488–500.

Aumann, R. J. (1995). Backward induction and common knowledge of rationality. *Games and Economic Behavior, 8*, 6–19.

Axelrod, R. (1984). *The evolution of cooperation*. New York: Basic Books

Bacharach, M. (2006). *Beyond individual choice*. Princeton: Princeton University Press.

Cho, I. K., & Kreps, D. M. (1987). Signaling games and stable equilibria. *Quarterly Journal of Economics, 102*, 179–221.

Durlauf, S., Blume, L. (eds.). (2008). *New Palgrave: A Dictionary of Economics (The)*, 2nd ed., vol. 8, Palgrave Macmillan, London.

Fishburn, P. (1970). *Utility Theory for Decision Making*. New York: John Wiley.

Chapter 11 · Games and Information

Fudenberg, D., & Maskin, E. (1986). The folk theorem in repeated games with discounting or with incomplete information. *Econometrica, 54,* 532–554.

Harsanyi J. C. (1967). Games with incomplete information played by Bayesian players, I, II and III. *Management Science, 14,* 159–182, 320–34, 486–503.

Gintis, H. (2000). *Game theory evolving.* Princeton: Princeton University Press.

Jehle G. A., Reny P. J. (2011). *Advanced microeconomic theory.* Haley, UK: Financial Times/Prentice Hall (Pearson).

Klemperer, P. (2004). *Auctions: Theory and practice.* Princeton: Princeton University Press.

Kreps, D. M. (1990). *A course in microeconomic theory.* New York: Harvester Wheatsheaf.

Mailath, G., Okuno-Fujiwara, M., & Postlewaite, A. (1993). Belief based refinements in signalling games. *Journal of Economic Theory, 60*(2), 241–276.

Mas-Colell, A., Whinston, M. D., & Green, J. R. (1995). *Microeconomic theory.* Oxford: Oxford University Press.

McMillan, J. (1994). Selling spectrum rights. *Journal of Economic Perspectives, 8,* 145–162.

Milgrom, P., Roberts, J. (1992). *Economics, organization and management.* Hemel Hempstead, UK: Prentice Hall International.

Muñoz-Garcia, F. (2017). *Advanced microeconomic theory. An intuitive approach with examples.* Cambridge, Mass: MIT Press.

Osborne, M. (2004). *An introduction to game theory.* New York: Oxford University Press.

Osborne, M. J., & Rubinstein, A. (1994). *A course in game theory.* Cambridge, MA: MIT Press.

Peters, H. (2015). *Game theory: A multi-level approach.* Berlin: Springer.

Rosenthal, R. (1981). Games of perfect information, predatory pricing, and the chain-store paradox. *Journal of Economic Theory, 25,* 92–100.

Salanié, B. (1994). *Théorie des contrats.* Paris: Economica.

Selten, R. (1975). Re-examination of the perfectness concept for equilibrium points in extensive games. *International Journal of Game Theory, 4,* 25–55.

Selten, R., & Stoecker, R. (1986). End behaviour in sequences of finite prisoner dilemma supergames. *Journal of Economic Behaviour and Organization, 7,* 47–70.

Spence, A M. (1973). Job Market Signaling. *Quarterly Journal of Economics, 87,* 355–374.

Tversky, A., & Kahneman, D. (1992). Advances in Prospect Theory: Cumulative Representation ofUncertainty. *Journal of Risk and Uncertainty, 5,* 297–323.

Varian, H. (1992). *Microeconomic analysis* (3rd ed.). New York: W. W. Norton.

Von Neumann, J., & Morgenstern, O. (1944). *Theory of games and economic behavior.* Princeton:Princeton University Press.

Product Markets: Pricing, Capacity, Investment, Imperfect Competition

Contents

12.1   Introduction – 1023

12.2   Two Types of Markets. Primary Products – 1024

12.3   Administered Prices and Capacity Utilization – 1027

12.4   Unused Capacity – 1029

12.5   Time-Specific Input Prices – 1030

12.6   Demand Variations – 1035

12.7   The Investment Decision of Firms – 1041

12.7.1   Neoclassical Investment Theory Without Full Labour Employment – 1041

12.7.2   The 'Array-of-Opportunities' Approach – 1046

12.7.3   The Adjustment Costs Approach – 1050

12.7.4   Investment Determined by Profits? – 1052

12.7.5   Investment and Sales Prospects – 1060

12.8   Administered Prices, Differentiated Products, and Competition – 1062

Electronic supplementary material The online version of this chapter (▶ https://doi.org/10.1007/978-3-030-62070-7_12) contains supplementary material, which is available to authorized users.

© Springer Nature Switzerland AG 2021
F. Petri, *Microeconomics for the Critical Mind*,
Classroom Companion: Economics, https://doi.org/10.1007/978-3-030-62070-7_12

12.9   **Full-Cost Pricing – 1063**

12.10   **Monopoly – 1067**

12.11   **Monopolistic Competition Versus Full-Cost Pricing – 1073**

12.12   **Duopoly – 1079**
12.12.1   Cournot Duopoly – 1079
12.12.2   Conjectural Variations – 1086
12.12.3   **Stackelberg (Quantity Leadership)** – 1086
12.12.4   Price Leadership – 1089
12.12.5   Bertrand – 1090
12.12.6   Bertrand-Edgeworth – 1092
12.12.7   Capacity Constraints and Bertrand Competition – 1094
12.12.8   Differentiated Products and Bertrand Versus Cournot Competition – 1095
12.12.9   Price Matching and the Kinked Demand Curve – 1096

12.13   **Repeated Interaction, Cartels, Tacit Collusion, Folk Theorems – 1098**

12.14   **Entry – 1102**

12.15   **Conclusions – 1109**

12.16   **Review Questions and Exercises – 1110**

           References – 1113

12.1 · Introduction

This chapter tries to reach a more realistic picture of how firms behave in more and in less competitive product markets. In it you will learn:
- that there are different types of product markets
- that many firms adopt full-cost pricing
- that capacity utilization is highly variable and this requires a reformulation of cost curves
- that the determinants of the investment decisions of firms are a controversial issue
- that the theory of monopolies is rather straightforward, that of oligopolies is not
- that competition is more active than one might think even in markets with few firms and differentiated products
- that free entry allows reducing the indeterminacies of oligopoly theory
- that advertising is more and more important.

12.1 Introduction

The study of firms and markets in ► Chap. 5 aimed at supplying what was needed to understand the neoclassical theory of general competitive equilibrium. In this chapter I try to get closer to a realistic picture of the working of firms and of product markets.[1] After a distinction between markets without or with administered prices, the chapter notes that the second type of markets needs a rather quick adaptability of supply to demand, and studies how this adaptability is ensured via variable capacity utilization. This raises the question, when do variations of demand induce decisions to change productive capacity and not just the degree of utilization of existing capacity? This brings to a discussion of the investment decision of firms, with some hints at macroeconomic implications. Then the chapter discusses the microeconomics of so-called imperfectly competitive markets, where firms are not price-takers, because products are differentiated, or because there are very few firms in the market. After an introduction to the standard theory of monopoly, the theory of full-cost pricing is compared with the theory of monopolistic competition. Then the standard models of oligopoly are presented; the indeterminateness of the conclusions emerging from these models disappears if full importance is given to entry. Barriers to entry are discussed in some detail. Entry also greatly reduces the relevance of tacit collusion. The chapter ends with a section on advertising, more and more important nowadays because it finances most of what can be seen on the Internet. The online

---

1 On how product markets actually work there is an enormous mass of empirical studies, surveyed in Industrial Organization textbooks; the wealth of acute observations and illustrative examples of these textbooks cannot be reproduced here. Some of the old textbooks, for example the one by Scherer, are particularly rich of enlightening examples. The underestimation of the importance of full-cost pricing in these textbooks can be corrected by reading F. Lee, *Post-Keynesian price theory*.

12.2 Two Types of Markets. Primary Products

Appendix to this chapter in the book's website page on SpringerLink includes a section supplying further details on monopoly theory, in particular on price discrimination and on natural monopoly, and a section with formal proofs of results on Bertrand competition.

12.2 Two Types of Markets. Primary Products

Let us leave monopoly for later, it is a very special market form which excludes entry; in the great majority of product markets, entry is possible. Let us distinguish product markets into two broad categories.[2] In the first type, the producer does not know in advance the average unit price her supply will fetch, and once the supply is there the producer sells it at whatever price she is able to get, through individual or organized bargaining. In the second type, the seller *fixes* the price and sells as much as the market will take at that price.

The first type of markets is found above all among perishable products that take a long time to be produced, e.g. agricultural products. It is nearly impossible to change the supply in the short period. Many small-scale producers produce for many final retail sellers, or for several industrial firms, usually with intermediaries in between (wholesale dealers). The good is rather homogeneous; its supply depends on decisions taken considerably in advance, and often also on accidental elements (e.g. irregularities of climate or of catch); supply is rather rigid in each market period; neither buyers nor sellers are organized in cartels; on each market day[3] buyers and sellers, on the basis of information as to that day's supply and of their cumulated experience, rapidly form an estimate of the price at which that day's supply can be disposed of, and, although each individual tries to get somewhat better bargains (e.g. by waiting if persuaded that by the end of the day the price will evolve favourably), exchanges are at very similar prices and one can reasonably speak of '*the*' price of the good on that day's market. This price changes from one market day to the next, sometimes considerably. In each market day, unless there have been novelties that oblige demand conditions to be discovered anew, on the basis of their past experience sellers and buyers rapidly converge to common expectations as to how price will evolve during the day, and the average price is reasonably close to the price that, if it held continuously during the day, would allow all intended supplies to find purchasers. Wholesale food markets of big towns are representative of this type of markets. Sometimes the market is organized, with an auctioneer.

The less perishable the product, the more it is possible to delay sales to the next market day or to anticipate purchases, and the more, as a consequence, expectations as to the future evolution of price affect daily demand: a speculative compo-

---

2 I acknowledge here the influence of Robinson and Eatwell (1973, pp. 148–58).

3 A 'market day' must be intended as the time stretch over which supply is fixed, therefore it may mean a whole month or even a longer period for seasonal agricultural products.

12.2 · Two Types of Markets. Primary Products

nent of price determination can appear. However, perishability, the carrying costs of inventories and past experience limit the size of speculative inventories.

Although slowly (it takes time to change quantities produced in agriculture, fishing, etc.) supply tends to adapt to demand at the average price at which entry or exit in the industry essentially stops (or rather, entry and exit roughly compensate each other, since there is always some entry and some exit), that is, at the normal long-period supply price. This tendency does not need a definite *demand curve*, it only needs that there be a quantity demanded at the normal long-period supply price, an effectual demand in Adam Smith's terminology, and that price tends to be below (above) this normal price when supply is greater (less) than effectual demand (see ▶ Chap. 5, Sect. 5.32).

Some specific aspects of the working of these markets are worth mentioning. Demand is often inelastic, so when supply increases considerably (e.g. because of an exceptional harvest), price might fall ruinously unless some intervention prevents it, and usually *there is* some intervention. In these cases a ruinous fall in revenue for producers is quite likely in the absence of protective institutions, because of the presence of intermediaries between producers and final consumers: wholesale dealers and retailers add a mark-up to the price at which they buy the good, to cover their additional costs and normal profits; when supply increases and the price to consumers falls, the presence of this relatively fixed addition renders the percentage fall in price for the producers greater, possibly much greater, than the percentage fall in price for final purchasers. For example, aggregate consumer demand for fruit is not very elastic, and a particularly good fruit harvest can cause fruit prices to consumers to drop even 50%, which can mean an 80% drop of the price to producers. Compulsory destruction of a portion of supply is often imposed; if possible, stockage with costs partially covered by the state. The situation of the small producers remains precarious, because wholesale dealers—fewer and bigger than individual small producers—are at an advantage in bargaining and can easily tacitly collude; their bargaining strength is estimated to have been increasing in recent decades (also because of increasing concentration in food-processing industries) and to be an important and often neglected cause of a reduction of the income of small agricultural producers.

Minimum efficient scale is small in the productions we are considering[4]; the undifferentiated nature of the product prevents scale or scope economies[5] connected with marketing. Thus little is gained by being a big producer. Entry is easy because of the rather small minimum efficient size and the absence of a need for marketing expenses. If, as is often the case in this type of industries, the product

---

4   In some agricultural productions that use tractors, mechanical mowers and other big machinery, minimum efficient scale is kept small by the possibility to *rent* these machines, rather than having to buy them.

5   *Scope economies* are the reductions in average cost obtained by enlarging the range of products produced by the same firm (or conglomerate). For example, reputation of high quality acquired through one product can help sales of other products by the same firm, reducing marketing expenses.

is perishable, in each market day the several sellers and buyers can be described as *price takers* because unable to affect the average price on that day, competition obliges them to accept the price that allows selling all the supply. Being price takers on each market day, sellers and buyers cannot but be price takers for long-period choices too, this time with respect to the *average* price they expect to fetch over a succession of market days.

Thus, for these markets Marshall's distinction between long-period, short-period and very-short-period supply curves is useful. Considerable increases in the production of apples, olive oil, or wine, require years because the new trees take years to grow; in the meanwhile, only very limited increases in production can be obtained by greater use of fertilizers, reduction of waste etc.; so for these productions only the very-short-period (given supply) and the long-period supply curves appear useful. For fish production, a well-known Marshallian example, supply can be increased in the short period by the use of less experienced fishermen and possibly of boats not originally intended for fishing, and/or by particular efforts (which will require higher wages); while in the long period an increase in the number of fish boats or of experienced fishermen can be obtained without appreciable increases in their supply prices, but fish catch will not increase in proportion with the number of boats because each boat catch reduces the catch of other boats, so the long-period supply curve of fish is upward-sloping. This example shows that the Marshallian notion of short period can refer to periods of several years.

Hence for these markets the traditional diagrammatic determination of partial-equilibrium price in perfectly competitive markets, at the stable intersection of an upward-sloping or horizontal supply curve and a downward-sloping demand curve, is not greatly misleading – except in suggesting a definiteness of the amount demanded at non-equilibrium prices which in fact is not there; the practical content of the diagram is nearly only that the equilibrium point is rather well defined and there is gravitation towards it. In the long period, entry and exit will ensure a roughly normal rate of return on investment.

If expectations about future prices have an important role, the behaviour of the market can be less regular. As pointed out in ▶ Chap. 6, ▶ Sect. 6.26, cobweb-shaped 'hog cycles' become a possibility, although the resulting instabilities can be expected to be only temporary owing to learning. When the product can be stored, wholesale dealers form expectations on the future price of the good, and increase their purchases in order to accumulate stocks when they consider the current price low relative to the expected future price, and disaccumulate stocks in the opposite instance. Then if the current price starts rising and this induces an expectation of a continuation of the price rise, demand rises and this exacerbates the price rise; so the intended changes in stocks often amplify swings in price. When instability is observed to be a real danger, institutional modifications are usually introduced to prevent it from occurring. But at times these modifications are introduced too late, and there are bubbles, 'tulip manias'. For some minerals (oil above all, but not only) there are highly organized markets, that afford the possibility to buy and sell 'futures' (promises of future deliveries), and then there is room for short sales and speculation; the similarities are great with financial markets.

12.3 Administered Prices and Capacity Utilization

The second type of markets is characterized by *administered prices*, that is, prices fixed by the seller. This does not necessarily mean prices that do not change for long periods (at petrol stations, price changes every day), but it does mean that the seller is not ready to bargain at each transaction: the price is fixed, and the buyer decides whether to buy or not. A price is called *administered* when it is kept fixed for all transactions in a period of time, in contrast with non-administered prices that are 'determined coincidentally with the market transactions' (Lee and Downward 1999, p. 861).

This type of prices is typical of manufacturing industry, of many services, and of retailing. The general case here is ***differentiated products***, that is, slightly different products in the same category, and such that if the price of the product of two different firms is slightly different, demand does not go entirely to the cheaper product. Breakfast cereals, toothpaste, beer are examples. Purchasers are not totally indifferent among the products of different sellers.

Very few products—nearly all of them raw materials—are not differentiated. Even kitchen salt is often differentiated: certain brands apparently are trusted more than others as supplying a salt free of chemical residues. (Fruits and vegetables too are more and more often sold packaged, with a brand name and an administered price.) The general situation for such markets is that the output of the single firm is limited by demand for its product, not by the need to incur higher average costs in order to increase production.

This was forcefully stated in Piero Sraffa's famous 1926 article:

» Everyday experience shows that a very large number of undertakings—and the majority of those which produce manufactured consumers' goods—work under conditions of individual diminishing costs. Almost any producer of such goods, if he could rely upon the market in which he sells his products being prepared to take any quantity of them from him at the current price, without any trouble on his part except that of producing them, would extend his business enormously. It is not easy, in times of normal activity, to find an undertaking which systematically restricts its own production to an amount less than that which it could sell at the current price, and which is at the same time prevented by competition from exceeding that price. Business men, who regard themselves as being subject to competitive conditions, would consider absurd the assertion that the limit to their production is to be found in the internal conditions of production in their firm, which do not permit of the production of a greater quantity without an increase in cost. The chief obstacle against which they have to contend when they want gradually to increase their production does not lie in the cost of production—which, indeed, generally favours them in that direction—but in the difficulty of selling the larger quantity of goods without reducing the price, or without having to face increased marketing expenses. This necessity of reducing prices in order to sell a larger quantity of one's own product is only an aspect of the usual descending demand curve, with the difference that instead of concerning the whole of a commodity, whatever its origin, it relates only to the goods produced by a particular firm; and the marketing expenses necessary for the extension of its market are merely costly efforts (in the form of advertising, commercial travellers, facilities to customers, etc.) to increase the willingness of the market to buy from it—that is, to raise that demand curve artificially.

....

The causes of the preference shown by any group of buyers for a particular firm are of the most diverse nature, and may range from long custom, personal acquaintance, confidence in the quality of the product, proximity, knowledge of particular requirements and the possibility of obtaining credit, to the reputation of a trade-mark, or sign, or a name with high traditions, or to such special features of modelling or design in the product as – without constituting it a distinct commodity intended for the satisfaction of particular needs – have for their principal purpose that of distinguishing it from the products of other firms. What these and the many other possible reasons for preference have in common is that they are expressed in a willingness (which may frequently be dictated by necessity) on the part of the group of buyers who constitute a firm's clientele to pay, if necessary, something extra in order to obtain the goods from a particular firm rather than from any other (Sraffa 1926, pp. 543–45).

For the near totality of differentiated products, prices are administered. The saving on time and transaction costs made possible by administered prices is the main reason for their fixity. Imagine what it would be like to have to bargain for the price of each item when you go shopping in a supermarket—and how many more sales clerks the supermarket would have to have. Even small shops generally have administered prices. Usually it is only for purchases involving considerable sums and for which there isn't a very close substitute readily available (e.g. houses, luxury carpets, second-hand cars, building contracts) that one turns to bargaining.

The given price requires some *flexibility of supply*: it must be possible to adapt supply to demand rather quickly. Producers maintain some spare productive capacity that permits rapid increases in production if necessary; the adaptability of sales to demand is further increased by the holding of product stocks both by the producer and by wholesale and retail dealers.

Supply flexibility is usually ensured by the fact that fixed plants and machines are never utilized 24 h a day at full volume. The very few firms that never shut operations down (metal foundries, electricity producers) produce at full pace only part of the day or of the month; most of the other firms are active only one shift (seven or eight hours) a day, five days a week, and if needed they can easily produce for a few more hours per week. So there is always room for increase in working hours and/or in product per hour, and hence in weekly production. Immediately after increases in demand, increases in production are obtained by the use of inventories of intermediate goods, and by overtime work or, if the increase is expected to be lasting, by hiring additional workers. The existence of overt or hidden unemployment, typical of capitalist economies, makes it generally easy to find the additional workers when these are needed. So generally there is very little problem with adjusting supply not only to decreases in demand but also

12.3 · Administered Prices and Capacity Utilization

to considerable increases. As pointed out already in ▶ Sect. 1.14.4, an initial run-down of product inventories, due to increased sales, is then corrected by increased production; this causes a rundown of inventories of the raw materials and other intermediate inputs needed for that production, and an increased demand for these intermediate inputs; then a similar process of initial rundown of product inventories and increased production goes on in the firms producing those intermediate goods; thus an increase in the flow of output in one industry propagates, accordion-like, to the industries supplying it with produced inputs, and the initially depleted inventories are rapidly reconstituted.[6]

This poses two questions. First, why do firms maintain unused margins of productive capacity? Second, at what level do firms fix product prices?

12.4 Unused Capacity

One must distinguish unused capacity due to sales inferior to expected sales, from unused capacity due to *planned* underutilization of productive capacity.

Let us ask why firms *plan* to underutilize their productive capacity, i.e. why they plan to produce, on average, less than the maximum production technically possible by utilizing 24 h a day the fixed plant and other durable equipment they plan to possess.

Main reasons:

(A) higher cost of some inputs at some hours of day or some days of the year (above all, labour wages for work at night or weekends, but not only, e.g. electric lighting may not be necessary at daytime);

(B) regular peaks of demand at certain hours of day or certain periods of year, e.g. for cafes, size must be sufficient for customers at peak hours; electricity plants must satisfy demand for electricity at peak hours; sale of turkeys increases for certain holidays;

(C) possible unexpected rises of demand, that firms want to be able to satisfy in order not to lose customers to other firms (the so-called goodwill of a firm, that is the customers who prefer to buy from it rather than from very similar firms, can be easily lost, and one reason may be the disappointment with finding that the firm does not supply the product immediately);

(D) expected gradual growth of demand for a few years that induces to build bigger plants than initially necessary.

Oligopoly theory argues that a fifth reason can be a desire for excess capacity as a way to discourage entry, but this argument (further discussed below, ▶ Sect. 12.12) can hold at most in a small minority of cases.

---

6   See Gandolfo (1971, Ch. 5, Sect. 3 and Ch. 7, Sect. 2) for some mathematical dynamical models of inventory adjustment. As nearly always with dynamical systems, stability is not always guaranteed, but for these models stability is very plausible.

1030   **Chapter 12** · Product Markets: Pricing, Capacity, Investment, Imperfect Competition

12.5 Time-Specific Input Prices

The clearest example of reason A is the higher cost of labour in night shifts or at weekends or holidays. Without such higher cost (whether due to higher hourly wage rates or to lower efficiency of night labour), it would be cost-minimizing to utilize durable capital 24 h a day, all days of the year; this would cause a quicker depreciation of the capital invested in durable items, i.e. less interest payments, hence lower average cost. (In this section 'time-specific' input and input price refers to the hour of the day, i.e. to the shift, or to the day of the week, i.e. working day or holiday, when the input is utilized.)

I prove this with an example. Suppose that both the efficiency and the cost of labour and of other circulating inputs are independent of the time when utilized, that the efficiency of durable equipment is constant during their lifetime, and that there is no demand constraint that reduces the product price if, given some minimum efficient scale, the firm produces with the 24-h method instead of the single-shift method. Consider a factory producing bread. Suppose producing at day and at night makes no difference to technical coefficients (inclusive of time-use of the durable machines *per unit of bread*); the firm can choose between producing with a single shift, 8 h a day, or with three shifts, 24 h a day; the sole difference is that the durable machines needed to produce bread last three years (with constant efficiency) if used with the single-shift method; they last one year with the 24-h three-shifts method. Suppose the firm's given yearly output of bread can be produced with the single-shift method by using 3 workers and 3 machines that last three years, or with the three-shifts method by using only 1 machine (that lasts one year) and 1 worker working on it in each shift (hence in total again 3 workers). Assume that all payments and earnings occur at the end of the year, even for machines: these are bought at the beginning of the year with borrowed money and therefore entail no cost at the beginning of the year but an interest cost plus a depreciation cost at the end of the year. Assume the cost of a new machine is given and equal to p and the yearly rate of interest is r; the cost of a unit of labour (which for the moment is assumed to be the same for all shifts) together with the cost of the circulating capital that goes with it in fixed proportion is α.[7] Then with the three-shifts method one new machine is bought every year and scrapped at the end of the year, and the average end-of-year cost of the given yearly production of bread is $3\alpha + (1 + r)p$.

That is, at the end of the year the firm pays labour and circulating-capital inputs, and reimburses the money p borrowed at the beginning of the year to buy the machine, plus interest on it. With the single-shift method the yearly cost of labour and circulating capital is still 3α, the difference is in the cost of capital. Each machine, lasting three years, entails an annual cost determined by formula (2.38) of ► Chap. 2, that gives the constant annual charge ρ to be paid for interest

---

7 I am assuming that bread is a non-basic whose price does not influence the prices of its inputs.

12.5 · Time-Specific Input Prices

and depreciation on a durable machine that lasts k years (with constant efficiency and sudden death) and has initial price p; for the reader's convenience the formula is repeated here:

$$\rho(k) = p \cdot \frac{r(1+r)^k}{(1+r)^k - 1}. \tag{2.38}$$

With a stock of k machines uniformly distributed by age, the yearly cost is $k\rho$. In our example, $k=3$ and there are three machines, hence at the end of each year the cost of the three machines is $3\rho(3)$. For $r>0$ and $k>1$ it is $k\rho(k) > (1+r)p$.[8] The reason is simple: the greater time taken by the machinery to produce its total potential output means that the capital employed in its purchase must pay interest for a longer time. To get an idea of the difference, an interest rate of 10% implies that $(1+r)=1.1$, while $3\rho(3)/p=1.206$, i.e. about 10% more; so if, e.g., the interest and depreciation charge on machinery is 40% of the total cost of bread, the one-shift method causes bread to cost 4% more than with the three-shifts method. If there were no difference in efficiency and in unit input costs between the single-shift and the three-shift method, utilization 24 h a day would be always preferred.

And yet, more often than not, one observes that single-shift methods are preferred. Leaving aside legal constraints that sometimes forbid working in certain hours or days, the reason is that either input costs, or productive efficiency, or both, are not time-invariant. The organization of social life and biological reasons make work at abnormal hours (e.g. at night hours or on weekends or holidays) more unpleasant and therefore requiring an extra compensation in addition to the ruling basic hourly wage. Thus hourly wages for overtime, night shifts and holidays include a wage premium, sometimes a very considerable wage premium, and if this overcompensates the saving on interest costs achievable with multiple shifts and/or no holiday closing, then firms will find single-shift methods, and shutting down during weekends and holidays, to be cost-minimizing.

The analysis of long-period choice of cost-minimizing production methods of ▶ Chap. 2 can be applied by distinguishing methods also according to which shifts a method uses, with labour at different hours treated as different types of labour if paid different wages (even if physically identical labour activities are required); alternatively one can 'reduce' all labour to equivalently paid labour, by counting one hour of night labour as 1.2 h of standard (i.e. day) labour if the night labour's wage is 20% greater than the standard wage; then processes utilizing equal amounts of differently paid labour will be formalized as utilizing different amounts of standard labour. The two alternatives will bring to the same result as to which method is cost-minimizing (Kurz 1990).

---

8 Remember from the proof of (2.37) that $(x^{k-1}+x^{k-2}+\ldots+1)=(x^k-1)/(x-1)$; setting $(1+R)=x$ the inequality $k\frac{R(1+R)^t}{(1+R)^t-1}>(1+R)$ can be written $k\frac{x^t}{x^{t-1}+x^{t-2}+\ldots+1}>x$, which is proved for $x>1$ and $k>1$ by multiplying both sides by the denominator of the fraction on the left-hand side.

Which method will be cost-minimizing can depend on income distribution, which now will mean not only the level of the standard wage, but also the wage premiums for labour in abnormal hours.

Thus consider the previous example. We found that if the wage rate is uniform, the three-shifts-one-machine method allows approximately a 4% reduction of average cost relative to the one-shift-three-machines method. Thus, an increase of wage costs in the two night shifts implying an increase of average cost greater than 4% would make the one-shift method preferable. Given our assumption that the portion of cost caused by wages and circulating-capital inputs is about 60% of average cost, supposing 3/4 of this is wages, that is, that the wage cost of the two night shifts is approximately 30% of total cost when wage rates are uniform, a rise of the night-shift wage rate by 14% above the day-shift rate would suffice. Usually the order of magnitude of the difference between day-shift and night-shift wages is above this (although often this is not very visible because workers take turns in working on night shifts); this contributes to explaining why single-shift production is largely dominant.

Changes in the rate of interest (rate of profit), with given ratios between different-shift wages, can change the relative convenience of the two methods, because changes of r change the savings from faster depreciation.[9] Furthermore, in all likelihood the methods will also differ in something else besides the wage, for example mistakes can be more numerous at night, requiring extra labour to discover defective products; or electricity costs can be greater.

In the short period, limited output increases can be obtained by some overtime work, e.g. a 10% increase can be obtained with a few hours of overtime per week. A firm with a given fixed plant that can be utilized with a single shift, somewhat less than a full single shift, a single shift plus overtime, or two shifts, or three, and with different wages for each shift and for overtime, can derive its marginal cost curve and its average variable cost curve by treating each shift as a separate 'plant' with its own marginal cost curve, and then deciding how to allocate each total quantity to be produced per week among these 'plants' in the same way as a firm that owns different plants of different efficiency and must minimize total cost by allocating output among the plants in the most convenient way. Increases in output beyond the level that minimizes average variable cost with a single shift will be obtained by adding overtime labour, or by passing to two shifts, depending on which solution minimizes average cost. If one assumes a constant variable input vector per unit of output (which is plausible in most industrial firms) the marginal cost curve can have discontinuities.

To derive the equivalent of the standard total cost curve C, total variable cost curve VC, average total cost curve AC, average variable cost curve AVC, marginal cost curve MC for the case of variable utilization including the possibility of multiple shifts, is no easy matter, because of the many possibilities about use of overtime, and because of the variation of depreciation depending on the extent of the use of

---

9 Kurz (1990) shows that re-switching is possible among techniques that differ in the number of shifts adopted in one industry.

12.5 · Time-Specific Input Prices

durable capital per week. Attempts at drawing these curves can be found in Shaikh (2016, pp. 133–151).[10] Below I supply one simpler attempt.

Imagine a firm that produces iron widgets from iron bars and plates that are given the desired form through the use of durable machines. The firm has a given number of these machines. One machine produces a maximum number of widgets per hour; it is not difficult for workers to produce at that rhythm. Output per week is obtained by activating part or all of the machines, for one shift, for two shifts, or for one shift plus some overtime. Because it takes some waste of inputs for a machine to start to produce after it is turned on, it is convenient to use for the entire length of the shift (or shift plus overtime) the minimum number of machines required for the desired output, and the corresponding number of labourers. Apart from the turning-on operations that absorb inputs with no output, inputs of labour iron electricity, etc. per unit of output are fixed. Assume one machine produces, during a single shift, 100 widgets per week. To produce 2000 widgets per week with a shingle shift, twenty machines will be activated; so there will be twenty turning-on costs to be added to the direct input cost of 2000 widgets. Therefore turning-on costs are roughly proportional to production and I include them in the variable cost per unit. Idle machines do not depreciate. Each machine has constant efficiency during its life and then sudden death; it lasts 1 year if used for two shifts (4000 h per year), 2 years if used for one shift (2000 h per year), and between 1 and 2 years in proportion to use, if used for 1 shift plus some overtime. Wage per hour is higher for second-shift work, and still higher for hours of overtime added to first-shift work. The efficiency of labour is constant. The two graphs below assume given hourly wages for the three types of work, and given costs of circulating-capital inputs; they depict total variable cost as a function of weekly output if output is produced by the first shift (40 h per worker, or more if there is overtime), or by the second shift (40 h per worker). Activating a second shift entails a fixed cost OA additional to the other fixed costs, due to the need for additional overhead labour (security men and repair technicians for the night shift, extra secretarial work, etc.)[11] and independent of how many machines are activated in the second shift. Then the total variable cost (inclusive of the additional fixed cost if the second shift is activated) is shown in the third ◼ Fig. 12.1c (where BC is equal to OA), which indicates that for q intermediate between q^* (output with full use of all machines for one shift) and $q^\wedge$ it is convenient to produce with only one shift plus some overtime, while for output beyond $q^\wedge$ it is convenient to activate the second shift. Marginal cost is a step function shown in the fourth Figure[12]; assuming the technically maximum output is $2q^*$,

---

10 But Shaikh complicates things by assuming labour efficiency changes depending on how many hours a shift lasts, plus other special assumptions, so his analysis is not easy to follow.

11 Overhead labour is the amount of labour that, once the productive capacity (fixed plant) of the firm is chosen, is independent of output; its wages are therefore a fixed cost as long as the firm is active (a quasi-fixed cost, in standard microeconomics terminology).

12 Shaikh's treatment is more complicated because it assumes a labour efficiency that varies with the number of hours worked by a worker; but this aspect disappears if, as assumed here, all workers work the same number of hours, a full shift, and what changes with output is their number, proportional to the number of activated machines.

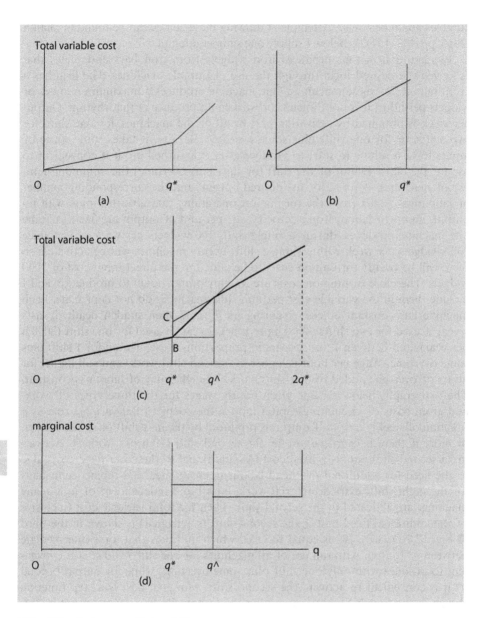

◘ Fig. 12.1 Cost curves with two shifts

at that output marginal cost becomes vertical (probably in reality it would be possible to increase output even beyond $2q^*$ with special incentives or a third shift).

The total average cost curve is not shown because its derivation is very complicated, owing to the varying relevance of depreciation that depends on the number of shifts and on the varying proportion of machines that are idle and hence do not depreciate. So from ◘ Fig. 12.1 it is impossible to know whether, at the given

12.5 · Time-Specific Input Prices

input prices and rate of interest, double-shift production is or not more convenient than single-shift production in the long period. Anyway to reach a result on this issue would require to take into account also the desired margin of unused capacity, which is absent in this example.

Can something be said about the connection between average total cost and marginal cost? In fact, yes. For $q < q^*$, since in the short period there is a positive addition (fixed cost) to be made to total variable cost to obtain total cost, it is $AC > AVC = MC$. For $q > q^\wedge$, AC can be greater or smaller than MC. In the example shown in ◘ Fig. 12.1c the reader can easily check, by drawing a straight line from the origin to the total variable cost curve, that for $q > q^*$ it is $AVC < MC$, so a sufficiently small fixed-cost addition to variable cost (such that at q^* fixed cost is less than BC) would imply that for $q > q^*$, even for $q > q^\wedge$, it is $AC < MC$; this would imply that AC is minimized at q^*, single-shift full utilization. Otherwise AC is minimized at $2q^*$. Since in the first case it is not convenient to use the double-shift method, we can conclude that with either method marginal cost is horizontal at normal capacity utilization and less than average cost, and remains less than marginal cost for increases in output up to full capacity utilization with that method, possibly crossing the average cost curve only with the use of overtime labour; see ◘ Fig. 12.1d.

One thing is clear: the standard Marshallian theory of the firm implicitly assumes single-shift production, and needs profound modification to make room for choice among one or more shifts with different input prices at different moments of the day, and so far we only have some beginnings of the necessary reconstruction.

Remembering that firms determine normal capacity utilization as leaving a margin of unused productive capacity, the important short-period implication of variable utilization of fixed plants is that, both for most firms (agriculture being the relevant exception) and for the entire economy, output from given durable capital (given fixed plant) can be varied in the short period, and can easily go *above* the normal level, because the *normal* monthly output level, that is, *the level of sales in the expectation of which the size of the fixed plant was decided*, is always abundantly less than the technically maximum output obtainable from the fixed plant. Even when to pass from one to two or three shifts is not convenient, generally it is possible to obtain increases in output beyond normal output even by 20% through the use of extra or overtime labour.

12.6 Demand Variations

Let time-dependent input costs be given. If the greater cost of labour at unusual hours or days were the only reason for partial idleness of durable inputs, one could conclude that, if capacity utilization is higher or lower than the planned one, then average cost of production is higher, because planned capacity utilization is the cost-minimizing one. However, there are other reasons too for planned capacity underutilization, and some of these can mean that a higher-than-planned capacity utilization causes a *lower* average cost.

Very few shops remain open during night hours because sales would be next to nil in those hours. Shop facilities remain unused for the greater part of each day because of the rhythmic variation in demand. Ski resorts as well as electrical power stations have capacity determined by peak demand, and are partially or totally unused at other times.

In these cases of regular, predictable fluctuations in demand the choice of capacity can again be seen as a problem of choice of cost-minimizing method per unit of output.[13] Now the possibility and costs of storage become very important. For example, suppose that demand for the product is concentrated in one week of the year (e.g. fireworks for New Year's Eve; specific greeting cards for St. Valentine's Day) and the product is not perishable. Suppose the entrepreneur is certain as to how much will be sold in that week; she can choose to produce the output in twelve months, and bear the interest cost and storage cost on the advance production, or in eleven months, or in ten months, and so on; furthermore, for each one of these production periods, she can choose whether to produce with a single-shift method, or with a double-shift method and half the machines, or with a three-shifts method and one third of the machines.[14] If storage and interest costs are very low and the additional labour costs due to interruption of labour for part of the year are very high and the additions to the basic wage for working in second or third shifts are high, production over twelve months with the single-shift method will be preferred. The greater the storage and interest costs and the smaller the costs of labour interruption, the more probable it becomes that production be concentrated in the months closer to the sales month; and the smaller the wage differentials among shifts, the more probable still it becomes that double or triple shifts and correspondingly fewer machines per unit of output be adopted for the months when the factory is operative. The alternatives are very numerous, but there seems no reason why cost minimization should not be capable of dealing with them.

But suppose now that the product must be produced in advance and cannot be stored from one year to the next (e.g. Christmas cakes), and peak demand fluctuates from year to year, so producers must form an estimate of the demand forthcoming in the big sales period. Suppose firms have a probability distribution of expected demand. We introduce now an important aspect: as long as there is no particular reason to turn to other suppliers, purchasers usually continue to buy from the same seller, because familiar with her/him, satisfied with the quality of the product, enjoying the small privileges of faithful clientele (even simply receiving a warm greeting when entering the shop can count). This is part of what is called the *custom* or *goodwill* of a firm. One of the reasons that can induce a buyer to turn to other sellers is that the usual supplier is out of stock with the good. Once a buyer has experimented another seller, there is the risk that she/he

---

13 In the case of shops which close down because of too few sales outside normal hours, the output is sales, so outside normal hours there is a lower productive efficiency because the same inputs produce fewer sales.

14 Of course other possibilities exist, e.g. a single-shift method plus some overtime.

12.6 · Demand Variations

does not go back to the previous seller. It is likely that, in order not to disappoint customary buyers, firms will plan to produce (or to be ready to produce, if differently from assumed here production can be quickly adjusted to demand) more than the expected value of demand, preferring to run a risk of unsold production rather than to leave part of demand unsatisfied. Since in this example unsold production goes to waste, if sales are greater than expected then profits are greater than expected too. In this case a level of demand higher than its expected value causes the rate of return on capital to be greater than the one on whose basis capacity decisions were taken (with no reduction in real wages; it is as if productive efficiency had increased).

This is not the only case in which a capacity utilization greater than normal can result in a higher rate of return than the one associated with normal utilization. The reason is that capacity is chosen with reference to average expected sales, but actual sales can come out to be greater than the expected average. Thus normal utilization is the cost-minimizing one relative to average expected sales, but in the short period greater-than-normal utilization is possibly associated with higher-than-normal profits.

Another case is when the plant is planned for a production greater than the expected one in order for the firm to be able to deal with unexpected peaks of demand without losing market share to existing or new competitors and without bearing sharp rises in marginal cost. As put by Jacob Steindl: 'The producer wants to be in a boom first, and not to leave the sales to new competitors who will press on his market when the good time is over' (Steindl 1952(1976) p. 9).

The available evidence on short-period cost curves is that generally in manufacturing industries marginal cost is more or less constant up to *full* capacity,[15] rising very steeply afterwards (see ❏ Fig. 12.4 in ▶ Sect. 12.9), and that planned *full* capacity is chosen greater than *normal* planned production, so as to leave room for increases of output if demand comes out to be greater than expected. Scherer (1980, p. 185), when describing as highly representative the pricing method followed by General Motors, writes: 'Since it does not know how many autos will be sold in a forthcoming year, and hence what the average cost per unit (including prorated fixed costs) will be, it calculates costs on the assumption of *standard volume*—that is, operation at 80% of conservatively rated capacity.' The US Bureau of Census periodic survey of capacity utilization shows firms seldom declare that they utilize more than 82% of full productive capacity, where what 'full' means is left to the firms to decide but clearly must be understood as 'desired', not as technically maximum, because firms also declare that in case of national emergency they could reach production levels even 60% greater than full productive capacity. The approximately 20% deficiency of utilization relative to 'full' that emerges on average between booms and depressions suggests that 'normal' utilization as I have defined it (i.e. planned) is less than 'full', and confirms Scherer's reference to GM as indeed representative.

---

15 Cf. e.g. Hay and Morris (1991), p. 54.

Therefore the AC curve reaches its minimum for a production $q^\wedge$ greater than expected production q^*. The firm's choice can be described as follows. Without necessarily assuming that the firm faces a well-defined demand curve, it can be assumed that the firm has an idea of how much it can sell at a price slightly above minimum average cost. The same minimum average cost can be reached for different volumes of output, by appropriately choosing the size of the fixed plant, i.e. the number of replications of the minimum-efficient-size plant. Once the plant is chosen, apart from low quantities of output marginal cost is constant up to a level of output where it starts rising very quickly, and for a level of output a little greater, $q^\wedge$, minimum average cost is reached. The firm prefers to build a fixed plant that reaches minimum average cost for a level of output $q^\wedge$ greater than the level q^* it expects to sell at a price slightly above minimum average cost; $q^\wedge$ exceeds q^* by a margin ensuring that unexpectedly favourable demand can be satisfied. Normal long-period price p^*, or price of production, is in this case slightly above true minimum long-period average cost because it includes the cost of carrying some unused capacity on average: this is a necessary cost in order to stand competition in the presence of irregularities of demand, therefore it is included by investors in the costs to be incurred and on which at least the normal rate of profit must be earned; it is not going to be undercut by competitors because they too find it advantageous to carry a safety margin of excess productive capacity. Then if sales are higher than expected, fixed costs are distributed over a greater amount of production and profits are higher than expected.

(All this will be taken up again in Sects. 12.8 and following. Standard microeconomics assumes the imperfectly competitive firm faces a definite inverse demand curve $p(q)$, from which one can derive the **marginal revenue curve** as the derivative with respect to q of total revenue $q \cdot p(q)$; it is a downward-sloping curve below the demand curve. As will be shown later in the section on monopoly, profit is maximized where marginal revenue equals marginal cost, so in this formalization q^* is chosen as the level of output where that equality obtains; but since long-period marginal cost is constant, and it has a long horizontal stretch even after plant size is chosen, that equality does not determine plant size univocally, it must be determined by introducing the firm desire for some safety capacity margin as argued in the text, and thus a $q^\wedge$ greater than q^*. That price is $p(q^*)$ is due to entry.)

Another reason (when capacity is given) for greater profits accruing if demand is greater than expected is the expectation of a growth of demand over time, that induces to plan a capacity level that for some time will be in excess of expected production because adapted to the greater future demand. If then demand turns out to grow faster than expected, capacity is utilized more fully than expected and profits are greater than expected. If the growth rate of demand persists in being higher than expected and there is little reason to expect it to slow down, full utilization of capacity is reached earlier than expected, but this is only welcomed; and further investment is anticipated.

Another possibility for greater profitability than expected is that, in the expectation of fluctuations in demand, capacity is built at the size that will satisfy peak demand, and then demand, without ever going beyond the expected peak, comes

12.6 · Demand Variations

out to be on average greater than expected because the falls in production with respect to the peaks are smaller than expected.

This flexibility of capacity utilization has relevant macroeconomic implications (that it would be silly not to stress even if this is not a macro textbook).

(i) First, it confirms the capacity of aggregate output to respond to changes in aggregate demand in the short period as argued by Keynes (see ▶ Chap. 1, ▶ Sect. 1.14).

(ii) Second, it is important for the evolution of productive capacity over time, because if demand for the firm's product comes out to be persistently different from the level in the expectation of which the size of plant was chosen, then the firm will try to adjust capacity, building a smaller plant (when the time comes to shut down the old plant) if demand is less than expected, or performing net investment (even before the old plant is scrapped) if demand is greater than expected.

(iii) Third, it shows that, at least as long as there is extra labour available, the traditional neoclassical idea that the amount of savings is a constraint on investment must be rejected; if an increase of investment requires an increased amount of savings, this will be supplied by the rise of aggregate output and incomes. And empirical evidence shows that extra labour is indeed generally available.

(iv) Fourth, it shows that it is generally perfectly possible to raise the growth rate of an economy with no decrease of the share of aggregate consumption in aggregate income, even if the starting point is a situation in which, on average, the economy's productive capacity is normally utilized. The point is that a sufficient rise in aggregate demand can raise capacity utilization beyond normal even for many years in a row; the increased level of the aggregate net income produced from a given capital structure creates room for an increase both of net investment (which is also an increase relative to the capital structure and hence an increase in the growth rate of productive capacity), and of aggregate consumption. This is less and less pointed out in standard macro textbooks, which assume the economy to be on an intertemporal full-employment equilibrium path. So students are generally not aware that, except in extreme situations (e.g. war times), increases in the growth rate of [the autonomous components of] aggregate demand causing rises of the average growth rate of the economy by two or three percentage points would be perfectly possible and *without necessity of decreases in aggregate consumption*. Numerical examples (e.g. Petri 2003) suggest that an increase in the growth rate of an economy by two percentage points would nowhere raise capacity utilization by more than 10%, not even in the capital-producing industries (where the accelerator effect is strongest, see ▶ Chap. 1, fn. 81, and below ▶ Sect. 12.7); and it is difficult to think of industries where an increase in production by 10% cannot be easily achieved. The capital-goods industries, where the increase in demand is likely to be greatest owing to the accelerator, can be presumed to be particularly well adapted to ample variations in production, precisely because aware of possible very ample variations of demand. And a growth rate higher by two percentage points makes an enormous difference to a nation over

1040   Chapter 12 · Product Markets: Pricing, Capacity, Investment, Imperfect Competition

periods of a decade or two. Agricultural production is less flexible, but it must be remembered that except for very poor nations, demand for food is the component of aggregate demand that rises least with rises in the general level of activity, because the unemployed eat even when unemployed.

(Imports can be a problem if revenue from exports is a constraint on import capacity, but this problem falls outside the scope of the present textbook, which implicitly assumes a closed economy.)

Generally, even long-lasting changes in the economy-wide average degree of utilization of productive capacity will not significantly affect relative product prices. For decreases of average utilization, price decreases are discouraged by the expectation that competitors will reduce price too, and by the generally low elasticity of demand for the ensemble of goods in a given category. For example, a decrease in the general price of toothpaste does not significantly increase total demand for toothpaste; a decrease in the price of just one brand of toothpaste might significantly raise the demand for that brand (and decrease demand for other brands), but the other brands will most likely react by reducing their price too, and then the relevant elasticity is the low one for toothpaste in general, so price decreases are no way to re-establish profitability in a recession. And then there is the general fear of 'spoiling the market' stressed by Marshall. For demand increases, price rises are made unnecessary by the generally constant marginal cost, and by the relevant possibility that the greater degree of utilization of capacity raises the rate of return; to which one must add the need not to encourage entry, which is a greater danger when demand is buoyant.

Thus, the thesis that prices are generally determined by costs *in new plants*, because it is new firms or more generally new plants that are best adapted to latest technical knowledge and income distribution (and taxation etc.) and can therefore impose lower prices, which older plants must grudgingly accept, remaining content with smaller residual quasi-rents—this thesis holds independently of the economy-wide average degree of utilization of productive capacity. Of course besides the presence of plants of different vintages and therefore embodying different technical knowledge, in any actual economy in each industry one must expect a co-existence of more and less efficient firms for a variety of reasons, with the most efficient firm probably reluctant to push the less efficient ones out of the market too quickly, because that would require a considerable lowering of price and would risk attracting new, more modern entrants; thus in each industry in each period the price-determining average cost is probably somewhat superior to the one corresponding to the frontier technology; the dominant, price-determining method to be included in the equations that determine prices of production is the one in new plants but generally not the one in the newest plant, it is best considered to be always a little behind the most advanced method, adopted by still too little a percentage of firms. But what is most important now is that the new plants can be presumed to be utilized closer to desired capacity than the economy-wide productive capacity, because built after observing the tendency of aggregate demand and built in the size that is expected to permit normal utilization. This reinforces their capacity to determine price.

12.6 · Demand Variations

These considerations imply that the gravitation of relative prices towards normal prices operates largely independently of what is happening to the economy-wide average degree of capacity utilization. Relative prices can be expected to be close to normal even in periods in which economy-wide average capacity utilization is not normal. Indeed, it has been noted with reference to economy-wide average capacity utilization that 'the achievement of a particular size of capacity relative to that of demand appears in itself to be a process that is liable to be frustrated for long periods of time' (Ciccone 1986, p. 25). This is because the attempts to eliminate excess capacity will consist of reductions of gross investment, but these reduce aggregate demand, possibly worsening the divergence of actual average capacity utilization from desired capacity utilization; conversely, attempts to reduce too high a utilization of capacity by increasing capacity and hence increasing investment raise aggregate demand, possibly increasing capacity utilization (See ▶ Sect. 13.9).

12.7 The Investment Decision of Firms

12.7.1 Neoclassical Investment Theory Without Full Labour Employment

With the considerations of the last sub-section we have entered the field of investment decisions. These are generally left out of microeconomics textbooks, but with little justification,[16] since investment decisions are decisions about plant size, which are as much microeconomic decisions as long-period decisions about how much to produce, in fact are one side of the latter decisions. So their discussion seems perfectly apposite in this textbook. And this seems a good moment to say something more about the implications for investment decisions of what this book has explained up to here.

We have already discussed some investment theory in ▶ Chap. 7, where we saw that the traditional neoclassical demand curve for 'capital' (the single factor of variable 'form') had as its main purpose to explain investment. The view of investment implicit in that approach was that, via direct or indirect factor substitution induced by changes in income distribution, investment in new plants absorbs the labour 'freed' by the shutting down of the plants that reach scrapping age, and combines it with the capital goods produced by the resources that gross saving decisions leave free from production of consumption goods; the flow of production of new capital goods is viewed as embodying the flow of 'free capital' corresponding to the flow of gross savings.

This neoclassical approach to investment falls down on the inconsistencies of the notion of 'capital' as a single factor analogous to a physically measurable

---

16 The separation between macroeconomics and microeconomics must be reconsidered if one adopts a classical-Keynesian approach, as argued in the Preface of this book.

factor in spite of being a quantity of exchange value. But it also suffers from a further grave weakness, which helps to understand the evolution of investment theory from Keynes onwards.

Keynes unwittingly threw the neoclassical theory of investment into disarray, because the derivation of the investment function from the demand-for-capital curve *needs the continuous full employment of labour*, as I will presently show; but after Keynes the full employment of labour could not be *assumed*, it had to *result*—if at all—from the analysis. The full employment of labour had been considered an unquestionable assumption before Keynes, but his model, by showing that it was possible to conceive persistent positions of the economy without the full employment of labour, made it necessary to determine investment without assuming the full employment of labour, and then matters became problematical. The (not clearly perceived) problem was the following.

Without an assumption of continuous full labour employment, neoclassical capital-labour substitution does not suffice to determine investment as a function of the rate of interest. The reason is that in the neoclassical approach income distribution, that is relative factor rentals, only determines the *proportion* in which factors must be optimally combined; thus in ▶ Chap. 3 when studying the neoclassical economy that produces a single good with labour and land according to a differentiable production function, it was shown that the wage–rent ratio only determined the optimal *proportion* L/T of labour to land; the demand for labour could be derived from this proportion only because of the assumption that land supply was fully employed, which ensured that in the ratio L/T the denominator was given. Analogously (and now neglecting land for simplicity), *even conceding to the neoclassicals the right to treat capital as a factor analogous to land*, the rate of interest (and associated real wage) only determines the optimal K/L *ratio* in new plants, which is the sole place where the K/L ratio can be changed.[17] Without the assumption of full labour employment, the denominator in this ratio is no longer given because it need not correspond to the flow of labour 'freed' by the closing down of the oldest plants. Investment in new plants can employ only part of the labour flow 'freed' by the closing down of the oldest plants, leaving the rest to swell the ranks of the unemployed; or it can employ more labour than that flow, taking the extra from the pool of the unemployed (or from immigration). Therefore without the assumption of continuous full labour employment a given rate of interest leaves investment indeterminate, *even if* one accepts neoclassical traditional capital-labour substitution.

This problem appears in Keynes's theory as a difficulty with justifying the decreasing *marginal efficiency of capital* (the term Keynes uses for what others would call the marginal product of capital). Keynes justifies this decreasing MEC as follows:

---

17 The reader will no doubt remember that in already existing plants the given capital goods prevent factor substitutability, see ▶ Chap. 7, ▶ Sect. 7.8.1.

12.7 · The Investment Decision of Firms

» If there is an increased investment in any given type of capital during any period of time, the marginal efficiency of that type of capital will diminish as the investment in it is increased, partly because the prospective yield will fall as the supply of that type of capital is increased, and partly because, as a rule, pressure on the facilities for producing that type of capital will cause its supply price to increase; the second of these factors being usually the more important in producing equilibrium in the short run, but the longer the period in view the more does the first factor take its place. Thus for each type of capital we can build up a schedule, showing by how much investment in it will have to increase within the period, in order that its marginal efficiency should fall to any given figure. We can then aggregate these schedules for all the different types of capital, so as to provide a schedule relating the rate of aggregate investment to the corresponding marginal efficiency of capital in general which that rate of investment will establish (Keynes 1936–1967, p. 136).

Keynes reasons here as if one could derive a separate investment function for each type of capital good by assuming that only investment in that type of capital good increases, with unchanged employed quantities of all other factors (capital goods as well as labour); then a decreasing marginal product of that capital good can be assumed, and it determines a decreasing rate of return on further investment in that capital good. But individual investors assume they can vary the amount of a capital good together with the amounts of all other factors needed for the efficient employment of the first capital good, and it is only if an additional amount of some of these other factors comes out not to be obtainable (e.g. labour, if it is already fully employed), that they will accept a decreasing marginal product of the first capital good. Now, in Keynes's framework, unless the economy is already at full employment, extra labour is available, and owing to the flexibility of production of the capital goods industries the supply of the other needed capital goods will increase if demand for them increases, so there is no reason why more aggregate investment should cause a decrease of the marginal efficiency of capital.[18] As to the short-period rising supply price of capital goods, it is Keynes himself who argues that in the longer period this reason loses importance; furthermore, the empirical evidence suggests that a rising supply price of capital goods is implausible, we have seen earlier in the chapter that most produced goods have constant price in the short period even for ample variations of quantity produced.[19]

---

18 Keynes seems not to have been clear about the impossibility to assume a given schedule of the marginal product of capital if labour employment is not given. This emerges in Chapter 14 of *The General Theory* (Keynes 1936–1967, pp. 178–180), where Keynes treats the demand curve for capital as given, unaffected by changes of the rate of interest, in spite of admitting that the latter changes affect the level of aggregate income, and hence *labour employment*, which affects the marginal product of capital.

19 Thus the rising supply price argument was dismissed as implausible by Kalecki (1937).

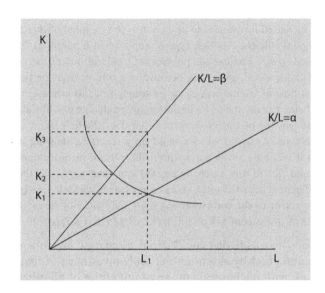

◘ **Fig. 12.2** Demand for capital along an expected-demand isoquant

Then we must turn to what emerged from the analysis of the choice of the K/L ratio in new plants: whether one concedes or not the traditional conception of 'capital'-labour substitution, the rate of interest can only influence the methods adopted in new plants[20] but not the *level* of investment in new plants. Its influence on the value of capital per unit of labour in new plants is anyway uncertain owing to the possibility of reverse capital deepening[21]; in all likelihood this influence is swamped by the influence of desired productive capacity (as determined in each industry by expected demand). To admit the latter influence only means to extend to all industries Marshall's partial-equilibrium argument that each industry tends to adjust its productive capacity to demand.

One is then brought to attribute the greater influence on investment to the ***accelerator***. Leaving to macro courses more detailed discussions of this influence,[22] I limit myself to illustrating with an example the reason for this name,

---

20 And the possibility of reverse capital deepening shows that the influence of the interest rate on adopted methods offers no guarantee that a lower interest rate will induce a rise of normal value capital per unit of net output.
21 Even traditional neoclassical capital-labour substitution is considerably weakened by taking desired productive capacity as given, rather than labour employment. In ◘ Fig. 12.2 if labour employment is given at L_1, the change in desired K/L ratio from α to β raises demand for capital from K_1 to K_3; if what is given is desired productive capacity (so that firms move along a given isoquant), the demand for capital rises only to K_2. Also, a lower real wage induces a lower desired K/L ratio in new plants, hence *less* investment; see Petri (2013, 2015).
22 A good introduction to the argument is Ackley (1978, Ch. 8 and Ch. 19).

12.7 · The Investment Decision of Firms

which refers to the influence of variations of expected aggregate demand on the demand for the products of the industries that produce capital goods. Several economists (among the first a French one, Aftalion) noticed around the 1920s that an increase of aggregate sales causes an 'acceleration', that is an increase by a greater percentage, of the demand for new capital goods. The reason can be made clear with a numerical example. Let me simplify by assuming production needs only durable machines all of the same type, and labour. Assume optimal capacity utilization requires one machine to produce in a year a net product of value 10, and that initially Y is constant at 1000; the economy uses 100 machines, which we assume last 10 years with constant efficiency and are uniformly distributed by age, so in order to maintain a constant productive capacity of the stock of machines firms buy each year 10 new machines. Now assume Y rises 10%, to 1100, and firms esteem this is a permanent rise. Then firms will desire to increase the stock of machines to 110; assuming they try to realize this increase rather gradually, over four years, then for four years the demand for new machines rises from 10 to 12.5, a 25% increase, much greater than the 10% increase of Y (and it would be even greater if firms tried to bring the stock of machines to 110 in less than four years). A similar 'acceleration' of the demand for capital goods would be caused by a rise of the *growth rate* of Y, the reader is invited to try some numerical example. The name 'accelerator' has become representative, more generally, of the influence of non-transitory variations of aggregate demand on gross investment, owing to the induced variation in desired productive capacity. This influence can have a very strong return effect on aggregate demand itself, owing to the multiplier effect of variations of investment on aggregate demand; this dynamic interaction with feedbacks between aggregate demand, capacity utilization, investment and aggregate demand again, already hinted at in Sect. 12.6, is studied in macroeconomics and growth theory under the name of multiplier-accelerator interaction, potentially a cause of macroeconomic instability as famously suggested by Harrod (1939).

It cannot cause surprise, then, that the empirical evidence is unable convincingly to support the thesis that the rate of interest exerts a significant influence on investment, and on the contrary strongly supports an influence of sales (i.e. demand). This conclusion of older empirical enquiries (cf. e.g. Ebersole 1938; Meade and Andrews 1938; Andrews 1940; Junankar 1972) has not been disproved by later econometric research. The 1993 survey of investment theory in the *Journal of Economic Literature* concluded:

> » While there is clearly no uniformity in the results and the role of shocks remains to be assessed, it appears to this author that, on balance, the response of investment to price variables tends to be small and unimportant relative to quantity variables (Chirinko 1993, p. 1906; also see *ibid.*, pp. 1881, 1883, 1897, 1899).

There has been no authoritative attempt, afterwards, to reject this double conclusion: very weak influence of 'price variables' (meaning, in fact, the interest rate), very clear influence of 'quantity variables' (sales). Rather, the great majority of analyses has further confirmed it.[23]

12.7.2 The 'Array-of-Opportunities' Approach

But the absence of a mechanism adjusting investment to savings would radically question the entire neoclassical approach. The tendency towards the full employment of factors of production, fundamental for the neoclassical determination of income distribution, could no longer be assumed. Then the tendency of factor rentals to decrease as long as there was unemployment of a factor could no longer be assumed either, since it might cause indefinite decreases, for example, of money wages, unobserved and incompatible with a regular functioning of economic activities. This problem has motivated a continuous search, after Keynes, for theories justifying a negative interest elasticity of investment, with an obstinacy that seems to me to betray an attitude like: 'the neoclassical approach is no doubt correct, therefore investment is no doubt a decreasing function of the rate of interest, we must only better understand how to prove it'.

This search has produced attempts to derive the decreasing investment function from bases other than a decreasing demand-for-'capital' function. Two of these attempts will be discussed here because marred by grave deficiencies and it is one purpose of this section to stop the consequent miseducation of students.

One approach, named 'array-of-opportunities' by Witte Jr. (1963), and popular in elementary and intermediate textbooks, argues that each entrepreneur has at each moment in front of her/him a series of investment projects, which can be ranked in order of decreasing expected rate of return; the entrepreneur starts all the projects with a rate of return (net of risk) not lower than the rate of interest; adding one after the other in abscissa, in order of decreasing rate of return, the investment volumes required by the different projects, with in ordinate their rate

---

23 Thus R. E. Hall (1993, pp. 278–9): 'established models are unhelpful in understanding this [1990–91] recession, and probably most of its predecessors....In spite of low interest rates, firms cut all forms of investment....Little of this falls into the type of behavior predicted by neoclassical models.' Chatelain and Tiomo (2003, p. 195): '... empirical estimates of the sensitivity of investment to cost of capital measures are very low and range from zero to 0.15 ... In fact, as is well known and indeed very well explained by Chirinko et al. (1999), one of the difficulties found in the empirical analysis of the relationship between investment and the user cost is that these estimates usually turn out to be very low.'. Sharpe and Suarez (2014) on the basis of the *Global Business Outlook Survey*, that reviews opinions of entrepreneurs and managers on the influence of the interest rate on investment, conclude that there is nearly no influence, only some limited discouragement of investment when the interest rate rises. Khotari et al. (2014) perform a panel analysis of aggregate investment of US firms from 1952 to 2010 and conclude that there is no relationship between interest rates and investment. And there seems to have been no visible stimulus to investment in the euro area coming from the considerable reduction in the European Central Bank's rate of interest in recent years.

12.7 · The Investment Decision of Firms

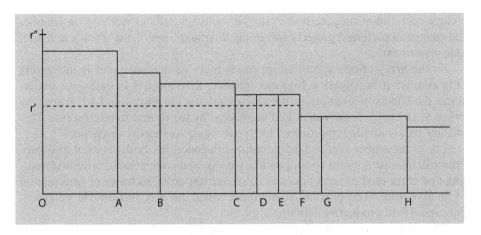

Fig. 12.3 'Array-of-opportunities' investment schedule. Each rectangle has as basis the investment required by the project, and as altitude the expected rate of return (net of risk) of the project. If the rate of interest is r', all the investment projects with a rate of return above r' are implemented and investment is OF

of return, one obtains a decreasing step schedule for each entrepreneur, and the horizontal sum of all these schedules yields the decreasing investment step schedule for the entire economy, see ◘ Fig. 12.3.

As Ackley (1978, Ch. 18) notes, it is true that at each moment there are investment projects with different expected profitability, because there is continuous emergence of novelties, and adjustments take time, so there are always temporary differences in profitability between investments in different fields; but this disequilibrium tells us nothing on the position and shape of the array-of-opportunities schedule (i.e. on how far to the right it extends at the several levels of the rate of return), which therefore is theoretically totally indeterminate. The approach might at most claim that, whatever the position of the schedule, it is decreasing and therefore a lower rate of interest will induce more investment. But this claim too cannot be derived from the approach. Even if the projects composing the schedule had some persistency, still the shape of the schedule would be strictly temporary, competition would tend to reduce the differences in profitability of existing projects by channelling investment into the more profitable projects and causing a reduction in the prices of their outputs, and conversely causing a rise in the price of the outputs of the least profitable projects; but at what level of rate of return will the convergence tend? As argued below, at a level equal to the rate of interest plus 'profit of enterprise' (risk coverage, essentially); but the approach does not tell us anything about the associated general level of investment. Above all, the schedule sums the investments that are the most profitable ones for the several firms at a certain moment, on the basis of the price vector and interest rate ruling at that moment; it does not indicate whether at a lower rate of interest and at the associated different relative prices these projects will remain the most profitable ones, or will be replaced by other ones not appearing in the original schedule—this second case being the usual one since changes in income distribution change cost-minimizing methods; but the approach tells us nothing on whether the change in preferred projects will imply a definite sign of the change in aggregate investment.

So the array-of-opportunities approach takes us nowhere, and is interesting only because it highlights a frequent mistake, that consists of trying to understand the effects of changes in the rate of interest on investment while treating prices as given, i.e. as persistent and unaffected by the change in interest rate. This mistake recurs in other approaches too, so it requires extensive discussion.

Let us remember that in traditional microeconomics, both classical and neoclassical, interest is a cost (or opportunity cost), and competition, price undercutting and entry tend to push prices to equal average costs, inclusive of interest and of an allowance to cover what Adam Smith called the 'risk and trouble' of investing capital into productive activities.

This 'risk allowance' has been often assumed absent for simplicity in previous chapters; it is opportune now to make room for it explicitly; nowadays it is usually referred to as **profit of enterprise**, and is the *excess* over interest that makes it convenient to invest capital in productive activities, running the risk of losses and perhaps bankruptcy and possibly special entrepreneurial efforts in case unexpected novelties and difficulties arise.[24] Profit of enterprise will differ as between industries owing to their different riskiness, and is one reason why a perfectly uniform rate of profit as the tendential result of gravitation is only a simplifying assumption; what can tend to uniformity (with free competition and free entry) is the rate of profit *net* of profit of enterprise. The difference between the rate of interest on loans to firms, and the expected rate of return or of profit (inclusive of profit of enterprise) necessary to induce firms to accept such loans, can be considerable, even 10% versus 25%. There seems to be a broad agreement in the history of economic theory that, given the characteristics of the period, profit of enterprise has a normal level in each industry, so it can be considered a given percentage to be added to the long-term rate of interest in each industry to obtain the normal rate of profit or of return in that industry. Note that the normal rate of interest itself can differ as between different fields of investment (and possibly as between different borrowers) depending on the riskiness of the loan.

If normal profit of enterprise and normal long-term rate of interest can be taken as given in an industry, and if an expected profit of enterprise greater than normal induces net investment in the industry (and conversely induces disinvestment, if profit of enterprise is less than normal), then if input prices and wages paid by that industry are given and the industry is competitive with free entry, the industry's output price must be expected to gravitate around the level that covers input costs, the normal rate of interest, and normal profit of enterprise. One can still speak of *tendency of price towards minimum average cost*, if the latter is

---

24 Profit of enterprise is the minimum such excess of revenue over costs inclusive of interest; it will generally differ depending on the field of investment, since risk, possibility of innovations, obsolescence, changes of laws etc. are not the same in all industries.

defined as also including normal interest on capital, and normal profit of enterprise per unit of output; for brevity, this notion of 'enlarged' normal average cost can be called *risk-inclusive normal average cost*.

This tendency implies the following. If the interest rate decreases, for given monetary costs other than interest charges the reduction of interest reduces the risk-inclusive normal average cost of the industry, and then competition will cause the output price to decrease too, even without an excess of supply over demand for the industry's output, because if competition is active a reduction in costs stimulates competitive price undercutting—possibly by new entrants. This output price decrease will tend to happen in all industries if the reduction in interest rate is general; then money costs decrease because produced input prices decrease, stimulating a further reduction in output prices, so there will be a general product price reduction relative to the monetary costs not due to produced inputs: essentially money wages, in a closed economy (and if one neglects land and fixed taxes); import costs too, in an open economy and if the exchange rate does not change, but here it is best to leave aside the complications of the open economy. So real wages rise, reflecting the reduction in the rate of return on capital (inclusive of profits of enterprise).

Of course the important thing is not that money wages be given, the important thing is that they rise *relative* to the general price level, which will be the case if the *real* rate of interest decreases.

The above implies that a change of the real rate of interest on loans to firms, then kept at the new level by opportune policies of the Central Bank, influences the rate of profit in the same direction, and hence influences real wages in the opposite direction. If this is how things work, then one cannot expect a reduction of the rate of interest to increase profit of enterprise except temporarily: competition will cause prices to decrease relative to money wages so as to reduce the rate of profit in step with the rate of interest, until profit of enterprise returns to its normal level. This adjustment will take time, perhaps considerable time, because it can be expected to operate on the same time scale as the tendency of profit rates (net of profit of enterprise) towards uniformity, entry being the main force behind the process. But the returns from an investment project are generally spread over several years, so entrepreneurs are not likely to be moved to invest by a *temporary* difference between rate of profit (net of profits of enterprise) and rate of interest; they know that the most probable effect of competition will be soon to eliminate this difference..

Note that these considerations are fully taken into account in the traditional neoclassical derivation of investment from the demand-for-'capital' function explained in ▶ Chap. 7: the influence of the rate of interest on investment is not derived from changes in the *difference* between rates of return and rate of interest: the influence is derived by assuming a *complete adaptation* of rates of return (net of profit of enterprise) to the rate of interest; a change of the rate of interest influences investment because it modifies cost-minimizing factor proportions owing to the change in relative normal factor prices, and modifies the composition of consumer choice owing to the change in relative normal prices of consumption goods. The possibility that, starting from a situation of normal prices with a certain income distribution, a decrease of the rate of interest creates

1050   **Chapter 12** · Product Markets: Pricing, Capacity, Investment, Imperfect Competition

a difference between rate of profit (net of normal profit of enterprise) and rate of interest that stimulates investment, is incompatible with the full-employment assumption of the approach, because any attempt at increasing output would cause an excess demand in the labour market that would raise wages,[25] reducing the rate of return on capital (net of normal profit of enterprise) back to equality with the rate of interest. The lower rate of interest can stimulate investment only by inducing a rise of the capital-labour ratio in new plants.

12.7.3 The Adjustment Costs Approach

The above considerations are totally absent from the other mainstream approach to investment theory that deserves discussion, the **adjustment costs** approach, currently dominant in advanced macroeconomics textbooks.

The birth of this approach was motivated by the following problem: assume a neoclassical decreasing demand curve for 'capital' $K^D(i)$; assume the 'capital' stock is K_1 and the rate of interest, after being for some time at the level i_1 such that $K^D(i_1) = K_1$, decreases to i_2 and demand for 'capital' rises to K_2. This, it was argued in the 1950s, leaves gross investment indeterminate, because the change in the *stock* demand for 'capital' does not tell us the speed with which firms want to pass to K_2: reaching K_2 in one, or two, or ten years means a very different monthly gross investment *flow*.[26] In the abstract, and in the absence of extra costs, the faster firms reach the new optimal 'capital' stock, the less the loss of potential profits; so investment should undergo a very high jump up (down) whenever there is an increase (decrease) in the desired capital stock. This was not empirically observed, so the idea was to look for obstacles that prevent an extremely quick adjustment of the entire 'capital' stock to the new optimal capital-labour ratio. The traditional answer, increasing short-period supply price of capital goods, was found empirically unsatisfactory, given the ample constancy of industrial product prices.[27] At the end of the 1960s a new proposal was advanced: to assume that when firms change the size

---

25 The same rise would happen to the rentals of lands, if land is admitted.

26 This indeterminacy problem arose because of a view of the whole of 'capital' as 'putty', easily re-adaptable to a different capital-labour ratio; the traditional neoclassical approach explained in ▶ Chap. 7 and briefly remembered in Sect. 12.8.1 implicitly took care of this problem, by admitting a putty-clay nature of capital, and a possibility to change the capital-labour ratio only in the new plants re-employing the flow of labour 'freed' by the gradual closure of the oldest plants. But this was not clearly perceived: at the time of Keynes's *General Theory* and in the following decades there was great confusion and approximation in the treatment of capital; and anyway even if the traditional neoclassical approach had been well understood, it could hardly be advocated: the continuous full employment of labour was impossible to assume after the Great Crisis of the 1930s and after Keynes.

27 As noticed for example by Kalecki (1937), who argued that replication of plants (including hired managers) is always possible, so firms have constant returns to scale, and then a price-taking firm with even only one project with an expected rate of return (net of profit of enterprise) greater than the rate of interest would plan to replicate the project indefinitely, that is, would plan an infinite investment, unless some extra cost prevents it. Kalecki found the solution in the 'principle of increasing risk', discussed later.

12.7 · The Investment Decision of Firms

of their 'capital' stock there is a disruption of routines that causes costs *additional* to those of purchasing and installing the extra capital goods, which increase in the speed of adjustment. The idea was formalized via dynamic optimization methods (a new advanced mathematical instrument! always good for winning publication in prestigious journals) by assuming that firms are price takers, and take the expected product prices both of the product and of capital goods as given *over the infinite future*; if the product price is greater than minimum average cost the firm would like to expand the capital stock[28] as fast as possible, but there are adjustment costs to changing the capital stock, which are increasing, and more than proportionately increasing, in the speed of change of the 'capital' stock[29]; so the firm adopts the growth path along which at each point the growth rate of the 'capital' stock is such that a marginal increase in the growth rate causes an increase in adjustment costs equal to the discounted value of the extra profits from that marginal increase in the growth rate. A lower rate of interest increases the gap between rate of return and rate of interest, raising the discounted value of the extra profits from growing faster, and this induces the adoption of a higher growth rate because the firm can afford higher adjustment costs; hence the firm's investment increases.

There is more than one totally unacceptable assumption in this approach (for more details see Petri (2015, 2004: Ch. 7):

- The price of each produced good is assumed given and constant through time[30]: it is unaffected by changes of the interest rate; if greater than average cost (inclusive of interest cost and normal profit of enterprise), it does not tend towards average cost even over very long periods, in spite of the growth of supply. Hence prices (and real wages) are not affected by changes of the interest rate.

- If there is excess of a product price over average cost, this excess persists, but there is no entry: the number of firms is given over the entire future. (If one were to admit entry, aggregate investment would be indeterminate even accepting the other elements of the approach, because it would depend on the rate of birth of new firms.[31] The possibility of entry condemns to sterility all approaches to investment based on the investment decision of the single firm.)

---

28 Up to the optimal dimension if the latter exists, or otherwise indefinitely.

29 The reasons for these costs and for their more-than-proportional increment have been found unpersuasive by many commentators. It is not clear why building two new plants, each one with the needed supervising expert managers to follow the operation, should cost more than twice the cost of starting only one new plant: the usual possibility of discounts associated with bigger orders would rather suggest the opposite. For further comments and for references see Petri (2004, pp. 277–280).

30 For example Heijdra and van der Ploeg (2002) assume 'that the prices of goods and labour … have no time index, because we assume that firms expect these to be constant over time' (p. 40).

31 The given number of firms is also assumed in the slightly different formulation of the adjustment costs approach in David Romer's advanced macro textbook (see e.g. the 4th edition, 2012, ► Chap. 9, but the treatment is the same in the earlier editions), which tries to avoid the given-for-ever product price by assuming that the firm is part of an industry facing a decreasing demand curve. But the number of firms in the industry is given, and they are identical. In Romer's treatment too (although the industry's demand curve makes it less visible) prices and wages are unaffected by changes of the interest rate, see Petri (2015). The definition of 'profit' is also very peculiar and potentially misleading.

- Firms have no problem with obtaining the inputs required by their optimal growth path, at fixed prices and rentals, in spite of the general framework of the analysis, which neoclassically assumes the economy fully utilizes all resources, and therefore should admit constraints on the availability of inputs, and changes in factor rentals if demand for factors changes.

These assumptions are absurd, contradicting the whole of microeconomics. The sole explanation I can find for the readiness of so many macroeconomists to accept this incredible theory is a desperate need to find some way to make investment adjust to savings. The result is a scandalous miseducation of students, who if persuaded to swallow this, will afterwards be ready to accept anything however absurd and contradictory.

As confirmation of the dire state of the mainstream theory of aggregate investment, a habit has spread in recent years of formulating macroeconomic models (growth models, in fact) without any investment function, replaced by the assumption that investment adapts to full-employment savings, without justifications except that this is what general equilibrium theory assumes. ▶ Sect. 8.17.2 has discussed this justification and found it unacceptable, so we need not stop on these models.

12.7.4 Investment Determined by Profits?

We need a non-dogmatic approach to investment decisions. There is plenty of room for further enquiries here; one finds a considerable diversity of opinions. The remainder of this section offers an overview of the basic ideas among non-neoclassical economists.

There is a broad consensus that a persistent difference between demand for the products of an industry and normal productive capacity of the firms in that industry will induce net (positive or negative) investment. If demand for the product of an industry—say, portable phones—increases considerably, producers will want bigger plants, or new entrants will build additional plants, in order to satisfy the increased demand at an average cost as close as possible to the minimum: net investment will be positive. If a trend of demand increase is observed which is expected to continue, net investment can be stimulated even before demand exceeds the productive capacity of the industry. An analogous consensus exists on the stimulus to investment coming from innovations: however, an innovation can discourage renewal of plants producing other goods that the better new product replaces, so the effect of innovations on *net* investment is not certain and it seems necessary to study it case by case; general conclusions such as are sometimes reached by 'Schumpeterian' growth models appear possible only on the basis of special and essentially arbitrary assumptions.

Much less agreement exists on the influence on investment of income distribution, and of the rate of interest.

Ricardo and Marx considered investment *generally* to depend on profits (classical meaning), increasing if the rate of profit increases. In Ricardo the idea seems to be simply that savings translate into investment without difficulty (Say's Law); in Marx the picture is more nuanced, but it is reinforced by the observation that firm owners (the capitalists) strongly want their firms to grow, not only because of a desire for more power, but also to exploit economies of scale: bigger firms win over smaller firms, so it is important for firms to grow, in order to avoid succumbing to the competition of bigger rivals; all must run, in order not to be left behind. This general picture is qualified in many ways: Ricardo admits the possibility that after a period of prosperity the next generation of capitalists become spendthrifts and allocate a lesser percentage of profits to savings and hence to investment; Marx admits the possibility of crises due to decreases of investment, owing to political fears (e.g. because of a wave of workers' protests), or to pessimistic expectations concerning future demand (e.g. because of an unusual wave of bankruptcies, or because of a decrease of demand for consumption goods after a decrease of real wages), or to credit crunches due to disruptions of the banking and financial sector. In spite of these qualifications, the dominant impression one derives from Marx is that a change in income distribution in favour of profits tends to increase investment and the growth rate of the economy. This view is rather popular among non-neoclassical economists nowadays, and brings to investment functions in which aggregate investment, besides depending positively on demand according to some version of the accelerator, also depends positively on the rate of profit. In ▶ Chap. 13 we will see that this view can be the basis for a theory of the long-run evolution of income distribution, associated with the name of Richard Goodwin.

One must not confuse a positive influence of the *normal rate* of profit on investment, with an influence of the *quantity* or mass of profits. For a given real wage (and hence a given normal rate of profit) the mass of profits depends on the level of economic activity; therefore an empirical evidence of more investment when there are more profits will be above all an indication of the influence of sales (aggregate demand) on investment (or possibly of a *reverse* influence of investment on sales and hence on profits via the multiplier—here we catch a glimpse of the difficulties that can arise in interpreting the causal connections behind empirical evidence). The difference becomes clearest when one neutralizes the influence of aggregate demand and capacity utilization by assuming continuous normal capacity utilization: then profits are normal profits, and the idea is that a higher rate of profit entails a greater share of investment in normal capacity output, hence faster growth.

However, there seems to be a common basic idea behind the positive influence on investment of the mass of profits, and of the rate of profit: the idea that investment is *constrained* by profits, that is, by the amount of money fully at the disposal of the class of persons who take investment decisions: capitalists in Marxist terminology, or more generally 'businessmen' (Kalecki), to include top managers too. The same idea is behind the thesis that investment positively depends on the cash flow of firms (when cash flow is not seen as simply an indicator of demand), or on the amount of retained profits (viewed as the main source of investment funds). Implicitly, the assumption is that capitalists would invest more, if only they had or could get the capital to do it.

This view is not found convincing by other non-neoclassical economists who insist on the influence of aggregate demand on output and capacity utilization. It is argued that the classical economists took aggregate output as given and corresponding on average to normal capacity utilization, because not yet fully aware of the considerable adaptability of production to demand and of the possibility that average capacity utilization may remain different from normal for many years[32]; then it was natural for them to conclude that the less of aggregate output goes to consumption, the more goes to investment (it must be so within this framework, since the given output is observed output, i.e. actual productions, which are produced because evidently they find purchasers). If one accepts that, certainly up to a limit but a limit from which economies generally remain far, investment is not constrained by the level of consumption because the level of aggregate output is variable and determined by the level of investment, then the views of the classics are not a solid basis for a theory of investment. And there is reason to think that an increase in the rate of profit is neither necessary, nor sufficient, for a stimulus to investment. It is not necessary, because investment can be financed by creation of purchasing power effected by the banking system or more generally by the financial system, or by mobilization of wealth kept until then as idle monetary balances for precautionary reasons, and *will* be so financed if needed and if the investment opportunities appear promising. It is not sufficient, because if it does not look easy to increase sales, a capitalist will not decide to build further productive capacity and will look for other ways to invest her/his profits, for example purchases of land, of mineral resources, of property abroad, of buildings, of gold, or of shares and other financial assets; such a purchase guarantees earning more or less the normal rate of return (net of risk), while investing in productive capacity which will be less than normally utilized would yield less. From such an employment of funds a bubble (of share prices, or of the price of land or of houses, etc.) may well originate, but hardly an expansion of capacity-creating investment, unless the conditions are favourable for the latter because demand has grown or is growing.

These considerations appear prima facie convincing.[33] Importantly, they hold whatever the rate of profit, because they request that investment in productive

---

32 In Chapter 1 it was argued that Marx too seems to have conceived of output in this way, as growing owing to the reinvestment of savings out of normal aggregate output, except for the interruptions due to crises.

33 The admission of an influence both of capacity utilization, and of the profit rate, on the propensity to invest has given rise to a distinction between *wage-led* and *profit-led* growth, depending on whether a greater share of wages in aggregate income, and hence a higher multiplier, stimulates investment via its positive influence on aggregate demand more (wage-led) or less (profit-led) than the discouragement to investment due to the lower rate of profit. The extremely informative book by Lavoie (2014, pp. 375–7) reports empirical enquiries that suggest that nearly all nations are wage-led if one neglects the generally negative influence of higher wages on the trade balance, while a few (heavily dependent on exports) become profit-led when one admits the latter influence. This empirical evidence strongly supports the influence of aggregate demand on investment, and appears to belittle the influence of the rate of profit, since the profit-led nations appear to owe this character only to the influence of the wage level on exports and imports, which is again an aggregate-demand influence.

12.7 · The Investment Decision of Firms

capacity offers a prospect of returns (net of risk) not less than in safer employments of investible funds, and since the several rates of return will tend to move in sympathy, tending to equality if taken net of differences in riskiness, liquidity, and need for profit of enterprise, a higher normal rate of profit in productive investment will go together with a higher rate of return on safer employments of investible funds, and therefore will not be a stronger incentive to investment.

However, it can be argued that this connection between rate of interest and rates of return (net of risk etc.) in more and less safe employments of investible funds need not always be verified. This will be the case, in particular, if one accepts the classical authors' view that the forces influencing income distribution act mainly by fixing the real wage, while at the same time one considers the rate of interest on loans to firms as modifiable by Central Bank policies. Then it can happen that the rate of interest is decreased by Central Bank policies, while the normal rate of profit does not decrease because it is determined by the given real wage. This will increase the difference between rate of profit and rate of interest beyond what is needed for profit of enterprise.[34] This can be argued to be a stimulus to investment.

A theory of investment as a positive function of the *difference* between normal rate of profit, and rate of interest, is precisely the proposal of Shaikh (2016, Ch. 13). He argues that investment is an increasing function of $r^e - i$, the difference between expected rate of profit (corresponding, over long periods, to the actual rate of profit), and rate of interest. The idea is not without *prima facie* plausibility: if one can borrow at 5% and invest for a rate of return which remains clearly higher than 5% even after subtracting from profits the coverage for risk and the other elements motivating the need for what has been called the '*profit of enterprise*' (the compensation for Adam Smith's 'risk and trouble' of entrepreneurial activity), one would be stupid not to do it. But this view can be extended from temporary situations to a general theory only if one denies that $r^e - i$ tends to become such as just to cover the necessary profit of enterprise. If rate of profit and rate of interest move 'in sympathy' (Pivetti), with the average difference only covering profits of enterprise, then investment cannot be explained by this difference. The majority opinion in the history of economic thought is precisely that in the long period rate of profit and rate of interest differ as required by 'profit of enterprise'. The influence can be from the rate of interest to the rate of profit as in neoclassical theory, where it is the rate of profit (called rate of return inclusive of risk coverage) that adjusts to the rate of interest if the latter is given, and then disequilibrium in the savings-investment market induces the rate of interest to gravitate towards the full-employment level; or it can be from the rate of profit to the rate of interest, as in Smith and Ricardo who took the rate of profit as given, determined by the given real wage, and argued that the rate of interest would rise to the maximum that investors were ready to accept, that is to the level sufficient

---

34 The non-neoclassical framework prevents the applicability of the argument used in ▶ Sect. 12.7.4 to deny that a divergence of profit of enterprise from its normal level can be other than strictly temporary.

to grant investors the necessary profit of enterprise. In recent years, Pivetti (1985, 1991) has argued that it is the rate of profit that adapts to the rate of interest via adaptation of product prices to given money wages, but rejecting the neoclassical approach and arguing that the rate of interest is determined by the policy of monetary authorities within a conflictual classical approach (see ▶ Chap. 13); a rise of the rate of interest compresses real wages by obliging firms to raise product prices in order to cover the higher interest costs, the Central Bank is fully involved in the conflict over income distribution.

For his different view, Shaikh refers to Marx, who argued that there is no such a thing as a 'natural' rate of interest, and that for a given rate of profit the rate of interest can be at any level between that rate of profit and zero. But above all, Shaikh refers to Marx's observation that the banking sector too is a sector with free entry, where therefore there must be a tendency towards earning the normal rate of profit (*Capital*, volume III, Part IV). Here Shaikh accepts, with minor modifications, the argument of Panico (1988) that the cost structure of banks implies that a given rate of profit univocally determines the rate of interest capable of yielding that rate of profit on the bankers' capital. The correctness of this view does not seem to have been sufficiently discussed yet, and therefore only an extremely simplified presentation of the basic Panico-Shaikh idea is provided here.

Suppose the creation of a new bank requires the anticipation of capital K for the initial expenses (buildings, furniture, machinery, etc.) plus as a collateral guaranteeing solidity to the bank. The bank is able to attract deposits and to use part of the money deposited to make loans. For simplicity assume there is no interest paid on deposits, on the contrary current accounts pay a yearly fee that covers the bank's running costs. Then the bank's net earnings are the interest on loans. Suppose there is a fixed ratio between the advanced capital K and the amount of loans the bank is able to emit, because K influences the attractiveness of the bank for people intending to open current accounts, and the loans issued are limited by the money collected as deposits, plus possibly Central Bank regulations oblige the bank to increase its own capital if it extends its loans. Let the volume L of loans be in the ratio λ to K, and let i be the rate of interest on loans. Under these extremely simplified assumptions, profit P is

$$P = iL = i\lambda K,$$

so the bank's rate of profit is

$$r = (i\lambda K)/K = i\lambda. \tag{12.3}$$

The conclusion is that a given r, equal to the normal rate of profit in the rest of the economy, univocally determines the 'natural' rate of interest needed for that rate of profit to be earned by the capital invested in banks. Entry and exit in the banking sector can then be argued to cause the rate of interest to gravitate around its 'natural' level in the same way as entry and exit in other sectors causes product prices to gravitate around their long-period levels.

Clearly the analysis can be complicated by admitting different rates of interest on deposits of different liquidity and on loans of different length, but these do not introduce degrees of freedom if interest rate differentials can be taken as given, determined by portfolio composition preferences due to riskiness, liquidity etcetera.

Shaikh assumes a more complicated cost structure of banks, with a fixed cost component that makes it necessary that the interest rate be positive to guarantee banks a zero rate of profit, and therefore a 'natural' rate of interest higher than the rate of profit in a neighbourhood of $r=0$; because of the fixed cost component, as the general rate of profit r rises, the rate of interest required to yield banks that rate of profit rises less, and soon becomes less than r, with two implications: first, there is a minimum (rather low) rate of profit below which capitalism cannot operate because it could not have a functioning banking system; second, above this minimum level if r increases the 'natural' rate of interest increases less, r^e-i increases, hence profit of enterprise of firms increases, and this brings to the classical view that a higher rate of profit stimulates investment and growth (Shaikh 2016, p. 623).

If one accepts Shaikh's argument and also the existence of a 'normal' profit of enterprise, then a given rate of profit implies two different 'natural' rates of interest: a rate of interest $i_F(r)=r-\eta$ guaranteeing *firms* the normal profit of enterprise (where η is the given difference between r and i required to that end), and a rate of interest $i_B(r)$ guaranteeing *banks* the given rate of profit (this rate of interest is given by r/λ in our supersimple example). Conversely, a given rate of interest (say, imposed by the monetary authorities) determines the 'normal' rate of profit required by firms to cover normal profit of enterprise, which can be presumed to be the rate of profit that determines product prices on the basis of given money wages owing to competition, but this 'normal' rate of profit may not be the rate of profit that banks earn with that rate of interest as the source of their earnings. Shaikh takes the rate of profit as given, determined by real wages that are determined, essentially, by the bargaining power of wage labour that depends on the rate of unemployment (see the Goodwin cycles in ▶ Chap. 13); furthermore he assumes that the rate of interest is determined by bank competition i.e. is $i_B(r)$; simplifying, as r rises r/λ increases less than $r-\eta$, that is $i_F(r)-i_B(r)$ increases, and investment is stimulated.

As I said, the field needs further study, and more confrontation with the empirical evidence. If I can hazard an opinion, it seems to me that the thesis that the rate of interest is determined by competition and entry in the banking sector on the basis of the cost structure of banks is empirically difficult to sustain, the role of Central Banks in determining rates of interest is more and more generally recognized, and Pivetti (1991) convincingly argues that this role is not a recent innovation but characterizes the last two centuries of history of capitalism. Therefore I find it difficult to accept that the rate of interest offered by banks to firms is $i_B(r)$ even assuming the rate of profit is given and not affected by the rate of interest. Secondly, Central Banks do not only directly influence rates of interest, they also continuously intervene on the cost structure of banks by changing reserve requirements, capitalization requirements, and what financial instruments banks are allowed to emit. Therefore if a given rate of interest fixed by the Central Bank causes problems in the banking sector (too low or too high earnings) the adjustments will be often determined by changes in the cost structure of banks rather than by changes in the rate of interest autonomously determined by the banking sector. Thirdly, if the notion of a given profit of enterprise (a given η) is accepted, and the powerful role of competition and entry argued so far in this book is accepted, then one must expect competition to oblige firms to accept a rate of profit not greater than the rate of interest plus η, and one must expect any excess of the rate of profit over this normal rate of profit to be temporary only, even though in this case 'temporary' may mean a rather long time stretch (see below on the euro area after 2008). If one accepts the tendency of prices towards minLAC owing to competition and entry, then a lower rate of interest cannot be expected to stimulate investment since firms will expect the rate of profit to decrease in step with the rate of interest, via reductions of product prices relative to money wages induced by price-cutting competition since now the costs due to interest costs have decreased. Even if the price reduction is slow (firms are reluctant to reduce prices!), investments must be profitable over a number of years so firms look at long-run forecasts in which the presumable tendency of profit rates to adjust to interest rates will be taken into account.

An adjustment at least partial of prices to changes of interest rates does appear to exist, as shown by the *Gibson paradox*, the rise in prices when the interest rate rises, 'one of the most completely established empirical facts within the whole field of quantitative economics' (Keynes 1930, II: 198), confirmed by more recent papers too. But the adjustment does not seem to be total, unless perhaps over a *very* long time interval. The experience of the Euro area after 2008 appears to show a persistently very low interest rate, but not a rise of real wages. It would seem that the rate of interest on own capital ('capitale di rischio') has decreased much less, owing to the banks' problems which induced them to increase the risk coverage on loans to firms. Also, a decrease of aggregate demand as observed in the Euro area after 2008 certainly slows down the tendency of the profit rate to decrease in step with the rate of interest, because it weakens the liveliness of competition. When there is no prospect of increased sales for an industry, an individual firm in that industry can increase its sales only by enlarging its market share to the detriment of other firms; this requires a lower price, but this runs the risk of retaliations, with the competitors reducing their prices too, with the result of a lower selling price with no sales increase; so incumbent firms are understandably hesitant to lower the product price, and the stagnant sales discourage new entry, so the competition from new entrants is missing too. The lower price would more easily come about in a situation of expanding demand, that reduces the risk that even a lower price does not increase sales. Without the expansion of aggregate demand, the lowering of prices (relative to money wages) because the rate of interest has decreased will likely be very slow. Also, the sales difficulties will increase the risk of capacity expansion, i.e. will increase the needed 'profit of enterprise'.

Still, one can object that, more generally, historically wage increases in the face of productivity increases have come from labour pressure, rather than from decreases in the price level as one should expect to observe according to Pivetti's theory when the rate of profit is increased by productivity increases. It is perhaps

12.7 · The Investment Decision of Firms

possible to reinterpret the Pivetti approach as entailing that an above-normal profit of enterprise reduces the resistance of firms to conceding wage increases; the rate of interest would then function as establishing a minimum rate of profit firms must earn, above which they are less capable or less willing to resist an always-present upward pressure of wages. But this wage pressure will be weaker when the low interest rates have been adopted to try to get the economy out of a recession, i.e. out of a situation of high unemployment. So, it seems, an influence of lower rates of interest on the rate of profit is less likely to be observed precisely in the situations in which lower rates of interest are more likely to be observed. But precisely because, I would expect, these will be situations of sales difficulties, an increased difference between rate of profit and rate of interest is not likely to stimulate investment in these situations.

Another approach to investment ultimately pointing to an influence of the difference between rate of profit and rate of interest is Kalecki's (1937) *principle of increasing risk*. The argument is that competitive firms should be treated as price-takers, hence facing a constant marginal efficiency of investment, and that the assumption of decreasing returns to scale is not credible because there is no reason why duplication of plant (including duplication of good management) should raise average cost. Therefore even if only one investment project has an expected marginal efficiency of capital greater than the rate of interest, the firm should plan to replicate it an indefinite number of times. This does not happen because more investment raises the leverage of the firm, i.e. the ratio of debt to assets, and this increases the risk of difficulties with repayment of debt (including the risk of bankruptcy) and more generally of liquidity problems. Therefore, in our language, in order to extend investment the firm needs a greater profit of enterprise to cover the increased risk; and also, owing to increasing risk for the lenders, a higher rate of interest must be offered to lenders. The rising marginal cost of debt and rising needed profit of enterprise put a limit to investment.

The approach has problems with reconciling the flow character of investment with the stock character of the degree of leverage, but here we can leave this problem aside. More importantly, the approach takes the rate of return on investment projects as given, and therefore is of no use if one believes that the rate of profit adjusts to the rate of interest, a lower (higher) rate of interest causing a decrease (increase) of product prices relative to money wages. Then a generalized expansion of investment that raised interest rates would be accompanied by a rise of prices relative to money wages, and the profitability (net of interest costs) of investment would be unaffected, and one would have to turn to other elements (demand!) to determine aggregate investment. But even if the rate of profit is taken as given, the approach suffers from its neglect of entry of new firms, and from its neglect of demand-side limits to what can be sold. If aggregate demand is rising and existing firms find they encounter limits to what they can borrow, this does not prevent the birth of new firms to fill the gap between aggregate demand and aggregate supply; to which one can add that it seems difficult to conceive situations in which a generalized excess of aggregate demand over aggregate supply is observed, and yet firms find it difficult to obtain credit for expansions of productive capacity that are clearly going to be successful; new firms too would find it easy to obtain credit. Conversely, the assumption that firms neglect demand-side limits to what they can sell appears difficult to accept. The empirical evidence is that productive capacity of industries is nearly always in excess of sales, that is, firms could easily produce more and do not do it only because they individually, or their industry, face a given demand. It is unconvincing to argue that, in such a situation, firms would want to expand productive capacity if only they could get a lower marginal cost of borrowing: they already have excess capacity! Also, the kind of percentage changes in economy-wide degree of leverage required for relevant changes of aggregate investment are quite small; a successful investment produces revenue, hence increases the firm's assets, the increase in degree of leverage is only temporary. In conclusion, credit constraints to investment, unless engineered by the Central Bank as a policy decision, appear acceptable only for specific firms or industries where demand has undergone an extremely quick expansion and entry is not easy; or are only a reflection of sales difficulties, of which lenders are aware.

12.7.5 Investment and Sales Prospects

I have discussed the possible connection between rate of profit and rate of interest, because of the thesis of Shaikh and, in a different form, of Kalecki, that investment depends on the difference between rate of profit and rate of interest. The issue certainly requires more theoretical reflection and more discussion of the historical evidence. But it seems to me that a point emerges again and again. *Ease of sale of the output resulting from an investment is a necessary condition for the investment to look attractive.* The impact on net earnings of 10% less sales than the expected ones is very strong, owing to the generally relevant weight of fixed costs[35]; to obtain an analogous but opposite impact on earnings of a reduction of interest costs with unchanged prices, even an enormous fall of the interest rate on loans to firms, say, from 15 to 5%, will not be enough in many cases. So even if a decrease of interest rates does not cause a decrease of product prices relative to money wages, the influence of expected sales on the desirability of investment must be expected to be much stronger than the influence of profit of enterprise.

The needed ease of sales can result from two things: first, expansion of demand, that at the level of the entire economy must mean *growth of aggregate demand*; second, creation of a new market via an *innovation*.

Growth of aggregate demand causes a desire to expand productive capacity in order to avoid increased costs due to excessive utilization of capacity (e.g. need to pay overtime wages) and ultimately also loss of market shares because of inability further to increase output. This is a well known and widely accepted consideration that motivates the accelerator approach to investment.

---

35 Even activities classified as services generally have relevant fixed or quasi-fixed costs, for example rent to be paid for office space.

12.7 · The Investment Decision of Firms

Innovative products, if successful, open up new markets; also, they stimulate investment, because if the innovation reduces production costs then other firms too are obliged to adopt it in order to resist price undercutting, perhaps with anticipated scrapping of durable capital goods; and if the innovation consists of a new attractive consumption good, investment will be stimulated because competing firms must come up with some similar product. But innovations do not come out of the blue; they require expenditure on research and development (R&D). Now, how much to 'invest' in R&D is not easy for firms to establish,[36] because the results of this expenditure are not easily predictable (here it is even less legitimate to assume rational expectations than for inflation or other macro variables). There seems to be little theory of what determines the amount of expenditure in R&D in private firms. In 1990, in the USA on average approximately 1% of sales revenue was allocated to R&D, with the pharmaceutical industry and the electronic industry being at the top of a list by industries, with respectively 11 and 9% of sales revenue allocated to R&D (Scherer and Ross 1990, Ch. 17). Why not less or not more, is a question which as far as I know has not received answers yet. Possibly, as for marketing expenses, in many industries the percentage is a historical accident, if some firm started spending more on R&D its competitors would feel obliged to spend more too, but no firm dares challenge the established routine.

Anyway it is clear that the importance of R&D expenditure for investment is enormous, because it produces innovation, and innovation, both among means of production and among consumption goods, is fundamental for investment. Among capital goods, innovation produces technological obsolescence, which is responsible for anticipated scrapping of durables which otherwise might continue in use for several more years. Among consumption goods the thing is even more evident, people change computers or portable phones or clothes much faster than required by the durability of these goods. And revolutionary innovations bring about enormous change in many industries and in infrastructures, which requires big waves of investment:

> » It seems obvious that major waves of investment demand often have had their origin in revolutionary changes in technology. The railroad, electricity, the automobile, and computers and automation, for example, have each been responsible for a great burst of investment, both in the industries directly involved and in subsidiary industries ... we can be quite sure that a technically progressive economy, and one that continually creates new products, will have a higher level of net investment than an economy in which the pace of innovation is more leisurely (Ackley 1978, p. 663).

This is frightening to some extent, suggesting we are actually slaves of a system which pretends continuous change and high consumerism. If innovation were

---

36 Expenditure in R&D is not considered investment in national accounting, but it has every right to be considered as autonomous an expenditure as fixed investment, which is why occasionally I will call it 'investment'.

1062   **Chapter 12** · Product Markets: Pricing, Capacity, Investment, Imperfect Competition

to slow down, investment would slow down, and aggregate output and employment with it. The capitalistic form of organization of production *needs* continuous emergence of new products and of people desiring them, if it is to give jobs to a majority of people. A more relaxed, slower, less consumistic lifestyle would need some drastic reorganization of what determines aggregate demand, and would certainly need a way to prevent the decrease in investment from causing disastrous rates of unemployment: a three-day working week might be a solution, but it can be adopted only if a strong majority desires it, and the pressure of the media (with the business world behind them) is against it.

If, as we seem obliged to conclude, investment depends above all on aggregate demand and its variations and on innovation, it is confirmed that there is no reason to believe in some automatic mechanism that adjusts investment to an independently determined level of savings, in particular to full-employment savings. Therefore the recent mainstream macroeconomic models that assume continuous equality between investment and full-employment savings are clearly unacceptable. And the so-called New Keynesian models that assume an acapitalistic economy are just as unacceptable, since the elimination of investment can only be justified with the argument that the introduction of capital and investment would introduce no new problem because investment adjusts to full-employment savings. It is to be hoped that the waste of intellectual energies on these models will rapidly decrease.

12.8 Administered Prices, Differentiated Products, and Competition

The reader may have noticed that in the considerations on long-period price determination, degree of utilization of capacity, and investment no distinction was made between highly competitive industries (composed of firms producing a homogeneous product, perhaps sold in an organized market via auction-like methods) and industries producing differentiated products; the reasonings were based essentially on free entry and hence on the tendency of product prices towards minimum average cost, and on the tendency towards a uniform rate of profit (apart from differences in the needed profit of enterprise) again due to free entry, the 'mobility of capital'. The desired degree of capacity utilization does depend to a greater extent on whether the firm is one of many that contribute to a total supply of a homogeneous product and therefore the single firm does not face a demand specifically for its own product (we can call this type of firm '*anonymous*'), or instead there is some even very minor market segmentation due to differences in location, goodwill, reputation of product quality, etc.; only in this second case the firm has the problem of catering to the demand specifically addressed to its own product, which can motivate a desire for some excess capacity so as not to lose market shares in case demand unexpectedly increases; the 'anonymous' firms generally will not want this excess capacity. But other aspects of the choice of capacity, for example the problem whether to use single-shift

12.8 · Administered Prices, Differentiated Products, and Competition

production or also night shifts, are problems that arise for both types of firm; 'anonymous' firms too will generally not utilize their productive capacity maximally, 24 h a day all days of the year, and so they too can usually increase production if the expected product price makes it convenient and if they do not hit against technical constraints (like the maximum production of corn obtainable from a given land surface).

It was therefore implicit in the considerations so far in the chapter that, apart from exceptions characterized by impossibility or great difficulty of entry,[37] it makes little difference to the important, long-period aspects of price and quantity determination whether prices are administered or not, whether product is differentiated or not. The remainder of this chapter will show the plausibility of this view in the face both of standard and of non-neoclassical microeconomic analysis of firms not classifiable as perfectly competitive, hence falling in the administered prices category—no doubt the ample majority of cases. It will emerge that frequently this analysis brings to indeterminate results, but the indeterminacy is greatly or totally reduced by the admission of entry. Apart from the mentioned exceptions, entry is possible everywhere, and even more so than in the past, because there are more and more big conglomerate firms with the financial and technical capability to open up firms able to compete with incumbent firms in any industry; see ▶ Sect. 12.14.

12.9 **Full-Cost Pricing**

There is convincing empirical evidence about the prevalence of *full-cost pricing* among the firms that practice administered pricing. The 'full cost' terminology refers to the inclusion into cost of not only variable cost but also fixed costs such as depreciation and normal interest costs (plus a risk coverage element). Full-cost pricing means that the firm calculates average total production cost at the normal rate of capacity utilization, and fixes the product price so as to cover this average cost, plus possibly an extra if the product has special characteristics that justify a higher price than for comparable products. There is considerable evidence that, outside primary production, firms generally fix prices precisely in this way, also called *cost-plus* pricing. This amounts, fundamentally, to accepting the dominant-technology normal price (minimum average cost, determined on recent plants embodying state-of-the-arts technology, inclusive of the normal rate of return and of necessary marketing expenses)[38] and sticking to it even when

---

37 The main ones are monopolies, to be studied presently, and productions with nearly zero marginal cost and/or strong network effects, increasingly important because common in the Internet, briefly discussed at the end of the chapter.

38 It will be explained below that this notion of normal price does not exactly correspond to the marginalist notion of long-period price although it seems to correspond well to the classical notion.

demand varies, adapting supply to demand without variation in price. A variety of reasons can be advanced to explain this absence of price change when demand changes, including:

- the costs of price changes,
- the preference of buyers for price stability (which reduces uncertainty),
- the seller's difficulty with distinguishing persistent changes in demand from stochastic fluctuations,
- the already noticed generally low elasticity of the demand for the category of goods to which the product belongs, together with a certainty that price reductions will be matched by the producers of the other goods in the category, while price rises will stimulate entry (including cross-entry, see below),
- the fear of 'spoiling the market' (Alfred Marshall), that is, fear of starting a downward price war that may be ruinous for the starter too; recently, particularly James Crotty has insisted on this element, renaming the result 'co-respective competition'.

What remains to explain is the level at which the price is fixed and then kept broadly unchanged in the face of variations of demand. Here the answer is entry, actual and potential. Abundant empirical evidence shows that firms are aware of strategic interaction with other firms and are very much worried by the danger of entry, of new firms or new products, that might cause difficult-to-recuperate losses of goodwill. What attracts entry is a price above normal average total cost, which means a possibility to undercut. The highest price that does not risk being undercut by new entrants is the price that covers normal average total cost (inclusive of normal marketing expenses and normal rate of profit), because new entrants too must cover costs. Of course, since we are talking of differentiated products, entry leaves room for price differences, but these will be explained by the greater cost of producing certain better varieties of the good.

The point is that in most cases buyers look for characteristics of products that are found, more or less identical although perhaps in different amounts, in other products (e.g. trucks have a carrying capacity, drills drill, shower foams clean and perfume), and then buyers—be they consumers, or other businesses—will opt for the product that produces those services at a lesser price; in most cases a product might be copied practically identical by other firms in the field, and *will* be copied and undersold if very profitable. So actual or potential entry (including what has been called ***cross-entry***, product imitation by other firms already in the field) allows one to describe long-period price formation as, in a reasonable sense, price taking, even in the presence of differentiated products. Even in the short period, price remains very close to the long-period normal price; some limited price variation is sometimes observed depending on demand: when demand is depressed, producers or retailers sometimes offer discounts, especially to get rid of excess inventories that built up before it became clear that the demand decrease was not a stochastic irregularity but was persistent, and production was accordingly reduced; but these discounts are limited in amount (to avoid price wars), and in time (becoming unnecessary once excess inventories have been reduced).

12.9 · Full-Cost Pricing

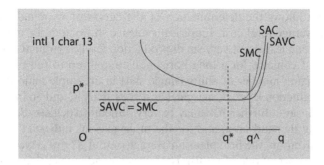

Fig. 12.4 Marginal cost constant up to full capacity. The firm chooses the capacity level so as to have the full-capacity, average-cost-minimizing quantity q^ greater than the expected sales q* at the price p* slightly greater than minimum average cost but covering average cost at q*. The excess capacity q^–q* is desired so as to have greater production flexibility in case of demand fluctuations

The usual graphical presentation of the above is shown in Fig. 12.4.[39]

Firms are not identical; they have plants, whose size was planned having in mind the firm's expected capacity to sell the product, which differed from firm to firm (and from product to product). Whether a bigger plant will allow a reduction of average cost, and by how much, is necessarily vague, because engineers solve problems only when called upon to do it, and it is unclear in advance how the problems posed by a bigger plant will be solved. Therefore the notion of long-period minimum average cost as the minimum of all the minimums reachable with plants of different sizes is enveloped in uncertainty; managers will refer to what is known, which is costs of *existing* plants, plus whatever is already clear about other kinds of plant, so as to estimate the possible minimum price charged by a new entrant. They will then refer to the dominant plant to determine the normal price.[40] The

---

39 The graph is from Koutsoyiannis (1975), pp. 272 and 275. Pages 256–282 of this textbook are highly recommended. Also see Elizabeth Brunner (1975); and Andrews (1949). These are attempts to complete and synthesize the views on industrial pricing developed by the Oxford Economists' Research Group in the 1930s on the basis of interviews of managers, views famously expounded in Hall and Hitch (1939), also highly recommended. The stress on cross-entry in the main text is from Andrews. No discontinuity of marginal cost due to higher overtime wages appears in this graph (nor in the graphs in the other two papers), probably because the issue of time-specific labour costs and utilizability of overtime had not yet conquered general attention. For a more recent survey of the evidence on the prevalence of full-cost pricing cf. Lee (1998).

40 This corresponds well to the idea of dominant method of production, which is the one that must appear in the 'Sraffian' matrix of technical coefficients that determines normal prices. The notion of long-period equilibrium of the industry, in the sense of a situation in which no firm has any more an incentive to change because they all have identical plants of the size that minimizes minimum average total cost among all plant dimensions, can then be dismissed as (i) indeterminable because the efficiency of plants of not yet experienced dimensions is not known, and (ii) anyway irrelevant because technology and preferences change too fast relative to the time required to approximate such an industry equilibrium. For this reason, Andrews and Brunner qualified their analysis as short-period; but the relevance of actual or potential entry in their analysis makes it a long-period one, albeit not in the neoclassical sense of complete adaptation of all firms in the industry.

dominant plant allows the determination of the curves of marginal cost, average variable cost, average total cost. Empirical evidence shows that for most manufacturing firms, if one leaves out very small production levels, marginal cost and average variable cost coincide for a long horizontal stretch, up to full utilization with the cost-minimizing number of shifts (single shift in an ample majority of cases). Beyond this production level $q^\wedge$, marginal cost rises sharply, and an increase in production beyond, say, a further 10% may be very difficult to achieve. So to be able to satisfy a varying demand level, and for the other reasons indicated when discussing capacity utilization, the firm plans an average output $q^* < q^\wedge$. Average total cost (inclusive of the normal rate of return) is decreasing and greater than marginal cost and average variable cost all the way to $q^\wedge$, hence a price equal to marginal cost at q^* would cause losses. But knowledge that competitors cannot afford a lower price allows maintaining a price equal to the average total cost of the dominant plant—or perhaps a little above that, to minimize complaints of unfair competition (predatory pricing[41]), and as long as entry does not oblige to a price reduction. (Economists have come to the habit of calling *predatory* any aggressive behaviour aimed at pushing competitors to exit or not to enter a market.[42])

This description of how administered price is formed in most manufacturing industries is confirmed by massive evidence based on interviews with managers, questionnaires, and other evidence on cost curves and prices.[43] It will be noted that nowhere in this description there appears the notion of a demand curve. Indeed its proponents argued that the demand curve is not a notion used by managers to decide price or quantity. This raised a hot debate, during which it was

---

41 Predatory pricing is the lowering of price by a firm, which is costly to the firm and dictated only by the desire to push competitors to exit the market.

42 'Predatory' conduct is condemned by antitrust law and juridical decisions, because aimed at reducing competition, but is an ambiguous notion. Consider the following effort to arrive at a clear definition: 'Considerable care is required in an investigation of predatory conduct. For example, we must be careful not to characterize actions by a firm either to improve its cost-efficiency or to promote its product as predatory, even if such actions have the effect of enhancing the firm's market position .... Economists define predatory conduct to be actions taken by a firm that are profitable *only if* they drive existing rivals out of the market or deter potential rivals from coming into the market. Predatory conduct is some costly action for which the only justification is the reduction in competition that such action is designed to achieve. If there is no cost to the firm to engage in some conduct, then that behaviour could simply be part of profit-maximizing strategy and, hence, not explicitly 'anti-competitive'. To put it somewhat loosely, predatory conduct must appear on the surface to reduce the predator firm's profit and seem to be 'irrational' (Pepall et al. 2005, pp. 266, 269). Now consider a firm with a cost advantage relative to competitors, which decides to undercut the price until then common, and there is a high chance that the competitors will match the price reduction. Relative to leaving price unaltered, the firm reduces its profit *unless* it enlarges its share of the market, which requires that some competitor exits and can be interpreted as a reduction in competition. So is this price reduction predatory? Plenty of leeway seems to be left for the judge to decide on the basis of personal opinion, or of money accruing to him/her on anonymous Swiss bank accounts.

43 ▶ https://socialdemocracy21stcentury.blogspot.com/p/there-is-mountain-of-empirical-evidence. html.

12.9 · Full-Cost Pricing

argued that the empirical evidence could be explained by the more traditional theory of ***monopolistic competition***, where the notion of a demand curve facing each firm is accepted. Let us present this theory and then discuss its difference from full-cost pricing. For this, we need first the standard theory of monopoly, so this is the subject of the next section.

12.10 Monopoly

Monopoly is the name of the market form with a single supplier of a product for which there are no close substitutes, and entry into the market is impossible. Standard monopoly theory assumes the monopolist firm has a given cost function, and faces a given *and known* downward-sloping continuous demand curve $q = f(p)$ for its product, generally assumed to be a consumption good.[44]

Consider profit π (neoclassical definition) as a function of the *quantity* q produced by the monopolist. The inverse market demand function[45] is $p(q) = f^{-1}(q)$, where the demand function $q = f(p)$ is assumed continuous and monotonically strictly decreasing (we neglect Giffen goods). Total cost is $C(q)$, based on given input costs, and measured at the same moment when output is sold, so input costs if paid in advance are increased by the interest cost for the time interval. The monopolist's problem is

$$\max_q \pi(q) = p(q)q - C(q) \text{ with } q \geq 0.$$

Assume $p(q)$ and $C(q)$ are continuous and differentiable at all $q \geq 0$. Then the solution must satisfy the first-order condition $d\pi/dq \leq 0$ with equality if $q > 0$. Thus if the monopolist finds it convenient to produce at all, the first-order condition is

$$qp'(q) + p(q) - C'(q) = 0.$$

Assume that a solution $q^* > 0$ satisfying this condition exists. Define ***marginal revenue*** as the derivative of revenue pq with respect to q:

$$MR(q) := qp'(q) + p.$$

The term $qp'(q)$ is negative, hence $MR(q) < p(q)$. As always, the definition for a discrete variation helps intuition: marginal revenue can be approximately defined

---

44 Here too the given demand curve, sufficiently persistent for the monopolist to have been able to discover its position and slope, needs given and persistent consumer incomes, which requires given and persistent aggregate employment level and income distribution. A demand curve for a capital good is a much more complicated notion, not by chance seldom mentioned in neoclassical literature, because it requires specifying how a change in the price of a capital good affects technical choice and product price in the industries that use it, and then how these price changes affect demand for the products of these several industries: the partial-equilibrium methodology is inapplicable, because many other prices cannot be assumed nearly unaffected by changes in the price under study.

45 If, as I assume, there is a p° such that q = 0 for p ≥ p°, then one avoids having to deal with correspondences by defining the inverse demand function as taking the sole value p° for q = 0.

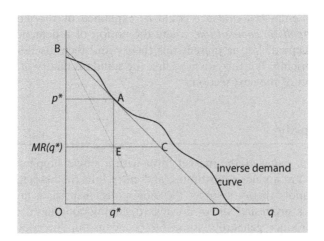

■ **Fig. 12.5** Graphical derivation of $MR(q*)$ from the inverse demand curve: given $q*$, draw the line tangent to the inverse demand curve in the corresponding point $A=(q*, p(q*))$; with B the intercept in ordinate of that tangent line, $|q*p'(q*)|$ is the length of the segment from B to $p*=p(q*)$; subtracting it from $p*$ one obtains $MR(q*) = p(q*) - |q*p'(q*)|$. Alternatively, draw from B a downward straight line with absolute slope twice that of the inverse demand curve in A, and find its point E vertically above $q*$; its ordinate is $MR(q*)$. Note that at $p*$ the elasticity of demand is $|\varepsilon| = \overline{AD/AB} = \overline{Op*/p*B}$ (prove it!)

as the variation in the value of sales if the firm lowers p enough to sell one more unit of output. Note that with this definition in terms of variation of output by one unit, **marginal revenue equals the new price (which is what the extra unit earns) minus the decrease in earnings on all previous units due to the fall in price**. If 100 units are sold at $p=100$ and 101 units are sold at $p=99.5$, total sales increase from 10,000 to 10,049.5, the loss on the previous 100 units is $100 \cdot 0.5$, this must be subtracted from the earning on the extra unit, 99.5, and the result is the marginal revenue, 49.5. Clearly, marginal revenue can easily be negative: in the previous example it suffices that to sell 101 units p needs to decrease to 99 or less.

Now indicate *marginal cost* $C'(q)$ as $MC(q)$; then the first-order condition for maximum profit can be written[46]

$$MR(q) = MC(q). \tag{12.1}$$

Actually this condition holds for the Marshallian competitive firm too, but in perfect competition $MR=p$ because p is assumed given, while here $MR<p$, so in monopoly at the optimum it is $MC<p$ (■ Fig. 12.6).

There is a graphical method for determining MR from the inverse demand curve if the latter is differentiable; it is shown in ■ Fig. 12.5. It shows that if the demand curve is a straight line, the function $MR(q)$ is a straight line too, with

---

46 *Exercise*: Assume profit is maximized with respect to *price*, $max_p \pi(p) = pq(p) - C(q(p))$, and show this yields condition (12.1) again.

12.10 · Monopoly

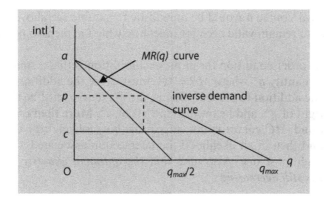

Fig. 12.6 Marginal revenue if demand is linear

the same vertical intercept as the demand curve and double the slope in absolute value, a result which can be confirmed algebraically: if $q = a - bp$, then $p = a/b - q/b$; hence:

$$MR(q) = p(q) + qp'(q) = a/b - 2q/b.$$

Then MR becomes zero for $q = q(0)/2$. If one represents the linear inverse demand curve as $p = \alpha - \beta q$, it is $MR(q) = \alpha - 2\beta q$. In this case if marginal cost is constant at c, the condition $MR = c$ implies the optimal price is half way between α and c.

If the demand curve is not a straight line, things can be less neat; MR may even not be a decreasing function of q, see Exercise 4 below. Or consider the connection between MR and the price elasticity of demand $\varepsilon = (dq/q)/(dp/p) = (dq/dp) \cdot (p/q)$. Divide and multiply $MR = p + (dp/dq)q$ by p to obtain

$$MR = p[1 + (dp/dq)(q/p)] = p\left[1 + \frac{1}{\varepsilon}\right] = p\left[1 - \frac{1}{|\varepsilon|}\right], \qquad (12.2)$$

where of course ε (a negative number) depends on p. This is a useful re-writing of MR in terms of elasticity of demand which will be used later (◘ Fig. 12.6).

The optimality condition $MR = MC$ implies that the monopolist will never choose a quantity whose elasticity is less than 1 (in absolute value) because that would cause MR to be negative, while MC is at most zero. So if the inverse demand curve is linear, the monopolist will never choose a price in its lower half. But now assume that the demand curve facing the monopolist has *constant elasticity*, which means (check it!)

$$q = Ap^\varepsilon = A/p^{|\varepsilon|}.$$

Suppose this constant elasticity is $|\varepsilon| = 1$; then MR is constant at zero, and if total cost is an increasing function of q the monopolist finds it convenient to reduce production as much as possible as long as that shape of the demand curve

1070   **Chapter 12 ·** Product Markets: Pricing, Capacity, Investment, Imperfect Competition

remains valid (of course it would be unrealistic to assume the above shape of the demand curve to remain valid even for indefinitely high p; then no optimal output would exists).[47]

The second-order condition for profit maximization is that a small increase of q beyond the quantity q^* where $MR = MC$ must cause the addition to cost to be greater than the addition to revenue, that is, the MC curve must be above the MR curve to the right of q^*, and below it to the left of q^*. More than one intersection between MR and MC curves is not impossible but unlikely (try to represent it graphically) and then in all likelihood the intersection associated with maximum profit is the rightmost one. Also note that *the optimum quantity can be where marginal cost is still decreasing*.

Exercise 1: Prove that if the inverse demand curve is a straight line the monopolist will never set the price below $1/2p(0)$.

Exercise 2: Using the device of ■ Fig. 12.1, derive the MR curve from an inverse demand curve which is the non-negative portion of a circumference centred in the origin. Where does MR become zero?

Exercise 3: Prove graphically, using the device of ■ Fig. 12.1, that a downward-sloping differentiable inverse demand curve need not imply an everywhere decreasing marginal revenue curve. (Hint: let the inverse demand curve have at a certain point a rapid decrease in absolute slope as q increases, which renders it almost horizontal for a short stretch.)

Exercise 4: Prove that if $q = A/pp^{|\varepsilon|}$ and $\varepsilon| > 1$ and $|\varepsilon| > 1$, then $d^2MR(q)/dq^2 < 0$, and conclude that in this case profit as a function of q is concave if marginal cost is convex.

In the long period, a monopolist can choose the MC curve by choosing the fixed plant. The long-period choice of plant by the monopolist can be understood as follows. Suppose the monopolist considers a plant A, with the associated marginal cost curve $MC_A(q)$ and average cost curve $AC_A(q)$. From the given demand curve the monopolist derives the optimal quantity q_A that yields $MR = MC_A$, and the associated $AC_A(q_A)$. If at *this* quantity there is another plant B such that $AC_B(q_A) < AC_A(q_A)$, it is more convenient to produce q_A with plant B; the monopolist then considers plant B, determines the optimal quantity q_B (generally different from q_A) and if at that quantity there is still another plant C with lower average cost than B at q_B, plant C replaces B; and so on, until all profitable replacements are exhausted. If the long-period production function has constant

---

47 With a demand function of constant elasticity for all values of p, when $|\varepsilon| = 1$ revenue is independent of output so the firm finds it convenient to minimize total cost by decreasing output indefinitely (price tends to $+\infty$) but at $q = 0$ revenue and profit jump discontinuously to zero, there is no maximum profit. Same problem with constant elasticity $|\varepsilon| < 1$, then marginal revenue is always negative. I have excluded these cases by assuming that $p(0)$ exists.

12.10 · Monopoly

returns to scale and perfect divisibility, but one can still distinguish variable factors from fixed factors not modifiable in the short period once adopted, then for each q there is a fixed plant that allows producing q at the same minimum average cost $MinLAC$; then the monopolist chooses the plant dimension such that the AC curve with that fixed plant reaches its minimum ($AC = MC$) where it crosses the MR curve, and produces the corresponding quantity, which now satisfies $MR = MinLAC$; hence average cost is minimized, long-period price is above average cost. If the monopolist can only choose among a few indivisible fixed plants, the long-period MC curve is the lower envelope of the MC curves corresponding to the different plants, and the intersection with the MR curve will not generally correspond to $MinLAC$.

Equation (12.2) shows that $MR = MC$ implies p must equal MC multiplied by the **mark-up** $1/[1 - 1/|\varepsilon|]$, a decreasing function of $|\varepsilon|$; if MC is constant, the optimal price is the greater, the less elastic is demand.[48] The same thing is shown by **Lerner's index of monopoly power**

$$\left[p(q*) - MC(q*)\right]/p(q*),$$

the percentage of price in excess of marginal cost, which equals $1/|\varepsilon|$ (prove it!).

Note that *a monopolist has no supply function*, the monopolist *chooses* the price.

The optimal employment of variable factors by a monopolist is easily determined: it requires that the factor rental be equal to the *marginal revenue product* of the factor, given by marginal product times marginal revenue; this is also true for the perfectly competitive firm, but for a price-taking firm marginal revenue equals p, here $MR < p$, so the product exhaustion theorem does not apply: with all factors variable, optimal factor employment implies that *a monopolist with CRS technology pays each factor less than the value (at the optimal output price) of the factor's marginal product, so in total pays less than her revenue, and is left with a profit.*

Without CRS, it is possible that profit is zero, this will be the case if the average cost curve is U-shaped and the demand curve happens to be tangent (from below) to the average cost curve where the latter is decreasing, cf. ◼ Figure 12.7a. In such a case, the optimal quantity is precisely the one corresponding to tangency, because at that quantity $q°$ one has average revenue (that is, price) $= AC$, and also $MR = MC$, because, as ◼ Fig. 12.4b shows, at $q°$ one also has tangency between the total cost curve and the total revenue curve,[49] which means their slopes are the same. This tangency, particularly important for the theory of monopolistic competition to be studied next, requires a U-shaped long-period average cost curve, hence either a fixed cost, or initially increasing returns to scale.

---

48 Here we have one example of the economists' habit to refer to the *absolute value* of the elasticity of demand: a less elastic demand means a smaller $|\varepsilon|$.

49 Simple proof: on both sides of $q°$ average revenue (that is, price) is less than average cost, so total revenue and total cost do not cross. Both curves are assumed smooth, so they must be tangent at $q°$.

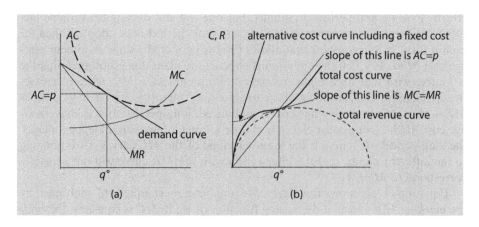

◘ **Fig. 12.7** Graphical proof that tangency of average cost curve and demand curve implies tangency of total cost curve and total revenue curve and thus equality of marginal cost and marginal revenue. But for the tangency to be possible, average cost must be initially decreasing, that is, there must be initially increasing returns to scale, possibly due to a fixed entrance cost, see ◘ Fig. 12.4b.

This analysis of monopoly assumes that the reaction of other firms to changes in the monopolist's price does not significantly affect the monopolist's demand curve; so there is no strategic interaction between firms. This is not necessarily the case even if the product in question is offered by only one firm. There may be only one amusement park in a town, but it competes with other ways to spend one's leisure time, e.g. cinemas: if the entrance ticket to the amusement park is lowered, cinema owners may respond by lowering the price of cinema tickets. In this case, the owner of the amusement park cannot be classified as a standard monopolist, the situation is one of strategic interaction, a duopoly in this example.

A monopoly causes the Marshallian surplus to be less than the one achievable if the monopolist firm produced the quantity satisfying $p = MC$. In ◘ Fig. 12.8 a Paretian improvement is achievable: the monopolist produces q_m; assuming standard measurement of consumer and producer surplus, if the monopolist increases output until the price reaches the competitive level $p(q) = MC(q)$, it loses the area FGDH and gains the area CEH, while consumers gain the area FGDC; if now lump-sum taxation collects the sum of money FGDH from consumers (in such a way as to make none of them worse off than under monopoly) and gives it to the monopolist, then relative to the monopoly solution the consumers have gained the area CDH, and the monopolist has gained the area CEH, a Pareto improvement relative to the initial monopoly situation. The potential surplus CDE, lost because of the lesser production of the monopolist, is called the *deadweight monopoly loss*.

Variations of consumer surplus correctly measure variations of utility only if one assumes a constant marginal utility of money, but the inefficiency exists even without this assumption, because the Pareto efficiency condition proved in ▶ Chap. 3, that all factors must have the same indirect utility in all uses, is violated. Consider labour employed in a competitive industry producing a prod-

12.10 · Monopoly

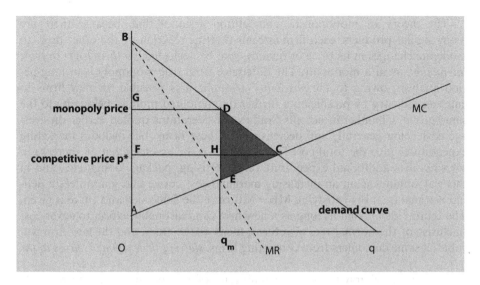

Fig. 12.8 Monopoly and Marshallian surplus: the potential (i.e. competitive) surplus is the triangle ABC, the reduction of production to q_m causes the loss of the triangle CDE. Consumers lose the area FCDG, the part FHDG of this area is transferred to the monopolist. The demand curve and the marginal cost curve are drawn as straight lines only for simplicity

uct C and having a marginal product MP_{LC}, and the same type of labour producing a product M in a monopoly firm where it has marginal product MP_{LM}. The wage is uniform. In the competitive industry $p_C = MC_C$ means $w = p_C \cdot MP_{LC}$ because cost minimization implies $MC_C = w/MP_{LC}$; the value marginal product or marginal revenue product of a unit of labour is $p_C \cdot MP_{LC}$. In the monopolistic firm too cost minimization implies $MC = w/MP_L$, but $p_M > MC_M$ means $w < p_M MP_{LM}$, hence $p_M MP_{LC} < p_M MP_{LM}$, the indirect marginal utility of labour (cf. ▶ Chap. 3) is higher in the monopolistic firm: hence moving a unit of labour from the competitive industry to the monopolistic firm would allow a Pareto improvement.

See the online Appendix to this chapter for a discussion of price discrimination and natural monopolies.

12.11 Monopolistic Competition Versus Full-Cost Pricing

Monopolistic competition is the name given by Chamberlin (1933) to the model of a market in which many firms produce differentiated products which are rather close substitutes, there is free entry, and the decisions of firms can be studied by assuming that each product (each firm, assuming one product per firm) faces a downward-sloping demand curve: a small rise in price does not cause a loss of *all* customers, so from this point of view the firm is similar to a monopolist (although the demand curve is rather elastic, because there are rather close substitutes for the firm's product).

The theory of monopolistic competition assumes that, because there are many similar products, each firm esteems that the reaction of the other firms to moderate changes in its price or quantity can be neglected, so *there isn't strategic interaction*, as in a monopoly. The difference from true monopoly is in long-period analysis, owing to the *possibility of entry*: it is possible for new firms to enter an industry by producing a further differentiated product belonging to the same group. Chamberlin accepts Sraffa's considerations quoted earlier on average cost being generally still decreasing for these firms, but includes marketing expenditures into the total cost function, that is, he assumes that an increase in sales requires additional expenditure on advertising, package design etc., and in this way obtains again an increasing marginal cost curve, that guarantees a definite optimal quantity satisfying $MR = MC$ once the firm's demand curve is given. The central idea is that as long as a new firm can reasonably expect to cover cost (inclusive of the normal rate of return), there will be entry, and the new firm will subtract some customers from competing firms, *shifting their demand curves to the left*.

The centre of gravitation, or equilibrium, of the industry[50] can be precisely characterized if one makes an assumption of *symmetry* both in costs and in demand curves for all firms in the industry. That is, assume that all products, if sold at the same price, are able to secure the same share of the total demand for products in that group, and that appearance of new products simply proportionately reduces the equal share of each product in total demand; furthermore, assume that all firms have the same cost curves, with initially decreasing average cost because of initial indivisibilities. Then entry will tend to eliminate profit: the equilibrium of the industry will consist of such a number of firms producing at such a scale, that all of them make zero profit, and are therefore in the situation depicted above in ◘ Fig. 12.7, of tangency between the demand curve faced by the individual firm, and its average cost curve (where it is still decreasing): hence zero profit, but price greater than marginal cost, and average cost greater than the minimum.

Of course this assumption of symmetry is only to obtain a clear image of the basic idea of the theory, which is that entry ends up bringing profit roughly to zero, except for the lucky producers of particularly appreciated varieties of the product, which are able to sell at a price somewhat above average cost (inclusive of marketing expenses) as long as no one is able to imitate the characteristics that make those varieties particularly liked.

Now let us compare monopolistic competition with the full-cost approach. In monopolistic competitive equilibrium, price is greater than marginal cost, and output is at a level where average total cost is still decreasing; so on these issues

---

50 Chamberlin avoided the term 'industry', preferring the term 'group', because of the traditional association of 'industry' with the production of a specified product. I think that 'industry' is still a useful notion, although more and more it must refer to connected products produced by multiproduct firms, e.g. generally toothpaste producers produce several types of toothpaste and also mouthwashes, toothbrushes, dental floss, shaving cream, aftershave lotions, etc.

12.11 · Monopolistic Competition Versus Full-Cost Pricing

the theory is in agreement with observation as much as the full-cost school of thought. But there are differences between the two approaches that are worth discussing.

First, monopolistic competition assumes absence of strategic interaction, that is, each firm neglects the fact that its decisions perturb the equilibrium of other firms and that their reaction will shift its own demand curve. This is generally implausible, there is always some product B more similar than others to a certain product A, and then the producer of A would be irrational to neglect the relevant dependence of its demand curve on the price of B. For example, the amount of advertising clearly is influenced by how much the more closely competing products are advertised. Full-cost theorists argue that firms are acutely aware of the possible reactions of competitors, so if strategic interdependence means oligopoly then the general industrial structure in manufacture is oligopoly; but the fear of entry or cross-entry pushes firms to a determinate behaviour all the same: the fixing of the normal price.

Second, monopolistic competition argues that firms decide quantity and price by setting $MR = MC$. Full-cost theorists categorically deny this, arguing that firms do not know the demand curve they face, and that in fact the notion of a decreasing demand curve facing the single firm must be rejected. On the basis of past experience and of whatever information is available on the industry, a would-be entrant attempts to calculate what its new product can hope to sell at a price comparable with that of similar products (of course when accompanied by a sufficient promotional campaign, whose amortization in the customary number of years enters the calculation of normal cost), and if this price comes out to be not less than the normal price with a plant adapted to that output, entry is decided; but this does not amount to determining a demand *curve* for the product, just a single quantity at a single price. To determine how much the product would sell at other prices is impossible because there isn't sufficient experience, so experimentation would be necessary, but (**a**) experimentation would require that the firm has already entered, so it cannot be part of the information on whose basis entry is decided; (**b**) the effect of price changes on demand would depend on the reaction of incumbent and potential competitors, which cannot be predicted with certainty: if the price is raised, one must expect at least some competitors not to raise their price, and furthermore one must expect the appearance of new nearly identical products if price rises (it is generally not difficult to imitate the important specifications of a product, e.g. to produce new models of lorries with performance similar to other models); and if the price is reduced, one can expect analogous reductions in the price of many similar products,[51] probably entailing nearly no change in the product's share in the total output of the category – which generally faces an inelastic demand. But all this is wrapped in uncertainty, and the economy changes. In conclusion, any dependence of quantity sold on price is too vague and too impermanent to be representable as a demand curve.

---

51 Or analogous increases in the marketing expenses of competitors if the product's price is not decreased but advertising or other marketing expenses are raised.

But without the demand curve there is no marginal revenue curve, so there is no way to reach $MR = MC$. This, it is argued by the full-cost theorists, also helps to explain another result emerging from interviews: that firms do not seem to know their marginal cost curve. They do not need it, so they make no attempt to calculate it; what they need is average cost.

Andrews and E. Brunner, in particular, insist forcefully on the role of actual or potential entry (see, e.g., Brunner 1975, pp. 22–23): if convenient, entry can generally be very quick, owing to *cross-entry* (term used to indicate an already existing firm that starts also producing products belonging to a different product group, e.g. a fashion-clothes firm that starts producing perfumes and cosmetics), and owing to the frequent possibility quickly to create products that nearly perfectly imitate the product sold at a particularly profitable price; and once entry has happened, it can cause significant earnings reduction for a long time to the firms previously dominating the industry. The pressure towards normal price thus created eliminates the indeterminacy that otherwise oligopoly would create (as discussed later in this chapter). Andrews indicated this result by coining the term 'competitive oligopoly'.

Entry pushes towards normal price also according to a different argument put forth by Harrod (1952). This is interesting, because at first Harrod fully accepted the theory of monopolistic competition, but later, as a member of the Oxford Economists Research Group, he was among the interviewers in the series of interviews to entrepreneurs then reported by Hall and Hitch (1939), and he changed his mind. In the 1952 paper he does not go so far as rejecting the theoretical notion of a demand curve facing the imperfectly competitive firm, but he admits that entrepreneurs do not know this curve: 'the great majority of entrepreneurs have scarcely any knowledge about the value of short-period marginal revenue. This applies even to those who conduct intensive market research. There appear to be few cases in which an entrepreneur could decide with confidence whether a drop in price of 10% would cause, other things being equal, an increase of sales of 10% or 15% or 20%' (Harrod 1952, pp. 153–4). These admissions imply that entrepreneurs cannot possibly determine output by setting $MR = MC$. But Harrod argues that even if they could, they would not, and would adopt what amounts to the full-cost solution. He notices that firms selling differentiated products can earn the normal rate of return in two ways: first, by fixing price where marginal revenue equals marginal cost, which is a price above minimum average cost, *in this way inviting entry*, and causing a leftward shift of the individual firm's demand curve up to tangency between demand curve and average cost curve as argued by the theory of monopolistic competition; second, by setting the product price directly equal to minimum average cost and thus discouraging entry; and he concludes that firms prefer the second case because it yields them a larger market, fewer competitors, and a much smaller danger of *further* entry, an always-present danger as long as price is above minimum average cost, which in the tangency case would cause losses to all firms until some firm dropped out.

These arguments of the full-cost school appear convincing. They agree, in many aspects, with the arguments advanced by Garegnani against the need for, and the possibility of, demand curves (see ▶ Sect. 5.32). They also agree with the arguments about variable capacity utilization and its macroimplications advanced in ▶ Sects. 12.3–12.5. More generally, the full-cost approach appears capable of explaining prices of differentiated products even if one does not allow enough time for entry to eliminate *all* less efficient firms because there is further innovation. Empirical evidence shows that firms want a rather quick amortization of initial expenditure on fixed plants and on new campaigns: in four-five years all debt must be repaid, longer delays imply too much risk of novelties, technical obsolescence, drastic changes in some input price, new laws, etcetera. This means that many firms that are a few years old need not worry any more about initial debt, so if they are able to maintain the same product prices as during the initial years they make fat profits; price reductions due to innovations may often not be able to push these firms out of the market for quite a few more years, even if they do not modernize.

The description of the effects of entry must be dynamical. There will generally be all the time some optimistic entrepreneurs attempting entry in a broadly defined industry, but if there is too much entry or capacity expansion some firms will not reach a sufficient level of sales and will exit. Successful entry attracts further entrants, too much entry increases exits, many exits discourage entry; so the gravitation of the industry's output towards effectual demand will operate not by reaching a point where entry stops, but rather via a continuing flow of entry that will tend to balance the flow of exits; with, however, new entrants often introducing better products or production methods, and hence obliging older firms to a gradual reduction of quasi-rents (unless they modernize, which is like a new entry).

To sum up: for the theory of value and distribution the important thing with respect to product markets is the *long-period* tendencies of relative prices and quantities; and these can be described as follows: because of active competition and entry, product prices tend to average cost (inclusive of normal marketing expenses), and quantities produced tend to adapt to *effectual demands* (the normal quantities demanded at those prices) even when products are differentiated. These tendencies need *free* competition, not *perfect* competition. On the existence of these long-period tendencies, there is little difference between classical-Keynesian and the *traditional* neoclassical approach. Relative to the Marshallian conception of competition and to monopolistic competition, full-cost pricing means less short-period price variations, and a choice of some excess productive capacity motivated by demand fluctuations rather than by tangency between demand curve and average cost curve,[52] but it does not appear incompatible with the long-period tendencies postulated by the traditional neoclassical approach: in an economy composed of full-cost firms and with free entry the neoclassical direct and indirect factor substitution mechanisms would be still operative in the long period, if the neoclassical conception of capital and of factor substitution were

---

52 So full-cost pricing entails less inefficiency due to underutilization of capacity than monopolistic competition, because excess capacity is due to a search for production flexibility which helps the economy's efficiency by making production capable of quick adaptation to demand variations.

acceptable: even full-cost firms would change factor proportions in favour of factors whose rental decreases, and relative consumption good prices would change with changes in income distribution. It can be concluded that traditional neoclassical theory too only needed classical free competition rather than perfect competition *in product markets*; it could admit time-consuming competitive rivalry, also operating via product differentiation. (In factor markets of course things are different, the neoclassical approach needs flexible factor rentals, which for labour markets the classical approach finds implausible.)

The real gulf between a classical and a neoclassical approach to competition in product markets arises when one moves to the *contemporary* neo-Walrasian approach to value and distribution. The latter approach, as explained in Chapter 8, cannot admit actual disequilibrium productions and exchange, otherwise the equilibrium itself is unpredictably modified by disequilibrium. Which explains the recourse to the fairy tale of the auctioneer-guided tâtonnement, from which the impression can be derived that *perfect* competition means total passivity, the *absence* of competition in the sense of the behaviours normally associated with 'to compete'. In the classical approach, the different determination of income distribution allows for true time-consuming dynamics, and for a conception of the competitive process well summarized in the following excerpt from an introductory economics textbook:

» ...as capitalists search for profits, competition drives them to change their operations almost continuously. This competitive scramble limits what any one capitalist can do, shapes what all capitalists are driven to do, and produces an enormous pressure for continual change in the capitalist economy as a whole.

This main idea is expressed in six main points:

1. Capitalists must compete for profits, and they do so by attempting to improve the determinants of their own profit rates. They are severely limited in what they can do, however, by the discipline of competition.
2. Competition among capitalists takes three principal forms: efforts to achieve a price advantage (*price competition*); efforts to create new situations in which potential competitors are at least temporarily left behind (*breakthroughs*); and efforts to eliminate competition (*monopoly power*).
3. For all three types of competition, firms must invest to compete. Investment is the primary way that firms achieve price advantages, breakthroughs, and monopoly power.
4. Because firms must invest to compete, competition is inherently dynamic. The process of competition among capitalists contains within itself powerful forces for change. This internal dynamic insistently changes every market situation even as competition occurs, and it imparts a powerful dynamic tendency to the economy as a whole.
5. The competitive scramble both continually generates new and divergent profit rates among firms and tends to equalize existing rates. Whether there is any overall equalization of profit rates depends on the balance between these opposing forces.

6. Competitive dynamics also lead to both economic concentration (large firms increasing their role in the economy) and the erosion of established positions of market power. Whether there is any continuing tendency toward economic concentration depends on the balance between these opposing forces.

(...............................)

Profit-making is a never-ending struggle by each firm to break out of the limits set by competition. The ensuing warfare among the combatants determines who the winners, and the losers, will be. (...) We need not wait until some external force disrupts the market – competition incessantly does that itself.

Moreover, this dynamic of competition continues *without an end or limit*. After all, the end of one period of competition is but the beginning of the next period. Those firms that fail to take advantage of every chance for growth will be outcompeted by other firms that will. There is no rest for the weary, nor even for the victors! (Bowles and Edwards 1985, pp. 128-9, 131)

The continual change correctly stressed by the authors does not mean that the idea that prices tend towards average costs loses validity. Strong confirmation comes from the fact that cost reductions provoke price reductions: think of computers, television sets, light bulbs. Technical progress may be fast, but competition and entry are fast too, and a product does not long remain priced much above average cost. The tendency of price towards average cost remains the explanation of why certain things persistently cost so much more than some other ones, for example why a medium-quality car costs the same as ten thousand ballpoint pens.

12.12 Duopoly

12.12.1 Cournot Duopoly

Now let me pass to other, more mainstream models developed for the study of imperfectly competitive markets *without entry*. These will be followed by a discussion of possible reasons for barriers to entry.

Let us start with models of *oligopoly*, Greek word for 'market with few sellers', in which the number of firms competing in the market is *given* (two—*duopoly*—in most models). Cases where there is little need to worry about possible further entrants can be easily conceived, although they are always somewhat special. For example, a tourist resort may attract too few tourists for more than two hotels to be profitable (account being taken of indivisibilities that make too small a hotel unfeasible); or entry may be impossible because it would require access to non-reproducible natural resources (springs, thermal baths, special personal abilities...[53]).

---

53 For example, two opera singers unanimously recognized as way superior to all others. Their agents can compete on how many performances per year to offer and at what price.

Initially let us leave aside competition through advertising, design, innovation. Assume competition can be only quantity competition, or price competition. Let us start with *quantity* competition for a *homogeneous* product. Assume that two or more producers supply amounts of the same good, and then 'the market' fixes the (uniform) price for all units of the good, that renders demand equal to total supply, on the basis of a given demand curve.

The nineteenth century French mathematician, Augustin Cournot (1801–1877), was the first formally to discuss such a situation, in a book, *Recherches sur les principes mathématiques de la théorie des richesses* (1838), which applied for the first time differential calculus to the theory of the firm, starting among other things the modern theory of monopoly. Here we are interested in his model of *duopoly*, in which two firms produce quantities q_1 and q_2 of two perfectly substitutable goods (mineral spring water of equivalent quality, in his example) with cost functions $C_1(q_1)$ and $C_2(q_2)$[54]; the price depends on total supply $Q=q_1+q_2$ according to a known downward-sloping inverse demand function $p(Q)$. There is no danger of entry of other firms. Cournot assumes that each firm decides how much to supply by taking as *given* the supply of the other firm, i.e. he assumes the existence of well-defined *reaction functions*

$$q_1 = f_1(q_2), q_2 = f_2(q_1)$$

that specify the *best response* of each firm to any supply of the other firm *treated as given*; Cournot assumes that each firm will indeed implement such best responses, then correcting them if it discovers that the quantity supplied by the other firm has changed. He then argues that the two firms will converge, through a process of repeated adjustments, to a situation in which neither has an incentive to alter its supply, i.e. such that $q_1 = f_1(f_2(q_1))$, which of course also implies $q_2 = f_2(f_1(q_2))$.

For firm i the profit function is $\pi_i = p(Q[=q_1+q_2])q_i - C_i(q_i)$, which must be maximized with respect to q_i. The reaction function is implicitly defined by how the optimal solution, determined by the first-order condition for profit maximization (assuming an interior solution), changes with the given output of the other firm, e.g. for firm 1:

$$[q_1 \cdot dp(Q)/dQ + p(Q)] - MC_1(q_1) = 0,$$

where $dp/dQ = dp/d(q_1+q_2) = dp/dq_1$, because q_2 is treated as given. The term in square brackets is the marginal revenue of firm 1; the equation is the familiar $MR=MC$. Once the functions $p(Q)$ and $MC_1(q_1)$ are given, one derives the *reaction function* of firm 1. For firm 1 the effect of its output on price when q_2 is given is shown by the market inverse demand curve shifted to the left by the amount q_2, or equivalently by a rightwards shift of the origin to q_2, see ◻ Fig. 12.9. Later we will show graphically the connection between reaction functions, and *isoprofit curves* in (q_2, q_1) space.

---

54 Cournot actually assumed zero cost but this makes no essential difference.

12.12 · Duopoly

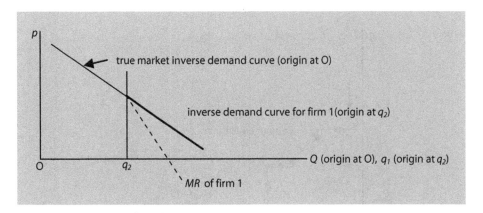

◘ **Fig. 12.9** Residual inverse demand curve for firm 1

For example if

$$p(Q) = a - bQ = a - bq_1 - bq_2$$

and if the marginal cost of firm 1 is a constant $c < a$, then the reaction function is

$$q_1 = f_1(q_2) = (a - bq_2 - c)/(2b),$$

a continuous linear function[55] with slope $-1/2$ and vertical intercept $a - c$ in (q_2, q_1) space (that is, with q_1 in *ordinate* because we are treating it as the dependent variable). In the same diagram we can also draw firm 2's reaction function, and if we assume that the firms are identical (*symmetric duopoly*), firm 2's reaction function has slope -2 in (q_2, q_1) space and the two reaction functions intersect: their intersection satisfies $q_1 = f_1(f_2(q_1))$ and is therefore the *Cournot equilibrium*.[56]

Cournot took it for granted that the equilibrium was unique, and saw it as reached through an iterative process in which firms take turns in adjusting the output to the output of the other firm treated as given. The successive steps of this iteration converge to the Cournot equilibrium if, with q_1 in ordinate, $f_1(q_2)$ is less steep than $f_2(q_1)$, see ◘ Fig. 12.10. In the symmetric duopoly case this slope condition is satisfied if, with q_1 in ordinate, the slope of $f_1(q_2)$ is negative and less than 1 in absolute value.

---

55 Actually this is the reaction function for $0 \leq q_2 \leq (a-c)/b$; it continues as $q_1 = 0$ for $q_2 > (a-c)/b$, where the condition $q_1 \cdot dp(Q)/dQ + p(Q) = c$ cannot be satisfied for non-negative values of q_1. Indeed the rigorous first-order condition is, $q_i \cdot dp(Q)/dQ + p(Q) \leq c$ with equality if $q_i > 0$.
56 **Exercise**: prove that, if both firms have zero marginal cost and demand is linear, then the Cournot outcome corresponds to each firm supplying 1/3 of the demand that would be forthcoming at price zero.

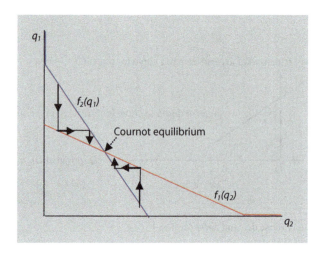

Fig. 12.10 Convergence to Cournot equilibrium

But in this process each firm repeatedly treats the output of the other firm as fixed, without learning from observation. Call it Cournot's *naive* adjustment process: it is not very plausible. Nowadays the usual justification of Cournot equilibrium is different, namely that it is a Nash equilibrium of the one-shot game in which the two firms *know* the two reaction functions and must decide in advance and simultaneously their output with no possibility to change it afterwards. The Cournot outcome is the (pure strategy) *Nash equilibrium* of this game, for this reason also called *Cournot-Nash equilibrium*.

To justify that the Nash equilibrium will be reached, one can assume hyper-rational reasoning plus the assumption that the Cournot naive adjustment process is stable. Assume that each entrepreneur, say, entrepreneur 1, reasons like this:

» I know my opponent's best response to each output of my firm, and I know she knows mine. So I can calculate the Nash outputs q_1^*, q_2^*. Now, my opponent cannot expect me to produce $q_1 \neq q_1^*$, because that would mean she expects me to expect her to produce the quantity $q_2 \neq q_2^*$ to which q_1 is a best response, which means she expects me to expect her to expect me to produce the quantity $q_1^\wedge$ to which q_2 is a best response, and this means she expects me to expect her to expect me to expect her to produce the quantity $q_2^\wedge$ to which $q_1^\wedge$ is a best response, and so on. Now, I see from the shape of reaction functions that the Cournot naive adjustment process is stable; then the path of quantities traced by my reasoning is divergent because it is just the reverse, so sooner or later it takes us to a negative output, which is impossible; so it is impossible to rationalize any expectation that I will produce $q_1 \neq q_1^*$, and therefore my opponent can only expect me to produce q_1^*, to which she will respond with q_2^*, so my best response is q_1^*.

This reasoning needs that the reaction functions are known; and furthermore that a Nash equilibrium exists, that it is unique, and that the Cournot naive adjustment process is stable. These conditions are not always satisfied.

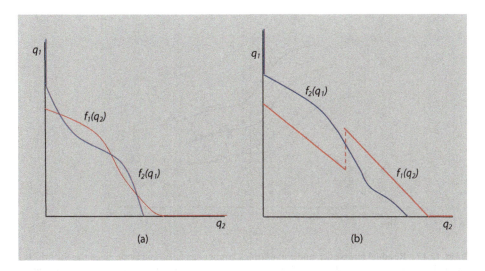

◘ **Fig. 12.11** Possible shapes of reaction curves

With more general inverse demand functions and marginal cost functions, reaction functions are generally not linear, can be considerably more elastic than in the above example, and can even have discontinuous jumps; so the cases shown in ◘ Fig. 12.11 are possible.[57] The literature studying these issues is advanced beyond our aims. I only give some intuition for the possibility of discontinuous reaction functions, with the help of a diagram, cf. ◘ Fig. 12.12.

Assume for simplicity that for both firms production is costless, and in a diagram with (q_1, p) on the axes draw a map of residual (inverse) demand curves faced by firm 1 for different given levels of q_2. In the same diagram draw a map of isoprofit curves for firm 1, which in this case coincide with isorevenue curves, i.e. are rectangular hyperbola. For each residual demand curve firm 1 chooses the point on it that touches the uppermost isoprofit curve. If the residual demand curves are straight lines, there is no problem, firm 1 chooses the midpoint. But if they are wiggly, the maximum-profit point on some residual demand curve may not be unique. Then as q_2 changes, and the residual demand curve shifts, the best response may change discontinuously, as shown by the red broken lines in ◘ Fig. 12.12. And we know from the Sonnenschein–Mantel–Debreu results that demand functions can have practically any shape.

---

57 If the reaction function of firm 1 is entirely above the other, the Cournot equilibrium has $q_2 = 0$, and q_1 equal to the monopoly amount; but the two reaction functions, if continuous, have nonetheless a point in common, because firm 2's reaction function continues upwards along the ordinate (i.e. with $q_2 = 0$) as q_1 increases beyond the level where q_2 becomes zero, so the vertical intercept of firm 1's reaction function is a point in common. The absence of a point in common requires a discontinuity. It has been proved, with numerical examples of general equilibria where the production side is a Cournot duopoly (Roberts and Sonnenschein 1977; Bonnisseau and Florig 2004), that there may be no Nash equilibrium even in mixed strategies.

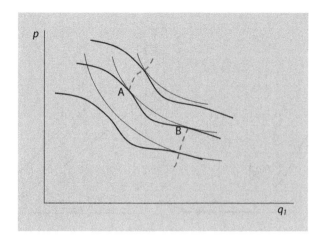

☐ **Fig. 12.12** Residual inverse demand curves (thick continuous lines) and isoprofit curves for firm 1. The path of best responses is the red broken line, downwards as q_2 increases, and with a discontinuity from A to B

Let us come to the assumption that reaction functions are known. In order to calculate them, each duopolist must know the market demand curve and the other duopolist's cost curve. In general, there seems to be no way to discover these curves except by *repeated* production and observation of the other firm's reaction and of how price changes with total supply. Thus *game theorists appear to make incompatible assumptions when in the Cournot duopoly model they assume complete knowledge and one-shot interaction*. So neither the Cournot naive adjustment nor the realization of the Cournot equilibrium as Nash equilibrium of a one-shot simultaneous game appear convincing; therefore the instances in which the Cournot equilibrium can be taken to correspond to what will be observed are still the object of discussion.

Cournot's analysis of duopoly can be interestingly extended to the case of *many firms*. With a given number of firms, the Nash equilibrium is the situation in which each firm's output is a best response to the other firms' total output, treated as given. Let q_{-i} stand for the aggregate supply of all firms except the i-th one, $q_{-i} = \sum_{k \neq i} q_k$; indicate the reaction function of the i-th firm as $f_i(q_{-i})$; the Nash equilibrium requires that for all i it is

$$q_i = f_i\left(\sum_{k \neq j} f_k(q-k)\right).$$

Let $p(Q)$ be the market inverse demand function and let $s_i = q_i/Q$ represent the *share* of firm i in total supply. The marginal revenue of firm i (with the outputs of the other firms treated as given) becomes, with ε the elasticity of market demand (a *negative* number):

$$MR_i = p + (dp/dq_i)q_i = p\left[1 + \frac{dp}{dq_i}\frac{q_i}{p}\right] = p\left[1 + \frac{dp}{dQ}\frac{Q}{p}\frac{q_i}{Q}\right] = p\left[1 - \frac{s_i}{|\varepsilon|}\right],$$

12.12 · Duopoly

where $dp/dq_i = dp/dQ$. Hence the condition $MR_i = MC_i$ implies that the difference between price and marginal cost is less than in the monopoly case, and is the smaller, the smaller the share of the firm in total supply. If the firms in the industry are all identical, the share of the firm is the reciprocal of the number N of firms, hence

$$MR_i = p(1 + 1/(N\varepsilon))$$

which tends to p as n grows large. Thus Cournot competition approaches the competitive result $p = MC$ as supply is divided among more and more similar firms.

For the symmetric case with furthermore all firms having the same constant marginal cost c, and assuming a linear inverse market demand function $p = a - bQ$, one can develop a very simple expression for how the deviation of price from marginal cost depends on the number of firms. Let there be N firms; then $Q = \sum_{k=1}^{N} q_k$. The profit of firm i is

$$\pi_i = pq_i - cq_i = \left(a - b\sum_{k=1}^{N} q_k\right)q_i - cq_i = a - b\left(\sum_{k \neq i} q_k\right)q_i - bq_i^2 - cq_i.$$

Its maximization with respect to q_i, treating all $q_{k \neq i}$ as given and taking into account how q_i affects p, requires as first-order condition:

$$a - 2bq_i - b\sum_{k \neq i} q_k - c = a - bq_i - b\sum_{k=1}^{N} q_k - c = 0.$$

In the Cournot-Nash equilibrium all firms must satisfy this condition, which can be rewritten as $bq_i = a - b\sum_{k=1}^{N} q_k - c$. This equality implies all q_k's must be the same: if two of them differed, the equality could not hold for both, because the right-hand side would be unchanged. Call q^* this uniform q_k, then the above equality becomes $bq^* = a - bNq^* - c$, which implies

$$q^* = \frac{a - c}{b(N + 1)}. \tag{12.4}$$

From $Q = Nq^*$ one easily derives, with p^* the Cournot-Nash equilibrium price:

$$p^* - c = \frac{a - c}{N + 1} > 0. \tag{12.5}$$

Thus $p^* > c$, but the difference decreases as N increases. These expressions hold for all N, even $N = 1$ (the monopoly case). The Cournot duopoly price is greater than the perfectly competitive price $p = c$, but smaller than the monopoly price ($N = 1$) which in this case is $p = (a + c)/2$, greater than c because $a > c$ by assumption. The single duopolist produces less, but the two duopolists produce more in total, $\frac{2}{3}\frac{(a-c)}{b}$, than the monopolist, who produces $\frac{1}{2}\frac{(a-c)}{b}$.

Admitting entry as long as there are profits, and a resulting decrease of the share of each firm, the tendential result is a price decrease as long as price is above minimum average cost, as in Marshallian partial-equilibrium long-period analysis.

1086   **Chapter 12 · Product Markets: Pricing, Capacity, Investment, Imperfect Competition**

12.12.2 **Conjectural Variations**

Back to the duopoly case without entry, the Cournot equilibrium has been criticized as assuming irrationality. Each firm finds its Cournot output optimal because it takes the output of the other firm as given. But a rational firm cannot ignore that if it changes its output the output of the other firm will change too, and its output optimization will take into account the expected reaction of the other firm. The optimal output of, say, firm 1, should be the solution, not of the problem $\max_{q_1} \pi_1(q_1, q_2)$ with q_2 treated as given, but instead of the problem

$$\max_{q_1} \pi_1(q_1, q_{2E}(q_1)),$$

where $q_{2E}(q_1)$ is the expected reaction, called **conjectural variation**, of firm 2's output to changes of q_1, or equivalently

$$\max_{q_1} q_1 p(Q^*) - c_1(q_1)$$

where $Q^* = q_1 + q_{2E}(q_1)$. This yields the first-order condition

$$p(Q^*) + q_1 \frac{dp}{dQ^*} \left(1 + \frac{dq_{2E}}{dq_1} \right) - MC_1(q_1) = 0 \tag{12.6}$$

The difference this makes can be seen by considering some possible conjectural variations. If firm 1 expects $\Delta q_2 = -\Delta q_1$ then it expects p not to change and finds it optimal to behave like a price-taking firm, i.e. as a perfectly competitive firm. If both firms have the same conjectural variation such that firm i expects $\Delta q_j / q_j = \Delta q_i / q_i$ (constant market shares) then in a symmetric duopoly with linear demand curve the first-order condition is the same as in a monopoly, and at the monopoly joint output (the collusive output)—half of it produced by each firm—no firm has an incentive to change its output (**Exercise**: confirm this conclusion).

The obvious question then is, which conjectural variation is plausible? No agreement has been reached on this issue. The approach then ends in indeterminacy.

12.12.3 **Stackelberg (Quantity Leadership)**

Suppose, as originally proposed by the Austrian economist Stackelberg in the 1930s, a Cournot duopoly except that firm 2, the *follower*, treats the output decided by the first firm as given, while firm 1, the *leader*, is conscious that its output decision influences the output decision of the second firm. The leader knows the market demand function and the reaction function of the second firm, and maximizes its profit by calculating what the quantity q_2 produced by the follower (and hence the market price) would be for each q_1. (One can see the Cournot model as assuming that both firms act as followers.) The leader's problem is

12.12 · Duopoly

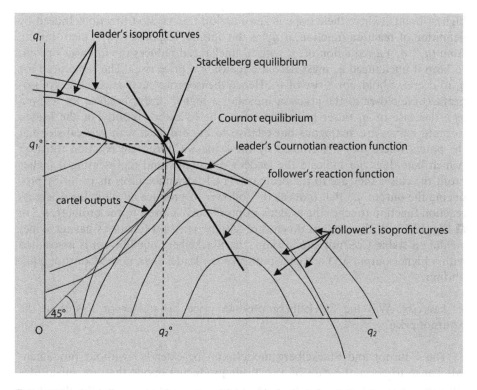

Fig. 12.13 Stackelberg versus Cournot equilibrium (the leader is firm 1, its output is in ordinate)

$$\max_{q_1} \pi_1(q_1) = p(q_1 + f_2(q_1))q_1 - c(q_1)$$

and the first-order condition is

$$p(Q) + p'(Q)(1 + f_2'(q_1))q_1 - MC_1 = 0.$$

This plus the first-order condition for the follower:

$$p(Q) + p'(Q)q_2 - MC_2 = 0$$

determines the two quantities. A graphical analysis helps to see the difference from the Cournot outcome.

In a diagram with q_2 in abscissa and q_1 in ordinate, see ◘ Fig. 12.13, assume linear best response functions, and draw isoprofit curves for the leader and for the follower. For the follower, isoprofit curves[58] are hill-shaped concave curves, whose

---

58 Careful: these isoprofit curves are in (q_2, q_1) space, differently from the isoprofit curves in ◘ Fig. 12.10 that are in (q_1, p) space.

highest points (where their slope is zero) are on the reaction function. Indeed by definition of reaction function, if $q_2^\wedge$ is the optimal response to $q_1^\wedge$, then starting from $(q_1^\wedge, q_2^\wedge)$ a reduction of q_2 with q_1 unchanged reduces the follower's profit; to keep it unchanged q_1 must decrease (causing a price rise). The same need for q_1 to decrease holds for a rise of q_2. Hence the isoprofit curve is concave. An isoprofit curve closer to the abscissa indicates a higher profit, because for a given q_2 a decrease of q_1 raises price and hence the follower's profit. For the leader, isoprofit curves are analogous but relative to the ordinate, with vertical slope at the points where they are crossed by the leader's Cournotian reaction function (which here does *not* indicate the leader's decisions), and representing a higher profit the closer they are to the ordinate. The leader maximizes its profit by producing the output q_1° that induces the follower to produce at the point where its reaction function touches the leader's isoprofit curve closest to the ordinate, q_2° in ◘ Fig. 12.13. With standard downward-sloping reaction functions having slopes yielding a stable Cournot equilibrium, the Stackelberg equilibrium is associated with a higher output and a higher profit for the leader than in the Cournot equilibrium.

Exercise: Will the Stackelberg product price be greater or less than the Cournot price?

The Cournot and Stackelberg models can be extended without fundamental change to cover the case of two firms producing goods that are substitutes but not perfect substitutes. The isoprofit curves still have the shape indicated, because if the quantity supplied of one product increases and as a result its price decreases, in order to sell a given quantity of the other product the latter's price must decrease (its inverse demand curve is shifted downwards).

The notion of Stackelberg leadership is perhaps applicable to those primary product markets where a single nation or a big cartel controls such a major share of the world production of the good (e.g. oil; diamonds) that the smaller independent producers feel they cannot influence its output decisions.

Stackelberg leadership can be useful to analyse entry problems. Suppose there is a single firm in a market, which produces the monopoly amount, and a second firm wonders whether to enter. Assume a linear demand function and that both firms have the same constant marginal cost. It can be shown (prove it as an *Exercise*) that if the monopolist decides to behave as a Stackelberg leader then it must continue to produce precisely the monopoly amount; then, barring price wars, the entrant must behave as a Stackelberg follower. If besides the variable cost the two firms have a fixed cost because of indivisibilities, it can be that the quantity the follower can expect to sell does not allow obtaining the normal rate of profit, so entry is blocked.

Of course Stackelberg leadership need not be accepted by the follower. If both firms produce as if they were Stackelberg leaders, total output considerably exceeds the Cournot amount, and the situation will not last, but how it will evolve is unclear.

12.12.4 Price Leadership

Another standard model assumes a homogeneous product produced by several firms, one of which is recognized by the others as price leader, perhaps because it has lower costs and could push the other firms out of the market if it so decided, but abstains from such a policy to avoid intervention of the Antitrust Authority. This dominant firm sets the price at a level that allows the other firms to survive, and the other firms accept that price and maximize profit as price-takers. These other firms, given in number, behave like Marshallian competitive firms that set $MC = p$ (and for this reason are collectively referred to as the *competitive fringe*) and are assumed to have upward-sloping supply curves. The price leader is assumed to know both the market demand curve, and the aggregate supply function of the competitive fringe, and determines its own residual demand curve by subtracting, at each price, the followers' supply from the market demand at that price. The leader maximizes profit by behaving like a monopolist facing that residual demand curve.

In ◘ Fig. 12.14 at each price the horizontal distance of the residual demand curve from the market demand curve equals the supply of the competitive fringe. At sufficiently low prices, the supply of the competitive fringe is zero and market demand and residual market demand coincide. The broken red line is the MR curve of the price leader derived from the residual demand curve; the leader's profit-maximizing output q^* is the one where $MR = MC$, with correspond-

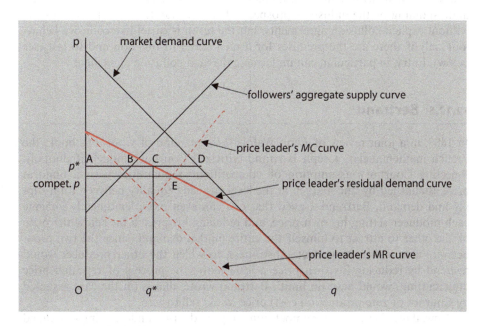

◘ **Fig. 12.14** Price leadership

ing price $p*$ that causes residual market demand to equal the leader's supply and therefore total demand to equal total supply (the competitive frige's supply AB is equal to segment CD by construction).

If the price leader were to set $MC=p$, it would produce where its MC curve crosses the residual demand curve (point E). Hence with price leadership, price is higher and output lower than in the competitive outcome. Thus, interestingly, the competitive fringe produces *more* than in the competitive outcome, but this is more than compensated by the price leader's restricted supply. Therefore, starting from a situation of generalized price taking, according to this model there is an incentive for any firm with a significant share of the market to try and take the role of price leader; since this raises the sales and profits of the followers too, the firm can expect not to encounter opposition; however, the aspiring price leader must be ready to restrict its output.

The analysis is only a short-period one for all industries where entry is possible: in the long period, free entry has the effect of making the competitive fringe's supply curve horizontal at the $p=minLAC$ level, undermining any advantage obtainable from price leadership.

A different kind of 'price leadership' consists of a firm announcing a rise in price (motivated, e.g., by a claimed rise in costs), and then waiting to see whether the competitors raise their price too; if they don't, after a while the first firm backtracks. Empirical evidence shows that this is not unusual; the firm proposing the price increase is not always the same (**barometric leadership**) although it is always a firm with a significant share of the market and reputation of good understanding of the industry's prospects. This is a way for firms to co-ordinate without explicit collusion agreements; but the result is cartel-like collusive behaviour only if there are the premises for a tacit cartel to function and to last (see below). Entry, in particular, can undermine the tacit collusion agreement.

12.12.5 Bertrand

In 1883, in a joint review of Léon Walras' *Eléments* and of Cournot's book, the French mathematician Joseph Bertrand criticized Cournot's model of duopoly. Rejecting Cournot's assumption of competition in quantities with a uniform price established by 'the market' at the level ensuring equality between total supply and demand, Bertrand argued that one can even more legitimately imagine each producer setting his own price, and reducing his price a bit below the price of the other to attract to himself the entire market demand (since the two products are assumed to be perfect substitutes), to which the other producer would respond by reducing his own price a little more; the process of repeated price undercutting 'would have no limit', Bertrand wrote, that is (in the case assumed by Cournot of zero production cost) price would fall to zero.

Nowadays this type of competition—repeated price undercutting—is called **Bertrand competition**; again the dynamic story is found implausible because there is no learning, and it is found preferable to describe the situation as a one-shot game, in which the price equal to marginal cost is the sole Nash equilibrium.

12.12 · Duopoly

To prove this statement, let us describe the assumptions in greater detail. There are two identical price-*making* firms with same constant marginal cost c and zero fixed cost. The firms find it convenient to produce as long as revenue covers cost. The two products are perfect substitutes, and each firm is capable of supplying the entire demand forthcoming at $p=c$. The demand curve $Q(p)$ is downward-sloping, at $p=c$ demand is positive and finite, it becomes zero for a finite sufficiently high price. If the two prices are unequal, demand goes entirely to the lower-price firm. If the two prices are equal, each firm gets half the demand: this usual assumption can be justified as describing the average result if consumers choose the supplier randomly. Each firm must set its price before knowing the other firm's price, and cannot change it afterwards. Then, if price is a continuous variable, *the sole Nash equilibrium in pure strategies is $p=c$.*

Proof

(i) $p_1=c<p_2$ cannot be a Nash equilibrium because firm 1 can earn a greater revenue by choosing $c<p_1<p_2$; the same holds for $p_2=c<p_1$;

(ii) $c<p_1<p_2$ cannot be a Nash strategy because firm 2's revenue is zero, while it would earn a positive revenue (and in excess of variable cost) by setting $p_2=p_1-\varepsilon$ with ε the smallest difference necessary to induce consumers to switch to firm 2; the same holds for $c<p_2<p_1$; indeed the best response to $p_i>c$ is $p_j=p_i-\varepsilon>c$;

(iii) $p_i<c$ cannot be part of a Nash equilibrium because at such a price firm i finds it convenient not to produce, but the other firm's best response to this is to fix the monopoly price which by assumption is greater than c, and the best response to this $p_j>c$ cannot be a $p_i<c$ because step (i) showed that a p_i such that $c<p_i<p_j$ is possible and it yields a revenue more than covering variable cost;

(iv) hence $p_1 \neq p_2$ cannot be a Nash equilibrium; if there exists a Nash equilibrium it must be $p_1=p_2 \geq c$; but $p_1=p_2>c$ is not a Nash equilibrium because each firm can, by lowering its price just a little bit, attract the entire demand and thus increase its profits; hence $p_1=p_2=c$ is the sole Nash equilibrium, called *Bertrand-Nash equilibrium.*[59] ∎

This proof is restricted to pure strategies; in fact the Bertrand-Nash equilibrium remains the sole Nash equilibrium even when one permits mixed strategies; the (long) proof is supplied in a section in the online Appendix to this chapter.

---

59 If price is not a perfectly continuous variable, being only divisible down to a smallest unit ε (or if ε is the smallest price difference that induces buyers to prefer a supplier to other suppliers), then $p_1=p_2=c+\varepsilon$ is another Nash equilibrium: if one firm charges $c+\varepsilon$, for the other it is not convenient to charge $p=c$ because it would make zero profit; if one firm charges $p=c$ the other firm is indifferent between charging $p=c$ or $p=c+\varepsilon$, because if $p_1=c$ and $p_2=c+\varepsilon$, firm 2 sells nothing and makes zero profit, but charging $p_2=c$ would mean zero profit too; since there is a possibility that, for the same reason, firm 1 may charge $p_1=c+\varepsilon$, firm 2 finds it preferable to charge $p_2=c+\varepsilon$ (it is a weakly dominant strategy); on the basis of the same reasoning, firm 1 too will charge the same price, hence, although $p_1=p_2=c$ is also a Nash equilibrium, the Nash equilibrium that one can expect to be established is $p_1=p_2=c+\varepsilon$.

A positive production when profit (neoclassical meaning) is zero is not absurd, because zero profit means revenue sufficient to pay costs inclusive of the normal rate of return on capital, therefore sufficient to induce production as much as in the usual analysis of long-period Marshallian competitive equilibrium, which too concludes to zero profit. So if there are no fixed costs the conclusion is that *Bertrand behaviour brings about the competitive price, equal to marginal cost, even with only two firms.*

The conclusion is not disturbed by assuming increasing marginal cost but I omit the proof.

A problem arises if there is a fixed cost: a price equal to marginal cost need not cover fixed cost (it certainly does not, if marginal cost is constant). If at the Bertrand equilibrium profit is negative, one cannot expect Bertrand behaviour. Indeed, as already noticed, Marshall stressed that entrepreneurs have high in their mind the need not to 'spoil the market', that is, not to start price wars that might be ruinous for all contenders. Or to put it differently, even in the short period entrepreneurs want price not to fall below the level needed to satisfy the long-period financing needs of the firm (except temporarily for clear reasons common to all competitors and therefore not interpretable as war declarations). Crotty (2002), mentioning Schumpeter, has stressed the same view and has termed **co-respective competition** the competition that avoids means susceptible of bringing contenders to bankruptcy. People know that price undercutting risks eliciting the same behaviour from their competitors, with potentially disastrous results, and avoid it.[60] This is a main reason in support of full-cost pricing.

12.12.6 Bertrand-Edgeworth

In oligopoly theory, results relevantly depend on the precise assumptions made. For example, capacity constraints coupled with Bertrand competition (i.e. with each firm treating the price set by the other firm as given) can cause the non-existence of a Nash equilibrium (in pure strategies).

Suppose a linear market demand curve for a product produced by two identical producers A and B with zero costs and with fixed productive capacity.[61] If price is uniform, each firm receives half the market demand. Draw symmetrically on the two sides of the ordinate the inverse demand curve facing each duopolist *if price is uniform*, hence each curve indicates *half* the market demand when price is uniform: DD_A is the curve facing duopolist A and DD_B the curve facing duopolist B, see $\blacksquare$ Fig. 12.15. Let $OA' < OD_A$ indicate the maximum quantity duopolist

---

60 Of course sometimes a firm does choose to start a price war, usually because it counts on winning it, and remaining for some time a monopolist, which will allow it to more than make up for the losses. Let me remember that **predatory pricing** is the name used for pricing at a level that would be unsustainable in the long run, in order to push competitors out of the market.

61 I follow the presentation in Marrama (1968, p. 321).

12.12 · Duopoly

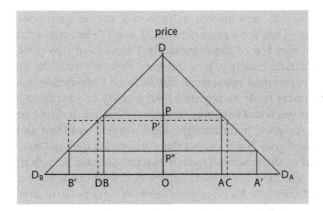

◘ **Fig. 12.15** Bertrand-edgeworth oligopoly

A can produce, and OB' (equal to OA') the analogous maximum quantity producible by duopolist B; these maximum quantities are less than half total demand at a zero price, but more than one quarter this total demand.

Price P is the monopoly price, with total demand one half of maximum total demand, and demands OA and OB (equal to 1/4 of total demand if price is zero) going to each firm if they collusively set that price. If there is no collusive agreement, then if one firm, say A, sets price at P then firm B, which by assumption treats the other price as given, finds it convenient slightly to undercut, setting price at $P' = P-\varepsilon$, which causes the demand for B's output to be DC which is a bit more than half the zero-price total demand. By assumption firm B can only produce OB' < DC; but by selling OB' at price P' which is only very little less than P it obtains a clearly greater revenue than at the collusive solution. Now it is firm A that finds it convenient slightly to undercut; to which B will respond with a further slight price decrease, and so on. The process of price undercutting cannot bring the price below P'' which if uniform allows both firms to sell their maximum production: if, say, firm B sets price at P'', at this price firm A sells its maximum output and therefore a lower price would not allow it to sell a greater quantity and would only cause a decrease of revenue.

But P'' cannot be an equilibrium common price, because now either firm, say A, can conclude that if it leaves firm B to produce OB' and sell it at price P'', there will be so many rationed customers ready to pay a higher price, that A can raise its price and sell enough to earn more than by accepting price P'' and selling OA'. This result can be reached in several ways, depending on what one assumes about which customers are rationed. To reduce complications I make a simple assumption: each demander demands only one unit of the good, differing from other demanders only in reservation price; for example six consumers are ready to pay up to 100 dollars for one unit of the good, two more (eight in total) are ready to pay up to 99 dollars, four more (twelve in total) are ready to pay up to 98 dollars, and so on; suppose also that if the demand that B satisfies at price P'' is a fraction α of total demand at that price, then satisfied demanders are sufficiently randomly drawn that they include a fraction α of the would-be demanders at each higher price. Then for a price between D and P″ the rationed demanders will demand the fraction $1-\alpha$ of the original total demand at that price. That is, continuing the numerical example, if at price P″<90 only half the market demand is satisfied, then rationed consumers will include 3 consumers ready to pay up to 100; 4 consumers ready to pay up to 99; 6 ready to pay up to 98; and so on. This is called *proportional rationing*; it implies that the residual inverse demand curve for firm A's good maintains the same vertical intercept D as the market demand curve and goes down steeper than the market demand curve,[62] indicating a demand equal to the fraction $(1-\alpha)$ of market demand at each price as long as A's price is not less than B's price (jumping discontinuously to coincide with the market demand curve as A's price goes below B's price). If firm B fixes its price at P″ it satisfies half the market demand at that price, so $\alpha=1/2$, for prices from D to P″ the residual demand curve facing A is half the market demand at those prices and therefore coincides with the DD_A curve; then the optimal price for A is the monopoly price P, which yields A a greater revenue than the revenue at price P″ (which is what firm B is earning).

But if A fixes the price at P, B finds it again convenient to raise the price to P′. So we are back where we started, and the price undercutting process starts again. There is no price couple where both firms have no incentive to change price.

Ysidro Edgeworth, the first one to analyse such a situation, concluded that the price would endlessly oscillate ("or rather will vibrate irregularly", Edgeworth wrote) between P and P″. Nowadays this dynamical interpretation is again found doubtful, because based on repetition without learning: as with Bertrand, the expectation that the other firm keeps its price unchanged is disappointed at every step. But the interpretation of Bertrand-Edgeworth competition as a one-shot game doesn't help either, since it has no pure strategy equilibrium. Actually the game has a mixed-strategy equilibrium (I omit the proof), but it seems even harder than for pure strategies to find a real-life equivalent of a *mixed*-strategy equilibrium for duopoly interactions analysed as *one-shot* games. In real life, interaction is *repeated* and one-shot games appear inappropriate. For example, if one tries to visualize the situation of two hotels in a small tourist resort where there is not enough tourism for three hotels, the repetition of interaction will likely allow developing a *modus vivendi* that will avoid price wars: perhaps collusion, perhaps co-respective competition with some differentiation that reduces competition for the same type of customers.

12.12.7 Capacity Constraints and Bertrand Competition

See the online Appendix to this chapter for a presentation of the argument advanced by Kreps and Scheinkman (1984) that if the two firms must first

---

62 And steeper than the DD_A curve if $\alpha>1/2$, which will be the case if the price of firm B is greater than P''.

12.12 · Duopoly

simultaneously choose a rigid capacity level, and then engage in Bertrand competition (a two-stages dynamic game), then there is a Nash equilibrium, that consists of the two firms choosing a plant with the Cournot quantity as capacity (i.e. maximum production), and then accepting the Cournot price and producing the Cournot quantities (that is, fully utilizing capacity). The presentation will also explain the notion of *efficient rationing*.

12.12.8 Differentiated Products and Bertrand Versus Cournot Competition

Consider a duopoly with no need to worry about entry, where the two products are substitutes but not perfect substitutes, and demand for each product depends on both prices (an example could be the two hotels mentioned earlier). Assume a constant marginal cost c for both firms, and the simple symmetrical linear demand functions

$$q_1 = 1 - p_1 + ap_2$$
$$q_2 = 1 + ap_1 - p_2.$$

Assume $0 < a < 1$, which means that the two products are substitutes, and that the own price effect is stronger than the cross price effect. This system of equations can be inverted to yield the prices equalizing supply and demand as functions of the quantities supplied:

$$p_1 = \alpha - \beta q_1 - \gamma q_2$$
$$p_2 = \alpha - \gamma q_1 - \beta q_2$$

where as the reader can check, $\alpha = (1 + a)/(1 - a^2)$, $\beta = 1/(1 - a^2)$, $\gamma = a/(1 - a^2)$, and $\beta > \gamma$.

With Cournot competition, firm 1 treats q_2 as given and maximizes

$$\pi_1 = (p_1 - c)q_1 = (\alpha - \beta q_1 - \gamma q_2 - c)q_1$$

with respect to q_1. The first-order condition is $\alpha - 2\beta q_1 - \gamma q_2 = c$ which, solving for q_1, yields the reaction function

$$q_1 = (\alpha - c - \gamma q_2)/(2\beta).$$

Its slope is $-\gamma/(2\beta) = -a/2$. Because of the symmetry assumption, the reaction function of firm 2 is the same with q_1 and q_2 interchanged. Hence there is a unique Nash equilibrium at

$$q_1 = q_2 = (\alpha - c)/(2\beta + \gamma) = \left(1 + a - c + ca^2\right)/(a + 2)$$

and the Cournot price is

$$p_C = \left[1 + c\left(1 - a^2\right)\right]/[(2 + a)(1 - a)].$$

With Bertrand competition, firm 1 maximizes

$$\pi_1 = (p_1 - c)q_1 = (p_1 - c)(1 - p_1 + ap_2)$$

with respect to p_1, treating p_2 as given. Now profit is a continuous function of p_1. The first-order condition is $1 - 2p_1 + ap_2 + c = 0$ which yields the price-reaction function:

$$p_1 = 1/2 \cdot (1 + c + ap_2).$$

The slope is now positive, and <1; and for $p_2 = 0$, $p_1 > 0$. Hence the symmetrical reaction functions cross at the unique Nash equilibrium price p_B:

$$p_B = p_1 = p_2 = (1 + c)/(2 - a)$$
$$q_1 = q_2 = [(1 - c(1 - a)]/(2 - a).$$

A dynamic naive process of repeated Bertrand adjustment of one price in reaction to change of the other price will be convergent (draw the diagram). In order to compare the Cournot price solution with the Bertrand solution, if $c > 0$ we can normalize prices by dividing all prices by c, so we obtain $c = 1$; then the expressions for prices simplify to

$$p_C = (2 - a^2)/(1 - a)$$
$$p_B = 2/(2 - a)$$

and by multiplying both by $(1 - a)(2 - a)$ and simplifying, one proves $p_C > p_B$ for $a > 0$: price competition brings to a lower price than quantity competition. The reason is that with Cournot competition a firm expects price, and hence the other firm's price, to decrease if it increases output; with Bertrand competition the other firm's price is treated as fixed, and therefore the expected gain in sales from a lower own price is greater, i.e. the incentive to reduce price is greater. Also interesting is that $p_B > 1$ if $a > 0$, i.e. $p_B > c$ since we have put $c = 1$. Thus, with differentiated products, Bertrand competition does not bring price down to marginal cost.

Of course we are dealing now with price-making firms, administered prices, so if one accepts full-cost pricing as the most plausible pricing theory for this situation, an excess of price over marginal cost is no surprise, it is indeed necessary in order to cover fixed costs.

12.12.9 Price Matching and the Kinked Demand Curve

An expectation of response by other firms to price changes, that reduces the risk of 'spoiling the market', and is supported by considerable empirical evidence, is that managers expect rival firms to *match* any price reduction susceptible of significantly affecting their sales. This strategy has advantages: it considerably decreases the attractiveness of price reductions for any single firm, while avoiding an indefinite war of price undercutting that might cause firms to go bankrupt.

Let us analyse the implications of price matching in a symmetric duopoly with product homogeneity. Let us suppose that if, starting from a situation of

12.12 · Duopoly

equal price, either firm changes its price, the other firm follows. What will happen? Under an equal sharing assumption, if the market demand curve is known, each firm receives one half the market demand, hence the two firms are like a cartel, and they maximize their profit where MC=MR, the marginal revenue being derived from a demand curve which is one half the market demand curve. If they are good at estimating the market demand curve and are certain that the other firm will match the price, the price will be the monopoly price.

However, the empirical evidence is that managers are often certain that price *reductions* will be matched, but are far less certain that price *rises* will be matched. Indeed a popular theory in the 1940s was the *kinked demand curve*, which assumes that a price reduction by a single firm will be matched, but a price rise will *not*. Hall and Hitch argued on the basis of their interviews that it was the normal case. A possible reason is that the other firms may want to profit for a while of the possibility to sell more. Another possible reason is an estimate that a general price rise is not advantageous for the industry (that is, that the price is already at the joint monopoly level). Another possible reason is not to encourage entry of new rivals who, once in, will not easily abandon the industry.

The kinked demand curve can help explain why a (moderate) shift of the demand curve need not alter price: in ◘ Fig. 12.16 the reader can check that a moderate rightward shift of the common-price demand curve with the kink at an unchanged price would still have the MC curve pass through the discontinuity at the kink quantity, so there is no incentive to change price.

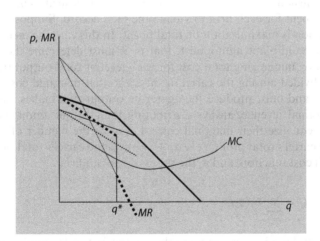

◘ **Fig. 12.16** Kinked (inverse) demand curve. The steeper portion is a common-price demand curve, it shows demand for the firm if all firms charge the same price. At the quantity q^* where the firm's demand curve (heavy continuous line) has a kink, the marginal revenue curve (the heavy dotted lines) has a discontinuity. If the *MC* curve passes through the discontinuity, the firm finds it optimal to produce q^*. At a different price (charged by all firms) the same situation can easily hold, so price must be explained on the basis of other considerations. A moderate shift of the demand curve maintains the *MC* curve inside the discontinuity, and then there is no incentive to change price, the kink can remain at the previous price

1098 Chapter 12 · Product Markets: Pricing, Capacity, Investment, Imperfect Competition

The price-matching behaviour of other firms if price is decreased can explain why Bertrand behaviour is not observed, but it does not explain at which level the price is fixed and the kink occurs. In the long period, the answer is entry.

12.13 Repeated Interaction, Cartels, Tacit Collusion, Folk Theorems

You don't need open agreements for collusion to be established. Willingness to collude can usually be signalled fairly easily if there are few firms in a market. Consider a duopoly with two firms A and B. The CEO of firm A can announce in an interview that high fixed costs and research expenses oblige the firm to fix a higher price for its product, starting in a week's time. Then firm A waits for firm B's reaction. If firm B does not announce in its turn an analogous price increase, firm A can cancel the announced price increase. This type of behaviour has been frequently observed (see *barometric leadership* in ▶ Sect. 12.12.4). It is difficult for anti-trust authorities to intervene against such procedures. In theory, an analogous behaviour is possible with output competition too; but generally it is more difficult to justify in advance an output decrease than a price increase. Firm A would have to actually reduce output below the Cournot output and accept a profit reduction during the interval before firm B responds, so it is more likely that the way to suggest a collusive increase in price and reduction in output takes the form of an announcement of a price increase.

If tacit collusion is possible, won't it be always established? The nag is that it may be convenient for each firm to violate the tacit accord. Suppose the purpose of tacit collusion is maximization of total profit. In this case the tacit cartel must behave like a multi-plant monopolist, that is, it must determine the cartel total cost function by minimizing total cost for each level of total output (total output must be subdivided among the cartel members so that marginal cost is the same for all firms), and must produce the aggregate output that makes marginal cost equal to marginal revenue, always distributing total output among cartel members so as to equalize their marginal costs. Let m be the number of firms in the cartel, Π the cartel's total profit, $Q = q_1 + \ldots + q_m$ the cartel's total output, $C_i(q_i)$ the i-th firm's cost function, and π_i the profit of the i-th firm:

$$\Pi = p(Q) \cdot Q - \sum_{i=1}^{m} C_i(q_i).$$

Maximizing total profit with respect to the q_i's, the first-order conditions are

$$\partial \Pi / \partial q_i = \left(\frac{dp}{dQ} \right) \cdot Q + p - MC_i(q_i) = 0, \quad i = 1, \ldots, m. \tag{12.7}$$

Suppose p is left to the market's determination. If at the cartel's optimum a single firm, say firm 1, is the sole one to increase its output, its profit increases, because:

12.13 · Repeated Interaction, Cartels, Tacit Collusion, Folk Theorems

$$\frac{\partial \pi_1}{\partial q_1} = \frac{\partial (pq_1 - C_1(q_1))}{\partial q_1} = \frac{dp}{dQ}q_1 + p - MC_1 = \frac{dp}{dQ}(Q - q_2 - \dots - q_m) + p - MC_1$$

$$= (\frac{dp}{dQ}Q + p - MC_1) - \frac{dp}{dQ}(q_2 + \dots + q_m) = -\frac{dp}{dQ}(q_2 + \dots + q_m) > 0.$$

$$(12.8)$$

(I have used condition (12.7) and the fact that $dp/dQ < 0$.) That is, if all other firms respect the cartel's pact, firm 1 has an incentive to violate it and produce more.

If on the other hand firms are price makers, then for each firm, since marginal cost is less than price, it is more convenient (Bertrand!) to sell at a price slightly lower than the cartel price (for example by offering secret discounts to some buyers) if it expects the other firms not to do the same. In both cases firms have an incentive to violate the collusive pact.

However, if a firm deviates and this is discovered, it is highly likely that the other firms in the cartel will change their behaviour too, in a direction that, intentionally or not, will punish the first firm. For example there may be a return to Cournot or to Bertrand behaviour, with a fall in profit for all firms. If conscious of this likely outcome, each firm will think twice before deviating, and it may well conclude that the best strategy is not to deviate. The formalization of the situation as a game must admit repeated interaction, hence must use the insights of the theory of repeated games.

Remember that one does not need the certainty of an infinite repetition of the stage game in order for the theory of infinitely repeated games to be applicable, one only needs that there is a probability not too far from 1 that there will be a next repetition; then the expected value of future payoffs is obtained by using a discount factor that includes not only the agent's preference for present income but also this probability. And the game is formally analogous to an infinitely repeated game with a discount factor.

So let us assume the firms in the cartel are in an infinitely repeated game; each firm must compare the profit from adopting collusive behaviour, with the profit from deviating. The latter profit will be initially higher than the collusive profit, but then it will decrease owing to the abandonment of collusive behaviour by the other firms. The result will often be that it is convenient not to deviate. I will only study one special case, a symmetric duopoly with price the strategic variable.

Both firms have constant marginal cost c, are capable of supplying the entire demand forthcoming at $p = c$, have a discount factor $\delta < 1$, and attempt to maximize the discounted value of profits $\sum_{t=1}^{\infty} \delta^{t-1} \pi_{it}$ with $i = 1, 2$. The δ can be interpreted as embodying both time preference, and the probability that repetition of the interaction will occur and future profits with it. If the firms charge the same price they share equally the forthcoming demand. Assume that the strategies considered by the firms are *Nash reversion strategies* of the following form, where price $p^\wedge$ will be further specified later:

Nash Reversion Strategy: $p_{it} = p^\wedge$ *if t is the first period* $(t = 1)$ *or if in all previous periods both firms have always charged* $p_1 = p_2 = p^\wedge$;
$p_{it} = c$ *otherwise.*

Thus the first period a firm adopting this strategy charges $p^\wedge$ and continues to do so in subsequent periods if the other firm has charged $p^\wedge$ in all previous periods. The term *Nash reversion strategy* indicates that if the cooperative strategy is not adhered to by some agent in some period, from the next period on and for ever firms revert to the Bertrand-Nash equilibrium strategy, which in this case is $p = c$. Now let us assume firms know the collusive optimal price that we indicate as p^{mon} because it coincides with the monopoly price. Then we have the following result, for which I supply the lengthy proof because it contains the indication of when it is convenient to collude:

*A **Bertrand folk theorem***: (*I*) *In the infinitely repeated symmetric Bertrand duopoly game without capacity constraints, when $\delta \geq \frac{1}{2}$ if both firms adopt the same Nash reversion strategy with the common price $p^\wedge \in [c, p^{mon}]$ then this couple of strategies is a subgame perfect Nash equilibrium path.* (II) *If $\delta < \frac{1}{2}$, the sole subgame perfect Nash equilibrium path has $p_1 = p_2 = c$ every period.*

Proof Part (I) of the theorem: If both firms adopt the same Nash reversion strategy, they will both charge $p^\wedge$ every period, but subgame perfection requires us to prove in addition that after any series of prices charged in previous periods, that is wherever the firms can be in the game tree when period t is reached, the strategies specified for that period and for the remainder of the game constitute a Nash equilibrium of the subgame that starts at t. The latter subgame is again an infinitely repeated Bertrand game. There are only two situations to consider, the one where in the previous period one price was not $p^\wedge$, and the one where both prices were $p^\wedge$ in all previous periods. Call the occurrence of a price different from $p^\wedge$ a *deviation*. The payoffs (to be discounted if in the future) are the profits per period.

If a deviation has occurred, the reversion strategy requires each firm to charge $p = c$ in t and in all subsequent periods. This is a Nash equilibrium because if a firm charges a price equal to c, the other firm cannot obtain a greater payoff than by setting its price equal to c (i.e. zero profit). If no deviation has occurred, the question is whether it is in the interest of a firm to comply with the strategy of charging $p = p^\wedge$ in every period if the other firm complies (if the answer were negative, the strategy would not be credible). We must compare the payoff from not deviating, with the payoff from being the sole one to deviate (that is, to charge a price less than $p^\wedge$: charging a price greater than $p^\wedge$ cannot be convenient). Let market demand be $q(p)$. If a firm deviates at time t, in that period it gets all the demand and earns a payoff which—by making the deviation extremely small— can be made as close as one wishes to $(p^\wedge - c)q(p^\wedge)$; but that is the sole payoff from deviating, because from $t+1$ on, it earns a zero payoff because the other firm charges $p = c$. If the firm does not deviate, its payoff is $1/2(p^\wedge - c)q(p^\wedge)$ per period from period t onwards for an infinite number of periods, which yields a value, discounted to t at the discount factor δ, equal to $[1/2 \, (p^\wedge - c)q(p^\wedge)]/(1 - \delta)$. This is more convenient than deviating if and only if $\delta \geq 1/2$ (the greater convenience is also there if $\delta = 1/2$ because the payoff from deviating is *less* than $(p^\wedge - c)q(p^\wedge)$, albeit by an arbitrarily small amount).

12.13 · Repeated Interaction, Cartels, Tacit Collusion, Folk Theorems

Part II): The proof of this part of the theorem, i.e. that if $\delta < \frac{1}{2}$ then the sole SPNE is $p = c$ always, is more involved (I follow the proof of Mas-Colell et al. 1995, p. 403, correcting a couple of misprints). Let π_t stand for the total payoff earned by the two firms in period t, $\pi_t = \pi_{1t} + \pi_{2t}$. Define $v_{it} \equiv \sum_{\tau \geq t}^{\infty} \delta^{\tau - t} \pi_{i\tau}$ as the value of payoffs obtained from period t onwards, discounted to period t, if the equilibrium strategies are played from period t onwards. The starting point of the proof is that, since we are looking for a SPNE, in every period $t \geq 1$ it must be

$$v_{it} \geq \pi_t, i = 1, 2, \text{ for all } t. \tag{12.9}$$

This is because if the discounted value of present and future profits of firm i were less than π_t, the firm would prefer to obtain a payoff arbitrarily close to π_t by deviating and slightly undercutting the lowest price in the market in period t, and then earning a zero payoff in all following periods; hence (12.9) is necessarily satisfied by optimal strategies. On this basis we can prove that if $\delta < 1/2$ the assumption, that there exists at least one period t in which $\pi_t > 0$, generates a contradiction. We must distinguish two cases. First case: suppose that there is a period T with $\pi_T > 0$ such that $\pi_T \geq \pi_t$ for all t. Then (12.9) implies that for $t = T$ it is $2\pi_T \leq (v_{1T} + v_{2T})$. But this is impossible if $\delta < 1/2$ because the definition of v_{it} implies $v_{1T} + v_{2T} = \sum_{\tau \geq t} \delta^{\tau - t}(\pi_1 \tau + \pi_{2\tau}) = \sum_{\tau \geq t} \delta^{\tau - t} \pi_\tau \leq \pi_T/(1 - \delta)$ and therefore if $\delta < 1/2$ and $\pi_T > 0$ it is $v_{1T} + v_{2T} < 2\pi_T$. Second case: there is no period T with $\pi_T > 0$ such that $\pi_T \geq \pi_t$ for all t. Then for any period t there is another period $T > t$ such that $\pi_T > \pi_t$. Define $T(t)$ recursively as the function yielding, for each date $t \geq 1$, the first date T after t such that $\pi_T > \pi_\tau$ for $1 \leq \tau \leq t$. The infinite sequence $\{\pi_{T(t)}\}$ that starts at $t = 1$ (but any other starting date would do) is monotonically strictly increasing and is bounded above by the maximum achievable payoff, the monopoly payoff level $\pi^{mon} \equiv (p^{mon} - c)q(p^{mon})$; hence it must converge to some $\pi^+ \in (0, \pi^{mon}]$ such that $\pi^+ > \pi_t$, all t. Hence it must be $v_{1T(t)} + v_{2T(t)} \leq \pi^+/(1 - \delta)$; but (12.9) implies $2\pi_{T(t)} \leq v_{1T(t)} + v_{2T(t)}$ for all t; hence it must be $2\pi_{T(t)} \leq \pi^+/(1 - \delta)$, which for $\delta < 1/2$ becomes impossible for t sufficiently large. ∎

Three observations are suggested by this result.

First, now we can discuss the price $p^\wedge$: it can be any price in the closed interval having the competitive price and the monopoly price as extremes. Other considerations must be brought in to reach a more determinate result.

Second, the critical value 1/2 for the discount factor comes from the number of firms in the market, two. With $n > 2$ identical firms in the market, and if it is assumed that, if the firms charge the same price $p^\wedge$, each one sells $q(p^\wedge)/n$, then the cooperative payoff per period is $\frac{1}{n}(p^\wedge - c)q(p^\wedge)$ instead of $1/2(p^\wedge c)q(p^\wedge)$, and the above proof carries through with the sole difference that now $\delta \geq 1/2$ is replaced by $\delta \geq (n - 1)/n$. Sustaining a cooperative payoff in the Bertrand repeated game becomes the more difficult, the more firms there are; with $\delta = 90\%$ there cannot be more than 10 firms.

Third, I have assumed that the deviation payoff lasts one period. If it lasts two periods, profit from deviating is $(1 + \delta)(p^\wedge - c)q(p^\wedge)$, and the convenience to collude requires $\delta^2 \geq 1/2$, more restrictive. Conversely, if the reaction to a deviation is very quick, say a few days, the profit from deviating is insignificant, and collusion is easier to sustain.

This last remark helps us to understand the frequent persuasion among managers of oligopolistic firms that if they lower their price, their rivals will *quickly* match the price reduction. This type of 'punitive' strategy has the advantage for the 'punishing' firms, relative to Nash reversion, that their variable profits do not fall to zero. Of course the 'punishment' is small for the deviating firm too; but since the increase in profits due to the deviation lasts very little, even a small decrease in subsequent profits relative to the non-deviation profits may well suffice to make the deviation not convenient.

In the quick survey of models of oligopoly of this and the preceding section a recurring conclusion was indeterminateness of results except under rather implausible assumptions. Furthermore in all these models the assumption of absence of entry is not easy to justify. Let us then discuss entry a bit more; it can be argued considerably to reduce, or even eliminate, the indeterminateness.

12.14 Entry

The empirical evidence shows strong irregularities and unpredictability of short-period behaviour of prices. For example, price wars or advertising wars between two firms do happen, and they start for non-generalizable reasons and last for lengths that vary greatly from case to case. But if one looks for broad trends, then entry is a very powerful equalizer. If investment in the production of a good offers prospects of yielding a higher rate of return than elsewhere, the likelihood that new producers will enter the industry is very high. The result is an increase in the industry's productive capacity and in the number of firms, and in all likelihood a price decrease, also because in order to conquer a sufficient share of the market in all likelihood a new entrant will charge a lower price (or will offer other advantages to customers), even up to suffering losses initially, and then the established firms will have to reduce price too—or entry will continue.

Entry is a very powerful and active mechanism in capitalist economies. It explains the observation (see ▶ Chap. 10) that differences among rates of return are usually confined within a range which is remarkably narrow. Entry is a main cause of dissolution of tacit collusion and of cartels, and of the scarcity of true monopolistic behaviour. As Schumpeter wrote: 'Outside the field of public utilities, the position of a single seller can in general be conquered—and retained for decades—only on the condition that he does not behave like a monopolist.' Some economists have argued that modern 'monopoly capitalism' is different from 19th-century capitalism owing to the much greater and growing presence of very large firms, which is argued to imply that the economy is becoming less and less competitive. But there is a powerful counterargument: although in many industries the minimum size necessary for successful entry has considerably increased, the number of giant conglomerate firms has in turn increased, capable of setting up a new firm (controlled by them) of the required minimum size in whatever industry one is considering: the capitals that a firm like Exxon or Nestle or Toyota or Walmart can mobilize would be sufficient to enter *any* industry. If this entry does not happen, the reason must be that it is not convenient because the rate of

12.14 · Entry

return obtainable by a new entrant in that industry is not greater than the one obtainable elsewhere. Accordingly, it can be argued that the pressure of actual or potential competition towards a roughly equal rate of return in different industries is *more* powerful today than in the nineteenth century (one possible exception, Internet industries with network externalities, is discussed in ▶ Chap. 14).

However, economists have long admitted that one cannot expect a tendency towards *complete* equalization of profit rates. Adam Smith recognized two causes of persistent differences in profit rates even with no obstacle to entry: 'the agreeableness or disagreeableness of the business, and the risk or security with which it is attended' (WN, Bk I, Ch. X, p. 99). But there are other reasons too, connected with *barriers to entry* that differ as between different fields of investment. A barrier to entry is anything that causes a new entrant in a trade to have higher average cost than established firms, thus allowing established firms to have profits in excess of normal profits without attracting entry. A useful classification distinguishes three broad groups of barriers: legal, economic and intentional.

Legal barriers to entry are exclusive concessions, patents, trade marks, copyrights. However, in this case a correct definition of profits would show that the rate of return need not be higher than the average. A patent guaranteeing exclusive exploitation of a superior production method, or a concession allowing exclusive access to an input (for example a toll bridge), is analogous to a property right on more fertile land; competition for the right to use that land causes differential rent to absorb any excess of profit over normal profit; analogously, the excess of profit over normal profit of a firm owning a patent should be considered differential rent earned by the owner of the patent, analytically to be distinguished from the profit of the firm as such, and to be included among the firm's costs, in the same way as one includes opportunity-cost rent among the costs in order to determine the profit of an agricultural firm that owns some of the land it uses. The same reasoning applies to politically granted exclusive concessions.

Economic barriers to entry are economies of scale, initial entry costs, knowledge barriers, dynamic advantages of established firms due to learning-by-doing.

Economies of scale are very important and have many causes.

A first technological cause of economies of scale is that the cost of containers increases less than in proportion with carrying capacity, at least until they become so big as to need special reinforcing structures. If one doubles the dimensions of a tank, the surface of its walls (hence the material needed for making the tank) quadruples, the volume becomes eight times the original one. Engineers have a rough 2/3 rule that says that costs can be expected to increase as 2/3 of carrying capacity. Here is the reason why sea gas tankers tend to be big. A similar reason causes costs per passenger to be lower, up to a limit, the bigger the airplane; however, big airplanes are only convenient if they fly nearly full, and this explains the smaller size of airplanes on less frequented routes.

A second technological cause is technical *indivisibilities*. Often, mechanization and automation can permit drastic reductions of average cost, but only for bigger production levels than when using simpler tools. Scherer and Ross (1990, p. 97) cite the case of ball bearings, where automated computer-controlled production achieves a reduction of average cost of 30–50% relative to medium-volume batch methods, but requires production levels around one million units a year of a single bearing design. They add that 'the crew needed to operate a large processing unit or machine is often little or no larger than what is required for a unit of smaller capacity, so labor costs per unit fall sharply with scale-up' (ibid. p. 100): an example is that both small and big tractors or small and big buses need one driver. This observation, based on indivisibilities of tasks or of human beings, can be extended: especially in small and medium-sized firms, savings in overhead labour costs can be substantial with increases in size, because the number of managers, accountants, receptionists, security guards, etc. need not increase with output, or not in proportion.

A third technological cause is *scale economies in distribution*, due to the smaller unit cost of bulk transport, and to smaller transport costs if production is so large that it can be split among several plants in different locations, which decreases the average distance from buyers.

A fourth cause which is technological and economic at the same time is the possibility of increasing the *division of labour* within the firm, which generally entails a decrease of the required skills and hence lower average wages.

A fifth cause is the possibility to obtain *discounts* from input suppliers: bigger orders give the supplying firms greater financial security as well as the possibility to obtain in their own turn reductions in average cost for the reasons already listed, and so can often obtain discounts.

A sixth cause is *cheaper access to credit* for bigger firms. Empirical evidence that borrowing, be it directly from banks or by issuing publicly traded bonds, costs bigger firms lower interest rates than it costs smaller firms. One reason is that transaction costs for these operations do not increase in proportion with the size of borrowing; another reason is that bigger firms generally produce many different products, and this spreads risk. Also, a firm producing a product in many different plants, perhaps located in different nations, is less likely to suffer a general production stoppage due to strikes or fires. *Very* big firms offer the additional security of being so important that one can expect government support for them in difficult times.

A seventh cause is that a given sum spent on *advertising* is a smaller percentage of unit cost the greater the number of units sold. A firm with ten times the sales of another firm that produces an equivalent product with the same productive efficiency can afford ten times the amount of advertising without having a higher advertising-inclusive average cost. And advertising does generally work. (For space reasons advertising is discussed in a section in the online Appendix to this chapter.)

An eighth cause, relevant above all for durable goods, is the ease with which customers can obtain *after-sale services* of revision, repair, refund etc., which is the greater, the greater the diffusion of the product (it is more difficult to find a nearby mechanic familiar with rare cars). These services are usually provided by other firms, so their price probably decreases with their volume because of economies of scale in the servicing firms, but even if their price were fixed the greater ease with obtaining them would make the product more attractive, and the producing big firm, knowing this advantage of its product relative to competing products, can sell it at a slightly higher price.

The list might be lengthened, but the message is clear: economies of scale are extremely important, and determine a minimum efficient size of firms which is often far from negligible. This means that often a new entrant in an industry cannot neglect the impact that its entry is going to have on supply, and hence on price or on probable reactions of established firms. However, it would seem that this impact, although not negligible, is seldom so strong as to discourage entry. If one leaves aside the natural-monopoly infrastructures (road systems, railways, water pipes, electricity and telephone cable networks) and network externalities, one finds that minimum average-cost-minimizing plant scale is almost never more than 6% of the market in the USA or Europe, generally much less (Scherer and Ross 1990, p. 115, find only one industry, refrigerators, where minimum efficient scale is above 6% of its USA market, at 14%; for the majority of other ones minimum efficient scale is 3% or less of the market). Also, only in industries where minimum efficient scale is less than 3% of the market does a reduction of production to one-third of minimum efficient scale raise average cost by more than 5% above its minimum. It must also be noted that a 5% increase in average cost can be highly significant for products that are perfect substitutes, but much less so for differentiated products, the much more general case: for these, a moderate price rise only causes a moderate reduction of sales. True, these data do not consider the advantages of bigger size in transport costs, commercial relations, credit cost, advertising and servicing, but these advantages do not appear to be so enormous as to prevent entry with diversified products: even rather small firms can often find profitable niches for specific products, for example very special cars, high-quality radios, different soft drinks; from this basis these small firms sometimes succeed in expanding to other products, exploiting the good reputation acquired with the first successful product. Even leaving small niche firms aside, Scherer et al. (1975) find that in only three of the twelve industries examined (refrigerators, brewing and perhaps cigarettes) the full exploitation of all the scale economies we have considered would clearly imply an oligopolistic industry structure, with the biggest *four* firms having more than 40% of the industry market in the USA. Since then, increasing international competition suggests that even in those industries entry would not be difficult.

Still another, and often very important, barrier to entry is the need for *intensive initial marketing effort* to make the new firm known, to build a favourable image, to persuade retailers to stock its products, to build a servicing network. These are sunk costs, necessary to start activity; they explain why, when demand for an industry's product expands, most of the expansion of productive capacity usually comes from already established firms. However, entry can be due to already existing firms that expand to nearby fields of activity (it is called **cross-entry**), and then this barrier is less relevant, because the entering firm already has a credit standing and an image: an example is Honda expanding from only motorcycles to automobiles too. For some products a big obstacle for a new entrant can be the limited capacity of retailers to stock many brands: for example small cafes have to choose which soft drinks to stock, and if they can stock only one cola drink they will generally not choose a little known brand, but either Coca-Cola or Pepsi; this reinforces the advantage of the more widely demanded brand.

Then there are cost disadvantages of new entrants due to their being *latecomers*. These are of two types. First, experience with producing a product is known to result in learning-by-doing, often consisting of informal know-how and organizational methods not easily transferable to other firms because embodied in specific workers' skills and team coordination methods; after some time this effect peters out, but generally for two–three years the learning-by-doing effect is quite significant; and in modern manufacture with differentiated products and continuous product innovation, product runs are seldom longer than a few years. Second, many firms keep the production methods that give them a quality or cost advantage at least partly secret; the trouble with patenting is that one discloses the invention and this may make it easier to develop competing inventions. To persuade technicians from established firms to pass their knowledge to a new firm can be very costly. For these reasons a new entrant, unless it can utilize some innovation or other cost advantage (e.g. in labour costs, because located in a nation where wages are lower), will have higher average costs or lower quality than long-established firms for a considerable period.

These considerations have given birth to the **infant industry** argument: newly industrializing nations must be protectionist for some decades, to allow firms to be born and learn how to lower costs and improve quality without initially having to stand the competition of the more experienced producers of advanced nations.

Intentional barriers to entry are all forms of discouragements of entry resulting from intentional choices by established firms, consciously directed to such an end.

I leave aside the discouragements consisting of illegal threats of violence, which are common in the criminal economy but appear to be an exception in the legal economy.

Other intentional barriers to entry are: threats of a price war or of a marketing-efforts war (or of a capacity war, see below) against new entrants; levels of established productive capacity chosen so as to cause expectations in the potential entrants of such a supply increase and price fall by the established firm after entry as to make entry unprofitable; brand proliferation; threats of legal attacks.

Brand proliferation consists of the same firm producing many varieties of a product, e.g. deodorants with different scents; it is a normal competitive weapon that aims at making it more difficult for competitors to be given room for their products on shelves in shops; as a side effect, it also discourages entry.

The *threat of lawsuits* against the entrant (e.g. for violation of patents, imitation of design), even if the lawsuit is most probably destined to be defeated, can nonetheless be effective because the lawsuit could be unbearably costly for the entrant, and could raise the cost of borrowing for the entrant because of the risk increase.

Excess capacity has been explored by game theorists as a way incumbent firms can signal to potential entrants that the incumbent firm is ready to increase supply, in case of entry of a competing firm, so as to cause price to fall to a level that causes losses to the entrant. This type of threat has been formally analysed in a famous contribution by Dixit (1980), which proved with the use of game theory and a Cournot approach that an incumbent firm, by choosing a capacity level in excess of the optimal one when it is the sole firm in the market, can credibly commit itself to producing such a high quantity in case a second firm enters, as to make entry not convenient. The basic intuition is that 'the incumbent commits to producing at least as much as the initial capacity it installs because to produce any less amounts to throwing away some of that investment, which is costly' (Pepall et al. 2008, p. 280). The quite complex Dixit model is not presented here because its Cournot approach, that is the assumption that the two firms leave the price of the common product to be fixed by the market on the basis of the two firms' joint output and of the market demand curve, is unconvincing. Nothing obliges either firm to avoid price competition; the firm with the lower minimum average cost can subtract demand from the other firm by fixing a price equal to average cost; the other firm cannot compete if it does not want to incur in losses. Then what is really relevant is whether there are strong increasing returns to scale and the incumbent firm is so large that, in order to resist price competition, the entrant would have to build a very large plant too, such that demand would be insufficient at a price covering fixed costs. The most likely result of entry would then be a price war (or a marketing-efforts war), both firms would suffer losses until one of the two exits, and the winner would not necessarily be the firm with the lowest average cost but rather the firm with greater capacity to resist a period of losses. But apart from natural monopolies (studied in the online Appendix to this chapter), there seems to be no industry where increasing returns to scale are so significant as to make entry practically impossible except at a scale that can only cause a price war. Let us also remember that entry can be cross-entry by conglomerates or anyway large firms with solid financial backing behind them. So entry prevention via excess capacity is not plausible unless accompanied by cost advantages: but then it is not the incumbent's excess capacity but its capacity to reduce price without incurring losses that discourages potential entrants. More plausibly, excess capacity of the established firms discourages entry *motivated by demand expansion*: the established firm, strong of its goodwill advantages and of its excess capacity, will satisfy a continuing demand increase for a long time without difficulty, in the meanwhile preparing a further capacity expansion; so the demand increase does not make entry by other firms look attractive. But this is so only as long as the established firm keeps price close to minimum average cost, otherwise entry *will* look attractive.

Increasing returns to scale and a limited market can allow a different 'productive capacity war' with advantages for the firm better able to tolerate temporary losses. In the town of Edmonton, Alberta, in the 1960s one firm initially owned all supermarkets, and wanted to prevent entry by other firms. When entry started to happen, simplifying a bit this firm acted as follows: the town was expanding, but whenever a new supermarket was opened up by another firm in a newly developed area, the first firm opened up a new supermarket just next to it. Supermarkets cannot be very small, they need a minimum amount of sales to be profitable. Since location is an important factor in the choice of where to go shopping, and nearby areas were already well served by other supermarkets, the two new supermarkets could not attract customers from a large enough area, and there was not enough custom for both supermarkets to be profitable. The first firm could absorb

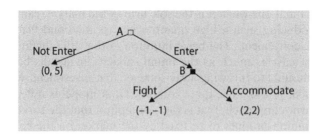

◘ **Fig. 12.17** Stage game of Selten's chain-store paradox

the losses because it owned already many other profitable supermarkets, but a new firm owning only one or two supermarkets could not, and exited. The Canadian antitrust authority recognized this behaviour as *predatory capacity expansion* although there was no *predatory pricing*, and forbade the first firm from opening up further supermarkets. Of course an even bigger firm (based in another town or region) could have resisted the capacity war; but this does not mean the intervention of the antitrust authority was unwarranted, a concern to defend the right of efficient but smaller firms to be born appears to deserve approval.

It is often difficult in real circumstances to reach clear-cut conclusions on the likelihood of being able to discourage entry, even leaving antitrust interventions aside. An example is the **chain-store paradox** (Selten 1978). Imagine a chain food store with 20 stores in as many different small towns. The owner realizes that in each town there is potential entry by a single competitor, and as each of these competitors takes time to raise the necessary capital, entry will be attempted in succession in the several towns. The owner must decide whether to fight or accommodate each attempted entry. She publicly announces that she will fight entry to the bitter end in each town. In each town the game has payoffs as in ◘ Fig. 12.17, with the payoffs of the local potential entrant A given first, while B is the local already established store. In each stage game of this repeated game, the subgame perfect Nash equilibrium is (Enter, Accommodate): if the potential entrant could be persuaded that the established store will keep the promise and choose Fight in case of entry, there would be no entry, but if the stage game is considered in isolation the threat is not credible. However, if by choosing Fight in the first and perhaps second stage game the chain-store owner is able to persuade future entrants that she will indeed fight entry, the loss in these initial stage games will be more than compensated by the avoidance of further entry.

But, Selten notes, repeated backward induction shows that the only subgame perfect Nash equilibrium of the entire repeated game is the repetition of (Enter, Accommodate) twenty times. This is because in the twentieth stage game there is no further entrant to be discouraged, so the threat is not credible: if entry happens B will choose Accommodate. Then backward induction proceeds as in finitely repeated Prisoner's Dilemma games. At any stage game in the succession of repetitions, backward induction shows that if A enters B will accommodate, independently of what happened in the previous stage games.

Selten speaks of paradox because the practice of an aggressive, *predatory* behaviour by the established firm looks like being unable to persuade successive potential entrants that it will continue to be adopted, independently of how many times it has been adopted already. And yet, after observing B fighting the first and the second time, would you enter?

In the discussion of repeated backward induction in ▶ Chap. 11 it was noted that its conclusions are not always persuasive. Furthermore, it is often not clear that the number of possible repetitions is given and known: the future is not known, a reputation of sticking by one's declarations might be useful to the firm in the future, so 'fight' might be chosen even in the twentieth stage game.

Examples of entry-prevention games were supplied in ▶ Chap. 11. As often with game-theoretic formalizations, a potential entry situation must be enormously simplified in order to be analysable as a game, so these games can only afford some initial insights. In particular, the capacity of the potential entrant to resist an initial period of losses seems fundamental, and it can depend on many different elements.

Anyway anti-trust authorities considerably limit the possibility of active entry-prevention strategies. But we have no time for more detailed discussion of the issue. The interested reader is invited to consult the chapters on predatory pricing in industrial organization textbooks.

12.15 Conclusions

It seems possible to conclude that barriers to entry do exist, but (except for natural monopolies) are unable to maintain significant differences in profit rates for a long time. Then entry allows us to reduce the indeterminateness we found in the analyses of oligopoly.

Cournot: In the cases in which quantity is the strategic variable and for a given number of firms the Cournot equilibrium is plausible, if the Cournot price allows extra profits (account being taken also of indivisibilities of fixed plant and of the connected fixed costs) entry will cause the number of firms to increase, and will stop when one more entrant at the minimum efficient size would cause a Cournot price below minimum average cost. That is, Cournot behaviour plus some fixed costs plus entry produce essentially the same tendency of price towards minimum average cost as standard long-period Marshallian analysis. It seems possible to conclude that, as long as minimum efficient scale is not very large relative to the industry's demand, the traditional conclusion that price tends to minimum long-period average cost remains valid even with Cournot behaviour.

Bertrand: The homogeneous-product Bertrand-Nash duopoly equilibrium (with each firm capable of supplying the entire demand) is implausible as a result of a one-shot game, and if one admits, as one must, repeated interaction one obtains indeterminacy owing to the folk theorem. A previous choice of capacity brings to a determinate result only under very restrictive assumptions (Kreps and Scheinkman, discussed in the online Appendix), among them that capacity is extremely rigid, which is generally not the case in real economies; but above all, there is no reason why the possibility to choose capacity and enter should be there for only two firms; the moment we admit entry, the tendency of the number of firms to increase if price is above average cost means that the probability of being undercut by some present or future competitor is very high. So Bertrand behaviour does not disturb the long-period prediction of a price determined by average cost.

Collusion: free entry makes the maintaining of collusion more difficult, because it is difficult to persuade each new entrant to join the cartel and the established members to accept the added member, each time renegotiating the cartel accord with all members. Strong support comes from the German experience: most of the thousands of German cartels formed between 1873 and 1933 collapsed quickly, often after only a few months of operation, and the reason was that 'if they succeeded in raising prices, new firms entered the industry, operating as outsiders, which led to a decline in sales by the cartel members; the cartel collapsed and a price war set in' (Voigt 1962, pp. 171–72, as quoted in Scherer, 1980, p. 242).

Kinked demand curve: the reactions postulated by this approach are very plausible, but the price at which the demand curve has the kink, that is to say, the ruling price, is not explained by the approach. Entry supplies the answer: the price will be the one that guarantees the normal rate of return on capital, otherwise there will be changes in industry supply via changes in the number and/or dimension of firms.

The conclusion is close at hand: product differentiation and economies of scale seem unable to prevent the tendency of product prices towards minimum average costs. Barriers to entry can exist but should not be overestimated, there are now such big conglomerates that they could create firms successfully entering even in fields requiring a very large minimum scale. Coca-Cola and Pepsi-Cola would probably see their joint domination seriously questioned if the price of their soft drinks rose to levels guaranteeing a rate of profit considerably higher than the average. And anyway if barriers to entry are such as to establish persistent differences in profit rate, price theory can treat the differences in profit rate as given, and price theory is little affected for questions like the effect of changes of real wages on the average rate of profit, or the effects of technical progress on prices. Network externalities (briefly discussed in ▶ Chap. 14) can cause exceptions, but these are precisely exceptions, deserving intervention much like natural monopolies. As a starting point, the old idea that product prices are fundamentally determined by cost of production seems still the best one.

12.16 Review Questions and Exercises

Review Questions
1. How can one motivate the decisions of entrepreneurs to plan firm size so as to have some excess capacity?
2. Prove that if all input costs are independent of whether the input is used in a day shift or a night shift, in weekdays or in holidays, then for firms that use

12.16 · Review Questions and Exercises

durable capital goods it would be cost-minimizing to produce 24 h a day, all days.

3. Explain why an over-normal utilization of capacity can improve profits for a firm in the short period.
4. Explain the argument that, in a partial-equilibrium framework, monopoly causes Pareto inefficiency.
5. Explain Harrod's criticism of the theory of monopolistic competition.
6. Explain why the frequent opinion that perfect competition means total passivity (i.e. no active competition) can be attributed to the shift of neoclassical theory to neo-Walrasian versions. Connect with the discussion of price taking and perfect competition in ▶ Chap. 5, in particular remember Arrow on the impossibility of perfect competition outside equilibrium.
7. Cournot duopoly. Prove that, if both firms have zero marginal cost and demand is linear, then the Cournot outcome corresponds to each firm supplying 1/3 of the demand that would be forthcoming at price zero.
8. Explain the notion of conjectural variation.
9. Show that firms in Bertrand competition have convenience in differentiating their products.
10. Illustrate the possible instability of Bertrand competition if there are capacity constraints.
11. Explain the difference between efficient rationing and proportional rationing.
12. Illustrate how the theory of repeated games can help understand the conditions for stable cartels.
13. Illustrate brand proliferation as a barrier to entry.
14. Discuss the criticisms of the theory that more profits stimulate investment.
15. Explain the importance of innovation for investment.
16. The derivation of the standard interest-elastic investment function from the traditional marginalist demand-for-capital function requires an assumption that labour is fully employed. Explain why without that assumption investment is indeterminate even accepting the demand-for-capital function.
17. Discuss increasing returns to scale as a possible barrier to entry.
18. Illustrate how entry eliminates indeterminacies otherwise resulting from imperfections of competition.
19. Full-cost pricing does not need the marginal revenue curve. This can be argued to be an advantage, why?

■ **Exercises**

1 to 4. In the Text.

5. Prove that if the inverse demand curve is a straight line with vertical intercept P, the monopolist will never set price below P/2.
6. Using the device of ▢ Fig. 12.3, derive the MR curve from an inverse demand curve which is the non-negative portion of a circumference centred in the origin. Where does MR become zero?

1112   **Chapter 12** · Product Markets: Pricing, Capacity, Investment, Imperfect Competition

7. Prove graphically, using the device of ◼ Fig. 12.3, that a downward-sloping differentiable inverse demand curve need not imply an everywhere decreasing marginal revenue curve. (Hint: let the inverse demand curve have at a certain point a rapid decrease in absolute slope as q increases, which renders it almost horizontal for a short stretch.)

8. Prove that $d^2MR(q)/dq^2 < 0$ if $q = A/p^{|\varepsilon|}$ and $|\varepsilon| > 1$, and conclude that in this case profit as a function of q is concave if marginal cost is convex.

9. Prove that **Lerner's index of monopoly power** $[p(q^*) - MC(q^*)]/p(q^*)$, the percentage excess of price over marginal cost relative to price, equals $1/|\varepsilon|$.

10. The condition for the successive steps of the Cournot iteration to converge to the Cournot equilibrium in the symmetric duopoly case is that, with q_1 in ordinate, $f_1(q_2)$ is less steep than $f_2(q_1)$, see ◼ Fig. 12.8. Prove that this condition is satisfied if, with q_1 in ordinate, the demand curve is linear and marginal cost is constant, and the slope of $f_1(q_2)$ is negative and less than 1 in absolute value.

11. Confirm that in a symmetric duopoly with linear demand curve if both firms have the same conjectural variation such that firm i expects $\Delta q_j/q_j = \Delta q_i/q_i$ (constant market shares) then the first-order condition is the same as in a monopoly, and at the monopoly joint output (the collusive output)—half of it produced by each firm—no firm has an incentive to change its output.

12. Will the Stackelberg product price be greater or less than the Cournot price?

13. A monopolist is unable to stop entry by another firm. Prove that if the monopolist decides to behave as a Stackelberg leader then it must continue to produce precisely the monopoly amount.

14. (Based on online Appendix, ▶ Sect. 12.3) A monopolist faces the inverse demand curve influenced by advertising $p = 20-q/A^{1/2}$, $c = 12$, $e = 1$; use the two FOCs to find the optimal A; check that the Dorfman-Steiner condition is satisfied at the optimum and indicate the advertising-to-sales ratio that satisfies it. (R. $A = 64$; 1/8.)(Hint: set $A^{1/2} = b$ and solve first for b.)

15. (Based on online Appendix, ▶ Sect. 12.1) Assume price discrimination between two categories of buyers, linear inverse demand curves in both markets: $p_1 = a_1 - b_1 x_1$, $p_2 = a_2 - b_2 x_2$, and a constant marginal cost, and prove that in this case the profit-maximizing combined output is the same as the output when the monopolist does not discriminate (thus in Fig. 12 Ap.10 it is $x^* = x_1^* + x_2^*$).

16. Assume the monopolist's profit is maximized with respect to *price*, $\max_p$ $\pi(p) = pq(p) - C(q(p))$, and show this yields the same condition as maximization with respect to quantity.

17. The indeterminate result of Bertrand-Edgeworth duopoly assumes neither firm is able alone to satisfy the demand at price equal to marginal cost. Without this assumption, what changes in the reasoning?

18. The kinked demand curve generates a discontinuity of the MR curve. Explain why.

References

Ackley, G. (1978). *Macroeconomics: Theory and policy*. New York: Collier Macmillan.

Andrews, P. W. S. (1949), A reconsideration of the theory of the individual business. *Oxford Economic Papers, New Series, 1*(1), 54–89.

Angeloni, I., Kashyap, A., & Mojon, B. (Eds.). (2003). *Monetary Policy Transmission in the Euro Area*. Cambridge: Cambridge University Press.

Bertrand, J. (1883). Théorie Mathématique de la Richesse Sociale. *Journal des Savants*, pp. 499–508.

Bonnisseau, J.-M., & Florig, M. (2004). Non-existence of Duopoly Equilibria: A simple numerical example. *Journal of Economics, 85*(1), 65–71.

Bowles, S., & Edwards, R. (1985). *Understanding capitalism* (pp. 128–9, 131). New York: Harper and Row

Brunner, E. (1975). Competitive prices, normal costs and industrial stability. In: P.W.S. Andrews & E. Brunner (Eds.) *Studies in pricing*. London and Basingstoke: Macmillan.

Chamberlin, E. H. (1933). *The Theory of Monopolistic Competition*. Cambridge MA: Harvard University Press.

Chatelain, J. B., & Tiomo, A. (2003). Monetary policy and corporate investment in France. In: Angeloni et al. (Eds.), pp. 187–197.

Chirinko, R. (1993). Business fixed investment spending: Modeling strategies, empirical results, and policy implications. *Journal of Economic Literature, 31*, 1875–1911.

Chirinko, R., Fazzari, S., & Meyer, A. (1999). How responsive is business capital formation to its user cost? An exploration with micro data. *Journal of Public Economics, 74*, 53–80.

Ciccone, R. (1986). Accumulation and capacity utilization: some critical considerations on Joan Robinson's theory of distribution. *Political Economy, Studies in the Surplus Approach, 2*(1), 17–36.

Clifton, J. A. (1977). Competition and the evolution of the capitalist mode of production. *Cambridge Journal of Economics, 1*(2), 137–151.

Cournot, A. (1838). *Recherches sur les principes mathématiques de la théorie des richesses*. Paris: Hachette.

Crotty, J. (2002). Why there is chronic excess capacity. *Challenge, 45*(6), 21–44.

Dixit, A. (1980). The role of investment in entry deterrence. *Economic Journal, 90*, 95–106.

Ebersole, J. F. (1938–39). The influence of interest rates upon entrepreneurial decisions in business. *Harvard Business Review, 17*, 35–39.

Gandolfo, G. (1971). *Mathematical methods and models in economic dynamics*. Amsterdam: North-Holland.

Hall, R. E. (1993). Macro theory and the recession of 1990–91. *American Economic Review, 83*, 275–279.

Hall, R. L., & Hitch, C. R. (1939). Price theory and business behavior. *Oxford Economic Papers, 2*, 12–45.

Harrod, R. F. (1939). An essay in dynamic theory. *Economic Journal, 49*, 14–33.

Harrod, R. F. (1952). Theory of imperfect competition revised. In R. F. Harrod (Ed.), *Economic essays* (pp. 142–190). New York: Harcourt Brace.

Hay and Morris. (1991). *Industrial economics and organization: Theory and evidence*. Oxford: Oxford University Press.

Heijdra, B. J., & Van der Ploeg, F. (2002). *The foundations of modern macroeconomics*. Oxford: Oxford University Press.

Junankar, P. N. (1972). *Investment: Theories and evidence*. London and Basingstoke: Macmillan.

Kalecki, M. (1937). The principle of increasing risk. *Economica, 4*(4), 440–447.

Keynes J. M. (1936). *The general theory of employment interest and money (1967 Papermac repr.)*. London: Macmillan.

Koutsoyiannis, A. (1975). *Modern microeconomics*. London and Basingstoke: Macmillan.

Kurz, H. D. (1990). Effective demand, employment and capital utilisation in the short run. *Cambridge Journal of Economics, 14*, 205–217.

Lavoie, M. (2014). *Post-Keynesian economics: new foundations*. Cheltenham, UK: Edward Elgar.

Lee, F. S. (1998). *Post Keynesian price theory*. Cambridge: Cambridge University Press.

Lee, F. S., & Downward, P. (1999). Retesting gardiner means's evidence on administered prices. *Journal of Economic Issues, 33*, 861–886.

Marrama, V. (1968). *Microeconomia*. Roma: Edizioni Ricerche.

Mas-Colell, A., Whinston, M. D., & Green, J. R. (1995). *Microeconomic theory*. Oxford: Oxford University Press.

Meade, J. E., & Andrews P. W. S. (1938). *Summary of replies to questions on effects of interest rates*. Oxford Economic Papers 1 (old series)(1): 14–31.

Steindl, J. (1952(1976)). *Maturity and stagnation in American capitalism*. New York, London: Monthly Review Press (a reprint of the 1952 edition, Oxford, Blackwell).

Panico, C. (1988). *Interest and profit in the theories of value and distribution*. London: Macmillan.

Pepall, L., Richards, D., & Norman, G. (2008). *Industrial organization* (4th ed.). Oxford: Blackwell.

Petri, F. (2003). Should the theory of endogenous growth be based on Say's Law and the full employment of resources? In N. Salvadori (Ed.), *Theory of Growth: A Classical Perspective* (pp. 139–160). Cheltenham, UK: Edward Elgar.

Petri, F. (2004). *General equilibrium, capital and macroeconomics: a key to recent controversies in equilibrium theory*. Cheltenham, UK: Edward Elgar.

Petri, F. (2013). The inevitable dependence of investment on expected demand: Implications for neoclassical macroeconomics. Palgrave Macmillan. In S. Levrero, A. Palumbo, & A. Stirati (Eds.), *Sraffa and the reconstruction of economic theory* (Vol. II, pp. 44–67). Basingstoke, Hampshire UK: Houndmills.

Petri, F. (2015). Neglected implications of neoclassical capital-labour substitution for investment theory: Another criticism of say's law. *Review of Political Economy, 27*(3), 308–340.

Pivetti, M. (1985). On the monetary explanation of distribution. *Political Economy: Studies in the Surplus Approach, 1*(2), 73–104.

Pivetti, M. (1991). *An essay on money and distribution*. London: Macmillan.

Roberts, J., & Sonnenschein, H. (1977). On the foundations of the theory of monopolistic competition. *Econometrica, 45*(1), 101–113.

Robinson, J. V., & Eatwell, J. (1973). *An introduction to modern economics*. New York: McGraw-Hill.

Scherer, F. M. (1970). *Industrial Market Structure and Economic Performance*. Chicago: Rand McNally College Pub.

Scherer, F. M., & Ross, D. (1990). *Industrial market structure and economic performance*. Boston: Houghton Mifflin.

Scherer, F. M., Scherer, I., Beckenstein, A., Kaufer, E., Bougeon-Massen, F., & Murphy, D. R. (1975). *The economics of multi-plant operations: An international comparisons study*. Cambridge MA: Harvard University Press.

Selten, R. (1978). The chain-store paradox. *Theory and Decision, 9*, 127–159.

Shaikh, A. (2016). *Capitalism*. Oxford: Oxford University Press.

Sharpe, S. A., & Suarez, G. (2014). *The insensitivity of investment to interest rates: Evidence from a survey of CFOs*. FEDS (Finance and Economics Discussion Series) Working Paper 2014-2, Federal Reserve Board, Washington, D.C.

Sraffa, P. (1926). The laws of returns under competitive conditions. *Economic Journal, 36*, 535–550.

Witte Jr. J. G. (1963). The microfoundations of the social investment function. *Journal of Political Economy*, **71**(5), 441–56.

Voigt, F. (1962). German experience with cartels and their control during pre-war and post-war periods. In: J. P. Miller (Ed.), *Competition, cartels and their regulation*. North-Holland, Amsterdam.

Labour Markets and Income Distribution

Contents

13.1   Introductory – 1117

13.2   The Labour Demand Curve Is Indeterminable – 1118

13.3   Search Theory – 1127

13.4   Implicit Contracts – 1140

13.5   Insiders–Outsiders – 1143

13.6   Efficiency Wages – 1146

13.6.1   Five Versions – 1146

13.6.2   Adverse Selection – 1149

13.6.3   Turnover Costs – 1150

13.6.4   Shirking – 1152

13.6.5   Gift Exchange, Fairness, Morale – 1164

13.7   Trade Unions – 1165

13.8   The Solow or Solow–Hahn Approach – 1180

Electronic supplementary material The online version of this chapter (▶ https://doi.org/10.1007/978-3-030-62070-7_13) contains supplementary material, which is available to authorized users.

© Springer Nature Switzerland AG 2021
F. Petri, *Microeconomics for the Critical Mind*,
Classroom Companion: Economics, https://doi.org/10.1007/978-3-030-62070-7_13

13.9	Long-Period Theories of Wages: Four Approaches. The Cambridge School – 1188
13.10	The Kaleckian Approach – 1200
13.11	The Classical–Marxian Approach. Goodwin. Investment – 1202
13.12	Pivetti – 1214
13.13	Concluding on Real Wages – 1216
13.14	Review Questions and Exercises – 1220
	References – 1223

13.1 · Introductory

This chapter discusses rather contentious topics, so it is fair to say that it will teach you *one perspective* on:

- why unemployment does not cause continuous wage decreases;
- why the demand-for-labour curve is indeterminable, and Keynes's arguments in its support are unconvincing;
- what explanations of wage rigidity in the presence of unemployment are offered by the main current theories of the working of labour markets: search theory, implicit contracts, insider–outsider theory, efficiency wages, trade unions, the Solow–Hahn approach;
- what explanation for the same question can be derived from the classical authors and Marx;
- the main theories of the long-run evolution of real wages not based on the demand-for-labour curve: the Cambridge approach, the Kaleckian approach, the Marx–Goodwin approach, the Pivetti approach;
- in the online Appendix to the chapter, some elements of bargaining theory.

13.1 **Introductory**

Generally, microeconomics textbooks do not contain a specific chapter on the labour market. They accept that 'The theory of the determination of wages in a free market is simply a special case of the general theory of value. Wages are the price of labour; and thus, in the absence of control, they are determined, like all prices, by supply and demand' (Hicks, *The Theory of Wages*, 1932, p. 1). Labour supply is studied in the chapter on consumer choice, but labour demand is treated as just one case of demand for factors, and there is no mention of special aspects of how labour markets function.

It is in *macro*economic textbooks that one discovers that there is a literature that treats the labour market as different from other 'factor markets', and introduces a rich array of *micro*economic new notions to study it: among them, search costs, implicit contracts, efficiency wages, trade unions, bargaining theory. This strange situation can be explained as due to the origin and nature of the distinction between microeconomics and macroeconomics, explained in the Preface. As also explained there, this distinction must be abandoned and is abandoned in the present chapter.

The chapter argues that a thorough reconsideration of the functioning of labour markets is rendered necessary by the impossibility to determine the standard neoclassical labour demand curve, owing to the problems with capital pointed out in ▶ Chaps. 7 and 8, whose destructive implications for the notion of a decreasing labour demand curve are pointed out at the beginning of the chapter. But if there is no labour demand curve, there is also no intersection between labour supply curve and labour demand curve: the notion of an equilibrium real wage towards which the free operation of competition would push actual wages must be dropped too. Two main questions then arise.

First, since the gravitation towards a full-employment level of real wages loses its foundations, one must conclude that, contrary to the views of Monetarism, of real business cycles and of most DSGE macroeconomics, the unemployment one nearly always observes in capitalist economies is not voluntary, and labour is not on its supply curve; but then how can we explain that wages do not decrease? Isn't it irrational for an unemployed worker ready to work at the going wage and then, generally, also at a slightly lower wage, not to offer to work for this slightly inferior wage?

Second, what determines the average level of real wages and its change over long periods if they cannot be explained on the basis of a gravitation towards an equality between supply and demand for labour?

The first question is discussed in Sects. 13.3–13.8. Search theory is unconvincing but offers interesting stimuli; implicit contracts and the insiders–outsiders approach are found to rely too much on a decreasing labour demand curve and to suffer from other weaknesses too. Efficiency wages, the role of trade unions and the Solow–Hahn approach are more promising although not fully satisfactory either.[1] The direction in which it seems reasonable to look for the answer is a view of income distribution as determined by the relative bargaining power of social groups with conflicting interests, with the different social groups forming explicit or tacit coalitions that try to resist unfavourable changes. The web of social ties that constitute the coalitional nature of the competing social groups causes competition to operate in labour markets in ways that differ from standard assumptions.

The chapter proceeds to survey the main theories that try to answer the second question. The Keynesian 'Cambridge approach', the Kaleckian approach, the Marxian approach as formalized by Richard Goodwin and the monetary approach of Massimo Pivetti contribute important insights which offer hope that their combination can produce a satisfactory theory.

13.2 The Labour Demand Curve Is Indeterminable

Workers need to survive, can decide how well to work, can individually or collectively fight the bosses up to using (or enduring) violence and can often resist without working for long periods; they entertain notions of fairness, reciprocity, status that influence their behaviour. More and more, these facts are admitted as important and useful to explain aspects of labour markets, in particular the coexistence of unemployment (excess supply of labour) and non-decreasing wages, against the neoclassical expectation of a tendency of a price to decrease as long as there is excess supply of the good or service.

Still, elements of the neoclassical theoretical structure remain extremely important in the dominant description of how labour markets function, both in textbooks and in research. Now, we have seen in previous chapters that the neo-

---

1 The treatment of these several approaches will be far from exhaustive, focused on how they contribute to explaining the downward rigidity or viscousness of wages in the presence of unemployment; for a fuller discussion of these approaches and of the empirical research stimulated by them the reader is invited to consult the impressive textbook on labour economics by Cahuc et al. (2014). On how these approaches fit in mainstream macroeconomics see Romer (2012), Heijdra and van der Ploeg (2002).

13.2 · The Labour Demand Curve Is Indeterminable

classical approach appears unconvincing. But what precisely of this approach seems indefensible for the study of labour markets?

The central notion questioned by the criticisms is the decreasing aggregate labour demand curve. (I will discuss it under the simplifying assumption of homogeneous labour.) This notion, although often absent in micro textbooks, is fundamental for the neoclassical approach, for the stability of the labour market, for traditional marginalist comparative statics and for the determination of the effect on employment of a wage fixed by minimum wage laws or trade unions.

The aggregate labour demand curve exhibits the relationship between real wage and aggregate employment if other factor markets and all product markets are in equilibrium and firms employ labour up to equality between money wage and marginal monetary revenue product of labour. As explained in ▶ Chap. 3, for a neoclassical competitive economy the traditional labour demand curve is the curve implied by the solution of a general equilibrium system where all factor markets apart from the labour market are in equilibrium, the equation 'demand for labour = supply of labour' is dropped, in its place the real wage is treated as a parameter, labour is employed up to equality between real wage and marginal product, and the labour income that goes to demand final goods is the income of the employed (i.e. demanded) amount of labour only, as if labour supply had decreased and become equal to labour demand. Hicks was quoted to this effect in ▶ Chap. 3, Footnote 17: the effect of a real wage above the full-employment level is that 'a final position must be reached which is precisely the same as that which would have occurred if there had been a direct reduction in the number of labourers available'.[2] In deriving the demand curve for a factor the incomes of the factor owners are the incomes earned by the *employed* amounts of factors, so if the real wage is higher than the full-employment level, the unemployed workers have no income and do not demand products (except with income from sources other than their labour), and if the real wage is *lower* than the full-employment level, the analysis hypothetically assumes the availability of the extra labour demanded by firms and their income too is used to demand produced goods.[3]

---

2 As these lines by Hicks make clear, the fact that the composition of demand might depend to some extent on *which* workers remain unemployed (or, if labour demand is *greater* than supply, on what is assumed about the tastes of the hypothetical workers in excess of actual labour supply) was traditionally considered of negligible importance.

3 Traditional marginalist/neoclassical authors must have felt that the assumption that the unemployed earn no income and can demand nothing, clear in Hicks' lines quoted in ▶ Chap. 3, was so obvious that there was no need to insist on it: Hicks seems to have been the sole one to make it so explicit, although careful analysis finds it implicit in other traditional authors too when they mention unemployment caused by too high real wages. In Keynes's *General Theory* the assumption remains implicit in the notion of the consumption function. Perhaps this made it easier to forget about it and not to realize the radical change entailed by the way the auctioneer-guided tâtonnement was formalized in the 1950s. In the latter, consumers transmit to the auctioneer demands for consumption goods based on full-employment incomes even at prices incompatible with full employment, which means the tâtonnement cannot even roughly mimic actual disequilibrium adjustments (▶ Sect. 8.16). So Clower's rediscovery of the traditional assumption under the name of 'dual-decision hypothesis'—cf. Clower 1967, 1969—was hailed as a great analytical advance, with no perception of it having been considered obvious by older authors.

Then *only one market is not in equilibrium*, the labour market; all other markets are in equilibrium at all levels of the real wage. When in my lectures to graduate students I reach this point and formulate the italicized statement, generally several students protest that it is impossible, because in contradiction of Walras' Law. But there is no contradiction, simply the 'balanced budget' assumption behind Walras' Law, namely that the incomes of consumers are the value of their *intended* factor supplies, has been replaced by the assumption that the incomes of consumers are the value of those, of their intended factor supplies, *that find purchasers*. In deriving the demand curve for a factor, the amounts employed of the other factors are assumed to be the equilibrium ones; but for the factor under study, only the employed amount generates incomes for consumers. In fact, one does a comparative statics exercise in which, for each rental rate of the factor whose demand curve is under study, one determines the supply of the factor that would make that rental rate an equilibrium one: the hypothetical factor supply curve thus obtained is the factor's demand curve.

This is the necessary way to make sense, in the neoclassical approach, of the effect of a real wage kept above its equilibrium level (by law or other causes). The unemployed workers will have to live on other incomes, or be supported by relatives or public subsidies, or emigrate.

The way to study the stability of equilibrium in the labour market on this basis is clear: if already there is full employment and the wage is below its equilibrium level, the competition of entrepreneurs will cause the wage to rise up to equilibrium, with a redistribution of aggregate income towards labour; more interestingly, if the real wage is *above* its equilibrium level and there is unemployment, then a lowering of the wage, by inducing firms to hire extra workers and increase output and incomes, *creates* the extra incomes that ensure that the increased production is sold (of course, Say's Law is assumed, and aggregate demand is assumed to remain equal to the value of aggregate output).[4]

(This picture of how full labour employment is reached according to traditional marginalist theory has been lost and largely forgotten with the adoption of the modern auctioneer-guided tâtonnement for the study of the stability of the Arrow–Debreu neo-Walrasian model. Within that fairy tale adjustment pro-

---

4   The mechanism ensuring Say's Law depends on whether the analysis is a long-period one, a Marshallian short-period one (as in Keynesian macroeconomics), or a very-short-period neo-Walrasian one. In long-period analyses under the static assumption, Say's Law is simply the equality between supply and demand for 'capital'. In short-period analyses one must assume (as in Keynes) that aggregate real savings increase with increases in labour employment and aggregate output, and then there must be some mechanism that maintains investment equal to the rising aggregate savings; since this will generally imply nonzero *net* investment, the economy cannot be assumed to be stationary, and then the mechanism must rely on the rate of interest as capable of adapting investment to the flow of 'loanable funds' (savings); it was argued in ▶ Sect. 7.5 that this adaptation actually needs the *assumption* of continuous full labour employment, but this was not clear to Keynes and subsequent macroeconomists, with confusions on investment theory discussed in ▶ Sect. 12.7. The neo-Walrasian versions, as explained in ▶ Chap. 8, assume Say's Law but have no mechanism ensuring it, they simply assume it.

13.2 · The Labour Demand Curve Is Indeterminable

cess, but only within it, it is not logically contradictory to assume that consumers count on an income equal to the value of their intended factor supplies, because if those supplies do not find purchasers equilibrium has not been reached and the tâtonnement continues. But the stability results are of no relevance for economies where generally incomes must first be earned in order to be used to demand goods. As further confirmation of its limitations, this tâtonnement is unable to study what happens if the real wage is fixed, e.g. by law, above the equilibrium level.[5])

The labour demand curve is also present in Keynes, and it is useful to understand what role it plays, given Keynes's different theories of what determines employment. Keynes in *The General Theory of Employment Interest and Money* (1936) accepts the neoclassical decreasing relationship between labour employment and real wage; but instead of viewing the real wage as what is determined by bargaining in the labour market, and employment and aggregate output as determined by it (with investment adapting to the corresponding level of savings), he reverses the direction of causality. He argues that wage bargaining determines only the money wage, not the real wage; output adjusts to aggregate demand, which is determined by investment (assumed here for simplicity to be the sole autonomous expenditure) and the multiplier; the adjustment of output is determined by the following mechanism: an excess of aggregate demand over output raises the general price level relative to *money* wages, and therefore *real* wages decrease; this makes it convenient for firms to increase labour employment, and this is the reason why aggregate output increases. The converse, he argued, happens when aggregate demand is less than output.[6] Then the labour demand curve indicates the real wage that must and will come to rule (through variations of the price level relative to the money wage) if a certain level of employment is imposed by the 'principle of effective demand' (savings adjust to investment via variation

---

5   After Clower a literature developed on 'fix price' economies where relative prices are rigid and agents are constrained in their purchases by the value of what they are able to sell, but this literature has petered out (and will not be discussed here) because it has added no significant insight to what had been already understood in Keynesian analyses (and with no recourse to fixed prices apart from the money wage) about the constraints deriving from the consumption function, a given autonomous expenditure, and the multiplier.

6   Therefore the frequent textbook presentations of the IS-LM model that assume a given *price level* are not faithful to Keynes, and are hard to reconcile with neoclassical principles. A presentation faithful to Keynes should assume the price level to vary with Y more than money wages (one can then for simplicity take money wages as given) so as to ensure that, for each level of Y, the real wage is the one that induces firms to employ the amount of labour required by that level of output. If, as textbooks generally accept, increases in labour demand require reductions of the real wage, and the price level is taken as given in the IS-LM scheme, then one must assume that money wages decrease as Y increases, which seems absurd. A given price level can be justified by a full-cost determination of prices; this is perfectly compatible with the principle of effective demand, but it is not easily combined with a decreasing labour demand curve, because this theory of price formation does not need changes in real wages in order to adapt outputs to demand. The decreasing marginal efficiency of capital too is not easily reconciled with this price theory.

of output) once autonomous expenditure is given. The direction of causality is no longer from the real wage to aggregate output to investment, it is from investment to aggregate demand to the real wage, via the effect of aggregate demand on the price level relative to the money wage.

But apart from this difference on the direction of causality, in Keynes too more employment requires a lower real wage; there is implicit in his analysis too a standard decreasing labour demand curve based on the decreasing marginal product of labour.

Let us then ask about the implications of the arguments of ▶ Chaps. 7 and 8 for the notion of labour demand curve. The main implication is a difficulty with determining this curve, because the demand curve for a factor must take as given the amounts employed of the other factors, but the given amount of capital or of capital goods seems impossible to specify when production uses heterogeneous capital goods.

Modern neo-Walrasian value theory would take as given the *vector* of endowments of the several capital goods, but this would cause the difficulties discussed in ▶ Chap. 8. Let us briefly remember them as specifically arising for the labour demand curve, which would then be a very-short-period labour demand curve. Let us start from the *impermanence problem*. The vector of capital endowments has *insufficient persistence*: before a given real wage were able to determine the labour employment indicated by this very-short-period labour demand curve (the thing would take some time, variations of labour employment cannot be instantaneous), the vector of capital endowments might considerably change. And we know from the *substitutability problem* that changes in the composition of capital can drastically alter the demand for labour based on a vectorial capital endowment. Therefore the effect on the equilibrium wage of, e.g., a change in labour supply would be indeterminable, because the labour demand curve might relevantly shift during the disequilibrium adjustments. Furthermore, in deriving this very-short-period labour demand curve, one would meet the *price-change problem* when trying to determine either the intertemporal equilibrium or the temporary equilibrium associated with each real wage in the current period; we have seen in ▶ Chap. 8 the enormous difficulties one would encounter.

Can one then take as given the amount of 'capital' conceived as a single factor of variable 'form'? No, because we have seen in ▶ Chap. 7 the illegitimacy of taking its endowment as a datum of equilibrium.

Is there a third way? Keynes in the *General Theory* assumed a decreasing marginal product of labour and hence increasing marginal cost curves of the several firms even in a Marshallian short period, that is, even on the basis of a given vectorial stock of *durable* capital goods and plants (the circulating capital goods or intermediate goods were on the contrary endogenously determined). Keynes does not explicitly discuss Hicks's earlier argument against such an assumption, based on the substitutability problem which evidently Hicks saw as arising also in the Marshallian short period (see ▶ Sect. 7.2). But some awareness of the issue emerges from how Keynes defends the increasing marginal cost curve. He adduces two reasons why 'in general, supply price will increase as output from a given equipment is increased' (p. 300), neither resting on factor substitutabil-

13.2 · The Labour Demand Curve Is Indeterminable

ity and neither persuasive. One is a need to employ, in order to expand output, labourers who are less and less efficient (*General Theory* pp. 42, 299). But this will cause an increasing marginal cost only if the firm pays the less efficient labourers the same hourly wage, which is implausible, because the less efficient workers are hired only when the supply of more efficient workers is exhausted; this means that the firm knows about the efficiency of workers, but then it will find ways to pay the less efficient ones less: there are many ways (productivity prizes, promotions, temporary contracts, etc.) to differentiate pay and to reward greater efficiency. A second reason is 'if equipment is non-homogeneous and some part of it involves a greater prime cost per unit of output' (*General Theory* pp. 299–300)[7]: that is, the firm is assumed to own both more efficient and less efficient machineries and to use the less efficient machinery only if full use of the more efficient machinery is insufficient. But cases of coexistence in the same firm of more and less efficient machinery (with the less efficient machinery maintained in good order and activated only when production is high) are very rare (when a new assembly line is built, the old one is scrapped); a main reason is that recourse to additional but older machinery is generally unnecessary to increase production, it is generally possible to produce more on the more efficient machinery by utilizing it more hours per week. So this reason is unpersuasive too.

It cannot cause surprise, then, that shortly after the publication of Keynes's *General Theory* two economists, Dunlop (1938) and Tarshis (1938, 1939), argued that one does not empirically observe that *real* wages move countercyclically, decreasing when employment increases, to which Keynes (1939) responded that his theory was, if anything, reinforced by the abandonment of the decreasing labour demand curve. Subsequent research has abundantly confirmed Dunlop and Tarshis: real wages are, if anything, slightly pro-cyclical (Abraham and Haltiwanger 1995; Brandolini 1995).

Thus, recourse to a Marshallian short period does not rescue the decreasing labour demand curve. Keynes himself wrote in the *General Theory* (p. 300):

> » It is probable that the general level of prices will not rise very much as output increases, so long as there are available efficient unemployed resources of every type.

which is in accord with what has been argued here. Keynes continued:

> » But as soon as output has increased sufficiently to begin to reach the "bottle-necks", there is likely to be a sharp rise in the prices of certain commodities.

But the evidence on capacity utilization mentioned in ► Chap. 12 suggests that market economies are generally quite far from 'bottlenecks' and could easily produce 10% more without any strain on fixed capital, provided the needed extra labour was available—and unfortunately generally it *is* available. 'Sharp rises in the prices of certain commodities' are not easily observed in the business cycle.

---

7   'Prime cost' is the Marshallian term for variable cost.

I conclude that the labour demand curve is not a defensible notion. But then wages cannot be considered determined by, or tending towards, the intersection of a labour supply curve with an indeterminable labour demand curve. We need an alternative theory of real wages.

The above also implies that the idea of a necessary connection between real wages and employment must be abandoned.

We have seen in ▶ Chap. 12 the flexibility and adaptability of production to demand. This holds also for the industries that produce capital goods; indeed this flexibility can be expected to be particularly great in those industries that produce capital goods for which the demand undergoes great fluctuations owing to the accelerator. (Think of firms producing airplanes, or trains, where demand can be low for long periods, and then can become very great when existing fleets are renewed with new models.) This means that only in exceptional circumstances (e.g. a war economy) the capital goods industries will not be able to produce whatever capital goods are demanded by expansions of aggregate demand or by the building of new plants according to new technologies. Therefore (if we leave aside constraints deriving from the balance of payments) there is generally no obstacle to having a rise in wages together with an increase in employment. In existing plants, it is possible to raise employment by increasing the degree of utilization of capacity. As to new plants, whatever the capital goods required for the building of new plants that employ more labour than before and with the production methods best adapted to the new wage, the capital goods industries will be able to produce them. It may be that the production of these new capital goods at the new prices requires a greater employment of savings, what the neoclassical economist would call a rise in the K/L ratio in new plants; no problem! this only means an increase of investment even greater than if the K/L ratio in new plants had not changed; this increased investment, through the operation of the multiplier, will raise aggregate income enough to generate the savings corresponding to it. So what is needed, for wages and employment to increase together, is only an increase of aggregate demand that can be obtained via an opportune fiscal policy.

This of course also implies that it is generally false that in order to produce more capital goods, as required by a faster growth rate, the economy must produce fewer consumption goods. The margins for increases of the degree of utilization of productive capacity that exist in all economies (leaving aside balance-of-payment constraints) up to levels from which usually advanced economies remain quite far mean that it is generally possible to have both more investment and more consumption. What is needed is the stimulus to produce more, coming from aggregate demand. Here we catch a glimpse of a view of economic growth that attributes a determining role to the evolution of aggregate demand rather than to supply-side determinants such as the given capital stock and the propensity to save at full employment.

If one maintains the Keynesian principle of effective demand (autonomous expenditure determines aggregate income via the multiplier) but one drops the decreasing labour demand curve, then real wage reductions have unclear effects on employment in the absence of policy interventions. According to some economists the resulting higher rate of profits stimulates investment, but other econ-

13.2 · The Labour Demand Curve Is Indeterminable

omists disagree. The lower real wages may favour net exports; this topic falls outside the arguments of this book, and it will only be noted that an appreciable effect may require very drastic falls in real wages; also, if what is desired is an improvement in the net export balance, it is unclear why only wages, and not other incomes too, should decrease. On the other hand, lower real wages reduce the demand for most consumption goods (the propensity to consume is generally higher for wage earners than for property income earners, so an income transfer from the former to the latter reduces the average propensity to consume), this reduces the multiplier, and it may also discourage investment in consumption good industries; this has a negative effect on employment. Except when net exports are very sensitive to real wages, one can plausibly assume, as a first approximation, that employment is little affected by moderate changes in real wages and is more probably *negatively* affected by their sharp reduction.

One might try to defend a supply-and-demand determination of real wages by arguing that (leaving aside as exceptional the case of such low wages that labour supply is strongly downward-sloping) a level of employment little affected by wage changes means a nearly vertical labour demand curve, but one still gets a unique and stable equilibrium if this curve crosses an increasing labour supply curve.

But in ▶ Chap. 4 it was pointed out that the assumption, usual in the macro-literature, that the labour supply curve is upward-sloping and rather elastic is contradicted by the available empirical evidence even at not-very-low real wages.[8] The male labour supply curve appears to be vertical or slightly backward-bending. The female labour supply curve is upward-sloping but only moderately so. The empirical evidence anyway refers only to moderate variations of real wages. In all likelihood, considerable *reductions* of real wages cause labour supply to *increase*, because housewives will look for a job, the young will leave school and start looking for a job earlier, and pensioners will look for a part-time job. Therefore in the Keynesian economy, given the generally inelastic (if not upward-sloping) labour demand curve, it is highly likely that an excess labour supply will not be eliminated by moderate real wage decreases, and that it will be made worse by drastic real wage decreases. A freely flexible wage would then fall to zero, or more concretely, to the level where most working people would turn to begging, crime, mass protests, violence; no normal economic activity would be possible.

One is brought to conclude that what allows market economies based on wage labour to function is that wages are *not* freely flexible.

This may seem to run counter the assumption of rationality and utility maximization: an unemployed worker who, at a wage slightly below the current wage, would prefer to work rather than remain unemployed, may appear irrational if

---

8   For example, Romer (2012, p. 456): 'there is little support for the hypothesis of highly elastic labor supply'. Nor is this empirical evidence in contradiction with what theory concludes, we saw in ▶ Chap. 4 that microeconomic theory gives no reason to presume that the labour supply curve is nearly certainly increasing. The assumption that it is, common in mainstream macro-models, must therefore be due to reasons other than its scientific robustness.

she does not make her readiness to accept a slightly lower wage manifest. The same rationality assumption that makes us conclude that in the market of a product, when supply is greater than demand, the suppliers who are unable to place their wares will find it convenient to ask for a lower price, should make us conclude—it is argued—that the unemployed workers willing to work at the current wage will also be generally willing to work at a slightly lower wage, and will then act to try and get a job by making their willingness clear.

Upon this argument the monetarist school concludes that if, in a situation in which unemployed people declare they would like to work at the current wage, wages do not decrease, then the reason must be that the unemployed workers (or more precisely, the ones in excess of *frictional* unemployment)[9] are not really interested in working at the current wage: if they were, they would also be ready to work for a slightly lower wage and would actively propose it. That is, at the current wage they really prefer leisure (or search; see the next section) to accepting currently available jobs and are waiting for some better work opportunity to turn up; all those who do want to work at the current wage are indeed working (or are just in frictional transition to a new job): so, the argument concludes, when the wage is not decreasing *there is* equality between supply and demand for labour (apart from inevitable frictional unemployment). If wages are not decreasing, unless there is something like minimum wage laws that prevent them from decreasing, unemployment (in excess of ineliminable frictional unemployment) is only apparent, it is voluntary; if it were involuntary, wages would decrease, which would tend to eliminate unemployment.[10] It is concluded that the government should not worry about unemployment, apart from trying to reduce the imperfect information and search time which make frictional unemployment greater than it might be.

This argument relies on a decreasing and rather elastic labour demand curve, because it needs that wage reductions raise employment appreciably; otherwise, in view of the inelasticity of labour supply, the workers' willingness to let wages decrease as long as there is involuntary unemployment would cause enormous wage decreases whenever labour demand became less than labour supply; now, a clear excess of labour supply is often observed, but not accompanied by enormous wage decreases. If the labour demand curve must be dropped, the empirical evidence obliges to drop downward wage flexibility too. But this raises the question, why don't wages decrease if really there are unemployed people ready

---

9 Frictional unemployment is the lowest level of unemployment obtainable, when account is taken of the firings inevitably occurring in a market economy owing to the continuous changes undergone by technology or composition of demand, or owing to mistaken decisions to set up firms that turn out to be unprofitable and are closed down, etc. Some time is necessarily taken by the fired workers to find a new job, and the same holds for new entrants into the labour market, so it is impossible to reach truly zero unemployment. More on this below, in the section on search costs.

10 Milton Friedman is known to have argued that trade unions are unable to prevent wages from decreasing if there is unemployment and some fraction of the unemployed labour supply are really ready to work for a lower wage. So it is only minimum wage laws that can cause persistent involuntary unemployment.

to work at the current real wage and then, in all likelihood, also at a slightly inferior real wage? In Spain in the 2000s unemployment was at 25%, and real wages stagnated but did not fall precipitously as standard competitive theory would lead us to expect. One could cite other similar empirical observations. Sections from 13.3 to 13.8 will examine the main proposed explanations of this phenomenon.[11] Many are associated with the neoclassical decreasing labour demand curve, and for them it will be necessary to ask how useful they remain if that notion is dropped.

13.3 Search Theory

Search theory has recently deserved for its main proponents, Mortensen, Pissarides and Diamond, the so-called Nobel prize in economics (this is assigned by the Swedish Central Bank, and its right to use Nobel's name has been disputed). Its basic idea (Mortensen 1970; Pissarides 2000) is that, because of imperfect information and of imperfect homogeneity both of jobs and of workers, it takes time for an unemployed worker to discover and contact firms with vacancies appropriate to her/his competences; it takes time for a firm to fill vacancies because the firm wants to examine a number of applicants before filling a vacancy; workers too are not indifferent among the job offers of firms and want to examine a number of job offers before accepting a job. Continuous changes in the economy oblige some firms to fire part of their workforce or even to shut down; thus there is a continuous flow of workers who lose their job; this flow plus the flow of spontaneous quits (except retirements for age reasons) plus the flow of newcomers to the labour market increase the pool of the unemployed. As against this, there is a flow of new vacancies opening up, because firms want to replace spontaneous leaves or to expand their workforce, and the filling of these vacancies (called 'job creation' in this literature) reduces the pool of the unemployed. Some time is required to fill the vacancies, so there are always workers who are looking for a job and will in time find it but have not found it yet. A basic hypothesis of the approach is that were it not for the search time of firms and of workers, there would be full employment. That is, the unemployed workers are in transition to a new job. Although the thing is never explicitly discussed, in this literature the implicit explanation why wages do not decrease in the presence of unemployment would appear to be that the unemployed workers do not feel the need to offer to work for a lower wage than the going market wage because the probability to find employment at the going wage in not too long a time is sufficiently high as to make it more convenient to wait than to shorten the expected waiting time

---

11 The reader is invited to read Stirati (2016) too, another critical discussion of much the same ground, and also of other influential views of the labour market not examined here, for example the views of the real business cycle school, which argues that the alternation of booms and busts is caused by fluctuations of the fully employed labour supply, that is, that when unemployment increases it is because people freely decide to enjoy more leisure—a sad manifestation of dogmatism and disregard for the evidence.

by asking for a lower wage, which would mean a lower income for a rather long period once a job is found. In order to grasp the presence of this implicit assumption, a presentation although brief of the approach is necessary.[12] It will be seen that some of the relationships on which the approach is based are independent of the neoclassical framework with which the approach is always combined, and interesting.

What I will briefly present is more precisely the *search-and-matching* approach in the version with wage bargaining. Another version, called *wage posting*, in which firms propose a take-it-or-leave-it wage which is not uniform (Burdett and Mortensen 1998), encounters serious difficulties with justifying the persistence of different wages: it must assume a continuum of infinitesimal workers and a continuum of wages, an absurdity in real economies where the number of workers and hence of wages is finite, and therefore I do not consider it.

Assume a stationary economy with a constant labour supply L, and assume only the unemployed look for jobs. We need the following notions and corresponding symbols:

L – labour force (labour supply, assumed constant: the flow out of the labour force (owing above all to retirement but also to other causes) is assumed equal to the flow of new entrants; thus, the participation rate is given. This simplifying assumption is sufficient to grasp the basic ideas of the approach);

N – number of employed workers or filled jobs[13];

$e = N/L$ – rate of employment;

---

12 Stirati (2016) correctly stresses the origin of search models in the desire to give foundations to the monetarist claim of 'misperception' as the explanation of changes of employment (assumed equal to labour supply) in the business cycle: the claim being that workers, mistaking a change in their money wage for a change of the real wage in the same direction (while in fact the price level is changing in the same direction even more and the real wage is decreasing), change their search efforts in the same direction, and thus hirings change in the same direction as the price level. I will not discuss changes of search efforts because my focus is on a largely different question—do these models help to understand downward wage stickiness? Anyway as Stirati notes there is abundant evidence that changes of the workers' search efforts cannot explain changes in hirings, the probability of acceptance of job offers has been shown to be generally close to one by numerous studies (see also the references in Andrews et al. (2008, p. 455)), and therefore hirings are determined by the demand for workers, not by their supply. Indeed Solow noted: 'It is thus legitimate to wonder why the unemployed do not feel themselves to be engaged in voluntary intertemporal substitution, and why they queue up in such numbers when legitimate jobs of the usual kind are offered during a recession' (Solow 1980 p. 7). The thing is further confirmed by the fact that a large portion, even one half, of hirings is of persons not up to then in the labour force, i.e. not considered unemployed, not (officially, at least) actively searching for a job.

13 Warning: symbology has not standardized in this literature. I follow the habit of Keynes and early macroeconomics of indicating employment as N and total labour supply as L. In recent years the meaning assigned to these two symbols is often inverted. Generally, apart from some exceptions that I will indicate, I try to adopt the symbols used in the basic reference in this literature, Pissarides (2000), so as to make it easier for the reader to refer to it. A first exception is that I find it useful to have a symbol for the hazard rate and the obvious one is h, Pissarides indicates it as $\theta q(\theta)$ (see below).

$u = 1 - e -$ rate of unemployment;

$U = uL$ – total unemployment; $L = N + U$;

λ – exogenous average rate of job terminations (relative to employment N) per unit of time, whether due to disappearance of workplaces or to workplaces losing their occupants; this is also the appearance of new vacancies because I am assuming the economy is stationary[14]; hence λN is the flow of job terminations (and hence, in a stationary state, it is also the flow of new vacancies filled up) per time unit;

v – ratio of vacancies relative to the total labour force;

$V = vL$ – total vacancies;

h – **hazard rate**, the instantaneous probability to exit unemployment, equal to the percentage per period of the unemployed who find a job; hence hU is the average number of new job occupancies, or vacancies filled up, per time unit.

Search theory assumes that the search process implies a **matching function**

$$M = M(U, V)$$

that indicates the average number of vacancies filled up per time unit (the creation of jobs) as a function of the number U of unemployed workers looking for a job and of total vacancies V. The matching function $M(U, V)$ is assumed increasing and strictly concave both in U and in V (i.e. with decreasing partial derivatives), zero if U or V is zero,[15] and, usually, homogeneous of degree 1[16]; hence we can divide by L and obtain new job filling as a *rate* relative to L, where, setting $m = M(U/L, V/L)$ we can write:

$$M(U, V) = m(u, v)L.$$

---

14 New vacancies are born in excess of job terminations in an economy where employment is growing; labour supply too can be growing. Technical progress can be a further complication. The formalization can easily be modified to take these growths into account, but the basic intuitions are not modified. Search intensity and readiness to reject job offers which differ in the proposed wage, the issues on which early search theory concentrated, again do not change the basic picture, and they can be treated as influencing the matching function.

15 This assumption, universal in this literature, seems too strong. Imagine an economy with well-organized employment offices that one can contact via Internet, where there are positive vacancies and when people lose their jobs or enter the labour market as newcomers, which always happens at 5.30 pm (the closing time of normal work days), they immediately contact the employment office (which stays open until late), are interviewed via Skype, are assigned to one of the vacancies and start working at the new job the next morning. In this economy unemployment is zero, and yet there is job creation. (This example shows that with adequate organization it would not be impossible to reach a rate of unemployment close to zero, which is in fact observed in some instances, e.g. Switzerland.) Conversely, in the presence of ample unemployment, vacancies might be filled the moment they are opened up.

16 One example is in Cahuc et al. (2014, p. 584). Often it is assumed that M(U, V) is linear in logarithms, i.e. is Cobb–Douglas.

1130   **Chapter 13** · Labour Markets and Income Distribution

This function $m(u, v)$ indicates the percentage of L that finds a new job per time unit.[17] It too is increasing in both u and v.

The flow of job terminations per period, as a percentage of L, is $\lambda e = \lambda(1 - u)$. Hence outside a stationary state the time derivative of employment is

$$dN/dt = L \cdot de/dt = M(U, V) - \lambda N = [m(u, v) - \lambda e]L. \qquad (13.1)$$

Therefore the time derivative of the employment *rate* $e = N/L$ is

$$de/dt = m(u, v) - \lambda e = m(u, v) - \lambda(1 - u).$$

Of course

$$du/dt = -de/dt.$$

In a stationary state both time derivatives are zero, therefore

$$M(U, V) = \lambda N \quad \text{or} \quad m(u, v) = \lambda(1 - u). \qquad (13.2)$$

The filling of new jobs depends on the resources dedicated by workers and by firms to search, and on the readiness of both to accept a match; these elements can be explicitly introduced (see Pissarides 2000, ▶ Chaps. 5 and 6) but they make little difference to the overall picture.

Since search is costly both for workers and for firms, from the side of firms the wage must be not greater than the marginal revenue product of labour minus the opportune fraction of the hiring cost corresponding to the expected length of employment of newly hired workers. Greater u means it takes less time on average for firms to fill vacancies, because the number of applicants rises and applicants, conscious of the greater competition, are readier to accept a job, and also because, the number of applicants being greater, the probability increases of finding in a short time a candidate matching the required skills.

New vacancies are assumed to be opened up for each job termination (if it is profitable to do so, an issue to be studied presently); they are filled at per-period rate (as a percentage of vacancies)

$$q = M(U, V)/V = M(U/V, 1) = m(u, v)/v = m(u/y, 1) = m(1/\theta, 1).$$

This is called the **vacancy-filling rate** or **arrival rate**. Here

$$\theta \equiv v/u = V/U,$$

vacancies per unemployed person, indicates the **degree of tightness** of the labour market from the firms' point of view: the tighter the market, the more difficult for a firm to fill a vacancy. Indeed if the matching function depends on θ as this approach assumes, then q does too and is decreasing in θ. The vacancy-filling rate $q(\theta)$ is the instantaneous probability that a vacancy be filled. The flow of job creation *per unit of unemployment*, that is the hazard rate, is

$$h(\theta) = M(U, V)/U = [M(U, V)/V] \cdot V/U = m(1, \theta) = \theta q(\theta).$$

---

17 Pissarides (2000) defines the matching function directly in the per unit of labour supply form $m(u, v)$; the form $M(U, V)$ is never used by him, but it helps intuition.

Of course $1/q$ is the average duration of a vacancy before it is filled: if every week $1/4$ of existing vacancies are filled on average, then on average a vacancy needs 4 weeks to be filled. Analogously $1/h$ is the average duration of unemployment. A rise of θ decreases q and raises h, increasing the average duration of an unfilled vacancy and decreasing the average duration of unemployment.[18] Note that the above implies $m(u, v) = hu$, useful below.

If job destruction at the exogenous rate λ and vacancy filling according to the matching function are the sole processes influencing the rate of unemployment u and its time derivative, then in a stationary state the flow of vacancy fillings $h(\theta)U$ must be equal to the flow of job destructions λN, and since labour supply L is given and $N = L - U$, unemployment is given once λ and θ are given: $h(\theta)U = \lambda(L - U)$ implies

$$U = L \cdot \lambda/(\lambda + h) \qquad (13.3)$$

or, in terms of *rate* of unemployment:

$$u = \frac{\lambda}{\lambda + h(\theta)} = \lambda/(\lambda + \theta q(\theta)). \qquad (13.4)$$

Equation (13.4) establishes a decreasing relationship between u and $h = \theta q$, and therefore between u and θ (because h and θ vary in the same direction, q in the opposite direction), or between u and v. A decreasing relationship between u and v/u by itself need not imply a decreasing relationship between u and v, but in this case it does. *Proof*: In order for u to increase, $h = m(1, \theta)$ must decrease, i.e. θ must decrease, which implies q increases. The flow of new job creations that in the stationary state must equal the flow of job destructions can also be characterized as $q(\theta)V$; that is, a stationary u must satisfy $q(\theta)v = \lambda(1 - u)$, which can be re-written as

$$u = (\lambda - q(\theta)v)/\lambda. \qquad (13.5)$$

A rise of stationary u requires a decrease of $q(\theta)v$; since we have seen from (13.4) that this requires q to increase, a decrease of qv requires v to decrease. ∎

This decreasing convex relationship between stationary u and v is identified by the search-and-matching approach with the **Beveridge curve**, a widely confirmed empirical relationship that states that higher rates of unemployment are generally associated with lower ratios of unfilled vacancies to employment. The Beveridge curve is interpreted as confirming the existence of a matching function increasing in v and u. However, the empirical Beveridge curve also reflects what happens to unemployment and to vacancies during the business cycle. When unemployment decreases because the economy is expanding, firms announce more new vacancies because they want to expand their workforce; conversely, in recessions firms do not wish to replace all job destruction and therefore the opening up of new

---

18 *Proof*: If v alone rises, h rises. If θ does not change, $h = \theta q(\theta)$ does not change. A rise of θ due to changes of both v and u can be decomposed into first a proportional change of v and u that brings u to the new level and leaves h unchanged, and then a rise of v alone, that raises h. ∎

1132   **Chapter 13** · Labour Markets and Income Distribution

vacancies decreases considerably. But an examination of how much empirical Beveridge curves confirm the existence of a matching function significantly elastic with respect to both u and v falls outside our interests here.

Equation (13.4) is an interesting relationship, independent of the theory of distribution one adopts, and useful even if one does not accept Say's Law. It says that if L, λ and θ (or h) are given, and there are no problems with selling the output from any level of employment (e.g. because the government ensures a sufficient level of aggregate demand), then the rate of unemployment can be constant at only one value; furthermore, the economy will gravitate towards that value: $u > \lambda / (\lambda + h(\theta))$ means $\lambda(1 - u) < hu$, the flow of job destruction $\lambda(1 - u)$ is less than the flow of job creation (flow of exit from unemployment) hu; therefore u decreases, employment increases and $\lambda(1 - u)$ increases with it; $h(\theta)u$ decreases; therefore the two flows tend to become equal at the level of u ensuring $hu = \lambda(1 - u)$. A persistent reduction of u requires a reduction of λ and/or an increase of θ or h.

The search-and-matching approach implicitly accepts Say's Law and argues that θ cannot be taken as given because it depends on v, so one must study how the amount of vacancies is determined.

The approach proceeds as follows. A first simple case is examined in which the rate of interest and of discount r is given, production uses only homogeneous labour, and each job produces the same flow p of output per unit of time and is paid the same flow of wage payments w per unit of time. Output is the numéraire.

A recursive approach is used to determine the value A_V for a firm of keeping an open vacancy. It is assumed that keeping the vacancy open costs the firm a flow pc per unit of time; the process that changes vacant jobs into occupied jobs is Poisson with rate q; therefore there is an instantaneous probability q that the vacancy be filled an instant later, becoming a filled job with value A_J. Hence over a very short time interval dt a vacant job 'earns' (in expectations) the sum in square brackets on the right-hand side of the expression below, and its value A_V is the discounted value of that sum:

$$A_V = \frac{1}{1 + rdt}\left[-pcdt + qdtA_J + (1 - q)dtA_V\right] \tag{13.6}$$

Multiplying both sides by $(1 + rdt)$ and rearranging and simplifying one obtains

$$rA_V = -pc + q(A_L - A_V). \tag{13.7}$$

A_V is the value at which an asset corresponding to property of a vacancy could be sold in a perfect capital market.[19] The firm finds it convenient to keep this asset as long as it yields the market rate of return r.

An occupied job yields the firm a profit $p - w$ per time unit if it keeps being occupied, but there is an instantaneous probability λ that it becomes unoccupied

---

19 Pissarides uses V for A_V and J for A_J.

13.3 · Search Theory

(job termination) an instant later, in which case it is assumed the firm replaces it with a vacancy (if it is not unprofitable to do so). Hence

$$A_J = \frac{1}{1 + rdt}\left[(p - w)dt + \lambda dt A_V + (1 - \lambda)dt A_J\right] \tag{13.8}$$

In the same way as for A_V, this can be re-written eliminating dt and it becomes

$$rA_J = p - w - \lambda A_J. \tag{13.9}$$

A_J is the price at which an asset giving right to the yield of an occupied job would be sold on a perfect capital market.

Free entry is assumed; firms enter (or expand) by opening new vacancies and will do so as long as a positive pure profit can be derived from it, consisting of opening up a vacancy and immediately selling it on the perfect capital market. This will stop only when the value A_V of a new vacancy is zero. Equation (13.7) shows that this implies

$$A_J = pc/q > 0. \tag{13.10}$$

So the value of an occupied job is positive; but to obtain an occupied job a firm must first open a vacancy and bear its cost for an average time interval $1/q$, and this brings the expected value of the vacancy (and of the firm, since it must borrow in order to pay the search costs) to zero.[20] Equation (13.10) can be used to eliminate A_J from (13.9), obtaining the wage as a function of q, i.e. of θ:

$$w = p - \frac{(r + \lambda)pc}{q(\theta)}. \tag{13.11}$$

This relationship too is independent of whether one adopts a classical or a neo-classical theory of income distribution. In a classical approach with the rate of profit r taken as given and assumed for simplicity identical to the rate of interest, Eq. (13.11) indicates that search costs on the firm's side must be recuperated by paying labour a bit less than the wage one would obtain in the absence of search costs, represented here by p since labour is the only input and wages are not advanced;[21] the subtraction from p is the one required by the cost of the average duration of a vacancy.

This average duration is $1/q$, increasing in θ. The implication is that w is a decreasing function of the level of employment even when r is given: in a com-

---

20 The debt incurred by the firm does not influence A_J because it is a sunk cost, but it does influence the value of the firm, which when negative should cause the firm to go bankrupt. This shows the model is too simple, the risk of bankruptcy cannot be left out, and firms cannot be risk neutral.

21 In the presence of capital goods p can be reinterpreted as the maximum wage that could be paid at the given r if there were no search costs; if r is endogenous, neoclassically determined by the marginal product of capital, then p can be reinterpreted as the marginal product of labour, as will be shown below.

parison among stationary situations a rise of u implies a decrease of θ and of $1/q$, and the decreased duration of vacancies reduces the firm's cost of search, allowing the payment of a higher wage. However, the change in w is *very* small, a point never stressed in this literature but indubitable.

Consider the following numerical example. Let us measure output in such units that $p=1$. Possible values, abundantly greater than the evidence suggests, for r, λ, c are (with the year as time unit) $r=20\%$, $\lambda=20\%$, $c=2\%$, yielding $(r+\lambda)c=0.8\%$; so if $1/q$, the average duration of a vacancy, passes from $1/50$ (about a week) to 1 (a full year), the percentage $(r+\lambda)c/q$ to be subtracted from the maximum potential wage $w=1$ passes from 0.016 to 0.2%, a nearly unnoticeable change in a w always extremely close to 1.

In this calculation the values for r and λ are almost double what empirical evidence would suggest. I decided the magnitude of c on the basis of the following reasoning. The average duration of a vacancy varies from a week or less for unskilled jobs to a month or less for clerical and skilled manual jobs, to even much more than a month for highly skilled jobs which however are a very small percentage of all jobs, so the average is usually estimated to be almost one month. If a firm with 1000 workers needs to hire on average 240 workers a year (generally an ample overestimation), and these vacancies last a month on average, the cost to the firm on a monthly basis is 240C where C is the cost per month of an open vacancy (C is not c which is the cost as a percentage of p). It seems difficult that for this recruiting (advertising, interviewing, paperwork, etc.) of approximately 5 workers a week this firm will need more than 4 workers assigned full time to recruiting: this means not more than 4 monthly wages for 240 one-month vacancies, or $c=1/60=1.66\%$ of the monthly wage as the cost per month of unoccupied vacancy. Generously increasing the recruiting expense per month of vacancy to 2% of the monthly wage to cover advertising, etc., we obtain $c=2\%$. Note that it can be interpreted as an expense equal to one month's wage to hire a worker for an average of 50 months, which confirms it is an overestimation.

The negligible value of $p-w$ even when vacancies last a year may explain why the influence of search costs on wages was traditionally neglected. But if one decides not to neglect this very small difference $p-w$, then Eq. (13.11) has a degree of freedom: one needs something determining $q(\theta)$ or w or establishing another relationship that ties them together.

To this end, the approach argues that w is within limits indeterminate because the filling of a vacancy is a gain both for the firm which hires the worker and for the worker who accepts the job; either side can then ask for a share of the gain of the other side and use as bargaining weapon the threat to exit the hiring deal. The w resulting from this bargaining is an *increasing* function of θ, and this supplies the needed extra relationship to be added to Eq. (13.11): the latter makes w a *decreasing* (although, I have argued, a nearly horizontal) function of θ, so we can trace two functions tying w to θ in the non-negative orthant of the (θ, w) plane, one decreasing and the other increasing; the point where they cross determines the equilibrium (θ, w) couple. (I will neglect the question whether they do cross.) Then Eq. (13.4) determines u.

13.3 · Search Theory

In order to determine the gain for the worker, the approach proceeds in the same way as for firms, determining the values of hypothetical assets A_U and A_W corresponding to having the status, respectively, of unemployed person looking for a job, and of employed worker.[22] An unemployed worker receives some benefit from leisure, the possibility of domestic production, unemployment subsidies or unemployment insurance; assume the flow of such total unemployment benefits per unit of time can be described as equivalent in value to a given flow z of output, the same for all unemployed workers independently of how long they have been unemployed. Assuming workers are risk neutral, to z one must add the value of the probability of getting a job, an instantaneous probability given by the hazard rate $h = \theta q(\theta)$, that must be multiplied by the value A_J of having a job. Then, going directly to the expression from which the dt terms have been eliminated, the value A_U of being unemployed satisfies

$$rA_U = z + h(A_W - A_U) = z + \theta q(\theta)(A_W - A_U). \tag{13.12}$$

The magnitude rA_U is called the reservation wage in this literature, in the sense of being the minimum (expected) income flow from accepting a job, needed to induce the worker to abandon the status of unemployed worker and accept the job. Of course it is the reservation wage in a sense different from the usual one, and it depends on the market wage, increasing with the latter; it does not measure the wage below which the worker prefers not to supply labour, but rather the wage below which the worker prefers to go on searching.

Once a worker gets a job, assuming for simplicity that workers are eternal the only reason why she/he may stop earning w is that the job terminates for reasons independent of the worker's decisions; job terminations occur as a Poisson process with instantaneous probability λ. Hence the value of an occupied job satisfies:

$$rA_W = w + \lambda(A_U - A_W). \tag{13.13}$$

These two equations allow determining the equilibrium values of A_W and A_U in terms of $z, r, h(\theta), w, \lambda$ (see Pissarides 2000, p. 16). One can then calculate $A_W - A_U$; the result measures the gain from obtaining a job:

$$A_W - A_U = \frac{w - z}{r + \lambda + h}. \tag{13.14}$$

The gain for a firm of filling a vacancy is $A_J - A_V$, but in equilibrium $A_V = 0$ so the gain equals $A_J = \frac{p - w}{r + \lambda}$ (from Eq. (13.9)).

The approach calls 'rents' these two gains and argues that at each 'match' there is room for bargaining about the wage, because filling the vacancy creates a surplus equal to the sum of the two rents, $(A_J - A_V) + (A_W - A_U)$, which might go entirely to one of the two sides, or be shared. Either side can threaten not to accept the recruitment deal and thus cause the other side to lose the potential gain. It is

---

22 Pissarides uses U for A_U and W for A_W. I prefer to use U for unemployment.

1136   **Chapter 13 · Labour Markets and Income Distribution**

assumed that the result of bargaining is the one indicated by *generalized Nash bargaining*. This requires the wage in each specific bargaining session to satisfy

$$w = arg\,max(A_W - A_U)^\beta (A_J - A_V)^{1-\beta}, \tag{13.15}$$

where β is a coefficient indicating the 'bargaining power' of the worker. No indication is given as to what determines β.

The first-order condition satisfies $(A_W - A_U) = \beta[(A_J - A_V) + (A_W - A_U)]$; hence w is such that β is the share of the worker's gain in the total surplus. From the expressions indicated above for the gains, one derives (see Pissarides 2000, Chap. 1 for the detailed derivation):

$$w = (1 - \beta)z + \beta p(1 + \theta c). \tag{13.16}$$

This bargaining-produced relationship between w and θ for given z and c that I will indicate as $w = \psi(\theta)$ shows w to be an increasing function of θ. Pissarides (2000) views this as meaning that when θ increases 'the workers' bargaining strength is then higher' (p. 17), but this is misleading, the 'bargaining strength' is represented by β which is taken as given; the reason why w rises is that generalized Nash bargaining imposes that the ratio between the worker's gain and the firm's gain is fixed (equal to $\beta/(1 - \beta)$); this ratio can be written as follows:

$$\frac{A_W - A_U}{A_J - A_V} = \frac{w - r}{r + \lambda + h} \bigg/ \frac{p - w}{r + \lambda}. \tag{13.17}$$

Treating w for a moment as fixed, we see that a rise of h affects only the worker's gain, decreasing it; so in order for the value of the ratio not to change w must increase. (The reason why the firm's gain is not affected is that $A_V = 0$ and A_J is independent of the vacancy-filling cost because the latter cost is a sunk cost when the job is filled.) But the assumption that β is fixed is purely arbitrary.

Now let us consider the derivative of $\psi(\theta)$:

$$\partial\psi/\partial\theta = d\psi/d\theta = \beta pc. \tag{13.18}$$

I have argued that $c = 2\%$ is an ample overestimation of its plausible value. The most common assumption about β is 1/2. Normalizing p to 1, the function $w(\theta)$ has slope not more than 0.01. Since, as argued, Eq. (13.11) implies that w is very close to 1, then the approach produces absurd results. Assume z is 80% of w (an overestimation in general), then the $\psi(\theta)$ function crosses the $w(\theta)$ function determined by Eq. (13.11) somewhere around $\theta = 60$. That is, equilibrium requires around 60 vacancies for each unemployed worker. Not credible.

Things do not change if one introduces capital. Pissarides unproblematically treats capital in the way of Solow's growth model, as homogeneous output which when used as capital depreciates radioactively at rate δ; gross output is produced by a CRS production function, the same for all firms, $F(K, E) = F(K, pN)$ where $E = pN$ is labour in efficiency units and p is no longer output per unit of labour, but rather a labour-augmenting coefficient, which we might neglect (Pissarides needs it later to formulate balanced-growth models with technical progress) but I will maintain, to minimize the modifications relative to Pissarides. Capital's *net*

13.3 · Search Theory

marginal product $\partial F/\partial K - \delta K$ equals the rate of interest r; indicating K/E as k and $F(K/E, 1)$ as $f(k)$ we obtain $f'(k) = r + \delta$. Note that capital per unit of actual labour is pk and net output per unit of actual labour is $pf(k) - \delta pk$. The single firm is price-taker, treats r as given and hires additional capital pk when an additional job is filled, so as to keep satisfying the profit-maximizing condition $f'(k) = r + \delta$. There is a perfect second-hand capital market so if the job terminates the associated capital is not lost, and if it was bought rather than rented it can be resold with no loss. Now the value of a job with capital at any given instant is $A_J + pk$, and the condition corresponding to (13.9) becomes

$$r(A_J + pk) = pf(k) - \delta pk - w - \lambda A_J. \tag{13.19}$$

Comparison with Eq. (13.9) shows that p has been replaced by $p[f(k) - (r+\delta)k]$, which is simply the marginal product of actual labour, since the term in square brackets is the marginal product of an efficiency unit of labour, $\partial[F(K, E) - \delta K]/\partial E$. It can be shown (see Pissarides 2000, p. 25) that p is simply replaced by this marginal product of actual labour in all expressions, except in the measurement of waiting cost for the firm per unit of time per unit of labour, which is kept equal to pc. The stationary equilibrium conditions for a given r (i.e. assuming provisionally an infinite supply of capital at the interest rate r) become:

$$f'(k) = r + \delta. \tag{13.20}$$

$$w = p[f(k) - (r+\delta)k] - \frac{(r+\lambda)pc}{q(\theta)} \text{ where } q(\theta) = M(U, V)/V \text{ is decreasing in } \theta. \tag{13.21}$$

$$w = (1 - \beta)z + \beta p[f(k) - (r+\delta)k + \theta c]. \tag{13.22}$$

$$u = \lambda/(\lambda + h(\theta)) \quad \text{where } h(\theta) = \theta q(\theta) = M(U, V)/U \text{ is increasing in } \theta = V/U. \tag{13.23}$$

The last three correspond to Eqs. (13.11), (13.16) and (13.4) which were the equations determining the stationary state when labour was the only input and r was given. The only difference is that the product per unit of labour has been replaced by the marginal product per unit of (actual) labour MP_L, here represented by $p[f(k) - (r+\delta)k]$. (The considerations advanced above hold here too: the difference $MP_L - w$ is practically negligible for plausible values of the parameters r, λ, c, $1/q$; the equilibrium value of θ is in all likelihood implausibly large.)

The step is now simple to a complete neoclassical model. Firms 'are assumed large enough to eliminate all uncertainty about the flow of labour' (Pissarides 2000, p. 68), and all adopt the same CRS production function; therefore the economy can be treated as a single giant CRS firm and all one needs to assume is a given fully employed total stock K of capital. For each r, the above four equations determine both pk as the amount of K per unit θ of labour employment and the rate of unemployment, i.e. the amount N of employment, the moment total labour supply L is given, thus determining the demand for K. The latter demand is decreasing in r, because k is decreasing in r, and the $w(\theta)$ and the $\psi(\theta)$ curves are both shifted upwards by the decrease of r, the second one exactly by the rise in MP_L, the first one slightly more, so θ is very nearly unaffected (it increases slightly) and hence u and N too. This decreasing demand for K ensures the stability of the market for capital. The only difference relative to the equilibrium of a standard Solow-type neoclassical model with K and L as rigidly supplied factors is that, as Eq. (13.21) shows, labour earns a bit less than its marginal product (the first term on the right-hand side) because of the need to cover the firms' search costs, represented by the second term on the right-hand side; there is some unemployment because of the time required to refill the terminating jobs.

Besides the implausible values of equilibrium θ, the model suffers from the implausibility of the marginal/neoclassical approach to capital and income distribution. It may appear that the simple model presented first, the one with labour the only input and r given, which is the way the search-and-matching approach is generally taught to students, is independent of the neoclassical approach to income distribution, but in fact it is not: it implicitly assumes Say's Law by assuming that the moment a new vacancy has a positive value, some firm will open it up and there will be no difficulty with selling the increased production deriving from the new hirings; since the simple model must inevitably be introduced into a more complete model where there are capital goods and investment, Say's Law is justified in the simple model only if it is in the complete model, and this requires the neoclassical approach to distribution and employment.

Anyway even conceding Say's Law the stability of the process that should bring to the stationary equilibrium is not proved. The idea of the approach is that, for each given r, the labour market reaches the equilibrium level of employment determined by Eq. (13.4), and this determines the demand for K; if this demand is less than the supply of K, then r decreases a bit, the labour market reaches the corresponding new equilibrium with a greater demand for K per unit of labour, and the process continues until equilibrium is reached in the capital market too. Therefore the important thing is to prove that if r is given, the labour market's equilibrium is stable. Pissarides proves it by assuming perfect foresight that ensures that the only indefinitely sustainable fulfilled expectation path from any initial conditions is the unique saddle path that converges to the stationary state (Pissarides 2000, p. 29). This means assuming *no disequilibrium at all* but rather that on the basis of any given initial conditions u, λ (not v, vacancies are assumed to be a jump variable) the economy instantaneously reaches a perfect foresight intertemporal DSGE, which is in this case the stable saddle path converging to a stationary state. We have here one example of the change of the term 'stability of equilibrium' to mean, not stability of disequilibrium adjustments, but convergence of the intertemporal equilibrium path to a steady state, mentioned at the end of ▶ Sect. 8.17.1. The fact that true disequilibrium is not discussed at all is hidden by renaming 'equilibrium' the steady state and 'disequilibrium' the equilibrium path to it. This proof of 'stability' is then as acceptable as the assumption that after any 'shock' the economy instantaneously reaches a perfect foresight intertemporal equilibrium. And given the novelty of the framework relative to traditional (pre-neo-Walrasian) neoclassical theory, even the implicit argument discussed in ▶ Sect. 8.18 appears not available to the neoclassical economist.

13.3 · Search Theory

In the classical–Keynesian approach, where aggregate output and employment depend on aggregate demand, search costs cause no difficulty. Then in Eq. (13.4) u is given, and θ is determined by it; hence $q(\theta)$ in Eq. (13.11) is determined, and it determines w. There is no indeterminacy of w to be 'closed' by bargaining. The adaptation of θ poses no problem: since firms want to be able to satisfy demand, they hire as much as needed to replace job terminations $\lambda(1 - u)$, and to this end they open up new vacancies as much as needed to obtain a flow of hirings $m(u, v) = q(\theta)v = \lambda(1 - u)$, so, given the matching function, θ adapts to the given u. It is not even necessary to assume a matching function; one could, for example, assume q, the flow ratio of hirings out of vacancies, to be given; it would still be the case that firms would open new vacancies up to obtaining $qv = \lambda(1 - u)$; as to the average hazard rate h of exit from unemployment, whose reciprocal $1/h$ is the average length of unemployment spells, it will be given by Eq. (13.4) as

$$h = \lambda(1 - u)/u \tag{13.24}$$

whether a matching function exists or not. An increased search effort by workers, if it makes for a quicker filling of vacancies, does not reduce u nor $1/h$, its effect is that by allowing for a somewhat smaller search cost by firms it permits a slightly greater rate of profit if w is given, or a slightly greater w if r is given, but the variation is minuscule, so if r is given the increase in w is certainly less than required to compensate the workers' increased search costs.

Do we get out of attention to search costs some help towards understanding why wages are downward sticky even in the presence of considerable unemployment? Yes, I would say, because we are stimulated to ask how correct the search-and-matching approach is, in assuming that, whatever the size of the gain $A_W - A_U$ and the probability $h(\theta)$ of obtaining it, the worker will passively accept the situation and wait for a job offer to arrive at the market wage. At most the approach admits that the worker can increase search efforts, with the result of somewhat raising the hirings the matching function produces per time unit for given U and V. The approach introduces no possibility for a worker to signal she/he is ready to accept a job at a wage less than the market wage. This possibility is certainly present in real economies, and it might shorten the expected unemployment spell for the worker if she/he is the sole one to propose a lower wage.[23] Then an offer of wage reduction may or may not be convenient for the worker depending on the expected shortening of the unemployment spell the offer can produce and on the magnitude of $w - z$. For example, suppose an offer by the worker to accept $0.95 \cdot w$ reduces $1/h$ from one year to zero: immediate hiring. The worker avoids losing $w - z$ for a year in exchange for a loss of 5% of the market wage for the expected length of employment. Assume this length is 10 years, neglecting discounting, etc., the wage reduction is convenient if z is less than a half of w. This suggests that unless $(w - z)/w$ is far from being only a few percentage points

---

23 This is important: if the worker expects other unemployed workers to do the same and the employed workers to respond by offering to accept themselves the lower wage rather than be replaced, things drastically change. The issue will be discussed later in the chapter.

and furthermore the length of the avoided unemployment spell is significant, the worker does not find it convenient to propose a wage reduction: it is better to wait for a job at the market wage.

No doubt this goes some way towards explaining downward wage rigidity. But it is not enough. The workers' condition is not uniform; some workers suffer very long unemployment spells, and some (e.g. elderly workers who lose their job close to retirement age) may even feel they are nearly unemployable at the market wage. Also, workers are not risk neutral as implicitly assumed in this approach, and risk aversion strengthens the incentive to propose wage reductions. And then, how easy do unemployed workers find it to resist and wait without an income? The search-and-matching approach implicitly assumes that it is easy, but the difficulty with resisting for even only a month without an income was the main cause of the bargaining weakness of workers according to Adam Smith, and certainly it is still relevant today in many cases, although less so if unemployment subsidies allow a bearable subsistence; but unemployment subsidies are often absent and have been missing for the greater part of the history of capitalism. So we should observe many more offers by unemployed workers to accept a lower wage than are actually observed. Let us then continue our search for explanations.

13.4 Implicit Contracts

An idea which was for a time very popular among mainstream labour and macroeconomists is the idea of implicit contracts, for which a basic reference is Azariadis (1975). It is an attempt to confirm that labourers are fundamentally on their supply curve all along the business cycle, surmounting difficulties of the real business cycle approach. The latter approach is unable convincingly to explain the evidence of considerable changes in employment with little changes in wages in the business cycle. The implicit contract approach focuses precisely on this issue and explains the constancy of wages as due to an implicit insurance function of the unchanging wage.

Suppose an industry whose labour force for some reason encounters high costs in looking for jobs in other industries. This may be due, e.g., to specialization, or to geographical distance from other job opportunities. The industry's homogeneous labour force can change owing to inflows and outflows, but only very slowly, so that in the short-period one can take its size m as given. Either one works full time, or one is unemployed. The industry's demand for labour n undergoes random fluctuations, due, for example, to climate or irregular abundance of fish, or to fluctuations in the position of the industry's demand curve due, e.g., to the business cycle. If $n < m$, hiring is random and the likelihood of being hired for the period is n/m. Labour hirings are for a limited time, say, a month, then hiring is repeated, so a labourer who remains unemployed has a good chance of being employed in the near future, both because there is a likelihood of n being greater next month and because of the random selection of hired workers each month. The fluctuations of n are known (which means an implicit assumption of rational expectations). Then for each level of m and of wages elsewhere there will be a constant wage w^*, higher than *permanent* wages elsewhere, that makes it as convenient for workers to stay in the industry as to go elsewhere, because the disutility of the random unemployment spells is compensated by the higher wage when employed. This constant wage is viewed in this approach as avoiding the wage fluctuations that would be associated with a supply-and-demand equilibrium of the labour market, given that there are fluctuations in the industry's productivity or product demand; thus, it is argued there is an element of insurance in the constant wage. Workers are risk averse; firms are risk neutral or at least considerably less risk averse than workers; therefore it is possible to have a constant wage with a present value *less* than the present value of the oscillating time path of the equilibrium wage, and yet preferred by workers to the fluctuating equilibrium wage, *even* when account is taken of the expected unemployment spells; so that both workers, and the industry, can be better off than with the fluctuating equilibrium wage. Azariadis was able to prove that it can be convenient for firms to lay off workers when revenue prospects are particularly low, and still there can be a constant wage preferred both by workers and by firms to the equilibrium wage path.

If the wage is fixed at a level different from w^*, m slowly changes tending towards the ratio to n that makes workers indifferent between staying in the industry or leaving. It may then seem that there is a degree of freedom in the fixation of the wage (a higher w will, although slowly, induce a higher m and hence a lower n/m that will compensate for the higher wage); but this is eliminated by considering firm competition in the product market, because if the wage is such that firms make positive pure profits, entry of further firms will reduce product price and profits, finally obliging firms to reduce the wage they offer. The 'implicit contract' element is the implicit agreement not to have wage competitively re-established every period at the supply = demand level, and to have re-employment of the fired workers as soon as possible. The result is a constant wage in all periods, for those workers who are employed. Workers implicitly accept to be occasionally unemployed, and it is all part of the implicit contract. The excess of w^* over a permanent employment constant wage depends also on the utility of leisure, which is influenced by the achievable household production and by unemployment benefits. In the short period, part of the potential welfare increase of workers may be absorbed by firms, as in all cases of risk sharing that allows both partners to be better off; but in the end the competitive tendency of profits to zero causes the gain to go to workers.

The actual formalizations are quite complicated because they must compare the fixed-wage situation with the period-by-period neoclassical competitive wage situation, but the basic intuition is as described. The conclusion is that habits and conventions will tend to establish a rigid wage for employed workers because they prefer it owing to risk aversion.

The intuition can be generalized to the entire economy. The basic idea is that labour mobility across industries is limited, and in each industry workers prefer a rigid wage when employed, to a fluctuating wage, and through conventions and custom this preference has been institutionalized.

1142   **Chapter 13** · Labour Markets and Income Distribution

Let us attempt an evaluation of the approach. It is not difficult to imagine situations in which the picture of a labour force specific to an industry or a firm and changing only slowly is realistic, and where workers remain there in spite of spells of unemployment, with a higher wage compensating for this fact relative to other industries where employment is more regular. This contributes to explaining *relative* wages, not the average wage level, because the convenience to remain in an industry depends on relative wages. We find here the third one of reasons indicated by Adam Smith as explaining persistent differences in wages: 'the constancy or inconstancy of employment' in different occupations (WN Bk I, x, iii; 1975 Dent ed., vol. 1 p. 89). Along this route one can also conceive a tendency towards an 'equilibrium' distribution of the employed labour force among various occupations; but not an explanation of unemployment, more unemployment will only mean a smaller n/m ratio in more or less all industries.

But the approach aims to explain above all why wages do not decrease when labour demand decreases and unemployment increases. The thesis is: (1) shifts of the labour demand curve are regular enough to be stochastically predictable; (2) given the fluctuating wage that would be established by regular supply–demand equilibrium, workers prefer a stable wage when employed as a way to bear less risk of income fluctuations; (3) some conventions have been able to develop that have caused such an arrangement to come about, and once in existence, it is convenient to maintain it.

Two fundamental perplexities arise concerning (1).

First, stochastic predictability of productivity or of product market conditions may perhaps hold in some industries for variations caused by climate or other natural causes, but most definitely not for variations caused by aggregate demand. The history of the evolution of aggregate demand is one of predictive mistakes. The assumption of rational expectations implicitly made in this approach rests on the thesis that the growth path of the economy is stochastically predictable, but this thesis has been amply falsified by historical experience: the growth rate of the euro area was systematically overestimated year after year for at least ten years after the birth of the euro zone; the Japanese nearly zero growth rate in the 1990s was not expected at all; the crisis that began in 2007 was unexpected, like most previous financial crises. The pace of technical progress too is not easily predictable, and the slowdown in the growth rate of labour productivity in the 1980s and 1990s was not predicted.

Second, the approach requires a (stochastic) predictability not only of aggregate demand, but of the labour demand curve; we have seen that this notion has no theoretical consistency. But without it, step (2) is impossible, because it is impossible to determine a supply-and-demand equilibrium wage; therefore the idea of a path of the equilibrium wage, relative to which a constant wage of the same expected value is preferred by workers, becomes impossible to sustain.

There are further weaknesses of the approach even relative to a neoclassical framework. First, variations of aggregate demand can be very long-lasting: a depression can last ten years, and it seems utterly unrealistic that firms maintain wages higher than the marginal product of labour for such long time stretches. Second, if there is such a capacity of markets to throw up implicit efficient contracts, it is unclear why one does not observe even more efficient contracts, e.g. explicit (i.e. legally enforceable) contracts including a specification of how firing and re-hiring will operate and under what outside conditions, thus reducing uncertainty and the possibility that the firm may default on the implicit contract.

In conclusion, the reason for a rather rigid real wage must be looked for elsewhere.

Another difficulty of the approach arises when one admits that Azariadis' assumption that each worker either works a fixed amount of hours or doesn't work at all is too rigid. In real economies there is some flexibility of hours per week, and the optimal implicit contract should utilize this flexibility by making workers work more when they are more productive. Subsequent work on implicit contracts has indeed assumed that the contract specifies the wage and hours for each possible state of the world (see, e.g., Romer 2012, pp. 479–481). But the result has been that, if labour is more productive of profits in booms than in busts, then hourly wages are *countercyclical*, in contrast to the empirical evidence that shows that they are constant or moderately pro-cyclical. Also unconvincing is that in this version unemployment disappears: all workers work the same variable number of hours, and no one is fired in downturns, against the empirical evidence. (This version is therefore unhelpful for the question we are posing, which presumes the existence of unemployment.)

13.5 Insiders–Outsiders

The central idea of the insider–outsider approach is that, owing to *turnover costs*, the *insiders* (workers who have already been working in a firm for some time) can ask for a wage higher than the minimum wage asked for by *outsiders* (workers still to be hired) without fearing to be replaced by *entrants* (newly hired outsiders). The outsiders are not ready to accept a wage low enough to make it convenient for firms to replace insiders with outsiders, and because of this the insiders can obtain a wage higher than the outsiders' reservation wage. The approach argues that turnover costs are made higher than they might be by the insiders' hostile attitude to entrants, which may include refusal properly to train them, harassment, mobbing, sabotage of the results of the work of the newly hired and even lower morale with general decrease of productivity if the firm replaces some insider with new entrants. The reservation wage of outsiders is in turn raised by the lesser attractiveness of getting a job owing to the hostility of insiders.

The approach couples this basic idea with the neoclassical decreasing demand curve for labour and argues that one must distinguish two demand curves, a first one reflecting the actual marginal product of a (trained) labourer and a second one which is the first one shifted downwards by the amount of turnover costs per labourer if one replaces an insider with an outsider. Given the amount of insiders, replacing one insider with an outsider is convenient for the firm only if the outsider's wage is not more than the marginal product of the stock of insiders minus the turnover cost. The addition of the costs caused by the insiders' hostility to the inevitable paperwork, search, training costs and severance costs causes the turnover cost to be considerable and renders plausible, the approach argues, that the outsiders' reservation wage be above the maximum outsiders' wage required to replace an insider. This is argued to explain why wages do not decrease in spite of the indubitable presence of unemployed workers more than willing to accept a job at the ruling market wage, the wage of insiders.

It is unnecessary for our purposes to enter a more detailed discussion of the way the approach combines the basic idea with the neoclassical labour demand curve at the level of a single firm (where the amounts of factors other than labour can be taken as given only in the short period, while the approach aims at long-period conclusions) and at the level of the entire economy (where the issue of formation of new firms cannot be avoided). The following observations appear relevant independently of whether the basic idea is combined with a neoclassical framework.

First, if the approach were valid it should be frequently observed that when an insider retires the firm does not find it convenient to hire an outsider and lets its workforce decrease; this is not observed.

Second, the history of the labour movement strongly suggests that if employed and unemployed workers are of the same race language and community (this is or has historically been the case in many European nations) then insiders' hostility towards outsiders is non-existent. Existence of this hostility is less implausible when a nation or region witnesses the arrival of many migrants of a very different culture, or suffers from deep racial divisions as the USA. However, even the existence of the hostility-based turnover costs seems insufficient to prevent the employment of the unemployed at a lower wage. The reason is that *new firms can be born with a workforce consisting entirely of outsiders*, in which case hostility-based turnover costs are absent. Nor can one counter that unless firms last only one year, these new firms after one year will find themselves with an insider workforce and hence with a tendency of wages to rise to the same level as in other older firms: the insiders of these one-year-old firms are of the same race or religion or nationality as the outsiders, so the reasons for hostility-based turnover costs are absent. This is important also for the following reason: Lindbeck and Snower (1988) argue that one effect of harassment is to raise the outsiders' reservation wage above what it would otherwise be, by making working conditions for the outsiders more unpleasant. But if so, then the wage asked by outsiders to join new firms composed entirely of outsiders is below the reservation wage to join firms with a hostile workforce, one more reason for these new firms to be born and to put pressure on the profitability of firms with an insider workforce.

Third, the relevance of turnover costs not due to hostility is doubtful too. Let us start with hiring and firing costs: these (apart from severance payments) are very small compared with the cost even only of one year of wages. Severance payments, when they exist, are generally proportional to the length of employment of the worker with the firm, they are actually a cumulated delayed wage payment, so the firm knows that if it does not fire the insider now it will have to pay a greater severance payment in future, and therefore it considers the wage cost of the insider to be the spot wage *plus* the sum to be set aside so as to be able to pay the increase in future severance payment; it is to *this* that the marginal revenue product of the insider must be equal. Therefore turnover costs should *not* include severance payments, and then hiring and firing turnover costs are in all likelihood of very little relevance.

As to training costs, it is a frequent element of labour contracts that newly hired workers go through a probation/training period, in which they are paid less because of their lesser efficiency and because of the cost to the firm of having to assign some other workers' time to assist and teach the newcomer. Training costs are therefore easily compensated by lower initial wages for a specified period. (Wages tied to seniority are another way of compensating for the initially lower efficiency of workers.) If the lesser wage during the probation period only compensates for the training costs, and there is a clear enforceable engagement by the firm to promote the newcomer to permanent employment with normal wage at the end of the training period, then the existence of training costs gives no bargaining power to insiders.

This is confirmed by the inevitable need to hire outsiders owing to retirement of the oldest insiders. Replacing workers who leave is indispensable for production to continue. Firms cannot but have developed ways to deal with the lesser efficiency of newly hired workers. As noted by Bertola (1990), all insiders started as entrants: how come they were hired? It seems plausible that outsiders, conscious of the fact that, once they become insiders, their wage will rise, are ready to accept an initial wage *lower* than the lowest wage they would be ready to accept if the latter were expected to remain unchanged in future. Then anything that raises the insiders' wage *lowers* the entrants' reservation *initial* wage, and a sufficiently lower initial wage for, say, a year will abolish the firm's resistance to new hirings without causing a refusal of the unemployed to accept.

Fourth, the insider–outsider approach explains the hostility of insiders towards newly hired outsiders due to the insiders' desire not to be *replaced*. But what about hiring an outsider in order to *add* a further worker to the already existing workforce? This would be the case, for example, when some insider reaches retiring age and the firm does not wish to reduce production. Firing costs would not be present, and the reasons for hostility due to fear of being replaced would not be present either. Only training costs would remain, but firms must be presumed to have a way to deal with them, since training costs are inevitable when some hiring of new workers is made necessary by the need to replace retiring insiders; it may consist of an initially lower wage, or of a wage calculated by the firm so as to cover training costs over the average length of a job: this is how presumably insiders too have been and are treated.

In a neoclassical framework where Say's Law avoids difficulties with selling increased amounts of output and where there is a decreasing demand curve for labour, the above considerations imply that the only obstacle to expanding the workforce by hiring outsiders ready to accept a lifelong wage somewhat below the market wage is costs caused by strong hostility of insiders; but the latter costs can be found at most in a small minority of the known historical situations.

The approach has so many and so glaring weaknesses that it appears to be the biased result of an ideological desire to accuse the employed workers of being selfish and nasty and of bearing all responsibility for unemployment, while absolving governments from any duty to intervene to cure unemployment.[24]

With respect to the question we are posing, the approach also suffers from having to take the reservation wage of the outsiders as given. A sufficient decrease of this reservation wage would make it convenient to replace insiders with outsiders even accepting the insider–outsider approach. Why isn't this reservation wage lower than the approach must take it to be? Where are the other opportunities for an income while unemployed, that prevent it from decreasing? Let me repeat again that unemployment benefits are a comparatively recent institution, and often not present, and that they are generally insufficient to make the unemployed indifferent between accepting a job and remaining unemployed: when a job is offered at the going wage, there is usually no problem with receiving ample numbers of applicants.

In conclusion, hostility of portions of the working class against other portions of the working class can of course have existed and exist, but offer no explanation of why wages do not decrease in the presence of unemployment.

13.6 Efficiency Wages

13.6.1 Five Versions

The basic answer of efficiency wage theories to our question is that it is *firms* that do not let wages decrease in the presence of unemployment, and refuse to hire workers proposing to work for a lower wage, because a lower wage reduces output per worker so much that profit *decreases*. Five very different reasons can cause this to happen:

1. *Nutrition.* Too low wages do not allow workers to eat enough to be strong and healthy.
2. *Adverse selection.* Lower wages induce lower-quality workers to apply for a job with the firm, thus lowering the average quality or quantity of the labour performed by the workforce per time unit.
3. *Turnover costs.* Higher wages reduce turnover, thus allowing savings on turnover costs (hiring and firing costs, and especially training costs).
4. *Shirking.* Lower wages decrease the incentive to avoid shirking, due to the threat of firing the workers caught loafing on the job, because the loss of utility associated with being fired decreases.
5. *Gift exchange.* Higher wages induce a feeling of gratitude towards the firm that stimulates workers to be more efficient in reciprocation.

---

24 Lindbeck and Snower (1986, 1988) insist that very little can be done to change the situation, owing to the strength of the cultural and customary elements that give strength to insiders: thus the responsibility for unemployment lies with the insiders' selfishness, *and* policy interventions are useless; we must resign ourselves to unemployment. A very convenient conclusion if what is really desired is that unemployment be not reduced, a Marxian or Kaleckian economist would say.

13.6 · Efficiency Wages

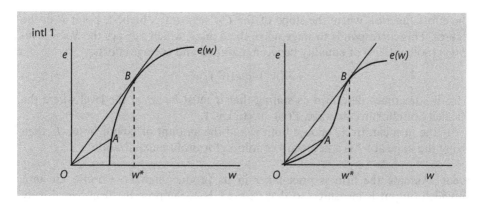

Fig. 13.1 Hourly wage, effort, determination of the efficiency wage with two different shapes of the dependence of effort on the hourly real wage

Reason 1 (Leibenstein 1957) is at the origin of the term 'efficiency wages' because it suggests that it is inefficient to pay very low wages that cause workers to be underfed, hence weak; it may be highly relevant in very poor nations, but seems irrelevant in less poor nations, and need not be further discussed. However, it supplies a very easy-to-grasp justification of the idea that the real wage per time unit can influence how much the worker produces in a time unit: heavy manual labour cannot be performed without a sufficient caloric intake; so the reader can provisionally adopt this as the reason for the basic idea of the approach. Assume a firm employs L units of labour (measured in time units, e.g. hours); all workers are identical, and the other factors are given; output from L units of labour varies depending on the effort, attention, conscientiousness of the workers during the L hours. This can be formalized as output $Y=F(eL)$, where e is 'quantity of effort per time unit' or also 'efficiency of labour'; eL can be interpreted as 'amount of effective labour services supplied', but for short I will call it 'amount of effort'.[25] If a smaller L produces the same Y, the reason must be a greater e. Assume e is a function of the real wage w per unit of time, the same function for all workers, and that this effort function $e(w)$ is smooth and increasing, $e'(w)>0$, and strictly concave, $e''(w)<0$, at least from a certain level of w onwards. Two possible shapes of the effort function are shown in ◘ Fig. 13.1.

The amount of effort per time unit obtained by the firm per unit of labour is $e(w)$; hence the cost of a unit of effort is $w/e(w)$, the reciprocal of the slope of the segment connecting a point of the effort function with the origin (OA is one such segment). The firm minimizes what it pays for each unit of effort at the point on

---

25 Bowles (2004) rejects the term 'efficiency wages' at least for the shirking version, arguing that it produces several inefficiencies (see ◘ Fig. 13.2 for one of them). I use the term because it is the accepted term and because it can be interpreted as not intended to deny the existence of inefficiencies, but only intended to point out that, given the institutional structure, it is efficient *for the capitalistic firm* to pay that wage and not less.

1148   **Chapter 13 · Labour Markets and Income Distribution**

the effort function where the slope of the OA segment is highest, point B in the figures. This corresponds to wage w^* in the figures, which satisfies the *Solow condition* (Solow 1979) of equality between marginal and average efforts:

$$e'(w^*) = e(w^*)/w^*. \tag{13.25}$$

This is sometimes described as stating that w must be set at the level where the elasticity of effort to the wage, $e'(w) \cdot w/e(w)$, is 1.

If the firm can freely choose both w and the amount of labour hours L, then fixing the wage at w^* is a necessary condition for profit maximization.

Proof Assume the firm is price-taker in its product market. Choose the unit in which output is measured so that its price is 1. Suppose the firm has already determined the amounts of other inputs so that function $F(eL)$ is well determined. The firm's profit is $\pi = F(e(w) \cdot L) - wL$, to be maximized with respect to w and L. The first-order conditions for a maximum are

$$\partial\pi/\partial L = F' \cdot e'(w) \cdot L - L = 0$$
$$\partial\pi/\partial w = F' \cdot e(w) - w = 0.$$

The first condition implies $F' = 1/e'(w)$; the second implies $F' = w/e(w)$; the two together imply the Solow condition. ∎

Thus $w = w^*$ is a necessary condition for profit maximization whichever the amounts of other factors; therefore it must also be satisfied if these other amounts are in turn chosen to maximize π. The reason is that whatever the output $Y = F(eL)$ to be produced, cost minimization requires that the cost of the required amount of effort eL be minimized, and this is obtained by setting $w = w^*$ which minimizes the cost of each unit of effort, and by then choosing L so that $e(w^*)L$ yields the needed amount of effort. Note that this holds for an imperfectly competitive firm too.

This means that w^* is independent of L and dependent only on the effort function $e(w)$. This is a possible explanation of wage rigidity. If an unemployed worker offers to work for a wage less than w^*, it will be the firm that will refuse to employ him/her, because the lower wage would cause such a decrease in the worker's productivity that the firm's profit would decrease. In the efficiency wage approaches, it is firms that refuse to let wages decrease in the presence of unemployment.

To describe the implication in a neoclassical framework, let us indicate amounts of effort, i.e. amounts eL of effective labour services, with the single symbol Λ (capital lambda) and the cost $w/e(w)$ of a unit of effort with the single symbol ω. Since it is effort that enters production functions as a factor of production, Λ takes the place of labour in the neoclassical factor substitution mechanisms. These, according to the neoclassicals, allow deriving a decreasing aggregate demand curve for Λ as a function of its unit cost ω; this implies a definite total demand for Λ once ω is given; since minimum ω^* is given once the effort function is given, there is no guarantee that the resulting demand for labour hours,

$$L^* = \Lambda(\omega^*)/e(w^*), \tag{13.26}$$

13.6 · Efficiency Wages

will equal the supply of labour hours: unemployment is a possible result.

The arguments leading to a rigid w^* do not require the neoclassical framework; in a classical–Keynesian framework the given $e(w^*)$ will determine the demand for labour determined by the given aggregate demand.

In both frameworks, depending on the reason for the influence of wages on effort the effort function can be made to depend on other things besides the hourly wage, and one important influence can be the rate of unemployment (the fear of the sack can induce more effort). In a neoclassical framework this will mean a simultaneous determination of aggregate demand, the rate of unemployment and w^*. In a classical–Keynesian framework with aggregate demand given, even with technical coefficients taken as little affected by the wage there will still be some (presumably minor) element of simultaneous determination of unemployment and of w^* because a given demand for total amount of effort Λ will not determine employment until $e(w^*)$ is determined, and w^* will also depend on the level of unemployment; the level of aggregate demand will anyway be treated as given at least in a first approximation (the level of w^* might influence the multiplier).

Let us briefly examine the four more relevant versions of the approach.

13.6.2 Adverse Selection

There is *adverse selection* when a good (or a worker) can be of different qualities, it is not easy for the buyer to ascertain its quality, and changes in the price offered for the good influence the average quality of the supply of the good in a direction which is not advantageous for buyers. A brief discussion of adverse selection was offered in ▶ Chap. 11.

Adverse selection can be argued to be one reason for efficiency wages. It is assumed that workers differ in the quantity of labour services they produce per time unit, which is a given quantity independent of the wage (as long as the worker accepts the contract); this quantity, indexed by η, is distributed according to a cumulative distribution function $G(h)$ defined over the interval $\left[\eta^-, \eta^+\right]$. Crucially, the reservation wage of labourers, ρ, is a strictly increasing function of η. The argument for this assumption is that 'Such a hypothesis seems natural, inasmuch as the most efficient individuals in the labor market generally have some way to make their competence pay off outside this market' (Cahuc and Zylberberg 2004, p. 268). This is not very convincing, because it means there must be some other productive activity where the difference in efficiency comes out clearly (or can be expected to come out clearly, e.g. because of past experience or education), then it should be in the interest of the worker to supply proof to the firm about her/his efficiency if it is above average, but this is assumed not to happen. Employers are unable to ascertain the η of each worker and only know the cumulative distribution function $G(\eta)$, so they must offer the same w to all workers, and labour supply will consist of those workers for whom $w \geq \rho(\eta)$. As w decreases, the average productivity of labour supply decreases because the highest $\rho(\eta)$ satisfying $\rho(\eta) = w$ decreases and hence the average η of those willing to work decreases: adverse selection. The expected productivity of a worker, conditional on the wage, is given by

$$E(\eta|w) = \frac{\int_{\eta-}^{\eta^\wedge} \eta dG(\eta)}{G(\eta^\wedge)} \quad \text{where } \eta^\wedge \text{is determined by } \rho\left(\eta^\wedge\right) = w. \tag{13.27}$$

The numerator of the fraction is the total amount of labour services produced by workers with productivity from η^- to $\eta^\wedge$, where $\eta^\wedge$ indicates the highest value of η compatible with workers' willingness to work at the given w. If one assumes that firms are big and employ a large number of workers randomly chosen among the applicants, average productivity in each firm sufficiently approximates $E(\eta|w)$.

It is then possible (if workers, conscious of the difficulty of proving their η, are ready to accept a wage somewhat below their actual productivity) that, as w rises, $E(\eta|w)$ traces a curve in the (w, η) plane with the same shape as the $e(w)$ curves in ◘ Fig. 13.1; then minimization of the cost of a unit of actual labour services will entail the solution reached there, the point of tangency (compare Weiss 1990, p. 20).

But the approach is not convincing because it needs to assume that workers are truly indistinguishable, even after they have been with a firm for some time. 'In a long-run perspective, the degree to which adverse selection problems affect the labor market must decline significantly. At that horizon, it is difficult to sustain the hypothesis that firms do not observe the productive characteristics of their employees' (Cahuc and Zylberberg 2004, p. 270).

Also, the approach encounters serious problems if applied to the general wage level. The best workers can refuse to work for a firm only if they have a way to obtain a higher income elsewhere, but if wages decrease everywhere, where can these best workers earn more? Must we suppose that they can earn more by turning to independent labour activities because they are good private detectives or tennis teachers? If competition operates, the incomes in these activities too will decrease if wage labour incomes decrease.

13.6.3 Turnover Costs

Turnover costs are due to the need to replace workers who leave their jobs, be it because they are fired or because of spontaneous quits. These costs include bureaucratic paperwork, the cost of advertising vacancies, the need to assign a few workers to the task of screening applicants and, above all, training costs, which include the need to assign some more expert workers to train newcomers, and the lower productivity of newcomers during the training period. The efficiency wage picture arises if wages negatively affect quits so much that a lower wage increases turnover costs to such an extent that the average cost of a given amount of labour services to the firm increases. This is no doubt possible, but it is not likely to be a main reason why a firm resists wage reductions. The problem is that turnover costs are seldom a significant component of labour costs for a firm; the wage reduction must cause a very great increase in turnover in order for the

13.6 · Efficiency Wages

cost decrease due to the lower wage to be more than compensated by the increase in turnover costs. It is much more likely that the wage reduction is not convenient because it worsens the quality of workmanship.

Let us consider the experience of Henry Ford (see Raff and Summers 1987). On 5 January 1914 he announced he would pass from offering a wage of 2.34 dollars a day for 9 h a day to offering 5 dollars a day for eight hours a day; this reduced turnover *very* considerably. But was this the reason for Ford's 20% higher profits? The year before Ford had an average workforce of 13,623 and 50,448 terminations (most of them spontaneous quits, since only 8490 were firings). This means workers lasted on average a little more than three months. It is known that a Ford superintendent claimed that 'two days is … ample time to make a first-class core molder of a man who has never seen a core-molding bench in his life'. There is little reason to expect training to have taken longer in the other jobs to which the 5-dollars-a-day wage offer applied (obviously it did not apply to managers and engineers), and probably some hirings were re-hirings of people who had already gone through training, but to be on the safe side let us assume a loss of production equivalent to zero production for three working days for each change of worker; this makes 1 day per month per occupied job of wage paid against no production, i.e. less than 5% extra wage costs for the same output than with zero turnover (assuming the same labour efficiency). The need for an average of about 200 new hirings each working day (assuming 250 working days in a year) cannot have required more than 20 workers assigned full time to recruiting, less than 0.2% of the workforce, a negligible increase in wage costs. This suggests that in order for the increase in turnover costs to have been the reason why the wage was not decreased below $2.34, Ford must have expected turnover costs to *double* if the wage was decreased by 5%. Not likely. It is much more likely that a wage reduction would have made it difficult to have enough applicants to replace the leavers (this is not a *turnover* cost, it is supply less than demand), and would have increased shabby work and absenteeism (which ran at about 10% each day). The importance of effort is highlighted by the fact that the wage increase did reduce turnover from 370% to only 16% a year, but that would have meant a huge loss if there had not been a strong increase in productivity, between 40% and 70% depending on the task. Absenteeism fell to 2.5%. Evidently at the previous lower wage the workers felt so little attracted by the jobs in Ford's factory that not only they did not stay long, but also worked very shabbily while there, and this was way more relevant than turnover costs.

When the wage offered by a firm is reduced, turnover costs can be expected considerably to increase (although in all likelihood still not enough to compensate the wage reduction) only if before the reduction the wage was the same as in other firms, and the other firms do not reduce their wages; then the workers in the first firm are ready to leave to other firms the moment these have open vacancies. The firm with the lower wage can be treated as a temporary parking space while waiting for the better-paid jobs. But the turnover costs will be significant only for jobs requiring a long and costly training period: the firm does not wish to lose trained workers to other firms, and this can prevent the firm from reducing their wage. But if there are unemployed workers offering to accept a lower wage, all firms will

1152 Chapter 13 · Labour Markets and Income Distribution

notice it, and it is difficult to think that no firm will dare be the first to propose a lower *entrance* wage: if competition works, the other firms will quickly follow, and then for the generality of new hires the entire wage path, including its seniority increases, will be lower than for the earlier hires. And when the wage decrease is generalized rather than only in one firm, there is little reason to expect a significant increase in turnover, apart from the case (from which advanced nations are far) of a wage becoming so low that workers are practically indifferent between working, and surviving in some other way: begging, scavenging rubbish dumps, petty crime.

On this basis, we can neglect turnover costs as a significant reason for refusals by the firms themselves to let wages decrease.

13.6.4 Shirking

The more widely accepted reason for downward wage rigidity in the efficiency wage approach is that a lower wage decreases the effort per time unit performed by workers, because it reduces the loss associated with being fired owing to being caught loafing on the job. The simplest version of this idea, due to Solow (1979), formally coincides with the nutrition version with which this section started: effort (actual labour services) is simply assumed to be an increasing, concave function of the wage. More complex versions have been elaborated afterwards. Here we study one of the more elaborate versions, the one by Samuel Bowles in his advanced textbook *Microeconomics* (2004, pp. 267–298), which is more complete than the popular version of Shapiro and Stiglitz (1984) in that it admits a continuously variable level of effort rather than just two levels.

The starting point is that the labour contract is necessarily *incomplete*, work effort cannot be established explicitly in the labour contract because it is *not verifiable* by an impartial third party and therefore is not usable in law suits, so it is useless to specify it in the contract; this is because it is only imperfectly ascertainable, both because of team production and because of excessive cost of continuous monitoring; nor can it be deduced with certainty from observed output, because of stochastic disturbances. So effort must be 'extracted' from workers by means other than an explicit level established by contract. The employer and workers are then in a *principal–agent* relationship (see ▶ Chap. 11).

Let $e \in [0, 1]$ be effort by one worker per unit of work time. This time unit will be called 'hour', but it can stand for any time unit; for example it will mean 40 h, if the time unit is the week and the contract establishes a working week of 40 h. The number L of 'hours' of labour employed by a firm is then also the number of workers employed per time unit. Workers are identical. Output per 'hour' or per worker is

$$y = y(e) + \varepsilon$$

where e is effort (actual amount of labour services) per 'hour' and ε is a mean zero disturbance term.

The employer monitors workers, with a monitoring level m per 'hour' of labour hired. The employer *knows* (has learned from past experience) the worker's best response function $e(w, m; z)$ where w is the real wage and z is the worker's fall-

13.6 · Efficiency Wages

back utility in case the job is not renewed; z depends on unemployment benefits, on the utility of leisure and possible homework production, and on the probable length of the unemployment spell before a new job is found. At the beginning of the period, the profit-maximizing employer selects and announces w, m and a (truthful) termination probability $t(e, m) \in [0, 1]$, dependent on the probability that the employer discovers shirking, with partial derivatives $t_e < 0$ and $t_m > 0$ over the relevant ranges. Each worker then decides on e for the period, so as to maximize the present value of her lifetime utility. At the end of the period, the worker is paid, and employment is terminated with probability $t(e, m)$. If there is termination, the worker obtains a present value z of lifetime utility and is replaced by an identical worker from the unemployment pool (*there is* an unemployment pool, as we will see). If there is no termination, the interaction is repeated identical next period. For simplicity, the possibility of job termination because of the firm's need to reduce production or close down is neglected, or considered included in $t(e, m)$.

Increased effort reduces the probability of termination, because it reduces the probability that one is discovered shirking; increased monitoring raises the likelihood that one is discovered shirking and therefore makes it convenient for workers to reduce shirking.

To determine the worker's best response function, we study the worker's utility maximization. The worker's per-period utility function when employed is

$$u = u(w, e)$$

with partial derivatives $u_w \geq 0$ and $u_e < 0$ over the relevant ranges. One can admit $u_e > 0$ initially, but clearly it will soon change sign as e rises. The worker has a rate of time preference i and at the beginning of the period chooses e to maximize v, the present value of *expected* utility over an *infinite* lifetime (i.e. the worker is assumed immortal; a given probability of death per period would change little; on the contrary, retirement for age reasons can have important consequences on which we will have to return). This present value is determined by a recursive definition (that resembles the one illustrated in the search approach, except that here time is treated as discrete); this sums to the utility to be obtained by the end of the current period the two possible values of subsequent expected utility depending on whether the job is terminated or not:

$$v = (1 + i)^{-1} \{u(w, e) + [1 - t(e, m)]v + t(e, m)z\}. \tag{13.28}$$

The interpretation is not difficult. At the end of the period under consideration the worker earns $u(w, e)$ and, being at the beginning of the next period, has an expected lifetime utility again of v if still with the job and of z if fired. VNM utility and risk neutrality are implicitly assumed, so these two expected lifetime utilities are weighted, at the beginning of the period under consideration, by their probabilities of occurrence.

For the moment z is treated as exogenous; in fact its determination requires the rate of unemployment, as explained below.

The worker selects e so as to maximize v, hence so as to obtain $v_e = 0$. The worker treats z as exogenous, and its difference from v depends on unemployment benefits and on the average length of the time spent as unemployed before finding a new job and returning to an expected lifetime utility v, all variables the worker cannot affect. Let us isolate v in (13.28) by using $(1+i)v = u + v - t(e,m)v + t(e,m)z$ to obtain $v = (i+t)^{-1}(u + t(e,m)z + iz - iz)$ and finally:

$$v = \frac{u(w,e) - iz}{i + t(e,m)} + z. \tag{13.29}$$

From this we can derive the numerator of v_e, to be set equal to zero: it is $u_e[i + t(e,m)] - (u - iz)t_e$, and one obtains $(i + t(e,m))u_e = (u + iz)t_e$ or, rearranging,

$$u_e = \frac{(u - iz)t_e}{i + t(e,m)} = t_e \left[\frac{u - iz}{i + t(e,m)} + z \right] - t_e z = t_e(v - z). \tag{13.30}$$

Thus the worker chooses the level of effort that equates the marginal disutility of effort u_e to the marginal benefit of effort, measured by the marginal decrease in the probability of losing the advantage $v - z$ of remaining employed over becoming unemployed.

Graphically, see ◘ Fig. 13.2, and let us consider the indifference curves (each one corresponding to a constant v) of the worker in non-negative (w, e) space. Given e, a higher w raises u and hence v, so v is the higher the farther to the right is the indifference curve. The indifference curves are U-shaped *relative to the ordinate*, because as e decreases the danger of termination rises, and so along the vertical line drawn for a given value of w, starting from a very high effort level it is convenient to reduce it, but not below a certain level, the one where further decreases of e raise the danger of termination so much that the disadvantage from this fact is greater than the advantage from less disutility of effort. Below this optimal effort level, a constant utility would require a greater w, to compensate with greater current utility the increase in the likelihood of becoming unemployed. Once w is established by

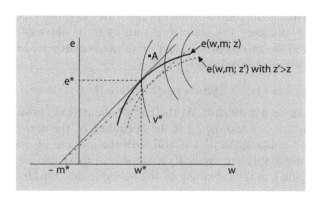

◘ **Fig. 13.2** Efficiency wage with shirking and monitoring. The straight lines that start at $-m^*$ indicate the effort associated with a constant cost per unit of effort (the latter is measured by the reciprocal of the slope of the line), and are called *constant-cost-of-effort lines*. Note that points like point A, above the straight line from $-m^*$ through point (w^*, e^*) and to the right of the worker's indifference curve through the latter point, are Pareto superior to (w^*, e^*): the worker is on a higher indifference curve, and the firm obtains more effort. Therefore (w^*, e^*) is Pareto inefficient; see Bowles (2004, p. 272)

13.6 · Efficiency Wages

the firm the worker wants to maximize utility, so she/he chooses e so as to obtain tangency between indifference curve and the vertical line starting at w. Therefore the best-effort response function $e(w, m; z)$ is the locus of leftmost points of the indifference curves; under plausible assumptions this is a rising concave curve. An increase of z makes the prospect of being fired less scary so this locus shifts downwards.

Relative to ◻ Fig. 13.1, there is a difference: here the point chosen by the firm on the best-effort response curve is of tangency with a line not from the origin, but from point $-m^*$ in abscissa, where m^* is the optimal expense on monitoring per worker. This is because what the firm must minimize is the cost per unit of effort, where the cost per time unit is the wage plus the monitoring expense. Note that for a given w the best effort depends on m, hence the optimal m depends on w, therefore m^* cannot be considered given before w^* is determined, but in ◻ Fig. 13.2 it is assumed that m^* is the finally resulting optimal value of m, and the $e(w, m; z)$ curve is drawn by treating m^* as given. In the figure the slightly illegitimate assumption is also made that m^* does not change when z changes to z'.

The presence of monitoring means the efficiency wage is not treated by the firm as given independently of its decisions. However, it is still independent of the single firm's decision as to how much to produce. The cost of effective labour input eL is $(w+m)L$, so the unit cost of effective labour input is $(w+m)/e(w, m; z)$.

Minimization of this cost with respect to w and to m requires now *two* 'Solow conditions' marginal effort=average effort, where effort can be marginal with respect to the wage or to monitoring; therefore the Solow conditions are:

$$e_w = e/(w+m)$$
$$e_m = e/(w+m).$$

The reasoning at the beginning of this section applies here too: these minimization conditions are independent of the amount eh of effective labour input the firm decides to use. So the firm decides w and m independently of the amount eL. In ◻ Fig. 13.2 only the first one of these two Solow conditions could be represented, the second one was behind the determination of m^*.

I confirm these Solow conditions by examining profit maximization. Suppose the firm takes prices as given, and let us measure output in such units that its price is 1. Assume the firm is risk neutral so the disturbance term ε can be neglected. The firm maximizes expected profit

$$\pi = y(Le(w, m; z)) - (w+m)L$$

The first-order conditions are

$$\pi_h = y'e - (w+m) = 0$$
$$\pi_w = y'Le_w - L = 0$$
$$\pi_m = y'Le_m - L = 0.$$

The second and third conditions imply $e_w = 1/y' = e_m$, and since the first condition implies $y'=(w+m)/e$, we obtain the Solow conditions.

However, the above does *not* mean that w and m are fixed independently of *total* labour employment in the economy. The reason is that the best-effort response function depends on z, and the latter is influenced by the rate of unemployment.

1156   **Chapter 13** · Labour Markets and Income Distribution

If at the end of the period the worker loses her job, she enters the status of unemployed; as long as she stays in that status she obtains a per-period income b that we can take as given, and that depends on unemployment subsidies and/or on whatever she can get with household production; hence she obtains a per-period utility $u(b, 0)$, where the 0 indicates she is performing no effort as a dependent labourer. At the end of each period she either remains unemployed, and then her expected future lifetime utility is z again, or she finds a job with probability h (as in ▶ Sect. 13.3), where h is the percentage of new job filling per period relative to total unemployment (assuming a random assignment of new jobs among the unemployed), and then she returns to having expected future lifetime utility v. Hence we have again a recursive determination:

$$z = (1 + i)^{-1}[u(b, 0) + hv + (1 - h)z] \qquad (13.31)$$

or, rearranging,

$$z = (i + h)^{-1}(u(b, 0) + hv).$$

Rewriting this as $(i + h)z - u(b, 0) - hv = 0$, the implicit function derivative rule proves that $dz/dh > 0$ if $v - z > 0$: that is, as long as having a job is preferable to being unemployed, the fallback position improves with a reduction of the average duration $1/h$ of unemployment status. And this duration is reduced by reductions of the rate of unemployment.

Now, we know from Eq. (13.30) that $u_e = t_e(v - z)$, that is, a rise of z reduces the marginal disutility of effort and hence reduces effort itself. That is, the best-effort response function shifts downwards, the same w corresponds now to a lower e, and this means a rise of the efficiency wage. The single firm treats z as given, but at the economy-wide level a decision by all firms to produce more raises the efficiency wage. Of course, once the neoclassical framework is abandoned, it will be some other theory that will determine unemployment and thus h; for instance, the Keynesian multiplier coupled with some theory of aggregate investment. An example is the paper by Bowles and Boyer in the very interesting 1990 book edited by Steven Marglin and Juliet Schor, *The End of the Golden Age*, a book whose reading I strongly recommend.[26]

---

26 How is equilibrium reached if one accepts a neoclassical general framework and hence a decreasing demand curve for labour (or rather for effort)? At a given rate of unemployment the resulting efficiency wage and associated effort and cost per unit of effort determine the demand for effort and hence for labour. If the resulting rate of unemployment is less than before, the efficiency wage rises, the cost of effort rises, the demand for effort decreases and plausibly the demand for labour too (only in extreme cases will effort per unit of time decrease so much when the rate of unemployment decreases as to imply a greater demand for labour time), hence unemployment rises, and contrariwise if the resulting rate of unemployment is greater than the initial one. Therefore the economy converges to the level of unemployment that determines such an efficiency wage as to cause that level of unemployment. The process requires of course not only the decreasing demand curve for labour but also Say's Law, as in the search approach, and it is surprising that Bowles (2004, p. 282) raises no perplexities on this account, in spite of having rejected Say's Law and accepted a Keynesian approach in several earlier articles, for example the 1990 article with Boyer mentioned in the text.

13.6 · Efficiency Wages

As z rises approaching v, Eq. (13.29) indicates that it becomes more and more difficult to obtain high levels of effort; the efficiency wage rises so much that at a certain point to pay it would render unprofitable for firms to produce. The rise of the efficiency wage is due to the fact that the lower the rate of unemployment, the shorter the period one remains unemployed (on average), and therefore the less effective the fear of being fired in inducing effort.

The shirking-based efficiency wage literature adds at this point that with full employment a fired worker would find a new job instantaneously, and then effort would be zero (or the maximum amount where the marginal utility of effort is not negative), which shows that capitalism intrinsically needs a positive rate of unemployment. Actually, the inevitability of a positive rate of unemployment derives already from the (near) inevitability of some frictional unemployment because of the time required for job matching, so we need not stop now on the doubtful legitimacy of identifying full employment with a *zero* delay between losing a job and finding another job. But that capitalism needs some unemployment in order to keep the working class under control is obvious to anyone who finds the classical approach more persuasive than the neoclassical one; it was argued in 1943 by Kalecki, it is a leitmotif in Marxist literature; it can be combined with forces determining wages different from the ones suggested by the shirking model.

Before passing to assess the shirking model, let us note why it can be classified as a type of hidden-action principal–agent model. The principal is unable to derive with certainty from observation of the output the action—the frequency of loafing—chosen by the worker, both because output is subject to stochastic influences and because of team production, so the action is (imperfectly) ascertained through monitoring, but the result is an imperfect signal of the action, as when output is affected by stochastic disturbances. The incentive payment too is a bit different from the one in the basic model of ► Sect. 11.24, in that it consists of a wage plus a probability of termination, but the result is still an expected utility of the agent dependent on the agent's choice of action. Note that the participation constraint does not bind, and the worker is not indifferent between working and remaining unemployed; according to the nowadays widespread usage of 'rent' to mean excess of the payment for a good or service over its minimum supply price, employed workers enjoy a rent, the first addendum on the right-hand side of Eq. (13.30).

One objection to the shirking model concerns the assumed difficulty with discovering that a worker shirks. The objection, essentially the same moved by Cahuc and Zylberberg against the adverse selection approach (see the end of ► Sect. 13.6.2), has been put as follows:

> » …this conveys an exaggerated impression of the importance of detection of employee inefficiency by shrugging off or ignoring some well-known facts of plant life. Shirking includes absenteeism and tardiness; neither is costly to detect. Workers with bad work habits can be detected and weeded out during short probationary periods. Moreover, discipline is 'graded' and applied 'progressively,' depending both on the gravity of the offense and the number of individual infractions. Hence the probability of dismissal — which is the ultimate punishment and the bottom line for the worker in this model — can be increased even if the probability and cost of detection are not. (Ulman 1990, p. 285)

If, as Ulman suggests, after a while the manager knows rather well the quality of the work performed by each labourer, then the manager can establish a definite level of e (possibly differing as between workers) below which the worker is fired, and will try to establish it as high as possible for each level of the hourly real wage. Assuming the manager is able to ascertain this maximum e, one can derive how it changes with w, and it will likely be increasing in w and increasing in the rate of unemployment. Then one obtains a maximum-effort response function $e_{max}(w)$ and there is no reason why it should not have a shape as in ◘ Fig. 13.1; the optimal 'hourly' wage w^* for the firm is again the one obeying the Solow condition, and in all likelihood it increases if the rate of unemployment decreases. That is, little changes relative to the shirking model, except that at $(w^*, e_{max}(w^*))$ the worker is indifferent between working and remaining unemployed; that is, there is no 'rent'. (But I will argue later that this does *not* mean that the worker does not prefer being employed to unemployed; 'indifferent' is misleading here, as I will explain.) Now the wage amounts in fact to a wage per unit of effort or of 'actual amount of labour', with the sole difference, relative to the standard case of absence of effort variability, that the amount of 'actual labour' is specified *per unit of time*. The term 'efficiency wages' would appear to be as legitimate here as in the Shapiro–Stiglitz–Bowles model.

Another objection to the shirking model is that firms have other possible ways to induce effort besides fixing the wage; in particular, they can use promises of a higher wage in the future (if the worker does not get her/him fired for loafing). This objection was first posed in the somewhat paradoxical form of a possibility for firms to bond the worker to the firm by asking the worker for a deposit at the moment of hiring, which the worker will get back in case of spontaneous leave, but will lose if fired because caught shirking (Carmichael 1985, 1989). In this case the incentive to supply an adequate level of effort is the risk of losing the deposit, not the risk of jumping down to the level of expected utility of an unemployed person. Without entering into the formal details, it should be intuitive that by raising the size of the deposit enough (and hence the expected value of the loss if one is fired), the expected utility of being hired can be reduced to equality with that of being unemployed; that is, the shirking model's employment rent can be made to disappear. This *bonding critique* has been countered by objecting that most workers would find it impossible to borrow the funds needed for the deposit, and that there is too much risk that the firm will not honour the contract, not necessarily because of malfeasance (e.g. it might go bankrupt). But it has been shown that essentially the same effect of bonding the worker to the firm can be obtained with a promise of higher wages in future (if the worker does not get herself fired in the meanwhile because caught shirking), assuming the firm is trustworthy in its promise i.e. (because of reputation or enforceable legal obligations) it does not 'cheat' by firing the worker at the end of the period of low wage. Initially the worker accepts a wage below its reservation wage in order to gain access to the higher wage in the future, and it is this prospect of a higher future wage that constitutes the incentive to produce effort. With contracts establishing a rising wage time path, be it because of seniority or because of a probability of promotion, again no rent needs to arise for employed workers (Cahuc et al. 2014, pp. 363–377).

Wages rising with seniority are rather common, and even more common are initial periods of 'apprenticeship' with a lower wage (or in recent years in Italy

13.6 · Efficiency Wages

even a *zero* wage, and with no guarantee of being hired into a permanent job at the end of this apprenticeship, truly a price to be paid for only a probability of being hired—a very evident proof of the effect of lack of jobs for new entrants). However, generally wages do not keep rising with seniority up to retirement (sometimes they *decrease* after a peak around the age of 55 or so), and then at some point the incentive of the expectation of higher future wages disappears. Also, there are jobs where wages rising with seniority are hard to conceive and indeed are seldom observed: if a job requires little training and replacements are easily found, then a firm would have too much incentive to replace more highly paid workers with new lesser-paid hires. Therefore a motivation for effort consisting of the fear of losing a 'rent' if one becomes unemployed seems to remain important.

But too much importance is attributed to whether a 'rent' exists or not. We need to discuss this point.

The ample success of the shirking-based efficiency wage approach among radical economists must be attributed to its *prima facie* success in finally proving that unemployment can be involuntary even in a neoclassical framework (i.e. in the presence of a downward-sloping demand curve for labour). The argument to be refuted was the monetarist one that if the unemployed really preferred working at the going wage to remaining unemployed, they would still prefer it for a slightly lower wage, and then they would offer to work at this slightly lower wage and one should observe wages decrease, which would reduce unemployment; if the wage does not decrease, then unemployment is voluntary. The shirking approach allowed arguing that the unemployed do prefer working at the going wage to being unemployed, and it is the firms that do not allow the wage to decrease, so unemployment is *involuntary*. But is it really?

Let us draw the effort supply curve of a worker as a function of the cost (wage plus monitoring cost per worker) *per unit of effort*, $e=f((w+m)/e(w))$, and for simplicity let us take monitoring costs per worker as given. Since it is effort that influences production, it is the cost per unit of effort that determines the optimal capital–labour ratio and hence the demand for labour in a neoclassical framework. Take z as given. If (to parallel the usual way to draw the labour supply curve) we measure e in abscissa and its price $(w+m)/e(w)$ in ordinate, the curve $e=f((w+m)/e(w))$ has the shape shown in ◘ Fig. 13.3: it can be derived from ◘ Fig. 13.2, where $e/(w+m)$ is the slope of the *constant-cost-of-effort line* that starts from point $-m$ in abscissa; treating m as given for simplicity, if $(w+m)/e$ is above $(w^*+m)/e^*$, this line crosses the $e(w)$ curve twice, and therefore for each value of the cost of effort there are two $(w, e(w))$ combinations associated with it (the higher $(w, e(w))$ corresponds to higher utility). Effort supply jumps discontinuously to zero when $(w+m)/e(w)$ goes below $(w^*+m)/e^*$. It is impossible to reduce labour cost per unit of effort below $(w^*+m)/e^*$; that is, a firm that pretends a lower labour cost per unit of effort faces a zero supply of workers.

A worker may well declare she accepts a lower hourly wage w, the firm knows that she will produce so much less effort at the lower w that it is more convenient to pay her w^*. The *aggregate* effort supply curve has the same shape (of course stretched horizontally), except that the discontinuity at $(w^*+m)/e^*$ is replaced by a horizontal series of separate points corresponding to the employment of 1, 2, 3, ... workers. So—in the neoclassical framework where there is a decreasing labour

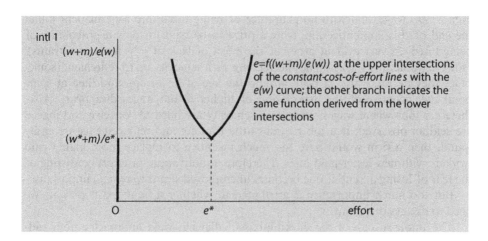

Fig. 13.3 Effort supply curve of a worker as function of the cost of a unit of effort

demand curve (or rather, here, an effort demand curve)—it is the workers' *voluntary* refusal to work sufficiently intensely at wages below w^* as not to let the cost per unit of effort go above $(w^* + m)/e^*$ that causes them to remain unemployed. The hourly wage payment masks the workers' refusal to accept to deliver the same productive contribution (actually, even a bit less) at a lower w. The neoclassical economist will find it only obvious that employment cannot increase, after all in standard traditional labour demand theory the capacity of wage decreases to increase labour demand depended on the possibility to reduce the unit cost of the productive contribution of labour.

One might argue that the unemployed are still involuntarily unemployed because they *prefer* to work rather than not work at wage per unit of effort w^*/e^*. But Keynes, for example, did not accept that unemployment is involuntary if the unemployed are ready to work at the going wage but not for anything even only slightly less. He wrote: 'Men are involuntarily unemployed if, in the event of a small rise in the price of wage-goods relatively to the money-wage, both the aggregate supply of labour willing to work for the current money-wage and the aggregate demand for it at that wage would be greater than the existing volume of employment' (Keynes, GT p. 15).[27] If one looks at the wage *per unit of*

---

27 In Keynes, the involuntary element is that workers are unable to reduce the real wage, because they can only reduce the money wage, and unless real aggregate demand increases, the result will be a parallel reduction of the price level that leaves the real wage, and hence labour demand, unchanged. So, according to Keynes, it is not the refusal of workers to let money wages decrease that is responsible for unemployment, in spite of the decreasing labour demand curve; then unemployment can be legitimately considered involuntary. The neoclassical synthesis criticized Keynes precisely on this point, arguing that according to Keynes's own theory the decrease in the price level brought about by decreases of money wages would reduce the demand for money and thus the rate of interest, which would stimulate investment and raise the demand for labour. Then unemployment becomes again voluntary, because due to the refusal to let money wages decrease.

effort, according to Keynes unemployment in the shirking model (coupled with a decreasing labour/effort demand curve) is voluntary.

If on the contrary the neoclassical labour demand curve is rejected, more specifically if one cannot assume that real wage decreases cause appreciable increases in employment, then the involuntary nature of unemployment is easily defensible. Now one can admit that there is a voluntary refusal by the unemployed workers to let wages decrease, but since such a wage decrease would not increase employment, its absence is not responsible for the existence of unemployment. The latter therefore is involuntary. In this case by refusing to accept a lower wage the unemployed worker is stating, not 'I know that by accepting a lower wage I would get a job but I prefer to remain unemployed rather than work at a lower wage', but rather 'a lower wage benefits you with no advantage for me, in this conflict I will resist as much as I can'. It cannot even be argued that the single unemployed worker, by offering to work for a sufficiently lower wage, can hope to obtain a job by *replacing* another worker, because the other worker would be compelled to accept the lower wage herself, in which case the firm would prefer not to replace her in order to avoid turnover costs.[28] The readiness to accept a lower wage would leave the unemployed worker unemployed, causing only a decrease of the wage of employed workers.

In such a non-neoclassical perspective, that having a job ensures a 'rent' over unemployed status is obvious, at least in advanced economies where the wage is abundantly above subsistence and generally also abundantly above unemployment income, which anyway is not always available and, even when it is, does not last for ever. Even in the Ulman approach and in the seniority wage approach, where the worker can be brought to what looks like indifference between work and unemployment, in fact a 'rent' will exist the moment one admits the presence of conflict behind wage determination. In order to understand why, we need further considerations on the shirking approach.

Let us start by noting that neither the Shapiro–Stiglitz–Bowles shirking approach, nor its modification according to Ulman, nor its modification to include an upward time path of wages, appear capable of explaining why, secularly, real wages have risen. The efficiency wage is determined by four things: worker preferences, utility level when unemployed, rate of unemployment and monitoring technology. Except for a possible but certainly minor influence via improvements in monitoring technologies, *technical progress has no effect at all on the efficiency wage* if the first three elements do not change. With the due modifications, the same holds for the average wage implied by a rising wage path. But if one looks at the evolution of real wages over very long periods, often after a couple of decades the same rate of unemployment is associated with considerably increased real wages. Changes in monitoring technology cannot explain such increases in real wages. There remain worker preferences and unemployment

---

28 In the neoclassical approach the lower wage obtains the unemployed worker a job because of the increase in labour demand, not because the worker replaces another worker.

utility level. It would be ridiculous to explain these higher wages as due to an *exogenous* change of worker preferences: it would mean that, decade after decade, for mysterious reasons people become less and less willing to work, then in order to induce them to work one must pay them more and more, and by a lucky coincidence technical progress has made this possible without the higher efficiency wage causing firms to go bankrupt. It is possible to advance a theory of *endogenous* preferences that adapt to higher levels of consumption, so that after a while a higher standard of living becomes as indispensable as the older lower standard of living, and therefore a fall (due to being fired) of monthly income from 2000 to 500 dollars a month is feared as much as, twenty years before, an income fall from 1000 to 250 dollars; but this leaves unexplained why the income when employed rose from 1000 to 2000 dollars a month. A neoclassical economist would explain it as due to the rightward shift of the curve of marginal productivity of labour, due to technical progress; a given efficiency wage then gradually raises the demand for labour, but this reduces the rate of unemployment and raises the efficiency wage, so consumption levels rise, and on this one can then superpose the endogenous adaptation of preferences. But if one does not accept the neoclassical approach, one must have recourse to some kind of conflictual theory of income distribution. On the other hand, increases of unemployment benefits may be adduced as reducing the fear of being fired and thus raising efficiency wages, but then—besides the difficulty with the periods and nations and worker categories for which unemployment benefits were or are absent—one must explain what caused the increase in unemployment benefits, and the political decisions behind this increase send us to the social forces that determined them, which in a classical perspective will be again the conflicting interests and strengths of different groups or classes. So one way or the other, inevitably one must admit conflict. Then there is no reason why one should not see conflict as directly influencing wages too.

Then one is pushed towards a different interpretation of 'efficiency wages': it becomes plausible that it is not mostly in order to prevent shirking due to too low a fear of being fired that firms refuse to let wages decrease in spite of the presence of unemployment; it is above all to prevent protests, strikes, work-to-rule, sabotage that would erupt if the firm tried to win back some of the wage increases obtained by the workers in the past. The fear of becoming unemployed is still operative, but largely as a greater or lesser brake on the willingness to risk the sack because of being a troublemaker. The likelihood of conflict, more than the likelihood of more shirking coming from tranquil individual utility maximization, is what plausibly lies behind the firm's choice not to let wages decrease. This different view is supported by Schor (1988), who in a paper based on the study of British data concludes that work intensity is influenced by unemployment rates but *not* by the real wage. Without this reinterpretation, the shirking approach risks presenting a false, too idyllic image of how labour relations operate, that underestimates conflict and the importance of collective forms of struggle and solidarity.

This perspective implies that even when, as in the Ulman-type approach, the formal model indicates that at the $(w^*, e_{max}(w^*))$ combination the worker is indifferent between working and being unemployed, this does not mean the worker is as well off in both states. The maximum effort a worker is ready to produce for a given hourly wage is not the result of utility maximization that concludes to indifference between working and being unemployed; rather it reflects the collective stand of workers in that period in the perennial conflict between the firm and the workers. The worker's decision to accept the sack rather than work more than $e_{max}(w)$ is a choice which one can describe as utility-maximizing only in the sense that the utility function by definition must assign a higher utility to what one chooses than to the alternatives not chosen, but it does not indicate a higher welfare, satisfaction, happiness; it reflects a determination to abide by certain collective standards of behaviour in the conflict over wages and working conditions, even at the cost of personal sacrifice. As a consequence, the worker who accepts $(w^*, e_{max}(w^*))$ and refuses any higher level of effort is not *indifferent* between having or not having the job, rather feels obliged by class solidarity to refuse to work more intensely, even at the cost of being fired or not hired. So there is a 'rent' here too: if there is unemployment, the lucky worker who obtains a job does prefer it to remaining unemployed, but this does not mean she/he would be ready to accept a lower wage—unless something changes the collectively reached explicit or implicit truce between workers and employers. Utility maximization as normally formulated is unable to grasp this distinction between preference (i.e. choice) and welfare; if a soldier prefers to die for his country rather than seeing it conquered by the enemy, one cannot conclude that dying means greater welfare. The identification of choice with welfare is legitimate in the study of tranquil, individualistic choice of what to consume (which is the problem for which utility theory was formulated), but not when there are fighting, strategic choices, collectively reached standards of behaviour, duties, pacts to be respected and so on.

One consequence of this perspective is the need to reinterpret the reservation wage (the fallback position z) as representing, not the utility of being unemployed, but the behavioural standards that workers accept as conscious or less conscious necessary components of the struggle over wages and working conditions. Unemployment benefits are only a part of what determines z. This means that the shirking approach is incomplete, it must assume some social process that determines the normal wage and working conditions below which the workers are ready to fight.

The same need arises for the versions relying on an increasing time path of wages. Once the neoclassical labour demand curve is rejected, these versions do not explain why this incentive to efficiency requires a wage path at a certain average wage level and not at a lower or higher wage level in a certain period, and at another wage level in another period, wage levels that tend not to decrease even in the presence of unemployment. Here too, it seems necessary to assume there is for each kind of job in each historical situation a certain wage level, the result of past struggles and of the present balance of bargaining power, below which it is extremely difficult to find workers who accept to be hired and to work with satisfactory levels of effort. The next group of versions of efficiency wage theories points in the same direction.

1164   Chapter 13 · Labour Markets and Income Distribution

13.6.5 Gift Exchange, Fairness, Morale

A worker will feel ready to retaliate with shabby workmanship or even sabotage if she/he feels she is being unfairly harassed or paid too little. It is well known that management considers the 'morale' of the workforce—by which one means the good or bad humour with which workers come to work, their greater or lesser readiness to put effort into what they do in the firm—a most important element contributing to the level of production, and that a behaviour by management that workers consider equitable, respectful, 'fair' (also in the wages paid) has been empirically confirmed to have great importance (Bewley 1999, 2005; Agell and Lundborg 1995). If workplace atmosphere is agreeable and workers feel the firm is not trying to overexploit them, workers may produce even considerably more than the norm fixed by management. Akerlof (1982), a recommended reading, proposed to view such behaviour as a gift by the worker to the firm, in exchange for the gift by the firm to the worker consisting of correct behaviour and of a 'fair' wage. The paper produced models with equilibrium unemployment two years before the paper by Shapiro and Stiglitz.

Reference to a 'fair' wage is frequent in the history of labour movements; for example Alfred Marshall cites the dictum 'a fair day's labour for a fair day's wage' as fundamental in bargaining over wages. But what exactly must one mean by a fair wage? The tendency in the literature seems to be that 'fair' wage means the normal, average wage. The assumption then is that workers tend to produce more effort when they get a wage above the 'fair' wage. Akerlof (1982), for example, assumes that effort tends to conform to a social norm, with normal effort determined as

$$e_n = -a + b(w/w_r)^\gamma, \quad b > a$$

where w_r is the reference 'fair' wage, w the actual wage, a and b positive parameters, and γ a positive parameter less than 1. The normal effort function then has the same strictly concave shape as in the shirking approach, and the firm chooses the wage that satisfies the Solow condition. An influence of the rate of unemployment is introduced by Akerlof via the assumption that the reference wage w_r is a weighted average of the wage paid by other firms and of unemployment benefits, with the weight of unemployment benefits increasing in the rate of unemployment. This is another way to obtain a positive influence of the rate of unemployment upon effort. The main difference relative to the shirking approach is that a rise of w does not raise effort, if w_r rises by the same percentage as w. This makes it possible to conceive effort as temporarily increasing when w rises, only to decrease again to a normal level as the rise in actual wages raises workers' idea of what constitutes a normal or 'fair' wage.

The approach justifies the reluctance of firms to decrease wages in the presence of unemployment as due to the fact that a wage decrease would worsen morale and hence productivity so much that the firm would lose in output more than it would save in wages.

The approach tends to admit, in a less sanguine language, much the same as the conflictual perspective suggested in the previous section. Indeed the most plausible interpretation of the adjective 'fair' in 'fair wages' is not 'according to justice and equity' but as in 'fair play', that is, respecting the rules, no cheating. But cheating on what? On the rules of the period's truce in the perennial conflict between labour and firms. A truce or armistice is a suspension of active fighting on the basis of a temporary accord or compromise; this temporary accord requires that if workers perform according to the rules of the stipulated compromise, the firms must pay them the agreed normal wage; 'a fair day's labour for a fair day's wage' means, if you the firm want us the workers to contribute 'a fair day's labour', then you must pay us the agreed normal wage; we will respect the truce if you do; otherwise there will be a resumption of active conflict. To talk of gift exchange depicts the thing is nicer colours but the essence is this. If an employer is nicer than the average to his workers these may reciprocate, but this requires a definition of the average, and the average is not the result of generosity on the part of employers, but of relative bargaining power in a situation of objectively conflicting interests.

Therefore, similarly as for the shirking approach, this fairness–morale–gift exchange approach needs social forces establishing a 'normal' or 'fair' level of wages and working conditions below which the truce is not respected and the latent inevitable conflict between wage labour and firm owners and managers becomes more open. On the side of labour, mostly conflict takes the form of *concerted action* by the entire workforce of a firm or of an industry, often but not always organized by trade unions, such as slowdowns, work-to-rule, strikes, sloppy workmanship, sabotage; these actions are opposed by actions by the firm and also by concerted actions by groups of firms, which may decide to oppose unionization, to fire troublemakers, to use other forms of retaliation. Often the conflict is heavily influenced by state intervention, as already noted by Adam Smith. Piore (1973), a recommended reading, has indicated that if the workforce is not ready to denounce their fellow workers, sabotageurs cannot be discovered by management, and the firm can be destroyed by its workforce. What prevents this last result from happening is the interest of workers to avoid the bankruptcy of the firm, because that would make them unemployed.

13.7 Trade Unions

If you consult the main advanced microeconomics textbooks, you will notice that none of them discusses trade unions, and the term 'trade unions' does not appear once. This is, the moment you stop to think about it, truly surprising. Consider this picture of the role of trade unions by an historian:

» For two centuries trade unions have led the struggle to achieve a more equitable distribution of the world's wealth and power. In virtually every country trade unions have battled at the workplace and in the community, in law courts and legislatures, at the bargaining table and in the streets to improve the living and working conditions of their members. As the principal institutions for the defence of workers' rights, they have played many roles and assumed many guises, at times operating as little

> more than lethargic bureaucracies on behalf of a minority of workers with leverage at the workplace, and at other times at the forefront of dynamic social movements for radical change. At their best, trade unions have championed campaigns for social justice and participatory democracy that have fundamentally altered national histories by giving voice to disenfranchised majorities. Whether as narrow vested interest for a privileged minority or the embodiment of the hopes for all workers, trade unionism has been a major feature of the modern world. (Phelan 2009, p. ix)

Such a fundamental component of the economies of all advanced nations cannot be left out of an advanced introduction to how markets work.

But I cannot dedicate to this issue the space of a labour economics textbook, so I must skip all discussion of the history of trade unions, of their several forms, of their sometimes strong, sometimes weak involvement in broader political campaigns, of their power to monopolize labour supply (in Great Britain closed-shop unionization, i.e. being a member of a trade union as a necessary precondition for being employable in an industry, was made illegal in the 1980s), and even of the question how many and why workers join a trade union. I will only remember that union membership and union coverage are very different things, union-bargained agreements often cover non-union members too; the extreme example is France, where in 2000 only 9% of workers were members of some trade union, but over 95% of workers were covered by a collective agreement signed by a trade union.

Nowadays unions bargain with firms (or confederations of firms) over wages, working hours, working conditions, sometimes pensions (especially in the USA where pensions are often provided by the firm itself); they provide assistance in case of grievances, for example, for mobbing or illegal firing, that often need a costly legal assistance that a single worker would be unable to afford. Their activities may be more or less limited by law; for example in the USA a union cannot call a strike unless the decision is approved by a majority of the firm's workers by secret ballot. Unions are sometimes actively opposed by firms, more so in the USA than in Europe. The efforts of many firms, particularly in the USA, to avoid unionization of their workforce are a clear indication that unionization decreases profits, which must mean it improves the income and/or the work conditions of the workforce.

Unions are generally seen by neoclassical economists as obstacles to full competition, and therefore as causes of inefficiencies relative to the Pareto optimality that unimpeded competition is argued to realize. A full treatment of welfare economics must wait for ▶ Chap. 14, but what was explained in ▶ Chap. 3 should suffice to grasp the basis for this view. In a neoclassical perspective, a real wage above the equilibrium level reduces employment, causing a loss to society because output is less than what would be produced by the full employment of labour supply; therefore if unions are able to raise wages above the equilibrium level, they cause a grave Pareto inefficiency. Actually this possibility is seldom explicitly discussed by neoclassical economists, and historically they have been very reluctant to admit the possibility of persistent unemployment and have generally preferred to assume that trade unions are active only in some industries: when they are able to raise wages above the competitive equilibrium level in those industries, reducing employment there, the effect is an increased labour supply in the other industries, and wages lower there than their competitive equilibrium level, with again some Pareto inefficiency (although less than when the higher wage is generalized and causes unemployment) because labour is inefficiently allocated.[29] Some neoclassical economists argue that trade unions have very little effect, because unable totally to monopolize the labour market, and competition from non-union workers forces wages down to the full-employment level; but then the resources absorbed by trade union activity are a waste, so trade unions damage the economy anyway. This seems to have been the view of Milton Friedman.

Because of the dominance of neoclassical theory, even economists who disagree with this view of the effects of trade unions often accept the decreasing labour demand curve, and refer to neoclassical competitive equilibrium as a benchmark. The abandonment of the neoclassical perspective in some cases has rather clear implications; in other cases it raises questions that call for future study.

'The conditions under which a union can achieve a wage rate greater than the competitive level are that there must be some surplus to be shared, and that the union must have some bargaining power to induce the firm to share the surplus'. (Booth 1995, p. 141). This quotation is representative of the dominant view: it assumes the existence of an equilibrium (full-employment) competitive wage, which workers would obtain in the absence of trade unions; only if imperfections of competition (absence of free entry) allow the firm to charge a product price higher than the minimum long-period average cost associated with the equilibrium competitive wage, there is a possibility to raise the wage above that level.

This view does not appear acceptable. First, apart from rare short-lived exceptions the normal situation in capitalist economies is that there is overt or hidden unemployment in excess of the frictional level. Second, the abandonment of the scarcity principle illustrated in ▶ Sect. 13.2 implies that even full employment does not entail a univocal real wage; there is always the possibility of redistributions of income (in either direction), with effects on aggregate demand and employment to be studied case by case.[30]

Third, at the level of a single *industry*, it is false that free competition implies no possibility to raise wages in that industry.[31] A single *firm* would be weakened relative to competitors if wages rose only for its workforce but not in competing firms (e.g. entrant firms with a non-unionized workforce), but the situation is very different if, as is often the case, the union stipulates agreements valid for

---

29 See Exercise 13.

30 I repeat that I am leaving aside the balance-of-payment constraint, since the working of the open economy depends on which general approach to value and distribution is considered correct, an issue more easily examined in a closed economy.

31 *Perfect* competition is a notion too much tied with the neoclassical approach and, nowadays, with the auctioneer. Free competition, based on entry but admitting that adjustments take time, is the older and more acceptable notion, present not only in the classical authors but also in Marshall.

an entire category of workers and therefore an entire industry, new entrants included; also, even when unions are firm-based it is often the case that the competitors of a firm have a unionized workforce too, and then the several firm-based unions will attentively watch what is happening in the other firms in the industry, and will be quick to claim wage rises similar to those in the competing firms since that will not endanger the firm's relative competitiveness; knowing this, even first-mover initiative will not be discouraged because it is certain that the unions in the competing firms will follow. Let us then consider the uniform-profit-rate (Sraffian) normal-price equations. These can admit different wages, and different wage changes, for different worker categories. A rise of real wages for a category of workers employed mainly or only in one industry causes a rise of the price of the industry's product (and a lesser rise of the prices of the industries that use that product as an input), and a slightly lower general rate of profit, and that's all. Therefore it is false that there must be a surplus at the firm or industry level (a barrier to entry, ultimately) in order for unions to make a difference.

Fourth, important effects of trade unions are at the economy-wide level, for example, because of political campaigns of the entire trade union movement for reforms, or for blocking proposed pejorative reforms, of labour legislation. Many strikes have precisely this kind of objectives.

Fifth, one must not forget the importance of trade unions in public employment, where no danger of entry exists, and where wage increases can motivate unions in the private sector to ask for similar wage increases.

Back to unions in the private sector, the room for potential effects of trade unions is confirmed by noting that, yes, the wage rise obtained by trade unions in an industry can have a negative effect on the demand for the industry's product, but this is easily very small because wage costs are, more and more often, a small share of total costs in modern industry (less so, however, in services). For example in the car industry some data suggest that wages count for 7% of the cost of production of cars; then increases of wages by 15% with unchanged productivity raise average cost by 1% only, requiring a product price increase that is nearly unnoticeable—and generally unnecessary, because demands for a relevant increase in wages are usually advanced *after* relevant increases in productivity not accompanied by product price decreases. In other words, when firms find ways to reduce costs they do not immediately reduce product prices, which would risk starting a price war; so firms will often prefer to maintain price unchanged and keep selling the same amounts as before. But when the increase in profits becomes evident, unions will see that there is room for a wage increase that does not push the firm out of the market. Unions do not want firms to go bankrupt, and they care a lot about employment as shown by their vigorous interventions whenever there is a danger of firings. But wages at the industry level have very little influence on employment. This explains why generally sectoral unions do not seem to worry about employment when advancing their wage demands, in spite of caring a lot about employment.

Anyway some knowledge of how unions are generally introduced into mainstream labour market theory can be useful to the reader. Under the influence of the US situation, the dominant theoretical approach takes as typical scenario a single union bargaining with a single firm, but the argument also applies to an industry. The union is assumed to behave as a single economic agent, endowed with a utility function which it tries to maximize. The labour force available for employment in the firm or industry is assumed limited by geographical and skill factors, and the union controls it totally: if the union decides a strike, there are no scabs, and if an agreement is reached, it applies to all hired workers (100% *coverage* of union contract). For space reasons I omit the theories of how the union's decisions are reached, and the theories of what determines union membership. (On this latter important issue, I note only that ideological motivations have been very relevant historically but seem to have become less important in recent decades; whether being a member of a trade union and paying the union fee is more advantageous than not being a member and not paying the fee seems to have become more important: union membership as a share of the workforce has tended to fall at least a bit practically everywhere except in the Northern European nations—Denmark, Finland, Sweden, Norway—and more so where *coverage* of the union contract is high, which favours free riding.)

The most popular theoretical model is as follows. Now effort variability is not considered, and effort per unit of time is independent of the wage. Symbols:

w – real wage;

$w^\wedge$ – reservation wage;

N – employment in the local labour market where the firm is the sole demander;

L – (given) labour supply in that market;

e – ratio of employment to total labour supply in the local labour market, $e = N/L$;

$V(\cdot)$ – concave subutility function of the union for the representative worker.

Two are the most frequently used classes of union utility functions:
(i) VNM expected utility function: $U = e \cdot V(w) + (1 - e) \cdot V(w^\wedge)$.
(ii) 'Utilitaristic' utility function: $U = N \cdot V(w) + (L - N) \cdot V(w^\wedge)$.

In the VNM function, $e = N/L$ is interpreted as the probability for a worker of being employed, and U can be interpreted as referring to a 'representative unionized worker', the *median* worker in one interpretation, whose VNM expected utility is what the union intends to maximize. The union cares about unemployment too, and the probability of unemployment influences the utility function as long as $w > w^\wedge$. The assumption of concavity of V intends to grasp risk aversion. Of course it is unrealistic to assume the same probability of unemployment for all workers in the local labour market, because the firm does not renew its entire labour force after signing the agreement, and it already has an employed labour force and will renew it only gradually owing to quits and retirements. But the function can be reinterpreted as describing the union's utility as depending on the share of L that is employed.

The utilitaristic function corresponds to this reinterpretation, and it sums up the expected utility of the employed and of the unemployed. Implicitly, the utilitaristic union assumes all workers have the same utility function, with a curvature (risk aversion) that determines the relevance of the difference between w and $w^\wedge$.

Clearly, these utility functions are not to be taken seriously in their detailed form, and they at most indicate what enters in the union's considerations. The maximization of either function brings to the same result if workers are all identical, because then the VNM function is the utilitaristic function divided by L (which is generally taken as given). In both approaches one obtains a map of the union's indifference curves in (N, w) space, clearly because it is assumed that w influences employment; the shape of the $V(\cdot)$ function determines the marginal rate of substitution between real wage and employment. There is no reason to expect such a rate of substitution to be similar for different trade unions and different historical periods, and the union's utility function cannot pretend to be more than roughly indicative; so the concrete content of either approach is simply that one expects the union to be ready to trade off some wage increase for some employment increase.

In order to reach results of some interest, one must add assumptions. Assume the union can perfectly control labour supply to the firm or industry in question, and uses this power to fix the wage. This is called the *monopoly union* model. The union has utility function $U(w, N)$. Given the wage, the firm determines employment according to a labour demand function $N(w)$, known to the union. The union wants to maximize $U(w, N(w))$. Assuming strictly convex indifference curves of the union, maximization requires the union to choose the point of tangency between indifference curve and labour demand curve in (N, w) space; see
◘ Fig. 13.4.

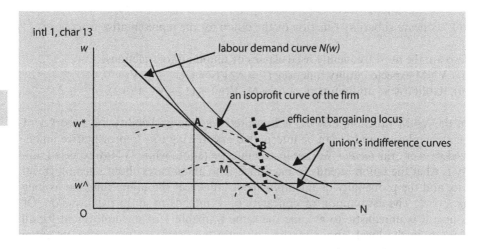

◘ **Fig. 13.4** Maximization of utility of a monopoly union at point A. In the same graph some concave isoprofit curves of the firm are drawn that represent (N, w) combinations that yield the same profit to the firm, derived from some assumption on how more employment affects the price at which the product can be sold. Of course each isoprofit curve reaches its maximum where it crosses the labour demand curve, and the higher the profit is, the lower the isoprofit curve. Note that point B is Pareto superior to point A because the firm's profit is the same and the union is on a higher indifference curve; clearly then there are (N, w) combinations which guarantee both higher profit and higher union utility than in A (e.g. along the straight segment from A to B); but the firm must employ more labour than on the labour demand curve

Evidently we are talking here of the labour demand curve of a single firm (or industry), in a *partial-equilibrium* analysis in which other prices (and incomes) are given; it is not clear whether the analysis is a short-period one in which the fixed plant is given, or a long-period one in which the imperfectly competitive firm has a definite idea of how much output can be sold at different prices if general conditions (number and prices of other firms, aggregate demand) do not change, and can derive from its demand schedule a decreasing long-period labour demand curve. The effect of the presence of the trade union is a lesser demand for labour than at the competitive wage.

Another model assumes again that the firm has the power to determine the employment level once the wage is fixed (hence the name: **right-to-manage** model), but now the union is unable to impose its preferred wage, it *bargains* with the firm over the wage. The literature generally assumes that this bargaining reaches the **generalized Nash bargaining solution**, which consists of maximizing the geometric average of the weighted utility *gains* of the players relative to *status-quo utilities*: see Appendix 1. (The weights are supposed to indicate bargaining power; see below.) The status-quo utilities indicate the utilities if no agreement is reached. For the firm, utility can be measured by profit, and the status-quo profit is generally assumed to correspond to zero production. The literature generally simplifies by assuming that production depends only on N; hence profit is

$$\pi = pq(N) - wN$$

where p is output price and $q(N)$ is quantity produced; the status-quo point is generally assumed to be zero because without agreement the firm has no access to labour and cannot produce. Which is an extreme assumption, generally there are ways to surmount the problem, and the firm can disavow the closed-shop agreement and bring in non-unionized workers, accepting conflict with the union (with picketing, appeals to authorities, etc.); if it is an entire industry that is bargaining with the union, the thing is even more likely. The problem would become very complex, but this seems to be a general characteristic of the effects of trade unions, and these can depend on so many things that the simple models elaborated by the literature appear of uncertain usefulness.

For example, continuing with the right-to-manage model, the gain of the firm relative to the status-quo point is its profit, which is a function of w. Even when the marginal product of labour is constant, N is a decreasing function of w because rises of w are assumed to cause rises of the product price and hence decreases of sales (the firm is imperfectly competitive). Therefore $p=p(q)$, and then it is convenient to put $pq = R(N)$, where R is sales revenue. The firm's gain is then

$$\pi(w) = R(N(w)) - wN(w)$$

Assume a utilitarian trade union. Its gain relative to the status-quo position is the total utility of the local labour force minus its status-quo or fallback utility, $G = Nu(w) + (L - N)u(w^\wedge)] - Lu(w^\wedge)$, that boils down to:

$$G(w) = N(w)\big[u(w) - u(w^\wedge)\big]. \tag{13.32}$$

The Nash bargaining solution asks to maximize the 'Nash product'

$$max_w G^\gamma \pi^{1-\gamma}. \tag{13.33}$$

The given γ is interpreted as 'bargaining power' but where this power comes from remains unexplained. Differentiating both sides of (13.32) with respect to w and indicating $\partial G/\partial w$ as G_w:

$$G_w = N'(w)\left[u(w) - u(w^\wedge)\right] + N(w)u'(w);$$

from the marginal increase in total utility if employment were constant, $Nu'(w)$, one must subtract the loss of total utility due to the marginal decrease in employment ($N'(w)$ is negative).

$$\pi_w = \left[R'(N) - w\right]N'(w) - N(w) = -N(w),$$

because the firm chooses N so as to have $R'(N)=w$ (so this is an alternative way to prove Hotelling's Lemma). The first-order condition for maximizing $G^\gamma \pi^{1-\gamma}$ is

$$\gamma G^{\gamma-1}\pi^{1-\gamma}G_w + (1-\gamma)G^\gamma \pi^{-\gamma}\pi_w = 0$$

or equivalently

$$\frac{G_w/G}{\pi_w/\pi} = -\frac{1-\gamma}{\gamma} \tag{13.34}$$

which highlights the ratio between elasticities implied by the generalized Nash bargaining solution. The sharing of the gains must be such that the proportional marginal gain of a wage *increase* for the union must be equal to the proportional marginal gain of a wage *decrease* for the firm, once these proportional gains are weighted by the respective bargaining powers. Again, this can only be roughly indicative.

The difference relative to the monopoly union model is that, with $\gamma<1$, the point corresponds to a lower wage and a higher employment level than in the monopoly union model. The bargained wage decreases with γ: when $\gamma=1$ we are back at the monopoly union case; when γ is zero the union is useless, and the firm decides the wage and fixes it as low as possible, that is, either at the wage ensuring full labour employment in the local labour market, or at the reservation wage, $w=w^\wedge$ (point C in ◘ Fig. 13.4), if at that wage the firm faces a horizontal labour supply curve.

But ◘ Fig. 13.4 makes it clear that at point A that maximizes the monopoly union's utility, the union's indifference curve is not tangent to the firm's isoprofit curve, so a Pareto improvement is possible, there is a 'lens' of employment-wage combinations where the union enjoys a greater utility and the firm enjoys more profit than at A. The same holds at the lower point (e.g. point M) on the labour demand curve emerging from the right-to-manage model, where the union's indifference curve is less steep than the labour demand curve, but is still downward-sloping by assumption, while the isoprofit curve is horizontal. The resulting Pareto inefficiency has prompted McDonald and Solow (1981) to propose a model which develops a *locus of **efficient bargaining***, the locus of wage employment combinations where there is tangency between the firm's concave isoprofit curves and the union's convex indifference curves; point B in ◘ Fig. 13.4 is one of these combinations. The authors assume that firm and union bargain simultaneously over wage and employment, agree to reach some point on this locus, and then agree on some 'fair share' rule, or use generalized Nash bargaining (again with a given unexplained γ) in order to select the point. The result is a point to the right of the labour demand curve; i.e. a labour employment greater than the firm would spontaneously choose for that wage. It is possible to derive the mathematical expression for this locus, but it adds nothing to the graphical determination. Anyway a widespread opinion is that 'The problem with the model appears to be its tenuous empirical relevance ... in the real world the relevant case appears to be that firms and unions negotiate over the wage rate, but that the firm can unilaterally determine the employment level' (Heijdra and Van der Ploeg 2002, p. 196). One reason is that an agreement about the size of the labour force is not easy for the union to defend, the firm can adduce many reasons for being slow at replacing workers who retire for age reasons, and a strike to oblige the firm to hire a few more workers is not easy to launch.

These models assume that the higher-than-reservation wage the union is able to obtain does not induce undercutting by other workers, and does not induce the firm to go non-union, fire all old unionized workforce and hire workers who accept a lower wage. The union certainly is aware of these dangers and takes them into account, so no doubt bargaining is a much more complex affair than these models depict.

But the main problem of these models is that they concern firm-specific unions, bargaining with a single imperfectly competitive firm enjoying above-normal profits and little danger of entry, and capable therefore of paying higher-than-elsewhere wages without being pushed out of the market by competitors: so at best these models apply to a minority of firms. One might think them applicable also to the determination of collective contracts valid for all firms in an ample industry (e.g. miners and chemical industry), but then in all likelihood the demand curve facing the entire industry is nearly vertical because substitutability is essentially between products of the same industry; then the union's worries about the dangers of too high wages will at most concern the international competitiveness of the industry; as argued, it is always possible for the industry to raise its prices in response to higher wages, and there is no need for a surplus in order for unions to be able to make a difference at this level. Industry-level bargains will anyway, if the industry is important, have repercussions on the entire economy and on subsequent bargaining in other industries; the government will seldom remain askance, without or with the occurrence of a strike. Often, renewals of important collective wage contracts fall in the same period, and then what is at stake is the entire general level of wages, and the danger of inflation, and the international competitiveness of the economy; the above models lose all relevance. A clear trade-off between wage and employment can only be argued on the basis of the neoclassical decreasing aggregate labour demand curve. If the latter notion is rejected, one shifts to a classical–Keynesian or Post-Keynesian framework and the issue becomes whether trade unions are able to influence the average real wage, the effects on employment depending on the effects on aggregate demand, which require separate study and cannot be discussed here—although they are certainly very much present to the leaders of national confederations of trade unions and can be part of negotiations. The historical examples are numerous of a trade union confederation which accepted to moderate its wage demands in order not to worsen its nation's trade balance. But when the external constraint does not bind,[32] a rise in wages may well help aggregate demand and employment.

The question becomes whether trade unions strengthen the general bargaining power of wage labour relative to capital, in a classical conflictual framework. It seems clear that the 'capitalists' (the 'industrial leaders' or 'captains of industry', in the terminology of Kalecki 1943) would answer yes without hesitation to such a question, and there must be good reasons behind their unceasing hostility towards trade unions. A quantitative estimate of this overall effect of trade unions is difficult, because it is unclear how to estimate what wages would be in the total absence of trade unions. What numerous contributions have tried to estimate is by how much (on average) trade unions raise wages relative to the wages of workers not covered by collective wage agreements. The difficulties of these empirical attempts are enormous, and a book might be written on them; anyway the estimates range from 4 to 20%, lower in countries like Italy, Germany, France or Sweden where union wage settlements spill over into the non-union sector, higher where unions are less strong overall, highest in the USA.[33] In spite of the problems with the several methodologies and with the comparability of the results of the studies owing to differences in databases, statistical methods utilized, institutional structure of the nations, a positive effect is undeniably present. This does not tell us whether trade unions reduce the average rate of profit or simply raise the wages of part of the labour force while reducing the wages of the remainder so that the rate of profit is not altered. Also, these studies cannot evaluate the overall effect of trade unions on the strength of the labour movement, which influences government policy, laws, work organization, general ideology; nor can they evaluate whether wage rises are started by trade unions and then drip down to the rest of the economy by processes of imitation, or trade unions defend wage differences relative to independently determined non-union wages.

The measurement of bargaining power is analogously difficult, and the notion itself is not clear. The dominance of the neoclassical approach and the desire not to stress the conflictual aspects of capitalism have not favoured attempts at analysing in detail what allows real wages to increase, or obliges them to decrease,

---

32 If the problem is not to endanger the international competitiveness of the economy, it is anyway unclear why it is only wages that must be contained or reduced. Higher incomes, and incomes from property, can be called upon to share in the effort; all will depend on political alliances and majorities.

33 See Cahuc et al. (2014, pp. 448–465) for an up-to-date survey of the empirical evidence.

13.7 · Trade Unions

taking into full account the multiplicity of relevant elements, including the possible recourse to private or public violence.[34]

Indeed it is possible to observe a tendency in the economic literature to treat situations of conflict and bargaining in labour markets as solved rather easily and pacifically by some 'fair rule' or other neat and 'equitable' agreement, for example generalized Nash bargaining, that avoids the eruption of open conflict, not to speak of recourse to violence. The tendency appears to be to argue that since players with conflicting interests are rational, they will try to avoid waste; conflict produces waste of time and resources; so players will use their knowledge of the situation to forecast the result of going on bargaining, and to assess what they can hope to obtain, and will then prefer to obtain it immediately and avoid the costs of conflict. An example of a theory that makes precisely this assumption is the bargaining model of Rubinstein (see Appendix 1). In this model of alternating offers on how to share a 'pie', players correctly forecast the result of drawn-out bargaining, realize what they can hope to achieve, and choose to agree on it immediately, saving the waste of time and utility entailed by going on bargaining.[35] The bargain agreed to in this model approximates a generalized Nash solution, with bargaining power (measured by the share of the 'pie' one obtains) decreasing in the relative *impatience* of each player to arrive at a solution. This bargaining game is accordingly viewed as supporting the assumption of generalized Nash bargaining and as providing an interpretation of the γ parameter as the reciprocal of a measure of relative impatience.

But in real life conflict does erupt. For example, there are strikes. The point is that the capacity of each side to resist in case of conflict is not generally clear in advance. Rubinstein's model assumes that each player knows the degree of impatience of the other player, but this is highly doubtful. And the generalized Nash solution cannot be reached if there isn't reciprocal knowledge of the 'bargaining power' of the players. In real life, when the union representative says 'then we will go on strike for as long as it takes' and the firm's representative answers 'we are not afraid, we can resist a strike of any length', neither side knows how much truth there is in either statement (including one's own). So it can easily be necessary to go and see.

A popular model of strikes is by Ashenfelter and Johnson (1969), then taken up and developed by other economists. The model assumes a firm that expects to produce a given quantity of output to be sold at a given price, needs for that a given amount of labour, and faces a closed-shop union, whose rank-and-file have excessively optimistic ideas about the firm's profitability and hence about what kind of wage increase they can obtain; the rejection of this increase by the firm and the firm's subsequent resistance in the face of a strike reduces their claims;

---

34 Some knowledge of the history of labour struggles and of the violence that often accompanied them should be part of the culture of all economists. Have a look at the Wikipedia entries 'Anti-union violence' and 'List of worker deaths in United States labor disputes', for a start.

35 See Kreps (1990, pp. 556–565) for a broader appraisal of Rubinstein-type bargaining.

the more so the longer the strike lasts. The authors assume that the union's leadership knows rather well how the length of the strike reduces the membership's aspirations, and also knows that the firm's management knows it. This means a decreasing convex 'union concession curve', with strike length s in abscissa and the proportionate wage increase $\mu = (w - w^\wedge)/w^\wedge$ in ordinate, where $w^\wedge$ is the pre-existing wage. This curve starts at time 0 at level μ^0, the initial aspiration of the rank-and-file; it decreases as strike length increases; it tends asymptotically to a minimum level $\mu^\wedge$, not necessarily positive, which if rejected by the firm causes the strike to go on indefinitely.

The firm maximizes the present discounted value V of its future profit stream

$$V = \int_0^\infty \pi e^{-rt} dt + H \tag{13.35}$$

where π is profit, which is decreasing in the negotiated wage rate; r is the firm's discount rate, t is time, and H is the given costs other than wages, treated as a fixed cost (i.e. to be borne even during a strike). Assuming a specific union concession curve $\mu(s)$, we can derive an explicit expression for V. Let

$$\mu(s) = \mu^\wedge + \left(\mu^0 - \mu^\wedge\right) e^{-\alpha s}$$

where α is the rate of decrease of the union's wage demand. The firm's profit is

$$\pi = R - wN - H$$

where $R = pq$ is revenue and N is employment. From $u = (w - w^\wedge)/w^\wedge$ we can derive $w = w^{\wedge(1+\mu)}$. Substituting this into π and the resulting expression for π into the V integral in (13.35), we obtain the value of V if the strike ends at time s, and assuming profits have been zero until then (because the firm could not produce):

13

$$V = \int_s^\infty \left\{R - Nw^\wedge\left[1 + \mu^\wedge + (\mu^0 - \mu^\wedge)e^{-\alpha s}\right]\right\} e^{-rt} dt - \int_0^\infty He^{-rt} dt.$$

Integrating, we obtain

$$V(s) = \left\{R - Nw^\wedge\left[1 + \mu^\wedge + (\mu^0 - \mu^\wedge)e^{-\alpha s}\right]\right\} \frac{e^{-rs}}{r} - \frac{H}{r}. \tag{13.36}$$

This yields V as a function of s; the firm's management, which somehow has a good grasp of the $\mu(s)$ function, can determine the s^* where $V(s)$ is maximized[36]; if $s^* > 0$, this implies equality between the firm's and the union's rate of substitution between wage increase and strike duration; when the union proposes the corresponding $\mu(s^*)$, the firm accepts and the strike ends. The thing is represented graphically in ◘ Fig. 13.5.

36 It requires only algebra to show that differentiating $V(s)$, setting the derivative equal to zero and solving for s yield $s* = -\frac{1}{\alpha} ln\left[\frac{R - Nw^\wedge(1+\mu^\wedge)}{Nw^\wedge(1+\frac{\alpha}{r})(\mu^0 - \mu^\wedge)}\right]$. Such a precise result is anyway as acceptable as the assumptions on which it is based, many of them (e.g. the given product price and the given quantity produced, independent of the contracted wage) very restrictive.

13.7 · Trade Unions

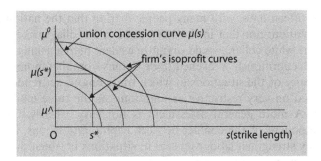

◘ **Fig. 13.5** Ashenfelter–Johnson model

Ashenfelter and Johnson assume that the union leaders know $V(s)$ and therefore they can determine $\mu(s^*)$; so at $t=0$ they would be ready to propose directly a μ a bit above $\mu(s^*)$ (which would be accepted, because of the profit loss the firm avoids by avoiding the strike); but they are unable to persuade the rank-and-file that that is the maximum that can be wrenched from the firm, and in order not to lose the support of their membership they launch the strike. As time passes and the strike continues, the rank-and-file gradually reduce their demands, until s^* is reached.

A frequent criticism of this model is that it assumes the rank-and-file behave irrationally. I disagree; the accusation of irrationality rests on the highly implausible assumption that the rank-and-file know the firm's isoprofit curves and their own $\mu(s)$ function.

The theoretical literature on strikes is generally puzzled by the occurrence of strikes because, it is argued, it is more efficient to agree immediately on the bargain that the strike would allow to reach, thus avoiding the profit loss and income loss the strike causes to the firm and to the workers. This viewpoint reflects a widespread propensity in recent economic modelling to assume 'perfectly rational' agents, that is agents who have complete knowledge of things it is actually impossible to know and a fantastic capacity to make actually impossible calculations and correctly to predict the future. (The road to such an absurd and totally illegitimate deformation of the meaning of rationality was probably opened by the need to assume perfect foresight in modern intertemporal general equilibrium theory.) In our case this viewpoint forgets that each situation is different, and that there is always considerable ignorance about the opponent's true capacity to resist in case of confrontation, or about the likelihood of outside intervention in support of one of the two sides. In all likelihood, either side has only vague and possibly wrong ideas even about *its own* capacity to resist. It seems only rational, in such a situation, to test the opponent. In situations of admitted partial ignorance, it is even unclear that one can talk of definite 'initial aspirations': during the struggle, social interaction can help the development of feelings of rage and solidarity that did not exist before, and the emergence of new demands. No one predicted, for example, that the general strike launched in France in May 1968 would develop into a generalized occupation of factories that paralysed France completely for fifteen days, with many people fearing that the nation was on the verge of a revolution; nor that in the 1980 FIAT blue-collar strike in Turin at a certain point the white collars would organize a silent march asking for an end of the strike, which enormously weakened trade unions from that moment on.

The complexity of the situations in which trade unions act renders all models necessarily based on very restrictive assumptions, as the three models presented make evident. A more general assessment is not easy. Clearly, unions are an important component of the conflict between capital and labour; it seems indubitable that they strengthen labour relative to situations in which they are absent; the empirical attempts to estimate the influence of unions on wages, for what they are worth, find that unionization raises wages by between 4 and 20%. The reasons are many but essentially reflect the greater bargaining power achievable via coordinated action. The damages that can be inflicted on a firm or industry are greater when all workforce acts in unison. An example: one reason why miners in Great Britain consistently won their struggles in the 1950s and 1960s was that when they went on strike, other trade unions went on strike too in order to support their demands; at the end of the 1970s, Margaret Thatcher defeated the miners after passing a law that prohibited supportive strikes.

I am not aware of serious attempts to develop a measure of the bargaining power of trade unions, connecting it to kind of union, degree of support from workers, fragmentation or co-ordination of unions, ideology, connections with political parties, legal framework (what it permits and forbids, how much it protects against unfair firings), government in office, unemployment benefits and so on. Perhaps such a task is even impossible, given the complexity and historical specificity of these determinants, and the vagueness of the notion itself of bargaining power. For the same reason, it is not easy to decide how much trade unions help to answer the two main questions motivating this chapter, that is,
(1) What prevents wages from falling (much) in the presence of unemployment.
(2) What causes (or has caused until recently) real wages secularly to rise.

Question (2) sends us to the long-period theories of wages that will be discussed in the second part of this chapter.

On question (1), what can be stated is that no doubt unions, in so far as they strengthen the workers' bargaining power, and help resistance to wage decreases when there is unemployment. But it is doubtful that their existence suffices to prevent wage decreases when unemployment is considerable. The point is that they are not able totally to sterilize the downward pressure on wages coming from the unemployed, if this pressure is strong. Take for example the USA: the law gives a union (if certified by the National Labour Relations Board) exclusive jurisdiction over the particular bargaining unit (a plant) that voted majority support for it; but employers are not obliged to reach an agreement or sign a contract with this union, and 'can effectively contrive to continue nonunion' (Booth 1995, p. 47). So in the presence of extensive unemployment, firms can decide to go 'non-union' and to hire at a lower wage, if the unemployed accept.

The inability of trade unions completely to prevent a negative influence of unemployment on wages is also highlighted by Blanchflower and Oswald's (1990) *wage curve*. This is an empirical finding confirmed by subsequent studies[37] that argues that, when comparing unemployment and wages in different regions of an advanced nation in the same period (the USA was studied first but then also UK, Germany and other nations), local unemployment rates do negatively affect local wages, with a rather constant elasticity, surprisingly similar in different areas and nations, usually not far from -0.1.

Blanchflower and Oswald argue that the plausible explanations of this finding are either efficiency wages (the shirking–gift exchange version) or bargaining (union bargaining, where there are unions). In the first case, the effort function $e(w)$ is shifted to the left by increases in the unemployment rate because more unemployment raises the dislike of workers for the sack, and workers shirk less; then the efficiency wage decreases. As to bargaining, less unemployment makes people less afraid of being fired and therefore readier to threaten the firm with strikes or other forms of conflict. Econometric discrimination between these two possible explanations is very difficult. But one paper (Blien et al. 2009) studies Germany, paying attention to institutional differences, and finds that a wage curve does exist except it is nearly non-existent for firms with *works councils* (a German institution, a firm-based board of worker representatives existing in almost half the firms with collective wage agreements, that has no power over wage bargaining or decisions to strike but has co-determination rights on many production aspects, e.g. overtime regulation or health and safety, and therefore certainly increases workers' bargaining power); the paper concludes that this capacity of works councils to dampen the adjustment of wages to the regional unemployment situation, jointly with the well-ascertained higher wages in firms with works councils, suggests that bargaining power is more important than efficiency wage considerations in determining wages.

The wage curve compares regional differences at the same moment, and this eliminates the difficulties that might arise with comparisons of effects of unemployment on wages in different years. One can conclude that unemployment is definitely an influence on what workers are able to obtain. The problem remains for standard supply-and-demand theory that unemployment (in excess of plausible frictional unemployment) only causes somewhat lower wages, not their continuing reduction as long as excess labour supply persists. So let us study one more approach to this issue in the next section.

But before leaving trade unions let me remember again that their influence is not only on wages but also on working conditions, on protection against unjustified firings and more generally on the political strength of the labour movement. Labour parties have often been, if not created, at least fundamentally financed and supported by the trade union movement. The capacity of trade unions to organize struggles to support political demands for better pension systems and more generally for an efficient welfare state has been fundamental to obtain the more civilized life conditions of Western Europe relative to the USA.

---

37 See Card (1995) for a careful review of the book *The Wage Curve*, which is often critical but concludes that the wage curve does exist.

1180   **Chapter 13 · Labour Markets and Income Distribution**

13.8 **The Solow or Solow–Hahn Approach**

The power of trade unions to impose wage agreements valid for all employed workers even in the presence of not irrelevant unemployment is not easily explained. Even when law establishes total coverage of the union agreement, firms might refuse to be part of the employers' federation that bargains with the union, and unemployed workers might offer to accept lower wages. But such behaviours are seldom seen, especially on the workers' side. As noted by many commentators, generally the unemployed seem reluctant to propose to *replace* the employed by offering to accept a lower wage; and it is plausible that, without this general attitude, trade unions would be much weaker in their bargaining.

So there is a puzzle to be explained. One approach to explaining it, that has raised much interest, has been proposed by Solow 1990 (and also by Weibull 1987; it is also taken up in Hahn and Solow 1992). I will call it *the Solow–Hahn approach* so as to make it clear that it is a different approach from the one of Solow's 1979 paper on efficiency wages, and I will present it taking into account the careful critical examination by De Francesco (1993), and also Levrero (2012).[38] The decreasing labour demand curve will be provisionally accepted, to check whether the approach has weaknesses even conceding this neoclassical element.

Solow admits that the reluctance of the unemployed to undercut is a social norm, analogous to other norms of behaviour historically developed by society and taught to the young as part of normal education (e.g. leave the seat to old people in a crowded bus, don't be smelly, don't go around naked). Norms of this type are followed not out of rational calculation of the advantage or disadvantage of so doing, but out of instilled habit. But Solow argues that the birth of norms that *prima facie* go against self-interest must in turn be explained as due to a realization that 'Behavior that has been found to be individually tempting but socially destructive is ... socially unacceptable' (Solow 1990, p. 43); and he proposes to explain the no-undercutting norm as resulting from the perception precisely of an 'individually tempting but socially destructive' nature of undercutting, that must therefore be replaced by a no-undercutting norm that brings general advantage to the community of workers. With time, this rational foundation may stop being a *conscious* reason for that behaviour but, without it, it is difficult to understand why the norm should ever have come into being.

So Solow proceeds to argue that it must be proved that no-undercutting can be advantageous for workers and rational as a norm, that is, capable of self-perpetuation because convenient, and proposes to prove it by showing that it can be a subgame perfect Nash equilibrium of an infinitely repeated game. He assumes a firm with a downward-sloping demand curve for labour, and an isolated, firm-specific labour market, with L workers each offering a fixed amount

---

38 Solow's 1990 book contains much more than the model to be discussed here. Levrero's 2012 booklet is rich of insightful observations on wage theory. Their reading is recommended. For those who can read Italian, De Francesco's paper is also recommended.

13.8 · The Solow or Solow–Hahn Approach

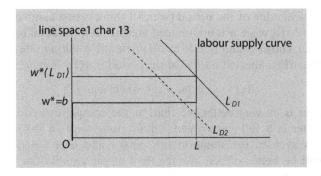

Fig. 13.6 Labour supply and labour demand in the Solow–Hahn approach. Here $w^*(L_{D1})$ is the equilibrium wage when the labour demand curve is L_{D1}

of labour hours (normalized to 1) per period, as long as the real wage is not inferior to a reservation wage b, equal to unemployment benefits. Since except in very special circumstances it is difficult to assume an isolated labour market without possibility of mobility into and out of it, De Francesco prefers to assume that the analysis refers to the entire economy's labour market, and therefore to the economy-wide neoclassical labour demand curve (assuming homogeneous workers). The labour supply curve has then the shape shown in ◘ Fig. 13.6. For $w<b$ labour supply is zero; for $w>b$ it is L; for $w=b$ workers are indifferent between working or not, and assuming that they accept to work if invited by some firm to do so (you can assume they are in fact offered b plus one cent a month), labour supply is any point on the horizontal segment between O and L.

The decreasing labour demand curve can cut this supply curve:

- in the horizontal stretch (the broken-line labour demand curve L_{D2}), and then the competitive equilibrium wage is $w^* = b$[39];
- in the vertical stretch (the continuous labour demand curve L_{D1}), and then the competitive equilibrium wage is $w^* > b$.

In both cases if w is greater than the competitive equilibrium wage, labour demand is less than supply, and in the first case this is so even at $w=b$. Solow assumes that if there is excess labour supply, all jobs are randomly reassigned every period among the L available identical workers. With N for employment, the probability of being employed is then $1 - u = N/L$, where u is the rate of unemployment. Assuming workers have risk-neutral VNM utility function in the sole variable income, it is possible to normalize their subutility so that it is measured by the wage if employed or by the unemployment benefit if unemployed.

---

39 Solow calls it the Walrasian wage, but this terminology is best avoided since if one really followed Walras in taking the 'form' of capital as given, then as admitted for example by Hicks (1932, 1980–81) the labour demand curve would be practically vertical.

Chapter 13 · Labour Markets and Income Distribution

Assume at the beginning of the period (which I think is best assumed rather long, at least six months) a wage w is announced greater than the equilibrium wage w^*, and each worker knows it and is able to calculate the resulting rate of unemployment $u(w) > 0$; her/his expected utility for the period is $w(1 - u) + bu$. If

$$w(1 - u) + bu > w^*, \text{ where } w > w^*, \tag{13.37}$$

then the worker is *ex-ante* better off than at the competitive equilibrium wage even if the latter is a full-employment equilibrium wage $(w^* > b)$, and if wage undercutting is avoided the situation can persist and over a series of periods all workers will be better off on average than at the equilibrium wage; but the worker is worse off *ex post* for the period if after the random assignment of jobs is effected the worker is among the unemployed. If (13.37) holds but before production commences the workers who discover they are going to be unemployed in that period can still offer to accept a lower wage, the question arises whether they will resist the temptation or not. If we can find reasons for them to resist, we have a possible explanation of wage rigidity.

As a preliminary, since condition (13.37) is necessary for the approach to make sense, let us study its likelihood. If $w^* > b$ (the labour demand curve is of type L_{D1}), at w^* there is full employment, then condition (13.37) can be re-written

$$\frac{w^* + \Delta w^*}{w^*}(1 - u) + \frac{b}{w^*}u > 1.$$

The second addendum on the left-hand side is positive if $b > 0$, so for the condition to be satisfied it suffices that the first term be 1 or at most a little less, that is, the (absolute value of the) elasticity of labour demand must be less than a value only slightly greater than 1. Therefore (13.37) is not guaranteed to hold.

If the equilibrium wage is $w^* = b$, which is what Solow (1990, p. 45) assumes (without explaining why he neglects the other case), then the expected utility of w^* is $w^*(1 - u^*) + bu^* = w^*$, where u^* is the rate of unemployment at $w^* = b$; then $w > w^*$ implies that condition (13.37) is *necessarily* satisfied. This may seem to allow for any elasticity of the labour demand curve; however, the empirical evidence suggests differently; given plausible values of u and of w/b, for the labour demand curve to cross the labour supply curve in its horizontal stretch its elasticity may have to be *very* low. De Francesco notes that a situation with a wage 30% greater than b and a 10% rate of unemployment does not seem implausible, but for the labour demand curve to pass through that point and to cut the labour supply curve in its horizontal portion, the (interval) elasticity of labour demand must be (in absolute value) less than 1/3. The elasticity would plausibly have to be even lower for the convenience, of a 'co-operative' behaviour of not proposing wage cuts even if you are unemployed, to become an accepted social rule of behaviour because, De Francesco observes, 'it seems plausible that some social stigma against the non-cooperative behaviour could arise and impose itself only where the advantages of cooperation were *substantial*' (1993, p. 18, my transl.).

So we find that the advantage in the long run, of a 'co-operative' behaviour of no-undercutting, is not guaranteed except under restrictive assumptions (var-

13.8 · The Solow or Solow–Hahn Approach

ying from case to case) about the elasticity of the labour demand curve. Now, the neoclassical approach gives no reason to presume that these assumptions will be satisfied in the near totality of cases. But unless these assumptions *are* satisfied in the near totality of cases, it seems difficult to view in the advantage of the 'co-operative' behaviour the origin of the no-undercutting social norm. The generalized absence of undercutting, in many cases, would *worsen* the condition of workers relative to the standard 'free play of competition'. This would counter the birth of a social norm.

Solow does not seem aware of this weakness of his argument. He notes:

> » You have to be pretty obtuse not to realize that very many of the unemployed would much prefer to be working at wage rates currently on offer … But then the belief that there is a stable and effective social norm against wage competition for jobs needs some reinforcement of a kind that might come from a showing that obeying such a norm is individually rational, besides performing a social function. (1990, p. 40)

That is, Solow wants to argue that conforming to the no-undercutting norm may be individually rational even in the absence of motivations such as internalized ethical norms or political ideals, or desire for social approval, or fear of sanctions (like losing friends, or being beaten up). To this end, he assumes workers take part in a repeated game. At the beginning of each period, each worker announces the minimum wage at which she/he accepts to work for the period (remember that work contracts are for only one period), and firms decide employment on that basis. If the game were a one-period non-repeated game, the only Nash equilibrium—in which each one chooses the most convenient wage, given the wages chosen by the others—would be that everyone proposes w^*: a complete proof would be long (it would consist of a generalization to L players of the argument applying to Bertrand competition; see ▶ Chap. 12), here it will suffice to note that if the other workers propose a wage $w > w^*$, a worker will find it convenient to propose a wage just a little bit less than w, in this way ensuring employment with a negligible income loss; and if there is an array of different wages greater than or equal to w^* proposed by workers, and firms hire the workers in inverse order to the w they propose, then there will be some worker whose wage choice is not a best response because she might have got employment at a wage higher than the one she proposed, therefore that array of wages is not a Nash equilibrium.

Things change if one assumes the game is an infinitely repeated one. If no-undercutting is indeed a co-operative behaviour at $w > w^*$, that is, if inequality (13.37) holds, then the *folk theorem* (see ▶ Chap. 11, Sect. 11.15) tells us that if the discount factor is sufficiently close to 1, then any vector of feasible average payoffs between w and w^* can be obtained as the result of a subgame perfect Nash equilibrium. The feasibility condition is that the average payoffs must indeed be reachable: and they are.

Solow argues that one such Nash equilibrium consists of all workers adopting the following strategy: ask for wage $w > w^*$ in the initial period, period 0 (note that because Solow assumes $w^* = b$, inequality (13.37) is satisfied); in all following

1184   **Chapter 13** · Labour Markets and Income Distribution

periods ask for the same w if all other workers in preceding periods have asked for it; otherwise ask for w^* for a sufficiently high (and agreed by all workers) number T of periods, and then go back to asking for w. If all workers conform to this strategy, the wage remains at w and workers' average income is indeed better than w^* (for a sufficiently low rate of discount). But will this strategy be *self-enforcing*, that is such that, if all other workers adopt it, a worker finds it optimal to adopt it?

Solow continues: 'Now suppose that the market wage is w and you learn that you will be unemployed this period. You must decide whether to undercut the market wage or to sit tight' (1990, p. 54). That is, he assumes that at the beginning of the period, after all workers ask for the same wage $w > w^*$, and after firms randomly decide whom to hire at that wage, there is still time for a worker who ends up unemployed to announce a change in her wage demand and, by asking for $w - \varepsilon$ (with ε positive but very small), to obtain a job *already for that period*, replacing one of the hired workers.[40] Then the alternative for this worker is between not undercutting, with income b in period 0 and expected income $w(1 - u) + bu$ in all subsequent periods, or undercutting, with income $w - \varepsilon$ in period 0, and w^* for T subsequent periods, which means a loss in each one of these periods, relative to the choice not to undercut, equal to $w(1 - u) + bu - w^*$. It is intuitive that for a sufficiently low discount rate there will exist a sufficiently long T that makes the (discounted) cumulative loss greater than the initial gain, thus discouraging undercutting; a rigorous proof seems unnecessary.

The picture remains essentially the same (only, less clearly explained) in Hahn and Solow (1992). I find it suggestive, but in need of improvement. A perplexing aspect is that the model assumes that after jobs have been assigned there is still time, for a worker who hasn't been hired, to reduce her wage demand to $w - \varepsilon$, and to displace someone else, before work activity commences. But if one accepts this, then it is unclear why one should not also accept that *there is time for the displaced worker to counter* by reducing her wage demand to $w - 2\varepsilon$, reconquering the job. And then it is unclear where to stop: it seems inevitable to admit that undercutting and quick counter-undercutting will go on until the wage falls to w^* *already in period* 0. There is no initial gain from undercutting, to be then compared with the subsequent loss due to w falling to w^* *the next period* and remaining at that level for some periods.

Now, it is strange that Solow does not admit the possibility of immediate counter-undercutting because it would strengthen his argument. If workers are clear that any initial undercutting will cause the wage to fall to w^* in that same period, then *if $w^* = b$ there is no incentive for the unemployed to undercut so there will be no-undercutting at all*, it would get the unemployed workers no advantage;

---

40 If the unemployed are more numerous than the jobs, and if all the unemployed change their wage demand to $w - \varepsilon$, they cannot all get a job by replacing the employed workers; but this seems an extreme possibility that can be neglected.

13.8 · The Solow or Solow–Hahn Approach

and if $w^* > b$, then undercutting is convenient only if condition (13.37) does *not* hold, that is, if anyway the full-employment wage is preferable for all workers.

If one drops the decreasing labour demand function and believes that there is no guarantee at all that wage decreases raise employment, the argument is strengthened: condition (13.37) certainly holds, and as already argued, wage undercutting will not get the unemployed a job because the wage reduction will be accepted by the employed workers themselves, in order to avoid being replaced. Popular culture will teach it to all workers, and wage undercutting will not be attempted.

Of course, this modification of the Solow–Hahn approach must be completed by a theory of what determines the level of the wage. The same need arises for Solow's own model, since the folk theorem leaves w indeterminate (within limits); Solow admits it and argues that w must be explained by 'the accident of history' (1990, p. 59). Which is disappointing, the evolution of real wages over time cannot be an 'accident of history', and the other sections of this chapter will deal precisely with this issue.

(Another weakness of the model is discussed in the online Appendix to this chapter in the book's web page.)

Four conclusions can be drawn from this examination of the Solow–Hahn approach, not only the model but also the rich considerations from which Solow (1990) starts.

First, it seems empirically undeniable that there is among wage labourers a strong social norm against undercutting; and it is difficult to explain its existence other than as reflecting a persuasion that indefinite wage undercutting for as long as there are unemployed workers must not be allowed, because it would have dire consequences for workers. (The neoclassical approach denies this conclusion on the basis of an assumed rather high elasticity of labour demand, but we have seen its inconsistencies.)

Second, within the neoclassical approach this explanation of the no-undercutting norm needs a low elasticity of labour demand (in some cases a low elasticity would not be needed, but it *is* needed in order for the explanation to be defensible for the generality of possible situations). Now, this poses a dilemma for the neoclassical economist, because this low elasticity would seriously undermine the plausibility of the neoclassical approach even apart from the capital-theoretic criticisms explained in ▶ Chaps. 7 and 8: it would mean the approach could generate multiple equilibria, or practically indeterminate equilibria, or implausible equilibrium income distributions and implausibly large changes in income distribution for very small changes in factor supplies (see ▶ Chap. 3). But this dilemma only arises if one desires to maintain the inconsistent neoclassical approach. If one abandons it in favour of a classical approach combined with the principle of effective demand, then the explanation of the no-undercutting social norm becomes easier, because the thesis of a significant positive influence of wage decreases on unemployment is deprived of foundations. Labour demand will depend essentially on aggregate demand, which is more likely to be negatively than positively influenced by decreases of real wages owing to the negative influence of income redistributions in favour of higher incomes upon the average propensity to consume.[41] As a first approximation, in the short period it seems legitimate to take labour demand as given when wages change; then a social limit to wage falls seems inevitable for an orderly functioning of the economy, and it is only to be expected that a social or even legal norm will have been born to enforce this limit. An unlimited downward flexibility of wages would not eliminate unemployment, and would continue until workers decided that it was preferable to turn to crime or revolt. As argued by several authors both in the past (e.g. Longe, Thornton; see Stirati 1999) and recently, it is in the interest not only of workers but of society at large to prevent such developments: an orderly functioning of the economy would become impossible (Garegnani 1990).

Third, a purely individualistic income motivation seems incapable of justifying the general acceptance of the no-undercutting norm: Solow's attempt in this direction is a failure, because unable to deal with the inevitable presence of cases where the incentive to undercut would be irresistible if individual selfish convenience were the sole motivation.[42] Bewley (1999a, b, 2005) reports that managers occasionally receive offers by unemployed workers to work at a lower wage than the current one, but they *reject them* because of fear it would worsen the morale of the workforce: this indicates the presence of social factors capable of countering the attempt by a few individuals to go against the norm. In all likelihood, compliance with the norm is helped by a consciousness by the unemployed that if they propose to *replace* the employed workers by offering to work for less, this would only oblige the employed workers to accept themselves the lower wage: which would leave the unemployed out in the cold, with as only result a reduction of the wage of employed workers, among whom probably there are also relatives of the unemployed. But moral, social and even physical (violent) sanctions against those who break the norm, resulting from social culture, neighbourhood ties, concerted action appear to be an indispensable support of the norm.

These reinforcing elements appear important also to explain why workers resist attempts by firms to lower wages. Concerted action, not necessarily in the form of trade union activities, seems universally present; it probably represents an innate tendency of human beings, who appear capable of grasping very quickly the possible results of concerted action and are ready to discuss it with potential allies. Piore (1973) insists that work groups in firms develop a set of rules of behaviour that become custom and allow effective threats:

---

41 In the open economy wage reductions can have a positive influence on net exports, anyway a slow one unable to prevent excessive falls of wages if these are freely downward flexible and uncertain because depending on many other circumstances too (e.g. the effect of the fall in wages on net exports must not be neutralized by an appreciation of the currency). However, if the trade balance prevents expansionary policies and the costs of producing exported goods must be reduced, there are many other ways of reducing these costs besides wage reductions, for example tax reductions to exporting industries financed by tax increases on higher incomes.

42 Besides the workers close to retirement age, there would be cases of desperate need for a job, for a variety of reasons.

13.8 · The Solow or Solow–Hahn Approach

» the moral character of custom permits the work group to punish violations through the imposition of sanctions which the moral code of the larger society proscribes and which the workers themselves would normally adjure as illegal and unethical. When directed against management, the available sanctions are legion. They range from petty individual sabotage to massive job actions. The vulnerability of society to attacks of this kind, particularly industrial sabotage, needs hardly be emphasized to-day (R. Walton). The costs of such attacks to a recalcitrant management are overwhelming. The costs to an individual who undertakes them depend almost completely upon the willingness of his fellow workers to deter such actions through group pressure and to co-operate with legal authorities. (Piore 1973 pp. 378–379)[43]

The historical and sociological literature on industrial conflict details the many possible situations and struggles; trade unions are a very important part of the story; certainly bits and pieces are already present to the reader's mind from readings and films; unfortunately for space reasons we must leave it to the reader to enrich the picture.

Fourth, in this way we obtain some understanding of the general absence of free downward wage flexibility, and this explains why wages seldom fall in the presence of unemployment, but it does not explain their *level*. This is the case even in Solow's own analysis, since the folk theorem leaves the wage level partly indeterminate; and certainly one cannot be content with 'the accident of history'. We find here the same need for a theory of the wage level, noticed in the more plausible versions of the efficiency wage approach: the shirking and the gift exchange (or fairness) versions. The same limit can be found in the dominant analysis of trade unions, which does not go beyond the formal analysis of a few special cases and the empirical observation that unions, it seems, are able to raise wages from 4 to 20% above the levels in non-unionized sectors. Fine, but what determines wages in the non-unionized sectors?

So, we must conclude, we still need a theory of what determines the average level of real wages. This question can be rendered clearer by asking what determines the *changes* in the average level of wages over decades.

The dominance of the neoclassical approach has helped economists not to be worried by this limit of the above analyses, because the labour demand curve supplied an initial answer, on which one could superimpose imperfections of competition, bargaining power of unions, reasons for downward wage inflexibility. The secular rise in wages could be explained by the upward shift of the labour demand curve caused by technical progress.

The rejection of the neoclassical labour demand curve leaves the non-neoclassical economist with a need for an explanation of the average level of wages and its secular changes. To this issue it is time to pass.

---

43 On R. Walton, see George Brown, *Sabotage*, 1977, p. xi; by the way, this is a book very much worth reading.

13.9 Long-Period Theories of Wages: Four Approaches. The Cambridge School

One can distinguish four main non-neoclassical approaches to the determination of real wages. In order of historical birth they are (with the name followed by an indication of the basic determinant of the evolution of real wages):

(1) Classical/Marxian/Goodwin: bargaining strength of wage labour depends above all on unemployment in a broad sense (the Marxian 'reserve army of labour'), the real wage determines the rate of profit; a broad tendency ensues to: more profits → more growth → less unemployment → rising wages → less profits → less growth → more unemployment → falling wages

(2) Kaleckian: degree of monopoly (capacity of firms to raise product price above production cost)

(3) Cambridge school: the growth decided by firms determines the profit share required for investment

(4) Pivetti: the rate of interest determined by Central Bank policy determines the rate of profit.

In the remainder of the chapter these four approaches will be presented and some synchretic conclusions will be drawn from their strengths and weaknesses.

It is more convenient to present the four approaches in a different order. I start with the third approach.

As a premise, 'workers', in the theories below, means dependent wage or salary earners, that is all persons whose income depends on wages or salaries paid to them by firms or the government (or by well-off families, in the case of servants), with the exception of top managers of corporations, who are formally workers but must be considered part of, or assistants to, the ruling elite, actively working in the interests of the latter. Independent professionals, be they plumbers or tailors or writers or musicians or lawyers or physicians, are a rather small group, close in lifestyle to that of dependent workers when their income is not high (although generally they hate taxes much more), and close to top managers when their income is very high and they work fundamentally as assistants to the ruling elite (top lawyers, very expensive surgeons, etc.). They are neglected in this chapter, or rather they are implicitly included either in the dependent workers, or in the ruling elite with their 'assistants'. Ratios between different wages and salaries are taken as given, so when the rate of profit rises all wages and salaries are assumed to decrease in roughly the same proportion. Of course the economic interests of the different subgroups in this big social amalgam 'the workers' do not perfectly coincide, and historically sometimes have radically diverged. But, although often they do not clearly perceive it, all workers have some important interests in common, for example they are all damaged by the opposition (remembered by Kalecki 1943) of the business community to policies aimed at reducing unemployment. Space constraints prevent a discussion of these issues. For the reader with limited time let me suggest, out of an enormous and fascinating literature, Strobel and Peterson (1997) as a short, lively paper on these problems.

13.9 · Long-Period Theories of Wages: Four Approaches ...

The Cambridge school develops the Keynesian principle of effective demand (savings adjusts to investment via variations of the level of aggregate output) into a theory of income distribution as ultimately determined by the forces that push for growth. I will discuss the views of Nicholas Kaldor, Joan Robinson, and Adrian Wood.

Suppose growth of national income is at a predefined rate g. In Kaldor (1956) this is the rate of growth of labour supply plus the rate of growth of average labour productivity: there is therefore an implicit assumption that in the long run the economy remains at, or very close to, full employment, and it is the need to maintain the full employment of labour that determines the growth rate of the economy (possibly through policy interventions). This means that, once the economy has got onto the growth path, in each year the level Y of income is given and the investment share in it is also given, it is the one required by the growth rate g. Assume a common average propensity s to net savings out of net income (net national product) Y; assume further that tranquil, persistent growth requires that productive capacity is normally utilized, and that this implies an average ratio v of value of capital K to value of net income Y, i.e. $K = vY$; neglect technical progress. Then capital K and income Y grow at the same rate g. Let the analysis be in continuous time. For K to grow at rate g, it must be $(dK/dt)/K = g$, where $dK/dt = I$, net investment, hence $I = gK$. Kaldor assumes that, spontaneously or through state intervention, investment I obeys this equation. Net savings S satisfy $S = sY$, and since savings is determined by investment, it is $I = S = sY$. It follows:

$$g = \frac{I}{K} = \frac{S}{K} = \frac{sY}{K} = \frac{s}{v}. \tag{13.39}$$

If g is given and v is given by the state of technology, s is univocally determined: $s = gv$ is the share of net income that *must* be assigned to savings (and investment) in order for Y and K to grow at rate g. Now suppose that net income is divided between wages and profits (classical meaning), $Y = W + P$, and that the average propensities to save out of these two incomes differ; indicate them as s_w and s_p; assume, as quite plausible, that $s_p > s_w$. The average share of savings in income depends on the share of the two kinds of income, increasing if the share of profits increases. Let $\pi = P/Y$ represent the share of profits in income, $1 - \pi$ the share of wages. The average propensity to save is then

$$s = s_w(1 - \pi) + s_p\pi = s_w + \pi(s_p - s_w), \tag{13.40}$$

an increasing function of π. If the share of savings in net income is to be $s = gv$ with g and v given, and assuming s thus determined is intermediate between s_p and s_w, this equation determines π, i.e. income distribution. A higher growth rate requires a higher s, i.e. a higher π, a lower real wage. The Cambridge approach argues that income distribution will tend to become such as to ensure $s = gv$. (Since the approach does not rely on neoclassical variability of the normal capital–output ratio v, it can neglect the fact that in value terms v will not be rigorously independent of changes in income distribution and output composition.)

The process that brings about such an income distribution is not very clearly illustrated by the authors in this group, but it would seem to have been inspired by Keynes's approach, that treats the wage bargain as fixing only money wages, while real wages are determined by the price level, which in Keynes is an increasing function of aggregate demand (because Keynes follows Marshall in having employment determined by the equality between real wage and marginal product of labour, and the latter is a decreasing function of employment). The Keynesian multiplier under our simplifying assumptions (no government, no exports) is $1/s$, a decreasing function of π. Suppose the economy has been for some time on the growth path required for continuous full labour employment, hence with K appropriate to produce the level of net income Y associated with full labour employment; suppose at a certain point π changes for some reason, becoming less than required for $S/Y = I/Y = gv$. But investment is still at the level required for a growth rate of K equal to g. Then the increased multiplier causes Y to be greater than the full-employment level; there is excess aggregate demand, and this causes prices to rise relative to money wages, which reduces real wages. The process continues until income distribution becomes such that the average propensity to save returns to $s = gv$. The forces pushing for growth at rate g determine the income distribution required for the savings needed by that growth rate.

This theory, in Kaldor's version (full labour employment!), is perhaps best viewed as a *normative* theory that tries to point out the need, for a government interested in *maintaining* continuous full labour employment and normal capacity utilization, to ensure a sufficient amount of savings: this, the model implies, may require an adjustment of income distribution, if saving propensities out of different income categories are given. As a positive theory, its assumption of continuous full labour employment is obviously contradicted by empirical observation. Nor can one try to defend the assumption by arguing that historically the rate of unemployment has remained rather small. The answer to this attempted defence is in a passage by Garegnani (1990) where he asks a Voltairian Candide (because of 'the irrepressible tendency of that character to compare what he is told with what he can see') whether unprejudiced observation makes neoclassical theory look persuasive:

> Indeed, it seems that Candide, turned economist, would not be easily led by observation to the conclusions of modern theory. Candide might start by noticing the presence in general, in a market economy, of the phenomenon of labour unemployment, at times a considerable amount of labour unemployment, a phenomenon that is *prima facie* of doubtful compatibility with modern theory, since, as Candide will be quick to remark, wages show nowhere the tendency to fall to zero.
>
> As for the possible counter-observation that experience shows some sort of long-run coincidence between labour employment and labour seeking employment, Candide might of course retort that such rough coincidence is only to be expected, to the extent that workers cannot live on air. That rough coincidence may in fact result from employment-seeking labour adjusting to employment opportunities rather than the reverse, with the labour 'endowment' being a determin*ed* rather than a determin*ing* magnitude of the system. Candide might indeed easily indicate the massive migrations of workers from country to country that have steadily accompanied the economic development of market economies in the last two

13.9 · Long-Period Theories of Wages: Four Approaches …

centuries. He might also, more subtly, and even more importantly, point to the adaptation implicit in the so-called 'dualism' of many economies, in which a sector using advanced techniques coexists with sectors using the traditional methods, which provide much lower incomes to the producers and release labour in step with the needs of the advanced sector. (Garegnani 1990, pp. 115–116)

The assumption of continuous normal utilization of capacity, or at least of normal utilization on an average over the business cycle, is also criticizable. Differently from the case with normal prices in price theory, in growth theory a tendency of firms to try and realize a normal utilization of capacity does *not* imply that one can assume that over sufficiently long periods capacity utilization is normal on average. Let us grasp why by delving a bit more into growth theory.

Assume a closed economy that produces a single output, corn, by employing labour and circulating capital (corn seed) in yearly production cycles. All firms are identical and behave identically. Land is free. The production cycle of year t begins with a given amount of capital K_t (seed corn) put into the ground at the beginning of the year; the amount of *gross* corn output at the end of year t, Q_t, is not univocally determined by K_t, it depends on how much labour is employed during the year; for simplicity assume Q_t is proportional to the amount of labour, $Q_t = \alpha L_t$, up to a maximum proportional to K_t, $Q_{max}(K) = 2(1 + \beta)K$. But assume that normally firms do not find it convenient to employ labour up to producing $Q_{max}(K)$, because it would require working at night too, and night labour pretends a higher wage; assume it is maximally convenient to stop at $Q^*(K) = (1 + \beta)K$, which therefore represents normal output when capital is K. $Q^*(K)$ can be called the *normal productive capacity* associated with a capital stock K; normal utilization of productive capacity, or normal utilization of the capital stock, means to produce Q^*. *Actual* output Q need not be equal to Q^* because it is determined by effective demand. Define the rate of (gross) capacity utilization as $u_t = Q_t/Q^*(K_t)$. Output adjusts to effective demand, and u can be smaller or (up to a limit) greater than 1. *Net* output $Y_t = Q_t - K_t$ goes to wages or to profits P, that is $Y_t = wL + P$. There is an average propensity to net savings s, and assuming the Keynesian multiplier completes its operation within each period, it is $I_t = S_t = sY_t$, where I and S are *net* investment and *net* savings. Note that K_t is capital at the *beginning* of year t, I_t is net investment at the *end* of year t. If capacity is normally utilized in each period, it is $Y_t^* = Q^*(K_t) - K_t = \beta K_t$. From the above we can derive the growth rate corresponding to *continuous* normal capacity utilization and to a net propensity to save s. With g_K the growth rate of K (also sometimes called rate of accumulation), and with $K_{t+1} = K_t + I_t$, it is

$$g_K = (K_{t+1} - K_t)/K_t = I_t/K_t = sY_t^*/K_t = s\beta. \tag{13.41}$$

Since Q^* and Y^* are proportional to K, they too grow at rate $s\beta$, and net investment too. This is **Harrod's warranted growth rate**, generally indicated as g_w (where the index w stands for *warranted*, not for wages): it is the growth rate of the capital stock that comes out to be justified, or warranted, by the subsequent evolution of aggregate demand because the investment required by that growth rate of capital causes a level of aggregate demand that allows a normal utilization of

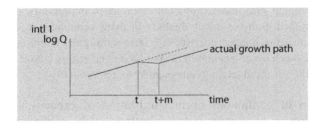

☐ **Fig. 13.7** Harrodian growth path shifted by a period of low growth

productive capacity. If the ratio of output to capital is the appropriate one (the normal one) to start with, then a ratio $s\beta$ of net investment to capital is the one that allows the growing capital stock to be normally utilized period after period. Equation (13.41) is formally the same as Eq. (13.39) with $\beta = 1/v$, but it refers to discrete cycles, and it does not assume that the growth rate is given, it *derives* the warranted growth rate from given β and s.

Let us assume this economy grows for a number of years at the warranted rate $s\beta$, with continuous normal capacity utilization. Then for some reason for a number of periods, say from t to $t+m$, investment grows at a lower rate, while the average propensity to save and hence the multiplier remain unchanged. At $t+m$ the growth rate of capital goes back to $s\beta$. The evolution of Q can be shown in semilogarithmic scale, in a Figure with time in abscissa and *log Q* in ordinate; a constant growth rate of Q shows as a straight line, with slope equal to the growth rate.[44] The periods in which investment's grow rate is less than $s\beta$ cause capital to grow at a lower growth rate, and cause capacity utilization to be less than 1. Indeed, given K_t, a growth rate of the capital stock $g_K < s\beta$ implies an investment I_t less than required for warranted growth, hence a net income $Y_t = I_t/s < Y_t^*$, and therefore $Q_t < Q^*(K_t)$, which implies $u_t < 1$. When g_K resumes at rate $s\beta$ (and capacity utilization goes back to $u=1$), the capital stock is less than it would have become along the warranted growth path; over any time interval including the periods from t to $t+m$ the average growth rate is less than g_w, and there is no reason to presume that there will be periods of growth faster than g_w to compensate (☐ Fig. 13.7).

The several elements that influence the actual growth rate of the economy—such as important innovations, government fiscal policy, evolution of net exports, anti-inflation restrictive policies of the Central Bank—may cause long periods of slow growth, or conversely of very high growth, associated with utilization below normal, or above normal, and with no reason to presume that deviations from normal utilization in one direction will be roughly compensated by deviations in the opposite direction.

Furthermore, the attempt by firms to bring utilization back to the desired, normal level can fail and actually make things worse: when the growth rate of

---

44 Assume $(dQ/dt)/Q = g$. It is $d \log Q/dt = [d \log Q/dQ] \cdot (dQ/dt) = (1/Q) \cdot (dQ/dt) = g$; hence if g is constant, *log Q* as a function of t has constant slope equal to g.

13.9 · Long-Period Theories of Wages: Four Approaches ...

investment is and has been for some years below the warranted rate, one obtains $I/K < g_w$ (an inequality that will sooner or later hold if investment keeps growing at a rate below g_w, because the growth rate of K converges to the growth rate of I), then $Y = sI$ is less than $Y^* = \beta K$, and Q is less than Q^*, that is, aggregate demand is less than required for the normal utilization of the capital stock; year after year firms discover they have invested too much, since the resulting capital is less than normally utilized; therefore firms have an incentive to reduce the growth rate of investment, *but this worsens the underutilization of capital.* Indeed define $u^\wedge = Y/Y^*$ to be the degree of utilization of *net* productive capacity, which is equal to u when $u = 1$, and is $\gtrless 1$ when $u \gtrless 1$ (I leave to the reader the derivation of the precise relationship between u and $u^\wedge$). When the growth rate of capital (equal to the growth rate of investment and hence of Y) is constant and can be different from g_w, Eq. (13.41) becomes[45]

$$g_K = (K_{t+1} - K_t)/K_t = I_t/K_t = sY_t/K_t = \frac{sY}{Y^*}\frac{Y^*}{K} = su^\wedge\beta = u^\wedge g_w. \qquad (13.42)$$

If $g_K < g_w$, it is $u^\wedge < 1$, capital is underutilized; the smaller is g_K, the smaller is $u^\wedge$.

Analogously, an overutilization of capital ($u^\wedge > 1$) that induces firms to accelerate the growth of investment has the effect of further increasing $u^\wedge$. This is the famous **Harrodian instability** of the warranted growth rate. Many economists think that this instability does not seem to show up in real economies (and debate possible reasons why), but for our purposes here all that is needed is that there is no guarantee that attempts to correct a generalized below-normal (or above-normal) utilization of capital quickly succeed in realizing the correction. This confirms that it is perfectly possible for an economy to exhibit for many years an underutilization (or, sometimes, an overutilization) of productive capacity. In conclusion, the Cambridge assumption that, at least on average, capacity is normally utilized (and therefore a faster growth requires a redistribution of net income from wages to profits) cannot be accepted; within limits, a stimulus to aggregate demand that causes it to grow faster can be satisfied by an increase in the degree of utilization of productive capacity with no need for income redistributions; and an underutilization of capacity can continue for years. (Also see ▶ Sect. 12.6.2, observation (iv), and ▶ Sect. 12.6.3.)

Let us pass to Robinson (1962). She maintains the idea that income distribution is determined by the growth rate determined by firms ('the central mechanism of our model is the desire of firms to accumulate', 1962, p. 128), and that, over long periods, capacity is normally utilized on average; but she does not assume the full employment of labour. Therefore she is in need of a determina-

---

45 This formulation is too simple, although useful as a first introduction to the importance of the variability of capacity utilization. Note that it implies that $g_K = 0$ requires $u^\wedge = 0$, that is, a zero net income, against the empirical evidence of economies with a zero growth rate but a positive net income. The introduction of an autonomous component in the aggregate consumption function, $C = c_0 + c_1 Y$, avoids this unrealistic result. The reader is invited to explore how this modification changes Eq. (13.42).

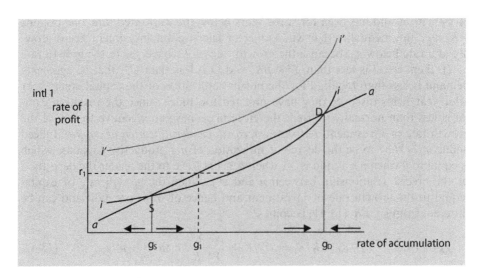

◘ **Fig. 13.8** Joan Robinson's banana diagram

tion of the growth rate. She achieves it on the basis of 'the relation between the rate of profit *caused* by the rate of accumulation and the rate of accumulation which that rate of profit will *induce*' (ibid. p. 129). This relation is represented by a famous 'banana diagram'; see ◘ Fig. 13.8.

This figure has the rate of accumulation in abscissa and the rate of profit in ordinate. Two functions are represented. The first function, the rate of profit as caused by the rate of accumulation, is line *aa*, an upward-sloping straight line because of the assumption Joan Robinson makes that savings come out only of profits (i.e. $s_p > 0$, $s_w = 0$; but it would make little difference to assume $s_p > s_w > 0$) and therefore a higher growth rate of capital (with a given $\beta = Y^*/K$) *requires* a greater share of profits in income,

$$g_K = I/K = (s_p P/Y) \cdot Y/K = (s_p P/Y)\beta, \qquad (13.43)$$

and, according to Joan Robinson, it also *causes*, i.e. *brings about*, the needed higher share of profits. The reason is not very clearly indicated, but from other writings of hers it seems to be that, when aggregate demand grows faster, owing to the better sales prospects firms are able to raise prices relative to money wages.

The second function, the rate of accumulation induced by the rate of profit, is curve *ii*, upward-sloping and strictly convex (the *i'i'* curve is discussed later). Its positive slope is explained as follows:

>> It seems reasonably plausible ... to say that ... to sustain a higher rate of accumulation requires a higher level of profits, both because it offers more favourable odds in the gamble and because it makes finance more readily available. For purposes of our model, therefore, the 'animal spirits' of the firms can be expressed in terms of a function relating the desired rate of growth of the stock of productive capital to the expected level of profits. (ibid. p. 118)

13.9 · Long-Period Theories of Wages: Four Approaches ...

The strict convexity of curve *ii* indicates that, beyond a certain level, to raise the growth rate by one more percentage point encounters increasing difficulties and needs therefore a greater and greater rise of the rate of profit. (Joan Robinson does not supply explanations why she assumes it is so.) There are now two growth rates, g_D and g_S in ◘ Fig. 13.8, that satisfy Eq. (13.41) by being associated with the needed income distribution (the needed rate of profit); the addition relative to Eq. (13.41) is the assumption of a propensity to invest dependent on the rate of profit, such that at a rate of growth different from those two, the rate of profit needed to generate the necessary savings does not induce entrepreneurs to invest as much as that rate of growth would require.

The case shown in ◘ Fig. 13.8 is not the only possible one: the *ii* curve might be in the *i'i'* position, i.e. entirely above the *aa* line; or it might cross the *aa* line from above (point S) but then remain always below it (i.e. no point D); or there might be a point D but no point S. But Joan Robinson considers the depicted case the more probable and more interesting one. In this case, if the rate of accumulation is greater than g_S and different from g_D, it tends to g_D. For example if it is g_1, intermediate between g_S and g_D, it causes a rate of profit r_1 that induces a rate of accumulation greater than g_1; the induced rate of accumulation raises the rate of profit, further raising the rate of accumulation. The reader can check that if the rate of accumulation is greater than g_D, it will tend to decrease. Point D is therefore stable. With the same kind of reasoning one concludes that point S is unstable. Then if for some reason the rate of accumulation falls below g_S, it continues to decrease, the economy falls into stagnation. This, says Joan Robinson, might explain why certain nations fall into a no-growth poverty trap.

It is a nice story, but it has weaknesses. I mention two. First, as mentioned in ▶ Sect. 12.7.4, it can be disputed that a higher rate of profit *induces* a higher rate of accumulation: without prospects of easy sales of the increased production there is no incentive to invest in production rather than in rent-yielding assets, real or financial; furthermore if, as argued by several authors (e.g. Pivetti, see below), in the long-run rate of profit and rate of interest move in sympathy, leaving entrepreneurial profit (the excess of profit over interest payments) just sufficient to compensate for the 'risk and trouble' of entrepreneurship, it is unclear why a higher rate of profit accompanied by a higher rate of interest should stimulate investment. Second, as already argued in ▶ Sect. 12.6, it can be disputed that a higher rate of profit (a lower real wage) is *necessary* for a higher rate of accumulation: in capitalistic economies it is generally possible, within limits, to have a higher rate of growth without a decrease of real wages, via a greater utilization of capital, a higher Y/K ratio. As shown by Eq. (13.42), a persistent rate of accumulation greater than the warranted rate is achievable by having $u > 1$ (or equivalently $u^\wedge > 1$). Now, it seems highly plausible that a rise in net investment above the previous growth path will have, at least initially, precisely this effect, because it will increase Y by a greater percentage than K, without any necessary effect on real wages. For example, suppose 2 years is the time required for the multiplier to complete its workings; if $I/K = 1/20$ initially (and hence $g_K = g_Y = 5\%$), a 10% rise of I/K from a certain year on, that causes g_K to rise to 5.5%, means, the first year, a 10% increase of I, which then continues to grow at 5.5% a year, and this

1196   **Chapter 13 · Labour Markets and Income Distribution**

means a rise of Y after 2 years around 10% more than along the previous growth path, while K has risen only 2% more than along the previous growth path. The resulting 8% increase in u appears perfectly compatible with the available data about the flexibility of capacity utilization: it is difficult to think of firms that would not be only too glad to increase production and sales by 8%. This more intense utilization of capacity can go on for many years. I conclude that, within limits (which actual economic growth does not reach), changes in the growth rate of the economy do not require changes in the share of profits, they can be achieved with unchanged real wages by changing the rate of utilization of capacity.

Actually, if one admits the presence in autonomous demand of non-capacity-creating autonomous expenditure, NCCAE (state consumption expenditure, or exports), then it is possible to change the long-run growth rate of the economy without changing the rate of utilization of capacity except temporarily, by changing the growth rate of NCCAE. Neglecting foreign trade, and without going into explicit formalization which is best left to courses on macroeconomics, open economies and growth, I will only note that a given growth rate $g_{NC} < s/v$ of NCCAE can be made to coincide with the growth rate of the capital stock and of Y, and with normal capacity utilization, via an opportune share of investment in total autonomous expenditure and an opportune ratio of K to NCCAE. Suppose the given capital stock K is normally utilized, hence Y is given; suppose private consumption is a fixed share of Y; this means the share of I + NCCAE in Y is given; by increasing the share of I in Y from zero and decreasing the share of NCCAE one raises the growth rate of K and hence (assuming continuous normal utilization of capacity) of Y until they reach the given growth rate g_{NC} of NCCAE. However the size of NCCAE thus determined may not correspond to its actual size. But if the actual size is larger, it will induce via the multiplier a greater-than-normal utilization of capacity that will stimulate investment, so K (and Y) will grow at a higher rate than g_{NC}, and as long as Harrodian instability does not arise the result will be a reduction of the share of NCCAE in Y, tending to the share that ensures a share of investment in Y that causes normally utilized K to grow at the same rate as NCCAE (Allain 2014). The converse will happen if the actual size of NCCAE is initially smaller than the one required, with the given K, for normal capacity utilization growth at rate g_{NC}. On this basis the so-called 'supermultiplier school' (Serrano, Cesaratto, DeJuan, Pariboni, Allain) argues that the 'animal spirits' of the government can take the place of the 'animal spirits' of private entrepreneurs and determine a different growth rate of the economy by changing the growth rate of NCCAE without changing the real wage and maintaining (except during the transitional adjustment) the normal utilization of capacity.

This means that it is not plausible to explain the behaviour of real wages in the way suggested by Joan Robinson. The growth rate of the economy may well have effects on real wages, but in all likelihood these will be rather different from those implied by Joan Robinson's approach: a faster rate of growth will generally entail a higher level of labour employment, which will tend to *strengthen* labour and therefore, sooner or later, probably (apart from neo-corporatist social arrangements) to *raise* the share of wages, rather than reduce it. It is possible that a sudden acceleration of aggregate demand may initially favour price rises relative to money wages, but as soon as the faster growth reduces unemployment one can expect wage demands to increase and to obtain some success, bringing about either higher real wages, or inflation—in which case further developments depend on policy decisions, on which we do not stop now. It is only in economies already at their maximum growth rate (perhaps USSR in the 1930s? or war economies) that a higher growth rate requires a decrease of consumption. Even the spectacular growth rates of China in the 1990s and 2000s do not seem to have been accompanied by lower real wages or more generally less per capita consumption.

After Robinson, Wood (1975) has insisted that the firms' aim is to grow as fast as possible, and that this is the main force determining profits (and hence real wages) by determining prices relative to money wages. His analysis has enjoyed considerable popularity among Post-Keynesian economists (e.g. see its favourable treatment in Lavoie 2014).

The basic idea is that growth is essentially financed by retained earnings, because firms are wary of developing an excessive leverage ratio (ratio of debt to own capital, also called gearing ratio), and then 'the company sector profit margin is uniquely determined by the need to finance company sector investment' (Wood 1975, p. 110). The thesis is that firms fix prices relative to costs so as to obtain the desired profit margin, motivated by the need to finance growth. What remains to be determined is growth. At the level of the individual firm, growth is determined by the intersection, in (g, r) space, between (i) a downward-sloping *opportunity frontier* that shows the profit rate determined by the firm's growth rate, a decreasing function because in order to grow faster the firm must spend more on advertising and R&D and must reduce the price of the product relative to competing products, and (ii) a linear upward-sloping *'finance frontier'* that indicates the minimum profit rate needed to finance each planned growth rate; see ◘ Fig. 13.9.

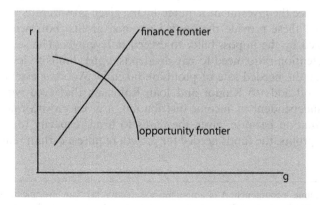

◘ **Fig. 13.9** Adrian Wood's finance frontier and opportunity frontier

This much-cited diagram (Wood 1975, p. 83) tells us less than it may seem. The firm's opportunity frontier is decreasing because the prices and the growth rates of other firms are taken as given: if *all* firms, including the one under examination, decide to grow faster and raise prices in order to obtain the needed retained profits, the diagram offers no reason why the profit rate of the firm under examination should decrease. But if the prices and the growth rates of other firms must be treated as given, the position of the opportunity frontier depends on them and tells us nothing until we know more about what determines them. For example, the position of the opportunity frontier and hence the chosen growth rate of each firm depend on the expected growth of demand for the industry's product, and on the competitiveness of the firm: the more competitive firms plan a higher growth rate than the industry's average, counting on subtracting market shares from the other competitors; but since this is a zero-sum game, the faster growth of some firms obliges other firms to grow slower, the industry's average growth rate cannot but be limited by the growth rate of the demand for its products, so it depends essentially on the growth rate of aggregate demand, which the diagram must take as given. That is, if one neglects differences in growth rates between firms, all one is left with is an aggregate 'finance frontier', that tells us that in order to finance a higher average growth rate a higher average profit rate is needed; but the average growth rate is indeterminate thus far. To determine it, Wood assumes that 'long run equilibrium prevails in the sense that stocks, the degree of capacity use, short term borrowing, financial asset holdings and the payout ratio are at their long run target levels' (ibid. p. 111). This is an assumption of continuous normal degree of capacity utilization, so Wood is simply *assuming* growth at Harrod's warranted rate. Given the normal Y/K ratio, that Wood takes as given as much as Kaldor and Joan Robinson, the warranted rate g_w depends on the average propensity to save out of income, and this is taken by Wood as given and independent of the share of profits in income (ibid. p. 112); the growth rate, equal to the warranted growth rate, is therefore fully determined independently of income distribution.[46] The real novelty of Wood relative to Kaldor or Joan Robinson is this degree of freedom with respect to income distribution, 'closed' by the thesis that the rate of profit must be sufficient for firms to be able to finance the investment required by the given growth rate, which requires profits because these provide the needed retained profits: borrowing is possible but it is limited by the impossibility to exceed in leverage. (The several financial variables—retention ratio, need to pay dividends, upper limits to leverage ratio—that determine the needed rate of profit are taken by Wood as essentially given.) Therefore Wood adds to Kaldor and Joan Robinson that even with a propensity to save independent of income distribution, a given growth rate determines income distribution because, given the limits to firms' capacity to get into debt and to retain profits, the funds needed for growth require a certain rate of profit.

---

46 Wood also admits a component A of autonomous demand other than investment, but the latter is implicitly assumed to grow at the same rate as investment in long-run equilibrium, so its presence does not alter the fundamental ideas of the approach and is neglected here.

The model is too rigid in its assumptions about the ratio between investment and share of profits. Investment need not be mostly out of retained profits: banks live off loans to firms; new firms cannot be born out of retained profits, and they do contribute to growth: corporations like Amazon were not born out of retained profits.[47] Also, the maximum acceptable leverage ratio depends on sales prospects.

But the main criticism of this approach is similar to one advanced against Joan Robinson: it offers no convincing reason why the equilibrium growth rate thus determined, 'which we may suppose to refer either to a single long period or to a situation of steady state growth' (p. 113), should indicate the actual average growth rate of the economy. To Wood's credit, differently from Joan Robinson he does advance two arguments to conclude 'that in practice modern capitalist economies will normally be sufficiently close to long run equilibrium to make our equilibrium model of the determination of the share of profits an acceptable description of reality' (p. 132); but he is not convincing. The first argument rejects Harrod's instability, on the basis of the thesis that 'since firms plan over a three to five year horizon, their expectations of demand growth are based on the extrapolation of secular trends and are very inelastic with respect to year to year changes in demand' (p. 130). A three to five year horizon is far from suggesting 'the extrapolation of secular trends', but above all, Harrodian instability does *not* need, as Wood seems to believe, that 'investment plans of firms are very sensitive to year to year changes in the level of demand and the degree of capacity use' (pp. 130–131). Equation (13.42) suggests that a persistent growth rate of demand different from the warranted one will not fail sooner or later to induce a change in the growth rate of investment, and the latter change even if very gradual will cause the economy's growth rate further to diverge from the warranted rate. Therefore unless the economy was already on the warranted path and therefore 'the extrapolation of secular trends' produces a belief in a continuation of the warranted path, the absence of incentives to alter the growth rate is not credible, and the incentives will be in the direction of Harrodian instability. But I have argued that there is no reason to assume that the actual growth path of market economies is the warranted path.

Wood's second argument is that governments will likely use economic policy to attain normal capacity use, 'to counteract autonomous deviations from the equilibrium growth path and to maintain the economy in a state of long run equilibrium' (p. 131). Were it so! One wonders whether Wood would have dared propose such an argument a few years later, with the oil crisis and then Margaret Thatcher's policies bringing industrial production in the UK down by over 15%, and unemployment rising to around 15% and staying at that rate for many years. But already the Great Crisis of the 1930s should have made him think twice. Anyway, with a few more decades of evidence in front of us, we can notice that from

---

47 Wood cites data about investment being internally financed for more than 3/4 in UK, but it is *gross* investment, and depreciation—for which internal finance is the obvious source—is the greater part of gross investment. So he unwillingly confirms that net investment is largely *not* internally financed.

1200   **Chapter 13 · Labour Markets and Income Distribution**

the 1980s onwards what can be observed in most advanced capitalist countries is a rise in the share of profits and a decrease of the share of wages, coupled with a decrease of growth rates relative to the 1960s—the opposite of what a warranted growth approach to the explanation of income distribution would suggest.

In conclusion, the idea is unpersuasive that historically the average real wage is ultimately determined by the growth rate of the economy and is a *decreasing* function of the growth rate because faster growth requires a greater share of savings, but then also of profits, in income.

13.10 **The Kaleckian Approach**

A number of non-neoclassical economists view income distribution as determined by the capacity of firms to fix higher or lower product prices relative to costs, a capacity that depends on the strength of competition. The basic idea is, that the weaker the competition owing to oligopolistic elements, the higher the product price relative to average cost, and hence, the lower the real wage for a given money wage. The main source of inspiration for this view is the writings of Michail (or Michał) Kalecki, a Polish economist who arrived autonomously, from the study of Marx and of Rosa Luxemburg, at the principle of effective demand around 1933, and from 1936 lived in England, working at Cambridge and then at Oxford, and published on growth, the trade cycle, investment, income distribution.

Kalecki, a self-taught economist, was not very rigorous as a microeconomist.[48] His view was that raw materials markets are often close to perfectly competitive, that is, have prices determined by supply and demand in Marshallian fashion; but the markets of industrially produced goods are imperfectly competitive; products

---

48 But he did have a knack for macro. Kaldor summarized his views with beautiful simplicity as 'workers spend what they get, capitalists get what they spend'. Let $S = s_p P$ where S is savings, P profits (classical meaning) and s_p the average propensity to save out of profits. Kalecki assumes that savings are only out of profits; workers don't save, and they spend on consumption all they get. What remains to illustrate is that 'capitalists get what they spend'. Let W be the total wage bill, Y national income, C consumption, C_p consumption out of profits, I investment. Assume a closed economy and neglect government taxation and expenditure. Then $C = W + C_p$; $Y = W + P = C + I = W + C_p + I$, hence $P = C_p + I$: profits equal capitalist expenditure. What we must show is that the causation is not from profits to capitalist expenditure but from capitalist expenditure to profits: an increase in autonomous capitalist expenditure increases profits by the same amount. It must be so since $P = C_p + I$, but let us grasp the way the multiplier implements this equality. Define $\omega \equiv W/Y$, the share of wages in income, that Kalecki takes as given; then $W = \omega Y$. Assume both investment and consumption out of profits are autonomous, decided by the capitalists independently of their income; then $Y = W + C_p + I = \omega Y + C_p + I$, i.e. $Y = [1/(1 - \omega)] \cdot (C_p + I)$; the multiplier is $1/(1 - \omega)$. If I or C_p increases, $\Delta Y = [1/(1 - \omega)] \cdot (\Delta I + \Delta C_p)$, and the increase of profits is $\Delta P = \Delta Y - \Delta W = \Delta Y(1 - \omega) = (\Delta I + \Delta C_p)$. That is, if capitalists increase their autonomous expenditure $C_p + I$, the multiplier raises Y until the difference between Y and W, that is profits, and becomes again equal to the new $C_p + I$. The striking conclusion is that *it is capitalist expenditure that creates profits*.

13.10 · The Kaleckian Approach

are differentiated, and firms have some room for fixing price. In each industry, he argues, prices are fixed by adding to 'direct cost' per unit of output (i.e. to average variable cost, also called *prime cost*) a markup 'to cover overheads and achieve profits'; on the determination of this markup Kalecki does not say much except that it is determined with an eye to the prices fixed by the competing firms in the same industry. Unfortunately this leaves the average size of markups indeterminate. Suppose differences in product quality and in cost-minimization efficiency determine certain differences between the prices of different firms in an industry, and differences in barriers to entry determine certain differences between average rates of return in different industries. This is what relative competitiveness and relative ease of entry can determine; but nothing changes in relative competitiveness if, given these differences, all prices rise relative to money wages. That is, Kalecki's vague reference to 'semi-monopolistic influences ... resulting from imperfect competition or oligopoly' (1971, p. 160) as the cause of the magnitude of markups cannot explain the average price level relative to money wages, i.e. cannot explain the real wage. The idea that markup-determined prices are rather insensitive to demand, and it is quantities produced that take the brunt of changes in demand, appears fully acceptable as argued in ► Chap. 12; but the idea, that seems to be what Kalecki was aiming at, that rises in money wages will be generally accompanied by *proportional* changes in prices, so that real wages do not change, cannot be justified on the basis of the degree of competitiveness of the several product markets. The latter can only explain the spread of rates of return of different firms around the average associated with the given real wage—which remains to be explained.[49] Imperfections of competition cannot explain why all prices do not rise more, or do not decrease more, relative to money wages, than one observes in any given situation. Note that one needs an answer to both questions: what prevents prices from being higher, and what prevents them from being lower. The standard answer to the second question is that prices must yield the average rate of return, modified for each firm according to its particular situation of competitiveness. The standard answer to the first question is that if a price is raised above the level determined by the first answer, the competition of other firms (possibly new firms) will cause the firm to go bankrupt.

Then we are back to needing a theory determining either the real wage, that determines the average rate of return, or directly the rate of return, perhaps via the rate of interest fixed by the Central Bank (see below, on Pivetti). Then imperfections of competition, in particular barriers to entry or network externalities, can cause the rate of return in some industries to be somewhat higher than the average, but the need remains for forces determining either the real wage, or the average rate of return. Once we have either, then and only then it becomes cred-

---

49 *Exercise*: Use the price equations of the corn–iron economy in ► Chap. 1 to show that if the rate of profit can be different in the two industries owing to a different ease of entry, a given real wage constrains the two rates of profit so that if one rises the other decreases.

ible that rises in money wages will not result in changes in real wages because prices will rise by the same percentage; but only if, and because, the forces determining income distribution have not changed.

It is possible to conclude that Kalecki's markup theory does not offer us a theory of what determines real wages, nor of why secularly they have increased in the advanced countries, nor of why this increase seems to have stopped in recent decades, especially in the USA.

13.11 The Classical–Marxian Approach. Goodwin. Investment

The classical–Marxian approach to wages was discussed in Sects. 1.3.1 and 1.12.1. It argued the tendency of wages to oscillate around a normal or 'subsistence' level which includes a customary element in excess of bare biological subsistence, rendered necessary by 'the established rules of decency'. The tendency of wages above this level to return to normal subsistence was due to variations in population, or (in Marx) to the tendency of wage rises to increase the 'reserve army of labour' by causing crises and intensifying the search for labour-saving technical innovations.

It was admitted that a durable rise in the workers' standard of living might induce a rise of subsistence itself, by making a higher standard of living customary, but (at least up to Ricardo included) this possibility was not given great attention since it was not easy yet to discern significant tendencies of wages secularly to increase; wages of unskilled workers (the great majority at the time) remained very close to bare biological subsistence: working-class families could afford very little more than barely sufficient food, minimal clothing, crowded housing, some protection against cold, some beer and tobacco. Nowadays, after two centuries of rise of real wages, the distance from bare biological subsistence is so great that the notion of a customary subsistence appears more difficult to define without arbitrariness. Probably most people would admit that a subsistence income must allow a family to pay for modest lodging, electricity, water, telephone, television, gas, winter heating, modest clothes, cheap food, school books for the children, some medicines; but even here there would be some arbitrariness, should having a television be part of subsistence? Smartphones? Winter heating? Wine? In the advanced nations, the working poor *could* live worse than they do, without becoming total wretches. Conversely, one might claim that decency requires that they be allowed to live better. Decency means different things to different people. As to attempts to define below-subsistence standards of living as those found *intolerable*, an analogous difficulty arises with attempting to define 'intolerable': popular mood might undergo quick changes in this respect, and it is also unclear how one could ascertain the limits of tolerability in a society in the absence of eruptions of protests and riots.

But above all, since at least the end of the nineteenth century the notion of subsistence has seemed unable to indicate the normal level to which real wages *return* when they move away from it, because the average level of wages has

13.11 · The Classical–Marxian Approach. Goodwin. Investment

kept rising although irregularly. Habitual, customary subsistence seems to have been determined by the evolution of wages more than vice versa. So one must go beyond Smith and Malthus, to the classical author who grasped the importance of technical progress: Marx. From his analysis of the causes and effects of changes in the reserve army of labour a theory of cyclical growth can be derived, which together with technical progress can perhaps explain the secular rise in real wages. This idea of a cycle, present in Marx and even more clearly in the Austrian Marxist Bauer (1986, 1936), was later formalized by Goodwin (1967) in a model that cleverly adapts Volterra's prey–predator equations to the interaction between growth and unemployment.

In 1931 the Italian mathematician Vito Volterra had proposed a formalization of the interaction between two populations of animals, one a predator and the other its prey, e.g. eagles and snakes. (It had been observed in some Norwegian fjords that in some years there were many eagles and very few snakes, and in other years the opposite.) Volterra assumes that the growth rate $\dot{y}_2/y_2$ of the size of the predator species is a linear positive function of the size of the prey population y_1 (good catch helps reproduction), $\dot{y}_2/y_2 = -(a_2 - b_2 y_1)$, while the growth rate $\dot{y}_1/y_1$ of the prey population is a linear negative function of the size of the predator species, $\dot{y}_1/y_1 = a_1 - b_1 y_2$, where all coefficients are positive constants and only non-negative values of y_1, y_2 are considered. This yields the system of two *nonlinear* differential equations

$$\dot{y}_1 = (a_1 - b_1 y_2) y_1, \quad \dot{y}_2 = -(a_2 - b_2 y_1) y_2.$$

For a mathematical study of this system the reader will have to turn to other textbooks (e.g. the extremely clear Gandolfo 1971, or subsequent editions; or Arrowsmith and Place 1982), here it will suffice to say that the solution yields time paths of y_1 and y_2 that, in the positive quadrant of plane (y_1, y_2), describe *phase paths* or *trajectories* that are closed quasi-elliptic orbits, the specific orbit depending on the starting point. For each given initial condition the system determines an identically repeated cycle, except when the initial condition is

$$y_1 = a_2/b_2; \quad y_2 = a_1/b_1$$

in which case the system remains there, it is the *fixed point* of the dynamical system. (There is another fixed point, $y_1 = y_2 = 0$, but it is uninteresting.) (◘ Fig. 13.10).

This type of dynamical 'equilibrium point' (as economists, but not mathematicians, prefer to call it), surrounded by closed orbits, is called a *centre*. It is neither *asymptotically* stable, nor unstable: a shock moving the point (y_1, y_2) a bit away from the centre causes the system to start a closed orbit around the centre, that is, the path neither tends to, nor tends indefinitely away from, the fixed point. Note also that when $y_1 = a_2/b_2$, it is $\dot{y}_2 = 0$ whichever the value of y_2; that is, each orbit's highest and lowest points are vertically above and below the centre; analogously, the leftmost and rightmost points of any orbit are horizontally at the level of the centre.

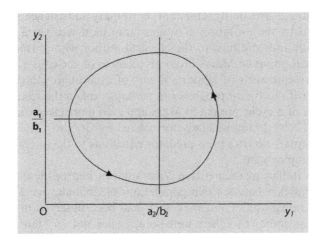

◘ **Fig. 13.10** One Volterra closed orbit. (See Arrowsmith and Place 1982, p. 19 ◘ Fig. 1.33 for a more rigorous phase portrait, with many orbits.)

Goodwin perceives that the Marx–Bauer theory of the cycle has elements implying a formal similarity with the Volterra system.[50] For simplicity the economy is treated as producing a single product using that same product and labour as inputs; land is neglected. The starting point is the assumption that the *rate of variation* of real wages depends on the rate of unemployment,[51] which at each given moment depends on aggregate output, the output–labour ratio, and labour supply, and therefore changes in time depending on the growth rate of output, the rate of growth of labour productivity, and the rate of growth of labour supply.[52] The second key assumption is that the growth rate of output is an increasing function of the rate of profit (and therefore *ceteris paribus* a decreasing function of the average real wage), because more profit means more investment, in accord with Marx's idea that competition obliges firms to grow as fast as possible, because bigger firms eliminate smaller firms, and therefore capitalists want their firms to grow and use profits to this end. (Goodwin obtains this positive effect of the rate of profit on growth by assuming that all profits are reinvested.) These two assumptions entail that if the wage rate increases, investment slows down and the growth rates of capital and output decrease; if the increase in wages continues, sooner or later output starts growing so slowly that unemployment starts increasing

---

50 Also called Lotka–Volterra system because of an earlier, less well known, formulation of much the same system by a mathematical biologist, A. J. Lotka.
51 Why a decrease of the rate of unemployment causes wages to increase, and to increase the faster the lower the rate of unemployment, is not explicitly discussed by Goodwin, it is implicitly considered to derive from Marx's view of the relative size of the reserve army of labour as influencing the bargaining power of workers.
52 The capital–output ratio is assumed constant; technical progress reduces the labour needed per unit of output and therefore also per unit of net output. Average labour productivity is net output per unit of labour.

13.11 · The Classical–Marxian Approach. Goodwin. Investment

(this does not require a negative growth rate of output, because labour productivity is growing, continually reducing labour demand per unit of output); this weakens labour and slows down the growth rate of wages, which can even turn negative. This raises the rate of profit and hence the growth rate of output, until the latter becomes again high enough to cause the unemployment rate to shrink, and the wage starts increasing again.

The analysis is in continuous time. More formally, Goodwin assumes:

(i)   homogeneous labour and homogeneous capital produce a single good which can be consumed or used as capital;

(ii)   capital does not depreciate (and it remains utilizable as consumption good), hence total output and net output coincide;

(iii) the capital/output ratio $k = K/Y$ is constant;

(iv)   the output/labour ratio Y/L (where L is *employment*, I am reversing now the meaning of L and N to remain close to Goodwin's symbols), or labour productivity, increases with time at a constant given rate $\alpha > 0$, that is $Y/L = a_0 e^{\alpha t}$[53];

(v)   labour supply N grows at a steady growth rate $\beta > 0$, that is $N = N_0 e^{\beta t}$; note that labour *employment*, L, can be (and will be) less than N;

(vi)   output is always at the level required for full (normal, optimal) utilization of the capital stock K;

(vii) capital accumulation is determined by income distribution: all wages are consumed, all profits are saved and invested;

(viii) the rate of growth of real wages is an increasing function of the employment ratio L/N.

The model assumes Say's Law (see assumptions (vi) and (vii)) and hence absence of crises as distinguished from periods of growth slowdown, and in this it is more Ricardian than Marxian; but it is more Marxian than Ricardian in its neglect of the Malthusian population mechanism in favour of a quicker, unemployment-based influence on real wages, and in admitting continuous technical progress.

Let us see how the above assumptions imply Volterra dynamics. Define:

w – real wage rate;

$u = wL/Y$ – share of wages in output (sorry about this change of the meaning of symbol u, used above for the rate of capacity utilization);

---

53 In the terminology of standard growth theory, there is pure labour-augmenting disembodied technical progress; 'disembodied' means that technical progress allows changing the capital–labour ratio in all plants and not only in new plants; 'labour-augmenting' means that labour counts as if it were a greater quantity of older labour, that is, as time goes on less and less labour time is necessary to produce the same amount of labour services; '*pure* labour-augmenting' means that this effect concerns only labour, and the capital–output ratio is unaffected; hence the proportion between labour *services* and capital is constant. Marx's stress on some endogeneity of labour-saving technical progress is not included in the model, but it might.

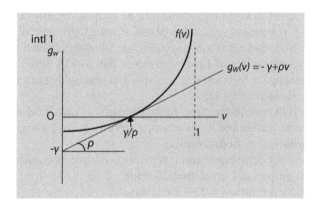

Fig. 13.11 Goodwin's linear approximation of g_W

g – growth rate of Y; g_L = growth rate of employment; $g_N = \beta$ growth rate of labour supply; g_W growth rate of real wage (sorry, now this symbol does *not* indicate the Harrodian warranted rate).

$v = L/N$ – employment ratio (the rate of unemployment is $(N - L)/N = 1 - v$)

$r = (Y - wL)/K$ – instantaneous rate of profit, equal to g by assumptions (vi) and (vii).

The central assumption (viii) states that $g_W \equiv \dot{w}/w$, the growth rate of the real wage, is an increasing function of v; Goodwin assumes that $g_W(v)$ has the shape shown in ◘ Fig. 13.11 as $f(v)$, but then takes a linear approximation of it at the point where $g_W = 0$, and assumes

$$g_W(v) = -\gamma + \rho v. \tag{13.44}$$

Now we can derive some implications:

$$r = g = (1 - u)Y/K = (1 - u)/k.$$

$\dot{Y}/Y - \dot{L}/L = g - g_L = \alpha$ (because α is the growth rate of Y/L, and the growth rate of a ratio is the difference between the growth rates of numerator and denominator): hence

$$g_L = g - \alpha.$$

Hence:

$$\dot{v}/v = g_L - g_N = g - \alpha - \beta = \frac{1-u}{k} - (\alpha + \beta). \tag{13.45}$$

$$\dot{u}/u = g_W - g_{Y/L} = -\gamma + \rho v - \alpha. \tag{13.46}$$

These can be re-written as

$$\dot{v} = \left[(\frac{1}{k} - \alpha - \beta) - \frac{1}{k}u\right]v$$

$$\dot{u} = \left[-(\alpha + \gamma) + \rho v\right]u.$$

13.11 · The Classical–Marxian Approach. Goodwin. Investment

Letting $(1/k) - (\alpha + \beta) = a_1$, $1/k = b_1$, $\alpha + \gamma = a_2$, $\rho = b_2$, $v = y_1$, $u = y_2$, one obtains the Volterra system.[54] So v, the employment ratio, has the same role as the prey population, while u, the share of wages, has the role of the predator population: a rise in the share of wages, by reducing r and hence g, slows down the growth of employment and ends up by causing a decrease of the employment ratio. Below I reproduce from Gandolfo (1971, p. 440) an approximate graphical representation of one orbit and of the corresponding time paths of u and v. (Here u, that is y_2, is in abscissa, and this is why the movement along the closed orbit is clockwise rather than counterclockwise.)

The centre or equilibrium, that corresponds to steady growth and also to the average values over the cycle whatever the orbit,[55] corresponds to

$$v^* = L/N = (\alpha + \gamma)/\rho, \tag{13.47}$$

$$u^* = wL/Y = 1 - k(\alpha + \beta). \tag{13.48}$$

An important implication of the model is that the cyclical behaviour of *the rate of profit* (and of the rate of output growth) repeats itself unaltered, but since technical progress goes on all the time and causes the same rate of profit to be associated with a higher and higher real wage (corresponding in a multigood economy to a continuous shifting upwards of the envelope of Sraffian wage curves), the average real wage is higher in each successive cycle. The growth rate of real wages oscillates around an average equal to the growth rate of labour productivity, and the rate of profit oscillates around a constant value; it is wages that on average appropriate the increase in production per unit of labour due to technical progress. This contradicts the thesis, frequent in the past among Marxist economists, of a tendential immiseration of the proletariat, both in the sense of a secular decrease of the real wage rate and in the sense of a decreasing share of total wages in income: the model predicts a secular *rise* of the real wage rate and an oscillation of the wage share around a *constant* average share.

Another important implication is the following. What is the effect of an upward shift of $g_W(v)$, that is, of a rise of the capacity of workers to win wage increases at each given rate of unemployment? This can be due to a decrease of γ, or to a rise of ρ, or to both; see (13.44). In either case there is no effect on u^*, and a negative effect on v^*. That is, a greater bargaining power of workers causes a worsening of the average situation of workers: a higher average rate of unemployment, the same average wage share, the same average growth rate and profit rate. The capitalist system responds to a greater fighting capacity of the working class by increasing the average rate of unemployment, and thus weakening the workers so as to reach the same average rate of profit and of growth as before, $r^* = \alpha + \beta$.

---

54 The formal similarity requires the four coefficients to be positive. Here b_1, a_2 and b_2 are positive by assumption; as to a_1, there is general agreement that $k < 5$, so $1/k > 0.2$, and $\alpha + \beta$ is certainly less than 20%, and it is in all likelihood not greater than 8%. Note that mathematically there is another fixed point at $v = u = 0$, of no economic interest.

55 See Gandolfo (1971, p. 441) for the proof of this result.

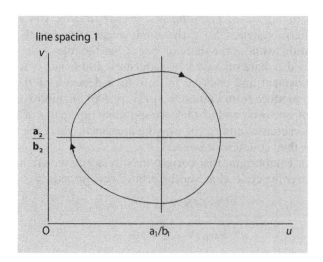

● **Fig. 13.12** Goodwin cycle in u (workers' share) and v (employment ratio)

One can sketch the dynamical process that brings this about if there is an upward shift of $g_W(v)$. It helps clarity to assume the initial situation to be one of steady growth. If in a Goodwin economy in steady growth there is a sudden jump up in the bargaining strength of workers (e.g. a decrease of γ), the result is a downward shift of v^* with no change of u^*, that is the new centre in ● Fig. 13.12 is vertically below the old one; the instant after this change the economy still has the employment ratio and the workers' share of the old centre, that is it is at u^* which has not changed, and at a value of v equal to the old v^* and therefore vertically above the new v^*, so it finds itself at the uppermost point of a new orbit around the new centre, and it starts circling on this new orbit; u initially increases because the real wage grows faster, but this slows down the growth of output and employment starts to decrease. In semilog scale, a representation of the path of Y is in ● Fig. 13.13. The new path is oscillatory, around the same u^* as before but around a lower average employment ratio than before, and the initial slowdown causes the path of average Y to shift downwards. So an increase in the fighting determination of workers results in a temporary increase in wage share, paid later by a persistently higher average unemployment rate with no gain in the average wage rate of the employed workers relative to the previous path.

The fact that in this model it is real wages that appropriate the rise in labour productivity means we have here one possible explanation of the secular rise of real wages. But several aspects of the model raise perplexities.

It may be best first of all to criticize the depressing conclusion that a strengthening of workers' fighting capacity only worsens their average condition. This conclusion depends on having left out of the model many important things. For example, the model includes no consumption of the capitalists; once this is introduced, the share of profit not going to investment can be affected by the bargaining power of the labour movement, it is possible to raise wages without reducing

13.11 · The Classical–Marxian Approach. Goodwin. Investment

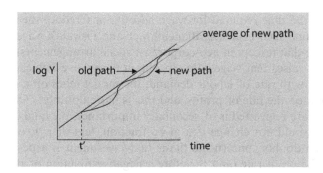

☐ **Fig. 13.13** New oscillatory path (the wavy line) due to a decrease at time t' of γ relative to a steady-state path: the dotted line indicates the corresponding new average path. The lower average Y (and hence L) after t' means a lower average L/N (i.e. more unemployment), because the growth path of N(t) has not changed

investment by reducing the share of consumption in profits. Also, there is no government in the model; a strong influence of the labour movement can obtain government policies (e.g. expansion of public firms) that maintain unaltered the growth rate in spite of a decrease of the rate of profit (and increase of real wages). Above all, a strong labour movement can *decrease* the need to prevent excessive wage rises through unemployment by imposing a ***neo-corporatist social accord***, as established for many decades after WW2 in European nations governed by social-democratic parties (Scandinavian nations, Austria, to some extent Belgium and Germany): the trade unions' confederation bargains with the employers' federation and the government, and asks for policies ensuring the near-full employment of labour offering in exchange 'social peace', that is, offering that the strength it derives from near-full employment will not be used to attempt to raise real wages so much as to induce firms to relocate abroad or raise prices (Rowthorn and Glyn 1990; Calmfors and Driffill 1988; Pekkarinen et al. 1992).

Besides not forgetting these possibilities of political intervention that can force the working of the basic mechanisms of the model to produce a different result, one must ask how convincing these basic mechanisms themselves are. The model rests on two basic ideas, a negative influence of unemployment on the rate of increase of wages, and a negative influence of the wage level on the growth rate of employment.

The first idea needs qualifications,[56] but there is ample evidence that increases in the rate of unemployment generally reduce absenteeism and turnover, reduce

---

56 The Goodwin model assumes that the rate of unemployment determines a given *rate of variation* of real wages that does not change as long as the rate of unemployment does not change. This has been found unconvincing by many economists. A high rate of unemployment, high enough to cause a fall of real wages, according to the Goodwin model continues to cause real wages to fall at the same rate indefinitely for as long as it lasts. And conversely, a low rate of unemployment that causes a growth of real wages greater than the growth of labour productivity will continue to squeeze the rate of profit indefinitely as long as it lasts. It seems difficult to accept this picture. Real wages did not continue to fall indefinitely during the Great Crisis of the 1930s, nor during the many years of an unemployment rate above 20% in Spain in recent decades.

strikes, reduce the time required for wage negotiations, reduce the average wage: above we saw one such evidence, Blanchflower and Oswald's wage curve. There is also evidence that (except in neo-corporatist social arrangements) a low rate of unemployment raises real wages. But to obtain a negative influence of the real wage on the growth rate of labour demand, the model relies on a strict dependence of growth on the rate of profits, and this is more doubtful. The assumption that *all* profits are reinvested is of secondary importance, the qualitative message of the model would not change if a given fraction, less than 1, of profits were reinvested. The doubts concern the thesis that investment is a positive function above all of the profit rate (and therefore a negative function of the real wage), and the assumption of continuous normal utilization of capacity.

The existence of a stimulus of lower wages to growth is found doubtful by many.

There is, first, the depressing effect of lower wages on consumption and hence on aggregate demand, which can discourage rather than stimulate investment. Second, the view, frequent among economists influenced by Marx, that if wages decrease then accumulation accelerates, rests on the thesis that if you give a capitalist more profits, he/she will invest more. The issue was discussed in ▶ Sect. 12.7. Briefly, the weakness of this view is that it is unclear why investment—in the sense of purchase of newly produced capital goods—should be the way investible funds are used, unless there is a prospect of fruitful use of investment funds in that direction: which requires an expectation that the product of the investment will be sold without problems, either because aggregate demand is growing, or because it is a promising innovation. If neither condition holds, a capitalist who has made unexpectedly large profits will prefer to use his funds to buy land, or shares of other firms, or bonds. That is, he will not use his profits for *productive* investment, but rather for *financial* investments that at least offer the prospect of the average rate of return. In this way he may help a financial bubble (which will further increase the preference for financial investments), but not real growth.

The negative effect of wage rises on the growth rate becomes doubtful too, the moment one admits a variable utilization of productive capacity. In Ricardo, aggregate output is given and Say's Law holds; the more goes to wages the less is left for profits; if the capitalists allot a given percentage of profits to consumption, or, worse, if they are not ready to reduce consumption, then a rise in the share of wages necessarily crowds out investment. If on the contrary aggregate output adapts to aggregate demand, there is no reason why a rise of wages should *crowd out* investment, a rise of aggregate output will make room for more consumption with no decrease of investment. There remains the possibility that the rise of wages reduces the *incentive* to invest by reducing the normal rate of profit; this seems highly unlikely too, if one accepts with Adam Smith and Ricardo that the rate of interest adapts to the rate of profit so as to leave a difference between the two rates capable of compensating for the 'risk and trouble' of entrepreneurship; then a lower rate of profit will go together with a lower rate of interest, but as long as the excess of the first on the second is sufficient, it is unclear why entrepreneurs should not invest. Indeed in Goodwin's model as in Ricardo, and it would seem in Marx too, it is the reduction of the *mass* of profits caused

13.11 · The Classical–Marxian Approach. Goodwin. Investment

by a wage rise that reduces investment (because it reduces the funds available for investment), not a reduction of the incentive to invest.

Further reasons to doubt this view of the determinants of growth are supplied by some historical evidence. The 1929 crisis and the 2008 crisis were not due to rises of real wages, but if anything to *too low* real wages, to an excessive redistribution in favour of profits and very high salaries, that favoured a financial bubble which hid the beginning of a slowdown of aggregate demand, which increasing indebtedness of the lower and middle classes could only temporarily counter in 2004–2006.

Another episode deserving attention is the end of the Golden Age. In USA and Europe after 1965 there was some (small) compression of the rate of profit due to wage rises slightly in excess of productivity growth, accompanied by an ample politicization of labour especially in Western Europe, but with no significant slowdown of growth; the growth slowdown and increase in unemployment that came after 1973 was due to a sharp rise in the price of oil occasioned by the Israel–Egypt Yom Kippur War, with consequent restrictive fiscal and monetary policies in several major countries aimed at reducing oil imports, and then at reducing inflation. The growth slowdown was therefore, to an extent, accidental, it might not have happened for many more years without the oil price increase and the consequent inflation. The growth slowdown continued (with Thatcher and Reagan) not as an automatic spontaneous negative reaction of investment to wage rises but as part of a conscious political attempt to sap (also via law changes) the strength acquired by the working class in advanced nations after WW2.

Margaret Thatcher's economic policy was particularly clear on this issue, although it hid its real intentions behind the smokescreen of monetarist economic doctrine. The following quotation from Palma (2009, p. 837) gives the picture:

» as Kalecki had analysed in 1943, both Keynesian-style liberalism and neo-liberalism are basically counter-cyclical, but each for a different phase of the cycle. Both seek to change the balance of power between income groups: Keynesianism in order to prevent the disruptive effects of crisis-ridden capitalism, neo-liberalism in order to return power and control to their 'rightful owners'—capital.

A summary along Kalecki's lines of this switching-cycles logic is given by Sir Alan Budd (a top UK Treasury civil servant, and strong supporter of monetarism at the time, who later became Provost of Queen's College, Oxford): "The Thatcher government never believed for a moment that monetarism was the correct way to bring down inflation. They did however see that this would be a very good way to raise unemployment. And raising unemployment was an extremely desirable way of reducing the strength of the working classes. [...] What was engineered—in Marxist terms—was a crisis of capitalism which re-created the reserve army of labour, and has allowed the capitalists to make high profits ever since." (quoted in Cohen, N., 2003. "Gambling with our future", *New Statesman*, 13 January, p. 13).[57]

---

57 The restrictive monetary policy of the Thatcher government caused a drop of industrial production by 15% in less than a year.

(Kalecki's 1943 paper 'Political aspects of full employment', to which Palma makes reference, is a beautiful short article whose reading I strongly recommend.)

One might argue that if when wages rise too much it is political interventions that recreate unemployment, in the end the result is the same as with the Goodwin model. But it is not easy to find before WWII historical episodes analogous to the policies of Reagan and Thatcher (Keynesian policies of control of aggregate demand were not used yet!). Also, the Goodwin cycles need not only something that weakens labour when it has become too strong, but also something that makes it stronger when it has become too weak; this second 'something' should be the stimulus of low wages to growth, and we have seen above reasons to doubt this stimulus. Indeed, the reduction of the wage share in most advanced nations from the 1980s onwards, for example the surprising stagnation of real wages of blue-collar workers in the USA in spite of considerable increases in productivity, did not cause a return to growth at pre-1970 rates.

The Goodwin model is therefore not very convincing both when it argues that wage reductions stimulate growth, and when it argues that wage rises slow growth down (except in rare instances of very high and drawn-out conflict, extensive strikes, political instability). Venturing outside my field of strongest competences, let me assert that this leaves us without a simple theory of long-run growth. Having rejected Say's Law and the neoclassical approach and having found unsatisfactory a theory that argues that in order that there be growth it is enough that there be profits, and that in order to have more growth it suffices that there be more profits, we seem obliged to turn to look for the changing elements stimulating the growth of aggregate demand in each nation and period: opening of new markets, innovations, the laying down of imposing infrastructures like railways, electric networks, motorways; state stimuli aiming at national industrial and military power, often at catching-up with more advanced nations; exports; and of course increases in per capita consumption too, sometimes wrenched, perhaps sometimes wisely conceded in order to have more demand for consumption goods, but never guaranteed to be such as required for continuation of smooth growth. In this perspective, growth is never guaranteed, it is always in need of supporting accidents or conscious interventions. Therefore one should not be surprised to find episodes of zero growth (e.g. Japan in the 1990s, Italy after 2008) or of negative growth (Argentina after WWII) for many years in a row.

The relevance of this perspective on growth for the evolution of wages is that the guarantee disappears of an automatic adjustment ensuring an average tendency of the unemployment rate to be so low as to allow dependent labour to appropriate most of the secular increase in productivity. And yet, this is more or less what has happened. How can we explain it? There seems to be ample room for further studies of when and why concretely wage rises are obtained: applied historical microeconomics. Just to throw out tentative suggestions, I dare advance two possibilities. (A third possibility is Pivetti's approach to be studied in the next section.)

One is that pressure for wage increases is greatly influenced by a conviction that increases in output and incomes should go at least in part to labour. Therefore when labour productivity has been rising for some time, visibly raising the standard of living of the well-off and the financial health of firms, wage (and salary) labour starts asking for part of the pie, and the pressure becomes the stronger, the greater the feeling of unfairness in the sharing of the pie. Working-class pamphlets in the nineteenth century are filled with declarations in this sense; according to some authors (e.g. Marglin and Schor 1990), in the 1950s–60s it was part of a social consensus in the US that wages should grow in step with productivity. This would imply that it is not only the rate of unemployment but also the way productivity increases have been shared in the recent past that influences the pressure for wage rises.

Another possibility is that rises in the rate of profit induce wage increases in the firms where such rises first happen, in order to reduce attrition with the workforce. A firm experiencing an increase in profits due to an increase in productivity may find it convenient to raise wages to its workforce, to exploit a comparative efficiency wage effect based on comparison with wages elsewhere: better-paid workers can be asked to work better. This wage increase will happen at different moments in different firms, depending on when technical progress increases profit in different industries and firms; and the negative comparative efficiency wage effect in the firms not directly benefiting from technical progress will oblige these other firms too to raise wages. The result will be staggered and ultimately general wage rises again directly due to technical progress.

I have expressed here my own tentative views, not necessarily shared by other non-neoclassical economists. For example in his impressive treatise *Capitalism*, Shaikh (2016) affirms a strong belief in Goodwin cycles. As remembered in ▶ Sect. 12.7, Shaikh defends the Marxian idea that a higher rate of profit implies a higher growth rate by arguing that investment is an increasing function of the *difference* between rate of profit and rate of interest: the stimulus to invest is argued to be the greater, the greater the amount remaining to the investor after paying interest on the borrowed capital (or an equivalent opportunity cost on owned capital). If the rate of interest is fixed, and the other elements of the Goodwin model are maintained, one obtains again a rate of growth increasing in the rate of profit, and hence a similar kind of cyclical behaviour as in the original model. However, this theory of investment does not seem (to me, at least) very persuasive. To the arguments in ▶ Sect.12.7 and in the present section let me add the empirical observation that in the euro area of Europe in recent years the rate of interest has been maintained close to zero while certainly the normal rate of profit has not decreased (real wages have not increased more than productivity), so there can be no doubt that the difference between normal rate of profit and rate of interest has increased considerably; still, investment has not responded.

To sum up. Fundamentally, the Goodwin model puts together two theses: that the capacity of real wages to rise is negatively affected by the rate of unemployment; and that the economy's growth rate is positively influenced by the rate of profit, and therefore it is negatively affected by wage rises in excess of the growth of labour productivity. The first thesis appears acceptable but must be integrated by some lower 'subsistence' limit to wages, which is positively influenced by the level of wages in the recent past, and can be broken only by exceptional events like war needs or an anti-labour military coup; also, the determinants of labour's bargaining power are still now not very clear, the details of what determines the extent of wage rises in different situations are not well understood, nor is it easy to reach generalizations because historically the legal framework and the degree of unionization and the fragmentation of the working class have changed greatly in the years. Certainly the laws limiting or reinforcing labour rights, and the political attitude of the government, have been and are of fundamental importance; and the neo-corporatist experiences show that even a very low level of unemployment need not determine wage rises in excess of productivity increases, so the Goodwin model's implication that a more militant working class only succeeds in worsening average unemployment need not be accepted. The second thesis is much less convincing, the admission of a variable degree of utilization of capacity influenced by aggregate demand and of a capacity of the financial system to create the monetary funds needed for investment breaks the classical strict connection between profits and investible funds, and makes the determinants of growth more mysterious. As a consequence, the secular growth of wages too becomes more mysterious, the thesis of a gravitation of the rate of profit around a more or less constant level, which would then determine a secular rise of real wages roughly in step with productivity, cannot be convincingly defended on the basis of the Goodwin model; and yet something not too far from this seems to have historically happened. There remains much to be better understood!

13.12 Pivetti

The classical view that the rate of interest is less than the rate of profit but moves in sympathy with the latter rests on the idea that there is a normal addition to the rate of interest, necessary to persuade investors to bear the 'risk and trouble' of investing in productive activities rather than in less risky bonds or in land. This difference between (real) rate of profit and (real) rate of interest can be called (real) *profits of enterprise*; in each industrial field, depending on the risks of the field (irregularity of demand, productivity influenced by weather, barriers to entry, risk of price wars, risk of change of legal regulations, risk of social turmoils, etc.), it has a minimum magnitude, above which entry in the field (and price undercutting) becomes convenient. The minimum average cost, towards which competition pushes the price of commodities, includes the rate of interest plus the minimum profit of enterprise upon optimal capital per unit of output. The notion of uniform rate of profit must be reinterpreted as uniform once differences in risk and therefore in profit of enterprise are taken into account.

Pivetti (1985, 1991) couples this view with the thesis that the Central Bank has the capacity to control the long-period real rate of interest. Then it is the Central Bank that determines income distribution, because the rate of profit is determined by the rate of interest, and real wages are determined residually, by the need for firms to fix such money product prices, relative to money wages, as will determine in each industry a rate of profit equal to the sum of rate of interest and profit of enterprise. This totally reverses the classical view that the real wage determines the rate of profit which in turn determines the rate of interest.

Pivetti's approach fits well with the Gibson paradox, the generally observed connection between a decrease (rise) of interest rate and a decrease (rise) of the price level (▶ Sect.12.7.7), which contradicts the expectation that a lower rate of interest, by stimulating investment and hence aggregate demand, should be accompanied by a tendential rise of the price level. But another very important reason behind his approach is his persuasion that in the modern world the workers' consumption cannot be considered physically determined by subsistence needs because it includes a surplus over subsistence, and what precisely the wage bargain can obtain depends on what determines the ratio of the price level to money wages: 'It seems to us that in the conditions of modern capitalism it is difficult to conceive of the real wage rate as the independent or given variable in the relationship between wages and profits—the difficulty, as we see it, arising from the fact that the direct outcome of wage bargaining is a certain level of the money wage, and that the price level cannot be determined before and independently from money wages … If instead the real wage rate is taken as given … what we are ultimately facing here is a conception of the ratio of prices to money wages as being determined by a magnitude—the real wage rate—which is not actually known before that ratio is known. This explains in our opinion why of the two alternative propositions—that the ratio of prices to money wages depends on the real wage rate, or that the real wage rate depends on the ratio of the price level to the money wage—the latter is easier to digest' (Pivetti 1985 pp. 94–95). One may disagree, but certainly Pivetti usefully puts the issue in very clear terms.

This approach raises two questions. The first is, why haven't we seen a decrease of the rate of profit in recent years in spite of a policy of very low interest rates by all main Central Banks, and especially by the European Central Bank? According to Pivetti (seminar at Università di Siena, November 2016), the explanation is precisely the increase in normal profit of enterprise caused by the uncertainties due to the 2008 crisis, that have not been allayed by the near absence of determined interventions to prevent the possibility of a repetition of financial crises. Maybe; but one might also suspect that rate of interest and rate of profit are not so intimately connected as Pivetti argues (Stirati 2013), or perhaps that the adjustment of the rate of profit to the rate of interest is so slow, especially when the rate of interest decreases, that one must also admit a direct influence of wages on the rate of profit and not only a residual role.

The second question is, what determines the real rate of interest that Central Banks aim at? Pivetti suggests a multiplicity of aims, among them support for the state's public debt, exchange rate policy, inflation policy, and influence upon growth and upon labour market conditions. The last aim implies an admission that the Central Bank takes into account the demands and strength of the labour movement, and may be ready to allow a decrease of the rate of profit for some years in order to avoid excessive social conflict, but in other situation may want to take back some part of what was conceded in the past.

Still, a question remains: why has the real rate of interest remained low, historically, thus allowing real wages to appropriate most of the secular income increase per labour unit made possible by technical progress? why haven't Central Banks—that certainly have historically leant more towards protecting the interests of banks and capital owners than those of wage labour—let the real interest rate on safe bonds gradually increase as labour productivity historically increased, so as to allow some rise of real wages but slower than historically observed, arriving at real interest rates on safe bonds much higher than observed, say 8% instead of the historical 2 or 3%? Certainly this would have still allowed a considerable increase in real wages relative to, say, those in the 1870s. One can perhaps suppose a strong desire of the state to avoid rises in the rate of interest that would make the payment of interest on public debt more difficult, and a strong state control on the Central Bank capable of imposing this desire. Maybe. But another possibility is that the Central Bank defends profits but within what the bargaining between labour and capital allows; in other words, according to this hypothesis the Central Bank would be unable to prevent increases in real wages, attempts to stop them via rises of interest rates would cause inflation and more social conflict; that is, ultimately the classical view that income distribution is fundamentally determined by what labour is able to win would remain the more correct one: the Central Bank would be only able to prevent falls of the rate of profit that would require so low a rate of interest as to block the smooth working of the financial apparatus and to cause excessive discontent of the rentier class. I do not think we are able yet to discriminate among these and other possible hypotheses.

13.13 Concluding on Real Wages

In labour markets it is not true that as long as there is excess demand (positive or negative) wages continue to change in the direction indicated by the sign of that excess demand. This makes it necessary to understand how concretely labour markets operate. Political motivations, concerted behaviour, laws, organizations such as trade unions are so important in the functioning of labour markets that the study of these markets is not very different from other studies of social phenomena, for example of political parties, campaigns for a change of some law, racial discrimination. Ideally, one would like to have a big book listing a high number of typical labour market situations, with theoretical and empirical reasons to expect each one of these situations to evolve in a certain way. Such a taxonomical classification of labour market situations is yet to come.

What we have is attempts to estimate Phillips curves connecting the rate of unemployment to the rate of change of money, or sometimes of real, wages, or attempts to estimate the NAIRU (non-accelerating-inflation rate of unemployment), a conflict-based version of the natural rate of unemployment which might even be given classical foundations (Stockhammer 2008). These topics are for macroeconomic courses, on them I will only note my opinion, for what it is worth, that these econometric estimates, even when not based on clearly indefensible theoretical foundations (as when assuming a neoclassical aggregate production function), assume a persistence, and independence from the institutional structure, of the determining forces which is on the contrary highly doubtful. The

13.13 · Concluding on Real Wages

NAIRU, for example, can be drastically changed by a change in how wage bargaining is organized and in the government's aims, as shown by neo-corporatism, or by laws weakening trade unions. Also, many more politically variable elements are relevant than one takes into account in these estimates. 'The complexity of the economic world might indeed justify some a priori scepticism about the validity of any theory where 'models' make, as Foley puts it, for 'routine predictions'' (Garegnani 2004, pp. 23–44).

Perhaps more long interviews with personnel managers, trade unionists, rank-and-file activists, government mediators in industrial conflict, similar to those performed by the Oxford Economists Research Group in the 1930s or more recently by Truman Bewley, would supply a colourful description of how typically things evolve in a number of cases. But history does not repeat itself; new ideas, new forms of struggle, new ways of organizing the labour process, new social divisions into groups with similar interests owing to changes in the kinds of jobs, will continually be born, and predictions will always be difficult, not to speak of quantitative predictions.

This is not surprising to an economist intent on resuming a classical approach. In that approach, as explained in ▶ Chap. 1, purely *deductive* reasoning is limited to the influence of a change in one distributive variable, or in technology, or in the extent of use of a scarce natural resource, on prices and on other distributive variables. More *inductive* reasoning, attentive to the peculiarities of each historical situation, is called for in order to explain what caused that change, and what effect that can have on further developments, on quantities, on growth.

Anyway it seem possible to deduce from historical experience and theoretical reflection a plausible answer to why often wages do not decrease even in the presence of considerable unemployment. The brief answer is that the wage decrease would not improve the situation of workers because unemployment would be little affected, and historical experience has taught this truth to workers; the result has been the development of forms of struggle and resistance, sometimes overt, other times absorbed through custom and culture so that one is not even conscious of them. Key to all this is the admission of the existence of conflict. From the history of labour movements and more generally of capitalist economies one derives the persuasions that allow one to formulate, for example, a table like the one next page, elaborated by Pivetti (2013), where a series of changes in labour market conditions are listed, and one plausibly assigns to these changes a positive or negative influence on the bargaining strength of wage labour.

The effect of the changes considered by Pivetti is indubitable: a weakening of wage labour's bargaining strength in advanced nations, probably destined to last owing to the product competition from low-wage countries, the pressure of immigrants, the absence of signals of a change in the political preferences of citizens in favour of more pro-labour parties (◘ Fig. 13.14).

No doubt the reader can add to this list (e.g. how technological change is influencing the capacity of workers to co-ordinate, or the monopolistic elements in the economy) or can suggest finer subdivisions of the factors (e.g. the extent of differences in unemployment rates and other work conditions among blue-col-

Table 8.1 Factors that have weakened wage earners' bargaining power since the early 1980s	
Factor	**Direction of change since early 1980s**
Factors whose increase weakens workers:	
Unemployment rates	↑
Privatiz ations	↑
Overall labour -market flexibility	↑
Restrictions of rights to strike	↑
Relative number of immigrant workers	↑
International capital mobility, interest rates/growth rates differentials and primary surpluses	↑
Trade from low -wage developing countries	↑
Direct investment flows (investment in plant and equipment) to low-wage developing countries	↑
Employment shift to lower-paying service -producing industries	↑
Factors whose increase strengthens workers:	
Share of full-time employment over all employment	↓
Rates of unionisation	↓
Minimum wages	↓
Indirect and deferred wages	↓
Overall progressiv eness of tax systems	↓

◘ **Fig. 13.14** Table from p. 181 of Pivetti (2013)

lar and white-collar workers can influence the political preferences of median voters and thus of governments). But even as it is, Pivetti's list sufficiently shows the need for analyses that cannot stay content with econometric exercises but must pay great attention to social and political aspects. A good example, on a less studied period (wages in Great Britain between 1870 and 1913), is Levrero (1999). Other examples are the studies of what has allowed after World War II the period of high growth rates in Western capitalism called the Golden Age, and what reasons have brought it to an end in the 1970s. On this period the best starting point is the 1991 book by Armstrong, Glyn and Harrison, *Capitalism Since 1945*, from which one can go on to the converging analyses of the French 'régulation' approach and the US 'Social Structure of Accumulation' approach (Boyer 1986; Boyer and Saillard 1995; Gordon et al. 1982; McDonough et al. 2010). Both approaches have argued that capitalism has gone through a series of stages distinguished by a different combination of institutions and mechanisms assigned to the control of labour, the development of technical progress, accumulation, international co-ordination; in some historical periods these combinations 'work well' and then one observes a period of rather smooth growth with little pressure for institutional change; but technology, industrial concentration, ideologies, demography, international relations change and end up destroying the compatibility among the several elements of the 'régulation', causing economic difficulties and the search for new institutions. A period of well-functioning 'régulation' has been precisely the Golden Age, characterized by 'Fordism', by which these approaches mean the generalization of the accord proposed by Henry Ford to his workers: higher wages in exchange for a readiness to work intensely on the assembly line without causing troubles. Extended to the entire economy, 'Fordism' means a tacit accord of policies of low unemployment and rising wages favouring mass consumption, in exchange for the workers' abandonment of the dream to overcome capitalism or even only relevantly to alter income shares. The pact ensured the rise in time of demand for consumption goods without a reduction of the rate of profit, favouring a high rate of capacity utilization and hence investment. The international domination of the US, and its supplying dollars to the rest of the world, ensured the absence of obstacles to accumulation deriving from difficulties of international co-ordination. But the long period of nearly full employment undermined the control over labour, and in the second half of the 1960s real wages rose more than productivity in the USA and Great Britain, while strikes increased. The rise in the price of oil in 1973, due to the Kippur War, is viewed as the occasion which, by justifying restrictive policies, permitted breaking the 'Fordist' accord, and the beginning of conscious policies of unemployment increase. Thereby a 'post-Fordist' period commences, with search for a new consistent structure of social accumulation or 'régulation', which so far has not been successful. These views have been criticized by Garegnani and co-authors (Cavalieri et al. 2004) who have argued that the idea of an 'accord' of high wages and high employment found convenient by capitalists (because it would guarantee a high rate of capacity utilization whose high rate of profit would allow paying higher wages) is unconvincing, because when making an investment the entrepreneur would be stupid to plan the new plant to have a size different from the one ensuring an expected *optimal* capacity utilization, and the rate of profit on optimally utilized plants is a decreasing function of the real wage; so a higher wage inevitably decreases the rate of profit expected on new investments. Therefore capitalists are always in favour of lower wages, and one should view the high wages and high-employment policies of the Golden Age as rather wrenched by the workers' bargaining strength, greatly aided by the high reputation enjoyed by the USSR after WWII: the high employment and the welfare state were conceded, the argument goes, to prevent the working class from becoming communist (this argument is also in the cited Armstrong, Glyn and Harrison 1991). In this view the abandonment of pro-labour policies after the 1970s was largely made possible by the loss of attractiveness of communism. The present book is not the place for an assessment of these contrasting views, they have been mentioned as confirmation of the need to take into consideration the complex interrelation between economic and political elements, and the differences between successive periods of the history of capitalism, in order for further research on the determinants of wages to be fruitful.

1220   **Chapter 13 · Labour Markets and Income Distribution**

13.14 **Review Questions and Exercises**

■■ Review Questions

1. Explain in what sense the standard neoclassical labour demand curve does not comply with Walras' Law.
2. Explain why an IS curve faithful to Keynes must admit a price level that is an increasing function of investment.
3. Keynes' arguments on why the labour demand curve is decreasing in the short period can be argued to reveal awareness of the substitutability problem. Explain.
4. 'Determination of the labour demand curve is impossible both in a long-period framework, and in a neo-Walrasian framework (without auctioneer)'. Explain.
5. Variability of capacity utilization can be argued to imply that, within limits, there is no obstacle to a simultaneous rise of real wages and of employment. Explain.
6. Motivate the inevitability of some frictional unemployment.
7. Explain why Pissarides' analysis of stability of his model is not about stability.
8. Explain why, in the search theory approach to wages, free entry can be argued to imply there is no surplus generated by a filled job and to be divided between the firm and the worker.
9. 'The Beveridge curve explained via the matching function tells us that *if* something determines the rate of unemployment and keeps it constant, *then* that same something also determines the corresponding volume of vacancies'. Explain.
10. List the main weaknesses of the insiders–outsiders approach.
11. 'In the efficiency wage approaches, it is firms that refuse to let wages decrease in the presence of unemployment'. Explain.
12. Reproduce and explain ◐ Fig. 13.2.
13. Why are two 'Solow conditions' necessary in the Bowles version of efficiency wages?
14. Illustrate the use of a recursive approach to determine consumer choice in the shirking model.
15. Explain how the shirking version of the efficiency wage approach is used to argue the inevitability of involuntary unemployment, and how the claim that the resulting unemployment is involuntary can be criticized.
16. 'One important weakness of the shirking version of the efficiency wage approach is that it neglects retirement'. Discuss and assess.
17. Explain why the monopoly union model assumes interpersonal comparability of cardinal utilities.
18. In the presentation of the right-to-manage model in the main text an alternative way to prove Hotelling's Lemma appears. Explain it.
19. Explain the difference between Nash bargaining and generalized Nash bargaining.
20. A frequent criticism of the Ashenfelter–Johnson model of strikes is that the rank-and-file behave irrationally. Explain the criticism and how it can be answered.

13.14 · Review Questions and Exercises

21. What can be derived from Blanchflower and Oswald's wage curve?
22. Explain the limit of the gift exchange approach to efficiency wages and how similar it is to the shirking approach.
23. Within the Solow–Hahn approach the no-undercutting norm needs a very low elasticity of labour demand, and the text argues that this poses a dilemma for the neoclassical economist. Explain.
24. Explain why Eq. (13.42) questions the Cambridge approach to the determination of income distribution.
25. The text concludes that 'it is not plausible to explain the behaviour of real wages in the way suggested by Joan Robinson'. Why?
26. Use Eq. (13.42) to illustrate the possibility of Harrodian instability.
27. Indicate some criticism of the thesis that investment is an increasing function of the rate of profit because it is an increasing function of the difference between rate of profit and rate of interest.
28. Summarize the reasons indicated in the text why the Goodwin model is not fully persuasive.

■ **Exercises**

(This chapter does not insist on detailed formalization of the approaches discussed, it concentrates on presenting their basic insights and in discussing their plausibility; so there is not much room for formal exercises based on variations of assumptions; hence the small number of exercises below. It will suffice as an exercise that the reader/student becomes able to reproduce by heart in a loud voice the reasonings and equations, as if preparing a lecture.)

1. In the simple labour–land neoclassical economy of ▶ Chap. 3, assume a real wage greater than the equilibrium level; land is fully employed; explain why, realistically, the excess supply of labour does not imply an excess demand on any other market, but would imply an excess demand for output in the Walrasian tâtonnement. In the first, more realistic case, without auctioneer, can you defend the stability of the full-employment equilibrium?
2. Prove that the Beveridge curve explained via the matching function is convex and is shifted outwards by increases of λ.
3. In ▶ Sect.13.3 when discussing the effects of search-and-matching costs in a neoclassical framework it is stated that a given real rate of interest (assimilated here to the rate of profit) does not univocally determine the real wage. Would the same hold in a classical framework? If your answer is yes, can you think of reasons why this fact is generally not mentioned in discussions internal to the classical framework?
4. In ▶ Sect.13.7, in connection with the inefficiency issue and ▣ Fig. 13.6, study the locus of efficient bargaining in a neighbourhood of $w = w^\wedge$. Since the union's indifference curves are convex and decreasing, and the firm's isoprofit curves are strictly concave and are horizontal when they cross the labour demand curve, can the tangency condition be satisfied at $w = w^\wedge$? Will the locus of efficient bargaining present a discontinuity as γ passes from 0 to slightly positive?
5. Modify Eq. (13.42) admitting an autonomous component in the consumption function.

1222 **Chapter 13** · Labour Markets and Income Distribution

6. Accept the Pivetti approach and take the real interest rate as given. Assume that, starting from a situation of general free competition and free entry, in a few industries directly or indirectly producing wage goods, barriers to entry increase. Argue that the real wage decreases.

7. (Nash bargaining) Suppose that utility depends on what one obtains of a certain 'pie', for example how much money one gets. Prove that, owing to axiom (ii) of Nash bargaining, it is always possible to set all $u_i^0 = 0$ and that changes in the a_i's do not change how the solution allocates the 'pie'.

8. Try writing down equations explaining Wood's determination of the rate of profit, first assuming investment is financed exclusively out of retained profits which are a certain proportion of profits, then assuming investment can also be financed by borrowing which cannot exceed a certain leverage ratio (ratio of debt to own capital).

9. In Bowles' model of efficiency wages, show graphically that for given workers' preferences and given unemployment benefits a lower rate of unemployment that shifts the $e(w, m; z)$ curve to the right causes e^*/w^* to decrease but does not necessarily cause w^* to increase. Find the condition for a rise of w^* to be guaranteed. Also, discuss the likelihood that e^* decreases.

10. In Goodwin's model the rate of wage increase depends on the rate of unemployment, but it is not explained why. Suppose you want to introduce in this model Bowles' efficiency wage model as a way to determine wages. There is continuous technical progress. If workers' preferences do not change, the $e(w)$ curve does not shift unless the rate of unemployment changes. But if the $e(w)$ curve does not shift, profits increase and then according to Goodwin's model, growth accelerates and sooner or later unemployment decreases. Conclude that in this Goodwin–Bowles model if workers' preferences do not change and if unemployment benefits do not rise, a continued secular rise of real wages is implausible.

11. The Goodwin model can induce pessimism on the advantages of trying to strengthen workers' organization and trade unions. Explain why, and discuss whether this pessimism is really justified.

12. (Cahuc and Zylberberg) Suppose that effort is a function of how 'fair' the wage is perceived to be by the worker, where fairness is measured by the ratio of this wage to the average wage in similar occupations. Assume all workers are identical and the worker's utility function is

$$u = R[1 + \beta e/\omega] - e^2/2$$

where β is a non-negative coefficient, ω is the average real wage, e is effort, and R is income, equal to the wage w if the worker is employed, and equal to the fallback income τ if the worker is unemployed. If a worker is unemployed, then $e = 0$. Workers are identical except that fallback income is not the same for all workers, it is characterized by a cumulative distribution function $G(\cdot)$ defined for the set of non-negative real numbers. Assume e is also output and it equals the wage. For $\beta > 0$, derive the choice of e via utility maximization under the assumptions that $R = w = e$ and that the worker treats ω as given; show that since all workers are identical and make the same choice, which they

13.14 · Review Questions and Exercises

change as it alters ω, finally at equilibrium the workers who offer themselves for work are those with $\tau \leq \beta + 1/2$.

This can be contrasted with the case in which there is no 'fairness' effect because $\beta = 0$. Prove that in this case fewer workers offer to work than when $\beta > 0$.

13. *Given real wage only in some industries.* Assume a neoclassical economy produces two consumption goods with land and labour in two separate industries. Assume different Cobb–Douglas production functions, given total supplies of labour and of land; good 1 is the numéraire, in terms of which real wages are fixed; the price of good 2 is p_2; trade unions are able to fix w_2, the wage in industry 2, while w_1, the wage in industry 1, adjusts so as to obtain equality between total supply and total demand for labour. Land is fully employed; factors are employed so as to equalize rentals and value marginal products. Write down the equations that determine quantities produced, employments of labour and of land in each industry, wage in industry 1, the uniform rent of land, and the price of good 2, if the composition of consumer demand is given or a (non-perverse) function of p_2. Argue that if w_2 rises, w_1 decreases and employment in industry 1 rises.

References

Abraham, K. G., & Haltiwanger, J. C. (1995). Real wages and the business cycle. *Journal of Economic Literature, 33*(3), 1215–1264.

Agell, J., & Lundborg, P. (1995). Theories of pay and unemployment: Survey evidence from swedish manufacturing firms. *Scandianvian Journal of Economics, 97*(2), 295–307.

Allain, O. (2014). Tackling the instability of growth: A Kaleckian-Harrodian model with an autonomous expenditure component. *Cambridge Journal of Economics.* ▶ https://doi.org/10.1093/cje/beu039.

Andrews, M. J., Bradley, S., Stott, D., & Upward, R. (2008). Successful employer search? An empirical analysis of vacancy duration using micro data. *Economica, New Series 75*(no. 299), 455–480.

Armstrong, P., Glyn, A., & Harrison, J. (1991). *Capitalism since 1945.* Oxford: Basil Blackwell.

Arrowsmith, D. K., & Place, C. M. (1982). *Ordinary differential equations.* London: Chapman and Hall.

Ashenfelter, O., & Johnson, G. E. (1969). Bargaining theory, trade unions, and industrial strike activity. *American Economic Review, 59*(1), 35–49.

Azariadis, C. (1975). Implicit contracts and underemployment equilibria. *Journal of Political Economy, 83*(6), 1183–1202.

Bauer, O. (1936). *Zwischen Zwei Weltkriegen?.* Bratislava: Eugen Prager Verlag.

Bauer, O. (1986). The accumulation of capital. *History of Political Economy, 18*, 88–110 (German original 1913).

Bertola, G. (1990). Job security employment and wages. *European Economic Review, 34*(4), 851–879.

Bewley, T. (1999a). *Why wages don't fall during a recession.* Cambridge MA: Harvard University Press.

Bewley, T. (1999b). Work motivation. *Review Federal Reserve Bank of St. Louis, 81*(3), 35–50.

Bewley, T. F. (2005). Fairness, reciprocity and wage rigidity. In H. Gintis, S. Bowles, R. Boyd, & E. Fehr (Eds.), *Moral sentiments and material interests. The foundations of cooperation in economic life* (pp. 303–338). Cambridge, MA: MIT Press.

Blanchflower, D., & Oswald, A. (1990). The wage curve. *Scandinavian Journal of Economics, 92*(2), 215–235.

Blien, U., Dauth, W., Schank, T., & Schnabel, C. (2009). The institutional contex of an "empirical law": The wage curve under different regimes of collective bargaining. LASER discussion paper no. 33, University of Erlangen-Nuremberg, Germany.

Booth, A. L. (1995). *The economics of the trade union*. Cambridge: Cambridge University Press.

Bowles, S. (2004). *Microeconomics. Behavior, institutions, and evolution*. Princeton, N.J.: Prrinceton University Press.

Bowles, S., & Boyer, R. (1990). A wage-led employment regime: Income distribution, labour discipline, and aggregate demand in welfare capitalism. In: *Margin and Schor*, pp. 187–217.

Boyer, R. (Ed.). (1986). *Capitalismes fin de siècle*. Paris: PUF.

Boyer, R., & Saillard, Y. (1995). *Théorie de la régulation: l'état des savoirs*. Paris: Editions La Découverte.

Brandolini, A. (1995). In search of a stylised fact: Do real wages exhibit a consistent pattern of cyclical variability? *Journal of Economic Surveys, 9*(2), 103–163.

Brown, G. (1977). *Sabotage*. London: Spokesman books.

Burdett, K., & Mortensen, D. (1998). Wage differentials, employer size, and unemployment. *International Economic Review, 39*, 257–273.

Cahuc, P., Carcillo, S., & Zylberberg, A. (2014). *Labor economics* (2nd ed.). Cambridge MA: MIT Press.

Cahuc, P., & Zylberberg, A. (2004). *Labor economics*. Cambridge MA: MIT Press.

Calmfors, L., & Driffill, J. (1988). Bargaining structure, corporatism and macroeconomic performance. *Economic Policy, 6*, 13–62.

Card, D. (1995). The wage curve: A review. *Journal of Economic Literature, 33*, 785–799.

Carmichael, H. L. (1985). Can unemployment be involuntary? The supervision perspective. *American Economic Review, 75*(5), 1213–1214.

Carmichael, H. L. (1989). Self-enforcing contracts, shirking, and life cycle incentives. *Journal of Economic Perspectives, 3*(4), 65–83.

Cavalieri, T., Garegnani, P., & Lucii, M. (2004). La sinistra e il problema dell'occupazione. *La rivista del Manifesto*, numero 48 (marzo).

Clower, R. W. (1967). A reconsideration of the microfoundations of monetary theory. *Western Economic Journal, 6*, 1–9.

Clower, R. W. (1969). Introduction. In R. W. Clower (Ed.), *Monetary theory* (pp. 7–21). Harmondsworth, England: Penguin.

Devine, T., & Kiefer, N. (1991). *Empirical labor economics: The search approach*. New York: Oxford University Press.

De Francesco, M. A. (1993). Norme sociali, rigidità dei salari e disoccupazione involontaria. *Economia Politica, 10*(1), 11–33.

Dunlop, J. G. (1938). The movement of real and money wage rates. *Economic Journal, 48*(No. 191), 413–434.

Elbaum, B., & Lazonick, W. (1986). *The decline of the British economy: An institutional perspective*. Oxford: Clarendon Press.

Gandolfo, G. (1971). *Mathematical methods and models in economic dynamics*. Amsterdam: North-Holland.

Garegnani, P. (1990). Sraffa: Classical versus marginalist analysis. In: K. Bharadwaj & B. Schefold (Eds.), *Essays on Piero Sraffa* (pp. 112–140). London: Unwin and Hyman (reprinted 1992 by Routledge, London).

Garegnani, P. (2004). Professor Foley and classical policy analysis. In: Foley et al. (2004), pp. 23–44.

Goodwin, R. M. (1967). A growth cycle. In C. H. Feinstein (Ed.), *Capitalism and economic growth* (pp. 54–58). Cambridge: Cambridge University Press.

Gordon, D. M., Edwards, R., & Reich, M. (1982). *Segmented work, divided workers*. Cambridge: Cambridge University Press.

Hahn, F. H., & Solow, R. M. (1992). *Macroeconomic theory*. Oxford: Oxford University Press.

Heijdra, B. J., & Van der Ploeg, F. (2002). *The foundations of modern macroeconomics*. Oxford: Oxford university Press.

Hicks, J. R. (1932(1963)). *The Theory of wages* (reprinted with additions, 1963). London: Macmillan.

Hicks, J.R. (1980–81). IS–LM: An explanation. *Journal of Post-Keynesian Economics*. As reprinted in Fitoussi, J. P. (1983a). *Modern macroeconomic theory* (pp. 49–63). Oxford: Basil Blackwell.

Kaldor, N. (1956). Alternative theories of distribution. *Review of Economic Studies, 23*, 83–100.

References

Kalecki, M. (1943). Political aspects of full employment. In: M. Kalecki (Ed.), *Selected essays on the dynamics of the capitalist economy 1933–70* (pp. 138–145). Cambridge: Cambridge University Press.

Kalecki, M. (1971). Class struggle and distribution of national income. In: M. Kalecki (Ed.), *Selected essays on the dynamics of the capitalist economy 1933–1970* (pp. 156–164). Cambridge: Cambridge University Press. Also published in *Kyklos*.

Keynes, J. M. (1936). *The general theory of employment interest and money* (1967 Papermac repr.). London: Macmillan. Cited in the text as *GT*.

Keynes, J. M. (1939). Relative movements of real wages and output. *Economic Journal, 49,* 34–35.

Kreps, D. M. (1990). *A course in microeconomic theory*. New York: Harvester Wheatsheaf.

Lavoie, M. (2014). *Post-Keynesian economics: New foundations*. Cheltenham, UK: Edward Elgar.

Leibenstein, H. (1957). *Economic backwardness and economic growth*. New York: Wiley.

Levrero, E. S. (1999). Worker bargaining power and real wages from 1870 to 1913: Phelps brown reconsidered. *Review of Political Economy, 11*(2), 183–203.

Levrero, E. S. (2012). *Four lectures on wages and the labour market*. Roma: Aracne.

Lindbeck, A., & Snower, D. J. (1986). Wage setting, unemployment, and insider-outsider relations. *American Economic Review, 76,* 235–239.

Lindbeck, A., & Snower, D. J. (1988). Cooperation, harassment and involuntary unemployment: An insider-outsider approach. *American Economic Review, 78,* 167–188.

Marglin, S. A., & Schor, J. B. (1990). *The golden age of capitalism*. Oxford: Clarendon Press.

McDonald, I. M., & Solow, R. M. (1981). Wage bargaining and employment. *American Economic Review, 71*(5), 896–908.

McDonough, T., Reich, M., & Kotz, D. M. (Eds.). (2010). *Contemporary capitalism and its crises: Social structure of accumulation theory for the 21st century*. New York: Cambridge University Press.

Mortensen, D. (1970). Job search, the duration of unemployment, and the Phillips curve. *American Economic Review, 60,* 505–517.

Palma, J. G. (2009). The revenge of the market on the rentiers. Why neo-liberal reports of the end of history turned out to be premature. *Cambridge Journal of Economics, 33,* 829–869.

Pekkarinen, J., Pohjola, M., & Rowthorn, B. (1992). *Social corporatism: A Superior economic system?*. Oxford: Clarendon Press.

Phelan, C. (2009). Introduction. In: C. Phelan (Ed.), *Trade Unionism since 1945. Toward a global history* (Vol. 1, pp. i–xxxv). Bern: Peter Lang.

Piore, M. J. (1973). Fragments of a sociological theory of wages. *American Economic Review, 63*(2), 377–384.

Pissarides, C. (2000). *Equilibrium unemployment theory* (2nd ed.). Cambridge, MA: MIT Press.

Pivetti, M. (1985). On the monetary explanation of distribution. *Political Economy: Studies in the Surplus Approach, 1*(2), 73–104.

Pivetti, M. (1991). *An essay on money and distribution*. London: Macmillan.

Pivetti, M. (2013). On advanced capitalism and the determinants of the change in income distribution: A classical interpretation. In E. S. Levrero, A. Palumbo, & A. Stirati (Eds.), *Sraffa and the reconstruction of economic theory* (Vol. I, pp. 176–191)., Palgrave Macmillan Basingstoke, Hampshire, UK: Houndmills.

Raff, D., & Summers, al. (1987). Did Henry Ford pay efficiency wages? *Journal of Labor Economics, 5,* S57–S86.

Robinson, J. V. (1962). *Essays in the theory of economic growth*. London: Macmillan.

Romer, D. (2012). *Advanced macroeconomics* (4th ed.). New York: McGraw-Hill Irwin.

Rowthorn, B., & Glyn, A. (1990). The diversity of employment experience since 1973. In: S. Marglin & J. Schor (Eds.), pp. 218–266.

Schor J. B. (1988). *Does work intensity respond to macroeconomic variables? Evidence from British manufacturing, 1970–1986*. Harvard Institute of Economic Research Discussion Paper no. 1379.

Shaikh, A. (2016). *Capitalism*. Oxford: Oxford University Press.

Shapiro, C., & Stiglitz, J. (1984). Equilibrium unemployment as a worker discipline device. *American Economic Review, 74*(3), 433–444.

Solow, R. M. (1979). Another possible source of wage stickiness. *Journal of Macroeconomics, 1*(1), 79–82.

Solow, R. M. (1980). On the theories of unemployment. *American Economic Review, 70*(1), 1–11.

Solow, R. M. (1990). *The labor market as a social institution.* Oxford: Basil Blackwell.

Stirati, A. (1999). Ricardo and the wages fund. In G. Mongiovi & F. Petri (Eds.), *Value, distribution and capital: Essays in honour of Pierangelo Garegnani* (pp. 204–229). London: Routledge.

Stirati, A. (2013). Alternative 'closures' to sraffa's system: Some reflections in the light of the changes in functional income distribution in the United States. In E. S. Levrero, A. Palumbo, & A. Stirati (Eds.), *Sraffa and the reconstruction of economic theory* (Vol. I, pp. 192–217). London: Palgrave Macmillan.

Stirati, A. (2016). Real wages in the business cycle and the theory of income distribution: an unresolved conflict between theory and facts in mainstream macroeconomics. *Cambridge Journal of Economics.* ▶ https://doi.org/10.1093/cje/beu088.

Strobel, F. R., & Peterson, W. C. (1997). Class conflict, American style: Distract and conquer. *Journal of Economic Issues, 31*(2), 433–443.

Stockhammer, E. (2008). Is the NAIRU Theory a Monetarist, New Keynesian, Post Keynesian or a Marxist Theory? *Metroeconomica, 59*(3), 479–510. ▶ https://doi.org/10.1111/j.1467-999X.2008.00314.x.

Tarshis, L. (1938). Real wages in the United States and Great Britain. *Canadian Journal of Economics and Political Science, 4*(3), 362–375.

Tarshis, L. (1939). Changes in Real and Money Wages. *Economic Journal, 49*(193), 150–154.

Ulman, L. (1990). Labor market analysis and concerted behavior. *Industrial Relations, 29*(2), 281–302.

Weibull, J. (1987). *Persistent Unemployment as Subgame Perfect Equilibrium.* Seminar Paper no. 381, Institute for International Economic Studies, Stockholm.

Weiss, A. (1990). *Efficiency wages: Models of unemployment, layoffs, and wage dispersion.* Princeton: Princeton University Press.

Wood, A. (1975). *A theory of profits.* Cambridge: Cambridge University Press.

Welfare, Externalities, Public Goods and Happiness

Contents

14.1   Introductory – 1229

14.2   Pareto Efficiency and Value Judgements – 1230

14.3   Externalities – 1234
14.3.1   The Coase Theorem – 1234
14.3.2   Production Externalities – 1236
14.3.3   Pollution Rights – 1241
14.3.4   Network Externalities and the Internet – 1241
14.3.5   The Tragedy of the Commons – 1246
14.3.6   Urban Segregation – 1248

14.4   Public Goods[15] – 1249
14.4.1   Non-rival Goods and Non-excludable Goods – 1249
14.4.2   When to Get an Indivisible Public Goods – 1250
14.4.3   What Quantity of a Divisible Public Good? – 1251
14.4.4   Lindahl Equilibrium – 1254

14.5   The Groves–Clarke Mechanism – 1255

14.6   The Fundamental Theorems of Welfare Economics – 1258
14.6.1   Does Competition Produce Pareto Efficiency? – 1258

Electronic supplementary material The online version of this chapter (▶ https://doi.org/10.1007/978-3-030-62070-7_14) contains supplementary material, which is available to authorized users.

© Springer Nature Switzerland AG 2021
F. Petri, *Microeconomics for the Critical Mind*,
Classroom Companion: Economics, https://doi.org/10.1007/978-3-030-62070-7_14

| 14.6.2 | The First Fundamental Theorem – 1260 |
| 14.6.3 | The Second Fundamental Theorem – 1265 |

14.7 Some Generally Accepted Limitations of the Two Fundamental Theorems – 1271

14.8 Pareto Efficiency: A Non-neoclassical Perspective – 1277

14.9 Cost–Benefit Analysis and the Compensation Principle – 1281

14.10 Cost–benefit Analysis Run Amok – 1287

14.11 Social Welfare Functions – 1292

14.12 Three Applications of Social Welfare Functions – 1301

14.13 Arrow's Impossibility Theorem – 1305

14.14 Happiness, and Externalities Again – 1322

14.15 Conclusions – 1330

14.16 Review Questions and Exercises – 1330

References – 1334

14.1 · Introductory

In this chapter you will be introduced to welfare economics and its application to several concrete issues, in particular to:

- why, in the presence of externalities and public goods, the market is unable to avoid inefficiencies, and how society can try to reduce them;
- the Coase theorem;
- some problems with network externalities and the Internet;
- under what conditions competitive markets can be argued to produce an efficient allocation of resources—the Fundamental Theorems of Welfare Economics;
- the use of social welfare functions and the relevance of Arrow's Impossibility Theorem;
- the contribution of happiness economics to an understanding of what is important for welfare.

14.1 **Introductory**

Welfare economics takes its name from Arthur Cecil Pigou's *The Economics of Welfare* (first edition 1920), a treatise in public economics and economic policy based on the Marshallian picture of how market economies function. Because of the neoclassical background, and with the Great Crisis and Keynes still to come, the subject matter was essentially microeconomic, starting from the assumption that a competitive economy with flexible wages would work very satisfactorily were it not for externalities, public goods, imperfections of competition and an equilibrium income distribution sometimes generally needing correction for reasons of equity. From this premise the analysis proceeded to examine how to correct for these unsatisfactory aspects of a market economy by using microeconomic instruments such as taxes, subsidies and regulation of natural monopolies.

If, as seems necessary, it is accepted that the spontaneous working of markets can produce unemployment and crises, then welfare economics in the sense of the study of how to correct for the malfunctioning of markets ought fully to include macroeconomic policies too; but since Keynes, in parallel with the distinction between microeconomics and macroeconomics, there has been a division of the theory of economic policy between a microeconomic and a macroeconomic branch, with the microeconomic branch assuming that the marginal/neoclassical approach is sound and neglecting Keynesian problems, therefore taking resources as fully utilized and prices and income distribution as determined by neoclassical theory. Welfare economics stands nowadays essentially for this microeconomic branch, extended however—relative to Pigou—to include a discussion of different criteria to arrive at a 'social' preference, which inevitably connects with political science and with moral and political philosophy.

After what was argued in previous chapters, one may legitimately ask for some indication of what difference it makes, in issues of economic welfare, not to accept the neoclassical approach. But the classical–Keynesian or more generally the Post-Keynesian school (of which the former can be considered part) has not built yet a comprehensive alternative welfare economics. So, differently from the situation in the theory of income distribution and in the theory of employment, in welfare economics there are not two radically different approaches to be compared; there are a mainstream approach, some criticisms, some suggestion for reorientation of the main priorities. This chapter selects for discussion some of the main issues in this situation.

The chapter starts with a discussion of the notion of Pareto efficiency, and with those aspects of standard welfare economics where this notion can be of help independently of the approach to value and distribution one finds more convincing: the analysis of (tractable) externalities, and of public goods. The Coase theorem is shown implicitly to assume the absence of relevant conflicts; the Internet is a new field where externalities are immensely important. (For space reasons I leave the interventions to correct monopoly distortions to courses in industrial economics.) Then I present the two neoclassical Fundamental Theorems of Welfare Economics, noting that they were originally intended for long-period equilibria and encounter problems if one tries to apply them to neo-Walrasian notions of general equilibrium; then I note a number of universally admitted limitations of the two theorems, which bring up limitations of the notion itself of Pareto efficiency. Of course the validity of the Fundamental Theorems is further questioned if one questions the neoclassical approach, in particular if one denies the tendency to the full employment of resources; this gives the opportunity to mention one alternative to Pareto efficiency, which has important implications for the evaluation of the institutions of the welfare state. Then an important tool used to assess public intervention, cost–benefit analysis, is found to be potentially independent of the approach to value distribution and employment one considers correct, and potentially very useful, although also potentially dangerous as evidenced by some examples. The notion of social welfare function is then discussed, distinguishing Bergson's original notion from subsequent SWFs; the issue is raised of the importance of Pareto's assumption of no externalities. Then Arrow's famous Impossibility Theorem is proved; the acceptability of its assumptions is discussed, and it is concluded that behind the search for 'nice' social choice rules there is a sort of utopian optimism which underestimates the harsh power conflicts that condition how social choices are actually reached. The chapter ends with a discussion of aspects of the economics of happiness that suggest that the importance of growth for welfare is overestimated, that unemployment is the most important economic cause of unhappiness in advanced economies and that the persons who do have a job work considerably more than welfare maximization would suggest. These results can be taken as indications of themes that a reformulated welfare economics ought to assume as central. The online Appendix raises the difficult issue of the optimal amount of resources to be allocated to innovation.

14.2 Pareto Efficiency and Value Judgements

It is inevitable to start from the notion central to mainstream welfare economics, the notion of Pareto efficiency. This notion is central because since Vilfredo Pareto the teaching of economic theory has insisted on the efficiency of market

14.2 · Pareto Efficiency and Value Judgements

economies, where efficiency is defined as Pareto proposed. The reader has already met the basic neoclassical argument in ▶ Chap. 3: competition is argued to push towards a state of efficient utilization of factor supplies, because these supplies (freely chosen by consumers) tend to be utilized.

(i) fully;
(ii) in efficient combinations;
(iii) for the production of a composition of output that reflects the desires of consumers.

The argument can be made more rigorous and generalized beyond the simple economies discussed in ▶ Chap. 3. But since doubts on (i) are raised by the criticisms of the neoclassical approach advanced in previous chapters, it is better to start with parts of welfare economics where those criticisms can be made not to apply by restricting the argument to partial equilibria: then the incomes of consumers as well as input prices can be taken as given, determined by a level of labour employment and by an income distribution which one is free to consider determined as one prefers, neoclassically or by other forces.

Of course if one takes labour employment as determined by aggregate demand and not generally at the full-employment level, then these partial-equilibrium welfare analyses must be viewed as reaching only provisional conclusions about the efficacy of any intervention, to be completed with an analysis of the *macro*-effects of the intervention (effects on aggregate demand, employment, balance-of-payment constraints) and of the effects on income distribution. For example, a welfare evaluation of a taxation increase needed to finance public goods must also take into account the effects on employment and on the balance of payments.

Let a *social state* be a situation specified in all the aspects relevant for each individual's assessment of whether it is preferable to other social states. Assume there are S individuals, and K possible social states; each individual s has complete, transitive preferences over these states described by a binary relation of weak preference denoted R_s or $\succsim_s$, with xR_sy or $x \succsim_s y$ indicating that individual s prefers social state x to social state y or is indifferent between the two. A social state x is considered (*weakly*) *Pareto superior* to a second social state y if everybody weakly prefers x to y and at least one person strictly prefers it. If everybody strictly prefers the first state to the second, then the first is *strictly Pareto superior*. A passage to a strictly Pareto superior state is called a *strict Pareto improvement*, a passage to a weakly Pareto superior state is called a *weak Pareto improvement*.[1] It is generally accepted in welfare economics that society should be in favour of Pareto improvements, even when only weak; this view will require comment later. If a social state is such that relative to it no other possible social state would imply at least a weak Pareto improvement, the state is said *Pareto efficient* or *Pareto optimal*.

---

1 The 'passage' in the text can be interpreted as the passing from one possible choice to another one in the ex-ante comparison of alternatives; or it can be interpreted as an actual transition in reality from a state A to a state B. In the latter case, state B is the final state that is reached taking into account all transition costs.

1232   Chapter 14 · Welfare, Externalities, Public Goods and Happiness

Apart from special cases such as lexicographic preference orders, relationship R_s can also be represented by a numerical utility function; this utility function will then depend on the vector of (quantifiable or not quantifiable) elements that distinguish social states, and each different vector will represent a different social state. This utility function is potentially very different from the usual utility function discussed in consumer theory, because the preference order between social states can also depend, for example, on which political coalition has the majority in Parliament, on whether gay marriage is legal or not, on the Gini index of income inequality, on the individual's estimation of how happy her child would be in each social state, on anything really. Even if one decides to restrict the comparison to social states differing only in economic variables such as consumption levels, implicitly assuming all other elements to be given, it seems necessary to admit *other-regarding preferences*, preferences among social states that are influenced by concern over the economic conditions of other people, be it because of affection, envy, altruism, emulation, reputation, moral feelings. These influences can be considered one kind of *externalities*. An *externality* is any influence of the condition or actions of a consumer or firm on the utility level of other consumers or on the outputs of other firms, for which no transaction occurs and no price is paid; examples are air pollution, traffic noise or the pleasure from seeing a beautiful building. In the presence of externalities, even restricting attention only to consumption baskets the conditions for Pareto efficiency illustrated in ▶ Chap. 3 do not hold; and externalities are everywhere. In particular, if one admits (as one must) other-regarding preferences, a social state x which assigns to each individual a greater consumption than a second state y need not be Pareto superior to y: envy or moral dislike of the income inequality associated with the new income distribution can cause some people to prefer y. Thus a change that raises the income of everybody by 2% except the very rich whose income is raised by 20% is certain to be a strict Pareto improvement only if one neglects other-regarding preferences: a majority of people might be against the change because they dislike the increase in inequality. Standard welfare economics, from Pareto onwards, considers generalized increases in consumption levels, even very unequally distributed, to be Pareto improvements and therefore deserving social approval because it disregards or underplays the importance of other-regarding preferences with their component of moral evaluations and desire for fairness and equality (especially in the distribution of *improvements*).

It must be added that even when, taking into account other-regarding preferences too and all other elements too, the passage from state a to state b is a Pareto improvement, to conclude that one should not oppose the passage from a to b is logically illegitimate because generally there will be other possible Pareto improvements too, differing in that some individuals will gain more and some others less with one Pareto improvement than with another, and then one needs other criteria to choose among the alternatives. It would be illegitimate to say that anyway to pass from a state a to a Pareto superior state b is an improvement, because the passage will generally exclude passing to other states c, d, etc., also superior to a and not Pareto-comparable with b, and possibly even superior to b.

14.2 · Pareto Efficiency and Value Judgements

The truth is that if all these considerations are fully taken into account, it becomes impossible in practice to ascertain whether a state is Pareto superior to another. A generalized uniform income increase may be disliked by someone because it allows more people to wear elegant clothes and the religious persuasion of this individual asks for generalized ascetic simplicity.

Probably the notions of Pareto improvement and Pareto efficiency would not have been born at all without the initial restriction of the variables influencing the utility of each individual to that individual's own consumption basket (inclusive of labour activities as 'consumptions' which may decrease utility), neglecting externalities and all moral or similar influences on the individuals' evaluations of social states—the neglect that allows the formulation of the Fundamental Theorems of Welfare Economics, and that allows Pareto to distinguish an 'economic point of view' concerned with efficiency, from considerations involving political or ethical evaluations.[2] On this rather unproblematic basis it was then possible to admit some reasons why public intervention can produce Pareto improvements: two big categories were (i) those externalities that appear ascertainable and modifiable by taxes and regulations,[3] and (ii) **public goods**. A **public good** is any good whose consumption by some consumer or firm does not decrease the possibility to consume it by other consumers or firms, for example radio transmissions. I proceed to examine the problems that (treatable) externalities and public goods create. Some terminology is necessary.

First let us redefine Pareto efficiency for the case of utility depending only on own consumption, in the absence of externalities and of public goods. An allocation $\mathbf{x}$ is a vector of vectors $\mathbf{x}^s$ that indicate the consumption basket of consumer s, $s = 1, ..., S$. Let us initially assume a pure exchange economy. An allocation is *feasible* in an exchange economy if the sum of all consumption vectors $\Sigma_s \mathbf{x}^s$ is not greater than the aggregate endowment vector $\omega = \Sigma_s \omega^s$. A feasible allocation $\mathbf{x}$ is *weakly Pareto efficient* if there is no other feasible allocation $\mathbf{x}'$ such that all individuals strictly prefer $\mathbf{x}'$ to $\mathbf{x}$. (This means that a strict Pareto improvement relative to $\mathbf{x}$ is not possible, but a weak Pareto improvement might be possible.) A

---

2 'When the community finds itself in a point Q from which it can depart to the advantage of all individuals, obtaining for all of them greater enjoyments, it is manifest that from the economical point of view and if one only researches the advantage of all the individuals who compose the community, it is convenient not to stop at that point, but to continue to move away from it as long as it is to the advantage of all. When afterwards one arrives at a point P where this is no longer possible, it is necessary, in order to stop or to continue, to turn to other considerations, extraneous to economics; that is, it is necessary to decide, via considerations of social utility, ethical, or of any other kind, in the interest of which individuals it is preferable to act, while sacrificing others. From the exclusively economic point of view, once the community has arrived at a point P, it had better stop' (Pareto 1968 (1917), p. 1339; my translation). A clear invitation to economists, qua economists, to abstain from suggestions implying more than Pareto improvements.

3 These externalities generally do not include the effects due to religious, political etc. persuasions.

1234   **Chapter 14** · Welfare, Externalities, Public Goods and Happiness

feasible allocation $\mathbf{x}$ is ***strongly Pareto efficient*** if there is no feasible allocation $\mathbf{x}'$ such that all individuals weakly prefer $\mathbf{x}'$ to $\mathbf{x}$ and at least one individual strictly prefers $\mathbf{x}'$ to $\mathbf{x}$. (That is, neither a strict nor a weak Pareto improvement relative to $\mathbf{x}$ is possible.) So don't get confused, a *strongly* Pareto-efficient allocation requires it to be only *weakly* Pareto superior to any other ('strongly' here is in the sense of requiring less unanimity, and therefore capable of existing in a greater number of instances, and more resistant to changes in preferences). By Pareto-efficient allocation it is usually meant a strongly efficient one. Note that if a weak Pareto improvement is possible, and goods are perfectly divisible and consumers are not satiated, then a strict Pareto improvement is possible too.

14.3 Externalities

14.3.1 The Coase Theorem

Let us see what welfare insights can be obtained from a partial-equilibrium framework, that is, by taking the determinants of income distribution and of the general level of economic activity as given, and asking whether within those givens the presence of externalities and of public goods means that public interventions should be advocated because capable of bringing about Pareto improvements. Within this framework, we will be able to ask only about *local* Pareto efficiency—this will hold if no further Pareto improvement is available in the restricted area of the economy under consideration and with the given givens. The wider effects of the public intervention, e.g. on employment and on income distribution, must be studied in a second stage of the analysis, not tackled here.

Given this restriction, it can be often acceptable to assume a *constant marginal utility of money*, i.e. quasi-linear utility, extensively discussed in ▶ Chap. 4.

An *externality* is an influence, for which no market payment occurs, of the choices of a consumer or firm on the utility of other consumers or on the production level of other firms.[4] Pollution of a river by a firm that damages downstream fisheries is an externality if the polluting firm does not pay the fisheries to have the right to go on polluting.

Fashion and similar externalities in consumption are not generally greatly resented and will be neglected here, except for the demonstration effect that pushes people to work a lot, discussed at the end of the chapter.

An important aspect of negative externalities such as noise that disturbs neighbours is that often they have the further negative effect of causing attrition and conflict; an important cause of these further negative effects is that *property*

---

4   To talk of choices can be occasionally strained. The owner of a beautiful palace on Canal Grande in Venice does not *choose* to let tourists enjoy the sight of the palace. The externality can be a consequence simply of the state of the individual's property (or looks).

14.3 · Externalities

rights are not clearly assigned. Suppose household A plays loud music at night in the top floor of an apartment building and disturbs the sleep of household B in the apartment below; if the law establishes a noise level that must not be surpassed, then household A has the right to be noisy up to that level, and household B will have to pay A if it wants less noise. If there is no regulation, it is unclear whether household B must pay A to avoid noise, or A must pay B to have the right to produce noise, and the result can be conflict, escalating even to violence.

In a famous article, Coase (1960) made it clear that, if one assumes quasi-linear utility (which may be legitimate if the money transfer needed to compensate for the externality has only a minor influence on the total income or wealth of the persons involved), and if there are no **transaction costs** (expenses caused by the process of arriving at an agreement), then as long as property rights are well defined and people can bargain about compensation to correct the externality, the same locally Pareto-efficient amount of externality will be reached *whatever the assignment of property rights*; the latter will only determine who pays whom, not the amount of externality. This is called the **Coase theorem** (although it is not properly a mathematical theorem, indeed its formulation differs from author to author; Coase did not use this term). The usual conclusion derived from this observation is that as long as property rights are well defined, the practical problems caused by externalities will find easy solution. Let us see how this is argued, and why this conclusion is open to doubt.

Assume that in our story of noise production the utility of household A is $u(n) + x$ where n is noise level, N is its maximum level ($N \geq n \geq 0$), x is A's monetary wealth, and $u'(n) > 0$, $u''(n) < 0$; the utility of the lower-flat household B is $v(n) + y$ where y is B's monetary wealth and $v'(n) < 0$, $v''(n) < 0$. The locally Pareto-efficient noise level n^* with money transfers is the one where the marginal utility of one less unit of noise for B is equal to the marginal utility of one more unit of noise for A, i.e. $-v'(n^*) = u'(n^*)$. If A has the right to produce noise, when $n > n^*$ it is $-v'(n) > -v'(n^*) > u'(n)$ and a price $p^* = -v'(n^*)$, paid by B to A for each unit of noise reduction, will induce A to reduce noise to n^*; further noise reductions would require a payment to A greater than p^* for each further unit of noise reduction, but B would not find it convenient. Note however that A might pretend more than p^* for the first units of noise reduction starting from N; if all units of noise reduction from N to n^* are paid p^*, B enjoys a surplus relative to having to pay for all units only the marginal disutility of the last one. In this bilateral bargaining situation there is no reason why all units of noise reduction should be paid the same, so whether some or all or zero of B's potential surplus will be appropriated by A remains undetermined. So there is a continuum of Pareto-efficient allocations, all with noise at level n^* and with money transfers from B to A between a minimum equal to $p^*(N - n^*)$ and a maximum equal to $v(n^*) - v(N)$. If it is A that must buy the right to produce noise, a price p^* for each unit of noise will induce B to accept n^*; again, for the first units of noise A is ready to pay more than p^*, so how much A will have to pay for the first units of noise remains undetermined within analogously determined limits. So in both cases there is some indeterminacy and then room for time-consuming bargaining

1236   **Chapter 14 · Welfare, Externalities, Public Goods and Happiness**

and conflict, i.e. for subjective or legal costs additional to the transfers. This difficulty will not arise only if the agents involved can be assumed to be price-takers and some market process causes the price of each unit of noise (or of noise reduction) to be $p*$, but in most situations this cannot be assumed.

Coase cunningly avoided the problem by specifying that transaction costs must be absent, which in our example would mean that A and B reach *some* agreement on the surplus split quickly and without bitter disputations. This shows that the role of the assumption of negligible transaction costs in the Coase theorem is more important than usually understood, because it implies, without making it explicit, no conflict over the split of the potential surplus—while conflict is what must be expected in the absence of clear rules imposing how to split it, and it can cause very high costs. A clear assignment of property rights is not enough, rules on the split of the surplus are necessary too.

Transaction costs can be prohibitive even apart from the potential for litigation, owing to the numbers involved. Take the case of several firms polluting the air of a vast valley: bargaining between all the consumers and firms in the valley would involve ascertaining how much each consumer suffers from the activity of each firm. Also, some consumers will be tempted to 'free ride' (enjoy the benefits of a pollution-reducing intervention that requires a contribution, by declaring pollution does not damage them), since a reduction of pollution benefits them anyway. The possibility to eliminate inefficiencies due to externalities via private bargaining is therefore often non-existent, and then public intervention is called for.

14.3.2 **Production Externalities**

Let us consider now externalities in production, again in a partial-equilibrium framework. Assume a firm plants fruit trees next to a wood used by another firm for honey production. Bees impollinate flowers, more bees means more fruit production *ceteris paribus*, and conversely more fruit trees means more pollen of the flowers of the fruit trees, which increases the production of honey. Let the production function of the fruit producer be $q = F(m, b)$, with decreasing returns to scale (owing to the presence of a given amount of land), where m is the labour employed by the fruit firm, which is proportional to the number of fruit trees, and b is the labour employed by the honey producer, which is proportional to the number of bees, so $\partial F/\partial b > 0$ and $\frac{\partial^2 F}{\partial b \partial m} > 0$. Analogously, let $h = G(b, m)$ be the honey production function, also with decreasing returns to scale, where a greater m means more fruit trees and therefore $\partial G/\partial m > 0$ and $\frac{\partial^2 G}{\partial m \partial b} > 0$. The two firms are price-takers, and fruit and honey are measured in units such that both their money prices equal 1. Labour receives the same given money wage w in both firms. If no account is taken of the reciprocal help of the two production levels, the fruit firm produces up to equality between price and marginal cost ($= w/MP_L$), where MP_L is determined by treating b as given; analogously, the honey producer treats m as given. So the fruit firm neglects the fact that an increase in its labour employment, besides having a direct effect $\partial F/\partial m$ on its output, has an

14.3 · Externalities

indirect effect consisting of an increase of the marginal productivity of the other firm's labour, which by reducing the marginal cost of the other firm induces it to employ more labour and thus to invest in more bees, which increases the marginal productivity of labour employed to produce fruit. Mathematically, the two independent firms satisfy the first-order conditions

$$\partial F(m,b)/\partial m - w = 0,$$
$$\partial G(b,m)/\partial b - w = 0$$

If they merged into a single firm, the profit of this firm would be given by

$$\pi(m,b) = F(m,b) + G(b,m) - w \cdot (m+b)$$

and the first-order conditions for profit maximization would be

$$\partial \pi/\partial m = \partial F/\partial m + \partial G/\partial m - w = 0,$$
$$\partial \pi/\partial b = \partial F/\partial b + \partial G/\partial b - w = 0.$$

So the merged firm would hire more labour than the two separate firms. This means that the indirect marginal utility of labour can be increased by merging the two firms, that is, the two separate firms use labour inefficiently—too little, in this case.

Conversely, let us consider a classical negative externality: river pollution by a firm S that produces steel reduces the product of a downstream fishery F. Let us change the method of analysis a bit by concentrating on cost functions. Let the cost function of S be $C_s(s, x)$ where s is steel production and x is quantity of pollutant going into the river, and let $C_f(f, x)$ be the cost function of the fishery, where f is fish production; assume $\partial C_f/\partial x$ is positive and increasing in x, while $\partial C_s/\partial x$ is negative and decreasing in absolute value in x, reaching zero for a finite level of x. The two firms, which I assume are price-takers, when acting separately maximize profit by satisfying

$$\partial C_s(s,x)/\partial s = p_s, \tag{14.1}$$

$$\partial C_s(s,x)/\partial x = 0 \tag{14.2}$$

$$\partial C_f(f,x)/\partial f = p_f. \tag{14.3}$$

Note that F treats the level of x as given, because it is decided by S, and fixed at the level, call it x_{max}, where further increases of x yield S no further advantage. If the two firms merge into a single one, the merged firm's profit maximization problem is

$$max_{s,f,x}\pi = p_s s + p_f f - C_s(s,x) - C_f(f,x)$$

and the first-order conditions (14.1) and (14.3) do not change, but condition (14.2) is replaced by:

$$\partial \pi/\partial x = -\partial C_s/\partial x - \partial C_f/\partial x = 0, \text{ that is, } \partial C_f/\partial x = -\partial C_s/\partial x. \tag{14.4}$$

That is, if the last unit of pollution decreases the cost of S by less than it raises the cost of F (which is precisely the case if the two firms decide separately), then x

1238   **Chapter 14** · Welfare, Externalities, Public Goods and Happiness

should be reduced.[5] So the merged firm, by choosing to produce less x than x_{max}, reduces the total cost of producing any vector (s, f), which means an increase in efficiency.

The correction of the inefficiency in the examples above consisted of *internalizing* the externality. This may be impossible. Air pollution, for example, easily involves a number of firms too great for a merger of all of them into a single firm to be realistic.

Another way to correct the externality, historically the traditional policy proposal, is to tax the cause of the negative externality, or to subsidize the cause of the positive externality, so as to induce firms to satisfy the optimality conditions. In the pollution example, suppose the merged firm's first-order conditions imply it would be optimal to produce amounts s^*, f^*, x^*. The important thing is to induce the steel mill to produce the amount of pollution x^*. This can be obtained by imposing a tax t per unit of pollution, that changes the firm's profit to sales revenue minus a tax-augmented total cost $C=[C_s(s, x) + tx]$:

$$\pi_s = p_s s - [C_s(s,x) + tx]$$

and by imposing that this tax satisfies

$$t = \partial C_f\left(f^*, x^*\right)/\partial x. \tag{14.5}$$

Note that t is given, it is not a function of x. Then profit maximization requires (14.1) plus:

$$-\partial C_s(s,x)/\partial x - \partial C_f\left(f^*, x^*\right)/\partial x = 0,$$

the same condition (14.4) satisfied by the merged firm.

Note that the determination of this kind of tax, known as a *Pigou tax* (or Pigovian tax), requires knowing $\partial C_f(s^*, x^*)/\partial x$, which requires determining x^*.[6] This may require very difficult-to-obtain information. Also, if x^* is calculable, the state might directly require the steel mill not to produce more pollution than x^*. This is indeed another method sometimes suggested to deal with externalities: direct quantitative regulation.

The Pigovian tax can be intepreted as raising the marginal cost of steel production for the steel mill so that when this tax-inclusive marginal cost is put equal to price, price is equal to the marginal *social* cost of steel. To understand this notion, start from the fact that the marginal cost of steel for the *untaxed* firm is not $\partial C_s(s, x)/\partial s$ but rather $dC_s(s, x(s))/ds$, where $x(s)$ is the level of pollution that minimizes cost for each level of s (i.e. that, for each s, satisfies $\partial C_s(s, x)/\partial x=0$), because the firm adapts x to s so as to minimize cost. From

---

5   The second-order condition for a maximum is ensured by the decreasing advantage for the steel mill, and the increasing damage for the fishery, of an increase of x.

6   Note that the tax must be directly on the emission of x. A tax on the steel mill's output will work well only if x is in a fixed, unchangeable proportion to steel output. Otherwise a tax on steel output would reduce output but not necessarily x.

14.3 · Externalities

$$dC_s = \frac{\partial C_s(s,x)}{\partial s}\,ds + \frac{\partial C_s(s,x)}{\partial x}\,dx$$

we obtain $MC(s) = dC_s/ds = \frac{\partial C_s(s,x)}{\partial s} + \frac{\partial C_s(s,x)}{\partial x}\frac{dx}{ds}$ where dx/ds is the derivative of $x(s)$. The variation of x caused by a variation of s imposes a cost on the fishery equal to $dx \cdot \partial C_f(f, x)/\partial x$. The marginal *social* cost of a variation of s is therefore $dC_s/ds + (dx/ds) \cdot \partial C_f(f^*(x),x)/\partial x$ where $f^*(x)$ is the optimal production of the fishery when pollution is x. When the steel firm maximizes profit it is $\partial C_s(s, x)/\partial x = 0$ and therefore only the first addendum of dC_s/ds survives, but dx/ds is not zero, and the marginal social cost is $MSC = \partial C_s(s,x)/\partial s + (dx/ds) \cdot \partial C_f(f^*(x),x)/\partial x$.

The Pigovian tax causes the cost function of the steel firm to become

$$C = C_s(s,x(s)) + tx(s) = C_s(s,x(s)) + x(s) \cdot \partial C_f(f^*,x^*)/\partial x.$$

Its total derivative with respect to s is $\frac{\partial C_s(s,x)}{\partial s} + \frac{\partial C_s(s,x)}{\partial x}\frac{dx}{ds} + \frac{dx}{ds}\frac{\partial C_f(f^*,x^*)}{\partial x}$. When x is optimized the second addendum disappears and we *almost* obtain the MSC: there is a discrepancy because the very last fraction should be $\partial C_f(f^*(x), x)/\partial x$, but this discrepancy disappears when the steel firm decides for a pollution level x^*. This confirms that the Pigou tax requires to take p_s as given and to know the optimal level of pollution and the tax that will cause the steel firm to choose x equal to the optimal level.

If the production of one firm has external effects on several firms, one can generalize this approach and calculate the marginal social cost of the output of the first firm by adding to its marginal cost all the marginal external effects on the cost functions of the other firms. If the external effect is on the utility of a consumer, we can assume quasi-linear utility because we are in a partial-equilibrium framework, then the marginal effect of, e.g., pollution is the marginal loss of utility (measured in money) due to one more unit of pollution. A well-planned tax on the polluting consumption good, transferred to the consumer, raises the price of the consumption good without decreasing the consumer's income, and by raising the price of the good reduces demand for the good and thus the external effect of pollution, so as to obtain that the marginal indirect utility (including the external effect) of factors employed in producing that good becomes the same as in producing other consumption goods.[7] At least in principle, an omniscient government would be able to determine the marginal social cost of a product, and one obtains ◘ Fig. 14.1.

Back to the steel mill and fishery case, relative to the Pigou tax the Coase approach to externalities raises the issue: why should the steel mill be the one that pays the tax? why couldn't the tax be paid by the fishery and passed to the steel mill as a subsidy to induce it to produce only the amount x^* of pollution?

---

7 A neoclassical economist can also formulate, at least for simple cases, a general equilibrium determination of the optimal tax when the external effect is of a produced good on utility; see, e.g., Blad and Keiding (1990, pp. 255–262).

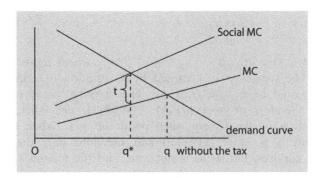

Fig. 14.1 Pigovian tax t that causes production of the socially efficient output q^*

Or, why couldn't the fishery pay the steel mill directly to induce it to pollute less? Note that if the fishery must pay the steel mill a price p_x for each unit of x less than x_{max}, the profit functions of the two firms become

$$\pi_s = p_s s - C_s(s,x) + p_x(x_{max} - x)$$
$$\pi_f = p_f f - C_f(f,x) - p_x(x_{max} - x)$$

and profit maximization implies

$$\partial C_s(s,x)/\partial s = p_s,$$
$$\partial C_f(f,x)/\partial f = p_f,$$
$$p_x = \partial C_f/\partial x = -\partial C_s/\partial x,$$

the same conditions realized by the Pigou tax, except that now $p_x = t$ is determined by the firms themselves (however, as in the two households case, an indeterminacy about the division of the surplus remains unless some institution ensures that the same price is paid for all units of $x_{max} - x$: this can result from a multifirm market for pollution rights with enough firms for price taking to hold; see below).

Coase (1960) raised this issue against Pigou's suggestion to apply his Pigovian tax to railways, whose locomotives produced sparks that caused fires in the woods the railways crossed. Coase asked why the cost had to be borne by the railways and not by the wood owners: if modification of locomotives to eliminate the sparks is less costly than the damage to woods, then that is the thing to do, but why should the cost be borne by the railways? So another main message of Coase is that, once the way to reach efficiency is found, this does not tell us who should bear the cost, and one must look for other considerations, of equity or convenience or custom, to find an answer. An implicit assumption in Pigou seems to have been that if a negative externality is created *by a novelty* (here the railways) that causes losses to pre-existing firms, it is the latecomer who must bear the cost of correcting the externality. Pigou's implicit assumption seems to have been that *pre-existing* economic activities must be compensated for the damage suffered owing to external effects of *new* economic activitives. This principle is applied when some state intervention (a motorway, a dam) damages the welfare of some consumers or the profitability of some firms and some compensation is granted them; but at other times it is not applied (in the absence of clear laws, courts oscillate on the issue—see Coase's article), and whether and when it should be applied is a very interesting 'law-and-economics' issue, that we cannot further discuss here.

14.3.3 Pollution Rights

When a negative externality, for example amounts of a pollutant, is produced by many firms and affects many other firms and consumers, a way to deal with the excessive information requirements of Pigou taxes is by creating a market for pollution rights. On the basis of some criterion (e.g. a cost–benefit analysis, see below), a maximum total yearly production of the pollutant is decided,[8] and tradable permits to emit pollution per year amounting in total to that level are initially distributed among firms on the basis of some criterion, e.g. in proportion to the firm's share of total pollutant production in previous years. Firms are allowed to trade the permits, and if some firm produces less pollutant than its permits allow, it can sell the excess permits to other firms, at a price determined by supply and demand. This is like a flexible quota system, which instead of imposing a rigid quota of pollutant to each firm allows more efficient firms to sell the right to emit pollution to less efficient firms. It has two advantages: first, it tends to establish an efficient distribution of pollutant production among firms, because all firms will tend to reach the same marginal cost of pollution avoidance[9]; second, it creates an incentive for firms to find ways to reduce the production of pollutant. In subsequent years the total allowed amount of pollutant can be decreased. Of course for a market for pollution rights to work, a control authority must exist that ascertains how much pollutant each firm produces, which is costly; but Pigou taxes or rigid quotas would require the same cost.

14.3.4 Network Externalities and the Internet

A very important category of externalities is *network effects*. They are particulary relevant in the commercial activities on the Internet, which have deeply changed everyday life in recent decades. The term *network effects* refers to the instances

---

8 Ideally, this total amount should be such as to make the cost of one less unit of total pollutant production equal to the net benefit. But especially the benefit will be inevitably arbitrary to some extent, in fact politically decided. For example, the health costs of long term exposure to certain pollutants are unclear, and furthermore are to a large extent arbitrary, because the economic value of life, or of good health, is inevitably a political decision (another law-and-economics issue!).

9 This was indeed achieved in the example of the steel mill and the fishery when the latter could pay the former to limit pollutant emission; the reader can easily prove that the same result would obtain if the fishery sells pollution rights to the steel mill (which means assuming that all pollution rights have been initially given to the fishery).

1242   **Chapter 14** · Welfare, Externalities, Public Goods and Happiness

when the utility of purchasing a good or service that connects to a network (e.g. a telephone) positively depends on how many other people or firms are connected to the network. (A telephone is useless if no one else has a telephone. Being a member of a social media like Facebook would have little value if it had only very few members with whom to communicate.) It is sometimes described as *demand-side increasing returns*.

A simple model (Rohlfs 1974) nicely grasps some consequences of this dependence of utility of a good or service on how many other people purchase it.

Suppose there is a total number T of potential buyers of the good. Each potential buyer i buys either one or zero units of the good and has reservation price nv_i, where n is the number of buyers who do buy the good, and v_i is different for different buyers. Let us order potential buyers in order of *increasing* v_i, and for simplicity let us assume $v_i = i$ dollars. So the least interested buyer is ready to pay at most n dollars for the good if the known number of buyers is n, the second least interested at most $2n$ dollars, and so on. Suppose the good's price is p. At this price, and if the number of people known to be currently purchasing the good is n, the people actually ready to pay p are those with $nv_i \geq p$, that is, under our simplifying assumption, $ni \geq p$. The *marginal buyer* is the one with the smallest i satisfying this inequality for the given n and p, let us indicate it as $i^*(p, n)$. This means that the number of people ready to pay p, for that n, is $T - i^* + 1$ (check it with some numerical example). As further simplifications (which can be shown not to affect the results), let us assume T is very large, so that it makes only a negligible difference if we forget about the $+1$, and furthermore that for the marginal buyer ni is very close to p. So it is approximately true that $ni^* = p$ and that the number of people ready to pay p is $T - i^*$. This number need not be equal to n, and if not, n will change: if $T - i^* < n$, necessarily some of the n present purchasers of the service are paying for it more than their reservation price, and will abandon the service the moment they become better informed about n, which we can assume will happen in a rather short time. If $T - i^* > n$, some potential buyers have not yet realized that they ought to buy, and we can assume that soon they will. The number of buyers n has no reason to change only when $n = T - i^*$, which, remembering $ni^* = p$, that is $i^* = p/n$, requires $T - p/n = n$. This implies that the value of p associated with an unchanging n is the following function of n:

$$p(n) = nT - n^2.$$

We are interested in p, $n \geq 0$. We obtain a bell-like shape of $p(n)$, that starts at zero for $n = 0$, and has derivative $dp/dn = T - 2n$, hence initially positive, reaching zero when $n = T/2$ (where p reaches its maximum value $p_{max} = T^2/4$), and then turning negative, with p again equal to zero when $nT = n^2$, that is, when $n = T$.[10]

Now suppose the service is supplied at a constant positive marginal and average cost less than p_{max}. Then there are three equilibrium values of n. Two are the

---

10 Exercise: Obtain the same result assuming the index i that distinguishes potential buyers is *decreasing* in v_i rather than increasing.

14.3 · Externalities

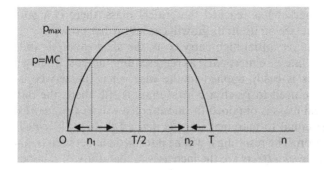

Fig. 14.2 Rohlf's model of demand for a network service. The curve represents $p(n)$

values where $p = MC$; call them n_1 and $n_2 > n_1$. The third is $n = p = 0$ where no one has any incentive to buy and therefore $n = 0$ does not change. Let us ask whether these equilibria are stable.

Stability here is a more complicated issue than in usual partial-equilibrium analysis because there is no standard demand curve, the quantity demanded does not depend only on p but also on n. Actually under our assumptions n can be taken to represent demand since each buyer buys one unit of the service. What we can say is that if the number of buyers is n, it (and hence demand) tends to increase if $p(n) > p$ and to decrease if $p(n) < p$. But we must also specify how p changes.

Let us assume a competitive supply side, with identical firms that gradually increase supply if p is *greater* than MC, and then decrease p when supply becomes greater than demand, i.e. than n. Then p sooner or later will decrease if it is greater than MC, because supply will increase and sooner or later will become greater than n, inducing firms to decrease p; the price decrease sooner or later causes p to become less than $p(n)$, so we have an increase of n. For p initially *less* than MC, in the previous sentence replace 'decrease' with 'increase' and vice-versa, 'greater' with 'less' and vice-versa, and conclude that n will tend to decrease. (It is conceivable that, starting from a situation where $p(n) > p > MC$, n increases and causes $p(n)$ to decrease faster than p, so p becomes equal to or greater than $p(n)$, and n stops increasing; but this is only temporary as long as $p > MC$, because supply keeps increasing so p keeps decreasing.) We can conclude that n tends to increase (decrease) as long as $p(n)$ is greater (less) than MC. This means that the equilibria at $n = 0$ and $n = n_2$ are locally stable, while the equilibrium at $n = n_1$ is unstable; see the arrows in Fig. 14.2.

This means that in order for the service to be bought persistently at a price covering costs, something must cause n to grow beyond n_1; then the market will spontaneously grow to n_2. This is expressed by saying that a ***critical mass*** $n_1 + 1$ of buyers is necessary. This can explain why when a new service with network externalities is offered, often initially it is free, and combined with other attractive offers for at least one segment of the market; a positive price is commercially feasible only when the market reaches the critical mass.

Once the market has reached the critical mass, there is a ***positive feedback effect*** of market size on itself: its growth causes further growth.

If entry requires initial high entry costs, the above analysis still applies if the MC horizontal line is reinterpreted as representing full-cost pricing.

The analysis is easily applied to the case when the service is offered by a monopolist; the need to reach a critical mass is still there, the difference is that once the critical mass is obtained the monopolist will fix price $p(n)$ so as to obtain marginal cost equal to marginal revenue derived from $p(n)$ treated as an inverse demand function. The resulting n will be intermediate between n_2 and T/2.

Indirect network effects are the increases in the utility of a good if more other people purchase it, not because the utility of the good directly depends on how many other people buy the good, rather because of a positive effect of the size of that good's market on the availability of ***complementary goods*** which raise the utility of the first good. A standard example is the attractiveness of an Operating System: to a considerable extent, it depends on how much software produced by other firms is available for it; Microsoft's success over Apple is often explained as largely due to its greater attention to the development of software useful to firms.

Direct and indirect network effects cause so-called ***tippy markets***. When two competing products satisfy the same need, if both enjoy network effects, and are offered by monopolists (e.g. because protected by patents), then the relative utility of the two products depends on the size of their clientele. Suppose the products have the same minimum price capable of covering cost, and that the competition between the two monopolists causes price to tend to this minimum price. There will be a relative size of the two customer groups that makes consumers indifferent between the two products. But if for any reason the relative size of the two customer groups is unbalanced in favour of, say, product one, this pushes some consumers to switch to it, so the relative size changes further in favour of good 1, which becomes even more attractive relative to product 2; the switch of consumers accelerates, sales tip towards product 1, and product 2 tends to be pushed totally out of the market. A classic example is Betamax versus VHS videocassettes, where VHS came totally to dominate once its greater diffusion caused a greater availability of recorded videocassettes.

As the above considerations show, competition among goods with network effects tends to favour the good which acquires the larger group of customers, with a ***winner-takes-all effect***. Once one product comes to dominate the market, entry is nearly impossible.

A very important indirect network effect is due to advertising. Take search engines for example. The more numerous the people using a search engine, the more attractive it is for firms to put ads on it, because more people see the ad. Then the bigger search engine obtains more earnings from advertising than its competitors, and this allows it to buy bigger and faster computers and to improve the quality of its services relative to its competitors, further attracting customers and thus advertising. Again, there is a tendency of the bigger firm further to increase its advantage over competitors.

Similar positive feedbacks due to network effects hold for booking services, or for platforms for selling second-hand goods like eBay. The more hotels one can

14.3 · Externalities

compare on a booking platform, the more the platform is preferred, and then the more hotels must and will appear on that platform. The greater the assortment of second-hand goods available on a goods exchange platform, the more attractive it is to turn to it to place a good or to look for a good, and then the greater the assortment. The push towards a winner-takes-all situation is very strong. The resulting monopolistic platform can ask for high prices for its intermediation. Booking.com asks for even more than 20% of the price obtained by the intermediated hotel.

This is why in ▶ Chap. 12 markets with network effects were listed together with monopolies as exceptions to the great prevalence of entry. Entry is made even more difficult by the tendency of the big incumbent firm to buy out the smaller firms that attempt entry by offering a diversified product; the smaller firm cannot resist. This raises the question how prices are determined for goods and services sold by these monopolistic firms, and what effect this has on income distribution. Not much has been done on these issues yet, but it seems clear that the big Internet firms are very profitable, and their profits are contributing to the increase of the relative income of the top 0.1% of the population.

There are also other aspects of the situation that are cause of worry. Google can practically destroy a firm by not letting it appear among the results of a search for firms in that category; how can we be sure that this power is not being or will not be used for socially undesirable ends? It seems clear that the bargaining power of these megafirms vis-à-vis governments is frightening, questioning the capacity of antitrust authorities really to defend the public interest. The problem concerns not only the dominators of the Internet, but also many other gigantic conglomerates.[11] Some way must be found to strengthen democratic social control on these firms which can take decisions of enormous impact on population (e.g. decisions to relocate plants in another nation), decisions that have no more right to escape the approval of elected political representatives of the nation than government decisions on economic policy. But this is a field not ripe yet for

---

11 'The revenues of large companies often rival those of national governments. In a list combining both corporate and government revenues for 2015, ten companies appear in the largest 30 entities in the world: Walmart (#9), State Grid Corporation of China (#15), China National Petroleum (#15), Sinopec Group (#16), Royal Dutch Shell (#18), Exxon Mobil (#21), Volkswagen (#22), Toyota Motor (#23), Apple (#25), and BP (#27) (Global Justice Now 2016). All ten of these companies had annual revenue higher than the governments of Switzerland, Norway, and Russia in 2015. Indeed, 69 of the largest 100 corporate and government entities ranked by revenues were corporations. In some cases, these large corporations had private security forces that rivalled the best secret services, public relations offices that dwarfed a US presidential campaign headquarters, more lawyers than the US Justice Department, and enough money to capture (through campaign donations, lobbying, and even explicit bribes) a majority of the elected representatives. The only powers these large corporations missed were the power to wage war and the legal power of detaining people, although their political influence was sufficiently large that many would argue that, at least in certain settings, large corporations can exercise those powers by proxy' (Zingales 2017, p. 113).

textbook treatment; if the essential role of conflicting interests at the very root of the determinants of value and distribution will be admitted more generally, this will probably also change the political tolerance towards megafirms.

So, back to the economics of the Internet: it is a developing and important new field, a fertile ground for doctoral dissertations. The problems are many, not all connected with monopolistic elements. For example, certain categories of firms can be discriminated against not because of any conscious intention of the intermediating platform, but because of customer prejudice emerging through customer evaluations: shops owned by blacks or Jews may receive unjustified bad evaluations simply because some customers are racist.

A further cause of worry is the increasing possibility to treat each consumer differently on the basis of the increasing information collected by search engines on her/his tastes, needs, health, purchases, probable spending capacity, etcetera, which can be utilized in tenths of a second. Already now, advertising is tailored to the person visiting a site, on the basis of her/his previous choices (not only on that site - these informations are exchanged across operators). And already now there are some cases of goods offered over the Internet to different customers at different prices, depending on the customer's presumed tastes and spending capacity; the tendency will no doubt spread.

There is clearly room, and need, for extensive public regulation and control.

14.3.5 **The Tragedy of the Commons**

Another case of external effects is, when there is a resource freely available for exploitation by everybody, but such that the output a firm can obtain from a given expenditure on this resource depends (negatively) on how many other firms are exploiting it. In many cases, an added complication is that the resource is a renewable stock consumed by use, so that whether the stock increases or decreases in time depends on how much it is exploited: examples are fish in the sea or in lakes; whales; pasture from grazing fields; wood from forests; game from hunting an animal species. Too great an exploitation of the renewable resource can extinguish it completely.

The renewable resource depletion effect can be very complex to treat formally and requires dynamical models. So let us concentrate on the effect of free access to the resource, assuming its total productive capacity is not depleted. Traffic congestion (increase in the time required to go to places by car) can be taken as an example, as it does not deplete (or almost) the resource 'roads'. We want to understand the effect of the fact that entry of one more firm or agent reduces the output of other firms or agents, an external effect.

A standard example is a village with a free-access vast field where milk-producing cows can pasture. Assume a cow produces an amount of milk that depends on how much grass it eats, which is negatively influenced by the presence of other cows. The price of milk is fixed on the national market and the village takes it as given; milk is measured in units such that its price is 1. The quantity of milk producible by all cows together is $f(n)$ where n is the number of cows graz-

14.3 · Externalities

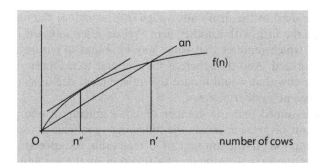

Fig. 14.3 Optimal and free-access number of cows

ing on the common field, with $f'(n) > 0$ and $f''(n) < 0$; $f'(n)$ reaches zero for $n = n^*$, the number of cows that maximizes total milk production. The milk produced by each cow is $f(n)/n$. A cow costs a fixed amount of money α (inclusive of interest charges). Assuming we can treat n and $f(n)$ as approximately continuous because n is large, maximization of the village's net income from milk production requires

$$max_n(f(n) - \alpha n).$$

The first-order condition is marginal value product = marginal cost:

$$f'(n) = \alpha.$$

If n is large, and if households decide independently, they will decide to own one more cow as long as the cow produces more income than it costs, neglecting the effect the extra cow has on the milk production of the other cows, that is, as long as $f(n)/n > \alpha$: if n is large, the extra milk produced by an extra cow is well approximated by average milk production. Then the number of cows will rise until

$$f(n)/n = \alpha,$$

average value product equal to unit cost, at which point no household gains anything from owning cows. In ◘ Fig. 14.3 the number of cows determined by independent choice is n', the number that would maximize the village's income from milk production is n''.

Plausibly (and historical experience confirms it) villagers will realize what is happening and will find ways to avoid it. But a collectively decided reduction of the number of cows from n' to n'' is not easy, because it requires deciding how the income from the n'' cows is to be allocated among the village members: again, as with the Coase Theorem and the night noise case, we see that *reaching efficiency requires solving equity issues* (see Bowles 2004, pp. 28–31). One way is to decide that only some families (the aristocrats?) can have cows. Another is to assign cows by lot and rotation (a rule adopted in some Turkish fishing villages for the allocation of fishing spots). Still another is to allow a single private firm to graze cows on the commons, paying a rent to the village: a single firm internalizes the externalities, profit maximization will induce it to hold the efficient number of cows; but the dependence of the village on this income gives the firm bargaining power,

1248   **Chapter 14** · Welfare, Externalities, Public Goods and Happiness

which might be used to the firm's advantage (e.g. to reduce the rent) if it is not easy to replace the firm with another firm. Yet another solution is to have this firm be public, which requires that some way be found to ensure that efficiency will be really pursued. And then there is the recourse to taxation: as an ***Exercise***, find the tax per cow that would induce the independent decisions of households to reach the efficient number of cows.

The above assumed that the number of cows grazing in one year does not affect the amount of grass available the following year. This is usually too optimistic an assumption. If the amount of a renewable resource (fish, grass, timber…) available one year is an increasing function of the amount surviving the previous year's outtake, there is a danger of the real tragedy of the commons, that consists of the complete disappearance of the resource. Even the private firm can be inefficient if its time horizon is not long enough.[12] But a more precise analysis of these ecological issues would require formalization in terms of dynamical systems, at mathematical levels beyond what this textbook assumes.

14.3.6 Urban Segregation

The next interesting example of externality (Bowles 2004, p. 66) would require dynamical equations for an exhaustive study, but its message can be grasped even without them. It shows that preferences over types of neighbours can result in a differentiation of neighbourhoods stronger than people actually desire.

Consider a single neighbourhood (one of many) called the Valley, where all houses are equally attractive to all members of the population in the broader region. There are two types of households, that we call the greens and the blues. The difference can be skin colour, or religion, or language, or education level, etc. Both greens and blues prefer a mixed neighbourhood to a homogeneous one; but greens like best a neighbourhood with a slight majority of greens living in it; blues like best a slight majority of blues. This difference entails that the price they are ready to pay to live in the Valley[13] depends on the composition of the inhabitants. Let p be the price everybody in the region would be ready to pay to live in the Valley if indifferent to who lives there. Let $f \in [0, 1]$ be the fraction of greens living in the Valley, let $\delta \in (0, 1/2)$ be a small scalar, and let p_g, p_b be the price a green, respectively a blue, is ready to pay to live in the Valley, which depends on f as follows:

$$p_g(f) = p + 1/2(f - \delta) - 1/2(f - \delta)^2$$
$$p_b(f) = p + 1/2(f + \delta) - 1/2(f + \delta)^2.$$

---

12 The inefficiency of non-regulated access to the commons has been used as an argument justifying ex post the enclosures in Great Britain as efficiency-improving. In fact the access to the agricultural commons was generally carefully regulated by custom and village regulations, because the consequences of overexploitation were well understood. But other cases (e.g. fishing, whale hunting) clearly exhibit elements of the tragedy of the commons.

13 You can assume this is the price to rent a house for a year, or that it is the price to buy a house, the analysis holds in both cases; in the first case 'house on sale' will mean 'house for rent'.

14.3 · Externalities

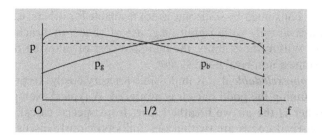

◘ Fig. 14.4 Neighbourhood preferences

For $f=1/2$ it is $p_g = p_b$ (check it). Maximization of p_g shows that it reaches a maximum for $f = 1/2 + \delta$, while p_b reaches a maximum for $f = 1/2 - \delta$; see ◘ Fig. 14.4.

So if $f > 1/2$, it is $p_g > p_b$, while if $f < 1/2$ it is $p_g < p_b$. Now assume that there is a flow of renewal of inhabitants in the Valley, some leaving and selling their house, and some from outside replacing them every year. Assume there is a very high probability that the owner of a house on sale, if only she is a bit patient, will be contacted both by greens and by blues. If $f = 1/2$, the owner will be unable to obtain more than p both from greens and from blues. But if for any reason f is different from 1/2, owners will know that one type is ready to pay more than the other, and will wait for prospective buyers of that type, in order to obtain more than p for the house.[14] The result will be a tendency of new inhabitants to be overwhelmingly of the type already in the majority in the Valley: f will shift towards one extreme. Even when at a certain moment it is $f = 1/2$, any accidental event causing it to increase or decrease a bit will start the process of gravitation towards an entirely green or entirely blue neighbourhood. The reason is the externality consisting of the influence, of previous choices to live in the Valley by different types, on the attractiveness of living there for newcomers. The result is inefficient, because a mixed neighbourhood would be preferred.

14.4 Public Goods[15]

14.4.1 Non-rival Goods and Non-excludable Goods

A good is called **public** if it is **non-rival**, that is, if its consumption by one individual (or firm) does not decrease the quantity consumable by others. Typical examples are (non scrambled) radio or TV emissions; street lighting; national defence.

---

14 The assumption that owners are aware of the situation can be replaced by an assumption that they ignore the situation but do not sell to the first comer and bargain with a few before deciding; if prospective buyers are random, it is possible that the ones contacting a seller are all of the minority type, but it is improbable; the probability is greater than 1/2 that the house will go to a buyer of the type already in the majority in the Valley.

15 It is possible to unify the treatment of externalities and of public goods by interpreting externalities as one type of (partially) public goods, but I will not pursue the topic here, see Winch (1971, pp. 117–131).

1250   **Chapter 14** · Welfare, Externalities, Public Goods and Happiness

A *rival* good, if consumed by someone, is not available for others: e.g. food. Some goods are non-rival only within limits, e.g. use of roads, of beaches, enjoyment of panoramas. Within these limits, the marginal cost of allowing one more consumer to consume a non-rival good is zero.

A good is **non-excludable** if it is impossible (or very costly) to prevent individuals from consuming the good once it is produced. A typical example is national defence. Another is the air we breathe (apart from special cases). Examples of excludable non-rival goods are (within the limits previously discussed) access to motorways, beaches, bridges; scrambled TV emissions; even football games (if the stadium is only partly filled up).

A *pure public* good is non-rival and non-excludable. This definition is very strict. A less strict definition of public good is a good 'for which use of a unit of the good by one agent does not preclude its use by other agents' (Mas-Colell et al. p. 359). With this definition, the public good can be excludable. Also, it may be a public good only up to a certain level of consumption, beyond which it ceases being enjoyable by further consumers because of congestion (think of roads).

Exercise: Compile a table with two rows: rival and non-rival goods; and two columns: excludable and non-excludable goods. Fill each box with at least four entries. In the upper left box you will have pure private goods. In the lower right box you will have pure public goods. The other two boxes are the most interesting ones.

A further interesting characteristic of public goods is whether they are *optional*, that is, whether an agent can decide how much of the public good to consume. Free radio transmissions are optional; national defence and public street lighting are not.

Separate individual choices in the market will seldom bring about the socially optimal amount of a public good, because the single individual who must decide whether and how much to buy of a public good has no incentive to take into account the positive externality, the fact that the good will be enjoyed (and for free) by other people too. Collective decision making, on the other hand, can raise difficulties.

14.4.2 When to Get an Indivisible Public Goods

Let us first discuss the case of an indivisible public good. A simple example can be the purchase of an air conditioning outfit by the graduate students who share an apartment. One outfit suffices for the entire apartment. It costs $1000. A *necessary* condition for a Pareto improvement to be *possible* is that the sum of the reservation prices of the students for the outfit be greater than $1000.

Proof   Remember that a consumer's reservation price for a good is the maximum amount one is ready to pay for the good rather than go without it: utility is the same without the good, or with the good and the payment of the reservation price. So if the air conditioner is made available and all students pay their reservation prices, each one of them is as well off as before; if the sum of the payments

14.4 · Public Goods

is greater than $1000, the excess can be redistributed to them (e.g. in equal parts), making them all better off, and therefore producing a strict Pareto improvement. If the sum of reservation prices is less than $1000, the purchase causes at least one student's utility to decrease. ■

But that a Pareto improvement is possible does not guarantee that it will be realized. Assume two students, A and B, share the apartment. Both have a reservation price of $600. Assume that at least a minimal utility increase must result for both students for the air conditioner to be bought, and that 1$ is the minimal money unit. Then any distribution of the $1000 expense between the two students that charges student A between 599 and 401 dollars ensures the purchase. So we have a hawk–dove (or chicken) game situation, in which each student has convenience to insist that she does not value the air conditioner more than $401, hoping to persuade the other student to contribute $599. Each student has an incentive to lie about her/his reservation price; there may result a waste of energies and time, a worsened social life in the apartment, and possibly no purchase. We see again that reaching efficiency requires solving equity issues.

If each student's reservation price is *greater* than $1000, each one can even try to be a free rider, denying any interest in the purchase, hoping to induce the other to pay the entire price: the hawk–dove element is even more evident. A *free rider* is a person who enjoys a public good while contributing nothing to its cost. The name comes from bus (or train) riders who don't pay the ticket. It is often the case that if no bus rider pays the ticket, the bus company goes bust and the free riders are worse off than if they had paid the ticket; but as long as many people do pay the ticket, the incentive to be a free rider is strong. One solution is to make buying the ticket obligatory and fines for the free riders nearly certain, but this requires resources to enforce the obligation.

14.4.3 What Quantity of a Divisible Public Good?

Now let us consider a non-optional public good whose quantity G is variable. Taking prices as given, let us ask what is the locally efficient amount of the good, leaving aside the macro effects of its production. I also leave aside income effects by assuming quasi-linear utilities, $u_i(x, G) = x_i + v_i(G)$ where x_i is the residual income of consumer i, spendable on private consumption goods (remember that with this utility function the marginal utility of money is 1, and the marginal utility of G is also the maximum amount of money one is ready to pay for the marginal unit of G). The public good is produced at a cost $C(G)$, with non-decreasing marginal cost $MC(G)$, and—assuming the public good cannot be financed by increases of public debt[16]—this cost must be covered by contributions (voluntary or through taxation) from the given incomes m_s of the S consumers involved ($s = 1, ..., S$).

---

16 This is the usual assumption, followed here in order to acquaint the reader with the standard analysis of public goods; but it is a highly debatable assumption; in a classical–Keynesian approach, deficit spending can be a very good policy.

1252   **Chapter 14 · Welfare, Externalities, Public Goods and Happiness**

Each consumer obtains from one more (small) unit of the public good a utility improvement equal to $v_i'(G)$, so this is the maximum amount she/he is ready to pay for that extra unit of G: we can call it *marginal reservation price* or *marginal willingness to pay* or also *marginal benefit*. For one more (small) unit of G the sum of the marginal reservation prices of the S interested consumers is $\sum_s v_s'(G)$. If

$$\sum_s v_s'(G) > MC(G),$$

then it is possible to cover the cost of the extra unit of G by having each consumer contribute less than her/his marginal reservation price, thus obtaining a Pareto improvement. If the inequality is in the opposite direction, G is too big and a Pareto improvement can be achieved by reducing it together with an opportune reduction of the contributions. Assuming the marginal utility of G is decreasing and the marginal cost of G is non-decreasing, absence of a possibility of Pareto improvement requires a level G^* of the public good satisfying

$$\sum_s v_s'(G^*) = MC(G^*),$$

which is therefore a necessary condition for local Pareto efficiency[17]: the marginal cost of the public good must equal the sum of the marginal willingnesses to pay of all consumers who benefit from the public good. (Of course this neglects the possible effect of a variation of G on employment, if the variation of G is part of a fiscal policy that alters aggregate demand.)

Note that the efficient level of G is uniquely determined, but not what each consumer must pay for it: the total cost of G^* can be distributed among consumers in any way that leaves each one with a non-negative consumer surplus; all such distributions will be weakly Pareto efficient. (For each given level of G, the situation—apart from the number of participants—is similar to that of the two students and air conditioning; the difference is that here G is variable, accordingly the reservation price of each consumer is variable, and furthermore we can determine the level G^* beyond which no further Pareto improvement is possible.) This indeterminateness is not due to quasi-linear utility, with any standard utility function the existence of G units of the public good yields a discrete utility increase (relative to $G=0$) for each involved consumer, and hence a positive maximum

---

17 But not a sufficient one, because it might be that the *total* willingness to pay for G^* (the sum of the maximum payments the consumers would be ready to pay rather than do without that amount of public good) is insufficient to cover the total cost of G^*. The production of the public good can nevertheless be convenient if, e.g. by being financed by money creation by the Central Bank, its production allows the utilization of resources that would otherwise remain unemployed. The considerations in the text implicitly assume that the resources needed for the production of the public good must be subtracted from other uses (the cost of G must be covered by contributions that mean less expenditure on other goods), an assumption deriving from the neoclassical thesis that the economy is normally fully utilizing its resources. A non-neoclassical approach will consider the standard analysis justified only when a trade-off does exist between more of the public good and more of other goods; which will often not be the case, in the presence of unemployment.

14.4 · Public Goods

willingness of each consumer to pay for that amount of public good rather than go completely without it (this maximum willingness to pay must not be confused with the *marginal* willingness to pay for one more unit of G); a Pareto improvement is possible when the sum of these maximum willingnesses to pay is greater than the cost of G, but the distribution of that cost among the individuals is indeterminate within limits. We obtain confirmation that there is always an equity issue involved in deciding who should pay for a public good.

The locally efficient level of G thus determined is not what independent individual purchases of the public good will tend to establish. Suppose each dweller in a street can contribute to night lighting of the street by setting up street lamps privately paid for, that cause a constant cost p per lamp per period. Let G be the total number of lamps in the street. Consumer s will decide to contribute one more street lamp if the (average and marginal) cost p does not exceed the private marginal benefit $v_s'(G)$ from more night lighting. Assuming we concede sufficient time for the number of lamps maintained by each inhabitant to be increased or decreased after looking at how many lamps are maintained by the other street inhabitants, in the final situation each consumer s does not wish to alter the number of street lamps if $v_s'(G)=p$. This means a smaller G than the efficient one, which requires $\Sigma_s v_s'(G)=p$. The reason for the inefficiency is that each consumer looks only at the advantage she/he derives from one more street lamp, neglecting the advantage for the other inhabitants, which, if monetized and paid to the first consumer, would reduce the cost of one more street lamp for her/him below p. It is again a case of neglected external effects. Of course community spirit might correct for this, but when the number of individuals involved is large, it is unlikely.

In fact, one should expect *free riding* to be rather common in such a situation, and even more so owing to our assumption of quasi-linear utility. Suppose all inhabitants have the same utility function. Then at each level of G they all have the same incentive to add to or subtract from the number of lamps, and then each one has an incentive to wait for the others to add one more lamp, or to rush to be the first to shut down a lamp. If at all levels of G the S inhabitants can be ordered in the same ascending order of marginal benefit, that is if a way of assigning indices $h_1, h_2, \dots h_S$ to them exists such that for all levels of G it is always $v_{h1}'(G)<v_{h2}'(G)<\cdots<v_{hS}'(G)$, then at the level of G at which $v_{hS}'(G)$ is barely greater than p while $v_{hS}'(G+1)<p$, no other consumer except h_S will want to maintain a lamp, consumer h_S will pay for all lamps, and all other consumers will be free riders.[18]

The inefficiency of private individual provision[19] can be corrected to some extent by public intervention. National defence, or law and order, clearly require

---

18 If marginal benefit is an increasing function of income, this means that the richest inhabitant pays for all lamps. This may be found pleasant if one dislikes income inequalities, but it must be remembered that the number of lamps remains inefficiently low.

19 Sometimes non-rival but excludable goods (which we have classified among the public goods) can be made available only on payment of a fee, and then can be provided by private firms, for example TV transmissions can be scrambled and decoders can be rented out by the TV company. Access to golf courses or to swimming pools (up to congestion limits) can be analogously considered a non-rival excludable good, for which one may have to pay; these goods are often obtainable by joining a private club, for which reason they are also called *club goods*.

1254   **Chapter 14 · Welfare, Externalities, Public Goods and Happiness**

the state to provide them; but some public agency is also required for the maintenance of streets, bridges, etc., and importantly, for controls on the quality of buildings, of food, of professional services, etc. But for efficiency to be at least approximated the public agency should know, at least approximately, the marginal willingness to pay of consumers. For most public goods, consumers should be much better informed about the effects of changes in order to form a reasonably clear marginal willingness to pay (or total willingness to pay, for indivisible public goods). Politicians seem to have very little desire to ascertain marginal (or, if more appropriate, total) willingnesses to pay; they have other criteria, for example, likelihood to get votes, for their decisions. Actually, often there may be excellent practical reasons for not attempting to ascertain the sum of the marginal or total willingnesses to pay: consider for example, in Italy, the project of the Messina Strait Bridge that should connect Sicily and Calabria: if realized, it would change transport costs for thousands of commodities and persons, causing price changes that would affect millions of citizens; furthermore, its construction would affect for years the welfare of the two hundred thousand people living on the two sides of the Strait, some of them suffering from the construction works, others obtaining an income increase from the new demand for labour and materials, but it would be impossible to specify with any precision how each person would be affected. Cost–benefit analysis (to be discussed below) attempts a more macro, aggregative evaluation, which has its drawbacks, but is useful if honestly performed—but politicians usually have other interests, and try to avoid impartial cost–benefit analyses that might render it more difficult to pursue their preferred policies.

14.4.4 Lindahl Equilibrium

One way to discover, in principle, the efficient amount of a public good without assuming omniscience on the part of the government was suggested by the Swedish economist Erik Lindahl and is called the *Lindahl process*. Assume a public agency presents each household s with the cost function of the public good $C(G)$ and with the proportion α_s of the public good's cost she/he will have to pay once its quantity G is decided, and the household *truthfully* indicates the level G_s of public good output she would prefer at that α_s. Assume the household's (quasi-linear) utility is $u_s = x_s + v_s(G)$, where $x_s = m_s - \alpha_s C(G)$, and m_s is the household's wealth or income endowment. So we can write

$$u_s = m_s - \alpha_s C(G_s) + v_s(G_s)$$

and its maximization with respect to G_s yields the G demanded by household s as solution to

$$v_s'(G_s) = \alpha_s MC(G_s).$$

The public agency is assumed to choose the α_s's so that $\Sigma_s \alpha_s = 1$. If all households agree on the same level G^* we obtain $\Sigma_s v_s'(G^*) = MC(G^*)$, the efficiency condition, and the cost of G^* is perfectly covered by the contributions. If the households indicate different levels of G, then the public agency raises α_s for the households which indicate a G_s greater than the average $(\Sigma_s G_s)/S$, and reduces it for the other ones, and iterates the procedure. The arbitrariness in the initial assignment of the α_s's disappears as this tâtonnement brings each α_s to become the one that induces household s to desire the same $G_s = G^*$ as everybody else. It is as if $\alpha_s MC(G_s)$ were the price of the personalized good «consumption of the public good by household s», whose α_s component changes according to the 'excess demand' $G_s - (\Sigma_s G_s)/S$.

Unfortunately the Lindahl equilibrium suffers from two drawbacks. The first is the concrete difficulty of carrying out the required 'tâtonnement' if the involved households are many. The second is that the Lindahl process requires truthful revelation of the G_s's, while it is convenient for a consumer to *misrepresent* preferences (if the other individuals are truthful), understating her demand for G and thus her $v_s'(G)$ curve, since for any G^* the α_s charged her is the higher, the greater the $v_s'(G^*)$ implied by the household's reported demand curve for G. There is thus an incentive to free ride: if consumer s always indicates $G_s = 0$ whatever is her α_s, then α_s goes to zero. If everybody free rides in this way, then $G^* = 0$, which is far from efficient; perhaps this may induce some consumers to reconsider and lie less, but the incentive to underreport G_s is always there, and will prevent the achievement of efficiency.

14.5 The Groves–Clarke Mechanism

If utility functions are quasi-linear, a truthful revelation of preferences for a public good can be obtained via an ingenious 'mechanism', resulting from the contributions of the two economists mentioned in the title of the section, and called the Groves–Clarke or also Vickrey–Clarke–Groves mechanism (some elements of it were anticipated by Vickrey 1961). Here only a simple introduction will be supplied. The approach assumes quasi-linear utilities of households. Again I adopt a partial-equilibrium perspective, with given prices.

Suppose a central authority (not necessarily the government, it could be the administrator of a condominium, because the builiding requires repainting) wants to decide whether to realize a public project whose total cost is C.

There are S households affected by this project, with quasi-linear utilities $u^s = x^s + v^s \gamma$, where x^s is residual income, γ takes value 0 if the project is not realized and value 1 if the project is realized, and v^s indicates the increase in the household's utility if the project is realized. Owing to quasi-linear utility, v^s is also the household's maximum willingness to pay, measured in money, for the realization of the project. The household may well lie about v^s. If the central authority is able to ascertain the sum of the willingnesses to pay it can verify whether it exceeds the cost of the project, and proceed with the project if that is the case. (So this is an example of cost–benefit analysis; see ▶ Sect. 14.12.)

The mechanism works as follows. The central authority communicates to each household s a sum z^s to pay if the project is realized and asks the household to declare a sum y^s it is willing to contribute, under the following condition:

*'If $\Sigma_s y^s \geq C$, the project will go ahead (i.e. $\gamma = 1$), and household s will have to pay the given sum z^s decided in advance by the authority minus, in case household s is a **pivot** [term to be explained presently], a sum D^s defined as follows:*

$$D^s := \Sigma_{j \neq s}\left(y^j - z^j\right).$$

The z^s's are chosen such that $\Sigma_s z^s = C$.

If $\Sigma_s y^s < C$, the project does not go ahead ($\gamma = 0$), and the household pays nothing if it is not a pivot, or pays D^s if it is a pivot'.

Definition of pivot: Once the intentions to contribute y^j, $j = 1$, ..., S, have been declared, the sign of $\Sigma_j y^j - C = \sum_{j=1}^{S}(y^j - z^j)$ determines, if non-negative, that the project is approved, i.e. $\gamma = 1$; otherwise $\gamma = 0$. Suppose that taking out household s from this sum, which therefore changes to $\Sigma_{j \neq s}(y^j - z^j)$, changes the sign of the sum from non-negative to negative or vice-versa;[20] that is, suppose that $\sum_{j=1}^{S}(y^j - z^j)$ and D^s have opposite sign. This means that, given the other declared intentions to contribute, household s is crucial in determining whether the project goes ahead or not. Then household s is **pivotal**, or a **pivot**.

A household can be a pivot either because with it $\gamma = 1$ and without it $\gamma = 0$ (a *positive* pivot), or because with it $\gamma = 0$ and without it $\gamma = 1$ (a *negative* pivot). In the latter case the declared intentions of the S–1 households with indices $j \neq s$ would suffice to get the project started, $D^s > 0$, but y^s is so much less than z^s that the result is reversed. Conversely, if household s is a positive pivot, it causes the project to go ahead while without its excess of y^s over z^s the project would not be approved.

In both cases the presence of pivotal household s causes the other households to be, in total, worse off than if household s had not been there (prove it), and the payment by household s of $D^s > 0$ if a negative pivot, and of $-D^s$ (again > 0—make sure you are clear as to why) if a positive pivot, is a penalty corresponding to the sum of the utility losses it causes the other households if these are truthful. Indeed if household s is a negative pivot and $v^j = y^j$, then $y^j - z^j$ is the utility variation household $j \neq s$ misses if the project does not go ahead: then $D^s > 0$ is the sum of the missed utility variations of all other households due to $\gamma = 0$. If household s is a positive pivot, it is $D^s < 0$, on balance the households other than s would prefer the project not to be approved, and household s pays $-D^s$ as a penalty. To summarize, household s will pay:

$z^s \qquad$ if $\gamma = 1$ and s is not a pivot
$z^s - D^s$ if $\gamma = 1$ and s is a (positive) pivot (then $D^s < 0$)
$0 \qquad$ if $\gamma = 0$ and s is not a pivot
$D^s \qquad$ if $\gamma = 0$ and s is a (negative) pivot (then $D^s > 0$).

The interesting thing is that *with the Groves–Clarke mechanism, truth telling is a (weakly) dominant strategy for the households.*

---

20 Note that the choice of the payments z^j can influence whether there are pivots, and which ones.

14.5 · The Groves–Clarke Mechanism

Proof Consider household s. Suppose initially

$$v^s - z^s + D^s = v^s - z^s + \Sigma_{j \neq s}\left(\gamma^j - z^j\right) \geq 0. \tag{14.6}$$

Then if household s declares $y^s \geq v^s$ this implies $\Sigma_j y^j \geq C$, hence $\gamma = 1$; if $v^s \geq z^s$ it is (weakly) preferable for s to declare $y^s \geq v^s$, so as to get the project approved and obtain a non-negative surplus (note that a declaration $y^s > v^s$ is not truthful but does not alter γ relative to $y^s = v^s$, so it does not damage the central authority's decision; but it brings no advantage to s relative to declaring $y^s = v^s$); and if $v^s < z^s$, household s would prefer $\gamma = 0$, but to declare $y^s < v^s$ is not convenient: either it has no effect on γ, or it causes $y^s - z^s + D^s < 0$ and $\gamma = 0$, in which case s is a negative pivot and must pay the penalty D^s which as (14.6) indicates, is (weakly) *greater* than the loss $z^s - v^s$ suffered if $\gamma = 1$.

Conversely, suppose $v^s - z^s + D^s < 0$. Then to declare $y^s \leq v^s$ implies $\Sigma_j y^j < C$, hence $\gamma = 0$; if $v^s < z^s$ it is convenient to declare $y^s \leq v^s$ (and to declare $y^s < v^s$ brings no improvement relative to $y^s = v^s$); and if $v^s > z^s$, household s would prefer $\gamma = 1$ but to declare $y^s > v^s$ is not convenient, the reader can complete the reasoning which is symmetrical to the one in case (14.6).

Thus not to tell the truth either reduces utility or leaves utility unaltered relative to truth telling, $y^s = v^s$: the latter is a (weakly) dominant strategy. ∎

Note that a truth-telling household who comes out to be a pivot and hence to have to pay a penalty does not wish that the opposite γ had come out and had saved her the need to pay the penalty. Suppose, to start with, that $\gamma = 1$ and household s is a positive pivot. Then $y^s - z^s + D^s = v^s - z^s + D^s \geq 0$, a possibly positive surplus, weakly preferable to $\gamma = 0$ that implies zero surplus. If $\gamma = 0$ and household s is a negative pivot, it is $v^s - z^s + D^s < 0$ and the household pays a penalty $D^s < z^s - v^s$, that is, the penalty is smaller than the loss the household would suffer if it were $\gamma = 1$. (I am assuming no free riding.)

A limitation of the Groves–Clarke mechanism is that what the individuals have to pay is generally greater than the sum of willingnesses to pay, hence greater than C: if there is one or more pivots, these pay a penalty in excess of the cost of the public good; this is particularly evident when the cost is zero because $\gamma = 0$ and the project is not implemented, and yet pivots pay a penalty. This penalty cannot be redistributed to the participants according to some prespecified rule, it would change their optimization and affect their choices. I cannot see this as a relevant deficiency of the mechanism: generally the excess payment will be small relative to C and it will be just one more small entry in the state's vast budget, contributing to some useful expense elsewhere with no clear connection with the decisions of the participants to Groves–Clarke mechanism.

Still, the Pareto efficiency condition is not rigorously respected; so theoreticians have looked for completions of the mechanism that allow the excess payment to return to the individuals involved in a way that saves the incentive to truth telling. Some completions have been found that maintain truth telling as part of a Bayes–Nash equilibrium (that is, if everybody else tells the truth then an individual cannot obtain more by lying than by telling the truth), but they no longer guarantee that truth telling is a (weakly) dominant strategy. I omit a discussion of the issue, it would be long and complex (see Jehle and Reny 2011, pp. 466–484).

Unfortunately the highly ingenious Groves–Clarke mechanism has other weaknesses too. First, there must be some criterion, for assigning the contributions z^s, that does not cause protests and litigations that would raise the cost of the project. Second, the mechanism is restricted to quasi-linear utility and therefore to projects that require only very small contributions relative to the incomes of participants. Third, at least for decisions about public projects the mechanism appears hardly realizable in practice, given the difficulty of finding out and reaching all the very many people touched by a public project: for example, who is *not* affected by a new motorway?

This mechanism has been presented here above all because capable of supplying some flavour of the general discipline of which it is part, **mechanism design**, that studies how to devise games with rules that induce participants to behave in a certain way desired by the designer, and can therefore be seen as 'mechanisms' producing a certain output. The search for general principles of mechanism design has been given great impetus in recent decades by the search for **revenue maximizing mechanisms**, a search stimulated by the sales (often via auctions) of radio frequencies, TV channel frequencies, advertising time on these channels, advertising inside Internet pages—sales where enormous sums are involved. This is an exciting field where apparently abstract theory (including most of auction theory) comes out to be very useful for issues of great concreteness. But the stakes are so big that both the theory and the cumulated empirical experience deserve a much more complete treatment than possible here, so the reader is invited to turn to specialist treatises—or specialist courses.

14.6 The Fundamental Theorems of Welfare Economics

14.6.1 Does Competition Produce Pareto Efficiency?

Now let us suppose absence of externalities and of public goods and let us discuss, in more general and rigorous terms than in ▶ Chap. 3, the traditional neoclassical claim that *a competitive market economy **produces** a Pareto-efficient allocation*.

This verb 'produces' requires comment. The formal result on which the claim is based, the *First Fundamental Theorem of Welfare Economics*, states that (under absence of externalities and of public goods) general competitive equilibria as defined by neoclassical theory *are* Pareto efficient. To pass from this to the claim that competitive markets *produce* Pareto-efficient allocations implies the claim that competitive markets do bring about a general equilibrium or a situation that closely approximates it. General equilibrium specialists usually hesitate to advance such a claim when asked about the descriptive, predictive capacities of general equilibria, and propose general equilibria as only idealized situations, 'benchmarks'. But when it comes to the theorems of welfare economics these cau-

14.6 · The Fundamental Theorems of Welfare Economics

tions are dropped, and understandably so: unless a competitive general equilibrium is what markets actually realize (or at least get quite close to realizing), one can only claim Pareto efficiency for an ideal benchmark, with no implication for the efficiency of actual economies. So one reads in popular textbooks: 'a competitive market system will give efficient allocations' (Varian 1992, p. 335); 'The first fundamental theorem of welfare economics states conditions under which ... any Walrasian equilibrium is a Pareto optimum. For competitive market economies, it provides a formal and very general confirmation of Adam Smith's asserted 'invisible hand' property of the market' (Mas-Colell et al. 1995, p. 549). The second sentence in the latter quotation implies that in a competitive market economy the working of markets, as if guided by an 'invisible hand', *brings about* a 'Walrasian equilibrium' under 'very general' conditions.[21] But on what basis can the authors of this prestigious textbook feel authorized to advance such a claim?

They admit that the Walrasian tâtonnement is unrealistic, and that anyway its stability is far from guaranteed. Furthermore they cannot ignore that nowadays the 'Walrasian equilibrium' of economies with capital goods can only be an intertemporal general equilibrium[22]; and it cannot have escaped them that, as noted in ▶ Chap. 8, the *definition* itself of such a 'Walrasian equilibrium' requires that there be either complete futures markets or perfect foresight. But then they must be aware that an actual economy cannot possibly attain, or gravitate towards, a 'Walrasian equilibrium' because the latter is impossible even to *define* for actual economies, which have neither complete futures markets nor perfect foresight; and something impossible to define does not exist. There is no 'Walrasian equilibrium' of an actual economy.

Then how can one make sense of the claim that competitive economies *produce* Pareto efficiency? I suggest that we need here the same interpretation advanced in Chap. 8, ▶ Sect. 8.18. When arguing the capacity of competitive markets to *bring about* Pareto efficiency, neoclassical theorists must have in mind a notion of *persistent* equilibrium approached by time-consuming trial-and-error adjustments. This notion can only be the traditional long-period equilibrium, with labour–land and 'capital' as factors, believed to describe the *average* state of an economy always in disequilibrium to some extent. The notion of Pareto efficiency is implicity referred to *this* notion of equilibrium, with no claim of perfect Pareto

---

21 Adam Smith's occasional statements that the market produces co-ordination 'as if by an invisible hand' cannot be interpreted as meaning that Smith thought that a competitive market economy produces a 'Walrasian equilibrium'. Adam Smith never thought of a decreasing demand curve for labour, and never claimed that the market economy produces the full employment of labour (cf. ▶ Chap. 1, fn. 13); nor did he claim the optimality of the results of markets, even apart from this issue; one can remember for example his observations on the negative effect of the division of labour on the intelligence of workers, more and more obliged to repetitive monotonous jobs that dull their intelligence. As his theory of wages clearly shows, he was internal to the surplus approach.

22 ▶ Chapter 8 noted that temporary equilibrium theory seems to have been abandoned as a research programme, and indeed Mas-Colell et al. do not mention it. Anyway, situations in which decisions are taken on the basis of expectations that will generally come out to be mistaken have little possible claim to Pareto efficiency.

1260   **Chapter 14** · Welfare, Externalities, Public Goods and Happiness

efficiency of the actual economy at each instant, but only of a good approximation to Pareto efficiency on average. There seems to be no other way to justify the claims advanced by welfare economics. For example we will see below that otherwise the Second Fundamental Theorem makes no sense. So we find here again the contradiction of modern neoclassical theory, whose applications presuppose a persistent equilibrium and time-consuming adjustments, in contradiction with the reformulations to which general equilibrium theory has been compelled.

14.6.2 The First Fundamental Theorem

The *First Fundamental Theorem of Welfare Economics* states that all competitive equilibria are Pareto efficient (in the absence of externalities and public goods). The *Second Fundamental Theorem* states that (in the absence of externalities and public goods) if preferences and production possibility sets are convex and no consumer's income (or wealth) is zero,[23] then all Pareto-efficient allocations can be supported as *equilibria* (*possibly with transfers*). We must define this last notion.

An *equilibrium with transfers* is an equilibrium in which each consumer s has at her disposal an income or wealth possibly different from the value of her endowments because each consumer s is assigned, through personalized lump-sum transfers[24] of purchasing power (taxes or subsidies), a wealth level W^s (in terms of the chosen numéraire). Each consumer maximizes her utility under the budget constraint $px^s = W^s$, and the sum of these wealth levels equals the value of the aggregate endowment:

$$\Sigma_s W^s = \mathbf{p}\boldsymbol{\omega}. \tag{14.7}$$

The theorem means that if for equity reasons it is found that the income distribution resulting from the given property distribution of endowments and the (neoclassical) working of competitive markets is not acceptable, then a series of lump-sum taxes, coupled with allowing the market to allocate resources, can correct the excessive inequalities and take the economy to an acceptable and efficient allocation.

By the way, why must wealth transfers be lump-sum taxes and subsidies in order to achieve Pareto efficiency? Taxes such that the tax burden is influenced by the choices of agents are *distortionary*, i.e. prevent the attainment of the equality between the marginal rates of substitution of different agents between the same couple of goods, a necessary condition for Pareto efficiency.

---

23   This last condition is needed to ensure that an equilibrium exists, avoiding the minimum-income problem (see ▶ Chap. 6).

24   A lump-sum *transfer* is the single taking away of part of a person's (or firm's) wealth, or the repeated taking away of a definite sum out of her periodic income, which is then given to another person, with the size of the transfer *independent of the choices of these two persons*. A lump-sum *tax* is a lump-sum transfer from a person or firm to the state; a lump-sum transfer can be seen as the combination of a lump-sum tax and a lump-sum subsidy. They do not introduce a wedge between pre-tax and post-tax price of commodities or factors, and thus avoid different individuals perceiving different prices for the same good, which would cause the rates of substitution between goods to differ among agents, against the requirements of efficient allocations.

14.6 · The Fundamental Theorems of Welfare Economics

One example may suffice. Consider a neoclassical exchange economy with two consumers and two goods, representable via an Edgeworth box as in ◻ Fig. 14.5. Assume smooth convex indifference curves and absence of corner solutions in consumer choices (e.g. Cobb–Douglas preferences). Assume in this economy there is a proportional income tax at rate t, which is then redistributed in equal shares to both consumers. Suppose that for each consumer the income on which the tax is applied is the value of the *net* or *excess* supply of the good of which the consumer is a net supplier. Assume that in the final equilibrium consumer A is a net supplier of good 1, and consumer B of good 2; then the equilibrium quantities are to the north-west of the endowment point, consumer A pays a tax equal to $tp_1(\omega_1^A - x_1^A)$ and consumer B a tax equal to $tp_2(\omega_2^B - x_2^B)$. The total tax revenue is equally divided among the two consumers; the budget constraint for consumer A is

$$p_1 x_1^A + p_2 x_2^A = p_1 \omega_1^A + p_2 \omega_2^A - tp_1(\omega_1^A - x_1^A) + (t/2)[p_1(\omega_1^A - x_1^A) + p_2(\omega_2^B - x_2^B)]$$

which implies that the budget line has slope $-(1-t/2)p_1/p_2$, hence is *less* steep than if $t=0$, and passes *above* the endowment point (if it were $x_1^A = \omega_1^A$, consumer A would pay no tax but would receive one half of the tax paid by consumer B, positive by assumption, hence $x_2^A > \omega_2^A$ when $x_1^A = \omega_1^A$). For consumer B, the same thing holds, hence *from his/her point of view* the budget line is again less steep than if $t=0$ and passes above the endowment point (hence it is steeper, and passes *below* the endowment point, in the Edgeworth box where B's axes are upside down). The two budget lines do not have the same slope, hence any allocation sustainable by prices will be a point where the indifference curves are not tangent to each other, and therefore not Pareto efficient, e.g. point x in ◻ Fig. 14.5.

Unfortunately in many cases taxes cannot be lump-sum taxes. Take the case of differently talented individuals whose (neoclassically determined) income derives only from their work. If one assumes they own no land nor capital, they can only pay taxes as a yearly payment out of their labour income. Suppose universally shared equity considerations suggest that the more fortunate individuals should pay more taxes than the unlucky ones. The yearly tax assigned to each individual can still be lump-sum, i.e. fixed once and for all independently of their possibly fluctuating income. But how can the government know in advance who is more and who is less talented? Only observation of market outcomes can show it, and since market outcomes do not remain constant, it may be inevitable periodically to revise the lump-sum tax. But then individuals will know that the tax is in fact influenced by their income, and this will influence their choice between labour and leisure: the tax is not lump-sum. Indeed it seems to be a majority opinion that there is no such thing as a truly lump-sum tax.[25]

---

25 This is sometimes called the *First Rule of Public Finance*, widely accepted among public finance economists. There is a literature on how to minimize the distortions caused by non-lump-sum taxation when lump-sum taxation is not available, that goes under the name of *optimal taxation*; its framework is general equilibrium, and furthermore it assumes knowledge of the shape of individual demand functions. If interested, look at Varian (1992, p. 410), Cowell (2006, p. 466).

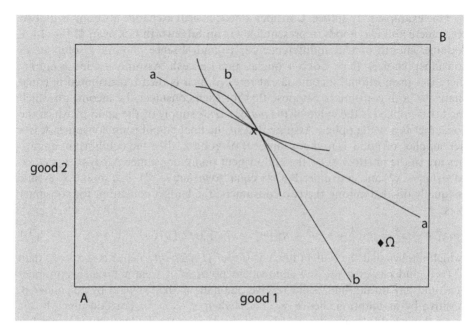

Fig. 14.5 Effect of income tax in an Edgeworth box. The endowment point is Ω; an income tax on the value of positive excess supplies, redistributed to consumers in equal parts, has the effect of shifting the budget constraint of consumer A in the way indicated by line aa, and the budget constraint of consumer B in the way indicated by line bb (see the text for the proof). When an equilibrium is found in point x, the indifference curves are not tangent to each other, hence x is not Pareto efficient

Of course, since equilibrium prices are not known in advance, the calculation *in advance of the establishment of equilibrium* of the lump-sum taxes and subsidies required for the desired vector of household incomes is impossible, it can only be achieved by repeated trial and error. This is particularly true for the production economy, where a redistribution of endowments does not indicate the new incomes of consumers until equilibrium prices are reached.[26] The equilibrium must be persistent (and indeed it was conceived as persistent when the first and second theorems of welfare economics were first formulated).

Since the First Theorem *assumes* an equilibrium to exist, it does not need assumptions that *guarantee* its existence. The sole assumption needed is local non-satiation. The reason is made clear by thinking of an Edgeworth box: without local non-satiation, indifference curves might be 'thick' strips, and then there might be an equilibrium where one consumer is in the interior of a strip, while on one of the edges of the strip the other consumer would be better off (draw the figure!). On the contrary, the Second Theorem needs that an equilibrium exists, and for this reason the minimum-income problem must be assumed not to arise (see below); furthermore it needs convexity for the reason shown in ◘ Fig. 3.17 in ▶ Chap. 3.

---

26 Again, we see that an equilibrium with transfers must be persistent in order to be useful.

14.6 · The Fundamental Theorems of Welfare Economics

I come to more formal statements.

Definition of exchange equilibrium. *An exchange equilibrium is an allocation and a price vector* $(x, p) = (x^1, .., x^s, .., x^S; p)$ *such that:*
(a) *the allocation is feasible,* $\Sigma_s x^s \leq \Sigma_s \omega^s$;
(b) x^s *is maximal for consumer s within her budget set, i.e. if* y^s *is strictly preferred by consumer s to* x^s, *then* $py^s > p\omega^s$.

T14.1. First fundamental theorem of welfare economics for exchange economies: *If* (x, p) *is an exchange equilibrium and preferences are locally non-satiated, then it is Pareto efficient.*

Proof Suppose not; suppose that there is an allocation y, feasible and which Pareto dominates x. Then there is at least one consumer, say consumer h, who strictly prefers y^h to x^h while the other consumers are at least indifferent; then by (b) in the definition of equilibrium it is $py^h > p\omega^h$ while for all other consumers $s \neq h$ it is $py^s \geq p\omega^s$; hence, summing over all consumers including h, it is $p\Sigma_s y^s > p\Sigma_s \omega^s$ which contradicts feasibility. ∎

Let us extend the theorem to production economies. Let x^s stand for the vector of consumptions of the sth consumer, and let $x^\wedge = \{x^s\}$ be a set of consumption vectors, one for each consumer, $s = 1, ..., S$, which describes a possible allocation of goods to the S consumers; let $y^\wedge = \{y^h\}$ be a set of netput vectors, one for each firm (h is the generic index of firms but their number is not given in advance); let p be a vector of prices, both product prices and factor rentals. Consumers and firms are price-takers. Consumers' preferences are not satiated; there is free entry, and firms either have constant returns to scale, or have a minimum efficient dimension sufficiently small relative to total industry demand that it is legitimate to assume that they minimize average cost; hence *industries* can be treated as if they were price-taking CRS firms.

An allocation $(x^\wedge, y^\wedge)$ is *feasible* if total consumption Σx^s can be satisfied from the available endowments through the production netputs $y^\wedge$, i.e. if $\Sigma_s x^s \leq \Sigma_s \omega^s + \Sigma_h y^h$.

Definition of general equilibrium with production. *A triplet* $(x^\wedge, y^\wedge, p)$ *where y is a vector of netputs is a production equilibrium if:*
(a) $\Sigma x^s = \Sigma \omega^s + \Sigma y^h$, *the allocation is feasible (s distinguishes consumers, h firms)*
(b) x^s *is maximal for each utility-maximizing consumer s within her budget set*
(c) *for each firm h,* py^h *maximizes profits within the production possibility set of the economy.*

In Chap. 6, ▶ Sect. 6.35, the conditions appear to be different (the content of the present condition (b) does not appear explicitly) only because they are expressed via excess demand functions, which already assume that each consumer is maximizing utility. With $y^\wedge = 0$ the definition defines a general equilibrium of pure exchange.

Let $z(p)=\Sigma x^s - \Sigma \omega^s$ stand for the excess demand vector of the aggregate of consumers, and $y(p)=\Sigma y^h$ stand for the excess supply vector of the aggregate of firms. Since we are assuming constant returns to scale for the industries and free entry, profits are zero for all firms. Hence $py(p)=p\Sigma y^h=0$. Because of balanced budgets, $pz(p)=0$. Hence $p[z(p)-y(p)]=0$, Walras' Law.

T14.2. First Fundamental Theorem of Welfare Economics for the production economy: If (x^*, y^*, p) is a production equilibrium and preferences are locally non-satiated, then the equilibrium is Pareto efficient.

Proof Suppose (x^*, y^*, p) is an equilibrium. If it is not a Pareto optimum, there is another feasible allocation $(x^\wedge, y^\wedge)$ Pareto superior to it, i.e. such that for each consumer s it is $x^{\wedge s} \succsim x^{*s}$ and for at least one consumer, say consumer r, it is $x^{\wedge r} \succ x^{*r}$. But if $x^{\wedge r}$ is strictly preferred by this consumer to x^{*r} and is not chosen at the prices p, it must not be affordable, i.e. $px^{\wedge r} > px^{*r}$; for the other consumers $px^{\wedge s} \geq px^{*s}$ for $s \neq r$; hence, summing over all consumers, $p\Sigma x^{\wedge s} > p\Sigma x^{*s}$. Firms are maximizing profits at p, hence it must be $p\Sigma y^{\wedge h} \leq p\Sigma y^{*h}$. Therefore $p\sum x^{\wedge s} - p\sum \omega^s - p\sum y^{\wedge h} > p\sum x^{*s} - p\sum \omega^s - p\sum y^{*h} = 0$. Hence $p\Sigma x^{\wedge s} > p\Sigma \omega^s - p\Sigma y^{\wedge h}$, which shows that $(x^\wedge, y^\wedge)$ is not a feasible allocation, because feasibility, i.e. $\Sigma x^{\wedge s} \leq \Sigma \omega^s + \Sigma y^{\wedge h}$, would imply $p\Sigma x^{\wedge s} \leq p\Sigma \omega^s - p\Sigma y^{\wedge h}$. Thus there is no feasible allocation that is Pareto superior to the equilibrium allocation (x^*, y^*), which is therefore Pareto efficient. ∎

The proof shows that here too fundamentally what is needed is local non-satiation of consumers, to guarantee $px^{\wedge s} \geq px^{*s}$.

The proof in ▶ Chap. 3 was longer because it detailed the conditions for Pareto efficiency for the differentiable economy and clarified their economic meaning (including the meaning of 'corner solutions'); the proof here is more general (it does not assume differentiability) but also less transparent.

This theorem allows a very quick proof of equilibrium uniqueness if there is a representative consumer with a strictly quasiconcave monotonic utility function. In this case it is easily proved that there is a unique Pareto optimum; every competitive equilibrium is a Pareto optimum; hence the equilibrium is unique. Here is the proof: Let (x, y), with x the consumer's consumptions and y the aggregate netput vector of firms, be a feasible Pareto optimum and assume there is another feasible Pareto optimum (x', y') with $x' \neq x$. The consumer's utility must be the same with both allocations, $u(x) = u(x')$. Since $x = \omega + y$ and $x' = \omega + y'$, where ω is the consumer's endowment, any consumption vector $x'' = tx + (1-t)x' = \omega + ty + (1-t)y'$ is feasible for $0 \leq t \leq 1$, and for $0 < t < 1$ owing to the assumed strict convexity of indifference curves it is $u(x'') > u(x)$ contradicting the assumption that x is Pareto efficient. I leave to the reader to show that this proof generalizes to the case in which the consumer demand is rigid for some goods (e.g. labour supply is rigid) and strict convexity of preferences only holds for the remaining goods. ∎

14.6 · The Fundamental Theorems of Welfare Economics

14.6.3 The Second Fundamental Theorem

This theorem too was explained in simple terms in ▶ Chap. 3, but for a more general and rigorous proof we need some new mathematical tools.

A function $f: R^n \rightarrow R^m$ is called *linear* if $f(a\mathbf{x} + b\mathbf{y}) = af(\mathbf{x}) + bf(\mathbf{y})$ for all scalars a, b and all vectors $\mathbf{x}, \mathbf{y} \in R^n$ in the domain of f.

A *functional* is the name of an application from a set S to R, i.e. to a scalar, where set S can be of any type. For example suppose you have m individuals and each one of them forms a list of the n English first-division football teams in increasing order of appreciation, called a Borda increasing order; given the m Borda increasing orders, assign to each team the Borda number equal to the sum of its order number in each list, for example if a team is best (i.e. last) in all lists its number is mn, if it is worst (i.e. first) in all lists its number is m. Let S be the set with elements the possible combinations of m Borda increasing orders, one per individual; the application from this set to the Borda number assigned to a certain team is a functional. In this example we have n functionals, from the elements of S to the Borda number of each team.

A *linear functional* is a linear function $R^n \rightarrow R$, that is, from vectors in R^n to a scalar. The **inner product** *or* **dot product** *or also* **scalar product** $\mathbf{p} \cdot \mathbf{x}$, with $\mathbf{p}, \mathbf{x} \in R^n$, is defined as $\mathbf{p} \cdot \mathbf{x} = \Sigma p_i x_i$; it is a linear functional if $\mathbf{p}$ is given and $\mathbf{x}$ variable. If $\mathbf{p} \neq 0$, and a is a scalar, the set of all vectors $\mathbf{x}$ such that $\mathbf{p} \cdot \mathbf{x} = a$ forms a **hyperplane** orthogonal to the direction of vector $\mathbf{p}$;[27] its intercepts with the Cartesian axes are given by a/p_i (because when $\mathbf{x}$ has all elements zero except for the ith element, then it must be $p_i x_i = a$); its distance from the origin is given by $a/\|\mathbf{p}\|$ (where $\|\mathbf{p}\|$ is the length of vector $\mathbf{p}$, i.e. $(\mathbf{p} \cdot \mathbf{p})^{1/2}$), because when $\mathbf{x}$ such that $\mathbf{p} \cdot \mathbf{x} = a$ is co-linear with $\mathbf{p}$—let us then indicate it as $\mathbf{x}^\wedge$ –, it can be expressed as $\mathbf{x}^\wedge = t\mathbf{p}$, hence $\mathbf{p} \cdot \mathbf{x}^\wedge = \mathbf{p} \cdot t\mathbf{p} = a$, so $t = a/(\mathbf{p} \cdot \mathbf{p})$; therefore $\mathbf{x}^\wedge = \frac{a}{\mathbf{p} \cdot \mathbf{p}}\mathbf{p}$ and its length, which is the distance of the hyperplane from the origin, is given by $\|\mathbf{x}^\wedge\| = \|\mathbf{p}\|\frac{|a|}{\mathbf{p} \cdot \mathbf{p}}\mathbf{p} = \|\mathbf{p}\| \cdot |a|/\|\mathbf{p}\|^2 = |a|/\|\mathbf{p}\|$. Therefore the distance of the hyperplane $\mathbf{px} = a$ from the origin is an increasing function of $|a|$. Given a vector $\mathbf{p} \neq 0$ and a scalar $a > 0$, the set of vectors $\mathbf{x}$ such that $\mathbf{px} \geq a$ is therefore the halfspace of R^n limited by (and including) the hyperplane $\mathbf{px} = a$ and not including the origin, while the set of vectors $\mathbf{x}$ such that $\mathbf{px} \leq a$ is the halfspace of R^n limited by (and including) the hyperplane $\mathbf{px} = a$ and including the origin. If $a < 0$, then it is the halfspace $\mathbf{px} \geq a$ that includes the origin (see ▶ Chap. 15 for the proof and a graphical illustration).

---

27 *Exercise*: as an easy mathematical exercise to acquire familiarity with hyperplanes, prove this orthogonality (hint: find out graphically what difference between vectors $\mathbf{x}, \mathbf{x}'$ produces a vector orthogonal to $\mathbf{p}$, and remember the connection between orthogonality and inner product of vectors).

1266   **Chapter 14 · Welfare, Externalities, Public Goods and Happiness**

A Separating Hyperplane Theorem: If $A \subset R^n$ and $B \subset R^n$ are two non-empty, disjoint, convex sets, then there exists $\mathbf{p} \neq 0$ and a scalar r such that $\mathbf{px} \geq r \geq \mathbf{py}$ for all $\mathbf{x} \in A$ and $\mathbf{y} \in B$.[28]

Now I can state and prove.

T14.3. Second Fundamental Theorem of Welfare Economics for the exchange economy, simplified version without transfers: Suppose that $\mathbf{x}^*$ is a Pareto-efficient allocation in an exchange economy where $\mathbf{x}^{*s} \gg 0$ for each consumer s and preferences are continuous, convex and monotonic. Then $\mathbf{x}^*$ is an equilibrium for endowments $\omega^s = \mathbf{x}^{*s}, \forall s$, i.e. there exist prices such that a distribution of endowments coinciding with the allocation $\mathbf{x}^*$ is itself an equilibrium.

Proof   Let $V^s \equiv \{\mathbf{x}^s$ in $R^n: \mathbf{x}^s >_s \mathbf{x}^{*s}\}$, where $>_s$ stands for 'is strictly preferred by consumer s to', be the open set of consumption bundles strictly preferred by consumer s to the bundle she receives in allocation $\mathbf{x}^*$. Let $V \equiv \Sigma_s V^s \equiv \{\mathbf{z}$ in $R^n: \exists$ an allocation $\mathbf{x}$ with, for each s, $\mathbf{x}^s$ in V^s, such that $\mathbf{z} = \Sigma_s \mathbf{x}^s\}$ stand for the set of vectors $\mathbf{z}$ representing total endowments which make it possible to reach allocations which strictly Pareto dominates $\mathbf{x}^*$. The symbol $\Sigma_s V^s$ here means 'sum of sets', that is the set whose elements comprise all possible sums of vectors, one from each set V^s. The sets V^s are convex by construction because preferences are assumed convex; and a *set sum of convex sets* is a convex set[29]; hence V is convex.

Now consider the economy's aggregate endowment $\omega = \Sigma_s \mathbf{x}^{*s}$. Since $\mathbf{x}^*$ is Pareto efficient, there is no redistribution of ω which Pareto dominates $\mathbf{x}^*$, hence ω is not in V. Then by the Separating Hyperplane Theorem, with V and ω the two non-empty, disjoint and convex sets, $\exists \mathbf{p} \neq \mathbf{0}: \mathbf{pz} \geq \mathbf{p\omega}$ for all $\mathbf{z} \in V$, which can be re-written $\mathbf{pz} \geq \mathbf{p}\Sigma_s \mathbf{x}^{*s}$, and rearranging:

$$\mathbf{p}(\mathbf{z} - \omega) = \mathbf{p}(\mathbf{z} - \Sigma_s \mathbf{x}^{*s}) \geq 0, \quad \forall \mathbf{z} \in V. \tag{14.8}$$

On the basis of this result I prove that $\mathbf{p}$ is an equilibrium price vector, in 3 steps:

(i) $\mathbf{p}$ is non-negative: consider an aggregate endowment $\omega + \mathbf{e}_i$ where $\mathbf{e}^i = (0, .., 1_i, .., 0)^T$ is a vector with zeros everywhere except in the ith place where there is a 1; so we are adding one unit of good i to the aggregate endowment ω. The endowment $\omega + \mathbf{e}^i$ belongs to V since by redistributing that 1 extra unit we can make everybody better off. Then (14.8) implies $\mathbf{p}(\omega + \mathbf{e}^i - \omega) \geq 0$, i.e. $\mathbf{pe}^i \geq 0$ which implies $p_i \geq 0$. By repeating for each good, we conclude that $\mathbf{p} \geq 0$.

---

28   Another version of the theorem differs only in that the two sets A and B are not necessarily disjoint, but no point of AB is *internal* to A, or to B (that is, no point of AB has a neighbourhood entirely contained in A, or in B). This version allows the sets A and B to have some point of their frontiers in common.

29   *Proof.* Let $A \subset R^n$ be the set *sum* of two sets $B \subset R^n$ and $C \subset R^n$ in the sense that for any $\mathbf{x_A} \in A$ and $\mathbf{y_A} \in A$, there exist $\mathbf{x_B}, \mathbf{y_B} \in B$ and $\mathbf{x_C}, \mathbf{y_C} \in C$ such that $\mathbf{x_A} = \mathbf{x_B} + \mathbf{x_C}$, $\mathbf{y_A} = \mathbf{y_B} + \mathbf{y_C}$, and conversely to each $\mathbf{x_B}, \mathbf{y_B} \in B$ and $\mathbf{x_C}, \mathbf{y_C} \in C$ there corresponds a couple $\mathbf{x_A}, \mathbf{y_A} \in A$ such that $\mathbf{x_A} = \mathbf{x_B} + \mathbf{x_C}, \mathbf{y_A} = \mathbf{y_B} + \mathbf{y_C}$. Let B and C be convex sets. Then $\alpha\mathbf{x_A} + (1 - \alpha)\mathbf{y_A} = \alpha(\mathbf{x_B} + \mathbf{x_C}) + (1 - \alpha)(\mathbf{y_B} + \mathbf{y_C}) = [\alpha\mathbf{x_B} + (1 - \alpha)\mathbf{y_B}] + [\alpha\mathbf{x_C} + (1 - \alpha)\mathbf{y_C}] \in A$ because the first term in square brackets is in B and the second is in C and therefore their sum is in A. Hence any convex combination of elements of A is in A, which is therefore a convex set.

14.6 · The Fundamental Theorems of Welfare Economics

(ii) let $\mathbf{y}^s \gg \mathbf{0}$ stand, not for a netput, but for another consumption vector of consumer s; if $\mathbf{y}^s \succ_s \mathbf{x}^{*s}$, then $\mathbf{p}\mathbf{y}^s \geq \mathbf{p}\mathbf{x}^{*s}, \forall s$. Consider consumer k and a consumption $\mathbf{y}^k$ such that $\mathbf{y}^k \succ_k \mathbf{x}^{*k}$; by continuity of preferences it is possible to take away a very small fraction $\theta > 0$ of every good from $\mathbf{y}^k$ and obtain a consumption vector $(1 - \theta)\mathbf{y}^k$ still strictly preferred by consumer k to $\mathbf{x}^{*k}$. Redistribute $\theta\mathbf{y}^k$ in equal parts to all other consumers; then for $r \neq k$, the consumption bundle $\mathbf{z}^r$ is $\mathbf{x}^{*r}$ plus a positive amount of each good and therefore is strictly preferred to $\mathbf{x}^{*r}$, while for consumer k too the consumption bundle $\mathbf{z}^k = (1 - \theta)\mathbf{y}^k$ is strictly preferred to $\mathbf{x}^{*k}$; the allocation $\mathbf{z}$ so constructed is therefore in V; then by (14.8) it is $\mathbf{p}\Sigma_s \mathbf{z}^s \geq \mathbf{p}\Sigma_s \mathbf{x}^{*s}$, which means $\mathbf{p}[(1 - \theta)\mathbf{y}^k + \Sigma_{r \neq k}\mathbf{x}^{*r} + \theta\mathbf{y}^k] \geq \mathbf{p}(\mathbf{x}^{*k} + \Sigma_{r \neq k}\mathbf{x}^{*r})$, which implies $\mathbf{p}\mathbf{y}^k \geq \mathbf{p}\mathbf{x}^{*k}$.

(iii) if $\mathbf{y}^s \succ_s \mathbf{x}^{*s}$, then $\mathbf{p}\mathbf{y}^s > \mathbf{p}\mathbf{x}^{*s}, \forall s$. Suppose not. By (ii), the sole possibility is that $\mathbf{p}\mathbf{y}^s = \mathbf{p}\mathbf{x}^{*s}$. By continuity of preferences there is a sufficiently small $\theta' > 0$ such that $(1 - \theta')\mathbf{y}^s \succ_s \mathbf{x}^{*s}$; then $\mathbf{p}(1-\theta')\mathbf{y}^s < \mathbf{p}\mathbf{y}^s$ if $\mathbf{p}\mathbf{y}^s > 0$, which is the case because we are supposing $\mathbf{p}\mathbf{y}^s = \mathbf{p}\mathbf{x}^{*s}$ and the theorem assumes $\mathbf{x}^{*s} \gg 0$. Hence $\mathbf{p}(1-\theta')\mathbf{y}^s < \mathbf{p}\mathbf{x}^{*s}$, but this contradicts (ii) because $(1 - \theta')\mathbf{y}^s \succ_s \mathbf{x}^{*s}$. Therefore we get a contradiction.

This proves that $\mathbf{p}$ is an admissible price vector and that (b) of the definition of general equilibrium is satisfied at $\mathbf{p}$. As to (a), it is satisfied by construction since $\omega = \Sigma_s \mathbf{x}^{*s}$. Therefore $(\mathbf{x}^*, \mathbf{p})$ is an exchange equilibrium for the endowments $\omega^s = \mathbf{x}^s, s = 1, ..., S.$ ∎

To summarize: through the Separating Hyperplane Theorem one proves that there is a price vector, such that all consumption baskets that Pareto dominate $\mathbf{x}^*$ are more expensive than $\mathbf{x}^*$ and therefore unattainable, and that at those prices, for each consumer s, $\mathbf{x}^{*s}$ is a possible demand vector[30] because it is utility-maximizing within the budget set; since $\mathbf{x}^*$ is such that, for each good, aggregate consumption equals aggregate endowment, excess demand is zero for all goods, hence we have an equilibrium.

An implication of this theorem, which extends to production economies, is that under the assumptions of the theorem *any Pareto-efficient allocation is a potential general equilibrium allocation.*[31]

The theorem asserts that, if the government redistributes physical endowments so that each consumer s gets $\mathbf{x}^{*s}$ as endowment vector, and if afterwards markets are allowed to operate and consumers are allowed to exchange and to reach a competitive equilibrium, the resulting equilibrium will entail no exchange: each agent will be satisfied with her/his endowment. So the government need not keep people under continuous control in order to maintain the desired allocation.

The idea expressed in the last paragraph is actually intended for the production economy, with the redistribution concerning the endowments *of factors.* In

---

30 A *possible* demand vector because we are not excluding demand correspondences.

31 It is easy to prove also the following (see, e.g., Varian 1992, p. 329): if $\mathbf{x}^*$ is a Pareto-efficient allocation and preferences are locally non-satiated, and if a competitive equilibrium $(\mathbf{p}', \mathbf{x}')$ exists for initial endowments coinciding with $\mathbf{x}^*$, then $(\mathbf{p}', \mathbf{x}^*)$ is itself a competitive equilibrium for those endowments. This theorem does not exclude the possibility of other equilibria, nor of non-convex preferences.

1268   **Chapter 14** · Welfare, Externalities, Public Goods and Happiness

a production economy factor redistribution needs to be performed only once, in an exchange economy in order to have the new allocation persist the government would have to intervene at the beginning of each market fair to which the several households arrived with their given endowments; and the theorem does need that the state intervention determines a *persistent* new equilibrium. This is because, since there is no auctioneer-guided instantaneous tâtonnement in actual economies, the effect of *any* state intervention can be evaluated only by reference to its final result determined by persistent forces, neglecting its initial impact that includes disequilibrium reactions to the novelty, reactions whose details cannot be predicted. The persistency of economic conditions is also required in order for the government to find out the optimal intervention by trial and error, because the government is not omniscient, it does not know the prices that goods and factors will have in the new equilibrium, so it cannot know in advance what endowment redistribution is appropriate to the income levels it would like the several consumers to reach. The redistribution of endowments can be replaced by a set of lump-sum taxes and subsidies that make consumers behave *as if* their initial endowments had been redistributed (this would avoid the need for repeated intervention at each fair in the exchange economy), the theorem can be modified accordingly, but in order to determine the taxes and subsidies capable of bringing about the desired consumption levels the government should be able to determine the equilibria corresponding to each set of taxes and subsidies, and the government does not have the necessary information, it can only arrive at approximating the desired equilibrium allocation by repeated trial and error, and this requires that the data of equilibrium other than taxes and subsidies be persistent. Therefore the Second Fundamental Theorem makes sense only inside the traditional conception of equilibrium as a persistent, long-period equilibrium, centre of gravitation of time-consuming adjustments, with the connected treatment of capital as a single factor illustrated in ▶ Chap. 7.

The extension of the theorem to the case of income transfers via taxes and subsidies can be made rigorous and extended to the production economy, by introducing the notion of **quasi-equilibrium with transfers**. To introduce it, let us first give a formal definition of an equilibrium with transfers, enlarging now the analysis to include (non-capitalistic) production. Now $\mathbf{y}$ without indices is an aggregate netput vector, sum of firms' netputs.

Definition of an equilibrium with transfers for the production economy: in an economy with S consumers with endowments $\boldsymbol{\omega} = (\omega^1, \ldots, \omega^s, \ldots, \omega^S)$, *an allocation* $(\mathbf{x}^*, \mathbf{y}^*)$ *and a price vector* $\mathbf{p}$ *constitute a price equilibrium with transfers if there is an assignment of income levels* $(m^1, \ldots, m^s, \ldots, m^S)$, *with* $\Sigma_s m^s = \mathbf{p}\Sigma_s \omega^s + \Sigma_h \mathbf{p}\mathbf{y}_h^*$, *such that:*

(i) *each firm is maximizing profit[32];*

---

32   To make it possible for the reader to connect the presentation here with other presentations that admit positive profits in equilibrium, here it is *not* assumed that profits are zero (this assumption would imply $\Sigma_h p y_h^* = 0$); but this assumption could be made, and it would change nothing in the reasonings that follow.

14.6 · The Fundamental Theorems of Welfare Economics

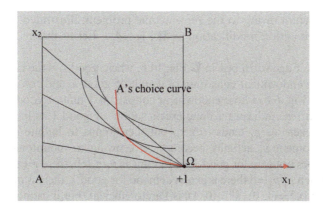

■ **Fig. 14.6** Zero-income problem in Edgeworth box. Ω is the endowment point. B's indifference curves are horizontal

(ii) *for each consumer s the basket* x^{*s} *maximizes utility under the constraint* $px^s \leq m^s$, *that is, if* $x^s >_s x^{*s}$, *then* $px^s > px^{*s}$;
(iii) *there is equilibrium in each market, that is,* $\Sigma_s x^{*s} = \Sigma_s \omega^s + \Sigma_h y_h^*$.

The words 'with transfers' suggest that the income levels m^s are obtained by transferring purchasing power across consumers in some way, but the definition does not specify how. The existence of an equilibrium with transfers only requires that *some* income assignment exists satisfying the conditions. The equality signs in (iii) assume free disposal.

In other presentations the vector $(m^1, ..., m^s, ..., m^S)$ is called vector of *wealth* levels, but the traditional notion of equilibrium is of an equilibrium of repeated *flows*, where therefore each period it is *income* that equals expenditure, not wealth.

Definition of a price quasi-equilibrium with transfers for the production economy: (i) and (iii) are the same as in the definition of a price equilibrium with transfers; condition (ii), *that any consumption basket* $\mathbf{x}^s$ *strictly preferred by consumer s to* $\mathbf{x}^{*s}$ *must cost more than* $\mathbf{px}^{*s}$, is replaced by the weaker condition that it must not cost less, that is, (ii′) if $x^s >_s x^{*s}$, then $\mathbf{px}^s \geq \mathbf{px}^{*s}$.

(So it is *not* certain that, at a quasi-equilibrium, consumers are maximizing utility: a zero price of a good does not imply, in a quasi-equilibrium with monotonic utility functions, that the demand for the good is infinite.)

Therefore:

T14.4. Existence of equilibrium with transfers: *an equilibrium with transfers exists if a quasi-equilibrium with transfers exists and in addition some condition holds which implies that in this quasi-equilibrium* $\mathbf{px}^s > \mathbf{px}^{*s}$ *if* $x^s >_s x^{*s}$.

Why this puzzling notion of quasi-equilibrium? Because there are cases where a Pareto-efficient allocation is a quasi-equilibrium, but cannot be sustained by prices as an equilibrium allocation. The typical such case is the case of non-exist-

1270   **Chapter 14** · Welfare, Externalities, Public Goods and Happiness

ence of equilibrium owing to the zero-income problem, illustrated in ◘ Fig. 6.6, reproduced here with a modification as ◘ Fig. 14.6. Let us briefly remember the problem.

Consider the Edgeworth box in ◘ Fig. 14.6, where good 2 is the numéraire, consumer B has an endowment consisting of 1 unit of good 2, and consumer A is the consumer of ◘ Fig. 6.6, whose endowment consists of 1 unit of good 1, and whose choice curve (in red) indicates a finite excess supply of good 1 as long as $p_1/p_2 > 0$, which tends to zero as p_1 tends to zero but then jumps to infinite positive excess demand the moment p_1 actually becomes zero, owing to monotonic preferences. Consumer B does not care for good 1, so as long as $p_1/p_2 > 0$, there is excess supply of good 1, and when $p_1/p_2 = 0$ there is excess demand for good 1: there is no equilibrium. The allocation: $[\mathbf{x}^A = (1, 0), \mathbf{x}^B = (0, 1)]$ is Pareto efficient, but it cannot be sustained as an equilibrium. But it is a quasi-equilibrium with $p = (0, 1)$ and $m^1 = 0, m^2 = 1$.

As observed in ▶ Chap. 6, in this case the non-existence of equilibrium would be avoided if consumer A had a positive endowment of both goods. This is indeed the key to the condition that guarantees that a quasi-equilibrium with transfers is also an equilibrium with transfers:

> **T14.5. Quasi-equilibrium with transfers and positive incomes.** *If in a quasi-equilibrium with transfers each consumer's income m^s is positive and preferences are continuous, then $\mathbf{x}^s >_s \mathbf{x}^{*s}$ implies not only $\mathbf{p}\mathbf{x}^s \geq \mathbf{p}\mathbf{x}^{*s}$, but also $\mathbf{p}\mathbf{x}^s > \mathbf{p}\mathbf{x}^{*s}$.*

Proof By contradiction. Suppose not, that is, suppose that for some consumer s there exists a $\mathbf{x}^s >_s \mathbf{x}^{*s}$ such that $\mathbf{p}\mathbf{x}^s \leq \mathbf{p}\mathbf{x}^{*s}$. By condition (ii′) of the definition of quasi-equilibrium, it is also $\mathbf{p}\mathbf{x}^s \geq \mathbf{p}\mathbf{x}^{*s}$, so it must be $\mathbf{p}\mathbf{x}^s = \mathbf{p}\mathbf{x}^{*s}$. By continuity of preferences, a sufficiently small $\varepsilon > 0$ exists such that $(1-\varepsilon)\mathbf{x}^s >_s \mathbf{x}^{*s}$; but $p(1-\varepsilon)\mathbf{x}^s < \mathbf{p}\mathbf{x}^{*s}$, so a basket exists that is strictly preferred to $\mathbf{x}^{*s}$ and costs less than $\mathbf{x}^{*s}$, which contradicts (ii′). ∎

The assumption $m^s > 0$ is necessary for the possibility of $\mathbf{p}(1 - \varepsilon)\mathbf{x}^s < \mathbf{p}\mathbf{x}^{*s}$. In the proof given above of the second welfare theorem for the exchange economy, the positivity of income was guaranteed by the assumption $\mathbf{x}^{*s} \gg 0$.

14

> **T14.6. Second Fundamental Theorem of Welfare Economics for the production economy.** *In an economy with S consumers with endowments $\omega = (\omega^1, ..., \omega^s, ..., \omega^S)$, and firms $h = 1, ...$ with production possibilities sets Y_h, suppose all firm production possibility sets are convex, and all preference relations are convex, continuous and locally insatiable. Then for any Pareto-efficient and feasible allocation $(\mathbf{x}^*, \mathbf{y}^*)$ there is a quasi-equilibrium with transfers, with associated price vector $\mathbf{p}$ and income vector $(m^1, ..., m^S)$, that establishes such an allocation. If furthermore the income vector is strictly positive, the quasi-equilibrium is an equilibrium with transfers.*

Proof The last statement in the theorem has been proved already. So we must only prove that there is a quasi-equilibrium with transfers. Let $Q^s(\mathbf{x}^{*s})$ be the set of consumption baskets strictly preferred by consumer s to $\mathbf{x}^{*s}$; by convexity of preferences, it is convex; therefore using the notion of set sum of sets (Footnote 26), $Q = \Sigma_s Q^s(\mathbf{x}^{*s})$ is convex because sum of convex sets.

14.6 · The Fundamental Theorems of Welfare Economics

Any element $\mathbf{q}$ of Q would make it possible to reach an allocation strictly preferred by all consumers to $\mathbf{x}^*$. Let F be the set $\{Y + \omega\}$ of all feasible aggregate consumption bundles $\mathbf{x} = \Sigma_s \mathbf{x}^s = \Sigma_s \omega^s + \Sigma_h \mathbf{y}_h$, not necessarily non-negative; this set is convex since all firms' production possibility sets are convex (and include free disposal). Since $(\mathbf{x}^*, \mathbf{y}^*)$ is Pareto efficient, Q and F are disjoint, because if an element of Q were an element of F, it would be possible to increase the utility of all consumers, contradicting Pareto efficiency. Then because of the separating hyperplane theorem there exists a vector p such that $\mathbf{p} \cdot \mathbf{q} \geq r \geq p \cdot x$ for all $\mathbf{q} \in Q$ and $\mathbf{x} \in F$.

Let us now consider allocations $\mathbf{x}^\circ$ of consumption bundles $\mathbf{x}^{\text{os}} \succsim_s \mathbf{x}^{*\text{s}}$ for all s: we can prove that $\mathbf{p} \mathbf{x}^\circ = \mathbf{p} \Sigma_s \mathbf{x}^{\text{os}} \geq r$, that is, $\mathbf{x}^\circ$ is included in the half-space $\mathbf{p} \mathbf{x} \geq r$; indeed, by local non-satiation for each consumer s we can choose a consumption bundle $\mathbf{x}^{\sim s}$ arbitrarily close to $\mathbf{x}^{\text{os}}$ such that $\mathbf{x}^{\sim s} \succsim_s \mathbf{x}^{\text{os}}$, so that $\mathbf{x}^{\sim s} \in Q^s$ and $\Sigma_s \mathbf{x}^{\sim s} \in Q$ implying $\mathbf{p} \Sigma_s \mathbf{x}^{\sim s} \geq r$; taking the limit as $\mathbf{x}^{\sim s} \to \mathbf{x}^{\text{os}}$ we obtain $\mathbf{p} \Sigma_s \mathbf{x}^{\text{os}} \geq r$. Note that this implies $\mathbf{p} \Sigma_s \mathbf{x}^{*\text{s}} \geq r$; but $\Sigma_s \mathbf{x}^{*\text{s}} \in F$, hence $\mathbf{p} \Sigma_s \mathbf{x}^{*\text{s}} \leq r$, therefore $\mathbf{p} \Sigma_s \mathbf{x}^{*\text{s}} = r$.

We can now prove condition (i) of the definition of quasi-equilibrium. Since $\mathbf{x}^* = \Sigma_s \mathbf{x}^{*\text{s}} = \omega + \Sigma_h \mathbf{y}_h^*$, it is $\mathbf{p}(\omega + \Sigma_h \mathbf{y}_h^*) = r$. Since $\Sigma_h \mathbf{y}_h \in Y$ for any collection of netputs (one for each firm h), it is $\mathbf{y}_h + \Sigma_{k \neq h} \mathbf{y}_k^* \in Y$; therefore $\omega + \mathbf{y}_h + \Sigma_{k \neq h} \mathbf{y}_k^* \leq r$ because it is in F; hence $\mathbf{p}(\omega + \mathbf{y}_h + \Sigma_{k \neq h} \mathbf{y}_k^*) \leq r = \mathbf{p}(\omega + \mathbf{y}_h^* + \Sigma_{k \neq h} \mathbf{y}_k^*)$, which implies $\mathbf{p} \mathbf{y}_h \leq \mathbf{p} \mathbf{y}_h^*$, i.e. profit maximization.

Now I prove condition (ii'). Take any $\mathbf{x}^i \succ_i \mathbf{x}^{*i}$. The allocation coinciding with $\mathbf{x}^*$ for $s \neq i$ and with $\mathbf{x}^i$ in place of $\mathbf{x}^{*i}$ is an $\mathbf{x}^\circ$ allocation, hence $\mathbf{p}(\mathbf{x}^i + \Sigma_{s \neq i} \mathbf{x}^{*\text{s}}) \geq r = \mathbf{p}(\mathbf{x}^{*i} + \Sigma_{s \neq i} \mathbf{x}^{*\text{s}})$, that implies $\mathbf{p} \mathbf{x}^i \geq \mathbf{p} \mathbf{x}^{*i}$.

Condition (iii), $\Sigma_s \mathbf{x}^{*\text{s}} = \Sigma_s \omega^s + \Sigma_h \mathbf{y}_h^*$, is simply the assumed feasibility of the Pareto-efficient allocation $(\mathbf{x}^*, \mathbf{y}^*)$. So all three conditions have been shown to hold. ∎

The associated incomes are of course, for each consumer s, $m^s = \mathbf{p} \mathbf{x}^{*\text{s}}$.

Note that again we find that any Pareto-efficient allocation can be the allocation of a general equilibrium, with such a distribution of endowments that every consumer has the income needed to obtain her allocation of consumption goods at the equilibrium prices. The distribution of endowments is not uniquely determined.

14.7 Some Generally Accepted Limitations of the Two Fundamental Theorems

This section discusses generally admitted limitations of the two Fundamental Theorems. These bring one to discuss some limitations of the Pareto efficiency criterion itself.

On the Second Fundamental Theorem, it is admitted (e.g. Mas-Colell et al. 1995, p. 556) that the amount of information needed to calculate the individual lump-sum taxes required to reach a desired allocation is enormous, impossible to obtain; and that the lump-sum wealth transfers must be enforceable, and *cos-*

tlessly enforceable, or their cost must enter the decision whether the transfers are desirable. In my view these limitations are not of fundamental importance, what is needed is a general direction of reallocation suggested by equity considerations, and even if the desired Pareto optimum is not perfectly reached, this is not such a big problem *if* the economy anyway tends to a Pareto-efficient state.

On the First Fundamental Theorem, it is usual to object that it neglects externalities, public goods, and imperfections of competition. But it might be replied that, more than criticisms, these are indications of the *usefulness* of the theorem, in that the violation of the conditions necessary for efficiency points to where public intervention is desirable. This defence of the theorem is questionable for externalities involving consumer preferences, as will be shown below. But it is acceptable (i) for imperfections of competition, which do admit corrective interventions and anyway appear to be of limited importance (Harberger 1954, 1959; natural monopolies are another issue, but it is obvious that regulation is required there); (ii) for public goods, which can be dealt with via public decisions possibly helped by cost–benefit analysis (on which see ► Sect. 14.9); and (iii) for externalities in production, which can generally be rather effectively dealt with (if there is the needed political determination), unless they involve more than one nation, for example global warming or seas invaded by plastic debris or whale hunting; the difficulty then is the absence of a supranational authority capable of deciding and imposing the tax or regulation; but then the inability to deal with these externalities can hardly be adduced as a criticism of the market economy, the problem would arise even if the nations had planned economies.

These defects of the market mechanism appear on the whole of minor relevance when compared with unemployment and crises, and with the relevance of certain other deficiencies to be discussed later. True, the complete correction of the mentioned violations of Pareto efficiency conditions can be impossible. We have seen that the Coase Theorem is not generally of great usefulness. Also, it is often the case that the government does not have at its disposal instruments capable of correcting *all* the inefficiencies relative to a desired Pareto-efficient allocation. For example, lump-sum taxes may be impossible to realize in practice. Then it is impossible to reach a ***first-best*** (FB) allocation, that is, one where all Pareto-efficient conditions are satisfied, even if the neoclassical approach were right; all the government can aim to achieve is a ***second-best*** (SB) allocation, the best one compatible with the desired income distribution and with the constraints that make it impossible to reach a FB allocation. But then a complication arises, called the ***Theorem of the Second Best***: it is far from guaranteed that reducing the number of violated Pareto efficiency conditions, but without being able to eliminate all violations, results in a socially better allocation in a generally neoclassical framework (Lipsey and Lancaster 1956–1957). For space reasons, and also because the theorem heavily relies on the neoclassical framework, on this issue I limit myself to quoting at length from a well-written little booklet of some years ago.

» The belief that it is better to fulfil some of the optimum conditions rather than none is false, as is the belief that it is better to depart from those conditions to a uniform extent rather than to different extents … Piecemeal welfare economics

14.7 · Some Generally Accepted Limitations …

based on achievement of the Paretian conditions in a partial equilibrium context may well lead to recommendations that would result in a reduction in welfare when viewed in a general equilibrium context of suboptimality … It is not true, for example, that public utilities or nationalized industries should price at marginal cost when other industries do not. Repeal of an apparently distorting marginal tax might reduce welfare if other marginal taxes remain in force. Repeal of tariffs on certain commodities, or on all commodities from certain countries by formation of a customs union, is not supported by the case for free trade unless free trade is universal, and the case for universal free trade is not substantiated on Paretian grounds unless all countries simultaneously achieve Paretian optimum positions internally. (Winch 1971, pp. 110–11)

These warnings induce caution on any policy proposal aimed at correcting one violation of Pareto efficiency conditions. One example of a policy intervention aimed at correcting a negative externality, that makes things worse because of the simultaneous presence of another inefficiency (monopoly) which is not corrected, is in Exercise 14.11. But caution must not mean paralysis, it must only mean careful study of the difficulties and of how to deal with them. And, as argued, anyway the inefficiencies caused by incomplete correction of the mentioned externalities and imperfections of competition pale in comparison with other defects of market economies.

Some other admitted but less often mentioned limits of the two Fundamental Theorems is that they need (i) *absence of a direct dependence of utility on the price of a good*, (ii) *absence of unnecessary ignorance about the effects of choices*. The phenomenon of a high price enhancing the attractiveness of a good because it turns it into a status symbol can be seen as a type of externality because it is the appreciation of others that one really is seeking, but it concerns a small minority of consumption goods and will not be further discussed; the proof that direct dependence of utility on price causes inefficiency is left as an ***Exercise***. As to (ii), ignorance about the quality of goods and about the consequence of consuming certain goods is an important reason for the existence of merit and demerit goods (defined below); it can also be due to conscious decisions of producers to remain silent, or lie, about some characteristics of the product, something that does happen and would be immensely more frequent without state checks on the quality of goods, a seldom remembered essential public activity. (Just think of the need for correct 'Best before' labels on packed foods. Clearly the ideology of the minimal state is wrong already for this reason alone.) Producers' imperfect knowledge of the best technologies is also a widespread phenomenon, and becomes relevant when public intervention might reduce it.

Another seldom mentioned limit of the Fundamental Welfare Theorems is the absence of consideration of technical progress. Admittedly, it is a big problem to find optimality conditions relative to the amount of resources to allocate to technical progress, given the logical impossibility of knowing what those resources will produce, even in probabilistic terms. But this does not justify forgetting to mention the issue, after all technical progress is perhaps the thing that changes life conditions the most. And it does not have only positive effects. One seldom mentioned effect is the unhappiness caused by seeing that one cannot afford (or cannot afford yet) all the just invented better consumption goods. When colour television had not been invented yet, people did not miss it. Once it was invented, people started suffering from not having it. And when they got it, they got accustomed to it and started suffering from not having the larger, better new models. Since one does not miss new consumption goods when they have not been invented yet, and one tends to grow accustomed to them once one has got them, it is possible to wonder whether perhaps it would be better to have *less* innovation in consumption goods.[33] The field is largely unexplored.

Now I come to another seldom mentioned limit of the two Theorems, which will require some extensive comment. The two Fundamental Theorems need that there be *no preferences unworthy of consideration and no need for paternalism*. This is because the notion of Pareto efficiency itself needs these conditions, and this makes it much less value-free that it is generally conceived to be.

The notion of Pareto efficiency is strictly associated with the **strong Pareto Principle**, that is the value judgement that a (weak) Pareto improvement—a change that raises the utility of at least one individual while reducing the utility of no one—is good, is something society should approve, if realized it indicates that the welfare *of society* (whatever that may mean) has increased. It is the Pareto Principle that gives importance to the notion of Pareto efficiency; without the Pareto Principle there would be little reason to be concerned with whether a state is Pareto efficient or not. There are several value judgements implicit in this value judgement, that it is useful to bring into the open.

The Pareto efficiency criterion produces vast incompleteness of the ordering of allocations, but it may seem to have the advantage of avoiding **equity** issues (issues about what allocations are equitable, that is, satisfy some criterion of justice), concentrating on evaluation of **efficiency**. The argument is that it would be silly to choose an allocation which is not Pareto efficient: efficiency can be considered a *value-neutral* aim; the choice of one among the Pareto-efficient allocations does not entail a *waste* of possible welfare for some individual. However, the application of the notions of Pareto efficiency and Pareto superiority to allocations embodies more value judgements than usually admitted:

(i) **Process irrelevance**. The exclusive attention to differences between allocations implies the value judgement that the process by which an allocation is reached does not matter. 'Procedural matters such as fairness or due process count only insofar as they affect outcomes' (Hausman and McPherson 2006, p. 218).

---

33 It is unclear that children have more fun with modern advanced expensive toys than with older, simpler, and generally more social games. This issue, which connects with the tendency of happiness economics to view increases in consumption levels as improving welfare less than normally thought (see the end of the chapter), is waiting for further examination. Anyway other effects of technical progress are no doubt positive: the reduction of the physical suffering due to heavy toil and to illness, and the potential for increases of leisure time. On the other hand, it is unclear whether technical progress in the development of more and more frightening weapons increases welfare ....

(ii) *Individualism* (sometimes called *welfarism*). What counts of an allocation is its effect on the utilities, or welfare, of individuals. Whether the allocation satisfies or not superior moral, political or religious principles is irrelevant, except in so far as individuals appreciate or dislike that the allocation does or doesn't satisfy them, and this influences their utilities. To clarify: excluding by law pork meat from consumption is a Pareto improvement only if this (weakly) raises the utilities of *all* involved individuals; this may be the case because the involved individuals are better off owing to their religious beliefs, but the reason why they are better off is irrelevant for concluding that the law causes a Pareto improvement, all that counts is that the individuals prefer it.

(iii) *Non-paternalism*. Individuals are the best judges of their own welfare. This is embodied in the Pareto criterion because if the condition of an individual changes, the evaluation whether this makes the individual better off or not must be made by the individual. This value judgement may appear eminently acceptable, but a moment's reflection shows that there is ample agrement that in many instances it must not be respected. Paternalism is inevitable towards children and mentally disturbed people; it is generally socially accepted vis-à-vis alcoholism, drug addiction, obsession with gambling, tendencies to run excessive risks, and similar self-destructive tendencies. Also, people may not know what is best for them out of ignorance. Non-paternalism is violated for *merit needs*, those needs that society judges must be met independently of individual preferences. *Merit goods* are the goods whose consumption satisfies merit needs; the government must intervene to increase their supply when individual preferences imply an underestimation of the personal or social usefulness of merit goods and hence too low a demand for them, for example because of ignorance, or of separation in time between cost and benefit, or of difficulty with appreciating their social usefulness which greatly depends on externalities: examples are education, health services, vitamin-rich food, preservation of artistic objects, in certain nations also provision of religious facilities. *Demerit* goods are overconsumed for the same reasons, e.g. tobacco smoking which produces not only negative externalities owing to air pollution but also health damages that are underappreciated because of separation in time between the enjoyment of smoking and the occurrence of lung problems. Demerit goods include forbidden goods whose consumption is treated as a crime (e.g. heroin). For merit and demerit goods, society decides to disregard the principle of non-paternalism.

(iv) *Right to neglect antisocial preferences*. Utility functions can be defined to depend on much more than simply own consumption bundles; they can be considered to depend on the climate, on how friendly people are, on the political system, on the prevailing religious persuasions of neighbours, on all sorts of externalities. The notions of Pareto improvement and Pareto efficiency can be applied in this case too, although the terms are somewhat improper because Pareto assumed the absence of externalities in defining efficiency as we will see. But even in the absence of externalities the application of the Pareto efficiency criterion is only effected after a previous application of value judgements aimed at a previous *exclusion of antisocial preferences* from the preferences to be considered in order to determine whether a Pareto improvement is achieved by a change. Greater satisfaction of certain preferences is not viewed as criterion for Pareto improvements because those preferences are condemned as crimes or anyway antisocial; examples are preferences for killing or raping other persons, stealing, driving dangerously; but the list greatly depends on the society and the individual, it can include certain sexual preferences, blasphemy, abortion, propagandizing certain political ideas.... The exclusion of such preferences from those considered for Pareto improvements is not paternalism (if this term is interpreted as meaning 'knowing better than you what is good *for you*'), it might perhaps be called ***moralism***. And of course if certain preferences are excluded as antisocial, the production of goods only demanded to satisfy those preferences is a waste, is an inefficiency. The limits within which individuals' preferences and connected productions can be accepted for the determination of Pareto improvements are among the most important value judgements, often the occasion for strong and politically relevant disagreements. This means that the separation between issues of efficiency and issues of equity supposedly achieved via the notion of Pareto efficiency is in fact illusory.

Only occasionally admitted is another limitation of the two theorems: they take preferences as given and do not question them (apart from preferences for demerit goods and antisocial preferences). But *satisfying given consumer preferences is a doubtful efficiency criterion if preferences are endogenously created by the economic system: and to a considerable extent, they are.* Extensive economic resources are consciously employed to influence preferences: ***advertising*** in many countries absorbs 3% or more of GDP, and it has not only a useful informative function but also an influence on people's preferences, aimed at increasing sales; therefore it *questions the right to take the observed preferences as the basis for welfare considerations.*[34] The problem goes even deeper: there is ample consensus among sociologists, ethnologists, psychologists that people's goals and desires are largely shaped by the kind of society they live in. In a society like capitalism, status is largely derived from income, so the choice between, for example, more leisure or more income might be very different in a different social organization that gave importance to other things. One can legitimately suspect that *consumerism* would be much less strong if there weren't so much pressure towards persuading people to spend (because firms need to sell).

Another deficiency of the two theorems is that they assume that uncertainty about the future is only 'risk', in the terminology of Frank H. Knight: the possible future states of the world are known, and individuals have a sufficiently defi-

---

34 See Chap. 5, ▶ Sect. 5.32, fn. 57. By the way, advertising, by *depriving preferences of the right to be considered data of general equilibrium (because endogenously modified by the choices of some individuals)*, questions not only the welfare implications but also general equilibrium theory, which needs *given* preferences among the data determining the equilibrium. And even if current preferences can perhaps be treated as given (although to base welfare evaluations on them would still be illegitimate), they certainly cannot be so treated for the future periods of intertemporal equilibria, where they will depend on advertising. One more reason why general equilibrium theory is untenable.

nite idea (correct or not) of their probability distribution. When it is admitted that the future is simply, to a large extent, unpredictable, it seems impossible to determine Pareto-efficient choices on all issues relevantly dependent on what will happen in the future. For example, it seems impossible to know the preferences of not-yet-born consumers: will they prefer more wealth (more capital accumulation) or less ecological problems? assuming we care about the welfare of future generations, we would need to know their preferences in this regard to decide how to allocate resources today between more accumulation or more reduction of pollution. Also, it seems impossible to know what novelties the future will bring, for example what new discoveries scientific and technical research will produce, or *could* produce depending on the resources allocated to it; but then an optimal allocation of resources to producing innovations appears impossible to determine. (Something more on this problem is said in Appendix 1) As far as I know, there have been admissions of these problems (e.g. Graaff 1957, Chap. VI), but there is no attempt concretely to circumscribe the issues on which it continues to make sense to discuss of Pareto efficiency in spite of these problems.

14.8 Pareto Efficiency: A Non-neoclassical Perspective

The two Fundamental Theorems assume *the full utilization of given resources*. Here the dependence on the neoclassical approach is clearest. In actual economies, labour unemployment in excess—sometimes in *considerable* excess—of frictional unemployment is the usual situation, and the deficiencies of aggregate demand that cause this situation are not efficiently contrasted, often because of conscious political decisions. This is the most obvious and most visible refutation of the claim that competitive markets bring about Pareto efficiency—a claim impossible to sustain not only in the face of the Great Depression of the 1930s but also in the face of unemployment above 10% in many developed economies at present. The previous chapters of this book have shown that the responsibility for unemployment cannot be attributed to labour.

Given the general presence of unutilized resources in actual economies, it is not even clear that the inefficiency due to (possibly) excessive expenditure in product differentiation and other marketing expenses is really to be condemned, since it causes less unemployment. Let us remember that Keynes argued that when there is unemployment a government decision to pay people to dig holes and then fill them up again—pure waste—is better than doing nothing. This gives a taste of the need for a different welfare analysis if market economies do not spontaneously tend to the full utilization of resources.

Some initial elements for a possible different welfare analysis can be gleaned from a 2001 Round Table, published in 2004, on the relevance of a resumption of the classical–Keynesian approach for economic policy. The anonymous editorial introduction argues that a resumption of classical theory entails radical changes in applied economics and policy analysis:

» The radical nature of those changes follows from two elements: (i) the compatibility between classical free competition and permanent labour unemployment; (ii) the

1278   **Chapter 14** · Welfare, Externalities, Public Goods and Happiness

relevance of the critique of neoclassical distribution [theory] in putting on a solid basis the possibility of aggregate demand deficiencies for a long period analysis, no less that for a short-period one. Once they have been solidly founded in theory, these two elements overturn the idea of a Pareto optimality of free competition. (Editorial Note, in Foley et al. 2004, p. 4)

The suggestion is further clarified in Garegnani's contribution to the Round Table, where it is argued that a main implication of the classical approach is *a principle of generalized underutilization of productive resources in a market economy*, based on the non-existence of the neoclassical mechanisms supposedly bringing about the full employment of resources:

» ... the full utilisation of productive capacity can be seen to occur only under special circumstances and for limited periods of time. Indeed there are reasons, which at times naked observation imposes in various forms even upon orthodox analysis, for believing that some underutilisation of resources, in particular unemployment of labour, is *systematically* required for the stability of a market economy. But what should above all be noted is that our "principle of underutilised resources" derives most of its strength not from the underutilisation of capacity which can be observed in the economy at any given time: it derives it from the compound-interest-rate-like effect which pertains to the missed potential increases of productive capacity entailed in the observable underutilisation of resources over the past. Thus, over a period of time of some length, observable unused capacity grossly understates the real underutilisation of resources in the economy, and the missed opportunities of growth due to the lack of aggregate effectual demand.[35]

... The Pareto optimality of a competitive economy vanishes: classical theory has no difficulty in recognising the presence of involuntary labour unemployment by which outputs could be increased, especially when we recognise the possibility of lost potential savings. It is thus recognized as altogether normal to have positions

---

14

35 (My footnote, F. P.) Here Garegnani refers to an argument put forth in earlier papers (Garegnani 1992; Garegnani & Palumbo 1998). Suppose in a past period—call it period zero—the economy could have increased its productive capacity by more than it did, by an amount of capital goods capable of producing, if normally utilized, 10 units of income (productive capacity is measured as equal to the units of yearly income it can produce if normally utilized; income distribution is given and determines prices). Had the economy done it, in period 1 by utilizing that extra capacity the economy could have produced 10 more units of income than it did. Suppose in this economy on average 1/5 of income is allocated to increase productive capacity and that 1 unit of income so allocated increases productive capacity by 1/2 unit; then in period 2 the economy could have had 11 more units of productive capacity than it did have, and by utilizing them normally and allocating 1/5 of the extra 11 units of output to increasing productive capacity, in period 3 the economy could have had 12.1 more units of productive capacity than it did. The lost potential increase of productive capacity keeps growing (at Harrod's warranted growth rate, under the assumptions made) even if after period zero the economy fully utilizes its productive capacity. The increase grows much faster if every period there is also underutilization of the productive capacity available in that period, which is the usual case. So the lost potential increase in productive capacity (and in employment) rapidly becomes enormous, but remains unperceived *because not visible*.

14.8 · Pareto Efficiency: A Non-neoclassical Perspective

of the economy where from a strictly technical point of view economic welfare in the sense of disposal of goods could increase for the many, without decreasing for any of the few.

… That breaks the magic circle within which policy analysis tends to be confined by the neoclassical preoccupation with distorting the Pareto-optimal allocation of resources allegedly effected by competitive prices. The circle, that is, is broken open for analysing the use of economic policy in order to influence the distribution of income and the growth of the economy. The focus of economic policy shifts from the *allocation* of productive resources to their *growth* and to the distribution of the resulting product. (Garegnani 2004, pp. 37–38)

In view of the contemporary worries with ecological problems, and of the indications coming from the economics of happiness on the limited contribution of growth to happiness (see the last section of the chapter), it is not even clear that the focus of economic policy should be on *raising* growth rates; a reduction of unemployment via a shortening of the working week would probably contribute more to a more civilized lifestyle. And I would add to Garegnani's indications the need to stimulate technical progress on socially useful issues.

An important implication of a turn to a classical–Keynesian approach is a much more positive assessment of the welfare state, against the criticisms addressed to it in recent decades. The topic would require an entire chapter but I think even the little I will say can be useful. The welfare state is the usual name for the ensemble of public institutions that supply health insurance, housing and pension services, unemployment insurance, and help for the invalid and the very poor. Sometimes the supply of free education is included in the activities of welfare state, but historically it is much older than the other components. Even within a neoclassical framework, public intervention in these fields, besides being often justifiable by ethical motives analogous to those which induce passers-by to help people wounded in an accident, can be justified as more efficient than reliance on voluntary private insurance or savings or education expenditure.[36] Universal health insurance pools risks, avoiding the tendency of private insurance providers to select applicants and to ask for exceedingly high insurance premiums, unaffordable except for the very rich, in order to insure the unlucky persons with a high likelihood of needing expensive cures; myopia can cause too little saving destined to private pensions; private providers of pensions or of unemployment insurance can go bankrupt, especially when there is a generalized economic crisis; pensions are unensurable against unexpected inflation because it affects all pensions simultaneously; there may be a tendency to free riding on the altruism of others.

---

36 'a welfare state is justified not simply by redistributive aims one may (or may not) have, but because it does things which private markets for technical reasons would either do inefficiently, or would not do at all … private insurance cannot cover contingencies such as unemployment, inflation and important medical risks' (Barr 1992, p. 754).

1280   **Chapter 14** · Welfare, Externalities, Public Goods and Happiness

But in recent decades the institutions of the welfare state have been attacked as causing inefficiencies by distorting market outcomes, as wasteful, and as discouraging production and growth. Milton Fredman's natural rate of unemployment has been used to argue that the unemployed are voluntarily unemployed, so the state should not worry about them. Subsidies to low-income families have been accused of reducing the incentive to work, shifting the labour supply curve to the left, thus reducing employment and aggregate output. Compulsory pension contributions have been accused of reducing savings and thus growth. Even when it is admitted that some public health insurance should be provided, the public direct provision of medical services is condemned as distorting market outcomes, medical services should be priced by the market and therefore at most the state can pay for privately supplied medical services priced at market prices. Public production of services and of goods is accused of being inefficient because there is no search for maximum profit; privatization should be pushed as far as possible. Public expenditure should be anyway minimized because it crowds out private investment and thus reduces growth.

These criticisms rest upon a faith in the validity of a neoclassical approach untainted by Keynesian elements.[37] They are unsustainable in a classical–Keynesian framework, as the arguments of previous chapters should have made clear. Unemployment is not voluntary, it is due to deficiencies of aggregate demand, that decreases of money wages or real wages are generally powerless to correct. A lower rate of unemployment does not generally accelerate inflation, and anyway there are institutional arrangements, like the neo-corporatist ones, which have shown themselves capable of avoiding wage inflation even at extremely low levels of unemployment. It is false that public spending crowds out private spending, precisely the opposite is the case. The percentage of people who prefer not to look for a job because they are obtaining unemployment benefits is extremely small when jobs are available, because having a job is fundamental for self-respect and a social role (on this see the last section of the chapter). Anyway since labour supply is never fully employed, their not working simply permits other unemployed workers to find a job. Compulsory contributions to a public pension system nearly certainly increase savings relative to allowing people freely to choose how much to save, because of widespread myopia or inability to resist consuming now especially at low-income levels. And anyway it is not savings that determine investment and growth, the causation goes the other way. The insistence that efficiency would require pricing health services (and other services too) at market prices rests on the belief that markets produce Pareto efficiency, which is wrong as just argued; furthermore, wages and salaries do not reflect relative contributions to utility, but relative social power; pricing a labour service at a political price may or may not be the best choice but cer-

---

37 Atkinson (1996) shows well the weakness of these criticisms even within a broadly neoclassical framework when one takes into account the many aspects that make real economies different from ideal first-best competitive general equilibrium. But such a defence always leaves room for counterarguments; if the basic neoclassical framework itself is rejected, the legitimacy of the welfare state is unassailable.

tainly one need not worry about Pareto efficiency nor about not rewarding a category according to what they deserve as indicated by the market. In the USA there is the added complication of a supply of physicians kept low by extremely costly medical schools, this adds to the bargaining power of the medical profession and makes it easier to justify high incomes of doctors as needed to repay educational expenses; in other countries like Italy where university education does not cost much, the direct provision of medical services by public hospitals allows health costs for the state and for the population to be one half what they are in the USA. And it is simply a myth that public firms are less efficient than private ones, on the contrary in the field of health there is much less danger of pecuniary-induced distortions of correct behaviour (like superfluous surgical operations), and in the commercial and industrial field there is much less risk of Enron-like scandals from public companies, and public managers are ofter superior to private managers: one should not underestimate the motivation that comes from working for the public interest as compared with the motivation from making a firm that you do not own earn profits and pay you a bonus. Renault and Volkswagen were for many decades very efficient publicly owned car producers; in Italy banks were all public after World War II up to the 1980s, and the Italian economy does not seem to have suffered at all from this fact. The requirement that public firms should be profitable and earn the market rate of profit or at least the market rate of interest cannot be justified as reflecting efficiency requirements, the rate of interest does not reflect a social rate of time preference; privatization of goods and services previously produced by non-profit public services means a rise in the price of these goods because now a rate of profit must be earned on the capital employed, that is, it raises the share of profits in national income, with no efficiency justification.

14.9 Cost–Benefit Analysis and the Compensation Principle

When the justification of decisions about a public economic intervention (e.g. building a new railway or bridge; fixing a maximum speed on motorways; choosing between two incompatible projects to avoid 'acqua alta' in Venice) includes an attempt at an evaluation of the impact on general welfare, the economic basis for this evaluation is generally found in *cost–benefit* (or *benefit-cost*) *analysis*. This is an ensemble of techniques aimed at comparing the *production cost* of an intervention (the necessary payments)[38] with its total *net benefit*, measured as the algebraic sum of the consumers' willingnesses to pay or to receive a compensation to have the intervention happen. Ideally these willingnesses to pay should be measured

---

38 These payments may be zero when the intervention is simply a new law that does not entail new public expenses.

by the compensating variations[39]; in practice they are generally measured as the expected changes in monetary incomes (modified to take into account externalities and the value change of non-marketed goods, e.g. panorama) due to the intervention[40]: the monetary gains enjoyed by some agents (e.g. if the intervention is a new railway reaching a previously isolated region, the increase of incomes of hotels and restaurants due to the new railway increasing tourism in the area) minus the (absolute value of the) monetary losses suffered by other agents or in other periods (e.g. loss of tourism during the works, loss of agricultural land occupied by the rails, esteemed monetary value of worsened panorama, or of increased noise and pollution). A total net benefit greater than the production cost of the intervention is taken to indicate that the intervention is beneficial. Unfortunately the concrete measurement of these expected benefits and losses must have recourse to many assumptions, that can considerably affect the final result according to their precise formulation; so the final result is often debatable, and is often accused (sometimes with good reason) of resulting from a priori aims.[41]

The theoretical welfare principle behind cost–benefit analyses is the ***compensation principle***, which for the purposes of cost–benefit analysis can be stated as follows: if an intervention causes the net benefit to exceed the production cost of the intervention, then in principle there is room for compensating those who suffered a loss, and for covering the cost, and a surplus would remain which, if distributed

---

39 Remember from Chap. 4, ▶ Sect. 4.17, that the compensating variation is the negative of the income variation that allows the consumer to reach at the new prices the same utility level as before the change, supposing an unchanged money income.; therefore it is the maximum *periodic* payment the consumer is ready to offer in order to obtain the change. If prices do not change, it is the income variation caused by the change, if the change would bring about an improvement in utility; therefore it can be interpreted as willingness to pay (periodically, because we are talking of income, i.e. income per period). To translate it into a single once-and-for-all payment. that the sign of the compensating variation is the sign of the balance variation of a hypothetical public institution which has to pay (or receive) the CV; so if the change brought about by the intervention makes a consumer worse off, and compensation requires that the consumer receive a positive sum, the sign of the CV is negative. A *negative* CV indicates that the consumer is made *worse off* by the intervention.

40 The neoclassical foundation of cost–benefit analysis implies that it is not necessary to include, into the net benefits, income changes of the factors of production utilized to produce the intervention: the assumption of full resource utilization implies that these income changes are negligible, since the factors are only transferred from some uses to other ones, with presumably only negligible changes in general income distribution since the change in the economy-wide composition of demand for factors will be, in all likelihood, very small. So one needs to include into the net benefits only the *other* economic effects of the intervention. Things are very different in an approach that considers the employment of resources to depend on aggregate demand; then if, e.g., an intervention reduces unemployment, there will be a willingness to pay in favour of the intervention by the newly employed workers too, and by the firms which increase sales. The main benefit will then be precisely the reduced waste of potentially utilizable resources.

41 'Cost–benefit analysis replaces the claim to know subjective satisfactions with ultimately arbitrary assumptions about hypothetical willingness to pay' (Campbell 2012, p. 2253).

14.9 · Cost–Benefit Analysis and the Compensation Principle

among all citizens, would make everybody better off; *this must be interpreted to mean that the total wealth of society has increased.*[42]

Note that *it is not required that the compensations be actually paid out.*

The compensation principle was proposed in the late 1930s by Kaldor (1939) and Hicks (1940) as a way to evaluate the allocative *efficiency* of a public intervention, leaving aside issues of *equity*, that is, of what modifications in income distribution deserve approval, which involves value judgements. The argument was that the economist can leave to politicians the issue of income distribution, limiting herself/himself to assessing whether *in principle* the intervention would allow making everybody better off; the politician is left with deciding whether to effect or not the compensations, a decision whether to make some people better off and others worse off, that arises in nearly all public decisions: these generally favour some and damage others (think, e.g., of forbidding smoking in public places).

The compensation principle was an attempt to escape the consequences of the rejection (argued in 1932 by Lionel Robbins) of *interpersonal comparisons of utility.* What happened has been concisely described as follows:

» Pigou had formulated the following proposition: '… it is evident that any transference of income from a relatively rich man to a relatively poor man of similar temperament, since it enables more intense wants to be satisfied at the expense of less intense wants, must increase the aggregate sum of satisfaction' (Pigou 1932, p. 89). According to him, this proposition was based on what he considered to be the more or less factual assumptions: that utility was cardinally measurable, that all individuals had similar tastes, that marginal utility of income diminished at the same rate for everybody and that social utility which was a sum of individual utility had to be maximized.

The assumption of similar tastes came to be known as that of equal capacity for satisfaction. Since this assumption involved interpersonal comparisons of utility, it was argued by Robbins (1935)[43] that it was a non-scientific, ethical assumption because inter-personal comparisons of utility could not be made scientifically. There was no commonly accepted apparatus to resolve disagreements of judgment on such comparisons. Robbins therefore concluded that Pigou's foregoing proposition was not scientific. He considered Pigou's more or less factual assumptions to be ethical, not judgments of fact but of value. Robbins' arguments sound perfectly legitimate to us today; nobody would seriously argue that Pigou's foregoing

---

42 This formulation actually assumes quasi-linear utilities, utility variations are measured by money variations, so a project is to be approved if it raises aggregate real income (modified to take into account effects not priced by the market). The compensation criterion as formulated by Kaldor (1939) did not measure benefits and costs in money, it was in terms of utility possibility frontier, see ◨ Fig. 4.6, but in the end it boiled down to the same thing since it is difficult to have compensations other than in money; indeed Kaldor said it very clearly: a policy satisfies the compensation principle if it 'leads to an increase in … aggregate real income' (Kaldor 1939, p. 549).

43 [Footnote by me] Robbins (1935) is the second edition, fundamentally unaltered, of Robbins (1932).

1284   **Chapter 14** · Welfare, Externalities, Public Goods and Happiness

assumptions are not in fact value judgments. Yet at that time Robbins' arguments gave rise to a great deal of dismay. ... Economists did not seem to want to admit boldly that no application of economic theory to any practical problem was possible without presupposing some ethical premises or other. (Nath 1969, pp. 94–95)

The dismay is visible in Harrod's reaction to Robbins:

» If the incomparability of utility to different individuals is strictly pressed, not only are the prescriptions of the welfare school ruled out, but all prescriptions whatever. The economist as an adviser is completely stultified, and unless his speculations be regarded as of paramount aesthetic nature, he had better be suppressed completely. (Harrod 1938)

Now, it is true that if 'incomparability of utility' is taken to mean that only the Pareto principle can be used to evaluate policies, then the economist is paralysed, because there are no cases in which a government decision can be expected to make *everybody* better off. But there is no need so to interpret it. Even if capacity for satisfaction were somehow measurable, a value judgement would still be necessary to decide how much less satisfaction by one individual can be accepted, from the viewpoint of 'society', if more satisfaction is enjoyed by another individual. But then, since the relative 'worth' of individuals requires value judgements, there is no need to base these value judgements on supposedly value-free measurements of utility. Value judgements can be used to *determine* what utility should be imputed to individuals depending on their situation, where utility will have to be specified so that its level has practical implications, for example corresponds to an income level—but then the term 'utility' can be dropped and one can talk directly in terms of income. One can decide, for example, that individuals should be treated as equally deserving of income when in equivalent situations and that when incomes are unequal society prefers that some units of income be tranferred from the richest to the poorest; or one can decide that it all depends on what caste you belong to, and that widows deserve no income at all, as in India until recently.

The compensation principle tries to re-establish the impartiality of the economist as adviser, by separating efficiency from equity: if the people who gain from a policy decision would be able to compensate those who lose and still be better off, then they could also slightly *over*compensate those who lose and still be better off; this means the decision has made the economy *capable* of generating a strict Pareto improvement; this is a clear gain in potential efficiency; whether the compensation should actually be implemented is a problem of equity, that can be left to philosophers and politicians.

The thing can be illustrated graphically with the help of the notion of ***utility possibility frontier***. This, if there are S households, is a (hyper)surface in R^S_+ determined as follows. Each household has a given positive utility function. To avoid the complications of intertemporal economies and of capital, assume a non-capitalistic economy. Given the economy's resources (the vector of total quantities of goods to be allocated among the several households, in an exchange economy; the vectors of possible consumptions once initial endowments and pro-

14.9 · Cost–Benefit Analysis and the Compensation Principle

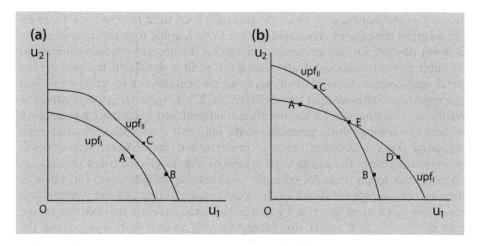

Fig. 14.7 Two possible utility possibility frontiers to discuss the compensation principle

duction possibilities are given, in a production economy), for each vector of utility levels of S-1 households the utility possibility frontier indicates the maximum achievable utility of the last household. For example with only two households, divisible goods, and monotonic utilities, the utility possibility frontier will be a downward-sloping continuous curve in (u^1, u^2) space, and there will be a different utility possibility frontier for each different vector of resources of the economy.

The compensation principle can be viewed as stating that a government intervention that shifts the utility possibility frontier outwards, as from upf_1 to upf_2 in ● Fig. 14.7a, creates at least the *possibility* of a Pareto improvement, and can therefore be recommended from this perspective even if the intervention results in a movement from point A to B, with a utility decrease for household 2; if the policy maker is in favour the reallocative tools already considered for the second Fundamental Theorem of welfare economics can then be used to reach a point representing a Pareto improvement relative to A, for example point C.

A logical weakness of Kaldor's compensation principle was soon noticed: if the intervention does not shift outwards the *entire* utility possibility frontier, the principle can run into difficulties. In ● Fig. 14.7b, an intervention causing the passage from A to B together with a shift of the utility possibility frontier from upf_I to upf_{II} is approved by the compensation principle because from B one can potentially reach C which is Pareto superior to A. But according to the same compensation principle the intervention should be undone and the economy should return to A, because from A one can potentially reach D, Pareto superior to B. The criterion is unable to conclude whether A is preferable to B or not.

Several economists (Scitovsky, Little, Samuelson and others) proposed more complex 'compensation principles' to eliminate this ambiguity, but the result was to restrict the number of interventions approved by the more exacting criteria. The initially intense debate on these criteria petered out because it was increasingly recognized that anyway the aim to avoid value judgements is not reached by

1286   **Chapter 14** · Welfare, Externalities, Public Goods and Happiness

the compensation principle. First, the principle is of little help because to ascertain whether the ex post compensation would be feasible is generally impossible: 'it is not possible for any government to obtain the necessary information about the subjective satisfactions of all those involved in a significant transfer. As the search and computations costs of doing so are tantamount to infinity, this is a task requiring omniscience' (Campbell 2012, p. 2252). Value judgements would be inevitable to compensate for the insufficient information in reaching a conclusion on how the compensation principle would judge an intervention. Second, even neglecting this fundamental practical problem and the abovementioned possible logical problem, the principle (i) is seldom able to give clear-cut indications, (ii) leaves too much room for ethically unacceptable decisions, and (iii) excludes ethically fully acceptable decisions. It would judge positively an intervention that raised the incomes of the rich by $10 billions and reduced the incomes of the poor by $9 billions; it would also judge positively an intervention that raised the incomes of the poor by 10 billions and reduced the incomes of the rich by 9 billions. If both interventions were possible, the compensation principle would offer no way to choose between them; and it is very seldom the case that there is only one alternative to remaining with the status quo. That the first of these two interventions is approved by the compensation principle raises of course the accusation that the principle concedes nearly everything to the more powerful. Even more so, since the compensation principle would eliminate, from the possible interventions the government should consider, an intervention reducing the incomes of the very rich by 10 billions and raising the incomes of the very poor by 9.9 billions.

The accusation that the compensation principle neglects equity considerations is answered by Frank (2006) with the argument that public initiatives are very numerous, and their costs and benefits are every time differently distributed; if we can be sure that every time the gains are greater than the losses, their rather random distribution will ensure that in the long run everybody will obtain a net gain.[44] This seems to forget that if in a society there are groups with conflicting interests and the stronger group has greater influence on political interventions, then there is no reason why the benefits of public interventions should be on average equally scattered over the entire population: the social groups with greater bargaining power or social strength will be able to get most of the benefits. The table by Massimo Pivetti reproduced at the end of ► Chap. 13 suggests that this is precisely what has been happening in the last thirty years, to the disadvantage of wage labour.

---

44 This argument accepts that, fundamentally, the important thing is whether the public intervention raises national income. Then the issue becomes whether national income is a good measure of the desirability of social states. There is a long series of criticisms of this criterion. Amartya Sen and others have forcefully argued that, more than income, what counts is how much people can develop their *capabilities*, how much they have the freedom and the means to become what potentially they can become and desire to become (see Fleurbaey 1996, pp. 136–138 for some distinction between several authors on this theme). And the economic literature on happiness, that has increased considerably in the last couple decades, argues that empirical evidence shows that the benefits of income growth for how happy people feel, at least for advanced nations, are much less significant than normally thought; see the chapter's last section. But welfare economics has not assimilated these findings yet.

14.10 Cost–benefit Analysis Run Amok

Cost–benefit analysis is strongly opposed by many owing to the difficulty with reaching objective monetary valuations of costs and benefits, which opens the door to arbitrariness and hidden aims, and to the possibility of ethically abominable conclusions. Barely a hint of these possibilities will be given here. Arbitrariness can easily slip in when one is to estimate the effects of the intervention (e.g. how many people will use a new flyover urban train, relieving traffic congestion?) and when one is to measure the value of non-marketed elements; for example, if a dam requires removing a number of people from areas that will be flooded, how is one to value the suffering because of having to abandon cherished familiar places and social networks? or, how is one to monetize the damage from the noise of a flyover? Arbitrariness also appears in forming estimates of future costs and benefits given the possibility of unexpected changes; in attributing monetary value to risks (e.g. of death, which also requires an evaluation of the value of life, on which more below; or of catastrophes, e.g. connected with nuclear plants); in the discounting rates used to compare costs and benefits extending over many periods; in circumscribing who must be considered as enjoying benefits or bearing damages from the intervention. Also very difficult, in some measure necessarily arbitrary, is deciding whether the intervention prevents other interventions, be it because of lack of funds or because of physical incompatibility; in both cases the net social benefit of one intervention should be determined taking into account what one renounces.

Then there are the dangers connected with the use of willingness to pay as a measure of benefits. The rich, having more money, can offer to pay more than the poor to have something approved; therefore when preferences differ, willingness to pay inevitably favours the desires of the rich. Proposals have been made to weigh willingnesses to pay taking into account the relative incomes of the individuals, but how to weigh them is arbitrary. The real solution of this problem would be drastically to reduce inequalities in wealth and income. And clearly, the compensation principle, that is the claim that it is not necessary that compensations be actually paid, is unacceptable; feasible compensations should be paid.[45] (But important problems arise at this point: *what* deserves compensation? Clearly, not all externalities can give a right to compensation, otherwise the persons who do not like women to wear bikinis, or do not like that there be doctors who earn money procuring abortions, should be compensated. Democracy cannot compensate all those who are against decisions democratically but not unanimously taken. Anyway compensations capable of really restoring the utility levels of all the persons damaged by a change are impossible to determine, even only conceptually, unless one very strongly circumscribes the elements of a social state to take into account; it is extremely doubtful that individuals would be capable of deter-

---

45 '...if compensations are not paid, it is not at all clear in what sense it can be said that this is a social improvement ("Don't worry, my dear loser, we can compensate you fully, and the fact that we don't have the slightest intention of actually paying this compensation makes no difference; it is merely a difference in distribution"). The compensation tests are either redundant or unconvincing' (Sen 2000, p. 947).

mining what compensation would make them indifferent between the status quo, and a change with compensation, when the change involves moral/political reactions. There may also be moral objections to such compensations.)

Although impossible to justify on the basis of the compensation principle, impossible to take as authorizing by itself political decisions, and certainly debatable in four out of every five evaluations made by its authors, a well-done cost–benefit analysis (accompanied by comments and criticisms) is better than not having it, because it contributes greater clarity about the possible effects of an intervention; it supplies useful information on who will benefit and who will suffer, with some even if contestable estimate of how much; thus helping politicians to decide, and even more importantly, helping democratic political pressure from below better to evaluate the issue. More and clearly explained cost–benefit analyses would be very useful to democracy. For example, in Italy where tax evasion is a relevant problem, it would be useful to have a cost–benefit analysis of the effects of increasing the personnel of Guardia di Finanza (the police body specialized in checking tax compliance); or, given the excessive time taken by both penal and civil Italian courts to adjudicate law cases, a cost–benefit analysis would be useful to estimate the convenience of having more judges. One is given to suspect a lack of political willingness behind the absence of cost–benefit analyses in these cases: perhaps there isn't a real desire of the ruling parties to fight tax evasion, nor to punish white-collar crime.

One serious problem with cost–benefit analysis, even in this role of simply supplying useful information, is that in too many instances in order to assess costs and benefits its present methods rely on neoclassical views of how to measure the contribution of individuals to welfare, that implicitly make the same assumptions as the two Fundamental Welfare theorems (income distribution reflecting relative factor scarcity, absence of externalities etc.), with sometimes grossly mistaken and even shocking consequences. Consider the following episode. In December 1991 a memorandum by Lawrence Summers, then the World Bank's chief economist (later to become President of Harvard University), was circulated to his staff. It was leaked out by an unknown source to a Brazilian newspaper which published it. It read:

» Just between you and me, shouldn't the World Bank be encouraging *more* migration of the dirty industries to the LDCs [less developed countries]? I can think of three reasons:

(1) The measurement of the costs of health-impairing pollution depends on the foregone earnings from increased morbidity and mortality. From this point of view a given amount of health-impairing pollution should be done in the country with the lowest cost, which will be the country with the lowest wages. I think the economic logic behind dumping a load of toxic waste in the lowest-wage country is impeccable and we should face up to that.

(2) The costs of pollution are likely to be non-linear as the initial increments of pollution probably have very low cost. I've always thought that under-populated countries in Africa are vastly *under* polluted; their air quality is probably vastly inefficiently low [sic—probably 'air quality' is a slip for 'air pollution level', F.P.] compared to Los Angeles or Mexico City. Only the lamentable facts that so much

pollution is generated by non-tradable industries (transport, electrical generation) and that the unit transport costs of solid waste are so high prevent world-welfare-enhancing trade in air pollution and waste.

(3) The demand for a clean environment for aesthetic and health reasons is likely to have very high income-elasticity. The concern over an agent that causes a one-in-a-million change in the odds of prostate cancer is obviously going to be much higher in a country where people survive to get prostate cancer than in a country where under-5 mortality is 200 per thousand. Also, much of the concern over industrial atmospheric discharge is about visibility-impairing particulates. These discharges may have very little direct health impact. Clearly trade in goods that embody aesthetic pollution concerns could be welfare-enhancing. While production is mobile the consumption of pretty air is a non-tradable.

The problems with the arguments against all of these proposals for more pollution in LDCs (intrinsic rights to certain goods, moral reasons, social concerns, lack of adequate markets, etc.) could be turned around and used more or less effectively against every Bank proposal for liberalisation.

Understandably, the document caused an uproar. And yet, Summers was correct in describing the implications of the economic logic applied in cost–benefit analysis.[46] Let us distinguish the arguments in the several paragraphs, and let us start with (1), the most shocking one.

---

46 Wikipedia reports that a member of Summers' staff, Pritchett, stated that the memo had been written by him and Summers had only signed it, and that it was intended to be 'sarcastic'; according to Pritchett, the memo as leaked was doctored to remove context and intended irony, and was 'a deliberate fraud and forgery to discredit Larry and the World Bank'. However, the original undoctored memo was never revealed, which makes these statements hard to believe. Also, a *Washington Post* article on February 10, 1992, reported as follows a subsequent clarification by Summers:

On Jan. 12, a month after the original memo appeared, Summers issued a clarification. He wrote that while the excerpt 'unfortunately makes it appear that I am seriously forwarding certain strong arguments', the statements were designed as a 'sardonic counterpoint, an effort to sharpen the analysis.' In an interview last week, he apologized for using 'inflammatory' language and stressed 'it is not my policy view that pollution is good anywhere.' Nevertheless, he insisted 'it is a legitimate question whether environmental standards should be the same worldwide,' and it is only because the question falls outside the bounds of 'political correctness' that it generated such a strong backlash. 'Free trade policies will have a real effect on the distribution of pollution around the world', said Summers, 37, who was an economics professor at Harvard until taking the World Bank job a year ago. 'Industries tend to locate in places where [production costs are the least]. The consequences need to be considered carefully.' His Jan. 12 clarification only deepened suspicion among the bank's environmental officials, long at odds with economists and their cost calculus of ecological protections. Summer's 'nuggets' seemed like a case of cost–benefit analysis run amok.

If the report is faithful, Summers did *not* deny the correctness of the economic reasoning remembered in the memo, he only denied he intended 'seriously' to push for the policies implied by that reasoning, but without explaining why, and on the contrary confirming that one can doubt that environmental standards should be the same everywhere—which brings to the memo's conclusions. Also, taking up even more explicitly the innuendos of the last paragraph of the memo, he stated that free trade policies help the process of pollution transfer, clearly implying: 'you moralistic critics must be stupid not to realize that if really you are against pollution transfers to low-wage countries then you and the World Bank should also be against free trade policies, which you are not'.

1290   **Chapter 14** · Welfare, Externalities, Public Goods and Happiness

In assessments in court of the damage caused by illness or death for compensation purposes, the standard method is to calculate the damage as the present value of income loss from past and future inability to work,[47] with the consequence that the illness or death of low-wage people is worth much less than the illness or death of high-wage people. The exclusive attention to the loss of labour income as the measure of the loss to society or to the household caused by death is terrifying enough; it confirms a tendency to give importance only to income and consumption as measures of welfare in capitalist societies, forgetting for example about the grief caused by the loss of a beloved person. But this criticism, although valid, does not get to the root of the strength of Summers' argument: which is the neoclassical theory of income distribution, which argues that the rental rate earned by a factor reflects its marginal contribution to production and ultimately to utility (see ► Chap. 3). Then the disappearance of a low-wage labourer means a smaller loss of utility to consumers than the disappearance of a high-wage manager. In paragraph (1) of the memo, Summers applies this approach: he implicitly asks to imagine the whole world as a single economy where income distribution is determined according to neoclassical theory, and where therefore the low wages in LDCs indicate a low contribution of their workers to worldwide welfare; and

---

47 In a manual (available on the Internet) prepared by the USA Center for Disease Control and Prevention to teach how to assess the efficiency of health policies, one reads:

The human capital approach for valuing indirect benefits in a benefit–cost analysis is based on the theory of investment. People are viewed as capital investments whose sole purpose is to produce for society at large. The value of their production potential in society is based on the wages they earn, including all the benefits associated with those wages, with some adjustments for their production potential within the household as well. The human capital approach assumes that workers have a value equal to their earnings because the fair market workplace would not pay workers more than they are worth. If a disease, injury, or illness affects a person's productivity, the cost to society is valued in terms of lost earnings. Thus, the human capital approach is fairly straightforward when valuing a death associated with a disease. The human capital approach would base the value of a death on the person's age, sex, and occupation because wages differ by these factors. The present value of future earnings, including gross earnings and fringe benefits, would be adjusted for non-market labor, such as household productivity. In some cases, you would subtract future consumption from this value because these goods and services would still be available to other members of society. You can use tables with calculated lifetime cost estimates using the human capital approach. See the Grosse chapter in the Haddix reference.

Despite its widespread use, the human capital approach for valuing indirect benefits of interventions has many limitations. First, because it's based on wages, it discriminates against low wage earners, such as the elderly; the very young; the disabled; and women, in comparison to men of the same age and occupation. Second, it assumes that the labor market has perfect equality in that people are paid at their true production potential, there are equal job opportunities for all, and people get paid the same wage for the same job. Unfortunately, we know these things aren't true. A teacher's salary may have more to do with geographic location than experience, quality, or productive potential. Finally, the human capital approach only values the indirect benefits associated with productivity losses and does not incorporate pain, suffering, and losses in leisure time.

Note the complete acceptance of the neoclassical view of factor rentals (wages, in this case) as measuring the factor's marginal contribution to social welfare.

then—'the economic logic is impeccable…and we should face up to that'—he renders some implications explicit which other people dare not utter so clearly but which it is difficult to escape once the logic of the approach is accepted. If somebody must suffer illness or death from pollution, it is preferable that it be the people who contribute less to worldwide welfare—the people whose labour costs less, evidently because it has a lower marginal revenue product.

This conclusion was harshly criticized by many as cynical and disgusting; but it is essentially the same as when a nation decides that medical treatments should only go to the people who can afford them, evidently because people deserve to be spared illness or death only if their willingness to pay (that to a large extent reflects their income, i.e. the contribution of their labour and of the capital and land they own to society's welfare) is up to the cost of the medical treatment.[48] Most people would counter that human life and human suffering should be given the same importance independently of whose life and suffering is in question. A discussion of this type of arguments would take us to complex issues of moral philosophy; but perhaps we can spare such a discussion, because the economics behind Summers' reasoning is radically wrong. The thesis that factor rewards are determined by the full-employment marginal contributions of the several factors to welfare derives from the neoclassical theory of income distribution, which is untenable. 'Factor rewards' in fact reflect relative bargaining power. As explained in ▶ Chap. 12, the adaptability of production to demand and the general possibility to produce more imply that it is income distribution that determines technology and prices; marginal revenue products adapt to—and so are determined by—the income distribution resulting from the relative bargaining power of the several social groups. Low wages in LDCs do not reflect a low marginal contribution to worldwide welfare, but a low bargaining power of those labourers in the world market. So no ethical justification for letting the poor bear more pollution can be derived from their being left poor by the market, except anti-democratic justifications such as 'the weak deserve to perish, the strong to dominate', that produce fascist dictatorships.

Arguments (2) and (3) are analogously undermined by a realization that what can make the proposed trades accepted by LDCs is their weakness. The argument is: LDCs would be ready to accept importing pollution if adequately paid, and

---

48 However, in the case of having to pay for medical treatment, capacity to pay includes property income, which is treated as reflecting a contribution to society's welfare analogous to labour's contribution (as explained in ▶ Chap. 3, the argument is that there is a sacrifice not only in working but also in allocating capital or land to production rather than to personal consumption). On the contrary, in the calculation of the loss due to death even a neoclassical economist can include only the disappearance of the future *labour* contribution of the dead person: the death of a person does not cause society to lose the non-labour factors she/he owns, these do not disappear but simply pass to other people via inheritance. So the death of a pensioner or of a person living entirely on property income causes zero loss to society; one reaches the conclusion that a welfare-maximizing allocation of pollution should consist of inducing non-working people (pensioners or people living on property incomes) to concentrate in certain localities, and dumping there as much pollution as possible.

1292   **Chapter 14 · Welfare, Externalities, Public Goods and Happiness**

rich countries would be ready to pay to export pollution, so most probably there would be room for mutually welfare-improving exchange here, if only pollution export were possible once pollution is produced, which unfortunately is not the case; so let us export pollution-producing industries instead, and let us consider the gain LDCs derive from the increased labour employment as a payment for importing pollution. The ethical evaluation of such a trade will be very different if one views rich and poor countries as deserving to be rich and poor, or one views the situation as analogous to that of a man offering at gunpoint to a woman to accept being raped rather than killed: if the woman accepts, this can be seen as mutually welfare-improving: the woman prefers to be raped rather than killed, the man prefers not to have to kill her.

For additional comments on Summers' shocking memo, read ▶ Chaps. 2 and 15 of Hausman and McPherson (2006). The authors are not aware of the possibility to criticize the entire neoclassical foundation of Summers' memo, but otherwise their comments are excellent. Another shocking use of cost–benefit analysis occurred in the case of the Ford Pinto, a 1971 car model which, because of design flaws, was liable to burst into flames in a rear-impact collision. It seems the problem was discovered by Ford before starting to sell the vehicle, but the company decided not to modify the car and to keep the problem secret. One estimate (by *Mother Jones*) attributes between 500 and 900 burn deaths to Pinto crashes. When the problem at last was discovered and made public, the company tried to argue that its cost–benefit analysis had estimated that, based on the number of cars in use and the probable accident rate, deaths due to the design flaw would cost it about $49.5 million to settle wrongful death lawsuits (taken to indicate the social cost of those deaths) versus recall costs of $137.5 million (considered the social cost of eliminating the defect), and therefore issuing a recall was inefficient from the point of view of society's welfare. The general reaction was of rage, forcing a recall *and* damaging sales of other Ford models too. Of course if the flaw had remained undiscovered Ford would not have paid the estimated $49.5 million compensation for wrongful deaths, so the decision not to divulge the problem was anyway callous, besides being theoretically contestable even on the basis of cost–benefit analysis and its estimate of the value of life because neglecting the value to consumers of knowing the risks that the use of a good entails. Also, there are serious doubts about Ford's calculation of recall costs, and the comparison should not have been with recall costs but with preventative costs: it seems that several possible modifications had been contemplated by Ford's engineers which would have avoided the car bursting into flames at a cost of little more than 10 dollars per car; and not more than 2.5 million defective cars were sold.) The episode is illustrative of the possibility to bend cost–benefit analysis to aims that general morality strongly rejects.

14.11 Social Welfare Functions

Much of the economists' discussion on welfare and economic justice uses the notion of social welfare function. Suppose society can find itself in a number of alternative social states, depending for example on policy decisions. Distinguish these social states by the economic activities in each, that is, the productive and consumption activities of each individual and of each firm, hence a long list for each household of what kinds of labour it performs,[49] what kinds of other factor services it supplies to firms, and what consumption goods and services it consumes, and for each firm what production activities it performs; other non-economic elements also count but are assumed constant and not explicitly considered. Call *socio-economic state* this list. Call X the set of the possible socio-economic states x. Assume there is some criterion that assigns a number to socio-economic states that indicates that between two states the one with associated the higher number is **socially preferred**. This means that the notion of a preference *of society* for one state over another can be conceived, evidently reflecting someone's view of what society *should* prefer—since what *society* in fact prefers is a highly problematical notion, clearly illegitimate for undemocratic societies, but doubtful also for modern democracies: what right do we have to say that *society* prefers what changing Parliamentary coalitions decide, or what a small part of it (sometimes less than a quarter of the people with the right to vote) has approved? and what about political decisions taken under the threat of a military coup, or even only of a flight of capital abroad, if the decision goes in a certain direction? Therefore when talking about social preferences we are talking about *political proposals* about what the community, or its rulers, should prefer.

The function, analogous to a utility function, that by attributing to each social state a number depicts a preference order among social states distinguished only by their economic characteristics (what is produced and how, and what is consumed by each individual), was proposed by Adam Bergson in 1938[50] as a tool to clarify 'the value judgments required for the derivation of the conditions of maximum economic welfare which have been advanced in the studies of the Cambridge economists [Marshall, Pigou, Kahn], Pareto and Barone, and Mr. Lerner' (Bergson 1969, p. 7). It was named the *Economic Welfare Function*. Bergson argued that the value judgements of those authors could be made clear in terms of different characteristics imposed on the Economic Welfare Function.

The idea that all these authors had been implicitly accepting an Economic Welfare Function which society should maximize was up to a point new, although at least the language of utilitarianism, which spoke of maximizing the sum of the utilities or happinesses of the members of the community, had presupposed some such notion.

---

49 Generally neoclassical equilibrium theory does not distinguish different working activities as generating different utility or disutility for the consumer; but it could. The creator of the notion of social welfare function, Bergson, made the distinction, and considered each type of labour activity a different 'consumption good'. The extension of consumer theory to include this distinction is not difficult and is left to the reader as an exercise; its use is above all to conclude that a consumer will decide which type of labour to offer depending on their disutility and wage.

50 At the time Bergson had not yet changed his last name, which was Burk, and the 1938 article was published as authored by Adam Burk. Later reprints changed the author's name to Adam Bergson.

1294   **Chapter 14 ·** Welfare, Externalities, Public Goods and Happiness

Bergson proceeds to assume that the Economic Welfare Function is differentiable and finds the maximum conditions subject to the limitations of the given technique of production and the given amounts of resources. He finds that one group of conditions is that 'the marginal welfare of each commodity and the marginal economic diswelfare of each type of work be the same with respect to each individual in the community'. For example, if the last unit of commodity 1 going to consumer h contributes less to Economic Welfare than the last unit of the same commodity going to consumer k, then one unit of commodity 1 should be transferred from h to k. Why a commodity going to a consumer has a certain 'marginal welfare' (i.e. marginal productivity of Economic Welfare) is not specified; note that this leaves room for valuing differently the contribution to Economic Welfare of the consumptions of different individuals, and also leaves room for all sorts of externalities and other-regarding preferences. Bergson then passes to production and finds 'that the economic welfare of the consumers' goods produced by a marginal increment of each type of work should equal the negative of the diswelfare of that increment of work, and that the increment of economic welfare due to the shift of a marginal unit of factors C and D from one production unit to another should equal the negative of the diswelfare caused by this adjustment' (ibid., p. 10). Again, these equalities leave undetermined the marginal contributions to Economic Welfare of all these variables, and leave room for all external effects.

These are more general conditions, Bergson continues, than in the welfare studies of the authors he is concerned with. 'Their derivation thus requires the introduction of restrictions on the shape of the Economic Welfare Function' (ibid., p. 11), that is, additional value judgements besides the one that Economic Welfare should be maximized. He derives from Lerner a *First Group of Value Propositions* that states that 'a shift in a unit of any factor of production, other than labor, from one production unit to another would leave economic welfare unchanged, provided the amounts of all the other elements in welfare were constant' (p. 12). Bergson shows that this implies that the marginal indirect contribution to Economic Welfare of a factor must be the same in all its employments, which implies that the ratios between marginal products of factors must be the same in all firms. This excludes externalities in production. From Pareto and Barone he derives the *Fundamental Value Propositions of Individual Preference*, also accepted by the Cambridge economists: 'if the amounts of the various commodities and types of work were constant for all individuals in the community except any i-th individual, and if the i-th individual consumed the various commodities and performed the various types of work in combinations which were indifferent to him, economic welfare would be constant' (p. 13). That is, as long as the utility of the ith consumer is constant and, not the other utilities, but the consumptions and labours of the other consumers are constant, Economic Welfare is constant. This excludes externalities in consumption, and together with the Lerner condition implies that the marginal rate of substitution of two commodities must be the same for all individuals. Then the Economic Welfare Function can be represented as a function of the vector of utility levels of the individuals; and all the conditions for Pareto efficiency we saw in ▶ Chap. 3 are shown to be implied.

14.11 · Social Welfare Functions

Finally, Bergson interprets the Cambridge economists as assuming the Propositions of Equal Shares, that is that, when the efficiency conditions just seen are satisfied, the total income from non-labour sources maximizes welfare when it is equally allocated among all individuals. Bergson admits in footnote that actually most Cambridge economists (not Kahn) require an equal distribution *of incomes*, not of non-labour incomes, but this conflicts with the Pareto efficiency conditions unless the amount of the various types of labour performed by different individuals is the same (p. 15). He then criticizes the Cambridge economists as obscuring the value judgement implicit in their position by using a comparison of utilities as if it were a factual comparison: 'Statements as to the aggregative character of total welfare, or as to the equality of marginal utilities when there is an equal distribution of Shares [incomes in excess of labour incomes], provided temperaments are about the same, do have the ring of *factual* propositions, and are likey to obscure the evaluations implied' (ibid., p. 20, italics in the text). But on the other hand, Bergson continues, Pareto and Barone give no reason why addition of utilities should be avoided and abstain from introducing value judgements about income distribution, but avoiding in this way the distributive problem *they undermine their own proposal* of what we have termed the Pareto principle, because 'unless the Cambridge Conditions, or a modified form of these conditions, are introduced there is no reason in general why it is more preferable to have the other conditions satisfied than otherwise. ... In general, if conditions regarding distribution are not satisfied, it is just as likely as not that any position for which $\sum \Delta_i$ does not equal zero [i.e. that not all Pareto efficiency conditions are satisfied, F. P.] will be *more* desirable than any position for which it does equal zero' (ibid., p. 22, italics in the text). Worth pondering, isn't it? (The paragraph following this quote is also extremely interesting but I will not report it here, I hope the reader will feel enticed to read this interesting article.)

Samuelson in *Foundations of Economic Analysis* (1947) proposed the name Social Welfare Function for Bergson's notion, and the currently dominant name is **Bergson–Samuelson social welfare function**. The different name is not entirely unjustified, because the function is now described as depending on the socio-economic state x exclusively via the utility levels this state determines, i.e. as having form

$$W(x) = W(u_l(x), \ldots, u_S(x)). \tag{14.9}$$

This *welfarist* form will be indicated below as *SWF*. It is not incompatible with externalities and it need not be restricted to considering utilities as depending only on consumption baskets. But it makes a restrictive value judgement that Bergson's Economic Welfare Function had not made: that what counts is the individuals' self-perceived utility. The Economic Welfare Function had not excluded that for example what each person consumes might be important for social welfare independently of the individuals' opinions. Bergson notes that a specific value judgement is needed, and is made by Pareto, to arrive at the SWF form; and the description of this value judgement is carefully made to reveal (although Bergson does not stress the thing explicitly) that Pareto implicitly assumes the absence of consumption externalities. The latter is not a value judgement, it is a restrictive assumption on the kind of states to which the analysis is applicable. We need to understand the importance of this assumption.

1296   **Chapter 14** · Welfare, Externalities, Public Goods and Happiness

Let us first be more precise about the connection between Pareto Principle and welfarism. Let $X = \{x, y, z, \ldots\}$ be the set of possible socio-economic states. There are S individuals. Suppose a binary reflexive transitive and complete relation R of weak preference is established among these states, where xRy means that state x is at least as good 'for society' as state y, and xR_sy means that state x is at least as good as state y for individual s. Strict preference can be represented with P, where $xPy \Leftrightarrow$ 'xRy and (yRx)'[51]; equipreference, that is indifference of society between two states, is indicated with the symbol I, where $xIy \Leftrightarrow$ 'xRy and yRx'. The absence of individual index signals social preference. It is usual to distinguish three versions of the Pareto Principle that connect individual preference to social preference:

Weak Pareto Principle: for all couple x, y of states in X, if for all individuals it is xP_sy, then xPy. Formally (it saves space): $\forall x, y \in X, [xP_sy, \forall s] \Rightarrow xPy$.

Strong Pareto Principle: for all couples x, y of states in X, if for all individuals it is xR_sy then xRy, and if for all individuals it is xR_sy and there is at least one individual i for whom xP_iy, then xPy. (Write yourself the concise formal expression.)[52]

Principle of Pareto Indifference: for all couples x, y of states in X, if for all individuals it is xI_sy, then xIy.

For the *strong* Pareto Principle a state x is socially strictly preferred to a state y if the *passage* from y to x would represent a *weak* Pareto improvement, while the weak Pareto Principle requires the passage from y to x to be a *strict* Pareto improvement. The apparent terminological contradiction is due to the fact that the words 'strong' and 'strict' are used here to indicate that the principle applies to a larger number of cases than the weak principle. The term Pareto Principle without qualifications is generally used for the strong principle. The reader will easily prove that the latter logically implies the other two principles. Also, below it will be useful to remember that if xIy then xRy.

Now let us assume the preferences of individuals can be represented by utility functions $U_s(x)$ defined over the states in X (thus for example lexicographic preferences are excluded). Define a binary relation R^* over vectors of utility levels of the individuals as follows. Let $\mathbf{u} = (u_1, \ldots, u_s, \ldots, u_S)$ and $\mathbf{u}' = (u_1', \ldots, u_s', \ldots, u_S')$ indicate utility vectors, and define

$$\mathbf{u}R^*\mathbf{u}' \Leftrightarrow \exists x, y \in X : \forall s, U_s(x) = u_s, U_s(y) = u_s', \quad \text{and} \quad xRy. \tag{14.10}$$

That is, when $\mathbf{u}$ is the vector of the S utility levels associated with state x, and $\mathbf{u'}$ the vector of utility levels associated with state y, and x is socially weakly

---

51 Symbols: $\Rightarrow$ means 'implies', $\Leftrightarrow$ means 'if and only if', $\neg$ means 'not',: means 'such that'. Note that P implies R.

52 A fourth principle is the **Strict Pareto Principle**: for all couples x, y of states in X, if for all individuals it is xR_sy and there is at least one individual i for whom xP_iy, then xPy. (This differs from the strong principle in that here if it is only xR_sy for all individuals this does not imply anything about the social preference.) It arises only in certain cases I will not discuss (see Fleurbaey 1996, p. 43).

14.11 · Social Welfare Functions

preferred to y, then the relationship $\mathbf{u}R^*\mathbf{u}'$ holds; conversely, one can say that $\mathbf{u}R^*\mathbf{u}'$ only if $\mathbf{u}$ and $\mathbf{u}'$ are vectors of utility levels associated the first to a state x and the second to a state y with xRy. This relationship can always be defined. It is transitive, if R is transitive.

Now assume the Principle of Pareto Indifference. I will prove that then

$$xRy \Leftrightarrow (U_1(x), \ldots, U_s(x), \ldots, U_S(x))R^*(U_1(y), \ldots U_s(y), \ldots, U_S(y)). \qquad (14.11)$$

That is, society's preference between two states translates into the same order applied to the vector of utilities associated with those two states, hence it suffices to look at the order relation R* between the vectors of utilities associated with two states to know society's attitude towards them. In other words, society's preference is entirely described by how it ranks the utility vectors associated with socio-economic states; therefore R is welfarist, and it can be described in the SWF form.

Proof I must prove (i) that the left-hand side of the above expression implies the right-hand side, and (ii) vice-versa. As to (i): we are given the couple of states (x, y) and the corresponding vectors of utilities, and we know that xRy, hence we have the right-hand side of the definition of R^* in (14.10), which implies $\mathbf{u}R^*\mathbf{u}'$ with $\mathbf{u}=(U_1(x), \ldots, U_s(x), \ldots, U_S(x))$ and $\mathbf{u}'=(U_1(y), \ldots U_s(y), \ldots, U_S(y))$. As to (ii), by the definition of R^* the given $\mathbf{u}R^*\mathbf{u}'$ with $\mathbf{u}=(U_1(x), \ldots, U_s(x), \ldots, U_S(x))$ and $\mathbf{u}'=(U_1(y), \ldots U_s(y), \ldots, U_S(y))$ implies that there exists a couple of states (x^*, y^*) such that for all individuals $U_s(x^*)=u_s$ and $U_s(y^*)=u_s'$ and x^*Ry^*. This means that each individual is indifferent between x and x^*, and between y and y^*. Then by Pareto Indifference xIx^* and yIy^*, and by transitivity xRy. ∎

Therefore the Principle of Pareto Indifference, or the Strong Pareto Principle which implies it, suffice for the social preference relation R to be welfarist, under the sole additional assumption that individual preferences can be represented by utility functions. If one assumes the Strong Pareto Principle, then the SWF is called Paretian.

A Paretian SWF does not prevent consideration of consumption externalities; but if one admits them the Pareto Principle seems to lose all practical relevance, while if one does not consider them, then the Pareto Principle would appear to lose whatever claim to general approval it can have after what was observed in ▶ Sect. 14.7. The (Strong) Pareto Principle states that if a change increases the utility of one individual while no other individual's utility decreases, then social welfare increases, that is, society should be in favour of the change. In order for this to be acceptable, a necessary condition would seem to be that utility functions include *all* external effects, for example the feelings of equity which may cause many people to dislike an increase in the income of one part of the population unaccompanied by any increase in the income of the rest of the population. But generally it is precisely the neglect of these external effects that makes the Pareto Principle capable of applicable implications. The Pareto Principle becomes totally inapplicable in practice if utility is admitted to depend also on how much social states agree with one's other-regarding preferences and value judgements. For example the introduction of a tax to correct a pollution externality would have to take into account the strength of the opposition of some citizens to the introduction of further taxes because they favour the ideal of a minimal state. Political decisions in a democracy do take such elements into account, but not because they try to apply the Pareto Principle, rather because of alliances, compromises, desire to be re-elected etcetera. The Pareto Principle is never applicable to political decisions, if utility is an index of the preference of social states defined to include all elements raising moral and political evaluations: there will always be someone who would have voted against a political decision. Pareto's neglect of externalities and of the role of political and moral preferences in the determination of utility levels was indispensable to giving his notion of efficiency practical relevance.

Therefore the usefulness of the notion of SWF can be debated. Bergson had the limited purpose of clarifying the value judgements implicit in the main writings on economic welfare up to then; and what he achieved was to make it clearer that these value judgements consisted of the Pareto Principle (from which, coupled with the assumption of absence of externalities, one can derive the conditions for Pareto-efficient allocations that authorize the Fundamental Theorems), to which the Cambridge economists added the value judgement that, the more equal the distribution of incomes or at least of incomes not deriving from personal labour efforts, the better. Whether the notion of SWF has usefulness beyond this, is not clear. I have already pointed out that it seems illegitimate to view actual collective decisions as expressing *social preferences* and therefore as reflecting a SWF. There is also the concrete difficulty that successive social decisions in a nation do not seem to reflect a persistent complete transitive ordering over possible alternatives. But if *social* value judgements in the sense of representative of the will of something named 'society' is not a defensible descriptive notion, then a welfare economics that postulates social value judgements can only be a *proposal* based on opinions of the proponent, 'I hope you will agree with me that it would be nice if….' But can a SWF interpreted as an individual's proposal be of great interest? For concrete problems, individual opinions on what to do will be derived from a theory of how the economy functions and from specific value judgements applied to the specific case, possibly derived from a general moral philosophy, but with no need for something as detailed, complete and non-contradictory as a SWF. A Paretian SWF allows certain statements about efficiency conditions, but then what one is assuming is the correctness of the marginal approach, and one stops precisely where the SWF should say something more, how to choose among the infinite Pareto-efficient allocations; any more specific thesis, for example a desire for more, or for less, equality, does not need the rigidity and vagueness of a SWF in order to become translated into practical opinions.

The notion of SWF seems to have only one clearly useful application: it allows a quick derivation of general conditions for Pareto efficiency (it was proposed by Bergson essentially for this purpose). Let us see.

*T14.7. **Welfare maxima are Pareto efficient**. Assume the SWF is strictly increasing in each of its arguments u_i. This is also expressed as 'W is strictly Paretian'. Assume society (or whoever decides for society) wants to maximize W over the*

14.11 · Social Welfare Functions

set X of socio-economic states, and therefore wants to choose a socio-economic state x^* that solves

$$Max_{x \in X} W(u_1(x), u_2(x), \ldots, u_S(x)) \quad s.t. \; x \in X. \tag{14.12}$$

If x^* solves this problem, then it is Pareto efficient.

Proof if x^* is not Pareto efficient, then a Pareto improvement is possible, so there is another state $x°$ where no one is worse off than in x^* and at least one individual is better off; then a strictly Paretian W will have a higher value in $x°$ than in x^*, contradicting the assumption that x^* maximizes W. ■

So, assuming a solution x^* exists, we have found a Pareto-efficient state. With a different W we would find another Pareto-efficient state. With a still different W, still another Pareto-efficient state. If we were to discover that, in a certain socio-economic choice problem, all Pareto-efficient states are solutions of problem (14.12) for some W, then we might look for conditions that characterize Pareto-efficient states in terms of *necessary* conditions that *all* solutions to some social welfare function maximization must satisfy.

In fact, there is a result that allows us to do exactly that, and for a particularly simple form of the SWF, a form to which the denomination 'Bergsonian social welfare function' is often restricted. To present this result, we need the notion of *set of possible utility imputations.*

A *utility imputation* is a vector of utility levels, one per individual, $\mathbf{u} = (u_1, u_2, \ldots, u_S)$. Since individual utility levels depend on the socio-economic state, to each element x of the given set X of possible socio-economic states there corresponds a utility imputation $\mathbf{u}(x)$. Let us indicate the set of utility imputations made possible by the elements of X as $U(X) = \{\mathbf{u}(x)\}$.

For example, consider an exchange economy where there is a given vector of total endowments of consumption goods that can be allocated in different ways among the S individuals in the economy; suppose individual utility depends uniquely on the vector of consumption goods the individual is allotted; then X is the set of possible allocations of the endowments of consumption goods among the individuals, and U(X) is the set of utility imputations (vectors of utility levels) corresponding to the possible allocations.

The result (whose proof I omit)[53] is the following:

T14.8. Pareto efficiency from SWF maximization. *Given a set of S individuals, a set $X = \{x\}$ of social states, and a vector of utility functions $u_s(x)$, $i = 1, \ldots, N$, suppose the social state x^* is Pareto efficient, and the utility imputation corresponding to x^*, $\mathbf{u}(x^*)$, is Pareto efficient in the convex hull of $U(X)$. Then for some selection of non-negative weights $(\alpha_1, \alpha_2, \ldots, \alpha_S)$ at least one of which is positive, x^* maximizes the social welfare function $W(x) = \Sigma_s \alpha_s u_s(x)$ over X.*

---

53 For a proof, that involves using the separating hyperplane theorem, see, e.g., Kreps (1990, p. 163).

1300   Chapter 14 · Welfare, Externalities, Public Goods and Happiness

Furthermore, if X *is a convex set and each* u_s: X→R *is concave, then if* x^* *is Pareto efficient in* X, *the utility imputation* $\mathbf{u}(x^*)$ *is Pareto efficient in the convex hull of* U(X).

The ***convex hull*** of a set is the smallest convex set that contains the original set; the convex hull of U(X) results from the convexification of the indifference curves that have non-convex portions. The condition of Pareto efficiency in the convex hull of U(X) does not exclude indifference curves with non-convex portions, but these portions must result irrelevant to the determination of efficiency; thus this condition excludes the possibility shown in ◨ Fig. 3.17. In order to be certain that this condition holds, one must assume concave utility functions, that imply convex indifference curves.

This theorem means that under its assumptions in order to locate Pareto-efficient states it suffices to restrict ourselves to the states which maximize social welfare functions that are weighted sums of individual utilities: having fixed the utility functions (i.e. having chosen for each individual the increasing transformation of her utility function that one prefers), if a state x is Pareto-efficient then there is a vector of weights for which the SWF is maximized at x. Conversely if, given the individual utility functions $u^s(x)$, there is no set of α_s weights that makes a given social state $x°$ satisfy the conditions requested for the maximization of a weighted sum of individual utilities, then $x°$ is not Pareto efficient.

Sometimes a distinction is made between a SWF which is a simple sum of utilities, called ***utilitarian***, and a SWF $\sum_s \alpha_s u_s(x)$ which is called ***weighed utilitarian*** or ***Bergsonian***, but if the positive α's are fixed the distinction is bogus, because preferences of an individual represented by $u(x)$ can also be represented by $v(x) = \alpha u(x)$ for any $\alpha > 0$, and with the second representation a weighed utilitarian SWF can be made to become utilitarian. Therefore it would be wrong to say that in a Bergsonian SWF the value judgements emerge in the α's, they emerge in them *and* in the scale of the utility functions; what is certain is that they are present.

The theorem as stated applies to social states broadly defined, but it also applies if utilities depends only on own consumption allocations, with no externalities, no other-regarding preferences. In this case, allocations that are general equilibria are Pareto efficient, so it can be concluded that general equilibrium allocations are maxima of some additive welfare function.

To sum up (Varian 1992, p. 335) in the absence of externalities and public goods:

- general competitive equilibria are Pareto efficient;
- under convexity assumptions, Pareto-efficient allocations are competitive equilibrium allocations for some distribution of endowments;
- maxima of SWFs are Pareto efficient;
- under convexity assumptions, Pareto-efficient allocations are maxima of some SWF, hence the same is true for general competitive equilibrium allocations.

No doubt there is an aesthetic elegance in all this. How useful it is to understand the working of real economies, is a different matter. But a question that arises is, how come in spite of the general lack of agreement among human beings on

14.11 · Social Welfare Functions

political and ethical values there has been such an ample accord among economists on one value judgement, the Pareto Principle, to the point of generally presenting it as natural and obviously acceptable, against what a more attentive analysis shows? (unless the principle is emptied of practical content). On this, one cannot escape being impressed by the temporal coincidence of the rise to prominence of the Pareto Principle and of the marginal approach, and by the possibility, given the belief in the marginal approach, to herald the satisfaction of the Pareto Principle as the great success of market economies.

14.12 Three Applications of Social Welfare Functions

Let us use T14.8 to confirm the conditions obtained in ▶ Chap. 3 for Pareto efficiency in the neoclassical differentiable exchange-and-production non-capitalistic economy, by deriving them from maximization of an additive SWF.

Because of CRS it is unnecessary to distinguish firms; the ensemble of firms can be treated as a gigantic single firm that jointly produces the several outputs. Indicate total factor i's input to the ensemble of firms as x_i, $i = 1, \ldots, n$. Differently from the indices in ▶ Chap. 5, let us indicate quantities of produced consumption goods as $q_{n+1}, \ldots, q_M$, and let us use $q_1, \ldots, q_n$ to indicate direct consumption of factor services by consumers. Then an M-vector $\mathbf{q}^s = (q^s_1, \ldots, q^s_n, q^s_{n+1}, \ldots, q^s_M)$ indicates quantities both of factor services and of produced consumption goods consumed by (or allocated to) consumer s. It is convenient to indicate input vectors $\mathbf{x}$ too as M-vectors, of course with all the elements indexed from $n + 1$ to M equal to zero. Each individual s has an M-endowment vector $\boldsymbol{\omega}^s$ of factors (a vector with elements from $n + 1$ to M all zero) that can be consumed directly or used to produce consumption goods. These individual endowment vectors are not given; we are only interested in Pareto-efficient allocations, unrestricted by property constraints or balanced budgets, so we are only interested (i) in the vector of *total* factor endowments $\boldsymbol{\Omega} = (\omega_1, \ldots, \omega_i, \ldots, \omega_n) = \Sigma_s \boldsymbol{\omega}^s$, (ii) in what can be obtained from them in terms of possible total consumption vectors (inclusive of direct consumption of the services of these factors), and (iii) in how these total consumption vectors can be allocated among the S individuals. A given allocation of consumptions of goods and services can be obtained with different distributions of the given total factor endowments among consumers: if there are two kinds of land, at the given equilibrium prices a consumer can derive the same land rent revenue and utility from different quantities of the two lands. Assume utility functions are monotonic (more is always better) and concave. To simplify the proof, assume that there is Pareto efficiency in production and so we can restrict attention to the transformation function that indicates all the alternative vectors of consumption goods efficiently producible from each given vector $\mathbf{x}$ of *total* factor inputs to firms; the feasible vectors of factor inputs are limited by total factor endowments, $\mathbf{x} \leq \boldsymbol{\Omega}$; if the amount of some input is less than its total endowment, the difference is available for direct consumption. So, if we indicate with $\mathbf{Q}^P$ the M-vector of quantities of *produced* consumption goods (with the first n elements all zero), production efficiency is described in implicit form

1302   **Chapter 14 · Welfare, Externalities, Public Goods and Happiness**

by an aggregate transformation function $T^\wedge(\mathbf{x},\mathbf{Q}^P)=0$, and to each point $(\mathbf{x},\mathbf{Q}^P)$ of the hypersurface thus determined there corresponds a complete vector of consumption goods and services $\mathbf{Q}=(\boldsymbol{\Omega}-\mathbf{x})+\mathbf{Q}^P$, the term $\boldsymbol{\Omega}-\mathbf{x}\geq 0$ being the M-vector of total direct consumptions of factor services (e.g. land used as pleasure gardens, time enjoyed as leisure rather than labour), again a vector with elements from $n+1$ to M all zero, for brevity indicated as $\mathbf{C}=\boldsymbol{\Omega}-\mathbf{x}$. We can obtain the Production Possibility Frontier of the economy (inclusive of 'production' of direct consumption of factor services)[54] as described by an efficient transformation function $T(\boldsymbol{\Omega};\ \mathbf{C},\ \mathbf{Q}^P)=0$ which is in fact the old $T^\wedge(\mathbf{x},\mathbf{Q}^P)=0$ with $\mathbf{x}$ replaced by $\boldsymbol{\Omega}-\mathbf{C}$ and $\boldsymbol{\Omega}$ given. The information contained in the two vectors $\mathbf{C}$ and $\mathbf{Q}^P$ is the same as in their sum $\mathbf{Q}$ owing to the zeros in those two vectors, so we can replace $\mathbf{C}$ and $\mathbf{Q}^P$ with $\mathbf{Q}$ in $T(\cdot)=0$; $T(\boldsymbol{\Omega};\ \mathbf{Q})=0$ renders each element of $\mathbf{Q}$ an implicit function of the others, determining the Production Possibility Frontier of the economy. Indicate as $\mathbf{q}^\wedge$ an allocation, that is a vector of s M-vectors of consumption baskets going to the s consumers, $\mathbf{q}^\wedge=(\mathbf{q}^1, \ldots, \mathbf{q}^s, \ldots, \mathbf{q}^S)$. The set X of social states over which the SWF must be maximized is then the set of all allocations $\mathbf{q}^\wedge$ that satisfy the constraints[55]

$$T\left(\boldsymbol{\Omega};\ \Sigma_s q_1^s, \Sigma_s q_2^s, \ldots, \Sigma_s q_M^s\right) \leq 0,$$

where for each good or service j what enters T is only its *total* availability $q_j=\Sigma_s q_j^s$, and the transformation function already includes the condition that efficient production of the produced consumption goods must require no more inputs than the available factor endowment minus direct consumption of factor services. Because the production functions behind $T(\cdot)=0$ are convex, X is convex too, and therefore the 'Furthermore' condition in theorem T14.8 is satisfied. We can conclude that every efficient social state can be found as the solution of

$$Max \quad W = \Sigma_s \alpha_s u_s\left(\mathbf{q}^s\right) \quad \text{s.t.}\ T\left(\boldsymbol{\Omega};\ \Sigma_s q_1^s, \Sigma_s q_2^s, \ldots, \Sigma_s q_M^s\right) \leq 0,$$

for some non-negative weights α_s, where the maximization is with respect to each q_j^s. If utilities are monotonic, the constraint is an equality.

To put an $\alpha_s=0$ means to give no relevance to the utility of individual s for the determination of social welfare, as if that individual did not exist; this normally will be considered unacceptable, so let us assume all weights are positive. Let us also assume that first-order conditions suffice to characterize the solution(s), that the constraint holds as an equality, and that we can neglect the non-negativity constraints that prevent negative consumptions. In other words, resources are fully utilized, and there are no 'corner solutions' in the consumers' utility maxima: all consumers consume positive quantities of all goods. Then the Lagrangian is

$$L = \Sigma_s \alpha_s u^s(\mathbf{q}^s) - \lambda T\left(\boldsymbol{\Omega};\ \Sigma_s q_1^s, \Sigma_s q_2^s, \ldots, \Sigma_s q_M^s\right)$$

---

54 In ▶ Chap. 3 it was unnecessary to consider consumption of factor services because for simplicity it was assumed that factor supplies were rigid.

55 Assuming $T(\cdot)$ is increasing in each of its arguments.

14.12 · Three Applications of Social Welfare Functions

and the first-order condition for each q_j^s, the amount of good j allocated to consumer s, is

$$\alpha_s \partial u^s / \partial q_j^s = \lambda \partial T / \partial q_j. \tag{14.13}$$

For another good h and the same consumer, the first-order condition is

$$\alpha_s \partial u^s / \partial q_h^s = \lambda \partial T / \partial q_h.$$

Dividing the first equality by the second, α_s and λ disappear, and we obtain the condition derived in ▶ Chap. 3 of equality between marginal rate of substitution in consumption and marginal rate of technical transformation in production; since the latter rate is independent of which consumer one is considering, we also find that the marginal rate of substitution in consumption for any couple of goods must be the same for all consumers. And we know that this is precisely what general equilibrium realizes (for goods both consumed in positive quantity by both consumers), with relative prices equal to ratios between marginal rates of substitution.

If instead we consider the same good consumed by two different individuals s and k:

$$a_s \partial u^s / \partial q_j^s = \alpha_k \partial u^k / \partial q_j^k = \lambda \partial T / \partial q_j.$$

Since the first two members in this double equality are $\partial W / \partial q_j^s$ and $\partial W / \partial q_j^k$ and they are equal, we see that when welfare is maximized, the marginal contribution of a good or service to 'social welfare', given by marginal utility of the good for consumer s times 'weight' α_s, is the same in all its uses. Hence marginal utilities of the same good for different consumers are inversely proportional to the 'weights' α_s. If the welfare maximum is achieved as an equilibrium, since we are assuming absence of 'corner solutions' equilibrium prices are proportional to marginal utilities: for each consumer s and good i it is $MU_i^s = \lambda_s p_i$ where λ_s is the marginal utility of income of consumer s. Since an increasing monotonic transformation of a utility function represents the same preferences, if we transform each utility function into $v^s(\mathbf{q}^s) = \alpha_s u^s(\mathbf{q}^s)$, we obtain $MU_i^s = p_i$, prices measure marginal utility; the SWF $W = \Sigma_s v^s(\mathbf{q}^s)$ yields the same social preference order among allocations as $W = \Sigma_s \alpha_s u_s(\mathbf{q}^s)$, the weight of each individual's welfare in the determination of social welfare is unchanged. Now prices directly measure the marginal contribution of each good or service to 'social welfare'.

At these prices, for factor services employed in production the 'price' (the rental) equals the indirect marginal utility of the factor: the sacrifice consisting of directly consuming one less unit of a factor service produces an increase in the output of some good, of value equal to the marginal revenue product of that factor and hence equal to the rental of the factor, and therefore of the same marginal utility to the factor supplier as the unit of the factor transferred from direct consumption to production.[56] The implication was pointed out in ▶ Chap. 3: in general equilib-

---

56 This is actually the ultimate meaning of Eq. (14.13) but to show it would require analysing the meaning of λ in that equation, a rather complicated issue that I skip.

rium, each (small) unit of the service of a factor receives a rental equal to its marginal contribution to social welfare, but also equal to the marginal disutility for the supplier of having to give up direct consumption of that service, therefore arguably equal to what the supplier *deserves* to receive, since marginal contribution = marginal sacrifice. Of course a classical approach views things very differently.

As a second use of T14.8, let us now assume one of the produced goods is a public good, whose enjoyment by one individual does not prevent its enjoyment by other individuals, e.g. a free TV channel with no advertising, to which all consumers have access. Let this be good M, the last one. With the same assumptions as in the first example, the Production Possibility Frontier is determined in the same way by the same transformation function $T(\Omega; Q)$; the sole difference arises when we specify the possible allocations $q^\wedge = (q^1, \ldots, q^s, \ldots, q^S) \in X$, now in each one of them all the vectors composing it have the same Mth element, equal to the available amount q_M of the public good. Therefore, with q_j total consumption of good or service j, the allocations must satisfy

$$T\left(\Omega; q_M, q_i = \Sigma_s q_j^s, \text{ for } j = 1, \ldots, M-1\right) \leq 0.$$

X is convex here too, so again we can conclude that every efficient social state can be found as the solution of

$$Max \quad W = \Sigma_s \alpha_s u_s(q^s) \quad \text{s.t. } T\left(\Omega; q_M; q_j = \Sigma_s q_j^s \text{ for } j = 1, \ldots, M-1\right) \leq 0,$$

for some non-negative weights α_s.

We can again assume that the constraint holds as equality. First-order conditions are unchanged for each q_j^s for any good j except the public good:

$$\alpha_s \partial u^s / \partial q_j^s = \lambda \partial T / \partial q_j, \text{ for } j = 1, \ldots, M-1.$$

It will be useful to rewrite this as

$$\alpha_s = \lambda(\partial T / \partial q_j) / \left(\partial u^s / \partial q_j^s\right), \text{ for } j = 1, \ldots, M-1. \tag{14.14}$$

For the public good the first-order condition is different:

$$\sum_{s=1}^{S} (\alpha_s \partial u^s / \partial q_M) = \lambda \partial T / \partial q_M.$$

In this equality, on the left-hand side replace each α_s with the right-hand side of (14.14):

$$\sum_{s=1}^{S} \left[\lambda \frac{(\partial T / \partial q_j)}{\partial u^s / \partial q_j^s} \cdot \frac{\partial u^s}{\partial q_M}\right] = \lambda \partial T / \partial q_M.$$

Now divide both sides by $\lambda \partial T / \partial q_j$:

$$\sum_{s=1}^{S} \frac{\partial u^s / \partial q_M}{\partial u^s / \partial q_j^s} = \frac{(\partial T / \partial q_M)}{(\partial T / \partial q_j)}.$$

14.12 · Three Applications of Social Welfare Functions

We have obtained on the right-hand side the marginal rate of technological transformation of the public good for private good j, and we see that this must equal the *sum* (over the individuals) of the marginal rates of substitution of the public good for this private good. This generalizes beyond quasi-linear utility the efficiency condition for the variable quantity of a public good.

Theorem T14.8 can also be used for some defence of the compensation principle (Varian 1992, p. 409). For simplicity consider an exchange economy (again without 'corner solutions'), and suppose this economy is at an equilibrium $(\mathbf{x}, \mathbf{p})$ where $\mathbf{x}$ is an equilibrium allocation of the economy's endowments among consumers, and $\mathbf{p}$ is an equilibrium price vector. The policy maker chooses on the basis of a social welfare function $W(u^1(\mathbf{x}^1), \ldots, u^S(\mathbf{x}^S)) = \Sigma_s \alpha_s u^s(\mathbf{x}^s)$. The question is whether an intervention that shifts the allocation to $\mathbf{x}^\circ$ is preferable to $\mathbf{x}$.

Suppose $\mathbf{x}^\circ$ is rather close to $\mathbf{x}$ so that we can use a Taylor expansion stopped at the first term. We have seen in Sect. 14.15.1 that we can transform utility functions u^s into $v^s = \alpha_s u^s$ and $W = \Sigma_s \alpha_s u^s(\mathbf{x}^s)$ into $W = \Sigma_s v^s(\mathbf{x}^s)$ with no effect on social preferences among allocations. Let us perform this transformation. For brevity let $W(\mathbf{x}) \equiv W(v^1(\mathbf{x}^1), \ldots, v^S(\mathbf{x}^S))$, and analogously for $W(\mathbf{x}^\circ)$. Indicate with $\nabla v^s(\mathbf{x}^s)$ the gradient of v^s. We can write:

$$W(\mathbf{x}^\circ) - W(\mathbf{x}) \approx \Sigma_s \nabla v^s(\mathbf{x}^s)(\mathbf{x}^{\circ s} - \mathbf{x}^s).$$

We saw in Sect. 14.15.1 that with these utility functions $MU_i^s = p_i$; therefore we can also write:

$$W(\mathbf{x}^\circ) - W(\mathbf{x}) \approx \Sigma_s \mathbf{p}(\mathbf{x}^{\circ s} - \mathbf{x}^s).$$

That is, the new allocation is preferable if at the old prices it raises the value of national income—precisely the criterion in practice adopted by the compensation principle and by cost–benefit analysis.

This conclusion depends on three things. First, that the initial allocation is Pareto efficient, with prices proportional to marginal utilities (no externalities!). This encounters all the problems we have seen if one tries to extend the analysis to production with capital goods and to intertemporal equilibria. Second, that the change is small. Third, that the SWF embodies interpersonal comparisons of utility plus the value judgement that what society must maximize is a (weighted) sum of utilities, and therefore a decrease in the utility (in fact, the income) of some people is acceptable if compensated by a sufficient increase in the utility (in fact, the income) of others, *with no need for compensations to be actually implemented*. This is a highly disputable value judgement, that would be rejected for example by Rawlsians, who argue that changes can only be approved if they do not worsen the welfare of the worst-off individual or more generally of the poorer strata of the population.

14.13 Arrow's Impossibility Theorem

In a society based on a market economy the bodies that take public decisions (government, local governments, parliament, the entire voting population in occasions like referenda, etc.) are inevitably called to take decisions that influence the economy.

Economists might limit themselves to act as consultants by trying to point out the *consequences* of alternative decisions and leaving the political decision makers to decide what to do. But economists have not resisted the temptation to try and supply general criteria for *evaluating* the economic consequences of decisions, or even for evaluating *procedures* to reach criteria for such evaluations. Their expertise with formalization and axiomatics has been used to explore general questions such as '*if* one has certain ethical values, are these contradictory? and how do they translate into criteria for deciding which economic policies are ethically just?'; for example, in which way being utilitarian, egalitarian, Rawlsian liberal, or libertarian affects how health problems, or old age, or immigration, or poverty, should be dealt with by society? There is a branch of welfare economics (in fact a branch of applied moral philosophy), called ***Economic Theories of Justice*** (Fleurbaey 1996), that by using axioms and theorems studies precisely the economic consequences of different broad ethical doctrines, with the aim of helping people to be clearer about the internal consistency and the implications of their declared general principles. My view is that in the present situation of economic theory more important than discussions about general ethical principles is to ascertain how the economy works, as a premise to grasping the *consequences* of different policies, dispelling wrong myths and intentionally devious analyses. Whether women should be allowed to work, to drive cars, to divorce is something about which religion and custom are so strong that it is not a discussion on ethics that is going to change people's attitudes. But on many issues it seems to me that at present in advanced democratic nations the disagreements more than on ethics are on how the economy works. Broadly shared ethical feelings can have deeply different practical implications depending on the theory of how the economy works. One example is the generally accepted idea that one should get paid for what one's contribution to the economy *deserves*. The attitude towards the acceptability of income differences is enormously dependent on whether one believes that each person earns the contribution of her/his factors to social welfare as argued by the neoclassical approach, or one views incomes as resulting simply from the relative power given to different social groups by the general institutions of capitalism and by the specific historical contingencies and laws, as a classical approach suggests. In fact, the economic theory one considers correct is often fundamental even for the general ethical system one prefers. For example it seems difficult to separate the absolute primacy given to freedom and the preference for a minimal state in Nozick (1974) from a strong faith in the unregulated market as producing optimal results and therefore not needing an active state to correct its malfunctionings. Not by chance, the fight against the socialist movements in the field of ideas criticized the idea that profits are unjust not by questioning the socialist moral principles but by arguing that the Marxist theory of capitalism was wrong. When the divergences are really about values, e.g. because due to religious differences, there is little alternative to political compromise, or civil war.

However, one element of the ensemble of economic theories of justice deserves mention, because it tries to deal with a different and, in some sense, a more practical question: 'what is a good set of rules (a '***constitution***') about how to reach public decisions?'

14.13 · Arrow's Impossibility Theorem

It is not clear that the economists' contributions in this field should appear in a microeconomics textbook, because they actually belong to political science, which extensively discusses whether it is best to have a proportional or a majority electoral system, a very powerful head of state or not, one or two legislative chambers, easy referendums or no referendums, and other issues on how best to reach collective decisions. The result I intend to present now, *Arrow's Impossibility Theorem*, is broadly part of this type of enquiries. It does not ask how various constitutions would work in practice, but whether it is possible to find a constitution obeying certain desirable criteria. So, both because it gives a taste of the axiomatic style much used in the field of economic theories of justice, and because tradition has its weight and one expects an economics graduate to know Arrow's theorem, I bow to the pressure of tradition and pass to explaining this political science result.

Imagine people debating what kind of procedure they would find acceptable about reaching social choices among alternative policies. Call *social state* the complete enumeration of characteristics, of the situation deriving from a policy choice, that may be relevant for individuals' assessment of their liking of the situation.

Let there be a finite set X of (at least three) mutually exclusive social states. There are H (at least two) individuals in the community. Each individual h has a complete reflexive and transitive *ordinal preference relation* or *preference pre-order* $\succsim_h$ over all the social states in X.[57] This can be conceived as a list from the least preferred to the most preferred social state, with equipreferred states appearing jointly in the list. A *preference profile* $\pi = (\succsim_1, \succsim_2, ..., \succsim_h, ..., \succsim_H)$ is a vector of preference pre-orders, one per individual, that order the states in the given X. Two preference profiles are different if for at least one individual the ordinal preference relation is not the same in the two profiles. Given X, let B(X) be the set of all possible preference profiles over X.

A *social* preference relation $\succsim$ (the absence of an index distinguishes it from preference relations of individuals) is a complete, reflexive and transitive ordinal preference relation over X, which indicates, for each couple x and y of alternative social states, which one *society* finds preferable (or equipreferred).

This is similar to what was said about the SWF, but here we remain at the level of preference orderings, without introducing utility functions, and we adopt a more general notion of social state, which is not restricted to only economic variables (consumption allocations) as in the SWF.

Arrow asks whether one can find a map (that he too calls a *social welfare function*, but since it is debated whether it is or not essentially the same thing as a Bergson–Samuelson SWF it is better to call it with a different name, for example *social preference function*, **SPF**) which maps preference profiles into social prefer-

---

57 A preorder is a reflexive and transitive binary relation over the elements of a set. If the binary relation is also complete, the preorder is called a total preorder. The order has only ordinal significance.

1308   **Chapter 14** · Welfare, Externalities, Public Goods and Happiness

ence relations—that is, a rule SPF(X, π) that, for each assigned preference profile π over a set X of social states, produces a social preference relation $\succsim = \text{SPF}(\pi)$ over that set of states—, and that furthermore, besides generating a pre-order among social states, obeys 'reasonable' criteria that presumably would meet general approval in a democratic society. The social state or states that a SPF puts on top of the list (given the individual preference pre-orders) is what society should choose if, by some procedure, that SPF has been chosen as the mechanism to arrive at social choices, once the individual preference pre-orders are ascertained (no mechanism is indicated to arrive at a single choice among socially equipreferred states). Because of its being a rule to arrive at social preferences, which can itself be an object of choice, Arrow has proposed the term 'constitution' for the SPF. Arrow (1963) proposes as reasonable the following four criteria a constitution should respect; I discuss them more after the proof of what they imply.

(1) **Unrestricted Domain**: There are at least two individuals and at least three alternative social states. Whatever the set X of alternative social states, the domain of the social preference rule is the set B(X) of *all* possible preference profiles on this set.

   Note that this condition imposes that a SPF that produces a pre-order over a set X for any possible preference profile π over X must be able to produce a pre-order also over any strict subset S of X and preference profile π(S) that restricts the individual pre-orders to the elements in S.

(2) **Weak Pareto Principle** (this is also called **Unanimity**): given a preference profile π(X), if between two social states x and y all individuals agree that x is *strictly* preferable to y, then the social preference relation produced by SPF(X,π) must have $x \succ y$.

(3) **Independence of Irrelevant Alternatives**: Let S be a subset of the set of possible social states X, possibly coinciding with X. Assume the social preference function satisfies universal domain and transitivity over any S containing at least three elements. Let π and π' be two different preference profiles over S; if for a couple x, y of elements of S for each individual the ranking of x relative to y is the same in π and in π', then the ranking of x relative to y must be the same in SPF(S,π) and in SPF(S,π').

   This definition can be concisely formalized as:

$$\forall x, y \in S, \forall \pi, \pi' \in B(S), \left[x \succsim_h y \Leftrightarrow x \succsim'_h y, \forall h \right] \Rightarrow [x \succsim y \Leftrightarrow x \succsim' y].$$

   This criterion's long name is often shortened to IIA. Its meaning can be clarified by saying that if the choice is among, say, four alternatives x, y, w, z and the preferences of individuals change so that for some individuals the preference order changes but not the preference order between y and z that remains for all individuals $y \succsim z$, then the preference order between y and z established by the SPF must not be altered by the change of preference profile. Arrow introduces this condition as translating the idea that if the social preference among four alternatives x, y, w, z is for x, then it should remain for x when one of the other alternatives drops out of the feasible alternatives. IIA also implies that the *introduction* of a further alternative v should not alter the order among the previous four. And, as Arrow explicitly admits, fundamen-

14.13 · Arrow's Impossibility Theorem

tally it serves 'to exclude interpersonal comparison of social utility either by some form of direct measurement or by comparison with other alternative social states' (Arrow 1963, p. 59).

(4) **Non-dictatorship**. There is no individual h^* such that, for every pair of social states x and y and for all possible preference profiles, $x \succ_{h^*} y$ implies $x \succ y$.

A social preference function SPF($\cdot$) is called *dictatorial* if there is such an individual. Note that for an individual h^* to be a dictator it is not enough that her *given* preference pre-order coincide with the one established by the SPF whatever the preferences of the other individuals; the coincidence must be there for *any possible* preference pre-order of h^*. That is, for any couple x, y of social states, going over all possible preference profiles whenever the profile π is such that $x \succ_{h^*} y$, SPF(π) establishes $x \succ y$, even when for everybody else it is $y \succ_h x$; and for all preference profiles π' in which $y \succ_{h^*} x$, SPF(π') establishes $y \succ x$. To exclude this emperor-like capacity to impose one's will upon society seems reasonable for modern democracies. Note that non-dictatorship does not exclude that, for *some* preference profiles, the social preference relation may perfectly coincide with the preference relation of an individual;[58] what it excludes is that the coincidence persists, however the preference profile of this individual (or of the other individuals) is changed. (Also note that for the pairs (x, y) among which h^* is indifferent, a dictatorial SPF($\cdot$) need not consider the two states equipreferred; so it is imprecise, although not really misleading, to say that a dictatorial Arrovian SPF produces social preference relations that *always* coincide with those of h^*.)

Now I present and prove the consequence of these four conditions (plus completeness and transitivity of all social preference orders produced by the SPF):

Arrow's (Im)Possibility Theorem[59]: *If X includes at least three social states, and there are at least two individuals, the above four conditions* (1) (2) (3) (4) *are incompatible: if the SPF satisfies Unrestricted Domain, Unanimity and IIA, then there is a dictator.*

This time I supply the, or rather one, proof (there are many different proofs; I follow the one in Kreps (2013, pp. 169–171), with a little more explanation of the logical passages) in spite of its length, because it is not difficult, it is fun (at each step the result is, at least to me, surprising), and it is a good introduction to the style of proofs in this field. See Sen (1970) for further examples of proofs in this style.

Proof Let X be given. Fix a social preference function SPF(X, π) obeying (1), (2), (3). As a matter of notation, when a specific preference profile, say π', is

---

58 This is the case, for example, when social choice concerns a one-dimensional issue, it is reached by pairwise majority voting, the number of voters is odd, and preferences are single-peaked (see below in the text for explanation of this term), in which case social preferences coincide with those of the *median voter*.

59 Arrow (1963) called it Possibility Theorem, but later the name Impossibility Theorem has become the more widely used.

1310   **Chapter 14 · Welfare, Externalities, Public Goods and Happiness**

assumed, the preferences under it are indicated as $x \succ'_h y$, or $x \succsim'_h y$, for the preference of individual h between x and y, and the symbol $\succ'_h$ alone stands for h's entire preference relation; without any h index, the same symbols refer to *social* preferences and to the entire social preference relation.

Let x and y be two different social states. Define *decisiveness* as follows. A subset $H' \subseteq H$ of individuals is said *decisive for x over y* according to SPF if, for *all* preference profiles in which $x \succ_h y$ for all $h \in H'$ and $y \succ_h x$ for all $h \notin H'$, SPF($\cdot$) establishes $x \succ y$.

Note that for all ordered pairs (x, y) there exists at least one decisive subset, the entire H, by the Weak Pareto Principle (Unanimity). Note also that a decisive subset contains at least one individual, the empty subset cannot be decisive because it contains no $\succ_h$ preference relation.

Six steps can be distinguished in the proof.

(i) For each ordered pair (x, y), there will exist a finite number of subsets of H that are decisive for x over y according to SPF; it is then possible to ascertain which of these has the smallest cardinality (= number of individuals in the subset); indicate this number as Min(x, y). It is then possible to find an ordered pair (x, y) whose Min(x, y) is smallest among all the Min(x, y) as we vary (x, y) over all possible couples of elements in X. (This pair need not be unique, but it doesn't matter which one we focus upon.) From now on in the proof, x and y will refer to this pair. Take the smallest decisive subset (or one of the smallest decisive subsets) of this pair, call it J. I prove that J contains a single individual.

The proof is by contradiction. If J contains at least two elements, partition it into subsets J' and J" such that both contain at least one element. Let z be any element of X which is not x and not y. Since SPF's domain is all possible preference profiles, it will contain a preference profile π where:

for all $h \in J'$, it is $z \succ_h x \succ_h y$;
for all $h \in J''$, it is $x \succ_h y \succ_h z$;
for all $h \notin J$, it is $y \succ_h z \succ_h x$.

Since J is decisive for x over y, SPF(π) establishes $x \succ y$; and then by negative transitivity[60] either $z \succ y$ or $x \succ z$. Let us examine these two cases in turn. Suppose $z \succ y$. Take any preference profile π'' such that $z \succ''_h y$ for $h \in J'$ and $y \succ''_h z$ for $h \notin J'$. The ranking between z and y in π'' coincides with the one in π, so by IIA the social welfare function SPF(π'') must establish the same order between z and y as SPF(π), hence $z \succ''y$. The set of preference profiles of type π'' includes all the ones (π among them) required to establish whether J' is decisive for z over y, so we conclude that J' indeed is decisive, contradicting the assumed size minimality of J. With analogous reasoning the reader can prove that if $x \succ z$, IIA implies that J" is decisive for x over z, again a contradiction. So J must contain only one member; indicate her/him as h^*.

---

60   If a weak preference relation $\succsim$ is complete and transitive, then *strict* preference is negatively transitive, that is, if $x \succ y$ then for any third element z either $z \succ y$ or $x \succ z$. Indeed if it is not $z \succ y$ then either $z \sim y$ or $y \succ z$, and then by transitivity $x \succ z$.

14.13 · Arrow's Impossibility Theorem

This is already rather bad, because it proves that for any social welfare function SPF(π) satisfying unrestricted domain, unanimity, and IIA, there is at least one pair of alternatives (x, y) for which a single individual is decisive, that is, in all profiles where this individual h^* strictly prefers x and everybody else strictly prefers y, the SPF sides with the individual, against the overwhelming majority. But worse is coming. Having proven that for any SPF we can find an individual h^* with dictatorial power over at least one couple (x, y), we can further prove that this individual has the same dictatorial power over any couple of alternatives.

(ii) We know that for any SPF there is an individual h^* who is the single member of the decisive set of the ordered pair (x, y) with smallest decisive set. I prove that for any profile π in which $x\succ_{h^*}z$ for arbitrary z, SPF must establish $x\succ z$. Assume first $z \neq y$. Among all possible preference profiles there will be a profile π' in which $x\succ'_{h^*} y\succ'_{h^*} z$, and where for all $h \neq h^*$, x and z are ranked in the same way as under π and $y\succ'_h x$, $y\succ'_h z$; since $J = \{h^*\}$ is decisive for x over y, it is $x\succ'y$; by unanimity, $y\succ'z$; hence by transitivity, $x\succ'z$; now note that in π each h ranks x and z in the same way as in π', hence by IIA, $x > z$. Now assume $z = y$ (we must discuss this case because J decisive for x over y does *not* mean that whenever $x\succ_{h^*}y$, SPF establishes $x\succ z$; it has this effect only in the profiles where in addition $y\succ_{hx}$ for all $h \neq h^*$). Take a social state w in X which is not x and not y. To this w we can apply the reasoning applied above to z when $z \neq y$, so for all π where $x\succ_{h^*}w$ it is $x\succ w$; this also holds when in addition $w\succ_h z$ for $h \neq h^*$, which shows that $J = \{h^*\}$ is decisive for x over w; then we can apply the reasoning applied above for $z \neq y$, replacing y with w, so now $z \neq w$, and that reasoning concludes to $x\succ z = y$.

(iii) I prove that for all π where $z\succ_{h^*}y$, SPF(π) must establish $z\succ y$. Assume first $z \neq x$. Consider a profile—that must exist—π' in which $z\succ'_{h^*} x\succ'_{h^*} y$ and for $h \neq h^*$ it is $z\succ'_h x$, $y\succ'_h x$ and z and y are ranked in the same way as under π; since $J = \{h^*\}$ is decisive for x over y, $x\succ'y$; by unanimity, $z\succ'x$; by transitivity, $z\succ'y$; then by IIA, $z\succ y$. Now assume $z = x$; by reasoning in the same way as for $z = y$ in step (ii), take a state w which is not z and not x; for all π where $w\succ_{h^*}y$, including those where $y\succ_h w$ for $h \neq h^*$, it is $w\succ y$, hence J is decisive for w over y, and by replacing x with w in the reasoning applied above to the case $z \neq x$ we conclude that in this case too $z = x\succ y$.

(iv) I prove that for any element w that is neither x nor y, $J = \{h^*\}$ is decisive for w over x. Let π be any profile in which $w\succ_{h^*}x$ and $x\succ_h w$ for $h \neq h^*$; and let π' be a profile that agrees with π on the ranking of w relative to x for each h, and where $w\succ'_{h^*}y\succ'_{h^*}x$ and, for $h \neq h^*$, $y\succ'_h x\succ'_h w$. By unanimity, $y\succ'x$. Because of (iii), $w\succ'y$. Hence $w\succ'x$ by transitivity and $w\succ x$ by IIA.

(v) I prove that for any profile where $z\succ_{h^*}x$ for arbitrary $z \in$ X, it must be $z\succ x$. This is because result (iv) implies that in step (iii) we can replace x with w, and y with x.

(vi) To conclude, suppose in a preference profile π it is $w\succ_{h^*}z$ for arbitrary w and z. If $w = x$, step (ii) implies $w\succ x$. If $z = x$, by step (iv) it is $w\succ x$. If x is neither w nor z, consider a profile π' such that each $\succ'_h$ agrees with $\succ_h$ on w versus z and $w\succ'_{h^*}x\succ'_{h^*} z$. By step (iv), $w\succ'x$. By step (ii), $x\succ'z$. By transitivity, $w\succ'z$.

1312   **Chapter 14** · Welfare, Externalities, Public Goods and Happiness

By IIA, $w \succ z$. So for each π' the social preference relation SPF(π') coincides with $\succ'_{h*}$. Individual h^* is a dictator. ∎

Some clarification of the meaning of the theorem can be obtained by considering some rules for reaching a social choice among alternatives.

Let us take the **Borda rule** or **Borda count**, which consists of each voter numbering the n alternatives in ascending order of preference, the worst one having number 1 and the best one number n, and assigning to each alternative as many points as its order number, so the preferred alternative gets n points, the second preferred one gets $n - 1$ points, and so on; if ties are admitted they are considered to occupy two consecutive positions and they share their points, for example if two alternatives tie in the second preferred place, they are considered to have numbers $n - 1$ and $n - 2$ and are assigned $n - 1.5$ points each. The social preference order is determined by the sum of the points each alternative gets. Clearly there is here an incentive to non-truthful revelation of preferences: each voter has an incentive to give top place to the alternative that she would like to be chosen (which may not be the really preferred one if the latter is considered too unlikely to win—game-strategic considerations come in) and to put lowest its strongest competitors. The Borda rule is then said **manipulable**, or **not strategy-proof**, that is, the choice it produces is affected by non-truthful revelation of preferences *and* there can be an incentive for voters to misreport their preferences. We see here an additional problem relative to the assumptions of the Arrow Impossibility Theorem: Arrow's social preference function is a map from individual preference profiles to a social preference relation, but it may be difficult to ascertain individual preferences except by asking individuals to indicate them, and if individuals have an incentive to misreport them, any map becomes untrustworthy. It is therefore desirable that the social choice rule implied by the adopted way to establish what is preferred by society be **strategy-proof**, that is, such that 'under no circumstance would any individual have an incentive to misreport his preferences ... if a social choice function is strategy-proof, no individual, no matter what his preferences might be, can ever strictly gain my misreporting his preferences no matter what the others report—even if the others lie about their preferences ... and so society's choice will be based upon the true preferences of its individual members' (Jehle and Reny 2011 p. 291). But 'under no circumstance ... no matter what his preferences might be' is a very strong double requirement that causes another negative result, the **Gibbard–Satterthwaite Theorem**, that states: 'If there are at least three social states, then every strategy-proof social choice function is dictatorial'.[61]

But let us suppose truthful voting, to see where the Borda rule, which is clearly non-dictatorial, fails the other Arrow conditions even neglecting manipulability. Note that which one of two alternatives is preferred can depend on the prefer-

---

61 See, e.g., Jehle and Reny (2011 p. 291), Mas-Colell et al. (1995 p. 874). The original sources are Gibbard (1973) and Satterthwaite (1975).

14.13 · Arrow's Impossibility Theorem

ence order. For example, assume $H = \{1, 2\}$ and $X = \{a, b, c, d\}$, and consider two preference profiles π and π':

π: $a \succ_1 b \succ_1 c \succ_1 d$ and $b \succ_2 c \succ_2 a \succ_2 d$ implies b has 7 points, a has 6; $b \succ a$.

π': $a \succ'_1 c \succ'_1 d \succ'_1 b$ and $b \succ'_2 c \succ'_2 a \succ'_2 d$ implies a has 6 points, b has 5; $a \succ' b$.

So the social ranking between a and b does not depend only on the individual rankings of a relative to b; this violates IIA.

The Borda rule violates two conditions called by Sen (1979) *ordinalism* and *non-comparable utilities*, that welfare economics tried to respect after Robbins' criticism. The numerical point system contradicts the requirement of paying attention only to the ordinal aspect of preferences because it establishes a measure of how much an alternative is preferred to another one by each voter; it also contradicts non-comparable utilities both because a one point difference by one voter is considered as relevant as a one point difference by another voter, and because the voters are all attributed an equal total amount of points to distribute among the alternatives, which is an equalitarian way of giving importance to their preferences, which by itself implies a way to compare their utilities.

The IIA condition has above all the effect, and purpose, of preventing comparison of the intensity of the preference of a social state x over another one y, by blocking the possibility to judge intensity by examining how these states are ranked relative to other states. For example suppose A and B have quasi-linear preferences, linear in income, and individual A prefers x to y and is indifferent between y and another state z that differs from x only in that in it A has 10,000 dollars less than in x, that is, A is ready to pay up to 10,000 dollars to get x rather than y; while B prefers y to x and is indifferent between y and another state w that differs from x only in that in it B has 1000 dollars more than in x. One might argue that social preference should go to x, because A would be ready to give B more than B needs in order to accept x. Of course there would be here a double value judgement: roughly, that social preference should go to the choice that causes the less total suffering; and that suffering is measured by the sum of what each individual is ready to pay to obtain the preferred state rather than the other state. In the second of these value judgements there would be an implicit acceptance of the capacity for sacrifice (in our example, capacity to pay) of each individual as not to be questioned; while the fact that B is ready to pay so much less than A might depend on B being much poorer. Also, if there isn't quasi-linear utility, there might be room for a surplus both if A bought from B the willingness to accept x, and if B bought from A the willingness to accept y (the reader is invited to produce an example). Furthermore, it would be unclear whether one should decide which state is preferable on the basis of willingnesses to pay *before* or *after* the choice between the two states is made: in the previous example, B might become very rich if y is chosen, and then might potentially more than compensate A.

This difference between two compensation tests, one based on potential compensation *before* the change from a status-quo x to y, and the other based on potential compensation *after* the change, was amply discussed in the 1940s and 1950s. But what interests us of this example in connection with Arrow's theorem is that in both cases the possibility to take into account readiness to compensate means that either the compensations are to be actually paid, and then the problem was ill formulated, the choice is not between x and y, but between them modified by the compensations; or the compensations are only potential, and then to take them into account violates IIA because one takes into account other states besides x and y, the states with compensation, which are 'irrelevant' in that they are not part of the set S of states among which one must choose.

More generally, IIA blocks considerations like the following. Assume society is divided into two equally numerous groups of people, M and N, and the criterion for social choice gives relevance to the intensity of preferences, measured in some way, perhaps by physical indices like anxiety, incidence of mental illnesses and so on. Suppose that according to preference profile π the people in M strongly prefer x to y, while the people in N very weakly prefer y to x. Social preference goes to x. According to preference profile π' the people in M very weakly prefer x to y, the people in N strongly prefer y to x. The criterion for socially preferring x in the first case suggests that society should prefer y in the second. IIA imposes that if social preference between x and y goes to x in the first case it must go to x in the second case too.

Since the first presentation (1951) of the Impossibility Theorem there has been debate on its implications for Bergson–Samuelson SWFs. The debate continues (see, e.g., Fleurbaey and Mongin 2005; Igersheim 2017). My view (a non-specialist's view) is the following. A Bergson–Samuelson SWF $W(x) = W(u_1(x), ..., u_H(x))$, where x indicates the social state, by assigning numerical values to social states such that a higher number indicates strict social preference, transforms a profile of individual utility functions into a social preference order. It is in the end irrelevant whether utilities depend only on economic allocations (as usually assumed for SWFs) or on other things too. If we treat $(u_1, ..., u_H)$ as just a vector of numbers, the value of W depends in some way on this vector of numbers (e.g. it might be the sum of these numbers; or the product of these numbers; and so on); let us call the way the value of W depends on this vector, neglecting how this vector depends on the social state, the *form* of W. For a given form of W, the social preference order over social states will generally change if the way social states determine the value of the individual utility functions changes. Therefore any W of given form *is* a social preference function in the sense of Arrow (if only one accepts to restrict the Universal Domain condition to preferences representable via utility functions, e.g. no lexicographic preferences): it translates any profile of individual preference relations over social states representable as utility functions into a social preference relation. But for assigned numerical utility functions, any given form of W does imply an interpersonal comparison of utilities: for example if $W(x)$ is the sum of the utilities associated with social state x, it changes as a function of social states if one decides that one utility function should be multiplied by 2 and another should be divided by 2, which can be interpreted as a different social weight assigned to the satisfaction of those two individuals, i.e. as a changed interpersonal comparison of utilities. The question then arises, when a SWF can be considered not to make interpersonal comparisons of utilities and to order social states exclusively on the

14.13 · Arrow's Impossibility Theorem

basis of the ordinal element implicit in the utility functions. The issue is subtle and requires many distinctions and lemmas, as shown by Mas-Colell et al. (1995, pp. 831–37). To make a long story short, I will only say that it seems possible to interpret a W as satisfying this ordinality requisite if the social preference pre-order that $W(x) = W(u_1(x)..., u_H(x))$ establishes among social states is not altered by non-identical affine increasing transformations of the utility functions (different changes of origin and of units operated on the several utility functions). It has been found out (see the proof in the cited pages of Mas-Colell et al.) that any such W is dictatorial. So one reaches the same result as Arrow: a complete and transitive rule for deciding which social state is preferable, that holds for any profile of utility functions but avoids dictatorship, cannot avoid value judgements that go beyond the Pareto principle and entail interpersonal comparisons of utility. The issue then boils down to why one should avoid interpersonal comparisons of utility. Samuelson, for example, has repeatedly insisted that concrete social decisions cannot avoid interpersonal comparisons of utility and that there is no problem with accepting them and thus avoiding a dictatorial SWF.

Sen (1979) concurs, arguing that the inability to avoid dictatorship is due to the *excessive* desire to avoid political or moral judgements implicit in the conditions postulated by Arrow.[62] Sen argues that the first three conditions imposed by Arrow imply a particularly strict form of *welfarism*, which restricts so much the information available for establishing social preferences, that one is forced 'to go relentlessly in the direction of recognising more and more information as unusable until we have the consistency of a dictatorial procedure, concentrating on the information in just one person's preference ordering' (Sen 1979, p. 543). This **strict-ranking welfarism** imposes that 'any two social states must be ranked entirely and solely on the basis of personal utilities in the respective states (irrespective of the non-utility features of the states) ... demands that the social ranking of any pair of states be *neutral* to the non-utility features of the states, i.e. the concentration must be exclusively on the utility information about the states' (Sen 1979, p. 538). Welfarism by itself does not forbid giving weight to intensity of preferences and giving weight to the preferences of some individuals more than to those of others, but if as in Arrow's theorem one adds *Ordinalism* (that only the ordinal properties of the individual utility functions are to be used in social welfare assessments) and *non-comparable utilities* (impossibility to decide whether an individual is better off than another one by looking at their utility levels) then it becomes impossible to derive, from utility levels, any information on how well off people are, and since utility levels are all that can be used, one is left with no criterion to prefer a state over another, except some version of the Pareto Principle, which does not supply the complete ordering over social states requested by Arrow, or voting procedures, which do not satisfy transitivity except under

---

62 Sen (1979) is a strongly recommended reading; it presents an unconventional proof of Arrow's Impossibility Theorem which allows him a thought-provoking discussion of its limitations.

1316   **Chapter 14** · Welfare, Externalities, Public Goods and Happiness

domain restrictions; so it is not surprising that the only way to reach a consistent (complete and transitive) criterion for social choice is to rely on some individual's own ordering.

The impossibility to use anything other than the ordinal individual rankings to reach a social evaluation of states is shown by the fact that the combination of restricted domain, Weak Pareto Principle, and IIA is proved by Sen to imply that if everyone's ranking of x vis-à-vis y in one situation is the same as his or her ranking of a vis-à-vis b in another, then the social ranking of x vis-à-vis y in the first situation must be the same as the social ranking of a vis-à-vis b in the second. The other characteristics of the two situations do not count. Thus if the community can be partitioned into two groups M and N, with everyone in M preferring x to y in case α and a to b in case β, while everyone in N prefers y to x in case α and b to a in case β, then if in case α it is $x \succ y$ (x *socially* preferred to y), it must also be $a \succ b$ in case β; similarly if $y \succ x$ in the first case then $b \succ a$ in the second, and if $x \sim y$ in case α, then $a \sim b$ in case β. This is the meaning of strict-ranking welfarism, 'the nature of the social states and their non-utility features should not make any difference to social preference as long as the utility information about them (in this case, the personal strict utility rankings) is the same' (ibid. p. 540). I proceed to report the proof.

Proof   Assume the two groups M and N postulated above with the described preference patterns in states α and β. Assume first strict personal preferences and, without loss of generality, that $x \succ y$ (strict *social* preference) in case α. We need to show that $a \succ b$ in case β. Consider a third set γ of individual preferences—admissible thanks to unrestricted domain—as follows (in descending order of preference): for group M it is $a \succ x \succ y \succ b$, for group N it is $y \succ b \succ a \succ x$. Since everyone's utility ranking of x vis-à-vis y in case γ is the same as in α, IIA requires $x \succ y$ in case γ too. By the Weak Pareto Principle, $a \succ x$ in case γ, and also $y \succ b$. Thus by transitivity $a \succ b$ in case γ. Now note that the individual orderings of a and b in the γ and in the β cases are identical, hence by IIA it follows that in the β case too it must be $a \succ b$. (This was proved assuming a particular third case γ, but this suffices, because if this case renders obligatory that $a \succ b$ in case β then the SPF must accept it for any other third case too otherwise it would not determine a single social ordering.) This suffices for the case of *strict* social preference[63]; there remains to consider the case in which $x \sim y$ in the α case. In this case we need to establish that $a \sim b$ in the β case too. Suppose not. Suppose without loss of generality that $a \succ b$ in the β case. Then reversing the roles of cases α and β in the above proof of strict-ranking welfarism for *strict* social preference, one proves that it must be $x \succ y$ in the α case, contradicting the assumption that $x \sim y$ in the α case. Reversing the roles of a and b the reasoning also applies to $b \succ a$ in the β case. This establishes strict-ranking welfarism in the case of social indifference as well. ∎

---

63 See Sen (1979, p. 541, fn. 1) for the case in which x, y, a and b are not all distinct; for example x and a might be the same good; then the same strategy of proof applies but it would be long to show it.

The effect of this result, Sen comments, 'is to combine the poverty of the utility information with an embargo on the use of non-utility information'. Sen supplies a nice illustration. Consider 'the principle of giving priority to the interests of the poor over the interests of the rich. Do we have the information necessary for the use of this principle in the Arrovian framework?' (ibid., p. 543). No! All the SPF can base itself upon is the ordinal aspects of the utility functions, but these utility functions are not comparable, so they tell us nothing at all on whether the individuals enjoy a high or low level of subjective welfare, nor whether one individual is better off than another, let alone whether they are rich or poor. The demand that social utility be a function only 'of the ordinally described personal utility levels without interpersonal comparisons robs us of our ability to 'tell' the rich from the poor' (ibid., p. 544).

One is brought to ask, if this is what they imply, should we care for these first three conditions posed by Arrow? Would grave consequences derive from not requiring them to be satisfied?

Let us consider traditional *utilitarianism*, which assumes interpersonal comparability and summability of utilities (in violation of IIA) and postulates that the sum of utilities should be maximized; it yields a complete and transitive non-dictatorial social welfare function the moment the effect of income and of the other most relevant variables on the utility of each individual is quantitatively specified. Nowadays utilitarianism is generally interpreted as the simple claim that the sum of utilities must be maximized coupled with a total 'indifference to inequality of well-being' (Blackorby et al. 2002, p. 546), 'aversion nulle pour l'inégalité' (Fleurbaey 1995, p. 76).[64] This is clearly a misinterpretation. Henry Sidgwick, the main advocate of utilitarianism at the end of the nineteenth century, clearly postulated that persons in the same objective condition (equal income, equal health) should be treated as having the same utility level; he spoke of 'the self-evident principle that the good of any one individual is of no more importance, from the point of view (if I may say so) of the universe, than the good of any other' and specified that 'individuals in similar conditions should be treated similarly' (Sidgwick 1973, pp. 223, 225). This egalitarianism with reference to *objective* conditions is forgotten by the critics of utilitarianism when they cite with approval Lionel Robbins' central critical argument, the impossibility to measure the difference in the utility obtained out of the same income by a person with simple tastes, and by a person with refined expensive tastes. This problem does not arise with utilitarianism, which, instinctively aware of the emptiness of relative utility levels unless referred to some common standard, assumes *as an ethical principle* that people in

---

64 A different kind of criticism of utilitarianism is that it does not consider ethical motives to judge certain actions as unacceptable even though apparently increasing total utility, for example killing a person who greatly disturbs an entire community with thefts, vandalism, sadistic acts. This problem is not neglected by utilitarian philosophers, but will not be discussed here except to note that this problem questions the Pareto Principle too, and therefore Arrow's theorem, so it cannot be a reason to judge utilitarianism unacceptable because it does not respect Arrow's conditions.

1318   **Chapter 14** · Welfare, Externalities, Public Goods and Happiness

the same objective condition must be treated as having the same level of utility. Clearly, further value judgements are needed, for example, if someone has lost a leg, to decide when this person has the same utility level as a person with both legs; and also, to decide how much more utility is created by more income so as to decide whether specific income reallocations are justified; but the important thing is that it will be tendentially equalitarian ethical principles that will decide. Sidgwick dealt with the income problem by stating that the best 'mode of distributing a given quantum of happiness' is an equal distribution, and although not having the notion of marginal utility and therefore unable to reach the notion of a decreasing marginal utility of income, nevertheless he found a way to argue that an equal distribution of the means to happiness would maximize total happiness: because men 'have an aversion to any kind of inferiority to others' (Sidgwick 1973, pp. 232, 244), that is, income inequalities cause sufferings. This equalitarianism is strengthened in the writings of Marshall and Pigou by the idea of a decreasing marginal utility of income, with the clear implication that income redistributions from the rich to the poor increase total utility, and that therefore optimal social states are equalitarian.[65] In conclusion, utilitarianism intelligently interpreted supplies a social welfare function that does not comply with IIA but appears neither irrational nor incompatible with a democratic society; it is not evident why its contradicting IIA should be seen as an obstacle to its acceptability.

Now let us consider *pairwise majority rule*, that is, the choice by majority vote between each *couple* of alternatives (note that voting for or against any law or policy implies a choice between it and the status quo, so it is a choice between two alternatives). Clearly it is not dictatorial. But suppose there are three social states a, b, c, and the voting body is divided into three equally numerous groups 1, 2 and 3 with the following preferences:

1. $a>b>c$
2. $b>c>a$
3. $c>a>b$.

Then between a and b sincere majority voting selects a (1 and 3 vote for it); between b and c sincere majority voting selects b; and between a and c sincere majority voting selects c, violating transitivity. That is, in a parliament that has approved a, which is therefore now part of the status quo, if each party votes sincerely, a law abolishing a and replacing it with c will be approved, and afterwards a law abolishing c and replacing it with b will be approved, and afterwards a law abolishing b and replacing it with a will be approved. This is called a **Condorcet cycle**. A potential Condorcet cycle can be avoided by forbidding the presentation

---

65 Except for inequalities of income that, for incentive reasons, ensure a greater total amount of happiness by stimulating efficiency: for example, prizes to the authors of socially useful inventions.

14.13 · Arrow's Impossibility Theorem

again of an already discarded alternative,[66] but then there is room for manipulation of the result through decision on the order of pairwise vote:[67] e.g. if the person who decides the voting order wants c adopted and is conscious of the situation, she must first propose the choice between a and b, and then the choice between c and the winning alternative, i.e. a. If neither a nor b nor c have been approved yet, manipulation can be blocked by a failure of any initial proposal of a, or of b, or of c, to be approved if all three groups decide to vote yes only for the alternative they prefer, and no against the others; then the status quo wins.

However, the possibilities of an endless cycle, of manipulation, of interlocking vetoes, are certainly defects of majority voting, but observation of reality suggests that they do not cause significant damage to the political decision process. First, no Condorcet cycle arises if decisions are about alternatives that can be ordered along a single left–right or up–down dimension and voters have *single-peaked preferences*, that is, each voter has a preferred point along this dimension and likes the alternatives less and less the farther they are from the preferred point; then sincere majority voting will be decided by the preference of the *median voter*.[68] And on many issues this is indeed the situation. Second, the anticipated possibility of cycles or vetoes induces bargaining and compromises among voters; proposals are modified; or agreements are reached among groups to give support to a *sequence* of decisions, some favouring one group and some favouring another group in the coalition (*log-rolling*). The possibilities of compromise are so many that some majority agreement will sooner or later be reached. As to manipulability, the voting process is sometimes manipulable, but by whom? By the people appointed to decide which proposals to put to vote and in which order. And how were these people appointed? By some decision process (e.g. a vote) in which the participants were obviously conscious of the power they were giving these appointees. So there is an initial acceptance of some power to manipulate, which is granted to some individual or group as part of the pacts behind the majority coalition. If manipulation goes beyond the limits implicitly assigned to it, there will be some change in alliances, perhaps the president is voted down and replaced.

Again, Arrow's conditions appear unnecessary. The real problems with majority voting lie elsewhere, above all in the risk that defeated minorities refuse to accept the result of majority voting without revolting, something about which no perfect rule can be found because the same risk arises that the rule be not respected. The limits to what majority voting can impose will depend in each

---

66 But small modifications of a law are always possible, which can make it very difficult to decide whether the same alternative is being proposed again.

67 Note that this is not the manipulability mentioned àpropos the Borda count, which concerns misreporting preferences.

68 Ordering voters along the dimension according to their preference peak, and assuming truthful voting, if there is an odd number $2n + 1$ of voters the median voter has n voters on either side, and her/his vote ensures majority to the proposal she/he prefers. If there is an even number of voters, a draw is possible, so what is required for unambiguous results is that the median *couple* of voters agree.

1320   **Chapter 14** · Welfare, Externalities, Public Goods and Happiness

historical situation on the strength of divergent interests and on the strength of repressive powers. Also relevant are the problems posed by the inevitability of a *representative* system due to the fact that ordinary citizens do not have the time to become sufficiently informed and to vote on the thousands of issues requiring collective decisions; then questions arise about the best electoral system, about the discretionality of the elected representatives, about the possibility that their votes be bought by powerful interest groups or gigantic corporations, and so on: very concrete problems untouched by Arrow's theorem.

Arrow's Impossibility Theorem is often considered a very depressing result for the search for a universally acceptable social choice rule.[69] My view is that the original mistake is the search for a rule that would be found acceptable by all whatever their preferences and their social role and power. The basic mistake is the idea that one can imagine the rules about how to reach collective decisions as resulting from a civilized conference similar to an academic debate, where discussion finally reaches some rational decision accepted by everybody. History shows that this is naive utopianism, blind to the inevitable conflict between individuals' aims, and to the power struggle behind every adoption and every change of a social choice rule. This utopianism is evident, for example, in the political theory of justice proposed by the moral philosopher Rawls (1971), which has enjoyed great interest in recent decades: it suggests that a just organization of society is the one people would approve in a hypothetical initial situation in which social arrangements must be decided under a ***veil of ignorance*** that prevents them from knowing in what social position they will end up. Rawls argues that in this case, owing to risk aversion, among the feasible social arrangements most people would prefer the arrangement that maximizes the welfare of the worst-off individual (some inequality of welfare is considered inevitable, even positive for incentive reasons), so he proposes this 'maximin' criterion of justice (how to measure welfare so as to decide who is worst-off is left vague). The utopianism of such a proposal is patent: people already have a social position, why should they worry about the theoretical possibility of having ended up in a different

14

---

69 Actually, a *social choice rule*, that is a rule that selects one among any set of alternatives, should be distinguished from a SPF: a SPF supplies a social choice rule, but to obtain a social choice rule one need not assume a SPF. A SPF produces a complete, reflexive *and transitive* preorder among alternative social states. If one replaces the transitivity condition with weaker conditions, then a complete and reflexive social choice rule can be found that satisfies all four conditions of Arrow's Impossibility Theorem (see Sen 1970, pp. 48–50, 52–55). One such weaker condition is *acyclicity*, that means that preferences are such that it is never possible to obtain a cycle of *strict* preferences over social states $x_1 \succ x_2 \succ \ldots \succ x_k \succ x_1$, or equivalently, that any subset of alternative social states has at least one maximal element (i.e. contains a social state such that no other state in the subset is strictly socially preferred to it). Acyclicity admits for example $a \succ b$, $b \succ c$, $a \sim c$. This need not be absurd; a helpful analogy is sports games, it can happen that a team a is able regularly to beat team b which is able regularly to beat team c, but the team multidimensional characteristics are such that a is only able to tie with c. It remains to decide which should be chosen among the three states a, b, c; under acyclicity a social choice rule can be found that always chooses a social state such that no other state is strictly preferred to it, in this case state a.

14.13 · Arrow's Impossibility Theorem

social state?[70] The acceptance of a social choice rule has a social decision process behind it, that involves complex combinations of values, interests, and power, always including the possibility of recourse to violence as a last resort. The disadvantaged groups may look like accepting the established rules for reaching collective decisions, but when they feel they have the strength, they will try to modify them. When a social choice rule runs into problems, the social decision process behind it is reactivated and social bargaining produces some new result: a compromise, a new constitution, sometimes a civil war. The underprivileged had better look for concrete ways and struggles to improve their lot, rather than hope in ideal social choice rules.

So, do we learn something useful from Arrow's theorem? Given his explicit indication that his conditions intended to forbid 'interpersonal comparisons of social utility', I interpret Arrow as wanting to find out the implications of the economists' search, after Robbins, for ways to reach comparisons between social states not relying on interpersonal comparisons of utility, because these, being value judgements, would destroy the impartiality of the economist as advisor. Arrow's theorem confirms, not surprisingly, that impartiality is impossible. A dismal result only for those who refuse to admit the logical inevitability of value judgements if one is to pass from statements of fact, 'this is the effect this intervention will have', to policy decisions, 'this intervention ought to be made'. Already in deciding what to study, a scholar is not impartial, the search for a better understanding of a problem is not without ethical or political motivations— and probable consequences. Well then, if taking sides is inevitable, let me take sides in favour of as much democracy and equality of political decisional power as possible, on the basis of the historical evidence that generally more democracy brings about a more civilized way of living for the average member of society, and let me express the opinion that the important problems in social choice are not the ones pointed out by Arrow's Impossibility result, but rather the highly unequally distributed capacity to influence collective choices, because of highly distorted and incomplete information, and because of several filters that make it difficult for the majority desires to become collective decisions if not approved by the ruling elites. Noam Chomsky should be obligatory reading.[71]

---

70 Also revealing is how Rawls starts a widely cited article: 'We may think of a human society as a more or less self-sufficient association regulated by a common conception of justice and aimed at advancing the good of its members'. (Rawls 1967, p. 319). I find it difficult to square historical societies with this idyllic description.

71 Noam Chomsky, emeritus professor of linguistics at MIT, for many decades has allotted half of his time to writing books denouncing how misleading is the information people receive about what the US government really does, especially in the international arena, and how ideological and false are the justifications of US government decisions produced by many intellectuals. Many of his writings are available over the Internet; they are extremely accurate and informative, based exclusively on publicly accessible information, which if cleverly searched out is surprisingly revealing. Economics students can start from his Davie Memorial Lecture 'Market Democracy in a Neoliberal Order: Doctrines and Reality', University of Cape Town, May 1997 (*Z Magazine*, November 1997; available over the Internet, and from my Google site web page fabiopetripapers).

14.14 Happiness, and Externalities Again

Much of this chapter has been critical of received welfare economics. But it has also been shown that many notions of welfare economics are quite useful. This chapter ends with a discussion of issues raised by the literature on economics and happiness, where again many notions of welfare economics show their usefulness.[72] The literature on happiness, combined with a more correct picture of the functioning of market economies that discards the full-employment assumption and the idea that income distribution reflects what people deserve, appears to be at present the most promising starting point for a reformulation of welfare economics.

The literature on happiness was started by Easterlin (1974) who concluded that growth of per capita income increases the happiness of households much less than generally thought. He found that, on the basis of a self-assessment of how happy they feel, in the 1950s people's happiness was an increasing function of household income, but twenty years later the considerable increase in income per capita that had occurred in the meanwhile had not increased the self-reported level of happiness, which remained roughly the same function of household income *increased by the average rise in per capita income* over those twenty years. Much research has been done since to check this result and to try to explain it, and the main results that interest us now are, first, the confirmation of Easterlin's finding; second, the confirmation that perceived levels of high happiness or welfare are not haphazardly subjective but do strongly correlate with physiological indicators of good health, relaxation, low frequency of mental disturbances, in a word indicators of what one normally associates with a satisfactory life; third, the need to include other elements besides consumption levels among the determinants of people's perceived level of happiness or welfare, especially three things:
- how the individual's consumption level fares in comparison with average consumption (of the entire society, and of the peer group);
- the quantity and quality of social interactions with others;
- the security of one's economic situation.

Unemployment has obvious relevance both for consumption levels and for the third of these elements because of the insecurity it causes; but it is also important because it damages social interactions: having a job is very important for having a recognized social role and social interactions. Its importance will be stressed later; now let us stop on less recognized inefficiencies of a market economy relative to this list.

The relevance of a comparison of one's consumption level with that of others, stressed by Thorsten Veblen and James Duesenberry but then neglected, is often summarized in the sentence 'keeping up with the Joneses',

---

72 I must thank professor Stefano Bartolini for the stimulus to study this literature and for important indications on the main problems needing reflection in this area. It is thanks to him that I have become aware of the importance of the comparative element in decisions about leisure time, which I have tried to highlight with the simple example of Sect. 14.17.2. I owe to professor Ennio Bilancini other very useful suggestions in this area.

14.14 · Happiness, and Externalities Again

that suggests that status seeking is important and that relative consumption levels are status symbols. The negative influence of a rise of the consumption levels of others on one's satisfaction levels has been often attributed to envy; but it might simply depend on a need for a consumption style similar to that of other people for a full enjoyment of social relations (a car, a smartphone become indispensable the moment shops, work, fun activities etc. become organized on the expectation that everybody has a car and a smartphone).

Whatever its causes, the existence of a comparative element is amply confirmed by empirical research. An important consequence of the comparative element in the utility one derives from a certain level of consumption is that a rise in the level of consumption *of others* reduces the pleasure obtained from one's own consumption, and raises the marginal utility of time allotted to raising one's consumption level, i.e. induces to work more and to enjoy leisure time less; this causes inefficiency in the aggregate.

This can be shown with a very simple example. Assume a single consumption good produced by labour as the sole input; all consumers are identical; consumption of relational goods is neglected. There are N consumers, each one has a utility function that depends on consumption C and leisure time L; non-leisure time is working time W which produces 1 unit of consumption good per hour of labour time, so $W = C$. Normalize the length of a day to 24 h; then $C + L = 24$.

Initially let us assume $U = C^\alpha L^{1-\alpha}$, no comparative element; utility maximization under the constraint $C + L = 24$ yields the Lagrangian function $L = C^\alpha L^{1-\alpha} + \lambda(C + L - 24)$. First-order conditions are

$$\alpha C^{\alpha-1} L^{1-\alpha} + \lambda = 0$$
$$(1 - \alpha) C^\alpha L^{-\alpha} + \lambda = 0$$

These imply $\alpha/(1 - \alpha) = C/L$ under the constraint $C + L = 24$.

Now let us introduce the comparative element: let M be the average consumption level of all other consumers, and let the representative consumer's utility be as before but multiplied by C/M; this raises utility if $C > M$, and decreases it if $C < M$. Now let us use u to indicate utility:

$$u = C^\alpha L^{1-\alpha} C/M \text{ which is equivalent to } u = C^{\alpha+1} L^{1-\alpha} M^1.$$

Consumers are all identical, hence they all maximize in the same way, hence $M = C$. For the single consumer M is given, outside her control, hence the first-order conditions are:

$$(\alpha + 1) C^\alpha L^{1-\alpha} M^{-1} + \lambda = 0, \text{ this for } M = C \text{ becomes } (\alpha + 1) C^{\alpha-1} L^{1-\alpha} + \lambda = 0$$
$$(1 - \alpha) C^{\alpha+1} L^{-\alpha} M^{-1} + \lambda = 0. \text{ this for } M = C \text{ becomes } (1 - \alpha) C^\alpha L^{-\alpha} + \lambda = 0.$$

These would be as for U except that the first condition is multiplied by $(\alpha + 1)$, not by α. It follows that $C/L = (\alpha + 1)/(1 - \alpha)$, instead of $C/L = \alpha/(1 - \alpha)$.

It makes a great difference. For example assume $\alpha = 1/4$: in the case without the comparative element one obtains $C/L = 1/3$, that is $C = 6$ and $L = 18$, or 6 h of work per day. With the comparative element and $M = C$ we obtain $C/L = 5/3$, that is $C = 15$ and $L = 9$. Even neglecting the probable consequences on health, since

$C/M = 1$ it is $u = C^{\alpha}L^{1-\alpha}$, as in the case without the comparative element, but now with a choice of C/L different from the optimal one when utility really depends only on C and L, and therefore yielding less utility, indeed now $u \cong 10.2$ while in the case without comparative element $U \cong 13.7$.

Note that if a law imposed a maximum working time less than 15 h per day (but not less than 6), then everybody would work that maximum number of hours, so again it would be $C/M = 1$, and utility would be given by $C^{\alpha}L^{1-\alpha}$, but now utility would be higher, increasing as the number of working hours decreased and the C/L ratio approached the optimal one obtained in the absence of the comparative element, 1/3 in our numerical example. The comparative element is an externality that the market does not correct; as usual with externalities, it induces an inefficiency, in this case an excessive amount of work; a public intervention can improve things by obliging people to work less. Alternatively, a tax on working time can reduce its marginal utility and have a similar effect.

Other utility functions have been proposed to grasp the phenomenon, and they all produce the same excessive amount of work, because of the extra incentive to consume, given by the comparative element.[73] For example, in one of the utility functions they propose, Clark and Oswald (1998) assume that utility depends on an 'action' which can be at various levels, indicated by a (to fix ideas suppose it is for example the choice of a level of consumption), which causes a convex cost $c(a)$ and influences utility both directly via an increasing concave subutility function $u(a)$ (that measures direct pleasure from consumption), and indirectly via an increasing subutility $v(a - a^*)$ that depends on the comparison of a with the average level a^* chosen by the others; the final utility is written

$$U = sv(a - a^*) + (1 - s)u(a) - c(a)$$

where s and $(1 - s)$ are weights that allow giving more or less importance to either subutility: $s = 0$ means no comparative element, $s = 1$ means only the comparison counts. Here we have an additive rather than a multiplicative influence of the comparison element. The authors show that an increase in a^* will cause a to increase if $s > 0$ and $v''(a - a^*) < 0$,[74] that is if the marginal subutility from comparison is decreasing in $a - a^*$, clearly a more plausible assumption[75] than the opposite one. The reason is that, starting from a situation where the marginal

---

73 Alvarez-Cuadrado (2007) estimates a consumption level 66% greater than the optimal one, i.e. that working time should be reduced to three-fifths of what it is today: a three-day working week!

74 Try proving it yourself as an exercise, before reading the rest of this footnote. The trick is to use the first-order condition for a maximum to obtain a as an implicit function of a^*. For an interior maximum the first-order condition is $sv'(a - a^*) + (1 - s)u'(a) - c'(a) = 0$. This makes a an implicit function of a^*, whose derivative is given by

$$da/da^* = [sv''(a - a^*)]/[sv''(a - a^*) + (1 - s)u''(a) - c''(a)];$$

The denominator is negative because it is the second-order condition for a maximum; so the sign of da/da^* is positive if the numerator is negative.

75 Indeed it means for example that, when $a < a^*$, the consumer becomes the more desirous to increase a, the greater the gap $a^* - a$ between average consumption level and her consumption level. Apart from a few hermits, it seems difficult to imagine people reacting the opposite way.

14.14 · Happiness, and Externalities Again

disutility of a (the derivative of $c(a)$) equals the sum of the two marginal subutilities, an increase of a^* reduces $a - a^*$: if this raises the marginal subutility from comparison $v'(a - a^*)$, the sum of the two marginal subutilities of a becomes greater than its marginal disutility, and an increase of a becomes convenient. If a is consumption and the cost of increasing a is having to work more, again we reach the conclusion that if $s > 0$ the consumer will go for more a than without the comparison element, hence more work and less leisure; in the same way as for the previous example, at least for the case of identical consumers it easily follows that this greater amount of work and of consumption is inefficient.

Let us turn to the relevance of social interactions; for this purpose the notion has been proposed of **relational** 'goods'. Relational 'goods' are those activities of interaction with others that supply emotional satisfaction, for example being member of an Escola de Samba in a Brazilian town; or meeting every weekend with friends to play cards; or having nearby a public garden where one goes and relaxes and chats with neighbours; or reading fairy tales to a child. The consumption of relational goods creates externalities, because the people with whom one interacts are also consuming relational goods; by itself, this fact suffices to indicate that, analogously to the case of fruit trees and honey, if it were the market the main determinant of relational activities then people would allocate to relational activities much less time than the optimal amount; and in all likelihood they indeed do, because the market does not supply the optimal amount of facilities for the exchange of relational 'goods'. Furthermore, it is widely accepted that the consumption of relational goods requires the existence of a 'stock' of social relations that make the interactions possible, and that this stock requires that it be maintained and reinforced by giving time to consuming relational goods, otherwise it deteriorates (friendships do not last if one never spends time with friends). Much and usually most of the time given to consuming relational goods must be leisure time; besides the direct positive effect on utility given by the consumption of relational goods, this consumption also has the effect of maintaining and possibly increasing the stock of social relations, an effect with some public good component because that stock helps other people too to enjoy relational goods.

The above considerations strengthen the conclusion that in modern individualistic society too much time is allotted to work: not only consumption is given too much importance because of the comparison element, but leisure is given too little importance because the direct external effects of the leisure time allotted to enjoyment of relational goods, and the effect of maintenance and increase of the relational stock, are not taken into consideration by individualistic choices.

Bartolini (2010; Bartolini and Bonatti 2003) has even advanced the provocative thesis that the development of modern society has enormously decreased the amount of relational goods that people consume, because of the smaller families and of the greater and greater isolation of people in modern urban neighbourhoods which offer little occasion for neighbourhood interaction (think for example of how different the social life of children is in modern cities relative to small villages where children spend much of their time playing in the streets together with other children). According to him this helps to explain consumerism and the abandonment of the aim of a shorter and shorter working week in

1326　**Chapter 14** · Welfare, Externalities, Public Goods and Happiness

recent decades: the insufficient social ties push people to look for compensation in individualistic consumption and hence to work more to raise income, with a vicious-circle effect. Bartolini has suggested that this desire to consume more has greatly facilitated modern economic growth, and in some papers he has used standard neoclassical growth models (that assume full employment and Say's Law) to depict economies where growth is *due* to people's increasing desire to consume more to compensate for the reduction of relational goods. If these models were intended to show not only a theoretical possibility inside the neoclassical approach, but actually an explanation of observed growth, I would disagree: it must be doubted that the reduction of relational goods and hence the increasing desire to consume more *cause* growth, because the criticisms of neoclassical theory presented in this book imply a rejection of a supply-side determination of growth; it is not the desire of population to work more that induces the economy to produce more, it is not the saving decisions of individuals that determine investment; growth is demand-determined, decided by the class of capital owners and managers, who want growth because it helps the survival and growth of their firms and enhances their power. But certainly the readiness to consume more has been a permissive and in all likelihood indispensable element in modern growth in advanced nations. And the conclusion that there should be much more leisure time and more attention given to favouring relational activities (which require not only leisure time allocated to them but also resources) remains fully valid in the Keynesian–Marxian explanation of growth that I would favour. The stress on giving less importance to growth also agrees with ecological preoccupations.

There is, however, a possible objection to the conclusion that a generalized reduction of the working week and correspondingly of incomes and per capita consumption would constitute a significant Pareto improvement. The objection is that the decrease of working time will generally, especially if the full employment of labour is assumed, entail a reduction of output, and this will generally mean a reduction of savings, hence less capital tomorrow than with the old amount of working time. This objection explains why most contributions on whether the externalities discussed in this section imply inefficiency go on to discuss what difference a correction of these externalities would make to the (discounted) present and future utility of consumers when one takes into account the effects in subsequent periods too.

I am not aware of studies of this question that do not accept the modern neoclassical macro theory of growth, which models the economy's behaviour as a full-employment path extending into the infinite future, with a representative infinitely lived consumer endowed with perfect foresight, and income distribution determined by marginal products: a standard Ramsey path. The procedure consists of comparing the 'decentralized' path, that takes no account of those externalities and is assumed to mimic the actual behaviour of the economy, with the path a perfectly efficient and perfectly informed benevolent planner would choose taking those externalities into account. The result is that the planner's path is Pareto superior.[76]

76　This is the procedure that brings Alvarez-Cuadrado (2007) to estimate that optimality would require a reduction of consumption by *two fifths* of its 'decentralized'-path value (supposedly indicating the actual behaviour of the economy), see footnote 73 above.

14.14 · Happiness, and Externalities Again

It does not seem necessary to reproduce the formal details of such a comparison, that would require a full introduction to modern neoclassical growth theory with Hamiltonians (or dynamic programming), transversality conditions etc., for which the reader will have to turn to other textbooks. The economic reason for the possibility of a Pareto improvement is clear and easily grasped. To explain it in the simplest possible terms, I leave aside the consumption of relational goods; but an extension of the reasoning to include them would not present difficulties and would only further confirm the conclusion.

Start from the 'decentralized' path that supposedly the unregulated market economy would take. Now suppose working time is reduced in one period by government fiat, and consumption with it, but not savings: by opportune state interventions the amount of gross savings and investment is maintained the same as in the 'decentralized' path; under this constraint, working time in the period is reduced and consumption with it, and this increases the period's subutility; to prove that a Pareto *improvement* is possible it is not necessary that the period's subutility be maximized by reducing working time to the level that would be optimal in the absence of the comparison element, it suffices that the reduction of working time does raise utility, which it will, as shown earlier. Now, the same procedure can be applied to each period; as a consequence, in each period the capital stock is the same as in the 'decentralized' path, so the consumption–leisure trade-off is the same, and the choice of leisure in one period does not alter the consumption–leisure trade-off in subsequent periods. It is therefore possible to obtain a Pareto improvement in each period without decreasing the utility achievable in subsequent periods. Then a Pareto improvement can be achieved in all periods. So there is no doubt that a new intertemporal path with reduced consumption and working time, and unchanged investment, can be reached via opportune state interventions which is Pareto superior to the 'decentralized' path. It is of course possible, indeed likely, that the perfect planner's path (which can alter the capital accumulation path too) would yield a still higher utility: this will only further confirm the Pareto inefficiency of the 'decentralized' path.

It remains to ask what relevance these exercises have, given the negative conclusion we have reached on the credibility of the neoclassical approach and hence also of the theory of growth based on it.

The trick of reducing working time while keeping investment unchanged is logically permissible with any theory of growth. So there is no need to accept neoclassical growth theory in order to argue that working less and consuming less would constitute a Pareto improvement (actually, not rigorously a Pareto improvement, because it would hold only for the vast majority, in all likelihood the ruling élite would prefer things to continue unchanged). Whatever the path the economy would spontaneously follow, an intervention that reduced working time and consumption without reducing investment would certainly, for a non-excessive such reduction, be a Pareto improvement (for the vast majority). One can extend the reasoning to include accumulation of knowledge: besides the amount of labour producing capital goods, one can assume that the amount of labour assigned to producing technical progress too is left unaltered, so the path of technical progress too is left unaltered.

This has implications for those, among the contributors to the literature that stresses that working time should be reduced, who appear from other writings of theirs not to share the neoclassical approach, but nevertheless present their analyses on this topic inside neoclassical growth models. There appears to be no need for such a concession to so highly questionable a theory.

The studies stimulated by the 'Easterlin paradox'—that growth of per-capita income apparently has little long-run effects on happiness—have concluded that once physical suffering is reduced by sufficient food, shelter, medical care against the more usual causes of pain, and reduction of the physical unpleasantness of work, then increases in material standard of living have nearly zero long-run effects on self-perceived happiness, and what counts most for happiness is good affective relations and a satisfactory secure job. It remains to explain how come a generation with bigger cars or larger houses or a television set in every room is not happier than the previous generation in spite of a preference for the wealthier life stile. The main explanation is that there is **habituation** to one's conditions and activities, in two senses; younger generations take their standards of living for granted; and even the same generation accustoms itself to changed conditions after a few years. We need not enter now into a discussion of the attempts at physiological explanations of this fact. As economists we are mainly interested in empirical confirmation of this fact, and in its implications.

The empirical confirmation is abundant. Recent empirical research has confirmed the presence of adaptation to changed circumstances in many fields, including marriage, divorce, loss of a close relative, loss of job: a vast survey repeated over a number of years in Germany (Clark et al. 2008) confirms that, at the time of the change, and even some time before if the change is expected, happiness rises with positive events (e.g. marriage, birth of a child), decreases with negative events; but after a couple of years the level of satisfaction goes back to what it was, with one important exception: unemployment, to which especially males do not seem to adapt.

The confirmation that adaptation exists and is quite relevant in fields other than standard of living confirms the plausibility of habituation as an explanation of the Easterlin paradox. This is a further confirmation that the importance of economic growth is overestimated.

The result that unemployment is something to which people find it very difficult to adapt confirms that fighting unemployment should be one of the top priorities of governments, and *the central concern of welfare economics*. 'The results in this paper suggest that, in a developed nation, economic progress buys only a small amount of extra happiness.... Unemployment appears to be the primary economic source of unhappiness. If so, economic growth should not be a government's primary concern' (Oswald 1997, p. 1827, 1828). It is worth remembering that after the fall of communism and the transition to a market economy in USSR and Eastern Europe in the 1990s, a significant fraction of the population expressed strong discontent and even a desire to go back to a planned economy, because of the loss of security due to the appearance of unemployment. Evidently the primary concern of governments should be to ensure as high a level of

14.14 · Happiness, and Externalities Again

employment as possible. Nor are full-employment policies difficult to conceive: the state could be an employer of last resort (e.g. employing the unemployed to recreate forests where they were destroyed by man), or it could compulsorily shorten the working week if one does not want to use expansionary fiscal policies. But full employment strengthens wage labour, and makes it more difficult to contain its demands for income redistribution and for a greater say in economic decisions; so as argued by Kalecki, 'Political aspects of full employment' (1943), one cannot expect governments in capitalist economies to operate persistently towards the realization and maintenance of full employment—unless, I would qualify, controlled by labour parties or socialist parties and with the economy organized according to *neo-corporatism*, a continuous bargaining between the confederation of industries, the confederation of trade unions, and the government, on what can be conceded to wage labour without stopping the good functioning of the economy; it seems to have worked well where adopted, e.g. in Sweden or Austria in the 1960s. One implication is that the European treatises connected with the euro, that insist on fighting inflation and state deficits even if it means increases of unemployment, are the opposite of what should be done.

Strictly connected with the great importance of having a job is the issue of *economic insecurity*. In recent decades legislation in most advanced nations has increased economic insecurity, by reducing protection against unjustified firings, reducing eligibility to unemployment subsidies, allowing unemployment to increase, reducing the average duration of jobs, favouring the replacement of permanent jobs with temporary jobs.[77] Having a job does not grant a feeling of peace and security if there is no guarantee that it will last. There is ample evidence that economic insecurity damages health, especially mental health.

So utility should be made relevantly to depend on economic security too; for the moment, as far as I know in the happiness literature no attempt to formulate a utility function that integrates this element has been attempted. Unfortunately, economic security is not something that can be easily bought, because for most people it depends on getting and maintaining a secure job, and the likelihood of such an event depends on overall economic conditions, institutions, laws and government policies. But the impossibility of purchase holds for most externalities and public goods too, and yet welfare economics does consider them important determinants of utility levels. It is time to extend welfare economics to considering economic insecurity too.

---

77 'There is evidence both at the macro and the micro economic level that there has been a growth of volatility [of incomes], and more income differentiation, and there is a lot of research to show that volatility has a negative effect on people's sense of well-being and causes great anxiety' (ILO 2004). The UN World Economic and Social Survey (2008), whose title was 'Overcoming Economic Insecurity', strongly condemned the dismantling, in the previous forty years, of the checks and balances of the mixed economy, which provoked what, with reference to the USA, was called 'the great risk shift' from capital to labour.

1330   **Chapter 14** · Welfare, Externalities, Public Goods and Happiness

14.15 Conclusions

Welfare economics needs a deep rethinking to make it independent of the unconvincing marginal/neoclassical approach in symbiosis with which it was born. The notion of Pareto efficiency was proposed and insisted upon because of the possibility to claim that general equilibrium is Pareto efficient, but this requires, besides the validity of the marginal approach, the restriction of utility to consumption allocations only, and without externalities. In fact the notion of Pareto improvement requires a preliminary series of value judgements on which preferences should be considered socially acceptable, and this deprives the notion of its claimed universal acceptability. Furthermore when one admits consumption externalities, the notion of Pareto improvement becomes unworkable, utility comes to depend on too many things, including the conformity of society and of other people's behaviour to one's value judgements and moral criteria; it becomes impossible to separate economic efficiency from political preferences. Anyway even neglecting externalities the First and Second Fundamental Theorems of Welfare Economics are unacceptable, market economies do not produce the full employment of resources, and income distribution does not reflect contribution to welfare. This permits a solid defence of the institutions of the welfare state against the attacks it is suffering. Cost–benefit analysis is potentially useful but it can be dangerous because it is manipulable and because it can bend neoclassical mistaken theses to horrible uses. Happiness economics indicates reasons to base a renewed welfare economics on making the elimination of unemployment, the reduction of insecurity, the increase of 'social capital' and the shortening of the working week the main priorities; the pursuit of economic growth appears less important because in advanced nations it does not increase happiness.

14.16 Review Questions and Exercises

- **Review Questions**
1. List the main objections to the relevance of the First Theorem of Welfare Economics.
2. Explain why the notion of quasi-equilibrium is important in the study of the Second Fundamental Theorem of Welfare Economics.
3. Let G be the quantity of a public good producible in different amounts. Explain why the condition of equality between sum of marginal willingnesses to pay, and marginal cost of G, is a necessary but not sufficient condition for a local optimum (neglecting macro effects).
4. Give examples to illustrate that reaching efficiency (in the cases where the market does not suffice) also involves solving equity issues.
5. Argue verbally why intertemporal efficiency is difficult to reach if for a good there is no futures market and expectations are not uniform among agents.
6. Explain why the Coasian thesis that a clear specification of property rights will allow solving most externality problems is too optimistic, even when the number of involved agents is small.

14.16 · Review Questions and Exercises

7. Distinguish transitivity from acyclicity of social preferences and explain why the latter is a weaker condition.
8. Explain why the Borda count does not comply with the requirements of Arrow's Impossibility Theorem.
9. What is criticizable about the thesis that the loss to society of a death is measured by the lost future earnings of the dead person? Distinguish labour earnings from property earnings.

- **Exercises**
1. In Sect. 14.9.2, suppose *nominal* wealth levels W^s are assigned; if Eq. (14.1) holds, this implicitly means the choice of which numéraire?
2. Compile a table with two rows: rival and non-rival goods; and two columns: excludable and non-excludable goods. Fill each box with at least four entries. In the upper left box you will have pure private goods. In the lower right box you will have pure public goods. The other two boxes are the most interesting ones.
3. Two goods, x and y, must be allocated between two individuals, A and B. The total quantities to be allocated are $x=600$, $y=400$. The utility functions are $U_A=x_A^{1/3}y_A^{2/3}$, $U_B=x_B^{1/2}y_B^{1/2}$.
   (a) Show that allocation $(x_A,y_A)=(x_B,y_B)=(300, 200)$ is not Pareto efficient.
   (b) Find the Pareto-efficient allocation corresponding to $y_B=200$.
4. (Cowell) In a two-commodity exchange economy there are two large equal-sized groups of traders. Each trader in group a has an endowment of 300 units of commodity 1, each trader in group b has an endowment of 200 units of commodity 2. Each type-a person has utility $U_a=x_{1a}x_{2a}$, each type-b person has utility $U_b=(x_{1b}x_{2b})/x_{1a}$.
   a. Find the competitive equilibrium allocation.
   b. Explain why the competitive equilibrium is inefficient.
   c. Explain what kind of redistribution (treating equally all individuals of the same type) would be a Pareto improvement.
   d. Explain why the inefficiency cannot be corrected by raising the price of commodity 1 for type-a people.
5. A seldom stressed assumption behind the First Theorem of Welfare Economics is that all goods must have markets. In an exchange economy with two consumers and three goods, assume that for one of the three goods there is no market (barter is forbidden), and show that this prevents reaching Pareto efficiency. (Hint: if for one good there is no market, will it be possible to consume an amount of the good different from its endowment?)
6. Externality. Individual A chooses x_A and y_A and has utility function $u_A=x_A+2y_A^{1/2}$. Individual B chooses x_B and y_B and has utility function $u_B=x_B+20y_B^{1/2}-y_A^{1/2}$. Prices are $p_x=1/10$, $p_y=1$.
   (a) find y_A and y_B if both individuals have enough income for income effects not to arise and they choose independently.
   (b) find optimal y_A and y_B using the principle of value maximization (Chap. 9, ▶ Sect. 9.16).

1332   **Chapter 14** · Welfare, Externalities, Public Goods and Happiness

7. Public good. In a condominium with two families A and B it is possible to build a condominium swimming pool, whose variable quality q is determined by its cost S according to q = S. The families have utility functions

$$u_A(x_A, q) = x_A + 6q - \frac{3}{2}q^2, \quad u_B(x_B, q) = x_B + 15q - \frac{1}{2}q^2.$$

   (a) Find optimal q according to the principle 'sum of marginal propensities to spend = marginal cost', assuming incomes high enough to avoid income effects and no transaction costs.

   (b) Show that the same result is reached by maximizing total value.

   (c) Find family A's maximum contribution $s_{A\max}$ and minimum contribution $s_{A\min}$ (corresponding respectively to B contributing its minimum and maximum), between which the distribution of S is indeterminate according to Coase's theorem.

8. Commons. In a village where cows graze on a common field owned by the village, the milk per year produced by m cows is $100\,m - m^2$ l, and the price of one litre is one euro. Maintaining a cow costs 10 euros per year. Indicate the number of cows if each family can freely bring one more cow to the field. Then indicate the maximum rent the village could ask a firm given exclusive licence to bring cows to the field, if a cow would have the same cost and there are many other firms ready to compete for that licence.

9. In a small town with 20 consumers, 10 of type A and 10 of type B, the local government must decide how many street lamps to instal. Each A-type consumer is ready to pay the additional sum 150–x for each additional street lamp, each B-type consumer 200–x, where x is the number of installed lamps. Each lamp costs 1000 but there is in addition a fixed cost of 500 to pose the electric cables. Determine the efficient number of street lamps.

10. Suppose there is a perfectly divisible public good G, and n agents with index i and identical Cobb–Douglas utility functions $u_i(G, x_i) = G^\alpha x_i^{1-\alpha}$. The price of x is 1. The public good has constant marginal cost c. The amount of G depends on the money spontaneously contributed towards it. A given amount W of wealth is divided in equal parts among $k \le n$ of the agents. Each agent i supplies the quantity of public good resulting from her independent decision (i.e. no attempt to free ride) to maximize utility by using wealth to buy an amount x_i of the private good and giving the remainder towards the public good. How does the amount of the public good change as k increases?

11. (Nicholson) Suppose a monopoly produces a harmful externality. Use the concept of consumer surplus in a partial-equilibrium diagram similar to the one used in ❏ Fig. 12.8 to analyse whether an optimal Pigovian tax on the polluter would necessarily be a welfare improvement.

12. (Varian) Suppose two individuals drive often on the same road. Individual i chooses speed x_i and gets utility $u_i(x_i) + y_i$ from this choice, where y_i is income; assume $u_i'(x_i) > 0$. The faster the individuals drive, the more likely it is that they get involved in a mutual accident. Let $p(x_1, x_2)$ be the probability of an accident, increasing in each argument, and let $c > 0$ be the cost, assumed given for simplicity, that the accident imposes on each individual i. Assume that each individual's utility is linear in money and $y_i > c$.

14.16 · Review Questions and Exercises

(a) Assuming each individual is conscious that her probability of accident also depends on the other individual's speed, suppose the chosen speeds are determined by a Nash equilibrium. Determine these speeds.

(b) Assuming comparability of utility, find the speeds that maximize social welfare. Show that each individual has an incentive to drive too fast from the social point of view.

(c) If individual i is fined an amount t_i in the case of an accident, how large should t_i be to internalize the externality?

13. (Cowell). A group of n identical schoolchildren know that at lunchtime they will receive a plate with a slice of pie. When they look through the dining hall window in the morning they can see that n plates have been prepared and the slices are not of equal size, and no child knows which plate she or he will receive. Taking the space of all possible plate allocations as a complete description of all the possible social states for these children, and assuming that ex-ante there are equal chances of any one child receiving any one of the plates, show that a utilitarian VNM utility function can be used as a social welfare function and, if with strictly concave subutility, it will rank more equal distributions as preferable to less equal distributions.

14. Discuss how prohibiting tobacco smoking might be justified (a) on the basis of paternalism, (b) on the basis of the compensation criterion.

15. Assume an atemporal non-capitalistic economy (several consumption goods produced by labour and land). Would levying an equal rate proportional purchase tax on all consumption goods violate the Pareto efficiency conditions?

16. (Usefulness of the Envelope Theorem) The steel firm on which a Pigou tax t is imposed in ▶ Sect. 14.3.2 has profit

$$\pi_s(s, x) = p_s S - c_s(s, x) - tx,$$

with s steel output, $c_s(\cdot)$ the cost function and x pollution. Maximization of profit relative to s and x produces $p_s = \partial c_s / \partial s$ and $\partial c_s / \partial x = -t$. Now define $C(s) = [c_s(s, x(s)) + tx(s)]$ as the tax-inclusive total cost function, in which x is determined by cost minimization for each given level of s. If we define profit as

$$\pi_s = p_s s - C_s,$$

maximization of profit implies $p_s = dC/ds$, so it must be $dC/ds = \partial c_s / \partial s$, in spite of the fact that $p_s = \partial c_s / \partial s$ treats x as given, while dC/ds does not. Still, $dC/ds = \partial c_s / \partial s$ seems inescapable. Prove it.

17. (Varian) Pollution from an upstream chemical plant damages a downstream brewery. The regulator is able to measure the amount x of pollution but not the damage it inflicts on the brewery, and organizes the following mechanism. The chemical plant must tell the regulator the subsidy s per unit of pollution which the brewery should receive from the regulator. The brewery must tell the regulator the tax t per unit of pollution the chemical firm should pay to the regulator. The regulator will impose t and s on the firms and in addition will impose a penalty of $\alpha(s - t)^2$ on the chemical firm. Let SPF(x) be the profit of the chemical firm apart from taxes, then the actual profit is $SPF(x) - tx - \alpha(s - t)^2$, while the profit of the brewery is $\pi^\circ + sx - D(x)$ where π° is independent of the level of pollution and D(x) is the damage caused by pollution.

Show that at the subgame perfect Nash equilibrium of the game induced by this mechanism there is an efficient level of pollution and the payments by and to the regulator sum to zero. (Hint: if t is given, what is the level of s the chemical plant finds it optimal to indicate? conscious of this, what is the level of t the brewery finds it optimal to indicate? Compare your answers with the conditions for an optimal level of x derived from integrating the two firms into one.)

18. Find which one(s) of the four conditions of Arrow's Impossibility Theorem is not respected by the Bergson–Samuelson standard SWF $W(\mathbf{x}) = \sum_{h=1}^{H} \alpha_h u^h(\mathbf{x})$.

19. (Muñoz-Garcia). (Free riding versus fairness concerns in public good provision.) Assume two players Alpha and Beta are asked to simultaneously and independently choose between contributing (C) and not contributing (N) to a public good. With selfish preferences and quasi-linear utility the game has a Prisoners' Dilemma structure with monetary payoffs indicated in the figure and obeying b > a > d > c.

	Beta	
	C	N
Alpha C	a, a	c, b
N	b, c	d, d

Now assume the monetary payoffs are the same but the two players have the following utility function with fairness concerns (Fehr and Schmidt 1999):

$$U_i(x_i, x_k) = x_i - \alpha_i \max [x_k - x_i, 0] - \beta_i \max [x_i - x_k, 0]$$

where i, k stand for the two players, x_i is the monetary payoff to player i and x_k the one to the other player, α_i measures envy for getting less than the other player, β_i measures embarrassment for getting more than the other player, and $\alpha > \beta$, $1 > \beta \geq 0$. Only one of the two other-regarding influences on utility operates when the payoffs are not the same. Rewrite the game with the new utility payoffs derived from this utility function, and prove that if for both players $\beta > (b - a)/(b - c)$, fairness transforms the game from a Prisoners' Dilemma game to a Hi-Lo game with two Nash equilibria in pure strategies, of which the cooperative one is superior and therefore presumably adopted.

References

Alvarez-Cuadrado, F. (2007). Envy, leisure and restrictions on working hours. *Canadian Journal of Economics, 40*, 1286–1310.

Arrow, K. J. (1951). *Social choice and individual values* 1st ed. (2nd modified ed., 1963). New York: J. Wiley.

Atkinson, A. B. (1996). The economics of the welfare state. *American Economist, 40*(2), 5–15.

Barr, N. (1992). Economic theory and the welfare state: A survey and interpretation. *Journal of Economic Literature, 39*(2), 741–803.

Bartolini, S. (2010). *Manifesto per la felicità*. Roma: Donzelli.

Bartolini, S., & Bonatti, L. (2003). Endogenous growth and negative externalities. *Journal of Economics, 79*, 123–144.

14.16 · Review Questions and Exercises

Bergson (Burk), A. (1938 (1969)) A reformulation of certain aspects of welfare economics. *Quarterly Journal of Economics*, 52, 310–334. As reprinted in American Economic Association. (1969). *Readings in welfare economics* (pp. 7–26). London: George Allen and Unwin.

Blad, M. C., & Keiding, H. (1990). *Microeconomics. Institutions, equilibrium and optimality*. Amsterdam: North-Holland.

Bowles, S. (2004). *Microeconomics. Behavior, institutions, and evolution*. Princeton, NJ: Princeton University Press.

Campbell, D. (2012). Welfare economics for capitalists: The economic consequences of Judge Posner. *Cardozo Law Review, 33*(6), 2233–2274.

Clarke, E. H. (1971). Multipart pricing of public goods. *Public Choice, 2,* 19–33.

Clark, A. E., Diener, E., Georgellis, Y., & Lucas, R. E. (2008). Lags and leads in life satisfaction: A test of the baseline hypothesis. *Economic Journal, 118*(529), F222–F243.

Clark, A. E., & Oswald, A. J. (1998). Comparison-concave utility and following behaviour in social and economic settings. *Journal of Public Economics, 70,* 133–155.

Coase, R. H. (1960). The problem of social cost. *Journal of Law and Economics, 3*(1), 1–44.

Cowell, F. (2006). *Microeconomics. Principles and analysis*. Oxford: Oxford University Press.

de Graaff, J. V. (1957). *Theoretical welfare economics*. Cambridge: Cambridge University Press.

Easterlin, R. A. (1974). Does economic growth improve the human lot? Some empirical evidence. In P. David & M. Reder (Eds.), *Nations and households in economic growth* (pp. 89–125). New York: Academic Press.

Fehr, E., & Schmidt, K. (1999). A theory of fairness, competition and cooperation. *Quarterly Journal of Economics, 114,* 817–868.

Fleurbaey, M. (1996). *Théories économiques de la justice*. Paris: Economica.

Fleurbaey, M., & Mongin, P. (2005). The news of the death of welfare economics is greatly exaggerated. *Social Choice and Welfare, 25,* 381–418.

Foley D. K., Garegnani, P., Pivetti, M., & Vianello, F. (2004). *Classical theory and policy analysis: A round table*. Materiali di Discussione (Vol. 1). Roma: Centro di Ricerche e Documentazione "Piero Sraffa", Università Roma Tre.

Frank, R. H. (2006). *Microeconomics and behavior*. New York: McGraw-Hill.

Garegnani, P. (1992). Some notes for an analysis of accumulation. In J. Halevi, D. Laibman, & E. Nell (Eds.), *Beyond the steady state: A revival of growth theory* (pp. 47–72). London: Macmillan.

Garegnani, P. (2004). Professor Foley and classical policy analysis. In Foley et al. (Eds.), (pp. 23–44).

Garegnani, P., & Palumbo, A. (1998). Accumulation of capital. In H. D. Kurz & N. Salvadori (Eds.), *The Elgar companion to classical economics* (Vol. I, pp. 10–18). Cheltenham, UK: Edward Elgar.

Gibbard, A. (1973). Manipulation of voting schemes. *Econometrica, 41,* 587–601.

Groves, T. (1973). Incentives in teams. *Econometrica, 41,* 617–631.

Harberger A. C. (1954) Monopoly and resource allocation. *American Economic Review, 44*(2)

Harberger, A. C. (1959). Using the resources at hand more effectively. *American Economic Review, 49*(2)

Harrod R. F. (1938) Scope and method of economics. *Economic Journal*, 48(191), 383–412.

Hausman, D. M., & McPherson, M. S. (2006). *Economic analysis, moral philosophy, and public policy* (2nd ed.). Cambridge: Cambridge University Press.

Hicks, J. R. (1940). The valuation of social income. *Economica, 7,* 105–124.

Igersheim, H. (2017). *The death of welfare economics: History of a controversy*. Working paper, no. 2017–03. CHOPE (Center for the History of Political Economy, Duke University).

ILO (International Labour Organization). (2004). World employment report 2004–05. Geneva: International Labour Office.

Jehle, G. A., & Reny, P. J. (2011). *Advanced microeconomic theory*. Financial Times. Haley, UK: Prentice Hall (Pearson).

Kaldor, N. (1939). Welfare propositions in economics and interpersonal comparisons of utility. *Economic Journal, 49,* 549–552.

Kalecki, M. (1971). (1943) Political aspects of full employment. In M. Kalecki (Ed.), *Selected essays on the dynamics of the capitalist economy 1933–70* (pp. 138–145). Cambridge University Press: Cambridge.

Kreps, D. M. (1990). *A course in microeconomic theory*. New York: Harvester Wheatsheaf.

Kreps, D. M. (2013). *Microeconomic foundations I. Choice and competitive markets*. Princeton: Princeton University Press.

Lindahl, E. (1958(1919)). Just taxation—a positive solution. In: R. A. Musgrave & A. T. Peacock (Eds.), *Classics in the Theory of Public Finance*. London: Macmillan. Originally published in German in 1919.

Lipsey, R. G., & Lancaster, K. (1956–1957) The general theory of second best. *Review of Economic Studies*, 24, 11–32.

Mas-Colell, A., Whinston, M. D., & Green, J. R. (1995). *Microeconomic theory*. Oxford: Oxford University Press.

Nozick, R. (1974). *Anarchy, state, and utopia*. New York: Basic Books.

Oswald, A. J. (1997). Happiness and economic performance. *Economic Journal*, 107(445), 1812–1845.

Pareto, V. (1968 (1917)) *Traité de sociologie générale*. Paris: Druoz.

Rawls, J. (1967). Distributive justice. In: P. Laslett & W. G. Runciman (Eds.), *Philosophy, politics and society* (3rd ed., pp. 58–82). Oxford: Blackwell (1967). As reproduced in Phelps, E. (Ed.). (1973). *Economic justice* (pp. 319–362). Harmondsworth, Middlesex: Penguin.

Rawls, J. (1971). *Theory of justice*. Cambridge, MA: Harvard University Press.

Robbins, L. (1932). *An essay on the nature and significance of economic science*. London: Macmillan.

Rohlfs, J. (1974). A theory of interdependent demand for a communications service. *Bell Journal of Economics and Management Science, 5*(1), 16–37.

Samuelson, P. A. (1947). *Foundations of economic analysis*. Cambridge MA: Harvard University Press.

Satterthwaite, M. A. (1975). Strategy-proofness and Arrow's conditions: Existence and correspondence theorems for voting procedures and social welfare functions. *Journal of Economic Theory, 10*, 187–217.

Sen, A. (1979). Personal utilities and public judgements: Or what's wrong with welfare economics? *Economic Journal, 89*(355), 537–558.

Sen, A. (2000). The discipline of cost#benefit analysis. *Journal of Legal Studies, 29*(S2), 931–952.

Sidgwick, H. (1973). The reasonableness of utilitarianism (excerpts from The method of ethics, Macmillan, 1907). In: E. S. Phelps (Ed.), *Economic justice* (pp. 222–244). Harmondsworth, England: Penguin.

UN. (2008). *UN world economic and social survey 2008: Overcoming economic insecurity*. New York: United Nations.

US CDC (Center for Disease Control and Prevention) (n.d.) *Economic Evaluation* Part IV: Benefit-Cost Analysis. At: ► https://www.cdc.gov/dhdsp/evaluation_resources/economic_evaluation/docs/Economic-Evaluation-Part4.pdf.

Varian, H. (1992). *Microeconomic analysis* (3rd ed.). New York: W. W. Norton.

Vickrey, W. (1961). Counterspeculation, auctions, and competitive sealed tenders. *Journal of Finance, 16*, 8–37.

Winch, D. M. (1971). *Analytical welfare economics*. Harmondsworth, UK: Penguin.

Zingales, L. (2017). Towards a political theory of the firm. *Journal of Economic Perspectives, 31*(3), 113–130.

Mathematical Review

Contents

15.1   Sets, Relations, Functions, Convexity, Convex Combination of Vectors – 1338

15.2   Logic: If, Only if, Contrapositive, Proof by Contradiction, Connection with Subsets – 1342

15.3   Vectors, Matrices, Hyperplanes. Definite Matrices – 1343

15.4   Analysis – 1353

15.5   Correspondences – 1364

15.6   Optimization – 1366

15.7   Linear Programming and Duality – 1381

15.8   Complex Numbers – 1382

15.9   Integrals – 1384

15.10   Probability and Statistics – 1385

15.11   Poisson Process – 1391

        References – 1394

© Springer Nature Switzerland AG 2021
F. Petri, *Microeconomics for the Critical Mind*,
Classroom Companion: Economics, https://doi.org/10.1007/978-3-030-62070-7_15

1338   **Chapter 15** · Mathematical Review

This chapter allows a quick review of the meaning of the mathematical notions used in this book and not explained in the course of the exposition. It briefly remembers for example the notions of

- set, convex set, logical implication as defining subsets, product set, preorder
- hyperplane, geometric interpretation of dot product, definite and semidefinite matrix
- open set, convergent sequence, limit, set of measure zero, differential and derivative of function of several variables, expansion in Taylor series, upper-hemicontinuous correspondence
- optimization without and with constraints
- complex numbers and solution of third-degree equations
- probability distribution, conditional probability, Bayes' Theorem, variance, correlation, order statistic
- and more.

15.1 Sets, Relations, Functions, Convexity, Convex Combination of Vectors

This chapter supplies a refresher of some undergraduate mathematical and statistical notions; it also gives brief introductions to some more advanced notions used in the main text and often not included in undergraduate mathematics courses for economists, as a temporary help while the reader completes attendance to a more advanced course in mathematics for economists. This chapter does not and cannot aim at substituting for such a course or for the study of equivalent manuals. In particular, proofs are generally not supplied of the results and theorems cited. The review of mathematical notions is generally very concise, I stop a little more only on some points generally not well understood by undergraduates, in particular the differential and the usefulness of expansion in Taylor's series. For a more extended treatment with proofs and examples, the reader unable or unwilling to go directly to mathematics textbooks or courses is referred to the mathematical appendices in Jehle and Reny (2011, pp. 495–617), which with their 120 pages and numerous exercises come close to being a synthetic substitute for a textbook in the mathematics for microeconomics (no matrix algebra though, and no dynamical systems).

Some mathematical notions are explained in the main text, because their relevance for the flow of the argument guarantees a good absorption if introduced at that point (for example decomposable matrices, eigenvalues, Perron–Frobenius theorem in ▶ Chap. 2; quasi-concavity, Kuhn–Tucker, envelope theorem in ▶ Chap. 4; fixed-point theorems, Liapunov's second method in ▶ Chap. 6; separation theorem in ▶ Chap. 14). An indication of where the notion is explained is supplied here.

A *set* is any collection of elements, which are called the elements of the set. It can be composed of a finite or an infinite number of elements. The number of elements in a set is the **cardinality** of the set. That an entity x is an element of a set S is indicated as $x \in S$. $S = \{x_i\}$ means that the set S has elements distinguished by an index, usually a numerical index, x_1, ..., x_i, ...; the symbol $\{x_i\}$ will be accompanied by an indication of the numbers over which the generic index i can vary, e.g. from 1 to n. A set that contains a single element is called a *singleton*. A set may contain no elements: one example is the set 'all the real numbers that are square roots of negative real numbers'; then it is called an *empty set* and is indicated as Ø (zero with a diagonal bar). The empty set is considered to be a subset of any set. If you take away from a set all its elements, you are left with the empty set.

A set S is a *subset* of another set U, denoted as $S \subset U$, if every element of S is also an element of U. If S is a subset of U, the *complement* of S in U is the set of elements of U which are not in S; it is indicated as S^C. If sets A and B are both subsets of a larger set U often called the universal set, then we can define:

- the *union* of the two sets, denoted $A \cup B$, as the set composed of all and only the elements of U which are elements of A or of B (or of both)
- the *intersection* of the two sets, denoted $A \cap B$, as the set of the elements of U which are both elements of A and of B.
- the *set difference* between a first set A and a second set B, denoted $A \backslash B$, as the set of elements of A which are not elements of B. (If A and B contain the same elements, they are called *equal sets* and the set difference is the empty set.)
- the *set product* of two sets A and B, denoted $A \times B$, is the set of *all* possible *ordered* couples of elements with as first element an element of A and as second element an element of B.

A set product can be defined analogously for more than two sets. R^n, the n-dimensional Euclidean space, is the set product of n sets $R_{(i)}$ each one corresponding to the real line, indexed with numbers from 1 to n; R^n has as elements all possible ordered n-tuples of real numbers, the first from $R_{(1)}$, the second from $R_{(2)}$ and so on. These n-tuples are called *n-vectors,* or also *points* of R^n with the elements of the vector representing Cartesian coordinates.

Ordered couples of elements of two sets can be used to define a *binary relation*. For example if A is a set of adult males and B is a set of adult females in a nation, the binary relation 'husband of' connects some elements of A with some elements of B. This relation is not complete, only a subset of the elements of $A \times B$ satisfy this binary relation.

A binary relation among the elements of the *product of a set S with itself*, called for brevity a binary relation *on S*, establishes a partial or complete order among the elements of S. A binary relation R on a set S is *complete* if for any couple (x,y) of elements of S it is xRy or yRx (or both). It is *transitive* if given three elements x, y, z of S, if xRy and yRz then xRz. It is *reflexive* if it holds for the couples whose two elements indicate the same element of S. If S is a set of numbers, the binary relation 'greater than' is transitive but is not reflexive, a number is not greater than itself; on the contrary the binary relation 'greater than or equal to' is reflexive. A transitive and reflexive binary relation on a set S is also called a *preorder*; a preorder on S is *total* if aRb or bRa for all a, b $\in$ S, that is, if the binary relation is complete besides being transitive and reflexive.

A *function* is a relation between two sets A and B, called respectively the *domain* of the function and the *range* of the function, that associates to *each* (non-empty) element of the domain a *single* (non-empty) element of the range, which is called the *image* under f of the element in the domain. A function is often indicated as f: A → B. Not all elements of the range need be images of some element in the domain. The reader is certainly familiar with functions that associate numbers to numbers, but the domain and the range of a function can be any sets. The typical element of the domain might be a vector $\mathbf{x}$ whose elements represent each a weapon arsenal of a different nation (i.e. $\mathbf{x}$ is a vector of vectors of stocks of weapons), so different elements of the domain differ for the stocks of weapons each nation has; the range might be the set of these nations, and the function might associate to each element in the domain the nation that would come out the winner in case of a simultaneous war of each nation against all the others. If the relation associates to each element in the domain a subset of elements in the range which in at least one case is not a singleton, the relation is not a function but a *correspondence*.

Convexity of a set and convexity of a function are very different concepts. I start with the former. I will only consider sets of *points* in Euclidean space R^n, with n a positive integer. A point in R^n is a vector $\mathbf{x}$ of n ordered numbers $(x_1,...,x_n)$; these numbers are the coordinates of the point, interpretable as distances from the origin along the the Cartesian axes of R^n. If a is a scalar, $a\mathbf{x} = (ax_1,...,ax_n)$; $\mathbf{x} + \mathbf{y} = (x_1 + y_1, x_2 + y_2,...,x_n + y_n)$. I assume the reader is familiar with the 'parallelogram rule' to interpret geometrically the addition of two vectors in R^2, viewing vectors as arrows starting at the origin and reaching the point of coordinates (x_1,x_2); with some effort the same rule can be applied to visualize the addition of two vectors in R^3.

Given a set V of k vectors $\mathbf{x}_i$ in R^n, $2 \leq k \leq n$, a vector $\mathbf{y}$ is a *linear combination* of these vectors if $\mathbf{y} = \sum_{i=1}^{k} t_i \mathbf{x}_i$, where the t_i's are scalars not all zero. (Do not confuse $\mathbf{x}_i$, the vector with index i among a set of vectors in V, with x_i, the ith element of a given vector $\mathbf{x}$.)

A (*linear*) *convex combination* of two vectors $\mathbf{x}$, $\mathbf{y}$ $\in R^n$ ('linear' can be omitted) is any vector $\mathbf{z} = \alpha\mathbf{x} + (1 - \alpha)\mathbf{y}$ with α a scalar satisfying $0 \leq \alpha \leq 1$. This can be generalized: given k vectors $\mathbf{x}_1,...,\mathbf{x}_k \in R^n$, the sum $\sum_{i=1}^{k} t_i \mathbf{x}_i$ is a convex combination of these vectors if the k scalars $t_1,...,t_k$ are non-negative and not all zero, and their sum is 1.

A set $S \subset R^n$ is a *convex set* if for any couple $\mathbf{x}$, $\mathbf{y}$ of points in S, *all* points $\mathbf{z} = \alpha\mathbf{x} + (1 - \alpha)\mathbf{y}$ obtainable for scalars α satisfying $0 \leq \alpha \leq 1$ are in S. That is, S contains all convex combinations of points in S. Or in other words, given any two points in S, the segment connecting them is entirely contained in S. The reader is invited to check graphically with the parallelogram rule that if $\mathbf{x}$ and $\mathbf{y}$ are two vectors in a plane, as α is varied from 0 to 1 the (tips of the) vectors $\mathbf{z} = \alpha\mathbf{x} + (1 - \alpha)\mathbf{y}$ trace the segment joining $\mathbf{x}$ and $\mathbf{y}$.

So a convex set not only must not have wavy borders (it cannot be star shaped) but also it must not have 'holes' nor consist of separate unconnected subsets (◘ Fig. 15.1).

15.1 · Sets, Relations, Functions, Convexity, Convex Combination of Vectors

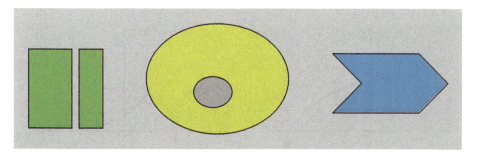

Fig. 15.1 Sets which are not convex

Let us pass to functions. The notion of convexity is only defined for continuous functions or portions of functions and is very different from the notion of convexity for sets. In economics a continuous function f (on a domain $S \subset R^n$ which is a convex set) is a **convex function** if, given any two points $\mathbf{x}'$ and $\mathbf{x}''$ in its domain, it is

$$f(\alpha \mathbf{x}' + (1-\alpha)\mathbf{x}'') \leq \alpha f(\mathbf{x}') + (1-\alpha)f(\mathbf{x}'') \quad \text{for any scalar } \alpha \text{ obeying } 0 < \alpha < 1. \tag{15.1}$$

As α goes from 1 to 0, the left-hand side of this inequality traces the value of f as point $\mathbf{x}$ in its domain travels along the segment connecting $\mathbf{x}'$ to $\mathbf{x}''$; the right-hand side traces the values f *would* take on this segment if it were linear (or rather, affine — see below) and its graph passed through points $(\mathbf{x}', f(\mathbf{x}'))$ and $(\mathbf{x}'', f(\mathbf{x}''))$ in R^{n+1}. Strict convexity obtains when the inequality is always strict. If $f(\mathbf{x})$ is convex, then $-f(\mathbf{x})$ is **concave**; a function $f(\mathbf{x})$ is concave if in (15.1) the inequality sign is inverted to $\geq$. If $f: R \to R$ or $f: R^2 \to R$, one can obtain a geometric visualization of the meaning of convex or concave function: a strictly concave function has a graph which stays above the segment joining two points of the graph (except of course at the extremes of the segment); a strictly convex function stays below this segment, see **Fig. 15.2**. Mathematicians ask that the *direction* of convexity and concavity be specified and would say that what economists call a convex function is a function that turns its concavity upwards (**Fig. 15.2**).

A function can be concave in some subsets of its domain and convex in other subsets, x^3 or $\sin x$ are examples for functions of one variable. A concave but not strictly concave function admits portions where it is affine; the same holds for convex but not strictly convex functions; a function $f: R \to R$ which is a straight line is both concave and convex, but not strictly so. Warning: economists often speak of concave or convex functions meaning *strictly* concave or *strictly* convex functions, you must deduce it from the context.

By the way, rigorously speaking a function $f(\mathbf{x}): R^n \to R^m$ is called a **linear function** if $f(a\mathbf{x} + b\mathbf{y}) = af(\mathbf{x}) + bf(\mathbf{y})$ for all scalars a, b and all vectors $\mathbf{x}$, $\mathbf{y} \in R^n$, which means that *its graph goes through the origin of a system of Cartesian coordinates*; a function $f(\mathbf{x}): R^n \to R$ is an **affine function** if $f(\mathbf{x}) - f(\mathbf{0})$ is

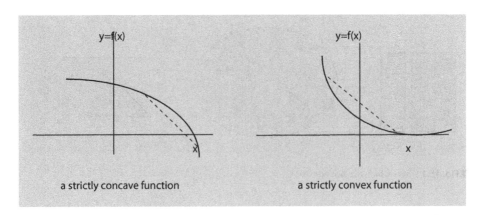

◘ Fig. 15.2

linear; for functions of one variable $f(x)$ is linear if it can be expressed in the form $f(x) = ax$, is affine if it can be expressed in the form $f(x) = ax + b$. *Warning*: frequently, affine functions are imprecisely called linear in the economics literature and in elementary mathematics; for example the consumer's budget constraint is called linear while it is in fact affine.

Quasi-concave functions are discussed in Chap. 4, ▶ Sect. 4.5.

15.2 Logic: If, Only if, Contrapositive, Proof by Contradiction, Connection with Subsets

Students sometimes are not totally sure about the difference between 'A implies B', 'A is sufficient for B', 'A if and only if B', 'A is necessary for B', etcetera. Here is a brief reminder. Let A and B be two statements of which it is possible to ask whether they are true or false, e.g. A: 'This town is in Italy', and B (referring to the same town): 'This town is in Europe'. It is possible that *if* a statement A is true, *then* another statement B is also true by logical necessity. This can be equivalently stated by saying that (the truth of) A *implies* (the truth of) B, in symbols $A \Rightarrow B$. And it can also be stated by saying that (the truth of) A *is sufficient for, or is a sufficient condition for* (the truth of) B. In the example just supplied, this is the case. Another example: that a number be greater than 10 is sufficient for the number to be positive. In set language, let us view A as a subset of a broader set S, B as another subset of S; 'if A then B', 'A implies B', 'A is sufficient for B' are interpreted as meaning 'whenever an element of S is in A then it is also in B', that is, A is a subset of B. Indeed the towns in Italy are a subset of the towns in Europe.

Let $\neg A$ indicate 'not A', meaning 'the negation of statement A' or 'A is false'. It is a basic logical result that if $A \Rightarrow B$, then $\neg B \Rightarrow \neg A$. Indeed if a town is not in Europe, then it is not in Italy. '$\neg B$ implies $\neg A$' is called the **contrapositive** of 'A implies B'. In set language, since 'A implies B' means A is a subset of B, then clearly if an element of S is *not* in B, then it cannot be in A.

15.2 · Logic: If, Only if, Contrapositive, Proof by Contradiction ...

The truth of a statement is *necessary* for the truth of a second statement if the second cannot be true unless the first is true. If A is a subset of B, it is necessary that an element of S be in B in order for it to be possible that it be in A. That is, if A is sufficient for B, then B is necessary for A. That a town be in Europe is necessary for the town to be in Italy. Another example: for a number to be greater than 10, it is necessary that it be positive. Thus, if B is necessary for A, that B is true does not guarantee that A is true; but if B is not true, then A cannot be true. That a number is positive does not guarantee that the number is greater than 10, but if the number is not positive then it cannot be greater than 10. Thus 'B is necessary for A' is logically equivalent to '¬B implies ¬A', which we know is logically equivalent to 'A is sufficient for B'. B necessary for A is also expressed by saying 'A only if B'. In conclusion, 'A only if B' and 'if A, then B' and 'if not B, then not A' are logically equivalent.

Therefore to say 'B if and only if A' is equivalent to saying 'A if and only if B' or 'B is necessary and sufficient for A' or 'B implies A and A implies B'. The relationship of implication is transitive, if $A \Rightarrow B$ and $B \Rightarrow C$ then $A \Rightarrow C$.

Now we can clarify the logical structure of a mathematical *proof by contradiction*. Suppose the aim is to prove that $A \Rightarrow B$. A proof by contradiction starts by assuming ¬B and shows that this contradicts the assumption that A is true because it implies some logical consequence C incompatible with the truth of A; actually what one does is to show that $\neg B \Rightarrow C \Rightarrow \neg A$, which means $\neg B \Rightarrow \neg A$ which is logically equivalent to $A \Rightarrow B$.

$A \Rightarrow B$ in terms of *properties* can generally be translated into a relation between *sets*. 'Property A implies property B' can be interpreted to mean: if x is an element of *set* A (the set of things that satisfy *property* A), then x is also an element of set B (the set of things that satisfy property B). Therefore, interpreting now A and B as names of sets, B contains all elements of A; therefore A is a *subset* of B; and if it is not true that property B implies property A, then A is a *strict* subset of B, that is, B is 'more inclusive' than A, property B is more general, includes more cases than the ones satisfying property A. 'If I am Italian then I am European' implies that 'European' is a broader category than 'Italian'. An important point is that if property A implies property B and property B implies property A, the things that satisfy one property also satisfy the other, so the two *sets* A and B coincide, but this does not mean that the two *properties* are the same property. Consider: 'this box contains red and blue balls; if a ball is red then it weighs 5 grams; if a ball weighs 5 grams it is red'. If this statement is correct, then the set of red balls in the box, and the set of balls weighing 5 grams in the box, are the same set of balls, but the two properties are not the same property.

15.3 Vectors, Matrices, Hyperplanes. Definite Matrices

Introductory courses of mathematics for economists generally include an introduction to vectors and matrices. This chapter cannot replace a course on these notions for readers without any previous contact with them; these readers are invited to consult at least the chapters on linear algebra and matrices of any

1344   **Chapter 15** · Mathematical Review

textbook on introductory mathematical economics, for example the ones mentioned at the end of this chapter. A useful quick review is offered by section A.1 of the Mathematical Appendix in Kurz and Salvadori (1995, pp. 492–505).

I assume the reader knows what a matrix is, as well as the rules for addition and multiplication of matrices. Mostly I will indicate vectors and matrices with bold characters, but not necessarily when no ambiguity can arise. When manipulating vectors and matrices, a single number is also called a *scalar*.

Interpreting vectors as points in R^n, the sum of two vectors can be given a useful graphical interpretation for vectors in R^2 and in R^3. In a system of Cartesian coordinates, a vector $\mathbf{x}=(x_1, x_2)$ in R^2 can be visualized as a pointed arrow from the origin to the point with those coordinates in abscissa and in ordinate. Given another vector $\mathbf{y}=(y_1, y_2)$ in the same plane, graphically the point $\mathbf{x}+\mathbf{y}=(x_1+y_1, x_2+y_2)$ is obtained by a parallel transposition of the $\mathbf{y}$ arrow until its origin comes to coincide with the tip of the $\mathbf{x}$ arrow; now the tip of the composite two arrows is point $\mathbf{x}+\mathbf{y}$. The same point is reached if it is the $\mathbf{x}$ arrow that is transposed 'on top of' the $\mathbf{y}$ arrow; if one draws both transpositions, one obtains a parallelogram, hence the name 'parallelogram rule' for this graphical method of summing two vectors. The same method works in R^3. It is used and illustrated below in the paragraphs on the angle formed by two vectors and on hyperplanes.

A matrix $\mathbf{A}$ is also indicated as $[a_{ij}]$, where a_{ij} is the number in the place corresponding to ith row and jth column. The ith row of this matrix, treated as a vector, is indicated as $\mathbf{a}_i$, the jth column as $\mathbf{a}^j$. The *transpose* $\mathbf{A}^T$ of a matrix $\mathbf{A}=[a_{ij}]$ is the matrix $\mathbf{B}=\mathbf{A}^T$ with $b_{ij}=a_{ji}$.

The *dot product* of two vectors $\mathbf{x}$, $\mathbf{y}$ in R^n, given by $\mathbf{x}\cdot\mathbf{y}=\sum_i x_i y_i$, is also called *scalar product* (especially for vectors in R^2 and R^3) and also *inner product*.

When dealing with multiplication of matrices, a vector in R^n can be treated as a $1\times n$ matrix (one row, n columns) if classified as a row vector, or as an $n\times 1$ matrix if classified as a column vector; the general convention is that a vector $\mathbf{x}$ is a column vector, and to indicate it is a row vector one represents it as $\mathbf{x}^T$, transpose of a column vector; but in most of this book this convention is not adopted, a vector is simply an ordered sequence of numbers; indeed the dot product of two vectors does not require that the vectors be interpreted as row or column vectors. But if needed, a vector is defined as a row or column vector the first time it is introduced, or the context shows it: if $\mathbf{p}$ and $\mathbf{x}$ are vectors the appearance in the text of the product $\mathbf{px}$ means that the two vectors have the same number of elements and that, even if this has not been said earlier, $\mathbf{p}$ is treated as a row vector, and $\mathbf{x}$ is a column vector. In the text the usual assumption is that price vectors are row vectors, quantity vectors are column vectors; but be careful, the opposite is assumed in other writings, for example in Kurz and Salvadori (1995).

To treat a vector as row vector or column vector or neither makes a difference when one comes to multiplication. If neither, then the multiplication between two vectors must be interpreted as their dot product in this book (in physics there are other vector products too). Otherwise, let me remember that two matrices $\mathbf{A}$ and $\mathbf{B}$ can be multiplied in the order $\mathbf{AB}$ if and only if the rows of $\mathbf{A}$ have the same number of elements as the columns of $\mathbf{B}$, that is, $\mathbf{A}$ must have as many columns

15.3 · Vectors, Matrices, Hyperplanes. Definite Matrices

as $\mathbf{B}$ has rows; that is, if $\mathbf{A}$ is an $m \times n$ matrix $\mathbf{B}$ must be an $n \times k$ matrix; indicating with $\mathbf{a}_i$ the ith row of $\mathbf{A}$ and with $\mathbf{b}^j$ the jth column of $\mathbf{B}$, matrix $\mathbf{C} = \mathbf{AB}$ has for element (c_{ij}) the dot product $\mathbf{a}_i \cdot \mathbf{b}^j$; if $\mathbf{A}$ is $m \times n$ and $\mathbf{B}$ is $n \times k$ then $\mathbf{AB}$ is an $m \times k$ matrix. Therefore a vector can premultiply an $m \times n$ matrix only if it is a row m-vector, and can post-multiply it only if it is a column n-vector. Hence if we are given a column vector $\mathbf{b}$ and a row vector $\mathbf{a}^T$ with the same number of elements, both the product $\mathbf{a}^T\mathbf{b}$ and the product $\mathbf{ba}^T$ are legitimate, $\mathbf{a}^T\mathbf{b}$ produces a 1×1 matrix and is treated as a dot product producing a scalar; $\mathbf{ba}^T$ produces an $n \times n$ matrix with element (i,j) equal to $b_i a_j$. If the product of two vectors is indicated without any transposition symbol, as $\mathbf{ab}$, then $\mathbf{a}$ is a row vector and $\mathbf{b}$ a column vector.

A set V of k vectors $\mathbf{x}_i$ in R^n, $2 \leq k \leq n$, is *linearly independent* if no vector in V can be represented as a linear combination of the other vectors in V, that is, if there is no set of k scalars $(t_1, \ldots, t_k)$ not all zero, such that $\sum_{i=1}^{k} t_i \mathbf{x}_i = \mathbf{0}$. If $k > n$ then necessarily the vectors are linearly dependent. A square matrix is said *non-singular* if its columns, viewed as vectors, are linearly independent (also see below on determinants).

Matrix representation of a system of linear equations. Suppose you have the system of three linear equations in three unknowns x_1, x_2, x_3

$$a_{11}x_1 + a_{12}x_2 + a_{13}x_3 = b_1$$
$$a_{21}x_1 + a_{22}x_2 + a_{23}x_3 = b_2$$
$$a_{31}x_1 + a_{32}x_2 + a_{33}x_3 = b_3.$$

Define $\mathbf{A}$ to be the matrix $[a_{ij}]$, $i,j = 1,2,3$, of coefficients of the above system; define $\mathbf{x}$ to be the *column* vector $\mathbf{x} := (x_1, x_2, x_3)^T$ of unknowns to be determined, and $\mathbf{b}$ the column vector $\mathbf{b} := (b_1, b_2, b_3)^T$ of known terms; then the system can be written more compactly as

$$\mathbf{Ax} = \mathbf{b} \tag{15.2}$$

where $\mathbf{A}$ and $\mathbf{b}$ are known and $\mathbf{x}$ is to be determined. Matrix $\mathbf{A}$ must be square and non-singular for the system of equations to yield a unique solution $\mathbf{x} = \mathbf{A}^{-1}\mathbf{b}$, where $\mathbf{A}^{-1}$ is the *inverse* of $\mathbf{A}$, defined below (see the paragraph on determinants). If $\mathbf{b}$ is considered variable, (15.2) becomes a system of equations $\mathbf{Ax} - \mathbf{b} = \mathbf{0}$ that implicitly determines $\mathbf{x}$ as a function of $\mathbf{b}$.

Linear map. A *functional* is the name of an application from a set S to R, i.e. from the elements of this set to scalars, where set S can be of any type. For example suppose you have m individuals and each one of them forms a list of the n English first-division football teams in increasing order of appreciation, called a *Borda increasing order*; given the m Borda increasing orders prepared by the m individuals, you assign to each team the *Borda number* equal to the sum of its order number in each list, for example if a team is best (i.e. last) in all lists its Borda number is mn, if it is worst (i.e. first) in all lists its Borda number is m. Let S be the set with elements the possible combinations of m Borda increasing orders, one per individual; the application from this set to R that for each m-combination of Borda increasing orders assigns to a given team its corresponding Borda number is a functional. In this example we obtain n functionals, one per team. A *linear functional* (over Euclidean spaces) is a *linear* (not an affine) function $R^n \to R$, that is, from vectors in R^n to scalars. An example of linear functional is the inner product or dot product $\mathbf{p} \cdot \mathbf{x} = \Sigma p_i x_i$ viewed as a function of $\mathbf{x}$ with $\mathbf{p}$ given. A linear functional $R^2 \to R$ is a function $y = f(x_1, x_2)$ represented by a plane in R^3 with equation $y = a_1 x_1 + a_2 x_2$, a plane that passes through the origin.

A more general linear function or *linear map* $R^n \to R^m$ is a vector of m linear functionals $R^n \to R$ indexed $1, \ldots, k, \ldots, m$, the kth one transforming each (column) vector $\mathbf{x} \in R^n$ into a scalar $y_k(\mathbf{x})$ according to $y_k(\mathbf{x}) = a_{k1} x_1 + \ldots + a_{kn} x_n = \mathbf{a}_k \mathbf{x}$. The linear map is accordingly fully characterized by the m row vectors $\mathbf{a}_k$ and can be compactly represented as

$$\mathbf{y} = \mathbf{A}\mathbf{x} \tag{15.3}$$

where $\mathbf{A}$ is an $m \times n$ matrix. This looks similar to (15.2) but it is a vectorial function, not a system to be solved; here $\mathbf{A}$ is given, and $\mathbf{y}$ is a vectorial function of $\mathbf{x}$; and $\mathbf{A}$ need not be square.

Length and distance. The **Euclidean norm** of a vector $\mathbf{x}$ in R^n is denoted by $\|\mathbf{x}\|$ and defined by $\|\mathbf{x}\| = (\mathbf{x} \cdot \mathbf{x})^{1/2} = \sqrt{x_1^2 + \ldots + x_n^2}$, the square root of the dot or inner product of the vector with itself. By Pythagoras' theorem, it is the length of vector $\mathbf{x}$ interpreted as a pointed straight arrow or segment starting at the origin of a system of Cartesian coordinates and reaching the point of coordinates $x_1, \ldots, x_n$; equivalently, it is the distance of point $\mathbf{x}$ from the origin. By the parallelogram rule, given two points $\mathbf{a}$ and $\mathbf{b}$ the distance between them is the Euclidean norm of vector $\mathbf{c} = \mathbf{a} - \mathbf{b}$.

Angle formed by two vectors and dot product. There is a useful connection between the dot or inner product of two vectors and the angle (the smaller of the two angles) they form.

Let $t\mathbf{x}$, with t a scalar, be the **projection** of a vector $\mathbf{y}$ onto a vector $\mathbf{x}$, cf. ◘ Figure 15.3: it is obtained by drawing from the end of vector $\mathbf{y}$ (point A) a segment towards $\mathbf{x}$ orthogonal to $\mathbf{x}$, that touches $\mathbf{x}$ (or its prolongation on the

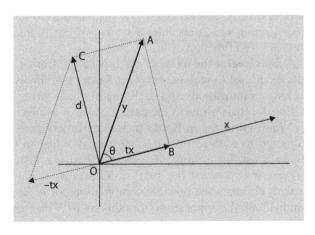

◘ **Fig. 15.3** Projection $t\mathbf{x} = OB$ of a vector $\mathbf{y} = OA$ onto another vector $\mathbf{x}$

15.3 · Vectors, Matrices, Hyperplanes. Definite Matrices

opposite side of the origin) in B; segment OB is the projection of **y** onto **x** and corresponds to **x** multiplied by an opportune scalar t which is positive if $t\mathbf{x}$ has the same direction as **x**, negative if it has opposite direction.

Segment AB has the same length as vector $\mathbf{d}=\mathbf{y}-t\mathbf{x}$ (that goes from O to C) which by the 'parallelogram rule' is also orthogonal to $t\mathbf{x}$; therefore the triangle with sides **y**, $t\mathbf{x}$, and segment AB is a rectangular triangle and, if θ is the angle between **y** and $t\mathbf{x}$, it is

$$\cos\theta = \|t\mathbf{x}\|/\|\mathbf{y}\| = t\|\mathbf{x}\|/\|\mathbf{y}\| = (t\|\mathbf{x}\|\|\mathbf{x}\|)/(\|\mathbf{x}\|\|\mathbf{y}\|) = t(\mathbf{x}\cdot\mathbf{x})/(\|\mathbf{x}\|\|\mathbf{y}\|) = (\mathbf{x}\cdot\mathbf{y})/(\|\mathbf{x}\|\|\mathbf{y}\|)$$

where in the last passage the result $t(\mathbf{x}\cdot\mathbf{x})=\mathbf{x}\cdot\mathbf{y}$ is used, derived from Pythagoras' theorem: $\|t\mathbf{x}\|^2 + \|\mathbf{y}-t\mathbf{x}\|^2 = \|\mathbf{y}\|^2$, that is, $t^2(\mathbf{x}\cdot\mathbf{x}) + \mathbf{y}\cdot\mathbf{y} - 2t(\mathbf{x}\cdot\mathbf{y}) + t^2(\mathbf{x}\cdot\mathbf{x}) = \mathbf{y}\cdot\mathbf{y}$, i.e. $2t^2(\mathbf{x}\cdot\mathbf{x}) - 2t(\mathbf{x}\cdot\mathbf{y}) = 0$, which simplifies to $t(\mathbf{x}\cdot\mathbf{x}) = \mathbf{x}\cdot\mathbf{y}$. Therefore:

$$\mathbf{x}\cdot\mathbf{y} = \|\mathbf{x}\|\|\mathbf{y}\|\cos\theta. \tag{15.4}$$

Thus the inner product **x·y** of two vectors has the same sign as $\cos\theta$, and the cosine function is positive for acute angles (reaching its maximum, 1, for a zero angle), zero at 90°, and negative for obtuse angles between 90° and 180° (the angle formed by two halflines having a common origin is by convention the smaller of the two angles formed by them). Hence if **x·y**=0 the two vectors are orthogonal, if **x·y** is positive the two vectors form an acute angle, if negative the two vectors form an obtuse angle.

Hyperplanes and halfspaces. If we are assigned a vector $\mathbf{p}\neq\mathbf{0}$ in R^n, and a scalar a, the set of all vectors or points **x** in R^n such that **p·x**=a forms a **hyperplane** orthogonal to **p**. To help visualization and intuition, let us see what this means in R^2 in ◘ Fig. 15.4, although the considerations that follow apply in higher dimensions too. Let **p** be any vector, e.g. **p**=(9, 12). By Pythagoras' theorem the length of **p** is 15. Choose vector **x^** colinear with **p**, i.e. **x^**=$t\mathbf{p}$, for example if $t=1/3$ it is **x^**=(3,4). Vector **x^** is part of the hyperplane **p·x**=a if $\mathbf{p}\cdot\mathbf{x}^{\wedge} = \mathbf{p}\cdot t\mathbf{p} = t\mathbf{p}\cdot\mathbf{p} = t\|\mathbf{p}\|^2 = a$,

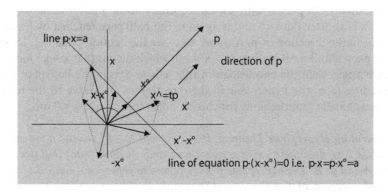

◘ **Fig. 15.4** When **x** is on the straight line of equation **p·(x − x°)**=0 then **x − x°** is orthogonal to **p**; if **p·(x'−x°)**>0, then **x'−x°** forms with **p** an angle less than 90°, so by the parallelogram rule **x'** must fall on the side of the straight line of equation **p·(x−x°)**=0 reached by proceeding from that line in the direction of **p**

1348   **Chapter 15 · Mathematical Review**

in our case $t\|\mathbf{p}\|^2 = 75$ so $\mathbf{x}^\wedge$ is part of the hyperplane $\mathbf{p}\cdot\mathbf{x}=a$ if $a=75$. The length of $\mathbf{x}^\wedge$ in general is $\|t\mathbf{p} \cdot t\mathbf{p}\|^{1/2} = t\|\mathbf{p}\| = a/\|\mathbf{p}\|$, in our case +5. Note that in this case *length* has a sign, indicative of a direction; it is a negative number if t is negative and hence a is negative, i.e. if $\mathbf{x}^\wedge$ points in the direction opposite that of $\mathbf{p}$. Now note that if you take any other vector $\mathbf{x}$ satisfying $\mathbf{p}\cdot\mathbf{x}=a$ one has that $\mathbf{x}^\wedge-\mathbf{x}$ is orthogonal to $\mathbf{p}$, because $\mathbf{p}\cdot\mathbf{x}=\mathbf{p}\cdot\mathbf{x}^\wedge$ implies $\mathbf{p}\cdot(\mathbf{x}^\wedge-\mathbf{x})=0$. The same holds for any other couple of vectors $\mathbf{x}^\circ$, $\mathbf{x}$ satisfying $\mathbf{p}\cdot\mathbf{x}=\mathbf{p}\cdot\mathbf{x}^\circ=a$. The hyperplane $\mathbf{p}\cdot\mathbf{x}=a$ (with $\mathbf{p}$ and a given, and $\mathbf{x}$ variable) is the locus of all points in R^2 obtained with the 'parallelogram rule' by adding to $\mathbf{x}^\wedge$ (or to $\mathbf{x}^\circ$) vectors orthogonal to $\mathbf{p}$; that is, it is the straight line orthogonal to $\mathbf{p}$ that passes through point $\mathbf{x}^\wedge$, i.e. through the tip of $\mathbf{x}^\wedge$ interpreted as an arrow from the origin. Here the hyperplane is a line; in R^3 it is a plane; in general it is of dimension $n-1$ if the vectors are in R^n. The standard consumer's Marshallian budget line with two goods is the hyperplane in R^2 generated by $\mathbf{p}\cdot\mathbf{x}=a$ where a is income; we see now that it is orthogonal to the price vector.

The intercepts of the hyperplane with the Cartesian axes are given by a/p_i, because when $\mathbf{x}$ has all elements zero except for the ith element, then it must be $p_i x_i=a$. The distance (i.e. the smallest distance) of the hyperplane from the origin is the (absolute) length of vector $\mathbf{x}^\wedge = t\mathbf{p}$ discussed above, which is $|a|/\|\mathbf{p}\|$, where we take the absolute value of a because distance is always positive. If $a=0$, the hyperplane passes through the origin. As a rises from zero, t does too, i.e. point $\mathbf{x}^\wedge$ moves on $\mathbf{p}$'s ray in the direction of $\mathbf{p}$: the hyperplane moves away from the origin in $\mathbf{p}$'s direction without changing its slope. If $a<0$, t is negative, that is, $\mathbf{x}^\wedge$ is on $\mathbf{p}$'s ray but in the direction opposite that of $\mathbf{p}$, and as the absolute value of a rises the hyperplane moves away from the origin in the direction opposite $\mathbf{p}$'s.

A hyperplane $\mathbf{p}\cdot\mathbf{x}=a$ divides R^n into two **halfspaces**, $\mathbf{p}\cdot\mathbf{x}\geq a$ and $\mathbf{p}\cdot\mathbf{x}\leq a$, closed convex sets that have only the hyperplane in common. Which halfspace is associated with which inequality? Consider vector $\mathbf{x}^\wedge = t\mathbf{p}$, colinear with $\mathbf{p}$ and such that $\mathbf{p}\cdot\mathbf{x}^\wedge=\mathbf{p}\cdot t\mathbf{p}=a$. Since a and t have the same sign, if $a>0$ then an increase of t to $t'>t$ causes $\mathbf{p}\cdot t'\mathbf{p} = t'\|\mathbf{p}\|^2 > a$, which means $\mathbf{x}=t'\mathbf{p}$ is longer than $\mathbf{x}^\wedge$ and is in the halfspace $\mathbf{p}\cdot\mathbf{x}\geq a$ reached by proceeding from the hyperplane in the direction of $\mathbf{p}$. If $a<0$, then $t<0$, $\mathbf{p}\cdot\mathbf{x}>a$ with $\mathbf{x}=t'\mathbf{p}$ requires t' to be *smaller in absolute value* than t, so $\mathbf{x}$ is shorter than $\mathbf{x}^\wedge$ and is again in the halfspace reached by leaving the hyperplane in the direction of $\mathbf{p}$. Another way (see the caption of ◘ Fig. 15.4) is to note that $\mathbf{p}\cdot\mathbf{x}>a$ and $a>0$ imply $\mathbf{p}\cdot(\mathbf{x}-\mathbf{x}^\wedge)>0$, which means that $\mathbf{x}-\mathbf{x}^\wedge$ forms with $\mathbf{p}$ an acute angle, then the parallelogram rule tells us $\mathbf{x}$ is in the halfspace reached by proceeding from the hyperplane in the direction of $\mathbf{p}$. I leave to the reader to confirm graphically that the same conclusion holds for the case $a<0$ too.

A Separating Hyperplane Theorem: *If $A\subset R^n$ and $B\subset R^n$ are two non-empty, disjoint, convex sets, then there exists a vector $\mathbf{p}\neq 0$ and a scalar c such that $\mathbf{p}\cdot\mathbf{x}\geq c\geq\mathbf{p}\cdot\mathbf{y}$ for all $\mathbf{x}\in A$ and $\mathbf{y}\in B$. The hyperplane $\mathbf{p}\cdot\mathbf{x}=c$ is said to separate A from B.*

Another version of the theorem differs only in that it replaces the condition that the two sets A and B are disjoint with the condition that no point of A∩B is *internal* to A, or to B (that is, no point of A∩B has a neighbourhood entirely contained in A, or in B). This version allows the sets A and B, if closed sets, to

15.3 · Vectors, Matrices, Hyperplanes. Definite Matrices

have some point of their *frontiers* in common. [1] The statement of the theorem following 'then' remains unchanged. That is, there exists a hyperplane $\mathbf{p} \cdot \mathbf{x} = c$ which 'separates' A from B, in the sense that A is entirely in one halfspace and B entirely in the other, at most they have in common points of the separating hyperplane.

If, in the first version of this theorem, set A is additionally assumed closed and set B is assumed to consist of a single point, one obtains the following:

Another separating hyperplane theorem: *If a set $A \subset R^n$ is non-empty, closed and convex and there is a point $\mathbf{x}^*$ in R^n which is not an element of A, then there exist $\mathbf{p} \in R^n$ and $c \in R$ such that $\mathbf{p} \cdot \mathbf{x} \geq c > \mathbf{p} \cdot \mathbf{x}^*$, for all $\mathbf{x} \in A$; that is, the halfspace $\{\mathbf{x}: \mathbf{p} \cdot \mathbf{x} \geq c\}$ contains all of A and does not contain $\mathbf{x}^*$; the hyperplane $\mathbf{p} \cdot \mathbf{x} = c$ (which does not contain $\mathbf{x}^*$) is said to separate A from $\mathbf{x}^*$.*

▪▪ Corollary

The intersection of all halfspaces of R^n that contain A coincides with A (*except if A coincides with R^n: there is no halfspace that contains R^n*).

This is because this intersection contains A but no other point, because for any x* not belonging to A there exists a halfspace that contains all of A but does not contain x*, and since the intersection of a number of sets contains only the elements that belong to *all* those sets, a point that does not belong to one of the sets cannot belong to their intersection.

If set A is closed but not convex, the intersection of all halfspaces that contain A is the ***convex hull*** of A, that is, the smallest convex set that contains A.

A convex hull can also be defined for a set of points. Given m points in R^n, the set of all their convex combinations is a convex set, called their ***convex polyhedron***, or also ***the convex hull of m points***. Given $n + 1$ points in R^n which do not all lie on the same hyperplane in R^n, their convex hull is called a ***simplex***. So a segment on a line, and a triangle in a plane, are simplexes. An often-used simplex is the following. Let R^3_+ be a space of non-negative price vectors $\mathbf{p} = (p_1, p_2, p_3)$; assume $\sum_i p_i = 1$; this means that any price vector is a convex combination of the vectors $(1,0,0)$, $(0,1,0)$, $(0,0,1)$, hence is a point of the triangle in R^3 with these three vectors as vertexes. The three vectors lie on a plane in R^3, so their convex hull (the triangle) satisfies the definition of simplex *relative to that plane, i.e. in R^2*, but economists find it more useful to call this triangle the ***unit price simplex in R^3***. Generalizing, economists intend by ***unit simplex*** in R^n the set of convex combinations of the n ***unit vectors*** $\mathbf{e}^1 = (1, 0, \ldots, 0)^T$, $\mathbf{e}^2 = (0, 1, 0, \ldots, 0)^T$, ..., $\mathbf{e}^n = (0, 0, \ldots, 0, 1)^T$. The sum of the unit vectors, the vector $(1,1,\ldots,1,1)$ is called the ***sum vector*** because its dot product with a vector sums the latter's elements.

Determinants, permutations, invertible matrix. It is not easy to remember what precisely a determinant is. To define it we need the notion of ***even and odd permutations***. Consider the ordered set of the first n integer numbers, that is the list $(1, 2, \ldots, n)$. A permutation of this set consists of a list of the same numbers in a different order, reached by starting from the original list and interchanging the place of

---

[1] A point of a set is part of its frontier if it is not internal, that is, if any neighbourhood of the point, however small, contains points that do not belong to the set. R^n is a closed set but it has no frontier.

1350   **Chapter 15** · Mathematical Review

a couple of (not necessarily contiguous) numbers, then interchanging the place of another couple of numbers, and repeating the operation several times if necessary. The original ordered set is called the *fundamental permutation*. It can be proved that the number of place interchanges required to reach a given permutation starting from the fundamental permutation is always either even, or odd, independently of what sequence of place interchanges is chosen. For example if the fundamental permutation is (1, 2, 3) then the permutation (2, 3, 1) can be reached by interchanging (2,3) obtaining (1,3,2), and then interchanging (1,2) obtaining (2,3,1); but it can also be reached by the sequence of one-interchange permutations (2, 1, 3), (3, 1, 2), (3, 2, 1), (2, 3, 1); in both cases the number of interchanges is even, 2 or 4. A permutation is called *even* or *odd* according as an even or odd number of place interchanges is required to reach it from the fundamental permutation (which is considered even). The notion of permutation also applies to ordered lists of n objects, by associating the numbers from 1 to n to the objects in the initial order, and then identifying each permutation of these numbers with a corresponding order of the objects. The number of different permutations of n different numbers is $n!$, read **n factorial** and defined as $n \cdot (n-1) \cdot (n-2) \cdot \ldots \cdot 3 \cdot 2 \cdot 1$.

The **determinant** of a square $n \times n$ matrix $\mathbf{A} = (a_{ij})$ is the sum of the $n!$ possible different products of n elements of the matrix so chosen: in each product each element is from a different row and from a different column, and no two products are equal; each product is of the form $(\pm)(a_{1,i1} \cdot a_{2,i2} \cdot \ldots \cdot a_{n,in})$, it includes an element from each successive row, the succession of column indices $(i_1, i_2, \ldots, i_n)$ forms one of the $n!$ permutations of the integers 1, 2, ..., n, and the product is multiplied by $+1$ or -1 according as the permutation is even or odd.

For example a 3×3 matrix has the following determinant, the sum of $3! = 6$ products:

$$a_{11} a_{22} a_{33} - a_{11} a_{23} a_{32} + a_{13} a_{21} a_{32} - a_{13} a_{22} a_{31} + a_{12} a_{23} a_{31} - a_{12} a_{21} a_{33}.$$

The column indices in each product, here in bold and underlined for better visibility, represent permutations of (1, 2, 3) differing from the preceding one by one interchange and therefore alternately even and odd, which explains the sign $+$ or $-$ in front of the products.

Two main reasons of interest in determinants are the following. First, a square $n \times n$ matrix $\mathbf{A}$ is **invertible** or **non-singular** if there is a matrix $\mathbf{A}^{-1}$, called the **inverse** of $\mathbf{A}$, such that $\mathbf{A}\mathbf{A}^{-1} = \mathbf{A}^{-1}\mathbf{A} = \mathbf{I}$ where $\mathbf{I}$, the **identity matrix**, is the $n \times n$ matrix with elements equal to 1 on the main diagonal and zero elsewhere; its name derives from the fact that $\mathbf{A}\mathbf{I} = \mathbf{I}\mathbf{A} = \mathbf{A}$. The existence of the inverse of a square matrix $\mathbf{A}$ is indispensable to find a vector $\mathbf{x}$ such that $\mathbf{y} = \mathbf{A}\mathbf{x}$ for assigned $\mathbf{y}$, problem solved by premultiplication of both sides by the inverse of $\mathbf{A}$, obtaining $\mathbf{A}^{-1}\mathbf{y} = \mathbf{A}^{-1}\mathbf{A}\mathbf{x} = \mathbf{x}$. A necessary and sufficient condition for $\mathbf{A}$ to be invertible is that its determinant be different from zero; this indicates that $\mathbf{A}$ has **full rank**, that is, its columns are linearly independent (the **rank** of a matrix is the maximum number of linearly independent columns of the matrix) and therefore its columns are a possible **basis** for R^n. (A basis for R^n is a list of n vectors in R^n such that each vector in R^n can be expressed as a linear combination of those vectors; the list must consist of linearly independent vectors.) If the determinant is zero then the matrix has rank less than n, its columns are not linearly independent.

15.3 · Vectors, Matrices, Hyperplanes. Definite Matrices

Second, one often meets homogeneous systems of n linear equations in n variables with typical equation $a_{j1}x_1 + a_{j2}x_2 + \ldots + a_{jn}x_n = 0$, $j = 1, \ldots, n$; this system can be written $\mathbf{Ax} = \mathbf{0}$; it has a solution $\mathbf{x} \neq \mathbf{0}$ only if $\det \mathbf{A} = 0$.

Eigenvalues and eigenvectors. On the definition of eigenvalues and eigenvectors and on the ***Perron–Frobenius theorem*** on non-negative matrices see ▶ Chap. 2. Remember that even if matrix $\mathbf{A}$ is real, its eigenvalues and eigenvectors need not be real; they can be complex; see below for a quick overview of complex numbers. But if matrix $\mathbf{A}$ is real and ***symmetric*** (that is, with $a_{ij} = a_{ji}$) then its eigenvalues are real, and therefore its eigenvectors are real too. Also remember that ***similar matrices*** have the same eigenvalues, where $\mathbf{A}$ and $\mathbf{B}$, both $n \times n$, are similar if there exists a non-singular (and hence invertible) matrix $\mathbf{X}$ such that $\mathbf{A} = \mathbf{X}^{-1}\mathbf{BX}$ (and therefore $\mathbf{B} = \mathbf{XAX}^{-1}$).

Determinants and definite matrices. Another use of determinants appears in the study of ***definite*** symmetric matrices.

When interested in characterizing concave or quasi-concave functions of several variables – this can be essential to solving maximization problems – in terms of their Hessian matrices (see below), we can use properties of these symmetric matrices, consisting of their being or not being *negative or positive definite or semidefinite*. A square symmetric matrix $\mathbf{A}$ is ***definite*** when, if postmultiplied by a column vector $\mathbf{x} \neq \mathbf{0}$ and premultiplied by the transpose $\mathbf{x}^{\mathrm{T}}$ of the same vector, it yields a scalar which is always of the same sign whatever the chosen vector $\mathbf{x}$. A definite matrix $\mathbf{A}$ is further classified as follows:
(i) *positive definite* if $\mathbf{x}^{\mathrm{T}}\mathbf{Ax} > 0$ for all $\mathbf{x} \neq \mathbf{0}$;
(ii) *negative definite* if $\mathbf{x}^{\mathrm{T}}\mathbf{Ax} < 0$ for all $\mathbf{x} \neq \mathbf{0}$;
(iii) *positive semidefinite* if $\mathbf{x}^{\mathrm{T}}\mathbf{Ax} \geq 0$ for all $\mathbf{x} \neq \mathbf{0}$ and $= 0$ for at least one $\mathbf{x} \neq \mathbf{0}$;
(iv) *negative semidefinite* if $\mathbf{x}^{\mathrm{T}}\mathbf{Ax} \leq 0$ for all $\mathbf{x} \neq \mathbf{0}$ and $= 0$ for at least one $\mathbf{x} \neq \mathbf{0}$.

If $\mathbf{A}$ falls into none of these four categories then it is said *indefinite*. An example of positive definite matrix is the identity matrix (try an example).

The expression $\mathbf{x}^{\mathrm{T}}\mathbf{Ax}$ with $\mathbf{A}$ symmetric is called a ***quadratic form.***[2] The same classification into five categories is applied to a quadratic form as to the matrix in it.

How can we ascertain whether a matrix (a quadratic form) is negative or positive semidefinite or definite? A *necessary* condition for a matrix to be positive semidefinite is that it has non-negative diagonal terms (otherwise, if $a_{ii} < 0$, when $\mathbf{x}$ has all elements zero except the ith one equal to 1 it is $\mathbf{x}^{\mathrm{T}}\mathbf{Ax} = a_{ii} < 0$, violating positive semidefiniteness). Otherwise for necessary and sufficient conditions one has recourse to the eigenvalues of $\mathbf{A}$, which are all real because $\mathbf{A}$ is symmetric.[3] A square symmetric matrix $\mathbf{A}$ is:
(i) positive definite if and only if all its eigenvalues are positive;
(ii) negative definite if and only if all its eigenvalues are negative;

---

2   A *form* is a polynomial function where all terms (all addendums) have the same degree; a quadratic form is a polynomial function where all terms are of degree two.
3   Unless otherwise specified, all matrices and vectors are here assumed to be real. The eigenvalues of a symmetric real matrix are real.

1352   **Chapter 15 · Mathematical Review**

(iii) positive semidefinite if and only if all its eigenvalues are non-negative with at least one equal to zero;

(iv) negative semidefinite if and only if all its eigenvalues are nonpositive with at least one equal to zero.

Calculating all the eigenvalues of a matrix can be a time-consuming affair (although now there are mathematical packages that can do it for you). Alternative necessary and sufficient conditions, often easier to verify especially for small matrices, can be given in terms of determinants of submatrices of A.

We need some terminology. The determinant of a $k \times k$ submatrix of A obtained by deleting $n-k$ rows and $n-k$ columns is called a **minor** of A. If the k non-eliminated rows and columns have the same indexes, the determinant of the submatrix is called a **principal minor of order k**. A principal minor of order k is called **leading** or **North-West** if the non-eliminated rows and columns are the first k ones. The NW principal minor of order 1 is simply a_{11}. The first k **naturally ordered principal minors** of a matrix A are the NW principal minors of order 1, of order 2, etc., up to order k, considered in this succession.

Now the determinantal conditions. A square matrix A is:

(i) positive definite if and only if all its naturally ordered principal minors are positive[4];

(ii) negative definite if and only if the naturally ordered principal minors of order k have sign $(-1)^k$ for k $= 1, \ldots, n$, i.e. alternate in sign starting from negative[5];

(iii) positive semidefinite if and only if all its naturally ordered principal minors are non-negative with at least one equal to zero;

(iv) negative semidefinite if and only if its naturally ordered principal minors of odd order are nonpositive and its naturally ordered principal minors of even order are non-negative (with at least one, of even or odd order, equal to zero).

Determinants and definite matrices for constrained maximization problems. Sometimes, again in maximization problems, one is interested in the sign of a quadratic form $x^T A x$ ($x \in R^n$) when vector x is constrained to satisfy an equality $Bx = c$, where B is a $k \times n$ matrix, $k < n$, and $c \in R^k$. Analogous conditions can then be applied to the *bordered* matrix A^+ so construed:

$$A^+ = \begin{bmatrix} O & B \\ B^T & A \end{bmatrix}, \text{ a } (k+n) \times (k+n) \text{ matrix where submatrix } O \text{ is a } k \times k \text{ matrix of zeros.}$$

Sending the reader to Takayama (1974, pp. 117–127) for further details, I limit myself to reporting that in order for $x^T A x$ to be positive for each $x \neq 0$ satisfying $Bx = c$, it is necessary and sufficient that the NW principal minors of A^+ of order

---

4   The NW principal minor of order n is det A, so a necessary condition for a positive definite matrix A is that its determinant be positive.

5   So a_{11} must be negative, and the determinant of A must be positive if n is even, negative if n is odd..

15.4 · Analysis

from $2k+1$ to $k+n$ be all negative, and in order for $\mathbf{x}^T \mathbf{A} \mathbf{x}$ to be negative for each $\mathbf{x} \neq 0$ satisfying $\mathbf{B} \mathbf{x} = \mathbf{c}$, it is necessary and sufficient that the NW principal minors of $\mathbf{A}^+$ of order from $2k+1$ to $k+n$ alternate in sign, starting from $(-1)^{k+1}$.

15.4 **Analysis**

The reader is assumed to have already encountered the notions of function, limit, continuity, derivative.

If may nonetheless be useful to remember the notions of neighbourhood and of open, closed, compact set. Given a vector $\mathbf{x}^*$ in R^n and a positive real number ε, an **open ball** of radius ε centred at $\mathbf{x}^*$ is the set $B_\varepsilon(\mathbf{x}^*) = \{\mathbf{x} \in R^n : \|\mathbf{x} - \mathbf{x}^*\| < \varepsilon\}$ where $\|\mathbf{x}\|$ is the Euclidean length or Euclidean norm of vector $\mathbf{x}$, $\|\mathbf{x}\| := \sqrt{x_1^2 + \ldots + x_n^2}$. A **neighbourhood** of a point $\mathbf{x} \in R^n$ is an open ball (usually a small one) centred at $\mathbf{x}$. A set $A \subset R^n$ is an **open set** if for every $\mathbf{x}$ in A there is some $B_\varepsilon(\mathbf{x})$ which is contained in A. Intuitively, all points of A are surrounded by points of A within a sufficiently small distance; all points of A are internal; for example on the line the open interval $(0, 1)$ satisfies this intuitive idea; however close a point is to 1 there is always a finite subinterval between the point and 1, and that interval is filled with points of the interval, so the point is internal. Open balls are open sets. If $\mathbf{x}$ is in a set A and there exists an $\varepsilon > 0$ such that all elements of $B_\varepsilon(\mathbf{x})$ are in A, then $\mathbf{x}$ is said to be in the **interior** of A.

Given a set S and a subset A of points in S, $\mathbf{x} \in S$ is called an **accumulation point** of A if every neighbourhood of $\mathbf{x}$ contains an infinite number of points of A. Note that $\mathbf{x}$ need not be $\in A$.

The **complement** of a set A in R^n, the set of all the points in R^n that are not in A, can be denoted by $R^n \backslash A$. If S is a subset of R^n and a set A is contained in S, we can analogously define the complement of A in S, and denote it as $S \backslash A$.

A set $A \subset R^n$ is a **closed set** if its complement $R^n \backslash A$ is an open set; another definition, in terms of convergent sequences, is given below. Note that a set can be neither open nor closed. A set A is **bounded** if there is some $\mathbf{x}$ in A and some $\varepsilon > 0$ such that A is contained in $B_\varepsilon(\mathbf{x})$. Given a system of Cartesian axes and an origin, if a set is bounded there is a scalar b such that no element of the set has a distance from the origin greater than b. If a non-empty set in R^n is both closed and bounded, it is called **compact**. (Compactness of a set has a different definition in more general spaces but for our purposes this definition suffices.)

A set $A \subset R^n$ is **bounded from above** if, with x_i the ith element of $\mathbf{x} \in A$, for each $i = 1, \ldots, n$ there exists a scalar b_i such that no x_i is greater than b_i. A set A is **bounded from below** if for each i there exists a scalar c_i such that no x_i is (algebraically) smaller than c_i.

Sequences. A **sequence** in R^k, usually denoted $\{\mathbf{x}^n\} := (\mathbf{x}^1, \mathbf{x}^2, \ldots)$, is an infinite set of points, indexed by the positive integers; it can be seen as a function from the integers to points of R^k. Of course the index n does not indicate the nth power of x, only its place in the sequence. Often a sequence is generated by a rule that specifies how to associate a number (or a vector) x^n to each integer n. A simple example of sequence in R is $\{x^n = 1/n\}$. A sequence $\{x^k\}$ is said to *converge* to a point x^* if for every positive number ε there is an integer N such that, for all $k > N$, x^k is in $B_\varepsilon(x^*)$. This means that however small the chosen ε, after the Nth element the sequence has all elements at a distance from x^* less than ε. We also say that x^* is the limit of the sequence $\{x^k\}$ and write $\lim_{k \to \infty} x^k = x^*$. If a sequence converges to a point, it is called a **convergent sequence**. $\{x^n = 1/n\}$ is one example, convergent to 0; $\{x^k = 1,\ \text{all } k\}$ is another example, convergent to 1; indeed a sequence which for $k > N$ becomes stationary, that is with all elements beyond the Nth one being identically the same point x, satisfies the definition of convergence to x.

Closedness of sets defined in terms of sequences. A set A *is closed if every convergent sequence of elements in* A *converges to a point in* A.

Convergent subsequences. A **subsequence** of a sequence $\{x^k\}$ is a sequence obtained from the original sequence by leaving out some elements of the original sequence. For example a sequence in R is $\{x^n = 1/n\} = (1, 1/2, 1/3, \ldots)$; one subsequence of this sequence is $(1, 1/3, 1/5, 1/7, \ldots)$, which leaves out the even-numbered elements of the original sequence. A subsequence can be convergent when the sequence is not. An important theorem on sequences states the following:

Existence of a convergent subsequence. If A *is a compact subset of* R^n, *then every sequence in* A *contains a convergent subsequence.*

Continuity of functions defined in terms of convergent sequences. A *function* $f(x)$ *is continuous at* x^* *if for every sequence* $\{x^k\}$ *that converges to some point, call it* x^*, *the sequence* $\{f(x^k)\}$ *converges to* $f(x^*)$.

Connected sets. The very intuitive notion of continuous curve or portion of curve allows us to define a notion that gets us close to topology and is useful in chap. 9, ▶ Sect. 9.2 and footnote 9 there. A set is **connected** if it is possible to connect any point of the set to any other point of the set with a continuous (portion of) curve consisting entirely of points of the set. In ◼ Fig. 15.1 the set on the left is not connected.

Sets of measure zero and genericity of properties. First we need at least some rough understanding of the notion of **countable sets**. A collection or set is countable if it contains either a finite number of elements, or an infinite one 'of the same power as' the set of integers in the sense that there exists a one-to-one function from the integers to the countable set. Examples of infinite countable sets are the elements of any sequence whose elements are all different, e.g. the set of numbers $\{1/n\}$ for n integer. The set of rational numbers (ratios between two integers) is countable. The infinity of real numbers on the real line, or on any segment of positive length of the real line, is uncountable: the integers are not sufficiently numerous to index them all, as proved by Cantor.

If $a = (a_1, \ldots, a_n)$ and $b = (b_1, \ldots, b_n)$ are points (vectors) in R^n such that $a_i \le b_i$ for $i = 1, \ldots, n$, then the **closed interval** $[a, b]$ is the set $\{x: a_i \le x_i \le b_i,\ \text{all } i\}$, the **open interval** (a, b) is the set $\{x: a_i < x_i < b_i,\ \text{all } i\}$. The **volume of an interval** $I = (a, b)$ or $I = [a, b]$ is defined as

$$v(I) = \prod_{i=1}^{n} (b_i - a_i).$$

15.4 · Analysis

This notion of *volume* is readily interpretable. An interval in R is a portion of the real line, and its *volume* is its length. An interval in R^2 is a rectangle with sides parallel to the axes, where **a** is the south-west corner and **b** is the north-east corner; therefore the basis is $b_1 - a_1$ and the altitude is $b_2 - a_2$, and its *volume* is its area. An interval in R^3 is a parallelepiped with $b_1 - a_1$, $b_2 - a_2$, $b_3 - a_3$ as its length, width and altitude, and its *volume* is...its volume. In spaces of dimension greater than 3 a geometric visualization is not possible but the meaning is the same.

*A set E in R^n is a **set of measure zero** if for each $\varepsilon > 0$ there is a countable collection $\{I_k\}$ of open intervals such that*

$$E \subset \bigcup_{k=1}^{\infty} I_k \quad \text{and} \quad \sum_{k=1}^{\infty} v(I_k) \leq \varepsilon.$$

In words: a set in R^n is of measure zero if it can be enclosed in a finite, or infinite but countable, number of intervals of total *volume* arbitrarily close to zero. (The intervals can overlap.) A finite or countable number of points in R, a curve or a finite or countable number of curves in R^2, a surface or a finite or countable number of surfaces in R^3 are examples of sets of measure zero.

The same definition applies if the set E is a subset, not of R^n, but of a subset of R^n not of measure zero (and therefore 'containing as many points' as R^n). Thus the intersection of a curve with a rectangle in R^2 is a set of measure zero relative to that rectangle as well as relative to R^2.

A property that elements of a set not of measure zero can have or not have is **generic** (or *holds almost everywhere*) if it holds for all elements of the set except a subset of measure zero. If a property only holds for a subset of measure zero, then the *absence* of the property is generic.

If a point is chosen at random in a set $S \subset R^n$ not of measure zero on which a uniform or at least a continuous non-atomic probability density is defined, then the probability is zero that the point belongs to a subset of measure zero of that set.

If in R^n, $n > 1$, from a point belonging to a subset S of measure zero one moves to a point in its neighbouhood and the direction of movement is chosen at random, the probability is zero that the point thus reached is in S; i.e. the probability that the point thus reached is not in S is one. This means that a very small movement in a random direction away from a point in a set $S \subset R^n$ of measure zero which is the only set of points enjoying a certain property causes the property no longer to hold with probability 1.

The differential for functions of a single variable. The *derivative* of a function of one variable $y = f(x)$ is indicated in many different ways, e.g. $f'(x)$, $Df(x)$, $df(x)/dx$, dy/dx. The last two ways represent the derivative as ratio between the differential of $f(x)$ and the differential of x. The notion of differential is not among the easiest to grasp, and students sometimes are not clear as to why $df(x)/dx$ is a legitimate alternative way to indicate the derivative, so here is a brief reminder. Let us start with functions of one variable. The differential of a function $y = f(x): R \to R$ at x is *defined* as

$$dy \equiv df(x) \equiv f'(x) \cdot \Delta x,$$

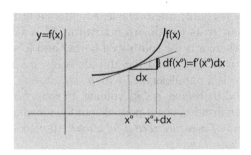

Fig. 15.5 Graphical illustration of $df(x)$ as differing from the actual variation of $f(x)$. Also see Fig. 15.13

where $f'(x)$ is the derivative of f at x, and Δx (which can be positive or negative) is a displacement of x to $x' = x + \Delta x$. The differential therefore is only defined if $f(x)$ has a derivative, and it is a function of *two* variables, x and Δx. But for x given, $df(x)$ is directly proportional to Δx, so one can write $df(x)/\Delta x = f'(x)$.

Now consider the function $f(x) = x$, called **the identical function**, and indicate its differential as dx; it is $dx \equiv \Delta x$ because the derivative of the identical function is 1; therefore in the definition of the differential of any $f(x)$ we can replace Δx with dx obtaining

$$dy \equiv df(x) \equiv f'(x) \cdot dx,$$
$$dy/dx \equiv df(x)/dx \equiv f'(x).$$

This explains why the derivative of $y = f(x)$ can also be written $df(x)/dx$ or dy/dx.

We can reach a better understanding of what $df(x)/dx = f'(x)$ means through a geometric interpretation, see Fig. 15.5. At the denominator of the fraction $df(x^\circ)/dx^\circ$ there is a variation of x from x°, and at the numerator there is the variation of y from $f(x^\circ)$, calculated *not* along the curve $f(x)$ but instead *along the straight line tangent to the curve $f(x)$ in x°*. The derivative $f'(x^\circ)$ measures the slope of this tangent line, so $df(x^\circ) = f'(x^\circ) \cdot dx^\circ$. Given x°, the magnitude of $df(x^\circ)$ depends on the magnitude of dx, but the ratio $df(x^\circ)/dx$ does not change because it is simply the slope of the tangent line.

One can treat $dx \equiv \Delta x$ and $df(x)$ as variables on which one can operate algebraically: for example the limit, for $\Delta x \to 0$, of the ratio between *proportional* variation of $f(x)$ and *proportional* variation of x that causes it, that is, the limit of $\frac{\Delta f(x)/f(x)}{\Delta x/x}$ for $\Delta x \to 0$, is also written $\frac{df(x)/f(x)}{dx/x}$ and is considered equivalent to $\frac{df(x)}{dx} \cdot \frac{x}{f(x)} = f'(x) \cdot x/f(x)$. This is the definition of the (point) **elasticity** of $f(x)$.

Functions of several variables. A *function of several variables* $f(\mathbf{x}) : R^n \to R$ is a rule to pass from a vector of values of independent variables to a scalar value of the dependent variable. A function of two variables $z = f(x, y)$, which if continuous generates a surface in three-dimensional space, helps to develop a useful geometric understanding of functions of several variables, and of the meaning of partial derivatives, see Fig. 15.6. The intersection of the surface with a vertical plane parallel to the x-axis and cutting the y-axis at y° is a curve that shows

15.4 · Analysis

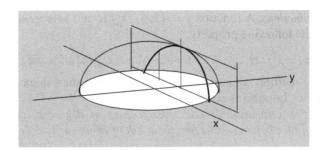

◘ **Fig. 15.6** Example of surface generated by a function $f(x,y)$ for $x,y \geq 0$, assumed to be a cupola; intersecting it with a vertical plane parallel to the x-axis, the intersection shows how $f(x,y)$ changes with x if y is kept fixed. The slope of this curve is the partial derivative of f with respect to x at the given level of y

the points of the surface $f(x,y)$ where $y=y°$; if 'smooth', this curve has a slope at each point, which indicates the speed with which $f(x,y°)$ varies when x alone changes, and which is called the partial derivative of f with respect to x if $y=y°$. The partial derivative of a function $f(x_1,x_2,...,x_k)$ with respect to, say, x_2 is calculated with the usual rules of derivation by treating all the other x_i's as constants. The differential of a function of several variables will be defined later, after defining *gradients*.

Implicit function. Given a continuous function of two variables $g(x,y)$, if we impose that this function must be equal to zero, we obtain an equation which (under conditions that are generally satisfied in economic applications at least in some subset of the domain of $g(\cdot)$)[6] obliges y univocally to change if x changes. (If we impose that a function $f(x,y)$ must be equal to a scalar t, this comes back to $g(x,y)=0$ by posing $g(x,y)=f(x,y)-t$.) Then $g(x,y)=0$ is said to render y at least locally an ***implicit function*** of x; let us indicate it as $y=\varphi(x)$; $g(x,\varphi(x))$ is constant at zero as x varies.

For example if $g(x,y)=ax+by-c$ with a, b, c given constants, then $g(x,y)=0$ means that it must be $y=\varphi(x)=(c-ax)/b$. In this case it was possible to make $\varphi(x)$ explicit in terms of elementary functions and elementary operations on them. This is not always possible; but even when possible, it is not necessary if one only wants the derivative $dy/dx=\varphi'(x)$; this is because if $f(x,y)$ has partial derivatives and the partial derivative with respect to y is not zero, there is a simple rule that yields $\varphi'(x)$ directly from $f(x,y)=0$. The rule is

$$\left.\frac{dy}{dx}\right|_{f(x,y)=0} = \varphi'(x) = -\frac{\partial f(x,y)/\partial x}{\partial f(x,y)/\partial y}.$$

---

6 The following ***implicit function theorem*** indicates the main restrictions. *Let $g(x_1,x_2): A \to R$, $A \subset R^2$, have continuous partial derivatives, and let $x^* := (x_1^*,x_2^*)$ be an interior point of A where $g(x^*)=0$, and $\partial g/\partial x_2^* \neq 0$. Then there is a neighbourhood N of x_1^* in which the equation $g(x)=0$ implicitly defines a unique function $x_1 \to f(x_1)$, that is $g(x_1,f(x_1))=0$ for all $x_1 \in N$, and it is $x_2^* = f(x_1^*)$. Furthermore $f(x_1)$ has continuous derivative df/dx_1 for all $x_1 \in N$.*

1358   **Chapter 15 · Mathematical Review**

Homogeneous functions. A function $y = f(x_1, \ldots, x_n)$ is said *homogeneous of degree* **k** if it satisfies the following property:

$$f(tx_1, \ldots, tx_n) = t^k f(x_1, \ldots, x_n) \quad \text{for all } (x_1, \ldots, x_n) \text{ and all scalar } t > 0.$$

In words: if you multiply all independent variables by t, the value of the function is multiplied by t^k. Important property:

If $f(x_1, \ldots, x_n)$ is differentiable and homogeneous of degree k, then its partial derivatives are in turn homogeneous functions, but of degree k–1.

■■ Proof

The proof will be given for $f(x_1, x_2)$ but it generalizes trivially to functions of n variables. Indicate tx_1 as x_1^*, and tx_2 as x_2^*; calculate the partial derivative with respect to x_1 of both sides of $f(tx_1, tx_2) = t^k f(x_1, x_2)$: the result, by the rule of derivative of function of function, is:

$$t \frac{\partial f\left(x_1^*, x_2^*\right)}{\partial x_1^*} = t^k \frac{\partial f(x_1, x_2)}{\partial x_1}$$

and dividing both sides by t we obtain

$$\frac{\partial f\left(x_1^*, x_2^*\right)}{\partial x_1^*} = t^{k-1} \frac{\partial f(x_1, x_2)}{\partial x_1}.$$

The same result holds for the partial derivative with respect to x_2. ■

A constant-returns-to-scale production function is homogeneous of degree 1, so its marginal products are homogeneous of degree zero, that is, they do not change if all inputs change in the same proportion; one can say that they depend only on the *proportions* among inputs.

If $f(x_1, x_2)$ is homogeneous of degree different from zero, only the *ratio between* partial derivatives is unaffected by proportional variations of all independent variables. This property also holds if $f(x_1, x_2)$ is a **homothetic** function—that is, a monotonic increasing transformation $f(g)$, $R \to R$, of a homogeneous function $g(x_1, x_2)$—because a monotonic transformation of a function does not alter the ratio between partial derivatives, as you can easily prove. Therefore homothetic non-constant-returns production functions share with constant-returns-to-scale functions the property that their isoquants are all radial expansions of any one of them; but do not share the property that along a ray from the origin the marginal product of a factor is constant.

Euler's theorem for homogeneous functions. *Assume $f(x_1, \ldots, x_n)$ is homogeneous of degree k. Then*

$$\sum_{i=1}^{n} \frac{\partial f}{\partial x_i} x_i = kf(x_1, \ldots, x_n).$$

15.4 · Analysis

■■ Proof

Differentiate with respect to t both sides of $f(tx_1,,,tx_n) = t^k f(x_1, \ldots, x_n)$.
On the left-hand side apply the 'total derivative' chain rule. The result is

$$\sum_{i=1}^{n} \frac{\partial f}{\partial(tx_i)} x_i = kt^{k-1} f(x_1, \ldots, x_n).$$

This holds for any t hence also for $t=1$, which yields $\sum_{i=1}^{n} \frac{\partial f}{\partial x_i} x_i = kf(x_1, \ldots, x_n)$. ■

In economics the most interesting case is $k=1$, constant returns to scale. Then we get

$$\sum_{i=1}^{n} \frac{\partial f}{\partial x_i} x_i = f(x_1, \ldots, x_n).$$

The economic interpretation is that if f is a production function and if its partial derivatives, the marginal products, equal the payments to factors effected with quantities of the product, the sum of these payments exhausts the product. If payments to factors are in money and they equal marginal *revenue* products and the firm is price-taker,[7] the payments exhaust the money revenue from sale of the product, because both sides of the equality are simply multiplied by p, the product's price. Therefore the result is also called the **product exhaustion theorem**.

Euler's theorem helps to understand how marginal products are related to the intensive representation of CRS production functions as indicating output per unit of labour. Assume a differentiable production function with two inputs, labour L and land T, and constant returns to scale. Then $Q=F(L,T)=F(1, T/L){\cdot}L$, and if we indicate T/L as t and $F(1,T/L)$, a function of only one variable, as $f(t)$, we can indicate output per unit of labour as $Q/L=q=f(t)$. How do marginal products appear in this reformulation of the production function much used in neoclassical growth models? Marginal products in this case depend only on the ratio between factors, hence

$$MP_T = \partial F(L,T)/\partial T = \partial F(1,T/L)/\partial(T/L) = f'(t).$$

So for land the marginal product is derivable directly as the first derivative of $f(t)$. For labour, the marginal product can be derived from $f(t)$ as follows. Because of Euler's theorem, $F(L,T)=MP_L{\cdot}L + MP_T{\cdot}T$, and dividing both sides by L we obtain $F(1,T/L)=MP_L + MP_T{\cdot}T/L$. Hence

$$MP_L = f(t) - t \cdot f'(t).$$

---

7 This addition is necessary because for a monopolistic firm the marginal revenue product of a factor is less than marginal product times product price.

1360   **Chapter 15 · Mathematical Review**

Gradient, Hessian, Jacobian. Let $\mathbf{x}$ stand for a vector $\in R^n$; given a function of several variables $f(\mathbf{x})=f(x_1,x_2,...,x_n)$ endowed with partial derivatives, one can associate to each point $\mathbf{x}$ in the domain of the function the vector of the partial derivatives of f in $\mathbf{x}$. Indicate these partial derivatives as $f_1(x), f_2(x),...,f_n(x)$; the vector $(f_1(x), f_2(x),...,f_n(x))$, generally treated as a row vector, is called **gradient** of f in $\mathbf{x}$, and is often indicated with the symbol $\nabla f(\mathbf{x})$. A graphical representation is easy with a function of two variables $f(x_1,x_2)$; the gradient is then a vector in the plane (x_1,x_2), conventionally represented as an oriented arrow with the origin in $\mathbf{x}$, it is the diagonal of a rectangle with sides parallel to the axes and of length proportional to the two partial derivatives $f_1(x)$ and $f_2(x)$, and with direction given by their signs. Thus the gradient points towards North-East if both partial derivatives are positive, towards South-East if $f_1>0$ and $f_2<0$, etcetera. Two very important properties of the gradient, proved later, are:

(i) *the gradient points in the direction of 'maximum speed of increase' of f (the direction in which f has maximum slope);*

(ii) *the gradient in $\mathbf{x}$ is orthogonal to the level curve or level surface through $\mathbf{x}$.*

Let us apply these two properties to consumer indifference curves. Let $u(x_1,x_2)$ be a utility function, take a given basket of goods $\mathbf{x}^*=(x_1{}^*,x_2{}^*)$, and draw the indifference curve through $\mathbf{x}^*$; if both marginal utilities are positive the gradient $\nabla f(\mathbf{x}^*)$ is an arrow pointing towards North-East in the direction of maximum steepness of the surface $f(\mathbf{x})$. Draw through $\mathbf{x}^*$ a straight line orthogonal to the arrow representing $\nabla f(\mathbf{x}^*)$; since by property (ii) the indifference curve through $\mathbf{x}^*$ is orthogonal to $\nabla f(\mathbf{x}^*)$, the indifference curve and this straight line are tangent to each other in $\mathbf{x}^*$; the slope of the straight line is the marginal rate of substitution in $\mathbf{x}^*$. If $\mathbf{x}^*$ is the consumer's optimum basket, the straight line is the budget line, which is therefore orthogonal to the gradient in $\mathbf{x}^*$.

The partial derivatives of $f(\mathbf{x})$ are functions of $x_1,...,x_n$, so one can calculate *their* partial derivatives (if these exist); they are called **second-order partial derivatives**; there are n^2 of them and they are indicated as $\frac{\partial^2 f(x)}{\partial x_i \partial x_j} \equiv \frac{\partial}{\partial x_i} \cdot \frac{\partial f(x)}{\partial x_j}$ where the second way of writing them indicates that one is calculating the partial derivative with respect to x_i of the partial derivative $\partial f/\partial x_j$. When $i=j$, $\frac{\partial^2 f(x)}{\partial x_j \partial x_j} \equiv \frac{\partial}{\partial x_j} \cdot \frac{\partial f(x)}{\partial x_j}$ is more simply indicated as $\frac{\partial^2 f(x)}{\partial x_j^2}$. Often one indicates second-order partial derivatives as $f_{ij}(x)$. When $i \neq j$ one speaks of *cross partial derivative*. These second-order partial derivatives can be calculated with the usual rules of derivation. They can be arranged in an $n \times n$ matrix called **Hessian matrix** (or simply the Hessian) of $f(\mathbf{x})$, which has $f_{ij} = \frac{\partial^2 f(x)}{\partial x_i \partial x_j}$ as its (i,j)th element. Thus the jth *column* of the Hessian of $f(\mathbf{x})$ is the gradient of the partial derivative $\partial f/\partial x_j$. The elements of the Hessian are functions of $\mathbf{x}$, so the Hessian can be viewed as a matricial function of $\mathbf{x}$.

An important result on second-order cross partial derivatives, generally called Young's theorem, is:

If $f(\mathbf{x})$ has continuous second-order partial derivatives (the case normally assumed in economics), then $f_{ij}=f_{ji}$.

15.4 · Analysis

In this case the Hessian, being a symmetric matrix, coincides with its transpose. Then the gradient of $\partial f/\partial x_i$ is represented both by the ith column and by the ith row of the Hessian of $f(\mathbf{x})$.

Suppose we have s functions of n variables $\left(g^{(1)}(\mathbf{x}),\ldots,g^{(k)}(\mathbf{x}),\ldots,g^{(s)}(\mathbf{x})\right)^T$, all of them defined on the same domain and endowed with partial derivatives. Each function $g^{(k)}(\mathbf{x})$ has a gradient; the matrix with these s gradients as its *rows* is an $s \times n$ matrix called the ***Jacobian matrix*** of the vector of functions.

If the functions of which one writes down the Jacobian are the partial derivatives $\partial f/\partial x_1$, ..., $\partial f/\partial x_n$ of $f(\mathbf{x})$, that is if they are the gradient of $f(\mathbf{x})$, then their Jacobian is the transpose of the Hessian of $f(\mathbf{x})$; but if the Hessian is a symmetric matrix as generally assumed in economic analyses, it coincides with its transpose and then it can be seen directly as the Jacobian of the gradient of $f(\mathbf{x})$.

Differentiability of a function of several variables. Consider a function of two variables $f(x_1,x_2)$; if continuous it can be seen as tracing a surface in three-dimensional space, with (x_1,x_2) a point in the horizontal plane, and $f(x_1,x_2)$ the vertical distance of the surface from that plane at that point. Suppose this surface is 'smooth', i.e. has no sharp edges or corners, and to help intuition imagine it is strictly concave; then if you rest a rigid plane upon a point $(x_1, x_2, f(x_1,x_2))$ of this surface, the plane will be tangent to the surface in the sense that it touches the surface only at that point and almost coincides with the surface in a neighbourhood of that point. This intuitive picture of a plane tangent to a surface can be made precise: such a plane exists if the function is *differentiable*. But this notion is not a very simple one, so after the definition of differentiability of a function $f(x)$: $R^n \to R$, I supply some interpretation in the easy-to-visualize case of a function of two variables. As a premise, remember that a ***linear map*** (a linear functional, in this case) $R^n \to R$ is a function $f(\mathbf{h})$ that transforms n-vectors $\mathbf{h} = (h_1,\ldots,h_n)$ into scalars according to $f(\mathbf{h}) = a_1h_1 + a_2h_2 + \ldots + a_nh_n$, for some given n-vector $\mathbf{a}$ that characterizes the linear map. If f is $R^2 \to R$, it generates a plane in R^3 which goes through the origin.

Definition of differentiable function. *A real-valued function f: $R^n \to R$ defined on a subset X of R^n is said to be **differentiable** at a point $\mathbf{x}°$ in the interior of X, if there exists a linear map $R^n \to R$ characterized by an n-vector $\mathbf{a}$ (generally dependent on $\mathbf{x}°$) such that*

$$\lim_{\substack{h \to 0 \\ h \neq 0}} \frac{f(x° + h) - [f(x°) + a \cdot h]}{\|h\|} = 0 \tag{15.5}$$

*for any n-vector $\mathbf{h}$; this vector is interpretable as displacements from $\mathbf{x}°$, $\mathbf{h} = (\mathbf{x} - \mathbf{x}°)$, and its tendency to zero is assumed not to change its direction, just its length (via an equiproportional reduction of all its elements). The linear map characterized by vector $\mathbf{a}$, when it exists, is also denoted $f'(\mathbf{x}°)$ or $Df(\mathbf{x}°)$ and is called the **derivative** of f at $\mathbf{x}°$; the dot product $\mathbf{a} \cdot \mathbf{h}$, a scalar dependent on $\mathbf{h}$, is called the **differential** of f at $\mathbf{x}°$ and is also indicated as df.*

A function $f(x_1,x_2)$ of two variables allows a geometric intuition of what this definition states. Remember that in R^3, with x_1, x_2 measured on the horizontal Cartesian axes and y measured on the vertical axis, the equation of an affine

1362   Chapter 15 · Mathematical Review

function $y=\varphi(x_1,x_2)$, i.e. of a plane is $y=a_1x_1+a_2x_2+b$. Back to $f(x_1,x_2)$, given a point $\mathbf{x}^\circ=(x_1^\circ,x_2^\circ)$ in its domain, let $y^\circ=f(x_1^\circ,x_2^\circ)$; the equation of a plane through point $(x_1^\circ,x_2^\circ,y^\circ)$ is

$$y = a_1\left(x_2^\circ + h_1\right) + a_2\left(x_2^\circ + h_2\right) + b$$

under the condition that the constants a_1, a_2, b satisfy

$$a_1x_1^\circ + a_2x_2^\circ + b = y^\circ = f\left(\mathbf{x}^\circ\right);$$

therefore the equation of any such plane can be written $y=f(\mathbf{x}^\circ)+\mathbf{a}\cdot\mathbf{h}$ where $\mathbf{a}=(a_1,a_2)$ and $\mathbf{h}=(h_1,h_2)$. This shows that the numerator in the above limit (15.5) is the error if one approximates the variation of $f(\mathbf{x})$, when $\mathbf{x}^\circ$ moves to $\mathbf{x}^\circ+\mathbf{h}$, by the variation along a plane through $f(\mathbf{x}^\circ)$. The differentiability condition then asks that the plane be such that, for any direction of displacement from $\mathbf{x}^\circ$, if the length of this displacement tends to zero the error *as a proportion of the length of the displacement* tends to zero: which means tangency. (See below, ► Sect. 15.6, ◘ Fig. 15.12, for a geometric illustration of the meaning of tangency along one direction.)

The derivative $\mathrm{Df}(\mathbf{x}^\circ)$ is then characterized by the vector of slopes of the tangent plane along the axes of the independent variables, that is by the gradient of $f(\mathbf{x})$ at $\mathbf{x}^\circ$. The derivative is not a vector, it is a *function*, a linear functional, a map that takes us from any vector $\mathbf{h}$ to the scalar $\mathbf{a}\cdot\mathbf{h}$, but to characterize this linear functional at $\mathbf{x}^\circ$ the vector $\mathbf{a}(\mathbf{x}^\circ)$ suffices, and it is the same vector as the gradient $\nabla f(\mathbf{x}^\circ)$; but the latter gradient characterizes the derivative only if the condition for the existence of the derivative is satisfied (for this it is not sufficient that the function has a gradient in $\mathbf{x}^\circ$, see below).

The equality $\mathbf{a}(\mathbf{x}^\circ)=\nabla f(\mathbf{x}^\circ)$ allows an easy proof of a statement made earlier: *the gradient of a function f points in the direction in which f increases most rapidly.* The proof is also the occasion to introduce the notion of *directional derivative*.

▪▪ Proof

The *directional derivative* at $\mathbf{x}^\circ$ in direction $\mathbf{h}$ of a differentiable function $f(\mathbf{x})$: $R^n \to R$ is the change in the value of f from $f(\mathbf{x}^\circ)$ if one moves from $\mathbf{x}^\circ$ along the tangent (hyper)plane in that direction and covers a segment of unitary length; in other words it is $Df(\mathbf{x}^\circ)\cdot\mathbf{h}$ with $\|\mathbf{h}\|=1$. Remembering the formula for the inner product of two vectors, we obtain

$$Df\left(\mathbf{x}^\circ\right) \cdot \mathbf{h} = \left\|Df\left(\mathbf{x}^\circ\right)\right\|\|\mathbf{h}\|\cos\theta = \left\|Df\left(\mathbf{x}^\circ\right)\right\|\cos\theta.$$

This reaches its maximum for $\cos\theta=1$, i.e. for $\mathbf{h}$ colinear with $Df(\mathbf{x}^\circ)$. ▪

The question, when a function of several variables is differentiable, that is, endowed with a derivative, in a point $\mathbf{x}^\circ$, is far from trivial. For a complete answer, turn to a good textboox on calculus in R^n; here it will suffice to say that it

15.4 · Analysis

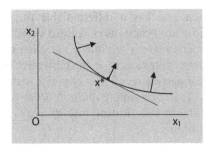

Fig. 15.7 Gradients along a convex 'smooth' indifference curve of a monotonic utility function. The gradient in **x*** is orthogonal to the indifference curve in **x***

is not enough that at **x°** the function is endowed with all partial derivatives, nor even that it has directional derivatives in all directions;[8] the basic result is:

*If $f: A \to R$, $A \subset R^n$, has partial derivatives in **x°**, an internal point of A, and these are continuous in a neighbourhood of **x°**, then f is differentiable in **x°**.*

If f(**x**) is differentiable at all internal points of its domain then it is called a **differentiable function** and it is endowed with partial derivatives and hence with a gradient. The domain can be chosen 'small' and identified with a neighbourhood of a point **x**. Then f(**x**) is said *differentiable in a neighbourhood of* **x**.

Contours, implicit functions, graphs. A **level set** or **contour** of a function $f(\mathbf{x}): R^n \to R$ is the set of all **x** such that the function takes an assigned value c, $f(\mathbf{x}) - c = 0$; if $f(\mathbf{x})$ has continuous partial derivatives different from 0 in a neighbourhood of **x**, this constraint makes each independent variable x_i an **implicit function** of the other ones. Indifference curves and isoquants are examples of level sets, respectively, of a utility function and of a production function. It is now possible to prove the orthogonality of gradients to level surfaces. The **graph** of a differentiable function $f: R^n \to R$ is a (hyper)surface in R^{n+1}; the hyperplane tangent to this surface at (**x°**,f(**x°**)) has level sets too, and the level set through (**x°**,f(**x°**)) maintains the value of the hyperplane on the f-axis equal to f(**x°**), i.e. is the portion of the tangent hyperplane corresponding to the **x**'s that obey $f(\mathbf{x°}) + Df(\mathbf{x°}) \cdot (\mathbf{x} - \mathbf{x°}) = f(\mathbf{x°})$, that is $Df(\mathbf{x°}) \cdot (\mathbf{x} - \mathbf{x°}) = 0$, which requires (**x** − **x°**) to be orthogonal to the gradient. This shows that *the gradient in **x°** is orthogonal to the level set through **x°*** (Fig. 15.7).

Again df and dx_i can be manipulated algebraically, and this allows reaching several results quickly, for example the derivative rule for implicit functions. If it must be $f(x,y) = 0$ then it must also be $df \equiv dx \cdot \frac{\partial f}{\partial x} + dy \cdot \frac{\partial f}{\partial y} = 0$; that is, the two variations of f caused by dx and by dy must neutralize each other, which can be rewritten $dy/dx = -\frac{(\partial f/\partial x)}{(\partial f/\partial y)}$ which is the derivative rule for implicit functions. If f is a function of several variables, the above holds for each couple of them treating the other variables as fixed.

---

8   This statement implies that a function can have all directional derivatives at **x°** without being differentiable there (see, e.g., Apostol, 1969, p. 257). This means that, differently from the definition given in the text, the notion of directional derivative can be defined without assuming differentiability, but I omit further details.

1364   Chapter 15 · Mathematical Review

Total derivative. When one has a differentiable function of two variables $f=f(x,y)$ and both x and y are functions of a third variable t, $x=x(t)$, $y=y(t)$, both differentiable with derivatives $x'(t)$ and $y'(t)$, then one can ask how f varies if t varies; f is an indirect function of t; the derivative of this function $f(t)$ is sometimes called the **total derivative** of $f(x(t),y(t))$ with respect to t, and can be indicated as $df(x(t),y(t))/dt$ or simply df/dt; in order to determine it one uses $dx=x'(t)\cdot dt$ and $dy=y'(t)\cdot dt$; substituting into $df = dx \cdot \frac{\partial f}{\partial x} + dy \cdot \frac{\partial f}{\partial y}$ and dividing both sides by dt one obtains

$$\frac{df(x(t),y(t))}{dt} = \frac{\partial f}{\partial x}x'(t) + \frac{\partial f}{\partial y}y'(t).$$

The right-hand side is also written $\frac{\partial f}{\partial x}\frac{dx}{dt} + \frac{\partial f}{\partial y}\frac{dy}{dt}$.

When $f=f(x,y(x))$, it is important not to confuse the total derivative $df(x,y(x))/dx$ with the partial derivative $\partial f/\partial x$. In this case $df(x,y(x))/dx = \frac{\partial f}{\partial x} + \frac{\partial f}{\partial y}\frac{dy}{dx}$.

15.5 Correspondences

A *correspondence* $R^n \to R^m$ is similar to a function but it associates to each point $\mathbf{x}$ in its domain an image which is a non-empty *set* $f(\mathbf{x})$ of points in its range; so now $f(\mathbf{x})$ indicates a set and not a single scalar or vector. The association is to be generally interpreted in the sense that any one of the points in $f(\mathbf{x})$ might be observed when $\mathbf{x}$ is observed. A correspondence is not a function even if the image consists of a single point for all points in its domain except for a single point whose image consists of two points. For example when at a certain price vector a consumer is indifferent between two consumption baskets and might demand either, her demand function is not a function but a correspondence, which associates to that price vector a demand set that comprises both baskets. A function can be seen as a special case of a correspondence. Some examples of correspondences $R \to R$ are graphically illustrated in ◘ Fig. 15.8.

A *function $f(\mathbf{x})$* is continuous in $\mathbf{x_0}$ if $\lim\limits_{x \to x_0} f(x) = f(x_0)$, i.e. if every sequence of values of $\mathbf{x}$, convergent to $\mathbf{x_0}$, generates sequences of values of $f(\mathbf{x})$ converging to $f(\mathbf{x_0})$. For a *correspondence $f(\mathbf{x})$* it may be possible to construct many different sequences of points $\in f(\mathbf{x})$ corresponding to the same convergent sequence of values of $\mathbf{x}$. Let us distinguish three types of continuity. For this we need the notion of *closed graph of a correspondence*.

The **graph**, of a correspondence $f\colon A \to Y$ which takes $x \in A$ to the set $\{y \in f(x) \subseteq Y\}$ (here and below in this section x and y can be scalars or vectors), is the set $\{(x,y) : y \in f(x)\}$; i.e. for every $x \in A$ it is the union of x and of the set $f(x)$. For a *function* $R \to R$ the graph is the set of points $\{x,f(x)\}$ in R^2 which is simply the formal definition of its graph in the usual graphic sense.

The graph is *closed* if for any sequence $\{x^m\} \to x_0$ (with x^m, $x_0 \in A$), *every* possible convergent sequence $\{y^m\}$ with $y^m \in f(x^m)$ converges to a point (not necessarily the same for different sequences) belonging to $f(x_0)$.

15.5 · Correspondences

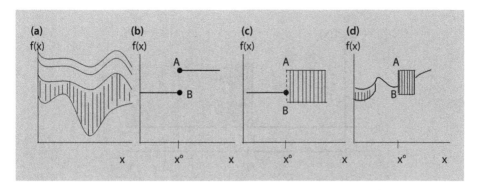

■ **Fig. 15.8** Examples of correspondences. In these drawings the convention is that a broken-line vertical segment above a certain x indicates points not belonging to the correspondence; thus in case (c), $f(x^\circ)$ consists of only one point, while $f(x^\circ + \varepsilon)$ is an entire vertical segment for $\varepsilon > 0$ arbitrarily small; one might say that $f(x > x^\circ)$ is open on the left

In ■ Fig. 15.8b the graph is closed: if $\{x^m\} \to x_0$ the only convergent sequences $\{y^m\}$ with $y^m \in f(x^m)$ converge either to point A (this is possible when $\{x^m\}$ converges to x° from the right) or to point B (this is possible when $\{x^m\}$ converges to x° from the left), and both points are in $f(x^\circ)$. In ■ Fig. 15.8c the graph is not closed: if $\{x^m\}$ converges to x° from the right, one can generate infinite sequences $\{y^m\}$ with $y^m \in f(x^m)$ converging to a point of segment AB which does not belong to $f(x^\circ)$. In ■ Fig. 15.8d the graph is closed because segment AB is all contained in $f(x^\circ)$.

A correspondence $f: A \to Y$ is ***upper hemicontinuous*** (or upper semicontinuous), ***uhc*** for short, if:
(i) its graph is closed
(ii) the images of compact subsets of A are bounded (in the sense that for any $B \subseteq A$ compact, the set $g(B) = \{y \in Y : y \in f(x) \text{ for some } x \in B\}$ is bounded).

The graph in ■ Fig. 15.9 might represent, with the price *in abscissa*, the demand for a good as a function of its price (with other prices given), of a consumer with strictly concave indifference curves. As for the case of ■ Fig. 15.8b, it is a uhc correspondence $R \to R$.

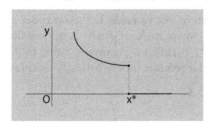

■ **Fig. 15.9** Upper hemicontinuous correspondence y(x) that could be a discontinuous demand curve of a consumer with concave indifference curves

1366   **Chapter 15 · Mathematical Review**

☐ **Fig. 15.10** This correspondence is uhc but not lhc

The correspondence defined below is not uhc because the graph is closed but $f(x)$ is unbounded for $x = 1$.

$$\begin{cases} f(x) = \left\{y : 0 \le y \le \frac{1}{1-x}\right\} & \text{for} \quad 0 \le x < 1 \\ f(x) = 1 & \text{for} \quad x > 1 \\ f(x) = R_+ & \text{for} \quad x = 1 \end{cases}$$

A correspondence f: $A \to Y$ is **lower-hemicontinuous** (or lower-semicontinuous), *lhc* for short, if, given $A \subseteq R^n$ and $Y \subset R^k$ with Y a compact set, for every sequence $\{x^m\} \to x_0$ with x^m, $x_0 \in A$, and for every $y \in f(x_0)$, it is possible to find a sequence $\{y^m\} \to y$ and a positive scalar M such that for $m > M$ it is $y^m \in f(x^m)$.

The correspondence in ☐ Fig. 15.10, where $f(x_0)$ is the vertical segment above point x_0, is uhc but not lhc because, for each sequence $\{x^m\}$ converging to x_0 from the left, the sequence $\{y^m\}$ with $y^m \in f(x^m)$ is univocally determined and it converges to point B, so it is not possible to find sequences of points in the images of x^m which converge to a point in the image of x_0 different from point B.

A correspondence is *continuous* if it is both uhc and lhc. Note that the correspondence in ☐ Fig. 15.8a is continuous.

15.6 Optimization

Maximization of functions of one variable. Let us consider a differentiable function of one variable $y = f(x)$ where $x \in X$. If $f(x^*)$ is no smaller than any other value $f(x)$ for $x \in X$, then $f(x^*)$ is called a maximum value of f; x^* maximizes $f(x)$ in that domain and is called a **solution** (not necessarily unique) of the problem

$$\max_x f(x) \; subject \; to \; x \in X.$$

15.6 · Optimization

The function $f(x)$ is the **objective function**. The x's are the **instruments**. The set of solutions, that is of elements of X for which $f(x)$ reaches its maximum value (these are called the **maximal elements** of the problem), is sometimes indicated as

$$\arg\max_{x} f(x) := \left\{ x \in X : f(x) \geq f(x'), x' \in X \right\}.$$

If a point x^* is internal to the function's domain[9] and it is $dy/dx^* \neq 0$, then it is possible to increase y by going to $x^* + \varepsilon$ or to $x^* - \varepsilon$, so x^* cannot be a solution. Hence a *necessary* condition for an internal x^* to be a solution is that $dy/dx^* = 0$. But this condition is not sufficient, x^* can be a point of minimum or of inflexion; for it to be a point of *local* maximum the function must be, in addition, such that neither small decreases nor small increases of x from x^* cause $f(x)$ to increase, and this means $f''(x^*)$ must be non-positive: a positive second derivative would mean $f'(x^* - \varepsilon) < 0$ and $f'(x^* + \varepsilon) > 0$ for sufficiently small ε, and therefore $f(x^* - \varepsilon) > f(x^*), f(x^* + \varepsilon) > f(x^*)$.

If $f''(x^*) \leq 0$ then $f(x^*)$ is not below the segment of its graph connecting the points corresponding to $(x^* - \varepsilon)$ and $(x^* + \varepsilon)$ for ε sufficiently small, so the graph is locally concave. Indeed *for twice differentiable functions concavity can also be defined as $f''(x) \leq 0$, and strict concavity as $f''(x) < 0$*, which means the slope of $f(x)$ decreases as x increases.

If $f(x)$ is everywhere concave then a local maximum at x^* is also a *global* maximum because to move away from x^* cannot cause $f(x)$ to increase (prove it). But if the function is not everywhere concave then it might reach greater values for other values of x, and the search for a *global* maximum must find all points of local maximum and compare them; and one must also find the values the function takes on the frontier of its domain: graphical analysis suffices to see that a function of one variable with a limited closed interval as domain can have a point of local maximum at the frontier, it will be so if $f(x)$ decreases when one moves away from the frontier towards the interior of the interval (see ◼ Fig. 15.11 to understand what that means for the sign of the derivative—it's easy).

The condition that the first derivative be zero is called the (necessary) *first-order condition* for a maximum or minimum; if it is satisfied, then the *second-order condition* of negative second derivative is sufficient for a local maximum. A zero second derivative requires to look for the sign of further derivatives (see below).

Maximum points are not necessarily unique nor finite in number nor locally isolated. A function $f(x)$ may reach its maximum where it has a horizontal segment, then there is a continuuum of solutions.

Careful: *a maximum does not always exist*. For example $f(x) = \ln x$, $x \in R_{++}$, is everywhere concave but does not have a maximum. Certainty that a maximum exists is obtained if the following theorem is applicable:

---

9   That is, if $f(x)$ is also defined for $x^* + \varepsilon$ and for $x^* - \varepsilon$, for a sufficiently small positive ε. If for any ε however small one of the two variations from x^* takes x out of the function's domain (e.g. $f(x)$ is defined only for non-negative x, and $x^* = 0$), then x^* is called a *frontier value* or an *extremum value* of the domain of f.

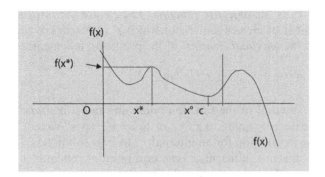

◘ **Fig. 15.11** A local maximum which is not a global maximum

Weierstrass' Theorem: *if $f(\mathbf{x})$ is continuous over a non-empty compact subset of R^n, then it reaches a maximum and a minimum in that subset.*

Note that the subset must be compact, i.e. closed and bounded. An unbounded domain is what allows the non-existence of a maximum for $f(x) = \ln x$. An open domain can easily cause trouble, $f(x) = x$ with domain the open interval $(0,1)$ has no maximum because for any value of $f(x)$ it is possible to find a greater value of $f(x)$ in its domain.

Maximization of functions of several variables. Maximization without constraints of a function of two variables $y = f(x_1, x_2)$ will supply the intuition for the cases with more variables. Graphically, f is a surface in R^3. One must find the point of maximum altitude of this surface. If the function is continuous and 'smooth' (differentiable) and concave, the point $f(\mathbf{x}^*)$ of maximum altitude of the surface, *if* internal, must have a horizontal plane tangent to it and elsewhere the surface must be below this plane (or at most not above it). For a local internal maximum at $\mathbf{x}$ the surface must be tangent to a horizontal plane through $\mathbf{x}$ and must be locally concave. Thus a first-order *necessary* condition is that both partial derivatives be zero (otherwise the tangent plane is not horizontal, there is a direction in which f increases); but it is not sufficient, the surface might be locally convex at $\mathbf{x}^*$ (which is then a local minimum), or the function might have all partial derivatives zero at $\mathbf{x}^*$ but one or both of them becoming immediately positive (or negative) on both sides of $\mathbf{x}^*$, in which case the surface has an inflection point (try drawing the graph of $f(x_1, x_2) = x_1^3 + x_2^3$ around the origin); or $\mathbf{x}^*$ might be a *saddle point* of $f(x_1, x_2)$.

A point $\mathbf{x}^*$ of $f(x_1, x_2)$ is called a saddle point of f in the assigned domain of f if there is a way of assigning indexes 1, 2 to the two variables such that

$$f(x_1, x_2^*) \leq f(x_1^*, x_2^*) \leq f(x_1^*, x_2) \text{ for all } x_1 \text{ and } x_2 \text{ in the assigned domain.}$$

That is, if the value of x_2 is fixed at x_2^*, then x_1^* maximizes $f(x_1, x_2^*)$, and if the value of x_1 is fixed at x_1^*, then x_2^* minimizes $f(x_1^*, x_2)$. The most easily visualizable saddle point of a surface in R^3 is the centre of a horse saddle aligned parallel to the x_2 axis. But the shape of the surface around a saddle point can be very different; for example it can remember a sixteeenth-century ruff. Or consider the following example: $f(x_1, x_2) = 1 - x_1 + x_2$, with domain $0 \leq x_1 \leq 1$, $0 \leq x_2 \leq 1$: draw it! point $(0,0)$ satisfies the definition of saddle point (Fig. 15.12).

15.6 · Optimization

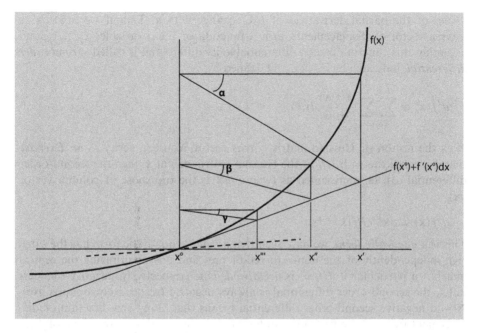

Fig. 15.12 Graphical illustration of the meaning of tangency in terms of proportional error for f: $R \to R$. Suppose that starting from $f(x^\circ)$ you approximate $f(x)$ by $f(x^\circ) + f'(x^\circ) \cdot dx$ where $dx = x - x^\circ$. The error as a *proportion* of $x - x^\circ$ is indicated by the trigonometric tangent of angle α when $x = x'$, of angle β when $x = x''$, of angle γ when $x = x'''$: it is graphically evident that it tends to zero as $x \to x^\circ$. An approximation along a non-tangent straight line such as the broken line does not produce this result: the error tends to zero as x tends to x°, but the error *as a proportion* of $x - x^\circ$ does not

A maximum at $\mathbf{x}^*$ requires that not only the partial derivatives be all zero but also that $f(\mathbf{x}^* + d\mathbf{x}) \leq f(\mathbf{x}^*)$ whichever the direction in which one moves away from $\mathbf{x}^*$. Since the partial derivatives are all equal to zero this second condition can be written

$$f(\mathbf{x}^* + d\mathbf{x}) \leq f(\mathbf{x}^*) + Df(\mathbf{x}^*)d\mathbf{x}. \tag{15.6}$$

This is the condition for a differentiable function to be concave at $\mathbf{x}^*$. Eschewing formal demonstrations (the present appendix does not aim at supplying general proofs but only results and intuitions on their validity), let us refer to a function of two variables. The above inequality (15.6) means that as one moves away from $\mathbf{x}^*$ in any direction $d\mathbf{x}$ the surface $f(\mathbf{x})$ does not go above the plane tangent to $f(\mathbf{x})$ in $\mathbf{x}^*$, plane obeying $g(\mathbf{x}) = f(\mathbf{x}^*) + Df(\mathbf{x}^*)d\mathbf{x}$: along any given direction, as one moves away from $\mathbf{x}^*$ the function's surface describes a curve which is locally concave. This must hold for all directions of displacement from $\mathbf{x}^*$. Hence $f(\mathbf{x})$ is locally concave at $\mathbf{x}^*$. Analogous reasonings can be advanced for functions of more than two variables; inequality (15.6) continues to characterize local concavity.

This inequality has connections with the nature of the *Hessian matrix* of $f(\mathbf{x}^*)$ (if it exists, i.e. assuming $f(\mathbf{x})$ is twice differentiable).

If the vector of displacements $d\mathbf{x}$ is treated as fixed, the differential $df(\mathbf{x}) \equiv \sum_{i=1}^{n} f_i(\mathbf{x})dx_i$ can be seen as a function of $\mathbf{x}$, changing with $\mathbf{x}$ because the

1370   **Chapter 15 · Mathematical Review**

values of the partial derivatives of $f(\mathbf{x})$ change with $\mathbf{x}$. Thus if we treat $d\mathbf{x}$ as a *given* vector of displacements, df is a function of the n variables $x_1,...,x_n$, and assuming this function is also differentiable its differential is called **second-order differential**, indicated by $d^2f(\mathbf{x})$, and defined by:

$$d^2f(\mathbf{x}) \equiv \sum_{j=1}^{n}\sum_{i=1}^{n} \frac{\partial^2 f(x)}{\partial x_j \partial x_i} dx_j dx_i.$$

Now the notion of Hessian matrix comes useful. You can verify as an **Exercise** that if we indicate with $Hf(\mathbf{x})$ the Hessian matrix of f at $\mathbf{x}$, then the second-order differential can be represented as (where $d\mathbf{x}^{\mathrm{T}}$ is the transpose of column vector $d\mathbf{x}$):

$$d^2f(\mathbf{x}) \equiv d\mathbf{x}^{\mathrm{T}} \cdot Hf(\mathbf{x}) \cdot d\mathbf{x}.$$

This is a **quadratic form**; we have seen that a *definite* quadratic form has the same sign independently of the non-zero vector pre- and post-multiplying the central matrix. In particular if $Hf(\mathbf{x})$ is *negative definite* (respectively, negative semidefinite), the second-order differential is always negative (respectively, nonpositive). Now a negative second-order differential means that along any direction of displacement from x^* the first-order differential decreases, that is, the slope of $f(x)$ along that direction tends to decrease; this means the surface bends away and downwards from the hyperplane tangent to $f(\mathbf{x})$ in x^*; that is, concavity. I conclude that if $Hf(\mathbf{x})$ exists then the condition that $f(x)$ be locally concave at x^* requires $Hf(\mathbf{x})$ to be negative semidefinite; if $Hf(\mathbf{x}^*)$ is negative definite then $f(\mathbf{x})$ is strictly concave at $\mathbf{x}^*$.

Thus if $f(\cdot)$ is a function of two variables, $f(x,y)$, and we indicate the partial derivatives with subscripts, $f_{xy} = \partial^2 f/\partial x\partial y$, then its Hessian is $\begin{bmatrix} f_{xx} & f_{xy} \\ f_{yx} & f_{yy} \end{bmatrix}$ where $f_{xy}=f_{yx}$ if f has continuous second-order partial derivatives, and $f(\mathbf{x})$ is strictly concave at $\mathbf{x}$ if $f_{xx}<0$ and $f_{xx}f_{yy} - \left(f_{xy}\right)^2 > 0$.

Drawing the implications of all this for the maximization of $f(\mathbf{x})$, we see that the necessary first-order condition for a point $\mathbf{x}^* \in R^n$, internal to the domain of the twice continuously differentiable function $f(\mathbf{x})$, to be a local maximum of that function is that the partial derivatives of $f(\mathbf{x})$ at $\mathbf{x}^*$ be all zero. Assume the first-order condition is satisfied. A *sufficient* second-order condition for $\mathbf{x}^*$ to be a local maximum is that $f(\mathbf{x})$ be locally *strictly* concave, which is guaranteed by a negative definite Hessian of $f(\mathbf{x})$ at $\mathbf{x}^*$; then $\mathbf{x}^*$ is a locally isolated maximum[10]; that the Hessian be negative semidefinite at $\mathbf{x}^*$ is a necessary but not a sufficient condition for $\mathbf{x}^*$ to be a local maximum, it is compatible with the second-order differential being zero for some directions of displacement from $\mathbf{x}^*$, in which case it is unclear whether along those directions the function is convex or concave or neither, the thing depends on higher-order differentials in analogy with the case

---

10 Note that a negative definite Hessian at a certain $\mathbf{x}$ is a sufficient but not a necessary second-order condition for a function to be strictly concave there: the function of one variable $f(x)=-x^4$ is strictly concave at $x=0$ but its Hessian, that is, its second-order derivative, is zero there.

15.6 · Optimization

of a function of a single variable $f(x)$: if at $\mathbf{x}^*$ it is $df/d(\mathbf{x})=0$ and $d^2f/dx^2 = 0$, then if $d^3f/dx^3 \neq 0$, $\mathbf{x}^*$ is a point of inflexion, i.e. neither a maximum nor a minimum (a single-variable example is x^3 at $x^*=0$), while $\mathbf{x}^*$ is a point of maximum if $d^3f/dx^3 = 0$ and $d^4f/dx^4 < 0$ (a single-variable example is $-x^4$ at $x^*=0$).

If the function is known to be everywhere concave, things become much simpler: the first-order condition, all partial derivatives equal to zero, is necessary and sufficient for a global maximum. A necessary and sufficient condition for a twice continuously differentiable function on an open convex set A in R^n to be concave is that its Hessian be negative semidefinite for all $\mathbf{x}\in A$, a global rather than local condition (see Takayama, 1974, p. 121).

The above can be applied to minimization, remembering that if $f(\mathbf{x})$ is convex then $-f(\mathbf{x})$ is concave, so $\mathbf{x}^*$ is a point of local minimum of $f(\mathbf{x})$ if it is a point of local maximum of $-f(\mathbf{x})$, the latter must be locally concave at $\mathbf{x}^*$. Or one can use the fact that if the first-order condition is satisfied, then a sufficient condition for $\mathbf{x}^*$ to be a local minimum is that $Hf(\mathbf{x}^*)$ be positive definite, in which case $f(\mathbf{x})$ is locally strictly convex.

The function to be maximized may contain one or more parameters and one may be interested in how the maximized value of the function changes with the value of these parameters. This maximized value of the function viewed as a function of the parameters is called the **value function** of the maximization problem. For example a firm is to produce a given output at minimum cost by choosing the optimal combination of factors at given factor rentals; the solution consists of the optimal quantities of factors, and associated with it there is the minimum cost of producing the given output; this minimum cost changes with the factor rentals, the function that associates the minimum cost to the factor rentals is the value function of this minimization problem with respect to the factor rentals considered as parameters. If the production function contains a parameter (e.g. the quantity of rain, in the production of a crop), one can treat the minimum cost as a value function with respect to this parameter too.

Expansion in Taylor series. Consider a differentiable function of one variable $y=f(x)$, with continuous derivatives $f'(x), f''(x),\ldots$ up to the order of derivation needed. Consider a value $x°$ and another value x different from $x°$; the displacement dx from $x°$ that reaches x is indicated as $dx=x-x°$. The variation $dy=f'(x°)dx$ is only an approximation to the true variation $f(x)-f(x°)$. Let the error be indicated as $e(x,x°)$:

$$f(x) - f\left(x°\right) = f'\left(x°\right)dx + e\left(x,x°\right).$$

Using $x=x°+dx$ this can be written as

$$f\left(x°+dx\right) - f\left(x°\right) = f'\left(x°\right)\left(x-x°\right) + e\left(x°,dx\right) = f'\left(x°\right)dx + e\left(x°,dx\right).$$

Many mathematics texts prefer to use h in place of dx to indicate the displacement, thus:

$$f\left(x°+h\right) - f\left(x°\right) = f'\left(x°\right)h + e\left(x°,h\right). \tag{15.7}$$

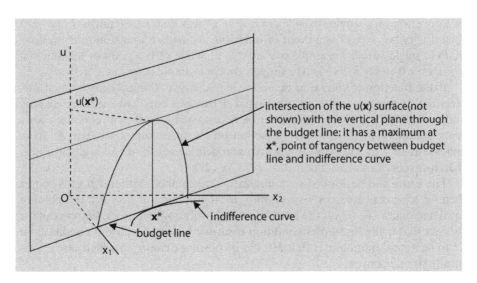

◘ Fig. 15.13 Constrained utility maximization with two goods

As h tends to zero, if $f(x)$ is differentiable then the error $e(x°,h)$ tends to zero 'more rapidly' than h, that is,

$$\lim_{h \to 0} e(x°, h)/h = 0.$$

In other words the error as a *proportion* of the displacement (the angles α, β, ... in ◘ Fig. 15.12) can be made as small as one likes by sufficiently reducing h; this does not happen if the straight line, whose divergence from $f(x)$ generates the error, is not tangent to $f(x)$ in $x°$. This is in fact the *meaning* of tangency.

The importance of this fact is that, as long as the derivative in $x°$ is not zero, in a sufficiently small neighbourhood of $x°$ the *sign* of the variation of $f(x)$ obtained from the differential indicates correctly the *sign* of the true variation of $f(x)$, which coincides with the sign of the derivative for $h > 0$: for small displacements the error is insignificant and therefore cannot alter that sign, so one can neglect the sign of the error. However, if in $x°$ it is $f'(x°) = 0$, then the sign of the variation of the function for displacements from $x°$ is determined entirely by the sign of the error, and one must determine that sign. For example, a local maximum requires the function to be locally concave, which means that the sign of the error must be nonpositive both for $h > 0$ and for $h < 0$. To determine the sign of the error, one decomposes the error into smaller fractions tied to higher-order derivatives according to **Taylor series expansion**.

I briefly remember this notion. Assume that $f(x)$ is differentiable n times in $x°$. In what follows, f'' is the second derivative, f''' the third derivative, $f^{(k)}$ the kth derivative, $e_k(x°,h)$ is the error or *remainder* (=residual) corresponding to Taylor's series developed up to the kth derivative of f; and $n!$ is **n factorial**, defined

15.6 · Optimization

as $n! = 1 \cdot 2 \cdot 3 \cdot \ldots \cdot (n-1) \cdot n$; so $1! = 1$, $2! = 2$, $3! = 6$, $4! = 24$, $5! = 120$, etc. Taylor proved that one can successively decompose the remainder as follows ($h = dx$):

$$f(x° + h) = f(x°) + f'(x°)h + e_1(x°, h).$$
$$f(x° + h) = f(x°) + f'(x°)h + f''(x°)h^2/2! + e_2(x°, h).$$
$$f(x° + h) = f(x°) + f'(x°)h + f''(x°)h^2/2! + f'''(x°)h^3/3! + e_3(x°, h).$$

. . . .

$$f(x° + h) = f(x°) + \sum_{k=1}^{n} f^{(k)}(x°)h^k/k! + e_k(x°, h).$$

To obtain the *variation* of f, $dy = df(x)$, one must only move the term $f(x°)$ to the left of the equality sign, with a minus sign of course. Error $e_k(x°, h)$ is the remainder of the Taylor series arrested at the k-th term (i.e. at the term where the kth derivative appears); the important part of Taylor's proof is that

$$\lim_{h \to 0} e_k(x°, h)/h^k = 0,$$

that is, *as h tends to zero the Taylor remainder tends to zero faster than h^k*. One has

$$e_1(x°, h) = f''(x°)h^2/2! + e_2(x°, h);$$
$$e_2(x°, h) = f''', (x°)h^3/3! + e_3(x°, h);$$

and so on. This means that for sufficiently small variations of x from $x°$ the sign of $e_1(x°, h)$ is the same as the sign of $f''(x°)$ if the latter derivative is different from zero; this follows from

$$e_1(x°, h)/h^2 = f''(x°)/2! + e_2(x°, h)/h^2;$$

only the second addendum on the right-hand side tends to zero as h tends to zero. So the error has the same sign as the sign of the second-order derivative both for $h > 0$ and for $h < 0$; hence *it is negative (indicating a locally strictly concave function and hence a proper local maximum) if and only if the second derivative, when not zero, is negative.*

Things become more complex if the second derivative is zero too. For $f(x)$ to be strictly concave in $x°$, its derivative must be decreasing there; so if f'' is zero in $x°$ where f' is zero, f'' must be negative both immediately to the left and immediately to the right of $x°$, and therefore it must be increasing to the left of $x°$ and decreasing to its right, hence f''' must be positive to the left of $x°$ and negative to the right, and hence if continuous it must be zero in $x°$; and $f^{(4)}$ must be negative in $x°$. The general result, of limited interest for economics, is that if the first $n-1$ derivatives are zero but not the nth one, then when n is even $x°$ is a local maximum (f is locally concave) if the nth derivative is negative, a local minimum if positive; when n is odd, $x°$ is neither a local maximum nor a local minimum.

1374   **Chapter 15 · Mathematical Review**

Let us move to differentiable functions of several variables. For $f(\mathbf{x})$ a function of several variables the differential is the approximation $df(\mathbf{x})$ to the true variation of $f(\mathbf{x})$ caused by a vector of displacements $d\mathbf{x} = (dx_1, \ldots, dx_n)$ from the initial vector $\mathbf{x}^\circ$, and it differs from the true variation of $f(\mathbf{x})$ by a remainder or error:

$$f(\mathbf{x}) - f(\mathbf{x}^\circ) = f_1 dx_1 + \ldots + f_n dx_n + e_1(\mathbf{x}^\circ, d\mathbf{x}) = Df(\mathbf{x}^\circ) d\mathbf{x} + e_1(\mathbf{x}^\circ, d\mathbf{x}) = df + e_1(\mathbf{x}^\circ, d\mathbf{x}).$$

If to get geometric intuition one considers a differentable function of two variables, $y = f(\mathbf{x})$ generates a surface in three-dimensional space, and the differential approximates the variation of $f(\mathbf{x})$ by calculating it along the tangent plane in $\mathbf{x}^\circ$ rather than along the true surface $f(x_1, x_2)$; the remainder measures the error. The basic result, that $e_1(\mathbf{x}^\circ, d\mathbf{x}) / \|d\mathbf{x}\| \to 0$ as the length of $d\mathbf{x}$ tends to zero, can be reformulated as follows. Let the *direction* of movement from $\mathbf{x}^\circ$ be determined by a vector of displacements $d\mathbf{x}^\circ$ of length 1; we can obtain a displacement from $\mathbf{x}^\circ$ in that direction of as small a length as we like by putting $d\mathbf{x} = t \cdot d\mathbf{x}^\circ$ and reducing t sufficiently; the result becomes $\lim_{t \to 0} e_1(\mathbf{x}^\circ, d\mathbf{x}, t) / t = 0$. As for functions of a single variable, if $dy \neq 0$ then the sign of the error is unable to affect the sign of the true variation of $f(\mathbf{x})$ for sufficiently small displacements. The sign of the error becomes fundamental if at $\mathbf{x}^\circ$ all partial derivatives are zero and therefore $dy = 0$.

In this case, to ascertain the sign of the error we decompose it into a function of the *second-order differential* plus a second-order error. For functions of several variables too it is possible to formulate Taylor expansions; the Taylor expansion arrested at the second term is

$$f(\mathbf{x}) - f(\mathbf{x}^\circ) = df(\mathbf{x}^\circ) + d^2 f(\mathbf{x}^\circ)/2! + e_2(\mathbf{x}^\circ, d\mathbf{x}) = \sum_{i=1}^{n} f_i dx_i + \frac{1}{2} d\mathbf{x}^{\mathrm{T}} \cdot Hf(\mathbf{x}^\circ) \cdot d\mathbf{x} + e_2(\mathbf{x}^\circ, d\mathbf{x}).$$

$$(15.8)$$

If $df(\mathbf{x}^\circ) = \mathbf{0}$ the variation of f is given by $\frac{1}{2} d\mathbf{x}^T \cdot Hf(\mathbf{x}^\circ) \cdot d\mathbf{x} + e_2(\mathbf{x}^\circ, d\mathbf{x})$. The ratio of the error e_2 to the length of $d^2 f(\mathbf{x}^\circ)$ tends to zero as the latter length tends to zero, and therefore for sufficiently small displacements the sign of the variation of $f(\mathbf{x})$ is the same as the sign of $d^2 f(\mathbf{x}^\circ)$; as we know, the latter sign will be negative if the Hessian matrix is negative definite, indicating that the surface is locally strictly concave and $\mathbf{x}^\circ$ is a point of isolated local maximum. If the Hessian is *not* negative semidefinite, $\mathbf{x}^\circ$ is not a local maximum; if it is negative semidefinite, $\mathbf{x}^\circ$ *may* be a point of local maximum but the second-order differential might be zero and then the sign of the variation of $f(\mathbf{x})$ would depends on the sign of e_2.

Constrained maximization. Cases of maximization without constraints are not very frequent in economics; much more frequent is maximization or minimization of a function $f(\mathbf{x})$ under constraints on the values the independent variables can take. One then speaks of **constrained maximum or minimum problem**. The constraints can be of several types.

For problems with f a function of n variables and n–1 **equality constraints** of type $g(\mathbf{x}) = 0$, it may be possible to eliminate the explicit consideration of the

15.6 · Optimization

constraints by deriving from them all variables but the first as functions of the first (this requires that the implicit functions can be rendered explicit), and replacing in f all variables but the first with these functions; then f becomes a function of a single variable without constraints. Often the implicit functions do not need to be made explicit, because the maximization only requires their derivatives. For example let $C = v_x x + v_y y$ be a production cost to be minimized, a function of the quantities employed of two inputs x and y which have rentals v_x and v_y. If this minimization, which is equivalent to $\max_{x,y} (-C)$, were without constraints except $C \geq 0$, it would be achieved by not producing at all! The problem becomes economically interesting when there is a constraint that one must produce a given quantity Q^* of output. Assuming a production function $Q = f(x,y)(x,y)$ we have the problem:

$$\max_{x,y} (-C) \text{ subject to the constraint} f(x, y) = Q^*.$$

The constraint renders y an implicit function of x, let us write it $y = y(x)(x)$; cost minimization requires to find the point (x,y) that minimizes C among the sole points $(x,y(x)(x))$ that allow producing Q^*. Replacing y with $y(x)$ in the C function we obtain an unconstrained maximum problem where C depends only (directly and indirectly) on x,

$$\max -C(x, y(x)),$$

and (for *internal* solutions) if the maximand function is differentiable the first-order necessary condition is that the *total* derivative $d(-C)/dx$ be zero. It is $d(-C)/dx = -dC/dx = -[\partial C/\partial x + (\partial C/\partial y \cdot dy/dx)]$; since $C = (v_x x + v_y y(x))$, it is $\partial C/\partial x = v_x$, $\partial C/\partial y = v_y$, and it is unnecessary to have the explicit function $y(x)$ because we only need its derivative, and the derivative rule for implicit functions yields $dy/dx = -\frac{\partial f/\partial x}{\partial f/\partial v} = -MP_x/MP_y$. The first-order condition then is $-[v_x - v_y MP_1/MP_2] = 0$ which can be rewritten as $v_x/v_y = MP_x/MP_y$. This is the well-known first-order condition of tangency between isoquant and isocost (remember that this is only a *necessary* condition for an optimum, and only for internal solutions, not for 'corner solutions').

As long as the solution is internal, the necessary first-order conditions for a constrained maximum of a differentiable function $f(x_1, x_2)$ under a single differentiable constraint $g(x_1, x_2) = 0$ (for simplicity I only consider this case) can also be obtained from the conditions for *unconstrained* maximization of a special function, called **Lagrangian function**. This function is composed as follows (where λ is a scalar to be determined, called *Lagrange multiplier*):

$$L = f(x_1, x_2) + \lambda g(x_1, x_2).$$

The three first-order necessary conditions for a maximum of this Lagrangian function are that the three partial derivatives with respect to x_1, x_2, λ be zero. The first two are

$$\partial L/\partial x_1 \equiv \partial f/\partial x_1 + \lambda \partial g/\partial x_1 = 0$$
$$\partial L/\partial x_2 \equiv \partial f/\partial x_2 + \lambda \partial g/\partial x_2 = 0.$$

1376   **Chapter 15 · Mathematical Review**

Move to the right of the equality sign the second term in each of them, then divide the first equality by the second so as to eliminate λ; one obtains:

$$\frac{\frac{\partial f}{\partial x_1}}{\frac{\partial f}{\partial x_2}} = \frac{\frac{\partial g}{\partial x_1}}{\frac{\partial g}{\partial x_2}}. \tag{15.9}$$

The third condition, $\partial L / \partial \lambda$, yields again the constraint:

$$g(x_b, x_2) = 0. \tag{15.10}$$

One obtains the system of two Eqs. (15.9) and (15.10), which generally permits the determination of the two variables x_1 and x_2.

If the constraint is not in the form $g(\cdot)=0$ called implicit form, it must be put in that form before being deprived of the $=0$ part and introduced into the Lagrangian function; for example if it is $g(\cdot)=h(\cdot)$ it must be put in the form $g(\cdot)-h(\cdot)=0$.

The cleverness of using the Lagrangian is that since its first-order condition with respect to the multiplier yields the constraint, the latter is satisfied, and therefore, the other first-order conditions indicate the conditions for a maximum of the objective function (with the variables constrained to respect the constraint).

For correspondences, maximization is obviously less simple and will not be discussed here; it is best studied case by case. One important theorem for maximization of correspondences is the following, in the version of a highly mathematical textbook.

Theorem of the maximum or Maximum Theorem

Let $X \subset \mathbb{R}^m$, $Y \subset \mathbb{R}^k$ and let $\gamma: X \to Y$ be a compact-valued correspondence. Let $f: Y \to R$ be a continuous function. Let the correspondence $\beta: X \to Y$ be defined by

$$\beta(x) = \{y \in \gamma(x) : y \text{ maximizes } f \text{ on } \gamma(x)\},$$

and let the function $M: X \to R$ be defined by $M(x)=f(x)$ for $y \in \beta(x)$. If γ is continuous at x, then β is closed and upper hemicontinuous at x and M is continuous at x. Furthermore β is compact valued.

Worry not! some interpretation is coming. There is a function $f(y): Y \to R$ to be maximized under constraints which limit y to be in a subset of Y, called $\gamma(x)$, which depends on a vector of parameters $x \in X$; for each x, the set $\gamma(x)$ is assumed compact; $\gamma(x)$ is the 'constraint set' (the set of elements of Y that satisfy the constraints) in the constrained maximization problem *max $f(y)$ over the set* $(y \in \gamma(x))$. We are interested in how the set of solutions and the value function of this maximization problem depend on the parameters x. The solution y needs not be unique, and the best-choice set β collects the solutions, all of course generating the same maximum value of $f(y)$. This maximum value of $f(y)$ considered as depending on the parameters x is indicated as $M(x)$, value function of the above maximization problem with respect to the parameters x. The theorem asserts that

15.6 · Optimization

if the 'constraint set' $\gamma(x)$ is a continuous correspondence of x, then the set β of the y's that are solutions to the maximization problem is a compact-valued[11] and upper-hemicontinuous correspondence of x, and the value function $M(x)$ is a continuous function of x.

Therefore the theorem can be reformulated as follows: *A continuous function* $f(y): R^k \rightarrow R$ *is to be maximized over a constrained domain which is a non-empty compact subset of R^k which is a continuous correspondence of a vector of parameters x. The best-choice set β, solution of the problem of finding the maximal elements of $f(y)$, is a compact-valued and upper-hemicontinuous correspondence of this vector of parameters, and the value function $M(x)$ is continuous.*

A further result usually considered part of the theorem is that this best-choice set β *is a continuous **function** of the vector of parameters x, **if** the best-choice set is always a singleton, i.e. contains only one element.*[12]

Applied for example to Marshallian utility maximization, $f(y)$ is utility as function of consumption baskets y, $\gamma(x)$ is the budget set, a set that depends on prices and income which are the elements of vector x. For each vector x of prices and income the best-choice set $\beta(x)$ is the set of utility-maximizing consumption baskets, as we know this set need not be unique and it need not be a *continuous* correspondence of the parameters, as made evident by the 'jumps' in consumer choice as prices change when indifference curves are concave; but it is an upper-hemicontinuous correspondence of the parameters *as long as prices are positive*: when a price becomes zero the budget set becomes unbounded along the dimension of the good whose price has become zero, $\gamma(x)$ is not compact, the theorem does not apply.

First-order conditions with inequality constraints. See ***Kuhn–Tucker theorem***, in §4.8. Nothing was said there on the fact that the solution (x^*, λ^*) of a constrained differentiable maximization problem can be seen as a ***saddle point*** of the Lagrangian $L = f(x) + \sum_i \lambda_i g_i(x)$, a point that maximizes the Lagrangian relative to the non-negative variables in x and minimizes it relative to the non-negative Lagrange multipliers λ_i. To make this evident would require, in the theorem as formulated in ▶ Chap. 4 (Proposition 4.7), a less simple reformulation of conditions (i) as separate groups of inequalities and equalities via the use of *slack variables*, as shown in Intriligator (1971, pp. 46–57); this would allow a better grasp of the theorem but at the cost of several pages of explanation; since this book does not require this clarification, I invite the interested reader to pursue the topic in Intriligator, and then to read also the very careful comparison of concave and differential programming in Takayama (1974, pp. 55–112).

Envelope theorem. *See §4.9, where an intuitive proof of the theorem is also supplied. I remember here how the envelope theorem allows an interpretation of Lagrange*

---

11 That a correspondence from $x \in X$ to a set $\beta(x)$ be *compact-valued* means that, for each x, the corresponding set $\beta(x)$ is a compact set. This is compatible with $\beta(x)$ containing a single element.

12 What is meant here by β being a function is that it always contains only one *vector*. For a rigorous statement and proof of the Theorem of the Maximum cf. for example Beavis and Dobbs (1990, pp. 83–4). A statement of the Theorem of the Maximum for topological spaces is in Ellickson (1993, p. 221).

1378   **Chapter 15** · Mathematical Review

multipliers. Suppose $f(x,y)$ *is to be maximized subject to an equality constraint* $g(x,y)=0$. *Rewrite the constraint as* $g(x,y)+\alpha$. The Lagrangian function is

$$L = f(x_1,x_2) + \lambda[g(x_1,x_2) + \alpha].$$

The envelope theorem states that the maximized value of $f(x,y)$ viewed as a function of α, indicate it as $M(\alpha)$, is a continuous function of α and it is $dM(\alpha)/d\alpha = \lambda$ even at $\alpha=0$. That is, λ indicates the variation of the maximized value of f if the constraint is rendered less strict by one (small) unit. For example in the utility maximization problem, if the constraint is rewritten 'income minus expenditure plus $\alpha=0$', then α is extra units of income, and λ indicates by how much utility is increased by one more unit of income, that is, at $\alpha=0$, λ is the marginal utility of income or of money when utility is maximized.

One can also ask how **solutions** of maximization problems (the optimal values of the 'instruments') vary as functions of parameters. One simple case can be analysed as follows. Assume the solution $\mathbf{x}^*$ of an unconstrained maximization problem is internal and depends on a parameter α. Consider one of the elements of $\mathbf{x}^*$, for simplicity indicate it simply as $x(\alpha)$. At the optimum it is $\partial f(x(\alpha),\alpha)/\partial x=0$. Differentiating both sides with respect to α we obtain

$$\frac{\partial}{\partial x}\frac{\partial f}{\partial x}\frac{dx}{d\alpha} + \frac{\partial}{\partial \alpha}\frac{\partial f}{\partial x} = 0.$$

Solving for $dx/d\alpha$ we obtain $\frac{dx(\alpha)}{d\alpha} = -\frac{\partial^2 f(x(\alpha),\alpha)/\partial x \partial \alpha}{\partial^2 f(x(\alpha),\alpha)/\partial x^2}$.

The denominator on the right-hand side must be negative, because it is the second-order condition for a maximum; hence the sign of $dx/d\alpha$ is the same as the sign of the derivative of $\partial f/\partial x$ with respect to α (at the optimum). For example, cost minimization for the production of a given output with two factors requires to maximize $-C=-(v_1x_1+v_2x_2)$ under the constraint $f(x_1,x_2)=q°$; we ask how the optimum employment of factor 1 changes with its rental v_1; reduce the problem to one of unconstrained maximization by using the fact that the constraint renders x_2 an implicit function of x_1, indicate it as $z(x_1)$; then the maximization is of $-C=-(v_1x_1+v_2z(x_1))$, hence $\partial(-C)/\partial x_1=-v_1-v_2\partial z/\partial x_1$, and its derivative with respect to v_1 is -1, negative; hence if v_1 increases, x_1 decreases.

Second-order conditions for constrained maximization. For an *unconstrained* local maximum at $\mathbf{x}^*$ of a differentiable function $u=f(x_1,...,x_n)$, assuming the first-order condition is satisfied, we have seen that the second-order sufficient condition for $\mathbf{x}^*$ to be a (local) maximum is that the function be locally concave at $\mathbf{x}^*$, i.e. that for small displacements from $\mathbf{x}^*$ in any direction it is $f(\mathbf{x}) \leq f(\mathbf{x}^*)$. A necessary condition for this is that the Hessian of f be negative semidefinite; a sufficient condition is that the Hessian matrix be *negative definite*, that is, that its principal minors alternate in sign, starting from negative; then $f(\mathbf{x})$ is strictly concave at $\mathbf{x}^*$. For a differentiable functions of a single variable, the first-order necessary condition is that the first derivative be zero, the second-order sufficient condition is that the second derivative be negative, or, if zero, that the third derivative be zero too and the fourth derivative be negative (a standard example for functions of one variable is $f(x)=-x^4$).

15.6 · Optimization

For a *constrained* maximum at $\mathbf{x}^*$ of $f(\mathbf{x})$ subject to a single *equality* constraint $g(\mathbf{x})=0$ (the case of greater usefulness in microeconomics), in addition to the first-order conditions (null partial derivatives of the Lagrangian function $L=f(\mathbf{x})+\lambda g(\mathbf{x})$) a *necessary* condition is that $f(\mathbf{x})$ does not increase for displacements from $\mathbf{x}^*$ *in the directions compatible with the constraint*; a *sufficient* condition is that, under the same condition, it decreases.

For example, consider utility maximization under local nonsatiation in the two-goods case, subject to the budget constraint formulated as an equality: utility is a surface in R^3, and for a certainty of maximum in $\mathbf{x}^*$, utility must decrease as one moves away from $\mathbf{x}^*$ *along the budget line*: then the point $u(\mathbf{x})$ moves along the intersection between the utility surface and the vertical plane passing through the budget line, cf. ◘ Fig. 15.13.

The second-order condition sufficient for a maximum is therefore:

$d^2 f(\mathbf{x}^*) < 0$ *for all* $(dx_1,...,dx_n)$ *not all zero and such that the constraint* $g(\mathbf{x})=0$ *is satisfied, that is, such that* $\sum_i (dx_i \cdot \partial g(x)/\partial x_i) = 0$.

That under the same assumptions it is $d^2 f(\mathbf{x}^*) \leq 0$ is only a necessary, not a sufficient condition for a maximum.

If there are several equality constraints, the sufficient condition is $d^2 f(\mathbf{x}^*) < 0$ when *all* constraints are simultaneously satisfied by the direction in which one moves from $\mathbf{x}^*$. This condition can be expressed (I omit the proof) in terms similar to the case of no constraints, if one replaces the Hessian of the objective function with the **bordered Hessian** *of the Lagrangian*, that is, the matrix of second-order partial derivatives of the Lagrangian considered as a function of the variables *and* of the multipliers. For concreteness let us consider a case with three choice variables and two equality constraints. Let the Lagrangian be

$$L = f(x_1, x_2, x_3) + \lambda g(x_1, x_2, x_3) + \mu h(x_1, x_2, x_3),$$

and indicate its second-order partial derivatives as L_{ij}, $i, j = \lambda, \mu, 1, 2, 3$; for example $L_{\mu 2} = \frac{\partial^2 L}{\partial \mu \partial x_2}$. The bordered Hessian consists of the Hessian matrix of the Lagrangian (the matrix of second derivatives of the Lagrangian with respect to the choice variables), 'bordered' on top by *row* vectors $L_{\lambda j}$, $L_{\mu j}$ $(j=\lambda, \mu, 1, 2, 3)$ and on the left by *column* vectors $L_{i\lambda}$, L_{ih} $(i=\lambda, \mu, 1, 2, 3)$ that are the transposes of those row vectors, as follows:

$$
\begin{bmatrix}
L_{\lambda\lambda} & L_{\lambda\mu} & L_{\lambda 1} & L_{\lambda 2} & L_{\lambda 3} \\
L_{\mu\lambda} & L_{\mu\mu} & L_{\mu 1} & L_{\mu 2} & L_{\mu 3} \\
L_{1\lambda} & L_{1\mu} & L_{11} & L_{12} & L_{13} \\
L_{2\lambda} & L_{2\mu} & L_{21} & L_{22} & L_{23} \\
L_{3\lambda} & L_{3\mu} & L_{31} & L_{32} & L_{33}
\end{bmatrix}
\equiv
\begin{bmatrix}
0 & 0 & \frac{\partial g}{\partial x_1} & \frac{\partial g}{\partial x_2} & \frac{\partial g}{\partial x_3} \\
0 & 0 & \frac{\partial h}{\partial x_1} & \frac{\partial h}{\partial x_2} & \frac{\partial h}{\partial x_3} \\
\frac{\partial g}{\partial x_1} & \frac{\partial h}{\partial x_1} & \frac{\partial^2 L}{\partial x_1^2} & \frac{\partial^2 L}{\partial x_1 \partial x_2} & \frac{\partial^2 L}{\partial x_1 \partial x_3} \\
\frac{\partial g}{\partial x_2} & \frac{\partial h}{\partial x_2} & \frac{\partial^2 L}{\partial x_2 \partial x_1} & \frac{\partial^2 L}{\partial x_2^2} & \frac{\partial^2 L}{\partial x_2 \partial x_3} \\
\frac{\partial g}{\partial x_3} & \frac{\partial h}{\partial x_3} & \frac{\partial^2 L}{\partial x_3 \partial x_1} & \frac{\partial^2 L}{\partial x_3 \partial x_2} & \frac{\partial^2 L}{\partial x_3^2}
\end{bmatrix}.
$$

It is an easy exercise to show that the border terms are indeed as shown by the right-hand matrix. The bordered Hessian matrix is therefore composed of four submatrices; on the main diagonal there is first a square matrix of zeros of dimension equal to the number of constraints, and then a square matrix $[L_{ij}]$ which is the Hessian of the Lagrangian with respect to the choice variables,

1380   **Chapter 15 · Mathematical Review**

with typical element $\frac{\partial^2 L}{\partial x_i \partial x_j} = \frac{\partial}{\partial x_i}\left[\frac{\partial f}{\partial x_j} + \lambda \frac{\partial g}{\partial x_j} + \mu \frac{\partial h}{\partial x_j}\right]$; above this Hessian there is the Jacobian of the constraints; and to the left of the same Hessian there is the transpose of that Jacobian. The second-order condition sufficient for $\mathbf{x}^*$ to be a maximum is the following:

Let n be the number of choice variables and let k be the number of equality constraints. Neglect the first 2 k naturally ordered (or leading, or North-West) principal minors; the last n–k naturally ordered principal minors of the bordered Hessian must alternate in sign, starting from $(-1)^{k+1}$.[13]

So one must neglect the first 2k North-West principal minors, and the signs of the successive ones must alternate, starting with positive if the constraints are odd in number, with negative if the constraints are even in number: in the case shown above with three variables and two constraints, the only relevant principal minor is the last one which coincides with the determinant of the entire bordered Hessian; it must be negative because there are two constraints.

When the constraints are inequality constraints, and the necessary first-order Kuhn–Tucker conditions are satisfied at $\mathbf{x}^*$, the second-order sufficient condition for a local maximum remains the same, except that the constraints to take into account are only the ones binding at $\mathbf{x}^*$; this is because the slack constraints pose no limitation to the possible direction of movement away from $\mathbf{x}^*$ (in a sufficiently small neighbourhood of $\mathbf{x}^*$).

I illustrate by applying the above to the problem of maximizing utility in the Marshallian two-goods case. The Lagrangian is $L = f(x_1, x_2) + \lambda(m - p_1 x_1 - p_2 x_2)$. *Assuming an interior solution*, there is only one principal minor to consider, the determinant of the entire 3×3 bordered Hessian. The first-order necessary conditions are:

$$L_1 = f_1 - \lambda_{P1} = 0$$
$$L_2 = f_2 - \lambda_{P2} = 0$$
$$L_\lambda = g(x) = m - p_1 x_1 - p_2 x_2 = 0.$$

The second-order sufficient condition is that the determinant of the bordered Hessian be positive; that is, remembering that $f_{21} = f_{12}$, it must be [14]

$$2p_1 p_2 f_{12} - p_1^2 f_{22} - p_2^2 f_{11} > 0.$$

This may seem unhelpful because depending on prices, but it can be reduced to a condition on the shape of $f(\mathbf{x})$ by using the first-order conditions: these allow replacing p_1 with f_1/λ and p_2 with f_2/λ, obtaining $\left[2f_1 f_2 f_{12} - f_1^2 f_{22} - f_2^2 f_{11}\right]/\lambda^2 > 0$; the λ^2 is positive, so the numerator must be positive. The expression we arrive at, more often written as:

$$f_{11}f_2^2 - 2f_{12}f_1 f_2 + f_{22}f_1^2 < 0, \tag{15.11}$$

---

13 If the problem is one of minimization, it suffices to multiply the maximand function by (–1) to obtain a maximization problem, to which this condition can be applied. For more on optimization see, e.g., Beavis and Dobbs (1990, Chaps. 1, 2, and 4), or Dixit (1990).

14 If the budget constraint is to have the form $g(\cdot) \geq 0$, then it must be formulated as $m - p_1 x_1 - p_2 x_2 \geq 0$. The reader can check that this is the version that generates first-order conditions implying $\lambda > 0$.

15.7 · Linear Programming and Duality

characterizes strictly quasi-concave increasing functions of two variables when these are twice continuously differentiable, as I proceed to show. Assume $f(x_1,x_2)$ is an increasing strictly quasi-concave function: its level curves are strictly convex, so if at $\mathbf{x}^*$ one considers the straight line tangent to the level curve through $\mathbf{x}^*$, then moving in either direction along this line, which means $dx_2/dx_1 = -f_1/f_2$ and $f_1(\mathbf{x}^*)dx_1 + f2(\mathbf{x}^*)dx_2 = 0$, one crosses level curves corresponding to lower and lower values of $f(\mathbf{x})$. This requires that, as one keeps moving away from $\mathbf{x}^*$ along that line, the variation df, which is zero at $\mathbf{x}^*$, becomes negative;[15] so it must be $d^2f < 0$. From $d^2f = f_{11}dx_1^2 + 2f_{12}dx_1dx_2 + f_{22}dx_2^2 < 0$ and from the constraint that it must be $dx_2/dx_1 = -f_1/f_2$ it is easy to arrive at expression [15.11].

15.7 Linear Programming and Duality

Linear programming studies a special case of the general problem of constrained maximization, the case in which both the constraints and the objective function are linear in the variables to be determined $x_1,...,x_n$ and furthermore $x_i \geq 0$, $\forall i$. The problem is therefore a problem with n variables (called *control variables*) and k constraints (besides the non-negativity constraints):

$$\max_{x_1,...,x_n} b_1x_1 + ... + b_nx_n$$

$$s.t.\ a_{11}x_1 + ... + a_{1n}x_n \leq c_1$$
$$a_{21}x_1 + ... + a_{2n}x_n \leq c_2$$
$$.........................$$
$$a_{k1}x_1 + ... + a_{kn}x_n \leq c_k$$
$$x_i \geq 0, i = 1,...,n.$$

In matrix terms, the problem is

$$\max_x \mathbf{bx} \quad s.t. \quad \mathbf{Ax} \leq \mathbf{c}, \mathbf{x} \geq 0$$

where $\mathbf{x}$ is a column n-vector and $\mathbf{A}$ is a $k \times n$ matrix. One can associate to this problem, which is called the **primal** problem, another linear programming problem called the **dual** of the primal problem, with k variables and n constraints. Let $\mathbf{y}$ be a row k-vector, then the problem, for brevity directly in matrix form, is:

$$Min_y \mathbf{yc} \quad s.t. \quad \mathbf{yA} \geq \mathbf{b}, \mathbf{y} \geq 0.$$

(One might also call primal this second problem, and then the first one would be its dual: thus each is dual to the other.) The **duality theorem of linear programming** states that if $\mathbf{x}$ solves the primal problem and $\mathbf{y}$ solves the dual problem, then $\mathbf{bx} = \mathbf{yc}$. In other words, if the *maximum* value V reached by the objective

---

15 Note that if f(x) is a decreasing quasiconcave function, the same result must hold because then level curves are concave.

function in the primal is $V = \mathbf{bx}$, then V is also the *minimum* value of the objective function $\mathbf{yc}$ in the dual. There are therefore two different ways to characterize the value V: as generated by the solution to a maximization problem, or as generated by the solution to a minimization problem strictly connected with the maximization problem.

The term 'duality', originally proposed in the theory of linear programming, has become used in microeconomics in a broader sense suggested by the last consideration. Two functions, usually one a function of quantities and the other of prices, are considered dual to each other if they represent two different ways of describing the same 'object': a set, or an ordered set, or a function, or a maximum value. This is the case, for example, for the utility function $u(\mathbf{x})$ and the expenditure function associated with it $e(\mathbf{p},u)$: as shown in ▶ Chap. 4, under certain assumptions a given expenditure function is said dual to the utility function from which it derives because it contains the same information about the consumer's preferences as the utility function. The same holds for utility function and indirect utility function, as shown, again, by the fact that either function can be derived from the other; so they too are said dual to each other. For the same reason one also speaks of duality between utility function and the Marshallian vectorial demand function derived from it: the utility function can be recovered from the latter function. Similar dualities exist in the theory of the firm between production function, cost function, profit function (when it exists), and derived factor demands.

There is the general mathematical theory of *Fenchel duality* behind this terminology. The interested reader can get a taste of it from Mas-Colell et al. (1995, pp. 63–67), and from the entries 'duality' and 'convex programming', both by L. Blume, in *The New Palgrave Dictionary of Economics, 2nd edition.*

15.8 Complex Numbers

The field C of complex numbers can be thought of as the set R^2 of all possible couples (x_1, x_2) of real numbers, enriched with further operations. A complex number is then a (row) vector $\mathbf{x} \in R^2$; the first element is called *real part*, the second element *imaginary part*. The field of complex numbers is treated as an enlargement of the field of real numbers by assimilating each vector $(x_i, 0)$ to the real number $x_i \in R$.

Equality, sum and difference between two complex numbers are defined in the same way as for vectors. The *multiplication* of two complex numbers $\mathbf{x} = (x_1, x_2)$ and $\mathbf{y} = (y_1, y_2)$ is on the contrary defined not as the dot product but as

$$\mathbf{xy} = (x_1 y_1 - x_2 y_2, x_1 y_2 + x_2 y_1).$$

This can also be obtained by agreeing to write any complex number (x_1, x_2) as

$$x_1 + ix_2$$

15.8 · Complex Numbers

where the symbol i is called the **imaginary unit**, and by agreeing to operate on these expressions according to the usual algebraic rules with only the special addition that $i^2 = -1$. Then

$$(x_1 + ix_2)(y_2 + iy_2) = x_1y_1 + ix_1y_2 + ix_2y_1 + i^2x_2y_2 = (x_1y_1 - x_2y_2) + i(x_1y_2 + x_2y_1).$$

This way of writing complex numbers can be justified in vectorial terms by interpreting the imaginary unit as the vector $(0,1)$ and interpreting any real number x, when one operates in the complex field, as equivalent to the complex number $(x,0)$; the multiplication rule specified above implies, with the symbol $\otimes$ indicating complex-number multiplication:

$$ix = (0,1) \otimes (x,0) = (0,x);$$

then $x_1 + ix_2 = (x_1,0) + (0,x_2) = (x_1,x_2)$. Also, x_1x_2, the product of two real numbers, in the complex field means $(x_1,0) \otimes (x_2,0) = (x_1x_2,0)$ and it remains interpretable as a real number. The writing of any complex number as the sum of two complex numbers, one with no imaginary part and one with no real part, is what allows operating on complex numbers with the usual rules of elementary algebra, plus $i^2 = -1$.

The convention that $i^2 = -1$ is no arbitrary trick, it derives from the definitions and the rule for multiplication. Indeed

$$i^2 = i \otimes i = (0,1) \otimes (0,1) = (-1,0).$$

Thus in the complex field -1 does have a square root, and then all negative real numbers do, because $-x = (-1)x = (-1,0) \otimes (x,0)$ and its square root is $i\sqrt{x}$ because $(i\sqrt{x})^2 = i^2(\sqrt{x})^2$. This means that when the solution of a real equation of degree two or higher implies square roots of negative numbers, no real solution exists, but a solution may exist if one reinterprets the equation as dealing with complex numbers. Indeed the following central result concerning polynomial equations of complex numbers is the **Fundamental Theorem of Algebra**:

The equation $\lambda^n + a_1\lambda^{n-1} + a_2\lambda^{n-2} + \ldots + a_{n-1}\lambda + a_n = 0$, with $a_1,\ldots,a_n \in C$ (which includes as a special case $a_1,\ldots,a_n \in R$) has, in C, n (possibly repeated) roots; that is, there exist n numbers $\lambda_1, \ldots, \lambda_n \in C$, not necessarily distinct, such that

$$\lambda^n + a_1\lambda^{n-1} + a_2\lambda^{n-2} + \ldots + a_{n-1}\lambda + a_n = (\lambda - \lambda_1)(\lambda - \lambda_2)\ldots(\lambda - \lambda_n).$$

Given a complex number $x + iy$, its **conjugate** is the complex number $x - iy$ (and the first is the conjugate of the second). The product of a complex number with its conjugate is a real number, $(x + iy)(x - iy) = x^2 + y^2$. Complex roots of polynomial equations with real coefficients come in conjugate couples.

Complex numbers can also be represented in *trigonometric form* and in *exponential form*. These forms are not explained here because not necessary for this textbook, but they are indispensable for the analysis of systems of differential or difference equations.

I add two elementary results on algebraic equations. The second-degree equation in standard form

$$ax^2 + bx + c = 0$$

1384   **Chapter 15 · Mathematical Review**

has real or complex solutions $x_1 = \frac{-b+\sqrt{b^2-4ac}}{2a}$, $x_2 = \frac{-b-\sqrt{b^2-4ac}}{2a}$. If the coefficients are all real but $b^2-4ac < 0$, the solutions are complex conjugate.

The third-degree equation in standard form

$$ax^3 + bx^2 + cx + d = 0$$

has real or complex solutions p, q, r that satisfy:

$$p + q + r = -b/a$$
$$pq + qr + rp = c/a$$
$$pqr = -d/a.$$

These three conditions do not immediately offer the solutions but allow more easily to reach them, for example two solutions allow determining the third.

15.9 Integrals

Given a continuous function of one variable $f(x)$, suppose that between x_0 and $x_1 > x_0$ it is $f(x) > 0$. The area below the graph of $f(x)$ down to the abscissa over that interval is called the (Riemann) **definite integral** of $f(x)$ between x_0 and x_1 and is indicated as $\int_{x_0}^{x_1} f(x)dx$. If x_1 is replaced by $x_2 > x_1$, then $\int_{x_0}^{x_2} f(x)dx = \int_{x_0}^{x_1} f(x)dx + \int_{x_1}^{x_2} f(x)dx$. If over the chosen interval it is $f(x) < 0$ and therefore the area is *below* the abscissa, the area is measured as a negative number. If over the chosen interval $f(x)$ is partly positive and partly negative, the integral of $f(x)$ over that interval is the algebraic sum of the positive and the negative areas (hence a zero definite integral does not necessarily mean that $f(x) = 0$ over the entire interval $[x_0, x_1]$).Given $f(x)$ and a point x_0, the definite integral $\int_{x_0}^{x_1} f(x)dx$ changes with x_1, increasing or decreasing as x_1 increases depending on whether it is $f(x) > 0$ or $f(x) < 0$. Therefore it can be seen as a function of x_1. If $x_1 < x_0$ then the definite integral is $-\int_{x_1}^{x_0} f(x)dx$. The function $F(x_1) = \int_{x_0}^{x_1} f(x)dx$ is called *a primitive* of $f(x)$. A primitive, not *the* primitive, because if one chooses a different point x_0' one obtains another primitive, equal to $F(x_1) + \int_{x_0'}^{x_0} f(x)dx$ which can be written $F(x_1) + C$, with the scalar C a constant. By changing C, one obtains all the primitives of $f(x)$. Note that all primitives of $f(x)$ have the same derivative with respect to x_1. It is usual to indicate the x_1 at the top of the integral simply as x, and then, to avoid confusion, to indicate the variable which determines the value of the integral by varying from x_0 to x_1 with a different symbol, e.g. t: then $F(x) = \int_{x_0}^{x} f(t)dt$. Having chosen a point x_0 one obtains two functions of x, $f(x)$ and its primitive $F(x)$ that takes value zero at $x = x_0$. The Fundamental Theorem of Calculus states that these two functions are intimately connected: the derivative of $F(x)$ is $f(x)$ for all points of the closed interval over which f(x) is defined. Note that this result implies that a continuous $f(x)$ need not be differentiable, but nevertheless has primitives which are differentiable. Also note that the result implies that, whichever the chosen primitive of $f(x)$, it is

$$\int_{x_0}^{x_1} f(x)dx = F(x_1) - F(x_0). \tag{15.12}$$

Indeed the choice of another primitive changes the right-hand side of this equality to $F(x_1) + C - F(x_0) - C = F(x_1) - F(x_0)$. And equality (15.12) becomes evident if you think of $F(x)$ as chosen so as to take value zero in $x_0^* < x_0$; then $F(x_0) = \int_{x_{0*}}^{x_0} f(x)dx$, $F(x_1) = \int_{x_{0*}}^{x_1} f(x)dx$. and therefore by the addition rule for definite integrals $F(x_1) = F(x_0) + \int_{x_0}^{x_1} f(x)dx$.

15.10 Probability and Statistics

Given a sample space S of (mutually exclusive) basic outcomes, the probability of an outcome is a measure of how likely it is that that outcome will occur when one conducts a random trial. An *event* A is a subset of S, hence a collection of basic outcomes; an event occurs when one of its outcomes occurs. For example at a roulette draw the basic outcomes are (for European roulette) the 37 integers from 0 to 36, the event 'an odd number' occurs if any odd number different from 0 comes out. The probability of an event is the sum of the probabilities of the basic outcomes composing the event. Pr(A) is therefore the probability that a random trial 'extracts' any one of the basic outcomes in subset A. Two events A and B can be mutually exclusive, or partially overlap, or one can be a subset of the other. Let us remember that, for sets, A∪B (the union of A and B) means the set of points that are elements of A or of B or of both; A∩B (the intersection of A and B) means the set of points that are elements both of A and of B.

Probability is assumed to satisfy

(1) $\Pr(A) \geq 0$.
(2) if the set of events $A_1, A_2, \ldots, A_K$ consists of mutually exclusive events then
$\Pr(A_1, A_2, \ldots, A_k) = \Pr(A_1) + \Pr(A_2) + \ldots + \Pr(A_K)$.
(3) $\Pr(A = S) = 1$.
These postulates imply many properties among which
(4) $\Pr(\neg A) = 1 - \Pr(A)$ where $\neg A$, also indicated as notA, means 'event A has not occurred', that is, the basic outcome that has occurred is not an element of A so it is an element of the *complement* of A in S, the set of all elements of S that are not in A, which is sometimes indicated as S\A.
(5) an impossible event (an event none of whose basic outcomes is in S) has probability zero; this is denoted by $\Pr(\emptyset) = 0$.
(6) $\Pr(A \cup B) = \Pr(A) + \Pr(B) - \Pr(A \cap B)$.
(7) If the set of events $A_1, A_2, \ldots, A_k, \ldots, A_K$ *partitions* the sample space (i.e. if these events are mutually incompatible and their union is the sample space), then for any event B it is $\sum_k \Pr(B \cap A_k) = \Pr(B)$. In particular this implies $\Pr(A \cap B) + \Pr(\neg A \cap B) = \Pr(B)$.

Conditional probability. If it is known that event B has a probability $\Pr(B) > 0$ of occurring, the probability that event A occurs in a random trial in which B occurs is called the probability of A conditional on B occurring, and it is given by

(8) $\Pr(A|B) = \frac{\Pr(A \cap B)}{\Pr(A \cap B) + \Pr(\neg A \cap B)} = \frac{\Pr(A \cap B)}{\Pr(B)}$.

1386 **Chapter 15 · Mathematical Review**

The denominator on the right-hand side can also be $\sum_k \Pr(B \cap A_k)$, from (7).

Bayes' theorem (Bayes' Rule). *If A and B are two events with $Pr(A) > 0$ and $Pr(B) > 0$ then*

(9) $\Pr(A|B) = \frac{\Pr(B|A)\Pr(A)}{\Pr(B|A)\Pr(A) + \Pr(B|\neg A)\Pr(\neg A)}$.

■■ **Proof**

Given the symmetry of A and B in $\Pr(A \cap B)$, (8) implies

$$\Pr(A \cap B) = \Pr(A|B)\Pr(B) = \Pr(B|A)\Pr(A) \Rightarrow \Pr(A|B) = \frac{\Pr(B|A)\Pr(A)}{\Pr(B)}$$

which is almost the theorem. With A_k in place of A we have $\Pr(A_k \cap B) = \Pr(B \mid A_k)\Pr(A_k)$ and we obtain from (7)

$$\Pr(B) = \sum_k \Pr(B \cap A_k) = \Pr(B|A_1)\Pr(A_1) + \ldots + \Pr(B|A_K)\Pr(A_K).$$

This, if S is partitioned into A and $\neg A$, yields the denominator in (9). Actually the proof shows that the denominator in (9) can also be $\sum_k [\Pr(B \mid A_k)\Pr(A_k)]$ for any partition $A_1, \ldots, A_K$ of S; this is sometimes useful in applications.■

Independence. Two events A and B are **independent** if the observation of the realization of one of them gives no indication about the probability of realization of the other. Formally, they are said independent if any of the following is satisfied:

$\Pr(A|B) = \Pr(A)$
$\Pr(B|A) = \Pr(B)$
$\Pr(A \cap B) = \Pr(A)\Pr(B)$.

Independence cannot hold if A and B are subsets of the same sample space in a single random trial: for example, if A and B have no point in common, then the occurrence of A means B cannot have occurred, so $\Pr(B \mid A) = 0 \neq \Pr(B)$. But consider the following random trial: blindly extract one ball from a bowl with 10 white and 10 black balls in it, while a friend blindly extracts one ball from a second bowl with 10 white balls and 50 black balls, and call A the extraction of a white ball from the first bowl and B the extraction of a white ball from the second bowl. In this case the probability of A is clearly independent from the probability of B.

Random variables. A **random variable** X is a function or rule that assigns a real number to each basic outcome in a sample space S on which a probability distribution is defined. Repeated random trials can be performed on this sample space, causing basic outcomes to occur with probabilities determined by that probability distribution,[16] and this causes the values of the random variable to be observa-

---

16 I am adopting here the frequentist interpretation of probability, the most easily understandable one, which says that the probability of an event is 20% if in 1000 trials in identical conditions the event happens very nearly 200 times. The reader must turn elsewhere for discussion of the various interpretations of probability. However, in ▶ Chap. 9 some introduction is given to the subjective interpretation.

15.10 · Probability and Statistics

ble with a probability distribution derivable from the first one. Attention will be concentrated here directly on this second probability distribution, which assigns probabilities to the occurrence of the several values the random variable can take, neglecting how these probabilities derive from the probabilities of occurrence of the basic outcomes in the sample space and from the connection between the occurrence of these basic outcomes and the values taken by the random variable. Then a random variable is simply a variable whose values are associated with a probability of being observed.

A *discrete* random variable takes on a finite or denumerable[17] number of distinct values, say (leaving aside the denumerable case) K values, which can be indexed in order of increasing magnitude, $x_1, \ldots, x_k, \ldots, x_K$. Capital-letter symbols are generally used to refer to samples resulting from random extractions, $X = x$ means one extraction produced value x. The symbol X is also used to indicate the entire random variable.

The **probability distribution** or **probability mass function** or *discrete density* of a discrete random variable that can take K values assigns a probability to each x_k, the sum of these probabilities being 1. It can be denoted $\psi(x_k) = Prob(X = x_k)$, $k = 1, \ldots, K$. Sometimes for brevity the expression $Prob(X = x_k)$ is abbreviated to $Pr(x_k)$.

The **cumulative probability distribution** of a discrete random variable indicates for each x_k the probability that $X \leq x_k$. Having numbered the possible values in order of increasing magnitude, the cumulative probability distribution for each x_k is equal to $Pr(x_1) + Pr(x_2) + \ldots + Pr(x_{k-1}) + Pr(x_k)$.

A *continuous* random variable can take any value on the real line or on a specified portion of the real line. The probability distribution of a continuous random variable yields the probability that X assumes a value within an interval; usually it is *non-atomic*, that is, it assigns a positive probability only to intervals, not to single values of X; the probability that a random extraction of a value of X precisely equals a certain real number is assumed to be zero.

Given a random variable X, let $f(x)$ be a continuous function such that the probability that X falls between two values $x = u$ and $x = v > u$ equals the area under the graph of the function between those values, i.e. equals the definite integral of f between u and v. That is,

$$Pr(u \leq X \leq v) = \int_u^v f(x)dx.$$

The function $f(x)$ is called the **probability density function**, or for brevity the *density*, of the continuous random variable X. The graph of the probability density function is called the **density curve**.

A function $F(x)$, everywhere continuously differentiable, which gives the probability that a continuous random variable X will assume a value less than or

---

17 This is synonymous with *countable*.

1388   Chapter 15 · Mathematical Review

equal to each number x is called the **cumulative density function** or, more often, the **distribution function** of X. That is,

$$F(x) = \Pr(X \le x) = \int_{-\infty}^{x} f(t)dt.$$

$F(x)$ is a primitive of $f(x)$, therefore $dF(x)/dx = f(x)$.

Be careful not to confuse the terms 'probability distribution' or 'probability function' referred to a *discrete* random variable, which are not cumulative unless the adjective 'cumulative' is explicitly prefixed to them, with the term 'distribution function' which refers to a continuous random variable and is cumulative.

The **median** of a random variable X is the number m satisfying the two conditions

$$\Pr(X < m) \le 1/2; \quad \Pr(X > m) \le 1/2.$$

Half the values assumed by X over a great number of random trials are expected to be larger and half smaller than m.

The **mode** is the value of X associated with the largest probability, for X discrete, or associated with the highest point of the density curve (if this point is unique), for X continuous.

The **mean** or **expected value** μ_X or $E(X)$ of a random variable is the *average* value one can expect from random trials repeated many times:

$$E(X) = \sum_{k=1}^{K} x_k \Pr(x_k) - \text{For a discrete random variable}$$

$$E(X) = \int_{-\infty}^{+\infty} xf(x)dx = \int_{-\infty}^{+\infty} xdF(x) - \text{For a continuous random variable.}$$

The expected value of a function g(X) of the random variable X is

$$E(g(X)) = \int_{-\infty}^{+\infty} g(x)f(x)dx.$$

$E(X^r)$ is called the rth **moment** of X about the origin.

$E\left[(X - \mu_X)^r\right]$ is called the rth **moment of X about the mean.**

The **variance** of a random variable, indicated as var(X) or as σ_X^2, is a measure of how dispersed the values of X obtained by repeated random trials tend to be. Its definition is

$$\text{var}(X) \equiv \sigma^2 x = \sum_k \left[(x_k - E(X))^2 \Pr(x_k)\right] - \text{For a discrete random variable.}$$

$$\text{var}(X) \equiv \sigma_X^2 = \int_{-\infty}^{+\infty} (x - E(X))^2 f(x)dx - \text{For a continuous random variable.}$$

Alternative equivalent expressions for the variance of X:

(i) $\text{var}(X) = E\left[(X - E(X))^2\right]$, that is, var(X) is the second moment of X about the mean.

(ii) $\text{var}(X) = E\left(X^2\right) - [E(X)]^2$ and therefore $= \int_{-\infty}^{+\infty} x^2 dF(x) - (E(X))^2$ for a continuous X.

By definition var(X) is non-negative, and zero only if X is constant. This can be confirmed by taking expression (ii) and using **Jensen's Inequality**, which states: *If*

X is a non-constant random variable and $f(X)$ is a strictly concave function of X, then $E[f(X)] < f(E[X])$. Indeed take $f(X)$ to be $-X^2$, and then multiply by -1 both sides of $E(-X^2) < -(E(X))^2$ to obtain $E(X^2) > [E(X)]^2$.

The **standard deviation** of a random variable X, indicated as σ_X, is the positive square root of var(X).

The calculation of the variance squares the deviations from the mean so as to avoid positive and negative deviations cancelling one another, but in this way it measures the average dispersion in a unit different from the unit in which the random variable is measured, for example if X is measured in kilograms the variance indicates the dispersion not in kg's but in squared kg's; the standard deviation avoids this defect.

Given two random variables X and Y, a **joint probability distribution** for discrete variables indicates the probability $\Pr(X = x_k, Y = y_j)$, for brevity $\Pr(x_k, y_j)$, that the values taken by the two random variables correspond to the couple (x_k, y_j); a **joint density function** for continuous variables tells us the probability that X is in a certain interval at the same time that Y is in another interval of the real line: the probability, that is, that the point (x, y) be in a certain rectangle in the (x, y) plane.

The **covariance** cov(X,Y) or σ_{XY} of two random variables X and Y is defined by

$$\text{cov}(X, Y) = E[(X - E(X))(Y - E(Y))] = E(XY) - E(X)E(Y).$$

In the last expression, the expectation $E(XY)$ of a product of two discrete random variables X and Y which can take respectively K and J values $x_1, \ldots, x_k, \ldots, x_K$ and $y_1, \ldots, y_j, \ldots, y_J$ is:

$$E(X, Y) = \sum_{x_k = x_1}^{x_K} \sum_{y_j = y_1}^{y_J} x_k y_j \Pr(x_k, y_j).$$

Analogously the covariance is determined as

$$\sigma_{XY} = \sum_{x_k = x_1}^{x_K} \sum_{y_j = y_1}^{y_J} (x_k - \mu_X)(y_j - \mu_Y) \Pr(x_k, y_j).$$

The covariance of two continuous random variables is determined by a double integral, see Chap. 9, ▶ Sect. 9.17.

A positive covariance indicates that when X takes values above the mean, the couples of values (x, y) in which Y too takes values above its mean tend to have higher probability than those in which Y takes values below the mean, and the same holds with 'above' replacing 'below' and 'below' replacing 'above'; so it is more probable that high (in the sense of above mean) values of X be observed together with high rather than with low values of Y, and low values of X together with low values of Y. A negative covariance means that it is more probable that high values of X be observed together with low rather than high values of Y.

If X and Y are independent then cov(X,Y)=0; the converse need not hold, the covariance between two non-independent variables can be zero.

1390   Chapter 15 · Mathematical Review

A useful connection between var(aX + bY) and cov(X,Y) is the following:

$$\text{var}(aX + bY) = a^2\text{var}(X) + b^2\text{var}(Y) + 2ab\,\text{cov}(X, Y).$$

The *correlation coefficient* is another measure of the direction and degree of dependence between two random variables; it is defined as

$$\rho(X, Y) = \frac{\text{cov}(X, Y)}{\sigma_X \sigma_Y}.$$

The correlation coefficient takes values between -1 and $+1$; relative to the covariance it has the advantage that, similarly to elasticity, it is unaffected by changes in the units used to measure the variables, while the magnitude of the covariance depends on the units.

Now the definition of two frequently used continuous probability distributions:

The *uniform (or rectangular) continuous probability distribution* has a constant density $f(x) > 0$ over a finite interval, say from $x=a$ to $x=b > a$, and $f(x)=0$ outside this interval. The area under $f(x)$ between a and b must be 1; it is a rectangle with basis $b - a$, hence $f(x) = 1/(b-a)$ for $a \leq x \leq b$, and is zero elsewhere.

The (continuous) *normal distribution* has density function

$$f(x) = \frac{1}{\sqrt{2\pi\sigma^2}} \exp\left[-\frac{1}{2}\left(\frac{x - \mu}{\sigma}\right)^2\right].$$

The symbols are justified by the fact that μ comes out to be indeed the mean of the distribution, and σ its standard deviation. The *standard or normalized form* of the normal distribution's density uses the transformation $y = (x - \mu)/\sigma$, which means to put $\mu = 0$ and $\sigma = \sigma^2 = 1$, so the density is

$$f(y) = \frac{1}{\sqrt{2\pi}} e^{-y^2/2}.$$

The density function of the normal distribution does not integrate into a simple closed expression of elementary functions. In spite of the formal complications thus arising, this function is central to statistics. One reason is the *central-limit theorem*, which states the following: given *any* density function $f(x)$ with finite variance, if from $f(x)$ by random trials one forms random samples of size n, then the sample mean M_n, which is itself a random variable, has a distribution that approaches the normal the more, the greater is n.

Law of large numbers. If we have a population with a measurable characteristic (e.g. weight) which is a random variable X with a probability distribution to be ascertained, an exact determination of E(X) would require ascertaining the entire empirical distribution of the values of X in the population, which would require either a totally exhaustive survey (impossible if the population is infinite), or an infinity of random trials (if one accepts the frequentist interpretation of probability). In any real-world problem we can observe only a finite sample of

15.10 · Probability and Statistics

values of X. The *law of large numbers* confirms the feeling that the larger the random sample, the more certain we can be that the sample mean is a good estimate of the population mean. In its so-called *weak* form the law states that, *given a random variable with density f(x) and mean μ, for any two chosen small numbers ε and δ where $\varepsilon > 0$ and $0 < \delta < 1$ there exists an integer n such that if a random sample of size n or larger is obtained from f(x), and the sample mean M_n is computed, then the probability is greater than $1 - \delta$ (and therefore as close to 1 as desired) that M_n deviates from μ by less than ε.* This can also be put as follows: $lim_{n \to \infty} Pr(|M_n - \mu| > \varepsilon) = 0$. In its form called the *strong law of large numbers*, it states that *as the number of trials composing the sample goes to infinity, the probability that the average of the observations converges to the expected value is equal to one: $Pr(lim_{n \to \infty} M_n = \mu) = 1$.* Another version, called *Borel's law of large numbers*, is not about means but about occurence of an event in repeated trials: it states that if an experiment is repeated a large number of times independently and under identical conditions, then the proportion of times that any specified event occurs approximately equals the probability of the event's occurrence on any particular trial, and the larger the number of repetitions, the better the approximation tends to be.

Order statistics. Suppose random trials produce a sample of numbers (e.g. weights of captured birds, prices of a good at random dates, roulette extractions). Having ordered the numbers in the sample from the smallest to the greatest, the kth *order statistic* of this statistical sample is its kth smallest value. Thus if a sample is composed of n numbers, the nth or highest order statistic is the greatest number in the sample. Chap. 11, ▶ Sect. 11.33, contains a derivation of the distribution function, density and expected value of the nth order statistic of a sample of n numbers drawn from a uniform distribution.

15.11 Poisson Process

A Poisson process describes a succession of discrete events on the time real line, where the average time between the arrival of events is known, but the exact timing of events is random, and the arrival of an event is independent of the time when the previous event happened (waiting time between events is *memoryless*). For example, statistical evidence might show that the number of ambulance calls per month in a region is remarkably constant, say 4320, but it is impossible to predict when exactly each ambulance call happens, and each ambulance call is the result of a history largely independent of the history of other ambulance calls (this implies I am excluding, for example, increases of ambulance calls on Saturday nights because of more car accidents); it seems reasonable to suppose the ambulance calls to be randomly distributed in the month, therefore on average 144 per day, or 1 every ten minutes. This is the average time between events, but the events are randomly spaced so it is impossible to predict with certainty the time between two successive events.

1392   Chapter 15 · Mathematical Review

A (stationary) Poisson process with rate lambda satisfies the following conditions:

(a) events are independent of each other; the occurrence of an event at time t does not affect the probability that another event will occur in a time interval $(t, t + \Delta t)$;

(b) the average rate of arrival of events per unit time period, λ, is constant; that is, the expected number of arrivals in any time interval of length T is λT;

(c) two events cannot occur at the same time.

(The rate λ may be a non-constant function of time, $\lambda(t)$, then the Poisson process is not stationary; turn to textbooks on probability models, e.g. Ross (2010), for this extension and for a more complete presentation.) The probability of a given number X of events per unitary time period, Prob (X), is determined by the Poisson Distribution probability mass function

$$\text{Prob}(X) = e^{-\lambda} \cdot \frac{\lambda^X}{X!}$$

where the symbol $n!$, pronounced n **factorial**, stands for the product of the first n integers, hence $X! = 1 \cdot 2 \cdot 3 \cdot \ldots \cdot (X-1) \cdot X$. It is useful to be aware that $n!$ increases *very* rapidly with n: $3! = 6$, $4! = 24$, $5! = 120$, $6! = 720$, $10! = 3{,}628{,}800$. If the length of the unit time period is changed, λ changes in the same proportion. So in the previous example we can calculate the probability of having 2 ambulance calls in an interval of 10 min by setting $\lambda = 1$, $X = 2$, and we find $\text{Prob}(2) = \frac{1}{2e} \approx 0.18$.

Suppose you start observing a Poisson process at time 0. The probability of having to wait a time T greater than an assigned t before observing an event is given by

$$\text{Prob}\,(T > t) = e^{-\lambda t}.$$

Therefore the probability of waiting less than or equal to an assigned time length y is given by

$$\text{Prob}\,(T \leq y) = 1 - e^{-ty}.$$

In other words, the duration T it is necessary to wait starting from a date t for an event X to occur is a random variable having an exponential cumulative distribution function defined by

$$F(y; t) \equiv \text{Prob}\{T(t) \leq y\} = 1 - e^{-\int_{t}^{1+y} \lambda(\xi)d\xi} = 1 - e^{-ty}$$

because $\lambda(t)$ is a constant, I am assuming the Poisson process is stationary. The corresponding probability density function of the random variable $T(t)$ is

$$f_t(y) = F_t'(y) = \lambda(t + y)e^{-\int_{t}^{t+y} \lambda(\xi)d\xi} = \lambda e^{-\lambda y}.$$

This corresponds to λ if we let y go to zero; hence λ is interpreted as the instantaneous probability of the arrival of event X at date t.

15.11 · Poisson Process

The unconditional expectation $E(T)$ of the random variable T is the *average* duration it is necessary to wait, starting from the date when one starts observing the Poisson process, for event X to occur. It is

$$E(T) = \int_0^\infty y\lambda e^{-\lambda y} dy = 1/\lambda.$$

Therefore if the arrival of an event causes a change of state, $1/\lambda$ represents the average duration of the state in which one starts before event X changes it. If, for example, λ represents the constant instantaneous probability that an unemployed person finds a job, and the time unit is the week, then λ is the probability that the person finds a job in the unit time period, i.e. in one week, $\lambda\Delta t$ is the probability that the person finds a job in the time interval Δt, and $1/\lambda$ is the average duration of unemployment, measured in weeks.

As an example of a stationary Poisson process, consider a worker who is working in a job at time t; the probability that the worker is still employed in the job at some later time $t+y$ is the probability that the event 'loss of job' requires arriving at a time greater than $t+y$, i.e. waiting for a duration T longer than y, that is, if the process is Poisson with rate λ,

$$\text{Prob}(t + T > t + y) = e^{-\lambda(t+y)-t)}, \quad \lambda > 0.$$

Since $e^{-\lambda((t+y)-t)} = e^{-\lambda y}$, we are assuming that the probability that the worker is still employed at time $t+y$ is independent of the moment t from which we start measuring the duration of unemployment and depends only on how much time y has passed since that moment; in other words, that probability does not depend on how long the worker has been employed *before* t. This is the meaning of the process being memoryless.

Parameter λ can be interpreted as the instantaneous probability, which actually means the probability per time unit, that the job ends, also called the **hazard rate** for job breakup.

- **Suggested Readings**

As this chapter and the whole book make clear, advanced microeconomic theory needs, at a minimum, mastery of the calculus of functions of several variables, basic linear algebra and matrix theory up to the Perron–Frobenius theorem, basic optimization theory, introductory probability and statistics. This last field requires its own courses and I will give no suggestion on it. For the other fields, if you need just a quick reminder of a notion and you find this chapter insufficient, a look at the very clear mathematical appendix in Muñoz-Garcia (2017) or at the more advanced mathematical appendices in Mas-Colell et al. (1995) or Jehle and Reny (2011) may be enough for the mathematics of mainstream economics; the Mathematical Appendix in Kurz and Salvadori (1995) may suffice for linear algebra and matrices. If you need more mastery of the basic maths, then study a good text on calculus of several variables, e.g. Apostol *Calculus* vols. 1 and 2; for a good text on linear algebra and matrices there is less choice if one wants it to cover the Perron–Frobenius theorem too, the latter is generally not included in books of mathematics for economists, so let me suggest Heal, Hughes and Tarling (1974), simple and conceived for economists, and then the Mathematical Appendix in Kurz and Salvadori (1995). From these you can go on to textbooks in mathematical economics, from the simpler ones such as Chiang and Wainwright (2004), Wade Hands (2004), Silberberg and Suen (2000), to more advanced ones like De La Fuente (2000), Sydsaeter et al. (2005), Takayama (1994). The old encyclopaedic Akira Takayama, *Mathematical Economics* (I ed. 1974, II ed. 1985), remains a very useful reference, interesting also for the many observations on the history of notions and of debates. If you want to get closer to the frontier of research on the issues discussed in this book, you will need advanced real analysis, theory of dynamical systems, topology, advanced game theory, advanced mathematical programming and combinatorial geometry; the entries in the *New Palgrave Dictionary of Economics*, and the references in the articles and books in the field you will choose to study, will tell you which textbooks can help you best; not being myself a specialist in mathematical economics, I do not feel I am the best source for suggestions. I will only say that for non-mainstream value theory the basic mathematically advanced references are Kurz and Salvadori (1995) and Bidard (1991, 2004). Duncan Foley has been proposing an entropy-based approach to price formation which is still of uncertain value, see his web page; if it takes hold then you will also need to understand entropy. For mainstream microeconomics the chapters in the *Handbook of Mathematical Economics* (vols. 1 to 3 edited by Arrow and Intriligator, vol. 4 edited by Hildenbrand and Sonnenschein) illustrate the mathematical level at the frontier.

References

Apostol, T. M. (1969). *Calculus Volume II*, 2nd edition. New York, John Wiley & Sons.
Beavis, B., & Dobbs, I. G. (1990). *Optimization and Stability Theory for Economic Analysis*. Cambridge: Cambridge University Press.
Bidard, C. (1991). *Prix, reprduction, rareté*. Paris: Dunod.
Bidard, C. (2004). *Prices, reproduction, scarcity*. Cambridge: Cambridge University Press.
Chiang, A., & Wainwright, K. (2004). *Fundamental Methods of Mathematical Economics* (4th ed.). New York: McGraw-Hill Education.
de la Fuente, A. (2000). *Mathematical Methods and Models for Economists*. New York: Cabridge University Press.
Ellickson, B. (1993). *Competitive Equilibrium*. Cambridge: Cambridge University Press.
Heal, G., Hughes, G., & Tarling, R. (1974). *Linear algebra and linear economics*. London: Macmillan.
Jehle G. A., Reny P. J. (2011) *Advanced Microeconomic Theory*. Financial Times / Prentice Hall (Pearson), Haley, UK.
Kurz, H. D., & Salvadori, N. (1995). *Theory of production: A long-period analysis*. Cambridge: Cambridge University Press.
Mas-Colell, A., Whinston, M. D., & Green, J. R. (1995). *Microeconomic Theory*. Oxford: Oxford University Press.
Muñoz-Garcia, F. (2017). *Advanced Microeconomic Theory*. An Intuitive Approach with Examples: MIT Press, Cambridge, Mass.
Ross, S. (2010). *Introduction to probability models* (10th ed.). Salt Lake City: UT, Academic Press.

Silberberg, E., & Suen, W. (2000). *The Structure of Economics*. New York, McGraw-Hill: A Mathematical Analysis.

Sydsaeter, K., Hammond, P., Seierstad, A., & Strom, A. (2005). *Further Mathematics for Economic Analysis*. New York: Pearson Education.

Takayama, A. (1974). *Mathematical Economics*. Hinsdale, Illinois: The Dryden Press.

Takayama, A. (1994). *Analytical Methods in Economics*. Hemel Hempstead, Hert., Harvester Wheatsheaf.

Classroom Companion: Economics

The Classroom Companion series in Economics features fundamental textbooks aimed at introducing students to the core concepts, empirical methods, theories and tools of the subject. The books offer a firm foundation for students preparing to move towards advanced learning. Each book follows a clear didactic structure and presents easy adoption opportunities for lecturers.

More information about this series at ▶ http://www.springer.com/series/16375

Fabio Petri

Microeconomics for the Critical Mind

Mainstream and Heterodox Analyses

Volume 1

Fabio Petri
University of Siena
Siena, Italy

ISSN 2662-2882 ISSN 2662-2890 (electronic)
Classroom Companion: Economics
ISBN 978-3-030-62069-1 ISBN 978-3-030-62070-7 (eBook)
https://doi.org/10.1007/978-3-030-62070-7

© Springer Nature Switzerland AG 2021
This work is subject to copyright. All rights are reserved by the Publisher, whether the whole or part of the material is concerned, specifically the rights of translation, reprinting, reuse of illustrations, recitation, broadcasting, reproduction on microfilms or in any other physical way, and transmission or information storage and retrieval, electronic adaptation, computer software, or by similar or dissimilar methodology now known or hereafter developed.
The use of general descriptive names, registered names, trademarks, service marks, etc. in this publication does not imply, even in the absence of a specific statement, that such names are exempt from the relevant protective laws and regulations and therefore free for general use.
The publisher, the authors and the editors are safe to assume that the advice and information in this book are believed to be true and accurate at the date of publication. Neither the publisher nor the authors or the editors give a warranty, expressed or implied, with respect to the material contained herein or for any errors or omissions that may have been made. The publisher remains neutral with regard to jurisdictional claims in published maps and institutional affiliations.

This Springer imprint is published by the registered company Springer Nature Switzerland AG
The registered company address is: Gewerbestrasse 11, 6330 Cham, Switzerland

Preface (Mainly, But Not Only, For Teachers)

> *We should regret that the truth only progresses slowly,*
> *but it shall surely triumph at last*
> (David Ricardo, letter to *Morning Chronicle*, 4 November 1810)

This is a textbook designed for first-year graduate lecture courses in microeconomics and suitable also for last-year honours undergraduate courses. It differs from other textbooks in that it aims at supplying as correct as possible a picture of the present state of the theory of value and distribution, arguably the most important part of the usual microeconomics curriculum because it gives the general picture of the functioning of market economies, which greatly conditions nearly all analyses, also in macroeconomics, growth theory, international trade.

Current micro textbooks are highly misleading on the state of the theory of value and distribution. They introduce students only to the supply-and-demand, or neoclassical, or marginal, approach (and, most of the time, trying not to mention the difficulties the approach encounters). The presentation of standard consumer theory, theory of the firm and partial-equilibrium analyses is a prelude to the presentation of general competitive equilibrium theory, that is, of the supply-and-demand approach to value and distribution. The chapters on oligopoly, imperfect information, externalities and public goods introduce several qualifications but do not question the basic insights derived from the general competitive equilibrium model. No other approach to value and distribution is presented. This is a misrepresentation of the present state of economic theory. The current situation in the theory of value and distribution (but then also, as a consequence, in the theories of the labour market, of growth, of taxation, of international economics, etc.) is one of frequent doubts about the correctness of the supply-and-demand approach to income distribution, employment and growth; and of attempts by a consistent and growing minority of economists to explore alternatives. The number of journals and of associations aiming at the exploration of non-neoclassical approaches (e.g. Post-Keynesian, Sraffian, Kaleckian, neo-Marxist, evolutionary, institutionalist approaches) has been growing rapidly in recent decades; also, even in Departments not greatly interested in these 'heterodox' approaches one observes a tendency to give the theory of general equilibrium very little space in graduate-level microeconomics courses, which suggests a tendency towards an agnostic stance on the validity of that theory (more on this below).

In this situation of scientific uncertainty and co-existence of competing approaches, the duty of serious teachers is to make students capable of understanding the writings of economists belonging to different schools of thought, and to stimulate them to form their own opinion as to which approach appears scientifically more promising. The situation requires open, critical minds. The present textbook is an attempt in this direction. Accordingly, its contents and structure are partly unusual.

The neoclassical (or marginal, or supply-and-demand) approach is explained in full detail, indeed in greater detail than elsewhere on many issues, because the need to compare it with other approaches requires careful discussion of aspects given little attention in other textbooks. For example, considerable space is given to the very important shift undergone by general equilibrium theory from traditional versions aiming at the determination of long-period prices to the nowadays dominant neo-Walrasian very-short-period versions. And the disappointing results on uniqueness and stability of general equilibrium are not only presented (contrary to the disconcerting choice, in some recent textbooks, to omit these topics completely, as if it were better for scientific progress to hide the problems under the carpet), but their relevance is discussed in greater depth than in any other textbook I am aware of.

But the neoclassical approach is not the sole approach presented. The classical or surplus approach of Smith, Ricardo and Marx is also presented, including its modern developments; and it is introduced *before* the marginal one: it has seemed opportune to start the book with the presentation of a non-neoclassical approach, so as to make it easier for students to look at the neoclassical approach (probably the sole approach they were previously introduced to) 'from the outside', that is, as only one possible way to explain the functioning of market economies, that must be compared with alternatives. The obvious choice has been the classical approach, not only because in this way students acquire a sense of the history of economic thought, but also because, when coupled with a Keynesian approach to the determination of aggregate output and employment, its framework appears capable of hosting many of the insights of other non-neoclassical schools of thought (e.g. Post-Keynesian, Kaleckian, evolutionary). The first chapter ends precisely with a simple sketch of how the classical approach to value and distribution can be combined with a Keynesian, demand-based approach to aggregate output. The reader is thus presented (albeit in simplified form) with a possible approach to the determination of quantities produced, income distribution and prices, against which the specificities of the neoclassical approach can be better perceived.

This has made it possible and opportune to contrast very early on (▶ Chap. 3) the marginal/neoclassical with the classical approach to value and distribution, and to highlight the central analytical difference between them. To such an end, in ▶ Chap. 3 the fundamental structure of the neoclassical approach to value and distribution is explained through very simple models *before* the chapters presenting advanced neoclassical consumer theory and producer theory, i.e. on the basis of simple intro-

Preface (Mainly, But Not Only, For Teachers)

ductory microeconomics only (which is itself concisely presented, so as to make the exposition accessible to readers coming from other disciplines). My teaching experience has shown that this is a very useful order of presentation; when, immediately afterwards, the student tackles rigorous consumer theory and producer theory and meets Kuhn–Tucker, upper hemicontinuity, Shephard's lemma, Gorman form, the weak axiom, etc., she/he has a stronger motivation and a greater capacity to grasp the role of the several assumptions.

The subsequent study of general equilibrium theory is unique at textbook level in that the various versions of the theory ('atemporal', long-period, intertemporal without and with overlapping generations, temporary) are distinguished, and the differences between the objections that can be advanced against them are clarified. In particular, care is taken to distinguish the criticisms based on the Sonnenschein–Mantel–Debreu results from the 'Sraffian' criticisms. These distinctions will spare students many confusions.

The several criticisms, when thus clarified, paint a rather negative image of the persuasiveness of the supply-and-demand approach. It would be misleading to hide this state of affairs, which is the reason behind important aspects of the present trend in scientific research and teaching. As one author has perceptively noticed,

> the Walrasian theory of market behavior or, as it is more commonly referred to, general equilibrium theory, has increasingly been abandoned by microeconomists ... an appropriately acceptable analysis of the uniqueness and global stability of Walrasian equilibrium has yet to be found ... The persistence of this gap along with the seemingly hopelessness of filling it has, to a considerable extent, led many microeconomists to forsake the general equilibrium conceptualization altogether. As a result, microeconomic theory has, by and large, been reduced to a collection of techniques and tricks for resolving narrow, isolated microeconomic problems and the study of, also narrow and isolated, strategic behaviors (Katzner 2006, p. ix).

This picture is correct; the content of many graduate microeconomics courses has indeed been evolving in this direction, avoiding discussion of the overall theory. The result is to leave students prisoners of whatever rather unrigorously presented picture of the functioning of market economies they absorbed as undergraduates. Nor is the present situation one in which either one teaches the supply-and-demand approach to value and distribution, or one can only remain silent, waiting for some new theory to emerge. Alternative approaches do exist. Thus, ▶ Chaps. 10, 12 and 13 go on to ask whether the classical approach to value and distribution, combined with a recognition of the importance of aggregate demand for the determination of quantities and employment, can be a fruitful alternative framework; they discuss in greater detail the notion of long-period prices (also in the presence of land rents), the functioning of competition in product markets, the determinants of the degree of utilization of capacity, the labour market, and some macroeconomic implications of the microeconomics thus surveyed. ► Chapter 14, on welfare economics, besides standard arguments includes an attempt to indicate elements for a non-neoclassical welfare economics. My own theoretical preferences inevitably emerge, but I have tried hard correctly to illustrate also the views I find unpersuasive. It is indispensable at present for prospective economists to understand all the main competing positions.

The aim of reflecting the richness (and uncertainties) of the present theoretical situation has suggested the inclusion of micro topics that are now generally relegated to 'macro' courses: efficiency wages and other theories of the labour market; the microtheory of the degree of capacity utilization; the investment decisions of firms. It would seem that the criterion for exclusion of these topics from standard microeconomics courses is not that they are not micro topics, but rather that they are associated with an admission of labour unemployment. This has historical reasons that appear now outdated. The distinction between microeconomics and macroeconomics was a consequence of the Keynesian revolution. Keynes did not question the marginalist/neoclassical 'real' factor substitution mechanisms behind the decreasing labour demand curve and the decreasing investment function; but he argued that those mechanisms were generally incapable of bringing about the full employment of labour, owing to various difficulties (on whose exact nature and relevance an intense debate has raged ever since). Anyway, in his theory, once investment and the multiplier determine aggregate production and hence labour employment, real wages are still determined by the marginal product of labour, and the marginal product of capital remains a fundamental determinant of investment. Keynesian theory became universally adopted for short-period macroanalyses, but the 'neoclassical synthesis' soon gave support to the faith that the long-run trend of the economy was reasonably well described by traditional marginalist analyses. The division between microeconomics and macroeconomics could then be proposed as a division between the study of the 'real' marginalist factor substitution forces determining long-run trends, and the study of the Keynesian mechanisms determining short-run deviations of labour employment and aggregate output from the full-employment long-run trend. Micro courses were accordingly confined, fundamentally, to the teaching of traditional marginalist/neoclassical 'real' theory, a theory of full-employment equilibrium, while the presentation of microeconomic mechanisms useful for the explanation of unemployment was mostly relegated to macro courses. The present existence of approaches that reject traditional marginalist 'real' theory (and thus also its predictions about long-run trends) obliges one to re-define the confines of microeconomics and macroeconomics. A considerable portion of modern economists argue that there is little reason to consider unemployment a regrettable but temporary lapse from a normal trend of roughly full employment, and that therefore the functioning of economies where significant unemployment is a normal state of affairs should be at least as central to micro courses as the study of full-employment situations. And this textbook wants to be an introduction to these views too.

The price to be paid for the inclusion of these topics is that less space is left for some other topics. For example auctions, and social choice, are treated in lesser detail than in other advanced micro textbooks; and regretfully there is nothing on the economics of crime, and too little on the economics of the Internet. Unfortunately space is a scarce resource; anyway given the enormous importance of these topics even a full chapter on each of them would not have done justice to their importance, they deserve full courses.

Much effort has gone into trying to make this text user-friendly, accessible to readers without advanced previous mathematical competences and/or without previous study of economic theory. Many graduate economics students do not have an undergraduate degree in economics; so this textbook does not assume a previously acquired familiarity with elementary microeconomics. ▸ Chapter 3 introduces the notions of production function, tangency between isoquant and isocost, utility function, tangency between budget line and indifference curve, marginal cost, in simple ways that should be understandable even to students totally new to economics. Simple models are used whenever possible to clarify the economic intuition before going on to more general formalizations. Even when more advanced mathematics are inevitable the treatment remains user-friendly, and this should make the textbook suitable also for semi-advanced third-year honours undergraduate courses.

The book should be of interest to economists too. ▸ Chapter 1 should help surmount misinterpretations of Marx. ▸ Chapter 7 should be of help if one wants better to understand why many heterodox economists attribute great importance to the Cambridge controversy in capital theory and dislike aggregate production functions. ▸ Chapter 8 clarifies the problems of intertemporal general equilibrium theory, including some which are seldom perceived, and can help to grasp the causes of the widespread dissatisfaction with modern general equilibrium theory. It also discusses temporary general equilibrium, a topic which has disappeared from modern teaching but cannot be totally neglected, younger economists must understand why it has been abandoned. ▸ Chapter 12 shows the enormous implications of variable capacity utilization for the effects of demand on aggregate production; in addition, it tries to bring sense back to the theory of investment, a field nowadays dominated in mainstream macroeconomics by theories in contradiction with all sensible microeconomics. ▸ Chapter 13 brings back to microeconomics the fundamental question, why wages do not decrease in the presence of unemployment. ▸ Chapter 14 presents a rather unusual view of welfare economics.

At the end of each chapter, before the exercises, the reader finds a list of review questions—the kind of questions that might be posed to students in traditional Italian university oral exams. I regret the general tendency to abandon oral exams, the preparation for this type of exams obliges students to become able to repeat the steps of each argument, aiding comprehension and rigour (and memorization too). The reader can check her/his grasp of the material by trying to answer these review questions in a loud voice.

This book has a web page on SpringerLink containing appendices that could not be included in the printed book for space reasons. My personal web page *fabiopetripapers* (that any search engine will locate) will contain a section dedicated to this book, where I will post errata and improvements suggested by the comments, criticisms, suggestions I hope I will receive.

I particularly thank for their comments Stefano Bartolini, Enrico Bellino, Christian Bidard, Ennio Bilancini, Sam Bowles, Mauro Caminati, Roberto Ciccone, Ariel Dvoskin, Heinz D. Kurz, Neri Salvadori, Antonella Stirati. I have not always followed their advice, and certainly many mistakes and weak points remain, but they would have been much more numerous without those comments. Again, thanks.

Siena, Italy   Fabio Petri

Reference

Katzner, D. W. (2006). *An introduction to the economic theory of market behavior. Microeconomics from a Walrasian perspective.* Cheltenham, UK: Edward Elgar.

Contents

1	**The Classical or Surplus Approach**	1
1.1	A Very Brief Historical Introduction	3
1.2	Social Surplus and Income Distribution	6
1.3	Income Distribution, Wages	12
1.3.1	The General Wage Level	12
1.3.2	Relative Wages	18
1.4	The Other Data in the Determination of the Surplus	19
1.4.1	Quantities	19
1.4.2	Technology	20
1.5	Land Rent	24
1.5.1	Extensive Differential Rent	24
1.5.2	Intensive Differential Rent	26
1.6	Rate of Profit and Relative Prices	30
1.7	Corn Model, Luxury Goods, the Decreasing w(r) Function	36
1.8	The Labour Theory of Value	39
1.9	Marx	46
1.9.1	Values, Surplus Values, Value of Labour Power	46
1.9.2	The Determination of the Rate of Profit	48
1.9.3	A Mistake in Marx's Determination of the Rate of Profit	51
1.10	The Marxist Tradition	52
1.11	The Standard Commodity as the 'average' Commodity Marx Was Looking For	57
1.12	More on Marx	59
1.12.1	Wages	59
1.12.2	Quantities	62
1.12.3	Growth, Technical Change, the 'law' of the Tendency of the Rate of Profit to Fall	64
1.12.4	Marx and the Future of Capitalism	69
1.13	'Core' and 'Out-of-Core' Analyses in the Surplus Approach	71
1.14	A Modern View of the Determinants of Aggregate Production	73
1.14.1	Going Beyond Marx on What Determines Aggregate Production	73
1.14.2	The Principle of Effective Demand	75
1.14.3	The Dynamic Multiplier	81
1.14.4	The Adaptability of Production to Demand	83
1.15	Conclusions	85
1.16	Review Questions and Exercises	85
References		88
2	**Long-Period Prices**	91
2.1	Long-Period Prices: Matrix Representation	93
2.2	Eigenvalues and the Perron–Frobenius Theorem	96
2.3	Applying Perron–Frobenius. The Standard Commodity	100

XII Contents

2.4	Non-basic Commodities	105
2.5	Leontief's Open Model	106
2.6	The Hawkins–Simon Condition	109
2.7	The Interpretation of the Leontief Inverse	109
2.8	Subsystems; Labours Embodied as Employment Multipliers	110
2.9	Pricing with Vertically Integrated Technical Coefficients	112
2.10	The Relationship Between Rate of Profit and Rate of Wages	112
2.11	Choice of Technique	119
2.12	Non-basics and Choice of Techniques	127
2.13	Techniques Including Different Commodities	129
2.14	The Samuelson–Garegnani Model and the Champagne-Whiskey Model	130
2.15	Fixed Capital	137
2.16	Conclusions	147
2.17	Review Questions and Exercises	148
References		151

3	**Introduction to the Marginal Approach**	153
3.1	Introduction	156
3.2	Equilibrium and Gravitation	157
3.3	The Labour–Land–Corn Economy: Direct (or Technological) Factor Substitutability	159
3.3.1	Production Functions, Isoquants and Marginal Products	159
3.3.2	Factor Demand Curves, Cost Function and Equilibrium in Factor Markets	163
3.3.3	Importance of Factor Substitutability	174
3.3.4	Comparative Statics	175
3.4	The Role of Consumer Choice: The Indirect Factor Substitution Mechanism	177
3.5	The Simultaneous Operation of Both Substitution Mechanisms, and the Importance of Highly Elastic Factor Demand Curves	180
3.6	Money	184
3.7	Efficiency, the Forest Exchange Economy, Choice Curves and Equilibrium in the Edgeworth Box	185
3.7.1	Elements of Consumer Theory: Utility Function, Indifference Curves, MRS	185
3.7.2	Exchange Economy, Edgewort Box, Pareto Efficiency	190
3.8	Pareto Efficiency in the Production Economy. Marginal Cost	196
3.9	Robinson Crusoe and Market Valuation as Reflecting 'Natural' Laws	206
3.10	Introduction of the Rate of Interest and of Capital in the Marginalist Theory of Distribution	209
3.10.1	The Rate of Interest in the Exchange Economy	209
3.10.2	The Rate of Interest in the Corn Economy	211
3.10.3	Capital and the Indirect Factor Substitution Mechanism	213
3.11	Money and the Rate of Interest	217
3.12	Accumulation	218

Contents

XIII

3.13	A Comparison Between the Classical and the Marginal Approaches to Income Distribution: The Basic Analytical Difference and Some Implications	219
3.13.1	The Different Data When Determining the Rate of Return on Capital	219
3.13.2	The Role of Social and Political Elements. Competition in Labour Markets	222
3.13.3	Exploitation?	224
3.13.4	Technical Progress, Relative Wages, Unequal Exchange	226
3.14	Intensive Differential Rent and the Marginal Approach	228
3.15	Final Elements of Differentiation: Supply of Capital, Say's Law	236
3.16	Conclusion	240
3.17	Review Questions and Exercises	241
References		245

4	**Consumers and the Exchange Economy**	247
4.1	Introduction	250
4.2	The Consumption Set, Time and the Role of Equilibrium	250
4.3	Preferences and Utility	253
4.4	Convex Preferences, Quasi-Concave Utility, Typical Indifference Curves	259
4.5	Optimization	261
4.6	Demand, Continuity and Upper Hemicontinuity of Correspondences	264
4.7	The Two-Goods Exchange Economy and the Importance of Continuity of Demand	268
4.8	First-Order Conditions. Corner Solutions. The Kuhn–Tucker Theorem	272
4.9	Envelope Theorem	280
4.10	Indirect Utility, Expenditure Function, Compensated Demand	282
4.11	Roy's Identity, Shephard's Lemma, Some Dualities and Some Utility Functions	287
4.11.1	Roy's Identity and Shephard's Lemma	287
4.11.2	Homothetic Utility Functions and Homothetic Preferences	289
4.11.3	Quasi-Linear Utility	290
4.11.4	The Cobb–Douglas Utility Function and the Elasticity of Substitution	291
4.11.5	The CES Utility Function	293
4.12	The Slutsky Equation	295
4.13	Given Endowments: The Walrasian UMP, The Walrasian Slutsky Equation	301
4.14	Labour Supply. Saving Decision	305
4.15	Some Notes on the Usefulness of Consumer Theory for Empirical Estimation	310
4.16	Money Metric Utility Function, Equivalent Variation, Compensating Variation	313
4.17	Constant Marginal Utility of Money. Consumer Surplus. Reservation Prices	319
4.18	Price Indices and Inflation	324

XIV   Contents

4.19	Hicksian Aggregability of Goods	326
4.20	Revealed Preference	328
4.21	Aggregability of Consumers: Gorman Aggregability and the Representative Consumer	333
4.22	General Equilibrium of Pure Exchange. Aggregability of Consumers....	337
4.23	Aggregate or Market Demand and the Weak Axiom of Revealed Preference	341
4.24	Conclusions	344
4.25	Review Questions and Exercises	344
References		351

5	**Firms, Partial Equilibria and the General Equilibrium with Production**	353
5.1	Introduction	356
5.2	Production Possibility Sets, Netputs, Production Functions	357
5.3	Axioms on the Production Possibility Set	364
5.4	Returns to Scale	365
5.5	Differentiable Production Functions and Value Capital	368
5.6	Homogeneous Production Functions and Returns to Scale	369
5.7	Activity Analysis	372
5.8	Marginal Product, Transformation Curve	373
5.9	Profit Maximization and WAPM	376
5.10	Optimal Employment of a Factor	378
5.11	Cost Minimization	379
5.12	WACm; Kuhn–Tucker Conditions and Cost Minimization	382
5.13	Supply Curves: Short-Period Marshallian Analysis, Quasi-Rents	384
5.14	From Short-Period to Long-Period Supply	388
5.15	The Product Exhaustion Theorem with U-Shaped LAC	393
5.16	Aggregation	394
5.17	Shephard's Lemma	395
5.18	The Profit Function and Hotelling's Lemma	395
5.19	Conditional and Unconditional Factor Demands, Inferior Inputs, Rival Inputs, Substitution Effect and Output Effect	397
5.20	Functional Separability: Leontief Separability	402
5.21	Duality	403
5.22	Elasticity of Substitution	404
5.23	Partial Equilibrium	405
5.24	Stability of Partial Equilibria	408
5.25	Welfare Analysis of Partial Equilibria	409
5.26	Price Taking, Perfect Competition, Tâtonnement	413
5.27	The Number of Firms in Modern GE	419
5.28	The Equations of the Non-capitalistic General Equilibrium with Production	423
5.29	The 'Reduction' to an Exchange Economy	427
5.30	The Role of Demand in Determining Product Prices: Why General Equilibrium Product Supply Curves Are Upward Sloping	429

Contents

XV

5.31	International Trade	430
5.32	On the Persistency of Preferences. Doing Without Demand Curves?	433
5.33	Conclusions	437
5.34	Review Questions and Exercises	438
References		441

6 Existence, Uniqueness and Stability of Non-capitalistic General Equilibria ... 443

6.1	Introduction. The Exchange Economy	446
6.2	Existence: Properties of the Market Excess Demand Correspondence	447
6.3	Continuity: Non-strictly Convex Preferences	450
6.4	Continuity: Non-convex Consumption Sets	453
6.5	Continuity: Survival	456
6.6	Continuity: The Zero-Income Problem	458
6.7	Continuity: Survival Again and Subsistence	460
6.8	Existence of General Equilibrium of Exchange: A Simple New Proof	463
6.9	Brouwer's Fixed-Point Theorem	465
6.10	Existence of Exchange Equilibrium with Strongly Monotonic Preferences	466
6.11	Uniqueness: The Non-uniqueness of Equilibrium in General. Possibility of Several Locally Stable Equilibria	469
6.12	Uniqueness: Regular Economies	471
6.13	The Sonnenschein–Mantel–Debreu Result	474
6.14	Uniqueness Through Conditions on Excess Demand: Gross Substitutes	475
6.15	Uniqueness Through Conditions on Excess Demand: WAM	478
6.16	Uniqueness: No-Trade Equilibrium and Index Theorem	481
6.17	Conditions on the Distribution of Characteristics	482
6.18	Stability: The Cobweb	483
6.19	Stability: The Samuelsonian Walrasian Tâtonnement	485
6.20	Stability: Some Mathematics and the WAM Theorem	488
6.21	Stability: Further Aspects of the Problem	492
6.22	On the Likelihood of Uniqueness and Stability	494
6.23	Production	498
6.24	Existence of a GE of Production and Exchange	499
6.25	Uniqueness of the Production Equilibrium	502
6.26	WAM and the Hildenbrand–Grodal Observation	509
6.27	Gross Substitutability not Sufficient for Uniqueness	511
6.28	Stability: The Tâtonnement in the Production Economy	512
6.29	Mandler's Factor Tâtonnement	515
6.30	Again on the Likelihood of Uniqueness and Stability	518
6.31	Conclusions	523
6.32	Review Questions and Exercises	523
References		527

XVI   Contents

7	**Capital: Long-Period Equilibria**	529
7.1	The Notion of Long-Period Equilibrium	531
7.2	The Endogenous Determination of Equilibrium Capital Endowments	534
7.3	The Equations of Long-Period General Equilibrium	539
7.4	The Quantity of Capital: Supply-Side Problems	548
7.5	The Quantity of Capital: Demand-Side Problems. Demand for 'capital' and Investment	551
7.6	Re-switching and Reverse Capital Deepening	558
7.7	More on Reverse Capital Deepening. Price Wicksell Effects	563
7.8	Stationary States and Hicks' Criticism of Long-Period Prices	569
7.9	The 'Austrian' Approach	572
7.10	On Substitutability in Modern and in Traditional Production Functions	575
7.11	Aggregate Production Functions	579
7.12	'Surrogate Production Functions' in a Non-Neoclassical Economy. Endogenously Determined Marginal Products	587
7.13	Perception of the Difficulties with 'Capital', and Shift Back to Walras—or Almost	591
7.14	Conclusions	595
7.15	Review Questions and Exercises	596
References		599

8	**Intertemporal Equilibrium, Temporary Equilibrium**	601
8.1	Introduction	605
8.2	The Intertemporal Reinterpretation of the Non-capitalistic Atemporal Model	606
8.3	Postponing to Chapter 9 on Uncertainty	609
8.4	The Consumer's Intertemporal Utility Function	609
8.5	Meaning of Prices; Own Rates of Interest	611
8.6	Production	612
8.7	The Reinterpretation Should not Hide a Difference	615
8.8	Different Own Rates of Interest and Effective Uniformity of Rates of Return	616
8.9	Uniform Effective Rate of Return Versus Long-Period Uniform Rate of Profit	618
8.10	UERRSP and URRSP	619
8.11	Radner Sequential Equilibria (Without Uncertainty)	620
8.12	Existence, Uniqueness, Stability	622
8.13	Really Only a Reinterpretation? Some First Problems	623
8.14	Money	625
8.15	Impermanence Problem, Price-Change Problem, Substitutability Problem	627
8.16	The Savings–investment Problem	632
8.16.1	The 'Further Assumption'	632

Contents

XVII

8.16.2 The Difference It Makes to Assume or Not the 'Further Assumption'......... 635
8.16.3 The Neoclassical Synthesis.. 640
8.17 **Equilibrium Over the Infinite Future** 641
8.17.1 The One-Good Growth Model... 641
8.17.2 The Old Problems Remain, Plus a New One 648
8.18 **Behind the Neoclassical Reliance on Intertemporal Equilibria** 650
8.19 **Overlapping Generations** 652
8.20 **Multiple OLG Equilibria** 656
8.21 **The Core of Allocations in the Neoclassical Economy** 661
8.22 **The Core Equivalence Theorem is not Valid for OLG Economies** 668
8.23 **A Continuum of Equilibria in OLG Models**.............................. 669
8.24 **Summing Up on OLG Models**.. 675
8.25 **Temporary Equilibria. An Informal Presentation of Some Problems**..... 677
8.26 **An Introductory Pure-Exchange Model** 679
8.26.1 General Description of the Exchange Economy 679
8.26.2 A More Detailed Description of the Household's Behaviour................. 680
8.26.3 Problems with the Introductory Model 685
8.26.4 A Perplexing Aspect of Green's Equilibrium............................... 689
8.27 **Extension to the Case of Economies with Production.**................... 691
8.27.1 The Extended Model 691
8.27.2 Discussion of the Extended Model 697
8.28 **Temporary Equilibrium in Economies with 'Money'.**.................... 702
8.28.1 Introduction of Money... 702
8.28.2 Existence of Monetary Equilibrium 707
8.28.3 Some Doubts on Grandmont's Characterization of the Function
       of Money... 713
8.29 **Conclusions on the Marginal/Neoclassical Approach, with Special
     Emphasis on the Labour Demand Curve and on the Investment
     Function** 714
8.30 **Review Questions and Exercises**.. 718
References.. 723

9 **Uncertainty and General Equilibrium.**.............................. 727
9.1 **Lotteries and Expected Utility**... 730
9.2 **Axioms for Expected Utility** 734
9.3 **Existence of Expected Utility** 738
9.4 **Risk Aversion and Prospects.**... 742
9.5 **Risk Aversion and Convexity of Expected Utility** 746
9.6 **Comparing the Riskiness of Lotteries: Stochastic Dominance.**.......... 748
9.7 **The St. Petersburg Paradox.**.. 749
9.8 **Cardinality of VNM Utility** 750
9.9 **Insurance**... 752
9.10 **Actuarially Fair Insurance and Risk Premium**........................... 753
9.11 **Unfair Insurance** 755
9.12 **Measuring Risk Aversion: Arrow–Pratt**.................................. 757
9.13 **Global Comparison of Risk Aversion** 759

XVIII   Contents

9.14	Decreasing Absolute Risk Aversion	760
9.15	Relative Risk Aversion	761
9.16	An Application of Arrow–Pratt: Efficient Risk Pooling in Absence of Wealth Effects	763
9.17	Diversification	767
9.18	Consumption and Saving Under Uncertainty	768
9.19	Firm Behaviour Under Uncertainty	769
9.20	Portfolio Selection: Two Assets	771
9.21	Portfolio Selection: Many Assets. Tobin	776
9.22	State-Dependent Utility	782
9.23	Subjective Expected Utility	784
9.24	Risk or Uncertainty?	787
9.25	Non-expected Utility: Allais' Paradox, Prospect Theory, Ellsberg's Paradox	790
9.26	Reducing Uncertainty Through More Information. Satisficing. Informational Cascades	796
9.27	Uncertainty and General Equilibrium in Traditional Marginalist Authors	801
9.28	Contingent Commodities	804
9.29	Equilibrium with Contingent Commodities	811
9.30	Radner Equilibrium (EPPPE)	814
9.31	Incomplete Markets	817
9.32	Conclusion. Final Considerations on the Supply-And-Demand Approach	821
9.33	Review Questions and Exercises	823
References		829

10	**Back to Long-Period Prices**	831
10.1	The Gravitation to Long-Period Prices in the History of Economic Theory, and Some Empirical Evidence	833
10.2	Objections to the Uniform Rate of Profit	839
10.3	The Traditional Explanation	842
10.4	Cross-Dual Models	844
10.5	The Possibility of a High Price and a Low Profit Rate	851
10.6	Joint Production and Sraffa	853
10.7	Graphical Representation: Single Production	858
10.8	Graphical Representation: Joint Production	865
10.9	Choice of Technique as a Linear Programming Problem	870
10.10	Piccioni's Contribution	879
10.11	No Gravitation to a Definite Technique?	885
10.12	Extensive Rent	889
10.13	Intensive Rent	895
10.14	External Intensive Rent; Rent Due to Consumer Demand	902
10.15	Given Quantities?	904
10.16	Constant Returns to Scale?	906
10.17	Lack of Consistency?	911

Contents

10.18	Conclusions	913
10.19	Review Questions and Exercises	913
References		916

11	**Games and Information**	**919**
11.1	Introduction, and Some Examples of One-Shot Simultaneous Games	921
11.2	Sequential or Dynamic Games	925
11.3	Extensive and Strategic (or Normal) Form	929
11.4	Mixed Strategies	931
11.5	Behavioural Strategies	933
11.6	Solutions. Elimination of Strictly Dominated Strategies. Some Doubts	935
11.7	Weakly Dominated Strategies, Dominance Solvable Games	939
11.8	Dominated Mixed Strategies	941
11.9	Nash Equilibrium in Pure Strategies	942
11.10	Nash Equilibria in Mixed Strategies	943
11.11	Existence of Nash Equilibrium. The Reasons for Interest in Nash Equilibria	944
11.12	Trembling-Hand Equilibria	950
11.13	Backward Induction and Subgame Perfection	951
11.14	Repeated Backward Induction and the Centipede Game	954
11.15	Infinitely Repeated Games	957
11.16	Finitely Repeated Games	962
11.17	Bayesian Games	963
11.18	Auctions as Bayesian Games. Revenue Equivalence Theorem. Winner's Curse	970
11.19	Dynamic Games of Imperfect Information	976
11.20	Sequential Rationality, Behavioural Strategies, Perfect Bayesian Equilibrium (PBE)	978
11.21	Limits of Perfect Bayesian Equilibrium. Sequential Equilibrium	983
11.22	Asymmetric Information. Signalling Games. Separating and Pooling Equilibria	985
11.23	Adverse Selection	994
11.24	Principal–agent Models	996
11.25	Screening	1003
11.26	Conclusions	1008
11.27	Review Questions and Exercises	1008
References		1019

12	**Product Markets: Pricing, Capacity, Investment, Imperfect Competition**	**1021**
12.1	Introduction	1023
12.2	Two Types of Markets. Primary Products	1024
12.3	Administered Prices and Capacity Utilization	1027
12.4	Unused Capacity	1029

12.5	**Time-Specific Input Prices**	1030
12.6	**Demand Variations**	1035
12.7	**The Investment Decision of Firms**	1041
12.7.1	Neoclassical Investment Theory Without Full Labour Employment	1041
12.7.2	The 'Array-of-Opportunities' Approach	1046
12.7.3	The Adjustment Costs Approach	1050
12.7.4	Investment Determined by Profits?	1052
12.7.5	Investment and Sales Prospects	1060
12.8	**Administered Prices, Differentiated Products, and Competition**	1062
12.9	**Full-Cost Pricing**	1063
12.10	**Monopoly**	1067
12.11	**Monopolistic Competition Versus Full-Cost Pricing**	1073
12.12	**Duopoly**	1079
12.12.1	Cournot Duopoly	1079
12.12.2	Conjectural Variations	1086
12.12.3	Stackelberg (Quantity Leadership)	1086
12.12.4	Price Leadership	1089
12.12.5	Bertrand	1090
12.12.6	Bertrand-Edgeworth	1092
12.12.7	Capacity Constraints and Bertrand Competition	1094
12.12.8	Differentiated Products and Bertrand Versus Cournot Competition	1095
12.12.9	Price Matching and the Kinked Demand Curve	1096
12.13	**Repeated Interaction, Cartels, Tacit Collusion, Folk Theorems**	1098
12.14	**Entry**	1102
12.15	**Conclusions**	1109
12.16	**Review Questions and Exercises**	1110
References		1113
13	**Labour Markets and Income Distribution**	1115
13.1	**Introductory**	1117
13.2	**The Labour Demand Curve Is Indeterminable**	1118
13.3	**Search Theory**	1127
13.4	**Implicit Contracts**	1140
13.5	**Insiders–Outsiders**	1143
13.6	**Efficiency Wages**	1146
13.6.1	Five Versions	1146
13.6.2	Adverse Selection	1149
13.6.3	Turnover Costs	1150
13.6.4	Shirking	1152
13.6.5	Gift Exchange, Fairness, Morale	1164
13.7	**Trade Unions**	1165
13.8	**The Solow or Solow–Hahn Approach**	1180
13.9	**Long-Period Theories of Wages: Four Approaches. The Cambridge School**	1188
13.10	**The Kaleckian Approach**	1200
13.11	**The Classical–Marxian Approach. Goodwin. Investment**	1202

Contents

13.12	**Pivetti**	1214
13.13	**Concluding on Real Wages**	1216
13.14	**Review Questions and Exercises**	1220
References		1223

14	**Welfare, Externalities, Public Goods and Happiness**	1227
14.1	**Introductory**	1229
14.2	**Pareto Efficiency and Value Judgements**	1230
14.3	**Externalities**	1234
14.3.1	The Coase Theorem	1234
14.3.2	Production Externalities	1236
14.3.3	Pollution Rights	1241
14.3.4	Network Externalities and the Internet	1241
14.3.5	The Tragedy of the Commons	1246
14.3.6	Urban Segregation	1248
14.4	**Public Goods**	1249
14.4.1	Non-rival Goods and Non-excludable Goods	1249
14.4.2	When to Get an Indivisible Public Goods	1250
14.4.3	What Quantity of a Divisible Public Good?	1251
14.4.4	Lindahl Equilibrium	1254
14.5	**The Groves–Clarke Mechanism**	1255
14.6	**The Fundamental Theorems of Welfare Economics**	1258
14.6.1	Does Competition Produce Pareto Efficiency?	1258
14.6.2	The First Fundamental Theorem	1260
14.6.3	The Second Fundamental Theorem	1265
14.7	**Some Generally Accepted Limitations of the Two Fundamental Theorems**	1271
14.8	**Pareto Efficiency: A Non-neoclassical Perspective**	1277
14.9	**Cost–Benefit Analysis and the Compensation Principle**	1281
14.10	**Cost–benefit Analysis Run Amok**	1287
14.11	**Social Welfare Functions**	1292
14.12	**Three Applications of Social Welfare Functions**	1301
14.13	**Arrow's Impossibility Theorem**	1305
14.14	**Happiness, and Externalities Again**	1322
14.15	**Conclusions**	1330
14.16	**Review Questions and Exercises**	1330
References		1334

15	**Mathematical Review**	1337
15.1	**Sets, Relations, Functions, Convexity, Convex Combination of Vectors**	1338
15.2	**Logic: If, Only if, Contrapositive, Proof by Contradiction, Connection with Subsets**	1342
15.3	**Vectors, Matrices, Hyperplanes. Definite Matrices**	1343
15.4	**Analysis**	1353
15.5	**Correspondences**	1364

15.6	**Optimization**	1366
15.7	**Linear Programming and Duality**	1381
15.8	**Complex Numbers**	1382
15.9	**Integrals**	1384
15.10	**Probability and Statistics**	1385
15.11	**Poisson Process**	1391
References		1394

The Classical or Surplus Approach

Contents

1.1   A Very Brief Historical Introduction – 3

1.2   Social Surplus and Income Distribution – 6

1.3   Income Distribution, Wages – 12
1.3.1   The General Wage Level – 12
1.3.2   Relative Wages – 18

1.4   The Other Data in the Determination of the Surplus – 19
1.4.1   Quantities – 19
1.4.2   Technology – 20

1.5   Land Rent – 24
1.5.1   Extensive Differential Rent – 24
1.5.2   Intensive Differential Rent – 26

1.6   Rate of Profit and Relative Prices – 30

1.7   Corn Model, Luxury Goods, the Decreasing w(r) Function – 36

1.8   The Labour Theory of Value – 39

1.9   Marx – 46
1.9.1   Values, Surplus Values, Value of Labour Power – 46
1.9.2   The Determination of the Rate of Profit – 48

Electronic supplementary material The online version of this chapter (▶ https://doi.org/10.1007/978-3-030-62070-7_1) contains supplementary material, which is available to authorized users.

© Springer Nature Switzerland AG 2021
F. Petri, *Microeconomics for the Critical Mind*,
Classroom Companion: Economics, https://doi.org/10.1007/978-3-030-62070-7_1

1.9.3	A Mistake in Marx's Determination of the Rate of Profit – 51
1.10	**The Marxist Tradition – 52**
1.11	**The Standard Commodity as the 'average' Commodity Marx Was Looking For – 57**
1.12	**More on Marx – 59**
1.12.1	Wages – 59
1.12.2	Quantities – 62
1.12.3	Growth, Technical Change, the 'law' of the Tendency of the Rate of Profit to Fall – 64
1.12.4	Marx and the Future of Capitalism – 69
1.13	**'Core' and 'Out-of-Core' Analyses in the Surplus Approach – 71**
1.14	**A Modern View of the Determinants of Aggregate Production – 73**
1.14.1	Going Beyond Marx on What Determines Aggregate Production – 73
1.14.2	The Principle of Effective Demand – 75
1.14.3	The Dynamic Multiplier – 81
1.14.4	The Adaptability of Production to Demand – 83
1.15	**Conclusions – 85**
1.16	**Review Questions and Exercises – 85**
	References – 88

1.1 · A Very Brief Historical Introduction

In this chapter you will learn:

- that the current prevailing approach to the theory of value and distribution, the marginal or neoclassical approach, was preceded by a very different approach, the classical or surplus approach, that many economists nowadays consider worth resuming;
- the views on wages, profits, land rent and growth of the three main representatives of the classical approach: Adam Smith, David Ricardo, Karl Marx;
- the notion of long-period relative prices and its connection with the labour theory of value;
- the difficulties of Ricardo and Marx on how to determine the rate of profits, and why against a long-dominant interpretation these difficulties can be surmounted without abandoning their overall approach;
- how the modern Keynesian approach to aggregate demand can be integrated with the classical approach.

1.1 A Very Brief Historical Introduction

The present chapter introduces to the views on value and income distribution of the classical or surplus approach, whose main representatives were Adam Smith, David Ricardo and Karl Marx. This approach is enjoying a considerable revival, and familiarity with it can help to realize that the dominant marginal/neoclassical approach is not the only possible way to conceive the working of market economies. The presentation adopts a historical-analytical approach, proceeding from Smith to Ricardo and to Marx, illustrating the needed notions when the theories of the author demand them. In this way the reader grasps the historical evolution of the approach and understands in particular the difficulties the three authors met in explaining the rate of profit. Those difficulties appear surmountable; however, the chapter finds the theories of classical authors on what determines quantities produced and employment not very satisfactory and concludes by noting the possibility to integrate the classical approach with a Keynesian determination of aggregate output (and employment) based on aggregate demand and the multiplier. In an online Appendix to the chapter, in the book's Website, you will find Ricardo's very interesting views on the possibility that technical progress increases unemployment and the essentials of national accounting for readers new to economics.

Microeconomics is the branch of economic theory where, from the study of the decisions of individuals and of their effects, one tries to answer the question: what is produced, how and for whom in a private-property economy. Historically, this set of connected questions used to be studied under a different name: 'theory of value and of income distribution'. The theory of value narrowly understood studies what determines the normal relative prices (or values) of the goods *produced* in a market economy; but from the inception of economic theory as a systematic enquiry, it was found that this study is intimately connected with the study of what determines wages, land rents, profits, interest, in other words, income distribution; hence an impossibility to separate the study of value from the study of income distribution. The latter study was found necessarily to involve also the study of the forces determining the quantities produced, and the overall utilization of resources, topics more often classified nowadays as part of *macro*economics; but the separation between microeconomics and macroeconomics cannot be rigid and actually needs a radical reconsideration (see this book's Preface).

In the history of economic analysis it is possible, albeit at the cost of drastic simplification, to distinguish two main successive approaches to the theory of value and distribution.

The earlier approach, the one of the Physiocrats, Adam Smith, David Ricardo, was called *classical* by Karl Marx. In order to avoid confusion with other current usages of the term 'classical', nowadays it is also called *surplus approach*, because centrally based on the notion of *social surplus*, the production *in excess of* what (inclusive of the necessary consumption of workers) must be put back into the production process in order to allow the repetition of production on an unchanged scale. The focus was on what determined the size, the distribution among the different social classes and the growth, of the social surplus. This approach was adumbrated by William Petty in the seventeenth century and took a clear form in the third quarter of the eighteenth century with the main Physiocrat, François Quesnay; it was developed by Adam Smith (his magnum opus, *The Wealth of Nations*, was published in 1776), and then by David Ricardo (who wrote between 1810 and 1823). When already a majority of economists was moving in another direction, the approach was resumed and further developed by Karl Marx (the first volume of *Das Kapital*, the sole one published in Marx's life, came out in 1867). His against-the-stream attempt to confirm and improve the surplus approach was not successful: the great majority of economists kept moving away from Ricardo's picture of the interests of the three main social classes (landowners, capitalists, wage workers) as strongly opposed. In the last quarter of the nineteenth century their search for a picture of capitalism as a fundamentally cooperative and harmonious form of economic organization solidified into a new approach that reduced to a decidedly minoritarian position whatever was left of the influence of the classical approach. The new approach was based on the notion of a tendency towards equality, or equilibrium, between supply and demand for the 'factors of production' labour, land and capital, a tendency due to technical and psychological factor substitution processes induced by changes in relative 'factor prices'. Anticipations of this approach are found, around the middle of the nineteenth century, in the German author Heinrich Von Thünen; the founders of the approach are generally considered to be Stanley Jevons in England, Carl Menger in Austria and Léon Walras in France, who with striking near-simultaneity proposed, little before or after 1870, to explain the exchange rates among consumption goods on the basis of marginal utility, and income distribution on the basis of an equilibrium between supply and demand for labour, land and capital; but Thünen should actually be seen as a co-founder. Alfred Marshall (who was to become the most influential economist for decades) published later but had autonomously reached essentially the same approach at

1.1 · A Very Brief Historical Introduction

about the same time, and largely under Thünen's influence. Because of the central role in it of the notions of *marginal utility* and *marginal product* (cf. ► Chap. 3), this approach was called *marginal* or *marginalist*, but it is nowadays more often referred to as *neoclassical* (a potentially misleading name, because, as ► Chap. 3 will show, it is rather *anti*-classical[1]). With the second generation of marginalist economists (Edgeworth, Wicksteed in Great Britain; Wieser, Böhm-Bawerk in Austria; J. B. Clark, Fetter, Irving Fisher in USA; Pareto, Barone, Pantaleoni in Italy; Wicksell, Cassel in Sweden, etc.) this approach came to dominate economic science nearly completely and is still largely dominant.

But, among value theory specialists, doubts about the validity of the marginal approach have considerably increased since the 1960s. The rigorous formulation of the approach—the theory of *general equilibrium*—is increasingly accused of having to rely on exceedingly implausible assumptions; furthermore, many economists have come to believe that a satisfactory treatment of capital

---

1 The approach is even sometimes called 'classical'. Thus the terms 'classical' and 'neoclassical' are susceptible of generating confusions, and some clarification is now necessary, albeit at the risk of mentioning notions still unfamiliar to some readers. Karl Marx had called 'classical' the body of economic theories from Petty through the Physiocrats and Adam Smith up to David Ricardo, but John Maynard Keynes, in his highly influential *General Theory of Employment, Interest and Money* (1936), extended the term 'classical' to cover also the marginal approach. He wrote: " 'The classical economists' was a name invented by Marx to cover Ricardo and James Mill and their *predecessors*, that is to say the founders of the theory which culminated in the Ricardian economics. I have been accustomed, perhaps perpetrating a solecism, to include in "the classical school" the *followers* of Ricardo, those, that is to say, who adopted and perfected the theory of the Ricardian economics, including (for example) J. S. Mill, Marshall, Edgeworth and Prof. Pigou" (Keynes, *GT*, 1936, p. 3, fn. 1). As this passage makes clear, Keynes based his use of the term 'classical' on Marshall's interpretation (the dominant one at the time) of marginalism as, not a radical rejection, but instead a development of, and improvement upon, Ricardo's approach; the phrase 'perhaps perpetrating a solecism' [Oxford Dictionary: 'solecism: 1. A violation of conventional usage and grammar. 2. A violation of etiquette. 3. An impropriety, mistake, or incongruity'] shows that Keynes was not certain he had the right thus to extend the meaning of 'classical school' to include the theories of employment he was really intent on criticizing, i.e. the *marginalist* theories of Marshall, Pigou and the generality of economists at the time. Keynes' usage, which essentially identifies 'classical' with 'marginalist', made it possible for Paul Samuelson to name 'grand neoclassical synthesis' the subsequent synthesis of Keynes' ideas with the marginal approach operated by Hicks, Modigliani, Tobin. During the intense debates of the 1950s and '60 s on the validity of this 'neoclassical synthesis', the term 'neoclassical' came more and more to indicate the 'real' forces that in the 'neoclassical synthesis' push toward a marginalist full-employment equilibrium if money wages are not downward-rigid; thus 'neoclassical' came to stand essentially for 'marginalist'. Keynes's usage of the term 'classical' occasionally reappears in macroeconomics, e.g. in the term 'New Classical Macroeconomics'. But nowadays the majority view, stimulated above all by the Italian economist Piero Sraffa's critical edition of the *Collected Works* of David Ricardo and in particular by his editorial *Introduction* to Vol. I of that edition (1951), rejects Marshall's claim of an analytical continuity between Ricardo and the marginal approach and argues that Marshall and Pigou did *not* adopt and perfect Ricardian economics, they *replaced* it with the marginal approach which was, if anything, anti-Ricardian. Thus, Keynes *did* perpetrate a solecism. In this book 'classical' is used in Marx's sense; the term 'marginalist' or 'marginal' will be often preferred to 'neoclassical'.

6 Chapter 1 · The Classical or Surplus Approach

in this approach is impossible.[2] Also, the approach is not easily reconciled with the empirical evidence: it forecasts a spontaneous tendency of market economies towards the full employment of all resources, a forecast which according to many economists is contradicted by the historical evidence of persistent labour unemployment. Thus, for both theoretical and empirical reasons, a number of dissident schools of thought have sprung up in recent decades, arguing in favour of alternative approaches. Nowadays the teaching of microeconomics must recognize that the situation is one of a plurality of approaches and of sharp disagreements among economists. The disagreements have profound implications for the characterization of the society in which we live; there is a wide spectrum of positions, from theories that view the market economy we live in—modern capitalism—as close to the best of all possible worlds, to theories that characterize it as more similar to a society based on slavery than one would tend to think on the basis of appearances. And these differences rest, not on different *ethical* judgements, but on different descriptions of the basic mechanisms and forces operating in a market economy, i.e. on *scientific* disagreements.

In this situation of uncertainty and debate about the very foundations of economic theory, a consistent group of economists argues that it was a mistake to abandon the classical or surplus approach in favour of the marginal/neoclassical approach, because the deficiencies of the analyses of the classical authors can be surmounted while remaining within their approach, while on the contrary the marginal/neoclassical approach has come out to suffer from insurmountable difficulties; a resumption of the classical approach, these economists argue, allows a great improvement in logical consistency and in the correspondence between the predictions of economic theory and empirical observation. We start precisely with a presentation of the classical approach, in order to allow students until now only familiar with the marginal/neoclassical approach to see that it is possible to view things differently. Also, the classical approach will be useful later in the book as a good basis for the study of other modern non-neoclassical economic theories.

The present chapter introduces to the classical approach in simple terms, assuming no prior acquaintance with it; more advanced analytical details are postponed to ▶ Chaps. 2 and 10. Readers particularly interested in understanding the difference between classical and marginal approach may skip ▶ Chap. 2 on a first reading and proceed directly to ▶ Chap. 3. However, a study of ▶ Chap. 2 must not be postponed too much, and it is indispensable for ▶ Chap. 7.

1.2 Social Surplus and Income Distribution

The surplus approach progressed considerably from the Physiocrats to Karl Marx. With hindsight, we can discern a common analytical structure in the analyses of classical economists. All these authors concentrate first of all on the

---

2   This development (see ▶ Chap. 7) is again largely due to the contributions of Piero Sraffa, who ranks therefore together with Keynes as one of the two most important economic theorists of the XX century.

1.2 · Social Surplus and Income Distribution

conditions that must be satisfied in order for the productive processes of the economy to be repeatable on the same scale period after period. To such an end, they distinguish the ensemble of the goods produced in an economy in a year in two parts:

(a) *total necessary consumption*, i.e. the part that must be employed again in the productive process in order to repeat it; in this part they include both the replacement of all means of production consumed in the productive process, and the necessary consumption, or *subsistence*, of the workers employed[3];

(b) the remainder, which we can call 'social surplus', whose value corresponds to the net income of the social classes other than the workers[4]; this surplus can be employed by society as it likes, without impairing the continuation of productive activity on at least the same scale.

The centrality of the notion of surplus and its connection with the theory of income distribution derives in the classical authors from their interest in the causes, and in the ways to increase, the 'wealth of nations'. The utilization of the surplus determines the evolution of the economy; and this utilization is seen as essentially depending on how the surplus gets distributed among the different social classes. Ricardo, for example, sees the surplus as constituting the income of capitalists and of landlords and is in favour of giving as great as possible a portion of the surplus to the capitalists rather than to the landlords, because according to him the capitalists reinvest the greater part of their income, thus favouring the growth of production, while the landlords consume their income in luxuries.

Let us grasp some of the central aspects of the classical approach via description of a simple economy, where the sole product is corn,[5] produced in yearly cycles by labour and corn (used as seed and as food for the labourers) over lands of different, or even of uniform, quality. Suppose that in a certain year 1000 tons of corn are produced by 1000 labourers who in the process have consumed 300 tons as seed and 500 tons as subsistence. Then the *net physical product* of that year (total product minus produced means of production used up as inputs[6]) is 1000–300 = 700; the *surplus product* is the net product minus the labourers' subsistence, 700–500 = 200. The *total necessary consumption* has been 300 + 500 = 800 tons.

If production is to be repeated on the same scale the following year, then 800 tons of the corn produced must be set aside to be used as seed and subsistence

---

3   Actually in this definition 'workers' should be interpreted to mean 'productive workers' only, cf. footnote 64 below.

4   Sometimes workers too can obtain a part of the surplus by raising their wages above subsistence, and this can change the subsistence itself; we will discuss these issues at several points in the chapter.

5   'Corn' in the classical authors is a generic name for all cereal grains, wheat barley, etc., and it is treated as the substance out of which most of the food of workers is made; and food was at the time such a preponderant part of the workers' consumption, that its consumption was often treated as representative of their entire necessary consumption.

6   'Input' means a good or service used in the production process of a commodity.

for the next production cycle; society is only free to use as it prefers the 200 tons of surplus, for example for consumption by landlords or warriors, or to maintain poets or musicians, or to build cathedrals, or for reinvestment. This last use means that part of the surplus is destined to increase the seed and the subsistence necessary for the production of corn. If for example 10% of the entire surplus is reinvested, then seed and subsistence employed in the next production cycle become 880 tons; if there is sufficient extra labour and extra land of the same quality as the land utilized up to then, and neglecting irregularities of agricultural yield, then in the subsequent production cycle production will be 1100 tons, obtained through the use of 1100 workers (who have consumed a total subsistence of 550 tons of corn) and 330 tons of seed. (This is assuming that the amount of labour performed on average by a worker does not change from one year to the next. Actually, how much on average a worker works might change, but for the moment let us leave this complication aside.)

So far the description might also apply to a society based on slavery, where the agricultural workers are slaves. For a capitalist society, the description is enriched as follows. Workers are wage labourers; the surplus is divided between land rents, obtained by landowners, and profits earned by the capitalists who organize production and anticipate seed-corn and wages. Suppose land rent is 100; then in our numerical example profits amount to 100 too, since the sum of rent and profit must equal the surplus, 200. The capitalist anticipated seed-corn and wages for which he needed to borrow (or to employ his own) capital equal in value to 800 units of corn; this capital yielded him a final product of 900, of which 800 replace the anticipated capital, and 100 are profits; the rate of profit, or rate of return on the anticipated capital, has been $100/800 = 12.5\%$.

Their own concrete experience suggested to classical authors that population is divided into three fundamental social classes: the landowners (generally *aristocrats*), whose income derived from the property of land; the *bourgeois* (ethimologically, inhabitants of towns) who are either professionals (lawyers, doctors, teachers, etc.) or businessmen (tradesmen, shopkeepers, industrialists, farmers, bankers, etc.); and the *labourers* or *workers* (mostly wage labourers, both agricultural, commercial and industrial). Dress, manners, values, everything sharply distinguished the members of these three classes. Slaves and serfs were given much less attention because, after the French Revolution, slavery was mostly abolished in the Western world (it survived in the USA, a sad record) and serfdom only survived in Russia and some other backward countries.

By the time of Adam Smith, and even more in subsequent decades with the Industrial Revolution, it became evident that the drive to economic development and change was coming above all from the *capitalists*, that is from the part of the bourgeoisie directly engaged as entrepreneurs-owners into obtaining an income from the employment of money sums (monetary *capitals*) in productive or commercial activities capable of yielding a revenue in excess of costs, i.e. a *profit*. This profit was in large part destined to enlarge the invested capital, i.e. it was reinvested into the creation of further farms, factories, shops, ships, trade ventures, etc., in an endless expansion process accompanied by an incessant search for technological innovations and entailing profound social transformations. This

1.2 · Social Surplus and Income Distribution

process is vividly portrayed by Karl Marx and Friedrich Engels in some deservedly famous pages of their *Manifesto of the Communist Party* (1848) that are worth quoting at length:

» The discovery of America, the rounding of the Cape, opened up fresh ground for the rising bourgeoisie. The East-Indian and Chinese markets, the colonization of America, trade with the colonies, the increase in the means of exchange and in commodities generally, gave to commerce, to navigation, to industry an impulse never known before, and thereby to the revolutionary element in the tottering feudal society a rapid development.

The feudal system of industry, in which industrial production was monopolized by closed guilds, now no longer sufficed for the growing wants of the new markets. The manufacturing system took its place. The guild-masters were pushed aside by the manufacturing middle class; division of labour between the different corporate guilds vanished in the face of division of labour in each single workshop.

Meantime the markets kept ever growing, the demand ever rising. Even manufacture no longer sufficed. Thereupon, steam and machinery revolutionized industrial production. The place of manufacture was taken by the giant modern industry, the place of the industrial middle class by industrial millionaires – the leaders of whole industrial armies, the modern bourgeois.

[......................................]

Each step in the development of the bourgeoisie was accompanied by a corresponding political advance of that class. [...] the bourgeoisie since the establishment of modern industry and of the world market, has at last conquered for itself, in the modern representative state, exclusive political sway. The executive of the modern state is but a committee for managing the common affairs of the whole bourgeoisie.

The bourgeoisie has played a most revolutionary rôle in history. Wherever it has got the upper hand it has put an end to all feudal, patriarchial, idyllic relations. It has pitilessly torn asunder the motley feudal ties that bound man to his 'natural superiors', and has left no other bond between man and man than naked self-interest, than callous 'cash payment'. It has drowned the most heavenly ecstasies of religious fervour, of chivalrous enthusiasm, of philistine sentimentalism, in the icy water of egoistical calculation. It has resolved personal worth into exchange-value, and in place of the numberless indefeasible chartered freedoms, has set up that single unconscionable freedom – Free Trade. In one word, for exploitation veiled by religious and political illusions, it has substituted naked, shameless, direct, brutal exploitation.

[......................................]

The bourgeoisie cannot exist without constantly revolutionizing the instruments of production and thereby the relations of production, and with them the whole relations of society. Conservation of the old modes of production in unaltered form was, on the contrary, the first condition of existence for all earlier industrial classes. Constant revolutionizing of production, uninterrupted disturbance of all social conditions, everlasting uncertainty and agitation distinguish the bourgeois epoch from all earlier ones.

10   Chapter 1 · The Classical or Surplus Approach

[................................]
The bourgeoisie, during its rule of scarce one hundred years, has created more massive and more colossal productive forces than have all preceding generations together. Subjection of nature's forces to man, machinery, application of chemistry to industry and agriculture, steam-navigation, railways, electric telegraphs, clearing of whole continents for cultivation, canalization of rivers, whole populations conjured out of the ground — what earlier century had even a presentiment that such productive forces slumbered in the lap of social labour?
We see then that the means of production and of exchange, which served as the foundation for the growth of the bourgeoisie, were generated in feudal society. At a certain stage in the development of these means of production and of exchange, the conditions under which feudal society produced and exchanged, the feudal organization of agriculture and manufacturing industry, in a word, the feudal relations of property became no longer compatible with the already developed productive forces, they became so many fetters. They had to be burst asunder; they were burst asunder.
Into their place stepped free competition, accompanied by a social and political constitution adapted to it, and by the economic and political sway of the bourgeois class.[7]

In an idealized picture that maximizes the difference among classes, the aristocrats, owing to their cultural formation of feudal origin (that stresses the lesser importance of money matters relative to courage and honour), mostly dislike the idea of becoming capitalists actively engaged in entrepreneurial activities and therefore generally rent out their lands to agricultural capitalists who create farms run for profit; the income of the aristocrats derives therefore from the *rent* of the land they own. The bankers, who lend money to the capitalists, are able to obtain an interest on their loans which depends on the profits of the capitalists; as Adam Smith explains, if an entrepreneur counts on earning a rate of return (rate of profit) of, say, 10% on an investment, he will be ready, considering the personal risk and fatigue, to borrow the capital necessary for the investment at a rate of interest perhaps of 5%, seldom of 7%, depending on the riskiness, etc., of the investment; if the expected rate of return is only 6%, then he will seldom accept to pay a rate of interest above 2 or 3%; in either case, interest is only a portion of profit, interest therefore determines a subdivision of profits between lenders and entrepreneurs, it can only be positive because profits are positive.

On this basis, classical economists concentrate on the forces determining three basic incomes: wages, profits and land rents, respectively the incomes of wage labourers, capitalists and landlords. Commercial exchanges are of course through money, but the classical economists perceived that the monetary value of things is

---

7   The *Manifesto of the Communist Party* is available in dozens of editions and in diverse translations. Here I have followed the version published by International Publishers, New York, 1932, which is the English translation authorized and edited by Friedrich Engels. These extracts are from chapter I, as reproduced in Freedman (1962, pp. 12–16).

1.2 · Social Surplus and Income Distribution

ultimately of little importance, what counts is which concrete goods are produced and who gets them. So they were interested in the *real* value of these incomes, i.e. their purchasing power in terms of **commodities** (the usual classical name for produced goods traded in markets). From the monetary values of commodities, the real value of a monetary income could be derived as its purchasing power in terms of some commodity or basket of commodities chosen as *measure of value* (or as *numéraire* in the more modern terminology deriving from Walras). (When I speak of value of something without further specification, it will mean the *real value*, i.e. the relative value in terms of the chosen numéraire.[8] The real value of a unit of the numéraire commodity is 1.) In the corn economy of our numerical example, the obvious measure of value or *numéraire* is corn itself and what must be determined is the real rate of wages (the amount of corn earned by workers per unit of labour time), the real rate of rent on each type of land (the amount of corn paid on an acre of land for its utilization for one time period)[9] and the real rate of profit (profits per unit of corn-capital anticipated). In our example all these magnitudes were real because specified in corn. (Note that for the rate of profit, which is a *ratio* between exchange values—the value of profits and the value of the capital advanced—the difference between 'real' and 'nominal' is not the same as for the rate of wages or the rate of rents; for the latter, 'real' means, purchasing power in terms of the good or bundle of goods chosen as *measure of value* or *numéraire*, and it changes if one changes numéraire; the rate of profit or rate of return on capital is unaffected by a change of numéraire, in its case 'real' means the rate of return *at constant money prices*, that is, eliminating the influence of inflation; as for the *real interest rate*. The reason is that if the rate of profit in terms of corn in our example is 12.5%, the rate of profit in terms of money can be very different if there is inflation. Suppose the money price of corn is 1 at the beginning of the year and 2 at the end of the year. A money wealth 800 anticipated as capital at the beginning of the year yields a money revenue 1800 at the end of the year; the monetary rate of return has been $1000/800 = 125\%$ which totally misrepresents how much richer the capitalist really is, which in this economy must mean in terms of his purchasing power measured in corn, which has increased by 12.5%.)

In this example the technology (the seed-corn, the labour and the land surface needed per unit of corn produced), the real wage rate and the real land rate were given. Profits could then be calculated as a residual, and the (real) *rate of profit* could be determined as the ratio of corn profits to the corn-capital advanced. We must now inquire into how these magnitudes, taken as given when determining the rate of profit, were determined according to classical authors.

---

8 If good 2 has money price p_2 and the numéraire, suppose it is good 1, has money price p_1, the price of good 2 in terms of numéraire, that is, how many units of the numéraire good must be given in exchange for one unit of good 2, is p_2/p_1. Check it with some example.

9 The acre is the old measure of land surface used in Great Britain at the time of Smith and Ricardo, equivalent to 4.046 m^2; a modern hectare (10,000 m^2) is equivalent to 2.47 acres.

12   **Chapter 1 · The Classical or Surplus Approach**

1.3 Income Distribution, Wages

1.3.1 The General Wage Level

In the classical approach the level of the real wage rate[10] is determined by a complex of social, demographic and economic circumstances, which can be classified in two groups.

A first group comprises those institutional and conventional elements that establish the level of the real wage considered normal in the period and in the society under discussion. This wage level, that the classical economists call 'natural' or 'subsistence wage', is the value of the 'necessaries', the consumptions indispensable to the worker's physical survival, capacity to work and reproduction, and also indispensable in the common (and historically specific) opinion of society for the worker's social role and membership in the social structure. A quotation from Adam Smith illustrates this perspective:

» By necessaries I understand not only the commodities which are indispensably necessary for the support of life, but whatever the custom of the country renders it indecent for creditable people, even of the lowest order, to be without. A linen shirt, for example, is, strictly speaking, not a necessary of life. The Greeks and Romans lived, I suppose, very comfortably though they had no linen. But in the present times, through the greater part of Europe, a creditable day-labourer would be ashamed to appear in public without a linen shirt, the want of which would be supposed to denote that disgraceful degree of poverty which, it is presumed, nobody can well fall into without extreme bad conduct. Custom, in the same manner, has rendered leather shoes a necessary of life in England. The poorest creditable person of either sex would be ashamed to appear in public without them. In Scotland, custom has rendered them a necessary of life to the lowest order of men; but not to the same order of women, who may, without any discredit, walk about barefooted. In France they are necessaries neither to men nor to women, the lowest rank of both sexes appearing there publicly, without any discredit, sometimes in wooden shoes, and sometimes barefooted. Under necessaries, therefore, I comprehend not only those things which nature, but those things which the established rules of decency have rendered necessary to the lowest rank of people. (*Wealth of Nations*, 1776, Bk V, Ch. 2, Part II, Article IV, Section "Taxes upon Consumable Commodities"; pp. 351–2 in the Dent and Dutton ed., Everyman's Library, vol. II, 1971 (1910). To help readers with different editions, it is customary to locate passages in *The Wealth of Nations* by indicating Book, Chapter and paragraph or Section.)

Note in particular the importance of being 'creditable': 'day-labourers' must show that they are not so poor as to make it probable that they are untrustwor-

---

10 The classical numéraire is often corn, at the time the main constituent of food, which absorbed most of the workers' income; sometimes it is gold, considered a produced good whose price is determined by cost of production in the same way as for other products.

1.3 · Income Distribution, Wages

thy. The idea applies more generally to lifestyles and makes lots of sense even for modern life. Acceptance by the others in modern social life requires, for example, being reasonably clean and not smelly.

An implication of this perspective is that, if wages rise above subsistence for a considerable period, subsistence tends to rise too; the new level of real wages tends to become the new subsistence, because of internalization of new consumption habits which, having become general, become part of what is socially expected.

The second group of factors affecting the real wage consists of the various elements influencing the relative bargaining strength of wage earners vis-à-vis employers and determining whether the actual wage level is above or below the normal, customary subsistence. To start to grasp these elements we can quote again Adam Smith (in this passage 'stock' means capital):

» What are the common wages of labour, depends everywhere upon the contract usually made between those two parties, whose interests are by no means the same. The workmen desire to get as much, the masters to give as little as possible. The former are disposed to combine in order to raise, the latter in order to lower the wages of labour.

It is not, however, difficult to foresee which of the two parties must, upon all ordinary occasions, have the advantage in the dispute, and force the other into a compliance with their terms. The masters, being fewer in number, can combine much more easily; and the law, besides, authorises, or at least does not prohibit their combinations, while it prohibits those of the workmen. We have no acts of parliament against combining to lower the price of work; but many against combining to raise it. In all such disputes the masters can hold out much longer. A landlord, a farmer, a master manufacturer, a merchant, though they did not employ a single workman, could generally live a year or two upon the stocks which they have already acquired. Many workmen could not subsist a week, few could subsist a month, and scarce any a year without employment. In the long-run the workman may be as necessary to his master as his master is to him; but the necessity is not so immediate.

We rarely hear, it has been said, of the combinations of masters, though frequently of those of workmen. But whoever imagines, upon this account, that masters rarely combine, is as ignorant of the world as of the subject. Masters are always and everywhere in a sort of tacit, but constant and uniform combination, not to raise the wages of labour above their actual rate. To violate this combination is everywhere a most unpopular action, and a sort of reproach to a master among his neighbours and equals. We seldom, indeed hear of this combination, because it is the usual, and one may say, the natural state of things, which nobody ever hears of. Masters, too, sometimes enter into particular combinations to sink the wages of labour even below this rate. These are always conducted with the utmost silence and secrecy, till the moment of execution, and when the workmen yield, as they sometimes do, without resistance, though severely felt by them, they are never heard of by other people. Such combinations, however, are frequently resisted by a contrary defensive combination of the workmen; who sometimes too, without any provocation of this kind, combine of their own accord to raise the price of their labour. Their usual pretences are, sometimes the high price of provisions; sometimes the great profit which their masters make by their work. But whether their combinations be offensive or defensive, they are always abundantly heard of. In order to bring the point to a speedy decision, they have always recourse to the loudest clamour, and sometimes to the most shocking violence and outrage. They are desperate, and act with the folly and extravagance of desperate men, who must either starve, or frighten their masters into an immediate compliance with their demands. The masters upon these occasions are just as clamorous upon the other side, and never cease to call aloud for the assistance of the civil magistrate, and the rigorous execution of those laws which have been enacted with so much severity against the combinations of servants, labourers, and journeymen. The workmen, accordingly, very seldom derive any advantage from the violence of those tumultuous combinations, which, partly from the interposition of the civil magistrate, partly from the superior steadiness of the masters, partly from the necessity which the greater part of the workmen are under of submitting for the sake of present subsistence, generally end in nothing but the punishment or ruin of the ringleaders (WN Bk. I, Ch. VIII, parr. xi–xiii; 1975, pp. 58–60).

Thus according to Smith the employers (the 'masters') are able normally to win in the wage disputes because of their capacity to resist longer in case of conflict, supplemented by the active support of the state in case of outbursts of revolt and violence by workers. The members of each class are united by a widespread consciousness of a common class interest: thus on the issue of the attitude towards workers there is a 'tacit, but constant and uniform combination' among the capitalists. Similar social mechanisms connected with a consciousness of a common class interest are active on the workers' side, and this tacit or sometimes vociferous alliance among workers can be expected to render the real wage rate fairly resistant to downward pressures, even in the presence of considerable unemployment, and even in the absence of trade unions or other explicit 'defensive combinations'. Indeed historical experience shows a great reluctance of workers to accept to work for a wage inferior to the one that, in the given historical situation, is considered 'fair' for their type of labour.

However, for Smith and the other classical authors the capitalists remain the stronger class; but then, one might ask, why don't they compress the wage rate even more?

Smith continues:

» When in any country the demand for those who live by wages … is continually increasing … the workmen have no occasion to combine in order to raise their wages. The scarcity of hands occasions a competition among masters, who bid against one another, in order to get workmen, and thus voluntarily break through the natural combination of masters not to raise wages;

....

where the funds destined for the maintenance of labour were sensibly decaying … the competition for employment would be so great …, as to reduce the wages of

1.3 · Income Distribution, Wages

labour to the most miserable and scanty subsistence of the labourer. Many would not be able to find employment even upon these hard terms, but would either starve, or be driven to seek a subsistence either by begging, or by the perpetration perhaps of the greatest enormities. Want, famine, and mortality would immediately prevail in that class, ... till the number of inhabitants in the country was reduced to what could easily be maintained by the revenue and stock which remained in it (WN, I, VIII, xvii, xxvi; 1975, pp. 61, 64–5).

One might derive from these observations a simple theory based on a population mechanism, and this theory was indeed derived by Ricardo's contemporary Thomas Malthus: if the real wage decreases below subsistence, then population decreases, labour supply decreases relative to labour demand, sooner or later a 'scarcity of hands' arises and competition among capitalists raises the real wage above subsistence; but then workers—Malthus argued—give birth to so many children and so many of these survive to working age that an excess of labour supply develops, which pushes the wage down, eventually below the subsistence level; thus the real wage oscillates around the subsistence level owing to its effect on population and hence on labour supply. The conclusion is very conservative: it is useless to raise wages, the labouring classes are condemned to remain poor by their tendency to have too many children as soon as the wage rises above subsistence.

Smith on the contrary, although arguing a tendency of population to adjust to demand,[11] admits that wage rises need not always cause increases in population: the newly available comforts can induce workers to have fewer children, so as better to defend their higher standards of living.[12] Thus persistent rises of real wages *are* possible, owing to the influence of the real wage itself on the social component of subsistence.

Note that, contrary to what modern supply-and-demand analysis would suggest, Smith does *not* say that wages keep decreasing as long as labour supply is greater than demand.[13] He classifies Great Britain as a country where demand for labour has been growing and wages have therefore tended to increase; and yet the

---

11 "…the demand for men, like that for any other commodity, necessarily regulates the production of men; quickens it when it goes on too slowly, and stops it when it advances too fast." (WN, I, 8, xl; 1975, p. 71). The whole of ▶ Chap. 8 of *The Wealth of Nations* makes for extremely interesting reading.

12 And Ricardo agrees: 'population may be so little stimulated by ample wages as to increase at the slowest rate – or it may even go in a retrograde direction' (in Sraffa, 1951–73, vol. VIII, pp. 168–69). The correctness of the usual attribution to Ricardo of a wholehearted endorsement of Malthusian wage theory can therefore be doubted.

13 In Smith 'supply' and 'demand' are always scalar quantities, *not* functions; accordingly the 'demand for labour' is the quantity of labour demanded in the given period (i.e., labour employment).

existence of unemployment in Great Britain (beggars, vagabonds and people on public relief or confined to workhouses) is not denied by him.[14]

But, if unemployment is generally present, why don't capitalists use their greater bargaining power to compress wages to the bare biological minimum that allows workers to have the energy to work? what is it that allows workers generally to defend the historical and customary excess of wages above bare biological subsistence? why does Smith speak of a 'lowest rate [of wages] which is consistent with common humanity' below which even capitalists do not find it convenient to compress wages? (WN, I, VIII, xxiv; 1975, p. 63).

The answer would appear to lie in Smith's description, quoted above, of the workers as 'They are desperate, and act with the folly and extravagance of desperate men'. 'Desperate' and 'extravagant' acts need not be caused by inability physically to survive; the same social habits, conventions and pressures that turn certain commodities into 'necessaries' can and will make it unbearable to live without them; thus, it would seem, Smith is implicitly admitting that it is the danger of ruptures of social peace and consequent disruptions of economic activity (both in the firm—e.g. sabotage—and in society at large: revolts, mobs), that makes it not convenient for the dominant class to try and depress the real wage below the historical subsistence level, i.e. below the level considered indispensable for a tolerable living by the great majority of workers.

Some such view of wages as considerably 'sticky' downwards is also implicit in the Malthusian wage theory based on the population mechanism. Variations of population are very slow; a decrease of real wages cannot but take many years before its influence on population can start being felt, but the influence of this decrease on population cannot but take *many* years to cause a significant decrease of unemployment; if one were to admit that, as long as there is excess labour supply, wages keep decreasing, one would have to conclude that real wages would fall enormously, even to nearly zero, against the empirical evidence; thus it is necessarily implicit in the Malthusian population mechanism that real wages only change very slowly, and that a high unemployment will cause *some* decrease in real wages below the previous customary subsistence level, but not indefinitely; and the reason must ultimately be the same as in Smith.

Thus in the classical approach real wages result from a continuous open or latent conflict and oscillate around a 'natural', or customary, real wage, which

---

14 An esteemed historian of economic thought indeed wrote, with reference to classical economists more generally, that 'in an era when the number of individuals on public relief hovered steadily around … 10 per cent of population … the existence of a hard core of surplus labour must have been taken for granted' (Blaug, *Ricardian Economics*, 1.1958, p. 75); and that 'Ricardo assumed the existence of Marxian unemployment' (*ibid.*, p. 179). Also cf. Smith's 'constant scarcity of employment' in WN, I, VIII, xxiv (1975, p. 63). Workhouses were sad quasi-prisons where the unemployed poor were obliged to live and work for a very low pay; their purpose was to decrease vagrancy and beggars.

1.3 · Income Distribution, Wages

labourers expect to earn (and consider therefore a 'fair' wage[15]) because it reflects the average balance of bargaining power between capitalists and wage labourers over the recent past; this customary 'subsistence' wage, which guarantees a standard of living which through habit has come to be regarded as indispensable to decent living, is the starting point of further bargaining. The latter, if conditioned by a changed balance of bargaining power,[16] can produce a lasting divergence of wages from their customary level, with a resulting slow change of the customary or 'natural' or 'fair' real wage itself. Unemployment does not necessarily exert a downward pressure on wages, except when it becomes very severe, and then it is still a *slow* and *not indefinite* downward pressure; more rapid and drastic decreases of real wages will only be observed in exceptional situations involving considerable political change (e.g.—to make a more modern example— after a right-wing military coup accompanied by bloody repression of workers' protests).

Such a perspective made it natural to consider the average real wage as something hardly susceptible of rapid change and to consider it an expense of production as inevitable as fodder for horses. Hence the treatment of the real wage as *given* when attempting the determination of the rate of profit and of land rents, and the conception of the incomes other than wages as a *surplus* over the necessities of reproduction. Given wages, not in the sense of exogenous with respect to economic analysis, but in the sense of explained by forces which allow one to consider wages as determined *before* profits and rents. Later we will see Marx's

---

15 . Historical evidence confirms the great importance, in the concrete behaviour of workers, of notions of 'a fair day's wage for a fair day's labour' (for recent evidence cf. the writings of Truman Bewley: Bewley T. F. (1999), *Why Wages Don't Fall During a Recession*, Cambridge, Mass., Harvard University Press; Bewley, T., (2005), 'Fairness, Reciprocity and Wage Rigidity', in H. Gintis, S. Bowles, R. Boyd, E. Fehr, *Moral Sentiments and Material Interests. The Foundations of Cooperation in Economic Life*, MIT Press.). The role and meaning of these notions is best appreciated, I would suggest, by viewing the normal real wage level as reflecting, in every period, an explicit or implicit armistice or truce in the continual latent or open conflict between wage labourers and employers. An armistice is a pact which saves losses and suffering to both parties to the conflict by suspending active fighting; pacts must be honoured; honouring a pact is 'fair', i.e. correct behaviour (remember that 'fair', in its basic meaning, does not mean ethically just, it means respectful of the rules, and giving each one its due, as in 'fair play' or 'fair decision'); a fair wage is then simply the wage that workers must get if they work correctly, according to the truce implicitly or explicitly signed by both parties; paying less would mean reneging on the armistice, and then workers too would not be bound to abide by their side of the pact. So, I would suggest, fair wages are fair, not in the sense of reflecting some perceived social *justice* of the resulting income distribution, but only in the sense that they correspond to the current truce, and must be paid if capitalists do not want a resumption of active conflict.

16 For an updating of what determines bargaining power to more modern situations, one can start from Smith's observations which stress the importance not only of unemployment but also of internal unity of either class, capacity of collective action, support of the state apparatus. One can then add what subsequent history shows, e.g. trade unions, enlargement of the electoral basis, discovery of new forms of struggle (e.g. work-to-rule; threat of dislocation of firms to other nations), unemployment benefits, military repression, political ideologies and so on.

views on the issue, and in ▶ Sect. 1.13 an important difference will be illustrated between the *inductive* classical approach to the real wage, and their *deductive* approach to the rate of profit and natural relative prices (prices of production).

1.3.2 Relative Wages

So far we have spoken of labour as if homogeneous,[17] with a single wage rate. Classical authors of course know that there are different kinds of labour, with differences in wage rates, and do discuss what determines these differences. Here too, a main reference is Adam Smith. He argues:

» The five following are the principal circumstances which, so far as I have been able to observe, make up for a small pecuniary gain in some employments, and counterbalance a great one in others: first, the agreeableness or disagreeableness of the employments themselves; secondly, the easiness and cheapness, or the difficulty and expense of learning them; thirdly, the constancy or inconstancy of employment in them; fourthly, the small or great trust which must be reposed in those who exercise them; and, fifthly, the probability or improbability of success in them (Smith, WN, I, x, I, 1: that is, Book I, Ch. X, Part I, par. 1).

Particularly interesting is the fourth circumstance, on which Smith adds: 'We trust our health to the physician, our fortune and sometimes our life and reputation to the lawyer and attorney. Such confidence could not safely be reposed in people of a very mean and low condition. Their reward must be such, therefore, as may give them that rank in the society which so important a trust requires' (WN, I, x, I, 19). (The complex sociological views behind these lines are still waiting for insertion into microeconomic theory.)

These circumstances render the ratios between wages very persistent, Smith argues, and a similar persistence exists for the differences in normal rates of profits:

» The proportion between the different rates both of wages and profit in the different employments of labour and stock,[18] seems not to be much affected ... by the riches or poverty, the advancing, stationary, or declining state of the society. Such revolutions in the public welfare, though they affect the general rates both of wages and profit, must in the end affect them equally in all different employments. The proportion between them, therefore, must remain the same, and cannot well be altered, at least for any considerable time, by any such revolution (WN, I, x, last par.; 1975, p. 130).

Thus it is possible, according to Smith, to treat *relative* wage rates (the 'proportion' between wage rates) as given when attempting the determination of the

---

17 This is the correct spelling (analogously, 'heterogéneous' = of a different *kind*), not the very frequent 'homògenous' which is erroneously imitated from the correct 'exogenous, endogenous' (= *coming from* outside, inside).

18 Remember that Smith calls 'stock' the capital advances.

1.3 · Income Distribution, Wages

other incomes and also when analysing the effects of forces that influence the *general* level of wages; analogous considerations apply to relative rates of profit.

Then in order to determine the wage costs of firms one can 'reduce' quantities of heterogeneous labour to quantities of a single type of labour on the basis of relative wage rates. Whenever classical authors speak of labour as if homogeneous and of 'the' wage rate, they are implicitly reducing quantities of heterogeneous labour to different quantities of homogeneous labour on the basis of given relative wages, generally to quantities of common, unskilled labour.

In conclusion, the existence of heterogeneous labour and of different wage rates does not prevent the treatment of wage costs as given when attempting the determination of land rents and of the average rate of profit.

1.4 The Other Data in the Determination of the Surplus

1.4.1 Quantities

Let us now briefly see how classical authors determine the other circumstances required to determine the amount and the rate of profit: quantities produced, production methods, rates of land rent.

We start with the *quantities produced*. The *composition* of production (an issue that did not arise in the corn economy example) is explained, for the part relative to the composition of *consumption*, as dependent on the historical development of consumption habits; the size and the composition of the production of capital goods are explained on the basis of the technical needs for reintegration of the capital stock and of society's propensity to accumulate; both consumption habits, and the propensity to accumulate, are considered historically variable and depending on the specific circumstances of the period. The *aggregate level* of production is considered to depend on the stage reached by the accumulation of capital, that is, on the past share of the surplus allocated to reinvestment rather than to consumption; and also, in the classical authors not accepting *Say's Law* (see below ▶ Sect. 1.9.2), on the factors determining fluctuations and crises, on which more later.

An important difference of these views from the later marginal approach is that one does not find in the classical authors the idea of a labour demand curve, establishing a *univocal* connection between real wage and labour employment and allowing a *simultaneous* determination of real wages and labour employment and hence level of aggregate production.[19] The effects of, for example, a change

---

19 As we will better see in ▶ Chap. 3, the marginal approach argues that lower wages increase the demand for labour even in the absence of growth of the capital stock; in the classical authors this notion is absent, in classical analyses increases in employment can only come about owing to capital accumulation, see this chapter's Appendix on Ricardo on machinery.

of the real wage rate on the composition of consumption, or on savings, or on employment, are considered sufficiently historically variable as to suggest a different method of analysis: in a first stage the effects of a change of the real wage on prices, on land rents and on profits are studied by taking the quantities produced as unchanged; this study is strictly analytical-deductive (see below); the results of this study can then be used in a second, more inductive stage of the analysis to try and estimate the probable effects on the quantities produced according to the specificities of the case.[20] Thus for example in Marx a rise of real wages definitely reduces the average rate of profit (the deductive, certain conclusion), but its effects on the quantities produced are to be determined according to historical circumstances, because sometimes a moderate increase in wages can stimulate aggregate production and employment owing to the workers' greater demand for consumption goods, at other times it can result in a discouragement to investment and to employment if perceived by capitalists as signalling a dangerous social strength of workers, capable of endangering the continuation of the capitalists' class domination.

1.4.2 Technology

The *production technology* adopted is explained by the classical authors as dependent on the stage reached by technical progress, and on the demand for natural resources, as we will see when we come to the determination of land rent. Initially for simplicity I neglect land rent.

The stage reached by technical progress determines the known alternative production methods for each commodity. The real wage, by determining costs, determines the relative convenience of these alternative methods, and this relative convenience determines the choice of production method on the basis of cost minimization; since real wages in general change only slowly, generally little attention is given to how their changes affect adopted methods. Great importance is given to the tendency to an increased division of labour, viewed as also affected by the extent of the market. According to Adam Smith:

» This great increase of the quantity of work which, in consequence of the division of labour, the same number of people are capable of performing, is owing to

---

20 The inductive character of the classical approach to consumer choice deserves a brief comment. We will see in ▶ Chap. 3 that in the marginal/neoclassical approach changes in the composition of consumer demand deductively derivable from changes in income distribution are very important for how the approach determines income distribution. In the classical approach the determination of income distribution is totally different, there is little interest in the general properties of how consumer choices change with changes in relative prices; the attention goes rather to the evolution of the *content* of consumer choices, for example, the evolution over time of preferences between income and leisure, the changing level of 'subsistence' and hence of the meaning of poverty, the importance of demonstration effects, the effects of new products such as railways (or, in modern times, the Internet and smartphones): questions connected with irreversible changes in tastes, to be studied with inductive, historical approaches.

1.4 · The Other Data in the Determination of the Surplus

three different circumstances; first, to the increase of dexterity in every particular workman; secondly, to the saving of the time which is commonly lost in passing from one species of work to another; and lastly, to the invention of a great number of machines which facilitate and abridge labour, and enable one man to do the work of many (WN, I, i, 5; 1975, p. 7).

The indivisibilities generally associated with machines require a minimum size of production in order for certain innovations to be profitable, so enlargements of markets help the introduction of more modern technologies.

Although not given great relevance by classical authors, the choice among alternative production methods for the same good and how it can be influenced by income distribution are issues that the approach must be able to tackle; modern analyses have greatly clarified the issues, let us illustrate the modern approach starting from the simplest case, the corn economy.

Assume labour is homogeneous and land is free because overabundant. A *production method* in the corn economy is defined by a_L, the **technical coefficient** of labour (i.e. the quantity of labour needed per unit of corn produced[21]), and by a_c, the technical coefficient of seed-corn input, i.e. the quantity of seed-corn per unit of corn produced. The overabundance of land allows the extension of production on more land with no need to change technical coefficients; so for each method, technical coefficients are assumed independent of the quantity produced: *constant returns to scale*.[22] Let z indicate the real wage rate, a quantity of corn, which, following the classical authors, we assume paid in advance; then total capital advanced at the beginning of the year as seed and as wages per unit of corn produced is $(a_c + za_L)$ and the rate of profit is given by

$$r = (1 - a_c - za_L)/(a_c + za_L).$$

If z changes, r changes. If z is zero the rate of profit is

$$r_{Max} = (1 - a_c)/a_c$$

which must be positive ($a_c < 1$) for the economy to function. An economy satisfying the condition $r_{Max} > 0$ is called *viable*, clearly an indispensable condition for the economy to be able to exist. Since $a_c < 1$, the wage rate associated with $r = 0$, i.e.

$$z_{Max} = (1 - a_c)/a_L$$

---

21 This quantity of labour is measured in time units, e.g. labour hours, and assumes a given intensity of labour effort. If labour intensity increases, then fewer hours of labour are necessary to obtain a given product, a_L decreases. The implicit assumption of a given labour intensity holds for the entire chapter. In fact, labour intensity results from bargaining between workers and firms as much as the daily wage and the number of hours of labour per day, so it will be taken as given only to maintain the analysis initially as simple as possible.

22 This means that if all inputs are increased in the same proportion, output increases in that same proportion. Different methods imply different technical coefficients. When only one method is known then one says that there are *fixed technical coefficients*.

22   Chapter 1 · The Classical or Surplus Approach

is positive. Furthermore it is easy to check that

$$dr/dz = -a_L/(a_c + za_L)^2 < 0,$$

well defined for $z \neq -a_c/a_L$, hence $r(z)$ is monotonically decreasing and invertible for $z \geq 0$. Following the usual practice in the literature I draw this function with the rate of profit in abscissa and the wage rate in ordinate and I limit the analysis to its portion in the non-negative orthant. Actually r can become negative, but I leave aside this possibility because it can only be strictly temporary, it discourages the employment of capital in a capitalistic economy where capital is employed to obtain profits: production would come to a halt.

The curve $z(r)$ is downward-sloping with positive intercepts. Its derivative

$$dz/dr = -(a_c + za_L)^2/a_L < 0$$

increases in absolute value with z, hence $z(r)$ is strictly convex.[23]

Let us compare $z(r)$ with the curve obtaining if wages are paid at the *end* of the year, i.e. *in arrears*, or *post-factum* (an assumption more appropriate to a majority of modern industries if by 'year' one means the length of a production cycle, often very short in manufacture). Then the capital advanced does not include the wages, and the relationship between rate of profit and wage rate— indicating now with w the real wage rate paid post-factum—is

$$r = (1 - a_c - wa_L)/a_c = (1/a_c) - 1 - w(a_L/a_c) \quad or \quad w = (1/a_L) - (1+r)a_c/a_L.$$

Thus $w(r)$ is a straight line with slope $-a_c/a_L$. The intercepts are the same as with advanced wages.

Let us now compare the equations establishing 'price of corn = cost of production of corn inclusive of profits' in the two cases, remembering that corn is the numéraire, i.e. the price of corn is 1. The 'cost of production inclusive of profits' of one unit of corn is the cost of seed-corn plus wages plus the rate of profit r on the capital advanced. We obtain, respectively:

$$1 = (1 + r)(a_c + za_L)$$

$$1 = (1 + r)a_c + wa_L.$$

Hence $z(r)(1+r) = w(r)$.

This means that in the *positive* orthant it is $z(r) < w(r)$, while at the intercepts with the axes the two curves coincide, cf. ◻ Fig. 1.1.

We can now compare the $z(r)$ or the $w(r)$ curve of two different methods. It is perfectly possible for a method to have a higher maximum rate of profit, and

---

23 A continuous function $f(x)$ is called strictly convex in economics if, given any two values x and x' of the independent variable, with t a scalar satisfying $0 < t < 1$ it is $f(tx + (1-t)x') < tf(x) + (1-t)f(x')$; in words and referring to the graphical representation of the function, a segment connecting two points of the graph of a strictly convex function is all above the graph (except of course at the extremes).

1.4 · The Other Data in the Determination of the Surplus

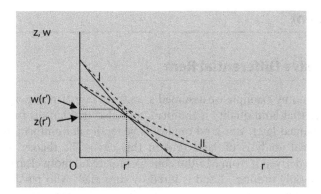

● **Fig. 1.1** Intersecting wage curves of two alternative methods in the corn economy. The continuous curves are the $z(r)$ curves of the two methods, and the broken straight lines are the $w(r)$ curves. The intersection of the $z(r)$ curves is vertically aligned with the intersection of the $w(r)$ curves (prove it!)

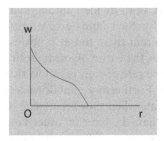

● **Fig. 1.2** Possible $w(r)$ curve for a multicommodity economy

a lower maximum rate of wages, than a second method: it suffices that the first method has a lower a_c and a sufficiently greater a_L than the second method. Then their $z(r)$ curves intersect in the positive orthant, and their $w(r)$ curves too, and for the same r. For each real wage, given whether the wage is advanced or paid in arrears, capitalists prefer the method yielding the higher r, hence the economy's wage–profit curve is the 'outer' or north-east envelope of the two curves. (Note that there is an interval of values of the real wage in which the preferred method depends on whether the wage is advanced or paid in arrears.) At the r where the two curves cross, the two methods can coexist. The analysis can be easily extended to more than two alternative production methods. It can well be that some method is never the preferred one because its wage curve is entirely below the outer envelope of wage curves.

In conclusion, given the institutional circumstances that determine whether the wage is advanced or paid ex post, a given real wage univocally determines the rate of profit even in the presence of technical choice. We will extend the study of choice of techniques to more complex cases in ▶ Chaps. 2 and 10.

24   Chapter 1 · The Classical or Surplus Approach

1.5 Land Rent

1.5.1 Extensive Differential Rent

In the corn economy example we assumed a uniform rate of rent per acre of land, which requires that land quality is uniform, and also that land is fully employed, as will be explained later. But land quality is generally *not* uniform, and we start with the classical analysis of land rent in this case. The theory we present is Ricardo's (who derived it from Malthus but formulated it more clearly).

Corn is the only product. Land is hired by capitalists who pay a post-factum yearly rent per acre to landlords for its use. The real wage rate is the same for all labourers, and given. Real wages are advanced, and therefore advanced capital includes wages and seed-corn. Only one production method (defined by quantity of seed-corn and of labour per unit of output, and quantity of output per hectare, or per acre) is known for each type of land.

Let us suppose that there are two types of land, a more fertile one, type A, and a less fertile one, type B, both divided among many owners. The landowners have no other employment for their lands except renting them out to capitalists for cultivation and prefer to rent them out at a positive rent however low, rather than leave them unused. Thus the entire quantity both of land A and of land B is offered for rent even when the rate of rent is so low that for practical purposes we can take it as equal to zero. Furthermore, landowners offer their land at a lower rate of rent than the going rate when they are unable to rent it, in order to induce capitalists to hire it rather than the land of other landowners; thus competition lowers the rate of rent on each type of land until either the rate of rent becomes *practically* zero,[24] or that type of land is fully employed.

If the rate of rent is zero on both types of land, then capitalists will only demand the land that yields the higher rate of profit, i.e. the higher surplus per unit of capital advanced. Let A be this land. Suppose initially the production of corn is so small that only land A is demanded, but not the whole of it, and competition among landowners causes the rate of rent on it too to tend to zero.

Now imagine that, from such an initial situation, corn production increases because demand for corn increases, and a point is reached where land A is no longer sufficient, and it is necessary to employ also part of the supply of land B. As long as some part of land B is unemployed, competition causes the rate of rent on it to be zero. But if no rent is paid on land A, the capitalists who use land

---

24 When the rate of rent is truly zero, plausibly land will not be offered for rent (unless it loses its fertility if left idle). So we should interpret the cases of zero rent as in fact meaning a very low rate of rent, not quite zero but very close to zero, below which landowners refuse to rent their land because some minimal rent is necessary to compensate them for the risk and trouble of signing the contract, checking that the farmers do not ruin the land, etc. By 'practically zero' we mean precisely a rate of rent positive but so low that it can be neglected; this being understood, from now on we drop 'practically'.

B obtain a lower rate of profit than on land A. Therefore they will offer to pay a positive rate of rent for the use of land A, as long as this rate of rent allows them to obtain a higher rate of profit than on no-rent land B. In order not to be displaced, the capitalists using land A have to accept themselves to pay that rate of rent. Because of competition, the rate of rent on land A will rise up to the point where the rate of profit on land A becomes equal to the rate of profit on no-rent land B.

A numerical example can illustrate. Assume that the yearly quantity of capital advanced *per acre* (seed-corn plus wages per acre[25]) and the yearly quantity produced *per acre* are as follows (the arrow stands for 'produce'):

A: $5 \rightarrow 9$ per acre.
B: $12 \rightarrow 18$ per acre.

If rent is zero on both lands, production yields a rate of profit of 80% on land A, of 50% on land B. Land A is therefore the first one put to cultivation. (Notice that the order of profitability when all rents are zero, i.e. of fertility *per unit of capital employed*, need not correspond to the order of fertility *per acre*: here land B is the one that produces the greater amount and the greater surplus per acre.). When the expansion of production brings land B into cultivation, competition causes a rent to appear on land A and to rise until it reduces the rate of profit on land A to 50%. This means profits per acre on land A must be 2.5, and a rate of rent per acre on land A of 1.5.

Suppose that further expansion of production brings to the full employment of land B too and requires in addition to utilize part of a third type of land, C, which when paying no rent yields a rate of profit less than 50%, for example:

C: $10 \rightarrow 12$.

The zero-rent rate of profit on land C is 20%. Competition will then bring down the rate of profit to 20% on both lands A and B. The rates of rent per acre that achieve such a result are 3 on land A and 3.6 on land B. Note the *higher* rate of rent *per acre* on land B: the order of profitability, although coinciding with the order of rent per unit of *capital*, does not necessarily coincide with the order of rent *per acre*, or order of *rentability*, which also depends on fertility per acre.

The existence of positive rates of rent derives from *differences* in the rates of profit obtainable on different lands when there is no rent: this is why these rents are called *differential* rents. And because they arise as cultivation is *extended* to less and less profitable lands, the rents thus arising are called **extensive differential rents**.

Note an important consequence of this theory. Apart from the transitional periods when the last land put into cultivation has just become fully utilized and

---

25 In this example it does not matter which portion of advanced capital is seed-corn and which portion is advanced wages. Corn is measured e.g. in tons.

26   **Chapter 1** · The Classical or Surplus Approach

soon one more land will be put into cultivation, there is always a type of land which is not fully utilized and whose rate of rent is therefore zero.[26] On this land the **supply price** of the product (the output price necessary to induce production of the quantity demanded) does not include rent; as classical economists used to put it, *rent does not enter* price. Do the **Exercise** in footnote in order fully to understand the meaning of this statement.[27] Given the wage rate, the determination of profits is as a residue, on the no-rent land. And as long as the no-rent land does not change, one can study the effects of changes in the real wage rate, or of technical progress, on the rate of profit without considering rent.

As long as there is a no-rent land which does not change with changes in quantities produced, nor with changes in production methods due to changes in income distribution or to technical progress, and this land is known, one can analyse the dependence of prices, and of technical choice, on income distribution totally neglecting land and land rent. This can be very convenient because then one can rely on the **non-substitution theorem**, which states: 'given either the rate of profit, or the real wage, if there are no scarce natural resources and no joint production then long-period prices and the other distributive variable are independent of quantities produced, they depend only on technical coefficients, which are either given or determined by cost minimization independently of the composition of demand'. If in fact there is land rent, but there is a given no-rent land, then the non-substitution theorem is **locally valid**, that is, valid as long as changes in quantities produced or in production methods do not require altering the no-rent land.

1.5.2 **Intensive Differential Rent**

Differential rent can arise for another reason. Let us again suppose that a type of land becomes fully utilized and the rate of rent on it starts to rise. There may be a different method for the production of corn on that land, which was not utilized up to then because it would have yielded a lower rate of profit when rent was zero, but which is more productive *per acre* than the first method, so that, when

---

26 The transitional periods mentioned in the text are analogous to the periods of transition to a new long-period price of a product, associated with the discovery of a way to produce it at a lower cost. Economic theory cannot aim at describing the details of these transitions, which depend on a myriad of accidental elements, but it can indicate the important things: the direction of change and the situation toward which the economy tends.

27 Of course this statement is intended for goods other than the measure of value, whose price is 1 by definition. To understand its meaning, as an **Exercise** apply the reasoning to another good, say potatoes, producible on lands A, B, C with the indicated technical coefficients (quantities of corn), and now with a *given* rate of profit (determined in the production of corn) equal to, say, 20%. The price of corn is 1. Determine the price of potatoes as the minimum price guaranteeing $r = 20\%$ on the no-rent land. Show that in this case it is the supply price of potatoes that rises as one extends cultivation to land B and then C, and determine how rents per acre change.

1.5 · Land Rent

the rate of rent rises, the rate of profit decreases slower for the second method than for the first. Then it can happen that at a still positive rate of profit a rate of rent is reached, at which the two processes are equally profitable; then they can be used side by side, and since the second method is more productive per acre than the first, a gradual extension of the part of land cultivated with this method and corresponding contraction of the part using the first method will assure a gradual increase in the amount of corn produced, up to the quantity demanded. In this case, rent has the function of rendering two different methods on the same land equally profitable; the second method utilizes land *more intensively*, i.e. produces more per unit of land by using more capital; one speaks of **intensive differential rent**.

Let us illustrate with an example. Now there is only one type of land, and A and B stand for two different productive methods on it. As before, wages are assumed advanced, given and summed up with seed so as to obtain the total corn-capital advanced *per acre*, and the corresponding quantities produced per acre are:

A: $5 \rightarrow 9$.
B: $12 \rightarrow 18$.

The numbers are the same as in the previous example, but now they refer to two different methods of production per acre *on the same land*. When rent is zero, the rate of profit is 80% with method A, and 50% with method B, so capitalists adopt method A. Suppose that demand for corn increases until all land is utilized and still insufficient to satisfy demand. Capitalists compete for land, and a positive rent is born and starts to rise. The rise in the rate of rent causes the rate of profit to decrease faster for the method that uses more land per unit of product, i.e. method A.

Let r_A and r_B be the rates of profit obtainable with the two methods, and let β stand for the rate of rent per acre, paid at the end of the year. If β is given, the rates of profit determined by the two methods will generally differ, they are determined by:

$$5(1 + r_A) + \beta = 9$$
$$12(1 + r_B) + \beta = 18$$

Thus for example if $\beta = 1$, it is $r_A = 3/5 = 60\%$, $r_B = 5/12 \cong 42\%$; if $\beta = 2$, it is $r_A = 2/5 = 40\%$, $r_B = 1/3 \cong 33\%$. The two methods become equally profitable for the value of β that solves the system assuming $r_A = r_B$; the solution is:

$$\beta = 18/7; \quad r_A = r_B = 2/7 \cong 28.6\%.$$

If β becomes greater than 18/7, r_B becomes greater than r_A, method B is more profitable and starts replacing A; the opposite happens if β is less than 18/7. This means that competition will ensure a gravitation of β towards 18/7, as I illustrate now.

We must now treat the demand for corn as a parameter, and corn is only one of the products in a larger economy. Then the demand for corn derives from the larger economy, so it can be taken as given from the viewpoint of the corn industry. Assume that no other production competes with corn for the use of land. Suppose initially that $\beta = 18/7$ and corn production equals demand; then for some reason corn demand rises. This stimulates an increase in the price of corn and hence in the rate of profit in corn production at the initially unchanged rent rate, thus investment in corn production rises, this enhances the competition for land, and β rises; the result is that method B is extended at the expense of A, and corn production increases until it equals the new greater demand.

As the expansion of the demand for corn proceeds, method B gradually replaces method A, while rate of rent and rate of profit do not change. When method B totally replaces method A, then corn production cannot be further increased, unless there is a third method which when $\beta = 18/7$ yields a rate of profit less than $r = 2/7$, but is more productive per acre such that a rise in the rate of rent makes it equally profitable with method B at a still positive rate of profit. For example:

C: $16 \rightarrow 23$.

The reader can check that B and C are equally profitable for $\beta = 3$, $r = 25\%$, while for $\beta = 18/7$ the rate of profit obtained with method C is less than 2/7.

The same process that caused B to become equally profitable with A will now cause a decrease of r to 25% and a rise of β to 3, rendering B and C equally profitable and thus allowing a further expansion of production by gradual extension of the use of C and contraction of B. Method A is no longer present: with intensive differential rent, only two processes coexist at each time.

Intensive differential rent is the possible justification of the assumption, made in our first presentation of the corn economy, of a uniform rate of rent on land of uniform quality: this land must be fully utilized. As production is increased, method C ends up by covering the entire land, then rent on it will be determined as extensive differential rent as production is extended to another land.

Of course, the simultaneous presence of extensive and intensive rent is possible. The gradual extension of corn production will use new lands, or new methods on already fully utilized lands, depending on what allows a smaller decrease in the rate of profit from its previous level. But since on each land the rates of profit at which two processes can coexist are well determined (they are isolated values, not intervals), then except for flukes[28] or transitional periods *there will never be more than one land on which two methods coexist and intensive differential rent is present, and it will be the last land put into cultivation.*

Is it possible to argue that intensive rent too 'does not enter price'? It might seem not, since all producers on this land pay a rent. But in fact it is still possible to argue that rent does not enter the 'cost of production inclusive of profits'

---

28 I.e. cases in which the coexistence of two processes requires exactly the same rate of profit on two different types of fully utilized land.

1.5 · Land Rent

of the last unit of corn produced, if one reasons as follows. Take the case when methods B and C coexist. Consider the 'differential method' that represents the *increase* in capital (seed plus wages) producing the *increase* in output if method C replaces B on one more acre. This is.

D: $4 \to 5$.

Notice that if this were an autonomous per-acre method *paying no rent*, it would yield a rate of profit $r_D = 25\%$, precisely the ruling rate of profit. Suppose total land surface is $x + y$ acres, method B is used on x acres and method C on the remaining y acres, and an intensive rate of rent β per acre is paid on all $x + y$ acres. Consider the farmer who extends method C from $y - 1$ to y acres, i.e. replaces method B with C on one more acre. She pays the same rent as before, so it is as if on that acre, besides applying method B as before, she were now additionally employing no-rent method D on top of method B. So we can visualize this producer as using method B on *all* the $x + y$ acres of available land and then adding no-rent method D on y acres. We might even visualize the producer as having at her disposal *two* lands both of surface $x + y$ acres, a first-quality land requiring method B, and a second-quality land on which method D can be employed. Then the rate of rent β can be viewed as the *extensive* differential rent rate earned by the first-quality land, when method D is used on the second-quality land which is not fully utilized and therefore earns no rent. With this visualization, all rent is extensive differential rent, and no-rent method D can be seen as determining the supply price of corn as including no rent. Thus it is possible with intensive rent too to conceive corn as produced by two different methods, one of which—the differential method—pays no rent, and in this way to argue that even with intensive differential rent, 'rent does not enter price'.[29]

According to this theory of rent, except during temporary transitions, there is always either a no-rent land, or a no-rent differential method. An implication is that moderate changes in quantities produced need not alter the rates of rent, because the lands and methods in use remain the same, what changes is only the extent of cultivation of the no-rent land, or the proportions between the two methods adopted on the intensive-rent land. Then for the study of problems in which changes in quantities produced can be presumed to be of minor importance, one can consider the no-rent production method not to change.

It must be added that Karl Marx did not follow Ricardo on land rent, he argued that there is also a rent which is not differential rent, but *absolute rent*, due to the capacity of landowners to pretend an income just for letting their land be utilized, so there is no no-rent land. But Marx's manuscripts on this issue and in general on rent theory are very provisional and not very clear, and a fairly unanimous consensus of modern scholars finds them unpersuasive if not plainly wrong. Therefore I skip Marx on rent.

---

29 The reader can apply to this case the same *Exercise* with potatoes as in fn. 25.

30   **Chapter 1 · The Classical or Surplus Approach**

1.6 Rate of Profit and Relative Prices

In the corn economy, product and capital are physically homogeneous; the rate of profit is determined as a ratio between physically homogeneous magnitudes. In real economies, on the contrary, there are many products, and relative prices are necessary to determine the rate of profit or rate of return on advanced capital. If a capitalist produces a good by employing capital, the rate of profit is

$$r = \frac{(value\ of\ product\ minus\ loss\ of\ value\ of\ the\ capital\ employed)}{(value\ of\ capital\ employed)}.$$

Unless there is product homogeneity, this ratio changes if the price of the product changes relative to the prices of the goods employed as capital. A simple example shows it. Suppose 1 ton of apples, with price p_2 per ton, come out at the end of the year and their production on no-rent land utilizes a units of seed-corn and L units of labour paid at the *beginning* of the year a corn wage w. Assume corn, good 1, is the measure of value or numéraire, so $p_1 = 1$. Advanced capital has value $a + wL$, nothing of it survives to the end of the year, so the capital consumption by the end of the year equals the capital advanced,[30] and the rate of profit in the production of apples is given by

$$r = \big[p_2 - (a + wL)\big]/(a + wL).$$

What we explained about the determinants of wages and of production methods authorizes us to take a, L, w as given. Still, we have one equation in two variables, r and p_2. Arguing that the same problem would arise for any product price, Walras accused Ricardo of trying to determine two variables with one equation, and therefore of not having an acceptable theory of price determination. Is that so really? Can we surmount this apparent indeterminateness?

First of all, let us be clear as to what prices we are talking about: the prices of products called **natural prices** by Adam Smith, that is the hypothetical product prices that would result from competition having brought to completion its tendency to render rates of wages, rates of rent and rates of profits uniform in all industries. Adam Smith distinguished between *market price* and *natural price*. Market prices are the actually *observed* day-by-day prices, influenced by transitory and accidental circumstances (and generally not even uniform, at each point in time, for all the units of the same commodity, so that to speak of 'the' market price of a commodity already presupposes some kind of averaging). Natural prices are a theoretical notion: the prices around which market prices gravitate, continually tending to come back to them after every deviation. This is because they are the prices that allow the payment of rent for the land used, the payment of wages to the labour employed, and the earning of profits on the capital advanced, *at their normal rates in the given situation, rates that Smith called* **natu-**

---

30 Advanced capital which at the end of the production cycle is entirely lost is called **circulating capital**. For durable or fixed capital, the value loss at the end of the production cycle is generally only part of its value, it is called **depreciation**. Here all advanced capital is circulating, because seed disappears, and wages once paid are lost to the capitalist.

1.6 · Rate of Profit and Relative Prices

ral rates. If the price of a commodity is above its natural level, then at least one of the three rates (of wages, of land rents or of profits) is above its natural rate, attracting further producers into that industry because by paying wages and land rents at their natural rate they earn a greater rate of profit than elsewhere. But the increased production and increased competition among suppliers of the commodity tend to lower its market price, which therefore tends towards its natural level. Conversely for a price below its natural level: production decreases, and this tends to raise its market price. Natural prices can also be called (Marx's preferred name for them) *prices of production*.

Nowadays they are also referred to as *long-period normal prices*. The reader who studied some economics will observe that she/he is already familiar with the notion, because it is introduced in any economics textbook when, in a partial-equilibrium framework, the tendency is studied, in competitive conditions with free entry, of the price of a product towards the long-period price corresponding to minimum average cost and hence to zero 'profits' according to the marginalist/neoclassical definition of profits.[31] But two observations are opportune here.

First, in these partial-equilibrium Marshallian analyses the tendency of market price towards long-period price equal to minimum average cost is studied on the basis of *given* input 'prices' or, as I shall prefer to call them, input *rentals*.[32] But the moment capital goods are admitted among the inputs of the good in question, the same tendency must be admitted to be simultaneously at work, and with a speed of the same order of magnitude, for the prices of these capital goods, *prices which therefore cannot be assumed given unless they in turn are equal to minimum average cost*. Now, many capital goods are, directly or indirectly, inputs to their own inputs: for example iron requires machines made of iron for its production. Then the minimum average cost of iron cannot be determined before determining the price of iron, because the minimum average cost of some of its inputs depends on the price of iron. So the Marshallian determi-

---

31 Profits are defined in marginalist theory as what is left of revenue after paying all costs *including* interest (gross of a risk-compensating allowance) on the capital employed. The classical authors did *not* include interest among the costs to be subtracted from revenue in order to obtain profits, in them the term 'profit' has a different meaning: 'profit' is what is left of revenue after paying all costs *except* interest. The classicals' rate of profit is what nowadays is called rate of return on the value of the capital employed. The tendency to zero 'profits' in the marginalist sense is expressed by the classical authors as the tendency of profits to become just sufficient to cover normal costs, and in addition the rate of interest on advanced capital increased to include a risk allowance. If for simplicity we neglect the risk allowance, zero neoclassical profits means classical rate of profit equal to rate of interest. To avoid ambiguities, where necessary the neoclassical meaning will be conveyed through the term 'extra profits'. The reader who is new to economics should come back to this and the next two paragraphs after studying ▶ Chap. 5.

32 The *rental* (or rental rate) of a factor is the price *of its services* per time unit: the rental of land is its rent per acre, the rental of labour is its wage per labour unit, the rental of a capital good is what each unit of that capital good can fetch per period if rented out. The reason for this terminology is that in this way there is no risk of confusing the price to be paid, e.g. for purchasing the *property* of a piece of land, with the price (the rent) to be paid for the *right to use* that land for a specified length of time. It is the latter price, i.e. the price of the services of land that enters the costs of production of commodities.

32   **Chapter 1** · The Classical or Surplus Approach

nation of long-period price as equal to minimum average cost is only legitimate for a good whose price does not enter the cost of production of its inputs (a pure consumption good), and as long as all input prices are given; a general consistent determination of the long-period price of a product requires the simultaneous determination of the long-period prices of all capital goods directly or indirectly entering its production,[33] and these can depend on the price of the good in question. Partial-equilibrium analysis is therefore generally insufficient for an explanation of the long-period normal prices of produced goods. We seem to find here again the indeterminacy denounced by Walras. We need a theory showing that the above simultaneous determination is possible, and at what conditions.

Second, these long-period prices must not only cover the costs of inputs and the wages of labour, but must also yield a uniform rate of profit, or rate of return, or—if one neglects risk—rate of interest on the capital advanced.[34] The way the costs of firms are usually described in standard microeconomics obscures the presence of this component of the cost that the long-period price must cover. Total cost is usually defined in standard microeconomics as:

$$C = v_1 x_1 + \ldots + v_n x_n, \tag{1.1}$$

where C is total cost, v_i is the rental (the price of the services) of the *i-th* 'factor of production' (the term used in marginalist theory for the inputs to production), x_i is the quantity employed of (the services of) the *i-th* factor of production.[35] No rate of interest or rate of return on capital appears among the costs; but it is not absent; it does not explicitly appear only because factor payments are implicitly assumed to be at the same moment as when revenue is obtained from the sale of output. Thus consider production of corn by means of seed-corn and labour, both paid at the beginning of the year while the product is sold at the end of the year. Let x_1 be seed-corn and x_2 labour in expression (1.1). Assume a rate of interest $i = 20\%$ (equal to

---

33 The time required for setting up new firms can sometimes be a year or even longer; and the entry process can take longer than that, if firms need time to make sure that demand is persistently greater than supply. In such a time span the relative amounts in existence of all capital goods can change considerably and must therefore be considered to have had the time to adjust so that their prices and rentals are at their natural or long-period values.

34 If investment is riskless, then ideally lenders will be able to ask for a rate of interest on their loans equal to the rate of profit, or rate of return, that borrowers are going to earn on their investments. This is the assumption that for simplicity I will generally make. Both classical and marginalist economists admit that the rate of interest that firms include in their costs is higher than the market rate on safe loans, the difference being necessary in order to cover the 'risk and trouble'—to use Adam Smith's expression—of entrepreneurial activity. Therefore profit in the marginalist sense does not actually tend to zero in the long period, but rather to that level that covers 'risk and trouble'; and the classical rate of profit tends to equality not with the rate of interest, but rather with the rate of interest increased by a percentage that must cover 'risk and trouble'. But I will generally neglect this complication and neglect risk.

35 It is common, although unrigorous, to speak of 'quantity employed *of a factor*', although what is meant is the quantity *of its services*, a quantity requiring for its specification also the indication of the time unit to which the unit of measurement refers. Thus when one says that the amount of labour employed is x, what one means is that the firm employs x units of labour time per period (how many labourers this means, depends on how many labour hours each labourer works per period).

1.6 · Rate of Profit and Relative Prices

rate of return or classical rate of profit because risk is negligible), a money wage rate $w=100$ paid at the beginning of the year, and a money price of seed-corn bought at the beginning of the year equal to 10. The standard representation of costs of Eq. (1.1) would have $v_1=12$, and $v_2=120$, the unit cost of seed-corn and of labour if the firm pays them at the *end* of the year, for example to an intermediary who has anticipated money to pay seed-corn and wages at the beginning of the year, and must then receive a 20% interest on this capital advance. Thus the absence of a rate of interest or rate of return on advanced capital in the usual specification of the cost of a firm does not mean that it is not there. The usual (neoclassical) textbook definition of profit means 'excess of revenue over a cost that *includes* the rate of interest over all costs that are advanced relative to when revenue is obtained'. Thus when the dominant microeconomics teaches that in the long period the price of produced commodities tends to equal average cost and profit tends to zero, a classical author would express the same idea by saying that in the long period price tends to become such as to make the rate of profit on the capital advanced equal to the rate of interest.

Let us then see how the insufficiency of the Marshallian determination of long-period prices can be surmounted.

Consider two commodities, corn (commodity 1) and iron (commodity 2), both produced in yearly production cycles by corn, iron and labour as inputs, with given production methods. Both corn and iron when used as capital goods are *circulating* capital goods, entirely consumed in a single utilization. They are called *means of production* to distinguish them from corn and iron not actually used as inputs but entering costs as wage goods. It is usual in the modern literature on long-period prices (prices of production) to indicate quantities produced with the symbol x, so forget the above use of $x_1, ..., x_n$ to indicate quantities of inputs, and let x_1, x_2 be the quantities produced of corn and iron; the production methods are described by technical coefficients a_{ij} where $i=1, 2, L$ indicates the input, while $j=1, 2$ indicates the output.[36] We can represent these methods as follows, where * stands for 'together with', and $\rightarrow$ stands for 'produce':

$$a_{11} * a_{21} * a_{L1} \rightarrow 1 \text{ unit of good } 1$$

$$a_{12} * a_{22} * a_{L2} \rightarrow 1 \text{ unit of good } 2$$

The labour technical coefficients are measured in labour-years per unit of output.[37] All inputs and all products are perfectly divisible[38]; if all inputs are varied

---

36 The reader must be warned that other authors (for example the basic reference treatise by Kurz and Salvadori, 1995) define a_{ij} to indicate the quantity of input j used per unit of output i, the opposite of the convention adopted here.

37 Of course the measurement of labour in labour-years assumes a given average number of labour hours in a year, with a given average intensity and dexterity of labour.

38 This assumption is to be intended as meaning that the smallest unit is sufficiently small as to allow neglecting indivisibilities. For example, cars are not perfectly divisible, but if a firm produces 10,000 cars of the same type a year, a variation of output by one unit is a variation of output by only one tenth of a thousandth, such a small fraction of total output that to treat output as a continuous variable in order to study, e.g., how cost varies with output is legitimate.

34   **Chapter 1** · The Classical or Surplus Approach

in the same proportion then output too varies in the same proportion (*constant returns to scale*). Of course technical coefficients indicate the *minimum* quantities needed per unit of output: firms, being interested in minimizing production costs, try not to use more inputs than necessary.

Land is overabundant and hence free, or alternatively we interpret the methods as referring to no-rent land or no-rent differential method.

Natural prices must cover wage costs and the cost of the means of production and in addition must cover the rate of profit which must be the same in both industries (we neglect here the elements admitted by Adam Smith which can determine persistent differences in rates of profit). Let p_1 be the price of corn, p_2 the price of iron, w the wage rate, i.e. the value of the physical wage basket which is a (column) vector $\mathbf{z} = (z_1, z_2)^T$ and r the rate of profit.[39] Then if wages are advanced, natural prices must satisfy

$$p_1 = (1 + r)(a_{11}p_1 + a_{21}p_2 + wa_{L1}) \tag{1.2}$$

$$p_2 = (1 + r)(a_{12}p_1 + a_{22}p_2 + wa_{L2}) \tag{1.3}$$

$$w = p_1 z_1 + p_2 z_2. \tag{1.4}$$

$$p_1 = 1. \tag{1.5}$$

The last equation indicates that corn is chosen as *numéraire* or *measure of value*. Without this equation, the system is indeterminate in the sense that if (p_1, p_2, w, r) is a solution, then (tp_1, tp_2, tw, r) is a solution too for any $t > 0$ as the reader can easily check; the system can only determine the *ratios* between p_1, p_2 and w.

We have here a system of four equations in four variables. ► Chapter 2 will prove that, dropping for a moment Eq. (1.4) and considering w measured in terms of the numéraire, if there is a range of values of w for which r is positive (in which case the economy is capable of producing a surplus, and is said **viable**), then r decreases if w increases in that range, and prices are uniquely determined and positive for each w. So what is needed to make natural prices determinate is either:

- the addition of Eq. (1.4), which takes as given what a wage can purchase (in a range for which r is not negative), or alternatively:
- a given rate of profit, determined for example by a given rate of interest (neglecting the elements that require the rate of return to be greater than the rate of interest to cover risk) and by the tendency of competition to undercut competitors by reducing product price if the price allows producers in that industry to earn a rate of return greater than the rate of interest.

Here we are concerned with classical authors, and they took the real wage as given, so we add Eq. (1.4). Alternatively we could replace this equation with just fixing w as equal to a positive scalar, then Eq. (1.5) would imply we are fixing the real wage in terms of the numéraire—how many units of corn the money wage can purchase.

---

39 Careful: the T in superscript indicates transposition, not elevation to the power T. In this book generally price vectors are row vectors, quantity vectors are column vectors.

1.6 · Rate of Profit and Relative Prices

It emerges that if the real wage is given, either as a vector of physical quantities or in terms of the numéraire, and such that $r \geq 0$, the moment all conditions price = natural price are simultaneously considered the indeterminateness, that seemed to appear when studying the price of apples, in fact is not there. A given real wage and given production methods do determine natural product prices and the rate of profit.

We can obtain an insight of the mathematical nature of the system by replacing w, in Eqs. (1.2) and (1.3), with the right-hand side of Eq. (1.4). The two equations come out to form a system of two equations linear and homogeneous in the two prices, if we treat r as a given parameter:

$$[1 - (1+r)(z_1 a_{L1} + a_{11})]p_1 - (1+r)(z_2 a_{L1} + a_{21})p_2 = 0 \qquad (1.6)$$

$$-(1+r)(z_1 a_{L2} + a_{12})p_1 + [1 - (1+r)(z_2 a_{L2} + a_{22})]p_2 = 0. \qquad (1.7)$$

Now, it is well known that a homogeneous linear system with as many equations as variables has a nonzero solution (that determines only the *relative* values of the variables) *if and only if the determinant of the matrix of coefficients is zero.* The rate of profit, which enters those coefficients, is therefore determined by the condition that it must render zero that determinant. In the present case this condition yields a second-degree equation, which determines two values r_1, r_2 which might be complex, but it can be proved (see next chapter) that if the economy is capable of producing a surplus then one and only one of these two values is real and economically significant because associated with real and positive prices. Note that prices do not enter the coefficients of the determinant, so we can see the rate of profit as determined *before* relative product prices. This confirms a certain intuition both Ricardo and Marx had, although they were unable to prove it rigorously for the general case: that the rate of profit depends on physical properties of the production system and there must be a way to determine it without needing simultaneously to determine relative prices, contrary to what Eqs. (1.2)–(1.3) seem to suggest. (Another way to determine the rate of profit before relative prices, that can be given a nice economic interpretation, is based on Sraffa's notion of *Standard commodity* and will be illustrated later.)

The generalization to more than two industries is immediate. For each additional commodity, one has one more variable, its price, but also one more equation, determining its natural price as equal to cost inclusive of the uniform rate of profit. So the number of equations remains equal to the number of variables. If the economy produces n different commodities, it suffices to know the technical coefficients a_{ij} and the vector representing the average physical wage basket or anyway the basket in terms of which the real wage rate is fixed[40] $(z_1, ..., z_n)^T$, and one can write the following equation for each ith price:

$$p_i = (1+r)[a_{1i}p_1 + a_{2i}p_2 + \ldots + a_{ni}p_n + (z_1 p_1 + z_2 p_2 + \ldots + z_n p_n)a_{Li}], \quad i = 1, \ldots, n. \qquad (1.8)$$

---

40 Once the real wage rate is fixed in terms of some good or composite basket of goods, then relative prices and the rate of profit are determined independently of how wages are actually spent.

36   **Chapter 1 · The Classical or Surplus Approach**

With n commodities one obtains a system of n price equations in the $n+1$ variables $p_1, ..., p_n$, r, and the system will determine *relative* prices and the rate of profit; the choice of a numéraire will fix prices.

We can also assume that w is paid in arrears, at the end of the production period, this only means that in the price equation of each commodity i the term wa_{Li} is not multiplied by $(1+r)$. The number of equations remains equal to the number of variables, and the nature of the mathematical problem remains essentially unchanged.

We can conclude that the magnitudes taken as given in the classical approach for the purpose of determining the rate of profit and normal prices do allow their determination. It must only be added that the quantities produced, which do not appear in Eqs. (1.2)–(1.8), are in fact implicitly present if land is not a free good, in that the corn industry technical coefficients appearing in them are those of the method on no-rent land or those of the no-rent differential method, and their determination requires to determine the no-rent land or the no-rent differential method, and this requires given quantities produced (together with the available quantities of the several types of land and the production methods on each type). The more complex analysis including land rent but valid beyond the very simple corn economy will be tackled in ▶ Chap. 10.

1.7 Corn Model, Luxury Goods, the Decreasing w(r) Function

Leaving for ▶ Chaps. 2 and 10 a more rigorous examination of the system of equations of natural prices or prices of production with n commodities, it is useful to point out two implications of that system of equations that even the simple corn–iron economy allows to illustrate.

Suppose in Eqs. (1.2)–(1.5) coefficients a_{21} and z_2 are zero. That is, production of corn has only corn among its inputs, both as means of production and as real wages. Then we have what is called the '*corn model*', an economy where one industry (here the corn industry, equal to the corn economy discussed earlier) uses only its product as input, both as means of production and as real wages, hence *the rate of profit is a material ratio*, profits and advanced capital are physically homogeneous.[41] Clearly, the rate of profit is determined in this industry: the iron industry can only adapt the price of its product so as to yield the same rate of profit. If the rates of profit are not the same in the two industries, investment will be directed in greater proportion to the higher-profit-rate industry, but the profit rate in the corn industry cannot change, it will be the change in production and hence in price in the iron industry that will change the price of iron until the iron profit rate becomes equal to the corn profit rate. The conditions of production of iron have no influence on the rate of profit, the price of iron is passive; for example, if technical progress reduces some technical coefficient in the iron

---

41 The '*corn model*' is an economy with several industries, in which the corn industry uses only corn as input. The *corn economy* is an economy that produces only corn.

1.7 · Corn Model, Luxury Goods, the Decreasing W(R) Function

industry, the rate of profit is unaffected, all that happens is that the price of iron decreases relative to the price of corn.

A good that enters neither the basket of goods in terms of which the real wage is fixed, nor the inputs of the industries directly or indirectly producing that basket of goods, is called a ***luxury good***. Iron is a luxury good in the corn–iron economy if both a_{21} and z_2 are zero; it is not, if only one of these two coefficients is zero. 'Directly or indirectly' refers to the fact that an industry *indirectly* contributes to the production of wage goods if it does not produce any of the goods in the wage basket but produces an input to one of the industries producing them (or to one of the industries indirectly producing them). If $a_{21} > 0$ and $z_2 = 0$, the iron industry indirectly contributes to produce the wage good, corn.

Given the real wage, the rate of profit is determined by the system of natural price equations of the sole industries directly *or indirectly* producing the basket of goods in terms of which the real wage is fixed; these are called ***the wage industries***. The other industries produce luxury goods. The prices of luxury goods can be determined in a second stage, after determining the rate of profit and the prices of the products of the wage industries. Thus if in the corn–iron economy $a_{21} > 0$, $z_2 = 0$, and if with no change in Eqs. (1.2)–(1.5) we add a third industry producing diamonds (good 3) whose price equation is

$$p_3 = (1 + r)(a_{13}p_1 + a_{23}p_2 + wa_{L3}), \qquad (1.9)$$

then this equation can be initially left aside because p_3 does not enter any other equation; p_3 is determined after the other equations are solved and supply p_1, p_2, w, r to insert into Eq. (1.9). The diamond industry is not a wage industry, the iron industry is.

Now let us show in a simple way that if r rises, the real wage decreases, a point on which Marx insisted as proving the conflict of interests between capitalists and wage labourers. Rewrite Eqs. (1.2)–(1.3) so that on their right-hand side the wage payments appear separately:

$$p_1 = (1 + r)wa_{L1} + (1 + r)(p_1a_{11} + p_2a_{21}) \qquad (1.10)$$

$$p_2 = (1 + r)wa_{L2} + (1 + r)(p_1a_{12} + p_2a_{22}) \qquad (1.11)$$

In the second addendum on the right-hand side of Eq. (1.10) let us replace p_1 and p_2 with the corresponding right-hand sides of Eqs. (1.10)–(1.11). We obtain

$$\begin{aligned}
p_1 &= (1 + r)wa_{L1} + (1 + r)\{[(1 + r)wa_{L1} + (1 + r)(p_1a_{11} + p_2a_{21})]a_{11} \\
&\quad + [(1 + r)wa_{L2} + (1 + r)(p_1a_{12}p_2a_{22})]a_{21}\} \\
&= (1 + r)wa_{L1} + (1 + r)^2w(a_{L1}a_{11} + a_{L2}a_{21}) \qquad (1.12) \\
&\quad + (1 + r)^2[p_1\left(a_{11}^2 + a_{12}a_{21}\right) + p_2(a_{21}a_{11} + a_{21}a_{22})].
\end{aligned}$$

This expresses the cost of production of commodity 1 as the wages paid to direct labour with the interest on them (because advanced), plus the wages paid to labour employed in the production of the direct means of production with the

38   Chapter 1 · The Classical or Surplus Approach

compound interest on them (because paid two periods before the output comes out), plus a residue (the third addendum on the right-hand side) where p_1 and p_2 appear again. Iterating the replacement of p_1 and p_2 with the corresponding right-hand sides of Eqs. (1.10)–(1.11), we can express the cost of production of commodity 1 as an infinite series of wage payments to the smaller and smaller quantities of labour employed to produce the direct means of production, their means of production, the means of production of those means of production, and so on indefinitely, each wage payment multiplied by $(1+r)^n$ where n indicates how many periods earlier that wage payment was made. If we write L_{-1}, L_{-2}, ..., L_{-t}, etc., for these 'dated' quantities of labour (e.g. $L_{-1}=a_{L1}$, $L_{-2}=a_{L1}a_{11}+a_{L2}a_{21}$), with $-t$ indicating that these amounts of labour are paid t periods before the output is obtained, we can rewrite Eq. (1.12) as

$$p_1 = w \cdot \left[(1+r)L_{-1} + (1+r)^2 L_{-2} + (1+r)^3 L_{-3} + \dots + (1+r)^n L_{-n} + \dots \right].$$

$$(1.13)$$

Let us now choose the wage as numéraire, i.e. let us divide p_1 and p_2 by w. The prices $p_1'=p_1/w$ and $p_2'=p_2/w$ thus obtained measure what Adam Smith called the **labour commanded** by each commodity, because they measure the amount of labour services that one can purchase (i.e. *command*, have at one's orders) with one unit of each commodity: if the money wage is \$100 and the price of a car is \$2000, the labour commanded by a car is 20, that is with the value of a car one can have at one' command 20 units of labour. Their reciprocals, $1/p_1'$ and $1/p_2'$, measure the purchasing power of the monetary wage rate, respectively, in terms of corn and of iron. Importantly, dividing both sides of the price equations by w does not determine income distribution, it only chooses the wage as numéraire, w becomes 1, but r is still not determined, nor the purchasing power of w in terms of goods. For example in the corn economy the price equation with advanced wages is

$$p_1 = (1+r)wa_{L1} + (1+r)p_1 a_{11}$$

and if we divide by w to obtain $w'=1$ the equation still has two variables,

$$p_1' = (1+r)a_{L1} + (1+r)p_1' a_{11}, \tag{1.14}$$

hence the real wage rate $1/p_1'$ is not determined yet, it depends on r, as r increases p_1' increases, indicating a lower real wage: when prices are measured in labour commanded, a rise in prices indicates a reduction of the real wage.

If we apply the measurement of prices in terms of labour commanded to Eq. (1.13) we obtain that p_1 becomes $p_1'=p_1/w$ and that w disappears:

$$p_1' = (1+r)L_{-1} + (1+r)^2 L_{-2} + (1+r)^3 L_{-3} + \dots + (1+r)^n L_{-n} + \dots \tag{1.15}$$

Now the sole variable on the right-hand side is the rate of profit. Clearly if r increases, p_1' increases because all terms on the right-hand side increase. An increase of p_1' means a decrease of the real wage in terms of commodity 1, which

1.7 · Corn Model, Luxury Goods, the Decreasing W(R) Function

proves that a rise of r reduces the real wage in terms of commodity 1. Exactly the same procedure would show that the same is true for p_2'. This shows that when r rises, the purchasing power of the wage decreases in terms of both commodities (although generally not by the same percentage, because p_2/p_1 changes). As will be shown in ▶ Chap. 2, the proof is generalizable to $n > 2$ commodities. This proves that when r rises, the real wage rate decreases in terms of any (simple or composite) commodity.

The assumption nowadays more common, that wages are paid not in advance but in arrears, does not affect the proof. In Eqs. (1.10)–(1.11) w is no longer multiplied by $(1 + r)$, so when one 'reduces' the cost of production of good 1 to dated wages the dated quantities of labour are all paid one period closer to when the output comes out than with advanced wages, and after division by w Eq. (1.15) becomes

$$p_1' = L_0 + (1 + r)L_{-1} + (1 + r)^2 L_{-2} + \ldots + (1 + r)^n L_{-n} + \ldots, \tag{1.15'}$$

where $L_0 = a_{L1}$, and L_{-n} corresponds to $L_{-(n+1)}$ of Eq. (1.15). Now the first term on the right-hand side does not increase when r increases, but all the other ones do. ▶ Chapter 2 proves that the series on the right-hand side of these equations are convergent.

We can conclude that, whichever the numéraire chosen, the real wage in terms of that numéraire is a strictly decreasing function of r; therefore we can draw in (r, w) plane a decreasing $z(r)$ curve or, if wages are paid in arrears, a $w(r)$ curve, similar for many-commodities economies to the curves in ◼ Fig. 1.1. Only, this curve can alternate convex and concave portions, it will be a straight line only in very special cases to be discussed later.[42]

1.8 The Labour Theory of Value

Classical authors were unable to reach the equations here illustrated (and expanded to more general cases in ▶ Chap. 2; they are generally called *Sraffian price equations*, because largely due to Sraffa 1960). Their theory remained defective on the proof that the magnitudes taken as given in the classical approach in order to determine the rate of profit (methods of production, real wage, and quantities produced if there are land rents to be determined) are in fact sufficient to determine it. The best exponents, Ricardo and Marx, got only close to the correct equations, through the *Labour Theory of Value*. It is opportune to explain the latter theory and especially how Marx made use of it, not only in order to have a sense of the historical evolution of economic theory, but also better to understand how the classical approach could be accused of being radically defective and deserving to be supplanted by the superior marginal or supply-and-demand approach.

---

42 In economics it is standard to intend concavity and convexity as referred to the abscissa, so a concave curve is what a mathematician would call 'concave downward', i.e. concave if looked at 'from below'.

40 Chapter 1 · The Classical or Surplus Approach

The labour theory of value is presented by Adam Smith, but only to be then immediately discarded. Smith observes that when 'the whole produce of labour belongs to the labourer', i.e. when there are no rents and no profit, then relative natural prices will equal ratios of labour 'embodied': commodities will tend to exchange in proportion to the labour required to produce them. The famous passage goes.

» In that early and rude state of society which precedes both the accumulation of stock and the appropriation of land, the proportion between the quantities of labour necessary for acquiring different objects seems to be the only circumstance which can afford any rule for exchanging them for one another. If among a nation of hunters, for example, it usually costs twice the labour to kill a beaver which it does to kill a deer, one beaver should naturally exchange for or be worth two deer. It is natural that what is usually the produce of two days' or two hours' labour, should be worth double of what is usually the produce of one day's or one hour's labour (Wealth of Nations Bk. I Ch. VI, vol. I p. 41–2).

The reason, not made explicit in this passage, is that if the exchange ratio was different from two deer to one beaver, it would be convenient for hunters to hunt only one of the two animals and obtain the other by exchange. For example if the exchange ratio is three deer to one beaver, all the hunters who desire to obtain deer but know how to hunt beavers will find it more convenient to hunt beavers, because by hunting beavers and then exchanging beavers for deer, with the labour time required to catch *two* deer they can obtain *three* deer; but the resulting increase in the supply of beavers and decrease in the supply of deer will cause beavers to become cheaper relative to deer. Thus the exchange ratio tends to gravitate towards two deer for one beaver.

There are a number of implicit assumptions in this argument, e.g. that there are no obstacles (e.g. taxes) to hunting either animal, and that a sufficient number of hunters know how to hunt either animal. Also, as already explained, if commodities are produced by different kinds of labour differently rewarded, for the argument to hold one must reduce the quantities of labour to homogeneity on the basis of relative wages. But within its assumptions the argument is convincing and can be extended.

The example of beavers and deer refers to goods produced by direct labour alone, but if rents and profits are zero, relative normal prices remain proportional to labour even if production uses capital goods besides labour; only, it is ***embodied*** labour that counts, i.e. the direct and indirect labour employed (or wages paid—the two are proportional, given that labour is reduced to homogeneity on the basis of relative wages) to produce a good *as net product*. It suffices to consider the corn–iron economy we already know. Assume homogeneous labour. The labour embodied or contained in a commodity is defined as the labour directly employed in its production (sometimes called the direct or living labour), plus the labour embodied in the produced means of production used up in its production. In the corn–iron economy the labours embodied in a unit of corn and in a unit of iron—let us indicate them as m_1 and m_2—are determined by:

$$m_1 = a_{L1} + a_{11}m_1 + a_{21}m_2 \qquad (1.16)$$

1.8 · The Labour Theory of Value

$$m_2 = a_{L2} + a_{12}m_1 + a_{22}m_2. \tag{1.17}$$

For example the first equation states that the labour embodied in one unit of corn, m_1, is the sum of the direct or living labour a_{L1}, and of the labour embodied in the means of production used up, $a_{11}m_1 + a_{21}m_2$.

Let us compare these equations with those determining natural prices. If profits are zero (and if there are land rents we consider the price equations on no-rent land), the natural price must cover only the wage costs and the cost of the means of production. Let p_1 be the price of corn, p_2 the price of iron, w the wage rate, i.e. the value of the physical wage basket (e.g. if the physical wage basket consists of z units of corn, it is $w = p_1 z$). Then natural prices must satisfy

$$p_1 = wa_{L1} + a_{11}p_1 + a_{21}p_2 \tag{1.18}$$

$$p_2 = wa_{L2} + a_{12}p_1 + a_{22}p_2. \tag{1.19}$$

If in both equations we divide both sides by w, we obtain equations identical to Eqs. (1.16)–(1.17) with the sole difference that in place of m_1 there is p_1/w, and in place of m_2 there is p_2/w. It follows that $p_1/w = m_1$, $p_2/w = m_2$, and therefore $p_1/p_2 = m_1/m_2$, *the ratios between natural prices coincide with the ratios between labours embodied*. The **labour theory of value** holds; values, i.e. natural prices are proportional to wages embodied and hence to labours embodied, and *coincide* with labours embodied—and are then called **labour values**—if one chooses as *measure of value* or *numéraire* a commodity embodying one unit of labour.

The reason is easy to grasp: the *labour embodied* in a commodity is the sum of (1) living labour employed in its production; (2) living labour employed in producing its means of production; (3) living labour employed in producing the means of production of those means of production; and so on indefinitely if necessary; in the absence of profits, wage costs are strictly proportional to quantities of labour, and they are the only costs that the natural price must cover, hence the natural price is the sum of these quantities of labour, each one multiplied by the wage rate. Therefore one can also say that in the absence of profits the natural price measures the *wages embodied* in the commodity; but since these are proportional to the labour embodied in the commodity, relative prices equal relative labours embodied.

There remains to clarify why in the definition given above of labour embodied it was said that it is the direct and indirect labour required to produce a commodity *as net product*. The reason is the following. Consider the corn–iron economy. Assume the quantities produced of corn and of iron in one production cycle are x_1 and x_2.[43] The net products y_1 and y_2 are obtained from these, subtracting the quantities of the same product consumed as means of production:

$$y_1 = x_1 - a_{11}x_1 - a_{12}x_2 \tag{1.20}$$

---

43 In Eq. (1.1), following prevalent textbook practice, I used x_i to indicated the quantity of input i. From now on, following the prevalent use in the literature on Sraffian price equations, x_i will indicate the per-period production of commodity i.

Chapter 1 · The Classical or Surplus Approach

$$y_2 = x_2 - a_{21}x_1 - a_{22}x_2. \tag{1.21}$$

Suppose the net product of the economy consists only of 1 unit of good 1, i.e. $y_1 = 1$, $y_2 = 0$. Then the system of Eqs. (1.20)–(1.21) can be solved and yields total quantities produced:

$$x_1^* = (1 - a_{22})/[(1 - a_{11})(1 - a_{22}) - a_{12}a_{21}]$$

$$x_2^* = a_{21}/[(1 - a_{11})(1 - a_{22}) - a_{12}a_{21}].$$

To produce these quantities, *total* labour employment, indicate it as L_1^*, is

$$L_1^* = a_{L1}x_1^* + a_{L2}x_2^* = [a_{L1}(1 - a_{22}) + a_{L2}a_{21}]/[(1 - a_{11})(1 - a_{22}) - a_{12}a_{21}]. \tag{1.22}$$

Now let us derive m_1 from the system of Eqs. (1.16)–(1.17). I leave to the reader the easy calculations: she will discover that $m_1 = L_1^*$! Analogously, it can be shown that $L_2^* = m_2$.

Thus, the labour embodied in a commodity is the total amount of labour time (total employment measured in units of labour time utilized—not in number of workers employed) needed to produce that commodity as net product, that is, the labour employment required to produce that commodity at the same time reintegrating all the means of production consumed, so that the economy can repeat the same productions the next production cycle. We can equivalently view the labour embodied in a commodity as the sum of direct labour and of the indirect labour earlier employed in producing its means of production, the means of production of those means of production and so on; or as the total labour simultaneously employed in an economy which produces that commodity as the sole net product. The second picture views as contemporaneous all those labour employments that the first picture views as successive in time.

I said that Smith immediately discards the labour theory of value. After noting the validity of the labour theory of value *if the natural price must only cover wages*, Smith observes that it is no longer valid when the natural price must also cover rents and profits. Let us leave rents aside for now, the Ricardian theory of differential rent (which Smith did not have at his disposal) shows that rents do not enter price. But Smith's objection remains valid even if we neglect rent. Assume the corn–iron economy, suppose (the 'corn model') that $a_{21} = 0$, $z_2 = 0$, and furthermore that $a_{22} = 0$, so iron too employs only corn both as means of production and as real wages (we obtain a 'corn model'). Let the remaining technical coefficients be

$$a_{11} = 0.2, \ a_{L1} = 1; \ z_1 = 0.3; \ a_{12} = 0.5, \ a_{L2} = 1.$$

Since in this case $m_1 = a_{L1} + a_{11}m_1$, it is $m_1 = 5/4$. Hence $m_2 = 13/8$, and $m_2/m_1 = 13/10 = 1.3$.

Now let us determine p_2/p_1. Choose corn as numéraire, $p_1 = 1$, then $p_2/p_1 = p_2$. The rate of profit is determined in the corn industry. Assume wages are advanced, then total capital advanced to produce 1 unit of corn is 0.5 units, hence

1.8 · The Labour Theory of Value

$r=100\%=1$. Therefore $p_2=(1+r)(0.5+0,3)=1.6$, different from 1.3. The labour theory of value does not hold.

But the divergence of relative natural prices from relative labours embodied will generally be small when the rate of profit is small and the ratio between value of means of production and wage costs does not greatly differ as between goods.[44] In the previous example, assume now that $a_{11}=0.609$, the other coefficients remaining unchanged. Then $r=10\%$, and $p_2=0.88$, while $m_1=1/0.391 \approx$ 2.56 and $m_2 \approx 2.28$, yielding $m_2/m_1 \approx 0.89$, very close to p_2/p_1. Without being able to produce such precise examples, David Ricardo sensed that, for realistic rates of profit (usually below 20%) the deviations of relative prices from relative labours embodied were going to be small: not greater than about 7%, he argued in one occasion. Furthermore some unpublished manuscripts of his show that he reasoned that, for the study of the problem he was centrally interested in—the sign of the effects of *changes* in the real wage rate on the rate of profit—those deviations would largely compensate one another when the big aggregates relevant for the determination of the rate of profit (the social surplus net of rents, and aggregate capital) were considered.[45] Being unable to get to a more precise determination of natural prices, he decided that the assumption of relative prices equal to relative embodied labours approximated the true relative natural prices sufficiently to prevent mistakes on the *sign* of the changes of the rate of profit caused by changes in the magnitudes determining it. Thus he assumed the labour theory of value as an approximation, well knowing that, rigorously speaking, it was not correct as a theory of relative natural prices. He was aware that relative prices depend on the rate of profit, but the rate of profit in turn depends on relative prices (except in the 'corn model'); to assume the labour theory of value allowed him to escape from this vicious circle because then relative prices are given independently of the rate of profit. Given

- (i) the quantities produced of each good, whose vector constitutes the *social product* physically considered,[46]

---

44 If the ratio between value of the means of production and wage costs is the same for all goods (a condition called by Marx *equal organic composition of capital*) then the labour theory of value holds. The reason is that, since the rate of profit is uniform, in this case the share of direct wages in the natural price is the same for all goods (prove it!), hence the ratio of direct labour to natural price is the same for all goods; so the succession of 'dated' quantities of labour in Eq. (1.15) is the same for all commodities; so a rise of r from zero raises the labour-commanded price of all commodities by the same percentage, and *relative* prices do not change, remaining the same as when r = 0, where the labour theory of value always holds. One special case of this assumption is when advanced capital consists only of advanced wages, which is what Smith and Ricardo mostly assume: then prices are greater than wage costs by the same percentage r. Also see ▶ Sect. 1.9.2.

45 The reason why Ricardo believed in this reciprocal compensation is much the same as in Marx and will be explained when we come to Marx.

46 We need this new term to distinguish the notion of 'all commodities produced in the economy in the given period' from the modern notion of gross national product, which includes the entire production of durable capital goods but includes only the *net* production of circulating capital goods.

44 Chapter 1 · The Classical or Surplus Approach

- (ii) the methods utilized to produce them,[47]
- (iii) the real wage,

he could derive the means of production and the wage goods constituting the physical advanced capital employed, and by difference, the physical goods going to profits (the surplus vector). Since relative prices were given (by the labour theory of value), he could then determine the rate of profit as

$$r = \frac{\text{aggregate } \textit{labour value} \text{ of the physical surplus (net of rent)}}{\text{aggregate } \textit{labour value} \text{ of the physical capital advances (inclusive of real wages)}}. \quad (1.23)$$

Without the labour theory of value, he would have encountered the problem that, since profits and advanced capital generally are of different composition, their relative value, that is the rate of profit, would depend on relative prices which depend on the rate of profit.[48]

The labour theory of value had then for Ricardo the role of allowing a measurement, of numerator and denominator of the fraction determining the rate of profit, independent of the rate of profit itself, surmounting the apparent danger of logical circularity due to the value of those aggregates depending on what they had to determine, the rate of profit.

The labour theory of value allowed Ricardo to reach a number of conclusions confirmed by modern equations. First of all, that if real wages rise, the rate of profit decreases. Second, that if, with an unchanged real wage, agricultural cultivation is extended, and less fertile lands must be put into cultivation, then land rents rise, and the rate of profit decreases. Third, that technical progress can reduce employment (see the section 'Ricardo on machinery' in the online Appendix to the chapter in the book's Website).

---

47 I am assuming here that commodities are produced according to normal conditions of production, so that the labour employed to produce them is what Marx would later call the *socially necessary labour* according to the dominant production technique of that period. If part of the production of a commodity comes from inefficient producers and uses more than the socially necessary labour, its labour value is nevertheless determined by the socially necessary labour. This is because labour values—in the conditions in which the labour theory of value would be a correct theory of relative prices—must determine the normal prices around which market prices gravitate, i.e. the prices that the more efficient producers tend to impose.

48 At first in the *Essay on Corn* (1815) Ricardo tried to surmount the danger of circularity by arguing that in agriculture there was nearly homogeneity between output, which at the time consisted for the greatest part of corn (the basic food for most of the population), and capital, consisting mostly of seed-corn and above all of wages in turn consisting essentially of corn. In other words he assumed the 'corn model'. But Thomas Malthus criticized the assumption of homogeneity between capital and product in the corn sector, pointing out that the workers' given subsistence also included manufactures. Ricardo, a very honest person, admitted that the 'corn model' did not apply if wages relevantly included non-agricultural products and started looking for a more general theory of the rate of profit, compatible with a lack of physical homogeneity between profits, and advanced capital. He concluded that he needed a way to determine relative prices *before* the rate of profit and adopted the labour theory of value as the best way he could find to answer that need.

1.8 · The Labour Theory of Value

Before leaving Ricardo, let us show how differential rents appear in the labour theory of value. In the absence of rents, the labour embodied in the aggregate *net product* of a year coincides with the total live labour performed during the year:[49] let L be the total labour performed during the year, and let C be the labour value transferred to the products by the means of production used up during the year (assume all capital is circulating capital); then the labour value of the social product is $C+L$, but the labour value of the *net* product is $C+L$ minus the labour value of the means of production used up, hence it is $C+L-C=L$. If capital is conceived to consist only of advanced wages as Ricardo often assumes, then C is zero, and the net product coincides with the social product, so it is even more immediate that its labour value is L. In either case, L is the labour value that must be divided between wages and profits; in the second case L is also the value of the social product.

Now let us see what difference it makes to admit rent. I leave aside intensive rent. When a commodity is produced on several lands, its labour value is determined by the production conditions on no-rent land[50]; on the lands that yield a positive rent, *less* labour is needed per unit of output. For simplicity let us treat, as Smith and Ricardo tend to do, capital as consisting only of wages advanced for one period; then the labour theory of value holds (can you confirm this?). To help intuition, fix at 1 the value of a good embodying one unit of labour. Then the value of the total production of a good produced on several different lands equals the quantity of labour that *would have been* necessary to produce it *if* all of it had been produced with the technology obtaining on no-rent land, therefore it is *greater* than the quantity of labour *actually* employed in its production, and the difference is the value going to rent. For example if corn is produced by labour alone on two lands, 100 units of labour producing 100 units of corn on no-rent land and 100 units of labour producing 120 units of corn on better land, then the labour embodied in the 220 units of corn is 220, but the labour employed is 200, and the difference of 20 is precisely the labour value of the 20 units of corn going as differential rent to the owners of the better land. Aggregating, we see that the total labour value of the social product is *greater* than labour employment by the amount corresponding to what goes to rent. If then we call L the labour *actually* performed, i.e. employment, the labour value of the *net (and here also social) product net of rents* will be equal to L. Thus, again, the labour value to be divided *between wages and profits* is measured by the total labour employment of the year. If we call V the labour value of the wage goods which have gone to L, then total profits in labour values are $L-V$, and if, as Smith and Ricardo tend to do, we identify V with the capital advanced, then the rate of profit is given by $r=(L-V)/V$.

---

49 I am using here the modern definition of net product that includes wages. Classical authors used 'net produce' to mean what is left after replacing all used-up advanced capital, hence wages too; so the net produce was the sum of profits and rents only—another confirmation of their view of wages as analogous to fodder for horses, i.e. as inevitable inputs to production.

50 This holds for Ricardo. Marx had a different view of land rent, on whose interpretation scholars don't fully agree yet, but which is generally found defective; it will not be discussed in this book.

46   Chapter 1 · The Classical or Surplus Approach

1.9 Marx

1.9.1 Values, Surplus Values, Value of Labour Power

Karl Marx (1818–1883) is an extremely important thinker whose writings are relevant for economics, sociology, political science, philosophy. We can only discuss Marx as an economist. His important analyses are often misunderstood; in particular, contrary to a common argument, Marx's general approach to the nature of capitalism and to the basic forces at work in the capitalist economy does not stand or fall with the labour theory of value. This is relevant for the validity of the entire surplus approach. The issue requires examining Marx's approach to value in some detail.

When around 1845 Marx starts a systematic study of economics, he discovers that the highest point reached by economic theory up to then is Ricardo. He starts therefore from Ricardo's labour theory of value and sets out to improve upon it. His study of the Physiocrats allows him to surmount an error of Smith and Ricardo, who had seen the natural price as the sum of wages, profits and (for products produced on land on which a rent is paid) rent, forgetting that price also includes a part corresponding to the value of used-up means of production, i.e. reasoning as if advanced capital consisted only of advanced wages.[51] Marx sees that the value of the social product (net of rent) does not resolve itself entirely into profits and wages: a part corresponds to the value of the used-up means of production and consists of goods which replace these used-up capital goods. This holds for the individual goods too. This allows him to reach a better understanding of why relative prices deviate from relative labour values, and autonomously to reach the idea (which, we have seen, Ricardo too was groping towards) of a *reciprocal compensation* of these deviations.

Let us provisionally assume—as Marx does in Volume I of *Capital*—that commodities exchange at ratios determined by the socially necessary labour they embody, and for the sake of simplicity let us consider the corn–iron economy,

---

51 Consider the corn economy: neglecting rents, and assuming advanced wages, the value of corn covers the value of wages, the value of profits *and* the value of seed-corn: Smith and Ricardo had difficulty perceiving the presence of this third part and viewed the value of corn as the sum of the first two parts only; which is correct only if seed-corn is zero (or such a small amount relative to wage costs as to be negligible), and advanced capital consists only of advanced wages. Smith argued, correctly, that the value of seed-corn can in turn be seen as the sum of the wages, profits and seed-corn used to produce it, and that proceeding backwards in this way the value of corn can be reduced to a sum of wages and profits only; but he did not clearly see that the part of these total wages and profits corresponding to the value of seed-corn was income earned in previous years and reasoned as if the entire value of the social product (the total gross income) of any year could be viewed as wages and profits entering the income *of that year*. So, again neglecting rent, his potentially correct intuition that natural price can be seen as a sum of wages and profits alone became the incorrect conclusion that the value of the gross income of a year is the sum of the wages and profits earned in that year, which is correct only if all capital advances consist of wage advances.

1.9 · Marx

where all capital is circulating capital. Corn, good 1, is the numéraire; choose as unit of corn the quantity that embodies one unit of labour, thus $m_1 = p_1 = 1$; then $p_2 = m_2$, prices *coincide* with labours embodied. Misleadingly, Marx calls 'values' these prices equal to labours embodied; I will call them **labour values**, in order to avoid confusion with Ricardo's notion of 'value', which is synonymous with 'natural price'.

Since seed-corn and iron are circulating capital, they transfer into their product all the labour embodied in them; therefore labour embodied is given by direct labour (*living labour*, as Marx calls it) plus the entire labour embodied in the seed-corn and iron used as means of production (*dead* labour, as Marx calls it because it has been already performed and cannot be changed). This is what Eqs. (1.16)–(1.17) told us. But Marx was unable to write down algebraic equations as disaggregated and simple as these. He was only able to separate living labour from the contribution to labour values of the means of production. Marx calls **constant capital** the labour embodied in the means of production of a commodity; and **variable capital** the labour embodied in the wage goods paid to the living labour employed. [52]He uses the symbol c for constant capital, v for variable capital, ℓ for living labour, and $s = \ell - v$ for *surplus labour*, the excess of the living labour performed over the labour embodied in the wage goods that living labour receives. For example if average subsistence per unit of labour includes z_1 units of corn and z_2 units of iron, then if we consider a firm producing 1 unit of corn, the labour value of its product is given by $c + \ell = c + v + s$ where .

$$\ell = a_{L1}, \tag{1.24}$$

$$c = a_{11}m_1 + a_{21}m_2, \tag{1.25}$$

$$v = (m_1 z_1 + m_2 z_2)a_{L1}. \tag{1.26}$$

In a firm producing x units of corn, the corresponding magnitudes $\ell,\ c,\ v$ are multiplied by x. (The reader should write down the analogous expressions for a firm that produces iron.)

Marx too, like Ricardo, conceives wages as advanced, and hence part of capital; therefore if a good's labour value is $c + \ell$, the labour value of advanced capital is $c + v$, where $v < \ell$ and the difference s (surplus value in Marx's terminology) is the labour value of profits.

Marx views s as measuring *surplus labour*, or *unpaid labour*; while v measures *necessary labour*. The reason is the following. Assume there is no rent. We have seen that the labour embodied in a good can be seen as the labour employment required to produce that good as net product. This applies also to composite goods, the labour embodied in a vector of goods is the employment required to produce that vector as net product. Let us then consider the net product of the economy, it consists of goods going to wages, with total labour embodied V, and

---

52 . As the real wage rate varies, v changes but c does not; this is why Marx calls v variable capital, and c constant capital.

48 Chapter 1 · The Classical or Surplus Approach

goods going to profits, with total labour embodied S. Total labour performed in the economy is $L = V + S$. Suppose $L = 100,000$ h of work a year corresponding to 50 workers each one working 2000 h a year, 8 h a day for 250 days. Suppose $V = 62,500 = 5/8$ L; this means that it would suffice for the 50 workers to work only 5 h a day (with possibly some redistribution of their employment between corn and iron industries) in order to produce the goods going to them as wages. The extra 3 h of work a day are what allows the production of the goods constituting the surplus or profits.

This explains why Marx calls surplus labour *unpaid labour*: for the 5 h of necessary labour, the worker receives goods embodying 5 h of labour; for the extra 3 h she/he receives nothing.

Marx distinguishes labour as an activity, from **labour power**. Labour power is the name Marx gives to the ability of workers to perform labour, an ability that will be utilized more or less depending on how many hours per year the labourer works. Marx calls the average wage (measured in labour embodied) the **value of labour power**, what the worker must receive every year to subsist and reproduce; note that a given wage and value of labour power does not tell us how many hours the labourer works in a year, so Marx distinguishes the labour value *of* labour power from the labour value *created by* the use of labour power, i.e. by the labour hours performed in a year. Value creation depends on the amount of *labour* performed, which can vary without variations in the value of labour power. This allows Marx to stress the importance of variations of the length of the workday, an issue previously given little attention by economists. Suppose the length of the workday is increased from 8 to 10 h a day. This means that now eight workers perform the amount of labour for which ten workers were previously required; if the daily wage has not changed, the cost of an hour of labour has been reduced by 20%, with a considerable increase of the rate of profit. If wages are established at a customary subsistence level, they are fixed at the level allowing a worker to subsist and raise a family with the customary living standards, but with the same wage that worker can work 8 or 10 or 12 h a day, so the capitalists will try to impose as long a workday as possible (sometimes 16 h a day in Marx's times), with dire effects on the health of workers; Marx stresses that the struggle for shortening the workday is very important. Now do Exercise 1.45.

1.9.2 The Determination of the Rate of Profit

Let us see how Marx uses these notions to determine the rate of profit. Suppose prices and labour values coincide, and that all capital goods are circulating capital; then the price p of a commodity can be represented as

$$p = c + \ell = c + v + s \tag{1.27}$$

where c, v, ℓ, s are the quantities of constant capital, variable capital, living labour and surplus labour in the production of one unit of that commodity; profit is s, and the rate of profit (with advanced wages and circulating capital goods only) is

$$r = s/(c + v) = \frac{\frac{s}{v}}{\frac{c}{v} + 1}.\tag{1.28}$$

Marx calls *rate of surplus value* or also *rate of exploitation* the ratio s/v, which tends to be the same in all industries if competition tends to impose a uniform wage and a uniform length of the workday.[53]

One last bit of terminology. Marx calls *organic composition of capital* the ratio c/v between constant and variable capital. Given the real wage basket, the organic composition depends on technology and is high in the industries where living labour is coupled with large fixed plants and machinery, low where labour is coupled with few and cheap means of production. So in the second expression for the rate of profit in Eq. (1.28) the numerator tends to be the same in all industries, but not the denominator. This allows Marx to see that at prices determined by the labour theory of value the rate of profit would not be the same in different industries, being uniform only if either $s = 0$, in which case $r = 0$, or the organic composition of capital is the same in all industries (see footnote 44).

Marx concludes that natural prices or prices of production as he prefers to call them, associated with a uniform rate of profit, cannot be proportional to labour values.

But then what determines the uniform rate of profit and the associated relative prices? By 1858, in manuscripts now referred to as *Grundrisse*, Marx reaches the following answer that he will never abandon. At prices proportional to labour values, the greater the organic composition of capital the lower is the rate of profit. So the relative prices yielding a uniform rate of profit must differ from ratios between labour values. If we start from prices proportional to labour values, then in order to reach a uniform rate of profit the price of the goods earning a lower-than-average rate of profit, i.e. produced with an organic composition higher than the average, must *increase* relative to the value of their means of production, and conversely the price of the commodities produced with a lower-than-average organic composition must *decrease* relative to the value of their means of production. Therefore, Marx reasons, there must be an intermediate or 'average' organic composition that does not require the price of the goods produced with that organic composition to increase nor to decrease relative to the value of its means of production. Relative to this 'average' organic composition, the function of these deviations of prices from labour values is to redistribute among the several industries the total social surplus value S, in such a fashion that the surplus value, created in proportion to the *variable* capital in each industry, is appropriated in proportion to the *total* capital of each industry and thus permits a uniform rate of profit. This redistribution, Marx reasons, cannot change the total which is redistributed, the deviations must compensate

---

53 Remember that labour is reduced to homogeneity on the basis of persistent relative wages, if skilled labour is paid twice as much as simple labour then one hour of skilled labour produces two hours of labour value, so the wage per unit of labour value is the same.

50   Chapter 1 · The Classical or Surplus Approach

one another, and therefore *the 'average' organic composition that does not require a change in the value of the product relative to the value of its means of production must be that of the social product*, whose organic composition is indeed the average one by definition, and whose total value cannot be altered by the redistribution.[54] Therefore according to Marx the general rate of profit is given by (if all capital is circulating):

$$r = S/(C + V) = [S/V]/[C/V + 1] \qquad (1.29)$$

where now C, V, S are, respectively, the labour value of *total* constant capital, of *total* variable capital and of *total* surplus in the entire economy. So according to Marx, Ricardo's formula for the determination of r (see Eq. 1.23) is not an approximation, it is *correct* when referred to the entire economy, one only needs to admit that advanced capital includes also the part C, constant capital, that Ricardo did not clearly perceive.

This rate of profit must then be applied to the advanced capital of each industry to obtain the *prices of production*, which are the prices corresponding to a uniform rate of profit and, because resulting from a redistribution of labour value across industries, are seen by Marx as 'transformed' labour values. How to determine the prices of production starting from labour values has accordingly been called in the Marxist literature the *'transformation problem'*.

For example, assume an economy that produces two goods, where all constant capital is circulating capital, and there is no rent; choose as unit for each good its *total* production; then prices equal to labour values must obey the following equations:

$$p_1 = c_1 + \ell_1 = c_1 + v_1 + s_1 \qquad (1.30)$$

$$p_2 = c_2 + \ell_2 = c_2 + v_2 + s_2 \qquad (1.31)$$

where now $p_1 + p_2$ is the total labour value of the economy's production, $c_1 + v_1 + c_2 + v_2$ is the total capital advanced, $s_1 + s_2$ is total profits. Unless $c_1/v_1 = c_2/v_2$, when $s > 0$ relative prices determined in this way yield different rates of profit in the two industries. Marx's 'transformation' of labour values into prices of production can be illustrated for this economy as follows. The rate of profit is

$$r = S/(C + V) = (s_1 + s_2)/(c_1 + v_1 + c_2 + v_2); \qquad (1.32)$$

---

54 In Marx a reciprocal compensation of deviations that leaves total value unchanged is explicitly mentioned in Volume III, Chap. 9, fifteenth paragraph; there Marx also admits that the 'transformation' of labour values into prices of production should also be applied to the means of production and real wages in the advanced capital (so Eqs. (1.33)–(1.34), which reflect a numerical example by Marx, are in fact mistaken because inputs should be valued at prices of production and not at labour values), but he concludes: 'However, this always resolves itself to one commodity receiving too little of the surplus value while another receives too much, so that the deviations from the value which are embodied in the prices of production compensate one another', and does not attempt to study the problem any further (p 119 of marxists.org online version of *Capital*, Vol. III, 1959 Institute of Marxism-Leninism version, International Publishers, NY).

1.9 · Marx

the *prices of production* are determined as

$$p_1^* = (1 + r)(c_1 + v_1) \tag{1.33}$$

$$p_2^* = (1 + r)(c_2 + v_2) \tag{1.34}$$

where r has the value determined by Eq. (1.32).

Thus, in Marx, relative prices of production are *ultimately* determined by labour values and are only 'transformed' (redistributed) labours embodied (indeed $p_1^* + p_2^* = C + V + S$: the exchange value of the social product evaluated at prices of production equals its labour value). The labour theory of value, Marx concludes, yields the correct rate of profit when applied to the whole economy's surplus value and advanced capital, and thus, although *not* correct as a theory of relative normal prices, it is the necessary basis for their determination.

In this way Marx is able to determine the rate of profit *before* relative prices and thus to escape the danger of circular reasoning that worried Ricardo, with significant analytical advances. First, the presence of 'constant' capital is fully recognized. Second, the consideration of constant capital permits a richer understanding of the causes of changes in the rate of profit. Ricardo saw only two such causes: changes in the real wage rate and in the productivity of labour. Marx recognizes a third influence: the ratio of constant to variable capital, C/V. Thus technical progress can influence the rate of profit also by affecting the 'mechanization' of production, the extent to which labour is replaced by machines and C/V changes: a theme that is very important in Marx's analysis of the secular tendencies of capitalist accumulation (see below).

On the reasons for the apparently aprioristic exposition of Volume I of *Capital*, where the labour theory of value is presented as correct and no hint is given that relative prices of production differ from relative labour values, I refer the interested reader to Garegnani (2018).

1.9.3 A Mistake in Marx's Determination of the Rate of Profit

But there is a mistake in Marx's determination of r. If commodities exchange at ratios different from relative labour values, why should this not be the case also for the two different composite commodities, physical profits and physical advanced capital, whose rate of exchange is the rate of profit? So we must expect Marx's formula $r = S/(C + V)$, with S, C, V measured in labour values, to be in general incorrect.

And indeed it is in general incorrect. One can distinguish two reasons. The first is that, as Ricardo had noted and explicitly declared, the production conditions of luxury industries cannot have a role in the determination of the rate of profit; in Marx on the contrary they do, their organic composition contributes to determining the average organic composition of the social product. So in Marx a change in the dimension of luxury industries relative to the rest of the economy changes C/V and hence r; this is wrong, as the 'corn model' makes clear, but

52   **Chapter 1 · The Classical or Surplus Approach**

Marx was never able to realize it. The second reason is that a change in the average organic composition can be due to changes in the relative dimensions of the wage industries too, and again this changes the rate of profit in Marx, but in fact in the correct equations determining the rate of profit and long-period prices the dimension of industries plays no role at all, only the technical coefficients and the wage count.

However, the modern advances in the theory of prices of production, exemplified by Eqs. (1.2)–(1.9), have shown that Marx was correct in this sense: the *data*—technical conditions of production, real wage basket and quantities produced if the no-rent land is to be determined too—from which he (and Ricardo) attempted to determine the rate of profit, are in fact sufficient *directly* to determine the rate of profit, with no need for labours embodied. This was shown precisely by those equations.

An important implication is the following. A number of marginalist authors (Böhm-Bawerk, Wicksteed, Pareto) argued that Marx's entire approach was fatally flawed owing to the deficiencies of the labour theory of value as a theory of relative prices and of the rate of profit; a totally different theory of value and distribution was needed, they argued. But they were wrong. The surplus approach does not fall with the defects of the labour theory of value; it *is* capable of satisfactorily determining rate of profit and prices. Walras's criticism of Ricardo (see above Sect. 1.6.1) was mistaken, because the indeterminateness at the level of a single price equation disappears once the real wage is given and the whole system of price equations is considered.

1.10 **The Marxist Tradition**

The irrefutable proof that Marx's determination of the rate of profit is defective has caused disconcert among many Marxist economists, who have been further aggrieved by the proof that the correct determination of the rate of profit and prices of production has no need for embodied labour magnitudes (these do not appear in Eqs. (1.2)–(1.9)). According to the historically dominant tradition among Marxist thinkers, the notion that exchange value is 'produced' by labour, is nothing but crystallized labour time, was essential to Marx's characterization of the capital–labour relation and to his argument that profits result from labour exploitation. But it can be convincingly argued that the replacement of Marx's labour theory of value with the more correct approach exemplified by Eqs. (1.2)–(1.9) denies nothing of Marx's insights on the capital–labour relation and on the origin of profits.

The Marxist tradition has tended to attribute two main roles to the conception of exchange value as crystallized labour. The first one is to unmask the alienated and fetishistic aspect of social relations in market economies.[55] According

---

55 Important names here are Hilferding, Rubin, Sweezy: cf. Howard and King, 1989–92, vol. I, ch. 3 and vol. II, chs 12 and 17.

1.10 · The Marxist Tradition

to this tradition, that value is crystallized labour shows that the worker's labour gets *alienated* from him/her: the worker's labour is not controlled by the labourer but by the capitalist, so it is no longer an expression of his personality but rather serves interests external to the worker; its result, the value created by a certain amount of labour, is that amount of labour itself, now crystallized in the product of that labour: but now this value stands in front of the worker as an alien thing, outside his control and endowed with a social recognition and power—the power to exchange with other things, and to command more labour than it was necessary to produce it—whose social origin becomes almost impossible to grasp, because resulting from nobody's conscious action; one result is that *commodities fetishistically appear to possess as natural qualities what in fact derives from the social structure*, e.g. gold appears as naturally endowed with great exchange value, rather than deriving it from the economy's need for money, which depends on how the social division of labour is organized: via private property and exchange. The labour theory of value is seen as allowing one to go beyond appearances and bringing out the subjugated, oppressed, alienated nature of the condition of the true producers under capitalism while at the same time explaining why it is difficult spontaneously to grasp it.

The second role is to prove that labour is exploited, by showing that, since value is produced by labour alone, capital does not contribute to the production of value, and therefore the part of value that constitutes profits has been produced by surplus labour alone with no contribution of capital, and is expropriated by capitalists owing solely to the greater bargaining power of capitalists.

But upon reflection, both roles need only the validity of the surplus approach with its conflictual picture of capitalism evident already in Adam Smith, not the notion that exchange values are crystallized labour time.

The discussion of fetishism in the first chapter of *Capital* aims at demonstrating that the form of *commodity* assumed by concrete use values in capitalism, that is, their coming with an exchange value and counting for their exchange value, 'is nothing but the definite social relation between men themselves which assumes here, for them, the fantastic form of a relation between things' (*Capital* vol I, p. 165 of Penguin ed.): men tend to treat the fact that physical objects have exchange values, and the relative exchange values themselves, as intrinsic, natural properties of these objects, without being aware of the historical specificity of the social structure that turns use values into commodities, nor of the complex social processes determining these exchange values as unintentional results of individual decisions. For example the capacity of land to yield a rent, that appeared to the Physiocrats to reflect natural powers of land, is due to the tendency to a uniform profit rate and thus to the historically specific social structure that causes that tendency to exist. And the extraordinary fascination of gold derives from society having chosen it as the money commodity, not from intrinsic qualities of the gold metal.

It is only because Marx sees exchange values as (redistributed) labours embodied that he characterizes the social process determining exchange values in these terms: 'The equality of the kinds of human labour takes on a physical form in the equal objectivity of the products of labour as values' (*Capital* I p. 164). The

54   **Chapter 1** · The Classical or Surplus Approach

more fundamental argument of Marx—that the commodity form of the products of labour is historically specific, not natural, and that the social processes determining exchange values result from the decisions of individuals but dominate individuals, bring to results that no one consciously wanted, and are therefore opaque—is independent of his view of exchange values as ultimately labour values. Exchange values, because resulting from competition, even if determined by a theory other than the theory of labour value will anyway reflect a historically specific social organization that produces social processes that are felt by the individual as *external forces that completely dominate her/him*, and whose social origin is not at all evident in how exchange values manifest themselves.[56] So the analysis of fetishism is perfectly compatible with Sraffian price equations.

Nor is the labour theory of value necessary to grasp the connection between changes of real wages, of labour intensity or of working hours, and changes of the rate of profit, and therefore to grasp the inevitable conflict of interests between capitalists and workers. This connection emerges also from Eqs. (1.2)–(1.9). Nor do the correct price equations deny the condition of subjugation and alienation of workers in the concrete labour conditions, in the determination of wages, and more generally in the running of capitalist society. The Sraffian determination of natural prices is perfectly compatible with descriptions of the condition of wage labourers as in these two passages by Marx:

» the worker always leaves the process in the same state as he entered it – a personal source of wealth, but deprived of any means of making that wealth a reality for himself. Since, before he enters the process, his own labour has already been alienated from him, appropriated by the capitalist, and incorporated with capital, it now, in the course of the process, constantly objectifies itself so that it becomes a product alien to him. Since the process of production is also the process of the consumption of labour-power by the capitalist, the worker's product is not only constantly converted into commodities, but also into capital, i.e. into value that sucks up the worker's value-creating power, means of subsistence that actually purchase humain beings, and means of production that employ the people who are doing the producing. Therefore the worker himself constantly produces objective wealth, in the form of capital, an alien power that dominates and exploits him (*Capital* I, p. 716).

within the capitalist system all methods for raising the social productivity of labour are put into effect at the cost of the individual worker; that all means for the development of production undergo a dialectical inversion so that they become means of domination and exploitation of the producers; they distort the worker into

---

56 Marx argues that exchange value takes 'the fantastic form of a relation between things' because the exchange value of a commodity *is a physical quantity of another commodity*, the commodity in terms of which the exchange value of the first commodity is measured: in its fully general form, it is an amount of money, generally of gold. Now, Marx notes, that the value of 20 yards of linen is a certain quantity of gold appears as a relationship among physical objects, it does not at all reveal by itself the social relationships and mechanisms from which it results. *All this is independent of how then Marx explains exchange values.*

a fragment of a man, they destroy the actual content of his labour by turning it into a torment; they alienate from him the intellectual potentialities of the labour process in the same proportion as science is incorporated in it as an independent power; they deform the conditions under which he works, subject him during the labour process to a despotism the more hateful for its meanness; they transform his life-time into working-time, and drag his wife and child beneath the wheels of the juggernaut of capital (*Capital* I, p. 799).

Let us come to exploitation. Here the worries of some Marxists derive from the belief that if it is not possible to prove that the exchange value appropriated by the capitalists as profits is created by surplus labour and by it alone, then it is no longer clear that the existence of profits reflects the exploitation of labour and not a contribution of capitalists to production and hence to value.

But the reasoning, from which such worries arise, confuses 'contribution to production', and 'cause of relative exchange values'—a confusion largely due to the influence of the marginal approach, where the two are intimately linked. As we will see in ▶ Chap. 3, in the marginal approach the relative values of goods result from the cost, of the 'factors of production' labour, capital and land, that their production requires, and the rewards of these factors measure the contribution of each factor to the production of social utility and therefore measure what these factors *deserve* to be paid. In such a perspective, if value derives solely from labour it must mean that the other factors give no contribution to social utility and therefore deserve nothing, labour deserves to receive all the value of the products, and if it does not receive it, then part of the value produced is being undeservedly appropriated by others, and labour can be described as exploited. But such a perspective is strictly connected with the marginal approach and stands or falls with it. Since the surplus approach is different, and its theory of income distribution is different, the question we must discuss now is not, whether labour is exploited if the marginal theory of income distribution is correct, but rather: does the defect of Marx's determination of r undermine the view of the origin of profits derivable from the overall surplus approach and in particular from its theory of wages? The answer is a clear no, as shown by the following considerations.

Why do we speak of exploitation of slaves, or of feudal serfs? Because another class takes away part of their product owing solely to its superior force. But then tracing the origin of profits to the exploitation of labour needs only the correctness of the classical approach to wages, which sees the positivity of profits as due simply to the power, given to the owners of the means of production by the institutional structure of capitalism, to appropriate part of labour's product, by virtue of their collective monopoly of the prerequisites for production (capital goods). This view makes it possible to retort against the bourgeoisie itself the accusation, moved by the bourgeoisie against feudal lords, that the latters' revenue was the fruit of exploitation, being due to their monopoly of land which obliged the serfs to accept performing *corvées* in order to have the possibility to produce for themselves and thus to survive.

56   **Chapter 1** · The Classical or Surplus Approach

In order to be convincing, such a view of income distribution does not need the labour theory of value, it only needs to show that it permits a satisfactory explanation of what determines relative prices and the rate of profit; and precisely the deficiencies of Ricardo's and Marx's solution of this problem made it possible for the subsequent marginalist economists to criticize the entire surplus approach and thus its view of the determinants of wages, and to argue for the superiority of their different explanation of value and of income distribution. But those deficiencies *can* be overcome without abandoning the classical view of wage determination, so the surplus approach's view of the origin of profits can be confirmed: part of the product of labour is appropriated by another class uniquely because of its bargaining power deriving from its collective monopoly of the possibility to produce, which requires ownership of capital. Equivalently, one can say that there is a surplus appropriated as profits because the workers are obliged to work more hours than needed to produce as net product only their wages. Neither way of explaining the origin of a surplus appropriated as profits requires or implies a labour theory of value.

The thing can be made clearer with the help of the following hypothetical example. Let us imagine a small nation, a competitive market economy where all firms are labour cooperatives, and there is no rate of profit nor rate of interest. Since $r = 0$, prices are proportional to labours embodied, and the labour theory of value is valid. Then this nation is conquered by an invader people, who imposes on the basis of its military domination that each firm must pay each year to the invaders' army a tax proportional to the value of its capital advances, at a tax rate r. This tax is a pure tribute, but it functions like a rate of profit, prices must cover it besides the other costs, and prices then gravitate towards the same relative prices of production as if there were a uniform rate of profit equal to r. Clearly the changes in relative prices due to the appearance of the $(1 + r)$ multiplicative term in the costs cannot be viewed as proof of a contribution of the invaders to production. The positivity of r is due solely to the capacity of the invaders to compress the real incomes of producers below the previous levels, and the changes in relative prices are only due to the need to pay a uniform tax rate on the capital advances. Now, according to the surplus approach, as evidenced already by Smith before Marx, the positivity of the rate of profit in capitalist economies has the same basic cause as the positivity of the tax in our hypothetical example: it reflects the capacity of the social group that appropriates the profits to compress real wages below their potential maximum[57]; and the fact that relative prices of production differ from relative labour values has only the function—Marx might have said—of *allowing all units of capital equally to share in the plunder*. If one finds it reasonable to describe the income of the invaders in this example as the fruit of the exploitation of the labour of the local inhabitants, and if one finds the classical theory of wages convincing, then one must also describe profits in capitalist society as the fruit of the exploitation of wage labour.

---

57 Or to oblige workers to work more hours for the same real daily wage, thus again reducing the real wage per unit of labour time performed.

1.11 The Standard Commodity as the 'average' Commodity Marx Was Looking For

When explaining the reasoning that brought Marx to conclude that $r = S/(C + V)$ in labour values, I argued that he was looking for a commodity of 'average' organic composition, for which there was no need to change its price relative to the value of its means of production when passing from prices proportional to labour values to prices associated with a uniform rate of profit. For such a commodity, the rate of profit would be correctly determined even when evaluating its product and its advanced capital at labour values. Marx was wrong in believing that the social product was such a commodity; but such a commodity does exist. It was discovered by Sraffa, and it is called the **Standard commodity**.

Here its illustration will be limited to the two-goods corn–iron economy, a more complete treatment will be offered in ▶ Chap. 2. Assume advanced wages, and define *subsistence-inclusive technical coefficients* c_{ij} (i input, j output) as follows: if the average real wage rate physically specified consists of the vector (z_1, z_2), then

$$c_{ij} \equiv a_{ij} + z_i a_{Lj}, \quad i,j = 1,2.$$

For example, if to produce one unit of corn (good 1) one needs 0.2 units of corn as seed, 0.1 units of iron and 0.8 units of labour, and if the real wage rate consists of 0.5 units of corn and 0.2 units of iron, then $c_{11} = 0.2 + 0.5 \cdot 0.8 = 0.6$, and $c_{21} = 0.1 + 0.2 \cdot 0.8 = 0.26$. Of course, for the economy to be able to produce a surplus, it must be $c_{11} < 1$ and $c_{22} < 1$.

Then the price equations can be written without any explicit appearance of labour quantities, by using the technical coefficients c_{ij}. The reader can easily check that Eqs. (1.2)–(1.3), once the real wage is specified by Eq. (1.4), are equivalent to the following ones:

$$p_1 = (1 + r)(c_{11}p_1 + c_{21}p_2) \tag{1.35}$$

$$p_2 = (1 + r)(c_{12}p_1 + c_{22}p_2). \tag{1.36}$$

The solution of these price equations is independent of the dimensions of industries as long as technical coefficients remain unaltered. Let us then imagine, as a mental experiment, to alter the relative dimensions of the two industries in

58 **Chapter 1 · The Classical or Surplus Approach**

such a way as to reach the proportions necessary for maximum potential growth of both industries at a common rate. To such an end, with x_1 the quantity produced of corn and x_2 the quantity produced of iron, define the *rate of physical surplus* of commodity $i = 1, 2$ as

$$\sigma_i \equiv (x_i - (c_{i1}x_1 + c_{i2}x_2))/(c_{i1}x_1 + c_{i2}x_2).$$

This is the ratio of the physical surplus of commodity i to the quantity of it employed in the entire economy as advanced capital (both as means of production and as part of physical wage advances). This ratio indicates the maximum percentage by which the employment of that commodity as advanced capital can be increased next period. It suffices to divide both numerator and denominator of this definition by x_2 to see that the rates of physical surplus depend on the composition of production x_1/x_2; also, it is easily shown that if x_1/x_2 increases then σ_1 increases and σ_2 decreases.[58] If the composition of production is *given* and constant from one period to the next, and if both industries are to grow at the same rate, then the lower one of the two rates of physical surplus is the highest common rate of growth achievable with that composition of production. The maximum common potential rate of growth g^* is therefore achieved when x_1/x_2 renders $\sigma_1 = \sigma_2 = g^*$.

For both industries to be able to grow at rate g^*, the quantity produced of each product must be $(1 + g^*)$ times the quantity of it advanced as wages-inclusive capital in the entire economy:

$$x_1 = (1 + g^*)(c_{11}x_1 + c_{12}x_2) \tag{1.37}$$

$$x_2 = (1 + g^*)(c_{21}x_1 + c_{22}x_2) \tag{1.38}$$

(Note carefully the difference from Eqs. (1.35)–(1.36) in the indices on the right-hand side.) In an economy satisfying these equations, the composite commodity 'social product', consisting of quantities x_1 and x_2 of corn and iron, and the composite commodity 'aggregate advanced capital' contain corn and iron *in the same proportion*, hence are two different quantities of *the same* composite commodity. The surplus product is again a quantity of the same composite commodity: Sraffa calls it *standard commodity*; the proportion x_1/x_2 associated with it is called the *standard proportion*.

The rate of profit in such an economy is necessarily the common rate of physical surplus, or of potential growth, $r = g^*$, a physical or material ratio, independent of relative prices, because the value of the social product is $(1 + g^*)$ times the value of advanced capital *whatever the prices*. It does not need to change its price relative to the value of its advanced capital when one passes from labour values to prices of production. The economy has become formally similar to the corn economy, because the standard commodity uses itself for its production.

The standard commodity shows that the rate of profit is the manifestation of the implicit maximum capacity of the economy to expand and can be determined without needing simultaneously to determine relative prices.

---

58 For example for x_1 given, a rise of x_1/x_2 means a decrease of x_2, which raises σ_1.

1.11 · The Standard Commodity as the 'average' Commodity ...

Note that, formally, labour does not appear in the determination of the rate of profit through the standard commodity or through Eqs. (1.35)–(1.36). That is, the rate of profit and prices of production would remain determinable even in a science-fiction economy where machines and robots produced and reproduced themselves with no human labour being used at all. This confirms that prices of production depend, not on quantities of labour, but on quantities of commodities used as inputs, with labour being only a way one part of these physical inputs is determined, via real wages. Of course the fact that work is produced by human beings and not by robots does have a crucial role, in that the bargaining strength and attitude of labour influences wages, the length of the working day, workpace, the efficiency with which production is carried out (e.g. the percentage of defective products); the choice of production methods too (e.g. amount of supervision) is influenced by the need to control workers, to prevent shirking or sabotage, to divide the workforce by introducing specializations and differentiations. But for the determination of exchange values and of r all these things ultimately count only through their determination of physical commodity inputs per unit of output.

1.12 More on Marx

1.12.1 Wages

Apart from some analytical issues on which Marx is inferior to Ricardo,[59] Marx's analyses are the highest point reached by the surplus approach before its resumption in modern times after a long period of neglect. They retain great interest, so something more will be said on them here.

On wages, Marx agrees with Smith and Ricardo on the importance of customary, social elements in the determination of normal wages or 'subsistence'. He is Smithian (or, one might say, Smith was Marxist before Marx!) in his stress on class conflict as a key element of capitalist society. The main purpose of *Capital* would appear to have been, to refute the apologetic picture of capitalist society which was becoming dominant at the time,[60] and to re-establish with theoretical argument and factual evidence the Smithian–Ricardian view of capitalism as a class society dominated by conflict, with the addition of:

---

59 Mainly, the inability to perceive that luxury industries do not influence the rate of profit, and the theory of rent.

60 In Marx's time Nassau Senior's thesis that profit was the necessary recompense for the capitalists' 'abstinence' (from consuming their entire gross income), abstinence that permitted the existence of capital, was more and more generally accepted among renowned economists. John Stuart Mill (whose *Principles of Political Economy*, 1st ed. 1848, supplanted Smith's and Ricardo's books as the basic reference treatise on economics), although declaring himself a Ricardian, accepted this non-Ricardian explanation/justification of profit, whose logic becomes clearer if one applies it to the income of slave owners: a slave owner too might argue that his income is justified by the fact that his abstinence (from consuming himself the slaves' subsistence, as well as from consuming the resources that keep whip and chains in good order) is what allows the slaves not to die of hunger.

60   Chapter 1 · The Classical or Surplus Approach

(1) a harsh denunciation of the conditions of the working class;
(2) a greater stress than in earlier classical authors on the importance of the length of the working day and of the struggles determining it, for the determination of the rate of profit[61];
(3) an important role assigned to technical progress, in particular to the stimulus given by wage rises to the search for ways to replace human labour with machines (a first formulation of the view of technical progress as at least partly endogenous and directed to specific ends);
(4) the prediction that the immanent laws of development of capitalism will pave the way for a proletarian revolution which would abolish the private property of means of production.

Many pages of *Capital* describe the role of violence and oppression in establishing and maintaining capitalism. Marx has greatly stimulated historical research on the origins of capitalism by arguing that there was a 'primitive accumulation' characterized by violence and forcible expropriation of the lower classes, not unlike the behaviour of conquerors towards natives in colonies.

However, once capitalism has established itself—Marx continues—open violence against the working classes, although always present in the background as a potential last resort, is not often used. As long as private property is respected, the spontaneous working of the laws of the capitalist economy suffices to maintain the capitalist domination over workers. In describing how these laws establish a tendency of wages to gravitate around a subsistence level, Marx is a harsh critic of Malthus. Marx accepts the influence of unemployment on the bargaining power of workers, although he qualifies that influence by giving great importance to ideological and organizational elements. But he rejects the Malthusian population mechanism as the explanation of the tendency of real wages to remain low, for two reasons.

First, agreeing in this with Adam Smith, Marx argues that it is by no means guaranteed that wage rises will induce the workers to have more children: actually Marx thinks that generally the opposite is the case; the main cause of the tendency of the poor to have many children is the firms' demand for child labour: this labour, although underpaid, helps poor families to survive, at horrible costs that Marx denounces in many angry pages of volume I of *Capital*.

The second and decisive argument against Malthus is that the latter's theory is unable to explain the length of the cyclical fluctuations in wages and profits, fluctuations that last much less than required by the Malthusian population mechanism, which requires two or more generations to produce a complete cycle. The average length of economic cycles in the first half of the nineteenth century had been, according to Marx, around 10–11 years.

---

61 Marx considers the normal daily wage to be largely independent of the length of the working day (except for the need for more nourishment in particularly heavy work); thus a lengthening of the working day decreases the wage per hour, i.e. the wage per amount of labour performed, raising the rate of profit. He views the legal limitations to the length of the working day as important results of labour struggles.

1.12 · More on Marx

Marx explains the tendency of wages to decrease back towards subsistence through the effect of changes in real wages on capital accumulation and technical progress, rather than on population. For Marx, the normal situation of capitalism is the existence of a vast *reserve army of unemployed labour* that includes not only the openly unemployed people but also vast amounts of disguised unemployment and potential labour supply (in agriculture, in petty commerce, among women and children). If rapid economic growth sufficiently reduces the size of this reserve army, the bargaining power of workers increases, and real wages rise. But when wages rise, profits decrease, and with them the rate of profit. The capitalists have both less profits to reinvest and a lesser incentive to invest them, since the expected rate of profit is lower. On the other hand, the purchasing power of workers has increased, consumption increases, and this is an incentive to invest; therefore it is by no means certain that wage increases always cause an economic crisis, sometimes they can be a stimulus to growth. But if the wage increase is strong, most probably the discouragement effect on investment is stronger than the incentive to invest deriving from the increase in consumption expenditures; the capitalists feel that their class domination is endangered; they stop investing. The money profits they obtain are hoarded, waiting for better times. The crisis is reinforced by the difficulties many firms encounter in repaying their debts, because the lower rate of profit makes it difficult to repay the rates of interest accepted when the rate of profit was higher.[62] In the meanwhile technical progress continues and even accelerates, because in order to avoid bankruptcies the capitalists become more than normally active in looking for and introducing cost-reducing innovations, and especially *labour*-saving innovations, since it is the rise in wages that is causing their difficulties. This causes further firings of labourers, besides those due to the decrease in quantities produced. The reserve army of labour swells again, and this sooner or later reduces real wages enough, and for a long enough time, to restore the profits and the self-confidence of capitalists; then accumulation starts again, and a new economic cycle begins.[63]

---

62 Thus for Marx the downturn in the cycle exhibits a sharp increase in bankruptcies. A first wave of bankruptcies is caused by the impossibility to repay a rate of interest now higher than the rate of profit; but the closed-down firms stop purchasing inputs from other firms, and this causes further bankruptcies. Thus, while in Ricardo an increase in wages simply slows down accumulation, in Marx it can cause a very sudden and violent crisis entailing a sharp drop in output.

63 'The rise of wages is therefore confined within limits that not only leave intact the foundations of the capitalist system, but also secure its reproduction on an increasing scale. The law of capitalist accumulation, mystified by the economists into a supposed law of nature, in fact expresses the situation that the very nature of accumulation excludes every diminution in the degree of exploitation of labour, and every rise in the price of labour, which could seriously imperil the continual reproduction, on an ever larger scale, of the capital-relation. It cannot be otherwise in a mode of production in which the worker exists to satisfy the need of the existing values for valorization, as opposed to the inverse situation, in which objective wealth is there to satisfy the worker's own need for development. Just as man is governed, in religion, by the products of his own brain, so, in capitalist production, he is governed by the products of his own hand'. (*Capital* I, pp. 771–2).

62   Chapter 1 · The Classical or Surplus Approach

The tendency of wages to decrease back towards subsistence is explained, in conclusion, through the influence of wage increases on the *demand* for labour rather than, as in Malthus, on the *supply* of labour.

1.12.2 Quantities

Differently from Ricardo, Marx did not accept *Say's Law*, the thesis that aggregate demand is never inferior to aggregate supply, nor was he alone in so doing among the classical economists.

The impossibility of 'general gluts', i.e. of generalized overproduction of commodities relative to demand, was strongly argued by Jean-Baptiste Say, a French economist contemporary of Ricardo, hence the name. Say was mainly concerned with denying that a continuous growth of production would hit against the limits of a given demand for commodities; he argued that one half of the social product necessarily buys the other half, clearly meaning by this that production produces the incomes which are then spent to buy the produced goods, so more production increases purchasing power in step with the increase in production; he concluded that there can be a glut in the markets of particular commodities if the composition of production is not well adapted to the composition of demand, but not an overall lack of purchasing power. Ricardo accepted Say's argument but reformulated it in a clearer way. On the basis of Adam Smith's argument that nobody will be so fool as to leave some of his income idle when he can employ it for a positive return, he stated that the value of production is distributed as gross income, and what of this income is not spent on consumption is, directly or indirectly (by lending it to others), invested in production; thus saving decisions *are* investment decisions, and aggregate expenditure is necessarily equal to the aggregate value of production because equal to aggregate gross incomes. Therefore except in cases of extreme perturbation of economic activity (such as the sudden cessation of a big war, which requires an enormous reorientation of economic activity; or a crazy decree suddenly suspending all banking operations), according to Ricardo *general* overproduction is impossible: there can only be overproduction in some industries, to which there will correspond underproduction in other industries.

The Ricardian theory of growth deriving from Say's Law is simple: capital accumulation does not meet obstacles from the demand side; the aggregate level of production is tendentially the one associated with the normal utilization of the existing productive capacity created by earlier accumulation; what is not consumed is invested.[64] Savings originate nearly exclusively from profits, because the workers

---

64 This is connected with a topic to which for space reasons I can allot only this footnote: the classical distinction between *productive* and *unproductive* labour. In the Introduction to *The Wealth of Nations* Adam Smith writes that the wealth of a nation is 'regulated by two different circumstances; first, by the skill, dexterity, and judgment with which its labour is generally applied; and, secondly, by the proportion between the number of those who are employed in useful labour and that of those who are not so employed … The number of useful and productive labourers, it will hereafter appear, is everywhere in proportion to the quantity of capital stock which is employed

are too poor to save, and the landlords are spendthrifts. Thus the share of savings in aggregate income depends on the share of profits: a higher profit rate entails a higher growth rate. If accumulation entails the extension of cultivation to less and less fertile land, since wages cannot fall below subsistence, the rate of profit will slowly decrease. Ricardo concludes that the rate of profit will tend to rise, remain constant or decline secularly, depending on whether its tendential decrease will be more than compensated, just compensated, or less than compensated, by the increase in the productivity of labour in agriculture due to technical progress.

Other authors of the period, for example Malthus and Sismondi, rejected Say's Law and admitted the possibility of generalized overproduction, on the basis first of all of empirical observation, which suggested that generalized selling difficulties could indeed be observed in certain periods. But they were unable to formulate convincing theoretical refutations of Say's Law. Malthus, for example, was a tenacious opponent of Ricardo on this issue but accepted as much as Ricardo that savings was synonymous with investment, and, because of this, Ricardo's logic came out as ultimately victorious in their debate.

Marx too rejects Say's Law, first of all on the basis of the historical evidence, which showed to him a tendency of capitalism to undergo periodic general crises; on the theoretical causes, although without arriving at the modern distinction between ex-ante (or programmed) and ex post (or realized) investment, Marx at

---

in setting them to work, and to the particular way in which it is so employed'. (WN, *Introduction and Plan of the Work*, iii, vi; 1975, pp. 1–2). Unproductive labourers are not set to work by capital but by revenue. In Book II, ▶ Chap. 3, Smith further clarifies the distinction: 'There is one sort of labour which adds to the value of the subject upon which it is bestowed, there is another which has no such effect. The former, as it produces a value, may be called productive; the latter, unproductive labour. Thus, the labour of a manufacturer adds, generally, to the value of the materials which he works upon, that of his own maintenance, and of his master's profits. The labour of a menial servant, on the contrary, adds to the value of nothing. Though the manufacturer has his wages advanced to him by his master, he, in reality, costs him no expense, the value of those wages being generally restored, together with a profit, in the improved value of the subject upon which his labour is bestowed. But the maintenance of a menial servant never is restored. A man grows rich by employing a multitude of manufacturers; he grows poor by maintaining a multitude of menial servants' (Smith, WN, II, 3, i; 1975, pp. 294–5). But Smith tends to identify unproductive labour with labour that produces no material product: Smith cites soldiers, musicians, artists, servants, lawyers, priests, politicians. More coherently, Marx calls productive all labour which is employed by capital and produces a profit; hence if the performances of actors and musicians working for a theatre or the work of temporary servants supplied by an agency produce profits for a firm, they are productive workers for Marx; indeed, those profits are indistinguishable in their effects (on competition, on class struggle, on growth) from other profits. However, Marx calls unproductive the labour employed in the *circulation* of commodities (e.g. shop-assistants, cashiers, bank clerks) although it is employed by capitalists and earns them a profit; here evidently other considerations enter, on whose reconstruction and reasonableness debate continues. More generally, the precise analytical aim and usefulness of the distinction between productive and unproductive labour are still open issues. See Kalmbach (1998) and the Wikipedia entry 'Productive and unproductive labour'.

64   **Chapter 1 · The Classical or Surplus Approach**

least notices that, since exchanges are against money, it is not guaranteed that whoever has sold will immediately use again the money thus obtained: he can choose to hold in monetary form the purchasing power thus obtained, if for some reason he does not expect to obtain from its immediate re-employment a higher profit than by waiting. Hence savings need not translate into investment. According to Marx this breakup of monetary circulation will happen for example when significant wage increases or social turmoils discourage capitalists from investing; an analogous breakup can happen when significant mistakes in the adaptation of the composition of production to the composition of demand cause crises simultaneously in a number of important sectors: the resulting difficulties of selling at cost-covering prices can extend to the firms and sectors selling inputs to the sectors in crisis, bankruptcies causing further bankruptcies; so the crisis of some sectors can become general.

In conclusion, the classical or surplus approach to distribution and prices is open on the issue of the determinants of the aggregate level of production, being compatible both with the acceptance, and with the rejection, of Say's Law. The rejection of Say's Law implies of course the need for an alternative theory of what determines the aggregate level of production, and one does not find in the classical authors, not even in Marx, a very satisfactory theory; but it will be argued later in this chapter that the Keynesian–Kaleckian *principle of effective demand* can be such a theory.

Importantly, note that in the classical approach the acceptance of Say's Law does *not* imply that aggregate production will tend to be at the level ensuring the full employment *of labour*, it only implies the normal utilization of capital. In each period labour employment depends on the level reached by capital accumulation and can only be increased by further capital accumulation. In the classical authors one does not find the notion of capital–labour substitution that, in the marginalist authors, motivates the thesis that labour employment can be increased *without a need for further capital accumulation* because the average capital–labour ratio can be varied. In the classical authors who accept Say's Law, employment will increase from a period to the next only if the increase in the scale of production, due to capital accumulation, more than compensates the tendency of labour-saving innovations to cause a decrease of labour employment. The online Appendix to this chapter contains a section on Ricardo on machinery that illustrates these statements.

1.12.3 Growth, Technical Change, the 'law' of the Tendency of the Rate of Profit to Fall

Marx's writings on crises do not amount to a full and coherent theory, they are mostly found in the manuscripts he left unfinished; anyway from them a clear prediction emerges of a tendency of capitalism to encounter greater and greater functioning difficulties, in particular to incur in crises of increasing gravity, owing to three main reasons:

1. increasing difficulties of coordination of a more and more complex economy, that is, greater and greater likelihood of imperfect adaptation of the composition of production to the composition of demand, with consequent bankruptcies;
2. the tendency of capitalism, owing above all to labour-saving technical progress, to increase the *reserve army of the unemployed* and to worsen the condition (at least the *relative* condition) of the working class, with a resulting tendential decrease of the share of workers' consumption in aggregate income, which makes it more and more difficult to avoid insufficiencies of aggregate demand;
3. a tendency, due to labour-saving technical progress, of the rate of profit to fall.

On the first reason, Marx produces attempts at a disaggregate treatment of the economy (his 'schemes of reproduction', on which we do not stop, but which have been the basis both of Soviet planning and of Wassily Leontief's input–output analysis), and concludes from them that it is very unlikely that 'disproportions' will be avoided. The growing complexity of the economy, due to the increasing division of labour and thus to the increasing number of sectors to be coordinated, is a first reason for the prediction of crises of increasing gravity, due to the tendency of bankruptcies to cause further bankruptcies of the firms which are suppliers to bankrupted firms.

The tendency of technical progress to cause a worsening of the conditions of the proletariat is derived from two causes, both based on developments of Smith's observations on the importance of the division of labour. One cause is the tendency of the increasing division of labour to cause a *deskilling* of labour. Here Marx utilizes observations of other writers, in particular Ure and Babbage, who had observed that, when the progress of the division of labour entails that the complex activities of an artisan are subdivided into different tasks assigned to different labourers, only a small part of these tasks will require advanced skills, while most of them will be fairly simple and repetitive operations which can be entrusted to unskilled workers. Thus the extension of the division of labour increases the proportion of unskilled workers and entails therefore a decrease of the average wage rate. The other cause is *mechanization*. The increasing division of labour makes the single, repetitive operations of unskilled workers more easily replaced by machinery. The result is a tendency of machines to replace workers; this causes an expulsion of workers from the productive process, hence unemployment. Marx argues that, because of increasing mechanization, unemployment tends to become worse at each successive economic cycle. The increased unemployment aggravates the tendency—already created by the tendential deskilling of labour—of average wages to decrease.

Thus Marx predicts a *growing immiseration* of workers. In his early writings Marx seems to have envisaged a tendency to *absolute* immiseration (decrease of the average real wage rate), in later writings he admits the possibility that immiseration be only *relative* (a worsening of the living conditions of the proletariat *relative* to the standard of living of the dominant classes), but even if only relative,

66   Chapter 1 · The Classical or Surplus Approach

immiseration still has two very important consequences in his view. First, it still means a worsening of the perceived living conditions of the proletariat[65] (this is important for the thesis of Marx that the proletariat will grow increasingly restless and dissatisfied with capitalism). Second, immiseration even if only relative still means a tendential decrease in workers' consumption as a *share* of the social product, which tends to create problems of overproduction, i.e. (in more modern terminology) of insufficient aggregate demand. This is, according to him, a difficulty of increasing relevance in the course of capitalist accumulation that tends to make the overcoming of crises more and more difficult. This contributes to the thesis that capitalism will undergo periodic crises of increasing gravity.

The third reason is the famous 'law of the tendency of the rate of profit to fall', considered by many Marxists the proof that capitalism is inevitably destined to function worse and worse and therefore to be sooner or later replaced by other forms of economic organization, but nowadays found unconvincing. There isn't complete agreement among interpreters as to what Marx meant by this 'law',[66] but the following seems to be the main idea in it. We have seen above that, according to Marx, technical innovation takes the prevalent form of replacing labour with machines, i.e., in Marx's terminology, of replacing living labour with dead labour. According to Marx this character of technical change means a tendency to an increase in the average proportion C/L of constant capital to living labour, which, even if the rate of exploitation is constant, results in an increase in the average composition of capital C/V. Owing to his approach to the determination of the rate of profit, Marx concludes that *technical progress tends to cause a decrease of the rate of profit*. The basic idea was, it seems, the following. When an innovation that replaces labour with machinery is discovered which is capable of reducing costs at the current prices,[67] it is introduced, because it allows higher profits for the capitalists who first introduce it; but when this innovation becomes generally adopted, by causing a rise in the economy-wide average organic composition of capital it causes—behind the back of capitalists, so to speak—a decrease of the rate of profit. True, this decrease might be neutralized for a time by a rise

---

65 'A notable advance in the amount paid as wages presupposes a rapid increase of productive capital. The rapid increase of productive capital calls forth just as rapid an increase in wealth, luxury, social wants, and social comforts. Therefore, although the comforts of the labourer have risen, the social satisfaction which they give has fallen in comparison with these augmented comforts of the capitalist, which are unattainable for the labourer, and in comparison with the scale of general development society has reached. Our wants and their satisfaction have their origin in society, we therefore measure them in their relation to society, and not in relation to the objects which satisfy them. Since their nature is social, it is therefore relative'. (Marx, *Wage Labour and Capital*, 1849, as repr. in Freedman (1961, p. 63)).

66 This 'law' (like the 'transformation of values into prices of production') is discussed in Volume 3 of *Capital*, assembled by Engels from provisional manuscripts after Marx's death; so ambiguities and contradictions are not surprising, and it remains unclear how much of the analyses in these manuscripts Marx would have endorsed for publication if alive.

67 Here Marx reasons in terms of labour values, so a cost reduction means a reduction of the total labour embodied in the product. But according to Marx the reduction of $c + v + s$ in the industry where machines replace labour goes together with a rise in $c/(v + s)$, and this affects in the same direction the economy-wide organic composition of capital.

1.12 · More on Marx

in the rate of exploitation S/V, but such neutralization cannot go on indefinitely, because $r = S/(C + V)$ can be rewritten as

$$r = \frac{\frac{S}{L}}{\frac{C}{L} + \frac{V}{L}} = \frac{1 - V/L}{C/L + V/L}. \tag{1.39}$$

Even with a wage (and V) tending to zero, and the numerator tending therefore to 1 and the denominator to C/L, an increase in C/L will sooner or later cause a decrease of the rate of profit.

This conclusion explains at least part of Marx's pessimism on the future of capitalist accumulation and on the possibility of increases of real wages: the tendency of the rate of profit to fall would eventually compel wages to fall and would eventually slow down capitalist accumulation, both through the effect on wages and thus on aggregate demand, and through the effect on the rate of profit, helping to cause crises of increasing length and gravity.

After Marx's death many Marxists advanced doubts on the validity of this 'law', observing that technical progress generally decreases the labour embodied in commodities, and can therefore result in a decrease in the labour embodied in the commodities composing the constant capital; therefore the adoption of more mechanized methods using less direct labour per unit of physical output does not necessarily imply an increase in C/L because the new ensemble of machines can embody less labour than the previous one. The tendency of the rate of profit to fall is a possibility, not a certainty, it was concluded. Modern analysis has added a stronger criticism in the shape of the following result (that will be proved in ▶ Chap. 2), usually called *Okishio's theorem*[68]:

» *Okishio's Theorem. Suppose that in a certain economy, at the going real wage rate and associated uniform rate of profit r and relative prices of production, a new method of production of a commodity directly or indirectly entering the real wage is discovered, which at the ruling prices yields a greater rate of profit. Then, if this new method replaces the old method for the production of that commodity and prices tend to the new prices of production, the new uniform rate of profit is necessarily higher than the old rate of profit r if the real wage rate has remained the same; if the rate of profit remains the same, then it is the real wage rate that becomes higher.*

The implication of Okishio's theorem is that the introduction of a new, more profitable production method cannot, when its adoption becomes generalized, cause a reduction in the rate of profit if the real wage rate has remained the same: if it concerns a 'wage industry', then the rate of profit *rises*; if it concerns luxury goods, the rate of profit is unaffected. Except in the latter case, the introduction of cost-reducing new methods opens up spaces for increases either of the rate of profit, or of the real wage rate, or of both.

---

68 The Japanese economist Nobuo Okishio was the first explicitly to prove this result, in 1961. In fact it was implicit in Sraffa's results in his 1960 book; some verbal statements by Samuelson in 1958 also allude to it.

This result can be illustrated graphically, cf. ◘ Fig. 1.3. Given the methods of production adopted in each industry, we have seen (cf. ▶ Sect. 1.7, and ▶ Chap. 2 for a more general proof) that, if one treats the real wage rate as variable, then, whatever the good or basket of goods chosen as numéraire, the real wage rate varies in a direction opposite to the rate of profit. Once a numéraire is chosen, the function $w(r)$ is a decreasing continuous and differentiable curve. If a method is changed in any one of the wage industries, the $w(r)$ curve changes. Okishio's theorem implies the following: suppose the $w(r)$ curve is given, and r (and hence w) is given. A new method is discovered which, at the ruling prices, would permit to sell at a lower price the good produced by one of the wage industries. If the new method replaces the old method in that industry and one calculates the new $w(r)$ curve (in terms of the same numéraire) and draws it in the same diagram as the old $w(r)$ curve, then at the old level of w the new $w(r)$ curve is *to the right* of the old curve, which, because it is a continuous curve, also implies that at the old level of r the new curve is *above* the old $w(r)$ curve. As ◘ Fig. 1.3 shows, this means there is room for a rise of w, or of r, or of both.

Marx's analysis of the cyclical tendency of wages to decrease after having increased must then be modified: if there is continuous technical progress, at each cycle the $w(r)$ curve is further 'outwards' than in the previous cycle at least in correspondence to the old (r, w) couple, so during a crisis the rate of profit needed to induce a resumption of accumulation requires the real wage to fall *less* than in the previous cycle.

Thus if for example the rate of profit necessary for the upturn to start is r' in ◘ Fig. 1.3, and in a crisis, the $w(r)$ curve being $w_I(r)$, the real wage must fall to w' in order for accumulation to resume, then if technical progress during the next

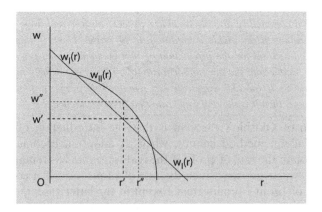

◘ **Fig. 1.3** Illustration of Okishio's theorem. The straight line $w_I(r)$ is the old $w(r)$ curve in terms of some given numéraire; initially $r=r'$ and $w=w'$; if a new method is more convenient at the associated prices, then its introduction shifts the $w(r)$ curve outwards at least in a neighbourhood of the point (r', w'), hence if the real wage rate remains unchanged the rate of profit rises, to r''; if r remains unchanged then w rises to w'''; or both r and w can rise. The new $w(r)$ curve might be entirely 'outwards' (i.e. to the North-East) of the old one; or it might be as the one indicated here as $w_{II}(r)$, that is outside the old wage curve at $w=w'$, but not for other values of w

cycle causes the $w(r)$ curve to shift to $w_{II}(r)$, the next upturn requires the real wage to decrease only to w''.

This result permits an explanation of the indubitable secular increase in the standard of living of the working classes in the main capitalist countries without a drastic fall of the rate of profit; and no doubt it weakens Marx's reasons for pessimism on the future of capitalism. On the tendency of capitalism to crises of increasing gravity, however, Marx's intuition appears not to have been off the mark, as the Great Crisis of the 1930s shows: afterwards, the discovery of Keynesian demand management techniques has changed the picture, but crises still happen.

1.12.4 Marx and the Future of Capitalism

Two more elements of Marx's predictions deserve mention.

One is the tendency towards an *increasing concentration of capitals*: bigger capitalists—Marx argues—tend to win in the competition against smaller capitalists because favoured by scale economies, so the smaller producers are pushed out of business or absorbed by takeovers; the winners in the competitive struggle become ever bigger. The development of the credit system significantly helps in this process of concentration of capitals, by making it easier to buy out other firms.[69] This prediction has been largely confirmed by historical experience. Indeed a modern problem is how to prevent the individuals who control giant corporations from having too much political influence.

The other prediction is the tendency towards an *increasing social polarization*: according to Marx, the advantage of big capital in the competitive struggle tends to destroy the independent middle class, by destroying petty commerce and small manufacture; thus a growing majority of population ends up having to sell their labour as wage labour, while the concentration of capitals decreases the number of capitalists. Wealth becomes more and more concentrated, while an increasing majority of the population falls into the proletariat. Marx includes in the working class all dependent, salaried workers, therefore well-paid technicians and managers too (the so-called workers' aristocracy), but owing to the process of deskilling mentioned above, he views this privileged portion of the working class as becoming less and less numerous; the tendency of capitalism according to him is towards an *increasing homogeneity of the working class*.

On these foundations, Marx views the class struggle as turning sooner or later decidedly in favour of the working class. A smaller and smaller minority of capitalists, weakened by a capitalist economy that encounters growing difficulties, is confronted by a working class that is more and more a majority of society, is

---

69 Thus Marx's conception of competition is very different from the perfect competition of modern neoclassical economics: it is a continuous, ruthless struggle that operates mainly through incessant innovations of products and of methods of production, and therefore continually revolutionizes markets and, also through its influence on the character and composition of the working class, the whole society.

70   **Chapter 1** · The Classical or Surplus Approach

more and more exasperated by its (at least relative) immiseration and by the worsening crises, is more and more homogeneous, and is more and more prepared by its work experience (the realization of the advantages of ex-ante coordination, made evident by the organization of giant firms) to appreciate the potential improvements in the running of the economy made possible by replacing the ex post coordination via markets with the ex-ante conscious coordination achievable via planning. The smaller and smaller minority of ruling class members will become sooner or later incapable of resisting the increasing rage, and the increasing clarity on an alternative project of social organization, of the vast majority of society.[70] In a justly famous passage in the penultimate chapter of *Capital* vol. I, Marx summarizes his predictions as follows:

» The expropriation of the direct producers was accomplished [in the process of primitive accumulation at the origins of capitalism] by means of the most merciless barbarism, and under the stimulus of the most infamous, the most sordid, the most petty and the most odious of passions. Private property which is personally earned, i.e. which is based, as it were, on the fusing together of the isolated, independent working individual with the conditions of his labour, is supplanted by capitalist private property, which rests on the exploitation of alien, but formally free labour.

As soon as this metamorphosis has sufficiently decomposed the old society throughout its depth and breadth, as soon as the workers have been turned into proletarians, and their means of labour into capital, as soon as the capitalist mode of production stands on its own feet, the further socialization of labour and the further transformation of the soil and other means of production into socially exploited and therefore communal means of production takes on a new form. What is now to be expropriated is not the self-employed worker, but the capitalist who exploits a large number of workers.

This expropriation is accomplished through the action of the immanent laws of capitalist production itself, through the centralization of capitals. One capitalist always strikes down many others. Hand in hand with this centralization, or this expropriation of many capitalists by a few, other developments take place on an ever-increasing scale, such as the growth of the co-operative form of the labour process, the conscious technical application of science, the planned exploitation of the soil, the transformation of the means of labour into forms in which they can only be used in common, the economizing of all means of production by their use as the means of production of combined, socialized labour, the entanglement of all peoples in the net of world market, and, with this, the growth of the international character of the capitalist regime. Along with the constant decrease in the number of capitalist magnates, who usurp and monopolize all the advantages of this process of transformation, the mass of misery, oppression, slavery, degradation and exploitation grows; but with this there also grows the revolt of the working class,

---

70 Owing to the increasing difference in numerosity of the two opposing groups, according to the mature Marx the revolution would not be necessarily violent. One of the tasks of trade unions was to contribute to the politicization of the working class in view of this final aim.

1.12 · More on Marx

a class constantly increasing in numbers, and trained, united and organized by the very mechanism of the capitalist process of production. The monopoly of capital becomes a fetter upon the mode of production which has flourished alongside and under it. The centralization of the means of production and the socialization of labour reach a point at which they become incompatible with their capitalist integument. This integument is burst asunder. The knell of capitalist private property sounds. The expropriators are expropriated (*Capital* I, pp. 928–29).

It is not important for the purposes of this book to discuss how correct Marx's predictions have come out to be—clearly, not quite correct; so far capitalist economies have been able to survive and grow, with changes in the advanced nations such as Keynesian demand management and elements (more in some nations than in others) of collective care for the sick, the old and the unemployed which, jointly with the rise in living standards, appear to have decreased the workers' hostility to capitalism. But these predictions, besides prompting admiration for their sheer vastness and radicality, remain of interest in that they show that in the classical approach there is no clear line of demarcation between economics, sociology and politics. A classical economist is naturally also a sociologist and a political scientist, because of the inevitable role that the approach attributes to social and political elements in the explanation of central economic phenomena. The difference here is great from the marginal approach, as we will see in ▶ Chap. 3.

1.13 'Core' and 'Out-of-Core' Analyses in the Surplus Approach

On the basis of what we have learned on the determinants of the real wage rate, of the quantities produced, and of the methods of production according to classical authors, it is possible to point out an aspect of the classical method of analysis that sharply distinguishes the classical approach from the marginal/neoclassical approach. The latter approach, as will be explained in ▶ Chaps. 3–9, argues that prices, income distribution, quantities produced, resources utilized are determined *simultaneously* and *interdependently* by the forces of supply and demand; deductive reasoning based on this interdependence allows univocal conclusions, e.g. on the effects of a change in the real wage on the demand for labour and on the general level of production. *The scope of purely deductive reasoning is much less wide in the classical approach.* Deductive reasoning holds full sway only in that part of the classical general analysis that has been called its analytical 'core' by Garegnani (1984, 1990b)[71]: the determination of the rate of profit on the basis of given real wage rate(s), given quantities produced, and given methods of production, and the comparative-statics study of the effects of changes in these data on the rate of profit. In the study of what determines these magnitudes and

---

71 This 'core' is of course not at all the cooperative-games notion of 'core' that will be met in ▶ Chap. 8, ▶ Sect. 8.21.

of the reciprocal influences among them, the classical approach admits such an importance of historical, social and political influences that the analysis must be much more inductive, attentive to historical specificities, and generally incapable of arriving on a purely deductive basis at univocal predictions analogous to those reachable in the marginal approach.

One can accordingly distinguish two different types of analysis in classical explanations and predictions. The analyses of the determinants of one or more of the data of the 'core' (real wages, quantities produced, technical conditions of production) are 'out of the core' analyses, rich in historically specific details and open to a variety of influences; the analysis of the effects of each such change on the rate of profit and relative prices is 'core' analysis, strictly deductive, and provisionally treating the other data in the 'core' as given and unaffected by the initial change; the analyses of the influences of these changes (both the direct influences, and the indirect ones operating through the change in profit rate and relative prices) on the other data of the 'core' are again 'out of the core' analyses and can also include an 'out of the core' analysis of repercussions on the magnitude(s) that changed first, or a second round of 'core' analysis if the other data of the 'core' are significantly affected to the point of requiring a new examination of the effects on the rate of profit.

Particularly striking to the modern economist is the absence, in the classical authors, of a simultaneous determination of changes in income distribution and in quantities produced. Quantities produced are studied separately, and the effects of changes in income distribution, or of technical progress, on them are studied only in a second stage, after keeping them initially given in order to study the effects on normal prices. The reason is the multitude of influences that can affect their change and therefore the difficulty with specifying general rules on how quantities produced will change when income distribution changes.

Thus for example Ricardo's discussion of the possible effects of abolishing the duty on corn imports motivated by the war with Napoleon started by considering the probable effects on the quantity of corn produced in England, an 'out of the core' analysis; the implication of the conclusion that British corn production would decrease (because some of the demand for corn would be satisfied by cheaper corn imports) was, that the least fertile lands would be abandoned and the new no-rent land would be more productive, a change in one of the data of the 'core'; the 'core' then allowed the conclusion that the rate of profit would rise (the real wage was taken as given). The initial deduction, that English corn production would decrease, depended on specific assumptions (e.g. no other war creating obstacles to corn imports, no great turbulence on foreign exchange markets, no failure of foreign corn harvests, no rise in wages).

Another example: in Marx's analysis of cyclical wage fluctuations the 'core' is used to demonstrate that, when the real wage rate rises, the rate of profit decreases; this is a purely deductive, univocal result; in the 'out of the core' analysis of the *causes* of rises in real wages, Marx admits the importance of social, organizational, ideological elements; on the 'out of the core' *effects* of the variation of the real wage rate *on accumulation*, again Marx is open to the possibility of different outcomes: a rise in real wages can discourage accumulation, but, if

1.13 · 'Core' and 'Out-of-Core' Analyses in the Surplus Approach

not excessive, in certain cases—depending also on political circumstances—it can stimulate accumulation by raising the demand for consumption goods.

The term 'core' can be misleading in that, in other contexts, it is used to indicate the most important part of an argument or analysis, a meaning *not* intended by Garegnani in this case. The term only refers to the 'central' position of this part of the classical approach, in the sense of being a node through which most reasonings in the surplus approach must pass in order to reach a conclusion on the effects of a change in one important variable on other important variables. It is indeed difficult to think of questions on the effects of changes for example in real wages, in technical knowledge, in extensions of cultivation, in the availability of oil, in exchange rates that do not require, for an answer, a study of the effects on the rate of profit and prices. The results of 'core' analyses are certainly indispensable to reach answers to most questions, but are only preliminary to answering the really important questions, which are 'out-of-core' questions, and concern the nature and tendencies of capitalism with respect to real incomes, employment, growth.

1.14 A Modern View of the Determinants of Aggregate Production

1.14.1 Going Beyond Marx on What Determines Aggregate Production

The main purpose of the present chapter is to make clear to readers acquainted (or who risk becoming acquainted) only with the marginal/neoclassical approach that there is an alternative way of looking at the functioning of capitalist economies, with a long tradition behind it. Its presentation can appear to go beyond microeconomics to typically macroeconomic issues that concern the working of the entire economy; but the same objection might be advanced against the presence in microeconomics textbooks of neoclassical general equilibrium theory, which can be seen as an eminently macroeconomic theory, since it studies how certain assumptions about the behaviour of individual agents produce economy-wide results. The classical approach too makes assumptions about individual agents, e.g. that workers try to act collectively to raise wages; that capitalists collude to counter the workers's requests; that capitalists invest to prevent their competitors from growing faster than them and to become more competitive by better exploiting scale economies; that investment goes in a greater proportion to the fields where the expected rate of return is higher; that a bankruptcy can cause further bankruptcies, etcetera. To ask about the overall effects of these microbehaviours is as legitimate for the classical as for the neoclassical approach.

An important overall effect is the general level of economic activity resulting from these microbehaviours. Here one must admit that the treatment of this issue by the classical economists, Marx included, is not very satisfactory. Subsequent

74   **Chapter 1** · The Classical or Surplus Approach

empirical episodes such as the Great Crisis of the 1930s, or the recession of 1973 and following years, or the nearly zero growth rate of Japan for ten years after 1990, or the 2008 financial crisis, have confirmed Marx's belief that capitalist economies are subject to crises and that labour unemployment and underutilization of plants can be high for many years in a row. Say's Law appears refuted by the evidence. But this makes it necessary to have a theory of what determines quantities produced and labour employment. Not even Marx gets close to a satisfactory such theory; he does grasp the possibility of non-correspondence between saving decisions and investment decisions; but he seems to have considered economic crises as episodes (even violent and long-lasting) that periodically *interrupt* an accumulation process of Ricardian type; he concentrates on the causes of these interruptions, without attempting to reach a theory of the level around which the social product gravitates when—for any reason—investment remains for a considerable time below the level required to absorb all the savings that would be forthcoming if the social product were at the Ricardian, normal-capacity-utilization level. So Marx's admission of obstacles to accumulation (for example, difficulties with selling the potential production of consumption goods owing to the tendency of capitalism to compress wages) has unclear implications for growth over longer periods; whenever there isn't a crisis, Marx's picture seems to be one of growth as *supply-determined*,[72] or if you like profit-determined: a higher rate of profit (lower real wages) favours growth, because it raises profits and hence savings and therefore investment; and capitalists do want to reinvest profits and to grow, because competition tends to eliminate the smaller capitalists. But what happens when this push towards reinvestment of profits meets obstacles remains unclear, apart from a suggestion that a crisis will unleash.

This view derivable from Marx, of output and growth as supply-determined except for periodic interruptions due to crises, is not always convincing. Let us consider Italy after 2008. The growth of public debt frightened financial markets and allowed a great pressure from the European Union upon the Italian government to cut down its deficit by raising taxes and reducing expenditure on public services. The Italian government complied, and this reduced consumer incomes and hence expenditure on consumption goods. This in turn made it difficult for firms to sell as much as before; many went bankrupt, and many others reduced investment, since there was no reason to increase productive capacity. The fall in

---

72 'Supply-determined' in the sense of determined, in each period, by the available supply of goods at the normal-capital-utilization level, hence given *before* the level of aggregate investment is determined, and *determining* investment as equal to the part of production not allocated to consumption. The causation goes *from* the social product to investment and growth. The Keynesian–Kaleckian approach to be presented next views the level and the growth of the social product as *demand-determined*, because adapting to an independently determined level and growth of aggregate demand. It is important to be clear that 'supply-determined' must not be intended in the marginalist/neoclassical sense of associated with full labour employment, because in the classical economists the normal utilization of existing plants means only the employment of the amount of labour required by existing capital, always less than labour supply.

1.14 · A Modern View of the Determinants of Aggregate Production

production went on for three years, but the reason was not a rise in real wages. Growth has not resumed since; industrial production in 2014 was 15% less than in 2007. This does not fit with either a picture of violent but temporary crisis, nor with a Ricardian picture of normal plant utilization. And anyway Marx's reasons for crises do not include a reduction in state expenditure: why should such a reduction cause a crisis? And why such a lasting one, with the economy's growth practically equal to zero for so many years, but without a further worsening of the crisis?

A theoretical development, due to John Maynard Keynes and to Michail Kalecki in the 1930s, supplies a theory capable of answering these questions, and compatible with the classical approach to value and distribution. In the remainder of the chapter you find an elementary and synthetic presentation of this theory. Readers familiar with traditional Keynesian macroeconomic theory will not learn much from it, except that here the central idea of this theory is separated from the neoclassical elements in combination with which it is usually presented, so its compatibility with the classical approach becomes evident. (For the reader who has not already studied them, Sect. 2 of the online Appendix to this chapter in this book's Website introduces the notions of national accounting needed for the remainder of this chapter.) This presentation will also be useful to students who only studied macroeconomics in those contemporary versions which assume continuous full labour employment, with savings automatically translating into investment.

1.14.2 The Principle of Effective Demand

The starting point of the Keynesian–Kaleckian theory is that each industry tends to adapt production to the demand for its products at a price sufficient to induce that production (this price is called *supply price*). Given sufficient time, this price is the natural price or price of production, imposed by entry. Let us assume no constraint coming from labour availability, owing to the existence of open or hidden unemployment (Marx's reserve army of labour). That production adapts to demand is accepted by neoclassical theory too, so no problem here. Then the question that arises is what determines demand.

The *composition* of demand can be taken as given, determined by income distribution and consumption habits for the part of demand addressed to purchase consumption goods, and by the preferred composition of investment, decided by firms in order to renew capital stocks and to expand them in the direction suggested by past trends plus innovations, for the part addressed to buy capital goods. Both compositions can be taken as fundamentally given for the purposes of the present analysis, and to be studied if necessary in a second stage of the analysis. As we will see, in value terms (all the magnitudes we will talk about in this section will be in value terms unless explicitly indicated otherwise) the ratio of demand addressed to investment to demand addressed to consumption can be taken as constant in a first approximation, so the difference in the two compositions does not cause indeterminateness of the overall composition of demand.

76   **Chapter 1** · The Classical or Surplus Approach

It is in the determination of the *aggregate level* of demand that the characteristic element of the theory emerges. We can distinguish the following steps in the argument:

First, *production creates incomes*: wages of the workers employed, interest on the capital employed, rents on the land utilized; also, the need to reconstitute the capital goods utilized creates demand for the products of the firms that produce those goods, and their production creates further incomes. By convention, national accounting identifies the value of the net product of a period with the net aggregate income perceived by members of the economy in the period. (Goods produced and not sold are counted as anyway having value at their normal prices, and contributing to the income created by the firm, which coincides with value added, as explained in Appendix 2.)

Second, *incomes create demand, but only one part of demand; as a result, aggregate demand can differ from aggregate production.*

Some part of aggregate demand is determined in autonomy from the aggregate level of incomes, and it is called *autonomous or exogenous* demand. At a first level of approximation, *programmed* or *ex-ante* gross investment (decisions to buy newly produced capital goods)[73] can be considered autonomous, that is, it can be treated as a given magnitude; indeed we have seen, studying Marx, that decisions to invest (that is, to purchase newly produced capital goods) are independent, moment by moment, from decisions to save (that is, decisions *not* to spend on consumption goods part of one's income), because previous accumulated monetary savings plus credit creation make it possible to invest without needing someone to save at the same time, and conversely one can decide not to spend part of one's income and hoard it, a saving decision without corresponding decision to invest.

The remainder of aggregate demand depends on the level of aggregate income, and it is called *endogenous or induced* demand. For the moment let us assume that aggregate demand consists of only two components: programmed investment and consumption. Consumption is very evidently dependent on income: when income decreases, a household generally spends less on consumption goods, when it increases, the household generally spends more.

By definition, the value of aggregate net production is aggregate net income, Y. Again by definition, the destination of net income is either consumption expenditure C (purchase of consumption goods), or net saving S (income not spent on purchasing of consumption goods, it does not matter whether employed to purchase new capital goods or simply hoarded). Hence

$$Y \equiv C + S.$$

Aggregate demand AD, on the other hand, is defined as the sum of consumption expenditure C and programmed net investment I:

---

73 The reader is invited to read Appendix 2 to the chapter that introduces to the necessary elements of national accounting and clarifies the difference between programmed or ex-ante investment and realized or ex post investment, dispelling possible doubts on whether savings and investment are, or not, identical by definition.

$$AD \equiv C + I.$$

Since Y is also the (value of) aggregate net production and C is (the value of) the part of it purchased for consumption purposes,[74] S can be interpreted as the part of aggregate net production *not* purchased for consumption purposes. It may have been sold or not.[75] If the net production corresponding to S is all sold, it coincides with net programmed investment. But it need not coincide with the latter. Part of the production of the period can remain unsold: one speaks then of *non-programmed accumulation of inventories*. Of it can be that net programmed investment (purchases of capital goods in excess of replacement of the used-up capital goods) exceeds S, implying a *decumulation* of inventories (in the aggregate; not necessarily at the level of each industry).[76] If $S > I$ then $Y > AD$, that is, aggregate net production is greater than aggregate net sales, there is a non-programmed accumulation of inventories. Conversely if $S < I$ then $Y < AD$, aggregate net production is less than aggregate net sales, on average firms are very glad to observe a decumulation of inventories that indicates they are selling more than expected.

Third, *aggregate production (aggregate income) tends towards aggregate demand*. When saving decisions are greater than investment decisions, that is, when $Y > AD$, firms on average find it impossible to sell all they intended to sell and *tend to produce less* (also to get rid of the undesired accumulation of inventories); the opposite happens when saving decisions are less than investment decisions. So when $Y > AD$, Y tends to decrease; when $Y < AD$, Y tends to increase; aggregate income tends towards aggregate demand.

Fourth, *when Y differs from AD, the change in Y alters AD in the same direction but the difference between the two decreases*, finally disappearing at the *equilibrium level of aggregate income*.[77] The reason is that when Y changes, by assumption only consumption C changes (we are treating I as autonomous, i.e. given), and it changes in the same direction as Y, but, as confirmed by statistical evidence, by

---

74 The words 'the value of' will be mostly omitted from now on but are implicit, the magnitudes Y, C, I, S, etc., are the value magnitudes of the corresponding physical aggregates.

75 In national accounting, it is also called *ex post*, or *realized*, investment. Ex post investment and savings are equal by definition (in a closed economy) according to standard national accounting, and this can induce confusion among students who, unless clear about the distinction between programmed and realized investment, remain wondering how investment can differ from savings, since it is equal to savings by definition. The key is not to confuse *programmed* investment, which is the one that can differ from savings, with ex post investment, which cannot.

76 If a firm decides to increase its product inventories, this is counted as programmed investment, i.e. as sales of the firm's product to itself. In this way all programmed investment can be viewed as purchases.

77 Here 'equilibrium' means only the disappearance of forces pushing Y to change, it does *not* mean the marginalist/neoclassical notion of general equilibrium on all markets that will be illustrated in ch. 3 (and includes the full employment of labour). To stress the difference, sometimes it is qualified as 'Keynesian' equilibrium level of Y; it may well be associated with considerable unemployment.

78   Chapter 1 · The Classical or Surplus Approach

a lesser *amount* than Y; that is, $\Delta C/\Delta Y < 1$. If Y increases, a part of the income increase is saved. The simplest function with this characteristic is the following:

$$C = c_1 Y, \text{ with } 0 < c_1 < 1,$$

for example $c_1 = 0.8$: this is called the *average propensity to consume*, and $1-c_1 = 0.2$ is called the *average propensity to save*. When Y increases, the increase of C is 80% of the increase of Y. Then $S = Y-C$ increases, if initially $S < I$, i.e. $Y < AD$, and therefore Y increases, this raises S, that tends towards the given I. The tendency of Y to change stops when $Y = AD$ or $S = I$, which in this example will happen when

$$Y_e = AD = I + c_1 Y_e = I \cdot \frac{1}{1 - c_1} = 5 \cdot I. \tag{1.40}$$

This is the equilibrium level of aggregate net income or aggregate net production.[78]

This is the basic new idea advanced by Keynes and Kalecki, generally called the **principle of effective demand**.[79] It states: *the level of aggregate production or aggregate income is variable and tends towards the level that brings savings to equality with investment, or more generally aggregate production to equality with aggregate demand.*

Given the production methods and the composition of production, this equilibrium level Y_e also determines labour employment. Thus we have here a simple theory of what determines the tendential level of aggregate production and of labour employment. A graphical illustration is in ◘ Fig. 1.4 which assumes $Y = S + C$, $AD = I + C$ and $C = c_1 Y$. Net income Y is in abscissa, AD and again Y in ordinate. To the left of Y_e it is $Y < AD$ so Y tends to increase, the opposite happens to the right of Y_e, so Y tends to Y_e.

Note that if I varies by the amount ΔI, Y_e varies by the amount $\Delta Y = \Delta I \cdot 1/(1 - c_1)$. The fraction $1/(1 - c_1)$ is called the **multiplier**, because it tells us by how much one must multiply a variation ΔI of autonomous expenditure in order to obtain the induced variation of equilibrium income. The multiplier is greater than 1, possibly much greater: it is 5 in our example with $c_1 = 0.8$.

The approach can be generalized by the consideration of further autonomous expenditures, such as an autonomous component of consumption, or exports, or state expenditure. If $C = c_0 + c_1 Y$, consumption includes a part which is independent of Y; then c_1 is called the *marginal* propensity to consume; the multiplier

---

78 All the reasoning has been expressed in terms of *net* aggregate income (and net aggregate demand), but it can be reformulated without difficulty in terms of *gross* aggregate income (GNP, GDP), the more widely used but theoretically somewhat unsatisfactory notion, see Sect. 2 of the online Appendix to the chapter.

79 Keynes called 'effective demand' the demand for goods that actually manifests itself in the markets, because voluntary *and* backed by purchasing power so that the intention to purchase can be translated into actual purchases. Unemployed workers, for example, would like to purchase goods but do not have the income to do so, therefore their demand is only potential, not effective.

1.14 · A Modern View of the Determinants of Aggregate Production

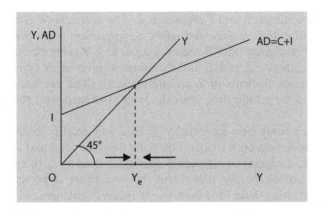

◻ **Fig. 1.4** Keynesian equilibrium income

remains $1/(1-c_1)$. If the State adds to the given investment I a flow of exogenous state expenditure on goods G, and if income is taxed at a uniform rate t, then $AD = C+I+G$, where consumption can be assumed to be determined as $C = c_0 + c_1(1-t)Y$, depending for the income-dependent part on *after-tax* (or *disposable*) income $(1-t)Y$. Putting all this together, Y will tend towards the level

$$Y_e = c_0 + c_1(1-t)Y_e + I + G = \frac{1}{1-c_1(1-t)}(c_0 + I + G). \tag{1.41}$$

(Prove it!) Now autonomous demand includes c_0, and the multiplier is different, but the analysis is similar, e.g. an increase ΔG of state expenditure causes an increase of equilibrium Y equal to

$$\Delta Y_e = \frac{1}{1-c_1(1-t)}\Delta G$$

State expenditure and taxation are seen as powerful regulators of national production and labour employment. Increases of taxation reduce equilibrium Y, because they reduce the disposable income of households $(1-t)Y$ and thus consumption expenditure out of any given Y.

This theory is very different from Say's Law. Coming back to the simplest case $Y = C+S$, $AD = C+I$, Say's Law can be expressed as follows: *whatever the level of aggregate net income and hence of net savings, net programmed investment adjusts to net savings*. Since investment is determined by savings, Say's Law implies that one must look for a theory determining the level of savings, and hence of aggregate income Y, *before* the determination of investment: the given Y and the given propensity to consume will determine S, and S will determine I. For example in the marginal/neoclassical approach, which accepts Say's Law, the equilibrium level of income is determined by the tendency towards the full employment of labour[80];

---

[80] Therefore 'equilibrium level of income' means different things in the marginal/neoclassical approach and in the Keynesian–Kaleckian approach.

80   **Chapter 1** · The Classical or Surplus Approach

this given Y determines S, and I adjusts to it. The principle of effective demand states the opposite: *it is savings that adjust to investment,* via *variations of Y;* a given I causes Y to change until S becomes equal to I. Y cannot be taken as given, it depends on aggregate demand, and therefore on investment or more generally on the autonomous elements in aggregate demand; these can cause Y to differ considerably and for a long time from the level associated with the full employment of labour.

One can then study how an initially given I may tend to change, by taking into account the convenience to invest deriving from the level and the changes of Y. For example, decreases of aggregate demand caused by a reduction of state expenditure G can discourage investment, because firms, if persuaded that the decrease will be lasting, have little incentive to invest in enlargement of productive capacity and even in replacing all the old plants that reach scrapping stage: they may well choose a reduction of plant size; I (which is net) can even become negative. Note that through the multiplier the decrease of I causes a *further* decrease of AD, which discourages investment further.[81] If the decrease of AD is considerable in all likelihood a number of firms will go bankrupt; this will create sales difficulties for the firms that were supplying them with raw materials and other circulating capital goods; and the workers who lost their job will decrease their demand for consumption goods; so bankruptcies can cause further bankruptcies. The crisis can become more and more serious.

Something like this happened in the 1930s, unleashing the most serious crisis known by the advanced market economies so far. In the USA the rate of unemployment went up to 25% or more (historians are not agreed on the precise number). That no analogously deep and long-lasting crisis has happened since is largely due to the fact that, precisely because of the discovery of the Keynesian–Kaleckian principle of effective demand, governments have understood that by intervening with increases of state expenditure, reductions of taxation, and direct stimulation of private investment, they can counter the tendency of aggregate demand to go on decreasing when it starts decreasing. For example U.S. government interventions in support of the economy after the 2007–2008 crisis were simply staggering.

---

81 This is one example of the application of the *accelerator theory of investment*. This theory states that gross investment is motivated by the desire of firms to adjust their productive capacity, and therefore their fixed plants, to normal demand; net investment will be positive when firms desire to enlarge their productive capacity, negative in the opposite case; gross investment is net investment plus depreciation (replacement of capital deterioration). The term 'accelerator' derives from the fact that changes in aggregate demand will tend to cause much greater percentage changes in investment. For example assume that on average firms wish to maintain a 1:1 ratio between their capital stock and yearly sales, and that from a stationary situation of capital adapted to sales (and gross investment equal to depreciation), there is a 10% increase of Y. Firms then wish to increase their capital stock by 10%, let us suppose in two years; assume depreciation is 10% of the capital stock per year; then net investment rises from zero to half the size of depreciation, which means an increase of gross investment by 50% for two years. (Of course this will have a big effect on Y, which may have further effects on desired capital stock and hence on investment, with dynamic consequences that you will have to study in macroeconomics courses and textbooks.).

1.14 · A Modern View of the Determinants of Aggregate Production

The view of the determinants of labour employment, aggregate production and economic growth, suggested by the principle of effective demand, is radically different from the one based on Say's Law. In the latter view, since Y is given and I adjusts to S, an aggregate decision to consume less and save more (a reduction of c_1) raises investment and hence accelerates capital accumulation. In the Keynesian–Kaleckian approach the effect is radically different: with investment given, a decision to save more causes a reduction of the multiplier and hence of Y, that causes *a failure of the attempt to save more*: savings increase *as a percentage* of Y, but of a smaller Y, so they *do not increase in total amount*, because at the new equilibrium Y_e they are again equal to the unchanged investment I. By trying to save more, consumers have only succeeded in *reducing aggregate income*. The effect can be represented in ◘ Fig. 1.4 as the AD curve becoming flatter (its slope is c_1), so its intersection with the 45° line shifts to the left. This is called the ***Keynesian paradox of thrift***. And this is what happens if investment is given; but as just illustrated, a reduction of Y tends to discourage investment, so the more probable effect of the attempt to save more is a tendency of investment to decrease, and hence a *reduction* of the amount of savings.

1.14.3 The Dynamic Multiplier

A clarification of the notion of *equilibrium* level of Y in this theory is necessary. *The equality of investment and savings in a period is not always sufficient to qualify the corresponding Y as an equilibrium Y.* Imagine an economy where programmed investment and savings are *always* equal, where production of each good is always perfectly adapted to demand *because all production is to order*, all that is produced is sold because it is only produced after receiving purchase orders. In such an economy there is no unprogrammed inventory variation, $Y = AD$ always. But this does *not* mean that Y is always an *equilibrium* Y, if one continues to mean by *equilibrium* Y the level at which *there is no incentive for Y to change*, and one explicitly takes into account a fact that was implicit in our earlier discussion of the dynamic tendency towards Y_e: generally one must *first* receive an income, and only after receiving it one can spend the part of it allotted to consumption; and *some time is needed for all this spending to go through*. In other words, *there is always some lag between earning an income and spending the fraction c_1 of it on consumption goods*. To understand the relevance of this lag, divide time into periods of length equal to the average length of this lag, and distinguish the periods with indices t, $t+1$, etc. Then, assuming $C = c_1 Y$ for simplicity, the consumption expenditure *caused by* the income Y_t obtained by consumers in period t, that is $c_1 Y_t$, is *not* C_t, it is C_{t+1}, and therefore it contributes to determining AD_{t+1}, not AD_t. Since we are now assuming that aggregate output perfectly equals aggregate demand in each period and treating investment as given and constant, so $I_{t+1} = I_t$, we obtain

$$Y_{t+1} = C_{t+1} + I_{t+1} = c_1 Y_t + I_t. \tag{1.42}$$

82 **Chapter 1** · The Classical or Surplus Approach

This equation implies that Y_{t+1} will be equal to Y_t only if $c_1 Y_t + I_t = Y_t$, that is, if $Y_{t+1} = Y_t = I_t \cdot 1/(1 - c_1) = Y_e$. In other words, if Y_t is different from Y_e, it tends to change. Now, *the true definition of equilibrium Y is the level of Y which no longer has a tendency endogenously to change (as long as autonomous expenditure does not change)*. Now that we admit a lag between receiving an income and spending it, we see that this equilibrium requires $Y_{t+1} = Y_t = I_t \cdot 1/(1 - c_1)$, the same equilibrium level we found in the previous static analysis.

Is this equilibrium level of Y stable in the present case, that is, is it the level towards which actual Y tends? A simple numerical example will show that the answer is yes.

Assume that $c_1 = 0.8$, that investment is initially constant at the level $I = 160$, and that Y is initially at the corresponding equilibrium level $Y_e = 800$. This situation, let us assume, goes on up to period -1; in period 0 investment increases to 200 and then remains at this level for ever. Assume that production adjusts perfectly to aggregate demand in each period, so from $t = 0$ onwards one has

$$Y_t = AD_t = C_t + I_t = 0.8 \cdot Y_{t-1} + 200 \quad \text{for } t \geq 0, \quad \text{and } Y_{-1} = 800.$$

The temporal evolution of C and Y is described by the following Table:

$$C_{-1} = (0,8) \cdot 800 = 640 \qquad \rightarrow AD_{-1} = Y_{-1} = 640 + 160 = 800$$
$$C_0 = (0,8) \cdot 800 = 640 \qquad \rightarrow AD_0 = Y_0 = 640 + 200 = 840$$
$$C_1 = (0,8) \cdot 840 = 672 \qquad \rightarrow AD_1 = Y_1 = 672 + 200 = 872$$
$$C_2 = (0,8) \cdot 872 = 697.6 \qquad \rightarrow AD_2 = Y_2 = 697.6 + 200 = 897.6$$
$$C_3 = (0,8) \cdot 897.6 = 718.08 \quad \rightarrow AD_3 = Y_3 = 718.08 + 200 = 918.08$$
$$C_4 = (0,8) \cdot 918.08 = 734.46 \rightarrow AD_4 = Y_4 = 734.46 + 200 = 934.46$$

$$\cdots\cdots\cdots\cdots\cdots\cdots\cdots\cdots\cdots\cdots\cdots\cdots\cdots\cdots\cdots\cdots\cdots\cdots\cdots\cdots\cdots\cdots\cdots\cdots\cdots$$

$$C_\infty = (0,8) \cdot 1000 = 800 \qquad \rightarrow AD_\infty = Y_\infty = 1000$$

The increase of investment by 40 units in $t = 0$ causes AD_0 and Y_0 to increase by 40 units relative to $t = -1$, and this causes C_1 (and Y_1) to increase by $0.8 \cdot 40 = 32$ units, and C_2 (and Y_2) to increase by a further $0.8 \cdot 0.8 \cdot 40 = 25.6$ units and so on: $\Delta C_t = C_t - C_{t-1} = 40 \cdot c_1{}^t$. The sum of the successive increases of Y_t equals the initial increase of autonomous expenditure, 40, times $(1 + c_1 + c_1{}^2 + c_1{}^3 + \ldots)$ which tends to $1/(1 - c_1)$ as long as $0 < c_1 < 1$. We obtain the same final increase of Y_e as in the static analysis. This process is sometimes called *the dynamic Keynesian multiplier*, while $1/(1 - c_1)$ is called the *static* multiplier.

The dynamic process just described is not very realistic: the lag from receipt of income to expenditure is different for different people, and the instantaneous adjustment of production to demand is often impossible, most firms must produce *before* knowing demand. In all likelihood Y tends towards Y_e both because of the gradual process of extension (with lags) of the effects of an initial change in autonomous expenditure described by the dynamic multiplier and because of discrepancies between Y and AD causing unprogrammed inventory variations. An idea of the speed of the adjustment? Some statistical evidence suggests that generally the greatest part (nearly 90%) of the variation of Y induced by a variation of autonomous expenditure and the multiplier is completed in 18 months.

1.14.4 **The Adaptability of Production to Demand**

The Keynesian–Kaleckian approach gives central role to the tendency of production to adjust to demand. This requires a *flexibility* of production, a capacity not only to reduce production, but also to *increase* it if demand increases, even considerably, and in relatively short time spans, weeks or at most months, that is, *without* needing first to enlarge productive capacity by building new plants. (We are now admitting durable capital goods too, as realism requires. The principle of effective demand remains perfectly valid.) What makes such a short-period upward flexibility of production possible?

The reason is the possibility to vary the *degree of utilization* of plants, increasing production from the same fixed plants by utilizing them for more hours per week; the existence of inventories of raw materials and of other circulating capital goods makes an initial increase of production possible, until the increase of production by the firms producing those raw materials and goods makes it possible to reconstitute those inventories. The economy behaves accordion-like, with the sectors where the increase in demand first arrives first increasing production and reducing their inventories of intermediate goods, and then their suppliers in turn increasing production and transmitting the increase to *their* suppliers, and so on.

As we will see in greater detail in ▶ Chap. 12, in most industries a considerable increase of production is perfectly possible, by increasing the number of hours per week the plant is operated; in emergency situations (e.g. a catastrophe, or war), even by working the weekends too and by introducing one more labour shift, passing, say, from 8 to 16 h of plant utilization per day. Even the very few firms with continuous production processes, e.g. iron furnaces, do not work at full capacity at all hours; furnaces are never shut off but raw materials are processed only in the amounts required to satisfy demand, the monthly production flow is generally considerably below the maximum possible one. Therefore the kinds of production increase from the same fixed plants that variations in aggregate demand can cause, say 10% more yearly production, appear perfectly possible. Over longer periods it will be convenient to expand productive capacity by building additional plant and thus reduce the need to pay higher wages for overtime or night shifts; but in the short period, considerable variations of production from the given plant will be implemented with no difficulty if demand makes them convenient. A constraint might come from lack of availability of extra labour; but generally market economies suffer from overt or hidden unemployment, and for short periods the already employed workers too will be generally ready to do overtime work if adequately paid. Over longer periods there are labour migrations and changes in the habits of the population (e.g. women can increase their participation to the labour market, or retirement age can be modified) that adapt labour supply to demand.

Firms producing durable capital goods are generally particularly well prepared for a great variability of production, because the demand for their products is often highly variable. Think for example of demand for new airplanes, or for new trains: it is high when better models come out and impose a general upgrading of the stock of airplanes, or of trains; but these periods can be followed by periods of very low demand.

Agricultural productions are of course less capable of varying the flow of supply in a few weeks or months; but of these goods, when durable (e.g. grains), considerable stocks are kept in reserve precisely for that reason; furthermore, agricultural food products, which are the main group of products of this kind, are mostly subsistence products, consumed by the unemployed and by the poor anyway, so the demand for them changes little with variations of Y and of employment.

I am insisting on these details because many economists seem not to be clear about this great variability of production in response to variations of demand and accordingly underestimate how much the level of Y and of labour employment and the rate of capital accumulation depend on aggregate demand. More aggregate demand means more production. More investment means more aggregate production through the multiplier, and thus also more consumption (*it is therefore generally false that more investment requires a reduction of consumption, as a given Y would imply*); furthermore, the greater production of capital goods stimulated by the higher investment means a greater expansion of the economy's productive capacity than it would otherwise have occurred, and this means that next period the economy can produce more than otherwise, which will in turn permit more investment than otherwise without any need to compress consumption, and so on in subsequent periods too, with a resulting higher rate of growth together with higher consumption.

Conversely, a reduction of aggregate demand means less production, a waste with no compensation. And the lower aggregate demand will also discourage investment, with loss of potential expansion of the productive capacity of the economy. This loss of what might have been produced, and of the potential expansion of productive structures, is much less perceived than unemployment because it is not visible, but it is there, and it can be gigantic. Conversely, China's exceptional growth rate has produced enormous increases of income and of productive capacity that would not have been realized if aggregate demand had not increased. China shows that most market economies could produce more and grow faster, they do not do so because aggregate demand does not increase faster; they would, if there were a higher level and growth rate of autonomous expenditure.

The above will have to suffice to show how radically the perspectives on the causes of aggregate production, employment and growth are changed by the Keynesian–Kaleckian approach relative to the ones based on Say's Law. To close the chapter we need only to clarify the connection between the Keynesian–Kaleckian approach, and the surplus approach to value and distribution.[82]

---

82 It is not possible to discuss here the marginalist/neoclassical elements present in Keynes in uneasy coexistence with the principle of effective demand. The latter principle does not in the least depend on them; in Keynes it is coupled with them for the determination of the effects of variations in labour employment on income distribution, and for the study of the determinants of investment, but it need not be.

1.14 · A Modern View of the Determinants of Aggregate Production

Clearly there is no difficulty with admitting a classical perspective on wages within the Keynesian–Kaleckian approach to employment and growth: in the other direction, the possibility of influences of government policy on aggregate demand enriches the classical perspective, indicating another way through which fluctuations of the 'reserve army of labour' can happen and can influence the bargaining power of the contending classes. As pointed out in a brilliant short article by Michail Kalecki, '*Political aspects of full employment*' (1943), whose reading is highly recommended, there is no reason why governments should be *always* interested in minimizing unemployment. The business community (the capitalists, in Marx's terminology) is against wage increases, because these reduce the rate of profit; and the business community has considerable influence over politics, owing to its capacity heavily to finance candidates in electoral campaigns, and to its capacity to put pressure on governments by threatening to invest less if government policies do not support the interests of business. The result, says Kalecki, is that governments will often consciously intervene on aggregate demand to *increase* unemployment, in order to reduce the bargaining power of wage labour and to re-establish discipline in the factories, discipline that full employment tends gradually to undermine because it makes workers less afraid of being fired.

1.15 Conclusions

This chapter has introduced you to an approach to the working of market economies which is not the dominant one at present, but is considered worth resuming by a consistent and growing number of economists. It realistically admits the presence in the economy of capitalist societies of sometimes violent conflicts of interests between different social groups. The different picture of capitalism emerging from the marginal/neoclassical approach will be contrasted with this classical picture at the end of ▶ Chap. 3.

The central notion of long-period prices remains central in marginalist economics too, we will see it emerge clearly in ▶ Chap. 5 when discussing the choices of firms and Marshallian long-period partial equilibrium, it will have a fundamental role in ▶ Chaps. 7 and 8, and it continues to be the basis of applied analyses even now when general equilibrium theory has taken a partially different direction. For this reason, before passing to the marginal/neoclassical approach, long-period prices are examined more rigorously in the next chapter.

1.16 Review Questions and Exercises

Review questions
1. Consider the determination of long-period prices (prices of production) in an economy that produces corn and iron using corn, iron (both circulating capital) and labour. Can the technical coefficients of the iron industry be totally irrelevant for the determination of the rate of profit, that is, such that if they change the rate of profit does not change?

86   Chapter 1 · The Classical or Surplus Approach

2. Why does Malthus' population-based theory of wages need considerably sticky wages?

3. Does Ricardo's acceptance of Say's Law imply a tendency to the full employment of labour? Explain.

4. Explain in what sense it can be argued that the theory of intensive differential rent too implies that rent does not enter price.

5. (Needs Appendix 1.3 in the Online Appendix) Explain the difference between realized rate of profit and normal rate of profit, and why it is the latter (at least) that investors aim to obtain, changes of the former being more an indication of changes of demand.

6. (Needs Appendix 1.2 in the Online Appendix) Explain the distinction between ex-ante and ex post investment, the connection with inventory variation, and how this distinction helps to understand why according to the Keynesian approach aggregate income Y gravitates towards the level where Y equals aggregate demand.

7. Explain the statement 'for the study of problems in which changes in quantities produced can be presumed to be of minor importance, one can consider the no-rent production method not to change'.

8. Explain why according to Ricardo a higher rate of profits usually implies a higher growth rate of the economy, and how this connects with Say's Law.

9. Explain why it is generally false that more investment requires a reduction of consumption.

10. Explain why the classical approach implies that governments can easily be against decreases of unemployment, and sometimes can even be in favour of increasing unemployment.

11. Explain why the equality of investment and savings is not always sufficient to qualify the corresponding Y as an equilibrium Y.

12. Illustrate graphically the Keynesian paradox of thrift in a diagram with Y in abscissa, and I and S in ordinate, assuming $Y = C + I$, $S = Y - C$, I given, $C = c_0 + c_1 Y$, and allowing first c_1 alone, and then c_0 alone, to decrease.

13. Illustrate graphically the plausible effect on equilibrium Y of a rise in real wages if investment is given and one accepts the Keynesian determination of Y.

14. Illustrate the danger of vicious circle that Ricardo tried to surmount by assuming corn production uses only corn as capital advance.

15. In the equations that determine relative prices and rate of profit in the corn–iron economy, how would you represent an increase in labour intensity per hour?

16. In the equations that determine relative prices and rate of profit in the corn–iron economy, suppose there are two different kinds of labour, paid different wages. Prove that there is a conflict of interest between the two kinds of labour, in that for a given rate of profit, one real wage rises if the other decreases.

17. In what case, in only apparent contradiction of Okishio's theorem, although the real wage stays fixed the discovery and introduction of a new more convenient method for the production of a good does not raise the rate of profit?

1.16 · Review Questions and Exercises

18. Show that if the *daily* real wage is given, a lengthening of the working day raises the rate of profit.
19. Suppose the average propensity to save out of profits is greater than the average propensity to save out of wages. Illustrate the plausible effect on equilibrium Y of a rise in real wages if investment is given and one accepts the Keynesian determination of Y.
20. The theory of extensive differential rent implies that rent does not enter price. Explain.
21. What danger of circular reasoning pushed Ricardo to accept the labour theory of value in spite of knowing it was not a correct theory of normal relative prices?
22. What is the main analytical advance of Marx relative to Ricardo on the determinants of the rate of profit?
23. Why did Smith or Ricardo find it natural *not* to assume an indefinite tendency of wages to decrease as long as there is unemployment?
24. Why does the extension, of the two-equations system that determines long-period prices for the corn–iron economy, to the case of more than two commodities pose no problem? (assuming all capital is circulating capital).
25. (Needs Appendix 1.3 in the Online Appendix) Why is the rate of profit one expects to earn on new investments decreased by a rise of the real wage even if the increased wage raises aggregate demand and thus *total* profits?

Exercises
1. In the caption of ◘ Fig. 1.1 it is stated that 'The intersection of the $z(r)$ curves is vertically aligned with the intersection of the $w(r)$ curves'. Prove it.
2. Corn is produced by seed-corn and labour with fixed technical coefficients. Choose coefficients such that, with advanced wages, the rate of profit is 20%. Explain how technical coefficients change if the unit in which corn is measured passes from 1 kg to 1 ton.
3. Corn is produced by seed-corn and labour. The labour embodied in one unit of corn is one unit. Find technical coefficients of seed-corn and of labour that produce this result. Are they uniquely determined?
4. In the equations that determine relative prices and rate of profits in the corn–iron economy, assume corn production does not need iron as an input $(a_{21}=0)$, but real wages (paid in arrears) are fixed in terms of iron. Prove that if the rate of wages rises, the rate of profit decreases.
5. Assume corn is produced by seed-corn and labour on no-rent land; suppose the length of the working day increases 10% with no change in the daily real wage; the quantity of seed and the number of hours of labour per unit of output do not change. Show how this affects technical coefficients depending on whether w is defined to mean the daily wage, or the hourly wage; then show how Marx's c, v, s change. (What is more convenient as a measure of the quantity of labour employed, labour hours or labour days?)
6. In the equations that determine relative prices and rate of profit in the corn–iron economy, suppose there are two different kinds of labour, paid different wages. Prove that there is a conflict of interest between the two kinds of

88   **Chapter 1 · The Classical or Surplus Approach**

labour, in that for a given rate of profit, if one real wage rises the other wage decreases.

7. Marx like Ricardo reduces heterogeneous labour to homogeneity on the basis of relative wages. Assume two kinds of labour, 'simple' and 'complex', with the corn wage of complex labour being $\alpha > 1$ times the corn wage of simple labour. Marx measures labour values in hours of simple labour and considers one hour of complex labour 'produces' α units of labour value. Prove with some simple example (e.g. assuming corn is the sole product, produced by corn and both kinds of labour) that with given technical coefficients and given quantities produced a rise of the sole real wage of complex labour (the real wage of simple labour does not change) raises the labour value of the social product and reduces the rate of exploitation of simple labour.

8. Luxury goods are goods that are neither components of the real wage basket nor directly or indirectly needed for the production of goods in that basket. Indicate the mathematical reason why Marx's own determination of the rate of profits is falsified by the existence of luxury goods.

9. Keynesian–Kaleckian paradox of cost. Suppose Y stands for *net* income and I stands for *net* investment, which is given; net $AD = C + I$, net income goes either to wages or to profits: $Y = W + P$; the (marginal equal to average) propensity to consume out of wages c_w is higher than the propensity to consume out of profits c_p. Assuming a given share of profits in net income (i.e. a given real wage), derive the static multiplier. Then show that with I given, an increase of real wages reduces unemployment.

10. Suppose aggregate consumption C is a function, not of Y, but of after-tax income $Y - tY$ where $t = 0.4$ is the average tax rate. Derive the multiplier.

References

Bewley, T. (1999). *Why wages don't fall during a recession*. Cambridge, MA: Harvard University Press.

Bewley, T. F. (2005). Fairness, reciprocity and wage rigidity. In H. Gintis, S. Bowles, R. Boyd, & E. Fehr (Eds.), *Moral sentiments and material interests. The foundations of cooperation in economic life* (pp. 303–338). Cambridge, MA: MIT Press.

Bharadwaj, K., & Schefold, B. (Eds.). (1990). *Essays on Piero Sraffa*. London: Routledge.

Blaug, M. (1958). *Ricardian economics, a historical study*. New Haven: Yale University Press.

Freedman, R. (1962). *Marx on economics*. Harmondsworth, Middlesex, UK: Penguin Books.

Garegnani, P. (1984). Value and distribution in the classical economists and Marx. *Oxford Economic Papers, 36*(2), 291–325.

Garegnani, P. (1990). Sraffa: classical versus marginalist analysis. In: K. Bharadwaj & B. Schefold (Eds.), *Essays on Piero Sraffa* (pp. 112–40). London: Unwin and Hyman (reprinted 1992 by Routledge, London).

Garegnani, P. (2018). On the Labour Theory of Value in Marx and in the Marxist Tradition. *Review of Political Economy*, online pub. November, ► https://doi.org/10.1080/09538259.2018.1509546.

Howard, M. C., & King, J. E. (1989–92). *A history of Marxian economics* (Volume I (1989), Volume II (1992)). London: Macmillan.

Kalecki, M. (1971). (1943) Political aspects of full employment. In M. Kalecki (Ed.), *Selected essays on the dynamics of the capitalist economy 1933–70* (pp. 138–145). Cambridge University Press: Cambridge.

References

Kalmbach, P. (1998). Productive and uproductive labour. In H. D. Kurz & N. Salvadori (Eds.), *The Elgar companion to classical economics, L-Z* (pp. 214–219). Cheltenham, UK: Edward Elgar.

Keynes J. M. (1936). *The general theory of employment interest and money* (1967 Papermac repr.). London: Macmillan (Cited in the text as *GT*).

Marx, K. (1976). *Capital, A Critique of Political Economy Volume I* (transl. Ben Fowkes). Penguin Books (in association with New Left Review), Harmondsworth, Middlesex, UK.

Kurz, H. D., & Salvadori, N. (1995). *Theory of production: A long-period analysis*. Cambridge: Cambridge University Press.

Smith, A. (1975). *An inquiry into the nature and causes of the wealth of nations*. In the text quoted as usual as WN, Book number, Chapter number, Part or Section number, paragraph number, in order to facilitate access to different editions. I have preferred to add page indications from *The wealth of nations* (Vol. I). London: J. M. Dent and Sons Ltd.

Sraffa, P. (1951). Introduction. In P. Sraffa (Ed.), *The works and correspondence of David Ricardo* (Vol. I, pp. 13–62). Cambridge: Cambridge University Press.

Sraffa, P. (with the collaboration of Dobb M. H.) (1951–73). *The works and correspondence of David Ricardo*. Cambridge: Cambridge University Press.

Sraffa, P. (1960). *Production of commodities by means of commodities*. Cambridge: Cambridge University Press.

Long-Period Prices

Contents

2.1   Long-Period Prices: Matrix Representation – 93

2.2   Eigenvalues and the Perron–Frobenius Theorem – 96

2.3   Applying Perron–Frobenius. The Standard Commodity – 100

2.4   Non-basic Commodities – 105

2.5   Leontief's Open Model – 106

2.6   The Hawkins–Simon Condition – 109

2.7   The Interpretation of the Leontief Inverse – 109

2.8   Subsystems; Labours Embodied as Employment Multipliers – 110

2.9   Pricing with Vertically Integrated Technical Coefficients – 112

2.10   The Relationship Between Rate of Profit and Rate of Wages – 112

2.11   Choice of Technique – 119

2.12   Non-basics and Choice of Techniques – 127

Electronic supplementary material The online version of this chapter (▶ https://doi.org/10.1007/978-3-030-62070-7_2) contains supplementary material, which is available to authorized users.

© Springer Nature Switzerland AG 2021
F. Petri, *Microeconomics for the Critical Mind*,
Classroom Companion: Economics, https://doi.org/10.1007/978-3-030-62070-7_2

2.13 Techniques Including Different Commodities – 129

2.14 The Samuelson–Garegnani Model and the Champagne-Whiskey Model – 130

2.15 Fixed Capital – 137

2.16 Conclusions – 147

2.17 Review Questions and Exercises – 148

References – 151

In this chapter you will learn the basic theory of long-period prices together with the mathematical tools in linear algebra and matrices needed for mastering it at a semiadvanced level; this will allow the study of the Leontief model too. You will learn:

- the notion of eigenvalues of square matrices;
- the economic interpretation of indecomposable matrices of technical coefficients;
- the fundamental Perron–Frobenius theorem on eigenvalues of non-negative matrices;
- the matrix form of the equations determining long-period prices;
- the difference between basic and non-basic commodities;
- the Leontief open model, the interpretation of its inverse, the notion of sub-system and the meaning of labour embodied in a commodity derivable from this notion;
- the relationship between rate of profit and real wage;
- how competition determines the long-period choice of production methods;
- how changes in income distribution affect the choice of production methods, and the important phenomenon of re-switching, illustrated with models by Samuelson and Garegnani which will be very important in ▶ Chap. 7;
- the extension of the theory of long-period prices to include fixed capital.

2.1 Long-Period Prices: Matrix Representation

This chapter presents a more mathematical treatment of the theory of long-period prices or natural prices or prices of production, supplying more rigorous support for their properties stated in the previous chapter, and adding other important issues: Leontief models, choice of technique, re-switching, simple fixed capital (general joint production, and land rent in multisector models, are discussed in ▶ Chap. 10).

The analysis presented in this chapter is relevant beyond the classical approach. The notion of long-period prices is important independently of whether one adopts the classical or some other approach. The thesis that in a competitive economy relative product prices gravitate toward long-period normal levels characterized by a uniform rate of return on the supply price of capital goods is also found in Marshall, Jevons, Walras, Wicksell, Samuelson…; although somewhat obscured by recent general equilibrium theory, this notion continues to dominate applied economics, and it is more and more reasserting its centrality also in theoretical work.

The present chapter uses matrices; the reader must know the basic elements of linear algebra, matrix theory, and complex numbers, as generally taught in the basic mathematics-for-economists undergraduate course; the chapter supplies the necessary minimal elements to understand eigenvalues and the Perron–Frobenius theorem.

Unless otherwise explicitly indicated, vectors are to be intended as column vectors, but once a vector is defined as a row vector then its symbol is not accom-

94   **Chapter 2 · Long-Period Prices**

panied by a transposition superscript T. Price vectors are generally row vectors, and quantity vectors are column vectors.

I consider an economy where production is in yearly cycles, and all produced means of production are *circulating capital* goods, i.e. goods which when used as inputs disappear in the course of a single year. I assume *no joint production* (i.e. each production method produces a single output), and only one type of labour. Land is overabundant, hence a free good which we need not explicitly include among the inputs.

Initially I take as given the productive methods of the several industries, represented by vectors of *technical coefficients*, i.e. amounts of inputs per unit of output. Competition is assumed to impose the same cost-minimizing productive method to all firms in the same industry. There are n products, and to produce one unit of the *jth* commodity it is necessary to use a_{ij} units of the *ith* commodity as means of production, $i = 1, ..., n$, and also a_{Lj} units of labour. The technical coefficients of the *jth* industry are represented by the *column* vector $(a_{1j}, ..., a_{nj}, a_{Lj})^T$, where the T indicates transposition. The technical coefficients of produced inputs form an $n \times n$ square matrix $\mathbf{A} = [a_{ij}]$, $i, j = 1, ..., n$. Labour technical coefficients form a *row* vector $\mathbf{a_L} = (a_{L1}, ..., a_{Ln})$. In the matrix $\left[\dfrac{\mathbf{A}}{\mathbf{a_L}} \right]$, formed by adding to matrix $\mathbf{A}$ the vector $\mathbf{a_L}$ as one more row, each *column* is the set of technical coefficients of one industry.[1]

Let us indicate the wage rate as w, prices as $p_1, ..., p_n$, the rate of profit as r. Let us initially treat the wage as advanced, i.e. paid at the beginning of the year while the products come out at the end of the year. The equations determining relative prices of production are (the degrees of freedom of these equations will be discussed presently):

$$(1 + r)(p_1 a_{11} + ... + p_n a_{n1} + w a_{L1}) = p_1$$
$$\cdots\cdots\cdots\cdots\cdots\cdots\cdots\cdots\cdots\cdots\cdots\cdots \quad (r, w, p_1, ... p_n \geq 0) \qquad (2.1)$$
$$(1 + r)(p_1 a_{1n} + ... + p_n a_{nn} + w a_{Ln}) = p_n$$

If vector $(r, w, p_1, ..., p_n)$ satisfies these equations, then also vector $(r, tw, tp_1, ..., tp_n)$, with $t > 0$, satisfies them: the system of equations only determines *relative* prices. If we choose a good or basket of goods as 'standard of value' or 'measure of value' or—the modern term—*numéraire*, we can specify the value of all other goods and of w as the number of units of this numéraire with which they can be exchanged; in practice, one assigns price 1 to the numéraire while maintaining *relative* prices as determined by the above equations. Using vectors and matrices, Eq. (2.1) can be written as

$$(1 + r)(\mathbf{p}\mathbf{A} + w\mathbf{a_L}) = \mathbf{p} \qquad (2.2)$$

where r and w are scalars, and $\mathbf{p} = (p_1, ..., p_n)$ is the *row* vector of prices. The addition of an equation fixing the price of the numéraire as equal to 1, e.g. $p_1 = 1$ if

---

[1] Other authors prefer to have *rows* represent different industries; then a_{ij} is the quantity of input j needed to produce output i, $\mathbf{a_L}$ is a column vector, and $\mathbf{p}$ is a column vector that post-multiplies matrix $\mathbf{A}$. For example Kurz and Salvadori (1995) prefer this representation to the one adopted in this book, which is the traditional one for Leontief models.

2.1 · Long-Period Prices: Matrix Representation

the chosen numéraire is good 1, or more generally, with a semipositive column vector of goods $\mathbf{v}$ as numéraire,

$$\mathbf{pv} = 1,$$

eliminates the indeterminacy of prices; there remains one degree of freedom (we have $n+2$ variables and $n+1$ equations) that can be 'closed' by taking r or w as given, as discussed in ► Chap. 1. Readers not thoroughly familiar with the matrix representation of linear systems of equations should check, by applying the rules about matrix and vector multiplication to Eq. (2.2), that from it one indeed obtains system (2.1). If one assumes wages paid at the end of the year, one obtains

$$(1 + r)\mathbf{pA} + w\mathbf{a_L} = \mathbf{p}. \tag{2.3}$$

Let $\mathbf{x} = (x_1, \ldots, x_n)^T$ be the *column* vector of quantities produced during the given period (this is often called the vector of *activity levels* of the productive processes) and let $\mathbf{y} = (y_1, \ldots, y_n)^T$ be the column vector of *net* products; the connection between the two is

$$\mathbf{y} = \mathbf{x} - \mathbf{Ax} = (\mathbf{I} - \mathbf{A})\mathbf{x} \tag{2.4}$$

where $\mathbf{I}$ is the identity matrix. The net product vector is obtained by subtracting from the vector of produced quantities the means of production used up, but not the physical goods going to workers.

Let $\mathbf{z} = (z_1, \ldots, z_n)^T$ be the *column* vector of 'subsistence', or average physical consumptions, per unit of labour. Then the *surplus product* is the vector $\mathbf{s}$ defined as

$$\mathbf{s} := \mathbf{y} - \mathbf{z}(\mathbf{a_L x}) \equiv \mathbf{y} - N\mathbf{z} = \mathbf{x} - \mathbf{Ax} - N\mathbf{z} \tag{2.5}$$

where $N := \mathbf{a_L x}$ is total labour employment, a scalar. (The symbol: $=$ means 'is *defined* as equal to' and serves to introduce a new notion.) The surplus product is obtained by subtracting from the quantities produced (the social product) both the vector of means of production used up, $\mathbf{Ax}$, and the vector of total subsistence consumption of workers, $N\mathbf{z}$.

Classical authors considered the subsistence consumption of workers to be as indispensable to production as the means of production, and, having in mind the yearly production cycle of agriculture, treated that subsistence consumption as necessarily advanced by society, because workers must subsist during the year before harvest. Define the $n \times n$ matrix $\mathbf{C}$ of technical coefficients of *inputs inclusive of the subsistence inputs required by labour* through the rule $c_{ij} := a_{ij} + z_i a_{Lj}$, i.e.:

$$\mathbf{C} := \mathbf{A} + \mathbf{za_L} \tag{2.6}$$

(For the reader not very familiar with matrices: note that $\mathbf{za_L}$ is an $n \times n$ matrix.) With this notation, Eq. (2.5) becomes

$$\mathbf{s} := \mathbf{y} - \mathbf{za_L x} = \mathbf{x} - \mathbf{Ax} - \mathbf{za_L x} = \mathbf{x} - \mathbf{Cx} \tag{2.7}$$

If the wage rate only allows the purchase of the subsistence bundle, i.e. if

$$w = p_1 z_1 + \ldots + p_n z_n = \mathbf{pz},$$

96   Chapter 2 · Long-Period Prices

and if wages are *advanced*, then one can rewrite Eq. (2.2) as $(1+r)(\mathbf{pA} + \mathbf{pza_L}) = \mathbf{p}$, or, since $\mathbf{pA} + \mathbf{pza_L} = \mathbf{p(A + za_L)} = \mathbf{pC}$:

$$(1+r)\mathbf{pC} = \mathbf{p}. \tag{2.8}$$

2.2 Eigenvalues and the Perron–Frobenius Theorem

Now a bit of mathematics. A real or complex number λ is said *eigenvalue* of a square $n \times n$ real matrix $\mathbf{A}$ if it satisfies the equation

$$\mathbf{Ax} = \lambda\mathbf{x}$$

for some real or complex column n-vector $\mathbf{x}$ different from the null vector $\mathbf{0}$. Since this equation is equivalent to $\mathbf{Ax} = \lambda\mathbf{Ix}$ where $\mathbf{I}$ is the identity matrix, another form for the same equation is

$$(\lambda\mathbf{I} - \mathbf{A})\mathbf{x} = 0$$

that makes it clear that we are dealing with a system of equations which is linear and homogeneous in $\mathbf{x}$. It is well known that a linear and homogeneous system of n equations in n variables has solutions different from the null solution only if the determinant of the matrix of coefficients is zero. An eigenvalue λ is precisely a real or complex number that makes the determinant of matrix $\lambda\mathbf{I}$–$\mathbf{A}$ equal to zero; that is, it is a real or complex root of the n-degree polynomial which is the determinant of $\lambda\mathbf{I}$–$\mathbf{A}$.

If λ and a column vector of real or complex numbers $\mathbf{x} \neq \mathbf{0}$ satisfy $\mathbf{Ax} = \lambda\mathbf{x}$, the vector $\mathbf{x}$ is called a *right eigenvector* of matrix $\mathbf{A}$, and the equation is called a *right-eigenvector problem*. For a given eigenvalue, an eigenvector is only defined up to a multiplicative scalar, because if multiplied by a scalar it still solves the equation. Thus two equi-proportional eigenvectors are considered to be the *same* eigenvector at different scales. To say that two eigenvectors are different means that they are not equi-proportional.

If the equation is $\mathbf{yA} = \lambda\mathbf{y}$, then a *row* vector $\mathbf{y} \neq \mathbf{0}$ solution of this equation is called a *left eigenvector* of $\mathbf{A}$, and the equation is called a *left-eigenvector problem*. The reader not very familiar with matrices is invited to check, by writing the explicit system of equations, that, with $\mathbf{A}^T$ the transpose of $\mathbf{A}$, *if* $\mathbf{y}$ *is a left eigenvector of* $\mathbf{A}$, *then* $\mathbf{y}^T$ *is a right eigenvector of* $\mathbf{A}^T$. It is *not* in general the case that if $\mathbf{y}$ is a left eigenvector of $\mathbf{A}$, then $\mathbf{y}^T$ is a right eigenvector of $\mathbf{A}$—unless $\mathbf{A}$ is symmetric, that is with $a_{ij} = a_{ji}$.

We need the following elementary facts about eigenvalues. An eigenvalue of square matrix $\mathbf{A}$ renders the determinant of the matrix $\lambda\mathbf{I}$–$\mathbf{A}$ equal to zero and is therefore a root of the equation that puts this determinant equal to zero; this equation is a polynomial equation of degree n if $\mathbf{A}$ is an $n \times n$ matrix; by the Fundamental Theorem of Algebra, the equation has n real or complex roots, possibly repeated. To each eigenvalue is associated an eigenvector; if an eigenvalue is repeated t times, there can be up to t linearly independent eigenvectors associated with it. The eigenvectors can be real or complex. The determinant of a matrix is the same as that of its transpose (check it on a 3×3 matrix); hence *a matrix and*

2.2 · Eigenvalues and the Perron–Frobenius Theorem

its transpose have the same eigenvalues. If A^T is the transpose of square matrix A, then $\lambda I - A^T$ is the transpose of $\lambda I - A$ (check it on a 2×2 matrix); so if $Ax = \lambda x$ has solution with eigenvalue λ^* and column right eigenvector $x \neq 0$, then there is a row left eigenvector $y \neq 0$ that solves $yA = \lambda^* y$.

Now consider the following equation:

$$pC = \lambda_C^* p, \tag{2.8a}$$

This is Eq. (2.8) rewritten with the substitution

$$\lambda_C^* := 1/(1+r). \tag{2.9}$$

So Eq. (2.8) is a left-eigenvector problem, and the vector p of prices of production is a left eigenvector of C. We ask whether there is an *economically acceptable* couple (λ_C^*, p) that solves (2.8a). In a realistic economy, the number n of different commodities can be hundreds of thousands, so C would have hundreds of thousands of eigenvalues and eigenvectors. Does this mean that the classical economists were wrong in believing that the rate of profit and the prices of production are uniquely determined? What helps us on this issue is that only *real and non-negative solutions* for the prices are economically acceptable: complex or negative prices would have no economic interpretation. We are also helped by the fact that C is non-negative. We can use a series of results on eigenvalues and eigenvectors of non-negative matrices, generally collected under the name of *Perron–Frobenius theorem* on non-negative matrices.

As a preliminary, we need the notion of *indecomposable matrix*. A square matrix A is called *decomposable* (or *reducible*) if it is possible, by a series of exchanges of place of rows and of the corresponding columns, to give the matrix a form

$$\tilde{A} = \left[\begin{array}{c|c} \tilde{A}_{11} & \tilde{A}_{12} \\ \hline 0 & \tilde{A}_{22} \end{array} \right]$$

with $\tilde{A}_{11}, \tilde{A}_{22}$ *square* submatrices, and 0 representing a matrix of zeros.

If A is not decomposable, it is called *indecomposable* or *irreducible*.

Decomposability of the matrix of technical coefficients has a clear and important economic meaning. To exchange the place of two rows and of the corresponding columns of a matrix of technical coefficients, say between places 1 and 3, simply means to re-number commodities,[2] giving number 3 to the commodity (and the industry) previously numbered 1, and number 1 to the commodity previously numbered 3. Check it with a 3×3 matrix. Suppose that by renumbering commodities the $n \times n$ matrix of technical coefficients A can be made to take the

form $\tilde{A} = \left[\begin{array}{c|c} \tilde{A}_{11} & \tilde{A}_{12} \\ \hline 0 & \tilde{A}_{22} \end{array} \right]$ with $\tilde{A}_{11}$ a *square* indecomposable $s \times s$ submatrix, with s

---

2   From now on I will generally use for produced goods the term 'commodities', traditionally used to indicate goods that are *sold* and therefore have a price.

98   **Chapter 2 · Long-Period Prices**

as small as possible. This means that the first s commodities are inputs, directly or indirectly, in the production of *all* commodities, while the other $n{-}s$ commodities are *not* inputs (neither directly nor indirectly) in the production of the first s commodities. (An *indirect* input of a commodity is, directly or indirectly, necessary for the production of some of its direct inputs.) The first type of commodities is called *basic commodities*, and the industries producing them are called *basic industries*. The other commodities are called *non-basic*. In ▶ chapter 1, Sect. 1.7, iron in the corn model, and diamonds in Eq. (1.9) were non-basics.

From now on, when a matrix is decomposable, unless otherwise specified it is assumed that the matrix has been given the above canonical form, that is, with the basic commodities listed first.

Which commodities are basic depends on whether one defines the technical coefficients as also including the subsistence of workers, or not. If one does and accordingly assumes that wages are advanced (i.e. if one uses matrix **C**), then— if one leaves aside science-fiction totally automated economies—all commodities included in the subsistence bundle z are necessarily basic, and the ensemble of basic industries can be called the ***wage industries***: it includes the industries that produce commodities included in the subsistence bundle or directly or indirectly necessary for their production. The other industries can be called non-wage industries or ***luxury goods industries***. Some wage industries can fall among the non-basic industries if one represents production methods via matrix **A**, whose technical coefficients only indicate the means of production. For example, assume that the economy produces, numbered in this order: corn, flour, bread and brioches. Corn is used as means of production in the production of corn and of flour. Flour is a means of production of bread and of brioches. Subsistence consists of bread only, that is, $z = (0, 0, z_3, 0)^T$.

$$\text{Then } \mathbf{A} = \begin{bmatrix} a_{11} & a_{12} & 0 & 0 \\ 0 & 0 & a_{23} & a_{24} \\ 0 & 0 & 0 & 0 \\ 0 & 0 & 0 & 0 \end{bmatrix} \text{ and with this matrix, only corn is basic.}$$

In matrix **C**, bread is an input in all industries if labour is required in all production. Matrix **C** has the form:

$$\mathbf{C} = \begin{bmatrix} c_{11} & c_{12} & 0 & 0 \\ 0 & 0 & c_{23} & c_{24} \\ c_{31} & c_{32} & c_{33} & c_{34} \\ 0 & 0 & 0 & 0 \end{bmatrix} = \begin{bmatrix} a_{11} & a_{12} & 0 & 0 \\ 0 & 0 & a_{23} & a_{24} \\ z_3 a_{L1} & z_3 a_{L2} & z_3 a_{L3} & z_3 a_{L4} \\ 0 & 0 & 0 & 0 \end{bmatrix},$$

thus only brioches are non-basic.

In the **C**-representation of technical coefficients (which assumes advanced wages) we can assume that basic commodities do exist.

With the **A**-representation, it can be that there are no basic commodities. This is the case with so-called '*Austrian*' technologies, which are such that for all commodities, by going from the inputs of a commodity to the inputs of those inputs and so on, in a finite number of steps one reaches inputs produced by labour

2.2 · Eigenvalues and the Perron–Frobenius Theorem

alone.[3] Then all goods are produced by processes which consist of a sequence of stages: in the first, some specific (possibly composite) capital good is produced by unassisted labour; the next period this capital good together with further labour produces another specific (possibly composite) capital good; the thing is repeated up to a final period that produces the final good. Then there are no basic goods if one uses the **A** matrix representation of inputs. This is logically possible, and it has been often postulated by theorists because it makes life simpler for the analysis of some problems, but it is clearly implausible (even primitive agriculture needs corn seeds to produce corn) and I will exclude it, except when specifically studying 'Austrian' models. I will also neglect consumption commodities produced by labour alone and not used as inputs in any industry; these are non-basics whose price does not influence and is not influenced by any other price, so it suffices to assume that they do not enter the real wage basket and it is unnecessary to consider them when the problem is the reciprocal interdependence of prices, the main problem of value theory.[4]

In what follows I will often assume that **C**, or **A**, is indecomposable. This can be interpreted in either of two ways:

(1) the economy does not produce non-basic commodities;

(2) the economy produces non-basics but we are restricting attention to the sole subset of basic industries and prices of basic commodities, and the numéraire and the real wage consist of basic commodities only.

The legitimacy of this second interpretation derives from the fact that—as already argued in ► Chap. 1—the prices of non-basics do not enter the price equations of basic commodities, so the latter can be determined first, and the prices of non-basics only afterwards.

A and **C** are non-negative matrices. Thus we can utilize the results of the Perron–Frobenius theorem (in fact a collection of theorems) on non-negative matrices. Below is a statement of the more important results contained in this theorem.

---

3   Or by labour and land. If there is some basic commodity (that uses itself, directly or indirectly, for its production) then the process of going from inputs to the inputs of those inputs never ends. Except when studying 'Austrian' models, I assume that no commodity is produced by labour alone. I do not deny that some paid productive activities that produce services, such as private maths lessons, or massage, come close to being produced by labour alone, but I choose to neglect them for the following reason: with wages paid in arrears (*post-factum*), the price of these services essentially coincides with their wage costs; thus these prices are immediately determined once the real wage rate is given; and if these services enter into the production of other goods, one can replace them with the labour that produces them, and therefore there is no need to make them appear in the list of the commodities for whose price determination we need a system of equations.

4   The case when $\widetilde{\mathbf{A}}_{12} = \mathbf{0}$ would also mean no basics, but then the economy consists of two entirely disconnected subeconomies, each one of which needs no input from the other. This case appears of no practical relevance and will be neglected.

100   **Chapter 2 · Long-Period Prices**

Perron–Frobenius Theorem.

Let $\mathbf{A}$ *be a square non-negative indecomposable matrix. Then:*

(i) $\mathbf{A}$ *has a real eigenvalue* $\lambda^* > 0$, *not repeated, and dominant (that is, not smaller in modulus than any other eigenvalue), and to it and only to it is associated a real non-negative, and in fact positive, eigenvector* $\mathbf{x}^*$;[5] *for each other eigenvalue* λ *of* $\mathbf{A}$, *it is* $\lambda^* \geq |\lambda|$, *and* $\lambda^* > |\lambda|$ *if* $\mathbf{A}$ *is positive*;[6]

(ii) $(\rho\mathbf{I}-\mathbf{A})^{-1} > 0$ *(where* ρ *is a real scalar) if and only if* $\rho > \lambda^*$;

(iii) λ^* *is an increasing function of each element* a_{ij} *of* $\mathbf{A}$;

(iv) *if* s *is the smallest, and* S *the greatest, of the sums of the elements of a row of* $\mathbf{A}$, *then* $s < \lambda^* < S$, *unless* $s = S$ *in which case* $s = \lambda^* = S$; *the same holds for the sums of column elements of* $\mathbf{A}$.

If $\mathbf{A}$ *is decomposable the previous results are weakened as follows:*

A has at least one non-negative real eigenvalue; to the highest non-negative real eigenvalue λ^* *is associated a semipositive[7] eigenvector; if* λ *is an eigenvalue of* A, *then it is* $\lambda^* \geq |\lambda|$;

$(\rho\mathbf{I}-A)^{-1} \geq 0$ *if and only if* $\rho > \lambda^*$;

λ^* *is a non-decreasing function of each element* a_{ij} *of* A.

2.3 Applying Perron–Frobenius. The Standard Commodity

Let us apply these results to the study of Eq. (2.8).

Sraffa in *Production of commodities by means of commodities* considers first an economy where the surplus product is zero. That is,

$$\mathbf{x} - \mathbf{Cx} = \mathbf{0} \quad \text{or} \quad \mathbf{Cx} = \mathbf{x} \quad \text{or} \quad (\mathbf{I} - \mathbf{C})\mathbf{x} = \mathbf{0}. \tag{2.10}$$

For Eq. (2.10) to have a solution $\mathbf{x} > 0$ simultaneously with a solution $\mathbf{p} > 0$ to Eq. (2.8), $\mathbf{C}$ must be a special matrix. In order to grasp its nature, let us change the units in which we measure each commodity (the choice of units is always arbitrary) and let us choose as unit of measurement for each commodity the total quantity produced of it, so that $\mathbf{x}$ becomes $\mathbf{e} = (1,...,1)^T$. Call $\mathbf{C}^*$ the matrix

---

5   I do not specify whether it is a right or left eigenvector because the statement, although traditionally intended for right eigenvectors, in fact applies to either, since a left eigenvector is a right eigenvector of $\mathbf{A}^T$, again a square non-negative indecomposable matrix, and with the same eigenvalues as $\mathbf{A}$.

6   The modulus of a real number is its absolute value; the modulus of a complex number $a + ib$ is $(a^2 + b^2)^{1/2}$, the length of a vector (a, b) in R^2 (see the Mathematical Appendix for a quick review of complex numbers). A matrix having a non-repeated eigenvalue of modulus greater than the modulus of all other eigenvalues is called *primitive*. The last result in (i) can be expressed as: every positive indecomposable matrix is primitive. But a matrix of technical coefficients is normally not positive, it contains zeros. An *imprimitive* non-negative indecomposable matrix $\mathbf{A}$, that is, having a second eigenvalue equal in modulus to λ^*, comes out to have a very specific structure: it can, by exchanging rows and the same columns, be brought to have all elements zero except $a_{12}, a_{23}, a_{34}, ..., a_{n-1,n}, a_{n1}$. For a matrix of basic technical coefficients it would mean that the product of each industry is used as input by and only by the next industry, and the product of the last industry only by the first, achieving a sort of perfect circle. Such a matrix has *all* eigenvalues equal in modulus to the only real one.

7   'Semipositive' means non-negative and with at least one positive element.

2.3 · Applying Perron–Frobenius. The Standard Commodity

that corresponds to $\mathbf{C}$ in these new units. Then (2.10) requires $c^*_{i1} + \ldots + c^*_{in} = 1$, $i = 1, \ldots, n$; that is, the sum of the elements of each row of $\mathbf{C}^*$ must be 1. A non-negative matrix with all row sums (or with all column sums[8]) equal to 1 is called a *stochastic matrix*. By property (iv) of the Perron–Frobenius theorem, if $\mathbf{C}^*$ is indecomposable then its dominant eigenvalue is 1.

Let us prove that under Eq. (2.10) this conclusion holds also for $\mathbf{C}$, where commodities are measured in terms of units such that the total quantities produced of the several commodities are not all equal to 1. We must understand the change $\mathbf{C}$ undergoes if we change the units in which commodities are measured. Suppose we want to change the unit in which commodity 1 is measured, passing to a unit that consists of x_1 old units; for example, the old unit might be kilograms and the new unit tons, then 1000 old units are 1 new unit, $x_1 = 1000$. To produce one new unit (a ton) of good 1 takes 1000 times the inputs needed to produce 1 old unit (1 kg) of good 1; also, you must divide by 1000 the technical coefficients of good 1 as input to other industries whose products are still measured in the old units, e.g. if industry 2 uses 100 kg. of good 1 to produce a unit of good 2, now a_{12} measured in tons becomes 0.1. So the first column of $\mathbf{C}$ must be *multiplied* by x_1, and the first row of $\mathbf{C}$ must be *divided* by x_1, where x_1 is the number of *old* units forming one *new* unit of good 1. As a result, c_{11} does not change, being multiplied and divided by 1000. Now assume x_1 is the number expressing the total quantity produced of good 1 in the old units, and we choose that total quantity as the new unit for good 1; then in the new unit the economy is producing 1 unit of good 1, and matrix $\mathbf{C}$ is altered as indicated. If for each commodity one chooses as unit its total production, $\mathbf{C}$ is altered as follows: in order to multiply each *ith* row of $\mathbf{C}$ by x_i we post-multiply $\mathbf{C}$ by the diagonal matrix

$$\mathbf{X} = diag\{x_i\} = \begin{bmatrix} x_1 & 0 & . & 0 \\ 0 & x_2 & . & 0 \\ . & . & . & . \\ 0 & 0 & . & x_n \end{bmatrix}$$ with on the main diagonal, for each commodity i,

the number of old units x_i corresponding to its total production and to its new unit; to divide each *ith* column of $\mathbf{C}$ by x_i we premultiply $\mathbf{C}$ by the diagonal

matrix $\mathbf{X}^{-1} = diag\{1/x_i\} = \begin{bmatrix} 1/x_1 & 0 & . & 0 \\ 0 & . & . & 0 \\ . & . & . & . \\ 0 & . & 0 & 1/x_n \end{bmatrix}$ which is the inverse of $\mathbf{X}$. Matrix

$\mathbf{C}^* = \mathbf{X}^{-1}\mathbf{C}\mathbf{X}$ expresses the same technical relations but in the new units.[9] If this

---

8 If we were to consider the transpose of $\mathbf{C}$, it would have the *column* sums equal to one. This is what one obtains if one prefers to have the *rows* of the matrix of coefficients represent the technology of each industry, i.e. if c_{ij} indicates the technical coefficient of input j in industry i. Then prices are a column vector, the price equation is $(1+r)\mathbf{Cp} = \mathbf{p}$, and the quantities produced are a row vector.

9 Sraffa (1960) does not adopt this change of units and represents each industry as producing a certain quantity of output with certain quantities of inputs (and this, not only for the economy without surplus but also in subsequent chapters). Therefore Sraffa's matrix of input uses corresponds to $\mathbf{CX}$ in terms of the symbols used here, where $\mathbf{X}$ is the diagonal matrix with total outputs on the main diagonal. Therefore for the no-surplus economy it suffices to premultiply it by $\mathbf{X}^{-1}$ to obtain $\mathbf{C}^*$.

102   **Chapter 2 · Long-Period Prices**

change of units is applied to the no-surplus economy of Eq. (2.10), that equation becomes

$$\mathbf{e} - \mathbf{C}^*\mathbf{e} = 0, \text{ where } \mathbf{e} = (1, \ldots, 1)^T,$$

and $\mathbf{C}^*$ has all row sums equal to 1, hence it is a stochastic matrix, with dominant real eigenvalue $\lambda_C^* = 1$, and it is indecomposable if $\mathbf{C}$ is indecomposable because it has zeros in the same places as $\mathbf{C}$.

$\mathbf{C}^*$ and $\mathbf{C}$ are *similar* matrices (two matrices $\mathbf{A}$, $\mathbf{B}$ are called similar if there is an invertible matrix $\mathbf{X}$ such that $\mathbf{B} = \mathbf{X}^{-1}\mathbf{A}\mathbf{X}$); and it is a theorem of matrix algebra that *similar matrices have the same eigenvalues*. Conclusion: a change in the units in which commodities are measured does not change the eigenvalues. Hence, the matrix of technical coefficients $\mathbf{C}$ of a no-surplus economy if indecomposable has a real dominant eigenvalue equal to 1 whichever the units in which commodities are measured.

Does this guarantee that there are prices capable of making this economy function, i.e. such that each industry is capable of purchasing its inputs with its output? *If* $\mathbf{C}$ is indecomposable, then the answer is yes because, by property (i) of the Perron–Frobenius theorem, to its dominant eigenvalue $\lambda_C^* = 1$, and only to it, is associated both a real and positive right eigenvector $\mathbf{x}^*$ and a real and positive left eigenvector $\mathbf{p}^*$; by Eq. (2.9) the rate of profit is zero; thus at prices $\mathbf{p}^*$ each industry makes no profit but no loss either, i.e. its output suffices to purchase the inputs it needs to go on functioning. Now, economic reasoning shows that $\mathbf{C}$ *must* be assumed indecomposable in this case of zero surplus. If $\mathbf{C}$ is decomposable, it includes non-basic industries producing luxury goods not used as inputs by the basic industries. The sole way to have a zero surplus in this case is that these non-basic industries, taken as a whole, absorb as inputs their entire production; but this would mean that the ensemble of these industries uses as inputs more than it produces, because it also uses some basic commodities: but then these industries make no sense, they simply destroy the surplus produced by the basic industries. With any positive prices and non-negative rate of profit, this ensemble of non-basic industries makes a loss and cannot go on existing. In conclusion, a zero surplus only makes economic sense if all industries are basic.

Then the left eigenvector of $\mathbf{C}$ associated with the dominant eigenvalue is unique (apart from scale) and positive, confirming the correctness of Sraffa's statement (1960, p. 4) that in an economy without surplus 'There is a unique set of exchange-values which if adopted by the market restores the original distribution of the products and makes it possible for the process to be repeated; such values spring directly from the methods of production'. These exchange values (*relative* prices) are associated with a zero rate of profit, because, the dominant eigenvalue being 1, from (2.9) it is $r = 0$; the price equation is $\mathbf{p} = \mathbf{p}\mathbf{C}$. With the change of units that transforms $\mathbf{C}$ into $\mathbf{C}^*$, the equation becomes $\mathbf{e}^T = \mathbf{e}^T\mathbf{C}^*$.

Consideration of the no-surplus economy is useful to Sraffa to stress that what makes a positive profit rate possible is the existence of a surplus product. This can be seen as follows. If, in the economy without surplus, one of the technical coefficients of matrix $\mathbf{C}$ decreases (either because of technical progress, or because the real wage rate decreases) without decrease in the quantities produced,

2.3 · Applying Perron–Frobenius. The Standard Commodity

a surplus arises for the corresponding commodity. By property (iii) of Perron–Frobenius theorem, λ_C^* decreases. Thus we obtain positive prices associated with $\lambda_C^* = 1/(1+r) < 1$, hence a positive rate of profit.

The rate of profit $r = (1/\lambda_C^*) - 1$ can also be interpreted as the growth rate the economy might achieve *if*, with no change in technical coefficients, the relative dimensions of industries became the ones needed for the entire surplus to be reinvested and all industries to grow at the same rate. Let g^* be this uniform rate of growth. Then for each product its production must be $1 + g^*$ times its total utilization as input in the entire economy, or:

$$x_i = \sum_{j=1}^{n} c_{ij} x_j \left(1 + g^*\right)$$

which, using matrices and vectors, becomes a right-eigenvector problem, with $\mathbf{x}^*$ a right eigenvector of $\mathbf{C}$:

$$\left(1 + g^*\right) \mathbf{C} \mathbf{x}^* = \mathbf{x}^*. \tag{2.11}$$

It must be $\lambda_C^* = 1/(1 + g^*)$ because the sole economically meaningful (i.e. real and nonnegative) right eigenvector $\mathbf{x}^*$ is the one associated with the dominant eigenvalue. Thus

$$g^* = r.$$

We can conclude that the rate of profit is positive if and only if, once the real wage rate is given and included in the technical coefficients, the economy is capable of positive uniform growth.

The rate of growth $g^* = (1/\lambda_C^*) - 1$ can be shown to be the maximum common rate of growth of all industries.

Proof Suppose the industries are initially in the proportions associated with a given vector of outputs $\mathbf{x}$. Define the ***rate of surplus*** of commodity i as

$$\sigma_i \equiv (x_i - \sum_{j=1}^{n} c_{ij} x_j) / \sum_{j=1}^{n} c_{ij} x_j, \tag{2.12}$$

that is, the ratio of its surplus to the quantity used of it in the entire economy; the rate of surplus of commodity i is the maximum percentage increase in its utilization from one period to the next. Hence the maximum *common* rate of growth of all industries, i.e. that maintains the proportions among outputs unaltered, is the minimum of the rates of surplus of individual commodities; a higher common rate of growth would hit against insufficient availability of at least one commodity. Dividing numerator and denominator on the right-hand side of (2.12) by x_i we see that σ_i is a decreasing function of x_j/x_i for $j \neq i$. This means that if one industry expands while the size of the other industries remains unaltered, all but one of the rates of surplus decreases. Thus, if one starts from the proportions $\mathbf{x}^*$ associated with g^*, which are such that all rates of surplus are the same, any

104   Chapter 2 · Long-Period Prices

change in the proportion among industries causes at least one rate of surplus to *decrease*. Therefore for all proportions among industries different from the ones associated with g*, the maximum common rate of growth is less than g*. ∎

Note that the unique proportions **x*** among *outputs*, associated with growth at the maximal rate g*, cause the proportions in which commodities appear in the (subsistence-inclusive) means of production to be the same as among outputs, because of the common rate of surplus equal to g*. The output vector, the vector of total inputs, the surplus can be seen as different quantities of the same composite commodity. This commodity has been called **standard commodity** by Sraffa, who has noticed that it allows the determination of the rate of profit $r = g$* as *a ratio between physically homogeneous quantities*, i.e. without having simultaneously to determine relative prices—Ricardo's dream. If output is a quantity of standard commodity its value is $(1+r)$ times the value of advanced capital *whichever the prices*, because a change in the price of a commodity changes the value of output and the value of advanced capital by the same percentage. The rate of profit thus determined holds for the actual economy too, where industry proportions are different, because notional changes in the dimensions of industries without alteration of technical coefficients do not require changes in prices in order for the rate of profit to remain uniform.[10]

In modern analysis, it is more common *not* to include the workers' consumptions in the technical coefficients and to assume that wages are paid at the end of the production cycle rather than at the beginning. Wages are normally paid *after* work is performed. This means a representation of technology through matrix **A** and the row vector of labour inputs $\mathbf{a_L}$. The price equations will then take the form

$$(1 + r)\mathbf{pA} + w\mathbf{a_L} = \mathbf{p} \tag{2.13}$$

and, beside some condition fixing the numéraire, they must be supplemented by some condition fixing the purchasing power of the wage rate, e.g. $w = \mathbf{pz} = p_1 z_1 + \ldots + p_n z_n$ where **z** is the average basket of goods purchased with the wage rate.

In the classicals' time it was natural to assume most production cycles to be yearly, given the prevalence of agricultural production; then even if wage was paid after work was performed, say on a weekly basis, it was anyway necessary for society to advance subsistence to workers for the entire year before the harvest, so

---

10 Actually the standard commodity is defined by Sraffa not as the commodity with the composition allowing the maximum common rate of growth, but as the composite commodity requiring for its production inputs of the same composition. For indecomposable **C**, the two definitions coincide, because only the dominant eigenvalue is associated with a positive right eigenvector. But what if the existence of non-basics is admitted? Clearly, if the standard commodity is defined as the one that maximizes potential growth, it cannot include non-basics: having determined g* on the basis of the basic industries' submatrix, if production of a non-basic good passes from zero to positive, it reduces the rate of surplus of at least some basics, reducing the potential maximum growth rate. But perhaps a composition of output including positive amounts of some non-basics might exist, that requires inputs of the same composition and therefore satisfies Sraffa's definition? The question is discussed in the online Appendix to this chapter in the book's Website.

2.3 · Applying Perron–Frobenius. The Standard Commodity

advanced wages were the natural assumption. Nowadays most commodities take a very short time to be produced, often they are sold even before the worker is paid; then to assume wages paid in arrears is more realistic, but then one must take as unit production period a period shorter than a year, possibly very short; for the minority of goods with a longer production process one can split it into a sequence of successive stages, each one lasting one period and producing an intermediate good that enters as input into the next stage. Thus the production of corn can be broken up into a succession of production processes of, say, one week length, each one producing a different 'product', consisting of a more and more advanced stage of ripeness of corn plants. The introduction of each one of these additional 'intermediate' products introduces an additional price equation, so the determinateness properties of system (2.13) are not altered. If the length of the production period is chosen sufficiently short, then even for continuous production flows the assumption that production is of the **point-input point-output** type, with inputs being all applied at the beginning of the period and the product of a period coming all out at the end of the period, is acceptable because the difference this assumption makes to revenues and profits will be negligible.

The standard commodity can be defined for the **A**-representation of technology too: it is the composite commodity with the composition of the eigenvector **x** solution of the right-eigenvector problem $\mathbf{A}\mathbf{x} = \lambda_A{}^*\mathbf{x}$. The previous reasonings apply unchanged, except for 'net product' in place of 'surplus', **A** in place of **C**, and λ_A in place of λ_C. The common proportion between net product and total input of each commodity now represents both the rate of profit if the rate of wages is zero, and the maximum rate of growth if workers receive no wage. Sraffa suggests that actually matrix **A** might include the basic subsistences of workers (i.e. might actually be matrix **C**), in which case w would indicate only the part of the wage which is a share of the surplus[11]: with such an interpretation, a zero wage would not be an absurd assumption [it would simply reduce the system of equations (2.13) to system (2.8)].

2.4 Non-basic Commodities

The existence of non-basics might create a difficulty for the determination of prices of production. We use now the **C**-representation. Let us number commodities so that the $m < n$ basic commodities are the first m ones, and let $\mathbf{C}_{11}$ represent the indecomposable submatrix of technical coefficients of the basic commodities. The system

$$(1 + r)\mathbf{p}_\beta \mathbf{C}_{11} = \mathbf{p}_\beta$$

where $\mathbf{p}_\beta = (p_1, \ldots, p_m)$ is the vector of prices of basic commodities, has been already discussed. It determines positive relative prices of basics, and a rate of

---

11 The reader is invited to read how Sraffa (1960, pp. 9–10), after initially adopting the C-representation, justifies passing to the A-representation at a certain point.

106   Chapter 2 · Long-Period Prices

profit which is positive if the dominant eigenvalue of $\mathbf{C}_{11}$ is less than one—as it must be, if the economy can afford to produce non-basics too.

The problem is that, when some non-basics directly or indirectly use themselves as inputs, it might be impossible for non-basic production to yield the rate of profit derived from (2.18), because the maximum rate of reproduction of some non-basics might be less than that rate of profit. An example will clarify the issue. Assume a certain type of fancy beans is a luxury good, and it needs itself as seed, and the planting of 100 beans as seed, plus all the needed other inputs, only yields the production of 120 beans at the end of the period. Clearly the production of these beans can yield at most a 20% rate of profit, in fact less since there are other costs besides seed. If the rate of profit established by (2.18) is greater than 20%, the production of these beans cannot yield it. Then either the producers of these beans stay content with a lower rate of profit than the normal one in the rest of the economy (for example because they *like* to produce those beans; or because the producers are also the wage workers employed by that production and the alternative is for the producers to remain unemployed), or those beans will not be produced. So either the production of those beans escapes the uniformity of the rates of profits and must be studied as a special case, or it will not be observed and we need not worry about it. Another peculiarity of these non-basics is that if the rate of profit r in the rest of the economy is initially inferior to the maximum rate of profit (rate of reproduction) r^+ that the beans can afford, but then rises approaching r^+, a uniform rate of profit implies that the price of these beans rises without limit, becoming infinite when $r = r^+$, and negative for $r > r^+$, impossible of course and resulting in either of the two possibilities indicated above. Anyway Sraffa observes that the non-basics that use themselves as inputs generally belong to animal or plant productions, where the potential rate of reproduction (when natural enemies are eliminated) is generally much higher than the average rate of profit; so he judges the problem negligible.

2.5 Leontief's Open Model

Leontief's open model (without durable capital) is formulated to answer the question: if capital is only circulating capital and technical coefficients are given, what is the vector of total outputs that must be produced during a year (or other accounting period) in order to obtain a given net product? in other words, what must the period's $\mathbf{x}$ be in order to obtain a given $\mathbf{y}$? does such an $\mathbf{x}$ exist?

The basis of the analysis is Eq. (2.4), $\mathbf{y} = \mathbf{x} - \mathbf{Ax}$; production is represented via matrix $\mathbf{A}$ because the interest is in the net product. But now $\mathbf{x}$ is the unknown to be determined, while $\mathbf{y}$ is a given vector.[12]

---

12 There is also a Leontief *closed* model that treats the net products as inputs to other sectors, e.g. families or the state sector or exports; *all* production is an input into something and there is no net output; these sectors contribute services to the other sectors. This model has been very important in the development of national accounting systems, but it is not relevant for the issues discussed in this book and will not be explained.

2.5 · Leontief's Open Model

As a preliminary, some clarification is opportune on the nature of the model, to avoid some frequent confusions. Differently from what we have assumed up to now, in the Leontief open model it is *not* assumed that all production processes take one period (the 'year'), with production starting at the beginning of the period and all products coming out at the end of the period. The Leontief model is perfectly compatible with this case, but it is more general.

Nothing, in the definition of $\mathbf{x}$ as the vector of produced commodity outputs that come out in an economy during a chosen period, obliges us to assume that the length of the *production period* is the same for all commodities and has the same length as the chosen *accounting period* used to calculate $\mathbf{x}$. Let us admit that in a year—the accounting period—for at least some commodities many production cycles can be performed. For example if for all commodities the production cycle takes one month, and in a year twelve identical production cycles are carried through, each one starting the first day and ending the last day of a month, $\mathbf{x}$ will be twelve times the vector of the amounts produced each month, and $\mathbf{y}$ will be twelve times the net output of each month; the relationships $\mathbf{y} = \mathbf{x} - \mathbf{A}\mathbf{x}$ and $\mathbf{s} = \mathbf{y} - \mathbf{z}\mathbf{a}_{\mathrm{L}}\mathbf{x}$, where all vectors refer to the year, remain valid. However, things become more complicated if, as is certainly the case, some production processes are not entirely contained in the accounting period. One must then be careful not to assume that if $\mathbf{x}$ was produced inside the period, the inputs used up inside the period are exactly $\mathbf{A}\mathbf{x}$. Some of the production processes that produced goods appearing in $\mathbf{x}$ have been started and half-completed in the previous period, and some of the inputs they consumed were used in that previous period; and some processes started in the given period are only half-completed by its end, their output will be included in next period's $\mathbf{x}$, and the inputs they have used did not contribute to produce goods in $\mathbf{x}$. This means that the commodities used up in a period as capital goods will differ somewhat from $\mathbf{A}\mathbf{x}$ (unless the economy is stationary). Statistically this difference can be so small as to be negligible, and below this is the assumption I will make, but theoretically this difference must not be forgotten.

More importantly, even assuming that all production processes producing $\mathbf{x}$ are started and completed inside the accounting period, a main difference remains relative to our earlier assumption of a yearly agricultural production cycle: with a yearly production cycle and all output coming out at the end of the year, the production of one year is *not* available for use as input, or for consumption, during that year: the goods used as inputs or for consumption during the year must be already available at the beginning of the year. Now that we admit that outputs are gradually coming out during the entire year, inputs and consumption during the year can and will often utilize commodities produced *during* the year. Thus $\mathbf{A}\mathbf{x}$ may well for the most part consist of goods produced during the year, i.e. goods that also appear in $\mathbf{x}$. The same is true for consumption: the goods consumed during the year can be largely goods produced during the year.

This difference can also be visualized in terms of what goods one finds in inventories at the beginning and at the end of the year. The economy with yearly production cycles finds in its inventories at the end of the year the entire production of that year, that is $\mathbf{x}$, not $\mathbf{x} - \mathbf{A}\mathbf{x}$; and in order to have produced $\mathbf{x}$, it had

108   Chapter 2 · Long-Period Prices

to have at least $\mathbf{Ax}$ as means of production in its inventories at the beginning of the year (and it had to have inventories of consumption goods too, for people to subsist up to the harvest). If we admit many production cycles during the year, the economy may need much smaller inventories than $\mathbf{Ax}$ at the beginning of the year and may find itself with much smaller inventories of produced goods than $\mathbf{x}$ at the end of the year, because part of $\mathbf{x}$ disappears during the year, being used as input for further production or for consumption. For example, let us assume that all goods are produced in very short production cycles, a year encompassing 100 of them, and that all production cycles during the given year produce identical quantities. Then each cycle produces the hundredth part of $\mathbf{x}$ and uses the hundredth part of $\mathbf{Ax}$ as inputs. In order to produce $\mathbf{y} = \mathbf{x} - \mathbf{Ax}$ as net product during the year, the economy needs to have at its disposal as means of production at the beginning of the year only the hundredth part of $\mathbf{Ax}$; the production cycles after the first one can use the products of the preceding cycle.

Thus the shorter the average production cycle, the smaller the amount of goods necessary at the beginning of the year to realize a given $\mathbf{y}$ during the year. However, since inputs *must* be available some time before outputs come out, some positive inventories of inputs must *always* be available at the beginning of the year in order for $\mathbf{y}$ to be produced.[13] It is impossible to assume that if $\mathbf{x}$ is produced during the year, the inputs utilized to produce that $\mathbf{x}$ are *entirely* produced during the same year.

The need for some initial inventories disappears only if $\mathbf{y}$ is produced with inputs directly or indirectly producible by labour alone (an 'Austrian' structure of production) and if these productive processes started by labour alone reach completion inside the year: then, at the beginning of the year, production is started by labour alone, which produces good which together with additional labour are used as intermediate products to produce the net products (or further intermediate products sooner or later used for the production of the net products), and the product at the end of the year consists only of the net products, all intermediate goods have disappeared in the course of production. Then each year's production is totally independent of what went on in the previous year; the sole input the economy must obtain from outside in order to produce a given yearly $\mathbf{y}$ is the necessary *labour* input (if we neglect land and other natural resources); no initial inventories of produced goods are needed. But real economies are not like that. At least a small part of the inputs of the period must have been available as inventories at the beginning of the period.

The *Leontief problem* is: 'given $\mathbf{A}$, find $\mathbf{x}$ such that a given semipositive net product vector $\mathbf{y}$ is obtained'. An economically significant, i.e. non-negative, solution to the Leontief problem exists if the matrix $(\mathbf{I} - \mathbf{A})^{-1}$, called the *Leontief inverse*, exists and is non-negative, because then from $\mathbf{y} = (\mathbf{I} - \mathbf{A})\mathbf{x}$ and $\mathbf{y}$ non-negative one obtains

$$\mathbf{x} = (\mathbf{I} - \mathbf{A})^{-1}\mathbf{y} \geq \mathbf{0}. \tag{2.14}$$

---

13 This has been lost sight of in much of the literature that has tried to determine the (neoclassical) general equilibrium of economies described by the Leontief model, see Petri (2016c).

2.5 · Leontief's Open Model

Matrix $\mathbf{A}$ is not assumed indecomposable, but obviously it is non-negative; then by property (ii') of the Perron–Frobenius theorem, it is $(\rho\mathbf{I}-\mathbf{A})^{-1} \geq 0$ if and only if $\rho > \lambda_A{}^*$, where $\lambda_A{}^*$ is the dominant eigenvector of $\mathbf{A}$; the Leontief inverse can be interpreted as assuming $\rho = 1$, therefore it must be $\lambda_A{}^* < 1$. The condition $\lambda_A{}^* < 1$ implies that the economy is capable of producing a positive net product, because it implies that the equation $\mathbf{x} = (1+g)\mathbf{A}\mathbf{x}$ has a positive solution $(\mathbf{x}, g)$: in other words, if the real wage rate was zero, the economy would be capable of growth, and the rate of profit would be positive. This condition is usually expressed by saying that the economy or the matrix A is *viable*.[14]

In conclusion, the Leontief problem has solution if $\lambda_A < 1$, or equivalently, if the uniform rate of profit is positive when real wages are zero. If $\mathbf{A}$ is indecomposable, it is $\mathbf{x} > 0$ always: since $\mathbf{y}$ is semipositive and all industries are basic, all industries must be activated at a positive level if a net product consisting even only of a single commodity is to be produced. The reason why (2.13) admits the possibility that some elements of $\mathbf{x}$ be zero (if $\mathbf{A}$ is decomposable) is that some non-basic industries may not need to be activated at all, if $\mathbf{y}$ does not include positive quantities of their products nor of the non-basics that need their products as direct or indirect inputs. Note that it is not required that $\mathbf{y}$ be semipositive, demand for some good in a period can be so low as not to allow reintegrating the inventories of that good.

2.6 The Hawkins–Simon Condition

See the online Appendix to the chapter in the book's Website.

2.7 The Interpretation of the Leontief Inverse

Let us grasp the economic meaning of the Leontief inverse $(\mathbf{I} - \mathbf{A})^{-1}$. As a preliminary, I remember the mathematical reason why, for a square non-negative matrix $\mathbf{A}$, the condition $\lambda^* < 1$ implies $(\mathbf{I} - \mathbf{A})^{-1} > 0$. For *any* square matrix the following theorem holds that permits to see the Leontief inverse as a matrix power series:

Let A be a square matrix. It is $(I - A)^{-1} = \sum\limits_{t=0}^{\infty} A^t = I + A + A^2 + A^3 + \dots$ *if and only if* $\lim\limits_{t\to\infty} A^t = 0$, *and it is* $\lim\limits_{t\to\infty} A^t = 0$ *if and only if all eigenvalues of A are less than 1 in modulus.*

If $\mathbf{A}$ has dominant eigenvalue $\lambda^* < 1$, the theorem's condition is satisfied. If furthermore $\mathbf{A}$ is non-negative then $\mathbf{I} + \mathbf{A} + \mathbf{A}^2 + \mathbf{A}^3 + \dots$ is non-negative; thus $(\mathbf{I}-\mathbf{A})^{-1} \geq 0$. If furthermore $\mathbf{A}$, an $n \times n$ matrix, is indecomposable, then $\mathbf{I} + \mathbf{A} + \dots + \mathbf{A}^n$ is strictly positive[15]; it follows that in this case $(\mathbf{I} - \mathbf{A})^{-1} > 0$.

---

14 Some authors are satisfied, for viability, with a non-negative rate of profit.

15 Let $a_{(t)ij}$ indicate element (i, j) of $\mathbf{A}^t$, and let $\alpha_{(t)ij} = a_{(0)ij} + a_{(1)ij} + \dots + a_{(t)ij}$, a sum of non-negative terms. Clearly $\alpha_{(t)ii} > 0$, so we only need to prove that if $i \neq j$ and $\mathbf{A}$ is indecomposable then at least one $a_{(t)ij}$ for t from 1 to $n - 1$ is positive. Let us use the economic interpretation of $\mathbf{A}$ to grasp why: deriving from the inputs of commodity j the vector of their inputs (step 2) and the vector of

110   **Chapter 2 · Long-Period Prices**

An immediate application of the result $(I–A)^{-1}=I+A+A^2+A^3+\ldots$ is the following. The vector of *labours embodied* $m=(m_1,\ldots,m_n)$, a *row* vector, is defined by

$$m = mA + a_L$$

hence

$$m = a_L(I - A)^{-1} = a_L + a_L A + a_L A^2 + a_L A^3 + \ldots \qquad (2.15)$$

i.e. the labour embodied in a commodity is the sum of the direct labour employed in its production, plus the direct labour necessary to produce its direct means of production, plus the direct labour employed to produce the direct means of production of those means of production and so on. Labours embodied are well defined if this infinite sum converges, which requires that $\lambda_A^* < 1$ (or equivalently that the Hawkins–Simon condition holds).

Let us now interpret the coefficients of the Leontief inverse.

Let $y=(y_1,\ldots,y_n)^T$ be the given vector of net products. We know that $x=(I–A)^{-1}y$. It is convenient at this point to indicate the Leontief inverse with the symbol $Q=[q_{ij}]$:

$$Q := [I - A]^{-1}.$$

Its columns are $q^1, q^2,\ldots,q^n$. Assume now that y has all elements zero except the first one, which is equal to 1. Then

$$x = (I–A)^{-1}y = Q \begin{pmatrix} 1 \\ 0 \\ \vdots \\ 0 \end{pmatrix} = q^1. \qquad (2.16)$$

Had the 1 been in the *ith* place of y, the result would have been $x=q^i$. We have found the following *interpretation of the elements of the Leontief inverse: its ith column indicates the total quantities that must be produced of the several goods if the net product is to consist of one unit of good i.*

2.8 Subsystems; Labours Embodied as Employment Multipliers

Let e^i be the *ith* column of the identity matrix I, a column vector with 1 in the *ith* place and zero elsewhere. In Eq. (2.16) we assumed $y=e^1$. More generally, assume only one element in y, y_i, is greater than zero. This net output vector y can be represented as $y_i e^i$, and the corresponding total output vector is $x=y_i q^i$. So we can write any net output vector y as

---

inputs to these inputs (step 3) and so on, within the n-th step one necessarily finds in one of these vectors a positive quantity of each commodity (and within the (n-1)-th step, for commodities different from *j* itself); when a commodity is indirectly necessary as input to a second commodity, it is not possible that more than *n* steps from the second commodity to its inputs and inputs of those inputs, etc., are necessary to find the first as one of the inputs.

$$\mathbf{y} = y_1 \mathbf{e}^1 + \ldots + y_n \mathbf{e}^n.$$

Since in order to produce a net product which is the sum of two net products $\mathbf{y}$ and $\mathbf{y}'$ the economy must produce a total output $\mathbf{Qy} + \mathbf{Qy}'$, it is clear that we can decompose the total output vector $\mathbf{x} = \mathbf{Qy}$ as follows:

$$\mathbf{x} = \mathbf{Qy} = y_1 \mathbf{q}^1 + \ldots + y_n \mathbf{q}^n.$$

Accordingly each industry can be, at least in imagination, decomposed into n subindustries, each one producing what is needed for the net product of only one commodity. If industries could be actually split into subindustries and these geographically relocated, we could imagine the economy's firms relocated into n 'industrial districts', the ith one of them including such a fraction of each industry of the original economy as is necessary to produce $y_i \mathbf{q}^i$ and thus to obtain a net product $y_i \mathbf{e}^i$ consisting of only commodity i. Such 'industrial districts' have been called *subsystems* by Piero Sraffa. Each subsystem produces all the means of production it needs; if the ith subsystem were installed on a separate island, one would observe only labour arrive on the island to work every morning, no other arrival of inputs being necessary in order for the subsystem to continue to operate and to send to the mainland the quantity y_i of the ith commodity every period.

Another term sometimes used to describe the notion of subsystem is *vertically integrated sector*, a term suggested by the notion of vertical integration in industrial economics, which refers to firms which own plants that produce the means of production of their main final product, and sometimes the means of production of those means of production too. However, in industrial economics vertical integration does not refer to complete auto-production of all the inputs the vertically integrated firm needs, so I prefer the term subsystem.

Let us determine labour employment in the subsystem whose net output is 1 unit of the ith commodity. The total quantities produced in it are $\mathbf{q}^i$. Let $\mathbf{a}_L$ be the row vector of labour technical coefficients of the production methods used in the economy; then total employment in the subsystem is given by $\mathbf{a}_L \mathbf{q}^i$. But *this is the labour embodied in the ith commodity* because

$$\mathbf{m} = \mathbf{a}_L(\mathbf{I} - \mathbf{A})^{-1} = \mathbf{a}_L \mathbf{Q} \text{ implies } m_i = \mathbf{a}_L \mathbf{q}^i. \tag{2.17}$$

Thus the labour contained or embodied in a commodity is the total employment in a vertically integrated sector producing one unit of that commodity as *net product*.

If labour is homogeneous, labours embodied can thus be seen as *employment multipliers* (relative to net products), in the sense that a net product $\mathbf{y}$ produced with technical coefficients $(\mathbf{A}, \mathbf{a}_L)$ implies a total employment $N = \mathbf{my}$, and, if technical coefficients can be supposed constant, a variation of the net product vector will imply a variation of total labour employment determinable in the same way. (This interpretation requires homogeneous labour; if labour is heterogeneous and 'reduced' to homogeneity in $\mathbf{a}_L$ on the basis of relative wages as in Ricardo or Marx, then $N = \mathbf{my}$ does *not* indicate labour *employment* in the sense of number of labour hours actually employed.)

112   **Chapter 2 · Long-Period Prices**

This result has a corollary of some interest. We know from ▶ Chap. 1 that, when the rate of profit is positive, exchange ratios are generally not proportional to labours embodied. If they were, variations in the total value of the net product would imply proportional variations of total labour employment. Since they are not, it is possible to have variations of the value of the net product caused by changes in the *composition* of the net product with no change in prices that cause a variation of opposite sign in labour employment.

2.9 Pricing with Vertically Integrated Technical Coefficients

See the online Appendix to the chapter in the book's Website.

2.10 The Relationship Between Rate of Profit and Rate of Wages

Let us study in greater detail the problem that Ricardo and Marx were much concerned with, the relationship between rate of wages and rate of profit.

Let us initially adopt the **C**-representation, assuming wages are advanced; and let us suppose **C** indecomposable. This can be interpreted as meaning that we concentrate on the sole wage industries, leaving for a second stage the determination of prices of non-basics. The price equations are

$$\mathbf{p} = (1 + r)\mathbf{pC}, \quad \mathbf{pv} = 1 \text{ where } \mathbf{v} \text{ is the numéraire vector.}$$

We know that $\lambda_C^* = 1/(1 + r)$ where λ_C^* is the dominant eigenvalue of **C**. Property (iii) of the Perron–Frobenius theorem implies that, if any element of the subsistence vector increases, then some elements of **C** increase, therefore λ_C^* increases and r decreases. The conflict between wages and profits is confirmed.

Note that the wage rate need not be actually spent on purchasing the vector **z** used to pass from matrix **A** to matrix **C**. If the money wage rate is just sufficient to purchase **z**, then wage costs are correctly indicated by **pz** per unit of labour employed, independently of how the money wage is actually spent. This means that the real wage rate might be determined by wage bargaining with reference to a basket of goods even considerably different from the average basket actually purchased by workers. For example, the real wage rate might be fixed by bargaining as the money wage capable of purchasing α units of the numéraire basket, which would mean $\mathbf{z} = \alpha\mathbf{v}$ and, since $\mathbf{pv} = 1$, we obtain $w = \mathbf{pz} = \alpha$.

If one assumes that wages are paid in arrears, the equations become

$$(1 + r)\mathbf{pA} + w\mathbf{a_L} = \mathbf{p}, \quad \mathbf{pv} = 1. \tag{2.18}$$

Now that the real wage is measured in terms of a basket that does not necessarily reflect how the wage is actually spent, a question arises: could it be that, when the rate of profit changes, whether the real wage rate increases or decreases depends on the good or basket of goods on which wages are spent? Could it be that an increase in the purchasing power of wages in terms of bread goes together with

2.10 · The Relationship Between Rate of Profit and Rate of Wages

a decrease in its purchasing power in terms of, say, cloth? In this case, if workers consume both bread and cloth, it would be unclear whether their lot has improved or not.

It can be proved that this ambiguity does not arise. Since relative prices in general vary with distribution, when r increases the *percentage* variation of the real wage will depend on the numéraire chosen, but not the *sign* which is always negative.

If one assumes advanced wages and adopts the **C**-representation and assumes advanced wages, this result can be proved as follows.

Proof Since we want to admit variations of z, let $C(z)$ indicate the matrix C obtained from (A, a_L, z). Assume that initially $z = z^\wedge \equiv (0,...,0, z^\wedge_j, 0,...0)^T$ and that the corresponding rate of profit $r^\wedge > 0$ determined by $(1+r^\wedge)p^\wedge C(z^\wedge) = p^\wedge$ is positive. If we increase z_j, r decreases. Let us now choose a different z, call it z^+, where the sole positive element is another one, e.g. the ith one. Let z_i in z^+ satisfy $p_i^\wedge z_i = p_j^\wedge z_j$. Then $p^\wedge z^+ a_L = p^\wedge z^\wedge a_L$ and therefore $(1+r^\wedge)p^\wedge C(z^+) = p^\wedge$: the rate of profit is the same, and here too if we increase z_i then r decreases. Thus to each higher and higher level of z_j in $z^\wedge$ there corresponds a higher and higher level of z_i in z^+ that obtains the same decrease in r. The same reasoning applies to any other couple of single or composite commodities. Therefore if r decreases (respectively, increases), the real wage rate increases (respectively, decreases) in terms of any single or composite good. ∎

Nowadays it is more common to assume wages paid at the end of the period (i.e. in arrears) and to adopt the A-representation of technology and price equations such as (2.18). Then let w_{adv} indicate advanced wages, and w wages paid in arrears. With advanced wages the equations are

$$\mathbf{p} = (1+r)(\mathbf{pA} + w_{adv}\mathbf{a_L}) = (1+r)\mathbf{pA} + (1+r)w_{adv}\mathbf{a_L}.$$

By comparison with (2.18) we obtain

$$(1+r)w_{adv} = w.$$

Thus if we prove that as r decreases, w increases, it is immediate that w_{adv} increases too. On the contrary having proved as we have done that as r decreases, w_{adv} increases, it is not clear whether w increases too. Therefore we study the relationship established by (2.18) between r and w directly.

Let us first study the cases $r=0$ and $w=0$. With $r=0$, it is $w=w_{adv}$ and (2.18) becomes

$$\mathbf{p} = \mathbf{pA} + w\mathbf{a_L} \quad \text{or,} \quad \mathbf{p} = w\mathbf{a_L}(\mathbf{I} - \mathbf{A})^{-1}. \tag{2.19}$$

Comparison with the equation that defines labours embodied, $\mathbf{m} = \mathbf{a_L}(\mathbf{I} - \mathbf{A})^{-1}$, shows that $\mathbf{p} = w\mathbf{m}$, i.e. that, when $r=0$, prices are proportional to labours embodied, thus *relative* prices are *equal* to ratios between labours embodied: the strict labour theory of value holds true. If one puts $w=1$, prices *coincide* with labours embodied. If A is viable, the Leontief inverse is non-negative, and in fact positive for all its elements denoting amounts of basic commodities, so all labours embodied are positive, and prices too.

114   **Chapter 2 · Long-Period Prices**

Note that if neither a condition $\mathbf{pv}=1$ is added, nor the rate of profit is given, then setting $w=1$ does *not* fix the purchasing power of the wage rate; it only amounts to establishing labour as the numéraire, so that prices measure *labours commanded*. When $r=0$, labour-commanded prices coincide with labours embodied.

If $w=0$, Eq. (2.18) becomes

$$\mathbf{p} = (1+r)\mathbf{pA},$$

identical to $\mathbf{p}=(1+r)\mathbf{pC}$ except that $\mathbf{A}$ has replaced $\mathbf{C}$; we know the mathematical properties of this system of equations; it can be rewritten $\mathbf{pA}=\lambda_A{}^*\mathbf{p}$, where $\lambda_A{}^*$ is the dominant eigenvalue of $\mathbf{A}$ (given our assumption that the dominant eigenvalue of the submatrix of coefficients of the basic commodities is also the dominant eigenvalue of $\mathbf{A}$). This maximum rate of profit $r=(1/\lambda_A{}^*)-1$ is also the maximum possible rate of growth if workers do not consume anything. This maximum rate of profit associated with the $\mathbf{A}$-representation is generally indicated with R; below it will be useful to remember that $1+R=1/\lambda_A{}^*$.

Let us now assume that $\mathbf{A}$ is indecomposable or that the dominant eigenvalue of the submatrix of coefficients of the basic commodities of $\mathbf{A}$ is also the dominant eigenvalue of $\mathbf{A}$. Choose a semipositive vector of goods $\mathbf{v}$ as numéraire, i.e. impose $\mathbf{pv}=1$. From $\mathbf{p}=(1+r)\mathbf{pA}+w\mathbf{a_L}$ we derive that, for $r<R$, it is

$$\mathbf{p} = w\mathbf{a_L}[\mathbf{I}-(1+r)\mathbf{A}]^{-1}, \tag{2.20}$$

where $[\mathbf{I}-(1+r)\mathbf{A}]^{-1}$ is semipositive as long as $r<R$, because we can treat $(1+r)\mathbf{A}$ as a new matrix, with dominant eigenvalue $(1+r)\lambda_A{}^*=(1+r)/(1+R)<1$ as long as $r<R$. Alternatively, from $[\mathbf{I}-(1+r)\mathbf{A}]=(1+r)\left[\frac{1}{1+r}I-A\right]$, matrix $[\mathbf{I}-(1+r)\mathbf{A}]^{-1}$ can also be rewritten $\frac{1}{1+r}\left[\frac{1}{1+r}I-A\right]^{-1}$, and therefore it is positive if $[\rho I-A]^{-1}$ is positive, where $\rho=1/(1+r)$, which requires that $\rho>\lambda_A{}^*$, i.e. that $r<R$. Post-multiplying both sides of (2.20) by $\mathbf{v}$ we obtain $1=w\mathbf{a_L}[\mathbf{I}-(1+r)\mathbf{A}]^{-1}\mathbf{v}$, or

$$w = \frac{1}{\mathbf{a_L}[\mathbf{I}-(1+r)\mathbf{A}]^{-1}\mathbf{v}}. \tag{2.21}$$

Equation (2.21) yields the real wage rate (measured in terms of $\mathbf{v}$) as a function of r.[16]

---

16 Sraffa prefers to consider the rate of profit, rather than the real wage, as the independent variable for the study of changes in income distribution, and explains the reason as follows:

"The choice of the wage as the independent variable in the preliminary stages was due to its being there regarded as consisting of specified necessaries determined by physiological or social conditions which are independent of prices or the rate of profit. But as soon as the possibility of variations in the division of the product is admitted, this consideration loses much of its force. And when the wage is to be regarded as 'given' in terms of a more or less abstract standard, and does not acquire a definite meaning unitl the prices of commodities are determined, the position is reversed. The rate of profit, as a ratio, has a significance which is independent of any prices, and can well be 'given' before the prices are fixed. It is accordingly susceptible of bein determined from outside the system of production, in particular by the level of the money rates of interest" (1960, § 44, p. 33).

A given r also has the mathematical advantage of making system (2.18) an affine system, easier to study.

2.10 · The Relationship Between Rate of Profit and Rate of Wages

It is possible directly to prove that this function has negative first derivative for $w > 0$, $R > r > 0$. But it is economically more enlightening to reach this result in the following way.

Proof that w (r) is decreasing Set $\mathbf{pv} = 1$, take Eq. (2.18), $\mathbf{p} = (1+r)\mathbf{pA} + w\mathbf{a_L}$, and on its right-hand side replace $\mathbf{p}$ with $w\mathbf{a_L} + (1+r)\mathbf{pA}$; in the right-hand side of the resulting expression

$$\mathbf{p} = w\mathbf{a_L} + (1+r)\big[(1+r)\mathbf{pA} + w\mathbf{a_L}\big]\mathbf{A} = w\mathbf{a_L}[\mathbf{I} + (1+r)\mathbf{A}] + (1+r)^2\mathbf{pA}^2$$

repeat the replacement of $\mathbf{p}$ with $w\mathbf{a_L} + (1+r)\mathbf{pA}$, and reiterate this replacement again and again, obtaining

$$\mathbf{p} = w\mathbf{a_L}\left[\mathbf{I} + (1+r)\mathbf{A} + (1+r)^2\mathbf{A}^2 + (1+r)^3\mathbf{A}^{3+} + \ldots\right]. \tag{2.22}$$

This equation shows that the price of each commodity can be seen as the sum of:
- wages paid to the direct labour employed in its production;
- wages paid to the direct labour employed in the production of its direct means of production, multiplied by $(1+r)$;
- wages paid to the direct labour employed in the production of the means of production of its means of production, multiplied by $(1+r)^2$;
- and so on, endlessly (if there are basic commodities).

In this way the price of each commodity is expressed as the sum of the wages paid to a series of *quantities of 'dated' labour* (labour employed a certain number of periods in the past), each quantity being multiplied by the power of $(1+r)$ corresponding to how many periods have passed between the payment of that labour and the sale of the commodity. For example for price 1 we can write

$$p_1 = w a_{L1} + w(1+r)L_{1(-1)} + w(1+r)^2 L_{1(-2)} + w(1+r)^3 L_{1(-3)} + \ldots \tag{2.22a}$$

where $L_{1(-t)}$ is the quantity of labour employed in the indirect production of commodity 1 whose wage has been paid t periods before the product comes out; with $\mathbf{a}^1$ indicating the first column of $\mathbf{A}$ (that is, the vector of inputs in industry 1), it is $L_{1(-t)} = \mathbf{a_L}\mathbf{A}^{t-1}\mathbf{a}^1$.

If now in Eq. (2.22) we put $w = 1$, i.e. if we measure prices in terms of labour commanded, w disappears

$$\mathbf{p} = \mathbf{a_L}\left[\mathbf{I} + (1+r)\mathbf{A} + (1+r)^2\mathbf{A}^2 + (1+r)^3\mathbf{A}^3 + \ldots\right], \tag{2.22b}$$

and $\mathbf{p}$ is determined as a sum of non-negative vectors which are certainly positive at least from a certain point on, and are (except for the first term) increasing functions of r. This proves that *all prices in terms of labour commanded are positive*

116   Chapter 2 · Long-Period Prices

and increase as r increases (except for a good produced by labour alone, whose production—since wages are paid in arrears—requires no capital advance: as explained, I assume there are no such goods). This means that all the *reciprocals* of labour-commanded prices, that indicate the purchasing power of the real wage rate in terms of each commodity, decrease as r increases. Therefore the function $w(r)$ is decreasing whatever vector $\mathbf{v}$ is chosen as numéraire. ∎

Of course this proof requires that $[\mathbf{I} + (1+r)\mathbf{A} + (1+r)^2\mathbf{A}^2 + (1+r)^3\mathbf{A}^3 + \ldots]$ converges, but this is guaranteed as long as $r < R$ because, as already noticed, matrix $(1+r)\mathbf{A}$ has dominant eigenvalue $(1+r)\lambda_A^*$, less than 1 as long as $r < R$, thus all eigenvalues of $(1+r)\mathbf{A}$ are less than 1 in modulus and therefore

$$\left[\mathbf{I} + (1+r)\mathbf{A} + (1+r)^2\mathbf{A}^2 + (1+r)^3\mathbf{A}^3 + \ldots\right] = [\mathbf{I} - (1+r)\mathbf{A}]^{-1}.$$

Therefore (2.20) and (2.22) are equivalent and have economically significant solution as long as $r < R$. When $r = R$ it is $w = 0$, prices cannot be expressed in labour commanded, one must use $\mathbf{p} = (1+R)\mathbf{p}\mathbf{A}$.

The Russian economist Dmitriev, an extremely brilliant mind stopped too early by tuberculosis, used this approach to prove in 1894 that Ricardo was not involved in a logical vicious circle, caused by a rate of profit depending on relative prices in turn depending on the rate of profit. He applied Eq. (2.22a) to the composite good $\mathbf{z}$ that represents the given physically specified wage basket, *chosen as numéraire*, so that not only $w = 1$ disappears from the right-hand side of Eq. (2.22a), but on its left-hand side there is a price set equal to 1, and the only unknown in the equation is r. Therefore, he concluded, r is determined once technology and real wage are given. Mathematically the proof was not watertight because Dmitriev should have proved that the infinite sum on the right-hand side did not diverge to infinity, and that the resulting polynomial equation did have a real solution and not only complex ones. Dmitriev did not have at his disposal the theorems we now have, he surmounted the first difficulty by assuming that the series of terms on the right-hand side could be stopped after a finite number of terms because the residue would become so small as to be negligible, and he neglected the possibility of only complex solutions; but we know now that his intuition was correct.

The function $w(r)$ expressed by (2.21) is called *wage–profit curve*, also $w(r)$ *curve*, or simply *wage curve*.[17] Note one thing that will be important later: the actual quantities produced in the economy have no role in Eq. (2.21), the shape of the function $w(r)$ depends only on $\mathbf{A}$, on $\mathbf{a_L}$ and on the numéraire vector $\mathbf{v}$.

If there is at least one basic commodity, and if the economy is viable ($\lambda_A^* < 1$), the $w(r)$ curve drawn in a Cartesian diagram has positive intercept with the

---

17 Some neoclassical economists have called it 'factor price frontier', thus implying that w and r are the prices of factors of production: w the price of labour, r the price of capital (viewed as in some sense a single factor). However, that capital can be considered a factor of production is hotly disputed (see Chap. 7), so I avoid this terminology.

2.10 · The Relationship Between Rate of Profit and Rate of Wages

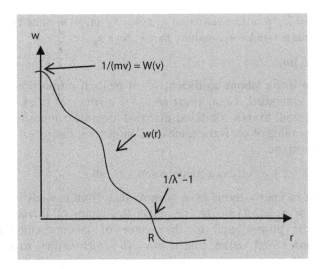

Fig. 2.1 Wage curve

abscissa at $r = R$, is decreasing[18] as long as $r < R$ and has positive intercept in ordinate determinable as follows.[19] If $r = 0$ then $\mathbf{p} = w\mathbf{m}$ where $\mathbf{m}$ is the vector of labours embodied; post-multiply both sides of this equality by the numéraire vector $\mathbf{v}$; since $\mathbf{pv} = 1$ we obtain $1 = w\mathbf{mv}$. Let us indicate as $W(\mathbf{v})$ this maximum wage rate measured in terms of $\mathbf{v}$:

$$W(\mathbf{v}) = 1/(\mathbf{mv}) > 0, \tag{2.23}$$

in other words, the wage rate corresponding to a zero rate of profit is the reciprocal of the labour embodied in the numéraire basket of goods.

The shape of the $w(r)$ curve can therefore be represented as for example in ◘ Fig. 2.1.

Nothing can be said in general in advance on the convexity or concavity of $w(r)$; it might be convex, concave, have inflexion points, because it is a polynomial function of degree n with n generally very great. The function $w(r)$ is a straight line only in two cases.

The first case is when the labour theory of value holds. This requires that $\mathbf{p}$ and $\mathbf{m}$ be proportional for all admissible levels of r, hence also for $r = R$, which

---

18 For $r > R$, the function $w(r)$ need not be decreasing, but r greater than R is not economically acceptable, it would mean a negative wage.

19 If by going from the produced inputs of a process to their inputs and repeating the procedure, sooner or later one reaches inputs produced by labour alone (an 'Austrian' structure of production), then the $w(r)$ curve does not cross the abscissa, but tends to it only asymptotically as r increases. Then as w tends to zero, r tends to $+\infty$. For example, let good 1, rabbits, be obtained by labour alone, and good 2, cooked rabbit meat, be obtained from rabbits and labour; with wages paid in arrears, it is $p_1 = wa_{L1}$, $p_2 = (1+r)p_1 a_{12} + wa_{L2} = (1+r)wa_{L1}a_{12} + wa_{L2}$ and it is easy (set $p_2 = 1$) to see that as w tends to zero, r rises without limit.

118   Chapter 2 · Long-Period Prices

implies that $\mathbf{pA} = \lambda_A{}^*\mathbf{p}$ can be rewritten as $\mathbf{mA} = \lambda_A{}^*\mathbf{m}$, so $\mathbf{m}$ must be a left eigen-vector of $\mathbf{A}$; since $\mathbf{m} = \mathbf{mA} + \mathbf{a_L}$, we have $\mathbf{m} = \lambda_A{}^*\mathbf{m} + \mathbf{a_L}$, i.e.

$$\mathbf{a_L} = \left(1 - \lambda_A^*\right)\mathbf{m},$$

the vector $\mathbf{a_L}$ of direct labour coefficients must be itself proportional to the vec-tor of labours embodied, i.e. $\mathbf{a_L}$ *must be a left eigenvector of* A, an extremely restrictive condition. Marx's condition of equal 'organic composition of capital' implies the same thing: if c/v is the same in all industries, since s/v is uniform then $(s+v)/c$ is uniform too, or

$$a_{Lj}/(a_{1j}m_1 + \ldots + a_{nj}m_n) = \text{a common scalar } \alpha, \text{ all } j;$$

this can be put in matrix terms as $\mathbf{a_L} = \alpha \mathbf{mA}$; then from $\mathbf{m} = \mathbf{mA} + \mathbf{a_L}$ we obtain $\mathbf{a_L} = \alpha(\mathbf{m} - \mathbf{a_L})$ or $\mathbf{a_L} = (\alpha/(1+\alpha))\mathbf{m}$, i.e. again the vector of direct labour coef-ficients must be proportional to the vector of labours embodied, hence $\mathbf{m} = \mathbf{mA} + \mathbf{a_L} = \mathbf{mA} + (\alpha/(1+\alpha))\mathbf{m}$, that is $\mathbf{mA} = [1 - (\alpha/(1+\alpha))]\mathbf{m}$, so $\mathbf{m}$ must be a left eigenvector of $\mathbf{A}$.

The second case in which $w(r)$ is a straight line is when the numéraire is some quantity of the standard commodity *defined for matrix* $\mathbf{A}$. (From now on, stand-ard commodity means the one referring to the $\mathbf{A}$-representation of technology.) To grasp why, start by assuming that the economy actually produces this stand-ard commodity *and* wages are paid in standard commodity: then, given the real wage, the rate of profit is determined as a material ratio, because the net prod-uct is a quantity of standard commodity, and the surplus too because wages are a quantity of standard commodity. Choose as unit of standard commodity and as numéraire the net product when total labour employment is 1 unit.[20] Then if $r=0$, it is $w=1$; w is the *share* of the net product; profits are the remaining share, $rk = 1 - w$ where k is the quantity of standard commodity employed as cap-ital per unit of labour. If $w=0$, $r=R$ which is the ratio of net product to capital advanced, the entire net product goes to profits so $Rk=1$, hence $k=1/R$, and if $r < R$ profits are $rk = r/R$; therefore

$$w = 1 - \frac{r}{R}, \tag{2.24}$$

a simple linear relationship.

The interesting thing is that it is not necessary that the economy be actually *producing* standard commodity for this linear relationship to hold, all that is necessary is that the *numéraire* be the standard net product: this is because, as noticed earlier, the shape of the $w(r)$ function is independent of the quantities produced, it depends only on the numéraire in which the wage is measured (once the technical coefficients are given).

Thus, if—having determined R by setting $w=0$ in the price equations derived from the given real economy—we impose the above linear relationship (2.24)

---

20 This corresponds to putting $\mathbf{pv}^* = 1$ where $\mathbf{v}^*$ satisfies (i) $\mathbf{Av}^* = \lambda_A{}^*\mathbf{v}^*$, and (ii) $\mathbf{a_L}\mathbf{x}^* = 1$ for $\mathbf{x}^*$ solu-tion of $\mathbf{v}^* = \mathbf{x}^* - \mathbf{Ax}^*$.

2.10 · The Relationship Between Rate of Profit and Rate of Wages

between w and r, we are de facto measuring the wage in terms of standard net product per unit of labour, even though we do not know the composition of this standard net product! (see Sraffa 1960, §43, pp. 31–32).

2.11 Choice of Technique

Now let us assume that, for at least one commodity, there are several alternative methods to produce it, each one represented by different technical coefficients. I keep assuming that all capital goods are circulating capital goods, that land is a free good, that labour is homogeneous, and that there is no joint production.

A *technique* (also called *production system* by some authors) is a set of *methods* of production, one for each commodity. It is represented by a couple $(\mathbf{A}, \mathbf{a_L})$ where $\mathbf{A}$ is square. Two techniques are different if they differ even in only one method. Two methods for the production of the same commodity differ if they differ even in only one coefficient.

Note that different techniques need not include the same number of commodities. Suppose for example that in the given economy tomatoes is one of the basic commodities produced, and call α the dominant method with which they are produced and (α) the technique of which it is part; then a new method β to produce tomatoes is discovered, which uses a specific new fertilizer only needed for that purpose. Technique (β) will then differ from technique (α) not only in the specific method that produces tomatoes, but also because it includes an industry not present in technique (α), that produces the special fertilizer.

We now study how competition selects the technique among the several available ones, and how this choice can depend on income distribution.

The starting point is the following: assume a given technique and given real wage rate, and assume competition has imposed a uniform rate of profit and the associated prices of production. Suppose new methods to produce a commodity become available. On the basis of the ruling prices, entrepreneurs will calculate the price at which each alternative method allows to sell the commodity if it is to yield the ruling rate of profit and will prefer the method associated with the lowest of these *supply prices*: if this lowest supply price is lower than the ruling price, the method can yield *extra profits*, by adopting it in place of the ruling one the firm can sell the product at a price slightly below the ruling price, subtract custom from its competitors and nevertheless earn a higher rate of profit. If it is the method until then dominant that guarantees the lowest supply price, the new methods are not adopted. We will call *cost minimizing* (at the given prices and distributive variables w, r) the method that yields the lowest supply price for the given commodity. If it is a new method, its generalized adoption changes the technique, then competition will cause relative product prices to tend toward the new values, and it can happen that at these new relative prices in the same industry or in other industries other methods until then not adopted come out to be the cost-minimizing ones. So the technique can change again. We must find out the final situation, if it can be determined, toward which this process of choice of technique tends.

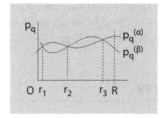

Fig. 2.2 Supply price of a non-basic commodity q as function of r according to two methods α and β, in terms of a basic numéraire

I start with the simplest case: two different methods are known to produce a non-basic commodity q that only needs, with either method, basic commodities (there are n of these) as means of production, and the real wage is fixed in terms of basic commodities. In this case all prices entering the cost of producing the commodity with either method are known once either the rate of profit, or the real wage rate in terms of the chosen basic numéraire, is given. Call the two methods α and β; the technical coefficients and supply price are distinguished by a superscript (α) or (β) according to the method. Then the supply prices are determined by:

$$p_q^{(\alpha)} = (1+r) \sum_{i=1}^{n} a_{iq}^{(\alpha)} p_i + a_{Lq}^{(\alpha)} w$$

$$p_q^{(\beta)} = (1+r) \sum_{i=1}^{n} a_{iq}^{(\beta)} p_i + a_{Lq}^{(\beta)} w$$

Competition will impose the adoption of the method with the lower p_q, which can depend on r. The relative prices of inputs will in general change with r, so if one traces the curves $p_q^{(\alpha)}(r)$ and $p_q^{(\beta)}(r)$ in the same diagram with r in abscissa, these curves can cross several times,[21] cf. ◘ Fig. 2.2. Where the two supply prices coincide, the two methods are equally convenient and therefore can coexist. Otherwise the method yielding the lower supply price will be preferred.

The precise shape of the curves $p_q^{(\alpha)}(r)$ and $p_q^{(\beta)}(r)$ depends on the numéraire, but not which curve is below the other one for a given r, this only depends on the ratio between the two supply prices, which is unaffected by the choice of numéraire because a change of numéraire changes all prices by the same percentage.

But if the price of a commodity enters, directly or indirectly, into its own costs, then when one wants to compare which of two methods for the commodity is cost minimizing, the complication arises that the two methods correspond

---

21 In this case the maximum number of intersections of the two curves, or 'switches', in the positive quadrant is $n+1$, where n is the number of commodities common to the two techniques producing q as net product; but if the alternative techniques differ in the goods they use, the number can be greater, see Bharadwaj (1970).

2.11 · Choice of Technique

to two different techniques; each technique determines a different set of relative prices and a different rate of profit for the given real wage (or a different real wage for the given rate of profit), so the prices at which to compare the supply price of the two methods are not univocally determined, they depend on the technique. This will require some additional notation.

Suppose all commodities are basic, and two methods α and β for commodity 1 are to be compared, while the methods of all other commodities are given. Depending on which method is included in matrix $\mathbf{A}$ and in vector $\mathbf{a}_L$, there are two techniques, $(\mathbf{A}_\alpha, \mathbf{a}_{L\alpha})$ and $(\mathbf{A}_\beta, \mathbf{a}_{L\beta})$, which generate different vectors of relative prices and different values of the residual distributive variable when the rate of profit, or the real wage rate, is given. It is customary in the literature to take r as the given parameter, so we write

$$p^{(\alpha)} = (1 + \bar{r}) p^{(\alpha)} A_\alpha + w^{(\alpha)} a_{L\alpha}$$
$$p^{(\beta)} = (1 + \bar{r}) p^{(\beta)} A_\beta + w^{(\beta)} a_{L\beta}$$

Therefore the situation is different for entrepreneurs if method β is discovered when α is the generally adopted one, or vice-versa. Suppose the numéraire is assigned, and that initially only method α is known, hence prices and income distribution are $(p^{(\alpha)}, r, w^{(\alpha)})$. Now method β is discovered. Entrepreneurs will find it convenient to adopt it in place of method α if at the *current* prices and distributive variables $(p^{(\alpha)}, r, w^{(\alpha)})$ method β yields extra profits, i.e. permits to sell commodity 1 at a supply price inferior to $p_1^{(\alpha)}$, that is if

$$(1 + \bar{r}) \sum_{i=1}^{n} a_{i1}^{(\beta)} p_i^{(\alpha)} + w^{(\alpha)} a_{L1}^{(\beta)} < p_1^{(\alpha)}. \tag{2.25}$$

The sum on the left-hand side of this inequality requires attention: it is the *supply price*[22] of commodity 1 produced with method β, with costs determined by the α prices and wage. We need a way to indicate it: let it be $p_1^{\beta(\alpha)}$. The first superscript indicates the method used to determine the supply price, the second superscript, enclosed in parentheses, indicates the technique determining the prices and wage used to determine the costs that sum up to the supply price. When the supply price refers to the same method as the one appearing in the technique determining the prices and distribution, then only one superscript suffices, in parentheses. Thus $p_1^{(\alpha)}$ is the price of production, i.e. the supply price, of commodity 1 produced with method α at the α prices and wage.

In this case method β is found more convenient than α and is introduced, if $p_1^{\beta(\alpha)} < p_1^{(\alpha)}$. The relevant comparison is between $p_1^{\beta(\alpha)}$ and $p_1^{(\alpha)}$. If on the contrary method β is the initially known one and method α is discovered later, then the prices and distribution used to determine which method is more con-

---

22 The supply price of a commodity is the minimum price necessary to induce it to be supplied; under free entry, it is the price that just covers costs inclusive of the normal rate of profit (in marginalist terminology, it is the price that yields zero profits).

venient are $(p^{(\beta)}, r, w^{(\beta)})$, thus the relevant comparison is between $p_1^{(\beta)}$ and

$$p_1^{\alpha(\beta)} = (1+\bar{r}) \sum_{i=1}^{n} a_{i1}^{(\alpha)} p_i^{(\beta)} + w^{(\beta)} a_{L1}^{(\alpha)}.$$

Can it happen that $p_1^{\beta(\alpha)} < p_1^{(\alpha)}$ and at the same time $p_1^{\alpha(\beta)} < p_1^{(\beta)}$? Then no method would be able definitely to impose itself, and it is unclear what would happen in the economy; perhaps it would indefinitely oscillate from adopting one method to adopting the other one. Luckily, except in a few special cases, this possibility can be excluded. In particular, it can be excluded when there is no joint production and no land, as we are now supposing. Under this assumption we can prove that the more convenient method is the same both at $(p^{(\alpha)}, r, w^{(\alpha)})$ and at $(p^{(\beta)}, r, w^{(\beta)})$, and furthermore that it is the method whose technique, for the given r, generates the higher w (or, for the given w, generates the higher r); the two wages will actually be the same, unless the alternative method concerns a **wage industry**.[23] Then, since as between any two alternative methods for the same commodity competition will tend to impose the one associated with the higher w,[24] it can be assumed that the economy will gravitate toward the technique yielding the highest w when r is given; or the highest r when w is given. This can be represented graphically in terms of $w(r)$ curves: the economy will tend to adopt the technique whose $w(r)$ curve is highest for the given r. This *dominant technique* can depend on the level of r, because the $w(r)$ curves can cross, even several times. The same reasoning applies to each choice between two methods, in any industry. However, if the industry is a luxury industry the $w(r)$ curve is unaffected by the change of method, the passage to a more convenient method has only the effect of reducing the price of the good.

Assume there is a number of alternative methods for each commodity. Having derived all the $w(r)$ curves corresponding to the different possible techniques concerning wage industries, the outer (or North-East) envelope of the $w(r)$ curves indicates the relevant long-period relationship between r and w, taking into account that the dominant technique may change as r changes when there is choice of techniques.

Let us prove the above statements. Assume two techniques that include the same commodities and differ in only one method, the method for commodity 1. We intend to prove that

---

23 When one adopts the **A**-representation of technology, an industry is a **wage industry** if it produces directly or indirectly one of the goods in terms of which the real wage is either fixed, or measured when treated as variable. Some industries can be wage industries without being basic relative to the **A** matrix, if the wage is fixed or measured in terms of a basket which includes commodities that are not basic relative to the **A** matrix. For example in the corn–iron economy, if $a_{21} = 0$ then corn is the sole basic good relative to the A matrix, but the iron industry is a wage industry if the real wage is measured in terms of a numéraire that includes iron.

24 The method capable of paying a higher w earns extra profits if it pays the old w, so the firms adopting it will undercut competitors by asking for a lower price at the old money prices and money wage; this lower price reduces costs in the industries using this commodity as input, inducing reductions of the prices of their products, and raises the purchasing power of the wage. Thus, if r is given and the new technique permits a higher real wage than before, price-cutting competition will tend to reduce prices relative to the money wage until the real wage becomes the one that the wage curve of the new technique associates with the given r.

2.11 · Choice of Technique

■ **Lemma 2.10.** (Okishio's Theorem).

If at the given $\bar{r}$ it is $p_1^{\beta(\alpha)} < p_1^{(\alpha)}$ and industry 1 is a wage industry, then $w^{(\beta)} > w^{(\alpha)}$.

(Of course the numéraire must be the same in determining both $w(r)$ curves.)

Proof I use a proof based on the C-representation of production; this will show that, for these issues, to assume that wages are advanced or paid in arrears makes no difference. Assume $p_1^{\beta(\alpha)} < p_1^{(\alpha)}$. We noted that for a given rate of profit r and a given technique it is $w_{adv} = w/(1+r)$, and relative prices of commodities do not change if one passes from advanced to paid-in-arrears wages (or vice-versa) respecting this condition. Therefore, with $r = r^\circ$ given, if technique (β) generates the higher w_{adv}, then it generates the higher w too. Let us restricts ourselves to wage industries and let us form the matrix $\mathbf{C}_\alpha$ by assuming the subsistence vector to be the numéraire vector $\mathbf{v}$ multiplied by the scalar $w^{(\alpha)}/(1+r^\circ)$, then the rate of profit determined by

$$\mathbf{p} = (1+r)\mathbf{p}\mathbf{C}_\alpha \tag{2.26}$$

is r°. Let us form a new matrix $\mathbf{C}_{\beta\alpha}$ in the same way, except with commodity 1 produced by method β; remember that this new matrix embodies in its coefficients the real wage $w^{(\alpha)}/(1+r^\circ)$ and differs from $\mathbf{C}_\alpha$ only in its first column. Applying to this matrix the prices determined by Eq. (2.26) one obtains for commodity 1 the supply price $p_1^{\beta(\alpha)}$ which is the same as with wage $w^{(\alpha)}$ paid in arrears, and therefore by assumption it is less than $p_1^{(\alpha)}$. Now imagine raising one technical coefficient of method β until at the prices (α) the supply price of good 1 becomes equal to $p_1^{(\alpha)}$. The resulting matrix, call it $\mathbf{C}^{\wedge}$, that includes this hypothetical new method, has the same dominant eigenvalue as matrix $\mathbf{C}_\alpha$ because it yields the same rate of profit. Since the matrix $\mathbf{C}_{\beta\alpha}$ has one lower technical coefficient than $\mathbf{C}^{\wedge}$, by result (iii) of the Perron–Frobenius theorem its dominant eigenvalue is lower, i.e. the rate of profit determined by $\mathbf{p} = (1+r)\mathbf{p}\mathbf{C}_{\beta\alpha}$ is higher than r°. We can therefore raise w_{adv}, and thus all the technical coefficients in $\mathbf{C}_{\beta\alpha}$ which include a subsistence component, until the rate of profit decreases back to its old level r°. The matrix $\mathbf{C}^*$ thus obtained is the matrix obtained from technique (β) when the advanced real wage $w_{adv}^{(\beta)} = w(\beta)/(1+r^\circ)$ is inserted into the technical coefficients of technique (β). This proves that $w_{adv}^{(\beta)} > w_{adv}^{(\alpha)}$; but then it is also $w^{(\beta)} > w^{(\alpha)}$. ∎

Assuming the starting point is technique (β) the same proof shows that if $p_1^{\alpha(\beta)} < p^{(\beta)}$ then $w^{(\alpha)} > w^{(\beta)}$. This means that if $p_1^{\beta(\alpha)} < p_1^{(\alpha)}$ (and hence $w^{(\beta)} > w^{(\alpha)}$) then it cannot be that $p_1^{\alpha(\beta)} < p^{(\beta)}$, which would imply $w^{(\alpha)} > w^{(\beta)}$. Therefore it cannot be that, once method β has replaced method α and prices and the real wage adapt to technique (β), method α comes out to be now the more convenient one; indefinite oscillations back and forth between two methods are excluded.

This result proves that if at the prices and distribution of a technique there is a wage industry method, not used in that technique, that yields extra profits, then if this method is introduced the new technique yields a higher wage rate if the rate of profit stays fixed, or a higher rate of profit if the real wage rate stays fixed.

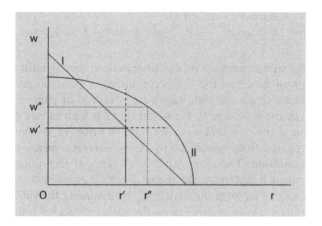

Fig. 2.3 Suppose the discovery of a new, more convenient method shifts the $w(r)$ curve from I to II; there is room for both the original rate of profit and original real wage rate (r', w') to increase, e.g. to r'', w''

Graphically, if the new $w(r)$ curve is *above* the old one at the old rate of profit, since $w(r)$ curves are decreasing and continuous for $r \leq R$, the new $w(r)$ curve is also *to the right of* the old one at the old rate of wages. There is therefore room also for an increase both of r and of w, cf. ◘ Fig. 2.3.

This result is independent of the choice of numéraire. A change of numéraire changes the shape of $w(r)$ curves and the vertical distance between the $w(r)$ curves of two techniques at the given rate of profit, but not which curve is the outer one, nor, therefore, the values of r at which they intersect.

The converse of Lemma 2.10 also holds, namely that, given the rate of profit, if by introducing the new method in place of the old one and allowing price to become the new normal ones the real wage rate rises, then at the old prices and distribution the new method yields extra profits and therefore it is convenient to introduce it. Therefore the possibility is excluded that a method which, if adopted, would raise the real wage rate is not introduced because not more convenient at the prices and distribution associated with the ruling technique. This is implied by the following result:

▪▪ Lemma 2.11.
If two techniques (α) and (β) are such that at the given rate of profit r it is $\mathbf{p}^{(\alpha)} \geq \mathbf{0}$, $\mathbf{p}^{(\beta)} \geq \mathbf{0}$, and $w^{(\beta)} > w^{(\alpha)}$, then there is a method in technique (β) which pays extra profits at the prices and distribution (α).

Proof By contradiction. Now we can use the A-representation of technology. Suppose $w^{(\beta)} > w^{(\alpha)}$ and $p^{(\alpha)} \leq p^{\beta(\alpha)}$. The expression

$$p^{(\alpha)} \leq p^{\beta(\alpha)} \equiv (1+r)p^{(\alpha)}A_\beta + w^{(\alpha)}a_{L\beta}$$

can be rewritten

2.11 · Choice of Technique

$$\mathbf{p}^{(\alpha)} \leq w^{(a)}\mathbf{a}_{L\beta}\left[\mathbf{I} - (1+r)\mathbf{A}_\beta\right]^{-1}.$$

Post-multiplying by the semipositive numéraire vector $\mathbf{v}$, since $\mathbf{p}^{(\alpha)}\mathbf{v} = 1$, it is.

$$1 \leq w^{(\alpha)}\, \mathbf{a}_{L\beta}\left[\mathbf{I} - (1+r)\mathbf{A}_\beta\right]^{-1}\mathbf{v} = w^{(\alpha)}/w^{(\beta)}.$$

The last equality derives from the fact that (cf. (2.21)) $w_\beta = \dfrac{1}{\mathbf{a}_{L\beta}[\mathbf{I}-(1+r)\mathbf{A}_\beta]^{-1}\mathbf{v}}$.

But $1 \leq w^{(\alpha)}/w^{(\beta)}$ implies $w^{(\beta)} \leq w^{(\alpha)}$ which contradicts the assumption $w^{(\beta)} > w^{(\alpha)}$. ∎

If the two techniques differ in the method of only one commodity, say of commodity 1, then the lemma says that $w^{(\beta)} > w^{(\alpha)}$ implies $p_1^{\beta(\alpha)} < p_1^{(\alpha)}$, the result we intended to prove.

Thus, as long as there are non-adopted methods capable of raising the wage rate, these methods will yield extra profits, and therefore competition will force their introduction, until a technique is reached whose $w(r)$ curve is on the outer envelope of the $w(r)$ curves. Given r, technical choice maximizes w; given w, r is maximized.

So far we have assumed given methods for the other commodities. But the same process of choice of methods on the basis of cost minimization will be going on for each commodity for which there is technical choice. This will push the economy finally to adopt some technique on the outer envelope of the $w(r)$ curves generated by all possible alternative techniques. A technique with $w(r)$ curve on the outer envelope for the given level of r is **cost minimizing** at that level of r, i.e. at its prices and wage rate there is no other method that generates a lower supply price or 'cost of production' for at least one commodity.[25] Formally, if technique (α) is cost minimizing at the rate of profit r, then for any other technique (β) it is $\mathbf{p}^{(\alpha)} \leq (1+r)\mathbf{p}^{(\alpha)}\mathbf{A}_\beta + w^{(\alpha)}\mathbf{a}_{L\beta}$.

Now let us prove:

■■ Lemma 2.12.

Two techniques (α) and (β) producing the same goods can coexist (i.e. competition does not cause either of them to be abandoned) if they are both cost minimizing at the given r, which implies that, in terms of any common numéraire $\mathbf{v}$, it is $w^{(\alpha)} = w^{(\beta)}$ and $\mathbf{p}^{(\alpha)} = \mathbf{p}^{(\beta)}$.

---

25 The term 'cost minimizing' can be criticized because it accepts the term 'cost of production' to refer to the sum of value of means of production used up plus wages plus profits; Sraffa (1960, pp. 8–9) prefers not to use this term because the marginalist tradition has tended to mean by 'cost of production' a quantity independent of the price of the product and *determining* it, while (except for non-basics not entering their own production) cost and price can only be determined simultaneously, because the price of the commodity directly or indirectly enters its own cost. My feeling is that, once the interdependence of costs and prices is grasped, 'cost minimizing' is not misleading.

Proof By definition of cost-minimizing technique the following inequalities are assumed to be simultaneously satisfied:

$$\mathbf{p}^{(\alpha)} \leq (1+r)\mathbf{p}^{(\alpha)}\mathbf{A}_\beta + w^{(\alpha)}\mathbf{a}_{L\beta} \quad \text{i.e.} \quad \mathbf{p}^{(\alpha)}\mathbf{v} = 1 \leq w^{(\alpha)}\mathbf{a}_{L\beta}[\mathbf{I} - (1+r)\mathbf{A}_\beta]^{-1}\mathbf{v} = w^{(\alpha)}/w^{(\beta)}$$
$$\mathbf{p}^{(\beta)} \leq (1+r)\mathbf{p}^{(\beta)}\mathbf{A}_\alpha + w^{(\beta)}\mathbf{a}_{L\alpha} \quad \text{i.e.} \quad \mathbf{p}^{(\beta)}\mathbf{v} = 1 \leq w^{(\beta)}\mathbf{a}_{L\alpha}[\mathbf{I} - (1+r)\mathbf{A}_\alpha]^{-1}\mathbf{v} = w^{(\beta)}/w^{(\alpha)}.$$

This can be the case only if $w^{(\alpha)} = w^{(\beta)}$. Then the left-hand inequalities can be written

$$\mathbf{p}^{(\alpha)} \leq w^{(\alpha)}\mathbf{a}_{L\beta}[\mathbf{I} - (1+r)\mathbf{A}_\beta]^{-1} = w^{(\beta)}\mathbf{a}_{L\beta}[\mathbf{I} - (1+r)\mathbf{A}_\beta]^{-1} = \mathbf{p}^{(\beta)}$$
$$\mathbf{p}^{(\beta)} \leq w^{(\beta)}\mathbf{a}_{L\alpha}[\mathbf{I} - (l+r)\mathbf{A}_\alpha]^{-1} = w^{(\alpha)}\mathbf{a}_{L\alpha}[\mathbf{I} - (l+r)\mathbf{A}_\alpha]^{-1} = \mathbf{p}^{(\alpha)}$$

which can be simultaneously satisfied only if $\mathbf{p}^{(\alpha)} = \mathbf{p}^{(\beta)}$. ∎

In view of the previous two lemmas, this lemma means that at the given r both $w(r)$ curves are on the outer envelope, i.e. the two curves either cross or are tangent to each other on the outer envelope. Then at that r the two techniques generate the same wage rate and relative prices, i.e. if the techniques differ in the method in more than one industry then for *each* commodity for which the methods in the two techniques differ, the two methods are equally profitable and can coexist. (This result is only valid on the outer envelope.) If two wage curves *cross* on the outer envelope at a certain r^*, that point is called a ***switch point*** because as r changes from a little less to a little more than r^* the economy 'switches' to a different technique.

In conclusion, if we are given all the $w(r)$ curves associated with all possible techniques that combine the available alternative methods, then their outer envelope will tell us how w changes with r, and which $w(r)$ curve, i.e. which technique (defined relative to wage industries only) will tend to be imposed by competition for each level of r.

Note that, if each method obeys 'constant returns to scale' (i.e. technical coefficients independent of the quantity produced), the technique imposed by competition depends only on r (or on the real wage, if it is the latter that is taken as given), not on the quantities to be produced, because only technical coefficients count in all the above lemmas about technical choice, and no limit to producible quantities (e.g. no limit to labour employment, or to utilization of free land) has

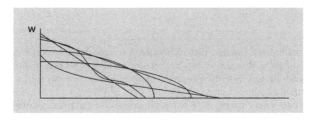

◘ **Fig. 2.4** Envelope of many $w(r)$ curves. Note that many of the intersections among wage curves can be below the envelope

been assumed. This independence of technical choice from quantities produced once the rate of profit or the real wage is given, is called the **non-substitution theorem**. It needs absence of joint production, and either no scarce land or changes in produced quantities small enough as not to alter the no-rent methods (in this last case for the commodities giving rise to extensive differential rent the method appearing in the price equations is the one on the no-rent land).

Another result of some practical relevance is the following: *if r is given, and if a more convenient method is discovered to produce a commodity, then its introduction causes the price of that commodity to decrease relative to all other commodities*. This result implies that, if r is given, and if the new method concerns a basic commodity, the purchasing power of the wage increases in terms of all goods but it increases most in terms of the good whose production method has improved. The proof is left as an *Exercise*; as a hint, put w = 1, so the commodity's price certainly decreases; now ask whether some other price can decrease by a greater percentage, by examining its price equation.

2.12 **Non-basics and Choice of Techniques**

Choice of production methods for wage industries is logically prior to choice of production methods for luxuries because the price equations of wage industries are not influenced by the prices of luxuries. Let us assume that wage industries and A-representation basic goods coincide. Given a numéraire basket consisting only of basic commodities, once either the rate of profit, or the real wage rate, is fixed the choice of methods for basics is determined and, with it, relative prices and residual distributive variable. Then in the equations determining the prices of non-basics all other prices and the two distributive variables are given; the choice of techniques for non-basics can then be studied in the following way. Assume that commodities have been numbered such that the first m commodities are the basic ones, thus $\mathbf{A}$ is formed by four submatrices $\mathbf{A}_{11}$, $\mathbf{A}_{12}$, $\mathbf{0}$, $\mathbf{A}_{22}$, with $\mathbf{A}_{11}$ being the $m \times m$ matrix of technical coefficients of basics in the production of basics, and $\mathbf{A}_{22}$ the $(n-m) \times (n-m)$ matrix of coefficients of non-basics in their production. The price equation of the t-th non-basic commodity $(m < t \leq n)$ is

$$p_t = (1+r)(p_1 a_{1t} + \ldots + p_n a_{nt}) + w a_{Lt}.$$

In this equation the terms $(1+r)(p_1 a_{1t} + \ldots + p_m a_{mt}) + w a_{Lt}$ are given. They can be summed up into a single constant scalar b_t (mnemonic for the *basic* component of cost). Therefore, if we indicate with $\mathbf{p}^{\wedge}$ the row vector of prices of non-basics, with $\mathbf{b}$ the semipositive row vector of constant terms b_t, $t = m+1, \ldots, n$, and with $\mathbf{A}^{\wedge}$ the matrix $(1+r)\mathbf{A}_{22}$, we can write

$$\mathbf{p}^{\wedge} = \mathbf{p}^{\wedge}\mathbf{A}^{\wedge} + \mathbf{b}. \tag{2.27}$$

It is $[\mathbf{I} - \mathbf{A}^{\wedge}]^{-1} \geq 0$ because of our assumption that either the dominant eigenvalue of the basics submatrix of $\mathbf{A}$ is also the dominant eigenvalue of $\mathbf{A}$, or anyway the rate of profit remains below the minimum among the maximum rates of self-reproduction of non-basics that use themselves in their production. Hence

128   Chapter 2 · Long-Period Prices

$$\mathbf{p}^{\wedge} = \mathbf{b}[\mathbf{I} - \mathbf{A}^{\wedge}]^{-1}.$$

It is strictly positive because all non-basics use, directly or indirectly, some basic commodity.[26] If at these prices some other method for some non-basic commodity yields extra profits, then it will be introduced, and it will lower the price of that commodity and of all non-basics in whose production it enters directly or indirectly. Therefore the choice of methods for non-basics can be analysed in very simple terms: those methods will be chosen, which minimize the prices of non-basics in terms of any numéraire consisting of basics only.

Here too, for the case in which there are non-basics that directly or indirectly use themselves in their production, we must prove that this choice of methods does not end up in indefinite oscillations back and forth between two methods. Thus we must prove that if, at the non-basic prices $\mathbf{p}^{\wedge(\alpha)}$ associated with $(\mathbf{A}^{\wedge}_{\alpha}, \mathbf{b}_{\alpha})$, a method β for the t-th non-basic commodity yields extra profits, i.e. $p_t^{\beta(\alpha)} < p_t^{(\alpha)}$, then at the prices $\mathbf{p}^{\wedge(\beta)}$ associated with $(\mathbf{A}^{\wedge}_{\beta}, \mathbf{b}_{\beta})$, (all other methods having remained unchanged) method α does not yield extra profits, i.e. it is not the case that $p_t^{\alpha(\beta)} < p_t^{(\beta)}$.

Proof The proof is by contradiction. With symbols of meaning analogous to those used earlier, since $\mathbf{A}^{\wedge}_{\alpha}$ and $\mathbf{A}^{\wedge}_{\beta}$ only differ in the t-th method we can write

$$\mathbf{p}^{\wedge(\alpha)} \geq \mathbf{p}^{\wedge\beta(\alpha)} = \mathbf{p}^{\wedge(\alpha)}\mathbf{A}^{\wedge}_{\beta} + \mathbf{b}_{\beta}$$
$$\mathbf{p}^{\wedge(\alpha)}\left[\mathbf{I} - \mathbf{A}^{\wedge}_{\beta}\right] \geq \mathbf{b}_{\beta}$$
$$\mathbf{p}^{\wedge(\alpha)} \geq \mathbf{b}_{\beta}\left[\mathbf{I} - \mathbf{A}^{\wedge}_{\beta}\right]^{-1} = \mathbf{p}^{\wedge(\beta)}$$

Thus $p_t^{\beta(\alpha)} < p_t^{(\alpha)}$ implies $\mathbf{p}^{\wedge(\alpha)} \geq \mathbf{p}^{\wedge(\beta)}$. Analogously, $p_t^{\alpha(\beta)} < p_t^{(\beta)}$ implies $\mathbf{p}^{\wedge(\beta)} \geq \mathbf{p}^{\wedge(\alpha)}$. These two inequalities can be simultaneously satisfied only if $\mathbf{p}^{\wedge(\alpha)} = \mathbf{p}^{\wedge(\beta)}$, but this would imply that at prices $\mathbf{p}^{\wedge(\alpha)}$ it is $p_t^{\beta(\alpha)} = p_t^{(\alpha)}$, a contradiction with the assumed $p_t^{\beta(\alpha)} < p_t^{(\alpha)}$. ∎

Now we can relax the assumption that the numéraire consists only of basic commodities. The numéraire is irrelevant for the determination of *relative* prices; the adoption of a different numéraire, possibly including non-basics, only changes all prices and w in the same proportion.[27] So it does not affect which of two methods is more profitable at the given r, and therefore which of two $w(r)$ curves is more 'outside' at the given r. These considerations extend to $w(r)$ curves based on numéraires including, or even exclusively consisting of, non-basic com-

---

26 Remember that I am neglecting the commodities produced by unassisted labour.

27 If we pass from a numéraire $\mathbf{v}$ to another numéraire $\mathbf{v}^{\wedge}$ such that it is $\mathbf{p}\mathbf{v}^{\wedge} = b\mathbf{p}\mathbf{v} = 1$, i.e. if b is the value of the new numéraire in terms of the old one, then passing from the old to the new numéraire only means dividing all prices and w by b.

2.12 · Non-basics and Choice of Techniques

modities. The intuitive reason is that if the real wage rate is measured in terms of a numéraire including non-basics, then by adopting the **C**-representation and putting $w_{adv} = w/(1+r)$ one renders those non-basics basic.[28] More formally, if the numéraire includes non-basic commodities, the function $w(r)$ is still given by (2.21), and the relationship between prices and the real wage can still be based on Eqs. (2.22) and (2.22b), with the sole difference that now **A**, **I**, $\mathbf{a_L}$ and **v** must be matrices and vectors of dimension greater than the number of basic commodities, because they must also include, besides all basics, all non-basics appearing in **v** and also all non-basics directly or indirectly required for the production of those non-basics.[29] With this reinterpretation of those symbols, expressions (2.21) and (2.22) are still valid, with the usual caveat about self-reproducing non-basics.

2.13 Techniques Including Different Commodities

Now let us discuss the important case of choice between two alternative methods α and β for the production of, say, commodity 1, when method β requires the use of commodities not appearing in technique (α).

To fix ideas, suppose that technique (α) includes n commodities, and that technique (β) has in common with technique (α) these n commodities, as well as the methods to produce all of them except commodity 1; method β for commodity 1 requires as inputs, in addition to some of the n commodities common to both techniques, some commodities indexed as $n+1$, $n+2$, ..., $n+h$, which do not appear at all in technique (α). Technique (β) must therefore also include industries producing these commodities, some of which might use themselves directly or indirectly in their own production. Therefore the determination of the supply price $p_1^{\beta(\alpha)}$ of commodity 1 at prices and distribution (α) requires the determination also of the supply prices of commodities $n+1,..., n+h$. This means that we have $h+1$ equations to determine the $h+1$ supply prices of these h commodities and of commodity 1. Formally, *these $h+1$ equations are like price equations of non-basic commodities* in technique (α), and therefore they can be solved. Thus $p_1^{\beta(\alpha)}$ is well determined and can be compared with $p_1^{(\alpha)}$. Now, the proof given above of Lemma 2.10 that *if $p_1^{\beta(\alpha)} < p_1^{(\alpha)}$, then at the given $\bar{r}$ it is $w^{(\beta)} > w^{(\alpha)}$*, did not need **A** to be indecomposable: the matrices $\mathbf{C}_\alpha$ and $\mathbf{C}_{\beta\alpha}$ were indecomposable anyway since all commodities need labour, directly or indirectly, to be produced. The key to that proof was that the subsistence vector was assumed to consist of

---

28 If $r = r°$ is given and determines the prices of basics and non-basics $\mathbf{p}(r°)$ and the wage rate $w(r°) = \lambda \mathbf{p}(r°)\mathbf{v} = \lambda$ in terms of a numéraire **v** consisting of basics only, then the real wage rate in terms of a new numéraire $\mathbf{v}^\wedge$ including non-basics is given by $w^\wedge(r°) = w(r°)/b = (\lambda/b)\mathbf{p}(r°)\mathbf{v}^\wedge$ $= \lambda/b$ where $\mathbf{p}(r°)\mathbf{v}^\wedge = b\mathbf{p}(r°)\mathbf{v}$. One can then determine **C** on the basis of the subsistence vector $(1+r°)^{-1}(\lambda/b)\mathbf{v}^\wedge$ so that $\mathbf{p}(r°) = (1+r°)\mathbf{p}(r°)\mathbf{C}$; the system $\mathbf{p}(r) = (1+r)\mathbf{p}(r)\mathbf{C} + w^+(r)\mathbf{a_L}$, $\mathbf{pv}^\wedge = 1$, yields $w(r)$ in terms of the numéraire $\mathbf{v}^\wedge$ (which now consists of basics) as $w(r) = w^+(r) + \lambda/b$.

29 All commodities included in the numéraire become basic if one adopts the **C**-representation of technology and one reasons in terms of the advanced wage rate w_{adv}.

130   **Chapter 2 · Long-Period Prices**

numéraire. All that is needed to apply the same proof here is that commodity 1, or one of the commodities which directly or indirectly use commodity 1 for their production, be included in the numéraire. (If commodity 1 is non-basic and not included in the numéraire not even indirectly, a method that decreases its cost has no effect on w.) Lemmas 2.11 and 2.12 too do not need an assumption that $\mathbf{A}$ be indecomposable. We conclude that those three lemmas are also valid for the case in which techniques differ in the commodities they include; only, the comparison of the profitability of alternative methods must be applied to the common commodities. Thus, the conclusion of Lemma 2.12 that if two techniques are both on the outer envelope at the given r, then $\mathbf{p}^{(\alpha)} = \mathbf{p}^{(\beta)}$, must be intended to apply to the prices of the common commodities only.

More generally, if two techniques differ in the commodities they include, we can always imagine to add, to the industries appearing in the first technique, new non-basic industries producing the commodities only utilized in the other technique; these new industries will use the methods with which they appear in the second technique. The first technique thus enlarged is called an ***enlarged technique***. The price equations thus added to the first technique will tell us what supply prices these added commodities *would* have if produced in the economy as non-basics, using the first technique's methods when possible.

Thus if two techniques differ in the production of tomatoes, and in the second technique the method for the production of tomatoes uses a specific fertilizer only used for the production of tomatoes and not used in the first technique, in the second technique there will appear an industry producing this fertilizer, which will not be present in the first technique. We can hypothetically imagine that a demand for this fertilizer arises from, say, some research laboratory even when the economy uses the first technique, in which case this fertilizer is produced in the first technique too, as a non-basic commodity. With this enlargement, all techniques can be made to include the same commodities; the difference will concern how these commodities are produced and which commodities are basic. Having 'enlarged' the techniques in this way, the criterion of choice of methods on the basis of cost minimization and of comparison of techniques differing in only one method becomes applicable. In the fertilizer example, enlarged technique α and technique β differ only in the method of direct production of tomatoes; the methods they use to produce the fertilizer and all other goods apart from tomatoes are the same; in (α), tomato production does not use the fertilizer; in (β) it does. The proof that cost minimization brings to a definite solution applies without modifications.

2.14 The Samuelson–Garegnani Model and the Champagne-Whiskey Model

As an important example of 'enlarged' techniques, let us study the model first proposed by Paul Samuelson in 1962 when presenting the notion of surrogate production function, and then much discussed in the Cambridge controversies in capital theory, in particular by Garegnani (1970), as discussed in ▶ Chap. 7. It is a two-industry model, where there is a single pure consumption good, which

2.14 · The Samuelson–Garegnani Model and the Champagne-Whiskey Model

can be produced by alternative methods; each different method for the production of the consumption good utilizes labour and *a different* circulating capital good, which is produced by itself and labour via a single method specific to it. Thus each technique uses a different capital good, the sole commodity common to alternative techniques is the consumption good, and the comparison of alternative *methods* for the production of the consumption good necessarily involves considering also the capital good utilized and how it is produced.

Let the consumption good be commodity 2, and the capital good be commodity 1α, or 1β, or 1γ, etc., depending on the method for the production of the consumption good, i.e. on the technique. Technique (α) is then a couple $(\mathbf{A}_\alpha, \mathbf{a}_{\mathbf{L}\alpha})$ where the 2×2 matrix $\mathbf{A}_\alpha$ has a positive first row $\mathbf{a}_{1\alpha} = (a_{1\alpha,1\alpha},\, a_{1\alpha,2})$ and a second row consisting of zeros. Choose the consumption good as numéraire. The price equations are

$$p_{1\alpha} = (1+r)p_{1\alpha}a_{1\alpha,1\alpha} + w^{(\alpha)}a_{L1\alpha} \tag{2.28}$$

$$p_2^{(\alpha)} = 1 = (1+r)p_{1\alpha}a_{1\alpha,2} + w^{(\alpha)}a_{L2,\alpha}. \tag{2.29}$$

The abundance of indices is necessary to make clear that, for each different production method adopted by the consumption industry, p_1 is the price of a different capital good, and the coefficients of the capital good industry are different. The indices need explanation: $a_{1\alpha,1\alpha}$ is the technical coefficient of capital good 1α in the production of itself; $a_{1\alpha,2}$ is the technical coefficient of capital good 1α in the production of the consumption good (which is good 2) when the latter is produced with method α and therefore by technique (α); $a_{L1\alpha}$ is the technical coefficient of labour in the production of capital good 1α; $a_{L2,\alpha}$ is the technical coefficient of labour in the production of the consumption good (good 2) with the method that uses capital good 1α. Formally the consumption good is a non-basic, but it is the numéraire so the consumption industry is a wage industry, its direct method of production influences the shape of the $w(r)$ curve. The latter curve for each technique is given by the function (where the coefficients are those of the technique in use, the index of the technique is omitted for simplicity):

$$w = \frac{1 - (1+r)a_{11}}{a_{L2} + (1+r)(a_{12}a_{L1} - a_{11}a_{L2})} \tag{2.30}$$

To compare the profitability of producing the consumption good with method α or with method β, let us take the rate of profit as given and let us use (2.30) with the α coefficients to determine $w^{(\alpha)}$. This wage is all we need to determine the supply price $p_2^{\beta(\alpha)}$ of the consumption good produced with method β at the prices and distribution (α); it is determined by the following two equations, where $p_{1\beta}^{(\alpha)}$ stands for the supply price of capital good 1β produced in technique α as a non-basic, hence produced by its sole known method with wage $w^{(\alpha)}(r)$ (don't confuse $p_{1\beta}^{(\alpha)}$ with $p_1^{\beta(\alpha)}$ that cannot be defined in this model since there is no good 1 producible with alternative methods).

$$p_{1\beta}^{(\alpha)} = (1+r)p_{1\beta}^{(\alpha)}a_{1\beta,1\beta} + w^{(\alpha)}a_{L1\beta} \tag{2.31}$$

$$p_2{}^{\beta(\alpha)} = (1+r)p_{1\beta}{}^{(\alpha)}a_{1\beta,2} + w^{(\alpha)}a_{L2,\beta}. \qquad (2.32)$$

Symbol $p_2{}^{\beta(\alpha)}$ is as usual the supply price of good 2 (the consumption good) produced with method β at the prices and wage of technique (α). These equations can be solved in succession: Eq. (2.31) determines the supply price of capital good 1β since the wage $w^{(\alpha)}$ is given, then the second equation determines $p_2{}^{\beta(\alpha)}$. These two equations are formally identical to the price equations of two non-basics.

In this case, the 'enlarged' technique (α) has capital good 1α as good 1, the consumption good produced with method α as good 2, and capital good 1β as a third good, whose index I will indicate not as 3 but as 1β; its 'enlarged' **A** matrix is $\mathbf{A}_\alpha = \begin{bmatrix} a_{1\alpha,1\alpha} & a_{1\alpha,2} & 0 \\ 0 & 0 & 0 \\ 0 & 0 & a_{1\beta,1\beta} \end{bmatrix}$ and its labour coefficients vector is

$\begin{bmatrix} a_{L1\alpha} & a_{L2,\alpha} & a_{L1\beta} \end{bmatrix}$. Given r, the price of capital good 1β is determined in enlarged technique (α) by Eq. (2.31) as the price of a luxury good that uses only itself as means of production. The 'enlarged' technique (β) includes the same three goods and differs in the sole production method of the consumption good, whose technical coefficients are now $\begin{bmatrix} 0 \\ 0 \\ a_{1\beta,2} \end{bmatrix}$ and $a_{L2,\beta}$. Capital good 1β is non-basic in the 'enlarged' technique (α), and capital good 1α is non-basic in the 'enlarged' technique (β), and since neither appears in the numéraire, the shapes of the $w^{(\alpha)}(r)$ curve and of the $w^{(\beta)}(r)$ curve are unaffected by their addition. In passing from one to the other 'enlarged' technique only the method of industry 2 changes but a capital good passes from non-basic to basic and the other does the opposite.

Our previous results imply that $p_2{}^{\beta(\alpha)}$ is greater than, equal to or smaller than 1 according as the rate of wages $w^{(\beta)}$ is less than, equal to or greater than $w^{(\alpha)}$.[30] Therefore in order to ascertain which method is more convenient in the long period, we need only trace the $w(r)$ curves and pick the technique whose wage curve lies above the other curve at the given level of r.[31]

In this very simple case, it is easy to show that two $w(r)$ curves can cross more than once. Assume that for all techniques $0 < a_{11} < 1$; $a_{L1} > 0$; $a_{12} > 0$.

---

30 The reader can check this result for the present case directly from Eqs. (2.28–2.32).

31 If this economy is using technique (α) and then technique (β) is discovered, in order to pass to it the economy will have to use some provisional method to produce the first units of capital good 1β; a more complete analysis would have to prove that, in spite of the need initially to use a provisional method later discarded because less efficient and therefore more expensive (which is the reason why it is not considered in the equations in the text), the greater cost of the production of the first units of capital good 1β does not prevent the shift in method from being convenient. We omit a rigorous analysis of this issue, but it should be clear that, as a longer and longer number of successive periods is considered in which the consumption good is produced by capital good 1β, the initial greater cost of producing the first units of that capital good becomes less and less relevant and, if prices and distribution remain determined by (α), the average rate of profit earned over the ensemble of periods by the use of the new method sooner or later rises above r. This explains why neither Samuelson nor Garegnani analyse this 'transition'.

2.14 · The Samuelson–Garegnani Model and the Champagne-Whiskey Model

Measure each capital good in such a unit that the labour coefficient is one unit, $a_{L1\alpha} = a_{L1\beta} = \ldots = 1$. The consumption good is the natural numéraire. Indicate the price of the capital good simply as p_α, p_β, etc., when produced in its technique; simplify the symbols by putting $a_{11} \equiv a$; $a_{12} \equiv b$; $a_{L2} = \ell$, so $a_{1\alpha,1\alpha}$ becomes simply a_α, and $a_{1\alpha,2}$ becomes b_α. The price equations of (non-enlarged) technique (α) are then

$$p_a = (1+r)p_\alpha a_\alpha + w_\alpha$$
$$1 = (1+r)p_\alpha b_\alpha + w\ell_\alpha.$$

Expression (2.30) becomes

$$w(r) = [1 - (1+r)a]/[\ell + (1+r)(b - a\ell)].$$

For $r=0$ it is $w = W = (1-a)/[\ell(1-a)+b] > 0$.
For $w=0$ it is $r = R = (1-a)/a > 0$.
Within these values, $w(r)$ is well defined, positive and differentiable, and the derivative is negative:

$$dw/dr = -b/[\ell + (1+r)(b - a\ell)]^2 < 0.$$

We further note that dw/dr is, respectively, a constant, a decreasing function of r (that is, increasing in absolute value: $w(r)$ is concave), or an increasing function of r, according as $b - a\ell$ is, respectively, zero, negative or positive, i.e. according as the proportion between physical capital and labour is, respectively, the same in the two industries, greater in the capital industry ($a > b/\ell$), or smaller in the capital industry ($a < b/\ell$). In these three cases $w(r)$ is, respectively, a straight line (with slope $-b/\ell^2 = -a/\ell$, and vertical intercept $W = (1-a)/\ell$), concave, convex.

Here is one way to show that two $w(r)$ curves can cross twice in the positive orthant. Assume the two wage curves $w^{(\alpha)}(r)$ and $w^{(\beta)}(r)$ have the same intercepts but the second is concave and the first a straight line. The same R requires that $a_\alpha = a_\beta = a$; then the same W requires that $\ell_\alpha(1-a) + b_\alpha = \ell_\beta(1-a) + b_\beta$; one can obtain a straight and a concave wage curve with the same intercepts by assuming these two conditions and in addition, for example, that $\ell_\beta > \ell_\alpha$, that $b_\alpha - a\ell_\alpha = 0$ which implies $w^{(\alpha)}(r)$ is a straight line, and that $b_\beta - a\ell_\beta < 0$ which implies $w^{(\beta)}(r)$ is concave.

These conditions are perfectly compatible as the following numerical example shows: $a = 1/2$, $\ell_\alpha = 1/2$, $b_\alpha = 1/4$, $\ell_\beta = 3/4$, $b_\beta = 1/8$: then $W = R = 1$ and $w^{(\alpha)}(r)$ has slope -1. ◻ Figure 2.5 illustrates; with these coefficients, $w^{(\beta)}(r)$ reaches slope -1 for $r° = 0.584$ which corresponds to $w^{(\beta)}(r°) = 0.87$, considerably greater than $w^{(\alpha)}(r°) = 0.416$.

Now reduce a bit the technical coefficients of technique (α) so as to leave its wage curve a straight line.[32] Call this new technique (γ) and $w^{(\gamma)}(r)$ its wage curve; this will have slightly greater intercepts than $w^{(\alpha)}(r)$ and will intersect $w^{(\beta)}(r)$ twice, cf. ◻ Fig. 2.5.

---

32 This requires that a_α decreases slightly, that $(1 - a_\alpha)/[\,l_\alpha(1 - a_\alpha) + b_\alpha]$ increases slightly, and that $b_\alpha - a_\alpha l_\alpha$ remains equal to zero; this is certainly achievable, e.g. let us suppose that l_α remains unchanged and let us remember that initially $b_\alpha = a_\alpha l_\alpha$, i.e. $W_\alpha = (1 - a_\alpha)/l_\alpha$; then a small decrease of a_α and of b_α by the same percentage obtains the desired result. If one wishes to maintain the slope unchanged, it suffices that l_α decreases in the same proportion as a_α, and that b_α decreases by the same amount as $a_\alpha l_\alpha$, so as to simultaneously maintain $a_\alpha/l l_\alpha$ unchanged and $b_\alpha - a_\alpha l_\alpha$ equal to zero.

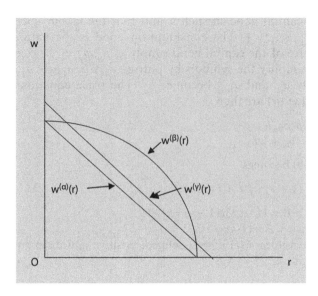

◘ Fig. 2.5 Decrease of technical coefficients of technique (α) produces technique (γ) that reswitches with technique (β)

We have here one instance of the phenomenon called **re-switching of techniques**: as r increases from zero, the technique chosen by competition at a certain point 'switches' from technique (γ) to (β), but at a higher rate of profit it switches back, or 'reswitches', to technique (γ). (See ▶ chapter 7 for the great importance of this phenomenon.)

The reason why re-switching can happen is that in economies with heterogeneous capital goods the relative price p_1/p_2 of two commodities need not be a monotonic function of r, it can first rise and then decrease and then rise again as r increases. This possibility becomes clear if we think of the reduction of labour-commanded prices to a series of dated quantities of labour each one multiplied by the opportune $(1+r)^t$ term. In the general case of many commodities, these dated quantities of labour tend to decrease irregularly as t increases. Let us neglect the terms after, say, $t=30$ as negligible. Then the ratio between two prices is the ratio between two polynomials of degree 30, which generally increase at different and changing speed as r rises. It is therefore perfectly possible that as r rises the ratio $p_1(r)/p_2(r)$ passes from being greater than 1 to less than 1 and then again to greater than 1 and then again to less than 1. Now reinterpret p_2 not as the price of a commodity different from commodity 1, but as the supply price $p_1^{\beta(\alpha)}$ of the same commodity 1 but produced with method β when the prices and wage are those of technique (α). Now $p_1/p_2>1$ means that commodity 1 is cheaper if produced with method β, $p_1/p_2<1$ means that method β is less convenient than method α. So an inversion more than once of the relative cheapness of two commodities as r rises means re-switching of techniques if the two commodities are actually two different ways to produce the same commodity.

What remains to show is that these phenomena can happen for economically acceptable values of r. Several numerical examples have shown that it is indeed

2.14 · The Samuelson–Garegnani Model and the Champagne-Whiskey Model

so. The reader is invited to examine on her own the first one, by Sraffa (1960, p. 37). Here I present a simpler one due to Samuelson (1966), based on 'Austrian' production techniques.

The example assumes that the production of 1 unit of champagne requires the payment of 7 wages two periods before the sale of the product, while the production of 1 unit of whiskey requires the payment of 2 wages three periods before, and of 6 wages one period before the product is sold. The long-period prices p_c of champagne and p_w of whiskey are given by

$$p_c = 7w(1+r)^2 \tag{2.33}$$

$$p_w = 2w(1+r)^3 + 6w(1+r). \tag{2.34}$$

Measure prices in labour commanded by putting $w=1$, then $p_c=7(1+r)^2$, $p_w=2(1+r)^3+6(1+r)$. The reader can check that

$p_c = p_w$ for $r = 50\%$ and for $r = 100\%$,

$p_w < p_c$ for $0.5 < r < 1$,

$p_c < p_w$ for $0 < r < 0.5$ and for $r > 1$.

At $r=0$ it is $p_c < p_w$ because cost consists only of wages and a unit of champagne requires the payment of 7 wages against 8 for a unit of whiskey; but the price difference decreases as r increases and is reversed as r becomes greater than 50%, because interest costs initially increase faster in the production of champagne than of whiskey; however, as r continues to increase, compound interest ends up by causing a greater increase of the cost of whiskey, so the price of whiskey starts approaching the price of champagne and the ratio between the two prices is reversed as r becomes greater than 100%.[33]

The reader can check that the derivative of the ratio p_c/p_w with respect to r is positive, zero or negative according as r is less than, equal to or more than $-1 + \sqrt{3}$.[34] Graphically p_c/p_w behaves as shown in ◘ Fig. 2.6.

---

33 **Exercise**: Choose a numéraire different from labour, and prove that with such an 'Austrian' assumption of absence of basic commodities there is no maximum rate of profit: when w tends to zero the rate of profit rises without limit, tending to $+\infty$. Then rewrite the production conditions of the two commodities in these terms: assume all production processes take one period, and each final commodity is produced by a process which is the last one of a series starting with a process where a (single or composite) commodity is produced by unassisted labour; the next period this commodity is used, alone (i.e. through ageing) or together with live labour, to produce another (single or composite) commodity, in turn used with or without labour the next period to produce another commodity, and so on up to the final champagne, or whiskey, commodity. (You must decide whether wages are advanced or paid at the end of the period. In this second case, the production of whiskey, for example, requires considering four successive production processes.) On this basis, assume the economy is stationary and produces each period a net product consisting of 1 unit of champagne; determine which productive processes must be going on every period in such an economy. Then do the same assuming the net product per period is 1 unit of whiskey.

34 The rate of interest is assumed to be non-negative, so the solution $r = -1 - \sqrt{3}$ is excluded.

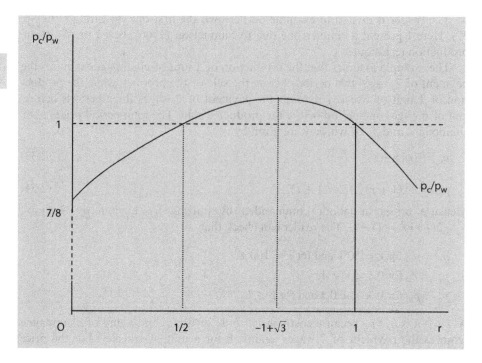

☐ **Fig. 2.6** Behaviour of the relative price of champagne to whiskey in Samuelson's example as r rises

If now we interpret the integrated production method[35] of whiskey as in fact an alternative way to produce champagne, this alternative integrated method is the more convenient one for $50\% < r < 100\%$ while the original integrated method is more convenient for $r < 50\%$ and for $r > 100\%$: as r rises from zero, at $r = 50\%$ the optimal technical choice switches to the alternative ('whiskey') integrated method, but at $r = 100\%$ there is re-switching back to the original integrated method.

The possibility of re-switching derives from the possibility of reversals in the direction of the movement of relative prices as the rate of profit or of interest rises. The latter possibility had not been suspected before Sraffa, and it questions some fundamental theses of the marginalist/neoclassical approach to capital, as will be explained in ▶ Chap. 7.

---

35 The term 'production method' refers to the method of an industry, while here we have been describing a series of production methods in temporal succession, as if the production of the final consumption good were operated by a vertically integrated firm, omitting the explicit indication of the product an earlier industry passes to the subsequent industry. Then a different term is needed to describe this vertically integrated production, and this is what the term 'integrated production method' refers to.

2.15 Fixed Capital

Many capital goods are not circulating but *durable*: a hammer, a tractor, a computer, a building do not disappear or become unusable after a single production cycle.

The way generally preferred nowadays to include these goods into long-period price theory is to treat them as goods that enter the productive process and also *come out of* the same productive process jointly with the main product, but one period older. Thus the productive process is visualized as *jointly* producing a main product and one-year-older durable capital goods. (I keep calling the length of the production period a 'year', but this is only to help intuition, in fact the 'year' or period can be assumed to have any length.)

In this way durable capital is viewed as a particular case of *joint production*, i.e. of productive processes that produce more than one commodity inseparably. Joint production is a broader category than production with durable capital: for example, wheat and straw or wool and mutton are examples of joint production independent of the use of durable capital, sometimes called 'pure' joint production. If there is no joint production one also says there is **simple production** or **single production**. The discussion of general joint production is postponed to ▶ Chap. 10. But durable capital will appear in ▶ Chap. 7, so it is useful to have an idea of how it can be treated in long-period price analysis. The discussion will also introduce an important new notion, *free disposal*.

Here I concentrate on *pure, or simple, fixed capital*, which is the case in which a durable capital good (or ensemble of several capital goods forming a fixed capital complex, a 'plant') is used in the production always of the same main product, and there is no joint utilization of durable capital goods of different ages,[36] nor any pure joint production.

Consider an economy that produces corn, iron and tractors, where corn and iron are circulating capital goods, while tractors are durable, last three years, and are used in the production of corn. The productive methods will use and produce commodities as follows (* stands for 'together with', → stands for 'produce'):

(1) corn * iron * labour → new tractors

(2) corn * iron * labour → iron

(3) corn * iron * new tractors * labour → corn * one-year-old tractors

(4) corn * iron * one-year-old tractors * labour → corn * two-years-old tractors

(5) corn * iron * two-years-old tractors * labour → corn (actually together with three-years-old tractors which however are no longer of any use and are thrown away as scrap at no cost, and can be neglected).

I avoid assuming that the scrap can be sold at a positive price because this would generally mean that, through some productive process, it can be recycled and become iron. Then process (5) would jointly produce corn and a product used as

---

36 Unless the efficiency of older capital goods is independent of the age of the capital goods jointly used in the method from which they emerge—as will be explained later.

138   Chapter 2 · Long-Period Prices

input in another industry, a case of pure joint production. On the other hand, getting rid of the useless three-year-old tractors might be costly, but I neglect this possibility too through an assumption of *free disposal*, namely that it is always possible to dispose costlessly of any amount of any product. In our case, free disposal means that this economy also has at its disposal the following possible methods, plus methods that use inputs and produce nothing at all:

(6) corn * iron * new tractors * labour → corn,

(7) corn * iron * one-year-old tractors * labour → corn,

(8) corn * iron * new tractors * labour → one-year-old tractors

(9) corn * iron * one-year-old tractors * labour → two-years-old tractors.

(The inputs are, respectively, the same as in methods 3, 4, 3, 4.) This means that the economy implicitly has a problem of choice of technique on how to produce corn. The economy will produce corn with method 6, and therefore will use methods 1, 2 and 6, if it is convenient to use tractors only if new; corn will be produced with methods 3 and 7, and therefore the activated methods will be 1, 2, 3, 7 if it is convenient to use one-year-old tractors but not two-year-old tractors. Methods 8 and 9 on the contrary can be neglected because they will always be less convenient than, respectively, methods 3 and 4, because the latter methods produce in addition another good, corn, which has positive value. For the same reason we can neglect the processes—mathematically assumed available by the assumption of free disposal—that use inputs and produce nothing, or that use the same inputs as other methods but produce less of outputs with a positive value.

It is generally possible to establish a maximum number of periods of use of a durable capital good, say k years, after which the 'machine', as one can call it, is certainly totally unusable. As that age approaches, the machine may require expenses due to maintenance and repair and may be of lower and lower efficiency. It might therefore be convenient to stop using the capital good *before* it reaches age k. There is a problem of choice of techniques: whether to go on using the capital good for k periods, or to stop before. All techniques in which the use of the capital good lasts less than k periods are called ***truncations*** (of the possible life of the capital good), but for simplicity the technique in which the capital good is used for k periods (and therefore has age k-1 in the last process in which it is used) is also called a truncation. In our example of the corn–iron-tractors economy it is $k=3$. Let us indicate a truncation with the number indicating the oldest age with which the capital good *enters* an activated process, then in this example the possible truncations are 0, 1 and 2. The number of successive processes in which the capital good is used is equal to the age at which it is thrown away, so it is the truncation number plus one. The earliest possible truncation is truncation 0, in which the capital good is used only when new.

This problem of choice of techniques is the sole one we analyse now; after showing that it is solved in a nice way, one will be able to add it to the usual problem of choice of techniques (that consists in choosing between two *alternative* methods, while here we have to choose whether to *add* an additional method or not).

2.15 · Fixed Capital

The steps to arrive at the optimal truncation are as follows.

(i) Solve the system of equations assuming that truncation 0 is used, i.e. assign price zero to the one-year-old tractors jointly produced, and assume that only new tractors are used. (In our example, this would mean solving the price equations associated with methods 1, 2 and 3 in which the price of one-year-old tractors is set at zero; or, equivalently, the price equations associated with methods 1, 2 and 6.) The resulting system of equations is identical to that of single production because only new tractors are used. In order to simplify proofs, assume that the given rate of profit r is not higher than the maximum rate of profit associated with that truncation, hence prices are all positive and the real wage rate is non-negative.

(ii) At the prices and real wage rate determined in step (i), calculate the rate of profit on the method using one-year-old tractors (method 4 in our example), assuming these tractors to have price zero, and assuming two-year-old tractors to have price zero too.

(iii) If this rate of profit is less than r, stop there: truncation 0 is optimal.[37]

(iv) If this rate of profit is greater than r, then the price of one-year-old tractors cannot be zero because then it would be convenient to set up firms using method 4, and demand for one-year-old tractors would increase until it raised their price from zero; so their price must be positive. But then to keep extra profits at zero in the firms using method 3 the price of corn must decrease relative to its cost of production, i.e. (since corn is the numéraire) the cost of production of corn must rise, which means the real wage and the price of iron and of new tractors must rise. The real wage must rise, because otherwise the price of iron and of new tractors would not change and then the cost of production of corn would not rise.

I prove now that indeed the price of *all* inputs to method 3 (other than corn, of course) increases when the real wage rises.

Proof The proof, formulated so as to apply to the general case (and therefore applicable to any number of inputs), is the following[38]: in the costs of any one of these inputs the real wage rate increases; then the price of this input can decrease only if the price of at least one of *its* inputs decreases by an even greater percentage[39]; considering the price of this second commodity one reaches the same conclusion that at least one of *its* inputs (different from both the first and the second commodity) must decrease in price by an even greater percentage; proceeding in

---

37 In order to keep proofs simple I am assuming that the efficiency of older durable capital goods does not increase with age.

38 This proof, inspired by an analogous proof by Sraffa, applies to all cases in which technical progress increases the amount produced of numéraire while the inputs remain unchanged.

39 To fix ideas suppose the input is iron. Since one component (the wage bill) of the cost of production of iron has increased, in order for its total cost and price to decrease by 1% the cost of the other inputs must decrease by more than 1%, and this requires that at least one of these inputs other than iron decreases in price by more than 1%.

140   **Chapter 2 · Long-Period Prices**

this way one necessarily exhausts the available commodities, and the last one of them cannot decrease in price because there is no commodity left whose price can decrease even more; but then the next-to-last commodity cannot decrease in price either, and so no one can. But if no commodity directly or indirectly used in the production of corn can decrease in price, then they must all rise in price since their costs have increased owing to the wage rise. ∎

Thus a positive price of one-year-old tractors and a rise of the real wage rate and of all other prices (except of course the price of corn and the price of two-years-old tractors which is kept at zero) are finally reached at which the rate of profit is r also in the production of corn with one-year-old tractors. Truncation 1 is feasible, it yields a higher wage rate than truncation 0, and at the prices of truncation 0 it is convenient to pass to truncation 1.

(v) Now we repeat the procedure for method 5, that uses two-year-old tractors, taking as starting points the prices and wage rate determined by truncation 1 and assuming a zero price of two-years-old tractors and of three-years-old tractors too. If at these prices method 5 yields a rate of profit less than r, then we do not introduce it and stop at truncation 1; if method 5 yields extra profits, then for the same reasons discussed under step (iv) a positive price for two-years-old tractors will exist that, together with a higher real wage rate and prices of all other goods, makes this method yield the rate of profit r; truncation 2 is feasible, it yields a higher real wage rate[40] than truncation 1, and at the prices of truncation 1 it is convenient to pass to truncation 2.

(vi) In this example truncation 2 is the last possible one, because by assumption three-year-old tractors have price zero *because useless*; in the general case the procedure can be repeated until either truncation $k - 1$ is reached, where the capital good is used in k processes and comes out of the last one totally useless, or a truncation t is reached in which at the prices of truncation $t - 1$ (which assigns price zero to the t-years old capital good coming out of it) there is a technically feasible process that uses the t-years old capital good but it yields a profit rate less than r, and then truncation t is not convenient. If truncation t were adopted, the price of the t-years old capital good would turn out negative.[41] At the last feasible truncation, all prices are positive, and the real wage rate is maximized for the given r: the economy is on the outer envelope of the $w(r)$ curves. End of the steps.

---

40 If a higher truncation is convenient, it is associated with a higher real wage; this means that cases can be conceived where at the given rate of profit truncation 0 yields a negative real wage but there is a higher truncation where the real wage is positive. For simplicity I neglect this possibility.

41 Put $w = 1$, i.e. measure prices in labour commanded; suppose truncation $t - 1$ is the optimal one; at its prices the method using the t-years old machine (priced zero) yields a rate of profit lower than r; raise its rate of profit to r by giving the t-years old machine a negative price; this lowers the profit of the method using the $(t - 1)$-years-old machine, as if it had suffered a loss of efficiency, and requires therefore a rise of its price, and then of all other prices; as prices rise, the negative price of the old machine rises too, i.e. gets closer to zero, but cannot reach zero (otherwise the methods using less old machines would have a rate of profit above r now that the real wage has decreased); the price rise stops when a uniform lower real wage is reached, with the old machine still with a negative price.

2.15 · Fixed Capital

Which truncation maximizes the real wage rate can depend on the level of the rate of profit. Also, just like two techniques can coexist on the outer envelope, so two successive truncations $t-1$ and t can be equally optimal—but in this case the capital good coming out of truncation $t-1$ has price exactly zero.

Simple fixed capital confirms therefore that competition tends to select the methods that, given one of the two distributive variables, maximize the other one.

Assuming competition to have already performed this function and that the result in our example is that truncation 2 is adopted, here are the price equations of that example, specified without the use of matrices and vectors in order to help readers to understand what is going on. Indices distinguishing commodities and industries can be kept reasonably simple, in this case, as follows. Technical coefficients refer to methods that produce 1 unit of main product, thus the three methods that produce corn all produce 1 unit of corn; the first two of them also jointly produce tractors, in amounts, respectively, b_{T1} for the output of one-year-old tractors, b_{T2} for the output of two-year-old tractors. The input technical coefficients of corn and of iron have a first index indicating which input it is: corn is good 1, iron is good 3^{42}; the second index indicates the industry (the main product): the iron industry is industry 3, the new tractor industry is industry T, the corn industry (which produces good 1) comprises three methods where the coefficients have second index 1 but followed by a further index 0, 1 or 2 indicating the age of the tractor used to produce corn. A new tractor is good $T0$, a one-year-old tractor is $T1$, a two-year-old tractor is $T2$; since tractors of age $h>0$ are only *used* as inputs in one method (the method that produces corn using tractors of age h), and are only *produced* in one method (the method that produces corn using tractors of age $h-1$), for their technical coefficients it is unnecessary to use three indices: thus for example a_{T0} is the input coefficient of tractors in the method that uses new tractors in order jointly to produce 1 unit of corn and one-year-old tractors in amount b_{T1}. (A natural but not obligatory choice of units makes $b_{T1}=a_{T0}$, and $b_{T2}=a_{T1}$.) Thus:

$$a_{11,0} * a_{31,0} * a_{T0} * a_{L1,0} \rightarrow 1 \text{ unit of corn} * b_{T1}$$

$$a_{11,1} * a_{31,1} * a_{T1} * a_{L1,1} \rightarrow 1 \text{ unit of corn} * b_{T2}$$

$$a_{11,2} * a_{31,2} * a_{T2} * a_{L1,2} \rightarrow 1 \text{ unit of corn } (* \text{three - year - old tractors of value zero})$$

$$a_{13} * a_{33} \qquad\qquad * a_{L3} \rightarrow 1 \text{ unit of iron}$$

$$a_{1T} * a_{3T} \qquad\qquad * a_{LT} \rightarrow 1 \text{ new tractor}$$

The price of corn is p_1, the price of iron is p_3, the price, respectively, of new, one-year-old and two-years-old tractors are p_{T0}, p_{T1} and p_{T2}. Three-years-old tractors

---

42 I give no new good index 2; iron is given number 3 to avoid confusion with two-year-old tractors which are indicated as $T2$.

142   Chapter 2 · Long-Period Prices

have price zero and do not appear explicitly. Wages are paid in arrears. The price equations are

$$(1+r)\left(a_{11,0}p_1 + a_{31,0}p_3 + a_{T0}p_{T0}\right) + wa_{L1,0} = p_1 + b_{T1}p_{T1}$$
$$(1+r)\left(a_{11,1}p_1 + a_{31,1}p_3 + a_{T1}p_{T1}\right) + wa_{L1,1} = p_1 + b_{T2}p_{T2}$$
$$(1+r)\left(a_{11,2}p_1 + a_{31,2}p_3 + a_{T2}p_{T2}\right) + wa_{L1,2} = p_1$$
$$(1+r)(a_{13}p_1 + a_{33}p_3) + wa_{L3} = p_3 \tag{2.35}$$
$$(1+r)(a_{1T}p_1 + a_{3T}p_3) + wa_{LT} = p_{T0}$$
$$p_1 = 1$$

The last equation specifies the numéraire. The other equations are as many as the goods produced, which include the older tractors: matrix A is square. With the inclusion of the numéraire equation, there are six equations in seven variables: five prices, r and w. If r or w is given, the system is determinate.[43] Earlier truncations eliminate one or more equations but they also eliminate the same number of products and of prices (the old machines no longer utilized, and their prices) so the system of equations remains determinate. In particular, matrix **A** remains square.

Note that these equations allow for different efficiencies of machines of different age. A special simple case, *constant efficiency* of machines independently of their age up to age k, will be considered later.

Another noteworthy result of the analysis of choice of truncation with simple fixed capital is that the outer envelope of the $w(r)$ curves is downward-sloping: if r increases, the real wage rate associated with the optimal truncation (which can change as a result of the change of r) decreases.

Proof   The analysis given above of how the optimal truncation is reached shows that since prices were assumed positive at truncation 0, they remain positive throughout, and also the prices of the older capital goods that it is convenient to use are positive. Thus we have proved that *on the outer envelope of the $w(r)$ curves* all prices are positive. Let us then assume that we are on the outer envelope and that r rises (by an amount such that the truncation does not change), and let us change numéraire, choosing as numéraire the wage rate, $w = 1$, i.e. expressing prices in labour commanded. To show that the real wage rate decreases we have to show that all prices thus measured increase. The proof is again based on the fact that if one price does not increase, then some other price must decrease, and it can do so only if some third price decreases by a greater percentage, which requires that some fourth price decreases by a still greater percentage, but when all commodities have been thus accounted for, the price of the last commodity cannot decrease because no other price can decrease by a still greater percentage, hence no price can decrease. (The reader is invited to apply this reasoning to the price equations of the corn and tractors example above, remembering that $w = 1$,

---

43   The given rate of profit can be higher than the R of truncation 0 if it comes out that higher truncations are feasible and raise R.

2.15 · Fixed Capital

and to verify that the joint production of corn and older tractors does not undermine the reasoning.) ∎

The optimal truncation can depend on income distribution. Then something unexpected can happen. Suppose the rate of profit is positive, and that at this $r>0$ the optimal truncation in our example of corn–iron and tractors is truncation 1, and this is in fact the truncation the economy is using. It might be that at $r=0$ the optimal truncation is truncation 0. This means that at $r=0$ truncation 1 yields a loss if $p_{T1}=0$, it can yield $r=0$ only by assigning a *negative* price to one-year-old tractors. That is, if we abolish the condition of non-negative prices and impose $r=0$ in the system of equations that includes the production of corn both with new and with one-year-old tractors, the solution determines a negative p_{T1}. Now, we have seen that in simple production the prices at $r=0$ are proportional to labours embodied. Must we conclude that in this economy one-year-old tractors, that at $r>0$ the economy utilizes without problems, embody a negative quantity of labour? Is it possible to give a meaning to a negative quantity of labour embodied? We will examine this issue in ► Chap. 10.

Now let us assume *constant efficiency* of durable capital until it reaches its scrapping age. Closely following Sraffa 1960, §76, suppose the durable capital good is a machine of constant efficiency for k periods after which it undergoes complete breakdown ('sudden death'). In this case, if it is convenient to use the machine at all, then it is convenient to use it for all k periods, combining it always with the same quantities of other inputs. Let us suppose this is the case for a machine T which is used to produce commodity 1. Apart from the machine, there are n circulating capital inputs. Then we have the following equations for these k methods that use the machine:

$$(1+r)(a_{11}p_1 + \ldots + a_{n1}p_n + a_{T0}p_{T0}) + wa_{L1} = p_1 + b_{T1}p_{T1}$$
$$(1+r)(a_{11}p_1 + \ldots + a_{n1}p_n + a_{T1}p_{T1}) + wa_{L1} = p_1 + b_{T2}p_{T2}$$
$$\ldots\ldots\ldots\ldots\ldots\ldots\ldots\ldots\ldots\ldots\ldots\ldots\ldots\ldots\ldots\ldots\ldots\ldots$$
$$(1+r)(a_{11}p_1 + \ldots + a_{n1}p_n + a_{Tk-1}p_{Tk-1}) + wa_{L1} = p_1.$$

Because of constant efficiency, the quantities of circulating capital goods and of labour are the same in all methods (this is why it was not necessary to use three indices). Furthermore $b_{T1}=a_{T1}$, $b_{T2}=a_{T2}$, etc., the same quantity of machines coming out of a method is transferred to the next method, so let us replace b_{Ti} with a_{Ti} on the right-hand side of these equations. Now multiply the k equations, respectively, by $(1+r)^{k-1}$, $(1+r)^{k-2}$, ..., $(1+r)$, 1; add their left-hand sides, and their right-hand sides: of course the two sums are equal, and the used machines of the same age, from 1 to $k-1$, appear on both sides and multiplied by the same profit term so they cancel out; we are left with

$$a_{T0}p_{T0}(1+r)^k + \left[(1+r)(a_{11}p_1 + \ldots + a_{n1}p_n) + wa_{L1}\right]\frac{(1+r)^k - 1}{r} = p_1\frac{(1+r)^k - 1}{r}.$$

Divide both sides by $\frac{(1+r)^k-1}{r}$, to obtain

$$a_{T0}p_{T0}\frac{r(1+r)^k}{(1+r)^k - 1} + (1+r)(a_{11}p_1 + \ldots + a_{n1}p_n) + wa_{L1} = p_1.$$

$$\tag{2.36}$$

144   Chapter 2 · Long-Period Prices

The first addendum in (2.36) represents the 'per-period rental' to be paid for the use of the machine, or the 'amortization' to be set aside, the constant annuity that allows earning the rate of profit r and reconstituting the capital invested in the purchase of the machine, which can then be used to repurchase the machine at the end of the k periods.

Assuming again a given truncation, now let us briefly inquire into the behaviour of **depreciation**. In practical life, depreciation is often estimated with very rough methods, usually as a constant. Often it is also unscrupulously played upon (using difficult-to-criticize estimates of future sales, future rates of utilization of plant, expected loss of value due to technological obsolescence)[44] to influence the prospects of the firm vis-à-vis investors, tax agents, etc. We here assume that the plant is normally utilized and that prices are long-period normal prices. Then the future profits that can be earned by processes that use older durable capital goods can be estimated with precision, and the value of the older capital goods can be obtained from the price equations that we have indicated. Correct depreciation is generally not constant.[45]

As the age of a durable capital good increases, its value will normally decrease; it can initially increase only if its efficiency initially increases with use, e.g. because a period of 'running in' is necessary in order to achieve full efficiency. Not much more can be said in general, owing to the possible diversity of the pattern of efficiency, maintenance, normal repairs, etc., over time as the capital good ages. Something more can only be said in the case of constant efficiency. In this case one must assume that the technical life of the capital good is limited, i.e. that after a given number of years it falls to pieces ('sudden death').

Following a common practice in the literature I refer for brevity to durable capital goods as 'machines'. If a machine has constant efficiency up to age k where it undergoes sudden death, then machines of age 0, 1, …, $k-1$ are technically perfect substitutes for one period, and therefore a producer will be ready to pay the same sum to *rent* a machine for one period, as long as its age is less than k years. The value of the machine will then vary with age only because the number of periods, for which that same yearly rent can be earned, decreases with age. At age k the value of the machine is zero. When new, the value of the machine equals its cost of production. If the machine can be profitably used for k years,

---

44 **Technological obsolescence** can be a cause of anticipated scrapping of a durable capital good relative to the case of absence of technical progress; and firms do try to take this fact into account in estimating the returns from an investment in durable capital; but a treatment of this extremely important aspect of real economies would require discussing expectations and uncertainty with regard to technical progress, a topic outside the standard theory of long-period prices although certainly not outside the theory of investment.

45 A non-constant *depreciation*—decrease in the value of the capital good as it gets older—is of course compatible with a constant *amortization* (i.e. the setting aside of a constant annuity each period, as in (2.42), re-employed so as to yield the market rate of interest, and whose cumulated value allows normal profits plus repurchasing the durable capital good by the time it must be replaced). But to determine the demand price of a partially worn-out fixed plant, it is depreciation that counts.

2.15 · Fixed Capital

if the price of the new machine is p, and if the rental per year (paid at the end of the year) is ρ, then the present value of the k rentals that a new machine will earn during its economic life must equal its purchase price p, hence for $r > 0$ we obtain[46]:

$$p = \rho/(1+r) + \rho/(1+r)^2 + \ldots + \rho/(1+r)^k = \rho \cdot \frac{(1+r)^k - 1}{r(1+r)^k} \quad \text{[if } r = 0, \text{ then } p = k\rho].$$

(2.37)

The rental ρ thus obtained is also the *constant* annuity to be set aside each year and invested so as to earn the rate of profit r, in order to have at the end of k years the sum $p(1+r)^k$, that is the compound profit at rate r for k years on the capital p invested in the purchase of the new machine, plus the capital itself p that can be used to replace the machine. Switching the place of p and ρ in (2.37) we obtain this annuity as given by the well-known accounting formula [already appearing in (2.36)]:

$$\rho = p \cdot \frac{r(1+r)^k}{(1+r)^k - 1}.$$

(2.38)

Let us use these formulas to study the evolution of the value of the constant-efficiency machine with age. At the end of the first year of utilization, only $k - 1$ future rentals remain, hence the addendum $\rho/(1+r)^k$ has disappeared from the sum in (2.37), the value of the machine has decreased from its initial value p by the amount of depreciation $D_1 = \rho/(1+r)^k$. From the end of the first to the end of the second year the value decrease is $D_2 = \rho/(1+r)^{k-1} = D_1(1+r)$; from the end of the second to the end of the third year the value decrease is $D_1(1+r)^2$; and so on. *The loss of value—the depreciation—increases with the age of the machine, being multiplied by $(1+r)$ each year.* Depreciation is constant only when $r = 0$.

The sum of the k terms D_t must equal p, i.e. $D_1(1 + (1+r) + (1+r)^2 + \ldots + (1+r)^{k-1}) = p$. This makes it possible to study the effect of *changes* of r on the *fraction* of the initial value p of a machine, represented by depreciation each year. For simplicity let us assume $p = 1$. If r increases to $r' > r$, the sole way for the sum $D_1(1 + (1+r') + (i+r')^2 + \ldots + (1+r'^{k-1}))$ to remain equal to 1 is for D_1 to decrease, i.e. it must be $D_i(r') < D_i(r)$. The growth of depreciation quotas is now faster since $r' > r$, and since the early depreciation quotas are now smaller, the last depreciation quotas must be larger. So at a higher rate of profit, initially the value of the machine decreases slower, and toward the end of its life faster, than at a lower rate of profit. This means that *at all intermediate ages, the value of the machine (as a fraction of its value when new) is the higher, the higher the rate of profit.*

One important implication of this result concerns the value of a constant stock of machines of constant efficiency and uniformly distributed by age.

---

46 *Proof*: put for brevity $(1+r) = x$; it is $1/x + 1/x^2 + \ldots + 1/x^k = \frac{x^{k-1} + x^{k-2} + \ldots + 1}{x^k}$; the numerator of this fraction equals $(x^k - 1)/(x - 1)$ because of the identity $(x^{k-1} + x^{k-2} + \ldots + 1)(x - 1) = x^k - 1$, verifiable by developing the product; hence $(x^{k-1} + x^{k-2} + \ldots + 1) = (x^k - 1)/(x - 1)$, valid for $x \neq 1$.

146   **Chapter 2 · Long-Period Prices**

Assume that a machine, of price 1 when new, lasts k years with constant efficiency and that k processes, each one using the machine at a different age, are
run side by side, each one using one machine. The previous result then means
that the value K of the uniformly age-distributed stock of machines is the greater,
the higher the rate of profit, being intermediate between $k/2$ and k. To prove this,
note that when $r=0$, depreciation is constant at $1/k$ per year, hence the value of
the stock of k machines is

$$K = [k + (k - 1) + (k - 2) + \ldots + 1]/k,$$

a sum rapidly tending from above to $k/2$ as k increases. As r rises, K rises
because each old machine rises in value, as shown above; if r could rise indefinitely, the rise of K would indefinitely approach its upper bound k, corresponding to machines that maintain a value practically equal to 1 very nearly up to
the end of their economic life. (Of course, in an economy with basic commodities, r cannot rise indefinitely.) Thus as long as durable capital is a significant
portion of capital goods, the normal value of the given stock of capital goods
present in an economy is relevantly affected by changes in income distribution
even when normal prices of *new* capital goods are little affected by changes in
distribution.

The reader is invited to read ▶ Chap. 10, §83, of Sraffa's *Production of Commodities*, where on p. 71 a beautiful Figure graphically depicts the above result.

This result is also useful to assess the connection between *persistent value of
capital* and *replacement gross investment*. Looking at the above result from the
opposite angle, as long as some of the capital goods are durable the *replacement
gross investment I*—the per-period expenditure needed to maintain this stock of
capital goods physically unchanged by replacing the scrapped ones[47]—is a smaller
fraction of the value of capital K, the higher the rate of profit; the fraction is
intermediate between 1, and a percentage less than 1 but not less than $2/k$ where
$k>2$ is the number of years of economic life of durable capital.

Let us conclude on simple fixed capital by asking whether the existence of
simple fixed capital creates difficulties in the Leontief problem 'find the vector of
total quantities to be produced in a period to obtain a given net output in that
period'. The answer is no, as long as the net product vector **y** contains positive
quantities only of new commodities. It *is* possible to produce a net product consisting entirely of new commodities: having found the truncation that determines
for how many periods a durable capital good is used, say k periods, all that is
necessary is that the total output of the final product for which that capital good
is used be divided among the k processes so that output and input of each aged
but still usable durable capital are equal and cancel out in the determination of
the net product of the economy. A net product of new capital goods is of course

---

47   This notion is what will allow us to derive a *long-period investment function* from the neoclassical
demand curve for capital in Chap. 7.

2.15 · Fixed Capital

obtainable by having the industry that produces them produce more than needed by the industries that use that new capital good. Therefore there are no difficulties with determining subsystems producing positive net outputs of 'final' commodities.

Difficulties can arise if one wants a net product consisting also of old capital goods *and* the assumption of free disposal is not made. Suppose that in our example of corn and tractors, the production of 1 unit of corn requires 1 tractor, whichever the age of the tractor; suppose that corn is not used as input in any industry, so any production of corn is production of a net output of corn; and suppose that it is desired to have a net output consisting only of 1 one-year-old tractor. This is impossible without free disposal, because the production of a one-year-old tractor requires the use of a new tractor to produce corn. In the absence of free disposal the sole way to have a zero net output of corn is to have some process run at a negative level of activity. If production of the desired net output of one-year-old tractors also entails a net output of x units of corn, this net output of corn can be reduced to zero by adding negative industries in the dimensions which, if positive, would form a subsystem producing x units of corn as its sole net product (we have seen that this is always possible).

Interestingly, this solution can be interpreted in a way that makes sense. Negative industries are of course impossible, but they can be interpreted as *variations* in the size of already existing industries: a diminution of the quantity produced of a good is perfectly conceivable. If we interpret a certain net output vector **y** as a vector of desired *variations* in net outputs, the dimensions of the industries associated with it can be interpreted as the *variations* in the size of industries necessary to obtain the desired variation of the net output vector; then negative industries can be interpreted as decreases in activity levels and make perfect sense; and they can arise even independently of the existence of durable capital goods, simply owing to negative components of **y**.

2.16 Conclusions

Now you are familiar with the notion of long-period prices, the decreasing relationship that ties the real wage and the rate of return on capital, the idea of long-period choice of production methods based on cost minimization imposed by competition, the useful notion of subsystem, the meaning of labours embodied, the nature of production with durable capital goods, the possibility to connect gross products and net products via the Leontief model, the phenomenon of re-switching whose importance may not be very clear now but will be appreciated in ▶ Chap. 7. The distinction between normal or long-period prices, moment-by-moment market prices, and intermediate notions of short-period prices, is central to economic theory and will be fundamental in what follows; even consumer choice means different things depending on what kind of prices it is referred to. The usefulness of the notions of this chapter will emerge even where you may not expect it, for example in showing a deficiency of the Marshallian determination of long-period partial equilibrium (in ▶ Chap. 5, §5.23, page 407).

148 Chapter 2 · Long-Period Prices

2.17 Review Questions and Exercises

❓ Review questions

1. Interpret the elements of $\mathbf{za_L}$ (Eq. 2.6).
2. Explain why, if wages are advanced and included in the coefficients matrix $\mathbf{C}$, if the economy is a no-surplus economy $\mathbf{C}$ must be indecomposable.
3. Explain the connection between the Hawkins–Simon conditions and the Perron–Frobenius theorem. (See the online Appendix to the chapter.)
4. It is often said that the modern Sraffian theory of value has shown that the rate of profit must be determined simultaneously with relative prices. In fact mathematically this is not quite correct, the rate of profit can be determined *before* prices although the converse is not true. Explain, both for the case of advanced wages and posticipated wages.
5. Interpret the elements of the Leontief inverse $[\mathbf{I} - \mathbf{A}]^{-1}$.
6. What does matrix $\mathbf{H} = \mathbf{A}[\mathbf{I} - \mathbf{A}]^{-1}$ represent? What is its relationship with the Leontief inverse? (Requires online Appendix 2.3)
7. Long-period prices $p = (1+r)p\mathbf{A} + w\mathbf{a_L}$ can also be determined as $p = rp\mathbf{H} + w\mathbf{m}$. Explain. (See previous question)
8. Prove that if r rises, w paid in arrears decreases in any numéraire.
9. Consider a good produced by labour alone; production takes one period, wages are paid at the end of the period and consist of a quantity of the good. Explain how the rate of profit depends on the real wage in this case. (Tricky question…)
10. Prove that the wage rate corresponding to $r = 0$ is the reciprocal of the labour embodied in the numèraire basket.
11. In what cases is w a linear function of r?
12. Prove that the labour theory of value (with circulating capital) requires that the labour vector be a left eigenvector of the matrix of input coefficients if industries are the columns of this matrix.
13. Explain why a uniform organic composition of capital (only circulating capital) implies the validity of the labour theory of value.
14. Explain the use of 'enlarged' techniques.
15. Distinguish non-basic goods from luxury goods.
16. Enunciate and prove the result that excludes the following possibility: a competitive economy does not tend to the outer envelope of the $w(r)$ curves because a method to produce good 1, which if adopted in place of the ruling method would raise w, is not adopted because at the prices of the ruling technique it is not cost minimizing.
17. Prove that the standard-commodity proportions are the ones that maximize the potential uniform growth rate.
18. Illustrate the procedure to find the optimal truncation with simple fixed capital.
19. Explain why the interpretation of labours embodied as employment multipliers requires that labour be homogeneous.
20. Illustrate how choice between two techniques in the Samuelson–Garegnani two-sector model can be analysed via 'enlarged' techniques.

2.17 · Review Questions and Exercises

21. Check that you are able to prove without consulting the textbook that with no technical change, just a change in income distribution, the value of a stock of durable machines of uniformly distributed age rises with r.
22. Explain why with fixed (i.e. durable) capital there is always a problem of choice of techniques.

✅ Exercises

1. The economy produces corn and iron. You are given the technical coefficients and the corn wage for a yearly production period. Suppose you want to pass to quarterly (three months) production periods. How will the coefficients and the prices be modified?
2. Assume a two-goods economy where corn and iron are produced by corn, iron and labour. Show the viability conditions in terms of the coefficients.
3. On the basis of the results of the section on choice of techniques, complete the proof, partially given below, of the following result: *if r is given, and if a more convenient method is discovered to produce a wage industry commodity, for example, without loss of generality, commodity 1, then the adoption of this method causes the price of commodity 1 to decrease relative to all other commodities.* Partial proof: Let r be given and put $w = 1$, i.e. prices are measured in labour commanded. Let $p_1^{(\alpha)}$ be the original price of commodity 1. At the old prices it is $p_1^{\beta(\alpha)} < p_1^{(\alpha)}$, so the introduction of method β reduces p_1 and hence reduces the prices of all commodities into whose costs p_1 enters directly or indirectly. No other price will decrease if commodity 1 is a non-basic not used as means of production in any other industry, in which case the demonstration ends here. If some other price decreases (if commodity 1 is basic, *all* other prices will decrease), we must prove that no price decreases by the same or greater percentage than p_1. Suppose that among the other commodities the price that proportionally decreases most is p_h. Prove that it must have decreased by a smaller percentage than p_1 by examining its price equation written as follows:

$$p_h = (1+r)p_1 a_{1h} + (1+r)(p_2 a_{2h} + p_3 a_{3h} + \ldots + p_n a_{nh}) + a_{Lh}.$$

4. The economy produces three goods and the sole positive coefficients of the **A** matrix are a_{12}, a_{23}, a_{31}. Prove that the three eigenvalues are all the same, and therefore matrix **A** is imprimitive.
5. Prove that changes of numéraire do not alter the switch points between two alternative techniques
6. In the Samuelson–Garegnani two-sector model, suppose a wage curve is convex and has given intercepts. Show that there are limits to its convexity, the curve cannot be very close to the axes. (Hint: first ascertain the condition for a convex wage curve; then study the conditions for positive prices in terms of the coefficients.)
7. The economy produces corn and iron. You are given the technical coefficients and the corn wage for a yearly production period. Suppose you want to pass to quarterly (three months) production periods. How will the coefficients and the prices be modified?
8. Explain how a switch of technique, that changes the capital goods adopted in the consumption industry because it introduces capital goods previously

150 **Chapter 2 · Long-Period Prices**

not utilized in any industry, can nonetheless be described as altering only one production method rather than the entire matrix $(\mathbf{A}, \mathbf{a}_L)$.

9. Formally distinguish non-basic goods from luxury goods.

10. Assume a two-goods economy where corn and iron (circulating capital goods when used as inputs) are produced by corn, iron and labour. Show the viability conditions in terms of the coefficients.

11. Rewrite the production conditions of each of the two commodities in the Samuelson example in §2.27 in these terms: assume all production processes take one period, and each final commodity is produced by a process which is the last one of a series starting with a process where a commodity (single or composite) is produced by unassisted labour; the next period this commodity is used, alone (i.e. through aging) or together with living labour, to produce another (single or composite) commodity, in turn used the next period with or without labour to produce another commodity, and so on up to the final production of champagne, or whiskey. (You must decide whether wages are advanced or paid at the end of the period. In this second case, the production of whiskey, for example, requires considering four successive production processes.) Determine the labour-commanded price of each one of the intermediate commodities thus implicitly postulated, and check that with such an 'Austrian' assumption of absence of basic commodities there is no maximum rate of profits: when w tends to zero the rate of profits rises without limit, tending to $+\infty$.

13. Having answered the previous exercise, assume the economy is stationary and produces one unit of whiskey as net product per year. Determine the gross output vector produced by the economy every year and the value of capital in terms of whiskey.

14. Corn is produced by seed-corn and labour. Wages are paid at the end of the year. Having fixed the technical coefficients, find the Leontief inverse, and prove that the labour embodied in a unit of corn is total employment in the subsystem producing a unit of corn as net product.

15. Study the condition under which the following *growth-modified Leontief problem* has solution: it must be possible to produce a vector of consumption goods $\mathbf{z}$, at the same time guaranteeing a uniform rate of growth $\mathbf{g}$ of inputs.

16. Corn is produced by seed-corn and labour. Wages are paid at the end of the year. Having fixed the technical coefficients, pass to the vertically integrated representation of income distribution.

17. Prove that with no technical change and no change in quantities produced, just a change in income distribution, the value of the stock of durable capital of the economy rises with r.

References

Debreu, G., & Herstein, I. N. (1953). Non-negative square matrices. *Econometrica, 21*, 597–606.

Dmitriev, V. K. (1974). The theory of value of D. Ricardo, an attempt at a rigorous analysis. In D. M. Nuti (Ed.), *Economic essays on value, competition and utility* (translation of a 1904 book in Russian), (pp. 37–95). Cambridge University Press: Cambridge. First published, 1898, in *Ekonomicheskie Ocherki*.

Garegnani, P. (1970). Heterogeneous capital, the production function and the theory of distribution. *Review of Economic Studies, 37*(3), 407–436.

Kurz, H. D., & Salvadori, N. (1995). *Theory of production: A long-period analysis*. Cambridge: Cambridge University Press.

Leontief, W. W. (1951). *The Structure of American Economy, 1919–1939* (2nd ed.). New York: OxfordUniversity Press.

Petri, F. (2016c). *Nonsubstitution Theorem, Leontief Model, Netputs: Some Clarifications*. Centro Sraffa Working Papers no. 20, Università di Roma 3.

Samuelson, P. A. (1966). A summing up. *Quarterly Journal of Economics, 80*, 568–583.

Sraffa, P. (1960). *Production of commodities by means of commodities*. Cambridge: Cambridge University Press.

Introduction to the Marginal Approach

Contents

3.1 Introduction – 156

3.2 Equilibrium and Gravitation – 157

3.3 The Labour–Land–Corn Economy: Direct (or Technological) Factor Substitutability – 159

3.3.1 Production Functions, Isoquants and Marginal Products – 159

3.3.2 Factor Demand Curves, Cost Function and Equilibrium in Factor Markets – 163

3.3.3 Importance of Factor Substitutability – 174

3.3.4 Comparative Statics – 175

3.4 The Role of Consumer Choice: The Indirect Factor Substitution Mechanism – 177

3.5 The Simultaneous Operation of Both Substitution Mechanisms, and the Importance of Highly Elastic Factor Demand Curves – 180

3.6 Money – 184

Electronic supplementary material The online version of this chapter (▶ https://doi.org/10.1007/978-3-030-62070-7_3) contains supplementary material, which is available to authorized users.

© Springer Nature Switzerland AG 2021
F. Petri, *Microeconomics for the Critical Mind*,
Classroom Companion: Economics, https://doi.org/10.1007/978-3-030-62070-7_3

3.7	**Efficiency, the Forest Exchange Economy, Choice Curves and Equilibrium in the Edgeworth Box – 185**
3.7.1	Elements of Consumer Theory: Utility Function, Indifference Curves, MRS – 185
3.7.2	Exchange Economy, Edgewort Box, Pareto Efficiency – 190
3.8	**Pareto Efficiency in the Production Economy. Marginal Cost – 196**
3.9	**Robinson Crusoe and Market Valuation as Reflecting 'Natural' Laws – 206**
3.10	**Introduction of the Rate of Interest and of Capital in the Marginalist Theory of Distribution – 209**
3.10.1	The Rate of Interest in the Exchange Economy – 209
3.10.2	The Rate of Interest in the Corn Economy – 211
3.10.3	Capital and the Indirect Factor Substitution Mechanism – 213
3.11	**Money and the Rate of Interest – 217**
3.12	**Accumulation – 218**
3.13	**A Comparison Between the Classical and the Marginal Approaches to Income Distribution: The Basic Analytical Difference and Some Implications – 219**
3.13.1	The Different Data When Determining the Rate of Return on Capital – 219
3.13.2	The Role of Social and Political Elements. Competition in Labour Markets – 222

| 3.13.3 | Exploitation? – 224 |
| 3.13.4 | Technical Progress, Relative Wages, Unequal Exchange – 226 |

3.14 Intensive Differential Rent and the Marginal Approach – 228

3.15 Final Elements of Differentiation: Supply of Capital, Say's Law – 236

3.16 Conclusion – 240

3.17 Review Questions and Exercises – 241

References – 245

156   **Chapter 3** · Introduction to the Marginal Approach

This chapter will introduce you via simple examples and models to the basic structure of the marginal/neoclassical approach to value and income distribution, both for an exchange economy and for an economy with labour, land and a single capital good as factors of production. You will become familiar with:

- isoquants, marginal products, indifference curves, choice curves, Edgeworth boxes, elasticities
- the two factor substitution mechanisms from which the marginal approach derives decreasing demand curves for factors of production
- why according to this approach a competitive economy is efficient and produces market evaluations that reflect 'natural' laws
- the main differences of the marginal from the classical approach, and their analytical roots in a generalization of the theory of intensive differential rent
- the implications of these differences for the issue whether labour is exploited, for the explanation of the different wages of different kinds of labour, and for the validity of Say's Law.

3.1 Introduction

Let us now compare the classical with the marginal (or supply-and-demand, or neoclassical) approach to value and distribution. To allow the comparison, first this chapter introduces to the fundamental structure of the marginal approach by using simple examples. The needed basic neoclassical microeconomic notions are introduced, so the reader without previous studies of microeconomic theory will be able to follow the argument. Of course more advanced formal details are omitted here and postponed to subsequent chapters, but the general marginalist/neoclassical picture of the functioning of market economies can be presented even through simple examples. After explaining the two factor substitution mechanisms that motivate the approach, the chapter illustrates the efficiency implications of the approach, introducing the Edgeworth box and the Production Possibility Frontier to reach a first proof of the First Fundamental Theorem of Welfare Economics; then it proceeds to compare the marginal with the classical approach; it ends by locating the origin of the marginal approach in a generalization of the classical theory of intensive differential rent.

The economists usually considered the founders of the marginal approach, that is Stanley Jevons, Léon Walras, Carl Menger, were all acutely conscious of the radical novelty of their approach vis-à-vis the Ricardian one. Alfred Marshall, who dominated the scene from the 1890s to the 1920s, tried to minimize the extent of the change, but nowadays it seems clear that the first three authors had got it right. The surplus approach views the capitalist economy as conflictual, unable to realize the full employment of labour except very temporarily, and, at least according to Marx, prone to crises; the income of capitalists is not the result of some productive contribution of theirs but only of their superior bargaining strength that allows them to keep wages below their potential maximum. The marginal approach, as we will see, views the capitalist economy as essentially efficient, views production as

3.1 · Introduction

characterized by cooperation between the efforts and sacrifices of the suppliers of productive services and views income distribution as obeying a criterion, 'to each according to his/her contribution to social welfare', which may need corrections but can hardly be found basically unfair. The difference is enormous.

One purpose of this chapter is to point out the analytical roots of this difference as simply as possible. These roots will be found in the thesis that the Ricardian theory of differential rent must be applied to *all* sources of income, and not only to income from property of land. It will be shown that it is from this difference that other important differences derive: for example the different conclusion as to whether labour is exploited.

3.2 Equilibrium and Gravitation

The marginal approach argues that in a market economy prices, quantities produced, and the distribution of the social product between wages, rents, interest[1] are determined by the interaction between supply and demand, which are functions of prices; this interaction—it is argued—causes the economy to gravitate toward a state of equality, or of *equilibrium*, between supply and demand for all goods and all [services of] productive factors.[2]

Equality between supply and demand in the market of a good or service is described as an *equilibrium* because demand (the presence of people who want to buy the good) is seen as a force tending to raise the price, supply (people trying to sell the good) as a force tending to reduce the price; when they are equal the two forces neutralize each other, and the price is therefore in equilibrium.

A physical analogy is a heavy object hanging by an elastic string: the weight of the object pushes it downwards, but the lower the object, the greater the upward pull exercised by the string, so the object, if disturbed, oscillates up and down until it comes to rest in a position where the downward and the upward pull are in equilibrium. In this case the physical system returns to the equilibrium when its state is perturbed, and the equilibrium is called *stable*. If the elastic string is attached to the branch of a tree, then wind causes the object to oscillate; the equilibrium indicates the average position of the object, in the proximity of which

---

1   In the marginal approach, the rate of interest takes the place that the rate of profits has in the classical approach. The meaning itself of 'profit' is modified, to indicate what is left of the firm's revenue after paying all costs *including* interest on the capital employed (and also the addition to interest necessary to cover risk, which here we neglect for simplicity); for the classical authors, on the contrary, profits are what is left *before* paying interest, they include interest; thus the marginal approach describes a situation, where the revenue of a firm is just sufficient to cover costs and interest, as a state of *zero* profits, while a classical author would describe it as profits equal to interests, i.e. rate of profit equal to rate of interest. In this chapter and the six following ones describing the marginal approach, 'profit' is used in the marginalist meaning unless otherwise specified.

2   In the marginal approach, what is actually offered and demanded is the *services* of land, labour and capital; but for simplicity one usually speaks of supply of, and demand for, land, labour and capital.

we can expect the object to be most of the time. The usefulness of the notion of equilibrium between supply and demand is similar, it indicates the average around which the day-by-day price and quantity gravitate—of course assuming the equilibrium is stable.

This stability in the case of the market of a single good, say, a local fresh shrimp market, is defended by arguing that demand (quantity demanded per unit of time, say, per week, by consumers and restaurants) is a *decreasing* function of the good's price, and supply (quantity supplied per week by fishermen) is an *increasing* function of the good's price; and that when price is such that they are not equal, the higgling and bargaining—with a lower price being proposed by sellers unable to find purchasers, and a higher price being offered by demanders unable to get the good—will cause the average price to increase if demand is greater than supply, and to decrease in the opposite case, and therefore to gravitate toward the value where supply and demand are equal, as the reader can check in ◘ Fig. 3.1 where, following the tradition imposed by Alfred Marshall, the price, which is actually the independent variable, is measured in ordinate, and the quantities demanded and supplied as functions of price are measured in abscissa.[3] (If one wants to maintain the mathematical convention that the variable in abscissa is the independent variable, then the curves are the graphical representation of the *inverse* demand function $p_d(q)$, and of the *inverse* supply function $p_s(q)$. The inverse demand function indicates, for each quantity demanded, what the price must be to cause such a level of demand; analogously for the inverse supply function.) The gravitation toward equilibrium is due to the fact that the shapes of the supply curve and of the demand curve are such that when p is above (respectively, below) the equilibrium value, supply is greater (respectively, smaller) than demand and therefore p tends to decrease (increase). The approach argues that supply-and-demand curves can be determined also for labour, land, capital, and are such as to determine stable equilibria in their respective markets.

We find here again the notion of a gravitation of market price toward a 'normal' position, extended now to the 'prices' that determine income distribution: wages, rents, rate of interest. But the determination of the 'normal' positions is different. The fundamental difference concerns the determination of income distribution, and to this we now turn.

---

3 The reference in this reasoning to some *average* price is made necessary by the fact that, during disequilibrium, not all units of the commodity will be sold at the same price.

3.2 · Equilibrium and Gravitation

3.3 The Labour–Land–Corn Economy: Direct (or Technological) Factor Substitutability

3.3.1 Production Functions, Isoquants and Marginal Products

The marginal approach calls 'factors of production' the production inputs: labour, land, capital. It argues that for these too, as for produced goods, there are supply functions and demand functions and a tendency toward an equilibrium between supply and demand.

Assume an economy where a single consumption good, corn, is produced by employing homogeneous labour and homogeneous land as factors of production. (The need for seed is neglected for the time being.) Free competition tends to establish the same price for all units of the same good or service; corn is the good in which relative prices are expressed, i.e. is the **numéraire** (modern term for the classical 'measure of value' or 'standard of value'); hence the price of a unit of corn is 1, and there are only two prices to be determined: the real rate of wages w (yearly corn wage per unit of labour time), and the real rate of rent β (yearly corn rent per unit of land).[4] The production of corn can be carried out according to a continuum of different methods, which can be represented via a continuously differentiable **production function** $q = f(L, T)$, which indicates the *maximum* quantity of corn producible in a year with the utilization of amounts L and T of [services of] labour and land.[5] Assume goods and input services are perfectly divisible; also assume the production function is characterized by **constant returns to scale**, CRS for short, defined as 'an increase of all inputs by the same percentage causes an increase of output by the same percentage', which means $f(cL, cT) = cf(L, T)$ for any real positive scalar c. Let us assume that if both inputs are positive then output is positive; then CRS implies that output can be increased indefinitely if inputs are sufficiently increased.

Let us grasp the connection between a production function and the representation of production methods through technical coefficients used in ▶ Chaps. 1 and 2. Suppose we fix the quantity to be produced at 1 unit. Each vector (L, T) such that $q = f(L, T) = 1$ is a vector of technical coefficients representing a production method of the corn industry according to the definition of ▶ Chap. 1; that is, if a_L, a_T are the technical coefficients of a production method for the production of corn as defined in ▶ Chap. 1, then $f(a_L, a_T) = 1$. If $q = f(L, T)$ is different from 1, then by dividing L and T by q we obtain quantities of labour and of land that produce 1 unit of corn and therefore are technical

---

4 The adjective 'real' is used to indicate purchasing power in terms of commodities rather than monetary value. In this economy the real rate of wages is how much corn one can buy with the monetary wage.

5 The notion of production function is generalizable to any number of inputs, but here for simplicity I assume they are only two.

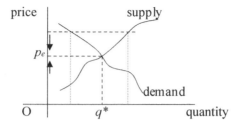

◘ **Fig. 3.1** Equilibrium quantity is q^*, and the equilibrium price is p_e. When $p > p_e$, quantity demanded is less than quantity supplied, so p decreases. Only the non-negative orthant is relevant because p and q cannot be negative

coefficients of a production method. The differentiability assumption means there is a continuum of alternative production methods.

These methods can be represented as points in the non-negative orthant of the (L, T) plane; under differentiability of the production function, these points form a curve which is called the ***unit isoquant*** of $f(L, T)$. Given a production function $q = f(L, T)$, having fixed a quantity q to be produced, the ***isoquant*** associated with q is the set of (L, T) vectors that when introduced into the production function produce q. The unit isoquant is the isoquant associated with $q = 1$. Our assumption of only two inputs allows us to represent isoquants geometrically as the projection onto the (L, T) plane of the contours (level curves) of the production function, which is a surface in R^3_+, see ◘ Fig. 3.2. A possible form of the unit isoquant is shown in ◘ Fig. 3.3, derived from the assumption of CRS plus the fundamental assumption of *decreasing partial derivatives of the production function*, which in the case of ◘ Fig. 3.3 can even become negative. The partial derivative of the production function relative to one factor, traditionally called ***marginal productivity*** or more recently ***marginal product*** of the factor, indicates—intuitively speaking and having chosen very small units to measure the quantity of the factor—the increase in corn output if the amount employed of the factor is increased by one unit while the amount employed of the other factor is kept fixed. Generally it depends on the quantities of both factors, as you can verify by considering for example the production function $q = L^{1/3} T^{2/3}$. Indicate the marginal products as $MP_L = \partial q / \partial L$, and $MP_T = \partial q / \partial T$. I assume that marginal products are positive for both factors only in the interior of the cone AOB of ◘ Fig. 3.3, and that the marginal product of a factor is a decreasing function of the amount of that factor (if the amount of the other factor is fixed), it is positive inside the AOB cone, reaches zero when the increase in the amount of the factor brings point (L, T) to touch an edge of the AOB cone and becomes negative if the factor is increased further.

This traditional assumption of *diminishing returns to increases of only one factor* is not arbitrary, because as noted by Sraffa ([1925: 288]; 1998: 332).

» diminishing returns must of necessity occur because it will be the producer himself who, for his own benefit, will arrange the doses of the factors and the methods of

3.3 · The Labour–Land–Corn Economy: Direct (or Technological) ...

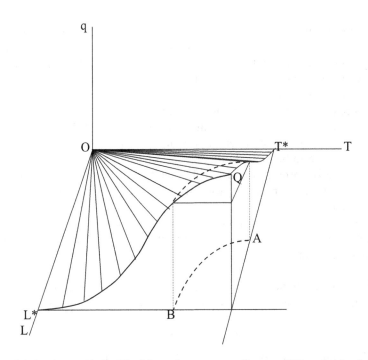

■ **Fig. 3.2** Portion for $L \leq L^*$, $T \leq T^*$ of the surface corresponding to a CRS production function $q = f(L, T)$ such that one marginal product is negative when (L, T) is outside the AOB cone. One isoquant (projection on the (L, T) plane of a contour of the surface) is shown as the broken AB curve. The L*Q curve is the *total productivity curve* of land (for T from zero to T^*) for $L = L^*$; this notion is defined in ▶ Sect. 3.3.2

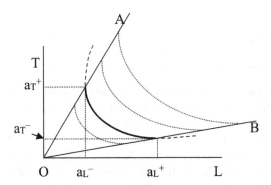

■ **Fig. 3.3** Unit isoquant (the thick curve) of corn production function with labour and land as factors; some other isoquants are also shown, assuming constant returns to scale. AOB is the cone inside which isoquants are decreasing curves, indicating that marginal products are both positive

use in descending order, going from the most favourable ones to the most ineffective, and he will start production with the best combinations, resorting little by little, as these are exhausted, to the worst ones.

The assumption that, at least after a certain point, MP_L decreases if T is fixed is inevitable: it is inconceivable that additional units of labour on a given amount of land produce the same addition to corn output indefinitely, unless land is not actually necessary for the production of corn. The assumption, that the marginal product of a factor becomes zero *and then negative* for sufficient increases of its amount, is realistic too: imagine a given land field, and visualize more and more labourers employed on it; when labourers are few they will be employed on the most useful tasks; as the number of available labourers increases, less and less useful tasks remain to be carried out; at a certain point an extra labourer becomes useless as there is nothing useful left for her to do; further labourers will even damage production by trampling too much on the field, it will be better not to employ them at all.

CRS implies that marginal products depend only on the *proportion* or *ratio* in which factors are employed, that is, do not change if both factors are increased by the same percentage.

Proof A CRS production function $f(x_1, \ldots, x_n)$ is a *homogeneous function of degree* 1, because it satisfies the definition of homogeneous functions

$$f(tx_1, \ldots, tx_n) = t^k f(x_1, \ldots, x_n) \, \textit{for any} \, t > 0$$

with k, the degree of homogeneity of the function, equal to 1. For differentiable homogeneous functions of degree k *the partial derivatives are themselves homogeneous functions, but of degree* $k - 1$. To show it, differentiate both sides of $f(tx_1, \ldots, tx_n) = t^k f(x_1, \ldots, x_n)$ with respect to any x_i, e.g. to x_1, to obtain

$$t \frac{\partial f(tx_1, \ldots, tx_n)}{\partial (tx_1)} = t^k \frac{\partial f(x_1, \ldots, x_n)}{\partial x_1}$$

and divide both sides by t. Since $k = 1$, the partial derivatives—the marginal products—are homogeneous of degree zero, i.e. are unaffected by multiplication of all inputs by the same scalar t, so they depend only on the *ratios* among the x_i's. ∎

This result plus the assumption of decreasing marginal products implies that for example MP_L is a decreasing function of L/T and decreases when L increases with T fixed, or when T decreases with L fixed. Now the form of the unit isoquant in ◨ Fig. 3.3 is easy to understand. If along it L is increased and we are inside the AOB cone, T must decrease otherwise q would increase because $MP_L > 0$; so inside the AOB cone the isoquant is decreasing. (Outside the cone, it is increasing because the marginal product of one factor is negative.) Inside the AOB cone, the isoquant is convex because its slope is the derivative of the function $T(L)$ implicitly defined by the condition $f(L, T) - 1 = 0$, and by the rule of derivation of implicit functions this derivative is $-(\partial f/\partial L)/(\partial f/\partial T) = -MP_L/MP_T$, where MP_L decreases and MP_T increases as T/L decreases as we move rightwards along the unit isoquant. This slope becomes zero when MP_L becomes zero as the unit isoquant reaches the lower edge of the AOB cone, and infinite as MP_T becomes zero at the upper edge of the cone.

3.3 · The Labour–Land–Corn Economy: Direct (or Technological) …

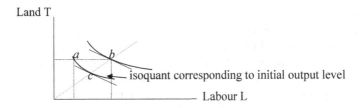

◘ **Fig. 3.4** With CRS, along a ray from the origin all isoquants have the same TRS

Also, all isoquants are radial expansions or contractions of the unit isoquant. The slope of an isoquant, constant along a ray from the origin, is called the ***technical rate of substitution*** between inputs, $TRS_{L,T}$; it indicates the decrease of T needed to keep q unchanged if L is increased by one unit; it is a negative quantity (if both marginal products are positive), but often economists use the same term to refer to its absolute value, MP_L/MP_T. Along a ray from the origin, TRS is constant (◘ Fig. 3.4).

3.3.2 Factor Demand Curves, Cost Function and Equilibrium in Factor Markets

Now let us proceed to study the determination of a simultaneous equilibrium in the three markets of this economy: the labour market, the land market and the corn market. Labour is all of the same quality, land too.

For simplicity assume that the aggregate supply of labour to firms, call it L^*, is rigid, that the same holds for the supply of land T^*, and that there are no savings: the income of a period is entirely spent on the product of that period.

Production is carried out by firms. The person who sets up a firm and owns the residual profits, if any, after factors have been paid, is called an *entrepreneur*.[6] The entrepreneur is not a factor of production, she/he is only the owner of the firm, who decides whether to set up the firm or close it down; if she also works in it, one separates logically the role as entrepreneur from the role as labourer (possibly as manager); as labourer, the person gets a wage; as entrepreneur, the profits.

For equilibrium to obtain, the supply of factors must be absorbed by the demand for factors. The assumption that the income of a period is entirely spent on the product of that period *guarantees equilibrium in the corn market*: by definition, the aggregate *income* per period of this economy is the value of aggregate corn production, which is distributed to some consumer or other as wages, as rents and as profits (possibly negative for some firms). Since this income is by assumption all spent in the purchase of the product, supply of corn and demand for corn

---

6   In this economy where there is no capital, profit is defined as revenue minus payments to labour and to land. It is the marginalist definition of profit applied to an economy where the sole factors are labour and land.

164   Chapter 3 · Introduction to the Marginal Approach

are necessarily equal whatever the level of factor employment and of corn production and whichever the rate of wages and the rate of rent. What remains to be studied is the forces acting in the labour market and in the land market.

Assume initially that landlords (the owners of land) and workers are two separate groups of people, and furthermore that the landlords act as entrepreneurs, each one setting up a firm with his own land and hired wage labour. Then equality between supply and demand for land is guaranteed; the sole market where equilibrium between supply and demand must be reached by price adjustment is the labour market.

For each firm, land supply is given, it is the entrepreneur's own land $T°$; the sole decision is how much labour to employ. The economy, let us assume, is competitive: there is no collusion, and firms are many and small, too small relevantly to influence prices and therefore *price-takers*, that is, treating prices as given parameters in their decisions. For each given corn wage w, each entrepreneur tries to maximize the income remaining after paying the labour employed, hence, with L representing the firm's *demand* for labour, each landlord solves

$$max_L f\left(L, T°\right) - wL.$$

The solution $L°$ requires, as first-order condition for a maximum,

$$MP_L - w = 0,$$

that is, *equality between the marginal product of labour and the given corn wage*. As long as $MP_L > w$, one more unit of labour adds to production more than to costs and therefore increases the income remaining to the landlord; as further units of labour are employed, the marginal product of labour decreases, until a point is reached when one more unit of labour would add to production less than its rental, and it is not hired.[7] If we reason in terms of *monetary* magnitudes, with p the given money price of corn and w_m the given *money* wage, the revenue to be maximized is the monetary one, $p \cdot f\left(L, T°\right) - w_m L$, the optimal employment of labour is the same.

Draw the curve representing MP_L (in ordinate) as a function of the amount of labour employed by the firm. This curve will have an initial horizontal segment, for the following reason. The marginal product of land becomes negative if $T°/L$ rises so much as to become greater than a_T^+/a_L^-, which will be certainly the case for L sufficiently close to zero. So for L very small it is better for the landlord to use only the amount of his land that has zero marginal product, leaving the rest unutilized. This corresponds to the T/L ratio along the OA ray in

---

7   In this book I will use the term 'factor *rental*' as the general short-hand term to indicate the price of one unit of *the service* of a factor, i.e. the rental rate, the price of *hiring* the factor for one period. Rental *rate* would be more correct, but for brevity I will simply say 'rental'. The rental of labour is the wage per unit of labour service. Most other textbooks use the term 'factor *price*' in the same sense (i.e. actually meaning 'price of the services of the factor'), but this creates confusion when one can purchase the factor itself: for example in common parlance 'price of land' means the purchase price, not the rental rate, of land.

3.3 · The Labour–Land–Corn Economy: Direct (or Technological) …

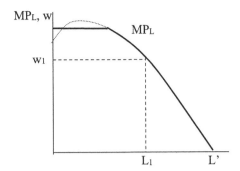

Fig. 3.5 Marginal product of labour as the landlord's demand curve for labour

Fig. 3.3. This T/L ratio maximizes the ***average productivity of labour*** (= output per unit of labour), because, for each given L, output is maximized when land use is increased up to the point where $MP_T = 0$. If L is so small that it is better to leave some land unused, output is L times the maximum average productivity of labour, and as L increases the marginal product of labour is constant and equal to the maximum average productivity of labour because the increase in labour is accompanied by an increase of actually utilized land. So initially the MP_L curve is horizontal: its height measures the maximum average productivity of labour. Of course as L increases from zero and actually utilized land increases in step, at a certain point land becomes fully utilized; from that point on, further increases of L cause reductions of MP_L, the MP_L curve becomes downward-sloping.

Measure w in ordinate in **Fig. 3.5**; for each level of w less than the maximum average productivity of labour, the $w = MP_L$ condition determines how much labour is demanded by the firm, e.g. when $w = w_1$ labour demand is L_1. The decreasing portion of the MP_L curve is the firm's demand-for-labour curve. As w decreases, the demand for labour by the firm increases. Given w, the optimal labour employment determines how much corn is produced; labour gets $MP_L \cdot L$, the landlord-entrepreneur gets the residual, $f(L, T^\circ) - MP_L \cdot L$. The total demand for labour is the sum of the demands for labour of the several landlords.

Suppose that learning and imitative processes cause firms to converge to a similar level of efficiency, i.e. all firms adopt the same CRS production function. This means that, if w is given, all firms want to reach the same MP_L, and therefore *all firms adopt the same T/L ratio*.[8] It is actually more convenient now to refer to the L/T ratio, the employment of labour per unit of land, indicating it for brevity as μ; let $\mu(w)$ be the ratio L/T that renders $MP_L = w$. Then if total land employment is T^*, the total demand for labour is $T^* \cdot \mu(w)$. Example: if all firms desire to employ 7 units of labour per unit of land, and in the aggregate they employ 100 units of land, the demand for labour is 700.

---

8 The relationship between factor proportion and marginal products is one-to-one and therefore invertible, a given MP_L determines the T/L ratio univocally.

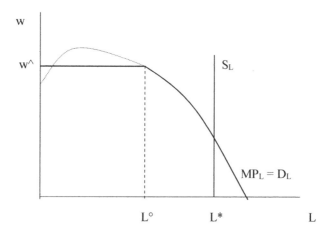

◘ Fig. 3.6 Aggregate labour demand curve and supply curve

Since, for each given w, $\mu(w)$ is the same in all firms, firm size is irrelevant to the determination of *total* labour demand: if land supply is 100 units and is fully utilized, it is irrelevant whether these 100 units are distributed among 100 identical firms each one demanding 7 units of labour, or among 10 identical firms each one demanding 70 units of labour, or in any other way. So we can determine the total demand for labour as if coming from a hypothetical single firm that employs the entire supply of land and has the same CRS production function $Q=f(L, T)$ as each firm, with Q now instead of q to indicate *aggregate* output, and L and T indicating total factor uses. The curve of the marginal product of labour of this mega-firm when land is fully utilized is the *economy-wide marginal product of labour curve*, and it coincides with the (inverse) total demand curve for labour, cf. ◘ Fig. 3.6. The initial horizontal section of this labour demand curve has been explained already, the dotted curve that crosses it indicates the marginal product of labour if *all* land is utilized even when L is very low, as I proceed to explain.

Textbooks generally prefer to assume that marginal products are always positive. This is very unrealistic, as noted above. Clearly the general case is that the marginal product of a factor becomes zero *and then negative* if the proportion in which it is combined with other factors increases too much. It is then convenient to leave part of the factor availability unutilized. Then it is useful to distinguish between *technological* and *economically relevant* isoquants and marginal products.

Define the **total productivity curve of a factor** for a given quantity utilized of the other factor as the curve that shows output of the firm as a function of the quantity employed of the first factor. If the given quantity of the second factor is fully utilized and marginal products can become negative, the curve has the S-like shape shown in ◘ Fig. 3.7b. Assume the firm's CRS production function generates isoquants as in ◘ Fig. 3.3, because as T/L increases MP_L increases and MP_T decreases, and marginal products remain both positive only for T/L internal to an interval, outside which the factor that has become relatively abundant has

3.3 · The Labour–Land–Corn Economy: Direct (or Technological) ...

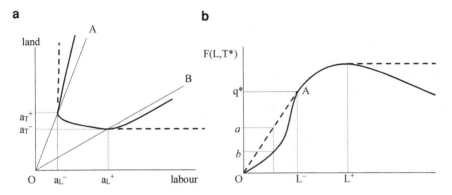

◘ **Fig. 3.7 a** Isoquant when marginal products can become negative. **b** Total productivity curve of labour

negative marginal product. Assume the firm fully utilizes a fixed quantity $T°$ of land. Let $T°/L^+$ be the factor ratio *below* which (that is, if L increases further) the marginal product of labour is negative. Then the total productivity curve of labour reaches a maximum at L^+: further increases of L cause output to decrease. Now let $T°/L^-$ be the factor ratio *above* which the marginal product of land is negative. This ratio can be surpassed by maintaining $T°$ fixed and decreasing L below L^-. This causes the S-like initial shape of the curve. Starting from L^+ let labour employment *de*crease: the ratio $T°/L$ increases, hence MP_T decreases and becomes zero at L^-, and negative if L is reduced below L^-. Now note that if, starting from $(L^-, T°)$ the firm reduces L and T in the *same* proportion, by CRS output decreases in the same proportion, that is, along the straight segment OA, leaving *average* labour productivity (output per unit of labour) unaltered. If on the contrary L is reduced below L^- but $T°$ is fully utilized, production decreases by more, because land has a negative marginal product, that is, leaving some units of land unutilized would allow output to be greater: e.g. production is b when L is one half of L^-, instead of a if actually utilized land is reduced in proportion with L. Therefore for L less than L^- we must distinguish the *technological* total productivity curve of labour, that indicates output if land $T°$ is fully utilized and has the S-like shape, from the *economically relevant* curve, that indicates output if for each L the entrepreneur chooses to use only the most convenient amount of land (the amount that maximizes output, i.e. that renders $MP_T=0$), and is the straight OA line. For $0 < L < L^-$ the marginal product of L if land is fully utilized is the slope of the technological total productivity curve and has the shape of the dotted curve in ◘ Fig. 3.6. The economically relevant marginal product of L is instead constant in that interval and equal to the maximum average product of labour; the definition of production function as indicating the *maximum* output obtainable from each vector of inputs implies that it must yield the economically relevant, and not the technological, marginal product of factors. Analogously, one must distinguish *technological* isoquants, based on full utilization of input availability, that can become upward-sloping (requiring an increase of

168 Chapter 3 · Introduction to the Marginal Approach

both factors to keep output constant because one of the factors has negative marginal product), from *economically relevant* isoquants, that keep marginal products non-negative by leaving one factor partially idle when its full utilization would make its marginal product negative, and therefore continue horizontally or vertically outside cone AOB (the broken straight lines in ◘ Fig. 3.7a).

Now draw in the same ◘ Fig. 3.6 the aggregate (inverse) labour supply curve, by assumption vertical at L^*. There is a single intersection of the two curves: the equilibrium wage w_e is unique.[9] Furthermore, when $w > w_e$ labour demand is smaller than labour supply, i.e. there is unemployment, and if the unemployed offer to work for a lower wage rather than go without a job, then w tends to fall; conversely when $w < w_e$ demand is greater than supply, and if the entrepreneurs who are unable to get the desired quantity of labour compete for workers by raising the wage they offer, then w tends to rise. Thus the competitive equilibrium is not only unique, it is also *stable* (there is tendency to reach it) if competition is allowed freely to operate.

Let us then assume the economy reaches the equilibrium aggregate output Q^* corresponding to the full employment of land T^* and of labour L^*. The equilibrium wage equals the full-employment marginal product of labour $MP_L^* = MP_L(L^*/T^*)$. The income of landlords is determined residually, it is

$$\text{landlords' equilibrium total income} = Q^* - MP_L^* \cdot L^* = f(L^*, T^*) - MP_L^* \cdot L^*. \quad (3.1)$$

Now, another important mathematical property of CRS differentiable production functions is the following:

▪▪ Product Exhaustion Theorem
If a differentiable production function has constant returns to scale (i.e. is homogeneous of degree one), then the payment to each factor of its physical marginal product exhausts (i.e. adds up to) the product.

It is proved in footnote.[10] Applied to our case:

$$f(L, T) = MP_L \cdot L + MP_T \cdot T. \quad (3.2)$$

---

9 It is possible that there be *no* intersection in the *positive* quadrant: labour demand might be less than supply even for $w = 0$; but even in this case the equilibrium wage exists and is uniquely determined as equal to zero. Note that a market where supply is greater than demand and price is zero is also considered in equilibrium, because the price has no incentive to change (it cannot become negative!).

10 This result is an immediate corollary of the *Euler theorem for homogeneous functions*, that states:
if $f(tx_1, \ldots tx_n) = t^k f(x_1, \ldots, x_n)$, then $\Sigma_i (x_i \cdot \partial f/\partial x_i) = kf(x_1, \ldots, x_n)$.
Proof Differentiating both sides of $f(tx_1, \ldots, tx_n) = t^k f(x_1, \ldots, x_n)$ with respect to t (applying the total derivative rule on the left-hand side) one obtains $\sum_{i=1}^{n} \left(\frac{\partial f(tx)}{\partial (tx_i)} \cdot x_i \right) = kt^{k-1} f(x)$ where $x = (x_1, \ldots, x_n)$; this must hold also for $t = 1$, in which case one obtains $\Sigma_i (x_i \cdot \partial f/\partial x_i) = kf(x)$. In our case $k = 1$, so if each factor is paid its physical marginal product, the sum of the payments equals the product.

3.3 · The Labour–Land–Corn Economy: Direct (or Technological) …

So if one factor is paid its marginal product, what is left of the product is just what the other factor would get if paid its marginal product. Applied to full-employment production, this means $Q^* = MP_L^* \cdot L^* + MP_T^* \cdot T^*$. The residual income accruing to landlords is what their land would receive as rent if it was paid its marginal product.

This means that *the equilibrium is not affected if the role of entrepreneurs is taken by someone else*, the labourers for example, or a third party hiring both labour and land. If labourers act as entrepreneurs (e.g. grouped in cooperatives), and hire land, then the land market is the sole market where equilibrium needs to be brought about by a price, now the rate of rent β. One obtains an aggregate demand curve for land coinciding with the marginal product of land in the economy as a whole, and equilibrium obtains when the rent rate β equals the full-employment marginal product of land, $\beta = \partial f(L^*, T^*)/\partial T = MP_T^*$. Landlords earn the same as when they are entrepreneurs; and workers too, because their residual income is $Q^* - MP_T^* \cdot T^* = MP_L^* \cdot L^*$. All factors tend to earn their full-employment marginal product independently of who acts as entrepreneur.

If entrepreneurs are a third party, hiring both labour and land, the analysis brings to the same result but is somewhat more complex because entrepreneurs must decide how much to employ of both factors, and it is now possible that there is unemployment of both factors.

Now the entrepreneur's profit is revenue minus both wages and rent. It is best now to visualize the entrepreneur as price-taker and facing a given money price p for corn, and given money rentals w_m for labour and β_m for land. The entrepreneur's decision as to how much to employ of the two factors in order to maximize profit can be usefully decomposed into two steps. First, for each given quantity of output q, the entrepreneur can ascertain whether profit is positive or negative by minimizing the cost of producing q and comparing it with the revenue pq that q yields. Second, the entrepreneur will expand or contract q if that increases profit. If the entrepreneur employs the vector (L, T) of inputs the cost is $w_m L + \beta_m T$; cost minimization requires finding the least costly vector of inputs that allows to produce q; profit is revenue pq minus the minimum cost required to produce q, let us indicate it as $C(q; w_m, \beta_m)$, below I discuss how to determine it. Because of CRS, doubling inputs doubles output, hence if a given q affords a positive profit because $pq > C(q; w_m, \beta_m)$, then doubling inputs and q doubles profit; the entrepreneur finds it convenient to increase output. The same holds for all entrepreneurs since they face the same technology and the same prices, and the result is an increase of demand for both factors; sooner or later one factor becomes fully employed, and then the demand function for the *other* factor is downward-sloping (as for the demand for labour when landlords are entrepreneurs); the rental of this still partly unemployed second factor decreases because of competition, demand for it increases, and a full-employment equilibrium is reached in its market too (in the meanwhile the first factor remains fully employed because its marginal product is raised by the gradually increasing employment of the second factor, this raises the demand for the first factor, which therefore remains fully employed while its rental tends to increase). If on the contrary profit at the given initial q, p, w_m and β_m is negative, then the entrepreneur decreases output,

170 Chapter 3 · Introduction to the Marginal Approach

the same holds for all entrepreneurs, demand for both labour and land decreases, both factors become partly unemployed, then both money rentals decrease, this reduces cost, profit becomes positive, and then the previously described expansion process starts, and as shown it will bring to full employment on both factor markets.

The adjustment I have described includes a variation of the demand for both factors when profit is not zero, and a variation of the *proportion* in which firms combine labour and land if the initial proportion does not permit the simultaneous full employment of both factors. Indeed when one factor becomes fully employed and the rental of the second factor, still partly unemployed, decreases and its demand increases, this is because the change in the relative price of the two factors entails a modification of the proportion in which firms wish to combine the factors, in favour of the factor which is becoming cheaper. This causes the proportion to be modified until it becomes compatible with the simultaneous full employment of both factors. This modification is called **the mechanism of direct or technological factor substitution**. In order to grasp it, we must understand cost minimization.

We have defined the **cost** $C(q; w_m, \beta_m)$ associated with given monetary factor rentals w_m and β_m and given output q as the minimum cost $w_m L + \beta_m T$ required to produce output q. It is the solution of:

$$\underset{L,T}{minimize}\, w_m L + \beta_m T \,.subject\, to f(L,T) = q.$$

This minimization determines the cost-minimizing vector (L, T). The Lagrangian is

$$L = w_m L + \beta_m T + \lambda[q - f(L,T)]$$

and the first-order conditions imply (confirm it!):

$$TRS = -w_m/\beta_m.$$

The meaning of this condition can be illustrated graphically by introducing the notion of **isocost**. Given the factor rentals, an isocost is the locus of all points in the non-negative orthant of the (L, T) plane that represent vectors (L, T) causing a same given cost. All the vectors of an isocost satisfy $w_m L + \beta_m T = C$ for the same C. Hence for each C the corresponding isocost is the function $T=(C-w_m L)/\beta_m$, a straight line with slope $-w_m/\beta_m = -w/\beta$ and intercepts C/w_m in abscissa and C/β_m in ordinate.[11] By changing C, one obtains a *map of parallel isocosts* which are the closer to the origin the smaller is C. The firm compares the isoquant associated with the given q with the map of isocosts and minimizes cost by choosing the point on the isoquant through which passes the isocost closest

---

11 Defining $w = w_m/p$ and $\beta = \beta_m/p$ as the *real* factor rentals, the ratio between money rentals is equal to the ratio between real rentals.

3.3 · The Labour–Land–Corn Economy: Direct (or Technological) …

to the origin. If the isoquant is smoothly strictly convex as we have assumed, an internal solution to cost minimization implies *tangency between isoquant and isocost*.[12] That is, $TRS = -w_m/\beta_m$, which can be written:

$$MP_L/MP_T = w_m/\beta_m. \tag{3.3}$$

In order to understand whether firms wish to expand or to contract at the given prices all we need is **average cost**, that is cost per unit of output, which is the minimum total cost to produce a given q, divided by q. Because of CRS, average cost is independent of q; if it is less than p, firms wish to expand, demand for the factors increases; if it is greater than p, firms make losses, factor demand decreases. The marginalist argument is that, if entrepreneurs are a third party, it is possible that neither factor is fully employed, but then sooner or later factor unemployment reduces factor rentals enough to cause average cost to go below p, then demand for both factors increases, sooner or later one factor becomes fully employed, and then *changes in relative factor rentals change the proportion in which firms wish to employ the factors* until both factors can be fully employed.

This change in proportions is shown in ◘ Fig. 3.8a, where if land rent decreases relative to real wages, then w/β rises, isocosts become steeper, and the tangency point shifts to the left along the given isoquant (and then along *any* isoquant, since they are all radial expansions or contractions of any one of them): that is, it is convenient to use more land and less labour to produce any given q; there is some *substitution* of land to labour in the production of q.

Behind the increase in labour demand when land is fully employed and the real wage decreases there is precisely this change in cost-minimizing factor proportions, i.e. some substitution of labour to land, only instead of taking q as given it is the quantity of land that is kept fixed, be it because the landlords are the entrepreneurs, or because entrepreneurs try to expand the employment of both factors and hit against the full employment of land first. The effect is shown in ◘ Fig. 3.8b. The relative factor rentals determine the cost-minimizing T/L and hence a ray from the origin in the (L, T) plane along which the given land employment determines the associated demand for labour; the given land employment determines point α when the ray is OA, point β when the ray becomes OB because labour has become cheaper relative to land and all isocosts have become less steep.

The only thing still to be clarified is how changes in the real wage affect relative factor rentals: the real wage does not determine relative factor rentals until we associate with it a univocally determined real land rent; is this univocal determination possible? The answer is yes, because when the real wage decreases and entrepreneurs demand labour up to equality between real wage and marginal

---

12 An *internal* solution is one in which both L and T are positive; a non-internal solution, that requires that only one factor be used, also called a 'corner solution', is possible but I neglect this case for the moment.

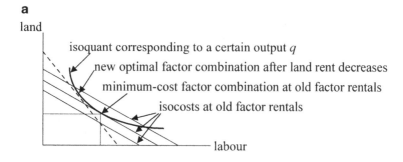

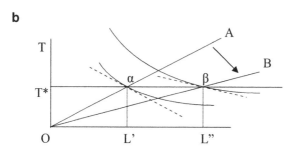

Fig. 3.8 a Tangency between isoquant and isocost as solution to cost minimization. b Factor substitution as labour becomes cheaper and land is given

product of labour, land rent must become such as to make entrepreneurs satisfied with employing the given amount of land; therefore land rent must be assumed equal to the marginal product of the given land corresponding to the labour employment that makes the marginal product of labour equal to the given real wage.

This last sentence was perhaps not so easy to absorb so here is a simple numerical example. Suppose corn is produced according to the production function $q = L^{1/3}T^{2/3}$; then $MP_L = 1/3 \cdot (T/L)^{2/3}$, $MP_T = 2/3 \cdot (L/T)^{1/3}$. Assume $T=1$, and that the real wage in terms of corn is $w=3$. This implies firms will employ labour and land in the proportion T/L such that $(T/L)^{2/3} = 9$, therefore $T/L = 27$, $L = L/T = 1/27$, $MP_T = 2/9$, so it must be $\beta = 2/9$. (With CRS and decreasing marginal products, the marginal product of one factor univocally determines the factor proportion and therefore also the marginal product of the second factor.)

Let us confirm that in equilibrium profit is maximized, hence entrepreneurs have no incentive to alter their decisions. The single entrepreneur can change both the labour and the land her firm employs, hence L and T must be chosen to maximize profit π which is given by

$$\pi = pf(L,T) - w_m L - \beta_m T.$$

The first-order conditions are

$$MP_L = w_m/p, \quad MP_T = \beta_m/p. \tag{3.4}$$

3.3 · The Labour–Land–Corn Economy: Direct (or Technological) …

These two conditions imply (3.3) but the latter alone does not imply them; it permits nonzero profits, but in that case there is expansion or contraction of factor demands, and factor rentals vary until real rentals equal respective marginal products. The thing that interests us now is that when the three prices p, w_m, β_m are such that conditions (3.4) *can be* simultaneously satisfied and *are* satisfied, then profit is indeed maximized: changes of q do not increase profit, which remains zero, so optimal q is indeterminate for the single entrepreneur (not for the economy, total q must be such that factor rentals do not change, i.e. must be associated with equilibrium in factor markets), but whatever q happens to be the entrepreneur has no incentive to change it, the condition of absence of incentives to change choices is satisfied.[13] (This zero-profit case is the only one where profit maximization is achieved, if the three prices p, w_m, β_m are such that profit is positive then there is no q that maximizes profit, by increasing q the entrepreneur increases profit indefinitely. But precisely the tendency to increase q will raise factor rentals until profit becomes zero.) The approach concludes that there is tendency toward an equilibrium in which all factor supplies are employed, each factor earns its full-employment marginal product independently of who acts as entrepreneur, and entrepreneurs as such make 'neither profit nor loss, *ni profit ni perte*', as Walras put it.[14]

The reader may find surprising that in this approach the role of entrepreneur yields nothing, in competitive equilibrium. But this derives from the fact that, as shown by the production function, entrepreneurial activity does not contribute to *production*. Clever entrepreneurs can earn profit in disequilibrium by adjusting faster than the others and exploiting opportunities for profit before the market adjustments wipe those opportunities out; but in equilibrium they only have the

---

13 (Readers unfamiliar with the notions presented in this footnote can skip it and wait for the explanation in ▶ Chap. 5.) No serious complication arises for the theory if one assumes that the production function of individual firms does not exhibit CRS but instead what, in Marshallian theory, is called a U-shaped long-period average cost curve. The idea then is that firms have an optimal size, beyond which they become less efficient because of difficulties with coordinating and supervising their workers' activities when production is on a large scale. Therefore firms tend toward a definite size, the one that minimizes average cost. Entry pushes the product price to equal this minimum average cost; total production will vary through variation in the *number* of identical firms, all of optimal size: as long as this optimal size is small relative to total demand one can assume competition and price taking, and then it is again as if *the industry*'s production (the whole economy's production, in our example where there is only one industry) came from a single giant CRS firm, because total inputs will change in the same proportion as total output, although now through variation *in the number of firms*. At the quantity where a firm minimizes average cost, it can be shown (see ▶ Chap. 5) that there are *locally constant* returns to scale, so the product exhaustion theorem applies, optimal factor employment is associated with zero profits (marginalist definition), and in equilibrium factors earn their full-employment marginal products. The total demand curve for labour can then be derived as before, as coinciding with the curve of the economy-wide marginal product of labour.

14 Equilibrium only determines the equilibrium *ratios* between the three money prices, another theory will be necessary to determine the *price level,* i.e. their monetary values, for example the quantity theory of money, see ▶ Sect. 3.6.

174 Chapter 3 · Introduction to the Marginal Approach

legal role of owners of the firm, a passive role requiring no special skills, hence not suffering from scarcity.[15] If, besides being the owners, they also work as managers/supervisors, then the entrepreneurs are contributing some labour to the production process and then will receive a salary for that labour, determined by supply and demand for that type of labour (For simplicity I have assumed only two factors but the theory can easily accommodate more than two factors and can thus distinguish different types of labour, or of land).

That entrepreneurs as such earn nothing in equilibrium is actually lucky for the theory. Let us see why. Suppose the product exhaustion theorem does not hold and that

$$F(L, T) > MP_L \cdot L + MP_T T.$$

Then the residual income of landlords-entrepreneurs is greater than the marginal product of their land, $F(L, T) - MP_L \cdot L > MP_T \cdot T$, and landlords will prefer to act as entrepreneurs rather than to rent out their land to others and earn its marginal product; but the same preference for acting as entrepreneurs holds for labourers, who by organizing in cooperatives and renting land can earn a residual income $F(L, T) - MP_T \cdot T > MP_L \cdot L$; so everybody wants to act as entrepreneur, nobody wants to supply their factors to others, and production cannot start. Conversely, suppose that

$$F(L, T) < MP_L \cdot L + MP_T \cdot T.$$

Then no factor owner wants to act as entrepreneur because she would earn less than by supplying her factor to other firms and earning its marginal product; and no third party wants to act as entrepreneur because she would incur losses; so again production cannot start.

3.3.3 Importance of Factor Substitutability

The tendency toward equilibrium simultaneously on both factor markets crucially relies on the fact that, if the amount employed of one factor is given, the demand curve for the other factor is *decreasing*. We have seen that this is a manifestation of the fact that the *proportion L/T* in which firms desire to use the two factors increases if labour becomes less expensive relative to land. If T is given, this means more demand for labour.

The variability of the proportion L/T means that one can *substitute* to some extent a factor with the other in the production of a certain output. Thus in this economy the reason for the existence of decreasing demand curves for factors is the existence of ***direct, or technological, factor substitutability***. Let us clarify its importance by showing the effects of its absence.

---

15 As Wicksell noted, if the entrepreneur 'could obtain a share of the product merely in his capacity of entrepreneur (a share not based on either labour nor land) then it might be thought that everybody would rush to obtain such an easily earned income' (Wicksell, *Lectures* vol. I, 1934, p. 126).

Suppose there is no substitutability between labour and land: only one fixed-coefficients method is known for the production of corn, which requires the use of 8 units of labour and 4 units of land per unit of output, i.e. the use of the proportion $L/T=2$. If the ratio between labour supply and land supply L^*/T^* is greater than 2, some labour is inevitably unemployed and if as long as there is labour unemployment the wage rate decreases, since we have assumed a *given* labour supply the equilibrium wage rate can only be zero and land rent absorbs the entire product. If $L^*/T^*<2$, land is necessarily partly unemployed and β falls to zero while wages rise to absorb the entire product. If $L^*/T^*=2$, the full employment of one factor entails the full employment of the other too, but income distribution is indeterminate; and the situation would in all likelihood not last, any change in population would destroy the equality. The thesis, that income distribution is determined by the tendency toward equality between supply and demand for each factor, becomes implausible: it would entail that generally one factor obtains a zero rental, against observation.

3.3.4 Comparative Statics

Comparative statics is the study of how changes in the data of equilibrium change the equilibrium. In the assumed labour–land–corn economy, the data are the known production methods (the production function), and the rigid factor supplies. For example, suppose migration alters the supply of labour. The marginal/neoclassical approach argues that the real wage will tend to the new equilibrium wage, at the new intersection of the shifted supply curve with the unchanged demand curve. Thus, if in ◘ Fig. 3.9 the supply of labour is initially L_1 and then owing to emigration it decreases to L_2, the real wage will gravitate toward the new higher equilibrium level w_2.

Another important example of comparative statics is the study of the effects of a real wage imposed by non-competitive forces, e.g. by legislation or by the bargaining strength of trade unions. If the real wage is given, firms will only demand the amount of labour which renders the marginal product of labour equal to that real wage. Thus if, again in ◘ Fig. 3.9, the supply of labour is L_1 and the real wage is rigid at the level w_2, the demand for labour will be L_2, and

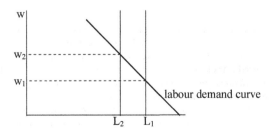

◘ **Fig. 3.9** Because the demand curve is downward-sloping, a decrease of labour supply raises the equilibrium wage

the amount of labour (L_1-L_2) will remain unemployed. If the real wage is left free to decrease, and at the given real wage the unemployed workers prefer to work rather than remain unemployed, then—marginalist economists argue—they will also be ready to work for a slightly lower wage, and then free competition will lower the wage, until the full employment of labour is reached.

Hence two conclusions, typical of the marginal approach:

- if there is labour unemployment in excess of the ineliminable frictional unemployment([16]), the cure consists of letting competition operate freely, bringing about a decrease of the real wage;
- unemployment might be only apparent, in that the workers registered as unemployed might in fact be hoping for job offers at a higher wage than the ruling one and might not be ready to work at the ruling wage (nor, of course, at a slightly lower one): in this case they are *voluntarily* unemployed, they are freely deciding not to supply their labour at the current or at a slightly lower real wage, and the labour market is then actually in equilibrium; if unemployment is involuntary and persistent, the responsibility must lie with what prevents the wage from decreasing: either trade unions (but then, ultimately, the workers' support of trade unions), or minimum-wage legislation (but then, ultimately, the workers' support for the political parties that have implemented that legislation). Hence the conclusion that it is the workers themselves who are collectively responsible for labour unemployment (in excess of frictional unemployment).

Note an implication of the above analysis of the effect of a real wage fixed above its equilibrium level. The output market is in equilibrium as explained in ▶ Sect. 3.3.2. The land market is in equilibrium too, and the labour demand curve is derived precisely under this assumption. Only one market is in disequilibrium, the labour market.

More experienced readers familiar with Walras' Law will perhaps protest that there must be a mistake somewhere in the argument, because Walras' Law implies that if prices are all positive and all markets but one are in equilibrium, then the last market is in equilibrium too; that is, either all markets are in equilibrium, or at least two markets are in disequilibrium. For these readers (the other ones will wait for the discussion of this Law in ▶ Chap. 5) I anticipate that there is no

---

16 In any concrete economy, there are continuous changes in the composition of demand, in technology, etc., and these entail closures of firms, geographical dislocations of firms, etc., and thus firings. Once some workers are fired, some time is necessary for them to find a new job; time is also needed for firms which need extra labourers to get applicants and to choose among them; hence the inevitability of some *frictional unemployment* even at the equilibrium wage, together with unfilled vacancies in firms; frictional in the sense that, if some mechanism existed for making the matching of vacancies with workers looking for a job extremely fast, at the same real wage there would be nearly zero unemployment. Full employment must therefore be realistically interpreted to mean that unemployment is only frictional. The determination of the rate of unemployment that may be considered frictional is hotly debated. Some put it as high as 4%, but some countries have been able to achieve unemployment rates as low as 1.5% for many years in a row.

mistake: the labour market may well be the sole market in disequilibrium if one assumes, as implicit here, that the income of factor owners corresponds, not to the value of the factor services they *would like* to supply, but to the value of the supply of factor services that does find purchasers. If there is labour unemployment, the unemployed have no income and therefore cannot demand the product. It is as if the supply of labour was equal to the employed amount of labour.[17] Therefore the demand curve for labour can be interpreted as indicating, for each level of real w, what the supply of labour *would have to be* in order to obtain equilibrium in the labour market at that w.

3.4 The Role of Consumer Choice: The Indirect Factor Substitution Mechanism

What difference does it make to introduce *consumer choice* into the analysis? If— as done up to here—one assumes no savings, only one product, and a rigid supply both of labour and of land, consumer choice has no role in the determination of equilibrium, nor in the arguments supporting a tendency toward it. The gravitation toward equilibrium relies only on technical substitutability.

Consumer choice *among different consumption goods* is important in the marginal approach because it is argued to entail a reason, for decreasing demand curves for factors, *alternative* or *additional to* technical substitutability among factors. It activates—the argument goes—an *indirect* factor substitution mechanism which can generate decreasing demand curves for factors *even in the absence of technical substitutability*, or adds its action to that of technical substitutability making demand for a factor more sensitive to changes of its rental, which increases the plausibility of the theory as will be explained in the next section.

Being based on consumer choice this mechanism needs at least two consumption goods. So let us assume that there are two consumption goods, corn (good 1) and meat (good 2), produced by labour and land in separate industries. In order to examine the working of this factor substitution mechanism in isolation, assume zero technical factor substitutability: in the production of each good only one method of production is known, characterized by given technical coefficients and therefore by a fixed L/T ratio, that differs as between the two industries. Let these technical coefficients be a_{L1}, a_{T1} in the corn industry and a_{L2}, a_{T2} in the meat industry. Assume $a_{L1}/a_{T1} > a_{L2}/a_{T2}$, i.e. the corn industry employs more labour per unit of land than the meat industry: corn is the *more labour-intensive* good.

---

17 '[W]hen, in a stationary closed community, the general level of real wages is raised, and maintained, at a height inconsistent with normal employment … a final position must be reached which is precisely the same as that which would have occurred if there had been a direct reduction in the number of labourers available … The final position thus reached is one of equilibrium, if the existence of the unemployed is left out of account' (Hicks 1932, pp. 198–199).

178   **Chapter 3 · Introduction to the Marginal Approach**

In a competitive economy, product prices gravitate toward the prices that cover costs and leave zero profit (marginalist definition) to entrepreneurs. Let now w, β represent *monetary* magnitudes. The long-period prices of corn and meat will satisfy

$$p_1 = a_{L1}w + a_{T1}\beta,$$

$$p_2 = a_{L2}w + a_{T2}\beta.$$

Then p_1/p_2 depends on w/β and, given our assumption that corn is more labour intensive, p_1/p_2 decreases when w/β decreases.[18] Example: suppose that with a certain income distribution, wages are 80% of total cost in corn production, and 20% in meat production, the rest of cost consisting of land rent. Suppose that money wages go down to one half what they were, while money rent does not change. The unit money cost, and hence money price, of corn goes down by 40%, while the money price of meat goes down by 10%: p_1/p_2 decreases. Thus, *the more labour-intensive good becomes relatively cheaper when the real wage decreases* and this causes w/β to decrease.[19]

Then the demand for labour is argued *generally* to be a decreasing function of the real wage, for the following reason. Assume as before rigid factor supplies and that land is fully employed. Suppose there is labour unemployment, and that this causes w/β to decrease. Corn becomes cheaper relative to meat, and then, it is argued, the composition of the demand for consumption goods *most probably* shifts in favour of corn.[20] The adaptation of productions to demands requires to shift some units of land from production of meat to production of corn; since in the corn industry each unit of land is combined with more units of labour than in the meat industry, this shift increases the demand for labour. (***Exercise***: given the technical coefficients a_{L1}, a_{T1}, a_{L2}, a_{T2}, by how much does labour employment increase for each unit of land shifted from the meat to the corn industry?).

The increase in the demand for labour is brought about, in this case, by variations *in the relative size of the different industries*; when labour becomes cheaper relative to land, the more labour-intensive industry expands and the other one

---

18 Formally, by dividing the first equation by the second we obtain $\frac{p_1}{p_2} = \frac{a_{L1}w+a_{T1}\beta}{a_{L2}w+a_{T2}\beta} = \frac{a_{L1}\frac{w}{\beta}+a_{T1}}{a_{L2}\frac{w}{\beta}+a_{T2}}$. The sign of the derivative of p_1/p_2 with respect to w/β is the same as the sign of $a_{L1}a_{T2}-a_{L2}a_{T1}$, i.e. it is positive if a_{L1}/a_{T1} is greater than a_{L2}/a_{T2}, negative in the opposite case. But the numerical example in the text suffices to clarify how the thing works.

19 In order to be rigorously defined the real wage requires the choice of a numéraire, but here it decreases for any product numéraire, because the money wage has decreased by 50% while the money price of corn decreases by 40% and that of meat by 10%. The real rate of rent increases in terms of both goods, so labour becomes cheaper relative to land. Note that the decrease in monetary product prices does not by itself cause an increase in total demand for the consumption goods, because monetary incomes decrease too.

20 On why 'generally' and 'most probably', see below in the text.

3.4 · The Role of Consumer Choice: The Indirect Factor Substitution

shrinks; part of the fully employed land is transferred to an industry where it requires to be combined with more labour than before.

This is called the ***indirect factor substitution mechanism***, because in changing the composition of their demand for consumption goods, consumers indirectly change the labour/land proportion in the economy as a whole, and in analogy with the case in which this change can be seen as a movement along an isoquant and hence a 'substitution' of one factor for the other, one speaks of factor substitution here too. (In fact one might speak of 'substitution' of labour for land along something similar to an isoquant: an indirect indifference curve; but we have not introduced this notion yet.)

Note that a plausible income distribution is not likely to emerge from the operation of the indirect substitution mechanism alone. The full employment of both labour and land is only possible if the ratio L^*/T^* between supply of labour and supply of land falls in the interval between the two ratios a_{L1}/a_{T1} and a_{L2}/a_{T2}, and these ratios might not differ much. And the extremes of this interval can be reached only if one of the two consumption goods is not produced at all, while consumer preferences might be such as never to let the demand for either good fall to zero, thus further reducing the maximum variability that can be obtained of the overall factor demand ratio. Furthermore, the composition of consumption might change little as p_1/p_2 changes. So this mechanism alone easily generates factor demand curves with little elasticity, with a high likelihood of an impossibility to reach the simultaneous full employment of both factors, and more generally of implausible equilibrium income distributions. But the argument is that this mechanism is above all a further aid to the direct substitution mechanism.

Also, this mechanism might sometimes work against technical substitutability because it is not guaranteed that when w/β decreases, consumer choice changes so that the demand for labour increases (hence the cautions earlier, the 'generally' and 'most probably'). Suppose in this economy labourers and landowners are two distinct groups of consumers, all identical within each group, and suppose labourers demand only corn (the more labour-intensive good), and landowners only meat. Land is fully employed. If there is labour unemployment and w/β decreases, we have seen that the real wage decreases in terms of corn, hence labourers demand *less* corn than before, and since they are the sole ones to demand corn, the demand for corn decreases; for an analogous reason, the demand for meat increases; so the corn industry contracts, and the meat industry expands, the opposite of what is needed for labour demand to increase. The assumptions in this example are extreme, but such a result can still happen if both groups demand both goods but the composition of labourers' demand is much more in favour of corn than the landowners', and if both groups do not alter much the composition of their demand in favour of corn when p_1/p_2 decreases. Marginalist authors considered this possibility highly unlikely. ▶ Chapter 6 will further discuss the issue, now let us accept the marginalist view, we want to understand the logic of the approach without stopping for the moment on its possible difficulties.

180   Chapter 3 · Introduction to the Marginal Approach

3.5 The Simultaneous Operation of Both Substitution Mechanisms, and the Importance of Highly Elastic Factor Demand Curves

I have examined the *direct factor substitution* mechanism and the *indirect factor substitution* mechanism separately so as to highlight their functioning as clearly as possible. But generally, the marginal approach argues, in a real economy *both* factor substitution mechanisms will be simultaneously at work. Their joint operation renders the aggregate demand for each factor more responsive to changes in its rental than if only one mechanism was active; in the economic jargon, each factor demand curve is more *elastic*.

The notion of *elasticity* of a function is a useful one in economics, and so I dedicate some space now to introducing it for newcomers to economics.

Let $y=f(x)$ be a continuous function of one variable. If x changes from x' to $x''=x'+\Delta x$, then y changes from $y'=f(x')$ to $y''=f(x'')=y'+\Delta y$. The *interval elasticity* of $f(x)$ is defined as the proportional (or percentage) variation of y divided by the proportional or percentage variation of x that causes it, i.e.

$$\frac{\Delta y/y}{\Delta x/x}, \text{ sometimes represented as } \frac{\%\Delta y}{\%\Delta x}.$$

If $f(x)$ is differentiable and we consider smaller and smaller variations of x, tending in the limit to an infinitesimal variation dx, the variation of y tends to $dy=f'(x)\cdot dx$, and the value of the interval elasticity tends in the limit to the *point elasticity* which is, for differentiable functions, what economists intend by elasticity:

$$\varepsilon = (dy/y)/(dx/x) = (dy/dx)\cdot x/y = f'(x)\cdot x/f(x).$$

In intuitive approximate terms, the elasticity measures the percentage variation of the dependent variable $y=f(x)$ caused by a 1% increase in the independent variable x. An elasticity greater than 1 in absolute value tells us that y varies percentwise more than x. When both x and y are positive—the usual case in economics—the sign of the elasticity is the same as the sign of dy/dx, so an elasticity equal to -2 tells us that y *decreases* by 2% if x increases by 1%.[21] The elasticity of a decreasing demand function is a negative number, but careful!, most economists have come into the habit of calling elasticity of a demand function the *absolute value* of this negative elasticity; so when an economist says that a demand function has elasticity 1, he means that a 1% increase in price causes a 1% *decrease* in demand, and when he says a demand function has become more elastic, he means the *absolute value* of that elasticity has increased.

A function is called elastic if its elasticity in absolute value is 1 or greater; inelastic if its elasticity in absolute value is less than one; anelastic if the elasticity is zero.

---

21   When x or y or both are negative, the sign of the elasticity need not coincide with the sign of dy/dx. For example y = –x has elasticity + 1, and yet when x increases, y decreases.

3.5 · The Simultaneous Operation of Both Substitution ...

Differently from the derivative, the elasticity of a function is independent of the units in which the independent and the dependent variable are measured, as the reader is invited to check by elaborating opportune examples.

If $y=f(x)$, with $y, x>0$, is differentiable, then elementary calculus shows that the elasticity $(dy/y)/(dx/x)$ is identical with the **logarithmic derivative** $d(\log y(x))/d(\log x)$:

$$\frac{d \log y(x)}{d \log x} = \frac{d \log y(x)}{d y(x)} \cdot \frac{d y(x)}{d x} \cdot \frac{d x}{d \log x} = \frac{1}{y(x)} \cdot \frac{d y(x)}{d x} \cdot \frac{1}{\frac{d \log x}{d x}} = \frac{1}{y(x)} \cdot \frac{d y(x)}{d x} \cdot x.$$

Thus if one graphs log y as a function of log x, the slope of the curve measures the elasticity of $y=f(x)$.

Now let us use the notion of elasticity to express more clearly the argument in the first paragraph of this section. Suppose that in the given economy a certain reduction in real wages would increase the demand for labour by 2% if the indirect substitution mechanism were the sole one allowed to operate; and that the same reduction in real wages would increase the demand for labour by 3% if only the direct substitution mechanism were allowed to operate; then if both substitution mechanisms are allowed to operate, the increase in the demand for labour can be assumed to be close to 5%.

This is important because the theory, in order to be a plausible explanation of how income distribution is determined in market economies, needs not only decreasing, but also *significantly elastic* demand curves for factors.

Without *decreasing* factor demand curves the theory would totally lose credibility: in ◘ Fig. 3.10, the increasing demand curve for labour entails that the sole equilibrium with positive rentals for both factors is unstable: if $w>w^*$ then wages keep increasing up to absorbing the entire output, if $w<w^*$ then wages keep decreasing down to zero; the economy therefore ends up with labour getting either the entire income or nothing, a result in obvious contradiction with the evidence.

The need for a *considerable elasticity* of the decreasing demand curve for each factor arises from the need to minimize the likelihood of four types of occurrence

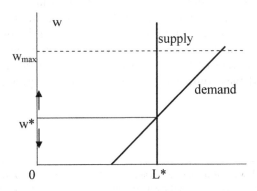

◘ **Fig. 3.10** If the labour demand curve is upward-sloping the only plausible equilibrium wage is unstable

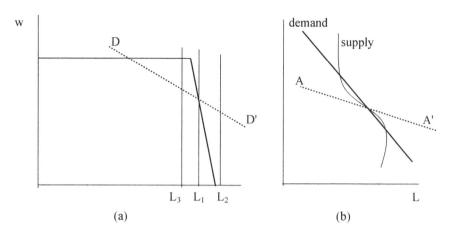

◉ **Fig. 3.11** Effect of a nearly vertical labour demand curve, and of a not very elastic labour demand curve if the supply curve can be partly 'backward bending'

which, unless extremely unlikely, raise doubts on the correctness of this theory as an explanation of what determines income distribution in market economies. The four types of troublesome occurrences are

- a zero or implausibly low equilibrium real wage;
- enormous changes in income distribution owing to small changes in relative factor supplies;
- multiple equilibria;
- *practically indeterminate* equilibria.

These possibilities are illustrated in ◉ Figs. 3.11 and 3.12, which also show how a higher elasticity of the demand for labour would render them less likely.

◉ Figure 3.11a illustrates how a decreasing but inelastic demand curve for labour (the heavy continuous line) can easily imply a zero equilibrium real wage, and implausibly large changes in income distribution owing to small changes in labour supply. The small increase in labour supply from L_1 to L_2 causes the equilibrium wage rate to fall from a high level to zero([22]); the small decrease from L_1 to L_3 causes the real wage to rise up to absorbing the entire product (the horizontal part of the labour demand curve is associated with a partly unutilized supply of land, hence the rent of land is zero). The more elastic labour demand curve DD' would avoid these outcomes which have no correspondence with empirical observation.

---

22 Even if for very low levels of the real wage the supply of labour fell to zero, and this prevented the real wage from reaching zero, still the equilibrium real wage might be so low as to result implausible anyway.

3.5 · The Simultaneous Operation of Both Substitution …

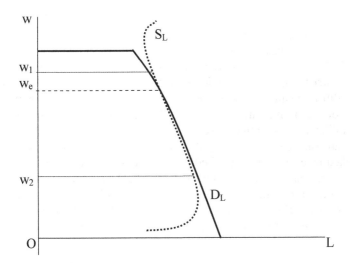

Fig. 3.12 Practically indeterminate equilibrium: between w_1 and w_2 the discrepancy between supply and demand is so weak that the tendency toward w_e is practically non-existent

Figure 3.11b illustrates the possibility of multiple equilibria due to a *backward-bending* labour supply curve, i.e. a supply of labour that for certain ranges of w is a decreasing function of the real wage. This is not at all implausible: when the main bread winner in a household has a rise in income the decision may well be taken to keep children studying for more years, or to have tired grandpa retire earlier. Then, unless the demand curve is highly elastic, there may well be three (or even more) equilibria in spite of a decreasing labour demand curve. This means that, if any shock pushes the labour market into a state of disequilibrium, the real wage toward which the economy will converge cannot be univocally predicted; in Fig. 3.11b the highest and lowest equilibrium wage are 'locally stable' equilibria, i.e. attract w if w is on their side of the central equilibrium, which is unstable. So the theory does not yield univocal predictions. A temporary disturbance to an equilibrium can push w into the 'basin of attraction' of another equilibrium, so after the end of the disturbance the economy need not go back to the previous equilibrium. And if there is a shift in the supply curve or in the demand curve, the new equilibrium reached by the economy can depend on the accidents of disequilibrium. The more numerous and the closer to each other the multiple equilibria, the more income distribution will be indeterminate and subject to variations for accidental and transitory reasons, depriving the theory of plausibility: historical evidence shows that the distribution of income among wages, rents and interest is considerably persistent, undergoing only very gradual changes. To be credible, the theory must exclude this indeterminateness by arguing that factor demand curves are highly elastic.

The possibility of *practically indeterminate* equilibria usually escapes attention but is as damaging to the theory as multiple equilibria. If the labour supply curve is backward-bending, it cannot be excluded that the decreasing labour demand curve and the labour supply curve are very close to each other for an ample interval of values of the real wage, cf. the interval between w_1 and w_2 in ◨ Fig. 3.12. In this case, even when the intersection between the two curves is unique and, strictly speaking, stable (as in ◨ Fig. 3.12), since the forces pushing toward equilibrium cannot but be the weaker the smaller the discrepancy between supply and demand, in an ample interval of values of the real wage the tendency toward equilibrium is extremely weak, and therefore in all likelihood unable to bring the real wage close to the equilibrium value in a reasonable time, and also easily blocked by even very weak rigidities: so the real wage would have to be considered indeterminate in such an interval of values, and one would have to have recourse to other forces in order to explain where it is located in that interval and what renders it usually quite persistent. Here too, the likelihood of such a phenomenon decreases as the elasticity of the labour demand curve increases.

3.6 Money

In the illustration of the factor substitution mechanisms that in this approach push the economy toward a full-employment equilibrium, the presence of money was nearly never mentioned. But this does not mean that we assumed that the economy functioned without the use of money. What was implicitly assumed was rather that the presence of money posed no obstacle to the working of those mechanisms, because the price level was such, and the distribution of money holdings among economic agents was such, as to make the behaviour required by those mechanisms possible.[23] For example, in the economy producing corn and meat with labour and land it was implicitly assumed that prices were money prices, people were paid in money, and used this money for their purchases; and that the total quantity of money present in the economy, and its distribution among agents, was appropriate to the level of money prices and to the transactions to be carried out in order for equilibrium behaviour to be possible. Then the quantity of money held on average by an agent needed not be specified because it was implicitly taken to be *endogenously* determined so as to make the actions of the agent be those that the analysis was specifying in terms of *relative* prices only.

This is why our analysis determined *relative* prices only, leaving money prices undetermined. To determine them an additional theory is necessary, capable of determining the price level. The oldest one is the **quantity theory of money**; in more recent times, theories of endogenous money are widely proposed. The study of these theories is not within the aims of this book. But a taste of the topic is

---

23 By *price level* one means the level of an index of monetary prices, e.g. the total monetary value of a representative basket of consumption goods. If all money prices and factor rentals double with no change in relative prices and rentals, one says that the price level has doubled but real factor rentals have not changed.

3.6 · Money

supplied by this quotation from Wicksell, which describes the functioning of the quantity theory of money:

>> Let us suppose that for some reason or other commodity prices rise while the stock of money remains unchanged, or that the stock of money is diminished while prices remain temporarily unchanged. The cash balances will gradually appear to be too small … I can rely on a higher level of receipts in the future. But meanwhile I run the risk of being unable to meet my obligations punctually, and at best I may easily be forced by shortage of ready money to forgo some purchase that would otherwise have been profitable. I therefore seek to enlarge my balance … through a *reduction* in my *demand* for goods and services, or through an *increase* in the *supply* of my own commodity … the universal reduction in demand and increase in supply of commodities will necessarily bring about a continuous fall in all prices. This can only cease when prices have fallen to the level at which the cash balances are regarded as *adequate*. (Wicksell 1936, pp. 39–40, italics in the original)

We see here one example of a process capable of causing the price level to tend toward an equilibrium level, such that 'cash balances are…adequate' for implementing the normal, equilibrium decisions as to demands and supplies. This should suffice to show that the reason why the consumers' and firms' equilibrium microeconomic decisions in the corn model or the corn-and-meat model are based only on relative prices and neglect to take money balances into account is that it is implicitly assumed that the consumer or the firm have at their disposal the 'adequate' cash balances needed to implement those equilibrium decisions; therefore it is implicitly assumed that there are processes that ensure that cash balances too tend toward equilibrium, together with the price level; so in equilibrium the price level and the distribution of money among the several agents are compatible with equilibrium behaviour, hence are endogenously determined. A more detailed analysis of the issue is a delicate matter that we cannot tackle here; the interested reader can consult Petri (2004, pp. 166–186).

3.7 Efficiency, the Forest Exchange Economy, Choice Curves and Equilibrium in the Edgeworth Box

3.7.1 Elements of Consumer Theory: Utility Function, Indifference Curves, MRS

The marginalist picture of the working of market economies implies that these tend to the full employment of resources and to reflect consumers' desires: all supplies find purchasers, the composition of production adapts to the composition of demand. Later we will see that capital accumulation too is viewed as reflecting consumers' preferences, in this case between consuming more today or tomorrow. This very positive picture of the working of market economies is synthesized in the so-called *First Fundamental Theorem of Welfare Economics*. This states: *a competitive equilibrium is Pareto efficient* (*in the absence of externalities*

186   **Chapter 3** · Introduction to the Marginal Approach

and public goods).[24]   We don't have yet the tools for a rigorous general proof of this theorem but it is worth illustrating the proof for some very simple cases, it will supply the concrete intuition without which the very general and abstract proof of the theorem to be given in ▶ Chap. 14 would remain of unclear content.

As a premise, I must introduce, for the newcomer to economics, some elements of the marginalist analysis of consumer choice and the famous concept of *marginal utility*. The reader familiar with standard consumer theory can jump to ▶ Sect. 3.7.2.

The marginal approach argues that consumers decide how much to work, whether to supply their land to firms or keep if for self-enjoyment, what to buy with their incomes, etcetera, on the basis of the fact that they prefer certain consumption baskets to other ones.[25]   These preferences, it is argued, can be described through the device of a *utility function*. This is a function of the amounts consumed of the several consumption goods and services to which the consumer can have access. If there are m different consumption goods and we indicate the amounts the consumer might get of them as $x_1, \ldots, x_m$, then the utility function $u(x_1, \ldots, x_m) : R^m \to R$ has the property that, between two consumption baskets, it assigns a greater numerical value to the consumption basket that the consumer prefers, and the same value to both baskets if the consumer is indifferent between them. It is a numerical device to indicate which basket the consumer prefers in a collection of baskets.

Although in fact simply a numerical representation of an ordinal preference order, a utility function is pretty much like a production function: each different basket of consumptions $(x_1, \ldots, x_m)$ might be viewed as a vector of inputs 'producing', within the individual's brain, reactions such that the individual can assess which of several alternative baskets she/he prefers; the preferred basket can be viewed as 'producing' more satisfaction or happiness or—the standard name—*utility*. This picture, that reflects the origin of the notion, helps intuition and is largely harmless. So let us interpret the utility function as a 'production function' of utility. It is indeed mathematically similar to a production function. If we restrict the analysis to only two goods, $u(x_1, x_2)$ is mathematically similar to $f(L, T)$: assuming the goods are divisible, it can be assumed to be a differentiable function, and then its partial derivative with respect to good i is called the *marginal utility* of good i and indicated as MU_i; when these marginal utilities are positive, an increase in the amount consumed of a good (with the other amount unchanged) increases utility, that is, a basket with more of that good and not less of the other than the original basket is preferred to the original basket. We can then define the equivalent of an isoquant, the set of consumption baskets associated to a given level of utility: the connected terminology is that when a consumer finds two different consumption baskets equally attractive, the consumer

---

24   These notions will be discussed in ▶ Chap. 14.

25   Among the 'goods' in these consumption baskets one also includes leisure time, or the amount of land kept for self-enjoyment.

3.7 · Efficiency, the Forest Exchange Economy, Choice Curves ...

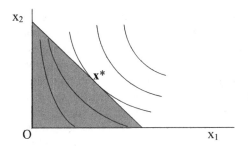

Fig. 3.13 Map of convex indifference curves and a budget set

is said *indifferent* between them, and the two baskets are said *equipreferred*; given a consumption basket, let $u°$ the utility level that the consumer's utility function assigns to it; the set of consumption baskets yielding utility $u°$ is called an *indifference set*; the consumer finds them all equipreferred. For example assume only two divisible goods and that the utility function is increasing in each good; then $u(x_1, x_2)$ is a surface in $\mathbb{R}^3_+$, and the set of baskets (x_1, x_2) yielding a given level of utility is a *contour* (level curve) of the utility function, just like an isoquant is a contour of a production function; its name is *indifference curve*.

A fundamental difference from production functions is that what is relevant of a utility function is only the *order* it establishes among consumption baskets. Let us indicate a consumption basket with vector **x**. If $u(\mathbf{x}') < u(\mathbf{x}'')$, it means the consumer prefers the second basket; it is irrelevant *by how much* according to that utility function she prefers $\mathbf{x}''$ to $\mathbf{x}'$. If $u(\mathbf{x})$ correctly describes the preferences of a consumer, any strictly increasing monotonic transformation of u, for example $v(\mathbf{x}) = 200u(\mathbf{x}) + 10$, or $z(\mathbf{x}) = [u(\mathbf{x})]^3$, will also correctly describe those preferences: indeed every time $u(\mathbf{x}') > u(\mathbf{x}'')$ it is also $v(\mathbf{x}') > v(\mathbf{x}'')$, so $v(\mathbf{x})$ too correctly indicates whether a basket is preferred to another or not.

If we assume only two goods, then indifference curves can be represented graphically in the non-negative orthant of the Cartesian plane, with x_1 and x_2 on the axes. Let us assume that goods are perfectly divisible, that indifference curves are decreasing, continuous, 'smooth' (i.e. differentiable) and strictly convex, and that the utility function that generates them has the property that 'more is preferred', that is, if two consumption baskets differ in the amount of only one good, then the basket where there is more of that good has greater utility. Such utility functions, that have partial derivatives (marginal utilities!) always positive, are called *monotonic*. Then indifference curves are indeed curves, and not thick strips (are you clear as to why?), are decreasing (are you clear as to why?), and the greater the utility they are associated with, the farther away from the origin they are along any one ray from the origin.[26] Some reason for the common assumption of strict convexity of indifference curves will be given in ▶ Sect. 4.8. A map of indifference curves can look, for example, as in ◘ Fig. 3.13.

---

26 If you are not sure as to why, just wait for ▶ Chap. 4.

188   **Chapter 3 · Introduction to the Marginal Approach**

To find general properties of how consumers change their choices when relative prices change, one first studies how a consumer chooses what to consume when prices are given, and then how the choice changes if prices change. The starting point is that the consumer chooses the consumption basket that maximizes her utility among the consumption baskets that she can afford. The latter baskets are those that, at the given prices (consumers are assumed to be price-takers), cost no more than what the consumer can spend: the consumer's income. In the Marshallian, partial-equilibrium approach to demand for consumption goods the consumer's income is taken as given; in general equilibrium theory, income is determined endogenously as the value of the resources (goods or factor services) the consumer owns and can sell.

For example, let us assume an economy where m types of goods are traded, and each consumer comes to a periodic market fair with a basket of goods she can sell or keep, and we do not care where that basket comes from, it is simply given, it is the consumer's **endowment**, a vector $\boldsymbol{\omega}$ of non-negative quantities ω_i, $i = 1, \ldots, m$, of the several goods. If prices are a vector $\mathbf{p} = (p_1, \ldots, p_m)$ the consumer's income is defined as $\Sigma_i p_i \omega_i$, that is, it is the purchasing power the consumer can obtain by selling her entire endowment. If the consumer chooses to supply to the market only part of her endowment, one treats this as equivalent to the consumer selling everything and then buying back what she in fact keeps. Then the consumption baskets the consumer can afford at prices $\mathbf{p}$ are all consumption baskets $\mathbf{x} = (x_1, \ldots, x_m)$ that satisfy $\mathbf{p} \cdot \mathbf{x} \leq \mathbf{p} \cdot \boldsymbol{\omega}$; they constitute the **budget set**.[27] Assume income cannot be transferred from one market fair to subsequent ones or vice-versa by borrowing and lending. Assume utility is monotonic; the consumer gets a higher utility by spending all her income rather than leaving some part of it unutilized, so the optimal consumption basket satisfies $\mathbf{p} \cdot \mathbf{x} = \mathbf{p} \cdot \boldsymbol{\omega}$. Assume two goods; then from this equality one obtains affordable x_2 as a function of x_1,

$$x_2 = (p_1\omega_1 + p_2\omega_2 - p_1x_1)/p_2,$$

a decreasing straight line in the same diagram in which one represents indifference curves: it is called the **budget line**. Its intercepts indicate the maximum amount of each good the consumer can afford to buy; its slope is $-p_1/p_2$.

The solution of the consumer's utility maximization problem consists of finding the point, on the budget line, that belongs to the indifference curve 'farthest' from the origin. With our assumption of strictly convex smooth indifference curves and monotonic utility, indifference curves farther away from the origin indicate higher utility, so the consumer chooses the point on the budget line through which passes the farthest indifference curve, basket $\mathbf{x}^*$ in ◘ Fig. 3.13 or ◘ Fig. 3.17a; if the solution is *internal* (i.e. if the optimal basket contains positive

---

27 We need not specify whether $\mathbf{p}$ or $\mathbf{x}$ or $\boldsymbol{\omega}$ are row or column vector if we indicate multiplication of two vectors as a dot product, as here. Anyway generally in this book a price vector is a row vector, and a quantity vector is a column vector.

3.7 · Efficiency, the Forest Exchange Economy, Choice Curves ...

quantities of both goods) it must be at the point where the budget line is tangent to the indifference curve through that point.

■ Figure 3.17a in ▶ Sect. 3.7.2 represents this tangency. In this two-goods case, the optimum consumption basket can be determined via a system of two equations: the first imposes that the basket be on the budget line:

$$p_1x_1 + p_2x_2 = p_1\omega_1 + p_2\omega_2, \tag{3.5}$$

the second imposes the tangency condition, that is, at the preferred point the slope of the indifference curve must be equal to that of the budget line[28]:

$$-p_1/p_2 = -MU_1/MU_2. \tag{3.6}$$

MU_1 and MU_2, the partial derivatives of the utility function, are traditionally referred to as the **marginal utilities** of the consumption goods. The slope of an indifference curve is $-MU_1/MU_2$ for the same reason why the slope of an isoquant is $-MP_L/MP_T$; it is called the **marginal rate of substitution**, $MRS_{1,2}$; intuitively, it indicates how many units of good 2 (the good in ordinate) one can give up if one is given one more unit of good 1 and utility is to remain unaffected; like the TRS, it is negative but economists often intend by MRS its absolute value.

The equality between MRS and slope of the budget line can be rewritten in a way that allows a useful economic interpretation:

$$MU_1/p_1 = MU_2/p_2. \tag{3.7}$$

Let p_1 and p_2 be money prices. Since $1/p_1$ is how much of good 1 can be purchased with one unit of money, MU_1/p_1 is, intuitively speaking, the increase in utility if one allocates one more unit of money to the purchase of good 1. It is then called the **marginal utility of money** (spent on good 1). As long as (3.7) is not satisfied, it is convenient for the consumer to reallocate some income toward the good with a higher marginal utility of money, until it is equalized.

This allows the study of how consumer choice changes if prices change. If *relative* prices change, the budget line rotates around the endowment point: the value of the endowment basket is of course always sufficient to buy the endowment basket, so the budget line necessarily passes through that point. Hence if all prices change in the same proportion, the budget line does not move. The point of tangency between budget line and indifference curve shifts as the budget line rotates, and its shift indicates how consumer choice changes with relative prices, cf. Figures 3.16 and 3.17b.

---

28 The budget line has equation $p_1x_1 + p_2x_2 = p_1\omega_1 + p_2\omega_2$ where ω_1 and ω_2 are given, hence $dx_2/dx_1 = -p_1/p_2$. The indifference curve at a given level $u°$ of utility satisfies $u(x_1,x_2) = u°$ and then along the indifference curve by the derivative rule for implicit functions it is $\partial x_2/\partial x_1 = -(\partial u/\partial x_1)/(\partial u/\partial x_2) = -MU_1/MU_2$. The two conditions (3.5), (3.6), only valid for interior solutions, can also be derived from maximization of $u(x_1, x_2)$ under the budget constraint with the Lagrangian method, see Chap. 4, ▶ Sect. 4.8.

190 Chapter 3 · Introduction to the Marginal Approach

3.7.2 Exchange Economy, Edgewort Box, Pareto Efficiency

Consider the economy in which each consumer h arrives at each periodic market fair with an endowment ω^h. There are H consumers. We neglect how the endowments of consumers are determined, we only concentrate on which exchanges happen at the market fair, so this is an **exchange economy**. At the end of the fair each consumer h has a basket $\mathbf{x}^h$ of consumption goods. An **allocation** is a vector of consumption baskets $(\mathbf{x}^1,\ldots, \mathbf{x}^h,\ldots, \mathbf{x}^H)$, one per consumer (so it is a vector of vectors); a **feasible allocation** satisfies the condition that, for each good, the allocation does not distribute in total more of it than its total quantity in the endowments; a **no-waste allocation** uses in total all the endowments, hence it is feasible and leaves no endowment unused. Given the endowments, a feasible allocation is **Pareto efficient** if no **Pareto improvement** is possible, that is, no reallocation or avoidance of waste is possible that would improve the utility level of at least one consumer without decreasing the utility level of any other consumer. Of course with monotonic utilities a Pareto-efficient allocation is a no-waste allocation. The notion can be illustrated with the help of the **Edgeworth–Pareto box**.[29]

Assume two consumers A and B who have given endowments of two consumption goods, good 1 and good 2, and can exchange these goods. The vector of endowments of consumer A is $\omega^A = \left(\omega_1^A, \omega_2^A\right)$ and that of consumer B is $\omega^B = \left(\omega_1^B, \omega_2^B\right)$. Draw the indifference curves of consumer A and those of consumer B in two separate diagrams; then rotate the diagram of consumer B by 180° and superpose it to the diagram of consumer A in such a way that the intersection of the axes forms a rectangle of length equal to $\omega_1{}^A + \omega_1{}^B$ and height equal to $\omega_2{}^A + \omega_2{}^B$. In this rectangle, called the Edgeworth box, the indifference curves of consumer A have the lower left-hand corner as their origin, and the indifference curves of consumer B are upside down, with the upper right-hand corner as their origin. The length of the sides of the box represents the total endowment $\omega_1 \equiv \omega_1{}^A + \omega_1{}^B$, $\omega_2 \equiv \omega_2{}^A + \omega_2{}^B$ of the economy consisting of these two consumers.

We interpret any point of the box as indicating simultaneously two consumption baskets: its coordinates relative to the lower left-hand corner indicate a consumption basket of consumer A; its coordinates relative to the upper right-hand corner indicate a consumption basket of consumer B; since these two baskets sum up to the total endowment, any point $\mathbf{x} = (x_1, x_2)$ of the box (using the coordinates relative to the lower left-hand corner to indicate a point in the box) represents a possible no-waste allocation of the total endowments between the two consumers.

Consider then the Edgeworth box of ◼ Fig. 3.14, where point $\Omega = \left(\omega_1^A, \omega_2^A\right)$ indicates the endowments of the two consumers. As before, I assume monotonic utility functions, and strictly convex and 'smooth' indifference curves. In the Fig-

---

29 This is usually called simply *Edgeworth box*, but in fact Francis Ysidro Edgeworth in 1881 used a different diagram, and the first one to draw the box as here was Vilfredo Pareto in 1906.

3.7 · Efficiency, the Forest Exchange Economy, Choice Curves ...

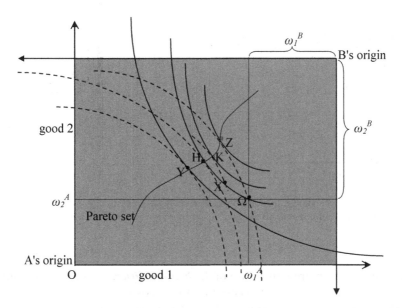

Fig. 3.14 Edgeworth–Pareto box. The lengths of the sides of the box are $\omega_1 \equiv \omega_1^A + \omega_1^B$ horizontally, $\omega_2 \equiv \omega_2^A + \omega_2^B$ vertically. The continuous heavy curves are indifference curves of consumer A, and the broken heavy curves are indifference curves of consumer B. They are drawn so as to make it clear that they extend outside the box. The Pareto set (actually, part of it) is the curve through Y, H, K and Z where there is tangency of indifference curves that are assumed strictly convex. Ω is the endowment point

ure, the initial allocation Ω as well as an allocation such as X are not Pareto efficient, because there exist allocations that make both consumers better off, for example allocation K. Allocation K is Pareto efficient because any movement away from it causes the utility level of at least one consumer to decrease. Allocations Z, H, Y are Pareto efficient too, for the same reason. Pareto-efficient allocations are therefore many, differing in the utility levels of the two consumers.

The locus of Pareto-efficient allocations in an Edgeworth box is called the ***Pareto set***.[30] As long as the Pareto set does not touch the edges of the box, its points must be of tangency between the convex indifference curves of the two consumers. But as points C and D in ◘ Fig. 3.15a show, the Pareto set can be partly along an edge of the box, in which case generally there will not be tangency between indifference curves along it.

---

30 Sometimes it is also called the ***contract curve***, but I, like most other economists, restrict the latter term to mean only the portion of the Pareto set where neither consumer is worse off than with her initial endowments; with convex indifference curves, it is the portion of the Pareto set included in the 'lens' formed by the indifference curves through the initial endowment point, the portion between points H and Z in ◘ Fig. 3.14. Only points in this portion can be reached by efficient contracting.

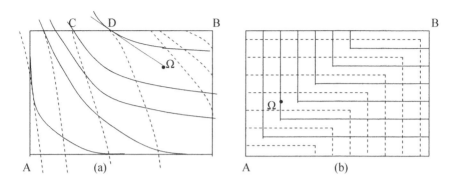

Fig. 3.15 Two less standard Edgeworth boxes. The indifference curves of consumer A are drawn as continuous lines, those of consumer B as broken lines. *Exercise*: Find the Pareto set in these Edgeworth boxes

Figure 3.15b represents a case of **L-shaped indifference curves** (monotonicity does not hold in this case), where the two goods must be consumed in fixed proportion, that is, if one good is in excess of that proportion the excess does not increase utility. In this case the goods are called **perfect complements**. The utility function has the form $u(x_1, x_2) = \min(ax_1, bx_2)$ with $a,b > 0$. Given x_1, any amount of x_2 in excess of ax_1/b is useless; given x_2, any amount of x_1 in excess of bx_2/a is useless. Isoquants too can be L-shaped, indicating that the inputs are perfect complements and if combined in a proportion different from the efficient one, at least one of the inputs is in excess and the excess is totally useless; this is in fact the implicit meaning of a fixed-coefficient method, if a fixed-coefficient method requires labour and land to be combined in the proportion 4:1, then one may combine 5 units of labour with 1 unit of land but the fifth unit of labour is useless.

If one assumes an economy with, say, 10,000 consumers identical to A and 10,000 consumers identical to B, then the Edgeworth box can be used to describe the outcome of their competitive interaction.

Assume these consumers are the active agents in an **exchange economy**, where they can exchange the goods in their endowments. It might be an economy consisting of households who live scattered in a forest and who once a month gather in a market place for a market fair. To be able to use the Edgeworth box we must assume that only two goods are exchanged, say, corn and meat. Assume each household always brings to each fair the same given quantities (specific to the household) of each good and decides on the basis of price how much to sell or keep of them. At the market fair there is competition and a free determination of prices on the basis of higgling and bargaining.

We treat each household as a single decision unit, and we call it a 'consumer'. There are H consumers distinguished by the index $h = 1, \ldots, H$. Each consumer h has a monotonic utility function $u^h(x_1, x_2)$ with strictly convex indifference curves. Corn is good 1, meat is good 2. Let us call endowment of consumer h the vec-

3.7 · Efficiency, the Forest Exchange Economy, Choice Curves ...

tor $\omega^h = (\omega^h{}_1, \omega^h{}_2)$ of quantities of corn and meat that she brings each month to the market fair. At each fair equilibrium is not reached instantaneously so not all units of each good will sell at the same price, and prices can change during the day, so one can at most speak of an *average* price of a good, and this average price can change from one fair to the next. But if endowments and utility functions do not change from one fair to the next, it is possible that prices tend to stabilize at a relative price p_2/p_1 which no longer changes from one fair to the next and must therefore be an equilibrium relative price. We want to find it.

Assume absence of loans and debts, so consumers want a **balanced budget**, i.e. want to exit each fair having spent on the purchase of other consumers' goods what they earn by selling all or part of their supplies in that fair. To leave unspent some part of what they earn would be stupid because getting more of something always increases monotonic utility and we assume one cannot carry unspent purchasing power from one fair to the next.

Let $x^h{}_1$, $x^h{}_2$ be the *demands* of consumer h, that is, the quantities the consumer wants to have at the end of the fair.[31] If $x^h{}_j > \omega^h{}_j$ the consumer wants to *purchase from* other consumers the difference; if $x^h{}_j < \omega^h{}_j$ the consumer wants to remain with less of the good than she starts with and sell the remainder $\omega^h{}_j - x^h{}_j$ to other consumers. The balanced budget assumption means that the value of the consumer's planned sales must equal the value of the planned purchases, i.e. her plans must satisfy the **budget constraint**:

$$p_1\left(x_1^h - \omega_1^h\right) + p_2\left(x_2^h - \omega_2^h\right) = 0.$$

Rearranging:

$$p_1 x_1^h + p_2 x_2^h = p_1 \omega_1^h + p_2 \omega_2^h.$$

This formulation states that *the value of demands must equal the income of the consumer*, where the income is the value of the endowments.

Graphically, if we measure the consumer's demand for good 1 in abscissa, and of good 2 in ordinate, the last formulation shows that the budget line necessarily passes through the endowment point $\omega = (\omega_1, \omega_2)$—for simplicity now let us drop the superscript h. So the position of the budget line is not altered by changes of all prices in the same proportion: it only depends on the endowment point and on *relative* prices.

The consumer maximizes her utility by choosing the point on the budget line through which passes the indifference curve 'farthest' from the origin, and therefore—if this point is internal and since we assume indifference curves are convex—the point where the budget line is tangent to an indifference curve. Given the slope of the budget line, the tangency condition determines the optimal choice (x_1, x_2). If indifference curves touch the axes, it may be that the consumer prefers a corner solution where she consumes only one good: this will happen when, moving along the budget line in the direction indicated by a difference

---

31 I assume that they are single-valued functions of endowments and of the relative price.

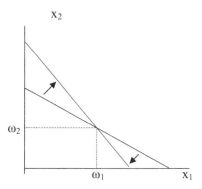

Fig. 3.16 Rotation of the budget line when income derives from given endowments and p_1/p_2 rises

between the two marginal utilities of money, she reaches an axis, i.e. demands only one good, without the difference having disappeared.

Now let p_1/p_2 change; the consumer's choice changes; the curve that indicates all the optimal consumption baskets corresponding to different relative prices is usually called the *offer curve* of the consumer. I find this term inappropriate, the curve indicates, if anything, the *demands* of the consumer, but the term 'demand curve' is reserved for another notion, so since the curve is the locus of optimal consumption choices of the consumer, I propose to call it *choice curve*; it is the heavy blue line in ◘ Fig. 3.16b. With smooth, strictly convex indifference curves, the choice curve is continuous and necessarily passes through the endowment point, where it is tangent to the indifference curve passing through that point, but more convex. For each slope of the budget line, the intersection of the choice curve with the budget line indicates the consumer's choice at that relative price. Note that a choice curve can have upward-sloping sections.

Suppose now that the economy comprises 10,000 consumers identical to A and 10,000 consumers identical to B. Then the Edgeworth box of ◘ Fig. 3.14 can be used to study the equilibrium of such an economy, because it reproduces in scale 1:10,000 what happens in the economy. The high number of consumers makes it plausible that each consumer is *price-taker*, i.e. treats prices as not influenced by her own decisions.

Equilibrium requires that relative prices be such that for each good i the sum of the demands of all consumers be equal to the sum of all endowments.

Given the relative price of the two goods, in the Edgeworth box for each relative price the budget lines of A and B coincide because both go through the endowment point and have the same slope. Let us trace the choice curves of A and B. They allow us to determine the equilibrium or equilibria without the explicit representation of indifference curves. Consider ◘ Fig. 3.18. For a given relative price and corresponding common budget line, the two choice curves give us the point indicating the demands of A, and the analogous point of B's demands. If the two points do not coincide, then one of the two goods is in excess demand (total demand greater than total endowment), and the other is in

3.7 · Efficiency, the Forest Exchange Economy, Choice Curves ...

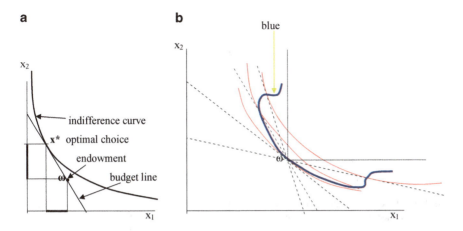

● **Fig. 3.17 a. b** Choice curve (offer curve). Indifference curves are red, budget lines are black and broken, the choice curve is the blue heavy line

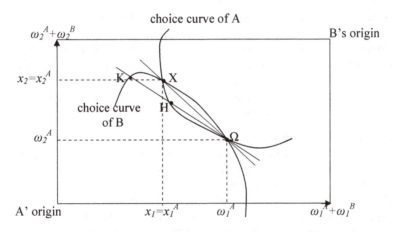

● **Fig. 3.18** Choice curves of A and of B allow finding the equilibrium at X

excess supply: for example when the two points are K and H, good 1 is in excess demand (then we can expect p_1/p_2 to rise and the budget line to rotate). If the two points coincide, as at X, then the relative price that causes the budget line to pass through that point is an equilibrium relative price, for each good what one consumer wishes to sell equals what the other consumer wishes to buy. Point X is an equilibrium allocation. **Exercise**: prove that in this example when p_1/p_2 is not the equilibrium relative price, the tendency of the good in excess demand to rise in relative price causes p_1/p_2 to tend to the equilibrium value: the equilibrium is stable.

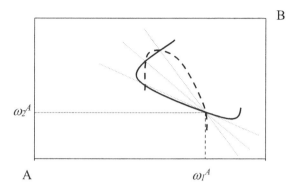

Fig. 3.19 Three equilibria in an Edgeworth box. Consumer A's choice curve is the heavy continuous line, consumer B's choice curve is the heavy broken line

By assumption the economy is only a replica, 10,000 times larger, of what is happening in this Edgeworth box, so if p_1/p_2 causes the budget line to pass through X the economy is in equilibrium.

We can now prove that the equilibrium is Pareto efficient.

Proof When the budget line goes through X, consumer A chooses X because that's the point of tangency between indifference curve and budget line. The same is true of consumer B. Hence the convex indifference curves through X of the two consumers, both tangent to the same budget line, are tangent to each other, which means the point is in the Pareto set. ∎

The choice curves also cross in the endowment point Ω but there is no equilibrium there, because the indifference curves of the two consumers through that point have the same slope as the respective choice curves and therefore have different slopes. An *interior* endowment point can be an equilibrium allocation only if the choice curves are tangent to each other in that point.

If the two choice curves cross more than once in points other than the endowment point (this is possible, cf. Figure 3.19), then all these points with the associated relative prices are equilibria, and if they are interior then in all of them the indifference curves of the two consumers are tangent to each other because tangent to the budget line; so all these points are Pareto efficient. An equilibrium can also be on the edge, see point D in Fig. 3.15a (note that in D only A's indifference curve is tangent to the budget line; try proving that this equilibrium too is Pareto efficient).

3.8 Pareto Efficiency in the Production Economy. Marginal Cost

Let us now extend the notion of Pareto efficiency and the First Fundamental Theorem of Welfare Economics to a simple production economy. Consider an economy where labour and land produce a variety of consumption goods in

3.8 · Pareto Efficiency in the Production Economy. Marginal Cost

single-product industries; assume monotonic utilities. Assume also (if you know what this means) no externalities, no public goods, no taxation.

Assume initially that factor supplies are rigid and equal to endowments; indifference curves and isoquants are smooth and strictly convex; all consumers demand all consumption goods in positive quantities; all firms employ both factors in positive quantities. Then it is necessary and sufficient for Pareto efficiency that three conditions be satisfied (the new terms that appear in these conditions will be explained in the course of the proof):

(a) Efficiency in *production*: it must not be possible to produce more of a good without decreasing the production of any other good. In other words, the economy must be on its **Production Possibility Frontier**, PPF, defined below. This requires (a1) full employment of all supplies of factors; (a2) efficiency within each enterprise (for each vector of amounts of factors employed by the firm, it must not be possible to produce more); (a3) equality among firms of the technical rate of substitution (TRS) between factors.

(b) Efficiency in the *allocation* among consumers of any given total production vector of consumption goods: all goods must be allocated to some consumer (no pure waste), and it must not be possible, by reallocating among consumers the *given* quantities available, to increase the utility of one consumer without decreasing the utility of some other consumer. This requires the equality among consumers of the MRS's.

(c) Efficiency in the *composition of production*: it must not be possible to increase the utility level of one consumer without decreasing the utility level of any other consumer by changing the composition of production (i.e. the point on the PPF). This requires that the **marginal rate of transformation** MRT between any two produced goods (the slope of the PPF restricted to those two goods) be equal to the MRS between them, for all consumers.

Let us prove it. The necessity of condition (a) can be shown as follows. The need for the full employment of factor supplies and for the efficient use of the best available technology is obvious, if waste is to be avoided. The need for the equality of the TRS of different firms can be shown through the analogous of an Edgeworth box. Take any two firms A and B which are employing given quantities L_A, T_A, L_B, T_B of labour and land. Draw an Edgeworth box with length equal to $L_A + L_B$ and height equal to $T_A + T_B$. In this box draw the isoquants of firm A with the lower left-hand corner as their origin, and (upside down) the isoquants of firm B with the upper right-hand corner as their origin; assume these isoquants are smooth and strictly convex. Remember that with labour in abscissa, $TRS = -MP_L/MP_T$. The picture is similar to the Edgeworth box of two consumers, so we can refer to ◘ Fig. 3.9 by simply reinterpreting it; each point in the box indicates a possible allocation between the firms of the labour and of the land employed in total by the two of them. We can analogously determine the Pareto set, i.e. the efficiency locus, as the locus of allocations such that it is not possible, by reallocating the factors, for a firm to produce more without the other firm producing less; at the interior points of this set there is tangency between isoquants. Efficiency requires that for any couple of firms the allocation

198   **Chapter 3** · Introduction to the Marginal Approach

between them of the factors they employ be Pareto efficient; given our assumptions, the allocation is interior, hence Pareto efficiency requires tangent isoquants and hence the condition of equal TRS. Let MP_{Li}, MP_{Ti} be the marginal product of labour and of land in the production of good i; the condition of equal TRS, $MP_{L1}/MP_{T1} = MP_{L2}/MP_{T2}$, can be rewritten $MP_{L2}/MP_{L1} = MP_{T2}/MP_{T1}$, a ratio (note well which good is at the numerator) that it will be useful to indicate with a symbol, μ.

When condition (a) is satisfied, the quantities produced are a point of the economy's **Production Possibility Frontier**, PPF, which is the locus (in R^n if there are n goods) of the combinations of quantities produced, such that it is impossible to produce more of a good without producing less of another good.[32] The PPF can be represented graphically as a curve if one takes as given all factor employments, and all quantities produced but two. For example, if the sole consumption goods produced are corn and meat, the PPF between corn and meat can be drawn as a curve once the total amounts employed of labour and of land are given; it will be decreasing, and generally strictly concave (cf. Appendix 1).[33] When there are more than two goods, one can assume that all quantities produced are given except two, and then one can draw the curve representing the PPF restricted to these two goods. The slope of the PPF restricted to two goods indicates, if units are very small, how many units of the second good (measured in ordinate) must be given up to obtain one more unit of the first good; hence it also indicates how many more units of the second good can be obtained by giving up one unit of the first good, and it is imaginatively named the (economy-wide) *marginal rate of transformation* of the first good into the second, $MRT_{1\to2}$.[34] I now show that if condition (a) is satisfied then $MRT_{1\to2} = -\mu$.

---

32 If factor supplies are not rigid, then the PPF is a surface in R^{n+m} if there are n goods and m factors, and it indicates the combinations of quantities produced and of factor endowments *not* employed in production (i.e. kept by consumers for self-enjoyment), such that it is not possible to produce more of a good or employ less of a factor without producing less of some other good or employing more of some other factor.

33 Some intuition for the strict concavity can be obtained through an example due to Samuelson. Suppose the two consumption goods are cannons and butter; cannons are produced by labour alone with fixed coefficients, one unit of labour produces one cannon; butter is produced by labour and land according to a differentiable production function with decreasing marginal products. The given supply of land is entirely used in the production of butter, hence if the production of butter is increased by transferring labour from the production of cannons, further units of labour have a lower and lower marginal product owing to the fixed supply of land, hence to a constant decrease in the production of cannons there corresponds a smaller and smaller increase in the production of butter, and the PPF is strictly concave.

34 Again, the MRT between two products is a negative number, but economists often use the term to refer to its absolute value. The qualification 'economy-wide' distinguishes this notion of marginal rate of transformation from the analogous notion defined for a single firm that produces more than one product jointly.

3.8 · Pareto Efficiency in the Production Economy. Marginal Cost

Assume two consumption goods. Let (x_1, x_2) be a point on the PPF. Suppose you reallocate a very small quantity of labour $dL > 0$ from producing good 1 to producing good 2; the (positive) change in the quantity produced of good 2 is $dx_2 = dL \cdot MP_{L2}$, the (negative) change in x_1 is $dx_1 = -dL \cdot MP_{L1}$, hence $dx_2/dx_1 = MRT_{1 \to 2} = -MP_{L2}/MP_{L1} = -\mu$. If a very small amount of *land* is reallocated from producing good 1 to producing good 2 we reach $dx_2/dx_1 = -MP_{T2}/MP_{T1} = -\mu$; if both a small amount of labour and a small amount of land are reallocated, then remembering that efficiency requires $MP_{L2}/MP_{L1} = MP_{T2}/MP_{T1} = \mu$, we obtain

$$dx_2/dx_L = -(dL \cdot MP_{L2} + dT \cdot MP_{T2})/(dL \cdot MP_{LI} + dT \cdot MP_{TI})$$
$$- \mu(dL \cdot MP_{LI} + dT \cdot MP_{T1})/(dL \cdot MP_{LI} + dT \cdot MP_{TI}) = -\mu.$$

Because of its coincidence with the absolute value of $MRT_{1 \to 2}$, the value of μ indicates the **opportunity cost** for society—in terms of good 2—of (the marginal unit of) good 1, that is, what society must give up to obtain the last unit of good 1. Conversely, $1/\mu$ is the opportunity cost for society of good 2 in terms of good 1. (The *opportunity cost* of something is what must be given up to obtain it, and therefore it depends on what one chooses to give up. If what is given up is money, then the opportunity cost of a good is its price, but if giving up money implies that one must buy less of a second good then the opportunity cost can also be expressed in terms of this second good. In fact, we will see shortly that in equilibrium $\mu = p_1/p_2$, so the opportunity cost of good 1 as price and as need to give up some amount of good 2 coincide.)

The proof of the need for condition (b) is similar. Take any two consumers A and B and let us suppose that they are allocated quantities x_1^A, x_2^A, x_1^B, x_2^B of two consumption goods. Draw, in the corresponding Edgeworth box, the indifference curves of the two consumers. Unless the point X corresponding to the given allocation is in the Pareto set, it is possible to raise the utility level of both consumers, therefore there is Pareto inefficiency. In our hypotheses, X is interior so in order for it to be in the Pareto set it must satisfy the tangency condition between indifference curves, i.e. the equality of their MRSs, which is condition (b).

Let us now show that (a) and (b) do not suffice for Pareto efficiency, condition (c) is necessary too. Assume that production is on a point of the PPF (condition (a) is satisfied) and that the resulting quantities are allocated efficiently among consumers so that condition (b) is satisfied, but the slope of the PPF between goods 1 and 2 is $MRT_{1 \to 2} = -4$, while for consumers it is $MRS = -3$. If we measure the goods in very small units, by giving up one unit of good 1 the economy can obtain 4 more units of good 2; suppose that this change in production is implemented, and one consumer receives 1 unit less of good 1 and 4 more units of good 2, while everybody else consumes the same as before; the consumer's utility increases because only 3 more units of good 2 were necessary to compensate her for the loss of 1 unit of good 1. A *Pareto improvement* has been achieved: the initial situation was not Pareto efficient.

A graphical representation of condition (c) can be obtained for the case of two produced consumption goods and two consumers, see ◘ Fig. 3.20. To each point of the PPF, e.g. to point Y, there corresponds an Edgeworth box with the

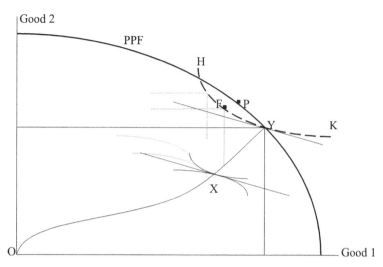

● **Fig. 3.20** Efficiency requires that the slope of the PPF equals the slope of indifference curves. If point Y indicates the quantities produced, and X their allocation among the two consumers, Pareto efficiency is not achieved in the case shown because curve HK that indicates the locus of quantities produced which would make it possible to leave the utilities of both consumers unchanged, goes below the PPF, indicating that it is possible to make both consumers better off, because its slope in point Y (equal to the common slope of the indifference curves in X) is different from the slope of the PPF in Y

upper-right corner in that point and the lower-left corner at the origin; each point in this Edgeworth box describes a possible allocation of the quantities produced between the two consumers A (with origin in the origin) and B with origin in Y; the Pareto set of this Edgeworth box describes the efficient allocations of the *given* quantities produced.

If we are given a point on the PPF and an efficient allocation of *these* quantities between the two consumers, e.g. points Y and X, then we can determine how the total quantities produced *should* change so as to make it possible to leave utility unchanged for both consumers, by moving the upper-right corner of the Edgeworth box (and hence shifting B's indifference curves) so that the indifference curve through X of consumer B slides along the indifference curve of consumer A while remaining tangent to it (cf. the red and the green indifference curves corresponding to the red and green upper-right corners); the upper-right corner of the Edgeworth box will then move along the convex curve HFYK.[35] The initial slope of this movement of the upper-right corner of the Edgeworth box is given by the MRS in X, and if the latter differs from the MRT in Y, the HK curve goes below the PPF; that is, in order to guarantee both consumers the same utility as

---

35 This curve is called a *Scitovsky community indifference curve*.

3.8 · Pareto Efficiency in the Production Economy. Marginal Cost

in X it suffices to produce quantities below the PPF, e.g. corresponding to point F; but then by producing the quantities of a point on the PPF between Y and H, e.g. point P, it is possible to improve the utility of both consumers. This is impossible only if the HK curve does not go below the PPF, which requires that it be *tangent* to the PPF in Y, i.e. that its slope in Y, equal—remember—to the MRS in X, be also equal to the slope of the PPF in Y.

The necessity of the three conditions has been shown. Their sufficiency for Pareto efficiency is easily proved (under our assumptions): the assumed strict convexity of isoquants and of indifference curves imply that both in a production and in a consumption Edgeworth box the interior points in the Pareto set and only those points exhibit tangency, respectively, of isoquants, and of indifference curves; hence common TRS plus interiority (plus full factor employment and technological efficiency, of course) implies that the given factor allocation is in the production Pareto set, and common MRS plus interiority (plus no pure waste, of course) implies that the given goods allocation is in the consumption Pareto set; hence the quantities produced are on the PPF and are efficiently allocated. The addition of condition c) guarantees that the convex curve HK in ◨ Fig. 3.13 is tangent to the concave Production Possibility Frontier, hence the HK curve does not go below the PPF, and it is impossible to increase the utility of one consumer without decreasing the utility of the other. This completes the proof of the necessity and sufficiency of (a), (b), (c) for Pareto efficiency under the stated assumption.

Now I prove that, under the assumptions made, these three conditions are satisfied by a competitive general equilibrium, and therefore the First Fundamental Welfare Theorem holds. For simplicity I continue to refer to the labour–land economy; w is the real wage, β the real land rent, in terms of the chosen numéraire.

In competitive equilibrium, factor supplies are fully utilized and in order to minimize cost all firms adopt $TRS = -w/\beta$, so condition (a) is satisfied. (Clearly an indispensable element of the argument is that the economy tends to employ all factor supplies.) All consumers maximize utility by setting $MRS_{i,j} = -p_i/p_j$, and since they face the same price ratios, they all choose the same MRS for the same couple of goods, so condition (b) is satisfied. There remains to prove condition (c), $MRT_{i \to j} = MRS_{i,j}$.

This requires another bit of standard microeconomics. So far we have considered the profit of a firm (for given product and input prices) as a function of the quantities employed of factors, so as to find the optimal employment of each factor; now let us look at profit (again at given product and input prices) as a function of output, so what must be maximized is profit as the difference between *revenue pq* and *total cost* as determined by the cost function $C(q)$ (that indicates the minimum cost for each q, for given input rentals). The first-order condition of the problem

$$max_q \, \pi = pq - C(q)$$

for a price-taking firm is

$$p - C'(q) = 0.$$

202 Chapter 3 · Introduction to the Marginal Approach

The derivative $C'(q)$ is called **marginal cost** and indicated as $MC(q)$; intuitively speaking it is the increase in total cost if output is increased by one (small) unit. Maximization of profit as a function of q requires marginal cost to be equal to the product price.

The conditions for profit maximization cannot be in reciprocal contradiction; therefore the condition $MC=p$ and the condition that each factor must be employed so as to equalize its rental with its marginal revenue product must come to the same. It is indeed so. If, in a firm, labour's marginal product is MP_L, then in order to increase output by 1 unit by increasing only L one must add $1/MP_L$ units of labour, so the increase in cost is w/MP_L. So if the unit increase in output is obtained by increasing only labour, marginal cost is given by $MC=w/MP_L$, and the conditions $MC=p$ and $w=p \cdot MP_L$ are the same condition. This equivalence continues to hold if the increase in output is obtained by increasing both labour and land by small amounts dL and dT that respect the cost minimization condition of tangency between isoquant and isocost. Then the increase in total cost is $dC=w \cdot dL + \beta \cdot dT$, the increase in output is $dq = MP_L \cdot dL + MP_T \cdot dT$, their ratio dC/dq is MC; efficiency imposes $-MP_L/MP_T = -w/\beta$, which can be rewritten as $w/MP_L = \beta/MP_T$; let us indicate either ratio as λ, so $w = \lambda \cdot MP_L$, $\beta = \lambda \cdot MP_T$; then

$$MC = dC/dq = (w \cdot dL + \beta \cdot dT)/(MP_L \cdot dL + MP_T \cdot dT) = \lambda.$$

Hence the condition $MC=p$ is the same as $\lambda=p$, i.e. $w=p \cdot MP_L$, $\beta=p \cdot MP_T$.

If increases in output are obtained by increasing only one factor (because the quantity of the other factor is fixed, a *short-period* analysis), at least after a certain point its marginal product decreases as output increases, so marginal cost is increasing, and the firm reaches the equality $MC(q)=p$ by varying output. If all factors can be varied (long-period analysis) and there are CRS, then marginal cost is constant and equal to average cost, because total cost is proportional to output; then the firm cannot reach equality of MC with the given output price through its own choices, it will be the change in industry total supply owing to entry and exit that, by causing the output price to change, will ensure equality between price and marginal cost, which in this case will also mean equality between price and average cost, another way to express the zero-profit condition that is brought about by free entry.

We are concerned with equilibrium, hence with a situation of equality between product price and marginal cost for each produced good. Hence the ratio p_i/p_j between any two product prices equals the ratio between their marginal costs. Since for all consumers $MRS_{i,j} = -p_i/p_j$, we obtain $MRS_{i,j} = -MC_i/MC_j$. So what we need is to prove that $-p_i/p_j = -MC_i/MC_j = MRT_{i \to j}$, because this implies $MRS_{i,j} = MRT_{i \to j}$ and condition (c) is satisfied.

Proof Suppose we decrease the production of good i and increase the production of good j, by transferring factors from one industry to the other. If the production of good i decreases by a small amount dx_i (a negative number), the industry's total cost C_i decreases by $dC_i = MC_i \cdot dx_i$, where MC_i is the marginal cost of good i. If the factors thus left free in the ith industry are employed in the jth industry, they determine an increase dx_j of its production. The slope of the PPF

3.8 · Pareto Efficiency in the Production Economy. Marginal Cost

restricted to goods i, j with good i in abscissa is dx_j/dx_i. For small variations in the composition of production, factor rentals can be treated as constant, hence the increase of C_j, the total cost in the jth industry, must equal the decrease of C_i, i.e. $dC_j = MC_j \cdot dx_j = - dC_i = -MC_i \cdot dx_i$. This implies $dx_j/dx_i \equiv \text{MRT}_{i \to j} = - MC_i/MC_j = - p_i/p_j = \text{MRS}_{i,j}$. ∎

(Note that through a simple reinterpretation this proof is also valid if we admit that the supply of labour and the supply of land are not rigid but depend on prices and on income distribution. We must only admit that among the goods that consumers demand there are leisure, and 'land for self-enjoyment', goods that are 'produced', respectively, by 'labour' alone and by 'land' alone on a one-to-one basis, the total endowment (and supply) of 'labour' being treated as equal to the sum of leisure and of actual labour, and the same for 'land'. For example, a consumer's decision to offer 6 h of labour and enjoy 18 h of leisure per day is formalized as a supply of 24 h of 'labour', 18 of which are employed by the consumer himself to produce 18 h of leisure, so only the remaining 6 h are offered to firms. The marginal cost and price of leisure is then w, the marginal cost and price of 'land for self-enjoyment' is β, and the total supplies of 'labour' and of 'land' can be treated as given.)

The above proof that the competitive equilibrium of our simple production economy is Pareto efficient assumed no '*corner solutions*', term indicating consumption baskets or vectors of factor employments where some good or some factor is zero (and therefore the consumption basket, or factor basket, is at a 'corner' of the indifference curve or isoquant with an edge of the non-negative orthant). In real economies with many goods and many factors it is normal that not all factors are employed by a firm, and that not all goods are demanded by a consumer. Let us see why these instances do not disturb the theorem.

The consumer's utility maximization condition $MU_i/MU_j = p_i/p_j$ can be rewritten as $MU_i/p_i = MU_j/p_j$. We noted that MU_i/p_i can be interpreted as *the marginal utility of the money spent on good i*, because the increment of utility obtained by a small addition dq_i of good i is given by $MU_i \cdot dq_i$, and $dq_i = 1/p_i$ is how much additional good i can be purchased with one additional unit of money spent on it. Accordingly, utility maximization requires that the *marginal utility of money* be the same for all goods *demanded in positive amount*: if $x_1 > 0$ and $MU_1/p_1 < MU_2/p_2$, utility can be increased by transferring one unit of money from buying good 1 to buying good 2. (The marginal utility of money is also called the marginal utility *of income*.) But it can happen that the inequality persists even when no money is allocated to demanding good 1: then utility maximization requires that her demand for good 1 be zero, it means that the marginal utility of even the first unit of money spent on good 1 is smaller than the marginal utility of money spent on good 2, $MU_1/p_1 < MU_2/p_2$ even when $x_1 = 0$. Then condition (b) does not hold; but this does not mean inefficiency, because it *is* efficient that the overall allocation assigns no amount of good 1 to this consumer: if a unit of good 1 is allocated to her, she can obtain a Pareto improvement by exchanging it for good 2 at the given market price ratio with a consumer for whom $\text{MRS}_{1,2} = -p_1/p_2$; the utility of the other consumer would not vary, but the utility of our consumer would increase.

204 **Chapter 3 · Introduction to the Marginal Approach**

Analogously, we can define *the marginal productivity of money* for a firm, and if a firm only employs one factor, e.g. only labour, it must mean that the marginal productivity of even the first money unit spent on land, MP_T/β, is smaller than for labour; condition (a) does not hold, but it is efficient not to allocate land to this firm, for the same reason as above.

Finally, if good 1 might be produced but is not produced because at a price equal to its marginal cost no one demands it, then for that good condition (c) (as well as condition (b)) does not hold, but here too there is no inefficiency, because it would be inefficient to employ factors to produce that good: they 'produce' more utility when employed for the production of goods in positive demand.

What does it mean that a factor 'produces' utility? The choice of units for the measurement of a magnitude is always arbitrary (e.g. length can be measured in metres, centimetres, yards, inches, etc.). Let us choose as unit for the utility of each consumer her equilibrium *marginal utility of money*, i.e. the common marginal utility of the last unit of money spent on any one of the goods she demands in positive amounts. E.g. suppose that with a certain utility function $u(\cdot)$ a consumer allocates her income to goods 1 and 2 and her marginal utility of money is 4, that is, $MU_1/p_1 = MU_2/p_2 = 4$. Let us operate on $u(\cdot)$ an increasing monotonic transformation by multiplying $u(\cdot)$ by 1/4; then all marginal utilities are multiplied by 1/4 and so $MU_1/p_1 = MU_2/p_2 = 1$. Doing the same for all consumers, for each consumer who demands good i in positive quantity it is $MU_i/p_i = 1$, that is,

$$MU_i = p_i:$$

when utility is scaled so that the equilibrium marginal utility of money is 1, the price of a good measures its marginal utility for all consumers who consume it. If a consumer does not demand good j, it must mean that for her $MU_j/p_j < 1$, that is, p_j is greater than marginal utility even of the first unit of the good, so the consumer correctly chooses not to buy any of it.[36]

This allows a useful interpretation of factor rentals. Take labour; it will be employed in the production of good i so that $w = MP_{Li} \cdot p_i$.[37] This can be written, owing to our having measured utilities so that $MU_i = p_i$ for all consumers who buy the good, in the following way valid for all these consumers:

$$w = MP_{Li} \cdot MU_{i_n},$$

where the product on the right-hand side is the *marginal indirect utility of labour through production of good i*; it indicates by how much the quantity of that good, produced by the last unit of labour employed to produce that good, increases the

---

36 It is possible that at a quantity equal to zero the marginal utility of the good is exactly equal to its price, but becomes less than the price for any positive amount, so the consumer finds it still optimal not to buy any amount of the good. I will neglect this unlikely fluke.

37 This is just another way to say that product price equals marginal cost, because producing one more unit of output requires the additional use of $1/MP_L$ units of labour, hence an additional cost w/MP_L, or an additional use of a combination of factors of the same cost.

3.8 · Pareto Efficiency in the Production Economy. Marginal Cost

utility of the consumer who gets it. The equilibrium conditions in our differentiable economy, plus our choice of units for utility imply that the marginal indirect utility of a factor for a consumer is the same in all productions of goods that the consumer demands and where that factor is utilized.[38] Then the reason why a good, say good k, is *not* produced can be expressed as follows: the marginal indirect utility of factors utilized to produce even the first unit of that good would be less than the marginal indirect utility they have elsewhere; therefore it is efficient *not* to employ them in the production of good k.

To close the section, a brief mention is useful, of a claim that will reappear a few times in later chapters, and will be studied in greater detail in ▶ Chap. 14. The First Fundamental Welfare Theorem states that a general equilibrium is Pareto efficient. There is a *Second Fundamental Theorem of Welfare Economics* that states something close to a converse result: *given a Pareto-efficient allocation, if indifference curves and isoquants are (strictly) convex and returns to scale are non-increasing, then that allocation can be obtained as a general equilibrium for an opportune distribution of endowments (or of purchasing power)*. In other words, it is not necessary to abolish the market and establish a command economy in order to obtain a desired Pareto-efficient allocation: a redistribution of endowments will be necessary, but then one can allow competitive markets to function, and they will maintain or produce the desired allocation.

The idea is illustrated for the exchange economy in the Edgeworth box of ◘ Fig. 3.21, where one is to imagine that there are, say, 1000 consumers like A and 1000 consumers like B. The continuous heavy curve is an indifference curve of representative consumer A, the broken heavy curve is an indifference curve of representative consumer B. Suppose the government desires that the allocation be H, which is Pareto efficient. The straight line through H is a budget line that induces the consumers to choices that render allocation H an equilibrium if that is indeed their budget line. If Ω is the initial endowment point, a redistribution of endowments so that Ω moves to a point on the straight line through H, e.g. to point K, followed by allowing market exchanges, will cause the economy to reach point H (assuming equilibrium H is unique and stable, as in the figure). One way to obtain allocation H is to redistribute endowments so that Ω comes to *coincide* with H. Other than this, reaching *precisely* H is practically impossible, because the indifference curves of consumers are not known with precision—but for the same reason the Pareto set too is only approximately determinable, and therefore whichever final allocation the government aims at, such as point H, cannot be known for sure to be Pareto efficient. However, the idea behind the importance attributed to the theorem is that what is generally sought is redistributions of income in a desired *direction* for equity purposes, rather than very precise results; and then the theorem suggests that such redistributions are better sought by changing incomes directly, than by trying to alter prices (e.g. imposing for some

---

38 Cf. Appendix 1 to this chapter for a definition of the marginal indirect utility of a factor when there is no technical substitutability.

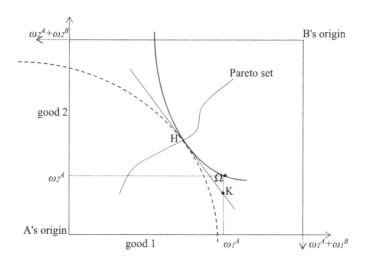

Fig. 3.21 Second Fundamental Theorem of Welfare Economics in the Edgeworth box. Allocation H can be obtained as an equilibrium if the endowment point is changed to H, or also if it is changed to K and the equilibrium is unique and stable

factor service a lower or higher price than the market would generate), because the latter type of intervention generally disturbs Pareto efficiency.

The next Figure shows why the convexity assumption is needed. The wavy shape of A's indifference curves causes allocation H not to be sustainable as an equilibrium because, at the associated relative prices, A finds it more convenient to choose point Z. The convexity must be strict if one wants to be *certain* that allocation H will be reached and maintained, because otherwise there might be a continuum of equilibrium allocations including H (◘ Fig. 3.22).

3.9 Robinson Crusoe and Market Valuation as Reflecting 'Natural' Laws

The marginal approach views the efficiency it attributes to the working of markets as satisfying *universal*, a-historical efficiency requirements. This is highlighted by how the approach compares the working of markets with the decisions of a single consumer–producer, Robinson Crusoe, who, alone on a desert island, must decide how much of his time he should dedicate to producing consumption goods rather than to leisure.

Let us assume that Robinson produces a single consumption good via a differentiable production function $q=f(L, T)$ where L is labour hours per month, T land and q consumption per month. The amount of land available to Robinson is given; Robinson must only decide how many hours to work per month on average, the remaining hours being leisure time. Robinson's utility depends on the amount of consumption good, and on the amount of labour: more consumption

3.9 · Robinson Crusoe and Market Valuation as Reflecting ...

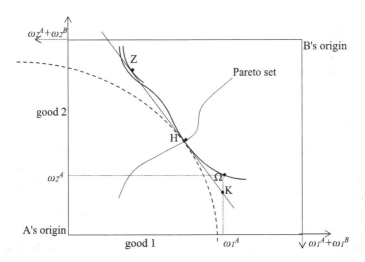

■ **Fig. 3.22** Convexity of indifference curves is required by the Second Fundamental Welfare Theorem. In this Edgeworth box consumer A's indifference curves are not convex, and as a result Pareto-efficient allocation H is not sustainable as a competitive equilibrium because at the corresponding relative price consumer A prefers point Z

means more utility; more labour contributes to utility indirectly by increasing consumption, but the direct effect of more labour is to decrease utility because it reduces leisure time and possibly because labour is intrinsically unpleasant. So we can write $u = u(q, L)$ and since q depends only on L because T is given, utility ultimately depends only on L: $u = u(q(L), L)$. Let MP_L be the marginal product of labour in the production of the consumption good, and let $MU_L := \partial u/\partial L$ be the *direct* marginal effect of an increase of L on u, which is negative. The *total* marginal effect of an increase of L on u is $du/dL = MP_L \cdot \partial u/\partial q - |MU_L|$. Note the difference between $\partial u/\partial L$ and du/dL.

It is reasonable to assume that the marginal utility of consumption is initially very high and decreases as q increases, that the marginal product of labour at least after a point decreases as L increases, and that the marginal *disutility* of labour—the absolute value of MU_L—increases as L increases; therefore du/dL initially is positive, decreases as L increases, becomes zero at a certain point, and then negative. The optimal amount of labour is where $du/dL = 0$, that is

$$MU_L/MU_q = -MP_L. \tag{3.8}$$

Let us now consider a consumer in a competitive economy who supplies labour, earning a *money* wage w per labour hour, and consumes a single consumption good q with money price p. It is usual in standard microeconomics to consider the utility of such a consumer to depend on q and on *leisure* time, but this changes nothing, because leisure time is simply total time minus labour time, so if L increases, leisure time decreases by the same amount, the direct marginal (negative) effect of more L on utility can be re-expressed, by changing its sign, as the direct marginal (positive) effect of more leisure time, and the marginal product of

208   Chapter 3 · Introduction to the Marginal Approach

L in the production of q can be expressed, by changing its sign, as the marginal negative product of leisure time. Let H indicate the total number of hours of the time period chosen, one month in our case, hence $30 \times 24 = 720$ h; let $\lambda = H - L$ indicate leisure time. Now the utility function of the consumer is $u = u(q, \lambda)$, and $wL = w(H - \lambda)$ is his money income. The budget constraint of the consumer, $pq = wL$ can be written

$$pq = wH - w\lambda.$$

This is just a special case of the budget constraint of a consumer with income deriving from given endowments: here the goods are leisure time (good 1) and consumption (good 2), and the endowment vector is $(H, 0)$, where H is total time, employable in leisure time or work time.

The graphical analysis of this case will be dealt with in ▶ Chap. 4. Now it suffices to remember that the consumer, assuming strictly convex indifference curves, maximizes utility by choosing the point in two-goods space where the budget line is tangent to an indifference curve. The slope of the budget line in this case, with leisure time in abscissa and consumption in ordinate, is $-w/p$: each additional unit of leisure time means one less wage, hence w/p fewer units of the consumption good. The slope of the indifference curves is $-[\partial u / \partial \lambda] / [\partial u / \partial q] = MU_L / MU_q$. Hence tangency requires

$$MU_L / MU_q = -w/p. \tag{3.9}$$

In competitive equilibrium a factor is used by firms in the quantity that renders its marginal revenue product equal to the factor rental, i.e. in our case $MP_L \cdot p = w$; hence $w/p = MP_L$ and therefore $(3.8) = (3.9)$.

So in a competitive market economy where the consumption good is produced by many firms, each one employing labour and with the same production function $q = q(L, T)$ as Robinson Crusoe and the same availability of land per person, the competitive equilibrium realizes the same efficiency condition that holds in Robinson Crusoe's case.

This is interpreted as meaning that Robinson the planner, when deciding how much labour to employ in production, obeys the same efficiency condition as a competitive economy would realize, implicitly attributing to labour the same price in terms of consumption as a competitive economy would.

The analogy can be easily extended to a case with several consumption goods, using the notion of indirect marginal utility of factors.

The conclusion marginalist economists draw from these observations is that efficient planning requires the same valuation of resources and goods as is brought about by competitive markets.[39]

---

39 '... no matter how technocratic the bias of the planner and how abhorrent to him are the unplanned workings of the free market, every optimal planning decision which he makes must have implicit in it the rationale of the pricing mechanism and the allocation of resources produced by the profit system' (Baumol 1965, p. 114).

On this basis, marginalist economists have argued that the market solves problems of allocative efficiency *that arise in any society*, and therefore equilibrium prices reflect the value that should be attributed to goods and to factors in *any* efficient type of social organization, i.e. reflect *natural*, a-historical, laws of evaluation.

Thus we find John Bates Clark starting the Preface to his treatise *The Distribution of Wealth* (1899) with these lines: 'It is the purpose of this work to show that the distribution of the income of society is controlled by a natural law'.

3.10 Introduction of the Rate of Interest and of Capital in the Marginalist Theory of Distribution

3.10.1 The Rate of Interest in the Exchange Economy

So far the rate of interest has not appeared. In order to determine it, the marginal approach once again refers to an equilibrium between supply and demand, this time supply and demand for *savings*, that is, for income not spent on consumption goods. Let us examine the logic of this explanation at first in the exchange economy where corn and meat are exchanged. Consider time as divided into 'periods', with only one market day in each period, for example (if the period is a month) only on the first day of each month. In this economy, let us now assume there is the possibility to transfer purchasing power from one period to another through loans and debts (but not through storage of goods). In a period a consumer can consume more than the income obtained from her endowments in that period by borrowing purchasing power from other consumers, i.e. by selling a (real) *bond*—a promise of repayment of a certain amount of some good in some future period—to some other consumer. Both corn and meat are perishable, and they cannot be stored from one period to the next.

Suppose corn, good 1, is the numéraire and only one type of bond can be emitted, a promise to give one unit of corn to the bond holder one period later. Purchasing such a bond in period t means to lend an amount of good 1 to the issuer of the bond, against a promise of repayment of 1 unit of good 1 in period $t+1$. If the price of the bond is 0.909, lending 0.909 units of good 1 yields 1 unit of the same good after one period, with a rate of interest $r = 10\%$. The price 0.909 of the bond is the price to be paid now for a unit of the good one period later, so it can be seen as the relative price of good 1 of period $t+1$ in terms of good 1 of period t. It is also called the *present value* at t of 1 unit of good 1 obtainable one period later. Because corn at $t+1$ will have price 1, this price 0.909 is also called the *discounted value* at t of a unit of good 1 at date $t+1$. The *discount factor* (the number by which one must *multiply* the price of the good at $t+1$ to obtain its discounted value at t) is $1/(1+r)$ with the rate of interest $r = 10\%$. The price of a bond in our economy coincides with the discount factor.

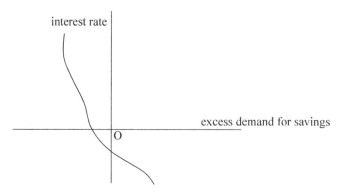

Fig. 3.23 Stable market for savings in the exchange economy, with a negative equilibrium interest rate

A consumer starts each period t with an endowment of corn ω_1 and of meat ω_2, and debts or credits b_{t-1} from the previous period, where b_{t-1} if positive indicates the number of bonds *bought* the period before (these mean the consumer will receive b_{t-1} units of corn at the beginning of the period as debt payments), if negative indicates the number of bonds *sold* by the consumer the period before (the consumer must pay $-b_{t-1}$ units of corn to other consumers in repayment for the loans obtained in the previous period). After payment of debts the consumer's income is $\omega_1 + b_{t-1} + p_2\omega_2$. (It can happen that debtors are unable to honour their debts and go bankrupt. Let us neglect this possibility.) The consumer demands corn and meat for the period for a value $x_1 + p_2 x_2$. If this is more than her income she demands savings, i.e. offers bonds b_t for a value $b_t/(1+r)$ equal to the difference, hoping these bonds will be bought by consumers who intend to demand corn and meat for a total value *less* than their income; the latter consumers demand bonds, i.e. supply savings.

Let us neglect how p_2 is determined and let us concentrate on what determines the price of bonds. This is $p_b = 1/(1+r)$, so it implicitly determines the rate of interest. If the number of bonds emitted by dissavers exceeds the number of bonds demanded by savers, the price p_b of bonds tends to decrease, which means that r tends to *increase*: indeed demand for savings (supply of bonds) is greater than the supply of savings (demand for bonds), so the rate of interest, which can be seen as the net price of savings, tends to increase (**Fig. 3.23**).

As r increases, the demand for savings by dissavers and the supply of savings by savers can change, and the difference, or *excess demand* for savings (excess supply of bonds), can increase or decrease and can change sign even several times. To graph the excess demand for savings as a function of r requires considering all four orthants, because it can be positive or negative, and negative values of the interest rate must be considered too: if nearly everybody in the economy would like to transfer income from period t to period $t+1$, they may have to accept to lend their savings at a negative rate of interest.

3.10 · Introduction of the Rate of Interest and of Capital in ...

As economists generally put price in ordinate and quantity in abscissa, let us draw the excess demand for savings in abscissa as a function of r in ordinate; the market is in equilibrium when the curve intersects the ordinate, i.e. when the excess demand for savings is zero. There can be more than one intersection; it is often assumed that the curve is decreasing because a rise of r discourages borrowing and stimulates lending, in which case there will be a single and stable equilibrium of the savings market; in fact, it need not be so, as we will see in ▶ Chap. 4; but now let us accept this assumption, since in this chapter I intend to present the marginal approach in the favourable light it enjoyed at its birth, when its possible weaknesses were not yet clearly perceived. The equilibrium interest rate can be positive or negative.

In a production economy without capital goods, such as the corn–meat economy with labour and land as factors of production, it is again true that in equilibrium some consumers can save only if other consumers dissave, because each period production is only of consumption goods and is independent of the production of the previous period. In each period there cannot be positive savings in the aggregate, the savings of some necessarily correspond to dissavings of others, they only entail a redistribution of consumption from some consumers to others. Some individuals can, but the economy as a whole cannot, transfer consumption from today to tomorrow.

3.10.2 The Rate of Interest in the Corn Economy

Things change once one admits production with capital goods, i.e. with produced means of production. Then society as a whole can consume less today and more tomorrow. For example consider an economy that produces only corn, by using labour, land and capital (seed-corn) as inputs according to a (gross) production function $Q = f(L, T, K)$. To fix ideas assume initially a stationary economy, which every period starts with the same stock K of seed-corn and reintegrates it at the end of the year, consuming all the rest of the full-employment corn production. If one period less corn is consumed, the economy ends the year with a greater stock of seed-corn, so next period the economy has more capital, and this means that the same amounts of labour and land produce more corn than before. The determinants of the rate of interest change too, because now savings can be used to purchase capital, lend it to firms, and earn the rate of return on its employment, so one will be ready to pay for a loan a rate of interest dependent on the rate of return on the productive employment of capital. Neglecting risk, the rate of interest will be determined by this rate of return, which corresponds to the *net* marginal product of capital.

This corn economy illustrates the basic marginalist view of the role of capital, but the presence of produced means of production considerably complicates the marginal/neoclassical approach, and we will have to dedicate many pages in subsequent chapters to studying these complications. Here we study only the case that raises the fewest problems: a single capital good.

212   Chapter 3 · Introduction to the Marginal Approach

In the corn economy the single capital good, corn used as seed (wages and rent are paid at the end of the year out of the harvest so do not require anticipations of capital), is homogeneous with the single consumption good the economy produces: let us further simplify the analysis by assuming land is overabundant and hence a free good, so we can neglect it. Capital is *circulating* capital, disappearing when used. We must distinguish the physical or *gross* from the *net* marginal product of capital. The latter is the increase in *net* corn production due to one more unit of corn-capital, i.e. the increase in total production minus the replacement of the additional used-up unit of capital. If by employing one more unit of corn-capital a farmer obtains 1.2 more units of corn, i.e. if the gross marginal product of capital is 1.2, she will find it convenient (leaving aside risk for simplicity) to borrow one more unit of capital if the real rate of interest does not exceed 20%, which is the net marginal product of capital. So the rate of interest r will tend to equal the *net* marginal product of corn-capital, i.e. its gross marginal product minus 1. Let us use MP_{KG} to indicate the *gross* or physical marginal product of capital, MP_K to indicate the *net* marginal product, and the condition of equality between net marginal product of corn-capital and rate of interest can be written $MP_{KG} = 1 + r$ or equivalently $MP_K = r$.

Similarly, one must distinguish the gross from the net total product; if the economy's gross product is 1000 and it has required the employment of 400 units of corn-capital, the net product is 600. Note that the gross product as I am defining it here does *not* correspond to the gross product, GNP, of the dominant national accounting conventions: the latter is defined *net* of the replacement of intermediate goods and only gross with respect to durable capital; thus in this economy, where no capital is durable, the usual national accounting definitions would make gross and net product coincide. It has been then proposed to call **social product** the total production in the given period, inclusive of production of intermediate goods or circulating capital goods. In this economy 1000 is the social product. But 'gross' remains useful to distinguish net from gross marginal product of seed-corn.

Apart from this need to distinguish gross from net magnitudes, the reasoning applied to labour and land is applied identically to labour and corn-capital. Thus assume initially that the capitalists (the owners of corn-capital) and the labourers are two different groups of people, and that the capitalists act as entrepreneurs. Competition ensures a tendency toward the same, most efficient production function in all firms. Let $Q = F(L, K)$ indicate the gross production function; the net product is $Y = Q - K = F(L, K) - K$. The gross marginal product of corn-capital, MP_{KG}, is $\partial F / \partial K$; the net marginal product is $\partial [F(L, K) - K] / \partial K = MP_{KG} - 1$. If $F(L, K)$ has CRS, so does $F(L, K) - K$. The same reasoning applied to labour with landlords as entrepreneurs can be applied here to derive the demand curve for labour. Conversely, if labourers are the entrepreneurs, the reasoning can be applied to corn-capital to derive a decreasing demand curve for capital; with K in abscissa and r in ordinate, the demand curve for K is the curve of the net marginal product of capital; plausibly it behaves similarly to the demand curve for land, hence also similarly to ◘ Fig. 3.6. Assuming a vertical capital supply curve corresponding to the given capital endowment of the economy, the equilibrium in the capital market is stable. The economy tends to the simultaneous full-employment equilibrium of both labour and corn-capital. The product exhaustion theorem becomes $Q = F(K, L) = MP_L \cdot L + MP_{KG} \cdot K = wL + (1+r)K$, or $Y = MP_L \cdot L + MP_K \cdot K = wL + rK$, and it can be used here too to demonstrate that it does not matter who acts as entrepreneur, and that in equilibrium the entrepreneur makes neither profit (neoclassical meaning) nor loss.

The assumption of a given supply (given endowment) of corn-capital can be criticized. In this economy, at the beginning of each year what is given is the corn harvest produced by the just completed production cycle; the stock of seed-corn available for the next production cycle will be determined by the consumers' decisions as to how much of the harvest to consume and how much of it to save and offer to firms as seed-corn, and it can be influenced by the rate of interest. It may seem more correct to determine the equilibrium of period t to take as given the harvest Q_{t-1} and determine K_t as resulting from consumer saving decisions. However, in order for this imaginary economy to mirror—albeit in simplified form—the working of real economies, one must remember that in real economies capital goods and consumption goods are mostly different goods and the stock of capital goods cannot be quickly transformed into consumption goods; so, if one wants to use this simple economy to obtain an initial understanding of how income distribution is determined in real economies, the assumption that in each given period the stock of corn-capital is *given* is the assumption that more closely mirrors the situation in more realistic economies.

This economy, where capital and product are the same good, and income distribution is determined by the technical substitution mechanism, illustrates the marginalist explanation of the income from the property of capital in the simplest way. The equilibrium rate of interest is the reward of the marginal contribution of capital to net production, equal to its full-employment net marginal product.

Adding land as a third production factor poses no difficulty. The demand curve for each factor can be determined once the employments of the other two factors are given and will be decreasing for the already known reasons. In equilibrium each factor receives its full-employment marginal product. Note the symmetry: all factors are on an equal footing, the same mechanism determines all rentals. This explains why labour, land, capital are all called 'factors of production': they are seen as having a similar role in the economy.

3.10.3 Capital and the Indirect Factor Substitution Mechanism

A bit more complicated is the study of the *indirect* substitution mechanism. Let us again assume an economy that produces two goods, corn and meat, but now produced by corn-capital and labour, with fixed technical coefficients. Corn is demanded both for consumption and for use as capital good. Let a_{K1} and a_{K2} be the technical coefficients of corn-capital in the production, respectively, of corn (good 1) as gross product, and of meat (good 2). Land is free. The technical conditions of production in the two industries are

214   **Chapter 3 · Introduction to the Marginal Approach**

a_{L1} units of labour$^*a_{K1}$ units of corn-capital $\rightarrow$ 1 unit of *gross* corn output

a_{L2} units of labour$^*a_{K2}$ units of corn-capital $\rightarrow$ 1 unit of meat.

Clearly it must be $a_{K1} < 1$ otherwise the economy cannot survive. The price = cost equations are now:

$$p_1 = wa_{L1} + (1 + r)p_1 a_{K1}$$

$$p_2 = wa_{L2} + (1 + r)p_1 a_{K2}$$

For each unit of corn-capital borrowed, the firm must repay $(1 + r)$ units of corn at the end of the year. If the firm owns the capital, it must anyway impute an *opportunity cost* equal to $(1 + r)$ to each unit of capital, because this is what it would earn by lending it to other firms.[40] If we choose corn as numéraire, $p_1 = 1$, the price equations become

$$1 = wa_{L1} + (1 + r)a_{K1} \tag{3.10}$$

$$p_2 = wa_{L2} + (1 + r)a_{K2}. \tag{3.11}$$

Let us study how the demand for corn for consumption purposes, and the demand for meat, determine the demand for labour and for capital. We want to determine the capital needed in order to obtain corn for consumption, or meat, as *net* products, that is, with the used-up capital being replaced. This is the way to determine the *persistent* demand for capital associated with a *persistent* demand for meat and for consumption of corn; which is what we need, because the equilibrium must be persistent, otherwise it cannot have the role of centre of gravitation, indicator of averages. This requires determining for each consumption good the *subsystem* or *vertically integrated industry* that produces one unit of it as *net* product.[41]

Suppose consumers demand 1 unit of corn per period for consumption purposes. In order for a repeated use of 1 unit of corn per period for consumption to be possible, the economy must produce more than 1 unit of corn, because it must also replace the corn-capital used up. The gross production of corn per period that satisfies such a condition is the quantity Q_1 that solves

$$Q_1 - a_{K1}Q_1 = 1 \quad \text{i.e. } Q_1 = 1/(1 - a_{K1}).$$

An ensemble of corn-producing firms producing Q_1 as total output is a subsystem producing a net product of 1 unit of corn. In this case the subsystem includes only corn-producing firms. This ensemble of firms employs (i.e. demands) $a_{K1}Q_1$ units of seed-corn; thus $a_{K1}Q_1 = a_{K1}/(1 - a_{K1})$ can be called the *technical coefficient of capital in the integrated production of corn as net product*. If this economy produced year after year a net product consisting of only 1

---

40 The **opportunity cost** of the employment of a factor in a certain use is what the factor could have earned in the best alternative use.

41 The notion of subsystem has been explained in ▶ Chap. 2 but it is also made sufficiently clear by the way it will be determined here, so ▶ Chap. 2 is not indispensable to understand what follows.

3.10 · Introduction of the Rate of Interest and of Capital in ...

unit of corn, one would observe that the corn-capital employed in this economy would be this amount. Let χ_1 indicate this coefficient: then $\chi_1 q_1$ is the demand for corn-capital associated with a demand of q_1 units of corn for consumption; the total demand for corn output caused by a consumption demand q_1 is therefore $(1 + \chi_1)q_1$.

The demand for labour associated with a consumption demand for 1 unit of corn, let us indicate it as λ_1, is the labour needed by the subsystem producing a *net* output of 1 unit of corn and hence producing a *gross* output of Q_1 units of corn, so $\lambda_1 = a_{L1}Q_1 = a_{L1}/(1 - a_{K1})$.

Now let us derive the demand for seed-corn of the subsystem producing one unit of meat as net product. This subsystem includes firms that produce meat and firms that produce corn. The firms that produce one unit of meat use a_{K2} units of corn, therefore overall corn production in the subsystem, let us indicate it as χ_2, must be such that after replacing the used-up seed-corn one is left with a_{K2} units of corn to pass to meat production. Hence it must be

$$\chi_2 - a_{K1}\chi_2 = a_{K2} \quad \text{i.e.} \quad \chi_2 = a_{K2}/(1 - a_{K1}).$$

This is also the quantity of corn this meat subsystem needs at the beginning of each production cycle, a_{K2} units for meat production and $a_{K1}\chi_2$ units for the production of χ_2 units of corn. So χ_2 is the *technical coefficient of capital in the integrated production of meat as net product*. Then the *technical coefficient of labour in the integrated production of meat as net product*, λ_2, is the labour employed in total in the subsystem, $\lambda_2 = a_{L2} + a_{L1}\chi_2 = a_{L2} + a_{L1}a_{K2}/(1 - a_{K1})$.

We can therefore write

λ_1 units of labour $^*\chi_1$ units of corn - capital $\rightarrow$ 1 unit of corn as *net* product

λ_2 units of labour $^*\chi_2$ units of corn - capital $\rightarrow$ 1 unit of meat as *net* product.

Now we can determine the demand for corn-capital, assuming the supply of labour to be fully employed. Let L^* be the supply of labour, let q_1 and q_2 stand for the *consumption* demands for corn and for meat that coincide with the net products of the two commodities (I am making the static assumption of no net savings, no net investment, the stock of corn-capital is simply reintegrated every period). The demand for labour is $\lambda_1 q_1 + \lambda_2 q_2$. The demand for capital is $\chi_1 q_1 + \chi_2 q_2$. Note that now the price equations can also be written as follows[42]:

$$1 = w\lambda_1 + r\chi_1 \tag{3.12}$$

$$p_2 = w\lambda_2 + r\chi_2. \tag{3.13}$$

These equations express the value of the net product of a subsystem as equal to the *value added* in total in the industries composing the subsystem; in this economy value added is the sum of the wages and interest paid to the labour and the

---

42 The reader should check as an ***Exercise*** that the two systems of equations are in fact equivalent.

216   Chapter 3 · Introduction to the Marginal Approach

capital employed in the subsystem. These equations are formally identical to the price equations when corn and meat are produced by labour and land, but the 'technical coefficients' have now a different interpretation, they are the factors needed for unit production of corn and of meat as *net* products.

Let us now see the indirect substitution mechanism at work. Assume labour is fully employed and that corn is the more capital-intensive good, that is, $a_{K1}/a_{L1} > a_{K2}/a_{L2}$; then also $\chi_1/\lambda_1 > \chi_2/\lambda_2$, because $\chi_1/\lambda_1 = a_{K1}/a_{L1}$, while the meat subsystem includes a production of corn, so its overall capital–labour ratio χ_2/λ_2 is intermediate between a_{K1}/a_{L1} and a_{K2}/a_{L2}, so it is less than a_{K2}/a_{L2}, but still greater than χ_1/λ_1.[43] Therefore we can apply the same reasoning as for the labour–land economy: assuming labour is fully employed, if the rate of interest decreases making corn cheaper relative to meat and shifting the composition of consumer demand in favour of corn, then some units of labour must move from the meat subsystem to the corn subsystem, where they are associated with a greater employment of corn-capital: the demand for corn-capital increases.

The reader might wonder whether it is acceptable to derive the demand curves for labour and for corn-capital under a static assumption (zero net investment): in real economies there often is positive net investment. In the present corn-and-meat economy it would mean a greater production of corn than under the static assumption, hence a different composition of net output, different demand curves, a different equilibrium income distribution. The answer supplied by traditional marginalist economists—a convincing one within their vision of how a market economy works—is that net investment causes only a very small alteration of the composition of demand for factors relative to a static economy, because it is a small fraction of net output; therefore the static assumption is a simplification that supplies a good approximation and also makes the basic mechanisms determining income distribution clearer.[44] It can be added that the capital demand function derived under the static assumption clarifies what allows capital accumulation in the marginal approach, as explained in the online appendix to the chapter. Anyway the analysis of economies with net investment in the marginalist framework requires further considerations owing to the presence of durable capital goods, but for this the reader must wait for ▶ Chap. 7.

It is important not to confuse the determination of equilibrium under the static assumption (which asks what equilibrium the economy gravitates toward on the basis of the given endowments of labour and capital, assuming it is little dis-

---

43 Therefore the difference in capital–labour ratio between the two *vertically integrated* industries is less than the difference between the industries directly producing those two goods.

44 'For the general fund of capital is the product of labour and waiting; and the extra work, and the extra waiting, to which a rise in the rate of interest would act as an incentive, would not quickly amount to much as compared with the work and waiting, of which the total existing stock of capital is the result' (Marshall 1920 (1970), VI, ii, 4, p. 443). 'In the case of capital, the normal case is a growing total stock; but this is so large that the net production in a short period of time will not make an appreciable difference in the demand price' (Knight 1946, p. 400). Note furthermore that, in order to make an appreciable difference, the factor proportions in the production of the goods included in net investment should be considerably different from average factor proportions.

3.10 · Introduction of the Rate of Interest and of Capital in ...

turbed by net savings) with the notion of *secularly stationary equilibrium*, where the capital endowment is *not* treated as given, but rather as a quantity that has had the time to change until it determines such a wealth of consumers and such a level of the interest rate that consumers spontaneously choose to have zero net savings in the aggregate. The stationary equilibrium one finds in traditional marginalist authors is based on the static assumption, it is not a secularly stationary equilibrium, and the reason is simple: a secularly stationary equilibrium does not allow the marginalist economist to explain the observed income distribution nor to predict how it would be modified for example by labour immigration, because the secularly stationary equilibrium would require a capital endowment and an income distribution *very* different from the ones corresponding to the capital stock of any concrete economy under study. It is the marginal product of labour with the *existing* capital stock that can be used by the marginalist economist to explain the average real wage, not the marginal product that labour would have when and if the capital stock became such as to induce the disappearance of net savings, perhaps seventy years from now, perhaps never. ▶ Chapter 7 will explain that the distinction between these two notions of stationary equilibrium is often not clearly perceived and the result is some important confusions.

3.11 Money and the Rate of Interest

The rate of interest has been determined so far by the equilibrium between supply and demand for corn-capital. In real economies, it might be objected, the rate of interest is the 'price' of credit, and loans are normally in money terms. Can the above theory apply to an economy where goods are exchanged against money and the rate of interest is the 'price' of monetary loans?

The basic idea of the marginal approach on this issue is that (if financial intermediaries do not disturb the process and if, for simplicity, we assume no inflation) the equilibrium rate of interest brings at the same time into equality the supply and demand for capital (stocks), and the supply and demand for monetary gross savings or 'loanable funds' (flows).[45] Gross savings are the sum of funds set aside to replace the used-up capital goods and net savings. Let us leave aside consumer credit which is a complication whose consideration adds little to the basic insight. If the supply of gross savings is greater than the demand for them coming from firms, the rate of interest decreases, and according to the marginal approach firms become ready to employ more capital per unit of labour than before, up to the point where the net marginal product of capital becomes equal (neglecting risk) to the rate of interest. There will be an increase of investment that will gradually increase the stock of capital until the stock of capital becomes such that its marginal product equals the rate of interest. Now, the greater the stock of capital, the greater the flow of loanable funds demanded by firms to replace the used-up

---

45 See ▶ Chap. 7 for more details.

218   **Chapter 3** · Introduction to the Marginal Approach

capital goods. For example, if each period the capital goods to be replaced are worth 1/10 of the value of the capital stock, then each period firms need to borrow loanable funds of a value equal to 1/10 of the value of the capital stock if they intend to keep it unchanged. This flow of borrowing increases if the capital stock increases. If the net savings are positive and gradually increase the stock of capital, then the flow demand for loanable funds by firms to replace used-up capital goods increases and finally swallows up the entire flow supply of gross savings, bringing net savings to zero. At that point the rate of interest that makes firms satisfied with the existing stock of capital—hence, the rate of interest equal to the marginal product of the existing stock of capital—also produces equilibrium between supply and demand for the flow of gross savings. The rate of interest will never go far above that level because firms will not be ready to borrow at a rate above the rate of return they can hope to earn on the capital bought with the loans, rate of return equal to the marginal product of capital. In other words, the demand for loans drops rapidly if the rate of interest goes above the marginal product of the existing stock of capital. As to decreases of the rate of interest below the current marginal product of capital, they too can be expected to be quite limited, as increases in the absorption of a flow of net savings will only very slowly reduce the marginal product of capital. The considerable elasticity of the flow demand for loanable funds implies that *the equilibrium rate of interest, although directly determined by the equilibrium between supply and demand for loanable funds, is in fact determined by the full-employment marginal product of capital, in the sense that it will always be very close to the latter.*

3.12 Accumulation

At this point we can ask: why does the quantity of capital tend to grow as time passes? In the marginal approach, the answer is: Because consumers decide not to spend on consumption goods their entire net income and lend the remainder to firms at a rate of interest that induces the firms to borrow those net savings and to use them to raise the capital/labour ratio in production by purchasing more new capital goods than required to replace the used-up capital goods. So the stock of capital grows. The increased demand for newly produced capital goods is satisfied by using the productive factors left free by the reduced demand for consumption goods.

For example, in the economy producing corn with corn-capital and labour, with wages paid at the end of the year, if 1100 units of corn are produced in a certain year with the employment of 400 units of corn-capital (hence the net product is 700), and if consumers decide to consume only 600 units of corn, they are left with 500 units of unspent income; they will offer it as loans to firms, and if the rate of interest becomes low enough firms will decide they want to borrow that income and use it to buy corn-capital raising the capital–labour ratio in production, employing 500 units of corn-capital instead of the old 400; so the net savings of consumers equal in value to 100 units of corn become net investment, and the stock of corn-capital grows from 400 to 500.

3.12 · Accumulation

In such a perspective, the capital stock of an economy is the result of the sum of past decisions by consumers to perform net savings out of full-employment production.

Evidently—marginalist economists conclude—since there has been and there continues to be capital accumulation, consumers have been having such preferences that, at the rate of interest corresponding to the full-employment marginal product of capital, in the aggregate they prefer to consume in each period less than the net product of that period, in order to consume more in the future. Nothing in the theory prevents consumers from preferring to consume more than the net product, in which case there would be decumulation of capital; but this has not happened. Evidently the rate of interest is such and preferences are such as to induce consumers to perform net savings, preferring to trade off some present consumption for more consumption in the future.

The marginalist view is that, were it not for the continuous growth of labour supply, and for technical progress that raises the marginal product of capital and contrasts the scarcity of land, this continuous capital accumulation would have caused a continuous decrease of the rate of interest, down probably to zero.

3.13 A Comparison Between the Classical and the Marginal Approaches to Income Distribution: The Basic Analytical Difference and Some Implications

3.13.1 The Different Data When Determining the Rate of Return on Capital

We now have the elements to grasp the radical difference between the classical or surplus approach, and the marginal or neoclassical approach.

The central difference is in the explanation of how the net product, net also of land rent, gets divided between wages on the one side, and on the other side income from the property of capital (profits in classical terminology, interest in marginalist terminology). The rent of land is explained on the basis of similar principles in the two approaches,[46] so we can concentrate on the differences in the explanation of wages and profits (interest), by assuming land is free. In the classical approach capitalists are able to appropriate part of the product owing to their bargaining strength that derives from their control of the means of production and their capacity to resist more in case of conflict; the sociopolitical elements that determine the relative bargaining strength of labour and capital fix the real wage, and profits are determined as the residue. In the marginal approach the real

---

46 When there are different qualities of land, in the marginal approach each one is treated as a different factor, and land rents will be determined as differential intensive and extensive rents in the same way as in the classical approach, once the rate of profits or the real wage are determined.

wage rate and the rate of interest are determined by a symmetrical mechanism, that determines both simultaneously, through the tendency toward an equilibrium between supply and demand.

The root of the difference does not lie simply in whether the labour market is seen as competitive (with each individual acting separately from the others) or not competitive (with labourers and capitalists acting as two coalitions). It lies in the presence in the marginalist authors, and absence in the classical authors, of the conception of production as a *cooperation* of factors of production which are *substitutable* one for the other, so that technical choices and consumer choices activate factor substitution mechanisms which engender a *decreasing demand curve for each factor*.

In the classical authors there is no notion of demand curves for factors. Only in the marginalist authors one finds a *necessary* (and decreasing) relationship between real wage and level of employment. Marginalist authors sometimes admit that the labour market may not be fully competitive, and that trade unions or other forms of labour coalitions can fix the real wage before the rate of interest. But the presence in the marginal approach of a decreasing demand curve for labour means that a given real wage renders the level of labour employment *endogenously* determined; increases in real wages have a negative effect on employment; persistent unemployment is due to too high a real wage. In the classical authors there is no necessary, univocal connection between real wages and labour employment: the same level of labour employment can correspond to different real wages depending on relative bargaining power, and a change in the real wage can have different effects on employment, depending on the specific situation. Thus in the marginal approach, if one were to observe two economies that differ only in the endowment of labour, not in the endowments of other factors nor in technology nor in average preferences, so that the labour demand curve is the same, then the observation of the same quantity of labour *employment* in the two economies (and hence of different rates of unemployment) would imply that the real wage is the same in both economies. On the contrary in the classical approach, if again in the two economies utilization of other inputs and technology and composition of demand and level of labour employment are the same but the rate of unemployment differs, there is no reason why one should expect the same real wage, there is rather an expectation of lower wages where unemployment is greater because this weakens workers *ceteris paribus*; but it is not excluded that on the contrary wages may be higher where unemployment is greater, because bargaining power depends on many other things too, e.g. legal protection against unfair firings, unity of the working class, strength of ideological motivations, political parties in power.

Another way to stress the difference is that in the classical approach the sole certain effect of a *change* in real wages is a change of the rate of profits in the opposite direction; its further effects, in particular its effects on employment, are not univocally determined, depending on the circumstances and possibly on the extent of the variation. E.g. in Marx an increase in wages can sometimes increase employment by stimulating demand for consumption goods, in other occasions— especially if it is a big increase accompanied by much social unrest—it can cause a crisis by frightening capitalists and discouraging investment. In Ricardo, who accepted Say's Law, a decrease in wages has no direct effect on employment; it may result in a decrease of unemployment only over a number of years and if the higher rate of profits stimulates a faster accumulation of capital; for marginalist economists on the contrary the increase in the demand for labour is brought about, without any need to increase the stock of capital, by the shift in methods of production and in the composition of consumption engendered by the lower real wage.

The absence of a univocal connection between income distribution and quantities produced also explains the classical separate determination of the quantities produced, and their treatment as given when one determines the rate of profits (cf. ▶ Chap. 1, especially ▶ Sect. 1.13): if a regular univocal connection existed between income distribution and quantities produced, a separate determination of quantities would make little sense, a *simultaneous* determination would be the natural approach.

The above explains the difference in the magnitudes taken as data in the two approaches for the determination of the rate of return on capital (rate of profit or, abstracting from risk, rate of interest). In the marginal approach the data are:

preferences ('tastes')

known production methods

factor endowments and their distribution among consumers.

These data allow the determination of the rate of interest *simultaneously* with the other factor rentals and with the quantities produced, all determined by the tendency toward a simultaneous equilibrium between supply and demand in all markets. In the classical approach the data are (cf. ▶ Sect. 1.13):

normal quantities produced

known production methods

real wage(s).

Only the second group of data is the same in the two approaches. The quantities produced and the real wage, which in the marginal approach, are determined simultaneously with the rate of interest, in the classical approach are taken as given (or as independently varying parameters) when the purpose is the determination of the rate of profit—given, not in the sense of unexplained, but rather in the sense of determined by complex forces best studied separately in a more inductive part of the overall analysis. So when analysing the effects of changes of the real wage on the rate of profit it is best first to take produced quantities as given, and only in a second stage to ask what the effect on quantities is presumably going to be depending on the specific historical circumstances, also asking in this second stage whether the effect on quantities (through its effect on no-rent land) suggests a modification of the conclusion reached in the first stage.

In the marginal approach, on the contrary, factor rentals, product prices and quantities demanded are all strictly interdependent owing to the factor demand curves. To each real wage there corresponds a definite level of labour employment and a definite demand for the several consumption goods, and if competition is

222   Chapter 3 · Introduction to the Marginal Approach

allowed to work freely the real wage will tend to a definite level, the full-employment level, and will change, and in a predictable direction, only if endowments, technical knowledge or tastes change.

3.13.2 The Role of Social and Political Elements. Competition in Labour Markets

The presence in the marginalist authors, and absence in the classical authors, of the notion of a negative elasticity of labour employment with respect to real wages entails a different role of social and political elements in the two approaches, and a different conception of how competition in the labour market operates.

In the marginal approach a wage fixed by sociopolitical elements is an *impediment* to the free working of competition, which if left free to operate would produce a fully determinate level of the real wages. The marginalist conception itself of the 'free working of competition' in labour markets relies on this: without a significant positive effect of decreases of real wages upon employment, the marginalist conception of competition in the labour market, entailing an indefinite downward flexibility of wages as long as there is unemployment, would clearly be unacceptable: its operation would bring wages to zero (or anyway to implausibly low levels) whenever unemployment persisted, with a clear contradiction with observation.

In the classical approach the absence of the notion of a decreasing demand curve for labour would have entailed precisely such implausible results, if competition had been thought to operate as the marginalists conceive it: the little response of labour employment to changes in wages and the nearly universal presence of unemployment in capitalist economies would have entailed a prediction of a tendency of wages to zero, clearly incompatible with observation. It is understandable then that in the classical approach one does not find the view that wages will decrease as long as the demand for labour is less than its supply, and one finds instead a stress on custom, on the need to defend social status, on relative bargaining power, on collective behaviours, on fear of popular revolts, and the like, as the elements capable of determining real wages and their variations. The social customs and political elements that in the marginal approach are, if at all, superposed upon a self-sufficient mechanism and *impede* its autonomous working are, to the contrary, *indispensable* in a classical approach and are accordingly viewed as an obvious component of an economy based on wage labour. Hence for a classical economist social, political, institutional and historical considerations are an integral part of economic analysis.[47]

Accordingly, in the classical approach the operation of competition in the labour markets is conceived as embodying those same social forces that establish

---

47 A modern example of such a classical approach is M. Kalecki, 'Political aspects of full employment', 1943.

the level of wages. Thus a skilled worker will not, only because he has been unemployed for a few months, accept a lower wage than the one social custom normally grants him. Unemployment will not necessarily mean a tendency of wages to decrease, and even when it does (because unusually high, and/or combined with other sociopolitical factors), the decrease will be slow and will not go below what Adam Smith called the (historically specific) lowest level 'compatible with common humanity' (that is, presumably, the level below which social peace is endangered).

Indeed, if one abandons the presumption of a significant negative elasticity of employment with respect to the real wage, then a stickiness of real wages in the face of unemployment becomes not only necessary in order to avoid absurd conclusions, but also easily understandable. If the level of employment is not significantly improved by real wage decreases, then it is only to be expected that historical experience will have taught workers that wage undercutting must be avoided. If the unemployed workers offer to work for less than the current wage, it suffices that the employed workers themselves accept the lower wage, and they will not be replaced by the unemployed, since labour turnover does imply at least some minimal costs. This is implicitly admitted also by the marginal approach, where the increased demand for labour ensures that the lower wage gets the unemployed a job *in addition* to the previously employed workers, not *in place of* previously employed workers. But if the resulting lower real wage does not increase employment, the unemployed workers have gained nothing by offering themselves for a lower wage—they are still unemployed, and have only made the employed workers worse off (and themselves too, in so far as they receive support from the income of their employed relatives). The presumption is then natural that popular culture will have developed a variety of ways ('fair wage' notions, a culture of solidarity, sanctions against blacklegs, etc.) to spare new entrants into the 'reserve army of the unemployed' the need to learn through experience—a learning process which would greatly damage their fellow workers in the meanwhile—that wage undercutting brings no advantage to the unemployed even from a strictly selfish viewpoint.[48] But in situations of particular weakness, or when there is reason to believe that only a decrease of wages will save jobs (e.g. a firm risking bankruptcy, foreign competition), or when a change in laws reduces the bargaining power of workers, wage decreases *can* be expected.

On the contrary in the marginal approach supply-and-demand functions are capable of determining prices, quantities and income distribution on the basis of a very restricted set of institutions: essentially, competition and the respect of private property and contracts. Apart from these institutional prerequisites, *the market is a self-sufficient sphere of social life*, capable of endogenously determining prices, quantities and income distribution. This is why classical theorists such as Adam Smith and Marx were also sociologists and political scientists, which is not generally the case with marginalist economists.

---

48 The customary element is so strong that usually the thought does not occur at all to unemployed people that they might try to replace already employed people by offering to accept a lower wage. The strength of this respect for social conventions and customs is often admitted even by neoclassical economists, see ▶ Chap. 13.

224   Chapter 3 · Introduction to the Marginal Approach

3.13.3 **Exploitation?**

The analytical differences just illustrated entail radically different answers to the question of the nature of income from the property of capital.

In the classical approach the answer that implicitly emerges to the question 'what is the origin of profits?' is: profits originate in the fact that, because of the capitalists' collective monopoly of means of production, workers can only work if capitalists give them permission by hiring them, and the permission will only be given if the workers' wages leave a surplus for the capitalists. Marx—re-expressing in more precise terms what had been already argued by other critics of capitalism, for example the so-called Ricardian Socialists Gray, Bray, Hodgskin—concludes that, behind the veil of the apparent freedom and formal (i.e. juridical) equality of the two parties to the wage contract, there is a substantial inequality of bargaining position that determines an exploitation of wage labour analogous to the exploitation of feudal serfs through corvées: only part of the labour time contributed by workers goes to produce what they get, the further labour time produces the profits of capitalists. In feudal society, however, the thing is more evident than under capitalism, where the apparent equality and freedom of the parties to the wage contract, plus the fact that the means of production are owned by the capitalist, makes it more difficult to perceive the reality of the situation; it may seem that the capitalist, because he contributes the capital goods to the productive process, does have a right to a share of output. In fact the capitalist class owns the capital goods only because it was able to appropriate the surplus in previous periods.

A marginalist author would reply that such a characterization of the origin of profits or interest derives from an imperfect comprehension of the forces that determine income distribution. Each unit of each factor receives a reward equal to the value of its marginal product, i.e. equal to its contribution to social production and to the utility of consumers, where this contribution is measured as what society would lose if that unit of factor were withdrawn from production. Indeed, if a worker stopped working, society would lose an output equal to the wage the worker earns, so the wage equals the worker's contribution.[49] Analogously, the owner of a unit of capital receives as interest the (net) marginal product of her capital, i.e. as much as her decision to abstain from consuming that

---

49   Or rather, nearly perfectly so, because the equality between marginal product and rental is rigorously true only at the margin; for example if a worker supplies 2000 h of labour a year, the real hourly wage equals the marginal product of the last hour; if this worker stops working completely, production decreases by a little more than the real wage multiplied by 2000, because the inframarginal labour hours have a (slightly) higher marginal product; thus the total income of the worker is slightly less than what society loses if the worker stops working entirely. But it can be plausibly argued that in most situations the total labour hours contributed by a worker are such a small fraction of total labour that the difference is negligible. Anyway all factors are in the same situation, so the (very small) difference between total income and 'total contribution' cannot be used to argue that labour is exploited a little bit, because then all factors would be thus exploited.

3.13 · A Comparison Between the Classical and the Marginal ...

unit of capital contributes to production; therefore it does not seem legitimate to argue that she is subtracting something from labourers. Factors cooperate in production and each unit of each factor is rewarded the value of its contribution. We can now complete the previous quotation from John Bates Clark:

» It is the purpose of this work to show that the distribution of the income of society is controlled by a natural law, and that this law, if it worked without friction, would give to every agent of production the amount of wealth which that agent creates.[50]

The cooperation is also highlighted by the fact that generally, and necessarily if there are only two factors, an increase in the amount employed of one factor increases the marginal product of the other factors[51]; this shows that *factors help one another to be more productive.*

It might be objected that the labourer contributes her/his own effort, the contribution of capital goods to production is not a contribution of their owners, so it is unclear why it should be the owners who appropriate that contribution. But the marginalist economist answers that the existence of capital is due to the past sacrifices of those who have renounced potential consumption and have thus allowed capital not to disappear through negative net savings or have even contributed to its increase. So behind the existence of each unit of capital there is *the sacrifice of abstinence from potential immediate consumption.* In the same way as the wage repays a sacrifice (labour's unpleasantness), so the rate of interest repays a sacrifice (abstinence from immediate consumption—this must be unpleasant too, otherwise more savings would be forthcoming), and in both cases each unit of sacrifice receives its (marginal) contribution to production, i.e. to social welfare.

Thus the marginal approach replaces the picture of capitalism as a conflictual society prone to unemployment and crises and where labour is exploited, developed by the classical critics of capitalism and motivating the left-wing parties' aspiration to a different society, with the picture of a harmonious and efficient cooperation among sacrifices, with each unit of sacrifice rewarded according to

---

50 J. B. Clark, *The Distribution of Wealth* (1899), p. 1. The importance Clark assigns to this conclusion becomes clear when we find him adding: "The welfare of the laboring classes depends on whether they get much or little; but their attitude toward other classes—and, therefore, the stability of the social state—depends chiefly on the question, whether the amount thay they get, be it large or small, is what they produce. If they create a small amount of wealth and get the whole of it, they may not seek to revolutionize society; but if it were to appear that they produce an ample amount and get only a part of it, many of them would become revolutionists, and all would have the right to do so. The indictment that hangs over society is that of 'exploiting labour'" (p. 4).

51 With three or more factors, it is not logically impossible that an increase in the employment of factor 1 reduces the marginal product of, say, factor 2 (this will happen if factor 1 in order to be optimally utilized must be combined with a large amount of the services of factor 3 so that, when the employment of factor 1 increases, it is convenient to leave a smaller amount of the services of factor 3 to cooperate with factor 2), but this phenomenon is judged implausible.

226   **Chapter 3 · Introduction to the Marginal Approach**

its usefulness to society.[52] Furthermore the approach argues that the contributions of these sacrifices are efficiently utilized, because fully utilized and with as little waste of potential satisfaction of consumers as one can concretely expect (Pareto efficiency). Finally, attempts on the part of labourers to obtain more than their full-employment marginal product cause a reduction of employment and hence a damage to society because total production decreases.

3.13.4 Technical Progress, Relative Wages, Unequal Exchange

According to the marginal approach, technical progress has no persistent negative effect on employment. Innovations can cause the bankruptcy of some firms and hence an increase in frictional unemployment, but only temporarily. As to the effect of an innovation on wages, this will generally be positive, owing to a generally positive effect of technical progress on the full-employment marginal product of labour. It is not inconceivable that technical progress may raise the product per person while at the same time reducing the full-employment marginal product of labour; this possibility is shown in ◘ Fig. 3.24, which illustrates two total labour productivity curves.

◘ Figure 3.24 shows a case in which technical progress alters the total productivity curve of labour such that the total product of the full-employment amount of labour L^* rises, but its marginal product (the slope of the total productivity curve) decreases. This is not impossible, but (it is argued) highly unlikely, and anyway soon to be reversed by the general tendency—shown, it is argued, by historical experience—toward a rise in the marginal product of labour. Thus technical progress is viewed as generally beneficial to workers.

In the classical approach, on the contrary, technical progress makes a rise in real wages without a decrease of the rate of profits *possible*, but its immediate effect is generally to cause firings because it allows the production of the same quantities with less labour, and the increase in unemployment will probably tend to decrease wages. This effect can be countered by increases in the quantities produced, but these increases need not happen, and especially so when technical progress takes the form of *process* innovation, i.e. of ways of producing the same final products in a cheaper way and therefore, most of the time, with less labour. The overall effect of technical progress on employment and wages can therefore

---

52 A weakness in this defence of income from the property of capital is that it does not justify the right to enjoy the fruits of sacrifices performed by one's parents or ancestors: it is unclear why one should be rich only because child or grand-grandchild of a rich person. The right to inheritance has been defended as the right of the parents to bequeath wealth as a gift to their children, a form of the right to make gifts; but society could decide that inheritance produces evils and could limit it for this reason, as it limits many other freedoms (e.g. the freedom to give heroin to others as a gift, or not to pay taxes). A society, where wealth could be accumulated but not bequeathed, and where the state would appropriate bequests and redistribute them by giving a sum to those who exit minor age, is certainly conceivable and it could work in interesting ways.

3.13 · A Comparison Between the Classical and the Marginal ...

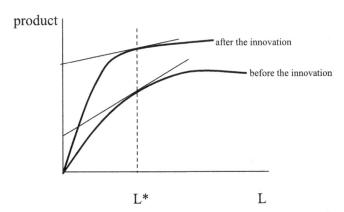

Fig. 3.24 Two labour total productivity curves in the corn economy, illustrating a case in which technical progress causes an upward shift of the total productivity curve of labour and therefore an increase of full-employment production, but together with such a change of the slope of the curve that the full-employment marginal product of labour falls. (The slope of the total productivity curve of labour is the marginal product of labour.)

be negative even for very long periods, and particularly so in periods of slow growth of aggregate production.

As to relative wages or wage 'differentials', the marginal approach explains the average real wage of each different type of labour as determined by its full-employment marginal revenue product, and so if the wage of a type of labour is twice the wage of another type, the marginalist explanation is that the first marginal revenue product is twice the second: the reason must be either a higher physical marginal product in the same production, or that one type of labour is capable of producing goods of greater value because esteemed more useful by consumers. Wage differences appear then justified by the different contribution to production or to social welfare.

According to the classical approach, wage differences may be due to the different cost and time require to acquire different skills, but nearly always differences in the bargaining strength of different types of labourers have great importance; certain categories of labourers are highly paid because they occupy positions in the production process from which they could easily cause great damages; this gives them great bargaining power. Other categories are well paid because it is convenient for the dominant groups to have them as allies in the class conflict. E.g. foremen, whose main task is to make sure that other workers work, must be paid more than the other workers, otherwise they will side with them rather than with the firm's owners. Marx, and later Lenin, argued that the so-called *labour aristocracy* (the more qualified and better-paid strata of the working class) is paid better than the rest of the workers above all in order to soothe its opposition to capitalism and make it more conservative.

An interesting version of the theory of the labour aristocracy, called the theory of *unequal exchange*, is the claim that nearly all labour in advanced econo-

228   **Chapter 3 · Introduction to the Marginal Approach**

mies is nowadays a labour aristocracy, whose high wages benefit from the fact that labour is paid much less in the rest of the world. The analytical basis of such a claim is simple. Consider a two-good economy producing corn and iron, and using both as inputs, such as the one described by Eqs. (1.2), (1.3) of Chap. 1, ▶ Sect. 1.6; but suppose now that the labour employed in industry 1 is located in nation 1 and receives a different real wage from the labour employed in industry 2, which is in nation 2. Assuming wages paid in arrears, choosing good 1 as the numéraire, we obtain

$$1(=p_1) = (1+r)(a_{11} + a_{21}p_2) + a_{L1}w_1 \tag{3.14}$$

$$p_2 = (1+r)(a_{12} + a_{22}p_2) + a_{L2}w_2. \tag{3.15}$$

Suppose international capital mobility renders the rate of profit the same in both nations. For a given level of r, it is easy to prove that there is a decreasing relationship between the two wage rates: a rise of w_1 in Eq. (3.14) requires that p_2 decreases, which in turn requires that w_2 decreases in Eq. (3.15). So if e.g. nation 2 is the less developed one (e.g. China), a low w_2 helps workers in advanced nation 1 (e.g. Europe) to enjoy a high real wage. Indeed many goods we buy in Europe would cost more (reducing our real wages) if wages in China were higher. If the rate of profit cannot be decreased, a rise of the real wage in less developed countries entails lowering the real wage in advanced countries; there is a conflict of interests between wage earners of the two nations. The name 'unequal exchange' refers to the fact that the goods produced in the low-wage nation have a lower exchange value relative to the goods produced in the high-wage nation than if wages were equalized, so the low-wage nation obtains less, in exchange for the products it exports, than with more equal wages.

3.14 Intensive Differential Rent and the Marginal Approach

Given its very different picture of capitalism, the effect on politics, on the choice of economic policies, on ideology and on other disciplines such as sociology and political science, of the dominance of the marginal approach since the end of the nineteenth century can easily be suspected to have been enormous. One more reason to try to answer the question: which approach is scientifically more solid?

In science, head counting of the opinions of scientists is no guarantee that the majority opinion is the correct one: new better theories are always initially held by a minority. Economic science is going through a period of debate and many criticize the dominant, neoclassical approach: they are a minority but they might be right. On the other hand, they might be wrong.

So, the sole way is to proceed scientifically, with an open mind, examining the logical consistency, and the correspondence with empirical evidence, of different approaches. For a number of chapters now we will examine in greater detail the marginal/neoclassical approach. The present chapter is intended as a premise to this more detailed study; it has supplied the general picture and noted the main

3.14 · Intensive Differential Rent and the Marginal Approach

differences from the classical approach that *derive from* the different analytical structure. The chapter ends with an attempt to go even deeper in understanding the difference between the two approaches, by tracing the new analytical discovery or advance relative to the classical approach that made the birth of the complex marginalist analytical structure possible.

The main impulse to the development of the marginal approach was the discovery of the possibility to argue that a decrease of the rental rate of a factor of production increases the demand for it. The argument rested in some authors upon the discovery of marginal utility, that allowed the formulation of the indirect factor substitution mechanism, but, given the not great substitutability that can be derived from this mechanism, even more important was the *direct* factor substitution mechanism. This mechanism was developed out of a generalization of the classical theory of *intensive* differential rent. It was the nearly exclusive basis of the marginal approach in the dominant Anglo-Saxon school (and also in Böhm-Bawerk and his pupils) well into the 1920s. Therefore it seems possible to state that the central analytical novelty of the marginal approach was the thesis, that *the theory of intensive differential rent can be applied, not only (as in Ricardo) to the division of the net social product between land rents on one side, and the sum of wages and profits (interest) on the other side, but also to the division of this second portion between wages and profits (interest), an issue that the classical economists had analysed on the basis of totally different principles*. The theory of rent, according to this thesis, explains *all* incomes.[53] Let us see how this can be argued.

We saw in ▶ Chap. 1 that in the presence of extensive or intensive land rent the production method on the no-rent land or on the no-rent 'differential' method determines what is left for wages and profits, that is for wages-inclusive capital (the classicals treat wages as advanced). To make it clear that capital cost includes the payment of wages, the term 'capital-cum-labour' is used to describe the composite input which together with land produces agricultural outputs. The classicals treated the proportion between labour and non-wage capital goods as given, and the real wage as given too, so there was proportionality between capital costs and labour employment in agriculture. Below for brevity capital-cum-labour is also called simply capital.

Suppose a single type of corn-producing land in fixed supply, whose total surface we choose as the unit of land surface, hence land supply is $T^* = 1$. Let us remember intensive rent theory. There are several known methods for producing corn, with land technical coefficient t_i and capital technical coefficient (a quantity of corn inclusive of advanced wages) λ_i:

$$t_i * \lambda_i \rightarrow 1 \text{ unit of corn.}$$

---

53 This was very clearly stated by John Bates Clark in an article named precisely 'Distribution as Determined by a Law of Rent': "The principle that has been made to govern the income derived from land actually governs those derived from capital and from labor. Interest as a whole is rent; and even wages as a whole are so. Both of these incomes are 'differential gains', and are gauged in amount by the Ricardian formula". *Quarterly Journal of Economics*, volume 5, (1890–1891).

230   **Chapter 3 · Introduction to the Marginal Approach**

As long as rent is zero, the most convenient method is the one with the smallest λ_j; let it be method 1. It allows a maximum corn production equal to $1/t_1$. When the need arises to increase production beyond $1/t_1$, demand for land becomes greater than supply, rent arises and starts increasing, and if another method has $\lambda_j > \lambda_1$ but $t_j < t_1$, there may be a positive rate of rent which makes the two methods equiprofitable. Suppose this is the case. Let $p_1 = 1$ be the price of corn produced with method 1; let p_j be the unit supply price (= unit cost inclusive of rent and profits) of corn produced with another method j when the rate of rent β is given and the rate of profit r is determined by method 1. Then consider the following system in which β is a parameter:

$$\begin{cases} 1 = p_1 = (1+r)\,\lambda_1 + \beta t_1 \\ p_j = (1+r)\,\lambda_j + \beta\,t_j, \quad j \neq 1 \end{cases}$$

Since $\lambda_j > \lambda_1$, it is certainly $p_j > 1$ when $\beta = 0$, but since $t_j < t_1$, as β increases and r decreases necessarily p_j decreases, and it may become equal to 1 before r becomes zero. Then method 1 and method j are equally profitable and can coexist, and a gradual extension of the portion of land cultivated with method j allows a gradual increase of corn production. Suppose method 2 is the first one to reach a supply price equal to 1 as β increases, and at a positive level of r. At that point β and r are determined by the system of two equations:

$$(1+r)\lambda_1 + \beta t_1 = 1 = (1+r)\lambda_2 + \beta t_2$$

Call $\beta_{1,2}$ the rate of rent which renders methods 1 and 2 equiprofitable. For each unit of land on which the method changes from 1 to 2, production increases by the amount $\frac{1}{t_2} - \frac{1}{t_1}$, and the surplus of corn (production minus capital consumption including wages) increases by $\frac{(1-\lambda_2)}{t_2} - \frac{(1-\lambda_1)}{t_1} > 0$.[54] By altering the fraction of land tilled with method 2, total production can vary from $q_1 = 1/t_1$ to $q_2 = 1/t_2$.

To increase q beyond q_2, the sole possibility is that there be a third method with $\lambda_3 > \lambda_2$ and $t_3 < t_2$ which becomes equiprofitable with the second method for a higher rent and a non-negative rate of profit. Assume this is the case and let us represent graphically the amount of corn produced as a function of the capital employed.

As long as only method 1 is employed, as the capital used increases production rises with slope $1/\lambda_1$, which is equal to $1+r$ because there is no rent so $(1+r)\lambda_1 = 1$. Let us indicate with K the employment of capital. The maximum amount of capital employable with method 1 is $K_1 = \lambda_1/t_1$. When method 2 is gradually replacing method 1, the slope is $(q_2 - q_1)/(K_2 - K_1) = (q_2 - q_1)/(\lambda_2 q_2 - \lambda_1 q_1)$. This slope again equals $1+r$ (of course at the new lower r).

---

54   When β renders the two methods equiprofitable, it is $p_2 = 1$, hence $\beta = [1 - (1+r)\lambda_1]/t_1 = [1 - (1+r)\lambda_2]/t_2$ that implies $(1+r) = (t_1 - t_2)/(\lambda_2 t_1 - \lambda_1 t_2)$; this ratio is >1, that is $r > 0$, if and only if $\frac{(1-\lambda_2)}{t_2} - \frac{(1-\lambda_1)}{t_1} > 0$.

3.14 · Intensive Differential Rent and the Marginal Approach

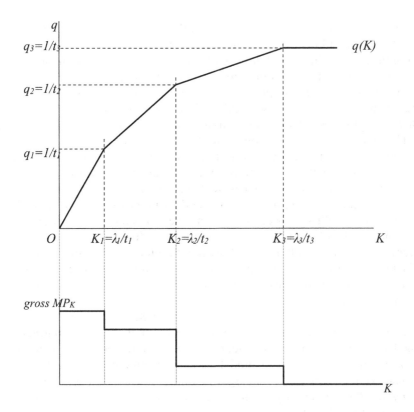

◘ Fig. 3.25 Output and gross MP_K as functions of K

Proof From $q_1 = 1/t_1$ and $q_2 = 1/t_2$ it follows that

$$\frac{q_2 - q_1}{\lambda_2 q_2 - \lambda_1 q_1} = \frac{1/t_2 - 1/t_1}{\frac{\lambda_2}{t_2} - \frac{\lambda_1}{t_1}} = \left(\frac{t_1 - t_2}{t_1 t_2}\right) / \left(\frac{\lambda_2 t_1 - \lambda_1 t_2}{t_1 t_2}\right) = \frac{t_1 - t_2}{\lambda_2 t_1 - \lambda_1 t_2}.$$

On the other hand from $(1+r)\lambda_l + \beta t_l = (1+r)\lambda_2 + \beta t_2 = 1$ it follows that $\beta = \frac{1-(1+r)\lambda_1}{t_1}$ and substituting into $(1+r)\lambda_2 + \beta t_2 = 1$ one obtains $1+r = \frac{t_1-t_2}{\lambda_2 t_1 - \lambda_1 t_2}$ (◘ Fig. 3.25). ∎

By the same reasoning, equality between slope and the new lower $1+r$ also holds true when the second and third method coexist. So (except at the kinks) $1+r$ equals the increase in output (net of wages) obtainable with one more unit of capital, increase that it seems natural to interpret as the form taken in this case by the notion of (gross) marginal product of capital-cum-labour; and r equals the net marginal product. *The theory of intensive differential rent determines the rate of profit as equal to the net marginal product of capital-cum-labour.*

232   Chapter 3 · Introduction to the Marginal Approach

Then we can interpret the $q(K)$ curve as the curve of the total gross productivity of capital, and from it we derive a step function representing the gross marginal product of capital, which for each level of K indicates the minimum rate of profit needed for that amount of K to be employable. (Beyond $q(K_3)$ further units of capital do not increase output and are simply wasted, so $r = -1$.)

Let us now ask how things would work if the total employed K were given, while the employment of land were variable. Let us assume the same three methods. The expansion of production from zero will initially not need the entire K, therefore competition among owners of capital brings $1 + r$ to zero.[55] All output goes to rent, and method 3 is preferred as yielding the highest output per acre since $t_3 < t_2 < t_1$, and hence the highest rent per acre; as production is increased, a point will be reached where the use of method 3 will fully utilize the given K, then r will rise until method 2 becomes as convenient as method 3, and production can be increased with r and $\beta = \beta_{23}$ constant, by gradually raising the fraction of the capital stock used with method 2; when all capital is used with method 2 and production is still less than demand, r rises again until methods 2 and 1 become equally convenient, with a reasoning perfectly symmetrical to the case with given land and variable capital.

Therefore the situation when, for example, methods 1 and 2 coexist can be seen as a point in the process of extension of method 2 and contraction of method 1 on a given amount of land, or as a point in the process of extension of method 1 and contraction of method 2 with a given amount of capital. Given the complete symmetry of the reasoning, the implication is that *it is simultaneously true that at all points $1 + r$ equals the gross marginal product of corn-capital, and β equals the marginal product of land.*

If one assumes more and more alternative methods which render the 'kinks' of the total productivity curves closer and closer, one approaches more and more the 'smooth' curve deriving from continuous substitutability between land and capital; the continuous-substitutability case is then revealed to be only an easier-to-treat version of a fact which also holds with a finite number of alternative methods.[56]

A marginalist economist, if asked about how he evaluates this result, would then argue that it confirms the marginal approach, the latter simply brings out clearly what was implicit in Ricardian rent theory (but was not clearly perceived by classical economists): that both the rewards of land and of capital-cum-labour are determined by a perfectly symmetrical mechanism that gives to each its marginal product.

---

55 That is, $r = -1$. This requires assuming that corn-capital if unused is totally perishable, so as long as $1 + r > 0$ it is better to lend it rather than store it even if $r < 0$. But even if the fall of r stops at zero (corn perfectly storable), method *3* is still the most convenient because it also produces the highest *surplus* product per unit of land.

56 Actually a formal difference remains: with 'smooth' substitutability the existence of 'true' marginal products (partial derivatives of production functions) entails that only one method is used in equilibrium, while the reinterpretation of Ricardian intensive rent defines what can be called 'marginal products' through changes in the proportion in which coexisting methods are used, and therefore it requires that a good be produced by *two* different methods.

He would add that therefore it would be one-sided to consider what goes to capital-cum-labour as *residually* determined, after first determining the income going to land as differential rent. With exactly the same legitimacy, he would insist, one could determine the income going to capital-cum-labour as differential rent and consider land rent as residually determined. The truth, he would argue, is that both incomes have their origin in the symmetrical application of the same mechanism, they are both determined by the marginal products of the respective factors, a result deriving from the substitutability between land and capital-cum-labour, and from the fact that the marginal product curves are in fact demand curves for the factors, pushing firms to employ more of a factor if its rental is below its marginal product; this generates a tendency toward the full utilization both of land, and of capital-cum-labour, if their rentals change in response to differences between supply and demand. If for example, in a situation of full utilization of the given land and given capital-cum-labour with methods 2 and 3 coexisting, there is an increase in land supply because a lord decides to offer for production his land previously reserved for fox hunting, then a slight reduction of β will induce the capitalist farmers to use method 2 more and method 3 less (the reduction of β makes method 2 relatively more profitable), which will induce them to demand more land in order fully to use their capital, until the increased demand for land absorbs the increased supply and β goes back to its previous level; if that is not enough to employ the extra land, a further reduction of β will induce the capitalists to pass to using methods 1 and 2, which will further increase the demand for land required for the full use of their capital. The labour–land–corn economy studied in ▶ Sect. 3.3 differs only in that, instead of the composite factor capital-cum-labour in which one factor, labour, is formally treated as similar to horses (the given real wage being treated similarly to necessary fodder) so that the rental determined by supply and demand is the rate of interest, we have simply labour, and its rental is the real wage.

Our marginalist economist would then draw a very important implication: there seems to be no reason why the same insight, about what determines the division of the social net product between rents on one side, and profits plus (given) wages on the other side, should not be applied also to the division between wages and profits of what is left after land rents are paid. Indeed, let us suppose land is overabundant and hence free, and let us separate seed-corn capital from wages, leaving only seed as capital by assuming wages are not advanced. Then, our economist would argue, there seems to be no reason why one could not apply the same kind of analysis to production with labour and seed-corn capital. Given their supplies and the alternative fixed-coefficients methods, both labour and capital will earn rentals determined as intensive differential rents, i.e. as marginal products; the net marginal product of a unit of capital, divided by that unit of capital, will yield the rate of profit, the wage will equal the marginal product of labour. And, he would conclude, the analysis can be extended to admitting land too, since the same intensive-rent logic can be extended to the simultaneous use of more than two factors (this is shown in the online appendix to this chapter).

Thus the discovery of the symmetry between land and capital-cum-labour entailed the idea, that Ricardian intensive rent theory could be 'generalized' also to the division between profits and wages of the part of the net product which is left after determining land rents.[57] This amounted to conceiving the *mechanism of direct factor substitution* as valid for all factors, also therefore for labour alone, and for capital alone (that is, not including wage advances). This can be considered the most significant analytical innovation of the marginal approach relative to the classical one. It appeared for the first time, applied to labour and capital, with land treated as a free good, in the second volume of Heinrich Von Thünen's *Die Isolierte Staat* (first volume, 1823; second volume, 1850), that is, *before* marginal utility was discovered around 1870, nearly simultaneously by Jevons, Walras, and Menger. It prompted Clark (1891)—who had studied Thünen—to state that the correct theory of distribution explained *all* kinds of income as determined by *a law of rent*. Marshall too read Thünen and reached the same conclusion.

The currently prevalent view is different, and it is that the great analytical novelty at the basis of the marginal approach was the notion of marginal utility. This notion was indeed a novelty and an important one; it supplied an explanation of the '*paradox of value*' (the fact that indispensable goods like water cost so little and superfluous goods like diamonds cost so much: as you increase the quantity supplied of a consumption good however useful, the desire for one more unit of it decreases, and it is this marginal desire that determines price); and it allowed the formulation of the indirect factor substitution mechanism, on which alone Léon Walras initially based the determination of income distribution, introducing direct factor substitutability only in the third edition (1897) of his treatise *Éléments d'économie politique pure*. But it is doubtful that the approach would have gained as much following as it did, if it had been based only on the indirect factor substitution mechanism. As pointed out at the end of ▶ Sect. 3.4, demand curves for factors based only on consumer choice cannot be presumed to be sufficiently elastic.[58] Therefore the *direct* factor substitution mechanism was in all likelihood the really decisive element in the success of the marginal approach.

---

57 The term 'generalization' is not really appropriate because some important changes occurred in the conception of capital. One was, that it was believed that capital could be treated as a single factor of production in spite of the fact that, apart from the imaginary case of the corn economy, capital consists of many heterogeneous commodities (▶ Chaps. 7 and 8 will discuss the implications of this fact). Another one was that the *endowment* of capital was treated as given in each period, resulting from previous accumulation. These changes, coupled with the marginalist forces making for full resource utilization, made it possible to include the endowment of capital among the data determining equilibrium income distribution. As explained below in the text, this was not the case in the classical approach.

58 The possibility of a zero or implausibly low equilibrium rental of labour or capital can be avoided by upward sloping and rather elastic supply curves of factors, but these in turn are far from guaranteed and definitely implausible for labour at low-wage levels: workers are going to offer more, and not less labour if wages fall considerably, in order to prevent their income from falling below subsistence.

3.14 · Intensive Differential Rent and the Marginal Approach

Actually, upon reflection the direct substitution mechanism comes out to supply the general picture, which also includes the indirect substitution mechanism, because utility can be seen as 'produced' by factors in analogy with the production of physical products. Imagine a firm where labour and land produce the final product, not directly, but indirectly, by first producing some intermediate products A, B, C, etc., which then produce the final product. An example might be a firm where labour and land produce grapes (good A), barrels (good B), and bottles and corks and labels (C, etc.), and these goods are used to produce bottled wine, so that one can view the wine bottles ready to be sold as indirectly produced by labour and land.[59] Assuming some substitutability between labour and land in the production of the intermediate products A, B, C... and some substitutability between the latter in the production of the final good, factor 'prices' (rentals) in terms of wine bottles will measure the (indirect) marginal products of labour and land in terms of final good.[60] Now reinterpret the amount of wine bottles as the utility of a consumer, and A, B, C... as consumption goods produced by labour and land, and you have the picture of labour and land indirectly 'producing' utility, and you also obtain the intuition of why factor rentals measure the indirect marginal utilities of land and of labour.

This picture, of the utility of a single consumer as indirectly 'produced' by the factor services that produce the goods consumed by the consumer, implies that, by supplying factor services and purchasing consumption goods, consumers are in fact exchanging factor services. This is very easy to visualize if factors are fully specialized: if strawberries are produced by land alone, and meat by labour alone, then by purchasing strawberries one indirectly purchases land services, and by purchasing meat one indirectly purchases labour services; so if a landowner sells strawberries and buys meat, he indirectly exchanges land services against labour services. The same picture can be reached when factors cooperate in production. Suppose you supply to the market 100 units of labour and that the goods you purchase with your wage income are produced by 60 units of labour and 60 units of land: then it is as if you consumed yourself 60 units of your labour and you exchanged the other 40 units of labour against 60 units of land.[61] We will see in ▶ Chap. 5 that the marginalist general equilibrium with production can indeed be reformulated as one of (indirect) exchange of factor services.

---

59 We can assume here the rate of interest to be zero, so that the lag between application of labour and land, and sale of the wine bottles, does not cause interest costs.

60 *Exercise*: define the indirect marginal product of labour and of land, and prove that cost minimization in the production of the final good requires that the ratio between the rentals of labour and land be equal to the ratio between their indirect marginal products.

61 If w is the wage rate and the land rent rate, your consumption goods must cost in the aggregate $60w + 60$, while your income is $100w$. Since we are assuming that you spend your entire income on these goods, it must be $60w + 60 = 100w$ i.e. $w/ = 3/2$, which is exactly the exchange ratio implicit in the exchange of 40 units of labour against 60 units of land.

3.15 Final Elements of Differentiation: Supply of Capital, Say's Law

The previous section illustrated the intensive-rent origin of the *demand* side of the marginal/neoclassical approach to equilibration in factor markets, i.e. the origin of the idea of decreasing marginal product curves of factors to be then interpreted as factor demand curves and combined, in a supply-and-demand framework, with supply curves in order to argue the tendency toward a simultaneous full-employment equilibrium in all factor markets. Now let us point out some differences of the *supply* side of this picture from the approach of the surplus theorists. The absence of an assumption of full employment of labour in the classical authors has been noticed already. Let us now point out the difference with respect to the supply of capital.

In the generalization of intensive rent theory to the division between profits and wages of the corn product net of rent in the simple corn–labour–land economy, the supply of capital is taken by the marginal approach as *given* and a *determinant* of income distribution and aggregate output; Ricardo would have considered it *to depend on* income distribution and aggregate output.

This corresponds to the difference between the two approaches in their general analysis and not just in the special case of an economy producing only corn with corn and labour. One of the data determining income distribution in the marginal approach is a *given* endowment of capital (differently specified in different versions of the approach, as will be explained in ▶ Chaps. 7 and 8, but always given). On the contrary in the classical approach in order to determine the rate of profit in the 'core', the capital employed is *derived* from the given social product and production methods and (if wages are advanced) from the given income distribution. The relevant difference is whether the *overall size* of the capital stock is given or endogenous; its composition is considered endogenously determined (by the composition of demand and the most convenient production methods) in both the classical approach and in the marginal approach (at least, in its traditional versions—the neo-Walrasian versions are different but the thing will need ▶ Chaps. 7 and 8 in order to be clarified).

At first sight this direction of causality from quantities produced to capital stock may seem untrue for Ricardo, who accepts Say's Law: in Ricardo, apart from exceptional circumstances, capital is fully and normally utilized, hence the general level of production (although obviously not its composition) appears to be the one corresponding to the normal utilization of the economy's productive capacity, and the latter capacity results from the stage reached by capital accumulation; so it may appear that it is the capital stock resulting from past accumulation (plus the normal utilization assumption) that explains the overall level of production rather than vice-versa. However, an examination of Ricardo's views on **wages fund theory** brings to a different conclusion.

Ricardo explicitly disagreed with the wages fund theory, whose first formulations already circulated while he was alive. This theory argued that in each period the capital available for wage advances is given, determined by the saving deci-

3.15 · Final Elements of Differentiation: Supply of Capital, Say's Law

sions of capitalists, and therefore the more numerous the workers among whom this given *wages fund* is to be divided, the smaller the real wage, with the implication that a given real wage *determines* the number of employed workers, and a lower real wage allows the employment of more workers (this was the first emergence of the notion of labour employment as a decreasing function of the real wage).[62] Ricardo rejected this theory and argued that a rise of real wages entails, not a reduction of employment and production as implied by wages fund theory, but rather an income redistribution from profits to wages, that is, the allocation of a greater portion of the net product to wages, which means an *increase* of capital advances; the implication being that the wages fund and hence total capital too is not given before the determination of the level of wages, it *results* from that level and from the desired production levels.[63] Ricardo implicitly rejects the idea

---

62 As explained in ▶ Chap. 1, capital advances at the time were often treated as if consisting entirely of advanced wages, so that wages fund and advanced capital coincided; but if capital advances also include means of production the theory's claim holds even more, because production methods being given, more labour employment requires more means of production and therefore out of a given total stock of capital (to be now conceived as of given labour value but of adaptable composition) less is left for total wage advances to more workers. (You can visualize the thing in terms of the simple corn–labour economy where corn-capital advances include both seed and wages.) After Ricardo's death, this theory was used by Nassau Senior (professor at Oxford) to argue that profits were a just reward for the capitalists' *abstinence* (the act of abstaining from enjoying more consumption than their net income would allow, a sacrifice that avoids reductions and allows increments of the capital stock). John Stuart Mill, the most respected economist in Great Britain in the 1850s and 1860s, declared himself Ricardian, but (until forced by criticisms to change his views in 1869) he accepted the wages fund theory and Senior's abstinence-based justification of profits and argued that the spontaneous working of competition in the labour market would ensure that wages would settle at the level permitting the full employment of the labour supply. The widespread acceptance of this theory at the time can be seen as a reaction to the rising socialist movement, which was making it essential for the dominant classes to refute the Smithian and Ricardian view of profits as originating only in the superior bargaining strength of capitalists, not in any contribution of theirs to production. As one historian of economic thought has written: 'Ricardo's system furnished no satisfactory answer to the arguments of the socialists. If anything, it opened the door to the destructive language of class warfare' (Blaug 1958, p. 149). The strength of the reaction against Ricardian analyses is exemplified by an author, Richard Scrope, who in 1831 convicted 'not merely of errors, but of *crimes*' Ricardo and his disciples: 'Surely the publication of opinions taken up hastily upon weak, narrow and imperfect evidence— opinions which, overthrowing, as they did, the fundamental principles of sympathy and common interest that knit society together, could not but be deeply injurious even if true,—does amount to a crime ... In their theory of rent, they have insisted that landlords can thrive only at the expense of the public at large, and especially of the capitalists: in their theory of profits, they have declared that capitalists can only improve their circumstances by depressing those of the labouring and numerous class ... in their theory of population, they have absolved governments from all responsibility for the misery of the people committed to their care ... In one and all of their arguments they have studiously exhibited the interests of every class in society as necessarily at perpetual variance with every other class!' (Richard Scrope, in the *Quarterly Review*, November 1831, p. 116, quoted in Blaug 1958, pp. 149–50).

63 The little right to assume a given wages fund in the face of changes of real wages was finally conceded by John Stuart Mill in 1869 after criticisms by F. D. Longe and W. T. Thornton.

238   Chapter 3 · Introduction to the Marginal Approach

that a capitalist will find it convenient to reduce production and employment only because the wage cost per unit of labour has risen.[64] He does not detail the reasons for this opinion, but a little reflection renders them evident. Suppose initially each year a capitalist produces 400 units of corn by advancing 200 units of corn: 100 as seed, and 100 as wages for 100 workers (1 worker must be combined with 1 unit of corn-seed to produce 4 units of corn); suppose the capitalist consumes all the 200 units of profits. The rate of profit is 100%. Now wages rise from 1 to 1.5 per worker. If the capitalist accepts to reduce consumption per period to 150, capital advances rise to 250 and production remains equal to 400; the rate of profit is now $150/250 = 60\%$. If the capitalist decides to maintain his capital advances equal to 200, then he can only employ 80 workers (seed $80 +$ wage advances $120 = 200$); production decreases to 320, so the first period after the wage rise the capitalist's consumption remains equal to 200, but in all subsequent periods his consumption falls to 120; the rate of profit is 60% anyway, and on a smaller capital. Furthermore, Ricardo admits that capital is partly sunk into durable capital goods; and capitalists will not like to underutilize these goods, as a reduction of labour employment would entail. And finally, there is the danger that total demand for the good produced by a capitalist who reduces production does not decrease and is satisfied by competitors, making him smaller and weaker. There is therefore no incentive for him to reduce production. The causality goes from sales and income distribution to capital advances and not vice-versa.

Note that the implied flexibility in capital advances also implies that a sudden surge of demand for the product of a capitalist might induce this capitalist to increase his capital advances and reduce his consumption for a period, in order to employ more labour and means of production, sell more, and not lose an opportunity for unusual profits and expansion. This potential positive effect of demand on capital *formation* with unchanged wages remains hidden in Ricardo, but the potential *negative* effect of sharp *falls* in demand is admitted by him; at the end of a war, when many outlets for production disappear and no clear new outlets immediately substitute for them, the result can be that 'much fixed capital is unemployed, perhaps wholly lost' (*Principles*, 1951, p. 265): a *destruction* of some capital, a diminution of the total capital stock. Here again we see a causation from sales to capital stock.

Say's Law (see ▶ Sect. 1.12.2) might be seen as a point of contact between the marginal approach and at least Ricardo, but there is an important difference. In Ricardo the thesis that all savings translates into investment and therefore aggregate output expansions do not risk meeting difficulties in a 'general glut' does not

---

64   For example, Ricardo argues that a tax on wages will cause a rise of the tax-inclusive wage that capitalists must advance, such as will leave the after-tax real wage unchanged because the tax 'does not necessarily diminish the demand compared with the supply of labour; why should it diminish the portion paid to the labourer?' (*Principles*, p. 166), where the undiminished demand for labour means *unchanged employment*; cf. Stirati (1999, pp. 219–221).

have explicit supporting arguments other than Adam Smith's weak one that no one will be so crazy as to hoard saved income rather than invest it.[65] The marginal approach on the contrary brings explicit analytical arguments, in fact the same mechanisms that determine income distribution, in support of Say's Law: the tendency toward equality between supply and demand in factor markets also applies to capital and implies an investment function which is negatively elastic with respect to the rate of interest (as will be explained in detail in ▶ Chap. 7); the rate of interest can then act as the price that brings the supply of credit or *loanable funds*, that is the flow of saved incomes offered for lending, into equality with the demand for credit coming from firms for investment purposes. Say's Law is now inseparable from the explanation of income distribution, also in the sense that the latter would be unsustainable without Say's Law: if labour is not fully employed, the marginalist argument is that a wage decrease will increase employment and therefore if the wage is not prevented from decreasing in response to unemployment, the economy tends to the full employment of labour; but the wage decrease and increased employment raise aggregate output and aggregate income; plausibly, this increases aggregate savings, therefore in order for the employment increase not to be undone by difficulties with selling the increased production, the increased savings must be absorbed by an equal increase of investment. Differently from the case in classical theory, in the marginal approach Say's Law and theory of income distribution need each other.

On the contrary as argued in ▶ Chap. 1 the classical approach to income distribution does not need nor entail Say's Law. The latter is accepted by Ricardo (for normal conditions), but rejected by other classical authors. Not only Marx but also David Hume, Henry Thornton, John Stuart Mill admit an influence of aggregate demand on aggregate production and employment, not only downwards but also upwards, and with very interesting observations on the stimulus coming from demand increases to a more intense utilization of resources. Quotations to

---

65 Caminati (1981) has argued that the given real wage implies a possible support for Say's Law coming from the mechanism determining the rate of interest in classical theory, although it is unclear that Ricardo was aware of it. Smith and Ricardo consider the normal rate of interest to be determined by the rate of profit minus whatever is necessary to compensate industrial investors for the 'risk and trouble' of their committing their capital to enterprises that might be unsuccessful. The mechanism determining the normal rate of interest must then be the following: if the rate of interest is greater than the given rate of profit minus this 'risk and trouble' margin, lenders are unable to find borrowers and the rate of interest tends to decrease; if it is less, demand for credit exceeds supply and the rate of interest tends to increase. If the flow supply of credit is given, this same mechanism will cause the rate of interest to function as the price that adjusts the demand for credit to this given supply and ensures that savings translate into investment. This stimulating interpretative proposal does not seem to have been widely discussed, so it is still waiting for further assessment.

240   **Chapter 3 ·** Introduction to the Marginal Approach

this effect are supplied in footnote.[66] With Keynes and Kalecki these admissions have been developed into a theory of the level of aggregate output and employment around and toward which the actual level *gravitates*, something still missing even in Marx, but in no way in contradiction with the classical approach to income distribution.

3.16 **Conclusion**

This chapter aimed at presenting the general picture of the functioning of market economies emerging from the marginal approach, highlighting the important differences from the classical picture. The presentation was based on simple models; the approach is actually richer and more complex; in order to be able to follow the literature you need to know much more, so let us move to a more detailed presentation of standard consumer theory, producer theory and general equilibrium theory. In particular after ▶ Chap. 6 we will have to dedicate much time to the question, how the approach can be generalized to more complex economies where capital does not consist only of corn but is a mass of heterogeneous capital goods.

---

66 Hume: 'in every kingdom, into which money begins to flow in greater abundance than formerly, everything takes on a new face; labour and industry gain life; the merchant becomes more enterprising, and even the farmer follows his plough with greater alacrity and attention' (*Of Money*, 1752). H. Thornton: 'For industry is excited, strictly speaking, not by paper, but by that stock which the paper affords the means of purchasing .... It may be said, however, and not untruly, that an encreased issue of paper tends to produce a more brisk demand for the existing goods, and a somewhat more prompt consumption of them; that the more prompt consumption supposes a diminution of the ordinary stock, and the application of that part of it, which is consumed, to the purpose of giving life to fresh industry; that the fresh industry thus excited will be the means of gradually creating additional stock, which will serve to replace the stock by which the industry has been supported; and that the new circulating medium will, in this manner, create for itself much new employment' (*An Enquiry into the Nature and Effects of the Paper Credit of Great Britain*, 1802). J. S. Mill: 'If every commodity on an average remained unsold for a length of time equal to that required for its production, it is obvious that, at any one time, no more than half the productive capital of the country would be really performing the functions of capital .... This, or something like it, is however the habitual state, at every instant, of a very large proportion of all the capitalists in the world ... every dealer keeps a stock in trade, to be ready for a possible sudden demand, though he probably may not be able to dispose of it for an indefinite period .... An additional customer, to most dealers, is equivalent to an increase of their productive capital ... if we suppose that the commodity, unless bought by him, would not have found a purchaser for a year after, then all which a capital of that value can enable men to produce during a year, is clear gain—gain to the dealer, or producer, and to the labourers whom he will employ, and thus (if no one sustains a corresponding loss) gain to the nation. The aggregate produce of the country for the succeeding year is, therefore, increased' (*Of the influence of consumption on production*, 1844).

3.17 Review Questions and Exercises

- **Review Questions**
1. Show that in the Ricardian theory of intensive differential rent the rate of profit is the net marginal product of capital-cum-labour.
2. Explain why it is lucky for the marginal approach that the product exhaustion theorem holds.
3. When deriving the demand curve for a factor, how legitimate is it to assume that the other factors are fully employed?
4. When one derives the demand curve for a factor, if the factor rental is not at the equilibrium level there is disequilibrium only on the market of that factor; what assumption allows this violation of Walras' Law?
5. Explain why the indirect factor substitution mechanism can work 'badly', and why even when working 'fine' it is rather weak and therefore needs the support of the direct substitution mechanism.
6. Explain why the fundamental analytical difference between classical and marginal approach does not consist of a different conception of wage flexibility (with the classicals taking the real wage as given while the marginalists allow competition to modify it according to excess demand for labour), but lies deeper and *explains* the different conception of wage flexibility.
7. Show that, with decreasing returns to scale, optimal factor employment yields positive entrepreneurial profits for a price-taking firm.
8. Prove that CRS production functions have partial derivatives that are homogeneous of degree zero, and the product exhaustion theorem.
9. Explain why in the marginal approach a rise in the demand for a consumption good generally raises its long-period value.
10. Explain why a backward-bending supply curve of a factor may imply that the demand curve for the other factor is in part upward-sloping.
11. Explain how the marginalist analysis of Robinson Crusoe suggests a natural, a-historical validity of the marginalist equilibrium evaluation of alternatives.
12. Reproduce by heart the Robinson Crusoe argument for the a-historical efficiency of markets.
13. When deriving the demand curve for a factor, how legitimate is it to assume that the other factors are fully employed?
14. In the fixed-coefficients economy producing corn and meat with labour and land, by how much does labour employment vary for each unit of land shifted from the meat to the corn industry?
15. When one derives the demand curve for a factor, if the factor rental is not at the equilibrium level there is disequilibrium only in the market of that factor; what assumption allows this apparent violation of Walras' Law?
16. Explain why the indirect factor substitution mechanism can work 'badly', and why even when working 'fine' it is rather weak and therefore needs the support of the direct substitution mechanism.
17. Explain why the fundamental analytical difference between classical and marginal approach does not consist of a different conception of wage flexi-

242 Chapter 3 · Introduction to the Marginal Approach

bility, with the classicals taking the real wage as given while the marginalists allow competition to modify it according to excess demand for labour, but lies deeper and *explains* the different conception of wage flexibility.

18. Show that, with decreasing returns to scale, optimal factor employment yields positive entrepreneurial profits for a price-taking firm.

19. Prove that CRS production functions have partial derivatives that are homogeneous of degree zero.

20. Prove the product exhaustion theorem with CRS production functions.

21. Explain why the marginal approach needs a *significantly* elastic labour demand curve.

22. Explain why a backward-bending supply curve of a factor may imply that the demand curve for the other factor is in part upward-sloping.

23. Show graphically that the marginal approach does not exclude the possibility that, in an economy with two factors (e.g. labour and land), technical progress raises output per unit of labour but reduces the equilibrium real wage.

24. Explain why 'corner solutions' in which a consumer does not demand all goods, or a firm does not demand all factors, do not disturb the First Fundamental Theorem of Welfare Economics.

25. In the Edgeworth box, are points of tangency of the indifference curves of the two consumers necessarily in the Pareto set? Is some assumption on the shape of indifference curves necessary for that condition to hold?

26. Reproduce by heart and illustrate the graph that shows that technical progress can worsen the rental of a factor.

- **Exercises**

1. In the neoclassical economy where corn is produced by labour and land according to a 'well-behaved' differentiable production function, assume that the supply of labour is backward-bending, and show that in this case there is no guarantee that the demand curve for land (assuming equilibrium on the labour market) is downward-sloping.

2. Derive graphically the form of the labour demand curve if labour and land produce only corn, when (a) only a single fixed-coefficients method is known, (b) two fixed-coefficient methods are known, which generate activity-analysis-type isoquants. Land is in fixed supply and fully employed.

3. Suppose that labour and land, inelastically supplied, produce corn and meat in two single-product fixed-coefficients industries. The labour–land ratio is higher in the production of meat. According to the marginal approach, if there is a shift in tastes in favour of meat, what will be the effect on quantities produced and on income distribution?

4. Suppose that labour and land produce corn, meat and silk in three separate industries, each industry having fixed coefficients, the labour–land ratio being lowest in the production of corn and highest in the production of silk. Explain the effects on income distribution, on the quantities produced and on the relative price of silk of a shift in preferences in favour of silk, according to the marginal approach (assume that the composition of consumer demand shifts in favour of a good whose relative price decreases).

3.17 · Review Questions and Exercises

5. Suppose labour and land produce two consumption goods, call them corn and meat, in two separate single-product industries, each one with fixed technical coefficients. Labour and land yield no direct utility. Show how one may derive indirect indifference curves for labour and land from the indifference curves for corn and meat of a consumer, and show that the wage–rent ratio will equal the marginal rate of substitution along the indirect indifference curve.

6. How would a marginalist economist analyse the determination of equilibrium in the following economy? Corn is the sole product and can be produced with labour and either one of two types of land, T and Z, according to different fixed technical coefficients:

$$L_T * T \rightarrow 1 \text{ unit of corn}$$
$$L_Z * Z \rightarrow 1 \text{ unit of corn}$$

Factor supplies are rigid and neither land is sufficient fully to employ the labour supply but if both are fully used labour demand is greater than labour supply. Write the system of competitive general equilibrium of this economy, discuss the possibility that not all three factors earn a positive rental, and conclude whether the difference between the rates of rent of the two types of land is or not a case of Ricardo's extensive differential rent.

7. In the fixed-coefficients economy producing corn and meat with labour and land, by how much does labour employment vary for each unit of land shifted from the meat to the corn industry?

8. Try to formalize the budget constraint behind the construction of the demand curve for labour in the labour–land–corn economy (assume rigid factor supplies for simplicity), so as to obtain that when the real wage is higher than its equilibrium level, it is possible that there be disequilibrium only in the labour market.

9. In the Edgeworth box, are points of tangency of the indifference curves of the two consumers necessarily in the Pareto set? (Hint: note that no assumption was made about the shape of indifference curves)

10. Prove that if $G = F(L,K)$ has constant returns to scale, so does $Y = F(L,K) - K$.

11. Check the correctness of Eq. (3.3), ▶ Sect. 3.3.2, for the so-called *Cobb–Douglas* production function $q = x_1^{\alpha} x_2^{1-\alpha}$, $0 < \alpha < 1$.

12. Use an Edgeworth box to confirm that efficiency in production requires that if the production functions of two firms are differentiable, the ratio between marginal products of labour and land must be the same in both firms.

13. (Nicholson-Snyder) Smith plus 99 other persons identical to him in tastes and endowments, and Jones plus 99 other persons identical to him in tastes and endowments, are stranded on a desert island. Each has in his possession some slices of ham (H) and of cheese (C). The Smiths eat ham and cheese only in the fixed proportion of 2 slices of cheese to 1 slice of ham, because their utility function is given by $U_S = \min(?, ?)$ (fill the parenthesis with the correct vector). The Joneses have a utility function given by $U_J = 4H + 3C$. Total endowments are 100 slices of ham and 200 slices of cheese for each couple formed by one Smith and one Jones.

244   **Chapter 3 ·** Introduction to the Marginal Approach

    a. Draw the representative Edgeworth box diagram that represents the possibilities for exchange between one Smith and one Jones in this situation. What is the only exchange ratio that can prevail in any equilibrium? (Choose cheese as numéraire.) (Hint: draw the indifference curves.)

    b. Suppose Smith initially has 40H and 80C. What will be the equilibrium basket obtained by Jones? And what if Smith's initial endowments are 80H and 50C?

14. Assume corn is produced by seed-corn and labour (wages are advanced and consist of corn) on fully utilized land. Show that in the Ricardian theory of *intensive* differential rent the rate of profit is the net marginal product of capital-cum-labour.

15. In the neoclassical economy where corn is produced by labour and land according to a 'well-behaved' differentiable production function, assume that the supply of labour is backward-bending, and show that in this case there is no guarantee that the demand curve for land (assuming equilibrium on the labour market) is downward-sloping.

16. Derive graphically the form of the labour demand curve if labour and land produce only corn, when (a) only a single fixed-coefficients method is known, (b) two fixed-coefficient methods are known, which generate activity-analysis-type isoquants. Land is in fixed supply and fully employed.

17. Suppose that labour and land, inelastically supplied, produce corn and meat in two single-product fixed-coefficients industries. The labour–land ratio is higher in the production of meat. According to the marginal approach, if there is a change in preferences in favour of meat, what will be the effect on equilibrium quantities produced and income distribution?

18. Suppose that labour and land produce corn, meat and silk in three separate industries, each industry has fixed coefficients, the labour–land ratio is lowest in the production of corn and highest in the production of silk. Labour and land are supplied in rigid quantities. Explain the effects on income distribution, on the quantities produced and on the relative price of silk of a shift in preferences in favour of silk, according to the marginal approach (assume that the composition of consumer demand shifts in favour of a good whose relative price decreases).

19. Suppose labour and land produce two consumption goods, call them corn and meat, in two separate single-product industries, each one with fixed technical coefficients. Labour and land yield no direct utility. Show how one can derive indirect indifference curves for labour and land from the indifference curves for corn and meat of a consumer, and show that the wage–rent ratio will equal the marginal rate of substitution between labour and land along the indirect indifference curve.

20. Try to formalize the budget constraint behind the construction of the demand curve for labour in the labour–land–corn economy (assume rigid factor supplies for simplicity), so as to obtain that when the real wage is higher than its equilibrium level, it is possible that there be disequilibrium only on the labour market.

21. With activity-analysis 'kinked' isoquants, except for very specific ratios of factor rentals generally cost minimization will be at a kink: it seems it would be an improbable fluke if the isocost had exactly the slope of one of the segments of the kinked isoquant. But a general equilibrium analysis of an economy with two factors, one product, and kinked isoquants brings to a different conclusion. Why?

References

Baumol, W. (1965). *Economic theory and operations analysis* (2nd ed.). Prentice-Hall (as reprinted 1968, Prentice-Hall, India).

Blaug, M. (1958). *Ricardian economics, a historical study*. New Haven: Yale University Press.

Caminati, M. (1981). The rate of interest in the classical economists. *Metroeconomica, 33*(1–3), 79–104.

Clark, J. B. (1890–1891) Distribution as determined by a law of rent. *Quarterly Journal of Economics, 5*, 289–318. ► https://doi.org/10.2307/1879611.

Clark, J. B. (1899). *The distribution of wealth*. New York: Macmillan.

Hicks, J. R. (1932(1963)) *The theory of wages* (reprinted with additions, 1963). London: Macmillan.

Knight, F. H. (1946). Capital and interest. In: *Encyclopaedia britannica* (Vol. IV, pp. 779–801) (reprinted in *Readings in the theory of income distribution*, edited by American Economic Association, Toronto, 1946).

Petri, F. (2004). *General equilibrium, capital and macroeconomics: A key to recent controversies in equilibrium theory*. Cheltenham, UK: Edward Elgar.

Sraffa P. (1925) Sulle relazioni tra costo e quantità prodotta. *Annali di economia* 2: 277–328. [English translation by J. Eatwell and A. Roncaglia, 'On the relations between cost and quantity produced', in L. Pasinetti, ed., *Italian Economic Papers*, vol III. Oxford University Press, London, and Il Mulino, Bologna, 1998].

Sraffa, P. (1998). See Sraffa (1925).

Stirati, A. (1999). Ricardo and the wages fund. In G. Mongiovi & F. Petri (Eds.), *Value, distribution and capital: essays in honour of pierangelo garegnani* (pp. 204–229). London: Routledge.

Wicksell, K. (1936). *Interest and prices*. London: Macmillan (originally *Geldzins und Güterpreise bestimmenden Ursachen*, Jena: G. Fischer, 1898) (Reprinted 1965, Kelley, New York).

Wicksell, K. (1934). *Lectures on political economy* (Vol. I). London: Routledge and Kegan Paul.

Consumers and the Exchange Economy

Contents

4.1   Introduction – 250

4.2   The Consumption Set, Time and the Role
        of Equilibrium – 250

4.3   Preferences and Utility – 253

4.4   Convex Preferences, Quasi-Concave Utility,
        Typical Indifference Curves – 259

4.5   Optimization – 261

4.6   Demand, Continuity and Upper Hemicontinuity
        of Correspondences – 264

4.7   The Two-Goods Exchange Economy and the
        Importance of Continuity of Demand – 268

4.8   First-Order Conditions. Corner Solutions. The
        Kuhn–Tucker Theorem – 272

4.9   Envelope Theorem – 280

4.10   Indirect Utility, Expenditure Function,
        Compensated Demand – 282

Electronic supplementary material The online version of this chapter (▶ https://doi.
org/10.1007/978-3-030-62070-7_4) contains supplementary material, which is available
to authorized users.

© Springer Nature Switzerland AG 2021
F. Petri, *Microeconomics for the Critical Mind*,
Classroom Companion: Economics, https://doi.org/10.1007/978-3-030-62070-7_4

4.11	**Roy's Identity, Shephard's Lemma, Some Dualities and Some Utility Functions – 287**
4.11.1	Roy's Identity and Shephard's Lemma – 287
4.11.2	Homothetic Utility Functions and Homothetic Preferences – 289
4.11.3	Quasi-Linear Utility – 290
4.11.4	The Cobb–Douglas Utility Function and the Elasticity of Substitution – 291
4.11.5	The CES Utility Function – 293

4.12 The Slutsky Equation – 295

4.13 Given Endowments: The Walrasian UMP, The Walrasian Slutsky Equation – 301

4.14 Labour Supply. Saving Decision – 305

4.15 Some Notes on the Usefulness of Consumer Theory for Empirical Estimation – 310

4.16 Money Metric Utility Function, Equivalent Variation, Compensating Variation – 313

4.17 Constant Marginal Utility of Money. Consumer Surplus. Reservation Prices – 319

4.18 Price Indices and Inflation – 324

4.19 Hicksian Aggregability of Goods – 326

4.20 Revealed Preference – 328

4.21 Aggregability of Consumers: Gorman Aggregability and the Representative Consumer – 333

4.22 General Equilibrium of Pure Exchange. Aggregability of Consumers – 337

4.23 Aggregate or Market Demand and the Weak Axiom of Revealed Preference – 341

4.24 Conclusions – 344

4.25 Review Questions and Exercises – 344

References – 351

250 Chapter 4 · Consumers and the Exchange Economy

This chapter introduces you to rigorous neoclassical consumer theory. You will learn about

- its application to the determination of the general equilibrium of a simple exchange economy;
- the connection between preferences and the utility function;
- the indirect utility function, the expenditure function and how to derive one from the other;
- substitution effects and income effects in demand changes;
- the difference between Marshallian and Walrasian demand functions;
- the application to choice about labour supply and about savings;
- consumer surplus, equivalent variation and compensating variation;
- revealed preferences and the Weak Axiom;
- consumer aggregability.

4.1 Introduction

The previous chapter described the basic picture of the functioning of a market economy that emerges from the marginalist/neoclassical approach to value and distribution, concentrating on the simplest cases and omitting many details and caveats. Now we embark upon a more systematic examination of this approach.

We start with the marginalist/neoclassical theory of consumer behaviour.[1] Our ultimate interest is in whether the effect of price changes on consumer behaviour, under as general assumptions as possible, offers reasons in support of the existence, uniqueness and stability of general equilibrium and therefore in support of the plausibility of the marginal/neoclassical approach. In this chapter the question is not fully tackled, we stop at how consumer theory allows *defining* the general equilibrium of an exchange economy; the possibility of problems in determining definite consumer choices is only hinted at, its study is postponed to ▶ Chap. 6 as part of a more general discussion of existence uniqueness and stability of the acapitalistic general equilibrium.

4.2 The Consumption Set, Time and the Role of Equilibrium

The consumer is assumed to be faced with *possible consumption baskets*, i.e. vectors of quantities of goods or services she may consume, which belong to a set X, called the **consumption set**, which includes all *admissible* consumption baskets.

---

1 This chapter assumes familiarity with functions of several variables, partial derivatives, differentials, Jacobians, Hessians and maximization of a function with equality constraints via the method of Lagrange. The same considerations apply, which were advanced at the beginning of ▶ Chap. 2: if the reader is not familiar with these notions and is attending, in parallel with the microeconomics course, a mathematics course but cannot wait for completion of the latter course before studying the present chapter, she/he is invited to study the Mathematical Review at the end of this book as a temporary stopgap.

4.2 · The Consumption Set, Time and the Role of Equilibrium

The consumption set is a subset of the ***commodity space***, the set of all possible vectors of quantities of the several commodities, which we take to be R^n_+, the n-dimensional non-negative Euclidean space (I exclude negative quantities), where n is the number of different commodities. Non-admissible consumptions are those vectors in the commodity space which, given the problem one is studying, *the consumer cannot possibly choose* owing to physical impossibility or conceptual inconceivability. The consumption set differs from the ***budget set***, which is the subset of the consumption set that the consumer can *afford* to purchase.

For brevity in what follows 'consumption goods' will also stand for consumption services directly provided by factors (e.g. labour services directly demanded by consumers, such as leisure time or a massage). Many consumption goods are indivisible, and the quantities in X relative to such goods can only be integer numbers; but the main insights derivable from an assumption of perfectly divisible goods essentially hold also for indivisible goods (cf. ▶ Sect. 4.17); so let us assume that all consumption goods are perfectly divisible.

The interpretation of the elements of X depends on the type of analysis.

One can be interested in determining the normal repetitive behaviour of the consumer in a situation of relative prices that remain unaltered through time or change sufficiently slowly to authorize treating them as unchanging. Then one aims at determining the *long period*, average behaviour of the consumer, i.e. the average quantities *per unit of time* ('flows') that the consumer demands in a situation of tranquillity. The equilibrium based on this type of analysis is called **long-period equilibrium**, and it is the type of general equilibrium that the first generations of marginalist economists aimed at determining and that we have considered in ▶ Chap. 3. The product prices determined by a long-period equilibrium are the equivalent, in the marginal approach, of the natural prices, or prices of production, of the classical authors; they are the centres of gravitation of day-by-day market prices when sufficient time is allowed in each industry for the tendency of price to minimum average cost. In the equations of equilibrium of an *exchange economy*, where consumers come to the market with given endowments of consumption goods to exchange them against other consumption goods, long-period prices are the prices that the economy tends to establish if sufficient time and repetition of market fairs with unchanged data are allowed, so as to allow agents to correct mistakes and come to the periodic market with more and more correct expectations as to the prices they will face.

A very different possibility—the usual one in the more recent versions of general equilibrium theory, reflecting an important change to be discussed at length in ▶ Chaps. 7 through 9—is that one may be interested in determining the **intertemporal** behaviour of the consumer, over a sequence of periods starting from a certain precise moment, under the assumption that the consumer knows with certainty the prices of both current and future goods, and her current and future endowments.[2] Then one considers time as subdivided into a succession of short periods, say, 'days', and one distinguishes goods not only by their type but also

---

2   Intertemporal equilibrium is discussed in ▶ Chap. 8. Uncertainty will be treated in ▶ Chap. 9.

252   **Chapter 4** · Consumers and the Exchange Economy

by their 'day' of availability. Then two elements x_i, x_j of the consumption set can be the same good on different 'days'. One then says that the analysis is in terms of **dated commodities**. One assumes that, at the beginning of the 'day' from which the analysis starts, the consumer decides simultaneously her consumptions for that 'day', and for a number of subsequent days.[3] Then it is useful to distinguish goods with two indices, one specifying the type of good and the other the date of availability. The price of a future good is interpreted as the price to be paid *in the initial day* for delivery of the good in the future; this can be seen as the price to be paid on delivery, discounted to the initial day, and it is therefore called *discounted price*; see ▶ Chap. 8. Now what is useful to note is that such an analysis does not aim at determining the average normal behaviour of the consumer over a number of periods, but rather the succession of precisely determined behaviours in each 'day', behaviours possibly changing radically from one 'day' to the next. For example it could be that in the first 'day' the consumer has just got out of an illness that obliges her to a diet for the initial day and a few more days: long-period analysis would neglect this transitory deviation from normal behaviour; intertemporal analysis takes it into account and tries to determine the different demands for food on each day. For this reason, the prices determined by intertemporal equilibria can be described as **very short-period equilibrium prices** because dependent on elements which can be as short lived and accidental— strictly dependent on the 'day'—as in the determination of prices in a local fish market in a given day, with the supply of fish determined by the accidents of the catch of the night before (a well-known Marshallian example).

Yet another possibility is that one is interested in determining all demands for consumption goods and supplies of factor services of the consumer in one period (usually viewed as the 'current' period), plus her positive or negative savings, consisting in purchases or sales of a bond which promises delivery of one unit of numéraire in the next period. Then X includes all current consumption goods and services and in addition the bond. The prices thus determined are again very short-period prices and dated (because referring to a precise 'day'), but in a framework of **temporary equilibrium** (see ▶ Chap. 8).

Now let us clarify the meaning of consumption set by discussing consumptions *not* in it. Example: more than 24 h of leisure time per day, a physical impossibility. The consumptions excluded from the consumption set can depend on the type of analysis. When one interprets consumer choices as intertemporal, i.e. as referring to dated commodities, then a consumption basket that includes a promise to supply labour in the future, but not enough food to have the energy to work on that future day, or a promise to supply labour after the date when one knows one will be dead, is excluded from the consumption set: 'A given consumption x_i may be possible or impossible for the ith consumer; for example, the decision for an individual to have during the next year as sole input one pound of rice and as output one thousand hours of some type of labor could not be carried out. The set X_i of all the consumptions possible for the ith consumer is called his *consumption set*' (Debreu 1959, p. 51).

---

3   In some analyses, an infinite number of subsequent 'days': then X is a subset of R^∞_+.

4.2 · The Consumption Set, Time and the Role of Equilibrium

There are problems here. Evidently Debreu is implicitly excluding the possibility of *default* on promises: he must be assuming that everybody in the economy knows that a consumer who plans to eat too little will be unable to honour promises of future labour supply, and the offer of such labour promises is therefore neither accepted nor attempted. This appears to imply that when accepting someone's offer of future labour supply, one knows how much that labourer is planning to eat, and her nutritional needs, not very realistic!

The traditional neglect of default is due to the fact that the original formalizations of equilibrium aimed at determining *long-period* equilibria. If what one intends to determine is a normal situation, in the sense of the average state around which markets oscillate, then it can be presumed that there will be an average number of non-honoured contracts, depending on elements that the analysis can take as given and that are implicitly taken into account in the determination of the agents' decisions, e.g. in an economy with production, an industry will include in its normal costs the fact that on average there is some worker absenteeism, that sometimes the raw materials sent by suppliers are not of the contracted quality, that some payments by customers arrive later than they should, that occasionally there are legal expenses because of the need to take defaulters to court, etc. A normal average situation, which is what long-period equilibria intended to depict, will include a normal, average number of disappointments, wrong decisions, thefts, etc., that will be included in normal cost. The neglect of the possibility of default is much less easy to justify in *intertemporal equilibria*.[4]

4.3 Preferences and Utility

The consumer is assumed to have a *preference order* over the consumption baskets in X, with the implication that if a choice must be made between two baskets of which the first one is preferred to the second, and then the first one is chosen. This order can be characterized either with the relationship of *weak preference*, or with the relationship of *strong preference* (also called simply preference). Weak preference is indicated with the symbols R or $\succsim$; xRy or $x \succsim y$ stands for 'basket x (a vector) is **weakly preferred** to basket y, i.e. either x is definitely preferred to y, or the

---

4 Involuntary default due to events the agent cannot control can be dealt with in the same way as other uncertain events, via insurance, see ▶ Chap. 9; *voluntary* default on the contrary raises problems. As we will see in ▶ Chap. 9, uncertainty is dealt within intertemporal equilibria through the notion of contracts in *contingent* commodities, promises of delivery of commodities conditional on the realization of a specific state of nature; the standard example is the purchase of a promise of delivery of an umbrella in a certain shop on a certain future morning if that morning it rains; a more realistic example is the purchase of insurance, e.g. against accidents during a trip. If one were to add to the things that distinguish states of nature whether there is voluntary default or not on a contract, one would fall into an infinite multiplication of contingent commodities, because contracts in contingent commodities that depend on whether there is default on other contracts could be in turn defaulted and would therefore enlarge the number of states of nature and hence of contingent commodities, but contracts in these further contingent commodities could in turn be defaulted, and so on endlessly.

254 **Chapter 4 · Consumers and the Exchange Economy**

consumer is indifferent as to which of the two baskets she obtains'. The expression $x \precsim y$ means 'y is weakly preferred to x'. If 'x $\succsim$ y and it is not the case that y$\succsim$ x', then x is said to be **preferred**, or **strongly preferred**, or **strictly preferred**, to y, and we write x $\succ$ y. If it is both the case that x$\succsim$ y and y$\succsim$ x, then the consumer is said **indifferent** between x and y and we write x~y; I shall also say that x is **equipreferred** to y. (Some authors describe x~y as 'x is indifferent to y', but this is an ugly deformation of the English language; only a *chooser* can be indifferent between two alternatives; 'equipreferred' is … preferable.) I assume that the weak preference relation is:

complete (over X): if x and y are in X, it is either x $\succsim$ y or y $\succsim$ x (or both);
reflexive: for all $x \in X$, x $\succsim$ x.

An example of a non-reflexive binary relationship among numbers is 'greater than': a number is not greater than itself. But how can a preference *relation*, that is, among two elements of X, apply to the same element taken twice? Formally, the reason is that the order relationship R is defined as the subset, of the set $X \times X$ of all ordered couples (x_i, x_j), for which the weak preference relation $x_i \succsim x_j$ holds; since the two Xs in $X \times X$ contain the same elements, the set of all ordered couples (x_i, x_j) includes couples (x_i, x_i) where the two elements are identical; we are stipulating that among these couples relationship R holds. Concretely, for many things it can also happen that one faces two identical things: for baskets of consumption goods it is possible that two baskets are completely identical, and yet the consumer must decide whether she prefers one of them or is indifferent. Many authors argue that completeness implies reflexivity which therefore is not a third independent assumption, because if we call X' and X'' the first and second X in $X \times X$, completeness implies that either $x_i \in X' \succsim x_i \in X''$ or $x_i \in X'' \succsim x_i \in X'$ or both, so necessarily $x_i \succsim x_i$. There are subtle arguments that this reasoning is not conclusive, but the issue appears of no interest in economics.

(weakly) transitive: if x, y and z are in X and if x $\succsim$ y and y $\succsim$ z, then x $\succsim$ z.[5]

One can also start from $\succ$, strong preference or simply preference, as the primitive concept;[6] then x $\succsim$ y is defined as 'not y $\succ$ x', and x~y is defined as 'not x $\succ$ y

---

5   Transitivity appears a natural assumption, only violated by mistake; but transitivity need not hold when decisions are made by a collective, e.g. if the decisions of a several members household are reached by majority vote, then it can be that a majority prefers choice A to B and a majority prefers B to C, but a majority prefers C to A. This is Condorcet's paradox, to be studied in ▶ Chap. 14.

6   Very briefly (and dispensing with bold characters since preferences can apply to any entity): if the starting point is (strong) preference, then the assumptions on it are that preferences are ***asymmetric*** (i.e. there is no pair x and y such that x $\succ$ y and y $\succ$ x) and ***negatively transitive*** (i.e. if x $\succ$ y then for any third element z, it is either x $\succ$ z or z $\succ$ y or both). It can then be proved that preferences are ***irreflexive*** (ti.e. for no x is x $\succ$ x), ***strongly transitive*** (i.e. if x $\succ$ y and y $\succ$ z, then x $\succ$ z) and ***acyclic*** (i.e. if for any finite integer n, it is $x_1 \succ x_2, x_2 \succ x_3, ..., x_{n-1} \succ x_n$, then $x_n \neq x_1$), cf., e.g. Kreps (1990, p. 22). The term 'negatively transitive' means that the *negation* of $\succ$ is transitive. Indeed 'If for some x, y, z neither x $\succ$ y nor y $\succ$ z, then it is not the case that x $\succ$ z': which is the contrapositive of 'if x $\succ$ z then for any y, either x $\succ$ y or y $\succ$ z or both'. Remember that the ***contrapositive*** of 'A implies B' is 'not B implies not A', which is logically equivalent. The weak preference relation is defined as 'x $\succsim$ y if it is not the case that y $\succ$ x', and indifference or equipreference is defined as 'neither x $\succ$ y nor y $\succ$ x'.

4.3 · Preferences and Utility

and not $y \succ x'$. The majority choice appears to be to start from weak preference. But what does 'preference' mean? The issue is debated. One interpretation is in terms of subjective feelings: if consumption basket x is strictly preferred to consumption basket y, then the consumer feels better, or is happier if she obtains x, than if she obtains y. Another interpretation is in terms of choice: the *meaning* of stating that a consumer strictly prefers x to y is considered to be that, if this consumer must choose between x and y, the consumer chooses x; then a preference order is derived from a **choice function** which, from any set S of possible consumption baskets (i.e. from any element of the **power set** of the consumption set X), selects a subset of baskets $C(S)$, called a **best-choice set**; the baskets in $C(S)$ are then renamed 'baskets among which the consumer is indifferent and each one of which is strictly preferred to any basket in S and not in $C(S)$'. A limit of this interpretation is that it does not make it possible to distinguish preference from choice, while there are cases (e.g. people who would like to stop smoking and are unable to; or mistakes) where the distinction appears useful; but I will mostly assume that choice never violates preference and therefore *reveals* preference.

A complete and transitive and reflexive relation among all elements of a set is called a **total (or complete) preorder**. There is a literature on non-transitive preferences and on incomplete preferences, but the cases where such preferences become relevant fall outside the issues that this textbook intends to discuss.[7]

Another common assumption is **continuity** of preferences.

*When goods are perfectly divisible, preferences are said to be **continuous** if, for all $x \in X \subset R^n$, the sets $\{y: y \succsim x\}$ and $\{y: x \succsim y\}$, called, respectively, the **upper contour set** of x and the **lower contour set** of x, are closed sets.*

Equivalently, if $\{y^{(t)}\}$ is a sequence of baskets such that for all t it is $y^{(t)} \succsim x$ (respectively, $y^{(t)} \precsim x$), and if it converges to a consumption basket y^*, then $y^* \succsim x$ (respectively, $y^* \precsim x$) (■ Fig. 4.1).

Note that since the *complement* in R^n of a closed set A is an open set, the complement $\{y: x \succ y\}$ of the upper contour set of x is an open set, and the complement $\{y: y \succ x\}$ of the lower contour set is an open set too. An *open set* S in R^n is such that for any element x in it there is a neighbourhood of it $B_e(x) \equiv \{y \in R^n: \|y - x\| < e\}$, that is an open ball centred at x and of sufficiently small radius $e > 0$, which is entirely contained in S. This implies:

■■ Proposition 4.1

Under continuous preferences if y is strictly preferred to x, then there is a neighbourhood of y, i.e. an open ball of centre y and of sufficiently small radius, whose elements are all strictly preferred to x.

---

7 Many authors call **rational** a preference relation that is complete and transitive, thus implicitly suggesting that otherwise preferences are irrational. But this terminology is arbitrary since no definition of rationality is supplied.

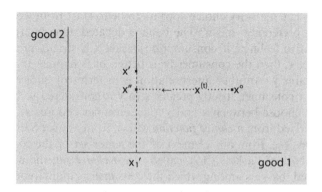

◘ **Fig. 4.1** Lexicographic preferences are not continuous: if the basket **x'** contains the same amount of good 1 as **x"** but contains more of good 2, and preferences are monotonic but lexicographic in good 1, then along any sequence {**x**$^{(t)}$} converging horizontally from the right to **x"** it is always **x**$^{(t)}$ ≻ **x'** as long as **x**$^{(t)}$ ≠ **x"**, so continuous preferences would imply **x"** ≿ **x'** while here **x'** ≻ **x"**

This allows us to understand one example of preferences that are not continuous: *lexicographic* preferences. Assume $X = R^2_+$, and **(strongly) monotonic** preferences, i.e. preferences such that 'more of even only one good and not less of the others is always strictly preferred'. Monotonic preferences in R^2 are lexicographic in good 1 when of two baskets $\mathbf{x} = (x_1, x_2)$ and $\mathbf{y} = (y_1, y_2)$, if $y_1 > x_1$ then **y** ≻ **x** independently of x_2 and y_2; only when $x_1 = y_1$ does the comparison between x_2 and y_2 become relevant, and then **y** ≻ **x** iff $y_2 > x_2$.[8] (The name derives from the analogy with the lexicographic order of words in dictionaries.) Then given two baskets $\mathbf{y} = (y_1, y_2)$ and $\mathbf{x} = (x_1, x_2)$ with $y_1 = x_1$ and $y_2 > x_2$, it is **y** ≻ **x** but *all* neighbourhoods of **y** contain vectors **y'** with less of good 1 than x_1 and therefore **x** ≻ **y'**: continuity is violated. ◘ Figure 4.5 shows the same thing in terms of sequences.

It may be possible to describe preferences by means of a numerical *utility function*, that is, a function $u: X \subset R^n \to R$ such that **x** ≻ **y** iff $u(\mathbf{x}) > u(\mathbf{y})$, and **x** ∼ **y** iff $u(\mathbf{x}) = u(\mathbf{y})$.

■■ Proposition 4.2

Preferences are representable by means of a utility function (and by means of a <u>continuous</u> utility function if goods are perfectly divisible) if the weak preference relation is complete, transitive and continuous.

I shall not give the full proof.[9] A simple proof under an additional assumption will be given in a short while.

---

8 The term 'iff' is shorthand for 'if and only if'.
9 Cf. Mas-Colell et al. (1995), pp. 47–49 for a proof for the case of monotonic preferences; or Barten and Bohm (1982), pp. 388–390, for a general proof.

4.3 · Preferences and Utility

Another frequent assumption on preferences is *local non-satiation* defined as follows: for any $\mathbf{x} \in X$ and for any neighbourhood $\{\mathbf{y}: \| \mathbf{y} - \mathbf{x} \| < \varepsilon \text{ with } \varepsilon > 0 \text{ a scalar}\}$,[10] this neighbourhood contains a consumption basket $\mathbf{y'} \in X$ such that $\mathbf{y'} > \mathbf{x}$.[11]

This means that, starting from any $\mathbf{x} \in X \subset R^n$, and assuming perfect divisibility of goods, there is always a continuous path in the consumption set X along which one moves to more and more preferred baskets. So *global satiation points* (i.e. baskets such that no basket in X is strictly preferred to them) as well as *local satiation points* (i.e. baskets such that there is a neighbourhood of them in X containing no basket strictly preferred to them) are excluded.

Given a consumption basket $\mathbf{x} \in X$, the set $\mathbf{y} = \{\mathbf{y} \in X: \mathbf{y} \sim \mathbf{x}\}$ is called the **indifference set** associated with $\mathbf{x}$. Under local non-satiation this set cannot be 'thick' (have interior points): in R^2 it can be at most a curve, in R^3 a surface. Otherwise there is a basket inside the 'thick' indifference set, with a neighbourhood of baskets all equipreferred to it, violating local non-satiation.

Another frequently made assumption on preferences is **strong monotonicity**: if $\mathbf{x} \neq \mathbf{y}$ and $\mathbf{x} \geq \mathbf{y}$, then $\mathbf{x} > \mathbf{y}$. In words, 'more is better': increasing the amount of even only one good in a consumption basket always entails that the new consumption basket is strictly preferred to the old one. A utility function representing strongly monotonic preferences is a strictly increasing function of each element of the consumption basket. Of course local non-satiation is satisfied.

In this book for brevity I use '**monotonicity**' to mean *strong* monotonicity.

If one adds the assumption of monotonicity to the assumption of complete, transitive and continuous preferences, then a simple proof is possible of the representability of preferences through a continuous utility function. It suffices to consider two goods. The assumptions imply that an indifference curve associated with any consumption basket $\mathbf{x}$ other than the origin exists, is decreasing and crosses the 45° line. Take two baskets along a ray from the origin, e.g. the 45° line, cf. ◘ Fig. 4.2: the basket which is farther from the origin is strictly preferred. We can therefore assign to the utility of each basket on the 45° line a numerical value equal to its distance from the origin and the same numerical value to the utility of all baskets on the same indifference curve. All points in R^2_+ are on some indifference curve which crosses the 45° ray, so all are assigned a utility. The resulting function is a function $u: R^2_+ \to R$ such that $\mathbf{x} > \mathbf{y}$ iff $u(\mathbf{x}) > u(\mathbf{y})$, and $\mathbf{x} \sim \mathbf{y}$ iff $u(\mathbf{x}) = u(\mathbf{y})$, hence it is a utility function that correctly represents the given preferences.

A terminological clarification: as common in economics, I call a utility function *monotonic* that a mathematician would call *monotonically strictly increasing* with

---

10 The symbol $\|\mathbf{x}\|$ stands for the Euclidean norm (i.e. length) of vector $\mathbf{x}$.

11 Some authors call this notion simply non-satiation; we prefer to follow the more common terminology and to distinguish *local* non-satiation, which excludes simultaneous satiation for all goods, but admits that the consumer may reach satiation for *some* good (i.e. may derive no further increase in utility from further increases in the consumption of that good), from *global* non-satiation, which excludes satiation for any good.

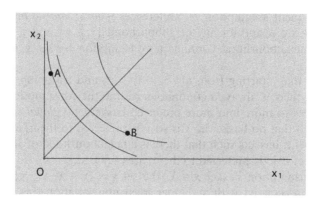

Fig. 4.2 Using the distance of an indifference curve from the origin along the 45° ray to assign utility values. Basket A has lower utility than basket B. (Indifference curves have been drawn here as strictly convex, but they need not be so.)

respect to each one of the variables on which it depends.[12] Preferences too are called monotonic if they are representable via a monotonic utility function (Fig. 4.2).

When preferences are representable through a utility function, the representation is not unique, because all that must be respected is the preference order, and if $u(\mathbf{x})$ does the job, so do $u(\mathbf{x})$ – a scalar, $2u(\mathbf{x})$, $(u(\mathbf{x}))^3$ and any other strictly increasing transformation $v(u(\mathbf{x}))$. The specific form can then be chosen on the basis of analytical convenience. Utility need not be positive: e.g. if $u(\mathbf{x})$ measures the distance from the origin of $\mathbf{x}$'s indifference curve and is positive, $v(\mathbf{x}) = -1/u(\mathbf{x})$ represents the same preferences and is negative.

The above means that all that is important about $u(\mathbf{x})$ is its ordinal properties.[13] In other instances (e.g. von Neumann–Morgenstern expected utility

---

12 Sometimes a distinction is proposed between increasing, *strictly* increasing and *strongly* increasing functions of several variables: then f(**x**) is defined increasing if **x**' ≥ **x** implies f(**x**') ≥ f(**x**), strictly increasing if it is increasing and in addition **x**' ≫ **x** implies f(**x**') > f(**x**), strongly increasing if **x**' ≥ **x** and **x**' ≠ **x** imply f(**x**') > f(**x**). That is, a strongly increasing function increases when any one of the independent variables increases; a strictly increasing function increases when all independent variables increase, but need not increase if not all independent variables increase. With these definitions, a monotonic utility function as defined in the text is strongly increasing.

13 This fact is sometimes misleadingly expressed by saying that the utility function is only ordinal. Mathematically, it is not so: an ordinal function is defined on an ordinal space, while a utility function is $R^n_+ \to R$, and these are not ordinal spaces. A utility function is numerical, so it implies a quantitative difference between the utility of a consumption basket and the utility of another basket. The point is that *we* are only interested in whether a consumption vector is preferred to another one, not by how much, so we are only interested in the ordinal *implications* of utility levels of different baskets, and therefore any monotonic increasing transformation of a utility function will do the job equally well; but a utility function remains numerical, i.e. cardinal. This also means that the marginal utility of one good in the consumption basket is arbitrary and hence uninformative except in comparison with the marginal utility of another good (according to the same utility function), because then their ratio indicates the slope of the indifference curve. The utility function is only a mathematical trick to obtain more quickly the same results on choice as one would derive from the preference preorder.

functions over lotteries see ▶ Chap. 9) the cardinal properties of $u(\mathbf{x})$ can be important too, but not in this chapter.

That preferences be representable via a utility function is not essential to the marginal approach, but it appears to cover most cases of interest. Lexicographic preferences in good 1 mean that the consumer will spend her entire income on good 1, not an interesting case. In what follows it will be assumed that preferences can be represented via a utility function.

4.4 Convex Preferences, Quasi-Concave Utility, Typical Indifference Curves

In the two-goods case (or in the n-goods case if we restrict ourselves to considering variations of only two of the goods), indifference sets are generally drawn as strictly convex decreasing curves. Which assumptions guarantee these properties? (◘ Fig. 4.3).

The absence of 'thickness' is guaranteed by local non-satiation. The negative slope is guaranteed by monotonicity. Convexity of downward-sloping indifference curves is not guaranteed by the assumptions listed so far, it can be obtained by *adding* to monotonicity the assumption of ***convexity of preferences***.

Preferences are ***convex*** if for every $\mathbf{x} \in X$, the upper contour set $\{\mathbf{y} \in X: \mathbf{y} \succsim \mathbf{x}\}$, i.e. the set of baskets weakly preferred to $\mathbf{x}$, is convex, that is, if for any $\mathbf{x}, \mathbf{y} \in X$ such that $\mathbf{y} \succsim \mathbf{x}$, it is $a\mathbf{x} + (1-a)\mathbf{y} \succsim \mathbf{x}$ for any $a \in [0, 1]$. Preferences are ***strictly convex*** if for any $\mathbf{x}, \mathbf{y} \in X$ such that $\mathbf{y} \succsim \mathbf{x}$, it is $a\mathbf{x} + (1-a)\mathbf{y} \succ \mathbf{x}$ for any $a \in (0, 1)$.

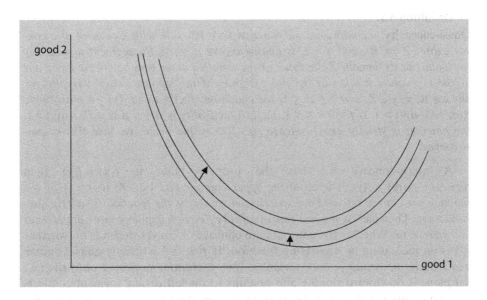

◘ **Fig. 4.3** Example of map of indifference curves exhibiting local non-satiation and convexity (the direction of the arrows indicates increases of utility) but not motonicity

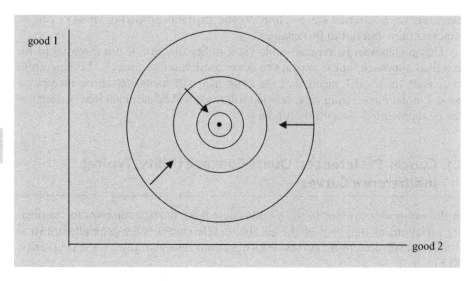

◘ **Fig. 4.4** Consumer with circular indifference curves and satiation. The direction of the arrows indicates increases in utility. Note that in this case indifference curves are not everywhere convex but *preferences* are convex. Thus, convex preferences do not imply convex indifference curves unless one adds monotonicity

◘ Figure 4.4 makes it clear that convexity of preferences without monotonicity does not suffice to establish convexity of indifference curves.

What does convexity of preferences imply for the utility function?

■■ **Definition 4.1.**

Quasi-concavity: *a continuous real function* $f(\mathbf{x})$: $R^n \to R$, *with* $\mathbf{x}$ *element of a convex subset* Z *of* R^n, *and* $n \geq 2$, *is* **quasi-concave** *if along the segment joining any two points in its domain* Z *the value of the function never goes below the lower one of the two values it takes at the two extremes of the segment; more formally, for any* $t \in R$, $\mathbf{x}, \mathbf{y} \in Z$, *and* $0 \leq a \leq 1$, *the conditions* $f(\mathbf{x}) \geq t$ *and* $f(\mathbf{y}) \geq t$ *must imply* $f(a\mathbf{x} + (1-a)\mathbf{y}) \geq t$. *If for* $0 < a < 1$, *the last inequality is strict,* $f(a\mathbf{x} + (1-a)\mathbf{y}) > t$, *the function is* **strictly quasi-concave**. *If* $-f(\mathbf{x})$ *is quasi-concave, then* $f(\mathbf{x})$ *is* **quasi-convex**.

A quasi-concave $f(\cdot)$ has the property that if $f(\mathbf{x}) = f(\mathbf{y})$ then $f(a\mathbf{x} + (1-a)\mathbf{y}) \geq f(\mathbf{y})$. Therefore *the upper contour sets* $\{\mathbf{x} \in Z: f(\mathbf{x}) \geq t\}$ *of the function are convex sets and are strictly convex sets if the function is strictly quasi-concave.* Then clearly *a quasi-concave utility function implies convex preferences and vice-versa.* Whether the contours are concave or convex depends on whether $f(\cdot)$ is an increasing or decreasing function. If $f(x_1, x_2)$ is strictly quasi-concave *and strictly increasing in both variables*, then a contour projected onto the (x_1, x_2) plane is downward sloping and remains to the left of any segment connecting two points $\mathbf{x}$ and $\mathbf{y}$ on it, because on that segment $f(a\mathbf{x} + (1-a)\mathbf{y}) > f(\mathbf{x})$ for $0 < a < 1$: so the contour is convex. Conclusion: convexity of monotonic pref-

4.5 · Optimization

erences implies quasi-concavity of the utility function that represents them, i.e. convex indifference curves; with strict convexity of preferences the utility function is strictly quasi-concave, with *strictly convex indifference curves*.

Quasiconcave *decreasing* functions have *concave* contours.

Concave functions are quasi-concave but the converse is not true. An example is the ***generalized Cobb–Douglas utility function*** $u(x_1, x_2) = x_1^c x_2^d$ with $c + d > 1$; it is quasi-concave (has strictly convex indifference curves) but it is easy to see that along the ray from the origin $x_1 = x_2$ the curve in R^3_+ generated by this utility function is strictly convex.

4.5 Optimization

Having assumed that the consumer has given preferences, we now assume that the consumer behaves according to them and acts so as to achieve a most preferred consumption basket among those that she can afford. The set of consumption baskets the consumer can afford is called the *feasible set* or ***budget set*** B. The budget set is the intersection of two sets: the consumption set (the set of *admissible* baskets) X and the set of *attainable* baskets given the ***budget constraint***. The set of attainable baskets is the set of consumption baskets that cost no more than what the consumer can spend. There are two standard specifications of this constraint. The Marshallian approach concentrates on demand for consumption goods of a consumer whose income is treated as given, determined in another part of the overall theory; the given consumer's income is m, and $\mathbf{p}$ is the (row) vector of prices of consumption goods, so with $\mathbf{x}$ the generic symbol for (column) vectors[14] representing consumption baskets the budget set is $B = \{\mathbf{x} \geq \mathbf{0}: \mathbf{px} \leq m\}$, i.e. is the portion of R^n_+ included between the origin, the no negative axes and the hyperplane $\mathbf{px} = m$ orthogonal to $\mathbf{p}$; the latter hyperplane is called the ***budget hyperplane*** (in the two-goods case, it is the ***budget line*** $p_1 x_1 + p_2 x_2 = m$). The general equilibrium approach (or Walrasian approach) treats the consumer as having a vector $\boldsymbol{\omega}$ of endowments (of goods or of factor services) and her income is the value of these endowments; the vector $\mathbf{p}$ is extended to include the prices or rentals of these endowments, and the budget set is $B = \{\mathbf{x} \geq \mathbf{0}: \mathbf{px} \leq \mathbf{p\omega}\}$.

Let the goods and factor services be perfectly divisible and the consumer's preferences be represented by a continuous utility function. The consumer tries to maximize her utility under the budget constraint plus the constraint that the quantities must be in the consumption set. Thus, in the Marshallian version the UMP, ***utility maximization problem***, has the form:

$$\max_{\mathbf{x}} u(\mathbf{x}) \text{ s.t. } \mathbf{px} \leq m, \mathbf{x} \in X, \mathbf{p} \in R^n_+ \text{ where } n \text{ is the number of goods considered.}$$

---

14 When a vector is defined as a row vector I do not use the transpose symbol to indicate it, I assume the reader will remember it. Unless otherwise indicated, vectors of quantities are column vectors, vectors of prices are row vectors.

262   **Chapter 4 · Consumers and the Exchange Economy**

Sometimes the last one of the goods in **x** is assumed to be *residual income*, with price 1, that is, money income left available for purchasing 'other goods', goods not listed among the first $n - 1$. Then the utility maximization problem is more complex than the UMP might suggest. Suppose $n = 2$, and good 2 is residual income which can be allocated among three goods that we will call goods 3, 4, 5; maps of indifference curves between good 1 and residual income must presume: (a) given prices of the other three goods, (b) that the consumer allocates the residual income among the other goods so as to maximize utility. Behind each point of such an indifference curve there is the solution of a Marshallian utility maximization problem: given a basket (x_1, x_2) the associated utility level, call it $u°$, is the highest one that the consumer can reach by using the amount of money x_2 to buy the other three goods; any other point of the indifference curve through (x_1, x_2) is determined by finding, for each given x_1, the *minimum* amount of money to spend on goods 3, 4, 5 that will allow reaching $u(x_1, x_3, x_4, x_5) = u°$. Of course the indifference curve thus obtained depends on the prices of the other three goods, it does not depend only on preferences.

If the consumer has a given vector of endowments $\omega \in R^n_+$, then she can obtain income (purchasing power) from selling these endowments, and her income is generally considered to be the *entire* value **pω** of these endowments, via the trick of imagining that, if the consumer chooses to keep part of her endowments for self-consumption, she in fact sells the whole vector of endowments and then buys back the part she consumes. Some authors call **pω** the *wealth* of the consumer. The endowment of a factor of production must be interpreted as the endowment of *services* that that factor can supply, and the corresponding price as the *rental*, or price of the services, of the factor. Thus the UMP, Walrasian version, is

$$\max_{x} u(\mathbf{x}) \quad \text{s.t.} \quad \mathbf{px} \le \mathbf{p}\omega, \mathbf{x} \in X, \mathbf{p} \in R^n_+.$$

▶ Chapter 3 had some intuitive discussion of the UMP.

Three comments are opportune before we study the formal aspects of the UMP.

First, implicit in these formulations of the UMP is the assumption of *price taking*: the consumer is assumed to treat prices as given, i.e. independent of her decisions.

Second, implicit in this way of formulating the UMP is an important restrictive assumption: *utility (i.e. the preference order among consumption baskets) depends only on the consumption basket* **x**. In reality, utility can also depend on what is being consumed by others, on how others appreciate one's consumption and on many other things. For example if the consumer worries about the envy of others, then depending on the intensity of this envy the consumer may or may not prefer a higher to a lower level of consumption of some goods. Some of these influences will be discussed in ▶ Chap. 14 under the rubric 'externalities'.

Third, *these formalizations of consumer choice aim at determining behaviour when there is no obstacle to implementing one's decisions, that is, in equilibrium*. Only in equilibrium all intentions to sell and to buy can be implemented.

4.5 · Optimization

In disequilibrium at least some consumer will be unable to act as the solution to her UMP would suggest. For example the consumer may not be able to buy a good for which supply is less than demand; then the consumer may turn to buying more of another good than indicated by the solution to the UMP. Or, in the Walrasian version, the consumer may find it impossible to sell labour services because demand for labour is less than supply: then the consumer has less income than required for her planned purchases so she cannot carry through the buying intentions resulting from the UMP. The solution to the UMP at given prices only aims at telling us what the behaviour of the consumer will be *if those prices happen to be equilibrium prices*; its purpose is to find out the equilibrium, that is, at which prices all intended actions of consumers are compatible; except under additional special assumptions it does *not* indicate behaviour when those prices are not equilibrium prices.[15]

We are interested in:

(a) under which conditions the UMP has a solution
(b) how this solution varies as a function of the vector of prices $\mathbf{p}$ and of income m or $\mathbf{p}\omega$; in particular it is important whether the solution varies *continuously* with $\mathbf{p}$ or not, and whether it is true that if the price of a good decreases, demand for that good increases.

A maximization problem is defined by a set $S = \{x\}$ of elements among which one must choose, called the ***choice set***, and by a function f from these elements to R; the elements of S for which f take the maximum value are called *maximals* or *solutions*. The set of solutions is called the ***best-choice set***, or ***solution set***, of the maximization problem. The best-choice set may be empty, in which case the maximization problem has no solution; it may contain a single element, in which case the solution is unique; it may contain several elements, a finite or infinite number of them.

We want to be sure that the best-choice set to the UMP is not empty. By ***Weierstrass' theorem***, a continuous function on a non-empty compact (i.e. closed and bounded) subset of a Euclidean space reaches there a maximum and a minimum. Our function to be maximized, the utility function, is continuous, so no problem here; then a solution certainly exists if the budget set is non-empty (which is the case), closed and bounded. Here problems can arise if a price is zero, then the budget set is not bounded, the consumer can demand unlimited quantities of a good whose price is zero. The problem can be avoided by assuming that prices are strictly positive, $\mathbf{p} \gg \mathbf{0}$ (the complications arising when some price can be zero will need discussion later). Then closedness of the budget set is not a problem, because the set $\{\mathbf{x}: \mathbf{px} \leq m\}$ of affordable consumption baskets is closed, so problems can only come from a not closed consumption set, but there seems to be no plausible reason why the latter should not be closed, it does not seem reasonable to assume that a consumer can get as close as she likes to consuming,

---

15 One such special assumption to be studied in ▶ Chap. 8 is that disequilibrium behaviour of markets is described by the Walrasian tâtonnement.

say, ten units of a perfectly divisible good, but cannot consume ten units. Boundedness requires that the budget set is limited above and below, and with positive prices this is ensured, because income is finite (endowments cannot be infinite), and hence what can be purchased is limited above, while the quantities of goods demanded cannot be negative, hence the budget set is limited below. Thus compactness of the budget set is an acceptable assumption when all prices are positive; then by Weierstrass' theorem the UMP has a solution.

However, the case of some zero price cannot be a priori excluded, in ▶ Chap. 6 we will study the zero-income problem that can arise if this case is not excluded.

4.6 Demand, Continuity and Upper Hemicontinuity of Correspondences

As **p** changes, the solution to the UMP changes. Does the UMP generate demand *functions* (i.e. a unique best choice for each **p**)? This is not guaranteed. One can show it graphically. Assume two goods and a consumer with a given income m. If one assumes a monotonic utility function, it is clear that the budget constraint can be written as an equality, $p_1 x_1 + p_2 x_2 = m$, $x_1 \geq 0$, $x_2 \geq 0$, because optimal consumption is necessarily on the budget line; in fact for this result we only need local non-satiation, because the consumer must choose the basket that yields the maximum utility among those baskets she can afford, and local non-satiation implies that any affordable basket **x** *not* on the budget line has a neighbourhood of affordable baskets that contains a basket strictly preferred to **x**, so the consumer does not maximize utility by choosing **x**. (Monotonic utility implies local non-satiation.) Uniqueness of the optimal choice of this consumer is only guaranteed by *strictly convex indifference curves*. If indifference curves are convex but not strictly convex, an indifference curve might have a flat portion lying on the budget line, then the consumer maximizes utility at any point of that portion of the budget line, she is indifferent among those baskets. Or, if the consumer has strictly *concave* indifference curves, it can happen that she is indifferent between two disconnected baskets. See ◘ Figs. 4.5, 4.6 and 4.7.

If the solution set of the UMP always contains only one element, then the function from (**p**, m) to the optimal choice vector **x** is called the *Marshallian demand function* **x**(**p**, m) of the consumer. This is a *vectorial* function, in fact a vector of functions x_i(**p**, m) each one indicating the demand function for good i.

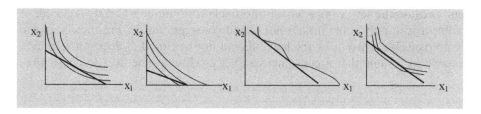

◘ **Fig. 4.5** Possible cases of optimal choice. The thick straight line is the budget line

4.6 · Demand, Continuity and Upper Hemicontinuity of Correspondences

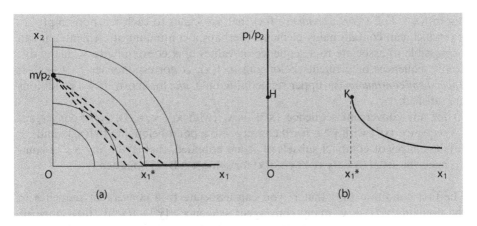

■ **Fig. 4.6** Marshallian demand for good 1 with strictly concave indifference curves when income is m and good 2 has price p_2; the demand curve for good 1 has two values (with a discontinuity in between) at $p_1/p_2 = OH$, the price ratio where, as shown on the left-hand side, the budget line touches the same indifference curve in abscissa and in ordinate

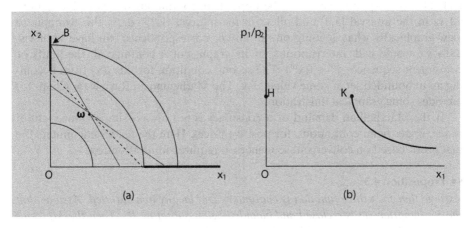

■ **Fig. 4.7** Choice curve in **a** is the thicker portions of the axes; **b** shows the corresponding demand curve for good 1 which has two values (with a discontinuity in between) at $p_1/p_2 = OH$, and is similar to the demand curve of ■ Fig. 4.6b although derived from a Walrasian UMP

If m is not given but is the value of the consumer's endowment vector ω, then we obtain the *Walrasian* vectorial demand function $\mathbf{x}(\mathbf{p}, \mathbf{p}\omega)$. If for at least some $(\mathbf{p}, m)$ the solution set of the UMP contains more than one element, then $\mathbf{x}(\mathbf{p}, m)$ is a multivalued function, or ***correspondence***.

For correspondences, the notion of continuity is more complex and one must distinguish several notions; see the Mathematical Review (▶ Chap. 15). Here we need the notion of *upper-hemicontinuous functions*, for short *uhc* functions.

A *function* $f(\mathbf{x})$ is continuous in $\mathbf{x}_0$ if $\lim_{\mathbf{x} \to \mathbf{x}_0} f(\mathbf{x}) = f(\mathbf{x}_0)$, i.e. if every sequence of values of $\mathbf{x}$, convergent to $\mathbf{x}_0$, generates sequences of values of $f(\mathbf{x})$ converg-

266   **Chapter 4 · Consumers and the Exchange Economy**

ing to $f(x_0)$. For a *correspondence* $f(x)$ that associates to each x a non-empty *set* $f(x)$ which can contain many elements (perhaps a continuum of elements), it can be possible to associate to a sequence of values of x converging to x_0 many different sequences of elements belonging to $f(x)$. A correspondence f: $A \to Y$ is ***upper-hemicontinuous*** (or upper-semicontinuous), *uhc* for short, if two conditions are satisfied:

(i) for any convergent sequence $\{x^m\} \to x_0$ (with $x_m, x_0 \in A$), *every* convergent sequence $\{y^m\}$ with $y^m \in f(x^m)$ converges to a point belonging to $f(x_0)$), and

(ii) the images of compact subsets of A are bounded, that is, for any $B \subseteq A$ compact, the set $g(B) = \{y \in Y : y \in f(x) \text{ for some } x \in B\}$ is bounded.

The first condition says that if you can associate to a convergent sequence in the domain $\{x^m\} \to x_0$ many convergent sequences $\{y^m \in f(x^m)\}$, then none of these can converge to an element not in $f(x°)$. This excludes for example the following case: $f(x)$ is a correspondence $R \to R$; for $x < 1$, $f(x)$ is the constant set $\{y \in [1,2]\}$, while for $x \geq 1$, $f(x) = \{y \in [3,4]\}$; then to any sequence $\{x^m\}$ converging to $x = 1$ *from below* it is possible to associate convergent sequences $y^m \in f(x^m)$ that converge to any value of y between 1 and 2, but none of these values is in $f(1)$. This correspondence would be upper-hemicontinuous if $f(1)$ included both all ys in the interval [3,4] and all ys in the interval [1,2]—draw this example to view graphically what is going on. So an *uhc* correspondence can have what visually we would call 'interruptions' of its graph, but it contains all the limits of convergent sequences $y^m \in f(x^m)$. The second condition forbids $f(x)$ from becoming an unbounded set at some value of x. The Mathematical Review ($\blacktriangleright$ Chap. 15) provides some graphical illustrations.

If the Marshallian demand of a consumer is not always single-valued, still it is *uhc*, upper hemi-continuous, for positive prices. Here the reader encounters the first proof based on convergent sequences, it requires some attention.

■■ Proposition 4.3
Assume that the utility function is continuous and locally non-satiated. Assume that the consumption set is a closed and bounded-below subset of R^n. Then the Marshallian demand correspondence $x(p, m)$ is uhc at all $(p, m) \gg 0$. Moreover if $x(p, m)$ is a function, i.e. single-valued, then it is continuous at all $(p, m) \gg 0$.

Proof   First, $x(p, m)$ is always bounded at all $(p, m) \gg 0$, because $x(p, m)$ is in the budget set which is compact. Hence condition (ii) of the definition of upper-hemicontinuity is satisfied.

Now I prove condition (i): given any sequence $\{(p^t, m^t)\} \to (p, m) \gg 0$, every possible convergent sequence $\{x^t\}$ with $x^t \in x(p^t, m^t)$ converges to an $x° \in x(p, m)$. Suppose not, i.e. suppose we had a sequence $\{(p^t, m^t)\} \to (p, m) \gg 0$ and a sequence $\{x^t\}$ with $x^t \in x(p^t, m^t)$ for all t, such that $x^t \to x° \notin x(p, m)$. Because $p^t x^t \leq m^t$ for all t, taking limits as $t \to +\infty$, we conclude that $px° \leq m$. So $x° \in B(p, m)$ but not being $\in x(p, m)$ it is not optimal, so there must exist a $x^\wedge \in B(p, m)$ such that $u(x^\wedge) > u(x°)$. By the continuity of u, there exists a $x' \neq x^\wedge$

4.6 · Demand, Continuity and Upper Hemicontinuity of Correspondences

arbitrarily close to $\mathbf{x}^\wedge$ such that $\mathbf{p}\mathbf{x}' < m$ and $u(\mathbf{x}') > u(\mathbf{x}^\circ)$. Now for t large enough, since $\{(\mathbf{p}^t, m^t)\} \to (\mathbf{p}, m)$, it must be $\mathbf{p}_t\mathbf{x}' < m$; hence for t large enough, it is $\mathbf{x}' \in B(\mathbf{p}^t, m^t)$ and $u(\mathbf{x}^t) \geq u(\mathbf{x}')$ because $\mathbf{x}^t \in x(\mathbf{p}^t, m^t)$. Taking limits as $t \to +\infty$, the continuity of u then implies that $u(\mathbf{x}^\circ) \geq u(\mathbf{x}')$, a contradiction. So it cannot be that $\mathbf{x}^t \to \mathbf{x}^\circ \notin x(\mathbf{p}, m)$.[16]

The same proof applies to the case when $x(\mathbf{p}, m)$ is a function; but for functions, upper hemicontinuity coincides with continuity, hence in this case $x(\mathbf{p}, m)$ is continuous. This can be obtained with strict convexity of indifference surfaces, which guarantees uniqueness of consumer choice as will be shown later: under this assumption $x(\mathbf{p}, m)$ is a demand *function* and hence it is continuous.[17] ∎

Exercise. Indicate where the assumption of local non-satiation enters the above proof.

The same proof can be used to show that the result applies also to demands derived from a Walrasian UMP. When income derives from given endowments, $x(\mathbf{p}, m)$ becomes $x(\mathbf{p}, \mathbf{p}\omega)$ and it depends only on $\mathbf{p}$; but the above proof continues to hold, it suffices to replace m with $\mathbf{p}\omega$ and m^t with $\mathbf{p}^t\omega$.

The above result can also be obtained as an application of the **Theorem of the Maximum** which, informally stated, says that, given the problem of finding the maximal elements of a continuous function $R^n \to R$ on a non-empty compact subset of R^n which is a continuous correspondence of a vector of parameters, the *solution set*[18] is an upper-hemicontinuous correspondence of this vector of parameters (and is a continuous **function** of the vector of parameters, if the solution set always contains only one element). In our case the solution set is the set of consumption baskets that maximize the (continuous) utility function in the budget set, and the latter set is easily shown to be a compact continuous correspondence of the prices-and-income vector as long as the price vector is positive.

As the above figures show, demand for a good can undergo discontinuities or not be univocally determined; one needs strictly convex indifference curves to avoid these possibilities. Let us see what otherwise can happen, by using the *choice curve* (my preferred denomination for the notion usually called offer curve) introduced in ▶ Chap. 3, ▶ Sect. 3.7.2, ◻ Fig. 3.17b. The choice curve collects the solutions to the two-goods Walrasian UMP as p_1/p_2 varies. Let us introduce here a bit of terminology useful for general equilibrium theory. Given the consumer's endowment $\omega = (\omega_1, \omega_2)$, assume x_1, x_2 are the demands of the consumer. The quantity $z_i = x_i - \omega_i$, $i = 1, 2$, indicates the quantity of good i the consumer

---

16 Note that the proof also applies to the cases in which, as the price of a good tends to zero, the demand for the good tends continuously to $+\infty$, because upper hemicontinuity only requires that the images of compact sets be bounded, and since we are assuming $\mathbf{p} \gg 0$, then compact sets of prices are closed sets of strictly positive prices.

17 Note that strict convexity of indifference surfaces excludes the possibility that a good yields no utility (this would generate linear segments in indifference curves) and more generally the possibility of satiation with any good.

18 The solution set of a maximization problem $\max_\mathbf{x} f(\mathbf{x})$ is the set of vectors $\mathbf{x}$ at which $f(\mathbf{x})$ is maximized.

intends to *purchase from* other consumers if $x_i > \omega_i$; if z_i is negative, its absolute value is the quantity that the consumer intends to *sell to* other consumers; z_i is called the (*individual*) **excess demand** or **net demand** for good i. The opposite of excess demand, $-z_i$, is called (*individual*) **excess supply**. The balanced budget assumption means that the value of the consumer's planned sales must equal the value of the planned purchases, i.e. her plans must satisfy the **balanced budget constraint**:

$$p_1 z_1 + p_2 z_2 = 0$$

Of course this is only a rearrangement of $p_1 x_1 + p_2 x_2 = p_1 \omega_1 + p_2 \omega_2$.

With strictly convex smooth indifference curves, the choice curve is continuous and necessarily passes through the endowment point (where it is tangent to the indifference curve through that point). But with other forms of indifference curves the choice curve need not be continuous. Suppose strictly concave indifference curves and an interior endowment point as shown in ◻ Fig. 4.7a. The choice curve consists of two disjoint half-lines along the axes, shown as thick lines in ◻ Fig. 4.7a. At one relative price the consumer is indifferent between two baskets.

In the Walrasian UMP of ◻ Fig. 4.7a there arises a discontinuity in the demand of the consumer, illustrated in ◻ Fig. 4.7b; the reader should prove that the discontinuity will also arise if the endowment point is point B as shown in ◻ Fig. 4.7a, which can also be taken to represent the budget constraint of a Marshallian UMP with p_2 given and $m = p_2 \cdot \overline{OB}$ (then we obtain ◻ Fig. 4.6a). The discontinuity can cause the non-existence of a general equilibrium.

4.7 The Two-Goods Exchange Economy and the Importance of Continuity of Demand

To illustrate that a discontinuity of demand functions can cause the non-existence of a general equilibrium, let us consider a simple example, an exchange economy like the forest economy of ▶ Chap. 3, with many consumers but only two goods. There are S consumers, and we distinguish them by a superscript $1,\dots,s,\dots,S$. Consumer s derives her purchasing power from her given endowments of the two goods, represented by a vector $\omega^s = (\omega_1{}^s, \omega_2{}^s)$, and is price-taker. Each consumer has a positive endowment of both goods and comes to the market to exchange part of the endowment and reach a higher utility; her budget constraint is:

$p_1 x_1{}^s + (1 - p_1) x_2{}^s \leq p_1 \omega_1{}^s + (1 - p_1) \omega_2{}^s$; or in terms of excess demands, $p_1 z^s{}_1 + p_2 z^s{}_2 \leq 0$.

Because of *local non-satiation* the constraint holds as an equality (*balanced budget*). For each given p_1/p_2 with both prices positive, the excess demands of the several consumers are, we assume, uniquely determined; their algebraic sum for good i is the *market excess demand* for that good, z_i (without index s). It is convenient to choose as numéraire a *basket* of goods comprising one unit of each good, so that $p_1 + p_2 = 1$, obviously with $p_1 \geq 0, p_2 \geq 0$. Then each price can vary

4.7 · The Two-Goods Exchange Economy and the Importance of Continuity of Demand

between 0 and 1, and once one price is fixed, the other one is determined too. So we can consider consumer demands and excess demands to depend only on p_1.

One property of market excess demands will be important below. Since for each consumer the balanced budget implies $p_1 z^s_1 + p_2 z^s_2 = 0$, then in the aggregate it is

$$p_1 z_1 + p_2 z_2 = p_1 \Sigma_s z^s_1 + p_2 \Sigma_s z^s_2 = \Sigma_s \left[p_1 z^s_1 + p_2 z^s_2 \right] = 0.$$

This property is called **Walras' Law for the exchange economy**.[19] Clearly it generalizes to n goods. In words:

■■ Proposition 4.4

Walras' Law. In an exchange economy, under balanced budgets, the algebraic sum, over all markets, of the exchange values of intended excess demands is necessarily zero whatever the prices.

Below, when it is clear from the context, I will refer to market excess demand as simply excess demand.

A market is said to be in equilibrium if competition does not tend to alter the price on that market according to the 'law of supply and demand', i.e. according to the principle that if market excess demand is positive (demand exceeds supply) the price tends to rise, if negative (supply exceeds demand) the price tends to decrease: but it cannot decrease below zero. It follows (under our assumption that prices cannot be negative) that *a market is in equilibrium if either excess demand is zero, or there is excess supply but price is zero.*[20] Now we can state an important corollary of Walras' Law:

■■ Proposition 4.5

Corollary of Walras' Law. Under Walras' Law, if there is equilibrium in all but one of the markets where price is positive, then there is equilibrium also in the remaining market where price is positive.

The proof is obvious. The qualification 'where price is positive' is often neglected, but is important. If there is equilibrium on all markets but one, and on that last market the price is zero, then Walras' Law does *not* imply that on that last market there is equilibrium: it only implies that the *value* (price times quantity) of excess demand on that market is zero, which will be the case even if excess demand is positive, since price is zero. We will see below that this is important.

In our two-goods economy Walras' Law has another obvious corollary: if both prices are positive and on one market there is excess demand, then on the other market there is excess supply.

---

19 Recently a questionable habit is spreading, of calling 'Walras' Law' the assumption of balanced budget, which is in no sense a law, it is an assumption, and only acceptable for equilibrium choices.

20 Note that it is not excluded that a market can be in equilibrium with a zero price and a zero excess demand.

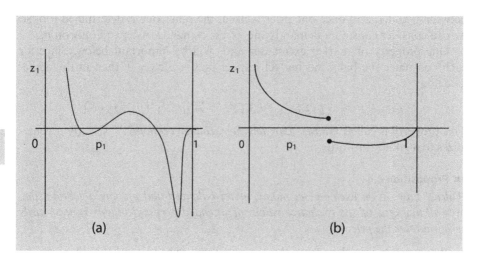

◘ **Fig. 4.8** Excess demand in the two-goods exchange economy

Let us represent graphically $z_1(p_1)$. Let us measure z_1 in ordinate and p_1 in abscissa; z_1 can be positive or negative, and p_1 varies between 0 and 1.

Assume that z_1 and z_2 are well-defined and continuous functions of p_1 as long as both prices are positive, and that when the price of a good is close to zero, any further decrease of this price raises the demand for the good, causing this demand to tend continuously to $+\infty$. (In ◘ Fig. 4.8a, z_1 obeys these assumptions.) Then *at least one equilibrium exists*.

Proof Remember that $p_1 + p_2 = 1$. By assumption, as $p_1 \to 0$, the aggregate demand[21] for good 1 tends to $+\infty$, but then the same is true for z_1, the aggregate *excess* demand for good 1, which is the aggregate demand for good 1 minus the finite aggregate endowment of good 1. Hence for p_1 sufficiently close to 0, z_1 is positive; applying the same reasoning to p_2 and z_2 we find that, for p_1 sufficiently close to 1 but not equal to 1, z_2 is certainly positive and therefore by Walras' Law z_1 is negative. So $z_1(p_1)$ necessarily changes sign at least once in the open price interval $(0,1)$, and being continuous it takes value zero (i.e. crosses the horizontal axis) at least once in that interval; at that positive value of p_1 it is $z_1 = 0$ and $p_2 > 0$, by Walras' Law it is $z_2 = 0$ too, so it is an equilibrium (not necessarily unique). ∎

Note that $p_1 = 1$ is not an equilibrium, here our caveat on Walras' Law when a price is zero is relevant: the market of good 1 is in equilibrium when $p_1 = 1$ because $p_2 z_2 = 0$ and $p_1 > 0$ imply $z_1 = 0$ owing to Walras' Law, but the other market is not in equilibrium, demand for good 2 is infinite.

---

21 'Aggregate demand' for a single good in microeconomics, differently from its use in macroeconomics where aggregate magnitudes are sums of exchange values, stands for the sum of the *physical* demands of the several consumers for the good; the same holds for aggregate supply, aggregate endowment. Aggregate excess demand and market excess demand are synonymous.

4.7 · The Two-Goods Exchange Economy and the Importance of Continuity of Demand

So in this economy if for the price of a good sufficiently close to zero the excess demand for the good is positive, and excess demands are continuous for positive prices, an equilibrium exists. But if for at least one consumer there is a price at which the composition of demand undergoes a discontinuous jump as shown in ◘ Fig. 4.7b, the case represented in ◘ Fig. 4.8b can arise, in which z_1 never crosses the horizontal axis, i.e. never takes value zero and therefore there is no equilibrium. This shows the relevance of continuity of excess demands. More on the issue is in ▶ Chap. 6.

The equilibrium must not only exist, but the economy must tend to it. Clearly, as particularly evidenced in the indirect factor substitution mechanism studied in ▶ Chap. 3, this needs that if the price of a consumption good decreases, the consumers' demand for that good increases. Does this always obtain? To study this important question, we need first to complete the study of the UMP. I will assume that the utility function is a continuous representation of complete, transitive, continuous and locally non-satiated preferences.

Two preliminary results will be of help.

First: the demand function or correspondence is homogeneous of degree zero[22] in $(\mathbf{p}, m)$. This is because the budget set is not altered by equi-proportional changes of all prices and of m. If the consumer's income derives from given endowments, $m = \Sigma_i p_i \omega_i$, then demand only depends on relative prices, i.e. it is homogeneous of degree zero in $\mathbf{p}$.

A second result is that strictly convex preferences guarantee single-valued demand.

■■ Proposition 4.6

If the preference relation is convex and u is monotonic and hence quasi-concave, then $x(\mathbf{p}, m)$ is a convex set, and if the preference relation is strictly convex, so that u is strictly quasi-concave, then $x(\mathbf{p}, m)$ is single-valued.

Proof We must prove that if $\mathbf{x}' \in x(\mathbf{p}, m)$ and $\mathbf{x}'' \in x(\mathbf{p}, m)$ and if $x''' = \lambda x' + (1 - \lambda)x''$, $0 < \lambda < 1$, then also $\mathbf{x}''' \in x(\mathbf{p}, m)$. It is $\mathbf{px}''' = \mathbf{p}\lambda\mathbf{x}' + \mathbf{p}(1 - \lambda)\mathbf{x}'' = m$ so $\mathbf{x}'''$ is feasible. Quasi-concavity means that if $u(\mathbf{x}') \geq u(\mathbf{x}'')$—which is the case here since the two are equal—then $u(\lambda\mathbf{x}' + (1-\lambda)\mathbf{x}'') \geq u(\mathbf{x}'')$, so $u(\mathbf{x}'') \geq u(\mathbf{x}'')$. Since $\mathbf{x}'''$ yields at least as much utility as $\mathbf{x}'$ and $\mathbf{x}''$ and is feasible, it must be $\in x(\mathbf{p}, m)$. If u is strictly quasi-concave, then in $u(\lambda\mathbf{x}' + (1-\lambda)\mathbf{x}'') \geq u(\mathbf{x}'')$ the inequality sign becomes strict, so we obtain $u(\mathbf{x}''') > u(\mathbf{x}'')$ which contradicts $\mathbf{x}'' \in x(\mathbf{p}, m)$: the implication is that there cannot be two distinct baskets $\mathbf{x}'$, $\mathbf{x}''$ both $\in x(\mathbf{p}, m)$. ■

---

22 A continuous function $f(x_1, ..., x_n)$ is *homogeneous of degree k* if, with t a positive scalar, $f(tx_1, ..., tx_n) = t^k f(x_1, ..., x_n)$. By differentiating both sides of this equality with respect to any x_i one proves that if a function homogeneous of degree k is differentiable, then its partial derivatives are homogeneous of degree $k - 1$; and by differentiating both sides with respect to t in $t=1$, one proves that $\Sigma_i (x_i \cdot \partial f/\partial x_i) = kf(x)$, a result sometimes called *Euler's theorem for homogeneous functions* (See ▶ Sect. 3.3.). The extension of the definition of homogeneous function to correspondences is obvious: the set $Y = \{y \in f(t\mathbf{x})\}$ coincides with the set $Y' = \{y \in t^k f(\mathbf{x})\}$.

4.8 First-Order Conditions. Corner Solutions. The Kuhn–Tucker Theorem

Let us now assume that the utility function is not only continuous but also twice differentiable, quasi-concave and monotonic. Then the indifference (hyper)surfaces are downward sloping, convex and differentiable; and indifference surfaces farther from the origin along a ray through the origin indicate a higher utility level.

Let us distinguish an *interior* maximum (i.e. a solution $\mathbf{x}$ in the interior *of the consumption set*, not of the budget set: demand strictly positive for all goods) from a 'corner solution' in which demand for one or more goods is zero. The consumer faces $n + 1$ constraints if there are n goods: the budget constraint 'total expenditure not more than total income', and the n constraints that the demand for each good cannot be negative. Under local non-satiation, the budget constraint 'binds', that is, is satisfied as an equality. At an interior maximum the non-negativity constraints do not 'bind', that is, they do not prevent a small change of any x_i in any direction, only the budget constraint 'binds', preventing changes in the quantities demanded that would cause expenditure to exceed income. If indifference curves are 'smooth', a necessary condition for an interior maximum is tangency between indifference surface and budget hyperplane; for each two goods, taking the quantities demanded of the other goods as given, there must be tangency between budget line and indifference curve restricted to that couple of goods. An indifference curve crossing the budget line would clearly mean that higher utility can be reached at other points of the budget line; see ◩ Fig. 4.9. (In ◩ Fig. 4.9 indifference curves are assumed convex, but if they were not the solution would not be interior.)

Then as explained in ▶ Chap. 3 for each couple of goods both demanded by the consumer there must be equality between their price ratio and their |MRS|. We need not repeat here the definition of MRS. Let us only remember that $p_1/p_2 = MU_1/MU_2$ can be rewritten $MP_1/p_1 = MP_2/p_2$ where these ratios measure the marginal utility of money or income. ▶ Chapter 3, ▶ Sect. 3.8, explained how this notion helps to understand why some goods are not demanded by the consumer.

On 'corner solutions' it is worth adding that they necessarily happen with concave indifference curves (cf. ◩ Figs. 4.6a and 4.7a), but can also happen with strictly convex indifference curves that touch the axes, as shown in ◩ Fig. 4.10 where at the optimum point $\mathbf{x}^*$ the demand for good 2 is zero. Generically[23] in

---

23 A property that is verified or not depending on the values of a parameter is said *generic* if the values of the parameter for which the property does not hold are a subset S of measure zero of the set A of possible values of the parameter; genericity is useful if there is reason to think that the parameter can take values in A with a non-atomic probability distribution (that is, there is no single element of set A with positive probability of occurrence): then the values of the parameter for which the property does *not* hold have probability zero of occurrence, and one can assume the property to hold. In Euclidean spaces, a subset of a set in R^n is of measure zero if its elements can be enclosed in hypercubes of R^n the sum of whose volumes can be reduced to a number as

4.8 · First-Order Conditions. Corner Solutions. The Kuhn–Tucker theorem

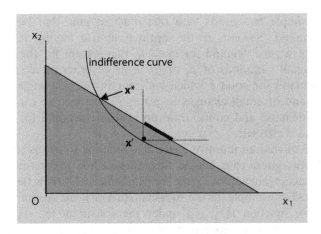

Fig. 4.9 If at **x*** the indifference curve crosses the budget line, then **x*** cannot be optimal: because of monotonicity the points on the thick line segment of the budget line yield a higher utility than **x**′ and hence than **x***. The grey area is the budget set

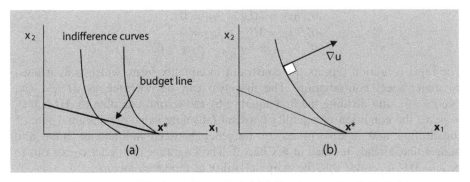

Fig. 4.10 'Corner solutions'. In **b** by fluke the indifference curve at **x*** has the same slope as the budget line. The usual case is the one in **a** where the two slopes differ

this case $MU_1/MU_2 > p_1/p_2$ at the optimum, a *proper* corner solution; but it might also be that, by a highly improbable fluke, there is tangency between budget line and indifference curve at the corner solution; see Fig. 4.10b.

But then *why is introductory economics so largely based on interior solutions?* Two reasons. First, generally one wants to study how a consumer alters the *composition* of her demand when income or prices change; then in the

---

close to zero as one likes. An (n-1)-dimensional object in R^n (a curve in R^2, a surface in R^3) is of measure zero. For example, if indifference curves relative to two goods are parallel straight lines (perfect substitutes), the case of non-coincidence of the slope of the budget line with the slope of indifference curves is generic; unless there is reason to suppose that there are economic forces tending to make the relative price of the two goods such that the consumer is indifferent between them, one can assume that only one of the two goods will be demanded.

274 **Chapter 4** · Consumers and the Exchange Economy

pedagogically simple two-goods case one must assume that both goods are in positive demand. Second, if the optimal choice among $n > 2$ goods is characterized by a zero demand for good k, then except for the fluke case of ◘ Fig. 4.10b, small variations of p_k or of m or of other prices are not going to alter the demand for good k which will remain zero; so when studying the effects on demand of small changes in prices or income, we can forget about goods in zero demand and concentrate on how the demand for the goods in positive demand is affected.

▶ Chapter 3 offered an intuitive analysis of interior solutions to utility maximization in the two-goods case. Let me illustrate here how to determine these solutions with the Lagrangian approach (see the Mathematical Review (▶ Chap. 15) for a quick review). For example, in the Marshallian UMP the consumer maximizes the differentiable function $u(x_1, x_2)$ under the constraint $m - p_1 x_1 - p_2 x_2 \geq 0$, which holds as equality under local non-satiation. The Lagrangian function is

$$\mathcal{L} = u(x_1, x_2) + \lambda(m - p_1 x_1 - p_2 x_2).$$

The first-order necessary conditions for a maximum are that the partial derivatives of the Lagrangian with respect to the three variables x_1, x_2, λ must be zero. This yields

$$\partial \mathcal{L}/\partial x_1 = MU_1 - \lambda p_1 = 0$$
$$\partial \mathcal{L}/\partial x_2 = MU_2 - \lambda p_2 = 0$$
$$\partial \mathcal{L}/\partial \lambda = m - p_1 x_1 - p_2 x_2 = 0.$$

The third condition repeats the constraint in equality form, which is as it must be under local non-satiation. The first two can be rewritten as $MU_1 = \lambda p_1$, $MU_2 = \lambda p_2$, and dividing the first equality by the second one obtains $MU_1/MU_2 = p_1/p_2$, the condition of equality between (absolute value of) marginal rate of substitution and relative prices, or tangency between indifference curve and budget line, already reached in ▶ Chap. 3. The Lagrange multiplier comes out to be $\lambda = MU_1/p_1 = MU_2/p_2$, the marginal utility of money or income.

But a general analysis must admit the possibility of corner solutions. Then we must use the ***Kuhn–Tucker theorem*** to obtain the first-order necessary conditions for a constrained maximum. (Second-order conditions are examined in the Mathematical Review.)

This theorem yields necessary conditions for maximization of a differentiable function of many variables $f(\mathbf{x})$, $\mathbf{x}$ a vector, under differentiable inequality and equality constraints. A constraint $g_i(\mathbf{x}) \geq 0$ is said *slack* at $\mathbf{x}^*$ if $g_i(\mathbf{x}^*) > 0$, it is said *binding* at $\mathbf{x}^*$ if $g_i(\mathbf{x}^*) = 0$. A '***constraint qualification condition***' (C.Q.C.) is any one of a number of conditions on the constraints that avoid some very special and rare cases in which the necessary conditions specified by the theorem do not hold; more on this below. The theorem can be presented in a variety of ways. I prefer the form in which all inequality constraints are of type $g_i(\mathbf{x}) \geq 0$.

▪▪ Proposition 4.7

Kuhn–Tucker theorem*. A necessary condition for* $\mathbf{x}^* \in R^n_+$ *to be a solution to* max $f(\mathbf{x})$ *subject to* $g_i(\mathbf{x}) \geq 0$, $i = 1,...,k$, *and to* $h_s(\mathbf{x}) = 0$, $s = k+1,...,m$, *(where* $f(\mathbf{x})$, $g_i(\mathbf{x})$ *and* $h_s(\mathbf{x})$ *are differentiable functions* $R^n \to R$), *assuming a*

4.8 · First-Order Conditions. Corner Solutions. The Kuhn–Tucker theorem

constraint qualification condition C.Q.C. is satisfied at $\mathbf{x}^*$, *is that there exist scalars* λ_i, $i = 1,...,k$, *called 'Kuhn–Tucker–Lagrange multipliers', and scalars* λ_s, $s = k + 1,...,m$, *called 'Lagrange multipliers', such that*

(i) $\dfrac{\partial f(\mathbf{x}^*)}{\partial x_j} + \sum\limits_{i=1}^{k} \lambda_i \dfrac{\partial g_i(\mathbf{x}^*)}{\partial x_j} + \sum\limits_{k+1}^{m} \lambda_s \dfrac{\partial h_s(\mathbf{x}^*)}{\partial x_j} = 0, \forall j$, *where all* λ_i, $i = 1,...,k$, *are* ≥ 0 (*on*

the contrary, the sign of λ_s, $s = k + 1,...,m$, is not a priori determined)[24];

(ii) $\lambda_i g_i(\mathbf{x}^*) = 0$, $i = 1,...,k$, *i.e. if* $g_i(\mathbf{x}^*) > 0$ *then* $\lambda_i = 0$, *and if* $\lambda_i > 0$ *then* $g_i(\mathbf{x}^*) = 0$.

The theorem states, among other things, that, if a constraint qualification condition holds, the gradient of the objective function at the optimum can be expressed as a linear combination of the gradients of the constraint functions. The original C.Q.C. postulated by Kuhn and Tucker is explained in Takayama (1974, p. 89); afterwards Arrow, Hurwicz and Uzawa found five more easily verified conditions (see Takayama, 1974, pp. 93–94) that imply the original one; each one of them guarantees that the constraints do not prevent the gradient of the objective function at the optimum from being a linear combination of the gradients of the constraint functions; one C.Q.C. with clear economic content is the *rank condition* that requires that the gradients of the constraints binding at $\mathbf{x}^*$ be linearly independent. For an example where this fails see the end of Sect. 4.9.6. In economic problems generally at least one of those five conditions holds, so the C.Q.C. can be assumed to be satisfied.

The function $f(\mathbf{x}) + \sum_i \lambda_i g_i(\mathbf{x}) + \sum_s \lambda_s h_s(\mathbf{x})$ whose partial derivatives are set equal to zero in (i) is the **Lagrangian function**, or simply the Lagrangian, of the constrained maximization problem. Conditions (i) are the first-order conditions.

A minimization problem must be turned into a maximization problem by multiplying the objective function by –1. The inequality constraints must be written in the form (*function*) ≥ 0; for example if one constraint is $x_1 \leq 0$, it must be put in the form $-x_1 \geq 0$. Each equality constraint $h_s(\mathbf{x}) = 0$ might be equivalently replaced with two inequality constraints, $h_s(\mathbf{x}) \geq 0$ and $-h_s(\mathbf{x}) \geq 0$.

Conditions (ii), which only concern the *inequality* constraints, are called **complementary slackness conditions**. They imply that if the ith inequality constraint is not satisfied as an equality at the optimum, i.e. if it is 'slack' (= not binding), then the corresponding Kuhn–Tucker–Lagrange multiplier is zero (note that it is not excluded that $\lambda_i = 0$ and $g_i(\mathbf{x}^*) = 0$ hold simultaneously). This often yields useful information on the characteristics of the solution, and one example is precisely the utility maximization problem, which as we now show is less simple than we have made it appear so far.

As an introduction to the application of the Kuhn–Tucker theorem let us analyse a case of maximization similar to the two-goods UMP but with a nonlin-

---

24 Actually there is also a Lagrange multiplier $\lambda^{\wedge}$ multiplying $\partial f(\mathbf{x}^*)/\partial x_j$, but it can be shown that, when the constraint qualification condition is satisfied, this multiplier is positive and can always be chosen equal to 1.

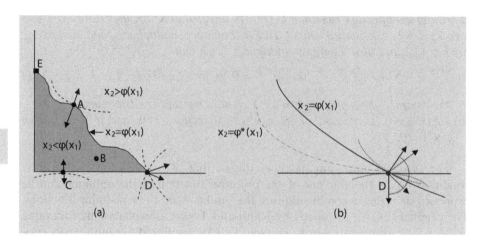

◘ Fig. 4.11 Kuhn–Tucker conditions and an example of failure of C.Q.C.

ear budget constraint $g(x_1, x_2) \geq 0$ and also with constraints $x_1 \geq 0$, $x_2 \geq 0$, hence three constraints in all. The function to be maximized is $f(x_1, x_2)$. The Lagrangian is

$$\mathcal{L} = f(x_1, x_2) + \lambda_0 g(x_1, x_2) + \lambda_1 x_1 + \lambda_2 x_2.$$

The function $f(x_1, x_2)$ is assumed differentiable but its shape is left unspecified in order to permit different possibilities. The constraints are such that the choice set is the grey area in ◘ Fig. 4.11a. This means that I am assuming (i) that $x_2 = \varphi(x_1)$, the implicit function defined by the first constraint holding as an equality, $g(x_1, x_2) = 0$, is decreasing, it is the curve EAD in ◘ Fig. 4.11a, and (ii) that the partial derivatives of the first constraint are $\partial g/\partial x_1 < 0$, $\partial g/\partial x_2 < 0$; then the constraint $g(x_1, x_2) \geq 0$ is satisfied below, or to the left of, the curve $x_2 = \varphi(x_1)$.[25]

◘ Figure 4.11a differs from the picture of the usual budget set of a consumer (as depicted, e.g. in ◘ Fig. 4.9) only in that the $x_2 = \varphi(x_1)$ line is curvilinear; to the left of this curve it is $g(x_1, x_2) > 0$, this constraint does not 'bind'. Let $\mathbf{x}^* = (x_1^*, x_2^*)^T$ be the solution. It can only be inside the grey area of ◘ Fig. 4.11a or on its edges. There are the following possibilities: $\mathbf{x}^*$ is at a point like point B where no constraint is binding; $\mathbf{x}^*$ is at a point where only one constraint is binding, e.g. point A where $g(\mathbf{x}) = 0$, or point C where $x_2 = 0$; $\mathbf{x}^*$ is at a point like D or E where two constraints are binding.

If $\mathbf{x}^*$ is at a point like B where $g(\mathbf{x}^*) > 0$, $x_1^* > 0$, $x_2^* > 0$, then we are free to move from $\mathbf{x}^*$ in any direction, but $f(\mathbf{x})$ does not increase, so we are at an unconstrained maximum, the first-order conditions must be the same as without the constraints; this is obtained by leaving only $f(\mathbf{x})$ in the Lagrangian through setting $\lambda_0 = \lambda_1 = \lambda_2 = 0$. If $\mathbf{x}^*$ is at a point like A, it is $g(\mathbf{x}^*) = 0$, $x_1^* > 0$, $x_2^* > 0$, then

---

25 Check that this is the case in the Marshallian UMP if the constraint is written $m - p_1 x_1 - p_2 x_2 \geq 0$.

4.8 · First-Order Conditions. Corner Solutions. The Kuhn–Tucker theorem

$\mathbf{x}^*$ is on the curve $x_2 = \varphi(x_1)$, the constraints $x_1 \geq 0$, $x_2 \geq 0$ can be neglected, so with hindsight we see that the problem is correctly solved as a maximization problem with the single equality constraint $g(\mathbf{x}) = 0$, so the Lagrangian must be $f(\mathbf{x})-\lambda_0 g(\mathbf{x})$ which is obtained by setting $\lambda_1 = \lambda_2 = 0$, and the first-order conditions are similar to those analysed above for the Marshallian UMP with interior solution.

Graphically we see that if the solution is at A then there must be tangency there between the contour of $f(\mathbf{x})$ and the $x_2 = \varphi(x_1)$ curve; the gradient of $g(\mathbf{x})$ at $\mathbf{x}^*$ must point to the South-West because it is orthogonal to the $\varphi(x_1)$ function in A and it points in the direction of fastest increase of $g(\mathbf{x})$; the gradient of $f(\mathbf{x})$ at $\mathbf{x}^*$ is co-linear but in the opposite direction (see the two arrows at point A), so it must point to the North-East implying $f_1 > 0$, $f_2 > 0$, hence $f_1/g_1 = -\lambda_0 < 0$ so λ_0 is positive as stated by the Kuhn–Tucker theorem.

Before analysing the other cases let us stop on the gradient of a non-negativity constraint on a variable. Take for example the second constraint, $x_1 \geq 0$; how can this have a gradient? The answer is that all inequality constraints have the general form $g_i(x_1,...,x_n) \geq 0$ (where i numbers the constraint, it does not indicate partial derivation), in our case the function g_i has taken the form $g_2(x_1, x_2) = x_1$, and therefore its gradient is the vector $(1,0)$. Analogously in the case of the third constraint, $x_2 \geq 0$, the general function g_i has form $g_3(x_1, x_2) = x_2$, therefore its gradient is $(0,1)$. If $\mathbf{x}^*$ is at a point like C, it is $g(\mathbf{x}) > 0$, $x_1 > 0$, $x_2 = 0$, then only the third constraint binds; evidently in this case $f_2(\mathbf{x}^*) < 0$, that is, decreases of x_2 would increase the value of the objective function; the contour of $f(\mathbf{x})$ through C must be as shown, with the gradient pointing vertically downwards; the binding constraint is $x_2 = 0$, its gradient $(0, 1)$ points vertically upwards, so again the gradient of $f(\mathbf{x}^*)$ is a linear combination of the gradients (only one in this case) of the binding constraints. The Lagrangian after eliminating the terms with a multiplier equal to zero is $f(x_1, x_2) + \lambda_2 x_2$, the first-order conditions are $f_1 = 0, f_2 = -\lambda_2$ which means $\lambda_2 > 0$.

There remains the case of more than one constraint binding simultaneously, as at point D, a vertex of the admissible region, where only the constraint $x_1 \geq 0$ is slack. The graphical illustration makes it clear that in this case the contour of $f(\mathbf{x}^*)$ through $\mathbf{x}^*$ can have various slopes; two possible slopes with the corresponding gradients are shown in ◻ Fig. 4.11a; b enlarges the picture and shows that any gradient of $f(\mathbf{x}^*)$ pointing in the arc limited by the two gradients opposite to the gradients of the binding constraints at D is admissible. Contours corresponding to the two extreme admissible gradients of $f(\mathbf{x}^*)$ are also shown in ◻ Fig. 4.11b, and they show that, except when the gradient is an extreme one, relaxing a little bit either constraint (i.e. shifting the $\varphi(x_1)$ curve to the right, or shifting downwards the horizontal line indicating the lowest admissible value of x_2) would allow reaching higher values of $f(\mathbf{x})$. Only if the contour is the red one will a lowering of the x_2 boundary leave $\mathbf{x}^*$ unchanged; only if the contour is the blue one will a rightwards shift of the $g(\mathbf{x})$ boundary leave $\mathbf{x}^*$ unchanged. Since the Envelope Theorem (to be presently illustrated) shows that the Lagrange multipliers indicate the effect on the maximum value of the objective function of a relaxation of the respective constraints, if the contour is the red one it will be $\lambda_0 > 0$, $\lambda_2 = 0$, if the contour is the blue one it will be $\lambda_0 = 0$, $\lambda_2 > 0$. For all other slopes of the gradient of $f(\mathbf{x})$ at D both multipliers will be positive.

278   **Chapter 4 · Consumers and the Exchange Economy**

In all these cases the gradient of $f(\mathbf{x}^*)$ can be expressed as a linear combination of the gradients of the binding constraints, *except* in the case where $\mathbf{x}^*$ is at a point like D and $\varphi(x_1)$ has slope zero there (the case $x_2 = \varphi^*(x_1)$, the green broken curve in ◘ Fig. 4.11b). Then the gradients of the two binding constraints are co-linear; so their linear combination cannot generate a gradient with a different slope. This is the exception where the constraint qualification condition is violated, in this case at $\mathbf{x}^*$ condition (i) of the Kuhn–Tucker theorem does not hold.

Let us apply the above to the Marshallian UMP, more rigorously formalized to include not only the budget constraint but also the condition $\mathbf{x} \in X$, with X the consumption set. For simplicity, let $X = R^n_+$. Then the conditions are $x_i \geq 0$, n inequality constraints. We know that under local non-satiation the budget constraint is satisfied as an equality, but this result too should come out of utility maximization, so let the budget constraint be the $(n + 1)$-th inequality constraint in the form $m - \mathbf{px} \geq 0$; then there are no equality constraints. We assume local non-satiation and $m > 0$, $\mathbf{p} \gg 0$. The *constraint qualification condition* is satisfied,[26] and the first-order Kuhn–Tucker conditions are (I leave the writing of the Lagrangian to the reader):

$$\partial u / \partial x_i^* - \lambda_{n+1} p_i + \lambda_i = 0, \quad i = 1, \dots, n, \text{ where } \lambda_1, \dots \lambda_n, \lambda_{n+1} \geq 0; \quad (4.1)$$

$$\lambda_i = 0 \text{ if } x_i^* > 0, \quad i = 1, \dots, n; \text{ and } \lambda_{n+1} = 0 \text{ if } m - \mathbf{px} > 0. \quad (4.2)$$

Thus for goods demanded in positive amount it is

$$MU_i = \lambda_{n+1} p_i; \quad (4.3)$$

hence if $x_i^* > 0$, $x_j^* > 0$ we obtain the standard result

$$-MRS_{ij} \equiv MU_i / MU_j = p_i / p_j.$$

For each good i demanded in positive amount, (4.3) implies $\lambda_{n+1} = MU_i/p_i > 0$ unless the marginal utility of all goods demanded is zero: this is excluded by local non-satiation,[27] which also implies that at least one good is demanded in positive amount, otherwise it would be $m - \mathbf{px} > 0$ and the last complementary slackness condition would imply that $\lambda_{n+1} = MU_i/p_i = 0$, i.e. all marginal utilities of goods would be zero contradicting local non-satiation; thus we have proved (i) that the marginal utility of money (measured precisely by λ_{n+1}) is positive and (ii) that all income is spent (otherwise it could not be $\lambda_{n+1} > 0$). If $x_i = 0$ there are two possibilities: $\lambda_i = 0$ and $\lambda_i > 0$; in the second case $MU_i = \lambda_{n+1} p_i - \lambda_i$ indicates that the

---

26 It suffices to look at the rank constraint qualification.

27 Local non-satiation, that is, a positive marginal utility for at least one good, does not exclude that the sole direction or directions in which the consumer can increase her utility starting from her optimal choice be exactly along the budget constraint; but the path along which utility increases must immediately curve outwards away from the budget constraint, otherwise the optimal choice would not be in fact optimal; therefore an outward shift of the budget constraint necessarily permits reaching a higher indifference curve.

4.8 · First-Order Conditions. Corner Solutions. The Kuhn–Tucker theorem

marginal utility of the first small unit of money spent on the purchase of the ith good, MU_i/p_i, is less than the marginal utility of the last unit of money spent on the goods demanded in positive amount, i.e. we are at a proper corner solution; if $\lambda_i = 0$ we are in the fluke case of ◘ Fig. 4.10b, a 'corner solution' with nonetheless tangency between indifference curve and budget line.

Let us briefly say something on second-order conditions. The first-order Kuhn–Tucker conditions are only necessary for a solution to a maximization problem, but not sufficient. For example, in the two-goods utility maximization problem if indifference curves are strictly *concave*, an interior point $x^* \gg 0$ satisfying both the budget constraint and the condition $MRS_{12} \equiv - MU_1/MU_2 = -p_1/p_2$ (tangency between budget line and indifference curve) satisfies the Kuhn–Tucker conditions but does not represent a point of maximum utility. We need, in addition, second-order conditions guaranteeing that a small movement from x^* in any admissible direction (i.e. in any direction that does not violate the budget constraint and the non-negativity constraints) does not increase utility. Under local non-satiation, we can restrict ourselves to movements along the budget line because optimal solutions are on the budget line. In this book an in-depth knowledge of second-order conditions is not needed, so the discussion here will be intuitive.

It is easy to see graphically that in the two-goods utility maximization case the second-order conditions must express the fact that, in a neighbourhood of the point x^* that satisfies the first-order conditions, along the budget line no higher indifference curve is reached than the one through x^*; if neither good is a 'bad', this will be the case if the indifference curve through x^* never goes below the budget line. If x^* is interior, this is guaranteed if the indifference curve tangent to the budget line in x^* is convex, which requires that the utility function be quasi-concave (cf. ▶ Sect. 4.5).

This generalizes to the n-goods case (proof omitted):

If the utility function is quasi-concave, monotonic and with partial derivatives everywhere positive, then the Kuhn–Tucker first-order conditions are sufficient for a global maximum of the UMP.

No easy sufficient conditions for x^* to be a global or even a local maximum are available if indifference curves are not convex, i.e. if the utility function is not quasi-concave.

Note that, since the utility function is ordinal and represents the same preferences if we change it via an increasing monotonic transformation, a quasi-concave but not concave utility function can generally be made concave by a transformation that causes it to increase at a sufficiently slower pace: if $u = x_1 x_2$, then $U = u^{1/2}$ is concave and $V = u^{1/4}$ is strictly concave. Thus at least for utility maximization we can assume that the objective function is concave; and the usual budget constraint is of the form $a - g(x) \geq 0$ where $g(x)$ is a convex function; then we need not worry about second-order conditions because we can utilize the following result (proved in any textbook on optimization):

280 Chapter 4 · Consumers and the Exchange Economy

▪▪ Proposition 4.8

Differentiable concave programming theorem. Consider the concave programming problem

$$max_x f(\mathbf{x}) \ s.t. \ a_1\text{-}g_1(\mathbf{x}) \geq 0, \ ..., \ a_k\text{-}g_k(\mathbf{x}) \geq 0, \ and \ \mathbf{x} \geq 0$$

with $f(x)$ concave and differentiable and $g_1(x),...,g_k(x)$ all convex and differentiable; then the necessary conditions (i) and (ii) of the Kuhn–Tucker theorem are necessary and sufficient for x^* to be a global maximum; if f is strictly concave, x^* is unique.[28]

Note that if $g_k(\mathbf{x})$ is convex (which includes linear), then $a_k\text{-}g_k(\mathbf{x})$ is concave, hence the name of the programming problem. In the consumer's Marshallian budget constraint a is income m and $g(\mathbf{x}) = \Sigma p_i x_i$; in the Walrasian budget constraint one puts $a = 0$ and writes the constraint as $-(\mathbf{px}-\mathbf{p\omega}) \geq 0$; so if the utility function is concave (and if it is quasi-concave it can be made concave by an opportune increasing transformation) the theorem is applicable. The theorem is not applicable if the utility function has strictly concave indifference curves and therefore is not quasi-concave, but the Kuhn–Tucker theorem supplies the first-order necessary conditions even in this case, and generally these are sufficient to restrict the possible candidates to very few.

See the Mathematical Appendix for more on second-order conditions for a maximum without and with constraints.

4.9 Envelope Theorem

The *value function* (also called *maximum value function* or *indirect objective function*) associated with a problem of free or constrained maximization is the scalar function that indicates how the maximum value of the objective function $f(\cdot)$, i.e. its value associated with the solution(s) of the maximization problem, varies with variations in the values of parameters entering f and/or the constraints. An example of parameter is income m in the Marshallian UMP. Let these parameters be $a_1,...,a_k$, and let $M(a_1,...,a_k)$ be the value function (with M mnemonic for *maximum* value). The ***Envelope Theorem*** concerns the partial derivatives $\partial M/\partial a_j$, if these exist, *assuming the constraints are equality constraints*. The last condition means that, in case there are inequality constraints, only the binding ones (whose Lagrange multipliers are not zero) must be considered. The ***Envelope Theorem*** states the following:

▪▪ Proposition 4.9

Envelope Theorem. Let $f(x_1,..., x_n, a_1,..., a_k)$ be the differentiable objective function (a scalar function) of a maximization problem $\max f$ without constraints or with equality constraints; let $g(\mathbf{x}, a_1,..., a_k) = 0$ be a differentiable vector function of equality constraints $g^{(1)}(\mathbf{x}, a),..., g^{(h)}(\mathbf{x}, a)$; let $(\mathbf{x}^*, \lambda^*)$ be a solution of

---

28 For a simple proof see Varian (1992, p. 504).

4.9 · Envelope Theorem

the maximization problem (with $\boldsymbol{\lambda}^*$ a vector of Lagrange multipliers), a solution dependent on the vector $\boldsymbol{a} = (a_1,...,a_k)$ of parameters and representable therefore as $\mathbf{x}^*(a_1,...,a_k)$, $\boldsymbol{\lambda}^* = \boldsymbol{\lambda}^*(a_1,...,a_k)$; and let $M(\boldsymbol{a}) \equiv f(\mathbf{x}^*(a_1,...,a_k))$ be the corresponding value of the value function. If a parameter a_j is changed, then generally $\mathbf{x}^*$ changes, and the value of M changes with it, and it is

$$\frac{\partial M(a)}{\partial a_j} = \frac{\partial f(\mathbf{x}^*(a), a)}{\partial a_j} + \sum_{s=1}^{h} \lambda_s^* \frac{\partial g^{(s)}(\mathbf{x}^*(a), a)}{\partial a_j}.$$

If one assumes that there are no constraints, the theorem states

$$\frac{\partial M(a)}{\partial a_j} = \frac{\partial f(\mathbf{x}^*(a), a)}{\partial a_j}.$$

In words, the effect on M of a very small variation of a_j is only the *direct* effect of the variation of a_j on f; *there is no further effect* due to the variation of $\mathbf{x}^*$ induced by the variation of a_j; the reason is that at a solution point the variation of f induced by a small variation of $\mathbf{x}^*$ is nil, because all partial derivatives $\partial f/\partial x_i^*$ are zero. With constraints, the effect on M is only the direct effect of the change of a_j on the Lagrangian: again there are no indirect effects due to the variation of $\mathbf{x}^*$.

Proof (sketch) Consider first the case of unconstrained maximization with one parameter. Define

$$M(a) = \max_x f(x_1, \ldots x_n; a) = f\left(\mathbf{x}^*(a); a\right)$$

where $\left(x_1^*(a),\ldots,x_n^*(a)\right) = \mathbf{x}^*(a)$ stands for the solution of $\max_x f$, solution in general depending on the value of a. Differentiating both sides with respect to a we get:

$$\frac{dM(a)}{da} = \sum_{i=1}^{n} \left(\frac{\partial f(\mathbf{x}^*, a)}{\partial x_i} \cdot \frac{dx_i^*}{da} \right) + \frac{\partial f(\mathbf{x}^*, a)}{\partial a} = \frac{\partial f(\mathbf{x}^*, a)}{\partial a}$$

because from the first-order conditions for a maximum one gets $\partial f / \partial x_i = 0, \forall x_i$.

Now let us consider constrained maximization, and if there are inequality constraints let us consider only the binding constraints (a 'slack' constraint remains slack for sufficiently small variations of a). Assume for simplicity a single constraint. Define

$$M(a) = \max_x f(x_1, \ldots x_n; a) \text{ subject to } g(x_1,\ldots,x_n; a) = 0.$$

The Lagrangian is $L = f(x; a) + \lambda g(x; a)$. Differentiate both sides of $M(a) = f(\mathbf{x}^*(a); a)$ with respect to a and use the first-order conditions $\frac{\partial f}{\partial x_i} = -\lambda \frac{\partial g}{\partial x_i}$ to obtain:

$$\frac{dM(a)}{da} = \sum_{i=1}^{n} \left(\frac{\partial f(\mathbf{x}^*, a)}{\partial x_i} \cdot \frac{dx_i^*}{da} \right) + \frac{\partial f(\mathbf{x}^*, a)}{\partial a}$$

$$= -\lambda \sum_{i=1}^{n} \left(\frac{\partial g(\mathbf{x}^*, a)}{\partial x_i} \cdot \frac{dx_i^*}{da} \right) + \frac{\partial f}{\partial a}$$

But the variation of $\mathbf{x}^*$ must continue to satisfy $g(\mathbf{x}, a) = 0$, and what this implies is ascertained by differentiating totally both sides of the constraint $g(\mathbf{x}, a) = 0$ with respect to a; one obtains:

$\sum_{i=1}^{n} \left(\frac{\partial g}{\partial x_i} \cdot \frac{dx_i}{da} \right) + \frac{\partial g}{\partial a} = 0$, that is, $\sum_{i=1}^{n} \left(\frac{\partial g}{\partial x_i} \cdot \frac{dx_i}{da} \right) = -\frac{\partial g}{\partial a}$, and therefore

$$\frac{dM(a)}{da} = \frac{\partial f(\mathbf{x}^*(a), a)}{\partial a} + \lambda \frac{\partial g(.)}{\partial a}.$$

The result is easily generalized to multiple constraints. If M depends on several parameters, $M(a_1,...,a_k)$, then the sole difference is that, if for example we consider the first parameter, we get $\partial M(a_1,...,a_k)/\partial a_1 = \partial f/\partial a_1 + \lambda \partial g/\partial a_1$; with several constraints $g^{(s)}(\mathbf{x}, a)$, one has $\partial M(a_1,...,a_k)/\partial a_1 = \partial f/\partial a_1 + \Sigma_s \lambda_s \partial g^{(s)}/\partial a_1$. ∎

Suppose in particular that there is a single parameter which appears only in the single constraint, and in the form $g(\mathbf{x}) = h(\mathbf{x}) + a = 0$. Then $\partial f/\partial a = 0$, $\partial g/\partial a = 1$. Hence $dM(a)/da = \lambda$. This has the following interpretation: any constraint $g(\mathbf{x}) = 0$ can be interpreted as meaning $g(\mathbf{x}) + a = 0$ with a set at zero; thus even when there appears no additive parameter a in the constraint, the derivative dM/da can be calculated, and it coincides with λ. The Lagrange multiplier measures the sensitivity of the value function to changes in the parameter.

Thus consider the UMP with the balanced budget constraint $p_1 x_1 + p_2 x_2 = m$. Rewrite the latter as $m + a - p_1 x_1 - p_2 x_2 = 0$. Here an increase of a from zero is equivalent to an increase of m, so it means a *relaxation* of the constraint (the admissible region of values of $\mathbf{x}$ becomes larger), that permits an increase of utility, and this increase is equal to λ. Indeed the first-order conditions yield $\lambda = MU_1/p_1 = MU_2/p_2$, that is, λ is the marginal utility of money or income, so it is the increase in utility permitted by one more unit of income.

4.10 Indirect Utility, Expenditure Function, Compensated Demand

Although utility maximization need not imply a unique utility-maximizing consumption basket, it is generally assumed that in most instances uniqueness will obtain. In particular, if the theory aims at determining the normal, *average*, long-period behaviour of consumers, then in the cases in which choice is not unique one can assume that, over a repetition of choices, the consumer chooses

4.10 · Indirect Utility, Expenditure Function, Compensated Demand

randomly among the equipreferred choices, with the result that on average the consumer chooses the average of the equipreferred baskets, and in this way one obtains uniqueness again. On this basis, unless explicitly indicated otherwise, I assume for the remainder of the chapter that demand is single-valued. I proceed to define some notions which introduce us to the core of standard consumer theory.

(1) The *ordinary, or Marshallian, vectorial demand function* $x(p, m)$ of a consumer is a vector function, i.e. a vector of as many functions as there are goods

$$\mathbf{x}(\mathbf{p}, m) = (x_1(\mathbf{p}, m), x_2(\mathbf{p}, m), \ldots, x_n(\mathbf{p}, m))^T$$

that indicates the optimal basket x associated with each given vector of prices and given income.

(2) The *Walrasian vectorial demand function* $x(p, \omega)$ or also $x(p, p\omega)$ differs only in that income m is not given but derives from given endowments, $m = \mathbf{p}\omega$.

Three more functions derivable from the Marshallian UMP:

(3) The *indirect utility function* $v(p, m)$ indicates the *maximum* achievable utility for each price vector and separately given level of income[29]:

$$v(\mathbf{p}, m) = max_x u(\mathbf{x}) \ s.t. \ \mathbf{px} = m. \tag{4.4}$$

It is called *indirect* because it indicates utility not directly as a function of x, but indirectly as a function of the p and m that determine the choice of x. By definition,

$$v(\mathbf{p}, m) = u(\mathbf{x}(\mathbf{p}, m)).$$

(4) The *expenditure function* $e(p, u)$ (called *cost function* by some authors because of its strict analogy with the cost function of firms, see ▶ Chap. 5) indicates the *minimum* expenditure necessary to reach an assigned utility level u when prices are p. It is a function $R^{n+1} \rightarrow R$.

(5) The *Hicksian, or compensated, (vector) demand function* $h(p, u)$ is a vector of demand functions that indicates how changes in p alter the vector of consumption goods that minimizes the expenditure necessary to reach an *assigned* utility level u. If there are n goods, it is a function $R^{n+1} \rightarrow R^n$.

Let us examine the last three functions in greater detail.

The *indirect utility function* $v(p, m)$ is a function $R^{n+1} \rightarrow R$. It depends on the specific utility function chosen to represent the consumer's preferences. An increasing transformation of u causes the same increasing transformation of v

---

29 Why 'separately given'? Because income might, as in Walrasian demand functions, not be given separately from prices but correspond to the value of the consumer's endowments and therefore depend on prices. The indirect utility function we are describing here corresponds to Marshallian demand.

284   Chapter 4 · Consumers and the Exchange Economy

$(\mathbf{p}, m)$. It can be shown that there is a one-to-one relationship between utility function and indirect utility function, a given $v(\mathbf{p}, m)$ derives from a unique $u(\mathbf{x}(\mathbf{p}, m))$ which is said *dual* to it because it satisfies the following minimization problem dual to maximization problem (4.4):

$$u\left(\mathbf{x}\left(\mathbf{p}^*, m^*\right)\right) = min_p\, v\left(\mathbf{p}, m^*\right)\ s.t.\ \mathbf{px}\left(\mathbf{p}^*, m^*\right) = m^*. \tag{4.5}$$

In words: let $v(\mathbf{p}, m)$ be the indirect utility function associated with $u(\mathbf{x})$; let $\mathbf{x}^* = \mathbf{x}(\mathbf{p}^*, m^*)$ be the demand vector determined by Marshallian demand for given prices $\mathbf{p}^*$ and given income m^* ; consider the set of prices $\mathbf{p}$ that satisfy $\mathbf{px}^* = m^*$; minimize $v(\mathbf{p}, m^*)$ over this set of prices; the minimum of v is $u(\mathbf{x}^*)$. This states that any price vector different from $\mathbf{p}^*$ but satisfying $\mathbf{px}^* = m^*$ allows the consumer to reach a *higher* utility level than $\mathbf{p}^*$, or at least the same. The reason is simple: for any such $\mathbf{p}$, since $\mathbf{x}^*$ remains affordable, the consumer will never choose a basket yielding less utility than $u(x^*)$.

The function $v(\mathbf{p}, m)$ is:

(i)   non-increasing in each p_i (and decreasing, if it was $x_i > 0$ before the increase of p_i, because the old consumption basket is no longer affordable);

(ii) strictly increasing in m (under local non-satiation), because the budget line shifts outwards;

(iii) homogeneous of degree zero in $(\mathbf{p}, m)$, because the budget line (or budget hypersurface) remains the same if all prices *and* income change by the same percentage;

(iv) continuous at all $\mathbf{p} \gg 0$, $m > 0$, because of the Theorem of the Maximum;

(v)   quasi-convex in $\mathbf{p}$, that is, for given m, $\{\mathbf{p}: v(\mathbf{p}, m)° \leq u°\}$ is a convex set for each given $u°$, and given that $v(\mathbf{p}, m)$ is (generally) decreasing in each p_i, it has convex contours. This can be proved as follows.

Proof By contradiction. Let $\mathbf{p}'$, $\mathbf{p}''$ be two vectors such that $v(\mathbf{p}', m) = v(\mathbf{p}'', m) = u°$, and let $\mathbf{p} = a\mathbf{p}' - (1 - a)\mathbf{p}''$, $0 < a < 1$, be any convex combination of these price vectors. We must prove that $v(\mathbf{p}, m)° \leq u°$; that is, that no consumption basket $\mathbf{x}$ that satisfies $\mathbf{px}° \leq m$ yields $u(\mathbf{x}) > u°$. Suppose on the contrary such a basket $\mathbf{x}$ to exist, then $a\mathbf{p}'\mathbf{x} + (1 - a)\mathbf{p}''\mathbf{x}° \leq m$; since by assumption a utility level greater than $u°$ cannot be achieved at prices $\mathbf{p}'$ or $\mathbf{p}''$, it must be $\mathbf{p}'\mathbf{x} > m$, $\mathbf{p}''\mathbf{x} > m$; but this implies $a\mathbf{p}'\mathbf{x} + (1 - a)\mathbf{p}''\mathbf{x} > m$, contradicting the initial assumption. So no such $\mathbf{x}$ can exist.

Since v is non-increasing in each price, and $v(\mathbf{p}, m)° \leq u°$ if $\mathbf{p}$ is a convex combination of $\mathbf{p}'$ and $\mathbf{p}''$, between these two points the contour $v(\mathbf{p}, m) = u°$ in $\mathbf{p}$ space must be closer to the origin than the segment connecting those two points, i.e. contours are convex. ∎

This property states that if a consumer is indifferent between two budget sets limited by budget lines $(\mathbf{p}', m)$ and $(\mathbf{p}'', m)$, then she will generally prefer either budget line to any convex combination of them.

One more observation: we have seen that the Lagrange multiplier λ is the marginal utility of income; this means $\lambda = \partial v(\mathbf{p}, m)/\partial m$.

4.10 · Indirect Utility, Expenditure Function, Compensated Demand

The *expenditure function* $e(\mathbf{p}, u)$ is the value function of the following minimization problem:

$$e(\mathbf{p}, u) = min \ \mathbf{px} \ such \ that \ u(\mathbf{x}) \geq u.$$

It has several properties of interest. It is:
(1) non-negative if $\mathbf{p} \geq 0$, and non-decreasing in $\mathbf{p}$;
(2) homogeneous of degree 1 in $\mathbf{p}$;
(3) continuous in $\mathbf{p}$ for $\mathbf{p} \gg 0$;
(4) strictly increasing in u as long as $\mathbf{p} \gg 0$;
(5) concave in $\mathbf{p}$.

Proofs
(1) Non-negativeness is obvious since both prices and quantities are non-negative. If some p_i increases and the old price vector $\mathbf{p}$ becomes $\mathbf{p'}$, the new optimal consumption basket $\mathbf{x'}$ guaranteeing the same utility as the old basket $\mathbf{x}$ cannot cost less than $\mathbf{px}$, otherwise the old expenditure was not the minimum possible one because $u(\mathbf{x}) = u(\mathbf{x'})$ could have been reached with basket $\mathbf{x'}$ which would have cost less than $\mathbf{px}$ since $\mathbf{px'}° \leq \mathbf{p'x'} < \mathbf{px}$.
(2) At prices $\mathbf{p}$, $\mathbf{x}$ is expenditure minimizing for reaching $u°$, that is, for all $\mathbf{x'}$ such that $u(\mathbf{x'}) \geq u°$ it is $\mathbf{px'} \geq \mathbf{px}$. These inequalities continue to hold if we multiply both sides by $t > 0$. Hence $\mathbf{x}$ is also expenditure minimizing at prices $t\mathbf{p}$, and therefore the minimum expenditure necessary to achieve u becomes $te(\mathbf{p}, u°)$.
(3) The continuity of e follows from the Theorem of the Maximum.
(4) Obvious: From local non-satiation, the consumer is on the budget constraint; in order to reach a higher utility level (a higher indifference curve), the budget constraint must move outwards.
(5) Let $\mathbf{p}^1$, $\mathbf{p}^2$ be two vectors of prices. We must prove that, for $0° \leq a° \leq 1$, it is

$$e(a\mathbf{p}^1 + (1-a)\mathbf{p}^2, u°)ae(\mathbf{p}^1, u°) + (1-a)e(\mathbf{p}^2, u°)$$

Define $\mathbf{p}^* \equiv a\mathbf{p}^1 + (1-a)\mathbf{p}^2$ and $\mathbf{x}^* \equiv \mathbf{h}(\mathbf{p}^*, u°)$, the demand vector that allows reaching utility $u°$ with minimum expenditure at prices $\mathbf{p}^*$. Then $e(\mathbf{p}^*, u°) = e(a\mathbf{p}^1 + (1-a)\mathbf{p}^2, u°) = \mathbf{p}^*\mathbf{x}^* = a\mathbf{p}^1\mathbf{x}^* + (1-a)\mathbf{p}^2\mathbf{x}^*$. Now, $\mathbf{x}^*$ is not necessarily the cheapest demand vector which allows reaching utility $u°$ when prices are $\mathbf{p}^1$ or $\mathbf{p}^2$; therefore $\mathbf{p}^1\mathbf{x}^* \geq e(\mathbf{p}^1, u°)$ and $\mathbf{p}^2\mathbf{x}^* \geq e(\mathbf{p}^2, u°)$. Hence $e(\mathbf{p}^*, u) \geq ae(\mathbf{p}^1, u) + (1-a)e(\mathbf{p}^2, u)$. ∎

The intuition why the expenditure function is concave can be obtained from ◻ Fig. 4.12. Let $e^* = e(\mathbf{p}°, u°)$, $\mathbf{x}^* = \mathbf{h}(\mathbf{p}°, u°)$ and suppose p_1 rises from $p_1°$ to $p_1° + \Delta p_1$; if the consumption vector remains $\mathbf{x}^*$, expenditure becomes $e^* + x_1^*\Delta p_1$, that is, it rises linearly, with slope x_1^*. This slope can be proved to be precisely the partial derivative of the expenditure function at e^* with respect to p_1; this will be proved below and is called Shephard's Lemma: $\partial e/\partial p_1 = x_1$. The new minimum expenditure needed to reach $u°$ cannot increase to more than $e^* + x_1^*\Delta p_1$ which allows reaching $u°$ by purchasing $\mathbf{x}^*$, at most it increases exactly by that much, or it increases less if the change in relative prices renders $\mathbf{x}^*$ no longer the expenditure-minimizing basket that achieves $u°$ (cf. basket $\mathbf{x}^+$ in

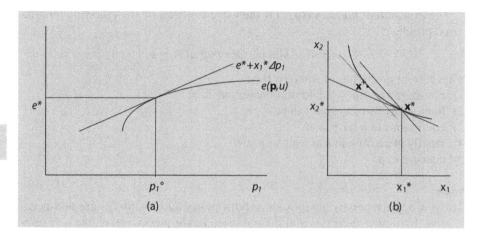

◘ **Fig. 4.12** Graphical intuition why the expenditure function is concave

◘ Fig. 4.12b), therefore the rise in expenditure as p_1 rises is either linear or, more probably, strictly concave.

The ***Hicksian or compensated vectorial demand function*** is strictly connected with the expenditure function:

$$e(\mathbf{p}, u) = \mathbf{p} \cdot \mathbf{h}(\mathbf{p}, u).$$

The term 'compensated' comes from the fact that, once u is assigned, $\mathbf{h}(\mathbf{p}, u)$ indicates how demand varies with prices, if income is adjusted or 'compensated' for the variation in prices such that the consumer can just reach utility level u.

Some further rather obvious connections among these functions are listed below. The proofs are easy (and left to the reader) except perhaps for one, supplied in footnote:

(A) $e(\mathbf{p}, v(\mathbf{p}, m)) = m$: the minimum expenditure, required to reach the maximum utility achievable with a given income m, is m.

(B) $v(\mathbf{p}, e(\mathbf{p}, u°)) = u°$: the maximum utility, achievable with the minimum expenditure required to reach a given level of utility $u°$, is $u°$. ([30])

---

30 Consider problem (I): max $u(\mathbf{x})$ such that $\mathbf{px} \leq m$, and problem (II): min $\mathbf{px}$ such that $u(\mathbf{x}) \geq u°$. Assume that $u(\mathbf{x})$ is continuous; that preferences satisfy local non-satiation and that answers to both problems exist. We wish to prove: (i) if $\mathbf{x}^*$ is a solution to (I) and we set $u°=u(\mathbf{x}^*)$, then $\mathbf{x}^*$ solves (II); (ii) if $\mathbf{x}^*$ is a solution to (II) and we set $m = \mathbf{px}^*>0$, then $\mathbf{x}^*$ solves (I). Proof of (i): by contradiction; suppose $\mathbf{x}^*$ does not solve (II), while $\mathbf{x}'$ does; then $\mathbf{px}'<\mathbf{px}^*$ and $u(\mathbf{x}') \geq u(\mathbf{x}^*)$; by local non-satiation there is a basket $\mathbf{x}''$ close enough to $\mathbf{x}'$ so that $u(\mathbf{x}'') > u(\mathbf{x}^*)$ and $\mathbf{px}'' < \mathbf{px}^*$; but then $\mathbf{x}^*$ cannot solve (I). Proof of (ii): again by contradiction; suppose $\mathbf{x}^*$ does not solve (I) while $\mathbf{x}'$ does; then $u(\mathbf{x}') > u(\mathbf{x}^*)$ with $\mathbf{px}' = \mathbf{px}^* = m$; because of the continuity of $u(\cdot)$, we can find a scalar t, $0 < t < 1$, sufficiently close to 1 such that $\mathbf{p}t\mathbf{x}' < \mathbf{px}^*=m$ and $u(t\mathbf{x}') > u(\mathbf{x}^*)$; but then $\mathbf{x}^*$ cannot solve (II). With (i) we have proved that the minimum expenditure, required to reach the maximum utility achievable with a given income m, is that same income m; with (ii) we have proved that the maximum utility, achievable with the minimum expenditure required to reach a given level of utility u, is that level u. ∎

4.10 · Indirect Utility, Expenditure Function, Compensated Demand

(C) $u(\mathbf{x}(\mathbf{p}, m)) = min_p\, v(\mathbf{p}, m)\ s.t.\ m=\mathbf{px}$ (this was proved above).

(D) $x_i(\mathbf{p}, m) = h_i(\mathbf{p}, v(\mathbf{p}, m))$: the ordinary or Marshallian demand associated with an income m coincides with the compensated or Hicksian demand when the utility level to be reached is the one achievable with that income.

(E) $h_i(\mathbf{p}, u) = x_i(\mathbf{p}, e(\mathbf{p}, u))$: the Hicksian or compensated demand associated with utility level u and prices $\mathbf{p}$ coincides with the Marshallian or ordinary demand at prices $\mathbf{p}$ and income m if m is the expenditure necessary, at those prices, to reach a utility level equal to u.

These connections will be useful below.

4.11 Roy's Identity, Shephard's Lemma, Some Dualities and Some Utility Functions

4.11.1 Roy's Identity and Shephard's Lemma

Several useful results can be obtained from the connections between these notions. Let us consider $\partial v(\mathbf{p}, m)/\partial p_i$, assuming an interior solution. By applying the Envelope Theorem for the case of constrained maximization, we obtain:

$$\frac{\partial v(\mathbf{p}, m)}{\partial p_i} = \frac{\partial u(\mathbf{x})}{\partial p_i} - \lambda x_i = -\lambda x_i$$

because $\partial u/\partial p_i = 0$. Using the result that the Lagrange multiplier λ is the marginal utility of income, this is often written as

■■ **Proposition 4.10**

Roy's Identity (first formulation): $\frac{\partial v(\mathbf{p},m)}{\partial p_i} = -x_i \frac{\partial v(\mathbf{p},m)}{\partial m}$.

Economic interpretation: if p_i increases by one unit, the consumer who used to buy x_i units of good i would need x_i more units of income to be able to purchase the same goods as before, so it is as if she had lost x_i units of income, and her utility decreases by x_i times the marginal utility of income.

By treating x_i as the Marshallian demand for good i, dependent on prices and income, Roy's Identity can be rewritten as

■■ **Proposition 4.11**

Roy's Identity (usual formulation): $x_i(\mathbf{p}, m) = -\frac{\partial v(\mathbf{p},m)/\partial p_i}{\partial v(\mathbf{p},m)/\partial m}$.

This indicates that, if one knows the indirect utility function, the Marshallian demands for the various goods can be obtained from its partial derivatives.

Let us now consider the function $-e(\mathbf{p}, u^*)$ as the value function of the maximization problem with constraint

$$max_x(-\mathbf{px})\ subject\ to\ u(\mathbf{x}) = u^*.$$

288   Chapter 4 · Consumers and the Exchange Economy

By applying the Envelope Theorem with $M = -e(\mathbf{p}, u)$, $f = -\mathbf{px}$, and $g = u(\mathbf{x}) - u^* = 0$, we obtain

$$-\frac{\partial e(\mathbf{p}, u*)}{\partial p_i} = -x_i - \lambda \frac{\partial u(\mathbf{x})}{\partial p_i} = -x_i \text{ (because } \frac{\partial u}{\partial p_i} = 0).$$

The quantity x_i that appears in this expression is the compensated or Hicksian demand for good i because it is the quantity demanded when u is kept fixed at the level u^*, so we obtain

■■ Proposition 4.12

Shephard's Lemma for the consumer: $\frac{\partial e}{\partial p_i} = x_i(\mathbf{p}, e(\mathbf{p}, u^*)) = h_i(\mathbf{p}, u^*)$.

In words: the partial derivatives of the expenditure function with respect to prices are the compensated demands $h_i(\mathbf{p}, u)$. So the Hicksian or compensated vector demand function $\mathbf{h}(\mathbf{p}, u)$ of a consumer can be obtained from her expenditure function's partial derivatives with respect to prices.

If we are also given the indirect utility function, then in $\mathbf{h}(\mathbf{p}, u)$ we can replace u with $v(\mathbf{p}, m)$ and we obtain the Marshallian vectorial demand function:

$$\mathbf{h}(\mathbf{p}, u) = \mathbf{h}(\mathbf{p}, v(\mathbf{p}, m)) = \mathbf{x}(\mathbf{p}, m).$$

Another connection: the indirect utility function can be obtained from the expenditure function. The reason is that the expenditure function $e(\mathbf{p}, u)$ and the indirect utility function $v(\mathbf{p}, m)$ are one the inverse of the other: at given prices the expenditure function is a one-to-one function of u hence invertible, and its inverse relative to u yields the utility—that is, the maximum utility—achievable with a given expenditure, i.e. yields $v(\mathbf{p}, m)$ since $m = e$; conversely, the inverse of $v(\mathbf{p}, m)$ relative to m yields the income m, i.e. the expenditure, needed to reach each given utility level; so all one needs is the mathematical operation of inversion of a function to obtain one of the two functions from the other.

Therefore from the expenditure function of a consumer one can derive not only the Hicksian or compensated demand function via Shephard's Lemma but also the Marshallian or ordinary demand function, by deriving the indirect utility function and then using Roy's Identity, or using the connection just written between Hicksian and Marshallian demand.

One more connection: one can derive from the expenditure function the utility function, by first deriving the indirect utility function and then remembering that if $v(\mathbf{p}, m)$ is an indirect utility function, the $u(\mathbf{x})$ that generates it is univocally determined as follows: for each $\mathbf{x}$, it is

$$u(\mathbf{x}) = min_p \, v(\mathbf{p}, m) \; s.t. \; m = \mathbf{px}(\mathbf{p}, m).$$

Thus recovering the utility function from the indirect utility function is possible, by solving a constrained minimization problem, if one knows the Marshallian vectorial demand function; and we have seen that the latter too can be derived from the expenditure function.

So one can start from a utility function and derive indirect utility function, expenditure function, Marshallian demand function and compensated demand function, but one can also start from the expenditure function (or from the indirect utility function) and derive all the other functions. And, although we will not show how in this text, one can also start from the Marshallian or from the compensated demand function and derive the expenditure function and the other ones with opportune *integration techniques*. These five functions are all *dual* to one another, in the sense that they contain the same information about the consumer's continuous convex preferences[31] over perfectly divisible goods.[32]

4.11.2 Homothetic Utility Functions and Homothetic Preferences

It is opportune that the reader becomes familiar with a number of utility functions often used in examples and articles. Many of these can also be production functions.

Two types of preferences permit to deduce the consumer's entire map of indifference curves from knowledge of just one of them: homothetic preferences and quasi-linear preferences.

A function is called **homothetic** if it is a strictly increasing transformation of a strictly increasing function homogeneous of degree 1. The partial derivatives of a function homogeneous of degree 1 are homogeneous of degree zero, i.e. only depend on the *ratios* between the independent variables; thus if a utility function is homogeneous of degree 1, marginal utilities only depend on the *proportions* between consumption goods, so (i) the MRS is constant along a ray from the origin, and (ii) indifference curves are all radial expansions or contractions of any one of them. These last two properties also hold for homothetic functions, because if the utility function homogeneous of degree 1 is $u(x_1, x_2)$ and the homothetic function is $g(x_1, x_2) = g(u(x_1, x_2))$ with $dg/du > 0$, then

$$(\partial g/\partial x_1)/(\partial g/\partial x_2) = \frac{\frac{dg}{du}\frac{\partial u}{\partial x_1}}{\frac{dg}{du}\frac{\partial u}{\partial x_2}} = (\partial u/\partial x_1)/(\partial u/\partial x_2).$$

The difference is that, for a utility function homogeneous of degree 1, along a ray from the origin utility is *proportional* to the distance from the origin; this need

---

31 If indifference curves are not convex, their reconstruction starting from the expenditure function only recovers the *convexification* of the utility function. I leave aside this issue.

32 The term 'duality' originally comes from the theory of linear programming, but the use of the term in microeconomics has broadened considerably. Two functions, usually one a function of quantities and the other of prices, are considered dual to each other if they represent two different ways of describing the same 'object': a set, or an ordered set, or a function, or a maximum value. This is the case, for example, for the utility function $u(\mathbf{x})$ and the expenditure function $e(\mathbf{p}, u)$ associated with it: a given expenditure function contains the same information about the consumer's preferences as the utility function from which it is derived, i.e. it allows the derivation of the consumer's indifference map, from which the utility function itself can be derived. The same holds for utility function and indirect utility function, as shown, again, by the fact that either function can be derived from the other one; so they too are said dual to each other.

290   Chapter 4 · Consumers and the Exchange Economy

not be so for its monotonic transformations, which can have that utility increases along a ray at varying speed. The preferences represented by homothetic utility functions are called homothetic too.

Consider the Marshallian vectorial demand function $\mathbf{x}(\mathbf{p}, m)$, with $\mathbf{p}$ fixed; as m grows the path traced by $\mathbf{x}$ is called the **income expansion path** of the consumption basket for the given $\mathbf{p}$. The income expansion paths of homothetic utility functions are rays from the origin. This means that, for a given price vector, the share of income going to each good does not change as income changes; the demand for a good can be written as $x_i(\mathbf{p}, m) = x_i(\mathbf{p}, 1) \cdot m$: *the demand functions derived from homothetic utility functions are linear in income.* In this case goods are normal and borderline between necessaries and luxury goods, notions to be explained in ▶ Sect. 4.12 below.

If the utility function is homogeneous of degree 1, then for given $\mathbf{p}$ if we know the utility level achievable for $m = 1$, i.e. $v(\mathbf{p}, 1)$, we can calculate the achievable utility level as m varies simply as $v(\mathbf{p}, m) = v(\mathbf{p}, 1) \cdot m$; and the expenditure needed to achieve utility level $u = \alpha v(\mathbf{p}, 1)$ is α; hence the expenditure needed to achieve $u = 1$ is $e(\mathbf{p}, 1) = 1/v(\mathbf{p}, 1)$, and the expenditure function takes the form $e(\mathbf{p}, u) = e(\mathbf{p}, 1)u = u/v(\mathbf{p}, 1)$.[33]

4.11.3 Quasi-Linear Utility

If by a suitable monotonic increasing transformation a utility function can be made to take the form $u(x_1, x_2, ..., x_n) = z(x_1, ..., x_{n-1}) + x_n$, then the utility function is said **quasi-linear (linear in good n)**. It is generally assumed that $z(\cdot)$ is strictly concave.

With this utility function the marginal utility of good n is constant and equal to 1, and the marginal utilities of goods $1, ..., n-1$ do not depend on x_n. If we restrict ourselves to two goods, $u = z(x_1) + x_2$, we obtain $|MRS| = dz/dx_1$, unaffected by x_2; all indifference curves are parallel vertical translations of any one indifference curve. If you assume $p_2 = 1$, then optimality requires $p_1 = \mathrm{MU}_1$, *the price of good* 1 *measures its marginal utility*; and if the budget constraint is $p_1 x_1 + x_2 = m$, for a given p_1 the demand for good 1 does not change as m changes, remaining constant at the level $x_1(p_1)$ such that $p_1 = \mathrm{MU}_1$ (the income expansion path is a vertical straight line), at least as long as $m \geq p_1 x_1(p_1)$.

This two-goods quasi-linear utility function is used—by interpreting the last good as *residual income* spendable on other goods not appearing in the utility function, see ▶ Sect. 4.5, and assuming the marginal utility of the first good to be decreasing—to formalize a hypothesis much used by Alfred Marshall to study the market of a single good in partial-equilibrium analyses, the hypothesis of a **constant marginal utility of money (or income)**. If my utility function when I buy candies is quasi-linear (linear in residual income; candies are good 1), then my demand

---

33 ***Exercise***: Confirm by application of Roy's identity to $v(\mathbf{p},1)m$ that the demand functions derived from homothetic preferences have the form $x_i(\mathbf{p}, m) = x_i(\mathbf{p}, 1)m$.

4.11 · 11. Roy's Identity, Shephard's Lemma, Some Dualities and Some Utility Functions

for candies is not affected by changes in my income; interestingly, this means that if I must pay for the first units of candy more than for further units, I demand the same total amount of candies as if I paid all candies the same final lower unit price, because the higher price on the first units is like a diminution of residual income together with paying all candies the same lower price. This means that if the price of candies is p_1 and I buy the amount x_1^* that satisfies $MU_1 = p_1$, in fact I would be ready to pay for that amount more than I pay, I would be ready to pay for each successive unit of candies an amount of money equal to the marginal utility of that unit. The difference from what I pay and what I would be ready to pay is called by Marshall *individual consumer surplus*. It can be interpreted as the maximum sum of money I would be ready to pay in order to obtain the right to enter the candies market and buy x_1^* at price p_1. Indeed under these assumptions on utility, I would be indifferent between being forbidden from buying candies, or obtaining x_1^* units of candies paying for them not only $p_1 x_1^*$ but also a sum of money equal to my consumer surplus. We will return to consumer surplus later.

4.11.4 The Cobb–Douglas Utility Function and the Elasticity of Substitution

The *standard* Cobb–Douglas utility function, assuming three goods, has the form $u(x_1, x_2, x_3) = x_1^\alpha x_2^\beta x_3^\gamma$ where the exponents α, β, γ are all non-negative and their sum is 1.

A monotonic increasing transformation of this function is its logarithm; the logarithmic form of the Cobb–Douglas is $U(x_1, x_2, x_3) = \alpha \ln x_1 + \beta \ln x_2 + \gamma \ln x_3$, legitimate when all x's are positive.

With this utility function, utility is positive only if all x_is are positive, so the function is monotonic only for strictly positive vectors of consumption goods. An important property of this function is that for no good demand is ever zero, because indifference curves are asymptotic to the axes, as the price of a good tends to $+\infty$ the demand for the good decreases but never becomes zero: there cannot be 'corner solutions'.

The *generalized* Cobb–Douglas has the same form but with the sum $q > 0$ of the exponents different from 1. Raising it to the power $1/q$ it becomes a standard Cobb–Douglas representing the same preferences; therefore here I restrict attention to the standard form.

In the two-goods case, $u = x_1^\alpha x_2^{1-\alpha}$, $1 > \alpha > 0$, it is particularly easy to derive the demand functions. Preferences are monotonic (as long as x_1, $x_2 \gg 0$) therefore the budget constraint holds as strict equality. The condition $MRS_{1,2} = -p_1/p_2$ implies

$$\frac{\alpha}{1-\alpha} \cdot \frac{x_2}{x_1} = \frac{p_1}{p_2}$$

which can be rewritten as $p_1 x_1 / p_2 x_2 = \alpha/(1-\alpha)$. The share of expenditure allocated to each good is independent of prices. So the Marshallian demand functions are

$$x_1 = \alpha m/p_1, x_2 = (1 - \alpha)m/p_2.$$

292   **Chapter 4** · Consumers and the Exchange Economy

If income is not given but derives from given endowments ω_1, ω_2, then one must replace m with $p_1\omega_1 + p_2\omega_2$. Then demands depend only on *relative* prices, and the reader is invited to derive them.

Exercise: Derive the standard Cobb–Douglas expenditure function (see exercise 2 for a hint).

Another special property of the Cobb–Douglas utility function concerns its *elasticity of substitution*, a notion originally invented for the study of production, but also applicable to utility functions. The *elasticity of substitution* ξ between two consumption goods x_1 and x_2 in a two-goods utility function is normally defined as the elasticity of the *ratio* x_2/x_1 of their *compensated* demands with respect to the absolute value of the marginal rate of substitution $|MRS| \equiv MU_1/MU_2$.[34] The latter ratio can be replaced by p_1/p_2, if the demand for the two goods is derived from utility maximization and hence $|MRS| = p_1/p_2$. For discrete variations of MRS it is

$$\xi := \frac{\frac{\Delta(x_2/x_1)}{x_2/x_1}}{\frac{\Delta|MRS|}{|MRS|}} = -\frac{\frac{\Delta(x_2/x_1)}{x_2/x_1}}{\frac{\Delta(p_1/p_2)}{p_1/p_2}}.$$

The elasticity of substitution thus defined (pay attention to the different order of the indices in the ratios x_2/x_1 and p_1/p_2) is non-negative since if MU_1/MU_2 increases, the ratio of the compensated demands x_2/x_1 cannot decrease. For infinitesimal variations one obtains

$$\xi \equiv [\partial(x_2/x_1)/\partial|MRS|] \cdot [|MRS|/(x_2/x_1)]$$
$$= [\partial(x_2/x_1)/\partial(p_1/p_2)] \cdot [(p_1/p_2)/(x_2/x_1)]$$

(One can equivalently define the elasticity of substitution as $\xi = \frac{d \ln(x_2/x_1)}{d \ln|MRS|}$. But this logarithmic form seldom permits shortcuts in calculations.)

Of course $-\xi$ is the elasticity of substitution of the ratio x_1/x_2 relative to $|MRS|$, but for this case economists usually refer to its absolute value.

Warning: the notion of elasticity of substitution was originally developed for the theory of production and long-period analyses and referred to homothetic functions with smooth strictly convex isoquants. Then ξ is certainly positive. In consumer theory, the definition of the elasticity of substitution as referring to compensated demands is of uncertain utility, because the variation of compensated demands is unobservable; if the elasticity of substitution is referred to *uncompensated* demands, then it is observable and illustrates the influence of relative prices on the share of expenditure allocated to different goods; but since utility functions are never homothetic it can happen that x_2/x_1 changes in the opposite direction to p_1/p_2, and this even when both goods are normal, see ◘ Fig. 4.17: then the elasticity of substitution is negative (◘ Fig. 4.13).

---

34 For a generalization of the definition to the n-goods case, cf. Blackorby and Russell (1989).

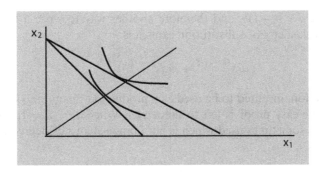

☐ **Fig. 4.13** That both goods are normal is compatible with an increase of x_2/x_1 when p_1/p_2 decreases; if the elasticity of substitution is defined with respect to uncompensated demands rather than with respect to compensated demands, it can be negative

A positive elasticity of substitution greater than 1 means that, if p_1/p_2 increases by 1% inducing some substitution of good 2 for good 1 in demand, x_2/x_1 increases by more than 1%, that is, x_1/x_2 decreases by more than 1%, so $(p_1x_1)/(p_2x_2) = \frac{p_1}{p_2} \cdot \frac{x_1}{x_2}$ decreases, and therefore the share of income going to purchase good 1, $(p_1x_1)/[(p_1x_1) + (p_2x_2)]$, decreases too: *when a good becomes relatively more expensive, the share of expenditure allocated to it decreases, increases or remains unchanged accordingly as the (positive) elasticity of substitution is greater than one, smaller than one or equal to one.*

The elasticity of substitution of a Cobb–Douglas function $u(x_1, x_2) = x_1^\alpha x_2^\beta$ is particular: it is constant and equal to 1. *Proof*: for this function, $|MRS| = MU_1/MU_2 = \frac{\alpha}{\beta} \cdot \frac{x_2}{x_1}$ which can be written $\frac{x_2}{x_1} = \frac{\beta}{\alpha} \cdot |MRS|$. Hence $\xi = (\beta/\alpha) \cdot (\alpha/\beta)(x_2/x_1)/(x_2/x_1) = 1$.

4.11.5 The CES Utility Function

The two-goods *constant elasticity of substitution* (CES) utility function is much used in models and in econometric research. It too was originally developed for production theory. It is the following:

$$u(x_1, x_2) = \left(a_1 x_1^\varrho + a_2 x_2^\varrho\right)^{1/\varrho}$$

with a_1, a_2 positive and $\varrho \leq 1$ and $\neq 0$. The name derives from the fact that the elasticity of substitution is constant, and given by $\xi = 1/(1-\varrho)$, as now I prove. The $|MRS|$ is given by $(a_1/a_2) \cdot (x_2/x_1)^{1-\varrho}$. Hence

$$d(x_2/x_1)/d|MRS| = (a_2/a_1)(1-\varrho)^{-1}(x_2/x_1)^\varrho$$

and thus

$$\xi = (d(x_2/x_1)/d|MRS|) \cdot (|MRS|/(x_2/x_1)) = 1/(1-\varrho)$$

294   **Chapter 4 · Consumers and the Exchange Economy**

It follows that $\varrho = (\xi - 1)/\xi$ and therefore another way to write a CES function that makes its elasticity of substitution explicit is

$$\left(a_1 x_1^{(\xi-1)/\xi} + a_2 x_2^{(\xi-1)/\xi} \right)^{\xi/(\xi-1)}.$$

The CES function, invented to be used as a production function, is homogeneous of degree 1: the easy proof is left to the reader. When $a_1 = a_2 = 1$, a monotonic transformation sometimes used which is not homogeneous of degree 1 but is very simple to use is

$$x_1^{\delta}/\delta + x_2^{\delta}/\delta.$$

Its elasticity of substitution is, again, constant and given by $\xi = 1/(1 - \delta)$.

As one lets ϱ vary, the CES approaches other well-known types of utility functions. For ϱ tending to 1 from below, the elasticity of substitution tends to $+\infty$, that is, to the case of perfect substitutes. Indeed if one sets $\varrho = 1$, one obtains the separable additive utility function of perfect substitutes, $u = a_1 x_1 + a_2 x_2$. As ϱ decreases, the elasticity of substitution decreases too, tending to 1 as ϱ tends towards zero.

For $\varrho = 0$ the CES function is not defined owing to division by zero, but if one lets ϱ tend to 0, the CES tends in the limit to have indifference curves identical to those of a Cobb–Douglas. Indeed, if ϱ tends to zero the MRS tends to $-a_1 x_2/(a_2 x_1)$ which is the same as for the generalized Cobb–Douglas $x_1^{\alpha} x_2^{\beta}$.

For ϱ tending to $-\infty$ the indifference curves approach the L-shaped indifference curves of the case of perfect complementarity.[35] The MRS, $-(a_1/a_2)\cdot(x_2/x_1)^{1-\varrho}$, tends to $-(a_1/a_2)\cdot(x_2/x_1)^{\infty}$ which has value $-\infty$ if $x_2 > x_1$, zero if $x_2 < x_1$; thus, indifference curves tend to become L-shaped with the corners on the 45° straight line through the origin (which can always be obtained with an opportune choice of units for the goods).

The CES Marshallian demand functions are derived as usual from the first-order conditions for utility maximization coupled with the budget constraint. It is left as an **exercise** to check that, if the two goods are given indices i, j:

$$x_i(p_i, p_j, m) = \left(\frac{a_i}{p_i} \right)^{\xi} \frac{m}{a_i^{\xi} p_i^{1-\xi} + a_j^{\xi} p_j^{1-\xi}}.$$

The CES form is often assumed in theoretical analyses of special models because analytically easy to manipulate; its frequent use in econometric analyses is less easy to justify, it is unclear why one should expect the assumption of a constant elasticity of substitution to have any correspondence with reality.

---

35 When the CES is a production function, L-shaped isoquants are called Leontief isoquants.

4.12 The Slutsky Equation

We finally tackle the issue of how the (Marshallian) demand for a good reacts to changes in prices. All the functions to appear below are assumed continuously differentiable, indifference curves are strictly convex, and the initial consumer choice is an interior basket, $x \gg 0$.

Let $\mathbf{p}^*$, m^* be prices and income in the initial situation, and let $u^* = v(\mathbf{p}^*, m^*) = u(\mathbf{x}(\mathbf{p}^*, m^*))$, $x_j^* = x_j(\mathbf{p}^*, m^*)$. Differentiate both sides of $h_i(\mathbf{p}, u) = x_i(\mathbf{p}, e(\mathbf{p}, u)) = x_i(\mathbf{p}, m)$ with respect to p_j:

$$\frac{\partial h_i(\mathbf{p}^*, u^*)}{\partial p_j} = \frac{\partial x_i(\mathbf{p}^*, m^*)}{\partial p_j} + \frac{\partial x_i(\mathbf{p}^*, m^*)}{\partial e(\mathbf{p}^*, u^*)} \cdot \frac{\partial e(\mathbf{p}^*, u^*)}{\partial p_j},$$

where $\frac{\partial x_i(\mathbf{p}^*, m^*)}{\partial e(\mathbf{p}^*, u^*)}$ can also be written $\frac{\partial x_i(\mathbf{p}^*, m^*)}{\partial m}$, because initially $m = m^* = e(\mathbf{p}^*, u^*)$ and under a balanced budget a variation in expenditure is the same thing as a variation in income. Furthermore, by Shephard's Lemma $\partial e(\mathbf{p}^*, u^*)/\partial p_j = h_j(\mathbf{p}^*, u^*) = x_j(\mathbf{p}^*, e(\mathbf{p}^*, u^*)) = x_j^*$. Hence

$$\frac{\partial h_i(\mathbf{p}^*, u^*)}{\partial p_j} = \frac{\partial x_i(\mathbf{p}^*, m^*)}{\partial p_j} + \frac{\partial x_i(\mathbf{p}^*, m^*)}{\partial m} \cdot x_j^*. \tag{4.6}$$

Let us indicate as $S(\mathbf{p}, m) \equiv [s_{ij}]$ the $n \times n$ Jacobian matrix of the vector of Hicksian demand functions for individual goods which form $\mathbf{h}(\mathbf{p}, u)$. Element (i, j) of this matrix is

$$s_{ij} = \frac{\partial h_i(\mathbf{p}^*, u^*)}{\partial p_j},$$

for which equality (4.6) holds. Matrix $S(\mathbf{p}, m) \equiv [s_{ij}]$ is called **Slutsky matrix** or also **matrix of Hicksian substitution effects**. It yields

$$\mathbf{dh} = S\mathbf{dp}^T$$

as the variation of compensated demands for infinitesimal variations $\mathbf{dp}$ of the price vector (the superscript T indicates transposition because we treat $\mathbf{p}$ as a row vector).

The usefulness of (4.6) is that, rearranging so as to isolate on one side of the equality sign the price effect on Marshallian demand, we obtain the **Slutsky equation for Marshallian demand**:

■■ Proposition 4.13

The Marshallian Slutsky Equation. The following equality connects differentiable Marshallian and Hicksian (or compensated) demand, where the asterisk indicates the variable is at the value where the derivation is performed:

$$\frac{\partial x_i(\mathbf{p}^*, m^*)}{\partial p_j} = \frac{\partial h_i(\mathbf{p}^*, u^*)}{\partial p_j} - x_j(\mathbf{p}^*, m^*) \cdot \frac{\partial x_i(\mathbf{p}^*, m^*)}{\partial m}. \tag{4.7}$$

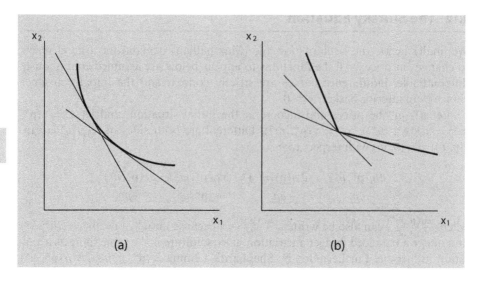

Fig. 4.14 Budget rotation to determine the substitution effect. Case (b) shows that if $\mathbf{x}^*$ is at a kink of the indifference curve the substitution effect is zero. But in the text I assume smooth indifference curves

This equation usefully decomposes the effect of a variation of p_j on the demand for good i into the sum of a ***substitution effect***—the first addendum on the right-hand side of the equality sign—which is the effect of a rotation plus shift of the budget constraint so as to keep it tangent to the original indifference curve or surface, and a residual effect called ***income effect***.[36] This allows useful conclusions on the possible effect of a price change.

The *own* substitution effect, $\partial h_i/\partial p_i$, is always non-positive and negative if indifference surfaces are differentiable (Fig. 4.14).

Graphical examples suffice to show it. But the mathematical reason is important: it is that *the Slutsky matrix is negative semidefinite*. To prove it, start from the fact that the expenditure function $e(\mathbf{p}, u)$ is concave in p_i. It is a result in the theory of matrices that *the Hessian matrix (i.e. the square matrix of second partial derivatives) of a concave function $f: R^n \to R$ is negative semidefinite and negative definite if the function is strictly concave.* (Cf. the Mathematical Review.) Hence the Hessian matrix of the expenditure function $e(\mathbf{p}, u)$ considered as a function of prices only (u is given) is negative semidefinite. But by Shephard's Lemma the Hicksian vectorial demand function $h(\mathbf{p}, u)$ is the vector of partial derivatives of

---

[36] In the second addendum on the right-hand side the representation of x_j^* as $x_j(\mathbf{p}^*, m^*)$ may cause perplexities because we saw that by Shephard's lemma the partial derivatives of the expenditure function with respect to prices are the *compensated* demands $h_i(\mathbf{p}, u)$ while here $x_j(\mathbf{p}^*, m^*)$ appears to be the Marshallian demand for good j. But here $x_j(\mathbf{p}^*, m^*)$ only indicates the single value taken by x_j at the initial price–income combination $(\mathbf{p}^*, m^*)$.

4.12 · The Slutsky Equation

the expenditure function. Hence *the Slutsky matrix, the Jacobian of* $h(\mathbf{p}, u)$, *is the Hessian matrix of the expenditure function, and therefore it is negative semidefinite.*

Another mathematical result is that *the main diagonal of a negative semidefinite matrix is non-positive.* This implies that *the own price substitution effects* $\partial h_i/\partial p_i$ *are non-positive (and in general negative), because they are the elements on the main diagonal of the Slutsky matrix.*

Since we are at it, let me add that if $e(\mathbf{p}, u)$ is twice continuously differentiable,[37] then $\partial h_i/\partial p_j = \partial h_j/\partial p_i$ by a theorem in the theory of functions of several variables (variously called *theorem of Schwarz,* or *of John,* or *of Young*) which states that *if a function* $f(\mathbf{x})$, $R^n \to R$, *is twice continuously differentiable, then* $\frac{\partial^2 f(\mathbf{x})}{\partial x_i \partial x_j} = \frac{\partial^2 f(\mathbf{x})}{\partial x_j \partial x_i}$. Then in the Slutsky matrix it is $s_{ij} = s_{ji}$, and we have proved:

■■ Proposition 4.14
If the Hicksian or compensated demand function $\mathbf{h}(\mathbf{p}, u)$ *is continuously differentiable (which means the expenditure function is twice continuously differentiable), then the Slutsky matrix is negative semidefinite and symmetric.*

This means that, when trying to estimate econometrically the vectorial demand function of a consumer, one should adopt a functional form of the demand functions for the several goods composing it, which implies that the Slutsky matrix is symmetric and negative semidefinite.

Another property of interest of the Slutsky matrix is $S(\mathbf{p}, m)\cdot\mathbf{p}^T = 0$.

Proof The Slutsky matrix is the matrix of price partial derivatives of the Hicksian demand function $\mathbf{h}(\mathbf{p}, u)$, which is homogeneous of degree zero in $\mathbf{p}$. Hence $\mathbf{h}(t\mathbf{p}, u)-\mathbf{h}(\mathbf{p}, u) = 0$ (the null vector) for all $t > 0$; differentiating the latter expression with respect to t yields the result. ■

In the only-two-goods case the sign of *cross*-substitution effects, $\partial hi/\partial p_j$, is non-negative, and positive if indifference curves are differentiable; again graphical examples suffice to see why. With more than two goods, the sign of cross-substitution effects becomes uncertain, and a classification is common: consider two out of three or more goods, call them goods 1 and 2, assume strictly convex and differentiable indifference curves, and let p_1 increase: assume the usual case, that the compensated demand for good 1 decreases; if the *compensated* demand for good 2 increases, goods 1 and 2 are said **net substitutes**; if it decreases, goods 1 and 2 are said **net complements**. The intuition is clear, a substitute for good 1 satisfies the same need and therefore competes with it for the consumer's expenditure, a complement of good 1 helps to enjoy good 1 and therefore is desired the more, the higher the consumption of good 1.

If in these definitions one replaces compensated demand with non-compensated demand, one obtains the definition of **gross substitutes** and **gross complements**. Income effects appear in this case, and in some instances this can make a

---

37 That is, $e(\mathbf{p}, u)$ is differentiable, its partial derivatives are differentiable, and their partial derivatives are continuous; this assumption appears acceptable, once one is ready to grant differentiable indifference curves.

298   **Chapter 4** · Consumers and the Exchange Economy

difference, but the basic intuition remains that a first good is a complement of a second good if a greater amount consumed of the second (e.g. because its price has decreased) raises the marginal utility of the first and this induces the consumer to demand more of the first good even though its price has not decreased. We can now define the *gross substitutes property*, GS, a special property important in general equilibrium theory:

> **Gross Substitutes Property (GS).** *GS holds if, when the price of a good increases, the demand for all other goods increases.*

In general equilibrium theory what is relevant is the Walrasian UMP, then GS holds if, when the price of a good or service increases, the consumer's demand for *all* other goods or services increases including the demand for factor services supplied by the consumer's own factor endowments, e.g. the demand for leisure, or the demand for land to be used as pleasure garden.

Coming to the ***income effect*** of a change of p_j on x_i, that is the second addendum on the right-hand side of (4.7), it is the product of two terms. Note that the first term $(-x_j)$ is the quantity of good j; so if $i \neq j$ it can be $x_j = 0$ (then there is no income effect) even when $x_i > 0$. If $x_j > 0$, the overall sign of the income effect is the opposite of the sign of the *effect of an income increase* (at fixed prices) on the Marshallian or ordinary demand for good i. A useful classification distinguishes goods according to this last effect in **normal** goods, if starting from a given income the demand for them (at the given prices) increases with income; and **inferior** goods if the opposite is the case. Mostly, inferior goods are poor-quality cheap goods which when income increases are replaced with more expensive but better-quality goods: examples are vacations at cheap but crowded seaside resorts; cheap clothes; small cars; cheap but not very tasty food. The balanced budget constraint implies that there is at least one normal good. Two useful subcategories of normal goods are **luxury goods**, whose demand increases more than in proportion with the increase in income, and **necessaries**, whose demand increases less than in proportion with the increase in income. A good can pass from one to another category as the level of income changes.[38]

The income effect, if different from zero, is negative for normal goods and positive for inferior goods. The reason is easy to understand: if p_j increases and the consumer used to buy a positive quantity of good j, then it is as if her income had decreased, and this induces her to demand less of good i if it is a normal good, more if it is inferior. Then for normal goods the **own price effect**

---

38 Plotting the quantity demanded as a function of income for given relative prices, one obtains the good's **Engel curve** for the individual: for necessaries the elasticity of the Engel curve is less than unity, for luxuries it is more than unity, for inferior goods it is negative. Engel curves are widely used, but one must distinguish *individual* Engel curves derived from *given* preferences and *given* prices, which are what we have just defined, from *historical* Engel curves, aggregated over individuals and also generally over categories of goods, which associate the changes in the composition of consumption with changes in income over very long periods; the changes described by historical Engel curves embody changes in preferences, in the vector of goods available, in wealth concentration, in relative prices, etc., therefore great caution is necessary before interpreting them as supplying insights into which goods are necessaries and which are luxuries.

4.12 · The Slutsky Equation

$\partial x_i(p, m)/\partial p_i$ is the sum of two negative (or at most zero) effects, so it is negative (or at most zero). For inferior goods, the own price effect is the sum of a negative substitution effect and a positive income effect; can the latter be stronger than the first and cause the consumer's demand for the good to increase when the good's price rises? Perhaps surprisingly, it can happen; the good is then called a *Giffen good for the individual*.

In this case the individual's demand curve for this good is in part an increasing function of its price: as ◘ Fig. 4.17b shows, a good can be Giffen for the individual at most in a limited price range, it stops being Giffen for a sufficient rise in its price. Note that the fact that a good is Giffen for some individuals does not necessarily question the uniqueness and stability of equilibrium in the market of the good, this would require that the good be a *market Giffen good*, one for which the *market* demand curve—the sum of the demands coming from *all* consumers—is, at least in some price interval, upward sloping. A good can be Giffen for some individuals without being a market Giffen good: when the good's price increases the increased demand by some consumers can be more than compensated by decreasing demand by other consumers for whom the good is not Giffen. The Slutsky equation shows that a Giffen good must be strongly inferior and absorb a considerable share of income; as well explained by Alfred Marshall when mentioning a nineteenth-century British member of the House of Lords from whom the term 'Giffen good' derives: '...as Sir R. Giffen has pointed out, a rise in the price of bread makes so large a drain on the resources of the poorer labouring families and raises so much the marginal utility of money to them, that they are forced to curtail their consumption of meat and the more expensive farinaceous foods: and, bread being still the cheapest food which they can get and will take, they consume more, and not less of it. But such cases are rare; when they are met with, each must be treated on its own merits'. (Marshall 1972, p. 109: Bk. III, Ch. VI, §4). Now, even if bread is a Giffen good for the poor, in all likelihood it is not for less poor families who can reduce expenditure on luxuries rather than on meat. Potatoes for the Irish poor in the nineteenth century, or rice for the Chinese poor, are practically the sole examples that have been adduced of goods that in all likelihood were Giffen goods for such a vast numbers of individuals as to make it possible that they were *market* Giffen goods for some price range.

Therefore market Giffen goods are highly unlikely, especially in advanced economies, and their absence can safely be assumed. I conclude that the Marshallian UMP broadly supports the so-called *Law of Demand*, the statement that when the relative price of a consumption good decreases, the demand for it (coming from consumers with given incomes) increases.[39] But when income m reflects the value of the consumer's endowments (Walrasian UMP), then m changes with **p**, and things change drastically as we will see later.

---

39 The Law of Demand must be distinguished from the statement that *compensated* demand functions can never be upward sloping, which is of course true if choice derives from a standard UMP (and the price of a good is not part of what makes it attractive for status reasons). Also note that nowadays by Law of Demand it is sometimes meant the Compensated Law of Demand defined in Proposition 4.19 below.

300   **Chapter 4** · Consumers and the Exchange Economy

Some graphical decomposition of the effect of a discrete change in one price into (discrete) substitution own effect and income own effect will give concreteness to these notions.

In ◘ Fig. 4.16a, at the initially high price of good 1, the consumer chooses point A; if the price of good 1 decreases, she moves to point B. The own price effect on the demand for good 1 is the shift from x_{1A} to x_{1B}. This shift can be seen as resulting from the sum of (i) a substitution effect, caused by a movement along the original indifference curve to point C, where |MRS| equals the new price ratio; and (ii) an income effect, caused by a movement from C to B, which, being due to a parallel upward shift of the budget line, can be seen as due to an income increase. The movement from A to C leaves utility unchanged and requires less income than initially because good 1 has become cheaper; it represents the change in demand if the consumer's incomes were reduced so as to allow her to reach only the initial utility level; it is the change in Hicksian or compensated demand if utility is kept at the same level as at A and prices become the new prices; for this reason it is called the **(*discrete*) *Hicksian substitution effect*.** The movement from C to B is the effect of bringing income back to the original level.[40] Of course Eq. (4.7) applies to infinitesimal price variations, it indicates that the vector representing the *direction* of change of $\mathbf{x}^*$ when $\mathbf{p}$ changes can be viewed as the composition of two vectors, one in the direction of the substitution effect (i.e. along the indifference curve through $\mathbf{x}^*$) and the other in the direction of the income effect.

Two extreme cases are of interest. Two consumption goods are called ***perfect complements*** if they are demanded in fixed proportions: then indifference curves are L-shaped, cf. the heavy lines in ◘ Fig. 4.15b. In this case utility is not monotonic. Two goods are called ***perfect substitutes*** if they can replace each other at a fixed rate without altering utility: then indifference curves are straight lines, cf. ◘ Fig. 4.17a.

The two-goods utility function of perfect complements is $u(x_1, x_2) = min(ax_1, bx_2)$ with $a, b > 0$; the two-goods utility function of perfect substitutes is $u(x_1, x_2) = ax_1 + bx_2$. In the latter case, the consumer will demand only one of the two goods except when the budget line has slope $-a/b$, in which case the consumer is indifferent between all baskets on the budget line.

◘ Figure 4.15b shows a case in which the change in demand is entirely due to the income effect: the L-shaped indifference curves of perfect complements cause the substitution effect to be nil.

In the case of perfect substitutes, the reader is asked to check graphically that, when a decrease of p_1 causes the consumer to shift from demanding only good 2 to demanding only good 1, the fall of the demand for good 2 to zero is entirely due to the substitution effect.

---

40 A different substitution effect is represented by the movement from A to D, the change in consumer choice if after the price change income becomes the one needed to buy the initial basket A. This is called the **(*discrete*) *Slutsky substitution effect*,** and it is commented upon in Exercise 4.31. Then the income effect is the shift from D to B.

4.12 · The Slutsky Equation

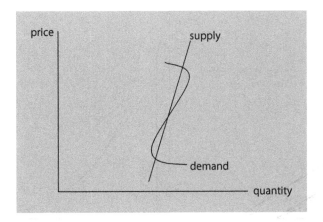

◘ **Fig. 4.15** Possible multiple equilibria in the market for rice, assumed to be a market Giffen good

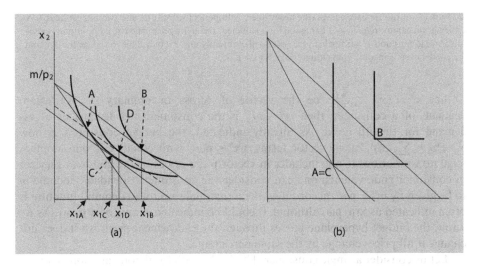

◘ **Fig. 4.16** Marshallian substitution and income effects

4.13 Given Endowments: The Walrasian UMP, The Walrasian Slutsky Equation

The income of a consumer, taken as given in the Marshallian approach, in fact depends on the prices of the goods or factor services that a consumer can offer. It is indispensable for the marginal approach not to stop at the Marshallian UMP, because factor prices cannot be taken as given in general equilibrium analyses.

Let $\omega^h = (\omega^h_1,...,\omega^h_n)$ be the vector of endowments of the hth consumer. These endowments are exogenously given (and, in a stationary economy, not changing from period to period). For land or labour or durable capital goods, the endowments must be interpreted as quantities of *services* that these factors can provide per unit of time.

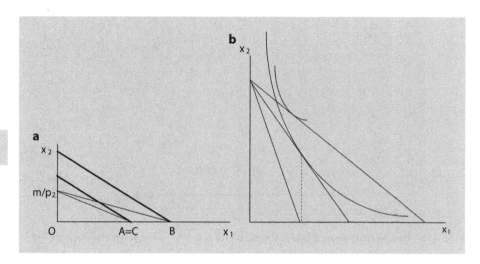

☐ **Fig. 4.17** **a** Indifference curves (the heavy lines) with perfect substitutes and two budget lines. **b** A Giffen good cannot remain a Giffen good for a sufficient rise in its price. The rise of p_1 initially raises the demand for good 1, but further price rises will eventually make it inevitable to reduce the demand for good 1 even if income goes entirely to purchase it

Let $\mathbf{x}^h = (x_1^h, \ldots x_n^h)$ be the vector of (**gross** or **ordinary** or **Walrasian**) **demands** of a consumer; then $x_i^h - \omega_i^h$ is the consumer's **net demand** or **excess demand** for the ith good. As already indicated, the budget constraint is now $\sum_j x_j^h p_j \leq \sum_j \omega_j^h p_j$ or, in vector terms, $\mathbf{px}^h \leq \mathbf{p\omega}^h$, with equality if one assumes local non-satiation. If one includes in vector $\mathbf{p}$ the prices of the goods or services in consumer endowments, one can consider the consumer's spendable income m to be given by $m^h = \mathbf{p\omega}^h$, accordingly the individual's vectorial demand function is often indicated as $\mathbf{x}(\mathbf{p}, \mathbf{p\omega})$ although it could be indicated simply as $\mathbf{x}(\mathbf{p}, \boldsymbol{\omega})$. As we know, the budget hyperplane passes through the endowment point, so it does not change if all prices change by the same percentage.

Let us consider a single consumer. The UMP with local non-satiation is now

$$max_x u(\mathbf{x}) \text{ such that } \mathbf{p\omega} - \mathbf{px} = 0.$$

The first-order conditions derived from the Lagrangian

$$\mathcal{L} = f(\mathbf{x}) + \lambda[\mathbf{p\omega} - \mathbf{px}],$$

assuming an interior solution are

$$\partial u/\partial x_i - \lambda p_i = 0, \quad i = 1, \ldots, n, \quad \text{implying } (\partial u/\partial x_i)/\partial u/\partial x_j) = p_i/p_j$$

$$\mathbf{p\omega} - \mathbf{px} = 0.$$

They are the same as for the Marshallian UMP if one puts $m = \mathbf{p\omega}$. The solution is homogeneous of degree zero in $\mathbf{p}$.

If we write the budget constraint as $\mathbf{p\omega} - \mathbf{px} + \Delta m = 0$, the Lagrange multiplier λ is the derivative of the value function of the UMP thus formulated, i.e. of the

4.13 · Given Endowments: The Walrasian UMP, The Walrasian Slutsky Equation

Walrasian indirect utility function, with respect to Δm, calculated in $\Delta m = 0$; it can still be interpreted as the marginal utility of money or income, in the sense of indicating the marginal increase in utility if, at the given prices, some extra money or income is given to the consumer, e.g. through a subsidy. Indirect utility is now a function of prices and of endowments, $v(\mathbf{p}, \mathbf{p\omega})$, and the Envelope Theorem yields $\partial v(\mathbf{p}, \mathbf{p\omega})/\partial p_i = \lambda(\omega_i - x_i)$; therefore Roy's Identity becomes

$$-\left[\partial v(\mathbf{p}, \mathbf{p\omega})/\partial p_i\right]/\lambda = x_i - \omega_i;$$

one obtains, not the demand for good i, but instead the *net* or *excess* demand for good i. The expenditure function and the Hicksian demand function are unaffected because independent of what determines actual income. Therefore the Slutsky *matrix* is unaffected. On the contrary the Slutsky *equation* must now take into account the fact that $m = \mathbf{p\omega}$. The effect of a price change on the demand for a good includes now an additional effect besides the ones already present when m is given as ◼ Fig. 4.24 illustrates.

Since now in $x_i(\mathbf{p}, m)$ it is $m = \sum_{i=1}^{n} p_i\omega_i$, differentiating this demand function totally with respect to any price p_j one obtains (on the left-hand side the symbol d is used instead of ∂ to stress it is a *total* partial differentiation):

$$\frac{dx_i(\mathbf{p}^*, m*)}{dp_j} = \frac{\partial x_i(\mathbf{p}^*, m*)}{\partial p_j} + \frac{\partial x_i(\mathbf{p}^*, m*)}{\partial m} \frac{\partial m}{\partial p_j}$$

where $m = \sum_{i=1}^{n} p_i\omega_i$. The first term on the right-hand side indicates how demand for good i would change if the consumer's income m was fixed, i.e. if after the price change from $\mathbf{p}$ to $\mathbf{p} + d\mathbf{p}$ income were compensated so as to remain equal to its initial value: this effect is the one given by the Marshallian Slutsky equation determined in ▶ Sect. 4.13, and we know it is the sum of:

(i) the substitution effect;
(ii) the income effect with m constant, called now the ***ordinary income effect***;

but now there is also:

(iii) a further effect, the second term on the right-hand side, due to the change in the value of the endowment, called the ***endowment income effect***.

The change in income (=value of endowments) is $\partial m/\partial p_j = \omega_j$ because if the price of good j rises by one unit, the value of the endowment of good j rises by ω_j units. Its effect on x_i is given by $\frac{\partial x_i}{\partial m} \cdot \frac{\partial m}{\partial p_j}$; therefore the endowment income effect is $\frac{\partial x_i}{\partial m} \cdot \omega_j$.

The sum of the ordinary income effect and of the endowment income effects is called the ***total income effect***. The new Slutsky equation (old Slutsky equation + endowment income effect) has on the right-hand side the sum of the substitution effect and of the total income effect; formally:

◼◼ Proposition 4.15

The Walrasian Slutsky equation is:

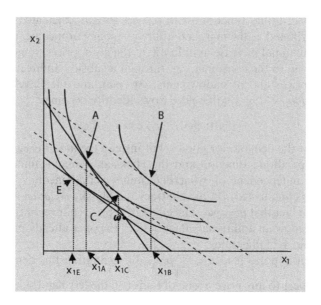

Fig. 4.18 This is similar to Fig. 4.15a except that $m = p\omega$. The initial budget line is through ω and point A; after p_1 decreases the new budget line is the one through ω and E, and the new optimal choice is point E. The Hicksian substitution effect (from A to C) is the same as before (the same holds for the Slutsky substitution effect, omitted in this Figure); the movement from C to B is now the *ordinary* income effect, obtained by assuming an unchanged m and hence an unchanged budget line intercept in ordinate; the movement from B to E is the *endowment* income effect. Note the enormous difference made by the endowment income effect, which causes the demand for x_1 to decrease rather than increase (although x_1 is *not* an inferior good, as shown by the increase in the demand for it as one passes to higher-income budget lines, see points E, C, B)

$$\underbrace{\frac{\partial x_i}{\partial p_j}}_{} = \underbrace{\frac{\partial h_i}{\partial p_j}}_{\text{substitution effect}} - \underbrace{x_j \frac{\partial x_i}{\partial m}}_{\text{ordinary income effect}} + \underbrace{\omega_j \frac{\partial x_i}{\partial m}}_{\text{endowment income effect}} = \frac{\partial h_i}{\partial p_j} + \underbrace{(\omega_j - x_j) \frac{\partial x_i}{\partial m}}_{\text{total income effect}}$$

As shown in Fig. 4.18, the presence of the endowment income effect can change the influence of price changes on demand drastically relative to the case when income is given. The reason is that the sign in front of $\partial x_i/\partial m$ is now positive if the good whose price changes is in excess supply, $\omega_j - x_j > 0$. Now *demand can be an increasing function of own price even for normal goods*.[41] This is because the price rise of an endowment in net supply *makes the consumer richer*, not poorer: the consumer's income is now greater than needed to consume the same basket as before.

---

41 A good for which this happens is *not* called a Giffen good; Giffen goods are so defined with respect to situations where m is given; they *must* be inferior goods.

4.13 · Given Endowments: The Walrasian UMP, The Walrasian Slutsky Equation

When income is given, $v(\mathbf{p}, m)$ is non-increasing in $\mathbf{p}$, and decreasing in p_j if the demand for good j is positive. This property no longer holds when income derives from given endowments: an increase in the (relative) price of a good *in net supply* allows the consumer to reach a higher indifference surface.

4.14 Labour Supply. Saving Decision

The Walrasian UMP permits the study of factor supply decisions. For many consumers, the income to buy consumption goods comes from supplying labour services. An important issue is how consumers decide labour supply. In real economies, often one must accept either a full-time job or nothing; but even then the average labour supply *of an entire household* can be varied by varying how many in the household work and how much during the period (part-time, overtime, vacation periods, etc.). So by interpreting the consumer as a household including several members, and referring to labour supply over not too short a period (say, a year), it is not too absurd to assume that labour supply can be varied more or less continuously.

Suppose that the consumer's endowment consists only of potential labour hours, i.e. of leisure hours usable to work; measure the supply of labour L per period (e.g. per week) as the difference between the endowment of leisure hours M per period (168 h per week) and the demand x for leisure hours per period.[42] (The supply of labour, $L = M - x$, is then identical with the *net supply* of leisure, and I am implicitly assuming that the consumer is indifferent between different types of labour.) Assume only two consumption goods, leisure x and consumption c;[43] the price of consumption is 1. The price of leisure is the real hourly wage w, because one less hour of leisure is one more hour of work, which yields the consumer w more units of income to spend on consumption. The budget constraint is $c = wL = w(M - x)$; if we assume that the consumer has in addition an initial endowment of non-labour income that permits the purchase of c° units of consumption, then the budget constraint is $c = w(M - x) + c^\circ$: in either case, with leisure measured in abscissa and consumption in ordinate, the slope of the budget constraint is $-w$. As long as labour supply is positive, $M > x$, for leisure the total income effect is positive if leisure is a normal good; thus as the real wage increases from an initial level where labour supply is positive, the demand for leisure may well increase, entailing a decrease in the supply of labour (cf. ◘ Figs. 4.19 and 4.20).

---

42 By 'spendable income' in this case I do not mean the value of endowments (here wM) which is our technical definition of income, I mean the flow of money that can be spent on goods other than leisure, and therefore if it comes only from labour, it is wL. By 'income', everyday language means spendable income; for this reason some economists prefer to use 'wealth' to indicate the value of endowments.

43 The good c can also be interpreted as spendable income, i.e. the money one can spend on goods other than leisure.

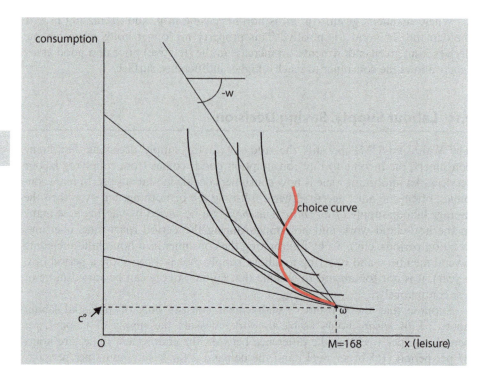

Fig. 4.19 Weekly leisure-consumption decision with an endowment including a non-labour spendable income $c°$ (sufficient to ensure survival: otherwise other things can happen as pointed out below). The choice curve (in red) starts from the endowment point and is initially negatively sloped, implying a supply of labour with, initially, positive slope. At higher wages the choice curve can turn upward sloping implying a 'backward-bending' labour supply curve

The Slutsky equation shows that, if the labour supply curve is continuous, this cannot happen in a neighbourhood of a zero supply of labour, because for $x = M$ the total income effect is zero, the own price effect coincides with the substitution effect; for $x < M$ one can be *certain* that labour supply is an increasing function of the wage rate *only if* leisure is *not* a normal good (prove it!). It is therefore possible that the consumer's labour supply curve is an increasing function of the real wage only initially and then becomes 'backward-bending' (see ◘ Figs. 4.19 and 4.21a).

Things will be different if there is a ***survival problem***. Suppose $c° = 0$, so at a zero wage survival is impossible. Then in all likelihood, as ◘ Fig. 4.20 shows, as w decreases to very low levels the consumer (the household) supplies more and more labour in order to avoid a fall of consumption below a socially or even biologically acceptable subsistence level; but for a sufficiently low w this becomes impossible, then the consumer gives up supplying labour and jumps discontinuously to no labour supply, turning to crime or begging or revolt (for more on survival cf. ► Chap. 6).

This type of discontinuity can cause a very significant discontinuity in the *market* labour supply curve, because in all likelihood it happens at the same w

4.14 · Labour Supply. Saving Decision

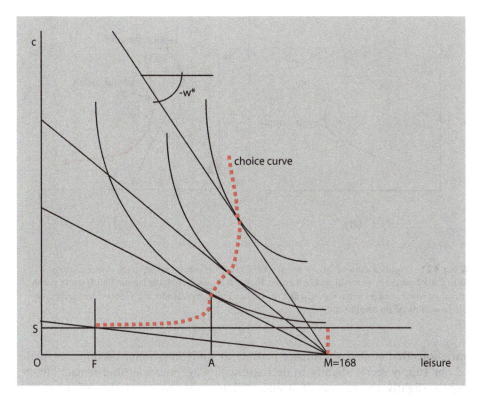

Fig. 4.20 Weekly leisure-consumption decision with a discontinuity due to a survival problem. The consumer's endowment consists only of 168 h of leisure per week. The choice curve is the broken red curve. When leisure is OA, labour supply is AM = 168–OA. In this example as w decreases labour supply increases, in order to permit consuming at least S, the minimum consumption required for survival; there is a maximum physically feasible supply of labour equal to FM; when w becomes so low that even a leisure reduced to the minimum OF does not permit consuming S, labour supply jumps to zero

for many consumers. This can prevent the existence of a labour market equilibrium: the labour demand curve (assuming its determinability)[44] might pass through the discontinuity of the labour supply curve and never cross the latter, see ▶ Fig. 4.21b. The term generally used to describe the possibility of a downward-sloping labour supply curve, 'backward-bending', presumes that initially the labour supply curve is positively sloped, and 'bends backward' when w rises considerably; but we see that it might behave quite differently.

Mainstream macroeconomic models generally assume a positively sloped labour supply curve; empirical evidence confirms the theoretical considerations that suggest that there is no reason to expect it. There is a wide consensus (see Cahuc et al. 2014, Chap. 1) that labour supply changes little for the limited wage

---

[44] We will see in ▶ Chaps. 7 and 13 reasons why a labour demand curve may be indeterminable.

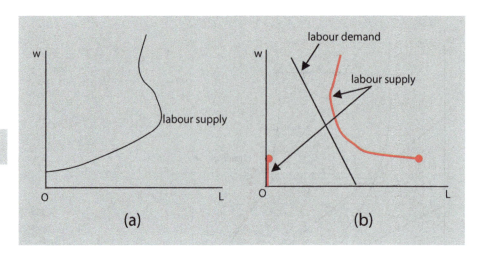

◘ **Fig. 4.21** Figure **a** shows a labour supply curve roughly corresponding to the choice curve of ◘ Fig. 4.19, where no survival problem arises. Figure **b** shows, in red, the labour supply curve corresponding to all workers behaving as in ◘ Fig. 4.20 and also, by introducing a labour demand curve, the possibility of no equilibrium

variations that empirical evidence permits to study in advanced economies; male labour supply seems slightly to decrease with wage increases and female labour supply slightly to increase. It would be interesting to see studies of what has happened to *intended* labour supply in Greece after the recent enormous fall of incomes caused by the European Central Bank, but for the moment we do not know (it will be difficult anyway to ascertain it, if aggregate demand constraints discourage looking for a job).

An analysis similar to the one used to analyse labour supply can be used for the saving decision. Consider a consumer who chooses between consumption in the current period, c_1, and consumption next period, c_2. For simplicity let us treat consumption as a single good and the consumer's endowments of consumption in the two periods as given. The consumption good today is also the numéraire, i.e. current consumption has price 1; consumption for delivery next period can be purchased or sold in the current period at a current price p, which implies a discount rate or interest rate. As already illustrated in ▶ Chap. 3, ▶ Sect. 3.10, suppose that $p = 0.909$. This means that one must give up 0.909 units of current consumption in order to purchase a promise of delivery of one unit of consumption after one period (promises are honoured). This is equivalent to a loan of 0.909 units of consumption today against payment of one unit of consumption after one period; this loan yields 0.091 units of consumption as interest, that is a real *rate* of interest $i = 10\%$. The number $i = 10\% = 0.1$ results from the equation

$$p(1+i) = 1,$$

which says that if today a person buys with p units of numéraire a bond promising to pay 1 unit of numéraire next period, then effectively that person is lending

4.14 · Labour Supply. Saving Decision

the sum p of numéraire for one period and i is the physical rate of interest (in numéraire) on the loan. Therefore we can equivalently say that the *present* price of *future* consumption is p, or that the rate of interest for one-period consumption loans is $(1 - p)/p$. This rate of interest need not be positive. We can also say that $p = 1/(1 + i)$ is the present value today of a unit of numéraire tomorrow, i.e. $1/(1 + i)$ is the **discount factor** which, multiplied by the value of a good tomorrow, yields its present value today.

Let us indicate the endowments of the consumer in the two periods as ω_1 and ω_2, respectively. The budget constraint is

$$c_1 + pc_2 = \omega_1 + p\omega_2$$

or equivalently, since $(1 + i) = 1/p$, it is

$$(\omega_1 - c_1)(1 + i) = c_2 - \omega_2.$$

This second form of the budget constraint expresses the fact that the current period's savings $\omega_1 - c_1$, if positive, can be lent at the rate of interest i and allow the consumer to consume in the next period in excess of her endowment of that period.

Graphically, we can represent the consumer's preferences between consumption today and tomorrow via indifference curves, with current period's consumption in abscissa and next period's consumption in ordinate. The budget constraint passes through the point $\omega = (\omega_1, \omega_2)$ and has slope $-1/p_1 = -(1 + i)$. If the consumer is a net saver in the current period, then an increase of the rate of interest may well cause her to consume more in the current period, i.e. to save less, cf. ◘ Fig. 4.22. In macroeconomics it is common to assume that the supply of sav-

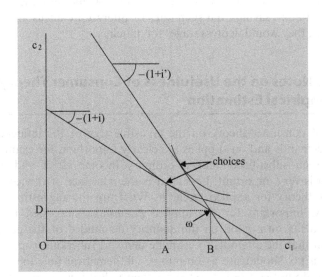

◘ **Fig. 4.22** Saving decision. When the endowment of current consumption is OB and of future consumption is OD, and the consumer demands OA of current consumption, then she is saving AB. Saving may decrease when the interest rate increases from i to i'

ings is an increasing function of the rate of interest, but there is little theoretical reason why it should be so. For example, if a sufficient retirement income must be privately obtained by the consumer by saving during working life, it is perfectly possible that if the rate of interest rises, the consumer decides to save less, since less saving is sufficient to ensure an unchanged income after retirement. This will not happen if the utility function is a Cobb–Douglas, which has the property that when income derives from given endowments even the demand for a good in excess supply decreases when the relative price of the good increases (prove it! it is easy). But with other utility functions it can happen.

There is an additional complication. The assumption we have made, that the saving decision can be reduced to a choice between consumption today and consumption tomorrow *where the consumption endowments today and tomorrow can be treated as independent of the rate of interest*, is generally unsustainable, because the rate of interest influences income distribution (the moment we admit capital). For example the consumption that a worker can afford depends on the real wage, and the real wage is not independent of the rate of interest or of profit, as argued in ▶ Chaps. 1 through 3. The same dependence of income on the rate of interest holds even more clearly for the owner of capital goods. Thus, a change of the rate of interest alters incomes and differently for different social groups; its overall effect on savings will depend on how the different incomes are influenced and on the different saving propensities of the different groups. Empirical evidence is disturbed by public pensions, by the fact that much saving is decided by firms (out of retained profits) rather than by consumers, and by the fact just pointed out that a rise in the real rate of interest (rate of return on capital) entails a decrease of real wages; so it is difficult to reach clear conclusions. Probably very high, usurious real yearly rates of interest, say 40%, would raise the average share of income allotted to savings, but such rates of interest are unsustainable in modern economies, they would depress wages too much.

4.15 Some Notes on the Usefulness of Consumer Theory for Empirical Estimation

The results of consumer theory on the plausible sign of the influence of price changes on demands and on supplies are clearly important, for example the distinction between substitution effect, ordinary income effect and endowment income effect is very important. Less clear is the relevance of the results reached by consumer theory for applied research. What are the suggestions from consumer theory, important for the applied economist interested in estimating the effect of a tax on a good on the quantity demanded of the good? Mainly, it would seem that the attempts to estimate demand functions, supply functions, the effect of a tax should use assumptions, mathematical functions, systems of functions that do not contradict consumer theory. But it is not easy to make this general idea more concrete.

Consumer theory is rich of results about the demand functions of a single consumer. We have seen in ▶ Sect. 4.12 that the Slutsky matrix derivable from

4.15 · Some Notes on the Usefulness of Consumer Theory for Empirical Estimation

these demand functions should be negative semidefinite and symmetric. The other restrictions that consumer theory imposes on the (Marshallian) system of demand functions of an individual consumer are that its demand functions must be homogeneous of degree zero in $(\mathbf{p}, m)$ and must satisfy the balanced budget restriction (expenditures on the several goods must add up to total income). It can be proved (I omit the proof) that homogeneity of degree zero, balanced budget and a negative semidefinite and symmetric Slutsky matrix are *all* the restrictions that standard consumer theory imposes on the system of differentiable demand functions coming from the choices of a consumer. (Actually it can be proved that homogeneity of degree zero is implied by budget balancedness plus symmetry of the Slutsky matrix, hence is not an additional restriction, cf. Jehle and Reny 2011, p. 85.) The implication is:

■■ **Proposition 4.16**
If a system of (continuously differentiable) putative Marshallian demand functions obeys homogeneity of degree zero in $(\mathbf{p}, m)$, budget balancedness and negative semidefiniteness and symmetry of the Stutsky matrix, then there exists a utility function reflecting 'well-behaved' preferences (i.e. complete, transitive, locally non-satiated and continuous preferences representable through a twice continuously strictly quasi-concave differentiable utility function) from which those function can be derived as Marshallian demand functions; therefore, whatever their other characteristics, those putative demand functions do not contradict standard consumer theory.

For a sketch of a proof, see, e.g. Jehle and Reny (2011, pp. 87–88).

An analogous question arises for the expenditure function and for the indirect utility function. A report of the main results for the expenditure function will give a taste of the issue.

A putative individual consumer's expenditure function $e(\mathbf{p}, u)$ can be shown to derive from some utility function and therefore not to contradict standard consumer theory, if it is:
- non-negative for $p \gg 0$;
- continuous;
- strictly increasing and unbounded above in u for all $\mathbf{p} \gg 0$;
- non-decreasing in $\mathbf{p}$;
- homogeneous of degree 1 in $\mathbf{p}$;
- concave in $\mathbf{p}$.

The utility function generating this $e(\mathbf{p}, u)$ is increasing and quasi-concave.

Having ascertained the properties that characterize *all* expenditure functions derivable from plausible utility functions, any function having those properties can be adopted as an expenditure function for empirical estimation, with no need to specify the utility function that generates it; it suffices to know that a utility function generating that expenditure function does exist, and therefore the proposed expenditure function does not contradict accepted consumer theory. Analogous conditions can be found that guarantee that a putative indirect utility function does not contradict accepted consumer theory. This can be convenient, because the partial derivatives of the expenditure function directly yield

312 Chapter 4 · Consumers and the Exchange Economy

the compensated demand functions (Shephard's Lemma), and from the indirect utility function one can directly derive the Marshallian demand functions via Roy's Identity. And analogous conditions guarantee that a system of functions $\mathbf{h}(\mathbf{p}, u)$ can be legitimately assumed to be a system of Hicksian demand functions, or that a system of functions $\mathbf{x}(\mathbf{p}, m)$ can be assumed to be a system of Marshallian demand functions. Once one estimates econometrically such a system, then integration techniques allow reconstructing the utility function.

But there is a problem, to be now briefly discussed, which motivates the decision not to go any deeper into integration techniques in this book: the decisions of a single consumer are not particularly interesting, the applied economist is interested in what happens to market variables, resulting from the decisions of very many individuals; and anyway the available data about demand only allow studying market variables, they are *aggregate* data, both in the sense of being the sum of choices of heterogeneous individuals and in the sense of generally concerning demand for aggregates of heterogeneous goods (e.g. meat); it is far from obvious that they can be usefully studied with the notions we have developed, which concern the demand for *single* goods by a *single* consumer.

Before discussing this issue, let me note other difficulties of the attempts at estimation of demand functions. *First*, any such attempt must be based on repeated observations over a time interval of considerable length, otherwise the observations are too few and/or the differences in prices and incomes are too small; and it is unclear that one has the right to assume that preferences have not significantly changed during that time. *Second*, when econometric estimation aims at prediction, e.g. of the effects of a tax, one must assume that the tax will not alter preferences, while preferences are often considerably altered by the change in social behaviours induced by the intervention itself; I do not think that people would have been as ready ten years ago as they are now to spend time to separate recyclable from non-recyclable rubbish; and certainly tolerance towards other people's smoking in public places has quickly decreased after laws prohibiting it were approved.

But if one decides to try anyway to arrive at econometric estimation of demand functions and of how a tax would change them, how does consumer theory help? We have ascertained that a complete system of demand functions deriving from a single locally non-satiated differentiable utility function satisfies budget balancedness, homogeneity of degree zero in prices and income and symmetry and negative semidefiniteness of the Slutsky matrix. Should market demand functions satisfy the same restrictions? The answer seems to be a clear no, because these conditions are satisfied by complete systems of demand functions derived from a single utility function, while estimated demand functions derive from choices of highly heterogeneous consumers, considerably different in income and tastes, and of a composition that does not remain unchanged; also, an estimated demand function generally concerns a category, a group of goods rather than single goods (with rare exceptions like electricity or petrol), and the conditions for aggregation over goods are stringent; and the demand functions never constitute a complete system, so the Slutsky matrix cannot be derived.

4.15 · Some Notes on the Usefulness of Consumer Theory for Empirical Estimation

Also, results in general equilibrium theory to be presented in ▶ Chap. 6 (the so-called Sonnenschein–Mantel–Debreu results) have shown that when the very restrictive assumptions guaranteeing the existence of a representative consumer are not satisfied, then market demand functions can differ drastically from the demand functions derivable from a single consumer and can have essentially any shape.

In conclusion, there seems to be very little reason to expect *market* demands to behave as if they came from a single consumer.[45] But unless they do, economic theory does not restrict the possible choice of functional forms for econometric estimation of market demand functions. Thus the relevance of Proposition 4.16 and of the analogous results mentioned immediately afterwards concerning expenditure functions, indirect utility functions etcetera is unclear.

4.16 Money Metric Utility Function, Equivalent Variation, Compensating Variation

Public policy decisions often require comparing their disadvantages with their advantages. To assess whether a public intervention should be approved, economists advocate the use of *cost–benefit analysis*, which tries to reach a one-dimensional quantitative measure (usually a *monetary valuation*) of the costs and of the benefits of a policy in terms of utility variations, so as to see whether the balance is positive or negative. Here I present one way to reach a monetary valuation of the effects upon consumers' utility of the change in a good's price; it may allow deciding whether the intervention that causes that price to change is good or bad. To such an end economists propose to use the consumers' own monetary valuation of the effect of the price change.

Imagine a price reduction will affect 1000 consumers, some of whom would be ready to pay up to 10 dollars a year in order to obtain the expected price reduction, some 20 dollars and some would on the contrary suffer a damage and would want a compensation of 5 dollars a year[46]; suppose the sum of these positive and negative amounts yields a *net* total of 10,000 dollars, then one possible valuation of the aggregate utility increase caused by the price reduction is 10,000 dollars. The *monetary valuation of the utility gains* of the several consumers makes them

---

45 It is then not surprising that Deaton and Muellbauer in their fundamental treatise on applied consumer theory, after surveying several empirical attempts at estimation of demand functions, should conclude: 'The Rotterdam, loglinear, and translog models all make different approximations and yet all obtain the same result: the restrictions of the theory do not hold, at least on aggregate data ... We have looked at different models, each embodying different approximations, and these have been fitted to different data sets from several countries, but the same conclusions have repeatedly emerged. Demand functions fitted to aggregate time series data are not homogeneous and probably not symmetric'. (Deaton and Muellbauer 1980, pp. 74, 78). Also page 80 of their book makes for very healthy reading.

46 For example because they sell services that are substitutes of the good whose price will decrease.

314   **Chapter 4** · Consumers and the Exchange Economy

commensurable, so one can add them and compare the result with the cost of the intervention (e.g. a public investment) that would cause the price reduction. Of course the use of this sum for policy evaluation implies a far from uncontroversial value judgement that an extra 1 dollar of benefit has the same social relevance independently of who gets it, with the implication that a 1 dollar benefit of one individual compensates a 1 dollar loss of another individual independently of who and of how wealthy they are. We do not discuss now this criterion and its proposed justifications (see ▶ Chap. 14); we only discuss how to determine a consumer's monetary valuation of a price change.

First, let us note a transformation of the utility function (Varian) that allows one to measure changes in utility in terms of money. Let us define the following new notion: the ***money metric utility function***, also called *direct compensation function*, defined as

$$M(\mathbf{p}, \mathbf{x}) := e(\mathbf{p}, u(\mathbf{x}))$$

where $e(\cdot)$ is an expenditure function and $u(\mathbf{x})$ the consumer's utility function. It answers the following question: how much money would the consumer need at prices $\mathbf{p}$ in order to reach the same utility level as obtained from the consumption basket $\mathbf{x}$. The function $M(\mathbf{p}, \mathbf{x})$ is for each $\mathbf{p}$ and $\mathbf{x}$ the solution to the problem:

$$min_y \mathbf{p}\mathbf{y} \ such \ that \ u(\mathbf{y}) \geq u(\mathbf{x}).$$

For fixed $\mathbf{x}$, $M(\mathbf{p}, \mathbf{x})$ behaves like an expenditure function because $u(\mathbf{x})$ is fixed. *For fixed $\mathbf{p}$, $M(\mathbf{p}, \mathbf{x})$ is a utility function* (whence the name) *representing the same preferences as $u(\mathbf{x})$*, because $e(\mathbf{p}, u)$ is strictly increasing in u, so if a change of $\mathbf{x}$ raises $u(\mathbf{x})$, $M(\mathbf{p}, \mathbf{x})$ increases too, while if the change of $\mathbf{x}$ leaves $u(\mathbf{x})$ unchanged, $M(\mathbf{p}, \mathbf{x})$ remains unchanged too; so for fixed $\mathbf{p}$, $M(\mathbf{p}, \mathbf{x})$ is a monotonic transformation of $u(\cdot)$ that measures changes in utility as changes in the amount of money needed to reach the different utility levels. But what really interests us is its indirect utility function, which is called the ***money metric indirect utility function*** and is defined by

$$\mu\left(\mathbf{p}^{\circ}, \mathbf{p}, m\right) := e\left(\mathbf{p}^{\circ}, v(\mathbf{p}, m)\right)$$

where $v(\mathbf{p}, m)$ is the indirect (Marshallian) utility function derived from the given $u(\cdot)$. It answers the following question: *How much money income the consumer would need at given reference prices* $\mathbf{p}^{\circ}$ *to reach the same utility level as she can reach with money income m at prices p?*

For given $\mathbf{p}$ and m (and hence given $u = v(\mathbf{p}, m)$), $\mu(\mathbf{p}^{\circ}, \mathbf{p}, m)$ behaves like an expenditure function. For given $\mathbf{p}^{\circ}$, it is a function of $\mathbf{p}$ and m and behaves like an indirect utility function, it is indeed only a monotonic transformation of $v(\mathbf{p}, m)$. If we choose it as indirect utility function, then it can be used to measure welfare changes expressed in amounts of money: suppose prices change from $\mathbf{p}$ to $\mathbf{p}'$; once one has chosen a reference price vector $\mathbf{p}^{\circ}$, the *difference*

$$e\left(\mathbf{p}^{\circ}, v(\mathbf{p}', m)\right) - e\left(\mathbf{p}^{\circ}, v(\mathbf{p}, m)\right) \quad that \ is, \quad \mu\left(\mathbf{p}^{\circ}, \mathbf{p}', m\right), \qquad (4.8)$$

4.16 · Money Metric Utility Function, Equivalent Variation, Compensating Variation

that is the change in the value of the money metric indirect utility, measures the change in utility as an amount of dollars.

By choosing the *initial* price vector $\mathbf{p}$ or the *new* price vector $\mathbf{p}'$ as the reference vector $\mathbf{p}°$, one obtains two monetary measures of welfare change due to a price change, the **equivalent variation** and the **compensating variation**, widely used in welfare economics.

Suppose prices change from $\mathbf{p}$ to $\mathbf{p}'$, while m does not change. The **equivalent variation** EV indicates the income *variation* that would allow the consumer to reach, at the *old* prices, the *new* utility level $v(\mathbf{p}', m)$ she reaches at the new prices. In other words, EV is the offer of an income variation *in place of* the price change that would make the consumer indifferent between accepting it and remaining at the old prices $\mathbf{p}$ or accepting the price change to $\mathbf{p}'$ with no change in monetary income. These definitions make it clear that if the price change would raise (respectively, reduce) the consumer's utility, then EV is positive (respectively, negative).

Formally, let $\mathbf{x} = \mathbf{x}(\mathbf{p}, m)$ be the consumer's (Marshallian) vectorial demand at the old prices and $\mathbf{x}' = \mathbf{x}(\mathbf{p}', m)$ the demand at the new prices with the same income m; let u stand for the initial utility level, $u = v(\mathbf{p}, m) = u(\mathbf{x}(\mathbf{p}, m))$, and let u' stand for the new utility level, $u' = v(\mathbf{p}', m) = u(\mathbf{x}(\mathbf{p}', m))$; initial and final actual expenditures satisfy $e(\mathbf{p}, u) = \mathbf{px} = e(\mathbf{p}', u') = \mathbf{p}'\mathbf{x}' = m$; the minimum expenditure allowing the consumer to reach the *new* utility level at the *old* prices is $e(\mathbf{p}, u')$, associated with a basket $\mathbf{x} = \mathbf{x}(\mathbf{p}, e(\mathbf{p}, u'))$ which for brevity I indicate as $\mathbf{x}_{EV}$ (cf. ◘ Fig. 4.23). Hence

$$EV(\mathbf{p} \to \mathbf{p}', m) := e(\mathbf{p}, u') - m = e(\mathbf{p}, u') - e(\mathbf{p}, u).$$

Rewriting it more explicitly as

$$EV(\mathbf{p} \to \mathbf{p}', m) = e(\mathbf{p}, v(\mathbf{p}', m)) - e(\mathbf{p}, v(\mathbf{p}, m))$$

we see that it is expression (4.8) with $\mathbf{p}° = \mathbf{p}$. So *EV is the change in money metric indirect utility when the reference price vector is the initial price vector, $\mathbf{p}°=\mathbf{p}$*.

Note that since $e(\mathbf{p}', u') = m$, we can also write

$$
\begin{aligned}
EV(\mathbf{p} \to \mathbf{p}', m) &= e(\mathbf{p}, u') - e(\mathbf{p}', u') \\
&= e(\mathbf{p}, v(\mathbf{p}', m)) - e(\mathbf{p}', v(\mathbf{p}', m)),
\end{aligned}
\tag{4.9}
$$

expressing EV as the change in expenditure made necessary by a *reversal* of the price change, that is by a price change from $\mathbf{p}'$ to $\mathbf{p}$, *if* utility is to remain at the *new* level u'.[47]

Let us now ask what income variation *after* the price change would cause the consumer at the new prices to reach the *old* utility level, thus 'compensating' her

---

47 If income too changes from m to m' when prices change from $\mathbf{p}$ to $\mathbf{p}'$, and $u'=v(\mathbf{p}', m')$, then
$EV(\mathbf{p} \to \mathbf{p}', m \to m') := e(\mathbf{p}, u') - m = e(\mathbf{p}, u') - e(\mathbf{p}, u) = e(\mathbf{p}, v(\mathbf{p}', m')) - e(\mathbf{p}, v(\mathbf{p}, m)) =$
$= e(\mathbf{p}, u') - e(\mathbf{p}', u')] + m' - m]$, because $e(\mathbf{p}', u') = m'$. I do not insist on this case.

316   **Chapter 4 ·** Consumers and the Exchange Economy

for the price change (in inverted commas because if the price change brought about a utility increase, the 'compensation' must *reduce* utility, against the usual meaning of the term). The **compensating variation** CV is usually defined as the *negative* of this income variation: the change in sign is made in order to make it directly comparable with the equivalent variation, otherwise they would be of opposite sign: for example if a price decreases and this makes the consumer better off, we have seen that EV is positive; since $u' > u$, to bring the consumer back to utility level u at the new prices it is necessary to decrease her income, the needed income variation is negative; to make it comparable with EV one puts a minus sign in front of it and makes it positive. One can interpret this positive sum as the *increase* in the funds of a public institution in charge of handing out or collecting money so as to bring the consumer's utility back to u after the price change. The CV is the maximum reduction in income a consumer would be ready to accept in order to obtain that the change is implemented.

Formally, the minimum expenditure that allows the consumer to reach the old utility level u at the new prices $\mathbf{p}'$ is $e(\mathbf{p}', u)$, associated with a basket $\mathbf{x}_{CV} := \mathbf{x}(\mathbf{p}', e(\mathbf{p}', u))$; hence

$$CV(\mathbf{p} \to \mathbf{p}', m) := -\left[e(\mathbf{p}', u) - m\right]$$
$$= m - e(\mathbf{p}', u) = e(\mathbf{p}, u) - e(\mathbf{p}', u).$$

Since $e(\mathbf{p}', u') = e(\mathbf{p}, u) = m$ we can also write

$$CV(\mathbf{p} \to \mathbf{p}', m) = e(\mathbf{p}', u') - e(\mathbf{p}', u)$$
$$= e(\mathbf{p}', v(\mathbf{p}', m)) - e(\mathbf{p}', v(\mathbf{p}, m)), \qquad (4.10)$$

which is expression (4.8) with $\mathbf{p}° = \mathbf{p}'$. Thus *CV is the change in money metric indirect utility when the reference price vector is the final price vector.*

Exercise: Prove that $EV(\mathbf{p} \to \mathbf{p}', m) = -CV(\mathbf{p}' \to \mathbf{p}, m)$. (Hint: remember expression (4.9).)

In general these two money measures of the change in welfare differ. Graphically, consider two goods and a decrease in the price of good 1, while the price of good 2 stays constant at 1 (through an opportune choice of units for good 2, or perhaps because utility is quasi-linear and good 2 is residual income); see ◨ Fig. 4.23. The EV alters m so that the budget line with the *old* slope touches the *new* indifference curve (the consumer passes from demanding $\mathbf{x}$ to demanding $\mathbf{x}_{EV}$). The negative of CV alters m so that the budget line with the *new* slope touches the *old* indifference curve (the consumer passes from $\mathbf{x}'$ to $\mathbf{x}_{CV}$).

Both variations can be read off as changes in the vertical intercept of the budget line, as explained under ◨ Fig. 4.23. It is then clear that, flukes apart, $EV = CV$ for a change in p_1 only if the map of indifference curves is obtained by shifting vertically any one of them, the case of quasi-linear utility function (linear in good 2, residual income) $u(x_1, x_2) = f(x_1) + x_2$, i.e. no income effects in the demand for good 1: Marshall's case of a constant marginal utility of money. Otherwise it can be proved that $EV > CV$ for normal goods, $EV < CV$ for inferior goods. We only prove the first inequality, for the case of a decrease of the sole

4.16 · Money Metric Utility Function, Equivalent Variation, Compensating Variation

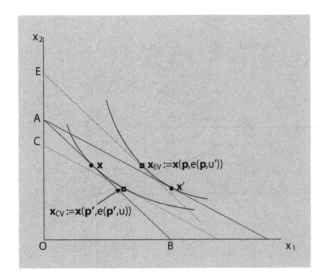

■ **Fig. 4.23** Equivalent and compensating variation when p_1 decreases and this does not affect the (Marshallian) income of the consumer. The initial budget line is AB, the consumer's initial choice is **x**, the new choice after p_1 decreases is **x**'; **p** is initial money prices, **p**' the new prices; $u = v(\mathbf{p}, m)$, $u' = v(\mathbf{p}', m)$ are the initial and final utility levels. Assume $p_2 = 1$ before and after the change, then $OA = m$, the equivalent variation is OE–OA (positive), and the compensating variation is OA–OC (positive too and smaller). Except for flukes, one obtains AE = CA only if all the indifference curves are parallel vertical shifts of one of them, in which case the vertical distance between them is constant, and $x_1 = x_{1EV}$, $x_1' = x_{1CV}$. Note that if **p**' is the initial price and **p** the new price, and therefore **x**' is the initial and **x** the final position of the consumer, then EV = OC–OA, negative, and CV = OA–OE, negative too and larger in absolute value, so in both cases *algebraically* it is EV > CV

price of good 1 from p_1° to p_1'. (Because we shall need to use p_1 to indicate the *variable* p_1, now we indicate its initial value as p_1°.)

In ■ Fig. 4.24, you find (with, as usual, quantities in abscissa) the two (inverse) compensated demand curves for good 1 corresponding to the initial and to the final utility level, and the (inverse) Marshallian demand curve for good 1 which obviously goes through points (x_1, p_1°) and (x_1', p_1'),[48] all three curves as functions of p_1. The normality of good 1 ensures that each compensated (inverse) demand curve for good 1 is steeper than the Marshallian (inverse) demand curve when the two demand curves cross, because the change in demand along a compensated demand curve only reflects the substitution effect, while the change in demand along a Marshallian demand curve also includes an income effect with the same sign (for normal goods) as the substitution effect, so it is greater. We prove below that CV can be shown to be the area of trapezoid $p_1^\circ ABp_1'$, EV the area of trapezoid $p_1^\circ HKp_1'$.

---

48 *Exercise*: If x_1 is a normal good, use the Slutsky equation to prove that the drawing in ■ Fig. 4.24 of the Marshallian demand function as less steep than the compensated demand functions is correct.

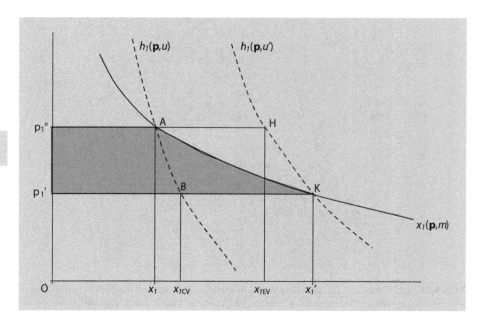

◘ **Fig. 4.24** Marshallian demand curve of the consumer for normal good 1 (when income is m) is the continuous-line curve through points A and K; the broken-line curves are the compensated demand curves. Initial demand for good 1 is x_1, final demand (after p_1 decreases to p_1') is x_1'. CV is the area of trapezoid $p_1°ABp_1'$, EV the area of trapezoid $p_1°HKp_1'$; SV (surplus variation, the variation in consumer surplus) is the area (highlighted in grey) of trapezoid $p_1°AKp_1'$. If price goes down to p_1' but the consumer's income m is decreased to $m - $ CV, the consumer demands x_{1CV}. If at the old price $p_1°$ the consumer's income is increased to $m +$ EV, the consumer demands x_{1EV}

The area $p_1°AKp_1'$ enclosed in ◘ Fig. 4.24 between the Marshallian demand curve, the vertical axis and the two horizontal price lines at $p_1°$ and p_1' measures a new notion, the *variation in consumer surplus* or **surplus variation**, SV. This is because *consumer surplus* is defined as the area enclosed between the Marshallian demand curve and the ordinate, above the price horizontal line; it was introduced in ▶ Sect. 4.12, I discuss it in greater detail in ▶ Sect. 4.22. ◘ Figure 4.24 shows that *for normal goods* EV > SV > CV; equality among the three variations obtains if EV = CV, which holds when the Marshallian demand curve is also the Hicksian one owing to absence of income effects.

Proof To prove the above statements, I use the connection between differentiation and integration, $f(x_0) - f(x_1) = \int_{x_1}^{x_0} f'(x)dx$. CV can be expressed as CV = $e(\mathbf{p}°, u) - e(\mathbf{p'}, u)$ where $\mathbf{p}° = (p_1°, 1)$ and $\mathbf{p'} = (p_1', 1)$, so the variation of $e(\mathbf{p}, u)$ is a function only of p_1; hence we can obtain CV as the definite integral, from $e(\mathbf{p'}, u)$ to $e(\mathbf{p}°, u)$, of the derivative of $e(\mathbf{p}, u)$ with respect to p_1, CV = $\int_{p_1'}^{p_1^0} \frac{\partial e(p, u)}{\partial p_1} dp_1$; by Shephard's Lemma it is $\partial e(\mathbf{p}, u)/\partial p_1 = h_1(\mathbf{p}, u)$; hence CV = $\int_{p_1'}^{p_1^0} h_1(p, u) dp_1$. Thus if in ◘ Fig. 4.31 we draw $h_1(\mathbf{p}, u)$, the compensated

4.16 · Money Metric Utility Function, Equivalent Variation, Compensating Variation

demand curve for good 1 at the *initial* utility level, it goes through point $(x_1, p_1°)$, and CV is the area between this compensated demand curve and the ordinate enclosed by horizontal lines at height $p_1°$ and p_1'. Analogously, since $m = e(\mathbf{p}', u')$, we can express the equivalent variation as $EV = e(p°, u')-e(p', u')$ and we can obtain EV as the definite integral of the derivative of $e(\mathbf{p}, u)$ with respect to p_1 from $e(\mathbf{p}', u')$ to $e(\mathbf{p}°, u')$, that is $EV = \int_{p_1'}^{p_1°} h_1(p, u')dp_1$, therefore EV is the analogous area but obtained from $h_1(\mathbf{p}, u')$, the compensated demand curve associated with the final utility and therefore going through (x_1', p_1'); this area is definitely larger than the CV area if $h_1(\mathbf{p}, u')$ is to the right of $h_1(\mathbf{p}, u)$, as must be the case if p_1 has decreased and good 1 is normal (if p_1 has increased, it suffices to note that by definition $CV(\mathbf{p} \to \mathbf{p}', m) = -EV(\mathbf{p}' \to \mathbf{p}, m)$, so since the signs are reversed it remains true that algebraically $EV > CV$). If good 1 is inferior, then $h_1(\mathbf{p}, u)$ is above $h1(\mathbf{p}, u')$, if $x_1' > x_1$ the Marshallian (inverse) demand curve is steeper than the two compensated demand curves, if $x_1' < x_1$ it is locally upward sloping (good 1 is a Giffen good). If there are no income effects, Marshallian and Hicksian demand curve coincide, $EV = SV = CV$. ∎

When EV and CV differ, which measure is more appropriate can sometimes be decided on the basis of the problem. I give two examples. Assume all consumers are identical. (i) Suppose the government can choose to allocate an unexpected revenue increase either to a lump-sum reduction in personal income taxation, or to policies whose effect will be a reduction in the price of a good. Here the relevant issue is the comparison of the lump-sum[49] tax reduction (= possible income increase) with the EV (= income increase equivalent to price reduction). (ii) Suppose a price reduction for a good can be achieved via public investments financed by a lump-sum tax. Here the relevant issue is whether the price reduction with income reduction makes each consumer better off: this will be the case if the lump-sum tax is less than the CV. Verify graphically!

Arriving at estimates of EV, CV, SV is one of the main purposes of attempts at estimation of demand functions. These will generally estimate the actual demand function, thus allowing a measure of SV only; compensated demand functions are not observable. But it is argued that for small variations SV is a good approximation to EV and to CV, and particularly so for goods whose demand is not very sensitive to income variations. Thus SV is used as a substitute for CV or EV.

4.17 Constant Marginal Utility of Money. Consumer Surplus. Reservation Prices

In this section the notion of consumer surplus is further clarified with the help of the notion of *reservation prices*.

---

49 A lump-sum tax is a fixed sum of money the consumer must pass to the state, independent of prices or of her income.

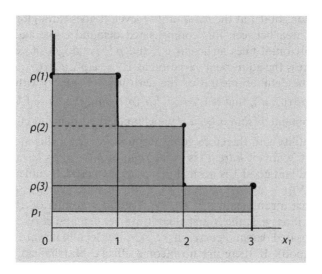

Fig. 4.25 Individual demand for discrete good 1 and reservation prices. The grey area is consumer surplus if all three units are paid p_1

Consider a consumer's (non-increasing) demand for good 1; assume her income m and all prices except the price of good 1 are given; we can consider her demand for good 1, x_1, to depend only on p_1. The **reservation price** $\rho(x_1)$ is the maximum unit price p_1 the consumer is ready to pay for the purchase of the quantity x_1 of good 1. If the good is divisible and $x_1(p_1)$ is a continuous decreasing function, then $\rho(x_1)$ is simply the inverse function of $x_1(p_1)$. If the good is discrete, e.g. bottles of whiskey, and can only be purchased in integer amounts, $\rho(n)$ is *the highest price at which the consumer buys n units of the good.* Clearly it is *also a price at which the consumer is indifferent between buying n−1 or n units of the good*, and I will assume it is the unique such price. Then the consumer's demand for bottles of whiskey (assuming there is a single brand) might have the shape of ◘ Fig. 4.25. A price so ever slightly above $\rho(2)$ induces the consumer to demand only 1 bottle. (The difference between two successive reservation prices will generally not be constant.)

If we represent the consumer's utility as $u(x_1, m - x_1 p_1)$, i.e. as depending on the units of good 1 and on residual income $m^R := m - x_1 p_1$, then $\rho(n)$ satisfies

$$u(n, m - n\rho(n)) = u(n - 1, m - (n - 1)\rho(n)).$$

This says that $\rho(n)$ is the price p_1 at which the consumer's utility is the same if she buys n units and remains with residual income $m - n\rho(n)$, or if she buys $n - 1$ units and remains with the greater residual income $m - (n - 1)\rho(n)$. In general (i.e. without quasi-linear utility), this equation need not determine a unique solution, as ◘ Fig. 4.26 shows; then $\rho(n)$ is the maximum of the prices that satisfy this equation. A maximum such price will exist, unless even when $p_1 = m/n$ and to buy n units of good 1 would absorb all of m, the consumer prefers to buy n units of good 1 to buying only $n-1$ units.

4.17 · Constant Marginal Utility of Money. Consumer Surplus. Reservation Prices

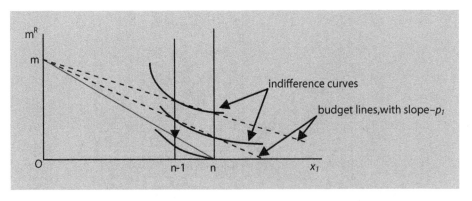

Fig. 4.26 Two different prices p_1 at which the consumer is indifferent between buying n or $n-1$ units of discrete good 1. A maximum such price exists if at the price $p_1' = m/n$ the indifference curve through $x_1 = n$ passes below the basket: $(x_1 = n-1, m^R = m - p_1'(n-1))$, indicated as ▼ in the figure

The meaning of a constant marginal utility of money for discrete goods is the following: reservation price $\rho(n)$ remains the same, whether all the n units are paid $\rho(n)$, or each successive unit is paid its reservation price; in the latter case in ◘ Fig. 4.25 the consumer pays for three units the sum of the vertical rectangles representing the payment, for each successive unit, of its reservation price. If all units are paid the same price, the consumer pays less than this, and consumer surplus is the excess of the payment of all reservation prices over what the consumer actually pays, in ◘ Fig. 4.25 it is the grey area when the consumer buys three units and pays p_1 for all three.

If utility is quasi-linear, $u(x_1, m^R) = z(x_1) + m^R$ with m^R residual income, then the above equation that determines $\rho(n)$ has a unique solution, and—prove as an *Exercise*—it simplifies to

$$\rho(n) = z(n) - z(n-1).$$

If the reservation prices for 1, 2, etc., units of a discrete good differ among consumers, and the total number of units demanded of the good is high, then the jumps up of market demand when price decreases are each time of only one unit, the market demand curve is a step function but the steps are so small and frequent that the market demand curve for the good can be treated as if continuous. This is the justification for the assumption that goods are divisible even when in fact they are not.

Then going back to the symbols of ▶ Sect. 4.16, assuming $u(x, y) = z(x) + y$ where y is residual income (with price 1) used to buy other goods and x is the quantity of the good under examination, whose price is p, individual consumer surplus is (◘ Fig. 4.27)

$$S(p) = \int_0^{x(p)} \frac{\partial u}{\partial x} dx - px(p) = z(x(p)) - px(p).$$

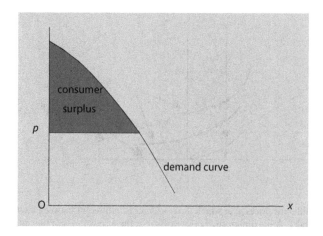

◘ **Fig. 4.27** Consumer surplus

It is the area enclosed between the ordinate and the consumer's (inverse) demand curve for the x-good, above the horizontal line at height p. The price of the x-good measures the marginal utility of the optimal x.

A different graphical representation is in (x, y) space: in ◘ Fig. 4.28, with $p_y = 1$. for given m and p the consumer's optimal choice is $(x^\wedge, y)$; the surplus, the maximum amount of income the consumer would be ready to give up rather than be excluded from buying x at price p, is the difference between m and the minimum income OA that would allow the consumer to reach the same utility $u = m$ as if $x = 0$, that is to reach the indifference curve through $(0, m)$; because of quasi-linear utility (all indifference curves are parallel vertical transpositions of any one of them), the latter indifference curve would be reached with minimum income at $(x^\wedge, y^*)$ and consumer surplus is $y - y^* = m - $OA.

So in this case the consumer surplus is really the compensating variation CV when the initial choice is $(0, m)$ (because p is so high that the demand for the x-good is zero) and the final choice is $(x^\wedge, y)$. If utility is not quasi-linear, the x-good optimal choice corresponding to the minimum income that allows the same utility as at $(0, m)$ will not in general be $x^\wedge$, nor will this minimum income be OA, see the red indifference curve and the explanation under ◘ Fig. 4.28.

Individual consumer surplus is a sum of money; this means that one can add the consumer surpluses of the several consumers, obtaining the *Marshallian aggregate consumers' surplus*, or *consumers' surplus* for brevity. This is the area under the *market* (inverse) demand curve for the good, down to the horizontal line at the height of the given price of the good. It measures the maximum total sum of money consumers would be ready to pay—under constant marginal utility of money—in order not to be forbidden from purchasing the x-good at price p. Marshall proposed to use it for policy evaluations, in the way we have seen one can use the compensating variation. Marshall himself stressed the difficulty with determining consumers' surplus because 'we cannot guess at all accurately how much of anything people would buy at prices very different from those which

4.17 · Constant Marginal Utility of Money. Consumer Surplus. Reservation Prices

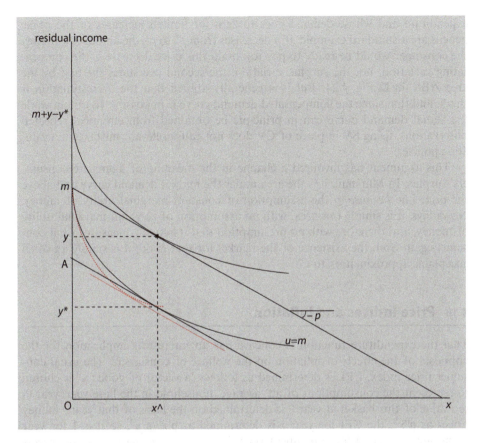

◻ **Fig. 4.28** Indifference curves (black) of quasi-linear utility $u = z(x) + y$, and consumer choice at price p. As long as the x-good is not indispensable for survival, indifference curves reach the ordinate. The consumer's initial endowment is $(0, m)$ and her optimal choice at the given price p is $(x^\wedge, y)$; if denied access to the x-good market, her utility is the one associated with the indifference curve through the endowment point, so (with strictly convex indifference curves such that $\partial u/\partial x > p$ at $x = 0$) we can find y^* such that she is indifferent between $(0, m)$ and $(x^\wedge, y^*)$; rather than be excluded from the x-good's market, the consumer is ready to pay up to m–OA, because OA is the minimum income that allows her to obtain $u(0, m) = u(x^\wedge, y^*)$; under quasi-linear utility m–OA $= y - y^*$ because all indifference curves are vertical translations of any one of them

they are accustomed to pay for it....Our list of demand prices is therefore highly conjectural except in the neighbourhood of the customary price' (*Principles* III, VI, 5; 1972 p. 110). But he added that this is not a great problem because what is important is not total consumers' surplus but rather its *variation* for limited variations of the price. The surplus *variation*, he argued, is a sufficiently well-defined notion.

But in general it is not legitimate to assume that the marginal utility of money is constant; it would mean that the consumer's demand for the good does not change if the first units of the good cost more than the last units; this can be approximately true only for goods that absorb a very small portion of total

324   **Chapter 4 · Consumers and the Exchange Economy**

expenditure and whose demand goes to zero for limited increases of the price: pencils are a standard example. If p decreases from $p°$ to p', the amount of money the consumer would be ready to pay to obtain this price decrease is the compensating variation, not the surplus variation: the second overstates the first by the area ABK in ◘ Fig. 4.24. But it is generally argued that the overestimation is small, and that since the compensated demand curve is impossible to obtain while the actual demand curve can in principle be obtained from empirical repeated observations, using SV in place of CV does not cause relevant mistakes in evaluating policies.

This argument has favoured a change in the meaning of aggregate consumers' surplus. In Marshall, it is the area under the market demand curve and above the price line *because of* the assumption of constant marginal utility of money. Nowadays, it is simply this area, with no assumption of constant marginal utility of money, and therefore with no presumption that it actually measures what consumers gain from the existence of the market for that good; it is simply an often acceptable approximation to CV.

4.18 Price Indices and Inflation

That the expenditure function is concave has an interesting implication for the appraisal of the effects of inflation on the welfare of consumers. The usual consumer price index, CPI, is determined as follows: a vector of goods x^0 is chosen to represent the consumptions of an 'average' household in the base year, year 0; the value of this basket at year 0 is determined on the basis of that year's money prices as $p^0 x^0$; the CPI for year t is determined as $p^t x^0 / p^0 x^0$, so it is 1 for year 0 and greater than 1 for subsequent years if money prices have risen, the excess over 1 yielding the percentage variation relative to the base year. This percentage variation measures the percentage by which the income of the average household should increase so as to allow purchasing the same consumption basket x^0, and it is usually argued that if the income increases by that percentage, the household is as well of as before.

The interesting observation is that, if *relative* prices change too, the household whose income increases sufficiently to buy $x°$ at the new prices will in fact be better off than before, because the money income sufficient to buy x^0 will be used to buy a different basket allowing a higher utility level (x^* in ◘ Fig. 4.29: in this Figure, the reader is asked to draw the budget line that at the new prices allows no change in utility). So if inflation is accompanied by changes in relative prices, in order for the utility of a household not to decrease its m needs to increase by a lesser percentage than CPI.

The CPI is an instance of a *Laspeyres* price index that measures the ratio of the new to the initial value of the *initial* basket:

$$\text{LPI}(t) = \frac{p^t \cdot x^0}{p^0 \cdot x^0}, \quad t > 0.$$

4.17 · Constant Marginal Utility of Money. Consumer Surplus. Reservation Prices

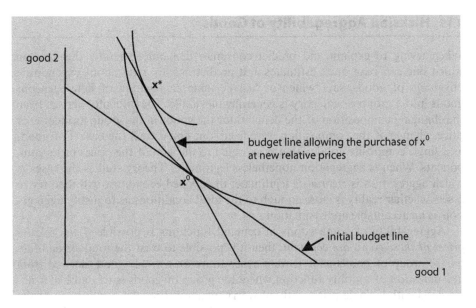

◘ **Fig. 4.29** If relative prices change, an income sufficient to purchase the old basket allows reaching a higher utility

It indicates how much monetary income is necessary to buy the old basket at the new prices if the initial year income is so measured as to be equal to 1. A *Paasche price index* on the contrary chooses as base basket the *final* one:

$$\text{PPI}(t) = \frac{p^t \cdot x^t}{p^0 \cdot x^t}, \quad t > 0.$$

and therefore if, e.g. it is equal to 1.2, and t is the current year while 0 is last year, it tells us that today's income is 20% greater than the income which at last year's prices would have allowed buying the basket bought today (and the latter income is the one chosen as the basis to determine the percentage variation).

There is a clear connection between Laspeyres price index and CV. Suppose a consumer at time 0 has income $p^0 x^0$ and demands x^0, and at time t has income $p^t x^t$ and demands x^t. If relative prices do not change, the Laspeyres price index minus 1 correctly measures the compensating variation as a percentage of the initial income $p^0 x^0$, because then a percentage change of money income equal to the percentage change in money prices leaves the budget constraint unchanged and hence allows reaching the same utility level. If relative prices change, the percentage variation of the Laspeyres price index overestimates the percentage CV, for the reason pointed out above.

326   Chapter 4 · Consumers and the Exchange Economy

4.19 Hicksian Aggregability of Goods

When trying to explain and predict consumer demand, generally the data on which one can base one's estimates and predictions are data about expenditure on *groups* of goods, say, 'wine', or 'meat'; some aggregation of heterogeneous goods into a group or category is generally inevitable. The difficulty derives from the changing composition of the demand for the goods in the group as income or prices change: if the composition were fixed, one could treat the basket of goods as a single composite good with a price equal to the sum of the prices of its components. When is aggregation nonetheless legitimate? Theory studies the cases in which aggregation is *rigorously* legitimate; the applied economist will then try to assess whether reality is close enough to the ideal conditions as to justify aggregation as an acceptable approximation.

Aggregability of some goods in demand functions *is* possible *if the relative prices of these goods are constant*; then it is possible to treat the total expenditure on the group of goods as if it were expenditure on a single good, derived from maximization of a utility function where the group of goods is treated like a single good with a single price, without worrying about how the *composition* of the demand for the goods in the group changes when other prices change. This result is called the ***Hicksian composite commodity theorem***,[50] The constancy of relative prices among a group of goods is called the ***Hicksian aggregability condition***.

Assume a consumer with given income, who maximizes utility over consumption goods that can be divided into two subvectors, x-goods (of which there are k) and y-goods; the demand for x-goods is represented by subvector $\mathbf{x}$ and the demand for the y-goods by subvector $\mathbf{y}$, with money price subvectors, respectively, $\mathbf{p}$ for the x-goods, and $\boldsymbol{\pi}$ for the y-goods. The (Marshallian) UMP is

$$\max_{\mathbf{x},\mathbf{y}} \ u(\mathbf{x},\mathbf{y}) \ \text{s.t.} \ \mathbf{px} + \mathbf{py} = m.$$

Let $\mathbf{x}(\mathbf{p}, \boldsymbol{\pi}, m)$, $\mathbf{y}(\mathbf{p}, \boldsymbol{\pi}, m)$ be the solution. Assume the *relative* prices of the x-goods among themselves are constant over time. Let $\mathbf{p}^\circ$ be the value of $\mathbf{p}$ in a base year; by assumption in another year $\mathbf{p} = \alpha \mathbf{p}^\circ$ with α a variable positive scalar. Define a new good X whose quantity is determined by $X = \mathbf{p}^\circ \mathbf{x}$, and define its price as $P = \alpha$. Good X can be interpreted as 'expenditure on x-goods at constant prices $\mathbf{p}^\circ$'; $PX = \alpha \mathbf{p}^\circ \mathbf{x}$ gives *actual* expenditure on the x-goods. It is $PX = \mathbf{px}$ by construction, and $X(P, \boldsymbol{\pi}, m) = \mathbf{p}^\circ \mathbf{x}(\alpha \mathbf{p}^\circ, \boldsymbol{\pi}, m)$. The expenditure function can be written $e(p_1,\ldots,p_k, \boldsymbol{\pi}, u) = e(\alpha p_1^\circ,\ldots,\alpha p_k^\circ, \boldsymbol{\pi}, u) = e^*(\alpha, \boldsymbol{\pi}, u)$ since $p_1^\circ,\ldots,p_k^\circ$ are fixed. If now we differentiate e^* with respect to α, by Shephard's Lemma we obtain:

$$\frac{\partial e^*}{\partial \alpha} = \frac{\partial e}{\partial p_1} \cdot \frac{\partial p_1}{\partial \alpha} + \ldots + \frac{\partial e}{\partial p_k} \cdot \frac{\partial p_k}{\partial \alpha} = \sum_i p_i^\circ x_i = X.$$

Thus α behaves like the price of a good whose quantity X is measured in such units that its quantity increases by p_i° units for each unit increase of x_i. It can be

---

50 I follow the treatment of the issue in Varian (1992) and in Deaton and Muellbauer (1980).

4.18 · Price Indices and Inflation

easily shown that $e^*(\alpha, \pi, u)$ satisfies all the properties of an expenditure function: it is non-negative, continuous, strictly increasing in u and non-decreasing in π and α, homogeneous of degree 1 and concave in π and α.[51] Since an expenditure function contains the same information on preferences as the utility function from which it derives, we can consider e^* to derive from a utility function $U(X, \mathbf{y})$ over the single good X and the y-goods.[52] In conclusion, P and X behave in the same way as ordinary price and quantity of a good. Note that aggregability does *not* imply that the proportions x_i/x_j between x-goods do not change with changes in α or π or m.

Hicksian aggregability is useful when one wants to study the demand for a single consumption good whose price is altered by something (e.g. taxation) which leaves other relative prices unchanged. Then all other goods form subvector $\mathbf{x}$, while subvector $\mathbf{y}$ is a scalar, the quantity of the single good under study. Hicksian aggregability says that we can consider the demand for good y to depend on its price π and on the scalar $\alpha = P$ that indicates the price level of all other goods (e.g. the consumer price index):

$$y = y(P, \pi, m).$$

---

51 The only property that may not be immediately obvious is that concavity also holds with respect to variations of α. But $e(\alpha p_1{}^\circ,...,\alpha p_k{}^\circ, \pi, u)$ is concave relative to $(\mathbf{p}, \pi)$ whatever the direction in which prices change, therefore it is concave also for simultaneous variations of some prices in the same proportion, which is the meaning of a change in α.

52 The same result can be reached via the indirect utility function. Let $v(\mathbf{p}, \pi, m)$ be the original indirect utility function, derived from $u(\mathbf{x}, \mathbf{y})$. Define a new indirect utility function as.
$$V(P, , m) = \max_{x,y} u(\mathbf{x}, \mathbf{y}) \text{ subject to } m - P\,\mathbf{p}^\circ\mathbf{x} - \mathbf{y} = 0.$$

Applying the Envelope Theorem for the case of constrained optimization, we obtain

$$\partial V(P, \pi, m)/\partial P = -\lambda \mathbf{p}^\circ \mathbf{x}\left(\alpha \mathbf{p}^\circ, \pi, m\right) = -\lambda X,$$
$$\partial V(P, \pi, m)/\partial \pi_i = -\lambda y_i\left(\alpha \mathbf{p}^\circ, \pi, m\right) = \partial v\left(\alpha \mathbf{p}^\circ, \pi, m\right)/\partial \pi_i,$$
$$\partial V(P, \pi, m)/\partial m = \lambda = \partial v\left(\alpha \mathbf{p}^\circ, \pi, m\right)/\partial m;$$

therefore by Roy's identity.

$$X(P, \pi, m) = -\frac{\partial V(P, \pi, m)/\partial P}{\partial V(P, \pi, m)/\partial m} = \mathbf{p}^\circ \mathbf{x}(\mathbf{p}, \pi, m)$$

$$y_i(P, \pi, m) = -\frac{\partial V(P, \pi, m)/\partial \pi_i}{\partial V(P, \pi, m)/\partial m} = -\frac{\partial v(p, \pi, m)}{\partial v(p, \pi, m)/\partial m} = y_i(\mathbf{p}, \pi, m).$$

Thus $V(P, \pi, m)$ yields the correct demand functions for the goods in subvector $\mathbf{y}$, and the correct aggregate index X for the demands for the goods in subvector $\mathbf{x}$. A given indirect utility function is associated with a unique direct utility function, called *dual* to it; therefore we can consider $V(P, \pi, m)$ to derive from a utility function $U(X, \mathbf{y})$ dual to it that satisfies:

$$U(X, \mathbf{y}) = \min_{P, \pi} V(P, \pi, m) \text{ such that } PX + \mathbf{y} = m.$$

And conversely we can see $V(P, \pi, m)$ as resulting from $\max_{X,y} U(X, \mathbf{y})$ s.t. $PX + \mathbf{y} = m$.

328   Chapter 4 · Consumers and the Exchange Economy

Because of homogeneity of degree zero of demand functions, we can write this demand function as

$$y = y^*(1, \pi \cdot 1/P, m/P)$$

In other words, we can consider the demand for good y to depend only on 'real' income and on its price relative to the price of 'all other goods'.

4.20 Revealed Preference

In 1938 Paul Samuelson argued that it is not necessary to base consumer theory on axioms about preferences that are only justifiable, if at all, by a process of introspection which concludes to the existence of a preference relation not amenable to direct observation by outsiders. He proposed to adopt a different approach which starts from axioms about observable entities: the observed consumption baskets demanded by consumers.

The aims of the proposal were not radical: there was no desire to subvert standard consumer theory, only to give it a foundation not requiring the existence of subjective unobservable entities. The main question therefore was what axioms made directly on observable choices allow one to obtain the *same* results on demand as derived from standard preference theory. Having found those axioms, if observable choices do comply with them, then consumers behave *as if* they had standard preferences representable via a utility function; then one can ask how these as-if preferences are at least partly *revealed* by observed choices.

Suppose a consumer has standard preferences[53] and behaves according to them, how does this restrict her observable choices?

When a consumer, endowed with an income m and faced with prices p, chooses a consumption vector $\mathbf{x}$ while she could afford another consumption vector $\mathbf{y}$ because $\mathbf{py} \leq m$, it must be the case that she prefers $\mathbf{x}$ to $\mathbf{y}$, or at least that she is indifferent between $\mathbf{x}$ and $\mathbf{y}$ and has chosen by tossing a coin. Thus the choice of the consumer *reveals* that $\mathbf{x} \succsim \mathbf{y}$. Define the ***revealed preference relation*** $\mathbf{x}R\mathbf{Py}$ as follows:

Revealed Preference. *A consumption vector* $\mathbf{x}$ *is revealed preferred to* $\mathbf{y}$, *and we write* $\mathbf{x}R\mathbf{Py}$, *if* $\mathbf{x}$ *is demanded when* $\mathbf{y} \neq \mathbf{x}$ *could have been demanded because affordable,* $\mathbf{py} \leq \mathbf{px}$.

Now assume that utility-maximizing baskets are always unique (strictly convex indifference surfaces or perfect complementarity—that is, L-shaped indifference curves—plus positive prices); then when $\mathbf{x}$ is chosen while $\mathbf{y}$ is affordable, i.e. when $\mathbf{py} \leq \mathbf{px}(\mathbf{p}, m)$, it cannot be $\mathbf{x} \sim \mathbf{y}$; revealed preference implies strict preference. Consistency then requires that, *if preferences do not change as between different observed choices*, if on one occasion the consumer reveals she prefers $\mathbf{x}$ to

---

53 That is, complete, transitive, continuous and locally non-satiated preferences.

4.19 · Hicksian Aggregability of Goods

y, then one must not observe that on other occasions she reveals she prefers **y** to **x** , i.e. when she chooses **y** it must not be possible for her to choose **x**). Then the following axiom is respected:

Weak Axiom of Revealed Preference (WARP). If **x***RP***y***, it is not observed that* **y***RP***x***. In other words, if* **x** *is demanded when income is enough to demand* **y***, then whenever the consumer demands* **y***, income is not enough to demand* **x***.*

Utilizing Marshallian demand symbols, let **x**(**p**, *m*) be the consumer's demand vector at (**p**, *m*), and with **x**(**p'**, *m'*) the choice of the consumer at (**p'**, *m'*). Then the WARP becomes:

WARP (equivalent specification): Let (**p'**, *m'*) *and* (**p''**, *m''*) *represent budget constraints, let* **x**(**p**, *m*) *indicate revealed choices, and assume* **x**(**p'**, *m'*) ≠ **x**(**p''**, *m''*). *If* **p'x**(**p'**, *m'*) ≥ **p'x**(**p''**, *m''*) *then* **p''x**(**p'**, *m'*) > **p''x**(**p''**, *m''*).

The WARP axiom as thus specified implicitly assumes that optimal choices are unique; its definition does not exclude (**p'**, *m'*) = (*t***p''**, *tm''*), then if at (**p'**, *m'*) the consumer is indifferent between two different consumption baskets **x** and **y**, one might observe the consumer choosing **x** at (**p'**, *m'*) and **y** at (**p''**, *m''*), violating the WARP as here specified[54] in spite of having 'standard' preferences.

But if optimal choices are always unique and nevertheless the choices of a consumer in one occasion show **x**RP**y** and in a second occasion show **y**RP**x**, this does not necessarily mean that the consumer does not have a 'standard' preference relation or does not act according to it. We can distinguish several reasons why.

Reason One: preference may be non-standard, for example the preference order can depend on prices (snob effect), or on what other consumers do (other-regarding preferences): between the first and the second observation the preference order between consumption baskets may have changed because, for example, fashion has changed.

Reason Two: standard preferences can have changed in the meanwhile because of new information or because experience alters tastes: between the first and the second observation, one can have learnt that a certain good damages health or can have developed a taste for good wine. And the observations cannot be very close in time if relative prices must sufficiently differ.

Reason Three: preferences may not have changed but circumstances may differ, an ice cream can be preferred or not to a cup of tea depending on how hot the day is, a restaurant can be preferred to another one or not depending on how recently it was last visited. That is, the WARP makes sense only for comparison of choices at different prices but in otherwise identical circumstances. (This

---

54 I am following the Houtthaker definition that assumes single-valued optimal choices. Different axioms of revealed preference that accept multiple-valued optimal choices or extensions of the domain of choice to more general sets than consumption goods budget sets can bring to results different from those here presented.

330   Chapter 4 · Consumers and the Exchange Economy

is the less easy to presume, the less one is concerned with average demand over long time periods. Yearly demand for ice creams or yearly visits to a restaurant need worry much less about different circumstances than choices over a day or a week. Accordingly, the conjecture can be advanced that the revealed preference approach could only be born in the framework of long-period analyses, in which one studies average choices over periods of some length.)

Thus it seems extremely difficult to derive from empirical observation evidence on whether preferences are or not such as to cause choices to conform to the WARP. But at a theoretical abstract level one can still ask, supposing the difficulties pointed out above do not arise (preferences do not change, etc.), whether the observation, that the choices of a consumer do not violate the WARP, suffices to conclude that the consumer has preferences representable through a strictly quasi-concave monotonic utility function.

The answer is yes, when there are only two goods and both are at least sometimes in positive demand;[55] not necessarily, when there are more than two goods. With three or more goods, it is possible to construct examples of a finite number of observed choices that do not violate the WARP but are impossible to rationalize on the basis of a utility function. The following example is due to Hicks. In a three-goods economy, let $\mathbf{p} = (p_1, p_2, p_3)$ and $\mathbf{x} = (x_1, x_2, x_3)$; a consumer with a constant income $m = 8$ makes the following choices, all of value equal to 8, in three different price situations:

A: when $\mathbf{p} = \mathbf{p}_A = (2,1,2)$ she chooses $\mathbf{x}_A = (1,2,2)$;
B: when $\mathbf{p} = \mathbf{p}_B = (2,2,1)$ she chooses $\mathbf{x}_B = (2,1,2)$;
C: when $\mathbf{p} = \mathbf{p}_C = (1,2,2)$ she chooses $\mathbf{x}_C = (2,2,1)$.

The WARP is not contradicted; e.g. $\mathbf{x}_A RP \mathbf{x}_C$ and when $\mathbf{x}_C$ is chosen it is $\mathbf{p}_C \mathbf{x}_A = 9 > \mathbf{p}_C \mathbf{x}_C$, but $\mathbf{x}_A RP \mathbf{x}_C$, $\mathbf{x}_C RP \mathbf{x}_B$ and $\mathbf{x}_B RP \mathbf{x}_A$ (check!), which violates transitivity of preferences.

It is possible to specify a condition implying that no such 'cycle' is exhibited by observed choices; it requires the notion of *indirectly* revealed preference. Let us now say that when prices are $\mathbf{p}$, if $\mathbf{x}$ is chosen and another basket $\mathbf{x}$' such that $\mathbf{p}\mathbf{x}$' $\leq \mathbf{p}\mathbf{x}$ is not chosen, $\mathbf{x}$ is *directly revealed preferred* to $\mathbf{x}$': this is what up to now we have simply called revealed preference and therefore I still indicate it as $\mathbf{x}RP\mathbf{x}$'. If basket $\mathbf{x}^a$ is directly revealed preferred to $\mathbf{x}^b$ and $\mathbf{x}^b$ is directly revealed preferred to $\mathbf{x}^c$, and $\mathbf{x}^c$ is directly revealed preferred to $\mathbf{x}^d$, ... we say that $\mathbf{x}^a$ is *indirectly revealed preferred* to $\mathbf{x}^c$, to $\mathbf{x}^d$, ... It is now possible to define a new axiom:

Strong Axiom of Revealed Preference, SARP: *Assume demand is always single-valued. If $\mathbf{x}$ is directly or indirectly revealed preferred to $\mathbf{x}$', and if $\mathbf{x}$ is not equal to $\mathbf{x}$', then $\mathbf{x}$' is not directly or indirectly revealed preferred to $\mathbf{x}$.*

The central result of revealed preference theory is

---

55   If a good is never demanded, preferences might be lexicographic.

4.20 · Revealed Preference

■■ Proposition 4.17

The SARP implies the existence of a complete and transitive preference relation rationalizing the observed choices.

For a proof, cf. Mas-Colell et al. (1995, pp. 91–92). If goods are perfectly divisible, then the SARP implies the derivability of observed choices from a strictly quasi-concave, monotonic utility function. The converse is obvious.

The SARP obviously implies the WARP; therefore if the WARP is violated, so is the SARP. The same caveats as to empirical observations 'contradicting' the WARP also apply to the SARP. The SARP too implicitly assumes demand is single-valued.

Another axiom requires a new notion. We have stipulated that when prices are $\mathbf{p}$, if $\mathbf{x}$ is chosen and $\mathbf{x}$' such that $\mathbf{px}' \leq \mathbf{px}$ is not chosen, $\mathbf{x}$ is *directly* revealed preferred to $\mathbf{x}$'. If in the same situation $\mathbf{px}' < \mathbf{px}$ let us say that $\mathbf{x}$ is *strictly directly* revealed preferred to $\mathbf{x}$' (then with locally non-satiated preferences $\mathbf{x} > \mathbf{x}$', because $\mathbf{x}$' is below the budget line). Let $\mathbf{x}DIRP\mathbf{y}$ indicate that $\mathbf{x}$ is *directly or indirectly* revealed preferred to $\mathbf{y}$. We can now state a new axiom that does *not* assume that demand is single-valued:

Generalized Axiom of Revealed Preferences, GARP: *If* $\mathbf{x}$ *is directly or indirectly revealed preferred to* $\mathbf{x}$'*, then* $\mathbf{x}$' *is not strictly directly revealed preferred to* $\mathbf{x}$*, i.e.* $\mathbf{x}DIRP\mathbf{x}$' *implies that when* $\mathbf{x}$' *is chosen and the prices at which it is chosen are* $\mathbf{p}$*, it is* $\mathbf{px}' \leq \mathbf{px}$*. In other words, one cannot construct a cycle* $\mathbf{x}^a RP\mathbf{x}^b$*,* $\mathbf{x}^b RP\mathbf{x}^c$*,…,*$\mathbf{x}^{k-1} RP\mathbf{x}^k$*,* $\mathbf{x}^k RP\mathbf{x}^a$*, where one or more of the direct revealed preferences are strict.*

With single-valued demands, the SARP clearly implies the GARP and vice-versa; but the GARP allows for demand *correspondences*, i.e. for the possibility that, when $\mathbf{x}$ is chosen and $\mathbf{y}$ is affordable, it is $\mathbf{x} \sim \mathbf{y}$, while both the WARP and the SARP as here formulated assume this is not possible. It has been constructively proved by Sydney Afriat (1967) that any *finite* collection of empirical observations obeying the GARP can be rationalized as deriving from a locally non-satiated, continuous, concave and monotonic utility function.

Exercise. Prove, in the two-goods case, that the GARP excludes 'thick' indifference curves (indifference 'strips').

But in order to be certain that a continuous *function* (not a correspondence) can be considered a demand function deriving from standard preferences, one would need an indefinite number of demand vectors derived from it to check that they never contradict the GARP; one must assume that this demand function satisfies the SARP.[56] Indeed it can be proved that:

■■ Proposition 4.18

Rationalizable demand functions. *If a Marshallian vectorial demand function* $\mathbf{x}(\mathbf{p}, m)$ *satisfies:*

(a) *homogeneity of degree zero in* $(\mathbf{p}, m)$*;*

---

56 A continuous demand function of perfectly divisible goods is equivalent to an infinite number of observations; so Afriat's proof, that assumes a finite number of observations, does not apply.

332   **Chapter 4 · Consumers and the Exchange Economy**

(b) *balanced budget, i.e.* $\mathbf{px} = m$;
(c) *the SARP.then there is a complete and transitive preference relation $\succsim$ that rationalizes* $\mathbf{x}(\mathbf{p}, m)$, *i.e. such that for all* $(\mathbf{p}, m)$ *it is* $\mathbf{x}(\mathbf{p}, m) \succ \mathbf{y}$ *for every* $\mathbf{y}$ *in the budget set different from* $\mathbf{x}(\mathbf{p}, m)$.

I omit the proof (cf. e.g. Mas-Colell et al. 1995, p. 92). In the other direction, it is clear that a demand *function* derived from a complete, transitive and non-satiated preference relation satisfies the SARP as well as the first two conditions.

The three properties of the demand function listed in Proposition 4.18 can be shown to be *all* the restrictions that a complete, transitive and locally non-satiated preference relation imposes on demand functions. Then comparison with Proposition 4.16 (in ▶ Sect. 4.15) shows that, *when preferences can be represented by a twice continuously differentiable utility function, the SARP is equivalent to the symmetry and negative semidefiniteness of the Slutsky matrix.*

Indeed, it can be proved that:

■■ Proposition 4.19

For a differentiable vectorial demand function implying the existence of a Slutsky matrix, the WARP implies the Compensated Law of Demand (definition in the Proof) and the negative semidefiniteness of the Slutsky matrix. Thus what the SARP adds to the WARP is the symmetry of the Slutsky matrix.

Proof Suppose that originally prices and income are $(\mathbf{p}, m)$ and the consumer's choice is $\mathbf{x}(\mathbf{p}, m)$, to be indicated as $\mathbf{x}$ for brevity. Then $\mathbf{p}$ changes to $\mathbf{p'}$ and we assume that m changes such that the consumer can still just purchase $\mathbf{x}$, i.e. $m' = \mathbf{p'x}$: then m has undergone a ***Slutsky income compensation*** (see point D in ◘ Fig. 4.15a), which is different from a Hicks income compensation but not for infinitesimal price changes, so the Slutsky matrix is the same; see Exercise 4ex31. Let $\mathbf{x'} = \mathbf{x}(\mathbf{p'}, m')$ be the new choice of the consumer, different from $\mathbf{x}$ and therefore revealed preferred to $\mathbf{x}$; under local non-satiation $\mathbf{p'x'} = m' = \mathbf{p'x}$, hence $\mathbf{p'}(\mathbf{x'} - \mathbf{x}) = 0$. The WARP implies that if $\mathbf{x'}$ was not chosen when prices and income were $(\mathbf{p}, m)$ it must be that $\mathbf{x'}$ was not affordable then, i.e. $\mathbf{px'} > m$; hence $\mathbf{px'} - \mathbf{px} = \mathbf{p}(\mathbf{x'} - \mathbf{x}) > 0$; this, together with $\mathbf{p'}(\mathbf{x'} - \mathbf{x}) = 0$, implies

$$\left(\mathbf{p'} - \mathbf{p}\right)\left(\mathbf{x'} - \mathbf{x}\right) < 0.$$

This is called the ***Compensated Law of Demand***: the vector of price variations and the vector of Slutsky-compensated quantity variations form an angle greater than 90°, a result usually expressed by saying that they point in 'opposite' directions. In particular, if only one price changes, say p_i, then $\mathbf{p'} - \mathbf{p} = (0,\ldots,0, \Delta p_i, 0,\ldots,0)$ and $(\mathbf{p'} - p)(\mathbf{x'} - \mathbf{x}) = \Delta p_i \Delta x_i$; in the latter expression it is better to write Δx_i^c to stress that we are considering *compensated* changes in demand. We have thus shown that if only p_i changes, it is $\Delta p_i \Delta x_i^c < 0$, the compensated own price effect is negative (as long as the change in p_i brings about a change of x_i; otherwise it is non-positive). For infinitesimal price changes, the

4.20 · Revealed Preference

Compensated Law of Demand becomes $dp \cdot dx^{c\circ} \leq 0$; we know from ▶ Sect. 4.12 that $dx^c = d\mathbf{h} = S \cdot dp^T$, where S is the Slutsky matrix; substituting, we obtain $d\mathbf{p} \cdot S \cdot d\mathbf{p}^{T\circ} \leq 0$. Since this result holds for any vector $d\mathbf{p}$, matrix S is negative semidefinite. ∎

If *market* demand satisfies all three conditions listed in Proposition 4.18, then it is *as if* it came from a single consumer, a 'representative consumer'. This has some nice implications for the uniqueness and stability of general equilibria. Actually, for those implications it suffices that market demand satisfies the WARP, but it will be seen that even this slightly weaker assumption, which will be referred to as *WAM (Weak Axiom of revealed preference holding for Market demand)*, is quite restrictive.

4.21 Aggregability of Consumers: Gorman Aggregability and the Representative Consumer

When one is interested in Marshallian demand, the existence of a representative consumer requires different conditions from those guaranteeing the existence of a representative consumer in the determination of general equilibrium. The difference is seldom stressed but is of some importance.

Let us start with the Marshallian perspective.

Suppose there are S consumers, distinguished by index $s = 1,\ldots,S$, each one with a Marshallian vectorial demand function $\mathbf{x}^s(\mathbf{p}, m^s)$, $\mathbf{x} \in R^k_+$. For each consumer, income is given, so the analysis does not examine what determines incomes; the prices and rentals of the goods and factors in the endowments of consumers are implicitly treated as given; vector $\mathbf{p}$ includes only a restricted set of prices, the prices of the consumption goods and services consumers demand. Indicate the market (vectorial) demand function deriving from the choices of these S consumers as

$$\mathbf{X}\left(\mathbf{p}, m^1, \ldots, m^S\right) := \sum_{s=1}^{S} \mathbf{x}^s\left(\mathbf{p}, m^s\right),$$

where $\mathbf{p} \in R^k_+$.[57] Four properties of individual demand functions are inherited by this market Marshallian demand function.

First, $\mathbf{X}(\mathbf{p}, m^1, \ldots, m^S)$ is homogeneous of degree zero.

Second, $\mathbf{X}(\mathbf{p}, m^1,\ldots,m^S)$ is continuous if the individual demand functions are continuous.

---

57 In this and subsequent chapters before ▶ Chap. 14, I implicitly assume that no good is a public good (such as street lighting, whose 'consumption' by one does not prevent others from 'consuming' it), all goods are 'rival' goods.

334   Chapter 4 · Consumers and the Exchange Economy

Third, market demand obeys an aggregate analogue of the balanced budget restriction: the sum of incomes equals the sum of values of demands.

Fourth, if for each consumer s it is $\partial x^s_i/\partial p_j = \partial x^s_j/\partial p_i$, the same holds for market demand.

Other properties of market demand require specific assumptions. For example, if when the price of a good decreases all individual demands for it increase, then market demand too increases.

Now let us ask when the Marshallian vectorial market demand function behaves as if coming from a single price-taking consumer endowed with the total income of the economy hence is unaffected by redistributions of a given total income among consumers. This hypothetical single consumer is called a *(**Marshallian**) **representative** **aggregate** **consumer***. By dividing this consumer's income and demands by the number S of consumers in the economy one obtains a *(**Marshallian**) **representative** **average** **consumer***. Both meanings of 'representative consumer' are present in the literature.

A representative consumer only exists in some very special cases. The basic result on this issue is due to Gorman (1953):

■■ **Proposition 4.20**
Gorman form. *Assume S consumers with incomes $m^1,\ldots,m^s,\ldots,m^S$ to be spent on k goods. A Marshallian market demand vector function $X(p, m^1,\ldots,m^S)$ can be written $X(p, m)$ with $m = \sum m^s$, and can be considered to derive from a single consumer with income equal to aggregate income m, if and only if for each consumer s the indirect utility function $v^s(p, m^s)$ has the* **Gorman form**: $v^s(p, m^s) = a^s(p) + b(p)m^s$.

Before the proof, note that the scalar function $a^s(p)$ can differ across consumers, but it must be independent of income; while the scalar function $b(p)$ must be the same for all consumers—or it must be possible, with an opportune choice of units in which to measure utility, to make it so. A complete rigorous proof is not easy and will not be supplied but some indication of how it proceeds will help to understand the meaning of the Gorman form and why it implies the existence of a representative consumer.

Proof (Partial)   To prove the necessity part (the 'only if' part)—that is, that if the Marshallian market demands for goods depend only on prices and on *aggregate* income then all the indirect utility functions of the several consumers can be given the Gorman form—is difficult beyond the aims of this book; the interested reader is referred to Gorman's articles. We can get close, by proving that Marshallian market demand functions depending only on prices and on aggregate income imply that *individual* demand functions have the form $x^s(p, m^s) = \alpha^s(p) + m^s\beta(p)$ which can be called a Gorman form of individual demand, and then supplying an intuition why this implies that individual indirect utility functions can be given the Gorman form.

In order for the total demand for each good to depend only on aggregate income and not on its distribution among consumers, a small redistribution of income among consumers at unchanged prices must leave total demands

4.21 · Aggregability of Consumers: Gorman Aggregability and the Representative Consumer

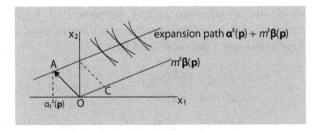

■ **Fig. 4.30** Gorman linear expansion path which is not a ray through the origin. Point A is $\alpha^s(\mathbf{p})$; $\mathbf{p}$ determines the slope of the budget lines tangent to indifference curves on the expansion path. Given money prices $\mathbf{p}$, the consumer is on the expansion path as long as m^s does not go below the level that makes $m^s\boldsymbol{\beta}(\mathbf{p})$ reach point C; a lower m^s would cause a negative quantity of good 1 because $\alpha_1^s(\mathbf{p})$ is negative

unaffected. Assume then a small redistribution of income from consumer s to consumer t that leaves aggregate income unchanged. Let $x^s(\mathbf{p}, m^s)$ be the demand function of consumer s. Aggregate demand $\sum_{s=1}^{S} x^s(\mathbf{p}, m^s)$ remains unchanged for changes of the individual income of consumers s and t if $dm^s \cdot \partial x_i^s(\mathbf{p}, m^s)/\partial m^s + dm^t \cdot \partial x_i^t(\mathbf{p}, m^t)/\partial m^t = 0$. Since the redistribution concerns only consumers s and t, it must be $dm^s = -dm^t$; this implies $\partial x_i^s(\mathbf{p}, m^s)/\partial m^s = \partial x_i^t(\mathbf{p}, m^t)/\partial m^t$. This equality must hold for all couples of consumers, for all goods, and for repeated small redistributions, i.e. for arbitrary m^s and m^t (as long as these remain above levels that will be pointed out below), so it implies that for given prices *the individual income effect for each good is the same for all consumers and is independent of their incomes*. Hence it must be $\partial x_i^s(\mathbf{p}, m^s)/\partial m^s = \beta_i(\mathbf{p})$ with $\beta_i(\mathbf{p})$ some function of prices, the same for all consumers. Note that then, for given prices, for each consumer the income effect on each good $\partial x_i^s(\mathbf{p}, m^s)/\partial m^s$ is a constant, hence the expansion path of consumer s is linear and has the same slope for all consumers; this means that the individual demand vector $\mathbf{x}^s(\mathbf{p}, m^s)$ must result from the sum of a vector $m^s\boldsymbol{\beta}(\mathbf{p})$ and of a vector $\boldsymbol{\alpha}^s(\mathbf{p})$, where $\boldsymbol{\alpha}^s(\mathbf{p})$ is some vectorial function of $\mathbf{p}$ independent of m^s. Because of balanced budgets, when $m^s = 0$ it must be $\mathbf{p}\boldsymbol{\alpha}^s(\mathbf{p}) = 0$: in the two-goods case vector $\boldsymbol{\alpha}$ corresponds to point A in ■ Fig. 4.30, where AO has the same slope as the budget line and as the MRS along the expansion path.

Given $\mathbf{p}$, what can differ among consumers is only point A, or equivalently the intercepts of the expansion path with the axes. In conclusion, in order for total demand to be (locally) independent of the distribution of income among consumers, individual vectorial demand functions must have the form $\mathbf{x}^s(\mathbf{p}, m^s) = \boldsymbol{\alpha}^s(\mathbf{p}) + \boldsymbol{\beta}(\mathbf{p})m^s$. It can then be proved that the preferences of consumers must be such that their indirect utility functions can be given the Gorman form. I omit the proof but it is intuitive that utility can be viewed as increasing in step with m along the expansion path, plus a fixed positive or negative amount depending on the position of point A relative to the origin.

Now I prove sufficiency: if the individual indirect utility functions have the Gorman form, $v^s(\mathbf{p}, m^s) = a^s(\mathbf{p}) + b(\mathbf{p})m^s$, then aggregate demand for each good

336 Chapter 4 · Consumers and the Exchange Economy

does not depend on the distribution among consumers of aggregate income. Using Roy's Identity we can derive the demand functions of each consumer. The demand function of consumer s for good i will be

$$x_i^s = -\frac{\partial a^s/\partial p_i}{b(p)} - \frac{\partial b/\partial p_i}{b(p)} m^s = \alpha_i^s(\mathbf{p}) + \beta_i(\mathbf{p})m^s. \tag{4.10}$$

Note that both $\alpha_i^s(\mathbf{p})$ and $\beta_i(\mathbf{p})$ are independent of income; $\beta_i(\mathbf{p})$, which measures $\partial x_i^s(\mathbf{p}, m^s)/\partial m^s$, can be called (remembering the Keynesian marginal propensity to consume as dependent on income) the constant *individual marginal propensity to consume good i* and is the same for all consumers. The division by $b(p)$ renders the two fractions independent of the choice of utility units.

Market demand for good i, let us indicate it as $X_i(\mathbf{p}, m^1, \ldots, m^S)$, is therefore:

$$X_i\left(\mathbf{p}, m^1, \ldots, m^s\right) = -\left(\sum_{s=1}^{S}\frac{\partial a^s/\partial p_i}{b(p)} + \frac{\partial b/\partial p_i}{b(p)}\sum_{s=1}^{S}m^s\right) \tag{4.11}$$

$$= \sum_s \alpha_i^s(\mathbf{p}) + \beta_i(\mathbf{p})m.$$

where $m = \Sigma_s m^s$ is aggregate income. Consider now the following indirect utility function:

$$V(\mathbf{p}, m) = \sum_{s=1}^{S} a^s(p) + b(p)m. \tag{4.12}$$

Applying Roy's Identity one verifies (***Exercise 50***: do it!) that this indirect utility function yields the market demands $X_i(\cdot)$ just obtained in (4.11). $V(\mathbf{p}, m)$ is itself in Gorman form, and therefore it can be seen as the indirect utility function of a possible consumer: the ***Gorman representative consumer*** of this economy. ∎

The above proof shows that Gorman aggregability can be expressed in a simpler way than through the form of the indirect utility functions:

▪▪ Proposition 4.21

Gorman representative consumer. *Marshallian market demand can be considered the vectorial demand function of a single individual with income equal to aggregate income if and only if for all prices individual demand functions have the Gorman form* $\mathbf{x}^s(\mathbf{p}, m^s) = \boldsymbol{\alpha}^s(\mathbf{p}) + m^s\boldsymbol{\beta}(\mathbf{p})$.

The aggregability conditions we have found are enormously restrictive: if one takes a unit of income away from any one consumer and gives it to any other consumer, market demands must not change. This will not be the case in an actual economy if one consumer is poor and the other rich.

Also note that, as ◻ Fig. 4.30 makes clear, the consumer's demand can have the Gorman form only as long as her income is sufficient to stay on the expansion path, which will not be the case for an income sufficiently close to zero unless $\boldsymbol{\alpha}^s(\mathbf{p})$ is the null vector. If one wants the representative consumer to exist not only

Consumers and the Exchange Economy

locally but for *any* positive income vector $(m^1,...,m^s,...,m^S)$, it must be $\alpha^s(\mathbf{p}) = \mathbf{0}$ for all consumers, i.e. for any given $\mathbf{p}$ all expansion paths must be the same linear ray from the origin, which means the preferences of all consumers can be expressed via *identical and homothetic* utility functions. This is called the *Antonelli theorem*, discovered in 1886 by the Italian economist G. B. Antonelli.

Gorman's analysis concerns the existence of a Marshallian representative consumer when both relative income levels and total income can change. A result called the *Eisenberg theorem* shows that if total income can change but not the *relative* income levels of consumers, then homothetic but not identical utility functions are sufficient for the existence of a Marshallian representative consumer (Eisenberg 1961). To understand the theorem, let total income be $M = \sum_s m^s$ and let the income of consumer s be $\lambda^s M$, where her share $0 < \lambda^s < 1$ of M is given, and $\sum_s \lambda^s = 1$. Suppose for all $s = 1,...,S$ the utility function $u^s(\mathbf{x}^s)$ is homogeneous of degree 1 (this can always be obtained by a monotonic transformation if the original utility function is homothetic) so its maximization under the budget constraint $\mathbf{px}^s = h^s M$ generates a demand function $\mathbf{x}^s(\mathbf{p}, \lambda^s M) = \mathbf{x}^s(\mathbf{p}, 1)\lambda^s M$, and indirect utility obeys $v^s(\mathbf{p}, \lambda^s M) = v^s(\mathbf{p}, 1)\lambda^s M$. We ask whether a representative consumer's utility function can be found which, if income is total income, generates the same demand functions for the several goods as the market demand functions generated by the sum of the individual demand functions. The answer is yes, the utility function is

$$U(\mathbf{x}) = \max_{\mathbf{x}^1,...,\mathbf{x}^S} \left[u^1\left(\mathbf{x}^1\right) \right]^{\lambda^1} \cdot \left[u^2\left(\mathbf{x}^2\right) \right]^{\lambda^2} \cdot ... \cdot \left[u^S\left(\mathbf{x}^S\right) \right]^{\lambda^S} \quad \text{s.t. } \mathbf{x} = \sum_s \mathbf{x}^S,$$

where $\mathbf{x}^s$ is the consumption vector of consumer s. Although it is not intuitively evident why, in fact, the vectorial demand function $\mathbf{x}(\mathbf{p}, M)$ of this hypothetical representative consumer can be shown to satisfy

$$\mathbf{x}(\mathbf{p}, M) = \sum_s \mathbf{x}^S\left(\mathbf{p}, \lambda^S M\right).$$

Hence the market demand vector function $\sum_s \mathbf{x}^s(\mathbf{p}, \lambda^s M)$ can be seen as deriving from the choices of this consumer, who is thus proven to be a representative consumer. I omit the interesting but complicated proof (see Shafer and Sonnenschein 1982, pp. 676–7).

4.22 General Equilibrium of Pure Exchange. Aggregability of Consumers

The issue of aggregability of consumers in general equilibrium requires a description of the latter. For the moment we can only discuss the general equilibrium of the exchange economy since we have not discussed production. This is often called *general equilibrium of pure exchange* in order to stress that the model admits no production at all. We need to generalize the simple economy discussed in ▶ Sect. 4.7. The intuition is provided by the 'forest economy' of ▶ Chap. 3.

338   **Chapter 4 · Consumers and the Exchange Economy**

The economy consists of a finite number of consumers, indexed $1,...,s,...,S$, and of a finite number of perfectly divisible perishable commodities indexed $1,...,i,...,N$. Each consumer s has given preferences and a given n-vector of endowments $\boldsymbol{\omega}^s = (\omega_1^s,...,\omega_n^s)$.

Consumers are *price-takers*; given a vector of prices $\mathbf{p}$, for each consumer utility maximization can determine a unique vector $\mathbf{x}^s$ of consumption demands that maximizes her utility under the budget constraint 'value of consumption basket $\leq$ value of endowments', or more than one such vector, among which the consumer is indifferent; let us indicate this best-choice set as $d^s(\mathbf{p})$, it can contain one vector $\mathbf{x}^s$, or a finite, or even an infinite, number of vectors. The consumer solves a *Walrasian* UMP. Note that we can imagine consumer s first selling all her endowment and obtaining $\mathbf{p}\boldsymbol{\omega}^s$ and then using this sum of purchasing power to buy the (or an) optimal $\mathbf{x}^s$; therefore the consumer's optimal consumption basket at prices $\mathbf{p}$ can also be obtained from a Marshallian UMP with $m^s = \mathbf{p}\boldsymbol{\omega}^s$, therefore $\mathbf{p}\boldsymbol{\omega}^s$ can be called the consumer's income or wealth at prices $\mathbf{p}$.

If $d^s(\mathbf{p})$ contains more than one vector, each one of them is a possible demand vector of the consumer,[58] to which corresponds a vector of **excess demands** $\mathbf{x}^s(\mathbf{p}) - \boldsymbol{\omega}^s$, whose elements can be positive or negative. The set of excess demands $d^s(\mathbf{p}) - \boldsymbol{\omega}^s$ changes with $\mathbf{p}$, generating the **excess demand correspondence** of consumer s. For each $\mathbf{p}$, unless each consumer's demand vector is unique, the *aggregate* or *market* excess demand for a good can be the sum of any combination of choices of the several consumers, so it can be considerably indeterminate: if at the given $\mathbf{p}$ all consumers but five have a uniquely determined demand for good 1 and those five different consumers have each two possible demands for good 1, there are 32 possible market demands for good 1. Clearly, to reach any definite result the theory of general equilibrium must assume that non-uniquely determined demands are an extremely rare occurrence; this assumption is universally tacitly made, with no discussion of its legitimacy, and I will conform to this habit, but the issue would deserve more discussion.

Having not-so-implicitly assumed that for each consumer utility maximization generates a vectorial excess demand *function* and not a correspondence, the sum of these functions over all consumers is the **market excess demand function**; if we change its sign we obtain the market excess supply function. The sum of the endowment vectors of the S consumers is the aggregate endowment vector $\boldsymbol{\omega}$. A distribution of this aggregate endowment among the consumers such that nothing remains undistributed is called a *no-waste allocation* but for brevity I will generally call it simply an **allocation** and indicate it as $\{\mathbf{x}^s\}$, a vector of S vectors $\mathbf{x}^s$, one for each consumer, such that $\Sigma_s \mathbf{x}^s = \boldsymbol{\omega}$. Barter, markets, theft, violence, etc., can determine the allocation. The theory assumes that market exchange is

---

58 . If set $d^s(\mathbf{p})$ contains a unique element, the consumer chooses that unique element; but if the consumer is indifferent among several possible consumption baskets which all equally maximize her utility, then how she will choose among these consumption baskets is a question not discussed in the literature, nor easily answerable. An assumption that seems as good as any other is that the choice will be random.

4.22 · General Equilibrium of Pure Exchange. Aggregability of Consumers

the only admitted way to modify allocations. Competition and arbitrage impose a uniform price for all units of a good. Consumers maximize locally non-satiated utility and cannot get into debt, so they try to have the budget constraint hold as an equality.[59] The general equilibrium for this economy can be defined at first in the following perhaps rather unusual way:

An exchange equilibrium is a price vector $\mathbf{p} \geq 0$ *and a no-waste allocation* $\{\mathbf{x}^s\}$ *such that* $\mathbf{x}^s \in d^s(\mathbf{p})$ *for each consumer s.*

This means that at prices $\mathbf{p}$ each consumer obtains a basket that maximizes her utility (under the budget constraint), i.e. does not wish to demand a different basket of goods. Supply and demand do not appear in this definition of equilibrium, but if $\mathbf{x}^s$ is different from ω^s the consumer must arrive at $\mathbf{x}^s$ via exchange, and since $\Sigma_s \mathbf{x}^s = \Sigma_s \omega^s$ by definition it follows that in equilibrium *the sum of the (positive or negative) excess demands of the several consumers for each good is zero, or at most negative (positive aggregate excess <u>supply</u>) but then the good must have price zero.* The reason is that we assume that as long as supply of, and demand for, a good is not equal the price of the good changes in the direction of the sign of aggregate excess demand for the good; then *an equilibrium is a situation where the interplay of supply and demand no longer causes prices to change*; now if a good remains in excess supply even when its price falls to zero, the pressure of excess supply would tend to cause the price to decrease, but a zero price cannot decrease further, so there is no tendency for the price to change, the market is in equilibrium.

The basic element in the search for equilibrium is the *aggregate or market (vectorial) excess demand function or correspondence,* $\mathbf{z}(\mathbf{p}) = (z_1(\mathbf{p}),...,z_n(\mathbf{p}))$ where $z_i(\mathbf{p})$ is the excess demand for good i obtained by summing the excess demands of the S consumers for the good. If excess demand is single-valued for all consumers, then $\mathbf{z}(\mathbf{p})$ is a function; unless otherwise specified I assume this is the case. Equilibrium requires $\mathbf{z}(\mathbf{p}) \leq \mathbf{0}$ and a zero price in the markets where equilibrium excess demand is negative (i.e. excess supply is positive).

Local non-satiated utility maximization implies $\mathbf{p}\mathbf{x}^s = \mathbf{p}\omega^s$, $\forall s$. Then a more formal definition of a price-taking equilibrium is

Definition of general competitive exchange equilibrium. *A price-taking general equilibrium of exchange when preferences are locally non-satiated is a vector of prices* $\mathbf{p}^*$ *and a set of demand vectors* $\mathbf{x}^{s*}$, *one for each consumer s, such that*
(i) $\mathbf{x}^{s*}$ *maximizes the utility of consumer s under her budget constraint, at the given prices* $\mathbf{p}^*$;
(ii) $\mathbf{z}(\mathbf{p}^*) \leq \mathbf{0}$.

It is not necessary to include in the definition that, if in some market there is excess supply, the equilibrium price in that market must be zero: the reason

---

59 Why do I say 'they try'? Remember the caveat that intentions to buy and sell can be all simultaneously satisfied only in equilibrium.

340   Chapter 4 · Consumers and the Exchange Economy

is that this condition *is implied by* **Walras' Law**. This law (also see ▶ Sect. 4.7) states that, as long as local non-satiation is assumed, the algebraic sum $\Sigma_i p_i z_i(\mathbf{p})$ of the exchange values of intended market excess demands is identically zero, i.e. $\mathbf{pz}(\mathbf{p}) = 0$, whether prices are equilibrium prices or not. This is because consumers' budgets are balanced, hence the sum of the exchange values of individual excess demands over all consumers, which is necessarily equal to the sum of the exchange values of market excess demands, is zero. (Note that this is true even when for some consumer the demand for a good is infinite because the good's price is zero.)

Proof that Walras' Law implies that if $z_i < 0$ then $p_i^* = 0$: from the definition of equilibrium $z_i(\mathbf{p}^*) \leq 0$ for all i, and by Walras' Law $\mathbf{p}^* \mathbf{z}(\mathbf{p}^*) = 0$, which is a sum of all non-positive terms, because equilibrium excess demands cannot be positive and prices cannot be negative; a sum of non-positive terms can be zero only if all terms are zero, so if $z_i(\mathbf{p}^*) < 0$ it must be $p_i = 0$. ∎

If we upgrade local non-satiation to an assumption that preferences are monotonic (i.e. marginal utilities are always strictly positive for all goods), then equilibrium prices can only be positive: there cannot be equilibrium with a zero price because the good with zero price would be demanded in infinite quantity and therefore the excess demand for that good would be positive. (If the *demand* for a good is infinite, the *excess* demand is also infinite because the total endowment of each good is finite.)

Something more on the general equilibrium of pure exchange has been said in ▶ Sect. 3.7.2 and in ▶ Sect. 4.7. For further discussion of its existence, uniqueness and stability, the reader must wait for ▶ Chap. 6. Here I add only what is needed to clarify the statement at the beginning of ▶ Sect. 4.21 on a difference between the conditions for aggregability of consumers into a representative consumer depending on whether one is interested in Marshallian demand or in general equilibrium.

So let us ask when the general equilibrium market excess demand function behaves as if coming from a single consumer having as endowment the total endowment vector of the economy. The Gorman conditions do *not* suffice because now incomes are functions of prices. There are three *sufficient* conditions:

(1) If the endowments of consumers are *co-linear* (i.e. are different amounts of the same basket of goods), their relative values are independent of prices, i.e. *relative incomes are given*. Then if in addition all consumers have *homothetic preferences* (possibly different across consumers), the Eisenberg theorem applies; a representative consumer exists.

(2) If endowments are the same for all consumers and preferences are the same too, then all consumers always make the same choices, each one of them is an average representative consumer.

(3) If endowments are different and not co-linear, then a representative consumer is guaranteed to exist only if indifference maps are the same *and* homothetic (and therefore all derivable from the same homothetic utility function). Then, given $\mathbf{p}$, all consumers' expansion paths are the same ray from the origin even if endowments differ, their demands can differ in

4.22 · General Equilibrium of Pure Exchange. Aggregability of Consumers

amounts but not in composition, and in total the value of their demands equals the total value of the economy's endowment, so a representative consumer exists with the same homothetic utility function as each consumer. This is the case of Antonelli's theorem, applied to an exchange economy.

To sum up, three cases guarantee the existence of a representative consumer in general equilibrium analysis: co-linear endowments and homothetic preferences; same endowments and same preferences; same and homothetic preferences.

4.23 Aggregate or Market Demand and the Weak Axiom of Revealed Preference

If the market demand vector function is as if coming from a representative consumer, then it satisfies the SARP and then also the WARP; this, as we will see in ▶ Chap. 6, makes for some nice results on uniqueness and stability of (acapitalistic) general equilibrium. But the conditions for the existence of a representative consumer appear to be not even vaguely approximated by real economies. What about being content with market demand satisfying only the WARP? Meaning, not that each consumer's demand function satisfies the WARP, this is implied by the assumption that consumers have standard utility functions; but that the *market* demand function does. It would mean the following: if at prices $\mathbf{p}$—that determine a *market* demand vector $\mathbf{x}(\mathbf{p})$—the total value of market demand $\mathbf{px}(\mathbf{p})$ would allow the purchase of the different vector $\mathbf{x}(\mathbf{q})$ which is the market demand vector at prices $\mathbf{q}$, then at the latter prices the total value of market demand $\mathbf{qx}(\mathbf{q})$ must be insufficient to demand $\mathbf{x}(\mathbf{p})$. This assumption will be indicated as *WAM* (Weak Axiom of revealed preference holding for Market demands). Let us state it formally:

> *Definition of WAM axiom*: $\mathbf{px}(\mathbf{p}) \geq \mathbf{px}(\mathbf{q})$ *and* $\mathbf{x}(\mathbf{q}) \neq \mathbf{x}(\mathbf{p})$ *imply* $\mathbf{qx}(\mathbf{p}) > \mathbf{qx}(\mathbf{q})$, *where* $\mathbf{x}(\mathbf{p})$, $\mathbf{x}(\mathbf{q})$ *are the market vectorial demands, respectively, at prices* $\mathbf{p}$ *and* $\mathbf{q}$.

Now we show with an example that the fact that individual consumers satisfy the SARP does not imply WAM. Assume two consumers, A and B, and 2 goods. The consumers derive their income from given endowments and have the same endowment ω but different non-homothetic preferences. Consider two different price vectors $\mathbf{p}$ and $\mathbf{q}$ implying different relative prices, and suppose the consumers' choices are $\mathbf{x}^A(\mathbf{p})$, $\mathbf{x}^A(\mathbf{q})$, $\mathbf{x}^B(\mathbf{p})$, $\mathbf{x}^B(\mathbf{q})$ which correspond to the points so labelled in ◘ Fig. 4.31. Point ω where the two budget lines cross represents the endowment of each consumer. At prices $\mathbf{p}$, the value of aggregate demand is $2\mathbf{p}\omega$, at prices $\mathbf{q}$ it is $2\mathbf{q}\omega$. Instead of representing aggregate demand, ◘ Fig. 4.31 represents *half* aggregate demand at $\mathbf{p}$, respectively, at $\mathbf{q}$, as the mid-point between the points indicating the demands of the two consumers at $\mathbf{p}$, respectively, at $\mathbf{q}$. Thus $\frac{1}{2}\mathbf{x}(\mathbf{p}) = (\mathbf{x}^A(\mathbf{p}) + \mathbf{x}^B(\mathbf{p}))/2$, $\frac{1}{2}\mathbf{x}(\mathbf{q}) = (\mathbf{x}^A(\mathbf{q}) + \mathbf{x}^B(\mathbf{q}))/2$. The figure shows that point $\frac{1}{2}\mathbf{x}(\mathbf{q})$ is below the budget line through ω at prices $\mathbf{p}$, hence $\frac{1}{2}\mathbf{px}(\mathbf{q}) < \mathbf{p}\omega = \frac{1}{2}\mathbf{px}(\mathbf{p})$, and analogously $\frac{1}{2}\mathbf{qx}(\mathbf{p}) < \mathbf{q}\omega = \frac{1}{2}\mathbf{qx}(\mathbf{q})$. Multiplying by 2 one obtains a violation of WAM: $\mathbf{px}(\mathbf{p}) > \mathbf{px}(\mathbf{q})$ but also $\mathbf{qx}(\mathbf{q}) > \mathbf{qx}(\mathbf{p})$.

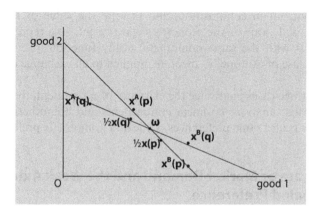

◘ Fig. 4.31 Example of violation of WAM due to different tastes of two consumers A and B

This example shows that, as long as consumers have different non-homothetic preferences, WAM need not hold even when endowments are identical. We can also show that identical but non-homothetic preferences do not guarantee WAM if endowments are different. An example can be based on same ◘ Fig. 4.31. Imagine that there are three consumers, A, C and C°. Consumer A is as in the previous example; consumers C and C° are two identical consumers with the same preferences as A, but each one with an endowment which is one half the endowment of A and therefore with an income which is one half the income of A. Since preferences are not homothetic, the composition of C's demand differs from the composition of A's demand, and it is possible that it differs such that twice C's demand is identical to the demand of consumer B of the previous example. But twice C's demand is the sum of C's and of C°'s demands, so in the (A, C, C°) economy aggregate demand is as in the previous example, and it does not satisfy WAM .

We can also grasp why Eisenberg's theorem implies that homothetic utility functions prevent a violation of WAM if consumers have co-linear endowments. Co-linear endowments hold in both the examples just illustrated, and it is easy to show that in these examples if preferences were homothetic the violation of WAM would be impossible. In ◘ Fig. 4.31, in order to obtain that ½x(q) is below the budget line through ω at prices **p** and that ½x(p) is below the budget line through ω at prices **q**, when prices change from **p** to **q** the ray representing the aggregate *composition* of demand must move from the right to the left of the ray from the origin to ω, and this requires that for at least one consumer the composition of demand x_2/x_1 increases: which is impossible with homothetic utility, because good 2 is relatively more expensive at prices **q** than at prices **p**, therefore the expansion path rotates clockwise, the new optimal consumption basket is for both consumers to the *right* of the ray from the origin to the old consumption basket.

But consumers in real economies are very far from having homothetic preferences or co-linear endowments, so changes in relative prices have relevant redistributive effects. I show graphically in ◘ Fig. 4.32 that non-co-linear endowments

4.23 · Aggregate or Market Demand and the Weak Axiom of Revealed Preference

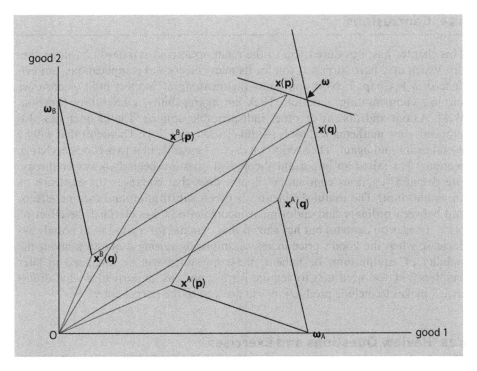

Fig. 4.32 Consumers A and B have homothetic utility functions but not co-linear endowments

can contradict WAM even when utility functions are homothetic. In ◘ Fig. 4.32 I represent the two-goods endowments and choices of two consumers, referred to the same origin (i.e. not as in an Edgeworth box): ω_A is the endowment of consumer A, consisting only of good 1, ω_B is the endowment of consumer B, consisting only of good 2; differently from ◘ Fig. 4.31 now ω stands for the sum of the two endowments, and $\mathbf{x(p)}$ and $\mathbf{x(q)}$ are the market demands at two different price vectors $\mathbf{p}$ and $\mathbf{q}$ that mean different relative prices; the market demands result from the sum of the choices of the consumers $\mathbf{x}^A(\mathbf{p}) + \mathbf{x}^B(\mathbf{p})$, $\mathbf{x}^A(\mathbf{q}) + \mathbf{x}^B(\mathbf{q})$; these choices are compatible with homothetic preferences because as relative price p_1/p_2 rises from $\mathbf{p}$ to $\mathbf{q}$ both consumers raise the ratio x_2/x_1 in which they demand the two goods. To reduce the complexity of the drawing, the budget lines of the two consumers have been drawn only from the endowment to the chosen basket; the vectors chosen by the two consumers at prices $\mathbf{p}$ are then summed up with the parallelogram technique to determine the market demand $\mathbf{x(p)}$, which is located to the left of ω on the aggregate budget line going through ω; the same is done at prices $\mathbf{q}$, and $\mathbf{x(q)}$ is to the right of ω on the steeper aggregate budget line through ω. WAM does not hold.

I conclude that WAM is highly restrictive. If it were to emerge that general equilibrium theory needs such an assumption in order to avoid results depriving it of plausibility, this would mean trouble for that theory. The issue will be discussed in ▶ Chap. 6.

344   Chapter 4 · Consumers and the Exchange Economy

4.24 Conclusions

This chapter has introduced you to the main notions in standard consumer theory, which may have surprised you for its many facets and complications, not evidenced in ▶ Chap. 3. Now you know the meaning of indirect utility, consumer surplus, compensating variation, Hicksian aggregability, CES utility function, Weak Axiom and dozens of other indispensable notions. The chapter has also supplied some mathematical tools (Kuhn–Tucker, Envelope Theorem) that will be useful again and again. The section on excess demands in a two-goods exchange economy has raised an important theoretical question behind consumer theory: Are demand functions continuous? if not, does that endanger the existence of an equilibrium? The useful distinction between substitution and income effects, and between ordinary and endowment income effects, has clarified the effect of price changes on demand but has shown that demand for a good need not always decrease when the good's price increases, implicitly raising a question about the stability of equilibrium. Be patient, these questions will be discussed in later chapters, but you need first to acquire further notions, in particular what difference it makes to include production—so proceed to the next chapter!

4.25 Review Questions and Exercises

Review questions
1. Distinguish individual Engel curves from historical Engel curves.
2. Explain why concave indifference curves cause discontinuities in demand 'functions' (an imprecise term in this case, why?).
3. Why is the Jacobian of the Hicksian demand function called Slutsky matrix? (First at least read exercise 31)
4. Define homothetic utility functions.
5. Discuss the likelihood of Giffen goods.
6. The Walrasian UMP can produce cases where demand for a good increases when the price of the good increases, and yet the good is not Giffen, because not inferior. Explain.
7. Explain the qualification to the statement that with quasi-linear utility all indifference curves are parallel translations of one of them.
8. Draw ◘ Fig. 4.26 bis and illustrate the kind of workers' behaviour that can justify it.
9. Which axiom about revealed preferences does not assume that demand is single-valued?
10. List the conditions required for the reconstruction of preferences from observed choices.
11. Attempts at econometric estimation of systems of *market* demand functions that do not satisfy WAM need not postulate functional forms that guarantee that the Slustsky matrix is negative semidefinite. Why?
12. Enunciate the Eisenberg theorem.

4.24 · Conclusions

13. The definition of general equilibrium of pure exchange in ▶ Sect. 4.22 does not specify that if in equilibrium in some market there is excess supply, the price in that market must be zero. Why is it superfluous to specify it?
14. With strongly monotonic preferences, exchange-equilibrium prices are all positive. Why?
15. Show that convex preferences by themselves do not suffice to guarantee convex indifference curves.
16. Why do textbooks nearly always assume internal optimal consumption baskets?
17. Prove that the expenditure function is concave.
18. Explain why the qualification 'in which price is positive' is important to a correct statement of Walras' Law
19. How can one recover the utility function from the expenditure function?
20. Show that without convexity of indifference curves, demand functions can have discontinuities.
21. Explain why Debreu's definition of the consumption set appears to exclude the possibility of default on contracts in futures.
22. Explain why the thesis, that the labour supply curve is necessarily increasing as w starts rising from zero, can be criticized.
23. Produce an Edgeworth box in which points of tangency between indifference curves of the two consumers are not in the Pareto set.
24. What is the addition the SARP makes relative to the WARP?

Exercises

1. A consumer has expenditure function $e(p_1, p_2, u) = (up_1p_2)/(p_1 + p_2)$. Find a direct utility function $u(x_1, x_2)$ that rationalizes this person's demand behaviour.
2. Find the indirect utility function $v(p_1, p_2, m)$ of the Cobb–Douglas utility function $u(x_1, x_2) = Ax_1^\alpha x_2^{1-\alpha}$. (Hint: derive from the UMP the demand functions for the two goods as functions of the two prices and of m, and plug them into the utility function.)
3. Confirm by application of Roy's Identity to $v(p, 1)m$ that the demand functions derived from homothetic preferences have the form $x_i(p, m) = x_i(p, 1)m$.
4. Find the total own income effect of a variation of p_1 on good 1 if the utility function is a (generalized) Cobb–Douglas $u = x_1^a x_2^b$, where a, b > 0 and the starting point is internal. (Hint: From the Marshallian UMP find the Marshallian demand function $x_1(p, m)$.)
5. Prove that the standard Cobb–Douglas expenditure function corresponding to $u = x_1^\alpha x_2^\beta$ with $\alpha + \beta = 1$ is $\alpha^\alpha(1-\alpha)^{\alpha-1}p_1^\alpha p_2^{1-\alpha}u$. (Hint: from the first-order conditions for expenditure minimization derive $x_1/x_2 = (\alpha/\beta)p_2/p_1$; from this and the constraint $x_1^\alpha x_2^\beta = u$ derive by substitution x_1 and x_2 as functions of p_1, p_2 and u; substitute into $x_1p_1 + x_2p_2$.) Prove that its inversion relative to u generates the indirect utility function.
6. Show that if, in the two-goods case, the consumer derives her income from an endowment consisting only of good 1, then as p_1 varies the consumer's demand for good 1 is an increasing function of p_1 if the utility function is CES with a negative ϱ (we know it is constant if the utility function is Cobb–

Douglas). Conclude on the possibility of an everywhere downward-sloping supply curve of labour.

7. (Blanchard and Kiyotaki 1987) Assume a CES utility function with n goods and $a_1 = a_2 = \ldots = a_n$. Assume that the prices of all goods are the same and equal to 1. Show that if the consumer allocates a given budget m to these goods, her utility increases as n increases. Show further that if the function is specified as $u = A^{1/(1-\sigma)}(\sum_i x_i^{(\sigma-1)/\sigma})^{\sigma/(\sigma-1)}$, where A is a positive constant, then the marginal utility of each good at the optimum does not vary if n varies.

8. Using the CES Marshallian demand function, prove that if the elasticity of substitution is >1 then the elasticity of demand for each good is >1 in absolute value.

9. Show graphically with reference to two goods the case in which a Walrasian and a Marshallian UMP coincide.

10. It is often stated that indifference curves cannot cross. Try to make this statement precise, listing the necessary assumptions (start from the fact that, without opportune assumptions, it is not a priori impossible that indifference curves be X-shaped).

11. Suppose the consumption set only includes integer amounts of goods 1 and 2:

Assume that preferences are monotonic and lexicographic in good 1. Show that the utility function $u(x_1, x_2) = 1 + x_1 - 1/(x_2 + 1)$ correctly represents these preferences.

Now modify the example by assuming that the consumption set includes only integer amounts of good 1 but all amounts of good 2, which is perfectly divisible. Represent graphically the consumption set for the first units of x_1. Preferences are monotonic and lexicographic in good 1. Show that, with the help of the arctang function, it is possible to find a utility function correctly representing these preferences.

12. (Guerrien) Deduce the two-goods utility function of a consumer whose indirect utility function is $v(p, m) = m/(p_1 p_2)^{1/2}$, by first finding the vectorial demand function x(p, m) through Roy's Identity.

13. Prove that if $x_1(p_1, p_2, m)$, $x_2(p_1, p_2, m)$ are the Marshallian demand functions derived from utility function $u = x_1^{1/2} + 2x_2^{1/2}$, then it is *not* true that $\partial x_1/\partial p_2 = \partial x_2/\partial p_1$. (Hint: by using the condition $MRS = -p_1/p_2$ and the budget constraint, derive the demand functions.)

14. After answering the preceding Exercise, find the Hicksian demand functions generated by $u = x_1^{1/2} + 2x_2^{1/2}$.

15. Find the substitution effect and the income effect in the own price effect of p_x on good x if $u = x^\alpha y^{1-\alpha}$ and income m > 0 is given. (Hint: from the condition

4.25 · Review Questions and Exercises

347 **4**

MRS $= -p_1/p_2$ and the budget constraint, find the demand functions; derive the substitution effect from the price effect and the income effect.)

16. (Varian). Consider the utility function $u(x, y_1, y_2) = x^{\alpha} y_1^{\beta} y_2^{\gamma}$. Is this utility function weakly separable in the y-goods, i.e. expressible as $u(x, z(y_1, y_2))$? If the answer is yes, find the function $z(\cdot)$, and find the conditional demands for y_1 and y_2, given m_z.

17. Show, by assuming sufficiently high values for α and β in the utility function $u(x, y) = x^{\alpha} y^{\beta}$, that strict convexity of indifference curves does not require decreasing marginal utilities.

18. The two-goods perfect-complements utility function is $u(x, y) = \min\{ax, by\}$. Find the indirect utility function and the expenditure function.

19. Prove that if the utility function is homogeneous of degree 1, then the indirect utility function has form $v(p, m) = f(p)m$ and the expenditure function has form $e(p, u) = \varepsilon(p)u$.

20. (Varian) Find the two-goods utility function whose normalized indirect utility function is $v(p_1, p_2, 1) = -\alpha \ln p_1 - \beta \ln p_2$, using the fact that $u(x(p^*, m^*)) = \min_p v(p, m^*)$ s.t. $m^* = px(p^*, m^*)$.

21. (Becker) Are rational preferences or WARP necessary in order for demand functions to exist? Assume two goods, a linear budget constraint, and that consumers (with given income) choose randomly among all points on the budget line. This means that, if there are many consumers, market demand will approximately correspond to consumers choosing the middle point of the budget line. With M the total income of all consumers, find the aggregate demands for x_1 and for x_2 and show that they satisfy homogeneity of degree zero and Walras' Law and that they are downward sloping.

22. (Mas-Colell et al.) Let $x(p_1, p_2, m)$ be the Marshallian demand function of a consumer for goods 1 and 2. From the fact that the elasticity of demand for good i with respect to price j can be written as $\varepsilon_{ij} = d \ln x_i(p, m) / d \ln p_j$, and the elasticity of demand for good i with respect to income can be written as $\varepsilon_{im} = d \ln x_i(p, m) / d \ln m$, conclude that if we estimate the parameters $(\alpha_0, \alpha_1, \alpha_2, \beta)$ of the equation $\ln x_i(p_1, p_2, m) = \alpha_0 + \alpha_1 \ln p_1 + \alpha_2 \ln p_2 + \beta \ln m$, the last three parameter estimates provide us with estimates of those elasticities.

23. (Mas-Colell et al.). Prove that if $x(p, m)$ is a Marshallian demand function that satisfies the WARP, then it is homogeneous of degree zero.

24. Verify, using Roy's Identity, that if a utility function has an indirect utility function with the Gorman form $v(p, m) = a(p) + b(p)m$, then it has income expansion paths which are straight lines.

25. Prove that, if $u(x)$ is homothetic, the income elasticity of demand is constant and equal to 1.

26. (Nicholson). Suppose a consumer obtains utility only from amounts of goods x and y that exceed minimal subsistence levels x°, y°, and more precisely that $u(x, y) = (x - x^{\circ})^{\alpha}(y - y^{\circ})^{1-\alpha}$.

(i) Is this utility function homothetic?

348   **Chapter 4 · Consumers and the Exchange Economy**

    (ii) Define *Supernumerary Income*, $m^*: = m - p_x x° - p_y y°$, as the income in excess of subsistence requirements. Find the demand functions for x and y and show that the share of m^* spent on each good is constant.

27. A consumer's expansion path (good 1 in abscissa, good 2 in ordinate) is a vertical straight line. Prove that the demand curve for good 1 is downward sloping.

28. Find the expenditure or cost function for each one of the following utility functions:

    A: $ax_1 + bx_2$, $a, b > 0$
    B: $ax_1{}^2 + x_2{}^2$, $a > 0$
    C: $\min[ax_1, x_2]$, $a > 0$
    D: $a \log x_1 + b \log x_2$, $a, b > 0$

29. Assume a quasi-linear utility function $U(\mathbf{x}, y) = u(\mathbf{x}) + y$, where y is residual income and $\mathbf{x}$ is a vector of consumption goods. The budget constraint is $\mathbf{px} + y = m$. Show that the indirect utility function has the form $V(\mathbf{p}, m) = v(\mathbf{p}) + m$, and that the expenditure function has the form $E(\mathbf{p}, U) = e(\mathbf{p}) + u$.

30. Draw the indifference curves of the following utility function: $u(x_1, x_2) = |x_1 - x_2|$. Find an interpretation. Indicate the direction in which utility increases.

31. ***Hicksian versus Slutsky compensation, and substitution effect.*** The notion of substitution effect illustrated in ◉ Fig. 4.15a was proposed by John Hicks and is therefore called the **Hicksian substitution effect**. It reflects the change in choice if relative prices change and the consumer's income is altered, or 'compensated', so as to have the consumer remain at the initial utility level. The original inventor of the distinction between substitution effect and income effect was not Hicks but the Russian economist Slutsky, who had defined the substitution effect differently, as the variation in the demand for a good if the consumer's income is altered, or 'compensated', *so that the consumer can still purchase, at the new prices, the original consumption basket.* This corresponds in ◉ Fig. 4.15a to the shift from point A to point D and thus to the change in demand for good 1 from x_{1A} to x_{1D} as p_1 decreases. The income effect is then defined as the shift from D to B.

The **Slutsky substitution effect** and the Hicksian substitution effect are different for discrete price variations. You are asked to prove that they coincide for infinitesimal price variations, implying that *the Slutsky equation is the same whether one adopts the Hicks or the Slutsky definition of the substitution effect.* Start with a discrete price variation. For a variation Δp starting from a given price-income vector (p, m) and associated demand vector $x(p, m)$, the *Hicksian compensation* (which is unobservable) is the variation in income Δm_H defined by $x_i(p + \Delta p, m + \Delta m_H) = x_i\{p + \Delta p, e[p + \Delta p, v(p, m)]\}$, where Δm_H is the income compensation necessary to remain on the indifference surface where one was before the price change; its determination requires knowing the shape of the indifference surface through $x(p, m)$, i.e. the utility function. The *Slutsky compensation* Δm_S is defined by $m + \Delta m_S = (p + \Delta p) \cdot x(p, m)$, i.e. income must become such as to allow purchasing the original consumption basket at

4.25 · Review Questions and Exercises

the new prices. The Slutsky compensation is therefore $\Delta m = \Delta p \cdot x$ and can be determined without knowing the utility function. The Slutsky compensated demand is accordingly defined by $x_i(p + \Delta p, m + \Delta m_S) = x_i[p + \Delta p, m + \Delta p \cdot x(p, m)]$. You are asked to prove that these income compensations become the same, for an infinitesimal variation of a price from p_j to $p_j + dp_j$, and to derive from this the announced identity of the two Slutsky equations (This result explains the use of the term '*Slutsky* matrix' for the Jacobian of the *Hicksian* demand function.)

32. Assume $u(x_1, x_2) = x_1{}^\alpha x_2{}^\beta$, a generalized Cobb–Douglas. Derive the Marshallian demand functions from the UMP and from them and the utility function obtain the indirect utility function. Then check the validity of Roy's Identity, and from the demand functions thus re-obtained derive the utility function.

33. Assume $x^2 + y^2 - c^2 = 0$, $x > 0$, $y > 0$, defines implicitly an inverse demand curve $y = \varphi(x)$, where x is quantity demanded and y is price. Clearly it is the portion of a circumference in the positive quadrant. Use the derivative rule for implicit functions to prove that $dy/dx = -x/y$, $dx/dy = -y/x$, and use these to find the price elasticity of demand.

34. Income is the value of given endowments of two goods; initially good 1 is in net demand; show graphically that even in this case it can happen that when the price of good 1 increases (sufficiently), the consumer can reach a higher indifference curve, but this requires that good 1 passes to being in net supply.

35. Provide a geometrical illustration of property (v) of $v(p, m)$ in Sect. 4.10.2, for the two-goods case.

36. Assume two consumption goods, $u(x, y) = x^\alpha y^{(1-\alpha)}$; income is m; the price of y is 1, of x is p; the demand functions are $x = \alpha m/p$, $y = (1 - \alpha)m$. Assume $m = b\sqrt{2}$ and $\alpha = 1/2$. Consider two prices of x, $p = 1/2$ and $p' = 1/8$. Determine SV and CV for the passage of p from 1/2 to 1/8; confirm that SV overestimates CV if utility is not quasi-linear.

37. The CES Marshallian demand functions are derived as usual from the first-order conditions for utility maximization coupled with the budget constraint. Prove that

38. Show that if, in the two-goods case, the consumer derives her income from an

$$x_i\left(p_i, p_j, m\right) = \left(\frac{a_i}{p_i}\right)^\xi \frac{m}{a_i^\xi p_i^{1-\xi} + a_j^\xi p_j^{1-\xi}}.$$

endowment consisting only of good 1, then as p_1 varies the consumer's demand for good 1 is an increasing function of p_1 if the utility function is CES with a negative ϱ (we know it is constant if the utility function is Cobb–Douglas). Conclude on the possibility of an everywhere downward-sloping supply curve of labour.

39. Assume a CES utility function with n goods and $a_1 = a_2 = \dots = a_n$. Assume that the prices of all goods are the same and equal to 1. Show that if the consumer allocates a given budget m to these goods, her utility increases as n increases. Show further (Blanchard and Kiyotaki 1987) that if the function is specified as $u = A^{1/(1-\sigma)}(\sum_i x_i^{(\sigma-1)/\sigma})^{\sigma/(\sigma-1)}$, where A is a positive constant, then the marginal utility of each good at the optimum does not vary if n varies.

350   Chapter 4 · Consumers and the Exchange Economy

40. Using the CES Marshallian demand function, prove that if the elasticity of substitution is >1 then the elasticity of demand for each good is >1 in absolute value.

41. (Slutsky) Find the total own income effect of a variation of p_1 on good 1 if the utility function is a (generalized) Cobb–Douglas $u = x_1^a x_2^b$, where a, b > 0. (Hint: From the Marshallian UMP find the Marshallian demand function $x_1(p, m)$.)

42. (Given endowments) Income is the value of given endowments of two goods; initially good 1 is in net demand; show graphically that even in this case it can happen that when the price of good 1 increases (sufficiently), the consumer can reach a higher indifference curve, but this requires that the good 1 passes to being in net supply.

43. (Choice curve) Assume $\omega_1 > 0$, $\omega_2 > 0$; show graphically both with convex and with concave differentiable indifference curves that as p_1 tends to zero, x_1 increases continuously towards $+\infty$, that is, the minimum-income problem does not arise.

44. Study the choice curve of a consumer with Leontief indifference curves and an endowment precisely at the kink of the indifference curve through it.

45. (Convexification) Show graphically that the expenditure function cannot distinguish between the case of everywhere strictly concave and the case of everywhere straight indifference curves.

46. Derive the expenditure function associated with the utility function $u(x_1, x_2) = x_1^\alpha x_2^\beta$, and prove that its inversion relative to u generates the indirect utility function.

47. Prove that $EV(p \rightarrow p', m) = - CV(p' \rightarrow p, m)$. (Hint: remember expression (4.9))

48. Prove, in the two-goods case, that the GARP excludes 'thick' indifference curves (indifference 'strips').

49. (Leontief aggregability) Unless the k goods are *all* the goods the consumers demand, the demand for the k goods will depend only on their prices if two conditions hold:

(i) *functional separability*: for each consumer the utility function $u(x_1,...,x_k, x_{k+1},...,x_n)$ has the form $u(f(x_1,...,x_k),x_{k+1},...,x_n)$, where $f(\cdot)$ has the same properties as a standard utility function;

(ii) the amount m_k^s to be spent on the first k goods has been separately decided by each consumer and can be treated as given.

Prove that if the two above conditions are satisfied, then for each consumer the demand for any one of the first k goods does not depend on the prices of the other n-k goods.

50. (Gorman aggregability) Consider the following indirect utility function:

$$V(p,m) = \sum_{s=1}^{S} a^s(p) + b(p)m.$$

Applying Roy's Identity prove that this indirect utility function yields the aggregate demands $X_i(\cdot)$ obtained in (4.11) in the course of the proof of the Gorman form Proposition 4.20.

References

Afriat, S. (1967). The construction of a utility function from expenditure data. *International Economic Review, 8*, 67–77.

Barten, A. P., & Bohm, V. (1982). Consumer theory. In: K. J. Arrow & M. D. Intriligator (Eds.), *Handbook of mathematical economics* (Vol. II, pp. 381–430). North-Holland, Amsterdam.

Cahuc, P., Carcillo, S., & Zylberberg, A. (2014). *Labor economics* (2nd ed.). Cambridge MA: MIT Press.

Deaton, A., & Muellbauer, J. (1980). *Economics and consumer behavior*. Cambridge: Cambridge University Press.

Debreu, G. (1959). *Theory of value*. New York: Wiley.

Eisenberg, E. (1961). Aggregation of utility functions. *Management Science, 7*, 337–350.

Gorman, W. M. (1953). Community preference fields. *Econometrica, 21*, 63–80.

Jehle, G. A., & Reny, P. J. (2011). *Advanced microeconomic theory*. Haley, UK: Financial Times/Prentice Hall (Pearson).

Kreps, D. M. (1990). *A course in microeconomic theory*. New York: Harvester Wheatsheaf.

Marshall, A. (1972). *Principles of economics*, 8th edn., 1920 (as reset and repr., 1949). London: Macmillan.

Mas-Colell, A., Whinston, M. D., & Green, J. R. (1995). *Microeconomic theory*. Oxford: Oxford University Press.

Shafer, W., & Sonnenschein, H. (1982). Market demand and excess demand functions. In: K. Arrow & M. D. Intriligator (Eds.), *Handbook of mathematical economics* (Vol. II, pp. 671–93). North-Holland, Amsterdam.

Takayama, A. (1974). *Mathematical economics*. Hinsdale, Illinois: The Dryden Press.

Varian, H. (1992). *Microeconomic analysis* (3rd ed.). New York: W. W. Norton.

Firms, Partial Equilibria and the General Equilibrium with Production

Contents

5.1 Introduction – 356

5.2 Production Possibility Sets, Netputs, Production Functions – 357

5.3 Axioms on the Production Possibility Set – 364

5.4 Returns to Scale – 365

5.5 Differentiable Production Functions and Value Capital – 368

5.6 Homogeneous Production Functions and Returns to Scale – 369

5.7 Activity Analysis – 372

5.8 Marginal Product, Transformation Curve – 373

5.9 Profit Maximization and WAPM – 376

5.10 Optimal Employment of a Factor – 378

Electronic supplementary material The online version of this chapter (▶ https://doi.org/10.1007/978-3-030-62070-7_5) contains supplementary material, which is available to authorized users.

© Springer Nature Switzerland AG 2021
F. Petri, *Microeconomics for the Critical Mind*,
Classroom Companion: Economics, https://doi.org/10.1007/978-3-030-62070-7_5

5.11	Cost Minimization – 379
5.12	WACm; Kuhn–Tucker Conditions and Cost Minimization – 382
5.13	Supply Curves: Short-Period Marshallian Analysis, Quasi-Rents – 384
5.14	From Short-Period to Long-Period Supply – 388
5.15	The Product Exhaustion Theorem with U-Shaped LAC – 393
5.16	Aggregation – 394
5.17	Shephard's Lemma – 395
5.18	The Profit Function and Hotelling's Lemma – 395
5.19	Conditional and Unconditional Factor Demands, Inferior Inputs, Rival Inputs, Substitution Effect and Output Effect – 397
5.20	Functional Separability: Leontief Separability – 402
5.21	Duality – 403
5.22	Elasticity of Substitution – 404
5.23	Partial Equilibrium – 405
5.24	Stability of Partial Equilibria – 408
5.25	Welfare Analysis of Partial Equilibria – 409
5.26	Price Taking, Perfect Competition, Tâtonnement – 413

5.27 The Number of Firms in Modern GE – 419

5.28 The Equations of the Non-capitalistic General Equilibrium with Production – 423

5.29 The 'Reduction' to an Exchange Economy – 427

5.30 The Role of Demand in Determining Product Prices: Why General Equilibrium Product Supply Curves Are Upward Sloping – 429

5.31 International Trade – 430

5.32 On the Persistency of Preferences. Doing Without Demand Curves? – 433

5.33 Conclusions – 437

5.34 Review Questions and Exercises – 438

References – 441

356   **Chapter 5** · Firms, Partial Equilibria and the General Equilibrium with Production

The present chapter introduces to the neoclassical theory of competitive firms so as to arrive at the general equilibrium of production and exchange, still without capital goods. It will familiarize you with:

- a more rigorous treatment of the notions introduced in earlier chapters of production function, isoquant, returns to scale, cost minimization, elasticity of substitution;
- the study of profit maximization via the Kuhn–Tucker approach;
- the notions, central in standard producer theory, of WAPM, WACm, Shephard's Lemma and Hotelling's Lemma;
- the curious effects of inferior inputs and rival inputs;
- the Marshallian approach to short-period and long-period partial equilibrium;
- the relevance of free entry for the notions of price taking and perfect competition;
- the system of equations of the non-capitalistic general equilibrium with production and its reducibility to an equilibrium of exchange (of factor services).

5.1 Introduction

The present chapter presents the standard marginalist/neoclassical analysis of competitive firms and competitive product markets and uses it to extend the marginalist theory of competitive general equilibrium to include production, for the moment without capital goods (i.e. without inputs to production that are produced goods). General equilibrium with capital goods will be discussed in ▶ Chaps. 7 and 8.

The chapter presents first the standard theory of *price-taking* firms. Price-taking behaviour means the economic agent treats prices as given parameters in her maximizations; hence a buyer (respectively, a seller) believes that the price at which she can purchase (respectively, sell) additional units of a good is the same as the price of the previous units; therefore, for a firm, revenue from sales of an output, or expenditure on an input, are linear functions of the quantity sold or bought.

The firms I study in this chapter produce *undifferentiated* goods: each product is so standardized that consumers are indifferent as between the output of the several producers. As a result, the only problem of the price-taking firm is how much to produce and with what combination of inputs. Firms producing differentiated goods are associated with imperfect competition and will be studied in ▶ Chap. 12.

The chapter then proceeds to the theory of partial equilibrium and the Marshallian distinction between very short-period, short-period and long-period partial equilibria. The last sections introduce the general equilibrium of exchange and production (without capital goods) and illustrate its reducibility to an equilibrium of pure exchange. Some brief hints are added on general equilibrium supply curves of products and on international trade. An Appendix discusses the possibility of doing without demand curves.

5.2 Production Possibility Sets, Netputs, Production Functions

The purpose of this chapter is to make more precise the study of ▶ Chap. 3 of how the marginal approach determines the competitive general equilibrium of an economy where a variety of consumption goods is produced through the use of unproduced ('original' or 'primary') factors: lands and labour (possibly, different types of labour, treated as distinct factors). But in discussing, as a premise, the marginalist/neoclassical theory of the competitive firm, the presence of produced inputs will be admitted in order to obtain a more general theory.

Some aspects of the economy to be considered are as follows. A production process generally produces first some intermediate stage good (e.g. corn plants, in the production of corn; shaped pieces of wood, in the production of furniture) but the production function does not describe this fact, it only describes the quantity of final product as a function of the quantities of inputs the firm starts with, because the intermediate product is entirely consumed inside the firm in order to produce the final consumption good.[1] All production processes last one period (often assumed to be one year); production is in separate cycles, labour and land are hired at the beginning of the period, and consumption goods come out at the end of the period.[2] The interest rate is zero, so production costs are the same as if all labour and land services were paid at the same moment when output comes out and is sold. The absence of capital goods means there is no production process where a good appears both among the inputs and the outputs (e.g. corn production, that uses seed-corn as one of its inputs: then it is necessary to specify that the corn used as input cannot be the corn output of that process, which appears later in time). Realistic disequilibrium adjustments take time, sometimes several periods are required for the quantities produced to adjust to demand at cost-covering prices. These adjustments can never be perfectly completed because there are always accidental or temporary disturbances and novelties. Therefore the general equilibrium has the role of central position towards which market prices and quantities gravitate, indicative of their averages over a sufficient number of periods, over which the irregularities largely cancel out or

---

1   All non-instantaneous production processes gradually transform something into something else and then into something else still. The name given to the things that appear in these intermediate stages, to be then further transformed and no longer being there when the final output of the firm's production process comes out, is *intermediate* goods (sometimes called 'work-in-progress'). But sometimes the production process is split into successive stages operated by separate firms, and then what would have been a proper intermediate good in the process carried out by one vertically integrated firm becomes an output of one firm, sold to be an input into another firm's production, that is, becomes a marketed *circulating capital good*; sometimes it is called an 'intermediate' good in this case too, but it is best to call it a circulating capital good.

2   This is called a flow-input, point-output production process. The amount produced of consumption goods is still a flow, because it is *per period*, but when it comes out at the end of a period it can be treated as a stock.

compensate one another.[3] This role of general equilibrium presumes of course that the data of equilibrium (factor endowments, tastes and technical knowledge) either remain constant for a sufficient time, or change sufficiently slowly (relative to the presumable speed of gravitation towards the equilibrium) for their change to be negligible. The effect of significant changes in the data, e.g. technical progress, or changes in labour supply due to migrations, must be studied via comparative statics.

There are two types of agents: consumers, with given endowments of factors and given preferences, and firms that buy factor services and produce consumption goods. In the background, there must be an institutional set-up ensuring respect of private property and of contracts, e.g. a state apparatus with laws, police and courts; these require resources; but I neglect this aspect. Consumer choices were studied in ▶ Chap. 4; in this chapter the attention will be first on firms, then on partial equilibrium, then on general equilibrium. The latter will be described as a non-capitalistic equilibrium with a zero interest rate, but in discussing production decisions of firms it is useful to consider more general production possibility sets than those of the 'non-capitalistic' economy, hence also with capital goods among the inputs and outputs and possibly with a positive interest rate. It is then useful to distinguish *durable* capital goods that last for several periods and provide a flow of services per time unit, from *circulating* capital goods that disappear in a single usage (e.g. ink, or parts to be assembled to obtain a product, or seed-corn). If there is a positive interest rate, and if costs must be borne before the revenue from the sale of the output is obtained, then the interest rate (if positive) must be added on top of these costs for the relevant time interval.

Firms have **production possibility sets**. The production possibility set Y of a firm is the set of all combinations of inputs and outputs that are technically possible for the given firm. These combinations are called **production processes** or **production plans**. A production process is a vector of physical quantities of inputs (factor services) and of outputs.

In this chapter inputs precede outputs by a finite, unitary time interval called a period; time is divided into periods, and all production processes active in period t are started at the beginning of the period and end at the end of the period.[4] Time

---

3 It suffices to think of the irregularity of productivity in agriculture depending on the year's climate, to realize that equilibrium can only aim at representing the average realized over a number of periods.

4 It would also be possible to conceive productions as continuous processes where flows of services of labour and land per unit of time produce flows of outputs per unit of time, simultaneous with the application of the services that produce them. With such a representation, the flows of input services can often be represented by the dimension of a stock, by choosing as unit for the service the quantity of service per unit of time supplied by a unit of the factor. A typical such formalization is the aggregate Solow growth model, where a single output, Y, is produced as a continuous flow per time unit by the contemporaneous flow of services supplied by two stocks of factors, a stock of capital K and a stock of workers L. (Note that with labour, the assumption that the flow of labour services is proportional to the stock of workers L requires a given average labour intensity and a given average number of labour hours per period per worker.)

5.2 · Production Possibility Sets, Netputs, Production Functions

is a continuous line, and points on this line are *dates* (real numbers); the line is divided into periods of unitary length, with *period* t starting at *date* or instant t and ending infinitesimally before date $t+1$.[5] An output coming out at date $t+1$ can be indifferently described as coming out at the beginning of period $t+1$ or at the end of period t. Inputs, applied all together at date t (e.g. seed planted into the earth) or applied as flows that start at date t and are applied *during* period t (e.g. labour services), produce the output at instant $t+1$. A one-period production process is then a non-negative vector in two parts $(a_1, a_2,...,a_n; b_1, b_2, ..., b_n)$ where a_i is an input applied (or that starts being applied) at the beginning of a period and b_j is an output that comes out at the end of the period. This representation, when there are capital goods, admits that the same kind of good can appear among the inputs and as an output, e.g. corn used as seed to produce corn; but corn output cannot be used as seed corn for processes within the same period, because it only comes out at the end of the period.[6]

To repeat: when production uses capital goods, it is assumed that the outputs of date-t inputs cannot be used *within period t* as inputs in other processes of period t. This avoids some dangers into which other formulations of production possibilities occasionally incur.

A different formalization of production processes, often preferred in modern general equilibrium theory, represents them as vectors of **netputs** (short for *net outputs*); a netput vector **y** has N elements if the economy has N goods and services, where a negative element indicates a *net* input of good i, and a positive element indicates a *net* output of good j. Then the production possibility set of the economy is the set of all netput vectors available to each firm, or to several firms combined, or even to *all* firms combined (i.e., to the entire economy). If a firm's production possibility set includes netput vector $\mathbf{y}^1$ and another firm's production possibility set includes netput vector $\mathbf{y}^2$, then the economy's production possibility set includes netput vector $\mathbf{y}^1 + \mathbf{y}^2$.

Netput vectors are a delicate notion that can create problems if the assumptions about timing of inputs and outputs are different from the ones adopted here. In a non-capitalistic economy the negative elements of a netput indicate services of labours and lands, and the positive elements are outputs of consumption goods; the qualification 'net' is actually superfluous, and no problem arises. But netputs are also used to describe production processes in economies that use and produce capital goods. Then consider corn production that uses seed corn and labour as inputs at the beginning of the period, and corn as output at the

---

5   This is different from the dominant usage, which, once an initial date 0 is assigned, calls 'year 1' the year that starts at date 0, while in the terminology proposed here that year must be called year zero.

6   In more general treatments, it is possible to consider production processes that take longer than one period, then one splits the production process into a sequence of successive processes of unitary length that produce 'intermediate goods' (circulating capital goods) which are then among the inputs to the next process, up to the production of the final good. More on this is in ▶ Chap. 8.

360   Chapter 5 · Firms, Partial Equilibria and the General Equilibrium with Production

end of the period. How will the netput look like? It is indispensable to distinguish seed corn from corn output; this can be done by distinguishing goods according to their date of availability; corn at date t must be treated as a different good from corn at date $t+1$. This is the representation of goods in intertemporal equilibrium theory (see ▶ Chap. 8). In this case to talk of *net* outputs is useful for situations like the following: consider a production plan that uses ten units of labour and of land at time $t-1$ to produce 100 units of corn at date t, then uses 80 of these units of corn and ten units of labour to produce 80 units of flour at date $t+1$. This production plan will be represented by the netput vector

$$(-10\,\text{labour}_{t-1},\ -10\,\text{land}_{t-1},\ 20\,\text{corn}_t,\ -10\,\text{labour}_t,\ 80\,\text{flour}_{t+1}).$$

The netput 20 of corn of date t indicates the excess over internal re-utilization, it's what the firm can sell of that corn to others. The remaining 80 units of corn of date t do not appear. Netput vectors are convenient here because (admitting now the possibility of nonzero interest rates) if $\mathbf{y}$ is a netput vector and $\mathbf{p}$ the vector of *discounted* prices of the goods in $\mathbf{y}$, the inner product $\mathbf{p}\cdot\mathbf{y}$ yields the discounted 'profit' (neoclassical definition) from adopting that production plan, with negative netput entries (amounts of inputs) contributing to discounted cost and positive netput entries (amounts of outputs) contributing to discounted revenue.[7] Netput and input vectors are column vectors when necessary but I will generally neglect to stick to this when it is not indispensable.

Netput vectors become dangerous for the neoclassical approach when production uses capital goods, and production processes can be of a length inferior to the length of the period, so it is possible that a good produced inside a given period is used as input of another production process whose output also comes out inside the period. This picture of production is the one in the Leontief model presented in ▶ Chap. 2 (where however production was not represented with netputs). In this model one admits that several production cycles may go on in a single period, the number measuring the output of a good is the total amount of the good produced during the period, and the number measuring use of an input analogously refers to total use of that input in all processes producing the outputs of the period (capital goods are all circulating). It is then perfectly possible that some outputs produced during the period are used as inputs within the same period. The period's net output of a good is defined as the output of the good during the period minus the consumption of the good as input during the same period. It is a perfectly legitimate definition, in fact it is the one adopted in national accounting. But troubles arise if one identifies this net output with the notion of netput and then uses these netputs to compare supplies with demands for the purpose of determining the equilibrium between them. An example will illustrate.

The renowned treatise on general equilibrium by Arrow and Hahn (1971) on p. 64 considers an economy with two industries and two goods: in one period,

---

7   Discounted prices are discussed in ▶ Chap. 8.

5.2 · Production Possibility Sets, Netputs, Production Functions

industry A produces two units of good 2 using as input one unit of good 1, and industry B produces two units of good 1 using as input one unit of good 2; this is represented by netput vectors $(-1, 2)$ and $(2, -1)$. This means that the two industries jointly considered, by using one unit of corn plus one unit of iron can produce 2 units of each good; this, the authors argue, means that the economy's production possibility set includes the aggregate netput vector $(1, 1) = (-1, 2) + (2, -1)$. This is correct if $(1, 1)$ is interpreted as the net output vector in the sense of Leontief. But it is clearly false if netput vectors are to describe production processes indicating the inputs the firm or industry or economy must get hold of in order to produce the outputs: in the aggregate netput vector $(1, 1)$ one loses sight of the true technical constraints and cannot specify the conditions for equality of supply and demand; for example, if both industries need their inputs at the beginning of the period while outputs come out at the end of the period, a net output $(1, 1)$ cannot be produced unless there is one unit of each good available at the beginning of the period, and this must not be made to disappear from the description of the production possibilities of the economy if one wants to keep correct track of input needs (and hence demands) and output supplies. This seems to escape the authors, who seem to interpret $(1, 1)$ as indeed indicating the *possibility of producing without inputs*; the possibility of infinite production is prevented only by arguing that of course production needs at least one non-reproducible input, labour, whose limited supply puts a limit to how much can be produced. Thus suppose labour is good 3, and that each one of our two processes also requires as input one unit of labour. Now the industry netput vectors are $(-1, 2, -1)$ and $(2, -1, -1)$, and the simultaneous activation of the two processes has netput vector $(1, 1, -2)$. This is interpreted to mean that the firm sector needs two units of labour per period *and nothing else* in order to supply one unit of each good per period to consumers. The trouble is that a netput vector thus obtained only indicates the net output of the period as defined by national accounting or in the Leontief model, *not* the demands for inputs and the supplies of outputs of the firm sector, to be confronted with the supplies of inputs to this sector and the demands for products from it so as to determine whether the economy is in equilibrium. If for example both production processes take one period and are activated at the beginning of the period on the scales that use one unit of labour, this means that the firm sector demands, besides labour, one unit of each good as inputs at the beginning of the period and supplies two units of each good at the end of the period; there will be equilibrium if there is the corresponding supply of inputs at the beginning of the period and the corresponding demand for the products at the end of the period. It is a grave mistake to interpret the netput $(1, 1, -2)$ as meaning that equilibrium needs only the supply of two units of labour at the beginning of the period, and the demand for one unit of each product at the end; and yet this is the interpretation one gets from Arrow–Hahn; nor are they the only ones to adopt it.

Note further that the determination of the beginning-of-period demand for the two goods as inputs depends on what one assumes as to how many production cycles take place in a period. Suppose that the two total productions of our example result from the repetition 100 times, within the period, of a cycle always performed by the same vertically integrated firm and consisting of two stages, first a production process producing 0.02 units of good 1 with 0.01 units of good 2 and of labour as inputs, then a production process producing 0.02 units of good 2 with 0.01 units of good 1 and of labour as inputs (0.01 units of each good are sold to consumers at the end of each cycle). This firm needs a positive initial supply of 0.01 units of good 2, and this is all the *initial* input supply other than labour that this firm needs to produce in total two units of each good in the period. Statistically, this initial supply can even be so small as to be practically irrelevant; but theoretically, for this economy an initial endowment of some produced input besides labour is ineliminable and cannot be neglected in the search for equilibrium conditions.

The way to avoid mistakes in the specification of the equilibrium supply = demand conditions is to represent production processes so as not to allow outputs of a period to be used as circulating capital inputs to production of outputs of the same period or date, by making the period short enough if necessary. In this book, this is guaranteed by assuming that production processes take a period, and that outputs of a period cannot be used as inputs in the same period. Correct netputs, when used to specify supplies and demands for economies with capital goods, will have to refer to *dated* goods as in the corn-and-flour example. When only two dates are considered, with inputs applied at date t and outputs coming out at date $t+1$, then it can be superfluous to append time indices and it can suffice to separate the inputs from the outputs of a date later with a semicolon; for example the netput vectors for the production of the goods 1 and 2 of the Arrow–Hahn example, assuming production to be point–input–point–output and to take one period, and treating labour as good 3, will be $(-1,0,-1; 0,2,0)$ and $(0,-1,-1; 2,0,0)$; and the netput vector representing their joint activation will be $(-1,-1,-2; 2,2,0)$. With these netputs the demand for inputs at the beginning of the period and the supply of outputs at the end of the period are clear and can be used correctly to specify equilibrium conditions between supplies and demands. Of course the absence of time indices will indicate that these production processes are available independently of the date the economy is at.

In the same way as in consumer theory, inputs and outputs can also be distinguished by the location in which they are available and (see ▶ Chap. 9) by the state of nature with which they are associated, but for the moment let us leave these complications aside. When goods are dated, it will be generally legitimate to assume that if a production possibility set Y includes a productive process with netputs distinguished by their dates, then it also includes the same sequence with all netputs' dates increased by the same number, indicating that what matters to distinguish production processes is the time lag between inputs and outputs, and not the moment when the productive process is started.

When the vector of outputs to be produced by a firm is given, its ***input requirement set*** is the set of input vectors that allow the production of (at least) that vector of outputs. Note that, differently from the case with netput vectors, in the input requirement set inputs are measured as *positive* quantities. If one assumes that some of the quantities of inputs can be left idle, the input require-

5.2 · Production Possibility Sets, Netputs, Production Functions

ment set for a certain output vector includes all vectors $\mathbf{x}$ of inputs that allow producing *at least* that output vector, plus all vectors $\mathbf{x}' \geq \mathbf{x}$.

Firms will try to utilize *efficient* production processes. In terms of *netput vectors* we say that $\mathbf{y} \in Y$ is efficient if there is no other $\mathbf{y}' \in Y$ such that $\mathbf{y}' \neq \mathbf{y}$ and $\mathbf{y}' \geq \mathbf{y}$: it is not possible to produce the same outputs with less of some input and no more of other inputs, or to produce more of some output with the same inputs and the same other outputs. If the output vector $\mathbf{z} \geq 0$ is given, an input vector $\mathbf{x}$ (inputs being measured now as positive quantities) is efficient if no vector $\mathbf{x}' \leq \mathbf{x}$, $\mathbf{x}' \neq \mathbf{x}$ exists that allows the production of $\mathbf{z}$.

When one considers production processes that produce only one output, it is often assumed that the *economically relevant* production processes that produce that output can be described by a **production function** $q = f(x_1, \ldots, x_n) = f(\mathbf{x})$ where output q is the *maximum* output obtainable from the vector of inputs $\mathbf{x} = (x_1, \ldots, x_n)$, the latter measured as *positive* quantities. In economics, when one speaks of output obtainable from certain inputs, one means the *maximum* output. The set of input vectors that a production function $q = f(\mathbf{x})$ associates with a given output $q°$ is called the **isoquant** associated with $q°$; it was already discussed in ▶ Sect. 3.3; see also ▶ Sect. 3.7.2 on L-shaped isoquants.

Note: 'q is the maximum output obtainable from an input vector $\mathbf{x}$' does *not* mean that no element of $\mathbf{x}$ can be reduced if q is to be produced. Given the other elements of $\mathbf{x}$, some element of $\mathbf{x}$ might be in excess of what is necessary for the production of q, without the excess helping production. L-shaped isoquants (inputs that are 'perfect complements') are a clear example; the isoquants illustrated in ▶ Chap. 3, ◘ Fig. 3.7a, are another example.

In the ***short period*** the quantity of some inputs to a production function cannot be varied; these are called *fixed inputs*. A **short-period production function** has two alternative representations: it can include among the inputs the given quantities of the fixed factors, but for brevity it can also describe output as a function of the sole *variable inputs*.

The equivalent of the production function for production processes that produce several outputs jointly is a ***transformation function*** implicitly defined by an equation $T(x_1, \ldots, x_n; q_1, \ldots, q_m) = 0$, where, again, inputs are measured as positive quantities.[8] The equation renders each output an implicit function of the quantities of inputs and of the other outputs. It is usually assumed that, if all inputs, and all outputs but two, are given, then the possible combinations of outputs of the remaining two goods form a decreasing concave curve, called a ***transformation curve***, and similar to the *Production Possibility Frontier* to be studied below, §5.29. The slope of the transformation curve is the ***marginal rate of transformation***, MRT.

---

8   *Exercise*: Obtain the transformation–function representation of a production function.

364   Chapter 5 · Firms, Partial Equilibria and the General Equilibrium with Production

5.3 Axioms on the Production Possibility Set

Economic literature uses both production functions, transformation functions and netput vectors, so the reader must learn to pass quickly from one representation of production possibilities to another. The main difference is that inputs are negative quantities in the netput representation. When the production possibility set Y is a set of netput vectors, some axioms that may be postulated on it are as follows:

1. $0 \in Y$, inactivity is one possibility.
2. $Y \cap R_+^n + \{0\}$, no production of outputs without some input.
3. $Y \cap -Y = \{0\}$, production is irreversible (the only element of $-Y$ which is in Y is zero production with zero inputs).
4. Y is convex.
5. Y is bounded above.
6. for any good i, and any positive scalar q, the vector $y = (0, \ldots, 0, -q_i, 0, \ldots 0)$ is in Y.

Axioms 1, 2 and 3 are unproblematic and are assumed in what follows. The other axioms may or may not be assumed. Axiom 4 implies perfect divisibility of all inputs and outputs; its connection with returns to scale will be discussed presently. Axiom 5 is counterintuitive, but sometimes it is useful temporarily to assume it in a first stage of some mathematical proofs and to remove it later.

Axiom 6 is called the *free disposal assumption*; it postulates that for each good there is a process available that uses that good alone as an input and produces nothing, so one can always get rid of any amount of any output or input without any cost. When the free disposal assumption is made, then any firm can couple any production process with free disposal processes, and the result is a property or assumption sometimes called *monotonicity of the production possibility set*,[9] which in terms of netputs states:

$$\text{if } \mathbf{y} \in Y, \text{ then any } \mathbf{y}' \text{ such that } \mathbf{y}' \leq \mathbf{y} \text{ is also} \in Y,$$

because $\mathbf{y}'$ is a process that employs at least as much of each input as $\mathbf{y}$ [10] and produces not more of each output than $\mathbf{y}$, and it is always possible to obtain $\mathbf{y}'$ from $\mathbf{y}$ by use of free disposal processes.

Free disposal may appear a questionable assumption in many situations (it is often costly to get rid of goods, or to prevent some output from coming out), but it can be argued to be fundamentally harmless. An ability costlessly to get rid of excess inputs is not needed as long as these inputs have a positive cost, because

---

9 Some authors call monotonicity the following slightly different assumption: let $\mathbf{q}$ stand for a vector of outputs and let $V(\mathbf{q})$ stand for the set of input vectors (measured as positive quantities) that allow the production of at least $\mathbf{q}$; if an input vector $\mathbf{x}$ is in $V(\mathbf{q})$, and $\mathbf{x}' \geq \mathbf{x}$, then $\mathbf{x}' \in V(\mathbf{q})$.

10 Remember that inputs are negative numbers, so a *greater* use of an input means a greater absolute value of a negative number, i.e. algebraically, a *smaller* number indicating input use.

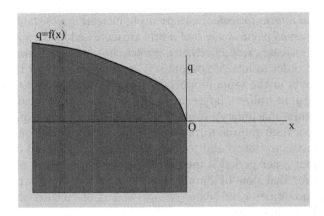

Fig. 5.1 Production possibility set resulting from a one-input one-output strictly convex *production function* $q = f(x)$ plus free disposal

then firms will not buy them to start with, so a free disposal assumption of costly inputs is superfluous but then also harmless; and if inputs are costless and with a negative marginal product, they can be left idle and all one needs is to distinguish the *technological* from the *economic* production method (as was done in §3.3). As to undesired joint outputs, if they must not be produced it can be assumed that, whatever disposal process is necessary in order to dispose of them, its inputs (and costs) are included among the inputs (and costs) of the desired output.

5.4 Returns to Scale

The convexity Axiom 4 stipulates that if $y \in Y$ and $y' \in Y$, then for $0 < a < 1$ all netputs $y'' = ay + (1-a)y'$ are also in Y. It requires divisibility of inputs and of outputs.

Exercise: α) Suppose a single output q is produced by two inputs x_1 and x_2 according to the production function $q = ax_1 + bx_2$, $a, b > 0$. Draw some isoquants and prove that the production possibility set is convex.

β) Suppose two outputs z_1 and z_2 are jointly produced by a single input x with transformation function $z_1^2 + z_2^2 - x = 0$. Prove that the production possibility set is convex and that for fixed x the locus of possible efficient combinations of z_1 and z_2 (the transformation curve) is concave.

γ) Suppose a single output q is produced by two inputs x_1 and x_2 according to the production function $q = x_1^2 + x_2^2$; draw some isoquants and prove that the production possibility set is not convex.

An assessment of the meaning and of the acceptability of Axiom 4 requires a discussion of increasing, constant and decreasing **returns to scale**, a notion given different meanings in the history of economic thought. The expression 'returns to scale' refers to the 'returns', in terms of output or of profit, a firm can expect from its activity when it changes the scale of its operations.

366 Chapter 5 · Firms, Partial Equilibria and the General Equilibrium with Production

Technological returns to scale are, respectively, increasing, constant or decreasing according as, when *all physical inputs* of a firm are increased by the *same* percentage, physical output increases, respectively, in a greater, the same, or a lesser percentage.

But often in order to increase output it is more convenient for the firm not to increase all inputs in the same proportion and possibly totally to change some of the inputs (e.g. to utilize a larger land surface it may be convenient to change type of agricultural machinery). It is still possible then to speak of increasing or decreasing or constant returns to the scale of the firm's operations by referring to returns in monetary terms and to the scale of *costs*. The **total cost** C of producing an output q per period is the (minimum) cost per period of the flows of inputs needed for that flow of output. For example if to produce q per period the firm needs quantities x_1 of labour services and x_2 of land services per period, and the rentals of these inputs are v_1 and v_2, total cost per period is $v_1x_1 + v_2x_2$. The monetary returns, if the firm is price-taker, are strictly proportional to output, so one can equivalently measure them directly in terms of output by choosing such a unit for output that its price is 1. Then **returns to the scale of total cost** are increasing, constant or decreasing according as an increase in total cost by a given percentage raises output by a greater, the same or a lesser percentage. This notion of returns to scale is much more flexible than technological returns to scale in that it allows changes in the types of inputs or in the proportions in which inputs are combined. But it needs either given input prices or input prices that change with output in a known way. If it is returns to scale of a single firm one is examining, then the normal assumption is given input prices. Then constant returns in this sense mean that the firm requires a doubling of total cost in order to double output. Let us define **average cost**, AC, as total cost per unit of output, $AC = C/q$. Then increasing returns to the scale of total cost, or for brevity increasing returns to cost, means that AC decreases if q increases. **Scale economies** is another term used to indicate increasing returns to cost, and **scale diseconomies** to indicate decreasing returns to cost, a rise of AC if q increases.

A third, still more complex notion of returns, was used by Alfred Marshall to refer to the returns an entire *industry* obtains from increasing its total output. Marshall allowed the average cost of an industry's output to change not only because of changes in the machinery used when output of each firm increases, but also because of (i) changes in the prices of some of the industry's inputs (e.g. a rise in the cost of a type of land used by the industry), and because of (ii) *external effects*, positive or negative influences on the production function of each firm in the industry caused by increases in the industry's output, for example greater facility in finding competent repair men and spare parts (a positive external effect) or more pollution that reduces productive efficiency (a negative external effect).[11] A constant returns industry in this Marshallian sense is an

---

11 *Externality* or external effect is the term denoting an influence of consumption or production decisions of some agents on the utility function or the production function of other agents. Listening to loud rock music, for example, may reduce the utility of neighbours and is then a negative consumption externality. When discussing production the terms *external economies* and *external diseconomies* are also used. See ▶ Chap. 14.

5.4 · Returns to Scale

industry which can expand output without incurring increases nor decreases of the long-period AC of the typical firm, so that the long-period normal output price, which as we will study tends to equal AC, does not change with changes in demand and its supply function is horizontal in partial-equilibrium analysis. But we are anticipating.

Standard microeconomics discusses only technological returns to scale, which can be defined in terms of properties of the production function. Let $\mathbf{x}$ be the vector of inputs to a production function $f(\mathbf{x})$. We say that $f(\mathbf{x})$ exhibits, with reference to technological returns to scale:

$$constant\ returns\ to\ scale(CRS) \quad if f(t\mathbf{x}) = tf(\mathbf{x}) \text{ for } t > 0;$$

$$increasing\ returns\ to\ scale(IRS) \quad if f(t\mathbf{x}) > tf(\mathbf{x}) \text{ for } t > 1;$$

$$decreasing\ returns\ to\ scale(DRS) \quad if f(t\mathbf{x}) > tf(\mathbf{x}) \text{ for } t > 1.$$

Returns to scale can be variable: for example a production function can exhibit returns to scale that are increasing at first, then constant, then decreasing. *Local* *technological returns to scale* for a given vector of inputs $\mathbf{x}$ are ascertained by checking which one of the three inequalities holds for small variations of t around 1 (cf. Sect. 5.6.1 below).

Technical returns to scale can also be defined in terms of netputs and of *frontier of the production possibility set F(Y)*, the subset of efficient netputs in Y. If netput $\mathbf{y} \in F(Y)$ implies $t\mathbf{y} \in F(Y)$, with t any positive scalar in a neighbourhood of 1, we say that Y exhibits local CRS. There are increasing returns to scale *at least locally*, if there is some $\mathbf{y} \in F(Y)$ and some scalar $t > 1$, such that $t\mathbf{y} \in Y$ and $t\mathbf{y} \notin F(Y)$, that is, $\exists\,\mathbf{y}' \in Y$ and $\neq t\mathbf{y}$ such that $\mathbf{y}' \geq t\mathbf{y}$.

Note that *if there are increasing returns to scale at least locally, then Y is not convex*.

Proof by contradiction. By Axiom 1, $\mathbf{y} = (0,...,0) \in Y$, so convexity requires that for any $\mathbf{y} \in Y$ also $t'\mathbf{y}$ with $0 < t' < 1$ is in Y; then consider netputs $\mathbf{y} \in F(Y)$, $t\mathbf{y}$ and $\mathbf{y}' \geq t\mathbf{y}$ of the above definition of locally increasing returns in terms of netputs: if Y is convex, $\mathbf{y}'' = t'\mathbf{y}'$ with $0 < t' < 1$ is in Y; choose $t' = 1/t$, then $\mathbf{y}'' \geq \mathbf{y}$ and $\mathbf{y}'' \neq \mathbf{y}$, so $\mathbf{y}$ cannot be in F(Y), contradicting the assumptions; hence Y cannot be convex. ∎

This shows that Axiom 4 excludes increasing returns to scale. Now, increasing returns to scale are argued by many economists to be often present in reality; therefore Axiom 4 is a restrictive assumption; in spite of this, I will generally assume it because it is necessary for the standard theory of general equilibrium.

Exercise: Prove that a convex production possibility set with a single output implies a *quasi-concave* production function. (Hint: prove first that the input requirement set is convex. The definition of quasi-concavity was given in Chap. 4, ▶ Sect. 4.5)

I will generally assume that all inputs and outputs are *perfectly divisible*, i.e. can be represented by continuous variables. This is a good approximation for land and for labour time, but it is obviously unrealistic for most capital goods and for many products; however, if the analysis deals with big quantities, the assumption

368 Chapter 5 · Firms, Partial Equilibria and the General Equilibrium with Production

can still be acceptable if the indivisibilities are small relative to total input use or total output of the industry.

5.5 Differentiable Production Functions and Value Capital

A common assumption is the **differentiability** of the production function, but here we come to a very important issue when we consider production functions with capital goods among the inputs. In most industries a different productive method requires, not different proportions among the same capital goods, but different capital goods in fixed proportions, and for each such method a rigid labour input per unit of output. For example the amount of labour services needed to assemble a car in an assembly line plant is strictly determined by how mechanized the production process is; and there is no substitutability between the parts to be assembled, a car needs exactly one engine, four wheels, etc., each one of these parts needing in turn, in order to be produced, rigid quantities of material inputs[12] and rigid amounts of labour determined by the machinery used. With the exception of some inputs in some agricultural production (where one can vary amounts of irrigation, fertilizers and pesticides per unit of land), there generally is no or nearly no variability of proportions among the *same* inputs when these include specialized capital goods: hence generally, differentiability of the production function is a *very* unrealistic assumption. But then how come the differentiability assumption is so widely accepted?

The reason is a historical one, namely the Marshallian habit, shared by the great majority of economists up to the 1960s, and still widespread today, to describe production functions with as inputs labour, land *and capital treated as a single factor K*, measured as an amount of *exchange value* (see ▶ Chap. 7). These production functions implicitly *take the prices of the several capital goods as given*, and the production function is determined as follows: the firm determines, for each given vector of non-capital inputs and each given K, the vector of capital goods of value K that maximizes production; given the amounts of labour and land, a small increase of K can well imply a totally different vector of capital goods[13]; thus along the **total productivity curve** of capital so conceived,[14] capital changes not only in quantity (total exchange value), but also in 'form' (physical composition of the vector of capital goods that are taken to represent the

---

12 Remember that raw materials are (circulating) capital goods too.
13 For example, in agricultural production, it can mean a different tractor.
14 Remember from ▶ Chap. 3 that, given a production function $q = f(x_1, x_2, \ldots)$, with divisible inputs, the *total productivity curve of a factor* represents output as a function of the sole amount of that factor, for *given* amounts of all other factors; it shifts if the amounts of the other factors are changed.

5.5 · Differentiable Production Functions and Value Capital

'quantity of capital' the firm is employing), generally discontinuously.[15] With such a specification of the capital input, the assumption of smooth variability of proportions between the inputs is no longer totally implausible: e.g. in car production if what can be coupled with a given amount of labour is the *value* of the capital goods employed, then it is likely that a way *can* be found to use an increase in capital so defined to increase the number of cars produced per period by a given number of workers. It is this treatment of capital that made the differentiability assumption acceptable.

In recent decades this traditional marginalist treatment of capital as a single factor of variable 'form', measured as a quantity of exchange value, has been replaced in advanced microeconomics by the treatment of the several capital goods as so many distinct factors; but the assumption of extensive factor substitutability is still generally made, with little awareness that it is no longer acceptable with this different treatment of capital. Nor is it possible to go back to the traditional treatment of capital as a factor whose quantity is a quantity of exchange value, because it has been realized that that treatment required *given* relative prices, while we know from ▶ Chap. 1 that even *normal* relative product prices cannot be taken as given before income distribution is determined; this means that the procedure described above, that for a given labour input finds the capital goods that maximize production for each given K, determines a different output for the same K if income distribution is different. This destroys the notion of production function as given independently of what it should help determine: demands for factors as functions of relative factor rentals. In ▶ Sect. 7.13 other traditional production functions where capital changes 'form' will be discussed; none justifies an assumption of substitutability among inputs including physically specified heterogeneous capital goods. In the present chapter I will not question the differentiability assumption but only because the aim is to introduce readers to the standard neoclassical theory of the firm.

5.6 Homogeneous Production Functions and Returns to Scale

In ▶ Chap. 4 we met homogeneous functions. Let us examine the connection between returns to scale and homogeneous production functions. CRS implies that the production function is homogeneous of degree 1.[16] If the production function is homogeneous of degree $k > 1$, it has increasing (technical) returns to scale;

---

15 Analogously an isoquant in terms of, say, labour and K indicates, for each level of labour, the minimum *value* of capital goods required to produce the given output; again, small movements along the isoquant can well mean a jump to a production method requiring a very different vector of capital goods. See ▶ Sect. 7.13

16 Let me remember two useful properties of a differentiable function $f(x_1,...,x_n)$ homogeneous of degree 1: first, the partial derivatives are homogeneous of degree zero; second, $\sum_i (x_i \cdot \partial f/\partial x_i) = f(\mathbf{x})$.

370 Chapter 5 · Firms, Partial Equilibria and the General Equilibrium with Production

if homogeneous of degree k < 1 it has decreasing (technical) returns to scale. Even when a production function $f(x($ is not homogeneous, we can determine its *local degree of homogeneity* by increasing all independent variables by a common small percentage, say, 1%, and observing whether $f(x)$ increases by more or less than 1%. The second percentage variation divided by the first is called **scale elasticity of output** or simply **elasticity of scale**. An elasticity of scale greater than (respectively, equal to, or less than) 1 indicates locally increasing (respectively, locally constant or locally decreasing) technological returns to scale. Let x be the vector of inputs in an initial situation with $q = f(x)$, and consider $f(tx)$ with $t > 0$; the scalar t measures the scale (of inputs) and the scale elasticity of output in $q = f(x)$ is

$$e_s = [df(tx)/f(tx)]/(dt/t) = (\partial q/\partial t) \cdot (t/q) = \partial \ln q / \partial \ln t \text{ evaluated in } t = 1 \text{ at the given } \mathbf{x}.$$

Note that this definition does not require differentiability of $f(x)$, it only requires differentiability of $f(tx)$ with respect to t, therefore it is also applicable to production functions where some of the inputs or even all of them must be combined in fixed proportions (perfect complements). But if $f(x)$ is differentiable, then by the derivative rule of a function of function it is

$$e_s = \frac{1}{f(x)} \sum_{i=1}^{n} [x_i \cdot \partial f / \partial x_i].$$

By Euler's theorem on homogeneous functions, if the production function has constant returns to scale then $\sum_i (x_i \cdot \partial f / \partial x_i) = f(\mathbf{x})$ so $e_s = 1$.[17]

If *all* relevant inputs are taken into account in the specification of the production function, then an exact doubling of all inputs should allow the exact replication of the same plant twice and therefore it should permit *at least* a doubling of production. Why do I say 'at least'? Consider the production function of a firm that extracts and transports oil and also produces all the pipes for the pipeline. The pipes are intermediate products in the overall production process and appear neither among the inputs nor among the outputs of the oil production-and-transport function. The inputs include the steel needed to make the pipes. Up to a point the carrying capacity of pipes increases more than proportionally with the increase in the steel utilized to make pipes, because the steel utilized is—within certain limits—roughly proportional to the diameter of the pipe but the carrying capacity is proportional to the square of the diameter. Doubling the amount of produced and transported oil may then require pipes of less than double diameter that use less than double the steel, with less than double the cost. This example shows that, when the production function reflects vertically integrated production processes

---

17 The extension of these definitions to **transformation functions** is left to the reader (*rays* of outputs will replace the single output; a complication is that, since with transformation functions generally a given vector of inputs does not uniquely determine the vector of outputs, it is possible to imagine cases where returns to scale differ according to which output ray one considers).

5.6 · Homogeneous Production Functions and Returns to Scale

which include the production and internal utilization of intermediate goods, a doubling of all inputs need not correspond to a replication of the same production process twice, and a doubling of output need not require a doubling of inputs.[18] Still, the replication of the same production process twice (the building of a second plant identical to the first one, in which the same method is applied) is always possible and therefore returns to scale for integer $t > 1$ are at least constant.

The result $f(t\mathbf{x}) \geq tf(\mathbf{x})$ need not hold for fractional increases in scale if there are indivisibilities. Below I will assume that this problem is of minor importance, presently we will see that when one considers an entire industry with free entry it is generally plausible to treat the industry output as coming from a CRS production function even when at the firm level there are relevant indivisibilities.

Plausibly, even if indivisibilities cause increasing returns at small scales of production, at each stage of technical knowledge there is a finite production scale beyond which returns to scale are no longer increasing: call it **minimum efficient scale**. (e.g. beyond a certain dimension, larger pipes are no longer convenient because they require specially reinforced structures.) Plausibly, competition with free entry will cause firms to reach at least the minimum optimal scale (less efficient firms will tend to disappear). As long as this minimum scale is small relative to total industry output, and time is given for competition and entry to impose efficiency, all firms in an industry will tend to adopt the same technology, and variations in the aggregate output of the industry will be obtained by variations in the number and/or dimension of efficient plants; then as pointed out in ▶ Chap. 3 the industry can be seen as having a production function exhibiting constant returns to scale—where the constancy is generated by variations in the number of efficient plants that use the same inputs per unit of output. For this reason, for long-period competitive analyses I will assume constant technical returns to scale for *industries*.

What about **decreasing** technical returns to scale? They are difficult to defend if the inputs appearing in the production function are really *all* relevant inputs, because then identical duplication of plant and process should yield double output. A production function with decreasing technical returns *to scale* must be interpreted as not including all the needed inputs, at least one input does not appear in the production function and is fixed in amount and causes decreasing marginal products of the other inputs. For example if a firm producing an output q with land T and labour L according to a CRS production function $q = L^{2/3}T^{1/3}$ has a fixed quantity of land $T^\circ = 64$, one can represent its production possibilities as $f(T^\circ, L) = 4L^{1/3}$, and the latter form has decreasing returns to scale. This is the typical representation of production possibilities in short-period analyses.

There is an argument contending that even in long-period analysis sooner or later a firm meets decreasing returns to scale owing to an increasing *difficulty of*

---

18 The same can happen if capital goods are aggregated into the single factor '(value of) capital' at given prices; then doubling the capital and the non-capital inputs need not correspond to purchasing twice as many of the same capital goods, it can mean the use of a different fixed plant that costs twice as much and employs twice as much labour but allows more than double the production.

control and coordination over the performance of subordinates: plant duplication, including duplication of managers, requires that managers must be controlled by a top manager to avoid subordinate managers shirking or embezzling, and this control becomes more difficult where there are many managers to be controlled; furthermore, the information that the top manager must process increases. According to this argument there is not only a minimum efficient scale but also a maximum efficient scale of firms. The persuasiveness of this argument is still an object of disagreement among theoreticians.[19]

But for the purposes of value theory what is important is the behaviour of *industries*, and then the moment one admits free entry, in long-period analysis *industry* output is varied by variation in the number of firms all producing at minimum average cost, so the industry can be treated as having approximately CRS anyway.

5.7 Activity Analysis

Let me clarify the difference between production *process* and production *method* when there are CRS. A production process is a production method applied on a certain scale or activity level. The production method (with CRS and divisibility) is defined by the vector of input technical coefficients *per unit of output*. The distinction between production *process* and production *method* comes useful when, given the general lack of substitutability between different capital goods, one esteems that it is a closer approximation to reality to represent the production possibilities of a firm as including only a finite number of CRS fixed proportions production *methods*, also called *activities* in older literature, which can be operated at any level. Assuming divisibility, the firm can also activate convex combinations of processes. In this case the production possibility set is a polyhedral convex cone, with the efficient methods as edges and the vertex in the origin; the isoquants are said to be *of the activity-analysis type*. ◘ Figure 5.2 shows one example of unit isoquant with three methods, the other isoquants are radial expansions or contractions of the unit isoquant.

---

19 For example, Scherer and Ross (1980, p. 106) agree with the traditional argument that the greater difficulty of control when firm size increases is a cause of ultimately decreasing returns to scale. Edith Penrose on the contrary writes: 'We do not know how effective the decentralization of authority can be as a means of keeping costs per unit of output from rising as a firm expands. Reliable empirical evidence does not exist and all studies of the matter are inconclusive, but there is no evidence that a large decentralized concern requires supermen to run it....Neither is there significant evidence that the ability to fill the higher administrative positions is excessively rare or that the demands on the men occupying these positions exceed their ability to cope with them effectively'. Penrose (1955, p. 542). Cases supporting Penrose, for example MacDonald's or CocaCola, easily come to mind. Perhaps *there are* increasing difficulties of coordination *but* in many cases the advantages of increasing size are so great (consider the scale economies in marketing, R&D, transport costs, etc.), as to more than counterbalance them; also, tying decentralized managers' pay to results may be often sufficient to motivate them.

5.7 · Activity Analysis

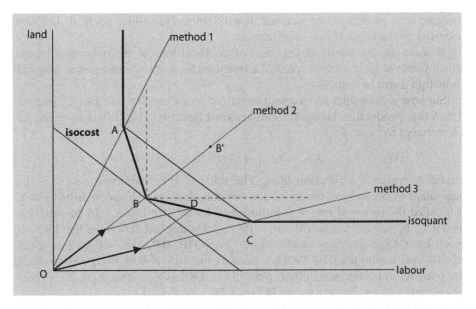

Fig. 5.2 Activity-analysis unit isoquant with three alternative methods, whose input vectors are points A, B and C. The red broken line is the unit isoquant associated with method 2 alone. A convex combination of methods 2 and 3 activated on the scales shown by the arrows allows producing one unit of output with the combination of the two factors indicated by point D. Any method corresponding to points above this isoquant, e.g. B′, will never be convenient. Hence convex combinations of methods A and C are not convenient

If only one method were available, the isoquants would be L-shaped, corresponding in the two-inputs case to a production function of type $q = min\{\alpha x_1, \beta x_2\}$. In ◘ Fig. 5.2 the unit isoquant of method 2 is shown in red.

With more than two methods, it can happen that one method is never convenient, the activity-analysis isoquant is the *lower envelope* of the segments uniting the points corresponding to the several methods, and some methods may be left out.

With activity-analysis isoquants it can happen that the *isocost* (defined in ▶ Sect. 3.3.2) associated with a given output is tangent to one of the segments of the isoquant; then input demands for that output are not uniquely determined, the firm can produce with any convex combination of the two production methods involved.

5.8 Marginal Product, Transformation Curve

I assume now that the firm produces a single output and its efficient production possibilities are represented by a production function $f(\mathbf{x})$ which is twice continuously differentiable (i.e. has partial derivatives that are differentiable, and *their* partial derivatives are continuous). Then we can define the **marginal product** of factor x_i as $MP_i \equiv \partial f / \partial x_i$; and the locus of input combinations which yield an assigned level of output, the **isoquant**, is a differentiable surface (in R^n if there are n inputs) by the implicit function theorem.

If some factors are fixed, the locus of combinations of the remaining inputs which yield the given output is called a **restricted isoquant** or **short-period isoquant** (note that it can be empty).

Suppose we consider an isoquant restricted to the two inputs i and j. The condition that production be equal to an assigned quantity $q^\wedge$ and that all inputs be given except for x_i and x_j:

$$f(x_1,\ldots,x_i,\ldots,x_j,\ldots,x_n) = q^\wedge; \text{ with } x_h \text{ given except for } h = i, j$$

implicitly makes x_j a function of x_i. The slope of this function $x_j = x_j(x_i)$ is the equivalent in production theory of the consumer's marginal rate of substitution; it is called the **technical rate of substitution** of factor j for factor i, to be indicated as TRS_{ji}; by the derivative rule for differentiable implicit functions the TRS_{ji} is given by $TRS_{ji} \equiv dx_j/dx_i = -(\partial f/\partial x_i)/(\partial f/\partial x_j) = -MP_i/MP_j$, the well-known result of first-year textbooks. The TRS is a *negative* quantity if both marginal products are positive; but economists often speak of the TRS as a positive quantity, implicitly referring to its absolute value (◘ Fig. 5.3).

In ▶ Chap. 3 we saw that marginal products need not be positive, and therefore *technological* isoquants need not be everywhere downward sloping. (The reader is invited to re-read in ▶ Chap. 3 the distinction between technological and economic isoquants.) I supply now a numerical example. Assume

$$q = \left(x_1 x_2 - .8x_1^2 - .2x_2^2\right)^{1/2}$$

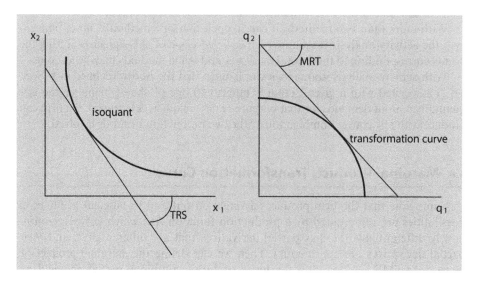

◘ **Fig. 5.3** Standard isoquant and standard transformation curve in R^2

5.8 · Marginal Product, Transformation Curve

The reader can check that this production function has CRS. Marginal products are given by

$$\partial q/\partial x_1 = \frac{1}{2q^{1/2}}(x_2 - 1.6x_1),$$

$$\partial q/\partial x_2 = \frac{1}{2q^{1/2}}(x_1 - .4x_2).$$

Provided it is $q > 0$, which will be the case as long as $1 < x_2/x_1 < 4$, the marginal product of factor 1 is positive as long as $x_2 > 1.6 \cdot x_1$, and the marginal product of factor 2 is positive as long as $x_2 < 2.5 \cdot x_1$. Hence both marginal products are positive and isoquants are negatively sloped only as long as $1.6 < x_2/x_1 < 2.5$. Outside this fairly restricted range of factor proportions, one of the two marginal products is zero or negative, implying an upward-sloping *technological* isoquant; it will be convenient to leave one of the factors partially unutilized.

For a differentiable transformation function $T(x_1,...,x_n;q_1,...,q_m) = 0$, since there is more than one output, an input has several marginal products, one for each output. The determination of the TRS between two inputs requires that all other inputs and all outputs be fixed. If all inputs, and all outputs but two are fixed, the locus of efficient combinations of the two remaining outputs (where efficiency means that one output is maximized when the other one is given) is called a **transformation curve**[20] and its slope is called the **marginal rate of transformation**, MRT, and is given by $\mathrm{MRT}_{ji} \equiv dq_j/dq_i = -(\partial T/\partial q_i)/(\partial T/\partial q_j)$.

Back to a single output, we know from ▶ Chap. 3 that with constant returns to scale marginal products only depend on factor proportions and not on the scale of production. Thus along a ray from the origin all isoquants have the same TRS, they are all radial expansions or contractions of any one of them.

No doubt the reader has noticed the resemblance between isoquants and indifference curves and between marginal products and marginal utilities. Thus, for example, convex isoquants imply that the production function is quasi-concave. However, there are some differences.

A first difference is the *cardinal* character of production possibilities versus the *ordinal* nature of preferences. Any strictly increasing transformation of an increasing utility function represents the same preferences; on the contrary, any transformation of a production function alters the production possibilities. Therefore returns to scale, which are arbitrary in ordinal utility theory, are quite significant in production theory.

Second, *as long as CRS and perfect divisibility of goods and differentiability of the production function are assumed, an isoquant is necessarily convex although it need not be strictly convex.* This is because under these assumptions if $\mathbf{x}$ and $\mathbf{x}'$ are two input vectors belonging to the isoquant associated with output q, then the firm can produce q with a convex combination of those two input vectors, as in

---

20 It is also called a Production Possibility Frontier *for the firm* (in order to distinguish it from the Production Possibility frontier for the entire economy).

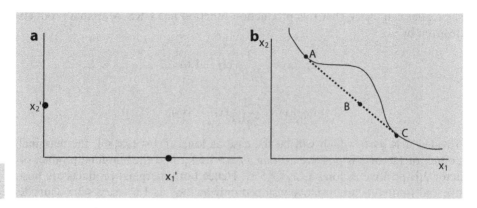

Fig. 5.4 Examples of isoquants

▶ Sect. 5.7. Any point on a concave portion of an isoquant will never be adopted because more costly than a convex combination of other points of the isoquant.

This is no longer necessarily the case with restricted, or short-period, isoquants. For example, with a given machine for chemical reactions, it might be possible to produce a given output by using one chemical process, or another chemical process based on different components, but any joint use (or even alternate use) of the two processes on the same machine might be impossible because the residues of the components of one process would damage the other process. In this case, assuming free disposal, a restricted isoquant will have the shape shown in ◘ Fig. 5.4a. The meaning of such an isoquant is that, given the other inputs, the desired output can be produced either with the quantity x_1' of input 1, or with the quantity x_2' of input 2, but *not* with a combination of both inputs. However, cases such as this one can be considered highly unusual and therefore I leave them aside.

5.9 Profit Maximization and WAPM

The standard assumption about the behaviour of firms is that they aim to maximize *profit*.[21] The meaning of 'profit' here and in the entire chapter is the marginalist/neoclassical one, i.e. in this chapter 'profit' stands for what is left to the 'entrepreneur' (the owner or owners of the firm) after paying all costs *including* interest on capital advances[22]. Even when the apparent aim of the firm is another

---

21 See A. Koutsoyiannis, *Modern Microeconomics*, 1975, Chaps. 15–18, for a survey of other views on what the firm aims to maximize; and more recently, Lavoie (2014), Chap. 3.
22 And including an allowance for risk too; but we are not considering risk for the moment. (The reader may be surprised by our mentioning interest here; but as explained in this chapter the treatment of firms aims to be general, the assumption that there are no capital goods and no interest rate will only be made when we come to the non-capitalistic general equilibrium model to be studied at the end of this chapter.)

5.9 · Profit Maximization and WAPM

one, e.g. sales maximization or maximization of growth rate, a case can usually be made that this does not entail significantly different choices from the ones aimed at maximizing long-run profit. Giving up profits today means to have less money to reinvest, and so to have one's wealth increase slower: so sales maximization entailing less profits today than with fewer sales seems reasonable only if this entails other advantages, e.g. an increase in market power which will allow raising price and hence profits in subsequent periods, but then it is part of a strategy of long-period profit maximization (in an imperfectly competitive market). Growth maximization entailing persistently lower profits than with a lower growth rate is analogously difficult to justify unless it brings other advantages, e.g. a greater chance of survival in a world with increasing returns to scale, but then again the ultimate reason is to avoid a loss of profits in subsequent periods. A different argument is that perfectly efficient profit maximization cannot be assumed, owing to limited managerial capacities and to the costs of maximization. But as long as management strives for profit maximization the fact that the goal is only imperfectly realized does not alter the broad pattern of industry behaviour. For example, the tendency to invest more in the industries that offer better profitability prospects will exist even if on average management is not very good at minimizing costs. And the occasional episodes of managers pursuing strategies of personal enrichment at the expense of the profitability of their firm usually end up rather quickly in the disappearance or takeover of the firm. I accept profit maximization as broadly valid as a survival condition in competitive industries.[23] A monopolist entrepreneur not threatened by takeovers might indulge in other aims, e.g. to have political influence, or play golf, or be generous towards employees; firms in competitive environments and under threat of takeovers end up being taken over or going bankrupt if they do not struggle to obtain good results, and this requires profit maximization or at least attempting it.

In what follows the prices of outputs are indicated as p_j, $j = 1, ..., m$; the rentals (prices of the services[24]) of inputs are v_i, $i = 1, ..., n$. The vectors $\mathbf{p} = (p_1, ..., p_m)$ and $\mathbf{v} = (v_1, ..., v_n)$ are *row* vectors if this must be specified, and the vectors of inputs $\mathbf{x}$ and of outputs $\mathbf{q}$ of a production process are *column* vectors. If, as I will mostly assume in what follows, the firm produces a single output, then vector $\mathbf{q}$ has only one nonzero element, in the netput representation a netput is a vector $(-x_1, ..., -x_n, 0, ..., 0, q_j, 0, ..., 0)$. At given prices $(\mathbf{p}, \mathbf{v})$, for each production process with netput $(-\mathbf{x}, \mathbf{q})$ total cost is $\mathbf{vx}$ and profit is $\pi := \mathbf{pq} - \mathbf{vx}$. If the process is a one-period process, with inputs applied at the beginning and output coming out at the end

---

23 A popular textbook states: 'From the voluminous and often inconsistent evidence, it appears that the profit maximization assumption at least provides a good first approximation in describing business behaviour. Deviations, both intended and inadvertent, undoubtedly exist in abundance, but they are kept within more or less narrow bounds by competitive pressures, the self-interest of stock-owning managers, and the threat of managerial displacement by important outside shareholders or takeovers'. (Scherer and Ross 1990).

24 As pointed out in ▶ Chap. 3, it is preferable to speak of input *rentals* to mean price *of the services* of inputs (e.g. wages for labour, rate of rent for land); but 'input price' is so often used to mean input rental that in this chapter I use the two terms interchangeably.

378   Chapter 5 · Firms, Partial Equilibria and the General Equilibrium with Production

of the period, **p** and **v** can be interpreted as payments at the end of the period (i.e. factors are paid in arrears). With the netput notation $\mathbf{y} = (-\mathbf{x},\mathbf{q})$, one can put all prices—of inputs as well as of outputs—into a single vector; if one uses the symbol $\mathbf{P} = (\mathbf{v},\mathbf{p})$ for this encompassing row vector, then profit can be represented more compactly as $\pi = \mathbf{Py}$. If inputs and outputs are paid at different dates, the several prices of the previous expression are to be intended as discounted or capitalized to a common date: I will assume it is the date at which output is sold.

Profit maximization implies a result usually formulated in terms of netputs: if at prices $\mathbf{P}^0 = (\mathbf{x}^0, \mathbf{p}^0)$ the firm chooses a netput vector $\mathbf{y}^\circ$, profit must be at least as great as with any other netput in the production possibility set Y, i.e. $\mathbf{P}^0\mathbf{y}^0 \geq \mathbf{P}^0\mathbf{y}, \forall \mathbf{y} \in Y$. This is called the *Weak Axiom of Profit Maximization*, WAPM. It has the following implication: if netput $\mathbf{y}^\circ$ is chosen at prices $\mathbf{P}^\circ$ and netput $\mathbf{y}^*$ is chosen at prices $\mathbf{P}^*$, it must be $\mathbf{P}^\circ\mathbf{y}^\circ \geq \mathbf{P}^\circ\mathbf{y}^*$ and $\mathbf{P}^*\mathbf{y}^* \geq \mathbf{P}^*\mathbf{y}^\circ$; rewrite these inequalities as $\mathbf{P}^\circ(\mathbf{y}^\circ-\mathbf{y}^*) \geq 0$, $-\mathbf{P}^*(\mathbf{y}^\circ-\mathbf{y}^*) \geq 0$ and add them to get

$$\left(\mathbf{P}^0 - \mathbf{P}^*\right)\left(\mathbf{y}^0 - \mathbf{y}^*\right) \geq 0,$$

which is often written

$$\Delta\mathbf{P} \cdot \Delta\mathbf{y} \geq 0.$$

In words: the inner or dot product of the vector of price changes and the vector of netput changes are non-negative and generally positive; geometrically, the two vectors form an acute angle. The interpretation requires to remember that inputs are negative numbers in the netput representation. Thus if price i is the only one to change and it increases, and if netput i is the only one to change, the WAPM implies that netput i must increase or at least not decrease: if netput i is an input, an algebraic increase of its negative quantity means a smaller absolute value, i.e. a lesser utilization of that input.

5.10 Optimal Employment of a Factor

Consider a competitive, i.e. price taking, firm that produces a single output and has a differentiable production function $q = f(\mathbf{x})$. Profit is $\pi = pq - \mathbf{vx} = pf(\mathbf{x}) - \mathbf{vx}$ where q is output (a scalar), p its price, $\mathbf{x}$ the vector of inputs (measured as positive quantities), $\mathbf{v}$ the vector of input rentals. How does the firm decide how much to employ of a single input? It must maximize π with respect to the employment of each factor i. Assuming an interior solution, $x_i > 0$, all i, the first-order condition for each factor is

$$(p \cdot \partial f / \partial x_i) - v_i = 0, \text{ or in the usual symbols}: p \cdot \mathrm{MP}_i = v_i.$$

i.e. the equality between **marginal revenue product** of the factor and 'price' (i.e. rental) of the factor. The marginal revenue product of a factor is, intuitively speaking, the increase in revenue due to the increase in output caused by one more small unit of the factor; under price taking it is $p \cdot \partial f / \partial x_i$. This first-order

5.11 · Cost Minimization

condition can also be expressed as $MP_i = v_i/p$ where v_i/p is the *real* rental of the factor measured in terms of the product.

A third way of writing this equality, $p = v_i/MP_i$, has the following interesting intuitive interpretation: the reciprocal of MP_i is the increase in input i needed for output to increase by one (small) unit; therefore v_i/MP_i is the increase in cost if the increase in output by 1 unit is obtained by increasing only factor i. Note that if profit is maximized the condition must hold for all inputs, which means

$$p = v_i/MP_{i,} = v_j/MP_{j,} = \alpha(v_i/MP_i) + (1 - \alpha)(v_j/MP_j), \quad \text{for } 0 < \alpha < 1.$$

This means that the increase in cost to obtain a very small output increase is the same whether obtained by increasing only one input, or two (or, generalizing, even all inputs). This increase in cost, the derivative of total cost relative to output, is called **marginal cost**, MC, and it must be equal to p for profit maximization. All this is of course rigorously true only for infinitesimal output variations, but it is sufficiently exact as long as output is measured in very small units. (The name 'marginal cost' reflects the fact that MC is the derivative of the *cost function* with respect to q, as explained in the next section.)

The second-order condition for the optimal employment of a factor, since p and v_i are given for the firm, is $\partial^2 f/\partial x_i^2 < 0$, that is, MP_i must be decreasing in x_i at the optimal employment of the factor.

It can happen that no positive value of x_i, however small, avoids a marginal revenue product inferior to the given v_i. In this case profit maximization implies a 'corner solution' with $x_i = 0$ and $p \cdot MP_i \le v_i$.

5.11 Cost Minimization

Above, profit was maximized by considering it *a function of factor employments* and finding the condition for optimal factor employments. A different procedure allows useful additional insights: since a necessary condition for profit to be maximized is that the total cost of producing the profit-maximizing output be minimized, one can first, for each level of output, minimize cost, and find how this minimized cost varies with output, i.e. find the *cost function*; then one can maximize profit by considering it *a function of output* and finding the condition for the level of output to maximize the difference between revenue pq and cost.

The **cost function** or total cost function is the minimum value function

$$c(\mathbf{v}, q) = \min \mathbf{vx} \text{ s.t.} f(\mathbf{x}) \ge q.$$

This will be a **short-run (or short-period) cost function** if some factors cannot be varied (then they are called **fixed factors**); if the other ones, called **variable factors**, are the sole factors that appear in $\mathbf{x}$, we obtain the **variable cost function**. The **total cost function** adds to the variable cost function $VC(q)$ whatever cost does not vary with q and therefore is a **fixed cost** FC. But since fixed cost is fixed, cost minimization concerns only variable cost. If all factors are variable, as in long-period analysis, then variable and total cost coincide. Dividing total cost by

380 Chapter 5 · Firms, Partial Equilibria and the General Equilibrium with Production

q one obtains **average total cost**, ATC; dividing variable cost by q one obtains **average variable cost**, AVC. The derivative of the cost function with respect to q is called **marginal cost**, MC.

Assume there is a unique cost-minimizing solution $\mathbf{x}$ for each given $(\mathbf{v},q)$ couple. Let $\mathbf{x} = h(\mathbf{v}, q)$ be the vector function indicating how this solution changes with $\mathbf{v}$ and q; $h(\mathbf{v}, q)$ is a (column) vector function called the **conditional input demand function**. Then

$$c(\mathbf{v}, q) = \mathbf{v} \cdot h(\mathbf{v}, q).$$

The **conditional demand for input** i, $x_i = h_i(\mathbf{v},q)$, is the demand for this input derived from minimizing the cost of producing each given output q; so it is an input demand *conditional* on the level of output; the **unconditional demand for an input** indicates the demand for the input associated with the profit-maximizing output, and it is defined only when the profit-maximizing output is well defined, which as we will see is not always the case.

There is a strict similarity between the cost function in production theory and the expenditure function in consumer theory,[25] and between the firm's conditional input demand function and the consumer's compensated (or Hicksian) demand function: mathematically they are just the same thing (this is why I use the same symbol h for both). Therefore I need not prove the properties I will now list because the proofs are the same as for the expenditure function, cf. Chap. 4, ▶ Sect. 4.17.

As long as $f(\mathbf{x})$ is continuous and $\mathbf{x}$ is such that $f(\mathbf{x})$ is strictly increasing in a neighbourhood of $\mathbf{x}$, the cost function has the following properties:

1. $c(\mathbf{v},q)$ is non-decreasing in v_i.
2. $c(\mathbf{v},q)$ is homogeneous of degree 1 in $\mathbf{v}$.
3. $c(\mathbf{v},q)$ is continuous in v_i, for $\mathbf{v} \gg 0$.
4. $c(\mathbf{v},q)$ is strictly increasing in q as long as $q > 0$.
5. $c(\mathbf{v},q)$ is concave in v_i.

Let me just remember the intuition behind the last result: if cost is minimized with respect to a given $(\mathbf{v},q)$ and this determines an input vector $\mathbf{x}$, and then v_i increases by an infinitesimal amount dv_i while $\mathbf{x}$ is kept fixed, then the increase in cost is $dc = x_i dv_i$, so $dc/dv_i = x_i$ as indeed Shephard's Lemma confirms (see below Sect. 5.17), so this is the local slope of c as a function of v_i, which remains constant if $\mathbf{x}$ does not change with v; if the change in relative factor prices makes it convenient to rearrange factor proportions, then for any finite increase of v_i the increase in cost is less, so the slope of $c(v_i)$ at most remains constant but generally decreases.

If the production function is continuous we can replace the constraint $f(\mathbf{x}) \geq q$ with the constraint $f(\mathbf{x}) = q$; if it is differentiable, for interior solutions ($\mathbf{x} \gg 0$) to cost minimization we can use the Lagrangian approach with equality constraint. Formulating the problem as one of maximization of $-c(\mathbf{v},q°)$ that is

---

25 Indeed a number of economists call 'cost function' the consumer's expenditure function.

5.11 · Cost Minimization

$$\max_{\mathbf{x}} -\sum_i v_i x_i \text{ subject to} f(\mathbf{x}) \geq q°,$$

the Lagrangian function is $-\mathbf{vx} - \lambda(q° - f(\mathbf{x}))$ where $q°$ and $\mathbf{v}$ are given. The first-order conditions for an interior solution yield

$$-v_i = -\lambda \partial f / \partial x_i, \quad i = 1,\ldots,n$$

from which one derives the well-known condition

$$v_i/v_j = \mathrm{MP}_i/\mathrm{MP}_j.$$

This is interpretable geometrically. Assume all input levels apart from those of inputs i and j are given and cause a given cost $B = \sum_{s \neq i,j} v_s x_s$. For each given total cost C, the expression

$$v_i x_i + v_j x_j = C - B$$

makes x_j a linear function of x_i. This function is called a restricted (two-dimensional) *isocost*. It is a downward-sloping straight line in (x_i, x_j)-space, with slope equal to $-v_i/v_j$ and intercepts $(C-B)/v_i$ in abscissa and $(C-B)/v_j$ in ordinate. It is the locus of quantities employed of the two factors that cause the same cost C, for a given cost B of the other factors. Increases in C induce a parallel outward shift of the isocost line. In this way one obtains a map of isocosts (◘ Fig. 5.5).

In the same (x_i, x_j)-space one can trace the restricted isoquant that indicates the combinations of factors i and j that, given the other inputs, allow producing the given $q°$. Cost minimization requires choosing the point on this isoquant through which passes the isocost closest to the origin. If the isoquant is 'smooth', the condition $v_i/v_j = MP_i/MP_j$ requires tangency between isoquant and an isocost. In order for this tangency to indicate a point of minimum cost, any isocost closer to the origin must have no point in common with the isoquant. This is ensured if the isoquant is convex. Furthermore the tangency point is unique if the isoquant is strictly convex.

With n factors, the isoquant is a surface (of dimension $n-1$) in R^n, and the isocost is a hyperplane; with a differentiable production function, the first-order

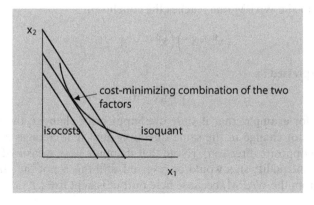

◘ **Fig. 5.5** Isocosts and cost minimization

conditions for an interior solution of the cost minimization problem imply tangency between isoquant and isocost, and the second-order sufficient condition is that the isoquant surface be convex. The difference from utility maximization is that now the curve (the isoquant) is given and the straight line (the isocost) must be found, while in the UMP the straight line (the budget line) is given and the curve (the indifference curve) must be found. In the same way as for indifference curves, isoquants are convex when the production function is quasi-concave and increasing (see ▶ Sect. 4.5): note that this does not exclude increasing returns to scale. In terms of second-order conditions for a maximum, we need (see the Mathematical Appendix) that at the solution $\mathbf{x}^*$ it is $d^2(-c)>0$ for displacements from $\mathbf{x}^*$ that satisfy the constraint $f(\mathbf{x})=q^\circ$, and it can be shown that this corresponds to the condition that the leading, or naturally ordered, principal minors (starting from the third one) of the bordered Hessian alternate in sign starting from positive (remember that the problem is formulated as the *maximization* of $-c$).

For the reasons explained earlier, for production functions convexity of the contours (the isoquants) is guaranteed when CRS and divisibility are assumed.

The profit-maximizing conditions for input use, $MP_i=v_i/p$, imply the cost minimization conditions $v_i/v_j=MP_i/MP_j$, but the converse does not hold. Cost minimization is only one part of what is necessary for profit maximization: one must also choose the optimal output level. I discuss this after exploring the cost function a little more.

5.12 WACm; Kuhn–Tucker Conditions and Cost Minimization

Cost minimization has an implication analogous to the WAPM. If for a given output q° and given input rentals $\mathbf{v}$ the firm finds it optimal to utilize an input vector $\mathbf{x}^\circ=h(\mathbf{v},q^\circ)$, it must mean that any other input vector capable of producing q° (or more) must cost at least $\mathbf{vx}^\circ$, in other words, $\mathbf{vx}^\circ \le \mathbf{vx}$ for all $\mathbf{x}$ such that $f(\mathbf{x})\ge q^\circ$, a result sometimes called *Weak Axiom of Cost Minimization*, **WACm** for short. If at input prices $\mathbf{v}^\circ$ the firm chooses input vector $\mathbf{x}^\circ$ and at input prices $\mathbf{v}^*$ the firm chooses input vector $\mathbf{x}^*$ *to produce the same output*, proceeding in the same way as for the WAPM one reaches the conclusion

$$\left(\mathbf{v^0} - \mathbf{v}^*\right)\left(\mathbf{x}^0 - \mathbf{x}^*\right) \le 0,$$

more often expressed as

$$\Delta\mathbf{v} \cdot \Delta\mathbf{x} \le 0.$$

This implies, for example, that if only one input price changes, the demand for that input cannot change in the same direction (and if it changes at all it must change in the opposite direction). (Note that if inputs were measured as negative quantities the inequality sign would be reversed, still this is not the same result as was derived from the WAPM, because here output is kept fixed.)

5.12 · WACm; Kuhn–Tucker Conditions and Cost Minimization

In general, not all possible inputs will be used in positive amounts by a firm; the condition $v_i/v_j = MP_i/MP_j$ must hold for inputs both used in positive quantities; the more general necessary first-order conditions for cost minimization are derivable from the Kuhn–Tucker theorem (▶ Sect. 4.8). In the present case, with $q°$ the given output, the function to be maximized is $-\mathbf{vx}$ and the constraints are $f(\mathbf{x})-q° \geq 0$, and $x_i \geq 0$, $i = 1, ..., n$. The Lagrangian is $-\mathbf{vx} + \lambda°(f(\mathbf{x})-q°) + \sum_i \lambda_i x_i$ indicating $\partial f/\partial x_i$ as f_i, the first-order conditions are therefore:

Kuhn–Tucker first-order necessary conditions for cost minimization:

$$-v_i + \lambda f_i + \lambda_i = 0, \quad i = 1, \ldots, n,$$

with complementary slackness conditions $\lambda°(f(\mathbf{x})-q°)=0$ and $\lambda_i x_i=0$, that is, if $(f(\mathbf{x})-q°)>0$, then $\lambda°=0$, and if $\lambda_i>0$, i.e. if $v_i>\lambda f_i$, then $x_i=0$.

If $x_i>0$, then $\lambda_i=0$ and the first-order condition $v_i=\lambda f_i$ can be rewritten

$$\lambda° = v_i/f_i = v_i/MP_i;$$

as already noted, v_i/MP_i is the increase in cost needed to increase output by one (small) unit through an increase of the sole factor i; this ratio is the same whatever the factor in positive use, since it is always equal to $\lambda°$; therefore the increase in cost is also the same if the increase in output by one small unit is obtained by increasing more than one of the inputs in positive use. Indeed, assuming $dx_i>0$ only if factor i is in positive use, and differentiating, we have $dc = v_1 dx_1 + \cdots + v_n dx_n$; $dq = f_1 dx_1 + \cdots + f_n dx_n$; hence for given v:

$$\frac{dc}{dq} = \frac{v_1 dx_1 + \cdots + v_n dx_n}{f_1 dx_1 + \cdots + f_n dx_n}$$

$$= [\textit{from the first-order conditions}] \quad \frac{\lambda° f_1 dx_1 + \cdots + \lambda° f_n dx_n}{f_1 dx_1 + \cdots + f_n dx_n} = \lambda°.$$

This ratio is **marginal cost**, MC[26]; and it equals the Lagrange multiplier $\lambda°$. This multiplier can be confirmed to be the marginal cost via the Envelope Theorem. Define the **marginal cost function** MC($\mathbf{v}$,q) as the derivative of the cost function with respect to q: $MC(\mathbf{v},q) := \partial c(\mathbf{v},q)/\partial q$. Now let M be the value function of the maximization problem with constraint

$$\max_x (-vx) \; s.t. \, f(x) = q;$$

hence $M = -c(\mathbf{v},q)$; the Lagrangian function of this problem is $-\mathbf{vx}-\lambda(q-f(\mathbf{x}))$, and the Envelope Theorem implies

$$\partial M/\partial q = -\lambda°, \text{ i.e. } \partial c/\partial q = \lambda° :$$

this confirms that the Lagrange multiplier $\lambda°$ in the cost minimization problem is the derivative of the cost function with respect to output, that is, is marginal cost.

---

26 Thus we have proved more rigorously what had been more intuitively shown in Sect. 5.10.

384   Chapter 5 · Firms, Partial Equilibria and the General Equilibrium with Production

Then the first complementary slackness condition is easily interpreted: it states that production will be greater than $q°$ only if it costs nothing to increase it beyond $q°$. The second slackness condition tells us that a factor will not be used at all if even its first unit yields such a low marginal product that, given its rental, to use this factor to increase output causes a greater cost increase than by obtaining the same output increase via an increase of other factors.

5.13 Supply Curves: Short-Period Marshallian Analysis, Quasi-Rents

The traditional, Marshallian approach distinguishes short-period from long-period profit maximization and short-period from long-period supply curves of firms. As Marshall puts it, the long-period or normal value of a commodity 'is that which economic forces tend to bring about in the long run. It is the average value which economic forces would bring about if the general conditions of life were stationary for a run of time long enough to enable them all to work out their full effect' (1972, V, iii, 6; p. 289). At the level of the single firm, the distinction between short-period and long-period decisions is traditionally described as follows: in the short period a firm cannot alter the quantities of some of the inputs, in the long period all inputs can be varied.

This is often put in terms of whether the more durable part of the capital goods used by the firm, its *fixed plant*, is given or variable. However, it takes very little time for a firm to sell or rent out its fixed plant to other firms, or to buy or rent the fixed plants of other firms (a firm is a legal entity, not to be confused with its plants): for example, a firm can rent a building or flat if needed for a particular production or period. So the idea that the short period is characterized by each *firm* having a given fixed plant is difficult to defend. If one re-reads the inventor of the short-period/long-period distinction, Alfred Marshall, one finds that the fixity he had in mind referred not to the individual firm but to the *industry*: the short period was the analytical period within which there was not enough time significantly to change the amounts available *to the entire industry* of specialized durable inputs necessary to the industry and requiring considerable time for their production. Thus Marshall's short-period analysis of the fishing industry takes as given the number of fishing ships (and of experienced fishermen), not the number of firms nor how the fishing ships are divided among different firms (1972, V, v, 4; p. 307). In the language of plants, one can say that in the short period the total number of fixed plants available to an *industry* is given, how they are divided among firms is secondary: a well-run firm owning two separate plants will behave in the same way as two firms each owning one of the two plants because it will want to maximize the profit from each plant.

However, once the point is grasped, then precisely because how the plants are divided among firms is secondary if all firms are efficient, to assume that the distribution of plants among firms is given will make no difference for the determination of the *industry's* supply decisions (which are what is relevant to determine

5.13 · Supply Curves: Short-Period Marshallian Analysis, Quasi-Rents

the equilibrium of the market one is studying.). Therefore we can follow the standard textbook approach after all.

So let us take the 'fixed plant' of the firm as given in the short period. The fixed plant includes all inputs whose quantity is given[27]; one can even omit the fixed plant from the inputs appearing in the production function; the other inputs, the sole ones affecting production in the short period, are the *variable inputs*; the corresponding production function is called the ***short-period, or restricted, production function***. Short-period cost minimization can only operate on the variable inputs.

Correspondingly, there will be fixed costs and variable costs. *Variable cost* is the total cost of variable inputs. The costs that are fixed (in the sense of not depending on the quantity produced) but only exist as long as the firm exists, i.e. disappear if the firm is shut down, are called ***quasi-fixed costs***. ***Fixed costs proper*** are those costs independent of the quantity produced that must be borne by the owners of the firm even if production is discontinued and the firm is closed down: debts, essentially. Quasi-fixed costs include, for example, those overhead labour costs (top manager's secretary, etc.) independent of the quantity produced but which can be eliminated by closing down the firm and firing all workers. Note that fixed costs do not necessarily coincide with the cost of fixed factors: a firm can have a debt to be repaid, that is due to past expenses and has no connection with the firm's present fixed plant, but if it causes a fixed repayment cost it will be part of fixed cost. For simplicity I mostly assume there are no quasi-fixed costs.

In what follows until differently specified the analysis refers to the short period. The **(short-period) variable cost function** $VC(\mathbf{v},q)$ results from the choice of variable inputs that minimizes variable cost for each assigned level of output.[28] Since there are fixed factors, the short-period production function will exhibit decreasing returns to scale at least after a certain level of output; as a result, at least beyond a certain level of output $VC(\mathbf{v},q)$ will increase more than in proportion with output. This is formalized by assuming that the ***short-period marginal cost***, i.e. the derivative of variable cost with respect to output,

$$MC(\mathbf{v}, q) := \partial VC/\partial q$$

is an increasing function of q at least beyond a certain level of output. In what follows I take $\mathbf{v}$ as given. The **(*short-period*) *average variable cost*** is

$$AVC(\mathbf{v}, q) := VC/q;$$

initially AVC can be a decreasing function of output, indicating that the fixed plant was intended for a certain level of production and up to that level variable cost increases less than in proportion with output. Assume all these magnitudes are continuous functions of output and let us study the relationships among them. For $q=0$ it is $AVC=MC$ because for the first unit of output average variable cost

---

27 It is possible not to use the entire amount of a fixed factor; this will be just one instance of the difference between technological and economic production function.

28 In Marshall and in the literature close to him (including Keynes) variable costs are called *prime costs*; fixed costs are called *supplementary costs*, and fixed factors *supplementary factors*.

coincides with the increase in cost. Then if AVC is initially a decreasing function of q, MC is a decreasing function of q too and is less than AVC (in order for the average cost to decrease, the additional units of output must cause an additional cost lower than the average). AVC remains a decreasing function of output as long as $MC < AVC$. But if MC becomes an increasing function of q at least from a certain level of output onwards, then sooner or later it becomes equal to AVC, and from that level of output onwards $MC > AVC$ and AVC becomes an increasing function of q. It follows that AVC reaches its minimum where its curve crosses the MC curve; if one knows the two functions, this minimum can be determined simply by solving $MC(q) = AVC(q)$ for $q > 0$. If MC is increasing from the very start, then AVC is increasing from the start too and is below MC except at $q = 0$. (The mathematical proof of these statements is trivial and left to the reader as **Exercise**, but be sure to check the second-order conditions.)

Now define **short-period average total cost** as $AC = (FC + VC)/q = AFC + AVC$. AFC is **average fixed cost**, defined as FC/q. If $FC > 0$, then $AC > AVC$; the vertical distance between the AC curve and the AVC curve decreases as q increases, because it measures AFC. For the same reason as for AVC, AC is a decreasing function of q when it is greater than MC, and an increasing function of q when it is less than MC, and as a result it too reaches a minimum where it crosses the MC curve. All these relationships are shown in ◘ Fig. 5.6: a particularly important point is X, where the

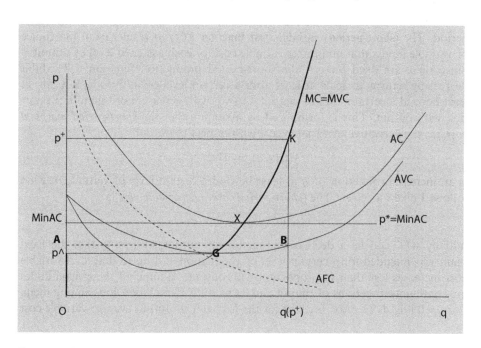

◘ **Fig. 5.6** Average cost AC and average variable cost AVC when marginal cost MC is initially decreasing; average fixed cost AFC is a rectangular hyperbola and equals AC–AVC. Note that if AVC included some quasi-fixed costs, then the AVC curve would not start at the same level as the MC curve, but would have initially a shape similar to that of the AFC curve. The thicker part of the MC curve and the segment Op^ in ordinate are the firm's short-period supply curve

5.13 · Supply Curves: Short-Period Marshallian Analysis, Quasi-Rents

AC and the MC curve cross each other; this point determines the *minimum average cost*, $MinAC$, associated with the given fixed plant and the given factor rentals, and the corresponding quantity of output $q^\wedge$. As long as the price at which the firm sells its output is greater than $MinAC$, the firm makes a positive profit.

Having calculated the cost function, if prices and rentals are given, profit can be treated as a function of output, being the difference between revenue $R: = pq$, and short-period total cost viewed as function only of q because **v** is given, let us indicate it as $SC(q)$. That is,

$$\pi(q) = R - SC(q) = pq - SC(q).$$

The first-order condition for a maximum is $p - MC(q) = 0$. The second-order condition is

$$-dMC(q)/dq < 0,$$

i.e. MC must be increasing where it equals the given output price.

Measure q in abscissa, and p, MC, AC, AVC, AFC in ordinate. If in ordinate we also measure p, the condition $p = MC(q)$ implies a **supply curve** of the firm which coincides with part of the MC curve. The part of the MC curve which coincides with the supply curve is the part above the AVC curve, so (if the AVC curve is initially decreasing) it also includes the portion GX of the MC curve between the minimum points of the AVC and of the AC curves; see $\blacksquare$ Fig. 5.6; for $p = MC$ in that range, $p < MinAC$ and profit is negative; but the firm finds it convenient to go on producing, because in this way it can at least minimize its loss: the excess of revenue over variable cost reduces the loss due to the fixed cost which must be borne anyway. If $p < AVC$, then the firm minimizes its loss by not producing at all.[29] At least, this is the usual textbook way of presenting the thing. In fact there is a way of understanding better what is being described in this way.

Consider $\blacksquare$ Fig. 5.6 and assume price is p^+. The firm finds it optimal to produce $q(p^+)$, earning a revenue $p^+q(p^+)$ and therefore a difference between profit and total *variable* cost equal to the area of rectangle $ABKp^+$. This excess of revenue over variable cost is the maximum a potential *leasee* of the fixed plant of the firm would be ready to pay for the right to use that fixed plant and produce with it. Therefore the fixed plant can be viewed as a special kind of (non-perennial) land whose property would allow, if rented out to utilizers, to earn a periodical 'rent' equal to the difference between revenue and variable cost. For this reason this 'rent' has been called by Alfred Marshall the **quasi-rent** earned by the fixed plant of the firm. A potential *buyer* of the firm with its fixed plant will be ready to pay, as maximum sum for the purchase, the discounted value of the future quasi-rents that the firm's fixed plant can be expected to earn for the remaining years of its economic life; the remainder of the future earnings of the firm-with-fixed-plant will pay the variable costs.

---

29 In concrete situations, a firm can decide to go on producing even when the price is below minimum average variable cost, if it esteems that this is a temporary situation and that the interruption by causing loss of goodwill would damage profit more than continuing to produce at a loss for a time.

388   Chapter 5 · Firms, Partial Equilibria and the General Equilibrium with Production

This has the following interesting interpretation. Fixed cost in the short period is a **sunk cost**, an irrecuperable cost to be paid whatever the entrepreneur decides to do. In the long period the part of cost due to fixed plants (interest cost plus depreciation) can be changed; being variable too, it must no longer be called fixed cost, in the long period all cost is variable. But in the short period fixed cost is given, inevitable, it can have little connection with the actual cost of the fixed plant because due to past contracts stipulated in particular conditions. Therefore it must not be included in the **opportunity cost** of decisions, which is the revenue obtainable from the best alternative and allows one to decide whether a choice is the most convenient one by comparing the revenue from the choice with its opportunity cost. If then one neglects fixed cost because it is a sunk cost, short-period profit must be calculated as the difference between revenue and variable cost only, that is, *profit in the opportunity cost sense (i.e. neglecting sunk costs) coincides with quasi-rent*. If one includes the quasi-rent of the fixed plant among the costs (as if the entrepreneur had taken the fixed plant on lease from other owners), profit is zero at all prices!

On this basis one can reach greater clarity on the meaning of the statement that the firm continues to produce even when price is below $MinAC$ but above $MinAVC$: the analysis is actually about when a *plant* will be shut down. The entrepreneur who first sets up the fixed plant and bears the cost of building it is in the same position as the person who purchases a land; she may go bankrupt if the plant's quasi-rent falls below the level expected at the time of purchase rendering it impossible to repay the debt incurred to purchase the plant. So the *firm* (legal entity) which sets up the plant will generally go bankrupt and close down much before the price goes down to MinAVC. But as long as quasi-rent is positive the *plant* will not be shut down, it will be bought by some other entrepreneur at its new value (the present value of its expected quasi-rents for its remaining economic life) and will be kept in operation. It will be closed down only when it no longer earns a positive quasi-rent.

In the short period the fixed plants of an industry, whose distribution among firms we assume given, are given, so the number of firms in the industry is given too, and we can determine the short-period supply curve of an *industry* as the horizontal sum of the parts, of the short-period marginal cost curves of the single plants, which lie above the respective AVC curves.

5.14 From Short-Period to Long-Period Supply

The short-period AC and MC curves were derived for a given fixed plant and given fixed cost and rentals of inputs. We can now extend the analysis to the **long period,** i.e. to the analytical situation where we treat *all* inputs as variable, by imagining that the price-taking firm can choose among a set of different fixed plants, each one entailing a certain fixed cost; input rentals are still given; for each fixed plant the firm can derive the AC and MC curves which have the shapes of ◧ Fig. 5.6. We need not assume perfect divisibility of the elements which go to

5.14 · From Short-Period to Long-Period Supply

form a fixed plant. For each level of q, there will be a fixed plant which allows producing it at the lowest *AC*. The locus of these lowest long-period *AC*'s as functions of q is the long-period average cost curve, *LAC*. The smallest of the minimum average costs associated with the several alternative fixed plants is the **long-period minimum average cost**, *MinLAC*; indicate the associated output as q^* (◘ Fig. 5.7).

The long-period average cost curve LAC is the lower envelope of the (short-period) average cost curves associated with different fixed plants, cf. ◘ Fig. 5.8. Along the LAC curve the type of fixed plant changes. If the different alternative fixed plants are so numerous and their short-period average cost curves change so gradually as to determine a differentiable lower envelope as in ◘ Fig. 5.8 (traditionally this was obtained by conceiving the possible short-period fixed plants to be a continuum, corresponding to the 'quantity of capital' embodied in each plant, where capital was the single factor of variable 'form' already encountered when discussing the differentiability of production functions), then each point of the LAC curve is tangent to one short-period average cost curve, but not at the point of minimum AC of that short-period average cost curve, except when the MinLAC is reached. The graphical representation shows this fact clearly enough, so I omit the mathematical proof.

It is of course possible that some fixed plants generate short-period AC curves having no point in common with the LAC curve, because less convenient than some other fixed plant whatever the output level is.

If there is perfect divisibility and constant returns to scale, then *MinLAC* can be reached for any *q*. If there are indivisibilities, but plants can be replicated (without loss of efficiency due to increasing difficulty of control), then there will be a most efficient plant whose minimum *AC* is the *MinLAC*, with a corresponding output q^*; a firm can reach the same *MinLAC* by replicating this plant and producing $2q^*$, or $3q^*$, etc. The *AC* and *MC* curves with two fixed plants are the curves with one fixed plant, 'stretched' rightwards so as to reach the same value in ordinate for a double value in abscissa. In ◘ Fig. 5.9 we see the *AC* curves and

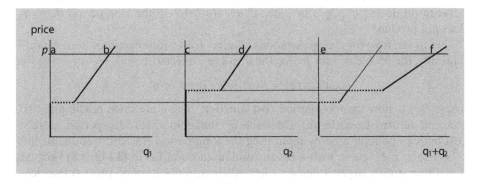

◘ **Fig. 5.7** Horizontal sum of the short-period supply curves of two price-taking firms having different minimum *AVC*. Aggregate supply at price *p*, the segment ef, is the horizontal sum of the supplies of the two firms, the two segments ab and cd

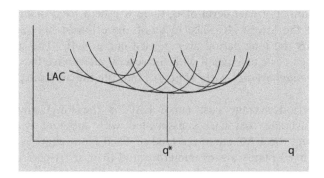

◘ **Fig. 5.8** Long-period average cost curve as lower envelope of the (short-period) average cost curves associated with different fixed plants

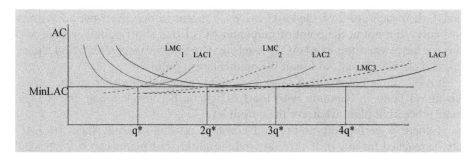

◘ **Fig. 5.9** Average and marginal cost curves with one, two or three identical plants

MC curves of a firm with one, two and three fixed plants of the same type. A price-taking firm considers that it can sell any amount of product at the given price, therefore as long as the output price p is greater than *MinLAC*, the firm finds it convenient to expand by replicating the plant associated with *MinLAC*; if $p = MinLAC$, then the firm's maximum profit is zero and the firm is indifferent between producing q^*, $2q^*$, $3q^*$, etc.; if $p < MinLAC$, in the long period the firm does not produce.

Let us see how these considerations connect with profit maximization. Mathematically, the problem, with $R = pq$ the firm's revenue, is

$$max_q \pi(q) = R(q) - c(q) = pq - c(q)$$

where $c(q)$ is now the long-period cost function. There are three possibilities: (i) constant returns to scale; (ii) a definite q^* that minimizes long-period average cost but can be replicated by replicating the long-period efficient fixed plant; (iii) a U-shaped *LAC* curve with a unique minimum point (as in ◘ Fig. 5.8) because if the firm grows larger it becomes less efficient, replication of plant causes loss of central control and difficulties of coordination, and average cost rises. With CRS, *MinLAC* can be reached at any q. In case (ii) we have the situation depicted in ◘ Fig. 5.9, then *MinLAC* is reached for output q^* and integer multiples of q^*

through replication of identical plants. In both cases (i) and (ii), if $p > MinLAC$ a price-taking firm wants to expand indefinitely, if $p < MinLAC$ the firm finds it convenient not to produce, if $p = MinLAC$ the firm is indifferent as to how much to produce or at least as to what multiple of q^* to produce, profit is zero anyway. Therefore there is no long-period supply *function* of the firm, the firm's long-period supply is either zero, or infinite, or indeterminate. In case (iii) the firm maximizes profit by setting the long-period marginal cost, LMC, equal to price, the firm's long-period supply function exists. However, if we are interested in the total supply function of the good under study, the sum of the supplies of the firms in the industry, and if we admit the possibility of entry of new firms (and we must, in long-period analysis!), then the replication of plants capable of producing at minimum long-period average cost remains possible via variation *of the number of firms*, each one with the optimal long-period plant, and competition and entry will push price to equal *MinLAC*. Since the possibility of entry exists also in cases (i) and (ii), we reach the conclusion that in all three cases the industry's supply function is (practically) horizontal at $p = MinLAC$; if price is greater, firms expand and new firms enter, causing supply to increase and p to decrease, and the less efficient firms are eliminated by competition; if price is lower, firms make losses and shut down; at $p = MinLAC$ supply is indeterminate.

Only the '(practically)' caution deserves further comment. I am anticipating here the notion of partial equilibrium of a single industry that will be discussed in greater detail later in the chapter. Briefly, we want to find the price that makes supply of the industry's product equal to demand, which is assumed to be a decreasing function of p. When firms do not have CRS but replication of efficient plant is possible (either by the existing firms or by new entrants), the industry *long-period* supply curve, that is the locus of possible quantity-price combinations in long-period equilibrium, is derived as follows. Let $LMC_n(q)$ stand for the horizontal sum of the marginal cost curves of n identical efficient plants (or firms, in case (iii)), as in ◘ Fig. 5.9; let q be their total output and q^* the single-plant minimum average cost output; the supply curve consists of a discontinuous series of upward-sloping segments yielding a saw-like shape, the nth segment being the portion of the $LMC_n(q)$ curve corresponding to q in the semiopen interval $(nq^*, (n+1)q^*)$, with n integer. The reason is that p cannot fall below $MinLAC$ in equilibrium, so if the industry faces a downward-sloping demand curve such that at $p = MinLAC$ demand is greater than nq^* but less than $(n+1)q^*$ then entry or plant replication by existing firms will bring the number of plants to n but there is no room for $n+1$ plants. Then equilibrium price will be a bit above $MinLAC$, but the less so the greater is n, because as ◘ Fig. 5.9 shows as the number of plants increases the $LMC_n(q)$ curve quickly becomes nearly flat. The industry long-period supply curve will have a saw-like shape: between q^* and $2q^*$ it will be the marginal cost curve of a single efficient plant; between $2q^*$ and $3q^*$ it will be the aggregate marginal cost curve of two efficient plants, and so on; each segment of it will start as equal to $MinLAC$ in ordinate and will have a smaller and smaller slope as n increases, approaching a horizontal line. If the downward-sloping demand function crosses this supply curve in more than one point, the equilibrium intersection is the one corresponding to the greatest output at a price not less than $MinLAC$,

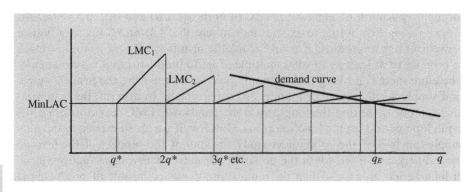

Fig. 5.10 Long-period industry supply curve with plants that reach minimum average cost at output level q^*, and a demand curve crossing the supply curve more than once. In this case in equilibrium there is room for six plants. The LMC curves are drawn as straight line segments only for simplicity. The slope of LMC curves has been exaggerated to make the drawing clearer; in real economies, already with three plants the aggregate marginal cost curve will generally be very close to horizontal in an ample neighbourhood of $3q^*$; see Fig. 5.9

q_E in Fig. 5.10. When n is great, the aggregate marginal cost curve is practically horizontal, the equilibrium price will be so close to $p = MinLAC$ that to assume that the equilibrium price is *equal* to $MinLAC$ is an excellent approximation.

The conclusion is that, with perfect replicability of plants and free variability of the number of plants (be it because existing firms change the number of plants they operate, or because of entry and exit of firms), as long as the output of a single efficient plant is only a small fraction of total output the long-period industry supply curve can be treated, to all relevant purposes, as a horizontal straight line (if input prices are given) at a level equal to minimum long-period average cost.

Note that quantity supplied so determined is not mathematically a *function* of price but if we interpret the curve as an *inverse* supply curve, or more precisely as a **supply-price curve**, that is a curve that for each quantity indicates the minimum price needed for the industry to supply that quantity, then it *is* a function (and this is the reason why clever Alfred Marshall preferred to have price in ordinate).

Some theorists have raised a problem about the above determination of the long-period partial equilibrium of a market. We have seen that with indivisibilities the long-period supply curve will not be rigorously horizontal, only approximately so, and then the equilibrium price can be slightly above $MinLAC$. For example if at $p = MinLAC$ demand is equal to $100.5 \cdot q^*$, it will cross the LMC_{100} curve at a price a bit above $MinLAC$. Supposing each firm runs only one plant, there is room for 100 firms; if there were 101 firms, price would go below $MinLAC$ and all firms would make negative profits. But with 100 firms profits are not zero; if we assume that firms enter as long as $p > MinLAC$, there will be entry; *no long-period equilibrium exists* if we define it as simultaneously requiring demand equal to supply *and* non-positive profits otherwise there is entry. However, let us remember that the role of a long-period equilibrium is to indicate the average situation around which the economy oscillates and to which the economy tends to come back whenever it gets noticeably far from it: then the above considerations do not raise a problem, because even if firms do enter and

5.15 · The Product Exhaustion Theorem with U-Shaped LAC

bring the total number of firms above 100, the number will subsequently decrease, and we can still assume that the average price over time periods sufficient for entry to operate will be very closely indicated by $MinLAC$, and it changes by the changes of the latter. Furthermore it is plausible that potential entrants try to make an estimate of the effect of their entry, and generally they will realize that it is likely that the very small excess of price above $MinLAC$ associated with 100 firms will disappear if they enter, and hence will not enter; but the main point is that the notion of equilibrium does not aim to indicate an actually reached situation, it only aims to indicate a good approximation to the observed averages of the market price and of day-by-day quantity that are influenced also by temporary and accidental causes.

5.15 The Product Exhaustion Theorem with U-Shaped LAC

In the previous section we admitted that firms might be able to reach $MinLAC$ at several levels of output, or at a single one. Disagreements among economists on this issue were mentioned in Sect. 5.6.3 and Fn. 19, with some, e.g. Edith Penrose, arguing that in many instances firms are able to grow to enormous sizes without any increase in average cost and therefore the limits to size must be found either on the demand side or on the need for own capital or collateral; and others arguing that the general case is U-shaped LAC curves because of control difficulties of management over subordinates that increase with size. In the face of the empirical evidence of more and more mammoth firms and increasing concentration in many industries, it would seem Penrose got it right.

Assuming now that maximum output is a continuous function of total cost and that the LAC curve is U-shaped, returns to cost are increasing where LAC is decreasing in q and are decreasing where LAC is increasing in q; hence $MinLAC$ is reached where the returns to costs, in passing from locally increasing to locally decreasing, are locally constant. If the production function is differentiable with respect to all inputs,[30] then the locally constant returns to costs at $MinLAC$, that is, the equality of average and marginal cost, imply locally constant technical returns to scale. I prove this for the two-factors case. At the point of minimum average cost it is

$$MC = \frac{v_1}{MP_1} = \frac{v_2}{MP_2} = AC = \frac{v_1 x_1 + v_2 x_2}{f(x_1, x_2)};$$

this can be rewritten

---

30 Then the local elasticity of output to the scale of inputs $e_s(\mathbf{x}) = [df(t\mathbf{x})/f(t\mathbf{x})]/(dt/t)$ evaluated at $t = 1$, can be defined (Sect. 5.6.1), and if the input vector $\mathbf{x}$ is cost minimizing at the given factor rentals $\mathbf{v}$ then $e_s(\mathbf{x}) = AC/MC$.
  Proof: rewrite the elasticity of scale as $e_s(\mathbf{x}) = \frac{\sum_{i=1}^{n} \frac{\partial f(\mathbf{x})}{\partial x_i} x_i}{f(\mathbf{x})}$. Since $\mathbf{x}$ is cost minimizing, it satisfies $v_i = p \partial f(\mathbf{x})/\partial x_i$, where the product price satisfies $p = MC$. Therefore $e_s(\mathbf{x}) = \frac{\sum_{i=1}^{n} v_i x_i}{pf(\mathbf{x})} = \frac{c(\mathbf{v},q)/q}{p} = \frac{AC}{MC}$. ∎
  This confirms that returns to scale are locally increasing or decreasing depending on whether AC is greater or less than MC.

$$f(x_1, x_2) = \frac{v_1 x_1 + v_2 x_2}{MC} = \frac{v_1 x_1}{\frac{v_1}{MP_1}} + \frac{v_2 x_2}{\frac{v_2}{MP_2}} = MP_1 x_1 + MP_2 x_2,$$

which implies that the production function is locally homogeneous of degree 1.

This implies that, if $p = MinLAC$, the payment to each factor of its marginal revenue product exhausts revenue. Thus *the fact that the long-period cost curve is U-shaped entails no contradiction between assuming zero profits of competitive firms in long-period equilibrium, and assuming that each factor is paid its marginal revenue product*, because in long-period equilibrium the firm produces where returns to scale are locally constant.

The assumption of competition with free entry implies an essentially horizontal long-period industry supply curve once input prices are given, as long as the minimum quantity that allows a firm to minimize average cost is small relative to the total demand forthcoming at a price equal to that average cost. When this is the case, since in the long-period competition tends to eliminate inefficient firms, one can assume a common technology within the industry. We can therefore treat the *industry's* long-period aggregate production function as exhibiting constant *technical* returns to scale even when we cannot do so for single firms. If input rentals are given, we can assume a constant MinLAC independent of the quantity the industry produces. This will be important when later in the chapter I formulate the neoclassical competitive general equilibrium with production.

5.16 Aggregation

When the number of firms in an industry is *given*, and for each firm a supply function exists, then the industry's competitive supply can be determined as if forthcoming from a single aggregate multiplant price-taking firm that operates all the individual plants and maximizes the profit from each plant.

If the analysis is a long-period one and competition and free entry push firms to adopt the same production function, then (assuming the individual plant's optimal output is small relative to aggregate output) the industry's supply curve can be derived with good approximation from a hypothetical aggregate firm with a CRS production function (and therefore it will be a horizontal line) even when individual firms do not have a CRS production function but rather a U-shaped average cost curve that determines an optimal output of the individual firm. The industry behaves like a single giant CRS firm, with a production function which, for each vector of relative factor rentals, yields the same optimal factor employments *per unit of output* as the average cost-minimizing choice of the individual firms or plants.

I illustrate with a numerical example. Assume two factors and that all firms have production function $q = x^\alpha y^\alpha$; returns to scale are locally increasing, constant or decreasing according as α is greater, equal or less than 1/2; we want a U-shaped long-period average cost curve, hence α must be initially greater than

5.17 · Shephard's Lemma

1/2 and decreasing in q; e.g. $\alpha = 4/10 + 10/(xy)$, which yields $\alpha > 1/2$ if $xy < 100$ and $\alpha < 1/2$ if $xy > 100$. Minimum average cost is achieved where returns to scale are locally constant, i.e. at $\alpha = 1/2$, $xy = 100$; hence all firms in the long period produce $q = 10$ with amounts of the two inputs such that $xy = 100$; the ratio x/y depends on relative factor rentals. The *industry* can be treated as a single firm with production function $Q = x^{1/2}y^{1/2}$; the number of firms is the greatest integer less than or equal to $Q/10$.

5.17 Shephard's Lemma

Now let us see a number of results in the theory of production of the same type as Roy's Identity, etc., in consumer theory.

Let us start by considering again the function $- c(\mathbf{v}, q)$ as the value function of the maximization problem with constraint, *max* $(-\mathbf{vx})$ s.t. $f(\mathbf{x}) = q$, and let us apply the Envelope Theorem to the derivative of this value function with respect to factor rentals; we obtain:

$$-\frac{\partial c(\mathbf{v}, q)}{\partial v_i} = -x_i + \lambda \frac{\partial f(\mathbf{x})}{\partial v_i} = -x_i \ (\text{because } \frac{\partial f(\mathbf{x})}{\partial v_i} = 0);$$

the quantity x_i that appears in this expression is the *conditional* demand for input i, because it is the quantity of this input demanded when output is kept fixed at q; so we obtain:

Shephard's Lemma for the firm: $\frac{\partial c(\mathbf{v},q)}{\partial v_i} = h(\mathbf{v},q)$.

In words: *The conditional factor demands are the partial derivatives of the cost function with respect to factor rentals.*

This is the original Shephard's Lemma, which was later extended to consumer theory.

5.18 The Profit Function and Hotelling's Lemma

Let us now define a new notion, the price-taking firm's ***profit function*** $\pi(p,\mathbf{v})$ defined as the value function of the (unconstrained) maximization problem with p and $\mathbf{v}$ as parameters

$$max_x \, pf(\mathbf{x}) - \mathbf{vx}.$$

The profit function must not be confused with the function $\pi(q) = pq - C(q)$, which is *not* called 'profit function', where profit is a function of output at *given* output price and factor rentals. The profit function describes how maximum profit changes with changes in output price or factor rentals.

The profit function is not always defined nor continuous. Suppose the firm has CRS and all factors are variable: for each given vector $\mathbf{v}$, marginal cost is constant and equal to minimum average cost; if $p > MC$ there is no maximum profit (the profit function is not defined), if $p = MC$ maximum profit is zero and output

396 Chapter 5 · Firms, Partial Equilibria and the General Equilibrium with Production

is indeterminate, if $p < MC$ maximum profit is zero and optimal output is zero; such a profit function is of very little use! The profit function has useful properties when, at least in an interval of output and input prices, profit-maximizing output and inputs are well defined and change continuously with (p,v); then the profit function allows useful conclusions on how output and inputs change with changes in p or in input rentals. This obtains if the analysis is a short-period one, output is positive, the factors considered are only the variable factors, and profit is defined as revenue minus variable cost, that is, without including quasi-rents into cost (otherwise profit would be zero always, as argued).

Properties of the profit function. *Suppose that the production function $f(x)$: $R_+^n \to R_+$ is continuous, strictly increasing and strictly quasi-concave and that the profit function $\pi(p,v)$, i.e. the value function of the problem $\max_x pf(x) - vx$ with respect to parameters p and v, is well defined for given (p',v') and continuous in (p,v) in a neighbourhood of (p',v'); then in that neighbourhood $\pi(p,v)$ is*
1. *non-decreasing in p and increasing if $q > 0$;*
2. *non-increasing in each v_i and decreasing if $x_i > 0$;*
3. *homogeneous of degree one in (p,v);*
4. *convex in (p,v);*
5. *differentiable in $(p,v) \gg 0$.*

Proof Properties (1) and (2) will be proved below as implications of Hotelling's Lemma. (3) is obvious. The proof of (5) is omitted. Here I give the proof of property 4, i.e. that for any scalar a, $0 \le a \le 1$, it is $a\pi(p,v) + (1-a)\pi(p',v') \ge \pi(ap + (1-a)p', av + (1-a)v')$. Define $p_a \equiv ap + (1-a)p'$ and $v_a \equiv av + (1-a)v'$. Let x, x', x_a and $q = f(x)$, $q' = f(x')$, $q_a = f(x_a)$ be the solution inputs and solution outputs associated, respectively, with $\pi(p,v)$, $\pi(p',v')$ and $\pi(p_a,v_a)$. Then it is

$$\pi(p,v) = pq - yx \ge pq_a - yx_a, \quad \pi(p',v') = p'q' - v'x' \ge p'q_a - v'x_a$$

which imply $a\pi(p,v) + (1-a)\pi(p',v') \ge a(pq_a - vx_a) + (1-a)(p'q_a - v'x_a) = p_a q_a - v_a x_a = \pi(p_a,v_a)$. ∎

Now let us apply the Envelope Theorem to the profit function. The latter is the value function of a maximization problem without constraints, so we obtain:

Hotelling's Lemma:
(i) $\partial\pi/\partial p = f(x) = q$
i.e. the partial derivative of the profit function w.r.t. the output price yields the optimal output;
(ii) $\partial\pi/\partial v_i = -x_i$
i.e. the partial derivative of the profit function w.r.t. input rental v_i yields the <u>unconditional</u> demand for input i measured as a negative number (i.e. in accord with the netput notation).

Hotelling's Lemma is sometimes called *the derivative property*.

5.18 · The Profit Function and Hotelling's Lemma

Thus the partial derivatives of the profit function, when the latter exists, give us the output supply function and the negative of the unconditional input demand functions when inputs are measured as positive quantities. Clearly (i) implies that if $q>0$ then profit is increasing in p, and (ii) implies that if $x_i>0$ then profit is decreasing in v_i; this proves properties (1) and (2) of the profit function.

The lemma has further implications. Since the profit function is convex (and strictly convex if output and inputs change with (p,v)), if we draw it as a function of only one variable we obtain an upward-sloping convex curve for $\pi(p)$ and a downward-sloping convex curve for each $\pi(v_i)$; that is, both $\partial\pi/\partial p$ and $\partial\pi/\partial v_i$ are non-decreasing and generally increasing in p, respectively, in v_i, conclusions which because of Hotelling's Lemma have two useful implications:

1. *output supply is a non-decreasing, and generally an increasing, function of output price;*
2. $-x_i$ *is a non-decreasing and generally an increasing function of* v_i; *that is,* x_i, *which is the unconditional demand for the input measured as a positive quantity, is a non-increasing and generally a decreasing function of the input own rental.*

Result 2 implies that, differently from the case in consumer theory, in production theory in all cases in which the profit function exists *there are no Giffen inputs*, a firm's demand for an input cannot increase when the sole rental of that input increases. (But things are different in long-period analysis, because then the change in the rental of an input means a change in income distribution and this can have complex consequences both on the composition of consumer demand and on firms' technical choices.)

Exercise: Prove that results 1 and 2 can also be derived from the WAPM (▶ Sect. 5.9).

5.19 Conditional and Unconditional Factor Demands, Inferior Inputs, Rival Inputs, Substitution Effect and Output Effect

When the profit function is well defined, for each output price p and vector of factor rentals $\mathbf{v}$ there is an optimal output and an associated vector of optimal factor utilizations: the latter vector need not be unique if isoquants are not *strictly* convex, but I will assume it is. In this case we can define the **supply function (of the individual firm)** $S(p, \mathbf{v})$ that indicates the optimal output as a function of factor rentals $\mathbf{v}$ and of the output price p; we also define the (vectorial) **unconditional factor demand function** $\mathbf{x}(p, \mathbf{v})$ that indicates the associated optimal factor employment vector. The connection between unconditional and conditional factor demand is

$$\mathbf{x}(p,\mathbf{y}) = h(\mathbf{y}, S(p,\mathbf{y})).$$

When the supply function and the unconditional factor demand function exist, what about the sign of their partial derivatives?

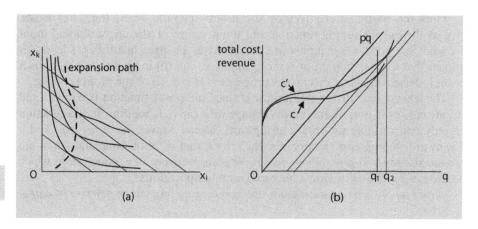

Fig. 5.11 Input x_i is inferior; an increase of its rental causes the cost curve c to become c', that is to shift upwards but to become less steep at the original output q_1, so that $p = MC$ is reached at $q_2 > q_1$

If profit is considered a function of q, we know that its maximization requires solving $max_q\ pq - c(\mathbf{v}, q)$, whose first-order necessary condition is $p = MC(\mathbf{v}, q)$; the second-order sufficient condition is that MC must be rising at the optimal q. If both conditions are satisfied it is:

$$\partial S(p, \mathbf{y})/\partial p > 0,$$

the supply function (graphically, the **supply curve**, usually drawn as an *inverse* supply curve, with p in ordinate and q in abscissa) is increasing. (Hotelling's Lemma proved it was non-decreasing, here we are proving it is increasing: why this difference? Here we are assuming an upward-sloping MC curve at the optimal q, i.e. we are excluding a vertical MC curve which would indicate that it is impossible further to increase output.)

On the sign of $\partial x_i(p, \mathbf{v})/\partial v_i$, Hotelling's Lemma plus the convexity of the profit function imply $\partial x_i(p, \mathbf{v})/\partial v_i \leq 0$: the own-rental effect is non-positive (and generally negative).

Does this result on input use imply $\partial S(p, \mathbf{v})/\partial v_i \leq 0$? that is, is it always the case that the optimal output, when it exists, does not increase and generally decreases if the rental of a factor in positive use rises? Surprisingly, not always. When the rental of a factor rises, supply *rises* if the factor is an **inferior input**. An input is (locally) inferior when its *conditional* demand falls as *output* increases, that is, when $\partial h_i(\mathbf{v}, q)/\partial q < 0$ (in a neighbourhood of the initial q), meaning that at the given input rentals the cost-minimizing way to increase q is by increasing some input other than i and *decreasing* input i.

In Fig. 5.11a input x_i is inferior for a certain interval of values of output, corresponding to isoquants whose points of tangency with isocosts move to the left as output increases beyond a certain level.[31] The locus of tangency points

---

[31] This is not possible with CRS and no other factors besides the two shown in the figure, but it is possible even with a CRS production function *if* there is a third factor in *given* amount.

5.19 · Conditional and Unconditional Factor Demands, Inferior Inputs ...

between isocosts and isoquants is called the *expansion path* of the firm, and it depends on the given relative input rentals. As the drawing helps to grasp, input inferiority is necessarily a local property: in order for the optimal use of an input to decrease as output increases, it must first have increased with output. An example of inferior input can be labour in some agricultural firms with a given land where, as long as the required output is not large, it is cost minimizing to achieve it with abundant use of labour nearly unassisted by machinery, but when output becomes large, it becomes convenient to mechanize production, which reduces the needed amount of labour.

The relevance of inferior inputs for the sign of $\partial S(p, \mathbf{v})/\partial v_i$ comes from the fact that locally *the increase in the rental of an inferior input shifts the MC curve downwards*, so the $p = MC$ condition is achieved *for a greater q* although at a smaller profit, as in ☐ Fig. 5.11b. This means that if factor i is inferior, then $\partial S(p,\mathbf{v})/\partial v_i > 0$, or equivalently

$$\partial S(p, \mathbf{v})/\partial v_i \leq 0 \; only \; if \; factor \; i \; is \; not \; inferior.$$

The proof that the marginal cost curve shifts downwards, that is, $\partial MC/\partial v_i < 0$ if input i is inferior, is an interesting non-trivial application of the notions studied thus far. The cost function is assumed twice continuously differentiable, so second-order cross-partial derivatives coincide.

Proof Let input i be inferior; differentiate both sides of $x_i(p, \mathbf{v}) = h_i(\mathbf{v}, S(p, \mathbf{v}))$ with respect to p, and apply Shephard's Lemma and the coincidence of cross-partials to obtain:

$$\frac{\partial x_i(\mathbf{v},p)}{\partial p} = \frac{\partial h_i(v,q)}{\partial q} \cdot \frac{\partial S(v,p)}{\partial p} = \frac{\partial}{\partial q} \frac{\partial c(v,q)}{\partial v_i} \cdot \frac{\partial S(v,p)}{\partial p}$$

$$= \frac{\partial}{\partial v_i} \frac{\partial c(v,q)}{\partial q} \cdot \frac{\partial S(v,p)}{\partial p} = \frac{\partial MC}{\partial v_i} \cdot \frac{\partial S(v,p)}{\partial p}.$$

Since $\frac{\partial S(\mathbf{v},p)}{\partial p} > 0$ and we are assuming that x_i is inferior, the conditional demand for factor i decreases when output increases at given input prices, so it is $\frac{\partial x_i(\mathbf{v},p)}{\partial p} < 0$, hence it must be $\frac{\partial MC}{\partial v_i} < 0$. Or also, the above shows that $\frac{\partial h_i(v,q)}{\partial q} = \frac{\partial MC}{\partial v_i}$, and the left-hand side is < 0 by the definition of inferior input.∎

I will not go into the intricacies of inferior inputs except to prove that when the production function is differentiable, a necessary (but not sufficient) condition for an input x_i to be inferior is that it be *rival* of some other input x_j, which means that an increase in x_j decreases the marginal product of x_i.[32] This proof is sup-

---

32 Rivalry can arise, for example, if there is some third input x_h, whose services cooperate with either x_i or x_j, and such that when x_j increases it is convenient to allocate x_h's services to cooperate mainly with x_j; or, one input can have direct negative side effects on the efficiency of another input, for example, owing to chemical interactions, pesticides might decrease the marginal productivity of fertilizers in fruit production. Of course when the production function is twice continuously differentiable the cross-partial derivatives coincide, so rivalry is reciprocal.

400   Chapter 5 · Firms, Partial Equilibria and the General Equilibrium with Production

plied both in order to introduce *rival inputs* that are interesting and will deserve some further consideration, and to give a further taste of the complex formal developments that the neoclassical theory of production can originate.

Proof   The proof will consist of showing that if no inputs are rival then the rise of the rental of an input cannot raise optimal output. Let $w = 1/p \cdot v$ be the vector of real factor rentals in terms of the firm's output; $f(x) = q$ is the firm's production function. Assume that marginal cost is locally strictly increasing so the profit function $\pi(w)$ is well defined at the optimal q. Maximization of $\pi(w)$ determines the unconditional factor demands $x(w)$. These satisfy the well-known condition $w_i = \partial f(x)/\partial x_i$, all i, that for brevity I indicate as

$$D_x f(x) = w,$$

where $D_x f(x)$ means the vector of partial derivatives of $f(x)$ with respect to the variables in x. Let us assume that $x(w)$ is invertible, i.e. to each input vector x there corresponds a unique vector w that renders it optimal. Let $w(x(w))$ be this inverse function.[33] Since $w = D_x f(x)$, it is $D_x(w(x(w))) = D_x^2 f(x(w))$. And by the derivative rule for inverse vectorial functions, the Jacobian $D_x(w(x(w)))$ is the inverse of the Jacobian $D_w x(w)$:

$$D_x\Big(w(x(w))\Big) = (D_w x(w))^{-1} = D_x^2 f(x(w)).$$

But then, inverting everything:

$$D_w x(w) = (D_x(w(x(w))))^{-1} = \Big(D_x^2 f(x(w))\Big)^{-1}.$$

Now we use a result in the theory of matrices (cf. Takayama 1974, p. 393, Theorem 4.D.3) that states that if the off-diagonal elements of a square non-singular matrix are all non-negative then its inverse is non-positive. If no inputs are rival, the marginal product of no input decreases when some other input is increased, so the Hessian (assumed non-singular) of the production function has non-negative off-diagonal elements, hence by this result its inverse is non-positive, and therefore $D_w x(w)$ is non-positive.

Now fix the product price p so we can return from w to v. It is $\partial S(p,v)/\partial v_i = \sum_j (\frac{\partial f(x)}{\partial x_j} \frac{\partial x_j(v,p)}{\partial v_i}) < 0$ because we have shown that the second term inside the parenthesis is non-positive for all j. Therefore absence of rival inputs implies that supply cannot increase when an input price increases, so no input can be inferior. ∎

---

33   As I have used $x(w)$ to represent the function that makes x depend on w, its inverse should be actually represented as $w = x^{-1}(x)$.

5.19 · Conditional and Unconditional Factor Demands, Inferior Inputs ...

The possibility of *rivalry* among inputs has some relevance for the marginalist or neoclassical approach to income distribution. As explained in ▶ Chap. 3, according to this approach each factor tends to earn, in the long period, a rental equal to the value of its full-employment marginal product. In the long period, competitive industries behave like firms with CRS production functions, and this prevents rivalry if factors are only two, as I prove below; but if factors are more than two, an increase in the equilibrium use of a factor because of an increase in its supply can cause a decrease of the long-period full-employment marginal product of a rival factor in fixed supply: thus the marginal approach *does not exclude the possibility that an increase in the supply of a factor causes a decrease of the equilibrium rental of another factor*. However, cases of rivalry appear rare and specific to certain industries, so marginalist/neoclassical economists unanimously exclude rivalry for those factors, e.g. most types of labour, for which demand comes from very many industries.

Proof *that with two factors and CRS there cannot be rivalry.* If factors are only two, call them x and y, since marginal products only depend on the proportion x/y owing to CRS, if an increase of x with y fixed causes a decrease of MP_y it must mean that an increase of y with x fixed causes an increase of MP_y, and this means a non-convexity of output as a function of y with x fixed; but such a non-convexity is excluded by profit maximization plus CRS: in ◘ Fig. 5.12, where the curve represents output as a function of y with factor x fixed, all points on the segment AB can be reached by a linear combination of the factor vectors (y_A, x) and (y_B, x); indeed it was argued in Sect. 5.8 that with divisibility production functions are necessarily convex, and we conclude that with CRS and two factors, increasing marginal products are impossible. This excludes rivalry. ■

Input rivalry can also cause counterintuitive effects of shifts in the composition of demand for consumption goods on equilibrium factor rentals. As illustrated in ▶ Chap. 3, if one leaves aside possible 'perverse' income effects then a shift in the composition of demand in favour of goods that use a factor in a higher-than-average proportion tends to raise that factor's equilibrium rental if technical coefficients are fixed, and if there is technical substitutability the effect on the factor rental is normally considered to be of the same sign, only weaker. But

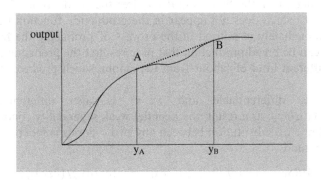

◘ **Fig. 5.12** Economic total factor productivity curve cannot have strictly convex portions

402   **Chapter 5** · Firms, Partial Equilibria and the General Equilibrium with Production

if a factor is specialized and used only by one industry and is rival of other inputs in that industry, then when demand for the industry's product rises the industry in order to produce more must increase the use of other inputs, and this can cause a decrease of the marginal product of the specialized factor and hence a decrease of the demand for it if its rental remains the same: the excess supply of the factor will then cause the rental of the factor to decrease; so it is possible that a rise in the equilibrium output of the industry, although associated with a higher output price, be associated with a lower equilibrium rental of the specialized factor. This possibility looks exceptional, but the marginal approach cannot exclude it.

Finally, returning to the firm in the short period, let us consider $\partial x_i(p, \mathbf{v})/\partial v_j$. It should be intuitive that its sign is ambiguous: if factor j is not inferior, optimal output decreases when v_j increases, and this would reduce the demand for x_i if factor proportions were fixed, on the contrary these proportions change (and in directions that depend on the specific production function) both because optimal factor proportions change with q even with fixed relative factor prices, cf. ◘ Fig. 5.11a, and because relative factor prices change and this alters optimal factor proportions for each level of q. The possibility that factor j be inferior adds further uncertainty by rendering the sign of the change in optimal q uncertain. All this could be confirmed more formally, but without great gains in clarification, so let us pass on.

5.20 Functional Separability: Leontief Separability

Suppose we can separate the $m+n$ inputs to a production function into two sub-vectors, $\mathbf{x}=(x_1,..., x_m)$ and $\mathbf{y}=(y_1,..., y_n)$, having, respectively, rental vectors $\mathbf{v}$ and $\mathbf{w}$, and that the production function satisfies

$$f(\mathbf{x}, \mathbf{y}) = f(z(\mathbf{x}), \mathbf{y}),$$

where the scalar function $z(\cdot)$ has the characteristics of a production function: then it is as if inputs $\mathbf{x}$ produced an intermediate good which then produces the final output in combination with inputs $\mathbf{y}$. This can be simply a mathematical property of the form of the production function, but it can also reflect the fact that the production of the final output requires the production of an intermediate good first, which does not appear in the production function because produced and immediately re-utilized in the process of producing the final output. An example can be bread production that requires first the production of dough, utilizing a different kind of labour from the labour which produces bread from dough.

If $z(\mathbf{x})$ is differentiable and $f(z, \mathbf{y})$ is also differentiable, then $\partial f/\partial x_i = (\partial f/\partial z)\cdot(\partial z/\partial x_i)$; as a result, the **Leontief weak separability** condition holds: the marginal rate of substitution between any two x-goods is independent of the amounts of y-goods:

$$MRS_{xj,xi} = -(\partial f/\partial x_i)/(\partial f/\partial x_j) = -(\partial z/\partial x_i)/(\partial z/\partial x_j).$$

Vice versa if the Leontief weak separability condition holds for the subgroup $\mathbf{x}$ of inputs, then a differentiable $f(\mathbf{x}, \mathbf{y})$ can be written as $f(z(\mathbf{x}), \mathbf{y})$ where $z(\mathbf{x})$ is a scalar function (I omit the somewhat complex proof; see Kreps 2013 pp. 39–42).

The term '*weakly* separable' is used to distinguish the notion from that of *strongly separable* production functions, which means *additively* separable, i.e. represented by an additive production function: $f(x_1,\ldots, x_n) = v_1(x_1) + v_2(x_2,\ldots, x_n)$. The term 'strong separability' is sometimes restricted to *completely* additively separable production functions $f(x_1, \ldots, x_n) = v_1(x_1) + v_2(x_2) + \cdots + v_n(x_n)$.

Under weak separability, the firm can adopt a two-stage cost-minimization procedure: it can first determine the cost-minimizing input combination of the x-inputs for each level of z, and the resulting cost of z; and then it can determine the cost-minimizing input combination of $(z,\mathbf{y})$ for each level of output. This is what a firm would do that produces itself some of its inputs in a separate plant. If $f(\cdot)$ has constant returns to scale, so does $z(\cdot)$; then the cost function for the 'good' z can be written as $\varepsilon(\mathbf{v}) \cdot z$, with $\varepsilon(\mathbf{v})$ representing the unit price of z.

5.21 Duality

I touch very briefly on the duality between some of the notions explained in this chapter. We have seen that cost function and conditional factor demands stand to the production function in exactly the same relationship as expenditure function and Hicksian (or compensated) consumer demands stand to the utility function: indeed, the utility function can be viewed as a sort of production function. It would be also possible to define an ***indirect production function*** $\varphi(\mathbf{v}, c)$ analogous to the indirect utility function that would specify the maximum production achievable for each vector of input rentals and total cost. The analogy with consumer theory shows that it is possible to pass from one to the other of these functions in the same way as for the parallel functions in consumer theory. Only the *unconditional* input demand function has no parallel in consumer theory, because it depends on profit maximization which is different from utility maximization in that there is no constraint analogous to a budget constraint. But among the other functions the same duality holds as among the parallel functions in consumer theory, and the same possibility exists to derive one from one of the others. For applied attempts at estimating these functions the same need arises as in consumer theory, to be certain that the functional form chosen for the function to be estimated is not in contradiction with theory. I will only list the needed conditions for a putative cost function. The conditions guaranteeing that a function could really be a cost function, because there exists a production function that generates it, are listed in the following proposition (I omit the proof, cf. e.g. Varian 1992, p. 85):

Let $c(\mathbf{v}, q)$ be a differentiable function which is
1. *non-negative if $(\mathbf{v}, q)$ is non-negative;*
2. *non-decreasing in $(\mathbf{v}, q)$;*
3. *concave in $\mathbf{v}$ and*

404   Chapter 5 · Firms, Partial Equilibria and the General Equilibrium with Production

4. *satisfying homogeneity of degree* 1 *in* **v**.*then* $c(\mathbf{v}, q)$ *is the cost function of a production function.*

It can be convenient, in applied work, to start directly from a cost function rather than from a production function.

As to conditional factor demands, they can be 'integrated' to yield the production function that generated them, with the same procedure that derives the utility function from a system of compensated demands for consumption goods.

5.22 Elasticity of Substitution

Cost minimization requires that firms intending to produce a *given* output locate themselves on the point of the corresponding (convex) isoquant touching the isocost closest to the origin—a point of tangency if the isoquant is smoothly convex. A change in the relative rental of two factors can induce no substitution, little substitution and extensive substitution. For example, if factors are perfect complements, then isoquants (with two factors) are L-shaped and cost-minimizing firms will locate themselves at the kink: changes in relative factor 'prices' induce no substitution. In order to measure the effect of changes in relative factor rentals on the proportions in which firms find it optimal to combine two factors, economists use the **elasticity of substitution**, already met in ▶ Sect. 4.11.3. The analysis here will be restricted to only two factors. When applied to production functions, this elasticity—to be indicated now with the symbol σ—is the ratio between the percentage change in x_2/x_1 along a *given* isoquant, and the percentage change (pay attention to the different order of the indices!) of MP_1/MP_2 or v_1/v_2:

$$\sigma_{21} = \frac{\frac{d(x_2/x_1)}{x_2/x_1}}{\frac{d(MP_1/MP_2)}{MP_1/MP_2}} = \frac{\partial(x_2/x_1)}{\partial(v_1/v_2)} \cdot \frac{v_1/v_2}{x_2/x_1}.$$

The second of the above two expressions for the elasticity of substitution is based on the assumption that the firm chooses the factor proportion that satisfies $-TRS_{2,1} = v_1/v_2$; therefore the elasticity of substitution measures the sensitivity, of the proportion in which factors are demanded, to relative factor rentals; it gives an indication of what happens to the *relative shares* of factors in total cost as relative factor rentals vary. The relative share of factor 2 in total cost is given by $(v_2x_2)/(v_1x_1)$, which can be rewritten as $(x_2/x_1) \cdot (v_1/v_2)$ or $(x_2/x_1) \cdot |TRS_{2,1}|$. When v_1/v_2 increases by 1%, x_2/x_1 increases by σ%; an elasticity of substitution equal to 1 means that relative factor shares in total cost do not change. An elasticity of substitution *less than* 1 means that when factor 1 becomes relatively *more* expensive, x_2/x_1 increases less than in proportion, so $v_2x_2/(v_1x_1)$ decreases: the relative share of factor 2 in national income decreases, and that of factor 1 increases. Note that a given percentage change in x_2/x_1 is the same (with the opposite sign of course) as the corresponding percentage change in x_1/x_2.

5.23 · Partial Equilibrium

405 **5**

The elasticity of substitution is used in one-output, two-factor general equilibrium neoclassical models (the factors are then generally labour, and capital treated as a single physical factor homogeneous with output—a treatment to be criticized in ▶ Chap. 7) to derive predictions on factor shares from changes in relative factor endowments. In these models the economy produces the single output with a CRS differentiable production function, and income distribution is determined by full-employment marginal products, hence the product exhaustion theorem holds. Changes in factor supplies alter factor shares in a direction that depends on the elasticity of substitution. Thus assume the factors are labour and land, rigidly supplied and fully employed. Suppose labour immigration raises labour supply, causing the real wage to decrease (while real land rent increases). Check your understanding of the issues with the following questions. If the elasticity of substitution is less than one, the percentage decrease of the ratio of wage to rent, needed to ensure the full employment of the increased supply of labour, will have to be greater or smaller than the percentage increase in labour supply? and the share of wages in full-employment national income will decrease or increase? The correct answers are given in a subsequent footnote, try your answer before turning the page.

▶ Chapter 7 will criticize this recourse to the elasticity of substitution by criticizing the recourse to aggregate production functions. But there is a vast applied literature that uses the elasticity of substitution to estimate demand curves for factors (especially labour) and in particular the elasticity of conditional demand for factors, so knowing more about these derivations can help readers to understand the applied literature. A section in the online Appendix to this chapter is dedicated to the issue.

5.23 Partial Equilibrium

As a first step towards the study of the competitive general equilibrium of production and exchange, let us discuss in greater detail the Marshallian construction often referred to in this chapter: the determination, via the intersection of a supply curve and a demand curve, of the *partial* equilibrium (or *particular* equilibrium, the original and more precise denomination) of a single competitive market studied in isolation.[34] A famous 1926 article describes this approach as follows:

» This point of view assumes that the conditions of production and the demand for a commodity can be considered, in respect to small variations, as being practically

---

34 Originally the term 'market' stood for a physical place where sellers and buyers would actually meet, and of course there still are markets in this sense, for example weekly markets in the main square of small towns, or stock exchanges; but nowadays in economics the term has a more abstract meaning. The market of a good or service is the collection of interactions among buyers and sellers of that good or service.

independent, both in regard to each other and in relation to the supply and demand of all other commodities. It is well known that such an assumption would not be illegitimate merely because the independence may not be absolutely perfect, as, in fact, it never can be; and a slight degree of interdependence may be overlooked without disadvantage if it applies to quantities of the second order of smalls, as would be the case if the effect (for example, an increase of cost) of a variation in the industry which we propose to isolate were to react partially on the price of the products of other industries, and this latter effect were to influence the demand for the product of the first industry. (Sraffa 1926, p. 538)

The motivation behind the partial equilibrium approach is that it allows the study of comparative statics of a market's equilibrium (e.g. how price and quantity change if some input cost decreases, or if consumers' tastes change and the desire for the good increases), and of some welfare aspects, without needing simultaneously to consider what is happening in all other markets. In ▶ Chap. 3 we saw that, rigorously speaking, in the neoclassical approach the simultaneous consideration of all markets cannot be avoided, because any change in some of the data of general equilibrium will have repercussions on all markets; for example, a change in tastes in favour of a good will alter equilibrium income distribution and hence all prices and quantities. However,

» when the expenditure on the good under study is a small portion of a consumer's total expenditure, ony a small fraction of any additional dollar of wealth will be spent on this good; consequently, we can expect wealth effects for it to be small. Second, with similarly dispersed substitution effects, the small size of the market under study should lead the prices of other goods to be approximately unaffected by changes in this market. (Mas-Colell et al. 1995, p. 316; "wealth effects" stands for income effects.).

So conclusions will not be far wrong if one treats the prices of all other goods demanded by consumers as unchanged in respect of small variations in the first good's price, and if then one uses Hicksian aggregability, that is, one treats expenditure on the other goods as a single commodity, 'residual income', with constant marginal utility, that ensures absence of income (or wealth) effects in the demand for the good. This means to follow Marshall in assuming a *constant marginal utility of money*, that is, quasi-linear utility (linear in residual income). Furthermore, if the industry's demand for inputs is, for each input, only a small fraction of its total supply, we can expect the prices of inputs to be nearly unaffected by limited changes in the output of the good, and so we can treat input costs as given too. Then the determinants of equilibrium on that good's market, and of its changes, become very clear.

Sometimes it can be legitimate to isolate not one, but two interdependent markets and maintain nearly the same clarity as to results: one example is the study of the effects of changes of the supply conditions and hence of the price of one product on the demand and hence on the equilibrium price of a complementary or of a substitute product; another example is the determination of the supply curve of an industry which is the sole one to use a specialized factor, whose rental

5.23 · Partial Equilibrium

rises when, owing to a rise in the demand for the industry's product, the industry's demand for that factor rises.

The partial-equilibrium *supply curve* of a competitive industry can be a long-period or a short-period one. The long-period supply curve is horizontal if factor rentals are given. The short-period supply curve is upward-sloping even with given factor rentals, owing to the given amounts of some factors. The derivation of these supply curves has been illustrated already.

The case with a specialized factor demanded only by the producers of the good under study requires further comment. (I will assume no factor rivalry.) The factor might be for example a special type of land indispensable to (and only demanded for) the production of a famous wine. In this case the land's rental will rise as the product price rises, so as to maintain the producers' profit at zero; hence the wine supply curve is upward sloping. The physical marginal products of the remaining factors (whose rentals are given) decrease as output increases, owing to the given amount of land; but their marginal *revenue* products remain equal to their given rentals because the product price rises. (The independence between supply curve and demand curve, necessary for meaningful comparative statics, additionally requires that the changes in the incomes of the owners of the specialized factor do not appreciably influence the demand for the product of the industry under analysis.)

Upon reflection, the short-period supply curve of an industry can be viewed as increasing for the same reason, with the sole difference that the non-augmentable factors are in fact augmentable but their increase takes such a long time that one can take their supply as given for the period under study. Indeed it was noted earlier that the short-period profit of a firm should be seen as the quasi-rent of the fixed factor that causes the short-period supply curve to be upward-sloping.

The supply curve is valid only for comparatively small variations of the quantity produced, because for considerable variations the *coeteris paribus* condition becomes doubtful.[35] Also, *it is only applicable to pure consumption goods*; for capital goods, it can easily be the case that the price of a capital good enters the cost of other capital goods, some of which are directly or indirectly inputs to the first capital good (e.g. iron needs for its production machines made of iron); *then the minimum average cost of the capital good cannot be determined before its price*, because the latter influences the cost of some of its inputs—a problem that requires going beyond the partial-equilibrium approach to a general theory of pricing such as was discussed in ▶ Chaps. 1 and 2 and will be taken up again in ▶ Chap. 7. The partial-equilibrium *demand* curve for a capital good too would be inconsistent with the requirements of partial-equilibrium analysis, because the price of the capital good significantly influences the prices of all goods in whose production that capital good enters directly or indirectly.

---

35 *Coeteris paribus* is Latin for 'other things equal'. A considerable expansion or reduction of supply entails a non-negligible effect on the demand for some inputs also used in other industries that will alter their rentals and hence production costs and prices of other goods. Answer to the questions on elasticity of substitution: greater; decrease.

Alfred Marshall attempted to argue that the long-period partial-equilibrium supply curve of a product can also be downward-sloping, owing to two effects of increases in the dimension of an industry: first, the possibility better to exploit scale economies (increasing returns to scale); second, an increase in *external effects* (or *externalities*). But in two famous articles, in 1925 (in Italian; only recently translated into English) and 1926, Piero Sraffa argued that the decreasing supply curve is incompatible with competitive partial equilibrium. He remembered that the existence of unexploited scale economies is incompatible with competition with undifferentiated products, because the perfect substitutability for the buyer of the products of the different firms in the industry implies that any small price reduction by a firm relative to competitors will make it possible to sell the increased output that allows the exploitation of scale economies; therefore, increasing returns to scale must have been all exploited in equilibrium; if this requires very large firms, then the competitive assumption must be dropped. As to externalities, he noticed that the positive external effects due to increases of the industry's output, e.g. greater ease with finding repairmen or transportation firms or skilled workers, are very seldom internal to a single industry, they generally concern large groups of firms belonging to different industries but connected by common location or by similar needed skills; these effects cannot be admitted in the partial-equilibrium analysis of one industry because they extend to other products, altering their costs as much as the costs of the industry under study, and therefore violating the *coeteris paribus* condition. Sraffa concluded, and subsequent economists have admired the cogency of his critique, that competitive long-period partial-equilibrium theory can admit only constant cost industries, or increasing cost industries in the sole case of an industry being the sole demander of a specialized factor. (When the expansion of an industry affects the rental of a factor also used by other industries, then the costs of these other industries are affected as much as in the first industry, and again the coeteris paribus condition does not hold.) This does not mean that unexploited scale economies do not exist in real economies, it only means that the study of their causes and effects requires a different approach: Sraffa suggested to abandon the assumption of perfect competition and admit that the general case is rather one of firms facing, each one of them, a downward-sloping demand curve. The thing will be discussed in ▶ Chap. 12.

5.24 Stability of Partial Equilibria

We have noted that the markets that can be studied with the partial-equilibrium methodology are consumption goods' markets. Then the partial-equilibrium demand curve for a product derives from consumer choices. It is based on given incomes of consumers and given other prices. So the partial-equilibrium approach presupposes a previous determination of income distribution—which determines the normal prices of other goods and the input costs of the industry under study—and of the general level of economic activity, which by determining

5.24 · Stability of Partial Equilibria

labour employment determines aggregate consumer incomes. In the marginal approach the implicit assumption is that there is general equilibrium, income distribution is the equilibrium one, and there is full employment of labour and of all resources. Some economists argue that other theories of income distribution and of labour employment too can be the background to the use of Marshallian partial equilibrium for the study of consumer markets. Other economists disagree, but this is not the place to study this debate, we are interested now in understanding the marginal/neoclassical approach.

Given the very low likelihood of Giffen goods, demand curves for produced consumption goods can be assumed decreasing. Short-period supply curves can be assumed upward-sloping, so the short-period equilibrium price is stable. If it is greater than $MinLAC$, in the long run there will be entry of new firms, or the existing firms will build new plants, and the short-period supply curve will shift to the right, and price will decrease. So the long-period partial equilibrium is stable too. If the good is homogeneous (undifferentiated), then on average all units of the good sell at the same price. Of course this can only be approximately true in actual markets, but, as already pointed out several times, the equilibrium position can only aim at describing the average position resulting over sufficient time from the trial-and-error higgling of the market.

There is a reason for representing price in ordinate and quantity in abscissa; then a supply curve and a demand curve represent *supply price* and *demand price* as functions of the quantity of the good—the prices that are necessary in order to obtain, respectively, convenience to supply, or to demand, the given quantity measured in abscissa. In this way a horizontal supply curve, or the saw-like supply curve of ◧ Fig. 5.9, are nonetheless functions.

In ▶ Chap. 6 it will be seen that the consideration of adjustment lags can raise doubts on the stability of the partial short-period equilibrium in spite of the decreasing demand curve and increasing supply curve, but it will be argued that these difficulties are not very serious. So the neoclassical economist has some justification for believing that the *assumptions* that will be made in the formulation of the general equilibrium equations, of equilibrium product prices equal to minimum average costs and of quantities produced equal to the demand for them at those prices, reflect actual tendencies. Of course the stability of the general equilibrium of an economy where there is production requires in addition the stability of factor markets, which raises a different set of issues, to be discussed in ▶ Chap. 6.

5.25 Welfare Analysis of Partial Equilibria

In the partial-equilibrium framework, once the demand curve and the supply curve of a consumption good are given, the competitive equilibrium of this market, determined by the intersection of demand curve and supply curve, is argued to be Pareto efficient, that is, it is not possible to obtain a Pareto improvement of the utility of the consumers and producers involved by producing a different amount of the consumption good or by allocating it differently.

410 Chapter 5 · Firms, Partial Equilibria and the General Equilibrium with Production

The argument goes as follows. There are two groups of maximizers: *consumers* maximize utility on the basis of their given incomes, and *producers* maximize their income, i.e. profit. Call x-good the good exchanged in the market; indicate the quantity produced as x, the price as p. The given prices of all other goods allow their treatment as a *Hicksian composite commodity*, whose price can be made equal to 1 by an opportune choice of units and whose quantity therefore can be identified with expenditure y on goods other than x, or 'residual income' y. Then the y-good is actually income or money. It is assumed that consumers have quasi-linear utility functions, linear in residual income; thus consumer h's utility function is

$$u^h(x_h, y_h) = z_h(x_h) + y_h,$$

and when a consumer pays p for one more unit of the x-good she gives up p units of y-good. A producer renounces amounts of y-good as cost to produce amounts of x-good; thus it is as if x were produced by using quantities of y as input. In (internal) equilibrium, all consumers have the same MRS between x-good and y-good; the equilibrium marginal utility of income is constant and equal to 1 for each consumer. This means that p^*, the equilibrium price of the x-good, equals the marginal utility of the x-good for all consumers active in the market. Producers are interested in maximizing their income, i.e. profit, so they equalize price and marginal cost; hence $MC(x^*) = MU(x^*)$ where x^* is equilibrium output.

■■ Proof of the Pareto efficiency of the perfectly competitive partial equilibrium

. In equilibrium, production is x^* and it is allocated among consumers so that the last unit has marginal utility $MU = p^*$ for all consumers and it is allocated among producers so that the last unit has marginal cost $MC = p^*$ for all producers. First let us prove that *production* of a quantity different from the equilibrium quantity x^* cannot be Pareto efficient. *Pareto efficiency* means that a *Pareto improvement* (a change that makes somebody better off without making anybody worse off) is impossible. If $x < x^*$, there will be some consumer ready to pay for one more unit of x a 'demand price' p^d greater than the equilibrium price p^*, and there will be some producer who can produce one extra unit at a marginal cost less than, or at most equal to, p^* (the second case holds with CRS and constant $MC = p^*$) and would be therefore ready to sell it at a 'supply price' $p^s \le p^*$, hence these two agents can strike a mutually advantageous bargain (to produce and exchange one extra unit of x-good at any p intermediate between p^d and p^s) without making anybody else worse off. If $x > x^*$, there will be some producer whose last unit cost him more than p^* or at most p^*, who is ready to pay p^* for the right to reduce production by one unit (this would reduce his expense by p^* or more); and there will be some consumer h with a marginal utility of the last unit of x^h less than p^*, hence ready to renounce one unit of x for a recompense equal to p^*, hence again these two agents can strike a mutually advantageous bargain, with the producer reducing by one unit his supply of x-good to the consumer in exchange for a payment slightly less than p^*. Thus $x = x^*$ is a necessary condition for Pareto efficiency.

Let us now prove that no different *allocation* of the production of x^* among producers can be a Pareto improvement, and no different allocation of x^* among

5.25 · Welfare Analysis of Partial Equilibria

the consumers can be Pareto efficient. A different allocation of the production of x^* among firms either leaves marginal costs unchanged, or causes an increase in marginal cost in at least one firm, whose profit decreases: in either case there isn't a Pareto improvement; in the first of these two cases Pareto efficiency does not uniquely determine the allocation of x^* among firms, but this does not disturb the Pareto efficiency of x^* and of its distribution among producers resulting from the equilibrium. A different allocation of x^* among consumers means that at least one has more x-good and at least one has less x-good than in equilibrium; this means that their MRS's between their quantity of x-good and income differ, so they can strike a mutually advantageous exchange. Hence the allocation of the production of x^* among producers realized by the competitive equilibrium, and its allocation among consumers, allow of no Pareto improvement and hence are Pareto efficient. ∎

We have seen in ▶ Chap. 4 the definition of consumer surplus in an industry. ***Producer surplus*** is analogously defined as the area above the supply curve up to the horizontal price line, cf. the triangle ADC in ◘ Fig. 5.13 if price is $p^* = D$.

Producer surplus intends to measure the maximum amount of money that 'producers', that is, the ensemble of the owners of the firms that supply the x-good, would be ready to pay in total rather than forgo the possibility to produce and sell the good at the given price. It too assumes a constant marginal utility of income.

In the short period, the producer surplus of a single firm, at a given product price and quantity supplied, is defined as total revenue minus total variable cost, which is the quasi-rent earned by the fixed plant (or the maximum rent another entrepreneur would be ready to pay for the lease of the firm's structures). This

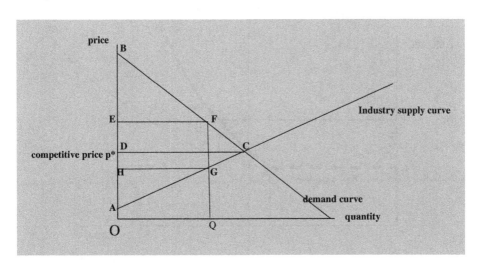

◘ **Fig. 5.13** Marshallian total surplus is the area of triangle ABC, the sum of consumer surplus (the area of triangle DBC) and producer surplus (the area of triangle ADC). If demand and hence production are Q because price is E, then consumer surplus is the area of EBF and producer surplus is the area of AEFG; if production is Q because price is H, then consumer surplus is the area of HBFG and producer surplus is the area of AHG; total surplus is the same in both cases, and less than at equilibrium by the area of triangle GFC

makes it clear that 'producer surplus' actually means income that the owner of the fixed plant can earn because owner. Considering fixed cost to be a sunk cost which cannot be avoided and hence can be neglected in valuing choices, the entrepreneur, rather than be excluded from the market, will be ready to pay up to the amount that would leave her with what is just sufficient to cover variable cost, hence revenue minus variable cost.

This is equivalent to the area above the firm's supply curve up to the horizontal price line: this is easily proved by remembering that total variable cost is the integral of marginal cost and therefore it is the area under the supply curve, cf. ◘ Figure 5.14. The sum of the areas 'above' each firm's supply curve up to the price line equals the area 'above' the industry's supply curve up to the price line.

If the single firm's supply curve is a straight line (because of CRS and all factors variable), and if p equals the firm's average and marginal cost, then variable cost and total cost coincide, profit is zero, producer surplus is zero. Hence in long-period analysis if the industry's supply curve is horizontal because all factor rentals are given, and it coincides with the price line as it must be in equilibrium, then total producer surplus is zero. But if the industry uses a specialized input whose rental rises with industry supply, the long-period industry supply curve is upward sloping, so producer surplus is positive if the rental of this specialized input is not included among variable cost (e.g. because that input is subdivided among firms in a way fixed by tradition and is therefore treated by firms as a fixed factor: this might be the case, e.g. for land, or mines). The profits of firms are

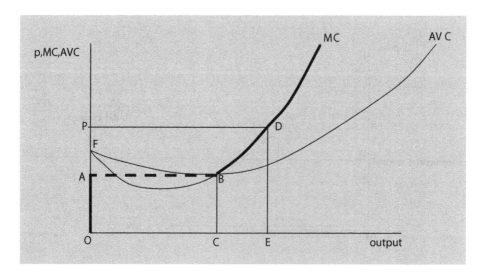

◘ **Fig. 5.14** Graphical proof that for a firm the area above the supply curve up to the price line (the trapezoid ABDP) equals revenue minus variable cost and therefore measures producer surplus. When price is P and therefore the supply of the firm is OE, revenue is rectangle OEDP, and the area under the supply curve OABD of the firm equals total variable cost, because the area of rectangle OABC is variable cost up to output OC, and, by integration, the area under the marginal cost curve from B to D is the addition to variable cost caused by increasing output from OC to OE

zero all the same, because at each point of the supply curve the specialized input's rental absorbs all the excess of revenue above variable cost. How is the positive producer surplus reconciled with the zero profits? The point is that the situation is the same as if all firms obtained their fixed plants on lease, in which case producer surplus would go to the owners of the fixed plants, treated now as different persons from the owners of the firms. The rise in the rental of the specialized factor due to the expansion of production implies an income gain for the suppliers of that factor, so *they* would be ready to pay rather than see production of the good forbidden. The maximum amount they would be ready to pay, rather misleadingly called producer surplus (it is in fact a consumer surplus of the consumers who supply the factor), is precisely the rental the factor earns.

Exercise: Assume wine V is produced by labour L over specialized land T in fixed supply according to the production function $V = T^{1/2}L^{1/2}$. Assume $T = 1$. Labour's wage in terms of other goods is fixed and equal to w. Prove that the industry's long-period inverse supply curve is $p = 2wV$ and that the area below it for any given V equals the wage payments to the labour employed to produce that V.

Marshallian aggregate producer surplus, or simply *producer surplus* for brevity, is the sum of the individual producer surpluses in a market. And the sum of consumer and producer surplus is called the *Marshallian aggregate total surplus*. It is the area of the triangle formed by demand curve, supply curve and ordinate axis.

It is easy to see graphically that *the competitive partial equilibrium maximizes total surplus*. In ◘ Fig. 5.13, a price higher than the equilibrium price would cause *demand* to be less than the equilibrium amount, and then supply too, since it would be useless to produce more than can be sold, and total surplus would be less than the equilibrium amount. A price less than the equilibrium price would cause *supply* to be less than the equilibrium amount, and then consumption too, and again total surplus would be less than the equilibrium amount.

5.26 Price Taking, Perfect Competition, Tâtonnement

We have studied the short-period and long-period behaviour of price-taking firms and industries. Before proceeding to the equations of the general equilibrium of the competitive production-and-exchange economy (without capital goods), some considerations on price taking and competition are opportune.

In neoclassical theory, a perfectly competitive *equilibrium* in a market is an equilibrium between supply and demand in which all agents, consumers as well as firms, are price-takers, that is, treat the equilibrium price as a *parameter* (a datum they cannot affect) in their optimizations. And a perfectly competitive *market* is a market where the equilibrium is perfectly competitive. This, as the more careful theorists admit,[36] does not require consumers and firms to be price-takers at *any*

---

36 See Mas-Colell et al. (1995 p. 315); Arrow 1959. Also see Kreps 1990 for a series of conditions that are often listed as defining perfect competition but that, as he observes, are not *proven* to imply price taking, which is therefore the real assumption that defines perfect competition, the other conditions being only intuitive arguments in support of the plausibility of price taking. Some of these

price—that would be an unsustainable assumption, implying that there would be no one to change a non-equilibrium price.[37] The realistic traditional argument for a tendency of price towards the equilibrium level is that when demand is not equal to supply, there are either sellers or buyers of the good who are unable to carry through their desired transactions and then have an incentive to propose a slightly lower price (if sellers) or a slightly higher price (if buyers) so as not to remain with unsold wares or unsatisfied demand; then other agents too are compelled to follow the change (e.g. if a seller asks for a lower price, other sellers are obliged to lower price too, otherwise no one wants to buy from them), and if the stability conditions hold, the price will gravitate towards the equilibrium level. So the gravitation towards equilibrium is due to at least some agents *not* being price-takers at disequilibrium prices. Is this incompatible with price taking? Price taking for all agents remains possible *in equilibrium*, but it must be *voluntary*, that is, there must be no incentive to propose a different price if at the ruling price there is equality between supply and demand.

This is not difficult to argue once one is clear that the previous argument for the tendency towards equilibrium is based on *repetition* of market interactions, as in the forest exchange-economy example in ▶ Chap. 3; equilibrium then is the situation towards which the price tends over a repetition of market 'days'. Imagine, for example, fruit stalls in a daily vegetable market in a town. Clearly, when sellers realize that at the going price they are able to sell all they desire, they have no incentive to propose a lower price and will reject occasional buyers' demands to pay less. Conversely, buyers who have realized that at the equilibrium price they are able to satisfy their demands have no incentive to propose a higher price and will reject occasional seller requests for a higher price. So in equilibrium sellers do not lower the price they demand and do realize they are unable to obtain a higher price, buyers do not raise the price they offer and do realize they are unable to obtain a lower price; learning makes all agents price-takers. The higgling and bargaining and learning and error correction take time and then there are always temporary disturbances, so there will always be transactions not at the equilibrium price, but traditional equilibrium analysis did not claim that a market would ever be perfectly in equilibrium, it only claimed that the equilibrium price is a good indication of the average over a sufficient time period. For such a conception of the role of the equilibrium price, there is no contradiction between price taking for the definition of equilibrium and price making for the description of convergence towards equilibrium.

---

conditions are: (1) homogeneity of the good on sale; (2) readiness of agents to take advantage of every opportunity to improve their condition by switching to trading with different agents and/or proposing a different price; (3) anonymity (indifference as to whom one is exchanging with); (4) perfect information about prices charged by other sellers or offered by other buyers; (5) atomistic market (numerosity of agents and smallness of their supplies or demands relative to the size of the market); (6) absence of collusion; (7) no transaction costs for resale of the good (hence easy arbitrage); (8) free entry and free access to state-of-the-arts technology, if the good is a product.

37 I am discussing traditional marginalist/neoclassical theory that does not assume the fairy tale of the auctioneer-guided tâtonnement, as explained below in the text.

5.26 · Price Taking, Perfect Competition, Tâtonnement

The realism of the above traditional considerations is not to be found in contemporary general equilibrium analysis, which assumes equilibrium is actually and instantaneously reached and continuously maintained and, to describe how this is realized, assumes a fairy-tale adjustment process: the auctioneer-guided tâtonnement to be described shortly, in which agents are price-takers in disequilibrium too. The reader will have to wait for ▶ Chaps. 7 and 8 in order fully to grasp the reasons for this momentous change, but I can anticipate that the reason is not to be found in problems with price taking.

Price taking, it will be noticed, concerns the *limit result* of competition rather than its actual operation (McNulty 1967). To compete in usual language means active research of advantage over competitors via a variety of possible actions. This is indeed the meaning it had in classical authors, where the common term was *free* competition, that meant unhindered possibility for labourers, land owners and capitalists, to move from one possible buyer to another and from one industry to another and to propose different prices; this would tend to equalize the reward for similar inputs across sectors and the price of all units of undifferentiated goods. Classical competition also included competition through marketing and through innovation; leaving these aside for the moment, a first big distinguishing element of classical competition relative to the modern notion of perfect competition is the absence of the need to suppose that agents are very small relative to the market, because a sufficient absence of market power is guaranteed by free entry, of firms as well as of labourers and landowners.

There is market power when a supplier by altering the amount supplied, or a buyer by altering the amount demanded, can relevantly affect price. This market power is generally rendered insignificant by assuming the agent's supply (or demand) is very small relative to total market supply (or demand). But this assumption is unnecessary if market power is destroyed by free entry and exit because a supplier's output reduction will be countered by entry of further suppliers, a buyer's demand reduction will be countered by exit of some suppliers. So price taking can be justified by assuming 'smallness' (absence of relevant market power) of a given number of agents, or by assuming free entry. The aim of general equilibrium theory to be applicable also to pure exchange economies has long given prominence to the justification of price taking based on smallness of agents; Aumann (1964) even assumed a continuum of infinitesimal agents (in an exchange economy) as a way rigorously to justify absence of market power. But, as rediscovered in recent decades by neoclassical theorists too, free entry of firms [38] can be a foundation, of absence of market power in product markets, *alternative* to smallness of agents (Novshek and Sonnenschein 1987). The reason is that, at given input prices, as long as in the industry there is room for several firms of minimum efficient size, the long-period supply curve of an industry with free entry is nearly perfectly horizontal (Sect. 5.20). Entry, actual or potential, obliges

---

38 We will concentrate on entry of *firms*, but free entry can be applied to any agent. Free entry of labourers, for example, will prevent the wage in an industry from going above the average wage elsewhere.

416 Chapter 5 · Firms, Partial Equilibria and the General Equilibrium with Production

firms to charge a price extremely close to minimum average cost, that is, to be price-takers.[39] Then *buyers too can be treated as price-takers*, because a change in their demand does not alter the supply price: they face a practically horizontal supply curve.

Of course the entry and exit of firms (or rather, of plants, even by already existing firms) take time, therefore the free-entry foundation of price taking concerns long-period choices. Actually, even in the instantaneous fairy tale tâtonnement the possibility of formation of new firms should be admitted, but it will have different effects, to be studied in the next section. Now let us study a bit more the industry's long-period supply curve.

Assume a U-shaped average cost curve of efficient firms, the same for all firms because competition eliminates inefficient producers. Let q^* be the efficient scale of production at the given input prices. With n firms, the industry supply curve for increases in total output beyond nq^* will have slope one nth the slope of the long-period supply curve (long-period marginal cost curve) of individual firms, up to when room appears for an extra firm. It is highly plausible that the *long-period* marginal cost curve of a firm is rather flat at the efficient output, cf. ❏ Fig. 5.9, because in long-period analysis the only element capable of causing decreasing returns to scale is the increasing difficulty of supervision and management, and there is no reason to think that this difficulty is increasing sharply at the efficient scale. But then the maximum deviation of the long-period supply curve from minimum average cost is likely to become insignificant rather quickly as the maximum number of efficient firms allowed for by the size of demand increases. Thus it seems plausible that, in most industries, room for ten minimum efficient size firms is already sufficient for the approximation to a horizontal long-period supply curve to be nearly perfect.

With a practically horizontal industry supply curve, even a single buyer, a monopsonist, cannot affect the equilibrium price in the long period because, at a lower price, supply would disappear (all firms would make losses). And even a (multiplant) firm supplying nearly the entire industry output would have no market power because if it tried to raise the price above minimum average cost it would cause entry or expansion of other firms. So in the long period, price taking is compatible with large constant returns to scale firms. Also, free entry makes it easier to *justify*, rather than simply to assume, absence of collusion: any collusion by existing firms can be undermined by entry of new firms.

Furthermore, a free-entry characterization of price taking allows a different interpretation of the horizontal *demand* curve that, according to the usual characterization of perfect competition, each firm faces. The approach based on entry

---

39 '...significant entry barriers are the *sine qua non* of monopoly and oligopoly, for as we shall see in later chapters, sellers have little or no enduring power over price when entry barriers are nonexistent' (Scherer and Ross 1990, p. 18).

5.26 · Price Taking, Perfect Competition, Tâtonnement

does *not* have the implication that a firm would have no difficulty with selling more at an unchanged price; it only implies that whatever different quantity from today a firm may sell will be sold at the same price, *once the market has gone back to long-period equilibrium*: but in order for one firm to sell more, some other firm must accept to sell less or exit the market, which is not going to be a painless process. Thus price taking with respect to the long-period price is perfectly compatible with a short-period inability to sell more at that price, and therefore also with price wars, and more generally with active competitive behaviour in its traditional classical sense.

The long-period nature of the analysis makes it easier to extend the analysis to markets where there isn't complete product homogeneity and where competition operates also through advertising, product design, servicing, location and innovation. The tendency towards a uniform rate of return on investment is not eliminated, for example, by the need for advertising or for continuous innovation, when these are necessary for survival; in those markets the cost of advertising and innovation will enter the calculation of the convenience of entry and of the cost-covering price. The notion of normal price will then have to be redefined to allow for (objective or perceived) differences in quality and in services.

It is often argued that a perfectly competitive firm faces a horizontal demand curve even in the short period, meaning that the firm can count on selling any quantity of output at the same price. One justification is that, owing to product homogeneity, if the firm reduces by a very small amount its price below the current price, then the demand for the firm's product will coincide with the entire market demand, allowing the firm to sell any output level less than market demand at practically the same price. This reasoning is defective, because it implicitly assumes that *the other firms do not match the price reduction*—but why shouldn't they? It will allow them to reduce losses, and probably to persuade the first firm to go back to the equilibrium price. So this justification of a horizontal short-period demand curve facing the single firm appears unacceptable. The other justification is that each firm's output is such a small part of total supply (and the presence of fixed factors limits the firm's output variability so much) that its changes do not affect the equilibrium price, or only negligibly. For this justification it is essential that the firm's short-period supply curve is upward-sloping and that price is free to vary; we must have in mind firms producing an undifferentiated product and ready to produce more only if price rises; that is, mostly, small producers of perishable agricultural products or fish, who do not know for sure the price their product will fetch, both because of natural variations in productivity and because they cannot be sure as to what other firms will do and therefore are price-takers in the sense that they have an expectation of the price that *on average* they will be able to obtain for their product over a number of future harvests or catches, a price they do not think they can relevantly influence. The picture is not inconsistent, but it applies to a very limited number of industries. Anyway it is important to be clear that, given that equilibrium can be at most indicative of the average of actual, fluctuating prices and quantities, price taking can only refer to an expected average price.

418   Chapter 5 · Firms, Partial Equilibria and the General Equilibrium with Production

The best neoclassical economists were aware that price taking cannot be assumed for disequilibrium situations, one of the most highly respected general equilibrium theorists, Kenneth Arrow, explictly noted that 'perfect competition can really prevail only at equilibrium' (1959, p. 41), because at a price at which supply exceeds demand 'the individual firm cannot sell all it wishes to at the market price; i.e., when suppy and demand do not balance, even in an objectively competitive market, the individual firms are in the position of monopolists as far as the imperfect elasticity of demand for their product is concerned ... the whole adjustment process is apt to be very irregular ... there can easily be a considerable dispersion of prices among different sellers of the same commodity' (*ibid.*, pp. 46-47).

The modern study (to which paradoxically Arrow himself has contributed) of the stability of price adjustments in competitive markets has taken a very different route: agents are assumed to be price-takers *always*, even in disequilibrium. This is because the adjustments are assumed to follow a peculiar process, derived from the one proposed in the 4th edition of Léon Walras's *Eléments d'Economie Politique Pure* (1900). It is imagined that economic activity is suspended, all agents meet as if in a big stadium (or connect through Internet), and there is a central institution, called the **auctioneer**, which goes through a series of 'rounds' in each one of which prices for all goods are proposed (are 'cried', Walras says); at these prices consumers and entrepreneurs write down promises of excess demands which become binding only if they generate an equilibrium and pass these *bons* (Walras' term, translated as 'tickets' or 'pledges') to the auctioneer. The latter calculates the excess demand for each good and for each factor, and, if a general equilibrium has not been achieved, declares the promises not valid and proceeds to cry out new prices, raising the price where demand has exceeded supply and lowering it (unless it is already zero) where supply has exceeded demand.[40] This process of price correction is repeated until an equilibrium is reached. Only then do promises become binding and exchanges are allowed and production processes are started. This adjustment process is nowadays referred to as a Walrasian or, better, neo-Walrasian **tâtonnement**.[41] It will be further commented upon in ► Chaps. 6 and 8.

This fairy tale is the reason why the notion of perfect competition is frequently criticized and even dismissed as irrelevant, because interpreted as paradoxically implying the *absence* of any competitive behaviour: all agents are price-takers always, passively accepting the ruling price, even at disequilibrium prices. This identification of perfect competition and neo-Walrasian tâtonnement

---

40 The modern formalizations of the tâtonnement generally describe price adjustments in continuous time via differential equations, implicitly assuming that one can treat as continuous a process which in fact could only consist of a series of separate rounds with discrete price variations from one round to the next; so difference equations rather than differential equations would appear more correct, but this can be considered a secondary issue.

41 . French word translatable as 'search by groping as if blindfolded', used by Walras to refer to the trial-and-error character of the disequilibrium adjustments of prices and quantities. Walras' description of the tâtonnement is very different from the usual modern formalizations, but we cannot discuss this issue here.

5.27 The Number of Firms in Modern GE

is unnecessary. As pointed out above, price taking realistically interpreted must only hold at equilibrium; it leaves room for price making and competitive rivalry in disequilibrium.

5.27 The Number of Firms in Modern GE

In the formalization of the general equilibrium of a market economy with production, traditionally the number of firms was treated as endogenously determined by the equilibrium itself (if not indeterminate, when firms themselves, and not only industries, have CRS). Modern theorists often adopt a different approach, and the issue requires some explanation.

Neoclassical value and distribution theory originally intended to determine the analogous for the entire economy of the *long-period* positions we have studied for partial equilibria. This notion of equilibrium appeared inevitable for the study of equilibrium on factor markets. The tendency towards an equilibrium rate of rent for lands of the same type or towards an equilibrium wage rate for labourers of similar skills cannot but be slow, both because factor rentals are usually fixed by contract for some time length, and because any change in the average rental of a factor alters relative production costs and hence relative product prices, hence product demands, hence factor demands; so the theory must admit that any state of rest temporarily reached by a factor market will be disturbed again and again before a general equilibrium can be sufficiently approached. During this time there is time for firms to alter their fixed plants, and for the number of firms in an industry to be altered, and therefore a long-period analysis of what happens to each industry is inescapable. Industries were treated as having constant returns to scale, and it was assumed that, in equilibrium, supplies of produced goods would equal demands at zero-profit (i.e. at *MinLAC*) product prices.

In modern articles and books on competitive general equilibrium it is on the contrary common (although not universal) to assume a *given* number of firms, each one with its own production function or production possibility set. Firm-level *decreasing* returns to scale are not excluded, indeed they are often assumed. Then the payment to each factor of its marginal revenue product can leave a profit.[42] These profits go to firm owners.

The first such treatment of the number of firms in general equilibrium theory is found in Hicks's *Value and Capital* (1939), where individuals are not only consumers but also potential entrepreneurs, each one with different 'entrepreneurial capacities' that influence the production function of the firms they own or might set up. Depending on prices, the potential firm a consumer might set up may be able to make non-negative profits, in which case it will be active; or

---

42 *Exercise*: Prove it for the case of decreasing returns to scale, using Euler's theorem on homogeneous functions. 'Profit' here stands for the neoclassical notion of profit.

it may not be able to make profits, in which case the individual will be only a consumer. Hicks also argues that as firm size increases the increase in coordination difficulties causes firms to have a U-shaped average cost curve. Depending on prices, individuals can choose different industries in which to employ their entrepreneurial capacities and set up firms. An implication is that even with given input prices and all factors variable, as the price of a product rises its supply never becomes infinite, the supply function is the sum of the gradually growing number of upward-sloping marginal cost functions of the (less and less efficient) firms that gradually join the industry. Supply functions of produced goods can be defined.

This approach treats 'entrepreneurial capacity' as a factor of production available in limited quantity, but this has been criticized as an illegitimate assimilation of 'entrepreneurship' to engineering knowledge or to managerial capacities, skills that can be hired on the market. Indeed, as already argued by, Kaldor 1934 there seems to be no decision traditionally considered the competence of the traditional 'entrepreneur-owner' that could not be assigned to a salaried manager (as indeed is the case with modern CEOs of corporations, who are not the owners). Therefore the idea that the production function differs depending on who is the owner of the firm is unacceptable in equilibrium analysis. A particularly good manager is like a particularly fertile land, she/he will be able to earn a differential rent, and the competition for good managers will raise the differential rent of the good manager until the firm hiring her makes zero profit, as in the case of agriculture and particularly fertile lands. Ownership as such cannot contribute to efficiency, therefore there is also no limit to the number of equally efficient firms that an entrepreneur *qua* owner can own in equilibrium. There is therefore no reason why there should be positive (neoclassical) profits in competitive equilibrium.

Many recent models of general equilibrium simply assume a given number of firms with decreasing-returns-to-scale production functions, so as to be able to derive supply curves for produced goods. But in this way they exclude the possibility that new firms be born, an aspect of market economies of such enormous importance that any theory excluding it for the study of economy-wide processes must be considered totally unacceptable. The assumption of decreasing returns to scale is also questionable, because if these decreasing returns derive from resources owned by the firm (i.e. by its owners) which do not appear among the inputs of the firm's possible netputs, then these resources must be tradeable and should be included among the inputs and priced at the price that others would offer for their services. If the reason is increasing difficulties of coordination, still to exclude entry is absurd.

(Note that a variable number of firms is not the same thing as a long-period equilibrium. Firms are legal entities that can demand factors and, if able to obtain factor services, can produce. The time required to set up a firm as a legal entity is very small, so the number of firms must be considered variable even in Marshallian short-period analyses in which a producible factor specific to the industry is given in amount, see Sect. 5.18. To treat *firms* as having a fixed factor in short-period analysis is only a didactical simplification, because a firm can rent the fixed plant of another firm. The real distinguishing element of

5.27 · The Number of Firms in Modern GE

long-period analysis is that the amounts in existence of all *producible* inputs can be modified.)

But since formulations of general equilibrium based on a given number of firms with possibly positive profits are frequent, a very brief description is now supplied of these versions—just so that the reader can recognize them when she meets them.

Consumers own factors and shares in the property of firms; they demand factor services for direct consumption, and consumption goods. Firms (given in number) may own resources, which do not appear in the firm-specific production function; firms hire the factor services not provided by their own resources; the more usual formalization, especially in textbooks, assumes that there are sufficiently decreasing returns (to the scale of *hired* factor services) for firms to have definite supply functions; but in other formalizations the possibility of firm-level constant returns to scale is admitted.[43] The 'profit' of a firm includes the implicit payment to (i.e. the opportunity cost of) the firm's own resources. Firms are active only if they are able to make non-negative 'profit'. Netputs are used to describe firms' choices, so firms' *supplies* of outputs appear as positive numbers in the determination of excess demands, while firms' demands for inputs are negative numbers. The excess demand on any market is defined as the aggregate excess demand of consumers for that good minus the aggregate excess supply of firms; this works for factor markets too, the consumers' aggregate demand for a factor is a negative number if it means a positive supply, the firms' aggregate 'supply' of a factor is negative too but it has a minus sign in front in the determination of excess demand and thus it becomes a positive number, representing the demand for the factor. It is assumed that there are S consumers with index $s=1,\ldots, S$ with endowments $\boldsymbol{\omega}^s$, and with vector excess demand functions $\mathbf{z}^s(\mathbf{p})$, and H firms with index $h=1,\ldots, H$, each one with a well-defined and continuous[44] excess *supply* vector function (in netput notation) $\mathbf{y}^h(\mathbf{p})$ (where if y_j^h is negative it indicates demand for input j, if positive it indicates supply of output j); then the aggregate excess demand for good i is:

$$z_i(\mathbf{p}) = \Sigma_s z_i^s(\mathbf{p}) - \Sigma_h y_i^h(\mathbf{p}).$$

---

43 Without free entry, to admit firms with CRS but possibly specific production possibility sets raises a little-noticed problem: the price-taking assumption may become illegitimate. There may be in an industry firms with different CRS technologies, yielding different minimum average costs; then for any given vector of input prices, in that industry the lowest *MinAC* will be generally associated with only one firm; this firm will notice that, at a price equal to its *MinAC*, it is the sole producer, and it will then stop being a price-taker, because it is a monopolist for the product price range between its *MinAC* and the one of the second most efficient potential firm in the industry; if the monopoly price falls in that range, it will be established; if it is above that range, anyway the two or three most efficient firms have an incentive to adopt collusive or oligopolistic behaviour.

44 ◘ Fig. 5.14 in ▶ Sect. 5.25 shows a discontinuity in the supply function, which is neglected in these models with little justification.

Each consumer s has a right to a percentage T_{sh} of the profit π_h of firm h, proportional to her given share in the ownership of the firm. (Obviously for most consumers only a few T_{sh} will not be zero.) The budget constraint of a consumer states that her income equals the value of her endowments plus the value of the profits she receives from her property of firms.

(Note the need for *given* property shares T_{sh} of the firms that make positive profits: otherwise the incomes of consumers are indeterminate. And yet in real economies there is continuous exchange of shares in the stock market; therefore the consumers' share ownerships in firms can hardly be considered given during any realistic disequilibrium adjustment process; the only way to prevent them from changing is to have recourse to the auctioneer-guided tâtonnement, now with an explicit additional assumption that shares cannot be traded during the tâtonnement, an assumption not easy to justify in view of the relevance of speculative behaviour in real economies. Trading of shares will be admitted in ▶ Sect. 8.27 where speculation arises owing to absence of perfect foresight.)

It is possible to prove, with techniques that have recourse to fixed-point theorems similar to those to be studied in ▶ Chap. 6 that an equilibrium exists for such a formalization.

The reader might perhaps try to defend the given number of firms and the given property shares as reflecting the intention to formalize a *short-period* equilibrium. But those assumptions are incompatible with a short-period equilibrium as well! Property shares in firms can change hands in a few minutes on the stock exchange. As to the number of firms, even if adjustments are the unrealistic ones assumed in the fairy tale auctioneer-guided tâtonnement, the attempt to form new firms buying or renting fixed plants cannot be excluded from the possible economic decisions taken during the tâtonnement—otherwise the theory would be excluding the birth of new firms and would be rubbish.

Perhaps in the mind of some the given number of firms is justified by the fact that in short-period analysis fixed plants are given and are owned by firms; from this premise the conclusion is probably inferred that firms are given too. Wrong! Firms (incumbent or newly formed) are *legal* entities that can be created in a very short time and can demand or supply the services of fixed plants of other firms too. So the number of potential demanders for the services of given fixed plants is indefinite, and this will cause the quasi-rents of fixed plants to absorb all profits.

I conclude that even under the assumption that the equilibrium is a very short-period one reached by an auctioneer-guided tâtonnement, the number and/ or dimension of firms must be considered variable. All the more so, then, for long-period equilibria. Thus the traditional formalization (that I will now present) appears to be the sole sensible one.[45]

---

45 A top general equilibrium specialist like Lionel McKenzie (2008 pp. 589–590) concurs with this conclusion.

5.28 The Equations of the Non-capitalistic General Equilibrium with Production

I illustrate now the traditional formalization of the general competitive equilibrium of production and exchange, still without capital goods. All produced goods are consumption goods. Factors are fully transferable across industries and firms; competition with free entry has had the time to eliminate less efficient firms; product prices equal minimum average costs; industries have constant returns to scale. The equilibrium is a long-period equilibrium. It is static, in that changes of its data over time (e.g. owing to population growth) are neglected as sufficiently slow relative to the presumable speed of gravitation towards equilibrium. In the traditional presentation of this kind of equilibrium it is generally further assumed (and I will assume) that one can neglect borrowing and lending among consumers, and hence no interest rate will appear in the equations; under these assumptions the equilibrium of a period has no need to include references to what happens in other periods, so in its equations no time index appears.

This fact has induced many recent theorists—no longer familiar with the notion of equilibrium as determining a normal (or long-period) position of sufficiently persistent flows, and rather accustomed by neo-Walrasian equilibria to the idea that equilibrium must refer to a precise instant and must distinguish prices and quantities of that instant from those of subsequent moments by dating them—to mistakenly interpret the non-capitalistic equilibrium as *atemporal* in the sense of referring to a world where time does not exist, or at least implicitly assuming that production and exchange as well as the adjustments to equilibrium prices and quantities are *instantaneous*. Thus a recent advanced microeconomics textbook declares: '[In the basic model of general equilibrium] each commodity has a price, with all trading seemingly done in a single instant. And, if we are going to adhere to the notion that all trade takes place simultaneously, any and all production by firms is also instantaneous' (Kreps 2013, p. 386). The reason is that the moment exchanges and production are admitted to take time, modern general equilibrium theory *dates* commodities and considers the same commodity sold today or tomorrow two different commodities with generally different prices; if commodities are not dated, it is inferred that one is referring to an equilibrium where there is a single date, so everything including production must be done 'in a single instant'. It is not grasped that traditional marginalist economists never entertained the idea of instantaneous production and exchanges; they fully accepted that economic activity takes time, but had no need to date commodities because they conceived equilibrium as a normal or long-period position, a persistent situation of equilibrium of flows repeating themselves essentially unaltered, with relative equilibrium prices unchanged from today to tomorrow. The assumption that the rate of interest is zero makes it also unnecessary to specify the length of production processes (a nonzero rate of interest would influence the cost of goods produced by labour and land paid in advance), so no reference to time appears in the equations, and for this reason I will occasionally refer to the general equilibrium system now to be presented as atemporal, but not in the sense of referring to a world where time does not exist or where exchanges and production are instantaneous. The references in this paragraph to modern or neo-Walrasian general equilibria will become clearer with ▶ Chap. 8.

The rate of interest is assumed to be zero only for simplicity, lending and borrowing could be admitted but would not change anything important in the equilibrium; as explained in §3.10 the absence of capital goods (and of a possibility of storage) means that lending and borrowing would only mean, within each period, a redistribution of some purchasing power among the period's consumers.

To help intuition I make a number of simplifying assumptions: no joint production; factors and (produced) consumption goods do not overlap: there are m products (consumption goods) and n factors (inputs: types of labour, types of land). Consumers have given endowments and utility function but these do not explicitly appear in the model, the utility maximization problem (UMP) of the several consumers is assumed already solved and to imply a definite market demand function for each consumption good and a definite market supply function of each factor service *to firms*. This last thing requires clarification. Consumers may well keep part of their endowments for their own consumption (e.g. leisure time; land used as garden), this is their *proper reservation demand*. Consumers also demand factor services directly from other consumers; the sum of the latter demands and of proper reservation demands is the portion of endowments that consumers as a whole keep for direct consumption, I will call it *overall reservation demands*; the remainder of the consumer endowments is offered to firms, and this is what the equilibrium equations need.

The factor endowments of consumers are to be interpreted as per-period endowments of *services* of the factors they own, for example if I own a hectare of type-B land and if the period length is a year, I have an endowment of 365 'days of use of one hectare of type-B land' per year.

I do not use the netput representation here; the quantities of inputs are positive numbers. For firms too the profit-maximization problem is assumed already solved, it is unnecessary to specify production functions, what is needed is the technical coefficients (inputs per unit of output) that cost minimization pushes free-entry CRS industries to adopt on the basis of the given factor rentals.

The symbols are as follows:

p_j $(j=1,\ldots, m)$ price of product j (a consumption good); $\mathbf{p}$ vector of these prices.

q_j market (i.e. total) supply by firms of produced good j; $\mathbf{q}$ vector of these quantities.

v_i $(i=1, \ldots, n)$ rental (i.e. price of the services) of factor i; $\mathbf{v}$ vector of these rentals.

x_i market (i.e. total) demand for factor i by firms; $\mathbf{x}$ vector of these demands.

a_{ij} *technical coefficient* of factor i in the production of good j, i.e. quantity of factor i employed per unit of product j, resulting from cost minimization; assumed to be a *function* of relative factor rentals, not a correspondence.

$Q_j(\mathbf{p},\mathbf{v})$ market demand function for good j, derived from the utility-maximizing choices of consumers; non-negative, homogeneous of degree zero and assumed to be a function and not a correspondence.

5.28 · The Equations of the Non-capitalistic General Equilibrium with Production

$X_i(\mathbf{p},\mathbf{v})$ consumers' total supply function of factor i *to firms*, derived from the utility-maximizing choices of consumers; non-negative and homogeneous of degree zero and assumed to be a function and not a correspondence. Consumers' total supply of a factor to firms is the total endowment of that factor minus the consumers' total demand for that factor, as reservation demand (retained endowment for self-consumption) and as direct demand for factors supplied by other consumers (e.g. domestic labour, medical services, paid access to private forests for mushroom picking).

Once a vector of factor rentals $\mathbf{v}=(v_1, \ldots, v_n)$ is assigned, cost minimization and the assumption of a common technology for all firms in the same industry univocally determine the minimum long-period average cost $MinLAC_j$ for each consumption good j, which—because of the assumption that industries can be treated as having CRS—is independent of the total quantity produced by the industry and only depends on factor rentals. The same process of cost minimization determines in each industry the choice of production method and hence technical coefficients $a_{ij}(\mathbf{v})$ (quantity of input i per unit of output j) as functions of the vector of factor rentals; obviously it is

$$MinLAC_j(\mathbf{v}) = \Sigma_i v_i a_{ij}(\mathbf{v}).$$

Equilibrium can be synthetically characterized by four groups of equations. First, profits (neoclassical meaning) must be zero in equilibrium owing to competition with free entry, hence product prices must equal minimum average costs:

(A). $\qquad p_j = MinLAC_j(\mathbf{v}) = \sum_i v_i a_{ij}(\mathbf{v}), \quad j = 1,\ldots,m.$

The technical coefficients $a_{ij}(\mathbf{v})$ result from this cost minimization, and I assume they are uniquely determined in each industry once $\mathbf{v}$ is given, hence are *functions* of $\mathbf{v}$ and not correspondences. The formulation admits fixed technical coefficients too.

Thus, once $\mathbf{v}$ is assigned, the vector $\mathbf{p}$ of prices of consumption goods is determined; therefore a given $\mathbf{v}$ suffices to determine consumer choices, as solutions to their UMP on the basis of their endowments and preferences; assuming these choices are functions and not correspondences of $(\mathbf{p}(\mathbf{v}),\mathbf{v})$, they determine for each vector $(\mathbf{p}(\mathbf{v}),\mathbf{v})$ the demand by each consumer for each consumption good j and the sum of these demands determines the market consumer demand for the good as $Q_j(\mathbf{p},\mathbf{v})$ and analogously they determine for each factor i the market supply to firms $X_i(\mathbf{p},\mathbf{v})$. Of course these functions indicate consumer choices *conditional on* $(\mathbf{p},\mathbf{v})$ *being indeed an equilibrium vector*, because they are derived on the assumption of balanced budgets, which cannot be satisfied for all consumers outside equilibrium (▶ Sect. 4.5). For example if labour is in excess supply the unemployed labourers, having no income, cannot buy consumption goods, so demands for consumption goods will not be correctly indicated by the functions $Q_j(\mathbf{p},\mathbf{v})$. The functions $Q_j(\mathbf{p},\mathbf{v})$ and $X_i(\mathbf{p},\mathbf{v})$ are not intended to tell us the actual disequilibrium consumer choices if the ruling prices $(\mathbf{p},\mathbf{v})$ are not equilibrium prices and the economy is in disequilibrium; they are only useful for the search for the equilibrium solution.

The next question in the search for equilibrium is: in order for $(\mathbf{p}(\mathbf{v}),\mathbf{v})$ to be equilibrium prices, what must the quantities produced be? Clearly, they must be the quantities consumers *would* demand if indeed $(\mathbf{p}(\mathbf{v}),\mathbf{v})$ were the equilibrium price vector. So equilibrium requires that the production of each consumption good be adjusted to the demand for it:

(B). $\quad q_j = Q_j(\mathbf{p},\mathbf{v}), \quad j = 1,\ldots,m.$

Since $\mathbf{v}$ determined technical coefficients, now we can determine the demand for factor i by industry j as equal to its technical coefficient $a_{ij}(\mathbf{v})$ times the quantity q_j produced by that industry. The sum of these demands over all industries yields, for each factor, the total demand for it coming from firms:

(C). $\quad x_i = \sum_j a_{ij}(\mathbf{v})q_j, \quad i = 1,\ldots,n, j = 1,\ldots,m.$

All that remains to specify is that there must be equilibrium in factor markets, i.e. the firms' total demand for each factor must equal its supply to firms.[46] However, it is possible that, for some factor, supply exceeds demand even when its rental falls to zero (e.g. lands no one is interested in), so we must introduce inequalities plus the side condition that prices cannot fall below zero:

(D). $\quad X_i(\mathbf{p},v) \geq x_i, \quad i = 1,\ldots,n,$ *and if for a factor the inequality is strict, then its rental is zero.*

Note carefully that, if $(\mathbf{p}(\mathbf{v}),\mathbf{v})$ is not an equilibrium price vector, the disequilibria one finds in equations (D) do *not* indicate the disequilibria one would actually observe in the factor markets of this economy at prices and rentals fixed at $(\mathbf{p}(\mathbf{v}),\mathbf{v})$ for any length of time. For example, if in equations (D) a factor comes out to be in excess demand, then firms would find it impossible to satisfy equations (B) because unable to obtain the needed amount of that factor, and then their demand for the factor (and for the other factors too) would not be the one determined in (C). These equations (A), (B), (C), (D) make sense only as conditions that must be satisfied in equilibrium; a realistic study of disequilibrium (e.g. in order to study the stability of equilibrium) would require different considerations and certainly could not assume the equilibrium budget constraint to be satisfied for all consumers, nor profits to be zero for all firms.

---

46 Equality between supply of a factor *to firms* and demand for the factor *by firms* implies also equality between total endowment and total demand for a factor, because supply to firms equals total endowment minus overall reservation demand, and total demand equals demand by firms plus overall reservation demand, and the endowments not kept by consumers as a whole for self-consumption as overall reservation demands are offered to firms. In the text for simplicity it will be assumed that consumers do not have a direct demand for factors of other consumers, they only have a proper reservation demand for part of their own endowments, but the case of overall reservation demand is discussed in footnote 49 below.

5.29 · The 'Reduction' to an Exchange Economy

These four groups of equations[47] are $2n + 2m$ equations, one of which is not independent of the others owing to Walras' Law [48]; hence $2n + 2m - 1$ independent equations in the $2n + 2m$ variables $(\mathbf{p},\mathbf{q},\mathbf{x},\mathbf{v})$. Are we one equation short? No, because the equations are homogeneous of degree zero in $(\mathbf{p},\mathbf{v})$ so they can only determine *relative* prices; hence we can add one more equation fixing the price of a numéraire commodity or basket of commodities as equal to 1, e.g.

$$\sum_j p_j = 1,$$

and then the number of independent equations is equal to the number of variables.

This is only an initial check of consistency, and a rigorous proof that an equilibrium exists requires more than this. But the rigorous proof will require little more than for the exchange economy, and it is useful to understand why.

5.29 The 'Reduction' to an Exchange Economy

The system of equations (A-B-C-D) can be reduced by substitution to a system of equations describing an equilibrium of (direct and indirect) exchange of factor services among consumers, formally equivalent to the equations of an equilibrium of pure exchange. This equivalence can be given a concrete interpretation. Suppose CRS is valid even for production on very small scale, and that, exploiting CRS, each household sets up minifirms producing all and only the consumption goods it demands. Then households do not purchase consumption goods from other agents; they only demand factor services and offer factor services to other households in exchange. Factor services would be the only things exchanged in such a hypothetical economy; equation (D**) below would be the standard representation of the equilibrium conditions. This makes it highly visible that, by demanding consumption goods, consumers indirectly demand factor services, and thus that the production-and-exchange economy is ultimately an economy of indirect exchange of factor services.

Let us start by remembering how everything depends on the vector of factor rentals. For any given $\mathbf{v}$, equations (A) determine $\mathbf{p}$, so we can consider $\mathbf{p}$ a function of $\mathbf{v}$ and write $\mathbf{p}(\mathbf{v})$. Then consumer demands for products and supplies of factors can be seen as functions only of $\mathbf{v}$: in vector notation, $Q(\mathbf{p}, \mathbf{v})$ and $X(\mathbf{p},\mathbf{v})$ can be rewritten as $Q^*(\mathbf{v})$, $X^*(\mathbf{v})$. Then, assuming equations (B) are satisfied, the vector of quantities to be produced $\mathbf{q}$ can be replaced by $Q^*(\mathbf{v})$; and therefore using equations (C) the demands for factors by firms can be seen as functions of $\mathbf{v}$ only:

---

47 Actually reducible to three groups, by rewriting equations (D) as $X_i(\mathbf{p},\mathbf{v}) \geq \Sigma_j a_{ij}(\mathbf{v})q_j$, and abolishing equations (C) and the x_i symbols. But the present formalization allows an easier discussion of the reducibility of the equilibrium equations to those of an exchange economy, see below, and an easier introduction of capital goods in ▶ Chap. 7.

48 *Exercise*: Prove Walras' Law for the present production economy, remembering that firm profits are zero.

428 Chapter 5 · Firms, Partial Equilibria and the General Equilibrium with Production

$$x_i^*(\mathbf{v}) \equiv \sum_j a_{ij}(\mathbf{v})Q_j^*(\mathbf{v}).$$

Hence both supplies and demands for factors are determined once $\mathbf{v}$ is assigned, and equations (D) suffice as equilibrium conditions if rewritten, using vectors, as

$$\left(\mathbf{D}^*\right) \quad \mathbf{X}^*(\mathbf{v}) \geq \mathbf{x}^*(\mathbf{v}) \quad and \; v_i = 0 \; if \; X_i > x_i.$$

Now define the *factor derived excess demand vector function* as

$$\boldsymbol{\zeta}(\mathbf{v}) \equiv \mathbf{x}^*(\mathbf{v}) - \mathbf{X}^*(\mathbf{v}),$$

where '*derived*' is to stress it is expressed as a function of $\mathbf{v}$ only; then equations (D*) become the standard equilibrium condition of an exchange equilibrium: excess demands must be non-positive, with factors having the role of the goods of the exchange economy:

$$\left(\mathbf{D}^{**}\right) \quad \boldsymbol{\zeta}(\mathbf{v}) \leq \mathbf{0}.$$

It might be objected that in the exchange economy excess demands are the demands for goods minus their *endowments*, while here so far endowments have not appeared. But actually $\boldsymbol{\zeta}(\mathbf{v})$ *is* the demands for factors by consumers minus their endowments, if by demands for factors by consumers we mean now the sum of their *direct* demands (overall reservation demands) and of their *indirect* demands implicit in their demands for produced consumption goods. For simplicity let us assume that consumers have no direct demand for the services of factors owned by other consumers, they only have *proper* reservation demands for parts of their own endowments. Define the *reservation demand* for factor services by consumer s as the vector of (non-negative) differences between her endowments of factor services and her supply of these services to firms, $\boldsymbol{\omega}^s - \mathbf{X}^{s*}(\mathbf{v})$; then the *aggregate reservation demand vector*, to be indicated as $\mathbf{R}_X(\mathbf{v})$, is defined by [49]

$$\mathbf{R}_X(\mathbf{v}) = \sum_{s=1}^{S} \left(\boldsymbol{\omega}^s - \mathbf{X}^{s*}(\mathbf{v})\right) = \boldsymbol{\Omega} - \mathbf{X}^*(\mathbf{v}) \quad where \; \boldsymbol{\Omega} = \sum_s \boldsymbol{\omega}^s.$$

The consumers' *indirect* demands for factors are $\mathbf{x}^*(\mathbf{v})$. Define the aggregate *direct and indirect* demand for factor services by consumers as the sum of their reservation demands and of their indirect demands and indicate it as $\mathbf{D}_X(\mathbf{v})$:

$$\mathbf{D}_X(\mathbf{v}) = \mathbf{x}^*(\mathbf{v}) + \mathbf{R}_X(\mathbf{v}).$$

---

49 The equation holds also if consumers exchange factors with other consumers, it suffices to interpret $\mathbf{R}_X(\mathbf{v})$ as referring to aggregate overall reservation demand, inclusive of all direct demand by consumers for factor services, because utility maximization requires that the endowments neither reserved by their owners nor demanded by other consumers be offered to firms.

Since $X^*(v) = \Omega - R_X(v)$, the condition of non-positive factor derived excess demand $\zeta(v) \leq 0$ means that aggregate direct and indirect factor demand minus endowments must be non-positive:

$$\zeta(v) \equiv x^*(v) - X^*(v) \equiv x^*(v) + R_X(v) - \Omega \equiv D_X(v) - \Omega \leq 0.$$

The parallel with the exchange economy is now complete.

5.30 The Role of Demand in Determining Product Prices: Why General Equilibrium Product Supply Curves Are Upward Sloping

We can now clarify the role of the composition of demand for consumption goods in the determination of equilibrium prices.

In the marginal/neoclassical approach to income distribution, demand is able to influence product prices only to the extent to which it influences factor rentals (i.e. income distribution). Once the vector of factor rentals is given, equilibrium product prices are given. The influence of the quantities demanded on product prices operates through its effect on factor rentals owing to its influence on the demand for factors.[50]

I illustrate the issue for the simple case of rigid factor supplies.[51] We are interested in equilibrium in all factor markets before and after the change in demand for a product. Assume equilibrium is unique. We can define the *general equilibrium supply curve of a product* as the function that indicates how the price of the product in terms of the chosen numéraire changes as we parametrically change the amount demanded (and hence produced) of the good in equilibrium. This curve will be upward sloping as long as the numéraire good is produced with average factor proportions while the product in question is not.[52] To fix ideas, suppose the product is labour-intensive. As the quantity demanded and hence produced of this good shifts upwards (because of a change in tastes), if neither relative prices, nor technical coefficients, nor the composition of demand for the other goods change, then demand for labour rises, becoming greater than supply (I am assuming the starting point was an equilibrium, then there is a change in tastes). The rental of labour rises, and this activates both the direct and the indirect substitution mechanisms: firms tend to use less labour per unit of land,

---

50 Even in short-period partial equilibrium analysis, we have seen earlier (Sects. 5.14 and 5.23) that the short-period supply curve is upward sloping only because of a rise in the implicit rentals (quasi-rents) of fixed factors as the quantity produced rises (which implies that even in short-period analysis profits are always zero when correctly computed).

51 Nothing fundamental changes if factor supplies are increasing in own rentals; on the contrary, much can change with 'backward-bending' factor supplies, but here I leave these complications aside, and furthermore I assume uniqueness of equilibrium.

52 Remember that what counts is *relative* prices, so when these change one does not know whether a price has increased or decreased until a numéraire is fixed.

430   Chapter 5 · Firms, Partial Equilibria and the General Equilibrium with Production

and consumers tend to reduce their demand for labour-intensive goods, but not for the good we are studying, whose demand by assumption has increased: the indirect substitution mechanism operates by changing the relative dimension of the industries producing the *other* consumption goods. Thus assume there are three consumption goods, corn, cloth and meat, produced by labour and land; corn is the good for which demand increases; cloth is more labour-intensive than meat; the rise in the price of labour causes the price of cloth to rise relative to the price of meat, causing (if the indirect substitution mechanism works 'well', aiding rather than endangering stability) a shift in favour of meat in the composition of that part of demand which goes to cloth and meat; this reduces the average labour–land proportion on the land employed in productions other than corn. The effect of both factor substitution processes is to counter the initial increase in the demand for labour, and the rise in the price of labour will go on until equilibrium is re-established in factor markets in the face of the increased corn production. But since the initial assumption was that corn is relative labour-intensive, the effect is to raise the relative price of corn. Thus the *general equilibrium* supply curve of corn, derived by assuming that equilibrium in factor markets is maintained as corn production increases,[53] is upward sloping even in the long period.[54] However, if the good only absorbs a very small portion of total factor use, moderate changes in the demand for it will be accommodated by only very small changes in relative factor prices, so the supply curve will be almost horizontal, and the partial-equilibrium horizontal supply curve can be considered a reasonable approximation.

5.31 International Trade

The basic insights the neoclassical approach reaches in the pure theory of international trade, i.e. in the explanation of what determines relative prices of commodities produced in different nations, derive from the application of reasonings similar to those presented above to cases in which factor supplies are not freely transferable across national boundaries.

---

53 The general equilibrium supply curve of a product traces the supply price of the good (in terms of the chosen numéraire) as a function of the quantity produced of it, assuming equilibrium on all markets and parametrically varying the demand curve for the good. Of course there is some arbitrariness in how one specifies how the demand for the other goods, and possibly the supply of factors, is affected by the resulting changes in prices. But this kind of analysis can seldom hope to reach more than conclusions on the *signs* of the changes, and the conclusion that the general equilibrium supply price of a product is an increasing function of the quantity produced appears hardly controvertible, as long as one assumes a unique and stable equilibrium (or at least, a locally stable equilibrium and only a small change in preferences).

54 *Exercise 5.4* discusses why for this result it is necessary that the numéraire good is produced with an average labour–land ratio. *Exercise 5.5*: discusses what would happen in the example if the consumption goods are only two, corn and meat, and there is no technical choice: fixed coefficients in both industries.

5.31 · International Trade

Thus, let us at first assume that good A is the sole good produced in one nation and good B the sole good produced in another nation. Each nation uses labour and land and is incapable of producing the other nation's good (perhaps because of climate differences), and there is no international factor mobility. (The analysis is very similar to the analysis of a neoclassical closed economy with four different factors, two of them only useful for the production of good A, the other two only useful for the production of good B.) We assume factor substitutability, otherwise the simultaneous full employment of labour and land in either nation would be generally impossible and one would reach the implausible result of all income in each nation going to only one factor. For simplicity assume rigid factor supplies. The basic argument then is, that in each nation technical substitution induced by changes in the wage–rent ratio will ensure the full employment of the nation's factor supplies; the supplies of good A and of good B are therefore determined, and the relative price p_A/p_B in international exchange must be such as to ensure that they are absorbed by total demand. If we can assume that, as p_A/p_B varies, in each nation the composition of demand varies continuously in the opposite direction, then there will be a unique value of p_A/p_B ensuring equilibrium, and the equilibrium will also be stable.[55] The real factor rentals in each nation will be determined in terms of the nation's product by the full-employment marginal products of the two factors; the purchasing power of these factor rentals in terms of the good not produced by the nation is determined by the equilibrium p_A/p_B ratio. The possibility to consume both goods raises the welfare in each nation relative to autarchy, if the consumers in a nation allocate part of their income to purchase the good produced by the other nation it must be because they prefer it to consuming only the good produced by their nation.

Let us now assume that both nations can produce both A and B, again with variable coefficients, but because of differences in the quality of their labour and/ or land the production functions are not the same in the two nations. There are therefore four factors, labour and land of nation I, and labour and land of nation II, not transferable across nations but transferable across industries within each nation. For each nation one can draw a **Production Possibility Frontier**, PPF, that describes the locus of possible efficient productions of goods A and B associated with the full employment of that nation's given factor supplies; it is a concave decreasing curve and its slope indicates by how much the production of good B (in ordinate) must decrease if production of good A increases by one small unit; the PPF was introduced in ▸ Sect. 3.83.8; its slope is called MRT, **marginal rate of transformation** (of one good into the other good). It was proved in ▸ Sect. 3.8 that competition ensures that the absolute value of this slope equals the relative price p_A/p_B of the two goods in the nation.

Assume that transport costs are negligible so p_A/p_B must be the same in both nations if trade is allowed. In each nation, as p_A/p_B increases, the composition of supply shifts in favour of good A. Thus if we can assume that the composition of the

---

55 Here we neglect the possibility that however low the relative price of one of the two goods becomes, the composition of demand never becomes equal to the composition of supply.

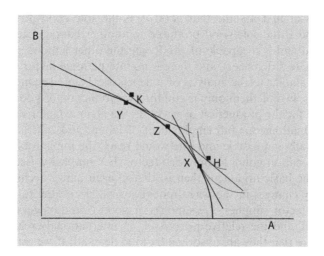

◘ **Fig. 5.15** Production Possibility Frontier and international trade

joint demand of the two nations shifts against good A as p_A/p_B increases, again there will be a unique equilibrium relative product price that equalizes aggregate composition of production and aggregate composition of demand, and in each nation relative factor rentals will be the ones associated with the point on the nation's Production Possibility Frontier determined by the equilibrium value of p_A/p_B.

This case suggests a favourable view of free international trade, which in fact characterizes marginalist/neoclassical economists. Let us compare the autarchic and the free trade equilibria. Both are full-employment equilibria, but, as long as in the autarchic equilibria the p_A/p_B ratio differs in the two nations, the introduction of free trade is equivalent to an outward shift of the Production Possibility Frontier: the trade with the other nation means that the economy reaches a point outside its Production Possibility Frontier.

Thus consider for simplicity the case of two nations having identical Production Possibility Frontiers but different tastes. In ◘ Fig. 5.15 the autarchic equilibrium of nation I is at point X, the one of nation II is at point Y. Thus p_A/p_B is higher in nation I; the initial impact of free trade, by allowing trade at some intermediate p_A/p_B, is to render it convenient for nation I to exchange B against A of nation II. The change in p_A/p_B will cause a change in the composition of production in both nations, and the free trade equilibrium will determine a p_A/p_B intermediate between the one at X and the one at Y. Thus nation I will locate itself on some point such as Z and will exchange part of its production of good B against good A produced by nation II, reaching for example point H. Analogously, nation II will reach a point like K. If one can neglect redistribution effects, for example by supposing that one can treat the consumers of each nation as a single representative consumer, there is an indubitable increase in welfare in both nations, shown by the higher indifference curve that both representative consumers reach. (In ◘ Fig. 5.15 indifference curves of the representative consumer of nation I have been drawn as dotted curves.) Actually, redistribution effects may be relevant: the change in the composition of production in each nation alters relative factor prices and it may well be that some factor rental decreases, making the owners of that factor poorer. But it remains possible to argue that if the nation can correct this effect with redistributive policies, e.g. through changes in taxation of personal incomes, then free trade makes it possible to increase everybody's welfare.

These arguments are heavily dependent on the marginal approach to distribution, and in particular on the thesis that the economy is always close to the full employment of resources. If, as argued in other approaches, market economies do not spontaneously tend to the full employment of labour, then the possibility arises that opening the nation to free trade causes an increase in unemployment, due to firms moving their production plants to other nations and importing what previously they produced domestically,[56] or due to the nation's firms being less competitive than foreign firms and losing market shares to another nation, which (since there is unemployment) can increase production and eat into the first nation's markets: then it would be unclear that free trade is preferable to autarky for the nation suffering the increase of unemployment.

5.32 On the Persistency of Preferences. Doing Without Demand Curves?

The general equilibrium model with production confirms that general equilibrium theory needs given consumer preferences. Even in the simplest model of ▶ Chap. 3 (given supply of labour and of land, no consumer desiring to save or dissave, a single consumption good) where income distribution was determined by the direct factor substitution mechanism alone, there were implicitly assumed certain consumer preferences, the ones causing rigid factor supplies and absence of savings. Of course in more realistic models consumer choice has a more extensive role, and changes in tastes can influence income distribution not only by affecting factor supplies but even if factor supplies are rigid. But even an assumption of totally rigid consumer choices (rigid factor supplies, rigid composition of demand for consumption goods) is a way of taking consumer preferences as given. What right does the approach have to include given consumer preferences among the data of equilibrium?

The data of equilibrium must be *data*, that is, not affected (not modified) by the decisions for which one searches for an equilibrium, and furthermore, at least in order for equilibrium to have its traditional role of centre of gravitation of time-consuming disequilibrium adjustments, the data of equilibrium must not be rapidly changing for non-economic reasons during the time required for the gravitation to cause the equilibrium quantities and prices to give a good indication of the observable average quantities and prices. The two conditions are often subsumed under the need that the data be *persistent*, but the distinction between economic and non-economic reasons for lack of persistency is useful. Preferences,

---

56 If a firm closes down a plant in nation A and opens up an identical plant in nation B that uses only unemployed factors of nation B, there has been no international factor movement, so the assumption of absence of international factor mobility is not violated.

434   Chapter 5 · Firms, Partial Equilibria and the General Equilibrium with Production

for example, might be irreversibly altered by economic decisions of some agents (e.g. a free distribution of wine to allow consumers better to appreciate how good-tasting wine is), or even without any such influence they might be rapidly changing in the economy under study (owing for example to the influence of religious or political preachers).

Now, on the persistency of preferences some first doubts are raised by no less an authority than Alfred Marshall, who admitted an influence of experience on wants, that can alter consumption habits and render the changes irreversible:

> » It must however be admitted that this theory is out of touch with real conditions of life, in so far as it assumes that, if the normal production of a commodity increases and afterwards again diminishes to its old amount, the demand price and the supply price will return to their old positions for that amount ... habits which have once grown up around the use of a commodity while its price is low, are not quickly abandoned when its price rises again ... many consumers will be reluctant to depart from their wonted ways. For instance, the price of cotton during the American wars was higher than it would have been if the previous low price had not brought cotton into common use to meet wants, many of which had been created by the low price. (Marshall, 8th ed., Appendix H, Sect. 3; 1972, p. 666).
> [any event] that increases the amount of English wares of any kind that are consumed in Germany, leaves behind it a permanent effect in an increased familiarity on the part of German consumers with English wares, and in this and other ways occasions permanent alteration in the circumstances of demand. (Marshall 1879 1930, Part I, p. 26)

The importance of fashion and of other tendencies to social conformity can only strengthen these observations on the tendential irreversibility of many changes in consumption habits. Also, the taste for foods or drinks or activities not previously experienced cannot be considered given before one starts experiencing them and can take a long time to stabilize. It is then unclear what can be assumed about the demand curve for a new consumption good, especially if this consumption good, like automobiles or smartphones, deeply changes many habits.

What we see here is that there are problems with including given preferences among the data of equilibrium: they may be involuntarily modified by disequilibrium actions, or they may be indeterminate when one attempts to predict the effect of a change. Or they may be modified by *voluntary* economic actions having precisely that aim: *advertising*. It is unclear how far preferences can be considered *data* of equilibrium, since several percentage points of national income are devoted to *influencing* preferences and in directions that can change quickly.[57]

---

57 In his popular intermediate textbook, Varian (2010, p. 571) writes: 'Conventional theory treats preferences as preexisting. In this view, preferences *explain* behaviour. Psychologists instead think of preferences as being constructed—people develop or create preferences through the act of choosing and consuming. It seems likely that the psychological model is a better description of what actually happens. However, the two viewpoints are not entirely incompatible ... once preferences have been discovered, albeit by some mysterious process, they tend to become built-into

5.32 · On the Persistency of Preferences. Doing Without Demand Curves?

The advocates of a resumption of the classical approach argue that, because of the different view of the forces determining income distribution, the classical approach does not need a simultaneous determination of income distribution, prices and quantities, and therefore does not need a considerable persistence of preferences; the two-stages structure of its explanations (cf. ch. 1, Sects. 1.4.1, 1.5.2, 1.11.4) allows a less ambitious, more inductive case-by-case approach to the determinants of changes in the composition of output, admitting possible irreversibilities and the complexity and historical variability of the causes influencing these changes. It might be argued that in the classical approach too some persistence of normal quantities demanded is necessary in order for them to indicate the averages of actually produced quantities; but the persistence needed in the marginal approach for equilibrium *income distribution* to function as centre of gravitation of actual income distribution is much greater, because it requires several *repetitions* of gravitation of quantities produced towards normal quantities as the latter are altered by the changes income distribution undergoes when it is not the equilibrium one.

The criticism has been extended from the persistence to the definiteness of demand curves. Often consumers themselves do not know how they would choose at prices considerably different from the ones they have experienced. Indeed Marshall wrote: 'the ordinary demand and supply curves have no practical value except in the immediate neighbourhood of the point of equilibrium' (1972, V, vi, 1, footnote; p. 318). For example, suppose a decrease in the price of a good makes it available to consumers who had never experienced it before: these consumers cannot know in advance how they like the good; demand for the good at the lower price cannot be considered well defined. The effect of a tax that raises the price of a good encounters a similar problem, if consumers are induced by that price rise to experiment for the first time with substitute goods.

One is induced to ask whether the notion of demand curves is really indispensable. It has been argued (Garegnani 1990b, pp. 128–131) that a non-neoclassical approach can do totally without the notion of demand curves: it can take the normal quantities demanded at normal (or long period) prices as the *observed* average ones and can be content with only rough guesses about the extent of changes in quantity demanded if price changes. The point is that the marginal/neoclassical approach needs a precise specification of how the composition of demand changes with changes in income distribution because it needs it in order to derive demand curves *for factors* and thus determine a well-defined equilibrium

---

choices'. But are preferences only 'discovered'? The fashion industry for example consciously plans to change fashion every year and systematically succeeds in inducing customers to dislike old models. As argued many decades ago: 'Nowadays consumers no longer act on their own free will. The demand-curve is no longer the product of spontaneous wants. It is manufactured ... The consumer is 'brain-washed' ... Consumer wants are no longer a matter of individual choice. They are mass-produced'. (Hansen 1960, p. 10.) If at all, in the 60 years since Hansen's paper things have gone further, not less, in this direction.

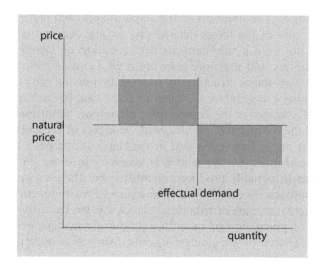

Fig. 5.16 According to Garegnani 1983 in the classical authors when the quantity supplied differs from the effectual demand the quantity-price point will be in the shaded areas but generally nothing more precise can be stated, nor need be stated, because the sign of the difference between natural price and market price suffices to stimulate capital movements that will push the quantity supplied towards equality with the effectual demand

income distribution; in the classical approach income distribution is determined differently, and there is no need for demand curves for that purpose.

Another purpose of demand curves is to argue that if, in a market, supply is less than the equilibrium amount, then price is above the long-period equilibrium level and this will stimulate an increase in the number of plants, which will increase supply and cause price to tend towards the long-period level and conversely for a supply greater than the equilibrium amount. Here Garegnani's argument is that the gravitation towards the long-period price does not need a definite demand *curve*: all one needs is the more flexible thesis that the market price will be in all likelihood above the long-period price if supply is less than **effectual demand**—that is, the demand at the normal price—and will be below the long-period price if supply is greater than effectual demand, but with no need to assume a precise functional connection between price and demand at prices different from the normal price. Indeed, Garegnani argues, in the analyses of classical authors there appears no notion of a demand *curve* specifying a precise relationship between price and quantity demanded; there is only the notion of *effectual demand* (the quantity demanded at the normal—or long-period, or natural—price) together with the thesis that if the quantity supplied is less than the effectual demand, the market price will be above the natural price and vice versa, a thesis representable as shown in ◘ Fig. 5.16 (from Garegnani 1983). The sign of the difference between natural price and market price suffices to stimulate changes in industry capacity that will push the quantity supplied towards equality with effectual demand, and thus the market price towards equality with the natural price. Of course it is not denied that price changes can affect quantities

5.33 · Conclusions

demanded, but the method illustrated in ▶ Sect. 1.13 can deal with the issue and remain open to the relevance of many unpredictable developments.

For example, let us suppose that a war elsewhere makes it more difficult for a nation to import oil for several months in a row. This situation can be considered to correspond rather well to a Marshallian short period. There will be in all likelihood a rise in the price of petrol (gasoline), but its extent and the change in oil demand will depend, not only on public policy such as changes in taxation, but also:

- on firms' decisions whether to postpone or not investments to when uncertainty will have decreased: these will influence aggregate demand and hence incomes;
- on public interventions on aggregate demand, e.g. restrictive fiscal policy to reduce oil imports, which again will influence incomes;
- on changes in consumption habits, not easily predictable because often influenced by fads or by declarations of politicians (e.g. calls for a spontaneous temporary decrease of certain oil-intensive forms of consumption in the name of national solidarity), and often affected by unexpected new ideas on how to reduce petrol consumption.

These considerations raise doubts on the right to assume a definite demand curve for petrol. But of course there is no impediment to utilizing whatever is known about how much less households tend to use cars or heating if petrol becomes more expensive: but always with an awareness of the extent of indeterminateness and readiness to change of any such behavioural inclination, and of the greater importance of changes in employment and incomes due to changes in aggregate demand.

5.33 Conclusions

This chapter has introduced you to standard producer theory, Marshallian partial-equilibrium analysis and the theory of non-capitalistic general equilibrium— the denomination I use to stress that, although this is the notion of general equilibrium usually presented to students, it is far from being sufficiently general, if the theory were unable to deal with capital goods it would be useless. The chapter introduced perhaps fewer new notions than the preceding chapter, but had many considerations on the theoretical meaning and justification of the assumptions, for example in Sects. 4, 5, 26, 27, 32. This should have given you a taste of the peculiarity of economic theory, which requires not only a good capacity at formal derivations, but also attention to the consistency and plausibility of the assumptions, which requires reasonings which must try to be as rigorous as possible in spite of having to deal with less precise notions such as 'sufficiently general', 'rather unlikely', 'not realistic', 'strongly suggested by empirical observation' and so on. Also essential is attention to the development of the theory, trying to understand the reasons for the changes it has undergone. You will amply need these qualities in the coming chapters.

438 Chapter 5 · Firms, Partial Equilibria and the General Equilibrium with Production

5.34 **Review Questions and Exercises**

Review questions

1. Produce an example where 'q is the maximum output obtainable from an input vector $\mathbf{x}$' does *not* mean that no element of $\mathbf{x}$ can be reduced if q is to be produced.
2. Obtain the transformation–function representation of a production function.
3. Explain why constant returns to scale and divisibility imply that isoquants are convex.
4. Prove the product exhaustion theorem for constant returns to scale differentiable production functions.
5. Consider a CRS production function $y = f(x_1, x_2)$. Prove that in a diagram with x_1 in abscissa and x_2 in ordinate, along a ray from the origin all isoquants have the same slope.
6. Prove that the cost function is concave in factor prices.
7. Explain why it is not always the case that the optimal output, when it exists, does not increase and generally decreases if the rental of a factor in positive use rises.
8. It is possible that a rise in the demand and in the output of the product of an industry which is the sole user of a specialized factor, although associated with a higher output price, be associated with a lower equilibrium rental of the specialized factor. Explain why.
9. Prove that the profit function, when it exists, is convex.
10. Explain why entry permits to consider *industries* as having constant returns to scale, even when *firms* have a definite optimal dimension because they have initially increasing returns to scale that after a point turn into decreasing returns to scale.
11. Suppose the marginal product of a factor can become negative if too much of it is employed. Show what will be the shape of the total productivity (or average productivity) curve of a factor in this case, assuming CRS.
12. Use the Envelope Theorem to prove Shephard's Lemma.
13. Use the Envelope Theorem to prove Hotelling's Lemma. Explain why this proof requires that the production function be strictly concave (=decreasing returns to scale).
14. Use Hotelling's Lemma to prove that when the profit function exists, there are no Giffen inputs.
15. In the problem of cost minimization, interpret the Lagrange multiplier.
16. Let $\mathbf{x}(w_1, \ldots, w_n, y^\circ)$ indicate the vectorial function of conditional input demands derived from a production function $y = f(x_1, \ldots, x_n)$ and cost minimization. Explain why the substitution matrix is symmetric and negative semidefinite. (What mathematical condition is implicitly assumed when one assumes symmetry?)
17. If the cost function of a two-inputs production function is $y w_1^a w_2^{1-a}$, prove that the production function has Cobb-Douglas form.
18. Define and interpret Leontief weak separability.

5.34 · Review Questions and Exercises

19. Explain how it is possible that there is a positive producer surplus in a market even if all firms make zero (neoclassical) profit.
20. Explain the reason for representing price in ordinate and quantity in abscissa.
21. Remember Sraffa's arguments against a decreasing supply curve.
22. Explain why when short-period price rises above average cost, and the firm increases output so as to obtain $p = MC$, it can be argued that the firm's profit (neoclassical definition) is only apparent, if rigorously defined it is zero.
23. Prepare an oral exposition of the difference between inferior inputs and rival inputs.
24. Explain why the profit function does not always exist.
25. Reproduce verbally by heart the formal reasoning that shows that the A-B-C-D general equilibrium with production can be 'reduced' to an exchange equilibrium.
26. (Also in the main text) Prove that a convex production possibility set with a single output implies a *quasi-concave* production function. (Hint: prove first that the input requirement set is convex. The definition of quasi-concavity was given in Chap. 4, ▶ Sect. 4.5)
27. In partial-equilibrium analysis, in which case does the sum of producer and consumer surplus coincide with the sole consumer surplus, and why?
28. Producer surplus can, perhaps more correctly, be called factor suppliers' surplus if the considerations are accepted that suggest that short-period profit is always zero even when it seems positive. Explain.
29. 'Perfect competition can really prevail only at equilibrium' (Arrow, see Sect. 5.24.3). Explain.
30. The text states that partial equilibrium cannot be used to study the determination of the prices of capital goods or of unproduced factors like labour or land. Why?
31. Explain why the fact that the analysis is short period does not authorize to take the number of firms as given.

Exercises
1. The production function is Cobb–Douglas with CRS, $q = Ax^\alpha y^{1-\alpha}$. Let factor prices be v_x and v_y. Find the cost function $C(v_x, v_y, q)$ and confirm Shephard's Lemma by showing that indeed $\partial C/\partial v_x = x$.
2. Suppose in an industry all firms have the same cost function, $c(0) = 0$, $c(q) = 8 + 2q^2$ for $q > 0$. Market demand is $D(p) = 100 - p$. Find the long-period partial-equilibrium price and quantity, and the number of firms.
3. Consider the production function (in terms of variable factors only) $q = (x+y)^\alpha - \beta y^2$, where $0 < \alpha$, $\beta > 1$. Prove that for some level of output and some prices, input y is inferior. (If you have difficulties, try G. S. Epstein and U. Spiegel, 'A Production Function with an Inferior Input', *The Manchester School*, vol. 68 no. 5 September 2000, 503–515, and 'Comment' by C. A. Weber, *The Manchester School*, vol. 69 no. 6 December 2001, 616–622.)
4. Remembering that the marginal product of a factor is the partial derivative of the production function, prove that with more than two factors an

440   Chapter 5 · Firms, Partial Equilibria and the General Equilibrium with Production

increase in the employment of a factor can cause the marginal product of some other factor to decrease. Check whether the following 'production function' can be of use: $q = x_1^\alpha x_{2A}^{1-\alpha} + x_{2B}^\beta x_3^{1-\beta}$, where $0 < \alpha < 1$, $0 < \beta < 1$, $x_{2A} + x_{2B} = x_2$. Explain why this is not yet a true production function (Hint: unless a condition is added—which one?—it does not yield the maximum output associated with given quantities x_1, x_2, x_3).

5. Check that the production function $q = x_1^\alpha x_2^{1-\alpha} - \beta x_1 - \gamma x_2$, with α, β, γ positive and less than 1, has constant returns to scale; show that it makes economic sense only if $\beta + \gamma < 1$; then find the interval of factor proportions outside which one marginal product is negative.

6. α) Suppose a single output q is produced by two inputs x_1 and x_2 according to the production function $q = ax_1 + bx_2$, $a, b > 0$. Draw some isoquants and prove that the production possibility set is convex.

β) Suppose two outputs z_1 and z_2 are jointly produced by a single input x with transformation function $z_1^2 + z_2^2 - x = 0$. Prove that the production possibility set is convex and that for fixed x the locus of possible efficient combinations of z_1 and z_2 (the transformation curve) is concave.

γ) Suppose a single output q is produced by two inputs x_1 and x_2 according to the production function $q = x_1^2 + x_2^2$; draw some isoquants and prove that the production possibility set is not convex.

7. (Quasi-concavity) Prove that a convex production possibility set with a single output implies a *quasi-concave* production function. (Hint: prove first that the input requirement set is convex. The definition of quasi-concavity was given in ► Chap. 4, ► Sect. 4.5)

8. Also in the text) (Hotelling's Lemma) Prove that results (i) and (ii) at the end of Sect. 5.18.2 can also be derived from the WAPM (Sect. 5.9).

9. (Also in the text) Assume wine V is produced by labour L over 1 unit of specialized land in fixed supply according to the production function $V = T^{1/2}L^{1/2}$. Labour's wage in terms of other goods is fixed and equal to w. Prove that the industry's long-period inverse supply curve is $p = 2wV$ and that the area below it for any given V equals the wage payments to the labour employed to produce that V.

10. Discuss the effects on distribution and on the composition of demand in a three-goods, two-factors economy if there is a shift of tastes in favour of good 1 but this good is produced with exactly the average labour–land proportion.

11. The production function is Cobb–Douglas with CRS, $q = Ax^\alpha y^{1-\alpha}$. Let factor prices or rentals) be v_x and v_y. Find the cost function $C(v_x, v_y, q)$ and confirm Shephard's Lemma by showing that indeed $\partial C / \partial v_x = x$.

12. Prove that if the firm is a multiproduct one and profit depends on inputs and outputs, then result (i) of Hotelling's Lemma generalizes to equality between the partial derivative of the profit function relative to any one output price, and supply function of that output.

13. Prove Walras' Law for the A-B-C-D production economy, remembering that firm profits are zero.

14. Consider a neoclassical economy where labour and land produce corn via a differentiable CRS production function. Land supply is rigid and fully employed. Trade unions would like to maximize the total wage bill (real wage times employment). Can the elasticity of substitution help them to decide whether it is opportune to raise the real wage above the full-employment level? (Careful: do not confuse the wage share with the wage bill.)
15. Reformulate equations A-B-C-D of non-capitalistic general equilibrium so as to eliminate equations C.
16. Reformulate the equations of non-capitalistic general equilibrium so as to allow demands for factor services coming from consumers to appear explicitly.
17. Consider the long-period equilibrium of an industry with free entry where each firm's production function is $q = 2(1 + \frac{1}{x_1 x_2})^{-1}$. Prove that the industry can be treated as a single firm with production function $Q = x_1^{1/2} x_2^{1/2}$.

References

Arrow, K. J. (1959). Toward a theory of price adjustment. In M. Abramovitz (Ed.), *The allocation of economic resources* (pp. 41–51). Stanford: Stanford University Press.

Arrow, K. J., Hahn, F. H. (1971). *General competitive analysis*. S. Francisco: Holden Day, and Edinburgh: Oliver and Boyd.

Aumann, R. J. (1964). Markets with a continuum of traders. *Econometrica, 32*(1/2), 39–50.

Cahuc, P., Carcillo, S., & Zylberberg, A. (2014). *Labor economics* (2nd ed.). Cambridge MA: MIT Press.

Felipe, J., & McCombie, J. S. L. (2013). *The aggregate production function and the measurement of technical change: 'Not even wrong'*. Cheltenham, UK: Edward Elgar.

Garegnani, P. (1983). The classical theory of wages and the role of demand schedules in the determination of relative prices. *American Economic Review, 73*(2), 309–313.

Garegnani, P. (1990b). Sraffa: classical versus marginalist analysis. In K. Bharadwaj & B. Schefold (eds), *Essays on Piero Sraffa* (pp. 112–40). London: Unwin and Hyman, (reprinted 1992 by Routledge, London).

Hansen, A. (1960). The economics of the Soviet challenge. *Economic Record, 36*(Issue 73), 5–12.

Kaldor, N. (1934). The equilibrium of the firm. *Economic Journal, 44*(173), 60–76.

Koutsoyiannis, A. (1975). *Modern microeconomics*. London and Basingstoke: Macmillan.

Kreps, D. M. (1990). *A course in microeconomic theory*. New York: Harvester Wheatsheaf.

Kreps, D. M. (2013). *Microeconomic foundations I. Choice and competitive markets*. Princeton: Princeton University Press.

Lavoie, M. (2014). *Post-Keynesian economics: New foundations*. Cheltenham, UK: Edward Elgar.

Marshall, A. (1879(1930)). *The pure theory of Foreign Trade, the pure theory of domestic values*./pKelley, Clifton.

Mas-Colell, A. (1991). On the uniqueness of equilibrium once again. In W. Barnett, B. Cornet, C. D'Aspremont, J. Gabszewicz, & A. Mas-Colell (Eds.), *Equilibrium theory and applications*. Cambridge: Cambridge University Press.

McKenzie L. W. (1987). General equilibrium. In: *(The) New Palgrave: A Dictionary of Economics* 1sted.

McKenzie, L. W. (2008). General equilibrium. In: *The new Palgrave: A dictionary of economics* 2nd ed.

McNulty, P. J. (1967). A note on the history of perfect competition. *Journal of Political Economy 75*(4 part 1), 395–399.

Novshek, W., & Sonnenschein, H. (1987). General equilibrium with free entry: A synthetic approach to the theory of perfect competition. *Journal of Economic Literature, 25*(3), 1281–1306.

Penrose E. (1955) Limits to the growth and size of firms. American Economic Review 45(2): 531–543.

Scherer, F. M., & Ross, D. (1990). *Industrial market structure and economic performance.* Boston: Houghton Mifflin.

Sraffa, P. (1926). The laws of returns under competitive conditions. *Economic Journal, 36,* 535–550.

Takayama, A. (1974). *Mathematical economics.* Hinsdale, Illinois: The Dryden Press.

Varian, H. (1992). *Microeconomic analysis* (3rd ed.). New York: W. W. Norton.

Varian H. (2010) *Intermediate microeconomics. A modern approach* (8th ed.). New York: W. W. Norton.

Existence, Uniqueness and Stability of Non-capitalistic General Equilibria

Contents

6.1   Introduction. The Exchange Economy – 446

6.2   Existence: Properties of the Market Excess Demand Correspondence – 447

6.3   Continuity: Non-strictly Convex Preferences – 450

6.4   Continuity: Non-convex Consumption Sets – 453

6.5   Continuity: Survival – 456

6.6   Continuity: The Zero-Income Problem – 458

6.7   Continuity: Survival Again and Subsistence – 460

6.8   Existence of General Equilibrium of Exchange: A Simple New Proof – 463

6.9   Brouwer's Fixed-Point Theorem – 465

Electronic supplementary material The online version of this chapter (▶ https://doi.org/10.1007/978-3-030-62070-7_6) contains supplementary material, which is available to authorized users.

© Springer Nature Switzerland AG 2021
F. Petri, *Microeconomics for the Critical Mind*,
Classroom Companion: Economics, https://doi.org/10.1007/978-3-030-62070-7_6

6.10 Existence of Exchange Equilibrium
with Strongly Monotonic Preferences – 466

6.11 Uniqueness: The Non-uniqueness of Equilibrium
in General. Possibility of Several Locally Stable
Equilibria – 469

6.12 Uniqueness: Regular Economies – 471

6.13 The Sonnenschein–Mantel–Debreu Result – 474

6.14 Uniqueness Through Conditions on Excess
Demand: Gross Substitutes – 475

6.15 Uniqueness Through Conditions on Excess
Demand: WAM – 478

6.16 Uniqueness: No-Trade Equilibrium and Index
Theorem – 481

6.17 Conditions on the Distribution
of Characteristics – 482

6.18 Stability: The Cobweb – 483

6.19 Stability: The Samuelsonian Walrasian
Tâtonnement – 485

6.20 Stability: Some Mathematics and the WAM
Theorem – 488

6.21 Stability: Further Aspects of the Problem – 492

6.22 On the Likelihood of Uniqueness and
Stability – 494

6.23 Production – 498

6.24   Existence of a GE of Production
and Exchange – 499

6.25   Uniqueness of the Production Equilibrium – 502

6.26   WAM and the Hildenbrand–Grodal
Observation – 509

6.27   Gross Substitutability not Sufficient
for Uniqueness – 511

6.28   Stability: The Tâtonnement in the Production
Economy – 512

6.29   Mandler's Factor Tâtonnement – 515

6.30   Again on the Likelihood of Uniqueness
and Stability – 518

6.31   Conclusions – 523

6.32   Review Questions and Exercises – 523

       References – 527

446 Chapter 6 · Existence, Uniqueness and Stability of Non-capitalistic General Equilibria

This chapter will teach you the main results on existence, uniqueness and stability of the general equilibrium of pure exchange and of exchange and production without capital goods. It will make you aware of:

- the problems with survival;
- the Sonnenschein–Mantel–Debreu results on uniqueness;
- the attempt to reduce the problems with uniqueness through the notion of regular economies and a limit of this notion;
- the importance of the Weak Axiom holding for market consumer excess demand, or *WAM*, for the uniqueness and tâtonnement stability of general equilibrium;
- why the gross substitutes assumption does not guarantee uniqueness in the production economy;
- a seldom noticed problem the tâtonnement encounters in the production economy;
- how Hicks and Harry Johnson argued that the problems with uniqueness and stability of equilibrium could be neglected.

6.1 Introduction. The Exchange Economy

The supply-and-demand (or marginal or neoclassical) approach to value and distribution argues that in a competitive market economy prices and quantities are determined by the competitive interaction of buyers and sellers, which pushes a market economy towards a situation of equality, or equilibrium, between supply and demand simultaneously on all markets. The theory's credibility requires:

1. that such a notion of general equilibrium is logically consistent: the system of equations or disequations that a general equilibrium must satisfy has a solution; this is the problem of *existence* of a general equilibrium;
2. that there isn't a multiplicity of solutions, so that the prices and quantities, that should result from the tendency towards equilibrium, are not left indeterminate (in real economies there does not seem to be any such indeterminateness); this is the problem of *uniqueness* of equilibrium;
3. that the spontaneous working of competitive markets causes the economy to *tend* towards the general equilibrium position; this is the problem of *stability* of equilibrium;
4. that the solutions of the general equilibrium system are not wildly in contrast with observation, for example equilibrium real wages should not be zero; this is the problem of *correspondence* of the theory's predictions with observation.

This chapter summarizes the main results reached on the first three issues by the theory of general equilibrium, first for the model of an exchange economy, then for the model of a *non-capitalistic* production economy, that is with only non-produced productive factors (types of labour, types of land). The latter model, according to modern general equilibrium theory, can be reinterpreted (in a way to be explained in ▶ Chap. 8) so as to accommodate capital goods too,

6.1 · Introduction. The Exchange Economy

but this reinterpretation introduces *dated* goods: bread today is treated as a different good from bread tomorrow; on the contrary the production economy to be analysed in this chapter has no need to date goods because its equilibrium is a long-period equilibrium, a persistent repetitive situation, and its determination determines the average quantities produced and consumed *per period* (traditionally, per year); this difference is sometimes underlined by qualifying the model as *atemporal*, not in the sense that there is no time in the model (production, for example, definitely takes time in the model) but in the sense that no time index is attached to goods, see ▶ Sect. 5.28.

I start with the exchange economy. The notion of general equilibrium of an exchange economy was met in ▶ Chap. 3 and again in ▶ Chap. 4. The reader is invited to re-examine in particular ▶ Sect. 4.22 for the definition (which will not be repeated here) of the exchange economy and of its general equilibrium and ▶ Sect. 4.7 for some first considerations on existence.

6.2 Existence: Properties of the Market Excess Demand Correspondence

The basic element in the search for equilibrium in the exchange economy is the (vectorial) *market excess demand function or correspondence,* $\mathbf{z}(\mathbf{p}) = (z_1(\mathbf{p}), \ldots, z_n(\mathbf{p}))$. This is guaranteed to be a *function* (i.e. uniquely determined for each $\mathbf{p}$) only if one assumes that, for each price vector, the choice of each consumer is uniquely determined. As we know from ▶ Chap. 4 (and most readers already knew from elementary microeconomics), this is only guaranteed if the indifference curves of consumers are *strictly convex*. If not, it is possible that at a price vector $\mathbf{p}$ certain choices of consumers out of their possible choices at that $\mathbf{p}$ guarantee a general equilibrium, but others do not; then the question arises, whether anything guarantees that the choices will be the equilibrium ones. This issue is discussed later. Now I assume $\mathbf{z}(\mathbf{p})$ is a function.

Several properties of $\mathbf{z}(\mathbf{p})$, all except the last one already proved in ▶ Chap. 4, are listed below.

1. $\mathbf{z}(\mathbf{p})$ is *homogeneous of degree zero in* $\mathbf{p}$, because for each consumer, since income or wealth is the value of the given endowments, the budget hyperplane passes through the endowment point and therefore the budget constraint does not move if all prices change in the same proportion. This makes it legitimate to restrict attention to *relative* prices, by choosing a numéraire, nowadays often consisting of a basket containing one unit of each good, i.e. one sets the sum of all prices as equal to 1 and then prices vary in the price simplex S^{n-1}.

2. $\mathbf{z}(\mathbf{p})$ satisfies *Walras' Law,* i.e. $\mathbf{p}\mathbf{z}(\mathbf{p}) = 0$ because local non-satiation is assumed and then consumers' budgets are balanced.

3. $\mathbf{z}(\mathbf{p})$ is *possibly not defined if some price is zero*: if there is even only one consumer who is never satiated of a good, then at a zero price the demand for that good is infinite, i.e. not defined.

448   Chapter 6 · Existence, Uniqueness and Stability of Non-capitalistic General Equilibria

4. $\mathbf{z(p)}$ is *bounded below*, because consumers cannot supply goods in excess of their endowments and therefore the excess supply of any good cannot exceed the aggregate endowment of that good.
5. $\mathbf{z(p)}$ is *continuous* on the *interior* of the price simplex S^{n-1} (i.e. as long as prices are all positive) if *preferences are continuous, strictly convex and locally non-satiated over a budget set which is compact and convex.* (The set of optimal consumption baskets and possible demand vectors of consumer s, $d^s(\mathbf{p})$, is an **upper-hemicontinuous correspondence** over the interior of the price simplex if *the strict convexity of preferences is relaxed to simple convexity*.) This was proven in Proposition 4.5, ► Sect. 4.6.
6. if one assumes in addition that preferences are strongly monotonic, then *if a sequence $\{\mathbf{p}^n\}$ of price vectors, with $\mathbf{p}^n \gg 0, \mathbf{p}^n \in S^{n-1}$, converges to $\mathbf{p}$ on the boundary of S^{n-1}(i.e. if the sequence converges to a price vector where some but not all prices are zero), then $\|\mathbf{z(p^n)}\|$, the length of the market excess demand vector, tends to $+\infty$* (i.e. at least one excess demand tends to $+\infty$).

This last property needs proof. Before, I remember the meaning of a number of terms which have appeared in these sentences. Preferences are *continuous* if for all $\mathbf{x}$ in the consumption set the set of consumption baskets weakly preferred to $\mathbf{x}$ and the set of consumption baskets to which $\mathbf{x}$ is weakly preferred are both closed sets. Preferences are *weakly monotonic* if $\mathbf{y} \gg \mathbf{x}$ implies $\mathbf{y} \succ \mathbf{x}$; this admits satiation for some goods but not for all goods simultaneously; preferences are *strongly monotonic* if $\mathbf{y} \geq \mathbf{x}$ and $\mathbf{y} \neq \mathbf{x}$ imply $\mathbf{y} \succ \mathbf{x}$. Preferences are *locally non-satiated* if, assuming all goods are perfectly divisible, for all $\mathbf{x}$ in the consumption set and for any $\varepsilon > 0$ there is in the consumption set, within a distance from $\mathbf{x}$ not greater than ε, a consumption basket $\mathbf{y}$ strictly preferred to $\mathbf{x}$. This admits that some goods may be 'bads', i.e. have negative marginal utility.[1] From the continuity (or, for correspondences, upper hemicontinuity) of the excess demand of each consumer the continuity (respectively, upper hemicontinuity) of the *market* excess demand follows trivially by summing over all consumers.

Proof of Property 6   Under the Assumption (i) that there is a positive aggregate endowment of each good for which a price is quoted, I prove Property 6 for the excess demand $\mathbf{z}^s(\mathbf{p})$ of a single consumer chosen so that (ii) *her endowment has positive value at the prices* $\mathbf{p}$ to which $\{\mathbf{p}^n\}$ converges. Note that because of (i) there will always be at least one consumer in the economy for whom (ii) holds, because in vector $\mathbf{p}$ the price of at least one good is positive, and at least one consumer

---

1   *Exercise 1*: Suppose there are only two goods; if one assumes local non-satiation, can both goods be simultaneously 'bads' everywhere in the consumption set, that is, such that a decrease of the amount of either of them raises utility? Prove your answer.

6.2 · Existence: Properties of the Market Excess Demand Correspondence.

has an endowment of that good; and if $\|\mathbf{z}^s(\mathbf{p}^n)\|$ tends to $+\infty$ for even only one consumer, then also $\|\mathbf{z}(\mathbf{p}^n)\|$ tends to $+\infty$ because endowments are finite.[2]

The proof of Property 6 is by contradiction.

We need first some intermediate results. Assume that $\|\mathbf{z}^s(\mathbf{p}^n)\|$ does *not* tend to $+\infty$ as $\{\mathbf{p}^n\}$ tends to a price vector with at least one price zero. Then there is a subsequence $\{\mathbf{p}^{n'}\}$ such that $\mathbf{z}^s\left(\mathbf{p}^{n'}\right)$ is bounded above, and hence bounded, for all n' (remember that $\mathbf{z}^s(\mathbf{p})$ is bounded below: excess supplies cannot be greater than endowments). A well-known mathematical result states that every bounded sequence in R^n contains a convergent subsequence. Therefore there is a subsequence $\{\mathbf{p}^m\}$ of $\{\mathbf{p}^{n'}\}$ such that $\mathbf{z}^s(\mathbf{p}^m)$ converges to a finite limit $\mathbf{x}$.

Now I use another result of consumer theory: *Let the preference relation be continuous, convex and (weakly) monotonic, let sequence $\{\mathbf{p}^m\}$ converge to $\mathbf{p}$, and let $\mathbf{p}\omega^s > 0$ where ω^s is the endowment of the consumer; if a sequence $\{x^m\} \in \mathbf{z}^s(\mathbf{p}^m)$ converges to $\mathbf{x}$ as $\mathbf{p}^m$ converges to $\mathbf{p}$, then $\mathbf{x} \in \mathbf{z}^s(\mathbf{p})$, i.e. no other element of the budget set $B(\mathbf{p})$ is strictly preferred to it.* The proof of this result is as follows. Since $\mathbf{p}^m\mathbf{x}^m = \mathbf{p}^m\omega^s$ and $\mathbf{p}^m \to \mathbf{p}, \mathbf{x}^m \to \mathbf{x}$, it follows that $\mathbf{p}\mathbf{x} = \mathbf{p}\omega^s$, i.e. that $\mathbf{x}$ is in the budget set $B(\mathbf{p})$. Now consider any other $\mathbf{x}' \in B(\mathbf{p})$. From $\mathbf{p}\omega^s > 0$ it follows that, for any scalar α in the open interval $(0, 1)$ it is $\mathbf{p}\alpha\mathbf{x}' < \mathbf{p}\omega^s$. Since $\mathbf{p}^m \to \mathbf{p}$, there is an m' sufficiently great such that for all $m > m'$ it is $\mathbf{p}^m\alpha\mathbf{x}' < \mathbf{p}^m\omega^s$; by the Weak Axiom of revealed preferences, since $\alpha\mathbf{x}'$ might have been chosen at the prices $\mathbf{p}^m$ but the consumer has chosen $\mathbf{x}^m$, this implies that for $m > m'$, $\mathbf{x}^m$ is weakly preferred to $\alpha\mathbf{x}'$. The continuity of preferences then implies that $\mathbf{x}$ is weakly preferred to $\alpha\mathbf{x}'$. Again because of the continuity of preferences, by making α tend to 1 we obtain that $\mathbf{x}$ is weakly preferred to $\mathbf{x}'$. Since this holds for any $\mathbf{x}' \in B(\mathbf{p})$, we obtain $\mathbf{x} \in \mathbf{z}^s(\mathbf{p})$.

On the basis of this result, the proof of Property 6 conthinues as follows. If $\|\mathbf{z}^s(\mathbf{p}^n)\|$ does *not* tend to $+\infty$, we obtain that the finite limit $\mathbf{x}$ is utility-maximizing at $\mathbf{p}$ (no other $\mathbf{x}'$ in $B(\mathbf{p})$ is strictly preferred to it). However, this is absurd since at least one price in $\mathbf{p}$ is zero, and by increasing the amount of the corresponding good in some consumer's demand, her excess demand is still in the budget set but her utility is greater owing to the strong monotonicity assumption. This contradiction shows that it is not possible that $\|\mathbf{z}^s(\mathbf{p}^n)\|$ does not tend to $+\infty$. ∎

Note that if more than one price tends to zero at the same time, not all the excess demands for the goods whose prices are tending to zero need tend to $+\infty$.

---

2 Is Assumption (i) defensible? To assume that there are prices for goods with zero endowment would cause problems to the existence of equilibrium: assume strictly monotonic preferences including preference for a good with zero endowment, and assume that demand for this good is positive however high its price as long as some other good has positive price (this will be the case, for example, with a Cobb–Douglas utility function); then there is no equilibrium because excess demand for the good is always positive for any price of the good as long as some other good has positive price, while when the prices of all other goods are zero demand for them is infinite. However, it seems reasonable to assume that, when the endowment of a good is zero, people will discover it and will give up attempting to buy it; this justifies the assumption that the only goods demanded and with quoted prices are goods with nonzero endowments.

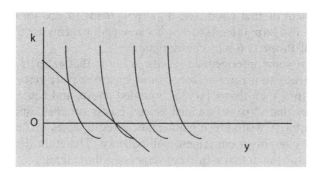

Fig. 6.1 Case in which demand for good k is zero and $MU_y/MU_k > 1$

Suppose there are three goods x, y, k and a consumer has utility function $u(x, y, k) = x^{1/2} + (y + v(k))^{1/2}$ with $v(k)$ such that the indifference curves between y and k are strictly convex but touch the y-axis and that $MU_y/MU_k > 1$ when $k = 0$ (see Fig. 6.1); this happens, e.g. if $v(k) = log(k + 1/2)$. Then if $\mathbf{p} \gg 0$ and $p_y/p_k = 1$ the consumer maximizes her utility by demanding a zero quantity of good k. Then a price sequence $\{\mathbf{p}^n\}$ where $\mathbf{p}^n = (1, 1/n, 1/n)$ does not cause the demand for good k to grow although its price tends to zero.

Therefore even with strong monotonicity, when the price of a good tends to zero one can be certain that the consumer's demand for the good tends to infinity only if that is the only price tending to zero or its ratio to all other prices tends to zero.

6.3 Continuity: Non-strictly Convex Preferences

In ▶ Chap. 4 it was shown that the certainty that a general equilibrium exists requires the continuity of $\mathbf{z}(\mathbf{p})$ for positive prices (▶ Sect. 4.7), and the absence of sudden 'jumps' of $\mathbf{z}(\mathbf{p})$ as some price becomes zero (▶ Sect. 4.15). Now let us go deeper into the problems raised by discontinuities of excess demand. It will take some time, as there are many issues to consider.

A first cause of discontinuities is non-convexity of indifference curves.

In the Edgeworth box in Fig. 6.2 consumer A has strictly concave indifference curves and as a result her offer curve or, as I prefer to call it, her *choice curve* consists of two separate segments on the axes, and then it can happen, as shown in the figure, that the two choice curves have no point in common: there is no equilibrium. There would then be a never-ending oscillation of the relative price: even if it were exactly at the discontinuity level where A is indifferent between two baskets, there would be either excess supply or excess demand for good 1 depending on A's choice.

Exercise Draw an Edgeworth box complete with the indifference curves of the two consumers, in which both consumers have discontinuous choice curves owing to strictly concave indifference curves, and determine whether an equilibrium exists.

6.3 · Continuity: Non-strictly Convex Preferences

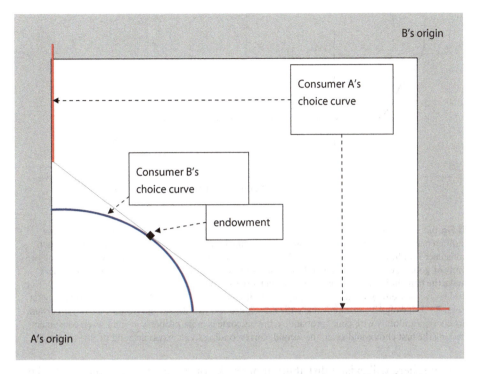

Fig. 6.2 Edgeworth box with no equilibrium owing to concave preferences of consumer A

This difficulty is generally considered negligible for economies with many different consumers, because, it is argued, the oscillation of relative price will be around the discontinuity price, so the latter will still function as an indicator of the average of market price, which is the traditional role of equilibrium prices; furthermore the price oscillation will be very small, hence nearly unnoticeable, if the discontinuity concerns only one consumer out of many.

But there might be many consumers with similar endowments and tastes and therefore a discontinuity at the same relative price. If there are k identical consumers who at the discontinuity price vector are indifferent between two baskets, then the usual argument to minimize the relevance of this case is the following (cf., e.g. Hildenbrand and Kirman 1988, pp. 40–41): consider the segment joining the two vectors of excess demands corresponding to all consumers demanding the same basket, e.g. in the two-goods case, segment MK in ◘ Fig. 6.3. Start from one extreme of the segment, e.g. in ◘ Fig. 6.3 the situation where all consumers are choosing the basket where the amount of good 1 is smaller: market excess demand for good 1 is M = −28. Now suppose that just one of the k consumers chooses the other basket; then suppose that two consumers do so, then three and so on; in this way we can make market excess demand correspond to either extreme of the segment, *or to any of the k − 1 intermediate equidistant points* on the segment MK. Thus, even when the discontinuity is relevant to equilibrium (it will *not* be, if equilibrium is at a price vector where there is no discon-

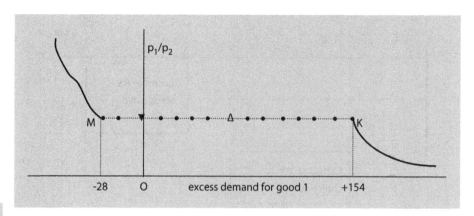

◘ **Fig. 6.3** Discontinuous excess demand for good 1 due to 14 identical consumers with concave indifference curves between goods 1 and 2. The figure assumes that at the price ratio at which each consumer is indifferent between two baskets, each consumer's choice is either an excess supply of two units of good 1, or an excess demand for 11 units of good 1. Depending on how many consumers make the first choice and how many the second, excess demand for good 1 can be $-28, -15, -2, +11, +24, \ldots, +154$. Zero excess demand is impossible, it would be possible to approach it considerably (at point ▼) by having 12 consumers make the first choice and two the second (result -2), but if consumers choose randomly with equal probability, the outcome is more probably around seven consumers making the first choice and seven the second, corresponding to an excess demand of $+63$ (point △)

tinuity), there will exist a distribution of the k consumers between the two baskets that makes market excess demand differ from zero by not more than if only one consumer presented the discontinuity—and therefore, it is argued, by a negligible amount.

This argument is not convincing. The problem remains, that it is unclear what might ensure that the discrepancy-minimizing distribution of choices is indeed achieved: if each price-taking consumer chooses randomly which of the two baskets to demand—and it is unclear how else they can choose—then, with many consumers, the most probable outcome is that approximately one half of them will demand each basket, in which case market excess demand will be approximately at the middle point of the segment, thus possibly significantly different from zero (cf. ◘ Fig. 6.3); the pressure on price to change can then be non-negligible, but as soon as the price changes however slightly, all consumers jump to the same choice, and a significant price oscillation becomes likely.

So the real way out of the difficulty is to postulate that consumers are not identical (a plausible assumption in many cases, but much less so in labour markets), so the discontinuities are many but happen at different prices for different consumers and are then unnoticeable because very small relative to total demand and therefore swamped by the irregularities and disequilibrium that anyway characterize real economies. If the tendency of price in a market is towards a *small oscillation* around a certain price rather than towards a precise price and quantity, this makes no difference to the explanatory and predictive power of the theory.

On this basis, the discontinuities or indeterminacies associated with non-convex or non-strictly convex preferences do not appear to be a reason seriously to

6.4 · Continuity: Non-convex Consumption Sets

question the validity of the supply-and-demand approach, as long as one can assume that the discontinuities occur at different prices for different consumers. This assumption is generally reasonable, but much less so in the labour market because very many people are in a very similar situation in that market; but then other problems appear even more relevant, as we will see.

6.4 Continuity: Non-convex Consumption Sets

Even with strictly convex indifference curves the continuity of the excess demand of a consumer is not guaranteed unless the *budget set* is compact (i.e. closed and bounded) and convex. If the budget set is unbounded (because of some zero price), then there may be no definite choice that maximizes the consumer's utility. What about convexity of the budget set? The budget set of the consumer is the intersection of the consumption set with the set of consumption vectors **x** that satisfy the budget constraint. If the budget constraint is not linear because the price of a good decreases with the quantity demanded, then the budget set need not be convex and discontinuities can arise (prove it graphically!) but nonlinear budget constraints are rare. But problems can be due to a non-convex consumption set. A consumer may find it possible to consume either good 1, or good 2, but no convex combination of them (e.g. hours spent in Paris or in Sydney in the same day). Then for given prices and given income to be spent on these two goods, the budget set restricted to these two goods consists of a single point in abscissa and a single point in ordinate, and a change in the prices of the two goods can cause a discontinuous jump from consuming only one to consuming only the other good.[3]

To overcome this problem it has been argued that the consumption set *can* include baskets including incompatible consumptions, because the consumption basket need not include the *acts* of consumption but only the *availability* for consumption, so one can purchase both a vacation in Australia and in Greece for the same day and then do only one of the two activities: the distinction between availability and actual consumption, plus a *free disposal assumption*,[4] makes this treatment possible.

---

3   In this example the difficulty is specific to intertemporal equilibria, which need to date every commodity, and does not arise if the equilibrium one is trying to determine is a long-period equilibrium. The latter type of equilibrium determines the demands per period, e.g. per year, not the demands on specific days, so one can always assume that the hours spent in Paris and the ones in Sydney are not in the same day. But in other cases the difficulty can arise in long-period equilibria too.

4   That is, one can get rid of goods at no cost. This assumption is formalized for firms as meaning that for each good there is available to all firms a process with that good as input and no output. To assume free disposal for consumers means to assume that consumers too have available for each good a 'production process' with that good as input and no output.

454   Chapter 6 · Existence, Uniqueness and Stability of Non-capitalistic General Equilibria

Indivisible (*or discrete*) *goods* too prevent convexity of the consumption set. But the problems raised by indivisible consumption goods can reasonably be considered of secondary importance. For an indivisible good, what one can determine is the **reservation price** of n units of it, i.e. the maximum price that the consumer is ready to pay in order to purchase 1, or 2, or 3,... units of the good, given all other prices (and income, if it is income that is given and not endowments).[5] In between two reservation prices, the number of units of the good demanded by the consumer does not change. The problem is that at the reservation price for n units of the good, the consumer is indifferent between demanding n or n–1 units of the good (for a slightly higher price she demands n – 1 units, for a slightly lower price she demands n units), and this affects her demands for the other goods which therefore have a discontinuity (two values) at each reservation price. Let us see this more formally.

Assume that utility is $u(x_1, x_2)$, good 1 comes in discrete units while good 2 is divisible, the consumer's income is m, and the given price of good 2 is p_2. The reservation price for 1 one unit of good 1, let us indicate it as R_1, is the price such that the utility from not consuming good 1 at all (and consuming therefore m/p_2 units of good 2) is the same as the utility from consuming one unit of good 1 and dedicating to the purchase of good 2 the residual income $m - R_1$:

$$u(0, m/p_2) = u(1, (m - R_1)/p_2).$$

(Also see ▶ Sect. 4.20.) Analogously, the reservation price R_2 for the purchase of two units of good 1 is determined by

$$u(1, (m - R_2)/p_2) = u(2, (m - 2R_2)/p_2)$$

and the reservation price for n units of good 1 is determined by

$$u(n - 1, (m - (n - 1)R_n)/p_2) = u(n, (m - nR_n)/p_2).$$

Assuming good 1 is not a Giffen good, it is $R_n > R_{n+1}$ and for $R_n > p_1 > R_{n+1}$ the consumer demands n units of good 1 and $(m - np_1)/p_2$ units of good 2. This means that, e.g. at prices (R_2, p_2) the consumer is indifferent between demanding $(m - R_2)/p_2$ and demanding $(m - 2R_2)/p_2$ units of good 2; demand for good 2 has two values here, with a discontinuity, cf. ◘ Fig. 6.4.

But, as for the discontinuities caused by strictly concave indifference curves, in all likelihood these discontinuities occur at different prices for different consumers and can be considered sufficiently small relative to total demand for good 2 as to be negligible.

Finally, the consumption of certain goods may be necessary to make it conceivable that certain other goods be desirable. For example, in intertemporal choices, it is impossible to consume a swim in deep water if one has not previously learnt to swim; it is impossible to climb mountains without sufficient phys-

---

5   The general definition of reservation price of a quantity x of a good (possibly perfectly divisible) is: the maximum price the consumer would be ready to pay for that quantity, given her income and the other prices.

6.4 · Continuity: Non-convex Consumption Sets

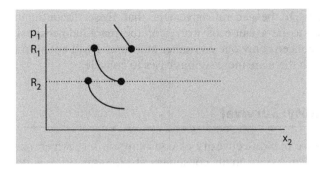

◘ **Fig. 6.4** Possible shape of the demand for good 2 (measured in abscissa) as a function of the price of discrete good 1

ical fitness, and the physical fitness depends on whether one chooses or not to do the needed previous physical exercise. Let us consider the shape of the consumption set restricted to the sole two goods 'physical exercise at time t', good 1, and 'mountain climbing at time t + 1', good 2; and let us suppose that as long as physical exercise is less than the amount OO' in ◘ Fig. 6.5, no mountain climbing is possible, but physical exercise as great as OO' or greater allows any amount of mountain climbing the following period. If one excludes impossible consumption baskets from the consumption set, then the consumption set in ◘ Fig. 6.5 is not convex because it consists of the segment OO' plus the grey area.

Again, the need to exclude from the consumption sets the baskets that include mountain climbing but not enough physical exercise is circumvented by arguing that, not mountain climbing as such should enter the consumption set but rather the clothes, shoes, socks, travel tickets, hotel nights, etc., which make mountain climbing possible, and that these things can be available without being consumed (free disposal again!).

This solution avoids the non-convexity of the consumption set, but raises another problem. In all likelihood the marginal utility of the goods useful for mountain climbing will not vary continuously, and it will jump to zero when previous exercise for physical fitness falls below OO'; thus the consumer's demand for the goods only useful for mountain climbing jumps discontinuously from a positive amount to zero when the demand for physical exercise goes below OO'. I conclude that when a certain minimum consumption level of a good is a prerequisite for another good to have any utility, then the assumption of continuity of preferences is unacceptable.[6]

A similar but more tragic case is that of suicide. A consumer (e.g. a finance speculator) may consciously *decide* to survive or not beyond a certain date depending on prices: a suicide decision causes her supply of labour and her demands for goods in subsequent periods to jump discontinuously to zero.

---

6   However, once again for most goods the resulting discontinuity in excess demand can be considered of secondary importance because, if consumers are numerous, the discontinuities are in all likelihood at different prices for different consumers.

There seems to be general agreement that these discontinuities can again be judged not to be a cause of worry for the marginal/neoclassical approach, because they concern only one consumer at a time. I will not stop to discuss this opinion because there are more serious cases to consider.

6.5 Continuity: Survival

A possible cause of non-convexity of consumption sets, which may cause a discontinuity of demand for many consumers at the same price, is that a minimum level of consumption is necessary in order to survive. Let me quote here a passage from Debreu (1959), which accompanies a drawing from which ◘ Fig. 6.5 has been copied:

» ...consider the case where there are one location and two dates; a certain foodstuff at the first date defines the first commodity, the same foodstuff at the second date defines the second commodity. Let the length of [O, O'] be the minimum quantity of the first commodity which that consumer must have available in order to survive until the end of the first elementary time-interval. If his input of the first commodity is less than or equal to this minimum, it might seem, on first thought, that his input of the second commodity must be zero. The set X_i [i.e. the consumption set of consumer i, F.P.] would therefore consist of the closed segment [O, O'] and a subset of the closed quadrant 1, O', 2'. Such a set has the disadvantage of not being convex in general. However, if both commodities are freely disposable, the set X_i is the closed quadrant 1, O, 2, which is convex: if the consumer chooses (perhaps

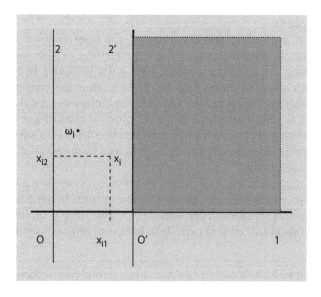

◘ Fig. 6.5

6.5 · Continuity: Survival

because he is forced to) a consumption x_i in the closed strip 2, O, O′, 2′, it means that x_{i1} of the first commodity is *available to him* and he will actually consume at most that much of it, and that x_{i2} of the second commodity is *available to him* and he will actually consume none of it.

The choice by the ith consumer of x_i in X_i determines implicitly his life span (Debreu, 1959, pp. 51–2).

(The last sentence in this quotation may appear disconcerting, but it refers to the fact that Debreu at this stage of his treatise is assuming no uncertainty, so consumers know the date when they will die and how that depends on their choices.)

Once again, the distinction between availability and actual consumption (plus the free disposal assumption) is used to avoid the *non-convexity* of the consumption set. But Debreu does not seem to perceive that this solution does not avoid another danger: of *discontinuity* in the excess demands for the goods after the initial period. Many people's endowment consists only of their labour/leisure. If the real wage gets sufficiently low for a number of periods, they may find it impossible to survive beyond those periods, and their supply of labour and demand for goods for the subsequent periods drops discontinuously to zero.[7]

Debreu has an intertemporal consumption set in mind, connected with the notion of intertemporal equilibrium which will be studied in depth here in ▶ Chap. 8; but the idea should be clear, the consumer determines simultaneously her demands for today and for tomorrow, and too low a demand for consumption today implies a sudden jump to zero of demand tomorrow (and also of labour supply tomorrow) because the consumer does not survive to tomorrow. And intertemporal equilibria too need a continuity of intertemporal excess demands in order for existence not to be endangered.

The problem actually arises for long-period equilibria too, which need market consumer demands to be the persistent normal repetitive ones in a situation of no change or very gradual change of exogenous data. The market labour supply function, for example, loses all persistence or even definiteness at too low a real wage, as people would not eat enough to be able to work, and perhaps population would start *rapidly* decreasing against the persistence of data required by a long-period equilibrium.

This problem motivates an assumption which is often made in general equilibrium theory: the **survival assumption**, i.e. the assumption that *the survival of each consumer is guaranteed*[8]; generally this is obtained by assuming that *each consumer has an endowment which is sufficient to survive without any trade*. This

---

7 This is a more serious problem than with mountain climbing, because as far as survival needs are concerned, many people are in a very similar situation.

8 Space reasons prevent further discussion of this assumption here, but the interested reader ought to read at least the entry 'consumption sets' by Peter Newman in *The New Palgrave Dictionary of Political Economy,* I edition. It may be noted that the assumption is implicit when the consumption set is assumed to be the entire non-negative orthant, this amounts to assuming that there is no need for some minimum consumption in order to survive.

458 Chapter 6 · Existence, Uniqueness and Stability of Non-capitalistic General Equilibria

is obviously extremely unrealistic except for the most primitive economies; most people are (and have always been) in need to get consumption goods, heating, etc., from other people and firms (there is *specialization*, in the terminology of Rizvi 1991). But this means that if the price of what they can offer to others becomes very low, their survival is endangered and with it the continuity of their excess demands. This problem is seldom mentioned in textbooks, but is serious.

6.6 Continuity: The Zero-Income Problem

Even if survival poses no problem, another kind of discontinuity due to income falling too much is possible. I call it the **zero-income problem**.

When income depends on the prices of endowments, a zero price can cause discontinuities of excess demand. Consider the following example. In a two-goods exchange economy a consumer has a monotonic utility function $u = x_1^{1/2} + x_2^{1/2}$ and has a positive endowment consisting only of good 1, i.e. $\omega_1 > 0$, $\omega_2 = 0$. Let us determine the demand function for good 1. Indifference curves have slope $MRS = -x_2^{1/2}/x_1^{1/2}$. Utility maximization requires tangency between indifference curve and budget line, i.e.

$$x_2^{1/2}/x_1^{1/2} = p_1/p_2 \tag{6.1}$$

under the budget constraint that we can initially specify in the Marshallian way:

$$p_1 x_1 + p_2 x_2 = m, \quad \text{where } m = p_1 \omega_1. \tag{6.2}$$

Solving these two equations in two variables, and assuming $p_2 = 1$ one obtains (check it!) $x_1 = m/(p_1 + p_1^2)$. Now we use $m = p_1 \omega_1$ to obtain

$$x_1 = \omega_1/(1 + p_1).$$

Thus as long as p_1 is positive, x_1 is positive and less than ω_1, the consumer is a net supplier of good 1. Let p_1 tend to zero: income tends to zero and x_1 tends to ω_1; as long as $p_1 > 0$ the consumer remains a net supplier of good 1, but when p_1 is zero the demand for good 1 is infinite. This means that $lim_{p_1 \to 0} x_1 = \omega_1$ but at $p_1 = 0$ the demand for good 1 jumps discontinuously to $+\infty$ as ◘ Fig. 6.6 illustrates.

This is called a **zero-income problem** because the discontinuity would not arise if the consumer's income did not tend to zero as p_1 tends to zero.

Then a general equilibrium of exchange can fail to exist. As long as $p_1 > 0$, our consumer is a net supplier of good 1 to the market. Suppose that no one else is interested in good 1; then at any positive p_1 there is excess supply of good 1 and p_1 decreases; as long as $p_1 > 0$ the excess supply does not disappear and there isn't equilibrium; when p_1 becomes zero, our consumer's excess demand for good 1 shoots up to $+\infty$, and there isn't equilibrium. There is no price at which there is equilibrium on the market for good 1; a general equilibrium does not exist.

To separate this problem from the survival problem, we can assume that even a zero income ensures survival (the consumption set coincides with R_+^n).

6.6 · Continuity: The Zero-Income Problem

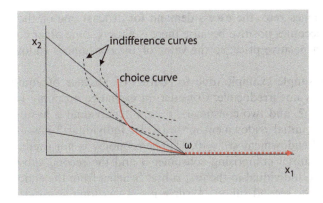

Fig. 6.6 Choice curve as p_1 tends to zero, when endowment is only of good 1

Exercise Find out why the numerical example used above to show the zero-income problem would not have worked if I had assumed a Cobb–Douglas utility function.

Three possible alternative assumptions surmount the zero-income problem:
1. **monotonicity**: *preferences are strongly monotonic for all consumers*;
2. **interiority**: *for each consumer the endowment is strictly positive, i.e. in the interior of R^n_+.*
3. **irreducibility**: *for any given allocation, whichever the way one divides the consumers into two non-empty subsets, there is at least one consumer in the first subset whose utility increases if all the endowments of the consumers in the second subset are added to her/his allocation.*

Assumption A surmounts the zero-income problem because at a zero price the demand for the good by all consumers is infinite, and as the price of a good tends to zero, before it becomes zero all consumers with a positive income develop a positive demand for the good, because the good has positive marginal utility for all of them. So no price can fall to zero.

Assumption B guarantees that the 'income (the value of the endowment) of each consumer is always positive (because at least one price is positive).

Assumption C, irreducibility,[9] is considered less restrictive than the first two. Since the second subset can consist of a single consumer, the irreducibility assumption implies that as the exchange value of the endowment of any con-

---

9   It is also called *indecomposability*; an essentially equivalent assumption is called *resource relatedness* in Arrow and Hahn (1971). The formal definition does not add to the given definition, but let me give it anyway. Let $\{1,...,s,...,S\}$ be the indices that distinguish the S consumers of the economy. Let us partition consumers into two mutually exclusive and exhaustive sets whose indices form two non-empty sets S1, S2 with S1∩S2= and S1∪S2={1,..,s,..,S}. The economy is *irreducible* if for any given allocation $\{x^s\}$ with for all s, $x^s \neq 0$, for any partition (S1, S2) there exists a consumer $s' \in S1$ such that $x^{s'} + (\Sigma_{s \in S2} \omega^s)$ is strongly preferred by consumer s' to $x^{s'}$.

460   **Chapter 6** · Existence, Uniqueness and Stability of Non-capitalistic General Equilibria

sumer approaches zero, the excess demand for at least one of the goods in her endowment becomes positive because there is always some other consumer *ready to pay* for it a positive price; so the value of the consumer's endowment cannot fall to zero.

Here is a simple example (due to Arrow) of absence of equilibrium when the economy is not irreducible. Consider an exchange economy with two commodities, $i = 1, 2$, and two consumers, $s = \alpha, \beta$. Individual α has utility function $u^{(\alpha)} = x_1^{(\alpha)}$ and initial endowment $\omega^{(\alpha)} = (1, 1)$. Individual 2 has utility function $u^{(\beta)} = x_2^{(\beta)}$ and endowment $\omega^{(\beta)} = (0, 1)$. The economy is not irreducible because, with the first subset comprising consumer α and the second subset comprising consumer β, no individual in the first subset benefits from the endowment of the consumers in the second subset. Assume $p_1 = 1$. As long as good 2 has positive price, it is in excess supply because consumer α offers the unit of it he owns but consumer β has no excess demand for it, so p_2 decreases; when good 2 reaches zero price, consumer β's demand for good 2 jumps to $+\infty$.

The generally accepted assessment of assumptions A (strict monotonicity) and B (interiority) is that they are extremely restrictive. This is obvious for B. As to A, it is difficult to find a consumption good which does not reach a satiation level sooner or later, beyond which utility decreases.

Irreducibility is more acceptable. It requires everybody to have something to offer that somebody else is ready to pay for. It fails with poor old people owning nothing and too old to work; but these people, in the absence of subsidies or pensions, have no income so their demands are zero to start with and remain zero at all prices, raising no danger of discontinuities. More importantly, irreducibility excludes that some consumer can only supply factors in so abundant supply that their marginal product is zero; so it implies that the marginal product of labour can be very low but never zero, there is always something a person can do which is useful to someone else.

It seems possible to conclude that the zero-income problem is not a serious problem for the theory. But the same cannot be argued for the survival problem, to which we must now return.

6.7 Continuity: Survival Again and Subsistence

The three possible assumptions that surmount the zero-income problem do not avoid the survival problem: they ensure that the income of each consumer will not be zero, but not that it will be sufficient for survival.

On the other hand, the assumption that each consumer has an endowment sufficient for survival does not suffice to avoid discontinuities, because another form of the zero-income problem, again a discontinuity of demand when a price becomes zero, can arise.

Consider a consumer with strongly monotonic preferences, who has an endowment of two units of good 1 and one unit of good 2 and needs one unit of both goods for survival. ◘ Figure 6.7 shows the consumption set defined as

6.7 · Continuity: Survival Again and Subsistence

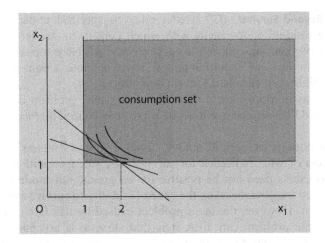

Fig. 6.7 Consumption set of a consumer with monotonic utility who needs 1 unit of both goods for survival, and has 2 units of good 1 and 1 unit of good 2 as endowment. As the price of good 1 decreases and becomes zero the demand for good 1 jumps discontinuously to + infinity

excluding non-survival baskets and the endowment $\omega = (2, 1)$ of the representative consumer. At any positive p_1/p_2 the consumer demands possibly less but never more than two units of good 1 because that would mean to consume less than one unit of good 2; when $p_1 = 0$ she jumps to demanding an infinite amount of good 1.

Note that monotonic preferences are not sufficient to avoid this problem, unless there are consumers who have an income in excess of what they need for survival and therefore can have a demand for good 1 in excess of their subsistence needs when p_1 approaches zero.

So some assumption ensuring no discontinuity at a zero price is needed in addition to something guaranteeing survival. There is no possibility here to illustrate the details of the literature on this issue (see Bryant 2010, ▶ Chap. 2), but it seems possible to say that, apart from a blunt assumption that each consumer's income is always above what is needed to purchase a survival level of consumption but without indication of what is required to ensure this, the two assumptions which surmount this more general minimum-income problem are as follows:

Interiority Beyond Survival (B′) Each consumer has an endowment where *all* goods are *in excess of* survival needs[10]; this guarantees that the consumer, after setting aside enough of her endowment to ensure survival, remains with a strictly positive residual endowment of all goods and is therefore in the same condition relative to market interactions as she would be under condition B if she had zero survival needs;

---

10 The survival assumption on the contrary only requires that the endowment be *sufficient* for subsistence needs. Assumption B, which is for example what is assumed by Arrow and Debreu (1954).

Irreducibility Beyond Survival (C′) Irreducibility as specified under condition C holds for the residual endowments with which consumers are left after setting aside enough of their endowments to ensure survival. Here too, consumers are assumed to be in the same condition relative to market interactions as they would be under condition C if they had zero survival needs.

How these assumptions avoid the minimum-income problem pointed out in ◖ Fig. 6.7 should be clear on the basis of what we have seen *à propos* the zero-income problem.

It will be noted that both B′ and C′ assume that consumers have endowments in excess of what is needed for survival, the sole gain with C′ relative to B′ is that this excess need not be positive for *all* goods. But modern economies are characterized by *specialization*, the general inability to survive with only one's own endowment. However, the main problem caused by this fact is not that the minimum-income problem can arise, it is that survival is not guaranteed, and this can cause *significant* discontinuities of excess demands, because it is highly likely that many consumers will have a discontinuity pretty much at the same relative prices, as noted in ▶ Sect. 4.15 for the labour supply curve.[11] It is possible now to be a bit more explicit on this issue. In modern market economies generally there is no risk of physical survival owing to starvation,[12] but the main reason why the notion of survival is important—as an indicator of conditions without which a person cannot participate in social life—is taken over by what the classical authors called *subsistence*: that is, the living standard, a fall below which is rendered unbearable by custom and social habits. As already suggested in ▶ Sect. 4.15, a discontinuity in the supply of labour can arise, not because of starvation, but because of a refusal to continue to supply labour and a preference for non-market choices such as crime or begging or—as shown by several historical examples—protests, riots, mobs, attacks on the property of the rich, armed rebellions and guerrilla activities. So one can speak more generally of a *survival/subsistence discontinuity problem* of the labour supply curve, but then also of consumer demands since incomes discontinuously change. This possibility is not contemplated in the usual formalization of consumer choices, but only because, with unclear legitimacy, attention is restricted only to situations in which markets work nicely and cause no social disruptions. The question however is, when is such an assumption of smooth working of markets legitimate? Clearly, not for very considerable falls in the income of large sections of the population. Wage labourers come to mind first, but other social groups too must not be neglected; a great fall in the incomes of dominant strata or of the middle class has often resulted in support for military coups and dictatorships. Anyway it seems clear that the neoclassical picture of a wage changing smoothly in response to excess demand for labour will be inapplicable if the danger of social disruptions is not remote: market societies develop institutions to avoid social problems for events of much smaller import, e.g. overproduction of agricultural

---

11 The same might happen for similar small farmers.
12 Medical assistance, however, can be at risk.

6.7 · Continuity: Survival Again and Subsistence

products; it is obvious that institutions, conventions and social mechanisms must be expected to exist to regulate labour markets in a way different from the one imagined by neoclassical theory, if disasters such as wage reductions bringing half the population below minimally decent living standards can be produced by the working of markets.

It seems clear, then, that a necessary condition for general equilibrium theory, in whichever formulation, to be a plausible description of real economies is that the equilibrium real wage must be above the minimum level felt by general consent to be necessary in order not to cause generalized disruptive behaviour. But the theory offers no reason to expect such a condition to be always satisfied. This indicates a considerable lack of generality of the theory.

This lack of generality does not seem to exist for the classical approach to wages, which took the existence of social conventions, custom, political pressures, etc., regulating wages for granted, as we saw in ▶ Chap. 1. This gives us a first reason to consider with attention the classical approach, whose different explanation of the real wage appears not to suffer from the lack of generality that seems inherent in a supply-and-demand explanation of wages.

After this discussion of aspects too often neglected in the usual introductions to the theory of general equilibrium, let us return to presenting this theory in standard form.

6.8 Existence of General Equilibrium of Exchange: A Simple New Proof

We have already seen (▶ Sect. 4.7) that in the case of only two commodities at least one equilibrium certainly exists if:

1. $z(p)$ is a continuous function on the interior of the price simplex $S^{n-1} := \{p \in R^n_+ : \Sigma_i p_i = 1\}$,
2. some $z_i(p) \to +\infty$ when some $p_j \to 0$, where it can be but it need not be $i=j$.

The proof that an equilibrium exists for a higher (but finite) number of commodities can be obtained, but the less restrictive the assumptions, the longer the proof and the more complex the mathematical tools. To go over the several possible proofs at different degrees of generality and with different methods would take an entire book. I present one very simple proof under restrictive assumptions and a less simple one to get a feeling of the kind of proof methods used in this area.

In all existence proofs it is assumed that *of all goods of which a price is quoted there is a positive aggregate endowment.*[13]

The first proof is, to the best of my knowledge, new; it is very elementary mathematically, it extends to many commodities the proof method used in

---

13 This assumption appears acceptable because it would become soon clear that there is no endowment of the good and then people would give up trying to obtain it. As long as they keep demanding the good there cannot be equilibrium because there will be excess supply of at least one of the other goods.

464 Chapter 6 · Existence, Uniqueness and Stability of Non-capitalistic General Equilibria

▶ Sect. 4.7 for the two-commodities exchange economy with strongly monotonic preferences, but it needs an additional assumption, Assumption 2 in the following theorem:

▪▪ Theorem 6.1

Consider an exchange economy with n goods where the consumption sets coincide with R_+^n (there is no minimum subsistence basket), and market excess demand is a continuous function on the interior of the price simplex; assume:

- *Assumption 1: Property 6 of $z(p)$ is satisfied, i.e. if some price tends to zero, the excess demand for some good tends continuously to $+\infty$;*
- *Assumption 2: having put the sum of prices equal to $+1$, for any good if its price tends to $+1$ then its excess demand sooner or later becomes and stays negative (before becoming zero owing to Walras' Law when the price becomes exactly $+1$). Then this economy has an equilibrium.*

Proof We can restrict the analysis to $\mathbf{p} \gg \mathbf{0}$ owing to Assumption 1. Start with any $\mathbf{p} \gg \mathbf{0}$, keep fixed the first $n-1$ prices so their ratios do not change: $p_2 = a_2 p_1$, $p_3 = a_3 p_1$, ..., $p_{n-1} = a_{n-1} p_1$, with $a_2, ..., a_{n-1}$ the initial ratios, $p_1 > 0$ by assumption; now reduce p_n; $\mathbf{z}(\mathbf{p})$ becomes a function of $\mathbf{p}_n$ alone. Owing to the budget constraints, if a convergent sequence $\{\mathbf{p}^t\}$ tends to the frontier of the unit simplex, the goods whose excess demands (by Assumption 1) tend to $+\infty$ can only be goods whose price is tending to zero; this is because, if without loss of generality we let $j = 1, ..., k$ be the indices of the goods whose price p_j tends to a limit p_j^* different from zero, then the excess demand for any one of these goods is eventually[14] bounded above, for example, by the value $\sum_{i=1}^n \frac{\omega_i}{2p_j^*}$. Therefore, if we let p_n tend to zero, since p_n is the sole price tending to zero, for p_n sufficiently close to zero it is $z_n(\mathbf{p}) > 0$. Now let $\mathbf{p}_n$ tend to 1: by Assumption 2, there is a $\mathbf{p}_n < 1$ such that $z_n(\mathbf{p}) < 0$. Therefore the sign of $z_n(\mathbf{p})$ changes in the open interval $p_n = (0, 1)$ and, since $\mathbf{z}(\mathbf{p})$ is continuous, there is a p_n^* such that $z_n(\mathbf{p}) = 0$. This is true for any ratios between the first $n-1$ prices. Now, p_n^* may not be unique; in this case, choose as p_n^* the smallest $p_n > 0$ for which z_n is zero. Clearly, p_n^* is a function of $a_2, ..., a_{n-1}$, implicitly defined by the system of two equations $\Sigma p_i = 1$, $z_n(p_1, a_2 p_1, a_3 p_1, ..., a_{n-1} p_1, \ p_n) = 0$; since both equations are continuous, by the implicit function theorem p_n^* is a continuous function of $a_2, ..., a_{n-1}$.

Now maintain fixed only the first $n-2$ prices and hence the ratios $a_2, ..., a_{n-2}$ and let p_{n-1} vary, but obliging p_n to vary at the same time in such a way as to maintain $z_n(\mathbf{p}) = 0$. Call p_n^* the value of p_n that maintains $z_n = 0$. I have shown that this is possible, with p_n^* so determined being a continuous function of $a_{n-1} = p_{n-1}/p_1$. As p_{n-1}/p_1 tends to zero, p_{n-1} tends to zero too; by Assumption 1 some excess demand tends to $+\infty$ and it must be z_{n-1}, because either p_{n-1} is the sole price tending to zero, or p_n tends to zero too but z_n does not tend to $+\infty$

---

14 I translate as 'eventually' the useful Italian mathematical term 'definitivamente' which means that there exists an n* such that a property is valid for all elements of a sequence $\{x^n\}$ with $n > n^*$.

6.8 · Existence of General Equilibrium of Exchange: A Simple New Proof.

because it is zero. By Assumption 2, for values of p_{n-1} sufficiently close to 1 it is $z_{n-1}(\mathbf{p}) < 0$. So $z_{n-1}(\mathbf{p})$ changes sign in the open interval $p_{n-1} = (0, 1)$ and therefore there exist positive values of p_{n-1} and $p_n{}^*$ such that simultaneously $z_{n-1} = 0$ and $z_n = 0$. If the value $p_{n-1}{}^*$ so determined is not unique, choose its smallest value. For the same reason as before, these values $p_{n-1}{}^*$ and $p_n{}^*$ are continuous functions of the ratios between the prices of the first n – 2 goods.

We can apply the same reasoning to p_{n-2}, assuming fixed the first n – 3 prices, and varying p_{n-2} imposing that p_{n-1} and p_n vary at the same time so as to maintain $z_n(\mathbf{p}) = 0$ and $z_{n-1}(\mathbf{p}) = 0$; again we can show that for any given ratios between the positive prices of the first n – 3 goods there exist positive prices p_n, p_{n-1}, and p_{n-2}, such that $z_{n-2} = z_{n-1} = z_n = 0$. Repeating the reasoning, one concludes that there exist relative prices p_n/p_1, $p_{n-1}/p_1,...,p_2/p_1$, all positive, that render the last n – 1 excess demands simultaneously equal to zero, and then by Walras' Law it is also $z_1(\mathbf{p}) = 0$, so there exists an equilibrium. ■

As shown above (Property 6), Assumption 1 is verified if, for all consumers, preferences are complete, transitive, continuous, strictly convex over a choice set (the budget set) which is compact and convex, and strongly monotonic (this of course implies local non-satiation). Assumption 2 appears plausible, but it is not completely clear yet which assumptions on preferences and endowments imply it (one assumption that implies it is interiority of endowments, see the online appendix to the chapter).

6.9 Brouwer's Fixed-Point Theorem

The next proof introduces to the use of fixed-point theorems, the common procedure in the proofs of existence of general equilibrium.

The method is to build an opportune continuous application $g(\mathbf{p})$, from the price simplex S^{n-1} to the same simplex, which is connected to excess demands in such a way that if a $\mathbf{p}^*$ exists such that $g(\mathbf{p}^*) = \mathbf{p}^*$, then the excess demands are all non-positive (and all zero, if $\mathbf{p}^* \gg 0$) and therefore $\mathbf{p}^*$ is an equilibrium price vector; and then to apply a fixed-point theorem to prove that at least one $\mathbf{p}^*$ exists such that $g(\mathbf{p}^*) = \mathbf{p}^*$.

I will need the following theorem.

■■ Generalized Brouwer's Theorem
Let $A \subset R^n$ be a non-empty, compact and convex set and let f: $A \to A$ be a continuous function. Then f has a fixed point $\mathbf{x} = f(\mathbf{x})$.

◼ Figure 6.8 shows a graphical illustration of the theorem for the one-dimensional case f: $[0, 1] \to [0, 1]$: any continuous function must touch the diagonal at least in one point. The theorem implies that any *continuous* deformation of a disc of pizza dough into a disc of same shape, or any continuous remixing of a liquid in a bowl, leaves at least one point in the initial position (in real-life examples this does not happen with molecules, which are not infinitely small).

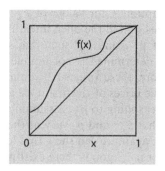

◘ **Fig. 6.8** Graphical illustration of Brouwer's theorem

6.10 Existence of Exchange Equilibrium with Strongly Monotonic Preferences

Now a less simple proof of existence of equilibrium, for an exchange economy with *strongly monotonic preferences*: now **z(p)** is not defined on the boundary of the price simplex, but for the existence of equilibrium this is not a problem because no equilibrium price vector can be on the boundary, if a price is zero demand for that good is infinite. The survival problem is not considered; the way to avoid the zero-income discontinuity problem is solution A. The method of proof adopted here is taken from Jehle and Reny (2011), and it makes use of Brouwer's fixed-point theorem.

▪▪ Theorem 6.2
(Existence of general equilibrium of exchange with strongly monotonic preferences) *Suppose* **z**: $R^n_{++} \to R^n$ *satisfies the following three conditions:*
1. $\mathbf{z}(\cdot)$ *is continuous on* R^n_{++}
2. $\mathbf{p} \cdot \mathbf{z}(\mathbf{p}) = 0$ *for all* $\mathbf{p} \gg 0$
3. *If* $\{\mathbf{p}^t\}$ *is a sequence of price vectors in* R^n_{++} *converging to* $\mathbf{p}^{\wedge} \neq 0$ *but with* $p^{\wedge}_k = 0$ *for some good k, then for some good k' with* $p^{\wedge}_{k'} = 0$ *(possibly k' = k) the associated sequence of excess demands in the market for good k', $\{z_{k'}(\mathbf{p}^t)\}$, is unbounded above.*

Then there is a price vector $\mathbf{p}^* \gg 0$ *such that* $\mathbf{z}(\mathbf{p}^*) = 0$.

(Comment: These are the relevant assumptions; the hypotheses on preferences are only relevant in so far as they justify these assumptions, e.g. strict convexity of preferences is required for **z(p)** to be a function, not a correspondence, and continuous, strongly monotonic preferences has the role of ensuring Assumption 3.[15]

---

[15] This was shown above as Property 6: strong monotonicity of preferences implies that, if some price tends to zero, $\|\mathbf{z}(\mathbf{p})\| \to +\infty$, which is equivalent to Max $(z_1(\mathbf{p}),\ldots,z_n(\mathbf{p})) \to +\infty$.

6.10 · Existence of Exchange Equilibrium with Strongly Monotonic Preferences

It is implicitly assumed—and it will be important in the proof—that *excess demand is bounded below* by the given endowments of consumers; note that when goods are distinguished according to date of delivery and it is possible to buy and sell today future goods, the possibility must be considered of a consumer *short-selling* goods forward, that is, selling a good for delivery in a future period in a quantity in excess of her endowment of that good in that period, so she will have to buy the good when the moment of delivery arrives; then unless some bound is imposed on the amount of short-selling, excess demand is not bounded below, and existence proofs—in order to be possible—will need different assumptions and tools.)

Proof Condition 3 implies that equilibrium is impossible unless the equilibrium price vector is strictly positive; this explains the insistence on $\mathbf{p} \in R^n_{++}$. (It also excludes the *minimum-income problem*, but I leave it to the reader to understand why.)

For each good k, define a 'bounded excess demand function' $z^\wedge_k(\mathbf{p}) = \min (z_k(\mathbf{p}), 1)$ for all $\mathbf{p} \gg 0$, and let $\mathbf{z}^\wedge(\mathbf{p})$ be the vector of these modified excess demands, which are bounded above by 1.

Choose a scalar $\varepsilon \in (0, 1)$ and define the following subset of the unit simplex:

$$S_\varepsilon = \left\{ \mathbf{p} : \sum_{k=1}^n p_k = 1 \text{ and for all } k, p_k \geq \varepsilon/(1 + 2n) \right\}$$

This leaves out of the unit simplex all points where at least one price is less than $\varepsilon/(1 + 2n)$, e.g. with three prices, it leaves out a 'strip' at the edges of the simplex triangle, which can be made narrower by reducing ε; see ❏ Fig. 6.9.

S_ε is closed and bounded, hence compact; it is clearly convex (easy to verify); it is non-empty because for example the price vector with all prices equal to 1/n is always a member since $\varepsilon/(1 + 2n) < 1/(1 + 2n) < 1/n$. So it satisfies the assumptions needed for a continuous function from S_ε to S_ε to have a fixed point by Brouwer's theorem.

Define then for each $k = 1,\dots,n$ and every $\mathbf{p} \in S_\varepsilon$ the function $f_k(\mathbf{p})$ as follows:

$$f_k(\mathbf{p}) = \left[\varepsilon + p_k + \max\left(0, z^\wedge_k(\mathbf{p})\right) \right] / \left[n\varepsilon + 1 + \sum_{m=1}^n \max\left(0, z^\wedge_m(\mathbf{p})\right) \right]. \tag{6.3}$$

Let $f(\mathbf{p})$ be the vector function $(f_1(\mathbf{p}),\dots,f_k(\mathbf{p}),\dots,f_n(\mathbf{p}))$. Note that $\sum_{k=1}^n f_k(\mathbf{p}) = 1$, and that $f_k(\mathbf{p}) \geq \varepsilon/(n\varepsilon + 1 + n) > \varepsilon/(1 + 2n)$, because the numerator of $f_k(\mathbf{p})$ is not less than ε (it equals ε if $p_k = 0$ and $z_k(\mathbf{p}) \leq 0$), and the denominator is not more than $n\varepsilon + 1 + n$ since $z^\wedge_m(\mathbf{p}) \leq 1$. Therefore each $f(\mathbf{p})$ can be interpreted as a price vector $\in S_\varepsilon$, that is, $f(\mathbf{p})$ transforms each $\mathbf{p} \in S_\varepsilon$ into another $\mathbf{p} \in S_\varepsilon$. We need to only prove that it is a continuous function and we will be able to apply Brouwer's theorem. And indeed $f(\mathbf{p})$ is continuous because by assumption $z(\cdot)$ is continuous and hence $z^\wedge_k(\mathbf{p})$ is continuous, so both numerator and denominator are continuous, and the denominator is never zero since it is ≥ 1.

Therefore $f(\cdot)$ is a continuous function from a compact convex non-empty set into itself and by Brouwer's theorem it has at least one fixed point, that we can indicate as $\mathbf{p}^\varepsilon = f(\mathbf{p}^\varepsilon)$, to stress it depends on ε.

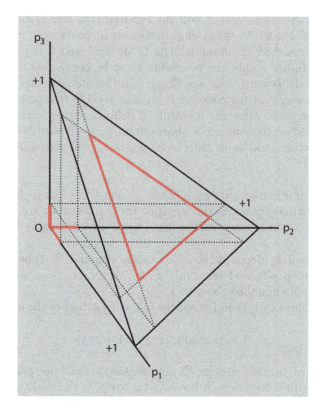

Fig. 6.9 Restricted price simplex with three goods. The red segments next to the origin have length $\varepsilon/(1+2n)$

Now note that $f_k(p^\varepsilon) = p^\varepsilon_k$ can be rewritten, using (6.3), as follows:

$$p^\varepsilon_k \cdot \left[n\varepsilon + 1 + \sum_{m=1}^{n} \max\left(0, z^\wedge_m(\mathbf{p})\right)\right] = \varepsilon + p^\varepsilon_k + \max\left(0, z^\wedge_k(\mathbf{p})\right).$$

Subtracting p^ε_k from both sides we obtain that for any k:

$$p^\varepsilon_k \cdot \left[n\varepsilon + \sum_{m=1}^{n} \max\left(0, z^\wedge_m(\mathbf{p})\right)\right] = \varepsilon + \max\left(0, z^\wedge_k(\mathbf{p})\right). \tag{6.4}$$

Now consider a sequence $\{\varepsilon^t\}$, with t numbering the elements of the sequence, that tends to $\varepsilon = 0$, and the associated price sequence $\{\mathbf{p}^{\varepsilon t}\}$, that satisfies (6.4). This price sequence is bounded, because $\mathbf{p}^\varepsilon \in S_\varepsilon$ implies p^ε_k lies between 0 and 1. Every bounded sequence has a convergent subsequence, hence there is a subsequence $\{\mathbf{p}^{\varepsilon\tau}\}$ that converges, let us indicate as $\mathbf{p}^*$ the price vector to which it converges.

Note that $\mathbf{p}^*$ cannot have some $p^*_k = 0$, because if it did, $\{p^\varepsilon_k{}^\tau\}$ would be tending to zero; then by Assumption 3 in the theorem there would be some good k′ with $p^*_{k'} = 0$ such that $z_{k'}(\mathbf{p}^{\varepsilon\tau})$ is unbounded above. This is incompatible with (6.4) applied to good k′, because the left-hand side would tend to zero as $\{\mathbf{p}^\varepsilon_{k'}{}^\tau\}$ tends

6.10 · Existence of Exchange Equilibrium with Strongly Monotonic Preferences

to zero, since max $(0, z^\wedge_m(\mathbf{p})) \leq 1$ by the definition of $z^\wedge_m(\mathbf{p})$, while the right-hand side would not tend to zero as $z^\wedge_{k'}(\mathbf{p}^\tau)$ would take value $+1$ for all τ's for which $z_{k'}(\mathbf{p}^\tau) > 1$, which would never stop happening. Hence $\mathbf{p}^* \gg 0$.

Since $z^\wedge(\cdot)$ inherits continuity on $\mathbf{R}^n_{++}$ from $z(\cdot)$, we can take the limit in (6.4) as ε tends to zero along subsequence τ, obtaining for any k:

$$p^*_k \cdot \sum\nolimits^n_{m=1} \max\left(0, z^\wedge_m(\mathbf{p}^*)\right) = \max\left(0, z^\wedge_k(\mathbf{p}^*)\right).$$

Multiply both sides by $z_k(\mathbf{p}^*)$, and sum over k to obtain:

$$\mathbf{p}^* \cdot \mathbf{z}(\mathbf{p}^*) \cdot \sum\nolimits^n_{m=1} \max\left(0, z^\wedge_m(\mathbf{p}^*)\right) = \sum\nolimits^n_{k=1} z_k(\mathbf{p}^*) \max\left(0, z^\wedge_k(\mathbf{p}^*)\right). \qquad (6.5)$$

By Walras' Law, $\mathbf{p}^* \cdot \mathbf{z}(\mathbf{p}^*) = 0$, hence the left-hand side of (6.5) is zero, but then the right-hand side must be zero too. Now, $z^\wedge_k(\mathbf{p}^*)$ has the same sign as $z_k(\mathbf{p}^*)$, therefore on the right-hand side the kth term of the sum is zero if $z_k(\mathbf{p}^*) \leq 0$, and positive if $z_k(\mathbf{p}^*) > 0$, so the sum is positive unless $z_k(\mathbf{p}^*) \leq 0$ for all k. So no excess demand can be positive, but none can be negative either, because then, prices being all positive, $\mathbf{p}^* \cdot \mathbf{z}(\mathbf{p}^*)$ would be negative contradicting Walras' Law. So it must be $z_k(\mathbf{p}^*) = 0$, for all k. Hence $\mathbf{p}^*$ is an equilibrium price vector: an equilibrium exists. ∎

Exercise Produce an example of non-existence of equilibrium when only condition 3 of Theorem 6.2 is not satisfied.

6.11 Uniqueness: The Non-uniqueness of Equilibrium in General. Possibility of Several Locally Stable Equilibria

An equilibrium is composed of two 'things', an equilibrium allocation and an equilibrium *relative* prices vector. An equilibrium is unique if both the equilibrium allocation and the equilibrium relative prices vector are unique. (Below I take it for granted that a numéraire has been chosen, so 'different price vectors' means non-proportional price vectors.) A unique equilibrium allocation may be supported by more than one relative prices vector, when indifference curves or isoquants have 'kinks' at the equilibrium allocation, such that—within limits— variations of relative prices or of relative factor rentals do not induce changes in the agents' decisions. But the more relevant cases are those of multiple equilibria differing in the equilibrium allocation.

Uniqueness of equilibrium requires restrictive assumptions, without which it is easy to produce examples with multiple equilibria. For example it is not difficult to draw an Edgeworth box with three equilibria, that is, three points other than the endowment point where the two choice curves cross, owing to the possible horseshoe-like shape of choice curves. The reader can try as an exercise to confirm, by drawing opportune maps of indifference curves that the choice curves can indeed have the shapes assumed in ◘ Fig. 6.10.

In ◘ Fig. 6.10 the three slopes of the budget line that cause it to go through a point where the choice curves cross indicate the three equilibrium relative prices.

It is also possible that the two choice curves be tangent to each other, in the endowment point or elsewhere, cf. ◘ Fig. 6.11; or that the two choice curves overlap over an entire stretch (cf. ◘ Fig. 6.15), in which case there is a *continuum* of equilibria differing in relative price and in allocation—but these two cases are flukes that disappear with any small change in tastes or endowments.

The figures show that in a two-goods economy, if the choice curves cross each other three times, the equilibria are alternatively locally stable or unstable. We can be content here with a simple intuitive description of the price adjustment process: *a price tends to rise if a good is in excess demand, to decrease if in excess supply*. This formulation is actually ambiguous in the general case, because

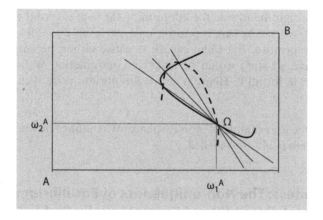

◘ **Fig. 6.10** Three equilibria in the Edgeworth box. Consumer A's choice curve is the thick continuous line, and consumer B's choice curve is the thick broken line

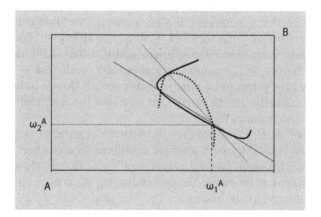

◘ **Fig. 6.11** Case of tangent choice curves causing an even number of equilibria. Consumer A's choice curve is the thick continuous line, and consumer B's choice curve is the thick broken line

6.11 · Uniqueness: The Non-uniqueness of Equilibrium in General...

what is relevant to equilibrium is *relative* prices, and what is happening to relative prices is not made clear by this formulation. But in the two-goods Edgeworth box no ambiguity arises, because if the budget line causes one good to be in excess demand then the other good is in excess supply. Turning then to the Edgeworth box of ◘ Fig. 6.10, it is easy to check that the central equilibrium is such that for a relative price a little different from the equilibrium relative price, the excess demands are such as to push the relative price *further away* from the equilibrium relative price, while the opposite is true for the other two equilibria. We see therefore that there can be more than one *locally stable equilibria*, i.e. equilibria such that the forces of demand and supply push the economy towards one or another of them depending on where relative prices start from.[16] Each locally stable equilibrium has an 'area of attraction', i.e. an open set of relative prices such that if initially prices are in that set, they tend to that equilibrium, but if they are outside that set, they do not.

Exercise Draw a square Edgeworth box with sides six units long. Both consumers have perfect-complement preferences; consumer A demands two units of good 1 for each unit of good 2; consumer B demands two units of good 2 for each unit of good 1. A's endowment is (5, 1). Show that there are three equilibria, of which the interior one is unstable.

The possibility of multiple locally stable equilibria questions not only the capacity of the theory unambiguously to indicate the result of a change in one of the equilibrium's data, but also the plausibility itself of the theory. If the equilibria are close to each other, the economy might move from one to the other simply because of transitory accidents which cause the economy to be pushed temporarily into disequilibrium. This does not seem to correspond to observations.

6.12 Uniqueness: Regular Economies

A particularly bad case for the theory would be a *continuum* of equilibrium allocations and of associated equilibrium prices, because then the indeterminateness of the equilibrium would be total within that continuum. Theorists have explored the likelihood of a continuum of exchange equilibria, and the following result has been proved. In the theorem below, $\partial z(\mathbf{p})$ is the Jacobian matrix of the market excess demand function $\mathbf{z}(\mathbf{p})$, with elements $\partial z_{ij} \equiv \partial z_i(\mathbf{p})/\partial p_j$; and an equilibrium price vector $\mathbf{p}$ normalized in the unit simplex is **locally isolated** (or **locally unique**) if there is no other equilibrium price vector in a sufficiently small neighbourhood of that equilibrium price vector.

---

16 This definition of local stability is based on the idea that when excess demand is positive (negative) for a good, the good's price tends to rise (to decrease). Later in the chapter we will be more precise on the adjustment mechanism.

472   **Chapter 6** · Existence, Uniqueness and Stability of Non-capitalistic General Equilibria

▪▪ Theorem 6.3

(Regular economies imply a finite number of equilibria) *Assume that the economy is one where each consumer's preferences are continuous, strictly convex and strongly monotonic and where the market excess demand function* $\mathbf{z}(\mathbf{p})$ *is continuously differentiable on* R^n_{++}. *Define* **regular** *this economy if its Jacobian matrix* $\partial\mathbf{z}(\mathbf{p})$ *has rank* $n-1$ *at all equilibrium price vectors. For every regular economy the equilibrium price vectors* (*normalized in the unit simplex*) *are finite in number and hence locally isolated.*

Proof I only give an intuitive proof. Note that $n-1$ is the maximal rank of the Jacobian matrix of $\mathbf{z}(\mathbf{p})$, because from the homogeneity of $\mathbf{z}(\mathbf{p})$, differentiating both sides of the equality $\mathbf{z}(t\mathbf{p}) = \mathbf{z}(\mathbf{p})$ with respect to t we obtain $\partial\mathbf{z}(t\mathbf{p})\mathbf{p}^T = \mathbf{0}$ and if we perform this calculation in $t = 1$ we obtain $\partial\mathbf{z}(\mathbf{p})\mathbf{p}^T = \mathbf{0}$; so $\partial\mathbf{z}(\mathbf{p})$ is always singular. The relevant property is that if the aggregate demand vector is considered a function of *relative* prices, then its $(n-1) \times (n-1)$ Jacobian matrix must be of full rank at all equilibrium relative price vectors. The interpretation of this condition is as follows. Put $p_n = 1$ (we have the right to choose a numéraire because we are only interested in strictly positive price vectors[17]), consider the aggregate demand vector a function of the first $n-1$ prices, $\mathbf{z} = \mathbf{z}^{\wedge}(\mathbf{p}^{\wedge})$ where $\mathbf{p}^{\wedge} = (p_1, \ldots, p_{n-1})$, and let $\partial\mathbf{z}^{\wedge}(\mathbf{p}^{\wedge})$ be its Jacobian matrix; if $\mathbf{p}^{\wedge *}$ completed with $p_n = 1$ is an equilibrium relative price vector, and if $\partial\mathbf{z}^{\wedge}(\mathbf{p}^{\wedge *})$ is of full rank, then there is no nonzero vector of variations of relative prices $d\mathbf{p}^{\wedge}$ such that $\partial\mathbf{z}^{\wedge}(\mathbf{p}^{\wedge *}) \cdot d\mathbf{p}^{\wedge} = 0$. Thus any infinitesimal change of $\mathbf{p}^{\wedge}$ causes the economy no longer to be in equilibrium; each equilibrium relative price vector is locally isolated. Hence the set of equilibrium relative price vectors is countable, and so is also the set of equilibrium price vectors normalized in the unit simplex. Because of Property 6 of $\mathbf{z}(\mathbf{p})$, equilibrium price vectors are bounded away from zero, so, going back to prices normalized in the unit simplex, there is a scalar s such that if $\mathbf{z}(\mathbf{p}) = 0$, then for all p_i it is $p_i > s$; therefore there is a closed (and obviously bounded) subset of the unit simplex $\{\mathbf{p} \in R^n_{++}: \Sigma_i p_i = 1 \text{ and } p_i \geq s \text{ for all } i = 1,\ldots,n\}$ that contains all equilibrium price vectors. A countable set of points of a closed and bounded (i.e. compact) subset of R^n is finite unless it has some accumulation point; but an accumulation point of equilibrium price vectors would have to be itself an equilibrium price vector by the continuity of $\mathbf{z}(\mathbf{p})$, and this would contradict the local uniqueness of each equilibrium. ▪

In the case of two goods for example (see ▶ Sect. 4.7), the rank of the Jacobian matrix is non-maximal, i.e. zero if at a point where $\mathbf{z}(\mathbf{p}) = \mathbf{0}$ it is $\partial z_1(\mathbf{p})/\partial p_1 = 0$, cf. points A and B in ◨ Fig. 6.12.

---

17 Nothing would change with a different normalization; in particular, if $\partial\mathbf{z}(\mathbf{p})$ is of rank $n-1$, then whichever the chosen numéraire that renders aggregate demand a function of $n-1$ relative prices the corresponding Jacobian will also be of rank $n-1$, and the sign of its determinant is independent of the numéraire chosen.

6.12 · Uniqueness: Regular Economies

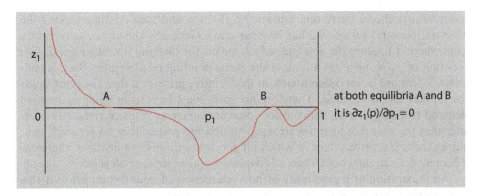

Fig. 6.12 Excess demand in a non-regular two-goods economy with $p_1 + p_2 = 1$

The above result has been greeted with great interest because of the following *Fundamental Property of Regular Economies* (which is intuitive enough to allow us to dispense with proving it): *if under the assumptions of Theorem 6.3 an economy is not regular, then by an arbitrarily small change in initial endowments, keeping preferences fixed, with probability 1 we obtain a regular economy* (see Hildenbrand and Kirman 1988, p. 223).

Therefore regular economies are the *generic* case among economies with continuously differentiable $z(p)$ (where a property is *generic* on a set if the property holds for 'almost all' the elements of the set, i.e. for all elements of the set except at most a subset of Lebesgue measure zero, so that, if an element in the set is selected at random according to a non-atomic probability distribution, the probability of selecting an element for which the property does *not* hold is zero). Hence, it is argued, the probability of encountering a non-regular economy among the economies with continuously differentiable $z(p)$ is zero.

Theorem 6.3, in view of the genericity of regular economies (among exchange economies with continuously differentiable excess demands), is interpreted to mean that there is no need to worry about the strong indeterminacy associated with a *continuum* of equilibria actually occurring.

But there are three reasons why the relevance of the result is actually very small. First, regular economies can well have *practically indeterminate* equilibria, which as noted in ▶ Chap. 3 are surrounded by a price neighbourhood in which the forces tending to change prices are so weak that practically it is as if the economy were in equilibrium.

Second, exchange economies very seldom have continuously differentiable $z(p)$ and therefore are very seldom regular. Differentiability of $z(p)$ requires that *for each consumer the goods in positive demand are the same at all prices*, that is, it must never happen that demand for a good is positive at some prices and zero at other prices. This seldom stressed implication derives from the fact that, except for flukes, differentiability of $z(p)$ fails at a price at which demand for a good becomes zero. This is easy to see with two goods. Suppose the consumer's convex indifference curves touch the axes, and as relative price decreases the

474   **Chapter 6** · Existence, Uniqueness and Stability of Non-capitalistic General Equilibria

(continuous) choice curve hits against the abscissa and then continues along the abscissa (demand for good 2 has become zero). Generally the choice curve has a kink where it touches the abscissa, which means the demand for either good, as a function of p_1/p_2, also has a kink at the corresponding relative price. So this consumer's demand is not differentiable at that relative price, and then the same holds for market excess demand. Therefore no good must pass from being in positive demand to being in zero demand for some consumer as its price rises. Note further that the theorem assumes strongly monotonic preferences, so for each consumer there is a price vector at which all goods are in positive demand; therefore Theorem 6.3 can only hold when *all consumers always demand all goods*.

An illustration of a possibility of non-uniqueness of equilibrium prices if this assumption is not made is in the chapter's online appendix.

Third, even granting the continuous differentiability of $\mathbf{z}(\mathbf{p})$, Theorem 6.3 only proves that the number of equilibria is finite. There might still be hundreds of equilibria, differing only by small differences in relative prices—nearly the same indeterminacy as with a continuum of equilibria. Can we exclude this possibility? Not without special assumptions, as shown by a famous result presented in the next section.

6.13 The Sonnenschein–Mantel–Debreu Result

It has been proved that there is no other property of the market excess demand function derivable from well-behaved[18] strictly convex preferences, except homogeneity of degree zero, continuity, Walras' Law and (if strong monotonicity is assumed) the boundary behaviour described in ▶ Sect. 6.2 as Property 6 of $\mathbf{z}(\mathbf{p})$. More precisely the result is the following:

▪▪ Theorem 6.4

(Sonnenschein–Mantel–Debreu) *Any function* $\mathbf{z}(\mathbf{p}) \in R^n$, *defined everywhere on a compact subset of the interior of the unit price simplex* S^{n-1} *(i.e. everywhere on* S^{n-1}, *except for a lower positive bound on each price which can be made as small as one likes), and with the properties of*
continuity on $S^{n-1} \times R^n_{++}$.

Walras's law: $pz(p) = 0, \forall p \in S^{n-1} \times R^n_{++}$
can be obtained.as the market excess demand function of an exchange economy with n goods and no less than n consumers with continuous, strictly convex and strongly monotonic preferences.

I omit the proof (cf. Hildenbrand and Kirman 1988; Shafer and Sonnenschein 1982; Mas-Colell et al. 1995 pp. 598–606). The name derives from having been proved first by Sonnenschein for a simple economy and then generalized more and more by the other two economists up to the final result.

---

18 I.e. complete, reflexive, transitive and continuous.

6.13 · The Sonnenschein–Mantel–Debreu Result

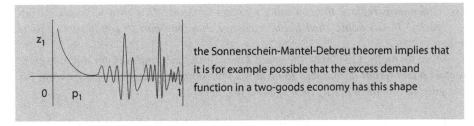

Fig. 6.13 Possible shape of excess demand as function of price

Thus if we neglect prices very close to zero, as long as consumers are at least as numerous as the number of goods there will always exist preferences and endowments generating any continuous market excess demand function we may choose. This means that it is possible for equilibria to be as many and as close to each other as we like. The risk of indeterminacy *is* therefore practically as high as with a continuum of equilibria (◘ Fig. 6.13).

One might hope that a very high number of equilibria are possible only if preferences and endowments are very peculiar, e.g. differing among consumers in special ways. But recent research has shown that even with consumers having (1) the same preferences, (2) co-linear endowments and (3) endowments differing in pre-assigned amounts, still the Sonnenschein–Mantel–Debreu result holds (Hildenbrand and Kirman 1988, p. 208).

6.14 Uniqueness Through Conditions on Excess Demand: Gross Substitutes

The Sonnenschein–Mantel–Debreu result has caused great discomfort among the followers of the supply-and-demand approach, because of the indeterminateness it shows to be possible in the results of the equilibration process. But the damage would be considerably reduced if assumptions could be found, capable of avoiding multiple equilibria, and such that one could argue that they are nearly always satisfied in actual economies. I proceed to list the main assumptions so far discovered that ensure (i.e. are sufficient for) uniqueness and then to assess their plausibility.

Two types of assumptions have been explored in this respect: assumptions on $z(p)$; and assumptions on *the distribution of characteristics (preferences and endowments) of consumers*. I list now the main results of the first type.

The oldest and most widely cited result is:

Proposition 6.5 (Gross substitutes) *Define the* **gross substitutes condition** *for consumers as follows: if the price of only one good varies, the consumer's excess demands for all other goods vary in the same direction, and this is true whichever the price that varies. The* **gross substitutes condition** *holds for the market excess demand function of an exchange economy if in the above definition the market*

476 Chapter 6 · Existence, Uniqueness and Stability of Non-capitalistic General Equilibria

*excess demands replace the consumer's excess demands. It is then indicated as **GS** for brevity. If GS holds, then if the exchange economy has an equilibrium, this is unique.*

More formally, GS states: *the goods are all gross substitutes if, for any two price vectors* **p** *and* **q** (***not*** *normalized to be in the unit simplex) such that* $p_i = q_i$ *except for one good, j, for which* $q_j > p_j$, *then* $z_i(\mathbf{q}) > z_i(\mathbf{p})$, $\forall i \ne j$.

The adjective 'gross' distinguishes this property from the usual, or Hicksian, definition of substitutes, which requires negative cross-derivatives of the *compensated* demand function.

In an exchange economy[19] $\mathbf{z}(\mathbf{p})$ is homogeneous of degree zero (because income derives from endowments); then GS implies that *the excess demand for a good decreases when its own price alone increases*: the reason is that, because of the homogeneity of degree zero of excess demands, the increase of the sole jth price has the same effect on excess demands as a decrease in the same proportion of all other prices; and if we keep the jth price constant and let the other prices decrease one at a time, GS implies that at each step the excess demand for the jth good decreases.

Another way to define GS, for differentiable excess demands, is that it must be $\partial z_i(\mathbf{p})/\partial p_j > 0$ if $i \ne j$. This again implies that the demand for a good decreases when the price of that good increases, because it implies $\partial z_j/\partial p_j < 0$: the proof is that the homogeneity of degree zero of excess demand functions and Euler's theorem on homogeneous functions imply $\sum_{i=1}^{n}(p_i \cdot \partial z_j/\partial p_i) = 0$, and all terms where $i \ne j$ are positive by assumption.

Proof of Proposition 6.5 This proof will be given here under the assumption of strongly monotonic preferences.[20] Let $\mathbf{p}^* \in S^{n-1}$ be an equilibrium price vector with $\{\mathbf{x}^{s*}\}$ the associated equilibrium allocation where $\mathbf{x}^{s*}$ is the vector of equilibrium demands of consumer s, $s = 1,...,S$ where S is the number of consumers. Let $\mathbf{p} \gg 0$, $\mathbf{p} \in S^{n-1}$ be another price vector; I want to show that it cannot be an equilibrium price vector. Since $\mathbf{p}^* \gg 0$ we can define $t = max_j \, p_j/p_j^* > 0$; suppose $t = p_i/p_i^*$. Consider the vector $t\mathbf{p}^*$; it is $tp_j^* \ge p_j$, with $tp_i^* = p_i$. Because of the homogeneity of $\mathbf{z}(\mathbf{p})$ it is $\mathbf{z}(t\mathbf{p}^*) = \mathbf{z}(\mathbf{p}^*) = 0$. Now in successive steps let us lower each price $tp_j^* \ne tp_i^*$ until it becomes equal to p_j. There is at least one such step, otherwise it would be $\mathbf{p} = \mathbf{p}^*$. At each step only one price decreases and GS implies that the excess demands for all other goods decrease, among them the

---

19 Or in the case of a consumer whose income derives from given endowments.

20 The general proof is based on the fact that *GS implies that in equilibrium* $\mathbf{p}^* \gg 0$ whether preferences are strongly monotonic or not; the proof of this result is complex and I omit it, and I stay content with obtaining $\mathbf{p}^* \gg 0$ from an assumption of strongly monotonic preferences. By the way, in ▶ Chap. 4 an intuitive proof was supplied that strongly monotonic preferences imply $\mathbf{p}^* \gg 0$, but I give here a simple rigorous proof. Suppose the contrary, i.e. that $\mathbf{p}^*$ contains a zero price, say p_k; let $\mathbf{e}_k$ be the k-th unit vector with as many elements as there are goods, $\mathbf{e}_k = (0,...,1,...0)^T$ with 1 in the k-th place; let $\mathbf{x}^{s*}$ and $\boldsymbol{\omega}^s$ represent the equilibrium demand vector and the endowment vector of consumer s; then $\mathbf{p}^*(\mathbf{x}^{s*} + \mathbf{e}_k) = \mathbf{p}^*\mathbf{x}^{s*} = \mathbf{p}^*\boldsymbol{\omega}^s$; thus consumer s can afford to demand vector $\mathbf{x}^{s*} + \mathbf{e}_k$, obtaining a higher utility than with $\mathbf{x}^{s*}$, against the hypothesis that at $\mathbf{p}^*$ the vector $\mathbf{x}^{s*}$ is an optimal choice. The contradiction shows that it cannot be that the equilibrium price vector contains a zero price.

6.14 · Uniqueness Through Conditions on Excess Demand: Gross Substitutes

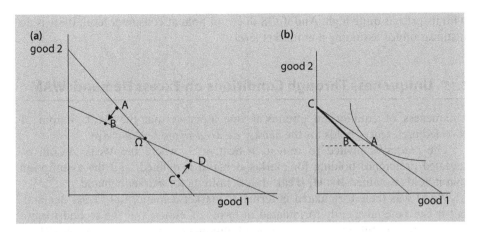

■ **Fig. 6.14** **a** Variations of the demand basket incompatible with GS. **b** where the endowment consists only of good 2, GS means that a rise in the price of good 1 must induce a rise in demand for good 2, i.e. the new choice must be on the BC segment

excess demand for good i which therefore becomes negative. When the equality to **p** has been achieved for all prices, it is $z_i(\mathbf{p}) < 0$ which is incompatible with equilibrium since $\mathbf{p} \gg 0$; hence **p** cannot be an equilibrium price vector. ■

GS is additive across excess demand functions; so if each consumer's excess demand function satisfies it, then the market excess demand function does as well; the proof is trivial, if as a price changes the sign of the change in individual excess demands for a good is the same for all individuals then the sign of the change of market excess demand for that good is the same.

The universal assessment of the GS assumption is that it is 'very restrictive' (Mas-Colell et al. 1995, p. 611) and rightly so. First, complementarity among goods is common and is incompatible with GS. Second, assume two goods and a consumer with strictly positive endowment of the two goods, point Ω in ■ Fig. 6.14a. Assume p_1/p_2 decreases and the consumer's choice changes from A to B: this is a violation of GS because the rotation of the budget line can be seen as caused by an increase of the sole price of good 2, in which case GS requires that the demand for good 1 increases. Analogously if the consumer's choices were C at the old prices and D at the new prices, this is a violation of GS because the rotation of the budget line can be seen as due to a decrease of the sole price of good 1, in which case GS requires that the demand for good 2 decreases. *For GS not to be violated, the choice curve of the consumer must be everywhere downward-sloping*, a most restrictive assumption.[21] In particular, when the consumer is a net supplier of a good, the likelihood that her demand for the good increases

---

21 There are two other conditions that ensure uniqueness, implied by GS but slightly more general: their names are diagonal dominance and negative definiteness, and they refer to properties of the Slutsky matrix. They will not be discussed here because they do not seem to have a meaningful economic interpretation when not associated with GS. Anyway they too, like GS, imply that choice curves are everywhere downward-sloping and are therefore very restrictive.

478   Chapter 6 · Existence, Uniqueness and Stability of Non-capitalistic General Equilibria

with its price is quite high. And if GS does not hold at consumer level, there is no justification for assuming it at market level.

6.15 Uniqueness Through Conditions on Excess Demand: WAM

Uniqueness of equilibrium obtains if one assumes that the Weak Axiom of revealed preferences holds for the *market excess demand function* $z(p)$.

The reader is invited to re-read ▶ Sect. 4.23, where the Weak Axiom of revealed preference holding for market demand is defined, and the assumption that it holds is named *WAM, Weak Axiom holding for market demand.

WAM was there formulated in terms of market demand, not *excess* demand, but it can be equivalently formulated in terms of either, and the second formulation is the useful one for the proof of uniqueness. Start from the WARP at the level of individual consumers. The WARP (implicitly assuming single-valued consumer choices) says that *if at prices* p *the consumer's demand vector is* $x(p)$ *and* $px(p) \geq px(p')$ *with* $x(p) \neq x(p')$, *then* $p'x(p) > p'x(p')$. Under balanced budget and a given endowment vector ω, it is $px(p) = p\omega$, $p'x(p') = p'\omega$, hence $px(p) \geq px(p')$ can be written $p[x(p')-\omega] \leq 0$, and $p'x(p) > p'x(p')$ can be written $p'[x(p)-\omega] > 0$; therefore the WARP can be formulated in terms of the consumer's *excess* demand vectorial function $z^s(p)$:

■■ Definition of WARP When Income Derives from Given Endowments
Assume consumer s has single-valued optimal choices; if $pz^s(p') \leq 0$ and $z^s(p') \neq z^s(p)$, then $p'z^s(p) > 0$.

In the above, $x(p)$, ω and $z^s(p)$ referred to a single consumer. Now replace them with, respectively, the *market* demand function; the sum of all individual endowments and the *market* excess demand function. The assumption that the WARP is satisfied by the market demand function can be analogously formulated in terms of market *excess* demand function; in either case, it is indicated as *WAM,* and it can be stated as follows:

Definition of WAM: With p and q two non-proportional price vectors, WAM holds if $px(p) \geq px(q)$ and $x(q) \neq x(p)$ imply $qx(p) > qx(q)$, where $x(p)$, $x(q)$ are market vectorial demands; equivalently, if $pz(q) \leq 0$ and $z(q) \neq z(p)$, then $qz(p) > 0$.

A useful implication of WAM, to be called *WAM Lemma*, is the following:

■■ WAM Lemma
Assume WAM. Consider its excess demand form: if $pz(q) \leq 0$ *and* $z(q) \neq z(p)$, *then* $qz(p) > 0$.. *For the exchange economy this implies that if* p^* *is an equilibrium price vector and* p *is any price vector such that* $z(p) \neq z(p^*)$, *then* $p^*z(p) > 0$.

Proof   By the definition of equilibrium it is $z(p^*) \leq 0$ and therefore $pz(p^*) \leq 0$ for any $p \geq 0$, so it suffices to replace q with p^* in the definition of WAM in terms of

6.15 · Uniqueness Through Conditions on Excess Demand: WAM

excess demands. (The condition '$\mathbf{p}$ is such that $\mathbf{z}(\mathbf{p}) \neq \mathbf{z}(\mathbf{p}^*)$' excludes that $\mathbf{p}$ and $\mathbf{p}^*$ represent the same vector of *relative* prices.) ∎

This lemma states that for the exchange economy, *under WAM if* $\mathbf{p}^*$ *is an equilibrium price vector, then any non-equilibrium* $\mathbf{z}$ *has positive aggregate value at prices* $\mathbf{p}^*$.

This further implies that *if* $\mathbf{p}^*$ *and* $\mathbf{q}$ *are both equilibrium price vectors but* $\mathbf{z}(\mathbf{p}^*) \neq \mathbf{z}(\mathbf{q})$, *then WAM does not hold*: if it held then by the WAM Lemma it would be $\mathbf{q}\mathbf{z}(\mathbf{p}^*) > 0$, contradicting the fact remembered at the beginning of the proof of the WAM Lemma that if $\mathbf{p}^*$ is an equilibrium price vector then $\mathbf{p}\mathbf{z}(\mathbf{p}^*) \leq 0$ for any $\mathbf{p}$. Thus we have:

▪▪ Corollary of the WAM Lemma

For the exchange economy, non-uniqueness of relative equilibrium prices is compatible with WAM only if $\mathbf{z}(\mathbf{p})$ *is the same at all equilibrium prices.*

Interpretation: Since in the markets where equilibrium price is positive equilibrium *excess* demand is zero, the only way that *excess* demands can differ as between different equilibria is that the goods in excess supply (and therefore with zero equilibrium price) can be different goods, or can be the same goods but with different excess supply. The Corollary of the WAM Lemma shows that not even these differences are allowed, if WAM holds. So if WAM holds, there cannot be two different allocations, equilibria can differ only in relative prices but generate the same allocation. How can this be? Evidently owing to the equilibrium quantities being at kinks of indifference curves.

The following result is then only to be expected:

Proposition 6.6 (Quasi-uniqueness of equilibrium in the exchange economy under WAM) *Under WAM the set of equilibrium price vectors of the exchange economy is convex.*

Proof Suppose $\mathbf{p}'$ and $\mathbf{p}''$ are two (non-proportional) equilibrium price vectors, i.e. $\mathbf{z}(\mathbf{p}') \leq \mathbf{0}, \mathbf{z}(\mathbf{p}'') \leq \mathbf{0}$. Let $\mathbf{q} = \alpha\mathbf{p}' + (1-\alpha)\mathbf{p}''$ for $0 < \alpha < 1$. We must prove that $\mathbf{q}$ is an equilibrium price vector, that is, $\mathbf{z}(\mathbf{q}) \leq \mathbf{0}$. By Walras' Law $0 = \mathbf{q}\mathbf{z}(\mathbf{q}) = \alpha\mathbf{p}'\mathbf{z}(\mathbf{q}) + (1-\alpha)\mathbf{p}''\mathbf{z}(\mathbf{q})$ for $\alpha \in (0,1)$; the terms on the right-hand side cannot both be positive, hence either $\alpha\mathbf{p}'\mathbf{z}(\mathbf{q}) \leq 0$ or $(1-\alpha)\mathbf{p}''\mathbf{z}(\mathbf{q}) \leq 0$ or both. If $\alpha\mathbf{p}'\mathbf{z}(\mathbf{q}) \leq 0$, then it is also $\mathbf{p}'\mathbf{z}(\mathbf{q}) \leq 0$; then the WAM Lemma implies that $\mathbf{z}(\mathbf{q})$ cannot be different from $\mathbf{z}(\mathbf{p}')$ and therefore it is an equilibrium excess demand, that is, $\mathbf{z}(\mathbf{q}) \leq \mathbf{0}$. If $(1-\alpha)\mathbf{p}''\mathbf{z}(\mathbf{q}) \leq 0$ then for the same reason $\mathbf{z}(\mathbf{q})$ cannot be different from $\mathbf{z}(\mathbf{p}'')$ and so $\mathbf{z}(\mathbf{q}) \leq \mathbf{0}$. So certainly $\mathbf{z}(\mathbf{q}) \leq \mathbf{0}$ and $\mathbf{q}$ is an equilibrium price vector. In fact because of the Corollary of the WAM Lemma it is $\mathbf{z}(\mathbf{q}) = \mathbf{z}(\mathbf{p}') = \mathbf{z}(\mathbf{p}'')$ (the goods in excess supply and with zero equilibrium price are the same, or are absent). ∎

Convexity of the set of equilibrium price vectors implies that either there is a continuum of relative equilibrium price vectors, or there is at most one. Thus *if the economy is regular, and therefore the number of equilibria is finite, WAM implies that if there is an equilibrium then it is unique.*

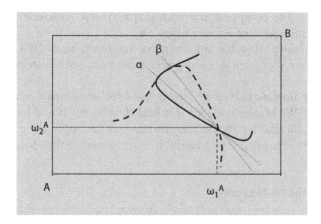

◘ **Fig. 6.15** Continuum of equilibria: all price lines through the origin and in between the α and the β lines are equilibrium price vectors. Consumer A's choice curve is the continuous line, and consumer B's choice curve is the broken line. The set of equilibrium relative prices is convex, in this case. Any small modification of the shape of either choice curve would cause the continuum of equilibria to disappear with probability 1

The case with three equilibria of ▶ Sect. 6.17, ◘ Fig. 6.9, is incompatible with WAM. The case of the Edgeworth box of ◘ Fig. 6.15 is incompatible with WAM too.

Exercise Show what precisely is incompatible with WAM in the case with three equilibria of ◘ Fig. 6.9 (in ▶ Sect. 6.17) and the case with a continuum of equilibrium prices of ◘ Fig. 6.15.

How plausible is WAM? If the market demand (or excess demand) vector function is as if coming from a single consumer holding the economy's entire endowment, that is if there is a representative consumer, then market demand satisfies the SARP, and then also the WARP, and WAM holds. If the representative consumer has a strictly quasi-concave and differentiable utility function, then equilibrium is unique; if his indifference hypersurfaces have kinks, it can be that equilibrium relative prices are not uniquely determined if the equilibrium allocation is precisely at a kink. But the conditions for the existence of a representative consumer are extremely restrictive as shown in ▶ Sect. 4.22. The slightly weaker WAM has been shown in ▶ Sect. 4.23 to be highly restrictive too: examples showed that WAM need not hold in all cases in which the conditions for the existence of a representative consumer are only partly satisfied: for example WAM need not hold when utility functions are homothetic, but endowments are not co-linear as Eisenberg's theorem would additionally require. In fact, to the best of my knowledge no economically meaningful condition sufficient for WAM and not implying a representative consumer is known. This strongly suggests that to assume WAM is no gain in generality relative to assuming a representative consumer.

6.16 Uniqueness: No-Trade Equilibrium and Index Theorem

Another result on uniqueness is the following:

■■ Proposition 6.7

If preferences are strongly monotonic and strictly convex and if the initial alloca-tion of endowments is itself an equilibrium allocation, then that is the sole exchange equilibrium allocation (there can be a continuum of equilibrium price vectors).

A rigorous proof appears unnecessary because the intuition is very clear. Consider the two-consumers two-goods Edgeworth box case: if the endowment point is an equilibrium, the indifference curves of the two consumers through the endowment point do not cross there, they are on opposite sides of the budget line and being strictly convex remain on opposite sides, and they are for each con-sumer the frontiers of the upper contour sets defined by the endowment point, sets which therefore have in common only the endowment point; the choice curves are each one contained in the respective upper contour set and therefore they never *cross*, they only have in common the endowment point (draw the dia-gram and check it!). If both indifference curves through the endowment point have a kink there, then the equilibrium relative price need not be unique.

A final result worth mentioning is that for regular exchange economies the uniqueness result based on GS and WAM can be derived (cf. Hildenbrand and Kirman, 1988 pp. 222–228) from the **index theorem**, a theorem based on differen-tial topology, which I state without proof:

■■ Proposition 6.8. Index Theorem

For a regular exchange economy, let $\mathbf{p}^*$ *be an equilibrium price vector and assign to* $\mathbf{p}^*$ *an index as follows: consider the determinant of* $-\partial z_{(-h)}(\mathbf{p}^*)$, *the Jacobian matrix of* $\mathbf{z}(\mathbf{p})$ *with inverted signs and deprived of any one row, say the hth row, and of the corresponding column; evaluate it at* $\mathbf{p}^*$, *and assign to* $\mathbf{p}^*$ *index* $+1$ *if this determi-nant is positive,* -1 *if it is negative; assume also that* $z_i(\mathbf{p}) > 0$ *if* $p_i = 0$, *all i (this implies* $\mathbf{p}^* \gg 0$); *then the sum of the indices of the finite number of equilibria is* $+1$.

The implication of this theorem for uniqueness analysis is that *if it can be shown that all possible equilibria have index* $+1$, *then equilibrium is unique*. (For a proof and considerations on the usefulness of the index theorem cf. Kehoe 1998.)

The index theorem does not greatly add to our knowledge of the conditions guaranteeing uniqueness, for two reasons. First, it is only applicable if the econ-omy is regular, and I have argued that this is a *very* restrictive assumption. Sec-ond, it states a mathematical condition which remains economically obscure until conditions implying it are found that have an economic interpretation: GS and WAM are the known conditions that do, and they had all been found before the formulation of the index theorem. However, the index theorem can be useful in order to produce examples of non-uniqueness, because if one proves that under the assumptions of the theorem the model has an equilibrium with index -1, then there are at least two more equilibria.

482   **Chapter 6** · Existence, Uniqueness and Stability of Non-capitalistic General Equilibria

To sum up on the assumptions on $\mathbf{z}(\mathbf{p})$ ensuring uniqueness, they are GS, WAM, and the existence of a representative consumer (which implies WAM). All are very special conditions.

6.17 Conditions on the Distribution of Characteristics

In more recent times some work has gone into trying to find assumptions, on the *distribution of characteristics* among agents, which might ensure the uniqueness of equilibrium. Some cases have been found in which a particular distribution of endowments and preferences ensures uniqueness. The literature is mathematically very advanced so I only summarize some results.

Hildenbrand (1983) opened the way, by showing that one can obtain WAM for the excess demand of an exchange economy with a continuum of infinitesimal consumers by assuming that

1. consumers have co-linear endowments (then the relative value of their endowments is independent of prices; choosing an endowment basked as numéraire, each consumer has an income m equal to the number of baskets in her endowment);
2. all consumers have the same demand function x(p, m);
3. if one orders consumers according to income, equal increases in income embrace decreasing numbers of consumers.

All three assumptions are *very* restrictive: this is obvious for the first two, and the third one is generally empirically false for very low-income classes. So certainly this result does not make uniqueness of equilibrium more plausible.

After Hildenbrand there have been other papers attempting to find other, possibly less restrictive, assumptions on the distribution of characteristics ensuring uniqueness of equilibrium; but no significant relaxation of the assumptions has been achieved; no reason exists to expect the assumptions to hold in the majority, let alone the quasi-totality, of cases.[22]

To conclude on uniqueness, there are no plausible assumptions ensuring equilibrium uniqueness and therefore capable of countering the Sonnenschein–Mantel–Debreu result that, without restrictive assumptions, equilibria can be

---

22 Cf. Billette de Villemeur (1998, 1999) for such an assessment. For example, Jerison (1999, p. 16) can only claim that his result holds 'in a broad class of economic models' (note the timidity of 'a broad class', that is, not even 'plausibly a majority'). Another example is Quah (1997) who assumes, among other things, (1) that consumers can be divided into a finite number N of classes, each class with such a dispersion of preferences that 'each class will behave approximately like an agent with a homothetic preference' (p. 1423), (2) that endowments are so randomly distributed that it is as if each one of these N representative consumers had an endowment equal to 1/Nth of the economy's endowment. This clearly amounts to assuming that the economy behaves as if there were a finite number of consumers each one with homothetic preferences and all with the same endowment. Then one does not need pages of mathematics! The assumptions of Eisenberg's theorem are assumed satisfied, a representative consumer exists. There is no reason to consider these assumptions as even vaguely plausible.

6.17 · Conditions on the Distribution of Characteristics

extremely numerous and the locally stable ones can be so many and so close to each other that even when there is no continuum of equilibria still to all practical effects there can be as much indeterminacy of equilibrium as with a continuum.

As already noted, this raises doubts about whether the supply-and-demand approach has correctly grasped the forces determining prices and quantities, since reality does not seem to exhibit the indeterminacy, or sudden jump to new persistent positions owing to accidental transitory disturbances, that multiplicity of equilibria should cause us to observe.[23]

6.18 Stability: The Cobweb

A caveat: stability is difficult to study because it is impossible to reach a universally valid model of detailed adjustments, given the wide differences in arrangements in different markets and the great variety of possible disequilibrium behaviours of agents. For example, consider a person who arrives at the market with corn to sell and the intention to buy cloth, but with no money, intending first to sell the corn and thus get the money to buy the cloth, and who has difficulties selling the corn; this person can wait, or can rush to borrow from a seller of short-term credit, or can offer to pay for the cloth with a promissory note, or can lower the price of his corn, etc.

Further complications are due to the difference that the precise specification of adjustments can make, e.g. the importance of lags. A well-known example is the following, based on partial-equilibrium analysis of a single market. Earlier we accepted the standard argument that if the demand curve in a market is downward-sloping and the supply curve is upward-sloping, then the tendency of price to increase if demand exceeds supply and to decrease if supply exceeds demand will cause a tendency towards the equilibrium price: the equilibrium is stable. But suppose there is some lag in the adjustment. Suppose that supply of an agricultural product adjusts with a lag, because production requires a year to be completed. We can then have the so-called hog cycle or *cobweb cycle*. Suppose a periodic market for this product, say once a year after the harvest; in each market fair there is a given supply determined by decisions taken the year before, and the price brings demand, determined by a demand function $D(p)$, to equal the given supply. Supply in each market fair depends on the production decisions taken the year before at the end of that year's market fair, on the basis of expectations as to the price the good would fetch in the next market. Suppose producers expect the price next year to be equal to the price determined in the market fair just concluded (*static price expectations*), and suppose they have an upward-sloping supply function $S(p)$. Then in the market in year t the equilibrium price is determined by $D(p_t) = S(p_{t-1})$.

---

23 '… our experience with real economies gives little support to the notion that there are multiple equilibria' (Gintis 2007, p. 1299).

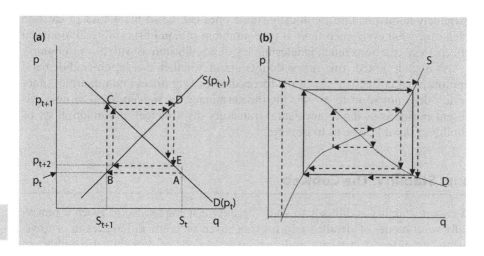

Fig. 6.16 Stable cobweb and a cobweb with an unstable equilibrium but tending to a limit cycle

Then ◘ Fig. 6.16 tells the story: in each period supply is given. Suppose at t supply is S_t, determined by p_{t-1} which is not shown. Then p_t, determined by $D(p_t) = S_t$ (intersection at point A of the demand curve with the vertical supply curve), determines $S_{t+1} = S(p_t)$, so in the next market p_{t+1} is determined by $D(p_{t+1}) = S_{t+1} = S(p_t)$ (intersection at point C) and so on; at t + 2 demand and supply intersect at point E. Joining the corresponding points on the supply-and-demand curves, one obtains a cobweb-like spiral which is convergent if the demand curve is less steep (in absolute terms) than the supply curve, as in ◘ Fig. 6.16a and divergent in the opposite case (check with a drawing). In the latter case, the equilibrium is unstable in spite of the 'well-behaved' slopes of the demand curve and of the supply curve. If the curves are nonlinear one can even obtain a limit cycle, as shown in ◘ Fig. 6.16b.

However, this type of instability does not appear to be a reason to expect more than some temporary instability, because in all likelihood learning processes will modify expectations in a direction favouring stability: for example suppliers, having observed that the price oscillates and that supply changes in a predictable direction from one period to the next, will no longer expect $p_{t+1} = p_t$ but rather $p_{t+1} < p_t$ if at t price was very favourable and therefore it can be expected that the subsequent year supply will be greater, and contrariwise if at t price was very low. This will make suppliers more cautious in altering their supply, which will greatly decrease the likelihood of instability. For example, suppose that in the situation of ◘ Fig. 6.16b producers from time t onwards decide to change their supply by only one half of the change suggested by static price expectations, no longer planning $S_{t+1} = S(p_t)$ but instead $S_{t+1} = S_t + \frac{1}{2}[S(p_t) - S_t]$; then the cobweb becomes stable (the reader is invited to check this graphically). We get here a glimpse of the possible diversity of disequilibrium behaviours depending on how people form their expectations.

6.19 Stability: The Samuelsonian Walrasian Tâtonnement

The modern developments concerning the stability of general equilibrium have not incorporated lags and are dominated by Paul Samuelson's proposal (1941, p. 102, p. 109) to formalize the dynamic adjustment of prices as a process in continuous time where for each good i the price change is regulated by excess demand:

$$dp_i/dt = H(D_i(\mathbf{p}) - S_i(\mathbf{p})),$$

with H an increasing function of the excess demand for the good, possibly $a_i(D_i(\mathbf{p})-S_i(\mathbf{p}))$ with a_i a positive scalar. Samuelson does not stop to discuss how the demand function $D_i(\mathbf{p})$ and the supply function $S_i(\mathbf{p})$ which he is assuming to exist are determined; he pays no attention to the fact stressed here repeatedly (e.g. Sects. 4.5, 5.28) that in disequilibrium these cannot be the functions that appear in a general equilibrium system because the latter functions are derived conditional on the prices being equilibrium prices and cannot indicate real demands and supplies in disequilibrium, nor is it clear what to replace them with; nor does he stop on the many problems connected with determining the supply function of a produced good even conditional on the prices being equilibrium prices—we have seen that a supply function may not exist at all if one admits entry or constant returns to scale. But production will be discussed later in this chapter, for the moment let us remain with the exchange economy. A careful historical reconstruction of the reasons for the evolution of equilibrium stability analyses does not exist yet; what seems clear is that soon after Samuelson's paper the accepted way to study the stability of equilibrium became Samuelson's approach coupled with the assumption that excess demands are the ones derivable from the general equilibrium behavioural equations. Thus in the paper that starts the modern formal studies of stability, Arrow and Hurwicz (1958), the excess demands are those derived from balanced budget consumer UMP's (see *ibid.* p. 526). That is, stability is studied in the fairy tale world of the Walrasian tâtonnement described at the end of ▶ Chap. 5, ▶ Sect. 5.26. In that setting, since the promises to sell or to purchase become binding only in equilibrium, consumers have the right to assume their excess supplies will find purchasers, so they can count on an income or wealth equal to the value of their endowments. At each proposed price vector consumers solve their UMP counting on balanced budgets. that is, counting on their decisions becoming effective only if those prices come out to be equilibrium prices.

The problem of course is that the neo-Walrasian tâtonnement is very different from the way markets operate in real economies, so the question arises, how applicable to real economies are the conclusions derived from the study of this tâtonnement?

For the moment only a first problem connected with this question will be discussed. Assume a unique equilibrium and that the tâtonnement converges to it, that is, the equilibrium is tâtonnement stable. But on the basis of the usual formalizations the tâtonnement process converges to equilibrium only *asymptotically*, because the smaller the excess demand in a market the lower the pressure on price to change, hence plausibly the slower the price change: $dp_i/dt = a_i z_i(\mathbf{p}(t))$ (or also $dp_i/dt = a_i z_i(\mathbf{p}(t))/x_i(\mathbf{p}(t))$) that considers the pressure on price to change to depend on excess demand relative to the dimension of the market) implies that excess demand z_i cannot become zero in a finite time interval, because the price adjustment slows down as excess demand approaches zero. So equilibrium is only asymptotically approached as $t \to +\infty$: equilibrium is *never* actually reached. Taken literally the auctioneer story, that assumes no exchange until equilibrium is reached, implies either that exchanges (and production) never start, or that the time flow indicated by t is only a 'logical' time but in fact the adjustment is infinitely fast.

The plausible way to avoid either absurdity is to interpret the tâtonnement as trying to mimic a process where exchanges (and production, if there is production) *go on during the adjustments*, so the economy is not paralysed; the equilibrium only aims at indicating the centre of gravitation of actual market behaviour which is always to some extent off equilibrium. The assumption of balanced budgets can then be defended as reflecting a repetition of transactions on the basis, at each round of price calling, of unchanged data.

For an exchange economy the picture might be something like the following. Remember the forest exchange economy of ▶ Sect. 3.7 where each household has a small farm producing certain goods, the same quantities every month, unmodifiable for technological reasons and differing across farms. For example some farms produce honey and fruit, other farms chicken and eggs, others wool and mutton. The monthly production is the household's endowment ω^s. Once a month the households meet in a one-day-long market fair in the central village, to exchange whatever part of their productions they have decided to bring to the fair. Suppose that, for any vector of goods brought to the market by each household, there is a unique equilibrium and that the tâtonnement, if it could be assumed to exist, would converge to it. The equilibrium prices sometimes can be predicted rather well on the basis of past experience, but at other times, after a novelty, they cannot. In the latter case the equilibrium prices will not be immediately hit upon: there will be tentative setting of different prices by different households for the same good, exchanges afterwards regretted, people unable to buy because they were unable to sell, prices changing during the market day and so on. The exchanges at prices different from equilibrium prices will alter the traders' endowments in ways incompatible with reaching, in that fair, the equilibrium corresponding to the initial endowments. But suppose that after the initial novelty the data (participants to the fair; production of their farms; tastes) remain unaltered for a number of successive fairs, and let us ask what will plausibly happen, over a *repetition* of market fairs, to the quantities brought to the fair, as well as to the *opening* prices; the experience of previous fairs suggests to families how to alter the amounts to bring to the fair and what opening prices to propose for their supplies and to accept for their purchases: if in one fair some sellers of a certain good have difficulty selling their inventory (and must lower the price a lot and earn much less than expected), in the next fair they can be expected to bring a lower supply and/or to start with a lower opening price than in the previous fair. The adjustment of quantities brought to the fair and of opening prices can then be considered to depend on the

6.19 · Stability: The Samuelsonian Walrasian Tâtonnement

'excess demands' experienced in previous fairs; one can suppose that temporary credits—based on the reputation of traders—will allow surmounting the problem that many participants may need to sell first their wares in order to become in turn demanders.

One can perhaps consider the process of adjustment of *opening* prices over the *repetition* of fairs to be reasonably approximated by the tâtonnement formalization. The fact, that during each fair the endowments of participants change, does not make convergence to the equilibrium based on the initial data impossible *over a repetition of fairs*, because the data are the same at the beginning of each new fair, so learning and error correction may well cause prices to tend to those that ensure equilibrium.

Thus the Samuelsonian tâtonnement appears perhaps not so absurd an idealization, if taken to describe the tendency of prices in an exchange economy over a *repetition* of market interactions to which agents arrive always with the same data.[24] But then, why isn't the tâtonnement justified in these realistic terms, rather than in terms of the fairy tale of an imaginary 'auctioneer' central office that stops everything and collects *bons* (pledges) in a congealed economy situation? A hint of the main reason—an anticipation of arguments to be presented in ▶ Chaps. 7 and 8—can perhaps be given here. Such a realistic justification would require that the equilibrium be defined on the basis of *persistent* data. This persistency can be perhaps assumed for the forest exchange economy or for a non-capitalistic production economy, but the theory must be capable of dealing with production economies with capital goods too. Now, for the latter economies modern general equilibrium theory includes, among the data determining the equilibrium, a given endowment of each capital good: in this case the needed persistence and independence of the equilibrium's data from disequilibrium actions cannot be assumed, disequilibrium productions can quickly alter the amounts in existence of the several capital goods, which alters the equilibrium itself. Then the auctioneer fairy tale becomes necessary to prevent the equilibrium from being relevantly altered by the disequilibrium adjustments that should bring to it. And since this fairy tale is necessary for the capitalistic economy, one assumes it even for the models where it is not indispensable, so as to accustom students to it.

If this raises more questions than it answers, please be patient, ▶ Chaps. 7 and 8 will clarify the issue, which is a complex one. Now let us survey the main results on the stability of the Samuelsonian tâtonnement, for the moment for the exchange economy. Some knowledge of these results is part of what all economists must know.

---

24 The economy just described seems to be the one to which the following lines from a renowned treatise on general equilibrium might apply: 'we could think of actual economies for which a tâtonnement would not appear to be so remote a description, for instance, in a world where all goods are perishable and where the goods agents have in possession after given time intervals are independent of the transactions they have carried out' (Arrow and Hahn 1971, p. 265).

488   **Chapter 6** · Existence, Uniqueness and Stability of Non-capitalistic General Equilibria

6.20 Stability: Some Mathematics and the WAM Theorem

We need a few mathematical notions that can be useful in other branches of economics too. Consider a subset S of R^n. A *dynamical system* $\{F, x(t)\}$ on S is a way of associating a vector $x \in S$ to each scalar t, usually interpreted as time, through a rule F: $S \times R \to S$ which starting from $x(t)$ and $h \in R$ representing a time interval, yields a unique $x(t+h)$. If x changes continuously as t increases, given an initial point $x(0)$ the dynamical system can be viewed as describing a trajectory of the point $x = x(t, x(0))$ in S as time passes.

For simplicity now I stop using bold characters for vectors, the context will make it clear. I shall only discuss dynamical systems consisting of systems of differential equations $\dot{x} = f(x(t), t)$ where $\dot{x} \equiv \frac{d}{dt}x(t) \equiv \begin{bmatrix} \frac{dx_1(t)}{dt} \\ \cdot \\ \cdot \\ \frac{dx_n(t)}{dt} \end{bmatrix}$. The vectorial function f is known, but the functions $x_i(t)$ are not; so what must be found are functional forms for $x_1(t), \ldots, x_n(t)$ that satisfy the system of equations. Such functional forms are called a *solution* of the dynamical system. Given an initial position $x(0)$, the solution[25] determines all subsequent values of the state variables $x_1, \ldots, x_n$ as t grows. I shall only use qualitative considerations on the character of the solutions, so no familiarity will be needed with the techniques to find solutions to differential equations.

What do we mean by *stability* of a dynamical system? Many meanings have been distinguished by mathematicians. Here we are concerned with the *asymptotic stability* of *equilibria*. An *equilibrium* of a dynamical system of the type we are concerned with is a point x^* such that $f(x^*, t) = 0$, i.e. such that $\frac{d}{dt}x^*(t) = 0$ for all t, and therefore if the system is in x^* it remains there. It is also called a *fixed point* or a *zero* of the dynamical system.

An equilibrium, or fixed point, x^* is *Liapunov stable* if, intuitively speaking, all solutions with initial conditions sufficiently close to x^* (i.e. in a neighbourhood of x^*) remain forever close to x^*. Formally:

An equilibrium x^* of a dynamical system is said to be *Liapunov stable* if for any scalar $\varepsilon > 0$ and any t° there exists a scalar $\delta > 0$ such that any solution x: $R \to R^n$ for which $\|x(t^\circ) - x^*\| \leq \delta$, $t^\circ \geq 0$, has the property that for all $t \geq t^\circ$ it is $\|x(t; x(t^\circ), t^\circ)) - x^*\| \leq \varepsilon$, where δ depends on ε and on t°. If δ can be chosen independently of t° then x^* is said to be *uniformly Liapunov stable*.

An equilibrium x^* is *locally asymptotically stable* if (i) it is Liapunov stable and (ii) $\lim_{t \to +\infty} x(t) = x^*$ for all $x(0)$ in a neighbourhood of x^*[26]; it is *uniformly asymptotically stable* if in (i) Liapunov stability is replaced with (i') uniform Lia-

---

25 Under certain conditions generally satisfied in economic applications, the solution is unique apart from a dependence on initial conditions.

26 It is possible to produce examples in which (ii) is satisfied but not (i); see Takayama (1974, p. 349).

6.20 · Stability: Some Mathematics and the WAM Theorem

punov stability; it is *globally asymptotically stable* if (i) holds and (ii) is replaced by $\lim_{t \to +\infty} x(t) = x*$, $\forall x(0) \in S$, where S is the set of possible states x of the dynamical system, called the *state space*; it is *uniformly* globally asymptotically stable if (i) is replaced with (i').

In the remainder of this chapter by stability I shall mean asymptotic uniform stability unless otherwise expressly indicated. With this meaning, a *globally* stable equilibrium x* is a point to which all trajectories converge, independently of where they start from.

An *equilibrium x* that is globally stable is unique*: any other equilibrium would be a point from which the dynamical system would *not* tend to x*, contradicting the global stability of x*.

Below I use the so-called **Liapunov's second method** (*or direct method*) for the study of the stability of an equilibrium x* of a dynamical system. This method consists of looking for a scalar function V(x(t)) of the state vector x(t), which:
1. is indirectly a *continuously differentiable* function of t, for any x;
2. always decreases for $x \neq x*$ as t increases, i.e. its chain-rule derivative with respect to t is always negative for $x \neq x*$;
3. reaches a minimum in x*.

If such a function can be found, then the dynamical system is globally stable because any trajectory reaches lower and lower values of V as t increases, so if V has a lowest value the dynamical system tends to it, and the lowest value of V is reached at point x*.

More formally, suppose we are given a dynamical system[27] {F, x(t)}, $x \in S$ with S compact (so the values that x can take are bounded), and suppose we know that x* is an equilibrium; suppose we can find a scalar function of x, V: $S \to R$, i.e. a function $v(t) = V(x_1(t), \ldots, x_n(t))$, with continuous partial derivatives $\partial V / \partial x_i$, and with the following properties:
1. it is positive except at most in x* and it reaches a minimum in x* and only there (without loss of generality this minimum can be assumed to be zero);
2. $\dot{V}(x(t)) \equiv \left(\sum \frac{\partial V}{\partial x_i} \frac{dx_i}{dt} \right) < 0$, $\forall x \neq x*$, while at x* it is$= 0$, i.e. as t increases, whichever the $x(0) \neq x*$ in S from which the system starts V(x(t)) always continuously decreases, except at x*.

Such a function V(x(t)) is called a **Liapunov function**[28] and it can be proved that, if such a function exists, then x* is *globally* stable.[29] An intuitive sketch of the proof is as follows.[30] Given that V has a unique minimum in x*, the positiveness and continuous partial differentiability of V imply the existence of a continuum

---

27 The dynamical system of differential equations given above in the text is one such system.
28 Liapunov was a Russian mathematician. His name is also written Lyapounov.
29 If in condition b the inequality <0 is replaced with the weak inequality ≤ 0, then x* is Liapunov stable but not necessarily asymptotically stable.
30 Cf. Arrowsmith and Place 1982, p. 200; Gandolfo 1971, pp. 369–375.

490   **Chapter 6** · Existence, Uniqueness and Stability of Non-capitalistic General Equilibria

of closed level curves (or more generally hypersurfaces) of V(x) in S around the equilibrium point, corresponding to lower and lower values of V as one approaches x*. For any x(0) the function V(x(t, x(0)) viewed as a function of t is decreasing and bounded below by zero so it must tend to a limit as $t \to \infty$. It follows that $\lim_{t \to \infty} \dot{V}(x(t, x(0)) = 0$ but since $\dot{V}$ is negative for $x \neq x^*$, this can only occur if $x(t, x(0)) \to x^*$ as $t \to \infty$.

With these minimal mathematics I can prove:

▪▪ Proposition 6.9

(WAM ensures the tâtonnement stability of exchange equilibrium) *Under WAM, if the equilibrium of the exchange economy is unique, then it is globally stable with respect to a tâtonnement adjustment process.*

Proof Let $p°$ and p^* be any two different and non-proportional[31] price vectors (not necessarily normalized in the price simplex). Assume p^* to be an equilibrium price vector; then by the assumption of equilibrium uniqueness $p°$ is not an equilibrium price vector; then as proved earlier, WAM implies $p * z(p°) > 0$: the value at equilibrium prices of any non-equilibrium excess demand vector is positive. Assume now that the price adjustment rule is the following (as usual, a dot over the symbol of a variable means the derivative of that variable with respect to time):

$$\dot{p}_i(t) = a_i z_i(p(t)) \text{(with } a_i > 0 \text{ scalar)}; \tag{6.6}$$

it can be shown that it makes no difference to the qualitative behaviour of the dynamical system if we assume simply all coefficients a_i to be equal to 1:

$$\dot{p}_i(t) = a_i z_i(p(t)). \tag{6.7}$$

These price adjustment rules imply the following. If an initial price $p(0)$ has been chosen and $p(t)$ is given by (6.6), then from $\frac{d}{dt} \left(\sum_{i=1}^{n} \frac{1}{a_i} (p_i(t))^2 \right) = \sum_i [(2/a_i)p_i(t) \cdot dp_i(t)/dt] = 2 \sum_i [p_i(t)z_i(p(t))] = 0$, where the last equality follows from Walras' Law, we derive that the quantity $\sum_{i=1}^{n} \frac{1}{a_i} (p_i(t))^2$ remains constant as t increases.[32] Therefore if we want to enquire whether an equilibrium is stable, we must choose a normalization for the equilibrium price vector p^* once $p(0)$ is chosen, or for $p(0)$ once p^* is chosen, which respects this constancy, i.e. such that $\sum_{i=1}^{n} \frac{1}{a_i} (p_i(t))^2 = \sum_{i=1}^{n} \frac{1}{a_i} (p_i^*)^2$. Since all that matters for excess demands is relative prices, this normalization condition is no restriction from the economic point of view. If with this normalization we can prove that

---

31 That is, it is not the case that $p° = cp^*$ for c a positive real scalar.

32 If all coefficients a_i are chosen equal to 1, then p(t) moves on the positive portion of a spherical hypersurface.

6.20 · Stability: Some Mathematics and the WAM Theorem

p^* is globally stable, the implication will be that a non-normalized $p(t)$ converges on the equilibrium ray $\{p = \alpha p^*\}$, with α any positive scalar. The adoption of this normalization has on the other hand an advantage: for $t \geq 0$, it cannot be simultaneously $p(t) \neq p^*$ and $p(t)$ equi-proportional to p^*, so we are certain that for $p(t) \neq p^*$ it is $p^* z(p(t)) > 0$.

Let us then adopt the price adjustment rule (6.6) with the above normalization of $p(0)$. I show that the function $V(p) = \sum_{i=1}^{n} \left[(p_i - p_i^*)^2 / a_i \right]$ is a Liapunov function for our dynamical system.

1. $V(p) > 0$ for $p \neq p^*$, and $V(p) = 0$ only if $p = p^*$, hence $V(p)$ reaches its minimum in p^* and only there:

2. $$\frac{dV}{dt} = \sum_{i=1}^{n} \left[\frac{2}{a_i} (p_i - p_i^*) \cdot \dot{p}_i \right]$$
$$= 2 \sum_{i=1}^{n} \left[(p_i - p_i^*) \cdot z_i(p) \right]$$
$$= 2 \sum_{i=1}^{n} \left(p_i z_i(p) - p_i^* z_i(p) \right) =$$
$$= 2(\underbrace{pz(p)}_{=0 \text{ by Walras' law}} - p^* z(p)) = -2p^* z(p) < 0$$

where the last inequality follows from $p^* z(p) > 0$. So the system has a Liapunov function and therefore p^* is globally stable.[33] ∎

Another case of global tâtonnement stability for exchange equilibria is GS. One can adopt for the proof exactly the same Liapunov function, because it can be proved (cf., e.g. Beavis and Dobbs 1990, pp. 195–196) that GS too implies that if p^* is an equilibrium price vector then $p^* z(p) > 0$ for all p different from and not proportional to p^*; therefore the proof that $V(p) = \sum_{i=1}^{n} \left[(p_i - p_i^*)^2 / a_i \right]$ is a Liapunov function is the same.

That global stability obtains only under very restrictive assumptions is not surprising. Let us remember that choice curves can have upward-sloping portions, which makes it easy to obtain three or more equilibria in an Edgeworth box; in which case global stability is impossible.

---

33 It is immediate that the proof still holds if $a_i = 1$, all i. So assuming (6.7) in place of (6.6) makes no difference. If the assumption, additional to WAM, that equilibrium is unique is dropped, and the possibility of a continuum of equilibrium prices is admitted, then V can be still defined in the same way and it remains true that it reaches a minimum at p^* and only there, but in step b) it is no longer guaranteed that $p^* z(p) > 0$ because p might be another equilibrium price vector, in which case $p^* z(p) = 0$ and $dV/dt = 0$; however, it remains true that $V(p(t))$ will go on decreasing as long as no equilibrium price vector is hit; therefore as t increases it remains true that $p(t)$ reaches lower and lower level curves of $V(p)$, so if it does not hit another equilibrium price it tends to p^*. Since any other equilibrium price vector might take the place of p^*, what is proved is that $p(t)$ reaches lower and lower level curves of $V(p)$ whichever the equilibrium price vector used to define $V(p)$, that is, it asymptotically approaches some element in the set of equilibrium price vectors.

6.21 Stability: Further Aspects of the Problem

Note that uniqueness of equilibrium, unless WAM or GS hold,[34] does not imply stability of the tâtonnement: numerical examples have been produced since 1960 by Herbert Scarf proving that, as long as there are at least three goods (hence a state space of dimension at least 2) and three consumers, there are cases not of measure zero, i.e. robust to small perturbations of the equilibrium's data, where the equilibrium is unique but unstable and the tâtonnement tends to a *limit cycle*: the time path of prices asymptotically approaches a closed orbit (cf. ■ Fig. 6.16); the auctioneer would never be able to stop!

Another possibility arises with four or more goods, and hence a state space of dimension 3 or greater: then a dynamical system can produce a path that wanders irregularly in the state space without converging to any point or limit cycle: the dynamical system is then called *chaotic*. It is possible to produce chaotic tâtonnements.

Recently, experiments have been made with real participants that mimic a multigood exchange economy that tries to reach an equilibrium *without* the auctioneer. In these experiments there is a repetition of trading periods, in each one of which the participants repeatedly propose exchanges and prices to other participants via a 'double auction' mechanism.[35] The endowments of consumers change *during* a trading period, but each participant starts each trading period with the same endowment, as in the forest economy of ▶ Chap. 3.[36] Convergence is not always obtained: sometimes there is instability, sometimes cycling without apparent equilibration (Anderson et al. 2004; Noussair et al. 2004, p. 50, footnote 1).

---

34 Or Diagonal Dominance or Negative Definiteness, mentioned in footnote 25 and practically as restrictive as GS.

35 'Trades in a double auction, in contrast, take place at discrete instances, and often at disequilibrium prices. 'Double auction' refers to the fact that price changes can come from both buyers and sellers of each commodity. At any time, an agent may tender a bid or an ask, accept another agent's bid or ask, or have a bid or ask accepted. Newly tendered bids and asks must improve (be higher or lower than, respectively) upon those in the market and cancel any previous bids or asks. The price discovery process can be observed as the prices at which trades are executed fluctuate through time. Allocations change with each transaction and can change no more only when the market closes due to expiration of trading time. The markets studied here have a number of such trading periods: after time expires and payoffs are calculated based on final allocations, endowments are reset to their initial values and another trading period begins. Within a period, trades depend on the patterns of bids, asks and acceptances. Therefore, there are within-period shifts in holdings that could cause deviations from the price adjustment paths predicted by tâtonnement models'. (Anderson et al. 2004 p. 213).

36 An older literature on non-tâtonnement models (see Hahn and Negishi 1962) studied what can be expected to happen in a *single* market fair of an exchange economy if transactions between agents go on as long as there is room for profitable exchanges; not surprisingly, the result is that—if no time constraint exists and search is costless—some situation will sooner or later be reached where no room for mutually profitable exchanges remains. The final allocation depends on the details of what transactions were made all during the trading period and will differ from the equilibrium corresponding to the initial endowments. Unfortunately the analysis cannot be extended to production economies, where changes in production decisions would require considerable time to yield changed outputs.

6.21 · Stability: Further Aspects of the Problem

When equilibrium is not unique, if the several equilibria are locally isolated there will generally be more than one locally stable equilibrium. In this case, the most one can hope for is *global quasi-stability*, also called (Mas-Colell et al. 1995, p. 623) *system stability*. An economy is globally quasi-stable or system stable if for any starting point the dynamical adjustment takes the economy to *some* equilibrium (generally a different one depending on initial conditions). If this condition holds and if furthermore the equilibria are few and far apart, then one can hope that, the economy having reached an equilibrium, transitory shocks and disequilibrium accidents will not push the economy into the 'basin of attraction' of another equilibrium, and also that small changes in the data (e.g. due to taxation, immigration, innovations) cause only a small shift of the equilibrium the economy was at, so the previous prices and quantities remain in its 'basin of attraction', and comparative statics remains possible. Unfortunately when the conditions guaranteeing uniqueness are not satisfied there seem to be no plausible general conditions ensuring that the equilibria be only few and far apart. Also, tâtonnement global quasi-stability is not guaranteed: Scarf's example suffices to show it.[37]

A further problem mentioned earlier, and definitely possible although neglected in the literature, is that of *practically indeterminate* equilibria: the ones where in an ample neighbourhood of the equilibrium price vector the excess demands remain very close to zero and therefore, even if mathematically the equilibrium is locally stable, still the forces tending to push towards it are very weak: then the equilibrium cannot be considered *really* stable for practical purposes, it is not an attractor over realistic time scales, it does not supply a good indication of the average of market realizations, because the tendency towards equilibrium is so weak that the economy can remain considerably far from equilibrium for very long periods, and the deviations due to temporary accidents can cumulate with little correction.

In conclusion, for exchange economies the *existence* of general equilibria does not appear to encounter serious difficulties, *except* for the survival–subsistence problem (▶ Sect. 6.8), which however is a serious problem and can arise in production economies too because it concerns the choices of consumers about labour supply. *Uniqueness* of equilibrium, traditionally considered essential to

---

37 A superpowerful central computer with complete information about the form of the market excess demand function $\mathbf{z}(\mathbf{p})$ and therefore about the numerical values of all its partial and cross-derivatives at all $\mathbf{p}$'s would be able to find a path of prices converging to equilibrium even when the tâtonnement was unstable, through the use of *global Newton methods*, which take into account the effect of the change of each price on *all* excess demands (cf. Mas-Colell et al. 1995, p. 624; Smale 1976). But when the tâtonnement is unstable the global Newton method, besides requiring such detailed information on the form of $\mathbf{z}(\mathbf{p})$ that the supercomputer would be able directly to determine the equilibrium, surmounts the instability by requiring some prices to move opposite to what excess demand would suggest, and this does not help the supply-and-demand approach, because no incentive is supplied capable of inducing individual agents to act in the way that brings to equilibrium.

494   Chapter 6 · Existence, Uniqueness and Stability of Non-capitalistic General Equilibria

the solidity of the approach, is guaranteed only under *very* restrictive hypotheses. As to *stability*, the results on tâtonnement stability are negative too (tâtonnement stability is not guaranteed even when equilibrium is unique; tâtonnement quasi-stability too may not obtain); the experiments without auctioneer assume repetition of trading periods always starting with the same data, which is not applicable to economies with capital goods, and do not always produce stability.

6.22 On the Likelihood of Uniqueness and Stability

The consequences of the above results (which as we will see are confirmed by the introduction of production) are seldom openly discussed. The tendency in textbooks and treatises is either (1) not to mention the problem at all,[38] or (2) to express some discomfort with the results which we have summarized, then briefly to hint at the need for some theory of equilibrium selection or for better theories of disequilibrium and to leave it at that and proceed as if in fact the problem could be neglected. This amounts to taking it for granted that there is no alternative to the neoclassical approach. But in fact there are alternatives.

More scientifically, one can try to minimize the problem by arguing that although a *guarantee* of uniqueness and stability is impossible to achieve, nonetheless multiple and unstable equilibria are *very unlikely*. This is precisely the argument in Hicks's influential *Value and Capital* (1939), and one can suspect that it continues to be accepted by many; so it is worthwhile briefly to consider it.[39] On uniqueness, Hicks starts by discussing the exchange of two goods; in this case as we know from ▶ Chap. 4 it suffices to look at the excess demand for only one of the two goods. Hicks distinguishes the net suppliers or sellers from the net demanders or buyers of the chosen good, and writes:

» A fall in price [of the good under consideration, starting from the equilibrium price] sets up a substitution effect which increases demand and diminishes supply; this therefore must increase excess demand. It sets up an income effect through the buyers being made better off and the sellers worse off. So long as the commodity is not an inferior good for either side, this means that the income effect will tend to increase demand and *increase* supply. Thus the direction of the income effect on excess demand depends on which of these two tendencies is the stronger. If the income effect on the demand side is just as strong as the income effect on the supply

---

38 For example the treatise on infinite-horizon economies by Aliprantis, Brown and Burkinshaw and the advanced microtextbook by Jehle and Reny (2011) do not discuss uniqueness of equilibrium, nor stability. The books which do discuss these issues usually only contain an exposition of some of the results also reported here, but with little attempt to discuss the implications. A partial exception is Hildenbrand and Kirman (1988, p. 239); perhaps not by chance, Kirman has ended up rejecting general equilibrium theory.

39 On this issue I found S. M. Fratini, *Il problema della molteplicità degli equilibri da Walras a Debreu* (Ph.D. thesis, Università di Roma La Sapienza, 2001), very useful.

6.22 · On the Likelihood of Uniqueness and Stability

side, then the income effect on excess demand will cancel out, leaving nothing but the substitution effect. In this case.... equilibrium must be stable." (Hicks 1946, p. 64; the reader can check that the income effect works as Hicks describes, using ◘ Fig. 4.24 in ▶ Chap. 4, ▶ Sect. 4.13).

Hicks admits that the cancellation of income effects is not necessarily the case and that the equilibrium might be unstable, in which case 'there may be more than one position of stable equilibrium' (p. 65). But, he argues, since income effects tend always at least partially to efface each other, the residual net income effect can be presumed generally to be fairly weak and therefore generally overpowered by the substitution effect. When Hicks goes on to discuss the exchange with more than two goods, he argues that 'There are just the same reasons [as in the two-goods case] ... for supposing that the income effect on excess demand will often be very small (since it consists of two parts which probably work in opposite directions)' (p. 68), and proceeds with 'Thus, if (as an approximation) we neglect the income effect...' (*ibid.*). So he concludes:

>> To sum up the negative but reassuring conclusions which we have derived from our discussion of stability. There is no doubt that the existence of stable systems of multiple exchange is entirely consistent with the laws of demand. It cannot, indeed, be proveda priori that a system of multiple exchange is necessarily stable.[40] But the conditions of stability are quite easy conditions, so that it is quite reasonable to assume that they will be satisfied in almost any system with which we are likely to be concerned. The only possible ultimate source of instability is strong asymmetry in the income effects. A moderate degree of substitutability among the bulk of commodities will be sufficient to prevent this cause being effective. (pp. 72–73).

Hicks' conclusion that instability requires 'strong asymmetry of income effects' can be made clear by drawing an Edgeworth box with the choice curves of two consumers A and B and looking at an equilibrium where the choice curves cross, with for example A a net supplier and B a net demander of good 1, hence an equilibrium to the North-West of the endowment point, see ◘ Fig. 6.17 which for simplicity only represents the equilibrium point, not the entire Edegworth box. Assume p_1/p_2 decreases. For each consumer one can draw vectors starting at the equilibrium point and representing substitution effect and income effect; the composition of the two effects gives the direction of change of the consumer's choice, which is the direction of the choice curve. For *both* consumers if both goods are normal the income effect vector is in a South-West direction (i.e. it increases B's demand and decreases A's supply; but if one measures supply as a negative quantity as required for the determination of excess demand, then it *increases*, as Hicks states in the first quotation). The equilibrium is unstable if at the equilibrium point the choice curve of consumer A is less steep than the choice

---

40 [Notice how Hicks considers 'stable' only a system with a *single* stable equilibrium. It is very clear that he considered the proof that equilibrium can be reasonably assumed to be unique as essential to the plausibility of the theory.—F. P.].

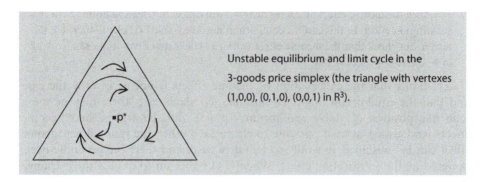

Fig. 6.17 Graphical illustration of limit cycle

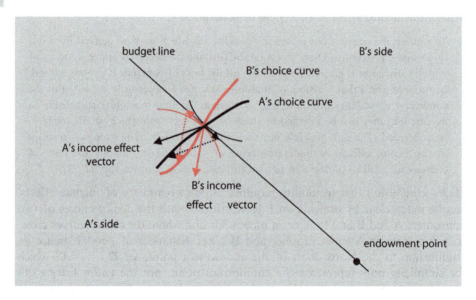

Fig. 6.18 Unstable equilibrium in an Edgeworth box (the figure focuses on the equilibrium point, the sides of the box are not represented). B's curves are in red. The equilibrium is unstable because A's income effect alters above all the demand for good 1, and B's income effect alters above all the demand for good 2. The price effects of a decrease of p_1/p_2 are the short arrows along the budget line, the composition of price and income effect results in the tip of the dotted-line arrows

curve of consumer B (the latter choice curve must be horseshoe-like). Since with smooth indifference curves the substitution effect vectors are along the budget line in opposite directions (towards the endowment point for A and away from it for B), if the income effect vectors are parallel there is no doubt that A's choice curve is steeper than B's and the equilibrium is stable. Instability can only arise from 'strong asymmetry of income effects', with B's income effect vector much less steep than A's, as in ◘ Fig. 6.18.

6.22 · On the Likelihood of Uniqueness and Stability

So Hicks was right on this point; but was he right when adding that 'a moderate degree of substitutability' would suffice to prevent this asymmetry of income effects from causing instability?

First, the degree of substitutability between the two goods might well be very low. One cannot substitute food with furniture; substitutability can be plausibly assumed only between goods that satisfy roughly the same need. Second, Hicks seems to underestimate the possibility of strongly asymmetric income effects: these do not require strange preferences, they can be due to different endowments even when preferences are identical and indifference curves guarantee extensive substitutability. This can be shown as follows. Assume a two-goods world, take a consumer with her map of indifference curves, and draw her choice curves (offer curves), assuming first that her endowment consists only of one good, then only of the other good. The resulting choice curves can be seen as the choice curves of two consumers with the same preferences but with different endowments. In ◘ Fig. 6.19 the reader can check, by drawing an opportune map of indifference curves, that indifference curves admitting high substitutability may well be such that curve A is the choice curve when the endowment consists of the quantity ω_1 of good 1, and curve B is the choice curve derived from the same indifference map when the endowment is quantity ω_2 of good 2.

If now we form an Edgeworth box with consumer A having endowment (ω_1, 0) and consumer B having endowment (0, ω_2) and both having the preferences of ◘ Fig. 6.19, we obtain ◘ Fig. 6.20 where the endowment point is the lower right-hand corner, and the choice curve of consumer B is choice curve B of ◘ Fig. 6.19, rotated 180°. The two choice curves cross three times.

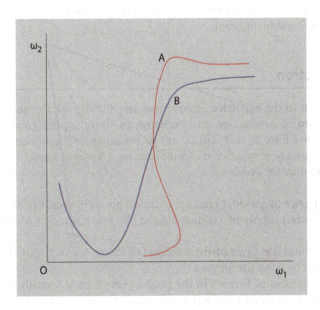

◘ **Fig. 6.19** Possible choice curves from same map of indifference curves but different initial endowments

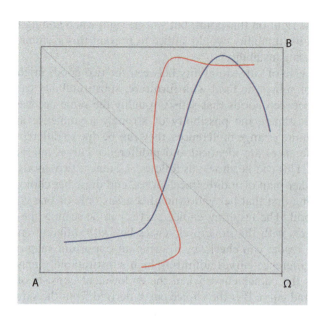

◘ **Fig. 6.20** Edgeworth box with the two previous choice curves

Thus it appears that Hicks was wrong to think that income effects would largely cancel out and that 'a moderate degree of substitutability' would suffice to prevent them from causing multiple equilibria. *Identical* preferences admitting considerable substitutability can cause 'strong asymmetry in income effects' and multiple equilibria if endowments are different. And in real economies endowments *are* considerably different.

6.23 Production

Now let us turn to the existence, uniqueness and stability of the general competitive equilibrium of production and exchange (without capital goods), presented at the end of ▶ Chap. 5, that will be called the atemporal non-capitalistic economy. Let me quickly remember its formalization. (Again it seems superfluous to use bold characters for vectors.)

Variables:

p_j ($j=1,\ldots,m$) price of product j (a consumption good); p vector of these prices.

q_j market (i.e. total) supply of produced good j by firms; q vector of these quantities.

v_i ($i=1,\ldots,n$) rental (i.e. price of the services) of factor i; v vector of these rentals.

x_i total demand *by firms* for factor i.

a_{ij} *technical coefficient* of factor i in the production of good j, resulting from cost minimization; assumed to be a *function* of relative factor rentals, not a correspondence.

6.23 · Production

$Q_j(p,v)$ consumers' total demand *function* for good j, derived from the utility-maximizing choices of consumers, assuming a balanced budget (hence only valid in equilibrium).

$X_i(p, v)$ consumers' total supply function of factor i *to firms*, derived like Q_j.

Equilibrium equations:

One numéraire equation, e.g. $\Sigma_j p_j = 1$.

Zero profits (neoclassical meaning):

(A) $p_j = MinLAC_j(v) = \sum_i v_i a_{ij}(v), \quad j = 1, \ldots, m$.

Quantities produced of consumption goods equal to demands:

(B) $q_j = Q_j(p, v), \quad j = 1, \ldots, m$.

Total firms' demands for factor services:

(C) $x_i = \sum_j a_{ij}(v) q_j, \quad i = 1, \ldots, n, \quad j = 1, \ldots, m$.

Factor supplies *to firms* equal to, or not less than, firms' factor demands (direct consumer demands for factor services either assumed non-existent, or assumed already satisfied so that supply to firms is the residual factor supply):

(D) $X_i(p, v) \geq x_i, \quad i = 1, \ldots, n$, and if inequality is strict, the corresponding rental is zero.

Because of equations (A), the vector p of prices of produced goods is given once the vector v of factor rentals is given; so both the vector X of factor supplies to firms and the vector x of firms' factor demands can be considered functions of v only and can be represented as $X^*(v)$, $x^*(v)$. Then the aggregate factor *derived* excess demand vector function is defined as $\zeta(v) \equiv x^*(v) - X^*(v)$.

6.24 Existence of a GE of Production and Exchange

The results on existence valid for the pure exchange economy are also valid for the atemporal GE of exchange and production, *if* the *derived excess demand for factors* $\zeta(v)$ defined in ▶ Chap. 5, ▶ Sect. 5.27 has the same properties as the excess demand $z(p)$ of the pure exchange economy.[41] Indeed since outputs are assumed equal to demands for produced goods, disequilibria can only appear in factor markets, where demand is direct demand by consumers plus the demand coming from firms, which is derived from the consumption goods consumers demand. $\zeta(v)$ must be continuous on the interior of the factor rental simplex, and there must not be discontinuities on the boundary of that simplex, or something must guarantee that no factor rental can be zero in equilibrium.

---

41 As in ▶ Chap. 5, I neglect joint production, except in ▶ Sect. 6.35 whose theorems are stated and proved so that they are also valid with joint production. With joint production the derived excess demand for factors $\zeta(v)$ cannot be obtained as simply as I obtained it, because generally the price of a jointly produced commodity cannot be determined independently of demand. The proofs of existence of equilibrium become rather involved.

500   Chapter 6 · Existence, Uniqueness and Stability of Non-capitalistic General Equilibria

Since $\zeta(v) = x(p(v),v) - X(p(v),v)$ the two terms on the right-hand side must be continuous on the interior of the factor rental simplex. $X(p(v),v)$ is a continuous function of p and v under the same hypotheses as for the pure exchange economy; p is a continuous function of v if minimum average costs are continuous functions of v, which can be proved to be guaranteed by the properties of the average cost function.

The general proof of the latter result is mathematically complex, because some borderline cases (e.g. Cobb–Douglas production functions when one factor rental is zero) create complications, and I omit it. But in order to make the complications disappear it suffices to assume that the subset of R^n_+ in which the isoquant hypersurface has negative slopes is bounded, i.e. that the marginal product of any factor becomes zero if the employment of the factor is sufficiently increased, a realistic assumption; then the relevant part of the isoquant is bounded, and one derives the continuity of minimum average cost from the theorem of the maximum, which it is convenient to write down here so we can easily see how it is of use here:

■■ Theorem of the Maximum
Let $f(x, \alpha)$, with x a vector and α a vector of parameters, be a continuous function with a compact range and suppose that the constraint set $G(\alpha)$ is a non-empty, compact-valued, continuous correspondence of α; then $M(\alpha)$, i.e. max $f(x,\alpha)$ such that $x \in G(\alpha)$, is a continuous function and $x(\alpha)$ is an upper-hemicontinuous correspondence.

This theorem yields the result we need with $-f(x, \alpha) = x \cdot \alpha$, $x \in G(\alpha)$ the inputs, and α the rental vector which if constrained to be in the unit simplex renders the range of $f(x,\alpha)$ compact because $G(\alpha)$, being the set of input vectors satisfying the constraint 'output $= 1$ unit', is non-empty by the assumptions of continuity and of CRS, is compact-valued by our assumption on marginal products because then only a compact region of the isoquant is admissible, and is a continuous correspondence of α because independent of α; $f(x, \alpha)$ is obviously continuous in x and α.

As to $x(p(v), v)$, it is a continuous function of p and v if (1) the quantities produced and hence the demands for consumption goods are continuous functions of p, which will be the case under the same hypotheses as for the exchange economy, and (2) technical coefficients are continuous functions of v, which is guaranteed by the assumption of strictly convex isoquants.

The assumption of strict convexity of isoquants is somewhat more restrictive than for indifference curves, in that in real economies the production possibilities of firms are often of the activity analysis type, in which case factor demands are upper-hemicontinuous correspondences, but this would only oblige one to have recourse to the kind of more sophisticated proofs of existence, already necessary for the exchange economy if strict convexity of preferences is not assumed.

On the contrary the *discontinuities* caused in the exchange economy by totally or partially strictly *concave* indifference curves have no parallel with firms as long as one assumes CRS and perfectly divisible factors, for the reason illustrated in ▶ Sect. 5.8.2: because of CRS and divisibility the firm can always produce along the segment joining any two points of an isoquant, so if the technological iso-

6.24 · Existence of a GE of Production and Exchange

quant is concave the concave part is replaced by a straight segment, the *economically* relevant isoquant is the *convexification* of the technological one. Factor demands are then correspondences, not functions, but are not discontinuous.

With entry, an industry can be treated as if it were a single firm with CRS. Therefore factor demands never present relevant discontinuities due to technical choices, the discontinuities can only derive from discontinuities in the demand for the products.

The problem remains that if the demand for a factor is a correspondence and not a function of factor rentals, then nothing guarantees that at the equilibrium prices the equilibrium demand will be chosen; here the problem seems more serious than for consumer demand because, owing to the tendency of firms in an industry to adopt the same technical choices, it concerns an entire industry, not a single consumer. Thus if, e.g. the corn industry has activity-analysis isoquants with flat segments and the isocost is tangent to one flat segment, this can mean a significant indeterminacy in the demand for certain factors. I am not aware of discussions of this problem in the literature and will neglect it.

As to the danger of discontinuities on the boundary of the factor rental simplex, these cannot be due to firm choices: the demand for an input never jumps up *discontinuously* when the input rental decreases to zero, because it is a *conditional* input demand, and the optimal employment of an input per unit of output, as its rental decreases towards zero, either reaches a limit at the zero marginal product level (the realistic case) or tends to grow continuously (the unrealistic Cobb–Douglas case). Discontinuous jumps in the excess demand for a factor can only be due to discontinuities in consumer choices for the goods that use that factor. Therefore for the existence of an equilibrium, production causes no problem additional to those posed by consumer choice.

But while no *additional* problem is introduced, the old problems with continuity remain. The discontinuities due to the survival/subsistence problem are even more relevant in the presence of production, because now we can have very many people who obtain their income only from labour and who start having survival problems at the same low level of the real wage.

Even leaving aside the survival/subsistence problem, there remains the zero-income problem as the following example shows.[42] Assume a production economy where two consumption goods, food and diamonds, are produced by the use of homogeneous labour and of two specialized lands, food-land and diamonds-land, with fixed coefficients: the production of one unit of food requires l_f units of labour and m_f units of food-land; the production of one unit of diamonds requires l_d units of labour and m_d units of diamond-land. Food is the numéraire. Because of competition and constant returns to scale, firms producing food or diamonds set prices equal to average cost. Population consists of labourers who own no land, and landowners who supply no labour. Utility only depends on consumption of food and of diamonds; labour supply and supply of either land are

---

42 The example is taken from a seminar by Burak Unveren (Ph.D., Siena, 2011).

502   **Chapter 6 ·** Existence, Uniqueness and Stability of Non-capitalistic General Equilibria

rigid (including at zero rentals; there is no survival problem). Maximum food production, associated with full utilization of food-land, is F. Labourers demand no diamonds when their income is low. Assume maximum labour employment, the one associated with the full utilization of both lands, is less than the rigid labour supply. Then a necessary condition for equilibrium is a zero wage. Consumers have a satiation level for food consumption, and the satiation level is such that total demand for food from landowners is always less than F, while *total* satiation demand for food (i.e. the maximum coming from both landowners and labourers), call it S, is greater than F. Then let the real wage (measured in terms of food) be zero as necessary for equilibrium: if the price of food is positive, demand for food is less than F because it comes only from landowners, so the price of food tends to zero (food-land rent is zero if demand for food is less than F) but as long as it is positive demand for food is less than F, and there isn't equilibrium; when the price of food reaches zero demand for food jumps discontinuously to $S > F$: there is no equilibrium. This discontinuity arises because none of the three conditions that would prevent the zero-income problem is satisfied. Monotonicity of utility functions and interiority of endowments are clearly not satisfied; irreducibility too is not satisfied, because when land is fully utilized the excess labour supply yields no additional utility to anyone else (clearly, in a production economy where endowments consist of potential supply of factor services, irreducibility must mean that the *utilization*, rather than the transfer, of the factor endowment of any agent increases the utility of at least one other agent).

In conclusion, we need not spend time on a formal proof of the existence of the general equilibrium of production and exchange: if the assumptions on consumer choice are such as to *guarantee* existence of an exchange equilibrium, then an equilibrium will also exist when production is introduced (only irreducibility must be modified in the direction indicated above).[43]

I postpone to ▶ Chap. 14 a more general proof than in ▶ Chap. 3 that (in the absence of externalities and of public goods) competitive general equilibria with production are Pareto efficient.

6.25 Uniqueness of the Production Equilibrium

I prove now that if WAM holds for the market excess demand function *derived from the sole choices of consumers*, then for a production economy the set of equilibrium price vectors is convex; furthermore, the equilibrium aggregate

---

43 The reason why in most textbooks the need is felt for an explicit proof of existence of the general equilibrium with production is the different formalization based on a given number of firms with decreasing returns to scale that determines well-defined firms' supply functions and nonzero profits which enter the consumers' budgets; then the production equilibrium cannot be so easily 'reduced' to an exchange equilibrium of factor services. I have argued that this different formalization is indefensible. A number of contemporary general equilibrium theorists, for example Lionel McKenzie and Michio Morishima, appear to agree with me (and with Walras) in that they assume constant returns to scale industries.

consumption vector is unique. The theorem will be proved for an economy where joint production is admitted, and intermediate goods (produced goods utilized as inputs in the production of other goods, capital goods in fact) are explicitly considered and priced. This allows a reinterpretation of the model as intertemporal, with *dated* commodities and discounted prices, describing therefore an intertemporal equilibrium (discussed in detail in ▶ Chap. 8). I introduce here the succinct formalization generally adopted in general equilibrium papers, where the choices of firms are indicated with the **netput** notation.

'Goods' must now be interpreted as referring both to commodities and to services of factors; the assumption of no overlap between the two categories is not made. For example, assume that the period within which the equilibrium's activities are performed lasts three time units; at the end of the first time unit a production of sugar comes out, which can be demanded both by consumers as consumption good and by firms as input (together with other inputs among which second-time-unit labour services and land services) to the production of jams that come out at the end of the second time unit; these jams can be demanded by consumers, or by firms which use them (together with other inputs among which third-time-unit labour services and land services) to produce cakes that come out at the end of the third time unit. 'Goods' are now also distinguished by the date in which they come out and are sold. There are n goods; now prices of goods are indicated by vector π, and if there is a positive interest rate then prices are *discounted* prices (referred to the beginning of the equilibrium's period), but this price notion has not been introduced yet, so the reader not acquainted with this notion should simply assume that the interest rate is zero. For the production decisions I use now the netput notation. Remember that the netput vector representing the production decision of a firm has a negative number for goods demanded by the firm, a positive number for goods offered by the firm for sale. Thus for example in the no joint production case the production by a firm of a quantity q_n of good n through the employment of quantities $a_{1n}q_n,...,a_{kn}q_n$ of inputs (with $k<n$) is represented by the vector $y=(y_1,...,y_k,0,...,0,\ y_n)$ where $y_1=-a_{1n}q_n,\ ...,\ y_k=-a_{kn}q_n,\ y_n=q_n$. In the intertemporal interpretation, the netput vector allows for inputs of different dates and outputs offered for sale at different dates. Produced goods are never the same goods as the goods directly or indirectly used as inputs in their production (in the intertemporal reinterpretation, produced corn is a different good from the corn-seed used to produce it, because it comes out at a subsequent date, so it is treated as a different good although physically both are corn, because goods are distinguished also by their date of availability). If a firm produces ten units of good j at date t and uses six units of the same good for further production effected by the firm itself, offering for sale at date t only four units, the netput vector only shows the number +4 at place j for date t; how much the firm is producing and re-utilizing of the good is not shown.

Consumers' individual excess demands $z^s(\pi)$—the demand vector $x^s(\pi)$ minus the endowment vector ω^s—are summed up to yield the consumers' *market* excess demand vector function $z(\pi)=(z_1(\pi),...,z_n(\pi))^{\mathrm{T}}$.

504 Chapter 6 · Existence, Uniqueness and Stability of Non-capitalistic General Equilibria

The firms' decisions are summed up to yield a *market* netput vector, actually a vector y of excess *supplies* of the ensemble of firms, where a negative y_j indicates that the aggregate of firms *demands* good j, and a positive y_k indicates that the aggregate of firms *supplies* good k. Production obeys constant returns to scale,[44] therefore firms are aggregable, and the production possibility set Y of the economy includes not only all netput vectors available to individual firms but also all their possible combinations; the market netput vector y is an element of Y. Y includes free disposal, i.e. if $y \in Y$ then any $y' \leq y$ (that is, that produces less of some output with the same or more inputs, or uses more of some input to produce the same or less outputs) is also $\in$ Y.

For given $z(\pi)$ and y, the *market* excess demand for good j is $z_j(\pi) - y_j$. Now equilibrium requires

$$z(\pi) - y \leq 0.$$

Note that if good j is a consumption good demanded by firms and supplied by firms, both z_j and y_j are positive and $z_j(\pi) - y_j \leq 0$ means demand does not exceed supply; if good i is a factor service supplied by consumers and demanded by firms, both z_i and y_i are negative, and again $z_i(\pi) - y_i \leq 0$, e.g. $-3 - (-2)$, means demand does not exceed supply. Therefore $z(\pi) - y \leq 0$ also means that with the aggregate netput y, sum of the netputs of all firms, it is possible to satisfy the desired consumption demands with the desired factor supplies. Note that since we assume free disposal, if the equilibrium condition $z(\pi) - y \leq 0$ is satisfied then there is some other y in the production possibility set Y such that $z(\pi) = y$, that is, $z(\pi) \in Y$.[45]

We need two preliminary results.

First, with this notation and the assumption of CRS, competitive equilibria—that is, situations where all agents are price-takers and are optimizing and no good is in excess demand, and a good has zero price if in excess supply—can be characterized in an extremely simple way:

▪▪ Proposition 6.10

(Necessary and sufficient conditions for equilibrium for the CRS production economy with the netput notation) *A price vector π^* is an equilibrium price vector for an economy with CRS production possibility set Y (that satisfies free disposal) if and only if, with π a price vector, y an aggregate netput vector, and $z(\pi)$ the consumers' market excess demand function, it is:*
1. $\pi^* y \leq 0$ *for all* $y \in Y$ (no possibility of positive profits), *and*
2. $z(\pi^*) \in Y$.

---

44 This can also be interpreted as variability in each industry of the number of identical efficient firms with U-shaped average cost curves but sufficiently small relative to total industry output.

45 For example if good j is only offered and demanded by consumers (e.g. baby sitting) and in excess supply, free disposal means that Y includes a process with good j as the sole input, and no output, and since the good will have price zero it is not illegitimate to assume that that process is operated at the scale that renders the market excess supply of the good equal to zero.

6.25 · Uniqueness of the Production Equilibrium

Proof *Only if* part: If π^* is an equilibrium price vector, then (i) is necessary for well-defined profit maximization when there are constant returns to scale, and (ii) is implied by market clearing. *If* part: we must prove that if (i) and (ii) hold, then π^* and $y^* = z(\pi^*)$ constitute an equilibrium, i.e. satisfy market clearing and profit maximization: indeed $y^* = z(\pi^*)$ implies market clearing, and y^* is profit maximizing because from Walras' Law $\pi^* y^* = \pi^* z(\pi^*) = 0$ and so from (i) we obtain $\pi^* y^* \geq \pi^* y$ for all y in Y. The reason, why one writes $y^* = z(\pi^*)$ even when some goods are produced in excess of demand (this might be the case with joint production), or some factors are supplied in excess of demand, is the assumption of free disposal. That in equilibrium goods in excess supply have price zero results from the same reasoning as for the pure exchange economy ($\blacktriangleright$ Sect. 6.11), applied to $z(\pi^*) - y^* \leq 0$. ∎

Second, because of the consumers' balanced budgets what can be called a *Walras' Law restricted to consumers' excess demands holds*: for any price vector it is $\pi \cdot z(\pi) = 0$. So the assumption I call *WAM* (the **Weak Axiom** of revealed preferences holding for **market** consumer excess demand), which states: *for any two different non-proportional price vectors π' and π'' such that $z(\pi') \neq z(\pi'')$, if $\pi' \cdot z(\pi') \geq \pi' \cdot z(\pi'')$ then $\pi'' \cdot z(\pi'') < \pi'' \cdot z(\pi')$*, can be reformulated for the production economy as follows:

▪▪ Definition. WAM for the Production Economy
If $\pi' z(\pi'') \leq 0$ and $z(\pi') \neq z(\pi'')$, then $\pi'' z(\pi') > 0$. Equivalently: if $\pi' z(\pi'') \leq 0$ and $\pi'' z(\pi') \leq 0$, then $z(\pi') = z(\pi'')$.

Now the result I intend to prove:

▪▪ Proposition 6.11
(Theorem of equilibrium quasi-uniqueness of prices in the production economy under WAM) *Assume preferences are continuous, strictly convex and strongly monotonic. Let $z(\pi)$ stand for the continuous excess demand function of consumers. Let Y stand for the set of production possibilities of the several industries that satisfies free disposal. I) Suppose that $z(\pi)$ is such that, for any constant returns technology Y, the economy formed by $z(\pi)$ and Y has a unique (normalized) equilibrium price vector π. Then $z(\pi)$ satisfies WAM. II) Conversely, if $z(\pi)$ satisfies WAM then, for any constant returns convex technology Y, the set of equilibrium normalized price vectors is convex (and so unique if finite), and all equilibrium price vectors are associated with the same vector z of excess demands of the ensemble of consumers and hence also with the same aggregate production vector y.*

Proof of (I) By the laws of logic, if statement 'A' implies statement 'B', then 'not B' implies 'not A': so we can equivalently prove that if $z(\pi)$ does *not* satisfy WAM, then there is a constant returns to scale production possibility set Y for which the economy formed by $z(\pi)$ and Y has more than one equilibrium. Suppose $z(\pi)$ violates WAM, i.e. there exist two normalized price vectors π', π'' such that $z(\pi') \neq z(\pi'')$, $\pi' z(\pi'') \leq 0$ and $\pi'' z(\pi') \leq 0$. Then there exists a CRS convex production possibility set such that netputs in it can be chosen so that both π' and π''

506 Chapter 6 · Existence, Uniqueness and Stability of Non-capitalistic General Equilibria

are equilibrium prices: this is $Y^* = \{y \in R^n: \pi'y \leq 0 \text{ and } \pi''y \leq 0\}$. Y^* is not empty since it contains the two vectors $y' = z(\pi')$ and $y'' = z(\pi'')$, because $\pi''y' \leq 0$ by assumption and $\pi'y' = \pi'z(\pi') = 0$ by Walras' Law restricted to consumers' excess demand, and the same holds for y''; this shows that condition (ii) is satisfied by both y' and y'', and by construction of Y^* the same holds for condition (i), hence there are (at least) two equilibria.

Proof of (II) Suppose π' and π'' are two different equilibrium price vectors, i.e. $z(\pi') \in Y$, $z(\pi'') \in Y$ and for any $y \in Y$ it is $\pi'y \leq 0$ and $\pi''y \leq 0$. Define $\pi = \alpha\pi' + (1 - \alpha)\pi''$ for $0 < \alpha < 1$. We show that π is an equilibrium price vector. By construction $\pi y = \alpha\pi'y + (1 - \alpha)\pi''y \leq 0$ for all $y \in Y$; it remains to show that $z(\pi) \in Y$. By Walras' Law restricted to consumers it is $0 = \pi z(\pi) = \alpha\pi'z(\pi) + (1 - \alpha)\pi''z(\pi)$; not both terms on the right-hand side can be positive so it is either $\alpha\pi'z(\pi) \leq 0$ or $(1 - \alpha)\pi''z(\pi) \leq 0$. Suppose $\alpha\pi'z(\pi) \leq 0$, then also $\pi'z(\pi) \leq 0$; but since $z(\pi') \in Y$ and we have shown that $\pi y \leq 0$ for all $y \in Y$, it is also $\pi z(\pi') \leq 0$, and WAM is violated unless $z(\pi) = z(\pi')$. If it is not $\alpha\pi'z(\pi) \leq 0$, then it is $(1 - \alpha)\pi''z(\pi) \leq 0$ and the same reasoning concludes to $z(\pi) = z(\pi'')$. Since either $z(\pi) = z(\pi')$ or $z(\pi) = z(\pi'')$ (or both), it is $z(\pi) \in Y$, so π is an equilibrium price vector and we have shown that the set of equilibrium prices is convex. In addition, since the proof that either $z(\pi) = z(\pi')$ or $z(\pi) = z(\pi'')$ holds for any $\alpha \in (0, 1)$, and since $z(\cdot)$ is continuous, it must be $z(\pi') = z(\pi'')$, otherwise there would be a discontinuity of $z(\cdot)$ somewhere as α varied over the interval $[0,1]$; so all equilibrium price vectors are associated with the same vector z of excess demands of the ensemble of consumers and hence also with the same market production vector y.[46] ∎

'Quasi-uniqueness' in the theorem's name stresses that equilibrium is not always unique but then there is a *continuum* of equilibrium price vectors that form a convex set, all associated with the same vector y of aggregate production decisions of the firm sector. In the exchange economy, the situations in which a unique equilibrium market excess demand does not uniquely determine the equilibrium relative prices (if one leaves aside the extreme flukes of zero probability in which the changes in the choices of one consumer are exactly compensated by the changes in the choices of other consumers) are due to 'kinks' in indifference curves, or to corner solutions, at equilibrium. For example, if the equilibrium is a no exchange equilibrium (everybody satisfied with her initial endowment) and there are kinks in the indifference curves of all consumers at their endowment point, the equilibrium prices may be indeterminate within an interval (draw the picture in an Edgeworth box!); the same can happen if the equilibrium entails for a certain good a corner solution for all consumers. But since either of these cases

---

46 Note that this does not mean that the equilibrium *allocation* is unique: different equilibria might be associated with different excess demands of the several consumers, which happen to sum up to the same consumer market excess demand vector. Of course it would be a fluke, but not a logical impossibility.

6.25 · Uniqueness of the Production Equilibrium

must concern *all* consumers, it is an extremely unlikely occurrence. With production, the situation is even less likely: leaving again aside the zero probability case of perfect compensation of the changes in factor supplies and consumption demands by one consumer with the changes by the other consumers, the equilibrium must be either a no production equilibrium (again with kinks in the indifference curves at the endowment points) or an equilibrium where factor supplies are rigid within a certain range of relative factor rentals (owing to kinks or corner solutions), and where furthermore consumption demands too are rigid for the corresponding range of relative product prices. When factor supplies are given but relative factor prices (and hence, in general, relative consumption goods prices) vary, a constant demand for consumption goods obtains in general only if for all consumers all consumption goods are perfect complements (or almost perfect complements, i.e. with kinks of the indifference curves) *in the same proportions*, so that the composition of the demand of all consumers is the same and remains unaltered as relative consumption goods prices vary. Since these cases are extremely unlikely, we can conclude that, in the pure exchange economy as well as in the production economy, under WAM the equilibrium is almost certainly unique. This result is strengthened if there is a single or representative consumer who owns the economy's endowment and has 'smooth' strictly convex indifference curves.

*If there is **a single consumer** with differentiable strictly quasi-concave monotonic utility function, equilibrium is unique.*

The proof is easy and very intuitive (and an exercise in the use of netputs). Remember the Production Possibility Frontier used when discussing international trade at the end of ▶ Chap. 5 or Pareto efficiency in ▶ Chap. 3. The PPF is the locus of all efficient consumption vectors the economy can produce; now let us include in these consumption vectors also possible direct consumptions of part of the endowments. It is possible to view any basket on the PPF as consisting entirely of 'produced' goods, if one treats the endowment of a factor directly consumed by its owner as a consumption good 'produced' by the same quantity of itself as sole input. For example in an economy with two factors, labour and land, and two produced consumption goods, corn and meat, produced by differentiable production functions, the PPF is the smooth concave surface in R^4_+ of vectors of quantities of corn, meat, leisure 'produced' by non-utilized labour time and gardens 'produced' by non-utilized land, such that it is not possible to obtain more of one of them without renouncing some of the others. It was shown that the slope of a smooth PPF restricted to two goods indicates their competitive equilibrium relative price (equal to relative average cost). In such an economy our single consumer owns all endowments, so her income is the value of endowments. The preferred consumption basket x^* is on the PPF, and, if strictly positive as I shall assume, it is at the unique point where PPF and indifference surface are tangent: there cannot be two tangent points since the PPF is concave and indifference surfaces are strictly convex. The hyperplane tangent to any point of the PPF, e.g. point E in ◨ Fig. 6.21, has slopes that indicate relative prices and is the consumer's budget hyperplane if those are the prices, because the cost of the basket indicated by that point is the value of the inputs utilized to produce it, which is the

508   **Chapter 6** · Existence, Uniqueness and Stability of Non-capitalistic General Equilibria

value of endowments,[47] the consumer's income; if the tangency is at the preferred basket x^*, the budget hyperplane is also tangent to the indifference curve through x^*, and at those prices the consumer chooses x^*, so there is equilibrium.

If you want more than a geometric-intuitive proof, then here is a more formal proof.

Proof   Let ω be the endowment vector. By assumption, x^* is feasible and efficient, that is, there is a netput vector y^* in the production possibility set Y such that $y^* + \omega \geq x^*$ and there is no other $y \in Y$ such that $y + \omega > x^*$ (remember that, for vectors, the notation in this book is $a \geq b$ does not exclude $a = b$; $a > b$ means $a \neq b$ and $a \geq b$; $a > > b$ means $a_i > b_i$, all i). Assuming sufficient substitutability among inputs we can assume $y^* + \omega = x^*$, so $x^* - y^* = \omega$. Now let v be a vector of prices of the goods appearing in the endowments. Cost minimization and zero profits (because of CRS industries) determine the vector p of prices of produced goods. Let $\pi = (v, p)$ be the resulting price vector. At these prices the cost of producing x^* with netput y^* is $-\pi(y^* - x^*) = \pi(x^* - y^*) = \pi\omega$. If the production methods in y^* are the cost-minimizing ones at factor prices v, then $\pi y^* = 0$, because profits are zero; hence $\pi x^* = \pi\omega$, x^* is on the budget hyperplane at prices π that reflect costs of production, so the hyperplane is tangent to the PPF in x^* and also tangent to the indifference curve through x^*, and x^* is the optimal choice. If at factor prices v the cost-minimizing methods are other ones, then prices p are, for at least some goods in x^*, less than the cost of producing them with the methods in y^*, so $\pi x^* < \pi(x^* - y^*) = \pi\omega$: the budget line passes outside x^*; then the consumer cannot choose x^*, otherwise monotonicity is contradicted; the chosen x is preferred to x^*, but then it cannot be feasible because by assumption x^* is the preferred basket among the feasible ones, so there is excess demand for some endowments, and there cannot be equilibrium. So there cannot be other equilibria except the one with x^* as quantities consumed and relative prices indicated by the slope of the PPF at x^*. ∎

But intuitive grasp of the reasons why a result obtains is important, so let us look at Fig. 6.21, where the economy produces a single consumption good with labour and land as inputs, and the concave curve is the PPF restricted to leisure and consumption, assuming a rigid (and fully utilized) supply of land to firms. Point D is x^* (restricted to leisure and consumption); for any point on the PPF, the tangent line is the consumer's budget line at the corresponding prices; for any budget line other than the one tangent at D, the preferred basket is outside the PPF. (To understand the figure, take the consumption good as numéraire; the slope of the budget line indicates the real wage; so if OA is leisure, then segment $A\lambda_{max}$ is labour, AE is the amount produced of the consumption good, AC is wage income,[48] and CE is land rent. If the budget line is tangent to the PPF in E, basket E is feasible and affordable, but the preferred basket cannot be E, it is B, necessarily unfeasible.)

---

47 Since the bundles on the PPF include the part of endowments not used in production, any point of the PPF requires for its production the entire endowment.

48 *Exercise*: Explain why segment AC in ▣ Fig. 6.21 is wage income.

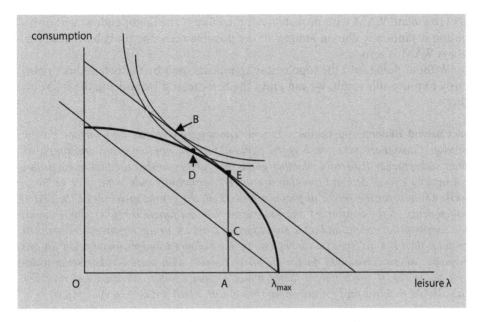

Fig. 6.21 Representative consumer with a PPF between leisure and consumption

6.26 WAM and the Hildenbrand–Grodal Observation

I have argued that it is unclear why WAM should hold apart from the case when there exists a representative consumer. Interestingly, the WAM assumption is even more restrictive for a production economy than for the exchange economy, for a reason highlighted by Hildenbrand and Grodal (Hildenbrand 1989, pp. 979–985; Grodal and Hildenbrand 1989, pp. 635–639). Consider a production economy with many consumption goods and at least two factors, where factors of production do not yield direct utility to consumers (they are then called *pure* factors of production and their supply by consumers coincides with their endowments—note that this excludes monotonic preferences). Assume there isn't a representative consumer. Take the total factor endowments as given; the set of allocations of these total endowments among the consumers which cause the consumers' market excess demand function $z(\pi)$ to satisfy WAM is a *negligible* subset (i.e. a subset of Lebesgue measure zero) of the set of possible factor endowment allocations; in other words, if, given the preferences of consumers, a certain distribution of factor endowments determines a $z(\pi)$ that satisfies WAM, then any very small redistribution of factor endowments among the consumers[49] will cause the new

---

49 In fact, any small change in factor endowments, even if it alters total endowments, because anyway the probability that the new allocation of the new total endowments be among those that guarantee WAM is again zero.

510   Chapter 6 · Existence, Uniqueness and Stability of Non-capitalistic General Equilibria

$z(\pi)$ to violate WAM with probability 1; therefore if the factor endowment distribution is randomly chosen among all the possible ones, the probability that $z(\pi)$ obeys WAM is zero.

Without going into the topological arguments used by the two authors rigorously to prove this result, we can grasp the basic reason by noticing the following *fact*.

Fact Behind Hildenbrand–Grodal   *Assume consumption goods and factors do not overlap. Consumers have non-negative demand for consumption goods and supply all their endowments of factors. Number goods and factors so that the first m goods in a consumer's excess demand function are the consumption goods, with price vector p, while v stands for the vector of factor rentals. Call $z^C(p,v)$ the m-vector of the first m components of the consumers' market excess demand function $z(p, v)$, the demands for consumption goods; and let ω stand for the n-vector of aggregate endowments of factors; then it is $pz^C(p, v) = v\omega$ because of the balanced budget assumption. In this economy where consumers' factor supplies coincide with factor endowments whatever the prices, if two different factor rental vectors v and v' are such that $v\omega = v'\omega$, then WAM requires that for any given (non-normalized) p it is $z^C(p,v) = z^C(p,v')$.*

Proof $v\omega = v'\omega$ implies $pz^C(p,v) = pz^C(p, v')$ owing to balanced budgets; since $z(p, v)$ is the vector with $z^C(p, v)$ as its first m components and $-\omega$ as its other components, it is $(p, v)\cdot z(p, v') = pz^C(p, v') - v\omega = pz^C(p, v) - v\omega = 0 = (p, v')z(p, v)$, hence it is both $(p, v)\cdot z(p, v') \leq 0$ and $(p, v')\cdot z(p, v) \leq 0$, and the only way WAM can hold is that $z(p, v) = z(p, v')$, that is, $z^C(p, v) = z^C(p, v')$. ∎

So for WAM not to be violated in this economy with rigid factor supplies, all changes in factor prices (with product prices unaltered) that leave the aggregate value of endowments unaltered must leave *all* market demands for consumption goods unaltered. But an unchanging aggregate value of endowments can always be obtained, by choosing the aggregate endowment vector as numéraire,[50] a choice that does not alter excess demands; so what is needed is that changes in relative factor prices leave all market demands for consumption goods unaltered. Generally a change in factor prices redistributes income across consumers, and then their demands for consumption goods change and thus market demands change too. This will not happen if there is a representative consumer, because she owns the entire economy's factor endowment, so her wealth does not change when v changes, and since p does not change, her demands do not change. Apart from this case, in this economy WAM can hold only in two special cases:
1. there is only one consumption good demanded by consumers;
2. changes in relative factor prices cause no redistribution of wealth, that is, the endowment vectors of consumers are co-linear: this is the case, of measure zero among all allocations of factor endowments among consumers, that saves WAM.

---

50   As noticed in the Ph.D. thesis of S. M. Fratini, *Il problema della molteplicità degli equilibri da Walras a Debreu* (Università di Roma 3, 2001), ▶ Chap. 7.

6.27 · Gross Substitutability not Sufficient for Uniqueness

A point apparently not noticed by Hildenbrand and Grodal, who assume that *all* factors are pure factors, is that the above fact—which is the key to their result—only needs that *at least two* of the factors are pure factors (i.e. yield no direct utility); the fact survives unaltered, if the consumers' excess demands for the other factors (the ones for which there can be demand for consumption purposes) are included in the vector $z^C(p,v)$, their rentals are included in the vector p, and ω and v are understood to refer only to the pure factors. Thus the existence of a variable reservation demand for labour (i.e. for leisure) does not render Hildenbrand and Grodal's result irrelevant, because the result only needs that there be at least two other factors which yield no direct utility to their owners, e.g. inhospitable lands of different types useful for production but unattractive for direct enjoyment, or—in capitalistic economies—pure capital goods; and this is *very* likely. Thus, recourse to the WAM assumption in order to ensure uniqueness of equilibrium is even less justifiable in production economies than in pure exchange economies.

6.27 Gross Substitutability not Sufficient for Uniqueness

The other main assumption guaranteeing uniqueness of equilibrium *in the pure exchange economy*, gross substitutability in consumer choice,[51] does *not* guarantee uniqueness of equilibrium in the production economy. Here is an example.

Consider the simple economy discussed in ▶ Chap. 3 to clarify the indirect factor substitution mechanism, where labour and land produce corn and meat with fixed coefficients (no technical choice). Corn is the more labour-intensive good. Assume that workers (all identical) are the sole suppliers of labour, landowners (all identical) are the sole suppliers of land, and for all relative factor rentals the proportion of corn to meat in the workers' consumption demand is higher than in the landowners' demand. We can call this the case of *self-intensive tastes of factor owners* in the sense that the income earned by a factor goes to buy a basket of consumption goods whose production uses that factor more intensively than on average. As pointed out in ▶ Chap. 3, ▶ Sect. 3.5.2, if factor supplies are rigid and the composition of demand of the two classes is also rigid, a decrease of the wage rate relative to the rent rate causes a *decrease* of the labour–land ratio in total factor demand, hence an upward-sloping demand-for-labour curve if land is assumed fully employed (as in ◻ Fig. 3.6), with, in all likelihood, three equilibria of which the full-employment one is unstable, while in the other two locally stable equilibria one factor is not fully employed and gets a zero rental. So far in this example consumer choices do not satisfy GS, which excludes rigid factor supplies and rigid composition of demand for produced goods; but we can modify the assumptions about preferences by assuming that all consumers have a very small direct demand for the services of both factors and that there is a very small

---

51 Of course what I mean is GS applying to each consumer's excess demand, and therefore also to the sum z(p, v) of the consumers' excess demands, but not to the economy-wide excess demands which also depend on firms' choices.

variability of consumer choices, such that if the sole price of one consumption good increases then all consumers increase by a tiny amount their demands for the other consumption good and their direct demands for the two factors, and if the sole rental of one factor increases then the owners of that factor decrease by a tiny amount their direct demand for that factor (i.e. increase a bit its supply), increase their demand for both consumption goods (by a common percentage) and increase by a tiny amount their direct demand for the other factor, while the owners of the other factor decrease by a tiny amount their direct demand for the first factor and increase by a tiny amount their demands for the two consumption goods and their direct demand for their own factor. Now GS holds for each consumer and hence for $z(p, v)$, but the variations in factor supply and in the composition of consumer demand relative to the rigid case can be made as small as one likes, hence the sign of the dependence of the composition of factor demand on relative factor prices can be left unchanged; thus if before this modification of preferences there were three equilibria there will still be three equilibria after the modification.

The point is that in the production economy the GS assumption constrains consumer choice but does not guarantee that a rise in the 'price' of the services of a factor—say, of leisure/labour—reduces the excess demand for it, because consumers demand less leisure, but they also demand leisure (i.e. labour) indirectly by demanding goods which require leisure (labour) to be produced, and GS poses no constraint on this indirect demand. Therefore, since the production economy, even the non-capitalistic one, is clearly closer to reality than the pure exchange economy, I find it strange that so much attention should have been paid to GS on the equilibrium uniqueness issue.

Strictly analogous considerations hold for diagonal dominance.

So sufficient conditions for uniqueness are even more difficult to reach for the production economy than for the exchange economy; essentially, we are left with WAM only.

6.28 Stability: The Tâtonnement in the Production Economy

For the perfectly competitive production economy formalized as required by economic good sense, that is with free entry and hence CRS industries, the supply of a product and the associated demands for factors are infinite or zero or indeterminate in the tâtonnement, depending on whether profits in that industry are positive, negative or zero. The infinite or zero production decisions indicate to the auctioneer the presence of positive or negative profits and oblige the auctioneer to find and announce, together with the vector v of factor prices, zero-profit product prices (i.e. prices obeying equations (A)). At these prices, equilibrium requires productions adapted to demands (see below for a problem that arises at this point). Then at the given $(p(v), v)$ price vector, nonzero excess demands arise only in factor markets. The resulting tâtonnement can be reduced to a tâtonnement acting exclusively on factor rentals v in response to disequilibria in markets of (non-produced) factors, and therefore it can be called a *factor tâtonnement* (Mandler 2005).

6.28 · Stability: The Tâtonnement in the Production Economy

But if a vector $(p(v), v)$ produces positive excess demand for a factor, the quantities of outputs behind that excess demand cannot actually be produced, there is not enough of that factor. So the disequilibrium as formalized by the tâtonnement cannot be given indications on the *actual* behaviour of an economy in disequilibrium unless one assumes the fairy tale auctioneer.

The results of tâtonnement studies are therefore of unclear relevance for ascertaining the stability of equilibrium in actual production economies. The founders of the marginal approach (with the sole exception of Walras, for reasons that will become clear in ▶ Chap. 7) studied the stability of the production equilibrium in another way, the one illustrated in ▶ Chap. 3: the argument was that, taking the employment of all factors but one as given, the demand curve for the last factor was decreasing, and in all likelihood this ensured the stability of the market of that factor; if then there was disequilibrium on some other factor market, the decreasing demand curve for that other factor would ensure stability there too. Interestingly, in this description of disequilibrium adjustments *no assumption of balanced budgets of consumers was made*. The incomes of consumers were assumed to depend on how many of them found purchasers for their factor supplies, and the output market was always in equilibrium. A decrease in the rental of a factor in excess supply was assumed to induce firms to increase the demand for the factor, which would raise the incomes of consumers and thus would make it possible to sell the increased product. The profession is still waiting for a careful reconstruction of this different, more sensible marginalist approach to stability and of when and why it was later abandoned in favour of the tâtonnement.

There is another serious problem for the tâtonnement in the production economy, which seems to have escaped attention so far. Assume, as one must, CRS industries, owing to free entry or to firms having themselves CRS production functions.[52] Then the prices proposed by the auctioneer must be such as to guarantee zero profits (neoclassical meaning), otherwise in each industry product supply is either zero or infinite. But at zero-profit prices each industry has a horizontal supply curve, supply is indeterminate. Since profits are zero, CRS firms are indifferent as to how much to produce, and firms with U-shaped average cost curves are indifferent as to whether to enter or not. They have no incentive to adjust the industry's output to demand. So there is no reason why entry and production-level decisions at the equilibrium prices, if taken separately by each entrepreneur, should be the ones indicated by equations (B). *The announcement by the auctioneer of equilibrium prices is not enough to ensure equilibrium.*

This difficulty did not arise in the traditional conception of adjustment of quantities produced to quantities demanded as gradual and taking time and involving actual productions—a conception associated of course with the conception of equilibrium as a long-period position. The reader will remember, for

---

52 The treatise on general equilibrium by Arrow and Hahn (1971) admits a given number of firms but admits that the theory must be able to deal with firms having constant returns to scale, in which case the problem I am going to point out does arise.

514   Chapter 6 · Existence, Uniqueness and Stability of Non-capitalistic General Equilibria

example, the Marshallian description of the long-period adjustment in product markets: in each product market, if price is not at the long-period level, the short-period supply curve shifts (because of gradual, time-consuming change in the number of plants in the industry); the tendency towards the long-period price operates through the gradual tendency of the quantity produced to adjust to the quantity demanded at that price. The tendency to satisfy equations (B) makes perfect sense in such a perspective.

In the tâtonnement setting, on the contrary, firms announce only *intentions* as to how much to produce, and since the auctioneer can only announce zero-profit prices, these intentions are *indeterminate*. (A given number of fixed plants in each industry do not avoid the problem, because firms are legal entities, which can demand fixed plants too: the auctioneer must announce rental rates for fixed plants too and determine product prices such that, also on the basis of these rental rates, profits are zero. So, since profits are zero anyway, a firm is indifferent between deciding to produce with one, or two, or ten leased fixed plants. If at the announced prices the total demand for fixed plants in an industry differs from the number of available fixed plants, that is no problem because intentions are only binding if an equilibrium results from them, so firms can ask for a number of fixed plants even vastly different from availability, it causes them no damage.) Of course factor demands are analogously indeterminate. In the economy of ▶ Chap. 3 that produces a single good with labour and land, at the equilibrium full-employment factor rentals firms are indifferent as to how much to produce, nothing guarantees the full employment of the two factors. Thus the auctioneer story in the CRS production economy obliges one to assume that, in order for equations (B) to be satisfied, the auctioneer must act as a true central planner, *imposing* how many and how big the firms must be in each industry so as to render production equal to demand, both at each stage of the tâtonnement and in equilibrium. The market as depicted in the auctioneer fairy tale needs a central planner!

The way out is to admit that *disequilibrium adjustments are not virtual but real, disequilibrium productions actually take place*, the Marshallian adjustments in each product market take time and entail actual productions and the actual building or closing down of fixed plants; then productions cannot become infinite at a price greater than *MinLAC* because production is limited by factor availability, production can only gradually increase as productive capacity is adjusted by building new plants, which takes time; and once the adjustment of the industry's short-period supply curve causes price to equal minimum average cost (i.e. the long-period price), supply is not indeterminate, it is determined by the short-period supply curve. It would seem that when, for reasons that will become clear in the next chapter, general equilibrium theory introduced the auctioneer-guided tâtonnement, it was not realized that the adjustment of quantities produced to the quantities demanded at zero-profit prices *had* to be time-consuming and gradual in order to make sense, while it could not be so in the tâtonnement, whose introduction had precisely the purpose of preventing disequilibrium productions from actually happening. So modern general equilibrium theory when it tries to study stability via the tâtonnement cannot do without the planner–auctioneer. One more reason to doubt the relevance of tâtonnement results.

6.29 Mandler's Factor Tâtonnement

If one still wants to study the tâtonnement in the (non-capitalistic) production economy, there seems to be little alternative to accepting that the auctioneer acts like a true planner, announcing, together with factor prices, product prices equal to minimum average costs and somehow ensuring the adjustment of the quantities that firms promise to produce to the quantities demanded at those zero-profit prices, so that there can be disequilibrium only in factor markets; then the tâtonnement can be called a *factor tâtonnement*.

Only one sufficient condition of clear economic interpretation is known that ensures the global stability of this tâtonnement: WAM. The proof becomes complicated if one assumes that isoquants can be of the activity-analysis type, because then it can happen that there is tangency between isocost and a segment of the kinked isoquant, and then the output corresponding to that isoquant can be obtained with a continuum of combinations of two methods, in which case factor demand is not uniquely determined, it is not a function but a *correspondence* of factor rentals and output. It is possible to prove that under WAM the tâtonnement is convergent even in this case; the proof, due to Mandler (2005), uses advanced results from the theory of Liapunov stability for dynamical systems with *correspondences* in place of functions; a simplified version of the proof, that assumes strictly convex isoquants and indifference curves, is supplied below. (Other sufficient—but still very restrictive—conditions for tâtonnement stability are known only for the unacceptable model of production economy with a given number of decreasing returns firms.)

The slightly simplified version of Mandler's (2005) proof of factor tâtonnement stability I will now present applies to equilibria of constant returns to scale production economies (reinterpretable as intertemporal economies with vertically integrated firms, see ▶ Chap. 8) whose consumers' market excess demand function satisfies the Weak Axiom (WAM). Here the equilibrium is interpreted as the long-period equilibrium of an acapitalistic economy whose factors are (types of) labour and (types of) land. In ▶ Chap. 8 this result is reinterpreted as applying to a neo-Walrasian intertemporal equilibrium (over a finite number of periods) of an economy with capital goods but vertically integrated firms.

Assume k non-produced *factors*, whose services can also be directly demanded by consumers.

The factors can serve as inputs to CRS production functions (no joint production) with *strictly convex* isoquants[53] that produce m different consumption goods.

---

53 This is my main simplification relative to Mandler's proof. Mandler admits the possibility of isoquants with straight segments (activity-analysis isoquants); then once output and factor prices are given, a firm's demand for factors can be a correspondence instead of a uniquely determined vector, and Mandler must have recourse to the theory of dynamical systems with correspondences in place of functions (cf. Aubin and Cellina 1984).

516 Chapter 6 · Existence, Uniqueness and Stability of Non-capitalistic General Equilibria

In this section I return to indicating vectors as bold characters.

Let $\mathbf{w}$ be the k-vector of factor prices or rentals, normalized by putting their sum equal to 1. For each $\mathbf{w} \geq 0$, minimum average production cost can be calculated for each product and it yields a k-vector $\mathbf{p(w)}$ of product prices yielding zero (extra)profit.

At each 'round' of the tâtonnement the auctioneer announces the vector of factor prices $\mathbf{w}$ and the vector of product prices $\mathbf{p(w)}$. At these prices each consumer determines her vectorial excess demand for products and for factors; the sum over all consumers of these excess demands we indicate as the $(k+m)$-vectorial function $\mathbf{z(w,p(w))}$ and for short as $\mathbf{z(w)}$. I assume that $\mathbf{z(w)}$ is continuous for positive prices. Its first k elements and last m elements are the two vectors $\mathbf{z_f(w)}$ and $\mathbf{z_p(w)}$ that indicate the consumers' market excess demands, respectively, for factors,[54] and for products: $\mathbf{z(w)} \equiv (\mathbf{z_f(w)},\mathbf{z_p(w)})$. It satisfies Walras' Law restricted to consumers (all consumers' budgets are balanced), that is, $\mathbf{w}\cdot\mathbf{z_f(w)} + \mathbf{p}\cdot\mathbf{z_p(w)} = 0$; since firms' profits are zero, consumers receive no income from the property of firms. Firms minimize cost, and each industry adapts its supply of product to the demand for it (this is where the planner–auctioneer is needed; Mandler does not discuss this problem); therefore, in the aggregate, firms produce a vector equal to $\mathbf{z_p(w)}$, with factor inputs $\mathbf{y_f(w,z_p(w))}$ determined by the technical coefficients reflecting cost minimization and by the quantities of consumption goods to be produced. I assume the cost-minimizing technical coefficients are uniquely determined by $\mathbf{w}$.

Consider the $(k+m) \times m$ matrix $\mathbf{A(w)}$, whose jth column $\mathbf{a^j}$ is the cost-minimizing vector of netputs associated with production of one unit of consumption good j at factor prices $\mathbf{w}$: the first k elements of $\mathbf{a^j}$ are non-positive and represent the negatives of the technical coefficients of factors required to produce one unit of product j; the other m elements are all zero except the jth one which is $+1$.

If the column vector of quantities produced, or 'activity levels', of the several industries is $\mathbf{x}$, the vector $\mathbf{A(w)x}$ yields the netput vector of the aggregate of firms, non-positive in the first k elements and non-negative in the last m. Actually $\mathbf{A}$ is composed of two matrices one on top of the other, $\mathbf{A} = \begin{bmatrix} A_F \\ I \end{bmatrix}$; the top one, that depends on $\mathbf{w}$, is the $k \times m$ matrix of factor inputs per unit of output (taken as negative) and the bottom one is a $m \times m$ identity matrix. If outputs are $\mathbf{z_p(w)}$ then input demand is $\mathbf{y_f} = A_F(\mathbf{w})\mathbf{z_p(w)}$. Thus for each $\mathbf{w}$ we obtain an excess *demand* vector for factors $\boldsymbol{\zeta}(\mathbf{w}) \equiv \mathbf{z_f(w)} - \mathbf{y_f(w)}$. (The signs on the right-hand side derive from the netput representation: the aggregate demand for factor j by firms is a negative number, and the minus sign in front of it turns it into a positive number, while an aggregate positive supply of factor j by consumers means z_{fj} is a negative number, so in this case factor j is in excess demand if $-y_{fj} > -z_{fj}$.)

The tâtonnement operates on $\mathbf{w}$ and is governed by

$$\dot{\mathbf{w}}(t) = [\alpha_1 \zeta_1(\mathbf{w}(t)), \dots, \alpha_k \zeta_k(\mathbf{w}(t))], \quad \text{with } \alpha \gg 0.$$

---

54 These will be *negative*, if consumers' demand for a factor is less than its endowment.

6.29 · Mandler's Factor Tâtonnement

In this equation t stands for the imaginary time outside real time in which the tâtonnement operates. For simplicity I assume that when a factor price gets sufficiently close to zero, consumers' direct demand for the factor service grows large enough to render its excess demand positive; this is to avoid the need to modify the tâtonnement rule to prevent prices from becoming negative; the proof could be modified so as not to need this assumption.[55] On this basis I proceed to prove:

■■ Mandler's Theorem

If the consumers' market excess demand function $\mathbf{z(w)}$ *satisfies WAM, then any path* $\mathbf{w}(t)$ *beginning from any positive* $\mathbf{w}(0)$ *and obeying* $\dot{\mathbf{w}}(t) = [\alpha_1 \zeta_1(\mathbf{w}(t)), \ldots, \alpha_k \zeta_k(\mathbf{w}(t))]\mathbf{z}$, *with* $\alpha \gg 0$, *converges to an equilibrium* $\mathbf{w}^*$.

Proof (I avoid zero initial factor prices in order to avoid the possibility of initially infinite, i.e. not defined, excess demands, as one would obtain under strongly monotonic preferences.) Let $\mathbf{w}^*$ denote an equilibrium and define the distance between $\mathbf{w}(t)$ and $\mathbf{w}^*$ as

$$V(t) = \sum_{j=1}^{m} \frac{1}{\alpha_j} (w_j(t) - w_j^*)^2.$$

$V(t)$ is positive for $\mathbf{w} \neq \mathbf{w}^*$, and it reaches a minimum, in fact zero, at $\mathbf{w}^*$ and only there. It is also a continuously differentiable function of t. So in order for it to be a Liapunov function yielding the stability of the tâtonnement, we must only prove that $\dot{V}(x(t)) \equiv \left(\sum \frac{\partial V}{\partial w_i} \frac{dw_i}{dt} \right) < 0$, for all $\mathbf{w} \neq \mathbf{w}^*$.

To this end what is needed is that the following condition holds: *if* $\mathbf{z(w)}$ *satisfies WAM and* $\mathbf{w}$ *is not an equilibrium factor price vector, then* $\mathbf{w}^* \cdot \zeta(\mathbf{w}) > 0$. Then the proof can repeat the argument used for the exchange economy in ▶ Sect. 6.20. Note that the fact that WAM holds for $\mathbf{z(w)}$ does not imply that it holds for $\zeta(\mathbf{w})$, but nonetheless it can be proved that the above condition holds. The proof is by contradiction. Suppose that, contrary to the condition we want to prove,

$$\mathbf{w}^* \cdot (\mathbf{z_f(w)} - \mathbf{y_f(w)}) \leq 0. \tag{6.8}$$

Profit maximization implies the WAPM (▶ Sect. 5.9; let us remember its meaning: at given prices, producing a given net output with a vector of inputs different from an optimal one yields less profit than with the optimal input vector, or at most the same) and therefore, since the assumption about product prices implies that profits with the optimal inputs are zero, if prices are the equilibrium ones we obtain:

$$\left(\mathbf{w}^*, \mathbf{p}(\mathbf{w}^*)\right) \cdot \left(\mathbf{y_f(w)}, \mathbf{z_p(w)}\right) \leq 0; \tag{6.9}$$

---

55 Mandler's proof does not make this simplifying assumption and is accordingly more complex.

518   **Chapter 6** · Existence, Uniqueness and Stability of Non-capitalistic General Equilibria

(6.8) and (6.9) plus the non-negativity of $\mathbf{w}^*$ imply $\mathbf{w}^* \cdot (\mathbf{y}_f(\mathbf{w}) + \mathbf{z}_f(\mathbf{w}) - \mathbf{y}_f(\mathbf{w})) \leq 0$, hence

$$\left(\mathbf{w}^*, \mathbf{p}\left(\mathbf{w}^*\right)\right) \cdot \left(\mathbf{z}_f(\mathbf{w}), \mathbf{z}_p(\mathbf{w})\right) \leq 0. \tag{6.10}$$

Because of the WAPM it is also

$$(\mathbf{w}, \mathbf{p}(\mathbf{w})) \cdot \left(\mathbf{y}_f\left(\mathbf{w}^*\right), \mathbf{z}_p\left(\mathbf{w}^*\right)\right) \leq 0; \tag{6.11}$$

and since $(\mathbf{w}^*, \mathbf{p}(\mathbf{w}^*))$ is an equilibrium price vector and therefore $\mathbf{w} \cdot (\mathbf{z}_f(\mathbf{w}^*) - \mathbf{y}_f(\mathbf{w}^*)) \leq 0$ (in equilibrium excess demands cannot be positive), by the same reasoning that brings to (6.11) it follows that

$$(\mathbf{w}, \mathbf{p}(\mathbf{w})) \cdot \left(\mathbf{z}_f\left(\mathbf{w}^*\right), \mathbf{z}_p\left(\mathbf{w}^*\right)\right) \leq 0. \tag{6.12}$$

If for brevity we indicate the complete price vector with a single symbol $\pi \equiv (\mathbf{w}, \mathbf{p}(\mathbf{w}))$ we have obtained $\pi^* \mathbf{z}(\pi) \leq 0$ and $\pi \mathbf{z}(\pi^*) \leq 0$, hence the only way for WAM to hold is $\mathbf{z}(\pi) = \mathbf{z}(\pi^*)$, but this is not the case because by assumption $\mathbf{w}$ is not an equilibrium factor price vector, hence WAM is contradicted. Since (6.8) yields a contradiction, it must be $\mathbf{w}^* \cdot \zeta(\mathbf{w}) > 0$.

Therefore we can apply exactly the same proof that $V(t)$ is a Liapunov function as in Sect. 6.29, with $\mathbf{w}$ in place of $\mathbf{p}$ and $\zeta(\mathbf{w})$ in place of $\mathbf{z}(\mathbf{p})$. ∎

The same considerations on the possibility of non-unique equilibrium prices for the unique equilibrium allocation apply as in the comment on Proposition 6.11 in ▶ Sect. 6.25.

Given that WAM is a highly restrictive assumption (remember also the Hildenbrand–Grodal observation), Mandler's proof may appear of little interest, but it has had some importance in certain debates in capital theory and will be taken up again in ▶ Chap. 8.

6.30 Again on the Likelihood of Uniqueness and Stability

Lacking a *guarantee* of uniqueness or (tâtonnement) stability of equilibrium in the production economy because WAM is unlikely, the neoclassical theorist can only try to argue that uniqueness and stability are *likely*. As for the exchange economy, one must turn to older authors to find some discussion of this likelihood.

Hicks in *Value and Capital* (1946 p. 104) suggests that there is less reason to worry about multiplicity and hence instability of equilibria in the production economy than in the exchange economy, because in production choices there is nothing analogous to the income effects which are the cause of instability in the exchange economy: the technical choices of industries know only a 'substitution' effect (a tendency to decrease the proportion in which the factor, whose relative rental has increased, is combined with other factors), and this always works in the 'right' direction and hence strengthens the likelihood of uniqueness and stability.

However, production introduces a new route through which income effects can work against uniqueness and stability: the indirect factor substitution mecha-

6.30 · Again on the Likelihood of Uniqueness and Stability

nism illustrated in ▶ Chap. 3, ▶ Sect. 3.5, is not guaranteed to work in the 'right' direction. Inferior goods can contribute to this, but I leave to the reader the task of exploring this possibility, and I only remember the possibility illustrated in ▶ Sect. 3.5, that what can be called *'self-intensive' demand* (wages spent mostly on labour-intensive goods, land rents spent mostly on land-intensive goods) can cause the demand for a factor to decrease when its rental decreases, because demand for the products using that factor more intensively comes mostly from the owners of that factor, whose income decreases.

This is one possible form of the income effects due to income redistribution from one group of consumers to another when income distribution changes. With 'self-intensive demand' this income effect works against the technical substitution effect and, if not neutralized by substitution within the choices of each consumer, it can even overpower the technical substitution effect if the latter is weak.

This new possibility of non-uniqueness and instability, which escaped Hicks, goes counter the claim that the introduction of production reduces the likelihood of non-uniqueness and instability.

However, even this problem has been considered of limited relevance. In the only extended discussion of the likelihood of multiple equilibria in the production economy of which I am aware, after presenting the neoclassical two-goods two-factors production economy[56] with rigid factor supplies, Harry Johnson (1973) admits that there can be multiple equilibria due to 'self-intensive demand' and comments: 'It can be shown, however, that the conditions required for multiple equilibrium are extremely restrictive'. (Johnson 1973, p. 61). His very dense argument in support of this statement amounts to the following.

Refer to the economy discussed in ▶ Chap. 3, which produces corn and meat with labour and land, with corn the more labour-intensive good. Johnson starts from this observation: for the indirect substitution mechanism to cause an equilibrium to be *unstable*, a rise in the relative price of a consumption good above its equilibrium value must cause an excess *demand* for it (this will induce this price to rise further). Assume initially fixed different factor proportions in the two industries and rigid factor supplies; then the outputs of the two goods that guarantee full employment of both factors are uniquely determined, so the corresponding equilibrium (assuming it exists) is unstable if a rise in the relative price of meat causes the demand for meat to increase. We have seen that this is what happens if the rise in the price of meat is due to a decrease of w/β, that is an income redistribution from wages to land rent, and the proportion in which a marginal income increase goes to buy meat is higher for landowners than for workers. Johnson's main point is that when consumer preferences are of this type but we admit technical substitutability, the decrease of w/β causes an excess demand for meat only if changes in relative factor prices have little effect on factor proportions, that is, if

---

56 Johnson calls the two factors labour and capital, with capital treated as perfectly analogous to land. Since in ▶ Chap. 7 I will argue that capital cannot be treated as analogous to land, it is better now to reformulate Johnson's analysis as referring to a non-capitalistic economy, where the factors are labour and land.

the elasticity of factor substitution is low. If the decrease of w/β raises the optimal labour-to-land proportion L/T in at least one industry (but corn remains the more labour-intensive good), then this fact by itself, in order for the full employment of both factors to be maintained (i.e. in order for demand for labour not to increase), requires a contraction of the more labour-intensive industry and expansion of the other industry, therefore an expansion of meat production. The *required* expansion of meat production may well be greater than the increase in demand for meat. Then, since the *actual* increase in meat production will be only equal to the increase in demand for meat, and therefore less than needed for labour demand not to increase, an excess labour demand will be created, and the wage will tend to increase back towards the equilibrium level: the equilibrium is stable.

As an example, suppose money rent is given, the money wage decreases 10%, and if technical coefficients are fixed this causes the money price of corn to decrease 8% because wages were 80% of its cost of production, while the money price of meat decreases only 2% because wages were 20% of its cost of production. If workers demand only corn and landowners demand only meat, demand for meat rises 2% and demand for corn decreases 2%; certainly the actual percentage changes will be smaller if (as is likely) landowners demand corn too and its relative price decrease will induce them not to allocate all their real income increase to meat; analogously in all likelihood workers will not allocate all the real income reduction to a decrease of demand for corn. It suffices then that, owing to the decrease of w/β, the optimal labour-to-land ratio in the two industries increases enough to require, in order to maintain both factors fully employed, an expansion of the meat industry, and contraction of the corn industry, by 2%, and the equilibrium will be stable. This is easily obtained if the elasticity of substitution is 1 in both industries. Then the 10% decrease of w/β raises L/T by 10% in both industries (are you clear as to why?), and this requires a decrease in corn production by *more* than 10% in order to bring the L/T ratio back to its equilibrium level: this is because, without a decrease of corn production i.e. with land still allocated to the two industries as before, demand for labour rises 10%; a decrease in corn production by 10% reduces by 10% labour employment in the corn industry, total labour employment reduction is less because the transfer of some land to meat causes meat production to increase: so corn production must decrease by more than 10%, while a 2% decrease suffices for stability. So, Johnson concludes, the elasticity of substitution must be less than 1 for stability not to obtain.

This conclusion is correct within this model, but does it mean the conditions for instability (and hence multiple equilibria) are 'extremely restrictive'? Evidently Johnson thought that the elasticity of substitution is considerable, 1 or greater, in actual economies.[57] There are empirical and theoretical reasons against any

---

57 Probably because of a widespread opinion at the time that the elasticity of substitution between labour and capital (derived from an aggregate production function describing national output as a function of labour and capital, with the latter treated as a single factor) was about 1, because of a roughly constant share of wages and of property incomes in national income. This constancy of relative shares has afterwards disappeared, in favour of property incomes. As to aggregate production functions, they are theoretically untenable as will be argued in ▶ Chap. 7.

6.30 · Again on the Likelihood of Uniqueness and Stability

such estimate. Theoretically, there is the problem that the factors considered in the empirical estimates of economy-wide elasticities of substitution are always labour *and capital*, with capital treated as a single factor, which is illegitimate as will be argued in ▶ Chap. 7, with the consequence that the estimates are entirely bogus. Furthermore, impressionistic evidence suggests a very low technical substitutability as measured by labour per unit of output: when multinational firms build plants to produce cars or computers in very-low-wage countries, production methods differ only little from those adopted in plants in higher-wage countries.

Also, as argued in ▶ Chap. 3, the plausibility of the neoclassical approach needs factor demand curves to be not only downward-sloping but also considerably elastic. Now, even forgetting the special difficulties raised by capital goods that I have not discussed yet, the fact remains that even if 'self-intensive' demand were unable to overpower the consumption and technical substitution effects, nonetheless it would have the effect of decreasing the elasticity of the factor demand curves, thereby increasing the risk of implausible results.

There appears therefore to be insufficient reason to think that the presence of (non-capitalistic) production renders the supply-and-demand approach more plausible than in the pure exchange case.

Before concluding, it is necessary to comment on a recent novelty, the paper by Herbert Gintis (2007) which, on the basis of simulations of an agent-based model of production and exchange, claims that the replacement of the auctioneer-guided tâtonnement with time-consuming adjustments including search for better prices, gradual adjustments of production to sales, imitation (both by consumers and by firms) of the more successful agents, and error-correction mechanisms, powerfully makes for stability, for example produces stability in the Scarf exchange example mentioned earlier where the tâtonnement converges to a limit cycle. The reported simulations show that, under a wide range of initial parameter values, there is convergence to a nearly full-employment steady state which closely approximates the quantities and relative prices of the Walrasian equilibrium of that economy. Gintis concludes that 'models allowing traders, consumers, workers and firms to imitate successful others lead to an economy with a reasonable level of stability and efficiency' (p. 1304), and that this result 'provides some justification for the importance placed upon the Walrasian model in contemporary economic theory' (p. 1303). In other words, according to Gintis a more realistic adjustment process than the tâtonnement, in particular admitting imitation, shows that there is little reason to be pessimistic about the stability of general equilibrium, but then, it would seem, about the solidity of the entire supply-and-demand approach.

This would be a very important conclusion, if acceptable. Unfortunately Gintis' model is so complex and different that its presentation would take too long; the reader is strongly invited to read his article to see that now it is possible to formalize rather realistic adjustment processes, with people who choose from which firm to buy and decide whether to buy or wait for more information, with firms which accumulate and decumulate inventories, with learning, error correction, imitation; certainly, although its thousands of equations and assumptions and its recourse to simulations make it difficult to verify the logical passages and to understand which assumptions are responsible for which result, the model opens the door to further interesting studies. But it does not seem to authorize a diminution of pessimism on uniqueness and stability of supply-and-demand equilibria, for two orders of reasons.

First, the model contains several assumptions that considerably aid uniqueness and stability. Consumers are endowed with CES consumption functions with random coefficients, and Gintis admits on the basis of studies by other economists and of his own simulations that this seems to imply that 'our model, without production, has a unique global steady state with very high probability' (p. 1291); he adds that 'it is unlikely that adding production changes this conclusion, since supply functions generally cannot have the unruly behaviour of demand functions' (*ibid.*), but in fact he has excluded by assumption the main possibility of "unruly behaviour" caused by non-capitalistic production, because his model does not admit the possibility of 'self-intensive consumption', the distribution of the property of the only production factor besides labour—a factor strangely called 'capital' but homogeneous, not deteriorating, and not produced, and therefore in fact land—is random, and anyway wealth has no effect on the composition of consumption of a consumer owing to the CES utility function, therefore there are no classes. So equilibrium is practically certainly unique, production is so introduced that it can cause problems neither to uniqueness nor to stability, and consumers have random preferences, which makes it highly likely that in the aggregate they behave like a representative consumer with average preferences, which would guarantee uniqueness and stability. Therefore there is very little reason why one should expect instability in such an economy, but that's because the reasons for instability have been neutralized; instability can only be due, it would seem, to cobweb-like phenomena caused by adjustment lags, or to unstable expectation formation processes, phenomena which might arise in a classical approach too and therefore are not reasons for questioning the neoclassical approach as such.

Second, and anticipating here issues to be discussed in further detail in the next chapter, Gintis presents his conclusions as applicable to market economies in general, but in fact they are not generalizable to economies with capital goods. The model is about non-capitalistic production, the factors are labour and land (illegitimately called 'capital' but not produced!), and this is what allows the model to take factor endowments as given and unchanging during the adjustments in spite of correctly admitting that adjustments take time and production continues during this time; if production uses capital goods, then the economy uses them up and produces them during the adjustments, this alters the vector of endowments of capital goods, so the model's *equilibrium* cannot include a given vector of capital goods among its data, at most the model's adjustment could *start* with a given vector of capital goods but then the model would need completion with something specifying what happens to this vector during the adjustments. This would necessarily require introducing production and sale of capital goods, hence how investment is determined and how equality between investment and savings is reached, issues totally absent in Gintis' model and which, unless a way is found to defend Say's Law, raise fundamental doubts about the capacity of market economies to guarantee 'a reasonable level of stability and efficiency'.

6.31 Conclusions

In conclusion, even neglecting the problems the marginal/neoclassical approach encounters with capital (to be discussed in the next two chapters), it appears that the supply-and-demand approach rests on shaky foundations: it needs an assumption of very high likelihood that, when relative factor rentals change, income effects working in an 'anti-neoclassical' direction are either absent or unable strongly to contrast substitution effects in the determination of the composition of the demand for consumption goods and do not cause significantly 'backward-bending' factor supply curves. My view—that it is difficult to consider realistic such an assumption—appears to be shared by many non-heterodox economists too. In the Preface of the present book a mainstream economist, Katzner, was quoted as saying that 'an appropriately acceptable analysis of the uniqueness and global stability of Walrasian equilibrium has yet to be found' and that 'The persistence of this gap' goes along with 'the seemingly hopelessness of filling it'. For this reason the esteemed general equilibrium theorist Alan Kirman openly declared in 1999 that general equilibrium theory must be abandoned, that economics needs to restart from scratch and to look for some different approach to value and distribution. Perhaps, as is often the case with neoclassical specialists, Kirman was not aware that the alternative is not necessarily between the neoclassical approach and restarting from scratch, there are already now other approaches to value and distribution, for example the several variants of a classical–Keynesian–Kaleckian approach. But anyway in order to understand the present complex situation in the theory of value and distribution the study of the marginal/neoclassical approach cannot stop at the non-capitalistic general equilibrium model, it must be extended to how the approach treats capital. This will be the subject of ▶ Chaps. 7 and 8 and, in part, of ▶ Chap. 9 too.

6.32 Review Questions and Exercises

❓ Review Questions

1. Explain why regular exchange economies are exceedingly rare.
2. Illustrate and prove by heart the WAM Lemma
3. 'The discontinuities or indeterminacies associated with non-convex or non-strictly-convex preferences do not appear to be a reason seriously to question the validity of the supply-and-demand approach, as long as one can assume that the discontinuities occur at different prices for different consumers'. Discuss, clarifying why the last assumption appears necessary.
4. Prove that under GS when the own price alone of a good increases the excess demand for the good decreases.
5. Why does the tâtonnement in the production economy with free entry need the planner–auctioneer?
6. Prove that GS does not hold if the choice curve of the consumer is not everywhere downward-sloping.

524 **Chapter 6** · Existence, Uniqueness and Stability of Non-capitalistic General Equilibria

7. What criticism can be moved to Hicks's argument intended to minimize the likelihood of multiple equilibria of pure exchange?

8. Explain what allows applying essentially the same proof of tâtonnement stability to the general equilibrium of exchange under WAM and under GS.

9. Explain why GS does not ensure stability in the production economy.

10. Show that Property 6 of excess demand (▶ Sect. 6.2) does not imply that when more than one price tends to zero at the same time, all the excess demands for the goods whose prices tend to zero tend to $+\infty$.

11. Show that the consumption set need not be convex. Explain why this creates problems.

12. Explain why the minimum-income problem due to survival can cause an equilibrium not to exist.

13. Explain the survival/subsistence discontinuity problem.

14. Even neglecting the limits of the argument that regular economies have a finite number of equilibria, a certain result shows that a finite number of equilibria does not reduce the risk of indeterminateness. Which result? and what is the argument?

15. Instabilities due to cobwebs are argued not to be a cause for serious worries. Explain.

16. Prepare an oral exposition of the Hildenbrand–Grodal observation on the WAM and its generalization.

✔ Exercixes

1. Suppose there are only two goods; if one assumes local non-satiation, can both goods be simultaneously 'bads' everywhere in the consumption set, that is, such that a decrease of the amount of either of them raises utility? Prove your answer.

2. Draw an Edgeworth box complete with the indifference curves of the two consumers, in which both consumers have discontinuous choice curves owing to strictly concave indifference curves, and determine whether an equilibrium exists.

3. In the Edgeworth box below, some indifference curves of consumers A and B are drawn. The indifference curves of consumer A are not convex; B's convex indifference curves are the broken curves. Ω is the endowment point. Some possible budget lines are shown. B's choice curve is shown in blue. Derive A's choice curve, and show it has a discontinuity, and that there is no equilibrium.

4. Find out why the numerical example used in ▶ Chap. 4, ▶ Sect. 4.15 to illustrate that the zero-income problem would not have worked if I had assumed Cobb–Douglas preferences.

5. Produce examples of non-existence of equilibrium when only condition 3 or only condition 4 of Theorem 6.2 are not satisfied.

6. Confirm, by drawing opportune indifference curves, that the choice curves can indeed have the shapes drawn in ◼ Fig. 6.10.

7. Show what precisely is incompatible with WAM in the case with three equilibria of ◼ Fig. 6.10

6.32 · Review Questions and Exercises

8. Draw an Edgeworth box with both sides six units long. Both consumers have perfect-complement preferences; consumer A demands two units of good 1 for each unit of good 2; consumer B demands two units of good 2 for each unit of good 1. A's endowment is (5,1). Show that there are three equilibria, of which the interior one is unstable.

9. Prove that if there is a *given* number of profit-maximizing firms, each one with a well-defined single-valued supply function, i.e. if for each price vector $\pi = (w, p)$ (where now p need *not* be the average cost-minimizing price vector corresponding to the given w) each firm supplies just one vector of netputs and therefore the aggregate netput supply vector $y(\pi)$ is single-valued, then if WAM holds for $z(\pi)$ it also holds for $z(\pi) - y(\pi)$, and therefore by setting $\dot{\pi}_i = \alpha_i(z_i(\pi) - y_i(\pi))$ and assuming that $z(\pi)$ satisfies WAM, one can prove tâtonnement stability.

10. Indicate how equations (A–B–C–D) of ▶ Chap. 5 should be modified, so as to arrive at the very concise redefinition of the equilibrium price vector in ▶ Sect. 6.35 that uses netputs.

11. Explain in what cases GS implies that the demand for a good is decreasing in the good's own price.

12. Suppose that in a two-goods economy the endowment of a consumer consists of an amount of good 2 only; the price of good 2 is given, the price the consumer must pay for good 1 is p_1 for a quantity of good 1 up to $x_1{}^*$, and is 20% lower (owing to a discount) for the quantity in excess of $x_1{}^*$. Then the budget line has a kink, the budget set is not convex if the consumer can afford to purchase more of good 1 than $x_1{}^*$. Draw how the budget line shifts as the price of good 1 decreases, and show that in this case the choice curve can have a discontinuity.

13. Explain why segment AC in ◻ Fig. 6.21 is wage income.

14. How would you define absence of income effects?

15. Prepare a clarification (with Powerpoint slides), for a 20 min. lecture at a course in advanced microeconomics, on the difference between the zero-income problem and the survival problem for the existence of general equilibrium.

16. Labour and land produce corn and meat in separate industries. Four units of labour and one of land produce one unit of corn. One unit of labour and one of land produce one unit of meat. Corn is the numéraire. The rigid supply of labour is 250 units, of land is 100 units. Find the full-employment outputs of corn and meat, and the associated rate of wage w and rate of rent β if workers only demand corn, and landowners only demand meat. Having shown that this is an equilibrium, show that it is unstable. (Hint: start from equilibrium w and β, and assume the immigration of one more worker causes the wage to become w-ε and the rate of rent to become such as to keep the price of corn equal to 1. Determine the excess demands for corn and meat if the extra worker is for the moment still unemployed, and assume production of the two goods tends to adjust to demand; observe the tendency of demands for labour and for land…)

17. In the marginal/neoclassical approach, it is spontaneous to think that an increased endowment of a good or factor must be associated with a reduction of its equilibrium price, since the good or service has become less scarce; but

526 **Chapter 6 ·** Existence, Uniqueness and Stability of Non-capitalistic General Equilibria

is this always true? Assume pure exchange, draw an Edgeworth box, choose an endowment point, determine the equilibrium; then assume the sole endowment of good 1 of consumer A increases (the right-hand side of the box shifts to the right) and show that the new equilibrium can be associated with a higher relative price of good 1, if good 2 is inferior for consumer A.

18. (Cowell) Consider the two-goods economy of ▶ Sect. 4.7 but do not assume monotonic utilities, and assume the numéraire is good 2. Let p be the price of good 1. Assume the excess demand for good 1, representable as z, is the following function of p:

$$z(p) = 1 - 4p + 5p^2 - 2p^3.$$

How many equilibria are there? Are they stable or unstable? Is the economy regular? (Hint: it is evident that $p=1$ is an equilibrium price, and $p=0$ is not. Use first and second derivative of $z(p)$ to understand the behaviour of z around $p=1$ and to derive information about possible other equilibrium values of p. You may find it useful to consult the Mathematical Appendix on third-degree equations; remember that solutions can be repeated.)

19 (Jehle and Reny) Consumer i *envies* consumer j if she likes consumer j's allocation strictly better than her own. In an exchange economy, an allocation is *envy-free* if no consumer envies any other consumer. If there are no externalities, there is at least one envy-free allocation if goods are divisible: the equal-division allocation in which each consumer has the same basket. But the equal-division allocation need not be Pareto efficient. Assume a two-consumers two-goods exchange economy with a strictly positive total endowments vector Ω; assume utility functions are monotonic and strictly quasi-concave. Prove that there is at least one envy-free allocation which is Pareto efficient. (Hint: Let E be the equal-division point in the Edgeworth box. The proof is only needed if E is not Pareto efficient. For any allocation assigning basket x^A to consumer A, let $x^{B \to A}$ indicate the corresponding basket of consumer B but represented in the Edgeworth box as if it were assigned to A: it will be a point symmetric to x^A relative to point E. If an allocation is Pareto efficient and gives A a basket x^A which is on the indifference curve through E, does A envy B?).

20. In an exchange economy with initial total endowments vector Ω, prove that the market excess demand vector function $\mathbf{z(p)}$ is independent of the initial distribution of endowments if and only if preferences are identical and homothetic.

21. *WAM and stability with a given number of DRS firms.* The symbols are those used in the Section on Mandler's theorem. Prove that if in the production economy there is a *given* number of profit-maximizing firms, each one with a well-defined single-valued supply function, i.e. if for each price vector $\mathbf{\pi}=(\mathbf{w,p})$ (where now $\mathbf{p}$ need *not* be the average cost-minimizing price vector corresponding to the given $\mathbf{w}$) each firm supplies just one vector of netputs and therefore the aggregate netput supply vector $\mathbf{y(\pi)}$ is single-valued, then if WAM holds for $\mathbf{z(\pi)}$ it also holds for $\mathbf{z(\pi)}$–$\mathbf{y(\pi)}$, and therefore by setting $\dot{\pi}_i = \alpha_i(z_i(\mathbf{\pi}) - y_i(\mathbf{\pi}))$ and assuming that $\mathbf{z(\pi)}$ satisfies WAM, one can prove tâtonnement stability.

References

Anderson, C. M., Plott, C., Shimomura, K.-I., & Granat, S. (2004). Global instability in experimental general equilibrium: The scarf example. *Journal of Economic Theory, 115,* 209–249.

Arrow, K. J., Block, H. D., & Hurwicz, L. (1959). On the stability of the competitive equilibrium, II. *Econometrica, 27,* 82–109.

Arrow, K. J., Hahn, F. H. (1971). *General competitive analysis.* S. Francisco: Holden Day, and Edinburgh: Oliver and Boyd.

Arrow, K. J., & Hurwicz, L. (1958). On the stability of the competitive equilibrium, I. *Econometrica, 26,* 522–552.

Arrowsmith, D. K., & Place, C. M. (1982). *Ordinary Differential equations.* London: Chapman and Hall.

Aubin, J.-P., & Cellina, A. (1984). *Differential inclusions. Set-valued maps and viability theory.* Berlin: Springer.

Beavis, B., & Dobbs, I. G. (1990). *Optimization and Stability theory for economic analysis.* Cambridge: Cambridge University Press.

Billette de Villemeur E. (1998). *Heterogeneity and stability: Variations on Scarf's processes.* European University Institute Working Paper ECO No. 98/38.

Billette de Villemeur E. (1999) *Aggregation of demand and distribution of characteristics: A difficulty in modelling behavioural heterogeneity.* Working Paper no. 9938, THEMA, Université de Cergy-Pontoise.

Bryant, W. D. A. (2010). *General equilibrium. Theory and evidence.* Singapore: World Scientific.

Debreu, G. (1959). *Theory of value.* New York: Wiley.

Debreu, G. (1982). Existence of competitive equilibrium. In: K. J. Arrow and M. D. Intriligator, eds., *Handbook of Mathematical Economics,* vol. II, North-Holland, Amsterdam, pp. 697–743.

Durlauf, S., Blume, L. (eds.). (2008). *New Palgrave: A Dictionary of Economics (The),* 2nd ed., vol. 8, Palgrave Macmillan, London.

Fratini, S. M. (2001). *Il problema della molteplicità degli equilibri da Walras a Debreu* (Unpublished Ph.D. thesis). Dip. Ec. Pubbl., Università di Roma La Sapienza.

Gandolfo, G. (1971). *Mathematical methods and models in economic dynamics.* Amsterdam: North-Holland.

Gintis H. (2007). The dynamics of general equilibrium. *Economic Journal, 117*(523), 1280–1309.

Grodal, B., & Hildenbrand, W. (1989). The Weak axiom of revealed preference in a productive economy. *Review of Economic Studies, 56,* 635–639.

Hahn, F. H., & Negishi, T. (1962). A theorem on non-tâtonnement stability. *Econometrica, 30,* 463–469.

Hicks, J. R. (1939a). *Value and capital.* Oxford: Clarendon Press.

Hicks, J. R. (1946). *Value and capital* (2nd ed.) Oxford: Clarendon Press (first edition, 1939).

Hildenbrand, W. (1983). On the 'Law of Demand.' *Econometrica, 51,* 997–1019.

Hildenbrand, W. (1989). The weak axiom of revealed preference for market demand is strong. *Econometrica, 57,* 979–985.

Hildenbrand, W., & Kirman, A. (1988). *Equilibrium analysis: Variations on themes by Edgeworth and Walras.* Amsterdam: North-Holland.

Jehle, G. A., & Reny, P. J. (2011). *Advanced microeconomic theory.* Haley, UK: Financial Times/Prentice Hall (Pearson).

Jerison, M. (1999). Dispersed excess demands, the weak axiom and uniqueness of equilibrium. *Journal of Mathematical Economics, 31,* 15–48.

Johnson, H. G. (1973). *The theory of income distribution.* London: Gray-Mills Publishing Ltd.

Kehoe, T. J. (1998). Uniqueness and stability. In A. Kirman (Ed.), *Elements of general equilibrium analysis* (pp. 39–87). Oxford: Blackwell.

Kirman, A. (1999). The future of economic theory. In A. Kirman & L. A. Gérard-Varet (Eds.), *Economics beyond the Millennium* (pp. 8–22). Oxford: Oxford University Press.

Mandler, M. (2005). Well-behaved production economies. *Metroeconomica, 56*(4), 477–494.

Mas-Colell, A., Whinston, M. D., & Green, J. R. (1995). *Microeconomic theory*. Oxford: Oxford University Press.

Newman P. (1987). Consumption sets. In *(The) New Palgrave: A Dictionary of Political Economy*, Ist ed.

Noussair, C., Plott, C., & Riezman, R. (2007). Production, trade, prices, exchange rates and equilibration in large experimental economies. *European Economic Review, 51,* 49–76.

Quah, J.K.-H. (1997). The law of demand when income is price dependent. *Econometrica, 65*(6), 1421–1442.

Rizvi, A. T. (1991). Specialisation and the existence problem in general equilibrium theory. *Contributions to Political Economy, 10,* 1–20.

Samuelson, P. A. (1941). The stability of equilibrium: Comparative statics and dynamics. *Econometrica, 9,* 97–120.

Scarf, H. E. (1960). Some examples of global instability of the competitive equilibrium. *International Economic Review, 1,* 157–172.

Shafer, W., & Sonnenschein H. (1982). Market demand and excess demand functions. In K. Arrow, M. D. Intriligator (Eds.), *Handbook of mathematical economics* (Vol. II, pp. 671–693). Amsterdam: North-Holland.

Smale, S. (1976). A convergent process of price adjustment and global Newton methods. *Journal of Mathematical Economics, 3,* 107–120.

Takayama, A. (1974). *Mathematical economics*. Hinsdale, Illinois: The Dryden Press.

Capital: Long-Period Equilibria

Contents

7.1 The Notion of Long-Period Equilibrium – 531

7.2 The Endogenous Determination of Equilibrium Capital Endowments – 534

7.3 The Equations of Long-Period General Equilibrium – 539

7.4 The Quantity of Capital: Supply-Side Problems – 548

7.5 The Quantity of Capital: Demand-Side Problems. Demand for 'capital' and Investment – 551

7.6 Re-switching and Reverse Capital Deepening – 558

7.7 More on Reverse Capital Deepening. Price Wicksell Effects – 563

7.8 Stationary States and Hicks' Criticism of Long-Period Prices – 569

7.9 The 'Austrian' Approach – 572

Electronic supplementary material The online version of this chapter (▶ https://doi.org/10.1007/978-3-030-62070-7_7) contains supplementary material, which is available to authorized users.

© Springer Nature Switzerland AG 2021
F. Petri, *Microeconomics for the Critical Mind*,
Classroom Companion: Economics, https://doi.org/10.1007/978-3-030-62070-7_7

7.10 On Substitutability in Modern and in Traditional Production Functions – 575

7.11 Aggregate Production Functions – 579

7.12 'Surrogate Production Functions' in a Non-Neoclassical Economy. Endogenously Determined Marginal Products – 587

7.13 Perception of the Difficulties with 'Capital', and Shift Back to Walras—or Almost – 591

7.14 Conclusions – 595

7.15 Review Questions and Exercises – 596

References – 599

In this chapter you will learn how traditional marginalist authors apart from Walras included capital goods into long-period general equilibrium, why their approach encounters problems which are still the object of debate, and how some perception of these problems favoured a shift to neo-Walrasian notions of general equilibrium. After studying the chapter you will be clear about:

- the endogenous determination of the composition of the capital endowment in long-period general equilibrium;
- that the same holds for the 'Austrian' or Wicksellian version of this notion of equilibrium, although the composition of the capital endowment does not appear explicitly in this version;
- why this notion of equilibrium needs a given endowment of capital treated as a single factor of variable 'form' and measured as an amount of exchange value;
- why this treatment of capital is not the same thing as assuming an aggregate production function;
- why this notion of capital suffers from supply-side and demand-side difficulties, relevant for the theory of investment;
- how some perception of the problems with this notion of capital helped the shift of the marginal/neoclassical approach to neo-Walrasian versions;
- the difference between traditional and modern production functions on the issue of factor substitutability.

7.1 The Notion of Long-Period Equilibrium

There is no unanimity in the history of the marginal/neoclassical approach on how to introduce heterogeneous capital goods into the theory presented in ▶ Chaps. 3–6. It is necessary to distinguish: (1) the long-period or *traditional* approach, whose clearest exponent is Knut Wicksell, and which is based on a conception of the capital goods as 'embodying' different amounts of a single factor capital of variable 'form'; (2) Walras; (3) the neo-Walrasian approach.[1] ▶ Chapter 8 will discuss (3). The present chapter discusses (1) and, very briefly, (2). It dispels a number of lingering confusions about the analytical role of this factor capital of variable 'form', the difference between its role in long-period equilibria and in aggregate production functions, the difficulties this notion of capital encounters in the determination of its endowment and in proving that its demand curve is downward-sloping, the connection with investment theory. The last section of the chapter explains, starting from Walras, why this long-period approach was abandoned in the 1930s by Lindahl, Hayek, Hicks in favour of neo-Walrasian versions that, in the formulation of general equilibrium, re-adopt Walras's treatment of each capital good as a separate factor with its given endowment; these versions are studied in ▶ Chap. 8.

---

1   I will use the term 'general equilibrium' for the equilibrium of all three approaches, but the reader should be warned that this term is often identified with the sole approaches 2 and 3.

The reader may wonder why it is necessary to spend so much time on the traditional versions of the marginal/neoclassical approach, versions that no neoclassical theorist seems intent on defending nowadays. A quick answer is that the view of the working of a market economy expressed by these versions is still dominant (it is for example clear in Solow's growth model); the conception of the capital goods as transient embodiments of a single factor 'capital' is still present and fundamental in contemporary applied neoclassical economics, from macroeconomics to international trade theory. Without a continuing acceptance of that conception one would not have Central Banks using models based on aggregate production functions. Capital as a single factor has apparently disappeared from the modern versions of general equilibrium theory, but whether the disappearance was real or only apparent is an important question that requires a full understanding of the analytical roles of that notion of capital in the traditional versions of the marginal/neoclassical approach.

The long-period approach can be called the *traditional* approach because shared by all founders and early developers of the marginal approach with the sole partial exception of Walras and his close followers (Pareto, Barone). Traditionally, equilibrium was conceived as the persistent situation towards which the economy continually gravitates, and close to which the economy will therefore be most of the time; the usefulness of equilibrium was that of approximately indicating the average values of economic magnitudes and of indicating, with its shifts, the shifts one can expect in the averages of observed prices and quantities. Equilibrium prices were not expected to be perfectly realized, *market prices* (the actually realized, observable prices) would nearly always be different from equilibrium prices, being affected by accidental and transitory events, but the averages of market prices would approximate equilibrium prices because market prices gravitate towards equilibrium prices. This is the role of the notion of equilibrium I have implicitly adopted in illustrating the adjustments postulated by the marginal/neoclassical approach from ▶ Chap. 3 onwards.

In order to have this role, equilibrium must be not only stable but also *persistent* (i.e. with sufficiently persistent data) relative to the presumable speed of the gravitation towards it. In common language the term 'stable' is sometimes used to mean 'not moving, resisting shocks, not undergoing changes', but in economic theory the term 'persistent' must be preferred to express this meaning; 'stable' is best reserved to indicate a state towards which there is a *tendency to return* when the system is pushed away from it; typical examples being the rest position of a pendulum, or the flat level of water in a pond when wind ceases.

A first sense in which equilibrium must be persistent in order to have its traditional role is that it must not be altered by the disequilibrium actions of agents; this independence of the equilibrium state from disequilibrium actions requires that *the data determining the equilibrium must not be modified by disequilibrium actions*. A second sense in which the equilibrium must be persistent is that its data must not (for exogenous reasons) change so frequently and so much relative to the speed of the tendency towards equilibrium, as to make it unlikely that the equilibrium state gives a good indication of the realized averages of market prices and quantities. This does not mean that no change in the data is allowed. In economics, very little can be considered as rigorously unchanging; sufficient persistence of the data of equilibrium must be interpreted to mean that the speed with which the data of equilibrium change is of a lower order of magnitude than the speed of the tendency towards equilibrium, or else the change is a once-for-all change after which the data no longer change or change sufficiently slowly for the economy to gravitate towards the new equilibrium.

This persistency requirement was interpreted by all founders of the marginal approach (with the sole exception of Léon Walras, to be discussed later) to mean that *the equilibrium cannot include, among the data determining it, given endowments of each type of capital good.* Let us remember the data on whose basis the marginal approach determines the general equilibrium:

1. given preferences of the several consumers;
2. the known production methods;
3. given total endowments of the several factors, and their distribution among consumers.

The need for persistence of the third group of data obliges to treat the endowments of capital goods differently from the endowments of the several types of land.

One might think that each capital good could be treated in the same way as a type of land: as a distinct factor with its given endowment. But most capital goods are continuously produced and used up in production, and their amounts can be quickly altered by differences between the flow of production and the flow of productive consumption of these goods; the endowment (=the amount present in the economy) of a capital good will tend to adapt to the demand by firms, and will stop changing quickly only when it has adjusted to the needs of firms, with the production of the capital good compensating its consumption by firms. *Any change in the demand for a capital good, be it due to change in production methods or in the outputs of industries that utilize that capital good or to accidental reasons, will quickly alter the amount of the capital good present in the economy.*

Thus suppose in a nation there is labour immigration and one wants to determine the equilibrium corresponding to the increased labour supply. One does not know what the amounts will be of the several capital goods in the new equilibrium. The wage decrease caused by the increased labour supply prompts technical substitution inside firms, and substitution in consumer choices; both substitutions alter the demands for most capital goods, possibly drastically (the demand for some capital good becomes zero, if that capital good is required only by production methods that are no longer optimal at the lower wage). So after a short while the amounts in existence of most capital goods will have changed. Now, the time required for the change in wages to reach an equilibrium between supply and demand on the labour market is considerable. Especially the change in labour demand cannot but take considerable time to manifest itself and reach an equilibrium: after a wage change, it takes time for product prices to change, for consumers to change their demands, for firms to change labour employment, for the productive methods in all industries to adapt to the changed real wage, for some plants to close down in the industries where sales considerably decrease and

534 Chapter 7 · Capital: Long-Period Equilibria

for new plants to be built in the industries where demand considerably increases. These adjustments take months at least; and yet, the result may well be that the wage change is not sufficient to ensure a labour demand equal to labour supply, so there are further changes of the real wage and further adjustments, taking more months. During these adjustments the amounts in existence of most capital goods can and *will* generally change. So in order to determine the equilibrium corresponding to the changed labour supply, the endowments of the several capital goods cannot be considered *given*, they must be considered *variables endogenously determined by the equilibrium itself.*

The same holds for the determination of the new equilibrium after a technological discovery, for example, smartphones: the new equilibrium will include production of smartphones, which requires a whole series of new capital goods,[2] while some other productions (e.g. of old-style telephones) will decrease and the demand for the capital goods specific for those productions will decrease if not disappear. We see again that the determination of the new position of rest the economy will tend towards, the new equilibrium, must include *an endogenous determination of the amounts of capital goods present in it.*

In the founders of the marginal approach (with the sole partial exception of Walras) the above considerations were considered obvious. In this, they did not differ from the classical economists who analogously treated the composition of capital as endogenously determined. But the classical authors took the real wage as given, which determined the production methods, and then the treatment of the quantities produced as given allowed the determination of the quantities of capital goods desired and hence present in the economy in the normal position. The marginal approach could take neither the real wage nor the quantities produced as given, and they had to be all simultaneously determined. But then how did it determine the composition of capital?

7.2 The Endogenous Determination of Equilibrium Capital Endowments

To determine the quantities of the several capital goods, traditional marginalist economists relied on two ideas.

The first idea was the tendency towards a *uniform rate of return on the supply price of capital goods.*[3] If the rate of return obtainable by purchasing a capital good is higher than for other capital goods, investors scramble to buy that capital good, the increase in demand for it induces an increased flow of production of that capital good, and this increases its endowment. Only when the rate of return

---

2 Remember that the capital goods that produce a product are not only the machines and fixed plants but also the parts that are assembled into the final product: these are capital goods too, so each new product necessarily involves the production of many new specific capital goods.

3 Remember that the *supply price* of a produced good is the price required to induce firms to produce it. In the long period, it coincides with MinLAC.

on supply price is the same as for the other capital goods, can the endowment of a capital good be taken to have reached an equilibrium. The product prices that analysis had to determine were therefore the relative prices guaranteeing a uniform rate of return on the supply prices of all capital goods (with positive equilibrium endowments).[4]

On this aspect there is no difference between these marginalist authors, and the older classical economists and Marx. In fact I will show that Wicksell's (or Walras's) equilibrium prices, if the assumptions about the type of technology are the same—e.g. only circulating capital goods—satisfy *exactly the same* price equations as the price equations presented in ► Chaps. 1 and 2, intended to determine what the classics called natural prices or *prices of production*. Marshall called these product prices *long-period normal* prices, so a general equilibrium aiming at determining this kind of product prices is called a *long-period general equilibrium*.

In the light of certain widespread confusions, it is as well to stress immediately that, just as in classical authors, the fact that in the long-period price equations of marginalist traditional authors (e.g. in Wicksell) a good has the same price as input and as output does not at all imply that relative normal prices are assumed to be rigorously constant through time in the economy under study, it only indicates that the slow changes that long-period prices may be undergoing over time—changes due, in the marginal approach, to the slow change in income distribution over time if the growth rate of labour supply is different from the growth rate of capital—are considered negligible in the determination of equilibrium (i.e. the equations of equilibrium are formulated *as if* relative prices were constant over time), precisely because of their slowness. The neglect of the changes that relative prices may be undergoing over time does not, therefore, mean that analyses determining long-period prices are only concerned with, or applicable to, a strictly stationary state or steady-growth states; Wicksell explicitly stated that his stationary state assumption was only a 'simplifying assumption' (1934, p. 155) and that 'The application to non-stationary conditions offers no difficulty in principle' (ibid., p. 154).

Thus the classical approach and the traditional marginal approach differ on the forces determining the distribution of income between wages and profits (interest), and also on the forces determining the quantities produced, but do not differ on the issue: what are the prices on which economic theory can usefully concentrate as starting points to grasp the averages and trends of observable prices? Pierangelo Garegnani (1976, pp. 27–28) put it as follows:

» As we all know, they [the Classical authors] understood the long-period position as the 'centre' towards which the competitive economy would gravitate in the given long-period conditions. …

---

4   This addition in parentheses is because the uniform rate of return on supply price is not on *all* capital goods, it does not obtain on the capital goods not demanded because inferior to others or only needed for productions for which there is no demand; in long-period equilibrium their endowments are zero.

536 Chapter 7 · Capital: Long-Period Equilibria

It was because of this 'gravitation' that the 'long-period values' of the variables (i.e. their values in the 'long-period positions' of the system) were thought to be those relevant for an analysis of lasting changes in the system. In the words of Ricardo (1951, Chap. IV, pp. 91–92):

> Having fully acknowledged the temporary effects which, in particular employments of capital, may be produced on the prices of commodities, as well as on the wages of labour, and the profits of stock, by accidental causes, without influencing the general price of commodities, wages or profits, since these effects are equally operative in all stages of society, we will leave them entirely out of consideration, whilst we are treating of the laws which regulate natural prices, natural wages, and natural profits....

where the argument for 'leaving entirely out of consideration' the deviations of market from natural values of the variables rests intimately on the 'temporary' nature of these deviations in contrast with Ricardo's concern with lasting changes.

And a similar argument about 'long-period normal' values was still used by Marshall (1920, V, iii, 7, p. 291) a century later:

> The actual value at any time, the market value as it is often called, is often more influenced by passing events, and by causes whose action is fitful and short lived, than by those which work persistently. But in long periods these fitful and irregular causes in large measure efface one another's influence so that in the long run persistent causes dominate value completely.

Therefore Marshall, one of the main *marginalist* economists, who wrote between 1870 and 1920, shared the classical thesis that, if one is interested in the causes that determine the value of products, one must first of all concentrate on *long-period positions*, where the rate of return on the supply price of capital goods is uniform because the tendency of investment to go where the rate of return is higher has adapted the composition of capital to the composition of the demand for capital goods. Such a study, according to Marshall as well as to Ricardo, will reveal the persistent causes acting upon value; further studies can then enquire into the reasons for the deviation at a certain moment of the market price from its normal long-period value, if such an enquiry is found useful for particular purposes.

An important implication of what has been argued in this section is that if land is neglected and capital goods are assumed to be all circulating, the analysis of the wage curve and of choice of techniques of ▶ Chap. 2 applies to long-period marginalist equilibria too; given the available techniques, a modern classical economist and a traditional marginalist economist would conclude to the same shape of the envelope of wage curves and therefore to the same real wage once the rate of return on capital (identified by the marginalist authors with the rate of interest) is given. This will be important later in the chapter.

The *second* idea, this one specific to the marginal approach, is the conception of the several capital goods as representing different amounts of a single factor of production 'capital', of which capital goods are only transitory embodiments, and whose services are rewarded by the rate of interest—the conception which will be indicated below with 'capital' in inverted commas. 'Capital' is measured

7.2 · The Endogenous Determination of Equilibrium Capital Endowments

in terms of exchange value, the amount of 'capital' owned by an individual is the value of the capital goods she/he owns, the quantity of 'capital' of which the economy is endowed is the total value of the capital goods present in it (why this measurement in terms of exchange value? it will be explained later). The specificity of this factor 'capital' is that it is continually consumed by being used, and is recreated by production of new capital goods, and this fact allows it to change its 'form' (the composition of the stock of capital goods in which it is 'embodied'), much as if capital goods were chunks of 'dry ice' (congealed carbon dioxide) of different shapes, which gradually evaporate, and are then re-formed by congealing more CO_2: the total amount of dry ice can change its 'form' without changing in 'quantity' (here weight), if the newly congealed CO_2 is equal to the amount lost through evaporation, but is congealed into pieces of dry ice of shapes different from the old ones.

The process through which the change in the 'form' of 'capital' is thought to operate is the utilization of the factors, which could reproduce the used-up capital goods, for the production of different capital goods, whose value will be the same because produced by the same resources; the total value of 'capital' will not change, but will be now 'embodied' in a different 'form', i.e. a different vector of capital goods. (See Petri 2004, p. 29.) Thus in 1893 (p. 103) Knut Wicksell wrote that though 'the forms of capital change, its total value remains unchanged, since, in place of the consumed capital goods, new ones of equivalent value enter successively'.

This conception of 'capital' as capable of changing 'form' is used to argue that 'capital' will take, in the several industries, the 'form' best adapted to the given technical knowledge and income distribution. This permits to assume the substitutability among factors needed by the theory. As noted in ▶ Sect. 5.5, substitutability among different capital goods is nearly zero in most industries: durable capital goods can be utilized more or less intensely (i.e. for more or fewer hours per month) but the proportions in which raw materials and labour must be utilized per unit of output are generally rigid. Except in rare cases it is not possible to change the amount of labour per unit of output in an industry by changing the proportion between labour and the *same* capital goods, one must have recourse to a different production method requiring *different* capital goods (e.g. a change of the entire assembly line of a car factory, using more robots and fewer workers). Therefore in most cases among physically specified capital goods and labour the *direct factor substitution mechanism* cannot operate.

The *indirect substitution mechanism* too is not able to operate if 'capital' is not able to change 'form', because many of the capital goods required by one industry are specific to it; therefore the contraction of some industries and expansion of other industries required by the indirect substitution mechanism cannot operate unless the 'form' of 'capital' changes, with a reduction of the endowments of the capital goods no longer demanded by the contracting industries, and an increase of the endowments of the capital goods needed by the expanding industries.

As a result, if the specification of the data of general equilibrium includes an arbitrary vector of given endowments of the several capital goods, then factor demand curves are nearly vertical, with the consequences pointed out in ▶ Chap. 3: implausible equilibrium factor rentals, for example, an impossibility fully to employ labour, and a zero price of most capital goods since most of them would not be fully employable. The variability of the 'form' of 'capital' avoids these problems.

The general presence in the first and second generation of marginalist authors of this conception of capital as a factor which can be treated as given in 'quantity' although variable in 'form' is indisputable. John Bates Clark is well known to have expressed this conception with the utmost clarity: 'Where there is a capital of five hundred dollars for each worker, that fund is in one set of forms; and where there is a capital of a thousand dollars per man, it is in a different set' (Clark 1925, p. 159; note the view of the concrete capital goods as 'forms' taken by the factor 'capital' viewed as a 'fund' and measured as an amount of value); 'As we take away laborers, we leave the capital everywhere unchanged in amount; but we change the forms of it in every one of the industries, so as to make it accurately fit the needs of the slightly reduced working force … The abandoned pick and shovel become, by miracle of transmutation, an improvement in the quality of horse and cart. There are fewer men digging; but they have as much capital as ever, and they have it in a form in which, with their reduced numbers, they can use it' (ibid., p. 170).

Note the implication of the last sentence: unless capital takes a 'form' adapted to the number of labourers with which it is to cooperate, these labourers cannot 'use it'. The variability of the 'form' of capital is indispensable to the variability of the proportions in which capital and labour can be efficiently combined. Hicks in *The Theory of Wages* (1932) puts the thing even more explicitly: allowing sufficient time for 'capital' to change its 'form' is indispensable for the determination of a curve of marginal product of labour endowed with sufficient elasticity:

> There can be no full equilibrium unless the wages of labour equal its marginal product….It does not follow, however, that because the marginal product of labour has changed, therefore the level of wages will change in the same direction at once … one of the co-operating factors - capital - is, at any particular moment, largely incorporated in goods of a certain degree of durability … In the short period, therefore, it is reasonable to expect that the demand for labour will be very inelastic, since the possibility of adjusting the organization of industry to a changed level of wages is relatively small….Since the whole conception of marginal productivity depends upon the variability of industrial methods, little advantage seems to be gained from the attempt which is sometimes made to define a 'short period marginal product' - the additional production due to a small increase in the quantity of labour, when not only the quantity, but also the form, of the co-operating capital is supposed unchanged. It is very doubtful if this conception can be given any precise meaning which is capable of useful application (Hicks 1932, pp. 18–21).

The conception of 'capital' as a factor of given endowment but variable 'form' reconciles the need to treat the endowments of the several capital goods as variable, with the theory's need for *given* endowments of factors of production. The solution is to treat as given the endowment of 'capital', while leaving its composition to be endogenously determined by the equilibrium. This factor 'capital' is treated as a factor of production on a par with labour or land; its 'price' or rental rate is the rate of interest (increased as necessary to cover risk; I will mostly neglect risk); the rate of interest is viewed as the price that brings about equilibrium between supply and demand for 'capital', because demand for 'capital' is a decreasing function of the rate of interest. In other words, the decreasing demand curve for corn-capital described in Chap. 3, ▶ Sect. 3.3, is assumed to hold for 'capital' too, in spite of the latter being an aggregate of heterogeneous capital goods measured by their exchange value.

As 'capital' is embodied in capital goods that wear out, a continuing demand for a certain quantity of 'capital' manifests itself as demand for the monetary funds needed to replace the part of this quantity of 'capital' that wears out; it is therefore a demand for a flow of funds to be used to buy replacement capital goods; a desire for additional 'capital' manifests itself as additional demand for funds, to be used for net investment. These funds available for lending, traditionally called 'loanable funds', are supplied by gross savings, which correspond to zero net savings if the existing quantity of 'capital' is equal to the quantity demanded. If the rate of interest is lower than the marginal product of the existing quantity of 'capital', firms wish to employ more 'capital', and the demand for 'loanable funds' (i.e. gross investment) becomes greater than needed for simple replacement of the used-up capital goods. If firms are satisfied with the existing quantity of 'capital', but the flow of savings is in excess of the level that maintains the quantity of 'capital' unchanged (i.e. if there are positive net savings), then the demand for loanable funds is less than their supply, the rate of interest decreases, firms desire to use more 'capital' and increase their demand for loanable funds (net investment becomes positive), and the rate of interest tends to the level ensuring equality between supply and demand for loanable funds. The net investment increases the stock of 'capital' reducing its marginal product, until the latter becomes equal to the decreased rate of interest. The conclusion is that— at least in the absence of malfunctioning of financial intermediaries—the rate of interest reflects the marginal product of the existing quantity of 'capital'.

7.3 The Equations of Long-Period General Equilibrium

The data of a long-period general equilibrium include then a given endowment of 'capital' (and an allocation of the property of this 'capital' among the several consumers, but to simplify I will neglect the differences that changes in this allocation can make to this equilibrium and will only pay attention to the aggregate supply and demand for 'capital'). In equilibrium this endowment of 'capital' is fully utilized and takes a 'form' determined by the needs for capital goods of the several industries.

The endowment of 'capital' is gradually used up by its utilization in production; its loss of value per period, i.e. its depreciation, coincides for circulating capital goods with their entire value since they disappear in a single utilization; it is only a fraction of their value for durable capital goods. The production of new capital goods can be of the same value as depreciation, in which case the endowment of 'capital' does not change; or it can be of greater value, and then the endowment of 'capital' grows; or it can be of lesser value, and then the endowment of 'capital' decreases. In terms of national accounting, remember that "gross national product" is anyway net of replacement of circulating capital goods, so gross (ex post) investment (equal by definition to gross savings) is the entire production of durable capital goods plus the net production of circulating capital goods. If the endowment of 'capital' grows, it means there are positive *net* savings.

It may be asked what is the legitimacy of including among the data of equilibrium a given endowment of 'capital', since in real economies net savings are often not zero, and therefore the endowment of 'capital' is not constant. But the data of equilibrium need not be strictly constant, it suffices that they be persistent, that is, changing very slowly relative to the speed of gravitation towards equilibrium of the variables that the equilibrium determines. So the traditional marginalist economist would reply to the above question that the potential speed, with which an economy can alter the relative proportions between the amounts in existence of the several capital goods, is generally much greater than the speed with which the total stock of 'capital' is altered by nonzero net savings: then in order to determine income distribution and normal prices one can treat the endowment of 'capital' as given with the same legitimacy with which one treats the endowment of labour as given (this too is generally not strictly constant, being slowly altered by population growth). For example, the quantity of car plants—not a quickly produced capital good!—in a nation can pass from 2 to 12 in a couple of years if the economy concentrates investment on that composite capital good, a 500% increase, while it is known that net accumulation practically never increases the overall stock of capital of an economy over two years by more than 15%, and generally by much less. The traditional marginalist economist will continue: the procedure can then be adopted, as in other sciences, of keeping fixed the much more slowly changing variables while studying the results of the adjustment of the more rapidly changing ones. Thus the endowment of 'capital' can be taken as given while leaving its 'form' free to adapt itself to the one desired by firms so as to allow product prices to tend towards long-period prices, equal to minimum average costs and yielding a uniform rate of return or rate of profits (net of risk) or rate of interest. In order to highlight as clearly as possible how the demand for 'capital' is determined, this demand will be assumed not to be changing over time, and therefore net savings are assumed to be zero.

How equations A-B-C-D of ▶ Chap. 5 must be modified in order to make room for capital goods can be explained in rather simple terms. I give the intuition before the equations.

Assume production is in cycles, each cycle takes one period. Assume that as explained in the previous section we can neglect the slow changes that the endowments of factors may be undergoing (for 'capital' this means neglecting net savings). Assume again the separation between consumption goods and factors, no consumption good is used as an input to production. There are h<n types of capital goods. Now assume at first that the endowments of the h different capital goods are given and can be treated as if they were kinds of lands because they are indestructible, eternal. Assume zero net savings, no debts, no loans (hence no interest rate). Since there is no depreciation of capital goods, zero net savings means

7.3 · The Equations of Long-Period General Equilibrium

zero gross savings hence zero production of new capital goods. The equilibrium is then perfectly analogous to that of a non-capitalistic economy: in equations A, B, C, D we must only stipulate that the first h of the n factors are capital goods. But under these assumptions capital goods are indistinguishable from lands.

Now let us drop the assumption that capital goods are indestructible and not produced; they deteriorate with usage (if circulating, they disappear entirely in a single production cycle), so they must be reproduced; and let us treat the endowment of each capital good and the quantity of it to be produced every period as variables that the equilibrium must determine. Relative to when the capital goods were identical to lands, not produced, and in given endowments, we are adding $3h$ variables:

- the h endowments of the several capital goods;
- the h quantities produced of them every period;
- their h prices.

Now that capital goods can be an investment, they yield a rate of return, and the rate of interest will be equal to it (if we abstract from risk) since one will not accept to lend money for a lower rate of return than one can earn by buying capital goods. So we introduce one more variable, the rate of interest r. In total $3h + 1$ new variables. We need $3h + 1$ more equations.

The h conditions 'selling price equal to minimum average cost for each newly produced capital good' give us the first h equations. We are neglecting the slow changes that population and capital may be undergoing, then the condition that for each capital good the quantity produced must maintain the endowment unchanged and therefore must just compensate for depreciation gives us h more equations (for example, for a circulating capital good the endowment must be entirely renewed each period, hence, the equation is: quantity produced $=$ endowment). This stationary assumption is not indispensable to the formulation of a marginalist long-period equilibrium but it simplifies things and allows a clearer picture of the determinants and the effects of a persistent income distribution. Then we have the long-period condition of uniform rate of return on the investment in the purchase of any newly produced capital good (at its long-period normal price, of course), which can be formulated as equality, for each capital good, between its rate of return and the rate of interest; this yields h further equations. For example if capital good h is a circulating capital, indicate its equilibrium price (equal to $MinLAC$) as P_h, and indicate as v_h the gross rental it earns at the end of the period if lent to a firm for the period; a saver-investor pays P_h to buy the capital good at the beginning of the period and receives v_h at the end of the period, so the net earning on the investment is $v_h - P_h$; the rate of return is $(v_h - P_h)/P_h$ and it must be equal to the rate of interest.

So far we have obtained $3h$ equations. There remains a degree of freedom, due to the fact that since we are treating all endowments of capital goods as variables, we have not said anything yet on whether the economy is richly or poorly endowed with capital goods: with the same endowments of labour and lands the economy might be poor because very poorly endowed with capital goods, or rich because abundantly endowed with them. The remaining degree of freedom is 'closed' through the conception of the several capital goods as embodiments of

542   Chapter 7 · Capital: Long-Period Equilibria

'capital', whose total endowment is given; the last equation will establish that the endogenously determined endowments of the several capital goods must be such that the total quantity of 'capital' embodied in them—that is, their total exchange value—is the total quantity of 'capital' of which the economy is endowed. The idea therefore is that the total 'capital' endowment, accumulated over the years owing to net savings, puts a limit to the concrete capital goods the economy can have at its disposal; the economy can have more of some capital goods only by having less of other capital goods. The total 'capital' will take the 'form'—will allocate itself among the several capital goods—so as to establish the uniform rate of return on supply price which, as in the analyses of classical authors, results from the tendency of investment to go where the rate of return is higher.

I proceed to list in detail the equations of one version of long-period general equilibrium. The formulation I shall adopt follows the intuitive explanation given above.

I maintain the simplifying assumption that consumption goods and capital goods are two separate groups of goods, so I neglect goods like sugar that are both capital goods and directly demanded by consumers. I also maintain the assumption of no joint production, and this entails that I ought to assume that all capital goods are circulating capital goods, because production with durable capital goods is a case of joint production: the production of the main product also produces, as a side product, older (but generally still usable) capital goods. But the complications of joint production can be avoided through an assumption (also made by Walras) of *radioactive depreciation*, i.e. an assumption that capital good k loses every period a constant fraction d_k of its efficiency; this permits to treat the case of circulating capital as the subcase where $d_k = 1$. I assume that capital goods are pure factors, i.e. yield no direct utility, so their endowments coincide with their supplies—which, remember, are unknowns that the equilibrium must determine endogenously.

The newly produced capital goods can be used for production only in the subsequent production cycle. It is equivalent to imagine that the newly produced capital goods are bought directly by consumers with their savings, or by firms which have borrowed the savings of consumers. In the first case, the endowments of capital goods at the beginning of the period belong to consumers who bought them with their savings at the end of the previous period; consumers lend these capital goods to firms in exchange for the payment of rentals equal to their value marginal products at the end of the period; in the second case the endowments of capital goods belong to firms, which bought them with savings lent to them by consumers; the firms must repay at the end of the period the money loans plus interest, and at long-period prices this costs them the same as if they had leased the capital goods from the consumers. In either hypothesis, there must be a uniform rate of return on all investments consisting of the purchase of a capital good, a rate of return equal to the rate of interest (I neglect risk).

I proceed by indicating how equations from A to D of the non-capitalistic economy must be modified and which new equations must be added. Remember that one more equation, that I will not list, must be added to fix the price of the numéraire good or basket of goods as equal to 1.

7.3 · The Equations of Long-Period General Equilibrium

There are m consumption goods with generic price p_j, and n inputs: kinds of labour, kinds of land, and capital goods (these cannot be called 'factors', because in this approach they are embodiments of the factor 'capital'). The rentals of these inputs are $v_1, \ldots, v_n$. (the rate of interest is not one of these rentals, and 'capital' is not one of these inputs.)

Assume the first h of the n different factors are capital goods; hence the first h elements of the rental vector v indicate (gross) rentals of capital goods. Below I use $i = 1, \ldots, h$ as the generic index for capital goods, and $\ell = 1, \ldots, n$ as the generic index for factors—both capital goods and other factors; the factors with index $h + 1, \ldots, n$ are types of land and types of labour. Consumption-industries technical coefficients (amount of input ℓ per unit of output j) are indicated as $a_{\ell j}$; as explained in ▶ Chap. 5 they can be treated as fixed, or as resulting from cost minimization, each industry being endowed with a constant returns to scale production function.

Equations A, price = cost for consumption goods, need no modification, but in order to make it clear that they are now part of a different system of equations I call them A':

$$p_j = MinLAC_j(\mathbf{v}) = \sum_{\ell=1}^{n} v_\ell a_{\ell j}(\mathbf{v}) \quad j = 1, \ldots, m; \quad \ell = 1, \ldots, n. \tag{A'}$$

To these an equation is added that fixes the numéraire price as equal to 1. Equations B must be modified to include the dependence of consumer choices also on the rate of interest r. Because in a long-period equilibrium the composition of capital has no reason to change quickly, and the endowments of total capital and of labour change only very slowly, relative prices and rentals can be assumed constant through time (or changing slowly enough that their change can be neglected). Hence there is no need to include, among the variables determining the choices of consumers in one period, the future evolution of relative prices; present prices and the rate of interest suffice. Furthermore, consumers need not pay attention to the prices of newly produced capital goods, because to a consumer all that matters is the rate of return on her savings, and in equilibrium that is the same whichever the way the savings are employed to purchase capital goods. Thus the demand for consumption goods depends only on vectors $\mathbf{p}$, $\mathbf{v}$, on r, and of course on the endowments of consumers which include endowments of 'capital', the value of the capital goods owned by the consumer (directly or through her/his property of firms). Hence:

$$q_j = Q_j(\mathbf{p}, \mathbf{v}, r), \quad j = 1, \ldots, m. \tag{B'}$$

Since for simplicity I assume a stationary economy, equations (B') are derived from utility maximization problems where it is imposed that each consumer performs no net savings and simply maintains the amount of 'capital' unaltered.

Equations C must be modified to take into account that the demand for factors also comes from the production of newly produced capital goods; indicate as q_{Ki}, $i = 1, \ldots, h$, the quantity produced of capital good i, and as $a_{K\ell i}$ the technical

544   Chapter 7 · Capital: Long-Period Equilibria

coefficient of input ℓ, that can be a capital good or a type of land or labour, in the production of capital good i:

$$x_\ell = \sum_{j=1}^{m} a_{\ell j}(v)_{q_j} + \sum_{i=1}^{h} a_{K\ell i}(v)_{q_{Ki}}, \quad \ell = 1,\ldots,n; \quad i = 1,\ldots,h. \tag{C'}$$

Equations D must be modified not only, like equations B, to take into account the rate of interest, but also because, owing to our assumption that the endowments of capital goods are entirely offered, for the first h factors we do not have a supply function $X_i(p, v, r)$ but simply a supply equal to the aggregate endowment, so X_i also stands for the aggregate endowment of capital good i, which is—remember—a variable and adapts to the demand for it, so the corresponding equations in (D') have the equality sign in it. Thus:

$$X_i = x_i, \ell \equiv i = 1,\ldots,h; \quad X_\ell(\mathbf{p},\mathbf{v},r) \geq x_\ell, \quad \ell = h+1,\ldots,n, \text{(and if } >, \text{ then } v_\ell = 0). \tag{D'}$$

So far we have added $2h + 1$ new variables: the quantities produced of capital goods, their endowments, and the rate of interest. Now I add h further variables, the prices of the newly produced capital goods. These are determined by h equations price = cost for the newly produced capital goods. Let P_{Ki}, $i = 1,\ldots, h$, be the selling price of newly produced capital good i; then

$$P_{Ki} = MinLAC_{Ki} = \sum_{\ell=1}^{n} v_\ell a_{K\ell i}(v), i = 1,\ldots,h. \tag{A'-K}$$

We are studying a stationary equilibrium, in which the given endowments of factors are not changing; so there is no net addition to the stocks of capital goods. This determines the quantities of new capital goods produced (and bought by consumers, if we assume that it is consumers who buy them in order to lend them to firms[5]) as those needed to replace the using-up of the existing ones. A simple way to determine the need for new capital goods is to assume a radioactive loss of efficiency equal for each capital good i to a percentage d_i per period; then the net rental of capital good i is $v_i - d_i P_{Ki}$, because $d_i P_{Ki}$ is the depreciation. If at the end of every period one adds to a given stock of, say, 100 units of capital good i the amount $100d_i$ of new capital goods—which requires a gross investment equal to $100d_i P_{Ki}$, the depreciation—the productive efficiency of the stock remains unaltered, as if one still had 100 units of the capital good. Hence we have the h equations:

$$q_{Ki} = d_i X_i \quad i = 1,\ldots,h. \tag{B'-K}$$

This assumption of **radioactive depreciation** greatly simplifies the meaning of the endowment of a durable capital good. We can now measure the endowment of a capital good in efficiency units; of each type of durable capital good there will be

---

5   The demands for new capital goods by savers cannot be considered functions of prices because savers are indifferent among them as long as all capital goods yield the same rate of return.

7.3 · The Equations of Long-Period General Equilibrium

in the economy new ones, one-period-old ones, two-periods-old ones and so on; but given the radioactive loss of efficiency and the stationariness assumption, the total stock of these capital goods of different ages will be equivalent, in efficiency units and in value, to a certain stock of new capital goods of that type, which in efficiency units our stationary economy keeps unchanged from one period to the next. It is this stock in efficiency units that is indicated as X_i. Alternatively, we can make the assumption that all capital goods are circulating, so $d_i = 1$ for all of them, in which case equations (B'-K) become simply

$$q_{Ki} = X_i \text{ for all } i = 1, \ldots, h.$$

With radioactive depreciation, the rate of return on the supply price of capital good i is $(v_i - d_i P_{Ki})/P_{Ki}$. In long-period equilibrium these rates of return must all be the same, and equal (since we are neglecting risk) to the rate of interest r. Hence h more equations:

$$(v_i - d_i P_{Ki})/P_{Ki} = r \quad i = 1, \ldots, h. \tag{E'}$$

If capital goods are all circulating, these become $(v_i - P_{Ki})/P_{Ki} = r$, i.e. $v_i = (1 + r) P_{Ki}$.

We have added $3h$ equations. There remains one degree of freedom, which reflects the fact that so far we have not determined whether the economy is poorly or richly endowed with capital goods, nor connected this fact with the rate of interest.

The remaining degree of freedom is 'closed' by the condition of equality between demand for and supply of 'capital', i.e. by the condition that the vector of endowments of capital goods $(X_1, \ldots, X_h)$ (in efficiency units), determined by the demands of firms (first group of equations D'), embodies the given quantity of 'capital' of which the economy is endowed. At any moment, this given quantity of 'capital' is embodied in the existing capital goods, and is not of the 'form' appropriate to the long-period equilibrium; but through the appropriate reinvestment of depreciation funds it tends to take the 'form' demanded by firms; equilibrium between supply and demand for it and for each capital good will require that 'capital' takes the 'form' (i.e. composition) demanded by firms, at the same time as its total demand becomes equal to its endowment.

This endowment of 'capital' is a quantity of exchange value, the value of the capital goods existing in the economy. This is made logically inevitable by the view of the rate of interest as the rental of 'capital'. The reason is that, for any factor, different amounts of it tend to earn rewards proportional to the amount of the factor they represent: e.g. if there are two fields A and B of land of the same quality and if field A earns a total rent twice as large as field B, we deduce that A's surface must be twice the surface of B. If now A and B are two capital goods, with capital good A earning a rental (net of depreciation) twice as large as B, and if we want to see these net rentals as earned by the productive contribution of a common factor 'capital' embodied in them, then we must conclude that A contains twice as much 'capital' as B; but, since the value of a capital good is the value of its net rental capitalized at the market interest rate, capital good A will also have a value twice as great as B. So necessarily the relative values of different capital goods must be a measure of the relative amounts of 'capital'

546   Chapter 7 · Capital: Long-Period Equilibria

embodied in them. It suffices to choose the unit, and the total value of capital goods will measure the economy's endowment of 'capital'.

(Nor is there any other alternative measure independent of relative prices. A physical, 'technical' measure of 'capital' such as the weight or volume of capital goods would not satisfy the condition that capital goods embodying the same amount of 'capital' earn the same rental, nor the condition, indispensable in order to determine the cost-minimizing choices of firms, that more 'capital' costs more and causes output to increase. Also, there would be no justification for the conception of 'capital' as a factor capable of changing 'form' without changing in amount.)

Thus there is a logical necessity behind the measurement of 'capital' as an amount of exchange value. This explains why Böhm-Bawerk, in a debate with the American economist John Bates Clark on what exactly capital consists of, wrote: "I, too [like J. B. Clark], believe that capital is a 'fund' or 'quantum' of matter. I think it clear that anyone who wishes to make an estimate of the size of this fund must measure it, not by counting the pieces or calculating their volume or weight, but by measuring it in terms of value—nowadays in terms of money." (Böhm-Bawerk 1906, p. 5).

Wicksell speaks of 'the amount of capital of the community, reckoned in terms of money' (Wicksell 1934, p. 174); J. B. Clark speaks of capital as a 'quantum of productive wealth' measured in money (Clark 1899, p. 119).[6]

The resulting conception of 'capital' is the generalization to the entire economy of the spontaneous view of capital of the single price-taking saver: 'capital' is conceived as the crystallization of accumulated past savings, i.e. of abstinence from consumption, to be therefore measured in the same units in which one measures savings or income; the value of the capital goods one owns, which changes 'form' without changing in amount if some of these capital goods are replaced by other capital goods of equal value, increases if one adds further capital goods bought with net savings. Thus we find Wicksell writing:

» The accumulation of capital consists in the resolve of those who save to abstain from the consumption of a part of their income in the immediate future. Owing to their diminished demand, or cessation of demand, for consumption goods, the labour and land which would otherwise have been required in their production is set free for the creation of fixed capital for future production and consumption and is employed by entrepreneurs for that purpose with the help of the money placed at their disposal by savings. (Wicksell, *Lectures on Political Economy*, vol. II, 1935, pp. 192–3).

---

6   Some marginalist authors, for example, J. B. Clark, and Marshall and his school, felt so confident about the possibility to conceive 'capital' as analogous to labour or land in spite of its being measured as a quantity of exchange value that they showed little hesitation about speaking of production functions with labour and 'capital' as factors, an illegitimate notion, see ▶ Sect. 7.13. Böhm-Bawerk and Wicksell avoided this mistake, and adopted production functions not implying the notion of 'capital', but had anyway to resort to a value measurement for the total endowment of capital of the economy.

7.3 · The Equations of Long-Period General Equilibrium

And Garegnani:

» Beneath the variety and, at times, the vagueness of the indications given in this respect [the unit in which capital is measured, F.P.] by the marginal theorists, there lies a common idea. The capital goods, and hence the quantity of capital they represent, result from investment; since investment is seen as the demand for savings, 'capital' emerges as something which is homogeneous with saving. Its natural unit is therefore the same as we would use for saving, i.e. some composite unit of consumption goods capable of measuring the subjective satisfaction from which (according to these theorists) consumers abstain when they save. 'Capital' thus appears as past savings which are, so to speak, 'incorporated' in the capital goods, existing at a given instant of time. (Garegnani 1978, p. 33).

The final equation must therefore impose the equality between the aggregate given endowment of 'capital' K^*, an amount of value, and the demand for it, the latter being the value at the equilibrium prices of the endowments of capital goods desired by firms, determined by the optimal technical coefficients at the equilibrium prices and by the quantities to be produced:

$$K^* = \Sigma_i P_{Ki} X_i. \tag{K'}$$

The system of equations A', B', C', D', A'-K, B'-K, E', K', plus the equation fixing the numéraire, has as many independent equations as variables (one supply = demand equation is not independent because of Walras' Law).[7] Of course this is only an initial check of mathematical consistency, but traditional marginalist authors did not go beyond this stage in the examination of the existence of a long-period equilibrium.

The reader must be warned against a frequent misunderstanding. Nowadays the logic of traditional marginalist long-period equilibrium is often not grasped. Because of a loss of familiarity with the notions of long-period equilibrium and more generally of long-period position, the presence in the old marginalist authors of the treatment of capital as a single factor, an amount of value, hence measured in the same units as national product or national income, has induced a belief that these authors were assuming that one could represent an economy via

---

7 To reformulate the system of equations without assuming that consumption goods and capital goods are two distinct groups of goods is not difficult. Now all produced goods can be both circulating or radioactively depreciating capital goods and consumption goods. Let us then assume there are h produced goods, with price p_i, $i = 1,\ldots, h$, produced quantity q_i, and rental $v_i = (r + d_i) p_i$ when used as capital goods. Equations (A') and (A'-K) merge into $p_i = MinLAC_i(\mathbf{v})$, $i = 1,\ldots,h$. Equations (B') and (B'-K) merge into $q_i = Q_i(\mathbf{p}, \mathbf{v}, r) + d_i X_i$, where the endowment of produced good i as capital good is $X_i = 0$ if good i is a pure consumption good. Inputs are in the number of n, with generic index ℓ; the first h of the n inputs are produced, i.e. capital goods (with technical coefficients and endowment zero if they are pure consumption goods); equations (C') become $x_\ell = \Sigma_j a_{\ell j} q_j$, $j = 1,\ldots,h$; $\ell = 1,\ldots,n$. Equations (D') become $x_i = X_i$, $i = 1,\ldots, h$, for the capital goods, and $X_\ell(\mathbf{p}, \mathbf{v}, r) \geq x_\ell$, $\ell = h+1,\ldots$, n, for labours and lands. Equations (E') and (K') are unchanged. So the system of equations is simpler, but less easy to grasp immediately in its meaning than if one assumes consumption goods and capital goods are two distinct groups of goods.

an *aggregate production function* $Y = F(K,L)$ where Y (the net national product or national income) and K are treated as made of the same single commodity, as if the economy were producing corn with labour and corn-capital as factors, totally neglecting the heterogeneity of outputs and of capital goods, and the dependence of relative prices on income distribution. This is a gross misinterpretation, traditional marginalist authors did not assume that the economy could be treated as if producing a single good with itself and labour as inputs, they had in mind a completely disaggregated general equilibrium, but with endogenously determined endowments of the several capital goods; the equilibrium would have remained indeterminate without something to fix whether the economy was richly or poorly endowed with capital goods: the idea that these capital goods were embodiments of the single factor 'capital', whose total endowment was given, rendered the equilibrium determinate, and allowed the equilibrium to have the persistency required for its role of centre of gravitation, indicator of the averages of market prices and quantities.

7.4 The Quantity of Capital: Supply-Side Problems

The conception of capital goods as quantities of the single factor 'capital' of variable 'form', and of the rate of interest as the price that brings the demand for 'capital' into equality with its given endowment, is still the conception used in the applications of the marginal/neoclassical approach to macroeconomics, growth theory, international trade, etcetera, as testified by the presence, in the models used in these applications, of a single quantity of capital K with a definite marginal product curve. But it has been abandoned, at least apparently, in modern neoclassical general equilibrium theory. The new notions of general equilibrium will be studied in ▶ Chap. 8; now let us see the reason for the abandonment.

We know that a long-period general equilibrium is determined by three groups of *data*: preferences of consumers; known production methods; endowments of factors (and distribution of these endowments among consumers, an aspect I neglect here as of secondary importance for the issues to be discussed now, the problems to be pointed out would arise even if all consumers had the same endowments and the same tastes). Among these endowments there is a given total endowment of 'capital'. The theory requires these data to be data, that is, given *before* the equilibrium is determined.

Can the amount of 'capital' be treated as one of the data determining the equilibrium? The given K^* can only be the observed value of the capital goods in the economy under study (in terms of the same numéraire one would use to measure savings, as clarified in the Garegnani quote in ▶ Sect. 7.3). Can this number be considered given as much as the amounts of lands or the number of labourers?

For example suppose one were able to collect sufficient information about preferences, technology, and labour and land endowments in the economy under study, and on the basis of these data and of the observed K^* one tried to determine how the economy's equilibrium would be modified by some labour immigration. In the simple corn-labour economy of ▶ Chap. 2 one would treat K, the

7.4 · The Quantity of Capital: Supply-Side Problems

stock of corn-capital, as given, one would derive the curve of the marginal product of labour, one would determine the initial equilibrium on the basis of the initial supply of labour; then one would shift the labour supply curve to the right to reflect labour immigration, and one would conclude that, in the new equilibrium, aggregate output is greater and the real wage lower. But in a realistic economy with heterogeneous capital goods we have the problem that the 'capital' endowment is the *value* of existing capital goods, which will change with labour immigration both because wages and prices will change and because the composition of the stock of capital goods will change during the several months the adjustments will take, as the composition of demand for capital goods changes owing to the changed choices of consumers and of firms. So it is impossible to consider the value K^* of the economy's capital goods as unaffected by the changes, therefore, we have no basis to conclude as to its value in the new equilibrium; but then it cannot be taken as given, and the equilibrium lacks one of the data it needs for its determination.

Actually, even in the situation before immigration, it would be impossible to view the observed income distribution and prices as determined by the observed K^*, because any change in prices would change the value of the existing capital goods; therefore this value, the observed K^*, cannot be treated as a datum independent of what the equilibrium should determine; it must be seen as *resulting from* income distribution, rather than as one of its determinants. Conclusion: *long-period general equilibria are indeterminable because needing a given endowment of 'capital', an amount of exchange value not determinable before prices are determined.*

We can use what we know from ▶ Chap. 2 about $w(r)$ curves to confirm a dependence of the *normal* value of a given stock of capital goods on distribution. To that, one will add that the value of the stock of capital goods in a real economy is also affected by all sorts of temporary disturbances, so it can change from one week to the next even without any change in its normal value.

◼ Figure 7.1 depicts the $w(r)$ curve corresponding to a given circulating capital technique, which we suppose in use in a closed economy with no scarce natural resources. As explained in ▶ Chap. 2, the wage curve results from the normal price equations

$$\mathbf{p} = (1 + r)\mathbf{p}\mathbf{A}(r) + w\mathbf{a}_\mathrm{L}(r)$$

where technical coefficients are the ones of the technique in use. Check that these are the price equations implied by the equations of long-period equilibrium if all capital goods are circulating and we do not separate capital goods from consumption goods, numbering all goods from *1* to *n*.

Assume all industries have adjusted their technical choices and dimensions to the given income distribution and quantities demanded. The quantities produced are given—they are the observed ones—hence the capital goods utilized are also given. Let $\mathbf{y}$ be the column vector representing the net product of this economy. Let us choose as numéraire a basket of goods with the same composition as $\mathbf{y}$; this basket by assumption has value 1, so if $\mathbf{y}$ consists of α such baskets the value of $\mathbf{y}$ is α. Labour is homogeneous; let us measure labour in such units that total

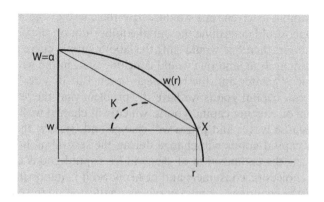

Fig. 7.1 How to derive the value of capital per unit of labour from the wage curve

labour employment is 1 unit (or else let us interpret **y** as net output vector per unit of labour). If $r=0$ all net product goes to labour, hence $W \equiv w(0)$, the vertical intercept of the wage curve, corresponding to a zero interest rate, equals α. Now let the rate of interest increase, assuming quantities and technique remain unchanged; **py** does not change, it remains equal to $\alpha = W$. Let K be the value of capital at long-period prices. The net product goes either to wages or to interest, the part going to interest being rK. Therefore

$$\mathbf{py} = W = w + rK.$$

Hence

$$K = (W - w)/r.$$

This has a simple graphical interpretation. Take $r>0$ as given; w is determined by the wage curve; in ◘ Fig. 7.1 $W-w$ is the segment in ordinate between $w(r)$, and the vertical intercept W of the wage curve. Therefore, with X the point $(r, w(r))$ on the wage curve corresponding to the given rate of interest or profit, K is the value of the trigonometric tangent of the angle wXW.

By varying the rate of interest and studying how the angle wXW changes, one obtains how the normal value of the given vector of capital goods changes in terms of the net product, when neither quantities produced nor technical coefficients change.

As r varies, K will remain constant only if the $w(r)$ curve is a straight line, which has been shown in ▶ Chap. 2 to be the case for arbitrary numéraires only if relative prices do not change with distribution, the pure labour-theory-of-value case.[8] In ◘ Fig. 7.1 the value of capital increases as r increases because the wage

---

8   When the pure labour theory of value does not hold, the w(r) curve is a straight line if the numéraire is the standard commodity. But this will mean a normal value of capital unaffected by changes in r only if the numéraire is proportional to the economy's net product, that is, the economy must produce the standard commodity (impossible: no non-basics, for example). It might be thought that the value of capital will not change with distribution if one chooses as numéraire the

7.4 · The Quantity of Capital: Supply-Side Problems

curve was drawn concave; in other cases or with a different choice of numéraire the value of capital might decrease or alternate increasing and decreasing behaviour as r increases. Thus the dependence of the normal value of capital on distribution, even when physically the capital vector remains unchanged, can be grasped visually.

The above determination of the value of capital per unit of labour was with circulating capital. With fixed capital, we have seen in ▶ Chap. 2 that the value of a stock of machines of the same type but different ages changes with r, one further reason for changes in the value of a given physical capital stock when income distribution changes. Furthermore, the degree of utilization of fixed capital can easily not be normal because it depends on demand, and this relevantly affects its value; a degree of utilization of a fixed plant below normal, and expected to remain below normal for some time, reduces the value of the fixed plant; so the value of durable capital depends on aggregate demand, and can relevantly change from boom to depression. Technical innovations also continuously modify the value of existing durable capital goods, creating technological obsolescence.

Thus the number K^* one obtains from observation *depends* on what the observed income distribution is, on aggregate demand, and on all the accidental temporary causes of deviation of market prices from normal long-period prices in the observed situation. Therefore the observed value of capital cannot be considered one of the *determinants* of that income distribution; to the contrary, the latter is one of the determinants of the observed value of capital. But then long-period equilibria cannot be determined, the datum relative to the endowment of 'capital' is logically indeterminable.

Traditional marginalist economists greatly underestimated the dependence of relative prices on income distribution, reasoning as if one could treat relative prices as given instead of as being among what equilibrium was intended to determine. This contradiction was gradually realized and caused increasing unease, and was a main reason for the shift to the third approach to capital, that will be illustrated in ▶ Chap. 8.

7.5 The Quantity of Capital: Demand-Side Problems. Demand for 'capital' and Investment

The impossibility to specify the endowment of 'capital' can be seen as a *supply-side problem* of long-period marginalist analyses, concerning the specification of the *supply* of 'capital'. But there is also a *demand-side problem*. Starting from certain results due to Sraffa, it has been shown that it is not necessarily true that the demand curve for 'capital' is downward-sloping.

---

existing capital vector; but equilibrium will generally require a composition of capital different from the given one, so during the gravitation towards equilibrium the composition of capital will change away from the initial one chosen as numéraire, and then the value of capital will depend on relative prices.

552   Chapter 7 · Capital: Long-Period Equilibria

The reader might ask, why should one worry about this problem if anyway the long-period equilibrium cannot be determined? Whether the demand for 'capital' comes out to be downward-sloping or not—the reader might continue—the conclusions on the stability or instability of the equilibrium resulting from such a demand function and from a given supply of 'capital' would seem irrelevant since that supply is indeterminable and hence so is the equilibrium.

The answer to this legitimate question will take some space, because it requires penetrating further the logic of the traditional conception of 'capital', and explaining the connection between demand for 'capital' and investment.[9]

The different points of the demand function for 'capital' corresponding to different levels of the rate of interest reflect different 'forms' (compositions) of the capital stock; but of course the approach admits that at each given moment the given quantity of 'capital' is not a malleable substance free to change its 'form' instantaneously; it is embodied, or 'crystallized', in concrete capital goods, and the change in 'form' can only happen as these capital goods are used up or scrapped and the resources that might reproduce them are used to produce other capital goods. Importantly, most capital goods are highly specific to a certain method of production and they (if circulating capital goods) or their services (if durable capital goods) must be generally combined in rigid proportions among themselves and with labour in order to obtain the product. Once the physical capital goods forming a 'plant' are chosen, at normal utilization the labour to be combined with them and with intermediate goods is rigidly determined. Therefore if labour is fully employed, and then there is a change in income distribution or in technical knowledge, the methods with which labour is utilized will not be quickly changed in the entire economy; in each period they will be modified only for the fraction of the labour force which in that period becomes 'free' to be combined with different capital goods owing to the closing down of the plants that in that period exhaust their usefulness and are scrapped. Only if all capital goods are circulating will the new methods take only one period to be applied to the entire labour force. In actual economies most production uses durable capital goods too, often very durable and combined in 'plants'. After the change, except for especially drastic changes, there will be little anticipated closure of plants, most of the labour force will continue to work in the already existing plants which, if no longer optimal in the new conditions, will be content with earning residual quasi-rents. A changed rate of interest will induce a change of methods of production, and of labour per unit of output, *only in new plants*, and therefore every period only for a fraction of the fully employed labour supply.[10]

---

9 For a more detailed discussion see Dvoskin and Petri (2017).

10 The approach assumes, at least on an average as between booms and slumps, the full employment of labour. An additional criticism advanced in Petri (2013, 2015) contends that this traditional neoclassical reasoning requires that the full employment of labour be *assumed* rather than derived from the analysis, and that if it is not assumed to start with, then even the traditional marginalist conception of capital–labour substitution does not suffice to obtain a tendency towards the full employment of labour. This criticism is summarized in ▶ Chap. 12, Sect. 12.7.1.

7.5 · The Quantity of Capital: Demand-Side Problems. Demand for 'capital' and Investment

This means that the demand for 'capital', if capital goods are largely durable, can only concretely present itself as a flow demand for the gross savings per period needed to replace the fraction of 'capital' due for renewal that period. Accordingly, the equilibrium between supply and demand for 'capital' can only concretely manifest itself as equilibrium between a flow supply of savings, and a flow demand for savings to be used for the gross investment needed to *maintain* the desired stock of 'capital'. The argument was traditionally put in terms of a credit market where a flow supply of 'loanable funds', corresponding to the part of gross income saved, must come into equilibrium with a flow demand for these funds to be then used to purchase newly produced capital goods. These two flows are flows of exchange value, and the rate of interest is the price considered capable of bringing them into equilibrium because the *demand* flow, i.e. gross investment demand, increases if the rate of interest decreases.

If production is in yearly cycles and all capital goods are circulating capital, and 'If the wage-rate and product-prices are assumed to adjust without appreciable delay to the equilibrium compatible with the new rate of interest …[then] the demand function for investment at the end of each year will simply be the demand function for 'capital' as a stock.' (Garegnani 1990, p. 59). In the presence of durable capital besides circulating capital, once 'capital' is of the quantity and 'form' adapted to a certain rate of interest, gross investment demand per period will consist of demand to replace the circulating capital, plus demand for the new durable capital goods which are to replace the scrapped ones. For example if the stock demand for 'capital' includes, besides circulating capital, demand for 200 durable machines all lasting 10 years with constant efficiency, and uniformly distributed by age, then each year 1/10 of the machines will need replacement, so yearly gross investment (demand for gross savings) will consist of the value of circulating capital plus the value of 20 new machines, which will re-employ the workers rendered 'free' by the shutting down of the plants whose machines have reached scrapping age. If this investment equals yearly gross savings, the economy is in equilibrium. The investment in new machines will be a fraction between 1/10 and 1/5 of the value of the part of the capital stock consisting of machines, depending on the rate of interest[11]; to that, one will have to add the value of circulating capital to obtain total gross investment.

---

11 Let me remember here a result shown in Chap. 2, ▶ Sect. 2.38. The gross investment that maintains unaltered a stock of durable machines of uniformly distributed age, constant efficiency and duration x periods, must buy each period a number of new machines equal to $1/x$ their total number; the value of these new machines, i.e. investment, is generally greater than the value of the stock of machines divided by x, because older machines are worth less than new ones. If $r=0$, the value of a machine decreases linearly with age, and gross investment per period is a bit less than the value of the stock times $2/x$ (if the machines last 10 years and a new machine costs 1, the beginning of period value of a stock of 10 machines of uniformly distributed age is 5.5). As r rises, the value of the stock rises relative to the cost of new machines, because a machine decreases in value at a slower pace initially, depreciation shifts towards the later years of the machine's life, and gross investment becomes a smaller fraction of the value of the stock, always greater than $1/x$ but possibly approaching it considerably. This explains why in the example investment in new machines is between 1/10 and 1/5 of the value of the fraction of the stock of capital that consists of durable machines.

554   Chapter 7 · Capital: Long-Period Equilibria

At a lower rate of interest, according to the marginal approach the circulating and the durable capital goods that firms desire to combine with the given labour supply will mean a demand for a greater total stock of 'capital', and hence a greater gross investment per period. The thing can be repeated for each rate of interest; the decreasing shape of the stock demand for 'capital' assumed by the marginal approach will imply a decreasing investment function. Garegnani concludes: 'The traditional theory implies that the delayed adjustments in the wages, rents, and prices of products do not fundamentally alter the terms of the question … Hence the significance of the demand and supply functions for capital as a stock, which would exhibit the basic tendencies destined to emerge from the multiplicity of forces acting at any given moment in the savings investment market. … the traditional analyses of the demand and supply for capital were in effect intended to be an analysis of the demand and supply for savings, abstracting from the complications likely to operate at each particular moment of time in the savings-investment market' (Garegnani 1990, p. 59–60).[12]

The gross investment function thus derived from the demand for 'capital' function abstracting from the 'complications' of each short period can be called the *long-period (gross) investment function*, a reduced-scale copy of the demand for capital function.

In this way the approach reconciles the need for variable capital–labour and labour–output proportions with the inevitable admission of a nearly total fixity of those proportions (at normal plant utilization) once certain durable capital goods and not other ones are in existence.[13]

Importantly, note that this notion of long-period investment function does not need, in order to be of use, that the capital stock of the economy has perfectly adapted its 'form' to the ruling rate of interest. Let us consider again the example of an economy with machines lasting 10 years with constant efficiency; and to simplify, let us assume that the capital stock consists only of machines, there is no circulating capital. Suppose that, starting from a previous equilibrium, an increase in the flow of gross savings to a new level (that remains constant from that moment on) reduces the rate of interest and induces the adoption of different production methods requiring different machines of greater value per unit of labour; the new methods will employ the flow of labour 'freed' by the shutting down of the oldest plants, i.e. 1/10 of the labour force every year, so (assuming the change in prices and rate of interest is not such as to cause an anticipated scrapping of old plants) each year one further tenth of the labour force becomes employed in plants using the new 'capital'-labour proportion, for 9 years plants embodying the new K/L ratio co-exist with old plants; but the real wage and the normal prices associated with the new rate of interest and the new optimal tech-

---

12 Also cf. Garegnani (1978, p. 352), which has inspired the example adopted in the text.

13 The parenthesis '(at normal utilization)' is needed because technological rigidities render short-period labour-output ratios and intermediate goods-labour ratios rigid, but not the degree of utilization of fixed plants: these can be utilized fewer or more hours per month (e.g. with overtime), but their normal utilization too is rigidly determined by long-period cost minimization that determines the optimal or normal utilization.

nology will come to rule after a much shorter time interval, the one required for the competition from the new plants to impose itself: at the new rate of interest, the new plants are the cost-minimizing ones so they can impose their product prices. So after perhaps only one year the new equilibrium rate of interest and associated real wage will be the ones inducing the adoption of a capital–labour proportion in new plants capable of maintaining the full employment of labour while absorbing the flow of 'free' capital corresponding to the increased flow of gross savings. Owing to competition, the real wage for the entire labour force will be equal to the marginal product of labour in these new plants even though a majority of the labour force works in old-technology plants.

This capital–labour proportion in new plants will have at the denominator the flow of labour 'freed' every period by the closing down of old plants reaching the end of their economic life, and at the numerator investment as determined by the long-period investment function and by the rate of interest needed for the equality of investment with the flow of gross savings per period.[14] Every year an additional 1/10 of the labour force will be employed in new-technology plants; after 10 years all the physical capital stock of the economy will consist of the new type of machines, and will stop changing; its value is the 'capital' indicated, for that rate of interest, by the demand for 'capital' function, which indicates the quantity of 'capital' firms wish to combine with the *entire* labour force. During the whole transition to this new stationary stock of 'capital' (apart from an initial period required for the new prices to impose themselves) it is the long-period investment function that, given the flow of gross savings, determines the equilibrium rate of interest. Thus the demand for 'capital' function through its influence on the investment function is seen by the marginal approach to govern the rate of interest even in periods in which a large part of the labour force is employed in plants no longer optimal in the new conditions. Income distribution is determined by the 'capital'-labour ratio in new plants.

In the terminology used in later growth theory, the 'capital' invested in new plants is treated as, *ex-ante*, malleable 'putty' adaptable to diverse technologies, but as rigid 'clay' *ex post*, requiring in each industry, once embodied in specific capital goods, a fixed labour input per unit of output.

These considerations clarify two aspects of the role of the traditional marginalist analysis of the supply and demand for 'capital' for the explanation of income distribution in actual economies.

First, given the little possibility to alter production methods once 'capital' has taken a certain 'form', apart from rare cases it is only when the 'capital' to be employed is still of 'free' form, that is, when the capital goods to be embodied in a new plant are still to be decided and produced, that a choice of the 'capital'-labour proportion can be conceived to exist. Income distribution is actually

---

14 The simplifying assumption that the new flow of gross savings remains constant at the new level implies therefore a constant ratio of 'capital' to labour in new plants. A graphical illustration of this process is provided in Petri (2004, p. 131). Note that the argument *assumes* the continuous full employment of labour rather than obtaining it as a *result* of the analysis; the moment this assumption is not made investment becomes indeterminate, as will be explained in ▶ Chap. 12.

determined by factor proportions 'at the margin of new investment', to use Frank Knight's expression.[15]

Second, the approach implies that the insights derivable from long-period analysis do not require, in order to be applicable, that the 'form' and even the 'quantity' of 'capital' has *completely* adapted to the ruling income distribution. In the above example, when the flow of gross savings increases and stabilizes at the new level causing, let us assume, an average doubling of the K/L ratio in new plants relative to the old K/L ratio, it can be that already after a year the new rate of interest will reflect the marginal product of capital associated with the doubled K/L ratio in new plants, that is, much before that ratio holds for *all* plants: the latter situation will be reached only when, after ten years in our example, the entire labour force is employed in plants with the new K/L ratio.[16] Interestingly, apart from the initial period of adjustments required for the new plants to impose the new income distribution, during the years required for the new K/L ratio to extend to all plants labour earns the wage appropriate to a quantity of 'capital' which the economy does not yet have.

Now we have the tools to answer the question posed by the imaginary reader at the beginning of the section. On the basis of the considerations just explained, it was possible for marginalist economists to view income distribution as determined by the marginalist factor substitution mechanisms even in situations in which the 'form' of 'capital' was largely given; the rate of interest was still determined by a supply–demand equilibrium, and precisely by the flow equilibrium in the savings–investment market, reflecting the marginal product of 'capital' *in new plants*. This was, essentially, the approach of Marshall and the Marshallian school, that Keynes inherited, and that has dominated macroeconomics after him.[17]

---

15 "Under conditions of perfect competition, or in an economic system in the position of the theoretical equilibrium (stationary or moving), all sources would yield a uniform rate of return on their cost of production, which would be equal both to their cost of reproduction and their market value ... Under real conditions, this rate 'tends' to be approximated at the margin of new investment (or disinvestment), with allowance for the uncertainties and errors of prediction" (Knight 1946, p. 396).

16 It is important to note that this approach implies that the total normal demand for labour cannot quickly change, because at normal utilization existing plants employ an essentially rigid amount of labour, as admitted by Hicks in the quotation in ▶ Sect. 7.3: in order for a decrease in wages significantly to affect the demand for labour, a large portion of existing productive structures must be modified, which will take years. Therefore the approach implies that unemployment requires a long time to be eliminated even when wages are fully downward-flexible, and then even the neoclassical economist must hope that they are *not* very flexible, because that could cause falls of wages to unbearable levels, with consequent disruption of orderly social life.

17 See Kaldor (1955–56, pp. 90–91) for a synthetic description, which makes it clear that the Marshallian school did not accept Hicks's observation of too little factor substitutability in the short period, and considered the labour demand coming from existing plants to be a rather elastic function of the real wage; the latter was determined by the intersection of this function with the labour supply curve, without an explicit connection with the rate of interest; a clear perception was missing (in Keynes too) that competition among new plants, by pushing profits (neoclassical definition) towards zero, made the real wage in new plants a function of the rate of interest, and

7.5 · The Quantity of Capital: Demand-Side Problems. Demand for 'capital' and Investment

In this approach, the short-period assumption of given fixed plants prevents the variability of the capital composition that requires the notion of a given total endowment of 'capital' of variable 'form' in order for equilibrium to be determinable. By treating the existing fixed plants much like given lands (although subject to deterioration), it was believed that one could determine a short-period equilibrium in which total income is determined by existing plants and by the full employment of labour, and the flow of savings, i.e. of 'free' 'capital' to be employed in new plants, determines the rate of interest as equal to the marginal product of 'capital' 'at the margin of new investment'. Such an approach at least at first sight avoids the criticism based on the indeterminability of the total endowment of 'capital'.[18]

But the conception of 'capital' as a single factor of variable 'form', an amount of value, remains indispensable. The demand curve for this factor 'capital' remains fundamental, because it indicates how the rate of interest determines the demand for 'capital' *per unit of labour* and therefore allows determining investment in new plants by applying this amount of 'capital' per unit of labour to the flow of labour gradually 'freed' by the scrapping of the oldest plants. *The decreasing demand curve for 'capital' is what allows to conclude that investment is a decreasing function of the rate of interest—which is indispensable for the stability of the savings–investment market.*

We see here why a demand-side criticism can be important. If the shape of the demand for 'capital' function does not support the stability of the savings–investment market, then even the short-period Marshallian version, perhaps less vulnerable vis-à-vis the supply-side criticism, is undermined. What the traditional marginal approach needs, and even now most neoclassical economists believe, is that 'capital'-labour substitution operates in the same way as labour-land substitution in a non-capitalistic economy, in spite of 'capital' being peculiar as a factor because physically heterogeneous and measured as an amount of exchange value: a lower rate of interest is believed to induce the adoption of techniques that use more 'capital' per unit of labour. Is it really so? Let us see.

---

that competition would then extend this real wage to the entire labour force, as I have assumed in the example with machines lasting 10 years. But this weakness would appear surmountable by assuming the short period to be long enough (a semilong period in fact) for new plants to impose the normal prices and real wage associated with the new rate of interest, as indeed I have assumed in the determination of the long-period investment function and in the example.

18 A full discussion of whether the criticism is really avoided would take too long. But certainly the notion of a total endowment of 'capital' is implicit in the view of savings as a flow of 'free' 'capital', which implies the stock of capital goods of an economy is the result of past savings translated into investments, hence, is a stock of cumulated savings, i.e. of 'capital'. Nor can the notion be avoided (and Marshall does admit it, see Dvoskin and Petri 2017): without reference to it, this Marshallian approach would be unable to conclude on the *persistent* effects of, say, changes in labour supply, that is, on the effects when sufficient time is allowed for the composition of the capital stock to become close to its long-period normal. For example if in an initially stationary economy there arise net savings for a few years, and then the economy returns stationary with the same labour supply as before, the approach would be unable to conclude on the new income distribution unless it could argue that the amount of 'capital' has increased and therefore output per unit of labour and real wage have increased, and the rate of interest has decreased.

7.6 Re-switching and Reverse Capital Deepening

To study how the demand for 'capital' per unit of labour changes with the rate of interest in as simple a case as possible, let us reduce complications on the choice of numéraire by assuming the economy produces a single consumption good, which is the net product of the economy, and is the natural numéraire since it is the sole answer to the search for 'some composite unit of consumption goods capable of measuring the subjective satisfaction from which consumers abstain when they save' (Garegnani 1978, p. 345, quoted above).

Let us further assume all capital goods are circulating, and all industries take a year to produce their products. Then gross investment per year coincides with the desired value of the capital stock, which must be entirely renewed every year. As the rate of interest rises, saving decisions can increase but also decrease, so in order to argue the stability of the savings–investment market the neoclassical economist must rely above all on a negative interest-elasticity of the *demand* side of the savings–investment market. What she/he needs is that the desired value of capital per unit of labour be a decreasing function of the rate of interest.

The phenomenon of *re-switching* with its implication of *reverse capital deepening* shows that things can be otherwise.

It was shown in ► Chap. 2 that two $w(r)$ curves can intersect more than once, the phenomenon called **re-switching** of techniques. Let us combine it with the possibility to derive, from the graphical procedure illustrated in ◘ Fig. 7.1, how the value of the capital goods employed per unit of labour changes with the rate of interest if the net product per unit of labour is given and is the numéraire. Assume we measure labour in such units that total labour employment is one unit. Then, given the assumption of circulating capital, the value of capital derived from the graphical procedure of ◘ Fig. 7.1 is the demand for 'capital'. The neoclassical approach needs this demand for 'capital' to be a decreasing function of the interest rate. This can be shown not to be guaranteed at all.

The method to show it is as follows. We know that for each rate of interest r, in the long period the economy adopts, among the set of alternative techniques[19] at its disposal, the corresponding dominant technique, that is, the one whose $w(r)$ curve is on the outer envelope of the wage curves for that r. Suppose the rate of interest is r_1 and the associated dominant technique, call it technique λ, has wage curve $w_\lambda(r)$ that determines a wage $w_\lambda(r_1)$ and has vertical intercept W_λ. Then the associated value of capital is

$$K(r_1, \lambda) = (W_\lambda - w_\lambda(r_1))/r_1.$$

For each r one can determine the dominant technique and derive K in this way, and one can plot K as a function of r.

---

19 I remind the reader that *technique* and *production method* are two different notions. A production method is a vector, a technique is a matrix (of technical coefficients). A production method refers to a single industry or firm. The technique that produces a certain net product is a set of production methods, one for each industry of the economy or subsystem producing that net product; two techniques are different if they differ by even only one production method.

7.6 · Re-switching and Reverse Capital Deepening

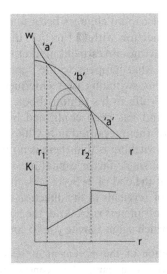

Fig. 7.2 In the upper diagram the value of capital per unit of labour at r_2 is represented by the angle in red for technique 'a' and by the angle in green for technique 'b'

Thus suppose that there are just two alternative techniques 'a' and 'b', which yield the $w(r)$ curves represented in Fig. 7.2, a case of re-switching. As r increases from zero, the economy will tend to adopt technique 'a' for $0 \leq r < r_1$, it will 'switch' to technique 'b' if r increases beyond r_1, only to 'switch back', or 're-switch', to technique 'a' as r, increasing still more, goes beyond r_2. Thus as r increases from infinitesimally less to infinitesimally more than r_1 there is a jump in the demand for 'capital' from the value of capital associated, at that rate of interest, with technique 'a' to the value of capital associated with technique 'b'; at r_1 the two techniques are equally profitable and can co-exist, the given net product can be produced by any linear combination of the two techniques, and accordingly the demand for capital can take any value in between those two values.

The same happens at r_2, except that the direction of the switch of techniques is the reverse one. In the case shown in Fig. 7.2, at r_2 the value of capital per unit of labour *increases* as the rate of interest *increases*: in this case the technical and price change induced by the change in distribution causes a behaviour of the demand for 'capital' that goes countermarginalist/neoclassical beliefs. This change in the value of capital contrary to what neoclassical tradition would expect is called ***reverse capital deepening***.[20] In the intervals in which the technique

---

20 Traditionally, marginalist authors distinguished two types of increases in the amount of capital employed by an economy: ***capital deepening*** indicated a rise in the average capital–labour ratio, due to a lower rate of interest; ***capital widening*** indicated an increase in the employment of capital with no change in the capital–labour ratio, and entailing therefore an increase of labour employment. This terminology has suggested the term 'reverse capital deepening' (or sometimes 'capital reversal') to mean a *decrease* in capital–labour ratio when the rate of interest decreases, hence, a change opposite to the 'capital deepening' change postulated by the marginal approach.

560   **Chapter 7 ·** Capital: Long-Period Equilibria

does not change, the value of capital changes because the wage curves are not linear, as already noted in connection with ◘ Fig. 7.1; the possible relevance of this fact for the stability of the savings–investment market is discussed later.

Before analysing further what happens to the demand for 'capital', let us see some other implications of re-switching of techniques. The possibility of such a case was pointed out by Sraffa in his famous book *Production of commodities by means of commodities*, and has been confirmed by subsequent analyses and numerical examples, some of them reported in ▶ Chap. 2.

A first implication of re-switching is that there is no way to consider the several capital goods as embodying a single factor capital measurable in units independent of distribution. As noticed at the end of ▶ Sect. 2.14, the possibility of re-switching derives from the possibility of reversals in the direction of the movement of relative prices as the rate of profit or of interest rises. After the numerical example mentioned in ▶ Sect. 2.14, p. 135, and which again I invite you to consult, Sraffa comments:

> **»** The reversals in the direction of the movement of relative prices, in the face of unchanged methods of production, cannot be reconciled with *any* notion of capital as a measurable quantity independent of distribution and prices. (Sraffa 1960, p. 38).

Why so? The reason is that when two goods are produced by fixed-coefficient methods that use two factors measured independently of distribution and prices, then a rise in the relative rental of a factor unambiguously raises the relative cost of production of the good produced with the method which uses that factor in a greater ratio to the other factor; this was the basis of the indirect substitution mechanism presented in ▶ Chap. 3, but it was also the basis of the direct substitution mechanism, by viewing the two goods as the *same* good producible with two different methods. Thus when the factors are labour and land, the relative cost of production of two goods is necessarily a monotonic function of the wage-rent ratio. When the two goods are produced by labour and 'capital',[21] and the rate of interest changes, if the capital goods embodied a quantity of a single factor capital[22] independent of distribution, the same monotonicity should obtain. Sraffa shows that monotonicity may easily not obtain; so when good A rises in price relative to a good B as the rate of interest rises, one should conclude that the

---

21   Actually in this case the way each good is produced cannot be called a *method* (with the exception of corn produced by corn and labour), because production of a good with labour and 'capital' means production of the good as *net* product, it involves an entire *subsystem*. Why 'as net product'? The logic of long-period equilibrium is that the use of a factor is the use *of its services*, and the factor is still there after production, ready to supply the same amount of services in the next production cycle. This is evident for labour and land. For production with labour and 'capital' too, the output of their use must be seen as the product one obtains after reintegrating the used-up capital goods, otherwise the amount of 'capital' has not remained the same. So one must assume that the production of a commodity is accompanied by the replacement of the capital goods used up in its production, and this means the commodity is the *net* product of a *subsystem*, see Chap. 2, ▶ Sect. 2.8. The thing is further clarified below, ▶ Sect. 7.10.

22   I am not using the inverted commas here because I reserve them for the conception of capital as an amount of value, while here the criticism holds for *any* possible conception of capital as a single quantity somehow 'embodied' in, or represented by, a vector of heterogeneous capital goods.

7.6 · Re-switching and Reverse Capital Deepening

capital–labour ratio is higher for good A; but at a different rate of interest good A can decrease in relative price as the rate of interest rises, which means that now A is produced with a lower capital–labour ratio than B, in spite of no change in the amounts of labour and physical capital goods used to produce each good. It is therefore impossible to treat the complex of methods producing a good as net product by the use of labour and capital goods as representing a definite capital–labour ratio independently of prices. Any theory based on such a notion is thereby shown to be unsustainable.

One implication is the following. Suppose the economy produces a vector $\mathbf{y} > \mathbf{0}$ of net products, utilizing technique $\mathbf{A}$. As shown in ▶ Chap. 2, we can decompose the economy into as many subsystems as there are commodities, and for each commodity i we can determine the quantity of labour and the vector of capital goods directly and indirectly utilized to produce one unit of that commodity as net product. If it were possible to consider this vector of capital goods to represent a definite, 'technological' scalar quantity of 'capital', then the 'capital'-labour ratio in the production of that commodity would be well determined, let us call it ξ_i. Let L_i be the total quantity of labour directly and indirectly utilized to produce the net output of commodity i, that is employed in subsystem i. Then the 'capital' employed in subsystem i would be $\xi_i L_i$, and the total 'capital' employed in the economy would be $\Sigma_i \xi_i L_i$. In other words, if the 'capital'-labour ratio adopted in the production of each commodity were a 'technological' magnitude independent of prices, then the given labour directly and indirectly employed in the production of each commodity (and therefore associated with a definite 'capital'-labour ratio in each subsystem) would imply a definite total quantity of 'capital' employed in the economy, and therefore also (neglecting as of minor importance possible inventories of idle capital goods) a definite total *endowment* of 'capital' of the economy. Re-switching, or the reversal in the direction of the movement of relative prices that makes re-switching possible, destroys this possible avenue to a well-defined total 'capital' endowment, because it shows there is no way to assign univocally, independently of distribution and prices, a 'capital'-labour ratio to the subsystem producing a commodity as net product. Therefore re-switching generalizes the supply-side criticism of the possibility of treating as given the endowment of value 'capital', by destroying all possibility that perhaps there is *another* way to conceive production with labour and heterogeneous capital goods as production with labour and a scalar quantity of a single factor 'capital'.

Re-switching also undermines in other ways the idea of a substitution between factors induced by changes of their relative rentals. Let us look at what happens to the demand for labour *per unit of net output* (a notion that does not require a measurement of capital) in the example of ◘ Fig. 7.2. As the rate of interest increases, the real wage decreases. According to marginalist theory, a *decrease* of the real wage rate, *if* it induces a change of technique, induces firms to switch to a technique that uses *more* labour per unit of net product. What happens at r_2 is the opposite: a decrease of w causing an increase of r from slightly less to slightly more than r_2 causes the economy to switch to technique 'a', which is the one that uses *less* labour per unit of net product, as shown by the greater vertical intercept of its $w(r)$ curve, i.e. by the greater net product per unit of labour. Here there is no aggregation problem or ambiguity connected with value measurements: labour and net output are measured in technical units. Of course if, to produce a given net output, less labour is used, more of something else must make up for it, so in this sense there is necessarily some substitution; but it is unnecessary to specify what the 'something else' is, what is clear is that at r_2 substitution works for labour in a direction opposite the one the marginal approach would need. So re-switching destroys the neoclassical idea of factor substitution operating in favour of the factor that becomes relatively cheaper, even without knowing *what* substitutes for labour when less labour is used to produce the same net output.

The indirect substitution mechanism, based on consumer choices, is also undermined. Let us take up again the example of champagne and whiskey of ▶ Sect. 2.33 and let us analyse its implication for the demand for labour, accepting that the composition of consumer demand shifts in favour of the good which becomes cheaper. At $r = 100\%$, champagne and whiskey cost the same (cf. ◘ Fig. 2.6), but the repeated production of one unit of champagne per period requires the employment of 7 units of labour against 8 units of labour for a unit of whiskey, so whiskey is the more labour-intensive of the two goods. Let the rate of interest increase above 100%, causing a decrease of the real wage; according to traditional marginalist reasoning, this should lower the relative price of the more labour-intensive good, i.e. of whiskey; on the contrary, it is champagne that becomes cheaper. Assuming for the sake of argument that one can treat 'capital' as a factor with a given fully utilized endowment, the decrease of w tends to cause a *decrease* in the demand for labour.[23] If labour is assumed fully employed, the demand for 'capital' rises. The indirect substitution mechanism is undermined too, and *not* because of income effects.

Indeed, the critical implications of these results appear to go deeper than the problems raised by income effects because they question *the substitution principle*, the thesis that substitution effects always operate in support of the tendency towards equilibrium. Problems for the uniqueness and stability of general equilibrium deriving from income effects were long admitted, but before the discovery of re-switching and reverse capital deepening it was believed that substitution effects would *always* support the factor substitution mechanisms on which the supply-and-demand approach rests, and this is what allowed not to worry too much about income effects because, the argument went (at least, before the Sonnenschein-Mantel-Debreu results), generally substitution effects would dominate (an example is the argument by Harry Johnson discussed in Chap. 6, ▶ Sect. 6.30). But re-switching shows that, in economies with heterogeneous capital, substitution effects need not work in the direction assumed—and needed—by the marginal approach. Pierangelo Garegnani concludes that 'those phenomena reflect the absence of a *factual basis* for the theory' (1990, p. 71). Later in the same paper he explains: "the dominant explanation of distribution was built on deducing from consumer choice, and from the existence of alternative systems

---

23 Now we cannot speak of labour demand per unit of output, because now net output is not a scalar, the composition of net output per unit of labour changes with distribution.

7.6 · Re-switching and Reverse Capital Deepening

of production, the idea that a fall in w (rise in i) would always raise in a regular determinable way the amount of labour employed with an amount of capital in some sense given. This provided what appeared to be a firm theoretical basis for the idea of 'demand and supply' as forces determining distribution, and therefore prices. That key logical deduction is what has been proved false by 're-switching' and 'reverse capital deepening'... had theoreticians realized earlier that the deduction in question was invalid, we would probably not be thinking today in terms of demand and supply functions for labour" (1990, p. 76).

7.7 More on Reverse Capital Deepening. Price Wicksell Effects

For the reader who wants a numerical example proving that reverse capital deepening is indeed possible, I show that the 'Austrian' Samuelson model of whiskey and champagne used in ▶ Chap. 2 provides it.

I repeat its assumptions. Production of 1 unit of champagne requires the payment of 7 wages *two* dates before the sale of the product (i.e. if labour is paid in arrears, if the product is sold at date t, that is at the beginning of period t, labour was utilized in period t − 3 and paid at its end i.e. at date t − 2). Production of 1 unit of whiskey requires the payment of 2 wages three dates before, and of 6 wages one date before the date when the product is sold. Then long-period prices p_c of champagne and p_w of whiskey must satisfy:

$$p_c = 7w(1+r)^2$$
$$p_w = 2w(1+r)^3 + 6w(1+r).$$

The example can be reinterpreted as describing the money price that a single final good, say, meat, must have in order just to cover production cost if the money wage w and the rate of interest r are both given, depending on which of two different 'Austrian' techniques 'C' and 'W' is used to produce it.[24] To determine the value of capital associated with the repeated production of one unit of meat with either technique, we must assume the economy produces meat as net product; prices and industry dimensions are fully adjusted to income distribution and to the given technique; so capital goods of a certain value are present each period in this stationary economy. Let us see how this value can be determined.

With technique 'C', if one unit of meat is produced every period then in each period the economy produces the unit of meat and furthermore replaces the used-up capital goods, hence the following production processes go on simultaneously in each period:
- 7 units of unassisted labour produce as output a capital good that we can indicate as $c1$;
- $c1$ alone, unassisted by labour, ripens into capital good $c2$;
- $c2$ alone, unassisted by labour, ripens into one unit of meat.

---

24 *Exercise*: explain why I call 'C' and 'W' *techniques*, and not methods.

564 Chapter 7 · Capital: Long-Period Equilibria

Thus at the beginning of each period the economy's stock of capital consists of $c1$ and $c2$. Taking the money wage w as given, the value of $c1$ is $7w$, the value of $c2$ is $7w(1+r)$. Hence the value of capital is $K_c = 7w + 7w(1+r)$ per unit of consumption good. Since a net output of one unit of consumption good implies the employment of 7 units of labour, the value of capital *per unit of labour* is $K_c/7 = w + w(1+r)$.

With technique 'W', each period the following production processes go on simultaneously:

- 2 units of unassisted labour produce as output a capital good that we can indicate as $W1$;
- $W1$ unassisted by labour ripens into capital good $W2$;
- $W2$ together with 6 units of labour produces capital good $W3$;
- $W3$ unassisted by labour ripens into one unit of consumption good.

At the beginning of each period the economy's stock of capital consists of capital goods $W1$, $W2$ and $W3$. Their respective values are $2w$; $2w(1+r)$; $2w(1+r)^2 + 6w$. The value of capital per unit of consumption good is $K_w = 8w + 2 w[(1+r) + (1+r)^2]$, and per unit of labour it is $K_w/8$.

These values of capital are the normal 'demands' for 'capital' per unit of labour implied by each technique for the production of meat. Because all capital goods are circulating, these values are also the values of gross investment per unit of labour per period if the economy is stationary. Let us calculate them at $r = 100\%$, where $w = 1/28$ for both techniques. It is $K_c/7 = 3/28 = 3w$, and $K_w/8 = w + 12w/8 = 5w/2$, which is less than $3w$. So as r *rises* from a little less to a little above 100%, technical choice is in favour of technique 'C' which implies a *higher*, and not a lower, value of capital per unit of labour: 'reverse capital deepening'.[25] Thus a *rise* of r causes an *increase* of gross investment.

This example illustrates how the demand for 'capital' associated with the production of certain goods as net products must be determined: it is the value of the capital goods that must be present and renewed each period in the economy, in order for the repeated production of that net product to be possible.

Now let us see other graphical examples confirming that there is no reason why the demand for 'capital', and hence the demand for savings to be employed for investment in new plants, should necessarily increase if the rate of interest decreases.[26]

---

25 Note also that as r rises above 100% (and the wage decreases), the switch is from technique 'W', that uses 8 units of labour per unit of net output, to 'C' that uses 7 units of labour: the wage decrease induces the use of *less* labour per unit of net output: again, substitution can work the opposite of neoclassical beliefs.

26 Another criticism is that the assumption used to derive investment from the K/L ratio determined by r, namely that there is a definite flow of labour to be employed in new plants, is derived from the full employment of labour; but this should not be assumed to start with, it should rather be a *conclusion* of the analysis. When the full employment of labour is not assumed, further problems arise for neoclassical investment theory, explored in Petri (2015).

7.7 · More on Reverse Capital Deepening. Price Wicksell Effects

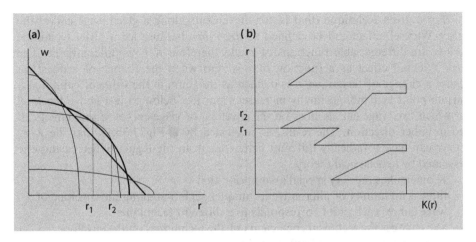

Fig. 7.3 **a** Example of several wage curves on the envelope. **b** How the value of capital per unit of labour changes with r, derived with the method illustrated in Figs. 7.1 and 7.2

Figure 7.3 presents a graphical illustration of a case with several alternative techniques. The value of capital per unit of labour, $K(r)$, is derived in the same way as in Fig. 7.2; its relationship with the rate of interest is represented on the right-hand side, Fig. 7.3b, where the rate of interest is measured in ordinate, to comply with the economists' habit of measuring quantity in abscissa and price in ordinate.

In Fig. 7.3a there are seven switches on the outer envelope, and as r increases the second, fifth and sixth switches cause the value of capital K to *increase*, owing to re-switching. The non-horizontal segments[27] of the $K(r)$ curve in Fig. 7.3b correspond to ranges of values of r where the technique is not changing, hence the vector of capital goods is constant, but its value in terms of the numéraire changes because relative prices change with r; these segments are downward-sloping when the corresponding wage curve is convex (a case not appearing in Fig. 7.3), upward-sloping when the corresponding wage curve is concave, vertical when the wage curve is a straight line. Knut Wicksell called attention to the change in the value of capital due purely to changes in income distribution while the technique remains the same, so this change is called *price Wicksell effect*. The seven horizontal segments of $K(r)$ correspond to the switch points (i.e. to the values of r at which two techniques are equiprofitable): at those values of r two techniques can be employed side by side and then, depending on which proportion of the unit of labour is used with either technique, K can take any value in between the values determined by each technique. As r increases from infinitesimally less to infinitesimally more than a switch point value, K jumps from one to the other extreme of the corresponding horizontal segment; this variation is sometimes called a *real Wicksell effect*, 'real' because corresponding to a change of the physical capital goods at unchanged prices. Re-switching entails a *positive* real Wicksell effect.

---

27 They are drawn as straight segments only for simplicity.

566   Chapter 7 · Capital: Long-Period Equilibria

For a given technique (that is, for movements along a given wage curve) the price Wicksell effect can be defined as $dK(r)/dr$, because for a given technique prices are differentiable functions of r and therefore $K(r)$ is differentiable. The *real* Wicksell effect as a function of r is zero when the change of r does not cause a change of technique, it is defined as the jump in the value of capital at a switch point as r infinitesimally increases from just below to just above the level at which two wage curves cross on the envelope of wage curves. Either effect can go in either direction. The result, as suggested by ◖ Fig. 7.3b, is that the $K(r)$ curve can have a radically different behaviour from the regularly decreasing one assumed by neoclassical theory.

If one makes the very special assumption that

— there is an infinity of alternative techniques such that along the envelope of wage curves each point corresponds to a different technique;
— as r changes the technical coefficients of the techniques on the envelope change continuously and differentiably,[28]

then the real Wicksell effect at a given value of r is the derivative of the value of capital with respect to r if one treats prices as given, and the price Wicksell effect is the derivative of the value of capital with respect to r if one treats technical coefficients as given. In this special case, one can define the actual total derivative dK/dr as the sum of the price Wicksell effect and the real Wicksell effect. Here too, the two effects can go in either direction and so can the total effect, as numerous examples have shown. One can understand why by starting from what can happen with a finite number of wage curves on the outer envelope, and then imagining more and more wage curves appearing on the envelope up to becoming 'dense'.

If some wage curves are concave, the $K(r)$ curve can have very anti-neoclassical shapes *even in the absence of any re-switching* among wage curves on, or below, the outer envelope.[29] ◖ Figure 7.4, where r is measured in abscissa, $K(r)$ in ordinate, illustrates one possibility: after the first switch, as r increases, although the discontinuous jumps of $K(r)$ at switch points (the real Wicksell effects) are all downwards in this case, the value of K increases in between switch points owing to the concave shape of the wage curves (positive price Wicksell effects), and this can more than compensate the downward jumps at the switch points, with a resulting upward-sloping saw-like shape of the $K(r)$ curve, which again is incompatible with the traditional view of 'capital'-labour substitution. By increasing the density of switch points the saw-like jumps can be made smaller

---

28 Assumption (i) does not imply assumption (ii). Garegnani (1970) assumes both (i) and (ii), but Bellino (1993) shows that it is possible to assume (i) but not (ii), and then a small change of r can cause a drastic change in the 'form' of capital.

29 *Exercise*: draw three wage curves such that at one switch point on the outer envelope there is a positive real Wicksell effect although there is no return of the same wage curve *on the outer envelope*. There is some disagreement in the literature on whether such a case, in which two wage curves cross twice but one of the crossings is not on the outer envelope, should be called a case of re-switching. I would say yes.

7.7 · More on Reverse Capital Deepening. Price Wicksell Effects

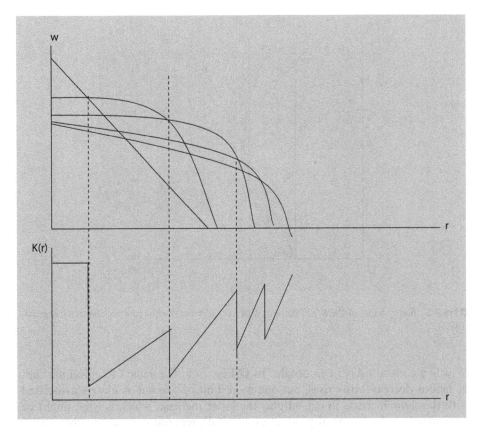

◘ **Fig. 7.4** Example of how the value of capital can tend to increase as r increases, owing to price Wicksell effects

and the behaviour of the envelope can be made to approach a continuous $K(r)$ curve that slopes upwards for part or even for most of its length.

This has been shown to be possible by Garegnani (1970). Using the Samuelson–Garegnani model (▶ Sect. 2.14), he has assumed that as r changes the cost-minimizing technique changes continuously and technical coefficients change continuously too. He has proved (Garegnani 1970, p. 433, Fig. 9; 1990, p. 42)[30] that in this way it is possible to obtain $K(r)$ functions totally in contradiction of traditional neoclassical beliefs and of stability needs, for example, constant, wiggly or all-the-way increasing $K(r)$ functions, see ◘ Fig. 7.5.

The possibility of these results is made evident by some further graphical examples. The shapes of wage curves in these examples can be obtained with opportune choices of the technical coefficients of the Samuelson–Garegnani model, or with more complex models. ◘ Figure 7.6a shows an example

---

30 The model was presented in Sect. 2.30??. The method is applicable to economies with any number of commodities and analogous results can be obtained.

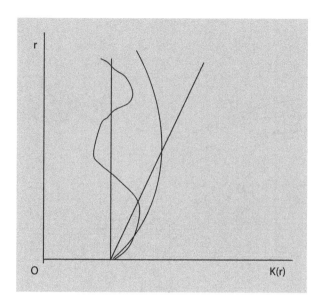

Fig. 7.5 Some shapes of the $K(r)$ function (with r in ordinate) shown to be possible by Garegnani (1970)

of why a constant $K(r)$ can obtain. In ◘ Fig. 7.6b, the value of capital per unit of labour decreases as r rises, but one more unit of 'capital' is always associated with the same increase in net output: the latter increase, which is what might be interpreted as the marginal product of 'capital', remains constant as the rate of interest and the quantity of 'capital' change, therefore, the rate of interest has no connection with the marginal product of 'capital'. Actually, often the latter notion cannot even be meaningfully defined. In the case of ◘ Fig. 7.6a one obtains the paradox of a constant quantity of the factor 'capital' which appears to lose efficiency owing simply to the rise of r, since the net output produced by the same amount of labour and of 'capital' decreases as r rises. Also, in this case there is no way to induce firms to use more 'capital', nor less, so how can one define its marginal product? Then the reader can try a modification of ◘ Fig. 7.6a in which the envelope is the same but, as r increases, the vertical intercepts of the wage curves decrease slower, obtaining a rising $K(r)$: now as r decreases the same quantity of labour and a *decreasing* amount of 'capital' are associated with an *increasing* amount of net output! Clearly in no way can 'capital' be considered a factor of production even vaguely analogous to physically measurable factors. No reasoning that treats 'capital' as a factor of production can have legitimacy.

Because of the connection between demand for 'capital', and investment function, the possibility of shapes of the demand for 'capital' curve such as these implies of course that *the traditional neoclassical thesis, that decreases of the interest rate regularly bring about increases in investment demand, is undermined, and the capacity of the interest rate to adjust investment to savings is questioned.*

7.7 · More on Reverse Capital Deepening. Price Wicksell Effects

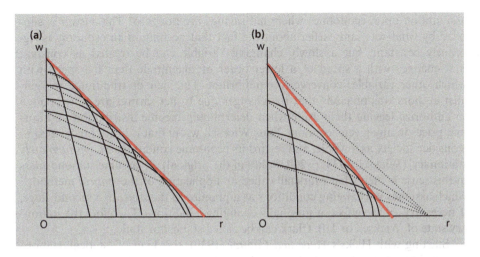

Fig. 7.6 Examples of envelope of wage curves (the red line). In the left-hand graph as r rises techniques change, output decreases as r rises, but the value of capital does not change. In the right-hand graph the value of capital is always proportional to net output, so as r decreases, value of capital and net output per unit of labour increase in the same proportion, which means the change in net output, brought about by an increase in the value of capital by one unit, is constant

Note that this result was reached while assuming the full employment of labour, of which a given fraction becomes 'free' to be re-employed in new plants every period, thus obtaining a given denominator of the fraction K/L in new plants. But if there is no guarantee that investment adapts to full employment savings then the assumption that labour is fully employed becomes unjustified too. The Keynesian thesis that it is savings that adjusts to investment via variations of aggregate output appears more credible.

7.8 Stationary States and Hicks' Criticism of Long-Period Prices

The relevance of re-switching and reverse capital deepening was debated in the so-called Cambridge controversy in capital theory in the 1950s and 1960s, but there were many confusions in that controversy. The most important obstacle to a fruitful debate was the imperfect understanding of the logic of traditional marginalist theory, by then most theorists had adopted the neo-Walrasian versions to be illustrated in ▶ Chap. 8 and were no longer aware of the logic of long-period equilibria. But there were other confusions too, and one can be usefully dispelled now. There was confusion between two different stationary-state assumptions one finds in traditional authors.

Both J. B. Clark and Wicksell assume, as done here, zero net savings when formulating the conditions of long-period general equilibrium, in this way *imposing* that the given endowment of 'capital' is not changing. Now, in most economies one observes nonzero net savings. How legitimate is it to force a stationary-state

570 Chapter 7 · Capital: Long-Period Equilibria

assumption upon economies where net savings are not zero? The answer is supplied by what was said earlier about the fact that nothing in an economy is rigorously constant, but a slowly changing variable can be treated as constant if it changes with a speed of a lower order of magnitude than the speed with which other variables converge to equilibrium. The view of traditional marginalist authors was precisely that the changes due to net savings are slow enough to authorize leaving them aside when determining income distribution and normal prices in any given economy. Thus Wicksell wrote that it is not far-fetched to 'consider society as a whole, and regard its economic conditions as *approximately* stationary' (Wicksell 1934, p. 209, italics in the original). To assume stationariness in this sense is then what Marshall called an application of the *statical* method,[31] which assumes unchanging conditions as a premise to the study in a second stage, if necessary, of the effect of gradually changing conditions. Therefore the stationary state of Wicksell or J. B. Clark can be called statical or static.

Starting with Hicks's *Value and Capital* (1939), this kind of 'statical' stationary equilibrium has been confused and is still often confused nowadays with the different notion of a stationary equilibrium as actually resulting from free choices of consumers to perform zero net savings because the rate of interest has become so low as not to encourage net savings. This notion of stationary equilibrium can be distinguished from the statical one by calling it a **secularly** stationary equilibrium: the secularly reflects the fact that this stationary equilibrium, once reached, would not change even over a century (if population, tastes and technical knowledge do not change), because it results from the fact that the quantities of capital goods have become such, and income distribution has become such, that zero net savings *result* from the given preferences of consumers.

The simple neoclassical economy of ▶ Chap. 3 where corn is produced in yearly cycles by labour and corn-capital (seed) can help to get the intuition. Assume that in this economy labour supply is stationary, technical knowledge does not improve, and net savings are positive, so period after period the stock of corn-capital increases, and the rate of interest decreases as the rise of the capital–labour ratio reduces the net marginal product of corn-capital. Suppose the average propensity to save of consumers depends positively on the rate of interest; then as capital accumulation proceeds, the decrease of the rate of interest makes net savings less and less attractive. Suppose a point is reached where net savings become zero, the capital stock stops growing: the economy has reached a secularly stationary equilibrium.

Two things must be noted about this kind of stationary equilibrium. First, it cannot be accused of needing for its determination an indeterminable *given* endowment of 'capital', because it doesn't; what it needs is that the rate of inter-

---

31 'In the stationary state all the conditions of production and consumption are reduced to rest: but less violent assumptions are made by what is, not quite accurately, called the *statical* method. By that method we fix our minds on some central point: we suppose it for the time to be reduced to a *stationary state*; and we then study in relation to it the forces that affect the things by which it is surrounded, and any tendency there may be to equilibrium of these forces'. (Marshall, *Principles*, VIII ed. reset, V, v, 4, pp. 306–7, Macmillan 1972; italics in the original).

7.8 · Stationary States and Hicks' Criticism of Long-Period Prices

est be so low that net savings become zero; the quantity of 'capital' will *result* from that rate of interest.[32] Second, the notion itself of 'capital' need not appear in the specification of the equilibrium: if a rate of interest exists which induces zero net savings, and if a way is given of univocally deriving the composition of consumption, the vector of capital goods required by the stationary equilibrium is determined by the rate of interest with no need to conceive the capital goods as crystallizations of a factor 'capital'.

This is important because Hicks in *Value and Capital* misinterpreted Marshall's statical equilibrium as a *secularly* stationary equilibrium (with no mention of the other notion of stationary equilibrium), and used the fact, that in such an equilibrium there is no given endowment of 'capital', to hide the presence and role of that endowment in the marginalist analyses up to then (including his own earlier writings). Hicks' misinterpretation was very successful, and obscured the central role of 'capital' in traditional marginalist authors.

Furthermore, the misinterpretation allowed Hicks to argue that Marshall's method had to be abandoned because the determination of long-period prices assumes them to be constant, which means—Hicks argued—to assume a stationary state, that is, a secularly stationary equilibrium; but real economies are far from a secularly stationary equilibrium. Hicks could then propose the method of temporary equilibria (which we will study in ▶ Chap. 8) as necessary to surmount the sterility of a method only applicable to secularly stationary economies.

The mistake in Hicks' argument—which, if valid, would undermine classical price theory too—is the claim that to write price equations in which price changes are neglected (as in the price equations of ▶ Chaps. 1 and 2, as well as in the long-period equilibrium presented earlier in this chapter) necessarily means to assume that the data determining these prices are *strictly* constant in the economy under study. To treat a long-period price or price of production as constant when studying the gravitation of the short-period price or market price towards it does not require that the long-period price be actually strictly constant; it only requires that the speed, with which this price changes, be of a lower order of magnitude than the speed with which the market price or short-period price can be presumed to tend to it. This holds in general in the study of variables gravitating around and towards more persistent variables. For example, to determine the average level of water at a pier in a wavy lake at a certain hour or a rainy day, one legitimately neglects the very slow change that this average level may be undergoing owing to rain: the oscillations due to waves are around an average water level which is perfectly determinable independently of the fact that it is very gradually changing.

The speed of change of the data of a marginalist long-period position, e.g. of the 'capital'-labour ratio, is of a lower order of magnitude than the potential speed of change of the *proportions* among capital goods; it is therefore legiti-

---

32 Plus of course the full employment of the given and unchanging labour supply. One difficulty is that the allocation of the ownership of capital goods among consumers is indeterminate. Another difficulty is that the secularly stationary equilibrium of a certain economy is determined on the basis of the preferences, technical knowledge, population of that economy, but to approach it would require many decades, and during such a long time stretch those data would change.

572   Chapter 7 · Capital: Long-Period Equilibria

mate to try and determine the long-period normal composition of capital while neglecting the much slower effects of capital accumulation or population growth. This is precisely what long-period equilibria tried to do, similar in this respect to the normal positions of the classical authors, which neglected, for example, the possible slow change in the rate of profit due to gradual expansion of corn production to less fertile lands.

The point is that, once the composition of capital has adapted to the composition of demand so as to yield a uniform rate of return on supply price, then normal relative prices will only change very slowly if at all, owing to the slow changes that income distribution may be undergoing owing to extension of cultivation to inferior lands, or—in the marginal approach—owing to the slow changes that the proportions between 'capital', labour and land may be undergoing owing to net savings and population growth.[33] The slowness of these changes implies that the treatment of the price of a capital good as unchanged between the beginning and the end of the period is a sufficiently good approximation.

7.9 The 'Austrian' Approach

The formalization of long-period equilibria of ▶ Sect. 7.5 is not to be found in this form in the traditional marginalist authors; it is a reconstruction of their notion of equilibrium in a way apt to be easily compared with Walras and modern general equilibrium. Very few marginalist authors attempted an explicit mathematical formalization of long-period disaggregated equilibrium admitting production with capital goods: the Swedish Knut Wicksell, who took up the 'Austrian' approach of Böhm-Bawerk—who had only described the approach verbally or with numerical examples—and some of his pupils (Lindahl, more recently Bent Hansen). They preferred to describe the production condition of consumption goods as if these were produced by vertically integrated firms whose production process starts with unassisted labour (and possibly unassisted land) and where the intermediate capital goods produced during the process do not appear explicitly in the production function, only dated inputs of labour (and possibly of land) appear.

Thus suppose flour F is produced by labour L and corn C utilized during the preceding year and paid at its end, i.e. at the same time the product comes out and is sold, according to a production function $F = F(L_P \ C_F)$; suppose that corn is in turn produced by labour and land applied two years earlier and paid one year earlier, according to a production function $C = C(L_C \ T_C)$; then Wicksell would adopt this representation of the production of flour:

$$F = \Phi(L_0, L_{-1}, T_{-1})$$

derived from

$$F = F(L_F, C(L_C, T_C)) = (F(L_0, C(L_{-1}, T_{-1}))$$

---

33 The occasional important changes due, e.g. to technical progress must on the contrary be studied via comparative statics, i.e. by assuming a transition towards the new long-period position.

7.9 · The 'Austrian' Approach

where the indices indicate how many periods earlier the inputs are *paid* relative to when the output comes out and is sold[34], and $L_0 = L_F$, $L_{-1} = L_C$, $T_{-1} = T_C$; and where

$$\partial\Phi/\partial L_0 = \partial F/\partial L_F, \partial\Phi/\partial L_{-1} = \partial F/\partial C_F \cdot \partial C/\partial L_C, \ \partial\Phi/\partial T_{-1} = \partial F/\partial C_F \cdot \partial C/\partial T_C.$$

It is intuitive that land too could appear among the dated original inputs. Thus if you study Wicksell (1934) you will find that the conditions of cost minimization and optimal factor employments are expressed in terms of production functions with amounts of dated labour and land as inputs, and no specification of which intermediate inputs are produced and consumed in the vertically integrated process. Cost minimization can be expressed in terms of equality between value marginal product of each dated input in terms of final output, and rental of that dated input with added onto it interest for the interval between payment of the rental and sale of the final output. For example the condition that the wage must equal the value marginal product of labour would appear in this example as the two conditions (with p_F the price of flour, and assuming wages to be paid at the end of the period in which labour is applied, i.e. at the same time as the sale of the final output for L_0 and one year earlier for L_{-1}):

1. $w = p_F \partial\Phi/\partial L_0$
2. $w(1 + r) = p_F \partial\Phi/\partial L_{-1},$

where w in the first equation is the wage paid to labour in the flour industry, and w in the second equation is the wage paid to L_{-1}, i.e. in the corn industry; since it is paid one year before the product comes out, interest must be added onto it to determine production costs at the time the product is sold. These two wages must be the same if labour is homogeneous.

The above shows that Wicksell's representation of production conditions and optimal factor employments in terms of dated inputs is implicitly *derived from* the more usual production functions in which produced intermediate inputs appear explicitly, and amounts to a representation of the production conditions and optimal factor employments of a *vertically integrated* firm, under the assumption of an 'Austrian' structure of production, i.e. that the vertically integrated production process starts with *unassisted* labour (and land). The restrictive character of this last assumption that excludes the presence of capital goods directly or indirectly used as inputs in their own production,[35] makes it preferable to formalize

---

34 The need to admit the presence of land besides labour among the original inputs is one of the reasons which induced Wicksell to abandon the notion of an average period of production, because it became impossible to arrive at a single average period of production. Another reason was the need, for the definition of the average period of production, to assume non-compound interest

35 If at least one capital good is, directly or indirectly, an input into its own production, the number of dated inputs is infinite, and it is impossible to alter only one dated input so as to determine its marginal product. Think of corn produced by corn-seed and labour; suppose one method is $a_{11}{}^* a_{L1} \to 1$ unit of corn in the usual formulation and assume wages paid in arrears: the Wicksellian production function would have final corn produced by $L_0 = a_{L1}$ units of current labour, $L_{-1} = a_{11} a_{L1}$ units of labour employed one period before, $L_{-2} = a_{11}{}^2 a_{L1}$ units of labour two periods

574 Chapter 7 · Capital: Long-Period Equilibria

the long-period equilibrium not in the Austrian way but rather via the more usual production functions and non-vertically integrated firms, as done in ▶ Sect. 7.3; this allows for the presence of goods that use themselves as inputs.

Note that as income distribution changes and the as-if-vertically integrated firms find it convenient to change the relative amounts of dated inputs used, the quantities of intermediate goods and even the *kinds* of intermediate goods produced may well radically change; in the above example of flour produced by current labour, advanced labour and advanced land, it could have been assumed that the *kind* of corn produced changes with changes in the proportion between advanced labour and land. It could also have been assumed that advanced labour and land produce a vector of intermediate goods, in proportions that change with the proportion between advanced labour and land. Therefore the Wicksellian production functions hide but do not eliminate at all the *endogenous* determination of the equilibrium composition of the stock of capital goods of the economy; simply, this composition remains implicit because the capital goods produced do not explicitly appear.

The reason for Wicksell's preference for his representation of production processes was the belief that the more the total quantity directly and indirectly employed of an input is advanced on average relative to when the output comes out, the greater the efficiency with which the input can be utilized: for example, that the output of wheat produced by 1 unit of labour is greater if, instead of using all labour as direct labour, one uses a part of it in advance to till and clear the ground, and even greater if a part is used even further in advance to prepare tools to till the earth more efficiently. If the rate of interest is positive, the more advanced on average is the amount of an input, the greater the capital advances required for its employment; so it is the availability of capital that allows advancing part of labour and land and thus increasing the efficiency of their utilization. This basic idea will not be formalized here (see Garegnani 1990; or Petri 2004, pp. 99–117). I will only say that this idea was believed to imply that a decreasing marginal product curve of 'capital' could be derived from the fact that one more unit of 'capital' allowed a greater average advancement of the available supply of labour (a longer 'average period of production' in the terminology of Böhm-Bawerk), with a consequent marginal increase of final output.

Wicksell, after initially following Böhm-Bawerk, later realized that the notion of average period of production had grave deficiencies. He abandoned the notion, but continued to think that the lags between application of original inputs and production of the output were fundamental in order to understand why a greater amount of 'capital' meant an increase of the production obtainable with a given amount of labour, and in order to make the lags evident he preferred to represent the conditions of production of goods in terms of production functions with

---

before, ..., $L_{-t} = a_{11}{}^t a_{L1}$ units of labour t period before, and so on endlessly; Wicksell would argue that one can neglect inputs employed many periods before because their quantity tends to zero; but it is arbitrary where to stop, and above all, since what can be altered is only a_{11} and/or a_{L1}, any such change alters *all* quantities of dated labour, it is impossible to alter only one of them.

7.9 · The 'Austrian' Approach

dated original inputs. The online Appendix to this chapter includes a presentation of a simple Wicksellian long-period general equilibrium system and its 'translation' into the more usual representation of production conditions in which intermediate inputs appear explicitly; the need for a given endowment of 'capital' in order to have as many equations as variables is confirmed.

Because 'Austrian' models are still frequent in the literature (one example is Samuelson's whiskey-and-champagne model in ▶ Chap. 2), it is useful to acquire some familiarity with their logic, and this was the purpose of this section.[36]

7.10 On Substitutability in Modern and in Traditional Production Functions

The loss of familiarity with traditional marginalist analyses has caused an inability to understand the fundamental role of the conception of 'capital' as of variable 'form' in justifying production functions with extensive factor substitutability in traditional marginalist authors. This assumption of production functions with extensive substitutability is still common nowadays, but it is applied to production functions where the inputs are not labour and 'capital', but labour and heterogeneous physically specified capital goods, where it is totally unrealistic. There is some limited variability of input proportions almost only in agriculture, where one can vary, within limits, amounts of irrigation and of fertilizers. A restaurant cannot change the proportions among inputs in producing food, or use more tables and fewer waiters. In most productions, labour and intermediate goods per unit of output are fixed, unless one changes the kinds of capital goods used. The smooth substitutability found in the production functions of traditional marginalist authors derived from allowing the 'form' of 'capital' to change as one changed factor proportions. It is worthwhile to stop on this point because it allows a better grasp of the traditional logic of neoclassical theory, which in fact is the one still used in applied neoclassical analyses.

We must distinguish three kinds of traditional production functions. (For simplicity I assume land is a free good.) The second kind will require notions that will be useful later in the chapter when discussing aggregate production functions.

The first kind of production function is found in J. B. Clark and in Marshall: in these authors one finds descriptions of *firms* having production functions in which capital, treated as a single factor (measured as a quantity of exchange value), is one of the factors on a par with labour (I neglect land for simplicity). The firm decides the amounts L to hire and K to borrow in order to produce any given output. Such a production function $q = f(L, K)$ is not illegitimate if one can assume *given* prices of capital goods. Then the isoquants are derived as follows

---

36 Re-switching and reverse capital deepening are perfectly possible even under the 'Austrian' assumption on technology that makes a Wicksellian representation of production functions possible; this is shown by Samuelson's whiskey-and-champagne model. On the deficiencies of the average period of production the reader is referred to Garegnani (1960, 1990).

(also see ▶ Sect. 5.5). Given the output level, for each L the entrepreneur asks, 'which vector of capital goods allows producing that output with the minimum employment of capital (that is, the minimum need for borrowing)?' The corresponding value K of that vector of capital goods, together with the given L, yields one point of the isoquant. Repeating the process for each value of L, one obtains an isoquant whose several points correspond to vectors of capital goods that generally differ in the amounts and in the *kinds* of capital goods. Less labour to build a road requires different machinery. In this way an entire isoquant map can be derived. The possibility to choose, for each level of L, the kinds of capital goods gives some plausibility to the assumption of substitutability between K and L: starting from a given $(L°, K°)$ point of the isoquant, if L is decreased, some more costly ensemble of capital goods may well exist, capable together with the reduced L of producing the given output.

Of course, this notion of production function is subject to a radical criticism. The purpose of an isoquant map is to indicate how the optimal factor combination changes with changes in the relative 'price' of the two factors. But here the 'prices' are the real wage, and the rate of interest: when they change, all relative product prices change, hence, the prices of capital goods change, so the isoquant map must be recalculated anew and one does not know how it shifts; hence it is of no use for the purpose for which isoquants are used (and the same applies to marginal productivity curves), *unless* relative prices are assumed unaffected by changes in income distribution. The use of such a production function reveals a belief in those authors that one can neglect the dependence of relative prices on income distribution, the same illegitimate belief ultimately lying behind the conception of 'capital' as a single factor of variable 'form'.

A second kind of traditional production function $q=f(K, L)$, not clearly distinguished from the first by these authors, refers to long-period variations, as income distribution changes, in the value of the capital goods and in the amount of labour employed in the *entire subsystem* that produces q units of that good as a *net* product. This production function extends to 'capital' the idea, obvious with labour and land, that production uses the *services* of factors but the factors *are still there, re-employable in another production activity,* after the output has been produced. The extension of this idea to production with 'capital' requires that the production of the final product goes together with production processes that reconstitute the used-up 'capital', so that, after the production of q, K is unchanged. Therefore now q in $q=f(K, L)$ is the *net* product of a *subsystem*, and L and K are the labour, and the value of the capital goods, used in the entire subsystem. I call this notion of production function the ***net-product K-production function***, where the K is a reminder of the presence of 'capital' as one of the inputs, in place of the variable vector of capital goods used in the subsystem. It is a long-period notion that admits the adaptation of all capital goods (fixed plants too) to changes in income distribution, and measures 'capital' in terms of long-period prices; apart from this, it is assumed to have the standard properties of a neoclassical production function (decreasing marginal products, convex isoquants, etc.), and to correctly yield the demand for the two factors if output and factor rentals are given, or the demand for one factor if its rental in terms of the

7.10 · On Substitutability in Modern and in Traditional Production Functions

product, and the employment of the other factor, are given. This notion of production function does not apply to a single firm, but rather to the complex of productive activities directly and indirectly contributing to the emergence of a good or basket of goods as net product; its purpose is to make clear the demand for 'capital' and for labour entailed by that net product.

This notion of production function is probably not familiar even to the reader with previous studies in economics, so let me stay on it a bit longer. It is important to realize what is independent of the marginal approach and what is not, in this notion of *net-product K-production function*. (A clear difference of this notion of production function from the first is that in the first kind of traditional production function the labour input is only the *direct* labour employed to produce a good, in this second kind of production function the amount of labour is all the labour directly and indirectly employed to produce the good as a net product.)

Let us remember from ▶ Chap. 2 that a subsystem is an ensemble of industries in such proportions that they, besides producing an amount q of a certain single or composite good every period, reproduce all the capital goods used up in the course of the period to produce q, see ▶ Sect. 2.16. Let us assume CRS, circulating capital, free land, a given set of available techniques. Then for each value of r or of w (this latter measured in terms of a given numéraire, of course), technical choice determines the adopted technique $(\mathbf{A}(r), \mathbf{a}_L(r))$, the other distributive variable, and relative prices; the subsystem producing a given net product vector[37] $\mathbf{q}$ per period produces each period total quantities $\mathbf{x}$ determined by $\mathbf{q}=\mathbf{x}-\mathbf{A}\mathbf{x}$, and hence determines the total labour L employed in the subsystem as $L=\mathbf{a}_L\mathbf{x}$ (it is in fact the labour embodied in $\mathbf{q}$) and, having fixed a numéraire, determines the exchange value K of the capital goods employed in the subsystem as $K=\mathbf{p}\mathbf{A}\mathbf{x}$, where $\mathbf{p}$, $\mathbf{A}$, $\mathbf{x}$ depend on income distribution. As r varies, for given $\mathbf{q}$ one can derive functions[38] $L(\mathbf{q}, r)$ and (having fixed a numéraire) $K(\mathbf{q}, r)$; the 'form' of K (i.e. the composition of the stock of capital goods) generally changes with r, often radically. This derivation of L and K from the production of a given *net* product once r (or w) is given can be applied to any net product vector $\mathbf{q}$; given two net product vectors $\mathbf{q}'$, $\mathbf{q}''$, and income distribution and adopted methods, the labour employment associated with their sum $\mathbf{q}=\mathbf{q}'+\mathbf{q}''$ is the sum of the labour employment in the two subsystems, and the same holds for the amount of 'capital'. Therefore the construction can also be applied to the net product vector of the entire economy. But now we are interested in production functions of single products, so let us suppose the net product consists only of 1 unit of commod-

---

37 To be able to use matrices and vectors, the net output is treated as a vector, with zeros for the goods not appearing in that net output; then if, for example, net output consists of q_2 units of the sole good 2 the vector will be $\mathbf{q}=(0, q_2, 0,..., 0)^T$.

38 Or rather, correspondences, since at switch points any convex combination of the equally profitable techniques capable of producing the given net product can be used—hence the horizontal segments as shown in ❑ Fig. 7.3b, which mean a value of 'capital' and a labour employment indeterminate within limits. One obtains functions (and no indeterminacy) only if one supposes that along the envelope of wage curves there is a continuum of techniques, with each point of the envelope corresponding to a different technique, so that there is no switch point *on* the envelope.

ity i; then the net product vector is $\mathbf{e}^i$, the ith column of the identity matrix $\mathbf{I}$, with elements all zero except 1 in the ith place. For given r and associated production methods, we can find L and K; as r changes, we can determine how L and K change, and we obtain *functions* $K(\mathbf{e}^i, r)$, and $L(\mathbf{e}^i, r)$ or $L(\mathbf{e}^i, w(r))$.

These functions derive simply from the analysis of long-period choice of technique, and they are independent of whether one adopts a classical or marginal approach. The marginalist element appears when it is argued that as income distribution changes the amounts of labour and 'capital' employed in the subsystem producing one unit of good i as net product change as indicated by a *net-product K-production function*: a production function $q_i = f^{(i)}(K, L)$ with standard neoclassical properties (CRS, decreasing marginal products, convex isoquants), from which those two functions $L(\mathbf{e}^i, r)$, $K(\mathbf{e}^i, r)$ can be derived as *conditional factor demands* for labour and for 'capital' when the net output of good i is 1 unit; so that as r varies, the functions $L(\mathbf{e}^i, r)$, $K(\mathbf{e}^i, r)$ trace the unit isoquant of this production function.

Since the functions $L(\mathbf{e}^i, r)$, $K(\mathbf{e}^i, r)$ have been derived directly from the available alternative production techniques, there is no guarantee that they may be seen as conditional factor demands derived from a production function $q = f(K, L)$, and indeed it will be shown in the next section that the conditions for this to be the case are extremely restrictive; but the point that interests us now is that in this notion of net-product K-production function the assumed substitutability is between labour and 'capital', where the 'form' of 'capital' (the capital goods employed in the subsystem) is left free to change as income distribution changes. So again, substitutability, for example, the variability of labour input per unit of output relies on changes in the kinds of capital goods employed.

The third kind of traditional production function is the differentiable production functions used by Wicksell in the *Lectures*, where the inputs are current labour and land, labour and land employed one period earlier, labour and land employed two periods earlier, and so on, as if firms were completely vertically integrated, as explained in ▶ Sect. 7.12. In these production functions 'capital' does not appear, the inputs are amounts of (dated) labour and land, all specified in technical units, in an 'Austrian' structure of production. The conception of 'capital' appears explicitly in Wicksell's system of general equilibrium equations only when he must 'close' the system, and then he specifies that the use of 'earlier' amounts of labour and land requires the anticipation of 'capital', hence, a demand for 'capital', and the total demand for 'capital' must equal its given endowment (see the simple Wicksellian model in the online Appendix to this chapter). In Wicksell's vertically integrated production functions with current and 'earlier' labour and land as inputs the assumed substitutability is among these inputs, and again it is not totally absurd because changes in the proportions among these inputs implicitly correspond to changes in the quantities and in the kinds of capital goods produced and utilized; for example in the production of pork a decrease in current labour and increase in current land along an isoquant will mean that the capital goods (fertilizers, tools, etc.) produced by 'earlier' labour and land are changed so as to allow the efficient utilization, in the final stage of the production process, of more land and less labour to produce the

7.10 · On Substitutability in Modern and in Traditional Production Functions

given output of pork. So here too the variability of the 'form' of capital is present although it remains implicit, and this renders the substitutability assumption not ridiculous.

In conclusion, the substitutability in traditional marginalist production functions is always between labour and 'capital', or between labour, land and 'capital', and it relies on the possibility to change the kinds of capital goods to be combined with labour or with labour and land; therefore it does not at all legitimize the modern production functions where smooth substitutability is admitted between physically specified capital goods and between them and labour. These modern production functions obscure the fact that factor substitutability could not have been assumed in the marginal approach if one of the factors had not been 'capital', a factor of variable 'form'. These considerations will be important when in ▶ Chap. 8 modern general equilibrium theory will be found to suffer from a *substitutability problem*.

7.11 Aggregate Production Functions

The notion of net-product K-production function allows clarity on the notion, much used in macroeconomics, macroeconometrics and growth theory, of *aggregate production function, APF*.

The neoclassical conception of the determinants of income distribution is sometimes argued to allow a simple, although only approximate, representation of the basic forces determining income distribution and growth in a market economy. This representation consists of models where the production possibilities of the economy, and the forces determining income distribution, are summarized via a single production function that represents the economy's net output as a scalar, Y, which is a function of a scalar quantity of labour L and of a scalar index K of the 'quantity of capital'. The aggregate production function $Y = F(K, L)$ is assumed differentiable and homogeneous of degree one; the real wage w and the rate of interest r are assumed to equal the marginal products of the two factors. Statistical data are argued to supply the numbers that illustrate how the five variables Y, K, L, w, r have changed over time; it is argued that from this information it is possible to derive information on the influence of technical progress and of changes in K/L on how net output per unit of labour and income distribution have changed, as well as on the form of the function $F(\cdot, \cdot)$. In this argument, the reference to statistical data implies that the index K in the APF is the exchange value of the economy's capital endowment; and the view of r and w as the marginal products respectively of K and of L shows that the traditional marginalist conception, of the capital goods as embodiments of a single factor 'capital' of variable 'form' measured in terms of value, is considered at least approximately acceptable, and in addition one is assuming, relative to traditional marginalist authors, that:

- (i) changes in the composition of the net product have only a very minor influence on factor demands, and therefore one can neglect them and treat the net output as a single composite good;

580   Chapter 7 · Capital: Long-Period Equilibria

- (ii) one can neglect the presence of natural resources, or rather, one can consider them as part of K (the value of land is such that rent yields the rate of interest on this value, so this value can be added to the value of capital goods to obtain the total value of interest-yielding wealth).

If one could neglect these two additional 'simplifying' assumptions, that is, if land could be neglected and if the composition of net output were constant, an aggregate production function would be a *net-product K-production function* as described in the previous section.

Two different critical attitudes can be held relative to aggregate production functions. First, one can deny the right to *simplify* in this way the neoclassical mechanisms that determine income distribution and net output per unit of labour, without denying the existence of those mechanisms; then one is not questioning the correctness of the supply-and-demand approach but only the right to simplify it in this way. Second, one can deny the correctness of the entire supply-and-demand approach and reject aggregate production functions as only one particularly unrigorous version of a mistaken approach to what determines income distribution and outputs.

The distinction between these two attitudes is important. The extent to which aggregate production functions are judged misleading depends on whether one believes or not in the neoclassical explanation of income distribution.

There are numerous different theoretical and statistical issues involved in the use of aggregate production functions and in the criticism of their use. Only a few points will be touched upon here.

Let us see some reasons why even a neoclassical economist might reject aggregate production functions—as indeed some have done, for example, Franklin M. Fisher (Felipe and Fisher 2003). First, the assumption of a single product means that the model cannot grasp the effects on income distribution of changes in the composition of demand as conceived by the supply-and-demand approach. Suppose labour and corn-capital, supplied in given amounts, produce cloth and corn (which is also demanded as a consumption good) in fixed-coefficient industries without technical choice, and distribution is determined according to marginalist theory, by the indirect substitution mechanism based on consumer choices. Suppose the equilibrium is unique, stable, with both the rigid supplies of factors fully employed, and stationary because consumers do not wish to perform net savings. A change in tastes (for example because it is discovered that one of the two consumption goods is excellent for health) will alter income distribution without any change in technology (by assumption there is no technical choice) nor in the quantities produced if both factors remain fully employed: the given technical coefficients plus the given factor employments uniquely fix the quantities produced. This change in income distribution without any change in technology nor outputs cannot be reflected in a model based on an APF where it is assumed that factors earn their marginal products. Now suppose the same economy and the same change in tastes but assume factor substitutability in each industry: both income distribution and the composition of net output change, and again, since neither technical knowledge nor factor supplies have changed, there is no

7.11 · Aggregate Production Functions

way to reflect this fact in a one-good model where as long as factor supplies and technical knowledge do not change, income distribution should not change. The economist using the APF will have to conclude that there has been a change in technical knowledge, i.e. in the production function, that has altered marginal products, thus misinterpreting the observation.

Second, consider the inference: if factor relative shares in Y remain roughly constant over a number of years in spite of changes in the ratio K/L, then the aggregate production function must have an elasticity of substitution equal to 1. This argument was used for many decades since the 1950s to justify the adoption of a Cobb–Douglas form for the APF for the US economy, for which it was argued that the share of wages had remained remarkably constant.[39] But over a number of years technical progress is no doubt relevant, and then even accepting that income distribution reflects the marginal products of an aggregate production function, it is unclear why technical progress should leave the elasticity of substitution unchanged at roughly 1 over decades.

Thirdly, there are problems connected with the inclusion of natural resources into K. Imagine an economy that produces corn with seed-corn and labour, over a given fully utilized land; rent is intensive differential rent due to the simultaneous activation of two processes, like B and C in Chap. 1, ▶ Sect. 1.5. An expansion of production can be achieved by expanding the portion of land cultivated with the more productive method per unit of land (method C), and restricting the portion cultivated with the other method. Rate of interest and real wage need not change, and then the value of land does not change because the rate of rent does not change and it is capitalized at an unchanged rate of interest, but the overall ratio of seed-corn to labour changes because seed-corn per unit of labour will in general differ as between the two methods. K/L, with K including the constant value of land, can change in either direction, and again an APF cannot grasp what is happening.

These deficiencies of APFs would exist even if net-product K-production functions were legitimate constructions for single products. In fact, generally there is no net-product K-production function describing how, given the set of available technologies, technical choices and the value of capital will change with income distribution, and this means an APF is illegitimate even when the economy's net product can be treated as a single good and land can be neglected.

I proceed to prove this statement. As a preliminary, let us be clear that we are interested in long-period choices: aggregate production function models are used to explain changes over periods of years. Therefore relative prices can be assumed to be on average sufficiently close to their long-period values, and the composition of capital can be assumed to have sufficiently adapted to the composition of demand and to the technique which is optimal at the given income distribution. So one can use the results of long-period price theory of ▶ Chap. 2 to inquire *how legitimate it is to represent the average wage and rate of interest 'as if' corre-*

---

39 In recent decades the argument—never fully accepted—has lost persuasiveness owing to the considerable reduction in the share of wages in the US economy.

582   Chapter 7 · Capital: Long-Period Equilibria

sponding to the marginal products of some net-product K-production function with the economy's net output as its product. In order to concentrate on this basic issue let us leave technical progress aside, and let us eliminate problems with aggregation concerning the net product by assuming that the economy is stationary and the net product consists of a single consumption good. Let us furthermore leave land and joint production aside (this last assumption implies all capital goods are circulating). Let us neglect risk and assume that r, the rate of return on capital (the classical rate of profits), coincides with the rate of interest. I report now some results from Garegnani (1970).

Assume that the consumption good can be produced with a number of different techniques involving the use of heterogeneous capital goods. The consumption good is the obvious numéraire; for each technique the $w(r)$ curve can be derived; all the $w(r)$ curves can be drawn in the same diagram; we know from ▶ Chap. 2 that long-period technical choice brings the economy on the outer envelope of the $w(r)$ curves.

Let us indicate as $w = e(r)$, with e mnemonic for 'envelope', the function describing how the real wage changes with r along this outer envelope; $e(r)$ is a continuous function, with kinks at the values of r corresponding to switch points. It is the outer envelope of the $w(r)$ curves corresponding to all available techniques. Each point of the $e(r)$ curve belongs to the $w(r)$ curve of the cost-minimizing or 'dominant' technique at that value of r, and the vertical intercept of that $w(r)$ curve indicates the net output per unit of labour at that value of r; therefore it is possible from the wage curves appearing on the outer envelope to derive how the *net output per unit of labour,* to be indicated as q (a quantity of the single consumption good) varies as r varies. Let $q = h(r)$ represent this function. With a finite number of alternative techniques, $h(r)$ is a correspondence; its graphical representation with q in abscissa and r in ordinate has vertical segments corresponding to intervals of values of r in which the dominant technique does not change, and horizontal segments at the values of r corresponding to switch points, see ◘ Fig. 7.3b.

But in order to make comparison with a differentiable aggregate production function possible, let us assume that an infinity of alternative techniques is available, such that the 'dominant' technique changes *continuously* along the envelope $e(r)$, which is smooth and with no switch points on it: each point of the envelope $e(r)$ corresponds to a different technique. Let us further assume that the corresponding relationship $q = h(r)$ is a continuous function.[40] One possible illustration is ◘ Fig. 7.7.

The question to be examined can now be formulated as follows: suppose a heterogeneous capital economy producing a single consumption good as net product has a given differentiable $w = e(r)$ curve and a corresponding continuous $q = h(r)$ curve, derived from the infinity of techniques available to this economy.

---

40 Bellino (1993) shows that this need not be the case: continuous change of technique along the envelope e(r) as r changes can correspond to discontinuous jumps of q. It is also possible (Garegnani 1970) that more than one w(r) curve be tangent to the envelope e(r) for each level of r, entailing that q(r) is not a unique value, but an interval, for each level of r.

7.11 · Aggregate Production Functions

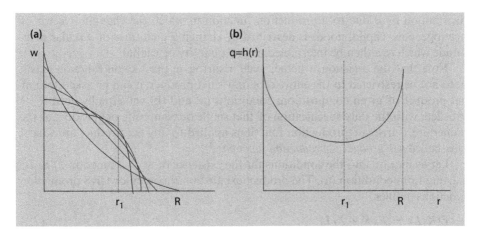

■ **Fig. 7.7** Example (Garegnani 1970) of a continuum of $w(r)$ curves along the outer envelope (only a few of the $w(r)$ curves are shown), obtained by assuming technical coefficients are continuous functions of a parameter. The example is obtained for the Samuelson–Garegnani two-sector economy where each different technique uses a different capital good; but analogous envelopes can be obtained with n-sector economies. Figure **b** shows the dependence of the net product per unit of labour on r, implied by the envelope $e(r)$ of the $w(r)$ curves of **a**

Can we obtain these $e(r)$ and $h(r)$ curves from a differentiable production function $Y = F(K, L)$, where Y is net product, such that w and r equal the marginal products of the two factors L and K?

More formally, we ask whether, given the functions $w = e(r)$ and $q = h(r)$ of a heterogeneous-circulating capital economy, it is possible to find a net output production function $F(K, L)$, homogeneous of degree one, yielding those same relationships between w, q and r if one assumes $w = \partial F/\partial L$ and $r = \partial F/\partial K$, and therefore such that
(a) $\partial F/\partial L = e(\partial F/\partial K)$, or more briefly $F_L = e(F_K)$
(b) $F(K,L)/L = h(\partial F/\partial K)$, or more briefly $F(K,L)/L = h(F_K)$.

Condition (a) is simply $w = e(r)$ under the assumption that $w = \partial F/\partial L$ and $r = \partial F/\partial K$. Condition (b) states that, since for a CRS production function with two factors the marginal product of a factor univocally determines the marginal product of the other factor and the factor ratio, and hence output per unit of either factor, $F(K, L)$ must be such that, once we assume $r = \partial F/\partial K$, the marginal product of K determines output per unit of labour as equal to $h(r)$.

If such a function $F(K, L)$ exists, then we can represent the way output per unit of labour changes with income distribution as identical to what one obtains assuming output produced by labour and by capital goods 'aggregable' into an index K that behaves like a quantity of a single capital good homogeneous with the consumption good. The function has been called '*surrogate production function*' by Paul Samuelson (1962), the term 'surrogate' indicating that it is not a true production function (because capital is not physically homogeneous, K is only an index), but that its existence would allow one to describe production and income

584   **Chapter 7 ·** Capital: Long-Period Equilibria

distribution *as if* due to a production function in which the changing vector of heterogeneous capital goods is described by changing quantities of a scalar magnitude which can then be interpreted as the 'quantity of capital'.

Note that the question, whether such a surrogate production function exists, need not be restricted to the entire economy's net product, it can be asked for any net product of given composition; conditions (a) and (b) will equally need to be satisfied, with the only specification of that single or composite net product as the numéraire. Surrogate production functions applied to any net product are what I have called *net-product K-production functions.*[41]

Let us inquire into the conditions for the existence of such a function $F(K, L)$ starting from condition (a). The product exhaustion theorem for CRS production functions implies

$$F(K,L) = F_K K + F_L L. \tag{7.1}$$

or, dividing by L:

$$F/L = F_K K/L + F_L. \tag{7.2}$$

Differentiating (7.2), or equivalently and more intuitively, differentiating (7.1) under an assumption that L is fixed and equal to 1:

$$dF = dF_L + K dF_K + F_K dK$$

which can be rewritten as

$$K = [dF - dF_L - F_K dK]/dF_K.$$

Remembering that it must be $F_L = w$, $F_K = r$, and hence $dF/dK - r = 0$, we obtain (again assuming $L = 1$, so that K in fact stands for K/L):

$$K = \frac{dF - rdK}{dr} - \frac{dw}{dr} = \frac{\left(\frac{dF}{dK} - r\right)dK}{dr} - \frac{dw}{dr} = -\frac{dw}{dr} = -e'(r). \tag{7.3}$$

Thus, condition (a) implies that, at each value of r, the index 'K per unit of labour' must equal the absolute value of the slope of the envelope $e(r)$. This excludes the existence of the APF if $e(r)$ has concave portions (see ◘ Fig. 7.1), because in those intervals of values of r the index K/L would *increase* as r rises, implying an increasing marginal product of factor K, which is incompatible with the idea of a production function. Furthermore, the same K/L ratio might

---

41   A surrogate production function is not the same thing as an APF; it assumes a single (or fixed-composition) net output, no land, and a composition of capital fully adapted to each rate of interest. An APF, since it is used for empirical estimations, besides neglecting changes in output composition over the periods of estimation and illegitimately incorporating land, implicitly assumes that the value of capital is a good indication of the productive potential of the stock of capital goods of the economy even though this stock is a mixture of optimal and of partially obsolete capital goods generally not well adapted to the composition of demand. But these are *further* objectionable aspects of the APF, which anyway needs as its foundation the validity of the notion of surrogate production function.

7.11 · Aggregate Production Functions

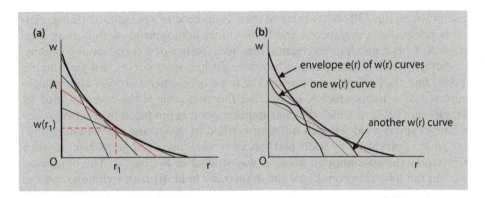

Fig. 7.8 Two cases in which condition (7.5) is satisfied

correspond to different values of r, again contrary to what a production function must represent. Since there is no reason why $e(r)$ should not have concave portions (it can even be strictly concave everywhere), this suffices to show the general non-existence of a surrogate production function.

But there is more.

Result (7.3) can be introduced into (7.2) to obtain:

$$F/L = -re'(r) + e(r). \tag{7.4}$$

Therefore the sole condition (a) completely determines how F/L, net output per unit of labour, must depend on the rate of interest; there is no possibility to adapt $F(K,L)$ so as to obtain condition (b); one can only check whether the function $F(K, L)$ that satisfies (7.4) does also satisfy condition (b), that is, whether it is

$$(-e'(r)) \cdot r + e(r) = h(r). \tag{7.5}$$

This will be the case only when $h(r)$ corresponds to an envelope $e(r)$ convex to the origin and generated by $w(r)$ curves which *either* are all straight lines tangent to $e(r)$ (therefore with slope $-e'(r_1)$ if tangent to $e(r)$ at r_1) as in ◘ Fig. 7.8a, *or* by an extraordinary fluke, all have the same vertical intercept as if they were the straight-line wage curves of the first case, as in ◘ Fig. 7.8b.

In ◘ Fig. 7.8(a), let us assume $r = r_1$ and that the wage curve corresponding to $e(r)$ at r_1 is a straight-line tangent to $e(r_1)$, with vertical intercept A; segment OA is the sum of segment $Ow(r_1)$ and segment $w(r_1)A$, where the ratio between the latter segment and segment Or is the slope of the wage curve, hence $A = (-e'(r_1)) \cdot r_1 + e(r_1)$ as already shown in ◘ Fig. 7.1. If A coincides with $h(r)$ for all r, condition (7.5) is satisfied.

The case represented in ◘ Fig. 7.8b is totally unrealistic: it would be already an incredible fluke if *one* curvy $w(r)$ curve tangent to $e(r)$ at a certain r^* had the same vertical intercept as a straight line tangent to $e(r)$ at r^*, it is clearly totally impossible that this be the case for *all* $w(r)$ curves forming the envelope $e(r)$. The first case, straight-line $w(r)$ curves, makes sense only if the economy produces a *single* good produced by itself and labour combined in variable proportions—the

586   Chapter 7 · Capital: Long-Period Equilibria

case in which the APF exists because there is no need to aggregate anything, capital is physically homogeneous and furthermore homogeneous with output; then $q = F(K, L)$ is a standard production function, the one of a corn-labour economy.

Actually, two other cases produce straight-line $w(r)$ curves, but they are so special that they offer no support to the hope of a general at least approximate existence of a net-product K-production function. One is the case assumed by Samuelson (1962) in which the consumption good is produced by a *different* circulating capital good for each different method of producing it,[42] and each capital good is produced by itself and labour *in the same fixed proportion* as when it produces the consumption good; it was studied in ▶ Chap. 2. The other case is when the following conditions simultaneously hold: (i) each technique can use several capital goods, possibly the same ones, but in each technique all industries have the same 'organic composition of capital' (different as among techniques), i.e. the same ratio of labour embodied in the capital goods to live labour, so relative prices do not change with changes in income distribution and equal relative labours embodied, (ii) for the goods that are common to two techniques the prices in terms of the consumption good are the same in both techniques. Then a technique with a higher 'organic composition' has a $w(r)$ curve which is a steeper straight line than for techniques with a lower 'organic composition' (prove it!); if at $r°$ two $w(r)$ curves cross, for $r < r°$ it is convenient for *all* goods to use the method of the higher-organic composition technique, the opposite is true for $r > r°$, and as r rises it becomes convenient at $r°$ to switch *simultaneously* for all goods from the method of the higher-organic composition technique to the method of the other technique. (This is an exceptional case in which it is false that at a switch point only one method of production changes. The techniques in this case have no method in common and at the switch point all methods are simultaneously changed.[43]) Actually Samuelson's case is the special subcase of this special case, in which only one capital good is used by each technique and it is not the same for different techniques. Clearly, such ultraspecial cases are only theoretical curiosities.

The conclusion must be that surrogate production functions, or as I prefer to call them *net-product K-production functions*, have no theoretical legitimacy and thus provide no support to the notion of 'capital'. It is also confirmed that to postulate that an APF exists for the entire economy and yields income distribution and its variations through its marginal products will necessarily produce mistaken inferences.

---

42 It must be noted that, in support of what has been argued here in ▶ Sect. 7.3, Samuelson admits that the theory must be capable of dealing with little or zero substitutability among physically specified capital goods: 'it would evade the issue to consider a model in which the capital goods were not highly specific to one use and to one combination of co-operating labour' (1962, p. 199).

43 Here is a numerical example. The economy produces corn (good 1) and iron (good 2). The technical coefficients with technique A are ($a_{11}{}^A = 0.1$, $a_{21}{}^A = 0.05$, $a_{L1}{}^A = 2$; $a_{12}{}^A = 0.2$, $a_{22}{}^A = 0.1$, $a_{L2}{}^A = 4$); with technique B, which has a higher-organic composition, they are ($a_{11}{}^B = 0.25$, $a_{21}{}^B = 0.125$, $a_{L1}{}^B = 1$; $a_{12}{}^B = 0.5$, $a_{22}{}^B = 0.25$, $a_{L2}{}^B = 2$); with both technique $p_2 = 2p_1$; technique B is dominant for $r < 1/4$, A is dominant for $r > 1/4$.

7.11 · Aggregate Production Functions

This conclusion undermines the models and the econometric exercises based on APFs, but as already said the use of APFs is only one particularly unrigorous version of the marginal/neoclassical approach to income distribution; it is possible to defend the latter while rejecting APFs. Still, this chapter has shown that the approach itself is not defensible in its long-period formulations. The functions $L(\mathbf{e}^i, r)$ and $K(\mathbf{e}^i, r)$ do not behave as the neoclassical approach needs. The question is not the same thing as the existence of APFs or surrogate production functions. Indeed suppose that for each commodity i, although they cannot be derived from a net-product K-production function still the function $L(\mathbf{e}^i, r)$ is increasing in r (that is, is a decreasing function of real w), and $K(\mathbf{e}^i, r)$ is a decreasing function of r. Then the same is true for $L(\mathbf{q}, r)$ and $K(\mathbf{q}, r)$ for any given composition of the economy's net product vector $\mathbf{q}$. Then for an economy-wide net product of given composition the K/L proportion is a decreasing function of r. Therefore, given L, we can determine a decreasing demand for K; and given K, we can determine a decreasing demand for L. If we add the assumption that it is legitimate to conceive the endowment of 'capital' as given and independent of income distribution, we have the elements needed in order neoclassically to determine income distribution on the basis of the direct factor substitution mechanism, even if net-product K-production functions do not exist for the single commodities nor for the economy-wide net product.

The decreasing shape of the 'demand functions' for L and for K thus obtained would be *guaranteed*, if for each commodity there existed a net-product K-production function; but it might obtain even without the latter condition. The mature Wicksell, for example, believed that it obtained, and considered it sufficient for the validity of the supply-and-demand approach, although after abandoning the average period of production he no longer believed in net-product K-production functions. This suggests that.

- (i) the decreasing shape of the functions $L(\mathbf{e}^i, w(r))$ or $L(\mathbf{q}, w(r))$, and $K(\mathbf{e}^i, r)$ or $K(\mathbf{q}, r)$;
- (ii) the legitimacy of a given endowment of 'capital'

are the really important things for the validity of the traditional marginal approach. Unfortunately on both issues (i) and (ii) this chapter has reached negative conclusions.

There remains the possibility to defend the marginal/neoclassical approach in its recent general equilibrium versions in which the notion of 'capital' does not appear (or at least seems not to): ▶ Chap. 8 will discuss the issue. Before passing to it, let us further see how misleading the use of APFs can be, if in fact a non-neoclassical approach to income distribution and quantities produced is the correct one.

7.12 'Surrogate Production Functions' in a Non-Neoclassical Economy. Endogenously Determined Marginal Products

Let us imagine an economy where income distribution and aggregate output and employment are determined according to a classical-Keynesian approach (see ▶ Chap. 1), for example, the real wage is determined by the bargaining power

588   Chapter 7 · Capital: Long-Period Equilibria

of the labour movement, the rate of interest adapts to the rate of profits as suggested by Adam Smith, the degree of utilization of productive capacity is flexible in the short run, aggregate output and employment are determined by autonomous expenditure and the multiplier, investment depends on the accelerator and on innovation (see ▶ Chap. 12), the productive capacity of the economy adapts in the long run to the evolution of aggregate demand. Now suppose that, by an extremely improbable fluke, the available techniques of this economy happen to be such that conditions (a) and (b) of the previous section are nearly satisfied and therefore the connection between income distribution and normal long-period net output per unit of labour can be nearly correctly described by a 'surrogate production function'. Would that mean the validity of the neoclassical approach for this economy? No, because the direction of causation is not from factor endowments to income distribution, nor from labour supply to employment. The value of capital, the index K in the 'surrogate production function', is a *derived* magnitude, with no constraining effect on income distribution nor outputs or employment. A decision of consumers to save a greater portion of their income does not cause the rate of interest to decrease and investment to increase and (given our assumption on the approximate existence of a surrogate production function) net output per unit of labour to increase and, after a while, the index K to be greater; on the contrary, because of the Keynesian *paradox of thrift* (▶ Sect. 1.14.2), the increased propensity to save reduces aggregate demand and employment, *discouraging* investment.

So if on the one hand the illegitimacy of APFs does not by itself undermine the neoclassical approach, on the other hand, even in the improbable cases in which a surrogate production function nearly existed, without the *additional* assumption of the correctness of the neoclassical approach this would tell us nothing on what determines income distribution, employment and growth.

An economist preferring a classical-Keynesian approach will conclude that for example the reasons for changes in average middle-class income relative to average lower-class income cannot be found in estimates based on aggregate production functions that point to changes in the marginal products of skilled labour versus unskilled labour due to the form of technical progress. This, not only because aggregate production functions always produce erroneous estimates, but above all because the determinants of wages are not marginal products at supply-equal-demand equilibria, but are bargaining power, social conflict, laws, etc. It is certainly possible that technological change has a role, for example, by decreasing the demand for unskilled labour, hence, decreasing the bargaining power of that category of workers, but the effect on wages cannot be grasped by trying to estimate marginal products, because production methods *endogenously adapt to the given real wages*, so whatever method one adopts to try and estimate the marginal product of labour from microeconomic data, one will find it has adapted to income distribution.

Indeed, let us suppose that, against the argument repeatedly advanced here that a short-period marginal product of labour is indeterminable because of insufficient substitutability (a long-period marginal product of labour is indeterminable because it would need a given endowment of 'capital'), in a number of competitive firms there is sufficient substitutability to allow asking whether these firms do employ labour up to equality between wage and marginal revenue product of labour at the given prices; and let us suppose empirical enquiries yielded a positive answer. This would be no confirmation that the marginal product of labour *determines* real wages, because the causality must be understood to go the other way: owing to the adaptability of production to demand (▶ Sect. 1.11.4; also see ▶ Chap. 12), the real wage will determine technical choices of firms and relative prices, so as to render the marginal revenue product of labour equal to the wage (when marginal products are determinable). This is not a very revolutionary claim: it is accepted by neoclassical theory too; in it, a given real wage *determines* the corresponding factor proportions adopted by firms and hence marginal products; the direction of causality becomes from full employment marginal products to factor rentals only because the marginal approach adds the tendency to the full employment of all factors. In actual economies the flexibility of production and the role of new plants in determining prices imply that marginal products in new plants (when determinable) are endogenously determined by income distribution.

So income distribution is not technologically determined; to understand the changes, for example, in relative wages, one must study in detail what has happened to demand for the several categories of labour, and all other things that influence relative bargaining power of different social categories. (One tends to suspect that the diffusion of APFs is also due to the comparatively little effort required by estimates based on them—some hours in front of a computer in one's office—relative to the difficulty of understanding the evolution of social conflict.)[44]

The above considerations can be further clarified by an example. This will also be useful to minimize the risk of misunderstandings concerning the meaning of the assumption made in ▶ Sect. 7.7 of a continuum of techniques along the wage curve. That assumption does not require smooth substitutability among inputs. Garegnani (1970), for example, obtains the continuum by assuming the Samuelson–Garegnani model and assuming that the technical coefficients of that model are continuous functions of a parameter, always under the assumption characteristic of that model that each technique uses a specific kind of capital good different from that of all other techniques, and each kind of capital good must be combined with labour in a fixed proportion: there is no substitutability between labour and each technically specified capital good.

However, it is also possible to obtain a continuum of techniques on the envelope of wage curves by assuming that, at the industry level, in at least one industry the available methods are described by a standard differentiable production function with labour and the several capital goods (*not* 'capital') as inputs. Above, in ▶ Sect. 7.10, the substitutability assumed by such a production function was judged totally unrealistic, but it is useful to understand what it would imply for

---

44 For further discussions of the errors in using APFs for explanation and prediction, and for a refutation of the estimates of so-called total factor productivity, space constraints oblige me to refer the reader to Appendix 9A in Petri (2004, pp. 324–340), and to Felipe and McCombie (2013).

590   **Chapter 7 · Capital: Long-Period Equilibria**

the formalization of long-period prices, in particular, for the thesis that cost minimization implies that factors *must* earn their (value) marginal products if marginal products can be defined.

Let us then assume an economy where two goods, say corn (good 1) and iron (good 2) are produced by CRS differentiable production functions with them and labour as inputs. Production takes one period, both corn and iron when used as inputs are circulating capital goods. Corn is the numéraire, its price is 1; the wage rate, paid at the end of the production period, is an amount of corn; p is the price of iron. $F(x_{11}, x_{21}, L_1)$, $G(x_{12}, x_{22}, L_2)$ are the production functions respectively of corn and of iron; if for both functions we fix output to 1 unit, the inputs appearing in F and in G are technical coefficients. Let F_i, G_i indicate the partial derivatives with respect to input $i=1, 2, L$. The long-period cost-minimization conditions are simple: the rental of each capital input in the production of corn, equal to its physical marginal product, must yield the rate of interest r on its purchase price, and w must equal the physical marginal product of labour; in the iron industry the rentals must satisfy the same conditions but must be equal to marginal *revenue* products, physical marginal products multiplied by p. Hence the cost-minimization conditions are as follows:

$$F(x_{11}, x_{21}, L_1) = 1$$

$$G(x_{12}, x_{22}, L_2) = 1$$

$$F_1 = 1 + r$$

$$F_2 = (1 + r)p$$

$$F_L = w$$

$$pG_1 = (1 + r)/p$$

$$pG_2 = 1 + r$$

$$pG_L = w/p$$

Because of the product exhaustion theorem, these payments to inputs imply zero profit (marginalist meaning), for example, for corn $x_{11}F_1 + x_{21}F_2 + L_1F_L = 1$. These are 8 equations in the 9 variables $x_{11}, x_{21}, L_1, x_{12}, x_{22}, L_2, p, w, r$. There is a degree of freedom: income distribution is not determined yet; we need a given w, or r, in order to determine the technique (the 6 technical coefficients). The marginal approach would determine income distribution by adding conditions of supply $=$ demand for labour, and for the endowment K of 'capital', the total value of the variable endowments of corn-capital and iron-capital, an illegitimate step as we know. But one can alternatively take w or r as given, determined by, say, class struggle. In either case, *in each industry the real wage in terms of the industry's output equals the marginal product of labour* and the same equality between marginal product and rental in terms of output holds for each capital good.

So if there is enough technical substitutability for the technical marginal products of labour and of each capital good to be determinable, then long-period cost minimization implies equality between rental and marginal (revenue) product at the given prices for these *physically measurable* inputs, independently of whether one adopts a classical or a neoclassical approach. But this equality between rental and marginal product does not determine income distribution, it simply reflects cost minimization; income distribution remains to be determined.

Once distribution and hence long-period prices are given, even the rate of interest can appear equal to the marginal product of value capital if one looks at single firms. The single *price-taking* firm, when deciding how many capital goods to combine with a given amount of labour, faces the first kind of production function discussed in ▶ Sect. 7.10 and employs capital goods up to a total value of employed capital that renders the rate of interest equal to the marginal value product of the last unit of value capital. But of course this does not mean that the rate of interest *is determined by* the marginal product of value capital, the opposite is the case, whatever the given income distribution and prices the firm will find it convenient to adjust the utilization of 'capital' so as to equalize its marginal product to the given rate of interest.

A last point deserves mention. When, as in the corn–iron differentiable economy above, industries have differentiable production functions with labour and the several capital goods as inputs, then there cannot be re-switching. Exactly the same technique cannot 'return' on the envelope of wage curves. The corn–iron differentiable economy helps to grasp the reason. Each technique implies a certain marginal product of labour in each industry, and cost minimization implies that, in the industry that produces the numéraire good, the wage equals that marginal product. If the same technique were on the envelope at two different values of r, that is, at two different values of w, it would mean that the same technical coefficients imply two different marginal products of labour, which is impossible.

But this result is of no help to the neoclassicals. First, smooth substitutability among physically specified capital goods is generally non-existent, so re-switching is perfectly possible in real economies. Second, even with smooth substitutability reverse capital deepening can happen (Burmeister and Dobell 1970, p. 290), so the regularly decreasing investment function is anyway undermined.

7.13 Perception of the Difficulties with 'Capital', and Shift Back to Walras—or Almost

This textbook intends to teach not only tools, but more broadly an ability to orientate oneself among the current disagreements in microeconomics and in the theory of value and income distribution. Then it is necessary to deal, however briefly, with Léon Walras and with the extent to which modern general equilibrium theory represents a return to Walras. This last section connects this chapter with the next one.

Wicksell in his *Lectures* (1934), after showing no doubt about treating the 'quantity of capital' as the *value* of capital goods when explaining how the use of 'earlier' inputs implies a demand for 'capital', reveals some hesitation on the specification of the endowment of 'capital' when he comes to writing down the complete system of equations of the long-period general equilibrium. There he admits that

» It would clearly be meaningless—if not altogether inconceivable—to maintain that the amount of capital is already fixed *before* equilibrium between production and consumption has been achieved. Whether expressed in terms of one or the other, a change in the relative exchange value of two commodities would give rise to a change in the value of capital, unless its component parts simultaneously underwent a more or less considerable change. (Wicksell 1934, p. 202).

Clearly Wicksell doubts that the 'more or less considerable change' would indeed happen and in such a way as to leave 'the amount of capital' unchanged, and indeed a few lines later he admits an 'indeterminateness' of the capital endowment. But a given endowment of 'capital' of variable 'form' is indispensable to render the system of equilibrium equations determinate, and we have seen that the measurement of this endowment cannot but be its exchange value; so in spite of that admission Wicksell, after listing the other equilibrium conditions, notes that there remains one degree of freedom and writes:

» If, for example, we now wish to impose the condition that in equilibrium the sum total of capital shall have a certain exchange value, measured in terms of one of the products, [the system of equilibrium equations becomes fully determinate]. (ibid., p. 204).

Wicksell is clearly hesitant and uneasy here: an author convinced of what he was doing would have written something like 'What we must *obviously* do now is add the condition that in equilibrium the sum total of capital shall have a certain exchange value', and would have written down the equation, which Wicksell on the contrary *refrains from doing*, limiting himself to this verbal statement. Indeed, there is clearly an arbitrariness in fixing the value of the 'sum total of capital … in terms of one of the products' *before* the equilibrium relative prices are determined: fixing the value of capital as equal to that of x units of corn or as equal to that of y units of rice means different things, depending on the relative price of corn and rice, which is unknown before equilibrium relative prices are determined.

Erik Lindahl, a pupil of Wicksell, and also Friderik (or Friedrich) A. von Hayek, an Austrian economist familiar with Wicksell's *Lectures* (whose first edition, written in Swedish in 1900, is translated into German in 1905), notice the hesitation of Wicksell on the value measurement of capital, and at the end of the 1920s develop it into an outright rejection of the notion of capital as a single factor, an amount of exchange value. But they are too deeply imbued with the supply-and-demand vision to be able to abandon it, also because no solid alternative approach to value and distribution exists at the time. They turn then to the treatment of the capital endowment one finds in Walras, as a given *vector* of endowments of the several capital goods. Under their influence, John Hicks too adopts the same solution and greatly contributes to its diffusion thanks to the success of his *Value and Capital* (1939). But these three economists cannot accept the whole of Walras's system of equations, so what they propose should be called neo-Walrasian rather than simply Walrasian. Let us understand what it is that they reject of Walras.

7.13 · Perception of the Difficulties with 'Capital', and Shift Back to Walras—or Almost

Walras' *Eléments d'Economie Politique Pure* starts from pure exchange, then discusses the equilibrium of production and exchange without production of capital goods, and finally passes to the general equilibrium of an economy with capital goods. In discussing the latter, alone among the founders of the marginal approach Walras includes among the data of general equilibrium the endowment of *each* capital good (each consumer is described as endowed with a given vector of capital goods). But he too aims at determining a long-period equilibrium. This is shown:

- by his characterization of equilibrium as the average situation around which the market oscillates, with adjustments that take a long time[45];
- by his assumption of a uniform rate of return on supply price and his description of the process which brings such a result about, a process involving changes in the endowments of capital goods[46];
- by his neglect of the changes that equilibrium relative prices may be undergoing over time; for example the purchase price of land is determined by dividing the rent rate by the rate of interest, the capitalization formula for assets yielding a constant coupon for ever, implying that both the equilibrium rent rate and the equilibrium rate of interest are extremely persistent;
- by his description, in the first three editions of the *Eléments* (1874–77, 1889, 1896), of the disequilibrium adjustments (the *tâtonnement*) that bring equilibrium about as involving the *actual* production and exchange of disequilibrium quantities, hence, requiring considerable time *and inevitably involving changes in the amounts of capital goods in existence*, something Walras does not seem to have realized before the fourth edition (1900).

---

45 'It never happens in the real world that the selling price of any given product is absolutely equal to the cost of the productive services that enter into that product, or that the effective demand and supply of services or products are absolutely equal. Yet equilibrium is the normal state, in the sense that it is the state towards which things spontaneously tend under a régime of free competition in exchange and in production' (Walras 1954, pp. 224–5) And even more clearly: 'Such is the continuous market, which is perpetually tending towards equilibrium without ever actually attaining it. ...Viewed in this way, the market is like a lake agitated by the wind, where the water is incessantly seeking its level without ever reaching it. But whereas there are days when the surface of a lake is almost smooth, there never is a day when the effective demand for products and services equals their effective supply and when the selling price of products equals the cost of the productive services used in making them. The diversion of productive services from enterprises that are losing money to profitable enterprises takes place in various ways, the most important being through credit operations, but at best these ways are slow'. (Walras 1954, p. 380). This passage is present from the first (1874) to the last (5th, also called 4th définitive) posthumous edition (1926).

46 'Capital goods proper are artificial capital goods; they are products and their prices are subject to the law of cost of production. If their selling price is greater than their cost of production, the quantity produced will increase and their selling price will fall; if their selling price is lower than their cost of production the quantity produced will diminish and their selling price will rise. In equilibrium their selling price and their cost of production are equal'. (Walras, 1954, p. 271). Walras's 'selling price' is what nowadays we would call demand price, the value obtained by capitalization of expected future net rentals, i.e. $(v_i - d_i P_{Ki})/r$, which, Walras says, must be equal to P_{Ki} in equilibrium. Our equations (E′) therefore can be seen as taken from Walras (with the sole difference that for simplicity we have neglected the insurance charges which Walras subtracts from capital rentals in addition to depreciation charges in order to obtain the net rentals, and which may be interpreted as a way to take account of risk).

594   Chapter 7 · Capital: Long-Period Equilibria

It would seem, therefore, that Walras was simply contradictory, not realizing that he should have left the composition of capital to be determined endogenously, if he wanted the equilibrium to be a long-period one, since the equality of rates of return on supply price he was assuming could only be brought about by an endogenous determination of the relative endowments of the several capital goods, as he himself admits.[47]

Some time between the third and the fourth edition, probably in 1899, Walras becomes better aware of the implication of a given vectorial endowment of capital goods. He realizes that disequilibrium productions would alter this vector, and that a uniform rate of return on supply price cannot be obtained. He tries to overcome these problems by assuming that economic activity is suspended during the tâtonnement, so as to avoid changes in the capital endowments during disequilibrium, and by admitting that the overabundant capital goods that offer a lower expected rate of return on their supply price than other capital goods will not be produced. He seems not to have perceived he was admitting an inability of his approach to determine what he aimed to determine, a long-period equilibrium; nor did he realize the further problems he was thus introducing. The admission that some capital goods will not be produced implies a quick change of the equilibrium's data, hence, a lack of persistency of the equilibrium, against the role of centre of gravitation Walras continues to attribute to it. And the assumption of unchanging prices implicit in the equations becomes indefensible if not all capital goods are reproduced, which implies a quick change of their relative endowments and hence of prices. But Walras, differently from the other founders of the marginal approach, never conceives the possibility to treat the several capital goods as variable embodiments of a single factor 'capital' of variable 'form'. So he has no alternative to treating each capital good as a separate factor with a given endowment.

Lindahl, Hayek and Hicks have all learned economics from authors (Wicksell, Böhm-Bawerk, Marshall) who believe in 'capital' and treat the composition of 'capital' as adapting to the equilibrium conditions; so, differently from Walras, they are clear that a long-period equilibrium needs an endogenously determined composition of capital. As a consequence, when, in order to avoid a value endowment of 'capital' and more generally the conception of capital as a single factor, these three authors decide to return to Walras's treatment of the capital endowment as a given vector—a given endowment for each capital good—*they know that they are abandoning the attempt to determine a long-period equilibrium.*

---

47   In the quotation in the previous footnote Walras implicitly admits that the equality between 'selling price' and 'cost of production' of capital goods is brought about by changes in the *endowments* of capital goods: the reason why the 'selling price' (demand price) falls when 'the quantity produced' increases can only be that the greater production lowers the rental of the capital good because it increases its quantity, i.e. decreases its scarcity. That is, in that sentence Walras contradicts his treatment of the capital endowments in the equilibrium equations as given. Why for so many years he did not realize the contradiction is discussed in Petri (2016a). In the online appendix to this chapter the reader will find a simple general equilibrium model that illustrates Walras' formulation.

This makes them fully aware of the need to admit that the prices and quantities which their notion of equilibrium determines cannot be supposed unchanging in time (since the composition of capital can be quickly changing), and that consumers and firms cannot be unaware of this fact. So they find it indispensable to include, in the equilibrium decisions of agents, an awareness that *equilibrium* prices may undergo quick change.

Two directions are explored to tackle this issue, and they characterize subsequent general equilibrium theory. The first is that of *intertemporal* equilibria, where the equilibrium prices of future goods are determined simultaneously with the prices of current goods, through an assumption *either* of complete intertemporal markets (futures markets) assumed to exist already in the initial period, *or* of perfect foresight; and what is attempted is simply a reinterpretation of the atemporal/non-capitalistic model in such terms. The greater part of ▶ Chap. 8 discusses this notion, leaving aside uncertainty, which is studied in ▶ Chap. 9. The second direction is that of *temporary* equilibria, where only current markets are assumed to exist, and agents take their decisions on the basis of *expectations* of what future prices will be, expectations which can differ among agents and will generally turn out to have been mistaken. Nowadays, owing to problems encountered by the attempts to give precision to the notion of temporary equilibrium and to prove its existence, the notion of temporary general equilibrium seems to have fallen out of favour and has disappeared from research and from textbooks. But it is opportune briefly to discuss it anyway, so that readers become aware of its difficulties; it will be done in the last sections of ▶ Chap. 8.

These new notions of general equilibrium tackle the need to admit non-constant equilibrium prices due to the changing composition of capital, but cannot abandon Walras' recourse to a tâtonnement that proceeds in a 'congealed economy' situation: it remains true in both these notions of equilibrium that time-consuming disequilibrium adjustments involving actual productions would alter the endowments of the several capital goods and hence the equilibrium itself. The theory of neo-Walrasian equilibria must maintain the fairy tale of the auctioneer-guided tâtonnement going on in a situation of suspended economic activity. ▶ Chapter 8 will discuss at length the implications of this aspect.

7.14 Conclusions

The contents of this chapter can be summarized as follows. All founders of the marginal approach aimed at determining a long-period equilibrium, and all, with the exception of Walras who was simply contradictory, treated the equilibrium composition of the stock of capital goods as endogenously determined by the equilibrium, and determined the quantities of capital goods by assuming a uniform rate of profit (a uniform rate of return on supply price) and by treating the capital goods as transient embodiments of a single factor 'capital' of variable 'form' whose endowment was given. Without this conception of capital the assumption of extensive factor substitutability would have been indefensible. Aggregate production functions reveal a persistent faith in this conception of capital, plus additional simplifying assumptions, but are illegitimate constructions and their use in applied analyses inevitably produces grave misinterpretations of the evidence. This factor 'capital' encounters logical difficulties in the determination of its endowment, and also grave problems (revealed by Sraffa) in the determination of a decreasing demand function for it, with consequences for the standard investment function. Some perception of the first problem in the 1920s and 1930s explains the shift to neo-Walrasian formulations that take the equilibrium's endowment of each capital good as given, and claim to have abandoned the conception of capital as a single factor. But this notion of capital continues to dominate applied neoclassical analyses, for example, it is used to explain changes in relative wages as due to technical progress having changed marginal products. In a non-neoclassical approach marginal products endogenously adapt to income distribution and so cannot explain it.

The arguments of this chapter are not universally accepted; in my view, the reason is an insufficient understanding of the evolution of the marginal/neoclassical approach and of its origin in long-period versions, largely due to Hicks' misrepresentation of traditional static equilibria as secularly stationary. Contemporary neoclassical theorists seem to have great difficulty in grasping the notion of long-period positions. I have tried to dispel the misunderstandings in Petri (1999, 2004, 2014, 2016b, 2019). See also Garegnani (2012).

7.15 Review Questions and Exercises

■ **Review Questions**

1. Recall the two senses in which equilibrium must be persistent in order to have its traditional role.
2. Explain why traditional marginalist economists considered the quantity of each capital good a variable that the equilibrium had to determine endogenously.
3. Explain why it is a logical necessity of the notion of capital as a single factor of variable 'form' that the quantity of this factor 'embodied' in each capital good must be proportional to the value of that capital good.
4. Explain how one can reformulate the system of equations from (A′) to (K′) without assuming that consumption goods and capital goods are two distinct groups of goods.
5. Explain why the determination of long-period equilibria encounters a supply-side problem that undermines their determinability.
6. Explain why in the traditional marginal approach the insights derivable from long-period analysis do not require, in order to be applicable, that the 'form' and even the 'quantity' of 'capital' has completely adapted to the ruling income distribution.
7. Explain why the Marshallian short-period determination of investment, as derived from the capital–labour ratio determined by the rate of interest and applied in new plants, needs the continuous full employment of labour in order for investment not to be indeterminate.

7.15 · Review Questions and Exercises

8. Clarify the quotation from Sraffa (1960, p. 38) in ▶ Sect. 7.9.1. (Read Sraffa, it is fascinating.)
9. Explain why price Wicksell effects add to the stability problem of the neoclassical savings–investment market.
10. Explain why in the Samuelson 'Austrian' example of production of whiskey or champagne I call 'C' and 'W' *techniques* and not methods.
11. Explain why the problem with determining the endowment of capital in long-period general equilibrium models destroys the possibility to determine a labour demand function.
12. Explain what is wrong with production functions with capital (i.e. the value of the capital goods employed) as one of the inputs.
13. Clarify why substitutability among the dated inputs of Wicksell's production functions in the *lectures* does not justify the substitutability assumption in modern production functions.
14. Illustrate how reverse capital deepening undermines the indirect factor substitution mechanism.
15. Explain why re-switching and reverse capital deepening can be argued to undermine the factual basis which was believed to support the marginal approach.
16. Explain how the demand for capital function becomes an investment function.
17. Clarify the functions $L(e^i, r)$, $K(e^i, r)$ defined in ▶ Sect. 7.11.
18. Explain why the legitimacy of production functions with 'capital' as one of the inputs can be argued not to be fundamental for the validity of the traditional marginal approach.
19. The text argues that 'Walras was simply contradictory'. Explain.
20. Why did Walras need to assume a tâtonnement with 'bons'?
21. Where is the mistake in Hicks' argument that a theory that neglects price changes can only deal with steady-growth situations in which relative prices are perfectly constant? (▶ Sect. 7.11)
22. Summarize in not more than half a page the message of Sect, 7.14.3.

- **Exercises**
1. Assume an economy produces a unit of food with this 'Austrian' technique: 3 wages must be paid 3 dates before the unit of food comes out, 1 wage must be paid 2 dates before, and 1 wage must be paid at the same date the unit of food comes out. If the price of food is 1, and the economy is stationary and produces 1 unit of food per period as net product, determine the value of capital in this economy as a function of r.
2. Draw three wage curves such that at one switch point on the outer envelope there is a positive real Wicksell effect although each wage curve has only one segment appearing on the outer envelope. (There is some disagreement in the literature on whether such a case, in which two wage curves cross twice but one of the crossings is not on the outer envelope, should be called a case of re-switching.)
3. In the 'Austrian' example in ▶ Sect. 7.12 of flour produced with corn and labour, assume the wage consists of corn which is the numéraire, and write down the equation determining the price of flour as a function of r and w; derive the wage curve; show there is no maximum rate of profit (rate of interest).

598 Chapter 7 · Capital: Long-Period Equilibria

4. Modify the long-period general equilibrium equations assuming that there is a positive propensity to net savings which causes a growth rate g of the capital stock, but because labour supply is also growing this positive growth rate of 'capital' is not believed significantly to alter next period's income distribution, so prices can be treated as constant. Assume investment ensures a common growth rate of all endowments of capital goods.

5. (Secular stationary state). Modify the system of equilibrium equations of the previous exercise assuming the common propensity to net savings decreases with the rate of interest and reaches zero for a positive r, and allow the endowment of 'capital' to become an endogenous variable which must become such as to bring the rate of growth to zero. Show that now equation (K') can be abolished, and the variable K* with it: the secular stationary equilibrium can be formulated without the notion of 'capital' appearing in the equations.

6. Assume an economy has at its disposal so many techniques that along the envelope of wage curves a different wage curve corresponds to each point. Draw some of the (concave) wage curves such that the envelope is a straight line and the value of capital per unit of labour is constant along the envelope. Draw the corresponding (inverse) demand curve for 'capital' if labour employment is given.

7. Write the equations of static long-period equilibrium of the following economy, in the style of the model in ▶ Sect. 7.12: there is is a single pure circulating capital good and a single pure consumption good; both are produced by labour and the capital good, according to different standard differentiable production functions (production takes one period, wages are paid at the end). The consumption good is the numéraire. In accordance with traditional marginalist theory, the endowment of capital is a given *value* endowment of 'capital', in spite of the physical homogeneity of capital goods. Check equality of unknowns and equations, without forgetting the numéraire's equation.

8. (Reverse capital deepening and fixed capital) Return to the treatment, at the end of ▶ Chap. 2, of the value of a stock of durable machines of constant efficiency for k years, uniformly distributed by age. Assume a new machine is produced with the same production coefficients as the single consumption good (which is the numéraire), therefore, its price is 1. If one assumes that the entire stock of capital goods of the economy consists of this machine, uniformly distributed by age, and that technical coefficients do not change with r, show that the demand for capital function of this economy is upward-sloping. Then study the long-period gross investment function.

9. Show that a change of numéraire alters the wage curves but not the value(s) of r at which two wage curves intersect.

10. Modify ◼ Fig. 7.6a so as to obtain that as r rises the value of capital per unit of labour increases.

11. ▶ Section 7.12 argues that even in the marginal/neoclassical approach marginal products adapt to income distribution. Confirm that it is so, by reference to the model in ▶ Chap. 3 of labour and land producing corn with a differentiable production function. What happens in this model if the real wage is different from the equilibrium level?

References

Bellino, E. (1993). Continuous switching of techniques in linear production models. *The Manchester School, 61*(2), 185–201.

Böhm-Bawer, E. (1906). Capital and interest once more: I. Capital Vs. capital goods. *Quarterly Journal of Economics, 21*(1), 1–21.

Burmeister, E., & Dobell, A. R. (1970). *Mathematical theories of economic growth*. London: Macmillan.

Clark J. B. (1925). *The distribution of wealth*. New York: Macmillan (New print. of the 1899 ed.).

Clark, J. B. (1899). *The distribution of wealth*. New York: Macmillan.

Dvoskin, A., & Petri, F. (2017). Again on the relevance of reverse capital deepening and reswitching. *Metroeconomica, 68*(4), 625–659.

Felipe, J., & Fisher, F. M. (2003). Aggregation in production functions: what applied economists should know. *Metroeconomica, 54*(2), 208–262.

Felipe, J., & McCombie, J. S. L. (2013). *The aggregate production function and the measurement of technical change: 'Not even wrong.'* Cheltenham, UK: Edward Elgar.

Fratini, S. M. (2008). Economic generality versus mathematical genericity: Activity-level indeterminacy and the index theorem in constant returns production economies. *Metroeconomica, 59*(2), 266–275. ▶ https://doi.org/10.1111/j.1467-999X.2007.00305.x

Garegnani, P. (1960). *Il capitale nelle teorie della distribuzione*. Milano: Giuffrè.

Garegnani, P. (1970). Heterogeneous capital, the production function and the theory of distribution. *Review of Economic Studies, 37*(3), 407–436.

Garegnani, P. (1976 (1983). On a change in the notion of equilibrium in recent work on value and distribution. In M. Brown, K. Sato, & P. Zarembka (Eds.), *Essays in modern capital theory* (pp. 25–45). Amsterdam: North-Holland. As reprinted in J. Eatwell & M. Milgate (Eds.), *Keynes's economics and the theory of value and distribution* (pp. 129–45). London: Duckworth, and New York: Oxford University Press, 1983.

Garegnani, P. (1978). Notes on consumption, investment and effective demand: I. *Cambridge Journal of Economics, 2,* 335–353.

Garegnani, P. (1990). Quantity of capital. In J. L. Eatwell, M. Milgate, & P. Newman (Eds.), *The New Palgrave Series: Capital theory* (pp. 1–78). London and Basingstoke: The Macmillan Press Limited.

Garegnani, P. (2008) On Walras's theory of capital. *Journal of the History of Economic Thought, 30*(3)

Garegnani, P. (2012). On the Present State of the Capital Controversy. *Cambridge Journal of Economics, 36,* 1417–1432.

Hicks, J. R. (1932(1963)). *The theory of wages* (reprinted with additions, 1963). Macmillan, London.

Hansen, B. (1970). *A Survey of General Equilibrium Systems*. New York: McGraw Hill Book Co.

Hicks, J. R. (1939). *Value and Capital*. Oxford: Clarendon Press.

Kaldor N. (1955–6) Alternative Theories of Distribution. *Review of Economic Studies* 23: 83–100.

Knight, F. H. (1946). Capital and interest. In: *Encyclopaedia Britannica* (Vol. IV, pp. 779–801) (reprinted in *Readings in the Theory of Income Distribution*, ed. by American Economic Association, Toronto, 1946).

Petri, F. (1999) Professor Hahn on the Neo-Ricardian criticism of neoclassical economics. In: G. Mongiovi. F. Petri (Eds.), *Value, distribution and capital: Essays in honour of Pierangelo Garegnani* (pp. 19–68). London: Routledge.

Petri, F. (2004). *General equilibrium, capital and macroeconomics: a key to recent controversies in equilibrium theory*. Cheltenham, UK: Edward Elgar.

Petri, F. (2013). The inevitable dependence of investment on expected demand: Implications for neoclassical macroeconomics. Palgrave Macmillan. In S. Levrero, A. Palumbo, & A. Stirati (Eds.), *Sraffa and the reconstruction of economic theory* (Vol. II, pp. 44–67). Basingstoke, Hampshire UK: Houndmills.

Petri, F. (2014). Blaug versus Garegnani on the 'formalist revolution' and the evolution of neoclassical capital theory. *Journal of the History of Economic Thought, 36,* 455–478.

600   Chapter 7 · Capital: Long-Period Equilibria

Petri, F. (2015). Neglected implications of neoclassical capital-labour substitution for investment theory: Another criticism of say's law. *Review of Political Economy, 27*(3), 308–340.

Petri, F. (2016a). Walras on capital: Interpretative insights from a review by Bortkiewicz. *Contributions to Political Economy, 35,* 23–37.

Petri, F. (2016b). Capital theory. Edward Elgar. In G. Faccarello & H. D. Kurz (Eds.), *Handbook of the history of economic analysis* (Vol. III, pp. 40–69). U.K.: Cheltenham.

Petri, F. (2019). What capital theory can teach us. In A. Moneta, T. Gabellini, & S. Gasperini (Eds.), *Economic Crisis and Economic Thought* (pp. 75–110). London: Routledge.

Ricardo, D. (1951). *On the principles of political economy and taxation.* iN: P. Sraffa (Ed.), *The works and correspondence of David Ricardo* (Vol. I). Cambridge: Cambridge University Press.

Samuelson, P. A. (1962). Parable and realism in capital theory: The surrogate production function. *Review of Economic Studies, 29,* 193–206.

Sraffa, P. (1960). *Production of commodities by means of commodities.* Cambridge: Cambridge University Press.

Walras, L. (1954). *Elements of political economy* (Jaffé translation). Homewood, Ill.: Richard D. Irwin (reprinted 1977 by Augustus M. Kelley, New York).

Walras L. (1988). *Eléments d'économie politique pure: ou théorie de la richesse sociale*, ed. Pierre Dockès et al., Economica, Paris.

Wicksell, K. (1935). *Lectures on political economy* (Vol. II). London: Routledge and Kegan Paul.

Wicksell, K. (1934). *Lectures on political economy* (Vol. I). London: Routledge and Kegan Paul.

Wicksell, K. (1893). *Uber wert, kapital und rente*, G. Fischer. English transl. 1954, *Value, capital and rent.* London: Allen and Unwin.

Intertemporal Equilibrium, Temporary Equilibrium

Contents

8.1   Introduction – 605

8.2   The Intertemporal Reinterpretation of the Non-capitalistic Atemporal Model – 606

8.3   Postponing to ▶ Chapter 9 on Uncertainty – 609

8.4   The Consumer's Intertemporal Utility Function – 609

8.5   Meaning of Prices; Own Rates of Interest – 611

8.6   Production – 612

8.7   The Reinterpretation Should not Hide a Difference – 615

8.8   Different Own Rates of Interest and Effective Uniformity of Rates of Return – 616

Electronic supplementary material The online version of this chapter (▶ https://doi.org/10.1007/978-3-030-62070-7_8) contains supplementary material, which is available to authorized users.

© Springer Nature Switzerland AG 2021
F. Petri, *Microeconomics for the Critical Mind*,
Classroom Companion: Economics, https://doi.org/10.1007/978-3-030-62070-7_8

8.9	**Uniform Effective Rate of Return Versus Long-Period Uniform Rate of Profit – 618**
8.10	**UERRSP and URRSP – 619**
8.11	**Radner Sequential Equilibria (Without Uncertainty) – 620**
8.12	**Existence, Uniqueness, Stability – 622**
8.13	**Really Only a Reinterpretation? Some First Problems – 623**
8.14	**Money – 625**
8.15	**Impermanence Problem, Price-Change Problem, Substitutability Problem – 627**
8.16	**The Savings–investment Problem – 632**
8.16.1	The 'Further Assumption' – 632
8.16.2	The Difference It Makes to Assume or Not the 'Further Assumption' – 635
8.16.3	The Neoclassical Synthesis – 640
8.17	**Equilibrium Over the Infinite Future – 641**
8.17.1	The One-Good Growth Model – 641
8.17.2	The Old Problems Remain, Plus a New One – 648
8.18	**Behind the Neoclassical Reliance on Intertemporal Equilibria – 650**
8.19	**Overlapping Generations – 652**

8.20	**Multiple OLG Equilibria – 656**
8.21	**The Core of Allocations in the Neoclassical Economy – 661**
8.22	**The Core Equivalence Theorem is not Valid for OLG Economies – 668**
8.23	**A Continuum of Equilibria in OLG Models – 669**
8.24	**Summing Up on OLG Models – 675**
8.25	**Temporary Equilibria. An Informal Presentation of Some Problems – 677**
8.26	**An Introductory Pure-Exchange Model – 679**
8.26.1	General Description of the Exchange Economy – 679
8.26.2	A More Detailed Description of the Household's Behaviour – 680
8.26.3	Problems with the Introductory Model – 685
8.26.4	A Perplexing Aspect of Green's Equilibrium – 689
8.27	**Extension to the Case of Economies with Production – 691**
8.27.1	The Extended Model – 691
8.27.2	Discussion of the Extended Model[84] – 697
8.28	**Temporary Equilibrium in Economies with 'Money' – 702**
8.28.1	Introduction of Money – 702
8.28.2	Existence of Monetary Equilibrium – 707
8.28.3	Some Doubts on Grandmont's Characterization of the Function of Money – 713

8.29 Conclusions on the Marginal/Neoclassical Approach, with Special Emphasis on the Labour Demand Curve and on the Investment Function – 714

8.30 Review Questions and Exercises – 718

References – 723

Intertemporal Equilibrium, Temporary Equilibrium

This chapter presents and critically assesses the neo-Walrasian notions of inter-temporal and of temporary general equilibrium. You will learn:

- the reinterpretation of the non-capitalistic general equilibrium model as an inter-temporal equilibrium referring to dated commodities and discounted prices;
- the possibility to avoid complete futures markets by introducing perfect fore-sight and Radner equilibria;
- four problems of intertemporal equilibria: impermanence problem, price-change problem, substitutability problem, savings–investment problem;
- which debatable assumption in the intertemporal-equilibrium tâtonnement guarantees the adjustment of investment to savings;
- whether intertemporal equilibria are really the microfoundation of macroeco-nomic models;
- the peculiarities of overlapping-generations intertemporal equilibria
- the notion of core of a competitive economy;
- the difficulties encountered by the attempts to formalize temporary equilibria.

The online Appendix to the chapter
- clarifies the difference between the long-period notion of uniform rate of return on all investments and the apparently similar notion valid in intertem-poral equilibria;
- briefly explains the 'neoclassical synthesis'.

8.1 Introduction

This chapter introduces to the neo-Walrasian notions of general equilibrium that since the 1970s are presented as *the* neoclassical theory of value: intertemporal equilibrium over a finite or an infinite horizon (including the overlapping-gen-erations versions) and temporary equilibrium. In this chapter it is assumed that there is no uncertainty about future states of nature; how this uncertainty is intro-duced into general equilibrium—through *contingent commodities*—is discussed in ▶ Chap. 9. Sects. 8.1–8.18 of the chapter discuss intertemporal equilibria *without* the overlapping generations (OLG) structure; the rather counterintuitive representation of the present and future prices as present-value prices is clari-fied, and it is explained that apparently different rates of return in equilibrium do not mean unequal convenience of different employments of savings, and yet this equal convenience of all investments does not mean the equilibrium is a long-period equilibrium. Some deficiencies of intertemporal equilibria noted by Garegnani are remembered, and the equality of investment and full-employment savings is found to lack justification; a recent new argument on this issue (Petri 2017) is remembered. Sects. 8.19–8.24 discuss infinite-horizon equilibria with the OLG structure and how they differ from Arrow–Debreu economies, especially with respect to Pareto efficiency, to the notion of core of neoclassical allocations, and to multiplicity of equilibria and how they need not be in the 'core' and can easily be a continuum. Sections 8.25–8.29 explain why the notion of temporary equilibrium has fallen out of favour. The chapter's online Appendix includes

606   Chapter 8 · Intertemporal Equilibrium, Temporary Equilibrium

sections on the tâtonnement stability of the finite-horizon intertemporal equilibrium; on a numerical example clarifying why an intertemporal equilibrium is not a long-period equilibrium; on discounted and undiscounted prices; on vertical integration; on the 'neoclassical synthesis'.

As explained at the end of ▶ Chap. 7, when in the 1930s Lindahl, Hayek and Hicks decide that one must do without the conception of capital as a single 'fund' and propose to return to Walras' treatment of the capital endowment as a given vector, differently from Walras they are aware that they are abandoning the attempt to determine long-period equilibria; they know that their very-short-period equilibria determine relative prices which may undergo rapid change, and they admit that agents cannot but be aware of this fact. To include this awareness into the agents' optimizations, they see only two possible roads. They are both discussed in this chapter. Sections 2–24 present the notion of *intertemporal equilibrium*, respectively without and with the OLG structure: future prices for a number of periods (or even for the infinite future) are determined simultaneously with current prices, through an assumption either of existence, already at the initial date when equilibrium is established, of complete markets for all future goods, or of perfect price foresight. The second road, *temporary equilibria* (without perfect foresight), assumes that for most goods only spot markets exist; equilibrium is established only on the current period markets, and agents take their decisions about the current period on the basis of *expectations* of future prices, expectations that will generally differ among agents and therefore will turn out to have been mistaken for most agents.

8.2 The Intertemporal Reinterpretation of the Non-capitalistic Atemporal Model

The notion of intertemporal equilibrium was formalized by Arrow and Debreu (1954) as a *reinterpretation* of the exchange and production non-capitalistic model without a rate of interest described in ▶ Chaps. 5 and 6. The variables and equations of that model are reinterpreted as referring to *dated* commodities: an umbrella delivered at date t is a different good from an umbrella delivered at date t + 1. Then the equilibrium can cover only a finite number of periods because the non-capitalistic model has a finite number of commodities. Nowadays, frontier research is on models extending into the infinite future, but I present the finite-periods model first.

Time is divided into short periods (Hicks called them 'weeks'); each period t starts at instant/date t on the timeline, and ends infinitesimally before instant/date $t + 1$; thus the number that identifies a period coincides with its initial date/instant.[1] The length of a period is not much discussed, but the idea seems to be

---

1   One must decide whether the period starting at date 0 and ending infinitesimally before date 1 is to be called period zero, or period 1. In common language it would be called the first period, hence period 1 (so the first year after Christ's birth is year 1, not zero). In economic literature, it is usually called period zero.

8.2 · The Intertemporal Reinterpretation of the Non-Capitalistic Atemporal Model.

that it is so short that it is legitimate to treat all units of a good sold during the period as having the same price, and to dispense with distinguishing the goods according to the precise moment of delivery within the period; so that it is permissible to imagine all deliveries and exchanges of the period's goods as happening at the beginning of the period. There are seldom discussed problems here, but for now it is best to leave them dormant.[2]

There is an initial date 0, where equilibrium is reached for all exchanges and productions to be carried out not only in that period but also for all subsequent periods up to a last period T called the horizon of the economy, at the end of which the economy terminates[3]; markets are assumed to exist at the initial date for all goods, present and future, over all periods up to the horizon. The markets for immediate delivery (that is, for goods of the initial period 0) are called **spot markets**; the markets for goods to be delivered in the future are called **markets in futures**, or futures markets. A 'future' is a contract for delivery of a good at a future date. All contracts for delivery of goods, both current and future, are signed at the initial date. The price of a future good is the price *at date 0* of a promise of delivery of that good when its date arrives; it can be seen as the *present value* at date 0 of the future good, or its spot value (its price if it were paid at its date of delivery and not in advance) *discounted* to date 0—see below for further explanations. Deliveries of goods of period t are assumed to happen at date t, i.e. at the beginning of the period.

How is equilibrium reached? The standard story relies on the auctioneer, the fairy tale institution described in ▶ Sect. 5.26 that suspends all exchanges and productions, announces tentative prices, collects intentions of supply-and-demand conditional on those prices being equilibrium prices, and then changes prices depending on excess demands, allowing exchanges and productions only when equilibrium is reached.[4] The auctioneer operates at date 0, crying out prices for all present and future goods. Distinguish prices by two indices, the second one indicating the date of delivery and the first one indicating the type of good or service; then p_{it}/p_{js} indicates the quantity of good j which at date 0 one must promise one will deliver at date s in order to obtain in exchange a promise of delivery of one unit of good i at date t. Equilibrium is reached at date 0 (the tâtonnement is

---

2 Just one hint: the longer the period, the less convincing it is to treat all units of the good as having the same price; the shorter the period, the fewer the agents interested in selling or buying a good, in the limit in continuous time there will generally be no more than one buyer and one seller contracting for a good at t, and then price taking is hardly defensible.

3 That is, it is known that something like a big asteroid hitting the Earth will happen. This assumption is hard to accept, but the alternatives are either to suppose equilibrium over the infinite future, which is just as hard to accept (see below); or to suppose that last period decisions are taken on the basis of expectations of what will happen later, as in temporary equilibria, but then the difficulties of temporary equilibrium to be mentioned later are not avoided, and the logical consistency of an equilibrium which is partly intertemporal and partly temporary is doubtful: why complete futures markets for goods up to period T and not up to period T + 1?

4 The auctioneer must also be supposed to check that consumers' plans respect their budget constraints and firms' plans respect their technological constraints.

608   **Chapter 8** · Intertemporal Equilibrium, Temporary Equilibrium

assumed to take no time), and then agents need no further opening of markets, they must only carry out the promises they signed. It is implicitly assumed that contracts will be honoured; this is the **no default** assumption. In this chapter let us neglect uncertainty about the state of the world in future periods, it is perfectly forecasted.

Endowments too are distinguished according to the date at which they start being available (which is always the beginning of a period); endowments of factors available at the beginning of period t supply services during that period. Suppose the equilibrium is over three periods and you own a land in all three periods. Then your endowment includes land-0, land-1 and land-2, each land supplying land services in its period. Analogously a consumer who can work from period 0 to period n has an endowment of labour or leisure time of date 0 (that is, of labour services deliverable during period 0), an endowment of labour of date 1, and so on. A produced good available at date t has a production process that starts at date $t - 1$ and is completed by date t, hence, utilizes services of period $t - 1$ and means of production available at date $t - 1$. Production processes last one period, if technically the process is longer it is considered a succession of one-period processes, with the product of earlier processes passed on as input to the next process.

The consumer's endowments at date 0 are called *initial endowments*. For capitalistic economies, the initial endowments include capital goods extant at date 0 because produced in the periods before date 0, and inventories of consumption goods just delivered to consumers; I will neglect the latter inventories in what follows. The capital goods extant at date 0 are treated like exhaustible natural resources, how they were produced is irrelevant; now they are, like labour and land, simply given quantities of **non-produced factors** (that is, not produced *inside the equilibrium's periods*). Thus, as in Walras and differently from long-period equilibria, the equilibrium's data include a given total date-0 endowment of *each* capital good, and of course a given distribution of this endowment among consumers. Equilibrium prices therefore depend on the accidents that determined the given initial composition of the capital endowment. Capital goods of date 1, 2 and so on are all treated as produced goods, if necessary produced by storing or (durable capital) by joint production, so they are not part of endowments; that is, from date 1 onwards the endowments consist only of labour(s) and land(s).

According to the Marshallian classification of equilibria as very-short-period, short-period, long-period, or very-long-period (or secular) depending on which supplies of produced goods are given and which are determined endogenously by the equilibrium, *an intertemporal equilibrium is a very-short-period equilibrium* because at date 0 there are given supplies of produced goods, as in Marshall's very-short-period partial equilibrium of a fish market.[5]

---

5   Warning: recently the short-period/long-period terminology has been sometimes used as referring to how many periods are covered by the equilibrium; then intertemporal equilibria are called long-period equilibria, a terminology rejected here because it obfuscates the traditional meaning of long-period equilibrium, which is analytically very important.

8.4 · The consumer's Intertemporal Utility Function.

8.3 Postponing to ▶ Chapter 9 on Uncertainty

In this chapter I leave aside the further reinterpretation of the same formal model that enlarges the interpretation to cover uncertainty about states of nature too. It consists of admitting that promises of delivery of a good can be conditional on the realization of a certain state of nature, in which case the goods traded are *contingent commodities*, i.e. promises of delivery of a commodity contingent on the realization of certain events, and prices are the prices one is ready to pay at the initial date for these promises, on the basis of the probabilities one attributes to the possible future states of nature, probabilities that can differ as between agents. This reinterpretation is for the next chapter, after an introduction to risk, expected utility and insurance. Now let us discuss the claim that intertemporal equilibria are formally identical to the equilibria of the atemporal non-capitalistic production economy studied in ▶ Chap. 5; only a reinterpretation is necessary of prices and quantities as *dated*. Let us examine this formal similarity.

8.4 The Consumer's Intertemporal Utility Function

The utility function of a consumer now depends on the consumption of present and future commodities. The consumer correctly forecasts the effects on her/his utility of future consumptions and decides everything at date zero. Indicate with Q_{jt} the quantity of good j consumed at date t (or, equivalently, in period t), and with p_{jt} the price, *to be paid at date zero*, of a promise of delivery of one unit of good j at date t. (Unless indispensable, in what follows I do not use an index to indicate which consumer we are talking of; otherwise we could write Q_{jt}^s for the amount of good (j, t) consumed by consumer s.) The endowment of the consumer consists of a vector ω of vectors ω_t of endowments of dated commodities or factors of date t.

The consumer's utility maximization problem is formally identical to the one in the non-capitalistic economy, with the sole difference that consumption goods and endowments have two indices instead of one:

$$\text{maximize} \quad u(Q_{10}, \ldots, Q_{n0}; Q_{11}, \ldots, Q_{n1}; \ldots; Q_{1T}, \ldots, Q_{nT})$$
$$\text{under the constraint} \quad \Sigma_{j,t} p_{jt} Q_{jt} \leq \Sigma_{j,t} p_{jt} \omega_{jt}.$$

Now it is better to drop the assumption that we can distinguish factors from consumption goods, because many consumption goods (e.g. sugar) are also used as inputs in the production of other goods, so let us simply assume n types of goods and services. Neglecting corner solutions, marginal rates of substitution will be made equal to price ratios; now they are possibly *intertemporal* MRS.

In the models utilized to study specific issues in intertemporal choice, often some specific utility function is assumed. Three are worth mentioning. The most widely used intertemporal utility function is separable, a discounted sum of the 'subutilities' derived from consumption in each period according to a constant subutility function. Let $\mathbf{Q}_t$ stand for the vector $(Q_{1t}, Q_{2t}, \ldots, Q_{nt})$ of consumptions in period t; subutility $u_t(\mathbf{Q}_t)$ is also called a *felicity function*; the utility function is

610   Chapter 8 · Intertemporal Equilibrium, Temporary Equilibrium

$$U(\mathbf{Q}_0, \ldots, \mathbf{Q}_T) = \sum_{t=0}^{T} \delta^t u_t(\mathbf{Q}_t).$$

Subutilities of period t are discounted to date 0 by multiplying them by the discount factor δ^t; δ is positive and less than 1, reflecting the assumption that consumers prefer present to future consumption.[6]

Of course this utility function is vastly unrealistic, its temporal separability neglects the dependence of the marginal utility of a good in a period on what was consumed in previous periods; the assumption of time-invariant felicity function is clearly contradicted by the different desires of young and old people; there is no reason why δ should be constant. Whenever such an intertemporal utility function is met, the reader should stop and ask what really the model tries to show, how much its conclusions depend on the particular and debatable form chosen for the utility function.

In macroeconomic models with a single consumption good c the following time-invariant felicity function is often assumed:

$$u(c_t) = \frac{c_t^{1-\sigma}}{1-\sigma}, \text{ for } \sigma > 0 \text{ and } \neq 1; \quad u_t(c_t) = \ln c_t \text{ for } \sigma = 1.$$

The resulting $U(\cdot)$ can be shown to have constant elasticity of substitution between consumption at any two consecutive dates, equal to $1/\sigma$. When the analysis admits uncertainty, this felicity function can be used as a utility function to describe attitudes towards risk, and then σ is the *coefficient of relative risk aversion*, a notion explained in ▶ Chap. 9; for this reason $U(\cdot)$ with the above felicity function is called the *constant relative risk aversion* (CRRA) utility function.

Another additive utility function frequently used in models with a single consumption good is the *constant absolute risk aversion* (CARA) utility function, which has the following felicity function:

$$u(c_t) = -\frac{1}{\alpha e^{\alpha c_t}}.$$

This function too is discussed in ▶ Chap. 9.

---

6   Empirical evidence suggests that a more appropriate theory of how consumers actually consider consumption at future dates is **hyperbolic discounting**: the discount factor from t to date zero is not $\delta^t < 1$ but $1/(1 + kt)$ with k > 0, which decreases with t slower than δ^t and implies **time inconsistency**: that is, given the felicity function and the consumptions at the several dates, when a consumer is at date 0, the marginal rate of substitution between consumption at date 2 and consumption at date 3 is different from the one when the consumer reaches date 1 (**Exercise**: prove it). This can occasion decisions about the intertemporal distribution of consumption, which afterwards the consumer regrets. The discount factor δ^t avoids time inconsistency, but this is no reason to prefer it if it does not correspond to how people choose.

8.5 Meaning of Prices; Own Rates of Interest

The prices appearing in intertemporal-equilibrium equations, sometimes called dated prices, present value prices, discounted prices, are counterintuitive for people only accustomed to market prices and natural prices; let us stop on their meaning.

All dated prices are prices quoted and to be paid at date 0 for purchases of present or future goods. Having fixed a numéraire, the price p_{it} of good (i, t) indicates the amount of numéraire to be promised at date 0 in exchange for the promise of delivery of one unit of good i when date t arrives. It is convenient, and usual, to fix as numéraire a date-0 good, so one can visualize it as actually paid at date 0 for any purchase.

The best way to penetrate the meaning of dated prices is to define *own* rates of interest. The relative price $p_{it}/p_{i,t+1}$ of the *same* physical good at two consecutive dates allows defining the (one period) **own rate of interest** r_{it} via the equation

$$p_{it}/p_{i,t+1} = 1 + r_{it} \text{ or equivalently } p_{it}/(1 + r_{it}) = p_{i,t+1}. \tag{8.1}$$

If the own rate of interest of good 1, gold, between periods 0 and 1 is 0.05, that is, 5%, it means that one can purchase 1 unit of date zero gold by paying with a promise of delivery of 1.05 units of gold at date 1; or equivalently, that with 1/(1.05) units of gold at date zero one can buy the promise to obtain 1 unit of gold at date 1. Assume $p_{10}=1$, that is, date-0 gold is the numéraire; then 1/(1.05) is the price in gold to be paid at date 0 for a unit of gold at date 1, i.e. $1/(1.05)=p_{11}$, *less* than 1 if r_{10} is positive. So r_{it} is the real rate of interest (measured in good i) on a one-period loan of good i from date t to date $t+1$ and to be repaid with an amount of the same good.

Dated prices are, in a sense we can make precise, discounted or present value prices. Suppose gold is good 1 and gold of date zero, good $(1, 0)$, is the general numéraire, hence, $p_{10}=1$; define the **undiscounted price** of good (i, t), to be indicated as π_{it}, as the amount of numéraire good (gold) *of date t* to be given in exchange for one unit of good (i, t)[7]; the undiscounted price of gold is 1 for all dates; and π_{it} can be seen as the amount of gold that would have to be paid for a unit of good (i, t) if the transaction were **spot,** i.e. if payment were made at date t. The price at date 0 of a unit of numéraire of date t can be seen as its undiscounted price 1, discounted to date 0 with its one-period own rates of interest:

$$p_{1t} = 1/(1 + r_{1,t-1}) \cdot 1/(1 + r_{1,t-2}) \cdot \ldots \cdot 1/(1 + r_{1,0}). \tag{8.2}$$

Then the dated price, i.e. price at date 0, of any date t good can be seen as the undiscounted price of the good—a quantity of date t gold—discounted to date zero in the way just indicated.

---

7   If one admits money and supposes money consists of gold, then π_{it} is the amount of money to pay for a unit of good (i, t) if the payment is spot, that is, made at date t.

612   Chapter 8 · Intertemporal Equilibrium, Temporary Equilibrium

But formally, the role of these prices in consumer choice is the same as that of the prices of non-capitalistic equilibria with zero rate of interest; only the interpretation changes.

(The online Appendix 3 on the chapter's website on SpringerLink can further help not to confuse *own* rates of interest with *money* rates of interest or with *real* rates of interest).

The intertemporal marginal rate of substitution between the *same* good at two consecutive dates can be seen as expressing a (one period) *rate of time preference* for that good. Consider an indifference curve with good (i, t) measured in abscissa and good $(i, t+1)$ in ordinate, and express its slope as $-(1+\rho_{it})$; then ρ_{it} is the (one period) **marginal rate of time preference** for good (i, t); if positive, the consumer wants more than one extra small unit of good $(i, t+1)$, and precisely $(1+\rho_{it})$ small units, in exchange for one less small unit of good (i, t). For specific goods, ρ_{it} can be positive or negative depending on many things; if $\rho_{it} > 0$ for the generality of goods, the consumer is said to exhibit *marginal impatience*. It is often assumed in macroeconomic models that intertemporal utility is the sum of discounted subutilities or 'felicities' of unchanging functional form, $U = \sum_{t=0}^{T} \delta^t u(x_t)$ where $u(\cdot)$ is strictly concave, x_t is consumption in period t, treated as a single homogeneous good, and $\delta < 1$. Then the intertemporal marginal rate of substitution $-\delta^{-1} u'(x_t)/u'(x_{t+1})$ is certainly in absolute value greater than one, that is, the consumer exhibits marginal impatience, as long as $x_t \leq x_{t+1}$.

When optimizing utility, apart from corner solutions the consumer chooses a point of tangency between indifference curve and budget line restricted to two goods; if the goods are (i, t) and $(i, t+1)$ this means $p_{it}/p_{i,t+1} = 1 + \rho_{it}$. Thus in equilibrium, for interior solutions of the consumer problem, it is $r_{it} = \rho_{it}$.

Exercise: Prepare an oral explanation and proof of this equality.

8.6 Production

Now let us see how the treatment of production in intertemporal equilibria can be formulated so as to make it formally identical to the one of the non-capitalistic model (A-B-C-D) of ▶ Chap. 5. To keep things simple assume no joint production, and constant returns to scale; in the discussion below all production processes last one period (inputs applied in period t produce their output at date $t+1$) and all capital goods are circulating capital goods which disappear in a single production cycle. The formalization of production functions is the same as in ▶ Chap. 5 with the sole added condition that inputs must precede outputs by one period.

The usual assumption that, in real economies, wages and rents are paid *after* the factor services have been utilized suggests that the rentals of these factors utilized in period t (factors whose *endowments* have date t as time index) would be paid at date $t+1$ if paid spot rather than at date 0, so if paid in some physical good they would be paid with a good dated $t+1$. Accordingly, factor *rental* $v_{i,t+1}$

8.6 · Production

is the discounted price at date 0 of the undiscounted payment at date $t+1$ of the services of factor i utilized during period t. For a circulating capital good of date t, in *undiscounted* terms one can suppose either that the firm buys it at date t paying a spot price P, or that the firm borrows the capital good and at the end of the period, i.e. at date $t+1$, the firm pays for it the spot sum $P(1+i)$ where i is the opportune rate of interest. In terms of date-0 equilibrium discounted prices, the two payments coincide, because the rate of interest is also the rate of discount, $P(1+i)$ is worth P when discounted to date t, so the date-0 value of date t spot price P and of date-$(t+1)$ spot price $P(1+i)$ is the same. Hence for a circulating capital good (j, t) we have that $p_{jt} = v_{j,t+1}$.

It is opportune to distinguish the factor services utilized by firms in the intertemporal economy into two categories:

- services of 'original' or 'non-produced' factors, which include both services of labour(s) or land(s) distinguished by the period of delivery of the service, and services of the capital goods already existing at date 0, which are treated as original factors, analogous to natural exhaustible resources, because how and why they were produced is no longer important;
- services of capital goods produced inside the equilibrium.

The endowments of factors in the first category are *data* that economic choices cannot modify[8]; they have the same role as the given endowments of labour and land of the non-capitalistic equilibrium. They are the factors that appear in the reinterpreted equations (C) and (D).

The services of the second category, supplied by capital goods produced inside the intertemporal equilibrium, can be made to disappear from the equilibrium equations by imagining all production of 'final' (i.e. consumption) goods to be performed by vertically integrated firms that produce internally, as intermediate non-marketed inputs, all the intermediate capital goods needed for their final output, and purchase only services of non-produced factors, including those of date-0 endowments of capital goods. An example will clarify.

Suppose that the production of bread coming out at date 3 requires flour and labour of date 2; that the production of flour of date 2 requires corn and labour of date 1; and that the production of corn of date 1 requires corn and labour of date 0 (for simplicity I neglect land). Labour of dates 0, 1, 2 and corn of date 0 are 'original' factors. Imagine the firm producing bread of date 3 to be completely vertically integrated, it internally produces and consumes the date-1 corn and date-2 flour it needs. Given the rentals of labour and the price of date-0 corn, this firm will produce date-1 corn and date-2 flour in exactly the same way as non-vertically integrated firms because (the same technical knowledge being accessible to all in a competitive economy) cost minimization will bring to the same technical

---

8 Actually how many children to have is largely a choice, so labour supply should be considered endogenous to an extent, and the more so the longer the time span covered by the intertemporal equilibrium. But the influence of economic variables on population growth is best studied separately, so here labour endowment will be assumed given in each period (not necessarily constant).

choices. Then the price of bread produced by the vertically integrated firm, and equal in competitive conditions to its minimum average cost, is the same as if the bread producer bought date-2 flour from other firms which bought date-1 corn from other firms: competition will impose that date-1 corn and date-2 flour are sold at prices equal to their minimum average cost, therefore, the bread producer has the same average cost whether internally producing date-1 corn and date-2 flour, or buying them from other competitive firms. Assuming relative factor prices determine cost-minimizing technical choices uniquely, once the rentals of labour of dates 0, 1 and 2 and the price of date-0 corn are given, the quantities of date-0 corn and date-0 labour, and of date-1 and date-2 labour, employed per unit of bread by the vertically integrated bread producer are the same as when date-1 corn and date-2 flour are produced in separate industries. Then bread can be considered produced by the production function of the vertically integrated producer, with as inputs only date-0 corn, and labour of dates 0, 1 and 2, even when in fact there are separate industries producing date-1 corn and date-2 flour.

The same reasoning can be applied to all produced goods of dates from 2 onwards that utilize capital goods produced inside the equilibrium's periods: these capital goods can be made not to appear at all in the equilibrium equations by imagining that the final goods are produced by completely vertically integrated firms which hire as inputs only 'original' factors. Then in the equations of intertemporal equilibrium the only outputs are consumption goods, and the only inputs are the services of 'original' factors whose endowments are data: the formal analogy becomes perfect with the non-capitalistic economy of equations (A-B-C-D) of ▶ Chap. 5.

Having established this result, one is free to avoid performing the vertical integration and to let the intermediate capital goods appear explicitly with their costs of production and their market prices. For simplicity I admit only circulating capital goods as intermediate goods. The list of goods becomes longer if these goods did not previously appear as consumption goods (sugar, for example, did); their price is determined by minimum average cost of production as for all produced goods; the inputs as well as the outputs of netputs, if one adopts the netput notation, now include produced capital goods too. The reader at this point should go back to ▶ Sect. 6.25 and Proposition 6.10 and should make sure that the necessary and sufficient conditions for equilibrium there specified continue to hold for the intertemporal reinterpretation with explicit intermediate goods. What changes in conditions (i) and (ii) in Proposition 6.10? In particular, if $\mathbf{y}$ is the equilibrium aggregate netput vector appearing in condition (i) when all firms are completely vertically integrated, how will it be altered by making the intermediate inputs be produced and sold by separate firms? will the element of $\mathbf{y}$ corresponding to sugar change? what will be the value of the element of the new $\mathbf{y}$ referring to an intermediate good not demanded as consumption good and therefore not appearing in the old $\mathbf{y}$? and if now the new price vector π includes the prices of intermediate goods absent from the old π, what will be the equilibrium partial derivative of $\mathbf{z}(\pi)$ relative to these prices?

8.7 The Reinterpretation Should not Hide a Difference

But the possibility to reinterpret the equations of an intertemporal equilibrium over a finite number of periods as equations of a non-capitalistic model and vice-versa, *must not hide a fundamental difference.*

The non-capitalistic model with only labour(s) and land(s) as factors aims at describing the normal, average result of the working (as conceived by the marginal approach) of competitive markets over a rather long period with unchanged data, hence, at determining a long-period equilibrium describing constant flows of quantities per time unit, with no dating of commodities; and it can have this aim because it has data that are sufficiently persistent and independent of disequilibrium events as to allow conceiving the equilibrium as unchanged during a repetition of disequilibrium productions and exchanges, and capable therefore (if stable) of having the role of centre of gravitation for market prices and quantities.

This is no longer true for the intertemporal reinterpretation that makes room for the presence of capital goods, because the intertemporal equilibrium describes a path of dated quantities and prices which is strictly dependent on a utilization and production of capital goods in each period perfectly corresponding to the one indicated by the path. Any deviation from the path in one of its periods causes the quantities of capital goods at the end of that period to be different from those indicated by the path, and then the path cannot be followed any more; *it has no persistence*, it is destroyed by disequilibrium productions, so it cannot be a centre of gravitation of trial-and-error disequilibrium productions and prices. This is an important point, so let me repeat it referring it, for concreteness, to the initial period of the path. Suppose the equilibrium path starts at date zero but, because there is no auctioneer, the economy does not behave in period zero as the path indicates; then at date 1 the economy has different capital endowments from those the equilibrium path predicted for date 1, so to continue along the original equilibrium path is impossible. Equilibrium theory can only say that on the basis of this different date-1 capital endowment vector, a new intertemporal-equilibrium path from date 1 onwards exists; but since there is no auctioneer, again the economy will not behave in period 1 as this new path would require, so at date 2 the economy will have capital endowments which, depending on two rounds of disequilibrium actions, can be very different from those predicted for date 2 by the original equilibrium path.[9] The only way one could defend the original path

---

9 The deviations can concern not only the composition of the capital endowment but also its average growth rate, which might be for many years considerably different from the one corresponding to the investment of full-employment savings; Japan's nearly zero growth rate in the 1990s, for example, greatly underutilized its output potential. In ▶ Chap. 12 it will be argued that durable overutilization of productive capacity is also a definite possibility.

616   Chapter 8 · Intertemporal Equilibrium, Temporary Equilibrium

as indicative of the average behaviour of the economy would be by arguing that there are forces tending to limit and to compensate the deviations of the vector of capital endowments from its original equilibrium path; but the theory is only capable of determining equilibrium paths, it has nothing to say on disequilibrium when it is not an auctioneer-guided tâtonnement, so it offers no reason to believe that the disequilibrium deviations of capital endowments from the original equilibrium path are not cumulative. So the intertemporal-equilibrium path cannot be viewed as a centre of gravitation of disequilibrium quantities and prices, because it is shifted by disequilibrium itself. This consequence (briefly noted already at the end of ▶ Sect. 7.13) of the Walrasian specification of the capital endowment as a given vector will be further explored below, in ▶ Sect. 8.15.

8.8 Different Own Rates of Interest and Effective Uniformity of Rates of Return

In an intertemporal equilibrium, the relative price of two goods of the same date does not in general remain the same from one date to another; in symbols, generally

$$p_{it}/p_{jt} \neq p_{i,t+1}/p_{j,t+1}. \tag{8.3}$$

The reason is that the arbitrary initial composition of the endowment of capital goods will be in general quickly altered. As a result, equilibrium relative factor rentals and costs of production of products will be changing over time.

But $p_{it}/p_{jt} \neq p_{i,t+1}/p_{j,t+1}$ implies $p_{it}/p_{i,t+1} \neq p_{jt}/p_{j,t+1}$, i.e. the change over time in equilibrium relative prices implies that in general *own rates of interest are not equal*; we obtain that $p_{i,t+1}/p_{j,t+1} > p_{it}/p_{jt}$ implies $(1+r_{it}) < (1+r_{jt})$; that is, in equilibrium *if from a period to the next a good rises in price relative to a second good, the own rate of interest of the first good is lower than for the second good*.

The reason is that there must be no **arbitrage opportunity**: it must be equally convenient to obtain a good $(i, t+1)$ by lending some amount of good (i, t), or by exchanging good (i, t) with good (j, t), lending the latter against good $(j, t+1)$, and then exchanging it against good $(i, t+1)$. So suppose that at date t good (i, t) and good (j, t) have the same value, 1 for both, and that $r_{it} = 10\%$; and suppose that from t to $t+1$ good i rises 20% in price relative to good j, i.e. $p_{i,t+1}/p_{j,t+1} = 1.2$; then it must be $r_{jt} = 32\%$, because at date $t+1$ the quantity of good j of the same value as 1.1 units of good i is 1.32 units. In equilibrium all possible indirect exchanges must bring to the same result.

When there are differences in own rates of interest, then the *real* rate of interest depends on the choice of numéraire. The *money* rate of interest indicates how much more money one obtains by lending money for one period; the *real* rate of interest indicates how much more purchasing power in terms of the good (or basket of goods) chosen as numéraire one obtains by lending purchasing power (measured in terms of numéraire) for one period. Suppose relative prices are constant from one period to the next; then the real rate of interest is the same which-

8.8 · Different Own Rates of Interest and Effective Uniformity of Rates of Return

ever the good chosen to measure purchasing power; the money rate of interest will coincide with the real rate of interest if the rate of inflation is zero. If relative prices are not constant, the real rate of interest depends on the good chosen to measure purchasing power, and coincides with the own rate of interest of that good as I proceed to show.

Assume that, from one period to the next, the money price of corn remains unchanged at 100, while the money price of iron rises from 100 to 120, and that the money rate of interest is 20%. Lending the 100 money units corresponding to the value, in the first period, of 1 unit of corn or of one unit of iron yields 120 units of money next period, which means 20% more purchasing power in terms of corn (the own corn rate of interest is 20%), but 0% more purchasing power in terms of iron (the own iron rate of interest is zero); the real rate of interest will depend on which good (or basket of goods) is chosen as measure of purchasing power, and will be 20% in terms of corn, zero in terms of iron. In intertemporal equilibria, the real rate of interest is determined once one chooses the numéraire: the real rate of interest one obtains on a loan is the own rate of interest of the numéraire, whatever the good one is actually lending and the good one is obtaining in exchange the following period. Thus in the example just given, suppose corn is the numéraire: by lending one unit of corn one obtains 20% more corn, by lending one unit of iron one obtains one unit of iron the next period, but the relative price of iron has risen 20% relative to corn so now the one unit of iron is worth 1.2 units of corn: *in terms of corn* one obtains 20% more purchasing power even by lending iron against iron; with corn as numéraire, the real rate of interest is 20%. Now choose iron as numéraire: lending iron against iron one obtains a zero rate of interest, lending one unit of corn one obtains 20% more corn, but the price of corn decreases by 20% relative to the price of iron, so in terms of purchasing power measured in iron to lend corn against corn yields a zero real rate of interest.

The relevance of all this is that differences in *equilibrium* own rates of interest do *not* mean that loans in different goods are differently convenient. In the previous example, to lend corn against 20% more of it the next period, or to lend iron against the same quantity of it the next period, are equally convenient: *in equilibrium the difference between two own rates of interest reflects and compensates the change in the relative price of the two goods.* This is relevant for productive investments too: in the above equilibrium price structure, to invest one's savings into a firm that produces corn by using corn as sole input, or into a firm that produces iron with iron as the sole input, is equally convenient even if the first firm obtains 20% more corn than it employed, while the second obtains the same amount of iron as it employed (in this case the second firm performs simply a storage operation; but the principle is valid in general). The numerical magnitude of the rate of return depends on the choice of numéraire, but this does not disturb the *equal convenience* of all employments of savings in an intertemporal equilibrium, and this finds expression in the equality of real rates of interest once one has chosen a numéraire. One can say then that in an intertemporal equilibrium there is an *effective* uniformity of rates of return on all employments of savings, for investment as well as for personal loans (Garegnani 2000). Only the numerical expres-

618 Chapter 8 · Intertemporal Equilibrium, Temporary Equilibrium

sion of this *uniform effective rate of return*, **UERR**, depends on the choice of numéraire.

8.9 Uniform Effective Rate of Return Versus Long-Period Uniform Rate of Profit

But then, is there no difference between an intertemporal equilibrium and long-period analysis? The distinguishing characteristic of long-period analysis was said to be, the need to leave the composition of capital to be determined endogenously, otherwise, a uniform rate of profits, or uniform rate of return in all investments, was not obtainable. But haven't we obtained this uniformity here too, in spite of the given initial composition of the capital endowment?

No. The uniform rate of profits of long-period analyses (classical as well as traditional marginalist) is not simply a UERR but a **UERRSP**, *uniform effective rate of return on supply price*, i.e. on the minimum average cost of production of capital goods. This means an additional condition relative to UERR. The additional condition is: the value of capital goods, obtained by *capitalization* of their future rentals (i.e. by discounting these and summing them up), and called their *demand price* because it is the maximum price at which one is ready to buy them, must be equal to their supply price or cost of production.[10]

In an intertemporal equilibrium where at date 0 there are given initial endowments of capital goods, at date 1 and usually also for a number of subsequent periods (in other words as long as the endowments of some capital goods remain largely exogenous) this additional condition does not generally obtain. If for example the given initial endowment of bricks (circulating capital) is so great that the gross marginal product of bricks is zero and is expected to remain zero for some periods because demand absorbs only a small part of this stock every period, then it is not convenient to produce bricks, it is more convenient to use already existing bricks until the decrease in the stock of bricks assures a rental from their use that covers their cost of production. In this case the demand price of bricks at date 1 is less than the supply price of bricks and they are not produced, there isn't UERRSP, although the equilibrium price of existing bricks ensures UERR. UERRSP needs that all capital goods are produced (except the obsolete ones that only survive because durable and not totally useless yet). The traditional expression 'uniform rate of profits' as a distinguishing characteristic of long-period positions must be intended as *on supply price*. This uniform rate of profits, or of return, does need that the existing quantities of capital goods be not given but rather adapted to the demand for them. A numerical example of intertemporal equilibrium without UERRSP is provided in the online Appendix 1 on the chapter's website on SpringerLink.

---

10 The distinction between UERR and UERRSP is due to Garegnani (2003).

The bricks at date 0 were not produced inside the equilibrium and therefore do not have a cost of production, which is why the above discussion concentrated on whether UERRSP is satisfied at date 1 (and subsequent dates). However, it is possible to impute to date-0 capital goods a cost of production, by imagining them produced with the same production methods and costs of inputs as when produced at date 1; when production periods are very short this is acceptable, and one can then compare supply price[11] and demand price; in general, if UERRSP does not obtain at date 1 it does not obtain at date 0 either.

The uniform effective rate of return on investment in an intertemporal equilibrium is on the *demand* prices of capital goods, which, for the capital goods already existing at the initial date, can be lower *or higher* than their costs of production.

The demand price of a capital good at date 0 can also be *higher* than its imputed cost of production (its supply cannot be increased); and the same can be true for some subsequent dates if the time required to produce that capital good is several periods. From the moment when it is possible to obtain the good by production processes started within the equilibrium's periods, the demand price of a capital good cannot be higher than its cost of production; it can be lower, see the bricks example, or consider capital goods rendered obsolete by technical progress; then the capital good will not be produced.

8.10 UERRSP and URRSP

One last observation is necessary on the issue. In earlier chapters, in the formulation of the notion of long-period positions and of neoclassical long-period equilibria, changes of relative prices over time were neglected (following the practice of both classical and traditional neoclassical authors), because absent or very slow once the composition of capital is given time to adapt to UERRSP. This is why in those chapters the acronym was URRSP; this stands for a uniform rate of return on supply price *in a situation of constant (or practically constant) relative prices*; the UERRSP condition admits changes of relative prices over time, therefore it is more general, it shows that one can define an equal convenience in the purchase of capital goods at their supply price even in a situation of (perfectly forecasted) non-constant relative prices. This generalization was useful in order to clarify the fundamental difference from neo-Walrasian equilibria. But this generalization appears of very limited usefulness beyond this specific purpose, precisely because once the composition of capital has adjusted to the firms' normal

---

11 Some date-0 capital goods may be also utilizable as consumption goods, for example, sugar. For them a supply price can be determined as the price at which consumers are ready to let (some part of the endowment of) the good be utilized by firms. To minimize complications I will neglect this possibility and assume that date-0 capital goods have no use as consumption goods and are entirely supplied to firms.

620   Chapter 8 · Intertemporal Equilibrium, Temporary Equilibrium

demands so as to yield UERRSP, relative prices are going to change only very slowly for endogenous reasons,[12] for example, because accumulation is extending cultivation to less fertile lands, or (in the marginal approach) because the capital stock grows faster than labour supply. It is highly doubtful that a uniformity of rates of return that takes such slow changes into account can be a better guide to average prices than the traditional uniformity based on constant relative prices; these slow changes are anyway to a considerable extent unpredictable, even the rise in urban estate prices sometimes stops and reverts its tendency. In conclusion, to assume unchanging relative prices appears the best assumption for the purposes for which a long-period position is useful; comparative statics of long-period positions in each one of which prices are assumed constant will be the tool to study the effects of significant changes in the data determining normal, average relative prices.

8.11 Radner Sequential Equilibria (Without Uncertainty)

For intertemporal equilibria over a finite number of periods, it would be ridiculous to assume that agents expect the economy to end in only a few years' time; the last period T must be far into the future. But then the equilibrium must extend to future periods where demands and supplies will also come from yet-to-be-born consumers, so the assumption of complete markets in futures requires that *yet-to-be-born consumers be present at the initial date* to exchange promises of delivery for the dates in which they will demand goods and will supply factor services. Which is impossible.

So it is impossible to assume complete futures markets. The usual way to surmount this difficulty is via a *reinterpretation* of the equilibrium—formally unchanged—as describing, not an economy in which at the initial date there are complete futures markets, but rather an economy where, at each date, there are only spot markets for goods of that date, plus a limited number of markets in futures, interpretable as markets where borrowers and lender can meet and transfer purchasing power across periods via purchase and sale of bonds that promise to deliver a good, e.g. gold, at a future date. At each date the gold bonds coming due are honoured, and markets re-open for spot transactions of goods of that date, and for new futures contracts in gold. The reinterpretation is completed by adding a fundamental assumption: that at the initial date there is **perfect foresight** of the spot prices and of the own rates of interest of gold that will rule at each subsequent date up to date t.

---

12 Exogenous changes, for example, due to technical progress, will have to be studied via comparative statics, assuming a gravitation to the new normal position.

8.11 · Radner Sequential Equilibria (Without Uncertainty)

The equilibrium is then called *sequential*, because it consists of a sequence of (correctly forecasted) one-period equilibria, with spot markets opening at the beginning of each period.[13]

In such a sequential economy, let gold be the only good for which at date 0 there are complete futures markets; in these markets agents buy and sell bonds promising delivery of gold at future dates, for example, *Arrow real securities*. An Arrow real security for date t promises delivery of 1 unit of gold at future date t. Suppose that at date 0 a consumer formulates a consumption plan as follows: for all dates except date t and date $t+1$, there is equality between her income of the date (i.e. the value of the endowments of that date) and the value of that date's consumption bundle; for date t the discounted value of planned consumption is less than the discounted value of that period's income (i.e. the consumer plans to save in that period), and for date $t+1$ the consumer plans to dissave (spend more than that period's income) for an equal discounted value. This consumer wants to transfer purchasing power from date t to date $t+1$. She can do it by selling (at date 0) Arrow real securities for date t in the amount that promises delivery of a quantity A of gold at date t whose discounted value equals that of her date t intended savings, and by buying Arrow real securities that promise delivery at date $t+1$ of a quantity B of gold for the same discounted value. The consumer need not have the quantity A of gold in her date t endowment. When date t arrives, having correctly predicted date t spot prices the consumer finds she has an excess of date t income over her planned purchases, that allows her to buy the quantity A of gold on the gold spot market and honour the securities she sold at date 0, and when date $t+1$ arrives she receives the quantity B of gold and by selling it she obtains the desired excess of purchasing power over her income at that date. In this way she can attain the same consumption plan as she would be able to attain if there were complete futures markets and she could directly use at date 0 her discounted date t excess of income over consumption to buy consumption goods of date $t+1$.

The bonds might even be promises to deliver (fiat) *money* if existence of the latter is admitted: then perfect foresight must mean correct foresight of future *money* prices too, and then there is no difference in the capacity to transfer wealth across dates relative to 'real' bonds that promise delivery of physical commodities. An *Arrow financial security*, also called simply an Arrow security, for date t is a bond that promises delivery of one unit of money at date t.[14] To purchase an Arrow security for date t means to lend money to the seller of the security, who will repay one unit of money at date t. With correctly forecasted money prices, complete markets in Arrow securities will allow consumers to reach the same consumption plans as with complete futures markets.

---

13 To contrast them better with sequential markets, complete futures markets existing at the initial moment have been described by Kreps (2013) with the nice expression 'all-markets-at-once'.

14 Here we are neglecting uncertainty; in an economy with uncertainty, an Arrow *contingent* financial security is a promise to deliver one unit of money at date t if and only if some specified event (ascertainable only when date t arrives) occurs. See ▶ Chap. 9, Sect. 9.6.

622   Chapter 8 · Intertemporal Equilibrium, Temporary Equilibrium

The same result can be achieved even if at each date of the sequential economy only *one-period Arrow financial securities*, i.e. bonds that promise one unit of money at the next date, are available. The sole difference is that a consumer, who wants to transfer purchasing power from period t to period $t+h$ with $h>1$, will wait for date t, will then buy one-period Arrow securities, at date $t+1$ will use the repayment of the securities to buy new Arrow securities, and will then renew the securities in subsequent periods up to period $t+h-1$, finally spending their value at date $t+h$. Perfect foresight means that her plans will not be frustrated by spot money prices at t, $t+1$, ... different from the ones she expected to rule when at date 0 she formed her consumption plan for the entire sequence of periods.

In the sequential economy thus described, futures markets are not complete but it is possible to achieve the same consumption and production plans as in the economy with complete futures markets. The resulting notion of sequential competitive equilibrium with perfect foresight (a sequence of one-period equilibria) is called an *equilibrium of plans, prices and price expectations, EPPPE*, or a *Radner equilibrium* without uncertainty, and it can be rigorously proved that in it agents make the same consumption (and production) choices as with complete futures markets at the initial date. This equivalence between Arrow–Debreu equilibria and Radner equilibria[15] allows the reinterpretation of intertemporal equilibria as sequential equilibria with perfect foresight.

8.12 Existence, Uniqueness, Stability

Once vertical integration of firms is performed, and assuming a neat separability of factors from consumption goods and absence of joint production, the equilibrium conditions of the finite-periods intertemporal-equilibrium model are the same equations (A), (B), (C), (D) as for the economy of ▶ Chap. 5; therefore the conclusion of the analysis of that chapter, that everything depends on factor rentals, and that once these are given all prices and quantities of produced goods as well as all supplies and demands for factors are determined, remains valid for the intertemporal economy, with the sole need to refer the term 'factors' only to the 'original' factors: labours and lands of the several periods, and *initial* capital goods endowments.[16]

---

15   The intuition behind the equivalence result appears so clear that I do not find it necessary to provide a more formal complete proof; but see Exercises 2 and 6; and Blad and Keiding (1990, ▶ Chap. 12) or Mas-Colell et al. (1995, pp. 695–8).

16   Of course, this is under an assumption that optimal production methods at the given factor prices are uniquely determined; and leaving joint production aside. Joint production adds no additional difficulty on existence of the non-capitalistic general equilibrium model; it can introduce additional causes of multiple and unstable equilibria, but these only marginally add to an already sombre situation, so it does not seem worthwhile to discuss them.

8.12 · Existence, Uniqueness, Stability

Since the equilibrium equations are the same, the conclusions on existence and uniqueness, and also on tâtonnement stability if the tâtonnement is so structured as to mimic that of the atemporal non-capitalistic economy, are the same too.[17] For existence of an equilibrium what is necessary is the continuity of excess demands and some assumption to surmount the minimum-income and the survival problems; among differentiable economies, regular economies are the generic case and thus the number of equilibria is generically finite; the Sonnenschein–Mantel–Debreu results remain valid; quasi-uniqueness is guaranteed by the assumption that the consumers' market excess demands obey the Weak Axiom of Revealed Preferences, WAM; tâtonnement stability is guaranteed by the same assumption, as long as one assumes a 'factor tâtonnement', that is, that at each stage of the tâtonnement, productions adapt to quantities demanded as assumed in equations (B), and that the same adaptation of productions to quantities demanded happens for the intermediate goods that do not explicitly appear in the formalization owing to the treatment of firms as vertically integrated. In this way the only markets on which there can be disequilibrium are the markets for 'original' factors. Hence the name 'factor tâtonnement' (due to Mandler 2005), whose stability under WAM was proved in ▶ Chap. 6; its reinterpretation for an intertemporal model is explained in the online Appendix to the present chapter.

8.13 Really Only a Reinterpretation? Some First Problems

The reinterpretation of the equations of the non-capitalistic equilibrium as describing an intertemporal equilibrium raises several problems due to the disappearance of the long-period nature of the equilibrium.

One problem is the neglect of default on promises, much less easy to justify in intertemporal equilibria than in long-period equilibria, as pointed out in ▶ Sect. 4.2.

A second problem is that the economy has a past, and it seems extreme to assume that there were no possibilities of debts and credits, or more generally of contracts in futures, in the periods preceding date 0. But then the endowments of agents at date 0 will include promises to be now honoured of repayment of debts or delivery of goods. This complication is neglected here for simplicity

---

17 A dissenting opinion has been expressed by Garegnani (1990, 2000, 2003, 2005a, b) who has argued that the presence of capitalistic production must necessarily make a difference relative to the non-capitalistic economy on uniqueness, stability and likelihood of implausible equilibria with zero wages: he has insisted that phenomena analogous to re-switching and reverse capital deepening cannot but be present in intertemporal equilibria too. His examples in (2000, 2003) have been found unpersuasive, but the results on convergence of relative prices to long-period prices as t increases in infinite-horizon intertemporal equilibria (Duménil and Lévy 1985; Dana et al. 1989a, b) suggest that the different approach Garegnani sketches in (1990, p. 70) might in the end prove him right. The issue remains open; see Petri (2011a).

624   **Chapter 8** · Intertemporal Equilibrium, Temporary Equilibrium

and following the general practice—budget constraints would otherwise be different from those of the non-capitalistic economy—but one must be aware of the problem one would otherwise have to face. If complete futures markets were not available nor was the future correctly forecasted in the periods before date 0, a danger arises of **bankruptcy** at date 0 of the agents who overestimated their capacity to honour their promises, and bankruptcy can create discontinuities of excess demand: depending on prices at date 0 and later, an agent may or may not go bankrupt; at the price at which the agent, for example, the single owner of a firm, goes bankrupt the firm disappears, the owner's properties pass to the creditors, these have different utility functions, the demands both of the bankrupted firm/owner and of the creditors undergo discontinuous jumps; a danger arises of non-existence of equilibrium.[18] Furthermore, since there were neither complete markets nor correct foresight in the past, what right is there to assume them at date zero? The only way to avoid these possibilities is to assume that complete futures markets or perfect foresight existed in the past, so the equilibrium established at date 0 is simply the continuation of an intertemporal equilibrium established earlier. *The theory seems to imply that either the economy was always continuously in intertemporal equilibrium, which is patently unrealistic, or we have no right to assume complete markets or perfect foresight at date 0*, which means the intertemporal equilibrium cannot possibly describe how the economy behaves at date 0; it can at most be some sort of ideal benchmark, something like 'oh how nice if the world were like that', but would it be of any use to explain how the economy really works?

A third problem is **inheritance**. The farther away the horizon (and we saw that it must be far away), the more the equilibrium will include bequests.[19] This could be neglected in the determination of long-period equilibria, because what was relevant there was the average aggregate demands and supplies of consumers, presumably only very slowly altered by deaths, births and bequests. On the contrary, intertemporal equilibria must determine the details of the behaviour of each agent in each period, and therefore cannot neglect bequests. The endowments of some consumers at some future date *are not given*, and they depend on decisions of 'earlier' consumers, a clear analytical difference from the non-capitalistic atemporal model. A frequently adopted solution consists of assuming that consumers are '**dynasties**': each household decides at date 0 for its offsprings too (perfect foresight of the latter's preferences is implied), so consumers are only those present at date 0, and it is as if they remained alive for all the equilibrium's periods; bequests are implicitly determined via utility maximization by each 'dynasty'. But this solution seems unacceptable: the children of one household will marry chil-

---

18 A similar problem arises in temporary equilibrium theory and will deserve comments in ▶ Sect. 8.26.

19 As in the equilibria of this chapter there is no uncertainty, consumers know when they will die, possibly depending on their choices. In OLG models it is often assumed that there are no bequests, but in the real world bequests exist and are very important.

8.13 · Really Only a Reinterpretation? Some First Problems

dren of other households, therefore, to which 'dynasty' will *their* children belong? Also, the living standard a child will enjoy after marriage will depend on the bequest to the spouse; then the bequest decision of the parents of a child can depend on how much the child's spouse inherits. We obtain what in game theory is called a *hawk-dove game* (see ▶ Chap. 11): if I let the parents of my son-in-law know that I am going to leave a very small bequest to my daughter, I may induce them to increase their bequest; but the same considerations hold for the parents of my son-in-law, we have a game with unclear solution,[20] what is clear is that utility maximization does not solve the issue. So the feudal idea of 'dynasties' makes no sense, and standard intertemporal utility maximization appears unable to determine bequests because price taking is not legitimate in this case.

8.14 Money

A fourth problem arises in connection with money.

As a preliminary, we must understand why in the equilibria illustrated in ▶ Chaps. 3–7 money (in the sense of fiat money, a token universally accepted as means of payment and desired for that use, not for an intrinsic utility of the physical substance of which it is made) did not appear at all. This was not due to an assumption that the economy was not using money. Traditional neoclassical authors took it as obvious that the economy uses money, but argued that the gravitation of relative prices and produced quantities towards a (long-period) equilibrium goes together with a gravitation of the money price level and of the distribution of money among agents towards an equilibrium. The normal price level was determined by the quantity theory of money, expressed, e.g. by a Fisherine equation $MV = PT$.[21] The 'real' part of the overall equilibrium, that is, the normal quantities and normal relative prices determined by the long-period equilibrium equations, *implicitly assumed* an equilibrium price level and an

---

20 ▶ Chapter 11 will show that this type of games has two Nash equilibria in pure strategies, hence, no clear solution; a mixed strategy makes no sense in this case, the threat of leaving a small bequest to induce the other parents to increase their bequest requires making one's choice known.

21 See ▶ Sect. 3.6 for the basic idea. The reader will have to turn to other sources for more on the quantity theory of money. Anyway M is the given quantity of (legal or base) money, V its *velocity of circulation* (the average number of times each unit of money changes hands in a period, because used for payments), P an index of the price level, T is not the horizon but an index of the volume of real transactions effected in the time period (often proxied by real GDP). M, V, T are given: M is determined by the quantity of gold, or by the Central Bank; V is determined by efficiency, the economy's structure, the desire for precautionary hoards; T is determined by the level of aggregate output (the full-employment level, in the marginal approach). If the average 'demand for money', i.e. average desired holding of money balances for transaction purposes, PT/V, is less than M, people hold on average more money than necessary for their transactions and will then increase expenditure, but T and V are given so the effect will be to raise P until the Fisherine equation is satisfied. Post-Keynesians deny that M, V, T can be taken as given.

equilibrium distribution of money balances among agents allowing them to carry through their desired transactions. This is why no constraint deriving from money holdings appeared in the decisions of consumers or firms: not because money was assumed absent, but because money holdings were assumed to have adapted to the needs of the agent (Petri 2004, Appendix 5A1, pp. 166–186). The analysis implicitly assumed the so-called *neoclassical dichotomy*: long-period equilibrium quantities and relative prices are independent of the quantity of money, which only determines money prices, the 'price level'. A doubling of M does not affect equilibrium quantities and relative prices, in the new equilibrium all money prices are twice what they were and that is all.

This dichotomy is no longer defensible in very-short-period analyses. The endowment of money of each economic agent at date zero can only be given, it is the amount of money the agent happens to have at that moment. Then, if money is indispensable for most exchanges, money holdings are an additional constraint on the agents' decisions. For example, if one assumes that a period is so short that it is not possible to utilize the money obtained from a sale in a period for a purchase within the same period, then in each period an agent can only purchase up to the value of the money with which she starts the period. The agent's decisions will be influenced also by her need for money balances in subsequent periods; for example an agent can decide to anticipate the sale of a good, relative to the date she would have otherwise chosen, as the only way to have enough cash for certain desired purchases.

But any attempt to take these *cash-in-advance constraints* into account in determining agents' optimal decisions encounters a serious danger of indeterminacy: how a given initial money balance constrains an agent's decisions depends on accidental elements (for example on how quickly she finds purchasers for her net supplies), on her possibility to postpone payments even only by a few hours, on her access to short-term credit, etc. Any assumption aimed at surmounting this indeterminacy would be largely arbitrary.

Now assume money is not indispensable for exchanges. This is a rather inevitable assumption once the need to assume that the intertemporal equilibrium is established instantaneously by the auctioneer-guided tâtonnement is interiorized (remember that time-consuming adjustments would take the economy to a date beyond date 0, and with an indeterminate vector of capital endowments, given the unpredictability of the accidents of disequilibrium). There seems to be no need for something functioning as means of exchange in the tâtonnement picture: agents simply announce their intentions at each round, and when equilibrium is reached they start honouring their promises.[22] But it is not only that money seems

---

22 Evidently—however, this is never made clear to students—the auctioneer also operates as a clearing house, carrying out the task of allocating the total equilibrium supply of each good among its several demanders: the tâtonnement does not ask agents to specify with whom they intend to interact, only their excess demands must be communicated to the auctioneer.

superfluous: at least for equilibria covering a finite number of periods, there is just no room for money, a money with positive exchange value cannot exist. By assumption the fiat money good has no intrinsic utility, then at the last date T no one will want to remain with a positive amount of it since there is no subsequent date in which to utilize it for purchases; as a result, at date T everybody will try to exchange the money she owns against goods, but no one will accept it, and the value of money will fall to zero; but then the value of money will also fall to zero at date $T-1$, because all agents, knowing that money will have value zero the next period, will want to get rid of all their money before the last date arrives, but no one will accept it; then the same fall of the value of money to zero will happen in the preceding period, and so on, and money will have value zero in all periods including the initial one.

In conclusion, intertemporal equilibria over a finite number of periods have great difficulty with making room for fiat money. If for some reason money is indispensable for exchanges and determines cash-in-advance constraints, this causes indeterminacy; if money is not indispensable for exchanges, this causes a zero value of money.

One thing we learn from this is that fiat money has positive value because it is believed it will keep having positive value in the future. The problem that its value is necessarily zero in the final period T can be surmounted through the extension of equilibrium to cover an infinite number of future periods. But this extension, besides being hardly conceivable (this will be discussed later), does not avoid the other difficulty, the indeterminacy of cash-in-advance constraints.

8.15 Impermanence Problem, Price-Change Problem, Substitutability Problem

The four problems illustrated in the previous two sections indicate that the equations of the non-capitalistic equilibrium would need modification in order to fit an intertemporal equilibrium. But assuming ways can be found to surmount these problems, one is faced with three more serious problems, which can be called problems of method because due to the abandonment of the traditional method of long-period positions, and concern the capacity of neo-Walrasian equilibria (intertemporal as well as temporary) to give indications on the behaviour of actual economies.

We owe to Pierangelo Garegnani (1976, 1990) clarity on these problems. All three have their root in the treatment of the vector of initial endowments of capital goods as given.[23] They will be first synthetically described, and then some further considerations will expand on their significance.

---

23 The main reference here is pp. 49–58 of P. Garegnani, 'Quantity of capital' (1990). This paper was to be an entry in *The New Palgrave* 1st ed. (1987) but was not completed in time.

628   Chapter 8 · Intertemporal Equilibrium, Temporary Equilibrium

1. *Impermanence problem*. Some of the data determining the equilibrium (endowments of the several capital goods and also, in temporary equilibria, expectation functions) lack persistence, being susceptible of radical modification during disequilibrium; the auctioneer is only a fairy tale; therefore the equilibrium itself can significantly change during disequilibrium adjustments, losing the capacity to indicate the average emerging from a repetition of transactions correcting or compensating the deviations from equilibrium. Then, since the theory is silent on what happens in disequilibrium and therefore offers no reason to exclude a cumulation of deviations of the actual path traced by the economy from the path traced by the original intertemporal equilibrium or sequence of temporary equilibria (even assuming this sequence does not itself suffer from indeterminacy), the path of the actual economy remains undetermined.

2. *Price-change problem*. The need to admit that equilibrium relative prices will generally change from one period to the next obliges to consider how awareness of this fact determines equilibrium decisions. Only two roads are available: intertemporal equilibria require complete futures markets or perfect foresight, obviously extremely unrealistic assumptions; temporary equilibria have to include expectation functions among the data of equilibrium and then suffer from an *indefiniteness problem* because the equilibrium of a single period as well as the path followed by a sequence of temporary equilibria come to depend upon arbitrary assumptions on unknowable initial expectations and on how these evolve over time.

3. *Substitutability problem*. In the initial periods of an intertemporal equilibrium (or in the single period of a temporary equilibrium) the composition of capital is largely given; then there is almost no substitutability among factors, because different production methods generally require different capital goods, not the same capital goods in different proportions; thus the demand for labour at least in the initial periods will be extremely inelastic and the equilibrium real wage can easily be totally implausible.

The impermanence problem was already pointed out in ▶ Sect. 8.7. It is the reason for the limitation of stability studies in general equilibrium theory to the auctioneer-guided tâtonnement, which prevents changes in the quantities of capital goods during disequilibrium adjustments. But realism requires admitting actual, time-consuming disequilibria. Then, as a highly esteemed neoclassical microeconomist has written:

》 In a real economy, however, trading, as well as production and consumption, goes on out of equilibrium … in the course of convergence to equilibrium (assuming that occurs), endowments change. In turn this changes the set of equilibria. Put more succinctly, the set of equilibria is path dependent … This path dependence makes the calculation of equilibria corresponding to the initial state of the system essentially irrelevant (Fisher, 1983, p. 14).

This is a striking admission, sufficient seriously to question the entire neo-Walrasian approach, and perhaps for this reason hardly ever quoted. Unique among mainstream economists, Fisher recognizes that disequilibrium actions not only redistribute endowments across individuals, but also change the endowments of capital goods, so that the equilibrium (or equilibria) corresponding to the initial data is 'essentially irrelevant': general equilibrium theory should try to determine the *final* equilibrium the economy will converge to, given time.

The trouble for the neoclassical approach is that, with the shift to neo-Walrasian general equilibrium theory, the traditional marginalist way to surmount the impossibility to predict the details of disequilibrium—by arguing that, through error correction or compensation, the economy's path gravitates around and towards *a persistent equilibrium defined independently of the accidents of disequilibrium*—is lost. Disequilibrium decisions cause the neo-Walrasian equilibrium itself to change, and in ways that equilibrium theory does not indicate; this renders the tendencies of the actual path of the economy impossible to establish. A theory of the average *actual* path would be needed to assess whether the intertemporal-equilibrium path gives an acceptable approximation to the behaviour of real economies, but the theory of intertemporal equilibrium does not supply it.[24]

The impossibility to conceive the equilibrium path as a centre of gravitation of disequilibrium prices and quantities also excludes the possibility to use comparative statics to analyze the effect of a change in one of the equilibrium's data; for example one cannot predict the effects of an increase in labour supply due to immigration by assuming an unchanged initial vector of capital goods since the disequilibrium caused by immigration will change that vector and in ways the theory cannot predict.

Let us come to the price-change problem. I leave for ▶ Sect. 8.29 a discussion of the form the price-change problem takes in temporary equilibria. For the determination of intertemporal equilibria, one must assume *either* complete futures markets existing already at date 0 (but one would need not-yet-born consumers present at the initial date), *or* a sequence of spot markets plus perfect price foresight.[25] An immediate criticism then is, that to arrive at *defining* the

---

24 Fisher (1983) has tried to escape the implications of his own admission by proposing a model of disequilibrium behaviour which, he argues, produces convergence to a rest point. But the model is extremely unrealistic. Besides assuming complete futures markets, a given number of firms, and no bankruptcies plus other questionable assumptions in order to avoid discontinuities, the analysis centrally rests on an assumption of *No Favourable Surprise,* that is, that during the disequilibrium process things never turn out to be better for any household or firm than she/he/it had expected. This assumption comes very close to assuming perfect foresight (Madden 1984), is patently contradicted by real-life disequilibria, and anyway leaves the final rest point amply indeterminate, not even necessarily a full-employment situation (Petri 2004, pp. 67–71). Fisher admits that the assumption is unrealistic and only a first step, but has not attempted afterwards further to explore the approach, thus implicitly admitting it is a dead end.

25 When one admits markets in contingent commodities, the perfect foresight assumption does not extend to the *probability* of occurrence of each state of nature, it holds for the spot prices that will rule once the state of nature has revealed itself. Different subjective probabilities on the occurrence of a state of nature can be admitted and influence consumers' willingness to pay for contingent commodities.

630   **Chapter 8 ·** Intertemporal Equilibrium, Temporary Equilibrium

equilibrium the theory must assume *the presence of elements with no correspondence with the real world*: neither complete futures markets, nor perfect price foresight are found in reality. Equilibrium cannot even be *defined* unless one assumes the world to be a fairy tale world radically different from the real world!

Perfect price foresight is unproblematically assumed in most recent mainstream macro-models. And yet, its absurdity should be obvious. First, one is assuming individuals to be better than the best economists at predicting equilibrium prices in situations different from the current one, for example, with a different labour supply or a different stock of capital goods; and such an assumption is certainly not made more acceptable by the fact that economists disagree on the correct theory of how prices are determined. The problem is recognized, of course, but its implications are seldom faced. For example Roy Radner, the important general equilibrium specialist, has written:

» Although it is capable of describing a richer set of institutions and behaviour than is the Arrow-Debreu model, the perfect foresight approach ... is contrary to the spirit of much of competitive market theory in that it postulates that individual traders must be able to forecast, in some sense, the equilibrium prices that will prevail ... this seems to require of the traders a capacity for imagination and computation far beyond what is realistic ... An equilibrium of plans and price expectations might be appropriate as a conceptualization of the ideal goal of indicative planning, or of a long-run steady state toward which the economy might tend in a stationary environment (Majumdar and Radner 2008, p. 444).

Radner admits in these lines[26] that, as part of a descriptive theory, the perfect foresight assumption is legitimate only for the determination of situations where relative prices *have no reason to change*, and where therefore past prices are an excellent guide to future prices. That is, situations where the composition of capital has so adjusted that prices no longer need to change. So Radner is implicitly admitting here that the perfect foresight assumption is in contradiction with the arbitrary given vector of initial capital endowments of neo-Walrasian intertemporal equilibria. Furthermore, since the sole situation in which a perfect-foresight equilibrium might reasonably describe the actual behaviour of an economy is a 'long-run steady state ... in a stationary environment', then an answer to the question, whether the economy *gravitates* towards a situation for which one could

---

26 These lines can be attributed to him alone because taken almost verbatim from Radner (1982, p. 942). Grandmont (1982, pp. 879–880) writes an extremely similar assessment of perfect foresight: 'In practice, economic agents have only a very imperfect knowledge of economic laws, and moreover their computing abilities are so limited that they cannot correctly forecast future economic events ... The perfect foresight approach is very useful as a tool for indicative planning or for the description of stationary states, where it seems natural to assume that agents correctly forecast their future environment ... However, it is surely an improper tool for the description of actual economies'. But differently from Radner, Grandmont does face the implications and concludes that one must *reject* the perfect foresight assumption, and turns to the temporary equilibrium approach.

assume perfect foresight, would require a theory *not* based on perfect foresight, that intertemporal-equilibrium theory does not provide. So one is left anyway with no help for the determination of the actual path of the economy.

Second, outside a stationary state correct price foresight can only mean a capacity correctly to *calculate* the equilibrium prices corresponding to the given evolution of the data that the equilibrium must take as exogenous. This requires a correct foresight of these future data, but this is impossible. No one can predict future novelties, not even in a statistical, probabilistic sense, because it is logically impossible to know what these novelties will look like. No one can predict new ideas, technical progress, political and institutional evolution, changes in fashions and in tastes, changes in the desire to have children, wars, new viruses, and so on. One can only make arbitrary assumption about them, e.g. about the pace of technical progress.

We see here that *two different kinds of perfect foresight are needed for the determination of intertemporal equilibria*. Agents need, first of all, perfect foresight of the exogenous data of each future period: state of technical progress, environmental conditions, tastes of the people living in that period, laws and so on; let us call it **perfect data foresight**. Only if these data are known can equilibrium prices be determined, and here we find the need for the second kind of perfect foresight, the **perfect price foresight** admitted by Radner to be legitimate only for states of constant prices. The need for the first kind of foresight is seldom discussed. One finds assumptions about future tastes equal to current tastes, about perfectly forecasted future technical knowledge, and so on, that no one questions because no one else does. The moment you stop to think about these assumptions, you realize they are totally arbitrary. One cannot even consider the *possible* future states of the world to be known, as assumed in ▶ Chap. 9, because possible novelties are unpredictable.

The substitutability problem emerges in the quotation from Hicks in Chap. 7, ▶ Sect. 7.3. Hicks admits the problem in *Value and Capital* too, where he states that in the first 'week' (his term for the short period over which a temporary equilibrium is established) but also in a few subsequent 'weeks' the level of output of most firms will be dictated by the amount of intermediate goods already in the pipeline ('work-in-progress'), and therefore 'The additional output which can be produced in the current week, or planned for weeks in the near future, will usually be quite small' (Hicks 1946, p. 206), and for the same reason the variation in inputs can only be very small (ibid., p. 211).[27]

Then factor demand curves cannot but be extremely inelastic; after some labour immigration, or after some labour-saving technical change, the equilibrium real wage might easily be so low for a number of periods that workers prefer to turn to looting and revolts. In *Value and Capital* Hicks tries to minimize the problem by arguing that wages are generally sticky and change only slowly in the

---

27 In a later article Hicks repeats that within a single 'week' 'The actual outputs of products, and probably also the actual input of labour, would be largely predetermined' (Hicks 1980–81, p. 55).

direction indicated by the excess demand for labour. That is, after any change in the neo-Walrasian equilibrium real wage the latter is *not* a good approximation to observable real wages, and this is what allows the economy to function! But then the same holds for labour employment too, and hence for aggregate income—and for savings, which (since the approach assumes that investment adjusts to savings) determine the growth rate: Hicks is actually admitting that the economy's growth rate can be for several periods considerably different from the one associated with full employment. One more reason not to trust the equilibrium path to give correct indications on the actual path of the economy.

8.16 The Savings–investment Problem

8.16.1 The 'Further Assumption'

Intertemporal-equilibrium models assume a continuous equality of investment and full-employment savings. What reasons does the theory of intertemporal equilibrium advance to conclude that this equality reflects the tendential result of markets, that is, that investment adapts to savings rather than, as Keynesian theory argues, the reverse?

As explained in ▶ Chap. 7, in long-period neoclassical theory the adjustment of investment to savings was based on the assumed capacity of the rate of interest to adjust the 'capital'–labour ratio in new plants in the direction needed for investment to absorb full-employment savings. This adjustment mechanism, based on the decreasing demand curve for 'capital', can be found unconvincing,[28] but at least *there was* an argument indicating forces pushing towards the equality of investment and full-employment savings. In the theory of intertemporal equilibrium, this argument can no longer be used because the notion of 'capital' has been abandoned: to dispense with that notion was the main reason for the shift to the neo-Walrasian versions! But then is there in this theory some other argument taking its place? It would seem not.

This conclusion is reached as follows (Petri 2017). The adjustments compatible with an intertemporal equilibrium must be adjustments that avoid disequilibrium productions, therefore, there is no alternative to some form of auctioneer-guided tâtonnement. So if we are to look for arguments that explain why investment adjusts to full-employment savings in intertemporal equilibria, we must find them in the way the tâtonnement is formalized. There is only one

---

28 In Petri (2013, 2015) I have contended that this traditional neoclassical reasoning requires that the full employment of labour be *assumed* rather than derived from the analysis, and that if it is not assumed to start with, then even traditional marginalist capital–labour substitution does not suffice to obtain a tendency towards the full employment of labour. See ▶ Sect. 12.17.

8.16 · The Savings–investment Problem

study of intertemporal tâtonnement that treats, as one must, the number of firms as variable and hence treats industries as having CRS: the 'factor tâtonnement' of Michael Mandler (2005), already described in ▶ Chap. 6. In that chapter it was applied to the atemporal economy, but Mandler intended it for the intertemporal economy (over a finite number of periods), and the online Appendix 2 on the present chapter's website on SpringerLink illustrates how the model and proof presented in ▶ Chap. 6 must be reinterpreted for the intertemporal case. In this factor tâtonnement, as I proceed to show, the adjustment of *total* investment (the sum of the discounted value of investment decisions in the several periods) to *total* savings is *not* justified, it is simply *assumed* to hold all along the tâtonnement, and total savings are determined before of, and independently of, investment because of a highly debatable 'further assumption' to be illustrated presently. With respect to savings and investment the tâtonnement has only the task of adjusting the *distribution* of total investment among the several periods to the distribution of total savings among the several periods; the equality among their totals is established *by assumption*. This is Say's Law applied to an intertemporal economy: there can only be mistakes in the (intertemporal) composition of production relative to the (intertemporal) composition of demand, not insufficiencies of overall demand.

This will become clear with an example. For the sake of argument, let us accept two assumptions implicit in the factor tâtonnement. First, at the initial date there are complete futures markets for all the periods covered by the equilibrium.[29] Second, at each round of the tâtonnement, for each product firms' production plans adapt perfectly to demand plans.[30]

---

29 This assumption seems inevitable, because the tâtonnement idea does not seem applicable to a Radner equilibrium: in the absence of futures markets, at each 'round' of the tâtonnement the auctioneer can only cry date-0 spot prices and prices of Arrow securities, and it is unclear how agents would derive future spot prices from the prices cried by the auctioneer: what can 'perfect price foresight' mean for *disequilibrium* date-0 prices? That is, not even the auctioneer-guided tâtonnement is able to supply a picture of how a Radner equilibrium might be reached. And what about the following argument: if perfect price foresight can be assumed to hold at date $t = 0$, it seems very difficult to deny that it must have held already at date $t = -1$; but then date-0 prices were correctly forecasted, then at date 0 there is no need for the auctioneer, people already know and accept the equilibrium prices; that is, the assumption of perfect foresight implies that the economy is and has always been in equilibrium; disequilibrium behaviour cannot be analysed under that assumption. Which confirms the inability of the approach to supply information on the behaviour of economies not perfectly in continuous equilibrium. Of course, a tâtonnement with complete futures markets is no better, since it requires the presence of yet-to-be-born consumers.

30 This second assumption is needed to surmount the indeterminate supply at product prices equal to average costs as required by constant returns to scale industries; as explained in ▶ Sect. 6.43, this assumption requires the *planner–auctioneer* who at each 'round' of the tâtonnement *imposes* to each industry a supply equal to demand—and one can doubt that then one is still talking of a market economy. This difficulty will be neglected in what follows, in order to highlight a further unacceptable aspect of the analysis.

634   Chapter 8 · Intertemporal Equilibrium, Temporary Equilibrium

At each 'round' of the tâtonnement, the auctioneer cries prices, consumers decide what consumption goods to demand, firms produce quantities of consumption goods equal to the quantities demanded; relative input prices determine the cost-minimizing production methods (already correctly determined by the auctioneer too, in order to determine zero-profit product prices); from these and the quantities of consumption goods to be produced the demands for produced capital goods are derived, and the productions of these capital goods are again assumed equal to those demands. Then disequilibria can arise only in the markets of 'original' factors (labour of the several periods, land of the several periods, initial endowments of capital goods). Owing to the assumed perfect adjustment of quantities produced to quantities demanded, all along the tâtonnement investment decisions raise no difficulty: *all* production decisions are *to order*, because decided on the basis of known demands; and therefore all gross investment decisions too—decisions to buy newly produced capital goods and to use them for production—are *to order*, because those capital goods will produce goods with guaranteed sale at cost-covering prices.

What is needed to make production decisions determinate at each 'round' of the tâtonnement is to determine consumer demands. This is done by making a *further assumption*: at each 'round' of the tâtonnement, the demands for consumption goods are based on ***consumer incomes corresponding to the full employment of all factor supplies***, independently of whether there is or not a demand for these supplies. That is, the demands consumers communicate to the auctioneer are based on the assumption that their factor supplies will find purchasers (▶ Sect. 6.27). Thus, at each 'round', once the auctioneer announces the complete price vector, consumer decisions are fully determined *independently of what firms decide*. Firm production decisions are derived from these given demands for produced consumption goods by assuming production adjusts to demand for each produced good, and owing to cost minimization, derived demands for inputs result. If these inputs are capital goods to be produced inside the equilibrium's periods, their production implies further derived demands, and by proceeding in this way one finally obtains the demands for the 'original' factors labour, land, initial capital goods. Since prices equal average costs owing to CRS and entry, the value of firms' factor demands equals the value of what they produce, that is, the value of consumers' demand for consumption goods, which is equal to the value of consumers' factor supplies to firms. Hence, on 'original' factor markets the total value of demand equals the total value of supply by assumption.

Therefore at each 'round' of the tâtonnement there can be excess supply of some 'original' factors, but counterbalanced by excess demand for other 'original' factors (possibly of another date): the problem is only one of possible non-coincidence of (intraperiod and intertemporal) *composition* of factor demand and *composition* of factor supply. On the ensemble of the periods (*not* for each single period), Say's Law, redefined for intertemporal complete markets to mean an aggregate (discounted) value of demand for factors always equal to the aggregate (discounted) value of factor supply, holds *by assumption* at each 'round'.

This means, at each 'round', an equality by assumption between total net savings and total net investment over the ensemble of periods; in fact, both will be

8.16 · The Savings–investment Problem

negative and equal to the value of the initial capital endowment, which in the last period(s) is not renewed because the economy is approaching its end. In disequilibrium, in each period there need not be equality between desired gross savings (excess of the period's gross income from intended factor supplies to firms, over the period's desired expenditure on consumption goods) and desired gross investment (planned purchase of new capital goods produced in the period), but the inequality will be compensated by inequalities of opposite sign in other periods.

8.16.2 The Difference It Makes to Assume or Not the 'Further Assumption'

Let us make these sentences concrete with a simple example. Assume a three dates intertemporal competitive economy where only one good, corn, is produced by many small firms, with labour and corn-capital as inputs, and with free entry. Corn is the numéraire. The economy starts at $t=0$ and ends at $t=2$ (plus the time needed to consume the consumption goods that come out at $t=2$); production cycles that take one period are started at $t=0$ and at $t=1$. Thus markets for labour, land and output exist at the two dates 0 and 1, while at date 2 there is only the output market. At date 0 the economy starts with a given initial endowment of corn G_0 produced the previous period; for simplicity I assume a rigid labour supply at dates 0 and 1, and a rigid propensity to *gross* savings s out of the real income at dates 0 and 1 (no savings and no labour supply at date 2, of course, since there is no production in period 2). Thus at date 0, sG_0 is offered as corn-capital for period-0 production, and $(1-s)G_0$ is eaten. It simplifies things to look at this economy assuming $(1-s)G_0$ has been eaten, so initial endowments are sG_0 and L_0, and consumer income goes to purchase consumption of dates 1 and 2.

Gross output at date 1 is $G_1 = F(K_0, N_0)$, at date 2 it is $G_2 = F(K_1, N_1)$, where K_t, N_t are respectively the corn-capital demanded (and utilized) by the aggregate of firms, and aggregate labour demand (and employment) at *date* t ($t=0$, 1) to be used during *period* t to produce G_{t+1}; these demands for corn-capital and for labour need not be equal to the respective supplies. Corn-capital is a circulating capital good.

Supplies of corn-capital at the two relevant dates are sG_0 and sG_1; labour supplies are L_0 and L_1. Corn supply at $t=2$, G_2, is only for consumption.

The gross production function $F(K, N)$, common to all firms and periods, is differentiable with constant returns to scale (CRS) and strictly convex isoquants; pure profits must be zero, so because of CRS the undiscounted real wages w_1, w_2 (quantities of corn to be paid at $t=1$ to each unit of N_0 and at $t=2$ to each unit of N_1) univocally determine factor proportions and the undiscounted *gross* rental rates earned by each unit of corn-capital $\rho_1(w_1)$, $\rho_2(w_2)$, so as to have real wages equal to the marginal products of labour, and gross rental rates equal to gross marginal products of corn-capital. For example if $F(K, N) = K^{1-\alpha}N^\alpha$, and $\alpha = 1/2$, it is $\rho = 1/(4w)$, the net rate of return on capital (the classical rate of profit) is $\rho - 1$.

636   Chapter 8 · Intertemporal Equilibrium, Temporary Equilibrium

In the standard tâtonnement, in this economy at each round the auctioneer need decide only w_1 and w_2 and call them together with the associated $\rho_1(w_1)$, $\rho_2(w_2)$; outputs G_1 and G_2 adjust to consumer demands determined by incomes equal to the value of their factor supplies, and to a capital demand K_1 derived from date-2 consumer demand. Demands are, in undiscounted terms, the right-hand sides of these supply-equals-demand equations:

$$G_1 = (1 - s)(w_1 L_0 + \rho_1 s G_0) + K_1 \tag{8.4}$$

$$G_2 = w_2 L_1 + \rho_2 s(w_1 L_0 + \rho_1 s G_0). \tag{8.5}$$

In Eq. (8.4), the first term on the right-hand side is the demand for date-1 corn for consumption purposes, while K_1 is the demand for investment purposes. K_1 is the amount of corn-capital of date 1 demanded by firms to produce the quantity demanded of G_2 with the optimal factor proportions determined by w_2, and the same holds for the other demands for factors. In Eqs. (8.6)–(8.9) below, the right-hand sides are the functions that determine the quantity of a factor needed for its marginal product to be the one determined by the given real wages when the output to be produced is the indicated one:

$$K_0 = F_K^{-1}(G_1, w_1) \tag{8.6}$$

$$N_0 = F_L^{-1}(G_1, w_1) \tag{8.7}$$

$$K_1 = F_K^{-1}(G_2, w_2) \tag{8.8}$$

$$N_1 = F_L^{-1}(G_2, w_2). \tag{8.9}$$

In each 'round' of the tâtonnement, once w_1 and w_2 are announced by the auctioneer, $\rho_1(w_1)$ and $\rho_2(w_2)$ are determined, and Eq. (8.5) determines G_2; then Eq. (8.8) determines K_1, and Eq. (8.4) determines G_1. Then the excess demands for the three 'original' factors, $K_0 - sG_0$, $N_0 - L_0$, $N_1 - L_1$, can be determined, and on their basis the auctioneer can determine the direction in which to change w_1 and w_2 for the next 'round'.

Note that, out of equilibrium, it is generally $K_1 \neq s(w_1 L_0 + \rho_1 s G_0)$; flukes apart, the optimal factor proportions in the production of G_2 will not be such as to cause firms to desire to invest at date 1 as much as consumers desire to save at that date. If $K_1 < s(w_1 L_0 + \rho_1 s G_0)$, possibly there can be excess supply on both date-0 factor markets, compensated by excess demand for L_1.

The above was in terms of undiscounted prices, which in my view makes things easier to grasp. Now let us pass to discounted prices, which allow comparing total value demand for 'original' factors with their total value supply. It

8.16 · The Savings–investment Problem

is possible to discount to a date different from date 0, I show it by discounting to date 1; if you multiply the expressions below by ρ_1^{-1} you obtain their value discounted to date zero. The value of consumers' factor supplies, that is their aggregate income, discounted to date one, is

$$w_1 L_0 + \rho_1 s G_0 + w_2 L_1 \rho_2^{-1}.$$

The cost of production of G_2 discounted to date 1 is

$$w_2 N_1 + \rho_2 K_1 \rho_2^{-1} = w_2 N_1 \rho_2^{-1} + K_1;$$

the cost of production of $(1 - s)G_1$ (the part of G_1 demanded for consumption), discounted to date 1 (that is, undiscounted), is

$$w_1 N_0 + \rho_1 K_0 - K_1;$$

we obtain the discounted total cost of production of the output of consumption goods:

$$w_1 N_0 + \rho_1 K_0 + w_2 N_1 \rho_2^{-1};$$

this is the discounted value of demand for factors. The discounted aggregate income of consumers goes to demand G_2 plus the consumption part of G_1; from Eqs. (8.4) and (8.5) we obtain a discounted total value of demand for final output (consumption goods):

$$(1 - s)(w_1 L_0 + \rho_1 s G_0) + w_2 L_1 + \rho_2 s (w_1 L_0 + \rho_1 s G_0)\rho_2^{-1}$$
$$= w_1 L_0 + \rho_1 s G_0 + w_2 L_1 \rho_2^{-1}.$$

Since production equals demand and average cost equals price, there is equality between discounted value of demand for factors, and discounted value of factor supplies; we obtain what I call *intertemporal Say's Law*:

$$w_1 N_0 + \rho_1 K_0 + w_2 N_1 \rho_2^{-1} = w_1 L_0 + \rho_1 s G_0 + w_2 L_1 \rho_2^{-1}.$$

That is, by assumption *at each round* of the tâtonnement, the (discounted) aggregate value of factor supplies is equal to the (discounted) aggregate value of factor demands; inequalities between supply and demand for some factor can only be due to a *composition* of demand for factors different from the *composition* of supply of factors; since we assume all markets to be open at date 0 to allow the tâtonnement to reach equilibrium simultaneously in all of them, we have exactly the situation imagined by Say or Ricardo: there can be disequilibrium due to a wrong *composition* of production, but there is no problem of insufficient or excessive *aggregate* demand.

638   **Chapter 8** · Intertemporal Equilibrium, Temporary Equilibrium

The 'further assumption' ensures Say's Law during the tâtonnement also in the labour–land economy producing a single consumption good studied in ▶ Chap. 3.[31]

As noticed, in this picture investment decisions are unproblematical, they are to order. Things radically change if one admits that investment decisions cannot be based on known future demands, because the incomes from which those demands will derive cannot be taken as given independently of firms' decisions.

The thing is evident already in the labour–land economy. Suppose that in this economy each consumer supplies one unit of only one factor, either labour, or land. Now suppose relative factor rentals are the equilibrium ones, but firms produce one half of the full-employment output. Half the supply of labour and half the supply of land remain unemployed. But there is no disequilibrium in the output market: earnings and hence the demand for the product equal the value of the product. This example makes it evident that consumer incomes cannot be assumed given before firms decide factor employments. *It is firms' decisions as to input use that determine consumer incomes and hence consumer demands for produced goods.* Therefore, if one wants to understand disequilibrium processes in real economies, one has no right to take consumer incomes as given and equal to full-employment incomes, to *derive* from these incomes their demands for consumption goods, and to derive demands for factors from these demands. If one wants the tâtonnement to try and mimic, however remotely, the functioning of markets, then one cannot assume that the incomes on which consumers can count in formulating their demands for consumption goods are the incomes corresponding to the value of their *intended* supplies of factors.

The moment this is accepted, the announcement of prices does not suffice to determine consumer demands; at least part of firms' decisions as to productions, and hence as to factor demands, must be determined first, and will determine what income consumers have at their disposal for consumption or savings. In an intertemporal economy this implies that investment decisions are necessarily partly indeterminate. To illustrate, we can use the same example of a three dates intertemporal economy.

---

31 Let the real wage w (measured in terms of output) be given and let output G be determined by a standard CRS differentiable production function $G = F(L, T)$. Marginal products are univocally determined by L/T, and the relationship is invertible, hence, $w = MP_L$ determines $L/T = \lambda(w)$ and this determines the real rent rate $\beta(w)$. Let L^* and T^* be the given supplies of labour and land. Given w, the total income of consumers determined under the '*further assumption*' is $wL^* + \beta(w)T^*$ and this is the demand for output, to which production is assumed to adapt, hence, $G = wL^* + \beta(w)T^*$. Demands for inputs are L^+, T^+ such that $G = F(L^+, T^+)$ s.t. $L^+/T^+ = \lambda(w)$. By the product exhaustion theorem, $G = wL^+ + \beta(w) T^+ = wL^* + \beta(w)T^*$, profit is zero. Actually if w is different from the equilibrium wage then demand for one of the factors is greater than supply, but we are considering a tâtonnement so $G = wL^* + \beta(w)T^* = F(L^+, T^+)$ can anyway be defined and factor demands can be derived from it; G is not in general equal to $G^* = F(L^*, T^*)$, it is greater (*Exercise*: confirm it graphically using isoquants), but for any real w, when supply of output equals demand for output, the demand price of output equals its supply price, hence, there is equilibrium in the output market (Say's Law holds), disequilibrium is only in the factor markets.

8.16 · The Savings–investment Problem

Let us then assume that consumer incomes correspond to the value of the factor supplies *that find purchasers*. Then these incomes are no longer determined once w_1 and w_2 are given. Equations (8.6) to (8.9) continue to determine demands for factors if G_1 and G_2 are additionally given, but now consumer incomes depend in turn on factor demands so it is not clear that the consumer incomes determined by production of G_1 and G_2 will cause a demand for G_1 and G_2 equal to production. Now (still assuming a given gross propensity to save s out of G_0 and of G_1) the supply = demand conditions for output at dates 1 and 2 are the following (where the demands for G_1 and G_2 are the right-hand sides):

$$G_1 = F(K_0, N_0) = (1 - s)(w_1 N_0 + \rho_1 K_0) + K_1 \qquad (8.10)$$

$$G_2 = F(K_1, N_1) = w_2 N_1 + \rho_2 K_1. \qquad (8.11)$$

Here K_0, N_0, K_1, N_1 are the quantities *demanded* of corn-capital and of labour. Equation (8.11) can raise perplexities, because it appears to express simply the necessary equality between value and cost of G_2, and therefore it does not appear to indicate what determines the demand for G_2. But this is precisely the point. G_2 *is indeed indeterminate*. For each level of G_2 taken as given, the given w_2 determines K_1 and N_1, and then the fixed propensity to save determines the level of G_1 required for equality between supply and demand for corn-capital at date 1,

$$K_1 = sG_1 = s(w_1 N_0 + \rho_1 K_0).$$

This is simply a rewriting of Eq. (8.10). Then G_1 determines N_0 and K_0 once w_1 is given.[32] And for each level of G_2 and connected level of G_1, the demand for G_2 is precisely the right-hand side of Eq. (8.11), because those are the incomes that go to demand G_2: previous incomes go to previous consumption expenditure, except for the savings sG_1 which correspond to K_1 and at date 2 earn an income $\rho_2 K_1$ which, together with $w_2 N_1$, is the income employed in demanding G_2. So demand for G_2 is always equal to G_2, it is determined by firms' decision to produce G_2, which evidently needs something else than the demand for G_2 in order to be determined.

This means that the announcement of factor rentals and prices does not suffice to determine excess factor demands, and the tâtonnement *cannot proceed*, unless some theory is supplied of what determines G_2 at each 'round'.

---

32 It is possible that, if G_2 is somehow given, demand for a factor at date 0 or at date 1 exceeds supply; since we are still assuming a tâtonnement albeit a non-standard one, we can assume that, in such a case, the auctioneer calculates herself what the incomes and decisions of consumers would be if, hypothetically, factor supplies were equal to demands, assuming a proportional increase of the number of each type of consumer if necessary; by comparing these demands with actual supplies she can derive the excess demands for 'original' factors so as to proceed to determine the wages to be proposed in the next round. (This tâtonnement does not pretend to be fully realistic, and it aims at being no more than an *initial* unveiling of the complications that the standard tâtonnement hides under the carpet. Realistic disequilibria should be admitted to involve actual productions.).

640   Chapter 8 · Intertemporal Equilibrium, Temporary Equilibrium

This shows the importance of the *'further assumption'*. This assumption hides an indeterminacy of disequilibrium incomes, due to their being in fact created by factor utilization decisions taken by firms. Its removal makes a theory of investment obligatory. G_2 depends on firms' decisions at $t=1$ as to how much corn to produce for $t=2$, that is, *it depends on investment decisions* at $t=1$.

These decisions are not to order, and they *determine* incomes and hence savings, so they cannot be determined by savings. It will be savings that will adjust to investment. Indeed, this is exactly what is indicated by Eqs. (8.10) and (8.11) once G_2 is given: G_1 adjusts so that sG_1 equals the investment K_1 motivated—we can assume—by the expectation that future sales will be G_2.

We can conclude that the existing theory of intertemporal equilibria is unable to prove that the adaptation of (overall) investment to (overall) full-employment savings is anything other than an arbitrary assumption. No proof is provided that this adaptation will result from some adjustment mechanism: the adaptation is assumed from the start, and is assumed to hold all along the tâtonnement, on the basis of a fairy tale assumption about consumer incomes that flatly contradicts how these incomes are determined in market economies.

8.16.3 The Neoclassical Synthesis

It might be countered that neoclassical theory does have arguments, in support of a tendency towards full employment, which accept that incomes are created by firms' production decisions: namely, the *neoclassical-synthesis* argument which, in the debates on Keynes in the years 1950s and 1960s, allowed concluding (on the basis of the so-called *Keynes effect*) that *there is* a tendency towards full employment if money wages are downward flexible in the presence of unemployment (and the money supply does not decrease with the price level). For the reader without previous studies of traditional macroeconomics, this argument is briefly remembered in the online Appendix to this chapter. But this argument rests upon the theory that investment is a decreasing function of the rate of interest, a theory derived from the traditional decreasing demand curve for 'capital'. If one appeals to this theory, one relies on the conception of 'capital' that the shift to neo-Walrasian equilibria was intended to avoid; furthermore, one relies on time-consuming disequilibrium adjustments that neo-Walrasian theory cannot admit (the traditional decreasing demand curve for capital is a long-period notion, derived from long-period choice of techniques, that takes time to be imposed by competition); so one is actually throwing overboard the presumed 'rigorous' microfoundation of the neoclassical approach, and one is returning to a theory admittedly without solid microbasis as shown in ▶ Chap. 7. To which it can be added that this theory of investment is notoriously contradicted by the empirical evidence.[33]

---

33 See Petri (2004, Chaps. 4 and 7, 2015) for more on mainstream investment theories; and here
   ▶ Sect. 12.7.

8.17 Equilibrium Over the Infinite Future

8.17.1 The One-Good Growth Model

Nowadays generally the assumption that the economy ends at a finite date is found not easily acceptable, and intertemporal equilibria over a finite number of periods are considered only pedagogical first steps towards equilibrium over the infinite future. One can wonder whether one is not jumping out of the frying pan into the fire. Let us see what evidence can be gathered on this issue by theoretical reflection.

Infinite-periods intertemporal-equilibrium models come roughly in two classes: the first assumes an infinitely-lived representative consumer who maximizes utility over the infinite number of periods (sometimes there is a finite number of infinitely-lived consumers or 'dynasties'), and is generally referred to as the Ramsey-Cass-Koopmans model; the second assumes overlapping generations (OLG). The second class is discussed in sections from ▶ Sect. 8.19–8.24. Here I comment on the first class, but without attempting a formal presentation, which would require advanced mathematical tools (see Aliprantis et al. 1989; Florenzano 2003). It seems possible to convey the main message of these models in simple terms. It is, after all, much the same message as one can derive from the model of a neoclassical economy presented in ▶ Chap. 3, where a single product, corn, is produced with the use of labour and corn-capital (seed) as inputs, in production cycles that take one period; one must only extend the model to cover successive periods, i.e. determine the economy's growth path.

Let us remember the model. Land is overabundant and hence free. Production is in yearly cycles; competition imposes the same production function to all firms, with CRS at least at the level of the industry (owing to free entry), which in this model coincides with the entire economy. Technical knowledge is given. Labour supply L is initially assumed given, and fully employed because wages are flexible. One passes from the gross output production function $G = G(K, L)$ to the *net* output production function $C = F(K, L)$ by subtracting capital depreciation; for simplicity let us assume circulating capital, then $F(K, L) = G(K, L) - K$ and $F(\cdot)$ too has CRS. Income distribution is determined by the full-employment net marginal products of labour and capital derived from $F(\cdot)$. What we must do is derive some implications of the model for growth theory.

A common simplifying assumption in neoclassical growth theory is the so-called ***Inada conditions*** on marginal products: it is assumed that as the amount of a factor changes while the amounts of the other factors are fixed and positive, its marginal product tends to $+\infty$ as the amount of the factor tends to zero, and decreases but remaining indefinitely positive, tending to zero only asymptotically, as the amount of the factor increases. However, always positive marginal products would be *too* unrealistic if assumed for the *net* output production function: it is hard to accept that, however great the amount of capital already employed with a given amount of labour, one more unit of corn-capital not only always increases output, but always increases it by more than one unit. When assumed to

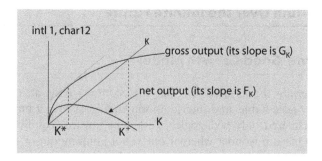

◘ **Fig. 8.1** Gross and net output as functions of corn-capital in the corn-labour economy with a fixed labour supply. The figure shows that if the Inada condition is satisfied by the marginal *gross* product of capital, this does not prevent *net* output from reaching a maximum (here for K = K*) and then starting to decrease, eventually becoming negative

apply only to the *gross* output production function, the Inada conditions do not prevent the marginal *net* product of capital from becoming negative, as shown in ◘ Fig. 8.1, where G_K satisfies the Inada conditions and yet F_K becomes negative for $K > K^*$.

Assume that initial K is less than K^*, and that tastes are such that every period a positive fraction $s<1$ of *net* output is saved, and re-invested: investment is, neoclassically, determined by full-employment savings. Let K_t be the corn-capital stock with which the economy is endowed at the beginning of period t. The economy reaches the full utilization of both capital and labour each period, with income distribution determined by the marginal products of labour and capital; so the qualitative paths of capital, output, and income distribution are easy to deduce. K grows from one period to the next; since $C_t = F(K_t, L)$, then, $K_{t+1} = K_t + sC_t$, therefore K grows, and as long as the net marginal product of capital is positive, net output grows too but by a smaller percentage than K owing to the decreasing marginal product of K^{34}; therefore net savings sC_t are less than required for an unchanged growth rate of K, and the rate of growth of K slows down gradually. As K grows, the real wage rises, and the rate of interest decreases. Since the net marginal product of capital, and hence the rate of interest, becomes zero when $K = K^*$, and then negative, sooner or later the assumption of a fixed s becomes implausible: one can plausibly assume that the community will realize the little or even negative effect of further net savings, and that the propensity to net savings s will decrease. For example one can assume that preferences are such that aggregate s is an increasing function of the rate of interest, that is, that s decreases as the rate of interest decreases; assuming that s becomes zero for a still positive interest rate r^*, we obtain that output growth slows down gradually, tending asymptotically to stop as the net marginal product of K, and hence

---

34 If an increase of K by 1% causes C to increase by 1% or more, and the marginal product of labour is positive, then an increase of both K and L by 1% causes C to increase by more than 1%, implying increasing returns to scale against the assumption of CRS.

8.17 · Equilibrium Over the Infinite Future

the rate of interest, approaches r^*. The economy tends to a stationary state with $K < K^*$.

Now assume labour supply grows at a given rate $n > 0$, and go back to assuming a given average propensity to net savings s. In a given period t, output is $C_t = F(K_t, L_t)$, net savings is sC_t and there results a certain K_{t+1}, that is, a certain growth rate of K_t, call it $g_{Kt} = sC_t/K_t$. As long as $g_K > n$, K/L grows at rate $g_k - n$; the marginal product of K decreases, hence, C grows slower than K, and this reduces g_K, which tends asymptotically towards n; conversely, if $g_K < n$, K/L decreases, therefore, C grows at a higher rate than K, so g_K rises, again tending towards n. When $g_K = n$, K/L is constant, the economy is on a steady-growth path. If s is an increasing function of the rate of interest, the tendency of g_K to approach n is faster, but the tendency towards a steady growth at rate n is still there; but the change of s is no longer necessary for a steady state to be reached.

Solow's 1956 growth model assumes that the same holds for a complex modern economy, where capital is a multitude of heterogeneous capital goods. Fully accepting the traditional marginalist/neoclassical conception of 'capital' as a single value factor, measured in the same units as national net output or income Y, Solow's model assumes that one can represent the entire economy's production possibilities via a CRS *net* aggregate production function $Y = F(K, L)$. Production is now described as a continuous process, so Y is a flow per unit of time and the analysis is in continuous time. Labour supply grows at rate n, i.e. is given by

$$L(t) = L_0 e^{nt}.$$

Assuming again a given average net saving propensity s, we have

$$dK/dt = sY.$$

Let $y = Y/L$ and $k = K/L$. Because of CRS, $Y/L = F(K/L, 1)$ or $y = F(k, 1)$ which we can represent as $y = f(k)$, where y is net output per unit of labour and k is capital per unit of labour, an increasing (and then decreasing)[35] strictly concave function. Note that since $dK/dt = sY$, net savings per unit of labour are

$$sf(k) = sY/L = (sY/K) \cdot (K/L) = (dK/dt)/K \cdot k = g_K k.$$

By definition $(dk/dt)/k = g_K - n$, and multiplying both sides by k one obtains

$$dk/dt = g_K k - nk = sf(k) - nk.$$

Representing graphically $sf(k)$ and two different values of nk as functions of k, one obtains ◘ Fig. 8.2.

For a sufficiently high initial net marginal product of capital,[36] $sf(k)$ is initially above nk and crosses it from above. It is clear that k grows if it is less than the value at the crossing point, and decreases in the opposite case, thus, tending

---

35 But many authors, including Solow (1956), neglect depreciation and implicitly assume that the Inada conditions hold for net output, and therefore, $y'(k)$ never becomes negative.

36 The Inada conditions state that $f(k)$ has infinite slope at $k = 0$; a less extreme assumption will do, what is necessary is that the slope of $f(k)$ at $k = 0$ be greater than n/s.

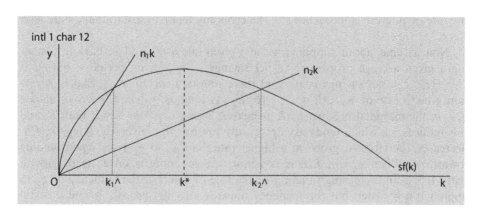

◘ **Fig. 8.2** Two possible steady-growth values of k in Solow's model, depending on n; the second one is a clear case of overaccumulation

to the value $k^\wedge$ that corresponds to steady growth. It is perfectly possible that this $k^\wedge$ be greater than k^* where y is maximized, it is what happens in ◘ Fig. 8.2 for $n=n_2$. In this case, clearly, consumption *per unit of labour* is not maximized in the steady state: a reduction of s would shift downwards proportionally the entire $sf(k)$ curve, shifting $k^\wedge$ to the left and thus ensuring both a higher net output per unit of labour, and smaller net savings per unit of labour. In fact, steady-state consumption per unit of labour keeps increasing for a while even if s is decreased beyond the level that causes $k^\wedge=k^*$.

A word of caution: in the real world, ownership of capital is unequally distributed, some people live on the interest earned by their capital without working, and the economy is possibly very far from a steady state (which, in this model, is approached very slowly, on a time scale of several decades), so the relevance of maximizing steady-state average consumption per *unit of labour* (which is not the same thing as per person) is unclear. But if you are interested in this maximization, then the problem is

$$max_{s,k}(1-s)f(k) \text{ subject to } sf(k) = nk.$$

Straightforward application of the method of Lagrange multipliers yields the Lagrangian function

$$\mathcal{L} = (1-s)f(k) + \lambda(sf(k) - nk);$$

if you set its partial derivatives with respect to s, k, λ equal to zero, you obtain (check this result as an ***Exercise***)

$$f'(k) = n,$$

the marginal net product of capital—that is, the interest rate—must equal the steady-state growth rate; this is the so-called *golden rule of accumulation*. We see from ◘ Figs. 8.1 and 8.2 that this implies that the $k^\wedge$ that maximizes steady-state consumption per unit of labour is less than k^* except if $n=0$; indeed $f(k)$

8.17 · Equilibrium Over the Infinite Future

is horizontal at k^*, that is, $f'(k^*)=0<n$, while 'optimal' $k^\wedge$ requires $f(k)$ to have slope n. The golden rule implies

$$f'(k^\wedge) \cdot k^\wedge = sf(k^\wedge);$$

that is, assuming the rate of interest equals the marginal net product of capital, *net savings must equal the income from capital ownership*, as if all wages were consumed and all income from capital ownership were invested.[37]

The Solow growth model is generally complicated with the introduction of technical progress: the latter is usually assumed to be **labour-augmenting**, that is, such that the production function instead of having the form $F(K, L)$ has the form $F(K, M)$ where $M=\tau(t)L$ (with $\tau>1$ and increasing in time) is *augmented labour*: the increase in labour productivity caused by technical progress is represented as causing each unit of labour to count as if it were more than one unit of labour, and more and more so as time passes. If labour grows at rate n and τ grows at rate μ, then augmented labour supply grows at rate $n+\mu$. The basic idea remains the same: the reinvestment of savings with a given net savings propensity will cause the capital–labour ratio and the corresponding income distribution variables to tend towards constant levels,[38] associated with a rate of growth equal to the growth rate of augmented labour supply.

Now assume that the same economy is controlled by a benevolent planner who knows the utility function of the infinitely-lived representative consumer, who is both worker and capital owner. Suppose this planner wants to find the accumulation path that maximizes the welfare of the representative consumer. The planner can do it by opportunely choosing what fraction of net output to save each period, and by thus choosing a time path of consumption (consumption per person, if population is growing) from the initial period for the infinite future. The task is not necessarily easy, as the utility function may be such that total (discounted) utility over an infinite consumption path is infinite, in which case maximization makes no sense. But supposing a criterion exists that allows deciding which one, of any two alternative consumption paths, is preferred by the representative consumer, the planner must choose the feasible consumption path that the representative consumer prefers. A consumption path is feasible if technology and factor availability permit at each date t such an output that consumption leaves room for the investment required by the continuation of the path. An optimal consumption path must be technically efficient, that is, such that it is not possible to increase consumption at some date without decreasing consumption at some other date; efficiency can be shown often to imply that the same path might be achieved as an infinite-horizon intertemporal equilibrium.

---

37 If $n=0$, $f'(k^\wedge)=0$ implies $k^\wedge=k^*$ and the fact that the rate of interest is zero implies zero net savings, as required by the zero growth rate. Thus, the golden rule of accumulation applies to the case $n=0$ too.

38 However, now a constant wage per unit of M will mean an increasing wage per unit of actual labour.

646   Chapter 8 · Intertemporal Equilibrium, Temporary Equilibrium

Even in the very simple case, the Ramsey model, that makes the same assumptions about production as the Solow model (a single product produced by itself and labour, utilizable as consumption good or as capital good), and even with a utility function that remains finite,[39] the determination of intertemporal optimal paths requires the use of considerably advanced mathematical tools not presupposed in this textbook, e.g. *optimal control* or *dynamic programming*. If certain assumptions are made, the maximization can be performed, and the outcome of the maximization can be *decentralized*, that is, it can be supported as an infinite-horizon intertemporal equilibrium. Under assumptions about labour supply and technical progress similar to those of the Solow growth model, the optimal time path of the economy can often be shown to converge to a steady-growth path. The difference from the Solow growth path is small: in both cases growth is supply-determined, investment is determined by full-employment savings, faster capital accumulation requires less consumption, and changes in the capital–labour ratio alter income distribution in the way indicated by neoclassical theory; the main difference is the endogenously determined propensity to save that changes along the time path.[40] But for practical purposes this difference is of little relevance: how the propensity to save changes in the model is anyway largely arbitrary, depending on the assumed form of the utility function of the representative consumer; above all, it is highly doubtful that the propensity to save in actual economies really reflects intertemporal optimization, people have only the foggiest idea of how the economy will evolve beyond at most a few years. When these weaknesses of the Ramsey model are taken into account, the main surviving messages are

- that market economies tend to the full employment of resources;
- that income distribution is determined by the marginal products of labour and capital, and these marginal products change in time if capital grows at a rate different from the rate of growth of (augmented) labour;
- that growth is supply-determined (investment adapts to full-employment savings) and a faster growth rate requires a greater share of savings and a smaller share of consumption in net output.

---

39 The usual assumption is that (if formalization is in discrete time) utility is the sum of countably infinite discounted *period utilities* (or **felicities**) $\sum_{t=0}^{\infty} \delta^t u(c_t)$, where $u(\cdot)$ is the time-invariant felicity function and $\delta < 1$ is the discount factor, and that the felicity function is sufficiently concave to ensure convergence of the sum even if output grows over time.

40 Another difference is that, owing to intertemporal utility maximization, overaccumulation is not possible. If consumers discount future consumption, i.e. if they prefer consumption today to consumption tomorrow, then the steady growth path to which the economy tends is associated with less capital per unit of labour than required by the golden rule: the extra savings that would bring the economy from this path to the golden rule capital stock per unit of labour require a decrease of current consumption, which is not counterbalanced, in terms of utility, by the future consumption increase, so consumers rest satisfied with a perennially lower consumption level per capita than at the golden rule. This lower level of capital per unit of labour is called the **modified golden rule** capital stock (see e.g. Romer 1996, p. 53).

8.17 · Equilibrium Over the Infinite Future

All these messages are derivable already from Solow's model.

Fundamentally the same messages emerge from the extension of the model to accommodate heterogeneous consumption and capital goods. Each period, the available factors (with the capital endowment now a heterogeneous vector) imply a Production Possibility Frontier, PPF, which—because of the full employment of resources—entails a trade-off between more consumption that period, or more capital goods (and hence a PPF plausibly shifted outwards)[41] the next period. The need to choose also the composition of consumption and the composition of investment every period does not introduce relevant additional problems for the benevolent planner (except the need to assume even more computational capacity); and again—under certain assumptions—it is possible to show that the outcome of the maximization can be supported as an infinite-horizon intertemporal equilibrium.

Of course this requires assuming the planner–auctioneer in order to avoid indeterminate firm supply decisions at equilibrium prices. This problem is not perceived; I will not attempt a discussion of other problems with existence and determinateness of infinite-horizon heterogeneous capital general equilibria because it would require advanced topology. I only report that the prevalent view seems to be that on these aspects the problems are not more serious than for finite-horizon general equilibria (except for determinateness in OLG models, see ▶ Sect. 8.24). Things are different with stability: it is not studied and not even mentioned. Footnote 29 offered some reasons why: if one tried to apply the tâtonnement, one could not avoid absurdities, made worse if possible by the infinity of periods (how can the auctioneer call an infinite number of prices?). The prevalent attitude is to avoid all allusion to the problem and to take for granted that the equilibrium path is a good indicator of the actual path of the economy, without bothering to give supporting arguments. For example: 'We will repeatedly exploit these classical connections between competitive equilibria and Pareto optima as a device for proving the existence of equilibria in market economies and for characterizing them. That is, we will solve planning problems, not for the normative purpose of prescribing outcomes, but for the positive purpose of predicting market outcomes from a given set of preferences and technology' (Stokey and Lucas with Prescott 1989, p. 31). The book from which this quotation is taken contains *no* discussion of whether the infinite-horizon intertemporal competitive equilibria it examines can be considered reliable 'for the positive purpose of predicting market outcomes'.

The meaning itself of the term 'stability' in the recent literature on intertemporal equilibria over the infinite future has changed. Nowadays, when the question is posed whether an infinite-horizon intertemporal equilibrium (or sequential Radner equilibrium) is *stable*, what is meant is not whether disequilibrium adjust-

---

41 Plausibly, because it might be that all capital goods are so abundant that their net marginal products are zero, and further net savings are unable to increase net output per unit of labour. This possibility is always excluded by assuming the Inada conditions, on *net* marginal products but it is an arbitrary assumption, those conditions are unrealistic.

648   **Chapter 8** · Intertemporal Equilibrium, Temporary Equilibrium

ments would converge to it, but the totally different issue whether the *equilibrium path* converges to a steady state.

8.17.2 The Old Problems Remain, Plus a New One

Disaggregated intertemporal equilibrium over the infinite future (with the addition of stochastic elements) is considered the rigorous microfoundation of current mainstream dynamic stochastic general equilibrium (DSGE) macroeconomic models, or more generally, DGE models (the acronym proposed by Wickens (2008), to include the models without stochastic elements, e.g. the Ramsey model): 'it is now widely agreed that macroeconomic analysis should employ models with coherent intertemporal general-equilibrium foundations' (Woodford 2009, p. 269). The premise of these models is therefore that infinite-horizon intertemporal general equilibrium theory is a robust starting point for a descriptive theory. But the extension of the equilibrium to cover an infinite number of future periods does not eliminate the impermanence problem, the price-change problem, the substitutability problem and the savings–investment problem, and furthermore creates a problem of impossibility to predict the state of the world.

The substitutability problem arises for the first periods of the equilibrium as much as for finite-periods equilibrium.

On the impermanence problem, it can be noted that the farther into the future the equilibrium path extends, the greater the potential cumulative deviations from it. Japan from 1990 to 2000 had a growth rate around 0.5% a year, after several decades of a growth rate approximating 5%, and with no visible decrease of the propensity to save; had Japan grown even only at 3.5% a year for those ten years, in 2000 its productive capacity and its output would have been 34% greater than it was—an enormous difference.

On the savings–investment problem, the dependence of consumer incomes on firms' decisions holds over infinite horizons too. To view this fact clearly, imagine a full-employment equilibrium over the infinite future, in an economy with many types of identical consumers, each type supplying only one non-produced factor, one unit per consumer. Now imagine that, at the same prices, firms produce of each good one half of the equilibrium quantity and employ one half of the equilibrium inputs, leaving one half of factor supplies unemployed. One half of each type of consumers is unemployed and with no income. Product markets are in equilibrium; investment equals savings. If firms decided to produce more, factor unemployment would decrease in spite of no change in relative prices. Equality of savings and investment *at equilibrium prices* does not determine production levels, because production decisions of firms determine incomes and hence savings, which are therefore *determined by* investment decisions. The general equilibrium requires an *additional* assumption of full employment of resources. But then different assumptions, for example, the Keynesian approach that postulates some autonomous expenditure plus the multiplier, appear to be clearly preferable, not only because with more support from the empirical evidence, but also because not needing complete markets nor perfect foresight nor the auctioneer.

8.17 · Equilibrium Over the Infinite Future

On the price-change problem, a correct foresight assumption becomes if possible even more absurd when the horizon is pushed far away, in view of the logical unpredictability of novelties, which makes the assumption of perfect data foresight the more ridiculous the farther in the future the horizon. To pretend anyone to be optimizing over even only the next twenty years although aware that she/he has no idea of the new inventions, new viruses and new wars waiting for us, is nonsense. Extend the horizon to infinity, and you get only nonsense upon stilts, to use Jeremy Bentham's famous expression.[42]

There is another problem too, that questions not only the logical possibility of perfect price foresight but more generally the determinability of infinite-periods equilibria: the need, in general, to solve mathematical problems with an infinity of variables. An infinitely-lived consumer must determine an infinity of optimal excess demands. This is mathematically impossible if it requires the execution of an infinite number of different operations.[43] The calculation of an infinity of different optimal decisions imposes a logically impossible mathematical task on this consumer, unless the calculation can be effected on the basis of a finite system of mathematical relations (e.g. a finite system of differential equations) whose solution determines the entire time path of the variables; this would require that the equilibrium's prices are constant or evolve in a simple determinable way. But this requires a regular time evolution of the equilibrium's data, which can only be arbitrarily *assumed*. For example ecological constraints might be perfectly predicted but follow an irregular development; even conceding knowledge of the entire infinite series of irregularly changing equilibrium prices, utility maximization would require the consumer to solve a problem with an infinity of different equations, which is impossible. The same would hold for perfectly predicted technological innovations, logically impossible as this is.[44]

So, to go from finite-horizon to infinite-periods intertemporal equilibria does indeed amount to jumping out of the frying pan into the fire.

---

42 Commenting on the French Declaration of the Rights of Man and the Citizen, Bentham wrote that '[N]atural rights is simple nonsense: natural and imprescriptible rights, rhetorical nonsense, – nonsense upon stilts' (Bentham 1843, p. 501).

43 This does not mean that mathematical results cannot be valid for an infinite number of different cases; but a correct interpretation of the proof will show that a finite number of operations is required to prove the result for each case. For example the proof that all natural numbers have a successive number, based on proving that 0 has a successive natural number and that for any n if n is a natural number then $n+1$ exists, only requires for each number n a finite number of applications of the principle of induction, so one needs a finite number of steps to prove the property for any number (so in reality one has *not* proved that *all* numbers have a successive number, one has only proved that one *would be able to prove it, if necessary*, for any assigned number with a finite number of operations; which is all we need).

44 Mas-Colell et al. (1995, p. 752) avoid this problem and the problem posed by the need for perfect data foresight by *assuming*, with no justification, no changes in the exogenous data of the economy as t tends to infinity (except possibly for given rates of population growth and of exogenous uniform technical progress in factor productivity—no new consumption goods). Unfortunately the world we live in is not like that.

650   Chapter 8 · Intertemporal Equilibrium, Temporary Equilibrium

8.18 Behind the Neoclassical Reliance on Intertemporal Equilibria

It is impossible that neoclassical economists are unaware of the criticisms presented above that radically question the ability of intertemporal equilibria to say anything on the distance between equilibrium path (even if this were determinable) and the behaviour of economies not continually perfectly in equilibrium.

But then, how can they go on attributing to disaggregated intertemporal equilibria the role of indicators of the tendencies of actual economies? I can see only one explanation (Dvoskin and Petri 2017). The economists attributing this role to intertemporal equilibria of course know that in actual economies there is no auctioneer, no instantaneous adjustments and no complete futures markets, rather there are time-consuming trial-and-error adjustments, mistakes, disequilibria, imperfect foresight, discovery of novelties; so they must be persuaded that the qualitative trends indicated by intertemporal equilibrium correspond to the trends in actual economies *in spite of* no auctioneer and no instantaneous adjustments, that is, in spite of the impermanence problem. Evidently these economists continue to believe in a tendency of firms to employ more labour if the real wage decreases, and to employ more capital per unit of labour in new plants (i.e. to invest more) if the rate of interest decreases; and in a tendency of the real wage and of the rate of interest to respond to excess demands in the respective markets. From these mechanisms they derive a tendency towards the full employment of resources and towards an income distribution determined by marginal products; this tendency is taken to imply that the economy evolves in the way described by the traditional neoclassical picture, that is (in simplified form) by Solow-Ramsey models. The explanatory-predictive capacity of intertemporal equilibria is then derived from their determining paths which are qualitatively similar to how one already believes the economy to behave, a belief deriving from the acceptance of the traditional neoclassical picture, not of neo-Walrasian theory. That the intertemporal equilibrium is not credible—in fact, indeterminate—on what will happen some years from now is evidently considered not important because what is important is the behaviour of the economy now and in a few subsequent years, which is little affected by what will happen farther in the future. Then the similarity between the trend described by Solow-Ramsey models, which is believed correct, and the path generated by disaggregated intertemporal equilibria (which is a full-employment path too, with income distribution determined by marginal products) authorizes the belief that intertemporal equilibria too have explanatory-predictive power.

If this interpretation is correct, then these economists still ultimately believe in capital–labour substitution as traditionally conceived, i.e. in 'capital' the single factor; that notion of capital has been only apparently abandoned, it is still fully accepted when it comes to the determination of the labour demand curve and of the investment function, and this explains the popularity of Solow-Ramsey one-good growth models.

8.18 · Behind the Neoclassical Reliance on Intertemporal Equilibria

But then the usual characterization of the aggregative neoclassical growth models used in mainstream macro-literature as simplified versions of the 'rigorous' disaggregated infinite-horizon intertemporal-equilibrium models, and deriving their legitimacy from the latter ones, appears to be *the opposite of the truth*. The neoclassical analyses based on the capacity of traditional capital–labour substitution to cause the economy to gravitate, through time-consuming adjustments,[45] towards full employment are the real microfoundation of the claimed validity of intertemporal-equilibrium theory as a positive theory, not the reverse. Without a faith in those analyses the implausible assumptions needed by neo-Walrasian equilibria would make it impossible to attribute descriptive relevance to these equilibria.

Support for this interpretation comes from the author who has insisted most on intertemporal general equilibrium theory as the only possible rigorous microfoundation for macroeconomic theory: Robert Lucas. Lucas has explicitly admitted that rational expectations and the connected optimal decision rules are what economic agents will converge to, *given time*, if the economic environment is sufficiently constant as to allow rational expectations to be learned.[46] This means accepting that, during the learning process, the economy does not behave as rational expectations would require, and therefore is in disequilibrium.[47] And in (1986) Lucas has admitted that the assumption of continuous market clearing

---

45 The legitimacy of the assumption of continuous equilibrium for a Solow-type model does not derive from intertemporal equilibrium theory, where this assumption is an unfortunate necessity, but from the long-period nature of the equilibrium of a Solow-type model, which only aims at describing the trend around which the economy gravitates, implicitly accepting the conception of 'capital' as a single factor. The quantity of capital in Solow's model is persistent enough to allow for time-consuming disequilibrium adjustments. So the 'momentary equilibrium' of Solow's model has no need for the auctioneer or instantaneous adjustment in order for the economy to *gravitate* towards it. The time scale over which the tendency towards it can be assumed to operate can well be years. So it is in fact a *long-period* equilibrium, a centre of gravitation of time-consuming adjustments.

46 'The economic interpretation of this assumption of rational expectations is that agents have operated for some time in a situation like the current one and have therefore built up experience about the probability distribution which affects them. For this to have meaning, these distributions must remain stable through time'. (Lucas 1974: 190). Later in the same article Lucas repeats that the probability distributions of the variables under examination "are learned by processing observed frequencies in some sensible fashion... which has the property that the 'true' distributions become 'known' after enough time has passed". (Lucas 1974: 204).

47 For example, if the government adopts a new systematic policy rule, 'it will take some time for individuals to learn the new rule, since initially they will tend to regard unexpected government behaviour merely as evidence of random deviations from the original policy rule. As time elapses, it will become less and less plausible to suppose the original rule remains in operation and only gradually will individuals discover the basis of the new policy. Not only will there be a transition phase during which perception of the model is incorrect and expectations irrational in the sense that forecasting errors are systematic, but in addition the discovery of the model through empirical econometrics is frustrated both by the need to model switches in policy and by the presence of transitional periods in which expectations bear little relation to the policy then in operation'. (Begg 1982, p. 66).

652 Chapter 8 · Intertemporal Equilibrium, Temporary Equilibrium

is only a simplification intended to depict the trend of markets in which there is no auctioneer but the time-consuming adaptive behaviour of agents in the setting of prices converges to the equilibrium prices.[48] Therefore the equilibria of the models formulated by Lucas and by other rational expectations macroeconomists are intended to determine the normal or average or trend situation of economies where disequilibria are in fact present but can be neglected because markets gravitate around and towards an equilibrium which is persistent and unaffected by the disequilibrium actions of agents: a long-period equilibrium. The composition of capital is necessarily endogenously determined in such an equilibrium, therefore what is taken as given as capital endowment is not a given vector of capital goods, but is capital conceived as a single amount of endogenously determined composition: the traditional marginalist conception of 'capital'. One understands better, then, why Lucas and other neoclassical macroeconomists always use models where capital is a single factor in spite of referring to Arrow–Debreu as the rigorous notion of equilibrium. Without such a traditional conception of capital their analyses would be unable to specify the data of the notion of equilibrium on which they are actually basing their analyses. Evidently the belief is still present that capital *can* be treated as a single factor of variable 'form', necessarily then an amount of value.

We can now reconsider what was stated in ▶ Sect. 8.15, namely, that a theory of the *actual* path would be needed to assess whether the intertemporal-equilibrium path gives an acceptable approximation to the behaviour of real economies. I suggest that behind the faith in the descriptive validity of intertemporal equilibria *there is* an implicit theory of the actual path, and it is the traditional neoclassical theory based on long-period tendencies, because the faith persists in capital the single factor. To put it in an expressive although imprecise way,[49] it is Solow's model with its traditional conception of capital–labour substitution that, if accepted, allows assigning some descriptive value to Arrow–Debreu, not the opposite. But this cannot be explicitly stated by the neoclassical theorist because officially the notion of 'capital' has been rejected, and indeed it cannot be defended after the discovery of re-switching and reverse capital deepening.

8.19 Overlapping Generations

I pass to illustrating the infinite-periods intertemporal-equilibrium model that dispenses with the assumption of infinitely-lived consumers and assumes instead an ***overlapping-generations (OLG) structure***. The models with OLG structure

---

48 '…decision rules are continuously under review and revision … Technically, I think of economics as studying decision rules that are steady states of some adaptive process, decision rules that are found to work over a range of situations and hence are no longer revised appreciably as more experience accumulates' (Lucas 1986, pp. S401–S402).

49 Imprecise, because 'Solow's model' should be replaced by "traditional marginalist theory relying on 'capital' the single value factor of variable 'form' ".

8.18 · Behind the Neoclassical Reliance on Intertemporal Equilibria

assume consumers who live for a finite number of periods, and whose lives partially overlap with the lives of other consumers. This is realistic, and it allows the neoclassicals to study many issues in a more realistic way than through models with infinitely-lived agents. For example, a pay-as-you-go system of social security assumes that each period retired people receive an income transfer from working people (who pay taxes which finance a pension system run by the state). The working persons accept this subtraction from their income, in exchange for receiving in their turn such a transfer when old. The overlap between generations and the infinity of periods are essential to this social arrangement; the implications of pay-as-you-go systems can only be studied in OLG growth models, neoclassical or not.

There are many studies of pension systems or education expenditure or public debt in non-neoclassical OLG frameworks. This book will not deal with them, as we would have to trespass onto the richly populated territory of non-neoclassical growth models. Here our interest is in whether the OLG structure saves the neoclassical approach from the problems encountered thus far.

No doubt an improvement in realism is obtained thanks to the absence of infinitely-lived consumers optimizing over a perfectly forecasted infinite future; each generation needs to worry only about what will happen during its presence in the economy. Bequests would re-introduce the need for foresight about what the bequeathed capital will yield to one's heirs, if one assumed bequests determined by maximization of utility functions also depending on the income of heirs; but we saw that these intertemporal utility functions encounter logical problems, and anyway it seems more realistic to assume socially determined given propensities to bequeath, determined by conventions and perhaps depending on social class (e.g. on income level relative to average income).[50] The most common assumption in OLG models is absence of bequests; this can be interpreted as reflecting the belief that bequests, if realistically introduced, would change nothing fundamental in the new results that emerge from the OLG structure.[51] The gain in realism comes together with a series of new and unexpected results: the First and Second Fundamental Theorems of Welfare Economics need not hold; equilibria need not be in the *core* of the economy (this notion will be explained in the course of the chapter); a continuum of equilibria can be robust, i.e. *not* made to disappear by any small change of parameters. Before attempting an evaluation

---

50 The strength of social conventions must not be underestimated. It explains, for example, fathers killing daughters who do not behave as social custom imposes, in muslim societies and not only.

51 The assumption of no bequests is the usual one in OLG models, but it obscures the important role of inherited wealth in capitalist economies. Inheritance plays a fundamental role in the maintenance of social structure, and social pressure to such an end is what, fundamentally, determines it. The rich must defend the existence and continuation of their class; this class will act against those of its members who do not conform to this social imperative: if a very rich person starts to spend like hell with a clear intention to leave nothing to her heirs, nine times out of ten the heirs will succeed in having her incapacitated. Analogous social pressures act on the bequest decisions of the middle class. The world would be *very* different if there were no bequests.

654   Chapter 8 · Intertemporal Equilibrium, Temporary Equilibrium

of this version of intertemporal equilibria, let us try to understand these novelties.

The simplest model of OLG general equilibrium assumes that each consumer lives two periods; at the beginning of each period, that is, at each date, there are the young, who will also be alive the next period, and the old, who know that the period just starting is their last period. In order to isolate the specificities originating in the OLG structure it is opportune to reduce other complications, so it is usual to assume that in each generation all agents are identical.

Already this simple model reveals something interesting. Time is divided into periods. Period t goes from date t to infinitesimally before date $t+1$. Suppose that in this economy population is stationary, and in each period income is produced only by the young; assume that a single *perishable, non-storable* consumption good, food, is gradually produced by unassisted labour, and is consumed the moment it is produced. Labour supply per person is rigid, and each person produces one unit of food. Assume an initial social arrangement where the young work and consume, while the old, unable to work, survive on theft or by scavenging rubbish dumps, or simply die of hunger. People are selfish, and the young do not care about the old. The equilibrium of this OLG economy consists of a separate extremely simple equilibrium for each period, where the young produce on the basis of their given labour supply, and consume what they produce, while the old lead a horrible existence at the margin of society. This equilibrium is not Pareto efficient. Now suppose at a date which we can call date 0 a political leader proposes a social pact: each young generation will pass to the old generation of the same period one-third of its production. By kind concession of the gods, all future generations are present when this proposal is made, and each generation can accept or reject it. Suppose that preferences (assumed to be the same for all generations) are such that the young prefer this split of their income over the two periods to enjoying the whole of it when young and then having a miserable old age; but if they are going to receive nothing when old, then they want as much income when young as possible. Suppose the pact is accepted; the young of date 0 pass one-third of the income they produce during period 0 to the old of date 0, and when old (during period 1) they receive one-third of the product of the young of period 1. By assumption, they prefer it to the previous situation, and all subsequent generations too. And the old of date 0 prefer it too. So the pact is unanimously accepted, and a Pareto improvement is obtained. (Who guarantees, and how, that the pact will be respected in the future is a problem I will not discuss.) The original equilibrium was not Pareto efficient; a pay-as-you-go social arrangement improves things for everybody.

Note that the pact is only possible because of the infinity of future periods. If the economy ends at a last period T, the young of that period reject the pact because they have no incentive to pass one-third of their food to the old of that period; then the young of period $T-1$ reject the pact too, ... and by repeated backward induction the pact is rejected by all generations (except the old of period 0). In order for the young freely to adhere to the pact, they must have faith that the pact will be respected in the future.

8.19 · Overlapping Generations

Now, there is nothing particularly neoclassical in this picture. Even if you replace the assumption that all the young work with an assumption that employment is determined by some other mechanism, the suffering of the old remains a problem, and a central authority capable of guaranteeing the respect of the pay-as-you-go pact in the future improves the situation for everybody independently of your theory of income distribution.

The trouble for the neoclassicals is that the situation without the pact is a legitimate intertemporal equilibrium, with everybody optimizing; and yet the equilibrium is not Pareto efficient; the First Fundamental Theorem of Welfare Economics does not hold. Nor is this attributable to absence of some markets, e.g. to absence of markets in futures: the young of date t can only produce the perishable consumption good, what can they offer to the young of date $t+1$ in exchange for some food when old? Nothing; there is no feasible desirable exchange, markets in futures will not operate even if open. Nor can the situation be changed by transfers *of endowments*, as considered in the Second Welfare Theorem. Here the sole endowment is labour, and it cannot be reallocated. So the Second Welfare Theorem fails. One needs a perennial state intervention: in each period a tax on the young and a subsidy to the old.

Absence of Pareto optimality does not always obtain in OLG equilibria, but it does not need such an extreme model in order to appear. Suppose the consumption good, call it food, is not totally perishable, it can be stored; if one unit of it is stored in period t then $1+r$ units survive to period $t+1$, where r can be negative (Weil 2008). The young of period t desire to transfer part of what they produce to period $t+1$ to consume it when old, but cannot obtain by trade more than by storing part of what they produce when young, because they cannot trade with other generations: there is nothing to exchange with the old of period t (to exchange one unit of food against one unit of food is useless) nor, when old, with the young of period $t+1$ (for the same reason), so they can only try to exchange food today for a promise of food tomorrow sold by other young people of their generation, but since we are assuming all individuals in the same generation are identical, no one will be ready to offer more than what can be obtained via storage; so the rate of interest on promises of food tomorrow against food today will be r. Labour supply is given, hence, one can treat the young as having an endowment of 1 unit of food when young and zero when old. Consumption when young and when old will be determined by utility maximization. If for example individuals have a Cobb–Douglas utility function $u=x_Y^a x_O^{1-a}$ (Y for young, O for old), since each one of them has budget constraint $x_O=(1+r)(1-x_Y)$, utility maximization implies $x_Y=a$, $x_O=(1+r)(1-a)$. Suppose all generations have the same number of individuals. If $r<0$ a pact establishing that each generation passes the fraction $(1-a)$ of its production of food to the old of the same period is a Pareto improvement: it allows all generations to consume as much as in equilibrium when young, but more than in equilibrium when old, $(1-a)$ instead of $(1+r)(1-a)$. Again, the equilibrium is not Pareto optimal. If population grows at rate $n>0$, and the young transfer the share $(1-a)$ of their output to the old of their period, since the old are fewer than the young each one of the old obtains

656   **Chapter 8** · Intertemporal Equilibrium, Temporary Equilibrium

even more, an amount of food equal to $(1 + n)(1 - a)$, so now an improvement can be obtained by transfers relative to the equilibrium even if $r > 0$ as long as $r \leq n$. Yes, even with $r = n$, if you are content with a weak Pareto improvement, because the young of all generations obtain as much as in equilibrium but the old of the first period obtain a transfer and are better off. If $r > n$, the equilibrium is Pareto efficient.

Which is the cause of the failure of the First Welfare Theorem? It would need some advanced maths to make it rigorously clear, but the intuition can be obtained from the famous example of the hotel with an infinite number of rooms, all occupied. Does this mean that if someone knocks at the hotel's door and asks for a room, the hotel director cannot accept her? No, because the guest in room 1 can be moved to room 2, the guest in room 2 can be moved to room 3, and so on ad infinitum, and this leaves room 1 free. There is no last room which makes it impossible for the guest who was occupying it to obtain another room. Let us extend the analogy to consumption. Imagine an infinite number of beggars sitting one behind the other; all except the first have a nice bowl of soup in front of them, and there are no bowls of soup not assigned yet. If each beggar passes the bowl to the beggar in front, the first beggar gets the soup and no one is left without.[52] The transfer of wealth from the young of generation t to the old of generation t − 1 compensated by an analogous transfer from generation t + 1 to generation t is analogous, it exploits the fact that there is no last generation which will not receive the compensating transfer.

8.20 Multiple OLG Equilibria

Let us now approach a different issue, multiplicity of OLG equilibria, via a slightly different model, a *two-ways-infinity* model.[53]

Consider a stationary exchange economy that not only will go on forever but has also forever existed, that is, t can take any integer value in the open interval $(-\infty, +\infty)$. Each generation comprises the same number of identical individuals (in preferences and endowments) so I aggregate them into a single individual: each generation is an individual who lives two periods. Generation t is the gen-

---

52 Why not repeat the transfer and have *two* bowls of soup arrive at the first beggar, and all the other beggars still with their soup? Or even better, after getting two bowls of soup to the first beggar, let us let the second beggar get two bowls by having the transfer stop at her, and then let us apply the same thing to the third beggar... The number of bowls is infinite, so we could take off an infinite number of bowls and still have enough bowls to give one to all beggars. (The natural numbers are infinite. Take away the infinite odd integers: the remaining numbers are still infinite.) This shows that the analogy is only an intuitive analogy, in OLG models one cannot neglect constraints on which transfers are possible. But the intuition remains valid, that sometimes the infinity of consumption goods makes it possible to give more to some without taking away from anyone else.

53 I will take the existence of OLG general equilibria for granted. Actually it requires to exclude a number of special cases, and to assume some condition equivalent, in the new framework, to irreducibility. See Geanakoplos and Polemarchakis (1991).

8.20 · Multiple OLG Equilibria

eration that is young in period t. Assume there is *a single perishable consumption good*, and at the beginning of each period each young person receives an endowment of this good as manna from heaven, and each old person too, generally a different amount from the young's. Each generation is only interested in her consumption over the two periods of her existence. The utility function of each generation is Cobb–Douglas in log form, with x^t_s consumption of generation t in period s:

$$U^t\left(\ldots 0, x^t_t x^t_{t+1}, 0 \ldots\right) = a_t \, ln \, x^t_t + (1 - a_t) ln \, x^t_{t+1}.$$

Marginal utilities are a_t/x^t_t and $(1 - a_t)/x^t_{t+1}$.

Each generation has a positive endowment only in the two periods of its life. The endowment of the generation that is young in period t is the two-vector $\omega^t \equiv (\omega^t_t, \omega^t_{t+1})$. The *overall* endowment of the good at the beginning of period t is $\omega^{t-1}_t + \omega^t_t$. There are no bequests.

Let us define an *allocation* as an infinite-dimensional vector with two elements per period $\mathbf{x} = (\ldots; x^{t-1}_t, x^t_t; x^t_{t+1}, x^{t+1}_{t+1}, \ldots)$ that specifies for each period the consumption of the old and the consumption of the young, and therefore also the consumption of each generation over the two periods of its life. An allocation is *admissible* if in every period t total consumption equals total endowment:

$$x^{t-1}_t + x^t_t = \omega^{t-1}_t + \omega^t_t.$$

Prices p_t are discounted prices of the single consumption good, for example, in terms of some date chosen as date 0 where $p_0 = 1$. An equilibrium is defined by a vector of discounted prices $\mathbf{p} \in L_{++}$ (the set of infinite strictly positive vectors, because preferences are monotonic) and by an admissible allocation $\mathbf{x}$ such that for each generation at the given prices utility is maximized (under a hypothesis of price taking), i.e. such that with $p_t \omega^t_t + p_{t+1} \omega^t_{t+1} < \infty$, $\forall t$ it is:

$$\mathbf{x}^t \equiv \left(x^t_t, x^t_{t+1}\right) \in ArgMax\left\{U^t\left(x^t_t, x^t_{t+1}\right)/p_t\left(x^t_t - \omega^t_t\right) + p_{t+1}\left(x^t_{t+1} - \omega^t_{t+1}\right) = 0\right\}.$$

The budget constraint is an equality because of non-satiation.[54]

If $\mathbf{p}$ is an equilibrium price vector then $k\mathbf{p}$ with k a positive scalar is also an equilibrium price vector; the normalization $\Sigma_t p_t = 1$ is not convenient because there is an infinite number of prices; a possible different approach is to define

$$q_t = p_{t+1}/p_t, \forall t \in Z \text{ (the set of positive and negative integers)}.$$

Since prices p_t are discounted prices, it is $(1 + r_t)p_{t+1} = p_t$, thus $q_t = 1/(1 + r_t)$ is the *discount factor* from period $t + 1$ to period t (if an amount of the consumption good at date 1 costs C in undiscounted terms, its value at date 0 is Cq_0); it is also the relative price of the consumption good of date $t + 1$ in terms of the

---

54 I will not discuss OLG models with fiat money having positive value, where the budget constraint must be specified differently.

658   Chapter 8 · Intertemporal Equilibrium, Temporary Equilibrium

consumption good of date t. This normalization makes it possible to redefine the equilibrium as a sequence of *relative* prices $\mathbf{q} = (\dots, q_{-1}, q_0, q_{+1}, \dots)$ and an admissible allocation $\mathbf{x}$ such that $\mathbf{x}^t \equiv (x^t_t, x^t_{t+1})$ satisfies

$$\mathbf{x}^t \in ArgMax\{U'(\mathbf{x}) \mid x^t_t + q_t x^t_{t+1} = \omega^t_t + q_t \omega^t_{t+1}\}$$

where the new expression for the budget constraint is obtained by dividing by p_t both sides of the original budget constraint. The maximization of the utility of generation t, once its endowments are given, depends only on q_t.

Let $z^t_t(q_t) \equiv x^t_t - \omega^t_t$ be the excess demand of generation t at time t, i.e. of the young at time t, and let $z^t_{t+1}(q_t) \equiv x^t_{t+1} - \omega^t_{t+1}$ be the analogous excess demand of the same generation when old, i.e. at time $t+1$. With this notation we can re-write the equilibrium condition as:

$$z^{t-1}_t(q_{t-1}) + z^t_t(q_t) = 0, \forall t \tag{8.12}$$

Let us study the case of a stationary economy, with the same preferences and endowments for all generations and the same number of identical agents in each generation. The parameter $a_t = a$ is the same in all utility functions, and the same goes for ω_t. We study the stationary solution, so we suppose that t goes from $-\infty$ to $+\infty$.

Let us set $w^{t-1}_t + w^t_t = 1$, and for brevity let us indicate the endowment when young as simply $\omega = \omega^t_t$, $\forall t$; therefore the endowment when old is $1 - \omega$. Let us also assume

$$\omega > a \geq 1/2.$$

Thus we are assuming that the young's endowment is greater than the old's endowment and furthermore that in the utility function consumption when young is given greater weight, or at most the same weight, than consumption when old.

Suppose each generation can transfer income across its two periods. The maximization problem of generation t is

$$max_{x_t, x_{t+1}} a \ln x_t + (1-a) \ln x_{t+1}, \quad \text{subject to } x_t + q_t x_{t+1} = \omega + q_t(1-\omega).$$

We can re-write the budget constraint as

$$x_t = -q_t x_{t+1} + \omega + q_t(1-\omega)$$

and use it to eliminate x_t from the objective function:

$$max_{x_{t+1}} u^t = a \ln \omega + q_t(1-\omega) - q_t x_{t+1} + (1-a) \ln x_{t+1}.$$

The sole variable is x_{t+1}. Given the shape of Cobb–Douglas indifference curves, the maximum is internal, so we can impose as first-order condition:

$$\partial u/\partial x_{t+1} = -q_1 a/\omega + q_t(1-\omega) - q_t x_{t+1} + (1-a)/x_{t+1} = 0$$

that is,

$$-q_t a/x_t + (1-a)/x_{t+1} = 0.$$

8.20 · Multiple OLG Equilibria

This yields the form taken in this example by the so-called **Keynes-Ramsey rule**[55]:

$$aq_t/x_t = (1 - a)/x_{t+1}. \tag{8.13}$$

The marginal utility of one more small unit of consumption tomorrow must just offset the marginal disutility of the decrease in consumption today, made necessary by the given rate of exchange q_t between consumption today and tomorrow. Now using jointly the budget constraint and Eq. (8.13) we eliminate x_{t+1} and obtain:

$$x_t = a\omega + (1 - \omega)q_t. \tag{8.14}$$

Thus consumption when young is a fraction $a \geq 1/2$ of the present value of the total endowment of the generation.

Let us look for the equilibria of this stationary economy.

First of all there is an *autarchic equilibrium* in which each generation consumes its endowments, with no exchanges nor intertemporal reallocations of consumption. This equilibrium is defined by the allocation $\mathbf{x} = \Omega$ and by a vector of constant relative prices $\mathbf{q} = (..., q^*, q^*, q^*, ...)$ determined as follows. Because the equilibrium is autarchic it is $x^t_t = \omega$ and $x^t_{t+1} = 1 - \omega$; by substitution in Eq. (8.13) we obtain

$$q_t a/\omega = (1 - a)/(1 - \omega)$$

and therefore

$$q_t = q^* = [(1 - a)/(1 - \omega)]/(a/\omega) > 1.$$

When $q_t = q^*$, it is $x^t_t = \omega$ from Eq. (8.14), and therefore $x^t_{t+1} = 1 - \omega$ from the budget constraint, so there is equilibrium. Note that $q^* > 1$ (which follows from the assumption that $\omega > a$) implies a negative interest rate. The interest rate must be negative enough to induce each agent to consume each period that period's endowment: owing to the assumed form of the utility function and the assumption $\omega > a \geq 1/2$, the marginal utility of consuming one's endowment when old, $(1 - a)/(1 - \omega) > 1$, is greater than the marginal utility of consuming one's endowment when young, $a/\omega < 1$: now, q_t is the relative price of the consumption when old with respect to consumption when young, and it must be equal to the ratio between the two marginal utilities.

But the autarchic equilibrium is not the only stationary equilibrium. Another equilibrium is the **golden rule** equilibrium (so-called because Pareto efficient, as we will see), with equilibrium relative price vector $\mathbf{q} = (..., 1, 1, 1, ...)$, hence, zero interest rate, and consumptions $(a, 1 - a)$ for each generation. The marginal

---

55 This rule takes a different form in different models, but it always expresses the need to balance, at the margin, the advantage of more consumption today with the disadvantage of the decrease in consumption in subsequent periods made inevitable by the assumption of full utilization of resources and therefore of a trade-off between consumption and savings in each period (in models with production, more consumption today means less capital tomorrow). In economies where this constraint does not hold because production is constrained by insufficient aggregate demand and not by the availability of resources, the rule does not apply.

660 Chapter 8 · Intertemporal Equilibrium, Temporary Equilibrium

utility of consumption when young and when old is the same, 1; the allocation is admissible. It is an equilibrium because for $q_t = 1$ the optimal choice of each generation is $x_t/x_{t+1} = a/(1-a)$ which, because of the budget constraint, imposes $x_t = a$, $x_{t+1} = 1 - a$. (We might also show that if population grows at rate g, then there is a golden rule equilibrium with interest rate equal to g, but we omit this demonstration.)

Now I prove that the autarchic equilibrium is Pareto inferior to the golden rule equilibrium.

Proof We have seen that in the autarchic equilibrium the marginal utility of consumption when young is less than the marginal utility of consumption when old, so for each generation a diminution of consumption when young, and increase by the same amount when old, increases utility until it brings the two marginal utilities into equality. Thus each generation is better off in the golden rule than in the autarchic equilibrium. ∎

This shows that the autarchic equilibrium is not Pareto efficient. We have confirmed what had been shown informally in ▶ Sect. 8.19: *the First Welfare Theorem does not hold for OLG equilibria.*[56]

I prove now that the golden rule equilibrium is Pareto efficient, by proving that, starting from it, any increase in the welfare of a generation implies that the utility of some other generation decreases.

Proof Assume, without loss of generality, that starting from the golden rule equilibrium the utility of generation 0 is increased via an increase of its consumption when old, x_1^0. (At least one of its two consumptions *must* increase if its utility is to increase.) This implies a decrease of x_1^1, and, in order to maintain the utility of generation 1 at least unchanged, the latter's consumption when old, x_2^1, must increase by a *greater* amount than the decrease of its consumption when young: this is because the starting situation is one of equal marginal utilities, i.e. of maximum utility achievable from a total two-period consumption, and then any reallocation of a *given* quantity of consumption from one period to the other decreases utility. So it must be $x_2^1 > x_1^0$; for the same reason, it must be $x_3^2 > x_2^1$, and so on; and the increase $x_{t+2}^{t+1} - x_{t+1}^t$ must itself increase with t, because, owing to decreasing marginal utility, even successive *equal* decreases of consumption when young would require greater and greater increases of consumption when old in order to leave utility unaffected, while here the decreases of consumption when young are themselves increasing as t increases; so at a certain point x_{t+1}^t becomes greater than 1 and therefore impossible. If the utility of generation 0 is increased by increasing its consumption when young, the same reasoning applies in the opposite direction. We have thus proved that it is inevitable that some generation's utility decreases if some other generation's utility increases starting from the golden rule equilibrium. ∎

---

56 On the contrary, it does hold for infinite-horizon economies with a finite number of infinitely-lived consumers, cf., e.g. Mas-Colell et al. (1995, pp. 766–68).

8.21 The Core of Allocations in the Neoclassical Economy

These are not the only equilibria of this economy; there are others, which we will now study as part of the study of the *core* in OLG models.

8.21 The Core of Allocations in the Neoclassical Economy

Another difference between the usual equilibrium models and OLG models concerns the *core* of the economy.[57]

The framework for this notion is an economy described in the marginalist way: there is a given number of individuals, each one with given endowments, and there is a given production possibility set; these determine a set of feasible allocations reachable via exchange and production.

The core of this economy is a subset of this set of feasible allocations; *an allocation is in the core if no subset of individuals in the economy (including the set that includes all the individuals in the economy) can, by using only their endowments plus production, reach an allocation for its members, that makes at least one individual in the subset strictly better off and no one worse off than in the initial allocation.*

(For exchange economies the notion of core is the same, except that there is no production.)

For example, an allocation in an exchange economy with three consumers is in the core if the following conditions are simultaneously satisfied: (1) no consumer can be better off counting only on her own endowments; (2) no couple of two consumers can, with the sole endowments of the couple, reach an allocation that makes both of them better off than in the given allocation; (3) no Pareto-superior economy-wide feasible allocation exists.

The last condition shows that only Pareto-efficient allocations can be in the core; but not all Pareto-efficient allocations are in the core. For example, in a standard two consumers exchange economy represented by an Edgeworth box with smooth strictly convex indifference curves, the core is only the portion of the Pareto set usually called the **contract curve**, the portion included in the 'lens' formed by the two indifference curves that pass through the endowment point. To be in the core an allocation must be Pareto efficient, but a Pareto-efficient allocation outside the contract curve does not satisfy condition 1.

In the theory of the core[58] the possible subsets of individuals are called **coalitions**, and if one of these coalitions can with its sole resources make all its members better off than in an initial allocation, then it is said that the coalition **can improve** on the initial allocation, or also that it **blocks** the initial allocation. The latter term implicitly refers to some social mechanism of coalition formation and

---

57 This notion of core *of a (neoclassical) economy* is totally different from P. Garegnani's notion of core *of the classical or surplus approach*, mentioned in ▶ Chap. 1.

58 As applied to economic allocations achievable (possibly through production too) from given total endowments; we are in the same framework as general equilibrium theory. The notion of core is more general, it is defined in terms of strategies in cooperative games, but here the term will be used in this more restricted sense.

662   Chapter 8 · Intertemporal Equilibrium, Temporary Equilibrium

suggests that the coalition will prevent the initial allocation proposal from being accepted *by mutual agreement*, if the members of the blocking coalition realize that they can reach another arrangement they unanimously prefer. *The core is the set of feasible allocations that are not blocked by any coalition.*

In Arrow–Debreu–McKenzie economies,[59] if an equilibrium exists, the core is not empty, because *equilibrium allocations are in the core*. I prove this last claim for exchange economies.

Proof By contradiction. Consider an exchange economy with n individuals where individual i has endowment vector ω^i. Let $\{x^*\} = \{x^{*1}, \ldots, x^{*n}\}$ be an equilibrium allocation at prices p^*. Let S stand for the set that collects the indices of members of a coalition. Suppose a coalition S can improve on $\{x^*\}$, that is, there is a feasible allocation $\{x\}$ such that for each $i \in S$ it is $x^i \succ x^{*i}$, and such that $\Sigma_{i \in S} x^i = \Sigma_{i \in S} \omega^i$, which implies

$$\Sigma_{i \in S} p^* x^i = \Sigma_{i \in S} p^* \omega^i.$$

By the theory of revealed preference, it must be $p^* x^i > p^* x^{*i} = p^* \omega^i$ for all i in S, otherwise, at the equilibrium prices p^* consumer i would prefer to use her equilibrium income to purchase x^i and not x^{*i}. This implies

$$\Sigma_{i \in S} p^* x^i > \Sigma_{i \in S} p^* \omega^i$$

that contradicts the previous equality. So the assumption that there exists a coalition that can block $\{x^*\}$ brings to a contradiction, hence there cannot be such a coalition, and $\{x^*\}$ must be in the core. ∎

The economic implication of this result is that consumers have no incentive to deviate from competitive behaviour and to look for other, non-market ways of redistributing endowments.[60]

The fundamental result of core theory (for which I will supply only some intuition) is that, as consumers become more and more numerous and smaller and smaller relative to the entire economy, the core 'shrinks' in a sense I will now clarify, and tends in the limit to coincide with the general equilibrium allocations.

'Smaller and smaller' is formalized as follows in the framework of a general equilibrium of exchange: starting from a given number N of consumers with given endowments, one assumes the appearance of N additional consumers who are an exact replica in preferences and endowments of the first N ones; the 'replication' is then repeated again and again; the initial economy including N consumers is called the first *replica economy*, the mth *replica economy* includes m groups of N consumers identical to the original group. Replication renders each

---

59 With this name one refers to general equilibria either with a given number of firms (Arrow–Debreu) or, as preferred here, with CRS industries and an implicit assumption of free entry (McKenzie).

60 Of course, barring non-voluntary redistributions based on extortion, violence, etc.

8.21 · The Core of Allocations in the Neoclassical Economy

consumer unambiguously 'smaller and smaller' relative to the entire economy. The equilibria of the mth replica economy are simply the equilibria of the first replica economy, only with all equilibrium market demands multiplied by m. The core, on the other hand, is *not* the same set of core allocations as in the first replica economy simply repeated identical for each group of N consumers. What has been proved is that each replication causes some of the symmetric replications of the original core allocations to fall out of the core, because further coalitions become possible at each replication, and some of them block some of the symmetrically replicated original core allocations. So the core allocations for each group of N consumers shrink at each replication, and converge in the limit to the set of equilibria. In the limit, as consumers tend to become infinitesimal relative to the size of markets, competitive equilibria tend to remain the sole non-blocked allocations. This is called the ***core equivalence theorem*** or also the *core convergence theorem*.

To understand why this theorem is found interesting, one must start from Francis Ysidro Edgeworth (1845–1926). Against his contemporary Stanley Jevons who had argued that the 'law of one price' (all units of a good sell at the same price) and price taking had to be *assumed* as part of the meaning of competitive markets, in 1881 Edgeworth argued that they would result from bargaining by price-*making* agents, as long as these were numerous. He started by pointing out that repeated barter between two persons with given endowments does not bring to a univocal result, because any point on the contract curve can be reached, depending on the succession of barters and on the barter abilities of the individuals. All one can say is that a barter proposal will be accepted only if neither individual is made worse off by it, and that if, as long as mutually more favourable exchange opportunities exist, they are discovered and a further barter is proposed, then barter will stop only when some point on the contract curve is reached; which point remains indeterminate. *But,* Edgeworth went on to argue, *this indeterminacy is reduced* when the number of exchangers increases, at least as long as one admits that '***recontracting***' is possible, that is, that 'contracts' are only tentative promises of exchange that can be cancelled when one of the partners finds that she/he can stipulate a more favourable contract with other exchangers. To prove this claim Edgeworth introduced indifference curves and an argument that, in more modern terms, can be formulated as follows.

Suppose two goods, x and y, and, initially, two individuals A and B with *strictly* convex indifference curves and given endowments. Draw the corresponding Edgeworth box, assuming that A's and B's indifference curves through the endowment point Ω are not tangent but form a 'lens' and therefore the contract curve is a portion of the Pareto set and not a single point, as shown in ◼ Fig. 8.3. Suppose initially that in contracting with A, B is always able to extract practically all possible advantage (and neglect for ease of exposition the very slight improvement in A's utility plausibly needed to induce her to accept the bargain). Then B is able to obtain the allocation corresponding to point α where A has the same utility level as with no exchange.

Now assume two more consumers appear, A_2 who is identical to A (in preferences and endowment), and B_2 identical to B. Measure A_2's allocation from

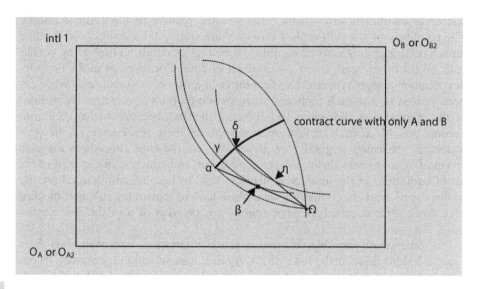

◘ Fig. 8.3 Edgeworth box and the core

the same origin as A, and B_2's from the same origin as B. A_2 has the same initial endowment as A, but A now has endowment α, and can exchange with A_2: a redistribution of their total endowment allows both to reach any point along the segment joining α and Ω, which raises the utility of both. Suppose they agree on the mid-point β. Now B is at α, A and A_2 are at β, and B_2 is at Ω. Now B_2 can offer A to recontract, that is, to undo all previous contracts and to bargain with him, and to reach some point on the contract curve where A is very slightly better off than at β, that is, practically at point γ on the contract curve, where A is on the indifference curve through β. Again suppose we can neglect the 'very slightly better off' and the 'practically'. A accepts and ends at γ. Now A and B_2 are at γ, while B and A_2 are back to their initial endowments Ω, and can bargain between them: A_2 will not accept a point on the contract curve worse than the point obtained by A, because she can get as close as she wants to γ by turning to contract with B and proposing him a very slightly better allocation than γ. So now all four agents are at γ. The replica has caused at least all symmetric Pareto-efficient allocations between α and γ to fall out of the core. But if the mid-point ε (not shown in Fig. 8.B.1) of the segment from γ to Ω touches an indifference curve of A (and hence of A_2) higher than at γ, A_2 can cancel previous agreements, go back to Ω, and contract with A to reach ε. This pushes B and B_2 back to their original endowments, but now they can propose respectively to A and to A_2 to reach a point on the contract curve yielding them only a very slightly higher utility than at ε.

Repeating the reasoning (always under the assumption that B or B_2 extracts practically all the advantage from contracts with A or A_2) we conclude that recontracting will go on until a point δ on the contract curve is reached by both couples,

8.21 · The Core of Allocations in the Neoclassical Economy

such that A's (and A_2's) indifference curve through it goes also through the midpoint η of the segment that connects δ to Ω, and therefore A and A_2 can no longer both increase their utility if one of them goes back to Ω and then they contract to redistribute their allocations among the two of them. This means that if we restrict attention to symmetrical allocations in which each group of 2 individuals, (A, B) and (A_2, B_2), reaches the same final suballocation, then suballocations in the interval [α, δ) of the contract curve cannot be in the core. By an analogous reasoning, assuming now that A and A_2 are able to extract all possible advantage from bargaining with B or B_2, an analogous portion at the other end of the contract curve can be shown to be out of the core. Now, I will not prove it, but it should be intuitive that if the allocation is not symmetric, in the sense that the suballocation going to each group of N individuals is not the same, then the allocation is not in the core: for example if (A, B) are at δ while (A_2, B_2) are at γ, then A and B_2 can obtain a mutual improvement by agreeing to reach with their endowments a point of the contract curve intermediate between γ and δ. Therefore I have indeed shown that the appearance of A_2 and B_2 has caused the core to shrink, in the precise sense that the set of suballocations, which symmetrically repeated for all groups of N individuals generate allocations in the core, has shrunk.

Edgeworth argued (and much later, in the 1960s, he was proved correct) that the appearance of further 'replica' competitors further restricts the indeterminacy; the core shrinks more and more as the number of replicas increases, and tends to coincide in the limit with the equilibrium allocations; and an analogous process happens with more than two goods too, as long as multilateral barter exchange is admitted.

Edgeworth concluded that the 'law of one price' and price taking need not be *assumed*; they can be derived from a description of competition as repeated bargaining, recontracting, and arbitrage among very numerous *price-making* competitors, a process that produces price taking at the same time as it produces a tendency towards an equilibrium allocation.

The modern theory of the core reformulates the same idea in terms of 'blocking coalitions', noting that all the successive stages of bargaining and recontracting in Edgeworth's process can be seen as the formation of coalitions that 'block' the previously reached allocation by proposing another allocation that, for the members of the blocking coalition, is an improvement. In the previous example the passage from the allocation with A and B at α, and A_2 and B_2 at Ω, to the allocation with B at α, A and A_2 at β, and B_2 at Ω, can be seen as B, A and A_2 forming a coalition that, when everybody is still at Ω, 'blocks' the formation of the first allocation because B, A and A_2 can be better off with the second allocation. And the subsequent contract between B_2 and A that reaches point γ is a coalition that 'blocks' the previous allocation. The theory of the core generalizes this insight by asking us to imagine agents engaged in a 'market game' in which agents do not use prices, 'simply wander around and make tentative arrangements to trade with each other' (Varian 1992, p. 388), and these tentative arrangements compete with one another, until no better arrangement can be found: a core allocation has been reached.

666   Chapter 8 · Intertemporal Equilibrium, Temporary Equilibrium

Some economists seem to think that the fact that general equilibria are in the core brings support to the thesis that economies get close to general equilibrium allocations: 'it would be surprising to find the economy settling on an allocation outside the core, since that would indicate there is a coalition which could have made each of its members better off, using only its own resources, but for some reason has failed to coalesce and do so' (Anderson 2008, p. 238 of Vol. 2). The surprising thing is rather that the author should be blind to the obvious fact that when an allocation not in the core is proposed, the members of a potential blocking coalition will find it far from easy—and clearly impossible if they are numerous—to discover that there is a coalition that can make them better off, to contact the other persons in this 'improving coalition', and to reach an agreement on how to allocate the improvement among them.[61] Varian notes that the idea that the core will be reached 'places great informational requirements on the agents—the people in the dissatisfied coalition have to be able to find each other. Furthermore, it is assumed that there are no costs to forming coalitions so that, even if only very small gains can be made by forming coalitions, they will nevertheless be formed' (Varian 1992, p. 388).

And there is an even worse problem, which not even Varian seems to perceive. Since long-period equilibria based on value capital have been rejected, and temporary equilibria with erroneous expectations do not generate Pareto-efficient allocations, the core equivalence theorem can only refer to the coincidence, in the limit, of the core allocations *with intertemporal-equilibrium allocations*. But then Varian's picture of agents 'simply wandering around and making tentative arrangements to trade with each other' would require yet-to-be-born consumers to take part in the formation of these tentative arrangements[62], an obvious impossibility. Neoclassical economists, it seems, find it hard to remember that now their notion of equilibrium is intertemporal.

What seems worth retaining of Edgeworth's analysis is the idea that the more numerous the price-*making* individuals competing in the same market, the more the indefiniteness due to price making is reduced by the presence of competitors, so that in the end agents behave as price *takers*. But this idea was already implicit in the traditional picture of how concretely, in a single market, price tends towards the level that makes demand equal to supply, a picture indeed based on price-*making* agents. This picture describes a time-consuming process, whereby a seller, who discovers she is selling less than what is necessary to dispose of all her supply, the next hour or day will propose a lower price to the buyers she is able to contact; then some more buyers turn to her; then in order not to lose their

---

61 The agreement can be difficult when the coalition can realize many suballocations, all better for its members than in the 'blocked' allocation, but such that members differ on which allocation they prefer—then conflict will arise among the coalition members. Also, an agent can find out she can be a member of several blocking coalitions.

62 Perfect *price* foresight would not be enough, perfect foresight would have to include knowledge of whether there are coalitions (including future consumers) that can block any given allocation, and this would require correct foresight of the complete preferences and endowments of future consumers.

8.21 · The Core of Allocations in the Neoclassical Economy

customers other sellers too reduce their prices ... In this picture, the participants are price-makers, and yet they are obliged by the counterproposals of the other participants finally to converge onto a single price, the one that equilibrates supply-and-demand flows in the market.[63] Now, one very important aspect of this picture is the ease with which more convenient actions are discovered, that cause small 'improving coalitions' to form when they exist (the passage of a buyer to a more convenient seller, for example) as the result of clear *individual* incentives to act in that direction, incentives activated by difficulties of sale or of purchase, or by arbitrage opportunities, or by discovery of more convenient prices elsewhere. These incentives stimulate *local* action, not the co-ordination of large coalitions: usually just one agent proposing a different contract to one other agent, or a firm deciding to produce a different quantity. So this capacity of price making and competition to bring price taking about in no way salvages core theory. A 'market game' of possibly extremely large coalitions is a fairy tale as much as the auctioneer-guided tâtonnement.

Also note that, in order for repeated barter along Edgeworthian lines to tend to the core, one requires **recontracting**, intending with this that 'contracts' are only tentative promises that one is free to cancel (analogous, in this respect, to the 'bons' in the Walrasian tâtonnement); this allows agents to start all over again with their initial endowments the moment they find it convenient. *If the change in endowments brought about by barter cannot be undone, then repeated barter need not reach the core.* This is shown by the following example due to Malinvaud (1971, pp. 139–140). Assume an exchange economy with two goods, 1 and 2, and three agents A, B, C. The initial endowments are $\omega_A = (0, 2)$, $\omega_B = (1, 1)$, $\omega_C = (1, 1)$. The utility function is the same for the three agents, $U(x_1, x_2) = x_1 x_2$. In a first barter exchange B gives A 1/4 units of good 1 and receives from A 3/2 units of good 2; now the endowments are $\omega'_A = (1/4, 1/2)$, $\omega'_B = (3/4, 5/2)$, $\omega_C = (1, 1)$; this improves the utility of A from 0 to 1/8 while the utility of B passes from 1 to 15/8. In a second barter exchange C gives B 1/4 units of good 1 and receives from B 1/2 units of good 2; B's utility passes from 15/8 to 2, C's utility passes from 1 to 9/8, because now the allocation is $\omega'_A = (1/4, 1/2)$, $\omega''_B = (1,2)$, $\omega'''_C = (3/4, 3/2)$. All consumers now have the same marginal rate of substitution, 2, so this allocation is Pareto-efficient, and once it is reached it is sustainable as a no exchange equilibrium at relative price $p_1/p_2 = 2$. But it is not in the core, because it is blocked by the coalition formed by A and C, who with their endowments can reach the following allocation: $x_A = (1/4, 1)$, $x_B = (3/4, 2)$, superior for both consumers to the allocation reached by the two assumed barter exchanges.

---

63 Note how this realistic picture implies that, except in organized auction markets, adjustments can take considerable time: the seller must realize she is selling less than expected, which takes time; then she must let buyers know her new price, the buyers must decide to turn to her, the other sellers must realize what is happening and must react...; and if changes of production flows are also involved, the time taken by the adjustments is even more obvious. Which is why now this picture is totally absent from advanced microtextbooks, replaced by the fairy tale of the auctioneer, and rare even in undergraduate textbooks: not because it is defective, but because of the new need, created by the shift to neo-Walrasian general equilibria, to exclude time-consuming adjustments.

668   Chapter 8 · Intertemporal Equilibrium, Temporary Equilibrium

So recontracting cannot be dispensed with. In an economy without capital goods, e.g. a pure-exchange economy in which each consumer comes to the periodic fair always with the same initial endowments, absence of recontracting is realistic for what happens *during a single fair*, but one could interpret 'recontracting' as the process of change of the proposed barters *from one fair to the next*, since the consumer starts each fair with the same initial endowments. But in an economy with production and capital goods, the data would be different at each fair; recontracting would require us to visualize the repeated bargaining and formation of blocking coalitions as an *ex-ante* comparison of possible allocations in a situation of 'congealed' economy, with no actual exchange of endowments nor actual productions during the 'market game' of coalition formation and allocation proposals; hence a process as fairy tale as the auctioneer-guided tâtonnement.

Therefore, what remains of Edgeworth's argument seems to be only that economic agents should be considered *price-makers*, and competition should be viewed not as passive price taking but as active rivalry, in which the interest of agents to exploit all advantageous opportunities causes (*if given time to operate*) a tendency towards a common price for all the units exchanged of a good, and towards the elimination of arbitrage opportunities. But this is the realistic notion of competition found not only in Marshall but also in Smith or Marx, and in the last two authors it does not imply the neoclassical theory of distribution and employment; so to accept this notion of competition leaves the question, of the overall working of a competitive economy, totally open.

8.22 The Core Equivalence Theorem is not Valid for OLG Economies

In conclusion, the widespread opinion among neoclassical theorists, that the core equivalence theorem brings additional reasons in support of the view that the economy will likely tend to a general equilibrium allocation, cannot be accepted. *Anyway this opinion cannot be advanced for OLG economies*, because the core equivalence theorem does *not* hold in OLG economies; in these the core can be empty in spite of the existence of competitive equilibria. This of course implies that *in OLG economies not all equilibria need be in the core*.

One example is supplied by the OLG stationary pure-exchange economy we have discussed. In it, besides the two stationary equilibria already discussed, there is a *continuum* of other equilibria; we will see in the next paragraph that for each $q°$ satisfying $1 < q° < q*$ (that is, strictly included in between the two constant q's corresponding to the two stationary equilibria) there exists a sequence of (non-constant) equilibrium prices $\mathbf{q} = (\ldots, q_{-1}, q_0, q_1, \ldots)$; there exists, in other words, a *continuum* of equilibria indexed on the value assigned to q_0. We will see that in these equilibria $q_t \to q*$ for $t \to +\infty$, and $q_t \to 1$ for $t \to -\infty$. I assert, omitting the proof, that these equilibria, plus the two stationary equilibria that we already know, are all the equilibria of this economy.

8.22 · The Core Equivalence Theorem is not Valid for OLG Economies

Now that we know all the equilibria, I prove that *none of them is in the core.*

Proof Let us start with perhaps the most unexpected result, concerning the Pareto-efficient golden rule equilibrium. In it, since $x^t_t = a < \omega$, each generation consumes when young less than its endowment when young, ω. Let us choose any t_0 and let us consider the coalition (with an infinite number of members) formed by the generations with index $t \geq t_0$. This coalition can make all its members better off than in the golden rule equilibrium, by exploiting the fact that, if it separates itself from the rest of the economy, it need not give a part of ω^{t0}_{t0} to the old of generation $t_0 - 1$. The utility of generation t_0 is increased by increasing x^{t0}_{t0} until it equals ω: this makes it possible to decrease somewhat that generation's consumption when old and still leave her utility higher than in the golden rule equilibrium; the consequent increase in the consumption of generation $t_0 + 1$ when young makes it possible to reduce this generation's consumption when old and still assure her a higher level of consumption than in the golden rule equilibrium; by doing the same for all subsequent generations, the utility of all subsequent generations can be increased too, although by a smaller and smaller amount (tending asymptotically to zero, but remaining eternally positive) as t tends to $+\infty$. Thus the golden rule equilibrium can be blocked.

Let us now consider the autarchic equilibrium. The proof given earlier that this equilibrium is Pareto inferior to the golden rule equilibrium implies that any coalition including the generations from any t_0 onwards can improve the well-being of all its members by redistributing its resources so as to consume a when young and $1 - a$ when old; so the equilibrium can be blocked. Note further that the reallocation among generations from t_0 onwards leaves an amount $\omega - a$ in period t_0 that can be given as a gift to the old generation of that period, and this allows this generation to distribute some part of its consumption when young to the old at time $t_0 - 1$, and the redistribution can proceed to the preceding generations similarly as above for the golden rule equilibrium but towards $t = -\infty$, so *all* generations can obtain a utility increase.

Let us finally consider any one of the equilibria with $1 < q_0 < q^*$. In this equilibrium too, like in the autarchic equilibrium, the marginal utility of consumption when young is less than when old, and therefore a coalition including all generations from any t_0 onwards can improve the well-being of all its members by redistributing its consumption so as to achieve the golden rule consumptions. Thus for all equilibrium allocations there exist blocking coalitions. ∎

8.23 A Continuum of Equilibria in OLG Models

As a premise to the proof in ▶ Sect. 8.22 that for the OLG model introduced in ▶ Sect. 8.20 no equilibrium is in the core, I have stated without proof that the model has a continuum of equilibria. Now I prove it.

Let us construct the excess demand functions. Let z^t_t stand for the excess demand of generation t when young, z^t_{t+1} its excess demand when old. It is:

670 Chapter 8 · Intertemporal Equilibrium, Temporary Equilibrium

$$z_t^t = x_t - \omega = a\omega + (1 - \omega)q_t - \omega$$

$$z_{t+1}^t = x_{t+1} - (1 - \omega) = \omega(1 - a)/q_t - a(1 - \omega).$$

Equation (8.12) can be rewritten as

$$\omega(1 - a)/q_{t-1} - a(1 - \omega) + a\omega + (1 - \omega)q_t - \omega = 0. \tag{8.15}$$

From this equation we can derive the equilibrium value of q_t as a function of q_{t-1}, or the equilibrium value of q_{t-1} as a function of q_t, obtaining two nonlinear first-order difference equations each one of which allows us to obtain all future or earlier equilibrium q_t's once any one equilibrium q_t is assigned:

$$q_t = \frac{\omega(1 - a)}{a(1 - \omega)} + 1 - \frac{\omega(1 - a)}{a(1 - \omega)q_{t-1}} = q^* + 1 - q^*/q_{t-1} \tag{8.16}$$

$$q_{t-1} = \frac{\omega(1 - a)}{a(1 - \omega) + \omega(1 - a) - a(1 - \omega)q_t}. \tag{8.17}$$

These equations (the same equation written in two different ways) imply that $q_t = q_{t-1}$ in two cases: when $q_t = 1$, and when $q_t = q^* = \frac{\omega(1-a)}{a(1-\omega)} > 1$. This shows that the autarchic and the golden rule equilibria are the sole stationary equilibria.

Now I prove that *for each q_0 such that $1 < q_0 < q^*$, there exists a non-stationary equilibrium in which $q_t \to q^*$ for $t \to +\infty$, and $q_t \to 1$ for $t \to -\infty$; which means a continuum of equilibria.*

Proof Equations (8.16) and (8.17) show that an infinite sequence $\{q_t\}$ with t from $-\infty$ to $+\infty$ can be obtained for any positive q_0; it remains to check whether this sequence is compatible with equilibrium (i.e. is non-negative). Equation (8.16) shows that the derivative of q_t with respect to q_{t-1}, that is $q^*/(q_{t-1})^2$, is positive, therefore, since $q_t = q_{t-1}$ for $q_t = 1$ and for $q_t = q^* > 1$, we obtain that, as we increase q_{t-1} from 1 to q^*, q_t increases too and cannot become greater than q^*; in other words, for $1 < q_{t-1} < q^*$ it is also $1 < q_t < q^*$, and vice-versa. Furthermore this derivative $q^*/(q_{t-1})^2$ is greater than 1 for q_{t-1} sufficiently close to 1: this result, given that $q_t = q_{t-1}$ when $q_{t-1} = 1$, implies that, as q_{t-1} increases starting from $q_{t-1} = q_t = 1$, q_t increases faster than q_{t-1}, so it is $q_t > q_{t-1}$, at least for q_{t-1} sufficiently close to 1, and this means that, in an open right neighbourhood of 1, q_t increases as t increases. On the contrary $q^*/(q_{t-1})^2 < 1$ for q_{t-1} sufficiently close to q^*, therefore, as q_{t-1} decreases starting from $q_{t-1} = q_t = q^*$, q_t decreases slower than q_{t-1} so again we obtain $q_t > q_{t-1}$, hence, q_t increases with t also in an open left neighbourhood of q^*. This also proves that for $1 < q_{t-1} < q^*$ it is always $1 < q_{t-1} < q_t < q^*$, because this is true in a right neighbourhood of 1 and it remains true as long as $q^*/(q_{t-1})^2 \geq 1$, and when the increase of q_{t-1} causes $q^*/(q_{t-1})^2 < 1$ this derivative no longer changes sign, so if as q_{t-1} increases it became $q_t < q_{t-1}$ before q_{t-1} reaches q^*, it would be impossible that $q_t = q_{t-1}$ when $q_{t-1} = q^*$. On the other hand as t increases or decreases from $t = 0$, q_t cannot go outside the interval $(1, q^*)$ if q_0 is internal to this interval, because we have seen that for $1 < q_{t-1} < q^*$ it is also $1 < q_t < q^*$ and vice-versa; therefore $q_t \to q^*$ for $t \to +\infty$ and $q_t \to 1$ for $t \to$

8.23 · A Continuum of Equilibria in OLG Models

$-\infty$. Hence q_t is always non-negative if $1 < q_0 < q^*$. (I omit the proof that if q_0 is outside this interval then there is no equilibrium. The proof is based on showing that in this case q_t diverges indefinitely as one gets farther away from $t = 0$, and therefore in one of the two directions it eventually becomes negative.)

I have thus proved that for any q_0 satisfying $1 < q_0 < q^*$, there exists a sequence $\{q_t\}$ of equilibrium prices that covers the infinite past and future. So there is a robust continuum of equilibria.[64] ∎

The reader might object that both Arrow–Debreu equilibria, and infinite-periods equilibria with a given number of infinitely-lived consumers, are not *two-way infinity* models, in them t does not extend to infinity from date 0 in both directions.

However, the possibility of a continuum of equilibria *has* been demonstrated also for *one-way infinity* OLG models. One proof is in ▶ Sect. 8.5 of the online Appendix to this chapter in the book's website on SpringerLink: it is there shown that the two-way infinity model discussed so far can be reinterpreted as formally equivalent to a one-way infinity model with two representative agents per period. A somewhat simpler model to be now presented supplies another proof.

It is not difficult to build one-way infinity OLG models with a continuum of equilibria, because it is possible to build OLG models in which fixing an action of the young in the first period, for example the young's choice of how much to save, requires—in order for the action to be optimal—certain prices in the second period, which can only hold if the young of the second period choose a specific action; and this action of the young in the second period in turn requires, in order to be optimal, prices in the third period that require a certain action by the third-period young, and so on for all subsequent periods. In this way one can recursively determine the entire infinite time path of the model's equilibrium on the basis of the arbitrarily fixed value of a first-period's variable. It can happen that at a certain point the path becomes unfeasible, for example, a quantity becomes negative; this means that the chosen initial value of the variable is not compatible with an equilibrium path over the entire future. But if the path determined in this way remains forever feasible, one has found an equilibrium of the model. Then it can be that there is an interval of values of the first-period variable, all of which determine an equilibrium: this means a continuum of equilibria. This is for example the case if the path asymptotically approaches a steady state (finding paths that asymptotically approach a steady state is the usual trick in the

---

64 Since we are determining equilibria without a beginning, the choice of $t = 0$ is arbitrary and therefore equilibria which have the same price at two different dates must be considered the same equilibrium; but this fact does not eliminate the existence of a continuum of equilibria, because infinitesimal variations of q_0 entail infinitesimal variations of all terms of the price sequence, whose terms differ by finite amounts; in other words, given a certain q_0' with the associated sequence $(\ldots, q_{-1}', q_0', q_1', \ldots)$, every q_0'' in the interval (q_{-1}', q_0') determines a different equilibrium.

672 Chapter 8 · Intertemporal Equilibrium, Temporary Equilibrium

examples produced so far of continua of equilibria), and the asymptotic tendency to the steady state exists for an interval of values of the first-period variable: then the economy has a continuum of equilibria, equilibrium is indeterminate in a strong sense.

A simple model exhibiting these characteristics (Mas-Colell et al. 1995, pp. 770–776) will be now presented.

Let us consider a one-way infinity OLG economy where each generation consists of a single type of individuals who live two periods and whose total endowment is one unit of labour when young. Each generation is equally numerous and can be treated as a single individual. The economy is also endowed with a given amount of indestructible land, which in each period belongs to the old of that period for the reason that I proceed to explain. In each period labour and land produce a single consumption good via a standard CRS production function which is the same in every period. The full-employment production of the consumption good is 1 unit. The good comes out *at the end* of the period and is immediately and instantly consumed; labour and land are paid (in kind, we may assume) their marginal products, which because of CRS exhaust the product; the young consume part of their labour income and use the remainder—their savings—to buy the land from the old at the end of the period, who immediately consume all their income; in this way the old add, to what they earn as marginal product of land, what they earn by selling their land to the young. If we indicate with w the labour income, with $\varepsilon = 1 - w$ the land income, and with c_{Yt} the consumption of the young at the end of period $t-1$ (remember our convention that period t goes from date t to date $t+1$, therefore the end of period $t-1$ is date t, and generation $t-1$ consumes at dates t and $t+1$), then the consumption of the old at the end of period $t-1$, to be indicated as c_{Ot}, is equal to the marginal product of land, ε, plus the savings of the young at the end of period $t-1$, $w - c_{Yt} = 1 - \varepsilon - c_{Yt}$. (In c_{Yt} and c_{Ot} the subscripts Y and O are mnemonic for 'young' and 'old'.) By assumption ε and w are constant.

Let π_t be the price of land at the end of period $t-1$, and p_t the price of the consumption good (all prices are to be interpreted as discounted prices; remember that the equilibrium is reached simultaneously for all periods from the beginning). Our description of the functioning of the economy implies that in equilibrium $c_{Yt}p_t + \pi_t = (1-\varepsilon)p_t$, which says that what the young consume, plus what they pay to purchase the land from the old, must equal their labour income; and $c_{Ot+1}p_{t+1} = \varepsilon p_{t+1} + \pi_{t+1}$. The sole decision in each period is the young's decision as to how much to save at the end of the period. The budget constraint of generation $t-1$ (for $t \geq 1$) is

$$c_{Yt}p_t + \pi_t + c_{O,t+1}p_{t+1} = (1 - \varepsilon)p_t + \varepsilon p_{t+1} + \pi_{t+1}$$

but in equilibrium it is

$$\pi_t = \varepsilon p_{t+1} + \pi_{t+1}$$

because in the absence of arbitrage opportunities the discounted price of an asset must equal the sum of the discounted prices of the future earnings it will earn. Therefore we can write the budget constraint as

8.23 · A Continuum of Equilibria in OLG Models

$$c_{Yt}p_t + c_{O,t+1}p_{t+1} = (1 - \varepsilon)p_t.$$

This is the standard intertemporal budget constraint for a consumer who must choose between consumption today and consumption tomorrow, with endowment $(1 - \varepsilon)$ today and zero tomorrow. Once we are given a utility function, we can derive the choice curve of the consumer as the locus of tangencies, of the budget lines that go through $(1-\varepsilon, 0)$ with parametric slope $-p_t/p_{t+1}$, with the indifference curves between c_{Yt} and c_{Ot+1}. This choice curve yields c_{Yt} and c_{Ot+1} once we are given p_t/p_{t+1}, but it can also be used to derive c_{Ot+1} and p_t/p_{t+1} once c_{Yt} is given.

Since choices only depend on relative prices, let us put $p_1 = 1$. In period zero land belongs to the old of generation (-1) and their consumption c_{O1} is residually determined once c_{Y1} is given, because $c_{Y1} + c_{O1} = 1$. (The rent earned by land can be supposed determined by contracts signed at the end of period -1 and equal to the marginal product of land, but the value at which land is sold at the end of period 0 depends on the young's savings.) Pick c_{Y1} and hence c_{O1} arbitrarily, and ask whether an equilibrium path exists corresponding to this initial choice of generation 0. In order for the given c_{Y1} to be chosen, p_1/p_2 must be such as to make it an optimal choice; if such a p_2 exists, then c_{O2} is also determined as the one corresponding to the given c_{Y1} on the choice curve. Consider now two possible shapes of the choice curve, as shown in ◘ Figs. 8.4 and 8.5. In each of these figures, besides the choice curve, there is also represented a negatively sloped 45° line with intercepts (1, 1) on the axes, which represents the points satisfying $c_{Ot} + c_{Yt} = 1$.

Let us initially examine the simpler case of ◘ Fig. 8.4 where c_{O2} is univocally determined. Then c_{Y2} is univocally determined too, as the one corresponding to the given c_{O2} on the 45° line; then the choice curve determines c_{O3} and from this, the 45° line determines c_{Y3}; recursively, we can therefore determine c_{Yt+1} from c_{Yt}. This determination in ◘ Fig. 8.4 shows that, unless $c_{Y1} = \gamma$ such that $c_{O1} = 1 - \gamma$ corresponds to the intersection of the choice curve with the downward-sloping 45° line, the sequence $\{c_{Yt}\}$ inevitably sooner or later becomes unfeasible (the reader is invited to check it on the figure for $c_{O1} > 1 - \gamma$); this shows that there is only one equilibrium path, the steady state with $c_{Yt} = \gamma$.

◘ Figure 8.5 differs from ◘ Fig. 8.4 in that the slope of the choice curve is *positive and less than* 1 when it crosses the 45° line, i.e. at the steady state. (It means that the utility function is such that at the steady-state relative prices the endowment income effect is strong, a rise of p_t/p_{t+1} induces an increase of both c_{Yt} and c_{Ot+1}, and larger for the first. We have seen choice curves with this shape in Chaps. 3 and 4.) The result is that, in a neighbourhood of $c_Y = \gamma$, the recursion yields a sequence $\{c_{Yt}\}$ that converges to γ. This means that there is an interval of values of c_{O1} within which an equilibrium path exists for each c_{O1}. There is a continuum of equilibria. (The reader is invited to explore what happens if the choice curve crosses the 45° line with a positive slope greater than 1.)

The continuum of equilibria of ◘ Fig. 8.5 is 'robust', it does not disappear with small modifications of the utility functions or of other parameters, contrary to the cases of continua of equilibria in Arrow–Debreu models, see ◘ Fig. 6.15.

Chapter 8 · Intertemporal Equilibrium, Temporary Equilibrium

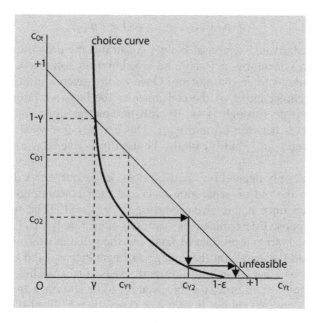

Fig. 8.4 OLG choice curve generating uniqueness

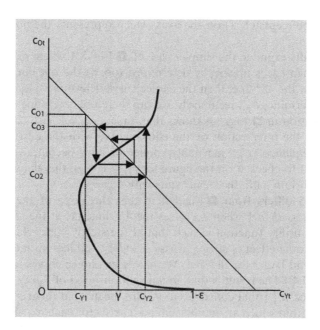

Fig. 8.5 Choice curve allowing convergence to a steady state for an interval of values of (c_{Y1}, c_{O1})

8.23 · A Continuum of Equilibria in OLG Models

Several other examples of robust indeterminacy in one-way infinity OLG models have been produced.[65]

This was an unexpected result of the research on OLG equilibria, and its causes are still not entirely agreed upon. One suggested explanation (Geanakoplos 1987) is *lack of market clearing at infinity*, that is, the presence of a disequilibrium whose elimination is indefinitely postponed.

But whatever the causes, at least according to a highly esteemed specialist the implication is that one must 'conclude that the forces of supply and demand are not sufficient to determine the rate of interest in the overlapping generations model' (Geanakoplos 1987, p. 768).

8.24 Summing Up on OLG Models

Geanakoplos' striking conclusion does not seem to have become popular in the over thirty years since it was published, but I am not aware of arguments refuting it; the tendency seems to be to avoid mentioning the problem (see e.g. Weil 2008).

But even if some way were found to conclude that Geanakoplos was too pessimistic, one would not be out of trouble. Rigorous theory cannot remain content with simple aggregate models; as claimed by Lucas, the aggregate neoclassical models must be interpretable as legitimate simplifications of disaggregated general equilibrium models. It is of course possible to formulate neo-Walrasian intertemporal disaggregated OLG general equilibrium models. But these will present all the problems pointed out in Sects. 8.13–8.18 of this chapter, only somewhat reduced (but not eliminated) on the issue of perfect foresight.

The other three main problems of neo-Walrasian general equilibria—the impermanence problem, the substitutability problem, the savings–investment problem—are not reduced. The neoclassical OLG literature makes these problems less easy to perceive because it is essentially modifications of widely accepted macroeconomic models, aggregate production function models when production with capital is admitted. Then apart from the OLG structure the models are standard neoclassical growth models similar to Solow's or Ramsey's, and the arguments in ▶ Sect. 8.18 apply to them too.

---

65 For example, indeterminacy can derive from the existence of many consumption goods and from assuming that the desired *composition* of demand when young is generally different from the one when old, and both depend on relative prices and therefore must be determined simultaneously: then relative prices at date 1 depend on relative prices at date 2, but these depend among other things on the composition of demand of the young generation of period 2, which depends on relative prices at date 3, and so on; the degrees of freedom in this case are n − 1 if there are n different consumption goods. For more detailed treatment of these and other aspects of OLG models, e.g. the possibility of *bubbles* (assets worth more than their 'fundamental value', the present value of their future returns), cf. at advanced textbook level Mas-Colell et al. (1995, pp. 769–777), and Heijdra and Van der Ploeg (2002, Chaps. 16 and 17); at a still more advanced level cf. Geanakoplos and Polemarchakis (1991).

676   Chapter 8 · Intertemporal Equilibrium, Temporary Equilibrium

Indeed, let us sketch how a neo-Walrasian disaggregated general equilibrium with overlapping generations would have to look like. One must choose a certain instant, call it date zero, assume a given endowment vector of capital goods at that date, and build an intertemporal equilibrium from that moment on, with consumers active over only a limited number of periods, say (assuming equal life length for all) for $60 \times 52 = 3120$ periods of one-week length if they are 'born' (or rather, reach adult age) inside the equilibrium, or for fewer periods if they belong to a cohort 'born' before date 0, hence, with an age attached to them at date 0, and then active for the remaining number of periods up to age 3120. At the beginning of each period a new cohort is born and the oldest cohort disappears. Although each cohort is active over only 3120 periods and (assuming no bequests) does not care about what happens outside its active periods, the equilibrium must extend over the infinite future because each consumer h faces prices influenced by the choices of consumers who will survive her/him, the choices of these consumers depend also on prices beyond h's lifetime, these are influenced by the choices of still subsequent cohorts of consumers, and so on endlessly: equilibrium *must* be established over the infinite future. How will equilibrium be established? The impermanence problem (the need for the auctioneer), the substitutability problem, the savings–investment problem are as present as in the infinitely-lived-consumer versions discussed in Sects. 8.2–8.18. And the dilemma about how to surmount the price-change problem is only slightly less serious: the assumption of complete futures markets at date 0 covering all future periods is of course just as absurd, since the not-yet-born consumers cannot take part in the establishment of the entire intertemporal equilibrium at date 0; but perfect foresight, although no one needs it over the entire future, is still needed by each newborn consumer for the next 60 years; the observations advanced on perfect foresight in ▶ Sect. 8.15 would seem fully to apply. In particular, in OLG models a generation may not need perfect data foresight over the infinite future, but *the theorist does*, otherwise the behaviour of subsequent generations is indeterminable and equilibrium is indeterminate: and the inevitable conclusion is that equilibrium *is* indeterminate, since no one can predict the tastes of future generations, nor technical progress and other novelties.

In conclusion, OLG models do not make the neoclassical approach more credible. The OLG structure reveals interesting possibilities of making everybody better off via state intervention on pensions, and is also extremely useful for other intergenerational issues, for example, the effect of public debt on future generations; the insights are relevant whatever approach to growth and distribution one adopts. But on the credibility of the marginal approach, nothing is gained: neoclassical OLG models are a little less absurd on the issue of perfect price foresight but can produce even worse indeterminacies of equilibrium than the Sonnenschein–Mantel–Debreu result.

Therefore the considerations advanced in ▶ Sect. 8.18 would seem to apply to these models too: they can be attributed credibility only on the basis of a faith in neoclassical *traditional* time-consuming mechanisms that rest upon the discredited treatment of capital as a single factor.

8.25 Temporary Equilibria. An Informal Presentation of Some Problems

The remaining five sections of the chapter describe the alternative way, within the neo-Walrasian approach, to deal with the price-change problem: the *temporary general equilibrium* (TGE) approach, where equilibrium is reached only for one short period, on the basis of *expectations* of future prices that can turn out to be mistaken and can differ from agent to agent.

The discussion of temporary equilibria extends over five sections. The first four have been prepared by Professor Fabio Ravagnani (see Ravagnani 2010, for an earlier version), the fifth is a joint work.[66] The present ▶ Sect. 8.25 is introductory. ▶ Section 8.26 presents a temporary equilibrium model of a pure-exchange economy. ▶ Section 8.27 introduces production. ▶ Section 8.28 summarizes the attempts to introduce money into temporary equilibria. ▶ Section 8.29 draws conclusions after pointing out some problems of temporary equilibrium theory which are less often discussed by the theorists who have worked on the topic.

To minimize complications, in the formal models to be presented in these Sections expectations will be mostly assumed to be point expectations, that is, the agent is assumed to be certain as to which future prices will occur; this permits to avoid probabilistic considerations almost completely. For the same reason we assume certainty about future states of nature, so we avoid having to consider contingent commodities.

The direction advocated by Lindahl and by Hicks, when they decided that the concept of long-period equilibrium had to be abandoned, was precisely the study of temporary general equilibria (and of their sequences); intertemporal equilibria were judged too unreal. But Lindahl's 1929 proposal (in Swedish) of the temporary equilibrium approach had little influence for many years; it was translated into English only in 1939. In that same year Hicks's *Value and Capital* was published and owing to the reputation of the author it was widely read, and had great influence. In the second part of that book the temporary equilibrium approach is proposed. Equilibrium is established for one 'week',[67] and the agents' supply-and-demand decisions for that 'week' are based on expectations of the prices at which it will be possible to buy or sell in subsequent 'weeks'. Hicks's discussion is only verbal; no formalization is supplied of the new notion of equilibrium. One must wait until the end of the 1960s for the first attempts to develop formal temporary equilibrium theory. The motivation, as in Lindahl and Hicks, was dissatisfaction with intertemporal equilibria and in particular with the assumption of perfect foresight.

---

66 I would like to exempt Professor Ravagnani from responsibility for the contents of subsections Sects. 8.26.4 and 8.28.3, which are my own addition.

67 Hicks defines the 'week' as a period short enough for the assumption of constant prices during the period to be legitimate: this leaves the length of the 'week' rather indeterminate. The choice of the term 'week' is anyway significant, it suggests less than a month. Hicks also assumes that equilibrium for the 'week' is reached on the Monday of the 'week'.

678   **Chapter 8** · Intertemporal Equilibrium, Temporary Equilibrium

The basic features of temporary equilibrium theory can be summarized as follows. Time is divided into a sequence of short periods. Spot markets for commodities are active at the beginning of every period, and there aren't complete futures markets nor perfect foresight; there is only a possibility of transferring purchasing power to the future via the hoarding of money, or via the purchase of securities promising future delivery of a restricted set of commodities or of money. Within this framework, the theory focuses on the behaviour of agents in the 'current' period, stresses the dependence of agents' choices on their individual expectations about future prices, and discusses the existence of general equilibrium on 'current' markets. No assumption of unanimity is placed on the expectations held by agents at the beginning of each period. Temporary equilibrium theory is thus ready to acknowledge that economic agents have limited predictive capabilities and for this reason may well base their choices on erroneous expectations.

Research in the field of temporary equilibrium theory attracted many distinguished scholars during the 1970s but was gradually abandoned in the subsequent decade. The work carried out in the field has since fallen into a sort of oblivion, as attested by the fact that temporary general equilibrium models[68] are not even mentioned in recent advanced textbooks in microeconomics. It is, however, our belief that knowledge of the basics of this area of research can be of use for a correct appraisal of the current situation in general equilibrium analysis. In accordance with this conviction, we shall endeavour to provide an accessible exposition of temporary equilibrium theory and highlight the analytical difficulties that emerged in the literature in the 1970s and were no doubt largely responsible for disenchantment with the approach. These difficulties can be called *difficulties of formalization*, that arise with regard to how to formalize the choices of individuals, and also with proving the existence of a temporary equilibrium. Other difficulties arise too, that can be called *difficulties of predictive capacity*, akin to those pointed out in Sects. 8.13–8.16 for intertemporal equilibria. The latter difficulties were responsible for a very significant change of mind by Hicks, who by the end of the 1950s (that is, *before* the emergence of the difficulties of formalization) started expressing very negative assessments of the method of temporary equilibria he himself had advocated in *Value and Capital* (Petri 1991). Afterwards, the difficulties of predictive capacity have been seldom mentioned by other scholars, so it is unclear how much they have contributed to the current disenchantment with the temporary equilibrium approach. Still, we think it is important that the reader be aware of them, so they will be remembered in ▶ Sect. 8.29.

---

68 This means, without perfect foresight. With perfect foresight, a temporary equilibrium is only the first-period equilibrium of a sequential Radner equilibrium, and it is not called 'temporary equilibrium'.

8.26 An Introductory Pure-Exchange Model

8.26.1 General Description of the Exchange Economy

Let us now proceed to a formal examination of some simple models of temporary equilibrium so as to grasp the formal problems that appear to have been more directly responsible for the abandonment of the temporary equilibrium approach. We first describe a pure-exchange model; then we extend it to the case of economies with production. Next we discuss the way money has been introduced in temporary equilibria; some concluding remarks follow.

Consider a pure-exchange economy with H price-taking households (indexed by $h = 1, ..., H$) and, in each period, $N \geq 2$ non-storable consumption goods[69] (indexed by $n = 1, ..., N$); assume this economy is active for only two periods of time, which following prevalent use in this literature we call period 1 (the present) and period 2 (the future). (That is, in this part differently from elsewhere in this book the initial period is period 1, not 0.) Assume that, at the beginning of period 1, there are N distinct spot markets for the different consumption goods *and* a futures market for good 1 of date 2, i.e. a market on which households can trade (against immediate payment) promises of delivery of physical units of good 1 at the beginning of the next period. Only the N spot markets for commodities are open in period 2.

Now assume that, at the beginning of period 1, each household observes the prices quoted on the $N + 1$ current markets and forms *definite* expectations of the future relative prices of commodities in terms of good 1 of date 2. Under these circumstances the generic household h will calculate that, by appropriately trading on the single forward market in existence, it can purchase or sell commodities for future delivery as freely as in the presence of a *complete system* of futures markets. To clarify this point, consider any of the $N - 1$ commodities different from good 1, say 'grapes', and assume household h expects that a unit of 'grapes' will exchange in period 2 for three units of good 1. Then the household will calculate that, if it wishes to purchase in the present a unit of grapes for future delivery, it can do so by buying forward[70] three units of good 1 *in the anticipation* of exchanging those units in period 2 for the desired unit of grapes. Similarly the household will calculate that if it wishes to sell in the present a promise of future delivery of one unit of grapes, it can do so by selling forward three units of good 1 *in the anticipation* of surrendering a unit of grapes in period 2 against three units of good 1 and then using those units of good 1 to honour its forward sale.

The above example shows that, for a household endowed with definite expectations of future relative prices, trading on the single forward market open in

---

69 Non-perishable goods would introduce the complication that it becomes possible to 'produce' goods of period 2 by storage; now we want to exclude any kind of production.

70 To avoid linguistic contortions, we will speak of 'buying or selling forward' as synonymous with buying or selling a promise of future delivery *against immediate payment* (in real economies forward contracts usually stipulate payment *upon delivery*), and we will occasionally use 'forward market' as synonymous with 'futures market'.

680   **Chapter 8** · Intertemporal Equilibrium, Temporary Equilibrium

period 1 allows transferring *purchasing power* across time, that is, saving or dissaving. By *buying* promises of future delivery of units of good 1 the household in fact performs a loan, transfers some present purchasing power to period 2, i.e. saves; and by *selling* promises of future delivery of units of good 1 the household can spend in the present the discounted expected purchasing power (in terms of good 1) of any commodity, or commodity bundle, that it plans to surrender in period 2, i.e. obtains a loan, dissaves. In order to highlight this aspect, from now on we shall refer to the single futures market in existence as a market for one-period *bonds* specified in terms of good 1, where the unit bond is defined as a promise to deliver one physical unit of good 1 at the beginning of the second period.

Given that the bond market allows intertemporal transfers of purchasing power, it is reasonable to assume that households will simultaneously plan both their present *and* their future consumption at the beginning of period 1. We shall accordingly assume that at the initial date, given the current and the expected prices, each household trades commodities for present consumption and bonds so as to attain the most preferred consumption stream over periods 1 and 2. By definition, a state of the economy in which all households trade in this way, and individual trades are such that all the $N + 1$ *current* markets clear, is a *temporary equilibrium* of the exchange economy for period 1.

8.26.2 A More Detailed Description of the Household's Behaviour

Let us now provide a more precise description of households' behaviour in the first period. It will be assumed that good 1 is each period's *numeraire* for the determination of relative spot prices, and good 1 of date 1 is the numéraire for the determination of discounted prices.

Let a *two-period consumption stream* of the generic household h be denoted by vector $x_{12}^h = (x_1^h, x_2^h)$, whose two elements are vectors, with $x_1^h \geq 0$, $x_2^h \geq 0$, where subvector $x_t^h = (x_{1t}^h, \ldots, x_{Nt}^h)$ denotes a consumption bundle for period t ($t = 1, 2$). Assume that the set of admissible consumption streams, or *two-period consumption set*, of the generic household is $X_{12}^h = \Re_+^{2N}$. Assume also that, at the initial date, the generic household h knows with certainty both its current commodity endowments $\omega_1^h = (\omega_{11}^h, \ldots, \omega_{N1}^h)$ and its future endowments $\omega_2^h = (\omega_{12}^h, \ldots, \omega_{N2}^h)$. In order to keep the model as simple as possible, we assume that the households' endowments are strictly positive and do not include credits nor debts,[71] and that its preferences can be represented by a well-behaved utility function:

---

71 Since the economy cannot have miraculously come into existence at date 1, it has a past, and there will have been sales of bonds in the previous period, which means that some households (the ones who sold bonds) have debts to be repaid at date 1, while other households (the ones who bought bonds) have credits, and the budget constraint should make room for this. The problem then arises that, since past expectations may have been mistaken, debtors may have overestimated the value of their period-1 endowments and may find it impossible to repay their debts, as mentioned in ▶ Sect. 8.13. For simplicity we neglect this issue and assume no debts inherited from the past.

■■ Assumption 8.1

(a) *The generic household h has a preference ordering over two-period consumption streams in X_{12}^h that can be represented by a continuous, strictly increasing and strictly quasi-concave utility function $U^h = U^h(x_1^h, x_2^h)$;*
(b) $\omega_1^h \gg 0$, $\omega_2^h \gg 0$ *for each h.*

Coming to the prices that guide households' choices, let the price system ruling in period 1 in terms of good 1 be denoted by vector $p = (p_1, q_1)$, where subvector $p_1 = (p_{11}, \ldots, p_{N1}) \in \mathfrak{R}_+^N$, in which $p_{11} = 1$, refers to the N spot markets for commodities, and scalar $q_1 \geq 0$ is the price of a unit bond, that is, the discounted price of good 1 of period 2, which implies an own rate of interest r_{11} determined by $q_1 = 1/(1 + r_{11})$. In p_{ij} the first index denotes the good, the second the period or date. As regards the future spot prices expected at the initial date, we assume that price expectations are subjective, and therefore likely to differ among agents, and 'certain', in the sense that each household believes that a definite price system will hold in the future with probability 1. Let us denote by $p_2^h = (p_{12}^h, \ldots, p_{N2}^h)$ the future relative spot prices in terms of good 1 *as expected by household h.* The first element of this vector is $p_{12}^h = 1$, independent of expectations because numéraire. In general, expected prices will depend on both the prices observed in the past and those currently observed; for the moment, however, let us assume that price forecasts do not depend on current prices (*fixed* expectations). Let us further assume that expected prices are strictly positive.

■■ Assumption 8.2

(a) *The system of future prices expected by the generic household h, p_2^h, is given at the initial date independently of current prices;*
(b) $p_2^h \gg 0$ *for each h.*

Let us now examine the behaviour of the generic household at the opening of markets in period 1. One way to understand its budget constraint is by assuming that the household in a *first stage* issues a quantity of bonds $\bar{b}_1^h$ corresponding to the maximum it expects to be able to repay in the future and adds the purchasing power thus obtained to the value of her period-1 endowments; in this way the household has available for expenditures the entire capitalized value of its incomes, i.e. its wealth; then in a *second stage* (always at the beginning of period 1) the household uses this total purchasing power to buy period-1 goods, and to buy bonds for a quantity $b_1^h \geq 0$ (it cannot *sell* further bonds because its expected income in period 2 is already just sufficient to repay $\bar{b}_1^h$ and we exclude *planned* bankruptcy). Since a bond entitles to the future delivery of one unit of *numéraire*, the number of bonds supplied by household h in the first stage coincides with the total spot value of the household's future endowments *as forecasted by the household itself.*

■■ Assumption 8.3

At the beginning of period 1 the generic household h in a first stage supplies a quantity of bonds $\bar{b}_1^h$ such that $\bar{b}_1^h = p_2^h \omega_2^h$.

682   Chapter 8 · Intertemporal Equilibrium, Temporary Equilibrium

By issuing bonds in accordance with Assumption 8.3, given the price q_1 of these bonds, the household obtains purchasing power equal to the discounted expected value of its future endowments. Since the current receipts from this operation are equal to $(q_1 \bar{b}_1^h)$ units of numeraire, the total wealth that the household can spend in the second stage in period 1 on goods for present consumption and bonds is $W_1^h = p_1 \omega_1^h + q_1 \bar{b}_1^h$. The *first-period budget constraint* of household h can therefore be written

$$p_1 x_1^h + q_1 b_1^h = p_1 \omega_1^h + q_1 \bar{b}_1^h \qquad (8.18)$$

where b_1^h denotes the non-negative quantity of bonds *demanded* by the household in the second stage, and the right-hand side indicates the value at date 1 of the household's endowments, where the second term is the discounted or present value of the future endowment according to the household's own *expectations* of future relative prices and to the market's price at date 1 of good 1 of date 2. On the other hand, the household is aware that in period 2 it will have to surrender its entire endowment ω_2^h in order to honour the bonds $\bar{b}_1^h$ issued in the first stage, and therefore calculates that the purchasing power it will be able to spend in the future for its own consumption is entirely determined by the income from the bonds purchased in the second stage. The *(expected) second-period budget constraint* of household h thus reads:

$$p_2^h x_2^h = b_1^h \qquad (8.19)$$

We see therefore that in (8.18) the term $q_1 b_1^h$ on the left-hand side is the discounted or present value of the possible future consumption; the budget constraint (1)–(2) states therefore that *the present value of present and future consumption must equal the present (expected) value of present and future endowments*. Each household chooses its current consumption of goods, current demand for bonds and planned future consumption so as to attain the most preferred two-period consumption stream subject to budget constraints (8.18)–(8.19). Formally we can say that the choice of the generic household h at given current prices p and expected prices p_2^h is a solution to the following problem:

I *Maximize $U^h(x_1^h, x_2^h)$ with respect to $x_1^h \geq 0,\ b_1^h \geq 0,\ x_2^h \geq 0$.*
   subject to constraints (1)–(2) and Assumption 8.3.

Let a solution to problem I be denoted by the triple $(x_1^{h*}, b_1^{h*}, x_2^{h*})$. It is clear that only the first two components will manifest themselves on current markets in the form of demand for commodities to be consumed in the present and demand for bonds, while planned consumption x_2^{h*} will remain, as it were, in the household's mind. It can therefore be stated that a solution to problem I identifies the corresponding *optimal action* $a^{h*} = (x_1^{h*}, b_1^{h*})$ taken by the generic household on period-1 markets after the action of Assumption 8.3. (So the complete action on period-1 markets should actually be indicated by a triplet: $(\bar{b}_1^h, x_1^{h*}, b_1^{h*})$.)

By substituting for b_1^h and $\bar{b}_1^h$ in constraint (8.18) according to constraint (8.19) and Assumption 8.3, one gets the equation

$$p_1 x_1^h + q_1 p_2^h x_2^h = p_1 \omega_1^h + q_1 p_2^h \omega_2^h \tag{8.20}$$

which by adopting the convention $q^h = q_1 p_2^h$ can be written in a way whose interest will emerge in the next paragraph:

$$p_1 x_1^h + q^h x_2^h = p_1 \omega_1^h + q^h \omega_2^h \tag{8.20'}$$

Equations (8.20) or (8.20′) express, as already indicated, that the present value of present and future consumption must equal the present *expected* value of present and future endowments. Note that in these equations the variables $\bar{b}_1^h$ and b_1^h do *not* appear. On the other hand, if household h determines a most preferred consumption stream $x_{12}^{h*} = (x_1^{h*}, x_2^{h*})$ by solving the problem

II   *Maximize $U^h(x_1^h, x_2^h)$ with respect to $x_1^h \geq 0$, $x_2^h \geq 0$*
   subject to constraint (3) or (3′),

the solution (x_1^h, x_2^h) is certainly also a solution, for these variables, of problem I.[72] It emerges then that problem I can be solved in two consecutive steps. In the first step the household determines the optimal two-period consumption stream by solving problem II, in the second step the household determines through the constraint (8.19) under Assumption 8.3 the quantity of bonds that in its opinion must be purchased (after selling $\bar{b}_1^h$) in order to finance planned future consumption, i.e. b_1^{h*} such that $b_1^{h*} = p_2^h x_2^{h*}$; this second step, if one assumes that the household does not actually first of all sell the amount $\bar{b}_1^h$ of bonds but only reasons as if it had, concretely means that the household determines and exercises on the market its *net* or *excess* demand for bonds, to be indicated as $z_b^{h*} = b_1^{h*} - \bar{b}_1^h = p_2^h(x_2^{h*} - \omega_2^h)$, whose present value $q_1 z_b^{h*}$ is the amount of savings (positive or negative) the household decides to perform in period 1. Then the optimal action of household h on current markets is the couplet $\alpha^{h*} = (x_1^h, z_b^{h*})$.

Let us examine the first step more closely. Constraint (8.20) or (8.20′) in problem II can be interpreted as the *single* budget constraint that household h faces when choosing its consumption stream at the initial date: recall that, in the presence of a bond market, household h considers that there is no impediment to its purchase of the quantity β_1^{h*} of bonds, which is not therefore something *constraining* its consumption choices, it is only an action necessary to implement those choices. Recall also that we have seen that the recourse to purchasing or selling bonds allows the household to trade goods for future delivery as if it faced a complete system of futures markets,[73] at the future prices it expects.

---

72 *Exercise*: prove it, by proving that (assuming U(·) differentiable, and interior solutions) the consumption variables are determined in problem I by the equalities between marginal rates of substitution and 'price ratios' $p_{it}/q_{it} p_{jt'}$, plus the budget constraints reduced to (3), without a need simultaneously to determine b_1^h, which is determined only afterwards, from the budget constraint (2) under Assumption 8.3.

73 This is the same principle behind the equivalence between Arrow–Debreu equilibria and Radner equilibria, mentioned in ▶ Sect. 8.11.

684   Chapter 8 · Intertemporal Equilibrium, Temporary Equilibrium

Let us then consider the budget constraint (8.20) in the form (8.20′). In the opinion of the household, the N components of the vector q^h appearing in (8.20′) are precisely the prices at which it would be possible to trade in period 1 promises of delivery of future goods if complete futures markets existed, i.e. they are the 'present or discounted prices' of future goods in the household's mind, given the discount rate q_1 supplied by the market. To see this it suffices to examine the first two elements of vector q^h. By the convention adopted, the first element is $q_1^h = q_1 p_{12}^h = q_1$, i.e. the 'present or discounted price' of a unit of good 1 for future delivery *as actually quoted* on the current bond market. The second element is $q_2^h = q_1 p_{22}^h$, where p_{22}^h is the future price for commodity 2 as expected by household h. By arguing like in the example that opens ▶ Sect. 8.26, we see that q_2^h is the 'present price' at which household h *esteems* it can trade a unit of commodity 2 of period 2, because it is the price that the household should pay in the present for buying forward p_{22}^h units of good 1 given its expectation that p_{22}^h is the quantity of good 1 that will allow the purchase of one unit of good 2 in period 2. (Reformulate the reasoning for the case of a forward *sale* of good 2.)

Because of this interpretability of q^h as a vector of esteemed or perceived 'present prices' for commodities to be delivered in period 2, the constraint in problem II is strictly analogous to the *intertemporal budget constraint* household h would face at the initial date in this economy if there were complete futures markets; the only difference is that it is the intertemporal budget constraint *perceived* by household h, owing to its expectation of future relative prices. It can therefore be concluded that, in the first step of the procedure indicated at the end of ▶ Sect. 8.26.2, the choice of the two-period consumption stream on the part of the generic household h at current prices $p = (p_1, q_1)$ and 'fixed' expected prices p_2^h is *formally equivalent* to standard consumer choice under complete forward markets at prices $p' = (p_1, q^h)$, where $q^h = q_1 p_2^h$.

In view of the abovementioned formal equivalence, and of Assumptions 8.1 and 8.2, the following results are immediate: (a) the first step of the procedure *univocally determines* the consumption stream $x_{12}^{h*} = (x_1^{h*}, x_2^{h*})$ chosen by the generic household h at any p such that $p \in \mathfrak{R}_{++}^{N+1}$; (b) each component of x_{12}^{h*} changes continuously with $p = (p_1, q_1)$ as the latter ranges in $\mathfrak{R}_{++}^{N+1}$. In other words, both the current and the planned future demands for consumption goods are *continuous functions* of period-1 prices, provided that the latter remain strictly positive. In what follows we shall respectively denote those individual demand functions for commodities by $x_1^h(p)$ and $x_2^h(p)$, $h = 1, \ldots, H$. A third result follows immediately, (c) the household's demand for bonds, to be indicated as $b_1^h(p)$, as well as its excess demand for bonds $z_b^h(p)$, are continuous functions of strictly positive current prices. In view of the foregoing discussion it can be finally concluded that, under the stipulated assumptions, the *optimal action* taken by the generic household on period-1 markets is well-defined and continuous for $p \in \mathfrak{R}_{++}^{N+1}$.

We have now what we need for the formal definition of temporary equilibrium for the exchange economy under examination. Let us restrict our analysis to strictly positive first-period prices, we can then define the excess demand functions for commodities of the generic household h as $z_1^h(p) = x_1^h(p) - \omega_1^h$

8.26 · An Introductory Pure-Exchange Model

, and we have defined the household's excess demand function for bonds as $z_b^h(p) = b_1^h(p) - \bar{b}_1^h$ (where $\bar{b}_1^h$ is a given parameter in view of Assumptions 8.3 and 8.2(a). Summation over the H households then yields the corresponding *aggregate excess demand functions* $z_1(p)$ and $z_b(p)$ that are obviously continuous.[74] A *temporary equilibrium* for period 1 is finally defined as a system of current prices $p^* \in \Re_{++}^{N+1}$ and a corresponding set of optimal actions $\{a^1(p^*)$, ..., $a^H(p^*)\}$ on the part of the H households, with $a^h(p^*) \in \Re_{++}^{N+1}$ for each h, such that the $N+1$ market clearing conditions $z_1(p) = 0$, $z_b(p) = 0$ are simultaneously fulfilled. (To drop Assumption 8.3 and to define the optimal actions as α^{h*} would make no difference since the several $\bar{b}_1^h$ are given parameters.)

It can be proved that temporary equilibrium of the exchange economy exists under Assumptions 8.1–8.3. Moreover, the existence of temporary equilibrium is preserved if it is assumed that individual expectations depend continuously on the current prices, i.e. if a continuous expectation function Ψ^h such that $p_2^h = \Psi^h(p)$ is introduced for each h. We shall refrain from substantiating these assertions, as the introductory model examined here is a particular specification of the temporary equilibrium model put forward by Arrow and Hahn (1971: ▶ Chap. 6), to which readers are referred for existence proofs. (See Footnote 83 for the relationship between the introductory model and the Arrow–Hahn model.) We shall instead focus in the remainder of this Section on showing that the introductory model, which has taken us quite comfortably from the Arrow–Debreu world with complete forward markets to the more realistic environment of temporary equilibrium theory, in fact contains a hidden problem and is not really robust.

8.26.3 **Problems with the Introductory Model**

The introductory model assumes that a single futures market is open in period 1 together with the spot markets for the N period−1 consumption goods. However, there is no reason why there should be a futures market for only one good (in real economies there are markets for many different types of bonds and futures markets for many financial, and some real, assets); nor does the notion of temporary equilibrium imply anything like it, it only postulates that futures markets are incomplete and there isn't perfect foresight; for the two periods exchange economy we are discussing, we have a temporary equilibrium if the number of futures markets is lower than N. It is therefore natural to ask whether the model is susceptible of generalization to economies with a larger set of futures markets. As we shall now see, unfortunately even a slight increase in the number of futures markets in existence has serious consequences for temporary equilibrium analysis.

Let us modify the introductory model by assuming that $N \geq 3$ consumption goods are traded in the economy and that *two* distinct futures markets are open at

---

74 *Exercise*. Prove that the aggregate excess demand functions defined in the text are homogeneous of degree zero in p and satisfy Walras' Law.

686 Chapter 8 · Intertemporal Equilibrium, Temporary Equilibrium

the initial date, say the futures market for good 1 and the futures market for good 2. (We could equivalently state that two distinct bond markets are open, one for bonds promising a unit of good 1 of period 2, and the other for bonds promising a unit of good 2 of period 2.) This change in market structure necessitates some adjustment of the formal description of the economy. To begin with, current prices in terms of good 1 will be denoted by vector $p = (p_1, q)$, where subvector $p_1 \in \mathfrak{R}_+^N$ refers to spot markets and subvector $q = (q_1, q_2)$, with $q \in \mathfrak{R}_+^2$, to forward markets (or bond prices). It will also be convenient to denote the quantities of goods that the generic household h trades on forward markets by the vector $b^h = (b_1^h, b_2^h)$, where by assumption $b_i^h > 0$ denotes a quantity of good i *demanded* and $b_i^h < 0$ a quantity of good i *supplied* by the household ($i = 1, 2$). In this notation, the *first-period budget constraint* of the generic household h reads:

$$p_1 x_1^h + q b^h = p_1 \omega_1^h \tag{8.21}$$

and the household's *expected budget constraint for period 2* can be written

$$p_2^h x_2^h = p_2^h \omega_2^h + p_2^{h'} b^h \tag{8.22}$$

where $p_2^h \in \mathfrak{R}_{++}^N$ denotes the future prices in terms of good 1 anticipated by the household, and $p_2^{h'} = (1, p_{22}^h)$ is the vector whose components coincide with the first two components of p_2^h.

Now the economy can be described along the same lines as in the introductory model. We accordingly assume that given the current and expected prices, the generic household h chooses its current consumption, current trading on forward markets and planned future consumption at the initial date so as to maximize the utility function $U^h(x_1^h, x_2^h)$ subject to budget constraints (8.21)–(8.22). Provided that it is well-defined, this choice in turn identifies the *optimal action* $a^{h*} = (x_1^{h*}, b_1^{h*}, b_2^{h*})$ taken by the household on period 1 markets, where $a^{h*} \in \mathfrak{R}^{N+2}$. Within this framework, a *temporary equilibrium of the modified exchange economy* is finally defined as a system of current prices and a corresponding set of optimal actions on the part of the H households such that the $N + 2$ current markets are simultaneously cleared.[75]

For this modified exchange economy a striking result is that a temporary equilibrium will generally not exist under Assumptions 8.1 and 8.2. As we shall see presently, the reason for this negative result is the possibility of speculative behaviour that can cause the household's demands and supplies to become unbounded.

The following example illustrates the nature of the problem. Assume that the price system ruling on futures markets at the beginning of period 1 is $\bar{q} = (\bar{q}_1, \bar{q}_2)$ such that $\bar{q}_2/\bar{q}_1 = 2$, while household h expects (with certainty) that the future price of good 2 will be $p_{22}^h = 3$. Under these circumstances the household will have a strong incentive to trade on forward markets for *speculative* purposes. Sup-

---

75 Under the notation adopted in the text, the market clearing condition on the forward market for good i is $\sum_h b_i^{h*} = 0$ ($i = 1, 2$).

8.26 · An Introductory Pure-Exchange Model

pose the household buys forward a unit of good 2 and simultaneously sells forward two units of good 1: under the postulated price conditions, the total cost of implementing that scheme would be zero; but the household calculates that in period 2 it will be able to exchange the unit of good 2 that it will then receive for three units of good 1, that is one *more* than the two units of good 1 that it has committed itself to deliver. The household will conclude that by carrying out the trading scheme under consideration *it can increase its future wealth at no cost* or, to use a concise technical expression, that trading on forward markets provides an opportunity for *profitable arbitrage*. Now recall that, by assumption, the household is price-taker and is never satiated in both present and future consumption: therefore it will tend to increase *without limit* the quantity of good 2 for future delivery demanded in the present and financed by selling forward good 1. This means, however, that at the assumed current and expected prices the household's optimal action *cannot be determined* and a temporary equilibrium cannot therefore exist.

The reader can check that the foregoing argument applies to all situations in which the current prices and the prices expected by the generic household h are such that $(q_2/q_1) < p_{22}^h$. By adapting that argument it can also be seen that, should the ruling and the expected prices be such that $(q_2/q_1) > p_{22}^h$, household h would tend to increase without limit the quantity of good 1 for future delivery demanded in the present and financed by selling forward good 2; as a consequence the household's optimal action cannot be determined in this case either, and for this reason $(q_2/q_1) > p_{22}^h$ too is incompatible with the existence of a temporary equilibrium. A system of period-1 prices can support a temporary equilibrium of the modified exchange economy only if at those prices profitable arbitrage is considered impossible by all households, i.e. only if the *non-arbitrage condition* $(q_2/q_1) = p_{22}^h$ holds *for each h*: which implies that all households have *exactly the same expectation* of the future price of good 2. But since perfect foresight is *not* assumed, one cannot expect a system of current prices generally to exist at which the required coincidence of forecasts could be fulfilled. This is quite obvious in the case of 'fixed' expectations, i.e. expectations independent of current prices: in this case it suffices that just two households disagree concerning the future price of good 2 to prevent the existence of a temporary equilibrium. But even assuming the expected prices to be *continuous functions* of current prices, it is perfectly possible that, for two or more households, the individual expectation functions be such that they generate different expected prices of good 2 of period 2 at any system of current prices, thereby preventing the existence of a temporary equilibrium; and even if some system of current prices existed rendering $(q_2/q_1) = p_{22}^h$ for each h, it would be a fluke if it were also capable of ensuring equilibrium on the current markets.

The problem that (perceived) arbitrage opportunities create for the existence of temporary equilibrium was pointed out by Green (1973) within the context of a pure-exchange economy close to that examined in this section. Green pointed out that the problem is reduced when expectation functions are 'probabilistic', i.e. take the form of probability distributions of future prices. However, Green made it clear that the problem is not completely ruled out under that formulation of

688   Chapter 8 · Intertemporal Equilibrium, Temporary Equilibrium

price forecasts, because, in order for an equilibrium to exist, unlimited arbitrage operations on forward markets must be prevented, and this requires an assumption that there be an 'overlap' of individual expectations. A simple example will illustrate the meaning of that 'overlap', and will also highlight a debatable aspect of the equilibrium whose existence is proved under that assumption.

Assume again the two goods, two periods economy with possibility of forward trading of both goods. Assume two price-taking households, A and B[76]; each one has an estimate, of the possible relative price of good 2 of period 2 in terms of good 1 of that period, which consists of a probability distribution over an interval. For simplicity, assume that A has a uniform probability distribution over an interval $(p_{22}^{A-}, p_{22}^{A+})$ which is independent of period-1 prices, while B has an analogous uniform probability distribution independent of prices, over the interval $(p_{22}^{B-}, p_{22}^{B+})$ generally different from A's interval. (Note that these are expected *relative* spot prices, i.e. $p_{12}^h = 1$.) Those intervals are the *supports* of the probability distributions and will be indicated as supp(A), supp(B). The expected value of p_{22} for household h, to be indicated as p_{22}^{hE}, is then the middle point of the relevant interval. Assume furthermore, again for simplicity, that both A and B have such endowments and preferences that they decide to perform no saving nor dissaving, i.e. $p_1 x_1^h = p_1 \omega_1^h$ for $h=$A, B; hence $q_1 b_1^h + q_2 b_2^h = 0$, that is, if a household speculates, it buys forward one good and sells forward the other good for the same value: *balanced speculative trading*. Remember that $b_i > 0$ indicates a purchase forward, $b_i < 0$ indicates a sale forward; under our assumption, b_1^h, b_2^h have opposite sign. When period 2 arrives, and actual spot prices p_{12}, p_{22} become known to a household, its budget constraint is

$$p_{12}x_{12} + p_{22}x_{22} = p_{12}b_1 + p_{22}b_2 + p_{12}\omega_{12} + p_{22}\omega_{22},$$

or rather, normalizing prices so that $p_{12} = 1$:

$$x_{12} + p_{22}x_{22} = b_1 + p_{22}b_2 + \omega_{12} + p_{22}\omega_{22},$$

where for simplicity the household index is omitted. If b_1 is negative, that is, if the household sold good 1 forward, then in period 2 it must give $-b_1$ units of good 1 to others, and if $-b_1 > \omega_1$ the household must buy some good 1 in order to be able to fulfil its contractual obligation; it is then possible that $b_1 + p_{22}b_2 + \omega_{12} + p_{22}\omega_{22} < 0$, which makes it impossible to satisfy the budget constraint. Green argues that this possibility must be excluded in order for the household's utility maximization problem to be well defined; actually, it may be possible to render the utility maximization problem well defined all the same, by stipulating that in that case the household goes bankrupt and there is a legal provision establishing what happens in this case, e.g. that $x_{12} = x_{22} = 0$; but the literature has preferred to assume that *no household ever wants to run the risk of going bankrupt* even with very small probability, and then for it to be possible that an equilibrium

---

76 Price taking can be justified by assuming that there are in fact 10,000 households identical to A and 10,000 identical to B.

8.26 · An Introductory Pure-Exchange Model

exists one obtains the same necessary constraints as Green on the household's speculative forward trades and on supp(A) and supp(B). To save on symbols, let $Q \equiv q_2/q_1$; then for each household $b_2 = -b_1/Q$, $b_1 = -b_2 Q$.

The result reached by Green, translated to our simple example, is that a necessary condition for an equilibrium to exist (under the stated assumption of no risk of bankruptcy) is that the intersection of supp(A) and supp(B) must be an interval of *positive* length. The reason is the following. If Q is not internal to supp(A), then A feels certain that it can speculate with no risk of bankruptcy; this is because there can be a subjective risk of bankruptcy only if it is esteemed that it can happen that $b_1 + p_{22} b_2 < 0$, which, remembering the connection between b_1 and b_2 under our assumptions, becomes $b_1(1 - p_{22}/Q) < 0$; but if $Q \le p_{22}^{A-} < p_{22}^{AE}$, A finds it convenient to speculate by selling good 1 forward and buying good 2 forward, and therefore $b_1 < 0$; and given Q and A's expectations, A is certain that $(1 - p_{22}/Q) \le 0$ and therefore is certain that $b_1(1 - p_{22}/Q) \ge 0$; the same result $b_1(1 - p_{22}/Q) \ge 0$ is reached if $Q > p_{22}^{A+} > p_{22}^{AE}$ (in which case the speculation requires $b_1 > 0$). So unless Q is *internal* to supp(A), A finds no reason not to engage in unlimited speculation, similarly to the case of subjective certainty (point expectation) on the future value of p_{22}; no equilibrium can exist. The same convenience of unlimited speculation applies to B if Q is not internal to supp(B). A necessary condition for an equilibrium to exist is therefore that there exists some Q internal to both supp(A) and supp(B): this requires that the two intervals overlap for some positive length. For an economy with several households and several forward markets, the equivalent condition is that the intersection of all supports of the price probability distributions of the households must have a non-empty interior. Therefore, in an exchange economy with many households and many goods tradable forward, it suffices that for at least one forward good (other than the numéraire one) there are two households whose probability distributions have supports that do not 'overlap' (i.e. that there is no price interval to which both households attribute a nonzero probability of containing the future spot price of that good), and a temporary equilibrium will not exist. The risk that no equilibrium exists appears considerable.

8.26.4 A Perplexing Aspect of Green's Equilibrium

Green is able to prove that, under the stated 'overlap' condition plus the no-risk-of-bankruptcy assumption plus various continuity assumptions,[77] an equilibrium does indeed exist.[78] But a perplexing aspect of this equilibrium seems to have

---

77 These are rather strong, for example, for each household h, supp(h) must be a continuous correspondence of period-1 prices; this excludes the possibility that a small change in present prices may induce some agent to expect some event, e.g. a state intervention, causing a discontinuous change in expected prices.

78 Green (1973) refers to other papers for important passages in his proof; cf. Grandmont (1982, p. 892) for a more complete proof.

690   Chapter 8 · Intertemporal Equilibrium, Temporary Equilibrium

escaped recognition: the equilibrium can require some household to engage in speculative trading from which it expects to gain *nothing*; this is implausible, the household has no reason to engage in it, and would actually incur a loss since transaction costs are never really zero in the real world. The need for this implausible assumption arises because equilibrium on the forward markets can require that Q equals a household's expected value of p_{22}. In such a case, assuming for example the household is A, it is $Q = p_{22}^{AE}$, hence A expects no profit from any extent of balanced speculative trading. To give an idea of why A may be nonetheless required to engage in some speculative trading for an equilibrium to exist, we study the implications of the no-risk-of-bankruptcy assumption on the amount of speculative balanced trading a household undertakes.

Without loss of generality consider household A. Suppose initially p_{22}^{A-} $< Q < p_{22}^{AE}$; the household finds it convenient to buy good 2 forward and to sell good 1 forward, hence $b_1 < 0$, $b_2 > 0$, and the no-risk-of-bankruptcy condition is $b_1 + p_{22}b_2 + \omega_{12} + p_{22}\omega_{22} \geq 0$ for all $p_{22} \in \text{supp}(A)$; using $b_1 = -Qb_2$ and with reference to the least favourable case ($p_{22} = p_{22}^{A-}$) this constraint becomes

$$b_2 \leq \left(\omega_{12} + \omega_{22}p_{22}^{A-}\right) / \left(Q - p_{22}^{A-}\right).$$

As Q tends to p_{22}^{A-}, the right-hand side tends to $+\infty$; as Q tends to p_{22}^{AE}, the right-hand side tends to a finite positive value that we may indicate as D^{A+}. Now suppose $p_{22}^{AE} < Q < p_{22}^{A+}$; the household finds it convenient $b_1 > 0$, $b_2 < 0$, and the no-risk-of-bankruptcy condition with reference to the least favourable case ($p_{22} = p_{22}^{A+}$) becomes

$$b_2 \geq -\left(\omega_{12} + \omega_{22}p_{22}^{A+}\right) / \left(p_{22}^{A+} - Q\right).$$

The right-hand side tends to $-\infty$ as Q tends to p_{22}^{A+}, and tends to a finite negative value D^{A-} as Q tends to p_{22}^{AE}.

We can conclude that the household's demand for b_2 as a function of Q has the shape of ◘ Fig. 8.6: it has no discontinuities because it is assumed that the household is ready to undertake no profit speculative arbitrage at $Q = p_{22}^{AE}$ within the vertical segment from D^{A+} to D^{A-}, where therefore its demand is multivalued; from the extremes of this segment two branches of hyperbola start, tending to positive infinity as Q decreases, and to negative infinity as Q increases. If the other household has a different probability distribution, its function $b_2(Q)$ will have the same type of shape, but the vertical segment will be of different length, and located at a different value of Q. One can then have a situation like that of ◘ Fig. 8.6, where the only equilibrium on the b_2 market is at $Q = p_{22}^{AE}$ and requires household A to locate itself on its vertical segment at a value of b_2 different from zero (point ■ in ◘ Fig. 8.6), while the household has no incentive to do so. Now, an equilibrium, which in order to be established requires an agent to choose one particular point in a continuum of points among which the agent is indifferent, cannot be presumed to be ever established if no reason can be found why the

8.26 · An Introductory Pure-Exchange Model

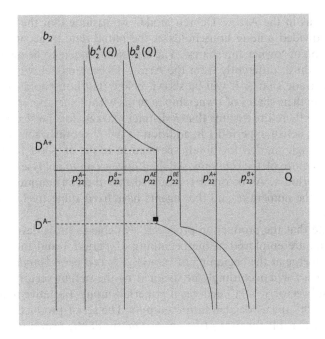

Fig. 8.6 Demand curves of consumers A and B. At price p_{22}^{AE} if consumer A's negative demand is as indicated by the small square, it compensates B's positive demand for b_2 and there is equilibrium

agent should be induced to choose that particular point. (Note that if one were to assume even minimal transaction costs, all points of the vertical segments different from zero would disappear, and in the case depicted the discontinuity would cause the non-existence of equilibrium.)

8.27 Extension to the Case of Economies with Production

8.27.1 The Extended Model

We shall now see how the introductory model with a *single* forward market can be modified so as to transform it into a model of exchange *and* production. This will allow pointing out some of the issues that arise in attempts to introduce production into the framework of temporary equilibrium analysis.

The first step towards the proposed extension consists of introducing the following basic changes in the model. To begin with, we assume that the N commodities traded in the economy include not only consumption goods but also goods and services susceptible of being used as production inputs. Second, we assume that a given number F of firms (indexed by $f = 1, \ldots, F$) are active in the econ-

692   **Chapter 8 · Intertemporal Equilibrium, Temporary Equilibrium**

omy.[79] Third, as in the Arrow–Debreu model, we assume that the ownership of each firm is divided among households at the initial date in accordance with a given allocation of 'ownership shares'. The last basic change to be made is closely related to the third: differently from the Arrow–Debreu model, we allow for the possibility to trade shares. It will be shown below that households are generally willing to trade their shares of ownership in firms within a temporary equilibrium framework. We therefore assume that F distinct markets for the shares in the different firms are active in period 1 in addition to the N spot markets for commodities and the single market for bonds specified in terms of good 1. Having thus altered the structure of the economy, we shall now go on to analyse the behaviour of agents in period 1. As before it is assumed that the consumption good listed as 'good 1' is the numéraire and that agents have fixed subjectively certain price expectations.

We assume that the production processes available to firms develop in cycles, i.e. that inputs are employed at the beginning of period 1 and the corresponding outputs emerge at the beginning of period 2. A *two-period production plan* of the generic firm f will accordingly be denoted by the netput vector $y_{12}^f = (y_1^f, y_2^f)$, where the subvector $y_1^f \in \mathfrak{R}_-^N$ denotes first-period inputs (negative numbers) and subvector $y_2^f \in \mathfrak{R}_+^N$ the associated future outputs. The set of production plans that are technically feasible for firm f (the *production set* of the firm for short) will be denoted by Y_{12}^f.

Due to the cyclical nature of production, the economy is endowed at the beginning of period 1 with given stocks of commodities derived from the activity of firms in the previous period. We assume that these stocks are part of the initial endowments of households; hence, firms do not own endowments and must finance their current input expenditure entirely by issuing bonds. We finally assume that each firm is run by a manager who is responsible for selecting the two-period production plan. Under these assumptions, the formation of production decisions can be described as follows.

Again for simplicity we assume certain and fixed expectations of future prices. At the beginning of period 1, the manager of the generic firm f is certain that the price vector $p_2^f = (p_{12}^f, \ldots, p_{N2}^f) \geq 0$ (which we normalize by setting $p_{12}^f = 1$) will obtain on future spot markets. Given these expected prices, the manager observes the prices $p = (p_1, q_1)$ quoted on current markets and assesses the profitability of the alternative plans in Y_{12}^f. In evaluating a hypothetical plan $y_{12}^f = (y_1^f, y_2^f)$, the manager realizes that the firm would have to issue a quantity of bonds b^f such that $q_1 b^f = -(p_1 y_1^f)$ in order to finance its current input expenditure and would accordingly have to repay $b^f = -(1/q_1)(p_1 y_1^f)$ units of numéraire at the begin-

---

79 In ▶ Chap. 5 it was argued that not even the assumption that the tendency towards equilibrium operates through an auctioneer-guided tâtonnement justifies taking the number of firms as given, because firms are legal entities, distinct from fixed plants (which are tradeable), and new firms can be created during the tâtonnement. But the literature on temporary equilibria has followed the Arrow–Debreu assumptions of a given number of firms and given (at least initially) property shares of households in each firm, and our intention here is to explain the results reached by this literature.

8.27 · Extension to the Case of Economies with Production

ning of period 2. At the same time, the manager anticipates that the plan would yield future receipts equal to $(p_2^f y_2^f)$ units of numéraire. According to the manager's subjective expectations, the hypothetical plan under consideration would therefore yield profits equal to $\pi_2^f = p_2^f y_2^f + (1/q_1)(p_1 y_1^f)$ in period 2. It is convenient to introduce an alternative formulation of these expected profits. Given that a quantity π_2 of the numéraire good for future delivery can be traded in the present on the bond market at the total price $\pi_1 = (q_1 \pi_2)$, the *present value* of the profits expected by the manager is $\pi_1^f = q_1 p_2^f y_2^f + (1/q_1)(p_1 y_1^f)$. By adopting the convention $q^f = q_1 p_2^f$, the present value of expected profits can be expressed in the equivalent form $\pi_1^f = (q^f y_2^f + p_1 y_1^f)$, where, it should be noted, the components of vector q^f are precisely the 'present prices' of commodities for future delivery *as calculated by the manager of firm f*. We assume that the manager of the generic firm chooses the production plan so as to maximize the present value of expected profits. In order for the analysis to continue, we assume (in accordance with this literature) that this maximization results in a finite dimension of the firm and hence in a finite maximum profit, i.e. that there are decreasing returns to scale at least beyond a certain scale of production.

■■ Assumption 8.4
Given the expected prices p_2^f and the current prices p, the manager of the generic firm f chooses a production plan that maximizes the 'profit function' $\pi_1^f(y_{12}^f) = (q^f y_2^f + p_1 y_1^f)$, where $q^f = q_1 p_2^f$, subject to $y_{12}^f \in Y_{12}^f$. The production plan is always finite.

Under Assumption 8.4, the choice of the production plan at current prices $p = (p_1, q_1)$ and fixed expected prices p_2^f is *formally equivalent* to standard producer choice under complete forward markets at prices $p'' = (p_1, q^f)$ and might be analysed in the same way. If we now use $y_{12}^{f*} = (y_1^{f*}, y_2^{f*})$ to denote the plan chosen by the manager of the firm f in accordance with Ass. 8.4, the manager's choice identifies not only the firm's current demand for inputs but also the current supply of bonds, where the latter is given by $b^{f*} = -(1/q_1)(p_1 y_1^{f*})$, and therefore determines the *optimal action* $a^{f*} = (y_1^{f*}, b^{f*})$ taken by the firm on period 1 markets.

Now let us go on to examine the household sector. As previously assumed, households are endowed at the initial date with given 'shares of ownership' in the different firms. We shall denote the share endowment of the generic household h by the vector $\bar{\theta}^h = (\bar{\theta}_1^h, ..., \bar{\theta}_F^h)$ and assume that $\bar{\theta}^h \geq 0$ for all h, $\sum_h \bar{\theta}_f^h = 1$ for all f. It should be clear from the description of firms' behaviour that the possession of an ownership share in a firm throughout period 1 entitles the holder to the same proportion of the profits accruing to the firm at the beginning of period 2. It should be noted, however, that when the firms' plans are announced at the initial date, households will estimate the associated receipts according to *their* individual expectations and will thus typically form *different opinions* concerning the amount of profit to be earned by holding shares in any given firm. In the presence of those different opinions, it is natural to assume that households will differ in the value they assign to the shares of a firm, and will find it advantageous to *trade* shares on the corresponding F markets in existence. Taking this aspect of

694   Chapter 8 · Intertemporal Equilibrium, Temporary Equilibrium

the economy into account, we shall now examine the behaviour of households on the markets at the beginning of period 1 *after* the announcement of the production plans selected by managers.

As regards trading on share markets, we shall drastically simplify our analysis by assuming that the shares of each firm are automatically transferred to the household (or group of households) expecting the highest amount of profit from the firm's plan, at a price exactly equal to the present value of those expected profits according to that household.[80] This assumption can be formally stated as follows. Define the present value of the profits that household h expects from the plan y_{12}^{f*} announced by firm f as $\pi_1^{hf} = q_1 p_2^h y_2^{f*} + (1/q_1)(p_1 y_1^{f*})$ and consider the equivalent formulation $\pi_1^{hf} = (q^h y_2^{f*} + p_1 y_1^{f*})$, where vector $q^h = q_1 p_2^h$ denotes the 'present prices' of commodities for future delivery *as calculated by household h*. Then denote by v^f the current price for the whole of firm f's shares, or *market value of the firm* for short. Finally, denote by θ_f^h the share in firm f that household h owns after the announcement of production plans and the transferral of firm shares to the households that value them most. The following assumption is then made:

---

80 This assumption is introduced for the sake of simplicity, but it might be acceptable in certain cases. Let us examine the demand for the shares of the generic firm f on the part of the generic household h at different prices. To begin with, let us assume that the price for the whole of firm f's shares coincides with $(q_1 \pi_2^{hf})$, i.e. with the present value of the amount of future profits π_2^{hf} that h expects from the plan announced by the firm. It is readily ascertained that in these circumstances, the question of whether to purchase the whole of firm f's shares or invest $(q_1 \pi_2^{hf})$ units of numéraire on the bond market will be a matter of indifference to h. It follows that in the event of the price for 100% of the firm's shares being *higher* than $(q_1 \pi_2^{hf})$, the household's demand for shares in firm f would be zero, as it would prefer to invest its savings in bonds; in the event of the price for the whole of the firm's shares being *lower* than $(q_1 \pi_2^{hf})$, household h would have an incentive to buy the firm outright and finance the purchase by borrowing on the bond market, because in the household's opinion the operation would ensure a positive profit in period 2 at no cost. Having established these preliminary results, let us assume for simplicity that there are only three households in the economy ($h = 1, 2, 3$) and that individual price expectations are such that $\pi_2^{1f} \geq \pi_2^{2f} \geq \pi_2^{3f}$. In those circumstances, it can be argued (a) that the equilibrium price for the whole of firm f's shares cannot be higher than $(q_1 \pi_2^{1f})$ and (b) that the equilibrium price cannot be lower than $(q_1 \pi_2^{2f})$, since at a price lower than $(q_1 \pi_2^{2f})$ at least two households would be interested in purchasing the whole of firm f's shares and an aggregate excess demand would accordingly appear on the market for those shares. It can thus be concluded that the equilibrium price for 100% of the firm's shares must lie in the interval $(q_1 \pi_2^{1f}), (q_1 \pi_2^{2f})$, the interval between the highest and the next-to-highest estimate by some household of the present value of expected profits. This in turn means that the assumption introduced in the text concerning the price for the shares of the generic firm can be justified in practice when the difference between π_2^{1f} and π_2^{2f} is very small, and can be *fully* justified when two or more households share the most optimistic expectation as regards the firm's profits (i.e. in the particular case in which $\pi_2^{1f} = \pi_2^{2f} \geq \pi_2^{3f}$). Thus that assumption requires that for each firm the two more 'optimistic' households have rather similar expectations. Note that if two or more households share the same most optimistic expectation about a firm's profits, the way the firm's shares are divided among these households does not affect their budget constraints because any division will result in the same (subjective) wealth for each household.

8.27 · Extension to the Case of Economies with Production

■■ Assumption 8.5

(a) *The market value of the generic firm f in period 1 is*

$$v^f = \underset{h}{Max}\, \pi_1^{hf} = \underset{h}{Max}\left(q^h y_2^{f*} + p_1 y_1^{f*}\right);$$

(b) *for all h and all f, $\theta_f^h \geq 0$;*

(c) *for all h and all f, $\theta_f^h > 0$ if and only if $\pi_1^{hf} = v^f$;*

(d) *for all f, $\sum_h \theta_f^h = \sum_h \bar{\theta}_f^h = 1$.*

As regards the market for bonds, we assume as before that each household initially issues bonds so as to capitalize its expected future wealth, which is given in the present context by the expected value of future endowments *plus* the household's expected profits from its shares of firms.

■■ Assumption 8.6

At the beginning of period 1 the generic household h issues a quantity of bonds $\bar{b}_1^h$ such that $q_1 \bar{b}_1^h = q^h \omega_2^h + \sum_f \theta_f^h \left(q^h y_2^{f*} + p_1 y_1^{f*}\right)$.

Under Assumption 8.6 the wealth at the disposal of household h after this issue of bonds is $W_1^h = p_1 \omega_1^h + \sum_f \bar{\theta}_f^h v^f + q_1 \bar{b}_1^h$, but part of this wealth must be used to pay for the share transfers carried out in accordance with Assumption 8.5; only the remainder can be spent on purchase of commodities for current consumption and on purchase of a quantity b_1^h of bonds. The *first-period budget constraint* of household h is therefore given by the equation

$$p_1 x_1^h + q_1 b_1^h = p_1 \omega_1^h + \sum_f \bar{\theta}_f^h v^f + q_1 \bar{b}_1^h - \sum_f \theta_f^h v^f \tag{8.23}$$

which, by substituting for $q_1 \bar{b}_1^h$ according to Ass. 8.6 and taking Ass. 8.5 into account, can be written[81]

$$p_1 x_1^h + q_1 b_1^h = p_1 \omega_1^h + q^h \omega_2^h + \sum_f \bar{\theta}_f^h v^f \tag{8.24}$$

This reformulation shows that what determines spendable income, besides the observed and expected prices and the endowments of goods, is the *initial*

---

81 By substituting for $q_1 \bar{b}_1^h$ the right-hand side of Eq. (8.23) becomes
$p_1 \omega_1^h + \sum_f \bar{\theta}_f^h v^f + q^h \omega_2^h + \sum_f \theta_f^h (q^h y_2^{f*} + p_1 y_1^{f*})$.
As θ_f^h is strictly positive if $\pi_1^{hf} = (q^h y_2^{f*} + p_1 y_1^{f*}) = v^f$ and must otherwise be zero (Assumptions 9.5 (b), (c)), the right-hand side can be rewritten in the equivalent form
$p_1 \omega_1^h + \sum_f \bar{\theta}_f^h v^f + q^h \omega_2^h + \sum_f \theta_f^h v^f$.
Once the right-hand side of Eq. (8.23) is reformulated in this way, elimination of the total expenditure for shares $\sum_f \theta_f^h v^f$ from both sides yields Eq. (8.24).

696   Chapter 8 · Intertemporal Equilibrium, Temporary Equilibrium

endowments of shares,[82] not the endowments after the transferral of shares to the households that value them most. On the other hand, the household anticipates that in period 2 it will have to surrender both its commodity endowments and its share of firms' profits in order to repay the bonds issued in accordance with Assumption 8.6. The household's *(expected) budget constraint for period 2* is therefore

$$p_2^h x_2^h = b_1^h \tag{8.25}$$

Comparison of budget constraints (8.24)–(8.25) and budget constraints (8.18)–(8.19) of ▶ Sect. 8.26.2 shows that once the firms' plans have been announced and share transfers have taken place, households are fundamentally in the same position as in the introductory pure-exchange economy. We therefore assume that in these circumstances, the generic household h will choose its current consumption, current demand for bonds and planned future consumption so as to maximize the utility function $U^h(x_1^h, x_2^h)$ subject to constraints (8.24)–(8.25). As in the introductory model, this choice will in turn determine the *optimal action* $a^{h*} = (x_1^{h*}, b_1^{h*})$ taken by the household on period 1 markets.

The description of agents' behaviour at given current prices and fixed price expectations is now complete. Given that share markets are 'automatically cleared' in view of Assumption 8.5, a *temporary equilibrium of exchange and production* can be accordingly defined as a system of current prices, a corresponding set of F optimal actions on the part of firms, and a corresponding set of H optimal actions on the part of households such that the N spot markets and the market for bonds are simultaneously cleared in period 1.

The model outlined in this paragraph corresponds essentially to the temporary equilibrium model with production put forward by Arrow and Hahn (1971: Ch. 6).[83] As regards the *existence* of temporary equilibrium we can therefore take

---

82 The assumption of given initial shares in spite of the admission of trading in shares can only be acceptable if either the equilibrium prices are struck at the first attempt, or the tradings in shares during the disequilibrium adjustments are provisional, the adjustments being a tâtonnement where tradings in shares too are done through 'bons' that are cancelled once the auctioneer announces that the prices were not equilibrium prices and the tâtonnement must continue. Of course any realistic adjustment will on the contrary alter share ownerships during disequilibrium, so we have here one more element of impermanence of the data of equilibrium.

83 Our repeated reference to the contribution of these authors calls for some clarification as regards the link that can be established between the temporary equilibrium model with production of Arrow and Hahn (1971), and the models presented in this and in earlier paragraphs. To start with the model outlined in this paragraph, even though all the assumptions concerning the behaviour of agents are either borrowed from the Arrow–Hahn model or compatible with it, there are two differences in the formulation adopted. As readers can check, in the model of Arrow and Hahn prices are expressed in terms of a fictitious currency of account ('bancors') and the unit bond is defined as a promise to pay a unit *of that currency* in period 2. However, these differences are immaterial. To see why, consider a version of the Arrow–Hahn model in which all agents expect that the future price of good 1 in terms of 'bancors' will be equal to 1. In these circumstances, which are fully compatible with Arrow and Hahn's formal treatment of expectations, the market

8.27 · Extension to the Case of Economies with Production

advantage of the results obtained by those authors, who prove that the temporary equilibrium of exchange and production exists under standard assumptions on preferences and production sets. They also show that this result holds not only in the case of fixed expectations but also if individual price expectations are continuous functions of current prices. Having thus briefly dealt with the question of existence, we shall now go on to a closer examination of the assumptions concerning production decisions and borrowing decisions made in the extended model. It will be argued that they are more problematic than they may appear.

8.27.2 Discussion of the Extended Model[84]

Let us first examine the production decisions of firms. In the intertemporal model of general equilibrium, the existence of complete forward markets for commodities permits a simple treatment of production decisions. Let us consider, within that model, the position of the households holding ownership shares in a generic firm at the initial date. On the one hand, each household is interested in receiving the highest amount of profit from the firm, as any increase in profit would correspondingly increase the household's initial wealth and therefore improve the household's consumption opportunities. On the other hand, the profitability of the alternative production plans that are feasible for the firm can be assessed *objectively* on the basis of the prices observable on the current system of spot and forward markets. It follows from these considerations that the households sharing the ownership of a generic firm at the initial date will *unanimously approve*

---

for bonds specified in 'bancors' becomes the same thing as a market for bonds *specified in terms of good 1*. As a result, the version of the Arrow–Hahn model under consideration coincides with the extended model outlined in this section except for the numéraire adopted. Given that the behaviour of agents in Arrow and Hahn's contribution is independent of the numéraire measuring current prices, we can safely modify that version by taking good 1 as numéraire.

Having thus established that the model with production presented in this paragraph is simply a version of the Arrow–Hahn model, we shall now show that further specification of that version makes it possible to obtain precisely the pure-exchange model of Sects. 8.C.2.1–8.C.2.4. Assume that there is only one firm in the economy ($F = 1$) and that its production set is $Y_{12}^1 = -\Re_+^{2N}$. The last part of the assumption states that the only processes the firm can operate are *free disposal* processes, through which any good available in any of the two periods is instantaneously destroyed by using no other input than the good itself. Under this particular specification of the productive sector, which is compatible with Arrow and Hahn's formal model despite its ad hoc nature, the single firm in existence will remain totally *inactive* in period 1 at every non-negative vector of current prices. As a result, the particular 'production economy' under consideration coincides in fact with the pure-exchange economy of Sects. 8.C.2.1–8.C.2.4.

84 This subsection is based on Ravagnani (1989, 2000).

698   Chapter 8 · Intertemporal Equilibrium, Temporary Equilibrium

the choice of a production plan that maximizes profits calculated at the currently observed spot and futures prices.[85,86]

By contrast, the treatment of production decisions encounters considerable complications in a temporary equilibrium framework. In order to discuss the main issues that arise, let us return to the Arrow–Hahn model as presented in ▶ Sect. 8.26.2 and focus on the position of households at the initial date. Jointly considered, budget constraints (8.24)–(8.25) show that the utility a household can plan to obtain by trading on current markets increases with the value of its period-1 wealth, which depends partly on the value of the household's initial endowment of shares. This means that any household holding an initial share in the generic firm f will favour the choice of the production plan that receives the highest market valuation for the firm's shares, i.e. the choice of the plan *that maximizes the market value v^f of the firm*. But according to Assumption 8.4 the manager of the firm will select the plan to which he *individually* attaches the greatest present value, so he does not try in general to act in the interest of the firm's initial owners. An unsatisfactory feature of the model is therefore that the criterion of choice attributed to managers has no clear rationale. We shall now show that this shortcoming is not easily remedied, as it is a symptom of an authentic analytical problem.

Suppose for the sake of argument that the manager of the generic firm, in an effort to serve the interests of the initial owners, forms a definite opinion as regards the production plan that will generate the highest market value of the firm and then announces that he intends to implement precisely this project. However, the manager's opinion is necessarily subjective: the firm's initial owners may happen to have a different opinion and wish to alter the manager's decision (perhaps by replacing the manager). But the initial owners may well have *conflicting opinions* as regards which plan will ensure maximization of the firm's market value; in these circumstances, no production plan could be unanimously approved by the initial owners and a sort of *social choice* problem would therefore arise within the constituency of the firm's owners. While this problem could be tackled in principle by assuming that some *institutional rule* leading to a definite production decision is at work within the firm, the fact that a variety of such rules can be conceived (e.g. different voting schemes) makes it hard to see how that assumption should be precisely specified.

On the other hand, it is possible to adopt a pragmatic attitude and argue that the assumption that managers choose production plans according to their own evaluation of future receipts provides a realistic representation of where control over firms actually resides (see, for example, Bliss 1976: 194–195). 'Manager'

---

85 Of course this argument presupposes that the owners of the generic firm are 'price-takers', i.e. they believe that prices are not appreciably altered by changes in the firm's production plan.

86 Note that, in the Arrow–Debreu approach where share ownership is relevant owing to the possibility of positive firm 'profits', complete futures markets or shared perfect foresight imply that households have no interest in trading shares at the equilibrium prices, because everybody agrees on the value of shares at those prices, so buying a share would not change the wealth of a consumer.

8.27 · Extension to the Case of Economies with Production

might also be interpreted (and can be so interpreted in the remainder of this Section) as indicating whatever expectations profile emerges as the decisions-determining one from the owners' expectations and preferences plus the institutional rule that governs the firm's decisional process. This attitude may explain why that assumption has been commonly adopted in temporary equilibrium models with production. However, as discussion of a further shortcoming of the Arrow–Hahn model will presently show, the assumption of production plans autonomously chosen by managers (or by shareholder assemblies) is hardly tenable in a temporary equilibrium framework.

The aspect we shall now discuss concerns the *financing* of the production plans selected by managers in accordance with their personal expectations of future receipts. As shown above, Arrow and Hahn assume that firms finance those plans by selling bonds on a *single* market where all bonds are traded at the same price and are therefore treated as perfect substitutes, who issued a particular bond being implicitly assumed to be irrelevant. It is highly doubtful, however, that rational households would be generally willing to treat bonds as perfect substitutes. A simple example will clarify this point.

Consider an economy with only two firms and assume that the manager of each firm selects a plan that maximizes the present value of profits calculated on the basis of his individual price expectations. Then assume that when the manager of firm 1 announces the chosen plan (from which he expects non-negative profits), all the other agents in the economy expect that the future price of planned output will be so low as to generate *negative* profits for the firm in period 2. Finally, assume that all households expect positive profits from the plan announced by firm 2. In such circumstances, the entire ownership of firm 1 would be transferred to the firm's manager when the markets open at the initial date. Moreover, the following situation would occur on the bond market. Except for the optimistic manager of firm 1, all households in the economy would calculate that firm 1 is going to issue bonds that cannot be repaid out of the firm's future receipts—and since they do not know whether the future wealth of the firm's new owner will be sufficient to guarantee repayment, those households would have to regard the bonds floated by firm 1 as *risky* assets. At the same time, they would regard the bonds issued by firm 2 as perfectly safe. The announcement of the production plans independently chosen by managers would thus signal to households that in the overall supply of bonds risky assets may coexist with others whose repayment is beyond doubt. In this situation it is unreasonable to suppose, as the Arrow–Hahn model implicitly does, that households may be disposed to purchase bonds on a single, 'anonymous' market where risky securities cannot be distinguished from safe ones.[87]

---

87 Problematic situations such as the one described in the text may also arise if the Arrow–Hahn model is modified by assuming that managers endeavour to select production plans that maximize the market value of their respective firms. For example, consider an economy with two firms, A and B, that can produce two different qualities of wine by employing grape must as the only input. Assume that each firm can produce any combination of wines by operating

700　Chapter 8 · Intertemporal Equilibrium, Temporary Equilibrium

In order to avoid the abovementioned shortcoming, the model would have to be reformulated so as to enable potential lenders to identify the agents issuing bonds and to learn how they plan to repay their debts. This could be done by introducing a *separate market* for the bonds issued by each individual agent, but then the hypothesis that managers autonomously select production plans could hardly be retained. For example, suppose that the manager of the generic firm f selects a definite plan $\bar{y}_{12}^f$ with the intention of covering the input cost through the sale of a sufficient quantity of bonds at price $\bar{p}_b^f$. When the plan is announced, households value future output according to their own price expectations (as well as the future wealth of the firm's owners, if the latter are legally responsible for the firm's debt) in order to assess the amount that can be paid back to lenders, and thus form an opinion about the rate of return that can actually be obtained on the bonds supplied by firm f. If this largely subjective rate of return proves to be lower than that expected on the bonds of some other firm, however, households will not buy firm f's securities. It would then be impossible to implement the plan chosen by the manager, and the theory would have to explain how the original project is to be revised.

---

two independent processes defined by the production functions $y_{12} = (-y_1)^{1/2}$ for wine of type 1 and $y_{22} = 2(-y_1)^{1/2}$ for wine of type 2, where y_1 (a negative number) denotes the quantity of must employed and y_{i2} the output of wine of type i ($i = 1, 2$). Assume further that there are four households in the economy characterized by the following fixed expectations. Household 1, which includes only the manager of firm A, expects that the price for wine of type 1 will be $\hat{p}_{12} > 0$ and that the price for wine of type 2 will be zero. Household 2 has the same expectations as household 1. Household 3, which includes only the manager of firm B, expects that the price for wine of type 1 will be zero and that the price for wine of type 2 will be $\bar{p}_{22} = \frac{1}{2}\hat{p}_{12}$. Finally, household 4 has the same expectations of household 3. Now recall that in the Arrow–Hahn model, the market value of each firm coincides with the present value of the profits that the most optimistic household (or group of households) expects from the firm's plan (Assumption 8.6). Taking this assumption into account, we can readily see that at any given positive price for grape must, there are always two distinct production plans that ensure maximization of the market value of the generic firm in the economy under consideration. The first involves producing only wine of type 1 in the quantity that maximizes the present value of profits calculated at the positive price expected for that wine by households 1 and 2. The second involves producing only wine of type 2 in the quantity that maximizes the present value of profits calculated at the positive price expected for that wine by households 3 and 4. Having established this point, assume that managers seek to maximize the market value of their respective firms and that if two or more plans ensuring this result are identified, each manager will choose the one that he thinks will yield the highest amount of profits (reasonable behaviour). Finally, assume for the sake of argument that both managers can correctly predict how individual households will evaluate any feasible production plan. Under these assumptions, each manager will be able to identify the pair of plans that ensure maximization of the market value of his firm when markets open in period 1. Moreover, the manager of firm A will choose and announce the plan that involves producing only wine of type 1, while the manager of firm B will opt for and announce the plan that involves producing only wine of type 2. On the other hand, every household will calculate that one of the announced plans will yield positive profits while the other is bound to bring about losses. The announcement of production plans will thus signal to households that risky bonds may coexist with safe ones in the overall supply.

8.27 · Extension to the Case of Economies with Production

Discussion of the Arrow–Hahn model thus shows that in the presence of subjective price expectations it is not reasonable to assume that managers or more generally firms can raise funds *freely* on capital markets. One is thus induced to explore different assumptions as to how firms finance their plans; e.g., as done by Grandmont and Laroque (1976), one can assume that firms own some wealth (some resources) and finance their input expenditure out of that wealth[88]; but this is unduly restrictive, in real economies firms do borrow; even when they own plants or mines or land they usually have obtained that property against indebtedness, so their *net* wealth is often not considerable and to restrict their plans to what can be financed with that net wealth would restrict their choices unrealistically. Or one may try to introduce collateral, but then the specification of equilibrium comes to depend on the specific assumptions as to what can be used as collateral, and how much collateral is needed, assumptions that cannot but be to some extent arbitrary, and furthermore do not avoid the loss of anonymity, with the unpleasant consequence that price taking can no longer be assumed in credit markets.

The considerations put forward thus far indicate that temporary equilibrium theory should admit that managers' decisions are subject to the ultimate judgement of savers, who may refuse to supply the required funds and thus force *revision* of the original projects. In this situation it would appear more appropriate to assume that managers, when selecting production plans, take into account the opinion of the agents who provide funds to the productive sector. However, this assumption gives rise to a new problem, because in order to develop a plausible notion of temporary equilibrium the theory would have to explain how managers can succeed in *correctly* interpreting the private opinions of the potential financiers of firms.

The problem with the assumption of indifference of lenders between potential borrowers arises also for lending to consumers. The assumption that shares end up to the household who values them most is only acceptable if the house-

---

88 This does not eliminate the possibility of conflict between manager and owners. Assume that the manager of the generic firm f, guided by his personal evaluation of future receipts, chooses a production plan that involves using the whole of the firm's initial wealth to finance input expenditure. Assume further that when the manager's decision is announced, all the households in the economy (except for the manager's) anticipate that the firm's planned output will have negligible value in the future. In these circumstances, it is reasonable to imagine that the current price for the whole of the firm's ownership shares would be very close to zero. Assume that this is indeed the case and consider the position of the initial owners of firm f. Apart from the negligible price they could receive from the sale of their shares in the firm, these owners would calculate that the manager's decision requires them to give up some of their potential period 1 wealth (corresponding to the value of the firm's commodity endowment) in order to finance a project that they regard as a sheer waste of resources. At the same time, each owner would calculate that he would be better off if the firm were instructed to close down, as then he could regain his share of the firm's initial wealth and improve his consumption opportunities. Even though there may be disagreements concerning the 'optimal' plan to put into operation, all the initial owners would thus prefer the firm not to engage in production, and in the presence of this *unanimously preferred option* it is paradoxical to suppose that they would passively agree to finance the manager's project.

702   **Chapter 8 · Intertemporal Equilibrium, Temporary Equilibrium**

hold can finance the purchase by issuing bonds, as assumed in the formulation of budget constraint (8.23). But bond purchasers may well not share the optimism of the issuer: and indeed in the real world we do not expect the entire ownership of General Motors to go to the individual—perhaps a lunatic—who is most optimistic about its future prospects. Thus one must admit limits to what individuals can borrow, and again one has difficulty with determining these limits without arbitrariness and with arriving at a definite theory of how shares will end up being allocated.

We find here some examples of the need of the approach, due to its very-short-period nature, to specify behaviours that in real economies depend on a myriad different elements, with a consequent indeterminacy (that arbitrary assumptions can reduce only at the cost of excluding many other plausible behaviours).

8.28 Temporary Equilibrium in Economies with 'Money'

8.28.1 Introduction of Money

The models discussed in the previous sections fail to capture one aspect of real-world trading processes, namely the fact that economic agents wish to keep stocks of a special good—(fiat) *money*—that has no intrinsic value and is used essentially in exchange against physical goods. It should be noted, however, that much of the research carried out by temporary equilibrium theorists had the precise aim of incorporating money into modern general equilibrium analysis. In this section we shall therefore illustrate some basic results emerging from that specific application of temporary equilibrium theory.[89] This will be done through reference to a simple model drawn from Grandmont (1983), whose basic features are summarized below.

The model considers an exchange economy in which spot markets are active in each period, no forward market exists, and agents can transfer wealth from one period to the next *only* by holding a particular asset, 'money', which is available in the system in a constant amount. By assumption, the existing stock of this asset is made up entirely of *outside* or legal or base money (i.e. not created against debt) and can therefore be seen as part of the households' net wealth. The stuff of which money is made has no intrinsic utility, so money is 'fiat money'. Since there are no forward markets, i.e. no bonds, money cannot be borrowed. The model is *exclusively concerned with the store-of-value function* of the asset (the possibility of using stored money as a way to transfer purchasing power

---

89 For an extensive treatment of the monetary issues addressed by temporary equilibrium theorists—which include the validity of the quantity theory of money, the possibility of monetary authorities to manipulate the interest rate, and the existence of a 'liquidity trap'—the reader is referred to Grandmont (1983).

8.28 · Temporary Equilibrium in Economies with 'Money'

across periods) and does not consider the other services performed by money in real-world economies, e.g. as a medium of exchange: the medium-of-exchange function of money does not appear in the model, in the sense that it poses no constraint on the agents' ability to transact. The behaviour of agents is analysed under the condition of strictly positive monetary prices, and money is chosen as numéraire. It should be noted that this choice of numéraire is incompatible with states of the economy characterized by aggregate excess supply of money, as the exchange value of money in terms of any commodity would be zero in such circumstances. The main issue addressed by the model is therefore whether a temporary equilibrium for period 1 exists in which households are willing to hold the whole stock of money in circulation, if only the store-of-value function of money is considered.

Let us then go on to develop a detailed formal exposition in order to try and answer this question.

As in ▶ Sect. 8.2, we shall refer to an economy with H households and N non-storable consumption goods that is active for two periods of time.[90] At the beginning of period 1, the generic household h has both a commodity endowment vector ω_1^h and an endowment of money $\bar{m}^h$ stemming from its past saving decisions, and knows that its future commodity endowment will be ω_2^h. The household observes the *monetary* prices $p_1 \in \Re_{++}^N$ quoted on current spot markets and expects the system of *monetary* prices p_2^h to obtain in period 2. (For the sake of economy of notation we continue to denote prices as in the previous sections even though they are now expressed in money.) Unlike the arguments developed in Sects. 8.2 and 8.3, we do not regard the vector p_2^h as fixed but assume that expected prices depend on current prices. To be more precise, we assume that $p_2^h = \Psi^h(p_1)$, where the expectation function Ψ^h can include past prices among its parameters. Finally we introduce the following assumption concerning the characteristics and expectations of households:

■■ Assumption 8.7

(a) *The generic household h has a preference ordering over two-period consumption streams in the set $X_{12}^h = \Re_+^{2N}$ that can be represented by the continuous, strictly increasing and strictly quasi-concave utility function $U^h(x_1^h, x_2^h)$;*

(b) *for all h, $\omega_1^h \gg 0$, $\omega_2^h \gg 0$;*

(c) *$\bar{m}^h \geq 0$ for all h, $\Sigma_h \bar{m}^h = M > 0$;*

(d) *for all h, the expectation function Ψ^h is continuous and such that $\Psi^h(p_1) \in \Re_{++}^N$ for every $p_1 \in \Re_{++}^N$.*

Note that by postulating that households expect strictly positive but finite monetary prices for period 2, part (d) rules out one case in which there is no reason to transfer money to that period, namely the case in which households are

---

90 The analysis that follows can be readily extended to economies in which markets are active for more than two periods and households formulate their plans accordingly (cf. Grandmont 1983, ▶ Chap. 1).

704   Chapter 8 · Intertemporal Equilibrium, Temporary Equilibrium

certain that future commodity prices in terms of money will be infinite (i.e. that money will have no exchange value in period 2); it also rules out the case in which households think that the future money prices of all commodities will be zero, a case of more difficult interpretability (can one use money to buy commodities in this case?).

Let us now examine the behaviour of households at the beginning of period 1. Given the ruling prices and the associated expected prices, the generic household h must choose a most preferred two-period consumption stream out of those it believes it can attain in view both of the value of its commodity endowments and of the possibility of transferring money to period 2. It can be stated in formal terms that at any given price system $p_1 \in \mathfrak{R}_{++}^N$, the generic household h must solve the following problem:

4.I *Maximize* $U^h(x_1^h, x_2^h)$ *with respect to* $x_1^h \geq 0, m_1^h \geq 0, x_2^h \geq 0,$
subject to the current and expected budget constraints:

$$p_1 x_1^h + m_1^h = p_1 \omega_1^h + \overline{m}^h \tag{8.26}$$

$$\Psi^h(p_1) x_2^h = \Psi^h(p_1) \omega_2^h + m_1^h \tag{8.27}$$

where the choice variable m_1^h, the 'demand for money' as this term is used in this literature, denotes the amount of money with which the household wants to end the period in order to carry it over to period 2 to finance future consumption.[91] Note that m_1^h must be non-negative because, by assumption, the household cannot borrow money in period 1. Note also that the household does not plan to demand money in period 2, as it is aware that economic activity is going to cease at the end of that period.[92]

---

91 [*footnote by F.P.*] This definition of 'demand for money', the amount of money *one wants to end the period with (and hence the money endowment one wants to start the next period with)*, is very different from the traditional meaning of 'demand for money' that refers to the *average* money balance holdings *over the period* that an agent desires in order to satisfy the motives (e.g. transaction, precautionary and speculative motive, in Keynes) for holding money. Consider a household which starts the period with zero money, sells labour services paid at the beginning of the period and thus obtains an amount of money m immediately after the beginning of the period, spends it at a constant rate over the period so as to finish it just at the end the period, and is satisfied with the situation. The traditional demand for money of this household is $m/2$, its demand for money as defined in the text is zero. Cf. Petri (2004, ▶ Chap. 5, Appendix 1).

92 The lack of incentives to demand money in period 2 creates a problem which we can neglect but it is opportune to remember, in fact the same problem with money as in the Arrow–Debreu model (which covers a finite number of periods), with expectations determining the same outcome as complete futures markets. If the generic household realizes that in period 2 all the other agents too have no reason to demand money (i.e. no reason to end the period holding a positive amount of money), it cannot reasonably expect money to have a positive exchange value in period 2 as stated by Assumption 8.7(d). The same problem arises when the two-period model put forward in the text is extended to economies that are active for a higher but *finite* number of periods. We already know the argument, which needs only to be reformulated in terms of plausible formation of expectations. Assume that economic activity comes to an end in an arbitrarily given period

8.28 · Temporary Equilibrium in Economies with 'Money'

Discussion of the solution to problem 4.I will be facilitated by focusing on budget constraints (8.26)–(8.27). To begin with, it should be noted that the outcome of the problem remains the same if those constraints are modified by replacing the equality signs with inequality signs, since U^h is strictly increasing. We can therefore consider the modified budget constraints

$$p_1 x_1^h + m_1^h \leq p_1 \omega_1^h + \overline{m}^h$$

$$\Psi^h(p_1) x_2^h \leq \Psi^h(p_1) \omega_2^h + m_1^h$$

On adding up the modified constraints and eliminating m_1^h, it becomes clear that the consumption stream chosen by the household must fulfil the inequality

$$p_1 x_1^h + \Psi^h(p_1) x_2^h \leq p_1 \omega_1^h + \Psi^h(p_1) \omega_2^h + \overline{m}^h \tag{8.28}$$

which we shall call the *intertemporal budget constraint* of household h. On the other hand, we know that m_1^h must be non-negative, i.e. that the household cannot borrow money in period 1. This means that the consumption stream chosen by the household must also fulfil the inequality

$$p_1 x_1^h \leq p_1 \omega_1^h + \overline{m}^h \tag{8.29}$$

which we shall call the *liquidity constraint* of household h.[93] It can be stated in the light of these considerations that Problem 4.I can be solved in two steps.

$T > 2$ and that all agents are aware of that future event. Then any non-stupid household operating in the economy at the beginning of period 1 will conclude that no agent will want to be left with money balances at the end of the terminal period T and that, for this reason, money will have no exchange value in that period. If the household assumes that the other households are not stupid, she will conclude that at the beginning of period $T - 1$ all agents in the economy will realize that money is going to be worthless in the terminal period, and therefore will want to end period $T - 1$ with zero money balances, causing the price of money to fall to zero in period $T - 1$ too, and then in all previous periods for the same reason—including the initial period. In order to avoid this problem the temporary equilibrium model with 'money' should be modified by assuming that economic activity extends *indefinitely* over time. Within that context, the fact that human life has limited duration could be taken into account by assuming an OLG structure with two generations of households co-existing in the economy in every period of time, an 'older' generation initially endowed with the whole money stock and purchasing goods produced by a 'younger' generation, who accepts the money in order to use it when old, in the belief that the new younger generation will do the same in the subsequent period (cf., for example, Grandmont and Laroque 1973). The structure of the temporary equilibrium model with 'money' would become more complex, since the maximization problem attributed to the younger generation should be distinguished from that attributed to the older one. However, there is no need to introduce this complex construction for our purposes, as the conditions ensuring the existence of temporary monetary equilibrium would remain essentially the same as those emerging from the simple model examined in this section.

93 Constraints (8.28), (8.29) can be interpreted in economic terms as follows. Assume for the moment that household h is not only able to transfer money balances to period 2 but also to borrow money at no interest in period 1 within the limit set by its expected future wealth. It is easy to ascertain that in these circumstances, the household will only be subject to the *intertemporal budget constraint* (8.28). Since we are assuming that the amount of money the household can actually borrow is zero, however, the *liquidity constraint* (8.29) on current consumption expenditure must also be introduced.

706   **Chapter 8** · Intertemporal Equilibrium, Temporary Equilibrium

In the first, the generic household determines its optimal consumption stream $x_{12}^{h*} = (x_1^{h*}, x_2^{h*})$ by solving the problem.

4.II   *Maximize* $U^h(x_1^h, x_2^h)$ *with Respect to* $x_1^h \geq 0$, $x_2^h \geq 0$,
     subject to constraints (8.28)–(8.29).

In the second, it determines its optimal 'demand for money' m_1^{h*} through the condition $m_1^{h*} = p_1 \omega_1^h + \overline{m}^h - p_1 x_1^{h*}$.

Let us focus on problem 4.II and define the *opportunity set* of household h as the set of two-period consumption streams in $X_{12}^h = \Re_+^{2N}$ that fulfil both the constraints (8.28)–(8.29). It is easily proved that this set is compact and convex under the assumption that both the current and the expected prices are strictly positive.[94] Given that U^h is strictly quasi-concave, it follows from the properties of the opportunity set that problem 4.II *uniquely determines* the consumption stream $x_{12}^{h*} = (x_1^{h*}, x_2^{h*})$ chosen by household h at any given $p_1 \in \Re_{++}^N$. In these circumstances, the amount of money demanded by the household is itself uniquely determined in the second step of the procedure. We therefore conclude that both the household's current consumption demand x_1^{h*} and its money demand m_1^{h*} can be represented as functions of (strictly positive) vectors of current prices, which we shall denote by $x_1^h(p_1)$ and $m_1^h(p_1)$ respectively. In this notation, the *optimal action* $a^{h*} = (x_1^{h*}, m_1^{h*})$ taken by household h at any given $p_1 \in \Re_{++}^N$ is univocally identified by the function $a^h(p_1) = (x_1^h(p_1), m_1^h(p_1))$.

Let us now consider the first-period *excess demand function* of the generic household h, defined as $z_1^h(p_1) = x_1^h(p_1) - \omega_1^h$, and the household's money demand function $m_1^h(p_1)$. It can be proved that they are both *continuous* functions (Grandmont 1983: App. B, p. 165). It should also be noted that since the household's optimal choice must fulfil budget constraint (8.26), the equality $p_1 z_1^h(p_1) + m_1^h(p_1) = \overline{m}^h$ necessarily holds at every strictly positive vector of current prices. It follows from this last consideration that first-period *aggregate* excess demands inclusive of the excess demand for end of period-1 money balances satisfy what can be called *Walras's Law with money*:

$$p_1 \Sigma_h z_1^h(p_1) + \Sigma_h m_1^h(p_1) = \Sigma_h \overline{m}^h = M \quad \text{for every } p_1 \in \Re_{++}^N \tag{8.30}$$

Given the above formal description of the behaviour of households, a *temporary monetary equilibrium* of the exchange economy for period 1 can be finally defined as a system of monetary prices $p_1^* \in \Re_{++}^N$, and a corresponding set of optimal actions on the part of households, such that the following market clearing conditions are simultaneously satisfied:

$$\Sigma_h z_1^h(p_1^*) = 0, \quad \Sigma_h m_1^h(p_1^*) = \Sigma_h \overline{m}^h = M \tag{8.31}$$

---

94 Key: under the assumption mentioned in the text, the opportunity set is the intersection of two convex and compact sets.

8.28 · Temporary Equilibrium in Economies with 'Money'

The second equality states that, in the aggregate, consumers must wish to end the first period with the same total amount of money they started with: if some consumer plans to spend in the first period more than his first-period income by using some of his initial money holding, some other consumer must wish to end the period with more money than he started with by spending less than his first-period income.

8.28.2 Existence of Monetary Equilibrium

Let us now address the question of the *existence* of temporary monetary equilibrium. Existence is *not* guaranteed under Assumption 8.7. To clarify this point, let us focus on the simplified case of an exchange economy with a single consumption good ($N=1$). In this case, the opportunity set of the generic household h at an arbitrary strictly positive price $\bar{p}_1$ for the consumption good can be represented as in ◘ Fig. 8.7.

By examining constraints (8.28)–(8.29) taken for $N=1$, it is easy to ascertain that the line going through points α and β, whose slope is $\bar{p}_1/\Psi^h(\bar{p}_1)$, represents the *intertemporal budget constraint*, while the vertical half-line going through β represents the *liquidity constraint*. The curve is the highest indifference curve with a point in common with the budget set; the optimal choice of household h therefore corresponds to point x_{12}^{h*}, which identifies both the household's current excess demand for the consumption good and the household's demand for money balances. We shall now use this graphic device to analyse how the optimal choice of the generic household changes as the current price of the consumption good changes from $\bar{p}_1$. We shall only deal with a rise in the price, as the analysis that follows is easily adapted to the case of a fall.

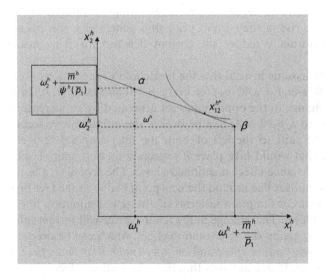

◘ Fig. 8.7 Optimal choice of household h in temporary monetary equilibrium

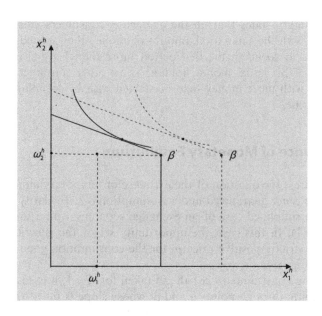

Fig. 8.8 How the choice of a consumer with unit-elastic price expectations shifts if current price rises

Let us first assume that the household has *unit elastic price expectations*, i.e. that $\Psi^h(\lambda p_1) = \lambda \Psi^h(p_1)$ for every positive value of p_1 and every positive number λ. In this case, an increase in the current price of the consumption good from $\bar{p}_1$ to $\lambda \bar{p}_1$, $\lambda > 1$, causes both the intertemporal budget line and the liquidity line to move to the left, without however altering the slope of the former. What basically happens is that the price rise proportionately reduces the purchasing power of the household's money endowment while leaving the 'relative price' of present consumption in terms of future consumption unchanged at the initial level $\bar{p}_1/\Psi^h(\bar{p}_1)$. The rise in the current price thus generates a *real balance effect* that will in turn normally reduce the current demand for the consumption good (Fig. 8.8).

Let us now assume instead that the household's expectations are not unit elastic, i.e. that $\Psi^h(\lambda p_1) \neq \lambda \Psi^h(p_1)$ for every $p_1 > 0$ and every $> \lambda 0$. In these circumstances, the change in the opportunity set generated by an increase in the current price from $\bar{p}_1$ to $\lambda \bar{p}_1$, $\lambda > 1$, can be broken down into two 'successive' changes. The first is the shift to the left of both the intertemporal budget line and the liquidity line that would take place *if* expectations were unit elastic. This is precisely the real balance effect mentioned above. The second is the *rotation* of the intertemporal budget line around the new point β' due to the fact that the 'relative price' of present consumption in terms of future consumption must now change from its initial level. This change in the relative price will further affect the household's choice by giving rise to a rotation effect, which can be decomposed into an *intertemporal substitution effect* and *an intertemporal income effect* whose sum is of uncertain sign. If one assumes that the substitution effect is stronger than the income effect (assuming both goods normal), when the elasticity of expectations

8.28 · Temporary Equilibrium in Economies with 'Money'

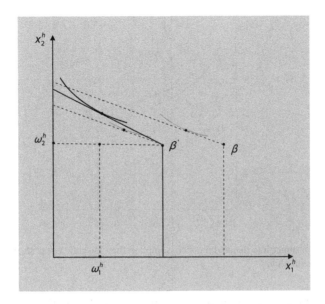

Fig. 8.9 The case with elasticity of price expectations greater than 1

is lower than 1 ($\Psi^h(\lambda\bar{p}_1) < \lambda\Psi^h(\bar{p}_1)$), and therefore the intertemporal budget line rotates *upward*, the intertemporal substitution effect reduces present consumption, thereby reinforcing the real balance effect (Fig. 8.9); when the elasticity of expectations is higher than 1, the budget line rotates downwards and the intertemporal substitution effect acts in the opposite direction to the real balance effect and the overall effect of the price rise on the household's choice cannot be assessed a priori.

In the light of the above analysis, we can now discuss the existence of temporary monetary equilibrium for the one-commodity exchange economy. We shall show first of all that existence is *not* guaranteed when expectations 'depend too much' on the currently observed price. This will be done by means of two examples taken from Grandmont (1983, pp. 22–24), in which it is implicitly assumed that $\bar{m}^h > 0$ holds for all h.

Example 1 A preliminary remark is necessary. Recall that the preferences of households can be represented by strictly increasing and strictly quasi-concave utility functions. It should thus be clear from Fig. 8.10 that at any given $\bar{p}_1 > 0$, the current consumption demand of the generic household h will exceed the endowment ω_1^h if and only if the 'relative price' $\bar{p}_1/\Psi^h(\bar{p}_1)$ is lower than the household's marginal rate of substitution[95] evaluated at point $\alpha = \left(\omega_1^h, \omega_2^h + \bar{m}^h/\Psi^h(\bar{p}_1)\right)$.

---

95 In this section for simplicity we intend by 'marginal rate of substitution' its absolute value.

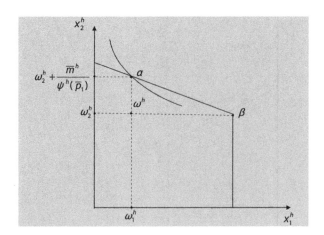

◻ **Fig. 8.10** For consumer h to demand more consumption than the endowment the tangency must be to the right of point alpha

Having established this preliminary result, let us assume that the households' utility functions can be written

$$w\left(x_1^h\right) + \delta^h w\left(x_2^h\right), h = 1, \ldots, H,$$

where $w(.)$ is strictly concave and differentiable and $0 < \delta^h < 1$ for all h. Let us further assume that the expectation function of household h is such that the following condition holds:

$$\frac{p_1}{\Psi^h(p_1)} \leq \frac{w'(\omega_1^h)}{\delta^h w'(\omega_2^h)} \text{ for every } p_1 > 0 \quad (8.32)$$

where the term on the right-hand side of the inequality is the household's marginal rate of substitution evaluated at the endowment point $\omega^h = (\omega_1^h, \omega_2^h)$. Given that the marginal rate of substitution increases as we move upward along the vertical half-line with origin $(\omega_1^h, 0)$ because $w(.)$ is strictly concave, it becomes clear that at any positive value of the current price, the household will be precisely in the position depicted in ◻ Fig. 8.10, and will therefore manifest an excess demand for the consumption good in period 1. If we finally assume that expectation functions are such that condition (8.32) holds *for all h*, it is clear that at every $p_1 > 0$ there will be an aggregate excess demand on the current commodity market, which will be accompanied in accordance with *Walras's Law with money* by a corresponding aggregate excess supply of money. This means that no temporary equilibrium exists for period 1, in which households are willing to hold the whole stock of money in circulation: assuming that the excess demand for the period-1 good causes an indefinite tendency of its money price to increase, it does not matter how high the price level becomes, in the aggregate consumers always wish to end the period with a smaller holding of money than they started with. In particular, the phenomenon described will occur when expectation functions are

8.28 · Temporary Equilibrium in Economies with 'Money'

unit elastic and such that, for all h, the (constant) 'relative price' $p_1/\Psi^h(p_1)$ fulfils condition (8.32).

Example 2 Let us assume that preferences are such that, for all h, the value of the marginal rate of substitution along the vertical half-line with origin $(\omega_1^h, 0)$ is bounded above by a strictly positive number v^h. Let us further assume that expectations are such that the following condition holds for all h:

$$\frac{p_1}{\Psi^h(p_1)} > v^h \quad \text{for every } p_1 > 0 \tag{8.33}$$

Under these assumptions, each household will be in a situation opposite to the one shown in ◘ Fig. 8.10 at any given $\bar{p}_1 > 0$. As a result, $z_1^h(p_1) < 0$, $m_1^h(p_1) > \bar{m}^h$ will hold for all h at every $p_1 > 0$ and temporary monetary equilibrium will not exist: however low the money price of the period-1 good, consumers still wish to end the period with more money than they started with. In particular, this phenomenon will occur when expectations are *unit elastic* and such that for all h, the (constant) 'relative price' $p_1/\Psi^h(p_1)$ fulfils condition (8.33).

Similar examples can be constructed for economies with a variety of consumption goods (cf. Grandmont 1983: 25). The simple examples put forward are, however, sufficient to develop the relevant economic considerations. To begin with, let us consider Example 1 on the hypothesis of unit elastic expectations. As we have seen, at an arbitrarily chosen $\bar{p}_1 > 0$ there is aggregate excess demand on the period 1 commodity market. We also know that an increase in the current price from $\bar{p}_1$ would generate a real balance effect that is likely to reduce that excess but cannot eliminate it completely. Similarly, on the hypothesis of unit elastic expectations, Example 2 shows that the real balance effect resulting from a fall in the current price may be not strong enough to compensate fully for an initial excess supply on the current commodity market. A negative conclusion therefore emerges from the temporary equilibrium model with 'money' as regards the effectiveness of the real balance effect as a mechanism capable of regulating the market. This negative conclusion attracted a great deal of attention when the original version of the model was published (Grandmont 1974), as its was commonly held among neoclassical economists at the time that the real balance effect would normally ensure market clearing in economies endowed with outside money (cf., for example, Patinkin 1965).

It should further be noted that conditions (8.32) and (8.33) in the examples presented are constraints on the variability of the 'relative price' $p_1/\Psi^h(p_1)$ and therefore impose limits on the strength of the intertemporal substitution effects that can be generated by changes in p_1. It can accordingly be conjectured that the introduction of restrictions on expectations capable of ensuring high variability of this 'relative price' could allow the intertemporal substitution effects engendered by changes in p_1 to become strong enough to reinforce the real balance effect and eliminate disequilibrium on current markets. The following argument indicates this is a reasonable conjecture.

712   Chapter 8 · Intertemporal Equilibrium, Temporary Equilibrium

Assume that in the single-commodity exchange economy with 'money' there is a household $\bar{h}$ whose expectations are 'insensitive' to large changes in p_1, in the sense that two numbers $\varepsilon > 0$, $\eta > 0$ exist such that $\varepsilon \leq \Psi^{\bar{h}}(p_1) \leq \eta$ for every $p_1 > 0$ (*bounded* expectations). Under this assumption, it can be stated (a) that for p_1 large enough an aggregate excess supply appears on the period 1 commodity market and (b) that for p_1 low enough an aggregate excess demand appears on that market. By continuity, a price $p_1^* > 0$ should then exist that leads to equilibrium on the current commodity market and, in view of *Walras's Law with money*, on the money market as well.

In the above argument, statement (a) can be justified on the grounds that when p_1 rises indefinitely, point β of the 'insensitive' household's opportunity set tends to the endowment point $\omega^{\bar{h}}$ and the slope of the intertemporal budget line rises with no limit. As a result, the household's planned demand for future consumption tends to infinity together with the household's current demand for money. Since by assumption the money demand of every household is bounded below by zero, this means that as p_1 progressively increases, an aggregate excess demand for money must eventually appear in period 1 with a corresponding aggregate excess supply on the current commodity market. As regards statement (b), note that when p_1 falls progressively towards zero, point β in the insensitive household's opportunity set shifts indefinitely to the right, while the slope of the intertemporal budget line tends to zero, thus giving rise to a strong substitution effect in favour of current consumption. As a result, the insensitive household's demand for present consumption tends to infinity. Since the current consumption demand of the generic household h is bounded below by $-\omega_1^h$, this means that with the progressive fall in p_1, an aggregate excess demand must eventually appear on the current commodity market.

The above heuristic argument indicating that the assumption of *bounded expectations* ensuring the existence of temporary monetary equilibrium can be rigorously formulated and generalized to exchange economies with any finite number of goods. The following theorem has indeed been proved for $N \geq 1$:

■■ Theorem

Let Assumption 8.7 hold in the exchange economy with 'money'. Assume further that there is at least one household $\bar{h}$, with $\overline{m}^{\bar{h}} > 0$, whose expectations are bounded in the sense that two vectors $\varepsilon \in \Re_{++}^N$, $\eta \in \Re_{++}^N$ exist such that $\varepsilon \leq \Psi^{\bar{h}}(p_1) \leq \eta$ for every $p_1 \in \Re_{++}^N$. Then a temporary monetary equilibrium exists.

Proof   cf. Grandmont (1983: Appendix B).

The assumption of *bounded expectations* has been generalized to the case of monetary economies in which agents' predictions take the form of probability distributions over future prices (cf., for example, Grandmont 1974). But is this really a *plausible* assumption? As noted, it postulates that price expectations are 'rigid' with respect to large variations in current prices and in particular that the price expected for any commodity remains practically unchanged when the current price keeps rising (falling) beyond a sufficiently high (low) level. It is quite doubt-

8.28 · Temporary Equilibrium in Economies with 'Money'

ful, however, that expectations would normally display this property. As an expert in the field has pointed out, 'price forecasts are indeed somewhat volatile, and are presumably quite sensitive to the level of current prices' (Grandmont 1983: 26). On the other hand, the examples presented in this section show that temporary monetary equilibrium may not exist under such circumstances. The conclusion that has been drawn is that 'the existence of a temporary equilibrium in which money has positive value is somewhat problematic' (Grandmont 1983: 27).

8.28.3 Some Doubts on Grandmont's Characterization of the Function of Money

Grandmont's conclusion is not fully convincing because money has other functions besides the only one considered by Grandmont (the transfer of purchasing power from one period to the next). In particular the transactions motive for holding money, the main motive traditionally advanced for the existence of money, that is, the need for a universally accepted medium of exchange to surmount the difficulties of indirect barter, plays no role in Grandmont's analysis. The present textbook does not intend to discuss money in any detail, but the quotation from Wicksell in Chap. 3, ▶ Sect. 3.6, permits some simple considerations. Let us take the first example studied in ▶ Sect. 8.28.2. This example applies specific hypotheses on utility to the idea of the model that the demand for end period money balances is determined exclusively by the desire to redistribute consumption across periods; what the example shows is that the wealth effect associated with changes in the purchasing power of the initial money holdings may have so little an influence on the desired redistribution of consumption, as not to correct an initial excess supply of (end of period-1) money holdings and excess demand for commodities. But suppose money holdings are also desired because money has a medium-of-exchange function (because goods exchange only against money—no barter—hence many transactions of goods against money must be carried out by each agent in each period, and the less money one has, the more difficult it is to perform the desired transactions); then the higher the price level expected for period 2 (i.e. the higher the price level observed in period 1), the more people will want to end the first period with a greater amount of money than they started with, in order to have fewer transaction difficulties in period 2, and this will tend to reduce demand for commodities in period 1; also, the higher the price level in period 1, the more the agents have transaction difficulties already in that period, which again contributes to a decrease in demand for commodities in period 1. We obtain a tendency in period 1 of demand for commodities to decrease and of demand for end period money balances to increase as the price level rises, independently of any desire to transfer consumption across periods; the excess demand for commodities and excess supply of money tend to disappear as the price level rises. Thus, the possible non-existence of monetary equilibrium in this model is caused by the neglect of this very plausible effect of changes in the price level.

714   Chapter 8 · Intertemporal Equilibrium, Temporary Equilibrium

Therefore one can conjecture that admitting a medium-of-exchange function of money would reduce the problems with existence of a temporary equilibrium with money. But as pointed out in ▶ Sect. 8.14, cash-in-advance constraints are incompatible with the neo-Walrasian framework, they create indeterminacy in agents' choices, and are also difficult to justify if equilibrium is reached without implementation of disequilibrium decisions by the auctioneer-guided tâtonnement. It would seem, therefore, that admitting a medium-of-exchange function of money would reduce the problems highlighted in this section, but would introduce other problems.

8.29 Conclusions on the Marginal/Neoclassical Approach, with Special Emphasis on the Labour Demand Curve and on the Investment Function

The studies in the field of temporary equilibrium theory carried out in the 1970s and early 1980s endeavoured to overcome the limitations of the Arrow–Debreu model by remaining inside the neo-Walrasian approach but focusing analysis on economies in which futures markets are limited in number or non-existent, trade takes place sequentially over time, and there isn't perfect foresight. As we have seen, the models put forward in that period examine the behaviour of economic agents in an arbitrarily chosen 'initial period', stress the dependence of agents' decisions on their subjective expectations about prices in subsequent periods, and analyse the conditions ensuring the existence of general equilibrium on the initial period's markets. According to the scholars who explored the field, the analysis concerning this isolated period was to be the first step of a more extensive research programme, whose ultimate goal was to model the evolution of the economy as a *sequence* of temporary equilibria without perfect foresight (Grandmont 1977: 542–543, 1989: 299).

However, the simplified exposition presented in the preceding three sections indicates that the very first steps of the programme pursued by temporary equilibrium theorists gave rise to serious problems. In particular, our presentation has shown that a major source of difficulties for the treatment of temporary equilibrium in a single market period is precisely the central role the approach must attribute to the subjective price expectations of economic agents. This point has been first illustrated with reference to economies with a numéraire commodity: ▶ Sect. 8.26 focused on the case of pure-exchange economies and showed that substantial difficulties arise in the determination of households' behaviour if individual expectations are not sufficiently uniform; ▶ Sect. 8.27 addressed the case of economies with production and argued that the divergence of individual expectations creates additional difficulties in the treatment both of the formation of production decisions within firms, and of the financing of production plans (and more generally of demands for loans).

▶ Section 8.28 went on to consider monetary economies and showed that a temporary equilibrium may not exist in those economies if expectations about

8.29 · Conclusions on the Marginal/Neoclassical Approach, with ...

the future level of money prices are rather sensitive to the level of current prices. However, differently from the cases studied in Sects. 8.26 and 8.27, it is unclear whether the non-existence of a monetary temporary equilibrium is due to the role of expectations, or to the restriction of the functions of money to the sole function of transferring purchasing power from one period to the next, to the neglect of the transactions motive for holding money, traditionally the main reason for the existence of money. But consideration of the transactions motive would introduce the indeterminateness caused by cash-in-advance constraints noted in ▶ Sect. 8.14.

The analytical difficulties highlighted in Sects. 8.26–8.28 are the ones that emerged more explicitly in the formal studies of temporary equilibrium, and they largely explain why research in the field of temporary equilibrium theory was abandoned. Thus they afford some insight into why general equilibrium theorists have since chosen to study economies with sequential trade only under the assumption of *correct* (or *self-fulfilling*) price expectations, along the lines indicated by Radner (1972). This assumption of 'perfect foresight' is normally taken for granted in advanced textbooks nowadays (cf., for example, Mas-Colell et al. 1995: 696). Basic knowledge of temporary equilibrium models makes us aware of the fact that modern general equilibrium theory can hardly dispense with that assumption.[96]

We can strengthen this conclusion by noting that there are further difficulties of formalization of temporary equilibria, less studied and less stressed but not less relevant, and two deserve a brief mention.

One is the problem of **bankruptcies**. This problem is occasionally admitted. Agents arrive at the 'current' period from a past in which they may have contracted debts, or conceded loans, to be honoured in the 'current' period. At each 'round' of the tâtonnement each indebted agent must calculate (also on the basis of her/his expectations about future prices) whether she/he will be able to honour the debt on the basis of the prices the auctioneer is calling, and may be obliged to declare bankruptcy; suppose for example wages gradually decrease during the tâtonnement, a 'threshold price vector' can be reached at which an indebted consumer declares bankruptcy; at this price vector the creditors suddenly become owners of assets belonging to the bankrupted consumer in place of the credit titles they held, and they will generally attribute to these assets a different value from the value they attributed to the credit titles; this causes a discontinuous jump in their wealth, hence, a discontinuity in their excess demands. And we know that discontinuities of excess demand functions create problems to the existence of equilibrium.

The other problem is that, even apart from the problems indicated in ▶ Sect. 8.27, serious problems arising in determining *firms' production decisions* if the product will come out and be sold in *subsequent* periods. A temporary equilibrium

---

96 And yet, the attempt to develop the temporary equilibrium programme was largely motivated by dissatisfaction precisely with the correct price expectations assumption, as shown by Grandmont (1982), quoted above, Footnote 26.

716 Chapter 8 · Intertemporal Equilibrium, Temporary Equilibrium

must refer to a rather short time period; therefore many production processes started in the equilibrium's period will produce products to be sold in subsequent periods, at prices that can only be guessed. Below, reference is to these products. Suppose firms in an industry have constant returns to scale, or there is free entry. The output of this industry is theoretically infinite if firms are price takers and expect a price higher than average cost; clearly such a result is unacceptable, but then how will firms decide how much to produce? and how is entry going to be determined? Since there is no unambiguous feedback of current industry supply decisions on future price, everything depends on (existing and potential) firms' expectations about future demand and future price, and there seems to be no way to restrict the arbitrariness of possible results depending on what is assumed about these (unknowable) expectations, unless one shifts to a totally different framework, e.g. a Keynesian one with production determined by demand and a sufficiently persistent situation in which expectations (at least short-period expectations about demand for one's product) have had time to become correct.[97]

Possibly, the resulting indeterminacy has been underestimated owing to the universal tendency, in this literature, to assume a *given* number of price-taking firms all with *decreasing returns to scale* (and hence with definite supply functions); then it suffices to assume that each firm expects a definite product price, and its supply decision is determined. But the exclusion of entry contradicts all sensible microeconomics of competitive economies and all available evidence, and new entrants would be irrational not to choose a size at which local returns to scale are not decreasing.

And then there are the impermanence problem, the price-change problem, the substitutability problem, the savings–investment problem. The first three were admitted by Hicks and considered by him so serious as to induce him to recant his earlier advocacy of the temporary equilibrium method (Petri 1991). It is worthwhile to discuss how these problems appear in the temporary equilibrium framework, because there are some differences from intertemporal equilibria.

Impermanence problem: there is one further group of data lacking persistence, price expectations, more precisely the *form* of the expectation functions that determine expected prices as functions of current prices. One possibility is to assume given expected prices, but clearly in general expected prices will depend to some degree on current prices, changing with the latter during the tâtonnement (which now operates only on current prices). The form of the functions deter-

---

97 Keynes to Kalecki, letter 12 April 1937: 'I hope you are not right in thinking that my General Theory depends on an assumption that the immediate reaction of a capitalist is of a particular kind. I tried to deal with this on page 271 *[? probably 261, F.P.]*, where I assume that the immediate reaction of capitalists is the most unfavourable to my conclusion. I regard behaviour as arrived at by trial and error, and no theory can be regarded as sound which depends on the initial reaction being of a particular kind. One must assume that the initial reaction may be anything in the world, but that the process of trial and error will eventually arrive at the conclusion which one is predicting' *(Keynes Collected Works, XII, p. 797)*. It is highly doubtful that in the very short time to which a temporary equilibrium refers this process of error correction can approach completion.

8.29 · Conclusions on the Marginal/Neoclassical Approach, with ...

mining expected prices from current prices will obviously be continuously revised on the basis of observation. It can be modified during the tâtonnement itself, if agents discover that their past expectations about current equilibrium prices were mistaken and try to learn from this new information (Petri 2004, Appendix 5.A.3). So in temporary equilibrium theory not even the auctioneer-guided tâtonnement is able to prevent a change in some of the data of equilibrium during disequilibrium adjustments.

Price-change problem: the way it is dealt with, given price expectation functions, introduces a problem of *indefiniteness* of the temporary equilibrium. The equilibrium depends on what one assumes about expectations, but—even if one leaves aside their impermanence—the problem remains that expectations are subjective, hence generally unobservable, so suppositions must be made about them; the theory can seldom do more than list a series of 'if ... then': for example, if expectations are optimistic, then investment ..., if on the contrary expectations are pessimistic, then investment....The same need for suppositions arises for specifying how expectations will change from one period to the next: in the temporary equilibrium framework any explanation or prediction of the path of the economy over several months or years, for example, any attempt to predict the result of a government policy, must be based on determining a *sequence* of temporary equilibria, which—even assuming uniqueness of each temporary equilibrium—will require assumptions as to how expectations will *evolve* from one 'week' to the next; absent a theory that makes expectations endogenous and therefore no longer part of the data (as in traditional analyses aimed at determining persistent positions in which on average expectations have had the time to be corrected, see Garegnani 1976), these assumptions would have to be largely arbitrary, confirming the indefiniteness.

On the substitutability problem there is nothing to add, Hicks's admissions on this issue mentioned in ▶ Sect. 7.3 and in ▶ Sect. 8.15 were formulated with reference to temporary equilibria.

Savings–investment problem: here the main difference from intertemporal equilibria is that there is no assumption turning investment decisions into decisions of production to order; investment decisions are motivated by expectations, so a theory of investment is indispensable, but the issue is not explicitly discussed in the temporary general equilibrium, the adjustment of investment to full-employment savings is taken for granted. Implicitly, ultimately the argument is the traditional one, in one way or the other an expression of the idea that the rate of interest is the price that brings supply and demand for savings to equality because the demand for 'capital' is a decreasing function of the interest rate. Nor are there other acceptable ways to derive a negatively interest elastic investment function, although this cannot be proved here (something will be said on the issue in ▶ Chap. 12 but the interested reader should consult Petri 2004, Chaps. 4 and 7, 2015; Dvoskin and Petri 2017). So here too behind the claim that the approach does without the notion of 'capital' one finds an implicit continuing faith in traditional substitution between 'capital' and labour.

It seems possible to conclude that the shift to neo-Walrasian versions, motivated by the desire to maintain a supply-and-demand explanation of income

718   **Chapter 8** · Intertemporal Equilibrium, Temporary Equilibrium

distribution in the face of the need to abandon the conception of capital as some-how a single factor, a 'fund', in fact did not abandon that conception, because without it there is no way to justify the claim that investment adjusts to full-em-ployment savings, and there is no way to argue that the path traced by intertem-poral equilibria or by sequences of temporary equilibria correctly describes the qualitative aspects of actual paths of market economies.

This conclusion will help the reader not to be confused by the oscillations of current mainstream economic theory between intertemporal disaggregated gen-eral equilibria and one-good growth models. Behind the apparent differences, the basic picture of the working of market economies is the same, and it is the tradi-tional marginalist one based on 'capital'–labour substitution.

8.30 **Review Questions and Exercises**

- **Review questions**
  1. '… the possibility to reinterpret the equations of an intertemporal equilibrium over a finite number of periods as equations of a non-capitalistic model, and vice-versa, *must not hide a fundamental difference*'. Illustrate this difference.
  2. Why is a neo-Walrasian intertemporal equilibrium a very-short-period equi-librium according to Marshall's classification?
  3. '… consumer theory makes more sense when interpreted as determining *aver-age* consumption decisions than moment-by-moment decisions'. How can this be argued?
  4. 'The theory seems to imply that either the economy was always continuously in intertemporal equilibrium, or we have no right to assume equilibrium can be established at date 0'. Explain.
  5. Date-10 bread can be bought in advance at date zero for a price equal to 20 units of the date zero numéraire. The production of a unit of date-10 bread requires the use only of a vector of circulating capital goods applied at date 9. What is the value at date zero of that vector of date-9 circulating capital goods?
  6. Produce a numerical example different from those in the text to illustrate the dependence of the real rate of interest on the choice of numéraire when rel-ative prices change from one period to the next. Show that the real rate of interest coincides with the own rate of return of the numéraire.
  7. Explain how circulating capital goods produced and utilized inside an inter-temporal equilibrium can be made not to appear in the equilibrium condi-tions.
  8. Explain the difference between UERR and UERRSP.
  9. Why in the equilibria illustrated in Chaps. 3–7 did money (in the sense of a commodity or token universally accepted as means of payment and desired for that use, not for an intrinsic utility of the physical substance of which it is made) not appear at all?
  10. Why is it impossible to assume complete futures markets?

8.30 · Review Questions and Exercises

11. 'Intertemporal equilibrium cannot even be *defined* unless one assumes the world to be a fairy tale world radically different from the real world'. What is the argument behind this statement?
12. (Substitutability problem) Explain why given initial endowments of the several capital goods impede the functioning also of the indirect factor substitution mechanism.
13. What is the aspect of the determination of consumer decisions in the tâtonnement, which is rejected as unacceptable in the argument of ▶ Sect. 8.16 (The savings–investment problem)?
14. Explain why the impossibility of demonstrations requiring an infinite number of mathematical operations is relevant for the significance of infinite-horizon intertemporal equilibria.
15. Prove that the First Welfare Theorem does not hold for OLG equilibria.
16. Prove that if the change in endowments brought about by barter cannot be undone, then repeated barter need not reach the core.
17. Explain ▣ Figs. 8.4 and 8.5. Explain in what sense the continuum of equilibria in ▣ Fig. 8.5 is 'robust'.
18. Explain why the possibility of speculative behaviour causes a temporary equilibrium generally not to exist.
19. Prove by heart that in the Solow growth model maximization of steady-growth consumption per unit of labour implies $f'(k)=n$, the so-called *golden rule of accumulation*.

■ **Exercises**

1. Prove that the CRRA utility function of §8.4 has constant elasticity of substitution between consumption at any two consecutive dates, equal to $1/\sigma$.
2. Write the budget constraints, one per period, faced by a consumer in each spot market of a finite-horizon Radner equilibrium without uncertainty and with real Arrow securities in good 1. Then add them up to obtain the final budget constraint: the condition that the algebraic sum of the discounted values of the Arrow securities bought and sold by the consumer must be zero. Derive from these constraints whether the Radner equilibrium determines or not the relative price levels of different dates.
3. Labour and land produce corn according to a differentiable production function. Assuming the standard factor tâtonnement (inclusive of its assumption about consumer incomes criticized in ▶ Sect. 8.16), show that an excess supply of labour necessarily implies an excess demand for land.
4. Consider an OLG economy where each representative consumer lives two periods and there is a single consumption good. Assume a standard intertemporal utility function, a separable constant elasticity of substitution function with CRRA subutilities and with intertemporal rate of time preference ρ:

$$U = \frac{c_1^{1-\theta}}{1-\theta} + \frac{1}{1+\rho} \cdot \frac{c_2^{1-\theta}}{1-\theta}.$$

720   **Chapter 8 · Intertemporal Equilibrium, Temporary Equilibrium**

Prove that the demand function for first-period consumption is

$$c_1(r) = w(r) \cdot \left[(1 + \rho)^{1/\theta}\right] / \left[(1 + \rho)^{1/\theta} + (1 + r)^{(1-\theta)/\theta}\right]$$

5. (Hyperbolic discounting) Empirical research suggests that a more appropriate
   theory than exponential discounting of how consumers evaluate future consumption is *hyperbolic discounting*: the discount factor from t to date zero is
   not $\delta^t < 1$ but $1/(1 + kt)$ with $k > 0$, which decreases slower than δ^t. Prove that
   this implies *time inconsistency*, that is, when a consumer is at date 0, the marginal rate of substitution between consumption at date 2 and consumption at
   date 3 is different from the one when the consumer reaches date 1. Prove that
   this can occasion regrets.

6. (Jehle and Reny) (Complete markets, spot markets, Radner equilibrium) This
   guided exercise confirms that in the intertemporal economy if there are complete futures markets at the initial date, there is no role left for spot markets.
   Once equilibrium prices and contracts based on initial date complete markets are reached, even if spot markets open up at some subsequent date, with
   prices for the goods of that date equal to the equilibrium prices, no additional
   trade will take place. Furthermore the endowments consumers have at date 1
   after the deliveries contracted at date 0 for date 1 are carried out allow one to
   conclude that if equilibrium is unique and price forecasts are correct, then the
   Radner equilibrium establishes the same relative prices at each date as would
   be determined by complete futures markets initial contracting.
   Consider an exchange economy with S consumers, N basic goods, and $T=2$
   dates: 0 and 1. There is no uncertainty. The goods are perishable and cannot
   be stored (a possibility of storage would mean that this is not an exchange
   economy, one kind of production is possible that transforms a good of date
   0 into a good of date 1). Let us focus on one consumer whose utility func-
   tion is $u(\mathbf{x}_0, \mathbf{x}_1)$, where $\mathbf{x}_t \in R^N_+$ is a vector of period-t consumption of the
   N goods. The intertemporal complete markets open an instant before date 0
   and reach the intertemporal-equilibrium prices (these I will call[98] Intertemporal Complete Markets Equilibrium prices, ICME prices for brevity), and the
   corresponding contracts are signed, so when date 0 arrives our consumer has
   already bought and sold promises of delivery of period-0 and period-1 goods.
   The spot markets that open at date $t=0$, 1 only allow exchanges among goods
   of that period (no borrowing and lending of date-0 goods against deliveries of
   date-1 goods).
   Suppose that $\hat{\mathbf{p}}=(\hat{\mathbf{p}}_0, \hat{\mathbf{p}}_1)$ is an ICME price vector ('an', in case equilibrium is
   not unique), indeterminate of course as to scale, but fixed by assigning price
   1 to a date-0 good whose date-1 corresponding good also has positive price.
   $\hat{\mathbf{p}}_t \gg \mathbf{0}$ is the price N-vector for period-t goods. Let $\hat{\mathbf{x}}=(\hat{\mathbf{x}}_0, \hat{\mathbf{x}}_1)$ be the vector of
   utility-maximizing consumptions resulting from the exchanges our consumer

---

98 Since I have argued that Walras was different, I cannot accept common usage and call these prices
    Walrasian.

8.30 · Review Questions and Exercises

has chosen when an instant before date 0 intertemporal complete markets have opened and the ICME price vector $\mathbf{p} = (\mathbf{p}_0, \mathbf{p}_1)$ has been called in them. Suppose now that at each date t, spot markets open for trade.

(i) Because all contracts are enforced, argue that our consumer's available endowment when date t spot markets open is $\mathbf{x}_t^{\hat{}}$

(ii)   Show that if our consumer wishes to trade in some period t spot market and if all goods have period t spot markets and the period t spot prices are $\mathbf{p}_t^{\hat{}}$, then our consumer's period t budget constraint is $\mathbf{p}_t^{\hat{}} \cdot \mathbf{x}_t \leq \mathbf{p}_t^{\hat{}} \cdot \mathbf{x}_t^{\hat{}}$

(iii)   Conclude that our consumer can ultimately choose any $(\mathbf{x}_1, \mathbf{x}_2)$ such that

$$\hat{\mathbf{p}}_0 \cdot \mathbf{x}_0 \leq \hat{\mathbf{p}}_0 \cdot \hat{\mathbf{x}}_0 \text{ and } \hat{\mathbf{p}}_1 \cdot \mathbf{x}_1 \leq \hat{\mathbf{p}}_1 \cdot \hat{\mathbf{x}}_1.$$

(iv)   Prove that at those prices the consumer can do no better than to choose $\mathbf{x}_0 = \mathbf{x}_0^{\hat{}}$ in period $t = 0$ and $\mathbf{x}_1 = \mathbf{x}_1^{\hat{}}$ in period $t = 1$, by showing that any bundle that is feasible through trading in spot markets was feasible in the complete markets initial reaching of ICME prices. You should assume that in period 0 the consumer has correct foresight of the spot prices she will face in the date-1 spot market, and that she wishes to behave so as to maximize her lifetime utility $u(\mathbf{x}_0, \mathbf{x}_1)$. Further, assume that if she consumes $\bar{\mathbf{x}}_0$ in period $t = 0$, her utility of consuming any bundle $\mathbf{x}_1$ in period $t = 1$ is $u(\mathbf{x}_1, \mathbf{x}_2)$. Conclude that in the spot markets there will be no exchange at those prices.

(v)   Now assume that the ICME is unique, but there aren't complete futures markets; at date 0 spot markets open for the goods of that period and for Arrow real securities promising one unit of gold at date 1 (gold has positive price at date 1); at date 1 spot markets open after enforcement of the contracts on Arrow securities, to establish trade in date-1 goods. At each date equilibrium on the spot markets is established by the auctioneer. Assume the consumer has correct foresight of the relative spot prices she will face in the date-1 spot market. Argue that the balanced budget constraints for date 0 and for date 1, inclusive of the trade in Arrow securities, allow our consumer to reach $\mathbf{x} = (\mathbf{x}_0^{\hat{}}, \mathbf{x}_1^{\hat{}})$ if prices are $\mathbf{p} = (\mathbf{p}_0, \mathbf{p}_1)$ (see Exercise 2); conclude that at those prices the consumer can do no better than use Arrow securities to obtain $\mathbf{x} = (\mathbf{x}_0^{\hat{}}, \mathbf{x}_1^{\hat{}})$. Derive that date-0 equilibrium prices are necessarily *proportional* (not necessarily equal) to $\mathbf{p}_0$ and date-1 equilibrium prices are necessarily proportional to $\mathbf{p}_1$. Conclude that the date-0 consumers' forecast of ICME prices for date 1 (more rigorously, forecast of prices proportional to $\mathbf{p}_1$) is confirmed as correct.

7. Consider the following intertemporal economy over two dates. The economy starts at date 0 with endowments G of corn, H of iron, L of labour. Iron is not desired for consumption and is entirely offered to firms for productive use. The economy produces corn and iron which come out at date 1. Consumers decide how much of G to consume, and offer the remainder, K, as corn-capital for production of corn and of iron. Both corn-capital and iron are circulating capital goods. The production of corn is according to a differentiable production function with corn-capital, iron and labour as inputs. Supposing the equilibrium (gross) marginal products of the three inputs in the produc-

722   Chapter 8 · Intertemporal Equilibrium, Temporary Equilibrium

tion of corn are determined, indicate them with MP_K, MP_H, MP_L. Date-0 corn is the numéraire. Determine the discounted price at date 0 of date-1 corn, and prove that the equilibrium price of date-0 iron is MP_H/MP_K. Also, determine the rate of profit (classical meaning) in this economy.

8. In the OLG model with each generation living two periods, assume the consumer's utility is additive, with each period's subutility of CRRA form:

$$U_t = \frac{C_{1,t}^{1-\theta}}{1-\theta} + \frac{1}{1+\rho} \frac{C_{2,t+1}^{1-\theta}}{1-\theta}, \quad \theta > 0, \rho > -1,$$

where ρ is the rate of intertemporal preference that discounts second-period utility to the first period, and θ is a coefficient that would be interpreted as the rate of risk aversion in an uncertainty framework (see ▶ Chap. 9); C_i, $i=1,2$, is consumption respectively when young and when old. Prove that the CRRA subutility is positive both for $\theta < 1$ and $\theta > 1$; then prove that as $\theta \to 1$, the CRRA subutility tends to $ln\ C$ (hint: first subtract $1/(1-\theta)$ from it, which only adds a constant and does not affect behaviour; then take the limit as $\theta \to 1$, applying L'Hôpital rule).

Assume the single output, corn, is produced at the end of each period by circulating capital and labour according to a differentiable CRS production function; the young work (each young consumer performs 1 unit of labour) and obtain the marginal product of labour, the capital is held by the old and earns its gross marginal product $1 + r$; consumption is performed at the end of each period; the output not consumed becomes capital. There are no bequests; when old, a consumer owns a capital stock equal to its savings when young. The consumer's budget constraint is therefore $C_{2,t+1} = (w_t - C_{1,t})(1 + r_{t+1})$. Prove that the consumer maximizes utility by satisfying the following condition:

$$\frac{C_{2,t+1}}{C_{1,t}} = \left[\frac{1 + r_{t+1}}{1 + \rho}\right]^{1/\theta}.$$

Now derive the share of w allotted to savings, if $\theta = 1$.

(We obtain here some initial inkling of the many mathematical passages necessary to complete the study of the dynamical behaviour of even a very simple OLG growth model: given an initial capital endowment, the young's savings, fully determined by their utility function and the production function, determine the next period's capital endowment, and then the next period's, and so on. One can add population growth, technical progress... Of course the conclusions strictly depend on the neoclassical framework, which has income distribution determined by marginal products, and capital accumulation determined by the reinvestment of full-employment savings.)

References

Aliprantis, C. D., Brown, D., & Burkinshaw, O. (1989). *Existence and Optimality of Competitive Equilibria*. Berlin: Springer-Verlag.

Anderson, R. M. (2008). Core convergence. In *(The) New Palgrave: A Dictionary of Economics* (II edn.)

Arrow, K. J., Hahn, F. H. (1971). *General Competitive Analysis*. S. Francisco: Holden Day, and Edinburgh: Oliver and Boyd

Bentham, J. (1843 (1995)). Anarchical fallacies. In: J. Bowring (Ed.), *The Works of Jeremy Bentham*, Vol. II (pp. 489–534). William Tait, Edinburgh. Repr. 1995. Bristol: Theommes Press.

Blad, M. C., Keiding, H. (1990). *Microeconomics. Institutions, Equilibrium and Optimality*. Amsterdam: North-Holland

Bliss, C. J. (1975). *Capital Theory and the Distribution of Income*. Amsterdam: North-Holland.

Bliss, C. J. (1976). Capital theory in the short run. In M. Brown, K. Sato, & P. Zarembka (Eds.), *Essays in Modern Capital Theory* (pp. 187–202). Amsterdam: North-Holland.

Dana R. A., Florenzano M., Le Van C., Lévy D. (1989a) Production prices and general equilibrium prices: A long run property of a Leontief economy. *Journal of Mathematical Economics, 18*: 263–80.

Dana R. A., Florenzano M., Le Van C., Lévy D. (1989b). Asymptotic properties of a Leontief economy. *Journal of Economic Dynamics and Control, 13*: 553–68.

Duménil, G., & Lévy, D. (1985). The classical and the neoclassicals: A rejoinder to Frank Hahn. *Cambridge Journal of Economics, 8*, 327–345.

Dvoskin, A. (2016). An unpleasant dilemma for contemporary general equilibrium theory. *European Journal of the History of Economic Though, 23*(2), 198–225.

Dvoskin, A., & Petri, F. (2017). Again on the relevance of reverse capital deepening and reswitching. *Metroeconomica, 68*(4), 625–659.

Fisher, F. M. (1983). *Disequilibrium foundations of equilibrium economics*. Cambridge: Cambridge University Press.

Florenzano, M. (2003). *General Equilibrium Analysis*. Kluwer, Boston/Dordrecht/London: Existence and Optimality of Equilibria.

Garegnani, P. (1976(1983)). On a change in the notion of equilibrium in recent work on value and distribution. In: M. Brown, K. Sato, P. Zarembka, eds., *Essays in Modern Capital Theory*. Amsterdam: North-Holland, pp. 25–45. As reprinted in J. Eatwell, M. Milgate (Ed.), *Keynes's economics and the theory of value and distribution* (pp. 129–45). London: Duckworth, and New York: Oxford University Press.

Garegnani, P. (1979). Notes on Consumption, Investment and Effective Demand: II. *Cambridge Journal of Economics, 3*, 63–82.

Garegnani, P. (1990). Quantity of capital. In J. L. Eatwell, M. Milgate, & P. Newman (Eds.), *The new Palgrave series: Capital theory* (pp. 1–78). London: The Macmillan Press Limited.

Garegnani, P. (2000). Savings, investment and capital in a system of general intertemporal equilibrium. In H. D. Kurz (Ed.), *Critical essays on Piero Sraffa's legacy in economics* (pp. 392–445). Cambridge: Cambridge University Press.

Garegnani, P. (2003), *Savings, investment and capital in a system of general intertemporal equilibrium*. In: Petri and Hahn (pp 117–173)

Garegnani, P. (2005). Capital and intertemporal equilibria: A reply to Mandler. *Metroeconomica, 56*(4), 411–437.

Garegnani, P. (2005). Further on capital and intertemporal equilibria: A rejoinder to Mandler. *Metroeconomica, 56*(4), 495–502.

Geanakoplos, J. (1987). Overlapping generations model of general equilibrium. In: *(The) New Palgrave: A Dictionary of Economics*, Ist ed. (Vol. 3, pp. 763–68)

724 Chapter 8 · Intertemporal Equilibrium, Temporary Equilibrium

Geanakoplos, J., Polemarchakis, H. (1991). Overlapping generations. In: W. Hildenbrand, H. Sonnenschein (Eds.), *Handbook of mathematical economics* (Vol. IV, pp. 1899–1960). Elsevier Science.

Grandmont, J.-M. (1974). On the short-run equilibrium in a monetary economy. In J. Drèze (Ed.), *Allocation under uncertainty: Equilibrium and optimality* (pp. 213–228). London: Macmillan.

Grandmont, J.-M. (1977). Temporary general equilibrium theory. *Econometrica, 45,* 535–572.

Grandmont J.-M. (1982) Temporary general equilibrium theory. In: K. Arrow, M. D. Intriligator (Eds.), *Handbook of mathematical economics* (Vol. II, Chap. 19, pp 879–922). North-Holland, Amsterdam.

Grandmont, J.-M. (1983). *Money and value: a reconsideration of classical and neoclassical monetary theories.* Cambridge: Cambridge University Press.

Grandmont, J.-M. (1989) Temporary equilibrium. In: J. Eatwell, M. Milgate, P. Newman (Eds.), *The new Palgrave series. General equilibrium.* London: Macmillan (pp. 297–304).

Grandmont, J.-M., & Laroque, G. (1973). Money in the pure consumption loan model. *Journal of Economic Theory, 6,* 382–395.

Grandmont, J.-M., & Laroque, G. (1976). On temporary Keynesian equilibria. *Review of Economic Studies, 43,* 53–67.

Green, J. R. (1973). Temporary general equilibrium in a sequential trading model with spot and future transactions. *Econometrica, 41,* 1103–1123.

Heijdra, B. J., & Van der Ploeg, F. (2002). *The foundations of modern macroeconomics.* Oxford: Oxford university Press.

Hicks, J. R. (1946). *Value and capital* (2nd edn.). Oxford: Clarendon Press (first edition, 1939).

Hicks, J. R. (1980–81). IS–LM: an explanation. *Journal of Post-Keynesian Economics.* As reprinted in Fitoussi, J.P. (1983a), *Modern macroeconomic theory* (pp. 49–63). Oxford: Basil Blackwell.

Kreps, D. M. (2013). *Microeconomic foundations I. Choice and competitive markets.* Princeton: Princeton University Press

Lindahl, E. (1929(1939)). The place of capital in the theory of price. In E. Lindahl (1939), *Studies in the theory of money and capital.* London: George Allen & Unwin (reprinted 1970 by Augustus Kelley, New York, pp. 271–350). Originally published in Swedish in 1929.

Lucas, R. E. (1974). Equilibrium search and unemployment. *Journal of Economic Theory, 7,* 188–209.

Lucas, R. E. (1986). Adaptive behavior and economic theory. *Journal of Business, 59,* S401–S426.

Madden, P. (1984). Review of Fisher (1983). *Economic Journal, 94*(4), 986–988.

Majumdar, M., Radner, R. (2008). Uncertainty and general equilibrium. In *(The) New Palgrave: A dictionary of economics* (2nd ed.).

Malinvaud, E. (1971). *Leçons de théorie microéconomique.* Paris: Dunod.

Mandler, M. (2005). Well-behaved production economies. *Metroeconomica, 56*(4), 477–494.

Mas-Colell, A., Whinston, M. D., & Green, J. R. (1995). *Microeconomic theory.* Oxford: Oxford University Press.

New Palgrave: A dictionary of economics (The) (1987) 1st ed. in 4 vols., edited by J. Eatwell, M. Milgate, P. Newman. London: Macmillan.

Patinkin, D. (1965). *Money, interest and prices* (2nd ed.). New York: Harper & Row.

Petri, F. (1991). Hicks's recantation of the temporary equilibrium method. *Review of Political Economy, 3,* 268–288.

Petri, F. (2004). *General equilibrium, capital and macroeconomics: a key to recent controversies in equilibrium theory.* Cheltenham, UK: Edward Elgar.

Petri, F. (2011a). On the Recent Debate on Capital Theory and General Equilibrium. In V. Caspari (Ed.), *The Evolution of Economic Theory* (pp. 55–99). Routledge, London: Essays in Honour of Bertram Schefold.

Petri, F. (2013). The inevitable dependence of investment on expected demand: implications for neoclassical macroeconomics. In: S. Levrero, A. Palumbo, A. Stirati (Eds.), *Sraffa and the reconstruction of economic theory: Volume II* (pp. 44–67). Houndmills, Basingstoke, Hampshire UK: Palgrave Macmillan.

Petri, F. (2015). Neglected implications of neoclassical capital-labour substitution for investment theory: Another criticism of say's law. *Review of Political Economy, 27*(3), 308–340.

Petri, F. (2017). The passage of time, capital, and investment in traditional and in recent neoclassical value theory. *Oeconomia. History, Methodology, Philosophy* [Online journal], 7–1|2017. ▶ https://oeconomia.revues.org/2596; ▶ https://doi.org/10.4000/oeconomia.2596

Radner, R. (1972). Existence of equilibrium of plans, prices, and price expectations in a sequence of markets. *Econometrica, 40,* 289–304.

Radner R. (1982) Equilibrium under uncertainty. In: K. J. Arrow, M. D. Intriligator (Eds.), *Handbook of mathematical economics,* vol. II (pp. 923–1006). North-Holland, Amsterdam.

Ravagnani, F. (1989). On conflicting expectations in temporary equilibrium models. *Political Economy. Studies in the surplus approach, 5,* 13–35.

Ravagnani, F. (2000). Decisions on production and the behaviour of savers in recent general equilibrium models. *Metroeconomica, 51,* 308–342.

Ravagnani, F. (2010). *A simple critical introduction to temporary general equilibrium theory.* Working Paper no. 136, Dipartimento di Economia Pubblica, Università di Roma La Sapienza.

Romer, D. (1996). *Advanced Macroeconomics* (1st ed.). New York: McGraw-Hill.

Solow, R. M. (1956). A contribution to the theory of economic growth. *Quarterly Journal of Economics, 70,* 65–94.

Stokey, N., Lucas, R., Prescott, E. C. (1989). *Recursive methods in economic dynamics.* Cambridge MA: Harvard University Press.

Varian, H. (1992). *Microeconomic analysis* (3rd ed.). New York: W. W. Norton.

Weil, P. (2008). Overlapping generations: The first Jubilee. *Journal of Economic Perspectives, 22*(4), 115–134.

Wickens, M. (2008). *Macroeconomic theory. A general equilibrium approach.* Princeton, NJ: Princeton University Press.

Woodford, M. (2009). Convergence in macroeconomics: Elements of the new synthesis. *American Economic Journal: Macroeconomics, 1*(1), 267–279.